ENCYCLOPEDIA OF THE

ROMANTIC ERA,

1760–1850

ENCYCLOPEDIA

OF THE

ROMANTIC ERA,

1760–1850

VOLUME 1

A–K

Christopher John Murray, General Editor

Fitzroy Dearborn

An Imprint of the Taylor & Francis Group
New York   London

Published in 2004 by
Fitzroy Dearborn
An Imprint of the Taylor & Francis Group
29 West 35th Street
New York, NY 10001

Published in 2004 by
Fitzroy Dearborn
An imprint of the Taylor & Francis Group
11 New Fetter Lane
London EC4P 4EE

10 9 8 7 6 5 4 3 2 1

Library of Congress Cataloging-in-Publication Data

Encyclopedia of the romantic era, 1760–1850/volume editor, Christopher John Murray.
     p. cm.
   Includes bibliographical references and index.
   Contents: v. 1. A–K – v. 2. L–Z.
   ISBN 1–57958–361-X (hb: set : alk. paper)-ISBN 1-57958-423-3 (hb: vol. 1: alk. paper)-ISBN
1-57958-422-5 (hb: vol. 2: alk paper)
   Romanticism—Encyclopedia. I. Murray, Christopher John.

   NX452.5.R64E53 2003
   700′.4145′03—dc21
                                                          2003042406

ISBN 1-57958-361-X (2-volume set)
ISBN 1-57958-423-3 (Volume 1)
ISBN 1-57958-422-5 (Volume 2)

BOARD OF ADVISERS

Contents

INTRODUCTION

Aims and Scope

The *Encyclopedia of the Romantic Era, 1760–1850* is a cultural encyclopedia covering the last decades of the eighteenth century and the first half of the nineteenth century in Britain, continental Europe, and the Americas. Its aim is to provide a broad-ranging guide to the profound changes in thought, sensibility, and expression that occurred during this era, a revolutionary period that saw many of the values and assumptions of the Enlightenment redefined, challenged, or rejected, and whose principal concerns—liberty, the individual, revolution and nationalism, nature, history and human identity—provided the foundation for the modern world.

The period covered is wide and, as with any such periodization, the defining dates are not precise. The early starting point of 1760 was set in order to include many of those developments seen as transitional. The end date was a little less contentious, given that the mid-nineteenth century was the era that saw the failure of so many uprisings across Europe. The intention was to choose a time span that allowed the inclusion of key features and developments, not to adhere to a strict and narrow chronology.

The *Encyclopedia of the Romantic Era* is not, therefore, simply an encyclopedia of Romanticism; many of the entries are on subjects that could not be described as Romantic in any sense. Nevertheless, a great majority of the entries analyze individuals, works, and themes that are still widely classified as Romantic. This focus on Romanticism and the Romantic is not based on the assumption that these terms can be adequately defined, or that a set of key characteristics or family resemblances can be identified. Editorially, the working principle was in effect a pragmatic nominalism: the terms Romantic and Romanticism may be of heuristic value, helpful in some contexts, but unhelpful in others. The contributors, who of course varied in their approach to this issue, were often asked to consider the value of these terms in analyzing their subjects.

The study of the period has gradually been transformed. During the early decades of the twentieth century, its distinctive cultural products were often viewed with suspicion. Pierre Lasserre (1907) in France and Irving Babbitt (1919) in the United States, for example, typified a deep skepticism: whatever their fascination or beauty, the works of the period were deemed as often expressions of a profound human failure, the products of the isolated ego's inability to relate to others or to the world. At their best, such works were seen as childlike in their sense of wonder and their emotional intensity; at their worst, as pathological and life-denying. (Such views were elaborations of Johann Wolfgang von Goethe's famous animadversion: "The classical is health, the Romantic sickness.")

Attitudes were to change radically, however, as a range of theories, methodologies, and critical approaches, such as archetypal criticism, deconstruction, feminism, Freudian psychoanalysis, Marxism, new historicism, phenomenology, queer theory, semiotics, and structuralism, were employed in several disciplines to produce a wealth of new insights and perspectives, particularly in the study of literature.

In the early twenty-first century, interest has turned increasingly to the relationship between the Enlightenment and the Romantic era (continuity/rupture), to the era's internationalism (the international significance of the French Revolution Jean-Jaogues Rousseau, and Sir Walter Scott, are among the most obvious examples), and to the close interaction among the arts, and among the arts and intellectual and political contexts (in Germany, for example, the links among Carl Gustav Carus, Johann Gottlieb Fichte, G. W. F. Hegel, Friedrich Hölderlin, Novalis, Friedrich Wilhelm Jospeh von Schelling, August Wilhelm and Frierich von Schlegel, Friedrich Danniel Ernst Schleiermacher, the French Revolution and Napoleon Bonaparte's career, the rise of nationalism, science, landscape painting, music, and so on). A good deal of contemporary interest is also based on the belief that the Romantic era's central concerns (notably the limits of rationality, and the urge to transcend boundaries) have a direct bearing on our self-styled postmodern world, which some see as having witnessed the final "failure of the Enlightenment project."

The *Encyclopedia of the Romantic Era* is a direct response to this ever-widening scope of study, and in its coverage of arts and ideas in Britain, continental Europe, and the Americas, it is unique. This ambitious range often made the selection of entries difficult, and even a hardened conscience would have been troubled by sins of omission. The aim, however, was not to create a comprehensive or definitive account of the era, but to provide a broad-ranging interdisciplinary resource that, rich in facts, ideas, and links, would act as a valuable point of departure for those who want to explore this era's extraordinary artistic and intellectual achievements.

After identifying the major entries, which were largely self-selecting, the aim was to provide a balanced selection that would be truly international in scope. Particular attention was paid to those subjects generally regarded as marginal (such as developments in Greece, the Netherlands, Scandinavia, South America, the Ukraine and so on), and also to Jewish culture—aspects that often emphasize the contrast with cultural phenomena traditionally defined as Romantic. Above all, the *Encyclopedia of the Romantic Era* is meant to reflect the era's cultural diversity.

Organization of the *Encyclopedia of the Romantic Era*

There are over 770 entries, arranged alphabetically. All the entries have bibliographies, and many have cross-references under the "*See also*" heading. Entries on individuals also have biographical outlines, and (in the case of writers, artists, and composers) a list of selected works. There are 116 illustrations.

There are four basic entry types:

Those on individuals—these form the bulk of the entries.

Those on works—works of literature, music, or art selected because they help to provide a fuller account of their creator, because they have a particular historical significance, or because they are representative (whether famous or not) of the period or an art form.

Surveys—that meant to provide a broad view of a subject, their scope complementing the detail provided by the more specifically focused entries. There are, for example, cultural and historical surveys of national developments.

Those on themes, concepts, approaches and events—a broad-ranging category. Some of the entries are specific to a particular art, discipline, or nation; others have a broad significance. Examples include the Dandy, Don Juan, Fragment, Gender, Genius, Homosexuality, Imagination, Irony, Orientalism, Progress, the Sublime, the Supernatural, Symbol and Allegory, and Volksgeist. This category also includes critical approaches to the period (Feminist Deconstruction and Romantic Literature, Approaches to Romantic Literature), and overviews of a number of key historical subjects, for example, French Revolution, Industrial Revolution.

In order to help readers explore this broad array of entries, three thematic lists have been prepared:

1. *A comprehensive alphabetical listing of entries.*
2. *A list of entries arranged in terms of subject.* There are entries on architecture, art, historiography, literature, music, philosophy, political and social thought, religion and theology, and scholarship. Science entries are on the whole restricted to those individuals and subjects directly influenced by developments in culture and thought (the close link between German idealism and science is a prime example). The aspects of economic, political, and social history included are those that that were closely related to cultural life (national and revolutionary aspirations, frequently expressed in artistic forms, made the links between culture and politics particularly close during this era). Historical surveys provide the background to cultural developments, and there are entries on a range of key historical subjects. These are listed under General Surveys and Themes.

    In the thematic listing, the categories are:
    Architecture
    Art
    Dance
    General Surveys and Themes
    Literature and Thought
    Music
    Science
3. *A thematic list based on national developments.* Here, countries are listed alphabetically; entries appear under the relevant nation, and are then subcategorized under the seven categories listed above.

Other research guides are the general analytical index at the end of volume 2, and the "*See also*" sections included with many of the entries.

Acknowledgments

A work of this size has depended on the generous advice, support, and hard work of many people. First and foremost, I need to thank the advisers and contributors. I would also like to thank Daniel Kirkpatrick for commissioning the project, Bridget Tiley for the picture research, and above all the Fitzroy Dearborn project editor, Anne-Lucie Norton, for her efficiency, patience, and unfailing good humor in bringing the project to life.

Christopher John Murray

List of Entries

LIST OF ENTRIES BY SUBJECT

Literature and Thought

LIST OF ENTRIES BY NATIONAL DEVELOPMENTS

Balkans

General Surveys and Themes
Balkans: Cultural and Historical Survey

Literature
Alecsandri, Vasile
Karadziz, Vuk Stefanovic
Kogalniceanu, Mihail
Petrovic, Petar Njegos
Radulescu, Ion Heliade

Bohemia and Moravia

General Surveys and Themes
Czech and Slovak Romanticism

Music
Dussek, Jan Ladislav

Britain

General Surveys and Themes
Britain: Cultural Survey
Britain: Historical Survey
Pre-Romanticism: Britain
Religion: Britain

Architecture
Pugin, Augustus Welby Northmore
Repton, Humphry
Soane, Sir John
Upjohn, Richard

Art
Bewick, Thomas
Bonington, Richard Parkes
Constable, John
Cotman, John Sell
Cozens, Alexander
Crome, John
Cruikshank, George
Dadd, Richard
Dedham Vale
Elohim Creating Adam
Flaxman, John
Gainsborough, Thomas
Gillray, James
Girtin, Thomas
History painting: Britain
Horse Frightened by a Lion
Landscape Painting: Britain
Lawrence, Thomas
Loutherbourg, Philippe Jacques
Martin, John
Mary, Duchess of Richmond
Nightmare, The
Ophelia
Palmer, Samuel
Portrait: Britain
Pre-Raphaelite Brotherhood
Reynolds, Sir Joshua
Sadak in Search of the Waters of Oblivion
Self-Portrait: Britain
Snow Storm: Steam Boat off a Harbour's Mouth
Stubbs, George
Turner, JMW
Wilkie, David
Wright, Joseph

Literature and Thought
Alastor: or The Spirit of Solitude
Austen, Jane
Baillie, Joanna
Barbauld, Anna Laetitia
Beckford, William
Bentham, Jeremy
Blake, William

Notes on Contributors

Henry Adams, Curator of American Art, Cleveland Museum of Art.
Author: ALLSTON, WASHINGTON.

Jeremy Adler, Department of German, King's College, London.
Author: EICHENDORFF, JOSEPH VON; KLOPSTOCK, FRIEDRICH GOTTLIEB.

Shona Allan
Author: DANCE: BALLET; DANCE: POPULAR; GISELLE; SYLPHIDE, LA; TAGLIONI, FILIPPO AND MARIA.

Joselyn M. Almeida, Department of English, Boston College.
Author: ECHEVERRÍA, ESTEBAN; SARMIENTO, DOMINGO FAUSTINO.

John M. Anderson, Department of English, Boston College.
Author: EPIC; TIGHE, MARY.

Norman Araujo, Department of Romance Languages, Boston College.
Author: HISTOIRE DE FRANCE; LAMARTINE, ALPHONSE LOUIS-MARIE DE PRAT; MAISTRE, JOSEPH-MARIE, COMTE DE; MÉRIMÉE, PROSPER; NODIER, CHARLES.

Monika Baar, Brasenose College, Oxford University.
Author: LELEWEL, JOACHIM; MOCHNACKI, MAURYCY.

David Baguley, Department of French, University of Durham.
Author: ADOLPHE; DUMAS, ALEXANDRE; SAINTE-BEUVE, CHARLES AUGUSTIN DE; TROIS MOUSQUETAIRES, LES.

Paul Baines, Department of English Language & Literature, University of Liverpool.
Author: BEWICK, THOMAS; FLAXMAN, JOHN; SOANE, SIR JOHN; VIOLIN; VIOTTI, GIOVANNI BATTISTA.

Tallis Barker
Author: HAMMERKLAVIER, DAS; SONATA.

Stuart Barnett, English Department, Central Connecticut State University.
Author: CRITIQUE OF JUDGEMENT; SORROWS OF YOUNG WERTHER, THE.

Thomas F. Barry, College of Foreign Languages, Himeji Dokkyo University.
Author: GERMAN IDEALISM; ITS PHILOSOPHICAL LEGACY; GERMAN ROMANTICISM: ITS LITERARY LEGACY; GRILLPARZER, FRANZ; GRIMM, JAKOB AND WILHELM; HAWTHORNE, HEBBEL, FRIEDRICH; NATHANIEL; KANT, IMMANUEL; MÖRIKE, EDUARD FRIEDRICH; NOBLE SAVAGE; SCARLET LETTER, THE; WIELAND, CHRISTOPH MARTIN.

Gerd Bayer, Department of Modern Languages and Literatures, Case Western Reserve University
Author: GRABBE, CHRISTIAN DIETRICH; JUNGES DEUTSCHLAND.

Roderick Beaton, Department of Byzantine and Modern Greek Studies, Kings College London.
Author: GREECE: CULTURAL AND HISTORICAL SURVEY; KALVOS, ANDREAS IOANNISIS; KORAÏS, ADAMÁNTIOS; SOLOMÓS, DHIONÍSIOS.

Bernard Beatty, Department of English Language & Literature, University of Liverpool.
Author: BYRON, GEORGE GORDON, LORD.

Nicolas Bell, Music Collections, The British Library.
Author: ALKAN, CHARLES-VALENTIN; CZERNY, CARL.

Lucy Bending, University of Reading.
Author: BARBAULD, ANNA LAETITIA; MORE, HANNAH.

Christine Berthin, Department of English Literature, University of Orleans.
Author: LEWIS, MATTHEW GREGORY; SHELLEY, MARY WOLLSTONECRAFT.

Paul Bishop, Department of German, University of Glasgow.
Author: DROSTE-HÜLSHOFF, ANNETTE; FICHTE, JOHANN GOTTLIEB; GOETHE, JOHANN WOLFGANG; SCHOPENHAUER, ARTHUR; WORLD AS WILL AND REPRESENTATION, THE; WIERTZ, ANTOINE JOSEPH.

Mette Bligaard, The Danish Cultural Institute.
Author: ABILDGAARD, NICOLAS ABRAHAM; CARSTENS, ASMUS JAKOB; KØBKE, CHRISTEN SCHJELLERUP; THORWALDSEN, BERTEL.

E. Douglas Bomberger, Department of Music, University of Hawaii at Manoa.
Author: Dichterliebe; Liszt, Franz; Program music and tone painting; Virtuoso.

Penny Bradshaw, Department of English and Drama, St Martin's College.
Author: Brontë, Charlotte; Opie, Amelia.

H. M. Brown, St Hilda's College, Oxford University.
Author: Hoffmann, Ernst Theodor Amadeus.

Helena Buescu, University of Lisbon.
Author: Castilho, António Feliciano de; Eurico, o presbítero; Garrett, João Baptista de Almeida; Herculano, Alexandre; Viagens na Minha Terra.

Ken A. Bugajski, Department of English, Rogers State University.
Author: Autobiographical writing: Britain.

William Burns
Author: Cuvier, Georges Baron; Dalton, John; Geoffroy Saint-Hilaire, Étienne; Industrial revolution; Ireland: historical survey; Science in Germany.

Edward Burns, Department of English Language & Literature, University of Liverpool.
Author: dadd, richard; Horse Frightened by a lion; Kean, Edmund; Mary, countess of Richmond; Nightmare, The; Sadak in Search of the Waters of Oblivion; Shakespeare: Britain; Shakespeare: Europe; Siddons, Sarah; stubbs, George.

James A. Butler, Department of English, La Salle University.
Author: Peaceable Kingdom, The; Peale, Charles Willson.

Kathleen L. Butler, University of California, Berkeley.
Author: Audubon, John James; Girtin, Thomas; Sully, Thomas; Travel writing: United States; Trumbull, Jonathan.

Michelle Callander, Department of English and Cultural Studies, University of Melbourne.
Author: Cruikshank, George; Gillray, James.

Suzannah Camm
Author: Crime and punishment.

Patricia Campbell, Department of Fine Art, University of Edinburgh.
Author: Cozens, Alexander and John Robert; History painting: Britain; Houdon, Jean-Antoine.

Brian Caraher, School of English, Queen's University of Belfast.
Author: Image and metaphor.

Roger Cardinal, School of European and Modern Language Studies, University of Kent.
Author: Fohr, Karl-Philipp; Friedrich, Caspar David; Hauff, Wilhelm; Kerner, Justinus; Moonrise Over the Sea; night.

Agnes Cardinal, Comparative Literary Studies, University of Kent.
Author: Günderode, Karoline von; Pestalozzi, Johann Heinrich.

Derek Carew, Music Department, Cardiff University.
Author: Dussek, Jan Ladisla; Études d'exécution transcendante; Fantasy in C major; Field, John; Hummel, Johann Nepomuk; Preludes; Romance; Schumann, Robert.

Brycchan Carey, School of English and Drama, Queen Mary and Westfield College, London.
Author: Day, Thomas; Slavery and emancipation; Yearsley, Ann.

Stephen Carver, School of English and American Studies, University of East Anglia.
Author: drugs and addiction; Gothic Revival; Maturin, Charles Robert; Pugin, Augustus Welby Northmore; Waverley.

Abigail Chantler, School of Music, Trinity College.
Author: Aesthetics and art criticism; Herder, Johann Gottfried; Literary criticism: German; Paul, Jean.

Susan Chaplin, Department of English, University of Salford.
Author: gender; Women.

William Christie, Department of English, University of Sydney.
Author: British Romanticism: approaches and interpretations; Hero; Lyric; Progress.

Daniel Chua, Department of Music, King's College London.
Author: Beethoven, Ludwig van.

Elvio Ciferri
Author: Catholicism; Minnardi, Tomasso; Pellico, Silvio; Rosmini Serbati, Antonio.

Keith E. Clifton, Department of Music, University of Central Arkansas.
Author: Halévy, Jacques François.

Edward Alan Cole, Department of History, Grand Valley State University.
Author: Russia: historical survey.

Philip Connell, Grange Rd, Selwyn College.
Author: Bentham, Jeremy; Peacock, Thomas Love.

Malcolm Cook, Department of French, University of Exeter.
Author: Bernardin de Saint-Pierre, Jacques-Henri.

Ian Copestake, Johann Wolfgang Goethe University, Frankfurt.
Author: Emerson, Ralph Waldo; Essays; American Romanticism: approaches and interpretation.

Heide Crawford, Dept. of German and Slavic Languages and Literatures, Pennsylvania State University.
Author: Brentano, Clemens; Folk literature: Germany.

Ceri D. Crossley, Department of French Studies, University of Birmingham.
Author: Historiography: France; Michelet, Jules; Thierry, Augustin.

Laura Dabundo, Department of English, Kennesaw State University.
Author: Christianity; Pforr, Franz.

Gregory Dart, Department of English, University College London.
Author: Martin, John; Rousseau, Jean-Jacques.

Frank Day
Author: Bingham, George Caleb; Concept of Anxiety; Constable, John; Dedham Vale; Fear and Trembling; Fur Traders Descending the Missouri; Sartor Resartus.

Juilee Decker, Art History, Case Western Reserve University.
Author: ART; ART ACADEMIES, EXHIBITIONS AND PATRONAGE; ART AND MEDIEVALISM; ARTIST, CHANGING CONCEPTIONS OF; GÉRICAULT, THÉODORE; BARYE, ANTOINE-LOUIS; LANDSCAPE PAINTING: BRITAIN.

Massimiliano Demata, St. Cross College, Oxford University.
Author: CHILDE HAROLD'S PILGRIMAGE; GALT, JOHN; SHERIDAN, RICHARD BRINSLEY.

Jane Desmarais, Department of Historical and Cultural Studies, Goldsmiths College.
Author: BAUDELAIRE, CHARLES; SALON DE 1846, LE; WRIGHT, JOSEPH.

Guillaume de Syon, Department of History, Albright College.
Author: FRENCH ROMANTICISM; ITS LITERARY LEGACY; SWITZERLAND: CULTURAL SURVEY; SWITZERLAND: HISTORICAL SURVEY.

Alex Dick, Department of English, University of British Columbia.
Author: DRAMA: BRITAIN; ECONOMICS; HUNT, LEIGH; MÜLLER, ADAM HEINRICH.

Sheila Dickson, Department of Modern Languages, Strathclyde University.
Author: ARNIM, ACHIM VON; NICOLAI, FRIEDRICH.

Margaret M. Doyle
Author: BIEDERMEIER; CARUS, CARL GUSTAV; KERSTING, GEORG FRIEDRICH; KOCH, JOSEPH ANTON; LANDSCAPE PAINTING: GERMANY; PORTRAIT: GERMANY; SELF-PORTRAIT: GERMANY.

Alexander Drace-Francis, School of Slavonic and East European Studies, University College London.
Author: ALECSANDRI, VASILE; KOGALNICEANU, MIHAIL; RADULESCU, ION HELIADE; ROMANIANS.

Osman Durrani, Department of German, University of Kent at Canterbury.
Author: GÖRRES, JOSEPH VON; HISTORY PAINTING: GERMNAY; LENAU, NIKOLAUS; RELIGION: GERMANY; RETHEL, ALFRED; RICHTER, ADRIAN; SCHADOW, JOHANN GOTTFRIED; SCHWIND, MORITZ VON; SPITZWEG, CARL; STIRNER, MAX; TRAVEL WRITING: GERMANY.

Sveinn Yngvi Egilsson, University of Iceland.
Author: HALLGRIMSSON, JONAS; THÓRARENSEN, BJARNI VIGFÚSSON.

Cliff Eisen, Department of Music, King's College, London.
Author: DON GIOVANNI; MOZART, WOLFGANG AMADEUS.

Clara Estow, Department of Hispanic Studies, University of Massachusetts, Harbor Campus.
Author: JOVELLANOS, GASPAR MELCHOR DE; LATIN AMERICA, CARIBBEAN AND THE WEST INDIES: CULTURAL SURVEY; LATIN AMERICA, CARIBBEAN AND THE WEST INDIES: HISTORICAL SURVEY; SAAVEDRA, ÁNGEL DE, DUQUE DE; SPAIN: HISTORICAL SURVEY; ZORRILLA Y MORAL, JOSÉ.

Frank Ferguson, Department of English, Queen's University Belfast.
Author: FOLK LITERATURE: BRITAIN.

Paul Fisher, Department of English, Wellesley College.
Author: LEAVES OF GRASS; PARKER, THEODORE; WHITMAN, WALT.

Michael Flavin
Author: BROWNING, ROBERT; LANDON, LETITIA ELIZABETH.

Katherine Fleming, New York University.
Author: PHILHELLENISM.

Luminita Florea, Robbins Collection, University of California, Berkeley.
Author: FOLK SONG; MENDELSSOHN-BARTOLDY, FELIX; MENDELSSOHN-HENSEL, FANNY; MUSIC, ROMANTIC.

Deborah Forbes
Author: SINCERITY.

Robert J. Frail, Departments of English and French, Centenary College.
Author: JULIE, OU LA NOUVELLE HÉLOÏSE; PRE-ROMANTICISM: FRANCE; SCHLEGEL, DOROTHEA.

Michael J. Franklin, School of English, University of Wales, Cardiff.
Author: ORIENTALISM: LITERATURE AND SCHOLARSHIP.

Camilla Fraser, SELC (Scandinavian Studies), University of Edinburgh.
Author: ALMQVIST, CARL JONAS LOVE; ATTERBOM, PER DANIELS AMADEUS; STAGNELIUS, ERIK JOHAN.

Denise Gallo, Music Division, The Library of Congress.
Author: ROBERT LE DIABLE.

Frederick Garber, Department of Comparative Literature, State University of New York, Binghampton.
Author: THOREAU, HENRY DAVID; WALDEN.

Nancy Garf
Author: LIEDER; LIEDER CYCLE; ORCHESTRA; SALIERI, ANTONIO; SYMPHONY.

Theodore L. Gentry
Author: CHOPIN, FRÉDÉRIC; NABUCCO; VERDI, GIUSEPPE.

Andrew Ginger, School of European Languages and Culture (Hispanic Studies), University of Edinburgh.
Author: CAPRICHOS, LOS; ESPRONCEDA Y DELGADO, JOSÉ DE; GARCÍA GUTIÉRREZ, ANTONIO; LARRA, MARIANO JOSÉ DE; SPAIN: CULTURAL SURVEY.

Wayne Glausser, Department of English, De Pauw University.
Author: DECONSTRUCTION AND ROMANTIC LITERATURE; MILTON AND PARADISE LOST.

Maxime Goergen, Institut de literature francaise moderne, Universite de Neuchatel.
Author: OLIVIER, JUSTE; TOPFFER, RODOLPHE.

George Gömöri, Darwin College, Cambridge University.
Author: HUNGARY: CULTURAL SURVEY; HUNGARY; HISTORICAL SURVEY; JÁNOS VITÉZ; JÓKAI, MÓR; KORDIAN; MALCZEWSKI, ANTONI; MICKIEWICZ, ADAM; NORWID, CYPRIAN KAMIL; PETOFI, SÁNDOR; SLOWACKI, JULIUSZ; BERNARD; SZÉCHENYI, ISTVÁN; VÖRÖSMARTY, MIHÁLY; ZALÁN FUTÁSA.

A.C. Goodson, Department of English, Michigan State University.
Author: LANGUAGE; WILHELM MEISTERS LEHRJAHRE.

Christopher Goulding
Author: COSMOLOGY; SCIENCE AND THE ARTS; SCIENCE OF THE PAST.

Peter Graves, Scandinavian Studies, University of Edinburgh.
Author: KALEVALA.

John Patrick Greene, Departmentof Modern Languages, University of Louisville.
Author: RESTIF, NICOLAS-EDME.

Daniel Greineder, Oxford University.
Author: ON NAÏVE AND SENTIMENTAL POETRY.

Matthew Grenby, Department of English, De Montfort University.
Author: BECKFORD, WILLIAM; CHILDREN'S LITERATURE; INCHBALD, ELIZABETH.

Gwendelin Guentner, University of Iowa.
Author: TRAVEL WRITING: FRANCE.

Santiago Rodríguez Guerrero-Strachan
Author: HARTZENBUSCH, JUAN EUGENIO; HEREDIA, JOSÉ MARÍA DE; JANE EYRE; SPANISH AMERICA AND BRAZIL: CULTURAL SURVEY.

Bonnie J. Gunzenhauser, English Department, Millikin University.
Author: BROWNING, ELIZABETH BARRETT; DICKENS, CHARLES; MIDDLE CLASS.

JD Guthrie, New Hall College, Cambridge University.
Author: DRAMA: GERMANY; GÖTTINGER HAIN; RÄUBER, DIE.

Li Sui Gwee, Dept. Of English Language and Literature, National University of Singapore.
Author: CONFESSIONS, LES; LAMARCK, JEAN BAPTISTE PIERRE ANTOINE DE MONET, CHEVALIER; LAPLACE, PIERRE SIMON DE; LESSING, GOTTHOLD EPHRAIM; SCHELLING, FRIEDRICH WILHELM JOSEPH VON; STRAUSS, DAVID FRIEDRICH,

Rafey M. Habib, Department of English, Rutgers University, Camden.
Author: EUROPE 1760–1850: HISTORICAL SURVEY.

Hans-Joachim Hahn, School of Languages, Oxford Brookes University.
Author: GERMANY: HISTORICAL SURVEY; HYMNEN AN DIE NACHT; HUMBOLDT, WILHELM VON; NOVALIS; ROMANTISCHE SCHULE, DIE; SCHLEIERMACHER, FRIEDRICH DANIEL ERNST; UHLAND, LUDWIG.

Martin Halliwell, Department of English, University of Leicester.
Author: AMERICAN ROMANTICISM: ITS LITERARY LEGACY; DOUGLASS, FREDERICK; IRVING, WASHINGTON; SKETCHBOOK OF GEOFFREY CRAYON, GENT, THE; TRANSCENDENTALISM; UNITED STATES: CULTURAL SURVEY.

Nicholas Halmi, Department. of English, University of Washington.
Author: ART AND CLASSICAL ANTIQUITY; BOULEE, ETIENNE-LOUIS; JACOBI, FRIEDRICH HENRICH; KLENZE, LEO VON; ROBINSON, HENRY CRABB; SCHINKEL, KARL FRIEDRICH; SYMBOL AND ALLEGORY.

Albert W. Halsall, Department of French, Carleton University.
Author: CHATEAUBRIAND, FRANÇOIS-AUGUSTE-RENÊ DE; DE L'ALLEMAGNE; FICTION: FRANCE; HERNANI; HUGO, VICTOR-MARIE; MÉMOIRES D'OUTRE-TOMBE; NOTRE-DAME DE PARIS; PIXÉRÉCOURT, (RENÉ-CHARLES-) GUILBERT DE; VIOLLET-LE-DUC, EUGÈNE-EMMANUEL.

Anthony John Harding, Department of English, University of Saskatchewan.
Author: MYTHOLOGY, CLASSICAL; WORDSWORTH, DOROTHY.

Gregory W. Harwood, Department of Music, Georgia Southern University.
Author: BERLIOZ, HECTOR; SYMPHONIE FANTASTIQUE.

Richard Haw
Author: UPJOHN, RICHARD; WATSON AND THE SHARK.

David Haycock, Oxford University.
Author: BIOGRAPHIA LITERARIA; COLERIDGE, SAMUEL TAYLOR; FUSELI, HENRY; HOGG, JAMES; KUBLA KHAN; RIME OF THE ANCIENT MARINER, THE.

Scott Hess, English Department, Earlham College.
Author: BEATTIE, JAMES; POETRY: BRITAIN; SELF AND SUBJECTIVITY.

Regina L. Hewitt
Author: LANDOR, WALTER SAVAGE.

Sarah Hibberd, Department of Music, Royal Holloway College, London.
Author: HUGUENOTS, LES; MEYERBEER, GIACOMO.

David Hill, Department of German Studies, University of Birmingham.
Author: STURM UND DRANG.

Terence A. Hoagwood, Department of English, Texas A&M University.
Author: ELOHIM CREATING ADAM; PRIESTLEY, JOSEPH; ROBINSON, MARY.

Pierre L. Horn
Author: BALZAC, HONORÉ DE; DRAMA: FRANCE; PÈRE GORIOT, LE.

Brian Horowitz, University of Nebraska.
Author: JEWS.

Jeremy Howard, School of Art History, University of St Andrews.
Author: BRÜLLOF, KARL; IVANOV, ALEXANDER ANDREYEVICH.

Peter Howell, Department of English, St Mary's University College.
Author: INDIVIDUALISM; REVOLUTION.

Ursula Hudson-Wiedenmann, Newnham College, Cambridge University.
Author: AUTOBIOGRAPHICAL WRITING: GERMANY; FICTION: GERMANY; FOUQUÉ, KAROLINE DE LA MOTTE; LETTERS: GERMANY.

Rowland Hughes, Department of English, University College London.
Author: COOPER, JAMES FENIMORE; DEERSLAYER, THE; FICTION: UNITED STATES; NEW WORLD; SIMMS, WILLIAM GILMORE.

Eleanor Sian Hughes, Department of Art History, University of California at Berkeley.
Author: PORTRAIT: BRITAIN; SELF-PORTRAIT: BRITAIN.

Timothy Hurley, Department of Philosophy, Furman University
Author: MILL, JOHN STUART.

John Irving, Department of Music, University of Bristol.
Author: CHAMBER MUSIC; CONCERTO; HAYDN, FRANZ JOSEPH (1732–1809); PRE-ROMANTICISM IN MUSIC.

Noel Jackson, Department of English, University of Chicago.
Author: HISTORIOGRAPHY: BRITAIN; SOLITUDE AND COMMUNITY.

Sara James
Author: DAUMIER, HONORÉ; SUE, EUGÈNE.

Jamie W. Johnson
Author: CARICATURE; REYNOLDS, SIR JOSHUA.

Adeline Johns-Putra, School of English, University of Exeter.
Author: BAILLIE, JOANNA; FEMINIST APPROACHES TO THE ROMANTIC LITERATURE; WILLIAMS, HELEN MARIA.

Christopher Jones, Department of English, University of Wales, Bangor.
Author: AUSTEN, JANE; BRITAIN: CULTURAL SURVEY; COBBETT, WILLIAM; HAPPINESS; MIDDLE AGES; OWEN, ROBERT; SENSE AND SENSIBILITY.

Susie Jordan, Department of English, Queen Mary and Westfield College, London.
Author: ALASTOR; BURKE, EDMUND; PAINE, THOMAS.

Christer Jörgensen
Author: BALKANS: CULTURAL AND HISTORICAL SURVEY; BALTIC: CULTURAL AND HISTORICAL SURVEY; FRANCE: 1760 TO THE REVOLUTION; FRENCH REVOLUTION: ITS IMPACT AND IMPORTANCE; KARADZIC, VUK STEFANOVIC; NETHERLANDS: HISTORICAL SURVEY; PETROVIC, PETAR NJEGOS.

Essaka Joshua, Department of English, University of Birmingham.
Author: BEDDOES, THOMAS LOVELL.

Andrew Kahn, St. Edmund Hall, Oxford University.
Author: BATYUSHKOV, KONSTANTIN NIKOLAYEVICH; KARAMZIN, NIKOLAY MIKHAYLOVICH; PUSHKIN, ALEKSANDR SERGEYEVICH.

Mark Kamrath, Department of English, University of Central Florida.
Author: HISTORIOGRAPHY: UNITED STATES.

Gary Kelly, Department of English, University of Alberta.
Author: FICTION: BRITAIN; HEMANS, FELICIA DOROTHEA BROWNE; PRE-ROMANTICISM: BRITAIN; SCOTT, SIR WALTER.

Malcolm Kelsall, Department of English, Cardiff University.
Author: BYRONISM; DON JUAN.

Christine Kenyon Jones, Department of English Language and Literature, King's College London.
Author: CHILDHOOD; DREAMS AND DREAMING.

James Kidd
Author: CHATTERTON, THOMAS; LAMB, CHARLES; MOORE, THOMAS.

David Kirby, Department of English, Florida State University.
Author: SCANDINAVIA AND FINLAND: HISTORICAL SURVEY.

Mark Knight
Author: BULWER-LYTTON, EDWARD; SATAN AND SATANISM.

Svitlana Kobets, University of Illinois at Urbana-Champaign.
Author: UKRAINE: CULTURAL AND HISTORICAL SURVEY.

Margarete Kohlenbach, School of European Studies (German), University of Sussex.
Author: BÜCHNER, GEORG; DANTONS TOD; LUCINDE; MESMERISM.

Astrid Köhler, Modern Languages (German) Department, Queen Mary and Westfield College, London.
Author: ARNIM, BETTINA VON; SALONS AND LITERARY SOCIETIES: GERMANY.

Charles S. Kraszewski, Department of English, King's College.
Author: DZIADY; KRASINSKI, ZYGMUNT; PAN TADEUSZ; POLAND: CULTURAL SURVEY; POLAND: HISTORICAL SURVEY.

Katharina Krosny, Department of German, University College London.
Author: DANDY; PAN-SLAVISM; VOLK(SGEIST); WACKENRODER, WILHELM HEINRICH.

Marie Lathers, Department of Modern Languages and Literatures, Case Western Reserve University.
Author: DELAROCHE, PAUL.

Thomas Lawrance
Author: SNELLMAN, JOHAN VILHELM.

Mark Ledbury, School of Art History and Archaeology, University of Manchester.
Author: ATALA AU TOMBEAU; GIRODET DE ROUCY-TRIOSON, ANNE-LOUIS; GOYA (Y LUCIENTES), FRANCISCO (JOSÉ) DE; INGRES, JEAN-AUGUSTE-DOMINIQUE; ROGER AND ANGELICA; THIRD OF MAY, 1808, THE.

David Lee
Author: COMTE, AUGUSTE; COUSIN, VICTOR; LAMENNAIS, FÉLICITÉ DE; POETRY: FRANCE; RELIGION: FRANCE; TOCQUEVILLE, ALEXIS DE.

Simon Lee, Department of History of Art & Architecture, University of Reading.
Author: DAVID, JACQUES-LOUIS; DELACROIX, (FERDINAND-VICTOR-) EUGÈNE; JOURNALS; LIBERTY LEADING THE PEOPLE; NAPOLEON CROSSING THE GREAT ST. BERNARD PASS.

Lauren Leighton
Author: BARATYNSKY, YEVGENY ABRAMOVICH; BESTUZHEV-MARLINSKY, ALEKSANDR ALEKSANDROVICH; SCHLEGEL, AUGUST WILHELM VON; SCHLEGEL, FRIEDRICH VON; ZHUKOVSKY, VASILY ANDREYEVICH.

Lisa Leslie
Author: CLAIRMONT, CLAIRE.

Anthony Levi
Author: MÉDITATIONS POÉTIQUES.

Kathryn L. Shanks Libin, Department of Music, Vassar College.
Author: MUSIC AND LITERATURE; SPOHR, LUDWIG.

Ed Lilley, History of Art Department, University of Bristol.
Author: ART AND POLITICS; GERARD, FRANCOIS (-PASCAL-SIMON), BARON; GROS, ANTOINE-JEAN; LANDSCAPE PAINTING: FRANCE.

Richard Littlejohns, Department of German, University of Leicester.
Author: ARNDT, ERNST MORITZ; FRANZ STERNBALDS WANDERUNGEN; GILLY, FRIEDRICH; HÜLSENBECK CHILDREN, THE; JOURNALS AND PERIODICALS: GERMANY; KAUFFMANN, ANGELICA; PRE-ROMANTICISM: GERMANY; RUNGE, PHILIPP OTTO; SCHILLER, JOHANN CHRISTOPH FRIEDRICH VON; TIECK, LUDWIG.

Charlie Louth, The Queen's College.
Author: HÖLDERLIN, (JOHANN CHRISTIAN) FRIEDRICH; HYPERION, ODER DER EREMIT IN GRIECHENLAND.

Tom Lundskær-Nielsen, Department of Scandinavian Studies, University College London.
Author: ANDERSEN, HANS CHRISTIAN; TALES BY ANDERSEN.

Ian Machin, Department of History, University of Dundee.
Author: BRITAIN: HISTORICAL SURVEY.

Robert Mack
Author: CASTLE OF OTRANTO; GRAVEYARD POETS; WALPOLE, HORACE.

Christopher MacLachlan, School of English, University of St Andrews.
Author: BURNS, ROBERT; OSSIAN.

Alison Martin, Christ's College.
Author: BEETS, NICOLAAS; POTGIETER, EVERHARDUS JOHANNES.

Laura Martin, Department of German, University of Glasgow.
Author: KLEIST, HEINRICH VON; MARQUISE VON O. . ., DIE; ÜBER DAS MARIONETTENTHEATER.

Bronwen Martin
Author: CHÉNIER, ANDRÉ; LITERARY CRITICISM: FRANCE; SENANCOUR, ETIENNE PIVERT DE.

Emma Mason, Department of English, Corpus Christi College, University of Cambridge.
Author: NEWMAN, JOHN HENRY; RELIGION: BRITAIN.

Pete Mauro, Department of Art History, City University of New York.
Author: LAVATER, JOHANN KASPAR.

Laurence W. Mazzeno, Office of the President, Alvernia College.
Author: BRONTË, ANNE; EDGEWORTH, MARIA.

Tilar Mazzeo, Department of English, University of Wisconsin, Oshkosh.
Author: COLE, THOMAS; VOLNEY, CONSTANTIN FRANÇOIS CHASSEBOEUF.

Renee McCachren, Music Department, Catawba College.
Author: EROICA.

Michael E. McClellan, Department of Music, The Chinese University of Hong Kong.
Author: CHERUBINI, MARIA LUIGI; MEHUL, ETIENNE-NICOLAS.

Mark R. McCulloh
Author: SOLGER, KARL WILHELM FERDINAND; VARNHAGEN VON ENSE, RAHEL.

Emma McEvoy, Department of English, Goldsmiths College, London.
Author: PICTURESQUE; RADCLIFFE, ANN.

Mitchell McNaylor
Author: AMERICAN REVOLUTION, THE; MACAULAY, THOMAS BABINGTON.

Peter McPhee, Department of History, University of Melbourne.
Author: FRANCE: 1815–1852.

Robert McVaugh, Department of Art and Art History, Colgate University.
Author: NAZARENE ART; OVERBECK, JOHANN FRIEDRICH.

Jennifer Davis Michael, Department of English, University of the South.
Author: CITY AND VILLAGE; COWPER, WILLIAM; SICKNESS.

Robert Mitchell, Department of English, Duke University.
Author: EDUCATION; FEUERBACH, LUDWIG; MELANCHOLY; UNCONSCIOUS.

Fátima Freitas Morna
Author: PORTUGAL: CULTURAL SURVEY; PORTUGAL: HISTORICAL SURVEY.

Robert Morrison, Department of English, Acadia University.
Author: HAZLITT, WILLIAM; POLIDORI, JOHN WILLIAM; SPIRIT OF THE AGE.

Christopher John Murray
Author: RAFT OF THE MEDUSA.

James Naughton, Oxford University.
Author: CZECH AND SLOVAK ROMANTICISM.

K. M. Newton, Department of English, The University of Dundee.
Author: HERMENEUTICS; PRELUDE, THE; SHELLEY, PERCY BYSSHE.

Marianne Noble, Department of Literature, American University
Author: FULLER, (SARAH) MARGARET; HOLMES, OLIVER WENDELL; STOWE, HARRIET BEECHER.

Michael S. O'Neill, Department of English Studies, University of Durham.
Author: KEATS, JOHN; LAMIA, ISABELLA, THE EVE OF ST AGNES, AND OTHER POEMS; PROMETHEUS UNBOUND.

Melanie Ord, School of English, University of Liverpool.
Author: TRAVEL WRITING: BRITAIN.

Peter Otto, Department of English and Cultural Studies, University of Melbourne.
Author: BLAKE, WILLIAM; FRANKENSTEIN; GOTHIC FICTION; IMAGINATION; LOUTHERBOURG, PHILIPPE JACQUES; MARRIAGE OF HEAVEN AND HELL, THE; SUBLIME, THE.

Lisa Paddock
Author: BRONTË, EMILY; WUTHERING HEIGHTS.

Brigida Pastor, Department of Hispanic Studies, University of Glasgow.
Author: GÓMEZ DE AVELLANEDA, GERTRUDIS.

David Patterson, Oxford Centre for Hebrew and Jewish Studies.
Author: MAPU, ABRAHAM.

Melissa Percival, Department of French, University of Exeter.
Author: SELF-PORTRAIT AT AN EASEL; VIGÉE-LEBRUN, ÉLISABETH.

Ralph Peters
Author: CLAUSEWITZ, CARL (PHILIPP GOTTLIEB) VON; WAR.

Anthony Phelan, Keble College.
Author: FAUST; HEINE, HEINRICH; POETRY: GERMANY; ROMANZERO.

Pamela Pilbeam, Department of History, Royal Holloway and Bedford New College, London.
Author: FOURIER, CHARLES; PROUDHON, PIERRE-JOSEPH; SAINT-SIMON, CLAUDE-HENRI DE ROUVROY, COMTE DE.

Johan Pillai, Department of English Literature and Humanities, Eastern Mediterranean University.
Author: FRAGMENT; IRONY, ROMANTIC; LITERATURE; MODERNITY; RATIONALITY AND IRRATIONALITY; SADE, DONATIEN-ALPHONSE-FRANÇOIS, MARQUIS DE; SUPERNATURAL, THE; TRANSLATION.

Lynne Press
Author: Alfieri, Vittorio; Canti; Foscolo, Niccolò; Leopardi, Giacomo; Ultime Lettere di Jacopo Ortis.

Fiona Price
Author: Dacre, Charlotte.

Roger Price, Department of History, University of Wales, Aberystwyth.
Author: Thiers, (Louis-) Adolphe.

Charles Pullen
Author: Bonington, Richard Parkes; Corot, (Jean-Baptiste-) Camille; Cotman, John Sell; Courbet, Gustave; Gainsborough, Thomas.

Paolo Rambelli, Department of Italian, University College London.
Author: Cuoco, Vincenzo; Piranesi, Giovanni Battista.

Alex Rehding, Joseph Henry House, Society of Fellows in the Liberal Arts.
Author: Symphony No. 9; Tannhäuser.

Johann Reusch, Department of Fine and Performing Arts, City University of New York, Baruch College.
Author: Forster, Georg.

Glynis Ridley, School of English, Queen's University of Belfast.
Author: Journals and periodicals: United States; Landscape and garden design; Letters: Britain; Letters: United States; Liberty; West, Benjamin.

Felizitas Ringham, Department of French, Birkbeck College, London.
Author: Bertrand, Aloysius; Desbordes-Valmore, Marceline.

Adam Roberts, Department of English, Royal Holloway and Bedford New College, London.
Author: Carlyle, Thomas; In Memoriam; Lady of Shalott, The; Tennyson, Alfred, Lord.

William S. Rodner, Department of History, Old Dominion University.
Author: Snow Storm: Steam Boat off a Harbour's Mouth.

Birgit Roeder, Department of German Studies, University of Reading.
Author: Fouqué, Friedrich Heinrich Karl de la Motte; Nachtstücke; Natchwachen des Bonaventura, Die.

Ekaterina Rogatchevskaia, Department of Slavonic Languages and Literatures, University of Glasgow.
Author: Griboedov, Aleksandr Sergeyevich; Hero of Our Time; Lermontov, Mikhail.

Andrei Rogatchevski, Department of Slavonic Languages and Literature, University of Glasgow.
Author: Bronze Horseman; Eugene Onegin; Overcoat, The (Shinel).

Joseph Rosenblum
Author: Brownson, Orestes Augustus; Literary Criticism: Britain; Longfellow, Henry Wadsworth.

Chris Routledge
Author: Melville, Herman; Moby-Dick; Poe, Edgar Allan; Tales (Poe).

Michael Rowe, School of Modern History, Queen's University of Belfast.
Author: Bonaparte, Napoleon; France: Revolution and Empire.

Nicolaas Rupke, Institut für Wissenschaftsgeschichte.
Author: Naturphilosophie; Oken, Lorenz.

Sharon Ruston, Department of English and Linguistics, University of Wales Bangor.
Author: Davy, Humphry; electricity and magnetism.

Christine Rydel, Department of Modern Languages and Literatures, Grand Valley State University.
Author: Gogol, Nikolay Vasilyevich; Journals and periodicals: Russia; Khomyakov, Aleksey Stepanovich; Russia: cultural survey; Tyutchev, Fyodor.

Jonathan Sachs, Department of English, University of Chicago.
Author: Niebuhr, Barthold Georg; Sismondi, Jean Charles Léonard Sismonde de.

Diego Saglia, Dipartimento di Lingue e Letterature Straniere, Universita di Parma.
Author: Berchet, Giovanni; Don Juan: themes and contexts; Repton, Humphry.

Roger Sales, School of English and American Studies, University of East Anglia.
Author: Clare, John; Duelling; Madness.

Robert Samuels, Music Department, The Open University.
Author: Schubert, Franz; Winterreise, Die.

Cherry Sandover
Author: Canova, Antonio; Lawrence, Thomas; sculpture.

Benedict Sarnaker, Goldsmiths College, London.
Author: Barber of Seville, The (Il Barbiere di Siviglia); Donizetti, Gaetano; Guillaume Tell (William Tell); onslow, George; Rossini, Gioacchino; Weber, Carl Maria Ernst.

Rachel Sauvé, Department of French Studies, Universite du Nouveau-Brunswick.
Author: Agoult, Marie d'.

Alexandra Schein
Author: Bulfinch, Charles; Napoleon in the Pest House at Jaffa.

Barry P. Scherr, Department of Russian, Dartmouth College.
Author: Belinsky, Vissarion Grigoryevich; Herzen, Aleksandr Ivanovich.

Esther Schor, Department of English, Princeton University.
Author: Mendelssohn, Moses; Nahman (Reb Nakhmen) of Bratslav.

Alison Scott, Collection Development, Harvard University.
Author: Bryant, William Cullen; Child, Lydia Maria; Sensibility; Vindication of the Rights of Woman, A; Wollstonecraft, Mary.

Elizabeth Ann Sears, Wheaton College.
Author: Bellini, Vincenzo; Fidelio.

Stephen Shapiro, Department of English and Comparative Literary Studies, University of Warwick.
Author: BROWN, CHARLES BROCKDEN.

Karl Simms, Department of English Language & Literature, University of Liverpool.
Author: GODWIN, WILLIAM; KIERKEGAARD, SØREN.

Karen Simons, Department of English, University of Alberta.
Author: CLASSICAL ANTIQUITY.

Christopher Smith
Author: CHATTERTON; CROME, JOHN; DESCHAMPS (DE SAINT-AMAND), ÉMILE AND ANTOINE; FREISCHÜTZ, DER; GLINKA, MIKHAIL IVANOVICH; HEBRIDES OVERTURE; LIND, JENNY; MURGER, HENRY; PAGANINI, NICCOLÒ; SPONTINI, GASPARE; VIGNY, ALFRED.

Robert C. Solomon, Department of Philosophy, University of Texas at Austin.
Author: HEGEL, GEORG WILHELM FRIEDRICH; PHENOMENOLOGY OF MIND.

Robert Southard, Department of History, Earlham College.
Author: HASKALAH; HESS, MOSES; JOURNALS AND PERIODICALS: JEWISH; JUDAISM; KROCHMAL, NACHMAN; LEBENSOHN, ABRAHAM AND MICHA JOSEPH; MAIMON, SOLOMON; SAVIGNY, FRIEDRICH KARL VON; ZUNZ, LEOPOLD.

W. A. Speck.
Author: SOUTHEY, ROBERT.

Erin Stapleton-Corcoran, University of Chicago.
MUSIC, ROMANTIC: AFTER 1850.

Henriette B. Stavis
Author: HAMANN, JOHANN GEORG; SONGS OF INNOCENCE AND EXPERIENCE.

Arne and Henriette B. Stavis
Author: BLICHER, STEEN STEENSEN.

Daniel Steuer, School of European Studies (German), University of Sussex.
Author: LICHTENBERG, GEORG CHRISTOPH; NATURE.

Kris Steyaert, Department of Dutch Studies, University of Hull.
Author: BILDERDIJK, WILLEM; CONSCIENCE, HENDRIK.

Benedikt Stuchtey, German Historical Institute.
Author: HISTORIOGRAPHY: GERMANY; HUMBOLDT, ALEXANDER VON; RANKE, LEOPOLD VON.

Andrew Swensen, Department of Germanic and Slavic Languages, Brandeis University.
Author: POLITICAL THOUGHT; THEOLOGY AND RELIGIOUS THOUGHT.

Barry Symonds, Department of English, University of Manchester.
Author: CONFESSIONS OF AN ENGLISH OPIUM EATER; DE QUINCEY, THOMAS.

Gurion Taussig
Author: FRATERNITY.

Julia Thomas, Department of English, Cardiff University.
Author: BOOK ILLUSTRATION; OPHELIA; WILKIE, DAVID.

Claire Thomson, School of Language, Linguistics and Translation Studies, University of East Anglia.
Author: GRUNDTVIG, NIKOLAI FREDERIK SEVERIN; INGEMANN, BERNHARD SEVERIN; NATIONALISM; OEHLENSCHLÄGER, ADAM GOTTLOB; PALUDAN-MÜLLER, FREDERIK.

Michael Tilby, Selwyn College, University of Cambridge.
Author: BÉRANGER, PIERRE-JEAN DE; BOREL, PETRUS; CONSTANT DE REBECQUE, (HENRI-) BENJAMIN; HUET, PAUL; STAËL, ANNE-LOUISE-GERMAINE (MADAME) DE.

Margaret Topping, School of European Studies, Cardiff University.
Author: CHASSÉRIAU, THÉODORE; VERNET, (ÉMILE-JEAN-) HORACE.

David McNeill Vallins, Department of English Language and Literature, University of Hiroshima.
Author: GENIUS.

Ton van Kalmthout, University of Groningen.
Author: NETHERLANDS: CULTURAL SURVEY.

William Vaughan
Author: TURNER, JMW.

Dietrich von Engelhardt, Institut fur Medizin und Wissenschaftsgeschichte.
Author: MEDICINE; NATURAL SCIENCES; OERSTED, HANS CHRISTIAN; STEFFENS, HENRIK.

Robert Ward, School of English, University of Leeds.
Author: CRIME AND PUNISHMENT.

Jeffrey Wasson, Barat College, DePaul University.
Author: GOUNOD, CHARLES; WAGNER, RICHARD.

Marie Wells
Author: ASBLJØTRNSEN, PETER CHRISTEN AND MOE, JØRGEN ENGEBRETSEN; DAHL, JENS (JOHANN) CHRISTIAN CLAUSEN; WELHAVEN, JOHAN SEBASTIEN; WERGELAND, HENRIK ARNOLD.

Nicolas White, Emmanuel College.
Author: ROUGE ET LE NOIR, LE; SAND, GEORGE; STENDHAL.

J. J. White, Department of German, King's College, London.
Author: PETER SCHLEMIHLS WUNDERSAME GESCHICHTE.

Peter J. Whyte, Chapel House.
Author: GAUTIER, THÉOPHILE; MADEMOISELLE DE MAUPIN.

Christopher J. Wickham, Department of German, University of Texas at San Antonio.
Author: CHAMISSO, ADELBERT VON.

Alexandra Wilson, Junior Research Fellow in Music, Worcester College.
Author: CHORAL MUSIC; MUSIC: PERFORMANCE AND PATRONAGE.

Susan Wolfson, Department of English, Princeton University.
Author: BRITISH ROMANTICISM: ITS LITERARY LEGACY; HOOD, THOMAS; LYRICAL BALLADS; WORDSWORTH, WILLIAM.

Susan Wollenberg, Lady Margaret Hall, Oxford University.
Author: CLEMENTI, MUZIO.

Sarah Wood
  Author: Crèvecoeur, Michel-Guillaume-Saint-Jean de; Portrait and self-portrait: United States.

Gregory Woods, Department of English and Media Studies, Nottingham Trent University.
  Author: Gay Approaches to the Romantic Period; Homosexuality.

Sarah Wootton
  Author: Palmer, Samuel; Pre-Raphaelite Brotherhood.

Karin A. Wurst, Department of Linguistics, Michigan State University.
  Author: Fashion; Lenz, Jakob Michael Reinhold; Love, Romantic.

Jennifer Yee, Department of French Studies, University of Newcastle.
  Author: Nerval, Gérard de; René.

Stephen Zank, School of Music, University of Illionois at Urbana-Champaign.
  Author: Moments musicaux; Piano; Violin Concerto.

ENCYCLOPEDIA OF THE

ROMANTIC ERA,

1760–1850

A

ABILDGAARD, NICOLAI ABRAHAM 1743–1809

Danish painter and architect

Nicolai Abraham Abildgaard occupies a prominent place in the history of Danish art at the time of transition from the neoclassicist era to the Romantic era. A competent linguist, well-read and acquainted with the doctrine of neoclassicism, Abildgaard intended to establish a Danish equivalent to the grand style in history painting, as advocated in England by his contemporary James Barry. Furthermore, Abildgaard was an exponent of the aesthetics of the sublime, inspired by and thoroughly familiar with the works of Edmund Burke, Johann Gottfried Herder, and Gotthold Ephraim Lessing. His subjects were found not only among the ancient Roman and Greek writers, but also in the works of William Shakespeare and Ossian, and he was among the first artists to deal with themes from Norse mythology and ancient Danish history, thereby paving the way for a Danish "national" iconography. Abildgaard expressed his talents in all areas of art, working as a painter, an architect, and a designer of interiors, furniture, and monumental sculpture. While occupying the positions of official court painter, and professor and director of the Royal Danish Academy of Fine Arts in Copenhagen, Abildgaard expressed himself as a pre-Romantic revolutionary artist. According to Patrick Kragelund, the Danish scholar whose studies of Abildgaard's work are the most thorough to date, the artist's subjects reflect a constant development of his attitude toward important contemporary events, and his choice of subject matter may be perceived as one continuous world vision.

In 1764, ten years after the establishment of the Danish Academy, Abildgaard was admitted as a student. He was awarded the academy's traveling scholarship in 1771, which lead to him finishing his studies with a stay in Rome from 1772 to 1777. While in Rome, he moved within a circle of artist friends, including Johan Tobias Sergel, the Swedish sculptor, and the Swiss-born artist Henry Fuseli; and apart from his study of classical sculpture, Abildgaard's main areas of interest were the work of Annibale Carracci, Michelangelo, Raphael, and Giulio Romano. Yet he was fascinated also by the aesthetics of Sturm und Drang, which attracted much attention from artists in 1770s Rome. His principal work from this period is a remarkable depiction of *Philoctetes* (1774–75; Statens Museum for Kunst, Copenhagen). Inspired by German philosopher Lessing's treatise *Laocoon* (1766), Abildgaard presents the wounded Philoctetes, who clearly conveys his suffering not only by means of his facial expression and tearful eyes, but also through his entire body, twisted in pain. Abildgaard's interpretation of this subject constituted a break with Johann Joachim Winckelmann's notion of serenity, which is supposedly characteristic of truly classical Greek art. Likewise, it contrasted sharply with Barry's version of this theme in a painting executed for the Accademia Clementina in Bologna in 1770. Abildgaard's *Philoctetes* has been conceived as a manifesto of art, reflecting pre-Romantic ideals in the art of painting. At this point, the presentation of ideal, heroic subjects is replaced by the description of individual frames of mind.

During his stay in Rome, Abildgaard was further introduced to other literary worlds, as found in the works of the three "original" geniuses: Homer, Ossian, and William Shakespeare. Inspired by Fuseli's great enthusiasm for Shakespeare, Abildgaard decided to illustrate the same set of tragedies as chosen by the Swiss artist, in particular works such as *Hamlet, Richard III,* and *Macbeth,* which contain supernatural events, ghosts, and omens, and he worked on dreamy scenes with a distinctly Gothic atmosphere, for example, *Richard III Waking from His Nightmare* (1787), *Richard III Threatened in His Dreams by the Ghosts of His Victims* (1780s), and *Hamlet and His Mother Seeing His Father's Ghost* (1770s?). However, the first scene from *Hamlet* treated by Abildgaard, *Hamlet Visiting the Queen of Scotland* (1776), had not been borrowed from Shakespeare: it was found in the bard's Danish source of inspiration, the medieval historian Saxo Grammaticus, whose principal work, *Gesta Danorum* (1185–1222), was sent to Abildgaard in Rome. For some time, subjects from Greek and Roman antiquity were thus replaced with Nordic characters, with the artist aiming to evoke a grim and brutal past through his use of imaginative modification of clothing, props, and highly emotional figures. Abildgaard's appreciation of the Ossianic poems was almost certainly a result of his associations with British artists in Rome, and he appears to be one of the first artists outside of Great Britain to have illustrated the work of the Celtic bard (the veracity of which was eventually disputed). His interest extended to the acquisition of several annotated editions of James Macpherson's poems of Ossian, in which Abildgaard had marked scenes suitable for artistic treatment. Time and again, Abildgaard returned to this circle of themes, choosing to depict somber, tragic scenes from the heroic poems *Fingal* and *Temora*, such as his *Cathmor by the Corpse of Fillan, Fillan's Ghost Appears before Fingal, Cathmor and Sulmalla*, and *Fingal Gives His Weapons to Ossian* (all c. 1790), in sepia drawings as well as paintings. In spite of his use of Gothic props, Abildgaard viewed the heroes of Norse mythology from a classical perspective. His masterpiece from this period is the eponymous, small painting of the blind Ossian (c. 1785; Statens Museum for Kunst, Copenhagen), a tremendously passionate portrayal of the bard as wild and primitive: a solitary figure, alone with his harp, singing into a snow-clad and windswept, wooded landscape.

Upon his return to Copenhagen in 1777, Abildgaard was commissioned to execute a series of paintings with subjects from the national history of Denmark, or, more specifically, the history of the Danish royal dynasty. This commission, painted for the royal palace of Christiansborg between 1778 and 1791, gave the artist an opportunity to devise a formula for modern history painting. He decided that the series should be a glorification of the ideals of the Enlightenment: education, instruction, and knowledge, expressed in both allegorical and quasi-realistic scenes. This picture poem on the history of Denmark, which was to become Abildgaard's most outstanding work, suffered a tragic fate: only three out of twenty-five original paintings survived a fire in 1794, although a number of oil sketches do remain.

With censorship in Denmark having been abolished in 1770, Abildgaard contributed to open public debate through allegories and social satire in different media and forms. As a prorevolutionary artist, he took a keen interest in the political and social conflicts of his time—for example, in 1788 as the originator and designer of draft plans for a monument to commemorate the abolition of serfdom in Denmark. The monument was executed as a cooperative piece by three sculptors after Abildgaard's design and, under his direction, was erected in 1797 outside one of the Copenhagen town gates; here it enjoys a unique status, having been built by the citizens of the capital to commemorate the emancipation of the peasants. On a 1792 medal, struck in remembrance of the abolition of slavery in the Danish colonies, Abildgaard uses classic imagery in his reference to the recently declared rights of man. In place of the king is a profile portrait of the black slave; on the reverse, a classic depiction of a winged

The Spirit of Culmin Appears to His Mother, from *The Songs of Ossian*. Reprinted courtesy of the Bridgeman Art Library.

nemesis. Contemporaneously, Abildgaard refers in another work to the cult of the noble savage, in a 1795 painting that forms part of a series of interior decorations in the royal palace of Amalienborg, Copenhagen. Here, in a suppraporte, he represented *Dance Scene from Tahiti* (1794), a South Sea motif inspired by an illustration in Captain James Cook's *Voyage to the Pacific Ocean* (1785). This motif has been introduced as representing the fifth continent, a subtle supplement to the current iconography linked to allegories on the four continents. Illustrations by the atheist Abildgaard for the classic Danish utopian novel *The Travels of Niels Klim* (1789), by Ludvig Holberg, constitute a bitter attack on the church. His illustrations for the *Collected Works* (1780) of the Danish poet Johannes Ewald caused much sensation and indignation at the time. This was due to the quite shameless approach taken by the artist in praising the naked human body and the "natural" relationship between man and woman in the Garden of Eden. Danish censorship was reintroduced in 1791. This was also the year in which Abildgaard was dismissed as court painter and director of the Royal Academy, and subsequently he undertook architectural and pictorial adornment of buildings such as the Levetzau Mansion at Amalienborg (for the royal family) and a citizen's house in Nytorv Square, Copenhagen. The latter was adorned with paintings of subjects from Voltaire's Roman tragedy *Le Triumvirat*. For his own home at the Academy (Charlottenborg, Copenhagen), Abildgaard executed four large paintings of scenes from Terence's comedy *The Woman of Andros* (1801–4; Statens Museum for Kunst, Copenhagen); as architectural pieces, these are most significant as visions of the Athens of antiquity.

Although Abildgaard was a professor at the Royal Academy for several years from 1778 until his death in 1809, he has no direct successors in the history of Danish art. Among his pupils we find Asmus Jacob Carstens (pupil, 1776–81), Caspar David Friedrich (pupil, 1794–98), and Philipp Otto Runge (pupil 1799–1801). All three were strongly influenced by their meeting with Abildgaard and his distinct views, with regard to the philosophical and poetic dimensions of pictorial art, as well as pertaining to the freedom of the artist as a "citizen of the republic of artists"; here, according to Abildgaard, the artist is his own master.

METTE BLIGAARD

Biography

Born in Copenhagen on September 11, 1743, the son of the painter Sören Abildegaard. Apprenticed as a decorative painter to J. E. Mandelberg. Entered the Royal Danish Academy of Fine Arts in Copenhagen around 1764. Won the academy's silver and gold medals 1765, 1766, and 1767. Awarded traveling scholarship to Rome, 1771. Lived and studied in Rome, associating with artists Johan Tobias Sergel and Henry Fuseli, among others, 1772–77. Returned to Copenhagen via Paris, 1777. Professor at the Royal Academy, Copenhagen, from 1778; director, 1789–91 and 1801–9. Commissioned to decorate Schloss Christiansborg, 1780–91, and later the Amalienborg Palace. Member of the Berlin Royal Academy, 1788. Engaged in design of interiors, furniture, and architecture from 1790s on. Member of the Accademia in Florence, 1808. Died in Sorgenfri (Frederiksdal?), near Copenhagen, June 4, 1809.

Bibliography

Kragelund, Patrick. *Abildgaard around 1800: His Tragedy and Comedy*. Analecta Romana Instituti Danici 16. Rome: L'Erma, 1987. 137–83.

———. *Abildgaard, Homer and the Dawn of the Millennium*. Analecta Romana Instituti Danici 17–18. Rome: L'Erma, 1989. 181–224.

———. *Abildgaard, kunstneren mellem oprørerne I–II*. Copenhagen: Museum Tusculanum, 1999.

———. "Nicolai Abildgaard and the Wounded Philoctetes," in *Art in Rome in the Eighteenth Century*. Philadelphia: Philadelphia Art Museum, 2000.

Sass, Else Kai. *Lykkens tempel*. Copenhagen: Gyldendal, 1986.

Swane, Leo. *Abildgaard. Arkitektur og Dekoration*. Copenhagen: Kunstakademiets Arkitektskole, 1926.

ADOLPHE 1816

Novel by Henri-Benjamin Constant de Rebecque

Like his unfinished novel *Cécile* and his *Journaux intimes* (diaries), with which its genesis is inextricably linked, Henri-Benjamin Constant de Rebecque's *Adolphe* is rooted in the emotional entanglement of the author's divided affections for two women, Charlotte von Hardenberg and Anne-Louise-Germaine de Staël during the second half of the year 1806, when, still living and working on treatises on politics and religion in the entourage of the latter, he fell passionately in love with the former. Though Constant and Hardenberg were to be (secretly) married in June 1808 and his final break with Madame de Staël would occur in 1811, he delayed publishing his novel, which was probably completed by 1810 if not before, until 1816—mainly, it is thought, to avoid offending Staël. Upon its publication the novel was naturally read as a roman à clef by a public familiar with its author's relationships, leading him to the dubious assertion in the preface to the second edition (1816) that "none of the characters drawn in *Adolphe* has any link with any individual."

Constant, who was closely associated with Staël and the Coppet group (Coppet was the name of Staël's estate in Switzerland, where her salon met), was a supporter of the incipient Romantic movement, and *Adolphe* is often considered to be a masterpiece of the Romantic or pre-Romantic novel. His preoccupation with the uniqueness of the individual; with the complexity and fluidity of human emotions; with the importance of nuances and the emptiness of general laws and principles; with the transitoriness of life and the insufficiency of language to express the subtleties of human feelings and thought are major themes of his works—and particularly of *Adolphe*—that link him to the Romantic movement. Indeed, the main protagonist and narrator of *Adolphe* is often held to be a characteristic Romantic hero in terms of his introspection, alienation, and sensibility. Critics have established links with other significant texts of the early Romantic canon: Jean-Jacques Rousseau's *Nouvelle Héloïse* (*The New Eloise*, 1761), Johann Wolfgang von Goethe's *Die Leiden des jungen Werthers* (*The Sorrows of Young Werther*, 1774), and François-Auguste-René, Vicomte de Chateaubriand's *René* (1802), as well as novels by Sophie Cottin and Madame de Staël. Closer affinities have been traced to a novel by Isabelle de Charrière, *Caliste* (1787), for Constant knew well and admired the work and the author. But the structural rigour of *Adolphe*; its concentrated and unified action, which are commonly compared to the essential features of classical tragedy; the lack of lyricism and concrete description; and the pellucid style have invited parallels with earlier traditions: the French *moralistes* of the seventeenth century and the analytical novel as represented notably by Marie-Madeleine de La Fayette's *La Princesse de Clèves* (1678) or l'abbé Prévost's *Manon Lescaut* (1731). On this question, Charles Bruneau's general assertion is frequently quoted: "Romantic in its ideas, the novel *Adolphe* seems to us today, in general, to be classical in its language." Such dichotomies do not, however, do justice to the complexity of Constant's novel. To take another familiar generic reading of *Adolphe*, it has been pointed out that it begins as a narrative of seduction in the manner of *Les Égarements du coeur et de l'esprit* (*The Wayward Head and Heart*, 1736) by Crébillon *fils* or of *Les Liaisons dangereuses* (*Dangerous Acquaintances*, 1782) by Pierre Ambroise François Choderlos de Laclos—both of which, in fact, could serve as alternative titles for Constant's text. But *Adolphe* is clearly written against the libertine moral, as it demonstrates the very opposite of the frivolous view of the hero's father on the virtues of the casual relation with women: "It does them so little harm, and gives us so much pleasure." Furthermore, the paratextual framing of *Adolphe*'s narrative by the third-person commentaries of the "publisher" and his correspondent not only rework the conventional authenticating and distancing device of the lost manuscript but also provide alternative readings of the story, to which the reader is implicitly invited to respond.

The confession of Constant's narrator, though orchestrated and articulated in the forms and language of prestigious literary traditions, gives expression to a more modern sensibility and system of values, as if he were playing original airs on antiquated instruments. Constant claimed to be representing in his novel a contemporary malaise: the lack of strength and direction among his contemporaries, their inability to love with constancy or believe with fervor. While denouncing the cynicism and scepticism of his society and its attachment to artificial conventions, the narrator admits agonizingly his own inability to transcend the constraints that society imposes. On the one hand, he condemns the self-seeking and hypocrisy of society and its representatives in favour of the higher demands of a "natural heart," but on the other hand, he reveals that his natural feelings are nonetheless subjected to self-interested calculation. His love is doomed to extinction even in the very throes of its conception. Neither commitment with its fetters nor freedom with its dreadful burden of loneliness provide a solution for his restless spirit.

When it was first published, *Adolphe* was not particularly well received by its author's contemporaries; Stendhal was lukewarm in his assessment and Charles-Augustin Sainte-Beuve at first quite hostile. Objective evaluations of the novel were usually hampered by speculation about its biographical sources and by commentaries on the conduct of its hero. Nevertheless, it prompted Honoré de Balzac—in *Béatrix* (1839) and especially in *La Muse du département* (*The Muse of the Department*, 1843) to write novels in reaction to Constant's text. Aleksandr Pushkin and Lev Tolstoy paid Constant the compliment of borrowing certain features of his novel in their own works. But generally, in France, it was only toward the end of the nineteenth century that the novel eventually received its due, when it was heralded as a supreme example of the psychological novel. In his preface to the 1889 edition of the novel, for example, Paul Bourget declared it to be "the masterpiece of the novel of analysis." However, as Dennis Wood has argued in his study of the novel, if

Constant's masterly exploration of such dualities as freedom and duty, egoism and unselfishness, alienation and social obligation, certainty and doubt, is "profoundly Romantic," its relevance applies as much to the modern era as to the age of the novel's conception.

DAVID BAGULEY

Text

Adolphe; anecdote trouvée dans les papiers d'un inconnu, et publiée par M. Benjamin de Constant (1816). Edited by C. P. Courtney. Oxford: Blackwell, 1989.
Translation: *Adolphe*. Trans. Alexander Walker, 1816. Trans. L. W. Tancock, 1964.

Bibliography

Alexander, Ian W. *Benjamin Constant: "Adolphe."* London: Arnold, 1973.
Bourget, Paul. *Essais de psychologie contemporaine*. Paris: Plon-Nourrit, 1924.
Cruickshank, John. *Benjamin Constant*. New York: Twayne, 1974.
Delbouille, Paul. *Genèse, structure et destin d' "Adolphe."* Paris: Les Belles Lettres, 1971.
Fairlie, Alison. "Constant," in *Imagination and Language: Collected Essays on Constant, Baudelaire and Flaubert*. Cambridge: Cambridge University Press, 1981.
Scott, Malcolm. "The Romanticism of *Adolphe.*" *Nottingham French Studies* 6, no. 2 (1967): 58–66.
Unwin, Timothy. *Constant: "Adolphe."* London: Grant and Cutler, 1986.
Valloton, François. *Bibliographie analytique des écrits sur Benjamin Constant (1980–1995)*. Paris: Champion and Geneva: Slatkine, 1997.
Wood, Dennis. *Benjamin Constant: "Adolphe."* Cambridge: Cambridge University Press, 1987.
———. *Benjamin Constant: A Biography*. London: Routledge, 1993.

AESTHETICS AND ART CRITICISM

It was not until the mid-eighteenth century that aesthetics emerged as an autonomous discipline concerned with the study of artistic creativity, aesthetic experience, and the interpretation and evaluation of art. Its definition in treatises, such as Alexander Baumgarten's *Aesthetica* (*Aesthetics*, 1752–58) and J. G. Sulzer's *Allgemeine Theorie der schönen Künst* (*General Theory of Fine Arts*, 1771), has to be understood as a product of the desire to gain a rational understanding of human experience that the philosophers of the Enlightenment inherited from their predecessors in classical antiquity. Indeed the aesthetic ideas expounded by many thinkers of the period illustrate the importance neoclassicism assumed in eighteenth-century thought. The association of beauty with formal balance and symmetry, perfect proportions, and simplicity was a reflection of Enlightenment thinkers' reverence for the art and culture of antiquity, which was inextricably linked to their reverence for nature. It was in accordance with Plato's view that the artistic representation of nature in an idealized state inspired moral virtue that the neoclassical doctrine of mimesis (imitation) was appropriated as the cornerstone of eighteenth-century aesthetic theory. The doctrine of mimesis—that the purpose of art is to represent or imitate nature—informed the critical reception of all the arts in the

mid-eighteenth century, as suggested by Jean-Baptiste Du Bos's statement that "just as the painter imitates the forms and colours of nature so the musician imitates the tones of the voice—its accents, sighs and inflections."

While the "back-to-nature" cult of Jean-Jacques Rousseau legitimized the artistic representation of nature in all its diversity, the neoclassical view, that only when represented in an idealized state could nature be deemed beautiful, resonated in the cult of *Empfindsamkeit* (sensibility), through which art became endowed with an expressive capacity. The aesthetic embodied in Jean-Honoré Fragonard's *The Swing* (1768), Carl Philipp Emanuel Bach's *Charakterstücken* (character pieces), and Laurence Sterne's *A Sentimental Journey through France and Italy* (1768) demanded that art display good taste and appeal to the delicacy of one's soul—a demand that was to provide a learned excuse for eroticism in art.

A more radical departure from neoclassicism, as a school of thought that ensured the hegemony of French culture for the first two-thirds of the eighteenth century, was the aesthetic articulated by thinkers of the Sturm und Drang movement of the 1770s, prominent among whom were Johann Wolfgang von Goethe, Johann Georg Hamann, and Johann Gottfried von

Herder. Their desire to revive German mysticism and their pantheistic view of nature informed their conception of art as "another nature, also mysterious like her but more intelligible" which, as an expression of the "divine inspiration" of the artist as a genius, awakens in the discerning recipient a sense of spirituality (Goethe, 1840). They rejected the view, propounded by Enlightenment philosophers, of the art and culture of antiquity as the benchmark against which to evaluate that of all ages, and celebrated the diversity of art as an expression of the diversity of the human spirit. Accordingly they championed Gothic architecture, Rembrandt's paintings, and William Shakespeare's plays, all of which were previously denigrated for their failure to conform to neoclassical standards of taste or eighteenth-century notions of beauty.

The aesthetic category invoked by thinkers of the Sturm und Drang movement to justify their reevaluation of such diverse art forms was the sublime, influentially formulated by Edmund Burke in 1757 to describe aspects of nature and art that inspire feelings of awe, fear, and terror. This enabled writers to explain the diversity of the aesthetic experiences to which art gives rise, experiences previously unaccounted for by the notion of the beautiful. Thus Goethe suggested that, on viewing Strasbourg Minster, his "soul was suffused with a feeling of immense grandeur" akin to that one associates with "the joys of heaven" (1772). This proto-Romantic aesthetic eclipsed the neoclassicism of the French Enlightenment and established Germany as the homeland of Romanticism.

The strong continuum in the history of ideas between the Sturm und Drang and Romantic literary movements is reflected in the kinship between the pantheism of thinkers like Goethe and the philosophical idealism of Friedrich Wilhelm Joseph von Schelling and Johann Gottlieb Fichte; in the concomitant view of art as the counterpart of nature that they shared; and in the Romantics' endorsement of the historical relativism of which Herder was the most lucid exponent. The view the Romantics shared with their literary predecessors of the art of genius as a metaphysical medium evocative of the sublime found embodiment in the paintings of Caspar David Friedrich.

The origin of the divergence of the aesthetic thought of the Romantics from that of thinkers of the Sturm und Drang movement was their assimilation of Immanuel Kant's insight that "a striving toward knowledge of the infinite, was a rational, and not merely irrational, striving." They reembraced the faculty of reason—the highest authority invoked by the philosophers of the Enlightenment—as the essential counterpart of emotion in spiritual and aesthetic experience, and in artistic creativity. Thus, E. T. A. Hoffmann propounded a twofold notion of an artistic genius, as one in possession of "divine inspiration" and "rational awareness"; and Jean-Paul Richter emphasized that "passive geniuses," gifted with the sensibility to appreciate art, "rule over their powers with reflective imagination."

The aesthetic thought of the Romantics was also informed by a more sophisticated sense of historical awareness than that of their literary predecessors. They did not merely champion art produced since antiquity in all its diversity (while bemoaning the spiritual poverty of much created in the eighteenth century), but maintained that contemporary artists ought to aspire to emulate the spirituality of art of bygone golden ages in an original form expressive of their individuality. This ideal was realized in much of Ludwig van Beethoven's late music, which in its

Strasbourg Cathedral. Reprinted courtesy of Bildarchiv.

contrapuntal complexity pays homage to Johann Sebastian Bach, and, arguably, in the paintings of the Nazarenes. In their insistence on the necessity for art to display originality, the Romantics, once again, betrayed their debt to Immanuel Kant, who stated that "the foremost property of genius must be originality." It was their appropriation of this aesthetic idea that underpinned the formation of a "canon" of artistic masterpieces of timeless aesthetic value.

The Romantics' view that art ought to be a product of the individuality of the artist was reflected in their conception of art as a form of personal emotional expression. This was voiced by William Wordsworth in the preface to *Lyrical Ballads* (1802), in which he famously described poetry as "the spontaneous overflow of powerful feeling," and by Robert Alexander Schumann, who conceived of art as an expression of the artist's personality. That *Sehnsucht* (longing)—for a higher realm, for the distant past, or for an unattainable beloved—was a central topos of Romantic art can be understood as a reflection of the Romantics' recognition of the close kinship of man's emotional and spiritual life, and of emotional expression as a means of endowing art with a spiritual meaning.

In the wake of the 1848 revolutions, the dominance of idealism, as the philosophy that underpinned the Romantic view of art as a metaphysical medium, gradually gave way to the emergence of realism and naturalism as the basis for aesthetic thought. The belief that art ought to depict ordinary people and everyday scenes in stark reality, rather than representing nature in an idealized state or attempting to evoke a higher, spiritual realm, was the aesthetic ideal to which Jean-François Millet and Gustave Courbet aspired in their paintings, and which the invention of photography made wholly realizable.

ABIGAIL CHANTLER

Bibliography

Abrams, M. H., ed. *The Norton Anthology of English Literature*, vol. 2. New York: Norton, 1993.

Ameriks, Karl, ed. *The Cambridge Companion to German Idealism*. Cambridge: Cambridge University Press, 2000.

Burke, Edmund. *A Philosophical Enquiry into the Origin of Our Ideas of the Sublime and the Beautiful*. Ed. Adam Phillips. Oxford: Oxford University Press, 1990.

Critchfield, Richard, and Wulf Koepke, eds. *Eighteenth-Century German Authors and Their Aesthetic Theories: Literature and the Other Arts*. Columbia, S.C.: Camden House, 1988.

Currie, Robert. *Genius: An Ideology in Literature*. London: Chatto and Windus, 1974.

Eagleton, Terry. *The Ideology of the Aesthetic*. Oxford: Blackwell, 1990.

Goethe, Johann Wolfgang von. *Essays on Art and Literature*. Ed. John Gearey, transl. Ellen von Nardroff and Ernest H. von Nardroff. Princeton, N.J.: Princeton University Press, 1986.

Harrison, Charles, Paul Wood, and Jason Gaiger, eds. *Art in Theory 1815–1900: An Anthology of Changing Ideas*. Oxford: Blackwell, 1998.

Hess, Jonathan M. *Reconstituting the Body Politic: Enlightenment, Public Culture and the Invention of Aesthetic Autonomy*. Detroit: Wayne State University Press, 1999.

Hoffmann, E. T. A. *E. T. A. Hoffmann's Musical Writings: Kreisleriana, The Poet and the Composer, Music Criticism*. Edited by David Charlton, translated by Martyn Clarke. Cambridge: Cambridge University Press, 1989.

Kant, Immanuel. *Critique of Judgment*. Translated by Werner S. Pluhar. Indianapolis: Hackett, 1987.

Le Huray, Peter, and James Day, eds. *Music and Aesthetics in the Eighteenth and Early Nineteenth Centuries*. Cambridge: Cambridge University Press, 1981.

Mattick, Paul Jr., ed. *Eighteenth-Century Aesthetics and the Reconstruction of Art*. Cambridge: Cambridge University Press, 1993.

Murray, Penelope, ed. *Genius: The History of an Idea*. Oxford: Blackwell, 1989.

Nisbet, H. B., ed. *German Aesthetic and Literary Criticism: Winkelmann, Lessing, Hamann, Schiller, Goethe*. Cambridge: Cambridge University Press, 1985.

Richter, Jean Paul. *Horn of Oberon: Jean Paul Richter's School for Aesthetics*. Translated by Margaret R. Hale. Detroit: Wayne State University Press, 1973.

Rosen, Charles, and Henri Zerner. *Romanticism and Realism: The Mythology of Nineteenth-Century Art*. London: Faber and Faber, 1984.

Sheppard, Anne. *Aesthetics: An Introduction to the Philosophy of Art*. Oxford: Oxford University Press, 1987.

Sheriff, Mary D. *Fragonard: Art and Eroticism*. Chicago: University of Chicago Press, 1990.

Simpson, David. "Commentary on the Sublime." *Studies in Romanticism* 26 (1987): 245–58.

———, ed. *The Origins of Modern Critical Thought: German Aesthetic and Literary Criticism from Lessing to Hegel*. Cambridge: Cambridge University Press, 1988.

Sterne, Laurence. *A Sentimental Journey through France and Italy*. Edited by Ian Jack. Oxford: Oxford University Press, 1998.

Vaughan, William. *German Romantic Painting*. New Haven, Conn.: Yale University Press, 1994.

Wheeler, Kathleen M., ed. *German Aesthetic and Literary Criticism: The Romantic Ironists and Goethe*. Cambridge: Cambridge University Press, 1984.

AGOULT, MARIE D' 1805–1876

French author

History and criticism retained Marie d'Agoult's name primarily as the companion of Franz Liszt and as an influential *salonnière*, but she was the author of over 150 articles; numerous essays, including her brilliant *Histoire de la Révolution de 1848*; intriguing memoirs on the Restoration; as well as thousands of letters to her numerous correspondents (Ralph Waldo Emerson, Georges Herwegh, Henri Lehmann, Giuseppe Mazzini, and Adam Mickiewicz). From the Monarchie de Juillet to the Second Empire she was a prominent figure of the Parisian intelligentsia. Although her position as a woman and an aristocrat did not allow her to enter the public sphere, she was close to those who shared her republican views, such as Émile de Girardin, Alphonse Marie Louis de Lamartine, Félicité Robert de Lamennais, and Charles-Augustin Sainte-Beuve, all of them important political and literary figures of her time. Her rehabilitation in literary history is still overdue, despite the publication of two major biographies in recent years. In fact, very few have been devoted to her works, which in turn have yet to be collected. Undoubtedly, George Sand's shadow was overbearing, and the genres Agoult exceled in (essay, history, journalism, and other nonfictional writings) have not been the focus of traditional or feminist literary criticism.

The first published works of Marie d'Agoult, who used the alias Daniel Stern, were articles signed by Liszt, her companion for nine years, as part of his series of *Lettres d'un bachelier ès musique*. She wrote her first literary review, on Sand's *Le Compagnon du Tour de France*, for *La Presse* in 1841. She took up her male, nonaristocratic pseudonym in 1843; outside literary circles, the true identity of Daniel Stern was to remain concealed for many years. Half German, she took a keen interest in the intellectual and religious effervescence of Germany that began in the 1830s, and she published a series of seven articles on this topic, as well as numerous literary and art reviews in *La Presse*, *La Revue des Deux Mondes*, and *la Revue indépendante* between 1841 and 1847. The interest in her novellas (*Julien, Hervé, Valentia*) stems mostly from the boldness of their themes (suicide, adultery, atheism), but Agoult would soon realize that her talent for fiction was limited and turn to other means of expression. In

1846 she published her only novel, *Nélida*, an autobiographical account, written in the third person, of her relationship with Liszt.

Agoult was the first to introduce Emerson's writings in France, and his influence is obvious in her daring *Essai sur la liberté* (1847), in which she postulates that the individual, the family, and the state are in chains, and that their evolution can only be achieved through their liberation from the institutions of the past. Her criticism of marriage, her stand for universal suffrage and for justice instead of charity, as well as her crude depiction of birth labor, were shocking for the times. Unlike the Saint-Simonians, to whom she was very close, she considered education, rather than sexual freedom, to be the cornerstone of women's emancipation. In 1849, she published her *Esquisses morales et politiques*, a collection of brief essays and aphorisms that summarized her opinions on the topics she had previously tackled.

Agoult's most important work is undoubtedly her *Histoire de la Révolution de 1848*, published between 1851 and 1853, and its main interest is the impartiality that she was able to maintain in the aftermath of the uprising of 1848. It can be argued that as a woman her incapacity to participate politically allowed her such a standpoint and made it possible for her to publish her work shortly after the revolution. Her research is based on newspaper articles, testimonies, archives, and police reports, and all points of view are represented, whether it be in her account of the shooting of the Boulevard des Capucines or of the abdication of Louis Philippe. Her substantial introduction constitutes an outstanding piece on the roots and the launching of the Revolution. Agoult published another historical study, *Histoire des commencements de la République des Pays-Bas*, in 1872, as well as plays on Marie Stuart and Jeanne d'Arc; the latter was performed in France and in Italy. In her later years she turned from politics to aesthetics in her writings, and her *Dante et Goethe* provides a brilliant synthesis of the various philosophical streams that nourished European civilization, revealing how Agoult was a tributary of both her Catholic and Protestant upbringing, of her travels through Europe, and of her epistolary contacts with other European thinkers. Unfortunately, she never finished her *Memoirs*, but the first book, recounting her childhood and her youth in the Faubourg Saint-Germain, renders with great perceptiveness the mores of the aristocracy during the time of the empire and the Restoration, and more particularly those related to marriage, which she criticizes openly and with great wit.

Marie d'Agoult is a truly modern European figure, and her writings, which are inspired by the thought of German, Italian, and French authors, call for a movement toward the unification and the democratization of an enlightened Europe. As a Romantic icon, she personified the power of passion both in her life and in her works, and she held on to her idealistic Romantic values while adjusting to the many political and social changes in France that she witnessed in her lifetime.

RACHEL SAUVÉ

Biography

Marie-Catherine-Sophie de Flavigny was born in 1805 in Frankfurt am Main to a German mother and a French father; she received an excellent education from her father. She was married to Charles d'Agoult in 1827, and had one living daughter when she separated from him in 1835 to join Franz Liszt in Switzerland. They had three children, the second of which, Cosima, was to marry Richard Wagner. In 1843, she came back to Paris and devoted herself to her writing while struggling with frequent bouts of depression, from which she suffered all her life, as well as with financial difficulties. She died in Paris in 1876.

Selected Works

Nélida. 1846.
Essai sur la liberté. 1847.
Esquisses morales et politiques. 1849.
Histoire de la Révolution de 1848. 1851–53.
Dante et Goethe. 1866.
Histoire des commencements de la République des Pays-Bas. 1872.
Julien, Hervé, and *Valentia*, la boîte aux lettres. 1883.

Bibliography

Bolster, Richard. *Marie d'Agoult, The Rebel Countess*. New Haven, Conn.: Yale University Press, 2000.
Stock-Morton, Phyllis. *The Life of Marie d'Agoult alias Daniel Stern*. Baltimore: Johns Hopkins University Press, 2000.
Vier, Jacques. *La Comtesse d'Agoult et son temps*. 6 vols. Paris: Armand Colin, 1963.

ALASTOR; OR THE SPIRIT OF SOLITUDE 1816

Poem by Percy Bysshe Shelley

Alastor, complete with its preface, was written in Bishopsgate, London, between September 10 and December 14, 1815. It was published, while Percy Bysshe Shelley was living in Rome, in his first volume of poetry, which took its title from the poem. The volume as a whole was originally not well regarded by its first reviewers (largely conservative periodicals), receiving its first lengthy favorable notice from John Gibson Lockhart in *Blackwood's Edinburgh Magazine* only in 1819. *Alastor* attracted most of the notice, and most of the blame. Favorable reviewers of *Alastor* drew their reader's attention to its place within a "new school" of poetry, that which we now think of as characteristic of the Romantic era. Its treatment of prominent Romantic themes and issues has meant it has maintained a position of importance and controversy within studies of the Romantic era, and within Shelley's corpus.

The poem tells the story of the solitary life and death of a poet. His mind is nurtured by nature ("Every sight and sound from the vast earth and the ambient air") and history ("all . . . which the sacred past / In truth or fable consecrates"). He remains alone, pursuing "Nature's most secret steps" through eastern countries that were associated by the eighteenth and early nineteenth centuries with the birth of human society and language. These two aspects of the poem—the study of nature and the eastern journey—have attracted much attention, as their apparent interests in living "naturally" and the formation of society seem to conflict with the habitual solitude of the poet. This sense is intensified as he rejects the advances of an "Arab maiden," preferring to pursue a vision he has seen in a dream of an ideal love in the form of a "veiled maid." The pursuit of this unreal love alienates him further from society until he embarks on a river journey in a "little shallop" into the Caucasus Mountains, where, still haunted by his vision, he dies.

These are the principal elements of the story, but *Alastor* is not a simple narrative. The story of the poet is framed at first by a preface, in which we are told (if obscurely) how we should read the poem, next by an epigraph from St. Augustine that comments ironically on the nature of a certain kind of love, and finally by the presence of a narrator who is similarly interested in the "deep mysteries" of nature and tells us the story. These framing devices encourage us to reflect critically: on them, their inconsistency with themselves and with the story, and on the ramifications they hold for our interpretation of the value of the poet's life, quest, and death. Their suggestion that the poem holds a complicated, even critical, relation to its protagonist is confirmed by its title: Alastor is not the name of the hero but a word derived from Greek meaning "avenging spirit"; the spirit of solitude, then, is not sanguine.

Alastor presents many interesting problems for interpretation and to a surprising degree the history of its critical reception is paradigmatic of changing attitudes to the literature of the Romantic era. In its treatment of common Romantic themes, particularly the poet's quest after the ideal, it is at once caught up with and departs from various Romantic formulations of the role of the poet and poetry. Most clearly, *Alastor* can be approached in terms of its engagements both with other works by Shelley and with that of other writers of the period. The time of the poem's composition marks the beginning of Shelley's most serious writing, where in poetry and prose he revisits the questions of the formation of the mind, the production and aim of the writing of poetry, and the involvement of the poet with society. It is read particularly frequently in conjunction with the later essays "On Life" and "On Love." The intensification in Shelley's writing is marked in *Alastor* by the emergence of characteristic stylistic and generic preoccupations—particularly his attention to the development of a narrative verse style. In terms of Shelley's engagement with his contemporaries, what is most apparent is that in the preface and the poem Shelley alludes particularly clearly, through direct and indirect quotation, to poems by Samuel Taylor Coleridge and William Wordsworth, whose poetic reputations were at this time already established. His language and themes have also been related to works by the poet Robert Southey, the French historian Constantine Volney, and the philosophers William Drummond, William Godwin, and Mary Wollstonecraft, among others. Because of this, critical approaches to the text frequently address the question of who, if anyone, the figure of the poet might represent or criticize.

Such attention to the role of the poet is invited particularly by the use that Shelley makes—to thematic and metaphorical effect—of the myth of Narcissus. The prominence of this myth of self-love in the poem suggests the self-destructive and selfish elements in the poet's quest. Critical attention has focused on the extent to which we can read this as Shelley deliberately ironizing the poet and his quest, or whether *Alastor* is implicated in such self-absorption. *Alastor* may be critical of the tendency of Romantic poetry to transcendentalize its goals, pointing to the lack of social and political engagement of the poet's quest, the self-defeating nature of his solitude (we may note that we only know the poet through the narrator's poetry, not his own; in fact, we rarely hear him speak at all). At the same time the reader may feel that it partakes of the narcissism it criticizes, particularly through its treatment of the women, real and imaginary, whom the poet encounters. The poet abandons the real "Arabian maid" for the "veiled maid" who is solely a construct of the poet's own imagination and is "like the voice of his own soul." Such an ambivalence further invites us to examine the ways in which the poem itself engages with the outside world: the social responsibilities of the poet in the wake of the wreck of radical hopes in the French Revolution; the implications of his journey through the east at a time when Britain was engaged in colonial domination of the east, as well as deeply interested in it as a place of its own history; and its implication in the sexual politics of the day. *Alastor* can be seen as Shelley's initial attempt to orient his own voice among those of his fellow contemporary poets and thinkers, to situate his own position critically in relation to their attitudes to the same poetic subjects; at the same time it is both interested, and implicated, in many of the problems of its contemporary world.

SUZIE JORDAN

Text

Alastor; or The Spirit of Solitude and Other Poems. London: Baldwin, Craddock, and Joy, and Carpenter and Son, 1816; reprinted in the standard edition *The Poems of Shelley*, edited by Geoffrey Matthews and Kelvin Everest. Vol. 1, 1804–17. London: Longman, 1989.

Bibliography

Barcus, James E. *Shelley: The Critical Heritage.* London: Routledge, 1975.

Birns, Nicholas. "Secrets of the Birth of Time: The Rhetoric of Cultural Origins in *Alastor* and 'Mont Blanc'." *Studies in Romanticism* 32, no. 3 (1993): 339–66.

Butler, Marilyn. "Shelley and the Question of Joint Authorship." Edited by Tim Clark and Jerrold Hogle. Edinburgh: Edinburgh University Press, 1996.

Clark, Tim. *Embodying Revolution: The Figure of the Poet in Shelley.* Oxford: Clarendon Press, 1989.

Crucefix, Martyn. "Ww, Superstition, and Shelley's *Alastor*," *Essays in Criticism* 33, no. 2 (1983): 126–47.

Day, Aidan. *Romanticism.* London: Routledge, 1996.

Gibson, Evan K. "*Alastor*: A Reinterpretation," *PMLA* 62 (1947): 1022–42.

Hamilton, Paul. *Percy Bysshe Shelley.* London: Northcote House, 2000.

Leask, Nigel. *British Romantic Writers and the East: Anxieties of Empire.* Cambridge: Cambridge University Press, 1992.

Mueschke, Paul, and Earl Griggs. "Ww as the Prototype of the Poet in Shelley's *Alastor*," *PMLA* 49 (1934): 229–45.

Ragan, Tillotama. "The Web of Human Things: Narrative and Identity in *Alastor*." In *The New Shelley: Late Twentieth Century Views*. Edited by Kim G. Blank. New York: St. Martin's Press, 1991.

ALECSANDRI, VASILE 1818-1890

Romanian poet, dramatist, folklorist, and politician

Born in Moldavia to a middle-ranking nobleman and a Romanianized Greek mother, Vasile Alecsandri was educated at first by a Greek monk but was then sent to Paris at an early age (in 1834), where time spent in boulevard theaters proved more decisive for his career than his unfinished studies in medicine and law. On his return to his home country he took up a sinecure in the Moldavian pensions office, but devoted most of his energy to writing plays put on in the Moldavian National Theater.

Having played a major role in the Moldavian Revolution of 1848, Alecsandri went into exile, returning to perform important diplomatic missions at the time of the union of the principalities of Moldavia and Wallachia in 1859. He was a founding member of the Romanian Academy in 1867, president of the Chamber of Deputies in 1869, and Romanian Ambassador to Paris from 1885 until his death in 1890.

Alecsandri's importance for Romanian Romanticism is basically threefold. From 1840, he played a crucial role in developing a local theatrical repertoire, transposing themes from French and Italian farces and satires into a Romanian setting, and sending up the conflict between the old orientalized nobility and the young Frenchified elite (the *bonjuriști*), and thereby dramatizing the conflicts and contradictions of social change and superficial Europeanization of local speech, manners, and forms. His most famous character is Chirița (the name is a Romanian feminine diminutive of the Greek *Kyr*, lord) a provincial boyar's wife who comes to the Moldavian capital, Iași, to educate and marry off her daughters. She ends up taking them to the West, but gets off the Danube steamboat too early at Belgrade, mistaking it for Paris. The social education of provincial Moldavians and their arrival in the capital stand synecdochically for the whole of Romania's relationship with Westernization. The role of Chirița was played by the famous Romanian actor Matei Millo, in female costume.

Alecsandri also contributed to the key Romanian journals *Propășirea* (*Progress*, 1840), and *România literară* (*Literary Romania*, 1855) and in his poetry and prose transposed themes from the French exoticism of Théophile Gautier, Victor Hugo, and Prosper Merimée (a man with whom he traveled in Spain and North Africa in the 1850s): this work both integrated stereotypes of the Orient into Romanian culture and placed the Romanians themselves in a comprehensible cultural geography somewhere between France and Constantinople.

Finally, Alecsandri published the most influential collection of Romanian folk poetry, *Poezii populare române* (1850–66). Ballads like "Miorița" ("The Ewe Lamb") and "Meșterul Manole" ("Manole the Master Builder"), which in fact treat universal folk themes and motifs, have always been touchstones in debates over a Romanian identity, interpreted in the light of Romantic theories of passivity and pastoralism, or, respectively, creativity and sacrifice. These and other poems collected or adapted by Alecsandri were included in all the first anthologies of Romanian poetry published in Western European languages during and after the Crimean War. His "adaptations" were later criticized by folklorists but defended by literary critics. Over a thousand different versions of *Miorița* were later collected throughout Romania.

After 1850, Alecsandri played an active role in politics, but continued to write, including a series of interesting lyrical *Pasteluri* (*Pastels*, 1875) and some rather overblown epic dramas, mainly on the theme of Romania's Latin heritage. His 1877 poem *Cîntecul gintei latine* (*The Song of the Latin Race*) won a prize from the Society of Romance Langauges at Montpellier, organized by Frederic Mistral and the Provençal group Félibrige, an event which was granted inordinate importance in Romania, and eventually came to symbolize a poetic recognition of the national dignity.

ALEXANDER DRACE-FRANCIS

Biography

Born in Bacau, Moldavia, June 14, 1821. Educated at Iasi and later in Paris, 1834–39. Worked in the Moldavian pensions office; wrote plays for the Moldavian National Theater in the 1840s. First collection of folk songs published, 1844. Participated in Romanian revolutionary cause from 1840s; engaged in the Moldavian Revolution of 1848. Went into exile, 1849–59. Published several volumes of poetry and songs from 1853; contributed to Romanian journals *Propirea* (*Progress*), 1840, and *Romania literatur* (*Literary Romania*), 1855. Minister for foreign affairs, Romania, 1859–60. Traveled to London as special envoy of Prince Alexandru Cuza on diplomatic mission to secure recognition for the United Romanian Principalities, 1860. Founder member of the Romanian Academy, 1867. President of the Chamber of Deputies, Romania, 1869. Romanian ambassador to France in Paris, from 1885. Died in Mircesti, Romania, August 22, 1890.

Bibliography

Alecsandri, Vasile. *Cântecul gintei latine . . . Il Canto della stirpe latina . . . Le chant de la race latine.* Translated into Italian by G. C. Mezzacapo. Roma: Tip. di Propaganda, 1878.

———. *Opere.* Vols 1–10. Bucharest: Minerva, 1966–85.

———. *Pastels: poésies roumaines . . .* Translated into French by Georges Bengesco. Bruxelles: 1902.

———, ed. *Poesii populare ale românilor.* 2 vols. Iași: Buciumul Român, 1852–53.

Cioranescu, Alexandre. *Vasile Alecsandri.* Translated into English by Maria Golescu. New York: Twayne, 1973.

Drouhet, Charles V. *Alecsandri și scritorii francezi.* București: Cultura națională, 1924.

Tappe, E. D. "Alecsandri and the English." *Revue des études roumaines,* 2 (1954): 153–68.

ALFIERI, VITTORIO 1749–1803

Italian dramatist, poet, and writer

While Vittorio Alfieri enjoyed a considerable reputation as a playwright and man of letters across Europe throughout his lifetime, in the turbulent years leading up to the unification of Italy in 1860 he was seen as a champion of liberty and a focus for Italian patriots. What is immediately striking about Alfieri is the force of his personality as it emerges in his writings, epitomizing a fundamental change of direction in European culture, from the age of reason to the Romantic era. His lifelong rejection of any type of authority may have had its roots in his reaction against his upbringing and education in Piedmont, then part of the rigidly repressive kingdom of Sardinia. In his autobiography he dismissed his experiences at the Royal Military Academy of Turin as years of miseducation, and no sooner had he left the academy than he sought permission from the king to travel throughout Europe. The next decade is described by him as one of journeys and dissipation, although it also afforded him the firsthand experience of a variety of forms of government, as well as the opportunity to study the Italian classics, French Enlightenment writers, and, most important, Plutarch. It was, above all, in Plutarch that Alfieri discovered the ideal of a heroic life, and, almost by corollary, his own sense of impatience with and antagonism toward contemporary society and culture.

With the success of his first tragedy, *Cleopatra*, in 1775, Alfieri decided to devote himself to literature and made an extended visit to Tuscany to perfect his Italian, as French was his first language. The choice of tragedy as most appropriate for the expression of poetic and political themes was driven by his desire to establish the genre in Italy and to rival the richer French tradition. In a letter to a friend, Alfieri hinted at a political subtext to the undertaking, writing, "I write with the one illusion that perhaps, if Italians are reborn, one day these tragedies of mine will be performed; . . . the presence of theater in modern nations, as in ancient ones, presupposes that they are truly nations and not ten little divided peoples."

The model on which Alfieri chose to structure his tragedies was clearly classical: five acts observed the Aristotelian unities of time, place, and, above all, action. He described his method of composition, which never varied, as three phases of invention, outline, and versification, but he held that the crucial element lay in the temperament of the writer: "in writing tragedies the prime requisite is passion, which is something that cannot be learned." The tragedies have a uniform, highly condensed structure in that the first and final acts tend to be very short, the number of characters is kept to a minimum, and all extraneous details are omitted. This streamlining is carried through to the language, which is concise to the point of telegraphic brevity, and the most famous example of this is found in the final scene of act 2 of *Filippo*, in which nine lines exchanged between two characters amount to twenty-two words.

The themes of the nineteen tragedies are taken from biblical, historical, and mythological sources, and George Steiner has described their range as "an index to the romantic imagination." The classical element of fate tends to be central, however, and his characters seem driven by forces beyond human comprehension. There are no preoccupations with realism, or the historical specifics of a given character's situation, but the lyricism of the language effectively evokes the inner life of the characters. The recurrent theme of the struggle for liberty is not posed in terms of a clash between individual and society, but rather of two titanic individuals—the hero and the tyrant—who occasionally show an uncanny psychological similarity. Two of his best plays, *Saul* (1782) and *Mirra* (1784), fall outside this scheme, as Saul is both tyrant and victim, while Mirra is at the mercy of her destiny.

There is, however, no real political dimension to Alfieri's notion of the power of the tyrant in the tragedies; it is, rather, an abstract concept that Alfieri analyzes in the treatise *Della tirannide* (*On Tyranny*, 1777). In this he explores various aspects of tyranny and suggests three remedies: solitude, suicide, or the murder of the tyrant, which are reflected in the various outcomes of the tragedies. It has been argued that Alfieri's concept of liberty is an absolute one that borders on anarchy in its refutation of all political systems.

Some of these themes are taken up in *Del principe e delle lettere* (*The Prince and Letters*, 1778–86), in which writers are seen as radical opponents of absolute power not so much through revolutionary activity as by the very nature of their vocation. The writer's task is to instill in his readers love of liberty and awareness of their rights and his superiority to the man of action lay in the fact that the work of art created would outlive him.

However, the impact of Alfieri on successive generations of Italian writers, such as Ugo Foscolo and Giacomo Leopardi, stems as much from the emotionally charged account of his life as his literary or political writings. *Vita* (his autobiography) was begun in 1790 and completed in 1803, and provides an intimate account of his travels through Europe and a somewhat idealized self-portrait, emphasizing his passionate nature.

The influence of Petrarch is evident in both the title and tone of his *Rime* (*Poems*, 1798–1804), some 350 compositions—mainly sonnets—that describe the physical and emotional characteristics of the poet. The language of his poetry bears traces of the peculiarities of his tragic style in the exclamations, sudden changes of register, and abrupt heartfelt cries that punctuate the lyrical flow.

A brooding, melancholy figure, Alfieri combined the disparate elements of contemporary culture in his reverence for the classical ideals of harmony and simplicity and his penchant for emotional self-indulgence and introspection, which explains Benedetto Croce's definition of him as a proto-Romantic.

LYNNE PRESS

Biography

Born in Asti, Piedmont, January 16, 1749. Attended Royal Military Academy, Turin, 1759–66. Traveled widely in Europe as an ensign, 1766–72, in, among other places, Austria, England, Holland, Russia, and Spain. Returned to Piedmont, 1772. Resigned his army commission, 1773. Studied and wrote full-time from 1775 after the success of his tragedy *Cleopatra*. Made an extended visit to Tuscany to perfect his Italian, 1776. Began lifelong relationship with Luisa Stolberg, Countess of Albany, wife of Charles Edward, Stuart pretender to the English throne, 1777. Lived in Florence with the countess from 1778, ceding most of his estate to his sister. Followed the countess to Rome, 1780; lived with her in Colmar, Alsace, 1784–90, then in Paris, 1790–92. Fled from revolutionary Paris to Florence with the countess, 1792; left Florence during the French occupation of the city, 1798. Important autobiographical work *Vita di Vittorio Alfieri scritta da esso* published posthumously in 1804. Died in Florence, October 8, 1803.

Selected Works

Collections

Opere. Edited by Vittore Branca. 1965.
The Tragedies of Vittorio Alfieri Complete. 2 vols. Edited by E. A. Bowring, 1876. Reprint 1970.

Essays

Del principe e delle lettere, 1795. Translated as *The Prince and Letters*, by Beatrice Corrigan and Julius A. Molinaro. 1972.

Della tirannide. 1800. 2 vols. Translated as *On Tyranny* by Julius A. Molinaro and Beatrice Corrigan. 1961.

Autobiography

Vita di Vittorio Alfieri da Asti scritta da esso. 1804. 2 vols. Translated as *Memoirs* anonymously, 1810. Revised by E. R. Vincent. 1961.

Bibliography

Betti, Franco. *Vittorio Alfieri*. Boston: Twayne, 1984.
Binni, Walter. *Saggi alfieriani*. Florence: La nuova Italia, 1969.
Croce, Benedetto. *European Literature in the Nineteenth Century*. New York: Haskell House, 1967.
Fido, Franco, "Alfieri and pre-Romanticism." In *The Cambridge History of Italian Literature*, edited by Peter Brand and Lino Pertile. Cambridge: Cambridge University Press, 1996.
Fubini, Mario. *Ritratto dell'Alfieri*. Florence: Lanuova Italia, 1963.
Megaro, Gaudence. *Alfieri: Forerunner of Italian Nationalism*. New York: Columbia University Press, 1930.

ALKAN, CHARLES-VALENTIN (MORHANGE) 1813–1888

French pianist and composer

Charles-Valentin Alkan's career as a pianist and composer spanned most of the nineteenth century. Though he was widely respected by some of his most famous contemporaries, his public appearances were few and far between, and his often idiosyncratic compositions remain largely unknown on the concert circuit.

Alkan was born Charles-Valentin Morhange, and assumed his father's first name, Alkan, from an early age, together with his sister and four brothers, all of whom were to establish successful musical careers in Paris. His father ran a musical boarding school in the Marais, the Jewish district of Paris, from which many proceeded to the Paris Conservatoire. Charles-Valentin was admitted to the Conservatoire at the exceptionally early age of six, and was awarded first prizes for solfège, piano, harmony, and organ in his time there. He was heavily promoted as a child prodigy, but never established himself on the international circuit of his contemporary virtuosi, and apart from two visits to London in 1833 and 1835, he apparently remained in Paris his whole life.

In 1839, with his career as a virtuoso progressing to great acclaim and several publications of piano music to his name, Alkan suddenly disappeared from the public eye. With the exception of six recitals in 1844–45 and 1853, he was not to make another public appearance until 1873, when he arranged the first of eight seasons of "petits concerts de musique classique," in which he performed an immensely wide range of then virtually unknown music from the seventeenth and eighteenth centuries, interspersed with compositions of his own and of his contemporaries.

In the meantime, Alkan had become deeply misanthropic. He gave piano lessons throughout his life, mainly to upper-class women, and published a substantial body of music, almost entirely for piano or pedal piano (an instrument that he came increasingly to champion later in life), but he rarely ventured outside his own circle of friends. His greatest work, misleadingly titled as a set of mere studies, the *Douze études dans tous les tons mineurs pour piano*, op. 39 (composed from 1846 onward, published 1857), runs to more than two hours in performance and includes within it a four-movement symphony and three-movement concerto, both for piano alone. In writing orchestral music for solo piano, Alkan developed bold new pianistic textures quite unlike anything written by any of his contemporaries. His "orchestral" piano music does not resemble a conventional piano arrangement of orchestral music, but sounds orchestral as a result of the number of different elements and textures heard simultaneously within a piece.

Despite the obscurity that Alkan cultivated, he occupies an important position within the Romantic movement. As a resident of the Square d'Orléans in the 1840s, his neighbors included not only some of the foremost Parisian musicians (Frédéric Chopin, Friedrich Kalkbrenner, Antoine Marmontel, Joseph d'Ortigue, and Pierre Joseph Zimmerman), but also an elite group of authors and artists including Eugène Delacroix, Alexandre Dumas, Victor Hugo, Felicité Robert de Lamennais, and George Sand. Marmontel records that Alkan was accepted by these neighbors as "un frère en poésie," and though he may have been an outsider to Parisian society at large, he had intimate acquaintance with many of the intellectual leaders of the French Romantic movement in art and letters.

Alkan's connection to the Romantic movement displays itself on two levels in his music. The intellectual concerns of his artistic compatriots were primarily literary, and references to literary subjects are very common in Alkan's music. It appears that the French translation of Johann Wolfgang von Goethe's *Faust*

(1828; part 1, with illustrations by Delacroix) inspired the second movement—entitled "Quasi-Faust,"—of one of Alkan's most imposing compositions, the *Grande sonate: les quatre âges*, op. 33 (1847), although Alkan points out in his introduction to this work that each movement, rather than being programmatically representative, corresponds to "une disposition particulière de la pensée, de l'imagination." There are several references to classical texts in this and other works, and biblical quotations precede several other compositions. In each case, it seems that individual words are not intended to be depicted so much as the sentiment of the quoted passage as a whole. On rare occasions, however, he descends to the banality of direct representation: *Le chemin de fer*, op. 27, a *perpetuum mobile* of 1844, depicts not only the fast-moving steam engine but even the sounding of its whistle.

Between the two extremes of a train's whistle and a musical depiction of the physical and mental suffering of the bound Prometheus (in the last movement of Alkan's *Grande sonate*), many aspects of the composer's wide-ranging musical style are concerned with the traditional Romantic concepts of fantasy and the macabre, as shown by such titles as *Les diablotins* (*The Little Devils*, 1861; from the *Quarante-huit esquisses*), *L'enfer* (*Hell*, c. 1841; the second movement of the *Duo concertant*), *La chanson de la folle au bord de la mer* (*The Song of the Mad Woman by the Seashore*, 1847; from the *Vingt-cinq préludes*), *Scherzo diabolico* (1857; from the *Douze études dans tous les tons mineurs*) and *Esprits follets* (*Will-o'-the-Wisps*, c. 1866; from the *Third Book of Chants*). Usually such pieces do not conform to the conventional nineteenth-century garb of the macabre, but seek to parody it. Thus, in *Les diablotins* Alkan employs not only the conventional device of *acciaccature* in the higher register, but also toys with note clusters fifty years before they became a feature of modernist piano music. Alkan's skill as a malicious parodist is best demonstrated in *L'opéra*, from the twelve-piece cycle of *Les mois*, op. 74 (c. 1840), which abounds in the worst clichés of piano reductions of grand opera, and in the *Marcia funebre sulla morte d'un pappagallo* (*Funeral March on the Death of a Parrot*, 1859), exposing the bathos in those grand funeral marches through which more extrovertly romantic French composers, Hector Berlioz included, displayed their supposed turmoil and anguish.

Paradoxically, Alkan's position as a Romantic composer is enhanced by his detachment from much of French musical Romanticism. His music often makes phenomenal demands of its performers, but never simply for reasons of show, as with so many pianists of the time. His idea of Romanticism existed on a higher, intellectual and philosophical plane, next to those of Lamennais and Sand.

NICOLAS BELL

Biography

Born Charles-Henri-Valentin Morhange in Paris, November 30, 1813, into a Jewish family; son of Alkan Morhange, head teacher of an elementary school and distinguished music teacher. Eldest of six children, all of whom became musicians; brother of the pianist, composer, and teacher Napoléon Morhange (1826–1910). Studied piano and composition at the Paris Conservatoire, 1820–34: awarded the *premier prix*, 1824. Published first composition, 1828; active as a virtuoso pianist, 1830 until 1838, after which time made only very rare public appearances. Visited London, 1833 and 1835. Lived in the Square d'Orléans, 1840s; gave piano lessons and associated with the literary circle of Victor Hugo, Félicité de Lamennais, and George Sand, and with the composers Frédéric Chopin and Franz Liszt. Became reclusive after the 1840s. Published his *Grand sonate*, op. 33, 1847; *Études*, op. 39, 1857. Organized "Petits concerts de musique classique" featuring seventeenth- and eighteenth-century music, 1873–80. Died in Paris, March 29, 1888.

Selected Works

Collections
The Piano Music of Alkan. Edited by Raymond Lewenthal. New York: Schirmer, 1964.
Œuvres choisies pour piano. Edited by Georges Beck. Paris: Hengel, 1969.

Piano Music
Trois grandes études pour les deux mains séparées et réunies, op. 74, c. 1839.
Grande sonate: les quatre âges, op. 33, 1848.
Douze études dans tous les tons majeurs, op. 35, 1848.
Douze études dans tous les tons mineurs, op. 39, 1857.
Chants, op. 38, 65, 67, 70, 1857–c. 1872 (five sets of six songs without words).
Sonatine, op. 61, 1861.
Quarante-huit motifs (*esquisses*), op. 63, 1861.
Impromptu sur le choral de Luther, Un fort rempart est notre Dieu, pour piano à pédales, op. 69, 1866.

Other
Duo concertant, for piano and violin, op. 21, c. 1841.
Trio, for piano, violin, and cello, op. 30, 1841.
Sonate de concert, for piano and cello, op. 47, 1857; edited by Hugh Macdonald. Kassel: Bärenreiter, 1975.
Marcia funebre sulla morte d'un pappagallo, for mixed chorus, three oboes and bassoon, 1859. Edited by Raymond Lewenthal. New York: Schirmer, 1972.

Bibliography

François-Sappey, Brigitte, ed. *Charles Valentin Alkan*. Paris: Fayard, 1991.
Marmontel, Antoine. *Les pianistes célèbres*. 2nd ed. Paris: Heugel et Fils, 1887.
Schilling, Britta. "Charles-Valentin Alkan: un solitaire dans le romantisme français," *Romantisme: revue de la société des études romantiques* 16 (1987): 33–44.
Smith, Ronald, *Alkan*. Vol. 1: *The Enigma*. Vol. 2: *The Music*. London: Kahn and Averill, 1976–87; reprinted in one volume, 2000.

ALLSTON, WASHINGTON 1779–1843

American painter

Washington Allston has been described by William Gerdts as "the most complete representative of the romantic age in American painting," but his significance, and the nature of his achievement, have long been open to debate. During his lifetime and in the period just after his death, Allston was viewed as master of major stature. An anonymous reviewer of 1850 declared, "As a painter he is acknowledged by all to stand at the head of American artists," and no less a figure than the poet Samuel Taylor Coleridge described Allston as a man of "high and rare genius" (see Griggs, 305–6). The art historian William Gerdts has noted that Allston's work received more praise and attention than that of any other American artist who worked before the Civil War.

By the late nineteenth century, however, reconsideration of Allston's critical and artistic significance began to appear. In 1893, William Coffin, writing in *The Nation*, declared that a display of Allston's work at the Columbian Exposition in Chicago proved "how little there was in his painting to justify the reputation ascribed to him by his biographers" (see Coffin, 116). Indeed, this fall from critical favor is recorded in the history of exhibitions of Allston's work. After a major retrospective of Allston's work in 1881, at the Museum of Fine Arts in Boston, no show of his work took place for sixty-five years, until 1946, when museums in Boston and Detroit staged an exhibition organized by Edward Preston Richardson. Although Richardson followed this venture with a full-scale biography, published in 1948, Allston is still generally considered a figure of historical interest rather than as an artist of the first rank. Indeed, even Allston's place in the Romantic movement seems problematic today, since most of his paintings appear to be not so much a full-blown expression of Romanticism as a kind of classicism overlaid with Romantic features.

Allston was born on November 5, 1779, on a plantation in Georgetown County, South Carolina, and he later recalled that the songs and ghost stories of the black slaves profoundly stirred his imagination. His father, a soldier in the Revolutionary Army, died two years after Allston's birth. Consequently, in 1787, around the time that his mother remarried, Allston was sent to live with his mother's brother in Newport, Rhode Island, where he attended the preparatory school of Robert Rogers; he seems to have first taken up painting in a serious way here, with the encouragement of the portrait painter Samuel King, as well as the young miniaturist Edward Greene Malbone.

In 1796 Allston entered Harvard College, where painting seems to have consumed much of his free time. Several paintings survive from this period. His work was already considered quite unusual by American standards, since rather than focusing on portraiture—which was the staple of all other American artists—Allston focused on narrative and literary themes, some humorous, and others of a romantic nature, often based on the Gothic novels of the period. Allston himself later recalled going through a phase of "bandittimania," and this is recorded in several studies of brigands in the manner of Salvator Rosa.

After graduating from Harvard, Allston sold his share in the family property to finance a trip to Europe for the purpose of studying art. In 1801 he sailed for England, introduced himself to Benjamin West, and was admitted to the school of the Royal Academy. In 1803 he left for Paris with the American painter John Vanderlyn, and after a stay of several months went on to Italy, where he spent the next four years (1804–8) living chiefly in Rome, but also visiting other cities, particularly Florence. During this period he befriended the American novelist Washington Irving, as well as the English Romantic poet Samuel Taylor Coleridge, with whom he associated in Rome for about six months.

Allston's first notable works are a group of landscapes created while in Italy, such as the large *Diana and Her Nymphs in the Chase* (1805), a painting greatly admired by Coleridge. These pieces are classical in their general format, and resemble contemporary works by northern artists in Rome—for example, those of the German painter Joseph Anton Koch (1786–1839). Allston's paintings, however, suffuse these classical motifs with a mood of nostalgia and reverie. Moreover, his paint handling was not crisp and hard, in the manner of Koch or of traditional classicists such as Nicolas Poussin, but was instead soft and Venetian. Indeed, Allston developed a complex and distinctive technique of using glazes over primer—and of applying paint in threadlike ribbons of incompletely mixed pigment—to create a glowing, opalescent paint surface that gives his paintings a mood of mystery and intangibility.

Along with such landscapes, while in Italy Allston also executed a remarkable self-portrait (1805), that initiated a new Romantic mode of self-fashioning for American artists. (This picture was later greatly admired by the American modernist Charles Demuth, who thus started but never finished an essay on Allston's work.)

In 1808 Allston returned to the United States, where he set himself up as a professional portrait painter in Boston. Such work does not seem to have been congenial to him, however, and in 1811 he returned to England, accompanied by the aspiring painter Samuel F. B. Morse, who became a lifelong admirer of Allston's work. Allston's second stay in England marked the high point of his productivity as an artist and of critical recognition of his work. In England, Allston resumed his friendship with Coleridge, and through him made contact with wealthy English connoisseurs, among them Sir George Beaumont, who commissioned one of Allston's major paintings, *The Angel Releasing St. Peter from Prison*. Most of Allston's paintings of this period were large figure compositions—modeled on those of Benjamin West and Henry Fuseli—that combine a generally classical treatment of the figure with otherworldly themes of a fantastic or religious nature. These included a much-admired painting, *Jacob's Dream* (1817), which was acquired by the Third Earl of Egremont and inspired a poem by William Wordsworth.

The most ambitious of these paintings was *The Dead Man Revived by Touching the Bones of Elisha* (1813), which received a prize of two hundred guineas when Allston first exhibited it at the British Institution in 1813. An academic tour de force and some thirteen feet high, this canvas contains seventeen carefully arranged figures based on famous prototypes, such as the Transfiguration of Raphael and the frieze of the Parthenon. Despite the overall classicism of the effect, however, Allston's underlying Romanticism is evident both in its subject (which deals with the connection between the material world, and that of soul, spirit, and afterlife), as well as in his paint handling, which is glowing and mysterious.

While no doubt remarkable, such efforts appear somewhat artificial and stilted to modern eyes. More appealing to contemporary taste is Allston's landscape *Elijah in the Desert* (1818–19), which he painted toward the end of his stay in England in just three weeks, applying the underpainting with skimmed milk mixed with pigment and then going over the result with oil glazes. Here, finally, Allston seems to have cast aside the straitjacket of classicism and to have produced a purely Romantic statement.

Despite many successes, Allston's stay in England was marked by difficulties and setbacks, including a near-fatal illness, the death of his wife, and mounting financial difficulties. In 1818, having exhausted his inheritance, Allston returned to the United States and settled in Cambridgeport, just outside of Boston. Shortly after his return, he produced one of his finest and most Romantic creations, *Moonlit Landscape* (1819), which shows a cluster of enigmatic figures in the moonlight and is filled with a spirit of restlessness and reverie.

In general, however, Allston's creative drive diminished after his return to the United States. In 1820 a group of ten Boston merchants contributed one thousand dollars each to enable Allston to complete his large painting *Belshazar's Feast*, which he had started in England in 1817. This painting shows the prophet Daniel interpreting handwriting that mysteriously appeared during a feast on the wall behind the Babylonian king Belshazar, foretelling his doom. But Allston was never able to complete the project, because he had either changed his mind about the composition, become distracted by other projects, or lost his creative drive in the unstimulating cultural atmosphere of Cambridge. At the time of his death, on July 9, 1843, the painting was discovered unfinished in his studio, marked up with chalk lines indicating compositional changes. Allston's inability to complete the painting became legendary, and inspired several literary treatments of the theme, including Henry James's novella *The Madonna of the Future*. As was the case with other romantic artists—one thinks of Coleridge's unfinished poem "Kubla Khan"—Allston's aspirations were so lofty that actually completing a work of art often became difficult, if not impossible.

In addition to his achievements as an artist, Allston also wrote verse, prose tales, a novel, and extensive art theory and art criticism. (Interestingly, he was the first to coin the term *objective correlative*, later taken up by T. S. Eliott). Allston's great reputation in his lifetime was clearly based not simply on his paintings but on his gifts as a conversationalist, which captivated all who knew him. As the actress known as Mrs. Jameson later recalled, "The vivacity of his conceptions, and the glowing language in which he could clothe them, rendered his conversation inexpressibly delightful and exciting. I remember, after an evening spent with him, returning home very late (I think it near three in the morning),—with the feelings of *one 'who had been magnetized* (see Jameson, 16).'" Indeed, in the end, Allston's greatness was probably based not so much on any actual accomplishment, as on a new set of Romantic ideals and yearnings that he introduced into American art and culture.

HENRY ADAMS

Bibliography

Coffin, William A. "The Columbian Exposition, II." *Nation*, August 17, 1893.

Coleridge, Samuel Taylor. *Unpublished Letters of Samuel Taylor Coleridge*. 2 vols. Edited by Earl Leslie Griggs. New Haven, Conn.: Yale University Press. 2: 305–6.

Flagg, Jared B. *Washington Allston, Life and Letters*. New York, 1892.

Gerdts, William H., and Theodore E. Stebbins Jr. *"A Man of Genius": The Art of Washington Allston (1779–1843)*. Exhibition catalog, Museum of Fine Arts, Boston, 1979.

Jameson, Anna. *Washington Allston*. London: Athenaeum. 1844.

Richardson, Edward Preston. *Washington Allston: A Study of the Romantic Artist in America*. Chicago: University of Chicago Press, 1948.

ALMQVIST, CARL JONAS LOVE 1793–1866

Swedish Poet

Carl Jonas Love Almqvist (the name Love is a romanticized version of Ludvig) is one of the few Swedish Romantic authors whose texts are still popular. His literary production was enormous; certain of the texts have achieved classic status and are constantly reprinted. Among his contemporaries, only Johan Stagnelius still belongs to the literature that is in circulation. Almqvist has become a symbolic figure in Swedish literary history and his life story reads like a literary creation in itself; a creation that encompassed both Romantic artistic life and the spirit of social revolt. Almqvist was, along with his primary rival Fredrika Bremer, one of the first Swedish authors to reach a position at the forefront of literature through prose rather than poetry. He was, however relatively primitive as a storyteller; his strengths lie in his skills of perception and observation, his original lyrics, and his unique stylistic tendencies.

Almqvist was the grandson of Carl Christoffer Gjörwell, himself an important figure in the literary history of Sweden through his work as a publisher and with several journals at the king's library in Stockholm. When Almqvist's mother died in 1806, his upbringing and education was overseen by Gjörwell. He was also influenced by his grandmother, apparently a favorite of King Gustav III, who sparked his interest in recent Swedish history. The interest in history was encouraged by Gjörwell, who wanted Almqvist to become a historian. When Almqvist attended Uppsala University (1808–15) he studied, among other subjects, philosophy and theology.

In 1815 he was employed at the ecclesiastic office; he worked there for eight years without getting to know his (later famous) colleague Stagnelius. The job was not enough to sustain him intellectually or financially, and he was eventually fired in 1823 for negligence. The following year Almqvist demonstrated his ability to put even his wildest ideas into practice, moving to Värmland to live as an idealistic farmer married to a suitable country wife. Almqvist was one of the few who lived out Romantic ideals so literally and fully. Although the project failed, the marriage continued, albeit unhappily.

He returned to Stockholm as a teacher and in 1829 he was appointed headmaster at the New Elementary School. A remarkable production of textbooks ensued, with *Svensk Rättstafningslära* (*Swedish Correct Spelling Teaching*) appearing in 1829 and *Svensk Språklära* (*Swedish Language Teaching*) in 1832. There would be later textbooks in subjects such as geometry, Greek, and French. The first of the textbooks became a commercial success; its innovative and absurd examples are famous.

Almqvist's literary debut was in 1833 with the first part of *Törnrosens bok* (*The Rose Tower Book*). The book is presented as a dream about the disappearing elite culture, an idea probably influenced by his grandparents, but the plot followed the modern Romantic preferences. The book did not bring him much financial reward, and Almqvist was still forced to retain other employment. He became a priest in 1837 in the hope of advancing himself, and the following year applied, without success, for a professorship in modern languages at Lund University.

Four new parts of *Törnrosens bok* came out in 1838, displaying an increase in realism and an attempt to introduce intrigue, in the style of the imported popular books. Most noteworthy is the introduction of a theme that would become especially strong in the following century, in an essay entitled *Svenska fattigdomens betydelse* (*The Importance/Meaning of Swedish Poverty*). The turning point in his career came in 1839 with *Det går an* (*It Will Do*), a short novel that examines feminist ideas through a detailed portrayal of everyday life. It was more shocking than any previous novel in that the main characters Sara and Albert decide to move in together without getting married, thus challenging the bourgeois attitude toward marriage. It is the oldest Swedish novel still read today and is constantly reprinted.

Det går an caused the first of the scandals surrounding Almqvist's reputation, and it forced him to retire from state employment and concentrate on increasing his literary production. He also reworked and published two of his youthful novels, *Orimus och Ariman* and *Amorina*, both in 1839. He was able to exploit his notoriety in the world of media by becoming a journalist for *Aftonbladet* (*Evening News*) in 1839, and this cemented his position as liberal-radical opposition man and also paid well. At the same time he began mass-producing novels, hoping to imitate the success of imported authors such as Charles Dickens. The awaited success was not forthcoming despite the anonymous reviews Almqvist himself wrote in the newspapers for which he worked. The publication of parts of *Törnrosens bok* continued. Noteworthy is the edition published in 1849 that contained *Songes*, poems set to music that are simultaneously the most Romantic and the most original pieces in the work.

The second great scandal in Almqvist's life arose from his attempt to poison von Scheven, an important moneylender to whom he owed great sums of money, in 1851. He fled to the United States and there entered into a bigamist marriage with his landlady in order to ease his financial difficulties. While in the United States he worked on the as-yet-unpublished *Om svenska rim* (*About Swedish Rhyme*). In 1865 he left his second wife. He died in obscurity in a boarding house in Bremen the following year. During his lifetime Almqvist was an extraordinarily prolific writer who left behind an extensive collection of works, and yet, despite the value of many of his books, his personal life and private escapes provide the most remarkable story of all.

CAMILLA FRASER

Biography

Born in 1793, studied philosophy and theology at Uppsala University 1808–15. In 1815 started work at the ecclesiastic office in Stockholm; fired due to negligence in 1823 and moved to Värmland to live as a farmer. Returned to Stockholm in 1829 and took a job as the headmaster of the New Elementary School. Published *Svensk Rättstafningslära* in 1829 and *Svensk Språklära* in 1832. Made his literary debut in 1833 with the first part of *Törnrosens bok*. In 1837 was ordained as a priest. In 1839, publication of *Det går an*; also reworked and published *Amorina* and *Orimus och Ariman* and became a journalist for *Aftonbladet*. In 1849 another part of *Törnrosens bok* published, containing, among other works, *Songes*. Fled from Sweden after attempt to poison von Scheven in 1851 and while in America entered into a bigamist marriage with his landlady. In 1865, ran away from his second wife; died in a boarding house in Bremen in 1866.

Selected Works

Amorina
Brev 1803–66
Det går an
Orimus och Ariman
Törnrosens bok, vols. 1–3

Bibliography

Balgård. *Carl Jonas Love Almqvist samhällsvisionären*. Stockholm: Svensk Radios förlag, 1973.
Berg. *Studier i C. J. L. Almqvists kvinnouppfattning*. Göteborg: Akademiförlaget-Gumperts, 1962.
Hägg. *Den svenska litteraturhistorien*. Stockholm: Wahlström and Widstrand, 1996.
Lageroth and Romberg. *Perspektiv på Almqvist*. Stockholm: Rabén and Sjögren, 1973.
Lönnroth and Delblanc. *Den svenska litteraturen: Upplysning och romantik 1718–1830*. Stockholm: Bonniers, 1988.
Olsson. *C. J. L. Almqvist*. Stockholm: Bonniers, 1927.
———. *Törnrosdiktaren*. Stockholm: Natur and Kultur, 1956.
Schück and Warburg. *Illustrerad svensk litteraturhistoria*. Stockholm: Natur and Kultur.
Tigerstedt, ed. *Ny illustrerad svensk litteraturhistoria*. Stockholm: Natur and Kultur, 1956.
Werin. *C. J. L. Almqvist: Realisten och liberalen*. Stockholm: Bonniers, 1923.

AMERICAN REVOLUTION 1775–1783

In 1815, John Adams argued (in a letter to Thomas Jefferson) that the real American Revolution had occurred in the minds of American colonists from 1760 to 1775. Several factors had contributed to this changing colonial mindset, characterized by distrust and resentment of the British presence in, and control of, the American colonies. Such factors included extensive reading in classical history by those who would become revolutionary leaders, and the writings of radical Whig authors, which encouraged extreme animosity towards British authority. In the period after the Seven Years War (also known as the French and Indian War), the British government struggled to assert greater control over the American colonies and to continue extracting tax revenue from them in order to pay off debts accumulated during the war. Arbitrary exercises of power, such as the Stamp Act and the Tea Act, provoked strong responses in the colonies, which for many years had hoped to heal the breach with Britain. But increasing taxes had created such strong currents of anti-British feeling that by March 1775 Virginian Patrick Henry could declare, "Our petitions have been slighted; our remonstrances have produced additional violence and insult; our supplications have been disregarded; and we have been spurned, with contempt, from the foot of the throne."

Unrest and threats of violence in the colonies led to the deployment of British troops to Boston. Fighting erupted in the spring of 1775, as General Thomas Gage ordered seven hundred British soldiers to seize caches of arms near Boston. The attempt failed, as armed colonists drove the British back to Boston and eventually descended upon the city. That siege, poorly conducted by the colonists, would continue until the following spring, when the colonists finally secured enough weapons to threaten British ships in Boston harbor.

Gage's career and reputation suffered irredeemable damage in 1775, when, despite being supplied with a superb professional force, he managed to lose the city of Boston to a ragtag band of colonials. His biographer John Alden concluded that while Gage's record in the early months of the American Revolution was dismal, he was certainly competent by European standards of the day and likely would have performed no more poorly than his successors had he remained in command.

For much of the eighteenth century, after the end of the War of Spanish Succession, Great Britain relied on its superb navy to maintain a powerful worldwide presence. During the campaigns against Quebec and Havana during the Seven Years War the Royal Navy placed British forces and their supplies in close proximity to the enemy, whom they then attacked in local towns. In the war against the American colonies, this ability to combine naval and military power offered the British a crucial advantage—namely, the ability to strike quickly and forcefully anywhere along the Atlantic seaboard. In New York, Savannah, and Charleston, British commanders would exploit their army's mobility and the surprise factor to their advantage. At Yorktown, Virginia, in 1781, however, the British army would be defeated by the colonial forces, while French ships defeated the British Navy and blocked the army's line of retreat.

Despite some victories, the colonial forces faced a variety of problems. In general they lacked any kind of military training other than militia duty; the good order, training, and discipline necessary to a successful eighteenth-century army was not immediately apparent in them. After a record of dismal defeats in 1776, American victories at Trenton and Princeton, New Jersey, helped to keep the cause of independence alive and boost morale. Then, a major victory at Saratoga, New York, in 1777 helped to secure the aid of France and Spain. Throughout the war, European forces remained relatively small and were supplemented by local militia. While militia troops were notoriously unreliable, tending to flee when faced with determined British soldiers, they did play an important role in victories at Saratoga and at Cowpens, South Carolina. American commanders were also plagued by an inefficient government composed of thirteen fractious colonies and the inefficient Continental Congress. Fortunately for the American cause, George Washington was named commander in chief of the continental army. While his battlefield performances lacked the tactical brilliance of Napoleon Bonaparte or Frederick the Great, he achieved the nearly impossible task of holding the army together through the grim years of war. By keeping his army intact, avoiding a decisive defeat, parrying British maneuvers, and attacking under favorable circumstances, he succeeded in thwarting a conclusive British victory.

The American victory at Saratoga induced France to enter the war against Great Britain. European intervention was essential for the colonists, since only a country with a powerful navy could neutralize British naval forces; also, France could provide the colonists with much-needed arms. French assistance proved crucial in the Yorktown campaign of 1781. George Washington's continental army held Lord Cornwallis's troops at Yorktown, while the French navy blocked a possible escape route by sea. Cornwallis surrendered, ending the conflict, although a formal peace treaty would not be signed until two years later.

The military struggle would ultimately decide whether the colonies would be ruled locally or from England. The political struggle in America proved intense as well. In 1776, the Continental Congress opened debate on a resolution by Richard Henry Lee that called for independence from Great Britain. After much contentious argument, the congress passed the Declaration of Independence in early July.

British historian Piers Mackesy has offered several causes for Britain's failure to maintain rule over the American colonies. British forces failed to ultimately put down the rebel armies when offered the chance. The royal navy was unable to secure command of the seas, and this would lead directly to the defeat at Yorktown. Mackesy also charges that British leaders were neither bold enough nor creative enough to meet the daunting challenges of the American Revolution.

MITCHELL McNAYLOR

Bibliography

Bailyn, Bernard. *The Ideological Origins of the American Revolution.* Cambridge; Mass.: Belknap Press of Harvard University Press, 1967.

Black, Jeremy. *Warfare in the Eighteenth Century.* London: Cassell, 1999.

Clinton, (Sir) Henry. *The American Rebellion; Sir Henry Clinton's Narrative of His Campaigns, 1775–1782, with an Appendix of Original Documents.* New Haven, Conn.: Yale University Press, 1954.

Commager, Henry Steele, and Richard Morris, eds. *The Spirit of 'Seventy-six: The Story of the American Revolution as Told by Participants.* Indianapolis: Bobbs-Merrill, 1958.

Duffy, Christopher. *The Military Experience in the Age of Reason.* New York: Atheneum, 1987.

Higginbotham, Don. *The War of American Independence: Military Attitudes, Policies, and Practice, 1763–1789.* New York: Macmillan, 1971.

Lee, Henry. *Memoirs of the War in the Southern Department of the United States.* New York: University Publishing, 1870.

Mackesy, Piers. *The War for America, 1775–1783.* Cambridge, Mass.: Harvard University Press, 1964.

Martin, Joseph Plumb. *Private Yankee Doodle: Being a Narrative of Some of the Adventures, Dangers, and Sufferings of a Revolutionary Soldier.* Boston: Little, Brown, 1962.

Royster, Charles. *A Revolutionary People at War: the Continental Army and American Character, 1775–1783.* Chapel Hill: University of North Carolina Press, 1979.

Shy, John. *A People Numerous and Armed: Reflections on the Military Struggle for American Independence.* New York: Oxford University Press, 1976.

AMERICAN ROMANTICISM: APPROACHES AND INTERPRETATIONS

Romanticism as a broad term is associated with the empowerment of the individual over and above forms of law and restriction. As a historical movement it emerged in the eighteenth and nineteenth centuries as a reaction to the more rational traditions of religion and philosophy. An important historical characteristic of American Romanticism is the lateness of its development, explained in part by the internal concerns of a newly defined nation in the fields of politics, economics, and religion. Not until 1836, with the publication of Ralph Waldo Emerson's *Nature*, was native expression given to the innovative ideas current in Europe at the turn of the century.

Historically, the realization of the freedom and independence of the individual, and the increasing valuation placed on it within Western society, goes hand in hand with the West's economic embrace of capitalist ethics from the early modern period. It is this factor which accounts for the contradictory sweep of its appeal, providing both secular and divine justification for economic expansionism as much as for ethical humanitarianism. American emancipation from British colonial rule marked a first stage in its openness to the influences of revolutionary Romanticism apparent in Europe. Yet the most clearly defined American response was against the perceived stagnation and corruption of a burgeoning Romantic spirit.

The ideals and enthusiasms of transcendentalism sought metaphysical justification for the social ideals embodied in the Declaration of Independence, and assimilated influences derived from French utopianism and German mysticism to bolster its assertion of the inalienable worth of man. The pivotal expression of this reaction arrived with the publication of Emerson's *Nature*, and the impetus for the subsequent movement which became associated with him, was its critique of America's institutionalized failure to aspire to the revolutionary values that its independence had embodied. Instead, as Margaret Fuller observed, mid-nineteenth-century America had become "spoiled by prosperity, stupid with the lust of gain, soiled by crime in its perpetuation of slavery, shamed by an unjust war, noble sentiments much forgotten even by individuals, the aims of politicians selfish or petty, the literature frivolous and venal."

The Romantic spirit had been used to embrace conflicting ideological ideals, on the one hand justifying the acquisitiveness of Jacksonian democracy, and on the other inspiring the transcendentalists' enthusiasm for the utopian ideals of Brook Farm.

The openness at the core of American Unitarianism, as it became institutionalized within Harvard University at the turn of the century, allowed for the belated reception and assimilation of continental ideals. As a form of liberal Christianity, Unitarianism had triumphed over the orthodoxies of puritan Calvinism, but had itself become an institution blighted by a conservative rationalism. The appeal of the philosophical and literary works of the German and English Romantic movements, and Emerson's assimilation of their influence, helped to revive America's own religious radicalism. A wide range of ethical, religious, and social interests were embodied by the transcendentalism of such figures as Bronson Allcott, Margaret Fuller, and Henry David Thoreau. Notably, they paved the way for a range of writers as diverse as Emily Dickinson, Nathaniel Hawthorne, Herman Melville, Edgar Allan Poe, and Walt Whitman, to take the lead in the creative realization and exploration of the self which transcendentalism revitalized.

The subsequent modernist debunkings of Emerson up to and beyond the 1920s, by T. S. Eliot, George Santayana, Yvor Winters, and others, obscured the fact that even these most resolute twentieth-century adversaries of Romanticism derived from the Romantic mainstream. For many American modernists and critics of the period, Whitman provided a more usable example than Emerson, the traditional figurehead of American Romanticism, for their reaction against Emerson was fueled by the cult of personality which had grown up around him subsequent to his canonization in the late Victorian period. The post–1945 revival of Emerson's critical reputation revealed the continual underlying importance of American Romanticism to a range of public and intellectual discourses and twentieth-century ideologies and theories; this continued up to the 1970s and 1980s, hinging on the recognition that Romantic discourses provided a deepened textual polyvalence and interrogation of the nature of textuality and rhetoricism. In the work of Harold Bloom, Stanley Cavell, Barbara Packer, Richard Poirier, and others, Emerson is a figure grappling with the central tensions which Romanticism underlines, including a profound skepticism about the capacity of language to embody truth. His reputation as a seer and seeker of unity is displaced by a recognition of his skepticism revealed in the ambiguities and contradictions of his rhetoric. This more disturbing underside of Romanticism is a vital part and subject of the deconstruction movement in America which, in the work of Paul de Man and J. Hillis Miller, foregrounds the profound uncertainty and skepticism of Romantic writing.

The Romantic inheritance can be seen to be vast and varied due to its provision of a basis for questioning which, in the 1960s, sees it informing the literature of the Beat poets, infusing the culture of youth rebellion and alternate lifestyles with

Romantic materials. Romanticism persists as an appropriate idiom for confronting the implications of modernity, providing a means for interrogating and interpreting a world characterized by increasingly rapid change and dislocation.

IAN D. COPESTAKE

Bibliography

Buell, Lawrence. *Literary Transcendentalism: Style and Vision in the American Renaissance.* Ithaca, N.Y.: Cornell University Press, 1973.

Chai, Leon. *The Romantic Foundations of the American Renaissance.* Ithaca, N.Y.: Cornell University Press, 1987.

Gura, Philip, and Joel Myerson, eds. *Critical Essays on American Transcendentalism.* Boston: G. K. Hall, 1982.

Jones, Howard Mumford. *Revolution and Romanticism.* Cambridge, Mass.: Belknap Press of Harvard University Press, 1974.

Morse, David. *American Romanticism.* 2 vols. London: Macmillan, 1987.

Parrington, V. L. *Main Currents in American Thought.* Vol. 2, *The Romantic Revolution in America.* New York: Harcourt, Brace, 1959.

AMERICAN ROMANTICISM: ITS LITERARY LEGACY

Romanticism is one of the strongest intellectual currents in American literature, starting with the burst of cultural activity in mid-nineteenth-century New England and continuing through to the more diffuse, yet still readily discernible, themes of late-twentieth-century writing. Numerous lines of influence can be traced in fiction and poetry, across different genres and from different regional perspectives. This can be demonstrated by four examples. First, the Romantic emphasis on imaginative expression connects the regional modernism of Thomas Wolfe's *Look Homeward Angel* (1929) with the poetry of Walt Whitman; Hart Crane's *The Bridge* (1930) and the urban modernism of Langston Hughes's poetry; and onto Allen Ginsberg's and Jack Kerouac's Beat writings of the 1950s. Second, the celebration of nature in Henry David Thoreau's *Walden; Or Life in the Woods* (1854) and Whitman's *Leaves of Grass* (1855) has found numerous outlets, from the twentieth-century poetry of Wallace Stevens, Robert Frost, and Robert Bly, to Native American writers attempting to preserve tribal customs and the sanctity of nature in an increasingly mercantile environment (for example, Louise Erdrich and N. Scott Momaday). Third, the Gothic writing of Charles Brockden Brown and Edgar Allen Poe has mutated into the ghost stories of Charlotte Perkins Gilman and Henry James; the "grotesque" stories of the modernist Sherwood Anderson in *Winesburg, Ohio* (1919); and the mid-twentieth-century southern Gothic of Carson McCullers and Flannery O'Connor through to popular horror writers such as Stephen King.

A fourth intellectual strain derives from the thought of Ralph Waldo Emerson, which provided the philosophical cornerstone for American Romanticism in the 1840s. Emerson himself was influenced by the British Romantic poets and German Romantic philosophy, but his essays ("First Series," 1841; "Second Series," 1844) offer a peculiar blend of New England spirituality and Kantian idealism, mixed with an assertion that American culture should no longer rely on European artistic models for direction. One aspect of Emerson's thought that has been particularly influential is his reconception of selfhood. In his essay "Circles" (1841) he shifts emphasis away from the "knowing" individual and the epistemological certainty of Enlightenment thought, to the "experiencing" individual and the "energizing spirit" that comes only by nurturing sensitivity to environment. This reformulation of the self can be seen as a direct influence on the work of the philosophers William James and George Santayana as they strove to question received notions of subjec-

tivity in the late nineteenth century, through to the cultural thinkers Stanley Cavell and Cornel West trying to revive the prophetic spirit of the early movement for the late twentieth century. Although versions of Emersonian Romanticism can still be detected in contemporary writing, such as Don DeLillo's interest in the technological sublime in *White Noise* (1984) and Paul Auster's explorations of postmodern identity in *New York Trilogy* (1989), it is in debates about the future of American literature in the late nineteenth century that the pervasive nature of Romantic thought began to emerge.

In his canonical study *The American Novel and Its Tradition* (1957), Richard Chase identifies two primary modes of American writing that emerged in the nineteenth century: the romance form, as a version of what Nathaniel Hawthorne called the "twice-told tale," existing at one remove from the everyday in an imaginative realm of fiction, and naturalistic writing characterized by the accurate study of social conditions. This polar view of American literature largely derives from the novelist William Dean Howells's argument in the 1880s that "the romance and the novel are as distinct as the poem and the novel." Howells separates the serious study of social values undertaken by realist and naturalist writers after the Civil War, from the earlier Romantic investigations of Hawthorne and Herman Melville into the inner life of characters troubled by, but partly transcending, their environment. While romance writers usually focused on the natural world and the morality of individuals at odds with their peers, naturalists tended to concentrate on the constraints that prevent moral action within the social and legal systems of urban America.

While Howells's distinction is true to a degree, another perspective on the realism of Henry James and the naturalism of Stephen Crane and Frank Norris suggests that American fiction around the turn of the century was more tightly interwoven than Howells acknowledges. Over a thirty-year period (from *Roderick Hudson* [1876] to *The Golden Bowl* [1904]) James worked with different strains of social realism, drawing as much from romance as from cool empirical observation. Similarly, although the naturalists were more direct than James in their depiction of urban conditions and class conflict, their exploration of the tensions between individuals and environment contain strong Romantic impulses. For example, Norris argued that it was the moral responsibility of the writer to rejuvenate refined and genteel literary forms (such as those of Howells and James) with the energy of "the Nature revival" in American literature. The strains of naturalism in Norris's major novels *McTeague* (1899), *The Octopus* (1901), and *The Pit* (1903) address the "realistic" issues of poverty and the effects of technology and business on the material conditions of life, but in each novel he delves "down deep into the red, living heart of things" rather than depicting only "clothes and tissues and wrappings of flesh." For Norris, the true writer takes realism away from the coziness of the middle class drawing room into the street, where it fuses with a dynamic Romantic spirit that is heedless of moral limits and literary propriety.

The modernist critics T. S. Eliot, in "'Romantic' and 'Classic'" (1934), and Philip Rahv, in "Redskin and Paleface" (1939), reinforced this notion of two competing traditions in American writing. For Eliot, the effusiveness of Romantic thought was inferior to the balance and poise of classical poetry, whereas Rahv compares "redskins" such as Whitman and Mark Twain and their celebration of nature and open spaces with the "paleface" writers James and Eliot, who are more cerebral and often drawn to European literary traditions. While Rahv's distinction holds for certain writers, his bipartite scheme lacks nuance, and does not take into account modernists such as Ezra Pound and Henry Miller, whose work reviles Romanticism (Pound expresses his dislike of Whitman in "A Pact" [1916] and Miller parodies Romantic expression at the beginning of *Tropic of Cancer* [1934]) but also displays sympathies with its spirit of nonconformism (Pound's poem ends by agreeing there should be "commerce between" Whitman and himself). Divisions in recent American writing can still be discerned in accordance with Howells' distinction, but critics such as Jonathan Levin have argued that the resistance to "definitive formulations" in Romantic thought is often expressed as "stylistic restlessness" and "unsettled possibility" that cannot be reduced to lists of generic characteristics. As such, the legacy of Romanticism forms a complex series of influences, revealing the tensions between nativist and international impulses while reinforcing the essential hybridity of American literary production.

MARTIN HALLIWELL

Bibliography

Chase, Richard. *The American Novel and Its Tradition*. New York: Doubleday, 1957.

Eliot, T. S. *Selected Prose*. Edited by Frank Kermode. London: Faber, 1970.

Emerson, Ralph Waldo. *Emerson: Essays and Lectures*, New York: Library of America, 1983.

Halliwell, Martin. *Romantic Science and the Experience of Self*. London: Ashgate, 1999.

Howells, William Dean. *W. D. Howells as Critic*. Edited by E. H. Cady. London: Routledge and Kegan Paul, 1973.

Levin, Jonathan. *The Poetics of Transition: Emerson, Pragmatism and American Literary Modernism*. Durham, N.C.: Duke University Press, 1999.

Norris, Frank. *The Literary Criticism of Frank Norris*. Edited by Donald Pizer. Austin: University of Texas Press, 1964.

Rahv, Philip. *Literature and the Sixth Sense*. London: Faber, 1970.

Ruland, Richard, and Malcolm Bradbury. *From Puritanism to Postmodernism*. London: Viking, 1991.

Weinstein, Norman. *Nobody's Home: Speech, Self and Place in American Fiction from Hawthorne to DeLillo*. New York: Oxford University Press, 1993.

ANDERSEN, HANS CHRISTIAN 1805–1875

Danish novelist, playwright, poet, and writer of fairy tales

Hans Christian Andersen was the first truly professional Danish writer in the sense that he earned a living from his writing and never had another occupation. Although his fame today rests on his fairy tales, his works cover every literary genre and many of them received great popular acclaim in his own time, both in Denmark and abroad.

There are few writers whose life and works are more inextricably entangled than those of Hans Christian Andersen. He grew up in great poverty in Odense, then the second largest city in Denmark, and was only eleven when his father Hans Andersen, a cobbler, died. His mother had to take odd jobs, and ended up an alcoholic. Some of his closest relatives had experienced imprisonment and madness, and the existence of an elder, illegitimate, half sister haunted him for much of his life. It is significant that the theme of a young man who has to overcome poverty before his innate talents are recognized—often with the help of benefactors—runs through Andersen's works. A loner, he always felt an outsider in the bourgeois and upper-class society to which he desperately tried to adapt. One of his own self-images was that of a "swamp plant" reaching for the light. From early childhood he did, however, believe strongly in his own artistic talents, and at the age of fourteen obtained his mother's reluctant permission to travel to Copenhagen to seek his fortune, without any contacts there and equipped only with a letter of recommendation to the leading ballerina at the Royal Theater.

From childhood, the theater was always Andersen's grand, if largely unrequited, passion, and his early visits to the Odense Theater left an indelible mark. In his first difficult years in Copenhagen, he managed to get minor parts at the Royal Theater and to have lessons in singing and ballet, but to no avail. Rejection as a performer only fueled his desire to become a playwright, but early derivative attempts were very crude and revealed an appalling lack of elementary education. Nevertheless, although the Royal Theater rejected them, it was at this point that some influential people there saw a few glimpses of potential in Andersen and offered him a free secondary education. Jonas Collin, the Royal Theater's director, oversaw this scheme, and in him and his family Andersen found the surrogate father and the bourgeois home that he yearned for, and subsequently referred to as the "home of homes." The actual school years were the most miserable of his life and haunted him long afterward, but they enabled him to move back to Copenhagen, and with the help of friends and protectors to embark on a literary career.

Strongly influenced by E. T. A. Hoffmann, Andersen's first major successful work (in 1829) was *Fodreise fra Holmens Canal til Østpynten af Amager i Aarene 1828 og 1829* (*A Walking Tour from Holmen's Canal to the Eastern Point of Amager in the Years 1828 and 1829*), a satirical, real and imaginary walking tour on New Year's Eve in Copenhagen. This tour de force brought Andersen's name to the attention of the public and the critics alike.

While still at school, Andersen wrote his first successful poem, "Det døende Barn" ("The Dying Child"), which was published anonymously. In the following years, Heinrich Heine became the main influence on Andersen's poetry, for example on *Digte* (*Poems*) in 1830, but most notably on his love poems in *Phantasier og Skizzer* (*Phantasies and Sketches*), 1831. In 1833 he published his *Collected Poems*, after which his lyrical writings become more incidental, appearing as part of his travelogues, plays and libretti, as occasional poems celebrating the nation or its regions, such as "I Danmark er jeg født" ("In Denmark I Was Born") and "Jylland mellem tvende Have" ("Jutland between Two Oceans"), or as humorous narrative poems like "Konen med Æggene" ("The Woman with the Eggs").

Despite his enthusiasm for the stage, Andersen was not a natural dramatist and he suffered more defeats and distress here than in any other area of his vast production. Plays accepted for staging at the Royal Theater often ran for just a few performances and professional criticism was usually harsh. Admittedly, most of his plays had a very loose structure and the verse did not always ring true, but the critics were at times unjustly severe on him on formal grounds and for deviating from the prevailing taste, not appreciating some of the novel elements that he brought to the stage. He had a rare success with *Mulatten* (*The Mulatto*) in 1840. With its exotic setting, its powerful portrayal of sexual passion, hate and revenge, its interracial conflicts and relationships, and its protagonist as an outcast with demonic characteristics that are dissolved through love, the play represents a peak in late-Romantic Danish drama and anticipates more modern treatments of some of these themes. However, his next play *Maurerpigen* (*The Moorish Maid*) was a spectacular failure, not helped when Johanne Luise Heiberg, the greatest Danish actress of her time and the wife of the influential writer and critic Johan Ludvig Heiberg, refused to play the title role. The following year Heiberg ridiculed both plays in his apocalyctic play, *En Sjæl efter Døden* (*A Soul after Death*). After the opening of the new Casino Theater in Copenhagen in 1848, Andersen achieved popular acclaim and commercial success with some fairytale fantasies, such as *Meer end Perler og Guld* (*More than Pearls and Gold*, 1849), *Ole Lukøje* (*Willie Winkie*, 1850), and *Hyldemoer* (*Mother Elder*, 1851), but from then onward his output for the theater was negligible.

Andersen wrote six novels. The first three appeared in rapid succession in the late 1830s, inspired largely by his grand tour of Germany, France, Italy, and Austria in 1833–34 and characteristically containing strong autobiographical elements. They are also in tune with the late Romantic period. Inspired by such European writers as Lord Byron, Heinrich Heine, E. T. A. Hoffmann, and Victor Hugo, Andersen was fascinated by the good-and-evil duality of human nature and the resulting disharmony, and of course by the role of the outsider, and he tried to explore

the underlying but fashionable spleen or *Weltschmerz*. However, the irony that is often found in the literature of that period is much more obvious in Andersen's fairy tales than in his novels. *Improvisatoren* (*The Improvisatore*, 1835), which brought him international fame, tells the story of a Roman boy from a poor background who achieves success through his talent for improvisation, helped by the members of a benevolent, wealthy family. This is often seen as the first Danish bildungsroman, but his next two novels are very different. In *O.T.* (1836)—which stands for the hero Otto Thostrup but also for Odense Tugthus (Odense Jail) where in his early childhood he and his mother had been (unjustly) imprisoned—the protagonist tries to overcome the traumatic childhood that haunts him later in life. The third novel, *Kun en Spillemand* (*Only a Fiddler*, 1837), is much more pessimistic, being an inversion of the familiar Andersen theme of the triumph of true talent despite a disadvantaged background since the musically gifted but passive hero, Christian, is crushed and rejected artistically, socially, and sexually. Today the novel is probably more famous for an extremely critical review by Søren Kierkegaard, the latter's first publication. A decade later came *De to Baronesser* (*The Two Baronesses*, 1848), with two female protagonists, in which Andersen shows that true nobility is a matter of mind and spirit, not birth. Another decade passed before the appearance of *At være eller ikke være?* (*To Be or Not to Be?* 1857), with a dedication to Charles Dickens. This is an even better example of a *bildungsroman* than *The Improvisatore*, and also poses a religious problem. The hero, Niels Bryde, influenced by David Strauss's *Das Leben Jesu* and the contemporary climate of religious scepticism, becomes a freethinker, but his experiences in the Schleswig-Holstein War in 1848–50 teach him the necessity of faith in God. Andersen's last novel, *Lykke-Peer* (*Lucky Peer*, 1870), once more features a seemingly autobiographical hero, an impoverished but musically talented man who achieves great success but dies at the peak of his career, artistically though not sexually fulfilled.

Few contemporary artists traveled as extensively as Andersen. He lived up to his own motto—"to travel is to live"—and experienced with excitement the change from the discomfort of stage-coaches to the relative speed and luxury of the railroad. After his 1833–34 grand tour he went on countless journeys throughout the whole of Europe, including two to England during which he visited Dickens. Many of these journeys resulted in published sketches or travelogues. The first of these was *Skyggebilleder af en Reise til Harzen, det sachsiske Schweitz etc. etc., i Sommeren 1831* (*Shadow Pictures from a Journey to the Harz Mountains, Saxon Switzerland, etc., etc., in the Summer of 1831*), inspired by Heine's *Harzreise* (1826) and the Danish writer Jens Baggesen's earlier, imaginative travelogue *Labyrinten* (*The Labyrinth*, 1792–93). The best of them is undoubtedly *En Digter's Bazar* (*A Poet's Bazaar*, 1842), the fruit of his long journey to Rome, Smyrna, Constantinople, Vienna, and Dresden, in which he blends travel information, impressions, fantasy, and poetry into a fascinating whole. Later travel accounts include *I Sverige* (*In Sweden*, 1851), *I Spanien* (*In Spain*, 1863), and *Et Besøg i Portugal* (*A Visit to Portugal*, 1866).

It is hardly surprising that a person of Andersen's sensibility should be a compulsive and prolific letter writer and diarist. Many books containing his correspondence with friends and acquaintances have appeared, and the diaries from 1825–75 have been published in twelve volumes. These offer a day-to-day account of Andersen's thoughts, opinions, emotions, and mood swings, and even more than his fiction they reveal his ambition, vanity, deference to his royal and noble acquaintances (some of them in Germany), and not least his profound insecurity and vulnerability.

His obsessive and persistent attempts to rearrange and reinterpret his life in retrospect, so as to reinvent himself, resulted in three autobiographies. The first one, *Levnedsbogen* (*The Book of My Life*), written as early as 1832 (in case of his premature death!), is the most immediate and honest account of his life up to that date. A second one appeared first in German as *Das Märchen meines Lebens ohne Dichtung* (1847) and later that year in an English translation as *The True Story of My Life*. His definitive version is *Mit Livs Eventyr* (*The Fairy Tale of My Life*, 1855); a more self-conscious work in which he tries to make his life story conform to the idea of a fairy tale and edits out some of the more uncomfortable details from the previous versions.

Even without the fairy tales, Andersen would thus have been an important figure in Danish and European literature.

TOM LUNDSKÆR-NIELSEN

Biography

Born in Odense, on the island of Funen, Denmark, April 2, 1805. Son of the cobbler Hans Andersen and Anne Marie Andersen, née Andersdatter. Left Odense for Copenhagen, 1819. Belatedly attended secondary school, 1822–27. Published *A Walking Tour*, 1829; *Shadow Pictures*, 1831; *Collected Poems*, 1833. First journey to Germany, 1831. Journey to France, Italy, Austria, and Germany, 1833–34. Published *The Improvisatore* and first collection of fairy tales, 1835; *O.T.*, 1836; *Only a Fiddler*, 1837; *The Mulatto* and *The Moorish Maid*, 1840. Journey to Italy, Greece, Turkey, Austria, and Germany, 1840–41. Published *A Poet's Bazaar*, 1842; *New Fairy Tales* (five collections), 1843–48. Journey to France and Germany; fell in love with Jenny Lind, 1843. First visit to England; met Charles Dickens; published *The True Story of My Life*, 1847. Published *The Two Baronesses*, 1848. Journey to Sweden, 1849. Journeys to Germany, Italy, Switzerland, 1851–52, 1854, and 1855. Published two collections of stories, 1852–53; *The Fairy Tale of My Life*, 1855. Second visit to England as guest of Charles Dickens; published *To Be or Not To Be*, 1857. Eleven collections of fairy tales and stories, 1858–72. Various journeys to Germany, Switzerland, Italy, France, Spain, and Morocco, 1860–63. Journeys to Sweden, Holland, France, and Portugal, 1865–66. Two visits to the World Exhibition in Paris; made honorary citizen of his home town, Odense, 1867. Journeys to Germany, Holland, France, Switzerland, and Austria, 1868–70. Published *Lucky Peer*, 1870. Journeys to Norway, Germany, Austria, Italy, and Switzerland, 1871–73. Died in Copenhagen, August 4, 1875; funeral in the cathedral of Copenhagen on August 11.

Selected Works

Fiction

Novels, Plays, and Poetry
A Walking Tour from Holmen's Canal to the Eastern Point of Amager in the Years 1828 and 1829 (novella). 1829.
Poems. 1830.
Phantasies and Sketches (poems). 1831.
Collected Poems. 1833.
The Improvisatore (novel). 1835.
O.T. (novel). 1836.
Only a Fiddler (novel). 1837.
The Mulatto; The Moorish Maid (plays). 1840.
The Two Baronesses (novel). 1848.
To Be or Not To Be? (novel). 1857.
Lucky Peer (novel). 1870.

Fairy Tales and Stories (156 in all)
Fairy Tales, Told for Children (first collection). 1835.
Fairy Tales, Told for Children (five further collections). 1835–41.
New Fairy Tales (five collections). 1843–48.
Stories (two collections). 1852–53.
New Fairy Tales and Stories (eleven collections). 1858–72.

Nonfiction

Shadow Pictures from a Journey to the Harz Mountains and Saxon Switzerland, etc., etc., in the Summer of 1831 (travelogue). 1831.
The Book of My Life (first autobiography). 1832.
A Poet's Bazaar (travelogue). 1842.
The True Story of My Life (autobiography; first in German as *Das Märchen meines Lebens ohne Dichtung*). 1847.
The Fairy Tale of My Life (last autobiography). 1855.

Bibliography

Andersen, Hans Christian. *The Fairy Tale of My Life*. Translated by W. Glyn Jones. New York: British Book Centre, 1954.
——. *H. C. Andersens Dagbøger 1825–1875*, vols. 1–12. Edited by H. Topsøe-Jensen and Kåre Olsen, Copenhagen: Gad, 1971–76.
——. *Romaner og Rejseskildringer*, vols. 1–7. Edited by H. Topsøe-Jensen. Copenhagen: Gyldendal, 1943–44.
——. *Samlede Skrifter*, vols. 1–12. 2d ed. Copenhagen: C. A. Reitzel, 1876–80.
Bredsdorff, Elias. *Hans Christian Andersen: A Biography*. Souvenir Press, London, 1993.
——. *Hans Christian Andersen—The Story of His Life and Work 1805–75*. London: Phaidon, 1975.
Conroy, Patricia L., and Sven H. Rossel. *The Diaries of Hans Christian Andersen*. Seattle: University of Washington Press, 1990.
Grønbech, Bo. *Hans Christian Andersen*. Boston: Twayne, 1980.
Marker, Frederick J. *Hans Christian Andersen and the Romantic Theatre*. Toronto: University of Toronto Press, 1971.
Mylius, Johan de. *H. C. Andersen—liv og værk. En tidstavle 1805–1875*. Copenhagen: Aschehoug, 1981.
——. *Hr. Digter Andersen. Liv Digtning Meninger*. Copenhagen: Gad, 1995.
——. *Myte og Roman. H. C. Andersens romaner mellem romantik og realisme*. Copenhagen: Gyldendal, 1981.
Prince, Alison. *Hans Christian Andersen: The Fan Dancer*. London: Allison and Busby, 1998.
Rossel, Sven Hakon, ed. *Hans Christian Andersen: Danish Writer and Citizen of the World*. Amsterdam: Rodopi, 1996.
Spink, Reginald. *Hans Christian Andersen and His World*. London: Thames and Hudson, 1972.
Wullschlager, Jackie, *Hans Christian Andersen: The Life of a Storyteller*. London: Penguin, 2000.

ARNDT, ERNST MORITZ 1769–1860

German historian, propagandist, and poet

At first sight, much of Ernst Moritz Arndt's work seems an affront to enlightened liberalism. Particularly during the period 1806–15, he published a series of essays, pamphlets, and poems expressing fanatical nationalism and xenophobia. He repeatedly glorifies the German *Volk* and fatherland. In his 1813 poem "Des Deutschen Vaterland" ("The German Fatherland"), he argues that the boundaries of Germany stretch from the North Sea to Switzerland and the Tyrol. Germany is "Wo Zorn vertilgt den welschen Tand, Wo jeder Franzmann heisset Feind" ("Where wrath wipes out foreign frippery, Where every Frenchie is a foe"). In the same year he declared "Ich hasse alle Franzosen ohne Unterschied im Namen Gottes und im Namen meines Volkes" ("I hate all the French without exception in the name of God and in the name of my people"). He pleads for a holy war against the French and by extension against all Latin ("welsch") races. In the poem "Vaterlandslied" ("Song of the Fatherland," 1812), he urges his compatriots literally to bathe their swords in French blood and hack to pieces those Germans serving in Napoleon's armies.

Such violent racism, while not excusable, is best considered in context. During the French hegemony in the German states, after Napoleon Bonaparte's defeat of Austria in 1805 and of Prussia in 1806, it appeared that Germany, which had never existed as a unified nation-state, might be permanently obliterated. To the Romantic generation, which had set about rediscovering the German cultural heritage, it seemed possible that a separate national identity could be lost before it had been properly established. In the face of political and military impotence, a trend arose among the German Romantics that might be described as cultural nationalism. This trend was reinforced by the increasingly exploitative French occupation and by economic hardship arising from the continental blockade. Arndt's hysteria is thus only an extreme variant on a Francophobia cultivated in the middle phases of German Romanticism by intellectuals as diverse as the formerly republican and cosmopolitan Friedrich Schlegel, and the devout Protestant painter Caspar David Friedrich. In 1806, even before Napoleon's decisive victories in Germany, Arndt published the first volume of his *Geist der Zeit* (*Spirit of the Age*), a collection of essays in which he denounced French expansion into German territory and the German rulers who had allowed it. He concluded that the Germans should rise up in a war of liberation and expel the French, the "archenemy."

In other respects Arndt's political creed was largely that of eighteenth-century liberalism and rooted in the egalitarian principles of the Enlightenment. His origins (his grandparents had been serfs in feudal Swedish Pomerania and his father had bought his own freedom) dictated his belief in social justice and reform, but he remained a monarchist till the end of his life and never advocated revolution. In his first major work, the treatise *Versuch einer Geschichte der Leibeigenschaft in Pommern und Rügen* (*An Attempted History of Serfdom in Pomerania and Rügen*, 1803), he argued that a repetition of the French Revolution on German soil could be prevented if serfdom were abolished and land made available to tenant farmers. In the first volume of *Geist der Zeit* (1806) he condemns particularist German princes

for putting dynastic ambitions before the interests of the nation, denounces bureaucratic and impersonal regimes such as that of Frederick the Great, and demands a greater involvement of the citizen in the processes of government. Therefore, it was natural for him to support the Prussian reformers, and through them Prussia itself. In *Der Bauernstand, politisch betrachtet* (*The Peasantry, Considered Politically*, 1810) Arndt expresses his approval of the agrarian reforms introduced after 1807 by the administrations of Karl vom Stein and Karl August von Hardenberg in Prussia, and calls for an end to hereditary privileges. The Pomeranian and once loyal Swedish subject had now evolved into a supporter of Prussia and a German nationalist.

In 1812, anticipating Napoleon's invasion of Russia, Arndt went to Saint Petersburg to act as private secretary to the now exiled Stein, who had been impressed with the second volume of *Geist der Zeit* (1809). Arndt soon became the principal propagandist in the campaign to expel the French from the German states and create a unified Germany. He then wrote his most influential work, the pamphlet *Kurzer Katechismus für teutsche Soldaten* (*Short Catechism for German Soldiers*, 1812; the *t* in "teutsch" is a deliberate archaism). Arndt visualizes an army of citizen soldiers motivated by patriotic enthusiasm and not by loyalty to ruling dynasties. It follows that Germans serving in Napoleon's *grande armée* at the behest of their particularist rulers do not in fact owe allegiance to these traitorous princes. Their loyalty is only to a united Germany, given that Germans from all regions are a single nation and should have a single ruler. Returning to Germany in 1813, at the height of the so-called Wars of Liberation, Arndt poured out bloodthirsty anti-French poetry.

By 1815 the *Katechismus* had been reprinted fifteenth times, but in later editions Arndt was compelled to tone down its subversive implications. He rapidly became disillusioned, as reformers and nationalists lost influence in the anti-French front and control was gained by legitimists supporting the restoration of the separate German monarchies. In 1813, following an attempt by Klemens Fürst von Metternich to negotiate peace by permanently ceding areas to the west of the Rhine to France, an outraged Arndt published *Der Rhein, Teutschlands Strom, aber nicht Teutschlands Grenze!* (*The Rhine, Germany's River but not Germany's Frontier!*). Political disappointment drove him increasingly toward religion and conservatism, and after the Congress of Vienna in 1815 he advocated an imperial but constitutional Germany based on a patriarchal and agrarian society. Such views began to appear in his periodical *Der Wächter* (*The Sentinel*, 1815–16) and in the fourth volume of *Geist der Zeit* (1818). Arndt was now considered a political loose cannon, and in 1820 the Prussian authorities forced his dismissal from the chair of history at the University of Bonn, reinstating him only in 1840. His intellectual development is typical of German Romanticism after 1806: resentment at the French occupation led, fatefully, to rejection of the democratic and cosmopolitan ideas with which the French were associated, and thence to nostalgic conservatism.

RICHARD LITTLEJOHNS

Biography

Born in Gross-Schoritz on the island of Rügen (then under Swedish rule) in Pomerania, Germany, December 26, 1769. Educated first in Stralsund. Studied Protestant theology in Greifswald and Jena to qualify for the Lutheran ministry, 1791–96. Private tutor and chaplain, 1796. Renounced the priesthood and traveled through Europe, 1797–99. Lectured in history at the University of Greifswald, 1800–1806. Lived in exile in Stockholm after fleeing from Napoleon, 1808–9. Returned to Germany, settling in Berlin, 1809: associated with Prussian reformist politicians and generals. Appointed to professorship at the University of Greifswald, 1810. Appointed private secretary to former Prussian chief minister Karl vom Stein, 1811. Joined Stein in Saint Petersburg to help organize the expulsion of the French from German states, 1812. Published his influential *Kurzer Katechismus fur teutsche Soldaten* (*Short Catechism for German Soldiers*), 1812. Returned to Germany, staying in Königsberg, Berlin, and Leipzig, 1813. Journalist and editor in Cologne, 1815–17. Married Nanna Schleiermacher, 1817. Appointed to the chair of modern history in the newly founded University of Bonn, 1818. Remained in Bonn until his death. Arrested for his seditious political views by the Prussian government, 1819; set free but removed from his teaching post, 1820. Reinstated in 1840 by Friedrich Wilhelm IV of Prussia. Served as an elected member of the abortive Frankfurt Parliament, 1848–49. Retired from public position after the refusal of Friedrich Wilhelm IV to take the German crown, 1854. Died of pneumonia in Bonn, January 29, 1860.

Selected Works

Collections

Ausgewählte Werke. 14 vols. Edited by Hugo Rösch and Heinrich Meisner. Magedeburg, 1892–1909.
Ausgewählte Werke. 6 vols. Edited by Hugo Meisner and Robert Geerds. Leipzig: Pfau, 1908.
Werke. 12 parts. Edited by August Leffson and Wilhelm Steffens. Berlin: Bong, 1912.
Ausgewählte Gedichte und Schriften. Edited by Gustav Erdmann. East Berlin: Union-Verlag, 1969.

Historical and Political Treatises

Versuch einer Geschichte der Leibeigenschaft in Pommern und Rügen, 1803.
Germanien und Europa, 1803.
Geist der Zeit, vol. 1, 1806; vol. 2, 1809; vol. 3, 1813; vol. 4, 1818.

Der Bauernstand, politisch betrachtet, 1810.
Ansichten und Aussichten der teutschen Geschichte, 1814.
Über künftige ständische Verfassungen in Teutschland, 1814.
Schriften für und an seine lieben Deutschen, 1854–55.

Political Pamphlets

Kurzer Katechismus für teutsche Soldaten, 1812. Revised under the title *Kurzer Katechismus für den deutschen Kriegs- und Wehrmann,* 1813.
Was bedeutet Landsturm und Landwehr? 1813.
Der Rhein Teutschlands Strom, aber nicht Deutschlands Grenze! 1813.
Drei Flugschriften. Facsimile reprints. Edited by Rolf Weber. East Berlin: Verlag der Nation, 1988.

Drama

Der Storch und seine Familie, 1804.

Poetry

Gedichte, 1803.
Lieder für Teutsche, 1813.
Geistliche Lieder, 1855.
Gedichte, 1860.

Travelogues

Reisen durch einen Teil Deutschlands, Ungarns, Italiens und Frankreichs in den Jahren 1798 und 1799, 1800–1803. Rev. ed. 1804.

Memoirs

Erinnerungen aus dem äußeren Leben, 1840.
Meine Wanderungen und Wandelungen mit dem Reichsfreiherrn Herrn K. F. vom Stein, 1858.
Erinnerungen 1769–1815. Edited by Rolf Weber. Berlin: Verlag der Nation, 1985.

Correspondence

Lebensbild in Briefen. Edited by Heinrich Meisner and Robert Geerds. Berlin: Reimer: 1898.
Briefe. 3 vols. Edited by Albrecht Dühr. Darmstadt: Wissenschaftliche Buchgesellschaft, 1972–75.

Bibliography

Kohn, Hans. *The Mind of Germany.* London: Macmillan, 1965. 75–80.
Kollektiv für Literaturgeschichte. *Erläuterungen zur deutschen Literatur: Befreiungskriege.* 5th ed. Berlin: Volk und Wissen, 1973. 57–76.
Scurla, Herbert. *Ernst Moritz Arndt.* East Berlin: Kongress, 1952.
Schäfer, Karl Heinz. *Ernst Moritz Arndt als politischer Publizist.* Bonn: Roehrscheid, 1974.

ARNIM, ACHIM VON 1781–1831

German writer

The importance of Achim von Arnim in German Romanticism has long been underestimated. During his lifetime, his works were known only to a small circle of friends (which included most of the major figures of the period) and were misunderstood by nearly all of them. This state of affairs has proven difficult to alter. Arnim's first writings were scientific; he contributed to contemporary debate in the prestigious journal *Annalen der Physik* (*Annals of Physics*) from 1799 until 1807, though his interests were always wide-ranging and his overriding concern was to unite all spheres of learning and culture. He came to believe that the reconciliation of all parts of life could only be achieved through poetry, which could present the eternal through the individual.

Arnim's understanding of the poet was of a gifted individual with the ability to see creatively and who felt responsible for others in society. Arnim's social engagement is demonstrated in his plans to found an academy for the popular arts, which would re-create a national folk consciousness, unite high and folk art, and foster a new golden age of German poetry; and in the numerous newspaper articles and essays he wrote on political (often patriotic), military, administrative, economic, geographic, agricultural, cultural, pedagogic, literary, and religious themes (themes that also play a major role in his creative works). He was a founding member in 1811 of the Christlich-Deutschen Tischgesellschaft (Christian-German Dining Society), a debating forum from which the members excluded "Jews and philistines." In the years 1813–14, during the Wars of Liberation, he edited the journal *Der Preussische Correspondent* (*The Prussian Correspondent*) and became captain in a unit of the National Guard in Berlin. His campaigns for reform were vigorous but nonsystematic and his ideas remained without influence, a major source of frustration which contributed to feelings of intellectual isolation. As an editor and journalist, he was strictly limited by censorship; as a political activist, he was irresolute and, ultimately, ignored. In 1814, he retreated to Wiepersdorf and tried to lift his estate out of debt and support his growing family. He continued to write but effectively removed himself from the literary and political stage.

Arnim is best known for his editorship, with Clemens Brentano, of the collection *Des Knaben Wunderhorn* (*The Boy's Magic Horn*, 1805–8), amalgamating traditional folk songs with new compositions, including the editors' own. Their creative editorial policy was criticized by Enlightenment figures such as Johann Heinrich Voss, and by close friends, particularly the brothers Jakob Ludwig Karl Grimm and Wilhelm Karl Grimm. Arnim defended it repeatedly as his central aesthetic principle. With Brentano, he also edited an unsuccessful and short-lived periodical, *Zeitung für Einsiedler* (*Journal for Hermits*, 1808), which appeared in book form as *Tröst Einsamkeit* (Solace for Loneliness, 1808), with contributions from Ludwig Tieck and Friedrich vom Schlegel, among others. This period, 1805–8, which Arnim and Brentano spent in Heidelberg with friends, has been christened the era of "Heidelberg Romanticism."

Arnim's attempts to write in the dramatic genre—for example, *Halle und Jerusalem* (1811)—were unconvincing due to his unwillingness to restrict himself in structure or content. Although any general statement on his work in this genre (as in all others) may have to be reassessed in the light of new material to be published in the ongoing Weimar critical edition of his works, undoubtedly Arnim's best works were written in prose, characterized by an often grotesque combination of surreal fantasy and historical and contemporary reality in a narrative of self-associating ideas. In a collection of novellas published in 1812, usually referred to as *Novellensammlung von 1812* (*The Novellas of 1812*), he tells in *Isabella von Ägypten* (*Isabella of Egypt*) the story of the gypsy lover of Emperor Charles V, and in *Melück Maria Blainville* of an Oriental prophet whose fate becomes entangled with events of the French Revolution. *Die Majoratsherren* (*Gentry by Entailment*, 1819) confronts visionary idealism with the philistine pragmatism of the bourgeoisie after the French Revolution. *Der tolle Invalide auf dem Fort Ratonneau* (*The Mad Veteran in the Fortress of Ratonneau*, 1818) was written for the financial benefit of invalid war veterans, and the story intertwines the serious political strand with popular psychology, supernatural curses, and exorcism.

Many of Arnim's writings are creative reworkings of old literature, in particular the collection of novellas *Der Wintergarten* (*The Conservatory*, 1809) and the dramas in *Schaubühne* (*Theater*, vol. 1, 1813). This tendency is also evident in his first published fictional work, the novel *Hollin's Liebeleben* (*Hollin's Love Life*, 1802), which places itself firmly in the tradition of Johann Wolfgang von Goethe's *Die Leiden des jungen Werther* (*The Sorrows of Young Werther*, 1774) and in which the protagonists act out Johann Christoph Friedrich von Schiller's *Maria Stuart* (1800). More significant in terms of Arnim's development as a poet is the novel *Armut, Reichtum, Schuld und Busse der Gräfin Dolores* (*Poverty, Riches, Guilt and Penance of Countess Dolores*, 1810) which depicts contemporary social and political turbulence symbolically through the institution of marriage, with an act of adultery on July 14 precipitating crisis and disaster. This novel is also a response to love and marriage as presented in Goethe's *Die Wahlverwandtschaften* (*Elective Affinities*, 1809) and Friedrich von Schlegel's *Lucinde* (1799). Arnim's *Metamorphosen der Gesellschaft* (*Metamorphoses of Society*) in the collection *Landhausleben* (*Manor House Life*, 1826) takes issue with Ludwig Tieck's *Die Verlobung* (*The Engagement*, 1823) on the theme of power struggles between church and state. In both works, Arnim preserves belief in the possibility of reconciliation and harmony. The unfinished *Die Kronenwächter* (*The Guardians of the Crown*, vol. 1, 1817) set in the Reformation period, intertwines the Romantic with the realistic and, typically for Arnim, uses the past to address the issues of the present day. In this and in other prose works, Arnim wove lyrical inserts into the fabric of the story. These are often the best examples of his poetry—another relatively unknown aspect of his work, which is substantial in volume and uneven in quality.

Arnim's contemporaries condemned his narrative world as chaotic, the only unity seeming to be the author's individual imagination, and subsequent readers have endorsed this verdict. Arnim justified himself explicitly against this criticism, responding that what he described was a true reflection of the complexities of the world. Moreover, his works are an attempt to draw together strands and reconcile opposites, enabling the unity of a higher world to shine through the fragmentary, imperfect, real world.

SHEILA DICKSON

Biography

Born Karl Joachim Friedrich Ludwig von Arnim in Berlin, 26 January 1781, into a noble Prussian family. Mother, Amalie Caroline, died shortly after his birth; father, Joachim Erdmann von Arnim, sold custody of Arnim and elder brother Carl Otto Ludwig to maternal grandmother, Caroline von Labes. Attended Joachimsthaler Gymnasium, Berlin, 1793–98; studied law, physics, mathematics, and chemistry at the University of Halle, 1798–1800, and at the University of Göttingen, 1800–1801. Published *Theory of Electrical Phenomena*, 1799; contributed to the prestigious scientific journal, *Annalen der Physik*, 1799–1807. Undertook grand tour of Europe, 1801–4. Edited the collection *Des Knaben Wunderhorn* (*The Boy's Magic Horn*) with Clemens Brentano, 1805–8. Cofounded the *Christlich-Deutsche Tischgesellschaft* (Christian-German Dining Society), whose membership included many influential Berlin men, and excluded "Jews and philistines," 1811. Married Bettina Brentano (sister of Clemens), 1811; they had seven children. Edited the journal *Der Preussische Correspondent* (*The Prussian Correspondent*); served as captain of a National Guard unit in Berlin, 1813–14. Moved to family estate in Wiepersdorf, Brandenburg, 1814. Wrote fiction, book reviews, and journal articles while managing the heavily mortgaged estate. Visited Bettina and their children regularly after their move to Berlin, 1823. Died of a stroke in Wiepersdorf, January 21, 1831.

Selected Works

Collections

Achim von Arnim: Werke in sechs Bänden. 6 vols. Edited by Roswitha Burwick, Jürgen Knaack, Paul Michael Lützeler, Renate Moering, Ulfert Ricklefs, and Hermann F. Weiss. Frankfurt am Main: Deutscher Klassiker Verlag, 1989–94.

Sämtliche Werke. 23 vols. Vols. 1–22. Edited by Wilhelm Grimm. 1839–56. Wemar: Kühn. Vol. 23 edited by Herbert R. Liedke and Alfred Anger. Tübingen: Niemeyer, 1976.

Sämtliche Romane und Erzählungen. 3 vols. Edited by Walter Migge. Munichi Herser, 1962–65.

Weimarer Arnim-Ausgabe: Ludwig Achim von Arnim: Werke und Briefwechsel. Historisch-kritische Ausgabe. Edited by Roswitha Burwick, Heinz Härtl, Lothar Ehrlich, Renate Moering, Ulfert Ricklefs, and Christof Wingertszahn. Tübingen: Niemeyer, 2000.

Novellas

Novellensammlung von 1812, 1812; translated as *The Novellas of 1812* by Bruce Duncan. Lewiston, N.Y.: Mellen, 1997.

Isabella von Ägypten, 1812; translated as *Isabella of Egypt* by Carl F. Schreiber. In *Fiction and Fantasy of German Romance: Selections from the German Romantic Authors 1790–1830.* Edited by Frederick E. Pierce and Carl F. Schreiber. New York: Oxford University Press, 1927.

Der tolle Invalide auf dem Fort Ratonneau, 1818; translated as *The Mad Veteran of Fort Ratonneau* by William Metcalf. In *The Blue Flower.* Edited by Hermann Kesten. New York: Roy, 1946. Retranslated by Helene Scher. In *Four Romantic Tales from Nineteenth Century Germany.* New York: Ungar, 1975.

Die Majoratsherren, 1819; translated as *Gentry by Entailment* by Alan Brown. London: Atlas, 1990.

Edited Collection

Des Knaben Wunderhorn. 1805–8. 3 vols. Edited by Achim von Arnim and Clemens Brentano. Translated (selections) by Margarete Münsterberg. New York: German Publishing Society 1915.

Bibliography

Andermatt, Michael, ed. *Grenzgänge. Studien zu L. Achim von Arnim*, Bonn: Bouvier, 1994.

Burwick, Roswitha, *Dichtung und Malerei bei Achim von Arnim.* Berlin: de Gruyter, 1989.

Burwick, Roswitha, and Bernd Fischer, eds. *Neue Tendenzen der Arnim-Forschung.* Berne: Peter Lang, 1990.

Burwick, Roswitha, and Heinz Härtl. eds. *"Frische Jugend, reich an Hoffen."* Der junge Arnim Tübingen: Niemeyer, 2000.

Härtl, Heinz, and Hartwig Schultz, eds. *Die Erfahrung anderer Länder. Beiträge eines Wiepersdorfer Kolloquiums zu Achim und Bettina von Arnim*, Berlin: de Gruyter, 1994.

Hoermann, Roland. *Achim von Arnim.* Boston: Twayne, 1984.

Knaack, Jürgen. *Achim von Arnim—Nicht nur Poet. Die politischen Anschauungen Arnims in ihrer Entwicklung.* Darmstadt: Thesen, 1976.

Ricklefs, Ulfert, ed. *Universelle Entwürfe—Integration—Rückzug: Arnims Berliner Zeit, 1809–1814.* Tübingen: Niemeyer, 2000.

Wingertszahn, Christof. *Ambiguität und Ambivalenz im erzählerischen Werk Achim von Arnims.* St. Ingbert: Röhrig, 1990.

ARNIM, BETTINA VON 1785–1859

German writer

Elisabeth Catharina Ludovica Magdalene von Arnim, née Brentano, known as Bettina or Bettine, was both an exemplary and an exceptional figure within the German Romantic movement. She was exemplary because many aspects of her life were typical of her time and because her works bear the hallmarks of her era; and exceptional because she achieved an unusual degree of independence and because she attained remarkable popularity as a Romantic woman writer.

Born into an affluent family in the comparatively liberal and cosmpolitan city of Frankfurt-am-Main, Bettina was educated first in the conventionally strict surroundings of a convent, and then at the house of her maternal grandmother, Sophie von La Roche, the celebrated author of the late Enlightenment sentimental novel *Die Geschichte des Fräuleins von Sternheim* (*The History of Lady Sophia Sternheim*, 1771). Bettina benefited from both the sociable atmosphere of her grandmother's house and its library, where she first made the acquaintance of Johann Wolfgang Goethe and Ludwig Tieck, among other contemporary authors. Her brother Clemens, seven years her senior, guided her reading and introduced her to fellow Romantics, including her future husband, Achim von Arnim. Before agreeing to marriage, however, Bettina spent some time furthering her artistic and philosophical education with the help of private tutors in Frankfurt, and undertook a number of journeys, sometimes disguised as a man, to visit friends and her newly married sisters. During these journeys she experienced and participated in various forms of sociability, most notably perhaps in the Romantic salons of Rahel Levin-Varnhagen and Henriette Hertz in Berlin and of Johanna Schopenhauer in Weimar. She did not consent to wed her brother's intimate friend and raise a family until the age of twenty-four.

A period of productivity began with the death of Achim von Arnim in 1831 during which Bettina was able not only to fully live up to her reputation for eccentricity, but also to set up her own salon and to elaborate her distinctive contribution to the literature of the Romantic era. Alongside instigating and overseeing the publication of her late husband's work, she began to publish in her own name, setting down among other things a memorial to her brother and Arnim's collaborator in *Clemens Brentanos Frühlingskranz aus Jugendbriefen ihm geflochten* (*Clemens Brentano's Spring Garland*, 1844).

As this title makes clear, Bettina's literary works developed out of her letter writing and the culture of conversation typical of the literary salon. It was this connection that had first allowed women access to the literary genre of the epistolary novel. In Bettina's case, however, the use of allegedly authentic material added an extra dimension to the practice. Her first book was *Goethes Briefwechsel mit einem Kinde* (*Goethe's Correspondence with a Child*, 1835). The child in question purported to be the author herself, and the novel is indeed partly based on her correspondence with Goethe. However, it also draws on Goethe's love letters to her mother Maximiliane and on her own friendship with Goethe's aging mother, and much of the material in it has been either rewritten or invented. Nonetheless, since the book was published shortly after Goethe's death in 1832, and coincided with the publication of many genuine collections of letters and volumes of reminiscences, it was initially taken at face value. Yet this arguable marketing strategy was also a genuine act of homage, which goes beyond the cult of the personality and pays tribute to Goethe's achievements as a writer. A closer look at the text reveals that both Goethe and Bettine are fictional characters that owe at least as much to Goethe's work as to his life. The role played by the Bettine of the book is prefigured in Goethe's own *Mignon*.

The narrative techniques used in the Goethe book were developed fully in *Die Günderode* (1840). This is based on Bettina's close friendship with Karoline von Günderode and makes reference to the correspondence between the two women and their meetings between 1804 and 1806. The title of the book draws attention to the life and work of a real and exceptional female poet. And yet, though the book clearly does have an autobiographical dimension, both the Bettine and the Günderode who appear in it are fictionalized characters. The correspondence between the two authentic women has been enlarged, restructured, and poeticized, and literary texts by both women have been included. What emerges is a new kind of composition that goes beyond the documentary and elaborates a philosophical discourse that owes as much to Plato (Günderode is even called "Platon" to Bettine's "Dion") as to any living person. In its insistence on the cognitive value of love, the novel validates a view of the world that is often seen as "feminine," and is also assimilable to Romantic antirationalism. But the shadow of a genuine suicide falls across the book and gives to Bettina's characteristic practice of erecting literary monuments a particular poignancy.

Die Günderode is dedicated to "the students," a group of young men who were part of the Junges Deutschland (Young Germany) democratic movement. In the times of political reaction and repression around 1840, this was an act of political bravery. Subsequent books such as *Dies Buch gehört dem König* (*This Book is for the King*, 1843) and *Gespräche mit Dämonen* (*Conversations with Demons, 1852*), are explicitly political and document Bettine's active concern for the underprivileged. The king in question is a caring patriarch, an idealistic construct that owes much to the concept of the enlightened monarch but is also informed by a Romantic urgency and Bettina's own firsthand experience of the life of the lower classes.

Certainly, the real king took scarcely any notice of the book that presented itself as his property. And though Bettina was constantly stretching the boundaries of what was possible for a woman of her time, she was careful never actually to overstep them. Perhaps this helps to explain why, unlike the famous poets with whom she is indelibly associated, she lived to a ripe old

Quartettabend bei Bettina von Arnim. Reprinted courtesy of AKG.

age and prospered. And certainly it ensures the enduring fascination of this exemplary and extraordinary woman.

ASTRID KÖHLER

Biography

Born in Frankfurt am Main, April 4, 1785. Seventh child of Peter Anton Brentano, an Italian merchant, and his second wife Maximiliane, a friend of the writer Johann Wolfgang von Goethe. Sister of poet Clemens Brentano. Following the death of her mother in 1793, attended an Ursuline convent school in Fritzlar. Went to live with her grandmother, the novelist Sophie von La Roche, during the French occupation of Fritzlar. Suffered loss by suicide of close friend Karoline von Günderode, 1806. Met and began a correspondence with Goethe, 1807. Married Romantic poet and novelist Achim von Arnim, 1811; they had seven children. Lived on the family's country estate in Wiepersdorf, Brandenburg, from 1814 and at Unter der Linden in Berlin from 1823. Lived as a writer and salon hostess in Berlin after Achim von Arnim's death in 1831; devoted herself to various charitable and political causes. Published *Die Günderode*, book based on letters written to Karoline von Günderode, 1840. Died in Berlin, January 29, 1859.

Selected Works

Goethes Briefwechsel mit einem Kinde. Seinem Denkmal, 1835. Translated by herself and "Mrs. Austin" as *Goethe's Correspondence with a Child. For His Monument*. 1837–38.
Die Günderode, 1840. Translated by Sarah Margaret Fuller as *Günderode* 1842 (incomplete). Translated by Sara Margaret Fuller and Mary Wesselhöft as *Correspondence of Fräulein Günderode and Bettine von Arnim*, 1861.
Clemens Brentanos Frühlingskranz aus Jugendbriefen ihm geflochten, 1844.

Dies Buch gehört dem König, 1843.
Gespräche mit Dämonen. Des Königsbuchs zweiter Band, 1852.
Bettina von Arnim: Werke. 2 vols. Edited by Heinz Härtl. 2 Berlin: Aufbau-Verlag, 1986–89.
Bettine von Arnim: Werke und Briefe. 3 vols. Edited by Walter Schmitz and Sibylle von Steinsdorff. Frankfurt am Main: Deutscher Klassiker Verlag, 1986–95.

Bibliography

Bäumer, Konstanze, and Hartwig Schultz. *Bettina von Arnim*. Stuttgart: Metzler, 1995.
Becker-Cantarino, Barbara. *Schriftstellerinnen der Romantik. Epoche—Werk—Wirkung*. Munich: Beck, 2000.
Drewitz, Ingeborg. *Bettine von Arnim. Romantik, Revolution, Utopie*. Düsseldorf: Eugen Diederichs Verlag 1969.
Frederiksen, Elke P, ed. *Bettina Brentano von Arnim. Gender and Politics*. Detroit: Wayne State University Press, 1995.
Goozé, Marianne. "Bettine von Arnim, the Writer." Ph.D. diss., University of California, Berkeley, 1985.
Hahn, Carl-Heinz. *Bettine von Arnim in ihrem Verhältnis zu Staat und Politik. Mit einem Anhang ungedruckter Briefe*. Weimar: Hermann Böhlaus Nachfolger, 1959.
Härtl, Heinz. *Bettina von Arnim 1785–1859. Eine Chronik. Daten und Zitate zu Leben und Werk*. Schloss Wiepersdorf, Stiftung Kulturfonds Künstlerheim "Bettina von Arnim," 1995.
Waldstein, Josefine. *Bettina von Arnim and the Politics of Romantic Conversation*. Columbia, USA: Camden House, 1988.

ART

Canonical art-historical surveys offer varying interpretations that obfuscate the perceived antagonism between Romanticism and its predecessors, particularly neoclassicism. Robert Rosenblum has referred to period markers as "semantic straitjackets," and Lorenz Eitner has offered a generational approach that avoided the period terms. Hugh Honour has deemed Romanticism problematic, arguing that no rubric existed by which to grade the artistic output from this era. He characterized Romantic art as lacking any linear, modernist progression, while calling neoclassicism a core movement with the varying trends or styles radiating outward. Rosenblum's definition comes closest to Lovejoy's assessment of romanticism as a series of interlinked variations, not a monolithic movement.

Without any linear progression, the varying threads of Romanticism were complex, integrated, and charged with a new emphasis on artistic freedom, originality, self-expression, and authenticity. Artists possessed a certain sense, often identified as genius, enabling them to merge the conscious and subconscious, the real and ideal, the natural and the fantastic. Just as romantic literature rejected classical dramatic structure, so too did the visual arts reject formalist constructs such as the superiority of line, classical motifs, and the primacy of historical and mythological subjects, favoring instead sensuous forms, rich colors, and varying textures as well as bizarre, pathetic, and visionary themes.

The hierarchy of genres ranked the significance of a composition according to its subject matter. While historical subjects were characterized as the highest of all art genres, this era witnessed an upheaval of this hierarchy so that historical and mythological portraits, genre, landscape, and still-life paintings were offered as acceptable subjects universally.

Genre scenes were popular in England, particularly when they came from the brushes of William Powell Frith, William Mulready, or David Wilkre. American frontier painter George Caleb Bingham championed Midwestern river life. Yet other works, such as John Lewis Krimmel's *Quilting Frolic* (1813), call to mind the scenes of everyday life painted by William Hogarth a century earlier. Here, instead of poking fun at English institutions and societal norms, Krimmel suggests nuanced relations among races and classes engaged in making a quilt. His painting calls to mind racial stereotypes, particularly physiognomical distortions that were reinforced with the introduction of the minstrel shows in the 1840s.

Nature, as an extension of the landscape, was defined in terms of mythical, unique interior visions as well as panoramic views and detailed glimpses of rusticity and ruin. Some artists shifted between these two modes. In the former group, James Barry, William Blake, and James Gillray created prophetic stories and prehistorical phantasmagoria where personal mythology was bound with limitless intellectual ambition. Samuel Palmer envisioned art's ability as spiritual vocation, while John Martin's landscapes combined borrowed narrative content with commentary on contemporary society (see, for instance, his *The Fall of Ninevah*, 1829). Artists also posed the landscape as the locus of spiritual reflection, material progress, and historical struggle. German landscape, painting like its poetry and philosophy counterparts, was linked with conceptions of the divine, thereby fostering the mystical and allegorical paintings of Karl Gustav Carus, Caspar David Friedrich, and Philipp Otto Runge. A renewed popularity of *plein-air* painting, later a hallmark of the impressionists, was championed by John Constable, the Barbizon school, Arnold Böcklin, and, later, Ford Madox Brown. Ever present in the minds of Americans, the boundaries of the United States dramatically expanded, and with it the rise of landscape painting. The Hudson River school, the first native school of American painting featuring Thomas Cole, Frederick Church, and later, Albert Bierstadt, portrayed the untouched landscape, nature's sublimity, and visions of utopia.

Visionary imagery was a new specialty of Romantic art, uncategorized by the traditional hierarchy. Henry Fuseli, enriched by an intellectual background rooted in the Sturm und Drang (storm and stress) movement, expressed occult, mythological, and visionary allusions in such works as *The Nightmare* (1790), where horse, spirit, and sleeping female reside. Francisco José de Goya y Lucientes's indeterminate images, particularly his prints, were satirical and horrific in contrast to English and French scenes. His *Caprichos* (1799) and *Disasters of War* (c. 1810–20) chastise the power of reason and instead merge the subconscious and the subculture. This visionary approach is akin to the sustaining, albeit subversive theme of Antoine-Louis Barye's *Tiger Devouring a Gavial* (1831), which has been interpreted as an allegory of the newly seated July Monarchy.

Paintings illustrating popular literature fostered a growing market for prints taken from these works. In contrast, politically charged lithographs portrayed social woes, such as Honoré Daumier's (1834) commentary on political uprising suppressed by the French government, *Rue Transnonain le 15 avril 1834*. Continuing the criticism and scrutiny of the July Monarchy, the foremost satiric journal of the time, *La Caricature*, led the attack on the constitutional monarchy of Louis-Philippe. Charles Philipon, founder of the journal, first portrayed the gradual transformation of Louis-Philippe into a pear. Censorship between 1835 and 1848, however, forced caricaturists to adopt more socially oriented topics.

Perhaps one of the most significant contributions to the visual arts during this era was the development of photography by William Henry Fox Talbot and Thomas Wedgwood in England and Joseph-Nicéphore Niépce and Louis-Jacques-Mandé Daguerre in France. Building upon earlier forms of graphic arts, photography added a scientific and mechanical element into art production, facets that Walter Benjamin has cited as those that liquidate the image and erode the aura of authorial presence.

Funded through government support and awarded by competition, public sculpture in England commemorating lives and accomplishments of significant persons emerged as a significant art form appear in gathering spaces. Equally symbolic though different in context, Harriet Hosmer's *Zenobia in Chains* (1859), according to Whitney Chadwick, embodied a new ideal of womanhood, particularly in consideration of her defiance of the male-defined institutions in which she engaged to advance her art.

In addition to changes in visual product, wider relationships among creators, patrons, critics, and the public contrasted with the central tenet of Romantic art: celebration of the cult of genius and originality that sought individual expression foremost. As Charles Baudelaire observed at midcentury, "Romanticism is precisely situated neither in choice of subjects nor in exact truth, but in a way of feeling," thereby championing the artist's reflexive inquiry as paramount. Major exhibitions in Europe and the United States were reported on and featured in newspapers and periodicals. These, in addition to the publication of belles lettres

and beaux arts, connected art with the public and the intellectual interests of the era. The visual language of artists, however, was under constant review, study, and revision by the public, critics, and artists themselves.

JUILEE DECKER

Bibliography

Baker, Malcolm. *Figured in Marble: The Making and Viewing of Eighteenth-Century Sculpture*, Los Angeles: J. Paul Getty Museum Publications for the Victoria and Albert Museum, 2000.

Baudelaire, Charles. *Curiosités esthétiques, L'art romantique et autres oeuvres critiques*. Edited by H. Lemaitre. Paris: Classiques Garnier, 1962.

Benjamin, Walter. "The Work of Art in the Age of Mechanical Reproduction." In *Illuminations*. Translated by Harry Zohn. New York: Schocken, 1968.

Chadwick, Whitney. *Women, Art, and Society*. New York: Thames and Hudson, 1990.

Eichner, Hans. *"Romantic" and Its Cognates: The European History of a Word*. Toronto: University of Toronto Press, 1972.

Eitner, Lorenz. *Neo-classicism and Romanticism 1750–1850: An Anthology of Sources and Documents*. Englewood Cliffs, N.J.: Prentice-Hall, 1970.

Guentner, Wendelin A. "British Aesthetic Discourse 1780–1830: The Sketch, the Non Finito, and the Imagination," *Art Journal* 52, no. 2 (1993 Summer): 40–47.

Hartley, Keith, Henry Meyric Hughes, Peter-Klaus Schuster, and William Vaughan. *The Romantic Spirit in German Art 1790–1990*. London: Thames and Hudson, 1994.

Hemingway, Andrew, and William Vaughan, eds. *Art in Bourgeois Society, 1790–1850*. Cambridge: Cambridge University Press, 1998.

Honour, Hugh. *Romanticism*. New York: Harper and Row, 1979.

Lovejoy, Arthur Onchen. *The Great Chain of Being*. Cambridge, Mass.: Harvard University Press, 1936.

Rosenblum, Robert. *Transformations in Late-Eighteenth-Century Art*. Princeton, N.J.: Princeton University Press, 1969.

Toreinx, F. R. de. *Histoire du Romantisme en France*. Paris: L. Dureuil, 1829.

ART ACADEMIES, EXHIBITIONS, AND PATRONAGE

The Romantic era may be categorized by the expanding possibilities within the hallmark institutions of the visual arts: systems of education, means of display, and commercial as well as critical exchange. These institutions were categorically monolithic; however, a thirst for inquiry among artists, and the emerging presence of the bourgeoisie as participants in the cultural discourse, proposed action, reaction, and renewal that in turn bred a spirited energy and gave birth to the avant-garde.

Academies, an extension of the guild system, were schools or studios where artists had basic instruction for drawing and learned by copying another's work or antique casts. Advanced direct study of the nude model was also a key aspect of academic education. The earliest academies, for example the Academia del Disegno in Florence, were established during the Renaissance as centers for drawing. The Académie Royale de Peinture et de Sculpture (Paris), although based in part on the Italian model, elevated its purpose by moving away from the craft tradition and focusing instead on the theoretical understanding of fine art. Founded in 1648 with the support of the government, the

Académie Royale underwent subsequent changes in name and character over the next two centuries, reflecting the oscillating importance of instruction at an established government-sponsored institution and education in independent studios and ateliers of academicians. By 1863, the École des Beaux-Arts, as it was now named, provided national and regional settings for art education to students of all nationalities, thereby shifting the focus away from the independent ateliers, and offered workshops in painting, sculpture, and architecture on the premises.

Paris was the center of artistic education in the eighteenth century, a responsibility it later shared with the Royal Academy, in London (established in 1768). These institutions were united in their aims: to offer education, exhibition space, and a level of professionalization. Other academies established their principles and organization on the French and English models (the Pennsylvania Academy of the Fine Arts, the Scottish Academy as well as regional art schools across England, the Academia de San Fernando in Spain, and centers of learning in Munich, Berlin, and Düsseldorf in Germany).

One goal of the academies was to promote a centralized, institutionalized, and authorized approach to artistic education. Artists trained there produced "academic" works, which fit the ideals of the institution's practice and exhibited uniform quality. *Academic*, however, has become a contested term embodying regularity and conservatism as well as adherence to institutional—and often governmental—authority without regard to individual expression. Among art historians, "academic" has been associated with aesthetic failure and juxtaposed against creative and dynamic oppositions to it, generally referred to as *avant-garde*. Avant-garde artists, however, were often heirs to academic training who nonetheless managed to create individualized manifestations of their art.

Public patronage was identified with the government, the monarchy, or religious institutions. The situation in England may be assessed from William Hogarth's frontispiece engraving for the *Catalogue of Pictures Exhibited in Spring Gardens* (1761), which featured a classically dressed figure as Britannia, who waters a tree that has intertwined branches of art (painting, sculpture, and architecture). An endless stream of water from a fountain featuring the bust of King George III reminds viewers of his support of the arts, foreshadowing his benefaction in founding London's Royal Academy seven years later. The popularity of the wealthy young Englishman's "grand tour" furthered the scholarship of, and taste for, continental art among English patrons throughout the eighteenth century; however, traditional sources of private patronage (the aristocracy and gentry) decreased significantly, replaced by a system of exchange between artists and/or their dealers and the public. The Grand Tour popularized travel and study of politics, geography, history, and culture of the continent. The taste for continental art increased throughout the eighteenth-century.

In addition to offering a system of education, academies offered space to display painting, sculpture, and graphic arts for public consumption. In regularly scheduled displays, one painting was placed above the next, from the floor to the ceiling, while sculptures were placed in between them or relegated to other galleries. The increasing inclusion of the middle class in the commercial exchange of art, a post-Napoleonic phenomenon, was furthered by the presence of art critics and arbiters of taste who reviewed exhibitions and offered descriptive, laudatory, or critical remarks. Published pamphlets (*livrets*, in France) listed the exhibited works in order to guide the viewer. The first critical essay (*salon*, in France), discussed the French academy's exhibition of 1746. Denis Diderot is perhaps best known for his salons from 1759–81, thereby ushering a wave of commentary from individuals presuming to represent as well as inform the public opinion. This integration of the public and private realms allowed them to make their way back into the fold as subjects of art, as Thomas Rowlandson observed in his satirical image *The Exhibition Stare Case* (c. 1800), where the subject is, in fact, the social spectacles that accompanied displays of art in the academies. Jürgen Habermas has identified such private individuals who come together to make up a corporate body as the "public sphere" that served to debate, negotiate, and build consensus among its practitioners.

Beyond, or perhaps in lieu of the academies, nontraditional modes of display emerged around topographical endeavors including the panorama, the *Eidophusikon*, and the diorama, which offered a triumvirate of spectacle: art, scientific invention, and theatricality. Individual artists often opened their homes and studios to encourage the circulation of artistic commodities. Caspar David Friedrich, for example, opened his studio in Dresden to display his Tetschner altarpiece; in 1855 Gustave Courbet built his Pavillion du Réalisme outside the Universal Exposition to offer his works to the public.

Critics shaped tastes while dealers and auction houses transacted much of the business between buyers and sellers. Many art dealers initially promoted continental art, particularly the work of the old masters; however, an increased interest in fostering the careers of emergent or established living artists focused attention upon the collecting contemporary works. By midcentury in France, as Harrison and Cynthia White have observed, auction sales and dealer activities facilitated much of the exchange between buyers and sellers of art; turning on its end the system of patronage. Academies, exhibitions, and patronage thus reflected as well as influenced broader social discourses of the Romantic era, in addition to aesthetic concerns.

JUILEE DECKER

Bibliography

Allen, Brian. *Towards a Modern Art World*. New Haven, Conn.: Yale University Press for the Paul Mellon Centre for Studies in British Art, 1995.

Altick, Richard D. *The Shows of London*. Cambridge, Mass.: Belknap Press, 1987.

Art Journal, Spring 1989. Entire issue of journal devoted to issue of art institutions in France.

Barrell, John. *Painting and the Politics of Culture: New Essays in British Art 1700–1850*. Oxford: Oxford University Press, 1992.

Becker, Howard. *Art Worlds*. Berkeley, London and Los Angeles: London University of California Press, 1982.

Bermingham, Ann. *Learning to Draw: Studies in the Cultural History of a Polite and Useful Art*. New Haven, Conn.: Yale University Press for the Paul Mellon Centre for Studies in British Art, 2000.

Boime, Albert. *The Academy and French Painting in the Nineteenth Century*. London: Phaidon, 1971.

Boschloo, Anton W. A., ed. *Academies of Art between Renaissance and Romanticism*. The Hague: SDU Uitgeverij, 1989.

Comment, Bernard. *The Painted Panorama*. Translated by Anne-Marie Glasheen. London: Reaktion, 1999.

Crow, Thomas. *Painters and Public Life in Eighteenth-Century Paris*. New Haven, Conn.: Yale University Press, 1985.

Denis, Rafael Cardoso, and Colin Trodd, eds. *Art and the Academy in the Nineteenth Century*. Manchester: Manchester University Press, 2000.

Fawcett, Trevor. *The Rise of English Provincial Art: Artists, Patrons and Institutions Outside London, 1800–1830*. Oxford: Clarendon Press, 1974.

Goldstein, Carl. *Teaching Art: Academies and Schools from Vasari to Albers*, Cambridge: Cambridge University Press, 1996.

Habermas, Jürgen. *The Structural Transformation of the Bourgeois Public Sphere*. Translated by Thomas Burger with the assistance of Frederick Lawrence. Cambridge, Mass.: MIT Press, 1996.

Holt, Elizabeth Gilmore, ed. *The Triumph of Art for the Public, 1785–1848: The Emerging Role of Exhibitions and Critics*. Princeton, N.J.: Princeton University Press, 1979.

Hutchison, Sidney C. *The History of the Royal Academy 1768–1986*. 2nd ed. London: Robert Royce Limited, 1986.

Jonker, Maria Anna. "Diderot's Shade: A Discussion on 'ut pictura poesis' and Expression in French Art Criticism, 1819–1840. Ph.D. diss., University of Amsterdam, 1994.

Oettermann, Stephen. *The Panorama: History of a Mass Medium.* Translated by Deborah Lucas Schneider. New York: Zone Books, 1997.

Orwicz, Michael. *Art Criticism and Its Institutions in Nineteenth-Century France.* Manchester: Manchester University Press, 1994.

Paulson, Ronald. *Breaking and Remaking: Aesthetic Practice in England 1700–1820.* New Brunswick, N.J.: Rutgers University Press, 1989.

Pears, Iain, *The Discovery of Painting: The Growth of Interest in the Arts in England, 1680–1768.* New Haven, Conn.: Yale University Press, 1988.

Perry, Gill, and Colin Cunningham, *Academies, Museums, and Canons of Art.* New Haven, Conn.: Yale University Press in Association with Open University, 1999.

Pevsner, Nikolaus. *Academies of Art, Past and Present.* Cambridge: Cambridge University Press, 1940.

Sloane, Joseph C. *French Painting Between the Past and the Present: Artists, Critics, and Traditions from 1848 to 1870.* Princeton, N.J.: Princeton University Press, 1951.

Sloane, Kim. *A Noble Art: Amateur Artists and Drawing Masters c. 1600–1800.* London: British Museum Press for the Trustees of the British Museum, 2000.

Solkin, David, ed. *Art on the Line: The Royal Academy Exhibitions at Somerset House 1780–1836.* New Haven, Conn.: Yale University Press for the Paul Mellon Centre for Studies in British Art and the Courtauld Institute Gallery, 2001.

Weinberg, Helene Barbara. *The Lure of Paris: Nineteenth-Century American Painters and their French Teachers.* New York: Abbeville Press, 1991.

White, Harrison C., and Cynthia A. White, *Canvases and Careers: Institutional Change in the French Painting World.* Chicago: University of Chicago Press, 1993.

Ziff, Jerrold, "Turner as Defender of the Art between 1810–20," *Turner Studies* 8, no. 2 (1998): 13–25.

ART AND CLASSICAL ANTIQUITY

Romanticism in the visual arts has traditionally and persistently been interpreted as a reaction against eighteenth-century neoclassicism, and hence as a rejection of reason, order, and inspiration from Greek and Roman antiquity in favor of emotion, and inspiration from the Gothic Middle Ages. Yet the antithesis of the classical and the Romantic, promulgated in the Romantic period itself for largely polemical purposes (most notably by Johann Wolfgang von Goethe, who defined the classical as "healthy" and the Romantic as "sick"), scarcely reflects the complexity of the historical facts. Artists conventionally labeled Romantic (such as William Blake, Eugène Delacroix, Théodore Géricault, Francisco José de Goya y Lucientes, and J. M. W. Turner) did not abandon classical themes and models, although they largely rejected the "orthodox" neoclassicism promoted in the writings of Johann Joachim Winckelmann and exemplified in the paintings of Anton Raphael Mengs: that is, a preference for line over color, the use of flattened perspectives and static poses, and a disdain for depictions of emotion. Goya's *Giant* (c. 1812), in which a male nude set against a darkened sky towers over a terrified peasantry, is as far from Winckelmann's ideal of "eine edle Einfalt und eine stille Grösse" (a noble simplicity and quiet greatness) as can be imagined, but the figure of the giant derives from the very sculpture that Winckelmann considered the fullest embodiment of that ideal, the Belvedere Torso.

The art historian Sigfried Giedion, who denied the existence of neoclassicism as an independent style, coined the term *Romantic classicism* to indicate that the reception and appropriation of classical antiquity was not incompatible with Romanticism. But there was neither a school nor even a distinctive style of Romantic classicism. Works that have been grouped under this heading range chronologically from Anne-Louis Girodet de Roussy-Trioson's *Sleep of Endymion* (1791) to Hans von Marées's *Diana Resting* (1863); thematically from Delacroix's *Medea* (1838), a depiction of a figure from Greek myth, to Pierre-Paul Prud'hon's *Crime Pursued by Vengeance and Justice* (1808), a personified allegory; and stylistically from Karl Friedrich Schinkel's Altes Museum in Berlin (1823–25), with its austere Ionic colonnade, to John Soane's house in London (1792–1825), with its mixture of classical and Gothic elements. Even if one rejects Giedion's

revisionist account of early-nineteenth-century art, it is undeniable that numerous artists of the period found their subject matter in the mythology and their formal inspiration in the art of ancient Greece and Rome. Among the foremost examples of such artists are Jacques-Louis David and Jean-Auguste-Dominique Ingres, whose mythological and historical paintings derived from and disseminated an idealized conception of Roman civic virtue; John Flaxman, whose illustrations to Homer were closely modeled on Greek vase painting; Antonio Canova and Bertel Thorvaldsen, who sculpted contemporaries in the poses and clothing of Roman portrait sculptures; and Leo von Klenze and Benjamin Henry Latrobe, whose public buildings sought to re-create the elegance and monumentality of Greek temples.

The attraction of classical antiquity may be attributed to a combination of factors. The first of these was the ubiquity of classical education among the European upper classes who collected and commissioned artworks: mythological themes would have been as familiar as biblical themes to those who had been steeped in Greek and Latin literature from childhood. The second factor, dating from the second half of the eighteenth century, was the remarkable visibility of ancient artifacts, not only through sight-seeing (as in the obligatory "grand tour" of wealthy young Englishmen, which might include a visit to the excavations at Herculaneum and Pompeii) but through illustrations (as in Giambattista Piranesi's *Antichità romane*, 1756, and William Hamilton's catalog of his own collection, 1766–67) and commercial reproductions (like Wedgwood jasperware and Sèvres statuettes) in well-known private collections (like that of Winckelmann's patron, Cardinal Alessandro Albani, much visited by *milordi inglesi*), and public museums (like the British Museum, founded in 1759, and Klenze's Glyptothek in Munich, completed 1830), and in the marketplace (in which important collectors like Hamilton and Albani doubled as unscrupulous dealers). The third factor was the inherent receptivity of classical antiquity—in particular, Greek myth—to reinterpretation and appropriation, which made it extraordinarily useful in serving contemporary needs. Projecting the realization of one's ideals and the fulfillment of one's hopes into the past as a state that has once existed (and by implication may be created again) entails less danger of contradiction than projecting them into the future.

Accordingly, the political uses of classical antiquity in Romantic-era art were multiple and disparate. While David's evocation of republican Rome in *The Oath of the Horatii* (1785) implied the value of defending the integrity of the civil state, Ingres's evocation of imperial Rome in his portrait of Napoleon Bonaparte on his throne (1806) implied the legitimacy and unlimited nature of the self-crowned emperor's power. Greek architectural styles represented monarchical absolutism in Munich (where Klenze's Walhalla, 1830–42, was commissioned by Ludwig I to glorify Bavaria), and republican democracy in Washington, D.C. (as Thomas Jefferson acknowledged when he proclaimed the U.S. Capitol, building, designed in part by Latrobe and begun in 1793, "the first temple dedicated to the sovereignty of the people, embellishing with Athenian taste the course of a nation looking far beyond the range of Athenian destinies"). Indeed, classical models could be used for contradictory political purposes in works by the same artist. Thus Canova on the one hand aggrandized members of Napoleon's family in his portrait sculptures of them, and on the other hand expressed support for Italian nationalism in his monument to Vittorio Alfieri (1806–10), which is dominated by a crowned and classically draped female figure who appears to be mourning not only the dead poet but the fate of Italy under the Napoleonic occupation.

NICHOLAS HALMI

Bibliography

Boime, Albert. *Art in the Age of Bonapartism, 1800–1815*. Chicago: University of Chicago Press, 1990.
———. *Art in the Age of Revolution, 1750–1800*. Chicago: University of Chicago Press, 1987.
Clark, Kenneth. *The Romantic Rebellion: Romantic versus Classic Art*. London: John Murray, 1973.
Constantine, David. *Early Greek Travellers and the Hellenic Ideal*. Cambridge: Cambridge University Press, 1984.
Eitner, Lorenz, ed. *Neoclassicism and Romanticism: Sources and Documents*. 2 vols. Englewood Cliffs, N.J.: Prentice-Hall, 1970.
Giedion, Sigfried. *Spätbarocker und romantischer Klassizismus*. Munich: Bruckmann, 1922.
Haskell, Francis, and Nicholas Penny. *Taste and the Antique: The Lure of Classical Sculpture, 1500–1900*. New Haven, Conn.: Yale University Press, 1981.
Honour, Hugh. *Neo-classicism*. 2d ed. Harmondsworth, England: Penguin, 1981.
———. *Romanticism*. London: Allen Lane, 1979.
Irwin, David. *Neoclassicism*. London: Phaidon, 1997.
Potts, Alex. *Flesh and the Ideal: Winckelmann and the Origins of Art History*. New Haven, Conn.: Yale University Press, 1994.
Rosenblum, Robert. *Transformations in Late Eighteenth-Century Painting*. Princeton, N.J.: Princeton University Press, 1967.
Trevelyan, Humphrey. *Goethe and the Greeks*. 2d ed. Cambridge: Cambridge University Press, 1981.
Webb, Timothy, ed. *English Romantic Hellenism*. Manchester: Manchester University Press, 1982.

ART AND MEDIEVALISM

Medievalism, a visual or philosophical acknowledgement of admiration for and emulation of pre-1500 art forms, began as an antiquarian endeavor and became an expression of cultural discourse that fueled subsequent endeavors by the arts and crafts movement and the Roycrofters, among others. Medievalism was part of a larger trend toward historicism that implied a conscious adaptation from any historical period. Neoclassicism, a type of historicism, was immensely popular in the visual arts during the late eighteenth century, stimulated by Johann Joachim Winckelmann's essays on the "noble simplicity and calm grandeur" of Greek art. Medievalism, aided by a general decline in the authority of classical forms and motifs, answered the Romantic search for identity through its nationalistic, religious, and sympathetic associations.

Historical novels and lyric poetry encouraged a renewed interest in ruins and their preservation, thereby summoning an interest in re-creating the spirit—if not the look—of them. Visually, medievalism took the form of flattened surfaces, denial of chiaroscuro, meticulous study outdoors, and the application of bold colors. Subject matter could have nationalistic overtones, highlighting events and myths (for example, the tale of Joan of Arc or the Arthurian legend) of a shared community. Sculptors and architects often imitated the aspiring forms of churches, promoting the Gothic revival, and other art forms such as stained glass, illustration, and publishing grew in importance.

Philosophically, the appropriation of historical subject matter could take two approaches. Borrowed subjects were re-presented for the contemporary audience. Examples include ephemeral gallery projects, such as the Milton Gallery decorated by Henry Fuseli (c. 1838), Jean-Auguste-Dominique Ingres's *Paolo and Francesca*, (1819), and Ary Scheffer's *Princess Marie d'Orleans in Her Studio* (c. 1838). While often not categorized as Romanticism, the troubadour style combined the format of Dutch genre paintings with subjects from French history, thereby presenting politically charged glances towards the past that reaffirm the French political climate. Literary justification of appropriation posits Alfred, Lord Tennyson's adaptation of medieval legend as historical and moral legitimation of imperialism; yet, nearly two centuries later, Edward Austin Abbey's murals for the Boston Public Library (1895–1904) uprooted this notion in their portrayal of the model of spirituality for American men.

Thoroughly mindful of the social context of borrowed style, the second strain of medievalism differs from pure admiration and the random borrowing or juxtapositions of many styles termed *eclecticism*. Here, medievalism lifts an earlier spirit, look, or style while also taking on the cloak of responsibility to challenge contemporary social constructs. In 1809 disgruntled academy students, including Johann Friedrich Overbeck and Franz Pforr, formed the Brotherhood of St. Luke, which was aimed at promoting alternative and more individualistic modes of study in contrast to the academy. The Lukasbrüder (soon the Nazarenes) sought to bring about a renewal of German art spiritually and formally, thus producing an art and offering an identity different from those generally available.

John Ruskin, a champion for the Pre-Raphaelites, saw a moral role for art, as explicated in his first volume of *Modern Painters*. The beginnings of the Pre-Raphaelite movement coincided with the entry of Jan van Eyck's *Arnolfini Marriage* (1434) into the national collection in London, an event that Ruskin anonymously chronicled. Exceptional brushwork, overt and covert symbolism, and the solemnity of Eyck's work (and much early Flemish painting) were matched by such works as Dante Gabriel Rossetti's *The Girlhood of Mary Virgin* (1848–49). Although the Pre-Raphaelites disbanded in the 1850s, their work influenced Les XX (the Twenty, an exhibition society based in Belgium) and symbolism. In contrast to Darwinian theories that refuted Christianity and mechanization of many aspects of life, these renewed medieval artistic communities (Nazarenes and the Pre-Raphaelite Brotherhood) share an affinity with later developments including the arts and crafts movement (England), the Roycroft arts and crafts community (East Aurora, New York), and movements categorized as "primitive", in terms of their dutiful absorption of previous eras.

As an architectural mode, initially medievalism revealed itself with a fanciful Rococo approach. Horace Walpole's house at Strawberry Hill (1749–76) featured the rococo Gothic of the eighteenth century, where forms are updated and enhanced, as did Sir Walter Scott's estate on the Tweed, which was transformed into a baronial mansion that he appropriately renamed Abbotsford. After 1830, however, the antiquarian revival kept to the purity of form, logic, and simplicity, maintaining a sense of archeological truth. In this vein, Henri Labrouste, Antoine Vaudoyer, and Eugène Emmanuel Viollet-le-Duc, reassessed the relevance of historical architecture in France. Benjamin Woolfield Mountfort, active in New Zealand from 1850, revived the forms and details of the Gothic style (Christchurch, Canterbury College) as well.

Augustus Pugin, known for his collaboration with Charles Barry to design Britain's Houses of Parliament, extolled the virtues of medievalism, and Gothic revival in particular, through his writing. *Contrasts* (1836) posited the superiority of the Gothic to the style of his present time, and *The True Principles of Pointed or Christian Architecture* (1841) laid much of the theoretical foundation for the national style of the building scheme around 1835–75 as well as the restoration of a number of buildings. However, English architects reevaluated and revived other styles. Concurrent with the medieval preference, the Ottoman, Italianate, Palladian, and Greek were favored, for example, by John Nash. Whatever the mode adapted, however, the goal of medievalism in particular and historicism in general aimed at sharing a kindred spirit with an earlier period draped in chivalric sensibility, nationalistic sensibility, spiritual values, and pure form.

While medievalism is evident visually through the appearance of a painting or building, its practitioners shared concerns of emulating a previous style or styles (as in the case of eclecticism) while also challenging contemporary authority and philosophy. Their appropriation of a subject, social structure, mode of instruction, or philosophical approach betrays their belief in the present in favor of a strengthened commitment to the past.

JUILEE DECKER

See also **Pre-Raphaelite Brotherhood**

Bibliography

Bann, Stephen. *The Inventions of History: Essays on the Representation of the Past*. Manchester: Manchester University Press, 1990.

Braysmith, Hilary. "Medievalism in German Romantic Art: Reading the Political Text of the Gothic Style," *Studies in Medievalism* 5 (1993): 38–47.

Brooks, Chris, ed. *The Albert Memorial: The Prince Consort National Memorial: Its History, Contexts, and Conservation*. New Haven, Conn.: Yale University Press for the Paul Mellon Centre for Studies in British Art, 2000.

Clark, Kenneth. *The Gothic Revival: An Essay in the History of Taste*. London: Constable, 1950.

Hearn, M. F. *The Architectural Theory of Viollet-le-Duc*. Cambridge, Mass.: MIT Press, 1990.

Kant, Immanuel. *The Critique of Judgment*. Edited by Paul Guyer, trans by Paul Guyer and Eric Matthews. Cambridge, U.K.: Cambridge University Press, 2000.

Kaufman, Edward, and Sharon Irish. *Medievalism: An Annotated Bibliography of Recent Research in the Architecture and Art of Britain and North America*. New York: Garland, 1988.

Mancoff, Debra N. *The Arthurian Revival in Victorian Art*. New York: Garland, 1990.

Marsh, Jan, and Pamela Gerrish Nunn. *Pre-Raphaelite Women Artists*. Exhibition catalog. Manchester: Manchester City Art Galleries, 1997.

Oberg, Charlotte. "Fra Elbertus and the Roycrofters: Medievalism in East Aurora," *Studies in Medievalism* 6 (1994): 69–84.

Pevsner, Nikolaus. *Ruskin and Viollet-le-Duc: Englishness and Frenchness in the Appreciation of Gothic Architecture*. London: Thames and Hudson, 1969.

Prettejohn, Elizabeth. *The Art of the Pre-Raphaelites*. Princeton, N.J.: Princeton University Press, 2000.

Ruskin, John. *The Works of John Ruskin*. 39 vols. Edited by E. T. Cook and Alexander Wedderburn. New York: Longmans, Green. 1903–12.

Scott, Sir Walter. *Minstrelsy of the Scottish Border: Consisting of Historical and Romantic Ballads, Collected in the Southern Counties of Scotland; With a Few of Modern Date, Foundd upon Local Tradition*. 2 vols. Edinburgh: Longman and Rus, 1803 (2 ed).

Staley, Allen. *The Pre-Raphaelite Landscape*. New Haven, Conn.: Yale University Press for the Paul Mellon Centre for Studies in British Art, 2001.

ART AND POLITICS

It is difficult to imagine, at least in the Western world postdating classical antiquity, a form of art with no connection to the political. If, however, there is a virtually necessary link between these two central areas of human activity, it exists in very different ways and often betrays its existence in subtle and complex fashions. It is no surprise that Francisco José de Goya y Lucientes's *Third*

of May depicts the reprisals on that date in 1808 by the invading French troops against the insurrection by the inhabitants of Madrid on the previous day. This is Romantic painting, the high pitch of emotional intensity guaranteed by the blood-drenched bodies of dead Spaniards, who lie in front of the next victim, kneeling uncomprehendingly as he awaits extinction at the hands of the faceless firing squad of French soldiers. It is also political painting, with a Spanish artist unsurprisingly showing his countrymen as hapless innocents, mown down by a military machine dedicated to the expansionist policies of the emperor, Napoleon Bonaparte. But this is not the only—perhaps not even the chief—political dimension of the work. Goya did not paint his picture in 1808, his imagination fired by recent atrocity. He first suggested the subject to the restored Spanish monarchy in 1814, asking to be commissioned to record, as he put it, "our glorious insurrection against the tyrant of Europe." He had produced portraits of French nationals during the invasion years and needed to clear himself of possible charges of collaboration. Here the political is both national and personal.

The years 1789 and 1848 must provide the beginning and end of this period. At the outset, the French Revolution overthrew autocratic monarchy and ensured the process by which the bourgeoisie would eventually become the dominant class. The year 1848 saw revolts, with different outcomes, affecting not only France, but also Italy and the German-speaking states. One aspect of the struggles was the emergence of the proletariat as the class most likely to challenge the developing hegemony of the bourgeoisie. The terminal dates, then, obey the logic of political history rather than of the history of art, but this is not to suggest the subservience of the latter to the former. Just as the power relationship between art and politics must be allowed as fluid, so too must be the links between particular political circumstances and individual works of art. The examples that follow are designed to show concrete examples of artistic and political interaction but they should be seen as particular, not as paradigmatic.

When Jean-Paul Marat was assassinated in 1793, he was deputy to the National Convention, a member of France's government. The call for a commemoration of this revolutionary martyr came from the floor of the convention in a speech by another deputy. The politician in question was the painter Jacques-Louis David, who duly produced the remarkable image of Marat breathing his last in his bloodstained bath. David had gained his artistic reputation through innovative manipulation of the classical tradition, an element retained in *Marat* through its similarity to antique deathbed scenes. But this is no mere classicizing schema, as was most eloquently recognized by the arch-Romantic poet and art critic, Charles Baudelaire, who wrote in 1846, "It is the bread of the strong and the triumph of the spiritual; as cruel as nature, this picture has all the perfume of the ideal." Baudelaire's opinion does not make this picture unequivocally Romantic, but it is nevertheless an unashamedly political image that moves triumphantly beyond mere cant and propaganda.

The German-speaking areas in Europe in the early nineteenth century were very different from France, both artistically and politically. Small principalities abounded, rather than a unitary nation state, leaving artists without the single focus that Paris provided for their colleagues across the border. Yet perhaps Paris was also a focus for Germans, albeit often in a negative sense. The development of Romanticism in German-speaking Europe derived from many factors, but particularly important was a determined rejection of classicism. This was seen as a French style, at a time of French military aggression. Some German art was overtly political, some more subtly so. In Caspar David Friedrich's *Chasseur in the Forest*, a lone soldier in identifiably French uniform stands lost in a vast German forest. As this was painted in 1813–14, during the War of Liberation (from the French invaders), its political meaning is unequivocal. Earlier, in 1812, Friedrich had exhibited in Dresden a picture titled *The Garden Terrace*. Here, a young woman sits reading in a formal garden occupying the foreground; beyond the garden wall is an unimproved hilly landscape. A contemporary critic referred to the painting as a "Garden Party in the French Style" Friedrich's work, in good Romantic fashion, allows enough latitude of interpretation for the critic to intuit that the picture might be contrasting (classical) French order with (Romantic) German feeling for unspoilt nature.

David, Friedrich, and Goya can all be considered political radicals, the latter two less violently so than their French counterpart. Perhaps there is indeed an expectation that artistic and political radicalism should go hand in hand. In England, where a constitutional monarchy prevailed throughout the period, circumstances could be very different. John Constable's evocations of a peaceful East Anglian countryside seem far indeed from the sanguineous streets of Madrid and Paris, far enough from any politics. His *Cornfield* (1826) shows a young shepherd slaking his thirst at a stream in the foreground while a reaper prepares to leave a field in the middle distance. Work here is done by isolated individuals, in line with Constable's arch-Tory beliefs, expressed in a letter of 1825, that the farm laborer "is only made respectable by being kept in solitude and worked for himself." Allowed to associate with his peers, the laborer might start discussing the possibility of improved working conditions, something recently made theoretically possible by the 1824 repeal of the Combination Acts, which had forbidden collective discussion for political purposes. The intensity of political opinion exemplified in Constable's apparent rural idyll turns out to be little weaker than that more obviously expressed by *Marat*. One cannot look for unanimity of political opinion in art of the Romantic period; one cannot look for the same means of expression. But all art will have its political dimension, and the best art will be "partial, passionate and political," as was Baudelaire's expressed wish in 1846 for the best art criticism.

ED LILLEY

Selected Works

John Constable, *The Cornfield*, 1826. Oil on canvas, 143 cm × 122 cm. National Gallery, London.
Jacques-Louis David, *Marat*, 1793. Oil on canvas, 165 cm × 128 cm. Musées Royaux des Beaux-Arts, Brussels.
Caspar David Friedrich, *The Garden Terrace* (*Die Gartenterrasse*), 1812. Oil on canvas, 54 cm × 70 cm. Staatliche Schlösser und Gärten, Potsdam-Sanssouci.
———. *The Chasseur in the Woods* (*Der Chasseur im Walde*), 1813–14. Oil on canvas, 66 cm × 47 cm. Private collection.
Francisco Goya, *Third of May* (*Tres de Mayo*), 1814. Oil on canvas, 266 cm × 345 cm. Prado, Madrid.

Bibliography

Barrell, John. *The Dark Side of the Landscape*. Cambridge: Cambridge University Press, 1980.
Baudelaire, Charles. *Curiosités esthétiques*. Paris: Michel Lévy, 1860. Translated by Jonathan Mayne as *Art in Paris 1845–1862* Oxford: Phaidon, 1965.

Clark, T. J. *Farewell to an Idea: Episodes from a History of Modernism*. New Haven, Conn.: Yale University Press, 1999.

Eisenman, Stephen, ed. *Nineteenth Century Art: A Critical History*. London: Thames and Hudson, 1994.

Rosenthal, Michael. *Constable: The Painter and his Landscape*, New Haven, Conn.: Yale University Press, 1983.

Thomas, Hugh. *Goya: The Third of May 1808*. London: Penguin, 1972.

Vaughan, William, Helmut Börsch-Supan, and Hans Heidhardt. *Caspar David Friedrich 1774–1840*. London: Tate Gallery, 1972.

Vaughan, William, and Helen Weston, eds. *David's "The Death of Marat."* Cambridge: Cambridge University Press, 2000.

Williams, Gwyn. *Goya and the Impossible Revulution*, London: Allen Lane, 1976.

Wolff, Janet. *The Social Production of Art*. London: Macmillan, 1981.

ARTIST, CHANGING CONCEPTIONS OF THE

The conception of the artist oscillates, rather than evolves, throughout the Romantic era to include learned, professional men as well as bohemian, antiestablishment individuals. Whether craftsman, courtier, or *salonnier*, eighteenth-century artists were recognized as professional *men* of training, part of an organized body (i.e, an independent atelier or state-sponsored academy). The Académie Royale den Peinture et de Sculpture in France, its English counterpart, and other continental variations taught young men (and occasionally women) techniques of painting and sculpture to further their hopes of becoming successful financially and intellectually as instructors for a new generation. Artists performed official roles; Francisco José de Goya y Lucientes who, as first court painter, was heavily occupied with a series of portraits of the royal family. Telling self-portraits by Jacques-Louis David (1794) and Jean-Auguste-Dominique Ingres (1804) attest to their composed, professional status as artists established in their field. Studio scenes provide a glimpse into working conditions and hint at self-appraisal. The portrait of Jean-Baptiste Isabey with his daughter (1795) featured the artist in his studio at the Louvre; J. P. Hasenclever (*Studio Scene*, 1836) and Léon Cogniet (*The Artist in His Room*) depicted themselves in their studio spaces (the former in Düsseldorf and the later at the Villa Medici, Rome). Often, essential ingredients for their profession—including figures in costume, canvases, a classical shield, helmet, swords, or a guitar—fill their surroundings. These works identify the perception of the artist as gained through the identity (nationality, social status, gender, and education). Equally interesting are their subjects, which signify their understanding of their roles as artists during the Romantic era.

The Romantic conception of the artist, while implying individuality and originality, precluded the existence of a singular style to hold together the forms of art. Instead, an artist developed approaches to art that, in turn, helped him to define his status and role as artist. For example, meditations on nature and religion by William Blake, Caspar David Friedrich, and Philip Otto Runge explained the artist in his role as mediator of the visual arts providing a highly personal, nondogmatic form of worship. Carl Gustav Carus's *Letters on Landscape Painting* embodied the distinct relationships among nature, its representations in art, and connections with God. Abandoning nature and seeking imagination and texts as the starting point for art, Blake offered his judgment on the errors and opacity of society rooted in reason. He sought to convey his belief in imagination and faith through his printed and painted media, including his illustrations for the Book of Job, Dante Alighieri's *Inferno*, and his own poetry.

Artists captured the pulse of contemporary society through portraiture, caricature, or commemoration. Jean-Pierre Pantan modeled caricatures of intellectuals, politicians, and others in the public sphere as paraphrases of the rigid, academic, and poised official portraiture espoused by Pierre-Jean David d'Angers. Honoré Daumier's graphic art and sculptures, particularly those from the series *Celebrities of the Juste Milieu* (1831) defined his conception of the artist as commentator. Artists were often called upon to commemorate a passing era, event, or person. Angelica Kauffmann's *Death of Leonardo* (1778) commemorates the Renaissance genius. Edinburgh's *Scott Monument* (1844) and London's *The Albert Memorial* (1863–72) exemplify the obsession to capture physical characteristics, as well as the interplay between social trends and individual character steeped in the iconography of Romantic and Victorian values.

Art and artists opened a discourse with contemporaries and predecessors in all fields. Eugène Delacroix, for example, felt akin to Michelangelo, describing him as a wild genius who fell victim to misunderstanding, a point of nexus they shared (*Michelangelo in His Studio*, 1850). In *Cenotaph* (1836), an enhanced view of the memorial to Sir Joshua Reynolds on Sir George Beaumont's estate park in Coleorton, John Constable inserted busts of Michelangelo and Raphael to surround the tablet inscribed with lines from William Wordsworth, thereby connecting Reynolds not only with his lineage in painting and the ability of poetry to explicate thoughts and feelings. Gustav Courbet, on the cusp of Realism, painted *The Studio* (1854–55) and explained the work in a treatise that described himself at work on a landscape with individuals and groups of supporters on either side. On the left are the commoners among the impedimenta of Romanticism including a plumed hat, guitar, and dagger; the right half of the canvas features those who supported Courbet, including the collector Alfred Bruyas, and Charles Baudelaire, Champfleury Pierre-Joseph Proudhon.

Such dialogues with writers and performing artists paved the way for intellectual inquiry and meditation upon the value of all arts. A correspondence among a community enabled artists to express their ideas with a new visual vocabulary. Renewed significance in literature was given to the autobiography through Jean-Jacques Rousseau's *Confessions*. Likewise, artists embraced this declaration of singularity and the cult of sensibility that allowed them to view and project themselves as individual creators attempting to express their unique point of view as individuals, and within their roles as mediators, inventors, reporters, and scientists that explored, extrapolated, and frequently rejected the notion of codified meanings.

While clearly appropriate during the eighteenth century, Samuel Johnson's definition of an artist as "the professor of an art, generally an art manual" (1755) represented, by the following century, only one categorization of the artist. Defined by their social milieu as court painters, academicians, or as independent agents, and bolstered by their individual points of view, artists became more self-reliant, less dependent on institutional prescriptions of what it meant to be an artist. The shift from community to individual is captured in the portraits of artists and commentary by critics and arbiters of taste, and is recorded in correspondence, journals, and marginalia found among disparate pages of notebooks from that time. All roads lead to the emergence of an autonomous figure whose work resonates with a spirit and energy that lessens the need for self-representation and furthers the idea of a correspondence among the arts, epitomizing Richard Wagner's *Gesamtkunstwerk*, or total work of art. Thus, the definition of an artist in the nineteenth century cannot be easily categorized; it embodies, rather an organic form that expresses the new consciousness of himself and his uniqueness, as explicated through word, image, chord or any variation in between.

JUILEE DECKER

Bibliography

Bermingham, Ann. *Learning to Draw: Studies in the Cultural History of a Polite and Useful Art*. New Haven, Conn.: Yale University Press for the Paul Mellon Centre for Studies in British Art, 2000.

Blühm, Andreas, Wolfgang Drost, Philip Ward-Jackson, Alison Yarrington, and Emmanuelle Heran. *The Colour of Sculpture 1840–1910*. Exhibition catalog. Amsterdam: Van Gogh Museum; Leeds: Henry Moore Institute; Zwolle: Waanders Uitgevers, 1996.

Brown, David Blayney. *Romanticism*. New York: Phaidon, 2001.

Clark, Kenneth. *The Romantic Rebellion: Romantic versus Classic Art*, New York: Harper and Row, 1973.

Crow, Thomas. *Painters and Public Life in Eighteenth-century Paris*. New Haven, Conn.: Yale University Press, 1985.

Denis, Rafael Cardoso, and Colin Trodd, eds. *Art and the Academy in the Nineteenth Century*. New Brunswick, N.J.: Rutgers University Press, 2000.

Eisenman, Stephen, ed. *Nineteenth Century Art: A Critical History*. London: Thames and Hudson, 1994.

Hamilton, George Heard. *Nineteenth and Twentieth Century Art: Painting, Sculpture, Architecture*. Englewood Cliffs, N.J.: Prentice-Hall, 1972.

Honour, Hugh. *Romanticism*. London: Allen Lane, 1979.

Holt, Elizabeth Gilmore. *The Triumph of Art for the Public, 1785–1848: The Emerging Role of Exhibitions and Critics*. Rev. ed. Princeton, N.J.: Princeton University Press, 1983.

Janson, H. W. *Nineteenth-Century Sculpture*. New York: Abrams, 1985.

———. *Rococo to Romanticism: Art and Architecture, 1700–1850*. New York: Garland, 1976.

Morton, Marsha L., and Peter L. Schmunk, *The Arts Entwined: Music and Painting in the Nineteenth Century*. New York: Garland, 2000.

Rosenblum, Robert, and H. W. Janson. *Nineteenth Century Art*. New York: Abrams, 1984.

Vaughan, William. *Arts of the Nineteenth Century*. 2 vols. New York: Abrams, 1989–99.

———. *Romanticism and Art*, Rev. ed. London: Thames and Hudson, 1994.

ASBJØRNSEN, PETER CHRISTEN 1812–1885, AND JØRGEN MOE 1813–1882

Collectors and publishers of Norwegian folktales

In 1840, when Peter Christen Asbjørnsen and Jørgen Moe tried to find a publisher, for their first collection of folktales, they were told that "there are few who would not regard folktales as mere nursery talk, and any attempt to publish a collection of them as childish folly." The first publisher they turned to tried to cover himself by suggesting that the public should be invited to subscribe to such an enterprise. The response was minimal, and possibly, it seems, even nonexistent. Eventually, however, a publisher was found, but when the first slim collection of tales was published in 1841 it appeared without a title page, table of contents, or the authors' names. Despite this wretched launch, the collection was well received, and Norway's leading historian, P. A. Munch, wrote in a major German newspaper that the collection "was the most successful product of our young culture." For the second volume, which had the title *Norske Folkeeventyr* (*Norwegian Folktales*, 1842), Asbjørnsen and Moe had collected more tales, and their names appeared on the cover. By 1844 two additional collections had appeared and the first volume was sold out. The first complete collection appeared in 1851–52 and the first illustrated edition in 1879.

Asbjørnsen and Moe had met and become close friends in their teens when they were both studying for their university matriculation examinations with the local clergyman at Støren in Ringerike. After that their paths parted for a time. Moe started studying theology, although with little enthusiasm, because he fostered aspirations to a literary career. Asbjørnsen had to support himself by becoming a private tutor in Romerike. Here his enjoyment of folktales, which he had maintained since childhood, developed into an interest in collecting them. He sent a sample of his work to the clergyman Andreas Faye, whose *Norske Sagn* (*Norwegian Legends*, 1833) had been the very first collection of Norwegian folktales. Moe, too, had developed an increasing interest in the folktales after suffering a nervous breakdown and having to interrupt his studies and return home to Ringerike. It was not till the mid-1830s, however—when Asbjørnsen and Moe became aware of the work of Jacob Ludwig Karl Grimm and Wilhelm Karl Grimm—that their interest blossomed into the realization that the collecting and publishing of folktales was a project of national significance. But some years were still to pass before the first collection saw the light of day. They needed more material (most of which they found in Valdres and Dalen, which like Romerike and Ringerike are areas of eastern Norway to the north of Oslo), and Moe wanted to finish his studies.

Two things made their collections a success: the fact that they were in step with the spirit of the age, and the language and style in which the tales were written down. Norway had gained a modicum of independence in 1814 when the Norwegians, had produced a written constitution that they had then used to defend their independence in relation to Sweden (with whom they were part of the twin kingdom of Sweden-Norway). Popular opinion held that being Norwegian was more than a political identity, and the people of Norway began searching for manifestations of a unique Norwegian culture. The folktales were one such manifestation. Here were stories that had been passed down from generation to generation in the farming community, which during this period was seen as representing the true essence of the Norwegian people, as the farming culture had continued in the valleys, with little influence from the culture of the Danish overlords.

The tales would not, however, have been the success they were if Asbjørnsen and Moe had not found exactly the right language for them. One of the reasons why Faye's *Norske Sagn* had not been a success was that Faye had had no desire to convey the mood or language of the tales but only the content, which he did in a rather dry and detached manner. Asbjørnsen and Moe, on the other hand, realized that if they wanted the educated reading public to accept them they could not go the opposite extreme and publish the tales in the dialects and speech patterns in which they had been told. Their solution was to try to retain the original flavor of the tales, which they believed they could do because of their intimate connection with the people who had told them, while at the same time lifting them and retelling them to the best of their literary and narrative ability. That they succeeded is clear from the endorsement they received from the Grimm brothers, "Die norske folkeeventyr sind die *besten* Märchen die es gibt" ("the Norwegian folk tales are the best folktales that exist"). What Asbjørnsen and Moe had managed to do was, as Olav Bø has put it, "retain a mood which is both native and imaginative. The naive alternates with the ambiguous, the delicate with the crude. Content, style and language work to the same end." Even so, many of the educated classes felt the result was too crude, and indeed some erotic tales were excluded altogther and only rediscovered in 1978.

Jørgen Moe, who was ordained in 1853, eventually abandoned his role as a folktale collector, but his son Moltke Moe was to become a leading folklorist who carried on his father's and Asbjørnsen's work, albeit with a more scientific approach. Asbjørnsen carried on as a collector of folktales and legends until his death, and made his own contribution with *Norske Huldreeventyr og Folkesagn* (*Norwegian Hulder Tales and Legends*; collected edition, 1870). These tales are set in frame stories that tell of the hikes and walking tours during which Asbjørnsen met his narrators, and are evocative of the Norwegian countryside and the people who live there.

MARIE WELLS

Biography

Peter Christian Asbjørnsen born, January 15, 1812. Matriculated 1833 and passed *andeneksamen* (general qualifying examinations) in 1837. Became government inspector of forests for the district of Trondheim in 1860 and head of the Government Survey of Peat Production in 1864. Retired 1876 and died, January 5, 1885.

Jørgen Moe born, April 22, 1813. Matriculated 1830 and completed his theological studies in 1839. University research fellow in folklore, 1849–50. Chaplain in Sigdal, 1853. Married February 2, 1854 and became vicar of Bragernes 1864–70 and of Vestre Aker 1870–75. Became Bishop of Kristiansands in 1875. Died, March 7, 1882.

Selected Works

Collections
Norske Folkeeventyr. Collected and told by Peter Christen Asbjornsen and Jørgen Moe, 1852.
Norske folkeeventyr, Ny samling. Told by Peter Christen Asbjørnsen, 1871.
Norske Huldreeventyr og Folkesagn. Peter Christen Asbjørnsen; collected edition, 1870.

Letters
Fra det nationale gjennembruds tid: breve fra Jørgen Moe til P. Chr. Asbjørnsen og andre. Edited and with an introduction by Anders Krogvig. Kristiania: Aschehoug, 1915.

Translations
Popular Tales from the Norse. Translated and with an introduction by Sir George Dasent. London: Bodley Head, 1969.
Norwegian Folktales. Translated by Pat Shaw. Pantheon Fairy Tale and Folklore Library. New York: Random House, 1982.

Bibliography

Bø, Olav. "Folkediktinga," in *Norges Litteraturhistorie*, edited by Edvard Beyer, Volume 2, Fra Wergeland til Vinje, Oslo, Cappelen, 1974.
Hodne, Ørnulf. *Jørgen Moe og folkeeventyrene: en studie i nasjonalromantisk folkloristikk*. Oslo: Universitetsforlaget, 1979.
Liestøl, Knut. *P. Chr. Asbjørnsen. Mannen og livsverket*. Oslo: Tanum, 1947.
Støverud, Torbjørn. *Milestones in Norwegian Literature*. Oslo: Tanum, 1967.

ATALA AU TOMBEAU 1808

Painting by Anne-Louis Girodet de Roussy-Trioson (known as Girodet)

Given Girodet's deep knowledge of and enthusiasm for literature, his penchant for ecstatic religiosity, and his friendship with François-Auguste-René, Vicomte de Chateaubriand, it is not surprising that he became the most profound interpreter in paint of a narrative that attracted and inspired many visual artists almost from its first publication.

Girodet's closeness to Chateaubriand during the period when he was working on *Atala au Tombeau* (known sometimes as *Les Funerailles d'Atala*) is attested to not only by his portrait of the writer (c. 1806–7) but by flattering references to Girodet in Chateaubriand's *Les Martyrs* (1809). *Atala au Tombeau* bears eloquent testimony not merely to this friendship, but to a remarkable sympathy on the part of the artist with the themes of the novel, and a complex understanding of its affective structures.

Chateaubriand's *Atala*, first published in 1801 to great public success and reprinted many times before Girodet created his painting, was set in Louisiana in the eighteenth century. It is the story of the doomed love between Chactas, an Indian taken captive by enemies, and Atala, a Christian Iroquois Indian who falls in love with him and frees him. They take refuge with a Christian hermit, Père Aubry (Father Aubry). However, Atala has sworn to her mother that she would give herself only to God, and as she realizes the extent of her love for Chactas, and thus the danger to her vow, she poisons herself. Between them, the grieving Chactas and the hermit accord Atala a Christian burial, and Chactas vows to become a Christian himself.

Girodet's painting, as has often been pointed out, is not an exact illustration of any one scene in the novel, but is actually a synthesis of three different moments: the burial, the mourning of Chactas and Père Aubry over Atala's body, and the last communion. The mournful but simultaneously highly eroticized tone of the painting reflects key aspects of the pervasive atmosphere of the novel, and its use of plant and moon symbolism is perfectly attuned to Chateaubriand's own aesthetic.

While Girodet gives reign to sensuality, exoticism, and even eroticism (as illustrated by the sensual depiction of Atala's face and body, and the detailed representation of flora and the landscape), he seems to restrain these notes within a conception that owes its overall clarity, and the modeling of its individual figures, to an aesthetic evolved during his early career. Indeed, Girodet seemed to have been very conscious of neoclassical discipline and the ideals of "la belle nature" as he worked from freer and more adventurous preparatory drawings (for instance the version Angers, at the Musée Turpin de Crissé, in which Chactas has tattoos and a pronounced hair knot, or the rather frenzied sketch in the National Gallery of Canada in Ottowa) toward the finished painting.

The pervasive religiosity of Chateaubriand's text, and its particular tension, which emanates from the conflict between desire and religious duty, is communicated forcefully in Girodet's canvas. The painting is even more steeped in religiosity feeling, and more indebted to religious painting as a genre, than Girodet's most celebrated religious work, the *Pietà* (1789).

It has been suggested that Girodet's pictorial construction in *Atala* was inspired by medieval imagery of the death of the Virgin. Scholars have pointed to specific examples, such as the *Death of the Virgin* tympanum in Strasbourg Cathedral, which may have helped shape Girodet's conceptions. The iconography of martyrs in ecstasy may have also provided inspiration for the creation of an image that was simultaneously religious and deeply emotional and sensual.

There is a subtle analogy to be drawn between the suffering of Atala and that of Christ in the way that Girodet styles and places his figures. In this sense, some of the profound Catholicity of the text is reflected in a rather uneasy role for Atala, hovering between the purity and self-sacrifice of Mary and the suffering of Christ.

The particular place and role of Atala in the painting, as in the novel, have drawn critical commentary from feminist scholarship. The composition of the picture perhaps inadvertently dramatizes the conflicts and expectations that serve to produce Atala's self-destruction. The heroine is in some ways the true prisoner of the tale and the painting, stretched lifeless and helpless even in life, between piety (represented by Père Aubry and the cross) and desire (as connoted in the picture by the bowed but unmistakeable physicality of Chactas and Atala's own sensuous beauty).

The critical reception for the painting was almost completely favorable, (a relief to Girodet after the rather lukewarm reception for his *Ossian* and *Deluge*), although most commentators commented on the fact that Atala did not really appear dead. They pointed to some of the tensions—between sensuality and the statuesque, between exemplarity and desire—that are evident in the canvas, but also remind us that the depiction of liminal, uncertain states was central to the affective power of some of the key canvases in French history painting, from Jacques-Louis David's *Socrates* and *Marat* to Theodore Géricault's *Raft of the Medusa*.

Girodet's painting did not escape the mania for visual and verbal parody; Louis-Leopold Boilly's *Flore au Tombeau* replaces the characters of the composition with dogs. Other, more conventionally related, compositions now in the public domain include a repetition of the painting (perhaps at least partially by Girodet's hand) in the High Art Museum, Atlanta, and a oil sketch in the J. Paul Getty Museum in Los Angeles that may be a model or draft for the painting.

MARK LEDBURY

Atala au Tombeau. Reprinted courtesy of AKG.

See also **Chateaubriand, François-Auguste-René de, Vicomte; Girodet de Roussy-Trioson**

Work

Atala au Tombeau, 1808. The Louvre, Paris.

Bibliography

Dube, Pierre H. "Chateaubriand et Girodet," *Revue de L'Universite D'Ottawa/University of Ottawa Quarterly* 54, no. 2 (1984): 85–94.

Guégan, Stephane. "De Chateaubriand à Girodet: Atala ou la belle morte." In *Chateaubriand et les arts.* Edited by Marc Fumaroli. Paris: Fallois, 1999, 139–45.

Lemonnier, Henri. "L'Atala de Chateaubriand et l'Atala de Girodet," *Gazette des Beaux Arts* 4, no. 2 (1914).

Levitine, George. "Some Unexplored Aspects of the Illustrations of Atala: The *Surenchères visuelles* of Girodet and Hersent." in R. Switzer, ed. *Chateaubriand*, pp. 139–45.

————. *Girodet: An Iconographical Study.* New York: 1978, 257–76.

Moffitt, John. "The Native American 'Sauvage' as Pictured by French Romantic Artists and writers," *Gazette des Beaux-Arts* 134 (1999): 117–30.

Violin-Savalle, Maryse. *Images croisées de la femme romantique à travers la littérature et la peinture en France de 1765 à 1833.* Paris, 1996.

Wakefield, David. "Girodet's *Atala* as a Source of Inspiration in Nineteenth-Century Art," *Burlington* 120 (1978): 13–22.

ATTERBOM, PER DANIEL AMADEUS 1790–1855

Swedish poet

Per Daniel Amadeus Atterbom was born into a vicarage family. He was an only child, and his doting mother sought to protect him from life's hardships. This sheltered upbringing did little to prepare him for the realities of the literary and academic world he was to enter. As a child he was an introverted dreamer and his companions were books, a situation that fostered his Romantic tendencies, evidence of which came in the addition of a third name, Amadeus, which he chose in his twenties. Many critics are of the opinion that Atterbom's literary talents have been overrated and his importance in literary history is primarily as a representative cultural icon. Nevertheless, Atterbom's name is remembered and proves significant in the Romantic era in Sweden.

Atterbom belonged to a group of student poets who joined the battle against the old school of classical poets started by Lorenzo Hammarsköld's spoof magazine *Polyfem* (1810–12). He never contributed to the magazine, but six months after the birth of *Polyfem*, the students started their own magazine *Phosphorus—Ljusbäraren* (*Phosphorus—Lightbearer*, 1810–13). The Phosphorists were, from the outset, serious; they shaped the form of Swedish Romanticism by following Friedrich Wilhelm Joseph von Schelling's philosophy and distinguishing it from German Romanticism by its close association to the Renaissance nature philosophy and aesthetics. Atterbom contributed to the first issue of *Phosphoros* with the essays "Prolog" ("Prologue"), "Gullåldren" ("The Golden Age"), and the poem "Erotikern" ("The Erotically Inclined Person"), which appears to be a Romantic advertisement in verse directed at a female reader.

Noteworthy among the poems he published in the following years are the suite *Blommorna* (*The Flowers*), published in the annual *Poetisk kalender* (*Poetic Calendar*) in 1811, and the incomplete *Fågel blå* (*Bluebird*). The *Poetisk kalender* seems to have reached a relatively wide audience while a second publication, *Swensk Litteratur Tidning* (*Swedish Literature Magazine*, 1813–25), where several of Atterbom's most important contributions were published, only had a very limited distribution. Atterbom was not one a poet who managed to exploit the mass market; his career was for the most part limited to academic circles. He met his audience in person in their homes and in salons, and it was left to other poets to publicize the work of the Phosphorists.

Atterbom spent the years 1817–19 in Italy and this resulted in a collection of letters that he later published. During this time the battle between the old and new schools of thought had taken an interesting turn, as the popular poet Esias Tegnér had entered the scene. He brought the new school to the attention of the public, but did so by picking apart their arguments and deriding

their leading figures. Atterbom tried to smooth things over by publishing a number of *Recensionsblommor* (*Review Flowers*) in *Poetisk kalender* (1821), which were dedicated to a number of poets, including Tegnér, and finishing with *Fridsrop* (*Cry for Peace*). His attempt failed to win any support.

Atterbom felt that it was necessary to consolidate his reputation as a poet by publishing a larger work; the first part of *Lycksalighetens ö* (*The Island of Happiness*) was therefore published in 1824, while the second part followed in 1827. It was not well received, even by his friends. The clumsy parody of democracy in the fourth section of the series laid him open to derision by the press. The publication of *Samlade dikter 1–2* (*Collected Poems 1–2*, 1837–38) was similarly ill-fated, as it received a bad review from his friend Erik Gustaf Geijer.

Atterbom progressed further in his academic career; he completed a doctorate in history and from there moved on to a professorship in theoretical philosophy, and later to a professorship in aesthetics and literature. He was voted into the Swedish Academy in 1839 which showed that his literary career was not a complete failure. It was in his academic role, however, that Atterbom showed real talent. He was a gifted interpreter of literature and had a feel for literary quality, especially in earlier authors and works. His work *Svenska Siare och Skalder 1–6* (*Swedish Prophets and Poets*, 1841–55) forms a strong basis for Swedish literary history, and it was Atterbom who championed the Swedish canon of poets before Olof Dalin (1708–63).

Atterbom's contemporaries said that to appreciate his poetry it was necessary to have met the man, whereas later critics have felt that it is Atterbom's personality that prevents appreciation of his work. Furthermore, his cowardly way of trying to get at rivals under a guise of friendship—perhaps a legacy of a solitary childhood—colors our perception of the poet. Nevertheless, it cannot be denied that his work on the literary history of Sweden displays real talent, and he remained true to the Romantic idealization of the poet as the manifestation of art and spirit. Atterbom was childlike throughout his whole life in many ways, with a sense of wonder that never left him and an endless fascination with everything around him. He remained close with all his friends from his youth, but in his later years he was left increasingly without company, as one by one his friends died. Finally, his much-loved wife also died in 1854 and he followed her to the grave in 1855, shortly after the reworked edition of *Lycksalighetens ö* was published in her memory.

CAMILLA FRASER

Biography

Born 1790. Contributed to first issue of *Phophorus* in 1810 with "Prolog," "Gullåldren," and "Erotikern." In 1811, published

Blommorna in *Poetisk kalender* and part of *Fågel blå*. Travelled in Italy 1817–19. In 1821, published *Recensionsblommor* and *Fridsrop* in *Poetisk Kalender*. Publication of first part of *Lyksalighetens ö* in 1824 and second part in 1827. In 1837–38, *Samlade dikter 1–2* published. In 1839, voted into Swedish Academy. In 1841–55, published *Svenska Siare och Skalder 1–6*. Died in 1855.

Selected Works

Atterboms samlade skrifter, vols. 1–6.
Samlade dikter 1–6.
Svenska Siare och Skalder 1–5.

Bibliography

Frykenstedt. *Atterboms sagospel Lyksalighetens ö.* Lund: Gleerups, 1951.
Hägg. *Den svenska litteraturhistorien.* Stockholm: Wahlström and Widstrand, 1996.
Lönnroth and Delblanc. *Den svenska litteraturen, Upplysning och Romantik,* Stockholm: Bonniers, 1988.
Santesson. *Atterboms ungdoms diktning.* Stockholm: Norstedt, 1920.
Schück and Warburg. *Illustrerad svensk litteraturhistoria.* Stockholm: Natur and Kultur.
Tigerstedt, ed. *Ny illustrerad svensk litteraturhistoria.* Stockholm: Natur and Kultur, 1956.
Tykesson. *Atterbom.* Stockholm: Bonniers, 1954.

AUDUBON, JOHN JAMES 1785–1851

Artist and naturalist

In 1788, at the age of three, Jean Jacques Audubon sailed in the care of the ship's captain from Haiti (his birthplace) to Fracce. This adventure set the tone for much of his later life. In France he received the education of a country gentleman, learning to read, draw, dance, and play music. Academic studies were of little interest, but observation of nature captured his attention, and from his youth, the natural world was the subject of his pastels and watercolors. Faced with his son's conscription into Napoleon Bonaparte's army, Jean Audubon sent his son to the United States to tend to his land in Pennsylvania, and to become John James Audubon, creator of *The Birds of America* and *The Viviparous Quadrupeds of North America*.

Upon arriving in the United States, Audubon began drawing birds in earnest and soon developed his method for observing, capturing, mounting, and drawing the birds that he would utilize in his later work. As was true of his academic studies, Audubon was not a dedicated businessman, and at a particularly low point he served a jail sentence for debt. Much of the time Audubon was able to get by on his charm, but he was plagued by financial insecurity. Realizing that he was neither an intellectual nor a financial genius, Audubon reflected upon his natural capabilities—and his personal interests—and decided to use his artistic skills to support himself and his family. At various times he received lessons and/or advice from the American painters John Wesley Jarvis, Thomas Sully, and John Vanderlyn, among others, but this was probably the extent of his mature artistic education. He had experienced limited success teaching drawing and selling paintings of birds and painting portraits when he met and saw the work of Alexander Wilson, author of *American Ornithology* (1808–14). Audubon's business partner, Ferdinand Rozier, commented that Audubon's ornithological drawings were better than Wilson's, sparking Audubon's ambition to create what would become *The Birds of America*.

America's ability to distinguish itself from Europe lay in delimiting the aspects of the landscape that could be most closely associated with the act of Creation. As a result, natural historical projects undertaken by individuals such as Wilson and Audubon, as well as Charles Willson Peale and his son Titian Ramsay Peale, among others, were recognized, discussed and supported by natural history societies and individuals, and to some extent by the federal government.

The Birds of America was an immense and at times overwhelming undertaking. Audubon spent months alone, away from his family, pursuing his quarry and capturing it on paper, leaving his wife to support herself and their two sons by teaching. It was this time that he spent observing the birds and their habits, that made his work unique and compelling. The authenticity of experience conveyed in the images was unparalleled. He worked with others to illustrate the backgrounds, and to create the final composition. Finding a printer in the United States proved impossible due in part to Audubon's overconfidence and lack of scientific pedigree, and also to the rivalry between Wilson and himself. Wilson had many supporters and was well respected in Philadelphia, the home of American natural science. Without support from this community, Audubon knew he could not hope to succeed.

Failing in Philadelphia, Audubon went to England to find a printer and patronage. Upon his arrival he was introduced to Liverpool society with great success. In marked contrast to his experience in Philadelphia, where the scientific community found his untutored persona ridiculous, the English gentry found Audubon's backwoods self-presentation enormously appealing. While in England he wore fringed buckskin and kept his hair long. Upon request he performed bird songs and animal calls, sang folk songs, and perhaps best of all told colorful stories about the places, and particularly the people, he met on his travels through the wilds of the American continent. Audubon has been likened to James Fenimore Cooper's character Natty Bumpo in the *Leatherstocking Tales*, popular in England and America at the time of Audubon's visit. The ladies were particularly charmed by Audubon's appearance, and he used this to his advantage. He wrote to his wife in 1826 that, "My hairs are now as beautifully long and curly as ever and I assure thee do as much for me as my talent for painting." Audubon knew quite well that while the scientific community might praise or criticize his work, it was the "wealthy part of the community . . . [that] will fill my pockets," thus enabling him to finish his project and return home.

While in Edinburgh and London he had success in securing a printer (first William H. Lizars and then Robert Havell Jr.), and patronage. The 29.5 by 39.5–inch elephant folio of *The Birds of America* containing 435 plates was published in five-print installments between 1827 and 1838. Audubon followed this with an enormously popular and less expensive octavo edition of 500 plates on 6.5 by 10–inch paper. To accompany *The Birds of America* he published his *Ornithological Biography* (1831–39), a series of natural histories of the birds pictured with "episodes" from Audubon's life in the wilderness inserted to sustain the attention of a popular audience. The narratives from his life are primarily based upon his letters to friends and family, and on his voluminous journals. They were edited by William MacGillivray, a Scottish scientist who cleansed Audubon's writing of its grammatical errors, but also, unfortunately, some of its immediacy.

After Audubon's death, a sanitized version of his journals was published by his Victorian-era granddaughter Maria R. Audubon, who felt compelled to free them of any sensual observation or overwrought emotion. His letters, however, remain in their original form and convey Audubon's arrogance, charm, skill, successes, and failures. Writing from Edinburgh in December 1826 to his wife Lucy he describes the self-doubt he felt upon meeting one of the learned ladies of the community: "I know that at one glance she had discovered my great inferiority." In another letter later the same month he compares himself to Napoleon, writing "Since Napoleon became, from the ranks, an Emperor, why should not Audubon be able to leave the woods of America a while and publish and sell a book?" This fluctuation between uncertainty and exuberant confidence continued through his second and final major work, *The Viviparous Quadrupeds of North America* (1845–48). Ultimately, the sacrifice that he and his family made to his creations was rewarded with popular praise and scientific approval.

KATHLEEN L. BUTLER

Biography

Born in Les Cayes, Santo Domingo (now Haiti), April 26, 1785. Illegitimate son of Jean Audubon, a French sea captain and plantation owner, and his Creole mistress. He was taken to Nantes, France, and formally adopted by Jean Audubon and his wife, 1794. Moved to his father's home near Philadelphia, 1803. Married Lucy Bakewell, 1808. Suffered a number of failed businesses and bankruptcy. Moved to New Orleans, 1821. Earned income by teaching art and doing commissioned portraits. Traveled to Scotland and England to seek a patron and publisher for his art, 1826. *The Birds of America* published in London in four volumes, 1827–38. *Ornithological Biography*, written with William MacGillivray, published in 5 volumes, 1831–39. Divided his time between Europe and the United States; settled in New York, 1839. Published *The Viviparous Quadrupeds of North America* in three volumes, 1845–48. Died 1851.

Selected Collections of Original Works

National Gallery of Art, Washington, D.C.
New York Historical Society. New York, N.Y.
New York Public Library. New York, N.Y.
Buffalo Bill Historical Center. Cody, Wyo.

Bibliography

Boehme, Sarah E. *John James Audubon in the West: The Last Expedition*. New York: Harry N. Abrams, 2000.
Bannon, Lois Elmer, and Taylor Clark. *Handbook of Audubon Prints*. Gretna, La.: Pelican, 1998.
Dunlap, William. "Audobon." In *The History of the Rise and Progress of Arts of Design in the United States*, 1834. Reprinted, New York: Benjamin Blom, 1965. 3: 202–9.
Ford, Alice. *John James Audubon: A Biography*. New York: Abbeville Press, 1988.
Lindsey, Alton A., ed. *The Bicentennial of John James Audubon*. Bloomington: Indiana University Press, 1985.
Sanders, Scott Russell, ed. *The Audubon Reader: The Best Writings of John James Audubon*. Bloomington: Indiana University Press, 1986.

AUSTEN, JANE 1775–1817

English novelist

Jane Austen's self-imposed restriction of "3 or 4 Families in a country village" enabled her to focus on the development and interplay of characters within narrowly discriminated classes in a provincial community presented in realistic detail. Austen herself, through her immediate family, had access to a far wider range of experience of the church, the navy, the large estate of her brother Edward, and the fashionable London life of her banker brother Henry. Deftly alluding to war, politics, slavery, religion, consumerism, medicine, the professions, and patronage, Austen extends the range of the "feminine" novel of the period to reflect the impact of the larger national world on courtship, family life, and local relationships. Her restricted settings also aid the careful plotting and structuring of her novels in which parallels of plot, situation, and character allow ironic juxtapositions and give the novels unity of theme. She combines the dramatic tradition of the epistolary novel with the potentially unifying power of a narratorial viewpoint in a mobile technique of presentation.

Austen's technical achievements recommended her to the Jamesian school of novelistic criticism of the early twentieth century. Though the Jamesian aesthetic was developed from Coleridgean ideas of unity and organization, Austen was, and often still is, regarded historically as the culmination of eighteenth-century novelistic art, due to her use of its novelistic conventions, her predominantly rationalistic viewpoint, and an apparent nostalgia for eighteenth-century certainties communicated through a solid language of shared moral and social values. Of particular interest was Austen's innovation in the customary courtship plot whereby the heroine has to undergo a process of education in self-knowledge, rather than merely learning how to comport herself in society as a respectable young lady. The emphasis on the heroine's subjectivity and on "timeless" inner virtues shadowed developments in the Romantic theory of the mid-century.

Marilyn Butler's study of 1975 inaugurated the modern school of Austen criticism by relating her work to the "war of ideas" of her time. Though her initial characterization of Austen as a Burkean conservative who found an ideal order in the landed gentry of her day has been substantially modified, the novels and their language have been opened up to the debates among historicists. Much recent criticism, taking its tone from Claudia Johnson's study of Austen's relation to feminism, sees her taking inherited forms and subtly undermining "from within" their conservative bias. Such approaches align Austen with Romantic writers like William Wordsworth, whose works suggest a reconciliation of aristocratic and middle-class values. It is characteristic, however, that the emphasis should be on the subversive quality of her art rather than on undoubted assertions.

Northanger Abbey (1805, published 1818) has a clear connection with Austen's exuberant juvenilia in which she parodies fictional modes and the literary conventions of character and behavior that reflect social constructions. The contrast between fiction and reality is established only to be destabilized, and the narrator, far from providing a reassuring authority, mimics several authoritative voices varying from the conventionally moralistic to the worldly wise, and becomes a surrogate author satisfying the expectations of readers with a patently manipulated conclusion. The misleading appearances and types of distress associated with sentimental/Gothic fiction reappear, toned down in the representation of "ordinary" social life, but still require in the character Catherine some of the qualities of a heroine.

Many of these disconcerting features appear to a lesser extent in Austen's later novels. The narrator's voice is infiltrated by other discourses and in turn infiltrates the represented thoughts of characters in the novelistic innovation of "free indirect discourse." Conclusions are hastily summarized in an ironic tone, with appeals to readerly desires, especially in *Sense and Sensibility* (1811) and *Mansfield Park* (1814). In general, the point of view of the narrator follows the physical possibilities of one main heroine and has privileged entrance only to her thoughts. Much of the comedy and moral seriousness of the novels arises from the limitations of such awareness, and the perceptions and judgments of the main character tend to become a central concern of the novel. Titles such as *Sense and Sensibility* and *Pride and Prejudice* (1813) might be reminiscent of the political conflicts of the 1790s, but if sensibility is a potentially subversive force it subverts not society but the perceptions and psychic health of the character Marianne. The character Darcy might initially suggest the pride and prejudice of rank justified politically by Edmund Burke, but Austen's characters have to struggle with the more personal and moral senses of the terms.

The three complete novels produced as an established author show approaches to more topical public themes, in conscious rivalry with authors such as Maria Edgeworth and Walter Scott. *Mansfield Park* can readily be taken as a metaphor for England's old "family" establishment, prey to the temptations of regency dissipation and political and financial corruption. Old forms of power, dependency, and moral obligation are put under stress by a pervasive spirit of exploitation. The character Fanny Price, as a woman and a dependant, feels the obligations and suffers the injustices of her situation but remains dedicated to what she believes Mansfield Park stands for. In *Emma* (1815), the heroine comes to terms with a fluid, enterprising society that challenges traditional hierarchies. Her idea of gentility is broadened socially and she becomes more morally sensitive to the exercise of patronage. In *Persuasion* (1818), the character Anne Elliot's new sense of self-worth, confirmed by her valued activities in different social settings, allows her to rise above the degenerate aristocratic values of her family and resist the modern glorification of the self-made man of talent.

The experience of Austen's heroines opens onto general aspects of "alteration, perhaps improvement." Female experience is strongly focused but is connected with the experience of other comparable social groups; even heroes have to follow parallel paths of self-education. General themes suggest the possibility of individual and social progress in integrity, sensitivity, and social responsibility, but Austen's heroines remain engaged in their passionate, individual struggles toward fulfilment, regarded with tolerant irony by the narrative voice.

CHRIS JONES

Biography

Born in Steventon, near Basingstoke, Hampshire, December 16, 1775, seventh of eight children of Rev. George Austen, a Church of England clergyman. Educated at home in Steventon and at Mrs. Cawley's School, Oxford. Lived in Bath with her family after her father's retirement, 1801. Moved to Southampton after her father's death, 1805; lived with her mother and unmarried sister Cassandra in a house owned by her brother Edward in Chawton, near Alton, Hampshire, from 1809. Published *Sense and Sensibility* (1811), *Pride and Prejudice* (1813), *Mansfield Park* (1814), and *Emma* (1815) anonymously, leaving another novel, *Sanditon*, uncompleted at her death. Died, after a lengthy illness, in Winchester, July 18, 1817. *Persuasion* was published posthumously (together with *Northanger Abbey*) in 1818 after its retrieval from publishers who had purchased but failed to publish it in 1805.

Selected Works

Novels
Sense and Sensibility. 1811.
Pride and Prejudice. 1813.
Mansfield Park. 1814.
Emma. 1815.
Persuasion. 1818.
Northanger Abbey. 1818.

Letters
Jane Austen's Letters. Edited by Deidre Le Faye. Oxford: Oxford University Press, 1995.

Bibliography

Butler, Marilyn. *Jane Austen and the War of Ideas.* Rev. ed. Oxford: Clarendon Press, 1975, 1987.
Copeland, Edward, and Juliet McMaster, eds. *The Cambridge Companion to Jane Austen.* Cambridge: Cambridge University Press, 1997.
Duckworth, Alistair M. *The Improvement of the Estate: A Study of Jane Austen's Novels.* Baltimore: Johns Hopkins University Press, 1971.
Johnson, Claudia L. *Equivocal Beings: Politics, Gender, and Sentimentality in the 1790s: Wollstonecraft, Radcliffe, Burney, Austen.* Chicago: University of Chicago Press, 1995.

————. *Jane Austen: Women, Politics, and the Novel*. Chicago: University of Chicago Press, 1988.

Kelly, Gary. *English Fiction of the Romantic Period*. London: Longman, 1989.

Kirkham, Margaret. *Jane Austen, Feminism and Fiction*. Brighton, England: Harvester Press, 1983.

Lascelles, Mary. *Jane Austen and Her Art*. London: Oxford University Press, 1939.

Looser, Devoney, ed. *Jane Austen and Discourses of Feminism*. New York: St. Martin's Press, 1995.

MacDonagh, Oliver. *Jane Austen: Real and Imagined Worlds*. New Haven, Conn.: Yale University Press, 1991.

McMaster, Juliet, and Bruce Stovel, eds. *Jane Austen's Business: Her World and Her Profession*. New York: St. Martin's Press, 1996.

Page, Norman. *The Language of Jane Austen*. Oxford: Blackwell, 1972.

Poovey, Mary. *The Proper Lady and the Woman Writer*. Chicago: University of Chicago Press, 1984.

Roberts, Warren. *Jane Austen and the French Revolution*. London: Macmillan, 1979.

Sales, Roger. *Jane Austen and Representations of Regency England*. London: Routledge, 1994.

Southam, Brian C., ed. *Critical Essays on Jane Austen*. London: Routledge, 1968.

Stokes, Myra. *The Language of Jane Austen*. Basingstoke, England: Macmillan, 1991.

Tomalin, Claire. *Jane Austen: A Life*. New York: Knopf, 1997.

Waldron, Mary. *Jane Austen and the Fiction of Her Time*. Cambridge: Cambridge University Press, 1999.

Wallace, Tara Goshal. *Jane Austen and Narrative Authority*. Basingstoke, England: Macmillan, 1995.

Watson, Nicola J. *Revolution and the Form of the British Novel, 1790–1825*. Oxford: Clarendon Press, 1994.

Wiltshire, John. *Jane Austen and the Body*. Cambridge: Cambridge University Press, 1992.

Wright, Andrew H. *Jane Austen's Novels: A Study in Structure*. Harmondsworth, England: Penguin, 1962.

AUTOBIOGRAPHICAL WRITING: BRITAIN

Between 1760 and 1850, the autobiographical genre grew both in number of publications and in popularity throughout Britain. Although Robert Southey is often credited with first using the word *autobiography* in an 1809 book review, it has been shown that forms of the word appeared in English as early as 1797 and before then in continental languages; thus, the development of the word and its use parallels the rise of the autobiographical genre as a whole.

Prior to the late eighteenth and early nineteenth centuries, British autobiographies tended toward one of two genres: the spiritual autobiography or the memoir. Although St. Augustine's *Confessions* still stands as the prototype of spiritual autobiographies, John Bunyan's *Grace Abounding to the Chief of Sinners* (1666) remains arguably the most well-known English work of this genre as it contains, like most spiritual autobiographies, a close focus on the writer's internal and emotional relationship with God along with comparatively little attention to the historical events of the writer's life. Inversely, memoirs, such as Edward Gibbon's unfinished *Memoir* (1796) and Mary Robinson's *Memoirs* (1801), concentrate primarily on the people, places, and events surrounding the author's life while the writer spends comparatively less time on his or her personal feelings.

In his *Confessions* (1782–89), Jean-Jacques Rousseau combines the elements of these two genres to create an autobiographical work that both recounts the historical events of the author's life and explores the deepest emotions the author felt while experiencing, causing, or even remembering those events. The *Confessions* afforded primacy to the author's thoughts and feelings, both positive and negative, which changed the focus and content of autobiographies, and its influence extended beyond the borders of France. Although spiritual autobiographies remained popular in England following the publication of the *Confessions* in English in 1783–90, many writers turned their attention toward describing their emotions as well as their relationships with themselves, other individuals, and society.

While the array of autobiographical works produced since 1760 is indeed diverse, the suggestion of a few basic categories may provide some means of understanding the variety. As writers turned inward, accounts of their literary growth and maturation often became the subject of their autobiographical writings. For example, William Wordsworth's *Prelude, or, the Growth of a Poet's Mind* (1805) provides a verse retelling of important emotional landmarks in Wordsworth's development. Other writers provide a more conventional and chronological retelling of the literary and nonliterary events of their lives, such as in Leigh Hunt's *Autobiography* (1850), while still others, such as Samuel Taylor Coleridge in his *Biographia Literaria* (1817), fuse personal recollections with literary theory and criticism.

Another branch of autobiography concerns authors whose life writing includes fictionalized incidents or autobiographical personas. Such is the case in Thomas de Quincey's *Confessions of an English Opium-Eater* (1822) in which de Quincey portrays his life only as it relates to his opium addiction and its effects; he thus recounts the poverty he experienced as a result of his addiction as well as fantastical opium-induced dreams. Thomas Carlyle's *Sartor Resartus* (1831) traces the intellectual development of Diogenes Teufelsdröckh, whose emotional struggles parallel those of Carlyle's own youth. In verse, Lord Byron's *Childe Harold's Pilgrimage* (1812–18) similarly creates a fictional main character whose adventures mirror those Byron himself experienced.

The use of fictional elements in writing about the self heavily influenced the development of the autobiographical novel: see, for example, Charlotte Brontë's *Jane Eyre* (1847) and Charles Dickens's *David Copperfield* (1849–50). In these and other autobiographical novels, specific events, people, and places from the author's life may be depicted in an exaggerated fashion, realistically, or even allegorically, but the author's experience remains the basis for the representation. Many critics have suggested that this genre has found its fullest artistic expression in such later works as James Joyce's *Portrait of the Artist as a Young Man* (1916).

A discussion of Romantic-era autobiographical writings must also include reference to the many writers whose journals and letters, which, although not published during their lives, have become important texts to contemporary scholars. The letters of John Keats are often considered among the most interesting literary letters of the nineteenth century, and they reveal his rapid poetic development and sense of humor in a manner his verse cannot. Keepers of journals have also offered important information about their lives, societies, and literary efforts. Dorothy Wordsworth's *Grasmere Journals* provide an interesting and informative counterpoint to her brother William's autobiographical poetry, and *The Journal of Sir Walter Scott* details the literary and financial struggles Scott faced after he found himself in debt following the collapse of his publishing house in 1809. Other notable journal keepers were Mary Shelley and George Eliot.

KEN A. BUGAJSKI

See also **Autobiographical Writing: Germany**

Bibliography

Buckley, Jerome Hamilton. *The Turning Key: Autobiography and the Subjective Impulse since 1800.* Cambridge, Mass.: Harvard University Press, 1984.

Danahay, Martin A. *A Community of One: Masculine Autobiography and Autonomy in Nineteenth-Century Britain.* The Margins of Literature Series. Albany: State University of New York Press, 1993.

De Man, Paul. "Autobiography as De-Facement." In *The Rhetoric of Romanticism.* New York: Columbia University Press, 1984.

Levin, Susan M. *The Romantic Art of Confession: De Quincey, Musset, Sand, Lamb, Hogg, Fremy, Soulie, Janin.* Columbia, S.C.: Camden House, 1998.

Nussbaum, Felicity. *The Autobiographical Subject: Gender and Ideology in Eighteenth-Century England.* Baltimore: Johns Hopkins University Press, 1989.

Spengemann, William C. *The Forms of Autobiography: Episodes in the History of a Literary Genre.* New Haven, Conn.: Yale University Press, 1980.

AUTOBIOGRAPHICAL WRITING: GERMANY

Autobiographical writing in Germany during the Romantic period, which stretched roughly from the mid 1790s to the second decade of the nineteenth century, is characterized by diversification. The hitherto established forms of pragmatic-historical autobiography, the then only recently introduced psychological-autobiographical novel (by Karl Philipp Moritz, with his *Anton Reiser*, 1785), and the widely debated model of autobiography as a radical personal account (as introduced in Jean-Jacques Rousseau's *Confessions* [1782–89]), all met with skepticism among the representatives of the early Romantic movement. Their critique of these forms of autobiography expressed general doubts about the possibility of an objective, valid autobiographical self-examination. Friedrich Schlegel's ironic aphorism on "pure autobiographies," whose authors he considers "mentally ill people obsessed with their Ego," and his further comments on this subject in the *Gespräch über die Poesie* (*Dialogue on Poetry*, 1800) display these fundamental doubts. Schlegel's views are in line with those of contemporary thinkers, such as his fellow contributor to the *Athenaeum* journal, the theologian Friedrich Schleiermacher and the philosopher Immanual Kant (1798). Schlegel's disapproval of the autobiography is at the same time accompanied by reflections on the close relationships among confessions, travelogues, letters and novels, and on his notion of Romantic poetry as rooted in historical truth, a concept that dissolves the distinction between historical truth and a fiction. Furthermore, he considers these other forms of autobiographical writing, along with the novel, as the main genres of the Romantic *Naturpoesie*. Within the concept of Romantic poetry as a "progressive and universal poetry" that reunites all literary genres and academic disciplines, and that proclaims an interchangeability of art and life, forms of autobiographical writing acquire the status of fiction and vice versa, since according to Schlegel, "novels are nothing more than barely disguised confessions of their author."

The effect of this detachment of autobiographical writing from the genre's typology is reflected in the wide use of autobiographical material in all forms of Romantic writing. An example of the use of autobiographical material, which was controversially discussed at the time, is Friedrich Schlegel's novel *Lucinde* (1799), perceived as a roman à clef about the relationship between Schlegel and his then partner and later wife Dorothea Veit-Mendelssohn. Schleiermacher's *Vertraute Briefe über "Lucinde"* (*Intimate Letters on "Lucinde,"* 1800) defended the novel publicly against the accusation of obscenity.

Other examples of German Romantic autobiographical writing are Sophie Mereau's epistolary novel *Amanda and Eduard* (1803), which incorporates whole passages of the correspondence between Mereau and her student lover from the years 1795–97, and the collaborative novel *Die Versuche und Hindernisse Karls* (1808) by Karl August Varnhagen von Ense, Wilhelm Neumann, Friedrich de la Motte Fouqué, and August Ferdinand Bernhardi; the main characters Karl and Warner are both modeled on Varnhagen.

Clemens Brentano, certainly one of the most ambivalent characters of the Romantic movement and one of its most prolific writers, pushes autobiography far beyond its status as source material. His work displays the manifold ways of blending autobiography and fiction in the early Romantics' programatic sense, taken to an extreme. His letters oscillate among diary, confession, and fiction (e.g., those to Sophie Mereau or Achim von Arnim) while his poetry and fiction draw on experiences and memories (e.g., *Romanzen vom Rosenkranz; Godwi*, 1802; "Preface to the Gockel fairy tale," 1838). Even his so-called religious works, such as the *Bittere Leiden unsers Herrn Jesu Christi* (1833) hover between fact and fiction according to the notion of art as life and life as art, and are in general models of self-presentation in poetry. Brentano's so-called general confession (*Generalbeichte*, 1817) as well as his confessional letters to Joseph Görres, Wilhelm Grimm, and Philipp Otto Runge, are to be seen within the wider context of a larger literary project, planned together with Achim von Arnim: the project of collecting biographies and autobiographies, and also writing their own (early 1810), although the latter aim was never realized.

Autobiographical forms of writing, such as journals, diaries and letters, have always been used particularly widely by women, during the Romantic period an increasing preference among women writers for these genres is apparent. Among these women the Berlin salonière of the turn of the century, Rahel Varnhagen, is probably the most interesting intellectually, and her literary oeuvre the most challenging. Her work, vast and consisting almost exclusively of letters and aphoristic diaries, offers a different, however no less characteristic aspect of Romantic autobiographical writing. Her autobiographical writings are, on the one hand, a measure and means of meticulous self-observation and self-analysis (here we see the tradition of autobiographical writing developed during the eighteenth century) but are simultaneously perceived as an art form. Rahel's autobiographical writing oscillates continuously between the pragmatic and the aesthetic. The posthumous publication *Rahel Ein Buch des Andenkens für ihre Freunde* (3 vol., 1834), prepared by herself and her husband Karl August Varnhagen von Ense, blends both pragmatic and aesthetic aspects in an artistic arrangement of edited text passages to give a rounded portrait of Rahel.

Parallel to this overtly Romantic autobiographical writing, the first decades of the nineteenth century saw the rise of the autobiographical genre in the sense of a continuous narrative account of one's life. In the first instance, there is a waning, from 1790 on, of the traditional forms of the scholar's or artist's autobiography, as well as of Rousseauesque self-analysis, as rejected by the Romantics. Autobiographies of that period, such as the composer Carl Friedrich Zelter's *Selbstbiographie* (*Self-Biography*, 1808), and the fifth volume of Johann Heinrich Jung Stilling's *Lebensgeschichte* in 1804, *Lehrjahre* (*Years of Apprenticeship*), neither engage exclusively in psychological self-examination nor address sequences of significant events or steps in a professional career. Examples such as Johann Gottfried Seume's *Mein Leben* (*My Life*, 1809) illustrate the new attempt to find a balance between individual and epochal analysis, a move that culminates eventually in Johann Wolfgang von Goethe's autobiographical writings, *Dichtung und Wahrheit* (1811ff) and his *Italian Journey* (1816f). Particularly in *Dichtung und Wahrheit*, Goethe's concept of the double mirror imaging of the individual, as well as the practice of treating the individual life as symbolic of human existence, found its most profound expression.

URSULA HUDSON-WIEDENMANN

See also **Autobiographical Writing: Britain**

Bibliography

Blackwell, Jeannine, and Susanne Zantop, eds. *Bitter Healing: German Women Writers 1700–1830*. Lincoln: University of Nebraska Press, 1990.

Feilchenfeldt, Konrad. "Nachwort." In *Clemens Brentano—Philipp Otto Runge. Briefwechsel*. Frankfurt: Insel Verlag, 1974.

Golz, Jochen, ed. *Edition von autobiographischen Schriften und Zeugnissen zur Biographie*. Internationale Fachtagung der Arbeitsgemeinschaft für germanistische Edition an der Stiftung Weimarer Klassik. Beihefte zu Editio, vol. 7. Tübingen: Max Niemeyer Verlag, 1995. Beihefte zu.

Niggl, Günther. *Geschichte der Autobiographie im 18. Jahrhundert: theoretische Grundlegung und literarische Entfaltung*. Stuttgart: Metzler 1977.

Ramm, Elke. *Autobiographische Schriften deutschsprachiger Autorinnen um 1800*. Hildesheim: Olms, 1998.

Schlegel, Friedrich. *Dialogue on Poetry, and Literary Aphorisms*. Translated by Ernst Behler and Roman Struc. University Park: Pennsylvania University Press, 1968.

B

BAILLIE, JOANNA 1762–1852

British dramatist and poet

Joanna Baillie was the leading British playwright of her day. She was widely praised by critics and was famously proclaimed by her fellow Scot, Sir Walter Scott, to be "the best dramatic writer whom Britain has produced since the days of Shakespeare and Massinger." Although she watched her popularity fade in her own lifetime, her work is now being reread in the context of Romantic recanonization. Both her plays and her poems place Baillie within a framework of Romantic egalitarianism and innovation.

Baillie is best known for her three-volume "Plays on the Passions," published as *A Series of Plays: In Which it is Attempted to Delineate the Stronger Passions of the Mind, Each Passion being the Subject of a Comedy and a Tragedy*. These appeared over a span of fourteen years and gained both popular appeal and critical acclaim. Her first volume, published anonymously in 1798, received highly favorable reviews and was variously attributed to William Cowper, Matthew Lewis, and Ann Radcliffe before Baillie put her name on the 1800 edition. This first volume contained a comedy on love (*The Tryal*), along with tragedies on love (*Count Basil*) and hate (*De Monfort*). Appearing in 1802 and 1812, the second and third volumes continued this project, providing a comedy on hate and also presenting comedies and tragedies on ambition and hope. In the space between these two later volumes, Baillie brought out two other volumes, *Miscellaneous Plays* (1804) and *The Family Legend* (1810).

As her preoccupation with the passions suggests, Baillie's plays are primarily psychological dramas. They unswervingly and insistently demonstrate the effect of a particular passion on an individual and on those around him, with much of their suspense and consequence deriving from what takes place in the hero's mind. For example, the character De Monfort in *De Monfort* struggles with an intense hatred for another that ends in murder and self-destruction; Basil in *Count Basil* is consumed by an unrequited love that drives him to suicide and his loved one to remorse and a nunnery; and Ethwald in *Ethwald* (1802) eventually finds that his ruthless ambition brings him military success but domestic and psychological ruin. Thus, the inner torments and eventual alienation faced by Baillie's protagonists foreshadow the misanthropy of the Byronic hero. Indeed, Lord Byron was a great admirer of Baillie's plays, which is especially significant in light of his open contempt for women writers.

On another level, however, Baillie is concerned with more than Romantic heroism. Her dramatic theory, outlined in the prefaces to *A Series of Plays*, demonstrates Baillie's commitment to having her plays performed and removes her from the phenomenon of the closet drama now associated with the Romantic age. This theory also provides a rationale for the psychological emphasis of her plays that goes beyond Byronic brooding. Baillie insists on the power of drama, and of literature in general, to effect a positive change in the life of the reader. In the "Introductory Discourse" to the first volume of *A Series of Plays*, Baillie suggests that, in representing the effect of the passions on an individual, her plays offer her audience the chance to observe human nature. Through this observation, which Baillie labels "sympathetic curiosity," the audience learns "the proprieties and decencies of ordinary life," since "i[n] examining others, we know ourselves." Central to Baillie's didacticism are her innovative ideas on acting and theatrical space. In the preface to the third volume of *A Series of Plays*, Baillie recommends the use of smaller and more intimate performance spaccs, and she reiterates her preference for more natural acting styles. For Baillie, the unadorned speech and actions of common life are more interesting and tragic—and hence, instructive—than grand theatrical gestures. In her desire to represent the speech of the everyday and the raw emotions of human nature, and consequently to provoke a sympathetic moral response, Baillie looks forward to the poetics that William Wordsworth would propose in the preface to *Lyrical Ballads*, a year after Baillie's first dramatic publication.

Although she was better known as a playwright, Baillie also published a small but significant body of poetry. Indeed, she began her literary career in 1790 with a volume of poetry entitled *Poems: Wherein it is Attempted to Describe Certain Views of Nature and of Rustic Manners; And Also, To Point Out, In Some Instances, the Different Influence Which the Same Circumstances Produce on Different Characters*. Poor sales, however, prompted her to channel her energies into drama. Later in her career, she published a set of poetical narratives, *Metrical Legends of Exalted Characters* (1821), an oriental romance, *Ahalya Baee* (1849), as well as a collection entitled *Fugitive Verses* (1840). Her poetry reifies the ideas propounded in her dramatic theory and practice. Her early poems are primarily realistic depictions of farm life, whose gently humorous descriptions of farm labor foreshadow Wordsworthian pastoralism and echo the rural lyrics of Baillie's compatriot Robert Burns.

In her narrative poetry, Baillie takes her interest in everyday heroism further and demonstrates her commitment to a gendered ideology of separate spheres. In *Metrical Legends*, for example, Baillie presents several poetic tributes to various heroes, such as William Wallace and Christopher Columbus, and pointedly adds her little-known ancestor, Lady Griseld Baillie, to the set. Baillie's point is that Griseld's domestic achievements are just as important as the epic deeds of the men she praises. Yet Baillie's celebration of female heroism was not a radical challenge to existing gender norms. As with Jane de Monfort in *De Monfort*, Griseld's female fortitude is meant to be complementary to, and not interchangeable with, masculine valor. Baillie herself practiced her ideal of respectable domesticity: her strict observance of household and philanthropic responsibilities and her preference for sober, quaker-like dress were well known to her readers and friends.

The impact that Baillie made in her time was due largely to the originality of her literary and dramatic ideas. The combination of natural blank verse, psychological tension, and direct didacticism resulted in influential and popular plays that today not only reveal much about the Romantic stage but retain, in works such as *De Monfort* and *Count Basil*, moments of dignity and poetic merit. Just as important, the democratic poetics and elegant realism of her poetry deserve a critical detailed reassessment, as does her discourse of domestic yet rational womanhood.

ADELINE JOHNS-PUTRA

Biography

Born at Bothwell, Lanarkshire, Scotland, September 11, 1762. Daughter of a Presbyterian minister, a professor of divinity at Glasgow University, 1776–78. Attended boarding schools in Glasgow from 1772. Moved with her mother and sister to Long Calderwood, Lanarkshire, after her father's death, 1778. Lived with her mother and sister in London from 1784; frequented the *conversazione* (salons) of her aunt, Anne Hunter. Moved with her mother and sister to Hampstead, 1802; met Sir Walter Scott, 1806. Published *Plays on the Passions*, 1798–1812. Remained unmarried but assumed the title of Mrs. Baillie from 1814. Died in Hampstead, London, February 23, 1851.

Selected Works

Collections

The Complete Poetical Works. 1832.

The Dramatic and Poetical Works of Joanna Baillie. 1851.

Joanna Baillie: A Selection of Poems and Plays. Edited by Keith Hanley and Amanda Gilroy. London: Pickering and Chatto, 1997.

The Selected Poems of Joanna Baillie. Edited by Jennifer Breen. Manchester: Manchester University Press, 1999.

Poetry

Poems: Wherein It Is Attempted to Describe Certain Views of Nature and of Rustic Manners; And Also, To Point Out, In Some Instances, the Different Influence Which the Same Circumstances Produce on Different Characters, as *Selected Poems*, 1790. Reprinted as *Joanna Baillie: Poems*. With an introduction by Jonathan Wordsworth, Oxford: Woodstock, 1994.

Metrical Legends of Exalted Characters, 1821. Reprinted, with an introduction by Donald H. Reiman. New York: Garland, 1976.

Fugitive Verses. 1840.

Ahalya Baee: A Poem. 1849.

Drama

A Series of Plays: In Which it is Attempted to Delineate the Stronger Passions of the Mind, Each Passion Being the Subject of a Tragedy and a Comedy. Vol. 1 (containing *De Monfort*, *Count Basil*, and *The Tryal*), 1798. Reprinted with an introduction by Donald H. Reiman. New York: Garland, 1977.

A Series of Plays: In Which it is Attempted to Delineate the Stronger Passions of the Mind, Each Passion Being the Subject of a Tragedy and a Comedy. Vol. 2 (containing *The Election*, *Ethwald*, and *The Second Marriage*), 1802. Reprinted with an introduction by Donald H. Reiman. New York: Garland, 1977.

Miscellaneous Plays (containing *Constantine Paleologous*, *Rayner*, and *The Country Inn*), 1804. Reprinted with an introduction by Donald H. Reiman. New York: Garland, 1977.

The Family Legend: A Tragedy, 1810. Reprinted with an introduction by Donald H. Reiman. New York: Garland, 1976.

A Series of Plays: In Which it is Attempted to Delineate the Stronger Passions of the Mind, Each Passion Being the Subject of a Tragedy and a Comedy. Vol. 3 (containing *Orra*, The Dream, The Siege, and The Beacon), 1812. Reprinted with an introduction by Donald H. Reiman. New York: Garland, 1977.

Other

A View of the General Tenour of the New Testament regarding the Nature and Dignity of Jesus Christ. 1831.

The Collected Letters of Joanna Baillie. Edited by Judith Bailey Slagle. Madison, N.J.: Fairleigh Dickinson University Press, 1999.

Bibliography

Brewer, William D. "Joanna Baillie and Lord Byron." *Keats-Shelley Journal* 44 (1995): 1658–81.

Burroughs, Catherine B. *Closet Stages: Joanna Baillie and the Theater Theory of British Romantic Writers*. Philadelphia: University of Pennsylvania Press, 1997.

Carhart, Margaret S. *The Life and Work of Joanna Baillie*. New Haven, Conn.: Yale University Press, and London: Oxford University Press, 1923.

Carswell, Donald. *Sir Walter: A Four Part Study in Biography (Scott, Hogg, Lockhart, Joanna Baillie)*. London: Murray, 1930.

Gilroy, Amanda. "From Here to Alterity: The Geography of Femininity in the Poetry of Joanna Baillie." In *A History of Scottish Women's Writing*. Edited by Douglas Gifford and Dorothy McMillan. Edinburgh: Edinburgh University Press, 1997.

Mellor, Anne K. "Joanna Baillie and the Counter-Public Sphere," *Studies in Romanticism* 33 (1994): 559–67.

Ross, Marlon B. *The Contours of Masculine Desire: Romanticism and the Rise of Women's Poetry*. New York: Oxford University Press, 1989.

Scullion, Adrienne. "Some Women of the Nineteenth-Century Scottish Theater: Joanna Baillie, Frances Wright and Helen MacGregor." In *A History of Scottish Women's Writing*. Edited by Douglas Gifford and Dorothy McMillan. Edinburgh: Edinburgh University Press, 1997.

BALKANS: HISTORICAL AND CULTURAL SURVEY

Turkish rule (established across the Balkans states since the late fourteenth century) had never extended to the autonomous principalities of Moldavia and Wallachia, which allowed its late seventeenth century rulers, Dimitri Cantemir and Constantin Brancoveanu, to retain a degree of native cultural independence not seen elsewhere in the Balkan Peninsula. Cantemir presided over a glittering Romanian court and wrote the first novel in the native language, while his Wallachian colleague was a brilliant patron of the arts and architecture. When they sided with the Russians against the Turks in 1711–12, the first Romanian renaissance was swept away. But even under the hated Greek-speaking princes known as the Phanariots, Romanian culture flourished.

During the Russo-Turkish War (1806–12) the last vestiges of de facto Ottoman rule were swept aside and replaced by imperial Russia's hegemony. To avoid being swallowed up by their giant northern neighbor, the Romanians tried to resurrect their culture, language, and history. Russia had forfeited her role as protector by annexing Bessarabia in 1812. The Romanians, as a Latin-speaking nation, were influenced by France in matters of taste and culture; they also looked to Italy, whose ideas of unification they adopted. Their nationalist leaders sought to unify the two principalities, which remained a dream until after the Romantic age. The one major attempt to unify the country came in 1848, but was crushed by a combined Russo-Turkish invasion. At least the Romantic era had produced two major writers, Costache Negruzzi and Vasile Alecsandri, and had lead to the establishment of a national theater by the 1840s.

Turkish rule had not extended to the principality of Montenegro, either, where a population of stubborn Serb-speaking mountaineers maintained a precarious existence and independence under the leadership of their prince bishops. It was under the most brilliant of these, Prince Peter II Njegosh, that Montenegro established an international reputation via the prince's poetry and political deeds.

Montenegro's example inspired the Serb population in Turkish-occupied Serbia to rise up against their overlords in 1804. This uprising was led by Kara Djordje (Black George) until Russia was distracted by the Napoleonic invasion of 1812, which allowed the Turks to reoccupy Serbia. Among the refugees that fled across the border to Austria was a private secretary to one of the rebel leaders, a young intellectual named Vuk Stefanovich Karadzic, who not only eventually established a modern Serb language, but would also go on to collect a great number of Serb folk songs. His fickle employer and patron, the new leader of the rebellion, Prince Milan Obrenovic, ruled Serbia long enough to secure de facto independence by 1830.

By that time, the Serb uprising was entirely overshadowed by the Greek war of independence (1821–29), which had been inaugurated by Prince Alexander Ypsilantis's invasion of Moldavia; his failure there served only to spark the uprising in Greece itself. The Greeks, although a trusted and privileged group in the Ottoman Empire, had by the late eighteenth century begun to look back to the glories of ancient Athens and the Byzantine Empire. The Phanariot princes in Romania proved to be generous patrons of the arts, and the first modern Greek play was staged in the Moldavian capital of Iasi (Jassy) in 1805.

As in Serbia, the question above all others was which language the Greeks were to speak and write in. Conservatives and the clerics wanted to keep ancient Greek, even though it was a dead language and quite inadequate to the needs of a modern nineteenth-century state. It was only in the latter part of the nineteenth century that modern Greek, established by Andreas Kalvos, was generally accepted.

The Greeks benefited from international support and sympathy, not least through the pointless yet heroic death of the British Romantic poet Lord Byron at Missolonghi in 1827. Count Ioannis Capodistrias, a Corfiate nobleman in the service of Imperial Russia, managed, as President of the Greek Republic (1821–33) to get all the great powers to support the fledgling country. The naval victory at Navarino, where the Turco-Egyptina fleet was sunk by the allied forces in 1829, paved the way for Greece's independence.

In the northwestern part of the peninsula, the struggle for independence during the Romantic era was not against the Turks, but against the Austrians and the Hungarians. In Slovenia the struggle to establish a national language, culture, and identity faced not only Italian cultural influence but also Austrian political oppression. Under the guidance of Baron Ziga Zois a group of intellectuals sought to promote the renaissance of the national language, culture, historical heritage, and ideas of Enlightenment. The first Slovene language paper was founded in 1797, and while Valentin Vodnik led a group of neoclassicists, the Slovene Romantics dreamed of a free, independent Slavic state. From 1830 onward France Preseren, founder and editor of the journal *Chelica* (*The Bee*), led a group of young intellectuals who freely mixed Romantic nationalism and writing. After the Hungarian uprising of 1848 was suppressed, the Austrian authorities visited censorship and arrests upon the Slovene nationalist and Romantic movement.

Slovenia's southern neighbor, Croatia, dreamed the same Romantic, nationalist dreams of independence, free from the grasp of imperial Austria. Part of the Kingdom of Hungary, as an autonomous principality the Croats were proud of their history and the fact that they had escaped Turkish rule. They were also proud of the fact that the city of Ragusa (Dubrovnik) had been the seat of Renaissance and baroque cultural developments, while the rest of the peninsula was under Muslim rule. Under Ljudevitj Gaj, the Croat language was Latinized and modernized as Gaj headed the romantic Illyrian movement. Ultimately the

Illyrians hoped to unify not only all the Croats, but also the Bosnian and Serbs in a south (Yugo) Slav union. He had the sympathy and support of Karadzic, who tried to unify the two languages of Serb and Croat into one. These attempts failed with tragic results, as seen during the last century in the Balkan region.

CHRISTER JÖRGENSEN

Bibliography

Clogg, Richard. *A Short History of Modern Greece.* Cambridge: Cambridge University Press, 1979.

Crampton, R. J. *A Concise History of Bulgaria.* Cambridge: Cambridge University Press, 1997.

Djilas, Milovan. *Wartime.* Translated by Michael B. Petrovich. London: Harcourt Brace and Jovanovich, 1977.

Glenny, Misha. *The Balkans 1804–1999: Nationalism, War and the Great Powers.* London: Granta Books, 1999.

Jelavich, Barbara. *History of the Balkans. Eighteenth and Nineteenth Centuries.* London: Cambridge University Press, 1983.

Judah, Tim. *The Serbs: History, Myth and the Destruction of Yugoslavia.* New Haven, Conn.: Yale University Press.

Malcolm, Noel. *Bosnia: A Short History.* London: Macmillan, 1994.

Norwich, John Julius. *Byzantium: The Decline and Fall.* London: Penguin, 1996.

Obolensky, Dimitri. *The Byzantine Commonwealth: Eastern Europe 500–1453.* London, Phoenix Press, 1971.

Palairet, Michael. *The Balkan Economies c. 1800–1914: Evolution without Development.* Cambridge: Cambridge University Press, 1997.

Stoianovich, Traian. *A Study in Balkan Civilization.* New York: Alfred A. Knopf, 1967.

BALTIC REGION: HISTORICAL AND CULTURAL SURVEY

Until the twelfth century, the Baltic region was outside the Catholic-Christian world of western Europe. Only Poland and Denmark were truly Christian by this time, and Sweden had only superficially become so. These newcomers to the faith set out to do their religious duties by instituting crusades against the pagan peoples on the southern and eastern shores of the Baltic Sea.

The Danes turned their attentions against the Slavic Wends and Finno-Ugrian Estonians. In the latter case they managed, by the thirteenth century, to conquer the northern half of Estonia while the Swedes turned their attentions against Finland. The Swedes had already colonized Åland, but went on to conquer the mainland of Finland by force. The Finnish tribes, including the Tavast, succumbed only after fierce resistance, while the more easterly Karelians were never conquered outright. The Karelians located in the more western part of their region became Catholic subjects of the Swedes, while the eastern tribes, converted peacefully by Orthodox missionaries, gave their loyalty to the Russian principality of Novgorod.

Further south, the Slav tribes of the Wends and Pomeranians, as well as the Baltic tribes of the Prusy, were conquered, colonized and eventually "Germanized" to such an extent that they became part of the German nation. The development in the Baltic region proper was somewhat different. Here the Teutonic crusader orders (the Livonian and the Sword) had, despite fierce resistance from the Estonians and Latvians, become masters of the entire region, with one vital exception. In the heavily wooded regions of Semgallia, the Lithuanians, under King Minduagas (d. 1263) resisted successfully the Teutonic onslaught and during the following century, under Vytautus the Great, expanded to the south and east to became a great regional power. In 1385 Lithuania, now a Catholic nation, entered into a dynastic union with Poland, which became a fully fledged political union in 1569.

Starting in 1561 when they occupied Reval (Tallin) the Swedes spread their influence and power across the Baltic in the wake of the decline of the Teutonic orders and the Hansa, which had predominated the Baltic during the Middle Ages. During several bloody wars the Danes and Poles sought to stem the Swedish tide. The Swedes had, since 1618 (the Peace of Stol-

bova), cut off Russia from the sea, and by 1629 they had gained control over the Baltic states. They also became the preeminent power in Northern Germany after 1648. Under Charles X (1654–60) the Swedish Baltic Empire reached its greatest territorial extent and pinnacle of power. Only the maritime powers' support of Denmark prevented the Swedes from making the Baltic their "mare nostrum."

Only Courland managed to retain her independence in the face of Swedish hegemoncy under several brilliant Dukes of the Kettler family. Under Duke Jacob (1642–82) Courland had a powerful fleet and even an overseas colonial empire in Tobago and Gambia. The rise of Russia under Peter the Great (1682–1725) ended Swedish hegemony in the Baltic by 1721 when it ceded, at the Peace of Nystad, Vyborg, and its Baltic provinces to Russia. The decline and political impotence of the commonwealth of Poland-Lithuania gave Prussia and Russia an opportunity for expansion. In 1772, 1793, and finally 1795 the commonwealth was divided between these two predatory powers. Imperial Russia, under Tsar Alexander I, conquered what remained of Swedish Finland in 1809, and Finland became an autonomous grand duchy within the Russian Empire.

The late eighteenth and early nineteenth centuries were a period of unprecedented cultural renewal in all of the Baltic states. Sweden under Gustavus III was, for the first time, a center of European arts. Tobias Sergel won prominence as a sculptor and Carl Michael Bellman was a national composer of songs of unsurpassed brilliance. In Finland the nineteenth century gave rise to a flourishing national culture. Johan Ludvig Runeberg (1804–77) became Finland's national poet, with his epic collection of poems entitled *Fänrik Ståls sägner*, published between 1848 and 1860. Zacharias Topelius (1818–67) was a poet of equal stature and an accomplished historian whose *Fältskärns berättelse* (1853–67) brought him popular and critical acclaim. Nevertheless, nothing did more to raise Finnish culture to as prominent a level as Swedish culture than the publication of the national epos, *Kalevala* (1835–48), under the supervision of Erik Lönnroth. Finland, it should be pointed out, was also the only Baltic state that had a composer of the same international stature as Norway's Edvard Grieg, in the person of Jean Sibelius (1865–1957), whose first symphony, *Kullervo* (1892), was inspired by the *Kalevala*. His first three symphonies were classical works, but his symphonies of 1919 and 1925 were more modern in tone.

Cultural life in the Baltic states was hampered by stricter Russian control and German cultural predominance. Estonia had a flourishing cultural life under Swedish rule, exemplified by such accomplished artists as Michael Sittow, who painted a portrait of Catherine of Aragon and Arent Passer. After the Russian occupation (1721) Peter the Great sponsored the building of Katrinental in the Russo-Italian baroque style. During the nineteenth century Estonian culture went through a renaissance: *Kalevipoeg*, the national poetry collection on a par with the Finnish *Kalevala*, was published despite Baltic German and Russian resistance. A host of talented artists appeared: Anton Köler (1826–99), Konrad Mägi (1878–1925), and Addo Vabbe (1892–1961), who introduced cubism and futurism to Baltic painting. In Lithuania, support for the Polish uprisings of 1830 and 1861 meant harsh Russian censorship and a stunted cultural life. In Latvia the first literary success in the vernacular, native tongue was the publication of *Dziesminas* (*Poetry*) in 1856 by Junis Alunans, who also published *St. Petersburgas Avizes*, with the support of the Latvian community in St. Petersburg. Owing to vehement Baltic German opposition, the Tsarist authorities censored it.

In the late eighteenth and early nineteenth centuries, the Baltic region was marked by artistic upheaval and development and a relatively placid political climate. That would change in the twentieth century, as the Russian Revolution, the two world wars, and recent independence (for Estonia, Latvia, and Lithuania) created a new set of political problems.

CHRISTER JÖRGENSEN

Bibliography

Barton, H. Arnold. *Scandinavia in the Revolutionary Era, 1760–1815*. Minneapolis: University of Minnesota Press, 1986.

Böhme, Klaus R., Göran Rydstad, and Wihelm M. Carlgren. *In Quest of Trade and Security: The Baltic in Power Politics 1500–1990*. 2 vols. Stockholm: Probus Förlag, 1994–95.

Derry, T. K. *A History of Scandinavia*. Minneapolis: University of Minnesota Press, 1979.

Hinden, John and Patrick Salmon. *The Baltic Countries and Europe: Estonia, Latvia and Lithuania in the Twentieth Century*. London: Longman, 1994.

Kirby, David. *Northern Europe in the Early Modern Period: The Baltic World*. 2 vols. London: Longman, 1990–94.

Loit, Alexander, ed. *National Movements in the Baltic Countries during the Nineteenth Century*. Stockholm: Almqvist and Wicksell, 1985.

Plakans, Andrejs. *The Latvians: A Short History*. Stanford, Calif.: Hoover Institution Press, 1995.

Raun, Toivo U. *Estonia and the Estonians*. Stanford, Calif.: Hoover Institution Press, 1987.

BALZAC, HONORÉ DE 1799–1850

French novelist and dramatist

Honoré de Balzac produced more than one hundred works of fiction and nonfiction, and is considered both a Romantic and a realist writer. This apparent contradiction is explained by the authors who influenced him and by his own acute observation of the world. First, the plays of William Shakespeare and Pierre Corneille provided him with complex human dilemmas. Second, the English Gothic novel and E. T. A. Hoffmann's fantastic tales revealed to him the importance of the supernatural. Third, through Johann Wolfgang von Goethe's *Faust* and Lord Byron's *Manfred*, he saw the necessity of a multiform pact—not with Satan, but through often nefarious associations. Fourth, Walter Scott and James Fenimore Cooper showed him how to resurrect the past through the accurate depiction of costumes and objects, the participation of historical figures, and the re-creation of daily existence.

In addition, Balzac borrowed techniques from scientists to develop his conception of human behavior. After Geoffroy Saint-Hilaire, he classified individuals according to their social class, profession, or marital status while keeping in mind that Georges Cuvier demonstrated how one bone could reconstruct an entire animal and thus that one ruin could evoke a whole civilization. Similarly, Franz Joseph Gall and Johann Lavater helped him understand personality through examining cranial and facial features, although Balzacian psychology is usually reduced to single, overpowering passions (monomanias).

After several potboilers in the Gothic manner written between 1819 and 1825, *Les Chouans* (*The Chouans*, 1829) was the first book to be published under Balzac's name. It already presented a number of themes and ideas that would be further explored later, such as those of a topographical milieu or historical context as determining influences on actions. *La Peau de chagrin* (*The Wild Ass's Skin*, 1831), however, is a better model for all the novels that would eventually comprise *La Comédie humaine* (*The Human Comedy*), since it asks the essential Balzakian question: How does one succeed? That is, how does one become famous and/or loved?

There are two ways to achieve fame: through the mind or through money. The thinker, the artist, the poet, the inventor each gives himself body and soul to an overriding idea he wants to impose on the world. That his work is at once the origin of martyrdom and of joy (often shared with a devoted companion) only underscores the Romantic notion of genius, and this despite the hero's ultimate failure (in, for instance, *La Recherche de l'absolu* [*The Quest of the Absolute*, 1834]), or madness (as in *Louis Lambert* [1832–35]). In fact, several of his characters are attracted to suicide as a way of escaping their acute *mal du siècle* (world-weariness). Therefore, it behooves superior human beings to try to overcome life's pitiless, even cruel, constraints through their will (in a Bergsonian sense) by bending in order not to break, by resisting without cracking, by withdrawing to fight another day.

To secure an eventual victory, they resort to vast conspiracies, criminal and otherwise: in so many cases, individuals are defeated—since *l'union fait la force* (strength lies in numbers)—by an actively aggressive collectivity converging, sometimes only temporarily, to destroy them: "[T]he entire society [was] armed against her and her cousins" (*Une ténébreuse Affaire* [*The Gondre-*

ville Mystery, 1841]). In fact, there were a number of occult organizations with such metaphorical names as The Thirteen (*Histoire des Treize* [*History of the Thirteen*, 1834–35]) or the Society of ten thousand, whose purpose was to defend and advance their members' ambitions.

Money, because it is the overriding personal and social motor, is the focus of many of Balzac's protagonists, who are bent on acquiring it by whatever means. Furthermore, as he states in *Le Père Goriot* (1834–35), "Money is life; money does everything." It is not just a source of power but also a condensation of energy in the modern world. This is why bankers, usurers, and politicians, in particular, and the ambitious young men out to conquer, are the exemplars of the new capitalist, highly mobile society. Admiring efficacy over morality and legalism over justice (not unlike Charles Dickens's novels), they struggle in their relentless drive toward gaining more and more wealth. To survive, they must keep control over their emotions, even hide them, and use anyone in order to succeed, for people are either "executioners" or "victims."

Love, and its concomitant marriage, are not totally selfless feelings. Like any emotion, love, too, can be based on financial considerations as another way of succeeding. A few exceptions

Honoré de Balzac. Reprinted courtesy of Bildarchiv.

prove the rule: *Les Chouans*; "La Bourse" ("The Purse, 1832); Part I of *Illusions perdues* (*Lost Illusions*, 1837–43); and *Le Lys dans la vallée* (*The Lily of the Valley*, 1835–36). Ironically, it often happens that the young lover—man or woman—misjudges the potential fortune of the intended as he or she then moves on to an apparently more lucrative liaison. This is how Charles rejected Eugénie in *Eugénie Grandet* (1833) or Emilie refused to consider young Maximilien de Longueville in *Le Bal de Sceaux* (*The Ball at Sceaux*, 1830). On the other hand, love also kills: Esther Gobseck dies of love (in *Splendeurs et misères des courtisanes A Harlot High and Low*, 1838–47), as does Père Goriot, killed by too much paternal love for his ungrateful daughters.

Goriot is the typical monomaniac whose *idée fixe* brings about his ruin. Like him, many become obsessed with some egocentric passion by which they live, and, sometimes, eventually die. Béatrix (in the eponymous 1839–45 novel) lives by the sadistic destruction she wreaks on others; Corentin by his cruel vindictiveness (in *Les Chouans*); and Cousin Bette (in *La Cousine Bette*, 1846) by her evil deeds. Bette is a monster in her unyielding pursuit of revenge against her family. From childhood on she had suffered constant humiliation from her relatives. However, when in her maturity she has at last found the one man who can make her happy and fulfilled and she loses him to her cousin's daughter, she lashes out in a rage—"I would have given him [Wenceslas] my blood"—as she plots all the culprits' downfall. Her keen but primitive intelligence, her will and her tenacity, the naturalness of her hypocrisy—these qualities make her a great, albeit wicked, heroine.

Two pivotal events occurred in Balzac's literary life. In 1834, he conceived the original idea of reappearing characters (first used in *Le Père Goriot*) to show the interrelatedness of human existence as well as to give a virtual density to his people. This quality is quite different from that found in the mere maturing and aging protagonists presented in "novels in sequence" (to use in John Galsworthy's phrase). Then, in 1842, after successive attempts at taxonomy, he organized all his fictional works published by that time under the overall title of *La Comédie humaine*, perhaps in contrast to Dante's *Divine Comedy*. Borrowing from ecology, he divided them into a series of six scenes—from private life, from provincial life, from parisian life, from political life, from military life, and from country life—and two studies, philosophical and analytical to which he added an *avant-propos* (preface). In this elaborate and well-argued general preface he laid out the rationale of the thought and purpose of his magnum opus.

The *Scenes from Private Life* depict childhood and youth, and the false steps to which they are prone. The *Scenes from Provincial Life* show the age of passion, calculation, self-interest, and ambition. The *Scenes from Parisian Life* portray finally the various tastes and vices, with all the unbridled forms of behavior of capital cities, for it is there that good and evil meet and have their strongest repercussions.

Balzac did not live to complete the *Scenes from Military Life*, and he had hardly begun the planned *Scenes from Political Life* and *Country Life*.

This monumental work, which can be read in any order, boasts that it easily competes with the Bureau of Vital Statistics. Not counting the few hundred real people, there are more than two thousand fictional characters, from whom emerge about thirty great starring and secondary roles whose universal stature and symbolic value (good or bad) compare favorably to those in Shakespeare or Molière: from the debauched Baron Hulot (in *La Cousine Bette*) and all his fellow amoral, egotistical roués to César Birotteau, symbol of business probity (in *Grandeur et décadence de César Birotteau* [*The Grandeur and Decadence of César Birotteau*, 1837]), and from the single-minded and naive collector Sylvain Pons (in *Le Cousin Pons* [1847]) to Dr. Benassis, a modern-day apostle of charity (in *Le Médecin de campagne* [*The Country Doctor*, 1833]). Women, too, play their part along the good and evil continuum: from the pure, generous, and self-denying Madame de la Chanterie (in *L'Envers de l'histoire contemporaine* [*The Seamy Side of History*, 1842–48]), and all the devoted and loving wives and companions, to the many femmes fatales who destroy families without pity or remorse.

Balzac depicts, among others, statesmen, speculators, tradesmen, journalists, army officers, policemen, traveling salesmen, courtesans, all manner of jurists and criminals, artists and writers, and physicians alongside representatives of the bourgeoisie, peasant class, and aristocracy. (In a wonderful epigram Oscar Wilde once declared, "It is pleasanter to have the entrée to Balzac's society than to receive cards from all the duchesses in Mayfair.")

To accomplish his sociological task, he usually visited the locales of his novels, interviewed knowledgable informants, compiled encyclopedic documentation, and, above all, observed real life, be it clothes, homes, furniture, or even food. Unlike his Romantic brethren who seldom show their characters sitting down for a proper meal, his people eat real food: "Does one eat in *René*?" he pointedly asked in an 1820 text. In his *Traité de la vie élégante* (*Treatise of Elegant Life*, 1830) Balzac elaborated the method he had already analyzed in *Code des gens honnêtes* (*Code for Respectable People*, 1825): "Speak, walk, eat, or dress, and I will tell you who you are."

Since he believed in determinism, moreover, milieu, profession, and gender became very important criteria in evaluating character, both socially and morally, as well as in explaining temperament, and thus required detailed descriptions. Even names were endowed with occult, portentous meaning: "Z. Marcas! The man's entire life is in the fantastic combination of these seven letters . . . This Z . . ., this last letter of the alphabet offered the mind something fatalistic" ("Z. Marcas," 1840).

Balzac's depiction of the various passions that can dominate and tyrannize the soul appealed to Fyodor Dostoevsky, William Faulkner, and Thomas Hardy, while his grand picture of a French society teeming with life greatly influenced later novelists, who also wanted to portray humanity and social environments as they really were: Émile Zola's twenty-volume *Rougon-Macquart* series (1871–93), Henry James (who called Balzac a "towering idol"), and Marcel Proust's *A la recherche du temps perdu* (*Remembrance of Things Past*, 1913–27) come readily to mind. Friedrich Nietzsche, for his part, admired several Balzac heroes (for example, *Le Père Goriot*'s Vautrin) as the precursors of his own theory of the "will to power."

Thus, in evoking an entire world from the French Revolution almost to the end of the July Monarchy, the self-styled historian and "secretary" of the nineteenth century went beyond Walter Scott's lessons. He not only presented dramatically historic crises but also the complexity and richness of contemporaneous social life, along with its chaos, brutality, and destructiveness. He analyzed the mores of his time through the confrontation and subsequent struggle of the individual and society in the vain hope of stopping their unstoppable downfall. Early in his career, Balzac realized that "vouloir nous brûle et pouvoir nous tue" ("will burns us and might kills us"), and that this monomaniacal urge creates an imbalance that itself triggers a fall. It is no wonder, then, that he himself should be felled by his overpowering desire for fame and wealth. Like Raphaël of *The Wild Ass's Skin*, he saw his own "skin" diminish into nothingness. He died at age fifty-one, calling for Horace Bianchon, the devoted physician of his *Comédie humaine*.

PIERRE L. HORN

See also **Pere Goriot, Le**

Biography

Born in Tours, France, May 20, 1799. Son of a civil servant working in army supply department. Educated at schools in Tours, Vendôme, and Paris. Attended lectures in law at the Sorbonne while working as a law clerk, 1816–19. Received baccalauréat of law, 1819. Abandoned studies to write full-time, 1819: worked as a novelist, journalist, and editor under a number of pen names, 1820s. Attempted unsuccessfully to establish a career as a publisher, 1826–28. Achieved first literary success with *Les Chouans* (*The Chouans*, 1829), prolific fiction writer and dramatist from 1829 on. Began intimate correspondence with Madame Eveline Hanska (née Countess of Rzewuska; d. 1882), a Polish noblewoman living in Ukraine, from about 1832 on; met Eveline secretly in Neuchâtel, Switzerland, 1833, continuing the relationship after she was widowed, 1841. Owner, *La Chronique de Paris*, 1835–36. Published *La Comédie Humaine*, 1942–48. Travelled in Europe with Eveline, 1845–46; fathered, with Evelyn, stillborn daughter, 1846. Stayed at Eveline's estate in Verkhivnia, Ukraine, 1847–50. Married Eveline Hanska, March 1850; one stepdaughter. President, Societé des Gens de Lettres, 1839; chevalier, Légion d'honneur, 1845. Died of cardiac hypertrophy in Paris, August 18, 1850.

Selected Works

Collections

Oeuvres complètes. Edited Maurice Bardèche *et al.*, 28 vols, 1956–63; as *Works*, 53 vols, 1895–1900 (incomplete).

La Comédie humaine, first edition under this general title, 1842–48, 17 vols; expanded to 20 vols, 1853–55; as *The Comedy of Human Life*, translated by Katharine Prescott Wormeley, 7 vols, 1885–93, later completed as *The La Comédie humaine*, 40 vols, 1896. Reprinted as *The Comédie Humaine*. 40 vols. Edited by George Saintsbury and translated by Clara Bell, Ellen Marriage, James Waring, and R. S. Scott. 1895–98.

La Comédie humaine. 12 vols. Edited by Pierre-Georges Castex et al. 12 vols, 1976–81.

Correspondance, edited by Roger Pierrot, 5 vols, 1960–69; as *The Correspondence of Honoré de Balzac*, translated by C. Lamb Kenney, 2 vols, 1878 (incomplete).

Lettres à Madame Hanska, edited by Roger Pierrot, 4 vols, 1967–71; as *Letters to Madame Hanska*, translated by Katharine Prescott Wormeley, 2 vols, 1900 (incomplete).

Théâtre, 1845, expanded, 1855; as *The Dramatic Works*, translated by E. de Valcourt-Vermont, 1901.

Fiction

Les Chouans. 1829. Translated by Marion Ayton Crawford as *The Chouans*. 1972.

Le Bal de Sceaux, 1830. Translated by Clara Bell as *The Ball at Sceaux*. 1895.

Le Chef-d'oeuvre inconnu, 1831. Translated by Michael Neff as *The Unknown Masterpiece*. 1984.

La Peau de chagrin, 1831. Translated by Herbert J. Hunt as *The Wild Ass's Skin*. 1977.

"La Bourse," 1832. Translated by James Waring as "The Purse." 1898.

Le Colonel Chabert, 1832. Translated by Carol Cosman as *Colonel Chabert*. 1997.

Le Curé de Tours, 1832. Translated by Clara Bell as *The Vicar of Tours*. 1900.

Louis Lambert, 1832–35. Translated by Katharine Prescott Wormeley. 1889.

Le Médecin de campagne, 1833. Translated by Ellen Marriage as *The Country Doctor*. 1911.

Eugénie Grandet, 1834. Translated by Sylvia Raphael. 1990.

La Recherche de l'absolu, 1834. Translated by Ellen Marriage as *The Quest of the Absolute*. 1908.

Histoire des treize, 1834–35. Translated by Herbert J. Hunt as *History of the Thirteen*. 1974.

Le Père Goriot, 1834–35. Translated by A. J. Krailsheimer as *Père Goriot*. 1999.

Le Lys dans la vallée, 1835–36. Translated by Lucienne Hill as *The Lily in the Valley*. 1957.

Histoire de la grandeur et de la décadence de César Birotteau, 1837. Translated by Robin Buss as *César Birotteau*. 1994.

Illusions perdues, 1837–43. Translated by Herbert J. Hunt as *Lost Illusions*. 1971.

La Maison Nucingen, 1838. Translated by Ellen Marriage as *The Firm of Nucingen*. 1897.

Splendeurs et misères des courtisanes, 1838–47. Translated by Rayner Heppenstall as *A Harlot High and Low*. 1970.

Béatrix, 1839–45. Translated by Beth Archer. 1970.

"Z. Marcas," 1840. Translated by Clara Bell. 1895.

Une ténébreuse Affaire, 1841. Translated by Ellen Marriage as *The Gondreville Mystery*. 1900.

La Rabouilleuse, 1841–42. Translated by Clara Bell as *A Bachelor's Establishment*. 1898.

L'Envers de l'histoire contemporaine, 1842–48. Translated by Clara Bell as *The Seamy Side of History*. 1895.

La Cousine Bette, 1846. Translated by Sylvia Raphael as *Cousin Bette*. 1992.

Le Cousin Pons, 1847. Translated by Herbert J. Hunt as *Cousin Pons*. 1968.

Plays

Mercadet, ou, Le Faiseur, 1851. Translated by E. de Valcourt-Vermont as *Mercadet*. 1901.

Other

Code des gens honnêtes [*Code for Respectable People*], 1825.

Traité de la vie élégante [*Treatise of Elegant Life*], 1830.

Les Contes drolatiques, 1832–37. Translated by Alec Brown as *Droll Stories*. 1967.

Bibliography

Affron, Charles. *Patterns of Failure in "La Comédie humaine."* New Haven, Conn.: Yale University Press, 1966.

L'Année balzacienne, 1960– (Annual journal).

Barbéris, Pierre. *Balzac et le mal du siècle*. 2 vols. Paris: Gallimard, 1970.

Besser, Gretchen R. *Balzac's Concept of Genius*. Geneva: Droz, 1969.

Farrant, Tim. *Balzac's Shorter Fictions: Genesis and Genre*. Oxford: Oxford University Press, 2002.

Hemmings, F. W. J. *Balzac: An Interpretation of "La Comédie humaine."* New York: Random House, 1967.

Kanes, Martin, ed. *Critical Essays on Honoré de Balzac*. Boston: Hall, 1990.

Pugh, Anthony. *Balzac's Recurring Characters*. Toronto: University of Toronto Press, 1974.

Satiat, Nadine. *Balzac, ou, La Fureur d'écrire*. Paris: Hachette, 1999.

BARATYNSKII (BORATYNSKII), EVGENII ABRAMOVICH 1800–1844

Russian poet

"Cold reason," "the reliability of naked truth," "cruel contradiction"—these are the Romantic poet Evgenii Abramovich Baratynskii's characterizations of his Weltanschauung. Aleksandr Pushkin said Baratynskii expressed thought well because he did so with feeling. Where other Romantic styles were emotive, Baratynskii undertook to express thought and feeling together, and to do so in a precise, harmonious style despite their tendency to negate one another. In his view, thought erodes the ability to feel, feelings interfere with rational thought. His struggle to overcome this contradiction, combined with thorough study of Friedrich Wilhelm Joseph von Schelling and August Wilhelm von Schlegel and Friedrich von Schlegel, culminated in a metaphysical poetry whose uniqueness revealed new possibilities for Russian literature.

Baratynskii matured with a rejection of escapism titled "Istina" ("Truth," 1823), in which he posited that "[p]ainful truth" is better than "easy deception." The poet, he felt, must express the truth, although that truth may be rejected by his readers, thus relegating the poet to obscurity. He expressed anxiety about this possibility in several poems and announced his decision to risk loss in "Moi dar ubog . . ." ("Poor Is My Gift . . .," 1828), in which he assured himself, "A reader in posterity I'll find."

Baratynskii's dedication to truth results in a generally pessimistic poetry characterized with a gloomy tone. "Dejection" is a favorite word, love lyrics are devoid of passion and trust in love, and happiness is impossible to attain.

This metaphysical Romantic articulated the schism between modern man and nature in compelling ways. He expressed a love of nature in "Vesna" ("Spring," 1820) and "Finlandiia" ("Finland," 1820, 1826). "Vesna, vesna! Kak vozdukh chist!" ("Spring, Spring! How Pure the air!" 1832) is a celebration of nature. Unhappily, however, spring is followed by "Osen" ("Autumn," 1836–37, 1841). The peasant "suffers life" but is fortunate to work and die close to nature, while the landowner suffers death *because* he is removed from nature.

Baratynskii's nature poetry realizes Schelling's Romantic teaching that the highest that a good man may achieve is dissolution of his ego in the Absolute, where contradictions between ego and nature disappear. He sought synthesis in antitheses: unity with, versus separation from, nature; primitive versus enlightened civilization; and natural beauty versus artificial order. He also expressed the Schlegelian teaching that modern man cannot commune with nature because his intuition has been weakened by his propensity to think. Anxiety over loss of contact with nature is expressed in "Primety" ("Signs," 1839): "As long as man loved nature, / So she loved him in turn" and her greatest gift was that "She blessed him with language." When man ignored his natural instincts, his harmony with nature was destroyed, and the terrible consequence of this schism is loss of the gift of prophecy that goes with language.

Baratynskii is saved from utter pessimism by beauty. As with Schelling, beauty is an ethical as well as aesthetic value. When Baratynskii's poetry achieves synthesis, it is due to beauty. In the lyric "V dni bezgranichnykh uvlechenii . . ." ("In my days of boundless enthrallments . . .," 1831) he is saved from the demon of "uncurbed passions" by an ideal of harmonious beauty in his soul. He illustrates harmony by shifting gracefully between "discordant raptures" and "proportionate measures of beauty." He does not doubt "the mysterious power of harmony" in "Boliashchii dukh vrachuet pesnopen'e" ("The lyric poem can heal an aching spirit," 1832), and here again he successfully synthesizes feelings and reason in harmonious verse. Still, where truth must be expressed, the demon of thought lurks. Baratynskii's concerns in the 1830s were alienation from nature, death, the end of a great age, and a dystopian future. In "Kogda ischeznet omrachen'e" ("When will the darkness vanish?" 1832) he wonders when he will be free of the darkness of his sick soul. Even in "Naslazhdaites': vse prokhodit!" ("Revel in pleasure: all things pass!" 1832) he writes that life is both joy and grief at once, and death is brought by demonic fate. In the Byronic–Shakespearian "Cherep" ("The Skull," 1826) death is repulsive—the skull bears clots of hair and decayed flesh—and so is humankind's lot in life.

As feelings are to nature, thought is to civilization. This is the basic theme of "Poslednii Poet" ("The Last Poet," 1835), a mythic poem of the four ages and the utopia of the golden age on which rests the myth of the golden age of Russian poetry. "The hearts of men" in a new iron age are filled with bourgeois, utilitarian concerns; men have no use for the "childish dreams" of poetry. In this age a poet has appeared, but his songs are ridiculed and he has buried his "useless gift." This poem is set in modern Greece (as opposed to the Hellenic golden age when man was supposedly unenlightened and natural). The poet longs for "those days of ignorance" when man lived joyfully in the "primeval bower" of nature. But in this Rousseauian—and Schlegelian—poem, nature, and beauty have been destroyed by enlightenment. "Posledniaia smert" ("The Last Death," 1827) is another poem about the golden age that denounces enlightenment. Like Lord Byron's "Darkness" (1816), to which it responds, it is an expression of despair. Here the poet does not long for a past utopia; instead, he looks with dread into a future damaged by extreme devotion to reason. Initially the future is seen as a paradise on earth, where magnificent cities spring from tamed nature. But generations pass, and at last the cities lie in ruin, people have vanished into their graves, and the sun rises on a moribund world covered with fog.

Baratynskii's Byronic verse tales are conventional, but they are beautifully written and notably draw heroines and heroes as equal. "Eda" (1824) is a Romantic tale about the seduction of a Finnish maid by a Russian hussar; its Ossianic landscape is striking. "Bal" ("The Ball," 1825–28) is a satire on Moscow society featuring both a dark southern and a fair northern beauty. In "Nalozhnitsa" ("The Concubine," 1831), later retitled "Tsyganka" ("The Gypsy"), the heroine kills her lover while trying to win him back with a love potion.

Baratynskii failed to compete with Pushkin in the narrative genre. By following his own path in his lyric poetry, he achieved a synthesis of thought and feeling and showed Russian poets how to express ideas in precise, harmonious language. He died believing himself a failure, but is today increasingly considered a major poet.

LAUREN G. LEIGHTON

Biography

Born in Viazhlia, Kirsanov district, Tambov Province, Russia, February 19, (March 2), 1800. Son of Abram Andreevich Baratynskii, a major-general who had been ennobled by Pavel I for service to his country. Educated at home by his mother and by an Italian tutor. Lived in Moscow, 1808–10; attended a German boarding school in Saint Petersburg, 1812. Entered Corps of Pages, 1813; expelled for involvement in Schillerian "robber band" theft, 1816. Returned to Tambov Province, 1816–18; Moved to Saint Petersburg, entered army as common soldier, 1818. Associated with young writers in Saint Petersburg, including Anton A. Del'vig and Pushkin. Began literary career as conventional poet of Romantic melancholy, 1818–19. During military service as a noncommissioned officer in Finland, assumed literary persona of martyred exile, affiliated with the formal poets of the Pushkin pleiad and with the Schellingian Lovers of Wisdom poets, 1820–25. Promoted to officer rank (ensign) and returned to Saint Petersburg, 1825. Retired from military service and settled in Muranovo, near Moscow, 1826. Married Anastasia L'vovna Engel'gardt, 1826: nine children, two of whom died in infancy. Worked in the government land surveying office, 1827–31. Maintained closer friendship with Pushkin; contributed to Del'vig and Pushkin's journal *Severnye tsvety*, 1826–29. Published lyric poems and Byronic verse tales. Association with the philosopher Ivan Kireevskii, 1829 to mid-1830s. Contributed to Kireevskii's *Evropeets*, 1832. Traveled with his family to western Europe, including Germany, 1843, and Paris, 1843–44. Met Alfred de Vigny, Prosper Mérimée, and George Sand, among others. Died suddenly in Naples, Italy, June 29 (July 11), 1844.

Selected Works

Sumerki. 1842.
Polnoe sobranie stikhotvorenii. 2d ed. Leningrad: Poet's Library, Large Series, 1957.
Selections in *The Ardis Anthology of Russian Romanticism.* Edited by Christine A. Rydel. Ann Arbor, Mich.: Ardis Publishers. 1984.
Polnoe sobranie stikhotvorenii. 3d ed. Leningrad: Poet's Library, Large Series, 1989.

Bibliography

Beaudoin, Luc J. "Evgenii Abramovich Baratynskii (1800–1844)." In *Russian Literature in the Age of Pushkin and Gogol: Poetry and Drama. Dictionary of Literary Biography.* Edited by Christine A. Rydel. Detroit: The Gale Group, 1999.
———. *Resetting the Margins: Russian Romantic Verse Tales and the Idealized Woman.* New York: Peter Lang, 1997.
Dees, Benjamin. *Evgeny Baratynskii.* New York: Twayne, 1972.
Frizman, L. G. *Tvorcheskii put' Baratynskogo.* Moscow: Nauka, 1966.
Khetso, Geir (Geir Kjetsaa). *Evgenii Baratynskii: Zhizn' i tvorchestvo.* Oslo: Universitetsforlaget, 1973.
Lebedev, E. N. *Trizna. Kniga o E. A. Baratynskom.* Moscow: Biblioteka "Liubiteliam rossiiskoi slovesnosti," 1985.
Pratt, Sarah. *Russian Metaphysical Romanticism: The Poetry of Tiutchev and Boratynskii,* Stanford, Calif.: Stanford University Press, 1984.

BARBAULD, ANNA LETITIA 1743-1825

British poet, essayist, and editor

Since she was born before the midpoint of the eighteenth century, many of Anna Letitia Barbauld's literary allegiances and influences were with her Augustan contemporaries, and in many ways it is helpful to think of her as a pre-Romantic rather than a full-fledged Romantic writer. Her poem "Corsica," published in her very successful 1773 collection, *Poems*, preempts Romanticism by lionizing the hero and leader of Corsican liberty, General Pasquale Paoli, as a solitary figure, with "eye sublime," striving for liberty and greatness against a backdrop of craggy, inhospitable mountains. It is clear, not just from her poetry, that Barbauld played an influential part in forming ideas that were to take off in the Romantic period, not least in her contributions to the important *Monthly Magazine*, edited by her brother John Aikin, and read by William Wordsworth and Samuel Taylor Coleridge, among others.

Rereadings of her work over the last decade have played a significant part in the recent renegotiation of Romanticism along gender lines. Barbauld's position as a woman writer is, however, in some ways anomalous, for while she was clearly one of the most respected figures of the late eighteenth century, it was also her supposed female presumption that was virulently attacked in Tory reviews of her major poem "Eighteen Hundred and Eleven" (1812). John Wilson Croker, who is said to have brought down John Keats's career with a bad review, also effectively put an end to Barbauld's poetic career. The poem "Eighteen Hundred and Eleven," a passionate, blank-verse poem about the disastrous state of the country, written from a liberal perspective, envisages the decline of the British empire, and the ruin brought about by war. In tone and form the poem owes much to Barbauld's eighteenth-century forebears: not just evoking James Thomson and Samuel Johnson by name, but also in the poem's style. But in writing this poem, Barbauld also presages Romantic poems—Lord Byron's "Darkness" (1816), or Percy Bysshe Shelley's "England in 1819" (1819) and "Ozymandias" (1817)—that envisage things falling apart, perhaps influenced by readings of Constantin François Chasseboeuf Volney's *The Ruins, or a Survey of the Revolutions of Empires* (1792), a book that had attained great popularity in England at the time. Croker specifically objected to Barbauld's use of satire, expressing his desire that "the empire might have been saved without the intervention of a lady-author," and her return to her "knitting needles," dropped in her hurry to write, was, for Croker, an absolute necessity. There are places within this poem that demonstrate Barbauld's own ambivalence, for while she is in many ways fulfilling the role of poet as prophet that was central to Wordsworth's vision, she also represents a collective voice, rather than a solitary one, fighting against oppression. Instead of the archetypal male Romantic vision of an individual ego that no chains can bind, Barbauld transfers this freedom to something she ambiguously designates "a spirit [that walks] o'er the peopled earth"—the spirit of civilization and imagination.

Barbauld's attitude clearly has as its backdrop the arguments over the education of women that raged from the 1780s onward, and, strangely, despite her connections to the Bluestocking circle of intellectual women, her attitude was in some ways aligned to that of Croker; she had strong reservations about the education of women and, despite her own highly trained mind, was certain that any knowledge gained, and displayed, by women would be "punished with disgrace." Her poem "The Rights of Woman" (1795) satirizes women's desires for "separate rights" and demands that women should "abandon each ambitious thought." It is an angry response to Mary Wollstonecraft's *Vindication of the Rights of Woman* written three years earlier, and embodies Barbauld's belief that there was "no bond of union among literary women."

This, however, makes her sound reactionary, which is far from the case. Brought up and educated by dissenters, she spent much of her career writing radical prose, including her *Address to the Opposers of the Repeal of the Corporation and Test Acts* (1790, published under the name A Dissenter), a pamphlet that profoundly irritated Edmund Burke because of its enthusiasm for the French Revolution.

By the 1790s Barbauld's attention was primarily focused on political and social matters, and like many of her contemporaries, including William Blake, Hannah More, and Ann Yearsley, she was deeply concerned about the abolition of slavery, a subject that comes to the fore in her *Epistle to William Wilberforce, Esq., on the Rejection of the Bill for Abolishing the Slave Trade* (1792), a poem, published in her own name, that as the title makes clear, deplores the failure of Wilberforce's abolition bill. The poem expresses Barbauld's anger that "still Afric bleeds; / Unchecked, the human traffic still proceeds."

Alongside these overtly political concerns were Barbauld's interests as an educationalist, stemming from the school that she ran until 1785 with her husband, a dissenting minister. A series of *Lessons for Children of* various ages, published between 1778 and 1779, and her *Hymns in Prose for Children* (1781) proved popular. They also demonstrate her engagement, once again, with contemporary concerns: her involvement in the "discovery" of childhood, often pinned to the eighteenth century, and growing out of the works of John Locke, Jean-Jacques Rousseau, and Isaac Watts. Almost a decade before Blake's *Songs of Innocence*, Barbauld was forming part of the cultural milieu that was to push the child so squarely to the fore in the writings of such poets as Wordsworth.

Barbauld's creative writing was balanced with a talent for the critical. She reviewed fiction for the *Monthly Magazine* and edited both prose and poetry for the publication. She was the editor of Samuel Richardson's correspondence (1804), as well as the works of Mark Akenside (1807) and William Collins (1797), and also entered into the increasingly important debate over the role of fiction and its function in her essay "On the Origin and Progress of Novel-Writing" written for *The British Novelists* (1820). It is perhaps ironic, in the light of Barbauld's critical prowess that, as her editors claim, her reputation, at least in part, fell because of the failure of male Romantic writers to include women in their political and poetical vision.

LUCY BENDING

See also **Blake, William; Childhood; Coleridge, Samuel Taylor; French Revolution; Keats, John; More, Hannah; Shelley,**

Percy Bysshe; Slavery and Emancipation; Sublime; Volney, Constantin François Chasseboeuf; *Vindication of the Rights of Woman, A*; Wollstonecraft, Mary; Wordsworth, William; Yearsley, Ann

Biography

Born at Kibworth, Leicester, the older child of Dr. John Aikin and Jane Jennings. She grew up at her father's academy for dissenters in Warrington, and, in 1774, married Rochemont Barbauld, himself educated at the academy. Barbauld and her husband set up a school for boys where she taught the younger children until 1775, when Rochemont Barbauld's poor mental health led to the closure of the school and continental travel. In 1802 they moved to Stoke Newington, where he lived until 1808 when he drowned, and she until 1825.

Selected Works

Poetry

Poems. 1773.
Epistle to William Wilberforce, Esq., on the Rejection of the Bill for Abolishing the Slave Trade. 1791.
Poems. A new edition, corrected. To which is added, An Epistle to William Wilberforce. 1792.

Prose

Miscellaneous Pieces in Prose. With John Aikin. 1773.
Devotional Pieces, Compiled from the Psalms and the Book of Job. 1775.
Lessons for Children of Two to Three Years Old. 1778.
Lessons for Children of Three Years Old. 1778.
Lessons for Children from Three to Four Years Old. 1779.
Hymns in Prose for Children. 1781.
An Address to the Opposers of the Repeal of the Corporation and Test Acts. 1790.
Sins of Government, Sins of Nation; Or, a Discourse for the fast, Appointed on April 19, 1793 By a Volunteer. 1793.
A Legacy for Young Ladies, Consisting of Miscellaneous Pieces, in Prose and Verse. 1826.

Critical and Edited Works

The Poetical Work of Mr. William Collins. With a Prefatory Essay, by Mrs. Barbauld. 1797.
The Correspondence of Samuel Richardson. 1804.
The Poetical Works of Mark Akenside. 1807.
The British Novelists; with an Essay; and Prefaces, Biographical and Critical, by Mrs. Barbauld. 50 vols. 1810.
The Female Speaker; or, Miscellaneous Pieces in Prose and Verse, Selected from the Best Writers, and Adapted to the Use of Young Women. 1811.

Bibliography

Aikin, Lucy, ed. *The Works of Anna Laetitia Barbauld, with a Memoir by Lucy Aikin.* London, 1825.
Barker-Benfield, G. J. *The Culture of Sensibility. Sex and Society in Eighteenth-Century Britain.* Chicago, 1992.
Chandler, James. *England in 1819: The Politics of Literary Culture and the Case of Romantic Historicism.* Chicago, 1998.
Curran, Stuart. "Romantic Women Poets: Inscribing the Self." In *Women's Poetry in the Enlightenment: The Making of a Canon, 1730–1820.* Edited by Isobel Armstrong and Virginia Blain. New York, 1999.
Favretti, Maggie. "The Politics of Vision: Anna Barbauld's 'Eighteen Hundred and Eleven.'" In *Women's Poetry in the Enlightenment: The Making of a Canon, 1730–1820.* Edited by Isobel Armstrong and Virginia Blain. New York, 1999.
Keach, William. "A Regency Prophecy and the End of Anna Barbauld's Career," *Studies in Romanticism* 33, no. 4 (1994): 569–77.
McCarthy, William. "'We Hoped the Woman Was Going to Appear': Repression, Desire, and Gender in Anna Letitia Barbauld's Early Poems." In *Romantic Women Writers: Voices and Countervoices.* Edited by Paula R. Feldman and Theresa M. Kelley. Hanover, N.H., 1995.
Moore, Catherine E. "'Ladies . . . Taking the Pen in Hand': Mrs. Barbauld's Criticism of Eighteenth-Century Women Novelists." In *Fetter'd or Free? British Women Novelists, 1670–1815.* Edited by Mary Anne Schofield and Cecilia Macheski. Athens, Ohio, 1986.
Ross, Marlon. *The Contours of Masculine Desire: Romanticism and the Rise of Women's Poetry.* New York, 1989.

IL BARBIERE DE SIVIGLIA (THE BARBER OF SEVILLE)

drama giccoso in four acts by Giovanni Paisiello, 1782
comedia in two acts by Gioachino Antonio Rossini, 1816

Pierre-Augustin Caron de Beaumarchais was the last great writer of comedy during the ancien régime. His *Figaro* trilogy (*Le barbier de Séville, ou La précaution inutile; La folle journée, ou Le marriage de Figaro*, and *L'autre Tartuffe, ou La mère coupable*) was a radical departure from contemporary dramatic conventions. It was a daringly original conception that not only dealt with aristocrats outwitted by meritocratic servants but also created stage characters who, across the three plays, grow older and change, and have to be seen as having "real" lives beyond their authorial texts. The trilogy was notorious and this, in turn, earned it considerable fame all over Europe. The wit and stylish

plotting of these plays gleaned enough support to overcome the strong censorship of most autocratic states. Being performed in French (and thus only accessible to the cultivated upper classes) also helped their progress across Europe, as did musical settings that deleted some of the most politically critical passages.

Originally, Beaumarchais's trilogy had been written as *opéras comiques* for the Comédie-Italienne, and would have been performed with numerous songs and incidental music. Even after revision into stage plays for the Comédie-Française, the plots still contained many incidents designed to be set to music, and this was how the first performances were delivered, with incidental music written by the principal violinist of the theater orchestra, Antoine-Laurent Baudron. The widespread fame of these plays, plus the innate musicality of the material, made them very attractive to composers. The most famous of these is the Wolfgang Amadeus Mozart–Lorenzo Da Ponte treatment of the second play as *Le nozze di Figaro* (*The Marriage of Figaro*, 1786), which they succeeded in staging despite strong opposition within the Viennese court.

The play of *Le barbier de Séville* begins Beaumarchais's exploration of the relationship between servants and masters. In it, Count Almaviva (disguised as a poor student) is courting Rosina, the beautiful (and potentially rich) ward of Dr Bartolo. Dr. Bartolo in turn is scheming to marry his ward, to which end he is using her music master, the dastardly Don Basilio, as his accomplice. After many entertaining setbacks, and by means of several disguises and with the help of his former servant Figaro (the barber of the title), Almaviva succeeds in outwitting Dr. Bartolo and marrying his beloved.

In 1780, a very successful performance of *Le barbier de Séville* in Saint Petersburg generated an opera based on this play by Giovanni Paisiello, the Italian chapel master to Catherine II. His opera was a setting of an Italian libretto (probably by Giuseppe Petrosellini) and it had its first performance in the Hermitage on September 26, 1782. Delivered by an excellent ensemble of Italian singers, it was a great success and quickly spread to major theaters throughout Europe, including those in Amsterdam, Lisbon, London, Madrid, Naples, Venice, and Vienna, it was also translated into German and French. This enormous success made it a staple of European opera houses and a model of its genre. Characteristically for its time, the orchestration is light, supporting (and sometimes doubling) the vocal lines. Paisiello's portrayal of humorous complexity is masterful. (See, for example, the wonderful trio in act 2 in which Dr. Bartolo is utterly frustrated in his attempts to discover who has been visiting his ward Rosina, because one servant constantly sneezes and the other cannot stop yawning.) In every way, the work's popularity was well merited, and by dint of music, its political message was softened.

In all, there were four operatic settings of *Le barbier*—by Georg Benda, Nicolo Isouard, Giovanni Paisiello, and Gioacchino Antonio Rossini. Although Rossini was greatly attracted by the subject matter, the huge popularity of Paisiello's setting was a major obstacle. Paisiello's setting was so famous, and his following so ardent, that when Rossini was invited to set the same drama for the 1816 season at the Teatro Argentina in Rome, he balked at the prospect. At first he tried to avoid the commission, and later issued numerous private and public statements in which he declared his admiration for Paisiello's opera and claimed that his work was new in manner, and not an attempt to compete with the earlier setting. Rossini was so concerned at the inevitable comparison that he even altered the title to *Almaviva* and did not restore the original title until after Paisiello's death.

The text that Rossini set was a reworking by Cesare Sterbini of Paisiello's original. The drama remains the same and Rossini even deliberately exploited similar effects. Although legend asserts that he composed the whole work in a matter of thirteen days, Rossini in fact devoted the greatest care on this composition. By modern criteria, all the comparisons are in Rossini's favor. However, this misconstrues the issues, for the treatment

The Barber of Seville. Reprinted Courtesy of the Lebrecht Collection.

of the two works is distinctively different and, if Rossini's work has endured, Paisiello's opera is unfairly eclipsed. Its lighter manner and lesser complexity also reveal an ability to project comic conflict and humorous dialogue with pointed ease. In the (admittedly eighteenth-century) context of the *opera buffa* of his age, Paisiello's setting of Beaumarchais's enduring comedy deserves to return to the stage.

Rossini's fears that Paisiello's popularity might make the audience antagonistic were well founded, the first night was a fiasco. Rossini was deeply upset by the audience's hostility and, despite his contractual obligations, refused to direct the subsequent performances; he even considered retiring from the operatic stage at that point.

Although *Il Barbiere di Siviglia* was not one of Rossini's most popular works with his contemporaries, its fame spread rapidly abroad. This popularity has continued unbroken; it has never left the stage, even when Rossini was out of fashion. This popularity has created many problems, both aesthetically and textually, over the years Singers have often made arbitrary alterations and took gross liberties, frequently turning the music lesson in act 2 into an extended cabaret of their favorite arias. If Rossini's score is respected, his setting is, in fact, a refined comedy of character, deftly colored by precisely pointed orchestration and exquisite dramatic timing. His exploitation of comic effects remains unsurpassed (as vividly exemplified in the aria "La calunnia," in which Don Basilio advises Dr. Bartolo to spread malicious rumors to discredit Almaviva).

In every dramatic, as well as technical, aspect (such as harmonic richness, vocal finesse, and orchestral brilliance), Rossini's opera is outstanding, its ethos sharp and penetrating. Ironically, the very brilliance and familiarity of the work rapidly diluted the biting social criticism of Beaumarchais's play and the opera has endured as a comedy of character rather than satire.

BENEDICT SARNAKER

Bibliography

Gatti, Guido M. *Le "Barbier de Séville" de Rossini*. Paris, 1925.

Hunt, J. L. *Giovanni Paisiello: His Life as an Opera Composer*. New York: National Opera Association, 1975.

Loewenberg, Alfred. 'Paisiello's and Rossini's "Barbiere di Siviglia," *Music and Letters* 20 (1939): 157–67.

Stendhal. *Vie de Rossini*. Paris: Auguste Boulland & Cie, 1824 [and various translations].

Tartak, M. "The Two 'Barbieri,'" *Music and Letters* 50 (1969): 453–69.

Weinstock, Herbert. *Rossini: A Biography.* London: Oxford University Press, 1968.

Zedda, Alberto. "Ancora sul belcanto, lo stile ed il Barbiere," *Rasegnia musicale Curci* 1 (1970): 3–10.

———. "Appunti per una lettura filologica del *Barbiere,*" *L'Opera* 2, no. 5 (1966), 13–16.

BARYE, ANTOINE-LOUIS 1796–1875

French sculptor, painter, printmaker

Son of a Parisian goldsmith, Antoine-Louis Barye, together with François Rude (1784–1855) and Pierre-Jean David d'Angers (1788–1856), forms the triumvirate of French Romantic sculptors. Rude's working class origins and neoclassical training gave rise to his monumental public art commissions (*La Marseillaise*, at L'Arc de Triomphe, Paris, 1833–36); David d'Angers was celebrated for his public commissions and numerous portrait medallions. Barye, however, was the earliest and most well known of the *animaliers*, artists who found their subjects in animals and beasts rather than historical or mythological narratives or portraiture. He created realistic portrayals of animals, monsters of legend and myth, as well as symbolical groups. Beyond these, Barye created monuments to historical figures, public sculptures for the Tuileries Palace and the Louvre, and interpretations from literature, including *Roger and Angelica* from Ludovico Ariosto's *Orlando Furioso.*

Like many visual artists in the Romantic era, Barye's training drew on the skills required of both the artisan and the fine artist. He took up metalworking before training in engraving, painting, and smithing, in addition to sculpture. After training under the sculptor François-Joseph Bosio and the painter Antoine-Jean Gros, Barye offered his work for competition at the École des Beaux Arts of the Academie Française, France's official school of art. Barye's entry received honorable mention, an impressive debut for an artist. To understand the intricacies of sculptural form, he made drawings after classical ancient sculptures and admired masters such as Titian and Caravaggio. In 1824, he sought training under Jacque-Henri Fauconnier, a goldsmith who encouraged him to produce small bronze bas-reliefs as ornamentation for furniture and clocks.

To create forms that evoked power and vigor, Barye studied animals inside and out. To observe their physical characteristics as well as their motion and poses, he visited the Jardin des Plantes, often with the Romantic painter Eugène Delacroix (1798–1863). To capture the movement and stasis in addition to melancholic confinement, they sketched in paint and pastel from direct observation. Additionally, Barye made rough sketches out of wax, to gauge modeling in three dimensions. To understand the anatomy of animals and the peculiarities of their fur, flesh, and bones, Barye attended lectures and observed dissections. Without traveling farther than Fontainebleau, he brought the title of *animalier* to one of distinction. His sketches, wax models, and later sculptural representations were the result of continuous anatomical study and, in the case of the bronzes, of tight control over casting techniques and reproductive technologies that yielded exquisitely detailed small sculptures.

He established his own studio in 1832, the same year that he exhibited *Lion Crushing the Serpent* (Tuileries) at the Salon.

This was later cast by Honoré Gonon by the lost wax (*cire perdu*) method. The work was celebrated for its realistic portrayal that captured the expression, gesture, and fierce movement of provoked animals. In fact, the painter Henri Rousseau told his pupil Jean-Antoine Letronne that Barye's lion was more realistic than if it had been modeled hair by hair. Barye's work was noted for this realism rooted in scientific study and direct observation, and that elevated animals to a worthy subject for sculpture.

His most important patron was, perhaps, the Duke d'Orleans, son of King Louis-Philippe. He created colossal architectural ornaments which were grandiloquently public, such as the personifications for the Louvre facade (*war, peace, strength*, and *order*) that show heroes attended by *putti* (winged angelic children) seated upon animal attributes. Commenting upon Barye's fantastic abilities at realistic and evocative portrayals, Maxime du Camp commented, in her review of the 1855 Exposition Universelle, that his work was beyond compare for its truth of form and spirited nature.

Barye was instrumental in technical advances in casting and patinating bronzes. Today subtle gradations in tone (patina) of the bronzes and variations of different casts of a work bear witness to the diversity of the sculptor's output. While Barye produced no new works after 1869, following his death in 1875 the works of his studio (over 230 models spanning a career of forty years) were purchased by Ferdinand Barbedienne, to be cast posthumously at the Barbedienne Foundry. While those sculptures cast after the artist's death are clearly marked with a different stamp than those done during his lifetime, the bronzes were cast with extreme attention to detail and attempted to carry on Barye's interest in patination and exquisite detail. Surprisingly, recent research has shown that the gradations of patina, difference in detail, and quality of bronze vary among the different editions of casts produced during Barye's lifetime and afterward.

Exhibitions have demonstrated Barye's skill as sculptor, teacher, and craftsman. In 1889–90 his work was featured at exhibitions at the École des Beaux Arts and the American Art Galleries in New York. During the twentieth century, two major exhibitions were held at the Louvre (1956, 1996) that sought to enlighten the public about the inspiration, creation, and reception of many of Barye's works.

Théophile Gautier complimented Barye, calling him "Michel-Ange de la Ménagerie" and found in his art a fiery and energetic spirit. Gautier praised Barye's resistance to the established tradition that elevated history painting above all other genres. Instead, Barye's works were heroic in their elevation of subject and dramatic, compact, and vigorous handling. Animal forms were transformed; intertwining torsos and interlocking paws resembled the entwined figures of medieval manuscript illumination. His artistic output was not limited in size or scope: the same sense of vigor, energy, and power greet the viewer, whether inside a home, strolling the entry of the Tuileries Palace, or gazing at the facade of the Louvre.

JUILEE DECKER

Biography

Born in Paris, September 24, 1796. Studied various arts and crafts; studied with sculptor François-Joseph Bosio (1768–1845); studied with the painter Antoine-Jean Gros (1771–1835); studied under Jacque-Henri Fauconnier (c. 1776–1839). *Lion Crushing Serpent* exhibited at French salon, 1831; opened his own studio, 1832. Director of casting at Louvre, 1848. Named professor of zoological drawing at the Musée d'Histoire Naturelle in Paris, 1854; exhibited at Exposition Universelle, 1855. Barye established a bronze foundry in the rue des Folies-Regnault of Paris, 1858. Died in Paris, June 25, 1875.

Bibliography

Ballu, Roger. *L'oeuvre de Barye*. With an introduction by Eugène Guillaume. Paris: Maison Quantin, 1890.

Benge, Glenn F. *Antoine-Louis Barye. Sculptor of Romantic Realism.* University Park: Pennsylvania State University Press, 1984.

Camp, Maxime du. *Les Beaux-Arts en 1855 à l'Exposition Universelle de 1855.* Paris: Librairie Nouvelle, 1855.

Cary, Elizabeth L. "Antoine-Louis Barye: His Methods of Work, part 2." *The Scrip* 2, no. 4 (1907): 110.

Kay, Charles, *Life and Works of Barye the Sculptor, with eighty-six wood-cuts, artotypes and prints, in memory of an exhibition of his bronzes, paintings, and watercolors held at New-York in aid of the fund for his monument at Paris.* New York: Barye Monument Association, 1889.

Lemaistre, Isabelle Leroy-Jay and Béatrice Tupinier Barrillon. *La griffe et la dent: Antoine-Louis Barye (1795–1875) sculpteur animalier.* Paris: Editions de la Réunion des musées nationaux, 1996.

Pivar, Stuart. *The Barye Bronzes, a Catalogue Raisonné.* Rev. ed. with improved photographs and twenty additional color plates. Woodbrige, Suffolk, England: Antique Collectors' Club, 1990.

Richarme, Alain and Michel Poletti. *Barye. Catalogue raisonné de l'oeuvre sculpté.* Paris: Gallimard, 2000.

Smith, Charles Sprague. *Barbizon Days: Millet, Corot, Rousseau, Barye.* New York: A. Wessels, 1902.

Zieseniss, Charles Otto. *Les aquarelles de Barye: étude critique et catalogue raisonné.* Paris: Charles Massin, 1954.

BATIUSHKOV, KONSTANTIN NIKOLAEVICH 1787–1855

Russian poet

Fluent in a wide range of languages, including French, Italian, and German, and steeped in European culture, Konstantin Nikolaevich Batiushkov achieved early prominence as one of the most accomplished of the poets belonging to the so-called school of harmonic accuracy. Together with contemporaries such as Vasilii Zhukovskii and Ivan Gnedich, Batiushkov perfected a style of lyric characterized by smoothness of sound orchestration and a meditative, near-solipsistic depiction of the lyric speaker. Batiushkov's first published poem, "Mechta" ("The Dream," 1804) is precocious and representative; it depicts the power of the imagination and of fancy to transport, and therefore celebrates the imaginative release that poetry affords from unfavorable circumstance. Much of the verse written before 1810 reflects an apprenticeship spent imitating the light verse of Jean-Baptiste-Louis Gresset, Évariste-Désirée de Forges de Parny, and Voltaire that broadened into an intertextual dialogue with Batiushkov's personal pantheon of great European lyric poets. Eventually his admiration for classical antiquity issued in the "Podrazhaniia drevnim" ("Imitations of the Ancients," 1821) epigrams that combine a timeless impersonality, simple linguistic perfection, and a lightness of philosophical touch. He was also the author of a number of distinguished essays on poetry, aesthetics, and psychology, which form an essential parallel oeuvre to his verse.

In his tragically brief mature period, Batiushkov produced a body of verse distinguished by verbal precision combined with suggestiveness, sparseness of metaphor with picturesque detail, balance and symmetry in syntax and skillful use of assonance and alliteration. The range of subjects and psychological complexity of the lyric speaker mark an advance on his precocious but somewhat precious early imitations. Apart from the epigram and elegy, where Batiushkov excelled, he left his mark on the verse epistle, which became a vehicle for Epicurean meditation on friendship and pleasure. In the only collection that he saw into print, the celebrated *Opyty v stikhakh i proze* (*Essays in Verse and Prose*, 1817), Batiushkov gave prominence to the theme of the ephemeral nature of pleasure and the anguish of disillusion once the poetic dream fades.

An interest in history was sparked by his military experience. His visit to Weimar proved an opportunity to immerse himself in Johann Wolfgang von Goethe, Johann Christoph Friedrich von Schiller, and Christoph Martin Wieland, and their aesthetics are reflected in Batiushkov's exalted sense of the poet and the importance of antiquity. He commemorated his experiences in "Perekhod cherez Rein" ("Crossing the Rhine," 1814) and "Na razvalinakh zamka v Shvetsii" ("At the Ruins of a Castle in Sweden," 1814). In the latter, Batiushkov, infused by Ossian, created a meditation on the nature of history set within features of a pre-Romantic landscape, including ruins, mist and gloom, inscription, and a passing traveler. In "Poslanie k Dashkovu" ("Epistle to Dashkov," 1813) shock at the devastation of Europe and Russia led to a crisis of faith in the legacy of the Enlightenment, the solution to which was a further celebration of friendship rather than the retreat into solipsism that marks the poetry of other early Russian Romantics.

Batiushkov is virtually the first Russian poet to give the status and role of the poet significant attention, and his treatment of the theme was to echo in later Russian poets from Aleksandr Pushkin to Osip Mandelshtam. In "Umiraiushchii Tass" ("The Dying Tasso," 1817) and the articles on Ludovico Ariosto and

Tasso (1815) and on "Petrarch" (1815), Batiushkov expressed a credo concerning the self-sacrifice of the poet whose gift was all-consuming and exclusive, and in some senses even tragic. His own biography seemed to assure for posterity the unique and fragile nature of poetic inspiration, and thus anticipated the later treatments by Pushkin and Evgenii Baratynskii, among others, of the theme of the poet's visionary powers. In his article "Nechto o poete i o poezii" ("A Word on the Poet and Poetry," 1815) Batiushkov attempted to expound a theory of poetic inspiration based entirely on the appreciation of a unique genius characterized by what he calls "active sensibility." At the height of inspiration he achieves a "freshness of reverie," and a unique perception of the beauty and moral order of life; and because these visionary moments are scarce and ephemeral, Batiushkov speaks, in an image that was to become more familiar in the Russian Romanticism of the next two decades, of the poet as a hierophant completely "taken over by poetry."

Yet the poet also wears another guise, now inspired by the poetry of Horace, dedicated to a modest Epicureanism in which simple pleasures and true friendships are celebrated. The locus classicus of this view comes in Batiushkov's famous "Moi Penaty" ("*My Penates*," 1814), where he describes the spirit of genius, stripped of wealth and worldly honors, that visits the poet at his ease in a humble country setting. His prose style is graceful, but lyrical and oblique, which means that intellectual sources for Batiushkov's views are diffused through his essays and remain difficult to pin down. At times he speaks of the poet as the product of factors akin to the forces in Charles de Secondat Montesquieu's theory of government. Poets are said to be shaped by climate and geography, but the ultimate purpose of such a theory is to assert the status of poets as speakers for individual national cultures. Batiushkov's belief in the centrality of the poet to a culture is most apparent in the remarkable elegy "The Dying Tasso," where the death of the poet occurs in a protracted monologue set on the Capitoline Hill in Rome. Traces of Jean-Jacques Rousseau's influence are also evident in the primacy that Batiushkov assigns to the natural goodness of individuals, which in the case of the poet is present in a higher degree. He argues his views on the basis of a series of idealized biographies, in which the lives of the poets, from the Roman Tibullus to the Russian Mikhail Lomonosov, are all meant to exemplify the timeless powers of the imagination that are the product of local culture and also transcend it. Nature remains a subdued presence in his poems until his remarkable last elegy ("There is Rapture even in the Wilds of the Forests") which ecstatically voices a romantic and frustrated yearning for oneness with nature and regrets the powerlessness of words to express feeling.

ANDREW KAHN

Biography

Born in Vologda, May 29, 1787, into landed gentry. Spent early years on his father's estate. Attended private boarding schools in Saint Petersburg; studied classics, French, and Italian. Lived with an uncle, the writer Mikhail Murav'ev, in Saint Petersburg, 1802. Served in the ministry of public education, 1803–7. Began to publish poetry, 1805. Joined Moscow literary circles; started publishing in Nikolay Mikhay Iovich Karamzin's journal *Vestnik Evropy*, 1809–10. Participated in Napoleonic campaigns, 1813–14, for which he was decorated, and visited Paris, England, and Sweden. Accepted into Nikolay Mikhay Iovich Karamzin's followers' Arzamas Society, 1815, and the Society of Lovers of Russian Letters at Moscow University, 1816. Transferred to the Household Guards; retired, 1816. Undertook diplomatic service in Italy, 1819–21. Granted indefinite leave owing to mental instability, 1821–22; suffered increasing and permanent insanity with intermittent periods in mental institutions, 1824–33. Stayed in the Maison de santé in Sonnenstein (Saxony), 1824–28 and in Moscow, 1828–33. Moved to Vologda and was released from official service and granted a life pension. Died in Vologda, July 19, 1855.

Selected Works

Collections
Sochineniia. 3 vols. 1885–87.
Polnoe sobranie stikhotvorenii. 19645.
Sochineniia. 2 vols. 1989.

Poetry and Essays
Opyty v stikhakh i proze. 2 vols. 1817.
Opty v stikhakh i proze. 1977.

Bibliography

Fridman, N. V. *Poeziia Batiushkova*. Moscow: Nauka, 1971.
Greenleaf, Monika. "Found in Translation: The Subject of Batiushkov's Poetry." In *Russian Subjects: Empire, Nation, and the Culture of the Golden Age*. Edited by Monika Greenleaf and Stephen Moeller-Sally. Evanston, Ill.: Northwestern University Press, 51–79.
Serman, Ilya. *Konstantin Batiushkov*. New York: Twayne, 1974.

BAUDELAIRE, CHARLES (PIERRE) 1821–1867

French poet, critic, and translator

Charles Baudelaire is best described as a writer whose work and career represent a transitional moment in literary history. In his poetry and prose written from the 1840s onwards he treats the notions of "Romantic" and "modern" not as discrete phases or styles but as complementary and intertwined. In his essay *Le Salon de 1846* (1846), he claimed that Romanticism is "l'expression la plus récente et la plus moderne de la beauté" ("the most up-to-date and the most modern expression of beauty"). For Baudelaire, Romantic was modern (and vice versa), and the artist must continually work his passage between the two, "de tirer l'éternel du transitoire" ("to distill the eternal from the transitory"). In Romantic pursuit of beauty and the higher forms of imagination (which he described as "the Queen of the Faculties" in his essay *Le Salon de 1859*), Baudelaire looked to the modern spectacle of contemporary Paris and the "l'héroïsme de la vie moderne" (the heroism of modern life); there, in the fashion and manners of individuals swarming the crowded boulevards, he found aesthetic pleasure and inspiration. Outside and at the same time within the crowd, Baudelaire's artist was a figure of ambiguity, a man (never a woman) of the fleeting moment: "Observateur, flâneur, philosophe, appelez-les comme vous voudrez. . . . Quelquefois il est poète; plus souvent il se rapproche du romancier ou du moraliste; il est le peintre de la circonstance et de tout ce qu'elle suggère d'éternel" (Observer, *flâneur*, philosopher, call him what you will. . . . Sometimes he is a poet; more often he comes closer to the novelist or the moralist; he is the painter of the passing moment and of all the suggestions of eternity that it contains"). This dualism is present everywhere in Baudelaire, and it is part of the reason why his work resists categorization. Like Lord Byron, Baudelaire was an outraged classicist with a penchant for themes of passion and exile, but unlike his aristocratic counterpart, Baudelaire's interest was in "le bric-à-brac confus" (the nameless jumble), described in his poem "Le Cygne" ("The Swan," 1859).

Subsisting on a family inheritance and revenue from his art criticism, Baudelaire inhabited the Latin Quarter of Paris and led a Bohemian life of brothels, Swedenborgian séances, and experiments with hashish and opium. Briefly, in February 1848, he was caught up in revolutionary activity, participating in the barricades, but from 1850 onward Baudelaire concentrated on his writing, creating a reputation and income from translating the tales of the American writer Edgar Allan Poe (1855), and later a *succès de scandale* in 1857 with his collection of poetry, *Fleurs du Mal* (*Flowers of Evil*). In this volume, which contains what critics have termed the *Vénus noire* (*Black Venus*) cycle of poems inspired by his mistress, Jeanne Duval, the provocative juxtaposition of symbols, images, and sensations conveyed more powerfully than any poet before the antagonism between evil and good (*spleen* and *idéal*). His notion of correspondences, whereby the poet is able to effect, through symbol and metaphor, a synthesis of different realities, sensations, and feelings was one that inspired later decadent and symbolist poets, including Arthur Symons and W. B. Yeats. From his Guernsey exile, Victor Hugo described Baudelaire's *Fleurs du Mal* as creating a "frisson nouveau" ("new shudder"), and apart from a few scattered accolades from the decadent novelist Barbey d'Aurevilly, and poet Algernon Charles Swinburne, *Fleurs du Mal* met with outrage and disgust from the bourgeois public for its depravity and focus on low life and suffering.

The seizure of *Fleurs du Mal* by the police in the year that it was published did not augur well for Baudelaire's literary career as a poet. He was ordered by the court to remove six poems from the collection. In spite of this setback, Baudelaire was highly productive in the late 1850s and early 1860s, writing a new section, "Tableaux Parisiens" ("Parisian pictures"), for a new edition of *Fleurs du Mal* that appeared in 1861, and publishing essays on topics as diverse as caricature ("Quelques caricatures françaises" ["Some French Caricaturists," 1857]) and music ("Richard Wagner et Tannhäuser," 1861). The subject matter of Baudelaire's poems and prose was undoubtedly modern, but his vision of the artist and his belief in the artist as a translator of perceived reality were Romantic. To distill experience into art, he argued, the artist must have the naiveté and curiosity of the child, while at the same time the sophisticated reflection of the philosopher or moralist. Abandonment to life's sensations was deemed by him a prerequisite to creativity and was a recurrent theme in his life and work. In his prose poem "Enivrez-vous!" ("Get Drunk!" 1855–67), for example, Baudelaire exhorts the reader to lose control and become inebriated on wine, poetry, or virtue. And yet, he was extremely attentive to matters of style and form, often preferring to work precisely within the strict classical meter of the Alexandrine to create suggestive tensions between form and content.

Baudelaire rejected realism on the whole because of the way it inhibited the key roles played by imagination and fantasy (this was also his objection against photography). He applauded the works of the Romantic history painter Eugène Delacroix in particular, for his suggestive use of color and for the way his paintings were "une espèce de mnémotechnie de la grandeur et de la passion native de l'homme universel" ("like a mnemonic device of the greatness and the inborn passions of universal man"). We might say, therefore, that his writing gathers momentum in the interstices of Romanticism and modernism, and that, paradoxically for Baudelaire, the activity of writing involved acknowledging both the Romantic conventions into that he was born and the modernity that he was living and by which he was inspired. Baudelaire's achievements were not recognized until some time after his death in the 1890s, when English and French symbolists adopted him as the figurehead of their movement. Since that time Baudelaire's life and work have continued to stimulate and perplex the critics. Many prefer to describe him as decadent or modern because of his obsession with beauty and style, and his preoccupations with the morbid and erotic aspects of contemporary life, but this is to deny him his interest in Romanticism, or what he described in *Le Salon de 1846* as intimacy, spirituality, and a sense of the infinite.

JANE DESMARAIS

Biography

Born in Paris, April 9, 1821. Son of François Baudelaire, a wealthy civil servant and amateur painter and poet who introduced his to art and literature. François Baudelaire died, 1827. Charles suffered a problematic relationship with his stepfather, Colonel Jacques Aupick (later a diplomat and senator), whom his mother married in 1828. Educated at the Collège Royal, Lyons, 1832–36, and the École Louis-le-Grand, Paris, 1836–39; expelled from the latter and completed studies at Pension Levêque et Bailly, Paris. Passed baccalauréat, 1839. Studied law at the École de Droit, University of Paris, 1839–41. Here he lived a Bohemian lifestyle, falling into debt and contracting syphilis from contact with prostitutes. Sent to India by his stepfather, 1841; left the ship at Mauritius and spent several weeks there and in Île Bourbon (now Réunion). Returned to Paris, 1842, taking up residence in the Hôtel Pimodan in the Latin Quarter. Began writing poetry and experimenting with opium. Took a mulatto woman, Jeanne Duval, as his mistress and inspiration; associated with artists Honoré Daumier, Eugène Delacroix, and Édouard Manet, and started writing art criticism. Access to his inheritance restricted by his stepfather, 1844, because of his profligate lifestyle. Started reading the work of Edgar Allan Poe, 1847. Associated with revolutionary insurgence in Paris, February 1848. Met Théophile Gautier, 1848. Liaisons with the actress Marie Daubrun and Apollonie Sabatier, 1850s. First edition of *Fleurs du Mal* published, resulting in trial and prosecution for indecency: fined for offenses against public morals, 1857–58. Lived in Honfleur intermittently with his mother, 1859. Published *Les Paradis Artificiels*, 1860; second edition of *Fleurs du Mal* (with thirty-five additional poems), 1861. Attempted unsuccessfully to gain membership of the Académie Française, 1861. Suffered further financial crisis when his friend and publisher, Poulet-Massis, was declared bankrupt. Became physically and mentally ill, dependent on alcohol and opium. Moved to Brussels, 1864; became increasingly ill and financially destitute. Returned to Paris suffering from general paralysis and aphasia; *Les Épaves* published, 1866. Spent his last months in a sanatorium in Paris, where he died on August 31, 1867.

Selected Works

Collections

Œuvres posthumes et correspondances inédites précédées d'une étude biographique par Eugène Crépet. Paris: Editions de la Pléiade 1887.
Correspondance. 2 vols. Edited by Claude Pichois and Jean Ziegler. Paris: Gallimard, 1973.
Œuvres complètes. 2 vols. Edited by Claude Pichois. 1975–76.

Poetry

Les Fleurs du Mal. 1857.
Les Épaves. 1866.
Petits Poèmes en Prose (later retitled *Le Spleen de Paris*), 1869.
    Translated by Arthur W. Symons as *Poems in Prose*, 1905. Edited

by David Scott and Barbara Wright (with the inclusion of *La Fanfarlo*). 1987.

Prose

Les Paradis Artificiels, opium et haschisch. 1860.

Translations

The Poems of Charles Baudelaire. Selected and translated with an introductory study by F. P. Sturm. 1906.
Selected Writings on Art and Literature. Translated and with an introduction by P. E. Charvet. 1972.
Selected Poems. Translated and with an introduction by Carol Clark. 1995.
Baudelaire in English. Edited by Carol Clark and Robert Sykes. 1997.
Complete Poems. Translated by Walter Martin. 1997.

Bibliography

Burton, R. D. E. *Baudelaire in 1859: a study in the sources of poetic creativity.* 1988.
Clements, P. *Baudelaire and the English Tradition.* 1985.
Coven, Jeffrey. *Baudelaire's Voyages.* 1993.
Evans, Margery A. *Baudelaire and Intertextuality.* 1993.
Hannoosh, Michele. *Baudelaire and Caricature.* 1992.
Leakey, F. W. *Baudelaire and Nature.* 1969.
Lecaye, H. *Le Secret de Baudelaire.* 1991.
Leoutre, G., and P. Salomon. *Baudelaire et le symbolisme.* 1971.
Sartre, Jean-Paul. *Baudelaire.* 1947.
Starkie, Enid. *Baudelaire.* 1971.

BEATTIE, JAMES 1735–1803

Scottish poet, moral philosopher, aesthetician, and man of letters

James Beattie spent most of his mature life as a professor of moral philosophy, rhetoric, and aesthetics at Marischal College in Aberdeen, where he played a central role in the Scottish Enlightenment and achieved fame as a poet, philosopher, defender of Christianity, and general man of letters. Beattie's 1770 *Essay on Truth* provided a popular and influential "refutation" of David Hume's philosophy and was quickly translated into German; it was widely read in Germany and contributed to Immanuel Kant's three philosophical critiques. At the same time, Beattie was one of the most influential poets in late-eighteenth-century Britain, as his poem *The Minstrel*, whose first and second cantos were published in 1771 and 1774, respectively, exerted major influence on British Romantic poetry and provided a precedent for a number of major Romantic themes, including the turn to nature, childhood, the quest narrative, and the central figure of the poet and his imaginative development. Beattie's later publications on aesthetics and rhetoric were similarly influential for the development of Romantic literary theory. In his own words a "friend to all," Beattie seems to have had a talent for friendship, making him central to the British literary and cultural circles of his time; he numbered among his friends David Garrick, Thomas Gray, Samuel Johnson, Lord Lyttleton, the aristocratic patron Lady Elizabeth Montagu, Sir Joshua Reynolds, and the Archbishop of York, to name only some of the more prominent.

The Minstrel narrates the childhood and imaginative development of its central hero, Edwin, amid the sublime natural scenery of the Scottish countryside. With a taste for solitude that marks

him apart from his companions and from society generally, Edwin wanders alone through the wild landscape, giving free reign to his own poetic imagination until he meets a hermit in a far-off, cultivated mountain glen who helps him complete his education in a variety of eighteenth-century physical and moral sciences. Beattie never wrote the projected third canto, in which an accident was to rob Edwin of his inheritance and cause him to take up the profession of wandering minstrel.

Subtitled *The Progress of Genius*, *The Minstrel* was one of William Wordsworth's favorite poems throughout his life; its depiction of the imaginative sensibilities and development of its hero provided a direct model for Wordsworth's account of his own imaginative progress in *The Prelude* (1850). Although not explicitly autobiographical, Edwin as a minstrel or poet was generally understood as a thinly veiled self-portrait of the poet Beattie himself, and as such provided the first major precedent and a continuing influence for a wide variety of Romantic poems focusing on the figure of the poet and his imaginative development, both fictional and autobiographical, including Lord Byron's *Childe Harold's Pilgrimage* (1812–18); François-Auguste-René Chateaubriand's novellas *René* (1802) and *Atala* (1808); John Keats' *Endymion* (1816); Sir Walter Scott's *Marmion* (1808); and Percy Bysshe Shelley's *Alastor* (1816), *The Revolt of Islam* (1818), and *Adonais* (1821). Appealing to late-eighteenth-century tastes for sensibility, melancholy, the minstrel or bard figure, medievalism, primitivism, and didacticism, *The Minstrel* popularized what would become the Romantic themes of solitude in a sublime natural landscape, the development of individual consciousness and imagination, the figure of the poet as aloof from society, and the importance of childhood—thus providing a kind of evolutionary bridge between neoclassical and Romantic poetics.

Beattie's greatest fame during his lifetime, however, derived from his *Essay on Truth*, an attempt to refute what he understood as the skepticism and atheism of David Hume's philosophy by asserting the clear and distinct "proof" of Christianity on the basis of its self-evidence to individual intuition. The essay's argument develops out of the commonsense school of the Scottish philosopher Thomas Reid, a fellow professor, and active member, together with Beattie and other prominent figures such as Alexander Gerard and George Campbell, of the Aberdeen Philosophical Society. The essay was quickly translated into French, Dutch, and German and was widely read in Germany at that time. Dismissed by Kant as a mere "appeal to the verdict of the multitude" and philosophically unpersuasive today, it was important in introducing Hume's philosophical positions to Kant and so awakening him from his "dogmatic slumber," as he later put it, thus leading to his formulation of his three critiques in the attempt to adequately respond to Hume's positions. Despite (or perhaps because of) its lack of merit as rigorous philosophy, the essay enjoyed huge public acclaim, continuing to appear regularly in new editions through the end of the nineteenth century. Lionized as a successful philosophical defender of Christianity by Samuel Johnson, among many others, Beattie continued his influential career as a moral philosopher and Christian apologist in later works such as *Evidences of the Christian Religion* (1786) and *Elements of Moral Science* (1790 and 1793).

In addition to his poetry and moral philosophy, Beattie wrote a number of essays on aesthetics that contributed significantly to the development of Romantic literary theory. In his 1776 essay "On Poetry and Music as they Affect the Mind" he wrote of poetry as "the language of nature" dictated by passion, although expressing a general rather than a specific human nature, a position that Wordsworth would recapitulate in his famous preface to the *Lyrical Ballads* (1798). In the essay, as well as in his later *Dissertations Moral and Critical* (1783), which were widely read at the time, Beattie celebrates individual genius as the source of great or sublime poetry and stresses the importance of imagination as a creative power distinct from the merely combinatory power of fancy (anticipating Samuel Taylor Coleridge's famous definition in *Biographia Literaria*, 1817). He also calls attention to the importance of sympathy in communicating the original consciousness of the creative artist to the consciousness of the reader or spectator, in what would become a general tenet of Romantic hermeneutic theory. The celebration of imagination and strong feeling in poetry and music is balanced by a stress on judgment and an insistence on the moral purpose of all art; none of Beattie's positions were radical in themselves, but Beattie's aesthetic and critical writings, like his poetry, estab-lished precedents for a wide number of Romantic critical positions and so provided an important evolutionary link in aesthetic theory.

SCOTT HESS

Biography

Born in Laurencekirk, Kincardineshire, Scotland, November 5, 1735; educated at Marischal College, Aberdeen, 1749–53. Schoolmaster and parish clerk, Fordoun, (near Laurencekirk) 1753–58; master at Aberdeen Grammar School, 1758–60. Professor of moral philosophy and logic, Marischal College, 1760–93; elected to Aberdeen Philosophical Society, 1761. Married Mary Dunn, 1767; they had two sons. Edited David Thomas Gray's *Poems* for Scottish publication; visited London: was celebrated by English social and literary elite and granted a pension by King George III, 1773. Declined offer of Edinburgh University professorship and various church livings, 1773; published subscription edition of *Essay on Truth*, 1776. LL.D., Oxford University, 1770. Died in Aberdeen after a series of strokes, 18 August 1803.

Selected Writings

Poetry
Original Poems and Translations, 1761. 2d rev. and enl. ed., 1766.
The Minstrel, Canto I. 1771.
The Minstrel, Canto II. 1774.

Essays/Nonfiction
An Essay on the Nature and Immutability of Truth, in Opposition to Sophistry and Scepticism. 1770.
Essays: On Poetry and Music as they affect the Mind; On Laughter and Ludicrous Composition; On the Utility of Classical Learning. 1776.
Dissertations Moral and Critical. 1783.
Evidences of the Christian Religion. 1786.
Elements of Moral Science. Vol. 1. 1790.
Elements of Moral Science. Vol. 2. 1793.
James Beattie's London Diary. 1773. Edited by Ralph S. Walker. 1946.

Bibliography

Forbes, Margaret. *Beattie and His Friends*. 1904; reprinted Altrincham, England: Martin Strafford, 1990.
Forbes, Sir William. *An Account of the Life and Writings of James Beattie, LL.D.* 2 vols. London: Roper, 1824.
King, Everard. *James Beattie*. Boston: G. K. Hall, 1977.
———. "James Beattie's Essay on Truth (1770): An Eighteenth-Century 'Best-Seller,'" *Dalhousie Review* 51 (1971): 390–403.
———. *James Beattie's "The Minstrel" and the Origins of Romantic Autobiography.* Lewiston, N.Y.: Edwin Mellen Press, 1992.
Land, Stephen K. "James Beattie on Language," *Philological Quarterly* 51 (1972): 887–904.
Phillipson, N. T. "James Beattie and the Defense of Common Sense," in *Festschrift für Rainer Gruenter*. Edited by Bernhard Fabian, Richard Alewyn, and Renate Schusky. Heidelberg, 1978.
Wolff, Robert Paul. "Kant's Debt to Hume via Beattie." *Journal of the History of Ideas* 21 (1960): 117–23.

BECKFORD, WILLIAM THOMAS 1760–1844

English writer and collector

William Thomas Beckford became the richest private citizen in Britain when his father died and he inherited the entire estate, at the age of nine, in 1770. This wealth had been founded on substantial slave-worked sugar plantations in Jamaica, but unlike Matthew Lewis, who found himself in a similar situation, Beckford never expressed any uneasiness about this legacy. Beckford also inherited from his father a name linked with political liberty. An impromptu rebuke to George III had made William Beckford senior a popular hero. Beckford junior was also groomed for high public office, but his political career amounted to nothing more than serving as member of Parliament for pocket boroughs (parliamentary constituencies owned by one man, known as the patron). Indeed, Beckford deliberately shunned the normal course of British patrician life and almost courted disapprobation. "I will seclude myself if possible from the World," he wrote in 1779. "I am determined to enjoy my dreams and my phantasies and all my singularity, however irksome and discordant to the Worldlings around." What the "Worldlings" found particularly irksome and discordant was Beckford's bisexuality, and particularly his liaison with Viscount William Courtenay, eleven years old when Beckford first met him and sixteen when their sexual relationship became public knowledge in 1784. Although it is not certain that Courtenay's family would have risked scandal by prosecuting him, Beckford fled abroad in 1785. He did not return to take up permanent residence at the family home at Fonthill Splendens until 1796.

Descriptions of the early part of Beckford's erratic exile are to be found in his *Italy; with Sketches of Spain and Portugal* (1834) and *Recollections of an Excursion to the Monasteries of Alcobaça and Batalha* (1835). The former was in part a reworking of *Dreams, Waking Thoughts and Incidents*, which had been suppressed by his family after its initial appearance in 1783. Beckford had been writing since his late teens. His *Biographical Memoirs of Extraordinary Painters*, a satirical commentary on European art and the pretensions of collectors, was written in 1777 and published in 1780. Many other fragments, often written in an Oriental or Arcadian vein, also survive from these years. Beckford regarded himself as a professional writer and as a scholar of Persian and Arabic. His commitment to his writing is evident from the history of the publication of *Vathek*. He claimed that the tale was composed in three days, but it probably took at least three months in early 1782 and he delayed publication for another four years while he worked on several additional "episodes." He also enlisted a collaborator, the Reverend Samuel Henley, to provide scholarly notes to elucidate the Oriental setting, and to translate *Vathek* from its original (rather impaired) French into English. It seems certain that Henley also made Beckford's prose much lighter in tone. Henley had a text ready for publication as early as 1783, and Beckford's prevarication over the "episodes" eventually pushed Henley into publishing his version of *Vathek* in London in June 1786. It was passed off as "An Arabian Tale from an Unpublished Manuscript with Notes Critical and Explanatory," and Beckford's name did not appear. Beckford, in Switzerland, was understandably angry, and quickly commissioned a translation of Henley's text back into

French, which was published in Lausanne under Beckford's name in December 1786, to be followed in June 1787 by a superior translation published in Paris. Beckford prepared a harmonized edition in 1816.

Based on the ostensibly historical account in Barthélemy d'Herbelot's *Bibliothèque Orientale*, Beckford's tale tells how the cruel Caliph Vathek became a servant of Eblis, the devil, in return for the treasures of the pre-Adamite kings. Vathek sacrifices fifty children and sets forth on a journey full of terrifying incidents until he finally reaches the halls of Eblis, where he is punished as his heart bursts into flames within his still-living body. Early reviews praised *Vathek* for Henley's notes and for its moral didacticism. The notes now seem turgid, and the final moral seems at odds with a tale that has enthusiastically celebrated the unrestrained appetite and the pursuit of forbidden knowledge. Lord Byron was an admirer of *Vathek* and acknowledged its impact on him in *The Giaour* (1813). Its influence may also be detected in the work of Benjamin Disraeli, Nathaniel Hawthorne, Walter Savage Landor, Thomas Moore, Edgar Allan Poe, Robert Southey, and many others. With its ambiguous morality and its celebration of the exotic and the sublime, *Vathek* developed the Oriental tale away from the neoclassicism of eighteenth-century versions like Samuel Johnson's *Rasselas*, yet the work is often considered as more properly pre-Romantic since it lacks any sustained insight into the protagonist's motivation.

Beckford published two other novels, both of which do little more than parody contemporary fashions in fiction, and from the late 1790s he devoted himself to collecting art and the construction of a new home, Fonthill Abbey. He patronized many contemporary artists, J. M. W. Turner and Benjamin West among them, and was responsible for bringing many works of art into Britain where they would remain after his collection was dispersed. Fonthill Abbey was to house the collection, as well as being his home and, he imagined, his mausoleum. First, as in Samuel Taylor Coleridge's *Kubla Khan*, he built a seven-mile wall to cut himself off from the world. The building James Wyatt designed in a series of uncoordinated phases over the next decades was one of the most important early examples of the Gothic revival. Its monstrous size was what set it apart from Horace Walpole's house at Strawberry Hill and all the other neo-Gothic edifices that had begun to appear in the late eighteenth century. Indeed, Fonthill might be considered more "performance art" than functional architecture. It was too stylized and impracticable to live in and, ultimately, too flimsy and too tall to remain standing. The tower, which eventually rose to almost three hundred feet, collapsed three times—the last, after Beckford had sold the building in 1822, and this time it destroyed the building almost entirely. Whether the monumental folly was approved of or not, Fonthill cannot have been ignored by later figures such as Charles Barry and Augustus Pugin, who were to do so much to make the Gothic respectable in the nineteenth century.

Though both took years to complete, *Vathek* and Fonthill were temporary projects. By contrast, Beckford ceaselessly cultivated his almost mythical self-image over the entire course of his life. He had always sought to portray himself as a solitary exile and persecuted aesthete, and ultimately, it is perhaps this Beckford myth, more than anything he wrote or designed, collected or commissioned, that contributed most to English Romanticism. His orientalism and medievalism, as well as his early love of nature, made him in many ways a Romantic archetype. His self-imposed exile from society made him a Romantic icon.

M. O. GRENBY

Biography

Born at Fonthill, Wiltshire, September 29, 1760, the only child of Sir William Beckford, member of Parliament and twice Lord Mayor of London, and Maria Beckford, formerly Marsh, née Hamilton. Educated at home privately; received lessons in drawing and architecture from eminent tutors and piano lessons from Wolfgang Amadeus Mozart. Inherited significant fortune upon the death of his father, 1770. Traveled to Geneva and Italy to complete his education, 1777–78; toured England and met Viscount William Courtenay, 1779. Undertook grand tour of France, Germany, Holland, and Italy, 1780–82 (Forced to leave England for Germany and Italy due to scandal over relationship with a cousin's wife, 1782?). Married Lady Margaret Gordon, daughter of the Earl of Aboyne, 1783; they had two daughters. Member of Parliament representing Wells, Somerset, 1784–90. Went to Switzerland to escape scandal over relationship with William Courtenay, 1785; Margaret Beckford died during childbirth, 1786. Lived in Portugal, Spain, France, and Switzerland, 1787–93, alternating residence between Paris and family home at Fonthill 1789–93. Member of Parliament representing Hindon, Wiltshire, 1790–94. Returned to Lisbon, 1793–96. Supervised construction of Fonthill Abbey, 1799–1822. Independently attempted to negotiate a peace treaty between Britain and France, 1797–98. Returned to Portugal, 1798. Entertained Nelson and Sir William and Lady Emma Hamilton at Fonthill, December 1800. Traveled to France and Switzerland, 1801–2. Reelected as member of Parliament for Hindon, 1806–20. Sold Fonthill Abbey and moved to Lansdowne Crescent, Bath, 1822; built Lansdowne Tower. Died of influenza in Bath, May 2, 1844.

Selected Works

The Long Story, 1777. Published 1930 as *The Vision*.
Biographical Memoirs of Extraordinary Painters. 1780.
Dreams, Waking Thoughts and Incidents. 1783 (suppressed).
Vathek. 1786, 1787.
Modern Novel Writing, or the Elegant Enthusiast. 1796.
Azemia: A Descriptive and Sentimental Novel. 1797.
Italy; With Sketches of Spain and Portugal. 1834.
Recollections of an Excursion to the Monasteries of Alcobaça and Batalha. 1835.

Bibliography

Alexander, Boyd. *England's Wealthiest Son*. London: Centaur Press, 1962.
Brockman, H. A. N. *The Caliph of Fonthill*. London: Werner Laurie, 1956.
Chapman, Guy Patterson. *Beckford*. 2 ed. London: Rupert Hart-Davis, 1952.
Lees-Milne, James. *William Beckford*. London: Century, 1990.
Mahmoud, Fatima Moussa, ed. *William Beckford of Fonthill, 1760–1844. Bicentenary essays*. Cairo: Cairo Studies in English, 1960.
Mowl, Timothy. *William Beckford: Composing for Mozart*. London: John Murray, 1998.
Parreaux, André. *William Beckford, Auteur de "Vathek" 1760–1844: Étude de la création littéraire*. Paris, 1960.
Redding, Cyrus. *Memoirs of William Beckford, of Fonthill, author of "Vathek."* London: C. J. Skeet, 1859.
Thompson, K. F. "Henley's Share in *Vathek*," *Philological Quarterly* 31 (1952): 75–80.

BEDDOES, THOMAS LOVELL 1803–1849

English poet and playwright

Thomas Lovell Beddoes, poet, physician, and writer of neo-Elizabethan tragedy, is best known for his literary fascination with death. The uniqueness of Beddoes's vision has left him predominantly on the periphery of Romantic studies, and he is often bracketed as a minor writer, with George Darley (who describes him as "a scion worthy of the stock from which Shakespeare and Marlowe sprung"), Thomas Hood, and Winthrop Mackworth Praed.

Beddoes's career began while he was in his first year at Oxford University with a volume of Gothic verse: *The Improvisatore in Three Fyttes* (1821), that introduces the themes of love, death, evil, and innocence that would be the main concerns of his later work. The poems employ the Romantic aesthetic of effortless composition, presenting the stories as songs performed by a minstrel with lyre accompaniment. The ornate language is reminiscent of John Keats and Edmund Spenser, and in content looks back to the Graveyard Poets (a group of early-eighteenth-century poets who were inspired by graveyards and contemplated death and mortality; chief among these were Robert Blair, Thomas Gray, and Edward Young). Beddoes later dismissed the volume as juvenilia, destroying almost every copy.

Beddoes's first major work, *The Brides' Tragedy* (1822), is an accomplished Gothic verse drama, though Beddoes believed at the time that "England can hardly boast anything that deserves to be called a national stage." The play links love with death, seeing the afterlife as the site of resolution of present dilemmas. The play can be viewed in the context of the novels of Matthew Lewis and Mary Shelley, as an expression of the darker side of the Romantic imagination. Daniel Watkins notes that it "painfully articulates the loneliness, fear, and dread which haunt Romantic literature particularly after 1815." *The Brides' Tragedy*, set in an undetermined feudal dukedom, focuses on the actions of the aristocratic antihero, Hesperus, whose father, Lord Ernest, is heavily in debt to Orlando's late father, the Duke. Orlando, Hesperus's friend and rival in love for Floribel, imprisons Lord Ernest ostensibly for the debt, but covertly in order to force

Hesperus to give up Floribel and marry Orlando's sister Olivia. Hesperus concedes, but is already secretly married to Floribel, a cottager who is keenly conscious of her humble life, and who longs for their marriage to be made public. Faced with abandoning his wife for another, Hesperus courts death, madness, and melancholy. Nevertheless, Hesperus, on becoming reacquainted with Olivia, whom he has not seen since childhood, falls in love with her and marries her. Olivia, schooled for her aristocratic position, submissively accepts her new husband. Feeling guilt at his abandonment of Floribel, Hesperus is left at the mercy of his imagination, becoming a solitary and brooding figure. He tries to end his torment by killing Floribel, stabbing her on the pretext that she may have been unfaithful to him. Hesperus's slaughter of the innocent Floribel is discovered and he is sentenced to death. Confessing to Floribel's mother, Lenora, that he truly loved her, Hesperus is pitied by Lenora, who poisons him with a bunch of flowers taken from Floribel's grave. He dies moments before he is due to be beheaded. Hesperus's body is melodramatically engulfed by "infernal flames," "serpents," and "hounds," and, Faust-like, he is claimed by hell.

Acclaimed by Beddoes's friend Bryan Waller Procter (the critic and poet known as Barry Cornwall) in the *London Magazine* (February 1823) as "undoubtedly one of the most promising performances of this 'poetical age,'" *The Brides' Tragedy* was well received, and identified as belonging to the tradition of William Shakespeare, whose *Macbeth* and *Hamlet* it echoes. As with Charles Lamb, Beddoes ascribes a vast and varied imagination to Shakespeare, encompassing the very particularities of existence. Beddoes's fascination with the Gothic aspect of Shakespeare recalls the paintings of Henry Fuseli; like Fuseli, Beddoes turns away from the natural world to a Gothic landscape inspired by twisted psychology and surreal terror.

After *The Brides' Tragedy*, very little of Beddoes's work appeared in print until Thomas Forbes Kelsall's posthumous editions in 1850 and 1851. Beddoes's departure for Germany in July 1825 removed him from the British literary scene, but his correspondence with Kelsall and Procter suggests that he continued to read the work of his contemporaries. In his lively and literary letters, Beddoes dismisses and celebrates the work of many writers of his day, greatly lamenting the loss of Percy Bysshe Shelley. Beddoes's letters also give an insight into the reception of English literature in Germany, and the English understanding and appreciation of German literature and ideas. The fragmentary nature of much of Beddoes's later work, and his increasing devotion to his medical studies, made it difficult for him to establish his literary reputation. While abroad, Beddoes read widely in German literature, translated poetry and medical texts, wrote poetry in German, and, in 1831–32 contributed political pamphlets to the radical journal *Bayerisches Volksblatt*. Inspired by the ideals of the French Revolution, Beddoes joined a university-based movement, the Burschenschaft, which sought to replace the small German states with a unified state governed by a constitutional monarch. Beddoes opposed censorship laws, and was a vigorous supporter of constitutional rights as well as education and freedom of the people.

Of the work that remained unpublished in his lifetime, the tragedy *Death's Jest-Book* (1850) is widely thought to be Beddoes's masterpiece. Begun in the 1820s and based on an unsubstantiated story that the Duke of Münsterberg was killed by his court fool in 1377, the play is complex. Isbrand, the fool and antihero, avenges the deaths of his father and brother by usurping the dukedom of their murderer. Isbrand rules tyrannically and is assassinated by Mario, a revolutionary. Much of the action is given over to necromancy and raising ghosts. Mandrake, a "zany" (jester or clown), persuaded to believe himself a ghost, muses on the lack of distinction between life and death. Isbrand mocks the "jester," death—"Let death wear the cap, let him toll the bells: he shall be our new court fool"—but death is no mere fool. Death mocks man's ambitious spirit, and the world is thus "death's jest-book." Regarded by its author as a "Gothic-styled tragedy," the play depicts a nihilistic world of shifting values in which characters switch allegiances and seemingly act arbitrarily. Mary Shelley, in a letter to Kelsall, describes *Frankenstein* (1818) as a "hideous progeny"; *Death's Jest-Book* is a similarly "gothic body," its "limbs being scattered and unconnected." Remaining unfinished, the play is dramatically not as tight as *The Brides' Tragedy*, but it is more ambitious. Beddoes's Romantic irony, derived from his reading of Ludwig Tieck, is exhibited in the play's mannered incongruity and antirealism. Beddoes calls the play his "sisyphean stone," and his frustration with it may have contributed to his suicide.

As a poet he is best remembered as the writer of the lyric "Dream Pedlary," and for "Pygmalion. The Cyprian Statuary," which has attracted critical attention because of its Romantic recasting of Pygmalion as a brooding solitary genius who attempts to dissolve the boundaries of life and art. The poem is a deliberate reworking of Jean-Jacques Rousseau's *Pygmalion* (1762).

Beddoes remains on the fringes of British Romanticism probably because of his unique interests and self-imposed exile in Germany for much of his writing career. Proclaimed by Lytton Strachey as "the last Elizabethan," Beddoes was admired by a range of poets. A collection of Beddoes's manuscripts was bequeathed to Robert Browning, and it is clear that Browning's interest in the grotesque was influenced by Beddoes. Browning writes in a letter to Kelsall that "the power of the man is immense and irresistible," and W. H. Auden, in his "Academic Graffiti" (1971), devote a clerihew to him: "Thomas Lovell Beddoes / Could never walk through meadows / Without getting the glooms / And thinking of tombs."

ESSAKA JOSHUA

Biography

Born in Clifton, Somerset (now in Bristol), June 30, 1803, son of the eminent scientist Thomas Beddoes (1780–1808) and nephew of the novelist Maria Edgeworth (1767–1849). Educated at Bath Grammar School, 1814–17, and at Charterhouse 1817–20; awarded prizes there for Latin and Greek composition. Studied at Pembroke College, Oxford University, 1820–25. Studied anatomy and medicine at the University of Göttingen, 1825–29; expelled from the university after a drunken incident. Worked on his poem *Death's Jest-Book: or, The Fool's Tragedy* (published posthumously, 1850). Studied Medicine at the University of Würzburg, 1829–31; received his M.D. Expelled from Würzburg and Bavaria for political activism, 1832. Attended the University of Zürich, 1833–37 and 1839–40. Fled from Switzerland, 1840; studied at the University of Berlin, 1840–42. Remained in Europe, returning to England briefly in 1846–47. Committed suicide, by poison, in Basel, Switzerland, January 26, 1849.

Selected Works

The Improvisatore in Three Fyttes, with Other Poems. 1821.
The Brides' Tragedy. 1822.
Death's Jest-Book: or the Fool's Tragedy. Edited by Thomas Forbes Kelsall. 1850.
The Poems, Posthumous and Collected, of Thomas Lovell Beddoes. Edited by Thomas Forbes Kelsall. 1851.

Bibliography

Donner, Henry Wolfgang. *Thomas Lovell Beddoes: The Making of a Poet.* Oxford: Basil Blackwell, 1935.
———, ed. *The Browning Box; Or the Life and Works of Thomas Lovell Beddoes as Reflected in Letters by his Friends and Admirers.* London: Oxford University Press, 1935.
———, ed. *The Works of Thomas Lovell Beddoes.* London: Oxford University Press, 1935.
Gosse, Edmund, ed. *The Letters of Thomas Lovell Beddoes.* London: Elkin Mathews and John Lane, 1894.
Gregory, Horace. "The Gothic Imagination and the Survival of Thomas Lovell Beddoes." In *The Dying Gladiator and Other Essays* (New York: Greenwood Press, 1968), 81–95.
Higgens, Judith and Michael Bradshaw, eds. *Thomas Lovell Beddoes: Selected Poetry.* Manchester: Carcanet, 1999.
Hoyt, Charles Alva. "Theme and Imagery in the Poetry of T. L. Beddoes," *Studia Neophilologica* 35 (1963): 85–103.
Thompson, James R. *Thomas Lovell Beddoes.* Boston: Twayne, 1985.
Watkins, Daniel P. "Thomas Lovell Beddoes' *The Brides' Tragedy* and the Situation of Romantic Drama," *Studies in English Literature 1500–1900* 29 (1989): 699–712.

BEETHOVEN, LUDWIG VAN 1770–1827

German composer

Ludwig van Beethoven, regarded by E. T. A. Hoffmann as a "purely romantic" composer, is paradoxically also a purely classical one. This contradiction is not simply a terminological confusion in music history where the term *Romanticism* appears somewhat belatedly, almost at the point of Beethoven's death in 1827; rather, it stems from the desire of Romanticism itself to formulate its own canon. Beethoven's classical status was conferred retrospectively as that of a Romantic icon, a modern classic. Indeed, after his death, Beethoven became a mythic figure, one immortalized by his music as the tragic genius and Romantic hero who summons composers into the pantheon of great masters. For many in the nineteenth century, his music stood as the monument of a new musical era to which they paid homage, both as a model to be emulated and as a spur for music's future. The symphony, in particular, lived under Beethoven's shadow; composers, including Johannes Brahms, Anton Bruckner, and Antonin Dvorák, felt compelled to allude to Beethoven's achievements in this genre as their point of departure; even Richard Wagner, who regarded the symphony as a compositional dead end, used Beethoven's Ninth Symphony with its choral finale to justify his advance into music drama.

Traditionally, Beethoven's life and works have been partitioned into three periods: early, middle, and late. Although such divisions tend to generalize the distinctiveness of Beethoven's oeuvre, they also underline significant biographical, political, and aesthetic changes that came in his lifetime. The early period is one of apprenticeship, or, in the words of Count Waldstein in an album to commemorate Beethoven's journey in 1792 from Bonn to Vienna, to "receive from the hands of Haydn the spirit of Mozart." Whatever misgivings Beethoven may have had about his sporadic counterpoint lessons with Franz Joseph Haydn, he seemed to have absorbed from his teacher two techniques of composition that were critical to his progress: first, the technique of motivic development, where tiny elements are constantly in a state of "becoming" as they change and combine with other ideas in shaping the form; and second, the ability to harness the tonal system to create large structures out of bold, and often dissonant, harmonic maneuvers in order to dramatize the conflict and resolution inherent in sonata form procedures. Both techniques, which require the synthesis of contrasting materials—motif to form or dissonant to tonic harmony—have been equated by scholars such as Theodor Adorno with the Hegelian dialectic, although the overtly philosophical ideas expressed in Beethoven's music stem from his rudimentary knowledge of Immanuel Kant and Johann Christoph Friedrich von Schiller.

Beethoven did not merely glean from Haydn a motivic and formal technique; he also adopted an aesthetic disposition. What hovers over the self-conscious manipulation of the material is a wit that plays with the illusion of art by thwarting the listener's expectations and revealing the music's construction; the music wears that wry and distant smile of romantic irony. In the opening movement of the Piano Sonata op. 10, no. 2 (1796–97), for example, Beethoven detaches the cadence at the end of the exposition, and manipulates this cliché of closure to contradict itself as a process of development, only to close that section with an illusion of closure—a false recapitulation. He also shares with Haydn an appetite for endless experimentation, perhaps in order to outwit his teacher; conventions are often reconfigured with striking originality, such as the unusual employment of the mediant key for the contrasting theme in the first movement of the Piano Sonata op. 31, no. 1 (1802).

The middle period is often described as the "heroic" period. Works such as the *Eroica* Symphony (1803), the Fifth Symphony (1807–8), the *Waldstein* Sonata (1803–4), the *Appassionata* Sonata (1804–5), and his opera *Fidelio* (1805, revised 1806 and 1814), capture the heroism of a revolutionary age inspired by Napoleon Bonaparte. It is apt that the *Eroica* Symphony marks the beginning of this period, for Beethoven famously dedicated the work to the first consul, only to scratch out the name when Napoleon proclaimed himself emperor. In this work Beethoven creates a revolution of his own, applying his motivic and formal technique to forge a symphony of hitherto unknown length and dissonance. Every thematic and harmonic implication seems to be consciously worked out with an inexorable logic that mirrors the psychological drama of a hero who presses ahead through danger and death to seize history as his moment of glory. Even the motivic technique enacts the hero's Bildungsroman; using the most basic musical element—the triad—

Beethoven forms the hero's identity through a struggle with the rhythmic and harmonic forces in order to create a full-fledged theme by the end of the first movement. This process of "becoming" is reinforced by the harmonic structure; Novalis's term, the *teleology of the revolution*, best describes the way in which the music masters time by exploiting each dissonant crisis to create vast trajectories that push ineluctably toward the harmonic goal. Similarly, the Fifth Symphony sets up a long journey that overcomes the ominous C-minor opening with a C-major finale of revolutionary victory; indeed, French audiences heard this moment as their own revolution. Yet, for Beethoven, it may also have symbolized something more personal, for the Promethean struggle that characterizes such heroic works coincides with his own struggle against deafness and his determination in his art to "seize fate by the throat," as he put it.

The Fifth Symphony is also the subject of a celebrated review by E. T. A. Hoffmann in 1810, in which he declares instrumental music to be "the most romantic of arts"; the organic structure of the symphony, which is constantly shattered by the "infinite yearning" of the sublime, is an expression of "the essence of romanticism," notes Hoffmann. This review highlights the pivotal role of Beethoven's music for early Romanticism: it confirms the Romantic vision of music as a pure language that speaks of the ineffable and gives an intimation of the absolute. What was regarded in the eighteenth century as merely an empty sign inferior to the articulations of vocal music has now become a metaphysical sign, pregnant with the meanings of what Hoffmann calls the "spirit realm." Beethoven establishes the content of instrumental music as a romantic utterance. Perhaps it was for this reason that he did not simply call himself a composer, but a "tone poet." His music poeticizes the world. Even a work as pictorial as the *Pastoral Symphony* (1808), with its bird calls, is, according to the composer, more about feeling than image. Part of Beethoven's power to communicate the Romantic aesthetic of "absolute music" derives from the fact that his life is a metaphor for his work: forced by his deafness to withdraw from performing his own pieces, Beethoven's music locates its meaning in the workings of the mind, as if it were deaf to the corruption of material reality; in Beethoven, music is seen to be pure, ideal, autonomous, and spiritual.

Ludwig von Beethoven. Op. 61, Violin Concerto. Reprinted courtesy of the Lebrecht Collection.

The years 1812 to 1817 were fallow years for the composer, no doubt partly as a result of the protracted and exhausting legal battles over the custody of his nephew, Carl. The crisis may have contributed to Beethoven's waning powers, but these years also witnessed a political and aesthetic transformation; the revolutionary ideals that inspired the "heroic" period had exhausted themselves and were finally muffled by the Congress of Vienna (1815). The congress itself signaled the beginning of a different Vienna, one with a less heroic but more honest, if somewhat mundane, Biedermeier taste. It is therefore ironic that it is in this declining moment of the middle period that Beethoven experienced the height of his popularity, with compositions as banal and bombastic as *Wellington's Victory* (1812). This work, which celebrates the defeat of the hero he had immortalized ten years earlier in the *Eroica*, is almost a parody of the heroic style, with its imitation of battle noises. As such, it marks the end of the heroic period, quite literally with a bang.

Perhaps the late works were forged in reaction to the facile adulation of the public, for the style that gradually emerged from these fallow years is an esoteric one. The String Quartet in F Minor, op. 95 (published 1816 but dated 1810) is the most prophetic; this work, said Beethoven, was "not to be performed in public"; its extreme contrasts and expressive contradictions give premonitions of a late style that neither panders to fashion nor courts popularity. The late works are mostly private chamber pieces; indeed, the last years of Beethoven's life were preoccupied solely with the composition of string quartets. But even public works such as the *Missa Solemnis* (1819–23) and the Ninth Symphony (1822–24), designed by Beethoven to convey universal messages to humankind, push the bounds of comprehensibility, seeming to demand a critical attention previously uncalled for. It is therefore not surprising that the late works were often denounced as the expression of a madman, and had little immediate influence on the generation after Beethoven. It was not until the late nineteenth century that these works assumed the spiritual aura they still have today.

With the *Hammerklavier* Sonata (1818) Beethoven discovers a resurgence of his creative energy. This time around, however, it is more violent and arcane; the fugue that closes the sonata is so abrasive and technically difficult that it almost damages the performer! But the music is also more lyrical; the monumental stillness of the slow movement is like an endless song that desires to communicate an inner experience. Such expressive extremes indicate that the late style is not really a single style but a questioning of the heroic music of his middle years, breaking up the organic and teleological structures with a diversity of elements that range from the arcane to the banal. Complex fugues, simple folk tunes, impassioned recitatives, and vast sonata-form structures all jostle with one another, seemingly without reason. It is true that sometimes these contrasting ideas share similar thematic material; it has even been suggested that the last five quartets revolve around two motifs. But in the late works, motifs do not necessarily stamp their identity on the piece; rather they tend to go underground, leaving a far more contingent surface that is prone to violent juxtapositions. The most extreme example of this is the String Quartet in B-flat Major, op. 130 (1825–26), which begins with a melée of dissociated fragments that contradict each other in tempo, texture, and character; the elements are held together by abstract thematic links that are hardly discernible. The tendency for oblique connections is also evident in Beethoven's renewed interest in variational forms that do not so much vary the themes as strip them down to their most abstract essence. Similarly, counterpoint is used as a hidden logic beneath the surface, as if the composer were laying bare the very basics of composition. For example, as the first movement of the E-flat Major String Quartet, op. 127 (1823–25), comes to a close, the composer peels away the ornamentation of the main melody to reveal the contrapuntal shapes that underlie the music.

These works are not merely late in Beethoven's compositional output. As with many Romantics, there is a sense that these compositions are late in history; instead of participating in the trends of their own time, they express a historical awareness that alludes to different epochs. In one quartet alone, op. 132 in A Minor (1825), Beethoven refers to the Renaissance, the baroque, the rococo, and his own revolutionary times; he even quotes one of his latest works, the Piano Sonata, op. 111 (1822), at the close of his *Diabelli Variations* (1823), as if the present were already old. In the late works, history is no longer organized teleologically; time is not seized by a heroic act to secure the future but is broken up into fragments that seem to transcend into the timeless past of a Romantic ruin.

DANIEL CHUA

See also **Hammerklavier, Das; Symphony No. 9**

Biography

Born in Bonn, December 15 or 16, 1770. Son of Johann van Beethoven, musician at the electoral court, Bonn, and Maria Magdalena van Beethoven. Studied with Christian Gottlob Neefe, court organist in Bonn; appointed assistant court organist, 1784. Stayed in Vienna, 1787; met Wolfgang Amadeus Mozart. Returned to Bonn to look after his two younger brothers after his mother's death, 1787–92. Met lifelong friend and supporter Count Waldstein; worked as music tutor in the Breuning household and also gave private music lessons. Moved to Vienna, November 1792. Father died, December 1792. Studied composition in Vienna with Johann Georg Albrechtsberger, Josef Haydn, Antonio Salieri, and Johann Schenk, 1792–1802; established a reputation as a virtuoso pianist and composer. Visited and performed in Prague, Dresden, and Berlin, 1795. First letters indicating his deafness, 1801. Relationship with Therese von Brunswick, early 1800s. Wrote the "Heiligenstadt Testament," addressed to his brothers, expressing despair over deafness (intended to be read after his death), October 1802. Established friendship and support of Count Andreas Razumovsky, c. 1805. Offered post of Kapellmeister by Jerome Bonaparte, King of Westphalia, at Cassel, 1807; refused and accepted instead an annuity from aristocratic patrons Prince Ferdinand Kinsky, Prince Josef Franz Maximilian Lobkowitz and Archduke Rudolph (son of Emperor Leopold II), on condition that he live and work in Vienna, 1809. Wrote the letter entitled "To the Immortal Beloved" (found after his death), addressed to an unknown woman, possibly Therese von Brunswick. Met Johann Wolfgang von Goethe in Teplice, 1810. Close friendship with Bettina Brentano (later von Arnim), 1810. Suffered increasing ill health and deafness from 1810. Visited his brother Johann in Linz, in an attempt to end Johann's immoral liaison with his housekeeper Therese (they married in 18??). After the death of his brother Caspar Karl, 1815, engaged in court battles with sister-in-law Johanna over custody of nine-year-old nephew Karl.

Achieved sole custody, 1820; problematic and unhappy relationship with Karl ensued, due in part to Karl's rebellious and dissolute lifestyle. (Karl attempted suicide, July 1826.) Visited Baden annually for treatment of recurring dysentery. Died of cirrhosis of the liver in Vienna, March 26, 1827.

Selected Works

Symphonies
Op. 55, *Eroica*, in E-flat. 1803.
Op. 68, *Pastoral*, in F. 1808.

Piano Concertos
Op. 15 in C. C. 1795.
Op. 37 in C. C. 1800.
Op. 73 in E-flat. 1809.

Violin Concerto
Op. 61 in D. 1808.

Piano Sonatas
Op. 10, nos. 1–3 in C, F, D (1795–98).
Op. 31, nos. 1–3 in G, D, E-flat. 1802.
Op. 53, *Waldstein*, in C. 1803–4.
Op. 57, *Appassionata*, in F. 1804–5.
Op. 106, *Hammerklavier*, in B-flat. 1817–18.
Op. 111, in C. 1821–22.

Piano Variations
Fifteen Variations and a Fugue on an Original Theme (*Eroica* Variations) in E-flat. 1802.
Thirty-three Variations on a Waltz by Diabelli, op. 120. 1819, 1822–23.

Violin Sonatas
Op. 12, nos. 1–3 in D, A, E Flat. 1797–98.
Op. 24, *Spring*, in F. 1800–1801.
Op. 47, *Kreutzer*, in A. 1802–3.

Cello Sonatas
Op. 5, nos. 1–2 in F. G. 1796.
Op. 69 in A. 1807–8.
Op. 102, nos. 1–2 in C, D. 1815.

Piano Trios
Op. 1, nos. 1–3 in E-flat, G, C. 1794–95.
Op. 70, nos. 1–2 in D, E-flat. 1808.
Op. 97, *Archduke*, in B-flat. 1810–11.

String Quartets
Op. 95, *Serioso*, in F. 1810.
Op. 127 in E-flat. 1823–25.
Op. 130 in B-flat. 1825–26.
Op. 132 in A. 1825.

Operas
Fidelio oder Die eheliche Liebe, op. 72. 1st version, 1804; 2d version, 1806; final version, 1814.
Missa Solemnis, op. 123 in D. 1812.
An die ferne Geliebte, op. 98. 1815–16.

Bibliography

Adorno, Theodor W. *Beethoven: The Philosophy of Music.* Edited by Rolf Tiedemann, translated by Edmund Jephcott. Cambridge: Polity Press, 1998.

Anderson, Emily, ed. *The Letters of Beethoven*. 3 vols. London: Macmillan, 1961.

Burnham, Scott. *Beethoven Hero*. Princeton, N.J.: Princeton University Press, 1995.

Chua, Daniel K. L. *Absolute Music and the Construction of Meaning*. Cambridge: Cambridge University Press, 1999.

Hoffmann, E. T. A. "Review of Beethoven's Fifth Symphony," *Allgemeine musikalische Zeitung* 12 (1810). Reprinted in *E. T. A. Hoffmann's Musical Writings: Kreisleriana, The Poet and the Composer, Music Criticism*. Edited by David Charlton, translated by Martyn Clarke. Cambridge: Cambridge University Press, 1989.

Kerman, Joseph, and Alan Tyson. *The New Grove Beethoven*. London: Macmillan, 1983.

Kinderman, William. *Beethoven*. Oxford: Oxford University Press, 1995.

Kinsky, Georg, and Hans Helm. *Das Werk Beethovens: Thematisch-bibliographisches Verzeichnis seiner sämtlichen vollendeten Kompositionen*. Munich: G. Henle Verlag, 1955.

Rosen, Charles. *The Classical Style*. London: Faber, 1971.

Solomon, Maynard. *Beethoven*. New York: Schirmer, 1977.

Thayer, Alexander Wheelock. *Ludwig van Beethovens Leben*. Berlin, 1866–79. Revised and edited by Elliot Forbes as *Thayer's Life of Beethoven*. Princeton, N.J.; Princeton University Press, 1970.

BEETS, NICOLAAS 1814–1903

Dutch pastor, poet, and writer

The vogue for Byronism that swept the Netherlands in the 1830s and 1840s was to be a crucial source of inspiration for the young student Beets, one of the most enthusiastic of the Lord Byron imitators in the Netherlands. Such was his veneration that he described Byron as "de zon der hedendaagse dichters, waaraan zij zich allen verwarmen" (the sun of contemporary poets, by whom they all warm themselves). This enthusiasm had already been expressed by Katharina Wilhelmina Schweickhardt, the wife of Willem Bilderdijk, who translated part of *Childe Harold* in 1819, and by Isaac da Costa, who published a Dutch version of the first act of *Cain* in 1822. The 1820s were also to see translations by Jacob van Lennep of *Marino Faliero* and *The Bride of Abydos*, as well as parts of *Don Juan* and *Manfred*. From the 1830s onward. Beets was to play a most active role in this group. He translated all the *Hebrew Melodies* into Dutch, as well as extracts from *Don Juan*. He also published a Dutch version of *Childe Harold's Pilgrimage*, which had previously been attempted by J. J. L. ten Kate and others. Beets's translated works also include passages from *Lara* and from *Beppo*, the "Sonnet to Chillon" and *The Prisoner of Chillon, Parisina, Mazeppa*, and sections from *The Lament of Tasso*.

In 1833, Beets went to Leiden to study theology. His student years coincided with his early Romantic phase, which he retrospectively dismissed as his "zwarte tijd" (black period). At this time, he wrote his first narrative poetry. His early works included *José: een Spaans verhaal* (*José, A Spanish Tale*), *Kuser*, and *Guy de Vlaming* (*Guy the Fleming*). These poems, published between 1834 and 1837, are essentially examples of the genre of ballads and romances that had come into vogue in the eighteenth century. In his protagonists, Beets had intended to create characters whose greatness was found in the self-control they exerted over their own emotions. In reality, though, the great passion they display seems empty and bombastic in comparison with their Byronic counterparts.

In 1837, Beets decided to put his Byronic period behind him. In the same year he published *Vooruitgang* (*Progress*), under the pseudonym Hildebrand in the newly established monthly literary journal *De Gids*. However, his decision to stop writing Byronic poetry did not allow him to escape ridicule in the critical journal *Braga*, to which poets such as J. J. L. ten Kate and J. Winkler Prins contributed in the period 1841–42. If anything, parody of the oversentimentality in Beets's early work reached a climax in 1856 when Piet Paaltjens, likewise a student at Leiden, published the collection of poems *Snikken en grimlachjes* (*Sobs and Snickers*).

Over the course of his studies, Beets had penned a series of miniatures in prose that primarily represented scenes from the daily life of the bourgeoisie. These he published in the work entitled *Camera obscura* (1839), again under the pseudonym Hildebrand. The title itself refers to a photographic device widely used at the time: a darkened box with a lens or aperture for projecting an external scene onto a piece of frosted glass inside the box; the scene could thus be observed as if the object were in the box itself. Hildebrand's aim, as a perceptive observer, is therefore to give a detailed and true-to-life portrayal of domestic scenes of the time. These are described with a subtle ironic humor in the tradition of Charles Dickens. Charles Lamb. and Laurence Stern. However, *Camera obscura* is not merely descriptive: it is also a highly moralistic work in which the good receive due reward while the bad meet similarly appropriate fates. The genre pieces in this collection can therefore be seen to characterize the Dutch Biedermeier. The caricatured portraits in *Camera obscura* include the bashful student Pieter Stastok in *De familie Stastok*, the cad Van der Hoogen in *De familie Kegge*, Mr. Bruis and Dr. Deluw in *Een oude kennis* (*An Old Acquaintance*), and Robertus Nurks in *Een onaangenaam mensch in den Haarlemmerhout* (*An Unpleasant Person in Harlem Wood*). The weakness of *Camera obscura* is widely considered to be the central first-person narrator (who is Hildebrand himself), a figure too obviously noble, sensible, and calm. E. J. Potgieter, the leading critic of *De Gids*, also criticized Beets for what he termed his "kopijeerlust des dagelijkschen levens" (desire to copy everyday life), taking exception to *Camera obscura* because it was critical of the bourgeois society with which Potgieter identified so entirely.

In March 1839 Beets completed his doctorate in theology (with a dissertation on Pope Pius II) and was ordained. In the next year he took up a pastorate at Heemstede, marrying Aleida van Foreest. In 1854 he became pastor at Utrecht and from 1874 to 1884 professor of ecclesiastical history at the State University of Utrecht. His career in the church was successful on two fronts. Beets was greatly appreciated by his congregation; he also published widely, producing *Lectuur van het ziekenvertrek*

(*Reading for the Sick-Room*, 1879) and composing hymns. He became a leading supporter of the ethical movement within the Reformed Church (the so-called Réveil), and contributed to the theological journal *Ernst en Vrede* (*Gravitas and Peace*), but avoided becoming embroiled in arguments regarding the different movements within the church's organization.

Among his contemporaries he was above all popular for his collections of anecdotal poetry. However, toward the end of the nineteenth century, the rather nonesoteric nature of his work again bore the brunt of critical scorn. This time it came from the *Tachtigers* (the "eighties" movement). Frederik van Eeden's poem "Grassprietjes" ("Grass Stalks," 1885) is a good example of a parody on Beets's "Korenbloemen" ("Cornflowers," 1853).

From his student period onward. Beets also contributed to discussions concerning developments in the Dutch language and the compilation of the *Woordenboek der Nederlandsche Taal* (*Dictionary of the Dutch Language*). Toward the end of his life he published *Verscheidenheden* (*Miscellanea*, 1858–74) and *Nieuwe verscheidenheden: meest op letterkundig gebied* (1885–1902); (*New Miscellanea: Chiefly in Literature*, 1858–74), although these works are not considered to have great literary merit.

ALISON E. MARTIN

Biography

Born in Haarlem, September 13, 1814. Studied theology at Leiden, 1833–39. Obtained doctorate in theology, 1839. Pastorate at Heemstede, 1840–53. Pastorate at Utrecht, 1854–74. Professor of ecclesiastical history at the State University of Utrecht, 1874–84. Died in Utrecht, March 13, 1903.

Selected Works

Fiction

Hildebrand (pseu.). *Camera obscura*. 1839.
Verpoozingen op letterkundig gebied. 1856.
Verscheidenheden meest op letterkundig gebied. 1858–74.
Gesprek met Vondel. 1861.
De Reizangen in Vondels treurspellen benevens andere opstellen. 1871.
Nieuwe verscheidenheden: meest op letterkundig gebied. 1885–1902.
Na vijftig jaar. Noodige en overbodige opheldering. Van de Camera obscura door Hildebrand. 1887.
Beets, Nicolaas, Willem van den Berg, Henk Eiyssens, Joost Klock, and Peter van Zonnevel. *Camera Obscura*. Amsterdam: Athenaeum; Polak and Van Gennep, 1998.

Poetry

Gedichten. 1844.
Verstrooide gedichten uit vroeger en later tijd 1831–1861. 1863.
Madelieven. 1870.

Ecclesiastical Works

Dissertatio de Aeneae Sylvii, qui postea Pius papa secundus, morum mentisque mutationis rationibus. 1839.
De christen by en op het ziekbed. 1846.
De herstelde kranke. 1847.
Beets, Nicolaas and Gustav Doré. *Bijbel bevattende al de canonieke boeken van het Oude en Nieuwe Testament volgens de Statenoverzetting*. 1868.

Biographical Work

Everhardus Johannes Potgieter: persoonlijke herinneringen. 1892.

Translations

Gedichten. 3 vols.: *Navolgingen van Lord Byron. De gevangene van Chillon. Mazeppa. Parisina. Fragmenten. Joodsche gezangen. Verscheiden gedichten* (vol. 2). 1848.

Bibliography

Dyserinck, Johannes. *Dr. Nicolaas Beets*. Haarlem: Bohn, 1903.
Rijn, G Van. *Nicolaas Beets*. Rotterdam: J. M. Bredée, 1911–16.

BELINSKII, VISSARION GRIGORIEVICH 1811–1848

Russian critic

The early years of Vissarion Grigorievich Belinskii's brief career coincided with the period when German Romantic and idealist thought came to exert an overwhelming influence on Russian intellectual life. Belinskii had little knowledge of foreign languages, but was part of a philosophical circle that had formed at the beginning of the 1830s under the inspiration of Nikolai Stankevich, and which numbered among its members Aleksandr Herzen and Mikhail Bakunin. Largely through this circle, Belinskii became acquainted with the ideas of Johann Gottlieb Fichte, G. W. F. Hegel, Friedrich Wilhelm Joseph von Schelling, and Johann Christoph Friedrich von Schiller, with Schelling's thought predominant for Belinskii in the middle of the decade and Hegel's assuming that role for roughly the period 1837–39. A restless and ever-evolving thinker, during the following decade Belinskii looked more to Ludwig Andreas Feuerbach and the French utopian socialists, although traces of his earlier outlook can still be discerned in his later writings as well.

Highly prolific, quick to absorb and apply the leading ideas in European thought, and possessing a knack for discussing the rapidly maturing Russian literary scene against the background of broad social and intellectual trends, Belinskii wielded an enormous influence on his contemporaries and on subsequent generations, through his more philosophical writings and through his practical criticism, which helped enshrine Aleksandr Pushkin and Nikolai Gogol as the great initiators of the nineteenth-century Russian literary tradition. Belinskii's unusually accurate ability to discern literary talent also enabled him to help bring early prominence to both Ivan Turgenev and Fyodor Dostoevsky, even though he did not live to see the novels that ensured their enduring fame. Indeed, it is hardly an exaggeration to say that Belinskii's opinions were to shape the appreciation of Russian literature into the twentieth century: his disinterest in neoclassical Russian writers of the eighteenth century as well as his aversion to what he saw as largely escapist literature helped push certain writers into the shadows, even as he helped secure Mikhail Lermontov's place as Pushkin's successor or, despite reservations, gave an early boost to the career of Ivan Goncharov.

Nearly all the concepts that shape his understanding and analysis of literature derive from German philosophy. In a series of ten articles that appeared under the collective title *Literaturnye mechtaniya* (*Literary Reveries*, 1834), Belinskii already expresses an organic view of art, in which the individual work serves as a microcosm of the larger world; the greater the artist, the closer the work will come to portraying the single, eternal "idea" that embraces the whole world. Early in these articles Belinskii makes the startling claim that Russia has no literature; his point is that a genuine literature must (as Russian literature did not) express the spirit of the people and depict their inner life—a notion that similarly has its origins in German idealism.

If the influences of Johann Gottfried von Herder, Schiller, and, most directly, Schelling, pervade the first writings of Belinskii, it was, as Victor Terras has shown, Hegel who was to make the most profound and lasting contribution to Belinskii's thought. In several reviews from the late 1830s through the early 1840s, Belinskii's Hegelianism appears in his insistence on a realistic and objective art, in a wholehearted embrace of historicism (and thus for a while his acceptance of the current Russian political and social situation as a "necessary" stage in the country's development), and a dislike of any art that seems to reproduce nature too directly without the assistance of an organic idea. Typical in this regard is Belinskii's review of *Hamlet* (1838), which both expresses his "organic" notion that the play's greatness results from the fullness with which it serves as a replica of the world, as well as the Hegelian notion that Hamlet's struggle involves a reconciliation with the real: he must pass from his naive idealism, through an inner disharmony caused by the struggle between reality and his ideal, to the point of accepting the world as it really exists. Similarly, in his review of Mikhail Lermontov's novel *A Hero of Our Time* (1840), Belinskii emphasizes the work's reflection of the universal; the appearance of disharmony if anything makes the work stronger, he claims, for in illustrating how harmony eventually results from struggle the novel in fact illustrates a universal law of life. The novel's hero Pechorin, much like Hamlet, is a person in need of becoming reconciled with reality. Pechorin's state, according to Belinskii, is understandable because it reflects the present situation in Russian society, and thus Lermontov's protagonist is indeed a "hero of our time." Belinskii often distinguishes between a work's historical and absolute artistic merit; thus, while admitting that Pushkin's *Eugene Onegin* (1823–31) is without doubt the greater artistic creation, he also holds that the Lermontov novel is a more valuable work for the present day.

As a corollary of the emphasis on art's need to reflect what is typical and real, Belinskii rejects any form of romantic escapism, of the irrational or fantastic, or of the abnormal. Hence, he has little appreciation for the trend in Romanticism that explored the supernatural or states of madness. This outlook explains his praise for Dostoevsky's first novel *Poor People* (1845), which depicts a downtrodden clerk, while he would criticize his later *The Double* (1846), despite admiring its artistry, for its focus on an insane protagonist.

Some of Belinskii's most important writings were devoted to Gogol and Pushkin. He followed Gogol's career closely, and there are key articles devoted to him from all of Belinskii's periods. In the early *O russkoy povesti i povestyakh g. Gogolya* (*On the Russian Story and the Stories of Gogol*, 1835), Belinskii confronts the stories' concentration on ordinary reality, which provided a challenge to the idealism that he had just been advocating in his *Literary Reveries*. By 1842, when Belinskii wrote his review

of Gogol's 1842 novel *Dead Souls*, he had moved beyond the notion of reconciliation with the existing reality, and now praised this work for its "subjectivity," its attack on the existing order, and thus its creator's willingness to affect developments in society, a goal elucidated by the French utopian socialists, who thus see the artist as not merely describing the world but as seeking to change it. Belinskii maintained his high view of Gogol's writings until the end, yet in his famous "Letter to N. V. Gogol" (1847) he castigated the great writer for the religious and political conservatism expressed in the latter's *Selected Passages from Correspondence with Friends* (1846). Conversely, the eleven articles on Pushkin (1843–46) all belong to a single period of Belinskii's career; here the critic attempts to define the greatness of Pushkin in his ability to reflect objectively the age in which he lived—albeit an age that has since passed.

That Hegelianism continued to pervade Belinskii's thought even in his post-Hegelian period is best evidenced by his unfinished article "Ideya iskusstva" ("The Idea of Art," 1841). Here he defines art as "the immediate contemplation of truth, or thinking in images." Art is thus a form of dialectical thinking; it has as its essence movement and development. Also expressed in this article are the notions that there are inner laws that bind together and determine the development of phenomena, and that the concrete work of art reflects a particular moment in history and represents a specific representation of the universal. Thus, at this central point in his career he defines art as revealing the truth; the artist, as the person who creates the specific work that embraces the universal, therefore holds a special place in society—a place that the Russian writer was to continue to hold for many generations to come.

BARRY P. SCHERR

Biography

Born in Sveaborg, Finland, May 30, (June 11), 1811, the son of a doctor. Educated at local school in Chembar, Penza, and gymnasium in Penza from 1825. Attended the University of Moscow, 1829–32; expelled, mainly for writing against serfdom without receiving a degree. Worked for the journal *Teleskop*, 1833–36, until it was closed for publishing Chaadaev's "Philosophical Letter." Editor of *Moskovskii nabluidatel'*, 1838–39. Moved to Saint Petersburg, 1839; appointed as literary critic of *Otechestvennye zapiski*, 1839–46, and then of *Sovremennik*, 1847–38. Married Mariia Vasil'evna Orlova, 1843: they had one son (died 1847) and one daughter. Suffered from consumption: traveled abroad for treatment, 1847. Died of tuberculosis in Saint Petersburg, May 26 (June 7), 1848.

Selected Works

Collections
Polnoe sobranie sochineniy [*Complete Collected Works*]. 13 vols. 1953–59.
Selected Philosophical Works. 1956.

Essays
Literaturnye mechtaniya, 1834; as *Literary Reveries*. In *Selected Philosophical Works*, Moscow: Foreign Languages Publishing House, 1956.
O russkoy povesti i povestyakh g. Gogolya [*On the Russian Story and the Stories of Gogol*], 1835. First part only translated by Lauren G. Leighton. In *Russian Romantic Criticism* as *On the Russian Prose Tale*. Westport, Conn.: Greenwood Press, 1987.

Ideya iskusstva, 1841. Revised translation by James P. Scanlan in *Russian Philosophy* as *The Idea of Art*. New York: Quadrangle Books, 1965.

Sochineniya Aleksandra Pushkina, 1843–46. Articles 8 and 9 as *Articles on the Works of Alexander Pushkin*. In *Selected Philosophical Works*, Moscow: Foreign Languages Publishing House, 1956.

Mysli i zametki o russkoy literature, 1846. Rev. transl. by Ralph E. Matlaw as *Thoughts and Notes on Russian Literature*. In *Belinsky, Chernyshevsky, and Dobrolyubor*. New York: Dutton, 1962.

Pis'mo k N.V. Gogolyu, 1847; translated by W. J. Leatherbarrow and D. C. Offord. In *A Documentary History of Russian Thought* as Letter to N. V. Gogol. Ann Arbor, Mich.: Ardis, 1987.

Vzglyad na russkuyu literaturu 1847 goda, 1848; translated as *A Survey of Russian Literature in 1847*, 1956; revised translation of part 2 by Ralph E. Matlaw, in *Belinsky, Chernyshevsky, and Dobrolyubor*. New York: Dutton, 1962.

Bibliography

Annenkov, Pavel. *The Extraordinary Decade: Literary Memoirs.* Translated by Irwin R. Titunik. Ann Arbor: University of Michigan Press, 1968.

Bowman, Herbert E. *Vissarion Belinski 1811–1848: A Study in the Origins of Social Criticism in Russia.* Cambridge, Mass.: Harvard University Press, 1954.

Masaryk, Thomas G. *The Spirit of Russia: Studies in History, Literature and Philosophy.* Vol. 1, 2d ed. Translated by Eden and Cedar Paul. New York: Macmillan, 1955.

Proctor, Thelwall. *Dostoevskij and the Belinskij School of Literary Criticism.* The Hague: Mouton, 1969.

Stacy, Robert H. *Russian Literary Criticism: A Short History.* Syracuse: Syracuse University Press, 1974.

Terras, Victor. *Belinskij and Russian Literary Criticism: The Heritage of Organic Aesthtics.* Madison: University of Wiscosnin Press, 1974.

Walicki, Andrzej. *A History of Russian Thought: From the Enlightenment to Marxism.* Stanford, Calif.: Stanford University Press, 1979.

Wellek, René. *A History of Modern Criticism, 1750–1950.* Vol. 3. New Haven, Conn.: Yale University Press, 1965.

Zenkovskii, Vasilii. *A History of Russian Philosophy.* Translated by George L. Kline. New York: Columbia University Press, 1953.

BELLINI, VINCENZO 1801–1835

Italian opera composer

Vincenzo Bellini chose to write primarily in one medium, the lyric theater, paralleling his contemporaries Gaetano Donizetti, a rival composer who also concentrated on opera, and Frédéric Chopin, the pianist-composer who focused almost exclusively on piano compositions. Bellini's reputation as a composer rests on the ten operas composed between his first student work of 1825 and his tragically premature death in 1835, most probably of amoebic dysentery, which was incurable at that time. Bellini's life story lends itself to a highly Romantic interpretation. Described by Heinrich Heine as a "sigh in dancing pumps," Bellini was tall, fair-haired, and blue-eyed, and considered by some to be a dandy. According to sensational contemporary reports, he engaged in a great many romantic involvements. The knowledge of this, added to his early death, tended to create an image of the tragic, beautiful but flawed, Romantic artist, one image that persisted well into the twentieth century.

Bellini's stature as an opera composer was affirmed by the enthusiastic popular response to his opera during his lifetime. After a period of neglect in the early twentieth century, his works have returned to the operatic repertoire, partly in response to bravura performances by great bel canto singers such as sopranos Maria Callas and Joan Sutherland. Bellini is now generally recognized as one of the greatest of nineteenth-century bel canto opera composers, alongside Donizetti and Gioachino Antonio Rossini.

Bellini was born into a musical family and given early piano instruction by his father. After age seven his musical education was in the hands of his grandfather, Vincenzo Tobia Bellini. During this time he wrote sacred music and ariettas, many of which were performed in the churches and aristocratic homes of Catania. By 1819 Bellini had exhausted local musical re-

sources, and with financial support from the municipal government of Catania he began advanced studies at Real Conservatorio di Musica in Naples. From 1819 to 1826 Bellini studied with Carlo Conti, Giovanni Furno, Giacomo Tritto, and the director of the conservatory, Nicola Zingarelli. His graduation piece was *Adelson e Salvini*, an opera performed at the conservatory in 1825. This work's success led to a commission from the Teatro San Carlo for the opera *Bianca e Gernando*, first performed in 1826.

Bellini spent the years between 1827 and 1833 mostly in Milan. His third opera, *Il pirata* (The Pirate, 1827), was performed at La Scala and established him as an opera composer. This opera was his first collaboration with librettist Felice Romani, who wrote the libretti for all of Bellini's subsequent opera except his last, *I Puritant* (The Puritans, 1833). *Il pirata* also signaled the beginning of Bellini's long, productive relationship with the tenor Giovanni Battista Rubini, who was already known for his interpretations of Rossini's opera. Other opera written during the Milan years include *La straniera* (The Stranger) and *Zaira* (both 1829); *I Capuleti e i Montecchi* (1830); *La sonnambula* (The Sleepwalker) and *Norma* (1831); and *Beatrice de Tenda* (1833). Of the opera written during this period, *Zaira* and *Beatrice de Tenda* were failures. However, *La sonnambula* was extremely well received, and *Norma*, though described by Bellini as a "total disaster" after the opening performance, was soon thereafter recognized as a masterpiece.

Bellini's personal life during these years was somewhat turbulent, owing to his passionate love affair with Giuditta Cantù, wife of merchant Ferdinando Turina, and a severe illness in 1830 from which he spent the entire summer recovering.

However, these difficulties were overshadowed by Bellini's growing success both in Italy and around Europe. In 1828 *Il pirata* was staged in Vienna, thus beginning Bellini's international reputation. Following Rossini's 1829 decision to cease writing opera, Bellini's place as an opera composer grew ever more secure.

Beginning in 1833 Bellini traveled abroad to prepare performances of his works in London. His close friend and favorite soprano Giuditta Pasta appeared in *Il pirata, Norma*, and *I Capuleti e i Montecchi*, and the great Maria Malibran was featured in *La sonnambula*. In August of 1833 Bellini went to Paris, hoping to arrange performances of his operas at the Paris Opéra or Opéra-Comique. These discussions never came to a satisfactory conclusion, but Bellini was able to get performances at the Théâtre-Italien for *Il pirata* and *I Capuleti e i Montecchi*. While in Paris, Bellini became friends with Rossini, and met Chopin and the great German poet and arbiter of the Romantic movement, Heinrich Heine. In 1834 he began composing *I puritani* to a libretto by Count Carlo Pepoli. (A second version composed for Naples was not used.) When in 1835 *La sonnambula* was performed to great acclaim, and the premiere of *I puritani* was a triumph, Bellini felt that he had reached a high point in his career. He began to contemplate new projects and again tried to have his operas staged at the Paris Opéra or the Opéra-Comique; unfortunately, none of these plans materialized because of his illness and subsequent death.

Bellini was profoundly influenced by Rossini, especially by a performance of *Semiramide* that he heard in 1824. He also absorbed characteristics of Sicilian and Neopolitan folk music. Yet, his music has a strong individual stamp apparent in his sensitive text setting. His work is characterized by the lyricism and melodic shapes that so impressed Giuseppe Verdi, his novel placement of the melodic climax of an aria toward the end of the piece, frequent shifts between major and minor harmonies, and striking modulations. Although the Romantic era viewed Bellini's gift for delicate, melancholy expression as his most representative voice, he is also capable of genuine drama and passion, which partially explains why his work has gone in and out of style. His music demands singers capable of breadth of expression in order to be successful on stage. With recent studies of his life and works in print and a discography of superb opera performances easily available, Bellini's importance in opera history is clearer than ever and his reputation appears assured.

ANN SEARS

See also **Chopin, Frédéric; Donizetti, Gaetano; Opera; Rossinim, Gioacchino Antonio, Verdi, Giuseppe**

Biography

Born in Catania, Sicily, November 3, 1801, into a family of musicians. Studied music initially with his father, an organist, and later with his grandfather, Vincenzo Tobia Bellini, organist and composer. Awarded a scholarship from the Decurionato (city council) of Catania to attend the Real Conservatorio di Musica (Collegio San Sebastiano), Naples, under Nicola Zingarelli, 1819–26. After the first performance of his *Adelson e Salvina*, 1825, gained patronage of the impresario Barbaia, manager of La Scala in Milan and the Teatro San Carlo in Naples. Lived and composed in Milan, 1827–33. Achieved first operatic success, *Il Pirata*, at La Scala, 1827. Began a love affair with a married woman, Giuditta Turina, after meeting her at the house of the Milanese singer Giuditta Pasta, 1828. Stayed in Venice while his sixth opera *I Capuletti ed i Montecchi* was performed at La Fenice, 1830. Suffered from dysentery in Venice; returned to recuperate in Milan and by Lake Como, 1831. Visited Milan with Giuditta Turina, 1832. Ended the affair after she left her husband, 1833. Lived in London, April to August 1833; met Countess Granville, who established professional connections for him in Paris. Moved to Paris, August 1833; with Rossini's influence, won commission to write an opera for the Théâtre-Italien, *Il Puritani di Scozia*, performed in January 1835. Died of dysentery and a liver abscess while visiting English friends in Puteaux, near Paris, September 23, 1835.

Selected Works

Il pirata. 1827.
La straniera. 1829.
I Capuletti e i Montecchi. 1830.
La sonnambula. 1831.
Norma. 1831.
I puritani. 1835.

Bibiography

Balthazar, Scott Leslie. "Evolving Conventions in Italian Serious Opera: Scene Structure in the Works of Rossini, Bellini, Donizetti, and Verdi, 1810–1850." Ph.D. diss. University of Pennsylvania, 1985.

Brauner, Charles S. "Textual Problems in Bellini's Norma and Beatrice di Tenda," *Journal of the American Musicological Society* 29 (1976): 99–118.

Cheskin, Jonathan. "Catholic-Liberal Opera: Outline of a Hidden Italian Musical Romanticism: Rossini, Bellini, Donizetti, Verdi." Ph.D. diss. University of Chicago, 1999.

Greenspan, Charlotte. "The Operas of Vincenzo Bellini." Ph.D. diss. University of California, Berkeley, 1977.

Kimball, David. *Vincenzo Bellini: Norma.* Cambridge Opera Handbooks. Cambridge: Cambridge University Press, 1998.

Maguire, Simon. *Vincenzo Bellini and the Aesthetics of Early Nineteenth-Century Italian Opera.* New York: Garland, 1989.

Orrey, Leslie. *Bellini.* New York: Farrar, Straus and Giroux, 1969.

Osborne, Charles. *The Bel Canto Operas of Rossini, Donizetti, and Bellini.* Portland, Ore.: Amadeus Press, 1994.

Rosselli, John. *The Life of Bellini.* Cambridge: Cambridge University Press, 1996.

Weinstock, Herbert. *Vincenzo Bellini: His Life and His Operas.* New York: Alfred A. Knopf, 1971.

Willier, Stephen A. "Madness, the Gothic, and Bellini's Il Pirata," *Opera Quarterly* 6 (1989): 7–23.

BENTHAM, JEREMY 1748–1832

British philosopher, jurist, and reformer

Jeremy Bentham's long intellectual career spanned the English Romantic period, exerting a powerful influence upon nineteenth-century politics, philosophy, and jurisprudence. Yet he has often been treated as the defining antitype of the Romantic sensibility, a coldhearted, philistine rationalist who once blithely declared that "the game of push-pin is of equal value with the arts and sciences of music and poetry." There is much that is unfair in such characterizations, for although Bentham's personal idiosyncrasies and visionary tendencies have always left him vulnerable to ridicule and opprobrium, he was in many respects a quite unselfish and even humane thinker. It remains clear, however, that Bentham could never be described as a *Romantic*, even allowing for the traditional imprecision of that term. His cosmopolitan ideals and resolute commitment to unfettered rational enquiry mark him out far more readily as a distinctive product of the eighteenth-century Enlightenment.

It is hardly surprising that Bentham was unhappy at Oxford University: he was only twelve years old when he arrived there. But he was equally disillusioned by his subsequent, short-lived experience in the legal profession. His first publication, *A Fragment on Government* (1776), was a devastating critique of the incompetence, obscurity, and corruption of the English legal system, along with its most celebrated eighteenth-century expositor, Sir William Blackstone. The *Fragment* proved something of a success, and brought its author to the attention of the Earl of Shelburne. It was at Shelburne's Bowood home that Bentham wrote the *Introduction to the Principles of Morals and Legislation* (1781), which remains arguably his single most important work. Bentham had already formulated, in the *Fragment*, the basic premise of utilitarian ethics, namely that "it is the greatest happiness of the greatest number that is the measure of right and wrong." In the *Principles* he went on to explore the means by which such an end could be pursued. "Nature has placed mankind under the governance of two sovereign masters, *pain* and *pleasure*," he wrote in the powerful first sentences of this work. "It is for them alone to point out what we ought to do, as well as to determine what we shall do." The pursuit of pleasure, and the avoidance of pain, thus became both a descriptive, psychological fact of human nature, and a moral imperative around which the wise legislator might construct an ideal body of laws.

In the mid-1780s Bentham spent two years in Russia with his brother Samuel. It was here that he composed his *Panopticon; or, the Inspection House* (1791). This novel architectural design for an ideal prison was intended to maximize both the visibility of the prisoner and the transparency of penal institutions to public inspection. In 1797–98, Bentham recommended a national reform of the English poor laws and the construction of workhouses on the panopticon model. His proposals were extremely ambitious, but seemed destined to remain unrealized. Bentham's disappointment was compounded by the government's decision to reject his proposals for a panopticon penitentiary after considering the idea for several years. However, his notorious "less eligibility" principle did eventually find embodiment in the controversial New Poor Law of 1834. The "less eligibility" principle required that the conditions of paupers supported by public relief should not be more "eligible" (attractive) than those of the independent poor. The principle was commonly associated with the harsh conditions of the Victorian workhouses. In this case, as in others, the influence of intellectual disciples such as the sanitary reformers Edwin Chadwick (one of the architects of the Poor Law Amendment Act of 1834) and Thomas Southwood Smith (a doctor and Unitarian minister) was essential to the diffusion of Bentham's ideas, particularly since his prose style showed an increasing tendency to degenerate into tortuous, mannered pedantry.

Bentham was made an honorary citizen of France by the revolutionary government (his writings on penal law and government procedure were published in French translation from the 1790s on). But he was repelled by the excesses of the French revolutionary Terror, and it was only in 1809 that he made a decisive turn to political radicalism, under the influence of James Mill. He soon attracted the attention of the radical journalist and poet Leigh Hunt, and thereafter Hunt consistently championed Bentham in his *Examiner* newspaper. The *Examiner* was also an important focus for the "second generation" of British Romantic writers, such as Percy Bysshe Shelley and William Hazlitt, who shared many of Bentham's political ideals, if not his suspicion of "fiction" and distaste for poetry and the arts. In the aftermath of the Napoleonic Wars, Bentham's "philosophic radical" party exerted a profound influence upon the middle-class reform movement, while his far-reaching *Plan of Parliamentary Reform* (1817) consolidated his standing within popular radicalism. In 1823, Bentham helped to establish the *Westminster Review*, in opposition to the established Whig and Tory reviews. He was by now convinced that a powerful and aristocratic "sinister interest," in both Parliament and the press, was working against the realization of the greatest happiness principle. But Bentham's radical commitments were also informed by a deep and abiding anticlericalism. His incautious attacks on the established church intensified during the postwar years, and represent some of the most extreme statements of secularist ideals expressed in this period.

Meanwhile, Bentham's reputation continued to grow abroad. He corresponded with politicians and heads of state in Latin America, Poland, Portugal, Russia, Spain, and the United States, offering his services as a legislative and constitutional codifier. His legislative ambitions inspired Bentham to begin work on the *Constitutional Code*, the first volume of which was published in 1827. He continued to write prolifically until his death in 1832. By this time he had inspired admirers around the world, as well as a committed group of followers in England, many of whom were to play significant roles in Victorian intellectual life. Bentham's most curious legacy, however, was the Auto-Icon, constructed from his preserved corpse (specifically, his skeleton and original clothing, upon which sit a wax head) and bequeathed to University College London. (When UCL was founded in 1826, it embodied many of Bentham's ideas on education, such as admission without regard to religious belief.) Bentham intended it to act as a permanent reminder of the Benthamite creed, and an inspiration to his successors. A bizarre, paradoxical product of quixotic idealism and uncompromising pragmatism, the Auto-Icon is perhaps a more revealing testament to his intellectual character than Bentham himself ever realized.

PHILIP CONNELL

Biography

Born in Houndsditch, London, February 15, 1748. Educated at Westminster School; studied at Oxford University, 1760–63; studied law at Lincoln's Inn, London, 1763–69; called to the bar, 1769; lived in Lincoln's Inn, 1766–92. Enjoyed patronage of Lord Shelburne (later First Marquess of Lansdowne), from c. 1780 on. Traveled to stay with his brother in Krichev, Russia, via Italy and Constantinople, 1785–87; returned to England, 1788. Published *An Introduction to the Principles of Morals and Legislation*, 1789. Made honorary citizen of France by revolutionary government, 1792. Engaged in prison reform, 1790s; proposed design for a "panopticon" penitentiary, 1797. Lived in Queen Square, Westminster, London from 1792. Influenced by the philosopher James Mill and associated with the poet Leigh Hunt, from c. 1809. Helped to found the *Westminster Review*, 1823. First volume of *Constitutional Code* published, 1827. Helped to found the nondenominational London University, 1828. Died in London, June 6, 1832.

Selected Writings

Collections
Works. 11 vols. Edited by John Bowring. 1843.
Collected Works. Edited by J. H. Burns and Fredrick Rosen. Oxford: Clarendon Press, 1968–.

Other
A Fragment on Government. 1776. Edited by J. H. Burns and H. L. A. Hart, with an introduction by Ross Harrison. Cambridge: Cambridge University Press, 1988.
An Introduction to the Principles of Morals and Legislation, 1781. Edited by J. H. Burns and H. L. A. Hart, with an introduction by F. Rosen and interpretive essay by H. L. A. Hart. Oxford; Clarendon Press, 1996.
Bentham's Theory of Fictions. Edited and with an introduction by C. K. Ogden. London: Kegan Paul, 1932.
Economic Writings. 3 vols. Edited by W. Stark. London: Allen and Unwin, 1952–54.
Bentham's Political Thought. Edited by Bhikhu Parekh. London: Croom Helm, 1973.
The Panopticon Writings. Edited with an introduction by Miran Božovoč. London: Verso, 1995.

Bibliography

Crimmins, James E. *Secular Utilitarianism: Social Science and the Critique of Religion in the Thought of Jeremy Bentham*. Oxford: Clarendon Press, 1990.
Dinwiddy, John. *Bentham*. Oxford: Oxford University Press, 1989.
Halévy, Elie. *The Growth of Philosophic Radicalism*. Translated by Mary Morris. London: Faber and Faber, 1928.
Harrison, Ross. *Bentham*. London: Routledge and Kegan Paul, 1983.
Hart, H. L. A. *Essays on Bentham: Studies on Jurisprudence and Political Theory*. Oxford: Clarendon Press, 1982.
Himmelfarb, Gertrude. "The Haunted House of Jeremy Bentham." In *Victorian Minds*. London: Weidenfield and Nicolson, 1968.
Mack, Mary P. *Jeremy Bentham: An Odyssey of Ideas 1748–1792*. London: Heinemann, 1962.
Steintrager, James. *Bentham*. London: Allen and Unwin, 1977.
Thomas, William. *The Philosophic Radicals: Nine Studies in Theory and Practice, 1817–1841*. Oxford: Clarendon Press, 1979.

BÉRANGER, PIERRE-JEAN DE 1780–1857

French poet and songwriter

Pierre-Jean de Béranger is now little more than a name, albeit one with a certain historical resonance. (He adopted the noble *de* during the Restoration, only to drop it after 1830, though by then it had stuck.) His works have long been out of print and are represented in only the most comprehensive anthologies of nineteenth-century poetry. The output of France's "national poet," as he once had the honor to be called, was not extensive, even considering the compositions he apparently destroyed, but he was without doubt the most well-known French poet of his day. One of Honoré de Balzac's characters, a bookseller, accurately states that during the Restoration there were only four poets of any consquence to the trade: Pierre-Jean de Béranger, Jean-François-Casimir Delavigne, Victor Hugo, and Alphonse Marie Louis de Lamartine.

Béranger's satirical and often scurrilous verses were not poems to be read, but songs to be sung to popular tunes that if not already known, were easily memorized. (He did not compose his own tunes but relied on established songs; those used by him from a separate volume in his *Complete Works*, 1875–76.) Although his songs were directed at the man in the street, they were also admired by such leading writers and intellectuals as

François-Auguste-René, Vicomte de Chateaubriand, Lamartine, and Stendhal, who placed him on a level with Lamartine. To Lamartine, Béranger was "the fiddler whose every pull of the bow had for its strings the hearts of thirty-six million men," while Johann Wolfgang von Goethe extolled him as the equal of Horace and Shams ud-din Muhammad Hafiz, the thirteenth-century Persian poet. In his prime, Béranger enjoyed a place at the center of Parisian literary life, but he was, above all, an influential figure in the liberal opposition to the restored Bourbon monarchy. He was also widely regarded as the key figure in the creation of the Napoleonic legend. Such was his potential as a beacon for popular dissent that his death in 1857 led Napoleon III's government to fear that his funeral would be a pretext for demonstrations by the populace.

Although the early-nineteenth-century French *chanson* is now equated almost exclusively with the songs of Béranger, the genre was by no means his invention. He was a member of Le Caveau moderne, a Parisian society of songwriters founded in the early eighteenth century and that met, since 1806, in the celebrated Rocher de Cancale restaurant in the rue Montorgueil. (His songs include tributes to such other *chansonniers* as Évariste-Desiré de

Forges de Parny and his closer contemporary, Émile Debraux.) It was from this association that Béranger derived the frank epicureanism that characterizes so much of his work. His first songs were drinking songs or compositions celebrating the pleasures apparently offered by the easygoing girls of his acquaintance, an idiom that would continue to attract both himself and his audience for the rest of his productive years. The fictional Lisette, to whom some of the songs refer, became fixed in the popular imagination.

In 1813, Béranger wrote his first political song, "Le Roi d'Yvetôt,"("The King of Yvetôt") which remained one of his best-known compositions. This imaginary king of a small town in Normandy, whose simple epicureanism was shared with the persona assumed by his creator, was a mild but clear response to the increasing self-aggrandizement of Napoleon Bonaparte. His initial response to Louis XVIII, like many other liberals with their belief in constitutional monarchy, was not notably hostile. He was ready to believe that the new king would strive to be a monarch in the popular mould of Henri IV, a figure he recalled in several of his songs. His songs from this period are either completely nonpolitical or are to be regarded as merely patriotic. (He would later claim that the love of his country had been the great and only passion of his life.) His targets were the nations of the Holy Alliance (particularly the English), the self-interested turncoats, and those who openly embraced the country's former enemies.

It was in the wake of a changing attitude on the part of other liberals that Béranger placed his pen in the service of opposition to the new regime. Even then, his venom was initially reserved for courtiers, priests (especially the influential Jesuits, but also the pope), magistrates, the police, and certain parliamentary figures (see, for example, the two songs entitled "Le Ventru" ["The Potbelly"]). Only subsequently was this directed at the monarchy itself. Despite being lampooned both for his obesity and his impotence, Louis XVIII was, by all accounts, not unappreciative of Béranger's art.

By the early 1820s Béranger had a prominent voice in a group consisting of the novelist, political theorist, and parliamentary deputy Benjamin Constant, the pamphleteer, Paul-Louis Courier, statesman Marquis Marie-Joseph-Paul de Lafayette, and Constant's fellow deputy Jacques-Antoine Manuel. Though he lacked his colleagues' intellectual capacities and was bound to them more by common targets for attack, it was an appropriate group for one who claimed to have taught himself to read from a copy of Voltaire's epic poem *La Henriade* (1723). The increasingly political content of his songs, together with their capacity to incommode a delicate notion of public decency, earned him spells of imprisonment in 1821 and 1828–29. He satirized the king's mistress, Madame du Cayla, both under her own name of Zoé and that of "Octavie" (wife of the Emperor Nero). The coronation of Charles X in 1825 was mocked in "The Coronation of Charles the Simple" (the sobriquet of Charles III, who died in Péronne in 929, the town in which Béranger had grown up), a song which was soon to be heard on the streets. Among his anticlerical poems, "Les Révérends Pères" ("Men in black, where have you sprung from?") was particularly popular. In retrospect, Béranger's satire may seem anodyne, but in the politically sensitive period in which they were written, it was not difficult for poems such as "Le Vieux Sergent" ("The Old

Pierre-Jean de Béranger. Reprinted courtesy of Bildarchiv.

Sergent") or "Le Vieux Drapeau" ("The old Flag") to become "thinly veiled incitations to rebellion." As opposition to the repressive ministerial regime increased in the closing years of the Restoration, Béranger's songs could become still more direct, as may be seen most clearly in his attack on the ruling gerontocracy, "Les Infiniment Petits" ("The Infinitely Small").

Béranger's increasing hostility toward the Bourbons (or the "Barbons" as he was apt to call them) led naturally to his reevaluation of the First Empire, and more especially to a glorification of its soldiers, who were now said to be dumbfounded by the mediocrity of the replacement regime. For a long time he was regarded as one of the founders of the Napoleonic legend, but as Jean Touchard has shown, he was relatively slow to write about the Emperor. In this, as in so much else, he followed the lead of others but through his successful formula for a popular art, he undoubtedly did much to disseminate the legendary image.

Béranger's concern with liberty also led naturally to involvement in the July Revolution, though his militancy has been exaggerated. More at home in opposition, he was unable to ally himself narrowly with any party or group. "Le Vieux Drapeau" nevertheless became the Revolution's unofficial anthem, with copies being handed out in the streets. The poet's initial assumption was that the chanson had been unseated along with Charles X, but he soon found himself revising his opinion (see "La Restauration de la chanson" ["The Restoration of the Song"]), thereby earning Stendhal's approval for not selling out to Louis-Philippe, as so many liberals had done. Béranger announced his retirement with the publication of his final collection in 1833, though he continued to write occasionally with posthumous publication in mind.

Much of the popularity of Béranger's chansons derived from the fact that they matched simple words to simple tunes. The effectiveness of the words stemmed largely from their demotic challenge to the norms of polite language. The political songs gave a new prestige to the genre and were easily admired for their boldness in taking on the powers that be, for a directness that was seen as a gauntlet laid down to the authorities. However, they were greatly dependent on the context in which they were written. Scarcely had they been composed than it became necessary to provide footnotes identifying some of the individuals and events to which allusion was being made. If they were widely enjoyed for their gaiety and for the Gallic humor with which they abounded, this could also be seen as a backward-looking form of national pride in a century that was intent on finding a modern idiom. As such, they may be regarded as the equivalent of the licentious "gay novels" of Béranger's contemporary, Charles-Antoine-Guillaume Pigault de l'Épinoy (Pigault-Lebrun). It is difficult to concur with Constant when he claimed that "Béranger had written sublime odes when he thought he was writing simple songs," or to accept Robert Louis Stevenson's view of the songs as "little chiselled toys of verbal perfection." Although it is of questionable legitimacy to read the chansons for the words alone, the ultimate impression is that Béranger's language, as even some of his contemporaries realized, comes dangerously close at times to being flat or banal.

A useful aid to an assessment of Béranger's popularity in his own times can be found in the references to him in Balzac's *Comédie Humaine* (1842–46), even if they are colored by the fact that Balzac's views placed him at the opposite end of the political spectrum. Béranger is said to have been the only effective liberal pamphleteer, precisely because he courted a mass appeal. Various Balzacian characters are given a penchant for Béranger's songs. Alongside the former Napoleonic officer Fleury (*Les Employés* [*The Clerks*, 1837–44]) and the admirable republican Michel Chrestien (*Illusions perdues* [Lost Illusions, 1837–43]) it is from the shopkeeper-commercial traveler class that Béranger is said to draw his principal admirers and on whom the influence is regarded as adverse. That said, Balzac—who knew Béranger personally—may have turned to him for the chanson sung by Lucien de Rubempré in *Illusions perdues*.

In more advanced artistic circles, Béranger's reputation was indeed associated with an irredeemably philistine (and, it might be added, male) commercial bourgeoisie. Thus, Gustave Flaubert's smug petit-bourgeois and self-styled progressive Homais proclaims, in *Madame Bovary* (1857), "My God is the God of Voltaire, the God of Béranger," thereby aligning himself with the equally self-important Crevel, who in Balzac's *La Cousine Bette* (*Cousin Bette*, 1846) declares himself to be "the admirer of Béranger, the friend of Lisette, and the child of Voltaire and Rousseau." For Charles Baudelaire, Bérenger was the incarnation of stupidity, the poet of the bourgeoisie whom he arraigned in his preface to *Le Salon de 1846* for understanding nothing of art. When his own poetry led him to be charged with obscenity, he instructed his counsel to remind the court of the licentious nature of Béranger's "Ma Grand'Mère" ("My Grandmother") and "Jeanette."

Béranger's songs were widely translated. William Makepeace Thackeray included four "imitations of Béranger" in his *Paris* *Sketch Book* (1840); it was necessary for "Le Roi d'Yvetôt," present in two separate versions, to undergo a degree of bowdlerization. Oscar Wilde was another admirer of a poet who "preferred the Pont Neuf to Parnassus." In the twentieth century Béranger was eulogized, often inappropriately, by a number of (non-French) Marxist critics.

In addition to his regular collections of songs, Béranger wrote others that may be regarded as erotica. From 1829 onward his songs inspired numerous works for the popular theater. In 1835, Hector Berlioz produced a short choral setting of "Le Cinq Mai," ("The Fifth of May") a poem Béranger had composed on the death of Napoleon in 1821. The less-than-perfect match of text and music confirms the view that the words of Béranger's songs rarely survive detachment from the simple tunes they were designed to accompany.

MICHAEL TILBY

Biography

Born Pierre-Jean Béranger in Paris, August 19, 1780. Largely self-educated. Brought up by grandmother, an innkeeper in Péronne (Somme). Active in revolutionary youth club, early 1790s. Apprenticed to printer. Worked in father's *cabinet de lecture* and did hack work for publisher while composing first songs, 1800–1809. Secured financial support from Lucien Bonaparte, 1803. Clerk at the Imperial University, Paris, 1809–21. Elected to Le Caveau moderne (club for songwriters); first political poem, 1813. First collection of songs published, 1815, followed by others in 1821, 1825, and 1828. Imprisoned for three months for offending public decency, religion, and the king's person and encouraging sedition, 1821. Sentenced to nine months in prison, on similar charges and for inciting opposition to the government, 1828. Involved in July Revolution, 1830. Published final collection of songs, 1833. Elected to Constituent Assembly, 1848; resigned shortly thereafter. Refused to accept membership in the Académie Française. Died in Paris, July 16, 1857.

Selected Works

Lyrical Poems. Selected and translated by William Anderson. 1847.
Béranger: Two Hundred of His Lyrical Poems, Done into English Verse. Translated by William Young. 1850.
Ma Biographie. Avec un appendice et un grand nombre de notes inédites de Béranger sur ses chansons. 2d ed. 1858.
Oeuvres complètes. 9 vols. 1875–76.
Correspondance de Béranger. Collected by Paul Boiteau. 4 vols. 1860.
Songs of Béranger. Translated by William Toynbee. 1886.
Pierre-Jean de Béranger. Selected and with commentary by S. Strowski. Paris: Plon-Nourrit, 1913.
Béranger et son temps. Selected and with commentary by Pierre Brochon. Paris: Les Editions sociales. 1956.

Bibliography

Brivois, Jules. *Bibliographie de l'oeuvre de P.-J. de Béranger.* Paris: L. Conquet, 1876.
Dauphin, F. and Émile Debraux. *Bréviaire du chansonnier, ou l'art de faire des chansons.* Paris: Hoquart jeune, 1830. A work dedicated to Béranger.
Dédéyan, Charles. "Balzac et Béranger," *L'Année balzacienne* (1995): 363–91.
Janin, Jules. *Béranger et son temps.* Paris: Pincebourde, 1866.

Quintus, Vera. *Karikatur als Wirkungsmittel im oppositionellen Chanson Bérangers.* Frankfurt: Peter Lang, 1983.

Stevenson, Robert Louis. "Pierre Jean de Béranger." In *Encyclopaedia Britannica*, 11th ed. 1911–12.

Touchard, Jean. *La Gloire de Béranger.* 2 vols. Paris: Armand Colin, 1968.

Wilde, Oscar. "Béranger in England," *Pall Mall Gazette*, April 21, 1886. Reprinted in *Reviews.* London: Methuen, 1908. 60–62.

BERCHET, GIOVANNI 1783–1851

Italian poet, essayist, and translator

An innovative poet and militant patriot, Berchet had been originally educated to work in his family's commercial business, receiving a thorough preparation in foreign languages, especially French, German, and English. His literary interests soon prevailing, however, he began to make contacts in the lively Milanese literary scene, publishing his first works in a period dominated by the neoclassical influence of Vittorio Alfieri, Ugo Foscolo, and Vincenzo Monti.

His knowledge of foreign languages enabled Berchet to obtain a post as a translator in the government of the French-occupied Milanese territories. At the same time, he worked at literary translation and published a version of Thomas Gray's "The Bard" as *Il bardo* (1807), in keeping with the Ossianic fashion (influenced by the "discovery" of the poems of the ancient Scottish bard Ossian, later dismissed as forgeries) much in vogue in Italy in this period, a translation that attracted Ugo Foscolo's attention. In addition, Berchet collaborated with the publisher Giuseppe Destefanis, who in 1809 started a series of modern novels. For Destefanis, Berchet translated Oliver Goldsmith's *Vicar of Wakefield* (1810) and, although the attribution is still uncertain, Johann Christoph Friedrich von Schiller's *Der Geistseher* (*The Ghost Seer*). Thanks to these first efforts and several later translations, he asserted himself as one of the major literary translators in Italian Romanticism, along with Silvio Pellico, the translator of Lord Byron's *Manfred*, and Giovita Scalvini, who produced a version of Johann Wolfgang von Goethe's *Faust*.

If Berchet's early literary activities were part of the neoclassical culture that flourished in Milan during the years of the Napoleonic occupation, his entrance into the Romantic literary scene, by contrast, corresponded with the restoration of the Austrians in Milan after the Congress of Vienna, and was closely linked with protorevolutionary movements in culture and politics. In a letter of October 30, 1816 to Ann-Louise-Germaine de Staël, Ludovico di Breme, one of the most active of the Romantic *literati*, asserted that his "faction" had recently made a new convert in Berchet, who promptly showed his allegiance by entering the polemics between classics and Romantics inaugurated by Madame de Staël's essay "Sulla maniera e l'utilità delle traduzioni" ("On the Manners and Usefulness of Translations," 1816). His major intervention in the debate was through the pseudonymous "Lettera semiseria di Grisostomo al suo figliuolo" ("Chrysostom's Half-serious Letter to his Son," 1816), published by Bernardoni in Milan, perhaps the best-known and one of the most effective assertions of Romantic poetics at the time. The "Lettera semiseria" opens with considerations on some technical points about translation, such as whether a poetic text is better rendered in verse or prose. Berchet exemplifies his views on translation by producing versions of Gottfried August Bürger's

ballads "Lenore" and "Der wilde Jäger" ("The Wild Hunter") that inspired the Italian Romantics' interest in ballads and "*romanze*." Even more importantly, the "Lettera semiseria" discusses a point till then largely unaddressed by Italian literary theory: the need for poetry to be truly "popular" and to address a specific audience—the "people"—which Berchet generally defines as the middle classes. In his analysis, if art must to be coeval with its times and not anchored to passed stereotypes, its main aim must be to discover and satisfy the interests of this broad and constantly expanding class.

Berchet's entrance into the Milanese Romantic circle effectively began with his collaboration with *Il Conciliatore* (*The Conciliator*), a periodical founded in 1818 with the support of wealthy, liberal figures such as Count Federico Confalonieri, and with the consent of the Austrian government. In his numerous contributions to this journal Berchet touched on a variety of subjects while putting in practice his own theory that the new culture must be keyed to the needs and interests of its (middle-class) public. Offering reviews and essays on a variety of national and international publications and issues, *Il Conciliatore* perfectly captures the opening up of Italian culture to contemporary European developments in the Romantic period. And Berchet's contributions are evidence of this cosmopolitanism, as he reviewed and discussed works by Friedrich Bouterwek, Pierre-Louis Ginguené, the Abbé Grégoire, William Roscoe, and Jean Charles Léonard Simonde de Sismondi, as well as the English, German, and French translations of the ancient Sanskrit play *Sakuntala* by Kalidasa. In the same period Berchet made the acquaintance of Alessandro Manzoni, becoming a member of his circle of Romantic intellectuals, but without sharing Manzoni's political cautiousness. By contrast, Berchet embraced political activism, entering the Carboneria secret society in the autumn of 1820, thus perfectly embodying the coincidence of political and cultural subversion typical of the early phases of Italian Romanticism.

After the failed revolution in Milan in 1821, Berchet went into exile to escape imprisonment. In this period he completed *I Profughi di Parga* (*The Refugees of Parga*, 1823), published first in Paris and then in London. This narrative poem evokes the terrible fate of the city of Parga, on the Ionian coast of Greece, ceded by the British to the Ottoman empire, against which the Pargiotes had long been fighting to keep their independence. The most outstanding example of Philhellenic poetry in Italian Romantic literature, the poem is both a commentary on the political climate of post-Napoleonic Europe and a coded reference to the subjugation of Italy by the Austrians after the Congress of Vienna. During his English exile, Berchet also began to compose a series of work in the "romanze" style, a poetic genre similar to the ballad, describing the political situation of Italy, the hatred for foreign oppressors, and the failure of patriotic resistance. These compositions—"Clarina," "Il Romito del Cenisio" ("The Hermit of Mount Cenis"), "Rimorso" ("Remorse"), "Matilde," "Il Trovatore" ("The Troubadour"), and "Giulia"—were eventually published in two editions, in 1824 with the title of *Poesie* (*Poems*), and as *Romanze* (*Ballads*) in 1826. After this date, probably due to the great number of long narrative poems on the English publishing market, Berchet turned to shorter poetry and started work on the *Fantasie* (*Fantasies*), which were published in Paris in 1829 and reelaborated national themes, especially the contrast between the grandeur of Italy in the medieval period and its present condition.

Generally, the bulk of Berchet's poetic output is distinguished by his predilection for narrative materials, a combination of "popular" rhythms and everyday expressions together with a recognizably poetic diction, the language and metrical structures of opera, and a variety of Romantic themes such as exile, ill-fated love affairs, virtuous figures, violence and revolutions, despairing and stoic freedom fighters. Critics have judged his medievalism as stilted, something akin to the French "genre troubadour" rather than Sir Walter Scott's more accurate reconstructions; but, when seen from an ideological perspective, Berchet's Middle Ages emerge as a time of lively social interaction, the idealized era of the *comuni* (central in the *Fantasie*) and the free spirit of the Italians. In terms of meter, he popularized the ballad and "romanza" forms, employed a variety of metrical schemes often in the same text, as in *I Profughi di Parga*, and, like Manzoni in the same years, widely experimented with decasyllables.

In his later years Berchet once more turned to translation. In 1829 he went to the University of Bonn to take its prestigious courses, and there he befriended August Wilhelm von Schlegel and started to translate the *Nibelungenlied* into Italian. The German epic, however, was left unfinished, and his major effort at translation appeared in 1837, in the collection *Vecchie Romanze Spagnuole* (*Ancient Spanish Ballads*), which not only responds to the more general Romantic vogue for Spanish poetry but also demonstrates Berchet's lasting interest in "popular" poetry. Once again, in this work Berchet confirms his central position as an important representative of an Italian Romanticism that is truly cosmopolitan, intent on introducing Italian culture to foreign literatures and developments, and making literature a fundamental instrument of historical and political intervention addressed to a specific, forward-looking public.

DIEGO SAGLIA

See also **Alfieri, Vittorio; Art and Medievalism; Foscolo, Ugo; Greece: Cultural and Historical Survey; Literature; Manifestoes; Nationalism; Orientalism: Literature and Scholarship; Ossian; Schiller, Johann Christoph Friedrich von; Schlegel, August Wilhelm von; Sismondi, Jean Charles Léonard Simonde de; Staël, Anne-Louise-Germaine (Madame) de; Translation**

Biography

Born in Milan, December 23, 1783. Abandoned his studies and joined his father's commercial activity; journey to Rome and Florence, 1811; took part in the foundation of *Il Conciliatore*, 1818; entered the Carboneria, 1820; went into exile in France, 1821; moved to London, 1822; joined the exiled household of Arconati at Gaesbeek, Belgium, 1829; studied at University of Bonn, 1829–30; went to Paris to follow the events of the July Revolution, 1830; in Geneva, 1831; in Berlin, 1833–34; in Edinburgh, 1837; returned to Italy, November 1845; became involved in politics but, after the failure of the 1848 revolutions, became an exile again. Died in Turin, December 23, 1851.

Selected Works

Collections
Opere. 2 vols. A cura di Egidio Bellorini. Bari: Laterza, 1911–12.
Lettere alla marchesa Costanza Arconati. 2 vols. A cura di R. O. J. van Nuffel. Rome: Vittoriano, 1956–62.
Opere. A cura di M. Turchi. Naples: Rossi, 1972.

Poetry
Il Bardo. 1807.
I Profughi di Parga. 1823.
Poesie, 1824. Revised edition as *Romanze*, 1826.
Fantasie. 1829.
Vecchie Romanze Spagnuole. 1837.

Other
Sul "Cacciatore feroce" e sulla "Eleonora" di Goffredo Augusto Bürger. Lettera semiseria di Grisostomo al suo figliuolo (*On Gottfried August Bürger's "Wild Hunter" and "Lenore." Chrysostom's Half-serious Letter to his Son*) 1816. New, rev. ed. by Mazio Scotti. Turin: UTET, 1979.

Bibliography

Ambrosio Mazziotti, Anna Maria D'. "L'apprendistato poetico di G. Berchet," *Critica letteraria* 12 (1984): 239–63.
Cadioli, Alberto. *Introduzione a Berchet.* Bari: Laterza, 1991.
Galletti, A., *et al., Studi sul Berchet pubblicati per il primo centenario della morte.* Introduction by Yoseph Colombo. Milan: Liceo Berchet, 1951.
Gotti, Ettore Lio *G. Berchet: la letteratura e la politica del risorgimento nazionale (1783–1851).* Florence: La Nuova Italia, 1933.

BERLIOZ, HECTOR 1803–1869

French composer, conductor, and music critic

Berlioz was a strikingly visionary and imaginative figure in nineteenth-century French musical Romanticism. His highly original approach to composition, strongly influenced by literature, produced works that often transcend the bounds of traditional genres, while his theatrical conception of performance emphasized massive ensembles and manipulation of the performance space to maximize the aural, visual, and psychological effects of his music. Writing about a performance of the *Sympho-*

nie fantastique in 1838, critic Stephen Heller noted: "With artists such as Berlioz, poetry, music, and painting exist simultaneously."

A true Romantic artist, Berlioz constantly placed himself at the center of his creative work, and many of his compositions have significant autobiographical levels of meaning. The most familiar example is the *Épisode de la vie d'un artiste* (*Episode from the Life of an Artist*, 1830), more popularly known by the title Berlioz himself generally used, *Symphonie fantastique*, whose written program depicts the composer's unrequited love for Shakespearean actress Harriet Smithson. *Roméo et Juliette* (1839) further portrays his passion for Smithson, who often played the role of Juliet; *Harold en Italie* (1834) recalls his sojourn on the Italian peninsula; while *La Damnation de Faust* (1846) manifests Berlioz's own brooding personality and reverential awe of nature.

Like Richard Wagner, Berlioz so closely identified himself with the totality of his compositions that he found it difficult to work with prepared texts and librettos, often substantially altering them or writing them himself. For example, in *Les Troyens* (composed 1856–58; Acts 3–5 first performed 1863) the grandest of his operas, Berlioz's literary contribution—his own translation of *The Aeneid* combined with original material inspired by Virgil—rivals the musical setting he created.

Berlioz's yearning for perfection led both to constant revision and polishing of "completed" works for many years after their premiers and to many abortive attempts at composition, the best parts of which he often reused in later works. As a conductor, Berlioz's insistence on polish often led him to omit challenging movements or sections that could not be performed to his satisfaction, and his scores abound with instructions regarding the number of performers, their physical placement, suggestions for rehearsing difficult passages, and special performance techniques.

Berlioz's flair for drama is manifest everywhere in his compositions, which often defy traditional genre expectations. Instead, his larger works that combine orchestra, chorus, and solo voice occupy various points along a continuum between operatic and concert music. For example, Berlioz vehemently asserted that *Roméo et Juliette* was a symphony, despite its inclusion of voices. The vocal text, he argued, was essential "to prepare the listeners' mind for the dramatic scenes whose feelings and passions are to be expressed by the orchestra." The succession of vocal, choral, and instrumental numbers in *La Damnation de Faust* is not far removed from *Roméo et Juliette*, yet its preponderant weight on vocal movements led Berlioz first to call it an *opéra de concert* and later a *légende dramatique*. *Harold en Italie* began as a *fantaisie dramatique* for orchestra, chorus, and viola, but eventually became a "symphony with viola soloist"; Berlioz described it as "a series of orchestral scenes in which the solo viola would be involved, to a greater or lesser extent, like an actual person, retaining the same character throughout." *La Fuite en Egypte* (1850), a nonliturgical religious work, was labelled a *Mystère*, while its expanded version, *L'Enfance du Christ* (1854), bears the appellation *Trilogie sacrée*. For one of his most radical works, *La Retour à la vie* (The Return of Life, 1832; revised end retitled *Lélio* in 1855), the composer adopted Thomas Moore's term *mélologue*. Its mixture of recitation with choral numbers, solo song, and instrumental music is so untraditional, and its subject so unabashedly autobiographical and topical to its period, that it has rarely been performed.

The spatial distribution of sound and visual placement of performers is a key component of Berlioz's aesthetics. The viola soloist in *Harold en Italie*, for instance, is instructed to sit "at front stage, near the public and isolated from the orchestra," representing the psychological distance between Harold the "narrator," and the orchestra. The act 1 finale of *Les Troyens* employs combinations of spatially divided stage bands to create the illusion of the passing of the Trojan horse. The Requiem spreads four groups of brass and percussion players apart from the main orchestra to represent, sonically and symbolically, the four quarters of the earth, while the spatial separation of the orchestra and organ in the Te Deum represents a "dialogue between church and state."

Berlioz's exquisite technical mastery and imagination in his use of orchestral tone color exerted a powerful influence on later composers such as Mily Balakirev, Nikolai Rimsky-Korsakov, Gustav Mahler and Richard Strauss, and his treatise on orchestration is still considered a fundamental source on the topic. Imaginative effects abound in Berlioz's music, ranging from softening the sound of a clarinet by encasing its bell in a silk bag to having a chorus sing from a room backstage while gradually shutting the door, creating a muting effect similar to that of the swell box on a pipe organ. While Berlioz's compositions have become known for massive sonic effects, these are balanced by many gossamer passages of transparent delicacy.

Berlioz's music criticism is insightful, barbed, and witty, in every way as colorful as his music, and like his compositions, firmly embraces the Romantic deification of the composer or author as creator. He directed particular outrage toward those who "mutilated" the works of artists he revered as special geniuses, such as Ludwig van Beethoven and William Shakespeare, to fit the tastes or whims of performers and the public, or the business interests of impresarios.

Partly due to his acerbic pen and his distance from official academic music establishments, Berlioz never achieved the amount of recognition he desired or deserved during his lifetime. In the later nineteenth and early twentieth centuries his music was largely overshadowed by that of German composers. Since the mid-twentieth century, however, Berlioz's music has experienced a renaissance, beginning with Jacques Barzun's impressive study of the composer in the context of the Romantic cultural milieu. Conductor Colin Davis championed the music of Berlioz in his concerts and recorded all of Berlioz's major works. Later in the century, John Eliot Gardiner made recordings of the symphonies using period instruments and nineteenth-century performance practices. Much outstanding research has now appeared from enthusiastic and dedicated Berlioz specialists such as Peter Bloom, David Cairns, D. Kern Holoman, and Hugh Macdonald, and a new complete edition of Berlioz's music, using newly discovered sources and modern critical techniques, is in progress.

GREGORY W. HARWOOD

See also **Music and Literature; Music, Romantic;** *Symphonie Fantastique*; **Symphony**

Biography

Born in La Côte-Saint-André, near Grenoble, December 11, 1803. Son of Dr. Louis-Joseph Berlioz, a physician. Educated in music and Latin by his father; learned the piano, flute, and guitar, and taught himself musical harmony. Sent to Paris by his father to study medicine, 1821. Published first songs at own expense, 1822; abandoned medical studies and began studying composition with Jean-François Lesueur at the Conservatoire National Supérieur de Musique in Paris, incurring the disapproval of his parents, 1823. Made many attempts at composition, which were mostly abandoned or reworked into later compositions, 1824–29. Witnessed Shakespearean actress Henrietta (Harriet) Smithson's first Parisian performance as Ophelia, 1827; although as yet unacquainted with her, adopted her as the inspiration for his work. Continued studying at the Paris Conservatoire. Began relationship with a professor of pianoforte, Camille Moke, c. 1829. First performance of the *Symphonie Fantastique*, 1829. Began career as journalist, 1829; won the Prix de Rome on third attempt, 1830. Engaged to Camille Moke, 1831, relationship broken off shortly afterwards when Moke became involved with the piano maker Camille Pleyel. Traveled to Rome; stayed there and in the Roman campagna, 1831–32. Returned to Paris via northern Italy, May 1832. Met Harriet Smithson, 1832; married her, 1833: they had one son, born 1834. First performance of *Harold in Italy*, 1834. Began writing music criticism for the *Journal des Débats*, 1835; completed his most influential prose writing, the *Treatise on Orchestration*, 1842. Began career as traveling conductor, 1842–43, continuing to tour intermittently until 1867. Began relationship with singer Marie Recio, c. 1840; separated from Harriet Smithson, 1844. Lived in London as conductor of the Drury Lane Theatre, 1848. Founded and became principal conductor of the Société Philharmonique in Paris, 1850. Member of the French delegation to the Great Exhibition in London, 1851. After Harriet's death, married Marie Recio, 1854 (d. 1862). Traveled frequently to Germany and London from 1855 on. Member of the Institut de France on fourth attempt, 1856. Actively promoted revival of operas by Christoph Willibald Gluck and assisted in editing new Gluck scores, 1859–66. Completed *Mémoires*, dedicating them to childhood sweetheart Estelle (Mme. Fornier), to whom he had renewed an attachment, 1865; had a number of copies of the book printed and bound for friends, family, and patrons. Son Louis Berlioz, a sea captain, died tragically of yellow fever in Havana, Cube, January 1867. Made his final tour, seriously ill and depressed by his son's death, to conduct concerts in Saint Petersburg and Moscow, 1867. Returned to France, attempting to recuperate in Nice briefly, 1868. Returned to Paris terminally ill. Died in Paris, March 8, 1869.

Selected Works

Collections

New Edition of the Complete Works. 20 of 25 projected vols. to date. Kassel: Bärenreiter, 1967–. Vol. 25, *Catalogue of the Works of Hector Berlioz*, edited by D. Kern Holomon, 1987, provides details about the origin, structure, and reception of each of Berlioz's compositions, as well as his books and newspaper articles.

Werke. 20 vols. Edited by Charles Malherbe and Felix Weingartner 1900–1907. Reprinted (New York: Edwin F. Kalmus) many times under several title variants and in a variety of formats.

Correspondance générale. 7 vols. projected. General editor, Pierre citron. Paris: Flammarion, 1972–.

Collected Literary Works. 7 vols. Facsimile reprints of first editions. Farnborough, England: Gregg, 1973.

Operas

Benvenuto Cellini. 1838; rev. version, 1856.
Les Troyens. 1863 (Partial performance of acts 3–5 *Les Troyens à Carthage*; first complete performance 1890).
Béatrice et Bénédict. 1860–62.

Secular Works

Huit Scènes de Faust. 1829.
Neuf Mélodies Imitées de l'Anglais (Irish Melodies), 1829; revised slightly and republished as *Irlande*. 1840.
Le Retour à la vie, 1832; revised and retitled *Lélio, ou Le Retour à la vie*. 1855.
La Captive. 6 versions with varying performance requirements. 1832–48.
Les Nuits d'été. Version for voice and piano, 1840–41. Revision for voices and orchestra. 1856.
La Damnation de Faust. 1846.

Sacred Works

Messe solennelle. 1828.
Grande Messe des morts (Requiem). 1837.
L'Enfance du Christ, Trilogie sacrée. 1854.
Te Deum. 1855.

Symphonies

Episode de la vie d'une artiste. 1830.
Harold en Italie. 1834.
Roméo et Juliette. 1839.
Grande Symphonie funèbre et triomphale, version for military band, 1840; revised for full orchestra and chorus *ad libitum*. 1842.

Concert Overtures

Grand Ouverture des Franc-Juges. 1828.
Grande Ouverture de Waverly. 1828.
Grande Ouverture du Roi Lear. 1833.
Intrata di Rob-Roy MacGregor. 1833.
Le Carnaval romain. 1844.
Ouverture du Corsaire, first called *La Tour de Nice*, 1845; revised as *Le Corsaire*. 1854.

Writings

Grande Traité d'instrumentation et d'orchestration modernes, 1843 (assembled from previously published articles in *La Revue et Gazette Musicale*); 2d ed. with a new section called *Le Chef d'orchestra; Théorie de son art*, 1855. Translated by Hugh Macdonald as *Berlioz's Orchestration Treatise: A Translation and Commentary*. Cambridge: Cambridge University Press, 2002. A translation by Theodore Front, *Treatise on Instrumentation* (New York: Edwin F. Kolmus, 1948; reprint, New York: Dover, 1991) is based on a revision of the treatise by Richard Strauss to reflect late nineteenth-century orchestral practices.

Les Soirées de l'orchestre, 1852. Translated by Jacques Barzun as *Evenings with the Orchestra*. New York: Knopf, 1956.

Les Grotesques de la musique. 1859. Translated by Alastair Bruce as *The Musical Mad house*. Rochester, N.Y.: University of Rochester Press, 2003.

A Travers Chants: Études musicales, adorations, boutades et critiques, 1862. Translated by Elizabeth Csicsery-Rónay as *The Art of Music and Other Essays* by Bloomington: Indiana University Press, 1994.

Mémoires, printed privately in 1865 and published in 1870. Translated by David Cairns; as *The Memoirs of Hector Berlioz*. London: Gollancz, 1969.

Bibliography

Barzun, Jacques. *Berlioz and the Romantic Century*. 2 vols. Rev. ed. New York: Columbia University Press, 1969.

————, ed. *The Cambridge Companion to Berlioz*. Cambridge: Cambridge University Press, 2000.

————, ed. *Berlioz Studies*. Cambridge: Cambridge University Press, 1991.

Bloom, Peter. *The Life of Berlioz*. Cambridge: Cambridge University Press, 1998.

Boulez, Pierre. "Berlioz and the Realm of the Imaginary." *High Fidelity–Musical America*, March 6, 1969, 43–46; reprinted in *Orientations: Collected Writings*. Edited by Jean-Jacques Nattiez. Cambridge, Mass.: Cambridge University Press, 1986.

Cairns, David. *Berlioz*. Vol. 1, *The Making of An Artist 1803–1832*. London: A. Deutsch, 1989. Vol. 2: *Servitude and Greatness 1832–1869*. London: Penguin, 1999.

Cone, Edward T. "Inside the Saint's Head." *Musical Newsletter* 1 (1971) and 2 (1972). Reprinted in *The Garland Library of the History of Western Music*. Vol. 9, *Nineteenth-Century Music*. New York: Garland, 1985.

Heller, Stephen. "Concert de M. Berlioz au Conservatoire de musique." *Revue et gazette musicale de Paris* 5, no. 48 (December 2, 1838): 492.

Holoman, D. Kern. *Berlioz*. Cambridge, Mass.: Harvard University Press, 1989.

Macdonald, Hugh. *Berlioz*. Rev. ed. London: Dent, 1991.

————. "Berlioz's Self-Borrowings," *Proceedings of the Royal Musical Association* 92 (1965–66): 27–44; reprinted in *The Garland Library of the History of Western Music*. Vol. 9, *Nineteenth-Century Music*. New York: Garland, 1985.

Rose, Michael. *Berlioz Remembered*. London: Faber and Faber, 2001.

Rosen, Charles. "Berlioz." In *The Romantic Generation*. Cambridge, Mass.: Harvard University Press, 1995.

Rushton, Julian. *The Musical Language of Berlioz*. Cambridge: Cambridge University Press, 1983.

BERNARDIN DE SAINT-PIERRE, JACQUES-HENRI (1737–1814)

French writer

Jacques-Henri Bernardin de Saint-Pierre was born in Le Havre in 1737 and died in Eragny in 1814. His life was long and exciting, taking him to Russia, Eastern Europe, and Mauritius (then called the Ile de France) before he finally settled in Paris, made the acquaintance of Jean-Jacques Rousseau, and became a major literary and cultural figure of the period from 1780 to 1800.

His first published work is the account of his journey to the Ile de France and a description of his life on the island (*Voyage à l'Ile de France* [*Journey to the Ile de France*, 1773]). The work was not a success, but it is considered today in the context of its relationship with the author's best-selling novel, *Paul et Virginie* (*Paul and Virginia*, 1788). This novel was first published in the third edition of *Les Etudes de la Nature*, the first edition of which appeared in 1784. Bernardin had compiled this major philosophical study of nature while living on the breadline in Paris and surviving through the generosity of a few friends and various charitable sources. The *Etudes* were a major literary success and brought about a change in his fortunes; he became a figure of note and received many letters from readers and admirers, most of which have survived in Le Havre library and which will form an important feature of the edition of his correspondence (in preparation). The *Etudes* represent, according to the author, an attempt to write the history of nature and to seek in nature the basis of morality and political and religious systems. Bernardin was greatly affected by the death of Rousseau in 1778; Rousseau's influence is felt throughout his writing. Bernardin was not a professional scientist, and he knew the botanical sciences only as an amateur observer. Nevertheless, he sought in the *Etudes* to demonstrate the harmony of nature and man's close relationship with the world in which he lived.

When the novel *Paul et Virginie* first appeared, it received immediate critical acclaim and encouraged many new readers to write to Bernardin. The novel was published independently in 1789 and it has been available in print ever since. The novel is a striking and beautiful love story set in an exotic paradise. Two young children are brought up close to nature, raised by their respective mothers and taught the virtues of frugal living and adoration of the divinity. Bernardin produced lavish poetic descriptions in this short novel, based on his firsthand knowledge of life on Mauritius. The idyllic love story has a tragic ending as the young heroine, Virginie, who is sent to France to see a rich aunt and is thus separated from her beloved Paul, returns to seek continued happiness on the island but is caught in a hurricane and is drowned in the sea within reach of safety, as she is unwilling to remove her clothes to allow a sailor to carry her to the beach. Critics have disagreed about the status of the ending; some believe that Virginie dies to preserve her modesty, others that she has been corrupted by her stay in Europe and cannot return, pure, to the island. Yet others believe that the conclusion is a religious one in which Virginie chooses to die to depart this world and live in a heavenly paradise. Whatever the interpretation of the conclusion, few critics would disagree that Bernardin has found the perfect recipe for a successful novel: a tragic love story, an exotic landscape, a serious political and religious message (there is a short episode on the fate of a female slave and a lengthy dialogue which involves serious criticism of contemporary France), and the finest example of poetic prose to be found in France in the eighteenth century. Bernardin is an evident precursor of François-Auguste-René de Chateaubriand, who was a great admirer of *Paul et Virginie*.

Such was the success of Bernardin's novel that a young writer, Etienne Pivert de Senancour, future author of *Obermann* (1804), wrote to him for advice about leaving civilization and settling on a tropical island that would offer him the benefits he read about in the novel. The letter survives in Le Havre, but we have no record of Bernardin's reply, if indeed there was one. In 1790, Bernardin wrote and published a short novel, *La Chaumière Indienne* (The Indian Cottage). The text is the account of a philosopher's journey in India, seeking happiness and the foundations for it. It is an overtly deistic account in which the author withdraws his support for organized religion and shows that the key to happiness is a simple life shared with a good companion and spent trusting in God's generosity. The influence of Rousseau is clearly visible here.

The Revolution found Bernardin working on other projects, in particular the *Harmonies de la Nature* and a play involving a white slave, *Empsaël et Zoraïde*. Neither was published in Bernardin's lifetime. Many projects remained unfinished, but survive in the vast archives in Le Havre. Bernardin's widow became the wife of his secretary, Louis Aimé-Martin; they initiated a vast publishing operation in the 1820s and Aimé-Martin set about producing an edition of the complete works of Bernardin. It is apparent to us now that many of the posthumous works were not edited according to today's standards and norms; it is hoped that a reliable edition will soon be planned.

Bernardin's influence was enormous; it is safe to say that no writer of the Romantic era was unaware of the novel *Paul et Virginie*, and references to his text are to be found in authors as diverse as Gustave Flaubert and Albert Camus.

MALCOLM COOK

Biography

Born Jacques-Henri Bernardin de Saint-Pierre in Le Havre, January 19, 1737, to a bourgeois family. Sailed on an uncle's ship to Martinique, 1749. Returned to Normandy: studied at a Jesuit school in Caen and the Jesuit Collège de Rouen, until 1757: awarded a prize in mathematics. Attended the École des Ponts et Chaussées, 1757–58. After the school closed, transferred to the military school at Versailles; obtained a commission as a military engineer. Joined the Rhine army under the Comte de Saint-Germain, 1760. Returned to France; appointed to Malta as engineer-geographer, 1761. Returned home destitute after commission was refused recognition. Traveled to Holland and on to Russia, 1762: served as sub-lieutenant in the engineering corps at Moscow; obtained the protection of the French ambassador, the Baron de Breteuil. Traveled to Finland on a captain's commission from Catherine II. Returned to France via Poland, Austria, and Berlin, 1765–67. Left penniless after inheritance from his father went in its entirety to his stepmother. Lived in Paris, virtually destitute, 1767. Commissioned as engineer captain to sail to Madagascar, 1767; after a quarrel with the head of the mission, refused to disembark and continued to Mauritius; stayed as a builder until 1770. Returned to Paris, 1771. Published *Voyages à l'Île-de-France*, 1773. Stayed with Breteuil in the Tuileries; began associating with philosophers in Paris, including Jean-Jacques Rousseau. Volumes 1–3 of *Études de la Nature* published, 1783. Third edition, including *Paul et Virginie*, published 1787. *Intendant* (head) of the Jardin du Roi, later the Jardin des Plantes, 1792. Installed the zoo at the Jardin, 1792. The post of *intendant* was suppressed; granted compensation by the Convention, 1793. Married Félicité Didot (died 1799), daughter of the publisher of *Études*, 1793: one daughter, Virginie, and two sons, both called Paul, one of whom died in infancy. Appointed Professeur de Philosophie Morale at the École Normale Supérieure, 1794 (school was closed, 1795). Member of the Institut de France, 1795; Académie française, 1803. Married Desirée de Pelleporc, 1800: one son (born 1802; died 1804). Chevalier, Légion d'honneur, 1806. President of the Académie française, 1807. Awarded pension from Napoleon in acknowledgement of his support. Completed *Harmonies de la nature*, 1812. Died in Eragny-sur-Oise, January 21, 1814.

Selected Works

Les Etudes de la Nature. 1784.
Paul et Virginie. 1784. Published as: *Paul et Virginie.* Edited with an Introduction, by Jean-Michel Racault. Paris: Livre de Poche, 1999.
La Chaumière indienne. 1790.

Bibliography

Maury, F. *Etude sur la vie et les oeuvres de Bernardin de Saint-Pierre.* Paris: Hachette, 1892; reprinted in Slatkine Reprints, Geneva: 1971.
Souriau, M. *Bernardin de Saint-Pierre d'après ses manuscrits*, Paris: Société Française d'Imprimerie et de Librairie, 1905.

BERTRAND, ALOYSIUS (LOUIS) 1807–1841

French poet

Aloysius Bertrand's short life coincided with the height of Romanticism in France, and in many respects he projects the typical image of the Romantic poet: young, suffering from ill health and poverty, passionate, and in search of recognition of his tortured genius. It is true that his major work was not published until after his death and was soon to be forgotten. Nonetheless its influence eventually extended well beyond the confines of the Romantic era and of France.

Bertrand's urge to write found an outlet in two media: poetry and journalism. He started composing poems before leaving school, and soon came to the attention of poets like Émile Deschamps, Victor Hugo (who admired his craftsmanship and finely perfected form), and Charles Nodier. His early work, how-ever, did not cause a lasting stir. Bertrand's renown, such as it was or is, rests almost entirely on one piece of writing: *Gaspard de la Nuit: Fantaisies à manière de Rembrandt et de Callot (Gaspard of the Night: Fantasies in the Manner of Rembrandt and Callot*, 1842). Written over a period of time around 1830, the work reflects both dominant trends in literary writing and innovative ideas.

Gaspard de la Nuit is composed of a collection of picturesque and bizarre prose poems demonstrating the revival of the taste for the medieval, the Gothic, and the grotesque. Using dreams and magic, its rhythmic language produces incantatory and nightmarish effects. At the same time, the prose poems resemble little tableaux; in fact the initial title of the work had been *Bambochades romantiques* (*Romantic small burlesque paintings*). Traces of the influence of, among others, François-Auguste-René, Vicomte de Chateaubriand, Johann Wolfgang von Goethe, E. T. A. Hoffmann, and Sir Walter Scott are clearly discernible.

The two prefaces reveal the poet's preoccupation with the question "What is art?" In this respect the work reflects the philosophical trend of negative transcendentalism as introduced by G. W. F. Hegel. The first introduction describes Bertrand's aesthetics: art is "sentiment" (feeling), God, and love; but the second condition of art, "ce qui dans l'art est idée" (that which in art is idea) belongs to Satan. Bertrand explores this duality by introducing the "new" poetic form. He seeks to convey ineffable aspects of the unconscious and the subconscious, the occult and the diabolic through the evocation of fantastic images and dreamlike qualities—in, for example, "Un Rêve" ("A Dream") or "L'Heure du sabbat" ("The Hour of the Sabbath") in the section "La Nuits et ses prestiges" ("The Night and its Marvels")— an approach that paved the way for surrealism. Nevertheless, he also initiated the modern prose poem. Charles Baudelaire called *Gaspard* the "mystérieux et brillant modèle" (mysterious and brilliant model) of his *Spleen de Paris*, and described prose poems as being musical without rhyme or rhythm. In fact, Bertrand's poetic prose is more defiant in its conception. Its novelty resides in its challenge to traditional and paradoxical assumptions about literary institutions: prose and poetry. He gave instructions to print his prose texts blocked like verse and interspaced with blanks to resemble couplets, making the empty spaces count as much as his words. Moreover, he attempts to "paint" with color and sound, rather than narrate his images, in the event inventing an "impressionnisme poétique" (poetic impressionism).

Bertrand first read excerpts of *Gaspard* to Hugo and to Charles-Augustin Sainte-Beuve in the salons he frequented while in Paris. Despite an initial show of interest in the work, however, he was unable to find a publisher. When the book finally appeared posthumously (1842), Sainte-Beuve was slow to write his foreword, and it did little justice to its generic novelty. Moreover, the few copies printed hardly sold. The *Revue des deux mondes* published a review of the book in 1843 that spoke of a certain charm and novelty, but remained skeptical. Deschamps in *La France littéraire* was more enthusiastic. But it was left to Baudelaire to draw proper attention to the poet and publicly announce his admiration. Bertrand's work achieved cult status with the symbolists. Several critics have pointed out Stéphane Mallarmé's affinity with Bertrand, whose "oeuvre exquis" (exquisite work) he revered. Jean Moréas took great interest in the poet and regretted that Paul Verlaine had not included him among his "poètes maudits" (accursed poets).

Bertrand's popularity was reawakened by the surrealists' taste for the cabalistic poetry at the heart of *Gaspard*. For André Breton, Bertrand was, together with Gérard de Nerval, one of the two fathers of the movement. Since then, Bertrand has intermittently been rediscovered. In fact, the interest in *Gaspard* has spread as far as Russia and Japan. Its topicality is confirmed by a 1993 conference in honor of Bertrand, as well as by the 2000 publication of the first edition of his collected works.

As a journalist, Bertrand started his career working for the *Provincial*, a short-lived literary journal founded by the Dijon Studies Society on the model of the (London) *Globe*. The paper was a convenient vehicle for the publication of Bertrand's early works. It also served the purpose of promulgating his ideas on writing. In an 1828 article in one of the last issues he places himself firmly on the side of the Romantics, proclaiming that classicism is useless and dead and that new times demand new poetry. The epic of the present, he maintained, should take the form of a drama written in prose. The article shows Bertrand as belonging to the avant-garde of French Romanticism. The poet did in fact also write several plays that until now had never been published. Only one play, *Monsieur Robillard [Le Sous-Lieutenant des Hussards]*, a comedy satirizing the bourgeoisie and the *juste milieu* (middle way), was produced in the theater (although it was performed only once, in 1832).

While working for *Le Spectateur* and then *Le Patriote de la Côte d'Or*, 1830–32, Bertrand gave vent to his political opinions. He produced strongly worded articles vilifying the royalists and fiercely supporting the republican cause. His polemical articles extend to subjects such as art and the École des Beaux-Arts in Dijon. During this revolutionary period he adopted the pen name Ludovic, just as he used Aloysius for his poetic compositions. His journalistic writings exhibit a great talent for irony, a feature that also marks *Gaspard* and the plays.

Literary history has marginalized Bertrand's work, underplaying the major impact it has had on modern French poetry. A true Romantic in his sources and inspiration, Bertrand also provided the starting point for a poetic revolution. Yet so far his originality, his modernity, and his genuine contribution to the aesthetic movements of the nineteenth and twentieth centuries have been neither fully recognized nor properly valorized.

FELIZITAS RINGHAM

Biography

Born Jacques-Louis-Napoléon Bertrand in Ceva, Piedmont, France (today part of Italy), April 20, 1807. Son of a lieutenant in the Imperial guard. Moved to Spoleto, 1812. Moved to Dijon, 1815. Attended the Collège Royal, Dijon, 1818–26; received the "prix de discours français," 1825, and the "premier prix de rhétorique," 1826. Joined the Société d'Études de Dijon (Dijon Studies Society), collecting historical archives, 1826–28. Manager of the periodical *Le Provincial*, Dijon, 1828. Worked as a writer in Paris; met Victor Hugo and Charles-Augustin Sainte-Beuve, among others, 1828–30. Adopted pen name Aloysius Bertrand. Worked for the liberal journal *Le Spectateur*, Dijon, 1830–31 until its suppression by the press laws of Charles X. Chief editor of the revolutionary journal *Le Patriote de la Côte-d'Or*, Dijon, 1831–32. Moved to Paris, 1833; worked in impoverished conditions as a writer and, for a time, as secretary to Baron Roederer; tried to find a publisher for his work; suffered first signs of tuberculosis. Engaged to Célestine F. [*sic*], 1834. *Gaspard de la Nuit* accepted for publication by Victor Pavie, a publisher in Angers, 1839. Died of tuberculosis exacerbated by malnourishment in Paris, April 29, 1841.

Selected Writings

Collections

Oeuvres Complètes. Edited by Helen Hart Poggenburg. 2000.

Le Keepsake Fantastique: Poésies, chroniques et essais, théâtre inédit, correspondance. Edited by Bertrand Guégan. 1923.

Poetry

Gaspard de la Nuit: Fantaisies à la manière de Rembrandt et de Callot. Foreword by Charles-Augustin Sainte-Beuve, 1842.

Gaspard de la Nuit: Fantaisies à la manière de Rembrandt et de Callot. Edited by Bertrand Guégan, with a review by Charles-Augustin Sainte-Beuve, 1925. Translated by John T. Wright as *Gaspard de la Nuit: Fantasies in the Manner of Rembrandt and Callot.* 2d ed. 1994.

Oeuvres poétiques: La Volupté et pièces diverses. Edited and introduced by Cargill Sprietsma. 1926.

Bibliography

Claudon, Francis, ed. *Les Diableries de la nuit: Hommage à Aloysius Bertrand.* Dijon: Éditions universitaires de Dijon, 1993.

Milner, Max. *Le Diable dans la littérature française de Cazotte à Baudelaire.* 2 vols. Paris: Corti, 1960.

Richards, Marvin. *Without Rhyme or Reason: Gaspard de la Nuit and the Dialectic of the Prose Poem.* London: Associated University Press, 1998.

Rude, Fernand. *Aloysius Bertrand.* Paris: Seghers, 1971.

Sprietsma, Cargill. *Louis Bertrand dit Aloysius Bertrand 1807–1841, une vie romantique.* Paris: Champion, 1926.

BESTUZHEV-MARLINSKII, ALEKSANDR ALEKSANDROVICH 1797–1837

Russian writer, poet, critic, and revolutionary

Aleksandr Aleksandrovich Bestuzhev-Marlinskii, led a Byronic life that Byron himself might have envied. He was a handsome officer of the dragoons whose seductions were legion. He was a polymath and a master of languages. His coeditorship of the literary almanac *Poliarnaia zvezda* (*Polar Star*, 1823 25) enabled him to champion "the new, so-called Romantic school." He was a key leader of the failed revolt of December 14, 1825 that spawned Decembrism. Bestuzhev spent the rest of his life in Siberia and the Caucasus Mountains, where he began a meteoric new literary career as Aleksandr Marlinskii, an ultra-Romantic writer whose popularity exceeded that of Aleksandr Pushkin and Nikolai Gogol. He was spied upon by the authorities and sent to remote posts, quarantine duty, and numerous battles. He suffered scandal when a young girl was accidentally shot in his bed. He may have been a government spy, a secret friend of rebels, or both. He was killed leading a charge against Circassian mountaineers; his body was not found, and immediately the legends of Marlinskii began. He was said to have sought death or to have used his contacts with bandits to escape abroad or to a free life in the mountains as a bandit, rebel, holy man, or lover of a beautiful maiden. He was quickly dismissed as a serious writer, but continued to enthrall adolescents for over a century.

Marlinskii's writing started in 1821 with a historical account of the Baltic, "Poezdka v Revel" ("Journey to Reval"), and a Gothic horror tale, "Zamok Venden" ("Castle Wenden"). This and two other "castle tales" of a Livonian cycle dramatize bloody revenge in the Baltic German age of chivalry. Sir Walter Scott's influence is strong in these and other historical tales, and "Revel'skii turnir" ("Tournament at Reval," 1825) is straight from *Ivanhoe.* In this tale the young merchant Edwin dons a knight's armor, defeats his haughty aristocratic rival, and wins the hand of Minna. For the tales of a Russian historical cycle Marlinskii relied on the national historian N. M. Karamzin. "Roman i Ol'ga" ("Roman and Olga," 1823) is an adventure tale about another socially unacceptable hero. Roman saves democratic Novgorod from autocratic Moscow and wins the hand of Olga.

The best early tale is "Izmennik" ("The Traitor," 1825), a Shakespearian-Schillerian tale of envy and lust for power in which the villainous Vladimir Sittsky sells his soul, betrays his homeland, and murders his brother. Among the later of Marlinskii's supernatural tales are "Strashnoe gadanie" ("The Terrible Divination," 1830) and "Latnik" ("The Cuirassier," 1831). In the former tale an impassioned young officer rushes to an illicit rendezvous. During a halt in a village he is subjected to a divination that saves him from his sinful ways. The latter tale dramatizes a murder mystery in a sinister mansion. This is a castle tale: the cuirassier returns and kills the villain who imprisoned and murdered his beloved.

Marlinskii wrote several Byronic society tales, the best of which are "Vecher na bivuake" ("An Evening at a Bivouac," 1823) and "Vtoroi vecher na bivuake" ("A Second Evening at a Bivouac," 1823). These are tales of love and duels over unworthy society darlings; both are composed of stories told around a campfire and framed by anecdotes. To these "tales of men and passions" Marlinskii later added "Ispytanie" ("The Test," 1830), a comic satire in which two hussars attempt to outwit each other while testing the fidelity of a beautiful woman and are saved from fighting a foolish duel.

Marlinskii also wrote naval adventures. In "Fregat *Nadezhda*" ("The Frigate *Hope*," 1832) a young captain of the finest Russian ship is carried away by his love for a society darling, allows her to use her husband's influence to sail aboard his ship, neglects his command, and is injured while saving the *Hope* in a storm. On his deathbed he confesses his betrayal of duty directly to the tsar. This elaborate tale is an allegory and an encoded confession of the author's role in the Decembrist conspiracy.

Marlinskii's fiction reaches its greatest extravagance in his tales of the Caucasus. "Ammalat-bek" (1831) is a story of terrible betrayal. A young Tatar chief is befriended by a Russian officer who hopes to show that Russians and Caucasians can learn to trust each other. Deceived by a mountain rebel into believing his Russian mentor plans to betray him, and lured by the villain's promise of his daughter's hand in marriage, Ammalat kills his benefactor, only to learn that he murdered a true friend. "Mulla Nur" (1836) is the tale of dreamy young Iskander Bey who undertakes to end a drought by bringing miraculous snow from a mountain top. He is aided in his quest by the famous bandit Mulla Nur.

Marlinskii's tales have been called transpositions of the Byronic verse tale into prose. This can be seen in his stylized authorial image, the heroes who hold themselves apart from crass society and have been betrayed by love, and the use of digression to negotiate narrative transitions. His skills show in quick, frequent shifts among narrative modes: now description, exposition, or declamation, suddenly direct authorial address sprinkled with witticisms, then digression or dialogue. His talent for telling a tale is undeniable. Marlinskii's specialty was *byt*—detailed, expert, and technical descriptions of cultural milieu. His tales are saturated with terms derived from his exceptional linguistic reserves. The castle tales are a lesson in medieval architecture. The Caucasian tales are enriched by explications of language and mores. His weakness, however, was his hyperbolic ultra-Romantic style, known as "marlinism"—a parade of metaphors, similes, epithets, personifications, and antitheses. Its syntax is made graceful by shifting rhythms, change of tone or pace, repetition, parallelism, and multiple clauses. Hyperbole and attention-getting word plays abound.

Marlinskii's poetry is conventional, with the exception of the revolutionary "Agitatsionnnye pesni" ("Agitational Songs") and "Podbliudnye pesni" ("*Under-the Saucer-Songs*") he co-authored in 1823–25 with the civic poet Kondratii Ryleev. Far better are Marlinskii's laments of exile, love lyrics, translations of Goethe, and imitations of Caucasian folk songs. He was also a superior critic, devastating "literary old-believers" with wit and demolishing their works with linguistic expertise. Marlinskii's Caucasian essays are models of political and military reportage. A theoretical essay, "O romantizme i romane" (1833; "On Romanticism and the Novel") is notable for its erudition and imaginative arguments for a Romantic view of history.

LAUREN G. LEIGHTON

Biography

Born in Saint Petersburg, October 23, 1797. Enrolled in Cadet Corps of Engineers, 1806; admitted to elite Light Dragoon Regiment, 1817. Critic, translator, polemicist, travel memoirist, writer of historical and Byronic society tales, 1817–23; coeditor with Kondratii Ryleyev of the literary almanac *Polar Star*, 1823–25. Member of secret revolutionary Northern Society, 1824–25, led mutinous regiment in failed revolt of December 14, 1825. Incarceration in Finland, 1826; Exile in Yakutsk, 1826–29. Service as common soldier, allowed to resume writing career under pseudonym Marlinskii; popular author of supernatural, naval, society, and Caucasian prose tales, 1829–37. Killed in battle at Cape Adler on Caspian Sea, June 7, 1837.

Selected Works

Ammalat-Beg, 1831; translated by J. B. Shaw as *Ammalat-Beg; or A Russian Colonel's Head for a Dowry*, 1845. Authorship as *Sultanetta* claimed by Alexandre Dumas.

Mulla Nur, 1836; translated from the French by Alma Blakeman Jones as *The Ball of Snow*, 1895, authorship claimed by Alexandre Dumas.

Vospominaniia Bestuzhevykh, edited by M. K. Azadovskii. 1951.

Sochineniia. 2 vols. 1958.

Polnoe sobranie stikhotvorenii. Poet's Library, Large Series, Proffer Anthology: Ann Arbor, Mich.: Ardis Publishers, 1961.

Selections in *Russian Romantic Prose: An Anthology*. Edited by Carl R. Proffer. Rydel Anthology: Ditto, 1979.

Selections in *Ardis Anthology of Russian Romanticism*. Edited by Christine A. Rydel. Leighton Anthology: New York, Westport, Conn., London: Greenwood Press, 1984.

Selections in *Russian Romantic Criticism*. Translated by Lauren G. Leighton. 1987.

Bibliography

Bagby, Lewis. "Aleksandr Aleksandrovich Marlinskii (Marlinskii) (1797–1837)." In *Russian Literature in the Age of Pushkin and Gogol: Prose. Dictionary of Literary Biography*. Edited by Christine A. Rydel. Detroit: The Gale Group, 1999.

———. *Alexander Bestuzher-Marlinsky and Russian Byronism*. University Park: Pennsylvania State University Press, 1995.

Kanunova, F. Z. *Estetika russkoi romanticheskoi povesti: A. A. Marlinskii-Marlinskii i romantiki-belletristy 20–30-kh godov XIX v*. Tomsk: Tomsk University, 1973.

Leighton, Lauren G. *Alexander Bestuzher-Marlinsky*. Boston: G. K. Hall, 1975.

———. *The Esoteric Tradition in Russian Romantic Literature: Decembrism and Freemasonry*. University Park: Pennsylvania State University Press, 1994.

Mersereau, John Jr. *Russian Romantic Fiction*. Ann Arbor, Mich.: Ardis, 1983.

Mordovchenko, N. I. "A. A. Marlinskii-Marlinskii." In *A. A. Marlinskii-Marlinskii, Polnoe sobranie stikhotvorenii*. Leningrad: Sovetskii pisatel', 1961.

Vatsuro, V. E. "Lermontov i Marlinskii." In *Tvorchestvo M. Iu. Lermontova*. Moscow: Nauka, 1964.

BEWICK, THOMAS 1753–1828

English printmaker and illustrator

Born in 1753 into a farming family, Thomas Bewick resisted conventional schooling, often playing truant, spending days (and nights) fishing, bird-watching, wandering, or wading in rivers and lakes. Though not without academic ability in school (he learned some Latin, for example), he was happier educating himself with rural ballads, ghost stories, and the recollections of retired soldiers—the kind of material that William Wordsworth observed and incorporated (from a gentlemanly perspective) in *Lyrical Ballads* (1798). Some exploits of Bewick's "active wild disposition" sound similar to the "glad animal movements" Wordsworth recalls in "Tintern Abbey." Bewick began drawing by instinct, filling in blank areas of his slate at school, and the margins of books, with tiny sketches. From here he progressed to drawing with chalk on grave stones, the church floor, and the hearth at home. Eventually he was given paper, pen, and painting materials, but he had no formal tuition and drew solely from "the Beasts and Birds which enlivened the beautiful Scenery of Woods & Wilds, surrounding my native Hamlet." In 1767

Bewick was bound apprentice to Ralph Beilby, an engraver in Newcastle, who taught him various methods of engraving on metal. Bewick took over the wood-engraving side of the business, developing it far beyond his master's abilities. In 1774, with his apprenticeship over, Bewick took a walking tour in Scotland before going to London to seek work. The metropolis disgusted him and he returned to Newcastle in 1777, becoming Beilby's partner. He visited London once more before his death, but otherwise remained determinedly provincial, visiting his family home at Cherryburn regularly and spending much of his spare time in solitary walking. He continued to frequent graveyards, on one occasion, in 1815, spending several hours talking to his own father's skull which had been disinterred during the excavation of a new grave.

His father had died on November 15, 1785. On that day, Bewick engraved a dromedary on a woodblock, thus initiating a long-cherished project to produce an accurately illustrated natural history. In 1790 he published a *General History of Quadrupeds*, with his own wood-engraved illustrations. It was confessedly unsystematic and derivative (from Georges-Louis Leclerc de Buffon in particular), but there was a strong concentration on animals that Bewick had actually seen himself. In 1797 a more ambitious work began to appear, with the first volume of his *History of British Birds*. This volume, devoted to land birds, contained descriptions compiled by his partner Beilby and derived from Buffon, Thomas Pennant, and Gilbert White; but Bewick corrected them on the grounds that his own habits led him "to a more intimate acquaintance with this branch of Natural History." The illustrations were a stunning success; Bewick had perfected the art of engraving on the end grain of very hard boxwood blocks with tools of his own construction, and the clarity of the results was unprecedented. In the second volume of *History of British Birds* (1804), devoted to water birds, Bewick wrote the descriptions himself and made great efforts to base his illustrations on observation. Two months at Marmaduke Tunstall's house in north Yorkshire allowed him to use that collection of stuffed birds; sportsmen and naturalists who had heard about the project brought him recently killed or living specimens to draw. Most of the descriptions are concluded with a small vignette engraving of some scene of rural life: boys playing in a churchyard, a man fishing, a snowman, a suicide, a goose pecking an old woman. These miniatures, humorous and Gothic by turns and without obvious connection with the texts, formed one of the most influential features of Bewick's books.

In his instinctive association with rural pursuits and nocturnal ramblings, Bewick resembled Wordsworth. In his combination of conventional engraving work with a highly developed sense of his individual craft, he was like his close contemporary William Blake, whose radical politics he also shared. But there was nothing of the hermetic visionary about Bewick, and his literary tastes remained conservative. His illustrated editions of poems by Oliver Goldsmith, Thomas Parnell, and William Somerville, and his quotations from James Thomson (whom he called "the naturalist's poet") indicate his true allegiances. Although he appears to have read nothing of the literature now regarded as Romantic, he was undeniably influential on the contemporary literature of his day: his natural history works were often cited in the notes to poems throughout the nineteenth century, and he may have been partially responsible for the remarkable number of poems about birds by Samuel Taylor Coleridge, John Keats, and Percy Bysshe Shelley, and William Wordsworth.

In Wordsworth's "The Two Thieves" (1800), Bewick's genius for vivid miniature characterization was celebrated as a kind of untutored wizardry, superior to the book-learned skills of writing. In the opening pages of Charlotte Brontë's *Jane Eyre* (1847) the heroine finds a Gothic strand in Bewick's *History of British Birds* that suits the loneliness and oppression of her condition. Reading about the bleak and remote habitats of sea fowl of the arctic circle, Jane forms a "shadowy . . . but strangely impressive" idea that she connects with the darker vignettes in the text: wrecked boats, isolated rocks, twilight churchyards, devils, and "the cold and ghastly moon glancing through bars of cloud at a wreck just sinking." The impressiveness of these mysterious images is later confirmed by Jane's own highly Gothic artwork.

Another admirer of the vignettes was the bird painter John James Audubon, who visited Bewick in 1827, and who declared that Bewick "was purely a son of nature, to whom alone he owed nearly all that characterized him as an artist and a man." The study of Bewick's natural history illustrations was recommended to all aspiring artists by Charles Robert Leslie, in his *Handbook for Young Painters* (1855), and John Ruskin celebrated Bewick's "magnificent artistic virtue" in several books. Bewick's autobiographical *Memoir*, begun in 1822 and recording his rural boyhood and political views in vivid detail, was published by his daughter Jane in 1862; a London exhibition was mounted in 1880, and a memorial edition of his major books, using the original blocks, came out in 1885, confirming the continued interest in his engravings through the nineteenth century.

PAUL BAINES

Biography

Born at Cherryburn, Eltringham, Northumberland, August 10 or 12, 1753. Son of John Bewick, farmer. Educated at Ovingham Parsonage, c. 1763–67. Apprenticed to metal engraver Ralph Beilby in Newcastle-upon-Tyne, 1767. First engravings on wood published in Charles Hutton's *Mensuration*, 1768. Undertook walking tour of Scotland; traveled to London to seek work, 1776. Returned to Newcastle; entered into business partnership with Beilby, with brother John Bewick as apprentice, 1777. Moved to Circus Lane, the Forth, Newcastle, 1781. Married Isabella Elliot (d. 1826), 1786: one son, three daughters. Published *A General History of Quadrupeds*, 1790. Started work on *A History of British Birds*, 1791. Moved to a new engraving studio in St. Nicholas's churchyard, Newcastle, 1795. Partnership with Beilby dissolved, 1797. Joined by his son Robert as apprentice, 1804. Became seriously ill; moved to Gateshead, 1812. Elected member of the Society of Dilettanti, Edinburgh, 1818. Visited by the painter John James Audubon; completed his *Memoir*, 1827. Traveled to London, 1828. Died in Gateshead, November 8, 1828.

Bibliography

Bewick, Thomas. *The Watercolours and Drawings of Thomas Bewick and his Workshop Apprentices*. 2 vols. Introduced and edited by Iain Bain. London: Gordon Fraser, 1981.

Rosen, Charles, and Henri Zerner. *Romanticism and Realism: The Mythology of Nineteenth-Century Art*. London: Faber and Faber, 1984.

Ruskin, John. *Aratra Pentelici*, 1872; *Ariadne Florentina*, 1876; *The Art of England*, 1883.

Schulz, Max F. *Paradise Preserved: Recreations of Eden in Eighteenth and Nineteenth Century England*. Cambridge: Cambridge University Press, 1985.

Weekley, Montague. *Thomas Bewick*. London: Oxford University Press, 1953.

BIEDERMEIER

The word *Biedermeier*, which combines an adjective meaning upright, conventional, and unpretentious (*bieder*) with a very common German surname (Meier), derived from the pseudonym Gottlieb Biedermaier used by the students Ludwig Eichrodt and Adolf Kussmaul for the satirical poems they published in the 1850s that mocked the philistine values of the *Spiessbürgertum* (petite bourgeoisie). The term was first applied in the later nineteenth century to the culture of German-speaking Europe and Scandinavia from the period spanning the peaks of Romanticism and realism—that is, approximately 1815–48. In this usage it referred to the simple, plebeian taste associated with the era's visual arts, especially furniture, decorative arts, and painting; subsequently it has been applied also to the literature and musical culture of the era, and has even come to denote the mood of the entire sociohistorical epoch. While it was intended as a derisive statement about the earlier period's unsophisticated aesthetics, it was tinged also with nostalgia for what was perceived to be an uncomplicated idyll of domestic comfort and family values that were lost with the arrival of the industrial revolution.

The turbulent beginning and end dates that mark the course of the Biedermeier epoch—two great upheavals of the Napoleonic wars and the March Revolutions—bolster its image as a time of tranquillity. However, it is telling that the period was interrupted and finally brought to an end by the outbreak of protest and insurrection. Percolating tensions were underlying the apparent complacency of the age of Metternich (1815–48; so named for Austrian statesman Clemens Lothar Wenzel Metternich, whose extreme conservatism marked the politics of time); these were brought about by censorship, crackdowns on liberal movements, and the suppression of attempts at political reform. Thus, the period's relative stability was sustained through force and repression, a factor that may be seen as informing many of the cultural trends of the day.

The Congress of Vienna (September 1814 to June 1815), with its conservative drive toward restoration, set in motion the prevailing monarchistic character of the Biedermeier era. Yet it was in fact the bourgeoisie that left its stamp on the period's taste and values, a phenomenon fostered by the high number of art, literature, and music *Vereine* (associations) that sprang up to accommodate the growing participation of the middle classes in the arts. Biedermeier culture bloomed especially in royal cities such as Berlin, Copenhagen, Munich, and Vienna, and the encroachment of the bourgeois aesthetic on the period as a whole is apparent in the way that the aristocracy adopted its understated sensibility in its own furnishings, fashion, and commissioned portraits.

The lines that demarcate what the term *Biedermeier* encompasses cannot be drawn too strictly, for much of what has been incorporated under its rubric can be ascribed also to Romanticism and realism. Biedermeier might be seen as a link between the two, overlapping both to some degree while resisting wholesale subsuming into either. While continuing many of the themes addressed by Romanticism, such as an introspective attachment to nature, the rediscovery of native folklore and homeland, and the exploration of inner life, Biedermeier culture was marked by a retreat from the grand visionary pursuits of Romanticism, reducing its lofty aspirations to a more manageable size. Indeed, an inclination toward small format characterizes Biedermeier cultural production in general. Pictures suitable for the scale of a bourgeois home, with favorite themes consisting of genre, landscape, still life, and portraiture, found a more willing audience than large historical or religious paintings. Mass-produced media such as lithographs and etchings made such images more accessible to a larger population. Folk and fairy tales, short stories, novellas, and one-act plays comprise much of Biedermeier literary work, while a thriving amateur writing culture found an outlet in journals, almanacs, guestbooks, and letters. *Lieder* (songs) and other short musical forms appropriate for performance by family and friends in the intimate setting of a private salon proved extremely popular.

A penchant for highly detailed description and rendering of the observed world is typical of the Biedermeier aesthetic. Works by artists such as Eduard Gaertner and Johann Erdmann Hummel, in their polished images of Berlin and its occupants, epitomize the smooth, tight handling of paint characteristic of much Biedermeier painting. Portraits were often particularly candid,

Die Familie des Malers Carl Begas. Reprinted courtesy of Bildarchiv.

depicting their subjects without embellishment, such as Johann Baptist Bastiné's frank depiction, *Frau Hasselbach* (c. 1820). Nature's tiniest details found their way into the writings of authors such as Annette von Droste-Hülshoff and Adalbert Stifter, or into the regional landscapes of artists such as Ferdinand Georg Waldmüller. The meticulous scrutiny of societal manners and morality also spoke to the Biedermeier sensibility, with an artist like Carl Spitzweg poking gentle fun at the ways of the bourgeoisie in his humorous anecdotal scenes (e.g., *The Love Letter*, c. 1845–46).

The bourgeois home was at the center of Biedermeier culture, and Gemütlichkeit, or coziness, was the principle behind its interior decoration. Households were furnished modestly with functional, simply ornamented, and comfortable pieces that deviated from the more formal Empire style prevalent at the beginning of the century. Rooms were arranged not with strict symmetry, but informally to allow for intimate socializing and to accommodate the comings and goings of daily living. The common accoutrements of the Biedermeier home (furniture, paintings, figurines, decorated glass, and porcelain) were lovingly rendered in countless paintings and drawings of interiors, and suggest the significant role played by the artist-craftsman in the decades just before industrialization firmly took root.

The child assumed a role of unprecedented importance in Biedermeier society, and the era saw a proliferation of children's literature and genre pictures of children at play. The Biedermeier esteem for the idea of domesticity is evident also in the numerous depictions of contented families relaxing at home, (e.g., Carl Begas's painting *The Begas Family*, 1821) and the vignettes of joyful domestic scenes that appear in literary works such as Eduard Mörike's poem "Der alte Turmhahn" ("The Old Weathercock," 1840–52). But alongside the idylls and contented scenes, much of Biedermeier literature conveys a tone of quiet resignation and general *Weltschmerz*, as in Franz Grillparzer's drama *König Ottokars Glück und Ende* (*King Ottocar, His Rise and Fall*, 1825) or Christian Dietrich Grabbe's *Don Juan und Faust* (1829). In light of the period's repressive atmosphere and shattered hopes for political reform, the emphasis on the security of the familial sphere might be read as a withdrawal into an interior world, away from the disillusionment experienced in the outside one.

The term *Biedermeier* cannot be used too sweepingly for an era that also produced the music of Ludwig van Beethoven, the poetry of Heinrich Heine, and the architecture of Karl Friedrich Schinkel. And despite similar trends elsewhere—that is, toward genre and a realistic impulse—there are no real analogues to the particularities of the political and social situation experienced in Germany. Just as the ending of the Napoleonic Wars marked the beginning of the Biedermeier period, it was the revolution and protests of 1830, and the awakening of dormant feelings across the European continent, that marked the beginning of its end. In the years before the March Revolution (the Vormärz), as the economic trauma left in the wake of Napoleon's occupation subsided, a more politically engaged literary culture was emerging. The simplicity of early Biedermeier style began to give way to more flourish and embellishment in furniture, fashion, and painting. Artists began to handle paint more loosely, and paid increasing attention to the effects of industrialization on their beloved landscape. A modest political awakening was underway, where Biedermeier's simplicity would seem less idyllic and more provincial.

MARGARET DOYLE

Bibliography

Biedermeier, 1815–1835: Architecture, Painting, Sculpture, Decorative arts, Fashion. Edited by Himmelheber, Georg, Munich: Prestel, 1989.

Historisches Museum der Stadt Wien. *Biedermeier in Wien 1815–1848: Sein und Schein einer Bürgeridylle*. Mainz: Ph. von Zabern, 1990.

Nemoianu, Virgil. *The Taming of Romanticism: European Literature and the Age of Biedermeier*. Cambridge, Mass.: Harvard University Press, 1984.

Norman, Geraldine. *Biedermeier Painting, 1815–1848: Reality Observed in Genre, Portrait, and Landscape*. London: Thames and Hudson, 1987.

Ottomeyer, Hans, ed. *Biedermeiers Glück und Ende: . . . die gestörte Idylle, 1815–1848*. Munich: Hugendubel, 1987.

Sengle, Friedrich. *Biedermeierzeit: Deutsche Literatur im Spannungsfeld zwischen Restauration und Revolution, 1815–1848*. 3 vols. Stuttgart: Metzler, 1971–80.

Roe, Ian F. and John Warren, eds. *The Biedermeier and Beyond: Selected Papers from the Symposium Held at St. Peter's College, Oxford, from 19–21 September 1997*. New York: Peter Lang, 1997.

BILDERDIJK, WILLEM 1756–1831

Dutch poet, jurist, scholar, and writer

Willem Bilderdijk's versatility as a scholar and writer was as phenomenal as his output, and his mastery of the Dutch language second to none. When he died in 1831, he left behind more than 300,000 lines of verse covering an extraordinary range of genres. His legacy further includes religious and legal treatises, numerous translations, linguistic studies on spelling and grammatical gender, annotated editions of medieval and Dutch renaissance poetry, a geological study on the formation of the earth, and a treatise on perspective. He corresponded with Jakob Ludwig Carl Grimm and Robert Southey, was an accomplished draftsman, engraver, and painter, and taught some of the most brilliant minds in the country while never failing to propagate his reactionary principles in word and deed. He was self-willed and full of contradictions, with a reputation that dwindled as fast after his death as it had risen in his youth.

Bilderdijk was born in Amsterdam on September 7, 1756, into a family of staunch defenders of the Dutch monarchy. Since the capital was mainly antiroyalist, the medical practice of Bilderdijk's father Izaäk did not do particularly well. Izaäk therefore accepted the post of tax inspector, offered to him at the intercession of Willem IV's widow. Willem Bilderdijk, who inherited his parents' unconditional support for the ruling House of Orange, had a prodigious nature, mastering French and Latin at a very young age. When he was six, he injured his left foot during a scuffle at school, and because of the deficient treatment he received would remain crippled for the rest of his life. Confined to his bed, the young boy turned into a shy recluse and passed the time by voraciously reading both literary and scientific works.

Because of his limp, the military career Bilderdijk had once aspired to was now out of reach. Instead, the precocious young man wished to continue with his studies but had to agree on a compromise with his father first: in 1776 he accepted a job as an accountant in his father's office until his brother was able to take over his duties. It was in the same year that Bilderdijk obtained the gold medal from a literary society in Leiden for a long Pindaric ode, "Invloed van de dichtkunst op het staetsbestuur" ("The Influence of Poetry on State Administration"). Similar prizes soon followed, turning the timid young man into something of a local celebrity. In 1779 he published an acclaimed translation of Sophocles' *Oedipus*, followed by a string of sensuous love poems collected in *Mijn verlustiging* (*My Delight*, 1781). Barely two years after enrolling at Leiden University, he graduated with a law degree in 1882. By then he had already been hailed as one of the foremost poets of the age, writing in an idiom that is instantly recognizable, but that must strike the modern reader as rhetorical and verbose. Technically flawless, his poetry has been characterized as "moving on stilts designed for giants."

Bilderdijk established himself as a successful barrister in The Hague and before long married Catharina Rebecca Woesthoven. In January 1795, when Napoleon Bonaparte's brother Louis was inaugurated as the new ruler of the kingdom of Holland, Bilderdijk, with typical stubbornness, refused to subscribe to the principles of the French Revolution and was forced into exile. He would never see his wife again. He eventually settled in London (1795–97), where he met Katharina Wilhelmina Schweickhardt, who became his second wife on May 18, 1797, without his original marriage having been dissolved first. Bilderdijk moved to Brunswick, Germany, 1797–1806, where he made a living as a private teacher in a wide range of subjects. During that period he still found time to publish more than ten volumes of poetry, including rhymed translations of James Macpherson's Ossian poems (1805), which number among his finest achievements. In 1806, Bilderdijk finally returned to the Netherlands, hoping in vain for a professorship in Dutch literature and linguistics. Despite the poet's fervent Orangist sympathies, King Louis Napoleon engaged Bilderdijk as his private tutor and offered him posts on a number of scientific and literary committees. In return, Bilderdijk wrote his notorious "Ode aan Napoleon" ("Ode to Napoleon," 1806), which his detractors saw as proof of the poet's rank opportunism. He also started work on an epic poem in alexandrines, *De ondergang der eerste wareld* (*The Destruction of the First World*), which is an account of the events leading to the biblical flood and Noah's rescue. The work breaks off in the middle of the fifth canto, never to be resumed; the unfinished work was published in 1820.

When Louis Napoleon was finally expelled by his own brother and the Netherlands became annexed to the French Empire, Bilderdijk lost his state pension and soon found himself in dire straits. Opium brought him only short-lived solace. Nonetheless he kept on writing, and in 1811 published *De kunst der poëzy* (*The Art of Poetry*), a curious, didactic poem in which he explains his poetological principles in terms that seem to link him firmly to the international Romantic movement, yet that also hark back to an older, more "rational" tradition. The work contains the famous line: "Uw hart, uw zelfgevoel, ô Dichter, is uw regel!" ("Your heart, your self-awareness, o Poet, is your dictum!") and ends on a defiant note: "Blaas me aan, gevoel der kunst! ik wil geen meesters meer" ("Inspire me, artistic feeling! I no longer wish for masters"). These quintessentially Romantic ideas, however, are offset in Bilderdijk's work by a proportionate depreciation of the role of the *verbeelding* (imagination) in the creative process: "Neen, 't is verbeelding niet (. . .) / Waar Dichtkunst in bestaat" ("No, it is not the imagination / That constitutes Poetry"). This makes it very difficult to categorize the poet as a Romantic *pur sang*.

Exactly half a century before Jules Verne's *Cinq semaines en ballon* (*Five Weeks in a Balloon*, 1863), Bilderdijk published one of his most original works, the *Kort verhaal van eene aanmerklijke luchtreis en nieuwe planeetontdekking* (*A Short Account of a Remarkable Aerial Voyage and Discovery of a New Planet*, 1813), purported to have been translated from Russian and relating the "shipwreck" of a balloonist on a small, unknown moon circling the earth. The tale can be read as the sublimation of his acutely felt loneliness and the sense of being an outcast that pervades much of his oeuvre. Another of Bilderdijk's liminal works of the same period is "De geestenwareld" ("The Spirit World"), a poetic discourse with strong Swedenborgian overtones on the nature of the afterlife, first published in the volume *Daffodillen* (*Daffodils*, 1814).

With the restoration of the Dutch monarchy in 1813, Bilderdijk produced an overwhelming amount of patriotic poetry. It did not help him to obtain a coveted professorship, however. From 1817 to 1827 he gave private lectures on national history and related subjects in his own home in Leiden, counting among his students Isaac da Costa, Jacob van Lennep, and Groen van Prinsterer. The last five years of his life were spent in Haarlem, where he died on December 18, 1831, at age 75.

KRIS STEYAERT

Biography

Born in Amsterdam, September 7, 1756; accountant in father's office, 1776; law degree at the University of Leiden, 1882. Married Catharina Rebecca Woesthoven, 1785; exiled from Kingdom of Holland, 1795; lived in London, 1795–97, and Brunswick, Germany, 1797–1806. "Married" Katharina Wilhelmina Schweickhardt, May 1797; later annulment of his first marriage, 1802. Returned to the Netherlands and appointed private tutor of King Louis Napoleon, 1806–10. Gave private lectures in Leiden, 1817–27; moved to Haarlem, 1827, where he died December 18, 1831.

Selected Works

Poetry

Mijn verlustiging, 1781. Edited by M. A. Schenkeveld van der Dussen. Zutphen: Thieme, 1975.
De kunst der poëzy, 1811. Edited by J. J. Kloek and W. van den Berg. Amsterdam: Prometheus/Bakker, 1995.
De ondergang der eerste wareld, 1820. Edited by J. Bosch, Zwolle: Tjeenk Willink, 1959.

Fiction

Kort verhaal van eene aanmerklijke luchtreis en nieuwe planeetontdekking, 1813. Translated by Paul Vincent as *A Short*

Account of a Remarkable Aerial Voyage and Discovery of a New Planet. Paisley: Wilfion, 1987.

Bibliography

Bavinck, H. *Bilderdijk als denker en dichter.* Kampen: Kok, 1906.

Eijnatten, Joris van. *Hogere sferen: De ideeënwereld van Willem Bilderdijk.* Hilversum: Verloren, 1998.

Hattum, M. van, L. Strengholt, and Peter van Zonneveld, eds. *Folia Bilderdijkiana.* Amsterdam: Bilderdijk Museum, 1985.

Johannes, G. J., "Bilderdijk draagt *De kunst der poëzy* voor in Felix meritis." In *Nederlandse literatuur: Een geschiedenis.* Edited by M. A. Schenkeveld-van der Dussen. Groningen: Martinus Nijhoff, 1993.

Zwaag, W. van der. *Willem Bilderdijk: Vader van het Réveil.* Houten: Den Hertog, 1991.

BINGHAM, GEORGE CALEB 1811–1879

American painter

Although Arthur Pope asserts that "[n]ot only in quality of surface but also in composition Bingham's paintings belong in the Renaissance tradition" (Nicolas Poussin, Giorgione, and Titian are three names cited), he also remarks of Bingham's "provincial" painting that "in good hands it achieved an extraordinary vigor." That "extraordinary vigor" in Bingham's good hands shines through in his river scenes celebrating the Romantic American frontier; in his role as recorder of the robust democracy that energized the American West; and in his skill as a landscape artist. While he was developing these rich subjects, he was, for almost half a century, making a living as a successful portrait painter.

After an erratic start that took him from his studio in Arrow Rock, Missouri, to Philadelphia, back to Missouri and a studio in Saint Louis, on to Washington D.C. and finally back to Saint Louis, Bingham exhibited his masterpiece *Fur Traders Descending the Missouri* (1845), an apparent companion place titled *The Concealed Enemy* (1845), and two landscapes at the American Art Union in New York City. Michael Edward Shapiro maintains that Bingham's rich genre paintings resulted from a fusion of elements derived from portraiture and landscape painting. The American Art Union, an outgrowth of the Apollo Association, was important to Bingham's career for it promoted American artists at a time when patronage was scarce. The Union's eastern audience was eager for scenes of the frontier, and Bingham fed its hunger by selling at least nineteenth paintings to the Union between 1845 and 1852.

Shapiro opines that *Fur Traders* and *The Concealed Enemy*, a portrait of an Osage Indian peering over a bluff with a loaded rifle, represent "a translation of European landscape styles into an American lexicon," with Claude Lorraine and Salvator Rosa cited by Henry Adams as probable influences. A succession of river paintings followed, including *Boatmen on the Missouri* and *The Jolly Flatboatmen* in 1846; *Lighter Relieving a Steamboat Aground* and *Raftsmen Playing Cards* in 1847; *Raftsmen on the Ohio* and *Watching the Cargo* in 1849; *The Woodboat* and *Fishing on the Mississippi* in 1850; *Mississippi Fisherman* in 1851; and *Jolly Flatboatmen in Port* in 1857. These genre paintings, scenes of everyday life lived robustly in the open air, earned Bingham the sobriquet of the "Missouri Artist."

In all of these works Bingham was contributing to the great outburst of creativity that can justly be described as the era of American Romanticism, marked by Ralph Waldo Emerson's proclamation of philosophical idealism, *Nature*, which preceded *Fur Traders* by only a decade. Bingham dramatized the river life that he knew so well, defining on canvas a truly American subject at the same time that James Fenimore Cooper was creating a frontier myth in fiction and Herman Melville was writing allegories of men at sea. And before Bingham died in 1879, Mark Twain would be at work on *The Adventures of Huckleberry Finn*, a romance of the Mississippi River that would rival Bingham's accomplishment.

Barbara Groseclose emphasizes the connection between Bingham, the "ardent Whig," and his election paintings *Country Politician* (1849), *Canvassing for a Vote* (1851–52), *The County Election* (1851–52), *Stump Speaking* (1853), and *The Verdict of the People* (1854–55).

In his works of social history, Bingham produced, Groseclose notes, "a pictorialized collective history of his region and, in turn, the activities of the people he delineated added to the framing of a national biography." The election paintings hardly suggest a genteel civic life, but rather a wide-open social process in which the drunk sprawled out in the foreground of *The Verdict of the People* bespeaks the heartiness of frontier democracy. The crowd gathered around the campaigner in *Stump Speaking* is clearly out as much for a diversion as for political oratory, and the listeners' expressions generally reveal their satisfaction with the speaker's tired rhetoric. The election paintings are not merely valuable historical documents but also superb demonstrations of Bingham's skill at compositions featuring many figures. In *The County Election* Bingham arranges his subjects in a progress from lower left to upper right, with bright light on several men in pale shirts in the center of the action. The background in the upper left quadrant presents a darker aspect, with trees, a steeple, and a tall signpost thrusting upward against billowing cumulus clouds. *Country Politician* arranges three men, the one in the middle as plump as a Buddha, beside a stove with a funnel reaching straight up through the roof, while a fourth man stands to the left reading a poster on the wall. In *Canvassing for a Vote* the men have moved outside and the Buddha sits as before except that he has a hat on. The politician sits in the same position, importuning his listeners with the exact hand gestures seen before. Bingham's familiar brindle dog snoozes at the left, a fourth figure has entered the scene, a chopping block has been added, clouds float in a darkening sky, and a tall post supporting a sign replaces the upright funnel in the center.

Other, nonpolitical, paintings include *The Squatters* (1850), in which a leathery older man leans on a stick and stares grimly at the viewer. A young man sits behind him, while a woman washes clothes in the background and a pot boils over an open fire. Two children appear in the background, and the brindle dog observes the painter. Their log home occupies the left side of the canvas, with a diagonal formed from the roof to the lower right, all in brown tones. The upper half of the scene depicts a vast sky with clouds moving to the right. *The Emigration of Daniel Boone* (1851–52) depicts the frontiersman striding straight ahead toward the viewer, emerging into the light on his way through the Cumberland Gap as the advance party for civilization. Boone's wife rides beside him on a white horse, his apparent second in command accompanies him at heel on his left, and a white dog trots along alertly in the left foreground. *Shooting for the Beef* (1850) records a frontier competition for the luckless beef creature tethered on the left. The composition is familiar: a dozen figures, seven of them massed on the left in front of a grocery store with several tall trees rising high behind the store. A man in the center aims a muzzle loader at the target nailed to a dead, twisted tree in the right background, and in the far distance pinkish clouds billow up into a blue sky. Painted in the same year, *The Checker Players* depicts an American ritual as the contestants face off across their board, while a kibitzer looms up between them as he leans against the counter of his store. In these paintings Bingham dramatizes American history as no one else ever has.

Bingham's appealing landscape paintings deserve more recognition than they sometimes receive. *Cottage Scenery* (1845) has Bingham's familiar browns in the center of a composition that swoops down to the lower right from a huge tree in the left background. The front yard of the cottage is bathed in sunlight that illuminates three figures in a triangle in the center, and massive white clouds dominate the right of the painting and provide a background for a gnarled and dying tree—all standard elements in a Bingham painting. *Landscape Rural Scenery* (1845), *Landscape with Cattle* (1846), and *Landscape with Waterwheel and Boy Fishing* (1853) generate the desired pastoral nostalgia, with the *Waterwheel and Boy Fishing* even reprising a Constable subject. Two of Bingham's most romantic landscapes are *The Storm* and *Deer in Stormy Landscape* (both c. 1852–53). Each is animated by a deer in the foreground, and the turbulence and blasted trees in each painting recall not only Salvator Rosa but also the "ghoul haunted woodland" in the poetry of Edgar Allan Poe, the Romantic genius who died just before these works were painted.

By 1856, the year he went with his family to Düsseldorf, Bingham's great achievement was behind him. His sensational protest painting *Order No. 11* (two versions, 1868–70), is a melodramatic mess in which Bingham lost all control. When Thomas Cole, one of the painters of the Hudson River school, left America for three years in Italy, William Cullen Bryant wrote in "To Cole, the Painter, upon Departing for Europe" that "Fair scenes shall greet thee where thou goest" and urged him to "Gaze on them, till the tears shall dim thy sight, / But keep that earlier, wilder image bright." Perhaps someone might have given Bingham similar advice when he went to Düsseldorf, but by that time Bingham's mission as the Missouri Artist was complete and he needed no further inspiration.

FRANK DAY

Biography

Born on March 29, 1811 in Augusta County, Virginia. Family moved to Franklin, Missouri, 1819; watched the painter Chester Harding in his Franklin studio, c. 1822; moved with widowed mother to farm near Arrow Rock, 1827; apprenticed to cabinetmaker in Boonville, c. 1828; began painting portraits, 1833. Married Sarah Elizabeth Hutchison, in Boonville, 1836; built a studio in Arrow Rock, 1837; studied in Philadelphia, 1838; took a studio in Saint Louis and exhibited six paintings at National Academy of Design in New York City, 1840. Shared studio in Washington, D.C., with John Cranch while painting portraits, 1841–44; exhibited *Going to Market* at National Academy, 1842; returned to Saint Louis; submitted *Fur Traders Descending the Missouri*, *The Concealed Enemy*, and two landscapes to American Art Union in New York City, 1845. Exhibited *The Jolly Flatboatmen* in Saint Louis and sold it to the American Art Union, 1846; exhibited *Lighter Relieving a Steamboat Aground*, *Raftsmen Playing Cards*, and *Stump Orator* in Saint Louis, 1847. Elected to state legislature from Saline County as a Whig; wife Sarah Hutchison died, 1848. Sold four paintings to Western Art Union; submitted *Raftsmen on the Ohio*, *Watching the Cargo*, *St. Louis Wharf*, *Country Politician*, and *A Boatman* to American Art Union; married Eliza K. Thomas, 1849. Painted *Shooting the Beef* and submitted *The Squatters* and *The Woodboat* to American Art Union, 1850. Painted *Emigration of Daniel Boone* while staying in New York City, 1851, exhibited *The County Election* in New Orleans, 1852. Exhibited *The Verdict of the People* in Saint Louis; took wife and daughter to Düsseldorf, 1856; returned to United States, 1859. Completed *Order No. 11*, 1868, and second version, 1870. Exhibited *Order No. 11* and *Washington Crossing the Delaware* at Louisville Industrial Exhibition, 1873; appointed adjutant-general of Missouri, 1875. Wife Eliza Bingham died, 1876; married Martha Livingston Lykins, 1878. Died in Kansas City, Missouri, July 7, 1879; first retrospective exhibition of work, University of Missouri, Columbia, April 9–24, 1910.

Bibliography

Bloch, E. Maurice. *George Caleb Bingham: The Evolution of an Artist.* 2 vols. Berkeley and Los Angeles: University of California Press, 1967.

———. *The Paintings of George Caleb Bingham: A Catalogue Raisonné.* Columbia: University of Missouri Press, 1986.

Demos, John. "George Caleb Bingham: The Artist as Social Historian." *American Quarterly* 17 (1965): 218–28.

Glanz, Dawn. *How the West Was Drawn: American Art and the Settling of the Frontier.* Ann Arbor: University of Michigan Press, 1982.

Groseclose, Barbara. "The 'Missouri Artist' as Historian." In *George Caleb Bingham.* New York: Abrams for The Saint Louis art Museum, 1990.

McDermott, James F. *George Caleb Bingham: River Portraitist.* Norman: University of Oklahoma Press, 1959.

Pope, Arthur, "Bingham's Technique and Composition." In *Four American Painters: George Caleb Bingham, Winslow Homer, Albert P. Ryder, Thomas Eakins.* New York: Arno Press, 1969.

Rash, Nancy. *The Painting and Politics of George Caleb Bingham.* New Haven, Conn.: Yale University Press, 1991.

Rusk, Fern. *George Caleb Bingham: The Missouri Artist.* Jefferson City, Mo.: Hugh Stephens, 1917.

Shapiro, Michael Edward, Barbara Groseclose, Elizabeth Johns, Paul C. Nagel, and John Wilmerding. *George Caleb Bingham.* New York: Abrams for The Saint Louis Art Museum, 1990.

Sunder, John E. *The Fur Trade on the Upper Missouri, 1840–1865.* Norman: University of Oklahoma Press, 1965.

Tyler, Ron. *American Frontier Life: Early Western Painting and Prints.* New York: Abbeville Press, 1987.

BIOGRAPHIA LITERARIA, OR BIOGRAPHICAL SKETCHES OF MY LITERARY LIFE AND OPINIONS 1817

Biography by Samuel Taylor Coleridge

Samuel Taylor Coleridge described the two volumes of his *Biographia Literaria* as a statement of his "principles in Politics, religion, and Philosophy, and the application of the rules, deduced from philosophical principles, to poetry and criticism." He aimed at the same time in this groundbreaking work of Romantic English criticism "to define with the utmost impartiality the real *poetic* character of the poet." Coleridge had begun work on the project in 1814; he described it then as book to be titled *Christianity the One True Philosophy*, and that it was to contain "fragments of *Auto*-biography." This moulding of self with criticism had been conceived early on in his literary career. As early as 1803 he had aired his intention "to write my metaphysical works, as *my Life*, & *in* my Life—intermixed with all the other events / or history of the mind & fortunes of S. T. Coleridge." The book is thus, in its finished form, a curious assortment of ideas and material—described, indeed, by its author both as "an immethodical miscellany" and as like "the fragments of the winding steps of an old ruined tower."

One of the major main aims of the *Biographia* was to establish a principled, unified approach to the major philosophical questions, particularly in respect to human knowledge, its limits, its relationship to morality, and to God. It is of major interest to modern scholars for its insights into poetry, criticism, and the operation of the imagination. However, it was also a political child of its times—the immediate aftermath of the end of the Napoleonic Wars, when economic depression, unemployment and the reemergence of radical politics once more seemed to threaten the Whig patriarchy. Coleridge and his friend and former poetic collaborator William Wordsworth were no longer the radicals they had been in their youth of the revolutionary 1790s, and in the *Biographia Literaria* he defended the canon of great literature (emblematized by Wordsworth) from the threat of impression into the radical cause.

Coleridge criticized contemporary critics and their "petulant sneers," declaring that "of all trades, literature at present demands the least talent of information." Instead, he called for a new code of critical practice, appealing to reviewers to "support their decisions by reference to fixed canons of criticism, previously established and deduced from the nature of man." The philosophical sections of the *Biographia*, in which he sought to establish a theory of mind on which to found his criticism, include discussions of Giordano Bruno, René Descartes, and the English philosopher David Hartley. But his ideas were particularly indebted to the work of German philosophers, including Emmanuel Kant, J. G. E. Maass, and F. W. J. von Schelling. In this section Coleridge also briefly elucidated his theory of imagination. However, what would have been a fascinating chapter on this subject was omitted, and perhaps never even existed. Coleridge declared, nevertheless, that he held the primary imagination "to be the living Power and prime Agent of all human Perception, and as a repetition in the finite mind of the eternal act of creation in the infinite I AM." The secondary imagination was "as an echo of the former," which "dissolves, diffuses, dissipates, in order to recreate." "Fancy," by contrast, was a lesser faculty. As he established in the book, poets of the imagination include John Milton, William Shakespeare, and Wordsworth, while those of fancy number the likes of Erasmus Darwin, John Dryden, and Alexander Pope.

In volume 2 of the *Biographia* Coleridge responds to the controversy surrounding the *Lyrical Ballads*, the joint collection of poems he had published with Wordsworth in 1798 and included his "Rime of the Ancient Mariner." This had been republished in 1800 with a foreword written by Wordsworth, of which Coleridge was particularly critical. He praised the language of "the educated man" over Wordsworth's acclaim for the language of the "low and rustic life." Coleridge defends metrical composition, and lays out his theory of meter as essential to poetry. Coleridge then dissected Wordsworth's poems, principally those in *Lyrical Ballads*, showing what he considers "the characteristic defects of Wordsworth's poetry," and those that he considers his "excellencies" The former included "inconstancy of style," Wordsworth's occasional "matter-of-factness," an "undue predilection for the *dramatic* form," and "thoughts and images too great for the subject." The "excellencies" include "an austere purity of language" and "a correspondent weight and sanity of the Thoughts and Sentiments. . . . They are *fresh* and have the dew upon them." The "perfect truth of nature" in Wordsworth's images and descriptions is equally picked out for praise, with his crowning virtue being "IMAGINATION in the highest and strictest sense of the word." Without Coleridge's chapter on imagination this praise is slightly hollow, and the volume ends uncomfortably with the autobiographical "Satyrane's Letters" and a critique of Charles Robert Maturin's recent play *Bertram*.

The work was not well received by reviewers. William Hazlitt and Francis Jeffrey, in the *Edinburgh Review*, a leading periodical (and one that Coleridge had attacked), pithily declared, "There are some things readable in these volumes;—and if the learned author could have been persuaded to make them a little more conformable to their title, we have no doubt that they would have been the most popular of all his productions. Unfortunately, however, this work is not so properly an account of his Life and Opinions, as an Apology for them." It was in the philosophical sections that the *Biographia Literaria* contained verbatim "borrowings," including, as Thomas de Quincey pointed out in an 1834, a long piece by Friedrich Wilhelm Joseph von Schelling. But de Quincey defended Coleridge, claiming that even with "the riches of El Dorado lying about him, he would condescend to filch a handful of gold from any man whose purse he fancied, and in fact reproduced in a new form." In an attempt to defend her father from these accusations, Sara Coleridge and her husband (the poet's cousin) Henry Nelson Coleridge published an important annotated edition in 1847, possibly based on a now lost copy corrected by Coleridge himself.

DAVID HAYCOCK

See also **Coleridge, Samuel Taylor**

Bibliography

Burwick, Frederick, ed. *Coleridge's Biographia Literaria: Text and Meaning.* Columbus: Ohio State University Press, 1989.

Coleridge, Samuel Taylor. *Biographia Literaria.* Edited by Nigel Leask. London: J. M. Dent, 1997.

Jackson, J. R. de J. *Coleridge: The Critical Heritage.* 2 vols. London: Routledge & Kegan Paul.

———. *Method and Imagination in Coleridge's Criticism.* London: Routledge & Kegan Paul, 1969.

Kearns, Sheila. *Coleridge, Wordsworth and Romantic Autobiography: Reading Strategies of Self-Representation.* London: Associated Universities Press, 1995.

Leask, Nigel. *The Politics of Imagination in Coleridge's Critical Thought.* Macmillan: Basingstoke, 1988.

Wallace, C. M. *The Design of Biographia Literaria.* London: George Allen and Unwin, 1983.

Wheeler, Kathleen M. *Sources, Processes and Methods in Coleridge's Biographia Literaria.* Cambridge: Cambridge University Press, 1980.

BLAKE, WILLIAM 1757–1827

English poet, painter, prophet, engraver, and illustrator

"Oh why was I born with a different face / Why was I not born like the rest of my race?" These plaintive questions, addressed by William Blake to his friend and patron Thomas Butts, evoke his sense of isolation from the dominant strands of late-eighteenth- and early nineteenth-century English culture. Although prompting periods of self-doubt and depression, isolation was, perhaps, an inevitable result of Blake's fierce independence and original genius.

Blake saw himself as a prophet, working in a radical tradition of liberty that reached back through John Milton and Edmund Spenser, to the biblical prophets Isaiah and Ezekiel. He believed that, rather than anticipating events in a preordained history, "Every honest man is a Prophet [when] he utters his opinion both of private & public matters / Thus / If you go on So / the result is So." In this role Blake pitted himself against the philosophies of Francis Bacon, John Locke, and Isaac Newton, prevailing sexual mores, hierarchical religious and political structures (he described state religion as "the source of all Cruelty"), and orthodox views on art established at the Royal Academy by Joshua Reynolds.

This critical impulse was not an end in itself. Blake believed that by giving form to error, the prophet opens up the possibility that error can be cast off. As Blake writes in *A Vision of the Last Judgment*, "Error or Creation will be Burned Up & then & not till then Truth or Eternity will appear." Prophecy is, therefore, the prelude to an ever-imminent apocalypse. At the same time, by demonstrating that what we take to be natural is actually constructed, Blake foregrounds the constitutive role of human imagination. Los and Enitharmon, the names given by Blake to the divided male and female portions, respectively, of the fallen imagination, produce the entire perceptual world. Still more dramatically, Blake asserts that "The Eternal Body of Man is The IMAGINATION. / God himself." The originality of Blake's oeuvre derives in part from this convergence of Enlightenment skepticism, aspects of millenarian thought and rhetoric, and Romanticism.

The synthesizing character of Blake's thought brings into dialogue a wide variety of canonical and noncanonical texts. The most important is the Bible, Blake's "Great Code of Art," though he warned his more conservative readers that "The Vision of Christ that thou dost see / Is my Visions Greatest Enemy."

Blake's Jesus is a figure of energy and imagination who preaches a gospel of radical freedom from the law.

The writings of the Swedish mystic Emanuel Swedenborg are the most significant noncanonical influence on Blake's work. Three of Swedenborg's books are among the thirteen books extant that were annotated by Blake, and the Swedenborgian New Jerusalem Church is the only religious group with which Blake was closely associated. Even after 1790, when Blake's enthusiasm for him turned to scorn, Swedenborg continued to exert an influence on the architecture and thematics of Blake's work. In "Milton" (1811), Blake described Swedenborg as the "Sampson shorn by the Churches," in part because he was unwilling to fully humanize religion.

Blake was the third son of James Blake, a London hosier, and his wife Catherine. William Blake married Catherine Boucher the daughter of a market gardener. Although critics have been eager to find a radical lineage for Blake, it appears that he came from an only mildly dissenting background. Blake received no formal schooling; however, at the age of fourteen he was apprenticed to James Basire, an antiquarian engraver, for seven years. In Basire's shop Blake learned the skills of etching and engraving that he used to support himself for the rest of his life. The bold, linear patterns characteristic of Basire's house style influenced Blake's own graphic work.

After completing his apprenticeship, Blake established a modest reputation as a reproductive engraver over the course of the next fifteen years. By 1790, the publisher Joseph Johnson was Blake's chief employer. Although at odds with their rationalism, Blake shared an enthusiasm for the French revolution with many of Johnson's authors, such as Thomas Paine and Mary Wollstonecraft. Blake's most overtly political poem, "The French Revolution," extant in page proofs but apparently never published, bears Johnson's name as publisher.

For much of his life, Blake struggled to balance the demands of his trade with his ambition to be recognized as an artist in his own right. In the same year that he completed his apprenticeship he commenced study at the Royal Academy and soon thereafter began to exhibit pictures on historical, literary, and biblical subjects at Academy exhibitions. Blake's first collection of poems, *Poetical Sketches*, was published in 1783, with the help of Reverend A. S. Matthew and his wife, Harriet.

William Blake, *The Echoing Green.* Plate 6 from *Songs of Innocence and of Experience.*" Reprinted courtesy of The Bridgeman Art Library.

portraying a world in which the structures of oppression have been internalized.

By 1794, England was at war with France; the millenarian hopes inspired by the French Revolution had been tempered by the Terror; and William Pitt's repressive policies had made the propagation of radical ideas a dangerous activity. It is hardly surprising, therefore, that the illuminated books published in that year and the next develop the second rather than the first of these strands, mapping the "mind-forged manacles" (as described in the poem "London") binding the present to the past. "The Song of Los" encloses the American Revolution (described in *America*) and the French Revolution (described in *Europe*) in the repetitive cycles of fallen history. Radically revising biblical accounts of creation, *The Book of Urizen*, *The Book of Ahania*, and *The Book of Los* offer a complex explanation of how the fallen world came into being. In their radical verbal and visual practices, these works look forward to his major prophecies: *Vala, or The Four Zoas* (c. 1796–1807), *Milton* (c. 1804–11), and *Jerusalem* (c. 1804–20).

In 1795, Blake was commissioned to design and engrave illustrations for a deluxe edition of Edward Young's popular *Night Thoughts*. Over the next two years, Blake produced 537 watercolor designs for Young; it was his largest project as a graphic artist. The first of a projected four volumes appeared in 1797, containing forty-three engravings by Blake, but no further volumes were published. This was a turning point in Blake's public reputation as an engraver and illustrator of books. Two years later, Blake complained in a letter to George Cumberland that "Even Johnson & Fuseli have discarded my Graver." Lack of employment, and the hope that the patronage of William Hayley might free him to work on his visionary art, may have prompted him to move to Felpham, Sussex, in 1800.

Blake claimed that, during the next three years, he "composed an immense number of verses on One Grand Theme . . . the Persons & Machinery intirely new to the Inhabitants of Earth." No extant work matches this description, although it is possible Blake was referring to *Vala or The Four Zoas*, the first of his major prophecies, which he worked on from 1796 until 1803. Although he continued to revise the poem until at least 1807, it was never completed, in part because of its remarkable scope and ambition: it sets out to map the course of fallen history, from the Creation to the Fall and, ultimately, the Last Judgment.

After three years in Felpham, Blake returned to London, frustrated with what he felt was Hayley's determination to keep him in a subservient position. His last year in Felpham was further soured by his arrest on charges of sedition and assault brought against him by a soldier he had thrown out of his garden. With Hayley's help, Blake was acquitted.

Blake's difficulties were not solved by his return to London. As he reported to Hayley, "Art in London flourishes. Engravers in particular are wanted. . . . Yet no one brings work to me." In 1805 Blake was commissioned by Robert Hartley Cromek to illustrate Robert Blair's *The Grave*, but he was disappointed when his designs were engraved by the more fashionable Louis Schiavonetti. Although *The Grave* sold well, it was harshly reviewed, with the *Anti-Jacobin Review and Magazine* describing Blake's designs as "the offspring of a morbid fancy." Insult was added to injury when, commissioned by Cromek, Thomas Stothard painted a picture of Geoffrey Chaucer's Canterbury pilgrims that Blake felt had been stolen from him. In 1809, Blake

Toward the end of the 1780s, Blake began to publish illuminated books, producing in quick succession thirteen works, including *The Book of Thel* (1789), *Visions of the Daughters of Albion* (1793), *Songs of Innocence and of Experience* (1794), *Europe* (1794), *The Book of Urizen* (1794), and *The Book of Los* (1795). The illuminated books were created by drawing and writing backward directly onto a copper plate, thus bringing invention and execution, the work of artist and engraver, into close relation. The work was printed on Blake's rolling press. Finally, each copy was colored by hand, often by Catherine Blake.

In the earliest of these books there are two distinct strands of thought. On the one hand, "The *Marriage of Heaven and Hell*", "Songs of Innocence" (1789), and *America* (1793) are marked by Blake's confidence that energy, whether the innocent energy of the child or the explosive energy of "Orc" (revolutionary energy), can sweep away injustice. As "A Song of Liberty" breathlessly announces, "Empire is no more! and now the lion & wolf shall cease." On the other hand, "The Book of Thel," "Visions of the Daughters of Albion" and "Songs of Experience" (1794) are more saturnine about the prospects of revolution, held an exhibition in his brother's hosiery shop, which featured his own version of the Canterbury pilgrimage. Few people attended, and Blake was described in *The Examiner* as "an unfortunate lunatic." Despite this debacle, many of Blake's most important works still lay ahead of him.

After a period of sixteen years during which Blake produced no new illuminated book, *Milton* was printed in 1811. The first complete copy of *Jerusalem* appeared in print in 1820. The former addresses the shortcomings of John Milton, the most important literary influence on Blake's own work. Although he saw him as divinely inspired, Blake felt Milton had rejected the feminine side of his identity. In this poem, Milton makes amends, returning from a dour heaven to be reunited with his female counterpart. This reunion sparks a moment of ecstatic vision in which the narrator glimpses an imminent reunion of heaven and hell, male and female, mind and body.

Jerusalem is the crowning achievement of Blake's work in illuminated printing. Its hundred pages provide a remarkable anatomy of fallen humanity, caught between Babylon and Jerusalem. The former is a city of violence and suffering, the latter the city of liberty; this vision is the "end of a golden string" that, Blake tells his readers, if wound into a ball "will lead you in at Heaven's gate, / Built in Jerusalem's wall."

In 1818 Blake met the landscape painter John Linnell, whose patronage enabled him to undertake the two most important projects of his later years: his illustrations to *Job* (1821–26) and to Dante Alighieri's *Divine Comedy* (1824–27). Through Linnell, Blake met the group of young artists called the Shoreham Ancients, among whom were Samuel Palmer, George Richmond, and Frederick Tatham, who admired Blake's early lyric poetry and visionary art though they distrusted his prophetic endeavors.

Despite Linnell's efforts, Blake died in poverty and obscurity. It was only with the publication of Alexander Gilchrist's biography, *Life of William Blake, 'Pictor Ignotus'* (1863) that interest in Blake's work began to grow. Modern Blake criticism takes as its starting point Northrop Frye's *Fearful Symmetry* (1947) and David Erdman's *Blake: Prophet against Empire* (1954), though recent historical and deconstructive studies have revised many of their assumptions. The visionary artist once dismissed as insane has been the subject of monographs in which he has been compared with Sigmud Freud, Isaac Newton, Friedrich Nietzsche, and, more recently, Jacques Derrida. The prophet isolated from his peers is now thought to have anticipated many of the insights of postmodernism.

PETER OTTO

Biography

Born in London on November 28, 1757. Attended Henry Pars's drawing school, 1767; apprenticed to James Basire, antiquarian engraver, August 1772; admitted to the Royal Academy Schools as a full student, October 1779. Married Catherine Boucher, August 18, 1782; attended first general conference of the Swedenborgian New Jerusalem Church, April 13, 1789. Moved to Felpham, Sussex, under the patronage of William Hayley, September 18, 1800; returned to London from Felpham, September 1803. Indicted on charges of sedition and assault, October 4, 1803; found not guilty, January 11, 1804. Exhibition of Blake's paintings at his brother's house, May 1809. Died August 12, 1827.

Selected Works

Blake's Illuminated Works. 6 vols. Edited by David Bindman. Princeton, N.J.: William Blake Trust and Princeton University Press, 1991–95.

The Complete Poetry and Prose of William Blake. Rev. ed. Edited by David V. Erdman, commentary by Harold Bloom. New York: Anchor-Doubleday, 1988.

"The Four Zoas" by William Blake: Photographic Facsimile of the Manuscript with Commentary on the Illuminations. Edited by Cettina Tramontano Magno and David V. Erdman. Lewisburg, Penn., and London: Bucknell University/Press Associated University Presses, 1987.

The Paintings and Drawings of William Blake. Edited by Martin Butlin. 2 vols. New Haven, Conn.: Yale, University Press, for the Paul Mellon Centre for Studies in British Art. 1981.

William Blake's Designs for Edward Young's "Night Thoughts": A Complete Edition. Edited by John E. Grant, Edward J. Rose, and Michael J. Tolley. Oxford: Clarendon Press, 1980.

Bibliography

Ault, Donald. *Visionary Physics: Blake's Response to Newton.* Chicago: University of Chicago Press, 1974.

Bentley, G. E., Jr. *Blake Records.* Oxford: Clarendon Press, 1969.

DiSalvo, Jacki, G. A. Rosso, and Christopher Z. Hobson, eds. *Blake, Politics, and History.* New York: Garland, 1998.

Essick, Robert N. *William Blake's Commercial Book Illustrations: A Catalogue and Study of the Plates Engraved by Blake after Designs by Other Artists.* Oxford: Clarendon Press, 1991.

Erdman, David V. *Blake: Prophet against Empire.* Rev. ed. Princeton, N.J.: Princeton University Press, 1969.

Frye, Northrop. *Fearful Symmetry: A Study of William Blake.* Princeton, N.J.: Princeton University Press, 1947.

Hilton, Nelson. *Literal Imagination: Blake's Vision of Words.* Berkeley and Los Angeles; University of California Press, 1983.

Mee, Jon. *Dangerous Enthusiasm: William Blake and the Culture of Radicalism in the 1790s.* Oxford: Clarendon Press, 1992.

Otto, Peter. *Blake's Critique of Transcendence: Love, Jealousy, and the Sublime in "The Four Zoas."* Oxford: Oxford University Press, 2000.

Schuchard, Keith. "Why Mrs. Blake Cried: Swedenborg, Blake, and the Sexual Basis of Visionary Art," *Esoterica: The Journal of Esoteric Studies* 2 (2000): 45–93.

Thompson, E. P. *Witness against the Beast: William Blake and the Moral Law.* Cambridge: Cambridge University Press, 1993.

Viscomi, Joseph. *Blake and the Idea of the Book.* Princeton, N.J.: Princeton University Press, 1993.

BLECHEN, CARL 1797–1840

German landscape painter

Carl Blechen's artistic career spanned only a decade and a half, yet during this brief period he created a diverse body of work that incorporated seemingly contradictory aspects of both Romanticism and realism, thus complicating wholesale assignment to either category. A proclivity for fantasy and melodrama, evidence of his early years as a theater scene painter, characterizes much of his production. Yet his work also reveals an uncompromising eye for recording the details of nature observed *en plein air*. Like Camille Corot and J. M. W. Turner, Blechen explored the topography of his native land but also surrendered to the lure of Italy, and like them, too, he demonstrated a facility for employing color and light as a means to expressive ends. However, a sense of irony or black humor often underlies even the brightest of his landscapes and prevents his somber, melancholic ones from assuming mystical overtones. While he often probed the conventions of European painting, at times his images feel quite modern: for instance, when they depict startlingly arbitrary scenes, as in *Blick auf Dächer und Gärten* (*View of Roofs and Gardens*, c. 1835), an almost unlovely picture of the view from his window in Berlin; or when they give an up-to-date inflection to traditional themes, as in *Park von Terni mit ba denden Mädchen* (*In the Park at Terni*, 1835), an apparently classical image of nude nymphs, who, however, turn out to be contemporary Italian ladies disturbed by the intrusion upon their bath.

In Berlin, where he studied under the landscapist Peter Ludwig Lütke, a foe of Romantic art, Blechen confronted a thriving Prussian classicism. However, his earliest works, with their Gothic ruins, gravestones, monks, and demons, seem more attuned to the work of Caspar David Friedrich (whom he most likely met on a trip to Dresden in 1823) and the fantastic imagery from some of the operas and plays he produced scenery for, such as Carl Maria von Weber's *Die Freischütz* (*The Marksman*, 1821) and E. T. A. Hoffmann's *Elixiere des Teufels* (*Devils' Elixir*, 1815–16) *Gebirgsschlucht in Winter* (*Ravine in Winter*, 1825), a depiction of a gnarled, defoliated tree set in a desolate grey landscape, produces an uncanny effect that even the nearby statue of Madonna and Child and the two tiny lights in the house in the background cannot alleviate. Such images richly illustrate Blechen's early engagement with a Romantic conception of nature as a powerful, potentially terrifying force, and the dreamlike, indeed nightmarish, qualities of this and other works suggest his fascination for the irrational phenomena of nature that Gotthilf Heinrich Schubert's *Ansichten von der Nachtseite der Naturwissenschaften* (*Views on the Dark Side of Natural Science*, 1806) had made a topic of popular conversation. Still, Blechen's landscapes often introduce an element of ironic jest that differentiate them from those of other Romantic painters. In his large canvas *Bau der Teufelsbrücke* (*The Construction of the Devil's Bridge*, c. 1835), the view focuses on the construction of a rickety bridge in the middle ground, rather than on the majestic peak of the mountain crowding the background. The scene is populated neither by reverential figures contemplating the grandeur of the Alps nor by shepherds tending idyllically to their flock, but by tired workers who pause for a nap, oblivious to the sublime landscape surrounding them.

Having left his position at the Königstädtisches Theater to work as an independent painter, Blechen made his declaration of artistic ambition with his 1828 contribution to the Konigliche Preussische Akademie der Künste (Royal Prussian Academy of Arts) exhibition, the immense *Blick von den Müggelbergen be: Köpenick gegen süden* (*Müggelberge Looking South toward Köpenick*). The work was both a landscape painting of a specific region and a history painting with patriotic overtones, monumentalizing Brandenburg's ancient past. The painting's success led to Blechen's first and only trip to Italy, a mecca for German artists, including the Nazarenes. There, he ignored the great churches and historic buildings of the cities in favor of the Roman Campagna and the landscape around Naples. A year's exposure to the sun and intense palette of the Italian peninsula led to a shift away from dark, northern motifs and toward a stunning application of color and rendering of light in the large canvasses of Italian scenes he painted upon return to Berlin. Yet even while he succumbed, like many other artists before and after him, to the intensity of its light, Blechen disregarded artistic convention in his depictions of the esteemed south. He gravitated toward scenes that defied received notions of beauty, and frequently emphasized the harshness of the land—rendering, for instance, the effects of the bright sun on the dried, scorched countryside. In *Das Kloster Santa Scholastica bei Subiaco* (*The Cloister Santa Scholastica at Subiaco*, c. 1832), a cloister, reflecting in its explosive brightness the fury of the sun, sits atop dark, rugged cliffs that occupy most of the composition, thus denying a sweeping view of the landscape. Critical reaction to Blechen's Italian paintings was one of admiration for the power and truth in the rendering, but also shock at the boldness of the palette and puzzlement at the mixture of imagination and reality, as well as at what was identified by one writer as the "schauerlichen" (horrific) humor.

Carl Blechen, *Gebirgsschlucht in Winter*. Reprinted courtesy of Bildarchiv.

Blechen's free handling of paint connects him more to French or English Romanticism than to the tightly woven constructions of many of his compatriots (for example, Caspar David Friedrich, Joseph Anton Koch, or Philipp Otto Runge), and after Italy his painterly style became even looser than before. His remarkable open-air oil studies (Johann Gottfried Schadow called him an "incomparable sketcher") have especially been valued for the freshness and immediacy of their vision; often they border on the abstract as he captures an entire panoramic view with just a few strokes of paint. Blechen's loose brushwork, his interest in the effects of light, and his practice of sketching from nature have led to the assessment of him by some latter-day critics as a kind of protoimpressionist. Although he frequently painted the environs of Berlin, however, he did not share the impressionists' keen interest in the contemporary urban scene, and his penchant for depicting narrative moments and *Stimmungslandschaften* (landscapes of mood) precludes too close a link with them.

Blechen's contemporaries recognized his enormous talent, and a host of influential figures, including Bettina von Arnim, Schadow, and Karl Friedrich Schinkel, fostered his work; in the early 1830s he even received a major commission from Friedrich Wilhelm III. Yet such connections could not hinder the opinion of many that his work was marred by a fondness for the bizarre, and, despite his critical acclaim, financial success eluded him. His tragic descent into mental illness has affected the perception of his achievement, as his agitated mind has been seen as informing not only the symbolic content of his work but also its characteristically furious brushwork. Blechen himself remained bitter about his perceived undervaluation, but today he is appreciated as an artist who both participated in and paved the way for many of the most significant currents of nineteenth-century painting.

MARGARET DOYLE

Biography

Born July 29, 1798 in Cottbus. His father intended for him to study theology or law, but financial constraints led instead to training in a Berlin bank in 1815. Worked as a bank clerk until 1822; completed landscape and drawing classes at the Berlin Academy Königliche Preussische Akademie der Künste 1822–24; met Johann Christian Clausen Dahl in Dresden in 1823, presumably also Caspar David Friedrich; married Henriette Boldt, 1824; worked as scenery painter in Berlin 1824–27; member of Berlinische Künstlerverein 1826; exhibited for first time at the Berlin Academy 1827; travel in Italy 1828–29, where he shared a house with landscape artists Joseph Anton Koch and Johann Christian Reinhart; professor of landscape painting at the Berlin Academy 1831–36; trip to Paris with art dealer Louis Friedrich Sachse 1835; mental breakdown and resignation from the Berlin Academy, 1836; died July 23, 1840.

Bibliography

Eberle, Matthias. "Karl Blechen oder der Verlust des Geschichte." In *Berlin zwischen 1789 und 1848. Facetten einer Epoche.* Edited by Sonja Günther. Berlin: Frölich and Kaufmann, 1981.

Emmrich, Irma. *Carl Blechen.* Munich: Beck, 1989.

Fontane, Theodor. *Aufsätze zur bildenden Kunst I.* Vol. 23 of *Sämtliche Werke.* Edited by Rainer Bachmann and Edgar Gross. Munich: Nymphenburger Verlagshandlung, 1970.

Möller, Heino. *Carl Blechen, Romantische Malerei und Ironie.* Weimer: Verlag und Datenbank für Geistesgewissenschaften, 1995.

Rave, Paul Ortwin, ed. *Karl Blechen. Leben, Würdigungen, Werke.* Berlin: Deutscher Verein für Kunstwissenschaft, 1940.

Carl Blechen: Zwischen Romantik und Realismus. Edited by Peter-Klaus Schuster. Munich: Prestel, 1990.

Vaughan, William, "Landscape and the 'Irony of Nature.'" In *The Romantic Spirit in German Art 1790–1990.* Edited by Keith Hartley. London: Thames and Hudson, 1994.

BLICHER, STEEN STEENSEN 1782–1848

Danish writer

In Denmark the Romantic era is also called the Golden Age because it was a time of cultural flowering for an entire spectrum of fine arts. Visual art had Christen Schjellerup Købke; sculpture had Bertel Thorvaldsen; music had Niels Wilhelm Gade; philosophy had Søren Kierkegaard; and literature had Nikolai Frederik Severin Grundtvig, Bernhard Severin Ingemann, Adam Gottlob Oehlenschläger, and, most prominently, Hans Christian Andersen. However, far from the glitter of the capital, in the deepest and darkest part of the Jutland heaths, one finds the solitary figure of Steen Steensen Blicher.

In Danish literary history it is customary to differentiate between *romantik* and *romantisme*: The first term originates from Germany and refers to the philosophical thinking of the Jena Romantics. It was brought to Denmark by Henrich Steffens, who had traveled extensively in Germany, where he had met and befriended a number of the most prominent members of the German "Frühromantik." Therefore, when he held a series of lectures in Copenhagen, he was able to inspire an entire generation of Danish poets and writers.

Among the listeners at these lectures was the young Blicher, who was in Copenhagen to study theology. Unlike Oehlenschläger, Blicher was unimpressed by Steffens's exposition of German Romanticism; he had just been presented with a copy of James Macpherson's *Poems of Ossian* and was enthralled. As opposed to many of his contemporaries, Blicher was heavily influenced by British literature. So instead of Johan Wolfgang von Goethe, Novalis, Johann Christoph Friedrich von Schiller, August Wilhelm and Friedrich von Schlegel, and Ludwig Tieck, Blicher found his literary inspiration in the works of Robert Burns, Oliver Goldsmith, Samuel Johnson, Alexander Pope, and Walter Scott.

In a Danish context Blicher is classified as an exponent of *romantisme*, which is understood as a more realistic and nontranscendental movement than that of the *romantik*. Transcendence is sought through aesthetics, thus leading to a heightened interest in poetic and fictional form. This focus on the world of materiality frequently found its expression in an exploration of the other in both colonial and domestic landscapes. In the first half of the nineteenth century Denmark still had its Atlantic, African, Caribbean, and Indian colonies; otherness was therefore a natural part of Danish identity, both overseas and in the homeland.

Blicher's most significant prose is set in the middle of the Jutland peninsula. Most of this prose is written in the form of short stories that reflect their regional setting in theme, characterization, and regional dialect. "En Landsbydegns Dagbog" ("The Diary of a Parish Clerk") was first published in 1824 in an Århus periodical called *Læsefrugter* (*Fruits for Reading*), whose nationwide circulation brought Blicher to the attention of readers outside his immediate geographical area. In this fictionalized diary Blicher uses a first person singular narrator, Morten Vinge, whose entire life is framed by his unrequited love for the noblewoman Miss Sophie. The diary relates how Morten is washed ashore on a Danish coast where he meets Sophie, now a fallen woman, tending the gardens at the Corselidse estate. The fictional status of the diary as a literary form is given an added dimension, because Sophie is a fictional reference to the historical figure of Marie Grubbe, an aristocrat who ended her life in poverty and degradation.

Not all of Blicher's prose is written in diary form, but most of his fiction includes historical and autobiographical elements that together create a multifaceted picture of rural Denmark. Some of his tales deal with Jutland as the center of domestic knitting production. The tale of "Hosekræmmeren" ("The Hosier and his Daughter," 1829) opens with a description of the heath and its people. It tells the story of the beautiful Cecil, who kills her one true love while clouded in madness; later when her sanity returns she tragically realizes her mistake, and this mercifully leads her back into madness. "The Hosier" is related by a first person singular narrator, but unlike the straightforward first person narration of the "Parish Clerk," "the Hosier" has two narrators: a narrative "I" who does not participate in the narrated events, and the hosier's widow, who is part of the plot. The narrative structure is like a set of Chinese boxes; the main events of the plot are narrated by the widow upon the request of the narrative "I," who in turn passes her story on to us, the readers.

The frame-story technique is refined further in Blicher's *E Bindstouw* (*The Knitting Room*). The narrative structure is reminiscent of Giovenni Boccacio's *Decameron* and Geoffrey Chaucer's *Canterbury Tales*, because inside an overall frame different narrators tell their tales. Each narrator tells his story in a genre befitting his person and the content of the story. The word *bindstouw* is dialect for a knitting room, which prior to the Industrial Revolution fulfilled a double function for the local peasantry. Knitting was common among both men and women in order to earn money; knitting together in a bindstouw combined the necessary with the social. Blicher's "bindstouw" narration has an overall first person narrator who tells of a particular gathering of knitters three days prior to Christmas Eve. The frame narrator describes the various knitters in indirect discourse; inside the frame, each subnarrator's contribution is in direct discourse—some tell tales, while others sing songs. Both frame and individual tales and songs are related in Jutland dialects.

Blicher's characteristic frame narration is not limited to his prose. His most successful poetry, *Trækfuglene* (*Birds of Passage*), subtitled as a "nature concert," is constructed using the same principle: each poem is titled as a bird and endowed with themes reflecting the bird's behavior. Bird symbolism is, however, not restricted to the thematic level, Blicher also captures the musical quality of the birds' song. The golden plover sings in a stately andante, the lark thrills with its allegro brillante, and the owl hoots like a bassoon.

Of all the poetic birds represented in the volume, it is the bird that sings the prelude that sings most beautifully. Unlike the other birds, this one is unnamed because this bird sings with Blicher's own voice. Written after a severe illness, the poem expresses the resignation and melancholy of departure. The bird sings of the freedom of God's nature and of the confines of its cage, and continues singing until the very end.

ARNE AND HENRIETTE STAVIS

See also **Andersen, Hans Christian; Britain: Cultural Survey; British Romanticism: Approaches and Interpretations; British Romanticism: Literary Legacy; German Romanticism: Its Literary Legacy; Germany: Cultural Survey; Grundtvig, Nikolai Frederik Severin; Ingemann, Bernhard Severin; Kierkegaard, Søren; Købke, Christen Schiellerup; Oehlenschläger, Adam Gottlob; Ossian; Scandinavia and Finland: Historical Survey; Scott, Walter; Thorvaldsen, Bertel**

Biography

Born in Vium, Denmark, October 11, 1782. Studied theology, University of Copenhagen, 1799–1809; doctorate, 1809. Worked as a grammar school teacher, Randers, 1810–11; married Ernestine Juliane, his uncle's seventeen-year-old widow, 1810; they had ten children, 1811–32; moved to his father's parish at Randlev as tenant farmer of father's land, 1811; vicar of Thorning-Lysgaard, 1819–25. Published first short story, "Brudstykker af en Landsbydegns Dagbog" ("Fragments from the Diary of a Parish Clerk") 1824. Vicar of Spentrup, 1825–48; published translation of Oliver Goldsmith's *The Vicar of Wakefield*, 1827; serious illness, 1837; published *Trækfuglene* (*Birds of Passage*), 1838. Died at Spentrup vicarage, March 26, 1848.

Selected Works

Ossians Digte. Translation of James Macpherson's *Poems of Ossian*. 1807–9.

Digte. Første Deel. 1814.

Digte. Anden Deel: Jyllandsrejse i sex Døgn. 1817.

"Brudstykker af en Landsbydegns Dagbog," 1824; rev. title, "En Landsbydegns Dagbog," 1833. Translated by Paula Hostrup-Jessen in *The Diary of a Parish Clerk and Other Stories*. Introduction by Margaret Drabble. 1996.

Trækfuglene: Naturconcert. 1838.

E Bindstouw: Fortællinger og Digte i jydske Mundarter. 1842.

The Diary of a Parish Clerk and other stories, 1996; translated by Paula Hostrup-Jessen, with an introduction by Margaret Drabble: "The Diary of a Parish Clerk" ("En Landsbydegns Dagbog," 1824), "The Gamekeeper at Aunsbjerg" ("Skytten paa Aunsbjerg," 1839), "Alas, How Changed!" ("Ak! hvor forandret," 1828), "The Hosier and His Daughter" ("Hosekræmmeren," 1829), "The Pastor of Vejlbye" ("Præsten i Vejlbye," 1829),

"Tardy Awakening" ("Sildig Opvaagnen," 1828), "Three Festival Eves" ("De tre Helligaftener," 1841).

Bibliography

Baggesen, Søren. *Den blicherske novelle*. Copenhagen: Gyldendal, 1965.

Brix, Hans. *Blicher-Studier*. Copenhagen: Gyldendal, 1916.

———. "Steen Blicher." In *Danmarks Digtere:Fyrretyve kapitler af dansk digtekunsts historie fra Saxo til Pontoppidan*. Copenhagen: Aschehoug, 1962.

Christensen, Jesper. "Steen Steensen Blicher (1782–1848)," *Kalliope-Digtarkiv*, September 5, 2001, online at http://www.kalliope.org/ffront.cgi?fhandle = blicher.

Høgh, Jon. *Kommentarer til Steen Steensen Blichers E Bindstouw*. Herning: Poul Kristensen, 1982.

———. *Kommentarer til Steen Steensen Blichers noveller: Hosekræmmeren og De tre helligaftener*. Herning: Poul Kristensen, 1979.

Jørgensen, Annemarie Gjedde, Charlotte Hviid, Anni Johansen, Connie Juul Jeppesen, and Mette W. Jønson. *St. St. Blicher: En bibliografi*. Copenhagen: Blicher-Selskabet and Danmarks Biblioteksskole, 1993.

Kristensen, Evald Tang, and M. A. S. Lund, *Steen Steensen Blichers Liv og Gerning*. Steen Steensen Blicher's Life and Work. Herning: Blicher-Selskabet and Poul Kristensen, 1991.

Nørgaard, Felix, Marie Stoklund, Gordon Albøge, and Eyvind Rafn, ed. *Omkring Blicher 1974*. Copenhagen: Blicher-Selskabet and Gyldendal, 1974.

Ostenfeld, Ib. *Blicher-Studier*. Herning: Poul Kristensen, 1989.

Sørensen, Knud. *St. St. Blicher: Digter og samfundsborger—En illustreret biografi*. Copenhagen: Gyldendal, 1984.

BONAPARTE, NAPOLEON 1769-1821

Emperor of France, 1804–1814 and 1815

Politically, Napoleon Bonaparte's career and legacy are distinguished by paradox. A product, if not personification, of the French Revolution, Napoleon perverted and even reversed many of the Revolution's principles. While his own regime was marked by increasing repression at home and the extension of a supranational empire abroad, following his exile and death he was admired by many liberals and nationalists throughout Europe who were dissatisfied with the conservatism of the Restoration. A similar gulf between reality and subsequent myth exists in the area of cultural politics: Napoleon, the representative of a regime that clad itself in a sterile neoclassicism and who found himself in conflict with the most talented literary figures of his age, was subsequently elevated by literature to Promethean status.

The horrors of the "revolutionary decade" (1789–99) were crucial in determining the policies pursued by Napoleon under the Consulate (1799–1804) and Empire (1804–14/15). However, no account of these regimes can neglect entirely the impact of Napoleon's Corsican upbringing, or education in the royal military school in Brienne, in shaping his character and outlook. Much indeed can be made of the "clannishness" and disturbed politics that distinguished the life of such Corsican (minor) noble families as the Bonapartes in the final decades of the Ancien régime, in endowing Napoleon with an understanding of power, in shaping his social outlook, and in explaining his policy when emperor of "providing" for his often treacherous and usually less capable siblings. In Brienne, Napoleon's qualities of self-reliance, toughness, and industry were further developed. He excelled in mathematics and Latin. He was an avid reader and worshipped the heroes he encountered in French translations of Tacitus, Livy, and Plutarch. He loved Torquato Tasso's Romantic epic *Jerusalem Delivered* (1581) and subsequently James Macpherson's *Lays of Ossian* (1765), though in his later teens his reading focused on histories (especially of his native Corsica) and political theory (he developed a liking for the authors of the French Enlightenment, notably Charles-Louis de Secondat Montesquieu and Jean-Jacques Rousseau).

The outbreak of the French Revolution found the young Napoleon in his native Corsica, a participant in the faction fighting on the island that only increased with the arrival of news of events in Paris. Subsequently a partisan of the Jacobins, Napoleon first gained nationwide fame in Toulon in 1793, where he distinguished himself as a young artillery captain in the expulsion of the British from France's Mediterranean naval base. With the overthrow of Maximilien de Robespierre, Napoleon also fell from grace and was indeed imprisoned for a brief period before being rehabilitated. In October 1795, as general, Napoleon crushed a royalist revolt in Paris through the ruthless deployment of artillery.

However, it was in March 1796, with his appointment as commander of the French army in Italy, that Napoleon's rise to glory began. In a brilliant campaign, Napoleon defeated the Habsburg army in a series of engagements culminating in the Battle of Rivoli in January 1797, forcing Vienna to sue for peace and thereby ending the first revolutionary war. Napoleon, who at the beginning of the campaign had been known only within a restricted circle in France, was now famous throughout Europe. Culturally, this fame manifested itself in a variety of forms, from James Gillray's scurrilous cartoons to Antoine-Jean Gros's painting of Napoleon leading the charge across the bridge at Arcole. It is this last image, that of the epic hero of the first Italian campaign, that would remain so powerful throughout the Romantic period and afterward. However, Napoleon the systematic "liberator" of Italian art treasures (which he transported in bulk from the peninsula to fill the cavernous galleries of the recently opened museum in the Louvre) was not associated with this image. Shortly after his return from Italy, Napoleon was elected to the Institut (after 1806, the Institut de France) as a member of the mechanics section in the sciences class.

Napoleon's courting of France's intellectual elite was cut short by his next military venture—namely, the 1798 expedition to Egypt. This was designed to strike a blow at British possessions farther east, thereby defeating the last great power still engaged in war against France. The expedition, including five hundred civilian experts (some of whom were members of the Institut who had gone along to study Egyptian culture), set sail in May 1798, landed in Alexandria on July 1, and defeated the assembled

Mameluk forces at the Battle of the Pyramids. However, the destruction of the French fleet by Lord Viscount Horatio Nelson at Aboukir a few weeks later proved a decisive strategic defeat. In cultural, if not military terms, the expedition had a greater impact, both in the short-term craze for Egyptian artistic themes and in the long-term development of modern Egyptology. British naval success encouraged the formation of a new anti-French coalition and the outbreak of a second revolutionary War in early 1799. Returning from Egypt, Napoleon arrived in a France that faced a domestic as well as military crisis. There he was co-opted by a group of politicians and intellectuals ("Brumairians," including, notably, Emmanuel Sieyès) dissatisfied with the seemingly inherent instability of the directorial regime established in 1795. These individuals required military might to effect a coup. This occurred on November 9–10 (Brumaire 18–19, under the Revolutionary calendar), and instituted Napoleon as first consul.

The institutional foundations of the new regime were provided for by the Constitution of the Year VIII (1799). Many of Sieyès's ideas were incorporated into this document and he was among the many "Brumairians" disappointed to see themselves marginalized as the first consul concentrated power into his own hands. While the principle of equal citizenship and universal (male) suffrage was respected on paper, in practice it was nullified by a complex indirect voting system and the weakening of the legislature through its division into three institutions—the senate, tribunate and legislative body, all with limited powers. Real power was vested in the hands of the first consul, who stood at the head of an administrative chain that ran from

Antoine Jean Gros, *Bonaparte au Pont d'Arcole, le 17 Novembre 1796.* Reprinted courtesy of the Bridgeman Art Library.

Paris to every city and town, along which instructions sped rapidly. Over time, and especially with the transformation of the consulate into the hereditary empire in 1804, this already rigid system grew progressively more inflexible. Napoleon believed that centralization best insured internal stability, while at the same time maximizing the mobilization of resources (conscripts and tax revenues) necessary to sustain the ongoing Napoleonic Wars.

Initially, at least, the Napoleonic regime raised the hopes of the many persecuted during the Revolutionary decade. Representative of those former émigrés who now returned from abroad and rallied to the new regime was the writer François-Auguste-René, Vicouete de Chateaubriand. His *Génie du christianisme* (*Genius of Charistianity*, 1802), which sought to demonstrate the intellectual and artistic creativity of Christianity, coincided with the conclusion by Napoleon of a concordat with the papacy that sought to reestablish the institutions of the Catholic Church in France. This represented the consulate's greatest achievement, and contributed to Napoleon's undoubted popularity at this stage. However, for Chateaubriand, the break came in 1804, with the abduction and assassination of the Duc d'Enghien. Already, the authoritarian tendencies of the regime were apparent with the progressive weakening of the one institution that had dared show some independence, the tribunate. This had become a forum for those, including Henri-Benjamin Constant de Rebecque (and, Napoleon believed, through him, Anne-Louise-Germaine de Staël and her salon), who were increasingly critical of the regime on the grounds that it was illiberal, and others—the so-called idéologues—who condemned it on the grounds that they resented being marginalized after Brumaire and because they opposed the Concordat. The Tribunate was successively purged and weakened institutionally before being finally extinguished in 1807.

The Napoleonic regime was essentially pragmatic, devoid of any overarching ideological foundation beyond the management of power and control of the vast forces unleashed by the Revolution. "Bonapartism" was neither revolutionary nor counterrevolutionary, but simply postrevolutionary. These principles, if they can be referred to as such, were reflected in Napoleon's educational and cultural policies. The progressive *écoles centrals*, set up under the directory at the secondary level, were replaced by the *lycées*, with their emphasis on Latin, mathematics, and military drill. Primary education was dumped on the communes, and consequently neglected. Higher education came in the form of special academies designed to train lawyers, engineers, and doctors useful to the society and state. As for special schools in nonvocational subjects, Napoleon was skeptical: for example, he dismissed the suggestion for a special school in literature as ridiculous, adding for good measure that in his own experience one had learned everything one needed to know about that subject by the age of fourteen.

Napoleon's attempt to enlist culture for political ends succeeded better in some art forms than others. In architecture, given the state's importance as patron and customer, the Napoleonic stamp was especially visible in neoclassical triumphal arches, columns, and memorials in Paris that were duplicated in more modest form throughout the empire. In sculpture, also, Antonio Canova created effigies of Napoleon. As for painting, Jacques-Louis David, with his *Bonaparte franchissant le mont Saint-Bernard* and *Le Sacre de Napoléon Ier et le Couronnement*

(*Napoleon Crossing the Alps at the Great St. Bernard Pass*), *de l'Impératrice Joséphine* (*The Consecration of Napoleon I and The Coronation of the Empress Josephine,* 1806), immortalized key events of the Napoleonic episode. With works such as Antoine Jean Gros's *Le Général Bonaparte sur le pont d'Arcole* (*General Bonaparte on the Arcole Bridge,* 1801), *Bonaparte visitant les pestiférés de Jaffa* (*Napoleon in the Pest House at Jaffa,* 1804) and *Napoléon sur le champ de bataille d'Eylau* (*Napoleon on the Battlefield of Eylau,* 1807) this genre produced a romanticized image of the Napoleonic legend well in advance of literature. For, as Napoleon himself admitted, the greatest writers of his age (Chateaubriand, Madame de Staël, Henri-Benjamin Constant de Rebecque, were all in opposition to him, and only the mediocre in favor. That this was the case was hardly surprising given the imperial regime's attempt to restrict the printed word to a "littérature dirigée" and to censor everything else. Under Louis XIV, the greatest writers had, on the whole, supported the state. In the second half of the eighteen century, they had become alienated from the state. This Napoleon failed to reverse.

Napoleonic propaganda worked in that when the end came it did so through invasion from without, not revolution from within. The loss of an army of over five-hundred thousand men in Russia in 1812 dramatically tilted the military balance in favor of a new coalition, the sixth, that now formed to defeat the ogre. By early 1814 it had done so, a verdict that Napoleon's attempt at a comeback during the so-called Hundred Days of the following year could not reverse. Yet, in many respects, the Napoleonic legacy proved more significant, both politically and culturally, than the episode itself. Politically, Napoleon bequeathed a legacy that liberals, both in France and elsewhere in Europe, could subsequently draw on; the same was true for nationalists, especially in northern Italy. In cultural terms also, the Romantic potential of the developing Napoleonic legend became apparent as a new generation, born during the Consulate and Empire, now looked back with nostalgia at an age that appeared the antithesis of the Restoration (1815–30), with its grubby place-seeking and intolerance, and the boring, bourgeois July Monarchy (1830–48). "The life of Napoleon is our century's epic for all the arts," wrote one of this new generation, Eugène Delacroix, a statement borne out by such works as Alfred-Victor de Vigny's *Servitude et grandeur militaries* (Servitude and Grandear of Arms, 1835), Louis-Charles-Alfred de Musset's *La Confession d'un enfant du siècle* (*Confession of a Child of the Century,* 1836), and Stendhal's *Le Rouge et le Noir* (*The Red and the Black,* 1830), not to mention those by Honoré de Balzac and Victor Hugo. Epics, of course, are generally more enjoyable to read about than to live through. The legend that emerged after 1815 was in reality a form of selective amnesia, and crucial in its spread was the *Mémorial de Sainte-Hélène,* ghostwritten by Emmanuel Dieudonné de las Cases and published in 1823. Ironically, in this work, Napoleon achieved greater success in shaping his image in exile than during his rule.

MICHAEL ROWE

See also **France: Revolution and Empire; French Revolution: Its Impact and Importance;** *Napoleon Crossing the Alps at the Great Saint Bernard Pass***;** *Napoleon in the Pest House at Jaffa*

Biography

Born in Ajaccio, Corsica, August 15, 1769, second son of Charles Marie Bonaparte and Maria Letizia Ramolino. Entered the military college of Brienne, May 1779, and then the École Militaire in Paris, September 1784. Commissioned as an artillery officer in the Royal French Army on September 1, 1785. Came to prominence as a captain of artillery at the siege of Toulon, December 1793, and promoted to brigadier-general. Briefly placed under house arrest following the fall of Robespierre, August 1794. Crushed royalist insurrection, October 5, 1795, and appointed commander of the Army of the Interior. Appointed general commanding the Army of Italy, March 2, 1796. Married Josephine Beauharnais, March 9, 1796. Italian campaign, March 1796 to April 1797. Embarked upon Egyptian campaign, May 1798; returned to France, October 1799. Seized power, November 9–10, 1799, and adopted the position of first consul. Crowned himself "Emperor of the French" in Notre Dame, Paris, December 2, 1804. Austerlitz campaign; 1805; Jena campaign; 1806; Intervention in Spain, 1808; Wagram campaign, 1809. Determined to father a legitimate heir, he divorced Josephine, December 1809, and married Marie-Louise of Habsburg, daughter of the Austrian emperor, March 1810. Birth of son, named the King of Rome, March 20, 1811. Russian campaign, 1812; German campaign, 1813; campaign for France, 1814. First abdication, April 1814. Exiled to the Mediterranean island of Elba; escaped and returned to France, March 1815. "Hundred Days" (Waterloo) campaign, followed by second abdication, June 22, 1815. Exiled to South Atlantic island of Saint-Helena. Died, May 5, 1821, aged 51. Remains reinterred in the Hôtel des Invalides, Paris, 1840.

Selected Works

Mémorial de Sainte-Hélène. Journal de la vie privée et des conversations de l'Empereur Napoléon, à Sainte Hélène. 4 vols. Edited by Marin Joseph Emmanuel August Dieudonné de Las Cases. 1823.
Mémorial de Sainte-Hélène, ou journal où se trouve consigné, jour par jour, ce qu'a dit et fait Napoléon durant dix-huit mois; par le Comte de Las Cases. 8 vols. Edited by Marin Joseph Emmanuel August Dieudonné de Las Cases. 1823–24.
Correspondance de Napoléon Ier publiée par ordre de l'empereur Napoléon III. 32 vols. 1858–69.
The Mind of Napoleon: A Selection from his Written and Spoken Words. Edited and translated by J. Christopher Herold. New York: Columbia University Press, 1955.

Bibliography

Draper, J. J. *The Arts under Napoleon.* New York: Metropolitan Museum of Art, 1969.
Ellis, Geoffrey. *Napoleon.* London: Longman, 1997.
Holtman, R. B. *Napoleonic Propaganda,* Baton Rouge: Louisiana State University Press, 1950.
Lefebvre, Georges. *Napoleon.* 2 vols. Translated by J. E. Anderson. London: Routledge and Kegan Paul, 1969.
Lyons, Martyn. *Napoleon Bonaparte and the Legacy of the French Revolution.* London: Macmillan, 1994.
Prendergast, Christopher. *Napoleon and History Painting: Antoine-Jean Gros's La Bataille d'Eylau.* Oxford: Clarendon Press, 1997.
Tulard, Jean. *Napoleon: the Myth of the Saviour.* Translated by Teresa Waugh. London: Weidenfeld and Nicolson, 1984.
———, ed. *Dictionnaire Napoléon.* Paris: Fayard, 1987.
Wilson-Smith, Timothy. *Napoleon and His Artists.* London: Constable, 1996.

BONINGTON, RICHARD PARKES 1802-1828

British painter

Richard Parkes Bonington is one of the tragic darlings of the Romantic movement, dying at twenty-five years of age, when his reputation was at its height and commissions for his paintings were plentiful. He was especially admired in France, although he had been born in England and had spent the first fifteen years of his life in Nottingham, where his mother ran schools and his father, a minor artist, worked in the lace trade.

Bonington is one of the triumphs of international Romanticism, and is unique in being claimed by both the British and the French. His work shows elements of both the British and the French Romantic traditions. He displayed early talent as an artist, and probably received some tuition from his father, but he had no serious professional instruction until his family settled in Calais in 1817; even that training was discouraged by his father, who had planned for him to be a designer in the lace business. He studied for a few months with François Louis Francia, a native Calais artist, who was himself influenced by the English watercolor artists of the period. Bonington moved to Paris to continue his education; it was during this time that his breezy seascapes and landscapes, such as *Shipping off Dunkirk* (1821), began to sell. These early works, often painted on site, have strong connections with the English watercolor tradition, and were widely appreciated in France for their bright, spontaneous liveliness. They often involved a further Romantic interest, the lives of the working class (for example, the fishing industry on the French coast as depicted in *Coast Scene*, 1825). He also had in interest in medieval ruins, a common Romantic enthusiasm, as shown in *Abbey of St. Bertin, St. Omer* (1823). Bonington possessed a totally assured grasp of a subject, expressed with bold, open brush strokes, brilliance of color, and a *plein aire* authenticity, wedded to a charmingly confident autographic style. It is these seascape and landscape paintings that have continued to be admired even as his general reputation has faded. Almost two-hundred years later he is considered to be only a very good minor artist.

Bonington was, however, not entirely satisfied with confining himself to the fresh, lively representations of topographical and architectural subjects popular with the Romantic painters. Another Romantic interest lay (somewhat perversely it might seem, given their theatrical clutter and staginess) in what was called "fancy subjects." Early in his Paris studies he became a close friend and professional associate of Eugène Delacroix, who was also just beginning to make his name as a painter, and it was from Delacroix that he picked up an interest in oriental themes, as seen in *The Arabian Nights* (1825). Another subject brought to his attention by Delacroix was French medieval history, (for example, in *Henry IV and the Spanish Ambassador*, 1826). He found some of his subjects, such as *Ann Page and Slender* (1826), in literature. From 1825 onward, landscape became a secondary interest for him as he reveled in an aristocratic, medieval world of rich furnishing and elegant costume, as seen in *The Great Staircase of a French Chateau* (1825). However, he continued to be interested in architectural themes, and a visit to Italy provided him with subjects that brought out the best in his topographical skills (perhaps best exemplified in *Street in Verona*, 1827).

Bonington was not a thinker, but a much simpler soul, precociously talented and interested in nature, travel, history, and the popular literature of the Romantic period. The "fancy" paintings have been judged, in the long run, of diminished value as the taste for nineteenth-century narrative painting has waned. A considerable number of topographical paintings (for example, *Bridge of St Maurice, Valais*, 1826), and cityscapes (such as the *Doge's Palace, Venice*, 1827) accumulated from his travels throughout Europe; many of these have retained their power with the public, possessing a bright, attractive ebullience and seemingly improvisational energy.

Although Bonington died very young of consumption, he experienced the satisfaction of early success, was praised by other artists, and was able to influence painters such as Jean Baptiste Corot. He was a thorough Romantic in his choice of subjects, in his commitment to *plein aire* painting, and in his artistic celebration of the pleasures and beauty of nature and the human condition.

CHARLES PULLEN

Biography

Born at Arnold, near Nottingham, October 25, 1802; his father was a minor artist and unsuccessful entrepreneur and lace maker, his mother a teacher. He was educated at home by his mother. Moved with his family to Calais, France, 1817. Destined originally for a career as a designer in the lace trade with his father. Studied for a short time with François Louis Francia; 1818. Moved to Paris; studied and made copies of Dutch and Flemish paintings in the Louvre; began a long association with Eugène Delacroix, 1819. Parents joined him in Paris, 1820. Studied at the École des Beaux Arts, in the atelier of baron Antoine-Jean Gros, 1820–22. Exhibited for first time at the Paris Salon, 1822; undertook a sketching tour of northern France and Flanders, 1821–23. Awarded gold medal at Paris Salon, 1824. Lived in Dunkirk, 1824. Visited England with Armand Cohn; met Delacroix there, 1825; on return to Paris shared a studio with Delacroix. Exhibited in London, 1826 and 1828. Enjoyed increasing popularity in France. Toured Italy with his friend Baron Rivet, 1826. Became seriously ill with tuberculosis, 1827–28. Traveled to London with his parents to seek medical treatment, 1828. Died of tuberculosis in London, September 23, 1828.

Bibliography

Cormack, Malcolm. *Bonington*. Oxford: Phaidon, 1989.

Gage, J. *A Decade of English Naturalism, 1810–1820*. Norwich: Castle Museum, 1969–70.

Hawes, Louis. *Presences of Nature, British Landscape 1780–1830*. New Haven, Conn.: Yale University Press, for the Paul Mellon Centre for studies in British Art, 1982.

Noon, Patrick. *Richard Parkes Bonington: On the Pleasure of Painting*. New Haven, Conn.: Yale University Press, for the Paul Mellon Centre for studies in British Art, 1991.

Pointon, Marcia. *The Bonington Circle: English Watercolour and Anglo-French Landscape*. Brighton: Hendon Press, 1985.

———. *Bonington, Francia and Wyld*. London: Batsford, 1985.

Shirley, Andrew. *Bonington*. London: Kegan Paul, 1941.

Wilton, A. *British Watercolours 1750–1850*. Oxford: Oxford University Press, 1977.

BOOK ILLUSTRATION

By the middle of the nineteenth century, European book illustration was unrecognizable by the standards of a hundred years earlier. Technological advances in illustrative techniques not only allowed more illustrated books to be published than previously had, but developed simultaneously with changes in the style of illustration and the relation of the image to the text. In the eighteenth century, France was at the forefront of these changes and played a major part in the development of illustration in Britain, Germany, and the Low Countries. These international cross-currents came about partly because of the movement of artists and engravers themselves. The French illustrator Hubert Gravelot, in his frequent trips between London and Paris, was one of the most important links between the two schools. Similarly, when wood engraving became popular in the early decades of the nineteenth century several British draughtsmen, including Charles Thompson, one of Thomas Bewick's pupils, went to Paris and trained French engravers.

Three main styles of book illustration dominated the years between 1760 and 1850, although the distinction between them was not always clear cut and illustrations often drew on a number of different influences. At the end of the eighteenth century, rococo designs, characterized by their florid borders and vignettes, were subsumed by the formality and symmetry of neoclassical illustrations undertaken by artists such as Anne-Louis Girodet de Roussy-Trioson and Antoine-Denis Chaudet. In France, the neoclassical illustrators looked to Jacques-Louis David for inspiration, but John Flaxman had more impact in Britain, where his illustrated books included *The Iliad* (1795) and *The Odyssey* (1805). Perhaps the most prominent shift in book illustration, however, came in the Romantic reaction against neoclassicism. Romantic illustrations were bound up in the revival of wood engraving, the appeal of which lay not only in its striking visual effects and the increased number of images that could be produced by the process but in the way that its origin in the medieval woodcut seemed to provide a historical link with the past. Wood engraving also allowed more freedom and spontaneity to the artist and engraver than copper or steel engraving, which relied on the drawing of more rigid lines.

The movement in favor of wood engraving was also a geographical one, shifting the emphasis from French to English illustrators, and in particular Thomas Bewick, who pioneered the technique. Bewick's images make a strong visual impact, with their extraordinary detail and the subtlety of the tones that are created alongside the sharp contrast between the black background (printed in relief) and the white lines. It is perhaps here in the ends of boxwood used in Bewick's engravings that one can identify the first grains of Romantic book illustration, and it is no coincidence that Bewick's most successful pictures were of the natural elements, like the wonderfully fresh images that appear in his *History of British Birds* (1797). Wood engraving also altered the relation between text and image in illustrated books, because when both words and pictures were produced using a relief process they could then be printed together and on the same page. It is not surprising that William Blake, with his own assimilation of text and image, often used this type of engraving. Blake's illustrations also owe much to medieval sources, with a sumptuous use of color and design that is reminiscent of the illuminated manuscript.

Although wood engraving was the most popular form of book illustration in the nineteenth century, illustrators continued to experiment with other ways of achieving a range of tonal effects, including mezzotint, aquatints, and stipple. Lithography (where prints are made by drawing on porous limestone, then dampening the stone and applying a greasy ink that only sticks to the drawn lines) was popular in France and Germany, where its successful practitioners included Adolf Menzel. One of the most important books of the period, a French translation of Johan Wolfgang von Goethe's *Faust* published in 1828 and illustrated by Eugène Delacroix, was embellished using this technique, and the power of its illustrations is testament to the fact that it is not wood engraving alone that makes a picture Romantic. The range of illustrated books that appeared in these years was strikingly diverse, leading to a strange but dynamic coexistence of different material. In England the satirical and often bawdy illustrations of Thomas Rowlandson appeared in the same years as Thomas Stothard's elegant and graceful designs for novels of sensibility such as Samuel Richardson's *Clarissa* (1784). Throughout Europe the illustration of novels and poetry increased in relation to the illustrated religious and scientific books that had formerly dominated the market, but there were also illustrated songbooks, keepsake annuals, sport and racing books, books of architecture, and topographical books, which often drew on the landscapes that characterized Romantic painting. Indeed, the period was dominated by illustrators who were also successful painters, a factor that strengthened the relation between the two arts. The role of the artist was not fixed in Romantic book illustration, however. In the majority of cases, one artist was employed to illustrate a book, but sometimes several different illustrators would work on a single text (a form that was especially popular in France). In some instances, the artist also undertook the engraving of the images, although it was becoming increasingly common, particularly with the revival of wood engraving, to send the designs out to a specialist engraver. Ultimately, the only way to define Romantic book illustration is in terms of its diversity. The imaginative brilliance and visual appeal of European books of this period influenced the art of illustration for decades to come.

JULIA THOMAS

Bibliography

Bland, David. *A History of Book Illustration: The Illustrated Manuscript and the Printed Book*. London: Faber and Faber, 1958.

Hodnett, Edward. *Five Centuries of English Book Illustration*. Aldershot: Scolar, 1988.

Katz, Bill, ed. *A History of Book Illustration: Twenty-nine Points of View*. London: Scarecrow, 1994.

Pre-Victorian Book Illustration in Britain and Europe. 8 vols. Bristol, England: Thoemmes 1998.

Ray, Gordon N. *The Art of the French Illustrated Book 1700 to 1914*. New York: Pierpont Morgan Library/Ithaca N.Y.: Cornell University Press, 1982.

———. *The Illustrator and the Book in England from 1790 to 1914*. New York: Pierpont Morgan Library/Oxford: Oxford University Press, 1976.

Slythe, R. Margaret. *The Art of Illustration 1750–1900*. London: Library Association, 1970.

BOREL, PETRUS (JOSEPH-PÉTRUS BOREL D'HAUTERIVE) 1809–1859

French poet and writer

Petrus Borel the Lycanthrope (or wolf-man), was the leader of a group of young writers and artists who sought to shock the Parisian literary world in the years following the July Monarchy of 1830. (The "e" of his forename Pétrus, which many reference works erroneously give as "Pierre," appears on his birth certificate with an acute accent, though Borel's apparent preference was for the more Latinate form.) Although he is sometimes remembered as much for his eccentric behavior and dress as for his writings, he was considered by Charles Baudelaire, whose poetry reveals him to have been an attentive and appreciative reader of Borel's work, to merit a secure place in history as "one of the stars of the dark Romantic sky." In his tales, the Lycanthrope drew on the legacy of the Marquis de Sade and the gothic novel (the fashion for which had reached its height in the mid-1820s), vying to produce ever more disturbing illustrations of animalistic violence. As such, he was one of the most distinctive exponents of the "frenetic" manner that, in the wake of the influence of Lord Byron, had attracted Charles Nodier and other French Romantic writers in the decade prior to the July Revolution before culminating in an ambiguous parody in the form of Jules Janin's scandalous novel of 1829, *L'Ane mort et la femme guillotinée* (*The Dead Donkey and the Gulliotined Woman*).

The group of which Borel was the leader became known as the Petit Cénacle, the post-1830 counterpart of the Romantic Cénacle that had formed around Victor Hugo and Nodier. Its other members, all of whom were in their late teens or early twenties at the time of the July Revolution, included Théophile Gautier and Gérard de Nerval and the painters and illustrators Joseph Bouchardy and Célestin Nanteuil. The group delighted in a parodic flaunting of their status as Romantic artists. With their extravagant pseudonyms (Philothée O'Neddy [anagram of Théophile Dondey]), Augustus Mac Keat [Auguste Maque]), Jehan [Jean] du Seigneur, Napoléon Thom [Thomas], also known as T. Napol) they both celebrated and mocked the Romantic cult of esoteric erudition, its fascination with the Middle Ages, and its status as a foreign (for example Scottish or Irish) import. They also became known as les Jeune-France (or, as Gautier flamboyantly and implausibly spelled it, les Jeunes-France), a group that, in contrast to La Giovine Italia, had no political overtones, but has often been confused with the Bousingos. The latter, who in the general atmosphere of parody and self-parody attracted various alternative spellings, were young republican political activists who appear to have taken their name from the waterproof hats worn by the volunteer force that came from Le Havre to support the July Revolution. Membership of these groups, however, often overlapped. Borel, whose portrait in bousingo "uniform" by Napoléon Thomas was exhibited in a tricolor frame at the Paris Salon of 1833, made no secret of his republicanism, alleging (in the eccentric preface to his first published work, *Rhapsodies* [1832]), "I've been a Republican since childhood, but not the kind that sports a blue or red garter on his *carmagnole*, a mob orator [pérorateur de hangar] or planter of poplar trees. I'm a Republican a lynx would recognize; my Republicanism is lycanthropy."

Rhapsodies (of which an extremely rare second edition was produced in 1833) is a hodgepodge of thirty-four poems. The choice of title has nothing to do with the more common meaning of the term in English—namely, an "excess of enthusiasm" (a meaning the French word does not possess). Instead, it harks back to the original Greek meaning of fragments of Homeric poems recited or sung by itinerant "rhapsodes" (in his prologue Borel uses the label *rhapsode* as a synonym for "poet") and exploits the word's subsequent connotations as "that which is disconnected or fragmented." The terms *Rhapsodize* and *rhapsodical* had, moreover, been given wider currency in Laurence Sterne's *Tristram Shandy* (1759–67), a work immensely popular in France at the time. Used by Sterne's narrator self-referentially, these words became readily associated with the humorous affectation of a self-deprecating manner. This represented a softening of Molière's earlier use of the term *rhapsodie*, in his *Critique de l'Ecole des Femmes* (*Critique of the School for Wives*, 1663), to designate a motley collection of bad prose or verse, but Maximilien-Paul-Emile Littré's *Dictionary* (1863–72) records that it was also used to refer to any ridiculous affair.

One of the two introductory epigraphs—three lines of which were taken from an unidentified poem by the seventeenth-century poet François de Malherbe—indirectly alludes to official censorship and ends with the provocative declaration, "ce livre se moque de vous" ("this book does not give a fig for you"). It is in the preface that follows, which enjoyed greater notoriety than the poems themselves, that the Lyncanthrope endeavors to scandalize the reading public. He alleges his poems to be "de la bave ["slaver"] et de la scorie" ["slag" or "scale"], and presents them as the work of a poet in opposition to the (official) poets of Romanticism, with "their would-be pasha-like poems and extravagance, their aristocratic profile, their ecclesiastical mummery, and their fussy and elaborate sonnets." A sense of camaraderie is promoted through the dedications to fellow members of the Petit Cénacle and the epigraphs taken from their works.

In the wake of such a preface, and the subsequent claim by Borel that the volume created a scandal, the poems are much less outrageous than the reader might expect. Yet Enid Starkie's view of the majority of them as "gentle and sentimental in character," poems that would not be out of place in a keepsake of the period, is to force the contrast unduly. A number of the poems display a rejection of polite convention and possess a directness that would have injured the sensibilities of the typical keepsake reader. The examples of early Romantic melancholy thus give way to a concern with the present, albeit filtered on occasion through some of the literary modes in vogue. The violence of the lycanthrope is given expression as part of a widespread tone of bitterness and sarcasm. There is a diatribe against Paris and materialism in a century that has spurned its offspring. A persistent theme is that of the impoverished artist (the final poem, entitled "Misère," ends with the bald statement "I am hungry"); Borel follows Alfred-Victor de Vigny in citing the examples of Thomas Chatterton and Nicolas-Joseph-Laurent

Gilbert, adds another example of his own, the poet Jacques-Charles Louis de Clinchamp de Malfilâtre, and elsewhere deplores the rejection of Louis-Candide Boulanger's *Death of Bailli* by the 1831 Paris Salon. Cudgels are taken up on behalf of liberty; the poems on 1830, which form a section entitled "Patriotes," invite comparison with those of Henri-Auguste Barbier. The poem "Sans-culottide" and the epigraphs from Louis-Antoine-Léon Saint-Just are a clear indication of the political stance of a poet who, according to Gautier, habitually wore a Robespierre-type waistcoat.

Champavert, contes immoraux was published in 1833, an ironic rejoinder to the immensely successful "contes moraux" of Jean-François Marmontel. (Champavert was a proper name common in Borel's home city of Lyons.) The collection was originally to be entitled *Graisse d'ours* (literally "bear fat," but an "ours" in French is also an uncouth being or boor, as well as printer's slang for a work that has done the rounds before finally finding a publisher). It is on the title page that Borel presents himself for the first time as the Lycanthrope, but in so doing he was merely adopting the ironic label attached to him by the reviewers of his *Rhapsodies*.

The seven stories are set variously in Havana, Jamaica, Lyons, and Madrid as well as in contemporary Paris, and exploit the contemporary fashion for morbid fictions that end with the dismemberment of human bodies in the dissecting room or under the blade of the guillotine. The female characters are invariably the victims of sexual violence, though this is only one of the ways in which the male characters take pleasure in acts of extreme and often calculated cruelty.

"Passereau l'écolier" is the gruesome tale of the effects of a medical student's conversion to violent misogyny. (At one point the student visits the celebrated executioner, Samson, to inform him, "I would most ardently have you guillotine me"—the French requires an eloquent imperfect subjunctive.) With its ironic show of learning, the story is a clear example of Jeune-France wit, but also an explicit account of spleen that left its mark on Baudelaire. In another story, the sixteenth-century anatomist Andreas Vesalius is made the subject of one of Borel's most macabre scenarios. The text at the heart of "Three-Fingered Jack" is a literal translation of the account of a Jamaican slave's death given by Dr. Benjamin Moseley in one of the "Miscellaneous Medical Observations" in *Treatise on Sugar* (second edition, 1800), a curious source in that, unlike that author's treatise on coffee, it appears not to have been translated into French. For the tale to be at home in *Champavert*, Borel needs to do little more than dub Jack a "lycanthrope," though, in an addition to his source, he describes him in a way that makes him a plausible ancestor of Honoré de Balzac's character Vautrin. In the closing story, Champavert dies in a suicide pact with his mistress.

It is, however, Borel's rambling but curiously compelling novel, *Madame Putiphar* (1839), that represents his supreme achievement. It is a reworking of the Old Testament story of Joseph, with the figure disguised by the title being none other than Madame Jeanne-Antoinette de Pompadour, who here persecutes a young Irishman for having spurned her advances. A striking example of Romantic prison literature, it incorporates an explicit evocation of the Marquis de Sade through its account of sexual violence, torture, sadistic jailors, and the widespread abuse of power by those in authority. It ends with the hero's madness and the heroine's death from grief. While ostensibly an extreme example of Gothic fiction (Baudelaire rightly detected a certain generic similarity with Charles Robert Maturin's *Melmoth the Wanderer*, 1820), the novel makes extensive, if cavalier, use of history. Culminating in an exploitation of the storming of the Bastille, it is an obvious expression of the author's virulent republicanism. More generally, as Victor Brombert has noted, it is a work in which Borel "with cruel insistence . . . lays bare human infirmity."

In addition, Borel made a number of contributions to magazines and keepsakes, and participated in the founding of various short-lived periodicals, notably *La Liberté, Journal des Arts* (1832), to which Eugène Delacroix was also a contributor. His 1836 translation of Daniel Defoe's *Robinson Crusoe* (1719) was the standard French version of the novel for a long time.

Baudelaire talked admiringly of the "bizarre lucubrations of the Lycanthrope" (*bizarre* being a positive term in his lexicon), but recognized that Borel was an "incomplete" writer, or "génie manqué." Gustave Flaubert had *Madame Putiphar* in mind during the composition of his *Salammbô* (1862). In the twentieth century, Borel was taken up by the surrealists, who approved of his political stance: for Louis Aragon, he was a "Colossus"; André Breton regarded him as an authentic revolutionary, while Paul Éluard situated him somewhere between the Marquis de Sade and Lautréamont in terms of influence and importance.

MICHAEL TILBY

Biography

Born Joseph-Pétrus Borel (also called Borel d'Hauterive) in Lyons, June 29, 1809. Twelfth of fourteen children of a successful ironmonger. Educated at religious schools in Paris after his father's retirement there. Architectural apprentice, 1823–28. Practiced as architect, 1823–28, then concentrated on literature. Militant participant in July Revolution, 1830. Assumed name of Lycanthrope (Wolf-man); formed notorious literary group known initially as the Petit Cénacle, later as les Jeunes-France and les Bousingos, which included writers Gérard de Nerval and Théophile Gautier. Published collection of poems, *Rhapsodies*, 1831. Founded short-lived journal *La Liberté, Journal des Arts*, 1832. Published *Champavert, contes immoraux*, 1833. Became financially destitute; moved to a small village in the country, 1835. Published translation of *Robinson Crusoe*, 1836. Returned to Paris, 1840. Edited the journal *Le Satan*, 1844, founded a publishing house with Nerval. Through the efforts of Gautier, obtained a post as inspector of colonization in Algeria, 1846. Dismissed from government service for intransigence, 1855; retreated to Mostaganem and lived in a Gothic mansion there until his death. Died in Mostaganem, Algeria, July 17, 1859.

Selected Works

Rhapsodies. 1832.
Champavert, Contes immoraux, 1833; translated by Tom Moran as *Champavert: Seven Bitter tales*. Chicago: Indigo Press, 1959.
Madame Putiphar, 1839; edited by Jean-Luc Steinmetz. Paris: Phébus, 1999.
Opera polemica. Edited by Bruno Pompili. Bari: Adriatica, 1979. Contains an important bibliography of Borel's journalism.
Écrits drolatiques, edited by Jean-Luc Steinmetz. Paris: La Chasse au Snark, 2002.

Bibliography

Asselineau, Charles. *Bibliographie romantique*. 2d ed. Paris: Rouquette, 1872.

Baudelaire, Charles. "Pétrus Borel," in Baudelaire, *L'Art romantique*. Paris: Michel-Lévy, 1868.

Bénichou, Paul. "Jeune-France et Bousingots. Essai de mise au point," *Revue d'histoire littéraire de France* 71, no. 3 (1971): 439–62.

Borel, Petrus. *Madame Putiphar*. Paris: Régine Desforges, 1972. This edition contains Jules Claretie's preface of 1877, and the essays "*Madame Putiphar*, roman sadien?" by Béatrice Didier and "Les Malheurs du récit" (by Jean-Luc Steinmetz).

Bourgeois, René. *L'Ironie romantique*. Grenoble: Presses universitaires de Grenoble, 1974.

Breton, André. *Anthologie de l'humour noir*. Paris: Le Sagittaire, 1943.

Brombert, Victor. *The Romantic Prison*. Princeton, N.J.: Princeton University Press, 1978.

Easton, Malcolm. *Artists and Writers in Paris: The Bohemian Idea, 1803–1867*. London: Edward Arnold, 1964.

Éluard, Paul. "L'intelligence révolutionnaire: Pétrus Borel le Lycanthrope (1809–1859)," *Clarté*, n.s., 5 (1927).

Gautier, Théophile. *Histoire du romantisme*. Paris: Charpentier, 1872.

Marie, Aristide. *Pétrus Borel le Lycanthrope, sa vie, son oeuvre, suivi d'une bibliographie*. Paris: Editions de la force française, 1922.

Pétrus Borel. Vocation: "poète maudit." Paris: Fayard, 2002.

Praz, Mario. *The Romantic Agony*. Oxford: Oxford University Press, 1933.

Starkie, Enid. *Petrus Borel: The Lycanthrope. His Life and Times*. London: Faber, 1953.

Steinmetz, Jean-Luc. *Le Champ d'écoute. Essais critiques: Nodier, Gautier, Borel, Rimbaud, Mallarmé, Zola, Verne*. Neuchâtel: La Baconnière, 1985.

———. *Pétrus Borel. Un auteur provisoire*. Lille: Presses universitaires de Lille, 1986.

BOULLÉE, ÉTIENNE-LOUIS 1728–1799

French architect

For several decades after his "rediscovery" by Emil Kaufmann in the 1930s, Étienne-Louis Boullée was commonly called a "revolutionary architect" and considered a precursor of several twentieth-century architects and architectural trends. But the label was doubly misleading, for he neither actively supported the French Revolution nor decisively rejected the academic conventions of French Neoclassicism. Boullée's place in architectural history is difficult to assess because his achievements were less tangible than those of the contemporaries with whom he had the strongest affinities. He shared with Sir John Soane a fascination with overhead lighting, Masonic symbolism, and funerary monuments, but it was Soane who used available building materials and techniques to express those interests. He shared with Jean-Nicolas-Louis Durand the distinction of being a long-serving and influential teacher, but it was Durand (himself one of Boullée's pupils) who secured a pedagogical legacy through widely used textbooks. Boullée's designs have been interpreted as prototypes both of modernist architecture (pure geometrical forms) and of Nazi architecture (monumental scale and abstracted classical ornamentation). However, his historical significance lies not in purported formal anticipations, but rather in his articulation and exemplification of the increasing separation, during the Romantic era, of architecture from construction, and of artistry from technology.

Before being forced by his father, an architect in the king's service, to study architecture, Boullée studied painting under Jean-Baptiste Pierre. This early training may have fostered his interest in dramatic lighting effects and the aesthetics of sublimity: the epigraph to his *Essai* is Antonio Allegri da Correggio's avowal, "Ed io anche son pittore" ("And I too am a painter"). Among his architectural teachers were Jean-François Blondel, from whom he derived the view that architecture is an art distinct from construction, and Jean-Laurent Legeay, from whom he acquired a knowledge of Roman architecture, particularly as illustrated in the manner of Grambattista Piranesi. (Boullée himself seems never to have traveled far from Paris.) In 1747, at the age of only nineteen, he began his teaching career. His first known commission, in 1752, involved redecorating three chapels in the church of Saint-Roch in Paris, but his original plans were rejected and he refused to execute his deliberately inferior revised plans. In the late 1750s, Boullée prepared plans for the reconstruction of the royal mint, his first attempt at a major public building. Although the commission was finally awarded to a rival, his restrained classical design helped win him election to the Académie d'Architecture in 1762.

From 1762 to 1777 Boullée's primary occupation, apart from teaching, was designing private houses. Only one has survived— the Hôtel Alexandre (built 1763–66)—but contemporary drawings and prints reveal certain characteristics common to all his house designs: a cubic central block fronted with columns or pilasters extending through more than one story, surmounted by an attic of some kind, surrounded by projecting wings in the Palladian manner, and perforated by French doors opening onto a carefully planned garden. Though not particularly original, Boullée's domestic architecture was widely admired in the eighteenth century. His most famous house was the Hôtel de Brunoy (built 1774–79); the garden, along the Champs-Élysées, was designed to frame the view of the central block, which featured an Ionic portico and a stepped roof topped by a statue of Flora. Such theatricality was to dominate his subsequent designs.

During his brief career as a government official, from 1778 to 1782, Boullée executed only minor public projects, such as converting a Parisian mansion into a prison (1780), and after 1785 he seems to have accepted no further private commissions, although he continued to be active as an academician and teacher. His remaining designs for major public buildings and for funerary monuments—none of which was built and many of which could not have been built with the technology of the time—were intended as contributions to an imaginary "museum of architecture containing all that can be expected of the art from those who cultivate it." Emphasizing the importance of emotional impact in architecture, Boullée argued in his *Essai* of the early 1790s that public buildings in particular "should arouse in us feelings that correspond to the purpose [*l'usage*] for which they are intended." Thus his Métropole (1781), a domed cathedral in the shape of a Greek cross, uses indirect overhead lighting, disproportionately large pendentives, and uninterrupted rows of closely spaced columns to induce a feeling of sublimity and awe (here, the influence of Burke's aesthetics is evident). The Palais de Justice (c. 1782) seeks to inculcate respect for the law by presenting "metaphorically the imposing scene of vice vanquished beneath the feet of justice": a cubic block of top-lit courtrooms, approached on each side by a formidable staircase, is set above a windowless plinth containing the prisons, the "shadowy lair of crime." The Bibliothèque Royale (c. 1785) is conceived as "a vast amphitheatre of books" in which stepped tiers of bookshelves face each other across a barrel-vaulted hall and seem to support the Ionic colonnade and coffered ceiling above them. In his perspective drawing of the interior, Boullée evokes Raphael's *School of Athens* by depicting the readers in togas.

While Boullée's designs for public buildings generally derive from ancient Roman models (e.g., the Pantheon, Hadrian's villa at Tivoli, the Temple of Jupiter at Baalbek), his funerary monuments, though influenced by illustrations of ancient ruins, employ his favored cubes, spheres, and pyramids in radically simplified form. Inspired by an intimation of his mortality during a moonlit walk past a wood, Boullée conceived what he called a "buried architecture" and "architecture of shadows." This "new kind of architecture," as he proudly described it in the *Essai*, was to be characterized by its "low and sunken proportions" and unadorned walls on which "the shadowy image of still darker shadows furnished the only decoration." Most of his drawings in this genre are of pyramids with semicircular portals, resembling half-buried archways, at ground level. But his best known funerary monument is the vast hollow sphere (perhaps inspired by Jacques-Étienne and Joseph-Michel Mongolfier's balloon of 1783) with which Boullée commemorates Newton. Perforated to admit small amounts of sunlight, the otherwise dark interior of the sphere, entered through a long tunnel, re-creates the appearance of the starry heavens, and hence, the architect proclaims, envelopes Newton in his own discovery.

NICHOLAS HALMI

See also **Art and Classical Antiquity; Burke, Edmund; Piranesi, Giovanni Battista; Soane, Sir John**

Biography

Born in Paris, February 12, 1728. Studied painting, c. 1740–44, then architecture, 1744–47. Began teaching at the École des Ponts et Chaussées, 1747. Designed private houses in and near Paris, 1762–78; elected to second-class membership of the Académie d'Architecture, August 1764; supervised building projects for the Comte d'Artois, 1775–77; appointed controller of buildings at the Hôtel des Invalides, October 1778, and at the École Militaire, 1780; elected to first-class membership of the Académie d'Architecture, December 1780; resigned his official positions, 1782; composed his *Essai*, 1790–93, became a founding member of the Institut de France and professor of architecture at the Écoles Centrales, 1795. Died in Paris after a long illness, February 6, 1799.

Selected Works

Buildings (with dates of completion)
Redecoration of Maison Tourolle, Paris. 1762 (subsequently altered).
Hôtels de Monville, Paris. 1766 (demolished).
Hôtel Alexandre, Paris. 1766.
Château de Chaville, Chaville. 1766 (demolished).
Hôtel de Pernon, Paris, 1771 (demolished).
Hôtel de Thun, Paris. 1771 (demolished).
Redecoration of Hôtel d'Évreux (now Palais de l'Élysée), Paris. 1774 (subsequently altered).
Hôtel de Brunoy, Paris. 1779 (demolished).

Unbuilt Designs
Hôtel des Monnaies. 1755–65.
Fortified Towers. Five designs, c. 1778–82.
Theatre, Place du Carousel, Paris. 1781.
Métropole. 1781.
Palais du Justice. c. 1782.
Cirque. 1782.
Museum. 1783.
Expansion of the Palais de Versailles. c. 1783.
Cénotaphe de Newton. 1784.
Funerary architecture. Eleven designs, early 1780s.
Bibliothèque Royale. 1785.
Palais National. 1792.
Temple à la Nature. c. 1792.

Writing
Architecture: Essai sur l'art, edited by Helen Rosenau, London: Arauti, 1953; Re-edited by Jean-Marie Pérruse de Montclos, Paris: Hermann, 1968 (reprinted) with additional texts the *Architecte visionnaire et néoclassique*, Paris: Hermann, 1993. Translated as *Architecture: Essay on Art* by Helen Rosenau in *Boullée and Visionary Architecture*. London: Academy, 1976.

Bibliography

Etlin, Richard. *The Architecture of Death: The Transformation of the Cemetery in Eighteenth-Century Paris*. Cambridge, Mass.: MIT Press, 1984.

Kaufmann, Emil. "Three Revolutionary Architects: Boullée, Ledoux, and Lequeu," *Transactions of the American Philosophical Society*, n.s., 42 (1952): 429–564.

Middleton, Robin, and David Watkin. *Neoclassical and Nineteenth-Century Architecture*. New York: Rizzoli, 1978.

Pérouse de Montclos, Jean-Marie. *Étienne-Louis Boullée*. Paris: Flammarion, 1994.

———. *Étienne-Louis Boullée (1728–1799): Theoretician of Revolutionary Architecture*. Translated by James Emmons. London: Thames and Hudson, 1974.

Picon, Antoine. *French Architects and Engineers in the Age of Enlightenment*. Translated by Martin Thom. Cambridge: Cambridge University Press, 1992.

Rosenau, Helen. *Boullée and Visionary Architecture*. London: Academy Editions, 1976.

Vogt, Adolf-Max. *Boullées Newton-Denkmal, Sakralbau und Kugelidee*. Basel: Birkhäuser, 1969.

BRENTANO, CLEMENS 1778–1842

German poet

Clemens Brentano was born to a wealthy merchant in Frankfurt, his father's business traded in citrus and tropical fruits and spices throughout Europe and was so successful that Clemens was able to live from the interest of his share of the family's wealth; he was not dependent upon the publications of his works in order to earn a living. His mother was Maximiliane von La Roche, the daughter of the German author Sophie von La Roche and Anton Brentano's second wife. Clemens was the third of twelve children from this marriage. In 1793 his mother died, and four years later his father died as well. He was then raised by a very strict aunt in Koblenz and attended a Jesuit high school there from 1787 until 1790. In 1791 he switched to the Mannheim Philanthropin School. His strict upbringing away from his home in Frankfurt and his fond memories of his childhood in Frankfurt were fundamental to his psychological development.

All attempts by his father and later by his stepbrother and guardian Franz, to train Clemens in the family business failed miserably. Brentano also made several attempts to study at the university. But he was not very serious about his academic endeavors in forestry, medicine, and philosophy. What was ultimately important for his development as a poet were the close contacts he had to the group of poets surrounding Friedrich and August Wilhelm von Schlegel and Ludwig Tieck in Jena from 1798 until 1800, and his friendships with the German poet Achim von Arnim and Jakob and Wilhelm Grimm.

Initially the group of early romantic poets in Jena that included the Schlegel brothers, their wives Dorothea and Caroline, and the author Sophie Mereau did not take Brentano very seriously. Against the wishes of his family Brentano married the divorceé Mereau on November 29, 1803, in Marburg. Each of their three children died and Sophie died during childbirth on October 31, 1806. Shortly after Sophie's death, Brentano married Auguste Bußmann, who was sixteen at the time, on August 21, 1807; in 1812 they divorced.

In two of his larger works, the dramatic satire *Gustav Wasa* (1800) and the novel *Godwi* (1801), Brentano attempted to demonstrate his creative ability by applying the early Romantic theoretical demands made by Novalis and Friedrich von Schlegel in the literary journal *Das Athenäum* (1798). For example, the dramatic satire *Gustav Wasa* combines dramatic satire with programmatic elements expressed in *Das Athenäum*. *Godwi* bears the subtitle *A wild novel*, referring, for example, to the aesthetics of productive chaos in Friedrich von Schlegel's novel *Lucinde* (1799). Schlegel and Tieck, however, critiqued both of Brentano's works as low-quality plagiarism even though the poetry in *Godwi* is considered to be much better than that of the Schlegel brothers. The poetry included in *Godwi* has mostly been published separately from the novel as a collection of Brentano's poems. Included among these poems is the story of *Lureley*, a legend that was created by Brentano. The echo effects of the cliffs along a dangerous passage on the Rhine River near Bacharach inspired Brentano to create the story of the siren Loreley.

In addition, Brentano also wrote several novellas, fairy tales and plays. In 1814 he published a mythological drama, *Die Gründung Prags* (*The Founding of Prague*), a prototype of the romantic historical drama. In 1817 he published the patriotic play, *Victoria und ihre Geschwister* (*Victoria and her Siblings*). He also published quite a few stories and novellas. Together with Achim von Arnim he published an anthology of folktales in 1805, *Des Knaben Wunderhorn* (*The Boy's Magic Horn*).

In Berlin Brentano experienced a personal crisis that led him to doubt his creative ability, he even briefly considered returning to the university to study architecture. In 1816 this personal crisis developed into a crisis of faith. As was common for other romantic poets, such as Joseph von Eichendorff and Friedrich von Schlegel, Brentano turned his interest to the Catholic faith. This trend of converting or reverting to Catholicism arose from initial pantheistic beliefs that glorified nature and focused on a godlike artist/creator of the world. Brentano's reversion to Catholicism marked a radical change in his life. He sold a large portion of his literary collection in December 1819 in Berlin and began collecting primarily theological literature on mystics, priests, and the lives of the saints. Not surprisingly, Brentano's crisis is closely connected to his love for a woman and his futile attempts to win her sympathies. In 1816 Brentano made the acquaintance of Luise Hensel, the daughter of a protestant minister. He fell in love with her, proposed marriage, and immediately tried to convert her. (By the end of 1818 she converted.)

In 1817 Brentano became intrigued by the signs of stigmata that a nun, Anna Katherina Emmerick, was exhibiting in the small town of Dülmen in northwestern Germany. He moved to Dülmen in 1818 to document Emmerick's visions and remained there until her death in 1824. During this time, Brentano's intention was to prove the reality of Emmerick's visions, while a commission appointed by the government attempted to prove fraud. Brentano devoted himself entirely to exhaustive investigations of the nun's visions. For example, he attempted to reconstruct Jesus' everyday life from the ecstatic dreams and visions of the nun.

Brentano remained productive as a poet in the last decade of his life. He contributed to Joseph Görres's journal *Historisch-politische Blätter* and worked together with his friend Johann Friedrich Böhmer to publish his works in a multivolume collection. Brentano's importance as a Romantic poet is not restricted to his literary oeuvre, but instead is demonstrated in his ability to integrate the ideals of Romanticism into his literature and his life. In doing so he built a bridge to the modern age, which was first noted by Hans Magnus Enzensberger in his 1967 dissertation on Brentano (1967). On July 28, 1842, Clemens Brentano died in his brother Christian's house in Aschaffenburg.

HEIDE CRAWFORD

Biography

Born Clemens Maria Wenzeslaus Brentano in Ehrenbreitatein, near Koblenz, September 9, 1778. Third of twelve children; brother of author Bettina Brentano (later von Arnim; 1785–1859). Father was a successful Frankfurt businessman; mother was Maximiliane von La Roche, daughter of German author Sophie von La Roche and friend of Johann Wolfgang von Goethe. Brought up in Koblenz by an aunt after his parents' deaths, 1797, educated at a Jesuit high school there, 1787–90, and later the Mannheim Philanthropin School, 1791–93. Attended the University of Bonn (1793–94), the University of Halle (1797–98), the University of Jena (1798–1801) and the University of Göttingen (1801). Met the poet Achim von Arnim in Göttingen, 1801; traveled along the Rhine with him, 1802. Married divorcée Sophie Mereau, 1803; she died during childbirth, 1806; they had three children, all of whom died in infancy. Published, with Achim von Arnim, *Des Knaben Wunderhorn*, 1805. Associated with the Heidelberg group of Romantics. Married Auguste Bußmann, 1807; marriage dissolved, 1810; divorced 1812. Established, with Achim von Arnim, the journal *Zeitung für Einsiedler* (later *Tröst Einsamkeit*), 1808. Lived in Bohemia, 1811–13, and Vienna, 1813–14. Moved to Berlin; fell in love with Luise Hensel, 1816. Converted to Roman Catholicism after severe depression, 1817, and became amanuensis for the nun Anna Katharina Emmerich in Dülmen, 1818–24. Died in Aschaffenburg, July 28, 1842.

Selected Works

Gesammelte Schriften. 9 vols. 1852–55.
Sämtliche Werke und Briefe. Historisch-kritische Ausgabe. Stuttgart: Kohlhammer, 1976.
Werke. 4 vols. Edited by Frühald, Gajek, and Kemp. Munich: Carl Hanser Verlag, 1978.

Bibliography

Enzensberger, Hans Magnus. *Brentanos Poetik.* Munich: Carl Hanser Verlag, 1964.
Janz, M. *Marmorbilder. Weiblichkeit und Tod bei Clemens Brentano und Hugo Hofmannsthal.* Königstein: Athenäum, 1986.
Kastinger Riley, Helene M. *Clemens Brentano.* Stuttgart: Metzler, 1985.
Rölleke, Heinz, ed. *Des Knaben Wunderhorn: Alte deutsche Lieder. Studienausgabe in neun Bänden.* Stuttgart: Verlag W. Kohlhammer GmbH, 1979.
Schultz, Hartwig. "Clemens Brentano." In *Deutsche Dichter Band 5: Romantik, Biedermeier und Vormärz.* Edited by Gunter E. Grimm and Frank Rainer Max. Stuttgart: Reclam, 1989.

BRITAIN: CULTURAL SURVEY

Several meanings of the modern term *culture* evolved during the Romantic period. Samuel Taylor Coleridge used the term *cultivation* for the development of spiritual and moral values essential for a just and progressive human society. Civilized values were attributed by Edmund Burke to a chivalric tradition, by Percy Bysshe Shelley to a tradition of imaginative creation perpetually remade in communal interaction, and by William Wordsworth to a rural tradition. Wordsworth produced the first criticism of sensationalist mass culture as an escapist reaction to the monotony of urban occupations. All three authors shared a concern for the quality of a way of life and its impact upon moral relations between people. In each a strong degree of imagination shaped the construction of the traditions they took as exemplary. A lesser, but still influential, degree of utopianism influenced their visions of social possibilities. If they drew authority from the past, they appealed confidently to the present (and future) vastly expanded public, who were now both the patrons and consumers of art. The roots of this optimism lay in eighteenth-century cultural history, with its praise of Britain's progressive traditions in politics, sociability, and commerce. But the reaction to the French Revolution opened rifts within the public, and between the public and the private, that Romantic culture struggled to unite.

Scottish philosophical historians, including Adam Ferguson, John Millar, and Adam Smith, abandoned classical paradigms of the rise and fall of civilizations, and saw Britain representing a new "commercial" stage of society. Commerce went together with sociability, and each was fostered by the freedoms gained under the British constitution. A money economy enfranchised men from feudal dependence and allowed them to interact as equals, extending the congeniality of polite society further down the social scale. The progress of society had loosened hierarchical structures of rank and subordination— especially those of gender—and developed unifying social feelings of sympathy and humanity. Walter Scott's novels chart the colonizing of Scotland by English progress, bringing an end to absolutism in nation

and clan and establishing equal laws that favor peace and commerce. Scott accepted this state of affairs as necessary, but echoed many theorists in their fears for the loss of classical civic virtues, and masculine values of military spirit and public service as credit replaced honor and contract supplanted loyalty. To base social and national cohesion on feelings was to dissolve the structure of the state and encourage individualism and materialism. Yet Scott's novels can be seen as establishing feeling as the guardian of national identity, feeling connected with traditions imaginatively conceived.

Burke championed traditional moral ideals more belligerently against the "inhuman" rationalism of Thomas Paine, Richard Price, and Joseph Priestley. In his *Reflections* (1790) he confronted the French Revolution and its threat to all social distinctions in defending the authority of the king and especially the aristocracy and upholding the prevailing power structure. He became an apologist for patriarchal, aristocratic practices under attack from the new egalitarian morality of humanitarianism, and valorized the honorable duel, maintaining that even vice loses half its grossness in the hereditary culture that distinguishes the aristocrat.

Burke, however, interprets precedent through sensibility, as linking family feeling with the hereditary principle and obedience to superiors with family affection and loyalty. He appeals imaginatively to a national tradition that has its roots in the "mixed system of opinion and sentiment" of the Middle Ages. British radicals such as Catharine Macaulay and Major John Cartwright looked further back to an Anglo-Saxon tradition and many, including William Godwin and Percy Bysshe Shelley, sought precedents in medieval culture for more progressive ideas. The current of medievalism, however, ran through predominantly conservative channels, through Robert Southey's *Colloquies* (1829), Samuel Taylor Coleridge's *On the Constitution of the Church and State* (1830), and Thomas Carlyle's *Past and Present* (1843).

In the early period commerce could be seen to aid sociability. Thomas Paine, followed by Robert Bage and Mary Wollstonecraft, held that free commerce was a pacific system with benefits for all, encouraging the cooperation and self-development of free individuals. Many hoped, with Thomas Jefferson, that slavery would decline because of its economic weaknesses. Most Romantic writers reacted against the new factory system, and Robert Owen attempted to replace exploitation and private profit with cooperative production, promising to let abundance loose. The motive of many efforts to alleviate hardship and maximize happiness, however, was sensibility, a development of sociability, but one that could be differentiated. Sociability was predominantly consumerist and emulative; it aspired to the same elegancies of life as the aristocracy. It followed them to theaters, pleasure gardens, spas, and seaside resorts in a free association at which continental visitors marveled. Sensibility was a more moralized movement, more liable to criticize fashion and to extend equality of concern to those below as well as claiming equality with those above. The educative, reformist humanitarianism of the period united Evangelicals, Dissenters, and radicals, and was often in conflict with commercial interests, as in the case of Jonas Hanway's efforts to regulate the conditions of child labor and in the antislavery campaign.

Sensibility prompted the revision of Burke's clichés of feeling molded by tradition. His privileging of the sublime (characterized by masculine power, greatness, and obscurity) over the beautiful (characterized by feminine weakness, compliance, and the social virtues of sensibility) was resisted by theorists such as Hugh Blair, who linked sublimity with moral magnanimity. Anna Laetitia Barbauld, Helen Maria Williams, and Mary Wollstonecraft claimed sublimity for women and brought sensibility to bear on the masculine subject of politics. Sensibility endowed man as well as woman with the quick feelings of sympathy and benevolence and, like Wordsworth, typically focused on the importance of the particular and the domestic. It created the wise child of Wordsworth's ballads and William Blake's child of innocence in a vision of universal reciprocity and harmony. William Godwin and Mary Wollstonecraft attacked Edmund Burke's idea of the hierarchical family and the restriction of his sympathies to the royal victims of the revolution in the name of a universal benevolence that valued independence. Wordsworth's rustics, in their industrious independence and practices of mutual assistance, carry criticism of an idle aristocracy and a fashionable, acquisitive society in a typical opposition of nature and art.

This radical sensibility produced tensions in the representation of domesticity and "low" subjects that were later associated with imagery of a harmonious, national society. Robert Burns's "Cotter's Saturday Night" (1786) was the subject of Victorian genre paintings, as a celebration of family values that linked the laborer to the queen; his contrasts of low and high society and his championing of an independent peasantry seemed then to be beside the point. Art that challenged traditional feelings largely gave way to sentimentality. John Constable produced "finished" landscape paintings for a taste that found more uncompromising renderings of nature incomprehensible. John Ruskin famously defended J. M. W. Turner, and prepared the way for the Pre-Raphaelites' fresh approach to nature and feeling. But he also valued the trite moralizing that replaced a tradition of history painting, continued in different ways by Blake, Henry Fuseli, and Turner, that attempted to use classical, national, and religious values to question contemporary life and sensibility more strenuously.

Sensibility's attempt to elevate private feeling into a socially unifying force, or to mobilize it as an agent of reform, foundered in the 1790s. Its basis in natural emotion smacked of democracy and also made it prone to "feminine" excess, an affair of the nerves and senses. Masculine control was necessary to brace a society threatened by the same lack of discipline that had plunged France into anarchy. Sensibility was also liable to exploitation. In the *Analytical Review* (1788–99) Wollstonecraft regularly criticized novels of sensibility for dressing up sensuality in fine-sounding phrases and for pale imitations of the masterpieces of Johann Wolfgang von Goethe and Jean-Jacques Rousseau. The raptures evoked by the harmony and sublimity of nature, or the new emotional intensities of Franz Joseph Haydn and Wolfgang Amadeus Mozart, could be reduced to vulgarization, dingy prints, and parlor versions played on the latest, English-produced pianos. The Romantic emphasis on individual self-development and original response always existed in a paradoxical relationship to commercial developments that might provide inspiration for similar cultural experience, but alternatively might reduce it to mere fashion. The passivity of a self-centered, consumerist sensibility, indulging in aesthetic visions and the luxury of sympathy with fictionalized distress, was a common reproach, and one that has been subsequently leveled at Romanticism as a whole. Wordsworth inveighed against the appetite of such sensibility for "outrageous stimulation" and saw Gothic modes as equally escapist, blunting people's reactions to real life. Coleridge wanted to turn the tea and sugar with which ladies of sensibility accompanied the reading of affecting novels into the realities of their production: lashes, cries, and blood. Such ideals of realism and sincerity demanded much of imaginative response.

Evangelicals lent their force to the establishment of traditional order, provoking Lord Byron's jibe that William Wilberforce was only interested in slaves abroad. They looked to the aristocracy to lead moral reform, in the process encouraging a class-based notion of moral respectability. While counseling women to abjure politics, Hannah More gave them a prominent role in the attempt to renew morality in the family and the poor. "Natural" sensibility could not be relied on to produce correct behavior, and women's moral and religious education was to be duplicated in their education of children, servants, and the working classes. The voice of sensibility, of spontaneous response and vulnerable, private feeling in public places, continued to be heard in the poetry of Letitia Elizabeth Landon and Felicia Hemans, but in the novel the first-person or epistolary form gave way to the controlling presence of a narrator. In poetry, Coleridge abandoned the poetic "effusion," with its undisciplined stream of consciousness, for a more controlled form. When the "cockneys" attempted to revive the extemporary modes of sensibility they were pilloried as feminized, though their informal, intimate modes of composition contributed a vogue for keepsakes and annuals. Scott can be credited with "remasculinizing" the novel form, not only by importing the masculine knowledge of history but by playing his part in the formation of a canon. Novels were republished in series such as those of James and John Ballantyne with prefaces by Scott, and favored the more realistic models that were becoming defined as novels as opposed to "feminine" romances. Here, specificity of context and probability of plot and character confine the presentation of individual sensibility, though in cases such as Emily Brontë's *Wuthering Heights* (1847) this was achieved with difficulty. The Gothic was the main challenge to this assertion of a common reality, a reminder of Romantic problematics of perception.

Gothicism and exoticism remained a staple of Romantic art, whether found in past eras by the "great enchanters" Ann Radcliffe and Walter Scott, or in images of the east conjured (with the aid of Sir William Jones's Asiatic researches) by Thomas Moore and Robert Southey. The encyclopedic ambitions of the Enlightenment were shared by Coleridge and Wordsworth in Wordsworth's proposed *Recluse: or, Views on Nature, Man, and Society*, and in the picture of the poet in his preface to *Lyrical Ballads* (1802 edition), using relationship and love to unite the whole empire of humankind. The expansion of the British Empire brought to England the natural and cultural products of the world to further such objectives. The comparative study of cultures could confirm ethnocentric Western ideas of progress; it could also produce a more challenging sense of unacknowledged kinship with the alien, as a barbarous but alluring "Asiatic luxury" or primitive spontaneity disturbed conventional moral notions in Lord Byron's tales. Wordsworth's enterprise of extending sensibility was based on the reader's perception of, and participation in, permanent, universal passions of human nature. Coleridge's exploration of the world of knowledge gave precedence to the sense-making powers of the mind. Empirical sensibility gave way to the creative imagination. The transformations of sensibility and the Gothic might show the indispensable necessity of art to unite the creative mind with the material of perception, but for Coleridge such creation was, or should be, governed by permanent shared values: rational ideas such as cause and effect, but also moral, aesthetic, and religious ideals. The experience of the 1790s was crucial to the search for permanent, controlling, and unifying powers as the threat of revolution from below drew the middle class and aristocracy together. Both Coleridge and Wordsworth praised Burke and his view of society as organic, maintaining its principle of integrity in its growth, but their productions were still exploratory of mysteries that defied complete mastery by a unifying and idealizing imagination, the demon-haunted fountain of creation in "Kubla Khan" (1797) or the mysterious gulf where the last book of the *Prelude* (1850) locates imagination. Coleridge's social theory, though dominated by the idea of a national church superintending education and culture, included independent professional and commercial interests as a necessary overbalance of the forces of progress.

The French Revolution provoked a hardening of political, religious, and social divisions in Britain. Reforms that had seemed imminent—removing the legal disabilities of Dissenters, a modest extension of the franchise, and the abolition of the slave trade—were postponed, apparently indefinitely. Extreme affirmations of constituted authority in family, society, and church construed any views of change as Jacobinic. British Jacobin writers described oppression similar to that of any absolutist continental state, as treason trials and a network of government spies gave credence to Gothic pictures of an organized persecution that destabilized the discourses of social identity. Burke's patriarchal society of traditional feeling betrayed its origins in Gothic violence. In France, reason and virtue were transformed into the Terror, with the accompaniments of anonymous accusations and tribunals reminiscent of the Inquisition. Civilized citizens turned into violent mobs, revolutionary or supportive of "Church and King." This confusion is echoed in the uncertain-

ties of Radcliffe's fiction and the disintegration of civilized restraint in Matthew Lewis's *The Monk* (1796). As Thomas Love Peacock noted in *Nightmare Abbey* (1818), the genre of the Gothic also included psychological studies of Byronic gloom and misanthropy, typically induced by the disappointment of benevolent social aspirations.

The social tensions of the 1790s greatly influenced the new institutions that were formed to control the increasing production and diffusion of knowledge. London-based professional associations, often with new buildings for their gentlemanly clubs, regulated what knowledge actually was. Sir Humphrey Davy, at the Royal Institution, lectured to a fashionable audience on investigations into a universe ordered by God, not to be marred by inconsiderate innovation. Networks of patronage and privilege provided barriers which reformist scientists, including Charles Babbage and William Lawrence, had to break in order to promulgate materialistic, utilitarian doctrines. They were assisted by the founding of University College London in 1826, envisaged as an academic institution unfettered by social or religious qualifications or restraints. Percy Bysshe Shelley, though no narrow utilitarian, incorporated their ideas in his imagery of universal liberation, while Mary Shelley's *Frankenstein* (1818), a Godwinian portrait of great gifts misapplied, questioned the disciplinary limitations of knowledge.

Government action to control literary and political publication, including the prosecution of radical publishers and ingenious use of libel law, established an atmosphere of circumspection. Much of the policing of the republic of letters was, however, carried out by those anxious to professionalize its institutions and establish the best standards. When John Stuart Mill commented in the *Westminster Review* (1824) that both the *Edinburgh Review* (1802–1929) and the *Quarterly Review* (1809–1962) were equally aristocratic in serving the status quo, he was perhaps too hard on the *Edinburgh Review*, which stood for moderate reform, but he accurately noted its emulative social tone. While even-handed in considering political writings, it lavished its judicial severity on literature that departed from social decorums in the Jacobinic way of the 1790s. The *Quarterly* and *Blackwood's Edinburgh Magazine* (1817–1980) were even more prone to social taunts, especially toward the "cockneys." The public they wrote for, and to some degree formed, was more fearful of being classed with the vulgar than indignant about being patronized. The age of the "making of the English working class" in the transient and often illegal publications that carried political education to the masses was also a time when the middle class was anxious to distinguish itself from them. Leigh Hunt's liberal *Examiner* (1808–81) ran the risks of social abuse and of prosecution in its wider appeal, shadowing William Cobbett's *Political Register* (1802–35) in its political commentary and attacking corruption and patronage. The wide sympathies of the Hunt circle, its spontaneous response to the moment, its foregrounded intimacy as a social group, and its concern for the "people" against a ruling oligarchy harks back to the attitudes of sensibility. Shelley gives a resounding reprise to its more radical doctrines in the *Defence of Poetry* (1821), defending the beauty of "equality, diversity, unity, contrast, mutual dependence."

While Jane Austen, Maria Edgeworth, Mary Russell, Mitford, and William Wordsworth registered the impact of national developments on rural and provincial communities, William Hazlitt and Leigh Hunt were metropolitan artists, responding, like Charles Dickens and Pierce Egan, to the vitality of the expanding imperial capital, with its multiplicity of subcultures. Increasingly, new printing technology provided a vigorous popular culture with cheap literature ranging from radical and aspirational works to prophetic almanacs, satiric and sporting prints, and sensational fiction. As the broadsheet and chapbook were superseded, so older rural pastimes died out or were transformed into the national sporting institutions that survive today. In "Signs of the Times" (1829) Thomas Carlyle attacked the "mechanism" of the culture-producing industry of London, the mart to which he and other literary aspirants had to come, like northern manufacturers, to exhibit their wares. The dangers of London dominance were highlighted by the suddenness with which Londoners were reminded of the problems of the north in 1839, by Carlyle's disclosures of industrial distress and a vacuum of authority. Countering Benjamin Disraeli's Gothic portraits of uncivilized, industrial troglodytes, Elizabeth Gaskell produced a more sympathetic picture that nevertheless did not minimize gaping social divisions. The character Thornton in Gaskell's *North and South* (1855) is a potential Carlylean leader, an industrial heir to Burke's aristocracy, yet to find a true social role. Northern independence is a bracing contrast to southern deference, especially in the situation of women, and affirms a localism under threat from the remote, centralized government legislating in the light of Benthamite theory. Gaskell points to Wordsworthian virtues of independence, mutuality, and family feeling among the working class. However, their unions have limited ideas of social unity and class distinctions and class-based morality divides community and families. The reconciliation and cooperation Gaskell produces in her novelistic conclusion is also a function of her form, the commercial production of art that attempts to unify society by extending knowledge and sympathy, a continuation of the embattled optimism of Romantic culture.

CHRIS JONES

Bibliography

Armstrong, Isobel, and Virginia Blain, eds. *Women's Poetry in the Enlightenment*. London: Macmillan, 1999.

Barker-Benfield, G. J. *The Culture of Sensibility*. Chicago: University of Chicago Press, 1992.

Barrell, John. *The Political Theory of Painting from Reynolds to Hazlitt*. New Haven, Conn.: Yale University Press, 1986.

Brewer, John. *The Pleasures of the Imagination: English Culture in the Eighteenth Century*. New York: Farrar, Straus and Giroux, 1997.

Butler, Marilyn. *Romantics, Rebels and Reactionaries*. Oxford: Oxford University Press, 1981.

Colley, Linda. *Britons: Forging the Nation 1707–1837*. New Haven, Conn.: Yale University Press, 1992.

Cox, Jeffrey N. *Poetry and Politics in the Cockney School*. Cambridge: Cambridge University Press, 1998.

Dickinson, H. T. *British Radicalism and the French Revolution, 1789–1815*. Oxford: Blackwell, 1985.

———. *Liberty and Property: Political Ideology in Eighteenth Century Britain*. London: Methuen, 1977.

Evans, Eric. *The Forging of the Modern State*. 2d ed. London: Longman, 1996.

Feldman, Paula R., and Theresa M. Kelley, eds. *Romantic Women Writers: Voices and Countervoices*. Hanover, N.H.: University Press of New England, 1995.

Fox, Celina, ed. *London: World City 1800–1840*. New Haven, Conn.: Yale University Press, 1992.

Fulford, Tim. *Romanticism and Masculinity: Gender, Politics, and Poetics in the Writings of Burke, Coleridge, Cobbett, Wordsworth, De Quincey, and Hazlitt*. New York: St. Martin's Press, 1999.

Gaull, Marilyn. *English Romanticism*. New York: W. W. Norton, 1988.

Harris, Tim. *Popular Culture in England 1500–1850*. London: Macmillan, 1995.

Hobsbawm, Eric, and Terence Ranger, eds. *The Invention of Tradition*. Cambridge: Cambridge University Press, 1983.

Johnson, Claudia L. *Equivocal Beings: Politics, Gender, and Sentimentality in the 1790s*. Chicago: University of Chicago Press, 1995.

Jones, Chris. *Radical Sensibility*. London: Routledge, 1993.

Kelly, Gary. *Women, Writing, and Revolution, 1790–1827*. Oxford: Clarendon Press, 1993.

Kerr, James. *Fiction against History: Scott as Story-Teller*. Cambridge: Cambridge University Press, 1989.

Klancher, Jon P. *The Making of English Reading Audiences, 1790–1832*. Madison: University of Wisconsin Press, 1987.

Langford, Paul. *A Polite and Commercial People: England 1727–83*. Oxford: Oxford University Press, 1992.

Leask, Nigel. *British Romantic Writers and the East*. Cambridge: Cambridge University Press, 1992.

———. *The Politics of Imagination in Coleridge's Critical Thought*. Basingstoke, England: Macmillan, 1988.

McCann, Andrew. *Cultural Politics in the 1790s*. Basingstoke, England: Macmillan, 1999.

McGann, Jerome. *The Poetics of Sensibility*. Oxford: Clarendon Press, 1996.

Mendilow, Jonathan. *The Romantic Tradition in British Political Thought*. Beckenham: Croom Helm, 1986.

Miles, Robert. *Gothic Writing, 1750–1820: a Genealogy*. London: Routledge, 1993.

Morse, David. *High Victorian Culture*. New York: New York University Press, 1993.

Pocock, J. G. A. *Virtue, Commerce, and History*. Cambridge: Cambridge University Press, 1985.

Punter, David. *The Literature of Terror*. 2d ed. London: Longman, 1996.

Thompson, E. P. *The Making of the English Working Class*. 1963. Reprint, Harmondsworth, England: Penguin, 1968.

Watson, Nicola J. *Revolution and the Form of the British Novel, 1790–1825*. Oxford: Clarendon Press, 1994.

Williams, Raymond. *Culture and Society, 1780–1950*. London: Chatto and Windus, 1958.

BRITAIN: HISTORICAL SURVEY

In the Romantic era, the triumphant Britain that emerged from the Seven Years' War (1756–63) was fundamentally challenged by the forces unleashed by the American and French Revolutions. Not only was British military power stretched to the limit, but new ideologies and bases for opposition were disseminated in Great Britain itself as well as in Ireland.

The British elite was politically challenged at home in the late eighteenth century, with the rise of radical movements for

Parliamentary reform, more frequent elections, and, in the most extreme formulations, suffrage. Radicals, often Protestant dissenters from the Church of England, charged the British ruling classes with subservience to royal despotism and, more credibly, with corruption. Despite the popularity of many reformers such as the notorious John Wilkes, and the embarrassment to British power caused by the success of the American rebels and the French in the American Revolution, the British establishment generally managed to contain dissent. The worst political disturbance in Britain itself during the American Revolution was the 1780 anti-Catholic riots in London. The riots, led by the Scottish demagogue Lord George Gordon, lasted four days with extensive property destruction, although little loss of life. Newgate Prison was razed, and the house of the prime minister attacked. Troops were called in to disperse the rioters.

Damaged by American defeat and civil unrest, Britain in the immediate aftermath of the American Revolution was often seen as a country in irreversible decline, although the rise in British power in India compensated somewhat for losses elsewhere. British recovery began in the long prime ministership of William Pitt the Younger, from 1784 to his death, with one interruption from 1801 to 1804. Pitt emphasized economical and administrative reform while leaving irregular and undemocratic Parliamentary franchises and the privileged position of the Church of England untouched. He relied on his own great ability and the support of King George III. Pitt's great rival, Charles James Fox, was forced to ally with the heir to the throne, the future George IV. Fox briefly came within sight of power in the "Regency Crisis" of 1788, when George III's madness nearly made his eldest son the regent. Fox's shrinking body of followers kept the designation Whig, while Pitt's followers were referred to by the revived term, Tory, and later as Conservatives.

The French Revolution added to the polarization of British politics. Many British people greeted the Revolution with the hope that France would now adopt a Parliamentary government on the British model, but horror at French excesses accelerated the conservative reaction that had begun with Pitt's coming to power. Sympathy for the exiled French Catholics and Catholic priests in Britain muted some British anti-Catholicism. On the political side, Pitt's government repressed dissenters, crushing the radicals in "Pitt's reign of terror" in 1793–94. The repression was particularly harsh in Scotland, with its different legal structure. On the religious side, the evangelical movement in the Church of England drew in many upper-class men and women. Evangelicals furnished much of the leadership for the popular movement for the abolition of slavery, but were conservative on other issues. Radicals, including the young William Wordsworth, sympathized with the French, and made Thomas Paine's *The Rights of Man* (1791–92) a best-seller, selling over 200,000 copies, far exceeding the antirevolutionary Edmund Burke's *Reflections on the Revolution in France* (1790).

The actual outbreak of war between Britain and Revolutionary France in 1793 caught the British military unprepared. Both the maintenance of a large military force and the endless subsidies required by Britain's continental allies strained the British treasury, forcing the adoption of an income tax in 1799. The need to effectively control Ireland, whose restiveness with British rule made it a target of French invasion, led to the act of Union of 1801, which joined Great Britain and Ireland into the "United Kingdom." The wars, which lasted until the British and allied victory over Napoleon at Waterloo in 1815 (with a respite from 1801 to 1803) cost fifteen billion pounds and 210,000 lives.

Victory in the Revolutionary and Napoleonic Wars enabled the British to vastly expand their empire. Viscount Horatio Nelson's defeat of the French navy at the Battle of Trafalgar in 1805 at the cost of his life won his country complete domination of the high seas. In addition to expanding their position in India and supporting the South American revolutions against Spain, which opened up new markets for British goods, the British acquired many new territories, including the Dutch colonies in Ceylon and South Africa and the Mediterranean island of Malta. Britain's Imperial predominance would not be seriously challenged until the late nineteenth century. The abolition first of the slave trade in 1807 and eventually of slavery in the British dominions in 1834 provided Britain with an ideological justification for naval predominance, as the Royal Navy took on the task of preventing slave trading, not always effectively. Caught up in Empire, the British in the post-Napoleonic period mostly refrained from active military and diplomatic involvement on the European continent, while fighting many wars outside Europe.

Domestically, the postwar period was marked by violent repression of dissent, most notably the massacre of "Peterloo" in 1819, when eleven peaceful demonstrators at a reform meeting outside St. Peter's fields in Manchester were massacred by the yeomanry, a local militia under the command of magistrates. The Parliament was dominated on both the Whig and Tory sides by landowners, and passed a series of protective tariffs, the Corn Laws, beginning in 1814, to maintain a high price for domestic grain. The Tory government at this time, personified by its foreign minister, Viscount Castlereagh, won the loathing of radical Romantics including Lord Byron and Percy Bysshe Shelley. Resentment of government's bondage to the landed interest was high throughout the country. George IV's accession in 1820 also produced a vast popular campaign in support of his estranged wife Caroline, although in the end it came to little.

The development of the steam locomotive railroad caused major changes in the British environment and way of life. The first public railroad began service in Britain in 1825. The major milestone in the early history of the locomotive railway was the inauguration of the thirty-mile run between the industrial centers of Manchester and Liverpool in 1830. The railway expanded dramatically over this period, with railway booms in 1835–37 and 1844–47 marked by speculative frenzies far in advance of actual profitability. The railway infrastructure itself grew from a few dozen miles in 1830 to over 8,000 by 1850

By the late 1820s, the reactionary qualities of British government began to moderate. A Tory government under the victor at Waterloo, the Duke of Wellington (1769–1852), repealed the Test and Corporation Acts in 1828, opening many positions in national and local government to Protestant dissenters. Despite vehement opposition from reactionary Tories, the so-called Ultras, Wellington also passed a Catholic emancipation law, granting political rights to Catholics in 1829. The law was passed mainly to appease the mass movement of the Catholic Irish led by Daniel O'Connell (1775–1847), but applied throughout the

British Isles, and together with the repeal of the Test and Corporation Acts dissolved the eighteenth-century Anglican "confessional state."

Reformers wanted more, specifically the reworking of Britain's archaic system of Parliamentary representation to more accurately represent the British people. This was a particularly sore issue in the industrial areas of the north, where vast urban agglomerations such as Manchester had tiny electorates and little representation. Scotland, too, had a very small electorate and disproportionately low representation in the House of Commons. The Tories, knowing that reform would alter the political landscape to their disadvantage, refused to budge, but the death of George IV in 1830 dissolved the Parliament, and the Whigs won the election on a platform of reform.

The passage of the Great Reform Bill of 1832 was difficult. The Whigs, led by the prime minister, Earl Grey (1764–1845) in an uneasy alliance with the radicals, got it through the House of Commons. Rejection of the Bill by the Tory-dominated House of Lords touched off riots and attacks on the homes of anti-Reform peers. In April 1832, after William IV had made his support for the Lords passing reform clear (despite his own doubts on the merits of the measure) the Lords gave way. The Reform Bill did not bring Britain democracy—nor was it meant to—but it increased the electorate and provided a more uniform set of qualifications for the franchise. Scotland's electorate increased fourteenfold, a stark contrast to that of England and Wales, which went up by only about a third. Other Whig reforms in the 1830s included the abolition of slavery in the British dominions in 1833, the very unpopular New Poor Law establishing the workhouse system for poor relief in 1834, and reform of local government in Scotland and England. The Factory Act of 1833 limited the hours of child labor and set up a system of factory inspectors. The Church of England lost some institutional and economic independence. Civil marriage was instituted in 1836, although divorce still required a specific act of Parliament dissolving the marriage, rendering it impossible for all but the very wealthy.

The Whigs in power continued to repress popular dissent. The "Captain Swing" riots of farm laborers in southern England were put down by force, as was the Grand National Consolidated Trades Union movement in 1834. The "Tolpuddle Martyrs," six working men sentenced to seven years transport to a penal colony in Australia for having administered illegal oaths to fellow union members, were brought back to England only after a massive petitioning campaign by workers forced the government to give in. The focus of working-class political activity shifted from trade unionism to politics with the goal of securing working class representation in Parliament. The six demands of the People's Charter, published by a London group dominated by skilled artisans in 1838 included annual Parliaments, manhood suffrage, equal electoral districts, the removal of property qualifications for Parliamentary membership, secret ballots, and payment for members of Parliament. "Chartism" dominated working class politics thenceforth.

The other grave political issue was free trade. A bad harvest in 1836 roused opposition to the Corn Laws, and the Anti–Corn Law League was founded in 1839. The League's base was in northern industrial communities, particularly Manchester. Its leaders, Richard Cobden (1804–65) and John Bright (1811–89) phrased their support of free trade in class terms, claiming to represent the intelligent and hard-working middle class against the corrupt landed aristocracy. Many supporters of free trade were industrialists who believed that cheaper grain would enable them to lower the wages of their workers, and there was little collaboration between the Anti–Corn Law League and the Chartists. The eventual victory of free trade was due to the conversion of the Conservative Prime Minister Sir Robert Peel (1788–1850), the first Prime Minister from an industrial background. Peel's support for the repeal of the Corn Laws in 1846, prompted by the beginnings of the Irish potato blight (to which British response was delayed and inadequate), cost him his office and divided the Conservatives into a Peelite faction and a larger but less distinguished protectionist one. One of the few major protectionist talents was the novelist Benjamin Disraeli (1804–81). Disraeli had previously been involved in "Young England," a group of young English aristocrats influenced by the romantic medievalism of Sir Walter Scott and the fantasy of an alliance between the aristocracy, the Church of England, and the working class against the Whigs and industrialists.

Despite glaring internal divisions, the British ruling class easily weathered the storm of 1848. There was a tense moment in April when the Chartists brought the last of their "monster petitions" to London. Ten thousand special constables were sworn in to deal with them, but the Chartists dispersed without violence. The Chartist movement declined rapidly thereafter. In 1851 the Great Exhibition, with its hordes of peaceful visitors, celebrated Britain's triumph both as the workshop of the world and as a model of social and political stability.

WILLIAM BURNS

Bibliography

Black, Jeremy. *British Foreign Policy in an Age of Revolutions, 1783–1793*. Cambridge: Cambridge University Press, 1994.

Colley, Linda. *Britons: Forging the Nation, 1707–1837*. New Haven, Conn.: Yale University Press, 1992.

Davidoff, Leonore and Catherine Hall. *Family Fortunes: Men and Women of the English Middle Class, 1780–1850*. Chicago: University of Chicago Press, 1987.

Drescher, Seymour. *Capitalism and Antislavery: British Mobilization in Comparative Perspective*. New York: Oxford University Press, 1987.

Duffy, Michael. *The Younger Pitt*. New York: Longman, 2000.

Gash, Norman. *Politics in the Age of Peel: A Study in the Technique of Parliamentary Representation, 1830–1850*. Rev. ed. Atlantic Highlands, N.J.: Harvester Press, 1977.

Lenman, Bruce. *Integration and Enlightenment: Scotland 1746–1832*. Edinburgh: Edinburgh University Press, 1992.

Morgan, Kenneth O., ed. *The Oxford History of Britain*. Rev. ed. Oxford: Oxford University Press, 1999.

Pares, Richard. *King George III and the Politicians*. Oxford: Clarendon Press, 1953.

Perkin, Harol. *The Origins of Modern English Society, 1780–1880*. London, 1969.

Thompson, Dorothy. *The Chartists*. London: Temple Smith, 1984.

Thompson, E. P. *The Making of the English Working Class*. New York: Pantheon, 1963.

Woodward, Llewellyn. *The Age of Reform: England 1815–1870*. 2d ed. Oxford: Oxford University Press, 1962.

BRITISH ROMANTICISM: APPROACHES AND INTERPRETATIONS

Contemporary Voices

There was no established criticism of Romantic poetry in Britain during the Romantic period itself, for the simple reason that the Romantic period did not see itself as Romantic. That came later, probably around 1863 and certainly by the time of Henry Beers's *A History of English Romanticism* (1899). Two important qualifications should be noted, however. The first is that there was indeed, during the period itself, a self-consciousness about its own collective aspirations and achievements. "The Literature of England," Percy Bysshe Shelley wrote in his *Defence of Poetry* (1821), "has arisen as it were from a new birth"; "our own will be a memorable age in intellectual achievements," he continued, establishing at the outset an essentially historical reading of Romanticism that saw it in intimate if vexed relationship with contemporary political and social revolutions: "we live among such philosophers and poets as surpass beyond any who have appeared since the last national struggle for civil and religious liberty." The second qualification is that, along with the celebration, a critique of certain assumptions and aspects of the poetry now identified as Romantic was launched during the period. While in Germany Johann Wolfgang von Goethe notoriously dismissed Romanticism as a disease, in Britain Francis Jeffrey began an attack on the poetry of William Wordsworth in the *Edinburgh Review* in 1802 that isolated its affected primitivism and egotism, its rejection of inherited forms and indifference to public opinion, its bid to create a private mythology, and its sheer difficulty, initiating a debate many of whose terms have remained unchanged to this day.

What is characteristic of the period about Jeffrey's criticism is its tendency to identify a distinct school of poetry. Wordsworth is condemned as the head of "a *sect* of poets" that Jeffrey would call "the lakers." Later, in the 1820s, Robert Southey vilified a "Satanic" school, with Lord Byron at its head, and *Blackwood's Edinburgh Magazine* attacked the presumption of what it called the "Cockney" school, including John Keats and the poet, editor, and journalist Leigh Hunt. By the 1830s, a cultural war between the supporters of Wordsworth and those of Byron was under way, fueled by arguments found in Jeffrey's rejection of Wordsworth on the one hand and, on the other, by principles and proscriptions developed in Wordsworth's prefaces, first to the *Lyrical Ballads* in 1800 and 1802, then to his *Poems* (1815), in the "Essay, Supplementary to the Preface" of 1815, and in Samuel Taylor Coleridge's *Biographia Literaria* (1817). Readers were being asked to make a choice: Wordsworth or Byron. Europe had chosen Byron, but the English-speaking cultural elite would ultimately choose Wordsworth.

Victorian to Mid-Twentieth-Century Romantic Criticism

Wordsworth's will to canonical supremacy never engaged more responsive collaborators than the Victorians (including Matthew Arnold, Thomas Carlyle, George Eliot, F. D. Maurice, John Shuart Mill, Walter Pater, John Ruskin, and Alfred, Lord Tennyson). For the Victorians, however, Wordsworth was not the archetypal Romantic poet he would become for the Anglo-American academy in the twentieth century. In the preface to his *Poems* (1853), for example, Arnold renounced what he saw as the "dialogue of the mind with itself" so characteristic of "modern" poetry, not least his own, arguing that it was a form of decadence to be overcome. Arnold's self-professed classicism, his dismissal of Shelley as "a beautiful *and ineffectual* angel, beating in the void his luminous wings in vain" became characteristic of the attitude toward Romantic poetry that prevailed in the first half of the twentieth century. Romanticism itself was a "spilt religion," according to T. E. Hulme, and a decadent obsession with the "inner voice," attitudes that were only reinforced by the recovery of metaphysical poetry effected by T. S. Eliot and I. A. Richards (among others), and by the subsequent development of the New Criticism of the American South and of the critical religiosity and disciplined exclusiveness that F. R. Leavis inherited from Arnold. Thanks largely to T. S. Eliot, Modernism built anti-Romanticism into its manifesto. Of the Romantics, only Wordsworth and Keats were thought to repay serious attention, although after A. O. Lovejoy's essay "On the Discrimination of Romanticisms" in 1924 students of intellectual history were debating whether one could talk intelligibly about Romanticism at all.

Occasional studies of individual poets and issues were still being published, however, such as Arthur Beatty's *William Wordsworth: His Doctrine and Art in their Historical Relations* (1922), John Middleton Murry's *Keats and Shakespeare* (1926), John Livingston Lowes on Coleridge in *The Road to Xanadu* (1927), Carl Grabo on Shelley in *Newton among the Poets* (1930), Joseph Warren Beach's *The Concept of Nature in Nineteenth-Century English Poetry* (1936), and Claude Lee Finney's *The Evolution of Keats's Poetry* (1936). From the continent, Mario Praz, in his *Romantic Agony* (1933), reminded scholars of the Gothic and oriental elements of Romanticism and of the immense influence of Lord Byron.

Out of these independent studies, especially in the United States, where the European influence on literary studies was much stronger and comparative literature existed as a distinct discipline, Romantic literature recovered its respectability. The 1940s and 1950s witnessed a number of important studies both of the Romantic period and of specific Romantic writers, including Walter Jackson Bate's *The Stylistic Development of John Keats* (1945), Carlos Baker's *Shelley's Major Poetry* (1948), W. H. Auden's *The Enchafèd Flood* (1951), M. H. Abrams's *The Mirror and the Lamp* (1953), F. W. Bateson's *Wordsworth: A Reinterpretation* (1954), John Jones's *The Egotistical Sublime* (1957), and Frank Kermode's *Romantic Image* (1957).

Particularly significant throughout these decades is the development of criticism on William Blake after the pioneering work of S. Foster Damon, in *William Blake: His Philosophy and Symbols* (1924). Blake was a latecomer to what had recently become the Romantic canon of six major poets (Blake, Byron, Coleridge, Keats, Shelley, and Wordsworth), and his reputation is indebted to work such as that of David Erdman (*Blake: Prophet against Empire*, 1954), Northrop Frye (*Fearful Symmetry*, 1947) and Geoffrey Keynes (*Blake Studies*, 1949).

Romantic Criticism in the 1960s

If the publication of M. H. Abrams's *Natural Supernaturalism* in 1971 failed to convert literary critics to Romanticism generally, to the centrality of the Wordsworthian "High Argument," or to the Shelley of *Prometheus Unbound*, it certainly gave students of British Romanticism a new pride and a new conviction. Abrams's second major study in fact marked a climax rather than a beginning. The 1960s had seen the entrenchment of the Romantics in the Anglo-American literary canon through such characteristic academic media as journals (*Studies in Romanticism* was founded in 1960), new and "definitive" editions, and a plethora of critical and biographical studies, like Geoffrey Hartman's brilliant study of loss, guilt, and the *via negativa* in *Wordsworth's Poetry 1787–1814* (1964). The first edition of Abrams's own extremely durable anthology of critical essays, *English Romantic Poets*, was published in 1960. Now seen as a major—if not *the* major—chapter in the history of Western humanism (a heroic chapter trumpeted in Wordsworth's "Prospectus to *The Recluse*"), Romanticism was conceived as the elevation of a transcendental subjectivity over revolutionary politics, which nevertheless still managed to retain a political relevance in spite of its renunciation of revolution. For all their reclusiveness, moreover, Abrams's Romantic poet-prophets were eminently public-minded and accessible—more accessible than, for example, their esoteric counterparts in Harold Bloom's earlier, equally influential *Visionary Company* (1961).

Individual and collective insight and research after 1971 conspired with the exigencies of publishing and the university promotion system to increase both the volume and the theoretical variety of academic criticism. As the 1970s went on, criticism of the Romantic—as of all periods—separated into distinct theoretical groupings. Concomitantly, the possibility of a literary criticism innocent of alignment of one form or another came to seem progressively more naive, and forms of skeptical relativism prevailed. One result of the revolutionary advent of literary theory was that the cultural and ideological continuity between the Romantic and our own enterprise (a continuity implicit and explicit in both Abrams's and Bloom's accounts) would within a decade or so become a source of critical embarrassment. Those Romantic values and motifs that we had inherited were identified as a constraint, indeed a form of "false consciousness," that needed to be recognized and overcome if Romanticism were to receive the critical attention that it deserved—or rather, the *critique* that it deserved, for where critical studies until at least the mid-1970s sought the secret of Romanticism's success and willingly recuperated what they saw as its creative optimism, since 1980 such critical studies have sought its secret, often unconscious, failure or guilt.

Psychoanalysis and Deconstruction

The act of mapping unconscious and inevitable breakdown is characteristic of deconstruction, in whose rigorous pursuit of linguistic self-sabotage intimations of authorial guilt are the legacy of a Freudian inheritance. Committed psychoanalytic criticism of the Romantics, whether Freudian, Lacanian or Kristevan, has been relatively rare, especially in light of speculation about unconscious activity and the role of memory and of childhood in the evolution of individual consciousness in the writings of the Romantics themselves. Psychoanalytic studies of all the major poets can be found, with Wordsworth again attracting most attention; see, for example, Richard Onorato's *The Character of the Poet: Wordsworth in "The Prelude"* (1971), Peter Manning's *Byron and His Fictions* (1978), Leon Waldoff's *Keats and the Silent Work of the Imagination* (1985), Douglas Wilson's *The Romantic Dream: Wordsworth and the Poetics of the Unconscious* (1993), and David Collings's *Wordsworthian Errancies: The Poetics of Cultural Dismemberment* (1994). However, skepticism about the accuracy and value of psychoanalytic paradigms like Sigmund Freud's Oedipal complex and "the family romance" more generally, or like the Lacanian law of the father, has inhibited the development of a systematic criticism.

The case against a literal reading of the Romantics was taken over by critical approaches like deconstruction. Sometimes the appraisal was positive. In Paul de Man's *The Rhetoric of Romanticism* (1983), for example, Romantic deconstruction derives from an anticlimax of the kind that, in the work of Immanuel Kant, affirms transcendental consciousness. By and large, however, deconstructive readings of the Romantics, such as of Cynthia Chase's *Decomposing Figures: Rhetorical Readings in the Romantic Tradition* (1986), are more negative, emphasizing only indeterminacy and irresolution. The same priorities are reflected in criticism's dealings with the canon after 1980 in which, for example, Shelley's darkly ironic, unfinished *Triumph of Life* often supersedes *Prometheus Unbound* (see Harold Bloom and colleagues' *Deconstruction and Criticism*, 1979, and Tilottama Rajan's *Dark Interpreter*, 1980).

The Romantic Ironists

In foregrounding the skepticism and uncertainties of Romanticism, and the ironies and vulnerabilities of subjectivity and desire, deconstruction is indebted less to Freud than to the Romantics themselves. The Romantics were aware that their own expressive or representational means were necessarily incommensurate with the ideas they strove to comprehend. In ironic readings of Romanticism (for example, David Simpson's *Irony and Authority in Romantic Poetry*, 1979, and Kathleen Wheeler's *Romanticism, Pragmatism and Deconstruction*, 1993), this awareness of the limits of human apprehension and creativity becomes identified as the recurrent subject matter of the work of art and, subsequently, of literary criticism.

Dialogism

A different form of contingency and disunity is featured in dialogical approaches to Romanticism. The influence of Mikhail Bakhtin on literary studies since the 1970s, particularly through the translation of his *Problems of Dostoevsky's Poetics* in 1973 and of *The Dialogic Imagination* in 1981, has been pervasive, and studies of the Romantic period are no exception. For Bakhtin, discourse is an essentially rhetorical affair in which words are shaped not just by the object or idea they would directly represent, but by their dialogical responsiveness to what has already been said about that object or idea. As language is insistently social and interactive, so texts are sites, not of any single or monologic assertion, but of a number of conflicting—or dialogical—discourses. As such, there can be no unity, no final authority.

Perhaps prematurely, a school of Romantic studies has been identified that centers on Don Bialostosky's work on dialogism in Wordsworth (*Making Tales*, 1984, and *Wordsworth, Dialogics, and the Practice of Criticism*, 1994). This school also embraces such works as Paul Magnuson's *Wordsworth and Coleridge: A Lyrical Dialogue* (1988), Gene Ruoff's *Wordsworth and Coleridge* (1989), and Michael Macovski's *Dialogue and Literature* (1994). So far, work in this area has concentrated on Wordsworth and hardly amounts to a radical rereading of the period, especially given that New Historicism continues to recover the extent and complexity of the dialogue of the period with itself, as Harold Bloom had once emphasized its dialogue with strong poets of the past. Indeed, the trope of literary "conversation" was a common one in the period and a fascination with the mutual (mis)-readings of Wordsworth and Coleridge, or of Byron, Shelley, and Mary Shelley, was a part of Romantic studies long before they were identified as Romantic studies. The real value of Bakhtin's work on Menippean satire and on carnival (from *Rabelais and His World*, 1965, onward), and of his valorization of the heterogeneous text, with its interactive voices, is yet to be felt. Not only will a variety of generically hybrid texts attract a new interest, but central texts of a once "monological" Romanticism, like Coleridge's *Biographia Literaria*, Thomas De Quincey's *Confessions of an English Opium Eater*, and Mary Shelley's *Frankenstein*, and will be valued and interpreted more and more as the immethodical and conflicted miscellanies they are.

Feminism

The ebullient, creative Romanticism of approaches and interpretations of the 1960s has fared least well under feminist criticism. One of the reasons is simple enough: women writers have suffered most from the mania for canonicity that Romanticism practiced and inspired. As with feminism generally, the first and in many ways least controversial task has been one of looking closely at what was happening at the time (see Marlon B. Ross, *The Contours of Masculine Desire: Romanticism and the Rise of Women's Poetry*, 1984), and then of recovering those women writers who had remained too long neglected. The first female writers recovered were Mary Shelly, Mary Wollstonecraft, and Dorothy Wordsworth, and because of their association with male writers (as discussed in Margaret Homans's *Women Writers and Poetic Identity*, 1980, and *Bearing the Word*, 1986; Susan M. Levin's *Dorothy Wordsworth and Romanticism*, 1987; and Anne Mellor's *Mary Shelley: Her Life, Her Fiction, Her Monsters*, 1988). Since that time, critical and scholarly work has been carried out on the writings of Joanna Baillie, Anna Laetitia Barbauld, Felicia Hemans, Letitia Elizabeth Landon, Mary Robinson, Charlotte Smith, and Helen Maria Williams, accessible if not readily available now in either new or facsimile editions and assured of a place in the syllabus, if not the canon. Monographs and journal articles are still hard to come by, though help has come from Anne Mellor's *Romanticism and Feminism*, (1988), Carol Shiner Wilson and Joel Haefner's *Re-Visioning Romanticism* (1994), Mary A. Favret and Nicola Watson's *At the Limits of Romanticism* (1994), and Paual R. Feldman and Theresa M.

Kelley's *Romantic Women Writers* (1995). What remains unresolved by feminist studies of the Romantic period is not so much the canonical status of these and other women writers, as the status of canonicity itself.

Just how masculinist the Romantic ideology was and is has been another focus of feminist revisionism. Studies scrutinizing the personal lives of the major male poets reveal their exploitation of the women close to them; studies of "the politics of desire" such as Mary Jacobus's *Romanticism, Writing, and Sexual Difference* (1989) and Julie Ellison's *Delicate Subjects* (1990) highlight an ambivalence in the Romantic exaltation of the feminine. Most of the work in recent years has moved beyond resentment, a fact registered by the number of male writers among the feminist revisionists of Romanticism. One possibility canvassed by scholars like Mellor in her *Romanticism and Gender* (1992) is of a feminine Romanticism distinct from its masculine counterpart, one that challenges the self-preoccupation and self-assertion of the creative visionary. Insofar as it shares certain social priorities with Marxism, Mellor's thesis suggests another reason for Romanticism's bad reputation among feminists. Along with the Marxists, feminism identifies in Romanticism an essentialism that encourages a series of related misrepresentations, including the idea of (male) genius and the (masculine) canon. But here, feminism joins forces not just with the Marxists, but with historical critics of a variety of persuasions.

(New) Historicism

Since 1980, much of the most interesting work on British Romanticism has been done under the banner of historicism: New or old, witting or unwitting. That historicism entered and transformed Romantic studies with the publication of Marilyn Butler's *Romantics, Rebels and Revolutionaries* in 1981 and Jerome McGann's *The Romantic Ideology* in 1983 is well recognized, as are its critical corollaries: a refusal of normative accounts of value, the systematic recovery (along with feminism) of a variety of texts obscured by the dominant aesthetic shared by the Romantics and their progeny in the twentieth-century academy, and the systematic discovering of contemporary meanings and of sociocultural constraints or motives that have been "occluded" by Romanticism's ideological investment in transcendental vision and the formal autonomy of art.

One type of new historicism is deconstruction in period costume, with the same sensitivity to acts of commission and omission, and the same focus on the instability—not to say illusion—of the self. The blindnesses, absences, and unwitting conspiracies so telling for the deconstructive critic, however, are now specifically historical and political ones. After the manner of Jerome McGann and Marjorie Levinson in *Wordsworth's Great Period Poems* (1986), Alan Liu, in his *Wordsworth: The Sense of History* (1989), discovers one after another ideological evasion of sociohistorical experience or reality. Wordsworth's own manifest unawareness is diagnosed as a form of "denial." What gives most offence to traditional Romanticists is New Historicism's reduction of the work of art to an object of contemporary cultural production and consumption only—a process of demystification that derives from Marxism. Against the arrogance of Romantic posturing, New Historicism directs an arrogance of its own, and one that cries out for the kind of psychobiographical and historical analysis offered by a syncretist like Peter J. Manning in his *Reading Romantics: Texts and Contexts* (1990), who notes that "our differences one from another can be historically illuminated but not construed into progressive mastery over the text."

As if taking up the period's own unending commentary on "the spirit of the age," there have been more historicist readings of Romantic literature since 1980 than could ever be represented proportionately here. Iain McCalman's *An Oxford Companion to the Romantic Age* (1999) draws together most of the issues and many of the major critics involved. The strongest work has come from scholars who go under the general label of *historicist* but are determined to collaborate with the historical sense of the Romantics themselves, such as Jon Klancher's *The Making of English Reading Audiences, 1790–1832* (1987), David Simpson's *Wordsworth's Historical Imagination* (1987) and *Romanticism, Nationalism, and the Revolt against Theory* (1993); Clifford Siskin's *The Historicity of Romantic Discourse* (1988) and *The Work of Writing* (1998); Jerome Christensen's *Lord Byron's Strength* (1993) and *Romanticism at the End of History* (2000), and James Chandler on "the politics of literary culture and the case of romantic historicism" in his *England in 1819* (1998).

For good *and* ill, we have lost the "interpretive community" reflected and promoted by so popular a collection as Abrams's *English Romantic Poets* (1960). Instead, the titles of (often excellent) critical anthologies over recent years reflect the skepticism, specialization, and restless revisionism of recent critical approaches and interpretations of British Romanticism: Stephen Copley and John Whale's *Beyond Romanticism* (1992); Karl Kroeber and Gene Ruoff's *Romantic Poetry: Recent Revisionary Criticism* (1993); and John Beer's *Questioning Romanticism* (1995). But while recent criticism may question the coherence of British Romanticism, it shares its doubts about the provenance, function, and adequacy of art with the Romantics themselves.

WILLIAM CHRISTIE

Bibliography

Erdman, David V., ed. *The Romantic Movement: A Selective and Critical Bibliography*. New York: Garland/West Cornwall, Conn.: Locust Hill Press, 1980.

Jordan, Frank, ed. *The English Romantic Poets: A Review of Research and Criticism*. 4th ed. New York: Modern Language Association of America, 1985.

McCalman, Iain, gen. ed. *An Oxford Companion to the Romantic Age: British Culture 1776–1832*. Oxford: Oxford University Press, 1999.

O'Neill, Michael. *Literature of the Romantic Period: A Bibliographical Guide*. Oxford: Clarendon Press, 1998.

Pirie, David B. *The Romantic Period*. Vol. 5, *The Penguin History of Literature*. London: Penguin, 1994.

Raimond, Jean, and J. R. Watson, eds. *A Handbook of English Romanticism*. Basingstoke, England: Macmillan/New York: St. Martin's Press, 1992.

Reiman, Donald H., ed. *The Romantics Reviewed: Contemporary Reviews of British Romantic Writers*. 9 vols. New York: Garland, 1972.

Shattock, Joanne, ed. *Cambridge Bibliography of English Literature*. 3rd ed., vol. 4 (1800–1900). Cambridge: Cambridge University Press, 1998.

Wu, Duncan, ed. *A Companion to Romanticism*. Oxford: Blackwell, 1998.

BRITISH ROMANTICISM: LITERARY LEGACY

As the Romantic era has been reexamined from a retrospect of two centuries, at least two things are clear. First, "Romanticism," a category codified in the late nineteenth century to describe a set of male writers, chiefly the poets William Wordsworth, Samuel Taylor Coleridge, Lord Byron, Percy Bysshe Shelley, John Keats, is a vital literary legacy. Second, "Romanticism," far from being a discrete, removed object available for interrogation, is entwined with the general cultural fabric. Whether in its original nineteenth-century definition, its more inclusive position in the twentieth century (taking in figures including William Blake, Mary Shelley, William Hazlitt, Charles Lamb, Thomas De-Quincey), or in its reconfiguration as "the Romantic era" (to include Edmund Burke, Thomas Paine, William Godwin, Mary Wollstonecraft, Jane Austen, Walter Scott, Anna Letitia Barbauld, Joanna Baillie, Maria Edgeworth, Dorothy Wordsworth, Helen Maria Williams, Mary Robinson, Felicia Hemans, and L.E.L.), Romantic-era literature has proven the the foundation of many of the issues and fascinations that are still with us: key character types such as the Byronic hero and the restless woman, the cult of literary celebrity (Scott, Byron, Robinson, Hemans), the idea and ideology of imagination, the birth of science fiction (Mary Shelley's *Frankenstein*), the millennial romance of political revolution and disillusion, and the first strong literary engagements with the controversies of the slave trade and women's rights.

Ironically, this late expansion beyond Victorian determinations of the field, its emblematic writers and preferred texts (works of subjective imagination and idealism, and the dynamics of male desire), has raised a question about "Romanticism" itself: how useful is this descriptor for the writing—even imaginative literature—from the 1780s to the 1840s? Is "Romanticism" most accurate as a reference to a strain coursing through a much wider, more various field? Along with this question, there has emerged a "critique" of "Romanticism," advanced under allied banners: "The Romantic Ideology" (identifying an evasion of historical contradictions and political turmoil), "feminism" (ideologies of gender generated by "masculinist" commitments), and a host of other identifications, in which Romantic traditions and texts are seen as implicated with imperialism, racism, orientalism, colonialism, sexism, misogyny, and homophobia. Literature once celebrated for imaginative explorations, political enthusiasm and traumatic disenchantment, love of nature and the common man aesthetic experimentalism, skeptical enquiry, oppositional critique, the infusion of the personal, and poetic self-consciousness was now seen as culpable, suspicious production.

Yet for all its global implications, these questions are mostly academic debates. In popular cultural reception, the literary legacy of "Romanticism" tends to be identified with the idea of "imagination." While eighteenth-century philosophy and science had insisted on objective, verifiable truth derived from concrete, measurable physical realities, there was a concurrent developing interest in individual variations, subjective filterings, and the mind's independence of physical realities, or even creative transformation of them: not just a tabula rasa or mirror, the mind was a source of active, synthetic, dynamic, even visionary power. Romantic writers, poets in particular, thus described "Imagination" in terms of binaries: imagination versus reality, reason, science, or even religious truth. Victorians reconsidered this debate in terms of delusory or escapist tendencies, or a futile nostalgia. Yet one way to grasp the question about what "Romanticism" includes and excludes is to review the gender alignments on "Imagination." Referring to the dream of Eve's creation in Paradise in John Milton's *Paradise Lost*, Keats compared "the Imagination to Adam's dream—he awoke and found it truth." Male Romantic imagination often described desires or fears in female forms, whether idealized, eroticized, or demonized: goddess, nature, Eve, the femme fatale. Women writers tended, though not always, to accent the practical dangers of imagination, described as a corruption of rational capacity and moral judgment, an invitation to destructive rather than creative passion. "The imagination should not be allowed to debauch the understanding before it has gained strength, or vanity will become the forerunner of vice," cautioned Wollstonecraft in *A Vindication of the Rights of Woman* (1792), a value inflected with Enlightenment rationalism; the best books were those "which exercise the understanding and regulate the imagination." When Austen wanted to indicate her heroine Emma's propensity to vain, egotistical illusions, she called her an "imaginist [. . .] on fire with speculation and foresight!—especially with such a ground-work of anticipation as her mind had already made."

As this gendered contrast on the subject of "Imagination" may indicate, one of the major legacies of Romanticism has been feminist literary criticism, its first remarkable exercise being Wollstonecraft's *Rights of Woman*. Wollstonecraft advances a critique of the "prevailing opinion" (as she calls it in the title of chapter 5) on the character of women. To treat the regulating forms of social existence as "opinion" and not as a dictate of divine or natural law, is to identify a human construction that may be subject to critical reading, revision, and rewriting. This critique is assisted and logically enabled by Wollstonecraft's literary criticism, applied to such prestigious works as Milton's *Paradise Lost* (and its biblical bases); Alexander Pope's epistle *To a Lady, Of the Characters of Women*; Samuel Richardson's epic novel *Clarissa*, Jean-Jacques Rousseau's influential "education" novels *Émile* and *Julie, ou la Nouvelle Héloïse*; and such literature of patriarchal advice as Dr. James Fordyce's *Sermons to Young Women* and Dr. John Gregory's *A Father's Legacy to His Daughters*. Reading the social text and its literary instances, Wollstonecraft sets her sights on key words by which women have been flattered into subjection: *innocent, delicate, beautiful, feminine*. "Why should [women] be kept in ignorance under the specious name of innocence?" she asks at the opening of "The Prevailing Opinion." At its root, *in-nnocence* means "free from harm" (cf. *innocuous*); behind the soothing logic of gallant protection lurks the material consequence of "ignorance." If Thomas Gray, looking back on his boyhood, famously intoned, "where ignorance is bliss, / 'Tis folly to be wise" (*Ode on a Distant Prospect of Eton College*, 1747), Wollstonecraft refines the syllogism with gender. Gray's college boys, after all, enjoy an education denied to girls in the name of preserving their innocence. When men tell women "to remain, it may be said, innocent[,] they mean in a

state of childhood": "in order to preserve their innocence, as ignorance is courteously termed, truth is hidden from them, and they are made to assume an artificial character before their faculties have acquired any strength."

By Wollstonecraft's critical terms, the Romantic legacy of "childhood" as a categorical, conceptual, metaphysical state of innocence to be looked back upon with rueful nostalgia is the construction of men weary of life in the world. For women, it is enforced intellectual feebleness and political impotence. Another dislocation of received understandings is the discourse of "Romantic Satanism." This was a line of sympathy that refused to see the Satan of *Paradise Lost* only, or even, as the architect of evil. Many Romantic-era readers (including Wollstonecraft) saw in Satan's language a poetry of imaginative, principled critique, subjective anguish, exile, and alienation: in sum, modern consciousness. Romantic Satanism, complicating moral judgment with other sympathies, proved a powerful legacy, spawning such darkly seductive figures as Charlotte Brontë's Rochester, Emily Brontë's Heathcliffe, obsessed protagonists such as Herman Melville's Captain Ahab, and a gallery of devilishly alluring antiheroes in twentieth-century literature and film.

One of the most durable specific legacies of Romanticism emerges from this complex Satanism: this is Shelley's *Frankenstein*, in which both a transgressive creator, Victor Frankenstein, and his alien and alienated creation suffer identification with Milton's Satan. The larger myth of "Frankenstein" names excesses of imagination and intellectual adventure idealistically engendered but disastrous in unforeseen consequences. In 1973, an article in the *New York Times Magazine* was sensationally entitled "The *Frankenstein* Myth Becomes a Reality: We Have the Awful Knowledge to Make Exact Copies of Human Beings." That awful knowledge took form recently in Dolly the cloned ewe, described as a "Frankenstein creation," as was another innocent creature of scientific manipulation, the "frankencat"—a work of breeding featuring furry stubs instead of legs—that made its debut at the New York Cat Show in 1995. It wasn't the creatures that seemed monstrous but the science that produced them in the face of questions about prerogatives of creation and miscreation, about consequences and misapplications. "Frankenstein" continues to name our fears about a human future in a world of technological experiment. In a 1997 op-ed piece for *The New York Times* William Safire confessed to "head-breaking thoughts about good and evil, God and humanity" provoked by "the creation of Dolly, the lamb formed by cellular biologists in Scotland and fused into life by electric shock, as was the Monster in Mary Shelley's *Frankenstein*." This partnering of lamb and monster summoned Gothic narrative: "Cloning, before it happened, was another one of those science fiction bugaboos, a prospect whose horror quotient ranked just below that of reanimated corpses or a walking, talking Frankenstein monster," began Ed Regis's review of Gina Kolata's *Clone: The Road to Dolly and the Path Ahead*. In popular imagination and in a steady stream of cinematic interpretations, the legacy of Frankenstein Romanticism endures. Mary Shelley, and the age that inspired her, created not just a novel (which has never been out of print) but a myth, even a meta-myth, of literary legacy.

SUSAN J. WOLFSON

Bibliography

Baldick, Chris. *In Frankenstein's Shadow: Myth, Monstrosity, and Nineteenth-Century Writing*. Oxford: Clarendon, 1987.

Beer, John, ed. *Questioning Romanticism*. Baltimore: Johns Hopkins University Press, 1995.

Bloom, Harold. *The Ringers in the Tower: Studies in Romantic Tradition*. Chicago: University of Chicago Press, 1971.

Bornstein, George, ed. *Romantic and Modern: Revaluations of Literary Tradition*. Pittsburgh, Pa.: University of Pittsburgh Press, 1977.

Eaves, Morris, and Michael Fischer, eds. *Romanticism and Contemporary Criticism*. Ithaca, N.Y. Cornell University Press, 1986.

Harrison, Antony H. *Victorian Poets and Romantic Poems: Intertextuality and Ideology*. Charlottesville: University Press of Virginia, 1990.

Levine, George, and U. C. Knoepflmacher, eds. *The Endurance of "Frankenstein": Essays on Mary Shelley's Novel*. Berkeley and Los Angeles: University of California Press, 1979.

Mellor, Anne K., ed. *Romanticism and Feminism*. Bloomington: Indiana University Press, 1988.

Ruoff, Gene W., ed. *The Romantics and Us: Essays on Literature and Culture*. New Brunswick, N.J.: Rutgers University Press, 1990.

Thorburn, David, and Geoffrey Hartman, eds., *Romanticism: Vistas, Instances, Continuities*. Ithaca: Cornell University Press, 1973.

Wolfson, Susan J., and William H. Galperin, eds. *The Romantic Century: A Forum. European Romantic Review* 11 (2000).

BRONTË, ANNE 1820–1849

British novelist

For most of her life, and for more than a century after her death, Anne Brontë lived in the shadow of her more famous sisters, Charlotte and Emily. The youngest of six children, she lost her mother before she was two. She was raised by her aunt and older sisters, who determined what games she would play, what literary amusements she would seek, and what work she would take up as a young woman. At the point in her literary career when she might have established independent status as an author she died. A sister who may have had ulterior motives for diminishing her accomplishments shaped early, slighting estimates of her literary prowess.

Brontë's life was quintessentially Romantic. As a child she learned the value of literature as a form of self-expression. Her upbringing on the Yorkshire moors exposed her to the landscape and rustic life celebrated by Romantic writers. Like the eighteenth-century Romantic poet Thomas Chatterton and the early nineteenth-century poet John Keats, she died before reaching her thirtieth birthday, leaving a modest canon. Not surprisingly, critics have found it interesting to speculate about what she might have done had she lived two or three decades longer.

From an early age, Brontë experienced the pleasures literature afforded as a diversion from the monotony of life on the moors. With sister Emily she was the principal creator of the imaginary land of Gondal, populated with characters drawn from the Middle Ages and from the sisters' fertile imagination. More than half of her extant poems deal with figures and themes emerging from the Gondal sagas. The Brontës were devotees of Sir Walter Scott, admired the poetry of Lord Byron and Percy Bysshe Shelley, and had a special fondness for the works of William Wordsworth. Much of Anne's early poetry is modeled—unconsciously, perhaps—on Wordsworth's. Many of the lyrics deal with highly autobiographical events, with the plight of a young girl growing to maturity and feeling the pangs of leaving family and friends, experiencing her first love, confronting the majesty of nature and the vagaries of human society.

It is no wonder that Brontë has often been classified, with her siblings, as a late Romantic novelist. Her elder sister Charlotte created one of the greatest Romantic figures in English literature, the brooding, secretive Rochester of *Jane Eyre*. Emily wrote what may be the most famous Romantic novel in the English language, *Wuthering Heights*. An examination of Anne's two novels reveals, however, that while she uses many of the familiar trappings of Romanticism, her fiction seems as firmly anchored in the Victorian tradition of social realism as it is inspired by such writers as Gregory "Monk" Lewis, Charles Maturin, Ann Radcliffe, Sir Walter Scott, and Horace Walpole. Like her predecessor Jane Austen, Anne Brontë found herself writing not paeans to Romantic ideals but criticism of the tradition.

Brontë's first novel, *Agnes Grey*, appeared in print in 1847 as the third volume of a set that included Emily Brontë's *Wuthering Heights*. Described as one of the many "governess novels" published in nineteenth-century England, *Agnes Grey* is based on experiences Anne had while working as a governess herself. Agnes Grey, the youngest daughter of a minister fallen on hard times, leaves home to work as a governess for two families who abuse her emotionally. She finds solace in the poetry she reads and writes and in her strong religious convictions. Fortunately, she meets an eligible and companionable parson, Edward Weston, and they marry. Set beside Emily's passionate lovers Cathy and Heathcliff, Agnes and Edward appear excessively tame. The novel's Romantic qualities are found in the rural setting, the quality of fantasy associated with Agnes's emergence from abused governess to independent wife, and in the portrayal of villainous squires and ladies of the gentry. Like many Romantic novels, *Agnes Grey* shares characteristics with the female bildungsroman; the heroine sets out from the security of her family and encounters the realities of a harsh society, and the experience shapes her character and prepares her for adult life.

The Tenant of Wildfell Hall (1848), published less than a year before Brontë died, is more notably Romantic than its predecessor. Using a narrative technique common to Gothic novelists, Brontë tells her story through a series of frame tales embedded in letters and diaries. The heroine, Helen Huntingdon, enters into a bad marriage with a man whom she hopes to save from his dissolute ways. Far from being amenable to reformation, her husband turns on her and on their young son to exercise his power. Helen escapes from her husband's home, taking up refuge near her brother in Wildfell Hall. There she is perceived by villagers as secretive, even sinister. For Helen, as for Agnes Grey, art becomes a way of expressing her inner thoughts and emotions. Unlike Romantic artists, however, Helen uses her talents to make a living.

It is possible to read *The Tenant of Wildfell Hall* as a bildungsroman, and its setting in the English countryside and among various old manor houses gives it some affinities with novels by writers such as Ann Radcliffe. Arthur Huntingdon has many qualities associated with Romantic heroes and villains. A comparison with Emily Brontë's Heathcliff, however, reveals that Huntingdon is not a larger-than-life character struggling against society's artificial and confining conventions; he is simply a self-centred, boorish, and cruel nobleman who asserts his privilege at the expense of his family. In this way, *The Tenant of Wildfell Hall* serves as a critique of *Wuthering Heights* and the Romantic tradition on which it is based.

Scholars have been late in recognizing Anne Brontë's artistic merits. Long linked critically as well as historically with her more famous sisters, she began to receive serious attention in her own right only after the feminist movement was firmly established in academic circles. Her blend of Romantic qualities with Victorian values make her novels intriguing and perceptive studies of human nature that modify the idealism of the Romantic movement with a realistic assessment of social conventions and restrictions that nineteenth-century women faced in trying to establish themselves as independent, sensitive, intelligent individuals in their own right.

LAURENCE W. MAZZENO

Biography

Born in Thornton, near Bradford, Yorkshire, January 17, 1820. Youngest of five daughters of Patrick Brontë, a clergyman, and Maria Branwell Brontë. Moved with her family to Haworth, Yorkshire, 1820; brought up by an aunt, Elizabeth Branwell, after mother's death from cancer in 1821. Two elder sisters, Maria and Elizabeth, both died of tuberculosis, 1825. Educated at home, and also at Miss Wooler's School, Roe Head, Yorkshire, 1835–37. Began writing "Gondal" saga with her sister Emily, 1831. Governess to the Ingham family at Blake Hall, Mirfield, near Huddersfield, 1839, and to the Robinson family at Thorp Green Hall, Boroughbridge, Yorkshire, 1840–45. Returned to Haworth, 1845. Under the pen name of Acton Bell, contributed to the Brontë sisters' collection *Poems by Currer, Ellis and Acton Bell*, published 1846. Published *The Tenant of Wildfell Hall* as Acton Bell, 1848; traveled to London shortly afterward with sister Charlotte to reveal their identities to publisher George Smith. Contracted tuberculosis, late 1848. Died from tuberculosis in Scarborough, Yorkshire, May 28, 1849.

Selected Writings

Poetry
Poems by Currer, Ellis, and Acton Bell (pseud. for the Brontë sisters). 1847.

Novels
Agnes Grey. 1847.
The Tenant of Wildfell Hall. 1848.

Bibliography

Allott, Miriam, ed. *The Brontës: The Critical Heritage*. London: Routledge and Kegan Paul, 1974.
Bell, Arnold Craig. *The Novels of Anne Brontë*. Braunton Devon: Merlin Books, 1992.
Berry, Elizabeth Hollis. *Anne Brontë's Radical Vision: Structures of Consciousness*. Victoria: University of Victoria Press, 1994.
Chitham, Edward. *A Life of Anne Brontë*. Oxford: Blackwell, 1991.
Frawley, Maria. *Anne Brontë*. New York: Twayne, 1996.
Gérin, Winifred. *Anne Brontë*. 2d ed. London: Allen Lane, 1976.
Langland, Elizabeth. *Anne Brontë: The Other One*. Totowa, N.J.: Barnes and Noble, 1989.
Liddell, Robert. *Twin Spirits: The Novels of Emily and Anne Brontë*. London: Peter Owen, 1990.
McNees, Eleanor, ed. The *Brontë Sisters: Critical Assessments*. 4 vols. Mountfield: Helm Information, 1996.
Scott, P. M. G. *Anne Brontë: A New Critical Assessment*. Totowa, N.J.: Barnes and Noble, 1983.

BRONTË, CHARLOTTE 1816–1855

English novelist and poet

Although Charlotte Brontë came of age during the Victorian period; her three major novels, *Jane Eyre* (1847), *Shirley* (1849), and *Villette* (1853), emerge in the middle of the nineteenth century with a complexity and intensity of vision that sets them apart from other fictional writing of the period. One of three literary sisters, Charlotte Brontë was the only one to achieve literary fame and success in her lifetime. Like her sister Emily's novel *Wuthering Heights*, Brontë's fiction initially shocked contemporary Victorian reviewers, who found it difficult to reconcile the intensely passionate, melodramatic, and imaginative content of the novels with their expectations of realist fiction. More recent critics have viewed Charlotte Brontë's appropriation of Romantic tropes while divorced from the revolutionary context of Romanticism as problematic, since in many ways bourgeois realism and an imaginative Romanticism sit uncomfortably together, both ideologically and stylistically. Yet more so than her sisters, Charlotte Brontë did strive to reconcile a Romantic concern with imaginative experience and the individual, with a Victorian emphasis on bourgeois realism and social responsibility, and in so doing developed Romanticism in new ways and challenged the simplistic historical demarcation of literary periods.

Brontë read a great deal of Romantic-era writing, in particular Lord Byron, Sir Walter Scott, Robert Southey, and William Wordsworth, and was heavily imbued with Romantic ideology. Her work draws extensively on Romantic imagery and language in both her novels and poetry. Her admiration for the Romantic poets is evident from her youthful gesture of sending a letter with some poems to Southey, then England's poet laureate, in December 1836, asking for his opinion on their poetic merit. When Southey replied in March of the following year, it was to tell Brontë that while she "evidently possess[ed], and in no small degree, what Wordsworth calls 'the faculty of verse'" she should not seek to cultivate this talent or look for publication, since "Literature cannot be the business of a woman's life, and it ought not to be. The more she is engaged in her proper duties, the less leisure she will have for it, even as an accomplishment and recreation."

While drawing on tropes inherited from male-authored Romantic literature in her writing, Brontë also problematizes certain Romantic constructs and ways of seeing. Her treatment of Romantic concepts like the self and nature are revised not simply from a Victorian perspective but from one that is specifically woman-centered. In her focus on individual subjectivity, for example, Brontë shifts the focus from a self-centred poetic "I" to heroines whose subjectivity is both at the center of the text, and yet is shown to be fundamentally fragmented and tortured. Brontë takes from the Romantics a fascination with the inner life, but in her novels and poetry shows that for women already living a buried life, further retreat into the self generates blank inertia and madness. She describes the day-to-day existence of her female characters in terms of burial and enclosure: "a black trance like the toad's, buried in marble . . . a long, slow death" (*Villette*). Further retreat into the self transforms the mind into another emblem of death: "That mind my own. Oh! narrow cell;/Dark—imageless—a living tomb!" (*Complete Poems*). To counter this potentially destructive inward-looking subjectivity, Brontë strives to return her heroines to society, seeking validation and experience in the world beyond their own minds. This same pattern is encountered in Brontë's treatment of nature: her novels are imbued with passages of detailed description of the natural. Her heroines are drawn to natural spaces as sites of contemplation, but these spaces, too, prove restrictive; we find them inhabiting narrow paths and inaccessible woods. Ultimately, Brontë's heroines seek instead validation within the public sphere.

Other key aspects of Brontë's writing that are clearly a product of her fascination with literature of the Romantic era are her creation of Byronic heroes and her use of the Gothic. Yet in her appropriation of these figures and genres, we can see Brontë rewriting and changing them in ways that are both a consequence of her Victorian bourgeois ideals and of her gendered response as a woman to a male literary inheritance.

Perhaps the most influential of the Romantic-era writers on Brontë is Lord Byron. All of the Brontë sisters were steeped in Byron's poetry, and Charlotte Brontë's characters have frequently been seen as types of the Byronic hero: dark, brooding, mysterious, and proud. However, while drawing on this literary figure, Brontë also subjects it to unexpected transformations, first in critiquing and negating the hero's power and second in projecting the characteristics of the Byronic hero onto powerful female protagonists. In the three novels published in her lifetime, Brontë creates a Byronic hero, only to reduce that figure to a condition of powerlessness and vulnerability at the end of the text. A similar transformation also takes place in a poem by Brontë entitled "Gilbert," in which she redefines the arrogant, proud Byronic male as "selfish." In her novel *Shirley*, Brontë goes furthest toward projecting these characteristics onto an empowered female heroine, Shirley Keeldar, who embodies the passion, pride, and visionary qualities of the Byronic hero, but who significantly rejects the more negative aspects of that figure—in particular, the tendency toward self-destruction.

Brontë also deploys Gothic mechanisms in her writing in new ways. She has been seen to move toward a more complex psychological development of the genre through a recontextualizing of supernatural imagery within a realist domestic framework. Her last novel, *Villette*, draws extensively on the Gothic genre; the Gothic elements disrupt the realist surface of the narrative. Yet the way in which the Gothic is used by Brontë demonstrates both a dissatisfaction with it simply as a mechanism for exciting fear, and an anxiety about the limitations of nineteenth-century realist fiction. Her combination of the two creates a profoundly disturbing narrative that allows her to express psychological depths not found elsewhere in Victorian writing.

PENNY BRADSHAW

Biography

Born in Thornton, near Bradford, Yorkshire, April 21, 1816. Third of five daughters of Patrick Brontë, a clergyman, and Maria Branwell Brontë. Moved with her family to Haworth, Yorkshire, 1820; brought up by an aunt, Elizabeth Branwell, after her mother's death from cancer, 1821. Educated briefly at the Clergy Daughters' School, Cowan Bridge, near Kirkby Lonsdale, Lancashire, with older sisters Maria and Elizabeth and younger sister Emily, 1824. Returned home when her two elder sisters, Maria and Elizabeth, both died of tuberculosis, 1825. Educated at home; with her brother Branwell, started writing fiction set in imaginary kingdom of Angria, 1825–31. Attended Miss Wooler's School, Roe Head, Mirfield, near Huddersfield, Yorkshire, 1831–32. Taught her sisters at home, 1832–35. Taught at Miss Wooler's School, 1835–38. Governess to the Sidgwick family, Stonegappe in Lothersdale, Yorkshire, 1839, and the White family, Upperwood House, Rawdon, Yorkshire, 1841. Attended Pensionnat Héger, Brussels, with sister Emily, 1842; teacher at Pensionnat Héger, Brussels, 1842–44. Returned to Haworth after unhappy and unrequited attachment to Constantin Héger. Attempted unsuccessfully to establish a school at Haworth, 1844. Under the pen name Currer Bell, published poems with those of her sisters Anne and Emily in a collection entitled *Poems by Currer, Ellis and Acton Bell*; attempted unsuccessfully to find a publisher for her novel *The Professor*, 1846. Published the novel *Jane Eyre* as Currer Bell, 1847. Traveled to London with Anne Brontë to reveal their identities as authors of *Jane Eyre* and *The Tenant of Wildfell Hall*, respectively, 1848. Returned to nurse sisters Emily (died December 1848) and Anne (died May 1849) at Haworth. Published *Shirley*, 1849, and *Villette*, 1853. Traveled to London, northern England, and Scotland, 1850–51; met the writers Elizabeth Gaskell, Harriet Martineau, and William Thackeray. Married her father's curate, Arthur Bell Nicholls, June 1854; honeymooned in Ireland. Died in Haworth from a tubercular condition aggravated by complications in early pregnancy, March 31, 1855.

Selected Writings

Collections

The Complete Poems of Charlotte Brontë. Edited by Clement Shorter, 1978.
The Poems of Charlotte Brontë. Edited by Tom Winnifrith. 1984.
The Letters of Charlotte Brontë, with a Selection of Letters from her Family and Friends. 2 vols. Edited by Margaret Smith. 1995–2000.

Novels

Jane Eyre. 1847.
Shirley. 1849.
Villette. 1853.

Bibliography

Boumelha, Penny. *Charlotte Brontë*. Bloomington: Indiana University Press, 1990.

Edwards, Mike. *Charlotte Brontë: The Novels*. Basingstoke, England: Macmillan, 1999.

Gaskell, Elizabeth. *The Life of Charlotte Brontë*. London: Everyman, 1997.

Gilbert, Sandra M., and Susan Gubar. *The Madwoman in the Attic: The Woman Writer and the Nineteenth-Century Literary Imagination*. New Haven, Conn.: Yale University Press, 1984.

Gilmour, Robert. *The Novel in the Victorian Age*. London: Edward Arnold, 1986.

Jacobus, Mary. "The Buried Letter: Feminism and Romanticism in *Villette*." In *Reading Women: Essays in Feminist Criticism*. Edited by Mary Jacobus. London: Methuen, 1986.

Linder, Cynthia. *Romantic Imagery in the Novels of Charlotte Brontë*. London: Macmillan, 1978.

Lyndall, Gordon. *Charlotte Brontë: A Passionate Life*. London: Vintage, 1995.

Padilla, Yolanda. "Dreaming of Eve, Prometheus and the Titans: The Romantic Vision of Shirley Keeldar," *Brontë Society Transactions* 21 (1993).

Stone, Donald D. *The Romantic Impulse in Victorian Fiction*. Cambridge, Mass.: Harvard University Press, 1980.

BRONTË, EMILY (JANE) 1818–1848

English novelist and poet

Although Emily Brontë produced what is unquestionably one of the masterpieces of English Romanticism, the novel *Wuthering Heights*, little is known about the actual biography of the second-eldest surviving Brontë sisters. One reason for the paucity of information about her is her early death at age thirty when she succumbed to tuberculosis, the disease that killed most members of her immediate family; another is her self-containment and reclusiveness. When in 1845 her sister Charlotte discovered a manuscript volume of her verse, Emily reacted by accusing her sister of invading her privacy. And although Charlotte ultimately prevailed upon Emily to publish her poetry, the former had learned a hard lesson, one that led, in all probability, to Charlotte's destruction of nearly all of Emily's correspondence and diaries upon her death.

In life Emily Brontë's society consisted almost exclusively of her family and its domestic help; she seems to have been particularly close to her sister Anne, with whom in youth she shared the imaginary world of Gondal, created as a counterpart to Charlotte and Branwell's fabulous Angria. But it is arguable that the members of the household to whom Emily felt closest were the Brontë animals, especially the hawk Hero and the dog Keeper. Some of the most memorable and telling anecdotes we have about Emily concern her relationship to nonhuman beings, as when she self-cauterized a wound incurred during an encounter with a strange dog or broke up a fight between Keeper and another large canine, using only her own strength and a box of ground pepper, which she liberally applied to both dogs' snouts. The latter incident was recorded by a local merchant, who could not help but comment on Emily's apparent obliviousness of the male audience who looked on but did not themselves dare interfere with the dogfight. He is only one of many observers to allude to the mannish quality that set Emily apart from her sisters and from her society. Constantin Héger, her teacher in Brussels in 1842, would later remark unequivocally, "She should have been a man—a great navigator. Her powerful reason would have deduced new spheres of discovery from the knowledge of the old; and her strong, imperious will would never have been daunted by opposition or difficulty . . ."

Emily's nine-month sojourn in Brussels, where she went with Charlotte to study, was the only time that she left England, and—aside from three months spent at a local boarding school and a six-month stint as a teacher, both of which ended when she returned home ill—the only extended period she spent away from her Haworth parsonage household. Away from the only domestic environment where she was comfortable and, more particularly, away from her beloved moorlands, Emily distinguished herself by her nonconformity and unsociability.

She apparently made no attempt to make herself likeable and refused to go along with her sister's adoption of more fashionable continental clothes. Her refusal to bend, to sacrifice a scintilla of her powerful sense of personal integrity, prompted her schoolmates to taunt her. Emily's response was angry and altogether characteristic: "I wish to be as God made me."

This wish to be in some sense "natural," illustrated by her physicality, her affinity with nonhuman creatures and for the outdoors, is part of what makes Emily Brontë an apt representative of the Romantic impulse. Numerous critics have remarked on her unwillingness or inability to break free of Gondal or, alternatively, her otherworldly, almost mystical nature, but such interpretations are not fully accurate. In fact, the ecstasy she experienced while dwelling in her imagination or in nature reflects the same desire to escape the self and individual identity expressed, for example, in William Wordsworth's "Snowdon vision" in *The Prelude*.

Unquestionably Emily was affected by art as well as the outdoors. One writer whose influence can clearly be seen in her work is the Scottish poet David Moir, whose verses extolling the beauties of the natural world she read in *Blackwoods' Magazine* during her youth. Echoes of Moir's lines appear throughout her poems, as do reflections of his predisposition toward the elegy. In what was to be her last great poem, Emily triumphantly declares, "No coward soul is mine / No trembler in the world's storm-troubled sphere." "There is not room for Death," she concludes, "Since thou art Being and Breath / And what thou art may never be destroyed." The speaker's sureness here results from her ability to see "Heaven's glories shine," but Emily's faith was far from the conventional sort this verse implies. Elsewhere she couples a longing for release from corporeal existence with a decidedly earthbound, sensual vision of eternity. A verse like "Yet none would ask a Heaven / More like this Earth than thine" leads us directly into *Wuthering Heights* and Cathy's dream of dying and going to heaven, only to beg the angels to let her come back to her earthly paradise amid the heath, where she and her beloved Heathcliff are one.

Wuthering Heights owes much to Gondal and, in turn, to Emily's lifelong passion for the romantic tales of Sir Walter Scott. But the strengths of Emily Brontë's unforgettable novel are those that inform the greatest Romantic poetry, which is characterized by the same sort of transcendental mingling of the sensual and the spiritual that leads Cathy to declare, "I *am* Heathcliff," and for both Cathy and Heathcliff to embrace death as the only state that will permit them total and eternal union. And like her doomed lovers, Emily herself seemed to yearn for a world beyond this one, whether it be Gondal, the moor, or some other place outside space and time. Charlotte Brontë never ceased to wonder at her sister's bravery in the face of early and certain death, but Emily clearly did not look on her demise as an end to anything. Charlotte's "Biographical Notice of Ellis and Acton Bell," written as a preface for the single-volume second edition of *Wuthering Heights* and Anne's *Agnes Grey*, conveys an attitude that is less like acceptance than anticipation. She notes that Emily "made haste to leave us. Yet, while physically she perished, mentally, she grew stronger than we had yet known her. . . . I have seen nothing like it; but, indeed, I have never seen her parallel in anything. Stronger than a man, simpler than a child, her nature stood alone."

LISA PADDOCK

Biography

Born in Thornton, near Bradford, Yorkshire, July 30, 1818. Fourth of five daughters of Patrick Brontë, a clergyman, and Maria Branwell Brontë. Moved with her family to Haworth, Yorkshire, 1820; brought up by an aunt, Elizabeth Branwell, after her mother's death from cancer, 1821. Educated briefly at the Clergy Daughters' School, Cowan Bridge, near Kirkby Lonsdale, Lancashire, with older sisters Maria, Elizabeth, and Charlotte; returned home with Charlotte after Maria and Eliza-beth both died of tuberculosis, 1825. Began writing the "Gondal" saga with her sister Anne, as a counterpart to the "Angrian" stories of Charlotte and brother Branwell, 1831. Attended Miss Wooler's School, Roe Head, Mirfield, Yorkshire, briefly, 1835; returned home when her health declined. Taught at Miss Patchett's School, Law Hill, near Halifax, 1838, until poor health again sent her home. Attended Pensionnat Héger in Brussels with sister Charlotte, 1842. Returned to Haworth on the death of Elizabeth Branwell; assumed role of housekeeper to the Parsonage, October 1842. Under the pen name Ellis Bell, contributed writing to the Brontë sisters' collection *Poems by Currer, Ellis, and Acton Bell*, 1846; published the novel *Wuthering Heights*, 1847. Contracted tuberculosis shortly after the death of her brother Branwell from the disease, late 1848. Died from tuberculosis in Haworth, December 19, 1848.

Selected Writings

Collection
The Complete Poems of Emily Jane Brontë. Edited by C. W. Hatfield. New York: Columbia University Press, 1941.

Novel
Wuthering Heights. 1847.

Bibliography

Barker, Juliet. *The Brontës.* New York: St. Martin's Press, 1994.
——. *The Brontës: A Life in Letters.* New York: Overlook Press, 1998.
Chitham, Edward. *A Life of Emily Brontë.* London: Basil Blackwood, 1987.
Fraser, Rebecca. *The Brontës: Charlotte Brontë and Her Family.* New York: Crown, 1988.
Gérin, Winifred. *Emily Brontë: A Biography.* Oxford: Clarendon Press, 1967.
Hewish, John. *Emily Brontë: A Critical and Biographical Study.* London: Macmillan, 1969.
Smith, Anne, ed. *The Art of Emily Brontë.* New York: Barnes and Noble, 1976.
Spark, Muriel, and Derek Stanford. *Emily Brontë: Her Life and Work.* New York: Coward-McCann, 1966.

"THE BRONZE HORSEMAN" ("MEDNYI VSADNIK")

Poem, 1833 (first published in 1837) by Alexander Pushkin

The title of the poem "The Bronze Horseman" refers to the equestrian statue of Peter the Great, erected in 1782 in the center of Saint Petersburg to commemorate the hundredth anniversary of his consecration as Russia's ruler. Designed by the French sculptor Etienne-Maurice Falconet after the famous statue of Louis XIV by Gian Lorenzo Bernini, the monument became a symbol of imperial Russia. One of Peter's controversial achievements was the founding in 1703 of a new Russian capital, which the tsar named in his own honor, on the marshy Finnish land retaken from Sweden in the Great Northern War (1700–1721). Severe floods have been a scourge of the city ever since. Using the disastrous flood of November 1824 as an example, Pushkin reassessed Peter the Great's legacy in the poem with an enigmatic message that is still very much a subject of debate.

"The Bronze Horseman" consists of two parts and a prologue. The prologue juxtaposes the dark and depressing sight of the thinly inhabited banks of the River Neva, described through the eyes of Peter himself, with a view of the same site one hundred years later, now a brightly illuminated grand city offering boundless excitement to its large population, fulfilling Peter's dream of Saint Petersburg as a "window onto Europe." However, the happiness and well-being of the Saint Petersburg dwellers are jeopardized by the elements in part 1, which describes the 1824 flood and the devastating effect it has on the life of an impoverished nobleman, Eugene. Separated from his fiancée Parasha by the overflowing Neva, he witnesses the raging waters (their wild attacks on the city are skilfully "mirrored" in the extensive use of enjambment) not far from the Bronze Horseman monument, and wonders whether Parasha and her mother, a widow whose house is situated in close proximity to the Gulf of Finland, have survived the disaster. Part 2 establishes the fact that they have not. Subsequently, Eugene becomes insane and one night, when suffering from an acute bout of madness, makes a threatening gesture toward the statue of Peter the Great, whom he holds accountable for the death of Parasha and her mother. (Although Pushkin does not provide the reader with detailed insight into Eugene's warped logic, the madman's grievances against Peter could be apparently summarized as follows: Had Peter not decided to build a city in such an inappropriate place, innocent people would not have perished as a result of ill-conceived urban planning.) The statue suddenly starts moving in response to the threats, and chases Eugene through the streets of Saint Petersburg. Presumably, this occurs only in Eugene's imagination, although Pushkin never makes a clear statement to this effect. The story ends with the dead body of Eugene being discovered in an abandoned house (supposedly, the same one that once belonged to Parasha's mother); he is given a pauper's burial.

This bleak finale, while raising awareness of the plight of ordinary people who are normally ignored by those in power, is in stark contrast with the panegyrical prologue. It is thus difficult to discern where Pushkin's sympathies lie, with the "little man" or the "higher interests of the empire." Tsar Nicholas I evidently believed that the empire came second on Pushkin's list of priorities, and suppressed the publication of the poem. Another, no less influential, school of thought posited that Eugene's pathetic revolt could not be treated seriously, and might only serve as an example of how pointless such protests are when they confront the power of the state itself. Some scholars even read the poem as an allegory of the Decembrists' rebellion of 1825 that unsuccessfully sought to overthrow Nicholas I.

An ideologically disengaged analysis of the poem demonstrates that Pushkin's attitude is consistently impartial. He expresses solidarity with the "poor madman" (it is not by chance that the next lodger in Eugene's rented accommodation is a poet who is also characterized as "poor") whose needs are neglected by the authorities (in the scene of the 1824 flood, Peter's statue is depicted as if symbolically turning its back on Eugene). However, Alexander I (the reigning emperor at the time of the 1824 flood, and of the same lineage as Peter), is accurately portrayed as a caring ruler who ordered his generals to try and save the drowning residents of Saint Petersburg. The significance of Peter's reforms is also done full justice in the poem, which compares both the River Neva and pre-Petrine Russia to a horse, and claims that Peter's mission was to break in the wild horse of Russia. The first-person singular statement in the prologue, evidently coming from Pushkin himself, expresses a wish for the "impregnable" Saint Petersburg and the "calmed" elements to live in peace and harmony with each other. It is also possible that Pushkin was not trying to make a political point, but was simply yielding to his fascination with the interaction between the mobile and the motionless, and in particular with the myth of a statue that comes to life.

ANDREI ROGACHEVSKII

Text

First appeared posthumously in an edited form in the *contemporary Review* (*Sovremennik*) 5 (1837); Pushkin scholars still argue over which version should be considered definitive. Translated as "The Bronze Cavalier" by Charles Edward Turner in *Translations from Poushkin in Memory of the Hundredth Anniversary of the Poet's Birthday*, Saint Petersburg: K L Ricker, and London: Sampson Low, Marston & Co 1899 and (in excerpts) as "The Copper Horseman" by C. A. Manning (South Atlantic Quarterly 25 (1926): 76–88). Other attempts include those of Oliver Elton (*Slavonic and East European Review* 13, no. 37 (1934): 2–14); Eugene M. Kayden (Colorado Quarterly 19, no. 3, (1971): 305–20); Charles Johnston, in *Talk about the Last Poet* (London: Bodley Head, 1981); and D. M. Thomas, in *The Bronze Horseman: Selected Poems of Alexander Pushkin* (London: Secker & Warburg, 1982).

Bibliography

Kahn, Andrew. *Pushkin's The Bronze Horseman*. London: Bristol Classical Press, 1998.

Panfilowitsch, Igor. *Aleksandr Puskins "Mednyj vsadnik."* In *Deutungsgeschichte und Gehalt*. Munchen: O. Sagner, 1995.

Briggs, Anthony David Peach. *A Comparative Study of Pushkin's The Bronze Horseman, Nekrasov's Red-Nosed Frost, and Blok's The Twelve: The Wild World*. Lewiston, N.Y.: Edwin Mellen Press, 1990.

Knigge, Armin. *Puskins Verserzahlung "Der eherne Reiter." In der russischen Kritik: Rebellion oder Unterwerfung*. Amsterdam: Hakkert, 1984.

Lednicki, Waclaw. *Pushkin's Bronze Horseman: The Story of a Masterpiece*. 1955. Reprint, Westport, Conn.: Greenwood Press, 1978.

BROWN, CHARLES BROCKDEN 1771–1810

American writer

Philadelphia-born, Quaker-raised Charles Brockden Brown belongs to the first generation of American writers who came of age after the American Revolution. Lacking any personal involvement with the struggle for political autonomy from England and growing up amid the financial depression and government instability of the 1780s, Brown experienced ambivalent feelings about the future success of the constitutional United States. After an unexpected trading boom in the 1790s produced relative ease for the educated elite, America suddenly appeared able to offer new opportunities. Brown abandoned a legal training that would have secured his career and attempted to become one of the new republic's first professional writers. Writing during a period of relatively minimal foreign immigration and in between phases of westward expansion, he concentrated mainly on how domestic, interpersonal conflicts damage human development and social betterment. His first published narrative writing, *Alcuin* (1798), discusses the limits to women's equality, and, although he withheld publication of the second half, its description of a journey to a land of female empowerment is one of the first examples of American utopian writing. *Wieland; or, the Transformation* (1798) is a tale about a man who murders his family after seeming to be duped by an itinerant ventriloquist. *Arthur Mervyn* (1799–1800) traces the journey of a backwoods youth into the city and through the yellow fever plague to document how prejudice affects the youth's conception of society. *Edgar Huntly* (1799), Brown's least urban novel, uses the backdrop of an Anglo-Indian frontier war to investigate the possibilities for male homosocial/homoerotic relations. *Ormond; or, the Secret Witness* (1799) charts a poor woman's survival challenges in a city replete with seducers, frauds, and rapists.

The ongoing French Revolution and the flowering of English literary radicalism encouraged Brown to write, but this optimism would be short-lived with the rise of reaction abroad (Napoleon Bonaparte) and the domestic emergence of insurgent capitalism. After the turn of the century, Brown abandoned novel writing in favor of editing magazines and annual digests of political events.

Brown's favorite fictional theme treats how an environment of social damage (poverty, family violence, epidemics, racial discrimination, and so forth) can act as the catalyst for overcoming corruption ("vice") and constructing a more equal and "virtuous" society. Since Brown's main target is the defects in conventional behavior rather than the tyranny of the state or inequity of the commercial marketplace, he represents an initial effort to critique what later critics call the bourgeois ideology of the everyday, the constricting practices of "normal" manners. Key to this project is Brown's belief in rational sentiment. Sentiment, or sympathy, believes in the unpremeditated, physical response to the sight, or imagination, of a body in pain. To this faith in instinctive benevolence Brown adds the notion that sentiment can be harnessed to Enlightenment ideals to overcome the passions of selfishness. The fusion of collective feeling and group progress exemplifies a strand of Romantic era culture that later "Romanticisms" often resist as they either disengage from a society viewed as irredeemably corrupt or celebrate the organic purity of a premodern folk.

Brown's aesthetic project develops from his understanding about the relation between historical and fictional (romance) writing. For Brown, history and literature are not different because one deals with factual rather than fictional materials. Histories describe and document the result of actions, but fiction investigates the possible motives that cause these actions. Fiction is hypothetical ratiocination; narrative experiments that explore possible preconditions for historical events. The most fitting subject for fiction is therefore the personal manners and intimate relations of women and men—what he calls "domestic history." The author's role in narrating the romance of real life is to hold up a mirror for readers to see things as they really are and to use storytelling about individuals as a testing ground for reconceptualizing larger, collective patterns. Brown's sensibility is not Romantic in the sense that it fetishizes the individual artist as the unacknowledged legislator of social change. It is "romanticist," however, in its belief that manners modify history and that writing can be potentially revolutionary as it educates its readers into critical thought.

Unlike contemporaries such as Matthew Lewis and Ann Radcliffe, Brown rejects familiar gothic devices such as ghosts and exotic locations (for example, castles) as pointlessly confusing because they rely on forces that are beyond human ability to manipulate and reform the world. Instead he uses situations of personal duplicity to emphasize how the examination of local, personal experience holds the key to social transformation. Likewise, Brown later denounced mythologizing historical romances, like those of Walter Scott, as invoking the "supernatural" spirit of nationalism, which he saw as a betrayal of the universal project for bettering the lives of humans, regardless of their location within global power structures.

In the American literary context, Brown turns away from Benjamin Franklin's idealism, which assumes private passions can be easily corrected and put to public good use. Brown's hesitation about Franklin's optimism becomes more pronounced by writers who follow his influence. Nathaniel Hawthorne acknowledges Brown's skill, but chooses to present his own writing as "romances," or tales of personal experience, rather than novels about private and public events. Edgar Allan Poe often revisits Brown's themes, but only to emphasize style over didactic social purpose. With George Lippard's *The Quaker City* (1845), dedicated to Brown, we return to the union of urban sensation and moral outrage at social injustice.

Beyond the United States, Brown's work is best read in relation to the Anglo-Jacobin writers (Robert Bage, William Godwin, Thomas Holcroft, and Mary Wollstonecraft); and the general contexts created by Scottish moral philosophy; physiological theories of sense perception (Erasmus Darwin, John Locke); Jean-Jacques Rousseau; and the young Johann Christoph Friedrich von Schiller (and August Friedrich Ferdinand Kotzebue, to a lesser extent). With his interest in European developments Brown sought to participate in a network of like-minded endeavors, a "republic of letters." He felt little or no need to emulate Europe as cultural superior. Additionally, his lifelong commitment to female education and equality means that he never considered literary production as belonging exclusively to either gender.

STEPHEN SHAPIRO

Biography

Born in Philadelphia January 17, 1771. Ends law apprenticeship, 1792; publishes first novel, 1798; leaves New York after friend's death from yellow fever, 1798. Return to Philadelphia, 1800; abandons novel writing for magazine editing, 1801. Dies from tuberculosis in Philadelphia, 1810.

Selected Works.

Alcuin: A Dialogue. 1798.
Wieland; or, The Transformation: An American Tale. 1798.
Edgar Huntly; or, Memoirs of a Sleep-Walker. 1799.
Ormond; or, The Secret Witness. 1799.
Arthur Mervyn; or, Memoirs of the Year 1793. 2 vols. 1799–1800.
The Novels and Related Works of Charles Brockden Brown. 6 vols. Edited by Sydney J. Krause. Kent, Ohio: Kent State University Press, 1977–87.
Somnambulism and Other Stories. Edited by Alfred Weber. Frankfurt: Peter Larg, 1987.
Literary Essays and Reviews. Edited by Alfred Weber and Wolfgang Schäfer in collaboration with John R. Holmes. Frankfurt: Peter Larg, 1992.

Bibliography

Barnard, Philip, Mark Kamrath, and Stephen Shapiro, eds. *Revising Charles Brockden Brown: Culture, Politics, and Sexuality in the Early Republic.* Knoxville: University of Tennessee Press, forthcoming.

Clemit, Pamela. *The Godwinian Novel: The Rational Fictions of Godwin, Brockden Brown, Mary Shelley.* Oxford: Clarendon Press, 1993.

Fleischmann, Fritz. *A Right View of the Subject: Feminism in the Works of Charles Brockden Brown and John Neal.* Erlangen: Palm and Enke, 1983.

Grabo, Norman S. *The Coincidental Art of Charles Brockden Brown.* Chapel Hill: University of North Carolina Press, 1981.

Rosenthal, Bernard, ed. *Critical Essays on Charles Brockden Brown.* Boston: Hall, 1981.

Watts, Steven. *The Romance of Real Life: Charles Brockden Brown and the Origins of American Culture.* Baltimore: Johns Hopkins University Press, 1994.

BROWNING, ELIZABETH BARRETT 1806–1861

English poet

When William Wordsworth died in 1850, Elizabeth Barrett Browning had achieved sufficient fame and renown so that she was thought a deserving successor to him as Britain's poet laureate. Browning had been publishing for nearly a quarter of a century by then, and in that time she had clearly established herself as a poet interested in poetry's relationship to aesthetics, politics, social justice, and everyday life. While her work registers clear connections to the Romantic poets who preceded her, her response to Romantic forms, themes, and subject matter also mark her as a poet deeply aware of the ways that historical location and gender shape literary production.

Browning greatly admired the second-generation Romantic poets (Lord Byron, John Keats, and Percy Bysshe Shelley), and shared with them an interest in classical and political subject matter. One of her most direct responses to Romantic aesthetic theory comes in her 1844 poem "The Dead Pan," in which she takes up the issue that Keats raised in his "Ode on a Grecian Urn": namely, whether classical mythology energizes or enervates modern art. While Keats suggests that pagan mythology is the clearest and most timeless route to truth and beauty, Browning takes the opposite position. In "The Dead Pan" she insists that antiquity is a time well lost, and that the "Truest Truth" is to be found by connecting art to the business of daily life. This insistence that poetry immerse itself in contemporary affairs is perhaps the guiding principle of Browning's work, and that she herself wanted it to be understood as such is evident from her demand that "The Dead Pan" be placed last, as a sort of concluding argument, in her collected *Poems, in Two Volumes*, of 1844.

Like Shelley and Byron, Browning became passionately involved in foreign politics, devoting herself to the cause of Italian independence after moving to Florence with new husband Robert Browning in 1845. Drawing on her claim for poetry's pragmatic value, Browning published two volumes of political poetry during her years in Italy—*Casa Guidi Windows* in 1851, and *Poems before Congress* in 1860. While Browning explicitly positions herself as observer in *Casa Guidi Windows*—Casa Guidi was the house she shared with Robert Browning and their son Pen in Florence—much of the volume belies such detachment, advancing such claims as "Heroic daring is the true success." And in *Poems Before Congress*—a volume named for an international summit that never actually took place—Browning offers still more direct political commentaries, speaking publicly about the corruption of the papacy, the need for international political coalitions, and the evils of American slavery. This collection of poems, her last, generated considerable critical censure; some objected to the politics, but more objected to the fact that a *woman* was writing about politics. As one reviewer for *Blackwood's Magazine* put it, "To bless not to curse is woman's function."

These reviewers may have been responding to more than *Poems before Congress*. Three years earlier, in 1857, Browning had published the "verse-novel" *Aurora Leigh*. With its frank treatment of a variety of issues related to what Victorians called "the Woman Question," *Aurora Leigh*—the longest narrative poem of the nineteenth century—was a highly controversial work. It was also the poet's favorite. Shortly before its publication she wrote to one correspondent, "I mean that when you have read my new book, you put away all my other poems . . . and know me only by the new." *Aurora Leigh* tells the story of its eponymous heroine's growth as an artist, and like "The Dead Pan," the poem shows Browning engaging with and responding to the Romantic tradition. In particular, she takes on the Wordsworthian *kunstlerroman*, *The Prelude*, using a similar epic structure to compare the lot of the male and female artist. Her formal choice was a daring one—epic verse was a highly masculinized form, associated with John Milton, William Shakespeare, Shelley, Alfred, Lord Tennyson, and, later, Robert Browning. But Browning does not simply feminize the epic form; she also provides a feminine perspective on epic content, repeatedly emphasizing the stark inequality of opportunity between men and women in contemporary British society. For example, while Wordsworth is educated, in nature and at Cambridge, to assume a position of importance in his society, Aurora Leigh is educated at home by a maiden aunt into quiet feminine "accomplishments"; while Wordsworth casts his relationship with Annette Vallon as a tragic love story, Aurora's friend Marian Erle shows the cost of illegitimate childbirth to the woman involved. Aurora Leigh does ultimately achieve a poetic vocation in the verse-novel, and this fact, too, added to the poem's controversy: the literary establishment had grown accustomed to female novelists, and had compensated by dismissing the novel as a lesser form of literature, but it had not yet made room for such phenomena as Browning's depiction of Aurora Leigh and of poetry as a legitimate female vocation.

Despite Browning's focus on difference between male and female poets in *Aurora Leigh*, the Romantic poets did influence

Elizabeth Barrett Browning. Reprinted courtesy of Bildarchiv.

her in significant ways. She wrote a very personal lament following the death of Byron, and praised Wordsworth quite publicly in essays and in an 1844 poem titled "On a Portrait of Wordsworth by B. R. Haydon." Perhaps most important, one of her earliest forays into topical poetry shows a strong Blakean influence. "The Cry of the Children," an 1842 poem written to draw attention to England's child-labor laws, uses the sing-song rhythm and simple ABAB rhymes of Blake's *Songs of Innocence and Experience*, and also gives body and voice to Innocence through Blakean child speakers who contrast their urban hardships with an idealized natural order, offering such laments as "all day, we drive the wheels of iron / In the factories, round and round." This early poem, like all of Elizabeth Barrett Browning's work, shows her consistent fascination with and focus on what she calls, in *Aurora Leigh*, "this live, throbbing age."

BONNIE J. GUNZENHAUSER

Biography

Elizabeth Barrett was born on March 6, 1806, in County Durham, England. The oldest of twelve children, she enjoyed a comfortable upper-class childhood. Though she received no formal education, she read voraciously and learned from her brothers' tutors; in this way she learned French, Greek, Hebrew, Italian, and Latin. Barrett kept a diary and wrote poetry throughout her childhood, and her father subsidized her first poetic publication, *The Battle of Marathon*, which was printed in 1820. Barrett displayed more of her classical and philosophical self-education in the long poem *An Essay on Mind*, published in 1826. With the decline of her father's fortunes in 1827 and the death of her mother in 1828, Barrett moved with the family to London. She suffered from a nervous disorder but continued to write, publishing a translation of *Prometheus Bound*, along with other poems, in 1833. In London, Barrett met various members of the literati, befriending in particular John Kenyon and Mary Russell Mitford. She published *The Seraphim and Other Poems* in 1838, published various poems in magazines in the late 1830s and early 1840s, and produced a two-volume set of poems in 1844. This set attracted the attention of the poet Robert Browning, who began an admiring correspondence with Barrett in 1845. The two met in 1845, and were secretly married in September of 1846; Barrett's father resisted the marriage, and died unreconciled to it in 1857. The Brownings left England for Italy immediately after the wedding, and settled in Florence, which would be their home base until Elizabeth Browning's death. In Italy, she published *Sonnets from the Portuguese* (1850), *Casa Guidi Windows* (1851), *Aurora Leigh* (1856), and *Poems before Congress* (1860). The couple had a son, Robert Wiedman (Pen) in 1849. Elizabeth Barrett Browning died on June 29, 1861, in the Browning's home of Casa Guidi in Florence.

Selected Works

An Essay on Mind, with Other Poems. 1826.
Prometheus Bound, and Miscellaneous Poems. 1833.
The Seraphim and Other Poems. 1838.
"The Cry of the Children." 1842.
Poems, in Two Volumes. 1844.
Sonnets from the Portuguese. 1850.
Casa Guidi Windows. 1851.
Aurora Leigh. 1857.
Poems before Congress. 1860.

Bibliography

Blake, Kathleen. "Elizabeth Barrett Browning and Wordsworth: The Romantic Poet as a Woman," *Victorian Poetry* 24 (1986): 387–98.
David, Deirdre. *Intellectual Women and Victorian Patriarchy: Harriet Martineau, Elizabeth Barrett Browning, and George Eliot.* Ithaca, N.Y.: Cornell University Press, 1987.
Donaldson, Sandra, ed. *Critical Essays on Elizabeth Barrett Browning.* New York: G. K. Hall, 1999.
Mermin, Dorothy. *Elizabeth Barrett Browning: The Origins of a New Poetry.* Chicago: University of Chicago Press, 1989.
Riede, David G. "Elizabeth Barrett: The Poet as Angel," *Victorian Poetry* 32 (1994): 121–39.
Rosenblum, Dolores. "Face to Face: Elizabeth Barrett Browning's *Aurora Leigh* and Nineteenth-Century Poetry," *Victorian Studies* 26 (1983): 321–38.
Stone, Marjorie. *Elizabeth Barrett Browning.* New York: St. Martin's Press, 1995.
Zonona, Joyce. "The Embodied Muse: Elizabeth Barrett Browning's *Aurora Leigh* and Feminist Poetics," *Tulsa Studies in Women's Literature* 98 (1989): 241–62.

BROWNING, ROBERT 1812–1889

English poet

The inheritor of a tradition, Robert Browning's relationship with Romanticism is a complicated one. He was undoubtedly influenced by the Romantics, most notably by Percy Bysshe Shelley, although he later distanced himself from his Shelleyan past when he learned about the earlier poet's desertion of his first wife, Harriet Westbrook. However, in his widespread use of the dramatic monologue technique, his allusiveness, and his perceived obscurity, it is also possible to regard Browning as a forerunner of modernism, and indeed he was championed by the modernist poet and theoretician Ezra Pound. The dramatic monologue technique itself, however, may be connected with Romanticism, as it is formally without designated boundaries (unlike the sonnet), and thematically it is intensely individualistic as it explores and exposes a personality.

Browning had little in the way of formal education. He attended boarding school in the early 1820s, and in 1828 he enrolled at the University of London, only to leave a few months later with no qualification. Browning's learning was not, however, thwarted by his lack of formal instruction. His father was a bibliophile and Browning read voraciously. We may therefore regard him as an autodidact. This may explain some of his perceived obscurity, with his choice of poetic subject matter and speakers being shaped by independent reading rather than by an institution.

Browning's writing career did not enjoy an auspicious beginning. In 1833, *Pauline* appeared anonymously, and not a single copy was sold. *Paracelsus* (1835) was better received, with John Forster stating, in March 1836, that "without the slightest hesitation we name Mr Robert Browning at once with Shelley, Coleridge, Wordsworth." *Paracelsus* attacks formal education, reflecting the Romantics' mistrust of institutions. In this sense, the eponymous subject of the poem is a Romantic hero, rebelling against authority. However, Browning's reputation incurred a setback with the publication of *Sordello* (1840), a poem about the life of a thirteenth-century Italian troubadour that was ridiculed by contemporary critics for its obscurity. Between 1841 and 1846, Browning published *Bells and Pomegranates*, a series of poetic pamphlets in eight volumes. He tried his hand briefly at writing for the stage, but none of his eight productions enjoyed critical or artistic success.

A political and moral liberal, Browning lived at home until the mid 1840s and his father paid for his publications. In 1845, however, he made contact with the poet Elizabeth Barrett. They married in September of the following year without her father's knowledge, and thereafter they left England for Italy, where Browning remained until after his wife's death in 1861.

Browning's most critically acclaimed work is *Men and Women*, first published in 1855. It was not well received on publication, however; there was a prevailing feeling that Browning was misusing his talent. The only favorable reception came from George Eliot, writing in the *Westminster Review*, and from the Pre-Raphaelites. Eliot defended the perceived lack of lyricism in the collection, stating, "Wordsworth is, on the whole, a far more musical poet than Browning, yet we remember no line in Browning so prosaic as many of Wordsworth's." The enduring appeal of *Men and Women* rests in Browning's skillful use of the dramatic monologue technique, with characters slowly revealing their true natures, often in little asides or slips. Browning's range of characters in *Men and Women* is certainly eclectic: we have two Italian Renaissance painters, a duke, a physician examining the Lazarus case, a biblical hero from the Old Testament, a tortured yet indomitable knight, and a Catholic bishop from the 1850s to name but a few. "Childe Roland to the Dark Tower came," arguably the most memorable poem from *Men and Women*, can be compared with Samuel Taylor Coleridge's "Ancient Mariner"; both present troubled narrators enduring suffering within a nightmarish landscape.

Browning did not enjoy significant commercial and critical success until the publication of *Dramatis Personae* in 1864. His reputation was enhanced by *The Ring and the Book* (1868–69), by which stage Browning was second only to Alfred, Lord Tennyson in the estimation of Victorian commentators. The Browning Society was founded in London in 1881, and Browning himself continued to publish prolifically until his death in 1889. His critical reputation remained intact until the publication of George Santayana's *Interpretations of Poetry and Religion* in 1900, which described Browning metaphorically as "a volcanic eruption that tosses itself quite blindly and ineffectually into the sky."

The introductory essay to the *Letters of Percy Bysshe Shelley* is Browning's only prose work of any real importance, though the book itself was withdrawn from sale when the authenticity of at least one of the letters was called into question. It is the only work of criticism that Browning published under his own name. Within the essay Browning adopts a popular critical belief of his day—namely, that literary periods are dominated by "subjective" and "objective" poetry in alternation. Within this pattern it would be fair to say that the first and second generation Romantic poets were subjective, focusing on themselves and their inner experiences, and that the inheritors of the tradition they founded—including Browning—were objective, focusing more on the world around them. This rather reductive critical strategy emerged out of German thought of the 1820s, and Samuel Taylor Coleridge received it enthusiastically.

Having discovered Shelley's poetry in 1826, Browning became an energetic devotee of a man he regarded as an unfairly impugned genius. A Shellyan influence is clearly detectable in *Pauline*, and, to a lesser extent, in *Paracelsus* and *Sordello*. However, by 1856 Browning had rejected Shelley; his separation from that influence was signaled clearly by his refusal of the presidency of the Shelley Society in 1885. Parts of the essay read like Shelley's own *In Defence of Poetry*, with Browning extolling the virtues of poets as visionaries and prophets. Browning talks of the poet's "double faculty of seeing external objects more clearly, widely, and deeply, than is possible to the average mind"; he also calls the poet a "seer."

Browning's poetry can be read as an attempt to adapt the principles of Romanticism to the mid-century. The individual is still important, but he now needs to be seen acting in relation to other aspects of his social life. The imagination is still relevant, but so are the facts. Thus we have Fra Lippo Lippi, the incorrigible painter from *Men and Women*, who performs for his patron Cosimo de Medici; his imagination is necessarily tempered by the demands of social life and the artistic market place.

MICHAEL FLAVIN

Biography

Born in Camberwell, London, May 7, 1812. Son of Robert Browning, a clerk at the Bank of England, and Sarah Anna Wiedemann. Educated at the school of Rev. Thomas Ready, Peckham, London, 1822–26, and at home, 1826–28. Studied Greek at the University of London 1828–29. Applied unsuccessfully for a diplomatic post, 1834. Travelled to Saint Petersburg, Russia, 1834, and to Italy, 1838. Lived with his parents in Camberwell until 1840 and in Hatcham, Surrey, until 1846. Began correspondence with Elizabeth Barrett after reading her *Poems* (1844), January 1845; met her in May 1845; married her in secret and eloped to Italy with her, September 1846. They had one son, Robert Weidemann "Pen" Barrett Browning (1849–1913). Lived in Pisa and later at Casa Guidi in Florence, 1846–61. Visited Paris and London, 1851–52; met writers Charles Kingsley, Dante Gabriel Rossetti, and Alfred, Lord Tennyson. Published *Men and Women*, 1855. Elizabeth Barrett Browning died, June 1861. Returned to England with his son, late 1861; lived in London with his father until his death in 1866, and later with his sister. Traveled frequently to France, Italy, Scotland, and Switzerland. Proposed marriage to Lady Ashburton and was rejected, 1869. Published *The Ring and the Book*, 1868–69. Honorary M.A., 1867; LL.D., Oxford University, 1882. Honorary fellow, Balliol College, Oxford, 1868. LL.D., University of Edinburgh, 1884. Governor of University College, London, 1871; correspondent, Royal Academy, London, 1886. Browning Society established, 1881. Died of bronchitis while staying in Venice, December 12, 1889.

Selected Writings

Collections

The Poetical Works of Robert Browning. 1888–94.
Men and Women and Other Poems. Edited by Colin Graham. 1975.
Robert Browning's Poetry. Edited by James F. Loucks. 1979.
Robert Browning: The Poems. Edited by John Pettigrew and Thomas J. Collins. 1981.
The Ring and the Book. Edited by Richard D. Altick. 1981.
The Oxford Authors: Robert Browning. Edited by Adam Roberts. 1997.

Letters.

The Letters of Elizabeth Barrett Browning. Edited by F. G. Kenyon. 1898.
Letters of Robert Browning. Edited by Thurman Hood. 1950.
The Letters of Robert Browning and Elizabeth Barrett Browning, 1845–46. Edited by Elvan Kintner. 1969.

Bibliography

Bristow, Joseph. *Robert Browning.* New York: Harvester, 1993.
Irvine, William and Park Honan. *The Book, The Ring, and the Poet: A Biography of Robert Browning.* London: Bodley Head, 1975.
Johnson, E. D. H. *The Alien Vision of Romantic Poetry.* Hamden, England: Archon, 1963.
Karlin, Daniel. *Browning's Hatreds.* Oxford: Oxford University Press, 1993.
Santayana, George. *Interpretations of Poetry and Religion.* New York: Scribner's. 1900.
St. George, E. A. W. *Browning and Conversation.* London: Macmillan, 1993.
Thomas, Donald, ed. *The Post-Romantics.* London: Routledge, 1990.
Woodford, John. *Browning the Revisionary.* London: Macmillan, 1988.

BROWNSON, ORESTES AUGUSTUS 1803–1876

American author

A self-taught voracious reader and prolific writer, Orestes Augustus Brownson could hardly be accused of consistency. In religion he ranged from Congregationalist to Presbyterian to Universalist, skeptic, and Unitarian before joining the Catholic Church. Politically he supported John C. Calhoun and then Abraham Lincoln. He opposed violence but predicted bloody class warfare. An early member of the Transcendental Club, Brownson in 1845 denounced its philosophy as "the Latest Form of Infidelity." Reviewing Brownson's 1857 autobiography *The Convert*, the New York *Herald* dubbed the author "Weathercock Brownson." Yet whatever his opinion was at the moment, Brownson placed himself at the center of the vital intellectual, religious, political, social, and philosophical debates that engaged the United States in the Romantic era. As one of his biographers, Arthur Schlesinger Jr., wrote, "Against the background of his time, Orestes Brownson stands an important and expressive figure. . . . There was hardly a question, large or small, that agitated the country from 1830 to 1870, on which Brownson did not make comment."

Raised by Congregational foster parents, Brownson in 1822 joined the Presbyterian Church. Unable to accept its Calvinist doctrines of total depravity and preelection, Brownson left that denomination two years later, and on June 15, 1826 was ordained a Universalist minister at Jaffrey, New Hampshire. He could no more accept the Universalist view that everyone would be saved than he could the darker Presbyterian vision, so in 1829 he left that church as well. He later recalled that at this time his true belief was in progress, his goal "man's earthly happiness." In the late 1820s and 1830s William Godwin's *Inquiry Concerning Political Justice* (1793) shaped Brownson's thinking, with Godwin's emphasis on the reform of the individual and his view of government as a corrupting force.

Brownson in *The Convert* elaborated on his beliefs in this period: "I had become a believer in humanity, and put humanity in the place of God. The only God I recognized was the divine in man, the divinity of humanity. . . . I regarded Jesus Christ as divine in the sense in which all men are divine, and human in the sense in which all are human." With the reformers Robert

Henry Owen (son of the Fourierist Robert Owen) and Fanny Wright, Brownson briefly supported the Workingmen's Party and edited the Genesee, New York, *Republican and Herald of Reform*, where he advocated radical positions on social and political matters.

Brownson's spiritual quest of 1830–31 is the subject of his 1840 novel *Charles Elwood*; the eponymous hero is the thinly disguised author. By late 1831 Brownson had returned to the pulpit, though as an independent preacher; the following year he joined the Unitarian Church. Still, he denied that any existing denomination possessed the truth. He therefore urged, as he wrote in *Charles Elwood*, "Range freely over all doctrines, analyze them all, and what you find in them which accords with human nature, . . . hold fast and cherish."

In 1836 Brownson left the Unitarian Church and moved to Chelsea, across the Mystic River from Boston, to establish the Society for Christian Union and Progress and to advocate a "church of the future." He set out his ideas in his first published book, *New Views of Christianity, Society, and the Church* (1836), and in his journal, the *Boston Quarterly Review* (1838–42). He chose this title for his magazine because it was indefinite, allowing him to range freely. In the first issue he announced the broad swath he would cut, "whether it be effecting a reform in the Church, giving us a purer and more rational theology; in philosophy seeking something profounder . . . than . . . heartless Sensualism . . .; or whether in society demanding the elevation of labor with the Loco foco, or freedom of the slave with the abolitionist."

Intellectually, Brownson for the moment allied himself with the Transcendentalists, sharing their beliefs in the spirit, intuition, and the unlimited potential of the individual. He attended meetings of the Transcendental Club and offered its members the use of his journal as their organ. Instead they created their own, *The Dial* (1840–44). In politics he supported the Democrats, whom he regarded as the party of humanity, as opposed to the Whigs, whom he saw as the party of property. He sought "the sovereignty of Man," with equal rights and equal worth for each person.

To support the reelection of the Democratic presidential candidate Martin Van Buren, Brownson wrote "The Laboring Classes," which appeared in the July and October 1840 issues of his journal. Five years before Friedrich Engels's *The Conditions of the Working Class in England in 1844* and eight years before Engels and Karl Marx's *Communist Manifesto*, Brownson analyzed the plight of the worker in the throes of the Industrial Revolution. Arguing that wage slavery was worse than chattel slavery, Brownson predicted a class war that would end in the liberation of workers. The only alternative was government action that would allow each person to become financially independent as a self-employed laborer or farmer.

Van Buren's defeat in 1840 shook Brownson's faith in democracy as the means to achieve this end. Under the influence of Pierre Leroux's *De l'humanité* (1840) Brownson now argued that each person can advance only as the group progresses. Hence he rejected the transcendental emphasis on the reformation of the individual. Brownson's religious views also underwent a metamorphosis. In June of 1842 he wrote an open letter to the Unitarian minister William Ellery Channing, "The Mediatorial Life of Jesus." Brownson here accepted the traditional Christian view of Jesus as both human and divine. In the final issue of his periodical (October 1842) Brownson similarly criticized his former religious ally Theodore Parker and claimed that the true church was "Catholicism without Papacy."

Two years later he was ready to accept the papacy as well, converting to Catholicism on October 20, 1844. Under the guidance of Bishop John B. Fitzpatrick of Boston he used his new journal, *Brownson's Quarterly Review*, to defend Catholics against nativist attacks. He maintained that only Catholicism could save American democracy and create a national literature. Becoming increasingly conservative, Brownson in an 1852 review of the fourth volume of George Bancroft's *History of the United States* rejected the positions he had supported in the 1830s: the supremacy of democracy as a form of government, the divinity of humanity, the belief in progress.

Quarreling with Bishop Fitzpatrick, Brownson moved to New York (1855) and then to Elizabeth, New Jersey (1857). Perhaps because he was now free from episcopal oversight, Brownson's views reverted to those he had held earlier. *The American Republic* (1865) restated those liberal ideas, and the April 1873 issue of his magazine declared his faith in democracy.

Brownson fit the New York *Herald*'s description of him, but a weathercock tells which way the wind is blowing. Addressing the crucial issues of his time, Brownson served as an indicator of the intellectual climate of America in the first three-quarters of the nineteenth century.

JOSEPH ROSENBLUM

See also **Emerson, Ralph Waldo; Transcendentalism**

Biography

Born in Stockbridge, Vermont, September 16, 1803. Taught school, 1822–25. Universalist minister, 1826–29. Married Sally Healy, 1827. Editor, *Gospel Advocate and Impartial Investigator*, 1828–29; *Republican and Herald of Reform*, 1829–30; *The Philanthropist*, 1831–32. Unitarian minister, 1832–36. Editor, *Boston Reformer*, 1836; *Boston Quarterly Review*, 1838–42; *Brownson's Quarterly Review*, 1844–64, 1873–75. Unsuccessful Republican candidate for Congress, 1862. Died April 17, 1876.

Selected Works

Collections

The Works of Orestes A. Brownson. 20 vols. Edited by Henry F. Brownson. Detroit, Mich.: T. Hourse, 1882–87.
The Brownson Reader. Edited by Alvan S. Ryan. New York: P. J. Kenedy, 1955.

Individual Works

New Views on Christianity, Society, and the Church. 1836.
Charles Elwood: Or the Infidel Converted. 1840.
Constitutional Government. 1842.
The Mediatorial Life of Jesus. A Letter to Rev. William Ellery Channing. 1842.
Essays and Reviews Chiefly on Theology, Politics, and Socialism. 1852.
The Spirit-Rapper: An Autobiography. 1852.
The Convert: or, Leaves from My Experience. 1857.
The American Republic: Its Constitution, Tendencies, and Destiny. 1865.
Conversations on Liberalism and the Church. 1870.

Bibliography

Brownson, Henry F. *Orestes A. Brownson's . . . Life*. Detroit: H. F. Brownson, 1898–1900.

Gilhooley, Leonard. *Contradiction and Dilemma: Orestes Brownson and the American Idea*. New York: Fordham University Press, 1972.

———, ed. *No Divided Allegiance: Essays in Brownson's Thought*. New York: Fordham University Press, 1980.

Lapati, Amerigo. *Orestes A. Brownson*. New York: Twayne, 1965.

Schlesinger, Arthur M. *Orestes A. Brownson: A Pilgrim's Progress*. Boston: Little, Brown, 1939.

Sveino, Per. *Orestes Brownson's Road to Catholicism*. New York: Humanities Press, 1970.

BRULLOFF, CARL (KARL BRYULLOV, BRULEAU, BRÜLLO) 1799–1852

Russian painter

As one of the first recipients of a scholarship for foreign study awarded by Saint Petersburg's newly founded Society for the Encouragement of the Arts, Carl Brulloff settled in Rome in May 1823 and within a few months had completed his *Italian Morning*, an image of a beautiful, luminous, and seminaked young woman collecting water from a spring in her cupped palms. It was to be succeeded by the anacreontic vision with which he transformed the history of Russian painting, whereby his unprecedented independence and personal immersion in the cult of art was expressed.

Brulloff's pictorial worship of love, wine, and conviviality was quintessentially Mediterranean. His relish for southern light and color harmonies, combined with an instinctive empathy for the bucolic and Bacchic, was displayed through the creation of a series of visual hymns to joy that echoed his own notorious preferences for drinking and sunny climes. This celebration of good living distinguished *Italian Noon* (1827), which formed a pair with *Italian Morning*, as well as *Dancing outside a Roman Hostelry* (1827–28), *Merry-Making in Albano* (1830–33), and *Young Girl Gathering Grapes in the Vicinity of Naples* (1827). These are scenes in which earthly bounty and human gratification are closely allied to intoxication, frivolity, and sensuousness. The break with the classical canon in which he had been immersed at the Saints Petersburg Academy of the Arts was radical enough to bring about the end of his relationship with the Society for the Encouragement of the Arts.

Italian Morning was created in the same year as Aleksandr Pushkin's elegaic love poem "Bakhchisarai Fountain," in many ways a literary counterpart to its novel Russian visualization of beauty as feminine, southern and subtly reflected, enlivened and ephemeralized through its contemplative association with the gently flowing waters of a marble fountain. The painting marked Brulloff's abiding concern with the tragic connections among beauty, human transience, and susceptibility to outer forces that was to be betrayed by his frequent recourse to themes in which the central characters are fatally drowned. Hence *Narcissus Looking into the Water*, his entry for the Saint Petersburg Academy's gold medal competition in 1819, *Hylas and the Nymphs* (1827); *Bathsheba* (1832) and *Bakhchisarai Fountain* (1838–49). Bathsheba is portrayed nude in her bath, helped by her black attendant. Brulloff suggests the biblical fragility and ominous nature of this moment of beautiful intimacy by softened dark tones and the inclusion of a dragonfly hovering over the two women. This tragisensual quality was highlighted in *Bakhchisarai Fountain*, upon which he worked for the twelve years that he remained in Russia following the death of Pushkin. In the atrophied months after losing his friend, Brulloff had initially considered, and sketched, a frontispiece to a proposed new edition of Pushkin's collected works. The poet was to be depicted, lyre in hand, on top of a craggy peak, enveloped by the majestic nature of the Caucasius mountains. According to Brulloff's program, written in Italian on the sketch, he "hears and is enraptured by Russia. He is crowned by Poetry. In the rays emanating from the lyre fragments of his verse are visible. Dante, Byron and Homer heed him from above." The realization of his tribute to Puskin was, however, to be a markedly different image in which he expressed a more emphatic and specific equivalence to the poet's transcendental aesthetic. In the early 1830s Brulloff had become the first Russian artist to gain international recognition, due to *The Last Day of Pompeii* (1827–33), whose sensational Vulcanian bravura was an incantation of fiery, universal doom in which the artist himself appeared as the only balanced figure with the possibility of a future. Now, back in cold, imperial Russia, *Bakhchisarai Fountain* lyrically encapsulated the mood of both era and artist. Gaiety, luxury and color are a hermetic center of activity juxtaposed with, and enshrouded by, the melancholic, dark and discordant. This tense, shaded, remote image of Maria Potocka and Zarema was the elegaic conclusion to the cycle that *Italian Morning* had introduced. *Bakhchisarai Fountain* depicts the harem of the Crimean Tartar Khan where East and West meet, where fate is a matter of incarceration.

Brulloff was the original Russian aesthete. His lifelong dedication to aesthetics was effected by his birth into a family of artists and court gardeners. His father, grandfather, and great-grandfather were ornamental sculptors who had arrived in Saint Petersburg from Germany in 1773, the Huguenot Bruleaux having originally left France after Louis XIV revoked the Edict of Nantes. Among his more successful Romantic images are portraits of his intimates, such as the brooding poet Nestor Kukolnik (1836) and cellist Matvey Vielgorsky (1828?), and his *Self-Portrait* (1848). During his late Saint Petersburg period, as his health declined, his marriage failed, court patronage increased, and his dislike of the cold north reached new heights, he also produced a series of orientalist pictures, the vivacity and subjects of which indicate a vicarious return to his Italian preoccupations: living well, farewells, and beautiful young women (now Turkish odalisques).

Ultimately, terminal illness brought about Brulloff's return to Rome. There, cared for and patronized by Angelo Tittoni, a wealthy activist in the Risorgimento movement, he embarked on his final image. Instead of the escapist Eastern images of his Russian years, *All-Destructive Time* (1850–52) confronted the viewer directly and attempted to portray the universal human tragedy. Unfinished when he died, the composition depicted Saturn casting mankind into the abyss. The great and the good, the religious and scientific—essentially, all of humanity—are reduced to small particles in the frenzied, downward cascade. This vision was not marked by pathos or terror, but rather by an inexorable subjugation to the omnipotence of the laws of nature. Though they cling to tokens of their identity, the figures are no longer separately engrossed in the elements; rather, they are integral to them. There appeared no place for the artist. *All-Destructive Time* was Brulloff's final testament to the dawn of the age of positivism, and to perdition.

JEREMY HOWARD

Biography

Born in Saint Petersburg, December 12 (23), 1799. Studied at the Saint Petersburg Academy of the Arts, 1809–22. Lived in Italy 1823–35. Professor of historical painting at the Saint Petersburg Academy, 1836–49. Due to ill health moved to Madeira, 1849–50, and Rome, 1850–52. Died in Manziana, near Rome, June 11 (23), 1852.

Bibliography

Bocharov, Ivan, and Yuliya Glushakova. *Karl Bryullov. Ital'yanskie nakhodki.* Moscow: Znanie, 1984.
Goldovsky, Grigory, and Yevgenia, Petrova. *Carl Brullov.* Saint Petersburg: Palace Editions, 1999.
Leontyeva, Galina. *Karl Briullov: Artist of Russian Romanticism.* Bournemouth, England: Parkstone/Aurora, 1996.

BRYANT, WILLIAM CULLEN 1794–1878

American poet and editor

William Cullen Bryant, the first and one of the finest American nature poets, was born in 1794 in Cummington, Massachusetts, the second son of Peter Bryant, a physician, and Sarah Snell Bryant. After attending local primary schools and receiving training in the classics from tutors, he studied at Williams College for one year. Unable to continue in higher education because of unstable family finances, Bryant turned to law, studying with attorneys in towns near his boyhood home until he passed the state bar in 1815. He practiced law in western Massachusetts until 1825.

The practice of law, though it was reasonably profitable and allowed him to marry and begin a family, was uncongenial. As a boy and young man, Bryant wrote poems that appeared in the regional newspaper, the *Hampshire Gazette*, and in the spring of 1808, at the height of the controversy over President Thomas Jefferson's interdiction of trade with England and the prelude to the War of 1812, his father had arranged the publication of his satiric poem, *The Embargo*, which enjoyed considerable popularity in Boston. While studying law and establishing his practice, he continued to compose verses, including the poem that earned him entrance to the world of professional letters, "Thanatopsis," published in 1817.

"Thanatopsis," a youthful work with an uncertain date of composition, is deeply indebted both to the "graveyard school" of poetry exemplified by Robert Blair's *The Grave* (1743) and to the nature poetry of William Wordsworth, yet its vision of the relationship of man to the natural world has led many critics to regard it as a landmark in the development of a distinctively American literature. Omitting mention of God or hopes of immortality in the face of omnipresent mortality, Bryant presents nature as both consolation and threat, writing of the world as an abode of beauty that is also "one mighty sepulchre"; he finally resolves the paradox by suggesting that man

sustain'd and sooth'd
By an unfaltering trust, approach thy grave,
Like one who wraps the drapery of his couch
About him, and lies down to pleasant dreams.

The poem was well received upon its appearance in the *North American Review* (September 1817) and upon its publication, with significant revisions in 1821 as part of Bryant's first collection of verses, *Poems* which also contained "To a Waterfowl," "The Yellow Violet," and "Green River." These verses celebrate the beauties of the New England landscape and the natural, divine order that they represent, and are characterized by classical restraint and impeccable diction. In Bryant's poetry the divine remains apart from creation, but it is always evident in nature, organizing, guiding, inspiring, and offering transcendant influence for proper moral action and purpose.

In 1824 Bryant was invited to contribute to the *United States Literary Gazette*, published in Boston, which led to his employment as the coeditor of the *New York Review and Athenaeum Magazine*. Though the *New York Review*'s precarious finances forced Bryant to continue part-time legal work, it did, in turn, lead to the chance to become subeditor of the New York *Evening Post* in 1826.

After three years' association with the *Evening Post*, Bryant became editor, also using the opportunity to gain part ownership of the company. He set a high standard of journalistic prose, and under his guidance the *Post* became one of the leading newspapers in the republic. The *Post*'s success in the highly competitive world of New York journalism made Bryant a wealthy man: he used his income from the paper to travel extensively in the United States and in Europe, drawing on his experiences and observations for his poetry and two volumes of prose, *Letters of a Traveller* (1859). As one of the leaders of American public opinion, Bryant used the forum of the *Post* to advance the moral and political causes that he supported, including abolition, John C. Fremont and the Republican Party in the election of 1855, Abraham Lincoln and the cause of national union in 1861, and emancipation and vigorous prosecution of northern efforts during the Civil War, 1861–65.

With his attention focused on journalism, Bryant became significantly less productive as a poet. Nonetheless, in 1832, Bryant published an expanded edition of *Poems*, which included the notable addition "To the Fringed Gentian," which was written in 1829 as a companion to "The Yellow Violet." This was followed in 1842 by *The Fountain and Other Poems, The White-Footed Deer and Other Poems* in 1846, and *Thirty Poems* in 1864.

Bryant's thematic interest remained focused on the poetry of nature throughout his career. His later verse may be best understood as refinements of his earlier work rather than as advances.

After his wife's death on July 27, 1866, Bryant returned to the classical studies of his youth; his translations of the *Iliad* and the *Odyssey* were published 1870–72. He died on June 12, 1878 of the effects of a head injury suffered in a fall: flags were flown at half-mast throughout New York City when news of his death became known.

Bryant's body of original work comprises only about 160 poems, of which more than one hundred are about nature, merging his observations of American, particularly New England, flora and fauna with his understanding of the unity of nature and mind, the significance of nature as symbol or metaphor of higher reality, and the high moral purpose of poetic representation. He made the tradition of Samuel Taylor Coleridge and William Wordsworth his own, and offered an inspirational example for succeeding generations of American poets, including Ralph Waldo Emerson and Walt Whitman, both of whom paid tribute to Bryant as the greatest American man of letters of his day.

ALISON SCOTT

Biography

Born November 3, 1794, in Cummington, Massachusetts. Attended Williams College in Williamstown, Massachusetts, September 1810–June 1811; studied law with attorneys in Worthington and Bridgewater, Massachusetts, December 1811–August 1815. Practiced law in Plainsfield and Great Barrington, Massachusetts, 1815–25. Married Frances Fairchild, June 11, 1821 (she died on July 27, 1866). Served as coeditor of *New York Review and Athenaeum Magazine*, January 1825–June 1826; subeditor of New York *Evening Post*, June 1826–July 1829; editor and co-owner of *Evening Post*, July 1829–April 1878. Died June 12, 1878 in New York City.

Selected Works

Poetry
The Embargo; or, Sketches of the Times: A Satire, by a Youth of Thirteen. 1808.
Poems. 1821.
The Fountain and Other Poems. 1842.
The White-Footed Deer and Other Poems. 1844.
Thirty Poems. 1854.
The Poetical Works of William Cullen Bryant. 2 vols. Edited by Parke Godwin. 1883.

Prose
Letters of a Traveller; or, Notes of Things Seen in Europe and America. 1850.
Reminiscences of the Evening Post. 1851.
Letters of a Traveller. 2d ser. 1859.
Letters from the East. 1869.
Orations and Addresses. 1873.
Prose Writings of William Cullen Bryant. 2 vols. Edited by Parke Godwin. 1884.

Translations
The Iliad of Homer Translated into English Blank Verse. 1870.
The Odyssey of Homer Translated into English Blank Verse. 1871–72.

Anthologies and Edited Volumes
Selections from the American Poets. 1840.
Picturesque America; or, The Land We Live In. 1872–74.
A New Library of Poetry and Song. 1876–78.
A Popular History of the United States. With Sydney Howard Gay. 1876–80.
The Complete Works of Shakespeare. With Evert A. Duyckinck. 1888.

Bibliography

Brodwin, Stanley and Michael D'Innocenzo, eds. "William Cullen Bryant and His America: Centennial Conference Proceedings, 1878–1989." *Hofstra University Cultural and Intercultural Studies* 4. New York: AMS Press, 1983.
Brown, Charles H. *William Cullen Bryant.* New York: Charles Scribner's Sons, 1971.
Godwin, Parke. *The Life and Writings of William Cullen Bryant.* 2 vols. New York: D. Appleton, 1883.
McLean, Albert F. *William Cullen Bryant.* Rev. ed., Boston: Twayne, 1989.

BÜCHNER, GEORG 1813–1837

German playwright, writer, scientist, and political activist

Georg Büchner's productive life as an adult only lasted from 1834 to 1837. Apart from several public speeches, the revolutionary pamphlet *Der Hessische Landbote* (*The Hessian Messenger*), illegally distributed in the Grand Duchy of Hessia in 1834, represents his first publication. He translated Victor Hugo's *Lucretia Borgia* and *Maria Tudor* into German, and wrote four plays, of which the last (and perhaps also the third, which is lost) remained unfinished: *Dantons Tod* (*Danton's Death*, 1835), *Leonce und Lena* (1838), *Pietro Aretino*, and *Woyzeck*. The novella *Lenz* was posthumously published in 1839. An important number of letters has been preserved, as well as philosophical notes (especially on René Descartes and Benedict Spinoza) and his doctoral dissertation, written in French, on the nervous system of fish. A lecture on cranial nerves, which four months before his death gained him the position of private lecturer (*Privatdozent*) at Zurich University, also survived.

Büchner's works exceed most of the contemporary productions of Junges Deutschland (Young Germany) in analytical rigor, intellectual breadth, and handling of literary effects and innovative techniques. Satirizing idealistic conceptions of experience, and translating the early Romantic dual postulate of levelheadedness (*Besonnenheit*) and enthusiasm into an almost scientific use of nonliterary documents and a moving, yet unsentimental expression of moral sensibility and political commitment, they occupy a pivotal position between the older traditions of German culture and twentieth-century modernity. Not widely received in his own time, most of Büchner's writings were (re)published by his brother Ludwig in 1850, but it was the first critical edition by Karl Emil Franzos in 1879 that provided the basis for the rediscovery and admiration of Büchner by naturalists and expressionists alike. Walter Benjamin held that this rediscovery was one of the very few cultural events before World War I that were not devalidated by 1918. The fact that Alban Berg used texts from Büchner's last drama for his opera *Wozzeck* (1925) may confirm this assessment. After 1951, the speeches accompanying the annual presentation of the Büchner award by the German Academy for Language and Literature gave outstanding writers and poets the opportunity to discuss their art in relation to Büchner's.

Although different in genre and intent, *Der Hessische Landbote* shares some of the major features of Büchner's literary works. Like *Dantons Tod*, the pamphlet insists on economic justice as the major issue of political change. With this position Büchner responded not only to the life of the peasants in his native Hessia, whom the pamphlet tried to induce to rebellion, but also to the persisting material misery of the lower strata of the former third estate in French society. The failure of the July Revolution to promote economic justice had strengthened radical—in part, early communist—positions in the political culture of Strasbourg, which Büchner had absorbed as a student from 1831 to 1833. To illustrate the fiscal exploitation of the peasantry, Büchner's pamphlet uses the drastic naturalist imagery which would be critically reflected in *Dantons Tod*, as well as statistical evidence on the budgets of the Hessian Grand Duchy between 1830 and 1832. The modern character of the latter device contrasts with the Romantic, theologicopolitical orientation in some parts of the pamphlet. Given Büchner's religious skepticism, the resort to religious language and traditions may reflect the attention he paid to the envisaged audience, or the stance of the rector and coauthor Friedrich Ludwig Weidig, a central figure of the political opposition in Hessia, who revised Büchner's original version and—probably after torture—allegedly committed suicide in prison in 1837. Since the unrevised version of the pamphlet has been lost, however, definite attributions of particular passages to either Büchner or Weidig are philologically problematic. Büchner's political agitation in Hessia followed his return from Strasbourg and an ensuing psychosomatic crisis in spring 1834, and it preceded his flight back to Strasbourg in March 1835 after the completion, with Büchner now under police observation, of *Dantons Tod*. In an oft-quoted letter of March 1834 to his Strasbourg fiancée, Büchner passionately evokes the feeling of human impotence in the face of history's "fatalism," a feeling that he writes has been triggered by his reading on the French Revolution. The question of how the apparent or real contradiction between such fatalism and his political activism is to be interpreted divides critical opinion to this day.

Leonce und Lena represents perhaps the least appreciated of Büchner's work. Friedrich Gundolf discarded it as a learned and belated adoption of the literary comedy of the German Romantics (notably Ludwig Tieck and Clemens Brentano), unfit for the stage. However, theatrical performances from the 1970s onward may have refuted this verdict. The play combines a wealth of literary allusions—to Johann Gottlieb Fichte, Johann Wolfgang von Goethe, Heinrich Heine, E. T. A. Hoffmann, Alfred de Musset, Jean Paul Richter, Friedrich Schlegel, William

Shakespeare, and Laurence Sterne, to name but the most important authors—with a playful insistence on the nonreferential qualities of language, which seems to reenvisage Novalis's ideal of an absolute language, concerned exclusively with itself. Yet placed in the context of Büchner's bitter satire of both idealistic philosophy and the social reality of contemporary German principalities, his evocation of the Romantic ideal no longer expresses a longing for the infinite. The theatrical self-reference, which his play shares with Romantic comedies, in the former represents less an instance of Romantic irony than an indirect, though forceful, demand for political and cultural change.

Redefining their respective genre, the novella *Lenz* and the unfinished tragic drama *Woyzeck* offer a literary psychogram of two outsiders, the Sturm und Drang writer Jakob Michael Reinhold Lenz, who died forgotten and depraved in Moscow in 1792, and the ex-soldier and murderer Johann Christian Woyzeck, publicly executed in Leipzig on August 27, 1824. Based on the notes of the pastor Johann Friedrich Oberlin about Lenz's stay with him in Waldersbach in 1779, *Lenz* describes and analyzes the writer's increasing alienation in the context of both Lenz's problematic position in the society and literary culture of the 1770s and Oberlin's efforts to provide help through religious and philanthropic practice. Drawing on medical and juridical documents concerning Woyzeck's questionable criminal responsibility as well as on similar court cases of the time, *Woyzeck* places a character from the lowest social stratum in the center of dramatic attention. Büchner forcefully depicts the soldier's abuse by his superior, by the doctor's scientific experiments, and by society in general, but forgoes the character's reduction to an argument in support of social determinism by expressing Woyzeck's suffering with much intelligent empathy. The simultaneous distance from both the mystical heights of Romantic *Naturphilosophie* and any merely technical approach to (human) nature—characteristic also of the underlying assumptions in the lecture on cranial nerves—in Büchner's literary work creates room for an expression of humane insight that is rarely matched in honesty, precision, and emotive power.

MARGARETE KOHLENBACH

Biography

Born in Goddelau, Grand Duchy of Hessia, Germany, October 17, 1813. Family moved to the capital, Darmstadt, where his father served as regional physician, 1816. Elementary teaching by his mother, attended a private school and a Darmstadt grammar school, public recitations, partly in Latin, 1821–31. Studied medicine in Strasbourg; participation in political meetings and discussions, 1831–33. Secret engagement with Wilhelmine Jaeglé before returning to Hessia because of legal restrictions of study abroad, 1833. Enrolled in medicine at Giessen University; illegal writing and distribution of *Der Hessische Landbote*; foundation of societies of human rights in Giessen and Darmstadt; repeatedly interrogated by the authorities; *Dantons Tod*; flight back to Strasbourg; 1833–35; graduated from Strasbourg University; started work on *Lenz*; *Leonce und Lena*; Private Lecturer at Zurich University, Switzerland; started work on *Woyzeck*, 1836–37. Died—probably of typhus—in Zurich, February 19, 1837.

Selected Works

Dantons Tod, 1835, incomplete, edited by Karl Gutzkow; *Dantons Tod: Dramatische Bilder aus Frankreichs Schreckensherrschaft*

(revised by Karl Gutzkow and Eduard Duller), 1835; in *Kritische Studienausgabe des Originals mit Quellen, Aufsätzen und Materialien*, edited by Peter von Becker, 1985. In *Complete Plays, "Lenz," and Other Writings*, translated with an introduction and notes by John Reddick. London: Penguin Books, 1993.

Leonce und Lena, incomplete, edited by Karl Gutzkow, 1838; in *Nachgelassene Schriften*, edited by Ludwig Büchner, 1850; in *Kritische Studienausgabe: Beiträge zu Text und Quellen*, edited by Burghard Dedner, text edition by Thomas Michael Mayer, 1987. In *Complete Plays, "Lenz," and Other Writings*, translated with an introduction and notes by John Reddick. London: Penguin Books, 1993.

Lenz: Eine Reliquie von Georg Büchner, edited by Karl Gutzkow, 1839; *Lenz* in *Nachgelassene Schriften*, edited by Ludwig Büchner, 1850; in *Sämtliche Werke und Briefe*, with Johann Friedrich Oberlin's report, edited by Werner R. Lehmann, vol. 1, 3d ed., 1979. In *Complete Plays, "Lenz," and Other Writings*, translated with an introduction and notes by John Reddick. London: Penguin Books, 1993.

Woyzeck, in *Sämtliche Werke und handschriftlicher Nachlaß: Erste kritische Gesamtausgabe*, introduced and edited by Karl Emil Franzos, 1879; *Kritische Lese- und Arbeitsausgabe*, edited by Lothar Bornscheuer, 1972. In *Sämtliche Werke und Briefe*, edited by Werner R. Lehmann, vol. 1, 3d ed., 1979. In *Complete Plays, "Lenz," and Other Writings*, translated with an introduction and notes by John Reddick. London: Penguin Books, 1993.

Der Hessische Landbote: Erste Botschaft in *Sämtliche Werke und handschriftlicher Nachlaß: Erste kritische Gesamtausgabe*, introduced and edited by Karl Emil Franzos, 1879; Georg Büchner, Ludwig Weidig, *Der Hessische Landbote: Texte, Briefe, Prozessakten*, with a commentary by Hans Magnus Enzensberger, 1965; in *Sämtliche Werke und Briefe*, edited by Werner R. Lehmann, vol. 2, 1972. In *Complete Plays, "Lenz," and Other Writings*, translated with an introduction and notes by John Reddick. London: Penguin Books, 1993.

Bibliography

Benn, Maurice B. *The Drama of Revolt: A Critical Study of Georg Büchner*. London: Cambridge University Press, 1976.

Georg Büchner Jahrbuch, vol. 1 (1981) to vol. 8 (1990–94).

Grimm, Reinhold. *Love, Lust and Rebellion: New Approaches to Georg Büchner*. Madison: University of Wisconsin Press, 1985.

Hinderer, Walter. *Büchner-Kommentar zum dichterischen Werk*. Munich: Winkler, 1977.

Knapp, Gerhard P. *Georg Büchner*. Stuttgart: Metzler, 1977.

Kurzenberger, Hajo. "Komödie als Pathographie einer abgelebten Gesellschaft: Zur gegenwärtigen Beschäftigung mit 'Leonce und Lena' in der Literaturwissenschaft und auf dem Theater." In *Georg Büchner III*. Edited by Heinz Ludwig Arnold. Special volume of the series *text + kritik*. Munich: edition text + kritik, 1981.

Lippmann, Heinz. *Georg Büchner und die Romantik*. Munich: Max Hueber, 1923.

Majut, R. "Georg Büchner and Some English Thinkers," *Modern Language Review* 48 (1953): 310–22.

Mayer, Hans. *Georg Büchner und seine Zeit*. Frankfurt/M.: Suhrkamp, 1972.

Mayer, Thomas Michael. "Büchner und Weidig/Frühkommunismus und revolutionäre Demokratie: Zur Textverteilung des 'Hessischen Landboten'." In *Georg Büchner I/II*. Edited by Heinz Ludwig Arnold. Special volume of the series *text + kritik*. Munich: edition text + kritik, 1979.

Reddick, John. *Georg Büchner: The Shattered Whole*. Oxford: Clarendon Press, 1994.

Schmidt, Henry J. *Satire, Caricature and Perspectivism in the Works of Georg Büchner*. The Hague: Mouton, 1970.

BULFINCH, CHARLES 1763–1844

American architect

Charles Bulfinch was the first American professional architect. He is most famous for his work in the Boston area, especially the Massachusetts State House, and his contributions to the Capitol Building in Washington, D.C. His works tended to be in the neoclassical style, one of the revival styles associated with Romanticism.

Bulfinch began his architectural career during the early years of American independence. Like many of the early American architects, Bulfinch did not abandon the cultural and architectural influence of England, despite his country's conscious break from England's political rule. Bulfinch's influences included the ancient Roman architect Vitruvius and the sixteenth-century Italian architect Andrea Di Pietro Della Gondola Palladio, and also English architects such as Robert Adam and William Chambers.

Bulfinch was born at a time when there were no art or architectural schools in the United States. He entered Harvard College in 1778 and graduated in 1781. Although he did not study architecture there, he was exposed to the ideas of neoclassicism and did receive some training in the fields of mathematics and perspective. In 1785, following the conclusion of the American Revolution, travel abroad was made easier, and Bulfinch left the United States for a journey to Europe. He visited England, France, and Italy, where he was able to study many architectural masterpieces firsthand. When he returned to Boston, in early 1787 he would take the lessons he learned from his years abroad and become one of the leading architects of his generation. His very first executed design, Hollis Street Church in Boston, was built in 1788 (now destroyed). In addition to his architectural influence on Boston, Bulfinch was also active in the civic and political life of the city, serving as the superintendent of the police, and the selectman.

Bulfinch's civic works included three state houses in the New England region. His first one, the Connecticut State House in Hartford, was built between 1793 and 1796 and was Bulfinch's first design for a public building to be executed. Bulfinch's most famous work in Boston, the Massachusetts State House, on Beacon Hill, the highest point in the city, is based on a plan he had submitted in 1787. The cornerstone was laid on July 4, 1795 and was completed on January 11, 1798. The original building was rectangular in shape, included an arcade at the ground level, a row of columns on the next one, a pedimented upper story, and a wooden dome (it was later covered in copper and gilded). The building was made of brick walls, a wooden portico and columns, and a wooden dome, materials more typical of American rather than European architecture. The design was heavily influenced by William Chambers's Somerset House in London, built, 1776–86. The Old Maine State House in Augusta, Maine, the last commission of Bulfinch's career, was completed in 1832. The design of this building echoes a number of features of the Massachusetts State House. As a whole though, the ornamentation is more austere.

Bulfinch also played a role in Boston's residential architecture. Between 1795 and 1806, Bulfinch designed three homes for the Boston lawyer and politician Harrison Gray Otis and his wife Sally Foster. Between 1793 and 1795 Bulfinch built a curve of sixteen, attached brick houses arranged around a garden area known as the Tontine Crescent (now destroyed). Bulfinch and his investors had hoped to achieve a profit from the sale of these individual homes. However, the project was a huge financial failure. Like many of Bulfinch's other works, this project was influenced by English architecture, including works such as John Wood the Younger's Royal Crescent, Bath, of 1767–75.

In 1805–6 Bulfinch was involved in the restoration and enlargement of Faneuil Hall in Boston, a work begun by John Smibert in 1740. In this work Bulfinch preserved the character of the colonial building, maintaining the market on the first floor, and the assembly room on the second, while adding a third floor and doubling the width of the building.

In 1813–14 Bulfinch built University Hall at his alma mater, Harvard College in Cambridge, Massachusetts. The building was intended to provide each of the four classes with a college commons, serviced by two kitchens in the basement. Another of Bulfinch's buildings, Massachusetts General Hospital in Boston, was built 1818–23. This building's dome and portico were features certainly influenced by the architects Robert Adam and John Soane. In this hospital, Bulfinch designed a clinical amphitheater to be housed under the dome, a feature that had been used in the Pennsylvania Hospital in Philadelphia ten years earlier, and that Bulfinch himself had seen firsthand.

In 1817, President James Monroe summoned Bulfinch to Washington, D.C., to replace Benjamin Henry Latrobe as architect of the Capitol building. Bulfinch's role was to continue the rebuilding of the Capitol, which had been torched by the British during the War of 1812. Bulfinch connected the chambers of the House of Representatives and the Senate with a domed rotunda that spanned the space between the two buildings. (The dome was later replaced with a much larger one.) In 1830, following his work on the Capitol, Bulfinch returned to Boston, where he spent the remainder of his life. He died there on April 15, 1844. Although many of his works have been destroyed over the years and are known today only through photographs and drawings, even in the twenty-first century, Bulfinch's architectural legacy remains.

ALEXANDRA SCHEIN

Biography

Born in Boston, August 8, 1763. Attended Harvard College, 1778–81. Traveled in Europe, 1785–87. Met Thomas Jefferson in Paris; on his advice, studied architectural works in Italy and France and the neoclassical work of Robert Adam in England. Returned to Boston to practice as an architect in the area, 1787. Active in promotion of the first American circumnavigation of the world by the *Columbia*, 1787. Designed the Massachusetts State House, 1787 (built 1795–98). Married Hannah Apthorp (died 1841), 1788; they had seven children. Selectman of Boston, 1791–95. Designed the Connecticut State House, Hartford (1793–96). Suffered financial ruin after failure of the Tontine Crescent development (1793–94), 1796. Accepted salaried office as Chairman of Selectmen of Boston and Superintendent of Police, 1799–1817. Architect of the Capitol in Washington D.C., 1817–29. Designed the Maine State House, Augusta (1829–32). Returned to Boston, 1830. Died in Boston, April 4, 1844.

Selected Works

Miscellaneous Works

Faneuil Hall, Boston. Originally built by John Smibert 1740–42. Rebuilt and enlarged by Bulfinch 1805–6; restored 1898–99.
University Hall, Harvard University, Cambridge, Massachusetts. Built 1813–14; altered 1842 and after.
Church of Christ, Lancaster, Massachusetts. Built 1816.
Bulfinch Hall, Andover, Massachusetts. Built 1818–19; restored 1936–37.
Massachusetts General Hospital, Boston. Built 1818–23; altered 1844 and after.

Civic Structures

Connecticut State House, Hartford, Connecticut, Built 1793–96, restored 1918–21.
Massschusetts State House, Boston, Massachusetts. Built 1795–97; restored 1896–98.
The Capitol, Washington, D.C. Built 1793–1827; altered after 1851. Work by Bulfinch began in 1829. Maine State House, Augusta, Maine. Built 1829–32; altered after 1851; enlarged and rebuilt 1909–11.

Residential Works

Tontine Crescent, Boston, Massachusetts. Built 1793–94; demolished c. 1858.
Harrison Gray Otis House (first), Boston, Massachusetts. Built 1795–96; restoration begun 1916.
Harrison Gray Otis House (second), Boston, Massachusetts. Built 1800–2.
Harrison Gray Otis House (third), Boston, Massachusetts. Built 1805–8.

Bibliography

Kirker, Harold. *The Architecture of Charles Bulfinch*. Cambridge, Mass. Harvard University Press, 1969.
———. *Bulfinch's Boston, 1787–1817*. Oxford: Oxford University Press, 1964.
Nylander, Richard C. "The First Harrison Gray Otis House, Boston, Massachusetts," *Antiques* 129 618–21.
Place, Charles A. *Charles Bulfinch: Architect and Citizen*. New York: Da Capo, 1968?
Roth, Leland M. *A Concise History of American Architecture*. New York: Harper and Row, 1979.

BULWER-LYTTON, EDWARD 1803–1873

English writer

In an article titled "Mr Thackeray and His Novels" published in *Blackwood's Magazine* in January 1855, a Mrs. Oliphant reflected upon the novel writers of the period and concluded that "the foremost figure of all . . . is Bulwer." While Oliphant's view was shared by many of her contemporaries, Bulwer-Lytton's reputation suffered a dramatic decline in the twentieth century. Nevertheless, he remains a vitally important figure for those seeking to understand British literary culture in the nineteenth century. Not only was he influential in literary circles (influencing writers such as Mary Braddon and Charles Dickens), and popular with the reading public; he also acted as a conduit for the transmission and development of various Romantic ideas in the Victorian period.

One of the most striking things about Bulwer-Lytton is the range of genres that we find in his fiction. As John Sutherland notes, "He can plausibly claim to be the father of the English detective novel, science fiction, the fantasy novel, the thriller, and the domestic realistic novel." Bulwer-Lytton's experiments with fiction often involved the revision of preexisting genres. This can be seen from his pioneering role in the development of the newgate novel. His newgate novels, which include *Paul Clifford* (1830), *Eugene Aram* (1832), and *Lucretia* (1846), built upon the Gothic interest in criminality. His enthusiasm for criminal psychology has led some critics to link Bulwer-Lytton with William Godwin, a link augmented by the polemic against capital punishment that runs through many of Bulwer-Lytton's newgate novels. Related to his interest in the heroic criminal was Bulwer-Lytton's fascination with Lord Byron. This reached a climax in 1824 when he had a brief, infatuated, and ultimately painful liaison with Byron's former mistress, Lady Caroline Lamb.

To many observers, the range of genres that we find in Bulwer-Lytton's work appears confused, even contradictory. Novels such as *Godolphin* (1833) and *Zanoni* (1842) are concerned with mysticism, while others, such as *Pelham* (1828), *The Caxtons* (1849), and *My Novel* (1852), are more interested in aspects of domestic realism. In an attempt to come to terms with this apparent dichotomy between tales of the supernatural and portrayals of dandyism and high society, Allan Christensen claims that the "epistemological opposition resembles the traditional one between idealism and empiricism." This is a helpful observation that reminds us of the range of philosophical ideas that can be found in Bulwer-Lytton's work. As Robert Lee Wolff points out, Bulwer-Lytton "read as they appeared the latest works on physiology, philosophy, and what passed for psychology, in French, German and English. Not only Bacon, Newton, Descartes, Locke, Condillac, Hume, Reid, Kant, Schelling, and Hegel, but Lamark, Laplace, Maine de Biran, Sir Humphrey Davy, Faraday, Darwin, Louis Agassiz—we shall find him citing all these and many others."

While the eclectic nature of Bulwer-Lytton's reading makes it difficult to locate him within a particular philosophical tradition, there seems little doubt that Johann Wolfgang von Goethe, Novalis, and Johann Christoph Friedrich von Schiller exerted a considerable influence upon him. His respect for Schiller is explicit in an extended essay that he wrote on the German philosopher, poet, and dramatist. His praise of Schiller's "combination of philosophy and poetry" is revealing in terms of Bulwer-Lytton's own philosophy of writing. His fiction reveals an ongoing attempt to engage with philosophical and scientific thought; unfortunately, this is often done in a cumbersome fashion, a weakness that is powerfully illustrated in the protracted discussions about the existence of the soul that dominate sections of *A Strange Story* (1862).

Idealism became increasingly central to Bulwer-Lytton's thought in the 1830s. In addition to reading the work of German idealists, he read widely in neoplatonism. The extreme notion of idealism that Bulwer-Lytton embraced provided the philosophical basis for his lifelong interest in the occult. Although he maintained a skeptical attitude to occult phenomena until he died, Bulwer-Lytton felt that the spiritual realm provided a better alternative to materialism. Indeed, he derided the materialism of the eighteenth century as "silly" in an essay "On the Spirit in Which New Theories Should Be Received" (1868). The desire to take the marvelous seriously encouraged Bulwer-Lytton to pursue investigations that can only be described as pseudoscience, as illustrated by the mesmerism that dominates the ghost story that he published in 1859, "The Haunted and the Haunters." In the story, the narrator outlines a theory of the supernatural that is typically seen as representative of Bulwer-Lytton's own position. He declares that "what is called supernatural is only a something in the laws of nature of which we have been hitherto ignorant."

As well as showing evidence of an interest in philosophy and science, Bulwer-Lytton's work frequently engages with history and politics. However, his political ideology is difficult to pin down: he began parliamentary life as a liberal reformer in the 1830s before switching to the Tory Party in the 1850s. Bulwer-Lytton's interest in issues of national identity found expression in some of the historical novels that he wrote—notably, *The Last Days of Pompeii* (1834) and *Harold: The Last of The Saxon Kings* (1848)—and in an interesting study called *England and the English* (1833). Further reflections can be found in his essay on the French Revolution, entitled "The Reign of Terror: Its Causes and Results" (1868). Bulwer-Lytton found a certain justification in the factors that led to the Revolution, but he censured the excesses of the events that followed. In this respect we can see a degree of similarity with the interpretation of events offered by Charles Dickens in *A Tale of Two Cities* (1859). Among other things, this reminds us of the way in which Bulwer-Lytton influenced the thinking of many of his contemporaries. It is largely in this that Bulwer-Lytton's importance lies as a key figure in the interpretation of Romantic events and ideas in the nineteenth century. As Sutherland comments, "Bulwer was the first nineteenth-century novelist to project himself as an intellectual, interested in ideas, and how fiction can be their vehicle."

MARK KNIGHT

Biography

Born Edward George Earle Bulwer in London, May 25, 1803. Youngest son of General William Bulwer and Elizabeth Lytton.

Educated at Dr. Ruddock's School, Fulham, London, and Dr. Hooker's School, Rottingdean, Sussex. Studied Latin, Greek, and history with Rev. Charles Wallington in Ealing, London, 1819–20. Entered Trinity College, Cambridge, as a pensioner, 1822, and Trinity Hall, Cambridge, as a fellow commoner, 1825. Chancellor's medal for verse, 1825; B.A., 1826, M.A., 1835. Traveled to Paris and Versailles, 1826. Married Rosina Doyle Wheeler, 1827 (legally separated, 1836); they had one daughter and one son. Lived at Woodcot House, near Pangbourne, Berkshire; wrote for various magazines, including *Quarterly Review, Keepsakes*, and *Books of Beauty*, 1827–29. Moved to London, 1829. Editor, *New Monthly*, 1831–32. Liberal member of parliament for St. Ives and Lincoln, 1831–1841: worked on the First Reform Bill, 1832. Traveled to Italy, 1833; first estrangement from his wife. Published *The Last Days of Pompeii*, 1834. Knighted, 1838. Retired from Parliament in protest at the repeal of the Corn Laws, 1841. Succeeded to family estate at Knebworth, Hertfordshire, and expanded his name formally to Bulwer-Lytton after death of his mother, 1843. Daughter Emily died of typhus, 1848. Joined Conservative Party, 1851. Conservative member of Parliament for Hertford, 1852–66. Rector, University of Glasgow, 1856, 1858. As secretary of state for the colonies (1858–59), named New Caledonia, Pacific crown colony now in British Columbia, Canada; established separate status for New South Wales and Queensland, Australia. Suffered increasingly from deafness from 1850s on LL.D., Cambridge University, 1864. Member of the Order of St. Michael and St. George, 1870. Raised to peerage as Baron Lytton of Knebworth, 1866. Died of an ear infection in Torquay, Devon, January 18, 1873.

Selected Works

Novels
Falkland. 1827.
Pelham. 1828.
The Disowned. 1829.
Devereux. 1829.
Paul Clifford. 1830.
Eugene Aram. 1832.
Godolphin. 1833.
The Last Days of Pompeii. 1834.
Rienzi. 1835.
Ernest Maltravers. 1837.
Night and Morning. 1841.
Zanoni. 1842.
Lucretia. 1846.
Harold: The Last of The Saxon Kings. 1848.
The Caxtons. 1849.
My Novel. 1852.
A Strange Story. 1862.
The Coming Race. 1871.

Poetry and Drama
Richelieu. 1839.
Money. 1840.
Poetical and Dramatic Works. 5 vols. 1852–54.

Essays
England and the English. 2 vols. 1833.
Miscellaneous Prose Works. 3 vols. 1868.

Bibliography

Campbell, James. *Edward Bulwer-Lytton*. Boston: Twayne, 1986.
Christensen, Allan. *Edward Bulwer-Lytton: The Fiction of New Regions*. Athens, Ga.: University of Georgia Press, 1976.
Lytton, Earl of, *The Life of Edward Bulwer, First Lord Lytton*. 2 vols. London: Macmillan, 1913.
Sadleir, Michael. *Bulwer and His Wife: A Panorama, 1803–1836*. London: Constable, 1931.
Snyder, Charles. *Liberty and Morality: A Political Biography of Edward Bulwer-Lytton*, New York: Peter Lang, 1995.
Sutherland, John, "Lytton, Edward Bulwer." In *The Longman Companion to Victorian Fiction*. London: Longman, 1988.
Wolff, Robert Lee. *Strange Stories and Other Explorations in Victorian Fiction*, Boston: Gambit, 1971.

BURKE, EDMUND 1729–1797

British statesman and political thinker

Edmund Burke, an Irishman, was an active member of the British Parliament for thirty years between 1765 and 1794. He was a political thinker whose thought was expressed not in a single theory but in response to the issues that he encountered during his political career. He wrote across a large number of genres, undertaking early works of aesthetics and political satire, and, later, a huge number of public and personal letters, speeches, and pamphlets. He is principally known for the influence of two works, the first his aesthetic treatise *A Philosophical Enquiry into the Origin of Our Ideas of the Sublime and the Beautiful* (1757, expanded 1759) and his account of the early stages of the French Revolution, the *Reflections on the Revolution in France* (1790). Other works, however—particularly his interventions in debates concerning the colonial administration of America and India— and later works on France—are of equal importance. His career cuts through the early stages of the Romantic era, and much of his influence took shape only after his death, but it is an influence that exposes many of the ambivalences inherent in any definition of "the Romantic."

A Philosophical Enquiry into the Origin of Our Ideas of the Sublime and the Beautiful was a youthful intervention into the fashionable eighteenth-century discussion of "taste," that sought to elucidate the criterion by which we should judge works of art. In the preface added to the second edition, Burke criticizes previous works on the subject, accusing them of allocating rules for the appreciation of art without first discussing the causes of our ideas of the sublime and the beautiful. The *Enquiry* undertakes to redress this, to find the unalterable laws of human experience, as Isaac Newton had found simple laws that governed the physical universe. True to the influence of this empiricism, the *Enquiry* takes the investigation of the sublime and the beautiful beyond the appreciation of art toward its origins in sense perception. Burke analyzes the effects on the human mind of the natural world, and borrows freely from contemporary physiological discoveries to explain them and breaking with essential tenets of eighteenth-century criticism that derived from classical literary theory. Notably, in the *Enquiry* Burke separates the sublime from the beautiful, giving each a basis in different sources of sensory stimulation and differing characteristics: the beautiful is associated with small, smooth, and gradually varying objects, and promotes social feelings of love and condescension; the sublime, by contrast, is caused by the mind being overpowered by objects greater than itself. It is based on fear in the face of such power, and is associated with the selfish emotions, but, paradoxically, one has at the same time to be aware that one is not imminently threatened by such displays of power. This double awareness produces the "delightful terror" of the sublime. The discourse on taste had frequently been used as a vehicle for the discussion of morality, and it may already be apparent that Burke's categorizations imply, if indistinctly, political ramifications, something that is confirmed by his analysis of the gradation of the sublime into the emotions of "awe, reverence, and respect." Initial reception of the *Enquiry* was mixed, but its influence was great, spanning new formulations of architecture, painting and gardening, aesthetics, theories of rhetoric, and particularly literature, where it fed into and expanded the vocabulary available to the language and referents of sensibility, gothicism, and natural description.

In Parliament Burke allied himself to various causes, such as the impeachment of the colonial administrator Warren Hastings and conciliation of the demands of the American colonies, which had given him a reputation as a friend of liberty. This had induced as different a thinker as Thomas Paine to believe that he would find a friend in Burke, and they sustained a correspondence for three years until Burke's publication in 1790 of the *Reflection on the Revolution in France*. Here Burke savagely attacked not simply events in France, but the reception of them by radicals in England. Response to *Reflections*, which was immediate and immense and included works by radicals such as William Godwin, Sir James Mackintosh, Thomas Paine, Helen Maria Williams, and Mary Wollstonecraft, showed the extent to which Burke's previous political thought had been misinterpreted, laying him open to charges that he had betrayed the liberal cause. Indeed, *Reflections*, while selling well (thirteen-thousand copies were sold in the first five weeks of publication), was seen unfavorably as an overreaction from all parts of the political spectrum largely because it was written at an early stage of the French Revolution, before terror and reaction had set in. Burke was always a fine prose stylist, yet the passionate and varied writing in *Reflections* did not help matters, distracting attention from his treatment of quite specific matters of political contention through dramatic, even inflammatory, description.

Reflections were written in response to a sermon delivered by Richard Price to the radical Revolution Society, an organization founded to celebrate the English "Glorious Revolution" of 1688. Burke argued that the revolutionaries in France and the radicals at home fundamentally misunderstood the nature of political society and particularly English liberty. Harking back to his scathing satire on Viscount Bolingbroke's theory of natural rights in the *Vindication of Natural Society* (1756), and centering on the propagation of similar views derived from Jean-Jacques Rousseau in the radical discourse surrounding the revolution, attacked the idea that natural rights existed in an abstract, theoretical sense, beyond their manifestation in any given society.

Burke argued that society is formed not through a written or even a formally agreed constitution, but through the long preservation of the bonds of local and hereditary society unwritten, and probably unable to be written. Implicit in this is an attack on what he saw as a secular intelligentsia who sought to divorce politics from conventional sources of authority, such as the church and the aristocracy, in favor of individual reason.

Burke's legacy is a complex one. This is largely because the issues that he addressed, particularly on the subjects of aesthetics and the French Revolution, were formative of, and were reformed in, the Romantic era. His influence is particularly in question concerning the political development of William Wordsworth and Samuel Taylor Coleridge, who from early criticism swiftly became firm admirers of Burke. It is also a paradoxical one, for his writings frequently galvanized opposition. While, personally this meant that he became increasingly isolated, these responses testify to the power and acuity of his interventions into some of the major aesthetic and political disputes of his day. Even those—such as William Blake—who despised his ideas did not overlook them.

SUZIE JORDAN

Biography

Born in Dublin, probably January 12, 1729. Son of a solicitor. Educated at Abraham Shackleton's school, Ballitore, County Kildare, 1741–43. Studied at Trinity College, Dublin, 1744–48; B.A., 1748. Entered the Middle Temple, London, 1750. Traveled in England and France, 1750s. Published first work, *A Vindication of Natural Society*, 1756, and *A Philosophical Enquiry into the Origin of our Ideas of the Sublime and Beautiful*, 1757 (expanded edition 1759), both anonymously. Married Jane Nugent, 1757; they had two sons. Established friendships with Oliver Goldsmith, Samuel Johnson, and other influential writers and artists. Founded the *Annual Register*, London, 1758. Private secretary to William Gerard Hamilton, 1759–64; accompanied him to Ireland, 1763–64. Member of Samuel Johnson's literary club from 1764. Whig member of parliament for Wendover, Buckinghamshire, 1765–74. Appointed private secretary to the Marquis of Rockingham, 1765; bought estate in Beaconsfield, Buckinghamshire, 1768. Published *Thoughts on the Cause of the Present Discontents*, 1770. Made speeches on American taxation and conciliation, 1774–75. Member of Parliament for Bristol, 1774–80; for Malton, Yorkshire, 1781–94. Paymaster general of the armed forces, 1782, 1783. Rector, University of Glasgow, 1784, 1785. Instrumental in impeachment of Warren Hastings, governor general of Bengal, 1786–95. Supported William Wilberforce in advocating abolition of the slave trade, 1788–89. Leading commentator on the French Revolution, 1790s: published *Reflections on the Revolution in France*, 1790; *Two Letters on Peace with the Regicide Directory of France*, 1797. Retired from Parliament, 1794; granted government pension. Helped with foundation of Maynooth College, Ireland, 1795; established school for French refugees at Penn, Buckinghamshire, 1796. LL.D., Dublin University, 1791. Died in Beaconsfield, July 9, 1797.

Selected Writings

Collections

The Correspondence of Edmund Burke. 10 vols. Edited by Thomas Copeland. 1958–78.

The Writings and Speeches of Edmund Burke. 12 vols. Edited by Paul Langford. 1981–.

Philosophy

A Philosophical Enquiry into the Origin of Our Ideas of the Sublime and Beautiful, 1757. 2d ed. with "Preface on Taste," 1759.

Reflections on the Revolution in France, and on the Proceedings in Certain Societies in London Relative to that Event. 1790.

Bibliography

Boulton, James T. Introduction to *A Philosophical Enquiry into the Origin of Our Ideas of the Sublime and Beautiful.* London: Blackwell, 1968.

Butler, Marilyn. *Burke, Paine, Godwin, and the Revolution Controversy.* Cambridge: Cambridge University Press, 1984.

O'Brien, C. C. *The Great Melody: A Thematic Biography and Commentated Anthology of Edmund Burke.* London: Sinclair-Stevenson, 1992.

Paulson, R. *Representations of Revolution (1789–1820).* New Haven, Conn.: Yale University Press, 1983.

Pocock, J. G. A. Introduction to Edmund Burke, *Reflections of the Revolution in France.* 3d ed. London: Penguin, 1976.

Reid, Chris. *Edmund Burke and the Practice of Political Writing.* Dublin: Gill and Macmillan, 1985.

Smith, Olivia. *The Politics of Language 1791–1819.* Oxford: Clarendon Press, 1984.

BURNS, ROBERT 1759–1796

Scottish poet

Scotland's national poet, Robert Burns, is the first major British writer whose life is as important as his writings and who consciously played the part of the poet genius. This was largely through force of circumstance. The son of a poor tenant farmer, brought up in a provincial part of Scotland, not uneducated by modern standards but lacking the classical training the eighteenth century deemed essential, Burns knew success would depend on presenting himself as an untutored rustic bard. In so doing, he almost accidentally anticipated much of British Romanticism, earning commemoration in William Wordsworth's "Resolution and Independence" (1802) as "Him who walked in glory and in joy / Behind his plough." Like Ann Yearsley, he had to negotiate, in both his life and his verse, with the contemporary admiration for uncultivated genius. Most of Burns's original poems were written in a marvelous burst of inspiration around the year 1785 and published in *Poems Chiefly in the Scottish Dialect* in 1786. The success of this collection was immediate; when Burns visited Edinburgh later that year, he was lionized as "The Ploughman Poet," a role he played not unwillingly (his capacity for role-playing is amply demonstrated in his varied and lively letters), even though he was never just a farm laborer. A few poems were added to the collection in the Edinburgh edition of 1787.

Writing of necessity out of his own experience, in *Poems Chiefly in the Scottish Dialect* Burns describes from a firsthand perspective the world of agricultural work, the face of nature, the changing seasons and the weather, and the lives of ordinary people. Though the lowliness of his social position should not be exaggerated, he offered an outsider's view of the upper classes, expressing egalitarian and radical opinions. Much of his thinking can be traced to Scottish Enlightenment sources, but his talent was for clothing abstract ideas in local particulars, as in his poem "To a Mouse, On Turning Her up in Her Nest with the Plough, November 1785," which combines generalizations on man's place in nature with graphic Scots language culminating in the now-proverbial lines "The best laid schemes o' *Mice* an' *Men,* / Gang aft agley." Many poems in the collection, such as "To a Louse" (1786) and "Address to the Unco Guid, or the Rigidly Righteous" (1787), are straightforward moralizing of experience in this way. Their neoclassical conventionality is disguised by

their pithy use of Scots, rooting them in a recognizable community, and by their frank, direct tone, "a man speaking to men," as Wordsworth later described the language of poetry. In other poems, such as "The Cotter's Saturday Night" (1786) and "The Twa Dogs" (1786) he offers detailed pictures of the social class to which he belonged.

Burns was steeped in the British literature of his time, freely acknowledging his admiration for James Macpherson's Ossian poems and Henry Mackenzie's sentimental novel *The Man of Feeling* (1771). As Carol McGuirk has shown, he is a poet of the sentimental era that preceded full Romanticism. He was one of the first to record his feeling for John Milton's Satan, and yet he also quotes frequently from the Augustan poetry of Alexander Pope. He might have remained a minor eighteenth-century versifier had he not encountered the poems, in Scots, of Robert Fergusson (1750–74), which put him in touch with traditions of Scottish verse reaching back to the fifteenth century. The Scots language and Scottish verse forms, together with the caustic humor Fergusson taught him, gave Burns's poetry strength and vitality. Fergusson also taught Burns how to apply these to contemporary life. It is safe to say that Burns's best work comes from the successful marriage of Scottish and English literary influences.

Excluded from *Poems Chiefly in the Scottish Dialect* were the satirical monologue "Holy Willie's Prayer" (1801), a definitive attack on Calvinist hypocrisy, and the cantata "Love and Liberty" (also known as "The Jolly Beggars," 1801), a celebration of low-life pleasures and amorality judged too revolutionary to appear in print. Burns's most substantial poem, "Tam o' Shanter," appeared in 1791. It is the mock-heroic tale of a drunken hero who stumbles on a dance of witches and narrowly escapes their wrath. Its gleeful use of folklore and the supernatural is undercut by its narrative irony, causing Thomas Carlyle to damn it in the *Edinburgh Review* as "not so much a poem, as a piece of sparkling rhetoric." As his poem about country superstition, "Halloween" (1786), shows in its humor and the detached scholarly tone of its footnotes, Burns's attitude to the dark mysteries of human nature, which would fascinate Lord Byron and Percy Bysshe Shelley, was more like the Enlightenment skepticism of David Hume and Samuel Johnson.

Burns's main poetical effort in his later years was in collecting, editing, and often rewriting Scottish songs. His interest was in short lyrics rather than long narrative ballads, but his collecting of folk poetry stands comparison with the work of Thomas Percy and Sir Walter Scott. Many of the songs he collected and improved became popular and remain so to this day; the best known is, of course, "Auld Lang Syne" (1788). His political song "A Man's a Man for A' That" (1795) remains one of the most uncompromising statements of egalitarianism. The success of his love songs and songs of conviviality added to his reputation as a lover of women and whisky. This image was reinforced by the knowledge that several of his songs were based on bawdy originals, which he also collected in *The Merry Muses of Caledonia* (1799). The legend of Burns the womanizer, inspired and finally killed by drink, rapidly took shape after his death, as did the custom of holding "Burns suppers" on the date of his birth to perform his poems and songs and toast his "immortal memory." Though the twentieth century saw some attempts by Scottish poets and academics to curb the excesses of the cult of Burns, he remains the icon of a working-class poet, the subject of novels, plays, and soon a Hollywood film, his birthplace a tourist shrine (visited by John Keats in 1818), and his works translated into many languages, notably in Russia and Japan. Many tried to emulate his achievement; the most successful of these in Scotland was James Hogg.

CHRISTOPHER MACLACHLAN

Biography

Born in Alloway, Ayrshire, Scotland, January 25, 1759. Educated at home and at a school in Alloway Mill, 1765–68. Moved with his family to farms at Mount Oliphant (1766) and Lochlea (1777). Became tenant of Mossgiel Farm, near Mauchline, after his father's death, 1784. Founded Tarbolton Bachelors' Club, 1780. Entered into a relationship with Elizabeth Paton, a servant; they had one child, born 1785. Fathered twins by Jean Armour, 1786; married her in 1788; they had six more children,

only three surviving to adulthood; fathered three children by other women. Published *Poems Chiefly in the Scottish Dialect* in Kilmarnock, 1786. Moved to Edinburgh; visited the Scottish borders and highlands, 1786–88. Began collecting songs and melodies for Johnson's *The Scots Musical Museum* (1787–1803) and Thompson's *Select Collection of Original Scotish Airs for the Voice* (1793–1818). Settled at Ellisland farm, Dumfriesshire, 1788. Gave up farming and moved to Dumfries to take up position as excise officer (tax inspector), 1791. Honorary member, Royal Company of Archers, 1792. Died in Dumfries, July 21, 1796.

Selected Works

Collections
Poems Chiefly in the Scottish Dialect. 1786.
The Merry Muses of Caledonia. 1799.
The Poems and Songs of Robert Burns. Edited by James Kinsley. London: Oxford University Press, 1968.
The Complete Letters of Robert Burns. Edited by James A. Mackay. Ayr: Alloway Publishing, 1987.
The Songs of Robert Burns. Edited by Donald A. Low. London: Routledge, 1993.

Bibliography
Bentman, Raymond. *Robert Burns.* Boston: Twayne. 1987.
Crawford, Robert, ed. *Robert Burns and Cultural Authority.* Edinburgh: Edinburgh University Press, 1997.
Crawford, Thomas. *Burns: A Study of the Poems and Songs.* Stanford, Calif.: Stanford University Press, 1960.
Jack, R. D. S. and Andrew Noble, eds. *The Art of Robert Burns.* London: Vision, 1982.
Low, Donald A., ed. *Robert Burns: The Critical Heritage.* London: Routledge and Kegan Paul, 1974.
Mackay, James A. *Burns: A Biography of Robert Burns.* Edinburgh: Mainstream, 1992.
McGuirk, Carol. *Robert Burns and the Sentimental Era.* Athens, Ga.: University of Georgia Press, 1985.
Simpson, Kenneth, ed. *Burns Now.* Edinburgh: Canongate, 1994.

BYRON, LORD GEORGE NOEL GORDON 1788–1824

British poet

For many throughout Continental Europe and America, Lord Byron was and still remains the quintessential Romantic poet both in virtue of his writings and his equally celebrated life. Much of his poetry, especially *Childe Harold's Pilgrimage* (1812–18) and the "Oriental Tales" (1813–16) were translated almost immediately into most primary European languages, and his verse and accompanying public image were widely imitated by José de Espronceda y Delgado, Heinrich Heine, Alphonse Marie Louis de Lamartine, Louis-Charles-Alfred de Musset, Alexandr Pushkin, and Alfred-Victor de Vigny and many others, and praised in extravagant terms by Johann Wolfgang von Goethe. This was partially because Byron identified with the history, culture, and civilization of Europe, which in turn he romantically projected in his writings. From 1809 to 1811, he traveled through Spain and Portugal to Greece and Turkey. From 1816, after the fateful collapse of his fifteen-month marriage to Anna-

bella Milbanke, which was accompanied by rumors of his incest with his half-sister, he lived in Geneva, Italy, and finally Greece, where he died in the Greek War of Independence, which has forever been associated with him. Thus, ten of his thirty-six years (and these the most productive) were spent outside Britain. Byron lived his restlessness on a "Titanic" scale (in Matthew Arnold's description) and was saluted by Percy Bysshe Shelley in an adaptation of Byron's own self-description, as the "Pilgrim of Eternity," but nevertheless he had an ability to decisively inhabit a place and speak from within its own history, like a native. By contrast Shelley, whom Byron lived alongside in Italy for a period of time, never assimilated into local life in a similar fashion. Byron's identification with national and liberal movements in Spain, South America (he had a ship, *Bolivar*, built for him in Italy), Italy, and Greece became an emblem for national or revolutionary movements in other countries. This effect was intensified by Byron's fascination with and (usually) support for Napoleon Bonaparte at a time when most English opinion was strongly critical of him. Byron's vignette of Napoleon in "Childe Harold's Pilgrimage III" (1816) is one of the most perceptive short accounts of Napoleon's character. Byron brackets him with Jean-Jacques Rousseau, but his contemporaries bracketed Byron with Napoleon himself. Byron accepted, but later reviewed, this identification in *Don Juan* (1819–24), referring ironically here to his later writings, *Don Juan* itself and to his plays *Marino Faliero* (1820) and *Cain* (1821). He was reckoned, he writes.

> a considerable time,
> The grand Napoleon of the realms of rhyme.
> But Juan was my Moscow, and Faliero
> My Leipsic, and my Mount Saint Jean seems Cain.

How does Byron embody Romantic qualities? First, he was seen primarily as an example of a new kind of public artistic figure, marked by a boundless sense of will. It is essential that his poetry and his personality are taken here as inseparable. English Romanticism, especially as considered by American critics such as M. H. Abrams, Harold Bloom, and Geoffrey Hartman, has been interpreted as understanding consciousness primarily as imagination, but Byron is always more interested in powers inherent in the will. Friedrich Nietzsche found in Byron's character Manfred (*Manfred*, 1817) a prototype for his conception of the superman (*übermensch*). Byron's understanding of will is linked with his Promethean stance of defiance (as in his poem "Prometheus," 1816), which has both political and religious overtones. Byron's mother, Catherine Gordon, was a Scottish heiress and Byron, abandoned early by his father who fled to France to escape his debts, was brought up in Aberdeen for the first ten years of his life, until he unexpectedly inherited the title of sixth Baron Byron of Rochdale and relocated to the Byrons' ancestral home of Newstead Abbey in Nottingham. His nurse and his early school education both in Scotland instilled Calvinism into him at a time when there was much dispute within Calvinism between its more liberal faction and those who wished to reinstate its more stern and rigorous aspects. For Byron, who carried on reading the scriptures assiduously throughout his life, will exists first within the echoes of the context of salvation through God's wholly originating will, and the possibilities of cosmic defiance that exist within human consciousness despite, or because of, predestination. Thus Byron says of Lara (in his tale *Lara*, 1814) "Till he at last confounded good and ill, / And half mistook for fate the acts of will." The dark coloring of Byron's poems derives from the force of these theological postulates. Roughly speaking, his contemporaries saw him as challenging these religious affirmations, but, from a later perspective, we note their survival, and indeed, revival in him and the weakness of his opponents' ostensible orthodoxy. This is particularly true of his mystery play *Cain*, which combines the biblical story via Salomon Gessner's *Der Tod Abels* (*The Death of Abel*, 1758) with elements of Goethe's *Faust* (1808). The play created a furor in England, where it was charged with blasphemy, but Byron's protestations of its orthodoxy are not entirely misleading.

Alongside and against this contemporary European reception of the "dark" Byron is his own self-conscious siding with classicism in the face of emerging Romanticism and the brightness of his comic sense of life. Goethe said of Byron that he was neither classic nor Romantic, but "Modern." He is, in fact, all three. It is almost impossible to keep track of this in a single vocabulary, for the cultural reception of Byron and Byronism has divided into a Continental perception that originally idolized him, then sought to sidestep or reevaluate this worship, and an English perception that was originally equally mesmerized (though appalled) but has subsequently sought to disavow its earlier relationship or try partially to recover it. It does so (it) in the guise of Byron as satirist (1930s–60s) or Byron as champion of history—the material fact, and relativism (1970s onward), as opposed to the pseudotranscendental Romantic project of the imagination associated with William Blake, Samuel Taylor Coleridge, William Wordsworth, and, to some extent, Percy Bysshe Shelley.

In approaching Byron as a Romantic writer, then, we cannot simply categorize him according to existing definitions of *Romanticism* but should see those definitions as derived partly from him. The simplest way of doing this is to stress contradictions. The French, especially Stendhal, had some sense of this from the beginning. Byron, far more than any other single figure, expresses the contradictions of Romanticism. The Napoleonic period saw a triumph of Enlightenment values carried out in a manner that belied their presuppositions. This in turn provoked a reactionary sense that the whole project was radically shallow and mistaken, or renewed the radical argument that the Revolution had been betrayed and still remained the future agenda. Byron, more than any other single figure, represents these contradictions, and this is a principal source of his astonishing and still continuing appeal. For example, when he died in Greece, he did so in the name of an approaching European nationalism fighting a dying imperial regime, in the name of mediaeval European Christendom versus Islam (here, the Turks), and in the name of ancient Greece and civilization versus the barbaric Persians. Byron had a classical helmet made for himself and understood immediately all the symbols that were in play. For convenience we will follow G. Wilson Knight's influential division of Byron's poetry into "bright and "dark" emphases ("eternities," in Knight's terminology).

Byron's dark poems (principally "Childe Harold's Pilgrimage," 1812–18; the "Oriental Tales," 1813–16; *Manfred*, 1817; and *Cain*, 1821) are centered on the new figure of the Byronic hero. This essentially new figure, sired by John Dryden's Achitophel, John Milton's Satan, and the villain in eighteenth-century novels by John Moore, Samuel Richardson, and others, combined with the sentimental heroes of Henry Mackenzie, Jean-Jacques Rousseau, and others, embodies a primal and fatal force of will together with a secret susceptibility to women and tenderness. Thus his corsair ("The Corsair," 1814) lives in both dark and bitter isolation and yet retains links with two different version of the feminine, passive Medora and murderous Gulnare. This means that his own sensibility is ambivalently both male and female, and critics thus often refer back to Byron's own bisexuality. These dark heroes live with a guilt that appalls them and yet is maintained by their own will. Dante and *Macbeth* are as much behind this as is Milton's Satan, and Byron here offers a glimpse of the intense reality of hell to a post-Enlightenment world that the Enlightenment had so busily denied. From here there is a straight route through to Charles- Baudelaire and Arthur Rimbaud, to Paul-Gustave Doré, and Franz Liszt' predilection for Dante Alighieri's *Inferno*, and to Fyodor Dostoevsky and Mikhail Lermontov.

Byron himself was ambivalent about this dark Romanticism which the public identified with his personality. He often repudiated it, or—as in his three carefully neoclassical tragedies modelled on Vittorio Alfieri's theater (*Marino Faliero* 1820; *Sardanapalus*, 1821; *The Two Foscari*, 1821)—situated it within a deliberately cool frame. Byron had a stronger sense of the theater than any of his major contemporaries and his eight major plays (in addition to the classical tragedies, *Manfred* and *Cain*, there are *Heaven and Earth*, 1821; *Werner*, 1822; and *The Deformed Transformed*, 1822) are a remarkable attempt to construct a new English drama at a time when the theater as such was in decline. Byron refuses to be simply part of the new Romantic consensus that patronized the customary classical insistence on the ideal fusion of purity of style with moral seriousness. Byron defends this in his championing of the poetry of John Dryden and Alexander Pope against attack by Samuel Taylor Coleridge, William Cowper, William Hazlitt, John Keats, Joseph and Thomas Warton, and William Wordsworth but, principally, by his poetic practice in his three great poems written in *ottava rima*—"Beppo" (1817), *Don Juan*, and "The Vision of Judgement" (1821). The choice of this verse form, hitherto little used in English, owes something to Hookham Frere, but a great deal to Byron's increasing familiarity with Italian and his reading of poets such as Giovanni Battista Casti. It is much more difficult to manage the contained rhymes of this form in English. Byron produces a comic *tour de force* in his extravagantly witty way

Lord Byron. Reprinted courtesy of AKG.

around these difficulties and, in this and other ways, suggests a sense of improvisation. We should see this as the shadow side of the insistence on will and constraint in his dark poems. In the *ottava rima* poems, especially *Don Juan* and "Beppo," Byron advertises the unexpected, and the relationship between spontaneity of consciousness and the containing energies of *life* (an insistent word in *Don Juan*; Byron was influenced by Henry Fielding and by Laurence Sterne here). But most important is his identification with women as embodying the priority of life over everything else, and his increasing sympathy with Catholicism. Beppo, the would-be dark hero, is ousted by the directed spontaneity of his cheerily adulterous wife, Laura, and Byron's Don Juan, unlike Tirso da Molina's and Molière' eponymous heroes, is seduced rather than seducer. Byron is absolutely serious in his claim that these poems are a novel but real continuation of the tradition of Dryden and Pope and thus deny the argument of Wordsworth in the Preface to the 1800 edition of the *Lyrical Ballads* that the greatest contemporary poetry must look elsewhere for its mode. He is equally serious in his claim that these poems are ethical in a sense that Samuel Johnson would understand and Byron's Romantic contemporaries would not. With some exceptions, these poems did not make the impact that Byron desired, although in the early nineteenth century *Don Juan* was widely circulated in cheap pirated copies as subversive reading. Goethe saw at once the huge importance of Byron's "cultured, comic language" in *Don Juan* but most English readers, already conditioned to find Byron shocking, were further shocked by its apparent license, and emerging critical opinion went in exactly the direction that Byron feared. Pushkin's *Eugene Onegin* (1833) is an obvious beneficiary of Byron's poem but, on the Continent, too, it was the dark and sublime Byron, not his comic reading of life, that was preferred. Only in the twentieth century has the poem been recognized as his masterpiece.

Byron was fully aware of his own contradictory tendencies. He justified them in *Don Juan* by writing, "But if a writer should be quite consistent, / How could he possibly show things existent?" Certainly he was a liberal populist, intensely proud of his aristocratic lineage, an arch-Romantic who was also a convinced classicist, a great poet who insisted on the superiority of the life of action to imagination, a skeptic who profoundly understood religious modes of being, a "citizen of the world" whose intense identification with the life of nations affected the course of European history, a famous lover of women who was also passionately in love with young men and, in many respects, an ascetic. He was a poet who wanted to be regarded, like the poets of the Restoration, as a gentleman who wrote rather than as a professional writer, but he remained profoundly concerned with the forms of poetry and drama, cultural tradition, and religious, political, and moral imperatives. He was also an incomparable letter writer. Byron is as much a European phenomenon as a British one, although in recent years interest in him on the continent has declined, whereas his status in Anglo-American criticism is now almost as high as it was in his lifetime. Virtually all the contradictions that have been discerned in Romanticism are embodied in him.

BERNARD BEATTY

Biography

Born George Noel Gordon Byron in London, January 22, 1788. Lived in Aberdeen as a child; attended Aberdeen Grammar

School, 1794–98. Inherited uncle's title and estate, Newstead Abbey, becoming the sixth Baron Byron, 1798. Attended Harrow School, 1801–5, and Trinity College, Cambridge, 1805–7. Traveled in southern Europe, July–December 1809. Took seat in House of Lords, 1809. Lived in Athens, 1809–11. Married Annabella Milbanke, 1815 (they separated, 1816); daughter, Augusta Ada (later Ada Byron King, Countess of Lovelace, mathematician), born 1815 (d. 1852). Ostracized for supposed incestuous affair with half-sister, Augusta Leigh: left England, 1816. Traveled in northern Europe, April–May 1816. Lived near Geneva and met the Shelleys there, 1816. Lived and traveled in Italy, 1816–23. Relationship with Claire Clairmont (stepsister of Mary Shelley), 1816–17; they had one daughter. Published *Childe Harold's Pilgrimage*, 1812–18; *Don Juan*, 1819–24. Took Teresa, Countess Guiccioli, as his companion, 1819; lived in Venice, following Guiccioli to Ravenna, 1820. Afterward lived in Pisa, Leghorn (Livorno) and Genoa, 1820–23. Actively supported Italian patriots from 1820. Editor, with Leigh Hunt, of the *Liberal*, 1822–23. Traveled to Argostoli, Cephallonia, Greece, August 1823, to organize an expedition to assist in the Greek War of Independence. Arrived in Missolonghi, Greece, January 1824. Died of fever in Missolonghi, April 19, 1824.

Selected Works

Poetry
The Complete Poetical Works. 7 vols. Edited by Jerome J. McGann. Oxford: Clarendon Press, 1980–93.

Prose
The Complete Miscellaneous Prose. Edited by Andrew Nicholson. Oxford: Clarendon Press, 1991.

Byron's Letters and Journals. 13 vols. Edited by Leslie A. Marchand. London: John Murray, 1973–94.

Bibliography

Beatty, Bernard. *Byron's Don Juan*. Totowa, N.J.: Barnes and Noble, 1985.

Beatty, Bernard and Vincent Newey, eds. *Byron and the Limits of Fiction*. Liverpool: Liverpool University Press, 1988.

Franklin, Caroline. *Byron's Heroines*. Oxford: Clarendon Press, 1992.

Gleckner, Robert F. *Byron and the Ruins of Paradise*. Baltimore: John Hopkins University Press, 1967.

Gleckner, Robert and Bernard Beatty, eds. *The Plays of Lord Byron: Critical Essays*. Liverpool: Liverpool University Press, 1997.

Graham, Peter W. *Don Juan and Regency England*. Charlottesville: University of Virginia Press, 1990.

Joseph, M. K. *Byron's Poetry*. London: Gollancz, 1964.

Kelsall, Malcolm. *Byron's Politics*. Brighton: Harvester Press, 1987.

Knight, G. Wilson. *Lord Byron: Christian Virtues*. London: Routledge and Kegan Paul, 1952.

———. *Poets of Action*. London: Methuen, 1967.

Manning, Peter J. *Byron and his Fictions*. Detroit: Wayne State University Press, 1978.

Marchand, Leslie A. *Byron: A Biography*. London: John Murray, 1957.

McGann, Jerome J. *Fiery Dust: Byron's Poetic Development*. Chicago: University of Chicago Press, 1968.

Rutherford, Andrew, ed. *Byron: Augustan and Romantic*. Basingstoke, England: Macmillan, 1990.

Stabler, Jane, ed. *Byron*. London: Longman, 1998.

Wood, Nigel, ed. *Don Juan*. Buckingham: Open University Press, 1993.

BYRONISM

George Sanders's double portrait of Lord Byron with Robert Rushton (1807–8) strikingly portrays the Romantic icon and namesake of Byronism. The young poet, in fashionable nautical costume, is landing on a windswept and gloomy mountain shore. His pose is that of the *Apollo Belvedere* (a Classical marble statue of the Greek god Apollo, notable for its heroic pose and as an epitome of the representation of male beauty). Behind him is his boat (which is flying the red ensign) in the care of a younger man who gazes up admiringly at Byron. This image became one of the most potent images of the poet for the nineteenth century. It suggests proleptically the most famous action of the poet's career: his voyage to Greece and subsequent death in the Greek War of Independence. Accordingly, the image of the admiring onlooker represents the subsequent generation of European nationalists and liberals who found inspiration in Byron.

But the icon also indicates the perplexities of Byronism as a kinetic myth. Sanders cannot have foreseen Byron's participation in the Greek war more than a decade later. His portrait, therefore, created its own Byronic image out of an already predetermining iconography of Romanticism, rooted in such idealized concepts as the wind of change, the darkness of the sublime, and the liberating hope of youth. But the predetermined imagery was subject to revision. Although the red ensign displayed was a patriotic signifier during the Napoleonic Wars, Byron never subscribed to British post-Napoleonic triumphalism. He became a nationalist hero in exile from his own nation. Byronism, accordingly, revised itself. This need to revise has become more acute recently in relation to the latent sexuality of the portrait. In its own time, the Sanders emphasis on masculine virtue suppressed the most notorious characteristic of Byronism, the poet's controversial romantic/sexual dalliances (including Lady Caroline Lamb, and the unsubstantiated rumors of an affair with his half sister Aurora Leigh). But in the late twentieth century, Rushton's presence draws attention to another aspect of Byronism known only to a covert circle: the fact that Byron is suspected of having maintained homosexual as well as heterosexual affairs.

The myth of Byronism, therefore, developed out of the preexisting matrix of Romanticism, but, like all myths, has been subject to continual reinterpretation. Byron himself participated in the process. His early poetry (until 1818) created the image of "the Byronic hero," a darkly Satanic figure who conceals the sentimental heart of a man of feeling behind a countenance wracked by unspeakable guilt, yet (paradoxically) stoic. The classic poetic texts are *Childe Harold's Pilgrimage* (1812–18), *Manfred* (1817), and the oriental tales. The literary genesis of the figure was complex. It is rooted in the Satan of John Milton's *Paradise Lost* but has strong affinities to Samuel Richardson's Lovelace in *Clarissa*, Valmont in Pierre Ambroise François Choderlos de Laclos's *Les Liaisons Dangereuses* and the villains of Ann Radcliffe's romances. The potent force of Byronism, however, was that in Byron's work the poet was identified with his creations and, like a sexualized star of the subsequent age of cinema, he played to that identification. He became the creature of his own fictions even as those fictions played into subsequent literature.

The theatricality of this interchange between life and art exposed Byronism as a target of satire, as a mere sham. Jane Austen's Captain Benwick in *Persuasion* (1818) and the morbidly atrabiliar Mr. Cypress in Thomas Love Peacock's *Nightmare Abbey* (1818) were typical literary manifestations of anti-Byronism, and the critical attitude represented by William Hazlitt's attack on Byronic flashiness in *The Spirit of the Age* (1825) culminated in Thomas Carlyle's notorious advice in *Sartor Resartus* (1833–34) to close one's Byron and open one's Johann Wolfgang von Goethe. Byronism as an affectation here became associated with those later aspects of Romanticism nominated as decadence and/or dandyism.

But Byron was the most effective critic of the cult of Byronism. His later satires, especially *The Vision of Judgement* (1822) and *Don Juan* (1819–23) separate the Byronic hero from the newfound comic voice of the narrator. This radical and skeptical deconstruction of Byronism makes it impossible to establish any essentialist norm. One of the many paradoxes of Byronism is that these late, self-subversive satires, through popular piracies, established themselves in a subculture among Victorian working-class readers. We know little of the reaction of that readership, however, beyond the fact that the Satanic aristocrat was adopted as a proletarian rebel.

Byron's death in Greece provided the final "spin" to the evolving myth. It was the guarantee of what Matthew Arnold called the poet's "sincerity" (*The Poetry of Byron*, 1881). The rebel without a cause had shown at last the ultimate commitment to principles with which liberal and nationalist sentiment could identify throughout Europe. Byron himself saw his actions in the tradition of other aristocratic freedom fighters, notably the Marquis de La Fayette (in Britain's American colonies) and Lord Edward Fitzgerald (in Ireland). For the subsequent generation Giuseppe Mazzini's idealization (in *Scritti Letterari*, 1847) provided a classic mythologization. Byron had been the friend of freedom and of the rights of the people everywhere against the forces of tyranny; but he was also a proud, self-doubting and suffering spirit who, even while existentially cursed, was always moved by the power of love. These complex elements were subject to continual reinterpretation in European Romanticism. Writers as diverse as the Brontë sisters and Alphonse Lamartine, Mikhail Lermontov and Afred Victor de Vigny took from the Byronic myth whatever elements they required. Aleksandr Pushkin's *The Queen of Spades* (1834) may serve as a typical example of this multivalency. The character Hermann is Byronic in his combination of the physical semblance of a hero (Napoleon) with the spirit of Satanism. Pushkin complicates the figure by treating him in the sardonic manner of *Don Juan*, but, subsequently, Pyotr Ilich Tchaikovsky returned the figure to the manner of *Childe Harold* darkly sentimentalizing him in his operatic reworking of Pushkin. In Goethe's *Faust* (book 2, part 3) Byronism achieved a form of apotheosis in the figure of Euphorion, the son of Helen of Greece, who leaves behind his mantle and his lyre while his aureole rises like a comet toward heaven: "Nun fort!/Nun dort/Eroffnet sich zum Ruhm die Bahn" (Now I go forth for there the way to glory opens). But in *Faust* (1808–32) the skeptical, unsatisfied, mocking spirit of Mephistopheles is as representative of Byronism as Euphorion. In that respect, Carlyle's injunction to close Byron and open Goethe returns one nonetheless to Byronism, for Byronism and the entire history of European Romanticism are inextricable.

MALCOLM KELSALL

Bibliography

Chew, Samuel C. *Byron in England: His Fame and Afterfame.* London: John Murray, 1924.

Elfenbein, Andrew. *Byron and the Victorians.* Cambridge: Cambridge University Press, 1995.

Moore, Doris Langley. *The Late Lord Byron.* John Murray, 1961.

Peach, Annette. *Portraits of Byron.* London: Walpole Society, 2000.

Praz, Mario. *The Romantic Agony.* London: Oxford University Press, 1933.

Thorslev, Peter Larsen. *The Byronic Hero: Types and Prototypes.* Minneapolis: University of Minnesota Press, 1962.

Trueblood, Paul Graham, ed. *Byron's Political and Cultural Influence in Nineteenth-Century Europe: A Symposium.* Basingstoke, England: Macmillan, 1981.

Wilson, Frances, ed. *Byromania.* Basingstoke, England: Macmillan, 1999.

C

CANOVA, ANTONIO 1757–1822

Italian sculptor

Antonio Canova was probably the best known and most influential neoclassical sculptor of the eighteenth century, his work steeped in the tradition of copying from antique sources. He was also influenced by the great Italian sculptors of the fifteenth century—Bandinelli, Michelangelo Buonarotti, Benvenuto Cellini, and Giambologna. Because neoclassical sculptors such as Canova sought to explore the traditional concepts of nobility, purity, and grandeur, it is not easy to label their work as Romantic. However, Canova's reputation as not only the saviour of Italian art, but as a symbol of Italian nationalist aspirations has meant that some of Canova's work has often been classified as Romantic. It is also possible to label the sculptor's own life as Romantic, in that though he was the son of a humble stonecutter from a small town in the Veneto, at the end of his life he could count among his many admirers prestigious patrons such as the Emperor Napoleon Bonaparte and members of his family, Pope Pius VII, the tsar of Russia, the emperor of Austria, and the Prince Regent.

Canova had received little formal education, but his early genius was recognized by a local Venetian Senator, Giovanni Falier, who commissioned Canova to carve two statues for the garden on his estate near Asolo. These works were *Orpheus* (1775–76; 203 cm × 85 cm, Museo Correr, Venice) and *Eurydice* (1775; 203 cm × 54 cm, Museo Correr, Venice). *Orpheus* was exhibited at the annual Fiera della Sensa, Venice, in 1777, and it received extravagant praise from the *Vicenza Giornale Enciclopedico*, which declared that the twenty-year-old Canova "need just make one final step to take his place beside Michelangelo Buonarotti, the most famous of Italian sculptors." This work had been inspired by the tragic love story of the legendary Thracian poet Orpheus and his wife Eurydice. It was a favorite theme with artists because Orpheus came to symbolize the immortality of the artist by virtue of his great skill. Canova's *Eurydice* has been described as owing a debt to the sentimentality of

the Baroque sculpture of Giovanni Bernini; and his *Orpheus* was admired for its "perfection of finish," a key feature of the intellectual style of neoclassical sculptors. However, Canova's emotive interpretation can also be seen as presaging the Romanticism of the subject by many nineteenth-century artists such as Frederic, Lord Leighton; Gustave Moreau; and Anslem Feuerbach, whose representations of the story also place emphasis on the tragedy of lost love through human weakness.

Though his most famous works were neoclassical in treatment and form, they often inspired truly Romantic reactions, and prompted many of his contemporaries, such as Lord Byron, to regard him as the one true heir to Italy's lost splendor. Stendhal stated that Canova was one of the greatest men he had ever met, and the German lyrical poet, Heinrich Heine, said that he had once dreamt that he had made love to Canova's *Venus Italica*. (1811). John Keats's *Ode to Pysche* was inspired by Canova's representation of young love requited, *Cupid and Pysche* (1787–93). The treatment of this work fully celebrates the neoclassical ideal of calm restraint. However, in choosing to depict the moment when the dying Pysche is about to be brought back to life by a kiss from her true love Cupid, the sculpture not only expresses but has also aroused great passion. The piece was originally commissioned by a British patron, John Campbell, in 1787, who had to leave it behind when he was forced to withdraw from Italy due to the French Revolutionary wars. It was seized by Napoleon's general, Joachim Murat, who took the statue to France; there it was later seen by the writer Gustave Flaubert, who declared that he had been unable to resist the temptation to kiss Pysche's armpit.

Canova's most famous patron was Napoleon Bonaparte, the soldier from Corsica who had, like the sculptor, risen to greatness and glory. Napoleon's considerable personal charisma not only roused his followers into battle but also inspired many poets, writers, and artists who helped to create his

Romantic cult status despite the reality of his physical limitations. Canova's colossal statue of the naked emperor, *Napoleon as Mars* (1803–6), towers over mere mortals as if in illustration of Jacques-Louis David's comment that he himself was greatly overwhelmed by the personality of Napoleon, "a man to whom altars would have been raised in ancient times." Canova's personification of Napoleon as a mythological figure reflects the neoclassical ideal of choosing a subject which would represent nobility, superiority, and greatness, but Canova's joyous celebration of this rags-to-riches story (which in turn reflected his own) is also profoundly Romantic.

Canova's decision to construct an enormous temple in his birthplace, the small village of Possagno, may have been taken in the spirit of this huge personal pride. It was completed by his heirs, and reiterates the notion that Canova was seen as not only an artistic genius, but was also honored in his own lifetime and beyond, as a symbol of Italian unity. When he died, his body was entombed in the temple according to his wishes, but his heart was buried in the church of Santa Maria Gloriosa, Venice. A pyramidal mausoleum was erected there by his pupils following a design he himself had made for an earlier monument (*Maria Christina of Austria*, 1799–1805). This funerary monument is neoclassical in the elegance of its treatment and the imposing nature of its form, but the inclusion of a procession of mourning figures lends a resonant and emotional emphasis reflecting the deep grief experienced by many of Canova's countrymen and his admirers from all over Europe. In a letter home, an English friend of the sculptor wrote about the effect the news of his death had on everyone in Rome: "The poor lament him as their liberal benefactor; the artists, universally, as their kindest patron and protector, the Roman public in general as the honour of their age and country; and all enlightened minds who knew him well, as one of the purest spirits that ever adorned human nature." This outpouring of human emotion, reflected in the design of Canova's mausoleum, is an aspect of Romanticism, as is the intense patriotism his work engendered at a time when many sought evidence of Italy's cultural greatness and identity.

CHERRY SANDOVER

See also **Alfieri, Vittorio; Art; Art and Classical Antiquity; Artist, Changing Conceptions of the; Bonaparte, Napoleon; Byron, George Noel Gordon, Lord; David, Jacques-Louis; Genius; Heine, Heinrich; Keats, John; Love, Romantic; Mythology, Classical; Stendhal**

Biography

Born November 1, 1757 in Possagno, Italy. Father was a stonecutter who died when Canova was four; mother remarried, 1762, Canova put in the care of his paternal grandfather, Pasino, a stonemason and owner of a quarry. Apprenticed to the Bernando family of sculptors, c. 1767. Moved to Venice to work in Bernando workshop in Santa Martina, 1768; copied from statues and casts from the Antique in the private gallery of Filippo Farsetti; attended life-drawing classes at the Venetian Academy. Two statues commissioned by Venetian senator Giovanni Falier, *Orpheus* and *Eurydice*, 1773–76. Opened his own studio in Calle de Traghetto, at San Maurizio, Venice, 1778. Received one hundred gold zecchini for his first sculpture in marble, *Daedalus and Icarus*, 1779. Left for study trips to Rome and other Italian cities. Settled in Rome, 1780; began to learn English and French; met the Scottish painter (also noted archeologist and dealer in classical antiquities) Gavin Hamilton, among other members of rising neoclassical movement. Hamilton had profound influence on Canova. Success of his sculpture *Theseus and the Minotaur* made him a celebrity in Rome, 1783. First biography published in Venice, *Le sculpture e le pittore di Antonio Canova* by Faustino Tadini, 1795. With fall of Venetian Republic following the French invasion, Canova returned to Possagno, 1797. Made a Knight of the Golden Spur by Pope Pius VII, 1801. Took up post of inspector general of antiquities and fine art of the papal state, previously held by Raphael. 1802: visit to Paris to model a bust of the first consul, Napoleon Bonaparte, that same year. Funeral monument to Maria Christina completed, 1805; considered to be Canova's most original sepulchre. Elected president of the Accademia di San Luca in Rome, 1810; elected perpetual president of the Accademia, an unprecedented honor, 1814. Nominated papal delegate to sue for and supervise the return of art looted by Napoleon and his generals, 1815. Invited in November 1815 to London to study the Parthenon marbles brought from Greece by Lord Elgin. Elevated to the peerage by Pope Pius VII as Marchese d'Ischia, 1816. Died on October 13, 1822 in Venice, of exhaustion due to overwork.

Selected Works

Orpheus. 1775–76. Vicentine stone, 203 cm × 85 cm. Museo Correr, Venice.
Eurydice. 1775. Vicentine stone, 203 cm × 54 cm. Museo Correr, Venice.
Daedelus and Icarus. 1777–79. Marble, 220 cm × 95 cm. Museo Correr, Venice.
Theseus and the Minotaur. 1781–83. Marble, 14.5 cm × 158.7 cm. Victoria and Albert Museum, London.
Monument to Pope Clement XIV. 1783–87. Marble. SS Apostoli, Rome.
Cupid and Pysche. 1787–93. Marble, 155 cm × 168 cm. Musee du Louvre, Paris.
Monument to the Archduchess Maria Christina of Austria. 1799–1805. Marble, 574 cm high. Augustiner-Kirche, Vienna.
Napoleon as Mars. 1803–06. Marble, 340 cm high. Apsley House, London.
Paulina Borghese as Venus Victrix. 1804–08. Marble, 1,200 cm. Galleria Borghese, Rome.
Monument to Vittorio Alfieri. 1806–10. Marble, 480 cm × 300 cm. Santa Croce, Florence.
The Three Graces. 1815–17. Marble, 173 cm × 97.2 cm. National Gallery of Scotland, Edinburgh.
Cenotaph to the House of Stewart. 1817–19. Marble. St. Peter's, Rome.

Bibliography

Clifford, Timothy. "Canova in Context: The Sculptor, his Reputation, his British Patrons and his Visit to England." In *The Three Graces*. Edited by Hugh Honour and Aidon Weston-Lewis. Edinburgh: Trustees of the National Galleries of Scotland, 1995.
Honour, Hugh. *Neo-Classicism*. Harmondsworth: Penguin, 1991.

Irwin, David. *Neoclassicism*. London: Phaidon, 1997.

Romanelli, Giandomenico. "Antonio Canova." In *The Glory of Venice: Art in the Eighteenth Century*. Edited by Jane Martineau and Andrew Robison. New Haven, Conn.: Yale University Press, 1994.

Vaughan, William. *Romantic Art*. London: Thames and Hudson, 1978.

Whinney, Margaret. *Sculpture in Britain 1530–1830*. Revised by John Physick. Harmondsworth: Penguin, 1988.

CANTI 1845

Collection of poetry by Giacomo Leopardi

The rally cry of the Italian patriots in 1848, "In chiesa con Manzoni; col Leopardi alla guerra" ("To church with Manzoni; to war with Leopardi") would have come as some surprise to the author of *Canti* (Songs), springing as it does from a very partial reading of his poetry. Patriotic sentiments are in evidence, particularly in the first three odes, which are constructed on a contrast between the former glory and contemporary wretchedness of Italy, but the patriotic vein is only one of several that appear, and is certainly not the dominant tone.

The collection contains some forty poems written between 1817 and 1837, arranged by Leopardi more thematically than chronologically. The first nine poems are civic and patriotic odes written between 1818 and 1822 whose titles give little indication of the themes they contain, such as the ode written on the occasion of his sister's wedding, which does not mention any of the usual topics associated with matrimony. A more personal note is sounded in two poems that deal with the theme of suicide: "Bruto minore" ("The Younger Brutus," 1821), which Leopardi claimed expressed his own attitude toward destiny; and "Ultimo canto di Saffo" ("Sappho's Last Song). In both poems, there is a strong identification with a noble but tragic figure who succumbs to fate without loss of moral dignity. The tone and expression of the odes bear witness to Leopardi's reading of Petrarch and Ugo Foscolo, but they also contain hints of the themes that would dominate his later poetry, which was characterized by the creation of the philosophical lyric, a new departure in Italian poetry.

During the same period that Leopardi was writing the odes, he also produced poems he called *idilli* (idylls), although they are quite different from the pastoral idylls of classical poetry in that depiction of the physical world in Leopardi always leads to meditation. One of his most famous poems, "L'infinito" (1819) expresses a feeling that is at the heart of Romanticism, as Leopardi moves in the course of fifteen lines from the representation of confined space and restricted vision to the imaginative evocation of infinity and eternity.

Contrast is at the heart of Leopardi's poetry, most markedly between past and present, whether that is explored on the level of social and civic mores as in the odes, or on a more personal level in the idylls. The longing for the glory of ancient Greece and Rome, a legacy of Leopardi's classical education and encyclopedic reading, becomes transmuted to nostalgia for the innocence of childhood and the illusions that were possible then. But Leopardi is no advocate of frivolous escapism, as he repeatedly confronts us with the misery of the human condition and the emptiness of life in terms that anticipate the existentialist philosophers of the next century.

A central concept in Leopardi's poetry is the sharp distinction between what Leopardi calls illusions of the imagination and of the intellect. The arrogance of man in general and his contemporaries' facile optimism, in technological advances in particular, typify illusions of the intellect, while the illusions of the imagination are notions such as love, virtue, and glory that imbue life with meaning and are to be cherished without losing sight of the fact that they are illusions.

The theme of love is featured in many of the poems, but it is usually unrequited and activated by the absence, rather than the presence, of the beloved. The situations evoked are built around reminiscence and imagination, with more emphasis on the emotions produced by the experience of love than descriptions of the love object, which remains generic and indistinct, in keeping with Leopardi's conviction that the essence of lyric poetry lies in the vague and the indefinite. The poems known as the *Aspasia Cycle*, written between 1831 and 1835, include the most impassioned celebration of the effects of love, in "Il pensiero dominante," and the moment of greatest disillusionment, in "Aspasia."

This duality of perspective, which has an element of the paradoxical, runs through *Canti*: some of the poems written in 1829 include "Le ricordanze" ("Memories"), which contains a strident invective against his birthplace, Recanati; while "La quiete dopo la tempesta" ("Quiet after the Storm") and "Il sabato del villaggio" ("Saturday Evening in the Village") offer finely observed and delicately evoked images of provincial life in his home town. In a similar vein, the various depictions of the consoling beauties of nature that feature in many of the poems end with "La ginestra, o il fiore del deserto" ("The Broom, or the Flower of the Desert"), the final poem set on the slopes of Vesuvius, in which the destructive aspect of nature is stressed, and the poet comes to the conclusion that nature is "madre di parto e di voler matrigna" ("our mother by birth and stepmother in affection"). However, Leopardi does not end on this negative note, but goes on to make a plea for solidarity, for the formation of a "social catena" (social chain) in acknowledgment of the fragility of human life and the need for mutual assistance.

Critical evaluation of Leopardi's poetry has not always been positive; in fact, all too often his message has been dismissed as gloomy and pessimistic. However, Francesco De Sanctis, one of the first critics to write about him, argued that the ultimate effect of Leopardi's poetry was to reconcile us to life and human nature with all its shortcomings. More recently, an Italian Nobel laureate of the twentieth century, Eugenio Montale, made a fitting tribute to the originality of Leopardi's poetic achievement in his remark that after Leopardi, it was almost impossible to write poetry in Italy. When Matthew Arnold measured Leopardi against his contemporaries, the English Romantic poets, he found that:

> Leopardi has the very qualities which we have found lacking in Byron; he has the sense for form and style, the passion for just expression, the sure and firm touch of the true artist . . . Leopardi is at many points the poetic superior of Wordsworth too. He has a far wider culture than Wordsworth, more mental lucidity, more freedom from illusions.

LYNNE PRESS

Text

Canti. First edition, 1831. Edited by A. Ranieri. 1845.
Translated as *The Poems of Giacomo Leopardi*, with introduction and notes, by Geoffrey L. Bickersteth. Cambridge: Cambridge University Press, 1923.

Bibliography

Binni, Walter. *La protesta di Leopardi.* Florence: Sansoni, 1973.
Bosco, Umberto. *Titanismo e pietê in Giacomo Leopardi.* Florence: Le Monnier, 1957.
Perella, Nicholas J. *Night and the Sublime in Giacomo Leopardi.* Berkeley and Los Angeles: University of California Press, 1970.
Press, Lynne, and Pamela Williams. *Women and Feminine Images in Giacomo Leopardi, 1798–1837. Bicentenary Essays.* Lewiston, England: Edwin Mellen Press, 1999.
Whitfield, John H. *Giacomo Leopardi.* Oxford: Blackwell, 1954.

LOS CAPRICHOS (THE CAPRICES) 1799

Etchings with aquatint by Francisco Jose' de Goya y Lucientes

Announced with a now famous advertisement in the *Diario de Madrid*, the eighty images of Francisco Goya's *Caprichos* are generally considered one of the key turning points of his art. A series of disparate visions of social and supernatural vice, they are at once innovative and rooted in convention. The etchings have their sources in folklore, especially witchcraft (then a subject of widespread fascination in educated Spanish circles), established satirical imagery, allusions to contemporary literature and slang, the tradition of the caprice as seen in Jacques Callot and Giovanni Battista Tiepolo, Horace's reference to monstrosities at the beginning of his *Ars poetica*, and long-standing representations of melancholy. The notion of a dreaming artist producing monstrous satires echoes the seventeenth-century satirist Francisco Gómez Quevedo y Villegas, and more still the eighteenth-century writer Torres Villaroel, whose *Visiones y visitas* (*Visions and Visits*, 1727–28) presents a fragmented panorama of a vice-ridden real-life Madrid transformed into fascinating grotesques.

The political intention of the work is a matter of debate: the assumption that the *Caprichos* reveal outright opposition to the government needs to be weighed against the latter's policies aimed at raising revenue and targeted against sectors of the aristocracy and the church, as well as royal enthusiasm for the painter. Janis Tomlinson has argued that the Inquisition may not have investigated Goya at this stage, and that the reason for the withdrawal of the prints from sale was lack of commercial success, followed by a favorable deal in 1803 under which the king purchased the plates.

Los caprichos were at the time the most striking product of Goya's interest in producing, alongside commissions, works that reflected his private interests. They dovetail with his attacks on neoclassical rules in his address to the Royal Academy of San Fernando in 1792, an attack fueled by wider trends in Spain. Alongside such daring creations as José de Cadalso y Vázquez's dialogue *Noches lúgubres* (*Lugubrious Nights*, 1770s) or Meléndez Valdés's distressed poem "A Jovino [Jovellanos], el melancólico" ("To Jovino, the Melancholic," 1794), the country's intellectuals witnessed an influx of ideas about the sublime, including José Luis Munárriz's influential version of Hugh Blair's *Lessons* (1798–1801).

Beginning (as had works by William Hogarth) with a portrait of the artist, the series appears to hinge around the most celebrated print, number 43, *El sueño de la razón produce monstruos* (*The Dream of Reason Produces Monsters*), and to terminate with

Francisco Jose' de Goya y Lucientes, *The Sleep of Reason Produces Monsters*, from the *Los caprichos* series. Reprinted courtesy of AKG.

something reminiscent of an ending with perhaps waking figures in print 80. There is not, however, a neat division before and after print 43, for on both sides the everyday and supernatural worlds blend together, though the latter perhaps predominates in the second part of the series. Although there is the sketchy outline of an overall pattern to the collection, what strikes one most is a relentless, hellish lack of progression, and a refusal of cogent development, its place taken by nightmarish fragments.

If Goya's sidelong glance initiates the procession of dark visions, it is the faceless artist of print 43, lying asleep in a melancholic posture on his desk, who emblemizes the transmutation of reality through the mind, a crowd of owls mutating into bats sweeping down to or shooting out of him, a lynx or gray cat watching alert in the night. Wisdom and dark impulses merge accordingly (owls at once symbolizing insight and ill omens), and we are left to wonder whether monsters arise when reason nods, or whether the monsters are the product of reason's own dreams; and, if the latter, whether this reveals a deeper truth or instead a distortion of true knowledge. That the artist has produced admirable depictions of monsters suggests a merit in such visions that sits uneasily with satirical condemnation of irrationality. In these intellectual concerns, Goya develops much more widely held preoccupations about the sublime. He questions the response of his audience by inserting grotesque onlookers in many images, disturbingly mirroring the viewer. The result stands in stark contrast to the parallel response to the occult in Tiepolo's *Scherzi di Fantasia* (*Scenes of Fantasy*, 1743–56); we are sunk in the murkier depths of experience.

Goya's central technical achievement was his use of aquatint to produce a visual world in which shapes loom out from mental darkness. In keeping with some of his European contemporaries' visionary departures from perspective, Goya's nightmares flout the natural laws of the universe in form as much as content, as Fred Licht has emphasized. Now, inside and outside are indistinguishable; now, outsized bodies defy physical limitations, and even merge; now, light falls expressively but not realistically; now, gravity does not apply; now, a corpse hangs inexplicably above a wall, the noose's rope not clearly joined to anything. The commentary running beneath the images frequently offers neither satirical nor epigrammatic elucidation; words and voices are left hauntingly and suggestively juxtaposed to the dream, their precise meaning often unclear. Loose, myriad associations of the mind are all that joins the images to each other, in patterns of unrelenting violence. Sex, knowledge, authority, and abuse headily and unnervingly fuse together. An owl in print 65 is a groin; a cat (slang for an officer of the law) has its head in the place of a monster's genitalia in print 48. It is not just social behavior that Goya portrays but the creatures of the human imagination: goblins, witches, winged beasts.

It ends with a cry of "Ya es hora" ("It is time"). But time for what?

ANDREW GINGER

Work

Los caprichos. Etchings with aquatint. 1799. Prado, Madrid.

Bibliography

Glendinning, Nigel. *Goya and His Critics.* New Haven, Conn.: Yale University Press, 1997.

Helman, Edith Fishtine. *Trasmundo de Goya.* Madrid: Revista de Occidente, 1963.

Ilie, Paul. *The Age of Minerva.* 2 vols. Philadelphia: University of Pennsylvania Press, 1995.

Licht, Fred. *Goya: The Origins of the Modern Temper in Art.* London: J. Murray, 1980.

Nordstrum, Folke. *Goya, Saturn, and Melancholy.* Stockholm: Almqvist and Wicksell, 1962.

Paulson, Ronald. *Representations of Revolution.* New Haven, Conn.: Yale University Press, 1983.

Tomlinson, Janis. *Francisco Goya y Lucientes.* London: Phaidon, 1994 (reprinted 1999), pp. 123–45.

Wolf, Reva. *Goya and the Satirical Print in England and the Continent 1730 to 1850.* Boston: D. R. Godine, 1991.

CARICATURE

The history and definition of caricature in Western art are intimately connected to the scientific, political, legal, and social developments of the eighteenth and nineteenth centuries. Caricature began in Italy as an exaggerated and thus humorous representation of the facial features of an individual, but soon developed into the depiction of whole scenes, often commenting upon a social or political issue. This latter form of caricature became an effective political tool in England and France in the late eighteenth and early nineteenth centuries. With the development of lithography at the end of the eighteenth century and the inception of illustrated periodicals such as *Le Charivari* and *Punch*, caricature reached a wider audience and played a more active role in shaping public opinion. This mass production, in addition to its emotional appeal and concern with contemporary events, made caricature a unique, entertaining, and effective means of communication.

The word *caricature* derives from the Italian *caricare*, meaning "to load," and first becomes connected to the exaggerated, or loaded, portraits of Annibale Carracci, who is often credited with originating the genre, in the sixteenth century. Artists such as Carracci, Il Guercino, and Giovanni Battista Tiepolo created *caricatura* to be circulated privately among aristocratic circles as a sideline to their main careers as painters. Later, in the first half of the eighteenth century, Pierleone Ghezzi would caricature gentlemen on the "grand tour," expanding the subject of caricature from specific individuals to general social types. Ghezzi, in conjunction with London publisher Arthur Pond, produced a collection of caricatures which then introduced the genre to an English public.

The concept of caricature gained widespread attention in Europe in the eighteenth century. It drew heavily upon another popular idea, that of physiognomy. Physiognomy, a supposedly scientific enterprise, drew correlations between facial features and human character. Upon understanding certain physiognomic principles, it was supposed, a person could literally read another person's face as a clue to his or her personality and morals. Though such famed physiognomists as Johann Kaspar Lavater stressed the complexities of the field, it soon entered popular culture in a simplified form. Artists then could draw upon the public's knowledge of physiognomy and use it as a code to communicate information about an individual through appearance.

In eighteenth-century England, caricature was most often associated with William Hogarth. Hogarth, in such series as *The Rake's Progress* (1733–34) and *Marriage à la Mode* (1743), explored and satirized contemporary English mores. In the first plate of *A Harlot's Progress* (1732), Hogarth foreshadows the decline of Moll Hackabout from naive country lass to mortally ill prostitute through the use of symbolism; the dead goose, crumbling wall of the tavern, and coffin-like shape of the trunk with Moll's initials indicate the downfall that awaits her if she succumbs to the attentions of the pockmarked procuress. However, Hogarth took great pains to differentiate between *caricatura*, the humorous Italian portraits, and his own "characters," which he believed were both realistic and moral.

The decades surrounding the turn of the nineteenth century have become known as the "golden age" of English caricature, as artists repeatedly addressed both social and political issues in thousands of prints. James Gillray, known for creating the standard image of Napoleon Bonaparte, or "Little Boney," produced caricatures of many of the leaders of the period, including George III and William Pitt. One of his most famous caricatures, *The Plumb-Pudding in Danger* (1805), depicts Pitt and Napoleon carving up the world with sword and fork, and knife and trident, respectively. Introducing another easily recognizable, though fictional, character, Dr. Syntax, Thomas Rowlandson and the poet William Combe explored social and often highly sexual themes in their caricatures in addition to standard political issues. These prints, generally published as single broadsheets and exhibited in print shops, reached an ever-expanding audience that became more sophisticated in its taste for caricature. In Spain, Francisco José de Goya y Lucientes produced collections of etchings which utilized caricature to comment upon the social and political atmosphere at the turn of the nineteenth century. In the series *Los caprichos* (1799), Goya explores the superstitions and follies of Spanish culture in the age of Enlightenment. However, his dark imagery belies the humor in such plates as "The Bogeyman is Coming," which makes manifest the terrifying creature a mother has used to scare a child. Similarly, *The Disasters of War* series (c. 1808–14) contains grim visualizations of the Napoleonic occupation of Spain and the devastation wrought by the ensuing conflict. Thus, Goya utilizes aspects of caricature—the exaggeration of human faces and contemporary social commentary—with little of the humor associated with it in other incarnations.

With the advent of lithography came the appearance of the illustrated newspaper, which reached an even larger audience than broadsheets. In France, Charles Philipon published such illustrated newspapers as *La Caricature* and *Le Charivari*. However, artists in France did not enjoy the political freedom of their English counterparts because of more restrictive press laws. Philipon and the artists who worked for him, including Honoré Daumier, Jean-Ignace-Isidore Gérard (Grandville), and Paul Gavarni, all suffered fines or imprisonment for their work in the newspapers during the reign of Louis Philippe. Most famous of these libelous images is Philipon's depiction of the king, who had forbidden the use in the press of his much-caricatured likeness, as a pear, with its double meaning of "fathead" and its resemblance to testicles.

James Gillray, *The Plumb-Pudding in Danger*. Reprinted countesy of AKG.

Daumier is perhaps the most notable of French caricaturists. He worked for Philipon throughout his career, creating approximately four thousand lithographs for different illustrated newspapers. Instead of depicting the king as a pear, Daumier drew Louis Philippe as François Rabelais's monster Gargantua, earning him six months in jail in 1832. When not addressing such political themes, Daumier often worked in series, introducing such characters as Robert Macaire and Ratapoil and focusing on such topics as lawyers and ancient history.

Following in the footsteps of France's *Le Charivari*, Henry Mayhew and others began to publish *Punch, or the London Charivari* in 1841. The caricatures, however, often lacked the biting political satire of the Golden Age of English caricature and instead addressed the social issues and later merely the social life of the paper's middle-class readership. The word *cartoon* took on its present meaning as a humorous picture within the pages of *Punch* when John Leech, in contrasting the lack of governmental provisions for the poor with the contemporary exhibition of cartoons, or drawings, for the decorations of the newly rebuilt Houses of Parliament, drew "Substance and Shadow: Cartoon No. 1" (1843). While in the early years many of its cartoons addressed political subjects, the cartoons in *Punch* in the second half of the nineteenth century addressed such topics as fashion and taste. But though the subject of the cartoons had changed, they still informed and entertained the public through the use of physiognomic details and humor.

While both German and American versions of *Punch* eventually existed, the development of illustrated periodicals and caricature in those countries lagged behind that of England and France. By 1850, however, audiences throughout Europe and the United States were accustomed to the use of caricature as a means for communicating views on contemporary events, issues, and customs through exaggeration and humor.

JAMIE W. JOHNSON

Bibliography

Cowling, Mary. *The Artist as Anthropologist: The Representation of Type and Character in Victorian Art*. Cambridge: Cambridge University Press, 1989.

Feaver, William, and Ann Gould. *Masters of Caricature*. New York: Knopf, 1981.

George, M. Dorothy. *Social Change and Graphic Satire from Hogarth to Cruikshank*, London: Viking, 1967.

Gombrich, E. H., and E. Kris. *Caricature*. Harmondsworth, England: Penguin, 1940.

Shikes, Ralph, and Steven Heller. *The Art of Satire*. New York: Pratt Graphics Center and Horizon Press, 1984.

Wechsler, Judith. *A Human Comedy: Physiognomy and Caricature in Nineteenth Century Paris*. Chicago: University of Chicago Press, 1982.

CARLYLE, THOMAS 1795–1881

Scottish essayist and historian

Thomas Carlyle is perhaps the best-known "Victorian sage," one of that strange, unofficial grouping of writers and thinkers whose essays, pamphlets, and books had such direct impact upon thought and culture in the later nineteenth century. We might bracket him with Matthew Arnold, John Ruskin, and John Stuart Mill in this capacity, except that of all of these Carlyle was the most Romantic, the one whose thought was most comprehensively informed, despite its occasional severity, with a passionate, imaginative, and stylistic Romanticism, especially as Duncan Wu has defined that problematic term as "an unquenchable aspiration for universal betterment, the reclaiming of paradise." Indeed, it is because of this that Carlyle was able to write, in *Sartor Resartus* (1833–34), the book that is often cited as marking the boundary between Romantic and Victorian literature, much in the way that pre-Romanticism and Romanticism are sometimes said to be marked off by William Wordsworth's preface to *Lyrical Ballads* (1800).

Carlyle was born into a serious, devout, and dutiful Presbyterian family in Dumfriesshire; he was so poor that, winning a scholarship to Edinburgh University in 1809, he had to walk to the city. After working as a teacher, he taught himself German in order first to study, and then to earn money translating, the works of Johann Wolfgang von Goethe, Johann Christoph Friedrich von Schiller, and the German philosophers. He wrote a life of Schiller for *The London Magazine* (1823–24), and translated Goethe's *Wilhelm Meisters Lehrjahre* (*Wilhelm Meister's Apprenticeship*, 1824) and *Wilhelm Meister's Travels* (1827), as well as compiling a four-volume anthology of German writing, *German Romance* (1827). He, together with Samuel Taylor Coleridge, was the chief channel by which German Romantic thought and writing found its way into mainstream British culture during the nineteenth century.

Sartor Resartus first appeared in installments in *Fraser's Magazine*, and was greeted by select admiration and more widespread bafflement and condemnation; one old subscriber to the journal wrote to the editor threatening to cancel his subscription if there was "any more of that damned stuff." This was a work of fictionalized autobiography and unconventional philosophy, written in a jarring and peculiar style, and presented as the biography of a fictional German writer of a history of clothes. The title, Latin for "the tailor retailored" (retailored in the sense of having the rents in his clothes patched over) refers to a spiritual allegory, in which clothes are the trappings and institutions of the world covering the naked spirit beneath. The tailor, in other words, is "man" in his social and political role, and this book "retailors" him in the sense of radically critiquing contemporary life. For all its idiosyncrasies, *Sartor Resartus* is a book that distils a Romantic fascination with the inner truth of the imaginative life as a validation for being in the world, in order to blend it with the tenets of duty and labor that are seen as crucially Victorian. A central series of chapters sees Carlyle moving from doubt to indifference to what he calls "The Everlasting Yea," where Carlyle, quoting Goethe, realizes that "doubt of any kind cannot be removed except by an action." Carlyle adjures his readers to "do the duty which lies nearest thee." And more important even than duty is work: "be no longer a Chaos, but a World, or even Worldkin. Produce! Produce! Were it but the pitifullest, infinitesimal fraction of a Product, produce it, in God's name!" Carlyle's book vigorously advocates the supersession of the old Greek philosophical precept "know thyself" with the Carlylean, Victorian one: "know what thou canst work-at."

Carlyle's reputation as a historian was established by his enormous *A History of the French Revolution* (1837), which configured the events in France as epic prose poetry. As an attack on "sham" society, and an extended demonstration that any culture that comes to be governed by blind custom, hypocrisy, falsehood, and indifference will necessarily fail bloodily, this is less history as we understand the term and more a moral text for the time. Something similar is true of *Past and Present* (1843), which contrasts the organic harmony of life in England in the Middle Ages, in the representative community of the Abbey at Bury St. Edmunds, with the alienation of life in the Industrial Revolution, where the "cash-nexus" had become the sole medium between human beings. A famous biographical incident associated with the composition of *The French Revolution* encapsulates the complex of Byronic Romanticism and dutiful Victorian work-ethic that best describes Carlyle. He had completed the first volume of this work after much labor, and had lent the manuscript to John Stuart Mill, whose servant inadvertently burnt it. After agonizing for a night, Carlyle resolved to write it all out again: "'*shall* be written again,' my fixed word and resolution to [my wife]. Which proved to be such a task as I never tried before or since." But while shouldering this duty with forebearance, and ultimately with success, Carlyle's sense of himself was melodramatically Romantic. He once wrote, in his *Reminiscences*,

> I was very diligent, very desperate . . . always heavy-laden grim of mood; sometimes with a feeling . . . of Satan's stepping the burning marl . . . Generally my feeling was, 'I will finish this Book, throw it at your [the public's] feet; buy a rifle and spade and withdraw to the Transatlantic Wildernesses—far from *human* beggaries and basenesses!'

This sort of grouchy misanthropy, present to one degree or another throughout Carlyle's career, becomes increasingly pronounced. A late conversation with Robert Southey, a friend, illustrates the apocalyptic pessimism characteristic of several of the Romantic figures who survived into the Victorian age. In *Reminiscences*, he wrote,

> We sat on the sofa together, our talk . . . the usual one, steady approach of democracy, with revolution (probably *explosive*) and a *finis* incomputable to man,—steady decay of all morality, political, social, individual . . . [until] noble England would have to collapse in shapeless ruin, whether forever or not none of us could know. Our perfect consent on these matters gave an animation to the Dialogue, which I remember as copious and pleasant. Southey's last word was in answer to some tirade of mine about universal Mammon-worship . . . to which he answered, not with levity, yet with a cheerful tone in his seriousness, 'It will not come, it cannot come to good!'

The gloomy joy at this imagined prospect is immensely expressive of Carlyle's view of the contemporary scene. His later life sees a calcification of political opinion into a rigid, and to modern sensibilities rather repellent, antidemocratic dogma, where increasing the franchise is intemperately attacked (*Shooting Niagara—and After?*, 1867), and great leaders of—to be anachronistic—quasi-fascist mold are valorized (*Oliver Cromwell*, 1845; *Frederick the Great*, 1858–65). The racism of his "Occasional Discourse on the Nigger Question" (1849) is especially unpalatable. After his wife's death in 1866 he wrote little, and lived a largely reclusive life until his own death in 1881.

ADAM ROBERTS

See also **Sartor Resartus**

Biography

Born a peasant in Ecclefechan, South Scotland, 1795. Entered the University of Edinburgh, 1809. Teacher at village school in Ecclefechan, 1814. Appointed tutor at larger school in Kirkcaldy, 1816. Returned to Edinburgh to become literary journalist, 1819. Existential crisis, 1822. First visit to London, 1823. Married Jane Baillie Welsh, 1827. Resident at remote farmhouse in Craigenputtock, 1827–33. Moved full-time to London, to earn a living writing and lecturing, 1833. *Sartor Resartus*, 1833–34. *French Revolution*, 1837. *Past and Present*, 1843. Death of Jane Welsh Carlyle, 1866. Death of Thomas Carlyle, 1881.

Selected Writings

Collected Works. Centenary ed. 30 vols. 1897.
The Collected Letters of Thomas and Jane Welsh Carlyle. Edited by C. R. Sanders, K. J. Fielding, and C. de L Ryals. Durham, N.C.: Duke University Press, 1970–present.
Sartor Resartus. Edited by Kerry McSweeney and Peter Sabor. Oxford: Oxford University Press, 1987.
Reminiscences. Edited by K. J. Fielding and Ian Campbell. Oxford: Oxford University Press, 1997.

Bibliography

Bloom, Harold, ed. *Thomas Carlyle: Modern Critical Views*. New York: Chelsea House, 1986.
Clubbe, John, ed. *Carlyle and his Contemporaries*. Durham, N.C.: Duke University Press, 1976.
Heffer, Simon. *Moral Desperado: A Life of Thomas Carlyle*. London: Weidenfeld and Nicolson, 1995.
Kaplan, Fred. *Thomas Carlyle: a Biography*. Cambridge: Cambridge University Press, 1993.
Moore, Carlisle. "Thomas Carlyle." In *The English Romantic Poets and Essayists*. Edited by C. W. and L. H. Houtchens. New York: New York University Press, 1966.
Wu, Duncan. *Romanticism: an Anthology*. 2d ed. Oxford: Blackwell, 1998.

CARSTENS, ASMUS JACOB 1754–1798

Danish-German artist

Throughout his career, Asmus Jacob Carstens asserted the independence of the creative genius and his freedom to produce art without regard to social applicability or relevance. His republican sentiments and strict antiacademism led to his being regarded as a rebel throughout his career. In relation to his break with the Berlin Academy of Fine Arts in 1796, he drew up a letter to his superiors, which contains this manifesto of the independent artist:

> I must inform your Excellency that I do not belong to the Academy of Berlin, but to the whole of mankind; and I have never fostered the thought, nor have I ever pledged, that in return for a certain allowance, which for some years I was granted towards the education of my talent, I would thus for the rest of my life enter into serfdom for an academy.

As the central figure in a group of German and Danish artists in 1790s Rome, Carstens greatly influenced German Romanticists and the young Danish sculptor Bertel Thorvaldsen, who arrived in Rome in March 1797. The generation following Carstens considered him an innovator, nothing short of the restorer of German art, along with Joseph Anton Koch.

Carstens was born in Schleswig (in present-day Germany). Being a Danish citizen, he went to Copenhagen in 1776 to study at the Royal Academy of Fine Arts. There he attended lectures in anatomy and practiced drawing from antique sculptures at the Royal Collection of Casts. Carstens's artistic career was strongly influenced by his meeting with Nicolai Abraham Abildgaard, the scholar, history painter, and professor at the academy. Carstens maintained, as did Abildgaard, the philosophical and poetic dimensions of pictorial art, with his entire oeuvre reflecting an urge to convert philosophical concepts into pictorial allegories. In his chosen circle of themes as well as his interpretation of figures, Carstens took inspiration from Abildgaard, and in light of this great example, Carstens eagerly embraced subjects from classical antiquity as well as Norse mythology and Ossian. Inspired by Johann Gottfried Herder's *Älteste Urkunde des Menschengeschlechts* (*Oldest Records of the Human Race*, 1774–

76) he worked on themes such as sleep, death, and the polarity between light and darkness, while aiming toward a renewal in the use of mythology in art.

After having been expelled from the academy in Copenhagen, Carstens spent some years in Lübeck, earning a living as a portraitist. In 1788 he moved to Berlin, where in 1790 he was appointed professor at the Berlin Academy of Fine Arts, though he undertook the duties of this office for no more than two years. An academy scholarship enabled him to travel to Italy and he arrived in Rome in 1792, where he remained until his untimely death in 1798. During these six years, he became the central figure in a group of German artists including Koch, Johann Christian Reinhart, and Eberhard Wächter. During April and May 1795, Carstens held an exhibition in the studio previously occupied by Pompeo Girolamo Batoni. The exhibition catalog, which contains the artist's own descriptions and information on the literary backgrounds of the works, provides an important source for our understanding of his world of ideas. Through an extensive paper written by Carstens's friend, the art critic Carl Ludwig Fernow, "Über eigene neue Kunstwerke des Hrn Prof. Carstens (Der Neue Teutsche Merkur)" ("Concerning Some New Works by Prof Carstens," 1795), the German public was offered its first-ever insight into Carstens's art. This gave further rise to a debate in which both Johann Wolfgang von Goethe and Johann Christoph Friedrich von Schiller took part. With his prorevolutionary, antiacademic points of view and his notion of the role of the artist, Carstens left a crucial mark on the dawning era of Romanticism. At the time of his death he had achieved the status of a cult figure, and his biography was written almost immediately afterward by Fernow.

In its entirety, Carstens's oeuvre is not particularly extensive, consisting mainly of work on paper in either tempera, watercolor, pencil, and black or red chalk. His more mature style is influenced by his studies of Michelangelo Buonarotti, Raphael, and Giulio Romano. Carstens shared the enthusiasm of the day for lines and shadowless contour drawing, which had created a sensation when first used by John Flaxman in the early 1790s. The drawing or cartoon, which had so far been used merely as an artistic aid, was, according to Carstens, a valid work of art inasmuch as the drawing is sufficient for the expression of an idea. Color was considered superfluous, working only to conceal the purest form. In his severe, linear style, Carstens depicted heroic themes from both the ancient Greco-Roman and Norse mythology. Among his principal works are the illustrations for *The Argonautic Expedition* (1797); after his death, this was etched and published by Carstens's friend, Koch, in 1799. In a series of twenty-four prints, using Apollonios of Rhodes as his source, the artist describes Jason the hero hunting for the Golden Fleece. Like Fingal in Carstens's painting *Fingal's Fight against the Spirit of Loda* (1797), Jason is represented as a symbol of the heroic resistance of the individual against obstinate, dark forces.

Following Carstens's death, his works were retained by Koch and Thorvaldsen, the Danish sculptor. Both artists copied numerous pieces, often in the form of contour drawings. Thus, it became difficult in later times to decide which were carried out by Carstens's own hand, and several of his works are known today only as copies made by Koch and Thorvaldsen. Carstens's work was inherited by Fernow, who in 1803, brought the works to Jena, Germany, where at the suggestion of Goethe they were acquired by Carl August, Duke of Saxony, and included in his Weimar art collections.

METTE BLIGAARD

Biography

Born Asmus Jakob or Erasmus Jakob Carstens in Schleswig May 10, 1754. Apprenticed to a wine merchant in Eckernförde 1771–76. Entered Royal Danish Academy of Fine Arts, Copenhagen, 1776. Expelled from the academy, April 1781. Worked as a portrait painter in Copenhagen 1781–83. Lived in Lübeck, 1783–88. Traveled to Mantua and Milan, 1783. Moved to Berlin, 1787. Appointed professor at the Berlin Academy of Fine Arts, 1790. Awarded a Prussian state grant to study fresco painting in Rome, 1792. Resigned his post in Berlin and remained in Rome after exhibiting his work with considerable critical success there, 1795. Died in Rome, May 25, 1798.

Selected Works

Bacchus and Cupid, 1786. Oil on canvas. Statens Museum for Kunst, Copenhagen.
Fingal's Fight Against the Spirit of Loda, 1797. Oil on canvas. Statens Museum for Kunst, Copenhagen.
Parcen Antropos. 1792–94. Plaster sculpture. Kunstsammlungen zu Weimar.
The Argonautic Expedition. Twenty-four drawings published 1799 by Joseph Anton Koch, entitled *Les Argonautes selon Pindare, Orphée et Apollonius de Rhodes en vingt-quatre planches inventées et dessinées par Asmus Jacques Carstens et gravées par Joseph Koch a Rome MDCCXCIX*. Department of Prints and Drawings, Statens Museum for Kunst, Copenhagen.

Bibliography

Asmus Jakob Carstens und Joseph Anton Koch: Zwei Zeitgenossen der Französische Revolution. Zeichnungen. Berlin: Staatliche Museen zu Berlin, Nationalgalerie, 1989.
Fernow, C. L. *Leben des Künstlers Asmus Jakob Carstens*. 1806.
Mildenberger, Hermann. *Asmus Jacob Carstens und die Französische Revolution: Asmus Jakob Carstens. Goethes Erwerbungen für Weimar*. Schleswig: Schleswig-Holsteinisches Landesmuseum, 1992. 47–60.
Miss, Stig, and Gertrud With, eds. *Asmus Jacob Carstens' og Joseph Anton Kochs værker i Thorvaldsens Museum*. Copenhagen: Thorvaldsens Museum, 2000.
Monrad, Kasper, ed. *Mellem Guder og Helte: Historiemaleriet i Rom, Paris og København 1770–1820*. Copenhagen: Statens Museum for Kunst, 1990.
Neuwirth, Markus. J. A. *Koch–A. J. Carstens: Die Argonauten. Ein Bildbuch als Document einer Künstlerfreundschaft*. Vienna: 1989.
Neuwirth, Markus. "Thorvaldsen im Spannungsfeld mytischer Bildfindungen um 1800." In *Künstlerleben in Rom: Bertel Thorvaldsen (1770–1844). Der Dänische Bildhauer und seine deutschen Freunde*. Nürnberg: Germanisches Nationalmuseum, 1991. 53–66.
Zeitler, Rudolf. *Klassizismus und Utopia: Interpretationen zu Werken von David, Canova, Carstens, Thorvaldsen, Koch*. Stockholm: 1954.

CARUS, CARL GUSTAV 1789–1869

German landscape painter, theoretician, physician, and scientist

One of the most multifaceted figures of the Romantic period, Carl Gustav Carus explored and integrated an astonishing range of artistic and scientific interests with keen insight. He was a physician by training, a professor well respected in his field of gynecology, and an expert in comparative anatomy and psychology. He also published a broad spectrum of scientific and medical articles and books, directed a major medical institution, and served as court doctor to the King of Saxony. Yet he was additionally an art theoretician and painter whose works explore the most prominent concerns of German Romanticism; author of several travel books who corresponded with the renowned explorer Alexander von Humboldt; occasional literary critic; and, not least of all, a philosopher-scientist of nature whose writings brought him the admiration of the equally versatile Johann Wolfgang von Goethe. Across all of these disciplines, Carus's observations of nature synthesized both the empirical and the speculative to forge a middle ground between the eighteenth-century rationalist search for knowledge and the subjective inclinations of early Romantics like Novalis, who felt that the poet understood nature better than the scientist. Carus instead preached the mutual benefit of art and science. He proposed that art should act as the "Gipfel der Naturwissenschaften" ("zenith of the natural sciences"); he developed and expressed his love of nature as both an artist and a scientist.

This link between scientific and aesthetic understandings of the world came to Carus early in life. As a boy he studied drawing under the artist Julius Dietz, who had him make careful, systematic studies of nature during long walks through the countryside. He was a precocious child and matriculated at age fifteen at Leipzig University, where he began a comprehensive study of the natural sciences before switching to medicine; six years later he earned both a doctoral and a medical degree. Having secured a reputation for himself with lectures on comparative anatomy, the young doctor accepted a post in Dresden in 1814. It was a pivotal decision, for it placed him among a dynamic group of writers, intellectuals, scientists, and artists.

A self-taught painter, Carus's early works, such as *Frühlingslandschaft im Rosenthal bei Leipzig* (*Spring Landscape in Rosenthal near Leipzig*, 1814), in which the first delicate spring buds of bushes begin to ward off the bleakness of winter's defoliated trees, demonstrate an initial preference for the staid, naturalistic rendering of quiet regional scenes typical of the Dutch landscape tradition. In 1817, Carus met Caspar David Friedrich, who became his artistic mentor and one of his closest friends. Their relationship had an immediate impact on Carus's approach to landscape painting, and he quickly adopted many of the more lugubrious subjects that have become the touchstones of the northern Romantic pathos: desolate winter scenes, moonlit seas, cemeteries, ruined cloisters, Gothic churches, and pilgrims. At times Carus approaches Friedrich's aesthetic so closely that works by each artist have been attributed to the other. In general, however, Carus's paintings are more literary and rarely attain Friedrich's emotional impact; the medievalism and musty symbolism that sometimes creep into his compositions give them a ponderous feel. His freshest works, such as the lovely *Kahnfahrt auf der Elbe* (*Boat Ride on the Elbe*, 1827), in which the view of approaching Dresden is framed through the open cabin of the boat, successfully incorporate recognizable Romantic subjects, such as the quiet figure seen from behind, in an intimate manner that verges on Biedermeier realism. Additionally, many of his most interesting landscapes are imbued with a scientific concern for geologic formations that takes them beyond the realm of metaphysical musings, as seen in the unmistakable rendering of a striking rock structure in Bohemia, *Die Dreisteine im Riesengebirge* (*The Dreisteine in the Riesengebirge*, 1826).

Carus did not earn a living as a painter; most of his paintings remained in the possession of his family. But he exhibited regularly at the Dresden Royal Academy of Art and took his painting quite seriously, for it was through landscape painting, he believed, that an audience first comes to a sense of nature's truth. The extent of Carus's devotion to landscape painting is evident in his *Neun Briefe über Landschaftsmalerei* (*Nine Letters on Landscape Painting*), written between 1815 and 1824, and published in 1831. These letters chronicle Carus's evolution in thinking about nature and its representations. In his early letters he argues that the purpose of landscape painting is to portray a certain mood corresponding to human emotions; a notable passage declares that from the view atop a mountain, "your ego vanishes, you are nothing, God is everything." This is a mystical, intuitive approach to nature, suggestive of an engagement with both Friedrich Wilhelm Joseph von Schelling's *Naturphilosophie* and Friedrich's art. Carus subsequently sought to combine the pleasure taken in the reflective encounter with nature with a more rigorous, scientific understanding of the world on its own terms. Sounding his departure from Friedrich's aesthetic program, he rejected the notion of landscape as "hieroglyph" and called instead for the objective depiction of it in the Goethean sense, based on the eternal laws of nature that govern its seemingly random phenomena.

Carus's shift in position, stimulated by his fruitful acquaintance with Goethe from 1818, and evident in the corresponding adjustment in the subject and manner of his later paintings, is highlighted by his proposition that the "trivial" term landscape (*Landschaft*) be replaced by the more descriptive neologism *Erdlebenbild* ("depiction of earth's life"). This concept, which he developed more fully in *Zwölf Briefe über das Erdleben* (*Twelve Letters on the Life of the Earth*, 1841), entails the belief that the landscape painter should convey the historical processes of nature. Carus reasoned that if an artist studied the physiognomy of mountains (a phrase paralleling Humboldt's idea of a physiognomy of nature), viewers could differentiate various types of rocks and strata in his paintings, thus gaining a sense of the earth's natural history. While many other artists, including Friedrich, Joseph Anton Koch, and counterparts in England such as John Constable, had used accurate studies from nature to construct their landscapes, Carus was distinct in his fervent aspirations to create what he called a "truly geognostic landscape," one that communicates the dynamics of geological structure through time.

Carl Gustav Carus, *Das Goethe-Deukmal*, 1832. Reprinted courtesy of the Bridgeman Art Library.

Despite this emphasis on the scientific, Carus did not abandon his Romantic reveries entirely, as demonstrated by the 1832 painting *Das Goethe-Denkmal* (*Monument to Goethe*), in which a sarcophagus topped with praying angels and harp is cast against a dramatic backdrop of craggy rocks and mist. Ultimately, he realized that there need not be a schism between science and poetry; the gulf between the desire for detailed, objective knowledge of nature's individual elements and the Romantic longing for a unified experience of the world and man's place within it could be resolved by opening up scientific inquiry to aesthetic reflection.

After 1840 Carus's painting production declined, and he devoted himself in his later years more assiduously to other aspects of his career as doctor and scientist, endeavors that brought him greater fame during his lifetime than either his paintings or his writings on landscape. Carus's reputation as a painter and art theoretician was not established firmly until the early twentieth century, when Friedrich was rehabilitated into the pantheon of German artists. The awakening of interest in Friedrich's circle of friends and followers has led to a belated acknowledgment of Carus's own contribution to the intellectual life of Romantic Germany. Indeed, the integration of art, science, and philosophy in so many of his pursuits speaks to the heart of the German Romantic achievement.

MARGARET DOYLE

Biography

Born January 3, 1789 in Leipzig. University of Leipzig, 1804–11. Birth of daughter Sophie Charlotte, 1810. Ph.D. and Dr. Med., 1811. Married Karoline Carus, 1811. First attempts at oil painting, c. 1811–13. Birth of son Ernst Albert, 1812. Professor of obstetrics and director of the Academy for Surgery and Medicine, Dresden, from 1814. Birth of daughter Mariane Albertine, 1814. Studied under Dresden professor of landscape Johann Christian Klengel, 1814. First exhibited at Dresden Royal Academy of Art, 1816. Birth of son Albert Gustav, 1817. Toured Rügen, 1818. Birth of daughter Caroline Cäcilie; travel in the Riesengebirge, 1820. Visited Goethe in Weimar, 1821; in Italy and Switzerland, 1821. Won prize at Royal Academy of Copenhagen, 1823. Birth of son August Wolfgang, 1824. Birth of daughter Johanna Eugenia, 1827. Appointed court doctor to King of Saxony from 1827. In Italy, 1828; in Paris, 1835; in Italy, 1841. Elected member of Academy of Arts in Florence, 1843; in England and Scotland, 1844. Elected president of Leopoldina Academy of Natural Scientists, 1869. Died July 28, 1869.

Selected Works

Frühlingslandschaft im Rosenthal bei Leipzig, 1814. Oil on canvas, 34 cm × 43.5 cm. Staatliche Kunstsammlungen, Gemäldegalerie Neue Meister, Dresden.

Pilger im Felsental, c. 1820. Nationalgalerie, Staatliche Museen Preussischer Kulturbesitz, Berlin.

Frau auf dem Söller, 1824. Oil on canvas, 42 cm × 33 cm. Staatliche Kunstsammlungen, Gemäldegalerie Neue Meister, Dresden.

Die Dreisteine im Riesengebirge, 1826. Oil on canvas, 64 cm × 92.5 cm. Staatliche Kunstsammlungen, Gemäldegalerie Neue Meister, Dresden.

Malerstube im Mondschein, 1826. Oil on canvas, 28.5 cm × 21.5 cm. Staatliche Kunsthalle, Karlsruhe.

Kahnfahrt auf der Elbe, 1827. Oil on canvas, 29 cm × 21 cm. Kunstmuseum, Düsseldorf.

Friedhof auf dem Oybin im Winter, 1828. Oil on canvas, 67 cm × 52 cm. Museum der bildenden Künste, Leipzig.

Das Goethe-Denkmal. 1832. Oil on canvas, 71.5 cm × 53.5 cm. Kunsthalle, Hamburg.

Bibliography

Carus, Carl Gustav. *Lebenserinnerungen und Denkwürdigkeiten*, 4 vols. 1865–66. Reprint Weimar: Kiepenheuer, 1966.

———. *Neun Briefe über Landschaftsmalerei*. 1831. Revised and edited by Dorothea Kuhn. Heidelberg: Schneider, 1972.

———. *Zwölf Briefe über das Erdleben*. 1841. Reprint Stuttgart: Freies Geistesleben, 1986.

Genschorek, Wolfgang. *Carl Gustav Carus: Artz, Künstler, Naturforscher*. Leipzig: S. Hirzel, 1978.

Kaiser, Konrad. *Carl Gustav Carus und die zeitgenössische Dresdner Landschaftsmalerei: Gemälde aus der Sammlung Georg Schäfer, Schweinfurt*. Schweinfurt: Sammlung Schäfer, 1970.

Meffert, Ekkchard. *Carl Gustav Carus: Arzt, Künstler, Goetheanist: eine biographische Skizze*. Basel: Perseus, 1999.

Mitchell, Timothy F. *Art and Science in German Landscape Painting, 1770–1840*. Oxford: Clarendon, 1993.

Müller-Tamm, Jutta, *Kunst als Gipfel der Wissenschaft: Ästhetische und Wissenschaftliche Weltaneignung bei Carl Gustav Carus*. Berlin: Walter de Gruyter, 1995.

Prause, Marianne. *Carl Gustav Carus: Leben und Werk*. Berlin: Deutscher Verlag für Kunstwissenschaft, 1968.

CASTILHO, ANTÓNIO FELICIANO DE 1800–1875

Portuguese poet, critic, and translator

António Feliciano de Castilho made himself known as a poet quite early, in 1821, with *Cartas de Eco e Narciso*, a work in which he would already manifest the characteristics that would lead a whole generation to consider him a major poet (although the generation after that would see him as a voice to contradict). His work is primarily characterized by a specific blend of the neoclassical heritage—displayed in his imagery, use of blank verse, incorporation of classical mythology, and diction—and a Romantic imagination, illustrated by melancholic laments for lost love, recollections of the past (both personal and historical), a taste for the Gothic, and a preference for nature. He is mainly remembered for his two narrative poems *A Noite do Castelo* and *Os Ciúmes do Bardo* (both published in 1836), two parts of a would-be trilogy that remained incomplete. Both pieces exerted a considerable influence on what would become the institutionalized Romanticism of his day, although this was not the same as the strain of Romanticism that would continue to exert a profound influence through the nineteenth and even twentieth centuries (represented by Camilo Castelo Branco, Almeida Garrett, Alexandre Herculano, and Antero de Quental).

Between 1840 and 1850, Castilho reached the height of his public success in the literary milieu as a poet (*Escavações Poéticas*, 1844), as the director of the influential literary periodical *Revista Universal Lisbonense*, and as the author of didactic prose pieces (*Felicidade pela Agricultura*, 1850) as well as historical ones (*Quadros Históricos de Portugal*, 1838). Castilho was also a major critic, a translator of classical authors (including Ovid, Virgil, Anacreon, and Sappho, as well as John Milton, Johann Wolfgang von Goethe, and Jean-Baptiste Molière), an essayist (*Tratado de Metrificação Portuguesa*, 1851), and a proponent of a (questionable) reading method (*Leitura Repentina*, 1850, then *Método Português*, 1853).

Castilho was involved in several polemical controversies, but the one with which he is mainly connected was the famous "Questão Coimbrã," which raged from November 1865 to July 1866, and which came to represent both a shift in Portuguese literature and the emergence of a new literary generation. This generation, known as the "Generation of 1870," made it their mission to, if not completely overthrow Romanticism, at least refashion it by incorporating certain realistic preoccupations. The controversy raged in letters, articles in several periodicals, satirical poems, and critical texts by several literary figures. It begins with an afterword, by Castilho, to a work written by one of his literary protegés, Pinheiro Chagas, a narrative poem entitled *Poema da Mocidade*. In the afterword, Castilho does not limit himself to specifying what he considers to be the best qualities of Pinheiro Chagas' work; he goes on to place it in opposition to what is called the "modern school," mainly identified with the students in Coimbra University, which according to Castilho shows neither "good sense" nor "good taste" (hence the name by which this controversy has become known, "Bom Senso e Bom Gosto"—"Good Sense and Good Taste").

Antero de Quental, then twenty four years of age but already recognized as the intellectual and symbolic mentor of the new generation (having published poetry since 1861 and publishing in that same year of 1865 the influential *Odes Modernas*), immediately reacted. After that, for almost a year, the Portuguese literary scene was divided into two camps: the Lisbon school, around Castilho (with names such as Pinheiro Chagas, Mendes Leal and Bulhão Pato, among others); and the Coimbra School, around Quental (including Teófilo Braga, Álvaro do Carvalhal, and Elmano da Cunha). Ramalho Ortigão, who would become one of the most important names of the next generation, also participated, with the publication of a balanced piece in which he tried to occupy a position situated equally between the two camps.

One cannot overstate the importance of this controversy in the context of the Portuguese literary and cultural scene at the time. It represented a major and decisive shift in literary taste, but also in ideological representations and preoccupations, in poetics (with the revolutionary role attributed to the poet), and in social issues (in terms of poetry's cultural, social, and political role). It brings to the forefront a number of philosophical (Johann Gottfried Herder, Giambattista Vico, Proudhon, August Comte), literary (Victor Hugo, Heinrich Heine, Jules Michelet, Edgar Allan Poe, Hippolyte-Adolphe Taine), and sociohistorical (Edgar Quinet, Charles Darwin) influences that will occupy a central position thereafter.

The literary evaluation of Castilho, by this generation and the following ones, remains an important factor in the evaluation of Portuguese literature of the nineteenth century, stressing the often paradoxical and ambivalent position he occupied in the literary and cultural scene. One thing remains clear, however: the discursive quality of Castilho's diction, both in poetry and in prose, has to be recognized, as does its unique derivation from sources of Romantic inspiration, combined with preponderantly neoclassical literary imagery.

The whole of Castilho's works, partly published posthumously, occupies more than eighty volumes, thus demonstrating the extent to which he influenced—even, for a time, dominated—the Portuguese literary scene.

HELENA CARVALHÃO BUESCU

Biography

Born in Lisbon, January 28, 1800. Became blind at the age of six. Completed degree in law at Coimbra University. Published first works at the age of sixteen. Liberal supporter in the Portuguese civil war, 1823–34. Occupied a central position in the Portuguese cultural scene after publication of his *Obras Completas*, 1837. Appointed director of the journal *O Panorama*, 1837. Responsible, with the poet Almeida Garrett, for the revival of Portuguese national theatre. Director of the *Revista Universal Lisbonense*, 1842. Commissioned to promote social reform in the Azores, c.1848–50. Suffered critical attack from younger generation of poets, 1850s and 1860s. Engaged in the literary polemic "Questão Coimbrã," 1865–66. Created a viscount, 1870.

Selected Works

Poetry
Cartas de Eco e Narciso. 1822.
Amor e Melancolia. 1828.
A Noite do Castelo and *Os Ciúmes do Bardo.* 1836.
Escavações Poéticas. 1844.

Other Works
Quadros Históricos de Portugal. 1838.
Tratado de Metrificação Portuguesa, 1851; 2d ed. 1858.
Leitura Repentina, 1850; 2d ed. 1853, under the title *Método Português.*
Casos do Meu Tempo. 1907 (posthumous).

Telas Literárias. 1907 (posthumous).

Bibliography

Chaves, Castelo Branco. *Castilho: Alguns Aspectos Vivos da sua Obra.* Lisbon: Seara Nova 1935.
Martins, A. Coimbra. "De Castilho a Pessoa: Achegas para uma poética histórica portuguesa." *Bulletin des Etudes Portugaises* 30 (1969): 323–45.
Mourão-Ferreira, David. "Ao encontro de Castilho." *Critério,* vol. 4 (1976): 27–32.
Rodrigues, Ernesto. "Castilho, António Feliciano de." In *Dicionário do Romantismo Literário Português.* Lisbon: Caminho, 1997.
Venâncio, Fernando. *Estilo e Preconceito: A Língua Literária em Portugal na Época de Castilho.* Lisbon: Cosmos, 1998.

THE CASTLE OF OTRANTO 1764

Novel by Horace Walpole

Considered by many critics to be the first Gothic novel in the English tradition, Horace Walpole's *The Castle of Otranto* first appeared in print in an edition of five hundred copies on December 24, 1764. A second edition of the novel followed in April 1765, and a third edition was readied for the press in 1766. The work was included in the second volume of the five-volume collection *Works of Horatio Walpole, Earl of Orford* in June 1798, which appeared just over one year after the death of its author at the age of seventy-nine. *The Castle of Otranto* has rarely been out of print since then.

Walpole's story was originally offered to the contemporary reading public, in its first preface, as having been discovered among the papers in the library of "an ancient Catholic family," and was said to have been printed "in the black letter" (a heavy form of type used by early printers) in the year 1529. It was averred on the same occasion to have been translated into English by one Onuphrio Muralto from "the purest Italian." In the preface to the second edition, however, Walpole owned up to his own authorship of the tale and argued that the work was in actual fact intended to be taken as a corrective to the kind of realism and realistic particularity that seemed by that date to have overtaken, and indeed completely to have superseded, many of the older and more established forms of Romantic and fantastic narrative fiction. *Otranto* was an attempt, as Walpole himself put it in the preface to the second edition, "to blend the two kinds of romance, the ancient and the modern. In the former all was imagination and improbability: in the later, nature is always intended to be, and sometimes has been, copied with success. Invention has not been wanting; but the great resources of fancy have been dammed up, by a strict adherence to common life. But if in the latter species Nature has cramped imagination, she did but take her revenge, having been totally excluded from old romances. ... The author of the following pages thought it possible to reconcile the two kinds."

Walpole's novel opens on an appropriately spectacular note. On the morning of his wedding, Conrad, the son of Manfred, Prince of Otranto, is suddenly killed when an immensely oversized helmet falls from the sky and crushes him. Manfred is suddenly left with the prospect of finding an heir for his kingdom. Undeterred by the fact that he himself is already married to Hippolita, Manfred decides to pursue his son's fiancée, Isabella. Isabella is horrified by Manfred's attempts, and, with the help of a peasant, Theodore, flees via an underground passage to seek sanctuary in the nearby church of St. Nicholas. A variety of supernatural horrors overtake both the pursuers and the pursued as the novel lurches toward its conclusion (Walpole later confessed that he had no preconceived plot in mind when he began writing the novel—"no, not even a plan," he protested, "until some pages were written"—and elsewhere commented that he had simply one evening "sat down and began to write, without knowing in the least what I intended to say or relate"). Gigantic body parts appear within the castle's precincts, and the skeleton of a ghostly hermit appears to warn the characters of the dangers still to come should the inexorable decrees of fate be ignored. At the end of the story, a giant ghost materializes from within the doomed castle, and smashes it to pieces. A seemingly happy (or at least conventionally comedic) ending is supplied when the transgressor Manfred abdicates his title and retires to a nearby convent; his wife Hippolita joins a neighboring order. The peasant Theodore, who marries Isabella, is discovered to be the legitimate heir to Otranto.

The contemporary success of *Otranto* can hardly be overstated. Its popularity was closely connected with the late eighteenth- and early nineteenth-century vogue for antiquarianism and for an increasing enthusiasm for all things Gothic. Walpole's novel was followed by early imitators with titles such as *The Spectre of the Chapel, The Castle of Olalla,* and *Mort Castle: A Gothic Story.* Later and more influential novels to some degree indebted to Walpole's story and its Gothic paraphernalia would of course include Clara Reeve's *The Old English Baron* (1778) and Ann Radcliffe's phenomenally popular *The Mysteries of Udolpho* (1794) and *The Italian* (1797). Ann Yearsley wrote a laudatory poem ("On Reading *The Castle of Otranto*") in 1784, and in the same year the novel was praised for its "delicate morality" by Eleanor Fenn in two papers in "Mrs. Teachwell's" *The Female Guardian*. Both Anna Laetitia Barbauld and Walter Scott wrote important introductions to *Otranto* in the earliest decades of the nineteenth century. William Hazlitt, on the other hand, while admitting *Otranto* to have been both popular and influential, dismissed the effects of the work as founded only on "the pasteboard machinery of a pantomime." The vogue for Gothic fiction had already been memorably parodied in Jane Austen's *Northanger Abbey* (1818).

ROBERT L. MACK

See also **Gothic Fiction; Gothic Revival; Walpole, Horace**

Text

Otranto, 1764, print run of five hundred copies; 2d ed., 1765; 3d ed., 1766. Included in vol. 2 of five-volume collection *Works of Horatio Walpole, Earl of Orford*, 1798.

Bibliography

Baldick, Chris. Introduction to *The Oxford Book of Gothic Tales*. Oxford: 1992.

Ketton-Cremer, R. W. *Horace Walpole*. 4th ed. New York: 1966.

Punter, David. *The Literature of Terror: A History of Gothic Fictions from 1765 to the Present Day*. London: 1980.

Sabor, Peter, ed. *Horace Walpole: The Critical Heritage*. London: Routledge and Kegan Paul, 1987.

CATHOLICISM

During the Romantic era, the Catholic Church was concerned with maintaining its traditions in the face of encroaching modernity while simultaneously attempting to undergo a process of spiritual renewal. The church leaders were preoccupied above all with preserving the temporal power they held in their small papal state. As a means of resisting the advances of Joseph II, the emperor of Austria (his government was characterized by an oppressive interest in church business), Pope Pius VI (papacy, 1775–99) visited Vienna, although he was not successful in reaching any sort of agreement with the emperor. Dissent over doctrine became particularly heated when the Jansenists (who promulgated a belief in predestined salvation or damnation, which the individual could do nothing to alter) summoned a synod at Pistoia in 1786, which was condemned by the pope.

The Catholic church was further weakened with the onset of the French Revolution, when it was heavily criticized and attacked. Little improvement came with the ascendancy of Napoleon Bonaparte. Although a Concordat was reached between the Holy See and France, Napoleon plundered precious works of art from the papal state. After Pius VI's death in exile, Pius VII (1800–23) lost temporal power from 1809 until 1814. This difficult phase was followed by the Restoration period, when the ecclesiastical hierarchy was preoccupied with restoring the Catholic Church and the papal state, in both material and spiritual terms, to its former glory. This phase concurred with the numerous patriotic European uprisings and found its ideal institutional expression, and peak, in Pius IX's (1846–78) condemnation of the modern world in the encyclical *Quanta Cura*, published in 1864.

Spiritual renewal was possible due to a revival of missionary and charitable activities carried out by institutions of new religious congregations. A long series of new foundations followed after the reestablishment of the Society of Jesus in 1814 (it had been suppressed in 1773). Antonio Rosmini Serbati (1797–1855), a philosopher, founded the Institute of Charity (the Rosminians) in 1828; he was guided primarily by only educational and philanthropic aims. His *Of the Five Wounds of the Holy Church* stresses that the internal divisions and the subjugation to a temporal power are hindrances to the spiritual mission of the church. In Turin, meanwhile, Giuseppe Benedetto Cottolengo (1786–1842) built the Little House of the Divine Providence in order to provide assistance to the poor and the sick. Several missionary congregations appeared, such as the Oblates of Mary Immaculate, founded by the archbishop of Marseilles, Charles Joseph Eugene de Mazenod (1782–1861) in 1816. Pauline Jaricot (1754–1836) organized the Faith Propagation Institute at Lion in 1822, taking it upon herself to provide financial assistance to missions in need. Pope Gregorio XVI (1831–46) stands out not only for his conservative politics, but also for his promotion of the revival of Catholic missions, at first as a prefect of the Congregation of Propaganda Fide, and then as pope.

The Romantic Age is also characterized by a renewed interest in the Catholic faith among the cultural elite and artists, a segment of society that had generally rejected religion during the Enlightenment period. The causes of this phenomenon are to be found in the spirituality and interest in medievalism that mark the Romantic era. Once again the Catholic Church was seen as a historical and living body in all its ascetical, mystical, spiritual, artistic, and devotional aspects. A number of key Romantic figures converted to Catholicism. The conversion of Prince Friederich Leopold Stolberg (1750–1819) was influential, as was his *Geschichte der Religion Christi* (1806–18) which portrays the Church's history as the history of salvation itself. In Vienna, the Redemptorist Clemens Maria Hofbauer (1751–1820) and Friedrich von Schlegel (1772–1829) played a significant role in bettering the image of Catholicism during Romanticism; the latter, converted in Colonia, became a professor of the history of religions in Vienna. These two individuals formed the basis of a group that embraced Romantic ideals (and Catholicism) while rejecting the tenets of the Enlightenment. Another convert, Karl Ludwig von Haller (1768–1854) from Bern, a professor of public law, argued that the Catholic Church, with its hierarchical organization, embodies the maintenance of the apostolic succession, which warrants its continuity.

The renewed interest in Catholicism extended beyond the German-speaking world. In Italy Alessandro Manzoni (1785–1873), Silvio Pellico (1789–1854), and Niccolò Tommaseo (1802–74) are only some of the many intellectuals who returned to Catholicism. In England the conversion to Catholicism of some English intellectuals in the so-called Oxford movement caused a sensation in 1845; among them was John Henry Newman (1801–90), then a cardinal. This is not to say that everyone embraced Catholicism wholeheartedly and unproblematically. Some converts abandoned it eventually, disillusioned by the church's conservatism and strict adherence to hierarchical structures. An example is Felicité de Lamennais (1782–1854), a French philosopher who rejected atheism to convert to Catholicism, joined the priesthood, and founded a newspaper, *L'Avenir*, in 1830, only to break with the church over its condemnation of his liberal ideas.

Catholicism in the Romantic era was not limited in its influence to the foundation of charitable organizations. A large amount of work, ranging from theology to literature, was produced that grappled with the concepts of charity and divine providence. These ideas find the most legitimate support and defense in the work of Rosmini and Manzoni.

Romanticism affected Catholic devotional practices in its exaltation of symbols of emotions, such as the heart, and its praise of maternal love. The devotion to Jesus's heart was included in the Catholic liturgy for the first time in 1765 by Clemens XIII. Pius VI approved the liturgical devotions to Mary's immaculate heart at this time, which would have drastic repercussions, even in holy art, in encouraging Mariology.

ELVIO CIFERRI

See also **Bonaparte, Napoleon Lamennais, Felicité de; Religion, France; Religion, Germany**

Bibliography

Aubert, Roger, Johannes Beckmann, and Rudolf Lill. "Die Kirche zwischen Revolution und Restauration." In *Handbuch der Kirchengeschichte*, Vol. 8. Edited by Hubert Jedin. Freiburg in Breisgau: Verlag Herder KG, 1971. (English edition: Roger Aubert et al. "The Church in the age of Liberalism." In *History of the Church*. Edited by Hubert Jedin and John Dolan. London: Burns & Oates, 1981.)

Aubert, Roger, Johannes Beckmann, Patrick. J. Corish, and Rudolf Lill. "Die Kirche zwischen Revolution und Restauration." In *Handbuch der Kirchengeschichte*, Vol. 8. Edited by Hubert Jedin. Freiburg in Breisgau: Verlag Herder KG, 1971.

Dizionario degli Istituti di Perfezione. 9 vols. Rome: Edizioni Paoline, 1974–97.

Bibliotheca Sanctorum. vols. 15 Rome: Pontificia Università Lateranense/Città Nuova, 1961–2000.

Leflon. Jean "La crisi rivoluzionaria, 1789–1815." In *Storia della Chiesa*, Vol. 20. Edited by Augustin Fliche and Victor Martin. Turin: SAIE/Edizioni Paoline, 1971.

———."Restaurazione e crisi liberale, 1815–1846." In *Storia della Chiesa*, Vol. 20. Edited by Augustin Fliche and Victor Martin. Turin: SAIE/Edizioni Paoline, 1975.

CHAMBER MUSIC

During the early classical period, chamber music genres such as the string quartet had been associated with informal entertainment, typically involving performance by amateurs and taking place within a private, domestic setting. However, by the time of Ludwig van Beethoven's earliest quartets and Franz Joseph Haydn's mature masterpieces, they had been embraced as suitable for the public concert. Chamber concerts organized by kapellmeister Karl Möser in Berlin rapidly became the centerpiece of Berlin musical life in the early nineteenth century, noted for their concentration on the works of "the classics." Surviving programs, diary entries, reviews, and reports from public concerts given in Berlin, Vienna, and Leipzig reveal a strong preference for the works of Beethoven, Haydn, Wolfgang Amadeus Mozart, and suggest an emerging core repertory consisting of solo, chamber, and symphonic music by these three great composers of what was to become the Viennese classical tradition. Repeated public performance helped give the various chamber music groupings (trio, quartet, quintet, octet, etc.) an unassailable cultural status. The earlier, quite limited *Gebrauchsmusik* (utility music, written for amateur performance) aspiration of chamber music was broken forever by this shift of focus, and works such as Haydn's late quartets (for instance, those of op. 76, 1797–99, and op. 77, 1799–1802) and Beethoven's "Rasumovsky" string quartets (op. 59, all composed and published in the span of just a few years around 1800), became cultural objects, intended to make a profound artistic statement. No longer inhabiting the naive world of the *divertimento*, they offered instead a more technically and intellectually challenging diet. The "Rasumovsky" quartets were actively promulgated in Vienna by the Schuppanzigh Quartet, and it was undoubtedly the prospect of reliable professional performances by this group that encour-

aged Beethoven to invest his quartets with their quasi-symphonic character, orchestral breadth of scale, and sonority, and that expanded technical demands, all likewise features of Franz Schubert's late quartets and other chamber works included in Schuppanzigh's chamber music concerts in the 1820s.

It is within this context of past "authority" that the chamber music of the early nineteenth century is best understood. It exhibits continuity with the timeless exemplars of the recent past (cemented by emerging concert traditions), while simultaneously setting out on new paths. Holding to the established classical genres, works such as Robert Schumann's Piano Quartet (op. 47, 1842); his string quartets (op. 41, 1842); the "Fantasiestück" Trio (op. 88, 1842); the trios (op. 63, 1847; op. 80, 1847; and op. 110, 1851); and the violin sonatas (opp. 105 and 121, 1851) were intended to be appreciated within the context of the "Viennese classics." The technical fabrication of Schumann's Piano Quintet (op. 44, 1842), is, without a doubt, masterly and classical in origin. The connecting passage emerging from the main theme utilizes the same material shapes (though contrasting in gesture) to create unity from diversity; but such technical fabrication now sits securely within the expressive character of the musical discourse, and the overall impression is of a vigorous, effervescent piece, tempered periodically by moments of repose. The respective boundaries of technique and expression have been redrawn.

Schubert's chamber music occupies a central place within this transition, and demonstrates a thorough revaluation of the high classical style, most especially as encountered in the work of Mozart, to whose symmetrical proportions and Italianate tunefulness Schubert's early string quartets openly refer. But this adolescent style, in which the significance of a movement is contained wholly within the materialist-formalist domain, unconcerned with the revelation of any deeper "spiritual" (or even extra-musical) quality, is one from which Schubert's later works (such as the "Death and the Maiden Quartet," D810, 1824) depart radically. This is apparent in the extra-musical associations of the quartet's slow movement, quoting Schubert's "Der Tod und das Mädchen," and thereby sacrificing the realm of "pure" chamber music for the dark poetic connotations of the earlier song. Schubert's late instrumental work increasingly imports associations from other genres such as the *lied*. A memorable illustration of this occurs at the start of the String Quartet in A Minor (D804, 1824), its two-bar introduction, *pianissimo*, featuring a memorable shuddering rhythmic pattern at the bottom of the texture, and creating an immediate association with Schubert's mood-setting song accompaniments. At such moments Schubert seems to be reaching out toward the expression of a realm beyond the notes themselves, echoing philosophical aspirations of the early romantic age described by G. W. F. Hegel and E. T. A. Hoffmann as *Das Geist* (spirit). Indeed, Schubert's later chamber music points to a genre whose meaning lies in an allusive play of images lying outside the purely musical structure, escaping, despite the survival of classical formal procedures, from the relatively "literal" mode of speech found in his early string quartets.

The more formalistic chamber music of Felix Mendelssohn-Bartholdy and Schumann increasingly demonstrates "cyclic" principles of organization, possibly suggested by the late quartets of Beethoven, most especially the Quartet in C-sharp Minor (op. 131, 1826), whose "sectional" rather than "movement" layout is reinforced by subtle motivic interconnections. Resonances of Beethoven's later quartets are encountered in the early string quartets of Mendelssohn, in E-flat (op. 12, 1829) and A Minor (op. 13, 1827), in both of which the separate movements are thematically interrelated. Op. 12's first movement borrows from

both Beethoven's "Harp" Quartet (op. 74, 1809) and from op. 127 (1823–24). But the debt to Beethoven does not stop with overt quotation. Formally, the movement is a hybrid, combining sonata conventions with rondo, and exploiting a novel ambiguity of content and setting, typically exposing new material within textural gestures suggestive of sonata development, challenging traditional structural assumptions. Such creative reinterpretation of conventions suggests the Beethoven of the late quartets, to which the subsequent movements also pay homage. Other chamber works of this period which rely to some extent on "cyclic'" procedure include Schubert's E-flat Piano Trio (D929, 1827), whose finale incorporates a reference to the slow movement's main theme; Mendelssohn's Octet (op. 20, 1825) (in which the finale and scherzo are interrelated) and his Piano Sonata (op. 106, 1827); and Schumann's Piano Quintet (op. 44, 1842), which combines the main finale theme with that of the first movement toward the end as an impressive peroration to the work as a whole.

JOHN IRVING

Bibliography

Hosler, B. *Changing Aesthetic Views of Instrumental Music in Eighteenth-Century Germany.* Ann Arbor: UMI Press, 1981.

Longyear, R. *Nineteenth-Century Romanticism in Music.* 2d ed. Englewood Cliffs, N.J.: Prentice-Hall, 1973.

Mahling, C. H. "Berlin: Music in the Air." In *Man and Music: The Early Romantic Period.* Edited by A. Ringer, London: Macmillan, 1990. 118.

Morrow, M. S. *German Music Criticism in the Late Eighteenth Century.* Cambridge: Cambridge University Press, 1997.

Neubauer, J. *The Emancipation of Music from Language: Departure from Mimesis in Eighteenth-Century Aesthetics.* New Haven, Conn.: Yale University Press, 1986.

Rosen, C. *The Romantic Generation.* London: Harper Collins, 1995.

CHAMISSO, ADELBERT VON 1781–1838

German author, poet, explorer, naturalist

A troubled and restless seeker of ultimate and immediate truths into his thirties, Adelbert von Chamisso found in science, at age thirty-one, the purpose and direction which determined the remainder of his life. He was acquainted with luminaries of German and Franco-German Romanticism, including Johann Gottlieb Fichte, Friedrich de la Motte Fouqué, Louis de la Foye, E. T. A. Hoffmann, Alexander von Humboldt, August Wilhelm Schlegel, and Madame Anne-Louise-Germaine de Stael, and was present in the salons of Ephraim and Cohen, but his work is peripheral to the Romantic enterprise. His representation of love and nature, his tendency to realism in his attention to detail, his political liberalism, and his cosmopolitanism set his work apart from the mainstream of German Romanticism.

The insecurities of a young man who, forced from his home in the French provinces, abandoned his noble upbringing for a circle of cultured, bourgeois friends and discovered new roots in a foreign city, inform Chamisso's early writing. Consistent with his restless and self-questioning disposition, his *Faust: ein Versuch* (*Faust: A Dramatic Sketch*, 1803) has an aging Faust

resolve the doubt regarding his destiny by taking matters into his own hands and precipitating his end. He takes his own life and thus, by imposition of his own will, eliminates doubt and makes the leap either into annihilation or into knowledge, but in any event into certainty. In *Adelberts Fabel* (1806), Chamisso similarly has his protagonist discover that life's path is determined by a synthesis of will and necessity. The author's acutely felt tension between wanderlust and a desire for a home is foregrounded in his dramatic adaptation of the 1509 chapbook *Fortunati Glückseckel und Wunschhütlein* (*Fortunatus's Lucky Purse and Wishing Hat*, 1806).

The fantastic magic purse recurs as a central motif in *Peter Schlemihls wundersame Geschichte* (*The Wonderful History of Peter Schlemihl*, 1813), in which Chamisso combines elements of the supernatural (diabolical agents, seven-league boots, disappearing shadows) with a familiar world of bourgeois logic and values. What appears to adhere to a quintessential Romantic formula detaches itself from that model when Schlemihl ultimately turns his back on the fantastic, refuses to barter his soul for the return of his shadow, rejects the advantages of wealth, and dedicates his life to rigorous scientific investigation. The alternative reality of the supernatural does not release him entirely, however, as his expeditions of scientific discovery are made possible only by the seven-league boots.

In February 1815 Chamisso failed in his attempt to become a member of the expedition of Prince Maximilian von Wied zu Neuwied to Brazil. Four months later, however, thanks to the mediation of his friend and mentor Eduard Hitzig, Chamisso was engaged as ship's naturalist for the 1815–18 voyage of the Russian brig *Rurik* to the Pacific, the Bering Strait, and around the world. The purpose of the voyage, captained by Otto von Kotzebue (son of dramatist and statesman August von Kotzebue), was ostensibly to seek a northwest passage from the Pacific. Chamisso's two published accounts of the voyage place him consciously in the company of Georg Forster and Alexander von Humboldt, and his subsequent correspondence with William J. Hooker, Humboldt, Karl Friedrich Philipp Martius, and others, ties him into the fraternity of scientist explorers of the early nineteenth century whose collections and taxonomic analyses constitute the foundations of the biological and geological sciences. The rigorous scientific account of the voyage, "Bemerkungen und Ansichten," published in 1821 as part of Kotzebue's official record of the voyage, represents a distanced, factual report on geographical, geological, zoological, botanical, meteorological, and ethnographic observations, organized by location. The *Tagebuch* (*Journal*, 1836), marks a deliberate turn to an anecdotal recounting of the events of the voyage "vor Freunden," arranged chronologically. Taken with the fictional narrative of Peter Schlemihl's scientific explorations, we may read these accounts as Chamisso's multigenre approach to representing scientific discovery in the era of Romanticism. In 1813 the Schlemihl tale connects exploration and documentation of empirical data with a fantasy world where phenomena often defy the observable laws of physics and matter. In 1821 the tenets of scientific rigor are observed in a sustained exercise of professional savoir faire. Most interesting of the three is the 1836 attempt to synthesize the objective with the personal and inject the subjective position of the narrator as an essential component. Though Chamisso is not subscribing to Fichte's abolition of the *Ding an sich* ("thing in itself") in adopting this strategy, he is acknowledging—as Forster and Humboldt had done—the experiencing subject as an essential mediator of scientific knowledge.

The breadth of scientific interest in these accounts notwithstanding, it is evident that the ethnographic yield of the voyage holds the greatest fascination for Chamisso. The most engaging episodes in the travel narratives involve human contact, customs, and behavior, and where the ways of Europeans are compared with those of Pacific Islanders, the Europeans are in most cases found wanting. European missionary activity and its cruelties are the target of repeated criticism. Informed by Jean-Jacques Rousseau, whose writings Chamisso knew well, these views recur in the poetry of the post-voyage years. Chamisso's reception of Rousseau is not founded in escapism and intellectual fascination with the exotic, but rather in the realities of the human condition, which he observed firsthand, and the quest for social justice. In his portrayals of lands and peoples in his travel writing as in his poetry, his descriptions betray little overt emotional investment but rather are detached; sources are documented (even

for poems), and he entertains the reader while simultaneously confronting intercultural and international issues.

The plant specimens collected during the voyage provided much of the raw material for two decades of scientific publication. As first assistant at the Berlin botanical garden in Schöneberg (since 1819) and second curator of the Royal Herbarium (under D. F. L. Schlechtendal), Chamisso named and described 763 plant species and 37 new genera, mostly in Schlechtendal's journal *Linnaea*. He named the California poppy (*Eschscholzia californica*) after his friend and conaturalist on the *Rurik*, the ship's doctor Johann Friedrich Eschscholtz. In addition, he authored or coauthored taxonomic publications for plants gathered by fellow botanists from around the world, including Wilhelm Schiede and Ferdinand Deppe (Mexico, 1830–31), Friedrich Sellow (Brazil, 1833–34), and Adolph Erman (Kamchatka, 1835). He further contributed to the scientific literature on salps (sea worms), coral reefs, peat moors, and the flora of northern Germany.

Settling into a stable family life and steady employment following his voyage, Chamisso seemingly adopted a lifestyle consonant with the Biedermeier preoccupations of the post-Napoleonic era. This impression is deceptive, however, since it is during the next thirteen years that Chamisso's poetry production reaches its most outspoken political pitch. His liberal voice was acknowledged as a stimulus by writers whose work prepared the way for the 1848 revolution (*Vormärz*), and Chamisso was an early champion of Ferdinand Freiligrath. Having supported the July Revolution in Paris (1830), he subsequently became less radical and more supportive of the economic and social status quo, criticizing the amorality of the *Junges Deutschland* (Young Germany) group.

Chamisso's verse rarely emerged directly from his personal experience; he processed topoi, themes, and subject matter culled from the lore and literature of many cultures. He composed German poetry using the traditions of Lithuania, Denmark, Russia, Greece, Arabia, China, and the South Seas, and translated poems and songs by Pierre-Jean de Béranger. Unlike the agenda of many German Romantics, his was neither nationalistic nor retrospective. His interest in the Middle Ages was limited to his youthful interest in Faust and Fortunatus. Like many Romantics, notably Jacob and Wilhelm Grimm, he was fascinated by the study of language and published the first Hawaiian grammar (1837).

The reception of his published work shows a falling curve. His poems were exceptionally popular and influential during the last decade of his life; Edvard Grieg, Karl Loewe, Robert Schumann ("Frauen-Liebe und Leben"), and Friedrich Silcher set his poems to music, and until World War I anthologists included his poems in collections for their solid nineteenth-century values. Most of his botanical names and the supporting classification work remain in use, but with the exception of *Peter Schlemihl*, his literary work was ignored for most of the twentieth century.

CHRISTOPHER J. WICKHAM

Biography

Born in Boncourt, France, January 1781. Emigrated to Prussia to escape the French Revolution, 1792; in the Hague, Düsseldorf, Würzburg, and Bayreuth; in Berlin, from 1796. Attendant to Queen Friederike Luise, 1796. Ensign in the Prussian army, 1798; lieutenant, 1801; active service in Hameln, 1806; discharged 1808. Cofounder of the literary club Nordsternbund, 1803. In France and Switzerland, 1806–12. Studied medicine, University of Berlin, 1812–13. Naturalist accompanying Otto von Kotzebue to the South Seas and Northern Pacific, 1815–18. Curator, Berlin Botanical Gardens, 1819. Coeditor, with Gustav Schwab, of *Deutscher Musenalmanach*, Berlin, 1833–38. Member Berlin Academy of Sciences; honorary doctorate, University of Berlin, 1819. Died August 21, 1838.

Selected Works

Collections
Sämtliche Werke. Edited by Jost Perfahl and Volker Hoffmann. 2 vols. Munich: Winkler, 1975.

Fiction
Peter Schlemihls wundersame Geschichte, edited by Friedrich de la Motte Fouqué, 1814. Translated as *Peter Schlemihl* by Sir John Bowring, 1823 (reprinted Columbia, S.C.: Camden House, 1993). Translated as *Peter Schlemiel: The Man Who Sold His Shadow* by Peter Wortsman (New York: Fromm International, 1993).

Poetry
Frauen-Liebe und Leben: Ein Lieder-Cyklus. 1879. Translated as *Women's Love and Life: A Cycle of Song* by Frank V. MacDonald. 1881.
The Castle of Boncourt and Other Poems. Translated by Alfred Baskerville. In *German Classics of the Nineteenth and Twentieth Centuries.* Vol. 5. 1913.

Plays
Fortunati Glückseckel und Wunschhütlein. Edited by E. F. Kossmann. 1895.

Other
"Bemerkungen und Ansichten auf einer Entdeckungs-Reise, unternommen in den Jahren 1815–1818 . . ." In Otto von Kotzebue, *Entdeckungsreise in die Südsee und nach der Berrings-Strasse zur Erforschung einer nordöstlichen Durchfahrt unternommen in den Jahren 1815–1818.* Vol. 3. 1821. Translated as "Remarks and Opinions of the Naturalist of the Expedition" by H. E. Lloyd, in *A Voyage of Discovery to the South Seas and Beering's Straits, for the Purpose of Exploring a North-east Passage, Undertaken under the Command of the Lieutenant in the Russian Imperial Navy, Otto von Kotzebue.* 1821.

Übersicht der nutzbarsten und der schädlichsten Gewächse, welche wild oder angebaut in Norddeutschland vorkommen: Nebst Ansichten von der Pflanzenkunde und dem Pflanzenreiche. 1827.
Salas y Gomez. 1830. In Karl Lentzner, *Chamisso: A Sketch of His Life and Work with Specimens of His Poetry and an Edition of the Original Text of "Salas y Gomez."* 1893.
Reise um die Welt mit der Romanzoffischen Entdeckungsexpedition in den Jahren 1815–1818. 1836. Translation: *A Voyage around the World with the Romanzov Exploring Expedition in the Years 1815–1818 in the Brig Rurik.* Edited and translated by Henry Kratz. 1986. Honolulu: University of Hawaii Press, 1986. Translation: *The Alaska Diary of Adelbert von Chamisso Naturalist on the Kotzebue Voyage 1815–1818.* Translated in part by Robert Fortuine. 1986. Anchorage: Cook Inlet Historical Society, 1986.
Über die Hawaiische Sprache: Versuch einer Grammatik der Sprache der Sandwich-Inseln. 1837.

Bibliography

Atkins, Stuart. "Peter Schlemihl in Relation to the Popular Novel of the Romantic Period," *Germanic Review* 21 (1946): 191–208.
Bois-Reymond, Emil Heinrich du. "Adelbert Chamisso as a Naturalist," *Popular Science Monthly* 38 (1890–91): 252–263.
Brockhagen, Dörte. "Adelbert von Chamisso," In *Literatur in der sozialen Bewegung.* Edited by Alberto Martino. Tübingen: Niemeyer, 1977.
Feudel, Werner. *Adelbert von Chamisso: Leben und Werk.* Leipzig: Reclam, 1988.
Kuzniar, Alice. " 'Spurlos verschwunden': Peter Schlemihl und sein Schatten," in *Aurora* 45 (1985): 189–204.
Liebersohn, Harry. "Discovering Indigenous Nobility: Tocqueville, Chamisso, and Romantic Travel Writing," in *American Historical Review* 99 (1994): 746–766.
Menza, Gisela. *Adelbert von Chamissos "Reise um die Welt mit der Romanzoffschen Entdeckungsexpedition in den Jahren 1815–1818": Versuch einer Bestimmung des Werkes als Dokument des Überganges von der Spätromantik zur vorrealistischen Biedermeier.* Frankfurt am Main: P. Lang, 1978.
Mornin, Edward, " '. . . viele Städte der Menschen gesehen und Sitten gelernt': Observations on Chamisso's Cosmopolitan Verse," in *Colloquia Germanica* 31 (1998): 55–65.
———. " 'Wie verzweifelnd die Indianer pflegen': American Indians in Chamisso's Poetry," in *Seminar* 33 (1997): 213–227.
Schneebeli-Graf, Ruth. *Adelbert von Chamisso . . . und lassen gelten, was ich beobachtet habe: Naturwissenschaftliche Schriften mit Zeichnungen des Autors.* Berlin: Reimer, 1983.
Wallach, Dagmar. "Adelbert von Chamisso: *Peter Schlemihls wundersame Geschichte.*" in *Erzählungen und Novellen des 19. Jahrhunderts. Interpretationen,* vol. 1. Stuttgart: Reclam, 1988.

CHASSÉRIAU, THÉODORE 1819–1856

French painter

Critics have traditionally viewed Théodore Chassériau as an eclectic artist who reconciled classicism and Romanticism, an artist who started out as a pupil of Jean-Auguste-Dominique Ingres, later to succumb to the influence of Eugène Delacroix. Yet Léon Rosenthal and many subsequent critics have shown that even from his early years, Chassériau was using the methods learned under Ingres's tutelage with skill and sensitivity, but was also bringing to them a Romantic temperament. Among his first submissions to the Salon in 1836 was *Caïn maudit* (*Cain Cursed*) (1839), a painting that reveals Chassériau's fusion of a classical style with, to borrow Marc Sandoz's analogy, an atmosphere reminiscent of the poetry of Alphonse Marie-Louis Prat de Lamartine. In this painting, too, the pathos of the landscape only enhances the Romantic mood. Chassériau's duality of artistic temperament is substantiated by his own professed aesthetic. He described, for example, how he wished, in his grand decorative projects, to discover the poetry in reality ("Trouver la poésie dans le réel"), but also to combine the monumental with the real ("Faire monumental mais réel"), the real being "des sujets tout simples, tirés de l'histoire de l'homme, de sa vie" ("simple subjects, drawn from man's history, from man's life"). And indeed, while maintaining a noble focus and epic scale in his choice of allegorical, historical, religious, and mythological subjects, Chassériau's work appears to blend the external, tangible world with the inner, psychological realm of the figures he portrays. Famously, he railed against the pleasant, soporific beatitude ("l'agréable béatitude qui vous endort") of the school of Jacques-Louis David and, by extension, of Ingres, their gazes turned toward the past instead of the present, and unredeemed by a modern sensibility.

Chassériau's submissions to the Salon of 1839 secured his reputation. These were *Vénus Anadyomène/Vénus Marine* (*Venus Anadyomene*, 1838) and *Suzanne au bain* (*Suzanna in her Bath*, 1839), paintings that stood out from his earlier work for their quality while also marking the birth of a new style in Romantic painting. Classical in inspiration and almost mannerist in form, *Vénus Anadyomène* is imbued with a new, modern sensuality and sensitivity, concentrated in the figure of Venus, but emphasized by the empathy between landscape and goddess. *Suzanne au bain* also shares the mood of indefinable emotion highlighted by Henri Focillon in relation to *Vénus Anadyomène*, and in Chassériau's portrayal of these two figures, Sandoz and other critics have pointed to the creation of a new female type, characterized by nostalgia and reverie. The originality of these paintings did not strike all contemporary critics, however. Théophile Gautier was one exception, and he was to become Chassériau's most faithful and perceptive critic. Throughout the 1840s, Chassériau, like many Romantic artists and writers, pursued his interest in mythological, biblical, and Shakespearian subjects; and during this period, the new melancholic female type inaugurated by *Vénus Anadyomène* reappears in the form of ill-fated heroines such as Andromeda, Esther, and Desdemona. Chassériau's duality of temperament is evident in these paintings and in his first large-scale decorative work, the decoration of the chapel of *Sainte-Marie-L'Égyptienne* in the church of Saint-Merri in Paris (1841–43). Unique among Chassériau's works of this period are the *Othello* engravings, which were commissioned by Eugène Piot and for the completion of which Chassériau mastered a medium previously unused by him. The *Othello* series was, however, surrounded by controversy, with critics accusing the artist of having copied Delacroix's *Hamlet* engravings.

Chassériau's largest-scale work was the decoration of the staircase of the Cour des Comptes in the Palais d'Orsay (1848). This work was largely destroyed by fire on May 23, 1871, although some fragments survived and were eventually moved to the Louvre in 1898. For further details of the work, we must rely on photographs taken by Baron Arthur Chassériau (Théodore's cousin) of what remained of the murals after the fire, and on Gautier's descriptions of them. Chassériau's decorations were allegorical, portraying, in a careful symmetrical structure, the subjects of war and peace. The work comprised three major sections: the first was war, the second, peace, while the third, force and order, provided a bridge between them. The movement, violence, and color of war were juxtaposed to the serene industry of peace, represented by such activities as study, meditation, the arts, and agriculture. Despite the grand scale of the project, Chassériau again reconciled an idealized, classical serenity reminiscent of a Renaissance decor with a Romantic identification with the ideas portrayed: as Léonee Bénédite argues, Chassériau enters into his subject and breathes modern life into his allegories.

Between the late 1840s and 1850s, Chassériau's style and method evolved to become freer and more assured: some of Ingres's rigor fades, for example, and fewer preparatory sketches exist from this period, as Chassériau frequently paints straight onto the canvas. Instrumental in this development was his visit to Algeria in 1846, a country which was also a revelation of color for Chassériau. The result of his fascination with all aspects of Arab life was a considerable corpus of orientalist paintings, dating from 1847–56, many of which were exhibited at the Salon. Most notable among these, to judge by Gautier's evaluation, was the massive *Le jour du Sabbat dans le quartier juif de Constantine* (*The Sabbath in the Jewish Quarter of Constantine*, 1847). This was Chassériau's first orientalist painting, its violent originality, to use Gautier's terms, born of its joyous use of color and its comparatively relaxed style, characteristics which are common to all of the orientalist paintings.

Chassériau continued to find inspiration in the religious, mythological, and Shakespearian themes he had previously favored, but traces of exoticism persisted in his work from the time of the trip to Algeria until his death. Among the great works of this period are Baigneuse endormie près d'une source (*Bather Sleeping by a Stream*, 1850) and *Tepidarium* (1853) (Paris, Musée d'Orsay). *Tepidarium* possesses a rigorous, classical structure, but the verve of the colorist of the orientalist paintings is present too. For this reason, many critics have interpreted the painting as an illustration of Chassériau's eclecticism, the successful alliance of Ingres's drawing with Delacroix's color. However, for Sandoz, one of Chassériau's most sympathetic modern critics, the *Tepidarium* is the fulfilment of his ambition to renew the painting of his time by freeing it from convention and imitation, and placing it at the centre of the artist's emotions. In the poetry of expression and situation thus evoked, the contemporary world would, for Chassériau, discover its own reflection.

MARGARET TOPPING

Biography

Born in Haiti, September 20, 1819. In 1822, the Chassériau family returned to France. In 1830, Théodore Chassériau entered the atelier of Ingres. Undertook the decoration of the Salon Pompadour in the old deanery of the Louvre, 1833, met Théophile Gautier at this time. In 1834, left Ingres's atelier because of the latter's departure to take up the directorship of the Académie de France in Rome. July 1840 to January 1841, visit to Rome, during which time he carried out a large number of studies that he later used in the decoration of the Cour des Comptes and other large-scale compositions. Decoration of the chapel of *Sainte-Marie-l'Égyptienne*, 1841–43. Decoration of the staircase of the Cour des comptes, 1844–48. Trip to Algeria, 1846, during which time he made a large number of sketches that he would use for the rest of his life. In 1849, he became Chevalier de la Légion d'honneur. Began the decoration of the St. Roch church with a number of other artists, 1851; his contribution was completed in 1853. From 1852 on, suffered from ill health. In 1855, exhibited five works at the Universal Exhibition. 1856, health deteriorated; died October 8, 1856.

Selected Works

Portrait du R.P.F. Dominique Lacordaire de l'ordre des frères prêcheurs (*Pater Lacordaire*). 1840. Oil on canvas, 146 cm × 107 cm. Paris: Musée du Louvre.
Mesdemoiselles Chassénau/Les Deux Soeurs (*The Sisters of the Artist*). 1843. Oil on canvas, 180 cm × 135 cm. Paris: Musée du Louvre.
Cavaliers arabes important leurs morts (*Arab Horsemen Reclaiming their Dead*), 1850. Oil on canvas, 167 cm × 248 cm. Cambridge, Massachusetts: Fogg Art Museum.
Intérieur du harem (*Harem Interior*). 1854. Oil on canvas, 67 cm × 55 cm. Strasbourg: Musée des Beaux-Arts.

Bibliography

Bénédite, Léonce. *Théodore Chassériau: Sa vie et son oeuvre.* Paris: Éditions Braun, 1931.

Focillon, Henri. "Théodore Chassériau ou les deux romantismes," in *Le Romantisme et l'art.* Paris: Laurens, 1928.
Guégan, Stéphane, Vincent Pomarède, and Louis-Antoine Prat. *Chassériau: un autre romantisme.* Paris: Réunion des musées nationaux, 2002.
Peltre, Christine. *Orientalism in Art.* Translated by John Goodman. New York: Abbeville, 1998.
Prat, Louis-Antoine. *Musée du Louvre: Cabinet des dessins. Inventaire général des dessins. École française. Dessins de Théodore Chassériau (1819–1856).* Paris: Éditions de la Réunion des Musées Nationaux, 1988.
Rosenthal, Léon. *L'Art et les artistes romantiques.* Paris: Le Goupy, 1928.
Rosenthal, Léon. *Du Romantisme au réalisme: essai sur l'évolution de la peinture en France de 1839 à 1848.* Paris: Laurens, 1914
Sandoz, Marc. *Théodore Chassériau 1819–1956. Catalogue raisonné des peintures et estampes.* Paris: Arts et Métiers Graphiques, 1974.

CHATEAUBRIAND, FRANÇOIS-AUGUSTE-RENÉ, VICOMTE DE 1768–1848

French novelist, critic, and statesman

Often called in France "le père du Romantisme" (the father of Romanticism), François-Auguste-René de Chateaubriand personified some aspects of the movement's first revolt against the Age of Reason, or of François-Marie Voltaire. A fervent Catholic who declared that his conversion resulted entirely from emotion rather than intellectual inquiry—"J'ai pleuré et j'ai cru" ("I wept and so I believed"), he declared in the first preface to his *Génie du christianisme* (*The Beauties of Christianity*, 1802)—he was also the scion of an ancient aristocratic family, never hesitant to avail himself of the privileges accruing to his class. His personal misfortune came from being a Catholic aristocrat as the Revolution exploded in Brittany. Dispossessed due to his religion, he left for America with no clear plan in mind. However, his rich imagination, nurtured by several years of adolescent leisure at the family estate of Combourg, during which he created the dream world realized in some of his literary creations, allowed him to exploit the short time he spent in the New World to the full. The *Génie du christianisme*, whose function was to convert readers by insisting on the "beauty of Christianity," contains the three stories, *Atala*, *René*, and *Les Natchez*, which together explain both his immense first success and much of his lasting reputation as a Romantic author.

Atala presents didactically the story of a Native American virgin whose Christian mother destines her for the convent. Ignorant of doctrine, Atala believes this vow of chastity, imposed without her consent, is in danger when she falls in love with the young Indian brave, Chactas, and so commits suicide. (Anne-Louis Girodet's picture, entitled *The Entombment of Atala* [1808], captures perfectly the pathetic appeal to nascent Romantic sensibility made by Chateaubriand's first fictional bestseller.)

The young Frenchman, *René*, while in the American wilderness, confesses to the missionary Father Souël the profound discontent preventing him from living either in the civilized European world or in that of the "savage" Natchez tribe that has adopted him. Many readers have understood his dissatisfaction

and boredom to be caused in part by the incestuous attraction he feels for his sister, Amélie. His confession outlines all the characteristics which made up what Chateaubriand's readers called the *mal du siècle* (world weariness). To the dismay of *René*'s creator, they also imitated its wilder sartorial aspects, personifying in the process the disheveled portrait of the young soulful Romantic idealist. (Once again it was Girodet who, in his windswept portrait of Chateaubriand gazing at the ruins of the Roman Colosseum [1809], created another of the icons most evocative of the early Romantic male ideal.) In *René*, Chateaubriand also embellished the Romantic view of autumn, season of impending doom and colorful fruitfulness, and many present-day travel agents and operators of "fall foliage tours" in New England and Eastern Canada owe something to the inspiration of such passages as,

> Autumn overtook me in the midst of my uncertainty: ecstatically, I entered the season of storms . . . During the day, I wandered over great heaths bordered by forests. How little it took to set me dreaming! A dead leaf that the wind swept in front of me, the smoke from a cabin rising into the bare treetops, the moss trembling in the North wind on an oak tree, an unfrequented rock, a lonely pond where the withered reed murmured! A solitary church tower rising up from some distant valley often drew my eye; often my eye followed flocks of migrating birds flying overhead.

In 1820, the young Charles Augustin Sainte-Beuve wrote in his personal notebook, "J'ai lu *René* et j'ai frémi. . . . Je m'y suis reconnu tout entier" ("I read *René* and I trembled . . . I recognized myself totally in it").

Les Natchez brings the cycle to a sentimental conclusion, recounting the death of René and the martyrdom of Souël, tortured by the "savages" for his beliefs. The Christian utopia he had founded in the virgin American forest, a village of hard-working, devout cultivators also martyred by tribes preferring to worship their own gods, illustrates the role that the "beauty of Christianity" played both in the French colonial ideal and in its destruction.

This brief plot summary gives little idea, however, why Chateaubriand's worldview became the craze of Romanticism's first youthful generation; nor why, for instance, Victor Hugo's ambition as an adolescent author was "to be Chateaubriand or nothing." For young writers it was the richness of his style, which incorporated vocabulary new to a France tired of neoclassical imitations, and his treatment of emotions capable of overpowering reason and the founding canons of eighteenth-century "good taste," that pointed them on their way.

His later political career disappointed his younger disciples and his long and ardent opposition to Napoleon lost him many of his first adherents, who, like Victor Hugo for instance, created their own grandiose "mythe de Napoléon," architect of France's imperial *gloire*. Only in his 1811 account of the Holy Land and of its religious value as the birthplace of Christianity, the *Itinéraire de Paris à Jérusalem* (*Travels in Greece, Palestine, Egypt and Barbary during the years 1806 and 1807*), did he succeed once more in seizing the imagination of French Romantics. Years later, in 1849–51, Gustave Flaubert's pilgrimage to the Near East shows the power of Chateaubriand's hold on the young realist's imagination during his "Romantic period."

In his final work, a model of monumental Romantic autobiography, *Mémoires d'outre-tombe* (*Memoirs from beyond the Grave*), written between 1809 and 1847, he returns to the lyricism of his early fiction, relying on his memory and imagination to reawaken the emotions of his youth. His old themes, the wellsprings of French Romanticism, are all revisited: the love of nature, and of the ocean; tragic human love; the celebration of youth; and, most of all, the poetry of memory and of death. In looking back over his own youth, Chateaubriand supplies the sources of René's melancholic self-absorption, pathological boredom, uncontrolled passion, and morbid contemplation of death, ruins, and charnel-houses. The author's anguished realization of the irrevocable passage of time leading to inevitable dissolution causes him to use the work to imagine what life will be "from beyond the grave." As might be expected from a world-weary Romantic, his vision of the future is almost unremittingly pessimistic. In his *Mémoires*, he also creates an enormous parallel between his own influence and that of Napoleon: his great opponent had dominated world history, just as he himself had been the fountainhead of the literature of his day in France.

ALBERT W. HALSALL

Biography

Born 1768 in Saint-Malo into an old Breton family, Catholic and aristocratic. Educated at the colleges in Dol and Rennes, 1777–82. The family settled in the Château de Combourg, 1778. In Brest to prepare exam for entry into the French navy, 1783. Time spent alone in Combourg reading and roaming the estate, 1784–86. Joined the French army in Cambrai, 1786. Presented to Louis XVI at Versailles; stayed frequently in Paris, 1787. Reduced to poverty after the local Revolutionaries occupied Combourg, 1789. April–December 1791, America; July, Baltimore; was received by George Washington; visited Niagara Falls; traveled as far south as the Mississippi. Married Céleste Buisson de la Vigne, 1792, left France, and joined the Army of the Princes to fight against the Revolution; wounded at Thionville. Emigrated to London, 1793. Lived in penury in England, 1793–1800. Back in France, published *Atala*, based partly on his travels in America, 1801. Published the *Génie du christianisme*; some success, 1802. Began career as diplomat in Rome as Secretary to French Legation, 1803. After Napoleon executed the Duc d'Enghien, Chateaubriand resigned his post and began long opposition to the emperor, 1804. Traveled to Jerusalem, 1806. Published *Les Martyrs*, 1809, began the *Mémoires d'outre-tombe*, published 1820–48. Published *L'Itinéraire de Paris à Jérusalem*, 1811. After the Restoration, became Peer of the Realm, 1815. Resumed diplomatic career, ambassador in Berlin, 1821. Ambassador in London, 1822. Minister of foreign affairs, 1823; dismissed, 1824. Published *Les Aventures du dernier Abencérage*, 1826. Ambassador in Rome, 1828. Published *Essai sur la littérature anglaise*, 1836. Published *La Vie de Rancé*, 1844. Died in Paris, 1848; buried on an islet in Saint-Malo harbor facing the ocean.

Selected Works

Le Génie du christianisme ou les Beautés poétiques et morales de la religion chrétienne. 1802. Translated as *The Beauties of Christianity* by Frederic Shoberl, 1813. In part translated as *Celuta or The Natchez* by Henry Colburn and Richard Bentley, 1832. In part translated as *Atala, René* by Rayner Heppenstall. Oxford: Oxford University Press, 1963.
Itinéraire de Paris à Jérusalem. 1811. Translated as *Travels in Greece, Palestine, Egypt and Barbary during the years 1806 and 1807* by Frédéric Shoberl. 1811.

Anne Louis Girodet-Trioson, *Portrait of Francois René, Vicomte de Chateaubriand.* Reprinted courtesy of the Bridgeman Art Library.

Mémoires d'outre-tombe. 1846 Translated as *The Memoirs of François-René, Vicomte de Chateaubriand* by Alexander Louis Teixera De Mattos. London: Freemantle, 1902.

Oeuvres romanesques et voyages. 2 vols. Edited by Maurice Regard. Paris: Gallimard, Bibliothèque de la Pléiade, 1969.

Bibliography

Barbéris, Pierre. *Chateaubriand, une réaction au monde moderne.* Paris: Larousse, 1976.

———. *"René" de Chateaubriand, un nouveau roman.* Paris: Larousse, 1973.

Blewer, Evelyne, et al., eds. *Victor Hugo raconté par Adèle Hugo.* Paris: Plon, 1985. Texte intégral établi et annoté par Evelyne Blewer, Sheila Gaudon, Jean Gaudon, Gabrielle Malandain, Jean-Claude Nabet, Guy Rosa, Carine Trévisan et Annie Ubersfeld sons la direction d'Annie Ubersfeld et Guy Rosa.

Goffic, Charles le. *Ombres lyriques et romantiques.* Paris: Nouvelle Revue Française, 1933.

Painter, George D. *Chateaubriand: A Biography. Vol. 1, 1768–93.* London: Chatto and Windus, 1977.

CHATTERTON 1835

Play by Alfred de Vigny

First performed in Paris at the Théâtre-Français before an audience that included King Louis-Philippe on February 12, 1835, *Chatterton* gave Alfred de Vigny one of his most striking successes in a literary career that had already covered fifteen years and was to continue for three decades more. Though no longer very highly rated even within the restricted canon of French Romantic drama, *Chatterton* remains nonetheless important for its exemplary embodiment of a major theme in the Romantic period, the poet's lot in a hostile world.

Like Victor Hugo and other French writers of his time, Vigny was attracted to the theater when he began writing, and his early works include historical dramas and versions of William Shakespeare, who was then all the rage in France. For *Chatterton,* however, Vigny turned to the *drame bourgeois.* Under the influence of such English plays as George Lillo's *George Barnwell* (1731), this theatrical form had been developed in France, notably by Denis Diderot, as a more realistic alternative, in prose, to the rigidity in form and verse of classical tragedy and comedy to express the emotions and aspirations of the rising middle classes with due seriousness. In 1831, turning momentarily from historical melodrama, Alexandre Dumas *père* had shown the potential of the drame bourgeois (drama of middle-class life) for Romantic themes in his *Antony,* and Vigny profited from his example. It allowed him to adopt a style of representation that was perceived as realistic by comparison with routine Classical evocations of antiquity, and as prosaically quotidian in contrast to the melodramatic exoticism of most of the French Romantic plays of the age.

The single setting, which serves, as in plays respecting the Aristotelian rule of place, to create a feeling that all the action is concentrated and confined to this one spot, is a London house. There John Bell lives and conducts his business. The standing commerce enjoys in England is revealed when none other than the Lord Mayor of London condescends to make a visit. Less attractive aspects of economic developments are shown with the arrival of a delegation of workers to complain about the excesses of newly introduced industrial practices. Obsequious to his betters, Bell is high-handed with employees.

He also bullies his wife. Sweet and meek, the mother of his two little children, Kitty lives in awe of Bell, taking care not to speak a word out of place and keeping her household accounts with scrupulous accuracy. To ensure that no opportunity for profit is neglected, Bell insists that spare accommodation in his house should be let out to a lodger. This is the start of difficulties, for Kitty has rented a room to a young man called Chatterton. Some mystery surrounds him, yet his good nature is shown by his affection for Bell's children. Unfortunately, however, he is penniless, but Kitty tries to persuade the increasingly irritated Bell to overlook his late rent payments. Throughout the play it gradually becomes more apparent that affection is growing between Kitty and Chatterton, and one of Vigny's neatest dramatic devices is the way this emotional development is left unspoken and unfulfilled. Both characters are crippled by timidity and repression, and their economic exclusion is an image of their incapacity to participate in the life of their time.

Gentle, sad, and depressed, the character Chatterton is modeled on the real Thomas Chatterton, who was born in Bristol in 1752 and died, it was then universally assumed, by his own hand in penury in 1770. Vigny was not, however, really interested in depicting the historical figure and the various problems arising m connection with the medieval poems he claimed to have discovered, which were ultimately determined to be forgeries written by Chatterton himself. The dramatist set out rather to develop the image of young talent stunted by an uncomprehending public and cut off before it had time to blossom. Vigny's Chatterton is never seen in the throes of composition. Instead, when confronted by erstwhile friends, who generally opt for the good things of life and see literature as no more than a social accomplishment, Chatterton expounds Shelleyan sentiments about the true role of poets as the leaders of society, reading in the stars the best course for the ship of state. It is a bold, deeply Romantic claim, but hardly one that the play is able to justify, and Vigny's hero comes across primarily as a sensitive misfit in despair.

Bell's ill-assorted household is completed by the Quaker, as he is called. Costume, hat, and manner of speech conjure up a type known well in France ever since 1734, when Voltaire had brought out his *Lettres sur les Anglais.* With stoic calm and the tolerance of human frailty that comes from a long life, the Quaker is a willing listener to Kitty as well as a disabused commentator on her husband's heartlessness. He understands Chatterton, but knows he cannot help him, which may be seen as an oblique comment on the limitations even of his pure religion. Permitted to live in Bell's house because he rescued one of his children from mortal danger, he serves at the end like a chorus, lamenting tragedy that he cannot avert.

The Quaker is also one of the elements contributing local color to this Romantic drama. Though some of it may seem stereotyped, especially to English readers, its contribution to the play's initial triumph was considerable, for it could be considered not merely a picturesque detail, but also fundamental to the theme, for Chatterton's suicide appeared as the typical desperate act of an English melancholic. Entering his bedroom, Kitty discovers his corpse. As she comes out on to the landing, she collapses and tumbles down the stairs in a swoon. The great Romantic actress Marie Dorval achieved the triumph by turning what might have been a mere stunt into the powerful conclusion of a drama that had generally made its impact more discreetly. In *Chatterton* a prosaic world is portrayed in which the poet has no place; only at the end do we appreciate what a tragedy that implies.

CHRISTOPHER SMITH

Text

Chatterton. 1835. Published as *Chatterton.* Edited by Liano Petroni. Bologna: Pàtron, 1962. Published as *Chatterton.* Edited by Armel Hugh Diverrès. London: University of London, 1967.

Bibliography

Buss, Robin. *Vigny: "Chatterton."* Critical Guides to French Texts, No. 34. London: Grant & Cutler, 1984.

Chatterton, Thomas. *Complete Works.* 2 vols. Edited by Donald Stewart Taylor. Oxford: Clarendon Press, 1971.

———. *Selected Works.* Edited by Grevel Lindop. Oxford: Carcanet, 1972.

Doolittle, James. *Alfred de Vigny.* Twayne World Authors Series. New York: Twayne, 1967.

Dorval, Marie. *Lettres à Alfred de Vigny.* Edited by Charles Gaudier. Paris: Gallimard, 1942.

Flottes, Pierre. *Vigny et sa fortune littéraire.* Tels qu'en eux-mêmes. Bordeaux: Ducros, 1970.

Lamoine, Georges "Thomas Chatterton dans l'œuvre de Vigny et dans l'histoire." *Dix-huitième siècle* 3 (1970): 317–30.

Taylor, Donald Stewart. *Thomas Chatterton's Art: Experiments in Imagined History.* Princeton, N.J.: Princeton University Press, 1978.

CHATTERTON, THOMAS 1752–1770

English poet

The life and writing of Thomas Chatterton acted as pervasive and significant influences on both generations of British Romantic writers. His brief existence and early suicide in obscurity provided them with a grim but potent symbol of the solitary artist's struggle with an uncaring society; meanwhile, his poetry and prose prefigured many of their own concerns, both formally and thematically. Although his current status owes much to the Romantics' admiration, expressed in verse, letters, dedications, and criticism, it was secured through a complex process of evaluation and reevaluation. The poet that William Wordsworth famously evoked in *Resolution and Independence* ("I thought of Chatterton, the marvellous boy / The sleepless Soul that perish'd in its pride"), the "poor Child" with whom Samuel Taylor Coleridge identified so strongly in *Monody on the Death of Chatterton*, and Thomas De Quincey saw in a dream ("I see his arm weak as a child's—languid and faint in the extreme") is only part of the picture. The later Romantics, and in particular John Keats and Percy Bysshe Shelley, recognized the social, cultural, and political dimensions of his work.

Nevertheless, Chatterton's biography has played a crucial role in establishing his reputation. It has provided posterity with a blueprint for the beautiful, brilliant, and misunderstood genius too sensitive to live beyond his youth. Chatterton's early death, in obscurity and a lonely garret, enhanced the indifference of an artistic world that was not ready to acknowledge the merits of an original and precocious talent. A published author by the age of ten (the Miltonic *On the Last Epiphany* was printed by his local newspaper, 1662), Chatterton was a prolific satirist and balladeer by the time he was fourteen. His youthful desire for artistic fame, expressed with religious zeal, displayed many of the characteristics that would later define the Romantics (his sister avers that, having been asked to propose an image for her to paint on a bowl, Chatterton replied, "Paint me an angel, with wings, and a trumpet, to trumpet my name over the world").

Most importantly, Chatterton had also begun to compose the modernized medieval romances that would guarantee his posthumous reputation: first, a satire on a vandal who destroyed a medieval cross at St. Mary Redcliffe church (1763); and then, playing a more sophisticated literary game (though aged only eleven), *Elinoure and Juga*, a pastoral eclogue in royal rhyme, which, Chatterton claimed, had been the work of a poet of the fifteenth century. Inscribed on parchment, and presented as genuine to a local hospital usher, the forgery demonstrated not only Chatterton's meticulous, if fallible, eye for detail, but also an intense awareness of the materiality of the text. This awareness extends to Chatterton's desire for financial rewards: knowing that his youth would prejudice his hopes of monetary and literary success, he turned to imitation and deception to make his name.

Thus, the seeds of the Rowley controversy were sown. Thomas Rowley sprang from Chatterton's imagination, in part as an allegorical representation from the past of his present situation: a fifteenth-century Bristol priest and poet, with an enlightened and wealthy patron (the real William Canynges), who wrote sonorous, dramatic verse in manifold moods, forms, and meters. The works Chatterton produced, claiming their author to be Rowley, ranged from the lengthy *Aella* ("a Tragycall Enterlude"), with its novel dramatic structure and manifold metrical variations, to the ballad, the *Bristowe Tragedie*. Presented as genuine medieval artefacts, their authenticity was the subject of heated debate (mainly after Chatterton's death); at the same time, "Rowley's" blurring of reality and artifice, his concentration on the self and nature, provided the Romantics with an inspirational artistic model for their own philosophical pursuits.

"Rowley's" works belong to the late eighteenth-century Gothic revival, which also included Horace Walpole's *The Castle of Otranto* and Thomas Percy's compilation of antique songs and ballads *Reliques of Ancient English Poetry*. However, Chatterton's self-consciousness as an imitator distinguishes him from his peers: laying the seeds of the Romantics' attraction, the verse displays an intense awareness of its own literariness, a playful engagement with its inauthentic originality, and a knowing investigation of the poetic traditions with which it engaged. By adopting a fictional poetic persona, Chatterton confronted the eighteenth century's anxiety of influence, and transcended its feeling that poetry had reached an impasse in form and content.

The combination of youthful idealism and calculated experience, both in the conception and execution of "Rowley," set a precedent that most Romantic artists would follow and admire. In 1803, Robert Southey collaborated with Joseph Cottle to produce an edition of Chatterton's verse. Critics were less kind than the poets (William Hazlitt, for example, thought Chatterton a prodigal, though unrealized, talent, but not a great poet), though Lord Byron is an exception to this rule. Chatterton's experimentation with Gothic imagery and the ballad form, which helped to revive it as a means of social and poetic expression, influenced William Blake's *Songs of Innocence and Experience*, and the *Lyrical Ballads*. Chatterton's *The Unknown Knight*, for example, anticipates Coleridge's "radical" use of four-stress lines in *Christabel* by a quarter of a century. He was, in addition, a role model for self-educated poets like John Clare, who identified with his use of traditional songs and verse forms, and with his autodidactic artistry.

However, it is perhaps Keats who has most warranted a comparison with Chatterton. Shelley explicitly connects the pair in *Adonais* for political ends, conceiving them as innocent victims of a literary establishment that is as cruel as it is reactionary: in Chatterton's case, the abrupt rejection of "Rowley" fragments by the initially enthusiastic Horace Walpole. Keats and Chatterton were self-educated poets for the most part, and incorporated this personal relationship with the canon in their verse: as Keats read George Chapman's Homer, so Chatterton absorbed the diction and symbolism of the "Rowley" poems by studying John Kersey's *Dictionarium Anglo-Britannicum*, Weever's *Ancient Funerall Monuments*, and Verstegan's *A Restitution of Decayed Intelligence*.

Henry Wallis, *The Death of Chatterton*. Reprinted courtesy of the Bridgeman Art Library.

However, although the biographical similarities appear compelling, they are more often than not misleading. Tuberculosis (with help from Joseph Severn) deprived Keats of the suicidal choice that Chatterton made; indeed, Keats's final months are characterized by optimism and misery in almost equal proportions. The dedication of *Endymion* to "the memory of Thomas Chatterton" was a valediction to that influence as well as an acknowledgment of it: it suggests Keats both bidding farewell to his immaturity and embracing it.

The true nature of Keats's debt, revealed by his poems, friends, and letters, expresses a widespread sea-change in the Romantics' attitude to Chatterton. Keats concentrates less on the story of the "marvellous boy" and more on the poetry he produced, and how he produced it. He endorses Chatterton as the "purest writer in the English Language," whose diction he calls, with perhaps a touch of irony, "genuine English Idiom in English Words"; Benjamin Bailey remembers how his friend loved the melodies of Chatterton's "Roundelay sung by the Minstrels of Ella [*sic*]," and would chant it aloud "in his peculiar manner." Keats's light, erotic poems recall the forms and language of his predecessor; and the Gothic and medieval conventions inscribed by *La Belle Dame Sans Merci* and *The Eve of St Agnes* explicitly echo Chatterton's use of the past to comment on the present and the future.

Keats's admiration, and that of the other Romantics, was just the beginning. Modern literary theory has found much to admire in the knowing playfulness of Chatterton's verse. This has helped to elevate the importance of his artistic achievement at the expense of the myth as of the tragic "boy" or idiot savant. This research owes much to the respect of the Romantics, and indeed has increased understanding of their importance to Chatterton and, at the same time, of his to them.

JAMES KIDD

Biography

Born in Bristol, November 20, 1752. Son of Thomas Chatterton, musician, poet, and occultist. Father died before his birth; brought up by his mother and an uncle, Richard Philips, sexton at church of St. Mary Redcliffe in Bristol. Encouraged by Philips to take an interest in writing and antique manuscripts. Educated at Colston's Hospital, c. 1760–66, but mostly self-taught. Apprenticed as a clerk to the offices of Bristol attorney John Lambert, 1767. Contributed to *Felix Farley's Bristol Journal* from 1767 on. Began to write "Rowley" poems: sent them to Horace Walpole who, after initial enthusiasm, rejected them as forgeries, 1769. Concentrated on political and satirical journalism: contributed to *Town and Country Magazine* and a number of other London journals. Coerced his employer to release him from his contract by writing a false suicide note; left Bristol for London, April 1770. Continued to write political articles and a burletta, *The Revenge*; discouraged by lack of critical and financial success. Moved from Shoreditch to Brook Street, Holborn, June 1770. Committed suicide by poison in London, August 24, 1770.

Selected Works

Poetry Collections

The Complete Works of Thomas Chatterton. Edited by Donald S. Taylor and Benjamin B. Hoover. 2 vols. Oxford: Clarendon Press, 1971.
Selected Poems. Edited by Grevel Lindop. Manchester: Fyfield, 1986.

Bibliography

Ackroyd, Peter. *Chatterton*. London: Penguin, 1993.

Browning, Robert. *Essay on Chatterton*. Edited by Donald Smalley. Cambridge, Mass.: Harvard University Press, 1948.

Dix, John. *The Life of Thomas Chatterton*. London: Hamilton, 1837.

Groom, Nick, ed. *Thomas Chatterton and Romantic Culture*. London: Macmillan, 1999.

Kaplan, Louise J. *The Family Romance of the Imposter-Poet Thomas Chatterton*. Berkeley and Los Angeles: University of California Press, 1989.

Kelly, Linda. *The Marvellous Boy: The Life and Myth of Thomas Chatterton*. London: Weidenfeld and Nicolson, 1971.

Masson, David. *Chatterton: A Story of the Year 1770*. London: Macmillan, 1874.

Mathias, Thomas. *An Essay on the [. . .] Poems Attributed to Thomas Rowley*. London: T. Becket, 1783.

Myerstein, E. H. W. *A Life of Thomas Chatterton*. London: Ingpen and Grant, 1930.

Taylor, Donald S. *Thomas Chatterton's Art: Experiments in Imagined History*. Princeton, N.J.: Princeton University Press, 1978.

CHENIER, ANDRÉ 1762–1794

French poet, writer, and political journalist

André Chenier's career was very brief, lasting only from 1778 to his death in 1794 at the hands of the Revolutionary Tribunal. Following the posthumous publication of his poems in 1819, he was adopted by the Romantics as a precursor of their movement.

A frequent visitor to the salon of his Greek mother, Chenier was further exposed to the works of classical antiquity at the Collège de Navarre in Paris (1773–81). At the same time, he came into contact with more contemporary French authors and with the theories of modern science. It was during this period that his poetic vocation emerged, and his first examples of writings in verse included an adaptation from Homer and an imitation of Virgil's eighth *Eclogue* (1778).

The fundamental tenets of Chenier's poetic theories are expressed in his *Essai sur les causes et les effets de la perfection et de la décadence des lettres et des arts* (*Essay on the Causes and Effects of Perfection and Decadence in the Letters and the Arts*) begun in the early 1780s and published several years later (exact date unknown). Here he elaborated the Romantic notion of naivete described as "an infallible erudition of nature, a profound and naive experience of the human heart." For Chenier, the artist's task was to express universal feelings, in particular the primary, primordial passions of love, hate, and fear. These feelings manifest themselves in different ways throughout history, and the modern writer must seek a new language through which to communicate them.

In the *Essai*, Chenier also focused on the relationship between literature and society. Foreshadowing Madame Anne-Louise-Germaine de Staël, he felt that literature can only be fully comprehensible when viewed against the background in which it evolved, and that the poet's function is to be the supreme interpreter of his age; also that writers have a moral obligation to fight social and political corruption.

Indeed, a large section of the essay is devoted to the discussion of an ideal society. Clearly influenced by Jean-Jacques Rousseau, Chenier posited a social system based on the principles of equality and justice. He expressed a particular preference for ancient Greek civilization and literature, which he saw as the embodiment of the good, the beautiful, and the simple.

Chenier's poetic theories are further developed in his controversial poetic manifesto *L'Invention* (1787). Here he saw the role of the poet as essentially that of inventor: by drawing upon the disparate elements in nature the artist can produce new associations or combinations, a process that in many respects recalls Charles Baudelaire's poem "Correspondances" (in *Les Fleurs du Mal*, 1857). Chenier also elaborated a doctrine of "inventive imitation": the artist should seek inspiration from the literature of classical antiquity as regards matters of form and aesthetic beauty, but the choice of subject matter must be modern: "sur des pensers nouveaux faisons des vers antiques" ("Let us graft ancient verses onto new thoughts").

Chenier attached particular importance to science among contemporary sources of poetic inspiration, notably to physics, the natural sciences, and astronomy. As an ideal source of color and of dazzling images, science can serve as an effective tool in realizing the poet's task, that of inventing a new world or poetic universe through the creation of a new language.

In 1787 Chenier also began his *Epitre sur ses ouvrages* (*Epistle on his Works*) describing his method of writing. This was followed by the poem "La République des lettres" ("The Republic of Letters," 1787), in which he further expounded his views on the relationship between the artist and society. His stress on the role of poet as seer guiding humanity towards a better life was to be echoed later in the writings of Victor Hugo.

Chenier composed his first series of poems, *Bucoliques*, from 1785 to 1787. The poems are set in a pastoral landscape reminiscent of ancient Greece, and evoke feelings later recognized as characteristic of the Romantic sensibility: love, friendship, solitude, death, nostalgia for a lost childhood, regret for the passing of youthful love. Particularly influential was the poem "La Jeune Tarentine" ("The Young Tarentine"), one of the first to be published after his death: in its musicality, power of suggestion, and focus on the visual and pictorial, it not only anticipated the writings of Baudelaire and of the Parnassians, but also those, much later, of Paul Verlaine. Equally significant was the poem "Le Malade" ("The Sick Person"), which, in its evocation of the ambivalent and the bittersweet, pointed to what the Romantics would uphold as a central aspect of love.

Also during the 1780s, Chenier composed many of his elegies, which are addressed to his lovers. Their principal themes include those of suffering and loss, of love as a dreamlike state and as a state of disequilibrium. A trip to Italy in 1787–88 marked a development in Chenier's concept of love, his poems now acquiring a more spiritual and philosophical dimension. The years he spent in England (1788–90) as secretary at the

French Embassy also had a strong impact on his work, his own experience of intense alienation in a class-ridden society expressing itself in the fundamental theme of solitude. It was at this time that he wrote his political poems "La Liberté" and "Hymne à la justice." It is also thought that he began his two philosophical epics "L'Hermès" and "L'Amérique" while in London. These were later to exert a profound influence on Alfred de Vigny and on Alfred de Musset.

Chenier's political writings were inaugurated with his article *Avis au peuple français sur ses véritables ennemis* (*Advice to the French People on Its True Enemies*, 1790), which condemned the corruption of the Ancien Régime and called for reforms within the framework of constitutional monarchy. The Reign of Terror, however, led him to alter his position. In his essay *Réflexion sur l'esprit de parti* (*Reflections of Partisan Spirit*, 1791) he pleaded for the restoration of basic human rights and attacked mob psychology. Later in 1793 he wrote several *iambes* in which he expressed indignation at the number of executions, and virulently satirized the Jacobins.

Many of the poems written during this period are considered among Chenier's finest works. These include the odes written for Fanny Lecoulteux, recognized as the quintessential expression of Romantic agony. An equally powerful work is the poem "La Jeune Captive" ("The Young Captive Girl," 1794), inspired by the Duchesse de Fleury, whom Chenier met while interned in Saint-Lazare. In its focus on the themes of life's brevity, the passing of youth, and the inevitability of death, this work stands out as one of the most striking examples of lyricism in French poetry, exerting a profound influence on generations to come.

BRONWEN MARTIN

Biography

Born in Constantinople, October 30, 1762. Moved to France, 1765. Student at the Collège de Navarre, Paris, 1773–81; fell in love with dancer "Lycoris," 1781; military service in Strasbourg, 1782; returned Paris, 1783. Began writing poems, essays, and epistles in eighties. Traveled to Switzerland, 1784; began relationships with Mme de Bonneuil and Marie Cosway, 1785. Traveled to Italy, 1786. Fell in love with Fanny Lecoulteux, 1787. Left for London to take up post as secretary at the French Embassy, 1787; returned Paris, 1790. Began writing numerous political articles, mainly for *Le Moniteur* and *Journal de Paris*, as well as continuing poetic output begun in the eighties. Arrested in Passy, March 7, 1794; imprisoned in Saint-Lazare; guillotined by Revolutionary Tribunal, July 25, 1794.

Selected Works

Avis au peuple français sur ses véritables ennemis. 1790.
Réflexions sur l'esprit de parti. 1791.
La Jeune Tarentine. Published by Marie-Joseph Chenier as *Elégie dans le goût ancien*, 1801.
Oeuvres complètes. 1819.
Oeuvres poétiques. 1862.
Oeuvres complètes d'André Chenier. 3 vols. Edited by Paul Dimoff. 1908.
Oeuvres complètes. Edited by Gerald Walter. 1958.
André Chenier, Poems. Selected and edited by Francis Scarfe. Oxford: Blackwell, 1961.

Bibliography

Dimoff, Paul. *La Vie et l'oeuvre d'André Chenier des origines jusqu'à la Révolution française, 1762–1790.* Paris: Librairie E. Droz, 1936.
Fabre, Jean. *André Chenier.* Paris: Hachette, 1965.
Kopf, Martin. *The Poetics of André Chenier.* New York: Columbia University Microfilms, 1972.
Mornet, Daniel. *French Thought in the Eighteenth Century.* Translated by Lawrence Levin. Hamden, Conn.: Archon Books, 1969.
Scarfe, Francis. *Andre Chenier: His Life and Work, 1762–1794.* Oxford: Clarendon Press, 1965.

CHERUBINI, MARIA LUIGI 1760–1842

Italian composer

Maria Luigi Cherubini lived the first half of his life in the eighteenth century and the second half in the nineteenth century. This fact is reflected in his music, which blends classical and Romantic aesthetic values. Of course, these stylistic labels oversimplify a complex situation, but the fact remains that Cherubini and his music offer us a good example of how musical Romanticism grew out of the traditions associated with composers like Christoph Willibald von Gluck and Wolfgang Amadeus Mozart. By nature, Cherubini was a conservative composer. His early musical education had been rigorous and thorough, and he held traditional compositional standards in high regard. His father, a keyboard player who worked for the Teatro della Pergola in Florence, began teaching his son music at the age of six. By the time he was nine, the boy had begun composition lessons with other Florentine musicians, eventually studying with the renowned opera composer Giuseppe Sarti in Milan and Bologna. All of these teachers insisted that Cherubini make a systematic study of the rules of counterpoint and figured bass, and they used the works of revered Renaissance and baroque composers as models to emulate. This education remained with Cherubini throughout his life and marked all of his musical output. Few musicians of his generation possessed such a high degree of technical facility, which to a large extent was the direct result of his fervent adherence to the skills he had learned while a student in Italy.

Cherubini settled in Paris in 1788. His greatest influence on the Romantic generation was through the operas he composed from 1791 to 1800. All these operas were composed for the Théâtre Feydeau (known as Théâtre de Monsieur prior to July 1791), a theater known for its excellent orchestra and singers. *Lodoïska* (1791), the first of Cherubini's operas for the Feydeau, is an early example of the rescue opera, a genre particularly popular during the early years of the Revolution, in which an innocent prisoner is liberated from confinement imposed by a tyrant (the best-known example is Ludwig van Beethoven's *Fidelio*). This opera also secured Cherubini his first major success in Paris. Audiences and critics alike praised the composer for his effective deployment of ensembles and the expansion of arias to accommodate greater emotional nuance. In this opera, elements of *opera buffa* and *opera seria* were incorporated within a French operatic idiom; the composer grafted Italian lyricism on to forms associated with *opéra-comique*. This amalgamation of stylistic elements owed much of its success to the formal balance that Cherubini managed to maintain throughout the work, further evidence of his training.

Of course, Cherubini's contributions to French opera extended beyond his deployment of Italianate features within a Gallic genre. With his friend and fellow composer Étienne-Nicolas Méhul, he participated in the development of operatic innovations that would transform French opera. The violent plot of *Médée* (*Medea*, 1797), in which the mythological sorceress Medea is rejected by her husband Jason and kills their sons in revenge, encouraged Cherubini to compose his most ambitious and, in many ways, satisfying music for the stage. Passionate vocal lines are accompanied by a seething orchestra that is symphonic in its conception. For example, in the duets for Medea and Jason, the two performers sing in a declamatory style while the orchestra develops short, rhythmically charged motives that build in momentum. Although some critics of the day found the work difficult, none doubted the music's force. A few years later, in *Les Deux Journées* (*Two Days*, 1800), Cherubini used recurring themes, or reminiscence motives, to great effect. A number of Parisian composers, including Méhul, had successfully exploited this technique in their operas of the 1790s, and it would eventually influence composers like Richard Wagner and Carl Maria von Weber. Although Cherubini was just one of many composers developing these musical devices in the 1790s, he stands out from his contemporaries by virtue of his superior musical technique. The counterpoint in his ensembles, as well as his ability to sustain a novel effect without rendering it cloying, set Cherubini's operas apart from those of other composers active in France.

The stage works composed after *Les Deux Journées* failed to achieve the same degree of success that the earlier operas had enjoyed. This fact contributed to a growing sense of depression that would periodically recur throughout the remainder of the composer's life. Whatever doubts he had concerning his career, Cherubini continued to compose, but he focused less and less on opera, turning to other genres instead. With the Bourbon Restoration (1814–15), he became interested in sacred genres. His approach to religious music is best exemplified by his two requiem masses. In them, he fused the dramatic vigor found in his best operas with liturgical texts. The role of the orchestra in these works equals, and on occasion overwhelms, the vocal writing. By means of these powerful statements of faith, Cherubini helped to reinvigorate French sacred music, which had suffered from neglect during the Revolution and Consulate, and earned lavish praise from composers like Beethoven, Hector Berlioz, and Johannes Brahms. At roughly the same time, Cherubini was also busy running the Conservatoire National de Musique in Paris, having been named its director in 1822. He devoted increasing amounts of his energy to this new position, carefully shaping the institution for future generations.

A wide array of nineteenth-century composers embraced Cherubini's music enthusiastically. His pupils, including Daniel-François-Esprit Auber, François-Adrien Boïeldieu, and Fromental Halévy, wrote admiringly of him. Even outside France his name was associated with music of the highest quality. Brahms, Anton Bruckner, and Wagner all studied scores by Cherubini. His operas from the 1790s continued to be performed throughout Europe for several decades after his death in 1842. Unfortunately, by the end of the nineteenth century, his music was more esteemed than performed, and his reputation rested on a single counterpoint treatise that he had written in collaboration with Halévy. *Médée* continued to receive occasional performances, but in an Italian translation, with extensive cuts and newly composed recitative replacing the original spoken dialogue. In the past two decades, however, Cherubini's music has enjoyed something of a revival. French versions of *Lodoïska* and *Médée* have been staged, while recordings of these and other works attest to the composer's achievement and place in opera history.

MICHAEL E. McCLELLAN

Biography

Born in Florence, probably September 8, 1760. First studied music with his father; studied under the renowned composer Giuseppe Sarti, 1778–81. Composer for the King's Theatre, London, 1784–86. Moved to Paris, 1786; hired at the Théâtre de Monsieur (renamed Théâtre Feydeau, 1791), 1789. Married Anne Cécile Tourette, 1792. Employed by the Institut National de Musique, 1793–95; named inspector of the Conservatoire National de Musique in 1795–1814, 1816–42; director of the Conservatoire, 1822–42. Died in Paris, March 15, 1842.

Selected Works

Modern Editions
Médée. Facsimile ed. 1971.
Requiem in C Minor. Edited by Wolfgang Hochstein. Stuttgart: Carus-Verlag, 1996.

Operas
Démophon. 1788.
Lodoïska. 1791.
Elisa, ou le voyage aux glaciers du Mont St-Bernard. 1794.
Médée. 1797.
L'Hôtellerie portugaise. 1798.
Les Deux Journées. 1800.
Anacréon, ou l'amour fugitif. 1803.
Faniska. 1806.
Les Abencérages, ou l'étendard de Grenade. 1813.
Ali-Baba, ou les quarante voleurs. 1833.

Sacred Music
Requiem Mass in C Minor. 1816.
Solemn Mass in G Major for the Coronation of Louis XVIII. 1819.
Mass in A Major for the Coronation of Charles X. 1825.
Requiem Mass in D Minor. 1836.

Other
Cours de contrepoint et de fugue [in collaboration with F. Halévy]. 1835. Translated as *A Course of Counterpoint and Fugue* by J. A. Hamilton. 1837.

Bibliography

Boyd, Malcolm, ed. *Music and the French Revolution*. Cambridge: Cambridge University Press, 1992.
Charlton, David. "Cherubini: A Critical Anthology, 1788–1801." *Research Chronicle* 26 (1993): 95–127.

Charlton, David. *French Opera 1730–1830: Meaning and Media.* Aldershot, England: Ashgate, 2000.

Deane, Basil. *Cherubini.* London: Oxford University Press, 1965.

Dent, Edward J. *The Rise of Romantic Opera.* Edited by Winton Dean. Cambridge: Cambridge University Press, 1976.

Heidemann, Oliver. *Luigi Cherubini: Les Abencérages, ou l'étendard de Grenade.* Munster: Waxmann, 1994.

Laudon, Robert T. *Sources of the Wagnerian Synthesis: A Study of the Franco-German Tradition in Nineteenth-Century Opera.* Salzburg: Katzbichler, 1979.

Mongrédien, Jean. *La Musique en France des lumières au romantisme, 1789–1830.* Paris: Flammarion, 1986.

Ringer, Alexander L. "Cherubini's Médée and the Spirit of French Revolutionary Opera," in *Essays in Musicology in Honor of Dragan Plamenac.* Edited by Gustave Reese and Robert J. Snow. Pittsburgh: University of Pittsburgh Press, 1969.

Russo, Paolo. "Visions of Medea: Musico-Dramatic Transformation of a Myth." *Cambridge Opera Journal* 6 (1994): 113–24.

Selden, Margaret. "The French Operas of Luigi Cherubini." Ph.D. diss. Yale University, 1951.

Willis, Stephen C. "Cherubini from Opéra Seria to Opéra Comique." *Studies in Music* 7 (1982): 155–82.

———. "Cherubini, Luigi (Carlo Zanobi Salvadore Maria)," in *The New Grove Dictionary of Music and Musicians,* vol. 4: 203–13. Edited by Stanley Sadie. London: Macmillan, 1980.

———. "Luigi Cherubini: A Study of His Life and Dramatic Music, 1795–1815." Ph.D. diss. Columbia University, 1975.

CHILD, LYDIA MARIA FRANCIS 1802–1880

American writer, editor, and activist

The youngest surviving child of a prosperous baker, Lydia Maria Childnée (Francis) received a modest education and briefly taught at school until she began her career as an author. From the publication of her first novel in 1824 until the appearance of her last essay in 1879, Child was one of a small handful of professional writers in the United States, and the foremost woman among them. Her significant contributions to American literature include pioneering works in a variety of genres, from the advice book and historical novel to children's fiction and the travel essay. Her enduring influence on American culture stems from her leadership in crusades to extend to all human beings the promises that democracy made to white, male Americans. Child was eclectic, writing fiction, nonfiction, and poetry, but several intertwining themes can be identified in her major works: abolition; religious toleration; education; and civil and social equality for women, African Americans, and Native Americans.

Her first novel, *Hobomok, A Tale of Early Times,* appeared in 1824. Set in frontier New England, it is the story of Mary Conant's flight into the forest in rebellion against puritan strictures, marriage to Hobomok, an "Indian . . . cast in nature's noblest form," and eventual reintegration into white civilization with her biracial child. Written in an effort to create a distinctly American historical novel, Child's narrative presented a radical revisioning of the history of New England's settlers' relations with Native Americans, and women's relations to patriarchal institutions, challenging the then-normative view of the inevitability of antagonism between races, and women's subordination to men.

Child also published a collection of children's stories in 1824, *Evenings in New England,* which led to the opportunity to edit the *Juvenile Miscellany,* the first American magazine for children. During her eight-year tenure as editor, Child wrote much of the material that appeared in the *Miscellany* herself (especially short stories that encouraged hard work, thrift, and democratic values), and published work by other leading American women writers, including Sarah Hale, Catherine Sedgwick, and Lydia Sigourney.

While editing the *Miscellany,* Child also wrote nonfiction for adults, which reiterated the values expressed in her children's fiction: *The Frugal Housewife,* the first manual of home economics intended for use by American women of limited means, appeared in 1829. It became an enduring best-seller, going through more than thirty printings during Child's lifetime. Child published other practical guidebooks for child-rearing and family management and textbooks for adult education, including *The Freedmen's Book* (1865), designed to offer freed slaves instruction in reading and civics while providing inspirational examples of the abilities and accomplishments of Africans and African Americans.

Child's groundbreaking work with *The Juvenile Miscellany* ended in the midst of public disapproval of her abolitionist activism. She had begun writing antislavery stories for the *Miscellany* in 1830, but reached a large adult audience in 1833 when she published *An Appeal in Favor of That Class of Americans Called Africans,* a wide-ranging and comprehensive argument for the rights of African Americans to the fruits of their labor, freedom, citizenship, and equality under the law. Abolitionists hailed *An Appeal* as a masterwork, but subscriptions fell dramatically in the following months, and Child resigned as editor in 1834. However, Child became a figure of national importance in the anti-slavery debate, earning William Lloyd Garrison's accolade as "the first woman in the republic." She published a number of short stories and books, including *Authentic Anecdotes of American Slavery* (1835) and *The Duty of Disobedience to the Fugitive Slave Law* (1860); served as the editor of the *National Anti-Slavery Standard* (1841–44); edited Harriet A. Jacobs's *Incidents in the Life of a Slave Girl* (1861); and participated in the national work of antislavery societies. During the Civil War, Child wrote pro-emancipation articles and letters, performed charitable work for "contrabands" (runaway slaves in the care of the United States Army) and for abolitionist-led regiments, and lobbied for education and land redistribution for freedmen.

Child joined the Swedenborgian Society of the New Jerusalem in 1822, breaking with the Calvinism of her childhood and the Unitarianism of mainstream Boston society. In 1855, Child published *The Progress of Religious Ideas,* an expansive discussion of world religions, which approached Christianity as one of many paths to religious truth, rather than the only gauge by which faith can be measured. Her continuing interest in world religions led her to join the Free Religious Association in 1876; one of her last published works, *Aspirations of the World* (1878), stressed the unity of diverse paths toward the divine.

It was in 1828 that she married David Lee Child, a Harvard-educated lawyer, who was at the time of their marriage editor of the *Massachusetts Journal*. David's poor judgment about money soon forced Lydia Child to bear financial responsibility for the couple, making her, by necessity, one of America's first self-supporting professional authors, which gave her a deep and painful understanding of the legal and civil disabilities imposed upon American women. In 1835, Child published *History of the Condition of Women*, a comparative analysis of women's place in society throughout world history. She often compares the situation of women to that of slaves, and emphasizes that women's "nature" is necessarily shaped by social and historical circumstances. Though not an explicit tract on women's rights, Child does argue that women neither deserve nor require the dependency idealized by the American ideas of genteel woman-hood and the sexual double standard. These themes had been evident in her 1825 bestseller, *The Rebels*, in which women's struggles for selfhood are depicted along with men's political struggles for nationhood during the Revolutionary War. After the Civil War, and the failure of the Reconstruction to ensure civil rights for African Americans, Child turned her energies to advocacy for women's suffrage. A generation older than many of the key figures in this struggle, Child did not live to see its success.

Throughout her life, Child used her pen to promote the causes inspired by her deepest beliefs—the fundamental equality of all human beings, the importance of education, and the diversity of true faith—which emerged from her own religious faith and political convictions as a Romantic humanist. Many of her causes were controversial, and her early adoption of radical political positions and her powerful advocacy made her a pioneer in the most significant American campaigns for human rights in the nineteenth century.

ALISON SCOTT

Biography

Born in Medford, Massachusetts, February 11, 1802. Educated in local day schools and female academies in Medford and Norridgewock, Maine. Taught school in Gardner, 1820–21; in Watertown, 1826–27; and Dorchester, 1830 (all in Massachusetts). Worked as writer, 1824–79. Editor of the *Juvenile Miscellany*, 1826–34. Married David Lee Child, attorney and newspaper editor, October 19, 1828. Editor of *National Anti-Slavery Standard*, 1841–44. Died October 20, 1880, in Wayland, Massachusetts.

Selected Works

Fiction
Hobomok, A Tale of Early Times. 1824.
The Rebels; or Boston before the Revolution. 1825.
The Coronal. A Collection of Miscellaneous Pieces, Written at Various Times. 1832.
Philothea. A Romance. 1836.
Fact and Fiction: A Collection of Stories. 1846.
Sketches from Real Life. Vol. 1, *The Power of Kindness.* Vol. 2, *Home and Politics.* 1850.

Autumnal Leaves: Tales and Sketches in Prose and Rhyme. 1857.
A Romance of the Republic. 1867.

Nonfiction
The Frugal Housewife. 1829.
The Mother's Book. 1831.
The Biographies of Madame de Staël, and Madame Roland. 1832.
The Biographies of Lady Russell, and Madame Guyon. 1832.
Good Wives. 1833.
An Appeal in Favor of That Class of Americans Called Africans. 1833.
The History of the Condition of Women, in Various Ages and Nations. 1835.
Authentic Anecdotes of American Slavery. 1835.
The Evils of Slavery, and the Cure of Slavery. The First Proved by the Opinions of Southerners Themselves, the Last Shown by Historical Evidence. 1836.
The Family Nurse; or Companion of The Frugal Housewife. 1837.
Letters from New-York. 1843.
Letters from New York. Second Series. 1845.
The Progress of Religious Ideas, through Successive Ages. 1855.
Correspondence between Lydia Maria Child and Gov. Wise and Mrs. Mason, of Virginia. 1860.
The Right Way the Safe Way, Proved by Emancipation in the British West Indies, and Elsewhere. 1860.
The Duty of Disobedience to the Fugitive Slave Act: An Appeal to the Legislators of Massachusetts. 1860.
An Appeal for the Indians. 1868.

Children's Books
Evenings in New England. Intended for Juvenile Amusement and Instruction. 1824.
Biographical Sketches of Great and Good Men. Designed for the Amusement and Instruction of Young Persons. 1828.
The First Settlers of New-England; or, Conquest of the Pequods, Narragansets and Pokanokets: As Related by a Mother to Her Children, and Designed for the Instruction of Youth. 1829.
The Little Girl's Own Book. 1831.
Anti-Slavery Catechism. 1836.
Flowers for Children. 3 vols. 1844–47.
The Gift Book of Biography for Young Ladies. 1847.
Rose Marian and the Flower Fairies. 1850.
The Childrens' [sic] Gems. The Brother and Sister: And Other Stories. 1852.
A New Flower for Children. 1856.

Edited Volumes
The Juvenile Souvenir. 1827.
Moral Lessons in Verse. 1828.
The Oasis. 1834.
The American Anti-Slavery Almanac for 1843. 1843.
The Patriarchal Institution, As Described by Members of Its Own Family. 1860.
Incidents in the life of a Slave Girl, by Harriet A. Jacobs. 1861.
Looking Toward Sunset. From Sources Old and New, Original and Selected. 1865.
The Freedmen's Book. 1865.
Aspirations of the World. A Chain of Opals. 1878.

Letters
Letters of Lydia Maria Child with a Biographical Introduction by John G. Whittier and an Appendix by Wendell Phillips. Edited by Harriet Winslow Sewall. Boston: Houghton Mifflin, 1882.
The Collected Correspondence of Lydia Maria Child, 1817–1880. Edited by Patricia G. Holland, Milton Meltzer, and Francine Krasno. Millwood, N.Y.: Kraus Microform, 1980.

Lydia Maria Child: Selected Letters, 1817–1880. Edited by Milton Meltzer, Patricia G. Holland, and Francine Krasno. Amherst: University of Massachusetts Press, 1982.

Bibliography

Baer, Helene. *The Heart is Like Heaven: The Life of Lydia Maria Child.* Philadelphia: University of Pennsylvania Press, 1964.

Clifford, Deborah Pickman. *Crusader for Freedom: A Life of Lydia Maria Child.* Boston: Beacon Press, 1992.

Karcher, Carolyn L. *The First Woman in the Republic: A Cultural Biography of Lydia Maria Child.* Durham, N.C.: Duke University Press, 1994.

————, editor. *A Lydia Maria Child Reader.* Durham, N.C.: Duke University Press, 1997.

Meltzer, Milton. *Tongue of Flame: The Life of Lydia Maria Child.* New York: Crowell, 1965.

Mills, Bruce. *Cultural Reformations: Lydia Maria Child and the Literature of Reform.* Athens: University of Georgia Press, 1994.

CHILDE HAROLD'S PILGRIMAGE 1812–1818

Poem in four cantos by Lord Byron

Lord Byron's *Childe Harold's Pilgrimage* embodied, perhaps better than any other poem of the age, that spirit of melancholy and disillusionment typical of the younger generation of English Romantics. The publication of the first two cantos of the poem in 1812 ensured immediate literary and social fame for Byron; as he put it, he woke one morning and found himself famous. The protagonist, Harold, is a solitary figure, alienated from society and haunted by guilt, who wanders around Europe in a series of secular "pilgrimages." Harold is the first example of the so-called Byronic hero, the egotistical and misogynist character of most of Byron's successive works, particularly the "Turkish Tales" *Manfred* (1817) and *Cain* (1821), as well as a central protagonist of English and European Romantic culture.

The subject of the poem was contemporary, but paradoxically was presented in Spenserian stanzas, a traditional meter that in Byron's opinion allowed greater flexibility and freedom of expression than other poetical forms. Despite Byron's claims to the contrary, Harold was identified by the majority of readers with Byron himself. In fact, in an early draft of the poem the protagonist was called Childe Burun, after an old version of Byron's family name. *Childe Harold* certainly has strong autobiographical elements, as the depiction of the protagonist's meditations occasioned by the view of places visited by Byron himself during his travels. In the first two cantos, Harold travels through Spain, Portugal, and the Near East, following very closely Byron's own itinerary during 1809–11, while cantos 3 and 4 deal with Harold's reflections on Belgium, France, Switzerland, and Italy, which Byron visited in 1816–17 following his final departure from Britain. Byron indeed wrote *Childe Harold* during these travels, thereby conferring upon it a sense of immediacy and descriptive accuracy.

The historical and literary associations of the places visited by Harold in his wanderings are given a particular significance in relation to Byron's own revolutionary ideals. The poem may be read as a series of political manifestos in favor of all the oppressed peoples of Europe. Harold raises his voice in support of Spain fighting Napoleon's invasion, Greece suffering under the Ottoman yoke, and Italy moving toward a second renaissance.

Central to the expression of Byron's radicalism is the image of the ruin. In particular, in cantos 1 and 2, the ruins of Greece, linking past with present, represent the potential for liberation of that enslaved people. Classical associations served to add force to Byron's plea for the freedom of "Fair Greece," the "sad relic of departed worth" (2.73), and made an immense contribution to the cause of Greek independence. The ruins, particularly those of Rome in canto 4, also stand as proof and symbol of man's transitory nature, and find their equivalent in the condition of Harold, a "fallen" individual admittedly satiated by vice, himself "a ruin amidst ruins" (4.25), standing as both Byron himself and the archetype of mankind. The silent majesty of the Greek past and the decadence of its present inhabitants are placed in deliberate contrast to the wild Albanians. A largely mysterious country ruled by the violent Ali Pasha of Ioannina, Albania struck a powerful note in Byron's imagination and inspired some of the best passages of the whole poem.

Byron resumed *Childe Harold* in 1816, in the first phase of his self-imposed exile on the continent, a period in which his social reputation and fame seemed to have vanished. In canto 3, the traumatic end of his marriage, the ostracism decreed by English society, the final defeat of Napoleon, and the apparent end of revolutionary hopes among European radicals give particular topicality to his description of the torments of Harold. While the first two cantos were characterized by a precarious balance between the narrator's voice and that of the protagonist, cantos 3 and 4 signal a deepening of the poet's subjectivity as the distinction between Harold and the narrator becomes increasingly blurred: Harold's voice progressively approaches that of the poet himself and finally merges with it.

Central to canto 3 are the portraits of Napoleon Bonaparte and Jean-Jacques Rousseau, two heroic figures whom Byron admires but nevertheless accuses of excessive ambition and egoism. Canto 3 also displays Byron's greater (albeit temporary) concern with the charm of nature's forms. Responding to the influence of Percy Bysshe Shelley, who was traveling with him in Switzerland, Byron is moved by the sublime landscape of the Alps and is prompted to declare, in pantheistic and almost Wordsworthian terms, that "I live not in myself, but I become / Portion of that around me" (3.72). However, Byron's apparent faith in nature and its healing powers is only short-lived, and unlike that of William Wordsworth, is never accompanied by a sympathetic drive toward mankind.

With the journey from Venice to Rome, the very long canto 4 (1818) brings Harold's wanderings to an end. This canto is largely a meditation on time and its work, and culminates with the address to the ocean, a symbol of eternity. From the canto's famous opening lines, "I stood in Venice, on the Bridge of Sighs; / A palace and a prison on each hand" (4.1), Byron operates a shift from nature to art in a celebration of Italian writers and painters. The canto, together with its long notes and the volume of *Historical Illustrations of the Fourth Canto of Childe Harold* (1818), written by Byron's friend John Cam Hobhouse, could be said to have the typical features of a tourist guide.

As a whole, despite its precise geographical locations, *Childe Harold's Pilgrimage* is much more than a topographical poem or a travel book in verse. The poem's historical associations and the places and landscapes described are given meaning only through Byron's personal perspective and his poetical rendition of Harold's misanthropic and solipsistic distance from mankind. At the same time, the revolutionary cosmopolitanism of the poem made it extremely popular among radicals throughout Europe.

MASSIMILIANO DEMATA

Text

Childe Harold's Pilgrimage, cantos 1 and 2. 1812.
Childe Harold's Pilgrimage, canto 3. 1816.
Childe Harold's Pilgrimage, canto 4. 1818.
Childe Harold's Pilgrimage, cantos 1, 2, 3, and 4. 2 vols. 1819.

Childe Harold's Pilgrimage, In Lord Byron, *The Complete Poetical Works*, Vol. 2. Edited, with prose notes and editorial commentary, by Jerome J. McGann. Oxford: Clarendon Press, 1980.

Bibliography

Gleckner, Robert. *Byron and the Ruins of Paradise*. Baltimore: Johns Hopkins University Press, 1967.
Hirsch, Bernard A. "The Erosion of the Narrator's World View in *Childe Harold's Pilgrimage*, I–II," *Modern Language Quarterly* 42 (1981): 347–68.
Joseph, M. K. *Byron the Poet*. London: Victor Gollancz, 1964.
Manning, Peter J. "Childe Harold in the Market Place: from Romaunt to Handbook." *Modern Language Quarterly* 52 (1991): 170–90.
McGann, Jerome J. *Fiery Dust: Byron's Poetic Development*. Chicago: University of Chicago Press, 1968.
Thorslev, Peter L., Jr. *The Byronic Hero*. Minneapolis: University of Minnesota Press, 1962.
Vicario, Michael. "The Implications of Form in *Childe Harold's Pilgrimage*." *Keats-Shelley Journal* 33 (1984): 103–29.
Woodring, Carl. "Nature, Art, Reason, and Imagination in 'Childe Harold.'" In *Romantic and Victorian: Studies in Memory of William H. Marshall*. Edited by W. Paul Elledge and Richard L. Hoffman. Rutherford, N.J.: Fairleigh Dickinson University Press, 1971.

CHILDHOOD

Childhood became an important theme in visual and literary art from the second half of the eighteenth century. This new interest was reflected in works featuring children and childhood themes, in the production of new educational theories, and in the first material written specifically for children to read.

Background

Until the third quarter of the eighteenth century, approaches to childhood in England were dominated by the ideas of John Locke. In his *Essay Concerning Human Understanding* (1690), Locke set out the notion of the blank page, or tabula rasa, of the mind, needing to be trained or "written on" by experience before it could become whole, while in *Some Thoughts Concerning Education* (1693), he provided a practical approach to implementing such training, essentially for the sons of the upper classes. Lockean ideas were challenged from the late 1760s onward in England and elsewhere by the thinking of Jean-Jacques Rousseau, particularly as expressed in his *Discourse on the Origin of Inequality* (1755), his educational guide *Émile* (1762), and the *Confessions* (1782–89). These works, which had a profound influence on Romanticism, presented childhood as a stage of life possessing uniquely valuable qualities of innocence and truth-to-nature that are lost as the effects of civilization encroach upon the growing child. "Everything is good as it comes from the hands of the Author of Nature: but everything degenerates in the hands of man," Rousseau claimed in *Émile, on de l'éducation* (*Emile, or On Education*).

The burgeoning of the middle classes extended education to a much wider section of society than ever before, and gave rise to the growth of a new and substantial market in educational material and writing specifically aimed at children. Samuel Taylor Coleridge, William Wordsworth, and their circle deplored the replacement of the older "wild" and "faery" tales by these new didactic children's books, characterizing this change as a struggle between imagination and instruction, and this notion in turn became a part of British Romantic ideology.

Jean-Jacques Rousseau

In *A Discourse on the Origin of Inequality*, Jean-Jacques Rousseau presented the capacity for self-improvement as "the source of all human misfortunes," since "it is this which, in time, draws man out of his original state, in which he would have spent all his days insensibly in peace and innocence" and "makes him at length a tyrant over both himself and nature." In *Émile*, therefore, Rousseau's plan for his pupil's education consisted in "well-regulated liberty"; "not in gaining time, but in losing it"; "doing nothing and allowing nothing to be done," so that the boy is brought "sound and robust to the age of twelve years without his being able to distinguish his right hand from his left."

The case for Sophie, Émile's female counterpart was, however, completely different: "The first and most important quality of a woman is gentleness," Rousseau maintained. "Made to obey a being as imperfect as man, often so full of vices, and always so full of faults, she ought early to learn to suffer even injustice, and to endure the wrongs of a husband without complaint." Mary Wollstonecraft reacted sharply against such a categorization of the roles of girls and women in *A Vindication of the Rights of Woman* (1792), but nevertheless made use of Rousseauian ideas in her own book for children, *Original Stories from Real Life* (1791).

Writing for Children

The spread of Rousseau's views on children led to a battle between different groups of English educators and writers for the minds of children in the 1780s, 1790s, and early 1800s. On the one hand, authors such as Thomas Day, a dedicated Rousseauist, wrote his popular children's book *Sandford and Merton* (1783–89) to demonstrate that childhood innocence is superior to sophistication, that a rough hardiness is preferable to polished manners, and that the country is better than the town. On the other hand, educators such as Sarah Trimmer, through her periodical *The Guardian of Education*, declared that "the greatest injury the youth of this nation ever received was from the introduction of Rousseau's system . . . which proposed to banish Christianity from the nursery and the school, to make room for a *false* Philosophy, which has no foundation in truth or reason." Trimmer responded to Day with her own famous children's book, *Fabulous Histories* (1786), later known as *The History of the Robins*, which inculcates staunchly conservative values for children, including kindness to animals, respect for one's social superiors, care and charity for one's inferiors, and belief in a God who has ordered the world for the benefit of humankind.

Imagination versus Instruction

Locke had recommended that if a child "had a poetic vein . . . the parents should labour to have it stifled and suppressed as much as may be," and within Romanticism the dichotomy between instruction and imagination was to some extent aligned with the difference between Lockean and Rousseauian thought.

Wordsworth and his sister Dorothy followed Rousseauian methods in their upbringing of little Basil Montague in the late 1790s, and Dorothy explained in 1797 that their "system" was to "teach him nothing at present but what he learns from the evidence of his senses." Within a month of the birth of his first child, Hartley, in 1797, Coleridge was already expressing his view that "children [should] be permitted to read Romances, & Relations of Giants and Magicians & Genii" since he knew "no other way of giving the mind a love of 'the Great,' & 'the Whole.' " Charles Lamb also reflected such views when seeking books for Hartley in London in 1802, complaining to Coleridge, about the *Evenings at Home* series of Anna Laetitia Barbauld and John Aikin (1792–93),

> Knowledge, insignificant and vapid as Mrs Barbauld's books convey, it seems must come to the child in the shape of knowledge; and his empty noddle must be turned with conceit of its own powers when he has learned that a horse is an animal, and Billy is better than a horse, and such like, instead of that beautiful interest in wild tales, which made the child a man, while all the time he suspected himself to be no bigger than a child.

This aptly satirizes items in *Evenings at Home* such as the one in which making tea is presented as "an operation in chemis-

try." In 1808 Coleridge claimed that "such books do not teach goodness, but—if I might venture such a word—goodyness": probably an allusion to one of the best-known children's books of the period, the anonymous *Goody Two-Shoes* (1765).

William Wordsworth

William Wordsworth similarly castigated these instructional volumes, and the attitudes they promoted, in book 5 of *The Prelude* (1800), where he satirically pictured the model child of the educational theorists as a "monster birth / Engendered by these too industrious times," a "child, no child / But a dwarf man." While "The wandering beggars propagate his name," and "Dumb creatures find him tender as a nun," such a child is nevertheless presented as one to be pitied for his "unnatural growth." Wordsworth contrasted this theoretical infant prodigy with the "race of real children," such as himself and his playmates: "not too wise, / Too learned, or too good; but wanton, fresh, / And bandied up and down by love and hate." His own mother is portrayed as "the parent hen amid her brood," who, rather than exercising the forceful educational interference which Wordsworth deplored, "doth . . . little more / Than move with them in tenderness and love."

The same attitude toward children and their view of the world is reflected in the series of poems Wordsworth later designated as "Referring to the period of childhood," which includes "Anecdote for Fathers," "We are Seven," "To H. C., Six Years Old," and "The Pet Lamb, a Pastoral," and this respect for the unique qualities of children and the mysteries of childhood is explored in depth in the "Intimations of Immortality" ode (1807). The ode, which is addressed to four-year-old Hartley Coleridge, is based on the premise of the existence of the soul before birth, and Wordsworth commented in 1843 to Isabella Fenwick that "though this idea is not advanced in revelation, there is nothing there to contradict it." Because the child has as yet traveled only a little way from the "immortal sea" of heavenly preexistence, and still remains close to the "eternal mind" from which he will inevitably become distanced as he grows up, he is characterized as our "best philosopher."

Samuel Taylor Coleridge

The place of childhood in the relationship between Wordsworth and Samuel Taylor Coleridge was a sensitive one. Wordsworth believed that his own country childhood had made a highly beneficial contribution toward his becoming a poet: a belief reflected through *The Prelude*'s status as the story of "the growth of poet's mind." Coleridge, however, felt he had been deprived of the influences of nature at a crucially formative time by being immured at school in London. Hartley's birth offered Coleridge the chance of overcoming his past; of living a Wordsworthian "natural" childhood vicariously through his son. "Frost at Midnight" (1798) explores these ideas, prompting "abstruser musings" both on Coleridge's schoolboy homesickness "in the great city, pent mid cloisters dim," and on his own "cradled infant" who is to "wander like a breeze / by lake and sandy shores" so that he will "see and hear / The lovely shapes and sounds intelligible / Of that eternal language which thy God / Utters."

By contrast, the "Rime of the Ancient Mariner" (1798) presents what is in some ways a childhood nightmare world, in which the refrain "He prayeth best who loveth best / All things both great and small" sounds as if it has been taken from one of the didactic children's stories Coleridge so much disliked.

William Blake

William Blake deplored both the values of the "rational" educators and the mercantile system which supported their books, and his *Songs of Innocence* (1789) and *Songs of Experience* (1794) expose and deconstruct contemporary instructional children's literature, schooling, and religious instruction by using subversive and resistant songs that parody the forms, rhymes, and rhythms of this writing. Although childless himself, Blake loved children; he much admired Wordsworth's "Intimations of Immortality" ode (1807), and in his own work, too, children are presented as still close to eternity and symbolizing the fecundity of the imagination. His position was also, however, ironic and paradoxical, and his use of multiple narrators in the *Songs* complicates the straightforward equation of childhood with innocence, nature, and divinity, and adulthood with experience, the city, corruption, and loss.

Visual art

Children were increasingly the subjects of portraits and other pictures during this period. While Jean-Baptiste Chardin's depictions of children seem always to have a moral message, the "fancy pictures" of Jean-Baptiste Greuze, Joshua Reynolds, Thomas Gainsborough, and others featured children as both angels and urchins, sometimes using beggars as models and presenting fables about children's lives that included religious themes and sometimes overtly erotic elements (as in some of Greuze's work, and Reynolds's "Cupid as a Link-boy" and "Mercury as a Cut-purse," 1774). In Spain, Francisco José de Goya y Lucientes created paintings of children that show childhood as a time of intensely threatened fragility, whereas in more prosperous England portraits of mothers playing with their children (such as that by Reynolds of the Duchess of Devonshire with her daughter, Lady Georgiana Cavendish, 1784), demonstrated the new overtness of affection between parents and children.

Germany

Johann Wolfgang von Goethe's *Wilhelm Meisters Lehrjahre* (*Wilhelm Meister's Apprenticeship*, 1795–96) provided a much-imitated example of the bildungsroman (novel of education) in which a young man is shown setting out in life and learning from experience. The new popularity of folk literature in Germany in this period was exemplified by the recording of folksongs and ballads by Achim von Arnim and Clemens Brentano in *Des Knaben Wunderhorn* (*The Boy's Magic Horn*, 1805–08) and in the *Märchen* (fairytales) collected by the brothers Wilhelm and Jakob Grimm. Their first volume of tales was published in 1812, while a "little edition" of fifty of the stories, issued in 1825, became an enormously popular children's book. Folktales were the source of inspiration for many of the early poems and stories

of Joseph von Eichendorff, which bridge the gap between naive poetry and conscious art. Eichendorff's work expresses a powerful longing for his own childhood in a fictionalized form, with an intense evocation of his lost home in Silesia, which idealized the claims of preindustrialized life.

Denmark

Folk tales were also the inspiration (and often the source) for the children's stories of Odense-born Hans Christian Andersen published between 1835 and 1875. Among the most famous are "Thumbelina," "The Little Mermaid," "The Princess and the Pea," "The Emperor's New Clothes," "The Ugly Ducking," "The Snow Queen," and "The Little Matchseller." The stories can be roughly classified into those that are based on existing folk tales, those deriving inspiration from Andersen's own life, those that make fun of human faults, and the philosophical tales. Andersen was not afraid of introducing feelings and ideas beyond a child's immediate comprehension, while remaining in touch with the child's perspective.

France

Jean de La Fontaine had addressed his *Fables* (1668–78) to the world of the French salons "which one must amuse like a child," and eighteenth-century children enjoyed both these and the French fairytales collected and recounted by Charles Perrault in *Contes de ma mère l'oye* (*Tales of Mother Goose*, 1697) and by Marie-Catherine d'Aulnoy in *Contes des fées* (*Tales of the Fairies*, 1698). Later in the century children were provided with their own highly didactic literature by Marie Leprince de Beaumont, who wrote *Magasin des enfants, contes moraux* (*The Children's Shop: Moral Tales*, 1757); Stéphanie-Félicité de Genlis in *Veillées du château* (*Winter Evenings at the Chateau*, 1784); Louis de Berquin in *Ami des enfants* (*The Children's Friend*, 1782); and by Nicolas Bouilly's *Contes à ma fille* (*Tales for my Daughter*, 1809) and *Contes aux enfants de France* (*Tales for the Children of France*, 1824–25). This didactic tradition gained new force from 1833 onwards, when François-Pierre-Guillaume Guizot enabled local communities to establish primary education facilities, and the resulting increase in childhood literacy was catered for by magazines, such as the *Journal des Enfants* (*The Children's Journal*).

By contrast, Rousseau was a major influence on Bernardin de Saint-Pierre's novel *Paul et Virginie* (*Paul and Virginia*, 1788), which recounts the idyllic and sentimental story of two Parisian children brought up in freedom on Mauritius; the novel became immensely popular both in France and abroad in this period. In early nineteenth-century France, the Rousseauian preoccupation with childhood innocence coincided with decades of high infant mortality and led to a somewhat mawkish sensibility about children in, for example, André Chénier's "Elégie sur la mort d'un enfant" ("Elegy on the Death of a Child," 1819), Émile Deschamps's "A une mère qui pleure" ("To a Weeping Mother," 1828), and "L'Ange et l'enfant" ("The Angel and the Child," 1830) by Jean Reboul. Alphonse de Lamartine included poems on childhood in his *Harmonies poétiques et religieuses* (*Poetic and Religious Harmonies*, 1830) and his epic *Jocelyn* (1836) evoked both the playful and the serious side of childhood. Victor Hugo's verse on this topic earned him later in the nineteenth century the title of "the poet of childhood." Some of Hugo's poems of this type were based on intensely recreated memories of his own childhood, for example "Ce qui passait aux Feuillantines" (What Happened at The Feuillantines) in *Les Rayons et les ombres* (*Sunbeams and Shadows*, 1840), while others, in *Contemplations* (1856), commemorated his beloved eldest daughter, who drowned just after her marriage.

In contrast with this sentimentalizing of childhood purity, autobiographical and other prose treatments of the theme, such as François-Auguste-René Chateaubriand's *René* (1805) and *Mémoires de l'outre-tombe* (*Memoirs from Beyond the Grave*, 1849–50), are much more realistic; and many authors, including Prosper Mérimée in "Mateo Falcone" (1829), Charles Nodier in *Mémoires de Maxime Odin* (*Memories of Maxime Odin*, 1832), Honoré de Balzac in *Louis Lambert* (1834) and *Le Lys dans la vallée* (*The Lily in the Valley*, 1836), and Gustave Flaubert in *Mémoires d'un fou* (*Memoirs of a Madman*), written in 1838 but not published until 1900, painted a predominantly bleak and suffering image of childhood.

Despite the widespread perception that the theme of childhood was of less importance in France than in England and Germany in the Romantic period, Charles Baudelaire could nevertheless deploy childhood as an image for summing up inspired literary achievement as a whole: "le genie," he wrote in 1863, "n'est que l'enfance retrouvée à volonté, l'enfance douée maintenant, pour s'exprimer, d'organes virils et de l'esprit analytique" ("Genius is merely childhood rediscovered at will, but a childhood now possessing, in order to express itself, adult organs and an analytical mind").

CHRISTINE KENYON JONES

Bibliography

Avery, Gillian, and Julia Briggs. *Children and Their Books: A Celebration of the Work of Iona and Peter Opie*. Oxford: Clarendon Press, 1989.

Brown, Penny. *The Captured World: The Child and Childhood in Nineteenth-Century Women's Writing in England*. London: Harvester Wheatsheaf, 1993.

Darton, F. J. Harvey. *Children's Books in England*. 3d ed. Cambridge: Cambridge University Press, 1982.

Goldstone, Bette P. *Lessons to be Learned: A Study of Late Eighteenth Century English Didactic Children's Literature*. New York: Peter Lang, 1985.

Hunt, Peter. *Children's Literature: The Development of Criticism*. London: Routledge, 1990.

Hughes, Glyn Teai. *Romantic German Literature*. London: Edward Arnold, 1979.

Lloyd, Rosemary. *The Land of Lost Content: Children and Childhood in Nineteenth-Century French Literature*. Oxford: Clarendon Press, 1992.

McFarland, Thomas. *Romanticism and the Heritage of Rousseau*. Oxford: Clarendon Press, 1995.

McGavran, James Holt Jr., ed. *Romanticism and Children's Literature in Nineteenth-Century England*. Athens, Ga.: University of Georgia Press, 1991.

Meigs, Cornelia, Anne Thaxter Eaton, et al. *A Critical History of Children's Literature*. New York: Macmillan, 1953.

Pickering, Samuel F. Jr. *John Locke and Children's Books in Eighteenth-Century England*. Knoxville: University of Tennessee Press, 1981.

Postle, Martin. *Angels and Urchins: The Fancy Picture in Eighteenth-Century British Art*. Nottingham: Djanogly Art Gallery, 1998.

Summerfield, Geoffrey. *Fantasy and Reason: Children's Literature in the Eighteenth Century*. London: Methuen, 1984.

CHILDREN'S LITERATURE

Building on the ideas of John Locke and, more immediately, Jean-Jacques Rousseau, Romantic writers developed a new understanding of childhood. Locke had been influential in suggesting that a child was a tabula rasa, a blank slate ready to be inscribed by education and experience. Rousseau made this blankness a virtue, seeing the child as being free from the mental impedimentia that children accumulate as they mature into adults. Poets like William Blake, Samuel Taylor Coleridge, and William Wordsworth seized on this, writing of the child before his or her acculturation as being closest to nature and to God and of childhood as being a state of sublime innocence. In their view, childhood ought to be celebrated for itself, not regarded only as a preparation for adulthood. These views helped to forge a new children's literature, one which rejoiced in the innocence, spontaneity, and unfettered imagination of childhood. Blake, for instance, designed his *Songs of Innocence* as songs that "Every child may joy to hear." But in fact few children had the opportunity to appreciate Blake's efforts on their behalf. During the Romantic era itself, children's literature was still dominated by the sort of improving books which provoked the disgust of Blake, Wordsworth, and others. A new children's literature that was sympathetic to the romantic view of childhood was not to develop until the middle of the nineteenth century.

This was hardly surprising, since a literature written expressly for children was a relatively new phenomenon. It had been able to emerge in the middle of the eighteenth century precisely because publishers, like John Newbery in England, had been able to prove to parents that their books improved their readers, both morally and materially. Until at least the 1820s the utility and morality of children's books were still their major selling points, and their principal aim, to the disgust of Romantic writers, was still to prepare children to become successful adults. Indeed, this kind of literature was able to exert its influence by defining itself in opposition to the recklessness of Romanticism, which seemed to upset existing hierarchies by suggesting that children ought to be free from the authority of their elders, and from the constraints of a prescriptive education, and free to make up their own minds about how society ought to be ordered. For those who lived in fear of the French Revolution—writers such as Sarah Trimmer, who surveyed and censured contemporary children's literature in her periodical *Guardian of Education*—such an ethos was a threat to be treated seriously.

However, just because some prominent Romantic poets dismissed moral tales and heavily didactic stories does not mean that these works are wholly without merit. The polarization between the Romantic ideal and the reality of children's literature may not have been as pronounced as some of the Romantic poets would have had their readers believe. Some recent scholarship has pointed to similarities between the attitudes of Wordsworth and Isaac Watts, who, besides being an influence on Blake, was one of the chief exponents of a supposedly constraining, puritan literature for children. Likewise, Coleridge seems to have welcomed moral didacticism in books for children, although his pantheistic approach would have been anathema to more conventional moralists. Moreover, a sympathetic reading of some of the texts supposedly reviled by the romantics reveals them to be more entertaining and well-written than one might expect. Charles Lamb may have been the one to write, in a letter to Coleridge, "Damn them!—I mean the cursed Barbauld Crew, those Blights and Blasts of all that is Human in man and child," but in fact Anna Laetitia Barbauld's poetry and prose for children, like Mary Martha Sherwood's or Barbara Hofland's, can be engaging and is just as readable as Lamb's own work for children.

During the late eighteenth century, the English and French traditions of children's literature had coalesced. Rousseau was the inspiration for both (although his insistence that the child should not be forced into adulthood too quickly was largely ignored, as was his conviction that all books were bad for children). His English and Irish disciples included Thomas Day and Maria Edgeworth, who were translated into French, just as Arnaud Berquin and Madame de Genlis routinely appeared in English. But it was for the renaissance of the fairy tale that Britain owed most to the continent. Many classic fairy tales had been collected and rewritten in France in the early eighteenth century by Charles Perrault and others. Along with the *Arabian Nights*, they were soon imported to Britain; and, although they came under attack from the moralists in both Britain and France in the decades on either side of 1800, they began to be republished in the early nineteenth century. The continued hostility of early-nineteenth century moralists in itself demonstrates that popular, indigenous tales like *Jack the Giant Killer* and *Valentine and Orson* had also survived in Britain, despite the claims of Lamb, Wordsworth, and others that they had been all but eradicated. Similar traditions of chapbook tales existed on the continent, and it was in Germany that such tales, and others which had never been written down, started to be collected, published, and valued as a pure expression of national culture. Clemens Brentano and Achim von Arnim, E. T. A. Hoffman, and J. K. A. Musäus brought out important collections, but it was the work of Jakob and Wilhelm Grimm that was most influential internationally. Although originally published with extensive notes and no illustrations, their *Kinder- und Hausmärchen* (Children's and Household Tales, 1812–22) quickly became a children's classic throughout Europe; the first English translations appeared in 1823–26. The Grimms inspired similar projects in almost every European nation—Peter Christen Asbjørnsen and Jørgen Moe in Norway, Nathaniel Hawthorne in America, Hans Christian Andersen in Denmark, Aleksandr Pushkin in Russia, to name just a few—and the fairy tale garnered a respectability it had never previously enjoyed. These collections succeeded in establishing the putative Romantic association between children and a pure, uncorrupted folk culture. When Johann Gottfried Herder wrote of folktales that they represented a people's "intuitive sense, creative energy and instinctive behaviour," that they emanated from "a stage of consciousness in which men dreamt

what they did not know, believed what they could not see and in which a man's actions involved his whole being because it was still untouched by any cultural influence," he might just as well have been expressing Wordsworth's views on childhood.

This Romantic revision of children's literature did not entirely purge bookshelves of serious, improving books. Moral tales continued to be produced, often under the aegis of religious societies, and the nineteenth century was the heyday of textbooks full of facts to be learned by rote (which, rather than moral tales, had probably been Wordsworth's primary target in his attack on children's literature in book 5 of *The Prelude*). Yet the work of authors like James Fenimore Cooper, Charles Dickens, Alexandre Dumas, Heinrich Hoffman, and Washington Irving demonstrated that children's literature was no longer to be so utterly dominated by didacticism.

M. O. GRENBY

Selected Works

Joachim Heinrich Campe. *Robinson der Jüngere*. 1779–80.
Stéphanie Félicité Ducrest de Saint-Aubin, Comtesse de Genlis. *Adèle et Theodore*. 1782.
Eleanor Fenn. *Cobwebs to Catch Flies*. c. 1783.
Thomas Day. *Sandford and Merton*. 1783–89.
Friedrich Justin Bertuch, ed. *Bilderbuch für Kinder*. 1790.
John Aikin and Anna Laetitia Barbauld. *Evenings at Home*. 1792–96.
Sarah Trimmer. *The Guardian of Education*. 1802–06.
Clemens Brentano and Achim von Arnim. *Des Knaben Wunderhorn*. 1805–08.
William Roscoe. *The Butterfly's Ball and the Grasshopper's Feast*. 1806.
Charles and Mary Lamb. *Tales from Shakespear*. 1807.
Ivan Andreyevich Krylov. *Fables*. 1809.
Clement Clarke Moore. *A Visit from St. Nicholas*. 1823.
Catherine Sinclair. *Holiday House*. 1839.

Bibliography

Darton, F. J. Harvey. *Children's Books in England: Five Centuries of Social Life*. Revised by Brian Alderson. Cambridge: Cambridge University Press, 1982.
Gaull, Marilyn. *English Romanticism: The Human Context*. New York: W. W. Norton, 1988
Grenby, M. O., "Politicizing the Nursery: British Children's Literature and the French Revolution." *The Lion and the Unicorn*.
Hürlimann, Bettina. *Three Centuries of Children's Books in Europe*. 2d ed. Translated and edited by Brian Alderson. London: Oxford University Press, 1967.
Hunt, Peter. *An Introduction to Children's Literature*. Oxford: Oxford University Press, 1994.
Hunt, Peter, ed. *International Companion Encyclopedia of Children's Literature*. London: Routledge, 1996.
Jan, Isabelle. *On Children's Literature*. Translated by Catherine Storr. London: Allen Lane, 1973.
McGavran, James Holt, Jr., ed. *Romanticism and Children's Literature in Nineteenth-Century England*. Athens, Ga.: University of Georgia Press, 1991.
Myers, Mitzi, "Reform or Ruin: 'A Revolution in Female Manners'," *Studies in Eighteenth-Century Culture*, 11, edited by Harry C. Payne, Madison: University of Wisconsin Press, 1982, 199–216
Pickering, Samuel F. *John Locke and Children's Books in Eighteenth-Century England*. Knoxville: University of Tennessee Press, 1981.

Sander, David. *The Fantastic Sublime: Romanticism and Transcendence in Nineteenth-Century Children's Fantasy Literature.* Westport, Conn.: Greenwood Press, 1996.

Tatar, Maria. *Off With Their Heads! Fairy Tales and the Culture of Childhood.* Princeton, N.J.: Princeton University Press, 1992.

Tucker, Nicholas. "Fairy Tales and Their Early Opponents." In *Opening the Nursery Door: Reading, Writing and Childhood 1600–1900.* Edited by Mary Hilton, Morag Styles, and Victor Watson. London: Routledge, 1997.

CHOPIN, FRÉDÉRIC FRANÇOIS 1810–1849

Polish composer and pianist

Frédéric François Chopin encapsulates the Romantic image of the musician-composer. Along with Franz Liszt, he revolutionized piano music and created much of the important repertoire for that instrument. His creative genius probed the expressive qualities of the piano with an inexhaustible array of compositional devices. Completely identified with the piano, he, perhaps more than any other individual, expressed Romanticism through that instrument.

Both Chopin and Liszt determined to do for the piano what Niccolò Paganini did for the violin. The results of their endeavors are extraordinary, but remarkably different. Both exploited the extreme technical possibilities of the piano. It is not too much of an overgeneralization to describe Liszt's solutions as exuberant and flamboyant, whereas Chopin's music tends to be somewhat more introspective and intimate. Exceptions do exist; some of Chopin's music is quite aggressive and loud, while that of Liszt can be quite subdued. However, the overall impression of their work generates this perception. Paganini visited Warsaw in 1829. Though there is no evidence that he ever met Chopin, his visit did inspire the young composer to commence work on his études, a monumental collection of pieces that demonstrate the technical intricacies and possibilities of the keyboard.

One of the first overtly nationalistic composers, Chopin's Polish identity permeated much of his oeuvre. His Polish heritage even appears in some of his early compositions. The mazurkas in B flat and G of 1826 were composed as direct result of a summer dance party in rural Poland. He consciously endeavored to flavor his music with Polish characteristics. By 1830 he was beginning to assume the mantle of a national composer because of the distinctively Polish character of his work, which included Polish folk dances and modal scales.

The political climate in Poland understandably generated this propensity for Polish music. Poland, like many European states at this time, seethed with unrest as independence movements gained strength and momentum. Chopin was surrounded by many young compatriots in the arts who viewed him as a bright hope for the future. The 1830 revolutions that swept many young radicals into patriotic fervor profoundly influenced the developing young artist. Though it cannot be proven, it is widely believed that the fall of Poland to Russia in 1830 probably inspired the passion of the Revolutionary Étude.

Chopin interacted with many leading figures of Romanticism, including Honoré de Balzac, Eugène Delacroix, and Heinrich Heine. He was acquainted with such musical luminaries as Liszt, Felix Mendelssohn, and Clara and Robert Schumann. His contact with the giants of Romanticism affected his artistic development and fired his imagination. Lesser-known people also influenced him, most notably Johann Nepomuk Hummel, an early exponent of Romanticism who laced his music with classical restraint and who encouraged Chopin's early musical efforts. John Field and Vaclav Tomasek also influenced Chopin, especially regarding the creative possibilities of character pieces such as the nocturne.

Like many fellow Romantics, Chopin's personal life was marked with mood swings and emotional upheaval. Many Romantic artists, Chopin among them, exhibited signs of melancholy tinged with a morbid obsession with death. Though some parallels can be drawn, in general there seems to be little correlation between the mood of a piece of Chopin's work and his state of mind at the time of composition. Some of his most exuberant mazurkas were composed during times of illness and depression, while some of his most pensive nocturnes were created during joyous periods of his life. However, there are several instances in which personal circumstances directly affected his work. His sister, Emilia, died at the age of fourteen of tuberculosis, the same disease that would claim his own life decades later. The brooding Nocturne in E Minor resulted from that tragedy. Romantic entanglements inspired some of his finest work. His adolescent love for Konstancia Gladkowska, an opera singer, inspired the second movement of the Concerto in F Minor, several études (from op. 10), as well as two waltzes (opp. 69 and 70). During the legendary affair with George Sand, he composed the B-flat and B minor sonatas and the F-sharp Impromptu, along with several other works. There is, however, no overt correlation between this music and the love affair. The most striking aspect of the Sand relationship concerns the paucity of output during the years he spent with her. They first met in 1836 and had become lovers within two years. The social life of Paris impeded his ability to focus on composition, and consequently much of his work was produced during summers away from Paris. His teaching schedule in Paris also hampered his creativity. Especially in the early Paris years, the temptation of high fees for teaching members of aristocratic families often interfered with composition. In addition, the debilitating effects of tuberculosis contributed to the diminished output in his later years.

Chopin's early decision to leave Poland permanently was pivotal to his career. He settled in Paris in 1831, but despite previous high-profile performances in Warsaw and Vienna he was not well known at first. After an 1832 concert in Paris, however, he emerged as a major musical force. Though a concert artist of the highest caliber, he gave only about thirty performances during his entire career. Teaching and composition generated a large income, freeing him from the stress of public performance. When he did perform, he preferred the intimacy of salons to the large public halls favored by Liszt and Paganini. Near the end of his life, the 1848 revolution forced him to perform more intensely than he liked. The political upheaval during that time effectively dismantled his lucrative piano-teaching studio. Thus the need for income prompted the physically draining tours of England and Scotland.

We cannot separate Chopin from the piano. No other major composer in history has been so associated with a single instrument. The cello is the only other instrument he favored, and even it appears only in collaboration with the piano. He seemed unable to separate composition from the keyboard and composed almost all works at the piano. Many compositions were written for purposes of self-expression. This trait is especially evident in his mazurkas, scherzos, and ballades. In keeping with this aspect, his music is improvisational in nature. Though some authorities have criticized this freedom in his work, it is not possible to separate it from his artistic being. The published versions of his works were never precisely duplicated in his public performances; no two performances of his compositions were ever identical. The Romantic ideal of self-expression and individualism finds its exemplar in Chopin.

As may be expected from improvisation-based work, most of Chopin's pieces are dominated by melody that is supported by a widely varied accompaniment. In fact, there seems to be an infinite variety of accompaniment figures. His ability to be constantly creative with accompaniment voices while producing simple melodies is perhaps his most notable accomplishment. That by no means diminishes the inventiveness and beauty of his melodic writing. It is his melodies that people are most likely to remember. Chopin's melodies are often compared to those of Vincenzo Bellini—especially his nocturnes to Bellini's cavatinas. The sweeping melodies are vocal in character. The similarities are striking, though there is no substantive evidence that either composer influenced the other.

Chopin revolutionized harmony. It is through harmony that he most impacted later composers. He pushed the boundaries of chromaticism and dissonance. He diluted a sense of key through chains of diminished seventh and ninth chords, often leading into remote key centers. Coloristic use of arpeggiated seventh and ninth harmonic structures was a common accompaniment device. Unusual modulations, often to foreign keys, permeate many pieces. Unresolved dissonances in works like the Prelude in F Major, where the E-flat in the final chord shakes tonal stability, anticipate Arnold Schoenberg and Richard Wagner. Chopin's chromatic movement, especially harmonic deviations from tonality through chromaticism, influenced many other nineteenth-century composers as well. It must be pointed out, however, that Chopin tended to limit his use of chromatic devices for decoration and color. Composers like Wagner, on the other hand, used chromaticism for fundamental structure. Nevertheless, Chopin's extreme chromaticism and colorful chordal structures paved the way for the future. Chromaticsm and unusual harmonies became the organic feature of a work.

The harmonies were emphasized through judicious use of pedal. More than any previous composer for the piano, Chopin exploited the pedal to extend the range and expressiveness of his work. The sustaining power of the pedal enabled him to spread the hand over the entire keyboard, thus transforming the technical possibilities of the instrument.

The opening of the Ballade in G Minor (op. 23) illustrates his penchant for tonal obscurity. The arpeggio that opens the piece is based on a Neapolitan sixth chord instead of the more traditional tonic or dominant. The tonic chord makes its first appearance in measure nine. The Prelude in E Minor uses yet another method to cloud the diatonic anchor. Though the piece begins in E minor, Chopin proceeds through a series of harmonic structures that at first seem to be dominant-seventh chords, but they do not function as dominants, thus creating tonal instability.

Chopin's orchestration and use of form have been subject to much criticism. It is true that his orchestration is rather simple and even clumsy when compared to other leading composers of his day. Whether this is due to inability or to a lack of interest cannot be determined. Lack of training may contribute to the deficiencies of his orchestration, but more than likely the improvisational nature of his work is the greater cause. It is unquestionably a great challenge to transfer the freedom of keyboard improvisation to the discipline required of detailed orchestration. One must also note that five of the six works for orchestra were completed before the age of twenty-one; if he had lived longer, it is likely that he would have demonstrated a more mature approach to orchestration.

The criticism of form is less justified. Chopin favored ternary form, sometimes strictly, but often in modified ways. He had little interest in the traditional boundaries of sonata form, thus placing him in the center of the Romantic ideal as opposed to the tenets of classicism. He and Liszt share this trait, though sonata form is arguably more evident in the work of Liszt. If classical form is the ideal by which music is judged, then Chopin fails the test. The complexity of his music arises less from adherence to formal outlines than from freedom of expression.

Though improvisatory liberty seems to pervade his work, when it is probed, we find that Chopin employed sonata form much more frequently than is often believed. Adhering to the spirit of the Romantic age, he placed his own stamp of individualism on traditional form. In the Ballade in A-flat Major (op. 47), he judiciously employs sonata form with creative subtlety. Initially, the work appears to have a free form, but the tonal scheme reveals an ingenious handling of sonata form. Even in his sonatas he departs from classical norms. The recapitulation consistently begins with the second theme group. In fact, one vital aspect of Chopin's genius lies in his ability to transcend the rules of form, sometimes with startling effect. The last movement of the Sonata in B-flat Minor (op. 35) is comprised of only seventy-five bars. In performance, it occupies less than ten per cent of the total length of the work. Yet the movement's extreme brevity functions well. Traditional thematic development is certainly not missed. One can persuasively argue that in Chopin's oeuvre, form serves the music in imaginative ways rather than dictating its structure. The mature polonaises all share similar organizing traits, such as accented second beats, triple meter, and a foundational accompaniment rhythm. However, Chopin is never straitjacketed by compositional principles. In these works he demonstrates incredible variety, ranging from the melancholy of the Polonaise in E-flat Minor to the virtuosity of the Polonaise in A-flat Major.

It is this seemingly infinite variety that sets Chopin apart from many lesser composers. The mazurkas particularly demonstrate his genius for variety. Chopin wrote mazurkas throughout his career. They not only reveal nationalistic pride, but also tremendous inventiveness in mood, harmony, and melody. He seems to have used this genre for experimentation, a laboratory for the practical working of his musical ideas. On a different level, one can see a similar objective in his collection of twenty-four preludes, completed while living on the island of Majorca with George Sand. Inspired by Johann Sebastian Bach's "Well-Tempered Clavier," Chopin created a relatively brief piece for every major and minor key. Every work in this collection is unique; no two are similar. Chopin revered Bach and devoted much time to the study of his music. It is interesting to note, however, that Chopin does not include a single fugue in the preludes. While paying great respect to Bach, Chopin accomplished a similar goal through completely different and inventive means.

Chopin's music has often been described as feminine. This designation is usually applied perjoratively; such terms as weakness, sentimentalism, restraint, and intimacy pervade descriptions of his work. Even today, many outstanding professional pianists strive to avoid association with the music of Chopin, preferring to be known as exponents of more "masculine" composers like Johannes Brahms or Liszt. Such reticence probably reflects the values of Western society, but may also display ignorance of some of his later and less frequently performed works.

Chopin's influence on succeeding composers is a great legacy. Claude Debussy, Franz Liszt, Arnold Schoenberg, Aleksandr Skriabin, and Richard Wagner are only some of the artists who learned from his work, especially in the area of harmony. The French school was particularly influenced by him. The remarkable use of texture and color as organizing principles, as well as the daring use of chromatic dissonance, impressed many French and Russian composers later in the nineteenth century. At times, Debussy seemed obsessed with Chopin; he intensely examined Chopin's music and admitted that his influence on him was profound. The nationalistic characteristic of his work, especially in the area of modality, served as a clarion model for a number of successors like Bedrich Smetana. Though he died in 1849, Chopin's creative genius influenced the remainder of the century and extended well into the twentieth century.

THEODORE L. GENTRY

Biography

Born in Zelazowa Wola, Poland, probably March 1, 1810. Studied piano with Adelbert Ziwny, 1816–22; studied at Warsaw Conservatory, 1826–29. Moved to Paris in 1831; first Paris concert, February 26, 1832. Met George Sand in 1836; Nov. 1838 to Feb. 1839, lived with her on Majorca; relationship ended in 1847. Last Paris concert, February 16, 1848; arrived in London, April 20, 1848; last public performance, November 16, 1848, at Guildhall, London. Died October 17, 1849.

Selected Works

Mazurkas, op. 6 (4), 1830–32; op. 7 (5), 1830–32; op. 17 (4), 1832–33; op. 24 (4), 1833; op. 30 (4), 1837; op. 33 (4), 1838; op. 41 (4), 1838–39; op. 50 (3), 1842; op. 56 (3), 1843–44; op. 59 (3), 1845; op. 63 (3), 1846; op. 67 (4); op. 68 (4); nine others without opus numbers.

Nocturnes, op. 9, 1830–32; op. 15, 1833; op. 27, 1835; op. 32, 1837; op. 37, 1838–39; op. 48, 1841; op. 55, 1842–44; op. 62, 1846.

Twelve Études, op. 10, 1830–32.

Twelve Études, op. 25, 1835–37.

Concerto No. 1 in E Minor, op. 11, 1830

Concerto No. 2 in F Minor, op. 21, 1829

Four Ballades, op. 23, 1835; op. 38, 1839; op. 47, 1841; op. 52, 1842–43.

Seventeen songs, 1827–47.

Polonaises, op. 26, 1835; op. 40, 1838–39; op. 44, 1841; op. 53, 1842–43; op. 71, 1827–29.

Twenty-four Preludes, op. 28, 1838–39

Impromptu, op. 29, 1837; op. 36, 1839; op. 51, 1842.

Scherzo, op. 31, 1837.

Scherzo, op. 39, 1839.

Waltzes, op. 34, 1835; op. 42, 1840; op. 64, 1846–47; op. 69, 1829–35; op. 70, 1829–32.

Sonata in B-flat Minor, op. 35, 1837.

Sonata in B Minor, op. 58, 1844.

Fantasy, op. 49, 1841.

Berceuse, op. 57, 1844.

Polonaise-Fantasy, op. 61, 1846.

Bibliography

Abraham, Gerald. *Chopin's Musical Style.* London: Oxford University Press, 1968.

Atwood, William G. *The Parisian World of Frederic Chopin.* New Haven, Conn.: Yale University Press, 1999.

Azoury, Pierre. *Chopin through His Contemporaries: Friends, Lovers, and Rivals.* Westport, Conn.: Greenwood Press, 1999.

Brown, Maurice J. E. *Chopin: an Index of His Works in Chronological Order.* London: Macmillan, 1972.

Eigeldinger, Jean-Jacques. *Chopin: Pianist and Teacher.* Translated by Naomi Shohet; edited by Roy Howat. London: Cambridge University Press, 1986.

Zofia, Lissa, ed. *The Book of the First International Musicological Congress Devoted to the Works of Frederick Chopin.* Warsaw: Polish Scientific Publishers, 1963.

Liszt, Franz. *F. Chopin.* Paris: 1852. English translation, 1877.

Samson, Jim. *The Music of Chopin.* London: Routledge and Kegan Paul, 1985.

Siepmann, Jeremy. *Chopin: the Reluctant Romantic.* Boston: Northeastern University Press, 1995.

Szulc, Tad. *Chopin in Paris: the Life and Times of the Romantic Composer.* New York: Scribner's, 1998.

Walker, Alan, ed. *The Chopin Companion.* New York: W. W. Norton, 1973.

Walker, Alan. *Frederic Chopin: Profiles of the Man and Musician.* New York: Taplinger, 1967.

Weinstock, Herbert. *Chopin: the Man and His Music.* New York: Alfred A. Knopf, 1959.

CHORAL MUSIC

For the Romantics, music was the ultimate art form, due to its ability to foster direct communication between musician and listener, without a need for a text or visual image as intermediary. In the nineteenth century, several prominent Romantic composers, notably Frédéric François Chopin, abandoned choral music altogether or preferred to explore the more intimate genre of solo song. Others, however, saw the potential for using the vocal ensemble as an effective medium for the expression of Romantic themes. The era witnessed change in the purpose, scope, and style of choral music, and while regional variations mean that it is not always easy to trace a clear sense of linear development, certain common features may be detected.

Ludwig van Beethoven's unprecedented use of voice in his Ninth Symphony was perceived by early critics as bewildering. However, it is regarded now not merely as having influenced Richard Wagner's music dramas and the choral symphonies of such figures as Gustav Mahler, but also as a turning point in the development of choral music. Many nineteenth-century composers adopted Beethoven's use of the chorus within a secular setting. As the social and political significance of ecclesiastical institutions waned, the composition of a mass came to be an exceptional rather than a quotidian event within a composer's career (Wolfgang Amadeus Mozart wrote copious masses, Beethoven a mere handful). As such, masses tended to become larger in scale and composers felt freer to impose their own interpretation, making cuts or additions to the text for dramatic motives. Beethoven's *Missa Solemnis* (1823), for example, was a personalized vision of Christianity, presenting a benevolent and amicable Jesus rather than a distant and inaccessible deity. His works marked a shift in focus within sacred music away from the established church and toward inner spirituality.

The partial divorce of choral music from the church was countered by its entry into the concert hall. While many works continued to be religiously inspired, composers no longer regarded the expression of devotion to God as the sole function of choral music. The Romantic enthusiasm for artistic synthesis led many to look toward literary sources which lent themselves to forward-looking musical forms. Such texts offered seemingly limitless possibilities for the expression of programmatic elements, and composers became aware of the theatrical potential of using massed voices in the concert hall.

Hector Berlioz was a major composer of dramatic choral works. Characters from Orpheus to Cleopatra stimulated his imagination, reflecting a typical Romantic fascination with myth, history, and exoticism. Berlioz made use of texts by contemporary Romantic writers (such as Victor Hugo) and by literary figures from former ages whose work held contemporary appeal—most notably, William Shakespeare. *La Damnation de Faust* (1845–46), after Johann Wolfgang von Goethe, was subtitled a "légende dramatique," and was part unstaged opera, part symphony. The work presented the preoccupations of its age, depicting the supernatural and the terrifying aspects of nature, and foregrounding the psychological experiences of a quintessentially Romantic hero—yearning, sensitive, and overpowered by emotion. Berlioz used the chorus not simply as commentators but as dramatic protagonists, metamorphosing into—among other things—peasants, drunkards, gnomes, soldiers, students,

and demons. The expression of personal experience, combined with innovative form and the intermingling of vocal and instrumental textures, was central to Berlioz's choral works.

Beethoven's setting of Johann Christoph Friedrich von Schiller's "An die Freude" in the Ninth Symphony was a hymn to brotherhood and unity, symbolic of the social and philosophical ideals of its era. This aspect of his work inspired many composers to appropriate the choral repertory for nation-building purposes. French composers in particular became interested in using choral music as an expression of the national spirit, influenced by the large-scale outdoor works of the French Revolution (such as the choruses of François-Joseph Gossec and Étienne Nicolas Méhul). This heritage is apparent in the ceremonial style of Berlioz's *Messe des morts* requiem (1837), its massed brass and percussion and 450-plus performers a testimony to the Romantic taste for the monumental. Conceived as an endeavor to restore the prestige of French sacred music, the inspiration for the work was not liturgical but self-consciously patriotic: its first performance was at a memorial service in the Invalides to commemorate the demise of a prominent French general. Berlioz's numerous other patriotic vocal works include the *Hymne à la France* (1844).

Another, rather more conservative, trend within nineteenth-century choral music was the continuation, particularly in Protestant countries, of the oratorio tradition. The main exponent of this movement was Felix Mendelssohn, and perhaps the most significant work his *Elijah*, first performed in Birmingham in 1846. Like other nineteenth-century choral works, *Elijah* was as much a theatrical as a religious piece, and incorporated much pictorial writing. Heavily derivative of baroque and classical styles, Mendelssohn's accessible music was an immediate success with the early Victorians, his works being appropriated as "national" treasures alongside such touchstones of Britishness as George Frideric Handel's *Messiah*. Mendelssohn was also a prominent figure in the contemporary revival of the choral works of Johann Sebastian Bach and Handel (the *St. Matthew Passion* was rediscovered in 1829), upon which the nineteenth century would stamp its own aesthetic, the vast performing forces out of keeping with the original Baroque spirit. (The fashion for massed performances was set by the Handel commemorations in London in the 1780s, at which there were reports of concerts involving one thousand players and singers.) Such works became the mainstay of the repertory of the amateur choral societies established as edifying organizations in Britain and Germany in the nineteenth century. Catholic countries also took inspiration from the music of earlier periods, the Cecilian Movement promoting a reform of church music centered on unaccompanied choral singing influenced by Renaissance polyphony. Thus, composers of choral music during the Romantic era looked both to the future and to an idealized past, and held the expression of social and political ambitions to be as crucial as purely aesthetic concerns.

ALEXANDRA WILSON

Bibliography

Abraham, Gerald. "Choral Music." In *The New Oxford History of Music, vol. 10, Romanticism (1830–1890)*. Edited by Gerald Abraham. Oxford: Oxford University Press, 1990.

Cone, Edward T. "Berlioz's Divine Comedy: the *Grande Messe des morts*," *Nineteenth Century Music* 4, no. 1 (1980): 3–16.

Cook, Nicholas. *Beethoven: Symphony No. 9.* Cambridge: Cambridge University Press, 1993.

Dahlhaus, Carl. *Nineteenth-Century Music.* Berkeley and Los Angeles: University of California Press, 1989. 160–168, 178–91.

Fiske, Roger. *Beethoven's Missa Solemnis.* London: Paul Elek, 1979.

Lewis, Anthony. "Choral Music." In *The New Oxford History of Music,* vol. 8, *The Age of Beethoven, 1790–1830.* Edited by Gerald Abraham. London: Oxford University Press, 1982.

Kinderman, William. "Beethoven's Symbol for the Deity in the *Missa Solemnis* and the Ninth Symphony," *Nineteenth Century Music* 9, no. 2 (1985): 102–18.

Rushton, Julian. *Berlioz: Roméo et Juliette.* Cambridge: Cambridge University Press, 1994.

CITY AND VILLAGE

Even as industry and commerce shifted more and more of Europe's population toward the cities, Romanticism generally deplored that move, depicting cities as alienating and dehumanizing places. In part, this aversion reacted against a classical emphasis on the city as the public sphere, where ideas, like goods, were exchanged in a rational fashion and the public good took precedence over the needs and desires of the individual. More directly, however, the backlash against urbanism derived from Jean-Jacques Rousseau's celebration of the "state of nature," in which virtue thrived without the interference of social institutions.

Views of the city during the eighteenth century alternated between admiration and disgust. Frequently the city was depicted as an organic body, or as a part of the body (head, heart, or stomach): this organic metaphor might tend to naturalize the city, but more often led to its representation as a monster, devouring people and resources from the surrounding countryside. William Cowper sums up the prevalent ambivalence thus:

Oh thou, resort and mart of all the earth,
Chequer'd with all complexions of mankind,
And spotted with all crimes, in whom I see
Much that I love, and more that I admire,
And all that I abhor.

In England, as enclosure and other agricultural innovations prompted migrations to London, many writers, notably Oliver Goldsmith, began to depict this migration as a moral lapse and a social loss. Goldsmith's "Deserted Village" participates in a pastoral mythology of the rural village that, in turn, is challenged by George Crabbe's "The Village." Prior to 1790, the alternative to the city was not the wilderness but a smaller, simpler community. Other poems and novels incorporate the "fall" of a young person (usually female) who is lured from the village to the city with the promise of love or employment, only to find moral and financial ruin. The city as seducer thus figures in the novels of Henry Fielding and Samuel Richardson. Yet, as the century wanes, we see more acceptance of London's inevitable place in the self-definition of a character such as Fanny Burney's Evelina. No longer is the city merely the realm of public discourse: London is full of threats to a young woman, but it is also her testing ground, without which she cannot come of age.

In Paris, where the city is defined by its revolutionary disorder (the rebuilding of Paris under the direction of Georges Haussman, 1852–70, was in part an attempt to make the city easier to control during times of political unrest), the novel becomes a means to contain its incoherence. Honoré de Balzac and Victor Hugo incorporate elements of the guidebook to make the novel a mode of urban exploration, with Hugo ultimately publishing a *Paris guide* (1867) as well. In general, French writers seem more willing than English ones to work with the city rather than against it. The younger Alexandre Dumas shocked audiences with his glamourization of the Parisian courtesan in *La Dame aux camélias* (1848), which became the basis for Giuseppe Verdi's *La Traviata* (1853). Even there, however, only the countryside offers the lovers a hope for the future; the city ruins them with its disease and moral hypocrisy.

The preeminent English Romantics Samuel Taylor Coleridge and William Wordsworth turned their backs on the city as a source of audience and validation, instead seeking communion with nature in the wilds of the Lake District and writing the stories of poor villagers and vagrants. In "Frost at Midnight," Coleridge clearly articulates the future he imagines for his infant son:

For I was reared
In the great city, pent 'mid cloisters dim,
And saw nought lovely but the sky and stars.
But thou, my babe! shalt wander like a breeze
By lakes and sandy shores, beneath the crags
Of ancient mountain, and beneath the clouds.

And Wordsworth, revisiting the banks of the Wye River after a five-year absence, testifies to the nurturing power of its remembered scenery:

These beauteous forms,
Through a long absence, have not been to me
As is a landscape to a blind man's eye:

William Daniell, *View of London with the Improvements of its Port and the Double London Bridge.* Reprinted courtesy of the Bridgeman Art Library.

But oft, in lonely rooms, and mid the din
Of towns and cities, I have owed to them
In hours of weariness, sensations sweet,
Felt in the blood, and felt along the heart.

William Blake, whose denunciations of "charter'd streets" and "dark Satanic mills" seem to mark him as the city's most vehement critic, nonetheless lived in London nearly all his life and transformed it, in his prophetic books, into an image (albeit fallen) of the New Jerusalem. Interposed between the London of history and the Jerusalem of eternity is a city Blake calls Golgonooza, the workshop of the artist, "ever building, ever falling." Blake thus challenges the flight from the city, reclaiming it as a work of human imagination even in its most flawed state. Nor is Blake alone in finding beauty in the city: Joanna Baillie admires the city from the suburb of Hampstead, and even Wordsworth speaks with awe of the "mighty heart . . . lying still" in his sonnet "Composed Upon Westminster Bridge." Friedrich Hölderlin, attempting to translate a Greek sense of national community to Germany, represents the city as a dwelling-place in harmony with its natural surroundings in such poems as "Heidelberg" and "Stutgard."

The ability to aestheticize the city, however, often depends on distance and the "prospect view" of the landscape painter. Villages fit more easily into the picturesque rural landscapes of John Constable, although J. M. W. Turner offers a few views of London. Paul Sandby produced some townscapes in the 1760s and 1770s, and Thomas Malton drafted a hundred aquatinted views of London buildings and streets in the 1790s. More often, following the example of Antonio Canaletto, painters turned to Rome or Venice to find the urban sublime. The depiction of ruins, especially Roman ones, conveyed respect for ancient cities and empires while simultaneously affirming the dominance of time and nature over manmade structures. The poems of Lord Byron and Percy Bysshe Shelley written on the continent similarly capture this contrast.

Russian treatments of the city show a similar ambivalence, as well as an instability that prefigures modernism. Aleksandr Pushkin's *The Bronze Horseman* (1833) presents Saint Petersburg as an Enlightenment city that uneasily bridges East and West, generating an uncanny sense of homelessness in sharp contrast to the village life that represents old Russia. In such works as *Dead Souls* and "The Overcoat" (both 1843), Nicolai Vasilyevich Gogol adds to this ghostliness a sense of the city as a commercial system unto itself, ungrounded in human values.

Arguably, it is in Paris that the Romantic spirit best comes to terms with the city. Balzac, Charles Baudelaire, and Gustave Flaubert create the figure of the flâneur, a product of urbanization and revolution, an observer and consumer of urban sights. When the flâneur is also an artist, he turns the city's unknowability into creative material, as does Baudelaire in *Le Spleen de Paris* (published 1869), when he identifies the city as generating a new poetic form. It is this figure that provides the link between Romanticism and modernism, as in the modern age city replaces nature as humanity's given environment.

JENNIFER DAVIS MICHAEL

Bibliography

Ahearn, Edward J. "The Search for Community: The City in Hölderlin, Wordsworth, and Baudelaire," *Texas Studies in Literature and Language* 13 (1971): 71–89.

Byrd, Max. *London Transformed: Images of the City in the Eighteenth Century.* New Haven, Conn.: Yale University Press, 1978.

Ferguson, Priscilla Parkhust. *Paris as Revolution: Writing the Nineteenth-Century City.* Berkeley and Los Angeles: University of California Press, 1994.

Johnston, John H. *The Poet and the City: A Study in Urban Perspectives.* Athens, Ga.: University of Georgia Press, 1984.

Lehan, Richard. *The City in Literature: An Intellectual and Cultural History.* Berkeley and Los Angeles: University of California Press, 1998.

Pinsky, Robert. "Skies of the City: A Poetry Reading." In *The Romantics and Us.* Edited by Gene W. Ruoff. New Brunswick, N.J.: Rutgers University Press, 1990. 168–83.

Sennett, Richard. *Flesh and Stone: The Body and the City in Western Civilization.* New York: W. W. Norton, 1994.

Spears, Monroe K. *Dionysus and the City: Modernism in Twentieth-Century Poetry.* New York: Oxford University Press, 1970.

Versluys, Kristiaan. *The Poet in the City: Chapters in the Development of Urban Poetry in Europe and the United States (1800–1930).* Studies in English and Comparative Literature 4. Tübingen, Germany: Gunter Narr, 1987.

Williams, Raymond. *The Country and the City.* Oxford: Oxford University Press, 1973.

CLAIRMONT, CLAIRE 1797–1879

British woman of letters

Claire Clairmont (born Clara Mary Jane Clairmont) has been known through her more famous associates: her stepfather William Godwin; her stepsister Mary Wollstonecraft Godwin Shelley; Percy Bysshe Shelley, one of her closest friends; and Lord Byron, the father of her illegitimate daughter Allegra. Although early in her life she began several works with an eye toward publication, all that remains of this ambition is one short story that she sent to Mary Shelley to finish. Mary Shelley wrote the final, bloody scene of "The Pole" (1832) and published it as "by the author of *Frankenstein*." Despite her lack of conventional literary production, Clairmont was a copious writer. She kept a journal from 1814 to 1827, and her surviving letters cover the years from 1815 to 1879. It is through these personal writings that Clairmont reveals herself as a woman of the Romantic era.

Clairmont accompanied her stepsister on her elopement with the married Percy Bysshe Shelley in 1814, and she remained a resident of the Shelley household for most of the years until Shelley's death in 1822. She was only seventeen years old when she left the Godwins to live with Shelley and his wife Mary, and Shelley directed her reading and shaped her character. Although this prepared her for life in the Shelley community, by 1826, working as a governess in Russia, she wrote in a letter that she felt that "I might have been understood in the time of Socrates, but never shall be by the moderns." (*Letters*, 1. 243).

Clairmont's earliest writing, a travel journal that she kept on the elopement tour, shows her to be conversant with the Romantic attention to landscape in terms of the beautiful, the sublime, and the picturesque. Many of her descriptions of the countryside through which they traveled in postrevolutionary Europe are carefully composed, noting arches of trees, rocks, or mountains that frame the scenes, and sometimes suggesting an almost Gothic atmosphere. Her account of her first view of the Alps gives a flavor of both her method of description as well as her enthusiastic style. "[T]hen come the terrific Alps," she writes in her *Journals*. "I thought they were white flaky clouds[;] what was my surprise when after a long & steady examination I found them really to be the snowy Alps—yes, they were really the Alps—Peaked broken, one jutting forward, another retreating, now the light airy clouds rested a few moments on their aspiring fronts & then fled away that we might better behold the sublimity of the scene" (*Journals*, 27). These early descriptions seem to be conscious attempts to display a certain aesthetic knowledge. By the time she assumed the post of governess in Russia in 1824, she had come to seek nature as a balm for the troubled soul and expressed frustration whenever she could not be in the countryside.

Clairmont's musings on the nature of poetry and of what makes a genius parallel much Romantic thinking. Naturalness in poetry had become the critical norm, in reaction to the artificial, mechanistic verse of the Enlightenment. The current belief was that a poem should come in a moment of inspiration, naturally and organically: William Wordsworth's "spontaneous overflow" "recollected in tranquility." Clairmont's eulogy of the death of John Keats asserts that he was the "brightest promise of genius" that England had seen in many years, and her language shows her sense of organicism in the finest romantic poetry; she believed that Keats's genius "needed the utmost tenderness to develope [*sic*]." She was not surprised that, as many thought, harsh criticism had brought about his death, his genius "withered by the poison of calumny." (*Journals*, 228).

Claire Clairmont felt strongly that the best poetry was poetry of the soul. She harshly criticized Byron, whom she had come to despise, by attacking his poetry in her journals. His poetry was "so entirely divested of any thing pertaining to the aerial voice of imagination, so sensual, so tangible that like every thing corporeal, it must die." (*Journals*, 225). Expressing a typical Romantic concern with nature, she states, "Nature[,] which is the unsubstantial food on which the soul feeds[,] is as equally neglected by this poet. . . . he looks upon her fair adorned breast, not as if it were the bosom of beauty . . . but as so much space allotted for the completion of his desires." (*Journals*, 226). To Clairmont, nature is capable of awakening the imagination only if it can speak "in full tones to the heart," and she believed that Byron as a man was too coarse to receive its inspiration. She always felt that Shelley never received the notice he deserved because Byron, who "had the world's voice within him," completely overshadowed him. Thinking probably of Shelley and his own poetry, and influenced no doubt by his *Defense of Poetry*, she believed that poetry "bursts into harmony inspired by mental perfection." (*Journals*, 226).

Clairmont went to Russia to earn her living as a governess, which, according to Elizabeth Gaskell's *Wives and Daughters*, was akin to taking the veil. But Clairmont found in the household of Russian lawyer Zachar Nicolaivitch Posnikov a degree of freedom to express her intellect. Her letters reveal that women's rights, philosophy, and politics were common topics of conversation with the German tutor, Chrétien-Hermann Gambs, a promising composer who later published volumes of poetry under the name of his muse, "C. Clairmont." Although Clairmont protested that she was not in love with Gambs, clearly he was extremely attached to her. And she appreciated his presence, admitting that "in such a country as Russia, where nothing but the vulgarest people are to be met, a cultivated mind is the greatest treasure." (*Letters*, 1. 230). During her spell in Russia, Clairmont wrote articles for the household's *Islavsky Gazette*, including "Reflections upon Women" and "Conversation between Man and Woman." Unfortunately, these private newspapers have not survived, but they provided intellectual stimulation and enjoyment for the entire household.

After her years in Russia, Clairmont worked as a governess in Italy, France, and England, and seems to have lived out what she once wrote in her journal: "think of thyself as a stranger and traveler on the earth, to whom none of the many affairs of this world, belong and who has no permanent township on the globe." (*Journals*, 180). Toward the end of her life, however, she settled in Florence with her niece, Pauline Clairmont. There she was sought out by an American, Edward Augustus Silsbee, a Shelley devotee, who was enthralled to find himself, for a time, an intimate of Shelley's "Constantia." The tale of Silsbee's visits to Claire and Pauline Clairmont eventually made its way to Henry James, who used it as the basis of his novella *The Aspern Papers*. Clairmont died on March 19, 1879 and was buried, with a shawl that Shelley had given her, in the Cemetery of Antella, just outside of Florence.

In her journals and letters, Claire Clairmont reveals herself as a thinker who was concerned about all the primary issues of the Romantic period: love, equality of the sexes, nature and romantic scenery, philosophy, and politics. She asserted to Mary Shelley in 1835 that "all the pupils I have ever had will be violent defenders of the Rights of Women. I have taken great pains to sow the seeds of that doctrine wherever I could." (*Letters*, 2. 323). But as she grew older and the culture shifted to Victorian conservatism, she, too, shifted, becoming Roman Catholic after her years of expressed atheism. She thought of writing a book using the exploits of Shelley and Byron to warn people about right conduct, but to the end she honored Shelley, the friend who had encouraged her in her challenge to conformity.

As literature in their own right, Clairmont's letters are outstanding. As Mary Shelley once noted in a letter to Clairmont, "you write the most amusing & clever letters in the world. . . . If your letters are ever published, all others that ever were published before, will fall into the shade, & you be looked on as the best letter writer that ever charmed their friends" (*The Letters of Mary Shelley*, 3. 48). Together, the letters and journals of Claire Clairmont provide a vivid panorama of the Romantic age, its writers, and its culture from the point of view of an intellectually liberated woman.

LISA LESLIE

Biography

Exact date and location of birth unknown; probably April 27, 1797, of Swiss ancestry. Moved into William Godwin's house when he married her mother, 1801. Left with Mary Wollstonecraft Godwin and Percy Bysshe Shelley when they eloped, 1814; lived with them almost continuously until Shelley's death, 1822. Worked as a governess in Russia, Italy, France, and England, 1824–40. Wrote her only published work, "The Pole" and sent to Mary Shelley to finish, 1832. Arranged an income from the Shelley estate and gave up teaching, 1841. Various residences in England, France, and Italy, 1841–75. Settled in Florence, 1876; remained there until her death in 1879.

Selected Works

Fiction

"The Pole," 1832.

Diaries and Letters

The Journals of Claire Clairmont. Edited by Marion Kingston Stocking. Cambridge: Harvard University Press, 1968.
"The Journal of Claire Clairmont, August 14–22, 1814." Edited by Sir Gavin de Beer. In *Shelley and His Circle.* Vol. 3. Edited by Kenneth Neill Cameron. Cambridge: Harvard University Press and London: Oxford University Press, 1970.
"The Journal of Claire Clairmont, January 17–18 (in Part), April 23–June 1818." Edited by Marion Kingston Stocking. In *Shelley and His Circle.* Vol. 5. Edited by Donald H. Reiman. Cambridge: Harvard University Press and London: Oxford University Press, 1973.
The Clairmont Correspondence: Letters of Claire Clairmont, Charles Clairmont, and Fanny Imlay Godwin. Edited by Marion Kingston Stocking. Baltimore and London: The Johns Hopkins University Press, 1995.

Bibliography

Blodgett, Harriet. *Centuries of Female Days: Englishwomen's Private Diaries.* New Brunswick, N.J.: Rutgers University Press, 1988.
Gittings, Robert, and Jo Manton. *Claire Clairmont and the Shelleys.* Oxford: Oxford University Press, 1992.
Grylls, R. Glynn. *Claire Clairmont: Mother of Byron's Allegra.* London: John Murray, 1939.
Leslie, Lisa D. " 'How Can I Exist Apart from my Sister?': Sisters in the Life and Literature of Percy Bysshe Shelley, Mary Shelley, and Claire Clairmont." Ph.D. diss., University of Liverpool, 2000.

CLARE, JOHN 1793–1864

British poet

John Clare was born into the agricultural working class in 1793. Although he received some formal education, he was self-taught as far as his knowledge of literature was concerned. He was variously employed as a thresher, plowman, gardener, nurseryman, lime burner, and agricultural laborer.

Clare began writing seriously around 1806, but only came to the attention of the reading public at the beginning of 1820 with the publication of his first volume, *Poems Descriptive of Rural Life and Scenery, by John Clare, A Northamptonshire Peasant.* This sold reasonably well and eventually went into four editions. It was published by John Taylor, who was associated with John Keats's poetry and went on to edit the *London Magazine.* Taylor and others marketed Clare as a peasant poet. Clare was seen as belonging to a tradition that included earlier English writers such as Robert Bloomfield, Mary Collier, and Stephen Duck, and Scottish writers such as Robert Burns and James Hogg. Clare was one of the last poets to be marketed in this way: during his literary life, much more notice was given to artisan-writers who appeared to offer answers to the "condition-of-England" question. The introduction to, and the reviews of, Clare's first volume paid as much attention to his background as to his poetry.

Clare's second volume, *The Village Minstrel* (1821), did not attract the same amount of interest as his first book. He could no longer be presented as an interesting curiosity. A third volume, *The Shepherd's Calendar*, was eventually published in 1827 after a long and dispiriting series of delays for which his publisher was partly responsible. It did not sell at all well, and Clare was reduced to hawking copies around his neighborhood. He visited London on four occasions: in 1820, 1822, 1824, and finally in 1828. He became a contributor to the *London Magazine* and got to know other contributors such Thomas De Quincey, William Hazlitt, and Charles Lamb. Clare was much influenced by the agendas of this magazine, for instance in his commitment to Renaissance writings. He was never able to establish himself as a professional writer, and often had to return to laboring jobs to support his large family.

After another long gap, a fourth volume, *The Rural Muse*, was eventually published in 1835. This attracted some good reviews, and Clare was awarded a small grant by the Royal Literary Fund. His health had never been strong, and having to combine the occupations of poet and laborer often placed him under further strain. He was placed in High Beach Asylum in Epping Forest (northeast London) in 1837, from which he escaped in 1841, walking almost all the way back home. He was nevertheless soon after confined to another asylum at Northampton, which was nearer to his home, where he remained until his death in 1864.

Much of Clare's work, in prose as well as in poetry, remained unpublished during his lifetime. This was sometimes because earlier on in his career he could not afford to alienate powerful patrons by publishing what might be seen by them as radical sentiments. Although writings from the asylum period were published in newspapers and elsewhere, the quantity and quality of this work remained largely unknown until after his death.

Works by Clare that were published in his lifetime were often edited to make them conform to what were seen to be the prevailing standards of taste. Although he often colluded in this editorial process, there were other times when he tried to resist the removal of profuse detail as well as some dialect expressions. Much of the recent debate about Clare, prompted by the publication of the Clarendon editions of his works, has centered on how his texts should be reproduced for modern readers. The Clarendon editors favor offering original, unmodified versions of these texts, with the detail and dialect present, and punctuation and standardized spelling absent. Others believe that unchanged texts are another way of reinscribing Clare as a peasant poet, and thus of continuing to condescend to him.

Although there are differences of opinion about editorial strategies toward Clare, the various recent editions of prose writings as well as of poetry show him to have been an extremely prolific and productive writer, despite the many disadvantages that he confronted. Some of the earlier criticism sought to establish links through his material, its expression, and the folk tradition. He was an avid collector of ballads. More recent criticism also suggests that he was much more literary, in a conventional sense, than has sometimes been supposed. He was very widely read, particularly in poetry, had a fondness for Renaissance writings, and was familiar with most of the important poets since then. He imitated earlier as well as contemporary writers and was able to demonstrate his technical mastery of forms such as the sonnet. There were times in the asylum period when he claimed that he was actually Robert Burns, Lord Byron, or William Shakespeare. He also sometimes claimed the identity of regency pugilists, which was partly an act of nostalgia for a sport that was no longer fashionable in the early Victorian period.

Clare wrote largely about rural society in his preasylum period. His notion of the pastoral was certainly nostalgic about the old customs associated with his childhood, and yet it could also be tough and uncompromising in the way in which it criticized the present and imagined better futures. Although Taylor found Clare's use of detail much too profuse, more modern readers have tended to see this as being one of the things that is distinctive about his work. His representations of birds, animals, insects, flowers, trees, and the land itself are sometimes seen as being part of an environmental consciousness which, although of its time, is also surprisingly modern. He was influenced by eighteenth-century writers such as James Thomson, but differs from them by often resisting the organizing gaze of the overseer. His landscapes are more cluttered because he is closer to them. His associations with the *London Magazine* and with writers like De Quincey meant that he experimented with Romantic themes; he wrote poems about dreams and became preoccupied with writing a prose autobiography. He recognized William Blake's talent and shared a publisher with Keats. He was an avid reader of Byron, and happened to be in London in 1824 to witness Byron's funeral procession setting off for Nottinghamshire. Clare connects with Romanticism in a number of ways, and yet was more influenced by earlier writers. In addition to eighteenth-century pastoral poets such as Oliver Goldsmith and Thomson, he was also influenced by Renaissance writers such as Christopher Marlowe and Edmund Spencer. Although he was placed within a tradition of "uneducated" writers, what is remarkable is just how well-read he was. This is demonstrated in the journal that he kept during the earlier part of the 1820s, as well as by the contents of his library.

Although sometimes shy and diffident, Clare was also an extremely ambitious writer. It was not his alleged madness talking when he compared himself to Byron in some of the asylum poetry. He felt that he should have been taken more seriously as a writer rather than just being seen as an oddity, and many modern poets and critics agree with him.

ROGER SALES

Biography

Born at Helpston, July 1793, into the agricultural working class; some elementary schooling. Various jobs as plowboy, gardener, and lime-burner. Started to write seriously after buying James Thomson's *Seasons* in 1806. Discovered as a writer in 1818 by a local bookseller, Edward Drury, whose cousin was John Taylor, an established London publisher. First volume published in 1820. Attracted notice largely because of what are felt to be discrepancies between the identity of the poet and the peasant. Conservative patrons such as Admiral Lord Radstock, a prominent member of the Society for the Suppression of Vice, tried to promote Clare as a conspicuous example of the deserving poor. Second volume published in 1821. Visited London and met writers attached to the *London Magazine*. Long delays with the third volume. Taylor, in common with others, stopped publishing poetry. Clare's third volume (often held to be his best) came out in 1827 after many delays. A fourth volume appeared in 1835 with a new publisher. Confined to an asylum in 1837. Escaped in 1841, but was placed in another asylum until his death in 1864.

Selected Works

The Clarendon Press (Oxford) editions of the poems, editor-in-chief Eric Robinson, consist of six volumes: two on the *Early Poems*, first published in 1989; two on the *Middle Period*, first published in 1996; and two on the *Later Poems*, first published in 1984. Robinson and his team have been responsible for collections of Clare's poetry, as well as editions of his autobiographical and political writings.

Bibliography

Barrell, John. *The Idea of Landscape and the Sense of Place 1780–1840: An Approach to the Poetry of John Clare*. Cambridge: Cambridge University Press, 1972.

Barton, Anne. "John Clare Reads Lord Byron," *Romanticism* 2 (1996): 127–48.

Brownlow, Tim. *John Clare and the Picturesque Landscape*. Oxford: Clarendon Press, 1983.

Clare, Johanna. *John Clare and the Bounds of Circumstance*. Kingston, Ont.: McGill-Queen's University Press, 1987.

Deacon, George. *John Clare and the Folk Tradition*. London: Sinclair Brown, 1983.

Goodridge, John, ed. *The Independent Spirit: John Clare and the Self-Taught Tradition*. Helpston: John Clare Society, 1994.

Haughton, Hugh, et al., eds. *John Clare in Context*. Cambridge: Cambridge University Press, 1994.

John Clare Society Journal; published annually since 1982.

Leader, Zachary. *Revision and Romantic Authorship*. Oxford: Clarendon Press, 1996.

Lucas, John. *John Clare*. Plymouth: Northcote House, 1994.

Pearce, Lynne. "John Clare's Child Harold: A Polyphonic Reading," *Criticism* 39 (1989): 139–57.

Sales, Roger. *John Clare: A Literary Life*. Basingstoke: Palgrave, 2001.

Website

http://ntu.ac.uk/Clare.

CLASSICAL ANTIQUITY

In 1765, in his *Dissertation on the Poems of Ossian*, Hugh Blair expressed the opinion of many readers when he described the ancient Celtic world as nobler and gentler than that of Homer. Though chronologically later than Homer's epics, the poems of Ossian reflected, according to Blair, a more primitive and thus more aesthetically pleasing stage of development. While this response indicates a preference for "native" literatures that would come to be called "Romantic," it also indicates a new interest in the worlds of ancient writers—both "native" and classical—as distant and qualitatively different periods of history.

The gap between classical antiquity and the present had been emphasized at the turn of the eighteenth century. Prompted by advances in scientific knowledge, intellectuals had argued the irrelevance of classics to enlightened society. Richard Bentley's discovery of the lost Greek letter, the digamma, in his studies of Homer in the 1720s reified this sense of distance by showing that the Greek language itself was subject to change. In contrast to the continuity and universality central to neoclassicism, "otherness" dominated the diverse and conflicting attitudes toward classical antiquity throughout the Romantic era.

Before 1760, Giambattista Vico in Italy and Thomas Blackwell in Scotland had linked myth, metaphor, and poetry to the earliest stages of human development. Drawing on Blackwell's work, Robert Wood traveled to Asia Minor to prove that Homer "copied what he saw." His *Essay on the Original Genius of and Writings of Homer* (1769) presented an illiterate, wandering bard similar to the Irish and Scottish bards being researched at the same time. In Germany, Johann Gottfried von Herder absorbed these theories on Homer, Robert Lowth's work on the Hebrew scriptures, and the research of British pre-Romantics on Celtic traditions focused on forging a theory of myth as a symbolic mode of thought rooted in the experience of a particular people (or *Volk*). This figure of the poet as the authentic voice of the people crystallized in F. A. Wolf's profoundly influential *Prolegomena to Homer* (1795) which asserted, as Vico had done seventy years earlier, that Homer had never existed; rather, the epics were formed of shorter ballads performed and passed down by many singers, and subjected to a long slow process of transcription, collation, and transmission.

The primitivism in Homeric scholarship provided an antidote to neoclassical artificiality. William Blake and Johann Wolfgang von Goethe seized upon symbolic mythopoesis. William Wordsworth presented a poetics of feeling and "natural" language. Percy Bysshe Shelley, echoing Blackwell, defended the role of poets as "legislators of the world" and rewrote Aeschylus's *Prometheus Bound* to reflect his hopes for the future of humankind. John Keats used myth to question the nature of memory, imagination, and art, and their relationship to the material world. The influence of these theories affected historical inquiry as well. Barthold Niebuhr, perceiving that Livy's early history of Rome must have drawn on traditional tales, recognized the need to sift firsthand through secondhand accounts. Thomas Babington Macaulay's *Lays of Ancient Rome* (1842) were an effort to imagine those original ballads.

Not all reconstructions of antiquity were text based. The Society of Dilettanti, founded in England in 1734 for the study of ancient art, had begun excavations of Herculaneum and Pompeii in 1738 and 1748, respectively. With the publication of Stuart and Revett's *Antiquities of Athens* in (1762), a journey into antiquity itself became a popular item on the "grand tour." Panoramic painting of the period suggests a preoccupation with ruins, and the grandeur of the ancients, rather than present-day Greece. Similarly, Edward Gibbon conceived the vision for his magisterial *Decline and Fall of the Roman Empire* as he sat "musing amidst the ruins of the Capitol."

Ironically, Johann Joachim Winckelmann, whose epoch-making *History of Ancient Art*, (1764) inspired a new Hellenism across Europe, ventured no further than Italy. His Greece, a world of serene beauty and simplicity, was shaped by distance and desire. This placid antiquity met with conflicting responses. Henry Fuseli translated Winckelmann into English, but explored a nightmare world of fear, pain, and repressed eroticism in his own art. For Blake, a friend of Fuseli, "Greece and Rome . . . were destroyers of all art. Grecian is Mathematic Form; Gothic is Living Form." But for others, tranquil Greece offered a welcome alternative to the obsessive rituals of Christianity. Gotthold Ephraim Lessing, Winckelmann's first interpreter and critic, saw calmer, more natural attitudes toward life and death in Greek art. While Coleridge disparaged Greek religion as merely containing a "Godkin or Godessling" in otherwise dead objects, Friedrich Hölderlin and Johann Christoph Friedrich von Schiller valorized the deities of ancient Greece as natural and joyful. The older Goethe, finding "health" in classicism and "disease" in Romanticism, dedicated a book of essays to Winckelmann in 1805.

The project of recovering antiquity was often seen as problematic. Schiller's *On Naïve and Sentimental Literature*, (1795) claimed that modern literature could never regain the unselfcon-

Robert Hubert, *The Maison Carrée with the Amphitheatre and the Tour Magne at Nimes*. Reprinted courtesy of the Bridgeman Art Library.

scious immediacy of ancient poetry. Friedrich von Schlegel expanded this observation, explicitly opposing *Romantic* (which he applied to medieval literature and Shakespeare) to *classic* and exalting the former for its energy and restlessness. Keats's "Ode on a Grecian Urn" reflects both Winckelmann's abstract antiquity and the contradictory experience of viewing the very concrete Elgin Marbles, acquired by Lord Elgin in 1816, in the British Museum. In Keats's poem a silent, unchanging antiquity is recognized as an imaginary construct that has no interaction with the world of time and process.

In France and the United States, revolutionaries turned to antiquity for political models. Jean-Jacques Rousseau found them less in Athens, the celebrated birthplace of democracy, than in the Sparta and republican Rome of Plutarch, who memorialized their ancient ideals of simplicity, equality, and hard work. The new republics identified with these values through publicly accessible symbols such as senates, architecture, and (in the United States) place names. Conversely, as the nineteenth century advanced into the imperial age, Britain's elite found a precedent for dominion over their colonies in the pax romana of the Roman Empire. Classics was now a rigorous academic discipline comprising philology, the legacy of Bentley and Richard Porson in England, and encyclopedic cultural reconstruction, exemplified by the work of German historian Theodor Mommsen. Synonymous with liberal arts, classics was prized for its separation from daily life; reserved for the best schools, it became a mark of status and a criterion for advancement. Nevertheless, aspects of antiquity remained available to the public through popular mythologies, burlesque theater, and fictional reconstructions such as Edward Bulwer-Lytton's *The Last Days of Pompeii* (1834) and Macaulay's *Lays*. And although women of all classes were generally excluded from Greek scholarship, and the age of great literary translations had long since ended, the year 1850 saw the publication of Elizabeth Barrett Browning's revised translation of Aeschylus's *Prometheus Bound*.

KAREN SIMONS

See also **Blake, William; Goethe, Johann Wolfgang von; Keats, John; Ossian;** *Prometheus Unbound***; Shelley, Percy Bysshe; Wordsworth, William**

Bibliography

Feldman, Burton, and Robert D. Richardson. *The Rise of Modern Mythology, 1680–1860*. Bloomington: Indiana University Press, 1972.

Ferris, David. *Silent Urns: Romanticism, Hellenism, Modernity*. Stanford, Calif.: Stanford University Press, 2000.

Grafton, Anthony, Glenn W. Most, and James E. G. Zetzel. "Introduction" to *Prolegomena to Homer*. F. A. Wolf. Princeton, N.J.: Princeton University Press, 1985.

Hall, Edith. "Classical Mythology in the Victorian Popular Theatre," *International Journal of the Classical Tradition* 5, no. 3 (1999): 336–66.

Highet, Gilbert. *The Classical Tradition: Greek and Roman Influences on Western Literature*. Oxford: Clarendon Press, 1949.

Larson, Victoria Tietze. "Classics and the Acquisition and Validation of Power in Britain's 'Imperial Century' (1815–1914)," *International Journal of the Classical Tradition* 6, no. 2 (1999): 185–225.

McNeal, R. A. "Athens and Nineteenth-Century Panoramic Art," *International Journal of the Classical Tradition* 1, no. 3 (1995): 80–97.

Pfeiffer, Rudolf. *History of Classical Scholarship from 1300–1850*. Oxford: Clarendon Press, 1976.

Rubel, Margaret Mary. *Savage and Barbarian: Historical Attitudes in the Criticism of Homer and Ossian in Britain, 1760–1800*. Amsterdam: North-Holland, 1978.

Webb, Timothy. "Romantic Hellenism." In *The Cambridge Companion to British Romanticism*. Edited by Stuart Curran. Cambridge: Cambridge University Press, 1993.

Weinbrot, Howard D. *Britannia's Issue: The Rise of British Literature from Dryden to Ossian*. Cambridge: Cambridge University Press, 1993.

CLAUSEWITZ, CARL VON 1780-1831

German philosopher

The only true philosopher of warfare the West has produced, Carl von Clausewitz's reputation rests primarily on one massive, unfinished work, *Vom Kriege* (*On War*) published after his death under his wife's supervision. His theories may be less important for the author's rich, sophisticated arguments than for the deadly misinterpretation of his writings by soldiers of lesser intellect. Often quoted, less often read in part, and rarely read in full, Clausewitz may be the most misunderstood of Europe's major thinkers.

Born into a family on the fringes of the German aristocracy, Clausewitz began his regimental apprenticeship at twelve and was a combat veteran at thirteen. His education was coincident with both the rise of Napoleon Bonaparte and the transition in the Germanic world from classicism in the arts to the triumph of the Romantic movement. The two developments shaped his life and thought. Unusually gifted, Clausewitz attracted the attention of Prussia's leading soldiers early on. By his mid-twenties, he had attended the select Allgemeine Kriegsschule in Berlin, won a place at court as adjutant to Prince August, and found a fatherly mentor in Germany's greatest soldier of the age, Gerhard von Scharnhorst.

Following Prussia's stunning defeat by Napoleon in 1806, Clausewitz endured a genteel captivity near Paris along with Prince August. Patriotism and wounded pride intensified his detestation of the French, yet Clausewitz, who read, among others, Johann Wolfgang von Goethe, Johann Christoph Friedrich von Schiller, and the leading continental poets of the day, developed a weakness for French sentimental novels and was quite taken with Madame Anne-Louise-Germaine de Staël, the reigning pop novelist, when he met her in Switzerland. Often assumed to be a regimented disciplinarian, Clausewitz married a blue-stocking wife, enjoyed table talk with philosophers and educators, and succumbed to the craze for attending highbrow lectures in Berlin. He was a valiant, smoldering man with a vibrant intellect, far removed from his dry and dusty image.

He also fought in the grimmest campaigns of his age. He could not abide Prussia's forced alliance with Napoleon, and accepted a commission in the Russian army to continue the struggle against the French. He participated, in multiple roles, in the campaign of 1812, which convinced him that the defensive is the stronger form of warfare, then helped negotiate the defection of a Prussian field army. It was nearly his professional undoing. The King of Prussia never quite forgave him for the perceived betrayal—though Clausewitz consistently saw himself as a Prussian patriot—and it took the lobbying efforts of Berlin's leading officers to regain Clausewitz his commission. First as a Russian liaison officer, then in his Prussian blue coat once again, he participated in the campaigns that liberated the Germanies, dethroned Napoleon, then finally ended the Emperor's ambitions at Waterloo.

Out of favor at court despite his service record, Clausewitz endured years of slow promotions, the denial of field commands, and assignment to military schools—where he was employed as a commandant responsible for administration, not in the more suitable role of pedagogue. Assisted by his wife, Marie, with whom he appears to have enjoyed a marriage of mutual devotion and remarkable intellectual companionship, he attended to duty in the mornings and wrote away the long garrison afternoons. He labored with Promethean ambition, allotting himself the impossible task of capturing the complexity, dynamics, and nature of warfare in one definitive work. His writing, though disciplined and precise, is complex, nuanced, and exploratory in nature. If he may be faulted as a thinker, it would be for his inability to explain his incomparable insights in prose that someone of lesser gifts could understand. Clausewitz wrote for an idealized reader, for an intellect comparable to his own.

Clausewitz seems to have feared publication of his great work and continued to tinker with it (few readers could distinguish between those sections he regarded as polished and those still "in progress"). His temperament—strict on the surface, Byronic underneath—also may have been drawn to the German cult of *das Unvollendete*, the eternally unfinished, the magnificent failure. We shall never know if he would one day have written his great work to a conclusion, since he died at age fifty-one, shortly after regaining royal favor, in the same cholera epidemic that killed the other great German philosopher of his generation, Georg Wilhelm Friedrich Hegel.

Attempts to summarize Clausewitz's thought have led to misguided wars and misfired campaigns, but several of his concepts have entered the marketplace of ideas, if in pauper's garb. He is best known for the observation usually rendered in English as "War is simply a continuation of politics by other means." His next-most-cited concept concerns the role of friction in war, which we may limn as a combination of chance, violent conten-

tion, and the likelihood that, if something can go wrong on the battlefield, it will. But his most profound hypotheses explore the dynamic relationship between the state, its military, and the general population, which he encapsulated as the trinity of reason (the state), chance (the military), and passion (the people).

Throughout Clausewitz's work, the reader familiar with other Romantic texts notes a recurrence of the trinities and dualities so popular in the German literature of the day. The doppelganger recurs in the discussions of warfare: only the relative strengths of the attack and the defense, war as a contest of opposing wills, the contrast between limited and absolute war, the tension between means and ends, and his fatally-ignored insistence on the gulf between theory and practice. The last point, especially, haunts his reputation, since his later acolytes in the German military willfully confused Clausewitz's abstract discussion of total war (*Vernichtungskrieg*) with a prescription for how to fight wars effectively.

Though not without its failings, the work of Carl von Clausewitz arguably retains a greater contemporary relevance than that of any other German philosopher of the nineteenth century. Certainly, he is still read and debated in military institutions, especially in the United States, where officers can become nearly professorial in their vitriol as they debate whether or not his insights remain applicable in the twenty-first century. Fortunately, the German military has stopped reading him entirely.

RALPH PETERS

Biography

Born in Burg, Prussia, 1780. Entered Prussian army, 1792. Fought against France, 1793–94. Attended war academy in Berlin, 1801–04. In army, captured by French, in captivity in France and in Switzerland, 1806–1808. Professor at war academy in Berlin, 1810. Left Prussian army, joined Russian army, 1812. Rejoined Prussian army, 1814. Appointed chief of staff, 1830. Died of cholera at Breslau, 1831.

Work

Vom Kriege (*On War*)

Bibliography

Aron, Raymond. *Penser la guerre, Clausewitz*. Paris: Editions Gallimard, 1976.

Bassford, Christopher. *The Reception of Clausewitz in Britain and America, 1815–1945*. London/New York: Oxford University Press, 1994.

Handel, Michael I., ed. *Clausewitz and Modern Strategy*. London: Frank Cass, 1986.

Paret, Peter. *Clausewitz and the State*. London/New York: Oxford University Press, 1976.

von Schramm, Wilhelm. *Clausewitz, Leben und Werk*. Esslingen: Bechtle Verlag, 1976.

CLEMENTI, MUZIO 1752–1832

Italian pianist, composer, music publisher, and piano manufacturer domiciled in England

Muzio Clementi began his career in the eighteenth century as an associate of Franz Josef Haydn and Wolfgang Amadeus Mozart, and ended it in the nineteenth century as a contemporary of Ludwig van Beethoven, Frédéric François Chopin, and Franz Schubert. This progression is emblematic of his role in the transition from the classical era to Romanticism, within the sphere of piano performance and composition especially. An early highlight of his performing career, the contest with Mozart before Viennese emperor Joseph II and his guests in December 1781 during the first of Clementi's many European journeys, was prophetic of the new pianism. As Leon Plantinga observes, "the great span of his career is strikingly illustrated" by his witnessing, in June 1824, the London debut of the twelve-year-old Franz Liszt. Like many foreign musicians, especially Italians, Clementi was drawn (in unusual circumstances—he was spotted by an English gentleman traveling in Italy) to adopt England as his country of residence. Although his earliest training as a keyboard player focused on the harpsichord, and his first documented public performances were as a solo harpsichordist, during the later 1770s his emergence on the London concert scene coincided with the transfer to the pianoforte as his main instrument at a time of increasingly high-profile status for the piano, and the concert pianist, in London's musical life. In the early nineteenth century, he was credited with having raised the piano's esteem, and was seen as a model for the new generation of pianists. Ignaz Moscheles referred to him as "the father of pianoforte playing"; François-Joseph Fétis identified him as the founder of the "brilliant school" of pianists.

Clementi's cosmopolitanism, his specialization on one instrument, and his pedagogical legacy combined to create a virtuoso pianist of a discernibly modern type when viewed in the context of the 1820s. Yet he cultivated a strong interest in music of the earlier eighteenth century, absorbing profoundly the influences of Johann Sebastian Bach and Domenico Scarlatti in particular. Far from alienating the younger generation, this historicism (to become a hallmark of the Romantic musical outlook) was of acknowledged benefit to his disciples; as Stephen Daw has noted, "the music of the past retained its power and its purpose for Clementi." His anthologies of pieces for study (in the *Introduction to the Art of Playing on the Piano Forte* and the *Selection of Practical Harmony for the Organ or Piano Forte*) put music of the past to practical purpose, in order to train musicians of the present.

Clementi's pedagogy was extensive and best known from his *Gradus ad Parnassum*, the vast compendium of keyboard pieces displaying the range of his styles, unfortunately perpetuated from the 1860s onward in the distorted selection by Carl Tausig. (Clementi also became known as a composer almost entirely by the Six Sonatinas for Solo Piano, op. 36, later added as a supplement to his *Art of Playing on the Pianoforte*, 1801.) The whole range of the original pieces in the *Gradus ad Parnassum* is distinguished by a combination of technically demanding keyboard figurations and polyphonic writing bringing their textures at times close to the piano style of Robert Schumann. His solo piano writing more generally has been compared with Johannes Brahms and Chopin. In specifically technical terms, he contributed to modern developments in such aspects as ornamentation and the use of the sustaining pedal. The extent of Clementi's pioneering exploration of piano technique and texture is especially apparent in his approximately seventy solo keyboard sonatas (published between the 1770s and 1820s). Although the three brilliantly virtuosic solo sonatas of opus 2 previously identified with his contribution to the rise of piano style are now known to have been primarily associated with the harpsichord, their emphasis on bravura passages of thirds and octaves, then a novelty, was nevertheless a factor in the development of pianistic idiom (famously, this aspect of Clementi's performance, acknowledged at the time as unrivalled, attracted adverse criticism from Mozart). Clementi was ahead of his time in the late eighteenth century in creating fiendishly difficult and stunning display. (Johann Samuel Schroeter said of Clementi's runs that "they could only be performed by the author himself or the devil." *QMMR*, 1820])

In 1803, the publisher Nägeli, reprinting the three solo sonatas, op. 2, commented: "It is well known that a most remarkable new epoch in this branch of the art, one that has had the greatest of consequences, began with Clementi." While Clementi was among the first to transform piano music, and piano playing, from the classical restraint represented by Mozart to the overt virtuosity of the Romantic age, the early emphasis on virtuosity (which he himself expressed a wish to modify later in favor of a "more noble" style of performance) should not mask other aspects of Clementi's compositional style. His piano sonatas, covering what Plantinga calls "a stylistic spectrum that extends from the most guileless *galant* writing to the rhetorical passion of romantic piano music" embody ideas of melody and sonata structures that were extremely influential, most significantly on Beethoven. Apart from specific thematic connections (notably the "Eroica" theme heard in Clementi and the anticipation of Beethoven's Arietta, op. 111, in Clementi's op. 13, no. 5), the scope of this influence ranges from a general tendency toward powerful and dramatic sonata writing (seen especially in minor-key sonatas such as op. 13, no. 6 in F Minor, op. 25, no. 5 in F-sharp Minor, and op. 34, no. 2 in G Minor) to structural experiments, including the integration of the slow introduction within the following movement, as in op. 34, no. 2, and the investing of motivic and thematic material with a network of unifying relationships. The overall effect, Plantinga notes, is to create "a whole much greater than the sum of its parts." In addition, Clementi's solo keyboard idiom is enriched by orchestral sound, reproducing what Simon McVeigh calls modern "orchestral drama" on the keyboard.

Clementi's acknowledged role as a pioneer in the development of piano style has overshadowed his activity in the orchestral sphere, with the patchy survival of the music (much of his symphonic work, as well as all but one of his concertos, has been lost) hindering appreciation of this side of his creativity. In accordance with English practice, he directed orchestral performances from the keyboard in both the earlier and the later phases of his symphonic production (in the 1790s stepping into Haydn's place in the Salomon concerts, and from 1813 conducting regularly for the Philharmonic concerts). The "keyboard conductor," notes McVeigh, formed a step on the way to the establishment of the nonplaying orchestral conductor.

While Clementi received critical acclaim as a pianist (celebrated also for his improvising) and symphonist, his career and his interests ranged more widely. His contemporaries admired his linguistic and classical learning; as Plantinga notes, "many who knew him spoke of his extensive studies in all sorts of subjects." Within the musical world, Clementi's international reputation and influence, achieved against the backdrop of the Napoleonic Wars, were unique among his English contemporaries in the range of activities they represented: playing, teaching, composing, conducting, publishing, arranging and editing, and piano manufacturing. After the late 1790s he moved away from performing and increasingly toward publishing and manufacture.

Among the distinguished achievements of his firm was their securing of the rights to some of Beethoven's music (Clementi negotiated personally with Beethoven in Vienna), resulting eventually in a series of first editions appearing in England of such works as the "Emperor" concerto (op. 73) and the Sonata, op. 81a ("Les Adieux"). Clementi was also a leading producer of internationally sought-after pianofortes. Here his knowledge of older music may have borne particular fruit if, as Daw suggests, Clementi's work as senior partner was "strongly influenced by the rich harpsichord [and clavichord] styles of Scarlatti and the Bach family." The *Allgemeine Musikalische Zeitung* reported in 1802 that Clementi could "produce without question the finest—but also, to be sure, the most expensive—instruments in the world, whose quality has been enhanced by Clementi's mechanical ability and artistic experience."

When Clementi "raised his terms for teaching" to the exceptionally high rate of a guinea an hour, the numbers applying to study with him increased. Several of his pupils left admiring testimony to his "art of tuition." His impact as a teacher was in both the nonprofessional sphere (as with Theresa Jansen, later Bartholozzi) and the aspiring professional (Ludwig Berger [later teacher of Felix Mendelssohn and Adolf Henselt], J. B. Cramer, and John Field). The *Berlinische Musikalische Zeitung* in 1805 referred to "the excellent young pianist Berger, who . . . surely will develop into a finished virtuoso from his association with Clementi. It is a real advantage for the art that such a great and profound musician as Clementi should establish a school of performance, and plant the seeds of his splendid and unique art in foreign soil as well." In recent literature Clementi has appeared alongside Jan Ladislav Dussek and others as representative of the "London Pianoforte School"; the documentation of his career suggests a more strongly individual role, and one that was of lasting importance in the formation of Romantic pianism.

SUSAN WOLLENBERG

Biography

Born Rome, January 23, 1752. Eldest of seven children of Nicolo Clementi, a silversmith, and Magdalena Kaiser Clementi. Stud-

ied music in Rome from an early age. Appointed organist at St. Lorenzo in Damaso, 1766. Brought to Dorset, England, as musician at the country estate of Peter Beckford, cousin of the writer William Beckford, late 1766 or early 1767. Studied music and played the harpsichord. Moved to London, 1774. Conducted operas (from the keyboard) at the King's Theatre, Haymarket, and made first solo appearances. Traveled as a pianist, 1780–83. Played for Marie Antoinette; took part in musical contest with Mozart staged by Emperor Joseph II at the Viennese court, 1781. Returned to London, 1783; performed as soloist for the Hanover Square Concerts. Embarked on brief elopement with Victoire Imbert-Colomés in France, 1784. Returned to London after staying in Bern, Switzerland; worked as composer, keyboard performer, and teacher in London, 1785–1802. Established music-publishing and instrument-making business in London, known under various names but generally referred to as Clementi and Company, 1790s. Made third European tour, 1802–10; traveled as his company's representative (initially with pupil John Field) to Germany, Russia, and Vienna. "Oeuvres complettes," launched by publisher Breitkopf and Härtel, 1803. Married Caroline Lehmann, 1804 (she died during the birth of their one son, 1805). Married Emma Gisborne, 1811; they had two sons, two daughters. Settled in London; later moved to Elstree; joined by his first son Carl, c. 1818. Founding codirector of the Philharmonic Society of London, 1813. Elected a member of the Swedish Royal Academy of Music, 1814. Retired from music business, 1830; moved with his family to Lichfield, Staffordshire, and later to Evesham, Worcestershire. Died in Evesham, March 10, 1832.

Selected Works

Pedagogical
Introduction to the Art of Playing on the Piano Forte, op. 42. 1801.
Gradus ad Parnassum, op. 44. 3 vols. 1817–26.

Bibliography

Collard, William. "Mr. Clementi," *Quarterly Musical Magazine and Review* 2 (1820): 308–16.

Cooper, Barry. "A Clementi Discovery," *Music Review* 44 (1983): 178–85.

Daw, Stephen. "Muzio Clementi as an Original Advocate, Collector and Performer, in Particular of J. S. Bach and D. Scarlatti." In *Bach, Handel, Scarlatti: Tercentenary Essays*. Edited by Peter Williams. Cambridge: Cambridge University Press, 1985.

McVeigh, Simon. *Concert Life in London from Mozart to Haydn*. Cambridge: Cambridge University Press, 1993.

Moscheles, Charlotte. *Life of Moscheles with Selections from his Diaries and Correspondence, by his Wife*. Translated by A. D. Coleridge. 2 vols. 1873.

Plantinga, Leon. *Clementi: His Life and Music*. London: Oxford University Press, 1977.

Ringer, Alexander. "Clementi and the *Eroica*," *Musical Quarterly* 47 (1961): 454–68.

Truscott, Harold. "The Piano Music I." In *The Beethoven Companion*. Edited by Denis Arnold and Nigel Fortune. London: Faber, 1971.

Tyson, Alan. *Thematic Catalogue of the Works of Muzio Clementi*. Tutzing: Germany: Schneider, 1967.

COBBETT, WILLIAM 1763–1835

English journalist

The grandson of a day-laborer, William Cobbett idealized the village life of his boyhood as unspoiled Old England, an Edenic agricultural community of abundance and traditional relations which he used as a yardstick to measure the impoverishment caused by economic and political corruption. His unexplained flight from this rural paradise led to a succession of miscellaneous employments, including six years soldiering in Canada. Influenced by Edmund Burke's praise of the historic organic community and appalled at the atrocities of the French revolutionaries, he published an attack on Thomas Paine and Joseph Priestley as English Jacobins upon the latter's emigration to America in 1792.

In England he initially supported the government in the *Political Register*, which he began in 1802, but soon turned to criticism of political corruption in both major parties and allied himself with the radical leader Sir Francis Burdett. The terms *Tory* or *Romantic radical* have been applied to him because of his reiterated contention that he wanted alteration but nothing new. While this may represent his early position, it became less convincing after the Napoleonic Wars, as he moved toward John Cartwright's idea of an Anglo-Saxon constitution that authorized universal manhood suffrage, annual elections, and secret ballot.

Nationalistic to the point of chauvinism, Cobbett presented himself as wishing to restore the customary relations between crown, parliament, and people. Bribery at elections, nepotism, and patronage in the distribution of sinecures, pensions, and appointments disfigured the ruling aristocracy; immorality and extravagance infected the court. Such corruption destroyed national unity and had rendered other regimes easy prey to Bonaparte. The remedies Cobbett supported were public opinion informed by a free press, a redistribution of parliamentary seats to eliminate "rotten boroughs," and an extension of the franchise to render more electorates as numerous and independent as those of London. Scandals involving naval procurement, secret and immoral influence in achieving commissions in the army, and mismanagement in the Peninsular war brought a resurgence of radicalism from 1806 which regrouped along these lines.

By establishing his series of *Parliamentary Debates* (later Hansard) and *State Trials*, Cobbett opened up the operations of government to the scrutiny of a new, vastly increased readership. In the *Political Register* he set the tone for popular radical journalism in his emphatic, colloquial style and his moralistic censure of abuses and vice in high places. He projected the character of a plain, blunt Englishman, speaking from experience and personalizing issues, as when he famously promised that if disaster did not come of the government's policies they could roast him on a gridiron. William Hazlitt relished this unaffected egotism that, like his own, exposed one to personal attacks. Cobbett's outspokenness led to imprisonment in 1810 (for condemning the flogging of British soldiers), and later to self-exile in America (he thought the Gagging Acts of 1817 were specifically directed at him), and, ultimately, to bankruptcy in 1820. He tended to focus more on personalities than on doctrines, but

followed Paine in trying to make economics intelligible to the layman, especially in his diatribes against the national debt and the taxes that serviced it. Through them the common laborer is seen as supporting the "dead weight" of government pensioners, sinecure holders, opulent churchmen, investors of ill-gotten colonial wealth, and those involved in managing the new financial system of the nation. He refused to see hardship as the result of ineluctible laws of political economy. David Ricardo might stigmatize rent as the root of economic ills, but rent was driven by taxes on landowners. Cobbett rejected fears of overpopulation and attacked Thomas Malthus for only targeting the reproduction of the poor. He came to see the war as fought at the people's expense for the purpose of stifling reform, and by 1817 his populism rivaled that of Henry "Orator" Hunt, and became too extreme for Sir Francis Burdett. Cobbett appealed directly to laborers and journeymen, demanding reform in twopenny pamphlets that, reprinted from the *Political Register*, avoided the stamp duty on newspapers, paving the way for future illegal "unstamped" radical papers. By explaining Luddism and rural riots as reactions to injustice, he often seemed to encourage violence. Percy Bysshe Shelley, while largely concurring with his economic analysis, referred critically to "Cobbett's snuff, revenge," but Raymond Williams praised him for his articulation of the nascent class struggle. Karl Marx saw Cobbett as charting a way from Old England to Young England. In his nostalgic view of "Merrie England," expanded in his *History of the Protestant "Reformation"* (1824–26), he contributed, with Thomas Carlyle, Walter Scott, and Robert Southey, to the revival of chivalric, even feudal, ideas among the Tory aristocracy of mid-nineteenth-century Britain.

Rural Rides (1830) is deservedly popular for Cobbett's personal response to the countryside in its picturesque and practical aspects, but it is also political in focus. Cobbett chronicles in Burkean fashion the passing of old estates into the hands of economists and bankers, and seems in full flight from the modern world as he avoids turnpike roads and curses canals, both seen as draining the life-blood of the countryside to swell the overpopulated "wens" (towns that had little connection with agricultural production, notably fashionable resorts such as Cheltenham and Bath; London was the "Great Wen"). He laments the passing of old farming customs, such as laborers eating at the farmer's table. Yet Cobbett also values the yeoman's and the villager's independence, secured by smallholdings and customary rights on the commons, both threatened by enclosure. Cash payments were a poor substitute for self-sufficiency. His *Cottage Economy* (1821–22), one of his series of self-help manuals, encouraged small cottage industries and sought to diminish dependence on fashionable imported commodities.

A nostalgic agrarianism has been seen as Cobbett's weakness as a radical, since the most substantial support for radicalism came from commercial interests and the new industrial areas, hardly likely to welcome his "Perish Commerce" articles or his reluctance to criticize the protectionist Corn Laws. In his own farming practice at Botley, however, Cobbett was innovative.

He introduced new crops and trees and even made a turnpike, while apparently maintaining good relations with his employees. His relish for local customs, including hunting, coursing, and robust physical contests, which affronted new humanitarian tastes, was shared by other radicals such as Samuel Bamford and William Hone. It testifies elegiacally to the perceived waning of an independent, indigenous culture and its communitarian values.

CHRIS JONES

Biography

Born in Farnham, Surrey, March 9, 1763. Son of a minor farmer and innkeeper. Worked as a farm laborer until the early 1780s. Gardener at the botanic gardens, Kew, and lawyer's clerk in London. Enlisted in the army; served in 54th Infantry Regiment, Chatham, 1784, and in Nova Scotia and New Brunswick, rising to rank of sergeant-major, 1784–91. Educated himself in his off-duty hours. Returned to England; after army discharge, brought charges of corruption against his former officers, 1791. Married Ann Reid, 1792: they had seven children. Escaped countercharges and court martial by traveling to France, 1792; fled the dangers of the French Revolution and sailed to America. Taught French emigrés in Delaware and Philadelphia, 1792–96. Became a bookseller and journalist under the pen name Peter Porcupine, supporting the federalist side, 1796–1800. Founded the monthly *Political Censor*, 1796–97, and its successor, *Porcupine's Gazette and Daily Advertiser*, 1797–1800. Convicted of libel, 1799; moved to New York; founded the magazine *The Rush-Light*. Returned to England, 1800. Farmer in Botley, Hampshire, 1804–17. Served a term in Newgate Prison, London, after criticizing flogging of militiamen, 1810–12. Editor, *The Porcupine*, 1801–02; bookseller, 1802–03; founding editor, *Cobbett's Weekly Political Register*, 1802–35. Fled to America to avoid arrest for sedition, 1817. Farmed on Long Island, New York, 1817–19. Returned to England, 1820; established seed farm in Kensington, 1821. Unsuccessful parliamentary candidate for Coventry, 1821, and Preston, 1826. Founded *Parliamentary Register*, 1822. Shareholder and contributor to the *Statesman*, 1822–23, and *Norfolk Yeoman's Gazette*, 1825. Published *Rural Rides*, 1830. Prosecuted for sedition after supporting agricultural laborers' protest, 1831. Member of Parliament for Oldham, 1832–34. Died of influenza in London, June 18, 1835.

Selected Works

The Soldier's Friend. 1792.
Observations on the Emigration of Dr Joseph Priestley. 1794.
The Life and Adventures of Peter Porcupine. 1796.
Cobbett's (Weekly) Political Register. 89 vols. 1802–35. (Also titled *Cobbett's Weekly Political Pamphlet.* 1817.)
Cobbett's Parliamentary Debates. 27 vols. 1804–14.
Cobbett's Complete Collection of State Trials. 33 vols. 1809–26.
A Year's Residence in the United States of America. 1818.
A Grammar of the English Language. 1818.
Cottage Economy. 8 vols. 1821–22.
A History of the Protestant "Reformation," 16 vols. 1824–26; part 2, 1827.
Cobbett's Poor Man's Friend, 5 vols. 1826–27.
Advice to Young Men, 14 vols. 1829–30.
Rural Rides. 1830.
Cobbett's Two-penny Trash, or Politics for the Poor. 2 vols. 1830–32.
History of the Regency and Reign of George IV. 2 vols. 1830–34.
Cobbett's Legacy to Labourers. 1835.

Bibliography

Chandler, Alice. *A Dream of Order: The Medieval Ideal in Nineteenth-Century English Literature.* London: Routledge, 1971.
Cole, G. D. H. *The Life of William Cobbett.* London: Collins, 1924.
Dyck, Ian. *William Cobbett and Rural Popular Culture.* Cambridge: Cambridge University Press, 1992.
Fulford, Tim. *Romanticism and Masculinity: Gender, Politics, and Poetics in the Writings of Burke, Coleridge, Cobbett, Wordsworth, De Quincey, and Hazlitt.* New York: St. Martin's Press, 1999.
Hazlitt, William. *The Spirit of the Age.* Edited by E. D. Mackerness. London: Collins, 1969.
Maccoby, Simon. *English Radicalism 1786–1832: From Paine to Cobbett.* London: Allen and Unwin, 1955.
Nattrass, Leonora. *William Cobbett: The Politics of Style.* Cambridge: Cambridge University Press, 1995.
Osborne, John W. *William Cobbett: His Thought and His Times.* New Brunswick, N.J.: Rutgers University Press, 1966.
Sambrook, James. *William Cobbett.* London: Routledge, 1973.
Spence, Peter. *The Birth of Romantic Radicalism.* Aldershot, England: Scolar Press, 1996.
Thompson, E. P. *The Making of the English Working Class.* London: Gollancz, 1963. Rev. ed., Harmondsworth, England: Penguin, 1968.
Williams, Raymond. *Culture and Society, 1780–1950.* London: Chatto and Windus, 1958.
Williams, Raymond. *Cobbett.* Oxford: Oxford University Press, 1983.

COLE, THOMAS 1801–1848

American artist and author

Thomas Cole was a primary member of the Hudson River school of Romantic landscape painting, and a prominent and popular figure in nineteenth-century American art. His images of grand landscapes, peopled by industrious and virtuous individuals, have been credited with helping to shape early public notions of American national identity.

Born in Bolton-le-Moor, Lancashire, England, Cole's family emigrated to the United States in 1818. Trained in England as an engraver, he began his career working as an artisan in his father's wallpaper manufacturing firm in Steubenville, Ohio. With no formal training in either painting or drawing but keenly interested in landscape, Cole soon began to teach himself the principles of composition, working from English chinaware patterns and copying a collection of mezzotint engravings of works by the British painter John Martin. In 1820, Cole became acquainted with a traveling portraitist named John Stein, who became his tutor; in addition to instructing him in painting, Stein taught Cole about the Romantic aesthetics of the sublime and the picturesque.

When his father's wallpaper business failed in 1823, the family moved to Pittsburgh, Pennsylvania, where Cole began his career as a professional artist. His early landscape studies, depicting the scenery along the banks of the nearby Monongahela River, show the influence of European painters Claude Lorrain and Salvatore Rosa. Soon thereafter, Cole enrolled as a student in the Philadelphia Academy of Fine Art, where he became acquainted with the works of painters Thomas Birch and Thomas Doughty, and where he began to develop a style that he considered distinctly American. This style flourished when Cole also found, on an 1825 sketching tour, his signature subject: the Hudson River Valley in New York State. At an exhibit of the works that resulted from the tour of the area, his paintings *The Falls of Caterskill* (1826) and *Lake with Dead Trees* (1825) attracted the attention of prominent artists Asher B. Durand and John Trumbull. Cole moved to the Catskill Mountain region (adjoining the Hudson Valley), where he was soon joined by several other aspiring artists. With the help of the publicity generated by the New York Knickerbocker writers, this informal group soon came to be collectively known as the Hudson River school.

Cole's early works interweave themes of landscape, solitude, and spiritual integrity, intending to represent nature as the visible hand of Providence. The portrait of Daniel Boone at home in the wilderness (1826) is a particularly fine example of Cole's developing interest in Romantic and Arcadian motifs. Another early work, *The Woodchopper* (1826), also reflects Cole's increasing anxiety about the destruction of America's wild spaces and, by extension, its loss of moral innocence. Like the British Romantics, Cole held that those "scenes of solitude from which the hand of nature has never been lifted, affect the mind with a more deep toned emotion than aught which the hand of man has touched . . . and the mind is cast into the contemplation of eternal things" ("Essay on American Scenery," 1836). A poet as well as a painter, two of Cole's finest verse compositions, "The Complaint of the Forest" and "The Lament of the Forest," reflect his familiarity with the Romantic tradition and his concern for environmental issues.

By 1827, Cole's career as an artist was securely established. In 1826, he had become one of the founding members of the National Academy of Arts, and he had completed his painting *Romantic Landscape* (1826), which identified American pastoralism with the abstract values of Romanticism. By 1827, Cole was the most popular painter in the United States, and this celebrity depended in large part upon his early interest in shaping and expressing a nativist American tradition. His *Scene from* [James Fenimore Cooper's] "*The Last of the Mohicans*" (1827), in particular, represents a visual history of early American national identity.

In 1829, Cole planned to travel through—and to mount an exhibition in—Europe, and in anticipation of this trip he went to Niagara Falls to sketch them, intending to impress European contemporaries with the grandeur of the American scene. In addition to completing twenty-three sketches of the falls, Cole also wrote a series of evocative travel letters. His painting *Niagara Falls* (1829) was completed in Europe.

Cole traveled in Europe from 1829 to 1832, studying landscape painting. He spent much of his first two years in London, where he visited James Fenimore Cooper and was introduced to the Romantic poet Samuel Rogers. While in England, he also sketched *A View of Rydal Water*, depicting "a spot near the dwelling of the poet Wordsworth," whose poetry he admired. From a professional standpoint, the most important part of his trip was the final two years Cole spent painting in Italy. In Rome, he worked in a studio that had once been occupied by one of his predecessors, landscape artist Claude Lorrain, and he completed several fine "Italian compositions," largely depicting pastoral scenery and classical ruins. During this time, Cole's technique gained considerable confidence and a new boldness, and he conceived the concept for *The Course of Empire* (1834–36), the didactic history sequence that was to become one of his most important works.

A series of five paintings, *The Course of Empire* was intended as an allegory on the dangers of imperialism, and may have marked a response to the autocratic administration of President Andrew Jackson. In the cycle, Cole chronicles society's progression from the *Savage State* (1834) to the *Arcadian State* (1834), and its eventual collapse into *The Consummation of Empire* (1835–36), *Desolation* (1836), and *Destruction* (1836). Suggested in part by Cole's reading of Lord Byron's *Childe Harold's Pilgrimage* and Edward Gibbon's *Decline and Fall of the Roman Empire*, the work seems to been influenced by the contemporary historical panoramas that Cole had viewed in London as well. In its development of thematic associations between the landscape and the moral and spiritual state of those who shape it, *The Course of Empire* represents Cole's continuing concern with the early commercialization of American culture.

Throughout the 1830s, Cole would continue concentrating on themes of warning and unrest. His pastoral paintings become more focused on turbulent landscapes, as in the *View from Mt. Holyoke, Northampton, Massachusetts after a Thunderstorm; The Oxbow* (1836). Cole also experimented with Gothic themes in paintings such as *The Departure* (1837) and *The Return* (1837), and in an unfinished work illustrating lines from Samuel Taylor Coleridge's poem "Love."

Cole traveled to Europe again in 1841–42, visiting Switzerland and Italy. In addition to several fine landscape paintings of Rome and Sicily, he also conceived plans for a second didactic painting series, depicting the soul's journey, entitled *The Voyage of Life* (1842). This sequence reflects Cole's increasing religiosity, which culminated in his conversion to Episcopalianism in 1842. Although he completed several minor paintings in the years after his return from Europe, Cole's last major work was *Home in the Woods* (1847), commissioned by the American Art Union and exhibited posthumously after his sudden death from pneumonia.

TILAR MAZZEO

Biography

Born in Bolton-le-Moors, Lancashire, England, February 1, 1801. Attended schools in Chester; trained as a textile printing engraver in Liverpool. Emigrated with his family to the United State, 1818. Lived in Philadelphia, moving to Steubenville, Ohio, 1819–23. Worked on designs and engravings for his father's wallpaper factory; learned portrait painting from itinerant painter John Stein. Stayed in Pittsburgh and Philadelphia, 1823–24; painted around city of Pittsburgh and studied work of Thomas Doughty and Thomas Birch at the Pennsylvania Academy of Fine Art. Moved to New York, 1825. Started walking and painting tours in the Hudson River Valley and the Catskill Mountains. Cofounder of the National Academy of Design, 1826. Traveled to Europe, 1829–32. Returned to New York; established studio in Catskill, 1832. Visited galleries and studied art in London, Paris, Rome, Florence, and Naples. Commissioned by businessman Luman Reed to paint the series *The Course of Empire*, 1834–36. Married Maria Bartow; moved permanently to Catskill, 1836. Second visit to Europe, 1841–42: visited France, Italy, and Switzerland. Completed *The Voyage of Life* series in Italy, 1841. Joined Episcopal Church, 1843. Took artist Frederick Church as apprentice, 1844. Died in Catskill, New York, February 11, 1848.

Selected Works

"Essay on American Scenery." 1836.
Thomas Cole's Poetry: The Collected Poems of America's Foremost Painter of the Hudson River School. Edited by Marshall B. Tymn. New York: George Shumway, 1972.

Bibliography

Callow, James T. *Kindred Spirits: Knickerbocker Writers and American Artists, 1807–1855.* Chapel Hill: University of North Carolina Press, 1967.
Cooper, James Fenimore. *Knights of the Brush: The Hudson River School and the Moral Landscape.* London: Art Books International, 2000.
Copplestone, Trewin. *The Hudson River School.* New York: Gramercy, 1999.
Driscoll, John Paul. *All That Is Glorious around Us: From the Hudson River School.* Ithaca, N.Y.: Cornell University Press, 1997.
Exhibition of the Paintings of the Late Thomas Cole: at the Gallery of the American Art-Union. Exhibition catalog. 1848.
Minks, Louise. *The Hudson River School.* New York: Barnes and Noble, 1999.
Noble, Louis Le Grand. *The Life and Works of Thomas Cole.* New York: Black Dome Press, 1997.
Orations and Addresses by William Cullen Bryant. New York: G. P. Putnam's, 1873.
The Scenery of the Catskill Mountains. New York: D. Fanshaw, 1850.
Thomas Cole: Paintings by an American Romanticist: Handlist and Comments. Exhibition catalog. Baltimore: Baltimore Museum of Art, 1965.
Truettner, William H., Alan Wallach, and Christine Stansell. *Thomas Cole: Landscape into History.* New Haven, Conn.: Yale University, 1994.
Veith, Gene Edward. *Painters of Faith: Spiritual Landscape in Nineteenth-Century America.* Washington: Regnery, 2001.
Wilson, James Grant. *Bryant, and His Friends; Some Reminiscences of the Knickerbocker Writers.* New York: Fords, Howard and Hulbert, 1900.
Yeager, Bert D. *The Hudson River School: American Landscape Artists.* New York: Todtri, 1999.

COLERIDGE, SAMUEL TAYLOR 1772–1834

English poet and philosopher

With his friend William Wordsworth, and with Lord Byron and Percy Bysshe Shelley, Samuel Taylor Coleridge forms one corner of the tetrarch of major English Romantic poets. As a child and a young man of latent genius, his adult life was marred by ill health, hypochondria, and an ever-increasing slavery to opium. Both in his own lifetime and subsequently he has been seen as a man of hugely unfulfilled potential, a dreamer, a talker, and a schemer, a "child of nature" brought low by the ordinariness and responsibilities of daily life.

Through his copious volumes of notebooks and letters, and his poems and other published works, Coleridge emerges as one of the great fashioners of the Romantic personality. This began with his own creation, or reflections, upon his childhood. A loved and cosseted child, in one autobiographical statement he declared that even before he was eight years old, "I was a *character*—sensibility, imagination, vanity, sloth . . . were even then prominent & manifest." The night he ran away from home after a family argument, at age seven, became a formative experience that lingered long in his imagination, and was a first example of his lifelong practice of escape and exile as a way to extract attention and emotional reactions. From an early age he was a voracious reader. *The Arabian Nights* was a favorite, and he reflected that "from my early reading of Faery Tales, & Genii etc etc—my mind had been habituated *to the Vast*." The death of his father in 1781, a teacher and clergyman, led to Coleridge being sent to school at Christ's Hospital in London, where he was friends with Charles Lamb. He proceeded from Christ's Hospital to Cambridge as a brilliant young student, winning the Brown Medal with his Greek Sapphic "Ode on the Slave Trade" at the end of his first year. The poem reveals Coleridge's early concern with political issues, and the ongoing revolutionary events in France, which were profoundly influential upon him.

Coleridge's time at Cambridge University was one of both brilliant success and squandered opportunity, of self-confessed debt, debauchery, indolence, and intoxication. In 1794 he met in Oxford another young poet, Robert Southey, and Coleridge soon abandoned Cambridge and his future career in the Church of England. Through Southey, who was strongly influenced by the ideas of William Godwin, Coleridge became closely involved in radical politics, Unitarianism, and journalism. An early collaborative work was the tragedy, "The Fall of Robespierre," which was published in Cambridge in 1794. However, the idealistic plan of Coleridge and Southey to establish a "pantisocratic" commune in America, in which private property would be abolished, inevitably failed.

Money would be one of the greatest troubles of Coleridge's life, and he often depended upon the generosity of patrons and the hospitality of friends. His financial responsibilities increased when he married Sara Fricker in 1795, a disastrous match engineered by Southey. Settling in the western English countryside, Coleridge made friends with the physician Thomas Beddoes and the young chemist Humphry Davy, and was immersed in the philosophy of George Berkeley and David Hartley (after whom he named his sons) and Joseph Priestley. Attempting to make a living from writing and lecturing, in 1797 he met Thomas Wedgwood, a wealthy son of the famous Staffordshire potter,

Josiah Wedgwood Sr. Coleridge was then toying with accepting a position as a Unitarian minister, but was soon offered an annuity of £150 by the Wedgwoods. This would allow him to work without the stress of pecuniary need, but it also put on him a pressure to perform great works that he found it hard to meet. The annuity would finally be withdrawn in 1811 after Coleridge failed to meet Josiah Wedgwood Jr.'s expectations. Coleridge's sometime friend, Charles Lloyd, gives a satirical impression of the young poet as he appeared around this time in his 1798 novel, *Edmund Oliver*. Oliver (i.e., Coleridge) is presented as "a character of excessive sensibility, and impetuous desires" who sinks into debt and opium.

In 1797 Coleridge met William Wordsworth, a major moment in the history of the English Romantic movement. In his poem *The Prelude*, Wordsworth recognized in Coleridge "The most intense of Nature's worshippers." They shared a similar vision of the world, and in 1798 they published a collaborative venture, the anonymously published *Lyrical Ballads*, which included Coleridge's poem the "Rime of the Ancient Mariner." This period of poetic work included the composition of the opium-induced poem *Kubla Khan*, though this was not published until 1816 in a short collection of unfinished poems, with the assistance and encouragement of Lord Byron. Supported by the Wedgwoods' patronage, in 1798 Coleridge traveled with the Wordsworths to Germany, with the plan of studying the works of Johann Christoph Friedrich von Schiller and Immanuel Kant. One of Coleridge's most important contributions to English philosophy would be his dissemination of the work of German thinkers. On his return to England in 1799 he once more attempted serious work as a journalist, but was too irregular a contributor to make a success of this profession. He also became increasingly conservative in his political views after 1800, to the subsequent disgust of William Hazlitt and other of his former associates.

It is impossible to make a review of Coleridge's life and work free from his reliance on opium—what he called in 1832 his "craving for the poison that has been the curse of my existence, my shame and my *negro-slave* inward humiliation and debasement." His habit increased considerably after his move to the damp environment of the Lake District in 1800, though he continued in his walking tours of the British countryside and his mountain climbs. In his youth he advocated the importance of a physical life, declaring in 1797 "I *will* be (please God) an horticulturist and farmer." An attempt to improve his health led to his two-year sojourn in the Mediterranean, during which time he visited Gibraltar, Malta, Sicily, and Italy. His friend the fellow opium-eater Thomas De Quincey wrote that opium "killed [Coleridge] as a poet," and perhaps significantly one of Coleridge's last major poetic works, the "Ode to Dejection," was written in 1802. Even prior to his opium habit, Coleridge was a man of profound action and inaction, but by 1810 Wordsworth wrote, "We have no hope of him—none that he will ever do anything more than he has already done. If he were not under our Roof, he would be just as much the slave of stimulants as ever."

After 1802 Coleridge became increasingly concerned with his philosophical interests, though he continued to give lectures in London and Bristol on literary subjects, and occasionally resumed his playwriting efforts. In August 1809 he began a metaphysical newspaper, the *Friend*, which ran only until April 1810. But much of his intellectual effort was put in to what he called his "Great Work." In 1820 he wrote that more than twenty years of his life had been devoted to its preparation, and that it was on this work that "my hopes of extensive and permanent Utility, of Fame in the noblest sense of the word, mainly rest." To this *opus maximum*, furthermore, he considered all his other work (except perhaps his poetry) "introductory and preparative; and the result of which . . . must finally be a revolution of all that has been called *Philosophy* or Metaphysics in England and France since the aera of the commencing predominance of the mechanical system at the restoration of our second Charles." This, in other words, was the philosophy of René Descartes, and its subsequent influence over "the present fashionable Views not only of Religion, Morals and Politics but even of the modern Physics and Physiology." Inevitably a project ever-spiralling in scope, by the late 1820s he was battling with the anxiety of arranging and editing a "huge pile of Manuscripts." Despite the assistance of his friend and future literary executor Dr. John Henry Green, his opus maximum was never published. But his *Biographia Literaria*, which appeared in two volumes in 1817, has been seen as one product of this unfinished greater work.

The unconnectedness of Coleridge's mind meant that his works, both philosophical and poetic, were often criticized for lacking a recognizable beginning, middle, and end. Wordsworth, for example, wrote of *The Ancient Mariner* "that the events having no necessary connection do not produce each other." This was a fair assessment, and a coherent system to his philosophical writing was also lacking, despite the attempts of his friend and literary executor J. H. Green to drawn them into a coherent work. A further criticism increasingly raised against Coleridge's philosophical work was that of plagiarism. Though Coleridge, Southey, and Wordsworth had borrowed freely from each other in the 1790s, Coleridge continued to make borrowings from other authors throughout his life, invariably without acknowledgment. This fact, and his estrangement from his wife, family, and many of his friends, due in part to his opium habit, led to a certain clouding of his reputation later in his life.

Coleridge felt that he had devoted his life to "unitermitted Reading, Thinking, Meditating and Observing," and for this he had "sacrificed all wor[l]dly prospects of wealth & advancement." However, despite his "affectionate exhortation" in the *Biographia Literaria* "to those who in early life feel themselves disposed to become authors" (that is, the advice "NEVER PURSUE LITERATURE AS A TRADE"), he considered his writing life a success: "I have not been useless in my generation," he reflected in 1820. Nevertheless, he also realized that his ambitions had been great, and that not all of these ambitions had been met. It is in this way that Coleridge's life and career have been seen by subsequent critics. But Coleridge also recognized that those things he had succeeded in achieving were great. Perhaps his greatest contribution to the Romantic, misunderstood in his own day, was the foundation of poetry upon vision, fantasy, and forceful imagination. As he rightly explained to Hazlitt, there is "a class of poetry built on the foundation of dreams."

DAVID HAYCOCK

Biography

Born the youngest of ten children of John Coleridge, a schoolmaster and vicar of Ottery St. Mary, Devon, who died when Coleridge was almost nine. Sent to school at Christ's Hospital, London, and then won scholarship to Jesus College, Cambridge

University, in 1791. Left Cambridge in debt and enlisted in the fifteenth Dragoons, but bought out by his brothers and discharged "insane." Left Cambridge in 1794 without taking his degree after meeting Robert Southey in Oxford. Together they became involved in Unitarian and radical politics and an unsuccessful "pantisocratic" scheme to found a utopian settlement in Pennsylvania based on self-rule and equality. Married Southey's friend Sara Fricker in "poor Chatterton's Church" in Bristol, 1795. Published his first volume of *Poems on Various Subjects* in 1796. Traveled in Wales, and canvassed in midland and northern towns for subscribers to his newspaper the *Watchman*. Settled at Bristol and then at Nether Stowey, Somerset, from where he wrote the first parts of "Christabel" as well as *Kubla Khan*, and occasionally preached in Unitarian chapels. Met and collaborated with William Wordsworth. Met William Hazlitt in 1798, and received annuities from Josiah and Thomas Wedgwood. Visited Germany with the Wordsworths in 1798–99, and studied German philosophy and literature. Settled at Greta Hall, Keswick, in the Lake District in 1800, but was becoming increasingly dependent upon opium. Traveled to Malta, Sicily, and Rome in effort to improve his health, 1804–06. Abandoned his wife and children on his return, became dependent on Wordsworth. Settled in London and then Bristol, living with friends and lecturing on philosophy and literature and writing for newspapers and journals, including his newspaper, the *Friend*. In an attempt to control his opium habit, he moved in to the house of Dr. James Gillman in Highgate, London, in 1816, where he remained for the rest of his life. Published *Biographia Literaria* in 1817; revisited Germany in 1828, and played an important role in promoting German philosophical thought in England. Died in 1834.

Selected Works

Lyrical Ballads, published anonymously with William Wordsworth. 1797.

Biographia Literaria: or Biographical Sketches of My Literary Life and Opinions. 1817.
Spiritual Philosophy, Founded on the Teaching of the Late S. T. Coleridge. 2 vols. Edited by Joseph Simon. 1865.
The Collected Letters of Samuel Taylor Coleridge. 6 vols. Edited by Earl Leslie Griggs. Oxford: Oxford University Press, 1956–71.
The Notebooks of Samuel Taylor Coleridge. 3 vols. Edited by Kathleen Coburn. 1957–73.
The Collected Works of Samuel Taylor Coleridge. Princeton, N.J.: Princeton University Press.

Bibliography

Ashton, Rosemary. *The Life of Samuel Taylor Coleridge.* Oxford: Blackwell, 1996.
Bate, Walter Jackson. *Coleridge.* London: Weidenfeld and Nicolson, 1969.
Beer, John, ed. *Coleridge's Variety: Bicentenary Studies.* London Macmillan Press, 1974.
Campbell, James Dykes. *Samuel Taylor Coleridge: A Narrative of the Events of His Life.* 1894.
Chambers, E. K. *Samuel Taylor Coleridge: A Biographical Study.* Oxford: 1938.
Cottle, Joseph. *Early Recollections: Chiefly Relating to the Late Samuel Taylor Coleridge.* 1837.
Ford, Jennifer. *Coleridge on Dreaming: Romanticism, Dreams and the Medical Imagination.* Cambridge: Cambridge University Press, 1998.
Fruman, Norman. *Coleridge, The Damaged Archangel.* New York: George Braziller.
Gillman, James. *The Life of Samuel Taylor Coleridge.* 1838.
Hall, G. K. *Samuel Taylor Coleridge: An Annotated Bibliography of Criticism and Scholarship.* Boston: 1983.
Holmes, Richard. *Coleridge: Early Visions.* London: Hodder and Stoughton, 1989.
Holmes, Richard. *Coleridge: Darker Reflections.* London: Harper Collins, 1998.
Lefebure, Molly. *Samuel Taylor Coleridge: A Bondage of Opium.* London: Quartet Books, 1977.
Lloyd, Charles. *Edmund Oliver.* 1798.

COMTE, ISIDORE-AUGUSTE-MARIE-FRANÇOIS-XAVIER 1798–1857

French philosopher and sociologist

The singular interest of Isidore-Auguste-Marie-François-Xavier Comte for the student of European Romanticism is that in one respect, he was the embodiment of the mental reflexes and gestures characteristic of the Romantic movement, but he was also one of the thinkers most directly responsible for its decline. In elevating the doctrine of positivism, with which he is primarily associated, to the status of a new religion, Comte displays one of the chief hallmarks of the French Romantic mind: the impetus in a postrevolutionary climate to compensate for the destruction of time-honored beliefs of a religious or moral nature by the elaboration of secular alternatives. His short but colorful life, dramatized by mental breakdown, failed suicide, and tragic passion, might even lead him to be regarded as the Thomas Chatterton of French thought in a period that sanctified the lonely, misunderstood genius. Yet his "système positif," to which he devoted his entire career in one form or another, is grounded in the rejection at once of Rousseauist individualism and of the

pursuit of the Absolute for which generations of Romantic youth had felt the longing. Comte is above all an antitranscendentalist whose ideas are closer to those of Ludwig Feuerbach and Karl Marx than Victor Cousin or Georg Wilhelm Friedrich Hegel; a cast of mind that, despite his generation being that of Honoré de Balzac, Alphonse Marie Louis de Lamartine, or Alfred-Victor de Vigny led him to become the emblematic thinker of the age that brought the Romantic period in France to a close, the Second Empire. The scientific and economic materialism that pervades the regime of Napoleon III, the naturalistic novels of Émile-Édouard-Charles-Antoine Zola, the associationist psychology of Hippolyte-Adolphe Taine, or the phenomenalist aesthetics of impressionism in the hands of Edouard Manet and his successors, are all expressions of the same intellectual *Zeitgeist* that Comte had conjured. By the same token, reaction against his thinking in the final two decades of the century was initiated by a second Romantic florescence—that of symbolism.

Born in Montpellier at the close of the eighteenth century, Comte would retain something of the exuberance of his meridional origins, just as he came to regard the Revolution of 1789 as a psychological horizon. Though constantly frustrated in his attempts to become an established academic, his association with the early socialist thinker Claude Henri de Rouvroy, Comte de Saint-Simon began in 1817, and provided the inspiration for eventual independent recognition. In the year after his marriage in 1825, he began delivering to a select audience a program of lectures that, published in stages between 1830 and 1842, would become the *Cours de philosophie positive* (*Course of Positive Philosophy*). Obsessive dedication to this work, or the effects of an unhappy domestic life, may explain the bout of mental illness that Comte suffered in 1826. The following year he attempted suicide by jumping from a bridge over the Seine, but the crisis passed and he progressively gained the respect of some of the chief minds of his day, including John Stuart Mill. His one-year relationship with Clotilde de Vaux, which ended upon her death in 1846, is sometimes held to account for the gradual expansion of a doctrine which, from its base in abstract theory, develops eventually to encompass the feminine and religious sensibilities latent in humanity.

Comte's starting point is epistemological, though his epistemology is inseparable from his sociological and political thought. The term *positivism*, which he began to exploit at the time of his rupture with Saint-Simon in 1824, denotes the selection from Immanuel Kant's dualist menu of the relative but usable knowledge of phenomena in preference to the contemplation of transcendent "things in themselves." While recognizing the limited field of his immediate perceptions, the positivist seeks to assimilate such practically-available truths as they provide. In this respect he is essentially an empirical scientist, concerned with the regularity of nature and society as it is manifested before us, rather than a speculative thinker preoccupied with its ultimate purpose or cause. As Comte himself puts it, introducing his classic *Cours de philosophie positive*, "[I]t is the nature of positive philosophy to regard all phenomena as subject to invariable natural *laws*, the discovery of which . . . is the aim of all our efforts, while causes, either first or final, are considered to be absolutely inaccessible, and the search for them meaningless."

The impact of such a manifesto on a Romantic culture wedded to philosophical or moral idealism was decisive, and we cannot read the novels of Zola's *Rougon-Macquart* series (1870–93) or view a canvas by Monet without the recognition that an intellectual sea-change has occurred, in the course of which enquiry about the ultimate meaning of life has given way to the simple recording of experience as it impresses itself immediately upon the mind.

It is from this immanentist matrix that Comte derived an analysis of society that earned him the title "founder of sociology." His celebrated "Loi des trois états" ("Law of Three States," from *Cours de philosophie positive*) invites us to view history as a process of socialization, whereby the successive social orders of the theological and metaphysical are finally replaced by a society founded on positivist principles and having complete consciousness of its own dynamics. Humanity, which initially relied on a fiction and then on an abstraction, would come to rely on the scientifically demonstrable, including the necessity of a free proletariat. It was then but a short, if controversial step, which Comte elaborated in his *Système de politique positive*

(*System of Positive Polity*, 1854), to proclaim the positivist doctrine as the true religion of humanity, having the founder of the movement as its high priest and in which women, as the guardians of the flame of affection, would play a prominent part. Comte was denounced by his erstwhile advocates—notably Maximilien-Paul-Emile Littré and Mill—for what appeared to be a retreat into mysticism, but his justification was that the emotional and devotional were equal constituents, with the rational, of humanity in its definitive positive state.

DAVID LEE

Biography

Born Isidore-Auguste-Marie-François-Xavier Comte in Montpellier, January 19, 1797. Son of Louis Comte, a tax official, and Rosalie Boyer. Studied at the Lycée de Montpellier, 1806–13, and at the École Polytechnique in Paris, 1814–16. Collaborated with social reformer Claude Henri de Saint-Simon from 1817. Married Caroline Massin, 1825 (they separated, 1842). Began a program of lectures, 1826, subsequently published as *Cours de philosophie positive* (*Course of Positive Philosophy*, 1830–42). Attempted suicide following mental breakdown, 1826. Failed to obtain academic posting under the July Monarchy, despite support of John Stuart Mill. Tutor, and later examiner, at the École Polytechnique, 1832–42. Involved in passionate relationship with Clotilde de Vaux, 1845 (died 1846). Founded the Positivist Society, 1848; established the Universal Church of the Religion of Humanity, 1849. Died of cancer in Paris, September 5, 1857.

Selected Works

Cours de philosophie positive. 6 vols. 1830–42. Translated and condensed as *Course of Positive Philosophy* by Harriet Martineau, 1853.
Système de politique positive, ou Traité de sociologie instituant la religion de l'humanité. 4 vols. 1851–54. Translated as *System of Positive Polity* by J. H. Bridges, Frederic Harrison, 1875–77.
Catéchisme positiviste, ou Sommaire exposition de la religion universelle en onze entretiens systématiques entre une femme et un prêtre de l'humanité. 1852. Translated by Richard Congreve, 1858.
Synthèse subjective, ou Système universel des conceptions propres à l'état normal de l'humanité. Tome premier, con tenant le Système de logique positive, ou Traité de philosophie mathématique. 1856. Translated by Richard Congreve. 1891.
Lettres . . . à John Stuart Mill. 1841–44, 1877.

Bibliography

Andreski, Stanislav, ed. *The Essential Comte*. Selected from *Cours de philosophie positive*. Translated by Margaret Clarke. London: Croom Helm, 1974.
Arnaud, Pierre. *Politique d'Auguste Comte*. Paris: Armand Colin, 1965.
Charlton, D. G. *Positivist Thought in France during the Second Empire*. Oxford: Clarendon Press, 1959
Gouffier, Henri. *La Vie d'Auguste Comte*, 1931; reprinted Paris: Vrin, 1965.
———. *La Jeunesse d'Auguste Comte et la formation du Positivisme*. 3 vols. Paris: Vrin, 1933–41.
Lacroix, Jean. *La Sociologle, d'Auguste Comtei*. Paris: P.U.F., 1956.
Littré, E. *Auguste Comte et la philosophie positive*. Paris: Hachette, 1863.
Mill, John Stuart. *Auguste Comte and Positivism*. London: Trübner, 1865.

THE CONCEPT OF ANXIETY (BEGREBET ANGEST) 1844

Philosophical treatise by Søren Kierkegaard

Søren Kierkegaard's *The Concept of Anxiety* (published under the pseudonym Vigilius Haufniensis and also translated as *The Concept of Dread*) is, in Gordon D. Marino's words, "a maddeningly difficult book," virtually opaque in many passages, and the first-time reader should circle around it several times, probing for a lighted entrance. But the futility of reason expressed throughout the book stresses the elements of intuition and irrationalism in Romantic epistemology, just as Søren Kierkegaard's intense preoccupation with individual psychology reflects that aspect of Romanticism.

Several points emerge in Kierkegaard's introduction, in which he rejects G.W.F. Hegel and his lockstep system making. Hegel identified actuality with necessity, whereas for Kierkegaard actuality allows freedom: "Actuality is not served by [inclusion in Hegel's *Logic*], for contingency, which is an essential part of the actual, cannot be admitted within the realm of logic." That is, there is a point where logic's usefulness stops, and the new science of dogmatics—a body of a priori truths evolved from faith—must take over. Establishing this argument right at the beginning clears the way for Kierkegaard's commentary on psychology and dogmatics. Psychology sheds light on the concept of anxiety, defined as the state that precedes the qualitative leap from freedom into sin. Dogmatics "presupposes" sin and explains it by hereditary sin. In a difficult passage well explicated by Reider Thomte and Albert B. Anderson in their 1980 translation, Kierkegaard alludes to the Greek teaching of a continuity from the ideal to the actual with an ethics that is, they note, "altogether ideal and proposes to bring ideality into actuality"; but this ethics was, in Kierkegaard's words, "shipwrecked on the sinfulness of the single individual." The new science, or ethics, "presupposes dogmatics, and by means of hereditary sin it explains the sin of the single individual," and it seeks ideality "not by a movement from above and downward but from below and upward."

Any reader not fixated on the relationship between sex and sin could be forgiven for losing interest in the steady rain of arbitrary assertions and clear absurdities that turn Kierkegaard's exposition into a soggy mass in many places. What, for instance, can one make of the claim that "In the moment of conception, spirit is furthest away, and therefore the anxiety is the greatest"? And, as might be expected, "In childbirth the woman is again at the furthest point of one extreme of the synthesis [of body and psyche]." These remarks come from a section in which Kierkegaard tortures the subject of "The Consequence of the Relationship of Generation," the main point of which seems to be that generations of procreation accumulate more and more sensuousness and hence anxiety: "The procreated individual is more sensuous than the original, and this *more* is the universal *more* of the generation for every subsequent individual in relation to Adam." In another passage Kierkegaard asserts of Eve, a "derived creature," that "she is created like Adam, but there is, as it were, a presentiment of a disposition that is not sinfulness but may seem like a hint of the sinfulness that that is posited by propagation." This is certainly a rich passage, as it were.

The first sin—Adam's sin—was a qualitative leap for the race, which has accumulated sin quantitatively since Adam's fall, but this accumulation produces no new qualitative sin, only repetition. As Kierkegaard says, sin "proceeds in quantitative determinations while the individual participates in it by the qualitative leap." If man were only psyche and body, then sin would not have come into the world with the sexual; but the third element in man's synthesis, spirituality, accounts for the appearance of sin with the sexual. Kierkegaard struggles in arguing that sin did not come into the world by necessity (then there would be no anxiety), and insists that attempting "a logical explanation of the coming of sin into the world is a stupidity that can occur only to people who are comically worried about finding an explanation." A corollary of this tenet is that although freedom causes anxiety, anxiety cannot be cited as a cause of sin. Given these dogma, the only conclusion is thus that man and man alone is responsible for his sin. The final step for the individual in this movement from anxiety through freedom into sin is an increased anxiety that drives the sinner back to God through another leap, a leap into faith rather than into sin.

Kierkegaard's commentary on the demonic explicates his notion of anxiety about the good, which the individual may experience once he is in sin: "The bondage of sin is an unfree relation to the evil, but the demonic is an unfree relation to the good." Kierkegaard's demonic appears to be a close relative of John Milton's Satan and Johann Wolfgang von Goethe's Mephistopheles, who described himself as "the spirit that denies," and "manifests itself clearly only when it is in contact with the good." The demonic's origins may lie in the "esthetic-metaphysical," in a stroke of misfortune that makes the demonic "analogous to being mentally deranged at birth." Kierkegaard rejects sympathy as appropriate to this demonic, for sympathy is "only a means of protecting one's own egotism." This leads to a hard conclusion: "If true human sympathy accepts suffering as a guarantor and surety, then it must first of all make clear to itself to what extent it is fate or to what extent it is guilt. And this distinction must be drawn up with the concerned but also energetic passion of freedom, so that a person may dare to hold fast to it even though the whole world collapses, even though it may seem that by its own firmness he brings about irreparable harm." A second view of the demonic, the ethical, has commonly demanded condemnation. Kierkegaard mistakenly cites St. Augustine for Tertullian, who recommended punishment for sinners. Did Tertullian lack sympathy, Kierkegaard asks, or "was his behavior different from that of our time because his sympathy had not made him cowardly . . . ?" And the demonic has been viewed "medically" and "therapeutically" to be treated "*mit Pulver und mit Pillen* and then with enemas." These different views of the demonic show that "it belongs in all spheres: the somatic, the psychic, and the pneumatic [or spiritual]," and the implications of the demonic for each sphere are worked out in much detail.

Kierkegaard reserves his most eloquent assertions for the short final chapter on "Anxiety as Saving through Faith." His target here is those who do not sufficiently appreciate the awfulness of the possible, especially when compared with the actual in life. That person who has never been in terror of the possible is explained by his spiritlessness, and Kierkegaard shares Milton's contempt in the *Areopagitica* for those whose virtue has been "fugitive and cloistered." One danger of being "educated by possibility" is a misunderstanding of anxiety that leads to suicide, but "Whoever does not wish to sink in the wretchedness of the finite is constrained in the most profound sense to struggle with the infinite."

At the end of his "simple psychologically orienting deliberation," Kierkegaard speaks clearly enough for anyone to understand the point of this difficult work: "So when such a person graduates from the school of possibility, and he knows better than a child knows his ABC's that he can demand absolutely nothing of life and that the terrible, perdition, and annihilation live next door to every man, and when he has thoroughly learned that every anxiety about which he was anxious came upon him in the next moment—he will give actuality another explanation, he will praise actuality, and even when it rests heavily upon him, he will remember that it nevertheless is far, far lighter than possibility was." Who would dispute that only a fool would not be anxious in this world?

FRANK DAY

See also **Kierkegaard, Søren**

Text

Published as *Begrebet Angest. En simpel psychologisk-paapagende Overveise i Retning af det dogmatiske Problem om Arvesynde.* Copenhagen, 1844.
Translation: Translated as *The Concept of Dread* by Walter Lowrie. 1957. Princeton: Princeton University Press, 1944. Translated and edited as *The Concept of Anxiety: A Simple Psychologically Orienting Deliberation on the Dogmatic Issue of Hereditary Sin,* with introduction and notes by Reidar Thomte in collaboration with Albert B. Anderson. Princeton, N.J.: Princeton University Press, 1980.

Bibliography

Beabout, Gregory R. *Freedom and Its Misuses: Kierkegaard on Anxiety and Despair.* Milwaukee: Marquette University Press, 1996.
Gardiner, Patrick. *Kierkegaard.* New York: Oxford University Press, 1988.
Marino, Gordon D. "Anxiety in *The Concept of Anxiety.*" In *The Cambridge Companion to Kierkegaard.* Edited by Alastair Hannay and Gordon D. Marino. Cambridge: Cambridge University Press, 1998.
Perkins, Robert, ed. *International Kierkegaard Commentary: The Concept of Anxiety.* Macon, Ga.: Mercer University Press, 1985.
Søren Kierkegaard's Journals and Papers: vol. 1. Edited and translated by Howard V. Hong and Edna H. Hong, assisted by Gregor Malantschuk. Bloomington: Indiana University Press, 1967.
Thompson, Josiah, ed. *Kierkegaard: A Collection of Critical Essays.* New York: Doubleday, 1972.

CONCERTO

Without a doubt, the early Romantics' grandest forum for the exhibition of musical virtuosity was the solo concerto. Concertos were written most often for piano or violin, less frequently for cello or for wind instruments such as the clarinet. Complementing music's function as a source of private solace amid the political turbulence of the 1830s and 1840s was its extraordinary ability to fulfil the public, sociopsychological need for "heroes," both on the operatic stage and on the concert platform. Virtuoso concertos rose superbly to that challenge. In these works the conventional forms (sonata, aria, ternary, variations, rondos) became backdrops against which the soloist could indulge in unabashed showmanship, conveyed by virtuosity of sometimes breathtaking proportions. Typically, Romantic concertos characterize the interaction of soloist and orchestra as opposing forces (a relationship that reaches an extreme form in the slow movement of Ludwig van Beethoven's Piano Concerto No. 4) in profound contrast to the closely integrated, quasi-chamber music textures of Wolfgang Amadeus Mozart's Viennese concertos, for instance, in which the character and use of material placed soloist and orchestra in an intimate relationship. In the piano concertos of Valentin Alkan and Franz Liszt, and in the violin concertos of Niccolò Paganini, the soloist assumes the status of the leading actor in a drama. In their virtuoso concertos the soloist is strikingly foregrounded against the orchestra, so much so that at times (in the two Frédéric François Chopin piano concertos, for instance) the function of the orchestra is reduced to near passivity. This generic shift was evidently a reflection of changing public tastes: within burgeoning early nineteenth-century Euro-

pean concert life, the concerto became more and more a vehicle for the display of virtuosity, a "competition" between composer and performer, acted out before an adoring public. During the mid- and later eighteenth century, virtuosity had always been aimed at the popular, rather than academic, taste. While it sat uncomfortably with the latter owing to the adoption of naturalness and simplicity of utterance as aesthetic articles of faith in the writings of Charles Batteux and Jean-Jacques Rousseau, it was substantially less problematic for the Romantics, whose adoption of the sublime discriminated positively in favor of the superhuman ability of Alkan, Liszt, and Paganini to encompass seemingly insurmountable technical feats at dizzying speed. These included a succession of exciting idiomatic gestures grounded in technical difficulty (including extreme register shifts, string crossings, digital dexterity), and rapid transitions between contrasting figurations demanding expert muscular control (and therefore uncomfortably beyond the ability of most amateurs). Through such gestures the soloist exercised dominance over the accompanying orchestra, and henceforth the actual thematic substance of a concerto existed as a counterpoint to the powerful, and occasionally overriding, element of display.

In Carl Maria von Weber's concertos, virtuosity takes center stage, anticipating trends that were to become typical of developments in the genre following Beethoven. Weber's two piano concertos (in C, op. 11, 1810, and in E-flat, op. 32, 1812) replace the musical "argument" that had typified Mozart's concertos with extensive and varied figurative passages founded on the most basic harmonic progressions (which, robbed of their scintillating surface, would appear quite banal). In the latter (overtly modeled on Beethoven's "Emperor" concerto), the soloist has to manage an extensive array of pianistic devices, moving sequentially through extremes of register in rapid arpeggiated contrary-motion patterns, flowing left-hand accompaniments to the major thematic presentations above, prolonged semiquaver passages in octaves between the hands, rows of double thirds, rapid chromatic scales, double trills, and numerous arpeggiated flourishes. Indeed, listening to a performance, it is these textural features that remain in the memory, rather than actual thematic material.

The centering of virtuosity within the concerto genre was to establish a tradition of embodying changing moods in the play of figurations that flitted across the music's surface. Among the most conspicuously successful illustrations of the early Romantic concerto of this type are those for piano by Chopin, Felix Mendelssohn, and Robert Schumann, and for violin by Mendelssohn. In none of these works does the sophistication of the sparkling figuration threaten structural comprehensibility, even when, as in the case of Mendelssohn, considerable liberties are taken with the form. Indeed, attention to the structure retained a key place in the thinking of these composers, even when engaged in sheer musical exhibitionism. The occasional linking of successive movements in a concerto is perhaps to be considered as an attempt to raise the "respectability" of a genre in danger of too much showmanship to the level of profundity characterized by the contemporary symphony. One means by which this was achieved was monothematicism, such as dominates the first movement of Schumann's Piano Concerto in A-Minor, op. 54, a work that began life in 1841 as a freestanding fantasy for piano and orchestra, and to which the remaining two movements, connected by a linking passage retrospectively referring to the opening theme of the first movement, were added in 1845. The main theme, first sounded by the winds at measure 4 and immediately answered by the soloist, returns in various guises during the course of the movement, and while there is much contrasting material, this theme regulates much of the movement. Arguably, the coordination of virtuosity and musical coherence is less satisfying in the concertos of Alkan, John Field, Johann Nepomuk Hummel, Frédéric Kalkbrenner, Liszt, Ignaz Moscheles, Paganini, and Weber, in whose work the overwhelming figurative assault undermines coherence. That is perhaps the price to be paid for the gain in expressivity offered by such works as Alkan's Piano Concerto, op. 39, or the two examples by Liszt, which portray a kaleidoscopic range of moods through their dazzling passagework.

JOHN IRVING

Bibliography

Downs, P. G. *Classical Music: The Era of Haydn, Mozart, and Beethoven*. New York: W. W. Norton, 1992.

Einstein, A. *Music in the Romantic Era*. New York: W. W. Norton, 1947.

Longyear, R. *Nineteenth-Century Romanticism in Music*. 2d ed. Englewood Cliffs, N.J.: Prentice-Hall, 1973.

Rosen, C. *Sonata Forms*. New York: W. W. Norton, 1980.

Rosen, C. *The Romantic Generation*. London: Harper Collins, 1995.

CONFESSIONS OF AN ENGLISH OPIUM-EATER 1821

Novel by Thomas De Quincey

In its two distinct forms (the text was significantly revised and enlarged in 1856), Thomas De Quincey's *Confessions of an English Opium-Eater* stands as one of the finest pieces of nonfictional prose in both the Romantic and mid-Victorian periods. Categorized in the 1850s by De Quincey as "impassioned prose"—aesthetically the most elevated branch of his opus—*Confessions* is a hybrid: part autobiography, part speculative philosophy, part prose poetry, and part spiritual meditation. It was originally conceived for *Blackwood's Magazine* in 1820, with a possible origin in autobiographical writings dating from 1818, and was published anonymously in two parts in the *London Magazine* in 1821.

This latter formal source is important. The periodical context served to determine the phenomenology of the work's first publication. The *Confessions* of 1821 is a carefully modulated exercise in irony. Its discursive mode embraces both the individualized "Reader" addressed at the opening of the work, and an audience recently introduced to the familiar tone and coterie exclusivity of an ideologically astute periodical. Intimacy of tone frequently gives way to ironic, not to say sardonic, banter as De Quincey seeks to match a professed didactic purpose—the work is to be "useful and instructive"—to an autobiographical account of the pathology of opium addiction.

Neither version of *Confessions*, however, offers a unified autobiographical subject or an internally coherent narrative focus. Structurally, each takes an essentially tripartite form. Moving from an opening autobiographical section dealing with De Quincey's early life (nearly four times as long in the 1856 text), through to the much briefer, more analytical sections outlining the "Pleasures" and the "Pains" of opium, the logic is clearly progressive. Traumatic adolescent experience, particularly the extreme privations of life on the run from parental authority in London, and more specifically the loss of his prostitute friend Ann, was possibly a formative shaping agent in De Quincey's eventual addiction. More significantly, this experience, it has been persuasively argued, shaped and colored the topography of the opium related dreams that are outlined in the "Pains of Opium" section of the work. Teleological purpose remains shadowy in the *Confessions*, and De Quincey's heuristic aims thwart formal closure. If opium was acknowledged as the "true hero of the tale" in 1821, then it would later become, as he put it in 1845, merely "the naked pole" around which are gathered the digressive "wandering musical variations" of his dreams.

Titling his work as he did, De Quincey was placing himself in an established literary continuum of confessional writing, most notably the *Confessions* of Jean-Jacques Rousseau and St. Augustine. Rousseau, in fact, is criticized by De Quincey for not offering grand moral judgments and pronouncements in his autobiography. Conversely, St. Augustine's book clearly sets a rhetorical pattern for establishing an atmosphere of nondramatic personal intimacy that also maintains a sense of inner privacy. New in De Quincey's text is the focus provided by a developing Romantic shift in the autobiography toward subjectivity, experiential discontinuity, and extreme solipsism. De Quincey's Romantic sensibility sought to round out an apparently fractured personal growth into organic reflective consciousness. More than one commentator has referred to the *Confessions* as a prose "Prelude"; in De Quincey, as in his great friend, mentor, and influence William Wordsworth, the power of childhood experience bears on the adult through the intuited rhythms of "spots of time," which serve to configure responses to subsequent experience. However, with De Quincey, the drug which offers unity of representation in the "Pleasures of Opium" is the same drug which disrupts psychological coherence in the "Pains of Opium." In this latter section the reader is presented with disparate sketches enacting the discontinuities of drug addiction. It is evident throughout that De Quincey's strict evangelical upbringing plays no small part in pushing rigorous moral self-scrutiny up against aesthetic self-representation, toward an ultimately indeterminate end.

One of De Quincey's aims in the *Confessions*, as he wrote in 1853, was "to clothe in words the visionary scenes derived from the world of dreams . . . Impassioned, therefore, should be the tenor of the composition." The complex of influences which structure this project is dense. Digression, paradox, absurdism, playfulness, and ontological self-exploration leading to an understanding of a "transcendental" self, all significant elements in *Confessions*, are primarily products of De Quincey's deep interest in the German Romantic ironists. Jean Paul in particular was a lifelong guide, and it is notable that De Quincey published a number of magazine pieces about him in the early 1820s.

As well as providing an extended psychological framework for *Confessions* as both a living presence and an aesthetic guide, Wordsworth is firmly integrated into the rich allusive structure of the work. Along with the poetry of John Milton, the figurative rhetoric of such prose writers as Thomas Browne, the speculative writing of Edmund Burke, and the metaphysics of Immanuel Kant, his work forms an intertextual matrix that grounds De Quincey's attempts to show the mind sensing its own perceptual infinitude. This latter is developed most fully in the final sections of the *Confessions*, and derives from theories of the Romantic (specifically Kantian) sublime. Heightened rhetorical language is used to construct a dreamlike only topography, which mimics the mind transcending every standard of sense within the temporal and spatial expansions of opium-related dreams. De Quincey famously references its architecture in terms of the "Imaginary Prisons" engravings by the Italian artist and opium-eater, Giovanni Piranesi: "vast Gothic halls . . . machinery . . . expressive of enormous power . . . aerial flight[s] of stairs . . . [the] power of endless growth and self-reproduction." It is an architecture suggestive of fully conscious sublimity and thus of elevated mental power.

Both versions of the *Confessions* met with great public acclaim; that of 1821 was published in book form in 1822, and went into many subsequent editions before De Quincey's exten-

sive revisions and expansions for his *Selections Grave and Gay* of the 1850s. The 1856 edition was reworked for both artistic and commercial reasons. A figure of some fame in that year, De Quincey tried to satisfy increased public interest in his life in the new, unevenly revised edition, as well as to correct the "imperfections" which he believed affected the quality of the original publication. He also foregrounded what he called the "medical character" of the work, rigorously assigning positive value to opium, and further emphasized the significance of "the power of opium . . . over the grander and more shadowy world of dreams."

Confessions proved a highly influential work in many ways. The version of 1821, along with its subsequent book publication, spawned numerous copies and burlesques; if one is to believe the medical profession, this "book . . . of universal ill tendency" was also a material cause behind a number of opium-related deaths in the 1820s. Despite the fact that opium addiction was common at this time, public fascination proved extreme for what was received like a narrative from some strange, exotic terra incognita. The small text of 1821 effectively assured De Quincey's career as a serious writer. It also marked the point of emergence of a career-long authorial persona, "The English Opium-Eater." Although the promised part 3 never emerged, De Quincey did produce a similarly "impassioned" prose-poetical "sequel," the *Suspiria De Profundis*, in 1845.

As an artistic influence, the seductive power of *Confessions* has inspired countless writers. It was an object of obsession for Edgar Allan Poe. Charles Baudelaire and Alfred de Musset produced creative translations of it (the latter's version in turn serving to feed Hector Berlioz's *Symphonie Fantastique*). Twentieth-century writers such as Jorge Luis Borges and D. H. Lawrence testify to the work's staying power. "I see," De Quincey noted of his text, "nothing transitory or less suited to the next year or century than to this."

BARRY SYMONDS

Text

Confessions of an English Opium-Eater, 1821. First published in two parts, in *London Magazine* (1821). One volume duodecimo, with added "Notice to the Reader" and "Appendix," 1822. Extensively revised and greatly extended in 1856 as Vol. 5 of *Selections Grave and Gay*.

Authoritative edition of 1821 and 1856: *The Works of Thomas De Quincey*. Vol. 2. Edited by Grevel Lindop. London: Pickering and Chatto, 2000.

Bibliography

Baxter, Edmund. *De Quincey's Art of Autobiography*. Edinburgh: Edinburgh University Press, 1990.

Clej, Alina. *A Genealogy of the Modern Self: Thomas De Quincey and the Intoxication of Writing*. Stanford, Calif.: Stanford University Press, 1995.

Hayter, Alethea. *Opium and the Romantic Imagination*. London: Faber and Faber, 1971.

Jack, Ian. "De Quincey Revises his *Confessions*," *PMLA* 72, (1957): 122–46.

Lindop, Grevel. *The Opium-Eater: A Life of Thomas De Quincey*. London: J. M. Dent, 1981.

Needham, Lawrence D. "De Quincey's Rhetoric of Display and *Confessions of an English Opium-Eater*." In *Rhetorical Traditions and British Romantic Literature*. Edited by D. H. Bialostosky and

Lawrence D. Needham. Bloomington: Indiana University Press, 1995.

Rzepka, Charles. *Sacramental Commodities: Gift, Text, and the Sublime in De Quincey*. Amherst: University of Massachusetts Press, 1995.

Whale, John C. *Thomas De Quincey's Reluctant Autobiography*. London: Croom Helm, 1984.

Snyder, Robert Lance, ed. *Thomas De Quincey: Bicentenary Studies*. Norman: University of Oklahoma Press, 1985.

LES CONFESSIONS (THE CONFESSIONS), 1764–1770

Autobiography by Jean-Jacques Rousseau

Jean-Jacques Rousseau's infamous first autobiography is often read as equivocally both self-justifying and self-inventing. On the one hand, it was composed during his years in exile following the condemnation of *Émile, ou l'education* (*Émile, or On Education*, 1762), his treatise on human nature and education, by the Parliament of Paris. His subsequent sojourns at various places in Switzerland, England, and France provided a vital psychological distance from his sense of self and belonging, but they also bred paranoid thoughts and a desire to address the injury done to his person. The *Confessions* is therefore not casually hagiographic in its allusion to St. Augustine's similarly named work; in his letters, as in how the book itself opens, Rousseau imagines how he will one day stand saintlike before a sovereign judge, clutching his writing, as indictment against his defamers.

On the other hand, as if Rousseau himself has not gone on to do enough justice to Rousseau, the work anticipates two further autobiographies, *Rousseau, juge de Jean-Jacques* (*Rousseau, Judge of Jean-Jacques*, 1772–76), otherwise called the *Dialogues*; and *Les rêveries du promeneur solitaire* (*Reveries of the Solitary Walker*, 1776–78). His second account violently divides his own being into an accuser, a defender, and their subject matter, a fragmentation already detectable in the first, while the third is more resigned in both tone and content as it reflects on an equally consistent inner tension between his yearning for solitude and for society. Taken together in this way, the trilogy may be characterized by innermost feelings that are sincere and intense, but it draws attention to the interpretive and narrative aspects of each effort to appear sometimes guilty but always innocent, socially corruptible but naturally good.

Such literary advantage emerges in the *Confessions* as how Rousseau can give belated reasons for what has resulted in guilt, the very clarification of his need to revisit some events. While the instances may include his improper affairs and bitter disagreements with peers, they certainly involve the abandonment of his own children and wrongful dismissal of a servant-girl. His blurring of a factual-fictional divide is itself symbolized by how the history of his hugely successful novel *Julie, ou la nouvelle Héloïse* (*Julie, or The New Eloise*, 1761) is described: we are told first that the book drew from both lived and imagined experiences, and then that it produced a fateful romance in reality. In a scenario in which it cannot be known whether Rousseau determines his own writing or whether his writing "writes" him, our writer can both claim not to be wholly responsible for his actions and yet to be true to his feelings, even while inventing fiction.

We should perhaps bear in mind the various visible influences here, like Daniel Defoe's *Robinson Crusoe* (1719), Alain René Lesage's *Gil Blas* (1715–35), Antoine Francois Prévost's *Cleveland* (1731), and Charles Pinot-Duclos's *Confessions du comte de *** (*Confessions of the Count of***, 1741). As with fiction making, the *Confessions* operates through a series of flashbacks and expectations to heighten a sense of linearity and present a coherent framework with cycles of happiness found and then lost. The larger structure itself embodies this cycle as it divides the work neatly into two parts of six books each, the first part spanning thirty-one years from 1712, and the second twenty-three years up to 1765—the former recording a relatively peaceful and modest period that was his youth, and the latter a period in which his nature was more frequently at odds with his circumstances. The story begins with an idyllic world, reaches its midpoint with Rousseau's departure for a new life in Paris, and ends in the midpoint of his time in exile, the "work of darkness" in which he has been "entombed for eight years."

The *Confessions* may moreover be read alongside Rousseau's familiar social philosophy and as, in fact, its verification. The confessor, from this perspective, becomes the very form of his natural man, who is not without faults or weaknesses but without malice and hence good; his opposite is the social man that society wants him to be and who, in living through its expectations, alienates himself from within. As such a philosophical tale of struggle, the autobiography shows how each individual must be judged by the depth of inner feelings alone, while as an empirical study of the subjective it offers specific examples for the exploration of innate goodness. Rousseau indeed later describes the whole project in terms of its methodical integrity: it can redeem both its author and itself, since no one can properly construe another except by how the other understands himself or herself, and this is true because no one can understand oneself better than oneself.

There are immediate paradoxes here, and our first question confronts the point of a confession if it wishes neither for another's understanding nor forgiveness, if confessing already absolves the speaker of the possible crime in its content. On a different level, if the message of a natural man's confession is that he is indeed justified in himself, then once again there is no need to confess aloud, unless to do so is a magnanimous gesture towards another and hence still no confession. These contradictions are themselves intensified by how, in opposition to his own thoughts, Rousseau really desires his acquittal in the minds of others; it is why he became greatly distressed when his public readings of the work were met instead with mixed reactions.

Other issues emerge: if at fifty-three Rousseau can still remain a child of nature as the natural man incarnate, then he must also strangely be himself and other than himself, literally himself and symbolically everyone—and thus ironically less of himself, for no one is wholly universal. As his own subject matter or as "simply myself," Rousseau is unique in the way all individuals are unique but, to account for himself through his radical philosophy, he must at once be less particular as not just an archetype but a paradox, a being who is uniquely universal. It is in this sense that David Hume's comment that "nobody knows himself less" than Rousseau must be reconceived; Hume is really challenging Rousseau's perception of himself as well as the philosophical ideas grounding his understanding of self.

Yet, by showing how a display of feelings can rival rational thought as an access to truth, the *Confessions* succeeds in fixing sincerity as an objective basis for evaluating subjective visions and providing an important counterpoint to the dominant Enlightenment values. Unsurprisingly, the book soon became a crucial cornerstone to the representation and vindication of inner reality from the Romantic period onward; it further established a useful genre for distinctive writers like Johann Wolfgang von Goethe, George Moore, Marcel Proust, Leo Tolstoy, and Anthony Trollope and political thinkers from John Stuart Mill to the revolutionary Aleksandr Ivanovich Herzen.

LI SUI GWEE

Text

Les Confessions. 1770. Part 1 posthumously published in 1782, and part 2 in 1789; first complete English translation as *The Confessions of Jean-Jacques Rousseau* in 1904 (Edinburgh: Oliver and Boyd); notable translations as *The Confessions* by John Michael Cohen (London: Penguin, 1953), Christopher Kelly (Hanover, N.H.: University Press of New England, 1994), and Angela Scholar (Oxford: Oxford University Press, 2000).

Bibliography

Broome, Jack Howard. *Rousseau: A Study of His Thought.* London: Edward Arnold, 1963.

Clément, Pierre Paul. *Jean-Jacques Rousseau, de l'éros coupable à l'éros glorieux.* Neuchâtel: Éditions de la Baconnière, 1976.

De Man, Paul. *Allegories of Reading: Figural Language in Rousseau, Nietzsche, Rilke, and Proust.* New Haven, Conn.: Yale University Press, 1979.

Derrida, Jacques. *De la grammatologie.* Paris: Éditions de Minuit, 1967.

France, Peter. *Rousseau: Confessions.* Cambridge: Cambridge University Press, 1987.

Grimsley, Ronald. *Jean-Jacques Rousseau: A Study in Self-Awareness.* Cardiff: University of Wales Press, 1961.

Kelly, Christopher. *Rousseau's Exemplary Life: The Confessions as Political Philosophy.* Ithaca, N.Y.: Cornell University Press, 1987.

Lejeune, Philippe. *Le Pacte autobiographique.* Paris: Éditions du Seuil, 1975.

Sassure, Hermine de. *Rousseau et les Manuscrits des Confessions.* Paris: Éditions E. de Boccard, 1958.

Starobinski, Jean. *Jean-Jacques Rousseau: La Transparence et l'obstacle suivi de sept essais sur Rousseau.* Paris: Gallimard, 1971.

Williams, Huntington. *Rousseau and Romantic Autobiography.* Oxford: Oxford University Press, 1983.

CONSCIENCE, HENDRIK 1812–1883

Flemish novelist

Born on December 3, 1812, Hendrik Conscience grew up to become the most prolific and celebrated novelist in nineteenth-century Flanders. His parents were Pierre Conscience, a French sailor-carpenter who had ended up in Flanders in the wake of the Napoleonic Wars, and Cordelia Balieu, a Flemish country girl from the Antwerp Kempen. Hendrik was barely eight years old when his mother died from consumption. As a child he was often ill and, despite being unable to attend classes regularly, became an assistant teacher when he turned sixteen. In this he followed the wishes of his determined stepmother, Anna Catharina Bogaerts, who had joined the Conscience household in 1826. Four years later, Hendrik enlisted as a volunteer in the army to safeguard Belgium's new and self-declared independence from the Dutch king Willem III. The move by the young Conscience should also be seen in the light of his attempts to escape the stern discipline at home and his desire to rise above the lowly milieu in which he was brought up.

Having read Victor Hugo in the 1830s, he discovered his own artistic calling and wrote the novel *In 't wonderjaer* (*Ludovic and Gertrude*, 1837). In it, Conscience gives an idealized account of the Flemish revolt in 1566 by the Protestant *Geuzen* (beggars) against the Catholic Philip II and his Spanish troops. As a member of the "Antwerp School," a group of Romantic writers that also included Johan Alfried de Laet and Théodoor van Rijswijk, Conscience made the momentous decision to write and publish his novel in Dutch. This was a very brave and even confrontational gesture, as cultural life in Flanders was almost entirely Francophone at the time.

His first major success came soon afterward with the publication of *De leeuw van Vlaenderen* (*The Lion of Flanders*) in December 1838. It narrates the battle of the Golden Spurs (1302) during which Philip the Fair's prestigious French army was defeated by Flemish commoners near the West Flemish town of Kortrijk. At this stage, Conscience was still struggling with his self-chosen tool: the Dutch idiom of *De leeuw* is awkward throughout, though the descriptions, which are full of *couleur locale* and based on research in medieval chronicles, make up for the clumsiness of the language. The characterization too is very rudimentary, and yet the novel did not fail to touch a nerve. Strongly didactic in intent, it urges the Flemish to draw inspiration from their glorious past for their linguistic and cultural struggles in newly-formed Belgium. *De leeuw*, therefore, has been rightly described as a historical novel turned national epic. For the Flemish, it remained the most popular novel until after World War II.

A work similar to *De leeuw van Vlaenderen* is *Jacob van Artevelde* (1849), which again jogged the Flemish collective memory and reminded them of the heroic deeds of their forefathers. Arguably the most accomplished of his novels, it describes how the weavers' guild in Ghent, under the leadership of the eponymous hero, takes up arms against the French oppressor in 1337. On a deeper level, the novel is also a commentary on the events of the revolutionary year of 1848. For this work, as for many others, it was of course the tradition of the British historical novel that provided Conscience with a ready-made model, as can be inferred from the title page of *The Iron Tomb* (1889), the English translation of *Het yzeren graf* (1860), which characterizes the writer as "the Walter Scott of Flanders."

Conscience also tackled contemporary issues in his work, and more particularly the everyday hardships of the (Flemish) proletariat. His social commitment, though often veering toward cloying sentimentality, is most outspoken in his rural novellas, many of which are set on the barren heathland of the Antwerp Kempen. In his *De plaeg der dorpen* (*The Curse of the Village*, 1855), for instance, he focuses on the bane of alcoholism, and in his famous *De loteling* (*The Recruit*, 1850), he describes how a poor, young farmer is drafted into the army, spends a miserable life in the barracks, turns blind, and is finally allowed to return home to rebuild his life.

In 1856, Conscience became the district commissioner for Kortrijk, which secured him a regular income. A steady stream of publications followed, some of them now set in a more urban milieu, for example *De koopman van Antwerpen* (*The Merchant of Antwerp*, 1863). He missed the hustle and bustle of Brussels and Antwerp, though, and in 1869 gladly accepted the post of curator at the Royal Museums in Brussels, which entitled him to live in the Wiertz Museum. He was involved in organizing several important art exhibitions, and with his fame and many connections managed to engage some of the foremost artists of the age (such as Camille Corot and Eugène Delacroix). Despite his comfortable position, Conscience was not spared his own personal tragedy: having lost two infant daughters already, his two sons Hildevert, aged twenty-five, and Hendrik, only twelve, died during a typhus outbreak in 1869.

Though Conscience's writings should be read in the context of the so-called Flemish movement and its fight for the emancipation of Flanders, the author himself never questioned the legitimacy of Belgium as a united state with Dutch-speaking Flemings living in the north and French-speaking Walloons in the south. Apart from a brief spell in 1851, Conscience also refused to side with any political party. Afraid to antagonize the establishment, he even took recourse to self-censorship, and expurgated in later editions all passages in *In 't wonderjaer* that might offend the Catholic reader. With his writings, Conscience clearly aimed at reaching the largest possible readership, and as the feted author turned more and more bourgeois in his lifestyle, so his work became increasingly conservative in attitude. Solidarity and charity toward the poor, rather than a fundamental overhaul of society, was the message he propagated.

Conscience's works were widely translated, turning the author into a novelist of European renown. His popularity spread in Germany and Britain as early as the 1840s. It was Alexandre Dumas *père* who introduced Conscience's writings to the French reader by incorporating (some say plagiarizing) two chapters from *De loteling* in his own *Conscience l'Innocent* (1853), also known as *Dieu et Diable* (*God and Devil*) and *Le bien et le mal* (*The Good and the Bad*), naming its main character after the Flemish writer. Special festivities were launched in Brussels when Conscience's hundredth work rolled off the press in 1881. On this occasion, the whole literary establishment of the Netherlands (including Nicolaas Beets, Geertruida Bosboom-Toussaint, and Piet Paaltjens) paid their tribute, showing that his work was also popular in the North—a real feat for a Flemish writer.

Conscience died of stomach cancer in September 1883, one month after he had had his own statue unveiled on the then renamed Conscience Square in Antwerp. His immense popularity gained him the slogan *hij leerde zijn volk lezen* ("he taught his people to read"), the words also engraved on his tombstone in the Schoonselhof cemetery in Antwerp.

KRIS STEYAERT

Biography

Born in Antwerp, December 3, 1812. Son of Pierre Conscience, a French sailor and carpenter, and Cordelia Balieu. Mother died of tuberculosis, 1820. Assistant teacher, 1828–30; volunteer in the Belgian army, 1831–36; clerk at the Antwerp Academy of Arts; gardener, 1841–53. Married Maria Peinen, 1842. District commissioner for Kortrijk, 1857–68; curator at the Royal Museums and the Wiertz Museum in Brussels, 1868–83. Died in Elsene, near Brussels, September 10, 1883.

Selected Works

Individual
In 't wonderjaer. 1837. Translated as *Ludovic and Gertrude* by J.S.F., 1895.
De leeuw van Vlaenderen. 1838. Translated as *The Lion of Flanders* (translator unknown), 1855.
Jacob van Artevelde. 1849.
De loteling. 1850. Translated as *The Recruit* by B. Mayer, 1854. Translated as *The Conscript* (translator unknown), 1856.
De koopman van Antwerpen. 1863. Translated as *The Merchant of Antwerp* by Revin Lyle, 1872.

Multivolume Collections in English Translation
Conscience's Tales and Romances. 6 vols. 1855–57.
Hendrik Conscience's Short Tales. 13 vols. 1856–75.

Bibliography

Bock, Eug. de. *Hendrik Conscience en de opkomst van de Vlaamsche romantiek.* Antwerp: De Sikkel/Amsterdam: Querido, 1920.
Lambin, Marcel. *Hendrik Conscience: Bladzijden uit de roman van een romancier.* Antwerp: De Vlijt, 1974.
Willekens, Emiel. *Hij leerde zijn volk lezen: Profiel van Hendrik Conscience 1812–1883.* Antwerp: Esco, 1982.
Willekens, Emiel, Marc Somers, and Antoon van Ruyssevelt, eds. *Hendrik Conscience en zijn tijd.* Antwerp: Mercator-Plantijn, 1983.

CONSTABLE, JOHN 1776–1837

English painter

Kenneth Clark's interpretation of John Constable's career as "a natural painter," as Constable judged himself, is clear from the title of his book *The Romantic Rebellion: Romantic versus Classic Art*. Comparing him with J. M. W. Turner, Clark finds in Constable representations of "comforting, health-giving nature" that contrast with the images of "destructive nature" commonly painted by Turner. Clark stresses the "Wordsworthian aspect of the romantic worship of nature" that gives such power to Constable's depiction of the Stour Valley region (East Anglia, England) so familiar to him. Both the painter and the poet rejected the clockwork metaphor of nature typical of the Age of Reason, and expressed in their art a feeling for the divine that their hearts told them was immanent in nature. Constable's Romanticism emerges in his remark that "Painting is for me another word for feeling," and he would have understood fully what the American Romantic philosopher Ralph Waldo Emerson meant when he declared that in a humble natural setting he could feel "glad to the brink of fear," a fear prompted by his overwhelming sense of spirit at work in nature.

By 1800, Constable was well on his way to creating a Romantic iconography of the Stour Valley, with four watercolor drawings, including *Dedham Church and Vale*. He returned to this subject around 1802 with *Dedham Vale, Road Near Dedham*, and *Wooded Landscape at Sunset, with a Figure*, three oils that reflect his decision to re-create the Bergholt region of Suffolk and to "endeavour to get a pure and unaffected representation of the scenes that may employ me with respect to colour particularly and any thing else. . . ."

By 1810 Constable was concentrating on the Stour Valley landscape studies in oil that preceded his greatest works. The two versions of *The Mill Stream* exhibited in 1813–14, for instance, look ahead to the so-called six-footers, like the *Dedham Vale* (1828) and the extraordinary *Salisbury Cathedral from the Meadows* (exhibited in 1831). The first of six large canal compositions was *The White Horse*, exhibited at the Royal Academy in 1819 under its original title, *A Scene on the River Stour*; a second, the canal scene *Stratford Mill*, was exhibited the following year. All of these works are saturated with Constable's feeling for the landscape of his childhood.

In 1819 Constable began a series of regular summer visits to Hampstead (north London), where he hoped to study the "chiaroscuro of nature," and the Heath (a large wooded park in Hampstead) became a favorite subject of several paintings over the next twenty years. *Hampstead Heath* (1824) depicts, in Constable's description, a "broken foreground and sand carts, [with] Windsor Castle in the extreme distance on the right of the shower." It was at Hampstead that Constable executed a series of important sky studies, many of them featuring windblown trees. Clark notes that Constable had been studying Luke Howard's classification of clouds, adding that "It is typical of the romantic conjunction of science and ecstasy that Constable should have written on the back of his cloudscapes the time, year, the hour of the day and the direction of the wind when they were painted."

Among the most important of the great works of the 1820s were four more large canal scenes: *The Hay Wain* (1821), *View on the River Stour* (1824), *The Lock* (1824), and *The Leaping Horse* (1825). Constable had done an earlier version of *View on the Stour near Dedham* titled *Landscape Sketch* (*View on the Stour near Dedham*), and he expressed his pleasure with the "rich centre" included in the revision, adding that he had "endeavoured to paint with more delicacy, but hardly anyone has seen it." The earliest of these large oils, all exhibited at the Royal Academy, so impressed the French painter Théodore Géricault that *The Hay-Wain, View on the Stour near Dedham*, and *View of Hampstead Heath* were exhibited in 1824 at the Salon in Paris, where Charles X awarded them a gold medal. The effects that Constable achieved in *The Hay-Wain* with impasto especially influenced another French painter, Ferdinand-Victor-Eugène Delacroix, who consequently repainted the background in his own *Massacre of Chios* (1824). Constable enjoyed considerable success with French dealers and critics, and *The White Horse* won high praise and a gold medal when he exhibited it at Lille in 1825. Probably only Constable's obstinate refusal to visit France limited the warmth of his reception there. His insularism emerges in this sneer: "Think of the lovely valleys mid the peaceful farmhouses of Suffolk forming a scene of exhibition to amuse the gay and frivolous Parisians." But it was precisely his provincialism that was the source of his Romantic genius, as is evident in this remark about his boyhood around the River Stour and his father's mill: "The sound of water escaping from mill dams, willows, old rotten planks, slimy posts and brick-work—I love such things."

Graham Reynolds has observed of the six large scenes of the canalized River Stour that much of their genius derives from Constable's "fixing upon an episode which contributed a narrative note," such as the horse leaping a barrier or the boys fishing in *Stratford Mill. The Leaping Horse*, in Constable's own words, was "full of the bustle incident to such a scene. . . ." It was, he remarked, "lively and soothing, calm and exhilarating, fresh and blowing." Reynolds notes that the canal scenes all present a horizon two-fifths of the way up the picture, but that despite their "complete homogeneity" of subject matter their skies become increasingly overcast. In fact, the mezzotints that David Lucas made of these paintings in the 1830s all had, at Constable's demand, more turbulent skies. Reynolds attributes this "progressive leaning towards the dramatic and morbidly romantic" to Constable's personal problems, especially the death of his wife Maria in 1828.

The canal did not occupy all of Constable's imagination in this productive decade. In 1826 he exhibited at the Royal Academy a large oil now known as *The Cornfield*, depicting a lane that he had walked many times in his childhood, another example of Constable's keen sense of place. Constable turned to *The Seasons*, by James Thomson, for an evocative quotation about "A fresher gale" that comes "Sweeping with shadowy gust the fields of corn." He later returned to *The Seasons* for quotations appropriate to a new large painting, *Hadleigh Castle*, exhibited in 1829. *Hadleigh Castle* portrayed a favorite Romantic subject, an impressive ruin, and it had been in Constable's mind since 1814, when he had sketched various scenes along the Essex coast and written to Maria: "I was always delighted with the melancholy grandeur of a sea shore. At Hadleigh there is the ruin of a castle which from its setting is a really fine place. . . ." In some respects, no work of Constable's was more Romantic than the large *Salisbury Cathedral from the Meadows* exhibited in 1831. The cathedral aspiring high to heaven in the center, seen against a wild sky and a magnificent rainbow, prompted Constable to include with the catalogue entry this passage, thick with pathetic fallacy, from James Thomson's *The Seasons*:

As from the face of Heaven the scatter'd clouds
Tumultuous rove, th' interminable sky
Sublimer swells, and o'er the world expands
A purer azure, through the lightened air
A brighter lustre and a clearer calm.
Diffusive tremble: while as if in sign
A danger past, a glittering note of joy
Set off abundant by the yellow sky
Invests the fields and nature smiles revived.

Salisbury Cathedral from the Meadows is Constable's closest visual equivalent of his remark to Maria in 1819 that "Everything seems full of blossom of some kind and at every step I take, and on whatever object I turn my eyes, that sublime expression of the Scriptures, 'I am the resurrection and the life', seems as if uttered near me." For Constable, as for Emerson, "natural facts are signs of spiritual facts."

In 1824 Constable took his family to Brighton for the healthier air, and even though he disliked the region he produced another fine six-footer, *Chain Pier, Brighton* (1827). The Chain Pier that stretched into the ocean caught his imagination, and the breakers gave him a new subject to complement his usual close attention to the sky. The last of the great large oils of the 1820s was *Dedham Vale* (1828), a subject he had first treated in 1802. *Dedham Vale* was universally liked, and Constable called it "perhaps my best."

The successes of the decade were capped by the great tragedy of Constable's life, the death of Maria Constable on November 23, 1823, at the age of forty-one, but he produced several distinctive works in his last years. *Waterloo Bridge from Whitehall Stairs* (1832), for instance, dramatized the opening of the Waterloo Bridge by the Prince Regent on June 18, 1817. *The Cenotaph* (to Joshua Reynolds), exhibited in 1836, was an unusual departure for Constable in its winter setting; it is an elegy to his great predecessor and a poignant allusion to the mutability of all things that must have occupied much of Constable's mind in these years. *Arundel Castle*, a final work, almost finished when he died, reverted to lifelong themes and was exhibited the year after his death. Graham Reynolds's summation of Constable's career is eloquent: "Outwardly his life was a tempestuous battle, but the world he entered in his painting-room was a secluded garden,

and no one has more completely communicated the euphoria of the English countryside."

FRANK DAY

Biography

Born on June 11, 1776 in East Bergholt, Suffolk, England. Met Dr. John Fisher, later Bishop of Salisbury, who encouraged him in his painting, 1798; quit working at his father's mill and enrolled at the Royal Academy Schools, 1800; bought a studio in East Bergholt, and exhibited his first work at the Royal Academy, 1802. Married Maria Bicknell, with whom he was to have seven children, 1816. Stricken by the death of Maria, 1828. Elected Royal Academician, 1829. Became member of Royal Academy's Hanging Committee, 1830. Published fifth and final volume of *English Landscape Scenery*, 1832. Died of a heart attack at home in Hampstead, March 31, 1837.

Bibliography

Beckett, R. B., ed. *John Constable's Correspondence*. 6 vols. Ipswich: Suffolk Records Society, 1962–68.

———. *John Constable's Discourses*. Ipswich: Suffolk Records Society, 1970.

Constable, Freda. *John Constable: A Biography—1776–1837*. Lavenham, Suffolk: Terence Dalton, 1975.

Cormack, Malcolm. *Constable*. Cambridge and New York: Cambridge University Press, 1986.

Fleming-Williams, Ian, and Leslie Parris. *The Discovery of Constable*. New York: Holmes and Meier, 1984.

Gadney, Reg. *Constable and His World*. New York: W. W. Norton, 1976.

Kroeber, Karl. *Romantic Landscape Vision: Constable and Wordsworth*. Madison: University of Wisconsin Press, 1975.

Leslie, C. R. *Memoirs of the Life of John Constable Composed Chiefly from His Letters*. 1843. (Reprinted Ithaca, N.Y.: Cornell University Press, 1980.)

Parris, Leslie. *Constable: Pictures from the Exhibition*. London: Tate Gallery, 1991.

Parris, Leslie, Conal Shields, and Ian Fleming-Williams. *John Constable: Further Documents and Correspondence*. 8 vols. Ipswich: Suffolk Records Society, 1975.

Paulson, Ronald. *Literary Landscape: Turner and Constable*. New Haven, Conn.: Yale University Press, 1982.

Peacock, Carlos. *John Constable: The Man and His Work*. London: John Baker, 1965.

Reynolds, Graham. *Constable: The Natural Painter*. New York: McGraw Hill, 1965.

———. *The Later Paintings and Drawings of John Constable*. New Haven, Conn.: Yale University Press, 1984.

Rosenthal, Michael. *Constable: the Painter and His Landscape*. New Haven, Conn.: Yale University Press, 1983.

Smart, Alastair, and Attfield Brooks. *Constable and His Country*. London: Elek, 1975.

Taylor, Basil. *Constable: Paintings, Drawings, and Watercolours*. London: Phaidon, 1973.

Walker, John. *John Constable*. New York: Harry N. Abrams, 1978.

CONSTANT DE REBECQUE, HENRI-BENJAMIN 1767–1830

Swiss-French political theorist and novelist

Henri's Benjamin Constant de Rebeque (known as Benjamin Constant) was a leading French intellectual and politician of the immediate postrevolutionary period who sought to elaborate a new concept of liberty at a time when existing alternatives had been widely discredited. His nonpolitical writings, which included works of fiction, were intimately related to his political theory by a shared respect for the self—contradictions that Constant explored in particular through the oscillating and ambivalent emotions he identifed in his own character, especially those discernible in his complex extended relationships with a number of widely contrasting women, including Madame Anne-Louise-Germaine de Staël. He was unable to resolve these contradictions on a personal level, and presented for scrutiny the spectacle of a self-alienation that in large measure reflected a troubled period in the history of Western European sensibility. This was a transitional moment when the intellectual confidence of eighteenth-century rationalism (and such offshoots as the *libertinage* practised by the author's father) found itself challenged by a new set of values embodied in a gentler, Romantic sensibility, and transmitted, in Constant's case, by the predominantly female environment with which he invariably surrounded himself.

As a creative writer, Constant is essentially remembered for the short first-person novel *Adolphe*, published in London and Paris in 1816, a work in which he drew on the paradoxes he encountered in his complicated love life, but which, together with François-Auguste-René de Chateaubriand's slightly earlier novel *René* (1805), is nonetheless a striking example of the Romantic malady that became known as "le mal du siècle." But unlike many such Romantic productions, *Adolphe* has steadfastly refused to age. It is an example of a genre sometimes known as "le roman personnel," in which the conflict within a (male) protagonist's personality is brought to the forefront by an emotional crisis, causing him to analyze his feelings with an apparent, but in fact often questionable, psychological confidence. It also occupies a prominent place in the broader French tradition of the "roman d'analyse," which stretches from Madame Marie-Madeleine de Lafayette's novel *La Princesse de Clèves* (1678) to André Gide's *récits* in the early twentieth century.

Constant had relatively little interest in the novel as a genre per se. If fiction was for him largely a medium through which to come to terms with the complications of his emotional life (which can be summarized as that of a failed libertine), a form in which he could deploy his natural self-awareness and skill in self-criticism to redefine the derogatory view of him presented by others, it was also a means of indirectly continuing his relationship with two of the women in his life, Madame Isabelle-Agnès Elizabeth de Charrière and Madame de Staël, both of whom were themselves accomplished novelists who saw the novel as a freer form of autobiography. With Charrière, who was twenty-seven years his senior, and with whom he enjoyed an "amitié amoureuse," he actually wrote an unfinished epistolary novel, *Lettres de d'Argillé fils*, the manuscript of which was discovered by Dennis Wood in 1980. By the time of the publication of *Adolphe*, Constant had not had direct contact with de Staël for five years.

Adolphe, the text of which was honed during a complex gestation spread over a number of years, reconfigures many of the landmark experiences of Constant's life and distills the ambivalence characteristic of many of his liaisons into the narrative of a single relationship that is depicted with almost mathematical precision. It is the story of Adolphe's seduction of an older woman whom he soon ceases to love and increasingly finds to be a burden, but from whom he has unexpected difficulty in parting. The parallel with Constant's tempestuous relationship with de Staël is evident, but Ellenore is separated from de Staël by more than a name. Adolphe's strikingly lucid account is given authority by its skilful rhetoric and its recourse to memorable maxims. But on further investigation, it is discovered to be a complex blend of a disconcertingly honest confession and an attempt at self-justification that is varyingly direct and oblique. (The most obvious attempts at self-exculpation redirect the blame toward his father, the prevailing culture of *libertinage*, and the inadequacies of language.) The incorporation of two imaginary documents at the end of the text, which advance very different views of the protagonist's behavior, compels the reader to continually question all judgments, both psychological and moral. Such questioning is rendered all the more imperative by the fact that Ellenore's thoughts, words, and actions are, inevitably, selected and presented by Adolphe.

Leaving aside the justifiable charge that Adolphe is seeking an alibi for his questionable behavior in the inherent coarseness of language, Constant's text is raised above the level of "anecdote" that its fictional discoverer claims it to be by the way language is revealed to be both the glory of the analytical novel, and a medium fundamentally incapable, at least as in its inherited forms, of giving authentic expression to emotional experience. It is this pinpointing of an irresoluble conflict that makes the dilemma embodied in *Adolphe* emblematic of its age. But it also renders the reader's attempt to formulate definitive conclusions highly problematic, and indeed may be seen as designed to accentuate the dangers inherent in such an enterprise.

It is likely that Constant intended *Adolphe* as criticism of Napoleon for having created a rigid and ungenerous society. The novel has certainly been seen to advocate strength of purpose, fidelity, human sympathy, and the need to avoid inflicting suffering on others. This broader interpretation is in line with Constant's social and political outlook; but instead of feeling enjoined to extract a lesson from the novel, perhaps it is more likely that modern readers will locate its worth in the experience of being embroiled in a medley of different perspectives that pose questions rather than offering answers.

Unsurprisingly, given the intensity of the debate the text stimulates with regard to Adolphe's character and his treatment of Ellenore, Constant's novel has engendered a number of "rewritings," beginning with Honoré de Balzac's *La Muse du département* (1843) and Sophie Nichault De Lavelette Gay's novel *Ellénore* (1844–46), and including, more recently, Eve Gonin's *Le Point de vue d'Ellénore* (1981) and Anita Brookner's novel

Providence (1982). The extensive commentary devoted to Constant's text in John Middleton Murry's *The Conquest of Death* (1951) is tantamount to a highly personal rewriting, the novel becoming a peg on which Murry hangs his gospel "of the liberation of the ego by simple love." Though not a rewriting as such, Maxim Gorkii's preface to a Russian translation of the work depicts Adolphe as epitomizing the situation of young men in capitalist societies.

While sharing the same origins in the author's personal life, the unfinished and unrevised novel *Cécile* (written, then abandoned in 1810–11, and finally published in 1951 from a manuscript long presumed lost) is much more directly autobiographical, tracing Constant's extended yet intermittent relationship with his future second wife, Charlotte von Hardenberg, against the background of a fluctuating devotion to de Staël, who in the novel appears unflatteringly as Madame de Malbée. Though written in a much more free-flowing manner than *Adolphe*, its admirers have included many prominent Constant scholars. The author's disinclination to complete it would nonetheless suggest that he had become aware of the way it represented only an intermediate stage in the process by which autobiographical material becomes transmuted into a more universal composition. Therefore, on one level, the successful recasting of the text we know as *Adolphe* may have rendered *Cécile* redundant.

Adolphe and *Cécile* were merely two of the products of an intense introspection that led to much other writing, notably the highly entertaining and self-mocking sketch of the first twenty years of Constant's life, *Ma Vie* (initially known as *Le Cahier rouge* after the notebook in which it was written; published for the first time in 1907), but also comprising his private diaries and letters, though not his correspondence with de Staël, both sides of which were destroyed by her daughter. His extensive concentration on the profound self-alienation he experienced has inevitably aroused considerable interest in Constant the man, ranging from the character assassination mounted by Charles-Augustin Sainte-Beuve to the extended psychoanalytical explanations of his personality advanced in more recent times.

If fiction represented the private domain for Constant, the contemplative dimension of his life, Constant gave priority, like Madame de Staël, to an active life in the public sphere. He was a powerful political theorist (and from his student days in Edinburgh, an eloquent public speaker), who turned his considerable intelligence to questions brutally raised by the French Revolution. Eventually he would become the undisputed intellectual leader of the liberal opposition whose successful overthrow of Charles X, just months before Constant's death in 1830, had the unpredicted consequence of crippling the French monarchy for good.

Constant's political thought was dominated by his concern with liberty, the origins of which can be related to his exposure to the Scottish Enlightenment, and in particular to the Scottish school of political economists. It was his belief that the individual's private life was the most precious part of his existence and needed to be protected against arbitrary interference by the state. Therefore he advocated explicitly liberty in religion, philosophy, literature, and industry, as well as in politics. Though he never repudiated the French Revolution, he rejected his earlier espousal of republicanism, which he had seen decline into despotism. His opposition to the equally despotic Napoleon Bonaparte remained more or less constant throughout the Empire. (The decision to rally to the Emperor during the Hundred Days and to assist in the drawing up of his new, liberal constitution laid him open therefore to charges of opportunism.) He considered the Empire to be a hedonistic continuation of the eighteenth-century cult of enlightened self-interest, and, as such, a threat to the very fabric of society. As with Madame de Staël, he was devoted to finding a viable alternative to extremism. He considered the way forward to be a representative form of government that reconciled the interests of the individual with those of the state, which would usher in a generous new age. In practice, this led to the advocacy of constitutional monarchy, the role of the monarch being confined to that of arbiter. Such a summary, however, irons out the conflictual forces within his thinking. As Biancamaria Fontana has emphasized, Constant's intellectual imagination was shaped by an "alternation between commitment and pessimism, idealism and scepticism," a fundamental uncertainty which has led to his reappropriation as a political thinker in our own times, when his "doubts and oscillations have seemed less the sign of exceptional individual volatility than a reasonable response to the tormented present and uncertain future of modern democracies."

If Constant's contribution to the making of the modern liberal state may be considered his most lasting achievement, his life's work may more properly be his five volume treatise on religion, *De la religion considérée dans sa source, sa forme et ses développements* (*On Religion Considered in Its Source, Its Forms, and Its Developments*, 1824–31), published in the last few years of his life and completed by the posthumous publication of *Du polythéisme romain* in 1833. Heavily marked by his Protestant inheritance, *De la religion* traces the continuity of the religious instinct and locates its proper modern manifestation within a free individual conscience that operates independently of priestly intervention. As such, it was in sharp contradistinction to the early Romantic Catholic revival spearheaded by such right-wing thinkers as Louis-Gabriel-Ambroise de Bonald and Joseph de Maistre.

MICHAEL TILBY

Biography

Born Henri-Benjamin Constant de Rebecque in Lausanne, Switzerland, October 25, 1767. Son of an officer in the Dutch army, originally from a family of French Protestant refugees. Mother died a fortnight after his birth. Privately tutored in Brussels, Switzerland, Holland, and England until 1782. Studied at Erlangen, 1782–83, and later at Oxford University and the University of Edinburgh, 1783–85. Lodged with Jean-Baptiste Suard in Paris, 1785. Began close long-term friendship with the writer Mme. de Charrière (b. Isabella van Tuyll van Serooskerken, 1740), 1786. Chamberlain to the Duke of Brunswick, 1788–95. Married Minna von Cramm, 1789. Relationship with Charlotte von Hardenberg, 1792. Started long-term affair with Mme. de Staël (b. Anne-Louise-Germaine Necker, 1766), 1794. Revolutionary sympathies caused divorce and abandonment of court position, 1794. Published first political pamphlets, 1796–97. Elected to the Tribunate through efforts of the abbé Sieyès, 1799. Friendship and correspondence with rationalist thinker Julie Talma, 1799. Affair with Anna Lindsay, 1800–01. Expelled (with others) from Tribunate, 1802. Lived at Mme. de Staël's estate at Coppet, near Geneva, and in Weimar. Traveled in

Germany, mainly with the exiled Mme. de Staël, 1803–04. Continued relationships with Charlotte and Anna, as well as Mme. de Staël, 1804–05. Married Charlotte von Hardenberg in secret, 1808; completed *Wallstein*, a version of Schiller's *Wallenstein*. Ended relationship with Mme. de Staël; took up residence with Charlotte in Göttingen, 1811. Met with Bernadotte (pretender to French throne) in Hanover, 1813–14. Met with Tsar in occupied Paris. Sustained unrequited passionate relationship with Mme. Récamier (b. Julie-Adelaïde Bernard, 1777), from 1814. Maintained initial hostility to Napoleon's return, 1815; later helped draw up Napoleonic liberal constitution ("La Benjamine," never implemented). Lived in semi-exile following Restoration, 1815. Lived with Charlotte in England, 1816. Published the novel *Adolphe* in Paris and London, 1816. Returned to France; elected deputy, and leader of the Liberal opposition, 1819. Lost his seat, 1822. Reelected in Paris, 1824. Reelected in Strasbourg, 1827. Called to Paris by La Fayette; with Sebastiani, composed declaration in favor of Louis-Philippe; appointed President of the Legislative Committee of the Council of State, 1830. Died in Paris, December 8, 1830.

Selected Works

Essai sur la Contre-Révolution d'Angleterre en 1660. 1798.
De l'esprit de conquête et de l'usurpation. 1813.
Réflexions sur les constitutions, la distribution des pouvoirs et les garanties dans une monarchie constitutionnelle. 1814.
Principes de politique. 1815. (Drafted in 1806.)
Adolphe. 1816.
Mémoires sur les Cent Jours. 1820–22.
De la religion considérée dans sa source, sa forme et ses développements. 3 vols. 1824–27.
Mélanges de littérature et de politique. 1829.
Du polythéisme romain. 1833.
Journal intime. 1895.
Le Cahier Rouge. 1907. Published as *Ma Vie*. Edited by C. P. Courtney. Cambridge: Daemon Press, 1991.
Cécile. 1951. (Edited, together with *Amélie et Germaine* and *Ma Vie*, by Paul Delbouille. Paris: Champion, 1989.)
Journaux intimes. Edited by Alfred Roulin and Charles Roth. Paris: Gallimard, 1952.
Political Writings. Translated and edited by Biancamaria Fontana. Cambridge: Cambridge University Press, 1988.
Oeuvres complètes. Edited by Paul Delbouille et al. Tübingen: Niemeyer, 1993– .
Correspondance générale. Edited by C. P. Courtney and Dennis Wood, with the collaboration of Peter Rickard. Tübingen: Niemeyer, 1993– .

Bibliography

Alexander, I. W. *Constant: "Adolphe."* London: Edward Arnold, 1973.
Annales Benjamin Constant. Journal in circulation, 1980– .
Bibliographie analytique des écrits sur Benjamin Constant (1796–1980). Compiled by Brigitte Waridel et al. under the direction of Etienne Hofmann. Lausanne: Institut Benjamin Constant/ Oxford: Voltaire Foundation, 1980.
Bibliographie analytique des écrits sur Benjamin Constant (1980–1995). Compiled by François Vallotton, Paris: Champion, 1997.
Berlin, Isaiah, *Four Essays on Liberty.* Oxford: Oxford University Press, 1969.
Charles, Michel. "*Adolphe* ou l'inconstance." In *Rhétorique de la lecture.* Paris: Seuil, 1977.
Courtney, C. P. *A Guide to the Published Works of Benjamin Constant.* Oxford: Voltaire Foundation, 1985.
Crossley, Ceri. "John Middleton Murry and *Adolphe*," *Annales Benjamin Constant* 7 (1987): 81–91.
Cruickshank, John. *Benjamin Constant.* New York: Twayne, 1974.
Deguise, Pierre. *Benjamin Constant méconnu: le livre "De la religion."* Geneva: Droz, 1966.
Delbouille, Paul. "*Adolphe* et *Cécile*: esquisse d'une comparaison stylistique." *Cahiers d'analyse textuelle* 17 (1975): 7–22.
Delbouille, Paul. *Genèse, structure et destin d'Adolphe'.* Paris: Les Belles Lettres, 1971.
Fairlie, Alison. *Imagination and Language: Collected Essays on Constant, Baudelaire, Nerval and Flaubert.* Edited by Malcolm Bowie. Cambridge: Cambridge University Press, 1981.
Fairlie, Alison. "Suggestions on the art of the novelist in Constant's *Cécile*." In *Literature and Society: Studies in Nineteenth and Twentieth Century French Literature Presented to R. J. North.* Edited by C. A. Burns. Birmingham: John Goodman and Sons, 1980. 29–37.
Fontana, Biancamaria. *Benjamin Constant and the Post-Revolutionary Mind.* New Haven, Conn.: Yale University Press, 1991.
Gonin, Eve. *Le Point de vue d'Ellénore: une réécriture d'Adophe.* Paris: José Corti, 1981.
Holdheim, W. W. *Benjamin Constant.* London: Bowes and Bowes, 1961.
Holmes, Stephen. *Benjamin Constant and the Making of Modern Liberalism.* New Haven, Conn.: Yale University Press, 1984.
Oliver, Andrew. "*Cécile* et la genèse d'*Adolphe*," *Revue des sciences humaines* (1967): 5–27.
Poulet, Georges. *Benjamin Constant par lui-même.* Paris: Seuil, 1968.
Segal, Naomi. *Narcissus and Echo: Women in the French "Récit."* Manchester: Manchester University Press, 1988.
Todorov, Tzvetan. *Benjamin Constant: a Passion for Democracy.* London: Algora Publications, 1999.
———. "La parole selon Constant." In *Poétique de la prose.* Paris: Seuil, 1971.
Waller, Margaret. *The Male Malady: Fictions of Impotence in the French Romantic Novel.* New Brunswick, N.J.: Rutgers University Press, 1993.
Wood, Dennis. *Benjamin Constant: a Biography.* London: Routledge, 1993.
———. *Benjamin Constant: "Adolphe."* Cambridge: Cambridge University Press, 1987.

COOPER, JAMES FENIMORE 1789–1851

American novelist

As James Fenimore Cooper was born just after the ratification of the American Constitution, his life spans a crucial period of American history during which the young nation was attempting to assert a cultural independence to mirror the political autonomy it had recently achieved. From the earliest appearance of his historical novels of adventure, set mostly on the American frontier or the high seas, Cooper was heralded as "the American Scott," a title which, as a staunch republican, he found increasingly irksome. The comparison was inevitable, however, as Cooper chose to write in the genre of historical fiction, which Walter Scott had created. The intellectual climate of the early American republic was generally hostile toward the practice of both reading and writing novels, which were commonly considered to be at worst morally degenerate, and at best, suited only for the tastes of idle women. Thus, Scott's fusion of romantic adventure with the more socially acceptable genre of history, especially when transplanted by Cooper to an American setting and dressed in the trappings of nationalism and republicanism, was perfectly suited to popularize novel reading in the United States.

Cooper's first major work was *The Spy* (1821), notable particularly for its setting during the American Revolution, and the central role played by Harvey Birch, the peddler and spy of the title, a nongenteel yet still loyally American representative of the "common man." Birch is a clear prototype of Cooper's most famous character, Natty Bumppo (or Leatherstocking), who would make his first appearance in Cooper's next novel, *The Pioneers* (1823). For this nostalgic re-creation of life in rural New York State during the 1790s, Cooper drew on his own boyhood memories of Cooperstown, New York, on the shores of Lake Otsego. His father, William Cooper, the founder of Cooperstown and a wealthy landowner, was the model for Judge Temple in *The Pioneers*. The plot of the novel, as with *The Spy*, is largely conventional, with a clear division of characters between "genteel" and "common." The tale is remarkable, however, for its insistence that the routine life of an American settlement can justify and sustain the whole narrative, and that the absence of Gothic castles and aristocratic protagonists need not render it devoid of interest. It was this that enthused contemporary American writers and reviewers, while its accurate and affectionate depiction of rural life made it acceptable even to British tastes.

Despite the popular and critical success of his naval adventure *The Pilot* (1824), Cooper soon realized that, in Natty Bumppo, he had created a figure of peculiar emotive power, able to encapsulate a very American contradiction. In *The Last of the Mohicans* (1826), he returned to the early life of Natty and his Delaware companions, Chingachcook and Uncas, before moving forward to his death, as a solitary old man transplanted to the plains of the Midwest, in *The Prairie* (1827). Cooper reiterates Natty's instinctive wisdom and his moral superiority over the more "civilized" characters who enter the wilderness environment. Natty is attuned to nature, at one with the American landscape that Cooper is so adept at depicting, but his "gifts," as he terms them, belong to a vanishing world. Natty is a scout, a forerunner for the forces of civilization that will eclipse him and destroy the environment to which he belongs. But though Cooper may lament the inevitability of his passing, just as he laments the fate of the Native Americans (split, in Cooper's simplistic scheme, into noble and ignoble savages), he cannot envision an alternative to the natural progress of white civilization. *The Last of the Mohicans* suggests fleetingly the possibility of a union between the genteel, white heroine Cora Munro and Uncas, the young Indian brave, but Cooper rejects the possibility of such miscegenation, and the novel ends with their deaths.

The Prairie was published after Cooper had departed for Europe in 1826, and the seven years that he spent there mark a distinct turning point in his career. When he left, he nurtured an idealistic belief in the perfectibility of the American republic, made explicit in *Notions of the Americans* (1828), a social, cultural, and political discourse upon his native country. The novels he wrote while in Europe abandon the American setting that had been the foundation of his success, but not the republican principles that underpinned it. He wrote *The Bravo* (1831), *The Heidenmauer* (1832), and *The Headsman* (1833), intending to impress upon his readers the advantages of the American system by highlighting the iniquities of what he witnessed in Europe.

Upon returning to America in 1833, however, he was horrified by the leveling tendencies he perceived in public life, so that the democratic system he so revered, rather than allowing talented men to rise, merely handed undue powers to the mob. Declaring his retirement from novel writing, Cooper spent the next six years experimenting with allegorical satire and travel writing, in which he warns of the dangers of basing the right to govern on the possession of property, and of allowing public opinion to dictate law. This culminated in the publication of a long political essay, *The American Democrat* (1838). Cooper's intention in all of this work was not to renounce his allegiance to the United States, but rather merely to outline his own brand of republicanism. However, his willingness to criticize American institutions earned him a reputation as a disloyal, bad-tempered has-been who should never have tried to mix politics and fiction. Cooper was constantly pilloried by the Whig press, although he was by no means a conventional Democrat either. A dispute with the citizens of Cooperstown over ownership of a tract of land further compounded his wholly undeserved reputation as an anti-Republican.

Cooper eventually began writing fiction again, despairing of communicating his democratic principles in any other way, and it was not long before he returned to familiar ground. But although *The Pathfinder* (1839), which reinstates Natty Bumppo at middle age, and *The Deerslayer* (1841), which depicts him at the age of twenty-two, received a warmer reception, Cooper never fully regained the widespread critical acceptance he had sacrificed to his stubborn adherence to principle in the 1830s. An astonishing burst of creative energy saw him produce a further sixteen novels in the last decade of his life, but although he remained popular with the reading public in this period, he was almost completely neglected by literary reviewers. Only after his death did his contemporaries finally give him his due, with writers including William Cullen Bryant, Ralph Waldo Emerson, Nathaniel Hawthorne, Washington Irving, and Herman Melville all belatedly acknowledging the extent of his influence on American literature.

Cooper's influence outside England and America was also significant. He had always been immensely popular in translation: in Germany, for example, between 1820 and 1853 there were 105 translations of individual works and five different collections of his tales. Johann Wolfgang von Goethe is known to have read and enjoyed *The Prairie*, and even to have incorporated some scenes from *The Pioneers* into his own *Novelle* (1826). There were similarly receptive readers in Spain, Italy, and particularly Russia, where Mikhail Lermontov and Alexandr Pushkin found echoes of their own steppes and Cossacks in Cooper's expansive prairies and noble Indians. But it was in France, where Cooper's republican values endeared him to the liberal intellectual community, that he was read with perhaps the greatest sympathy. His Byronic novel *The Red Rover* (1827) inspired Hector Berlioz's overture *Le Corsair Rouge* (1831–52), and he could number Honoré de Balzac and George Sand among his admirers.

In the seventy years or so after his death, Cooper's reputation went into further decline. Although his popular frontier and sea novels were still read, he was mainly known as the author of adventure stories suitable for children, and his social criticism was totally neglected. The age of literary realism could find little place for the stilted artificiality of much of Cooper's writing, and this attitude was both summarized and immortalized by Mark Twain's brilliant, hilarious, but slightly unfair critique, "Fenimore Cooper's Literary Offences" (1895). As Twain points out, Cooper writes dialogue badly, his attempts at humor are largely unsuccessful, his sentences are often unwieldy or even ungrammatical, and he pays little attention to consistency or plausibility in the construction of his plots. But Twain's view, while caustically accurate in many ways, is not entirely fair. Cooper is not generally concerned with the minutiae of sociohistorical detail (although, as *The Pioneers* demonstrates, he was perfectly capable of communicating such concerns). Although Twain's detailed analysis reveals many flaws, the pace and breathless excitement of Cooper's narratives often mask these failings. Cooper's ear for dialogue is poor, but his scenes of action and pursuit are masterful. His capacity to convey the grandeur of the American scene without dwelling on particulars (he never actually visited the Western plains of *The Prairie* in his whole life), infusing the landscape with republican values, proved an inspiration to a generation of later American authors. In short, Cooper's greatest achievement was to give substance to the very notion of "American literature."

ROWLAND HUGHES

Biography

Born merely as James Cooper (the Fenimore was added in 1826) in Burlington, New Jersey; family founded Cooperstown, in upstate New York, a year after his birth. Entered Yale University, 1803, but expelled in 1805 for a youthful prank gone wrong. Became a common sailor in 1806; entered the U.S. Navy, 1808–11. Married Susan Augusta DeLancey in 1811, with whom he had five daughters (including the author Susan Fenimore Cooper) and two sons. Moved to Westchester County, New York, 1817. Began literary career with *Precaution*, 1820. Relo-cated to Europe with his family, 1826, and spent the next seven years traveling extensively. Developed a friendship with Lafayette while in Paris. Returned to the United States, and to Cooperstown, 1833. Successfully sued several Whig newspaper editors for libel, 1837–43. Continued to live and work in Cooperstown, where he died September 14, 1851.

Selected Works

Fiction
Precaution. 1819.
The Spy. 1821.
The Pioneers. 1823.
The Pilot. 1824.
The Last of the Mohicans. 1826.
The Prairie. 1827.
The Red Rover. 1827.
The Bravo. 1831.
The Heidenmauer. 1832.
The Headsman. 1833.
The Monikins. 1835.
The Pathfinder. 1840.
The Deerslayer. 1841.
Wyandotté. 1843.
Satanstoe. 1845.
The Sea Lions. 1849.
The Ways of the Hour. 1850.

Social Criticism
Notions of the Americans. 1828.
A Letter to His Countrymen. 1834.
The American Democrat. 1838.

Travel Writing
Sketches in Switzerland, Parts 1 and 2. 1836.
Gleanings in Europe: France. 1837.
Gleanings in Europe: England. 1837.
Gleanings in Europe: Italy. 1838.

Bibliography

Dekker, George. *James Fenimore Cooper: The Novelist.* London: Routledge and Kegan Paul, 1967.

Dekker, George, and John P. Williams, eds. *James Fenimore Cooper: The Critical Heritage.* London: Routledge, 1973.

Dyer, Alan Frank. *James Fenimore Cooper: An Annotated Bibliography of Criticism.* New York: Greenwood, 1991.

Fields, Wayne, ed. *James Fenimore Cooper: A Collection of Critical Essays.* London: Prentice-Hall, 1979.

Franklin, Wayne. *The New World of James Fenimore Cooper.* Chicago: University of Chicago Press, 1982.

Lawrence, D. H. *Studies in Classic American Literature.* London: M. Secker, 1924.

McWilliams, John P. *Political Justice in a Republic: James Fenimore Cooper's America.* Berkeley and Los Angeles: University of California Press, 1972.

Slotkin, Richard. *Regeneration through Violence.* Middletown, Conn.: Wesleyan University Press, 1973.

Ringe, Donald. *James Fenimore Cooper.* Boston: Twayne, 1962.

Test, George A., ed. *James Fenimore Cooper: His Country and His Art.* Oneonta: State University of New York Press, 1991.

Twain, Mark. "Fenimore Cooper's Literary Offences." Reprinted in *The Shock of Recognition: The Development of Literature in the United States Recorded By The Men Who Made It.* Edited by Edmund Wilson. New York: Farrar, Straus and Cudahy, 1955.

Verhoeven, W. M., ed. *James Fenimore Cooper: New Historical and Literary Contexts.* Amsterdam: Rodolpi, 1993.

COROT, JEAN-BAPTISTE-CAMILLE 1796–1875

French painter

Jean-Baptiste-Camille Corot has been called the last neoclassical painter; he has also been called the first impressionist. There is truth in both statements. It is also true that there are traces of naturalism, realism, and Romanticism in his work. These five, sometimes merging, styles in nineteenth-century painting are not all present at the same time, but combinations of them can show up. The question of his possible Romantic tendencies is complicated by two further problems: Romanticism can mean a number of things, many of which might as well be indications of other forms of intellectual, artistic, and moral intentions. However, Corot did say that the feelings should be an artist's guide in painting, and emotion is one of the touchstones of the Romantic movement.

Corot began to paint, as a hobby, in his late twenties. Prior to that he had spent several years as a shop attendant. He turned to art with professional intent, taking instruction from two well-known neoclassical painters. He traveled to Italy to finish his education in the study of Roman and Renaissance art and architecture, the usual practice of young painters at the time. He continued to paint into the 1870s, long after the Romantic period had passed. He would not have thought of himself as a Romantic, and his artistic allegiance was always in the first instance to the painters of the neoclassical style in the seventeenth and eighteenth centuries. However, he also admired the more realistic, natural style of landscape painted in the early nineteenth century by artists such as the English painters Richard Bonington and John Constable, who were determined to paint what they saw, and who often painted on site rather than artfully arranging their landscapes in the studio. A gregarious bachelor, helpful to younger painters, he only occasionally commented on the intellectual nature of his craft, and it is possible to think of much of his work as quite untouched by Romanticism. Since his death, however, there has been much critical debate over how to classify his work.

In his own time, the work of his middle years was his most popular, and those paintings can, in general, be categorized as neoclassical. Since his death, his early plein air sketches, not made for sale but as part of his early training, and some of his late work, much of it again not meant for sale, have been seen as his finest painting, and these paintings are often atypical of his neoclassicism. In both cases, the work might be defined, in part, as Romantic. Some critics see these paintings as attempts to infuse the work with personal feeling, to explore character, and to paint subjects popular with Romantic artists. It might also be argued that the work of his mature years was unconsciously tinged with Romanticism, and that its enormous popularity in the middle of the nineteenth century can be ascribed not simply to a bourgeois taste for traditional landscapes, but for landscapes rich with Romantic connotations. These sweetly gentle paintings, basically neoclassical in structure, are charged with quiet emotion. The public adored his landscapes: silvery, dewy sylvan scenes, often lit from the back, populated by figures of fuzzy definition, often peasants, sometimes young lovers, sometimes characters from mythology, often modestly cavorting nymphs, making innocent music; see, for instance *A Morning* (1850). The restrained palette and the loose brush strokes made for a distinctive landscape style; so much so that imitations of Corot's *paysage composé* were a commonplace in the art market. He became known as the "Poet of the Landscape."

The later figure paintings, often of simple folk, usually young women, reveal an interest in personality and in the lower social orders, common subjects of Romantic enthusiasm, as in *Lady in Blue* (1874). His early Italian oil sketches, done in the open air, seemingly innocent of intent save to record the exact object, thus possessed elements of naturalism and realism that were to make them attractive to the impressionists; see, for example, *View of the Farnese Gardens: Morning* (1826). This simple, realistic style occasionally shows up in other paintings throughout his career, such as *Soissons: House and Factory of Mr. Henry* (1833). Very late in his career, he produced impressive paintings that are stylistically and tonally similar to those of the young impressionists, whose work was deeply imbued with Romantic influences, as in *The Belfry at Douai* (1871).

CHARLES PULLEN

Biography

Born in Paris, July 17, 1796. Son of successful milliners. Brought up by a nursemaid in L'Isle-Adam, near Paris. Educated in Paris and in boarding schools in Rouen and Poissy. Apprenticed to a Paris cloth merchant; worked in the cloth trade, 1815–22. Started to paint as a hobby in his twenties; supported in serious art study by parents from 1822. Studied with Jean-Victor Bertin and Achille-Etna Michallon, 1822–25; painted at Saint-Cloud and in the forest of Fontainebleau. Traveled, painted, and drew in Italy, visiting Rome, Naples, Ischia, and Venice, 1825–28; traveled in France, 1828–34. Started exhibiting at the Paris Salon, 1827: awarded second-class medal, 1833. Stayed in Italy for several months, 1834. Continued to exhibit at Paris Salons to increasing critical acclaim, 1830s and '40s. Traveled to Switzerland, 1842; the Netherlands, 1854; London, 1862. Named chevalier, Légion d'honneur, 1846. Established friendship with the painter Jean-François Millet, 1850. Awarded first-class medal for painting, Paris Exposition Universelle, 1855. Promoted to officier, Legion d'honneur, 1867. Exhibited at the Royal Academy, London, 1869; appointed knight of the Order of Saint Michael by the King of Bavaria; medal of honor, Paris Salon, 1874. Died in Paris, February 22, 1875.

Bibliography

Brenson, Michael. "French Landscape Painting: The Seeds of Impressionism," *New York Times* August 2, 1991.
Brookner, Anita. "The Eye of Innocence." In *Soundings*. London: Harvill Press, 1997.

Clark, Kenneth. *Landscape into Art*. Rev. ed. New York: Penguin, 1979.

Conisbee, Philip. *In the Light of Italy: Corot and Early Open-Air Painting*. New Haven, Conn.: Yale University Press, 1966.

Hughes, Robert. "Bringing Nature Home," *Time* April 29, 1996, 84–85.

Leymarie, Jean. *Corot*. Translated by Stuart Gilbert. Geneva: Skira/New York: World, 1979.

Galassi, Peter. *Corot in Italy: Open-Air Painting and the Classical Landscape Tradition*. New Haven, Conn.: Yale University Press, 1991.

Robert, Keith. *Corot*. London: Spring Books, 1965.

Tinterow, Gary, and Michael Pomarede Pantazzi. *Corot*. New York: Metropolitan Museum of Art and Harry N. Abrams, 1996.

COSMOLOGY

Isaac Newton's demonstration in his *Principia* (1687) that all motion in the solar system took place according to immutable, absolute, abstract laws that could be calculated and understood by humankind had tremendous philosophical and theological implications. Hitherto, the course of history and human destinies had been assumed to lie in the hands of a divine providence. In Newton's wake, such beliefs became seriously overshadowed by doubt, and throughout the eighteenth century explanations of the creation and mechanics of the universe at large were to become the province of science rather than religion.

A picture of a vast, sublime, and seemingly infinite universe was being pieced together by the observations of astronomers such as William Herschel, while philosophers such as Immanuel Kant developed theories to explain the births of star systems and their grouping into galaxies. Even the possibility of exotic celestial features, such as what are now called black holes, were imagined by theorists in the late eighteenth century: for example, John Mitchell mooted the idea of light being unable to escape from sufficiently massive and dense stars in *Philosophical Transactions* (1784). The early nineteenth century saw the opening of the first fully equipped observatory in the southern hemisphere on the Cape of Good Hope in 1821. Thus the era of exclusively European-based astronomical observation came to an end, and for the first time the wonders of the Milky Way visible only from the other side of the Earth were revealed.

However, it was the controversial implications of works such as *Exposition du Monde* (1796) and *Mecanique Celeste* (1799–1825, translated into English by Nathaniel Bowditch) by French astronomer and mathematician Pierre Laplace that were to most arouse Romantic sensibilities. Laplace pointed out that the Newtonian universe must be an entirely deterministic one in the purest mathematical and logical terms. In a universe set in motion by some primordial first cause, and continuing its movement according to rigid and calculable laws, he argued, it was theoretically possible for a powerful enough intelligence to calculate and predict every event in the future, each one of which was scientifically inevitable. "Nothing would be uncertain," he said, "and the future, as well as the past, would be present to our eyes."

Ironically, it was the remaining perceived necessity for a first cause to set such a universe in motion that was to offer the church its only hope. Indeed, demotion of God to the status of divine clockmaker in a mechanistic universe was to be a source of salvation for the theological cause. Church scholars such as William Paley in *Natural Theology* (1802) developed "the Argument from Design," whereby it was argued that such a perfectly ordered system was, paradoxically, evidence of the design of a divine creator rather than a denial.

Jean D'Alembert had raised further questions in his *Traité de Dynamique* (1758), proposing that the matter of which the universe was made might possess inherent properties of its own, irrespective of the influence of any natural laws or a god. He added that matter and its creation might in some way have existed prior to the advent of natural laws, and God and universal influence thus continue to remain separate for eternity.

This radical standpoint was taken to what was probably its furthest atheistic extent by Baron D'Holbach in his work *Systeme de la Nature* (1770), one of the key textual foundations of Romantic cosmological philosophy. In this work, Holbach took Newton at his word in attributing properties such as mass, momentum, inertia, and gravity entirely to matter, and extrapolated this to deduce that there was thus no need for a divine prime mover or first cause, as matter possessed its own inherent ability to move. As matter had also existed for all eternity and had no beginning in a universe infinite in terms of both space and time, nor was there, he said, any requirement "to have recourse to supernatural powers."

However, the prevailing cosmological beliefs of most educated people during the Romantic era remained essentially deistic, and are typified by the philosophical commentator Sir William Drummond in *Academical Questions* (1805), who wrote, "The boldest atheist, who ever hurled defiance against heaven, may not consider, unawed, the comparative insignificance of the whole earth with the suns and the planets of a thousand systems. It is surely, when we survey the order, and meditate the motions and the magnitude of the celestial bodies, that we obtain the most sublime notions of infinite power, and most readily confess the existence of a supreme Intelligence." This book, and other popular digests such as the best-selling *Astronomy Explained upon Sir Isaac Newton's Principles* by James Ferguson (1773), brought the latest scientific discoveries to the notice of the reading public at large. Equally popular were public lectures on astronomy and natural philosophy by figures such as Adam Walker, who appeared regularly at the Drury Lane Theatre and who taught Percy Bysshe Shelley at Eton College.

Even so, Romantic thinkers were always to have a problematic relationship with ideas of the universe at large; on the one hand its overall appearance of beautiful, benign simplicity; on the other, its awesome size and incomprehensible complexity. Imagery of the cosmos would gradually begin to replace the sea and other earthbound features of the natural world as preferred metaphors for concepts of the sublime.

In a manner similar to present-day postmodernist thought, Romanticism had a tendency to distrust objective scientific concepts of totality, synthesis, and empiricism. Eventually, subjective Romantic perceptions of the nature of matter, ontological idealism, and the primacy of human consciousness were to lead to a rejection of the mechanistic Newtonian universe, in favor of a more organic and holistic model.

Despite Newton, it was to be many years yet before the Western mindset would shrug off the ghost of the Aristotelian universe so beloved of Geoffrey Chaucer, John Milton, and William Shakespeare. Indeed, the lingering influence of classical tradition is illustrated by the fact that when astronomer William Herschel discovered a new planet in 1781 (the first in recorded history) names suggested for it, including Herschel or Georgium Sidus ("the Georgian Planet"), were rejected in favor of Uranus, a mythological deity.

CHRISTOPHER GOULDING

Bibliography

Abrams, M. H. *The Mirror and the Lamp.* New York: Oxford University Press, 1953.
Hoskin, Michael, ed. *The Cambridge Illustrated History of Astronomy.* Cambridge: Cambridge University Press, 1997.
Piper, H. W. *The Active Universe.* London: University of London/ Athlone Press, 1962.

COTMAN, JOHN SELL 1782–1842

British watercolorist

John Sell Cotman was an artist committed to recording nature in an immediately identifiable personal style. He also had artistic interests in the antique architecture of England and in the picturesque aspects of ancient ruins. At the time of his early career, oil paintings of the British countryside had become firmly established in the public taste; but it was Cotman, and a handful of other British artists, who established the watercolor as a Romantic medium.

There is a tendency to think of Romanticism as a movement of emotional and intellectual expansiveness, of the grand gesture in art. Cotman is of the British school of restraint and modesty, and the British watercolor was the perfect medium with which to express this quiet Romanticism. In the early nineteenth century, however, the watercolor did not have the kind of public credibility that the oil painting possessed, despite the fact that major artists, such as John Constable and J. M. W. Turner, occasionally used it.

Cotman's work exemplifies one aspect of Romanticism influenced by aesthetic theories developed in the eighteenth century by several theorists, culminating in Sir Uvedale Price's *An Essay on the Picturesque as Compared with the Sublime and the Beautiful* (1796). Price suggested that the attempt to paint nature need not necessarily involve the wide-open landscape, but could be expressed in the intense contemplation of the smallest details of nature, and that such focus could suggest an implicit significance, a metaphysical comment upon the nature of all life. This focus upon the most unprepossessing natural scenes is a mark of Cotman's work, and particularly so of watercolors made early in his career. Greta Bridge in North Yorkshire, the subject of his most famous watercolors, was painted on two occasions, once in 1805 and again in 1810; these paintings are examples of the quiet, muted, stylized apprehension of country beauty. On occasion, the point of view can be more intensely focused, manifesting the close scrutiny suggested in the Uvedale Price thesis (*The Study of Burdock*, c. 1813).

A general enthusiasm for nature was a Romantic commonplace of English middle- to upper-middle-class society, and it was often expressed by laymen not only in serious nature walks and in landscape gardening, but also in drawing and painting from nature. This enthusiasm was to be both a help and a hindrance to Cotman. The artist might make a modest living as a teacher of drawing and painting, and Cotman spent much of his life as such. However, he wanted to concentrate on working as a watercolor painter of topographical and architectural scenes, although he occasionally worked in oil. If it is Romantic to contemplate the artist's struggle, Cotman qualifies as something of a tragic figure, since his life was a continual battle to make a living. When his work as a watercolorist failed to support him, he branched out into etching, taking as his subject, in the main, antique architectural ruins. He published several volumes of this material that included studies of sites in England (*Norman and Gothic Architecture in the County of Norfolk*, 1816–18) and in Normandy, a main source of architectural influence on English churches. Much of this work with the ruins of churches and country houses has a medieval aura about it, consistent with the Romantic enthusiasm for Gothic themes (*Crosby Hall*, 1831). None of this work was sufficiently popular to keep him and his family on solid monetary footing. He was always in financial difficulty, a situation complicated further by his tendency to slip into deep depression as one enterprise after another failed. Eventually he found steady employment as the drawing master at King's College in London. He was well respected in artistic circles, but his work never sold well; when it did sell, it sold cheaply. Some forty years later, watercolors had become popular and Cotman was recognized as a major Romantic artist; there was a brisk trade not only in his work, but in imitations of it. A handful of his early watercolors, such as *Greta Bridge*, with their highly stylized, balanced masses of light and dark, their simplicity, their harmony of softened colors, and their Poussin-like *gravitas* seemed to express truths about nature that transcended the particular and became the visual poetry prized by the Romantic movement.

Cotman had a wide range of interests, many of them thematically Romantic and rendered with a focused emotional tonality. In his Yarmouth days, he produced seascapes (*Barmouth Estuary*, 1801), and there are touches of the sublime in his mountain scenes (*Snowdon, with the lake of Llanberis from Dolbaddern Castle, North Wales*, c. 1802). But the best and most popular examples of his quiet tenderness and gravity are in his honey-toned watercolors of church ruins and his close, sumptuous, spiritually charged views of what Price had suggested as the proper subject of painting: the most mundane elements of nature. Price claimed that even the tracks on a muddy road were picturesque (*The Drop Gate, Duncombe Park*, c. 1805), and Cotman understood what he meant.

CHARLES PULLEN

Biography

Born in Norwich, May 16, 1782. Son of a successful silk merchant. Educated at Norwich Grammar School; taught himself drawing. Moved to London to establish a career as an artist, 1798; worked as an aquatint colorist; later enrolled in academy of Dr. Thomas Munro. Exhibited at the Royal Academy, 1800–06. Joined Thomas Girtin's sketching club; met J. M. W. Turner, early 1800s. Spent summers drawing and painting at the estate of patron Francis Cholmely in Yorkshire, 1803–5. Painted *Greta Bridge*, c. 1805. Moved back to Norwich, 1806; joined and exhibited with Norwich Society of Painters; taught drawing. Married Ann Miles, 1809; they had four sons, including the painters Miles Edmund Cotman and John Joseph Cotman; and one daughter. Moved to Great Yarmouth, taught there and in Norwich, and worked as an archeological draughtsman, 1812–23. Published *Specimens of Architectural Antiquities of Norfolk*, 1812. Worked on antiquarian etchings in Normandy, 1817. Returned to Norwich and opened drawing school, 1823. Member of the London Water-Colour Society, 1825. Moved to London, 1834: taught drawing at King's College, London, 1834–42. Died in London, July 24, 1842.

Bibliography

Binyon, Laurence. *Crome and Cotman*. London: Seeley, 1897.
Cundall, H. M. *The Norwich School*. London: The Studio, 1920.
Kitson, Sydney. *The Life of John Sell Cotman*. London: Faber, 1937.
Mallalieu, Huon. *The Norwich School: Crome, Cotman and Their Followers*. London: St. Martin's Press, 1974.
Oppe, A. P. *Water-colour Drawings of John Sell Cotman*. London: The Studio, 1923.
Pevsner, Nikolaus. *The Englishness of English Art*. London: Penguin, 1956.
Quennell, Peter. *Romantic England: Writing and Painting 1717–1851*. London: Weidenfeld and Nicolson, 1970.
Reynolds, Graham. *A Concise History of Watercolours*. London: Thames and Hudson, 1971.
Rienaecker, Victor. *John Sell Cotman 1782–1842*. Leigh-on-Sea: F. Lewis, 1953.

COURBET, GUSTAVE 1819–77

French painter

The critics describe Gustave Courbet as a realist. Courbet, a man of considerable vanity, described himself as "Courbetist, that's all," denying all influences, although there is clear evidence of his debt to several artists, including Titian and Rembrandt van Rijn. Realism, the movement that developed from Romanticism, has, like its predecessor, many meanings. This is particularly true when considering Courbet, who should be viewed predominantly as a member of the Romantic movement. His early career in particular was heavily Romantic. His early paintings of professional quality were patently Romantic, especially his dramatic self-portraits (*Portrait of the Artist*, called *Courbet with a Black Dog*, 1842); and he is inclined to use medieval settings, a common Romantic practice in, for example, *The Sculptor* (1845). Extreme states of the human condition were popular with Romantic artists, and Courbet often paints himself in emotional situations. Madness is displayed in *The Desperate Man* (1843–44); death is explored in *Portrait of the Artist*, called *The Wounded Man* (1844–45) with the added touch of Romantic action suggested by the sword, tucked in the corner of the painting, hinting at mortal combat *Portrait of the Artist*, called *The Man with the Leather Belt* (1846), places the painter in Titian's world of the Spanish or Venetian nobility. Music as an entrance to the spiritual world appears in *The Portrait of the Artist* (1847).

In the late 1840s, he became interested in socialist politics, and supported the political struggles of 1848. Paintings of fantastic, elaborate, emotionally charged celebrations of the past, the imagination, extravagant posing, and bohemian excess lost their appeal for the mature painter; see for example, *Portrait of the Artist—The Man with the Pipe* (1849). He was never a great intellectual, although he associated with radical intellectuals and artists such as Charles Baudelaire and Pierre Joseph Proudhon, the socialist thinker; but he recognized the power of his art and how it could be used for public statements. The realist painter emerged in the very late 1840s after nearly a decade of practicing his craft in paintings that were thematically and tonally Romantic.

Realism in its most rigorous form was, in part, a repudiation of several aspects of Romantic painting: a rejection of grand historical or mythical moments in favor of contemporary subjects, a refusal to romanticize or sentimentalize, and a determination to paint subjects exactly as they were, rather than to manipulate them artistically. There were aspects of Romantic painting, however, that were deemed acceptable by the realist painters, such as the interest in the difficult life of the working classes, and the determination to paint landscapes exactly as they appeared. The realists' intention was to expunge any subjectivism, any emotion from the recording of contemporary life and nature. The difficulty lay in the fact that, particularly in the hands of Courbet, realism could have political intent, a determination to show that the French working classes were worthy of being subjects of artistic representation. This elevation of modest subject matter often carried tonal intent that did not simply record life, but gave it an emotionally charged gravitas, as in *Funeral at Ornans* (1849–50). Courbet used his mature gift not only to support the cause of the common man, and to celebrate the virtues, pleasures, and pain of provincial life, but to produce a great deal of first-class work as a landscapist who looked at the real world and attempted to realistically portray it, with all its three-dimensional breadth and weight, in a two-dimensional medium; see, for instance, *The Grotto of the Loue* (c. 1865). He was also a formidable painter of sexual subjects, sometimes with embarrassing frankness. His studies of animals, both wild and domestic, such as that of a simple fish caught on a line and being pulled to its death (*The Trout*, 1872), are heartbreakingly tender. *Realist* may be a convenient category, but it does not adequately suggest the emotional power of Courbet, and it could be argued that the best aspect of Romanticism, its expression of human feeling, remains present in his work throughout his career. His life was a Romantic journey from innocent rural simplicity to the bohemian improprieties of Paris, the physical excesses of high living, and the excitement and the dangers of political adventurism, with consequences in imprisonment, financial disaster, a decline in artistic quality, ill health, alcoholism, and, finally, death in unhappy exile.

CHARLES PULLEN

See also **Art and Politics; France: 1815–1852; Landscape Painting: France**

Biography

Born in Ornans, France, June 10, 1819. Son of Eléonor-Régis Courbet, a farmer of substantial means. Educated locally and at the Little Seminary, Ornans; studied drawing with "Père" Beau, former pupil of Antoine-Jean Gros, in Ornans. Studied under Charles-Antoine Flajoulot at the Collège Royal, Besançon, 1837–39. Moved to Paris; studied law briefly, 1839, later deciding to concentrate on artistic study. Rejected formal study for private copying of the old masters at the Louvre; drew and painted models in the Académie Suisse. Exhibited for the first time at the Paris Salon, 1844. Visited Holland and the major Dutch art galleries, 1848. Associated with artistic and political intellectuals; supported the 1848 radical political disturbances. Painted *The Stone-Breakers* and *Funeral at Ornans*, 1849. Awarded the Second Class Gold Medal at the Paris Salon, 1849. Exhibited regularly at the Paris Salon; traveled to Germany, Normandy, and Switzerland, 1850s. Patronized by Alfred Bruyas; briefly opened an atelier to train students, 1861. *Return from the Conference* refused by the Paris Salon because of its antichurch bias, 1863. *The Awakening*

rejected as indecent, 1864. Traveled to paint at Trouville and other Normandy seaside resorts with the painters Claude Monet and James Whistler, 1865. Traveled in Germany; decorated by the King of Bavaria, 1869. Refused the rank of chevalier of the Légion d'honneur when it was offered in 1870. Elected president of the Federal Commission of Artists after the proclamation of the Third Republic, 1870. Took part in activities of the Paris Commune, 1871; upon its failure, arrested as a scapegoat, fined, and imprisoned for six months at the Sainte-Pélagie prison; after his health failed, taken to a clinic near Paris. Paintings rejected by the Salon, 1872. Fled to Switzerland to live in exile after his property confiscated by the Bonapartists, 1873. Lived in Fleurier, Vevey, and La Tour-de-Peilz. Died in La Tour-de-Peilz, Switzerland, December 31, 1877.

Selected Works

After Dinner at Ornans. 1848–49. 195 cm. × 257 cm. Musée des Beaux-Arts, Lille.
Funeral at Ornans. 1849–50. 315 cm. × 668 cm. Louvre, Paris.
The Bathers (*Women Bathing*). 1853. 227 cm. × 193 cm. Musée Fabre, Montpellier.
Woman by a Spring or *La Source*. 1868. 128 cm. × 97 cm. Louvre, Paris.
The German Hunter. 1859. 118 cm. × 174 cm. Musée des Beaux-Arts, Lons-Le-Saunier.
The Gour de Conches. 1864. 70 cm. × 60 cm. Musée des Beaux-Arts, Besançon.

Bibliography

Brookner, Anita. *Soundings*. London: Harvill Press, 1997.
Callen, Anthea. *Courbet*. London: Jupiter Books, 1980.
Clark, T. J. *Image of the People: Gustave Courbet and the 1848 Revolution*. London: Thames and Hudson, 1973.
Fernier, Robert. *Gustave Courbet*. New York: Praeger, 1969.
———. *La Vie et l'oeuvre de Gustave Courbet: Catalogue raisonné*. 2 vols. Lausanne: Bibliothèque des Arts, 1977.
Fried, Michael. *Courbet's Realism*. Chicago: University of Chicago. 1990.
Lindsay, Jack. *Gustave Courbet: His Life and Art*. New York: Harper and Row, 1973.
Mack, Gerstle. *Gustave Courbet*. New York: Alfred A. Knopf, 1951.
Nochlin, Linda. *Gustave Courbet: A Study of Style and Society*. New York: Garland, 1976.

COUSIN, VICTOR 1792–1867

French philosopher

Although largely neglected today, Victor Cousin was France's most influential thinker from 1815 to 1848, crucial years in the history of French Romanticism. His glamorous academic career, which the coup d'état of Louis Napoleon in December 1851 brought to a close, mirrors precisely the artistic and political trajectory and aspirations of the canon of Romantic poets, painters, and novelists in France. His system of ideas, including the considerable debt that it owes to contemporary German thought, provides at every point the intellectual framework beneath other more familiar forms of Romantic self-expression. In

many respects, philosophical enquiry in Cousin's hands is also to be considered a form of romance.

Cousin's early career affords a remarkable example of the social revolution initiated by the events of 1789 and institutionalized by the educational reforms introduced under Napoleon Bonaparte. The son of Parisian artisans, the future philosopher's prospects seemed, until the age of twelve, no different from those of any other city street urchin. However, a chance encounter with a group of schoolboys bullying one of their fellows would provide the young Cousin, who came to the aid of the victim, with a grateful parental benefactor prepared to support his entry to the Lycée Charlemagne from where, in 1810, he graduated to the newly established École Normale Supérieure. The completion of his academic apprenticeship by 1815, which coincided with the end of twenty years of war, ensured that he was perfectly placed to profit from his nation's revived appetite for intellectual discourse, particularly of a spiritual nature. In the three years after, he rose rapidly to academic stardom as a stylish presenter of his doctrines to a widening public. The first of three visits to Germany in 1817 led him to a meeting with G. W. F. Hegel, whose ideas he progressively incorporated into his own. In 1820, there was a temporary halt to his career when the assassination of the Duc de Berry provoked a skittish Restoration government into suppressing the proliferation of liberal ideas, and in 1824 he even found himself briefly incarcerated in a Prussian jail on conspiracy charges. However, during the reign of Louis-Philippe following the 1830 Revolution, he was made titular professor of philosophy at the Sorbonne, director of the École Normale, a member of the Académie Française and of the Académie des Sciences Morales, and eventually given a peerage. Cousin continued to be a prominent figure in the politics of higher education until, with the fall of the July Monarchy in 1848, he became one of many with a reforming outlook to be progressively relegated to the margins of public life.

The contradiction between heroic self-confidence and anxiety for past securities typical of the Romantic period in France is always alive in Cousin's public stance and intellectual makeup. A martinet and a showman by character (his mistress was the iconic Louise Colet), he was a constitutional monarchist by political persuasion, and a conciliatory, historically conscious thinker who turned into a doctrine the belief that all preceding philosophical systems were valid in what they affirmed. Cousin was born into an era of international and social conflict, an heir to the intellectual schism between rationalist and empirically-based systems of thought created in the course of the Enlightenment and fanned into crisis by Immanuel Kant. He looked instinctively for a solution on a philosophical level that was be comparable to the political compromise of the Restoration Charter. Inspired by Hegel (whom he claimed to have "discovered" for the rest of Europe), he found it in a syncretism, which, in positing the complementarity of reason and the senses, would release reason from the Kantian confines of its own subjectivity and the senses from their function as mere receptacles of random data. "The basis of our doctrine," he declared, "is an idealism tempered by a just measure of empiricism." Cousin authenticates this alliance by reference to what amounts to a third faculty in the form of a prereflexive intuition, simultaneously guaranteeing consciousness from the contingency and succession of sensual experience and protecting the reasoning mind from excessive sophistry. It is in this faculty, identified with sentiment and with conscience, that "nature's true logic" is to be found, allowing for the discernment of truths which are universal and disinterested. Cousin classified these absolutes into his celebrated trilogy of "le vrai, le beau, le bien" (truth, beauty, good), and argued that their origin and perfection was to be found in the divine being. "The voice of the heart," he declared, "is the voice of God."

To the extent that he distanced himself from the notion of a supernatural creator and chose to identify divinity with the life of the universe and the supreme aspirations of humankind, Cousin was at heart a rationalist who, with Hegel, sought to replace traditional Christian teaching by a form of pantheism. In reverting to the instinctual and spontaneous as the basis for philosophical certitudes that an age of scepticism had thrown into disarray, he also owed much to the "commonsense" doctrines of the then-fashionable Scots thinker Thomas Reid, and to Reid's French disciple and his own predecessor at the École Normale, Pierre-Paul Royer-Collard. However, the term *eclecticism*, which Cousin used to describe the reconciliation of existing thought systems, originated in Potamon of Alexandria, and there are further vestiges of Hellenism in the fundamentally Platonist cast of his mind.

Not unjustly castigated by his critics such as Pierre Leroux and, later, Hippolyte-Adolphe Taine, as a vague-minded rhetorician on the side of the preservation of public order and morality, Cousin nonetheless provided the intellectual soil in which Romantic optimism in relation at once to history, to affectivity, and to a more broadly spiritualized view of the universe was able to flourish. Always more of a historian of ideas than an original thinker and, in his later years, a tireless administrator convinced of the importance of providing his country with a recognizably national system of thought, he established the model of an alliance between philosophy and the institutions of state which is still reflected in French political life.

DAVID LEE

Biography

Born Paris, November 28, 1792, son of a goldsmith and a laundress. Educated at the Lycée Charlemagne, 1803–1810, and at the École Normale, 1810–1812. Appointed acting professor of Greek literature, 1812, and of philosophy, 1815, École Normale. Traveled in Germany, 1817; met G. W. F. Hegel, Jacobi, and Friedrich Schelling. Deposed from his academic position following the assassination of the Duc de Berry, 1820. Arrested in Germany (on suspicion of plotting against the Holy Alliance?), 1824. Published *Fragments philosophiques*, 1826. Reinstated to academic post in philosophy at the École Normale, 1828, and to full chair of philosophy, 1830. Appointed member of the Académie Française, 1831; and the Académie des Sciences Morales et Politiques, 1832. Named a peer of France, 1832. Director of the École Normale, 1834. Minister for Public Instruction, 1840. Retired following the Bonapartist coup d'état, 1851. Died in Cannes, January 13, 1867.

Selected Works

Cours de philosophie de l'année 1818 . . . sur le fondement des idées absolues du vrai, du beau et du bien. 1836. Revised as *Du vrai, du beau et du bien.* 1853. Translated by O. W. Wright, 1854.
Cours d'histoire de la philosophie morale au dix-huitième siècle, professé . . . en 1819 et 1820. (Part 1, *Ecole sensualiste*, 1839; Part 2, *Ecole écossaise*, 1840; Part 3, *Philosophie de Kant*, 1842. Translated by A. G. Henderson, 1854).
Fragmens philosophiques. 1826.
Cours de l'histoire de la philosophie . . . Introduction a l'historie de la philosophie. 1828.
Cours d'histoire de la philosophie moderne. 1841. Translated by O. W. Wright, 1852.

Bibliography

Bernard, Claude. *Victor Cousin ou la religion de la philosophie.* Toulouse: Presses Universitaires de Mirail, 1991.

Janet, P. A. R. *Victor Cousin et son oeuvre.* Paris: Calmann-Lévy, 1885.

Leroux, Pierre. *Réfutation de l'éclectisme.* Paris: Gosselin, 1839.

Renan, Ernest. "M. Cousin." In *Essais de morale et de critique (1859), Oeuvres complètes*, vol. 2. Edited by H. Psichari. Paris: Calmann-Lévy, 1947.

Simon, Jules. *Victor Cousin.* Paris: Hachette, 1887.

Taine, Hippolyte. "Cousin." In *Les Philosophes français au dix-neuvième siècle.* Paris: Hachette, 1857.

Vermeren, Patrice. *Victor Cousin: Le jeu de la philosophie et de l'état.* Paris: Editions l'Harmattan, 1995.

Wyzewa, T. de, ed. *Pages choisies des grands écrivains: Victor Cousin.* Paris: Perrin, 1898.

COWPER, WILLIAM 1731–1800

English poet

William Cowper is best described not as a pre-Romantic, but as an early Romantic who exemplifies a central Romantic theme and method: the contemplation of nature by a conscious, individual self, narrated in a conversational blank verse that embodies the processes of the mind. His long poem *The Task* heavily influenced William Wordsworth's *Prelude* in style and structure, while his general themes of retirement and the beneficent power of nature are clearly shared by Samuel Taylor Coleridge and Wordsworth. Like his contemporaries William Collins, Thomas Gray, and Christophor Smart, he shows signs of the poet's alienation from society, partly due to his own mental instability (which he shares with Collins and Smart), but also attributable to an instability he finds in the world.

It is difficult to extricate Cowper's work fully from his life, not only because of the unusual nature of his biography, but also because he himself described his writing as "therapy" for his chronic depression. Yet here, too, he bears much in common with Coleridge, who enacts his own recovery in a poem such as "Dejection: An Ode," or Wordsworth, who narrates a therapeutic encounter in "Resolution and Independence." The Romantic stereotype of the mad poet encourages some distortion of Cowper's story, because he shares with both Augustans and Romantics a calling to legislate for mankind, even in retreat: "Content if, thus sequester'd, I may raise / A monitor's, though not a poet's praise." At the same time, Cowper clearly saw a public purpose in personal narrative: his *Memoir* of his early life and *Adelphi*, describing his brother's deathbed conversion, were both circulated privately but published after his death.

Cowper is further set apart by his Calvinist faith, which played a large and complex part in both his initial recovery and his subsequent relapses (because he believed himself to be damned for his first suicide attempt). Certainly his *Olney Hymns* (1779), with their psychological clarity and powerful symbolism, constitute some of his most influential work. His religion sets him apart from his Augustan predecessors as well as from most Romantics (even William Blake had a very different notion of God). Yet arguably it is this faith that sanctions both his inward meditations and his physical retreat from the world: both themes the Romantics would adopt, even if most preferred to leave God out of it.

Cowper's early moral satire *Table-Talk* (1782) applies a style not unlike Alexander Pope's, as well as the structure of the Horatian epistles, to ask why poetry does not serve God as well as it might. But in *Retirement*, published at the end of the same volume, Cowper begins to demonstrate the theme, if not yet the style, that will come to maturity in *The Task* (1785). Here Cowper defines melancholy as a real disease, to be healed through faith in God, and only then will nature "Impart to things inanimate a voice, / And bid her mountains and her hills rejoice."

Cowper's poetic range is impressive, encompassing not only the didactic satires and hymns but also playful poems about domestic animals and *The Diverting History of John Gilpin* (1782). His highly personal poem "On the Receipt of My Mother's Picture" effectively links the elegiac mode of Gray and Oliver Goldsmith with the Romantic conversation poem. Among his last major works was a translation of Homer (1791, with later revisions), and he also translated the Latin and Italian poems of John Milton (1794). By far his most influential work, however, is *The Task*. This didactic-descriptive poem, often loosely grouped with James Thomson's *Seasons*, John Dyer's *Fleece*, and Edward Young's *Night-Thoughts*, differs from all these predecessors in its underlying egotism. As a public and (some would say) quintessentially English poem about the virtues of the countryside, it is equally a poem about the self and the problems of individual existence. In the end, the didactic purpose is overshadowed by autobiography: even in the famous passage that begins "I was a stricken deer, that left the herd," the healing power of Christ is invoked not to praise Christ but to help establish a stable identity for Cowper himself. What further sets his poem apart from *The Seasons* and other descriptive poems of the eighteenth century is the presence of self in the landscape, not merely as an objective eye but as a dweller in a familiar spot, so that a location such as the Ouse River Valley becomes a place in the mind, prefiguring Wordsworth's "spots of time." The descriptions are not only presented through the mind, but follow the mind's associations: the poem is famous for its intentional, journal-like formlessness, whereby, as Cowper puts it in a letter, "the reflections are naturally suggested always by the preceding passage." Cowper thus pioneers what one critic has called "the domestic sublime," making everyday experience a fit subject for poetry.

On the didactic side, the poem seems ambivalent toward civilization, as its playful opening, "I sing the SOFA," traces the evolution of furniture along with the rise of luxury. Cities become the object of some praise as "nurseries of the arts," but more of condemnation, especially in the pronouncement that "God made the country, and man made the town" (1749). "Art" thus is set in opposition to nature and associated with the contrived fashion of the unproductive rich. Yet the very reference to "making" implies not idleness, but labor: a task. The relation of work and leisure to the city and the country thus becomes a recurring problem in the poem: the city is berated for idleness, but the country is sought for retirement. Nonetheless, the poem has been aptly described as "restless," and its antipastoral rural descriptions are closer to George Crabbe than to Oliver Goldsmith.

Critics disagree as to how far Cowper anticipates a Wordsworthian pantheism. Certainly he finds God diffused through nature in a way that departs both from Deism and from the Evangelicalism of his religious mentors and even his own hymns. In the self-narrative of *The Task*, both nature and God exist only as perceived by the individual self, whose experience becomes the measure of truth and reality. Conversely, the God-forsaken isolation of this self when perception is darkened appears tragically, yet powerfully, in Cowper's last poem, "The Castaway" (1799).

JENNIFER DAVIS MICHAEL

Biography

Born in Great Berkhamsted, Hertfordshire, November 26 (?), 1731. Fourth child of Rev. John Cowper, chaplain to King George II. Mother and four siblings died before he was six years old. Educated locally as a boarder at Dr. Pittman's School and then at Westminster School, 1741–48. Entered Middle Temple, 1748; apprenticed to Mr. Chapman, solicitor, in Holborn, 1749; suffered first attack of depression. Engaged to his cousin Theodora Cowper, 1752; admitted to the bar, 1754. Suffered second, more serious, breakdown before examination for a clerkship in the House of Lords; made three suicide attempts and confined to the Collegium Insanorum asylum at St. Albans, 1763. Moved to Huntingdon with family of evangelical clergyman Rev. Morley Unwin, 1765; moved with the Unwin family again to Olney, Buckinghamshire, after death of Morley Unwin, 1767. Came under influence of evangelical curate Rev. John Newton in Olney: collaborated with him on religious verse compilation *Olney Hymns*, (published 1779). Engaged to Mary Unwin, Morley Unwin's widow, 1767, but suffered third attack of mental instability, 1772. Published *Poems*, 1782. Moved to village of Weston Underwood, Buckinghamshire, 1786; worked on translations of Homer. Moved with Mary Unwin to Norfolk, settling at East Dereham, 1795. Mary Unwin died, 1796. Suffered from further depression until his death in East Dereham, Norfolk, April, 25, 1800.

Selected Works

The Poetical Works of William Cowper. Edited by H. S. Milford. 4th ed. London: Oxford University Press, 1980.
The Poems of William Cowper. 3 vols. Edited by John D. Baird and Charles Ryskamp. Oxford: Clarendon Press, 1980–95.
The Letters and Prose Writings of William Cowper. 5 vols. Edited by James King and Charles Ryskamp. Oxford: Clarendon Press, 1979–86.

Bibliography

Feingold, Richard. *Nature and Society: Later Eighteenth-Century Uses of the Pastoral and Georgic.* New Brunswick, N.J.: Rutgers University Press, 1978.
Free, William Norris. *William Cowper.* New York: Twayne, 1970.
Golden, Morris. *In Search of Stability: The Poetry of William Cowper.* New York: Bookman Associates, 1960.
Hartley, Lodwick. *William Cowper: The Continuing Revaluation. An Essay and a Bibliography of Cowperian Studies from 1895 to 1960.* Chapel Hill: University of North Carolina Press, 1960.
Hutchings, Bill. *The Poetry of William Cowper.* London: Croom Helm, 1983.
King, James. *William Cowper: A Biography.* Durham, N.C.: Duke University Press, 1986.
Newey, Vincent. *Cowper's Poetry: A Critical Study and Reassessment.* Liverpool: Liverpool University Press, 1982.
Perkins, David. "Cowper's Hares." *Eighteenth-Century Life.* New series, vol. 20, no. 2 (1996): 57–69.
Priestman, Martin. *Cowper's Task: Structure and Influence.* Cambridge: Cambridge University Press, 1983.
Quinlan, Maurice J. *William Cowper: A Critical Life.* Minneapolis: University of Minnesota Press, 1953.
Ryskamp, Charles. *William Cowper of the Inner Temple, Esq: A Study of His Life and Works to the Year 1768.* Cambridge: Cambridge University Press, 1959.
Spacks, Patricia Meyer. *The Poetry of Vision.* Cambridge, Mass.: Harvard University Press, 1967.

COZENS, ALEXANDER 1717–1786, AND JOHN ROBERT 1752–1797

Landscape artist, theorist, teacher; Landscape painter, draughtsman, and printmaker

Alexander Cozens truly had Romantic origins: he was born in Russia and had early contact with the Russian Court through his father, superintendent of building the Russian fleet, who was favored by the tsar, Peter the Great. Cozens probably learned the principles of accurate, systematic drawing from draftsmen and designers in the shipyard. He studied in Italy, where he made topographical pen and wash drawings of the Roman *campagna* and landscapes in oil which were influenced by his master, the popular and successful Claude-Joseph Vernet.

As a teacher of drawing, Alexander Cozens became interested in systems of draftsmanship, using pattern books as models. He influenced the tastes of a wide range of aristocratic pupils who later became important patrons of art, influential in the picturesque and Romantic movements. These pupils included adult members of the Harcourt, Grey, and Grimston families, the influential amateur landscapist Sir George Beaumont, the Etonian William Beckford and, latterly, members of the Royal family. Cozens made many lifelong friends from among his pupils, and was Beckford's confidant. Professional artists such as George Romney and Joseph Wright of Derby, and literary leaders of the picturesque movement like the Gilpins, seriously considered his methods for ideal composition.

In order to stimulate the powers of invention and to develop speed and spontaneity in execution when creating an ideal or picturesque landscape, Alexander Cozens instructed the artist first to "possess your mind strongly with a subject" and then, while the idea persists, to take a large brush dipped in ink and as rapidly as possible make a variety of shapes and strokes on prepared, crumpled paper. This process should be repeated and then the paper with the most promising set of accidental marks should be used to work up an imaginary landscape conveying a particular mood. Practical instructions on how to prepare tracing paper are given, and his text is illustrated with some of the most fresh and attractive examples of his own work. His empirical efforts to establish a useful system of distinguishing between cloud formations predates Howard Luke's more scientific writings and greatly interested John Constable.

Much of Alexander Cozens's own work in oil is lost, but his very personal style of wash-drawings consciously evoke different moods in nature, largely dispensing with line and relying on masses of shade and color. His own notes reveal his experiments with the relationship between creating an imaginary composition, drawing from nature, and working up an outline, masses, tone, and color in the studio. The arbiter of taste, Horace Walpole, approved wash drawings exhibited by Alexander Cozens at the Royal Academy in 1770. Contemporaries admired the boldness, composition, tonality, and Romantic effect of his "commanding situations, and bold projections; in masses of racks and mountains; or whatever nature presents as solemn and stupendous; in noble fabrics, temples, palaces; in ruins of capital buildings; and the most magnificent executions of art, the lofty turret, the ivy-mantled tower, the consecrated aisle, the melancholy tomb."

A precocious artist, John Robert Cozens was taught the principles of landscape composition by his father, and he exhibited at the Incorporated Society of Artists from 1767 to 1771 and at the Royal Academy in 1776. He combined the imaginative and technical innovations of his father Alexander with a uniquely poetic vision, and was admired by the major landscapists and cognoscenti of the day. Between 1776 and 1778 he traveled through Switzerland and Italy with Richard Payne Knight, at first recording features of the rarely seen, inaccessible waterfalls, gorges, and landscapes in clear monochrome washes. Gradually his ability to take a wider-ranging topographical scene and invest it with an elegiac or dramatic mood developed. Some of his most limpid and personal visions are serene valley scenes with lakes, winding rivers, and spacious skies. His most subjective visions are of the Swiss mountains and valleys, where the power of massed, towering mountain ranges and elemental forces are confidently expressed with a breadth and freedom of handling which captivated John Constable, Thomas Girtin, J. M. W. Turner, and William Wordsworth. His most Gothic watercolors are of subterranean view from inside Italian caverns—almost totally obscure sheets saving only a strip of light at the entry fissure to the cave.

John Robert Cozens's capacity to interpret the ominous lowering ranges of Italian mountain ranges was dramatically extended on his second journey to Europe with William Beckford and his entourage in 1782. In Naples he stayed with Sir William Hamilton, who thought him to be a good cello player but an indolent artist. The ninety-four drawings from this tour are contained in seven quarto sketchbooks.

Like his father Alexander, John Robert Cozens appreciated the role that an expressive sky could play in creating mood in a landscape, and made attentive studies of cloud formations and light effects. *Part of Padua from the Walls* (1782) depicts one of his most unusual skies with black storm clouds torn by jagged lightning to reveal a livid view of the town. He rarely enhanced his work with artificial architectural forms or obtrusive, additional staffage, relying almost entirely for his emotional effects on instinctively placed organic forms expressed through a balance of pale, luminous washes of gray, green, and blue.

Although his surviving work is executed entirely in watercolor and within quite a restricted palette range, Cozens conveyed a sense of power in this medium which exactly suited contemporary literary taste for the sublime. Sir George Beaumont recognized no imbalance when he hung a J. R. Cozens watercolor beside his oil paintings by Claude, and Constable called John Robert Cozens "the greatest artist that ever touched landscape." When John Robert's insanity required medical attention, Dr. Monro, already a collector of his and his father's drawings, became his physician. Drawings from Dr. Monro's collection were copied by Girtin, Turner, and other young landscapists who met in his house to study. In this way the experimental systems of Alexander and the imaginative vision of John Robert provided the foundation for the development of confident interpretations of place, mood, and time of day in British landscape in the nineteenth century.

J. P. CAMPBELL

Biography: Alexander Cozens

Born in Saint Petersburg, Russia, 1717. Wrongly rumored to be an illegitimate son of the tsar. Son of Richard Cozens, a master shipbuilder to Peter the Great. Educated in London, from 1727. Studied painting from 1735. Probably in Russia, early 1740s, then sailed from Saint Petersburg to Livorno (Leghorn). Studied in Rome with Claude-Joseph Vernet, 1746–48. Returned to London; drawing master to Christ's Hospital school, 1749–53. Private drawing tutor to William Beckford, among others. Married daughter of John Pine, engraver; one son, artist John Robert Cozens, born 1752. Member of the Society of Arts and the Free Society of Artists, 1760. Published four important works on art theory, including his *New Method of Landscape* (1759–86). Died in London, April 23, 1786.

Biography: John Robert Cozens

Born in London, 1752. Son of painter Alexander Cozens. Exhibited in the Society of Artists 1767–71. Worked in London, Suffolk, Derbyshire, lived in Bath, 1779–82. Exhibited *A Landscape with Hannibal, in his March over the Alps, showing his Army the fertile plains of Italy* at the Royal Academy, 1776; became an associate of the Royal Academy. Traveled in Switzerland and Italy with Payne-Knight, 1776–78; met Sir William Hamilton. Visited Italy with William Beckford 1782–83. Married and had two children by c. 1789. Presumed to have earned a living in London by teaching and selling worked-up versions of his Swiss and Italian drawings. Published sets of fourteen etchings of trees, late 1780s. Associated with Thomas Girtin and J. M. W. Turner.

Taught Princes Ernest and Augustus 1787–88. Incapacitated by mental illness from 1794 on. Confined under the care of Dr. Thomas Monro, supported by funds from the Royal Academy, 1794–97. Died in London, December 13, 1797.

See also **Beckford, William Thomas; Constable, John; Girtin, Thomas; Turner, Joseph Mallord William; Wordsworth, William**

Selected Written Works by Alexander Cozens

Essay to Facilitate the Inventing of Landskips (later called *The Various Species of Landscape Composition in Nature*). 1759.
The Shape, Skeleton and Foliage of Thirty-two Species of Trees. 1771.
Principles of Beauty, Relative to the Human Head. 1778.
A New Method of Assisting the Invention in Drawing Original Compositions of Landscape. 1786.

Bibliography

Blunt, Anthony. *Catalogue of Seven Sketch-books by John Robert Cozens.* Sale cat. with introduction. London: Sotheby's, 1973.
"A Cozens Album in the National Library of Wales, Aberystwyth," *Walpole Society* 57(1995):.
Hardie, Martin. *Watercolour Painting in Britain.* Vol. 1. London: 1966.
Hawcroft, F. W. *John Robert Cozens.* Exhibition catalog. London: University of Manchester, Whitworth Art Gallery and Victoria and Albert Museum, 1971.
"A New Chronology for Alexander Cozens" *Burlington Magazine* 127, no. 983 (1985): 70–75; and no. 987 (1985): 355–63.
Oppe, A. P. *Alexander and John Robert Cozens.* London, 1952.
Sloan, Kim. *Alexander and John Robert Cozens: The Poetry of Landscape.* London, 1986.
Wilton, A., ed. *The Art of Alexander and John Robert Cozens.* Exh. cat. New Haven, Conn.: Yale University Press/Paul Mellon Center for British Art, 1980.

CRABBE, GEORGE 1754–1832

English poet

Born in Aldeburgh in 1754, a few decades before the tiny Suffolk seaport had begun its gradual development into the fashionable resort that was to become a cultural center in the second half of the twentieth century, George Crabbe had a father of some intelligence, if only limited education, whose ambition was to rise from a lowly position and secure material and social advantage. The boy was sent away to nearby towns to attend schools which, if without distinction, at least provided an education better than the mere training in the rudiments available in his home town. Though the need to earn a living obliged him to work for a time on the wharves at nearby Slaughden Quay, that was only an interlude, and in 1768 apprenticeship to an apothecary marked his first steps in the medical profession. Ten years of study, some of it in London, interspersed with practice, mainly in Aldeburgh, followed, until he resolved to abandon medicine. In a sense, Crabbe had made a false start, finding scientific interest only in botany, yet his aspirations to benefit from his talents were clear.

Crabbe was determined to develop a certain ability in versification into a literary career. For this he needed financial support. It took the typical eighteenth-century form of patronage when the great political orator Edmund Burke made the necessary arrangements for him to be ordained deacon in the Church of England and appointed curate to the rector of Aldeburgh. In 1782 Crabbe, by now in priest's orders, became chaplain to the Duke of Rutland at Belvoir Castle in Leicestershire. A year later he married Sarah Elmy, to whom he had long been engaged. After the death in infancy of some of their children, Sarah lapsed into incurable nervous disorder. In 1789 Crabbe was presented to become the priest in charge of parishes in West Allington, Lincolnshire, and Muston, Leicestershire; they provided an income, and his bishop did not insist on his residence and fulfillment of parish duties until 1805. After devoting his energies to natural history in the mid-1790s, Crabbe turned to verse again,

bringing out *The Parish Register* in 1807 and *The Borough* three years later. In 1814 Crabbe became rector of Trowbridge, in Wiltshire; he did not neglect opportunities of contacts with the leading writers of the age at nearby Bath and further afield. *Tales of the Hall* of 1819 were followed by a collected edition of Crabbe's *Works* in 1822. The opium that Crabbe took to alleviate chronic neuralgia may have had psychological side effects. He died in 1832; his *Posthumous Tales* appeared in 1834, the same year as *Life*, written by his son George.

Crabbe is known above all as a narrative poet who set his characters and their lives in the coastal region of Suffolk. Perhaps this reflects nostalgia for the region where he spent his childhood and, with considerable interruptions, his early years until moving away in his late twenties. It is, however, also possible that he glimpsed the artistic potentialities of regionalism and, like William Shenstone and Thomas Gray, for example, knew that the annals of the poor could be appealing to an eighteenth-century sensibility. Owing much to direct observation and, at least to some extent, to personal experience, Crabbe's writing is domestic and realistic (as opposed to classical and idealistic or else metropolitan and fashionable); it offers a quite detailed account of the local scene, and shows, moreover, not only the mores and pleasures of provincial society, but also the grim moral and material problems faced by the poor and disadvantaged classes. Crabbe's writing also owes a lot to cultural tradition. This is shown by his habit of presenting his poems with a selection of quotations that insert them in a literary context different from the background from which they more obviously spring. Crabbe's chief medium is the heroic couplet, though he can also handle with ease a more complex repeated stanzaic form; in either case rhyme plays an important role, shaping the verse and maintaining a certain tension in the linked lines, and often bringing out a certain irony.

Though narrative forms the basis of his best poems, Crabbe is generally content with a simple story. He needs only a few incidents, often not very surprising ones. Not troubling to develop them very far, he uses them to introduce a handful of characters within a context that is invariably social and sometimes natural. Though he evokes location, his descriptions are not particularly developed and can on occasion seem stiff and rather mannered, even within the context of the remainder of his work. When he is most successful, however, every story paints a picture that is peopled with strongly-drawn characters.

The work of Crabbe was largely admired by his contemporaries, who found its realism invigorating even if the language and poetic manner belonged rather to the past than to the period after the preface to Samuel Taylor Coleridge and William Wordsworth's *Lyrical Ballads*. A revival of interest in Crabbe following a period of comparative neglect is connected with the success of Benjamin Britten's opera *Peter Grimes*, first performed in 1946. Himself a Suffolk man, the composer was inspired to take an interest in the Aldeburgh poet after reading the text of a World Service radio broadcast talk by E. M. Forster, and Montagu Slater devised a powerful libretto from two of the tales in *The Borough*. From *Peter Grimes* comes an impoverished and lonely fisherman who becomes an outcast after the suspicious deaths of the boys he employs to help him in his back-breaking, soul-destroying toil, while his unfulfilled relationship with the spinster schoolmistress evoked in "Ellen Orford" raises the question whether Peter should be seen as hero or antihero. Though the opera has helped restore Crabbe's reputation, it represents only one side of his work. Much of it is gentler in tone, and in its depiction of everyday events in Georgian society there is engaging wry humor. A rather different outlook comes across in such poems as *The Voluntary Insane*. Perhaps it was mental illness in his family and his own reliance on opium that led Crabbe to explore the theme of dreams, hallucinations, and even madness that was becoming fashionable in literature at the time.

CHRISTOPHER SMITH

Biography

Born Aldeburgh, Suffolk, December 24, 1754. Attended schools in Bungay and Stowmarket, 1763. Briefly employed on wharf at Slaughden, near Aldeburgh, 1767. Apprentice to apothecary and surgeon in nearby towns, 1768. First poems, 1775. Medical study in London, 1776. Returned to Aldeburgh, 1777. Obtained patronage of Edmund Burke; ordained as a deacon and was curate in Aldeburgh, 1781. Ordained priest; became chaplain to Duke of Rutland at Belvoir Castle, 1782. Married Sarah Elmy, 1783. Presented to become priest in charge of the parishes of West Allington, Lincolnshire, and Muston, Leicester, 1789. Botanical publications, 1795. Began *The Parish Register*, 1804 (published 1807). Required to reside in his parish of Muston, 1805. Publication of *The Borough*, 1810. Death of his wife; Crabbe's health deteriorated, 1813. Became rector of Trowbridge, Wilts, 1814. Publication of *Tales of the Hall*, 1819. Died February 3, 1832.

Selected Works

The Complete Poetical Works. 3 vols. Edited by Norma Dalrymple-Champneys and Arthur Pollard. Oxford: Clarendon Press, 1988.
Selected Poems. Edited by Gavin Edwards. London: Penguin, 1991.
The Voluntary Insane. Edited by Felix Pryor. London: Richard Cohen, 1995.
Selected Letters and Journals. Edited by Thomas C. Faulkner. Oxford: Clarendon Press, 1985.

Bibliography

Bareham, Tony, and Simon Gatrell. *A Bibliography of George Crabbe.* Folkstone: Dawson, 1978.
Chamberlain, Robert Lyall. *George Crabbe.* English Authors Series, vol. 18. New York: Twayne, 1965.
Crabbe, George, Jr. *The Life of George Crabbe.* London: John Murray, 1833. Reprinted in *The World's Classics*, introduction by Edward Morgan Forster. London: Oxford University Press, 1932.
Huchon, René. *George Crabbe and his Times, 1754–1832.* Translated by Frederick Clarke. London: Murray, 1907.
Pollard, Arthur, ed. *Crabbe: The Critical Heritage.* Critical Heritage Series. London: Routledge and Kegan Paul, 1972.

THE CREATION 1798

Oratorio by Franz Joseph Haydn

Born in 1732, Franz Joseph Haydn spent most of his adult life in the employment of Prince Nicolaus Esterhazy, but on the death of his Hungarian patron he resolved never again to accept a court appointment. Almost before having time to enjoy greater artistic freedom in Vienna, he seized his opportunity when Johann Peter Batsmen, a German violinist and impresario settled in London, proposed a concert tour in England. Arriving in January 1781, Haydn stayed eighteen months. His compositions, some of the most ambitious of which were written specially for performance in London, were warmly applauded, he was himself treated with great respect, and his financial rewards were considerable. Not surprisingly, he undertook the arduous journey to England for a second time in 1794.

Haydn's visits marked an important stage in the modernization of musical life in England, which had tended to stagnate since the death of George Frideric Handel. They also triggered highly significant developments in the compositional style of Haydn, though he was already in his sixties. Before even setting out, he had begun to rethink his symphonic practice. It was not just a matter of writing something to impress the London public; he seized too the opportunity of experimenting with larger orchestral forces and more extended musical forms. While in England, Haydn had become familiar with the works of Handel, which had particularly impressed him at the 1791 Handel Festival, and on returning to Austria he was to achieve great successes with large-scale oratorios.

The first of these was *The Creation*. On leaving England for the last time in August 1795, Haydn had been presented by the impressario Johann Peter Salomon with an English libretto on the theme of the creation of the world. It was said to have been prepared originally for Handel, though there is no evidence he ever contemplated setting it to music. The drafting of the English text with its echoes of John Milton and the Bible is doubtfully credited to Thomas Linley, Richard Brinsley Sheridan's father-in-law. It was translated into German by Baron Gottfried van Swieten, and he encouraged Haydn, who did not know English well enough to cope with the original to set his version to music. The son of Maria-Theresa's personal physician and himself a force in Austrian culture, Swieten had already been pursuing a policy of encouraging the production of large vocal works for the Viennese public, commissioning Wolfgang Amadeus Mozart to revise, for instance, the orchestration of Handel's *Messiah*. Now he wished to add a new work to the repertory, and Haydn did not disappoint him. Ever since its first performance in Vienna on April 29, 1798, *The Creation* (in German *Die Schöpfung*) has maintained a favored place in the repertory.

Familiarity can cause modern audiences to overlook what a remarkable work *The Creation* is. Its origins in an English libretto may be seen as reflecting the extent to which England had become the trendsetter first in the intellectual, then in the cultural domain in the course of the eighteenth century, in the final decades of which interest in Milton was rising on the Continent. Though the Book of Genesis is plainly the foundation of *The Creation*, the oratorio is deistic in concept rather than wholeheartedly Christian. God is envisaged as the prime mover of the cosmos and the creator of the earth and all living things, but does not intervene to regulate the destinies of peoples or to procure the salvation of individuals. In the phraseology of Psalm 19, the heavens proclaim the glory of God, and man's duty, as we are reminded in later parts of the oratorio, is to return thanks to a beneficent and impersonal creator. The creed of the libretto, if not its wording, is rational, derived from the contemplation of nature without the intervention of church or clergy. Haydn became a Freemason, so he is likely to have responded to interpretations of the deity as the supreme craftsman responsible for constructing the cosmos and setting it in perpetual motion. Such ideas were, however, widespread in eighteenth-century intellectual circles; there are, moreover, plainly links between rational deism and the pantheistic attitudes of Romanticism, which found God, if not so much in astronomy, then in nature more generally.

The image of man in *The Creation* belongs largely to the optimistic Enlightenment. Man is seen at the end of the part 2 of the oratorio as the last and greatest work of creation, standing "in native worth, and honour clad, with beauty courage, strength adorn'd." Woman is hailed too, but less enthusiastically: her happiness will consist only of following her husband. Joy in pristine creation and pure nature is diminished to pastoral contentment that is in turn darkened by the long shadow of Eve's sin. The conclusion, if by no means tragic, is less triumphant than the endings of part 1 or part 2; humanity is the problem, as well as the summit, of creation.

To set all this to music, Haydn employs agile soloists in the roles first of archangels, then of Adam and Eve, a chorus that raises its voice in praise, and an orchestra with a range of instruments unusual at the end of the eighteenth century that is used to evoke events and situations as they occur. There was ample precedent for such sound painting, particularly in pastoral scenes on the one hand and in the depiction of battles on the other. Haydn, however, goes to unusual lengths with musical scene painting, thus participating in late-eighteenth-century debates on relationships among the various arts. The evocation of birdsong was already a cliché of baroque opera, and the vivid orchestral effects that accompany the creation of various animals—"the tawny lion," "the flexible tiger," and "the nimble stag"— appear so naive as to invite a smile. There is, however, nothing unsophisticated about the startling construction of the "Representation of Chaos" or the highly impressive and imaginative interpretation of the music of the spheres at the start of "In Splendour Bright." This is in effect the inauguration of the Romantic tone poem, with instrumental music conveying as precise a meaning and as exact a description as any text, whether spoken or sung.

CHRISTOPHER SMITH

Bibliography

Robbins Landon, Howard Chandler *Haydn: The Years of "The Creation" (1796–1800)*. London: Thames and Hudson, 1977.

"The Creation" and "The Seasons": The Complete Authentic Sources for the Word-Books. Foreword by Howard Chandler Robbins Landon. Cardiff: University College of Cardiff Press, 1985.

Temperley, Nicholas. *Haydn: The Creation*. London: Cambridge University Press, 1991.

CRÈVECOEUR, J. HECTOR ST. JOHN (MICHEL-GUILLAUME-JEAN) DE
1735–1813

French-American writer

Appearing at a time when European interest in North America was especially keen, J. Hector St. John de Crèvecoeur's seminal work, *Letters from an American Farmer* (1782), was published in London to great acclaim, securing the literary reputation of its author and enshrining the Romantic myth of the "great American asylum," and the agrarian idyll inhabited by "this new man," the American. Although initially treated as autobiography, *Letters* is a fictional work made up of twelve epistles from one Farmer James to an educated English correspondent, each letter describing the various customs and manners of colonial America. The felicitous condition of the industrious farmer, the whaling community of Nantucket, Martha's Vineyard, and the decadent lives of Charlestown planters are all discussed in the course of the correspondence. The final letter, "Distresses of a frontier-man," sees Farmer James expressing his dismay at the prospect of revolution and announcing his decision to shelter himself and his family in an Indian village.

A dedicated naturalist, with an eye to the seemingly insignificant minutiae of the natural world (hornets, bees, and humming-birds are all topics of discussion), Farmer James can be seen as a prototype for Henry David Thoreau's narrative persona in *Walden* (1854). His depiction of the "noble savage" and the "uncontaminated" Indian community offering "a refuge from the desolation of war" anticipates the Romantic fiction of James Fenimore Cooper. However, unlike the peripatetic heroes of nineteenth-century Romance, Crèvecoeur's Farmer James glorifies domesticity and extols a settled way of life. The issue of identity is also central to the text: the opening letter is preoccupied with the construction of authorial identity, while letter 3, famously titled "What is an American?" discourses upon the emergence of a national identity. "Description of Charles-town," in bleak contrast, exposes the inhumane repression of black identity in the Southern colonies, while the final letter charts the subjective collapse of an almost hysterical Farmer James.

Focusing on the opening letters, critics have until recently viewed *Letters* as a Utopian vision of rural America, though even George Washington was forced to concede that Crèvecoeur's America was in places "embellished with rather too flattering circumstances." D. H. Lawrence was less circumspect in his appraisal of the author whom he termed America's "emotional" prototype: observing that "Hazlitt, Godwin, Shelley, Coleridge, the English romanticists, were, of course, thrilled by the *Letters From an American Farmer*"; he immediately dismissed Crèvecoeur's "stuff about nature and the noble savage and the innocence of toil" as pure "Blarney!" More recently, critics have argued that the sinister images of the later letter (the caged and mutilated slave, the warring snakes, James's own fears of marauding rebels) deliberately undermine the farmer's early Utopianism and instead reveal an irresolvable tension between the American dream of agrarian independence and the living nightmare of actual experience.

Crèvecoeur's *Sketches of Eighteenth-Century America* was first published in 1925, following the discovery of unpublished manuscripts in Caen. "The American Belisarius," "The English and the French Before the Revolution," and the six short plays called "Landscapes" betray Crèvecoeur's loyalist sympathies, presenting portraits of self-seeking patriots who expose the violent impulses and latent depravity unleashed by the American Revolution. Sketches such as "A Snow-Storm as it Affects the American Farmer" and "The Man of Sorrows" explore the American's relationship with landscape and with a stormy and volatile nature, exhibiting a visual quality and interest in the picturesque that would later become associated with works such as Washington Irving's *The Sketch Book of Geoffrey Crayon, Gent* (1819–20).

Crèvecoeur was advised by friends to undertake a French translation of *Letters*, and *Lettres d'un cultivateur américain* was published in Paris in 1784. *Lettres* was more than a simple translation: it was twice the length of the original *Letters*, a sprawling compilation of autobiographical sketches, newspaper clippings, and public documents. It had also undergone an ideological transformation, for Crèvecoeur had erased the pro-British sentiments of *Letters* and proclaimed instead the abuses of imperialism and the benefits of American independence. While *Letters* had been dedicated to Abbé Guillaume-Thomas de Raynal (and many of Farmer James's Enlightenment ideals can be traced to the Frenchman's influential *Histoire philosophique et politique* [1770]), *Lettres* was dedicated to the Marquis de Lafayette, the general who had helped to secure American victory in the War of Independence. So incendiary was *Lettres* perceived to be, such a paean to political and religious freedom, that Crèvecoeur experienced great difficulties procuring a license for his work in the tense political climate of prerevolutionary France. Transformed from a persecuted loyalist into a champion of the revolutionary cause, he had shrewdly assessed the audience for his book, and once more successfully made himself over as a new man.

Published in Paris in 1801, Crèvecoeur's *Voyage dans la Haute Pennsylvanie et dans l'état de New-York* (*Travels in Upper Pennsylvania and New York*) attracted little notice in Napoleonic France, a beleaguered nation which had lost faith in republican values and preferred the Romantic primitivism of François-Auguste-René de Chateaubriand's *Atala*, published in the same year and featuring a mythical America peopled by noble savages. A lengthy analysis of American society and manners, Crèvecoeur's *Voyage* moves toward a more complex and less generic representation of Native American identity, as it follows the travels of S.J.D.C. (Saint-Jean de Crèvecoeur, the "translator" of this autobiographical work) through the northern states of the United States, recording "the awe-inspiring majesty" of the American landscape while acknowledging the harsh realities of American life.

As the French gentleman who refashioned himself as an "American Farmer," and the dedicated consul to New York who initiated the first regular packet service between France and the United States, Crèvecoeur worked hard to foster deeper cultural and commercial relationships between the two nations. A salesman in his youth, Crèvecoeur the writer sold the New World to the Old, an epitome of the transnational, cross-cultural interplay that was so integral to the Romantic era.

SARAH F. WOOD

Biography

Born Michel-Guillaume-Jean de Crèvecoeur in Caen, France, January 31, 1735. Son of Guillaume-Augustin Jean de Crèvecoeur and Marie-Anne-Therese Blouet, substantial landowners from the Nornandy nobility. Educated at the Jesuit Collège Royal de Bourbon, c. 1746–50; moved to England and continued studies in Salisbury, until 1754; probably also visited Lisbon. Sailed to Canada, 1755; served in French forces as cartographer and surveyor during French and Indian War; fought in battle at Fort George, 1757; achieved rank of second lieutenant, 1755–59. Wounded and hospitalized after the English siege of Quebec; resigned commission and moved to New York, 1759. Under the name of J. Hector St. John, traveled extensively through British North America as explorer, surveyor, and Indian trader; naturalized as citizen of colony of New York, 1765. Married Mehitable Tippet (d. 1781), 1769: they had one daughter, two sons. Purchased land in Orange County, New York; named the settlement Pine Hill. Farmed and wrote sketches and essays,

1769–78. Remained neutral when hostilities with Great Britain broke out, resulting in fines and imprisonment, 1776; applied for permission to go to France with his son to establish his children's inheritance, 1778; imprisoned for three months as suspected spy in British-occupied New York, 1779. Sailed to Dublin, 1780; traveled to England, sold manuscripts to publishers Davies and Davis, and returned to France, 1781. Lived in Normandy; associated with French intellectual circles. Published *Letters from an American Farmer*, 1782. Appointed French consul to New York, 1782; arrived in New York to find his farm destroyed, his wife dead, and his two younger children missing, 1783. Reunited with children in Boston, 1784. Lived in New York, 1783–85: established packet-boat service between America and France to facilitate trade, initiated scientific and cultural exchanges, and was instrumental in founding of botanical gardens, medical school, and first Roman Catholic Church in New York. Returned to France on leave, 1785–87: cofounded the Société Gallo-Americaine; published botanical treatise on the American acacia; elected to Royal Agricultural Society, Paris, 1786. Resumed consular duties in New York, 1787–90; elected to American Philosophical Society, 1789; corresponded with George Washington and James Madison. Published on agricultural and botanical matters under pen-name "Agricola." Returned again to France 1790; retired from public life, living in obscurity in Normandy and Paris during French Revolution. Elected to Institut Français, 1796. Lived with family in Munich, 1806–09. Fled to Paris at Austrian invasion of Bavaria. Died in Sarcelles, France, November 12, 1813.

Selected Works

Letters From an American Farmer. 1782.
More Letters From the American Farmer: An Edition of the Essays in English Left Unpublished by Crèvecoeur. Edited by Dennis D. Moore. 1995. Athens, Georgia: University of Georgia Press
Letters From an American Farmer and Sketches of Eighteenth-Century America. With an introduction by Albert E. Stone. Harmondsworth: Penguin, 1981.

Voyage dans la Haute Pennsylvanie et dans l'état de New-York. 1801. Translated as *Journey into Northern Pennsylvania and the State of New York* by Clarissa S. Bostelmann. Ann Arbor: University of Michigan Press, 1964.
Lettres d'un cultivateur américain. Paris: Cuchet, 1784; extended edition, 1787.

Bibliography

Allen, Gay Wilson, and Roger Asselineau. *St. John de Crèvecoeur: The Life of an American Farmer*. New York: Viking, 1987.
Goddu, Teresa A. *Gothic America: Narrative, History, and Nation*. New York: Columbia University Press, 1997.
Grabo, Norman S. "Crèvecoeur's American: Beginning the World Anew," *William and Mary Quarterly* 48, no. 2 (1991): 159–72.
Huysseune, Michel. "Virtuous Citizens and Noble Savages of the New World: The Contamination, Juxtaposition and (Mis)Representation of Cultural Models in Enlightenment France." In *Images of America: Through the European Looking Glass*. Edited by William L. Chew. Brussels: Free University Brussels University Press, 1997.
Lawrence, D. H. *Studies in Classic American Literature*. London: Secker, 1924.
Philbrick, Thomas. *St. John de Crèvecoeur*. New York: Twayne, 1970.
Plumstead, A. W. "Hector St. John de Crèvecoeur." In *American Literature, 1764–1789: The Revolutionary Years*. Edited by Everett Emerson. Madison: University of Wisconsin Press, 1977.
Rice, Grantland S. "Crèvecoeur and the Politics of Authorship in Republican America," *Early American Literature* 28, no. 2 (1993): 91–119.
Robinson, David M. "Community and Utopia in Crèvecoeur's *Sketches*," *American Literature* 62, no. 1 (1990): 17–31.
Rucker, Mary E. "Crèvecoeur's *Letters* and Enlightenment Doctrine," *Early American Literature* 13 (1978): 193–212.
Saar, Doreen Alvarez. "The Revolutionary Origins of Thoreau's Thought: An Examination of Thoreau in Light of Crèvecoeur's *Letters From an American Farmer*," *Mid-Hudson Language Studies* 7 (1984): 29–38.
Stone, Albert E. "Crèvecoeur's *Letters* and the Beginnings of an American Literature," *Emory University Quarterly* 18 (1962): 197–213.

CRIME AND PUNISHMENT

As the eighteenth century progressed, levels of crime appeared to rise, so that criminality was increasingly perceived as a threat to social stability in America, Britain, and continental Europe. A significant development in dealing with crime occurred during the Romantic era. By the middle of the nineteenth century, the consensus of opinion had settled on prison as the preferred solution.

The apparent increase in crime has been explained by the social effects of industrialization and urbanization. That the majority of criminal offenses were minor property thefts is unsurprising given the close proximity of the rich and poor in the growing cities of Europe and America. The problem of crime has often been related to poverty, and especially the displacement of large groups of people due to changing working and living patterns. In prerevolution France, for instance, there was much fear of roving bands of rural vagrants and vagabonds. In this context, the development of the prison can be linked to other

institutions aimed at the poor, including the work-house, the poor-house, hospitals, and asylums.

Before prisons were established as the proper site of punishment, criminals were subjected to public displays of humiliation and pain. Minor crimes were often dealt with by whippings and floggings, with the death sentence reserved for more serious offences. A public hanging provided a widely attended spectacle. Whether such events deterred potential criminals, or merely provided a dramatic and morally dubious form of entertainment, remains debatable. It is certain, though, that as time went on, public execution was increasingly thought of as distasteful, and doubts were raised as to its effectiveness as a deterrent. The gradual disappearance of this practice has been widely credited to changing sensibilities within this period.

The search for a new approach to crime was a shared one involving many European countries as well as America. An early influential figure for the British and European criminal systems was John Howard. *The State of the Prisons* (1777) recounted his travels across Britain and Europe, where he observed different types of prisons and systems of punishment. Howard held up the Dutch system as a model for its emphasis on productive work and the provision of a clean and ordered environment. These features would play an important role in the development of penal studies debate. An important contributor to the debate on the Continent was the Italian Ceasare Beccaria, who published *On Crimes and Punishment* (1764). Reformers such as Howard and Beccaria have been seen as epitomizing the Enlightenment approach toward crime and punishment. This current of thought suggested that criminal legislation should be coherently and systematically established, with structured definitions of crime and appropriate punishments. Punishment would consist of prison itself, rather than bodily pain, and the length of sentences could be altered to reflect the seriousness of the offense (punishment to fit the crime). The prison would serve a dual role: punishment for wrongdoing and rehabilitation enabling the prisoner to rejoin society on release. In theory at least, a comprehensive judicial and penalogical structure offered a humane and effective solution to crime.

The European movement became particularly interested in the American approach. The French government sent Gustave de Beaumont and Alexis de Toqueville to report on the American prison system, resulting in the publication of *On the Penitentiary System in the United States and its Application in France* (1833). Here, the writers observed that a country supposedly based on an ideal of personal liberty also displayed the world's most advanced prison system, the primary purpose of which was to deprive individuals of their freedom. Two methods had been tried and tested in America: the separate system and the congregate system. The separate system grew out of America's religious tradition, which regarded crime as a product of individual sin, as well as reflecting the innate sinfulness of humanity. In 1776, Jonas Hanway had published *Solitude in Imprisonment*, in which he argued that the isolated prisoner would undergo internal spiritual struggle resulting in religious conversion. It was first tried out in the Quaker State of Pennsylvania. Here, at the prison house at Walnut Street Gaol, Philadelphia, prisoners were to be kept in solitary cells all the time, their solitude occasionally punctuated by visits from spiritual advisors. In 1842, when Charles Dickens saw the separate system at Philadelphia in practice, the devastating effects of prolonged solitary confinement upon the inmates appalled him. The alternative congregate system was developed in Auburn Prison, New York. Here, the prisoners slept in separate cells at night, but during the day would be occupied with work in a communal area with other prisoners. They were expected to work in silence to avoid "contamination." The greater emphasis on work was controversial. While it helped to alleviate the costs of an extensive penal structure, it was seen as threatening the livelihoods of legitimate workers. Despite this, the congregate system became popular in northern states and proved influential in many parts of Europe.

The movement for prison reform may have proclaimed its humanitarian credentials, but recent critiques have highlighted some of the more disturbing aspects of their work. Jeremy Bentham's utilitarian ideals and design of the panopticon have been held up by Michel Foucault as epitomizing the sinister consequences of Enlightenment rationalism. Bentham proposed that the prisoner should be convinced of the "myth of perpetual surveillance," with control of the prisoner's body and mind taken to its logical extreme. Another persistent feature of penalogical debate since the early nineteenth century has been the prison's apparent failure. The initial aim of the prison was to rehabilitate the offender, with the ultimate goal of virtually eliminating crime from society. In this respect, early enthusiasm for the prison reveals a utopian vision of society in which crime, and the consequent need for punishment, no longer exist. Accordingly, the prison's continual presence would seem to be testament to the failure of the early ideals of penalogical thought. This apparent failure was recognized as early as the 1820s, yet in the decades that followed, no alternative presented itself.

SUZANNAH CAMM and ROBERT WARD

Bibliography

Dickens, Charles. *"American Notes" and "Pictures from Italy."* Oxford: Oxford University Press, 1957.

Foucault, Michel. *Discipline and Punish: The Birth of the Prison.* Translated by Alan Sheridan. Harmondsworth: Penguin, 1991.

Garland, David. *Punishment and Modern Society: A Study in Social Theory.* Oxford: Clarendon Press, 1990.

Gatrell, V. A. C. *The Hanging Tree: Execution and the English People 1770–1868.* Oxford: Oxford University Press, 1996.

Hirsch, Adam J. *The Rise of the Penitentiary: Prisons and Punishment in Early America.* New Haven, Conn.: Yale University Press, 1992.

McLynn, Frank. *Crime and Punishment in Eighteenth-Century England.* London: Routledge, 1989.

Melossi, Dario, and Massimo Pavarini. *The Prison and the Factory: Origins of the Penitentiary System.* Translated by Glynis Cousin. London: Macmillan, 1981.

Morris, Norval, and David J. Rothman, ed. *The Oxford History of the Prison: The Practice of Punishment in Western Society.* New York: Oxford University Press, 1998.

CRITIQUE OF JUDGMENT 1790

Philosophical treatise by Immanuel Kant

Immanuel Kant considered the *Critique of Judgment*, the third work in a philosophical trilogy, to be a treatise on the principles structuring judgments in general. Having delineated reason in its pure and practical senses in the first two Critiques, *Critique of Pure Reason* (1781) and *Critique of Practical Reason* (1788), Kant felt it necessary to outline what made the application of reason possible: the power to judge (*Urteilskraft*). Therefore, the *Critique of Judgment* was to be the bridge between the other critiques.

Kant broke judgment down into two distinct forms: determinant and reflective. Determinant judgment was the application of an existing concept to a particular. Reflective judgment was the judgment of a particular for which no concept existed. As a result, judgment circled back upon itself, and was thus held back from completion. The *Critique of Judgment* is concerned with exploring reflective judgment in two intriguingly problematic domains: aesthetic and teleological judgment. Most discussions of the *Critique of Judgment*—especially those having anything to do with aesthetic or artistic issues—make virtually no mention of what amounts to half of Kant's treatise. However, it should be noted that Kant considered both forms of judgment equally vexing and thus necessitating consideration. In the second half of *Critique of Judgment*, Kant wanted to demonstrate that judgments about the purposiveness of nature were necessary but heuristic attempts to ascribe a teleology to nature. This ascription of teleology, which was derived necessarily from an idea of reason and not from a concept that could be in accord with nature, is what made these judgments reflective. Therefore, the discussion of the teleology of nature was to serve as a counterpart to the discussion of art, for the former dealt with reflective judgment in a supposedly objective realm while the latter dealt with reflective judgment in a supposedly subjective realm.

The section of the *Critique of Judgment* that was to have a greater cultural impact dealt with questions of aesthetics. According to Kant, before the artwork, the imagination synthesizes sense data into a coherent image for which the understanding can provide no concept. What fuels the search for a concept is the apparent purposiveness of the work of art that nonetheless serves no purpose. As a result, understanding is put into a state of free play with the imagination. It is in this state of free play that the mind is to become aware of its own constitutive role in the act of judgment, and thus the production of knowledge. Because a concept is lacking to be applied in the instance of art, the mind comes to realize that in determinant judgment, it does not achieve a correspondence with an external reality; rather, it generates the concept to which the thing has to submit. What is disclosed in art thereby is the power and freedom of the mind.

However, Kant's claims about the function of aesthetic judgment extend much further, for he argues that aesthetic judgment, far from being individual and idiosyncratic, is profoundly universal in nature. In order to make this claim, Kant argues that the pleasure in art is necessarily a disinterested pleasure, oriented only towards the formal purposiveness of the artwork. The disinterested nature of aesthetic judgment allows it to make a universal claim for validity, for it appeals not to specific aspects of the artwork, but to a sense held in common (*sensus communis*). In this way the formal properties of the artwork are be isotropically linked to the form-generating properties of the mind. In the appeal to a sensus communis, moreover, awareness of the mind's legislative function in constituting perceived reality is linked to an awareness of the universally-shared nature of this legislative function. The judgment employed in art can thereby serve as preparatory guide to ethics, in that aesthetic judgment is but the purely formal version of self-application of ethical norms that is to take place in the exercise of practical reason.

Kant's *Critique of Judgment* is arguably one of the foundational texts of the aesthetics of Romanticism. It had both an overt and a subterranean impact on Romanticism. However, precise determinations of intellectual causation are difficult with Kant, in that at each stage his thought inspired heated debate and reformulation, all of which acquired a life of their own. Overtly, Kant's thought was carefully considered and addressed by writers such as Novalis, Johann Christoph Friedrich von Schiller, and Friedrich von Schlegel. In more oblique ways, writers such as Samuel Taylor Coleridge absorbed Kantian thought and served to disseminate it further, so that one could plausibly argue, for example, that there is a Kantian dimension to William Wordsworth's poetry.

It is no exaggeration to claim that Kant not only founded aesthetic modernism, but also enabled Romanticism to establish an aesthetic paradigm that continued on through the twentieth century. Kant brought the philosophical weight that was necessary to dismantle the centuries-old ideal of mimesis in European culture. The Copernican revolution that Kant sought to bring about in philosophy was something that he also catalyzed in aesthetic thought. Kant excluded consideration of the "thing in itself" from epistemology, and excluded slavish fidelity to an external object from aesthetics. No longer was mimetic accuracy an aesthetic ideal; rather, art was to connect to the generative, world-making activity of the mind. This shift had enormous implications for art.

Henceforth art was not to display virtuosity in a rule-bound medium. Since the understanding was to have no concept to apply to the work of art, it was essential that it not correspond to any known instance of art. In other words, the work of art had to be truly original, and not be characterized by the application of artistic rules. It ideally did not fit any existing concept of art. Art was now to be created by a genius *ab ovo*. The only rule was to avoid rules and any existing, accepted forms of art. Such notions are now seen to be commonplaces of Romanticism, and can indeed be found articulated in programmatic texts such as the preface to Coleridge and Wordsworth's *Lyrical Ballads* (1798). However, it is in the context of the *Critique of Judgment* that such notions of artistic autonomy and originality acquire their full philosophical import. Accordingly, Romanticism can be seen as a repudiation of a longstanding Platonic-Christian heritage that consigned art to a peripheral status at several removes from the realm of philosophical or theological truth. Instead, Romanticism presents art as part of an activity that is closer than anything else to the action the mind itself undertakes in the construction of the world as it is perceived. In this way, art is more central to human self-understanding than either philosophy or theology.

Finally, it can also be argued that Kant's work helps to make clear that Romanticism establishes an aesthetic paradigm that extends through the twentieth century, for, in its pursuit of formal purposiveness, art in the Kantian sense was to focus on the form and the mode of presentation as opposed to mimetic fidelity. This emphasis manifested itself initially in the prominent role that irony assumed in Romanticism. However, the concern with form continued to be a central concern well beyond Romanticism. Indeed, the history of art subsequent to Romanticism could be said to be the story of the liberation of form from content. There is arguably a clear trajectory from Immanuel Kant to James Joyce, Vasilii Kandinsky, and Arnold Franz Walter Schoenberg. While this increasing formalism is in a dialectical relationship with an increasing materialism in art—as is evident from Marcel Duchamp to Joseph Beuys and Damien Hirst—the counterpart to formalism is likewise dependent upon Kantian aesthetics in its prioritization of originality and conceptuality over the very idea of art. *The Critique of Judgment* is thus in many ways foundational to diverse modes of artistic production and appreciation that remain very much in effect.

STUART BARNETT

Text

Critique of Judgment. Translated by J. H. Bernard (New York: Free Press), 1986; by Werner S. Pluhar (New York: Hackett), 1987; and by J. C. Merdith (Oxford: Oxford University Press), 1997. Translated as *Critique of Power of Judgment* by Paul Guyer and Eric Matthews. Cambridge: Cambridge University Press, 2000.

Bibliography

Burnham, Douglas. *An Introduction to Kant's Critique of Judgment.* New York: Columbia University Press, 2000.
Guyer, Paul. *Kant and the Claims of Taste.* Cambridge: Cambridge University Press, 1997.
Lyotard, Jean-François. *Lessons on the Analytic of the Sublime.* Translated by Elizabeth Rottenberg. Stanford, Calif.: Stanford University Press, 1994.
Makreel, Rudolf A. *Imagination and Interpretation in Kant: The Hermenuetical Import of the Critique of Judgment.* Chicago: University of Chicago Press, 1990.
Menninghaus, Winfried. *In Praise of Nonsense: Kant and Bluebeard.* Translated by Henry Pickford. Stanford, Calif.: Stanford University Press, 1999.
Zammito, John H. *The Genesis of Kant's Critique of Judgment.* Chicago: University of Chicago Press, 1992.

CROME, JOHN 1768–1821

English artist

Born in Norwich on December 22, 1768, John Crome, an innkeeper's son, grew up in limited circumstances, receiving little education. Employment as errand boy for Dr. Edward Rigby, a noted physician, gave Crome his first glimpses of a better life. Apprenticeship to a sign and coach painter offered some scope for developing talent, though deficiencies in his painting technique cast doubts on this training. Once out of his indentured servanthood, Crome resolved to make his living as an artist, drawing master, and picture dealer. Friendly rivalry with Robert Ladbrooke was one factor in this decision. Others were persuasion and support from Thomas Harvey, a local businessman and amateur painter who allowed Crome access to his art collection at Catton Hall, just north of Norwich. In his early years the untutored and, by some accounts, uncouth Crome sowed his wild oats. The Quaker banker John Gurney nonetheless took him on as drawing master for his daughters, allowing him both to teach them at Earlham Hall and to accompany family parties to the Lakes and Wales to enjoy and, of course, sketch picturesque scenes. Mainly, though, Crome spent his life in Norwich. In 1803 he was a cofounder of the Norwich School of Artists; the first provincial society of its sort, it brought together professionals and amateurs, aspiring to enhance art appreciation and mounting annual shows until the 1830s. Crome also exhibited in London at the Royal Academy of Arts intermittently in the first two decades of the nineteenth century. In 1814, during the First Restoration, he joined the throngs hurrying to Paris to view the art looted by Napoleon. Crome's death in Norwich in 1821 prompted a wave of undiscriminating enthusiasm for his work.

Establishing a reliable catalog of Crome's work—oil paintings, watercolors, sketches, and some etchings—has been difficult. Scholars have also had to contend with traditional interpretations that promoted Crome as a largely self-taught artist, responding directly to the local scene. Despite (or conceivably because of) the scantness of his formal training, he was adept at absorbing hints or suggestions from artists with whom he had contacts and from works that he saw, sometimes only in engravings. Crome's relationship with classical traditions, as developed by Thomas Gainsborough and Richard Wilson, is now seen as significant. In later years Crome also reflected something of Joseph Mallord William. Turner's awareness of the pictorial possibilities of light.

The Slate Quarry (c. 1805) responds boldly to a wild landscape. A wisp of cloud adds mystery to the rocky summit rising from a complex foreground with the land falling away; the colors are dark, with even the lightest parts a rich ochre. This is not the picturesque, but wild nature. But for all its quality, this canvas, probably reflecting Crome's visits to the Lake District, is, except for the lack of emphasis on quarrying activities, not typical. Nor are *Paris: Italian Boulevard* or *Fish Market at Boulogne* (1814) related to his visit to France, or the two paintings from 1807–8 and 1810–14 called *Yarmouth Jetty*. Journeys, even if only to the seaside twenty miles away, apparently prompted unusually elaborate pictures, filled with people going about their business. Crome is, in both senses, more at home in Norwich and nearby. The early *Carrow Abbey* (1805), with towering outlines stark against stormy skies, is unusually dramatic. Generally the mood is calmer, serene even, and tinged with nostalgia. Crome rarely paints broad vistas in the grand tradition that was to be continued among Norwich painters, and especially by his gifted pupil George Vincent (for example, *Distant View of Pevensey*). Instead, in Norfolk's relatively uneventful scenery Crome will pick out a single feature, as in *The Poringland Oak*, and confer significance by isolating it in timeless space. Only occasionally, as in *The Beaters*, do rural sports add a dimension, and Crome does not assay much by way of figure drawing. Though Hannah Gurney records how at Ambleside, Crome and his charges sketched a "beautiful waterfall," in Norfolk he was content with placid rivers, though he responded to a Romantic theme in *Moonrise on the Yare*, where stillness is emphasized by the motionless windmill and the sails of craft becalmed in the distance. The buildings in his pictures are for the most part attractively ramshackle (for example, in the watercolor *The Blacksmith's Shop, Hingham*. Crome's nostalgia is evident too in his depiction of Norwich and the Wensum.

In the second half of the eighteenth century, the city witnessed a strong intellectual and artistic revival. It was particularly linked to the professional middle classes with Huguenot connections in the Colegate district near Crome's home. But apparently

Crome did not notice Thomas Ivory's Octagon Chapel of 1754–56, or John Soane's Blackfriars Bridge of 1783–84, just as he likely ignored developments in industry and transport. Instead, he captured what was passing away. The *New Mills*, which he repeatedly painted (1814–17), date from Elizabethan times; they were not dark or satanic. Though the river craft in Crome's pictures are generally all identified as "wherrie," most were in fact old-fashioned square-sailed "keels." He neglected the pictorial possibilities of the first steamers on the river and the fashionable water frolics that caught Joseph Stannard's eye.

A final phase of Crome's development is represented in a number of paintings, of which the best is the picture from about 1819 known as *Norwich River: Afternoon*. The low angle of the golden radiance from the setting sun, in fact, suggests a rather later time of day, and a major feature is the handling of light, not so much dramatically as lyrically in the creation of mood. Confident now in the handling of more complex groups of buildings with characteristic Norwich gables, Crome frames them with a delicate filigree of leaves and conveys scale with four rather sketchy figures in a boat. Pervading all is a great air of calm, as in a privileged moment when time stands still, subsuming the essential realism of yet another nostalgic scene into a regional idyll.

CHRISTOPHER SMITH

Biography

Born December 22, 1768, son of an innkeeper. First employed as errand boy by Dr. Edward Rigby, then apprenticed to a sign and coach painter. About 1786, set up as drawing master and art dealer in Norwich; befriended by local businessman, Thomas Harvey, of Catton, near Norwich. Around 1790, met Sir William Beechey, from whom he learned about painting. Around 1793, married, had large family. Founding member of the Norwich Society of Artists, 1803. Traveled to Wales on sketching tour with Robert Ladbrooke, 1804; about this time also traveled to Lake District as drawing master of daughters of John Gurney. First exhibited at Royal Academy, London, 1806, showing another fourteen works in the next twelve years. To Paris in 1814. Died April 22, 1821 in Norwich.

Bibliography

Brown, David Blayney, Andrew Hemingway, and Anne Lyles. *Romantic Landscape: The Norwich School of Painters*. London: Tate Gallery, 2000.

Clifford, Derek, and Timothy Clifford. *John Crome*. London: Faber and Faber, 1968.

Goldberg, Norman L. *John Crome the Elder*. 2 vols. Oxford: Phaidon, 1978.

Hemingway, Andrew. *The Norwich School of Painters, 1803–1833*. Oxford: Phaidon, 1979.

John Crome, 1768–1821. Bicentenary exh. cat., with introduction by Francis W. Hawcroft. London: Arts Council, 1968.

Mottram, R. H. Ralph Hale *John Crome of Norwich*. London: John Lane, 1931.

Walpole, Josephine. *Art and Artists of the Norwich School*. Woodbridge: Antique Collectors' Club, 1997.

CRUIKSHANK, GEORGE 1792–1878

English artist, caricaturist, and illustrator

George Cruikshank was born in London on September 27, 1792, the younger son of Scottish caricaturist Isaac Cruikshank and Mary McNaughton. His earliest drawings date from 1799, and by the age of eleven George was contributing to his father's engravings; by twelve he was commissioned to sketch a series of designs for children's lottery prints. Briefly a set painter at the Drury Lane Theatre, Cruikshank abandoned his early ambitions to act and settled into engraving.

He illustrated the monthly magazines the *Scourge* (1811–16), which featured Cruikshank's many caricatures of the "Royal Circle," with its secret wives and mistresses; as well as *Town Talk* (1812–13); the *Meteor* (1813–14); and the *Humourist* (1819). In 1815, Cruikshank began a fruitful collaboration with radical publisher and bookseller William Hone. During his years with Hone, Cruikshank gained a reputation as a political satirist in the tradition of James Gillray, whose drawing table he bought when the elder artist died, insane, in 1815. Like Gillray, his designs were dynamic, overflowing with active figures and intense movement, and featuring witty, intelligent verbal captions; and like Gillray, Cruikshank displayed no single allegiance; following the orders of those who commissioned his works, he criticized conservatives, royalists, radicals, and French Republicans alike. He picked up with Napoleon Bonaparte where Gillray left off, caricaturing the French emperor as "Little Boney," a dwarfish man in oversized hat and boots. His satires of the royal family, particularly the Prince of Wales (later George IV), were legendary; many, including his satirical reflections on Queen Caroline's trial (an attempt by her husband to find proof of infidelity and grounds for divorce), including *Non Mi Ricordo* and *The Queen's Matrimonial Ladder* (1820), cemented his standing as a preeminent caricaturist. Despite accepting a royal "donation" in 1820 "in consideration of a pledge not to caricature His Majesty in any immoral situation," Cruikshank continued to find ingenious, often subversive, ways to lampoon the king. Cruikshank also delighted in satirizing fashionable men and women, lampooned in his series *Monstrosities* (1816–29). His designs were popular instances of social and political observation: in the case of the *Bank Restriction Note* (1818), inspired by the sight of men and women hanged for forging one-pound notes, the sketch, circulated through parliament, contributed, Cruikshank believed, to the abolition of hanging for forging currency.

In 1820 Cruikshank, his brother Richard (also an artist), and writer Pierce Egan produced *Life in London*, a series designed to warn young men of the dangers of "seeing life" (drinking, profligacy, and prostitution), featuring three autobiographical characters: Corinthian Tom (George), his country cousin Jerry Hawthorn (Robert), and Bob Logic (Egan). While in his youth, Cruikshank was intemperate, impulsive, and adventurous; but his reputation as such was, for the most part, a romanticized exaggeration drawn largely from his connection with *Life in London*. While the text was intended as a moral lesson against profligate living, the public preferred to imitate Tom, Jerry, and Bob; groups of young men, led astray by their heroes, flooded into London streets drinking, brawling, and, in the manner of the naughty trio, tormenting "Charleys," the parish watchmen, by knocking over their sentry boxes and trapping them inside. Despite (or perhaps because of) these imitators, *Life in London* became incredibly popular, spawning souvenirs, a "Corinthian" fashion, songs, and a stage play.

After single-sheet satires declined in popularity in the 1820s, Cruikshank changed his medium (to the wood engravings he had begun experimenting with in the previous decade), and moved into the burgeoning market of book and magazine illustration. Many of these illustrations were thinly veiled political and social satires. He illustrated more than 860 books, among them Jakob and Wilhelm Grimm's *Fairy Tales* (1823), Roscoe's *Novelist's Library* (1831–33), Sir Walter Scott's *Waverley* novels (1835–45), and his long-time friend Charles Dickens's *Sketches by Boz* (1836–37) and *Oliver Twist* (1839). Cruikshank and Dickens shared a love of theater and an interest in the popular but controversial practice of mesmerism. Cruikshank, writing in 1872, claimed Dickens had "borrowed" from him the idea for *Oliver Twist*; he also argued that his sketches of prisoners in Newgate (a notorious London prison, where the condemned were held before being publicly hanged) and young London pickpockets inspired the characters of Fagin and the Artful Dodger. In these illustrations, particularly those for the brothers Grimm's *Fairy Tales*, Cruikshank transformed the fashionable taste for Gothic monsters and ghosts into a collection of anthropomorphic furniture, happy hobgoblins, and cheeky fairies and pixies.

In 1826 Cruikshank became his own publisher, producing works including *Phrenological Illustration; Illustrations of Time* (1827), *Scraps and Sketches* (1828–32), and the enormously popular *Comic Almanack* (1835–52), an annual publication with an etched plate for each month of the year and a number of smaller woodcuts. By the 1830s, politics had long ceased to be Cruikshank's cause; he was an established member of the literary and artistic community. By the 1840s, however, he had found another cause; one which radically changed his lifestyle. In his early years a drinker (although never to the excess of his father), Cruikshank later became a teetotaler, and produced for the temperance movement a series of eight plates titled *The Bottle* (1847), sketches warning against the dangers of gin drinking and the effect on the drinker's family and friends. The series was a great success, running to several editions, and spawned a stage play. He also painted a large oil work, *The Worship of Bacchus* (1860–62), an epic collection of figures whose lives are ruined by drink. Cruikshank's literary forays were not so successful. In 1853, Cruikshank's *Fairy Library* became a thinly veiled

temperance tract: drinkers were punished with poverty, abstinence rewarded with the destruction of ogres. In 1854 *George Cruikshank's Magazine*, featuring Cruikshank's sermons against tobacco, ran to only two issues.

Cruikshank's zealotry cost him work and friendships. Dickens tired of his behavior after Cruikshank had tried to snatch the drink from the lips of one too many dinner guests. A victim of his own bad economic sense, the changing tastes of Victorian audiences, and the financial demands of his cause, Cruikshank ended his career in relative poverty. He died in London on February 1, 1878.

MICHELLE CALLANDER

Biography

Born in London, September 27, 1792. Son of Isaac Cruikshank, Scottish caricaturist and illustrator, and Mary McNaughton. Started contributing drawings to his father's engraving collections by 1803. Contributed illustrations to periodicals the *Scourge*, 1811–16; *Town Talk*, 1812–13; the *Meteor*, 1813–14; and the *Humourist*, 1819. Began collaborating with publisher and bookseller William Hone, 1815. Worked with brother Richard Cruikshank and writer Pierce Egan on *Life in London*, 1820. Published *Comic Almanack*, 1835–52. Illustrated Charles Dickens's *Sketches by "Boz,"* 1836–37, and *Oliver Twist*, 1838. Enrolled to study painting at the Royal Academy Schools, 1856. Active in the temperance movement later in life, resulting in conflict with friends, notably Charles Dickens. Suffered financial hardship in later years: received financial support from John Ruskin and others and a Turner annuity from the Royal Academy. Died in London, February 1, 1878.

Bibliography

Bryan, M. *Dictionary of Painters and Engravers*. New ed. 2 vols. 1886.

Cochrane, R. *The Treasury of Modern Biography*. 1873.

Dabundo, Laura, ed. *Encyclopaedia of Romanticism: Culture in Britain, 1780s–1830s*. New York: Garland, 1992.

Knight, C. *The English Encyclopaedia*. 7 vols. 1856.

McCalman, Iain, ed. *The Oxford Companion to Romanticism and the Age of Revolution*. Oxford: Oxford University Press, 1999.

Men of the Time. Biographical Sketches . . . Also . . . of . . . Women of the Time. 1856.

Newman, Gerald, ed. *Britain in the Hanoverian Age, 1714–1837*. London and New York: Garland, 1997.

Otley, H. *A Biographical and Critical Dictionary of Painters and Engravers*. 1866.

Redgrave, S. *A Dictionary of Artists of the English School*. 1878.

Sanders, L. C. *Celebrities of the Century . . . Men and Women of the Nineteenth Century*. 2 vols. 1887.

Wood, Marcus. *Radical Satire and Print Culture, 1790–1822*. Oxford: Clarendon Press, 1994.

Wynn Jones, Michael. *George Cruikshank: His Life and London*. London: Macmillan, 1978.

CUOCO, VINCENZO 1770–1823

Italian historian and politician

The contribution of Vincenzo Cuoco to the renovation of early-nineteenth-century political thought is bound, on the one hand, to his reflections on the concept of "nation" and, on the other, to the central position he acknowledged to the moral and educational function of state organizations.

Cuoco did not limit himself to uphold his theses in theory, but he directly applied them by making use of all literary genres, from essays (*Saggio storico sulla rivoluzione di Napoli* [*Historical Essay on the Revolution of Naples,*] 3 vols., 1800 and *Osservazioni sul Dipartimento dell'Agogna* [*Observations on the Agogna Département,* 1802]) to letters (*Frammenti di Lettere a Vincenzio Russo* [*Fragments of Letters to Vincenzio Russo,* 1801]), to articles (published in the *Redattore cisalpino* and in the *Monitore Italiano*) to reports (*Rapporto al Re G. Murat e Progetto per l'Ordinamento della Pubblica Istruzione nel Regno di Napoli* [*Report to King G. Murat and Project for the Organization of State Education in the Kingdom of Naples,* 1809]) and to novels (*Platone in Italia,* [*Plato in Italy*], 1804–6).

Moreover, by asserting the need to educate more segments of society and by taking on this task as an intellectual, Cuoco paved the way for the vatic figure of the artist typical of Romanticism. It is emblematic from this point of view that he always placed his work as a journalist next to his essays and literary work; periodicals were, in fact, the privileged means for late eighteenth- and early nineteenth-century intellectuals who wanted to take part in contemporary debates.

His career began at the end of the 1780s, with his collaboration with the *Descrizione Geografica e Politica delle Sicilie* (*Geographic and Political Description of Sicily,* 1787) by Giuseppe Maria Galanti, who had already published his *Saggio sopra la Storia dei Primi Abitatori d'Italia* (*Essay on the History of the First Inhabitants of Italy,* 1783), which was inspired by Giambattista Vico's *De Antiquissima Italorum Sapientia* (*On the Ancient Wisdom of the Italians,* 1710). This was how Cuoco became acquainted for the first time with Vico's concept of "primacy," according to which the ancient Italians had already developed the main principles of philosophy, arts, and sciences before the Greek and Roman invasions, and therefore had a cultural tradition which justified their requests for independence.

Nevertheless, Cuoco did not take an active part in the revolution which led to the first Neapolitan Republic in 1799, even if subsequent involvement (writing influential reports) helped to delay the return of the Bourbons. Cuoco was not in fact against revolutions as such ("The revolution of Naples might just have been able to bring about the independence of Italy" he was to write two years later in his *Saggio*), but he realized that, given the way this revolution was carried out, it could not be successful. It fitted in with Napoleon Bonaparte's strategy of "sister republics"—that is, in the creation of French-type republics in Italy. But the people of Naples did not have the same problems as the French, neither were they prepared to accept and sustain ideas too different from their own. The Neapolitan revolution, as Cuoco defined it, was a "passive" revolution, so it could have succeeded only if it had been able to obtain public support.

These reflections about revolution, and about its correspondence to people's history and needs, enabled Cuoco to deepen the concept of nation. Unlike those revolutionaries who identified the nation with the more active part of the population (as Francesco Maria Pagano did in his *Rapporto premesso alla Costituzione* [*Report Introducing the Constitution,* 1799] of the Neapolitan Republic), Cuoco referred to the whole population. In fact, he identified the reason why the revolution failed as its attempt to act against the will of the majority in order to fulfill the wishes of the radically progressive minority. The secret of revolutions, according to Cuoco, is just "knowing what the whole nation wants and doing it."

The concept of nation is also at the root of the other works he wrote during his exile in Milan. After the Bourbons' return in June 1800, he was banished from Naples, and settled in the capital city of the Cisalpine Republic where, besides publishing the *Saggio*, he actively took part in the political debate by writing for the revolutionary magazine *Redattore cisalpino* (*Cisalpine Editor,* 1801–3). From 1804 on he edited the *Giornale Italiano* (*Italian Journal,* 1804–6), in which he ascribed to Napoleon the merit of reconciling order and freedom in a France fallen prey to anarchy. During this period he was also working on the *Statistica della Repubblica Italiana* (*Statistics of the Italian Republic,* 1802–3) on behalf of the Vice-President Melzi d'Eril, and publishing the *Osservazioni sul Dipartimento dell'Agogna* and the epistolary novel *Platone in Italia.*

In this last work, inspired by the successful *Voyage du jeune Anacharsis en Grèce* (*Travels of Young Anacharsis in Greece,* 1788) by Jean-Jacques Barthélemy, Cuoco advanced the excuse of Plato's imaginary travel through the Magna Graecia in order to unify and make more pleasant (according to the poetics of *utile dulci*: the useful with the agreeable) his different political and philosophical reflections. Therefore, in the letters by Plato and by his interlocutor Cleoboulos (openly an alter ego of the author himself), Cuoco reasserted that the Italians were a nation more civilized and learned than the Greeks and the Romans, and that they were the founders "of almost every knowledge which adorns the human mind."

This evocation of a primitive Italic golden age did not only aim at awakening the national pride required for shaping the self-consciousness of the Italian citizens to be, but also at offering them a new model for a war of independence.

Cuoco did not want the Italians to look to the French model again for revolutionary guidance. He preferred to create an Italian model by recasting the war between Romans and Samnites as a war between Italian populations, engaged in defending the independence of the peninsula, and the Roman invaders, who provoked the decadence of the ancient Italian civilization.

Faced with the danger of new invasions and with the threat of a new decadence, Cuoco stated the need for the independence and unification of Italy, referring to Niccolò Machiavelli's theories and anticipating both the neo-Ghibelline (a political movement that aimed to unify and confederate Italy under the Pope's authority) and the Mazzinian (republican) ideals of nation which were to inspire Italian Romanticism.

The concern for the education of people as citizens is also at the heart of the last important work by Cuoco, the *Rapporto al re G. Murat* (1809), written after his return to Naples, reconquered by Napoleon in 1806.

According to the Enlightenment view of the perfectibility of man and of his right to be educated, Cuoco based his project on three principles: universality (arts and sciences should not be distinct, but one had to serve the other), openness (primary education had to be free and it had to be open to women as well), and uniformity (all schools had to follow the same plans).

PAOLO RAMBELLI

Biography

Born in Civitacampomarano, Campobasso, Italy, October 1, 1770. Moved to Naples, where he contacted Giuseppe Maria Galanti, whom he helped to complete the *Descrizione Geografica e Politica delle Due Sicilie*, 1787. Took on a marginal role in the revolution, but thwarted the pro-Bourbon conspiracy promoted by Gennaro and Gerardo Baccher, 1799. Once Bourbons seized power again, he was banished from Naples for twenty years, and all his possessions were confiscated, 1800. Moved to Milan, where he wrote for the *Redattore cisalpino* and published anonymously the *Saggio storico sulla rivoluzione napoletana del 1799* and the *Frammenti di lettere a Vincenzio Russo*, 1801. Published under the name of Lizzoli the *Osservazioni su Dipartimento dell'Agogna*, 1802. Edited the *Giornale italiano* and published the *Platone in Italia*, 1804–6. Returned to Naples, where he edited the *Corriere di Napoli*, 1806–11; drew up the *Rapporto al re G. Murat e Progetto per l'ordinamento della pubblica istruzione nel regno di Napoli*, on behalf of the government, 1809; edited the *Monitore delle Due Sicilie*, 1811–15. His mental conditions worsened to the point of insanity, 1815. Died as a consequence of a fall, December 14, 1823.

Selected Works

Saggio Storico sulla Rivoluzione Napoletana del 1799, followed in the appendix by the *Frammenti di Lettere a Vincenzio Russo*. 1801.

Osservazioni sul Dipartimento dell'Agogna. 1802.
Platone in Italia. 1804–6.
Rapporto al Re G. Murat e Progetto per l'Ordinamento della Pubblica Istruzione nel Regno di Napoli. 1809.

Bibliography

Acton, Harold. *The Bourbons of Naples, 1734–1825*. London: Methuen, 1956.
Battaglia, Felice. *L'Opera di Vincenzo Cuoco e la Formazione della Coscienza Nazionale in Italia*. Florence: Giunti, Bemporad, Marzocco, 1972.
Cariddi, Walter. *Il Pensiero Politico di Vincenzo Cuoco*. Lecce: Milella, 1981.
Croce, Bendetto. *Studi sulla Rivoluzione Napoletana del 1799*. Rome: E. Loescher, 1897.
Francesco, Antonino de. *Vincenzo Cuoco: una Vita Politica*. Rome: Laterza, 1997.
Gentile, Giovanni. *Vincenzo Cuoco*. Rome: C. De Alberti, 1924.
———. *Vincenzo Cuoco: Studi e Appunti*. Venice: La Nuova Italia, 1927.
Johnston, R. M. *The Napoleonic Empire in Southern Italy*. London: MacMillan, 1904.
Merola, Alberto. "Saggio Storico sulla Rivoluzione Napoletana del 1799." In *Letteratura Italiana—Le Opere*. Vol. 3. Edited by Alberto Asor Rosa. Turin: Einaudi, 1995.
Palmieri, Giorgio, ed. *Contributo alla Bibliografia Cuochiana*. Campobasso: Enne, 2000.
Romano, Michele. *Ricerche su Vincenzo Cuoco Politico, Storiografo, Romanziere, Giornalista*. Isernia: Colitti, 1904.
Ruggieri, Nicola. *Vincenzo Cuoco*. Rocca San Casciano: Cappelli, 1903.
Stefano, Lino di. *Vincenzo Cuoco e la Rivoluzione del '99*. Rome: Serarcangeli, 1998.
Tessitore, Fulvio. *Vincenzo Cuoco tra Illuminismo e Storicismo*. Naples: Morano, 1971.
Tessitore, Fulvio. "Vincenzo Cuoco e le Origini del Liberalismo 'Moderato'." In *Storia della Società Italiana—L'Italia giacobina e napoleonica*. Vol. 13. Milan: Teti, 1985.

CUVIER, GEORGES 1769–1832

French scientist

Georges Cuvier dominated European, and especially French, zoology in the Romantic era. Interested in natural history from childhood, Cuvier was one of the many intelligent young men who took advantage of the social and intellectual opportunities available in Revolution-era Paris, as leading scientists were put to death or exiled, and centralized scientific institutions, such as the Academic Royale des Sciences, were abolished. Modeling his lecture style on the acting of his contemporary, the tragedian François-Joseph Talma, and making extensive use of visual aids, Cuvier was a popular lecturer at both the Museum of Natural History and the College of France. He was also adept at comparative anatomy and animal classification. Although he grew up in the French-speaking town of Montbeliard, Cuvier was born a subject of the Duke of Wurttemberg, and retained strong connections to the Germanic world throughout his career.

Throughout the duration of the consulate and the empire, Cuvier produced dozens of papers, as well as several multivolume studies. He was named Inspector General of the Imperial University, which required extensive travel throughout Europe. In Paris, he amassed the most complete collection of animal specimens in Europe (Cuvier carried out all of his work on dead specimens, rather than living creatures). He thought of an animal as a functioning whole; each part is subordinated to the needs of the whole, thus ensuring maximum systemic functioning. Essentially, the physical structure of an animal is determined by its function. Cuvier was an admirer of Aristotle's work on biology, and adopted his teleological view of zoology. Cuvier's functionalism led him to deny the possibility of a species changing or evolving; he argued that any significant variation would destroy the ability of the animal to function. Cuvier's functionalism (unlike that of the British natural theologians who were his contemporaries) was not connected to an argument from design or any other religious context, but the natural theologians eagerly seized on his work, adapting it for their own needs. So strong was Cuvier's belief in the subordination of the part to the whole, and the functional nature of the animal body, that he boasted (incorrectly) that he could deduce the entire structure of an animal from one bone.

Cuvier's study of fossils, collected in the four-volume *Recherches sur les ossemens fossiles de quadrupedes* (*Researches on the Fossil Bones of Quadrupeds*, 1812), founded the discipline of paleontology. His research led him to accept the concept of extinction, and also to integrate the fossil record with the geological history of the earth. The *Discours préliminaire* (*Preliminary Discourse*) section of the study, frequently reprinted separately, set forth the influential theory of "catastrophism." According to catastrophism, catastrophes in the earth's past, affecting large portions of its surface, account for the extinction of many species. Although the Flood of Noah was recognized as the last of these catastrophes, Cuvier, always wary of mixing science and religion, did not present his theory to support religion. Although Cuvier himself was not a Romantic, his portrayal of an earth millions of years old, and his history of the rise and fall of its numerous species, did appeal to some Romantics. Honoré de Balzac, an admirer and intellectual supporter of Cuvier's scientific rival Étienne

From Georges Cuvier, *Le regne animal distribue d'apres son organisation*, vol. 4, plate 131. Reprinted courtesy of AKG.

Geoffroy Saint-Hilaire, referred to Cuvier as "the greatest poet of the nineteenth century." Cuvier's other great work was the five-volume *La Regne Animal* (*Animal Kingdom*, 1817). This set forth a new classification scheme, dominant through most of the nineteenth century, that divided animals into four large groups, or *embranchements*, based on the differing structures of their nervous systems. The groups were the vertebrates, marked by a spinal cord; the mollusks, marked by separate neural centers; a group of *articulata*, or jointed creatures with a nervous system consisting of two ventral cords (including insects, spiders, and crustaceans); and the *radiata*, a group consisting of animals with rudimentary nervous systems or none at all, and defined by radial organization, such as starfish. The gaps between these four groups were, for Cuvier, near absolute. He strongly opposed a number of ideas that could link them, including the theory of the chain of being (which arranged all animals and other natural entities in a single hierarchy), Geoffroy Saint-Hilaire's view of all animals as variations on a single master plan, and Jean Baptiste Lamarck's evolutionary scheme to derive one species from another. Cuvier's antievolutionary argument that the fossil record shows no evidence of transitional forms from one species to another continues to be used by creationists.

Cuvier's experiences in the French Revolution had made him a strong supporter of the principle of authority, which transcended his allegiance to any particular regime. He had no difficulty adjusting to the Restoration of the Bourbons, and served the government as a liaison to the French Protestant community, of which he was a member. As a Protestant and believer in administrative efficiency, he had no sympathy with the reactionary Catholics who dominated the reign of Charles X, but he was willing to work with them if the alternative was social chaos. His administrative and political tasks led him to almost completely give up teaching from about 1814, but he continued to be an active scientist, publishing eight volumes on the natural history of fish. Cuvier acquired a somewhat undeserved reputation as a reactionary, and was seen by his contemporaries, both within and beyond the scientific community, as a scientist obsessed with garnering patronage, who would force all of accepted science to reflect his theories. He gained a significant victory for his views in a famous debate between himself and Geoffroy Saint-Hilaire at the Academy of Sciences in 1830, in which Cuvier successfully defended his four-part scheme of natural history against Geoffroy Saint-Hilaire's unitary model. Outside the scientific community, however, Cuvier was continually ridiculed as a tyrant and pedant. He adapted to the Revolution of 1830 as easily as he had to the Bourbon Restoration, and was made a peer of France in 1831, an extremely rare honor for a Protestant.

WILLIAM BURNS

Biography

Born Georges Léopold Chrêtien Frédéric Dagobert Cuvier in Montbéliard, Wurttemberg (later France), August 23, 1769. Attended Académie Caroline (Karlsschule), Stuttgart, 1784–88. Tutor at Académie Caroline, 1788–95. Became French citizen on annexation of Montbéliard, 1793. Secretary to the Commune of Bec-aux-Cachois, 1793–95. Joined staff of Museum of Natural History, Paris, 1795. Collaborated with zoologist Étienne Geoffroy Saint-Hilaire, 1795. Appointed assistant professor of animal anatomy at the Institut de France, 1796. Declined to travel as naturalist on Napoleon Bonaparte's Egyptian expedition, 1798–1801. Professor at the Collège de France, 1800; imperial inspector of public instruction, 1802–3; permanent secretary of the physical sciences at the Institut de France (later the Acadèmie des Sciences), 1803. Married Anne-Marie Duvaucel (d. 1849), 1804; they had four children. University councillor, 1808; chevalier, Légion d'honneur, 1811. Councillor of state, 1813; vice-president, Ministry of the Interior, 1817. Published *La Regne Animal*, 1817. Member of the Académie française, 1819; created baron Cuvier, 1820. Grand Officier, Légion d'honneur, 1824. Director of non-Catholic religious affairs, 1827; peer of France, 1831. Died in Paris, May 13, 1832.

Selected Works

Lecons d'anatomie comparee de G. Cuvier. 1805. Translated as *Lectures on Comparative Anatomy* by William Ross. 2 vols. 1802.
Le Regne Animal distribue d'apres son organisation, pour servir de base a l'histoire naturelle des animaux ed d'introduction a l'anatomie comparee. 4 vols. 1817. Translated and expanded as *The Animal Kingdom Arranged in Conformity with its Organisation by the Baron Cuvier* by Edward Griffith. 15 vols. 1827–1834.
Recherches sur les ossemens fossiles de quadrupedes, ou l'on retablit le caracteres de plusieurs especes des animaux que les revolutions du globe paroissent avoir destruites. 4 vols. 1812. Partially translated as *Researches into Fossil Osteology*, 1826.

Bibliography

Appel, Toby A. *The Cuvier-Geoffroy Debate: French Biology in the Decades before Darwin*. New York: Oxford University Press, 1987.
Coleman, William. *Georges Cuvier, Zoologist: A Study in the History of Evolution*. Cambridge, Mass.: Harvard University Press, 1964.
Gould, Stephen J. "The Stinkstones of Oeningen." In *Hen's Teeth and Horse's Toes: Further Reflections in Natural History*. New York: W. W. Norton, 1984.
Outram, Dorinda. *Georges Cuvier: Vocation, Science and Authority in Post-Revolutionary France*. Manchester: Manchester University Press, 1984.
Smith, Jean Chandler. *Georges Cuvier: An Annotated Bibliography of His Published Works*. Washington and London: Smithsonian Institution Press, 1993.

CZECH AND SLOVAK ROMANTICISM

Czech Literature

The reigns of Maria Theresa (1740–80) and her son Joseph II (1780–90) are traditionally taken to mark the beginning of a new era in Czech literature, though the continuities with the preceding age are much greater than usually admitted, especially in popular reading matter and religious publications. The end (or rather, beginning of the end) of the period that began with the Counterreformation in Central Europe and now generally known in the arts as "the baroque," is signaled by a series of radical state initiatives, including the institution under the Empress Maria Theresa of universal primary schools in her Ordinance of 1774. Joseph II's decrees enlarging peasant liberties and permitting Protestant worship followed in 1781.

One symptom of the modern era, crucially linked with wider general literacy, was an increasingly dominant tendency to attempt to equate language community with political nation. German was taught everywhere, and required for entering secondary schooling and universities (where it had only recently begun to replace Latin), but the primary schools also brought about general basic literacy in Czech; for the policy also encouraged the use of local vernaculars for lower popular education. Thus, central policy simultaneously both Germanized and vernacularized.

At first, much of the innovative literary activity toward the end of the eighteenth century was aimed at catching up with, and emulating, recent German and foreign models, whether in drama, poetry, fiction, or historical and linguistic scholarship. At this point, the Bohemian upper classes did not habitually speak Czech among themselves or write in the language; they were generally more comfortable with German, while cultivating French in the salon.

Elements in writing that would eventually fall under the label *Romantic*, especially in terms of imaginative vision, heightened subjectivity, the nonconventional depiction of natural landscape, and overturning of literary rules and conventions, appear later. Even then individual writers (most notably Karel Hynek Mácha) constitute isolated examples within a Czech-language movement that espoused values of community and patriotic solidarity, enjoyed some modest aristocratic support, was usually politically cautious, and only inclined to reject the malcontent and the socially alarming radical or openly revolutionary spirit.

The Czech patriotic writers' sentimental focus upon native history and native folk traditions, with the concomitant espousing of certain Rousseauist and ruralist ideals of "natural man," bring a partial shift away from classical texts and models; but such attitudes may perhaps be more acceptably labeled, as they often are, *pre-Romantic*. At the same time, however, touches of Sturm und Drang, imaginative nostalgia for the glories and sufferings of the past, graveyard sentiments and atmosphere of horror and the like, when they occur, can bring one much closer to subjective Romanticism, even though much of this type of writing equally has its roots in the religious baroque. (And again, the baroque heritage is much in evidence in the works of later authors, such as Mácha and Erben.)

Czech authors of the revival period and later decades of the nineteenth century both adopted the inherited literary standard and gradually evolved a new educated language by elaborately creating further intellectual, poetic, and technical vocabulary required to compete with other more powerful and esteemed literatures such as French, English, and now, their archcompetitor, German. German language and literature had itself entered a period of intellectual and literary resurgence only a few decades before. Czech literature, however, though practiced by enthusiasts, busily writing and translating and earnestly attempting to emulate middle-class German culture, nevertheless took a few decades to produce a poet or novelist of clearly European stature.

The influence of German culture was considerable. According to the contemporary historian F. M. Pelcl, "ladies who previously knew only French literature, now read Gellert, Hagedorn, Rabener, Gleim, Gessner, Kleist and others . . . In gardens, on walks and even on public streets one could meet [young people] with Wieland or Klopstock in their hands. Thus amongst the Czechs not only German language, but also German taste and German literature, spread more and more."

This period is more secular in literary outlook than before, and there is a growing rationalist reaction against the earlier devotional Roman Catholic literature, leading to an active dislike of the baroque mentality, and rejection of its literary output, style, and language. Enlightenment scholars now condemned uncritical baroque historiography, and sought to acquire a more empirical view of Czech history (but themselves were affected by mythopoeic patriotism and in due course by Romantic nationalism).

In his pioneering history of Czech literature, *Geschichte der böhmischen Sprache und Literatur* (1792), the grammarian and historical linguist Josef Dobrovský (1753–1829) saw the time of Veleslavín before 1620 as the high point in Czech literary culture, and he was skeptical about the future for Czech, due to the compulsory use of German in secondary and higher education. In verse he rejected classical quantitative meters (which some earlier poets had attempted), and recommended improving on traditional syllabic versification by adopting the stress-based meters that became the nineteenth-century norm.

A vitalizing new ingredient in Czech cultural life was the arrival of the permanent stage theater in Prague. From 1738 there was the Theatre V. Kotcích, and from 1783 the large Estates Theater (Stavovské divadlo), but most performances were in German (and opera in Italian). The Estates Theater in Prague opened in 1783 with a play by Gotthold Ephraim Lessing, and the premiere of *Don Giovanni* took place in the same theater four years later.

A Czech translation (in light verse) of a German farce was performed in 1771. A more extensive series of Czech productions began in 1785, and in 1786 a wooden theater called the Bouda (Hut) was erected on present-day Wenceslas Square which put on regular Czech performances for three years, until it was demolished. Most of the plays were successful pieces from Vienna by authors now long forgotten, but there were also versions of Johann Christoph Friedrich von Schiller's *Die Räuber* (The Robbers), and William Shakespeare's *Macbeth*.

The tale of horror was also a significant source for later Romantic writing (see Mácha below). Prokop Šedivý, a writer of local Prague farce, later owner of a traveling peepshow, produced texts of horror stories with the typical titles *Krásná Olivie aneb Strašidlo v Bílé věži* (*Lovely Olivia, or the Ghost in the White Tower*) and *Zazděná slečna* (*The Walled-Up Maiden*), while another lesser-known writer, Václav Rodomil Kramerius, produced the story "Železná košile" ("The Iron Shirt," 1831), which shares the same literary model as Edgar Allan Poe's "The Pit and the Pendulum."

An anthology entitled *Básně v řeči vázané* (*Poems in Metrical Verse*, 1785), edited by another theater man, Václav Thám, is generally regarded as marking the beginning of modern Czech verse. It offered some secular adaptations of the baroque religious poet Kadlinský, as well as specimens of light Anacreontic verse.

Somewhat more substantial are the anthologies edited by the priest Antonín Jaroslav Puchmajer (1769–1820, also author of a rhyming dictionary, a Russian grammar, and even a Romany grammar). There were five volumes of his anthology, entitled *Sebrání básní a zpěvů* (*Collection of Poems and Songs*, 1795, 1797), and *Nové básně* (*New Poems*, 1798, 1802, 1814). Its authors now used stressed meters, as recommended by Dobrovský. Among the verse types included are the neoclassical ode, fable, and mock-heroic narrative; the writing shows some Polish influence. More attractive perhaps today than Puchmajer's "Ode to Jan Žižka" or "Ode to the Czech Language" are his animal fables, which follow an old Czech tradition, but also localize Jean La Fontaine via the influence of Polish texts.

The next phase is associated above all with the name of Josef Jungmann (1773–1847). Born near Beroun, he studied in Prague, then became a grammar school teacher in Litoměřice, and moved to the Old Town Gymnasium in Prague in 1815. His literary achievements are above all as a translator, exercising and expanding the expressive powers of Czech.

Apart from smaller English and German works—Alexander Pope and Gray's "Elegy in a Country Churchyard" (in iambics), Johann Wolfgang von Goethe and Schiller, Herder, Bürger, Klopstock—and also Russian, he is particularly remembered for his translations of the Frenchman François-August-René de Chateaubriand's Romantic prose work *Atala* (1805) and John Milton's *Paradise Lost* (translation 1811), the latter a translation of impressive monumentality (helped by German and Polish versions). Later, he also translated Goethe's middle-class idyll *Herrmann und Dorothea* (translation 1841). Jungmann's original poems are few, but include two of the first Czech sonnets.

In order to achieve the stylistic range of vocabulary he desired, for poetic effect, and in order to expand the lexical resources of Czech, Jungmann revived archaic words, created neologisms, and borrowed from Russian and Polish. He also compiled a large anthology of Czech writing for school use, which provided a presentation of literary theory (*Slovesnost*, 1820), and, above all, a huge and fundamental five-volume Czech–German dictionary (*Slovník česko-německý*, 1834–39), still consulted to this day.

In the works of Jungmann's circle, the Enlightenment neoclassicist outlook blends with elements of Romanticism (for example, contemplation of nature, cultivation of a folkloric idiom); the term pre-Romantic is often applied to this era. One of the most notable poets of this circle was Milota Zdirad Polák, an army officer, famous in his day for his long nature poem *Vznešenost přírody* (*The Sublimeness of Nature*, 1813, revised 1819).

Simultaneously, the current vogue for ancient nonclassical literatures (influenced by works such as James Macpherson's rewritings of Ossianic ballads, etc.) led to the production of the so-called Dvůr Králové and Zelená Hora Manuscripts, named after their alleged places of discovery. The former, presenting itself as a thirteenth-century manuscript, contained a number of pseudo-ancient unrhymed narrative and lyrical verses with plenty of Slav and national flavor; the lyrical compositions in fact archaized current sentimental folk song. It was published by the librarian of the National Museum Václav Hanka in 1819, after its discovery in 1817. The second, sent to the Museum not long after, contained a version of "Libuše's Judgment over Chrudoš and Šťáhlav," purporting to be from the tenth century.

These texts helped to bolster Czech national pride and enlarged the corpus of national myths; their themes inspired a number of later authors and artists. Their bogus character was finally exposed to scholars in the 1880s, although doubts had existed much earlier (Dobrovský, for example, had rejected the Zelená Hora Manuscript from the start).

The originators of these pseudo-medieval texts are thought to be Václav Hanka himself and his friend Josef Linda, although direct proof is lacking. Hanka, as well as being respected librarian and archivist of the museum, was one of the first imitators of folksong, while Linda produced a rather Ossianic historical novel on the coming of Christianity to Bohemia, *Záře nad pohanstvem* (*Light over Pagandom*, 1818), with expressive use of landscape.

The first more widely celebrated Czech poet of the nineteenth century was a Slovak. Born in 1793, Jan Kollár studied Protestant theology in Jena, where he became enamored of the daughter of a Protestant pastor, Friderike Wilhelmine Schmidt, whom he eventually married, after a long gap in their contact, sixteen years later. Meanwhile he had become a pastor in Pest, writing a collection of sonnets, first published in 1821, in which his beloved metamorphosed into Mína, an ideal Slav maiden from territory once Slav, now German.

In an expanded edition of 1824, now entitled *Slávy dcera* (*Daughter of Slavia*), Kollár poetically elevated her to daughter of the goddess Sláva, liberator of the Slavs from past wrongs and oppression. The poet goes on a pilgrimage round the historic sights of Slavdom, with the sonnets divided into three sections, each named after a partly Germanized river: the Saale, the Elbe, and the Danube. The whole cycle is prefaced by a grand Prologue in classical-meter elegiac couplets, in which Kollár compares the lamentable present state of Slavdom with its ancient glories, and erects a vision of a future of Slav and universal human cooperation and liberty. The next edition of 1832 added new sections, Lethe and Acheron, portraying Slav figures residing in heaven and hell. By now Kollár had more or less overwhelmed the volume with didactic historicism. The best sonnets, if generally staid and four-square, still display some genuine versifying skill. Some strike notes of playful eroticism and pithy moral and national ardor, and display neat, memorable diction, using antithesis, paradox, and conceit.

Kollár's fervently expressed (but for him basically unpolitical) pan-Slav national pathos was a large part of the appeal. His ideas of Slav literary and cultural mutual cooperation are expounded in his treatise "On Literary Mutuality among the Slav Peoples and Dialects" (1836), best known under its German title: "Über die literarische Wechselseitigkeit." He was also a notable collector and publisher of Slovak folk song.

Folk-song gathering and imitation were widespread activities at this time. Collection of this material began on a larger scale in the late eighteenth century, and has had an enormous influence on poetry writing ever since, initially and most notably on the Romantics, who loved to identify elements of ancient pagan customs and myths, as often as not more imaginary than real. A great deal of the folklore they collected had its immediate roots in the baroque era—though there are embedded survivals of older material. Some of the orally transmitted songs and ballads have a pithy and compact emotional simplicity and power of language inextricably enmeshed with melody.

One collector who was also a poet was František Ladislav Čelakovský (1799–1852), who collected not only Czech, but Slav folksong and folklore generally. The Czech (and wider contemporary European) cult of "natural" spontaneous poetry, of "organic" and autonomous national culture, tended to idealize a certain limited view of "uncorrupted" peasant values. The sources of such ideas are various, but include of course the French Jean-Jacques Rousseau, and Herder, whose German writings also influenced those Kollárian ideas of Slav cultural unity (whether as imaginary glorious past, present needs, or visionary future). Indeed, both the folklore and pan-Slav cults rather precisely mirror German intellectual attitudes. Čelakovský embodied such concerns in two volumes of skillful imitations or "echoes," his *Ohlas písní ruských* (*Echo of Russian Songs*, 1829) mainly narrative pieces, and *Ohlas písní českých* (*Echo of Czech Songs*, 1839) mainly lyrical pieces, but also with the opening ballad of the collection, "Toman a lesní panna" ("Toman and the Forest Maiden"), with its melancholy thwarted lover who encounters a fairy femme fatale and his nemesis, powerfully anticipating the ballads of Erben.

Simultaneously intimately involved in and transcending the general provincialism around him is the work of Karel Hynek Mácha (1810–36), regarded today as the outstanding Czech poet of this period, and one of the few openly subjective and radical Romantic writers in Czech before 1848. Born in Prague of unprosperous parents, he studied law and became briefly a lawyer's assistant in Litoměřice, where, however, he soon prematurely died, not long after his fiancée had given birth to a short-lived baby son. His first poetic attempts were in German, while still at the Gymnasium, but he switched to Czech. He was also active as an amateur actor. In the spirit of historicist sentiment and love of scenery, he enjoyed visiting old castles full of the gloomy pathos of the past, and he traveled widely on foot, to destinations such as the Krkonoše mountains, or across the Alps to northern Italy. His sexual passion for the daughter of a Prague bookbinder, Eleonora (Lori) Šomková, is poetically transformed in that high Romantic interfusing of life and art into an agony of awareness of the gulf between the ideal and the actual.

His prose writings draw on elements of the historical novel, as exemplifed by the work of Walter Scott (for example, "Křivoklad," depicting the figures of Wenceslas IV and his executioner companion), the Gothic novel and lyrical speculative prose ("Pout' krkonošská" ["Pilgrimage to the Krkonoše Mountains"]), typically Romantic tales of outsiders, and the love tale with a contemporary setting ("Marinka"). He is also influenced by his readings of Polish poetry (for instance, Mickiewicz).

Mácha's various rebels, outsiders, and outcasts are typical Romantic self-images; but at his best, most obviously in his verse masterpiece, *Máj* (*May*, 1836), Mácha eludes easy literary-critical definitions and philosophizing summaries. In this poem, Mácha combines grotesquely exploited Gothic-Romantic (baroque-derived) clichés of prison, execution, gallows, skulls, robbers, dying lovers, and graveyards, with musical, ostensibly idyllic evocations of nature—in which he ambivalently employs further lyrical clichés of the cycle of seasons: doves, roses, nightingales, and the like.

In the story (exiguously sketched out in the poem), Vilém is imprisoned and executed for killing his own father, unrecognized—his father, seducer of his own beloved. (Is this fatal destiny or classical-mythicized Oedipal psychology? Mácha was later adopted by the Surrealists as one of their outstanding predecessors.) Man is envisioned as prisoner of enigmatic nature and time, subject to metaphysical agony and agnosticism. Seasonal, cyclical nature, the sensory may be received as pure sensory beauty, but also as beautiful illusion, and harsh mockery of human desire and ideals. The text plays with illusive (and elusive) sensual effects, ironic contrasting of nature and man, mind and matter, speculative lyrical meditations, and partly submerged eroticism. It expertly exploits lyrically (yet simultaneously deconstructs) the pathetic fallacy of empathy in nature. Possible sentimental or "Victorian" misapprehensions of his conceptions of "love," cosmic and human, are disrupted by inspection of his sexually explicit diary.

The patriotic community of Czech writers was, at the very least, uneasy as to whether this was the sort of poetry required by the nation to further its aspirations. The dramatist and novelist Josef Kajetán Tyl, author of the Czech national anthem, caricatured Mácha in his *Rozervanec* (*The Malcontent*, 1840). The contemporary humorist František Jaromír Rubeš likewise pokes fun at a Mácha-like figure in his vaguely Pickwickian travel story *Pan amanuensis na venku aneb Putování za novelou* (*Mr. Amanuensis in the Country, or In Search of a Novella*, 1842).

By the brink of that "Year of Revolutions," 1848, Czech revival literature had passed through a series of overlapping phases, all of which would continue to make themselves felt in the following decades: sensibility and rationalism, popular moralizing narratives, Gothic horror, folklorism and national historicism, nature-lyricism, and subjective Romanticism. There were also stirrings of a more sociological or descriptive concern with contemporary life in fiction, which one can at least partly assign under the category of nineteenth-century realism.

At least two authors from the 1850s should, nevertheless, be mentioned here. The most significant poet of the 1850s was Karel Jaromír Erben (1811–70), who was employed as archivist of the city of Prague. He was an outstanding collector of folk songs and tales, seeking for survivals of ancient pagan myth and wisdom in the spirit of the German brothers Jakob and Wilhelm Grimm, and he was also an important editor of older Czech literature. His poetic masterpiece was a slender collection of literary ballads *Kytice z pověstí národních* (*Bouquet of National Legends*, 1853; enlarged 1861). The core of the book is formed by twelve ballads (with a prefatory poem "Kytice"), based on various Slav legends, but also stimulated by German literary ballads, and even English ones. The earliest, "Záhořovo lože" ("Záhoř's Bed"), was begun in 1836, evidently under the influence of Mácha, especially in its early draft form, with its pilgrim figure and evocation of night landscape; but Erben polemicizes with Mácha's sensibility of revolt.

Another outstanding Czech author of the 1850s, Božena Němcová (1820–62), struck a balance between Romantic ideals and realist depictions in her harmonizing portraits of rural life. Her prose fiction may be placed alongside the ballads of Erben, especially her fairy tales and her classic idyllic novel *Babička* (*The Grandmother*). Her personal letters are also much read and admired. One might also fruitfully compare the approaches and attitudes of her fiction to the writings of the German Bohemian author Adalbert Stifter (1805–68), born in Horní Planá (Oberplan) in the Šumava region of southern Bohemia, which he depicts in some of his stories, such as *Der Waldsteig* (*The Forest Path*, 1845).

Němcová's masterpiece, the delightfully written novel *Babička* is a therapeutic metamorphosis of her childhood into an idealized, selectively realistic, poetically convincing vision of children growing up in a happy rural setting, presenting the cycle of the seasons, the lovingly and vividly enumerated minutiae of daily human life, its round of traditional observances and pious customs, in which even tragedy—disastrous flood, for example, or the seduction by an outsider, illegitimate pregnancy, and madness of the village girl Viktorka—is accommodated by human mutuality into a sense of order and harmony. The grandmother, from a poor upland district, brings her simple morality and pious wisdom to the household to help those around her, even the elevated family of the countess: a delicate advocacy of traditional simple existential values and moral egalitarianism, in which disharmony, urbanizing social change, and loss of older communal values and Christian verities are present to the reader either just beneath the surface or in their eloquently poetical near-erasure.

In this decade of political reaction, of bureaucratic neoabsolutism, and of renewed censorship, Erben and Němcová's works continued to appeal in their various ways to Romantic ideals, to man's relationship with nature, and to notions of "natural man."

Slovak Literature

In Hungary, of which modern-day Slovakia was the northern part, Hungarian elites aspired to achieve a homogeneous, Hungarian-language political nation, initially in opposition to the Habsburg ambitions to have German be the dominant elite medium, supplanting Latin. Already, by the late eighteenth century, certain authors enunciate the theme of the Slovaks as co-creators of the early Moravian state and of medieval Hungary, in which the Slovak element is seen as playing a civilizing role vis-à-vis the Magyar invaders. Views such as these feed into the historicist ideas of future Slovak nationalism.

Up to the mid-nineteenth century, Czech was generally used by Slovaks as the written form of their vernacular, with varying degrees of Slovakization. The first really systematic codification of a distinct Slovak written standard was the work of the Catholic priest Anton Bernolák (1762–1813), but it was short-lived and failed to be adopted by the Protestant Slovak writers who wrote in Czech, such as Jan Kollár.

Its outstanding author was another Catholic priest, Ján Hollý (1785–1849), who translated Virgil's *Aeneid* (1828) and then went on to produce his own verse epics in classical hexameters, on Slovak–Slav themes such as the Moravian prince Svatopluk (*Svatopluk*, 1833), or Cyril and Methodius (*Cyrilo-Metodiáda*, 1835). Hollý is venerated as the founding father of Slovak poetry, and there are strong touches of lyric freshness in his fusion of classical and Slovak idiom, especially in his Theocritan pastoral verse.

By the 1840s, however, a young energetic group of Lutherans led by Ľudovít Štúr (1815–56) became attracted by the idea of a separate Slovak literary language (to which the poet Kollár remained strongly opposed). Instead of Bernolák's Western Slovak, they forged a new standard based on Central dialects, and the modern language is based on this.

Štúr started a Slovak-language daily paper in 1845. During the 1848–49 revolution, he participated in the Slav Congress in Prague, but then took Vienna's side against the Hungarians, organizing military volunteers, in hope of winning Slovak autonomy. However, Vienna's victory inaugurated a period of centralism, and Štúr moved on toward Messianic faith in Tsarist Russia's mission to liberate.

In literature, Štúr stressed native originality, influenced by Herder, and believing that the Slavs were destined to give great poetry to human civilization. Poetry, the highest product of the human spirit, should take folksong as its starting point, not its goal; it should match spirituality with objectivity, espouse high ideals. Štúr died suddenly and prematurely, after a hunting accident in 1856, but his new standard language had begun to take root and soon found writers, especially poets, who made an immediate impact. Of these, three poets (Janko Kráľ, Andrej Sládkovič, and Ján Botto) are of undoubted eminence, and all may be seen as Romantics in various ways.

Janko Kráľ (1822–76) has become celebrated both for his poems and for his biography. In 1848, he joined a teacher friend in southern Slovakia, rousing the local villagers to overthrow the landowners. Held in Šahy and Budapest, after release he later became involved with pro-Habsburg anti-Hungarian volunteers. After the Hungarian defeat, Kráľ joined government service and virtually stopped writing. His best known poems are ballad-inspired verses, in which folk idiom combines with a central Romantic figure, divný Janko, "strange Janko," a solitary withdrawn hero, alienated from his surroundings, aspiring to soar eagle-like to freedom, but falling into suicidal melancholy.

Another, more staunchly optimistic, poet was the Protestant pastor Andrej Sládkovič (1820–72). His best work is perhaps the long poem *Marína*, written in lyrical sonnet-like ten-line stanzas, inspired by his unhappy love for a Banská Štiavnica burgher's daughter. Where for Jan Kollár (see above) erotic and patriotic love are divided, in some sense incommensurate, here they harmonize. Love for Sládkovič is not a mere intoxicating, sensual adventure of youth; it is a divine gift that enables Man to transcend his physical being, a force that enables one to contemplate and embrace truth through beauty, that joins in harmony body and mind, the physical world and the world of the spirit. All this is colored by a Hegelian vision of progress toward freedom and harmony. Sládkovič's second famous long poem *Detvan* (published in 1853) celebrates the uplanders of Detva, an area beneath Poľana, a vision of unspoilt innocent vigor.

The youngest of the three, Ján Botto (1827–76), is most remembered for his allegorical balladic poem *Smrť Jánošíkova* (*The Death of Jánošík*, 1862, revised 1870s), the most famous Slovak work on the theme of the executed robber bandit Jánošík. Throughout the text, a tension is maintained between fairy-tale–like visions (blended with messianism) and gloomy realism (almost)—a sense that ideals of freedom exist in a world apart from the world of men; there is a chasm between the mythic dream-world represented by Jánošík and the portrayal of passive Slovak peasants (or between ideals and mankind's lot).

Slovak fiction stood somewhat in the shadow of poetry. However, one might at least mention the notable writer Ján Kalinčiak (1822–71), whose masterpiece *Reštavrácia* (*Country Elections*, 1860) describes humorously, in a fictional setting, underhand goings-on during a Hungarian county election in the pre-1848 period. The overall tone is humorous, nontendentious, almost apolitical—but the lack of reverence amounts to a form of attack on the myth of the Slovak gentry as a force to be reckoned with in the national cause. Kalinčiak uses his material for humorous fiction as a vehicle for story telling and stylistic virtuosity—with sharp figure painting and flamboyant use of idiom, colorful sayings, and proverbs. The whole book may be seen as a display of verbal and narrative technique, just as much as it is a heightened portrayal of gentry types.

JAMES NAUGHTON

See also **Pan-Slavism**

Bibliography

Brock, Peter. *The Slovak National Awakening*. Toronto: University of Toronto Press, 1976.

Demetz, Peter. *Prague in Black and Gold*. London: Allen Lane, 1997.

French, A., ed. *Anthology of Czech Poetry*. Ann Arbor: Department of Slavic Languages and Literatures, University of Michigan, 1973.

Harkins, W. E., ed. *Anthology of Czech Literature*. New York: King's Crown Press, 1953.

Jakobson, Roman. "Notes on Myth in Erben's Work." In *Language in Literature*, ed. Roman Jakobson. Cambridge, Mass.: Belknap Press of Harvard University Press, 1987.

Jelínek, Hanuš, *Histoire de la Littérature Tcheque*. 3 vols. Paris: Éditions du Sagittaire, 1930–35.

Kovtun, George J. *Czech and Slovak Literature in English*. Washington, D. C.: Library of Congress, 1988.

Macura, Vladimír. "Problems and paradoxes of the national revival." In *Bohemia in History*. Edited by Mikuláš Teich. Cambridge: Cambridge University Press, 1998. 182–97.

Naughton, James. "Czech and Slovak." In *The Oxford Guide to Literature in English Translation*. Edited by Peter France. Oxford: Oxford University Press, 2000. 196–200.

———. *Traveller's Literary Companion to Eastern and Central Europe*. Brighton: In Print, 1995.

Novák, Arne. *Czech Literature* (1946). Translated by Peter Kussi. Ann Arbor, Mich.: Michigan Slavic Publications, University of Michigan, 1976.

Pynsent, Robert B. *Czech Prose and Verse: A Selection with an Introductory Essay*. London: Athlone Press, 1979.

———. "Characterisation in Mácha's *Máj*." In *Czech Studies: Literature, Language, Culture*. Edited by M. Grygar. Amsterdam: Rodopi, 1990.

Pynsent, R. B., and S. I. Kanikova, eds. *The Everyman Companion to East European Literature*. London: Dent, 1993.

Ripellino, Angelo Maria. *Magic Prague*. London: Macmillan, 1994.

Sayer, Derek. *The Coasts of Bohemia: A Czech History*. Princeton, N.J.: Princeton University Press, 1998.

Schamschula, Walter. *Geschichte der tschechischen Literatur*. Bd. 1. *Von den Anfängen bis zur Aufklärungszeit*; Bd. 2. *Von der Romantik bis zum Ersten Weltkrieg*. Cologne: Böhlau, 1990–96.

Selver, Paul, trans. *An Anthology of Czechoslovak Literature*. London: Kegan Paul, 1929.

Seton-Watson, R. W. *A History of the Czechs and Slovaks*. London: Hutchinson, 1943.

Součková, Milada. *The Czech Romantics*. The Hague: Mouton, 1958.

Wellek, René. *Essays on Czech Literature*. The Hague: Mouton, 1963.

CZERNY, CARL 1791–1857

Austrian pianist and composer

As Ludwig van Beethoven's most famous pupil, Carl Czerny played an important role in establishing the Beethovenian tradition of piano performance and composition. He was influential and prolific as a teacher, pianist, and composer, and his many theoretical writings are a rich source of information on nineteenth-century piano technique.

Czerny was the only son of Wenzel Czerny, a musician born and brought up near Prague, who had established himself as a music teacher in Vienna. He had an isolated childhood, and under his father's rigorous training was able to play most of the standard repertoire by the age of ten. In the winter of 1799–1800, young Czerny was introduced to Beethoven by a mutual friend, the violinist Wenzel Krumpholz. Beethoven immediately took him on as his pupil, and Czerny quickly became a champion of his tutor's music, both in performance and in editorial work for his publications.

A concert tour was planned in 1805 but never took place, probably because of the political situation in Europe at the time. Instead of a career as a traveling virtuoso, Czerny became very prominent as a piano teacher, and by 1815, when Beethoven became guardian to his nephew Carl, he entrusted the boy's musical education to Czerny. In 1816 Czerny began to hold Sunday concerts in his house for his pupils, at which Beethoven was often present. He continued a very heavy teaching schedule until 1836, when he stopped teaching completely, and his pupils included the young Franz Liszt (from 1821 to 1823) and many of the leading virtuosi of the day.

Though he occupied all his free time with composition, Czerny published comparatively few compositions in the earlier period of his life. In 1819 he was the first to send Anton Diabelli a variation on his waltz for the collection published by the *Vaterländischer Kunstlerverein*, the project that was to result in 1823 in Beethoven's *Diabelli Variations*; and by the time of the original collection's publication in 1824, he had added a thematically developed coda to the set. He was well aware of the ephemeral nature of his early compositions, and when in the mid-1820s Beethoven encouraged him to turn to more substantial works, he explained that he composed so quickly that he thought of his works primarily as a means of acquiring printed music by exchange with publishers.

Czerny was a torchbearer in Beethoven's funeral procession in March 1827, and helped in sorting through his *Nachlass*. In later years he was to devote an increasing amount of his time to composition, editing, and other publications. His final years were beset by illness, and on his death in 1857, with no family of his own, he left his considerable fortune to the Gesellschaft der Musikfreunde (which also houses his library and his own manuscripts) and other institutions in Vienna, which had remained his home throughout his life.

Czerny was one of the most productive musicians of the Romantic era. His published compositions reach as far as an opus 861, and there are several hundred unpublished works as well as several hundred arrangements and editions of the works of other composers and writings on music. Apart from eleven piano sonatas and twenty-eight sonatinas, a large proportion of the published compositions are pedagogical, either in the sense of being simple compositions for students or technical exercises and studies. These studies are generally études in the literal sense: their function is not to provide musical interest, but to improve manual dexterity, often in one very specific aspect, such as trills (op. 151), *legato* and *staccato* (op. 335), or thirds (op. 380). Unlike Frédéric Chopin's *Etudes*, opp. 10 and 25, they were never intended for public performance.

Czerny reserved his most prominent opus numbers for more substantial and systematic schools of piano playing. The *Systematische Anleitung zum Fantasieren auf dem Pianoforte*, op. 200, and *Die Kunst des Präludierens*, op. 300, are manuals for the improvisation of fantasias and preludes, and provide valuable information about an often forgotten aspect of music-making in the Romantic era. *Die Schule des Fugenspiels*, op. 400, deals with contrapuntal playing. The *Vollständige theoretisch-praktische Pianoforte-Schule* (*Complete Theoretical and Practical Pianoforte School*), op. 500, dedicated to Queen Victoria, with whom Czerny played duets in 1837, covers every conceivable aspect of the concert pianist's professional life; and the *Schule der praktischen Tonsetzkunst*, op. 600, is a treatise aimed at the composer.

Czerny's exercises remain widely used to this day. His more "serious" compositions (as he himself described them) include many piano sonatas, as well as piano trios, concertos, overtures, symphonies, and a large number of sacred choral pieces, many of which are unpublished and virtually none of which is heard today. Czerny was widely berated as a mere technician of the piano (notably by Robert Schumann, in several reviews in the *Neue Zeitschrift für Musik* in the 1830s), but his compositions did on occasion attract the interest of such figures as Chopin and Liszt, who dedicated his *Etudes d'exécution transcendante* to Czerny. It cannot be denied, however, that Czerny's primary importance was as an instructor in the art of piano playing in the tradition of Beethoven. Czerny arranged large numbers of Beethoven's orchestral and chamber works for piano solo, piano duet, or two pianos, thus enabling their performance off the concert platform. His editions of earlier composers' works, such as Johann Sebastian Bach's *Well-Tempered Clavier* (c. 1850), may bring us closer to Beethoven's conceptions of these works, and his published comments on Beethoven interpretation are an immensely valuable source for the study of Beethoven's own performance practice.

NICOLAS BELL

Biography

Born in Vienna, February 21, 1791. Son of Wenzel Czerny, a music teacher and piano repairer. Studied the piano with his father, 1794–1800; gave first public performance at Augarten Hall, Vienna, 1800. Studied with Beethoven, 1800–1802. Published first composition, 1805; piano teacher and composer in Vienna, 1805–36. Closely associated with and influenced by Muzio Clementi and Johann Nepomuk Hummel. Died in Vienna, July 15, 1857.

Selected Works

Systematische Anleitung zum Fantasieren auf dem Pianoforte, op. 200. 1829. Translated as *A Systematic Introduction to Improvisation on the Pianoforte* by Alice L. Mitchell. New York and London: Longman, 1983.

Die Kunst des Präludierens in 120 Beispielen, op. 300. 1833. Translated as *The Art of Preluding* by John Bishop. London: Robert Cocks & Co., c. 1840.

Die Schule des Fugenspiels und des Vortrags mehrstimmiger Sätze und deren besonderer Schwierigkeiten auf dem Piano-Forte in 24 grossen Übungen, op. 400. c. 1836. Translated as *The School of Fugue-Playing* by John Bishop. London: Robert Cocks & Co., c. 1890.

Vollständige theoretisch-praktische Pianoforte-Schule, op. 500. 1839–46. part III edited by Ulrich Mählert, 1991; chapters 2 and 3 of part IV with an introduction by Paul Badura-Skoda as *Über den richtigen Vortrag der Sämtlichen Beethoven'schen Klavierwerke*, 1963; Translated as *Complete Theoretical and Practical Piano Forte School* by J. A. Hamilton. London: Robert Cocks & Co., 1839.

Schule der praktischen Tonsetzkunst, op. 600. c. 1849–50. Translated as *School of Practical Composition* by John Bishop. London: Robert Cocks & Co., 1848 or 1849.

Bibliography

Barth, George. *The Pianist as Orator: Beethoven and the Transformation of Keyboard Style*. Ithaca, N.Y.: Cornell University Press, 1992.

MacArdale, D. W. "Beethoven and the Czernys," *The Monthly Musical Record* 88 (1958): 124–35.

Mählert, Ulrich. "Die Vortragslehre von Carl Czerny," *Musica* 44 (1990): 4–11.

Mahr, Justus. "Carl Czerny: das Genie des Fleisses," *Neue Zeitschrift für Musik* 130 (1969): 520–28.

Mandyczewski, Eusebius. *Zusatzband zur Geschichte der k.k. Gesellschaft der Musikfreunde in Wien: Sammlungen und Statuten*. Vienna: Adolf Holzhausen, 1912.

Pazdírek, Franz. *Universal-Handbuch der Musikliteratur*. Vienna: Pazdírek, 1904–10.

D

DACRE, CHARLOTTE c. 1772–1825

English novelist and poet

The novelist and poet Charlotte Dacre, born Charlotte King, associated herself with the excessive emotion of the Della Cruscan school that achieved literary notoriety at the end of the eighteenth century. Although they were later mocked for their sentimentality by the English Romantics, Dacre exploited their emphasis on emotion to produce contributions to the Gothic genre which contained highly unconventional portrayals of sexuality and race. Combining a disconcertingly radical emphasis on subjectivity and sexuality with conservative condemnation, Dacre's novels form an important contribution to the debate on social authority for which the British Gothic novel became a vehicle after the French Revolution.

After completing *Trifles of Helicon* (1798) with her sister, Dacre associated herself with the Della Cruscans by adopting the pseudonymns "Rosa" and "Rosa Matilda." Writing occasional verse for *The Morning Post* from 1802 to 1815, her choice of periodical publication reflected the growing importance of the literary newspapers and periodicals for women writers of occasional works. Dacre chose a paper that, under Nicholas Byrne's editorship, supported William Pitt and the Prince of Wales.

Reinforcing her connection to the Della Cruscans, Dacre opened her most important volume of poems, *Hours of Solitude. A Collection of Original Poems* (1805) with an engraving entitled "Rosa Matilda." She also included "To the Shade of Mary Robinson," a reference to one of the most celebrated poets of the circle who was also the scandalous "Perdita," former mistress to the Prince of Wales. Dacre's association with the Della Cruscans was similarly double-edged. Described as "stimulating love verses" (by a reviewer in the *New Annual Register*, 1806), her poetry could be criticized for Della Cruscan sentimentalism, as Lord Byron demonstrated in *English Bards and Scotch Reviewers* (1809):

Far be't from me unkindly to upbraid
The lovely Rosa's prose in masquerade,
Whose strains, the faithful echoes of her mind,
Leave wondering comprehension far behind.
Though Crusca's bards no more our journals fill,
Some stragglers skirmish round the columns still;
Last of the howling host which once was Bell's,
Matilda snivels yet, and Hafiz yells . . .

He adds, in a footnote, "This lovely little Jessica, the daughter of the noted Jew K[ing], seems to be a follower of the Della Cruscan School, and has published two volumes of very respectable absurdities in rhyme, as times go; besides many novels in the style of the first edition of *The Monk*."

In fact, while the use of horror and sensationalism in Dacre's novels indicates the influence of Matthew Lewis and the Della Cruscans, her work also contains conservative overtones which link her more closely to Ann Radcliffe. Her first novel *Confessions of the Nun of St Omer* (1805) was dedicated to Lewis and appeared under the name "Rosa Matilda," referring to the demonic Matilda of *The Monk*. The sexual passion, exuberance, and independence of the novel's youthful heroine, though condemned by the older narrator, retain some attractiveness. However, the novel's exploration of education reflected the fact that, during the post-French Revolution debate, conservative interpretations of women's education connected romance reading with illicit sexuality and, ultimately, social collapse.

Published in 1806, Dacre's most successful novel, *Zofloya; Or, the Moor: A Romance of the Fifteenth Century* also showed the influence of both Radcliffe and Lewis, and, perhaps as a result, contained an extremely unusual presentation of female sexuality. Initially placed in a Radcliffean situation of confinement, the novel's heroine commits a series of horrific crimes in her search to fulfill her desires. This connection between female sexuality and violence is complicated when Victoria's adviser and servant, Zofloya, is revealed to be the Devil. The heroine's resultant punishment indicates *Zofloya*'s conservatism; given this, the extensiveness of its portrayal of female desire is unexpected. Conservative authors often treated female sentiment and sexuality in far less detail than radical writers. Dacre's portrait of sexuality, on the other hand, led *The Annual Review* of 1806 to describe the work's contents as "an exhibition of wantonness of harlotry."

Like her presentation of sexuality, Dacre's treatment of politics also contained contradictions. Despite signaling its critique of radicalism by its deployment of the philosophical language of cause and effect, *Zofloya* provides no clear explanation of Victoria's behavior, and hence no hope of any social solution. Her crimes are not triggered by infernal temptation, and other causes (including maternal example, education, disposition, and social structure) are put forward with equally little conviction. This lack of causation gives the novel's violence the pornographic quality which led Algernon Charles Swinburne to liken it to the work of the Marquis de Sade. Significantly, this reluctance to provide social solutions makes it a forerunner to Mary Shelley's *Frankenstein* (1818), as does its examination of otherness and race. The novel certainly influenced Percy Bysshe Shelley, as his early romance *Zastrozzi* (1810) and the Gothic novella *St. Irvyne; Or the Rosicrucian* (1811) show.

Despite Dacre's confused political agenda, her work ultimately makes the common conservative connection between female desire, revolution, and social collapse. However, it persistently differs in its explicit examination of such sexuality. This can be detected in the criticisms of extravagance leveled at her third novel, *The Libertine* (1807). *The Annual Review* of 1807 argued that the novel was exaggerated enough to give "to truth the garb of fiction." The reviewer suggested that although Dacre recommends the moral benefits of accuracy, she neglects her own advice to provide a sensationalized narrative: "Libertinism . . . is the vice here traced from its polluted source through all its wild and capricious meandrings [sic]." Nonetheless, in the year of its publication the novel went through three editions.

Dacre again drew upon the post-French Revolution debate in her last novel, *The Passions* (1811). The work depicts an ideal domestic community which is revolutionary in its reliance upon affection rather than authority. Using the epistolary form associated with subjectivity and emotionalism, Dacre argues that the group is doomed by the willfulness of individual desire. Significantly, the name of one of the novel's most important female characters, Julia, refers to the heroine of Jean-Jacques Rousseau's *Julie, ou la nouvelle Héloise* (1761). Although *The Passions* contains similar ambiguities to those found elsewhere in Dacre's work, its ending, like other responses to Rousseau's novel, suggests the destructive effects of sexual desire.

FIONA PRICE

See also **Edgeworth, Maria; France: Revolution and Empire; *Frankenstein; or, the Modern Prometheus*; Gothic Fiction; Robinson, Mary; Rousseau, Jean-Jacques**

Biography

Born c. 1772, daughter of John King, also known as Jacob Rey, an infamous London Jewish moneylender, radical writer, and blackmailer; Rey divorced Dacre's mother, Deborah Lara, by Jewish law in 1785; from 1802 to 1815 Dacre wrote occasional verse for *The Morning Post*; in July 1806 she published a series of poems on contemporary political figures in the *Morning Post* known as "The Dream; Or, Living Portraits"; the father of Dacre's three children was Nicholas Byrne, the paper's editor from 1803–33; their first son was born in 1806 and named William Pitt; in 1807 and 1809 two further children, Charles and Mary, were born and all three were baptized in June 1811 at Saint Paul's, Covent Garden; Dacre married Byrne July 1, 1815 at Saint James, Westminster; she died November 7, 1825; Dacre's husband remained editor of the *Morning Post* until 1833, when he was supposedly murdered because of his opposition to the Reform Bill; however, announcements of his death suggest that he died at the age of seventy-two after a long illness.

Selected Works

Prose
Confessions of the Nun of St. Omer. A tale. Edited by Devendra P. Varma. 1972.
The Libertine. Edited by Devendra P. Varma and John Garrett. 1974.
The Passions. Edited by Devendra P. Varma and Sandra Knight-Roth. 1974.
Zofloya; or, The Moor: A Romance of the Fifteenth Century. Edited by Devendra P. Varma and G. Wilson Knight. 1974.
Zofloya or, The Moor. Edited by Kim Ian Michasiw. 1997.
Zofloya; or, The Moor: A Romance of the Fifteenth Century. Edited by Adriana Craciun. 1997.

Works in Translation
Zofloya, ou le Maure, historie du Xveme siècle, traduite de l'anglais par Mme. De Viterne. 4 vols. 1812.
Angelo, comte d'Albini, ou les Dangers du vice, par Charlotte Dacre Byrne connue sous le no, de Rosa Matilda, traduit de l-anglais par Mme. Élizabeth de B***. 3 vols. 1816.

Other
The Dæmon of Venice. An Original Romance. 1810.

Poetry
Trifles of Helicon. By C. and S. King. 1798.
George the Fourth. 1822.
Hours of Solitude: A Collection of Original Poems, Now First Published by Charlotte Dacre, Better Known as Rosa Matilda. Edited by Donald H. Reiman, 1978.

Bibliography

Craciun, Adriana. " 'I Hasten to Be Disembodied': Charlotte Dacre, the Demon Lover, and Representations of the Body," *European Romantic Review* 6, no. 1 (1995): 75–97.
Dunn, James A. "Charlotte Dacre and the Feminization of Violence," *Nineteenth-Century Literature* 53, no. 3 (1998): 307–27.
Erdman, David. "Byron's Mock Review of Rosa Matilda's Epic on the Prince Regent—A New Attribution," *Keats-Shelley Journal* 19 (1970): 101–17.
Hoeveler, Diane Long. "Charlotte Dacre's Zofloya: A Case Study in Miscegenation as Sexual and Racial Nausea," *European Romantic Review* 8, no. 2 (1997): 185–99.
Jones, Ann H., "Charlotte Dacre." In *Ideas and Innovations: Best Sellers of Jane Austen's Age.* 1986.

Miles, Robert. "Avatars of Matthew Lewis' *The Monk*: Ann Radcliffe's *The Italian* and Charlotte Dacre's *Zofloya, or The Moor*." In *Gothic Writing 1750–1820: A Genealogy*. 1993.

Peck, Walter Edwin. Appendix A, "Shelley's Indebtedness in *Zastrozzi* to Previous Romances." In *Shelley: His Life and Work*. Vol. 2. 1927.

Pollin, Burton. "Byron, Poe, and Miss Matilda," *Names* 16 (1968): 390–414.

Wilson, Lisa M. "Female Pseudonymity in the Romantic 'Age of Personality': The Career of Charlotte King/Rosa Matilda/Charlotte Dacre," *European Romantic Review* 9, no. 3 (1998): 393–420.

DADD, RICHARD 1819–1887

Born in 1817 to a family that ran a chemists shop in Chatham, Kent (southeast England), Richard Dadd was a precocious draftsman who gained a place in the Royal Academy School at the age of twenty, in 1837. His father had by then moved to London, where he changed his trade to ormolu and silver gilding. In the process, Dadd made contact with an upper-class clientele that was useful to him at the beginning of his writing career. Within the group of ambitious young artists from the academy who met regularly in London's Soho and called themselves "The Clique," Dadd distinguished himself with his artistic focus on purely imaginative subject matter; his friends (who included the latterly eminent Victorian painters Augustus Egg and William Powell Frith) preferred realist depictions of daily life or literary scenes.

Dadd was beginning to achieve some success with fanciful illustrations derived from folklore and paintings on fairy themes, when he accepted, in 1842, an invitation to travel with Sir Thomas Phillips in the eastern Mediterranean. He returned the following year with watercolor sketches, and a repertoire of exotic imagery that he could draw on later in his career. He also brought back, it seemed, the beginnings of the mental illness, probably schizophrenia or bipolar manic depression, which would eventually lead to the events that overshadow his fame as an artist. Friends were disturbed by his erratic behavior, which his father ascribed (in public, at least) to sunstroke. On one occasion, a friend found him covered in blood; Dadd had just cut out a birthmark, which he said was a mark put on him by the devil. Later in the year he proposed to his father a trip to Cobham, in Surrey, during which, Dadd said, he would explain himself and his recent behavior. As they walked through the park at night, Dadd attacked and killed his father with a razor he had purchased just before the trip.

He fled to France, but was arrested at Fontainebleau after trying to kill a fellow passenger in a coach; he was subsequently brought back to England. On August 22, 1844, he was declared mentally unfit to stand trial, and committed to Bethlehem Hospital (the later, infinitely more progressive descendent of the medieval Bedlam Hospital). He was treated humanely there and encouraged to paint as a form of therapy. Dadd was transferred in 1864 to the recently built Broadmoor Asylum (originally Broadmoor Criminal Lunatic Asylum, located in Berkshire) where his painting was further supported by the doctors supervising him. He produced much of his most interesting work as an inmate of the asylum, including extensive decorative painting, murals, and theatrical sets. Bethlehem hospital still retains and exhibits a selection of his work in its gallery. Dadd died in Broadmoor in 1886.

It is impossible to disentangle Dadd's art from his psychosis, and not simply in the unfortunate aptness of his name to his crime. His asylum paintings in particular offer constant reflections on his own psychosis, often in elaborately schematized and symbolic form. In the watercolor *The Child's Problem* (1857), for example, the head of a small boy appears over the back of the table which forms the lower foreground of the design. He stares, in terror, at an abandoned chess match, while his monstrously ugly, ambiguously sexed guardian snores behind him. On the wall behind are images of a manacled slave, with hands stretched up and out in a plea for mercy, and a cowering marble nymph. Both images of subjection echo the black and white of the chess pieces. In *The Packet Delayed* (1854), another dramatically diagonal composition, one small boy, hanging onto a fence of writhing, tightly bound branches, holds the hand of another, who lunges precariously toward a toy boat. But the boat is depicted as if an actual full-scale vessel, and the pond has been turned into a stormy sea, perhaps an effect of the boys' imagination. The delayed boat, which may not survive the storm, and its distance from the boy's grasp arc images of strain and desperation of a kind that runs through much of the asylum work (as is also visible in the series of figures in often grotesque situations: see the *Sketches to illustrate the passions*). The convention is superficially realist, but the intricately symbolic internal narratives are matched by a pictorial space without depth and normally without sky, and an almost hypnotic patterning of detail. With hindsight it is possible to read the pre-travel fairy pictures in a similar way. Henry Fuseli had established a tradition of grotesquerie and eroticism in illustrations to William Shakespeare's *A Midsummer Night's Dream*. However, Dadd's circular compositions, with suggestions of hysterical movement, and his settings of caverns that open on to nothing or darkness, seem to dramatize a sexual panic, emphasized for example by the phallic mollusk emerging from its shell in the foreground of *Come unto These Yellow Sands* (1842), unseen by the nearly naked fairies.

Dadd's masterpiece, worked on obsessively in the asylum over a long period, is *The Fairy-Feller's Master Stroke* (1855–64). The title figure, his back to the viewer and his face unseen, holds an axe raised and ready to fall on a pile of chestnuts. He is watched in this action by over thirty tiny figures (the painting measures only 21.25 by 15.5 inches) all elaborately dressed, some in Victorian, some in Elizabethan costume, some insect- or gnome-like, all individualized and busy. The fairy king and queen stand watching from a bank, and a dragon fly blows a trumpet. The "feller's" action is clearly profoundly significant, but the meaning of the blow poised to fall was known only to Dadd, as the fable was his own. But the surface of the picture is crossed by carefully rendered stems of grass, pulled aside as if by the viewer, and the bank is studded with minutely rendered daisies, moss, and nuts, to suggest scale and emphasize the claustrophobia of the fairy kingdom. To even glance at the picture is to share Dadd's hyper-aware and enigmatic gaze.

EDWARD BURNS

Biography

Born, in Chatham, Kent, England, 1817. Accepted into the Royal Academy Schools, London, 1837. Traveled with Sir Thomas Phillips around the Meditaranean as a watercolorist, 1842, returned exhibiting the first symptoms of severe paranoia. Persuaded his father to go with him to Cobham, Surrey, then murdered him with a razor, 1844. Was arrested in Fontainbleau, France, after attacking a fellow coach passenger. Found unfit to stand trial, and committed to the Bethlehem hospital (Bedlam) for the criminally insane, 1844. Moved to the new government-built psychiatric prison Broadmoor, 1864; died there in 1879.

Selected Works

Puck and the Fairies. c. 1841. Private collection.
Titania Sleeping. c. 1841. Private collection.
Come Unto These Yellow Sands. 1842. Private collection.
Portrait of a Young Man. 1853. Private collection.
The Fairy-Feller's Masterstroke. 1855–64. Tate Museum, London.
The Flight into Egypt. 1855. Leicester Gallery.
The Child's Problem. 1857. Tate Museum, London.

Bibliography

Carter, Angela. *Come unto These Yellow Sands.* Newcastle upon Tyne: Bloodaxe Books, 1985.

Frith, W. P. *My Autobiography and Reminiscences.* 3 vols. London: Richard Bentley and Son, 1887–8.

Greysmith, David. *Richard Dadd: The Rock and Castle of Seclusion.* London: Studio Vista, 1973.

Maas, Jeremy. *Victorian Painters.* London: Barrie and Rockliff, 1969.

Sitwell, Sacheverell. *Narrative Pictures.* London: Batsford, 1937.

St. Pierre, Isaure de. *L'Oeil d' Osiris* (novel). Paris: Pierre Belfond, 1980.

DAHL, JOHAN CHRISTIAN CLAUSEN 1788–1857

Norwegian Painter

Johan Christian Clausen Dahl is both the father of Norwegian painting and Norway's first internationally acclaimed painter. As a landscape painter, he is most immediately associated with depictions of the dramatic mountain landscapes of western Norway, and there was a time when these landscapes were considered typical of Norwegian landscape as a whole. While in the past Norwegians tended to be most interested in the cultural-historical significance of Dahl as the painter who first showed them what they believed was the essential nature of their country, those who looked at Dahl's work from a purely artistic and painterly point of view tended to stress the significance of his sketches and the naturalism of his best work. In recent years there seems to have been a tendency for the two approaches to come together.

Dahl's early years were spent in Bergen, a lively fishing town on the west coast of Norway, but culturally a backwater, because the country as a whole was small, poor, and under the control of Denmark. Although Dahl started his career as an apprentice to a house painter and decorative artist, it soon became clear that he had talent and ambitions for something more. In 1811 a travel grant from some of the wealthier citizens of Bergen enabled him to move to Denmark where he enrolled at The Academy of Fine Arts in Copenhagen, which was the capital and cultural center of Denmark-Norway.

Dahl was not overimpressed with the academy. The masters of an earlier generation, Jens Juel and Nicolai Abraham Abildgaard, were dead, and the academy was going through a rather mediocre phase, though Dahl became friends with, and was influenced by, Christoffer Wilhelm Eckersberg, who became professor there in 1818. Dahl attended drawing classes (the only tuition offered by the academy), but seems to have derived more benefit from his visits to the galleries. There he studied both Danish and Dutch masters, particularly Allaert von Everdingen and Jacob van Ruisdael, whose rocky landscapes with waterfalls and old trees and forests helped Dahl to find a painterly means through which to interpret the wild nature of his native Norway. In addition he did a great many studies from nature, and in fact maintained that he had been a "naturalist" even before he came to Denmark. Originally these studies were executed in graphite or watercolor, but eventually oil sketches became more and more important to him. An early and important full-scale painting of a corner of the Danish landscape entitled *View near Prestø* (1816), which Dahl said was "a study from nature," is, however, not so much a study as an early example of a painting probably executed largely on the spot.

In 1818 Dahl left the academy, planning to spend some years traveling to perfect his art, but when he reached Dresden he abandoned his plans to move on, for the city was at that time the hub of German Romanticism, with such eminent residents as the writer Johan Ludwig Tieck and the painters Carl Gustav Carus and Caspar David Friedrich. Dahl formed a close friendship with Friedrich and in 1823 moved into his house, where he lived until Friedrich's death in 1840. Dahl quickly became involved in the artistic circle and in fact gained quite a prominent position in it because of his artistic maturity, clear sense of purpose, and what was seen as his striking faithfulness to nature, as in the painting *Norwegian Mountain Landscape* (1819), which in relation to his later work, strikes one today as being far from true to the nature of Norway.

After two years in Dresden, Dahl was invited by Danish Crown Prince Christian Frederik to travel with him to his villa, Quisisana, outside Naples in Italy. Dahl accepted, and in the two years he spent in Italy his development reached its culmination. He developed greater freedom in his handling of artistic means and it was during this period that the quality and number of oil sketches increased dramatically. Dahl, who in true Romantic fashion was fascinated by the dramatic, was also lucky to be in Naples when Vesuvius was erupting and several of his paintings have views of the eruption as their motif.

After one highly influential year in Italy, Dahl returned to Dresden, where he settled and worked for the rest of his life, from 1824 as professor at the Dresden Academy of Arts. Despite not having been back to Norway since he left in 1811, Dahl had never stopped painting "Norwegian" landscapes (dramatic imaginary landscapes with realistic detail). Now, however, he felt the need to return and, with the mastery of the means of expression that maturity had given him, record his subjective encounter with the landscape of his home district of western Norway. In all he made five study trips back to his home country, but the one in 1826 seems to have been the most important, and he returned to Dresden with 250 sketches, which became the basis for future paintings. In fact one of his most famous paintings, *View from Stallheim*, which was started in 1836 and completed in 1842, is based on sketches made in 1826.

This painting exhibits many characteristics of Dahl's art, for example, the closeness to the sketches (Dahl chose the best angle for his compositions at the sketching stage and did not like to alter more than necessary later). The painting also shows Dahl's fondness for the combination of storm clouds with shafts of sunlight coming through, the use of alternating areas of light and shade to break up the surface plane and give the impression of distance, and the attention to detail. Norwegian scholar Knut Berg maintains that it was Dahl's faithfulness to nature that enabled him to maintain the standard of his work well into later life (as in *Stugunøset in Filefjell*, 1851) and in his best work to avoid the banal or routine. It is also Berg who has summed up Dahl's position in relation to the two artists closest to him, saying that in his view of nature Dahl was more subjective than Eckersberg, and more concrete than Friedrich. Dahl did not, however, only paint mountainscapes; his oeuvre also contains coastal landscapes (several with storm clouds and a wreck), and views of Dresden (often in moonlight) and the surrounding countryside.

MARIE WELLS

Biography

Born February 24, 1788 in Bergen. Apprentice in the painter workshop of Johan G. Müller, 1803–9. Left Bergen in 1811 to train at the Academy of Fine Art in Copenhagen. Completed his studies in 1817 with the Great Silver Medal. Left for Dresden in 1818. Married Emilie von Bloch, June 1820, before traveling to Rome to join Danish crown prince Christian Frederik in Naples. Returned to Dresden, July 1822. Made Professor Extraordinary at the Academy in Dresden, 1824. First summer sketching tour to Norway, 1826 (subsequent tours in 1834, 1839, 1844, and 1850). Third child born, but wife died nine days later, 1827. Death of two other children, 1829. Married Amalie von Bassewitz, 1830; she died during childbirth that same year. Death of child by wife Amalie, 1835. Dahl died October 14, 1857.

Bibliography

Bang, Marie Løstrup. *Johan Christian Dahl, 1788–1857. Life and Works.* 3 vols. Oslo: Universitetsforlag, 1987.

Berg, Knut, Nils Messel, and Marit I. Lange, eds. *Norges Kunsthistorie.* Vol. 4. Oslo: Gyldendal, 1981.

Kent, Neil. *The Triumph of Light and Nature: Nordic Art 1740–1940.* London: Thames and Hudson, 1987.

Munro, Jane, ed. *Nature's Way, Romantic Landscapes from Norway.* Exhibition. Manchester: Whitworth Art Gallery and Cambridge: Fitzwilliam Museum, 1993.

DALTON, JOHN 1766–1844

English scientist

John Dalton, probably the most gifted scientist working in northern England in the early-nineteenth century, was the first scientist to establish a quantitative chemical system based on an atomic theory. Unlike most English scientists, who were Anglicans and working in London, Dalton was a Quaker from England's industrial north who spent most of his career in Manchester. His formal education was extremely limited; as a Quaker, he was barred from attending English universities. There was, however, an active scientific culture where he lived and worked, and he gained a great deal of knowledge through discussion and study. The Quaker school where he first taught, Kendal Friends School, possessed an adequate scientific library and a reasonable collection of laboratory apparatus, and he had access to more resources when he moved to Manchester in 1792.

Dalton's first scientific interest was meteorology (he kept a weather diary, beginning in 1787 which only ended on the day of his death) and his first published book was entitled *Meteorological Observations and Essays* (1793). His intellectual journey from meteorology to chemistry began when he became interested in the question of the atmosphere's composition. Dalton wanted to understand how water vapor, and by extension other gases, exist in the atmosphere. During the eighteenth century, chemists such as Joseph Priestley and Antoine-Laurent Lavoisier had divided the air into its component gases, such as oxygen and nitrogen. For Dalton the primary issue was how these gases physically mix, and why the atmosphere resists separating into distinct layers by gas. Many chemists believed that the atmosphere was a chemical compound, but Dalton theorized that the particles of the separate gases repelled each other and only each other; thus, atmospheric gases are independently suspended in an overall mixture. Dalton's exposition of his theory of mixed gases (presented in three papers delivered to the Manchester Literary and Philosophical Society in 1801) was debated and discussed throughout English chemistry and scientific circles.

Dalton's work on atmospheric composition led him to develop a theory that all basic elements are composed of these repelling particles, or atoms, and that atoms combine in fixed ratios to form compounds. Dalton proposed that elemental atoms can be neither created nor destroyed. They also cannot be transmuted into another element, because atoms of different elements have different weights (the notion of differently-weighed atoms was one of Dalton's most important theoretical achievements). Dalton surmised that elemental atoms combine to form what he called "compound atoms" and what we refer to now as molecules. Since particles of the same element repulse one other, the most common form of compound would be one combining one atom of one element with one atom of another element. The most common compound of hydrogen and oxygen is water; thus, Dalton reasoned, it is most likely comprised of one hydrogen atom and one oxygen atom. He further proposed that, because water is only formed when a given weight of hydrogen combines with eight times that amount of oxygen, the ration of oxygen to hydrogen in water is eight to one. These theories were set forth in the first volume of Dalton's *A New System of Chemical Philosophy* in 1808, and subsequent volumes appeared in 1810 and 1827.

Atomic theory had first been developed in ancient Greece. Many of Dalton's peers still considered elements in terms of ultimate particles of differing weights. Dalton was the first English scientist to employ chemical atomism as the quantitative basis for chemistry. Although a large portion of his contemporaries found Dalton's system useful for describing chemical phenomena, they were generally not willing to invest as much belief in or importance to his theories of atomism. Dalton's system of chemical notation (in which circles representing elemental atoms are grouped together to depict the composition of compound atoms), was rejected in favor of Jacob Berzelius's system of letters (still in use today); Dalton's system would force chemists to speculate on how elemental atoms are arranged in a compound atom, something they were generally unwilling or unable to do.

Dalton's other scientific interests included color blindness, of which he was a victim. In a 1794 paper delivered to the Manchester Literary and Philosophical Society, he argued that his own inability to see the color red was the result of the blueness of his eye's aqueous medium.

As Dalton became a prominent scientist, he supplemented the income he derived from teaching with delivering lectures all over Britain, mainly in the north of England. The numerous honors Dalton received late in his life partially resulted from the concurrent development of the new role of the scientist, once merely an amateur talent, now considered a professional and respectable member of society. Dalton, neither a physician nor a clergyman nor a gentleman amateur, was seen as a model example of the new professional scientist. The cultural gap between Dalton and the London-based, more amateur scientific establishment is illustrated by his late admission to the Royal Society in 1822. Dalton had never shown much interest in becoming a fellow of the Royal Society, declining admission when fellow chemist Humphry Davy had offered to sponsor him in 1810, and his ultimate admission was made without his knowledge. Even after admission, the Royal Society played only a minor role in his career, despite awarding him a Royal Medal in 1826. He submitted only four papers to the Society, and did not present himself to be enrolled until 1834. The British Association for the Advancement of Science, which he helped found in 1831, was specifically devised as an alternative to the Royal Society, which would recognize the value and accomplishments of more provincially-located and commercially-oriented professional science. He was a much more active member of the British Association, although his activity was curtailed by two severe strokes in 1837. Dalton's funeral in 1844 was a great state occasion in Manchester, as over forty thousand people filed past his displayed coffin over the course of four days. On the day of the funeral, shops and offices were closed as a gesture of respect. His will directed that his eyes be dissected, in order to prove his theories of color-blindness; the procedure disproved his theory instead.

WILLIAM BURNS

Biography

Born in Eaglesfield, Cumberland, England, September 6, 1766. Son of a Quaker weaver. Remained in the Quaker faith until his death. In charge of local Quaker school, 1778. Taught at the Quaker Friends School, Kendal, 1781–93. Professor of mathematics and natural philosophy at the New College, Manchester, 1792–1800. Admitted to Manchester Literary and Philosophical Society, 1794: secretary, 1800–1808; vice president, 1808–17; president from 1817 on. Opened private mathematical academy, Manchester, 1800. Corresponding member, Académie des Sciences, France, 1816; foreign associate, 1830. Fellow of the Royal Society 1822. Awarded gold medal, Royal Society, 1826. Instrumental in founding of the British Association for the Advancement of Science, 1831. Honorary degrees from Oxford University (1832) and University of Edinburgh (1834). Awarded government pension, 1833; appointed fellow and member of the Senate of London University, 1836. Died in Manchester, July 27, 1844.

Selected Works

Meteorological Observations and Essays. 1793.
A New System of Chemical Philosophy. 3 vols. 1808, 1810, 1827.

Bibliography

Brock, William H. *The Norton History of Chemistry.* New York: W. W. Norton, 1992.
Greenaway, Frank. *John Dalton and the Atom.* Ithaca, N.Y.: Cornell University Press, 1966.
Patterson, Elizabeth Chambers. *John Dalton and the Atomic Theory: The Biography of a Natural Philosopher.* Garden City, N.Y.: Doubleday, 1970.
Smyth, A. L. *John Dalton, 1766–1844: A Bibliography of Works by and about Him, with an Annotated List of His Surviving Apparatus and Personal Effects.* Aldershot, England, U.K. Brookfield, Vt.: Manchester Literary and Philosophical Publications in association with Ashgate, 1998.
Thackray, Arnold. *John Dalton: Critical Assessments of His Life and Science.* Cambridge, Mass.: Harvard University Press, 1972.

DANCE: BALLET

If Romanticism was rather late in exerting its influence on the world of ballet, this takes nothing from its effect in transforming ballet completely from the soulless classicism, evident at the beginning of the nineteenth century, to an emphasis on emotion and a more expressive style. This period of transition from Baroque dance to Romantic ballet was as revolutionary as the recent social and political developments of the day, especially in France, and changes in technique, costume, makeup, music and technical innovations, not to mention the choreography and the subjects for the ballets themselves, essentially developed the model for ballet as we know it today: for example, *Giselle, La Sylphide*, and *Napoli*, all popular Romantic ballets, are still performed today.

The Paris Opera saw the majority of these ballets premiered and initiated the careers of ballerinas such as Fanny Elssler, Carlotta Grisi, and Marie Taglioni. In order to attract audiences, the director of the newly-privatized opera, Dr. Louis Véron, was happy to import the supernatural creatures that were already populating smaller theaters. The inspiration for this change in subject matter was provided primarily by German Romanticism, and led to the swift replacement of classical heroes by otherworldly figures in what was to become known as the *ballet blanc*. Yet in *La Sylphide* and *Giselle*, these ethereal creatures were presented side by side with a much more realistic world, and thus one of the other facets of Romanticism was also highlighted on the ballet stage; touches of exoticism were frequent as choreographers looked to give their productions hints of local color. This gave dancers the opportunity to reveal their talent in different styles of dancing, and emphasized the contrast between the otherworldly sylphs and the fiery passion of the Spanish *cachucha*, for example, made famous by Fanny Elssler in *Le Diable Boiteux* (1836).

The use of pointe work in these ballets was one of the most significant ways in which the dancer and the choreographer were able to achieve the image of weightlessness so important to the depiction of these ethereal creatures. No longer was this recent innovation an act of virtuosity, rather, it was a pragmatic means to an end; the ballerina's contact with the floor was minimal and this contributed to her aura of lightness. Pointe work was not the only development in technique at that time, although it was clearly one of the most important in expressing the otherworldliness required. Since the publication of Jean-Georges Noverre's *Letters on Dancing and Ballets* in 1760, technique had advanced significantly and teachers Auguste Vestris and Carlo Blasis were very influential. Blasis's *An Elementary Treatise upon the Theory and Practice of the Art of Dancing* (1820) provided the basis for many contemporary ballet teaching methods (Guest, 1994). Technique improved generally, grew in complexity, and became a means of depicting emotion from within, rather than an end in itself. These advances in technical virtuosity and the expressive and fluid nature of Marie Taglioni's style made it possible to make these supernatural figures come to life.

Costume, makeup, and the set itself played a role in creating this illusion of spirituality too. The high-heeled shoes of the seventeenth and eighteenth centuries had been replaced by soft satin slippers, which allowed greater movement and let the ballerina rise onto pointe. Corsets had been abandoned and dresses shortened, again giving more freedom. These flimsy calf-length dresses of white muslin only added to the illusion of otherworldliness, and if exotic touches were needed for character dances, then bodices could be adorned with ribbons or colorful material, or a head-dress could be worn. The use of masks had been discarded in the 1770s, and the conventionalized use of makeup allowed the dancer to use a variety of expressions appropriate to this new emphasis on emotion. Arms and shoulders were whitened, and together with the floating, lightweight dresses, they convincingly suggested the unearthly illusion. These sylphs appeared even more ethereal due to the rather ghostly gas lighting which had recently been introduced at the Paris Opera, and the more elaborate scenery, made possible by the practice of lowering the curtain between acts, enhanced the illusion yet further.

Music also played a role in the Romantic ballet, with the advent of music being composed particularly for the ballet rather than vice versa, and ballet no longer being merely interval entertainment in opera. The music became more descriptive and successful in reflecting the illusion of ethereality in the world of the sylphs, or at hinting at local color through the tunes for the character dances. The music of Adolphe Adam in particular, and especially the score for *Giselle*, paved the way for the ballet music of Léo Delibes and Pyotr Ilich Tchaikowsky later in the century.

It was not one of these aspects in isolation which accounted for the revolution on the ballet stage at that time, but a combination of various innovations. What is also clear is that the Romantic ballet stage was the domain of the ballerina; the acrobatic feats of the male dancers had vanished, as had the anachronistic practice of categorizing dancers as either *danseur noble* (the serious dancer), *demi-caractère* (the semi-serious dancer) or the *danseur comique* (the dancer who performed grotesque and folk dances). The male dancer was relegated literally to a supporting role. Indeed, this went even further in some ballets where the male roles were also danced by women. Jules Perrot was one of the few male dancers to make a name for himself at that time, but he is perhaps better known as co-choreographer of *Giselle* and choreographer of the successful *Pas de Quatre* (1845), which Ivor Guest calls "perhaps the most sublime ballet that was produced throughout the whole of the Romantic period."

As Deborah Jowitt notes, some critics have denounced the significance of Romantic ballet within the phenomenon of Romanticism, accusing it of freely adding just a few Romantic touches to that soulless classical technique of earlier times. Perhaps it was indeed not as groundbreaking within the wider context of Romanticism as a whole, but within the context of ballet, the influence of these developments and innovations in bringing emotion, fluidity and elegance to the dance, and a much wider range of technical prowess and stage apparatus to the whole spectacle of the Romantic ballet, cannot be underestimated.

SHONA M. ALLAN

Bibliography

Babsky, Monique. "France: Theatrical Dance, 1789–1914." In *International Encyclopedia of Dance*. Vol. 3, pp. 67–72. Edited by Selma Jeanne Cohen. Oxford: Oxford University Press, 1998.

Blasis, Carlo. *An Elementary Treatise upon the Theory and Practice of the Art of Dancing* (1820). Translated by Mary Stewart Evans, New York: Dover, 1968.

Chapman, John V. "Great Britain: Theatrical Dance, 1772–1850." In *International Encyclopedia of Dance*. Vol. 3, pp. 257–61. Edited by Selma Jeanne Cohen. Oxford: Oxford University Press, 1998.

Cohen, Selma Jeanne and Katy Matheson, eds. *Dance as a Theatre Art: Source Readings in Dance History from 1581 to the Present*. 2d ed. Princeton, N.J.: Princeton Book Company, 1992.

Garafola, Lynn. *Rethinking the Sylph: New Perspectives on Romantic Ballet*. Middletown, Conn.: Wesleyan University Press, 1997.

Guest, Ivor. *The Dancer's Heritage: A Short History of Ballet*. 6th ed. London: Dancing Times, 1994.

Jowitt, Deborah. "In Pursuit of the Sylph: Ballet in the Romantic

Period," In *The Routledge Dance Studies Reader*. Edited by Alexandra Carter. London: Routledge, 1998.

Noverre, Jean-Georges. *Letters on Dancing and Ballets*. Translated by Cyril W. Beaumont. London: C. W. Beaumont, 1930.

Rameau, Pierre. *The Dancing Master*. Translated by Cyril W. Beaumont. London: C. W. Beaumont, 1931.

Winter, Marian Hannah. *The Pre-Romantic Ballet*. London: Pitman, 1974.

DANCE: POPULAR

Popular social dance did not remain immune to the effects of the political, social, and industrial revolutions of the nineteenth century, even if the influence of Romanticism on popular dance, and the role played by popular dance in the phenomenon of Romanticism, is perhaps less easy to perceive. Just as theatrical dance was transformed by the advent of Romantic ballet, so too new dance forms, styles, and techniques swept the ballrooms of Europe. Romanticism was but one influential factor among many.

If the eighteenth century had been the century of the minuet, then the nineteenth most certainly belonged to the waltz. The contrast between this German/Austrian turning dance, whose origins are obscure, and the refined minuet of the preceding century is striking. Although the minuet was by far the most flexible of the Baroque dances, it was still extremely formal and offered little opportunity for freedom of expression. This formality did not appeal to the Romantic sensibility, but the "potentially intoxicating momentum of circle dancing" (Schneider, 1998) and the close physical contact necessary in the waltz most certainly did.

All waltzes—for example, the Slow French, German, Viennese—had their own distinct choreography and the music, in either 3/8 or 3/4 time, had as many names as there were different waltzes. *Allemande, Deutsche, Ländler*, and *Walzer* appeared frequently and were to be found among the works of Ludwig von Beethoven, Frédéric Chopin, Wolfgang Amadeus Mozart, and Franz Schubert. The most significant composers of waltz music, however, were Joseph Lanner and the Strauss family. As instruments, instruction, and printed music became less expensive, so music became more easily accessible to all classes, and the small, touring bands and orchestras did much to popularize this and other dance music.

The middle of the century saw an increase in the popularity of the *deux-temps* waltz at the expense of the *trois-temps* version. This simplification in choreography was indicative of the trend in technique and style in nineteenth-century popular dance as the split between social and theatrical dancing became more marked. The precise and competent execution of complicated classical ballet steps was no longer of prime importance, and the stress was placed firmly on the effect of the dance group as a whole rather than the individual's technical virtuosity. Thus the practice of dance became more widespread as it was no longer open only to those who could afford tuition in classical ballet technique.

As a consequence of this less complex choreography, the need for dance teachers dissipated and they were forced to rely on emphasizing the moral and physical benefits of dance in order to attract more pupils and make a living. Life was also not made any easier by the ready availability of dance instruction manuals as printing techniques improved, though again this did much to fuel the public's enthusiasm for these new social dances.

Yet the waltz was not the only dance which gained in popularity as these developments took place: the galop, mazurka, polka, polonaise, and quadrille, to name but a few, all enjoyed a share of the limelight too.

For a short time the waltz found a worthy rival in the mazurka, originally a Polish national dance in 3/4 or 6/8 time. Romanticism's interest in nationalism, nostalgia, history, folklore, and the exotic assisted in promoting dances such as the mazurka. It was a fast dance with much clicking of heels and stamping of feet, and was led by the first man while the other couples followed in a circle. Like the waltz, the mazurka gave dancers much more freedom of movement and this surely also appealed to the Romantic frame of mind. The mazurka was exported successfully, together with Frédéric Chopin's music, to ballrooms throughout Europe, even if its reception in England was less enthusiastic. Although it challenged the waltz for a time, it ultimately proved too difficult for ballroom dancers. Nevertheless it did become fashionable on the ballet stage and can famously be seen later in the century in *Coppelia*.

The only other serious competition to the waltz was provided by the polka. Probably originating in Bohemia, the polka was a lively dance in 2/4 time. Enthusiasm for the polka grew rapidly, not only because of the nationalistic sentiments it aroused, but also because the dance steps were already familiar to ballroom dancers. The steps were rather similar to the Scottish Strathspey step of eighteenth-century reels, and the dance itself was rather similar to the slightly faster galop. The polka was fashionable in both European and American ballrooms and, in the 1840s, enjoyed success on the ballet stage too. Such was its triumph that polka steps soon infiltrated other dances, and dances such as the polka-redowa (polka plus waltz), polka-mazurka, polka-quadrille, and the Esmeralda glide (polka plus galop) and many others were born.

Rather than playing a revolutionary role in shaping Romanticism, it appears that the developments in popular dance in the

Waltz, *La vie Parisienne*. Nineteenth century. Reprinted courtesy of the Lebrecht Collection.

nineteenth century were more influenced by Romanticism. The success of the waltz, mazurka, and polka was aided by the appeal of these dances to contemporary Romantic preoccupations—nostalgia, nationalism, history, folklore, exoticism—but the influence of political, economic, and social factors should not be forgotten.

SHONA M. ALLAN

Bibliography

Au, Susan. "Mazurka." In *International Encyclopedia of Dance*. Vol. 4, pp. 343–44. Edited by Selma Jeanne Cohen. Oxford: Oxford University Press, 1998.

Carner, Mosco. *The Waltz*. London: M. Parrish, 1948.

Cellarius, Henri. *The Drawing-Room Dances*. 1847.

Emmerson, George S. *A Social History of Scottish Dance: Ane Celestial Recreatioun*. Montreal: McGill-Queens University Press, 1972.

Richardson, Philip J. S. *The Social Dances of the Nineteenth Century in England*. London: H. Jenkins, 1960.

Schneider, Gretchen. "Social Dance: Nineteenth-Century Social Dance." In *International Encyclopedia of Dance*. Vol. 5, pp. 623–26. Edited by Selma Jeanne Cohen. Oxford: Oxford University Press, 1998.

Strobel, Desmond F. "Polka." *International Encyclopedia of Dance*. Vol. 5, pp. 221–23. Edited by Selma Jeanne Cohen. Oxford: Oxford University Press, 1998.

———. "Waltz." In *International Encyclopedia of Dance*. Vol. 6, pp. 359–62. Edited by Selma Jeanne Cohen. Oxford: Oxford University Press, 1998.

DANDY

Derived from the Scottish diminutive for Andrew, the word *dandy* rose to popularity throughout the American colonies in the 1770s when English soldiers used the song "Yankee Doodle Dandy" to ridicule the shabby dress worn by American troops. However, from its roots an abusive term attacking American provincialism it soon came to denote the pretentious behavior and extravagant dress sense of the aristocratic English, which was best represented by the members of the Macaroni Club established in London in 1764.

In Regency England, the dandy style stood for an amoral, superficial attitude toward life and the rejection of middle-class responsibilities in favor of aristocratic detachment, pedantically observed decorum, and a general decay in morals. The dandy's world revolved around stylish clothing, drawn-out toilettes, extravagant dinner-parties, the London season, the newest dances, horse racing, and the Jockey Club. His social behavior was characterized by capricious favoritism, dry wit, sangfroid, and a tendency to turn on those fallen from grace.

The most prominent dandy of the period was the commoner George Bryan Brummell (1778–1840), known as Beau Brummell. Educated at Eton and Oxford Universities and endowed with an inheritance, Brummell enjoyed the Prince of Wales's confidence and friendship before the latter became Prince Regent in 1811 and was forced to assume a more responsible public demeanor. This gesture was meant to allay the skepticism and contempt of his middle-class subjects, who disagreed with the aristocracy's lavishness, most prolifically symbolized by the Brighton Pavilion, although the later George IV maintained his loyalty to the fashionable world throughout his life: "I care nothing for the mob but I do for the dandies." Having spent his fortune and exhausted his credit with shopkeepers and tailors, Brummell, like many other dandies, found himself forced to leave England for the continent in 1816, where he set up residence in Calais and was later made British consul at Caen, France, by the Duke of York, where he finally died, utterly impoverished, in a charitable asylum.

Brummell and his circle put particular emphasis on taste, fashion, and refinement, and insisted on the exclusiveness of their world, which they maintained by patronizing certain clubs that were Whig in outlook and situated in Saint James's Street close to Prince Regent's London residence of Carlton House. They met at Brook's, Crockford's, and most importantly White's, with its bow window on the front facade from which the most famous dandies watched the goings-on of fashionable London. Contact with the opposite sex was catered for by Almack's, whose patronesses bestowed tickets upon ambitious mothers anxious to secure a good match for their daughters at the weekly Wednesday Ball. By breeding within its own circle, London's fashionable society endeavored to keep out the upstarts of their time, made rich by advancing industrialization. With neither high birth nor wealth acting as guarantors of initiation into the world of the so-called exclusive, the dandies and their female pendants regarded high style, impeccable manners, and exuberant unconventionality as the attributes necessary for precluding vulgar egalitarianism from entering their sphere. They answered notions of middle-class respectability with the worship of some indefinable chic excellence, a certain *je ne sais quoi*.

With the exception of Lord Byron, who was an accepted member of the dandy world, there was no overlap between Regency high-society and the Romantic poets, who were mostly of middle or lower class decent. For their literary media, Regency literature relied on magazines, journals, and the fashionable novel. The latter, also known as the "Silver-Fork School," owed its success to the publisher Henry Colburn, to whose catalog belonged Lady Morgan's travel book on *France* (1817); Robert Plumer Ward's *Tremaine* (1825), whose title hero is closely modeled on Brummell, and works by Theodore Edward Hook, a friend of Prince Regent's who translated his admiration for the fashionable world into his novels. Colburn also founded the anti-Jacobin *New Monthly Magazine* (1814) and the *Literary Gazette* (1817), which discussed a wide range of books, fine arts, and sciences. Two other major works of the period were Benjamin Disraeli's *Vivian Grey* (1826) and Edward Bulwer-Lytton's *Pelham* (1828). These novels and periodicals were enjoyed by the members, both male and female, of the in-group, who took pleasure in finding their world portrayed so flatteringly, as well as the aspiring middle classes longing to make their way to such lofty airs of society.

The dandy's obsession with dress and appearance coupled with physical hyper-sensitivity and the rejection of all bodily exertion provoked the wit of the Regency Period's satirists and caricaturists (for example, George Cruikshank) at the same time as it raised questions with regard to the sexual preferences of men like Brummell, who appeared widely indifferent to the fe-

DANDIES and DANDYZETTES.

Reprinted courtesy of Topham Picturepoint.

male sex. Contrary to popular belief, however, Brummell's costume was masculine and marked by simplicity, restraint, and an austere lack of extravagance. Rather than indulging in jewels, perfumes, frills, and colorful fabrics, Brummell limited himself to silk, cotton, and leather, and the colors navy, black, and white, and put the greatest emphasis on cleanliness, thus in fact revolutionizing the male outfit.

Social historians usually attribute the emergence of the dandy phenomenon to the prolonged period of overseas wars under George III and the boredom and frustration felt by the men left behind in Britain. With the end of the Napoleonic Wars in 1815 came the dandy's infiltration of Restoration France, when the French aristocrats returned from English exile and brought with them their dandified manners and a taste for Anglomania. This cultural cross-fertilization was reinforced by the resumption of tourism as well as Lord Wellington's discovery and Lady Blessington's guardianship of the young French count Alfred d'Orsay, who soon replaced Brummell as London's foremost dandy.

Thus, while England saw an anti-dandy reaction following the death of George IV and the appearance of *Fraser's* magazine in 1830 and found its two major condemnations of dandyism

in Thomas Carlyle's *Sartor Resartus* (1833–34) and William Makepeace Thackeray's "Yellowplush Papers" (1837), France produced the three principal manifestos of the dandy style: Honoré de Balzac's "Traité de la vie élégante," published in the journal *La Mode* in 1830; Barbey d'Aurevilly's *Du dandysme and de George Brummell* in 1844; and Charles Baudelaire's "Le peintre de la vie moderne" published in the newspaper *Le Figaro* 1863. Baudelaire introduced the hybrid creature of the artist-dandy, the "observateur passionné" and "parfait flâneur," later adopted by Huysmans and Oscar Wilde, who is characterized by outstanding sensibility and inherently good taste, which makes him the only fit analyst of modern culture and society, and whose aim in life is to experience every kind of sensation, including that afforded by sinful beauty and crime.

Dr. Katharina Krosny

See also **Balzac, Honoré de; Baudelaire, Charles (Pierre); Britain: Cultural Survey; Britain: Historical Survey; Bulwer-Lytton, Edward; Byron, Lord George Noel Gordon; Carlyle, Thomas; Chateaubriand, François-Auguste-René de Vicomte; Cruikshank, George; Daumier, Honoré (Victorin); Dickens, Charles; France, 1815–1852; France: Revolution and Empire; Sensibility**

Bibliography

Adams, James Eli. *Dandies and Desert Saints. Styles of Victorian Masculinity.* Ithaca, N.Y.: Cornell University Press, 1995.

Barbey d'Aurevilly, J. Jules. *Of Dandyism and of Beau Brummell.* London: Dent, 1897.

Calder, Angus. *Byron and Scotland. Radical or Dandy?* Edinburgh: Edinburgh University Press, 1989.

Garelick, Rhonda K. *Rising Star: Dandyism, Gender, and Performance in the Fin-de-Siècle.* Princeton, N.J.: Princeton University Press, 1998.

Moers, Ellen. *The Dandy.* London: Secker and Warburg, 1960.

Pine, Richard. *The Dandy and the Herald: Manners, Mind and Morals from Brummell to Durrell.* Basingstoke, England: Macmillan, 1988.

Stanton, Donna C. *The Aristocrat as Art: A Study of the Honnête Homme and the Dandy in Seventeenth and Nineteenth Century French Literature.* New York: Columbia University Press, 1980.

DANTONS TOD (DANTON'S DEATH) 1835

Play by Georg Büchner

Arranged in four acts and occurring over approximately two weeks, the action of Georg Büchner's play represents those events of the French Revolution that led to the execution of Georges-Jacques Danton and his followers on April 5, 1794. Danton had himself helped to create the Terror that brought about his downfall; he had supported, or at least tolerated, the massacre of a large number of prisoners, mainly royalists and clergy, when the coalition armies were threatening to overturn the Revolution in September 1792. When the action of the play begins, Maximilien de Robespierre and Louis-Antoine-Léon Saint-Just are in control of the Committee of Public Safety, the effective organ of the Terror. Having already killed various opposing factions, including that of the ultraradical Jacques René Hébert, they seek to

secure their power by eliminating the moderate faction around Danton, which now advocates the end of the Revolution and the beginning of a republic without further bloodshed. However, the moderates take no action to realize this political objective. Even when his own life and those of his friends come under threat, Danton remains a passive critic of the Terror, haunted by the memory of the September massacres, and seized by a general *ennui* of politics and life. Asserting his impotence to abolish the rule "kill or be killed" and relying on his apparent invulnerability as a symbol of the revolution, after a half-hearted readoption of his earlier heroic postures, he dies without resistance.

Büchner represents the "political" actions during the Terror as a mixture of heroic rhetoric and slaughter. Neither the radical

Jacobin leaders nor the people of Paris possess a social strategy to realize equality in the sense of economic justice. Throughout, the abolishment of privileges is taken to consist in the killing of the privileged. The magic assumption that social hierarchy is rooted in the body of those who are rich or at the top thwarts the successful abolition of hierarchical structures. Action is rhetorically conceived as a magic force, emanating directly from the revolutionary body. "My voice was the hurricane that buried the satellites of despotism under a tidal wave of bayonets," Danton says in act 3, scene 4. The moderates indulge in the liberal vision of a constitution that, as a transparent "garment" loosely flowing around the naked body of the people, is unrestricted by state control or moral rules (1.1). Yet to the extent that the revolutionary ideal of equality is not actually revoked in their liberalism, they must share Saint-Just's conviction that equality somehow already exists in the state of nature (1.7); for they reject the radicals' attempt to eradicate actual inequality by the violent restitution of that state, without offering an alternative to deal with persistent social injustice and the suffering of the poor, which Büchner emphasizes in his picture of the Revolution.

The public events of the play are complemented by a variety of successfully dramatized reflections, for example concerning the nature of historical necessity, the (non)existence of God, the shallowness of traditional drama, competing conceptions of (political) morality, or the inadequacy of revolutionary posturing itself. In act 2, scene 5, Danton responds to the traumatic memory of the September massacres with a fatalistic, mythic, or metaphysical conception of history. Although reminiscent of the wording in Büchner's so-called "fatalism" letter of March 10, 1834, the existential depth of Danton's imagery may be questioned in view of its self-exculpating function in the drama, or of Danton's rather dry, concluding remark to his wife Julie: "Come to bed!" In act 3, scene 1 Thomas Payne entertains the prisoners with a demonstration of atheism. A brilliant philosophical performance goes hand in hand here with Büchner's insistence on the irreducible experience of pain: "The least twinge of pain splits creation from top to bottom." By contrasting it to the plenitude of life, Danton's friend Camille Desmoulins caricatures idealistic theatre (2.3), describing its deficiencies partly with the same imagery of dead puppets which Danton will use to evoke the fatalism of history. The famous confrontation of Robespierre and Danton at the end of the first act opposes the former's "Roman" insistence on virtue and sacrifice with the latter's "Greek" sensualism and rejection of any imposed morality. Danton's simple statement "I don't understand the word 'punishment'" surpasses the moderates' sometimes grandiloquent display of antimoralism in both rational insight and anarchic force. His (anti)hero's pursuit of sensual pleasure and political forgetfulness permits Büchner to present different aspects of sexuality and love. While Danton seeks in his wife the peace of death (1.1), the prostitute Marion attracts this unbalanced political dandy and cynicist with the quasi-cosmic unity and wholeness of the Romantically stylized "female" (2.5). In the grisettes of the Palais Royal, Danton seeks the classical beauty of the Medici *Venus*, judging the various parts of their body accordingly and, as he is said to have put it, "playing mosaic" (1.4–5). His ostensible sensuality, against which Robespierre's virtue appears as a grotesque contortion of human nature, thus actually figures within a neoclassical perception of beauty that reduces the living body to a dead vehicle of formal perfection. It is Camille, Lucile's passionate lover, who shortly before their

execution applies Danton's criticism of Robespierre to Danton's own heroic posturing: "He is making a face as if he meant to petrify and be excavated by posterity as an antique." (4.5) And it is Lucile who, in her despair about Camille's death, performs what is perhaps for all its alienation and sadness, the only authentic action in this drama. Subverting the windy rhetoric and heroic rules of the power game, her cry "Long live the King!" provokes her own arrest, with which the play concludes.

Danton's Death sweeps away Hegelian evaluations of the French Revolution, the German neoclassical and Romantic replacement of French politics with aesthetic education or, respectively, Romantic literature and an emphasis on "volk." Although still organized into acts, the play is remarkably modern in its multiperspectivism and intertextuality. To a considerable extent, it presents a both imaginative and analytically fruitful montage of historiographical and literary source material. Especially important is Büchner's use of Louis-Adolphe Thiers' *Histoire de la Révolution Française* (1823–27), Louis Sébastien Mercier's *Le Nouveau Paris* (1799) and the popular journal *Die Geschichte Unserer Zeit* (*The History of Our Time*, 1826–30), the latter of which was read in Büchner's family long before those five weeks at the beginning of 1835 in which he claimed to have written the play. Büchner's classical education and schooling in rhetoric, which provided a forum for republican aspirations in a time of political censorship, enabled him to recreate *and* critically reflect the "Roman" self-presentation of the French Revolution. Literary sources he used comprise folk songs as well as works by Clemens Brentano, Johann Wolfgang von Goethe, Christian Dietrich Grabbe, Heinrich Heine, Jean Paul, and William Shakespeare. It is possible that French literary influences—for example, that of Charles Nodier—can contribute to the explanation of that puzzling impression of singular modernity which distinguishes Büchner's work from most of the German literature of the early nineteenth century.

MARGARETE KOHLENBACH

Text

Dantons Tod. One thousand eight hundred thirty five, incomplete, edited by Karl Gutzkow; *Dantons Tod: Dramatische Bilder aus Frankreichs Schreckensherrschaft*, revised by Karl Gutzkow and Eduard Duller, 1835; translated with an introduction and notes by John Reddick in Georg Büchner's, *Complete Plays, "Lenz" and Other Writings*. London: Penguin Books, 1993.

Bibliography

Benn, Maurice B. *The Drama of Revolt: A Critical Study of Georg Büchner*. London: Cambridge University Press, 1976.

Dedner, Burghard. "Legitimationen des Schreckens in Georg Büchners Revolutionsdrama," *Jahrbuch der deutschen Schillergesellschaft* 29 (1985): 343–80.

Grimm, Reinhold. *Love, Lust and Rebellion: New Approaches to Georg Büchner*. Madison: University of Wisconsin Press, 1985.

Holmes, T. M. "The Ideology of the Moderates in Büchner's 'Dantons Tod,'" *German Life and Letters* 27 (1973–74): 93–100.

Horton, David. "'Die gliederlösende, böse Liebe': Observations on the Erotic Theme in Büchner's 'Dantons Tod,'" *Deutsche Vierteljahresschrift für Literaturwissenschaft und Geistesgeschichte* 62 (1988): 290–306.

Mills, Ken, and Brian Keith-Smith, eds. *Georg Büchner: Tradition and Innovation: Fourteen Essays*. Bristol: University of Bristol Press, 1990.

Reddick, John. *Georg Büchner: The Shattered Whole*. Oxford: Clarendon Press, 1994.

Richards, David G. *Georg Büchner and the Birth of Modern Drama.* Albany: State University of New York Press, 1977.

Schaub, Gerhard. *Georg Büchner und die Schulrhetorik: Untersuchungen und Quellen zu seinen Schülerarbeiten.* Bern: Herbert and Peter Lang, 1975.

Schings, Hans-Jürgen. *"Der mitleidigste Mensch ist der beste Mensch": Poelik des Mitleids von Lessing bis Büchner.* Munich: C. H. Beck, 1980.

Wender, Herbert. *Georg Büchners Bild der Großen Revolution: Zu den Quellen von "Danton's Tod."* Frankfurt: Athenäum, 1988.

DAUMIER, HONORÉ(-VICTORIN) 1808–1879

French graphic artist, painter, and sculptor

Over a career that spanned more than forty years, and in which he produced over four thousand lithographs, wood engravings, paintings, drawings, and watercolors, Honoré Daumier became known as the Michelangelo of the nineteenth century. Famous in his own lifetime for his biting political caricature and as a perceptive comic satirist of urban life, his lesser-known paintings and drawings gained increasing acclaim posthumously, and the twentieth century has accorded justice to Charles Baudelaire's claim that he was "one of the most important men . . . of modern art." Closely involved in the artistic and literary milieux of his day, Daumier participated in many innovative publishing ventures of the Romantic era, and his achievements in lifting popular art forms like lithography from the realm of the ephemeral to the realm of works of art cannot be overestimated.

Daumier's first published lithographs bore witness to his strong Republican views and his disappointment in the outcome of the July Revolution. Together with Charles Philipon, the founder of the satirical journal *La Caricature,* Daumier waged a political battle against Louis-Philippe, frequently depicting him as a pear (*la poire,* fool). He was imprisoned for six months, from August 31, 1832 to February 14, 1833, for creating *Gargantua,* in which the king was depicted eating cartloads of gold and then defecating commissions. Political caricature, which emerged in England with James Gillray, was also practiced by Eugène Delacroix and Victor Hugo, but in his use of violent, contrasting forms, local color, and mixing of genres, Daumier was unequalled. *Rue Transnonain, le 15 avril 1834* (1834), for example, is generally acknowledged as a masterpiece for its vigorous but unheroicized image of state violence, showing the influence of Francisco Goya y Lucientes and Théodore Géricault in its composition. Daumier was also the first to experiment with caricatures in sculpture, creating for Philipon, in 1832, forty-five small busts of political figures, notable for their apt exaggeration of prominent characteristics. *Ratapoil* (c. 1851), later typified the corruption and egotism that led to the election of Louis-Napoleon. Daumier's democratic ideals and social conscience permeated all his political lithographs, culminating in the powerful indictments of the Franco–Prussian War in the late 1860s and early 1870s.

Daumier's work centers around human beings. He believed steadfastly that "one must belong to one's own time" and devoted much of his talent to depicting scenes of everyday life, particularly after he was forced by the September Laws of 1835 to abandon political caricature. His aptitude for seizing the ridiculous made him a firm favorite with the bourgeois readers of *Le Charivari* and other illustrated magazines. It led also to the creation of such enduring figures as Robert Macaire, a self-seeking entrepreneur based on a popular character played by Frédéric Lemaître at the Folies dramatiques and on the greed encouraged by François Pierre Guizot's slogan "Enrichissez-vous!" ("Get rich!"). Like Molière, whom he acknowledged as a lasting inspiration, Daumier frequently targeted hypocrisy in any shape or form, and doctors and lawyers became particular objects of his satire, set against his idealized symbol of the common man. The thity-one series he produced between 1837 and 1851 offered a vibrant and comprehensive panorama of Parisian life in which married couples, blue-stockings, bathers, and the worthy bourgeois all became the subjects of his own "human comedy." Comparisons with Honoré de Balzac have often been drawn, but Daumier's series were not deliberately planned and represented mainly the urban bourgeoisie, emphasizing the universal aspects of human behavior rather than the "realist" aspects of the moment. His caricatures encompassed irony, sarcasm, and even a sense of the tragic in their wit. Baudelaire praised the emotive power derived from Daumier's technique of observing then drawing from memory, and ranked him in the same league as Delacroix and Jean-Auguste-Dominique Ingres, while Champfleury likened his technique to the subjective powers of the camera.

Like many other Romantics, including Delacroix and Géricault, Daumier drew inspiration from classical painting, particularly from sixteenth-century Venetian and seventeenth-century Flemish art, and from the eighteenth-century painter Jean-Honoré Fragonard. He admired Rembrandt von Rijn and Peter Paul Rubens and learned from their use of color and tone. This is especially clear in his watercolors and paintings, to which Daumier devoted increasing time after his oil sketch *The Republic* was successfully exhibited at the Salon of 1848. This marked a shift to the realm of high art. Although he accepted some commissions, and also continued to paint scenes of everyday life, such as passengers in an omnibus or on trains (*Third-Class Railway Carriage,* 1864), the independence thrust on him by his summary dismissal from *Le Charivari* in 1860 allowed him to diversify into other subject areas, such as mythology (*The Drunkenness of Silenus,* 1863) and literature.

One theme Daumier returned to time and time again was that of Don Quixote and Sancho Panza. He produced around thirty paintings, often variants of similar scenes, contrasting Cervantes's knight—who in the Romantic era was revalorized as a symbol of spiritual creativity—with the more prosaic and sensual Sancho. In these works, and in his depictions of clowns and street performers, which at mid-century were held to be symbolic of the artistic life, Daumier achieved greater luminosity and a deep concentration of emotion and meaning. It has been suggested that the figures of Don Quixote and the saltimbanque personified Daumier's own struggle for artistic recognition at a time when ill health, financial troubles, and the threat of war darkened his existence.

A year before his death in 1879, a major retrospective exhibition of Daumier's work was held at the Galerie Durand-Ruel. It was mounted by friends, with Victor Hugo as the honorary president, and, though not financially successful, it brought the full range of his artistic power to public attention for the first time. Daumier's contribution has frequently been overshadowed by his reputation as a "popular" artist and cartoonist. However, he had a far-reach influence in writers and artists as different as Gustave Flaubert, Paul Cézanne, Vincent Van Gogh, and Henri de Toulouse-Lautrec. His importance in the Romantic era can perhaps best be judged by the praise accorded to his work by Balzac, Baudelaire, Delacroix, and Jules Michelet.

SARA JAMES

Biography

Born in Marseilles, February 20 or 26, 1808. Son of a glazier. Moved with his family to Paris, where his father attempted to establish literary career, 1816. Attended schools in Paris; after father suffered mental breakdown, worked as errand boy for a bailiff and as assistant in a bookshop at the Palais-Royal, c. 1820–21. Studied drawing with Alexandre Lenoir, c. 1822; attended Académie Suisse, 1823–28. Apprenticed to lithographer and publisher, Zéphirin Belliard, c. 1825; first lithographs for *La Silhouette* published, c. 1829. Produced around four thousand lithographs from 1830 on. Prosecuted and later imprisoned for *Gargantua*, lithograph in *La Caricature*, 1832. Changed to less overtly political caricature after laws prohibiting political satire passed, 1835. Contributed to the journal *Le Charivari*, 1836–60. Married Marie-Alexandrine Dassy (Didine), dressmaker, 1846. Dismissed from *Le Charivari*, 1860; concentrated after this on painting and drawing. Reinstated at *Le Charivari* after death of its director, Philipon. Moved to Valmondois, outside Paris, 1865; eyesight began to fail, 1867. Elected to the artists' committee of the commission to safeguard works of art threatened by the siege of Paris; fine arts delegate to the Paris Commune, 1871. Held retrospective exhibition at Galerie Durand-Ruel, 1878. Died in Valmondois, February 10, 1879.

Bibliography

Adhémar, Jean. *Honoré Daumier*. Paris: Tisné, 1954.

Campbell, Douglas, and Ushes Caplan, eds. *Daumier, 1808–1879*. Exhibition catalog. Ottawa: National Gallery of Ottawa/Paris: Réunion des Musées Nationaux/Washington, D.C.: The Phillips Collection, 1999.

Delteil, Loys. *Le Peintre-graveur illustr.* Vols. 20–29. Paris: chez l'anteu 1925–30.

Ives, Colta, Margret Stuffmann, and Martin Sonnabend, eds. *Daumier Drawing*. New Haven, Conn.: Yale University Press, 2000.

Larkin, Oliver W. *Daumier: Man of His Time*. London: Weidenfeld and Nicolson, 1967.

Laughton, Bruce. *Honoré Daumier*. New Haven Conn.: Yale University Press, 1996.

Loyrette, Henri, Henry Loyrette, and Michael Pantazzi, eds. *Daumier*. New Haven, Conn.: Yale University Press, 2000.

Maison, K. E. *Honoré Daumier: Catalogue Raisonné of the Paintings, Watercolours and Drawings*. 2 vols. London: Thames and Hudson, 1968.

Passeron, Roger. *Daumier*. Trans. Helga Harrison. Oxford: Phaidon, 1981.

Ramus, Charles F., ed. *Daumier—120 Great Lithographs*. New York: Dover, 1978.

DAVID, JACQUES-LOUIS 1748–1825

French painter

Jacques-Louis David was arguably the single most important European painter between 1785 and 1815. His working life spanned the Enlightenment, the French Revolution, the abolition of the monarchy, the Napoleonic era, and the return of the Bourbon kings to France. During the 1780s he perfected a form of dramatic and noble painting that answered demands for serious and morally elevating pictures, a style that was later termed neoclassicism. During the Revolution, he became involved in politics and painted for the revolutionary cause, although it almost cost him his life and caused him to be imprisoned. When he returned to work, he vowed never to engage in politics again, but the lure and attraction of Napoleon was enough to galvanize him to become the Emperor's painter, capturing the pomp and magnificence of the Imperial Court. After Napoleon's defeat, David left France for Brussels where he continued to paint until his death in 1825.

Born into a family of Parisian tradesmen, in 1765 David entered the studio of Joseph-Marie Vien and a year later enrolled at the Académie de Peinture et de Sculpture. He won the Prix de Rome at his fifth attempt in 1774, his previous setbacks leaving him with grievances against the Académie and its teaching system. Between October 1775 and July 1780, David was a student at the Académie de France à Rome and created a synthesis of the real and the ideal based on precise draughtsmanship from the life model and borrowings from seventeenth-century sources such as Nicolas Poussin and Michelangelo Merisi da Caravaggio.

David became an associate of the Académie Royale in 1781 with *Belisarius Asking Alms*, and a full member in 1783 with *Andromache Mourning Hector*. His neoclassicism reached its clearest expression in the *Oath of the Horatii* (1784), a painting on the theme of patriotism and the sacrifice of the individual for the good of the nation. At the following two salons he continued his austere neoclassicism with *The Death of Socrates* (1787) and *The Lictors Bringing Brutus the Bodies of His Sons* (1789). Exhibited at the time of the storming of the Bastille, the republican nature of Brutus meant that in following years the painting acquired a political significance that David had not originally intended.

As a liberal, David welcomed the promise of social change that the French Revolution offered, and from September 1790, when he joined the Jacobin Club, he became directly involved in politics and worked on the unfinished project for *The Oath of the Tennis Court* to commemorate the National Assembly's oath on June 20, 1789, to remain in session until a constitution was assured. David also agitated against the privileges and elitism of the Académie Royale and was instrumental in its abolition in 1793. Elected a deputy of the Convention in September 1792, he allied himself closely with the Montagnards, led by Maximilien de Robespierre, and in 1793 he voted for the death of King Louis XVI. He served a term as president of the Convention in January 1794.

Most significantly, he produced paintings that glorified three Republican martyrs, notably the moving and iconic *Dying Marat* (1793), in which the radical journalist was transformed into a revolutionary saint, and Christian iconography was utilized to excite revolutionary fervor. Although the ugly Marat was idealized in this picture, the overall realism of the work served as an example to later Romantics, such as Théodore Géricault with his studies of the heads and limbs of the executed. In Paris, David also organized great revolutionary festivals that worked as a powerful instrument of propaganda to unify the new Republic in celebrations of brotherhood and liberty.

David narrowly avoided the guillotine at the fall of Robespierre in 1794 and spent a total of six months in prison, during which time he painted a self-portrait (1794), in which he is shown with palette and brush in hand, staring out at the spectator. He also started an ambitious history painting, *The Intervention of the Sabine Women* (1799), an image of reconciliation as the Sabine women separate their warring menfolk and the Roman soldiers who have come to reclaim their females. The picture demonstrated a change from the muscular Roman bodies of the Horatii to smoother and more sculptural forms, which David described as being "more Greek."

David quickly came under the spell of Napoleon. He became the favored artist of Bonaparte as he rose from brilliant general to first consul and finally to emperor. David first painted Napoleon early in 1798, but only completed a fragment in the three-hour sitting granted. After Napoleon's coup of Brumaire (November 10, 1799), he painted the first consul crossing the Alps (1801). When Napoleon became emperor in December 1804,

David was appointed his first painter and was charged with commemorating the events of the coronation. Four subjects were planned but only two, *The Coronation of Napoleon* (1805–8), and *The Distribution of Eagle Standards* (1810), were completed. For *The Coronation*, David turned to the example of Peter Paul Rubens to find an appropriate style to celebrate the empire. As such, *The Coronation* was so far removed from his previous neoclassicism that it is considered to represent a new "Empire" style; certainly no other image captures so perfectly the glitter and opulence of Napoleon's Imperial Court. However, David's demands for payment were considered excessive and later commissions were given to less expensive artists. David painted Napoleon for the last time in 1812, for the Englishman Alexander Douglas (later the tenth Duke of Hamilton); it was a life-size portrait that depicted the emperor as lawgiver working on the Napoleonic Code into the small hours of the morning.

David treated the topical theme of military defeat, albeit in ancient history, in *Leonidas at Thermopylae* (1814), where Leonidas and his Spartans had to defend a pass against the Persians, knowing that certain death awaited them. However, as an image of war it was considered outdated to those who had experienced the carnage of modern, industrialized warfare.

Following Napoleon's defeat and exile, David moved to Brussels in 1816. His later pictures appear rather different due to a change in artistic direction. In his last large-scale painting, *Mars Disarmed by Venus and the Three Graces* (1821–24), the unsettling combination of the real with the ideal replaced the element of fantasy that usually underpinned mythological works. The overall effect was one of parody, and David's later works may be seen as attempts to reinterpret mythology. In July 1825 David suffered a stroke, and he died in December of that year. Denied burial in France, an impressive funeral was arranged for him by the Belgian government.

David managed to encapsulate exactly the differing aspirations of successive regimes and created his own stylistic parameters. But his style was by no means static, and significant changes did occur. Through his teaching, David had an enormous influence on art in France and elsewhere in Europe. Although neoclassicism, a revolutionary art form in the 1780s and 1790s, became a highly orthodox and conservative form of academicism in the nineteenth century, David's productions remained inventive and his work does not reflect the supposed divide between neoclassicism and Romanticism. With his passionate and individual response to the Revolution and later interest in Rubensian color, to some Romantics (such as Eugène Delacroix, Théodore Géricault, and Horace Vernet) David's works provided lessons in how the universal and the personal could interact to produce an ethical yet deeply felt response.

SIMON LEE

Biography

Born in Paris, August 30, 1748. Son of Louis-Maurice David, prosperous cloth merchant, killed in a pistol duel 1757. Brought up by two uncles. Attended the Collège des Quatre-Nations, Paris, 1758–64. Trained in studio of history painter Joseph-Marie Vien, 1864–66. Enrolled in Académie Royale de Peinture et de Sculpture, 1775–80. Unsuccessful four times in official competitions; attempted suicide (date?). Won Prix de Rome for his *Antiochus and Stratonice*, 1774. Studied in Rome, 1775–80. Associate member (*agrée*) of the Académie Royale, 1781. Married Marguerite Pécoul, 1782 (they divorced in 1793), and had

The Oath of Horatii. Reprinted courtesy of the Bridgeman Art Library

two sons and twin daughters. Full member of the Académie Royale, c. 1783. Returned to Rome; painted *The Oath of the Horatii*, 1784–85. Exhibited *The Lictors Bringing Brutus the Bodies of His Sons* at the Paris Salon, 1789. Joined the Jacobin Club, 1790. Elected as deputy for Paris at the National Convention, 1792. Voted in favour of the execution of Louis XVI; appointed dictator of the arts and abolished the Académie Royale, 1793. President of the National Convention, 1794. Designed public festivals and monuments. Arrested and imprisoned twice after the execution of Maximilien de Robespierre, 1794–95. Remarried Marguerite Pécoul, 1796. Taught painting in Paris; pupils included François Gerard, Girodet, Antoine-Jean Gros, and Jean-Auguste-Dominique Ingres. Met Napoleon Bonaparte and started work on his portrait, 1797. Appointed as first painter to the emperor, 1804. Worked on *The Coronation*, 1805–8. Exiled to Switzerland after the fall of Napoleon, 1814; settled in Brussels, 1816. Completed *Mars and Venus*, 1824. Died in Brussels, December 29, 1825.

Bibliography

Brookner, A. *Jacques-Louis David*. London: Chatto and Windus, 1980.

Crow, T. *Painters and Public Life in Eighteenth-Century Paris*. New Haven, Conn.: Yale University Press, 1985.

"David contre David." *Proceedings of 1989 David Colloqium*. 2 vols. Paris: La Documentation Française, 1993.

David, J. L. J. *Le Peintre Louis David, 1748–1825. Souvenirs et documents inédits*. Paris: Victor Havard, 1880.

Delécluze, E. J. *Louis David, son école et son temps*. Paris: Didier, 1855. Reissued with introduction and notes by J. P. Mouilleseaux. Paris: Macula, 1983.

Dowd, D. L. *Pageant-Master of the Republic: Jacques-Louis David and the French Revolution*. Lincoln: University of Nebraska Press, 1948.

Lajer-Burcharth, E. *Necklines: The Art of Jacques-Louis David after the Terror*. New Haven, Conn.: Yale, 2000.

Lee, S. *David*, London: Phaidon Art and Ideas, 1999.

Schnapper, A. *David: Témoin de son temps*. Fribourg: Office du Livre, 1980.

Schnapper, A, and A. Sérullaz. *David*. Exhibition catalog. Paris: Louvre Versailles: Château; Editions de la Réunion des Musées Nationaux, 1990.

Weston, H., and W. Vaughan, eds. *David's The Death of Marat*. Cambridge: Cambridge University Press, 2000.

Wildenstein, D., and G. Wildenstein. *Documents complémentaires au catalogue de l'oeuvre de Louis David*. Paris: Fondation Wildsenstein, 1973.

DAVY, HUMPHRY 1778–1829

During the Romantic era, Humphry Davy was the "Man of Chemistry," as Lord Byron called him. His career is interesting for many reasons, not least because it witnessed eighteenth century notions of imponderable fluids give way to a modern nomenclature and atomic weights. Davy benefited from, and encouraged, increased specialization in the sciences, which saw chemistry emerge as an independent discipline and, specifically, a "gentleman's science." Davy can be seen as a bridge between eighteenth- and nineteenth-century science. His career began in the radical Pneumatic Institute in Bristol with Thomas Beddoes, and with the society of Samuel Taylor Coleridge, Robert Southey, and Thomas and Josiah Wedgwood, and ended with his entrenchment in the conservative establishment as president of the Royal Society. His work spanned some of the most important events that the Romantic era witnessed, and he responded to the prevailing mood of the times. He was also a socially transitional figure, with his humble origins in Penzance eclipsed by his later self-made gentleman status, with which he never felt entirely at ease. His most recent biographer, David Knight, identifies these oppositions in Davy: "brilliant and enigmatic, he was one of the most respected and most disliked men of science ever."

Though Davy's contributions to science were considerable, he is mostly remembered today for his miner's lamp, still known as the "Davy lamp." This was one example of his work being put to a practical use to help ordinary people. Yet, as science historian Jan Golinski has noted, he was partly responsible for the move away from Priestlian-style science where a general public could replicate experiments with little technical expertise or expensive instruments, to a more elite science practiced for, and among, the landed classes. Even the lamp has been seen as primarily permitting mine owners to attempt deeper and more dangerous lines, thus increasing the danger to miners.

Davy's early work was bold, inventive, and wildly speculative. In his first essay, published in a collection brought together by Thomas Beddoes, Davy asserted that Antoine-Laurent Lavoisier's "caloric" was a misnomer; he claimed that heat should instead be called "phosoxygen," identifying it as the result of combined light and oxygen. The essay brought him to the attention of Joseph Priestley, who expressed great interest in his ideas, but it encountered harsh criticism from others, by whom he was denounced as a hot-blooded materialist. The essay was purely theoretical and its lack of empirical proof exposed him to ridicule. This was a formative experience; he was careful never to speculate publicly again, and by the time of Beddoes's death Davy wrote coldly of his former mentor, having decided that he was responsible for these premature publications.

When Davy began his research into nitrous oxide at Bristol, he was already a budding poet. Southey published Davy's "Sons of Genius" in his 1799 *The Annual Anthology* and Davy continued to write, if not always publish, poetry throughout his life, becoming in later years a great admirer of Byron. In Bristol Coleridge befriended Davy and believed that, had he not been a scientist, he would have been an equally successful poet. Davy was engaged by William Wordsworth to correct the proofs of the second edition of *Lyrical Ballads* (1801). The inhalation of nitrous oxide was likened to poetic inspiration, and Davy himself announced that he had made a grand discovery while under its influence, reporting, "Nothing exists but thoughts!—the universe is composed of impressions, ideas, pleasures and pains." Davy's work with nitrous oxide at Bristol was considered to be quackery by conservative practitioners in the medical profession, a claim encouraged by the theatrical nature of its experiments and identification with radical politics, materialism, and atheism.

When Davy was appointed lecturer at the The Royal Institution of Great Britain, Coleridge worried that his friend would change. Davy was injured by his dealings with the conservative scientific press, and as a result became increasingly more conformist in his own philosophy and ideas. The institution was changing as well; originally it had been set up under the philanthropic ideals of Benjamin Thompson, Count Rumford, but in more recent years had revealed the agenda of its landed gentry members. From the outset Davy was a skillful lecturer. His introductory courses on chemistry were well attended by both women and men of the educated classes. It seems likely that Mary Shelley either attended or later read some of these lectures, since her character, Victor Frankenstein and his teacher Mr. Waldman share some of Davy's phrases and sentiments.

Davy made some of his most important contributions to science during his years at the Institution. His use of electricity in chemistry enabled him to discover new elements by identifying their alkaline form. Davy then turned his attention to agricultural chemistry and tanning, reflecting the interests of the institution's sponsors. Symbolic of his international status, he was decorated by Napoleon and the Institute of France while Britain and France were still at war. He was involved in the formation of the Animal Chemistry Society; this was significant because at the time organic chemistry was under-researched in Britain.

Davy was by this point recognized as the most famous scientist of his day. Yet Jons Jacob Berzelius remembered Davy for "brilliant fragments" rather than any single significant find. Perhaps his greatest contribution to science was his patronage of Michael Faraday, whose work was to prove of more lasting importance than that of his mentor.

As his final illness consumed him, he allied himself with other Romantic poets—Lord Byron, John Keats, and Percy Bysshe Shelley—who within the last ten years had died young and on the Continent. In his last work, *Consolations in Travel* (1830), he returned to concerns that had occupied him in his younger days at Clifton. Michael Neve highlights the "curious link between the beginning and the end of Davy's career, connected as they are by [a] commitment to establishing a Romanticist view of life."

SHARON RUSTON

Biography

Born in Penzance, Cornwall, December 17, 1778. Son of middle-class landowning parents. Educated at Penzance Grammar School and Truro (1793). Apprenticed to John Bingham Borlase, a Penzance surgeon, 1795. Began studying science in earnest, 1797. Appointed superintendent in the Pneumatic Institute, Bristol, 1798. Assistant lecturer at the Royal Institution, 1801; professor of chemistry there, 1802; elected Fellow of the Royal Society, 1803. Delivered first of annual series of lectures in Dublin, 1803. Awarded Copley medal from Royal Society, 1805. Secretary of the Royal Society, 1807. Honorary LL.D., Trinity College, Dublin, 1811. Knighted, 1812. Married Jane Apreece, a widow, 1813. Undertook European tour, 1813–15. Created a baronet, 1818. Elected president of the Royal Society, 1820; resigned that presidency in 1827. Lived in Europe, settling in Rome in 1829. Died in Geneva, May 29, 1829.

Selected Works

"Experimental essays on heat, light, and on the combinations of light, with a new theory of respiration, and observations on the chemistry of life." In *Contributions to Physical and Medical Knowledge, Principally from the West of England*. Edited by Thomas Beddoes and James Watt. 1799.

Researches, Chemical and Philosophical; chiefly concerning nitrous oxide, or dephlogisticated nitrous air, and its respiration. 1800.

A Discourse, Introductory to A Course of Lectures on Chemistry, delivered in the theatre of the Royal Institution on the twenty first of January, 1802. 1802.

Elements of Chemical Philosophy. 1812.

Elements of Agricultural Chemistry. 1813.

Salmonia; or, Days of fly fishing. In a series of conversations, with some account of the habits of fishes belonging to the genus Salmo. By an Angler. 1828.

Consolations in Travel; or The Last Days of a Philosopher. 1830.

Bibliography

Crouch, Laura E. "Davy's *A Discourse Introductory to a Course of Lectures on Chemistry*: A Possible Scientific Source of *Frankenstein*," *Keats-Shelley Journal* 27 (1978): 35–44.

Fullmer, June Z. "Humphry Davy: Fund Raiser." *The Development of the Laboratory: Essays on the Place of Experiment in Industrial Civilisation*. Edited by Frank A. J. L. James. Basingstoke, England: Macmillan, 1989.

Golinski, Jan. *Science as Public Culture: Chemistry and Enlightenment in Britain, 1760–1820*. Cambridge: Cambridge University Press, 1992.

Hoover, Suzanne R. "Coleridge, Humphry Davy, and Some Early Experiments with a Consciousness-Altering Drug," *Bulletin of Research in the Humanities* 81 (1978): 9–24.

Jenkins, Alice. "Humphry Davy: Poetry, Science and the Love of Light." In *1798: The Year of the Lyrical Ballads*. Edited by Richard Cronin. Basingstoke, England: Macmillan, 1998.

Knight, David. *Humphry Davy: Science and Power*. Oxford: Blackwell, 1992.

Lawrence, Christopher. "The Power and the Glory: Humphry Davy and Romanticism." In *Romanticism and the Sciences*. Edited by Andrew Cunningham and Nicholas Jardine. Cambridge: Cambridge University Press, 1990.

Levere, Thomas. "Dr Thomas Beddoes and the Establishment of His Pneumatic Institution: A Tale of Three Presidents," *Notes and Records of the Royal Society of London* 32 (1977): 41–49.

Neve, Michael. "The Young Humphry Davy: or John Tonkin's Lament." In *Science and the Sons of Genius: Studies on Humphry Davy*. Edited by Sophie Forgan. London: Science Reviews, 1980.

Sharrock, Roger. "The Chemist and the Poet: Sir Humphry Davy and the Preface to *Lyrical Ballads*," *Notes and Records of the Royal Society of London* 17 (1962): 56–76.

Stansfield, Dorothy. *Thomas Beddoes, M.D., 1760–1808: Chemist, Physician, Democrat*. Dordrect: D. Reidel, 1984.

Treneer, Anne. *The Mercurial Chemist: A Life of Sir Humphry Davy*. London: Methuen, 1963.

DAY, THOMAS 1748–1789

British essayist, novelist, and poet

Thomas Day is best remembered as the author of *Sandford and Merton* (1783), one of the earliest novels intentionally written for children, but during his lifetime he was equally known as a philanthropist, poet, and political essayist. Early on, Day demonstrated charity toward the poor and kindness to animals. At Oxford University he came under the influence of Jean-Jacques Rousseau, denounced the luxurious lifestyles of other students, and lived ascetically. He became close friends with Richard Lovell Edgeworth (father of Maria Edgeworth), who shared his enthusiasm for Rousseau's educational theories. Day decided to educate two orphan girls on Rousseau's principles, in the hope that one of them would make him a suitable wife, but the experiment was a failure. In Lichfield, Day and Edgeworth joined a literary circle that included Anna Seward and Erasmus Darwin. Traveling to Paris, they visited Rousseau, exhibiting Edgeworth's son as the picture of Émile.

In 1773, Day moved to London, where a newspaper article about a slave who had committed suicide rather than be sent to labor in the plantations inspired Day and his friend John Bicknell to produce *The Dying Negro* (1773). The poem, one of the earliest literary attacks on slavery and the slave trade, is influenced by the polite genre of sensibility, but also represents Africans as "noble savages," uncorrupted by the "sordid gold" of "Christian traffic." These themes are united early on in the poem:

In their veins the tide of honour rolls;
And valour kindles there the hero's flame,
Contempt of death, and thirst of martial fame:
And pity melts the sympathising breast,

The poem's debt to Rousseau is clear, and the 1775 edition, to which Day added an essay opposing slavery, is formally dedicated to the philosopher. The essay contains an attack, among the first of its kind, on the hypocrisy of the British colonists in America, "whose clamours for liberty and independence are heard across the Atlantic ocean." As long as the colonists keep slaves, Day argues, these are "wild inconsistent claims." The poem was popular, and, although it appeared some 15 years before the widespread anti–slave trade agitation of the 1780s, it is an important early document of the movement.

Having attacked the American colonists in 1775, Day rose to their defense with *The Devoted Legions* (1776) and *The Desolation of America* (1777). In the latter he drew a gruesome portrait of the despoilation of America by British and Hanoverian troops, concluding that "o'er the wasted fields and dreary plains, / In silent horror desolation reigns." These were understandably less popular than his attack on slavery, although the defeat for the British which he predicted appeared increasingly likely. During this period, Day met Esther Milnes, who admired his principles. The two courted, but at first Day refused to marry her, as one of those same principles dictated that he could not marry a wealthy woman. They eventually reached an agreement whereby Milnes's fortune was put legally beyond Day's reach, and they were married in August 1778. They lived frugally, in accordance with Day's belief that "we have no right to luxuries while the poor want bread." During the Political crisis of 1780, Day established himself as a speaker and writer, sharing a platform with John Wilkes and a pamphlet with Charles James Fox. His politics, though radical, were not original, and his contribution lay more in his skill as a propagandist and public speaker. At the general election, he was urged to stand, but declined to join the "tribe of begging, cringing, shuffling, intriguing candidates." He dropped out of politics and retired to his new estate at Anningsley in Surrey, where he lost money conducting agricultural and social experiments, employing the very poorest parish inhabitants and promoting (on his own terms) their physical and spiritual welfare.

Here he produced his most significant achievement, *The History of Sandford and Merton*, inspired by Edgeworth's complaint that there was no suitable reading for his children. The novel is essentially a collection of short stories, usually with a moral, linked by a unifying narrative. Young Tommy Merton, the son of a rich Jamaica planter, has been grossly spoiled by life in a corrupt slave-owning society. Sent to England to be educated, he is rescued from a poisonous snake by Harry Sandford, the virtuous son of a "plain, honest farmer." Despite their differences, the two become friends, and Tommy is introduced to Mr. Barlow, the local clergyman. Under Barlow's directions, Tommy's innate good nature is revealed, and he learns the virtues of patience, self-reliance, and respect for others. The book thus plainly inculcates the values proposed by Rousseau in *Émile* while illustrating Rousseau's belief that man is by nature good, though corrupted by society. However, in his preface Day denies that *Sandford and Merton* is a treatise on education, claiming "it is from [children's] applause alone I shall estimate my success." The work sold extremely well, was praised by the critics, and in response Day produced two further volumes (1787 and 1789). The whole forms the first substantial work for older children, and it remained popular for over a century.

Day produced other children's literature during the 1780s, but none matched the success of *Sandford and Merton*. Always true to his principles, he published anonymously and continued with the secluded philanthropy of his life at Anningsley. In 1789 he was thrown from an unbroken horse that he had attempted to train by kindness, and died shortly afterward from his injuries. His death reflects his life. By all accounts a generous and good-hearted man, Day's devotion to rigid, and sometimes eccentric, philosophical principles often led him to work against his own best interests. His contribution to the Romantic era was rather more positive. *The Dying Negro* was frequently imitated over the following years, and *Sandford and Merton* inspired countless children's novels. Rousseau is frequently cited as a central influence on early Romanticism. Day's contribution ensured that philosophy inspired by Rousseau formed the very earliest reading of most literate English-speaking people during the Romantic era.

BRYCCHAN CAREY

Biography

Born London, June 22, 1748. Educated Charterhouse and Corpus Christi College, Oxford, 1767; formed friendship with Richard Lovell Edgeworth, 1767–73; lived variously in England and France, 1773; wrote *The Dying Negro* (with John Bicknell), 1776–77; wrote poetry in support of the American revolution, 1788; married Esther Milnes, 1780; briefly involved with radical politics, 1783; first volume of *Sandford and Merton*, 1787; second volume, 1789; third volume, 1789. Died after a fall from a horse, September 28, 1789.

Selected Writings

The Dying Negro. 1773.
The Devoted Legions: A Poem Addressed to Lord George Germaine and the Commanders of the Forces against America. 1776.

The Desolation of America. 1777.
The History of Sandford and Merton: A Work Intended for the Use of Children. 3 vols. 1783–89.

Bibliography

Gignilliat, George Warren. *The Author of Sandford and Merton: A Life of Thomas Day, Esq.* New York: Columbia University Studies in English and Comparative Literature, 1931.
Rowland, Peter. *The Life and Times of Thomas Day, 1748–1789: English Philanthropist and Author; Virtue Almost Personified.* Studies in British History, 39. Lewistown, Queenston, and Lampeter: The Edwin Mellon Press, 1996.

DE L'ALLEMAGNE (ON GERMANY) 1810

Critical work by Anne-Louise-Germaine de Staël

De l'Allemagne (*On Germany*, 1810), the third of Madame de Staël's treatises on critical theory after *De l'Influence des passions sur le bonheur des individus et des nations* (*On the Influence of Emotion on the Happiness of Individuals and Nations*, 1796) and *De la Littérature considérée dans ses rapports avec les institutions sociales* (*On Literature and Its Relationship to Social Institutions*, 1800), had, despite the circumstances surrounding its publication, a great influence on French Romanticism, far greater than any of her other works. Napoleon Bonaparte who detested her for what he saw as her intrusion on French imperial politics, had the entire first edition of ten thousand copies destroyed. As a result, the first published edition of a seminal work in the history of French Romanticism initially appeared in London in 1813. Madame de Staël did not endear herself to the emperor when she wrote, in the preface, that the French should no longer surround themselves with a "Wall of China" to protect themselves from foreign influences; her position became even less favorable when she compared contemporary France to Rome in its decadence. And when she celebrated, in the text itself, the Romantic talents of Johann Wolfgang von Goethe, Gotthold Emphraim Lessing, Jean Paul Richter, and Johann Christoph Friedrich von, Schiller, French critics interpreted such praise as implied disdain for eighteenth-century French neoclassical masters such as Voltaire, and considered her espousal of August Wilhelm von Schlegel's Romantic theories a rejection of Boileau and neoclassicism.

Divided into four parts—"De l'Allemagne et des moeurs des Allemands" ("On Germany and German Customs"), "De la Littérature et des arts" ("On Literature and the Arts"), "De la philosophie et de la morale" ("On Philosophy and Morals"), and "La religion et l'enthousiasme" ("Religion and Enthusiasm")—*De l'Allemagne* mapped out, as did François-Auguste-René, Vicomte de Chateaubriand's *Génie du Christianisme* (1802), the route that the French Romantics were to follow. She indicated four principal approaches that would become characteristics of French Romantic literature. These are: rejection of the imitation of ancient Greco-Roman models in favor of "modern," (i.e., medieval and later) subjects, exploitation of the author's own emotions (which would find expression in French Romantic autobiographical and confessional literature, both historical and

fictional), use of specifically French subjects, and a recognition of Christian belief, rather than "fate," a pagan notion, *pagan-influence fate*, as the ruling power in Romantic psychology. To assist French authors in the development of their new, specifically French, voice, she advised them to look to Germany and England, not as models, but as sources of the new sensibility, as when she wrote, "The name *Romantic* has been introduced recently in Germany to designate poetry whose source is the songs of the troubadours, poetry born of chivalry and Christianity . . . Romantic poetry [is] the kind that derives in some way from the traditions of chivalry." (part 2, chapter 11).

Madame de Staël argued that the new Romantic poets should find inspiration in their own inner sensibility, which the Christian institution of confession had taught them to analyze. This position was a rejection of the neoclassical dictum to writers to follow the external "rules" derived from Aristotle's *Poetics*, Horace's *Art of Poetry*, and other classical sources. She believed classical heroes were creatures of action, rather than reflection, and classical works were dominated by plot, as opposed to characterization. Thus, she argued, French Romantic writers should focus their efforts on character development and analysis. Christianity, with its emphasis on self-analysis, offered Romantic writers a method of psychological scrutiny based on religious morality. Finally, she argued, French Romantic writers should choose distinctly French subjects. Such a choice would produce a popular literature; classical subjects, she felt, had never appealed to the people because they were foreign. "The literature of the Ancients," she wrote, "is for us moderns a transplanted literature; whereas Romantic or chivalric literature is indigenous to us, brought to blossom by our religion and our institutions. . . . Poetry on the Antique model, however perfect it may be, is rarely popular, because in the present day it relates to nothing native to us."

A. W. HALSALL

Selected Works

De l'Allemagne, nouvelle édition d'après les mss. et les éditions originales avec des variantes. 5 vols. Edited by Jean de Pange, and Simone Balayé. Paris: Hachette, 1958–60.
Madame de Staël on Politics, Literature, and National Character. Translated, edited, and with a general introduction by Morroe Berger. Garden City, N.Y.: Doubleday, 1964.

Bibliography

Gutwirth, M., A. Goldberger, and K. Szmurlo, eds. *Madame de Staël: Crossing the Borders*. New Brunswick, N.J.: Rutgers University Press, 1991.

Naudin, Marie. "Madame de Staël, précurseur de l'esthétique romantique," *Revue des sciences humaines*, fasc. 139 (juillet-sept. 1970), 391–400.

Solovieff, Georges. *L'Allemagne et Madame de Staël*. Paris: Klincksieck, 1990.

Winegarten, Renée. *Madame de Staël*. Leamington Spa: Berg, 1985.

DE QUINCEY, THOMAS 1785–1859

English essayist and critic

The cultural span of Thomas De Quincey's life is broad, and his connection with Romanticism perplexed and convoluted. Traditionally, he is integrated into its nexus of values through his threefold obsession with the circle of William Wordsworth and Samuel Taylor Coleridge, with opium, and with autonomous systems of knowledge. Despite this self-evident focus, De Quincey's was always a contemporary voice. A true polymath, he would, as an essayist, embrace many of the major cultural and sociopolitical issues of his age, as well as experiment widely with a variety of aesthetic principles in his fictional and semifictional publications. Early, Enlightenment-based classicist interests were soon modified by the sensibilist, radical-humanist strain encountered in (for one) the *Lyrical Ballads* of Coleridge and Wordsworth. This was itself rapidly to be drawn through the critical epistemologies offered by Kantian metaphysics and German Romantic irony. Much of De Quincey's earlier writing would concern itself with clarifying and disseminating these cultural features in the pages of the great periodicals of the age, most extensively in the politically disparate *London* magazine, *Blackwood's*, and *Tait's*. While these journals were significant social determinants, offering topical immediacy, they conjointly threatened ephemerality, a fact which often led the ambiguously ultra-Tory De Quincey simultaneously to universalize, personalize, and ironize topics as varied as animal magnetism, a life of Hannah More, and the 1850s Anglo-Chinese Opium Wars.

If his original aesthetic lodestar was Wordsworth, then De Quincey's seminal philosophical guide would be that fixation of so many writers of the Romantic age, Immanuel Kant, whose work he was one of the first (along with Coleridge) to introduce into Britain. His early writings for *London* magazine and for *Blackwood's* practically cover the entire range of important European Romantic figures. Among other subjects, De Quincey would deal with the work of Johann Wolfgang von Goethe, Johann Gottfried von Herder, Immanuel Kant, Gotthold Ephraim Lessing, Jean Paul Richter and Johann Christoph Friedrich von Schiller, offering original translations of their writings in a number of cases, some representing a first British appearance.

As with so many fellow Romantic and Victorian writers, De Quincey was passionately interested in political economy, "that philosophy of society [and] profound social binding agent," as he called it. Ricardian economics, which De Quincey aligned epistemologically with Kant's metaphysical system, formed the subject of many articles as well as of a book publication, the *Logic of Political Economy* (1844), a work favorably mentioned by both Karl Marx and John Stuart Mill. Conversely, as a historian, De Quincey's major interest was the rise and fall, or "disrupted linearity" as he put it, of great civilizations, a process examined at length, for example, in the "Caesars" series of 1832–34. Like so many writers of his generation, very much post-Edward Gibbon, it was the form of ruin, the psychological growth and degeneration of the power-base of empires, that proved an irresistible fascination.

That evolving line of Romantic aesthetics that analogized artistic subjectivity and object of characterization found new direction in De Quincey's writings on crime. As a social entity, factual crime-writing "concreted . . . social duties" and served to anchor a number of his essays. Fictively, violent crime became a matter for poetic anatomization, the focus of a quite different form of publication. Kant's principle in the *Critique of Pure Reason* (1790) that aesthetic experience is essentially amoral would be applied in the latter, with considerable irony, "to the composition of a fine murder." The most accomplished result can be seen in the papers "On Murder Considered as One of the Fine Arts" (1827 and 1839; with a "Postscript," 1854). Extending the theme to the still-fashionable genre of gothic fiction, De Quincey (following Matthew Lewis and Ann Radcliffe) outlined a psychopathology of paranoia and social paralysis in, for example, *Klosterheim* (1832) and "The Avenger" (1838).

Much of De Quincey's periodical writing was to develop the artistic possibilities of prose discourse far beyond the bounds of the traditional essay form, as a brief comparison with, for example, the magazine work of Charles Lamb and William Hazlitt, no timid experimenters themselves, shows. When he came to categorize his writings in the 1850s, he evaluated those essays formalized through the topology of what he called "impassioned prose" most highly. Here he placed, for example, the essentially autobiographical *Confessions* (1821; greatly enlarged in 1856), "The English Mail-Coach" (1849), and "more emphatically" the *Suspiria de Profundis* (published incompletely in 1845). With its aesthetic roots in the work of such German Romantic ironists as Novalis, Richter and Ludwig Tieck, this latter category approximates the Romantic hybrid of prose poetry. Here the speculation is philosophical, and autobiography often seems more like a poetic attenuation of lived experience than the thing itself. The works listed here are paradigmatically linked to opium. They deal, in very different ways, with the social, personal, and artistic context to ingesting the drug, and, especially in the *Suspiria*, with the incarnation of patterns of experience in the enriched, organically interconnected ("involuted," as De Quincey called it) phenomenology of opium-induced dreams. If Coleridge tried to live his life in denial of his opium addiction, De Quincey was to make a virtue of it. All of those elements of the Kantian, and thus Romantic, sublime can be found integrated into the topology of oneiric and subreptitious landscapes in De Quincey. Time and space expand infinitely within a hyperaesthetic mental landscape as the "dreamer" enacts exquisitely sensuous and nightmarish experience by turn. This paradigm, which in Wordsworthian fashion occludes the empirical and the metaphysical in a sort of allegory of the unconscious, proved influential with a number of subsequent writers, including Charles Baudelaire, Alfred de Musset, and Edgar Allan Poe. Such would also appeal to twentieth-century artists as varied as Jorge Luis Borges and Sid Vicious.

After the *Confessions* it is for his rather solipsistic biographies of Wordsworth and Coleridge, certainly the most notable portraits of the Romantic age, that De Quincey is best known. He was on intimate terms with both men, "the deep deep magnet . . . of William Wordsworth" (whose daily life at Grasmere he at one point shared) particularly, and didn't scruple to detail this knowledge in his many writings on the subject. As critics note of De Quincey, it is his defiance of traditional generic conventions that has often served him ill with readers. "Samuel Taylor Coleridge" (1834–35) and the numerous, variously subtitled installments of the "Sketches," "Autobiography," and "Lake Reminiscences . . . William Wordsworth" of the 1830s and 1840s are no different: an intertextual "English Opium-Eater" moves analytically by the side of those large number of "Lakes" figures under review. Revealing Coleridge's plagiarisms along with the extent of his opium addiction and detailing Wordsworth's egoism and domestic habits won De Quincey few literary friends at the time. However, the cultural determinants of the two writers are also outlined in fine detail: a self-reflexive construct, once again, since one can also see the epistemological influences of De Quincey's own writings taking evolutionary shape in these articles.

De Quincey's main affiliation was always with first-generation Romantic writing, his long life notwithstanding. If he also appreciated John Keats, Shelley and others of their generation, then the interest was limited if no less sure. Of Victorian novelists and poets one hears very little, even though article after article shows a concentrated awareness of the major moving forces of an advanced industrial society. Virginia Woolf described De Quincey as both "an angel with wings of flame and eyes of fire [and] a gentlemen in black who talks sense." It is this curiously bifurcated cultural consciousness which makes him simultaneously a child of Romanticism *and* a representative Victorian: ultimately taxonomy and epistemological organicism inhabit the same intellectual endeavours in his work. When the authoritative Manchester-based collected edition has cohered as a cultural construct, the vast depth and extent of these endeavors will be fully evident and a persisting critical part-picture of De Quincey will at last stand complete.

BARRY SYMONDS

Biography

Born in Manchester, August 15, 1785. Educated at Bath Grammar School, 1796–99; private school in Winkfield, Wiltshire, 1799–1800; Manchester Grammar School, 1801–2. Lived incognito in London, 1802–3. Studied at Worcester College, Oxford University, 1803–8. First took opium, 1804. Met and became close friend of Samuel Taylor Coleridge, Robert Southey, and William Wordsworth, 1807. Moved to Grasmere, Westmorland; lived at Wordsworth's former home there, Dove Cottage, intermittently from 1809 on. Entered Middle Temple, London, 1812. Married Margaret Simpson: five sons, three daughters. Edited the *Westmorland Gazette*, 1818–19; contributor to *Blackwood's Edinburgh* magazine, 1821, 1826–34, 1837–45, 1849; to *London* magazine, 1821–24; to *Hogg's Instructor* (later *Titan*), 1850–58. Published "Confessions of an English Opium-Eater" in *London* magazine, 1821. Lived permanently in Edinburgh from 1828. Became eccentric and reclusive after his wife's death, 1837. Died in Edinburgh, December 8, 1859.

Selected Works

Collections
Selections Grave and Gay. 14 vols. Edited and revised by Thomas De Quincey. 1853–60.
The Collected Writings of Thomas De Quincey. 14 vols. Edited by David Masson. 1896–97.
The Works of Thomas De Quincey. 22 vols. General editor Grevel Lindop. 2000– .

Separate Publications
"Confessions of an English Opium-Eater." 1821; first book publication, 1822. Edited by Grevel Lindop.
Articles on and translations of Kant and other German cultural figures lie scattered throughout a number of periodical sources. They can be found primarily in *London* magazine, 1821–24, and in *Blackwood's,* 1826–27 and 1830. See also collected works above.
New Essays by De Quincey. (Contributions to the *Edinburgh SaturdayPost/Edinburgh Evening Post,* 1827–28. Edited by Stuart M. Tave. 1966.
"On Murder Considered as One of the Fine Arts." 1827, 1839; "Postscript." 1854.
"The Caesars." 1832–34.
Klosterheim, or the Masque. 1832. Edited by John Weeks. 1982.
"Samuel Taylor Coleridge." 1834–35. "Lake Reminiscences." 1839; published as *Recollections of the Lakes and the Lake Poets,* (with selections from the *Sketches* and the *Autobiography,* 1834–41). Edited by David Wright. 1970.
"The Avenger." 1838.
Logic of Political Economy. 1844.
Autobiographic Sketches. 1853.
A selection of De Quincey's critical writings can be found in *De Quincey as Critic.* Edited by John E. Jordan. 1973.

Bibliography

Barrell, John. *The Infection of Thomas De Quincey: A Psychopathology of Imperialism.* New Haven, Conn.: Yale University Press, 1991.
Baxter, Edmund. *De Quincey's Art of Autobiography.* Edinburgh: Edinburgh University Press, 1990.
De Luca, V. A. *Thomas De Quincey: The Prose of Vision.* Toronto: University of Toronto Press, 1980.
Lindop, Grevel. *The Opium-Eater: A Life of Thomas De Quincey.* London: J. M. Dent, 1981.
McDonagh, Josephine. *De Quincey's Disciplines.* Oxford: Clarendon Press, 1994.
Roberts, Daniel Sanjiv. *Revisionary Gleam: De Quincey, Coleridge, and the High Romantic Argument.* Liverpool: Liverpool University Press, 2000.
Russett, Margaret. *De Quincey's Romanticism: Canonical Minority and the Forms of Transmission.* Cambridge: Cambridge University Press, 1997.
Rzepka, Charles. *Sacramental Commodities: Gift, Text, and the Sublime in De Quincey.* Amherst: University of Massachusetts Press, 1995.
Snyder, Robert Lance, ed. *Thomas De Quincey: Bicentenary Studies.* Norman: University of Oklahoma Press, 1985.
Whale, John C. *Thomas De Quincey's Reluctant Autobiography.* London: Croom Helm, 1984.

DECONSTRUCTION AND ROMANTIC LITERATURE

The critical method known as deconstruction has a number of important affiliations with Romanticism. It is no doubt appropriate that deconstruction, a method associated with paradox and aporia, can be said to have both revitalized and undermined the study of Romanticism in late-twentieth-century scholarship. On the one hand, deconstructive critics helped to restore the prestige of Romantic literary texts that had been demoted somewhat by modernist and new critical judgments. On the other hand, deconstructive arguments effectively called into question the validity of Romanticism as an historical and conceptual entity, and led many scholars to de-emphasize the term Romantic in favor of some looser period distinction, such as "the long eighteenth century."

Although deconstructive interpreters worked with literature from all periods, in many ways Romanticism is the source and center of deconstruction as a critical movement. The most prominent deconstructive theorists focused their attention on texts associated with English, French, and German Romanticism. Jacques Derrida, the French philosopher usually cited as the founding voice of deconstruction, wrote about G. W. F. Hegel, Immanuel Kant, Jean-Jacques Rousseau, and Percy Bysshe Shelley. Paul de Man, the Belgian-American literary theorist who was the leader of the so-called Yale school of deconstruction in the 1970s and early 1980s, did his most important work on Romantic writers, including Friedrich Holderlin, Rousseau, Shelley and William Wordsworth. The other celebrities of the Yale school included Geoffrey Hartman, best known for his rereading of Wordsworth; Harold Bloom, who articulated his theory of the anxiety of influence primarily through readings of English Romantic poets; and J. Hillis Miller, who increasingly focused on Romantic topics as he adopted a deconstructive approach. Bloom, de Man, Derrida, Hartman, and Miller collaborated on *Deconstruction and Criticism* (a manifesto of sorts for the Yale school), which takes Shelley's *Triumph of Life* (1979) as its primary textual focus. Despite their apparent gathering into a critical school, these five were united more by an interest in Romanticism and a dense, revisionary critical style than by any stable interpretive credo. Bloom was never very comfortable with the style of reading made popular by Derrida, and increasingly he denounced deconstruction as unproductive. Notably, the most influential scholarly antagonist of deconstruction, M. H. Abrams, was also a Romantic scholar.

If some Romantic scholars have denounced deconstruction as vigorously as others have devoted themselves to it, there are nevertheless substantive connections between deconstruction and Romanticism. Several theorists have attempted to show that the roots of deconstruction can be traced back to the philosophical and poetic expressions of European Romanticism. There do appear to be compelling links between the intellectual strategies of the two movements. Both Romanticism and deconstruction reacted against the dominant position of reason and science in their respective intellectual environments. This is not to say, of course, that Romantic and deconstructive writers simply disavowed the legacy of the Enlightenment, but they both questioned the abstract, systematic reasoning that had displaced alternative intellectual modes. Part of the challenge to reason had to do with the concept of objectivity in interpretation. Blake, for example, repeatedly denied the privileged status of reason, which he argued is neither objective in its own right nor superior to other mental acts (in particular, desire, and imagination) from which reason draws its constituent ideas. In a parallel way, deconstructive critics repeatedly look for the implicit assumptions or rhetorical tropes that subvert an apparently straightforward rational argument or poetic statement. Enlightenment faith in objective, determinate truth was challenged in the late eighteenth and early nineteenth centuries by Romantic irony, and in the late twentieth century by deconstructive indeterminacy. According to deconstructive interpreters, no text has a stable, foundational meaning that competent readers can accurately decode. Any text necessarily calls forth a multiplicity of meanings. Implicit within the language that frames an idea are the tropes and contradictions that subvert it. Furthermore, readings will vary as interpretive contexts vary, and there is no way to limit the variety of interpretive contexts.

One of the most heated debates surrounding the deconstructive interpretation of Romantic poetry centered on one of Wordsworth's so-called Lucy poems, titled "A Slumber Did My Spirit Seal." Miller published an essay in which he presented a number of questions about the poem that were previously considered out of bounds, either because they lacked proper textual evidence, or because they went against generally accepted assumptions about who Wordsworth was and what he was writing about. Miller teases out from the poem a host of contrary positions, including some that involve sexuality and incestuous desire. He deconstructs the surface meaning of this "apparently simple poem" that will not allow itself to be resolved or decoded as a settled message. The usual method of determinate interpretation, "does not work. Something is always left over, a plus value beyond the boundaries of each such interpretation" (p. 102). Several other critics weighed in on the interpretation of this poem, including M. H. Abrams, who stoutly defended a determinate reading: "I am reassured, however, by the stubborn capacity of construed texts to survive their second-order deconstruction." The poem offers not "a regress of deadlocked double-binds," but a beautiful expression of "the suddenness, unexpectedness, and finality of death" (p. 158).

Deconstructive interpretations of Romantic and other texts dominated literary studies until the mid-1980s, when two complaints against the method began to take hold. One criticism had to do with the predictable, almost mechanical plot of most deconstructive arguments, along with a tendency of many practitioners to employ puns and neologisms. A second criticism had to do with the way deconstructive interpretations minimized or erased political and historical content. (This criticism gained especial attention with the revelation that de Man had covered up his activities during World War II, when he wrote articles sympathetic to anti-Semitic positions.) The same accusation has been made about the so-called Romantic ideology of John Keats, Wordsworth, and others who appear to privilege private acts of imagination above political awareness and action. However, it is important to note that both Romanticism and deconstruction have been vindicated from this charge, at least to some degree. Romantic poets, including Keats and Wordsworth, have been reexamined in context to emphasize their political engagements; and most of the postdeconstructive critics known as the new historicists make heavy use of interpretive strategies borrowed from deconstruction.

WAYNE GLAUSSER

Bibliography

Abrams, M. H. "Construing and Deconstructing." In *Romanticism and Contemporary Criticism*. Edited by Morris Eaves and Michael Fischer. Ithaca, N.Y.: Cornell University Press, 1986. 127–82.

Bloom, Harold, Paul de Man, Jacques Derrida, Geoffrey Hartman, and J. Hillis Miller. *Deconstruction and Criticism*. New York: Continuum, 1979.

Culler, Jonathan. *On Deconstruction: Theory and Criticism after Structuralism*. Ithaca, N.Y.: Cornell University Press, 1982.

de Man, Paul. *Allegories of Reading: Figurative Language in Rousseau, Nietzsche, Rilke, and Proust*. New Haven, Conn.: Yale University Press, 1979.

———. *Blindness and Insight: Essays in the Rhetoric of Contemporary Criticism*. New York: Oxford University Press, 1971.

Derrida, Jacques. *Of Grammatology*. Translated with a preface by Gayatri Chakravorty Spivak. Baltimore: Johns Hopkins University Press, 1976.

Miller, J. Hillis. "On Edge: The Crossways of Contemporary Criticism." In *Romanticism and Contemporary Criticism*. Edited by Morris Eaves and Michael Fischer. Ithaca, N.Y.: Cornell University Press, 1986. 96–126.

Wang, Orrin N. C. *Fantastic Modernity: Dialectical Readings in Romanticism and Theory*. Baltimore: Johns Hopkins University Press, 1996.

Wheeler, Kathleen M. *Romanticism, Pragmatism and Deconstruction*. Oxford: Blackwell, 1993.

DEDHAM VALE 1828

Painting by John Constable

John Constable's long engagement with Dedham Vale, or the Stour Valley (East Anglia, England), begins with four watercolors he had completed by 1800, one of them entitled *Dedham Church and Vale*. Two years later he had completed *Dedham Vale; Road near Dedham*; and *Wooded Landscape at Sunset, with a Figure*—three small oils treating the region of his birth and upbringing, the Bergholt district of Suffolk. An important factor in his development at this time was his acquaintance with the amateur painter Sir George Beaumont, whose collection included the work *Hagar and the Angel* by Claude Lorraine. All students of Constable's work comment on the influence of Claude's *Hagar* on the *Dedham Vale* of 1802, citing the imposing tree on the right and the distant view dominating the center. Another identifiable borrowing, the rustic lolling in the foreground of another, smaller *Dedham Vale* oil of 1802, was inspired by the technique of Thomas Gainsborough, who commonly inserted such figures in his landscapes.

Karl Kroeber has written perceptively of Constable's 1802 painting, finding in Claude "theatrical dream visions" that Constable then transposed into "a new manner of representing immediate realities as temporal phenomena." Constable discarded Claude's iconography but kept his pattern of composition, striving for a "coalescence of subjective view and objective reality." His emphasis on the dramatic foreground departed from Claude's practice, illustrating one of Constable's maxims as a landscapist: "Get your foreground right and the rest will follow." Constable's foreground is "richly textured," in the words of Kroeber, who relates Constable's originality to the rise of English landscape poetry in the eighteenth century.

Two more small oil sketches of *Dedham Vale* in 1810 were climaxed by Constable's exhibition in 1811 of *Dedham Vale, Morning*, much larger (31 by 51 inches) than the earlier apprenticeship works, and perhaps the first of the great works that were to exemplify Constable's distinctive Romanticism. In the center foreground, a boy is driving cattle home from pasture, while a man and a woman approach from the right. The vale recedes in the center to a horizon suffused with early morning light; and angular, leafy trees on the left and on the right frame and complete the pastoral harmony. Leslie Parris notes that "The Claudean composition and the stone [in the foreground] inscribed, like some antique fragment, 'DEDHAM VALE,' add a further, Arcadian, dimension to the picture."

Constable once declared that "Painting is with me another word for feeling," a feeling largely identified with the "lovely valleys and peaceful farm-houses of Suffolk" that he said made him a painter. In this respect he was perhaps a provincial, but a provincial of the sensibility that Carlos Peacock has in mind when he instances Paul Cézanne, Constable, Dante Alighieri, and Charles Dickens as "geniuses of place" who have "achieved greatness in art not by straining at horizons, but by narrowing their range in order to understand profoundly a single fragment of locality." It is this sense of a familiar locale that inspires the great "six-footers," as Constable called them, of the 1820s, the large canal scenes of the River Stour. Finally, in the *Dedham Vale* exhibited at the Royal Academy in 1828, Constable painted the large oil that capped two decades of a loving engagement with that subject.

Constable's early patron, Sir George Beaumont, died in 1827 and left his *Hagar* to the National Gallery, where Constable may have seen it once more and been inspired to paint his last *Dedham Vale* as a tribute to his friend. In a discussion of "Landscape as Divested History Painting," Ronald Paulson quotes from Constable's lectures on landscape given in 1836, citing the assertion that "landscape is the child of history" (that is, of history painting). Paulson suspects that one of Constable's examples, Titian's *Martyrdom of St. Peter Martyr*, may have been in Constable's mind when he painted *Dedham Vale* and the other large upright compositions. John Walker points out that the heavy shadows in the foreground and the brilliant light in the distance were common in seventeenth-century landscapes, as were the framing foliage and the elevated perspective of the valley beyond as seen from Gun Hill, Dedham. Walker speculates that although such an arrangement of elements was not frequent with Constable, it was this traditional composition that may have accounted for *Dedham Vale*'s "excellent reception" at the Royal Academy show in 1828. The gypsy mother nursing her baby in the foreground has been criticized as sentimental bad taste, but Graham Reynolds defends this detail on the grounds that "gyp-

John Constable, *Dedham Vale, View to Langham Church, from the Fields just east of Vale Farm, East Bergholt.* Reprinted courtesy of AKG.

sies were and are frequently to be seen in East Anglia, and this group does not infringe Constable's rule that only actual or probable figures should be shown." Comparing it to the *Dedham Vale* of 1802, Kenneth Clark finds "sparkling details that would not have fitted into Claude's ideal scheme." The realistic elements in the painting—for example, Dedham mill, Dedham assembly rooms, Wrabness Point, and Mistley Church—have been scrupulously identified by Attfield Brooks, who reproduces a helicopter photograph of the tree-covered region now known as Langham Coombe.

Most critics have found much to praise in *Dedham Vale*. Walker singles out the "masterly handling of broken light," the "beautiful rendering of a showery day," a landscape that "seems to glitter in the sunshine," and "one of the loveliest skies in art." He concludes, "The great sweep of space, so magnificently depicted, is exhilarating." Walker's observations support Carlos Peacock's judgment that Constable was a thoroughgoing Romantic whose lifelong aim was "truth to nature, not truth in the photographic sense as we tend to think of it now, but truth as a kind of dual vision in which the outward forms of nature were seen as imbued with a spiritual significance, that 'something far more deeply interfused' of which Wordsworth so eloquently speaks."

Constable was certainly satisfied with his accomplishment. Speaking of *Dedham Vale*, he wrote to his friend John Fisher

on June 11, 1828, that he had "painted a large upright landscape (perhaps my best)." Of this opinion, Reynolds wryly observes that "For Constable, his most recent picture (with the odd exception of *The Hay Wain*) was always his best." Constable was so pleased by the reception of *Dedham Vale* that he exhibited it in 1834 at the British Institution and the Royal Hibernian Academy in Dublin, and again the next year at the Exhibition of Modern Works by British Artists at the Worcester Institution. Despite its popularity and wide showing, *Dedham Vale* remained unsold.

FRANK DAY

Work

Dedham Vale, 1828. Oil on canvas, 55-1/2 × 48 in. National Gallery of Scotland.

Bibliography

Beckett, R. B., ed. *John Constable's Correspondence.* 6 vols. Ipswich: Suffolk Records Society, 1962–68.

———, ed. *John Constable's Discourses.* Ipswich: Suffolk Records Society, 1970.

Cormack, Michael. *Constable.* Cambridge: Cambridge University Press, 1986.

Gadney, Reg. *Constable and His World.* New York: W. W. Norton, 1976.

Kroeber, Karl. *Romantic Landscape Vision: Constable and Wordsworth.* Madison: University of Wisconsin Press, 1975.

Leslie, C. R. *Memoirs of the Life of John Constable Composed Chiefly from His Letters.* 1843. Reprint, Ithaca, N.Y.: Cornell University Press, 1980.

Parris, Leslie. Conal Shields, and Ian Fleming Williams, eds., *John Constable: Further Documents and Correspondence.* 8 vols. Ipswich: Suffolk Records Society, 1975.

Paulson, Ronald. *Literary Landscape: Turner and Constable.* New Haven, Conn.: Yale University Press, 1982.

Peacock, Carlos. *John Constable: The Man and His Work.* London: John Baker, 1965.

Reynolds, Graham. *Constable: The Natural Painter.* New York: McGraw-Hill, 1965.

———. *The Later Paintings and Drawings of John Constable.* New Haven, Conn.: Yale University Press, 1984.

Rosenthal, Michael. *Constable, the Painter, and His Landscape.* New Haven, Conn.: Yale University Press, 1983.

Smart, Alastair, and Attfield Brooks. *Constable and His Country,* London: Elek, 1975.

Taylor, Basil. *Constable: Paintings, Drawings, and Watercolours.* London: Phaidon, 1973.

Walker, John. *John Constable.* New York: Harry N. Abrams, 1978.

THE DEERSLAYER; OR, THE FIRST WAR-PATH 1841

Novel by James Fenimore Cooper

The Deerslayer was the final published novel in the set that comprised James Fenimore Cooper's *Leatherstocking Tales* (1823–41), but the order of their publication differs from the order of the events they describe. *The Deerslayer* depicts Cooper's iconic frontiersman Natty Bumppo (nicknamed Leatherstocking, also the deerslayer of the title) at the age of twenty-two, and is therefore the first of the tales in terms of the chronology of his life.

It abandons the conventional, Scott-like structure of the earlier Leatherstocking novels, and owes much to the older tradition of pastoral romance which fascinated Cooper as a boy, and which was later to influence the romances of Nathaniel Hawthorne and Herman Melville. The allegorical patterns of such romances allowed for an amplification of meaning beyond the literal limits of the story onto a broader social, moral, and political scale. As with its precursor, *The Pathfinder* (1839), *The Deerslayer* is less overtly political than most of Cooper's output from the 1830s, but remains engaged with his self-imposed mission to preserve republican ideals and to promote private and public virtue.

The novel has an Aristotelian unity of time and place unusual for Cooper, whose previous frontier novels range over hundreds of miles of forests and plains. In *The Deerslayer*, the action takes place exclusively on and around tranquil Lake Otsego—referred to here as the Glimmerglass—the lake on which Cooper's father would establish Cooperstown in New York State some fifty years after the period in which the novel is set. The dramatis personae is correspondingly small. "Hurry" Harry March, a hot-tempered, vain frontiersman, is contrasted with Natty Bumppo throughout the novel; Harry's prejudice and greed act as a counterpoint to Natty's wisdom and restraint. The lake is occupied by Tom Hutter, a former pirate, though he now lives in seclusion, he, like Harry, is a morally unscrupulous man. Hutter's eldest daughter Judith (whom Harry has come to court) is beautiful and intelligent, but "overgiven to admirers and light-minded," by which Cooper implies her vanity and possible sexual promiscuity. Her sister Hetty, on the other hand, is "weak-minded," and Cooper casts her as a godly fool, a mouthpiece for pious but naive Christian virtue. Bumppo is on his "first warpath" with his Delaware friend, Chingachgook; they are searching for Chingachgook's intended wife, Wah-ta!-Wah (translated rather unhelpfully into English as "Hist-oh!-Hist"), who has been captured by a band of Mingos, or Hurons, the tribe frequently cast as the "bad" Indians in Cooper's works.

The plot consists of a series of narrow escapes and captures, interspersed with passages of reflection and conversation, in which Natty's flexible, natural views of religion and morality, which are drawn from his close observation of nature, are shown to be superior to the self-interest of Hutter and Harry, or the naive orthodoxy of Hetty. After an initial fortunate escape, Hutter and Harry are captured on a raid for scalps, for which they want the bounty; Natty negotiates their release, but is captured while rescuing Hist. Hutter is scalped during an attack by the Hurons, and dies after revealing that he is not the real father of the girls. Judith learns the history of her mother from a collection of old letters, and Harry goes for help to the British garrison. After a brief furlough, from which he voluntarily returns, and a failed escape attempt, Natty Bumppo is about to be executed when he is rescued by Chingachgook and a party of British soldiers. Hetty, however, is killed by a stray bullet. Judith declares her love for Natty, who rejects her. The story ends with a brief epilogue, which is set fifteen years later. Natty, Chingachgook, and the young Uncas indulge in a nostalgic return to the scene of their "first warpath"; and we learn that Judith probably became the mistress of a British soldier after her rejection by Natty.

In many ways *The Deerslayer* is unrepresentative of the *Leatherstocking Tales* as a whole. It eschews the painterly representation of landscape that had been so conspicuous a feature of Cooper's earlier work; in this novel we usually experience the landscape through the eyes of the characters, particularly Natty himself. The effect of this is to align the moral or social position of the viewer with their perception of their environment, generating a more complex, layered impression of the positive and negative aspects of frontier existence. Through *The Deerslayer*'s eyes we experience the sublime beauty of the lake and its environs—and, by extension, the inspiration of Natty's "natural religion"—but we are also made to feel the isolation of the wilderness through Judith, and the potential for its commercial exploitation through Hurry Harry and Tom Hutter.

The treatment of Judith has been problematic for readers since the novel's first appearance; and undermines (to good effect) the didacticism inherent in Cooper's scheme. Judith's resourcefulness and energy, so unusual for a Cooper heroine, seem to compensate for her moral failings; although her character is in stark contrast to the excessively saintly Hetty (Cooper's own favorite) she was intended as an example of the dangers of being "admirable in person, clever, filled with the pride of beauty, erring and fallen." George Dekker has argued convincingly that the novel is, in a sense, about Natty the deerslayer gaining a name, and about Judith losing one. The passage of Natty Bumppo from youth to full manhood is accompanied by the conferment of a new name: Hawkeye. Judith, by contrast, is dogged by the tarnished reputation she has acquired before the novel's start, for her dalliance with the officers of a nearby regiment. It is in this way that she is described to Natty by Harry, and in this instance, his opinion of her never fully recovers, despite her many commendable actions throughout the book. She loses the name of Hutter by discovering that Tom Hutter is not her real father, but cannot replace it with anything; her mother's letters all have the name of her father neatly cut out. It is one of the novel's ironies that Judith's hope of moral salvation is invested in Natty, a man with perpetually shifting titles, largely ignorant of his origins but—if he could be made to marry her—a man who has the unflinching integrity necessary to keep her from straying into dishonor. Here, it is Judith who sees past his youthful lack of reputation to his real internal worth, but Natty is too dogmatic, blind, and constrained by his previously formed opinion of her to see any potential in her.

Of course, Cooper had no choice, as his readers already knew from the previously published *Leatherstocking Tales* (whose action takes place chronologically after that of *The Deerslayer*) that Natty will never marry. In the preface to the first edition of *The Deerslayer* in 1840, Cooper wrote of Natty that "the pictures of his life, such as they are, were already so complete as to excite some little desire to see the 'study' from which they had all been drawn." The implication here is that the youthful hero of *The Deerslayer* is the culmination, as well as the original pattern, of the events which had already defined his character, in the minds of both the novelist and his readers. However, the story of Natty Bumppo's initiation into manhood is no less fascinating for this. Rather, it gains an added tension from the ways in which he is forced by circumstance to adapt the abstract morality by which he has led his life, as surely as he must make the physical transition from the slayer of deer to the killer of men.

ROWLAND HUGHES

Text

The Deerslayer; or, The First War-Path. 1841. Historical introduction and explanatory notes by James Franklin Beard, with text established by Lance Schachterle, Kent Ljungquist and James Kilby. Albany: State University of New York Press, 1987.

Bibliography

Clark, Robert, ed. *James Fenimore Cooper: New Critical Essays.* London: Vision, 1985.

Dekker, George. *James Fenimore Cooper: The Novelist.* London: Routledge and Kegan Paul, 1967.

Person, Leland S., Jr. "Cooper's Queen of the Woods: Judith Hutter in The Deerslayer," *Studies in the Novel* 21, no. 3 (1989): 253–67.

Ringe, Donald. *James Fenimore Cooper.* Boston: Twayne, 1962.

Slotkin, Richard. *Regeneration through Violence.* Middletown, Conn.: Wesleyan University Press, 1973.

DELACROIX, (FERDINAND-) EUGÈNE (-VICTOR) 1798–1863

French painter

Eugène Delacroix was a highly important and influential French Romantic painter, embracing new subject matter and fully exploiting the expressive possibilities of color and form. Although considered by some the champion of Romanticism and color in opposition to the linear classicism of his rival Jean-Auguste-Dominique Ingres, Delacroix disliked being associated with Romanticism; when called "the Victor Hugo of painting," he replied "I am a pure classicist." He sought to create a new language of color, gesture, and expression that was based on a profound knowledge and understanding of the art of the past. Delacroix treated subjects ignored by the neoclassicists, primarily literature and the Orient. Such subjects provided an opportunity to explore areas of experience previously neglected by the decorum and universality of classicism: death and suffering, high emotion, melancholy, and ennui. Delacroix used color and dynamic effects to communicate directly to the spectator and to extend the emotional appeal of painting, which could now emulate the effects of music and poetry in its ability to trigger the emotions and the imagination. He rarely painted modern life and was one of the last painters who felt neither the need nor the obligation to depict the events of his own time. His tendency to become intensely involved with artistic endeavors meant that, arguably, his best works depicted subjects into which he could project himself. In his quest for serious literary art, he became the final exponent of grand history painting in the European tradition. But while his early works vividly assert an ascendant and positive form of Romanticism, his later works became more introspective and muted.

Controversy surrounded Delacroix's paternity and a rumor spread that his natural father was the French statesman Charles-Maurice de Talleyrand, though there is no documentary evidence to support this. With the death of his father Charles Delacroix and the family's financial ruin due to a fruitless property claim, Delacroix was forced to earn his living from painting and entered the studio of the neoclassical painter Pierre-Narcisse Guérin in 1815. He became friendly with Théodore Géricault and posed for one of the figures for *The Raft of the Medusa* (1819). In 1821, Géricault passed on a commission for a depiction of the Virgin Mary to Delacroix and they shared the fee.

Delacroix's salon debut came in 1822 with his *Barque of Dante*, which shows Virgil leading Dante Alighieri across the River Styx in a boat piloted by Phlegias. Borrowing from Michelangelo and Peter Paul Rubens, the work was highly praised; Antoine-Jean Gros called it "Rubens chastened" and it was bought by the French government. Two years later, Delacroix exhibited *Scenes from the Massacres at Chios* to a mixed reception; this time Gros called it "The massacre of painting." Following Géricault's example, Delacroix chose a subject from very recent history, the Turkish massacre of the peaceful Greeks on the Island of Chios (Scio), in which all but nine-hundred of the ninety-thousand inhabitants were killed or sold into slavery.

Delacroix took a trip to England from May to August 1825 and, although finding London melancholy and lacking in good architecture, he appreciated English landscape painting and portraiture and attended the theater. For the 1827–28 salon, Delacroix exhibited his most frankly passionate and romantic painting, *The Death of Sardanapalus*, taken from Lord Byron's play. As all his treasure and concubines are destroyed, the defeated Assyrian king sits impassive. A violent, fiery, and disconcerting work, it was too much for even ardent Romantics, and Delacroix was warned that no more government commissions would be given if he maintained this style.

In 1830, when the reactionary Charles X was removed from power and replaced by the July Monarchy of Louis-Philippe, Delacroix painted *Liberty Leading the People*, which was a combination of the real and the allegorical with a female personification of Liberty rallying the rebels at the barricades. It was bought by the Ministry of the Interior and earned Delacroix the Legion of Honor. Under the July Monarchy (1830–48) Delacroix was a favored official artist receiving commissions for easel paintings and for public buildings, notably the Salon du Roi (1833) in the Palais-Bourbon (now Assemblée Nationale) in Paris and the library of the Chambre des Députés (begun 1838) in the same building, and in 1840 he decorated the cupola and half-dome in the library of the Senate in the Palais du Luxembourg. In 1837 his successes prompted him to apply for membership of the Institut de France, but he was not elected until 1857, at his eighth attempt.

Unlike the majority of his predecessors, Delacroix never visited Rome. Instead, between January and July 1832, he traveled to Algeria, Morocco, and Spain, with the Comte de Mornay, Louis-Philippe's ambassador to the Sultan of Morocco. He was fascinated by the color and light of the Middle East and discovered a civilization that had continued unbroken since classical times. The notes and sketches he made on this journey provided him with material for the rest of his life; the major paintings to emerge from this material were *The Women of Algiers* (1834) and *The Jewish Wedding* (1841).

Although Delacroix liked to cultivate the persona of a misunderstood artist, he was well patronized, but he never achieved the immense financial success of contemporaries such as Horace Vernet. His pivotal position in the French art world was recognized at the 1855 Exposition Universelle when, like Alexandre Decamps, Ingres, and Horace Vernet he was given a one-man exhibition. In his final years he continued to paint literary subjects, but his brand of Romanticism seemed outdated when confronted with the naturalism of the Barbizon school and the Realism of Gustave Courbet. Delacroix's last testament to painting was the decoration of the Chapel of Holy Angels at Saint Sulpice, where two canvases on the side walls showed Jacob's encounter with the angel and Heliodorus being expelled from the temple—both scenes of anguish and struggle with which he readily identified.

A prolific writer on art, Delacroix kept a journal from 1822 to 1824 and from 1847 until his death, recording his inner feelings and responses to the art, music, literature, and theater of his time. In addition, he wrote articles on Gros, Michelangelo, and Raphael; aesthetics; and art criticism, and he planned a dictionary of fine arts that was never completed. He was also interested in scientific theories of color and light and was aware of Michel Chevreul's law of simultaneous contrast, although Delacroix's application of theory remained empirical and he was a poor technician. His color researches influenced the Impressionists in their quest for a more naturalistic rendition of light and its effects on the surface of objects.

SIMON LEE

Biography

Born Ferdinand-Victor-Eugène Delacroix in St. Maurice-Charenton, France, April 26, 1798. Fourth child of Charles Delacroix, government official and ambassador to Holland (later prefect of Bordeaux; died 1805) and Victoire Oeben, from Oeben-Riesener family of furniture designers. Attended Lycée Louis-le-Grand, Paris, from 1806 on. After the death of his father and family financial difficulties, trained as a painter in atelier of Pierre-Narcisse Guérin, 1815. Attended École des Beaux-Arts, 1816–?? Received patronage of statesman Louis Thiers, from 1822. Influenced by Theodore Géricault, 1830s on. Exhibited *Dante and Virgil in Hell* at Paris Salon, 1822. Visited England; met painters John Constable, Thomas Lawrence, and J. M. W. Turner, 1825. Completed *The Death of Sardanapalus*, 1827. Toured Algeria, Morocco, and Spain as part of government delegation from King Louis-Philippe, 1832. Painted *Women of Algiers*, 1834. Commissioned to paint murals for several public buildings in Paris: Salon du Roi at the Palais-Bourbon, 1833–36; Library, Palais-Bourbon, 1838–47; and Palais Luxembourg, 1840–47. Decorated the Galerie d'Apollon, Louvre, 1850; Salon de la Paix, Hotel de Ville, 1849–53; and Church of Saint-Sulpice, 1849–61. Maintained close friendship with composer Frédéric Chopin and novelist George Sand, 1830s and 1840s. Held major one-man exhibition at Exposition Universelle, Paris, 1855. Elected to the Institut de France, 1857. Died in Paris, August 13, 1863.

Bibliography

Baudelaire, Charles. "The Life and Work of Eugène Delacroix." In *The Painter of Modern Life and Other Essays*. Edited by J. Mayne. London: Phaidon, 1964.

Delacroix in Morocco. Exhibition catalog. Institut du Monde Arab, Paris. Paris: Flammarion, 1994.

Huyghe, R. *Delacroix*. London: Thames and Hudson, 1963.

Jobert, B. *Delacroix*. Princeton, N.J.: Princeton University Press, 1998.

Johnson, L. *The Paintings of Eugène Delacroix*. 6 vols. Oxford: Oxford University Press, 1981–89.

Sérullaz, A. and V. Pomerade. *Delacroix: The Late Work*. London: Thames and Hudson/Philadelphia: Philadelphia Museum of Art, 1998.

Spector, J. *The Death of Sardanapalus*. London: Allen lane, 1974.

———. *The Murals of Eugène Delacroix at St. Sulpice*. New York: College Art Association, 1967.

Trapp, F. *The Attainment of Delacroix*. Baltimore: Johns Hopkins University Press, 1971.

DELAROCHE, PAUL 1797–1856

French painter

Although considered a major, if not always innovative, painter in his day, Paul Delaroche was virtually ignored throughout the last four decades of the nineteenth century and much of the twentieth century. He remains, however, an important artist for understanding the many facets of Romanticism, as well as the complex interaction of neoclassicism, Romanticism, and emergent Realism in the early to mid-nineteenth century.

He was probably the most famous painter in the Western world around 1850 (according to Stephen Bann) and he was certainly the most widely reproduced artist in his day, due to amiable collaborations with engravers and a keen interest in photography. Rediscovered by Frances Haskell and Norman Ziff in the 1970s, Delaroche and his work have most recently been the subject of a comprehensive study by Bann.

Born in 1797, Delaroche was a student of history painting in the studio of Antoine-Jean Gros. He first exhibited at the Salon of 1822. He was best known for his history paintings of national (especially French and British) scenes, such as *Joan of Arc in Prison* (1824), *Death of Elizabeth* (1828), *Children of Edward IV in the Tower* (1830), *Execution of Lady Jane Grey* (1834), and *The Assassination of the Duc de Guise* (1834). Toward the end of his life he turned to portraiture and religious painting. Delaroche's most recognized work was, however, a mural for the Hémicycle amphitheater of the École des Beaux-Arts in Paris, completed in 1841 and engraved by Louis-Pierre Henriquel-Dupont in 1853. This mural, which draws on Raphael's *School of Athens* and Jean-Auguste-Dominique Ingres's *Apotheosis of Homer*, represents the history of painting, sculpture, and architecture from antiquity to the seventeenth century.

Two incidents marked Delaroche as a painter who was more inclined to follow his own convictions rather than those of Beaux-Arts officials and the public. In 1833, Delaroche was named to decorate the Madeleine with seven large paintings, but he withdrew after learning that another painter would receive part of the commission. (Similarly, he accepted to do five paintings of French history for the Versailles Museum in 1838, but only completed one of them.) Then, due to the hostile criticism generated by his 1836 *Charles I Insulted by the Soldiers of Cromwell*, Delaroche never exhibited at the annual salon after 1837, and in fact rarely showed his works at all after this date.

Ziff notes Delaroche's predominant theme as usurpation versus rightful rule, and it is true that the painter favored stories of national heroes who lost power or their lives in tragic ways. As a *juste milieu* (golden mean) or compromise painter, one often mentioned alongside Ary Scheffer, Delaroche was said to have combined neo-classicism (Ingres) and Romanticism (Delacroix), in an effort to reconcile the two schools. The painter may therefore be seen to have found middle ground between those who would usurp, and those who would hold on to power. Some critics suggested that his compromise status accounted for his election to the Académie des Beaux-Arts at the age of thirty-five making him the youngest artist ever elected to this official body. The label of "juste milieu" painter carried an aura of mediocrity and banality with it, however, and contemporary critics have begun to dispute this label as regards Delaroche.

Delaroche was much praised (by Henri Delaborde, Alexandre Dumas, and Ingres—with some reservations), but also much maligned (by Charles Baudelaire, Théophile Gautier, and Gustave Planche). He was alternately lauded for reconciling the two schools of painting and condemned for not choosing an original path. He was further criticized for confusing painting and literature—that is, for placing too much emphasis on the narrative potential of painting. Following the lead of others, Edward and Jules de Goncourt have called Delaroche a "painter of prose." They note that Scheffer and Delaroche "could set up a studio, produce students; but the nature of their temperaments, the sterility of their works, condemned them to being unable to create a new school." Still, most agree that Delaroche was a master instructor, he took over Gros's studio after his death, and was an extremely popular instructor. He taught some of the more well-regarded artists of the nineteenth century, including Thomas Couture, Charles-François, Daubigny, Jean Léon Gérôme, and Jean-François Millet. (The studio was closed in 1843 following the death of a young student from a hazing incident.)

Delaroche, who had married Louise Vernet, daughter of the painter Horace Vernet, died in 1856. An important and very successful retrospective exhibit of his work was held at the École des Beaux-Arts in the year of his death.

MARIE LATHERS

Biography

Born Hippolyte-Paul Delaroche in Paris, July 17, 1797. His father was an art expert; his brother, Jules-Hippolyte Delaroche, a painter. Student of the landscape artist Louis-Étienne Watelet; trained in the studio of history painter Antoine-Jean Gros, 1818–20. Exhibited at the Paris Salon, 1822–37. Elected to Académie des Beaux-Arts in 1832; professor at the École Nationale Supérieure des Beaux-Arts from 1833. Officier, Legion d'honneur, 1833. Took over studio of Baron Gros in Paris until 1843. Commissioned to decorate the church of the Madeleine in 1833; later declined the commission. Traveled in Italy, 1834–35. Married Louise Vernet, 1835 (she died 1845). Commissioned to paint Hémicycle mural in the École Nationale Superieure des Beaux-Arts, 1836 (completed 1841); commissioned to provide five paintings for the Museum at Versailles completed one, 1838–39. Passed over for directorship of French Academy in Rome, 1840. Died in Paris, November 4, 1858.

Selected Works

Filippo Lippi Falling in Love with His Model. 1822. Disan, Magnin Museum.
Joan of Arc in Prison. 1824.
Death of Elizabeth. 1828. Louvre.
Cardinal Richelieu. 1829.
Cardinal Mazarin is Last Sickness. 1830. 57.2 × 97.3. Wallace Collection.
Children of Edward IV in the Tower. 1830. Louvre.
Cromwell and Charles I. 1831.
The Assassination of the Duc de Guise. 1834. Musée Candé, Chantilly.
Execution of Lady Jane Grey. 1834. 246 × 297. National Gallery, London.
Charles I Insulted by the Soldiers of Cromwell. 1836.
Saint Cecilia. 1836.
Hémicycle of the École des Beaux-Arts. 1841. 390 × 2470. École des Beaux-Arts, Paris.
Childhood of Pico della Mirandola. 1842.
Bonaparte Crossing the Alps. 1848. Louvre.

Bibliography

Allemand-Cosneau, Claude, and Isabelle Julia, eds. *Paul Delaroche, Un Peintre dans l'histoire.* Exhibition catalog. Nantes: Musée des Beaux-Arts, 1999.
Bann, Stephen. *Paul Delaroche: History Painted.* Princeton, N.J.: Princeton University Press, 1997.
Boime, Albert. *The Academy and French Painting in the Nineteenth Century.* London: Phaidon, 1971.
Delaborde, Henri, and Jules Godelé. *Oeuvre de Paul Delaroche.* 1858.
Dumas, Alexandre. "Paul Delaroche." In *Mes Mémoires.* Vol. 5. Edited by Pierre Josserand. Paris: Gallimard, 1968.
Goncourt, Edmond, and Jules de. *Manette Salomon.* Paris: L'Harmattan, 1993.
Halévy, F. E. *Souvenirs et portraits. Etudes sur les beaux-arts.* 1861.
Haskell, Frances. *Rediscoveries in Art.* Ithaca, N.Y.: Cornell University Press, 1976.
Heine, Henrich. *The Exhibition of Pictures of 1831. Delaroche.* In *The Works of Heinrich Heine.* Vol. 4. Translated by Charles Godfrey Leland. New York: E. B. Dutton, 1906.
Mirecourt, Eugène de. *Les Contemporains. Paul Delaroche.* 1856.
Ziff, Norman D. *Paul Delaroche. A Study in Nineteenth-Century French History Painting.* New York: Garland, 1977.

DESBORDES-VALMORE, MARCELINE 1786–1859

French poet

A known and acclaimed poet during her lifetime, Marceline Desbordes-Valmore fell into obscurity soon after her death and, although rediscovered sporadically, her name is today largely ignored even by scholars of the Romantic period. Yet her work undoubtedly influenced the development of nineteenth-century French poetry and, in some instances, can be said to have pioneered changes.

Desbordes-Valmore's life was plagued with hardship and tragedy. She was born shortly before the French Revolution, and the ensuing upheaval affected her upbringing and home life. Her father went bankrupt, the family split up, and, at the age of sixteen, she began working on the stage, as an actress and singer. It was this experience—learning verse through reciting and rhythm through song—that formed her lyric training.

Despite the troubles and suffering of her early years, love for her native Flanders and longing for her childhood reoccur incessantly in her poems, often expressed in effusions of nostalgia and closeness to nature. She also composed a semi-autobiographical novel about her youth, *L'Atelier d'un peintre* (*A Painter's Studio*, 1833). The story recounts her stay, in 1808, with her uncle, the painter Constant Desbordes, in the old Capuchin monastery that he shared with other artists among whom were Girodet de Roussy-Trioson and François Gérard. Apart from giving an insight into the life of the young Marceline and the artistic milieu, the novel, in its melodramatic ending, also reveals the lingering influence of Johann Wolfgang von Goethe's *Die Leiden des jungen Werther* (*The Sorrows of Young Werther*, 1774).

Her stormy affair with the poet Henri de Latouche (c. 1809–15) brought her into contact with the new ways in poetry and allowed her talent to find passionate expression. Her poems describing love, fulfilled and later scorned, are imbued with an intensity of emotion, tears, and pain. Many of them are entitled "elegy" according to contemporary lyric fashion. Yet they already differ from the general trend in the chaste sensuality they portray, in their dramatic rather than literary conception, and in their musical composition.

Shortly after her marriage to Prosper Valmore, she published her first collection of poetry, *Élégies, Marie et Romances* (*Elegies, Marie and Ballads*, 1819). Although poverty and domestic tragedy continued to afflict her (four of her five children died during her lifetime) she went on turning her misfortunes into poetry, publishing *Les Pleurs* (*Tears*, 1833) and the collection *Pauvres Fleurs* (*Poor Flowers*, 1839) both of which are intimate reflections of family life. She also made friends in the literary community. Sophie Gay introduced her to Delphine Gay, Jeanne Françoise Récamier, and Amable Tastu, among others. Her friend Pauline Duchambge set some of her poems to music. She had a long and lasting friendship with Charles-Augustin Sainte-Beuve, who wrote an introduction to the 1842 edition of her poetry in which he refers to her as "André Chénier femme" (a female André Chénier). He also compares her to Alphonse de Lamartine and points out that Marceline's lyrical inspiration precedes the *Méditations poétiques* (*Poetic Meditations*, 1820) and thus represents one of the first manifestations of the new poetry.

Marceline was brought up a Catholic and remained throughout her life a believer, as illustrated by the title of her 1843 poetry collection, *Bouquets et Prières* (*Bouquets and Prayers*). In the last years of her life particularly, she seemed to understand her faith in terms of charity, human solidarity, and hope of an afterlife; this is evident in of her best known and most beautiful poems, "Renoncement" (Renunciation) and "La Couronne effeuillée" (The Stripped Crown).

Contemporary appreciation was favorable and indulgent. Her earlier collections were very popular, certainly until 1830. Popularity waned when her intimate poetry no longer corresponded to prevailing taste. Victor Hugo called her a "reine" (queen) in the "monde des pensées et des sentiments" (in the world of thought and feeling); Alfred-Victor de Vigny considered her "le plus grand esprit féminin de notre temps" (the greatest feminine mind of our time); Alexandre Dumas confessed to being deeply affected by *Les Pleurs*, for which he wrote a preface. Lamartine addressed a poem to her; Pierre-Jean de Béranger spoke of her "sensibilité exquise" (exquisite sensibility). Many comments concentrate on her as the poet of the doleful sentiment, loving and good, but without any special originality or art.

Marceline was certainly aware of discrimination because of her gender. In *L'Atelier d'un peintre* her heroine dreams of "un nom de femme parmi les lauréats" (a woman's name among the great). In her poetry she is neither excessively ambitious nor feminist. She simply states the situation as she perceives it: "Les femmes, je le sais, ne doivent pas écrire; / j'écris pourtant" (Women, as I know well, should not write; / and yet I write) are the first lines of "Une lettre de femme" ("A Woman's Letter"). Altogether she conceives her art as instinctive, part of an energy and love of life she needs to express.

Posthumous acclaim was intermittent. Her poetic originality was recognized by Charles Baudelaire, Arthur Rimbaud, and the symbolists; Paul Verlaine underlined in particular her musical technique. Nonetheless, as the modern poet Yves Bonnefoy points out, literary history does not really know where to place Desbordes-Valmore in the context of French Romanticism. She never developed or advocated a poetic theory. Interest, such as it was, often focused more on the person than on critical analysis of her work. Her output is uneven in quality. Some of her early pieces abound in flowers, interjections, and sobs, so fashionable at the time. She is sometimes careless in composition, even clumsy; perfection of form was not all-important to her. And yet, despite her lack of literary culture, her talent is unique. Her poems move by their directness, by the powerful sensibility they express, and their songlike quality. She seems to be giving of herself. Some of her strongest poems were written in response to the silk workers' revolt in Lyons, 1834, though from commiseration rather than political conviction. In contrast to many of the better-known male Romantic poets in France who opt for mysticism and visionary ideas, Desbordes-Valmore, in her mature work, has eschewed the dreamworld of illusion; instead she attempts to portray what *is*, the essence of ordinary things and events in their modest elementary existence. In this sense she is perhaps a precursor of modern poetry. She is also the first to reconcile intensity of lyric emotion with the simplicity of song. Her most important achievement, however, is the introduction into poetry of a diversity of rhythm and irregular verses which led directly to Guillaume Apollinaire and Arthur Rimband. Bonnefoy, as a result, calls for a complete revaluation of French Romantic poetry, which would give Desbordes-Valmore a prominent position.

FELIZITAS RINGHAM

Biography

Born Marceline Félicité Josèphe Desbordes in Douai, France, June 20 (30?), 1786; her father was a coat-of-arms maker. Following the family's bankruptcy after the French Revolution, she went to Guadeloupe with her mother, 1801–2. She returned to Europe after her mother's death; worked intermittently as singer and actress at provincial theaters in France and in Paris and Brussels, 1802–23. Took singing lessons, 1805; abandoned singing, 1813. An affair with Eugène Debonne brought one child, 1810 (d. 1816); an affair with Henri de Latouche followed, c. 1812–15. She married actor Prosper Lanchantin (stage name Prosper Valmore) in 1817: they had five children, of whom four died before her own death. Published first collection of poetry, *Elegies, Marie et Romance*, 1819. Introduced to the literary circle La Muse Française; maintained friendships with Madame Récamier and Charles-Augustin Sainte-Beuve. Granted a small government pension, 1826, suspended by the 1830 revolution and reinstated in 1840. Awarded prize by the Académie Française, 1859. Died of cancer in Paris, July 23, 1859.

Selected Works

Collections
Les Oeuvres poétiques de Marceline Desbordes-Valmore. 2 vols. Edited and introduced by Marc Bertrand. 1973.
Marceline Desbordes-Valmore: Poésies. Edited and introduced by Yves Bonnefoy. 1983.

Poetry
Élegies, Marie, Romances. 1819. Revised and augmented editions 1820, 1822, 1825.
Poésies. Revised edition of the earlier collection with additional material, 1830; with an introduction by Charles-Augustin Sainte-Beuve, 1842; revised and augmented, 1860.
Les Pleurs, 1833. With an introduction by Alexandre Dumas.
Pauvres Fleurs. 1839.
Bouquets et Prières. 1843.
Poésies inédites. 1860.

Other
L'Atelier d'un peintre: Scènes de la vie privée. 2 vols. 1833.

Bibliography

Ambière, Francis. *Le Siècle des Valmore.* 2 vols. Paris: Le Seuil, 1987.
Boulenger, Jacques. *Marceline Desbordes-Valmore, sa vie et son secret.* Paris: Plon, 1926.
Descaves, Luicien. *La Vie douloureuse de Marceline Desbordes-Valmore.* Paris: Editions d'Art et de Littérature, 1910.
Jasenas, Éliane. *Marceline Desbordes-Valmore devant la critique.* Paris: Droz-Minard, 1962.
Moulin, Jeanine. *Marceline Desbordes-Valmore.* Paris: Seghers, 1955.

DESCHAMPS, (ANNE-LOUIS-FRÉDÉRIC) EMILE 1791–1871

Emile Deschamps receives attention today primarily because of the verses, uninspired though they are, that serve as the libretto for Hector Berlioz's *Roméo et Juliette*. First performed in 1840, it is a "choral symphony" in which the words are very distinctly secondary to the music. By the same token, Deschamps's younger brother Antoni (or Antony or Antoine; the variant spellings of whose first name reflect alternately his Italian or his English predilections) is remembered as the author of the scanty and conventional verses sung by the choir in the "Apothéose" concluding Berlioz's *Grand Symphonie funèbre et triomphale*, also first heard in 1840. Though these two collaborations are by no means the most significant contributions made by the Deschamps brothers to French cultural life in the first half of the nineteenth century, they aptly draw attention to the essentially secondary roles they played. Always in contact with the great creative poets, painters, and musicians of the period, they never challenged their preeminence. Some diffidence may be seen too in the readiness of both brothers to devote much effort to translations and to writing lyrics and librettos.

They came from a privileged and cultured background. Their father, a rich fiscal administrator who was fortunate to emerge from the Revolutionary period unscathed and still wealthy, was a man of wide reading who liked the company of men of letters. He admired Voltaire, knew something of English literature and maintained a salon where major literary figures gathered regularly in the second decade of the nineteenth century. The father's example set the pattern for his two sons. Emile's earliest recorded literary work was the ode "La Paix conquise" ("Peace Won"); dated 1811, it breathes patriotism and defiance of "Folle Albion" ("Mad England") in fourteen six-line strophes. However, the poet would generally avoid overt politics in the future, probably because of some unease about royalist principles in France. His idiom, like his versification, remained loyal to the French tradition of limpidity, elegance, and charm, at a time when some of his contemporaries were beginning to attempt something more daring.

Deschamps was one of the founders of La Muse Française. Launched in July 1823, with monthly issues appearing for just one year, it served as a rallying point for the new writers of the day, and marked Deschamps as one of their number. In 1828 he tried his hand at drama in collaboration with Henri de Latouche, who was his elder by half a decade and already had some experience of writing for the theater. Premiered without success in Paris at the Théâtre Favart on June 23, 1818, *Selmours* is a three-act comedy set in England, written in alexandrines. First performed in the same theater five months later, the one-act *Le Tour de faveur* was produced a hundred times, amusing audiences with its satire of contemporary developments in drama.

Deschamps was to make a more important contribution as a translator of English drama. Though known in France, albeit more or less imperfectly, especially thanks to versions of his plays prepared by Jean-François Ducis in the final decades of the eighteenth century, Shakespeare was to become the center of what Deschamps called feverish interest in Paris during the

Restoration. Late in 1826 Deschamps began work on *Romeo and Juliet*, sharing the work with his friend Alfred de Vigny, who took responsibility for the last two acts. Though hopes of acceptance by the Comédie Française were dashed, Deschamps, not uncharacteristically, found consolation in what others might well regard as his unequal collaboration with Berlioz on *Roméo et Juliette*. In 1844, in a rather different cultural atmosphere, Deschamps tried again, this time translating both *Romeo and Juliet* and *Macbeth* in a manner that he characterized as more literary and much more literal. Though he was setting out to produce a text for reading rather than for the stage, his *Macbeth* was performed in Paris at the Odéon in 1848 with considerable success, but only after cuts and changes had been made so that it accorded "with the demands of the French stage," which still could not take its Shakespeare unadulterated.

Before then Deschamps had become associated, above all, with translations of foreign poets, thus widening the scope of French Romanticism. Arguments for such literary cosmopolitanism form the basis of the excellent polemical preface to his *Etudes françaises et étrangères* (*French and Foreign Studies*) of 1828. The highly impressive range of material that Deschamps translated compensates for any disappointments about French versions that may on occasion appear somewhat anemic. Specimen German, English, Scottish, Russian and, in particular, Spanish lyrics and ballads appear in French here alongside versions of Horace that reveal a certain catholicity in Deschamps's taste.

His willingness to cross boundaries between cultures and nations is paralleled by his readiness to bridge genres. His pen was always at the service of musicians; they, in their turn, were perhaps attracted by a certain directness and simplicity in his style that was well suited for musical setting. As well as writing lyrics for many contemporary song composers, Deschamps worked on several librettos besides that for *Roméo et Juliette*. In 1826, for instance, he collaborated with G. de Wally on *Ivanhoé*, later performed in London as *The Maid of Judah*. The music for this opera was not original; it was arranged by Antonini Picini from passages quarried from *Semiramide, Mosè, Tancredi*, and *La gazza ladra*. This testimony to the popularity of Scott in Paris during the Restoration is all the more remarkable since neither Gieotchino Antonio Rossini nor Sir Walter Scott complained at the treatment of their respective work. In 1836 Deschamps was requested by Giacomo Meyerbeer to help remodel act 4 of *Les Huguenots*, and in 1837 he provided Louis Niedermeyer with the libretto of *Stradella*.

Deschamps was never, despite his efforts, elected to the Académie Française. Afflicted with blindness and somewhat re-moved from affairs, he spent his later years in Versailles, taking an interest in new developments in poetry until his death in April 1871.

The high point in the career of his brother Antoni Deschamps had come with the publication of his poems along with those of Emile in 1841, but Antoni had caused a stir with his Dante translations as early as 1829. They revealed to France, as Victor Hugo put it, a poet on a par with Shakespeare. Antoni's mental health was, however, never robust, and in October 1869, after twenty years of living as a recluse, he died in a private asylum at Passy.

CHRISTOPHER SMITH

Biography

Born on February 20, 1791 at Bourges, son of a senior tax collector. 1799: to school at Orléans. Birth of brother, Antoni, 1800. Father takes responsibility for his education, 1806. Emile publishes *La Paix conquise*, 1812; first mature works, two plays—*Selmours de Florian* and *Le Tour de Faveur*, 1818. Helps found La Muse Française, 1823. Contact with the Romantic circle around Victor Hugo, 1825. Translates, with Alfred de Vigny, Shakespeare's *Romeo and Juliet* (not performed), 1827. Publishes *Etudes françaises et étrangères*, with important Romantic preface, 1828. Awarded Légion d'Honneur, and brother Antoni publishes his translations of Dante, 1829. Antoni suffers mental illness, 1834. Emile composes verses for Berlioz's *Roméo et Juliett*, and Antoni writes verses for his *Grande Symphonie funèbre*, 1840. Emile translates Shakespeare's *Macbeth*; performed at Odéon, Paris, 1844. Emile retires to Versailles, 1845; suffers nervous breakdown, 1847. Publishes collections of fantastic stories, 1854. Antoni dies, 1869. Emile dies, after being blind for some years, at Versailles, 1871.

Bibliography

Berlioz, Hector. *Grande Symphonie funèbre et triomphale*. Edited by Hugh Macdonald. vol. 19 of *Hector Berlioz: New Edition of the Complete Works*. Kasel: Bärenreiter, 1990.
————. *Roméo et Juliette*. Edited by D. Kern Holoman. Vol. 18 of *Hector Berlioz: New Edition of the Complete Works*. Kasel: Bärenreiter, 1990.
Deschamps, Emile. *Oeuvres complètes* (1872–74). 6 vols. Reprinted, 1 vol. Geneva: Slatkine, 1973.
————. *La Préface des "Etudes françaises et étrangères": Un manifeste du romantisme*. Edited by Henri Girard. Paris: Press Françaises, 1923.
Girard, Henri. *Un bourgeois dilettante à l'époque romantique: Emile Deschamps*. Paris: Champion, 1921.
————. *Emile Deschamps dilettante: Relations d'un poète romantique avec les peintres, les sculpteurs et les musiciens de son temps*. Paris: Champion, 1921.

DICHTERLIEBE 1840

Lieder cycle by Robert Schumann

The year 1840 is known as Robert Schumann's *Liederjahr*, or "year of song." As he awaited the decision of the Leipzig court on his appeal to marry Clara Wieck, he concentrated on the genre of the solo song with piano accompaniment with a manic intensity that would characterize the creative periods of the rest of his life. He produced over 140 lieder before the year's end. Among the songs of 1840 are his greatest efforts in songwriting, including several important cycles: the Heine *Liederkreis*, op.

24; *Myrthen*, op. 25; the Eichendorff *Liederkreis*, op. 39; *Frauenliebe und -leben*, op. 42; and *Dichterliebe*, op. 48, perhaps the most popular lieder cycle of the Romantic era.

Dichterliebe is at once an intensely moving work and the ideal illustration of Schumann's views on poetry and music. The most literary of the Romantic composers, Schumann valued good poetry and had up to then resisted the urge to combine it with music. The songs of the Liederjahr were on the one hand a pragmatic response to Friedrich Wieck's claim that he could not earn enough from his compositions to support Clara, and on the other, a reconciliation of the inherent conflict that he had previously felt between the literary and musical aspects of his creative personality.

The texts of the sixteen songs (twenty in the composer's original manuscript) were selected from the sixty-five poems of Heinrich Heine's *Lyrisches Intermezzo* (1823). This work proved to be an inexhaustible source for the Romantic lieder composers, who found Heine's melodious use of language and vivid, simple images to be ideal for setting to music. The resulting cycle is loosely narrative, beginning with the awakening of love in the poet and moving through rejection and disillusionment to eventual acceptance of his plight. The story of unrequited love seems to contrast with Schumann's successful wooing of Clara, but the qualities of yearning that pervade the work are prevalent throughout his *oeuvre*.

The work is strongly cyclical, as the composer repeatedly underscores the importance of performing the entire work at once. Many of the songs are so short that they would be ludicrous if performed separately. Moreover, Schumann elides the songs through key relationships and other devices. The first song, "Im wunderschönen Monat Mai" ("In the Lovely Month of May,") is illustrative of this technique. The two stanzas of text are set strophically:

Im wunderschönen Monat Mai	In the lovely month of May,
Als alle Knospen sprangen	when all the buds were bursting,
Da ist in meinem Herzen	then within my heart
Die Liebe aufgegangen.	love broke forth.
Im wunderschönen Monat Mai,	In the lovely month of May,
Als alle Vögel sangen,	when all the birds were singing,
Da hab ich ihr gestanden	then I confessed to her
Mein Sehnen und Verlangen.	my longing and desire.

From the numerous images in these two picturesque strophes, Schumann chooses the longing and desire of the last line as the predominant mood. The accompaniment begins with the intense dissonance of a major seventh interval, which is reiterated when the voice enters, four measures later. The song is full of dissonant intervals in the form of suspensions that reinforce a sense of longing. The final chord of this first song is an unresolved dominant seventh that simultaneously leaves the poet's confession of love unanswered and propels the listener forward musically to the resolution in the second song.

Schumann's principal innovation is an intimate interdependence of piano and voice that had not been achieved by previous lieder composers. For Schumann, the piano is integral to telling the story, transcending the traditional role of accompanist to become an equal partner. The use of the piano ranges from the obvious (as in the nightingale calls in song two) to the subtle motivic interconnections between songs. Over half of the songs contain piano postludes that are as long as or longer than individual stanzas of the preceding vocal melody. These postludes may simply serve to give the listener time to process what has just been heard, as in song four. The first three songs tumble one after another with little or no postlude, but after the ironic and unexpected final couplet of song four—"Doch wenn du sprichst: Ich liebe dich / So muss ich weinen bitterlich" ("But when you say: I love you / Then I must weep bitterly")—Schumann provides over twenty seconds of soft chords in the piano, allowing time to reflect on what has just transpired. At the end of the final song, the poet relinquishes his yearning for the beloved by figuratively burying his love and pain in a large coffin in the sea. After the singer concludes this bitter, ironic song, the piano plays the longest postlude of the set, which reprises the accompaniment of song twelve. The astute listener recalls the final couplet of that song, in which the flowers whisper, "Sei unserer Schwester nicht böse, / Du trauriger blasser Mann!" ("Don't be angry with our sister, / you doleful, pale man!"). The piano thus has the last word, contradicting the mood of the vocal part and replacing bitterness with forgiveness.

Dichterliebe is in many ways Schumann's masterpiece in the genre of the lieder cycle and one of the seminal works of musical Romanticism. In it he achieves a rare balance between poetry and music, between piano and voice, and between individual song and cycle.

E. DOUGLAS BOMBERGER

Bibliography

Daverio, John. *Robert Schumann: Herald of a "New Poetic Age."* New York: Oxford University Press, 1997.

Hallmark, Rufus E. "The Sketches for *Dichterliebe*," *Nineteenth-Century Music* 1 (1977): 110–32.

Heine, Heinrich. *Buch der Lieder.* 1827; rev. edn., 1844. Translated by J. E. Wallis as *Book of Songs*, 1856. Translated by Hal Draper in *The Complete Poems of Heinrich Heine*. Oxford: Oxford University Press, 1982.

Schumann, Robert. *Dichterliebe: An Authoritative Score.* Edited by Arthur Komar. New York: W. W. Norton, 1971.

DICKENS, CHARLES 1812–1870

English novelist

Charles Dickens was born in 1812, one year after Jane Austen published *Sense and Sensibility*, and two years before Sir Walter Scott revolutionized the novel—and the publishing industry—with *Waverley*. Dickens's writing career began in 1832, and during the nearly forty years that followed, he edited five different periodicals, traveled widely, wrote a book about his American experiences, gave countless public readings, and published fourteen novels. Posterity remembers Dickens chiefly for his novels, and in them, Dickens shows clear debts to the Romantic novel tradition. He shares Austen's fascination with human relationships, for example, as well as Scott's deep interests in history and publishing. But the novels also clearly mark Dickens as a distinctly post-Romantic figure. With their panoramic sweep, stylized characters, and focus on social issues, Dickens's novels are firmly planted in Victorian-era British society.

Dickens rejected the three-volume format for novel publishing that had been pioneered by Sir Walter Scott, and broke new ground by publishing all of his novels serially. This move had important implications, both for the publishing industry and for Dickens's own authorial practice. Prior to the appearance, in monthly installments, of Dickens's 1836 *Pickwick Papers*, serial publication was, as an anonymous *Edinburgh Review* writer put it, "synonymous with literary ephemerae . . . the lightest kind of light reading." But by the time of *Pickwick*'s fifteenth installment, in 1837, Dickens was selling over forty thousand copies per issue.

While Dickens almost single-handedly ensured the popularity and esteem of serial publication during the Victorian period, the format did present him with certain constraints: he was compelled to create plots that would draw readers into a story quickly, for example, and to create characters who would be memorable from one installment to the next. Dickens began the novels with character and plot sketches, but he often altered his own plans as the stories unfolded—and as readers wrote him with their reactions. But the personal relationship allowed by serial publication was more apparent than real. As Mary Poovey points out, "the absolute standardization of the form—the fact that each serial part had to contain exactly thirty-two pages, which had to be produced according to an inflexible schedule and internal form—[meant that] the writer was constructed not as an individual, much less a 'genius,' but as just one instance of labor, an interchangeable part subject to replacement in case of failure or to repair in case of defect." In some ways, then, serial publication implicated Dickens in the very Victorian "system" that he so often criticized in the novels.

The critique of systems—judicial, educational, or other—is a pervasive theme in Dickens's novels, and a crucial link between Dickens and his Romantic counterparts. While Romantic figures such as William Blake and Percy Bysshe Shelley create abstractions (Urizen for Blake, Queen Mab for Shelley) to dramatize the evils of social systems and the possible ways to reform them, Dickens's critiques and solutions are more immediate. Often he develops a single character or plot device that precisely focuses a particular novel's social issue. In *Bleak House* (1853), for example, he illustrates the destructiveness and futility of the British legal system with *Jarndyce v. Jarndyce*, a never-ending estate-settlement case; by the time a resolution is reached, the estate's entire value has been consumed by the legal fees required to adjudicate the case. In *Hard Times* (1854), Dickens attacks Utilitarian social and educational philosophy and practice through the character of Thomas Gradgrind, an entrepreneur and father who handles both business and family matters in a completely dispassionate way; when Gradgrind's world begins to crumble, he renounces his Utilitarian practices, learns from the example of the generous-hearted Cissy Jupe, and is redeemed. These two examples capture a significant truth about Dickens's novels, one that sets him apart from his Romantic counterparts: neither the critiques he makes nor the means through which he makes them

are overly subtle. Instead, Dickens adopts very populist strategies for his social commentary, couching his lessons in memorable characters and entertaining story lines.

Thematically, Dickens shares more than a suspicion of system with the Romantics. Novels such as *Oliver Twist* (1839) and *David Copperfield* (1850) clearly demonstrate that, like Wordsworth, Dickens privileges childhood as a time of particular innocence and vision. To be sure, not all of Dickens's juvenile characters are possessed of youthful innocence; *Oliver Twist*'s Artful Dodger and *David Copperfield*'s James Steerforth, for instance, are both capable of serious misdeeds. Still, Dickens is careful to show that their corruption stems less from a defect in nature than in society—those two characters illustrate once again that too little or too much privilege can have seriously corrupting consequences in the world of Dickens's novels.

Unlike his Romantic counterpart Jane Austen, who declared "three or four families in a country village" as the appropriate scope for a novel, Dickens operates on a much larger scale. He creates large communities in his novels, employing multiple settings and large casts of characters. Readers both in Dickens's day and in our own have suggested that Dickens sacrifices depth for breadth, particularly in characterization. Dickens does rely upon superficial devices such as verbal tics (e.g, *David Copperfield*'s Uriah Heep, ever "umble"), repetitive activities (e.g. the continuous knitting of *A Tale of Two Cities*'s [1859] Madame Defarge), or allegorical names (e.g., *Our Mutual Friend*'s [1865] villain Rogue Riderhood) to create unique and memorable characters. However, serial publication requires that minor characters who do not appear in every part have some distinguishing characteristic to prompt a reader's memory. Dickens's characters thus provide one more illustration of how his innovations in serial publication, so central to his career, both informed and constrained his authorial practice.

BONNIE J. GUNZENHAUSER

Biography

Born February 7, 1812 at Portsmouth, England, the son of a British Navy pay clerk. He received minimal schooling at Chatham, near London, but was sent to work at a shoe-blacking warehouse in London in 1824 after his father was put in debtor's prison. Dickens returned to school in 1825 as a pupil at Wellington House Academy in London, and began working as a solicitor's clerk and studying shorthand in 1827. In 1829, he began working as a freelance reporter at the Doctor's Commons courts, and in 1831 he began making shorthand reports of Parliament meetings for the London newspapers *Mirror* and *True Sun*. He published short stories in literary miscellanies from 1831, and in 1836 accepted the editorship of a new miscellany, *Bentley's*. Dickens also married Catherine Hogarth in 1836, and the couple went on to have ten children. He resigned from *Bentley's* in 1839, and started his own monthly magazine, *Master Humphrey's Clock*, in 1840. For much of his later career Dickens was to move from one periodical to the next, editing and often publishing his novels serially in them. *Pickwick Papers* [1837] and *Oliver Twist* [1839] appeared in *Bentley's*; *The Old Curiosity Shop* (1841) and *Barnaby Rudge* (1841) appeared in *Master Humphrey's Clock*, and later in his career, *Hard Times* (1854) appeared in his periodical *Household Words*, and *A Tale of Two*

Cities (1859) and *Great Expectations* (1861) appeared in his periodical *All the Year Round*. In addition to his novel writing and editing, Dickens also acted in amateur theatricals and, from 1858, gave numerous public readings of his works. He maintained this schedule until June 8, 1870, when he suffered a stroke at his Gad's Hill home in London. He died on June 9, and was buried in Westminster Abbey on June 14, 1870.

Selected Works

Pickwick Papers. 1837.
Oliver Twist. 1839.
Barnaby Rudge. 1841.
The Old Curiosity Shop. 1841.
American Notes. 1842.
A Christmas Carol. 1843.
Martin Chuzzlewitt. 1844.
Dombey and Son. 1848.
David Copperfield. 1850.
Bleak House. 1853.
A Child's History of England. 1853.
Hard Times. 1854.
Little Dorritt. 1857.
A Tale of Two Cities. 1859.
Great Expectations. 1861.
Our Mutual Friend. 1865.
Mystery of Edwin Drood. 1870.

Bibliography

Altick, Richard. *The English Common Reader: A Social History of the Mass Reading Public, 1800–1900*. Chicago: University of Chicago Press, 1957.

Collins, Philip, ed. *Dickens: The Critical Heritage*. New York: Barnes and Noble, 1971.

Devries, Duane. *General Studies of Charles Dickens and His Writings and Collected Editions of His Works: An Annotated Bibliography*. New York: AMS Press, 2001.

Henkle, Roger B. *Comedy and Culture: England 1820–1900*. Princeton, N.J.: Princeton University Press, 1980.

Herst, Beth F. *The Dickens Hero: Selfhood and Alienation in the Dickens World*. New York: St. Martin's Press, 1990.

Marcus, Steven. *Dickens: From Pickwick to Dombey*. New York: Simon and Schuster, 1965.

Poovey, Mary. *Uneven Developments: The Ideological Work of Gender in Mid-Victorian England*. Chicago: University of Chicago Press, 1988.

Stone, Harry, ed. *Dickens' Working Notes for His Novels*. Chicago: University of Chicago Press, 1987.

Watkins, Gwen. *Dickens in Search of Himself: Recurrent Themes and Characters in the Work of Charles Dickens*. Basingstoke, England: Macmillan, 1987.

Welsh, Alexander. *From Copyright to Copperfield: The Identity of Dickens*. Cambridge, Mass.: Harvard University Press, 1987.

Young, Arlene. "Virtue Domesticated: Dickens and the Lower Middle Class," *Victorian Studies* 39 (1996): 483–511.

DON GIOVANNI

Opera in two acts by Wolfgang Amadeus Mozart

Don Giovanni, the second of Wolfgang Amadeus Mozart's collaborations with the poet Lorenzo da Ponte (after *Le nozze di Figaro* in 1785; it would be later followed by *Così fan tutte* in 1790), was commissioned in 1787 by the Prague impressario Domenico Guardasoni; it premiered in Prague's National Theater on October 29, 1787. Like *Figaro* before it, *Don Giovanni* was a success: the *Prager Oberpostmtszeitung* of November 3 reported that "Connoisseurs and musicians say that Prague had never yet heard the like. . . . The unusually large attendance testifies to a unanimous approbation." But it was less successful in Vienna, where it was presented at the Burgtheater on May 7, 1788. Karl Count Zinzendorf, an astute theatrical observer, reported that "Mme. De la Lippe finds the music learned, little suited to the voice," while Archduchess Elisabeth Wilhelmine wrote to her husband Archduke Franz, "I was told that it did not have much success." Even the emperor, Joseph II, was disappointed. He remarked to Count Franz Orsini-Rosenberg that "[the] music is certainly too difficult for the singers."

Mozart had made several changes for the Vienna production: Don Ottavio's Act II aria "Il mio tesoro" was replaced by the duet "Per queste tue manine," sung by Zerlina and Leoporello; in compensation he was given the aria "Dalla sua pace" in act 1. And Donna Elvira gained the recitative and aria "In quali eccessi—Mi tradì quell'alma ingrata," also in act 2.

The modest afterlife of the opera in Vienna, where it was performed only infrequently for several years after its premiere, is explained, at least in part, by contemporary Viennese taste, the new theatrical policies instituted by Joseph II's successor, Leopold II, and by the unwillingness of the local nobility to embrace a German national art. But that was not the case outside of Vienna, where the opera was soon translated and performed: at Mainz, Frankfurt, Hamburg, and Bonn in 1789 (Beethoven played in the orchestra at the Bonn performance), and at Berlin in 1791. At least three translations were probably made by 1789, including versions by Christian Gottlob Neefe, Heinrich Gottlieb Schneider, and Friedrich Ludwig Schroeder. Vienna did not likewise embrace *Don Giovanni* until 1806, when the breakup of the Italian troupe there led to a renewed interest in German opera. The earliest Paris performance dates from 1805; the opera was also presented at Moscow in 1806, Rome in 1811, Naples in 1812, Milan in 1814, and London in 1817.

The most influential translation was by Friedrich Rochlitz, published in the 1801 edition produced in Leipzig by Breitkopf and Härtel. Rochlitz was motivated in part by the need to compensate for what was seen as an inferior libretto as well as by a nationalistic concern to free German opera from Italian traditions. More important he attempted to transform the opera from a work of action to one of drama. To this end, whole scenes were inserted for Don Giovanni, including brooding, self-reflective

Manuel Garcia (1775–1832) in Wolfgang Amadeus Mozart's *Don Giovanni*. New York Park Theater, May 23, 1826. Reprinted courtesy of the Lebrecht Collection.

works based on the Don Juan story. Wolfgang Robert Griepenkerl's *Das Musikfest oder die Beethovener* (*The Music Festival or The Beethovenian*, 1838) describes a Don Giovanni who "personifies a vital principle, the need, unconditionally, to dare that which was most extreme," while Gustav Kühne's *Eine Quarantäne im Irrenhaus* (*A Quarantine in a Madhouse*, 1835) claims that Mozart "so richly endowed this sinner that . . . he was not able to celebrate the life-principle, the personified vital urge, in any other way"; the principle itself became "an incarnate demon." For Nikolaus Lenau (*Don Juan*, 1844), this "vital urge" leads the protagonist, disgusted with life, to seek death in a duel. Even more radically, Søren Kierkegaard (*Either/Or*, 1843) attributes to Don Giovanni a "genius of sensuality," a transcendental "desire which desires." With this formulation, the opera comes to encapsulate the romantic ethos: it is an "infinity of passion."

Alexander Ulibischeff, in his *La vie de Mozart* (1843), may have been the first to see Mozart's self-portrait in the character of Don Giovanni, imposing on the work a critical reading grounded in the biography of the composer as it was then understood while at the same time celebrating the idea of the Romantic artist. A flawed character, irresponsible both financially and personally, Mozart represents both a tragic figure (witness the decline, poverty, and isolation of his later years) and a lawgiver, establishing "the rules of art, an art which had hitherto been incomplete." As the creative genius of an undefined "absoluteness," Mozart's life and works are joined with the Romantic ethos, complete in one man and one work. This was an idea challenged as early as 1802 in Franz Horn's *Musikalische Fragmente*, which rejects the overtly pictorial element in music. In describing *Don Giovanni* he asserts that Mozart presents "a spirit in the spectator's mind," effectively traversing the finite to the infinite, both incomprehensible and ineffable. It is not contradictory that Wagner later described *Don Giovanni* as a work for which there was "no understanding any more." As absolute music it transcends time, place, and tradition.

CLIFF EISEN

Bibliography

Abert, Hermann. *Mozart's Don Giovanni*. London: Eulenberg, 1976.

Allanbrook, Wye J. *Rhythmic Gesture in Mozart: Le nozze di Figaro and Don Giovanni*. Chicago: University of Chicago Press, 1983.

Barzun, Jacques. *Pleasures of Music*. New York: Viking Press, 1951.

Bitter, Chrstoph. *Wandlungen inden Inszenierungsformed des Don Giovanni 1787 bis 1928: zur Problematik des musikalischen Theaters in Deutschland*. Regensburg: S. Bosse Verlag, 1961.

Forsberg, Michael. "Don Giovanni and Romanticism," *Opera* 13 (1962): 790–96.

Gounod, Charles. *Mozart's Don Giovanni*. New York: Da Capo Press, 1970.

Gruber, Gernot. *Mozart and Posterity*. London: Quartet, 1991.

Hoffmann, Ernst Theodor Amadeus. "*Don Juan*. Eine fabelhafte Begebenheit, die sich mit einem reisenden Enthusiasten zugetrage," *Allgemeine musikalische Zeitung* 15 (1813): 213–20.

Kierkegaard, Søren. *Either/Or*. New York: Doubleday, 1959.

Kunze, Stefan. *Don Giovanni vor Mozart*. Munich: W. fink, 1972.

Rushton, Julian. *W. A. Mozart. Don Giovanni*. Cambridge: 1981.

Werner-Jensen, Karin. *Studien zur Don-Giovanni-Rezeption im 19. Jahrhundert (1800–1850)*. Tutzing: Hans Schneider Verlag, 1980.

meditations, while the role of Leporello was downgraded, and the problematic final sextet cut; the work ends with the destruction of the "hero."

The idea of Don Giovanni as hero—a characteristically Romantic conceit—has its origin in the writings of E. T. A. Hoffmann, in particular his novella *Don Juan. Eine fabelhafte Begebenheit, die sich mit einem reisenden Enthusiasten zugetrage* (*Don Juan. A Fabulous Incident That Befell a Traveling Enthusiast*, 1831). The enthusiast's description of the overture speaks for the whole opera: "I could see, clearly before my mind's eye, the conflict between human nature and the hideous, unseen powers which sought to destroy it." But it is not so much the hero himself who is the catalyst for change, as it is Donna Anna, who is "chosen by Heaven, in her love for Don Juan, to make him aware of those immanent springs of divine nature within him." Through her, Don Juan becomes mythical, a tragic Romantic artist, "yearning for perfect love." (Apparently the first singer to interpret Donna Anna this way was Wilhelmine Schröder-Devrient, who had made her debut in Vienna in 1821 as Pamina in Mozart's *Die Zauberflöte*.)

Hoffmann's successors took his reading several steps further, both in their understanding of the opera and in their literary

DON JUAN 1819-1824

Book-length poem by Lord Byron

Lord Byron's *Don Juan* radically changed English Romantic poetry. Its effect was like that of Ludwig van Beethoven's "Eroica" symphony in Romantic music. Both works were provoked by disappointment that the Napoleonic era had not established a brave new world in Europe. Instead, to the Romantic artist fell the task of transforming the human spirit. "I want a hero . . .," wrote Byron in the first words of canto 1. His extraordinary and provocative choice was to reject the conventional heroic protagonist of epic and to offer as "a hero of our time" (Mikhail Lermontov's phrase, the title of his celebrated novel) the libertine figure of Don Juan.

The poem was not planned, but like Byron's earlier self-confessional meditation, *Childe Harold's Pilgrimage* (1812–18), evolved over a period of time. Byron began *Don Juan* in the summer of 1818, and continued work on it sporadically until May 1823, when his involvement with the War of Independence in Greece provided an active outlet for his political idealism. The initial reaction of his immediate circle to canto 1 (published 1819) was one of shocked disapproval. The libertine story read too much like an account of Byron's disastrous marriage, and the ferociously satirical dedication of the poem to the once republican sympathizer then reactionary poet laureate Robert Southey had to be suppressed. Eventually Byron took the poem away from his "respectable" London publisher, John Murray, and from canto 6 (1823) onward, the poem was issued by the "radical" John Hunt. Subsequent piracy of the poem in multiple cheap reprints finally transformed *Don Juan* into one of the icons of working-class chartism after Byron's death.

The adventures of the hero are merely a device to take the poem first on a satiric tour through Europe on the verge of the French Revolution and then to England, where the uncompleted poem ends at a country house party at Norman Abbey, a thinly disguised re-creation of Byron's ancestral home, Newstead Abbey. If Byron had lived, one option he considered at this juncture was to expel Juan (like himself) from English society because of sexual scandal and to involve him as an "Anarchasis Cloots" figure (an anarchic spokesman for human rights) in the revolution in France, where he would be guillotined.

Although the poem is set in the 1780s, the poet's commentary is, with deliberate anachronism, located in his own reactionary epoch after the fall of Napoleon Bonaparte and the Congress of Vienna. Accordingly, the revolutionary idealism and disasters of the period 1789–1815 color the narrative. Byron brings to the poem a passionate commitment to the cause of "liberty" (political and sexual), and yet a world-weary recognition that "the ancient social order" (the phrase of Viscount Castlereagh, notorious for his violent opposition to reform) had re-established itself in Europe with little change. In one of his great outbursts, Byron declares, in Jeffersonian mode, that he "will war at least in words (and should / My chance so happen -deeds) with all who war / With Thought . . ." (9.24), yet the poem ends with the corrupt aristocracy of Norman Abbey as securely in place as ever.

This discrepancy between imaginative ideal and mundane imperfection is fundamental to the "Romantic irony" of the poem, which, in its serial progression, is always open-ended to the transient multiplicity of human experience and to the necessary coincidence of opposites and contradictions in ideology. The preeminent Romantic ironist of the poem is the narrator himself, whose commentary on the adventures of Don Juan frequently overwhelms the storyline. Consistent only in his own inconsistency, he is both comic and serious, relativistic in his awareness of human imperfections yet at the same time absolute in his claims for the liberty of all to pursue the happiness that the imagination desires but experience can never deliver.

These ironies, accordingly, make it difficult to define the ideology of the poem. The narrator, for instance, is both the opponent of monarchical oppression, yet hostile to the tyranny of the majority which democracy entails; he is the advocate of passionate romantic love (in the desert island episode of cantos 2–4) and yet cannot condemn serial promiscuity. Even the most famous declaration of nationalist anti-colonialism in the poem, the lyric "The Isles of Greece," is set in the mouth of a hypocritical Southey figure who, we are told, gives his audience whatever they want to pay for (3.78f.). There is, thus, an element of anarchic nihilism in the poem which debunks everything (not least Byron and Byronism). Or, more positively, this disruption of polarized ideological positions suggests an affinity between Byron and Friedrich Nietzsche, for only by going beyond conventional ideas of good and evil can an authentic selfhood be made. Bertrand Russell suggested a connection between Byron and Nietzsche in his *History of Western Philosophy* (1946), and although this argument has been hard to digest, *Don Juan* has not infrequently been interpreted by subsequent criticism as a great existential text in search of liberation from all systems of constraint.

The key question remains, as it was for Byron's original readers, what is the relation of *liberty* to *libertinism*? The poem now, as then, challenges the social morality that has used the Don Juan myth to condemn male promiscuity. In Byron's version, the promiscuous male is represented as a man of feeling and of idealistic longings, often the innocent victim of female aggression, and never the cruel seducer of the traditional legend. The moral inversion is that marriage is the equivalent of the "hell" to which the Don Juan of legend is condemned. In its refusal to condemn male promiscuity, the poem might seem to challenge the prevalent orthodoxies of modern feminism today as it once offended the Christian piety of Byron's age. But, paradoxically, the poem has attracted a number of sympathetic feminist interpretations. The sexual politics of the poem demand the liberation of women as concomitant to the liberation of men. "Love is for the free!," Juan exclaims in the very heartland of the oppression of women: a Turkish harem (5.127). It is a sign of the capacity of Romantic irony to renew itself that Juan, via Byron, here becomes, for our time, a type of "new man."

MALCOLM KELSALL

See also **Byron, Lord George Noel Gordon; Byronism; Don Juan: Themes and Contexts**

Text

Don Juan.
 Cantos 1–2, 1819.

Cantos 3–5. 1821.
Cantos 6–14. 1823.
Cantos 15–16. 1824.
Canto 17 (incomplete). 1903.
The Complete Poetical Works. Vol. 5. Edited by Jerome J. McGann. 1986.

Bibliography

Barton, Anne. *Don Juan.* Cambridge: Cambridge University Press, 1992.
Beatty, Bernard. *Byron's "Don Juan."* London: Croom Helm, 1985.

Donelan, Charles. *Romanticism and Male Fantasy in Byron's "Don Juan": A Marketable Vice.* Basingstoke, England: Macmillan, 2000.
Graham, Peter. *"Don Juan" in Regency England.* Charlottesville: University Press of Virginia, 1990.
Haslett, Moyra. *Byron's "Don Juan" and the Don Juan Legend.* Oxford: Clarendon Press, 1997.
McGann, Jerome J. *"Don Juan" in Context.* Chicago: University of Chicago Press, 1976.
Wood, Nigel. *Don Juan.* Buckingham, England: Open University Press, 1993.

DON JUAN: THEMES AND CONTEXTS

The first documented literary version of the myth of Don Juan is the seventeenth-century play *El Burlador de Sevilla* (*The Trickster of Seville*) by Tirso de Molina (Gabriel Téllez), first published in Barcelona in 1630. This text reworks a story originally dispersed in a variety of popular narratives and, whether directly or indirectly, it is the source of all subsequent literary versions. The myth was mostly reelaborated in dramatic forms in the seventeenth century, quickly migrating from Spain to Italy (Giacinto Andrea Cicognini, *Il convitato di pietra* [*The Stone Guest*], 1640s), France (plays by Pierre Corneille, Dorimon, Rosimond, Villiers, and Molière's *Dom Juan*, 1682), and England (Thomas Shadwell's *The Libertine*, 1675). In these early versions Don Juan appeared as an entertaining figure, distinguished by a mocking and defiant attitude, and characterized by the repetition of similar types of adventure. Also in the eighteenth century, Don Juan featured in a large number of theatrical adaptations and, especially, operas by composers such as Giuseppe Calegari (1777), Giuseppe Gazzaniga (1787), and Giovanni Paisiello (1790). Da Ponte and Mozart's *Il dissoluto punito ossia il Don Giovanni* (*The Punished Libertine, or Don Juan*, 1787) the climax of this tradition, was to have a primary influence on Romantic literary versions.

In particular, Mozart's opera inspired E. T. A. Hoffmann's novella "Don Juan, eine fabelhafte Begebenheit" ("Don Juan, a Fabulous Incident," 1813), which had a profound impact on numerous Romantic-period revisions of the myth. A fantastic story set against a representation of Mozart's masterpiece in an unnamed small town, the novella contains a critical interpretation of *Don Giovanni* that stresses the individualism of the protagonist, removing him from the plot of "exemplary punishment" typical of previous versions. In addition, Donna Anna becomes the embodiment of pure femininity and Don Juan's superior ideal, both characters sharing the same desire for the unattainable.

Hoffmann's reelaboration of the Don Juan character was very quickly taken up by his contemporaries. His tale, together with Mozart's version, were familiar to Aleksandr Pushkin, whose tragedy on this theme, *Kamennyj gost'* (*The Stone Guest*), was written in 1830. Eduard Duller's poem "Juan" (c. 1835) seems to be the first German text directly influenced by Hoffmann, followed by Braun von Braunthals's play *Don Juan. Drama in fünf Abtheilungen* (*Don Juan, Drama in Five Parts*, 1842). On the basis of Hoffmann's transformation of Don Juan, writers also began to create links between this figure and Faust. Nikolaus

Lenau's *Don Juan: dramatische Szenen* (*Don Juan, Dramatic Scenes*), written in 1844 and published posthumously in 1851, was a companion piece to his *Faust* of 1836. In his tragedy *Don Juan* (1840) Sigismund Wiese also made explicit references to the *Faust* story as set down in Johann Wolfgang von Goethe's version. By contrast, Christian Dietrich Grabbe's play *Don Juan und Faust* (1829) located the figure of the Spanish libertine between Hoffmann's idealized character and the more mundanely motivated figure of the seventeenth- and eighteenth-century versions. In France, Hoffmann's novella was translated in the *Revue de Paris* in 1829, and traces of its influence emerge in Alfred de Musset's oriental tale *Namouna* (1832) and in Théophile Gautier's *La Comédie de la Mort* (*The Comedy of Death*, 1838). The image of a "dandified" Don Juan, later surfaced in Charles Baudelaire's "Don Juan aux Enfers" ("Don Juan in Hell"), composed in 1846, and in his unfinished play *La Fin de Don Juan* (*The End of Don Juan*, c. 1853).

Reactions against this idealized interpretation of Don Juan were voiced by George Sand in her novel *Lélia* (1833) and by Gustave le Vavasseur's one-act play *Don Juan Barbon* (1848), where the hero, a respectable elderly gentleman, has to defend his daughter Dolorès from the attacks of a young libertine who has modelled his seduction techniques on Don Juan's youthful exploits. The mythical hero as an old man was also portrayed in Jules Viard's 1853 drama *La Vieillesse de Don Juan* (*Don Juan's Old Age*).

However, the transfiguration of the character into a tormented figure was prevalent. In Ange-Henry Blaze de Bury's play *Le Souper chez le Commandeur* (*The Dinner at the Commendatore's*, 1834), Donna Anna is transformed into the pure woman who ultimately reconciles Don Juan with heaven and ensures his spiritual salvation. This shift announces José Zorrilla y Moral's *Don Juan Tenorio* (1844), in which Don Juan is saved from damnation by Donna Anna's self-sacrificing love. Deeply read in contemporary French literature, Zorrilla wrote also from within the Spanish tradition traced by Tirso, Antonio de Zamora and José de Espronceda's recent narrative poem *El estudiante de Salamanca* (*The Student of Salamanca*, 1840). A concentration of the traditional seducer and the tormented Romantic hero, Zorrilla's Don Juan is a contemporary figure and a lost soul saved by the power of love. Moreover, the fact that the last woman seduced by Zorrilla's hero is a nun is a point of contact with Alfred de Musset's dramatic fragment "Une matinée de Don Juan" ("A Morning of Don Juan," 1833), which extends the traditional motif of the "catalog" by providing a hyperbolically long list of women's names, the last of which is an anonymous nun. Zorrilla's play therefore presents obvious links with the tradition, greatly favored by the Romantics, of the historic Miguel de Mañara (also called Manara or Marana), a seventeenth-century libertine who, near the end of his life, repented and became a monk. The Mañara story converged with the Don Juan myth in Prosper Mérimée's *Les Ames du Purgatoire* (*The Souls of Purgatory*, 1834) which, in turn, inspired Alexandre Dumas's five-act "mystery" *Don Juan de Marana, ou la Chute d'un Ange* (*Don Juan de Marana, or the Fall of an Angel*, 1836). Traces of the Mañara story are also present in Espronceda's *Estudiante de Salamanca*.

The Romantic period produced one of the most innovative versions of the Don Juan myth in Lord Byron's unfinished seventeen-canto poem *Don Juan* (1819–24). In this highly digressive narrative, Byron takes Don Juan from his native Seville on a tour across Europe between the 1780s and the 1820s. There are several attempts to retain a connection to the Spanish sources of the myth, but it is actually the Don Juan of the contemporary London stage that Byron is reelaborating. More a passive, seduced man than the indefatigable seducer of tradition, Byron's Juan is an endlessly mutable figure, ultimately the best example of the adaptability of a myth reworked and reinterpreted by Romantic-era writers and announcing later nineteenth- and twentieth-century revisions of the myth.

Much like Faust, Don Juan was not a Romantic creation. And yet, between the eighteenth and the nineteenth centuries, authors across Europe made this figure their own, transforming him into one of the most powerful icons of Romantic cultural concerns. In spite of the variety of versions and interpretations, the Romantic Don Juan nevertheless presents some recurrent features, as he alternatively embodies the figure of the damned hero (or antihero) brought down by fate or an inherently flawed nature, the eternal wanderer, man's material aspirations, and the eternal search for love. Don Juan thus personifies the several facets, as well as the extremes of light and darkness, that characterize Romantic subjectivity.

DIEGO SAGLIA

See Also **Baudelaire, Charles (Pierre); Byron, Lord George Gordon; Dandy;** *Don Giovanni; Don Juan;* **Drama: France; Drama: Germany; Dumas, Alexandre Davy de la Pailleterie; Espronceda y Delgado, José de;** *Faust;* **Gautier, Théophile; Goethe, Johann Wolfgang von; Hero; Hoffmann, Ernst Theodor Amadeus; Individualism; Lenau, Nikolaus; Mérimée, Prosper; Mozart, Wolfgang Amadeus; Musset, (Louis-Charles-) Alfred de; Opera; Pushkin, Aleksandr; Sand, George; Zorrilla y Moral, José**

Bibliography

Boyd, Elizabeth French. *Byron's Don Juan: A Critical Study*. New Brunswick, N.J.: Rutgers University Press, 1945.

Gendarme de Bévotte, Georges. *La Légende de Don Juan*. 2 vols. Paris: Hachette, 1911.

Graham, Peter. *Don Juan and Regency England*. Charlottesville: University Press of Virginia, 1990.

Haslett, Moyra. *Byron's* Don Juan *and the Don Juan Legend*. Oxford: Clarendon Press, 1997.

Macchia, Giovanni. *Vita, Avventure e Morte di Don Giovanni*. Bari: Laterza, 1966.

Rousset, Jean. *Le Mythe de Don Juan*. Paris: Armand Colin, 1978.

Singer, Armand Edward. *The Don Juan Theme: An Annotated Bibliography of Versions, Analogues, Uses and Adaptations*. Morgantown: West Virginia University Press, 1954.

Smeed, John William. *Don Juan: Variations on a Theme*. New York: Routledge, 1990.

Weinstein, Leo. *The Metamorphoses of Don Juan*. Vol. 18, *Stanford Studies in Language and Literature*. Stanford, Calif.: Stanford University Press, 1959.

DONIZETTI, (DOMENICO) GAETANO (MARIA) 1797–1848

Italian composer

Donizetti most typically represents Italian operatic life in the second quarter of the nineteenth century. While not the most individualistic composer of his age, he was master of a wider range of operatic types than any of his contemporaries, and in comedy, he defined the genre for the rest of the century. He could handle satire (*Le convenienze teatrali*, [*The Conventions of the Theater*], 1827) and neoclassical tragedy (*Belisario*, 1836); he mastered the French stage (*La fille du regiment* and *La favorite*, 1840) and impressed the Viennese in the highest degree. Generally, Donizetti's work displays a wide-ranging invention within the traditions established by Gioacchino Antonio Rossini. He skillfully refined the procedures within all the operatic genres, constantly revitalizing them with elements of surprise and by transforming its structures. He frequently combined two forms within a section, thus transforming the rhythm and trajectory of the drama. His treatment of the voice followed the patterns established by Rossini and evolved by Vincenzo Bellini. As a meticulous craftsman, he paid the closest attention to the individual qualities of the singers for whom he wrote. His writing was florid for a singer such as Fanny Tacchinardi-Persiani (in *Lucia di Lammermoor* and *Rosmonda d'Inghilterra*) or showed simpler dramatic force for singers with more thespian talents, such as Giudita Pasta and Ronzi de Begnis in *Anna Bolena, Maria di Rudenz*, and *Roberto Devereux*. With male voices he mostly abandoned the florid style in favor of an eloquent declamation, often using syncopation (rather than ornament) for emphasis. Especially the tenor roles of Donizetti's operas show a sharpness and power of vocal characterization achieved by deceptively simple means.

Together with Bellini, Donizetti represents the epitome of Italian opera's response to the Romantic movement. However, unlike Bellini, Donizetti worked under the constant pressure of the operatic market place. His unceasing involvement with the writing, rehearsing, and production of his works—most completed and rehearsed within a period of weeks—developed a more finely-honed sense of theatrical effectiveness and a wider range of feeling and dramatic resource than his younger contemporary. These sensibilities were supported by a great fluency of technique and musical invention—both nurtured by a very thorough training under his beloved teacher (and quasi-father), the Austrian ex-patriot Giovanni Simone Mayr. Above all else, as a practical man of the theater, Donizetti was always prepared to modify and rework operas to fit the resources of every revival. This often resulted in the compromise of dramatic ideals to performance exigencies. To serve such needs, individual numbers were often reworked for different vocal ranges—or were transferred wholesale from one opera to another. This makes the specification of a Donizetti opera highly problematic and runs counter to the Romantic ideal of the unique, definitive masterpiece. Such pragmatism brought contumely to Donizetti—especially from such an archromantic as Richard Wagner.

Donizetti started his operatic career in 1818, in a marketplace dominated by the style and achievements of Rossini. Despite a personal predilection for change, Donizetti still conformed to the current vogue and, by his thirty-third year had successfully produced some thirty operas in the *seria, buffa*, and *semiseria* genres. He showed his earliest (and greatest) finesse in the comic genre, in which he achieved a special blend of tenderness and humor that became the hallmark of the genre.

During the late 1820s Donizetti's manner broadened—partly a reflection of the influence of Rossini's French operas and partly a clearer vision of his own dramatic needs. This resulted in a wider range of vocal delivery: Donizetti's vocal lines became more extended lyrically (in the manner of Bellini) and acquired a sharpened variant of Rossini's declamatory manner that anticipated the work of Verdi. This extended range now penetrated Donizetti's serious works and with *Anna Bolena* (1830) Donizetti produced a highly charged, swift, and powerful drama. More radical was *Lucrezia Borgia* (1833), which displayed a new melodramatic intensity as well as extensive changes to the conventions and structures of *opera seria*. With *L'elisir d'amore* (*The elixir of love*, 1832) Donizetti produced a supreme example of pastoral comedy that remains the touchstone of the genre—its only rival being his own late (and radical) masterpiece, *Don Pasquale* (1843). In *L'assedio di Calais* (*The Siege of Calais*, 1836), Donizetti created a patriotic grand opera on the French model, in which he hoped (with some success) that he would bring a new genre to Italian opera. These transformations and extensions of Italian opera are highly significant responses to trans-alpine Romanticism and sharply modulated the heritage of Italian culture and its conventions, which in turn greatly influenced Giuseppe Verdi. However, Donizetti was not an overt radical, nor was his progress uniformly coherent. A busy career left little leisure for theory or dramatic revolution. *Lucia di Lammermoor* (1835), while validly (along with Bellini's *Norma*) as the epitome of Italian Romantic opera, remains an uncomfortable mixture of the old and the new.

Patchiness remained a feature of Donizetti's sixty-five completed operas. Lacking Rossini's unquestioned position (and financial independence) or Bellini's patronage (which enabled the latter to be highly selective in subject matter and to take very extended periods in composing and staging his works), Donizetti worked at a frantic pace throughout his career. This, combined with his willingness to accommodate the idiosyncrasies of singers and the practicalities of production, generated a multitude of compromises.

In his latter years, Donizetti spent extended periods in Paris and Vienna where, in response to the local conventions and expectations of the audiences, he extended the structural scope and dramatic drive of his works. For Paris, he created such works as *Les Martyrs* (*The martyrs*), *Roberto Devereux*, *La fille du regiment* (*The Daughter of the Regiment*), and *La favorite*—all in 1840—and *Don Pasquale* in 1843. These works show clear evidence of French operatic resources and influence, without fundamentally changing Donizetti's methods or dramaturgy. For Viennese commissions he wrote *Linda di Chamounix* (1842)—his most mature and subtly varied example of the semiseria genre—and *Maria di Rohan* (1843), his most concentrated tragedy. So highly were these operas regarded that Donizetti was appointed *Hofkapellmeister*—an honor seldom given to foreigners.

Donizetti's reputation as a composer of *opera buffa* has never wavered. His serious works drifted from the repertory and still, despite many merits, fail to compete against the later, more concentrated achievements of Verdi. Notwithstanding, his contribution to the development of Italian opera and its rapprochement with Romanticism is central and crucial.

BENEDICT SARNAKER

See also **Bellini, Vincenzo; Rossini, Gioacchino Antonio; Verdi, Giuseppe; Wagner; Richard**

Biography

Born in Bergamo, Italy, November 29, 1797. Son of Andrea Donizetti, pawnshop caretaker. Studied with Simon Mayr, the *maestro di cappella* at the church of Santa Maria Maggiore Bergamo. Awarded a scholarship to the Lezioni Caritatevoli, Bergamo, 1806. Studied at Liceo Filarmonico Comunale under Padre Stanislao Mattei, 1815–17. First operatic work, *Enrico di Borgogna*, performed in Venice, 1818. Lived mainly in Naples from 1822 on; composed thirty-one operas for theaters there. Appointed director of the Teatro Nuovo, Naples, 1827. Married Virginia Vasselli, 1828; they had one son (died at eleven days old). Director of the Royal Theaters of Naples, 1828–38. Directed performances of his works in Milan, Rome and Genoa, 1833–34. First performance of *Lucia di Lammermoor*, 1835. Virginia died, possibly of syphilis, after the stillbirth of a child, 1837. Moved to Paris, 1838; composed works for theaters in Paris, Bologna, and Rome. Appointed *Hofkapellmeister* to Hapsburg court in Vienna, 1842. Suffered increasingly from symptoms of syphilis; mental instability caused confinement in asylum in Ivry, Paris, 1846. Returned to Bergamo at the request of family and friends; lived in the palace of Baroness a Rosa Rota-Basoni. Died of syphilis in Bergamo, April 8, 1848.

Selected Works

Anna Bolena. 1830.
L'Elisir d'amore. 1832.
Lucrezia Borgia. 1833.
Lucia di Lammermoor. 1835.
Maria Stuarda. 1835.
L'assedio di Calais. 1836.
Roberto Devereux. 1837.
La favorite. 1840.
La fille du regiment. 1840.
Linda di Chamounix. 1842.
Don Pasquale. 1843.
Maria di Rohan. 1843.

Bibliography

Allitt, John. *Donizetti and the Tradition of Romantic Love*. London: The Donizetti Society, 1975.

Ashbrook, William. *Donizetti and His Operas*. Cambridge: Cambridge University Press, 1982.

Barblan, Guglielmo. *L'Opera di Donizetti nell'età romantica*. Bergamo: Banca Populare di Bergamo, 1948.

Black, John. *Donizetti's Operas in Naples 1822–1848*. London: The Donizetti Society, 1982.

Commons, Jeremy. *Contribution to a Study of Donizetti and the Neapolitan Censorship*. Bergamo, 1977.

Duprez, Gilbert. *Souvenirs d'un chanteur*. Paris: Calman Lévy, 1880.

Donati-Petténi, G. *Donizetti*. Milano: Fratelli Treves, 1930.

Florimo, Francesco. *La scuola musicale di Napoli e i suoi Conservatorii*. Bologna: Forni Editore, 1881–83.

Gavazzeni, Gianandrea. *Gaetano Donizetti: vita, musiche, epistolario*. Bergamo: Istituto Italiano d'Arte Grafiche, 1948.

Gossett, Phillip. *Anna Bolena*. Oxford: Oxford University Press, 1985.

Weinstock, Herbert. *Donizetti and the World of Opera in Italy, Paris and Vienna in the First Half of the Nineteenth Century*. New York: Pantheon Books, 1963.

Zavadini, Guido. *Donizetti: vita, musiche, epistolario*. Bergamo: Istituto Italiano d'Arti Grafiche, 1948.

DOUGLASS, FREDERICK 1818–1895

African American spokesman, leader, activist, and writer

Frederick Douglass was the single most important African American public voice in nineteenth-century America. Born into slavery in Maryland in 1818(?), only to escape at age twenty to eventually become a prominent public orator and anti-slavery activist in New England in the 1840s and 1850s, Douglass used his life experience (recounted in the autobiographical works *The Narrative of the Life of Frederick Douglass, An American Slave* [1845], *My Bondage and My Freedom* [1855], and *Life and Times of Frederick Douglass* [1881, revised 1892]) to authenticate his representative status as a nineteenth-century American. It is difficult to generalize about the ideological weight of Douglass's work: the late-nineteenth-century black leader Booker T. Washington argued that his life exemplified the democratic fight for black industrial education, while his love of liberty could be seen as essentially Republican, embodied in his short story "The Heroic Slave" (1853), and Waldo E. Martin Jr. focuses on his ambivalence towards his African heritage. As Eric J. Sundquist has argued, there is a "protean character" to Douglass's thought and a "willingness to adapt" political and narrative strategies "to exploit most effectively the [prevailing] ideological crosscurrents." Although Douglass cannot be considered an exponent of Romanticism in the fullest sense, there are strong Romantic impulses in his thought, and it is useful to contrast his work with prominent Romantic thinkers on antislavery issues such as Ralph Waldo Emerson and William Lloyd Garrison.

Douglass's first major publication, *The Narrative of the Life of Frederick Douglass, An American Slave*, sold 4,500 copies between May and September 1845 rising to a total of 30,000 in the nineteenth century and helped raise public awareness of the plight of African American slaves. Douglass begins his life story by stressing his ignorance of his background: he had the briefest contact with his mother Harriet Bailey, a black slave, and he never knew with any certainty if his white father was in fact his owner Captain Aaron Anthony. The book avoids the sentimental style that was often associated with a certain type of Romantic narrative (as evidenced in Harriet Beecher Stowe's *Uncle Tom's Cabin* [1852]), and Douglass is terse and hardheaded in his accounts of himself and the treatment of his family and fellow slaves. He attempts to arouse the reader's indignation not with excessive sentiment, but through candid representations that are

often drained of emotion, such as his beating by his later master Edward Covey, which caused his "blood to run . . . raising ridges on my flesh as large as my little finger." At times, Douglass demystifies Romantic preconceptions, such as slavery songs that express "the sorrows of the heart" (not spiritual contentment) and the collusion between religious revivals and the slave trade. However, in other sections, his voice is more obviously Romantic: he praises Providence as his guiding force on the road to freedom and he relates his dreamlike vision of ships at sea "robed in purest white," which would be "so delightful to the eye of freemen," but were to him "so many shrouded ghosts, to terrify and torment me with thoughts of my wretched condition." Indeed, although Douglass does comment on other slaves, the individualistic trajectory of his journey from bondage to freedom, achieved by combining heroic courage with literacy and learning, reflects the exemplary American narrative form established in Benjamin Franklin's *Autobiography* (written in the 1770s and 1780s, but not published in its entirety until 1868) and developed in Horatio Alger's popular rags-to-riches stories, such as *Ragged Dick* (1867). However, while all Douglass's autobiographical narratives are deeply American in their focus on exceptional individualism, the upward sweep of *The Narrative* also parallels the European *bildungsroman* as a novel of social education and intellectual growth, as represented by Johann Friedrich von Goethe's *Wilhelm Meister's Apprenticeship* (1795–96) and Charles Dickens's *David Copperfield* (1850).

While certain distinctive aspects of *The Narrative* clearly reflect nineteenth-century American Romantic writing (such as Emerson's essay "Self-Reliance," 1841), other features of Douglass's thought resist incorporation into mainstream culture. For example, although his early intellectual awakening was stimulated by reading William Lloyd Garrison's abolitionist journal the *Liberator* (and Garrison wrote a long preface to *The Narrative* praising its eloquence, its modesty and its Romantic "union of head and heart"), Douglass deals with his experiences of slavery on his own terms; they are not filtered through prevailing conceptions of the moral inferiority of Africans. In the early 1850s Douglass fell out with Garrison and the Massachusetts Anti-Slavery Society, mainly due to their belief that although he was in a privileged position to present the realities of slavery, as an

African American he was incapable of analyzing and interpreting them. Douglass could not tolerate such patronizing attitudes nor any claims for intellectual superiority, as evident in the defiant motto for his own journal *The North Star*: "right is of no sex—truth is of no color." In the wake of the Fugitive Slave Act of 1850, Douglass maintained that, whether in the North or South, the black American remained in bondage, and even the liberty of freed slaves was precarious, as he claimed in his speech "what to the Slave is the Fourth of July?" (1852): "The Fourth [of] July is *yours*. not *mine*. *You* may rejoice *I* must mourn." In his "Lecture on Slavery" (1855) Emerson responded to these ideas by insisting on "the doctrine of the independence and the inspiration of the individual" and the supreme importance of "social action," but Emerson differed from Douglass in shifting away from the topic of the enlightenment of all Americans toward stressing the need to "elevate, enlighten" and "civilize" the people of the "semi-barbarous" Southern states.

Douglass's two subsequent autobiographies update his life and provide extra details, focusing on his success story as an emancipated African American and stressing the rights of revolution. In *My Bondage and My Freedom* he emphasizes his independence from the abolitionists by replacing Garrison's preface with that of the prominent black medical practitioner and reformer James McCune Smith, who calls Douglass "a Representative American man" (with an ironic nod to Emerson's *Representative Men* from 1850) and praises the book as "an example of self-elevation under the most adverse circumstances." The tensions between realism and Romanticism in Douglass's thought continued throughout his life, with his Enlightenment belief in "the indestructable and unchangeable laws of human nature" sitting uncomfortably with his intuitive conviction that different races had distinctive natural gifts, his argument for cultural hierarchy, and his call for black leadership. These tensions are also evident in *Life and Times of Frederick Douglass*, published after his active work in the Civil War, in which the democratic style of the book contrasts with Douglass's dislike of popular culture and his ongoing narrative of heroic self-creation.

MARTIN HALLIWELL

Biography

Born Frederick Augustus Washington Bailey in 1818(?) on a plantation in Tuckahoe, Maryland, to a slave mother and white father. In 1825 sent to Baltimore; in 1831 purchased a copy of *The Columbian Orator*, which helped him to read; learned the trade of caulking under supervision of his owner in the Baltimore shipyard; escaped in 1838 to New York, where he changed his name and married a freewoman, Anna Murray; in 1839 em-

ployed as lecturer by antislavery society in New Bedford, Massachusetts; published *Narrative of the Life of Frederick Douglass, An American Slave* in 1845; fathered four children between 1841–45; spent two years in Ireland and England as a fugitive slave; in 1846 his freedom was purchased by Ellen and Anna Richardson from Newcastle, England; returned to the United States in 1847 where he established an antislavery journal, *The North Star*, in Rochester, New York (later called *Frederick Douglass' Paper*, 1847–64); founded a second journal, *Douglass' Monthly*, in 1858; organized two black regiments for the Union during the Civil War; served as secretary of the Santo Domingo Commission in 1871; marshal of the District of Columbia, 1877–78; recorder of deeds for the District of Columbia, 1881–86; and as U.S. minister to Haiti, 1889–91.

Selected Works

Life and Writings of Frederick Douglass. 5 vols. Edited by Philip S. Foner. New York: International, 1950–75.
Life and Times of Frederick Douglass. Edited by Rayford W. Logan. New York: Collier, 1962.
My Bondage and My Freedom. Edited by William L. Andrews. Chicago: University of Chicago Press, 1980.
The Narrative of the Life of Frederick Douglass, An American Slave. Edited by Houston Baker Jr. New York: Penguin, 1982.

Bibliography

Andrews, William. *Literary Romaniticism in America*. Baton Rouge: Louisiana State University Press, 1981.
———. *To Tell a Free Story: The First Century of Afro-American Autobiography, 1760–1865*. Urbana: University of Illinois Press, 1986.
Foner, Philip S. *Frederick Douglass: A Biography*. New York: Citadel Press, 1964.
Huggins, Nathan Irvin. *Slave and Citizen: The Life of Frederick Douglass*. Boston: Little, Brown, 1980.
Martin, Waldo E. Jr. *The Mind of Frederick Douglass*. Chapel Hill: University of North Carolina Press, 1984.
McFeely, William S. *Frederick Douglass*. New York: W. W. Norton, 1991.
McKivigan, John R., and Stanley Harrold, eds. *Anti-Slavery Violence: Sectional, Racial, and Cultural Conflict in Antebellum America*. Knoxville: University of Tennessee Press, 1999.
Miller, Douglas T. *Frederick Douglass and the Fight for Freedom*. New York: Facts on File, 1988.
Stepto, Robert B. *From Behind the Veil: A Study of Afro-American Narrative*. Urbana: University of Illinois Press, 1979.
Sundquist, Eric J., ed. *Frederick Douglass: New Literary and Historical Essays*. Cambridge: Cambridge Unniversity Press, 1990.
Washington, Booker T. *Frederick Douglass*. Philadelphia: G. W. Jacobs/London: Hodder and Stoughton, 1907.

DRAMA: BRITAIN

For most of the eighteenth century, only two London theaters, the Royal Drury Lane and Covent Garden, were licensed to stage "serious" tragedy and comedy. The public, however, demanded spectacle. Spurred on by the innovations of Drury Lane's designer, Louis de Loutheburg, each set was more elaborate than the last. Audiences clamored for the star actors, Edmund Kean, John Phillip Kemble, Eliza O'Neill, and Sarah Siddons. By 1800, each house seated more than three thousand patrons. A

theatrical evening could last five hours, including the main play and a pantomime or farce. Smaller houses, including the Haymarket, Sadler's Wells, and the Aldwych, and many provincial theaters and touring companies, offered "illegitimate" theater at cutthroat prices.

Since the passing of the Theatre Licensing Act in 1737, the scope of drama had been curtailed by rigorous censorship. But the theaters were still hotbeds of political debate. The Revolution of 1789 was commemorated with a number of spectacular theatrical celebrations. As the political climate cooled, anti-revolutionary drama countered with plays discrediting such anti-authoritarian festivities and with displays of British military prowess. The audiences were not immune from political skirmishes. When Covent Garden audiences rioted for sixty three days in 1809–10 against price increases, the Whig press castigated the managers as tyrants, while the Tory papers accused the audiences of insurrection.

Domestic and sentimental comedy thrived, though altered by the political tensions of the revolutionary age. Gothic spectacle and themes of incest and imprisonment were instrumental to the anti-revolutionary campaign to shock audiences, and then placate their awakened sensibilities with scenes of domestic bliss. Adaptations of German Sturm und Drang (storm and stress) plays were very popular in the 1790s, but so were parodies of the German tragic style, echoing the charges of "Jacobinism" levied against them in the popular press. William Shakespeare was of course a great favorite, although *Julius Caesar* was banned because it depicted regicide. In an effort to outwit the censors, many playwrights used historical settings to diffuse the political topicality of their plays. Slavery was a popular vehicle for tragedy, farce, and pantomime alike, and frequently the most outrageous performances expressed the fiercest abolitionist sentiments. The result was a mixture of styles, genres, and ideologies, continually adapting to the social and political climate. By the 1820s the form settled into a generic pattern of psychological tension and domestic harmony, now loosely called melodrama.

Romantic verse tragedy does not reject the drama outright as much as experiment with available forms. These plays were inspired by Sturm und Drang, the Gothic, and William Shakespeare, and most were submitted to the royal theaters. When William Wordsworth's dark Schillerian tragedy of betrayal and revenge *The Borderers* (1797) was rejected by Covent Garden on the grounds of "moral obscurity," Wordsworth took it to Drury Lane. William Godwin's *Faulkener* (1802) and Charles Lamb's *Woodvil* (1807) were both staged, disastrously, at the royal houses. Samuel Taylor Coleridge's *Osorio* was written on commission and rejected by Richard Brinsley Sheridan in 1797, then rewritten and staged to great acclaim as *Remorse* in 1813. Innovations with dramatic form could also reflect political temperament. Leigh Hunt's *The Descent of Liberty* (1814), subtitled *A Mask*, hardly celebrates courtly ritual, though it borrows from the old aristocratic form a spirit of collaborative jubilation. This tendency is much accentuated in Percy Bysshe Shelley's *Prometheus Unbound* (1819), and later in Thomas Lovell Beddoes's difficult and outrageous *Death's Jest Book* (1825–49), as both plays seem to resist formal and generic constraints altogether. Shelley's *The Cenci* (1819), by contrast, was written with actors Kean and O'Neill in mind, and was submitted to Covent Garden. Hinting at the Renaissance tyrant Cenci's rape of his daughter and dramatizing his murder and her trial, the dramatic tension of this play derives as much from its careful stylization of theatrical poise as it does from its poetic intensity. Lord Byron served on the board of Drury Lane in 1815–16, and although he grew to despise the audiences' fickle attraction to spectacle and farce, his metaphysical tragedies *Manfred* (1818) and *Cain* (1820) and the historical intrigue *Sardanapalus* (1821) were staged throughout the nineteenth century. Byron's plays provide stirring vehicles for his trademark character, the antisocial genius, wanderer, or despot. Interestingly, the plays offer the clearest illustration of how much the dynamics of the Byronic hero owe to their theatrical embodiment.

The Romantic "antitheatical prejudice" lies mainly in the theater criticism of Coleridge, William Hazlitt, Hunt, and Charles Lamb. Lamb, for instance, argued that the plays of Shakespeare should not be performed on the public stage because the overbearing emotionalism and outlandish spectacles of the theater could not sustain the "excellence" of Shakesperean verse. Lamb also argued, however, that in the body of a genius like Kemble, a tragic figure like Macbeth was too real, too alive, to be understood with necessary critical judgement. Hazlitt also criticized the leading actors for not appreciating the subtleties of the drama. Yet he defined the ideals of dramatic action and its political implications with reference to the talent of Kean, Kemble, and Siddons.

Important advances in drama were introduced by women playwrights. Familiar authors, such as Sophia and Harriet Lee, Mary Shelley and Charlotte Smith all wrote plays with varying degrees of success. Two women playwrights in particular define the characteristic tensions of Romantic drama. Elizabeth Inchbald was a successful actress in the 1770s and 1780s; she wrote a number of domestic comedies, farces, and tragedies; she was also a noted theater critic and editor. Her plays reflect a keen interest in such issues as slavery and sexual equality. Joanna Baillie's dramatic series *The Plays on the Passions* (first published in 1798), with their remarkable "introductory discourse," represent the most systematic effort to stage the private self-reflection characteristic of Romanticism proper. Her most famous tragedy, *De Monfort*, featuring the typically reclusive hero harboring a secret hatred, inspired Lord Byron and William Wordsworth. Like Inchbald, however, Baillie draws particular attention to the way in which such behavior is the product of social forces.

ALEX DICK

Bibliography

Burroughs, Catherine B. *Closet Stages: Joanna Baillie and the Theater Theory of British Romantic Women Writers.* Philadelphia: University of Pennsylvania Press, 1997.

Burwick, Frederick. *Illusion and the Drama: Critical Theory of the Enlightenment and Romantic Era.* University Park: Pennsylvania State University Press, 1991.

Carlson, Julie A. *In the Theater of Romanticism: Coleridge, Nationalism, Women.* Cambridge: Cambridge University Press, 1994.

Cave, Richard Allen, ed. *The Romantic Theater: An International Symposium.* Totawa, N.J.: Barnes and Noble, 1986.

Conolly, L. W. *The Censorship of English Drama 1737–1824.* San Marino, Calif.: Huntington Library, 1976.

Cox, Jeffrey N. "Ideology and Genre in the British Antirevolutionary Drama of the 1790s," *ELH* 58 (1991): 579–610.

———. *In the Shadows of Romance: Romantic Tragic Drama in Germany, England and France.* Athens: Ohio University Press, 1987.

———. "Staging Hope: Genre, Myth, and Ideology in the Dramas of the Hunt Circle," *Texas Studies in Literature and Language* 38 (1996): 245–64.

Donohue, Joseph W. Jr. *Dramatic Character in the Romantic Age.* Princeton, N.J.: Princeton University Press, 1970.

Fletcher, Richard M. *English Romantic Drama: A Critical History.* New York: Exposition, 1966.

Hoagwood, Terence. "Prolegomenon for a Theory of Romantic Drama," *Wordsworth Circle* 23 (1992): 49–64.

Moody, Jane. "'Fine Word, Legitimate!' Toward a Theatrical

History of Romanticism," *Texas Studies in Literature and Language* 38 (1996): 223–44.

Richardson, Alan. *A Mental Theater: Poetic Drama and Consciousness in the Romantic Age.* University Park: Pennsylvania State University Press, 1988.

Simpson, Michael. *Closet Performances: Political Exhibition and Prohibition in the Dramas of Byron and Shelley.* Stanford, Calif.: Stanford University Press, 1998.

Watkins, Daniel P. *A Materialist Critique of English Romantic Drama.* Gainesville: University Press of Florida, 1993.

DRAMA: FRANCE

French Romantic drama reacted against the neoclassical theater of the seventeenth to early nineteenth centuries. Already, Denis Diderot, among other Enlightenment playwrights, wrote "bourgeois dramas" that no longer portrayed kings and princesses, but middle-class people and their psychological and familial problems discussed in everyday prose, rather than in inflated verse. Furthermore, thanks to the essays of Benjamin Constant, Anne-Louise-Germaine Staël, and Stendhal, newly translated foreign authors from Spanish golden-age dramatists to Johann Christoph Friedrich von Schiller resonated with the new generation. William Shakespeare, above all, was revered because his plays showed the struggle between good and evil and emphasized melancholy and feelings over reason and moderation: this with a felicitous mix of grotesque and sublime, fearful and farcical, tragic and comic, as well as a maximum of local color and realistic historical re-creation.

As a result, in 1809, Népomucène Lemercier tried to free himself from the neoclassical unities of time and place and to have his characters use a more contemporary French in his *Christophe Colomb* (Christopher Columbus). His experiment was followed by Jean-François Ancelot's *Louis IX* (1819) and Casimir Delavigne's *Les Vêpres siciliennes* (*The Sicilian Vespers*, 1819), both of which broached historical subjects. Other tragedies in the nascent mode were successfully produced: Pierre Lebrun's *Marie Stuart* (1820) mixed genres, and Alexandre Soumet's *Clytemnestre* and *Saül* (both 1822) included touches of local color. In addition, *Théâtre de Clara Gazul* (1825) by Prosper Mérimée is an excellent collection of prose plays. Inspired by Shakespeare and Pedro Calderón de la Barca, they depict violent passions against a backdrop of cruel eroticism, in a natural style and with a historical ambience.

Mention should also be made of melodrama, which as the avant-garde genre of the early nineteenth century, had already abandoned the unities and devised sensational but simple plots in exotic locations enlivened by spectacular scenic effects. Guilbert de Pixérécourt, the uncontested master, was hugely popular, with a repertoire of over hundred works. Through this influence, Romantic drama has duels, poisons, blood, disguises, last-minute recognitions, adulteries, kidnappings, secret passageways, hidden staircases, and sliding panels galore.

By the time Victor Hugo published his preface to *Cromwell* in 1827, therefore, many of his ideas were in the air. In rejecting imitation and the two unities and rules of propriety required in neoclassical theatre, he was advocating greater historical truth (through local color and modern material) and inner truth (through emotions). He and like-minded playwrights demanded freedom in form and content: to portray life in its entirety, drama had to include comic elements with tragic ones, and individualized characters, not abstract types, must participate in the action. Finally, favoring verse, he eventually also wrote several plays in prose. Another key text was Stendhal's *Racine et Shakespeare* (1823–25), in which he argued in favor of a literature that responded to contemporary life and so rejected traditional forms.

Alexandre Dumas's *Henri III et sa cour* (*Henri III and His Court*, 1829) portrays characters lacking depth and substance while it presents a very imaginative, if brutal, historical truth; yet it is full of unbridled vitality and dramatic pacing. Little wonder the drama was an immediate success when it premiered. More ambitious but no less well received was *Antony* (1831). It owes much to Lord Byron and to Charles Nodier not only for the somber, immoral, haughty, illegitimate hero, but also the passionate and violent love between Antony and the married Adèle.

When *La Tour de Nesle* (*The Tower of Nesle*) was staged in 1832, spectators loved it, but reviewers attacked its numerous acts of murder, incest, adultery, as though these had not occurred in Greek tragedy or Racine. What Dumas contributes is not just a melodramatic plot, but a breathless rush of action and an accumulation of horrors that overcome any thought that we are watching (or reading) a ludicrous tale. This is why Heinrich Heine could write, "Dumas is not so great a poet as Victor Hugo, but he possesses gifts which in the drama enable him to achieve far greater results than the latter."

Except for *Hernani* (1830), Hugo's plays were either banned or lukewarmly received. In fact, *Les Burgraves* failed in 1843, marking the end of Romantic drama in France, due in part to the public's renewed interest in Corneille and Racine and to the success of François Ponsard's neoclassical *Lucrèce* that same year. *Hernani* is rightly celebrated for its fresh style, its original Alexandrine lines full of bold images, a dialogue combining low and high language, a daring verse form, a picturesque historical framework. Moreover, all Hugo's plays show a dual conception of protagonists based on antitheses. For example, we have in Hernani the accursed bandit with a heroic soul, in Marion Delorme the fallen woman with a pure soul, in Ruy Blas the commoner ennobled by a queen's love, in Triboulet a deformed jester uplifted by his paternal love, and in Lucrezia Borgia a monster of immorality redeemed by maternal love.

Alfred de Musset's *Lorenzaccio* (written in 1834, but not performed until 1896, with Sarah Bernhardt in the title role), more than any other, fulfilled the requirements of Romantic dramaturgy and sensibility. Lorenzaccio, "pure as gold" in his youth, now finds vices "glued to my skin." So, despite the probable futility of his act, he must assassinate Duke Alexander de Medici: "This murder (. . .) is all that remains of my virtue," he acknowledges ruefully.

Chatterton (1835), by Alfred de Vigny, is "the examination of a wound of the soul." The play's eighteen-year-old (but going on "one thousand years") English poet is a lonely and misunderstood victim of society, who wears the fatal mark of genius on his forehead, and signifies "perpetual martyrdom and perpetual immolation [of] a spiritual man strangled by a materialistic society." His compatriots have only contempt for him, yet he finds both joy *and* misery in being chosen by the Muses since it proves his innate superiority (an important theme in Vigny's poetry as well).

French Romantic drama threw off the shackles of an exhausted neoclassical literature and took the great events of modern history as its inspiration in order to validate the supremacy of feelings over too-cool intellect. On the other hand, the French consider themselves rational, even Cartesian: perhaps, this explains why Romantic drama had no remarkable follow-up. The one notable exception is Edmond Rostand's *Cyrano de Bergerac* (1897), a sublime spectacle in five acts and in verse, full of verve, emotion, humor, and panache.

PIERRE L. HORN

Bibliography

Affron, Charles. *A Stage for Poets: Studies in the Theatre of Hugo and Musset.* Princeton, N.J.: Princeton University Press, 1971.

Buss, Robin. *Vigny: "Chatterton."* London: Grant and Cutler, 1984.

Carlson, Marvin. *The French Stage in the Nineteenth Century.* Metuchen, N.J.: Scarecrow Press, 1977.

Cox, Jeffrey N. *In the Shadows of Romance: Romantic Tragic Drama in Germany. England, and France.* Athens: Ohio University Press, 1987.

Crossley, Ceri. *Musset: "Lorenzaccio."* London: Grant and Cutler, 1983.

Daniels, Barry V. *Revolution in the Theatre: French Romantic Theories of Drama.* Westport, Conn.: Greenwood Press, 1983.

Descotes, Maurice. *Le Drame romantique et ses grands créateurs.* Paris: Presses Universitaires de France, 1955.

Halsall, Albert W. *Victor Hugo and the Romantic Drama.* Toronto: University of Toronto Press, 1998.

Howarth, W. D. *Sublime and Grotesque: A Study of French Romantic Drama.* London: Harrap, 1969.

Laurent, Franck, and Michel Viegnes. *Le Drame romantique.* Paris: Hatier, 1997.

Wren, Keith. *Hugo: "Hernani" and "Ruy Blas."* London: Grant and Cutler, 1982.

DRAMA: GERMANY

German drama in the period 1760–1850 presents a very heterogeneous picture. It developed from a traditional style inspired by neoclassicism to a form of drama drawing increasingly on native traditions in the 1770s, through to a synthesis of this with the neoclassical style in the last decades of the eighteenth century, and the erratic beginnings of realism and modernism in the first half of the nineteenth century.

Theatrical life in early eighteenth-century Germany had seen the enlightened pedagogue Johann Christoph Gottsched propounding neoclassical aesthetics and attempting to follow French models. His serious efforts to reform the theater (in which he was assisted by his wife Luise and Friederike Neuber's troupe) included the banning of the clown figure, but were marred by a degree of narrowness and prescriptiveness. He was attacked by Gotthold Ephraim Lessing, who became the liberator of German drama. Lessing was engaged as a theater critic in Hamburg, writing a large number of reviews of productions, which he grouped together in the *Hamburg Dramaturgy* (1767–68). He reassessed the role of fear and pity in tragedy, arguing that *Mitlied* (sympathy) was paramount. The work of William Shakespeare rather than French drama became important; Lessing's own mature plays established new directions in German drama: *Miss Sara Sampson* (1753) in domestic tragedy; *Minna von Barnhelm* (1767) in comedy; *Emiila Galotti* (1772) in tragedy; and *Nathan der Weise* (1779) in didactic drama. Lessing also laid some of the foundations for Sturm und Drang (storm and stress) drama by liberating the writer from normative poetics, turning toward Shakespeare, and using contemporary reality as a subject for drama.

The Stürmer und Dränger were more radical in their approach. Theoretical precursors were Heinrich Wilhelm von Gerstenberg (who also wrote a seminal tragic drama, *Ugolino*, in 1768), Johann Georg Hamann, and Johann Gottfried von Herder. Writing mainly in Strasbourg in the early 1770s, they reassessed Germany's cultural roots and made important contributions to drama, though their plays retain an element of literariness and their connections with the theater were in most cases not strong.

Johann Wolfgang von Goethe's *Götz von Berlichingen* (1773) was the first historical drama in Germany, but Goethe turned to his own times with scenes of stark realism in *Urfaust* (c. 1775; the "original" version of *Faust*). Similarly, Jakob Michael Reinhold Lenz and Heinrich Leopold Wagner addressed problems of their own time in their dramas (education, celibacy of the militia, class society, family relationships, and infanticide) while Friedrich Maximilian von Klinger and Johann Anton Leisewitz dealt with fraternal enmity and generational conflict. The high point of the Sturm und Drang was 1776, when plays by a number of dramatists were performed. After this time, the movement subsided, but its influence continued, especially on Johann Christoph Friedrich von Schiller's early plays, which are strongly indebted to it in terms of themes and style.

After a period of relative inactivity as a dramatist in the 1780s, Schiller emerged as Germany's preeminent writer of drama in the 1790s. He perfected an elevated style and turned to classical models to write historical tragedy, as seen in the *Wallenstein* trilogy (1800–1801) and in *Maria Stuart* (1801). Although he was at loggerheads with Romantics like Friedrich von Schlegel, Schiller's works, notably *Die Jungfrau von Orléans* (*The Maid of Orléans*, 1801), were influential in the Romantic movement. Through his collaboration with Goethe in Weimar, Schiller raised the standard of theater in Germany significantly.

Goethe's career as a dramatist stretches over two-thirds of the period in question. After his youthful Sturm und Drang works, he too developed toward a more chastened, classical style, first with the historical drama *Egmont* (1788), then in the tragedy of the artist, *Torquato Tasso* (1790), and his statement of humanist feminism in *Iphigenie auf Tauris* (1787). The first part of an uncompleted trilogy, *Die natürliche Tochter* (*The Natural Daughter*, 1804) shows more than anything else that Goethe's mature dramatic works are to a considerable extent alien to the theater. The writing of *Faust I* and *Faust II* stretches over his entire lifetime; sprawling and heterogeneous as the works are, they include everything that was possible in the German language along with scenes of great dramatic power. However, alongside the high literary standard achieved by Goethe and Schiller, one should remember that the most popular plays of the day were those of August Wilhelm Iffland and August von Kotzebue.

Though the German Romantics (Achim von Arnim, Clemens Brentano, August Wilhelm, Friedrich von Schlegel, Ludwig Tieck, and Zacharias Werner) did not create drama of lasting interest, they were still intensely engaged with the theater and the theory of drama. Friedrich von Schlegel argued for a synthesis of tragic and comic, ancient and modern, and for drama as a vehicle of a new mythology; the great interest in Shakespeare continued and Pedro Calderón de la Barca's works became an inspiration. The variety of plays produced by the German Romantics is impressive, though their stageworthiness is often questionable. They were not without considerable influence on later dramatists and on the composer Richard Wagner.

Heinrich von Kleist, though also eschewing realism in his dramatic works, went in a different direction and is in some respects more akin to Romanticism: his highly effective dramatic language is instilled with a far greater degree of tension, expressing disjunction between the self and the world. In Austria, Franz Grillparzer built on the legacy of Weimar classicism, often allying this with the Viennese popular theatrical tradition (with Johann Nestroy and Ferdinand Raimund continuing to keep this alive with their satires and comedies), while Friedrich Hebbel, also adhering to some neoclassical notions of form, wrote the last *Bürgerliches Trauerspiel* (middle-class tragedy) in German, *Maria Magdalene* (1844), combining social criticism with an all-embracing pessimism. Though in some respects similar to him in this, Georg Büchner marks a watershed in the development of German drama and the onset of modernism. His uncompromising realism, attack on class society, and rebellion against humankind's predicament are expressed in three dramatic works of outstanding power and immense influence, only really felt in the twentieth century: *Dantons Tod* (*Danton's Death*, 1835) the comedy *Leonce und Lena* (1836), and the fragmentary *Woyzeck* (posthumously published in 1879). Another radical voice who had brief success in its own lifetime was that of Christian Dietrich Grabbe, author of a number of historical plays and exponent of the grotesque.

JOHN GUTHRIE

Bibliography

Benn, Maurice B. *The Drama of Revolt: A Critical Study of Georg Büchner.* Cambridge: Cambridge University Press, 1976.

Boyle, Nicholas. *Goethe: "Faust, Part One."* Cambridge: Cambridge University Press, 1987.

Brown, Hilda M. *Heinrich von Kleist: The Necessity of Art and the Ambiguity of Form.* Oxford: Clarendon Press, 1998.

Lamport, Francis J. *German Classical Drama. Theater, Humanity and Nation 1750–1870.* Cambridge: Cambridge University Press, 1990.

———. *Lessing and the Drama.* Oxford: Clarendon, Press, 1981.

Paulin, Roger. "Drama." In *The Romantic Period in Germany.* Edited by S. S. Prawer. London: Weidenfeld and Nicolson, 1970.

Purdie, Edna E. *Friedrich Hebbel: A Study of His Life and Work.* Oxford: Clarendon Press, 1930; reprinted 1960.

Reed, Terence J. *The Classical Centre: Goethe and Weimar 1775–1832.* London: Croom Helm, 1980.

Sharpe, Lesley. *Friedrich Schiller. Drama, Thought and Politics.* Cambridge: Cambridge University Press, 1991.

Yates, W. Edgar. *Grillparzer: A Critical Introduction.* Cambridge: Cambridge University Press, 1972.

DREAMS AND DREAMING

The Romantic period saw a heightened interest in dreams and dreaming. The mechanical and psychological associationistic explanations of dreams offered by Étienne de Condillac, David Hartley, John Locke, and others were now regarded as unsatisfactory. The development of phenomenology and empiricism, primarily through the works of David Hume and Immanuel Kant, cast doubt on whether the evidence of the senses alone could ensure an accurate perception of the world and of the self. Interest was also raised through burgeoning medical theorizing about the links between mind and body; and dreams were widely discussed both by those such as Dr Thomas Beddoes, Dr. Erasmus Darwin, and Sir Humphrey Davey, who had professional scientific backgrounds, and by those who, like Samuel Taylor Coleridge, read and studied widely in the medical field as amateurs.

Medical Theories

Medical theories ascribed the cause of dreams to the physical condition or constitution of the dreamer, including in particular problems in the digestive process and difficulties in breathing. Added to these was the loss of will over bodily functions in sleep, which in itself was believed to cause nightmares. Leigh Hunt wrote facetiously in 1820 that "dreams in general proceed from indigestion. . . . The inspirations of veal, in particular, are accounted extremely Delphic; Italian pickles partake of the same spirit of Dante; and a butter-boat shall contain as many ghosts as Charon's." Nightmares were also sometimes believed to be the prelude to epilepsy, insanity, or apoplexy. From the late 1770s on, Friedrich Anton Mesmer used "animal magnetism" (now identified with hypnosis) to send subjects into a trance (often called "artificial somnambulism") and supposedly to cure disease.

Philosophical Theories

Philosophical theories about dreams and dreaming were numerous. Some emphasized the ethical dimension of dreams, claiming they could impart moral lessons. Other theories (such as those of Andrew Baxter, which interested Coleridge) drew on ancient and Renaissance ideas that dreams were miraculous, potentially divine, events with prophetic powers, perhaps caused by (good or evil) spirits or demons taking possession of the dreamer during sleep. Such theories imply that dreamers are distanced from any moral awareness of or responsibility for their dreams. Ideas of dreams as prophetic and as introduced by demons were supported by John Milton's influential presentation of dreams in

Paradise Lost (1667), including the dream of Adam (book 8), of which John Keats said "he awoke and found it truth," and the scene in which Satan, "squat like a toad close at the ear of Eve" (book 4), is shown insinuating the first dream of discord into the human race. Mary Shelley's description of the genesis of her novel in the 1831 preface to *Frankenstein*, in particular, seems to draw on this latter passage. William Shakespeare's widespread use of dreams to show states of mind and as prophecies was also highly influential, both in England and abroad.

Dreams and Imagination

Romantic poets often explored the creative process through dreams, and an analogy between the creative imagination and the power of dreaming was made by writers such as Samuel Taylor Coleridge, John Keats, and Thomas de Quincey. Coleridge and William Wordsworth, in particular, were interested in how dreams could enable them to escape from the "tyranny" of the senses, or, in the tradition of the European Romantic poets, might be a means of transcending the limitations of the senses. Dreams also offered an escape from strict realism, and an introduction to the mysteries of the folk tale and old romance. However, the title of Francisco José de Goya y Lucientes's etching of 1799, *The Sleep of Reason Produces Monsters*, encapsulates the negative side of this concept, and Lord Byron in 1820 accused Keats of "viciously soliciting his own ideas into a state which is neither poetry nor any thing else but a Bedlam vision produced by raw pork and opium."

The ability of dreams to provide, in Sigmund Freud's phrase, "a royal road to the unconscious," and their association with his concept of "the uncanny," have been applied (some would say anachronistically) by twelfth-century critics to work of the Romantic period, including the ubiquitous nightmares of Gothic novels, such as Matthew Lewis's *The Monk* (1796), Ann Radcliffe's *The Romance of the Forest* (1791), and the works of Edgar Allen Poe, and to poetic material such as Coleridge's *Kubla Khan* and "The Pains of Sleep" (both 1798), and Wordsworth's turbulent and visionary "spots of time." This aspect of dreams has also been linked with Freidrich Nietzsche's contrast, in *Die Geburt der Tragödie aus dem Geiste der Musik* (1872; *The Birth of Tragedy from the Spirit of Music*), between the Apollonian spirit of order, rationality, and intellectual harmony, and the Dionysian spirit of ecstatic, spontaneous will to life, with the Apollonian dream surface providing a means of incorporating the otherwise unbearable Dionysian depth.

Samuel Taylor Coleridge

Samuel Taylor Coleridge wrote, "I have long wished to devote an entire work to the Subject of Dreams, Visions, Ghosts, Witchcraft, &c", and although he never carried out this project he recorded and commented on his dreams throughout his life and is particularly well known for his use of dreams in his poetry. He presented *Kubla Khan* as having been entirely composed during an opium-induced dream, and dreams or nightmares play a crucial part in, for example, "Christabel," "The Rime of the Ancient Mariner," and "Frost at Midnight" (all 1798), and "De-

jection: An Ode" and "Chamouny; the Hour before Sunrise" (both 1802).

William Wordsworth

Notable among William Wordsworth's use of dreams is the sequence in book 10 of *The Prelude* (1850), where the poet pleads for his life before "unjust tribunals" recalling those of the French Revolution, and the apocalyptic nightmare in book 5, drawn from Descartes and Miguel de Cervantes Saavedra, in which an Arab struggles to rescue a stone and a shell (representing books of poetry and geometry) from a world-engulfing deluge. Equally threatening is the reverie of druids and human sacrifice on Sarum Plain recorded in book 13. The childhood dream in the "Intimations of Immortality" ode (1807) describes a fall from a privileged prenatal state, while in "Resolution and Independence" (also 1807) the solitary poet's waking dream of the leech-gatherer serves to check his suicidal tendencies. In "Elegiac Stanzas" (1805) Wordsworth reluctantly defines his earlier visionary imagination as an illusion: a dream which is unable to withstand the pain of his brother's death at sea.

John Keats

John Keats recorded that when he met Coleridge in 1819 they talked about different types of dreams and nightmares. Keats makes frequent use of the sexual dream in, for example, *Endymion* (1818), "The Eve of St Agnes" (1820), and "La Belle Dame sans Merci" (1820). He often equates dreaming with the imagination: sometimes as a beneficent escape from the cares of reality (as in the "Ode to a Nightingale"), but increasingly often as a relentless striving to see beyond human limits (as in "The Fall of Hyperion"). This demonstrates a tendency, which increases as the Romantic period progresses, to subject the dream to skepticism and fierce criticism.

Thomas de Quincey

Thomas De Quincey claimed that he wrote his *Confessions of an English Opium-Eater* (1821) more to reveal the mysteries and potential grandeur of dreams than to outline the dangers and pleasures of opium. His battle with his dreams, here and in the Dream Fugue from "The English Mail Coach" (1849), also reveals the underlying assumption that the dream can possess the dreamer: he asserts on more than one occasion that he has "triumphed" over his dreams. One of his most famous dream sequences is that which recounts Coleridge's description of Giovanni Battista Piranesi's series of etchings *Carceri* (*Prisons*, 1745–61), whose plates show nightmare visions of vast Gothic halls with Piranesi himself pictured standing on aerial flights of stairs, apparently about to plunge into the abyss below.

William Blake, Lord Byron, Percy Bysshe Shelley, and Others

The area in which "dream," "vision," and "prophecy" overlap is the basis of almost all of William Blake's poetry. For Blake, the imagination represents God's creativity as manifested in the poet's vision, which is often presented as a dream deploying elements from Miltonic, biblical, and cabalistic sources. Lord Byron's poem "The Dream" (1816) has an uncanny dimension and expresses three central Romantic beliefs about dreams: that they represent the waking world, that they have a profound effect on the dreamer's daily life, and that dream activity is analogous to poetic creation. The apocalyptic scenes of his "Darkness" (1816) are also presented as "a dream which was not all a dream." Percy Bysshe Shelley began to write an essay on dreaming, but was allegedly forced to stop because he was "overcome by thrilling horror"; many of his works contain elaborate dream sequences and visionary moments, notably *Alastor* (1815) and *Prometheus Unbound* (1820), while "Marianne's Dream" (1820) reflects his knowledge of medical theory in this area. Thomas Love Peacock satirized the vogue for dream and nightmare subjects in novels including *Nightmare Abbey* (1818). Robert Southey kept meticulous records of his dreams at several periods of his life, and George Crabbe and William Hazlitt also joined in speculation as to the origin and meaning of dreams.

Germany

The German Romantics brilliantly exploited the substrata of consciousness, of which the dream is a striking manifestation. Novalis expressed the character of much German literature of this time when he said, "Die Welt wird Traum, der Traum wird Welt" ("The world becomes the dream, and the dream becomes the world"). Characteristic of German dream literature is Ludwig Tieck's *Der Blonde Eckbert* (1796) a *Märchen* (fairytale) in which everything is relative, uncertain, and dreamlike, and may indeed be entirely a dream. Also intensely dreamlike are Novalis's *Hymnen an die Nacht* (*Hymns to the Night*, 1800) in which dreams (and, eventually, death) are presented as an annihilation of space and time and a release from the human condition. Likewise, in Novalis's unfinished novel *Heinrich von Ofterdingen* (1802) everything comes to assume a dreamlike quality, and an extended dream experience introduces the important symbolism of the blue flower. In *Märchen* such as E. T. A. Hoffmann's "Der Goldene Topf" ("The Golden Pot," 1814), elements of the fairytale, the myth, and the dream are fused when the student Anselmus lives simultaneously in two worlds: that of the everyday, where nothing goes well, and a fantastic and allegorical dream world, where everything succeeds.

Following the influence of Anton Mesmer and "occultism," particularly influential on the later Romantic movement in Germany was a series of lectures, *Symbolik des Traumes* (*Symbolism of the Dream*) by Gotthilf Heinrich von Schubert, published in 1814. Schubert suggested that the spiritual world, that borders this one, reveals itself through psychic anomalies such as clairvoyance, déja-vu experiences, dreams and reveries, animal magnetism, telepathy, somnambulism, prophetic inspiration, ecstasy, and fever. He called the language of dreams a "hieroglyphic language": one that is innate and spoken by the soul when it is released from its imprisonment in the body. The realm of the subconscious was more systematically explored by Karl Gustav Carus, a painter and writer as well as a doctor of medicine, whose work *Psyche* (1846) was later acknowledged by Sigmund Freud and by Carl Jung to be a precursor of their own systems.

France

François Marie Voltaire observed in his *Dictionnaire Philosophique* (1764), "If the wisest of men wishes to understand madness, let him reflect on the movement of his ideas in dreams"; and Denis Diderot self-protectively presented his dialogue on materialistic philosophy, completed in 1769, as the ravings of a disordered mind in *Le rêve de D'Alembert* (*D'Alembert's Dream*). But it was Jean-Jacques Rousseau's treatment of reverie in his *Confessions* (1781) that first began to explore dreams as an opportunity to transcend the senses, and the problematic relationship between dreams and madness preoccupied many nineteenth-century French thinkers, doctors, and writers, including Honoré de Balzac, Charles Baudelaire, Victor Hugo, Gérard de Nerval, and Arthur Rimbaud, who all grappled in different ways with the problems raised by dreams and dreamlike states and particularly with the question of whether dreams were a source of creativity.

In the earlier part of the century Honoré de Balzac and Charles Nodier wrote particularly vividly on dreams and dreaming, within a tradition that attributed an unusually high value to sleep. Nodier's 1831 article, "De quelques phénomènes du sommeil" ("On Some Phenomena of Sleep") was a bizarre mixture of philosophical and medical reflection and fantastic storytelling that mimicked the effects of dreaming, and also claimed, "Only in dreams can the universe of imagination be mapped." It has been suggested that Nodier's experience of seeing decapitations as a child during the Revolution made him a particularly violent dreamer and gave rise to some of the nightmare and dream effects in his fantastic *contes* (tales), including *Smarra ou les démons de la nuit* (*Smarra or the Demons of Night*, 1821) and *La Fée aux miettes* (*The Crumb Fairy*, 1832). In the latter, which is set in a Glasgow insane asylum, the borderline between dreams and madness is challenged by the narrator's discovery that a particularly dangerous-seeming maniac he meets is in fact a distinguished doctor.

Balzac, who was familiar with Nodier's article, used a similar link between dreams and madness, with the addition of the characteristic Balzacian anxiety about sexuality and creativity, in *Louis Lambert* (1834). This tells the story of a brilliant student who is writing a "treatise on the will" and who starts by experiencing a prophetic dream and ends in cataleptic madness. In later works, notably *Le Cousin Pons* (1847) and *Ursule Mirouët* (1841), Balzac sketches the history of Franz Mesmer, animal magnetism, and "artificial somnambulism."

CHRISTINE KENYON JONES

Bibliography

Barth, J. Robert, and John L. Mahoney, eds. *Coleridge, Keats, and the Imagination: Romanticism and Adam's Dream. Essays in Honor of Walter Jackson Bate*. Columbia: University of Missouri Press, 1989.

Clark, Timothy, and Mark Allen. "Between Flippancy and Terror: Shelley's 'Marianne's Dream,'" *Romanticism* 1, no. 1 (1995): 90–105.

Coyne, Frank. *Nightmare and Escape: Changing Conceptions of the Imagination in Romantic and Victorian Dream Visions.* Ann Arbor, Mich.: University Microfilms International, 1984.

Cunningham, Andrew, and Roger French, eds. *The Medical Enlightenment of the Eighteenth Century.* Cambridge: Cambridge University Press, 1990.

Ford, Jennifer. *Coleridge on Dreaming.* Cambridge: Cambridge University Press, 1998.

Hayter, Alethea. *Opium and the Romantic Imagination.* London: Faber, 1968.

Huet, Marie-Hélène. *Monstrous Imagination.* Cambridge, Mass.: Harvard University Press, 1993.

Hughes, Glyn Tegai, *Romantic German Literature.* London: Edward Arnold, 1979.

James, Tony. *Dreams, Creativity, and Madness in Nineteenth-Century France.* Oxford: Oxford University Press, 1996.

La Cassagnere, Christian. "Dreams." In *A Handbook to English Romanticism.* Edited by Jean Raimond and J. R. Watson. Basingstoke, England: Macmillan, 1992.

Magnuson, Paul. *Coleridge's Nightmare Poetry.* Charlottesville: University Press of Virginia, 1974.

Schneider, Elizabeth. *Coleridge, Opium, and Kubla Khan.* New York: Octagon, 1975.

Watson, J. R. *English Poetry of the Romantic Period 1789–1830.* 2d ed. London: Longman, 1992.

Wilson, Douglas B. *The Romantic Dream: Wordsworth and the Poetic of the Unconscious.* Lincoln: University of Nebraska Press, 1993.

DROSTE-HÜLSHOFF, ANNETTE VON 1797–1848

German poet

In a letter composed in the summer of 1843, Annette von Droste-Hülshoff wrote that she did not want to be famous then, but she did want to be read in a hundred years' time. Not just one hundred, but over two hundred years after her birth in 1797, Annette von Droste-Hülshoff is not only read, but recognized as one of Germany's most important poets (and, arguably, its most important woman writer). Born into an aristocratic household in Hülshoff, near Münster in Westphalia, Droste grew up in a small castle that her ancestral family had inhabited for several centuries, and a sense of a tradition informs much of her work. Encouraged by Anton Matthias Sprickmann, a professor of law at Münster who had earlier been close to the *Göttinger Hain* poets, she wrote her first poems in the early 1800s. In 1819, she began work on a sequence of religious poems, one for each Sunday and feast day of the year, written for her maternal step-grandmother. Supported by Christoph Bernhard Schlüter, professor of philosophy at Münster, Droste revised these texts, and Schlüter subsequently published them as *Das geistliche Jahr* (*The Spiritual Year*, 1851). Although devotional poems, they are neither simple nor complacent, and some of them anticipate the kind of religious despair later expressed by Gerard Manley Hopkins. Whereas Immanuel Kant had written that he had found it necessary to deny knowledge in order to make room for faith, in the Droste, in her poem for the third Sunday after Easter, was unable to make this move: "Mein Wissen musste meinen Glauben töten!" ("My knowledge had to kill my faith!") Of direct importance for her poetic output was her relationship with Levin Schücking, which began in 1837, inaugurating a period when Droste experienced a great surge of creativity. In 1835, she had written to Schlüter of the "violence" that she had to do to herself in order to control the "thoughts and images" that "poured upon her," comparing them to "frightened horses" (a trope recalling the ancient Pindaric motif of the horse and the charioteer). Her best poems show her fully in control of both her intellectual and physical impulses. Collaborating with Schücking on his study of Westphalian art and culture, Droste in turn integrated local themes, motifs, and dialect expressions into many of her ballads, for example "Der Heidemann" ("The Heath Man," 1841–42), and especially into her prose works, including the famous novella *Die Judenbuche* (*The Jew's Beech Tree*, 1842). In 1838, she published a volume of her early *Gedichte* (Poems), and in 1844 she published a second volume consisting of poems written in the intervening period. Due to her deteriorating health, she had moved in 1841 to Meersburg, living in a castle overlooking Lake Constance, and in 1843 she bought the Fürstenhäuschen, a little house with a vineyard attached. Sometimes looking out at the water, sometimes the earth, the soil, and the vines, Droste produced her most celebrated poems during this period, including "Am Turme" ("In the Tower," 1841–42):

Ich steh' auf hohem Balkone am Turm,	I stand on the tower's high balcony,
Umstrichen vom schreienden Stare,	Sweeping around me the starling that shrieks,
Und lass' gleich einer Mänade den Sturm	And, just like a maenad, I let the storm
Mir wühlen im flatternden Haare	Blow through my fluttering hair

Distressed by Schücking's marriage to another woman in 1843, and still in poor health, Droste lived alone in the castle in Meersburg until her death five years later; in the last two years of life, she wrote no more poetry.

Because some literary criticism, especially that from a feminist perspective, has constructed Droste as a "victim" of the patriarchal order in general and of Schücking in particular, the extent to which in her own way—and within the historical constraints of the age in which she lived—she was a remarkable (and a remarkably strong) individual can sometimes be overlooked. Equally, by attaching the label "poetic realism" to her work, the extent to which Droste engages with the epistemological problematic of Romanticism can become obscured. In "Lebt wohl" ("Farewell," 1844), the lyrical "I" speaks of how "jedes wilden Geiers Schrei / In mir die wilde Muse weckt" ("the cry of the wild vulture / awakes in me the wild muse"). The world of which this "wild muse" sings is often an uncertain one: is there really a ghost in "Der Fundator" ("The Founder," 1841–42) or is the old servant just imagining things? In "Der Knabe im Moor" ("The Lad on the Moor," 1841–42), the fantastic figures of folklore and local legend take on a terrifying reality in the mind of the child, while in "Mondesaufgang" ("Moonrise," 1843–44) the discrete sense-impressions of the opening stanzas become less and less precise until, in the fourth stanza, the poetic "I" is left alone and isolated, awaiting "ein fremdes, aber o! ein mildes Licht" ("so strange, but oh! so mild a light"). As Droste put it in a letter of 1840, we might reject the supernatural, but it can still make us afraid. While her interest in local life, custom, and legend, and the depiction of a lonely self in a world full of uncanny experiences and uncertain conclusions, reflect one aspect of the Romantic legacy, what also emerges very powerfully from Droste's lyric poetry is the role of the imagination in redeeming the everyday and overcoming the inevitable transience of experience. Just as she realized that the only way for her to break through the constraints of the time was through art, so, in such poems as "Carpe Diem!" (1843–44), "Halt fest!" ("Hold On!" 1843–44), and "Im Grase" ("In the Grass," 1844–45), Droste attempts to redeem the moment through the aesthetic. Hence, in "Leb wohl" it is the gift of the poetic *Zauberwort* (magic word) that enables her to overcome the precariousness of humankind's position in the world, the fear of the unknown, and the frustrations of a life spent on one's own: "Verlassen, aber einsam nicht, / Erschüttert, aber nicht zerdrückt" ("Alone, but not lonely, / Dismayed, but not distraught").

PAUL BISHOP

Biography

Born Anna Elisabeth Franziska Adolfine Wilhemina Louise Maria, Freiin von Droste zu Hülshoff, in Schloss Hülshoff, near Münster, Westphalia, January 12, 1797 into a Roman Catholic aristocratic family, educated privately by tutors. Worked on poems for *Das geistliche Jahr* (*The Spiritual Year*, 1851), from 1819 on. Had love affairs with August von Arnswaldt and Heinrich Straube, in an emotional year, 1820. Following the death of her father, moved from Schloss Hülshoff to Rüschhaus with her mother and sister, 1826. Started long-term unrequited relationship with novelist Levin Schücking, 1837, collaborating with him on literary projects. Lived in Meersburg, near Lake Constance, and at Hülshoff, 1841–45. Moved permanently to Meersburg (after Shücking's marriage to Luise Gall in 1843), 1846. Died, probably from tuberculosis, in Meersburg, May 24, 1848.

Selected Works

Collections
Sämtliche Werke. 4 vols. Edited by Karl Schulte-Kemminghausen. Munich: B. Müller, 1925–30.
Sämtliche Werke. Edited by Clemens Heselhaus. Munich: Carl Hanser, 1952.
Poems. Edited by Margaret E. Atkinson. London: Oxford University Press, 1964.
Sämtliche Werke. 2 vols. Edited by Bodo Plachta and Winfried Woesler. Frankfurt am Main: Deutscher Klassiker Verlag, 1994.
Sämtliche Gedichte. Edited by Karl Schulte-Kemminghausen. Frankfurt am Main: Insel, 1998.

Fiction
Die Judenbuche. 1842. Edited by J. R. Foster, 1955. Translated by Michael Fleming and Andrew Webber in *Eight German Novellas*. Oxford and New York: Oxford University Press, 1997.
Westphälische Schilderungen aus einer westphälischen Feder. 1845.
Bei uns zu Lande auf dem Lande. 1860. Edited by Elmar Jansen, Weimar: Kiepenhauer with *Ledwina*, 1966.
Joseph, 1886.
Ledwina. 1886. Edited by Elmar Jansen, 1966; translated by David Ward, Jeannine Blackwell, and Susame Zantop in *Bitter Healing*. Lincoln: University of Nebraska Press, 1990.

Play
Perdu! oder, Dichter, Verleger, und Blaustrümpfe. 1860.

Letters
Briefe von Annette von Droste-Hülshoff und Leven Schücking. 3d ed. Edited by Reinhold Conrad Muschler. Leipzig: F. W. Ourow, 1928.
Die Briefe der Annette von Droste-Hülshoff. 2 vols. Edited by Karl Schulte Kemminghausen. Jena: E. Diederichs, 1944.

Bibliography
Bennet, E. K., revised by H. M. Waidson. "Annette von Droste-Hülshoff." In *A History of the German Novelle*. Cambridge: Cambridge University Press, 1961.
Berglar, Peter. *Annette von Droste-Hülshoff in Selbstzeugnissen und Bilddokumenten*. Reinbek bei Hamburg: Rowohlt, 1967.
Gaier, Ulrich. *Annette von Droste-Hülshoff und ihre literarische Welt am Bodensee*. Marbach am Neckar: Deutsche Schillergesellschaft, 1993.
Guthrie, John. *Annette von Droste-Hülshoff: A German Poet between Romanticism and Realism*. Oxford: Berg, 1989.
Heselhaus, Clemens. *Annette von Droste-Hülshoff: Werk und Leben*. Düsseldorf: Bagel, 1971.
Kraft, Herbert. *Annette von Droste-Hülshoff*. Reinbek bei Hamburg: Rowohlt, 1994.
Pickar, Gertrud Bauer. *Ambivalence Transcended: A Study of the Writings of Annette von Droste-Hülshoff*. Columbia, S.C.: Camden House, 1997.

DRUGS AND ADDICTION

That drugs might aid the creative process remains a contentious issue; what is clear is how drastically public opinion has changed regarding a number of specific drugs. In 1790 the clergyman and poet George Crabbe was prescribed opium medicinally, which he continued to take for the rest of his life. At the time of Crabbe's first prescription, the East India Company was already employing entire Indian villages in the cultivation of opium.

One might buy laudanum, a suspension of opium in alcohol, quite legally at any street apothecary's. Thomas De Quincey once wrote that "happiness might now be bought for a penny." The Opium Wars (1839–42, 1856–60) also indicated a reliance on the drug by the British economy not unlike that of the addict; Queen Victoria herself was a regular user until she developed a taste for cocaine.

Like Crabbe, the Romantic figures we most associate with laudanum, Samuel Taylor Coleridge and Thomas De Quincey, first came to the drug for medicinal purposes. Coleridge first took the drug to relieve rheumatism in 1791, then to relieve stress, for toothache and, most famously, for a bout of dysentery. By the turn of the century, Coleridge was addicted, and remained so for the rest of his life. De Quincey similarly records that he first used laudanum for a toothache in 1804; he continued to experiment with the drug, for pain and for pleasure, over the course of the next decade, becoming completely addicted by 1813. Conversely, Charles Armitage Brown wrote that his friend John Keats was secretly taking laudanum for depression in the winter of 1819–20, but had promised to stop the habit when discovered. Whether Keats was a regular user or not remains a matter of conjecture. The relationship between Edgar Allan Poe and laudanum is similarly mysterious (although many seem to feel that he *ought* to have been an addict). Although the central characters in "Ligeia," "The Fall of the House of Usher," "A Tale of the Ragged Mountains," and the original "Berenice" are addicts, any traceable references to intoxication in the author's own life probably refer to his alcoholism.

Coleridge's 1816 preface to the "fragment" of *Kubla Khan: Or a Vision in a Dream* explains that the poem came to him in a dream engendered by a prescribed "anodyne." Coleridge then attempts to convey a semihallucinogenic experience. While in a deep sleep "at least of the external senses" (opium sends the user into a profound slumber and causes intense and vivid dreams), two to three hundred lines of verse came to him "without any sensation or consciousness of effort." Upon waking, Coleridge put pen to paper until he was distracted "by a person on business from Porlock"; reality thus destroyed the vision. Coleridge rarely admitted that opium altered his mind, however, and did not consider its potential in relation to the "shaping spirit of imagination" so crucial to Romantic poetics.

De Quincey went much further in his original *Confessions of an English Opium Eater* (1821), inaugurating a genre of confessional, addict-narrated literature, although his writing has more in common with a narrative of religious conversion such as the *Confessions* of Saint Augustine. De Quincey took a household remedy and presented it as a revelation, casting himself as the "only member" ("Pope" in the revised edition of 1856, by which time the members' name was Legion) of "the true church on the subject of opium." To the creative temperament will be revealed in dreams the most stunning landscapes, but a man "whose talk is of oxen" will simply "dream about oxen." The drug leads to hell as well as heaven, however, and the section entitled "The Pleasures of Opium" is followed by "The Pains," where, in increasingly chaotic prose, the addict describes withdrawal pains and terrible nightmares, eventually achieving something like a resolution after a final, epiphanic dream. By exploring this surreal inner world, De Quincey is also employing the techniques of psychoanalysis (as had Jean-Jacques Rousseau in his *Confessions* of 1765) thirty-five years before the birth of Sigmund Freud. Coleridge and De Quincey had a love-hate relationship with laudanum, but it unquestionably informed their artistic vision while, paradoxically, undermining their ability to write.

De Quincey's English disciples included Branwell Brontë and Francis Thompson, and Charles Baudelaire's meditation on hashish, *Paradis Artificiels* (1860), translates him at length in the belief that there is nothing to add. The French symbolists were the obvious successors to De Quincey's project. Baudelaire recorded the similarities and differences between opium and hashish and, like De Quincey, believed that such drugs could influence the literary imagination of those whom already had the gift, but that they could equally rob the artist of the ability to create. When Baudelaire refers to opium in his poetry it is as a symbol of a heightened awareness, both illuminating and terrifying. In the 1870s, Arthur Rimbaud continued to explore the visionary possibilities of systematically "disorientating the senses," anticipating the "automatic writing" experiments of the surrealists; he ceased to write before turning twenty.

By the end of the century, references to opium in English literature tended to signal corruption by Oriental otherness. The exploration of the relationship between drugs and art continued in postwar America, most fully realized in the writing of William S. Burroughs.

STEPHEN CARVER

Bibliography

Abrams, M. H. *The Milk of Paradise: The Effect of Opium Visions on the Works of De Quincey, Crabbe, Frances Thompson, and Coleridge.* 1934; reprint New York: Harper and Row, 1970.

Barrell, John. *The Infection of Thomas De Quincey: A Psychopathology of Imperialism.* New Haven, Conn.: Yale University Press, 1991.

Baudelaire, Charles. *Complete Poems.* Translated by Walter Martin. Manchester: Carcanet, 1997.

———. *Selected Letters of Charles Baudelaire: The Conquest of Solitude.* Translated by Rosemary Lloyd. Chicago: University of Chicago Press, 1986.

Burroughs, William. "Letter from a Master Addict to Dangerous Drugs," *The British Journal of Addiction* 53, no. 2 (1956). Appended to William S. Burroughs, *The Naked Lunch.* London: Flamingo, 1993.

Coleridge, Samuel Taylor. *Biographia Literaria: or, Biographical Sketches of My Literary Life and Opinions.* London: W. Pickering, 1847.

———. *The Complete Poems.* Edited by William Keach. London: Penguin, 1997.

Cornell, Kenneth. *The Symbolist Movement.* Hamden, Conn.: Archon Books, 1970.

De Quincey, Thomas. *Confessions of an English Opium Eater.* 1821. Edited by Alethea Hayter. London: Penguin, 1986.

Ebin, David, ed. *The Drug Experience.* New York: Orion Press, 1961.

Gautier, Théophile. *The Collected Works of Théophile Gautier.* New York: Walter J. Black, 1928.

Hayter, Alethea. *Opium and the Romantic Imagination.* London: Faber and Faber, 1968.

Hodgson, Barbara. *Opium: A Portrait of the Heavenly Demon.* London: Souvenir Press, 2000.

Holmes, Richard. *Coleridge: Early Visions.* London: Hodder and Stoughton, 1989.

Lyon, Judson S. *Thomas De Quincey.* New York: Twayne, 1969.

McDonagh, Josephine. *De Quincey's Disciplines.* Oxford: Clarendon Press, 1994.

Motion, Andrew. *Keats.* London: Faber and Faber, 1998.

Rimbaud, Arthur. *Complete Works.* Translated by Paul Schmidt. New York: Harper and Row, 1976.

Schneider, Elisabeth. *Coleridge, Opium and Kubla Khan.* Chicago: University of Chicago Press, 1953.

Symons, Arthur. *The Symbolist Movement in Literature.* London: Constable, 1911.

DUELING

A duel took place on the evening of February 16, 1821 at Chalk Farm in north London, which was a popular location for such activities. It was between a young lawyer called Jonathan Christie and John Scott, the editor of *London* magazine. Scott died ten days later from the wounds that he had received. The inquest declared that Christie and the two seconds involved were guilty of murder, indicating the illegality of dueling. Christie and his second were nevertheless acquitted at the subsequent trial at the Old Bailey, showing that although it was illegal dueling was nevertheless also condoned.

The quarrel between Scott and Christie arose out of the literary warfare of the period. Scott had objected to the way in which a rival journal, *Blackwood's Edinburgh* magazine, had attacked members of the Cockney School, including John Keats. Literary figures had always been involved in duels (Ben Jonson killed another actor in 1598), and this continued throughout the Romantic period. The poet Thomas Moore was also involved in a duel at Chalk Farm in 1806, with an influential critic who had questioned the morality of his work. This duel, in which the pistols may not even have been loaded, descended into farce and was ridiculed by Lord Byron in his *English Bards and Scotch Reviewers* (1809). Byron avoided fighting a duel with Moore as a result of this representation, and generally seems, through a mixture of luck and judgment, to have steered clear of dueling grounds despite priding himself on being an excellent shot. He nevertheless threatened to stand in for Percy Bysshe Shelley when the latter was challenged by John Polidori. Byron's friend Richard Brinsley Sheridan had made the impetuous duelist a figure of fun when he created the character of Sir Lucius Trigger in *The Rivals* (1775). Sheridan himself nevertheless fought two duels in 1772, and was badly wounded in the second one.

One of the reasons why duelists were often treated leniently by the courts was that many of the leading politicians often settled their quarrels on the dueling ground, sometimes with each other. Those involved in this practice included George Canning, Lord Castlereagh, Charles James Fox, William Pitt the Younger, and the Duke of Wellington. Members of the royal family, such as the Duke of York, also fought in what were known as affairs of honor. Although the courts tended to be lenient, some duelists preferred not to put this to the test and fled to France or elsewhere. This is what Sir Mulberry Hawk does in Charles Dickens's *Nicholas Nickleby* (1838–39) after he has killed somebody in a duel.

Dueling began to go out of fashion in the earlier Victorian period. It was banned by the army in 1844 and, according to some accounts, the last recorded duel in Britain took place in 1852. Moves to reform the army, together with Evangelical pressure, led to its demise. Although it had been supported by the upper classes (and those who copied them), it had never been as widespread in Britain as in some other European countries. British students often preferred to settle quarrels with their fists (pugilism) rather than with either pistols or swords. In contrast

dueling fraternities played an important part in student life in Germany, Russia, and elsewhere. Karl Marx fought a duel in 1836 while he was studying at Bonn. Various later German nationalistic movements, including Nazism, saw dueling as an important part of the national character.

Two major Russian writers were killed in duels: Aleksandr Pushkin in 1837 and Mikhail Lermontov in 1841. In some ways this was a case of life imitating art, since duels feature in the works *Evgenii Onegin*, (completed 1831) and *Geroy nashego vremeni* (*A Hero of Our Time*, 1840). Lermontov sees dueling as being the product of the ennui of life in a military outpost. Later Russian writers such as Anton Chekhov, Fedor Dostoevsky, Lev Tolstoy, and Ivan Turgenev also represent duels as being a feature of masculine codes of honor. British literature of the Romantic era does not foreground the practice of dueling to the same extent, although references to it can be found in the work of Jane Austen, Robert Bage, and Maria Edgeworth. For instance, Colonel Brandon is involved in an offstage duel with Mr. Willoughby in Austen's *Sense and Sensibility* (1811).

Joseph Conrad's short story "The Duel" (1904) is set during the Revolutionary and Napoleonic Wars and is partly responsible for the way in which this period continues to be associated with dueling. There was a film version of it in 1977, which romanticized the encounters between the characters Feraud and D'Hubert. Conrad's story, by contrast, often highlights the absurd and grotesque aspects of the duel, which are seen as playing out in miniature the insanity of war more generally. Duels figure prominently in modern historical romances set in the Romantic era, more particularly the Regency period, as signs of a more simplistic and chivalric world that has been lost.

ROGER SALES

Bibliography

Andrew, Donna T. "The Code of Honour and Its Critics: The Opposition to Duelling in England, 1700–1850," *Social History* 5 (1980): 409–34.

Atkinson, John A. *Duelling Pistols and Some of the Affairs They Settled*. London: Cassell, 1964.

Baldick, Robert. *The Duel: A History of Duelling*. London: Chapman and Hall, 1965.

Frevert, Ute. Translated by Anthony Williams. *Men of Honour: A Social and Cultural History of the Duel*. Cambridge: Polity Press, 1995.

Kelly, James. *That Damn'd Thing Called Honour: Duelling in Ireland 1570–1860*. Cork: Cork University Press, 1995.

Kiernan, V. G. *The Duel in European History: Honour and the Reign of Aristocracy*. Oxford: Oxford University Press, 1989.

Loose, Jacqueline. *Duels and Duelling: Affairs of Honour around the Wandsworth Area*. Wandsworth, England: Wandsworth Borough Council, 1983.

Myers, Jeffery. "The Duel in Fiction," *North Dakota Quarterly* 53 (1983): 129–50.

O'Leary, Patrick. *Regency Editor: Life of John Scott*. Aberdeen: Aberdeen University Press, 1983.

DUMAS, ALEXANDRE DAVY DE LA PAILLETERIE 1802–1870

French dramatist, novelist, and travel writer

Alexandre Dumas (known as Dumas père) followed the example of his father, one of Napoleon Bonaparte's generals, by taking on the surname of his grandmother, a Haitian slave girl rather than Davy de la Pailleterie, his grandfather's name. He was one of the Herculean spirits like Honoré de Balzac, Victor Hugo, and George Sand engendered by the Romantic movement in France. Everything about him was massive, boundless, and excessive: his appearance, his personality, his conversation, his way of life, his love life, and above all his prodigious achievements as a playwright and novelist.

Inspired in his youth by the productions of William Shakespeare's plays that he saw in the provinces and in Paris and prompted by the opportunities provided by the vogue of the melodrama in the 1820s, he began writing vaudevilles and melodramas based on historical themes. Dumas then turned to historical dramas, achieving an outstanding success with *Henri III et sa cour* (*Henry III and His Court*), which premièred on February 10, 1829 at the Comédie-Française. With this remarkably innovative Romantic drama, which combined love and political intrigue, local color and violent action and flouted all the precepts of the classical theater, Dumas became a leading figure in the Romantic revolution in the theater. Though far too independent ever to attach himself to any particular literary group, he did frequent Charles Nodier's soirées, where he came into contact with the rising generation of Romantics—notably, Hugo, Afred-Victor de Vigny, Alfred de Musset, Gérard de Nerval, Balzac, and Prosper Mérimée, but he much preferred the company of actresses. Marie Dorval, who was one of his favorites, starred in Dumas's second major success, *Anthony*, it was a tragic Romantic drama about adultery to which, contrary to prevailing conventions, he boldly gave a modern setting. On the opening night at the Porte-Saint-Martin Theater (May 3, 1831) and throughout the following year, the play was greeted with rapturous applause, particularly for its ending, in which Anthony stabs his mistress to preserve her honor and claims that he has done so because she was resisting his advances. Of the other numerous dramas that Dumas wrote with remarkable rapidity in the 1830s, the most notable successes were *Richard Darlington* (1831), based on Sir Walter Scott's novel *The Surgeon's Daughter*, with Frédérick Lemaître in the leading role, and *La Tour de Nesle* (1832), which, along with Hugo's *Notre-Dame de Paris*, contributed to the fashion for medieval settings during these years.

Dumas would continue writing for the theater until the end of his career, but in the 1840s his main interest shifted to the novel as he took full advantage of the financial opportunities provided by the vogue for the *roman feuilleton* (serial novel) in the newly, established mass circulation newspapers. He flung himself energetically into the task of feeding the new steam-driven presses that rolled out thousands of copies of newspapers with the *feuilleton*, their major selling feature, in the bottom panel, often writing novels for several newspapers simultaneously. In the heyday of the trend, 1842–48, he produced massive amounts of text, including his most famous historical romances, *Le Comte de Monte-Cristo* (1844–45), *Les Trois Mousquetaires* (*The Three Musketeers*, 1844), and its sequels *Vingt Ans après* (*Twenty Years After*, 1845) and *Le Vicomte de Bragelonne* (*The Viscount of Bragelonne*, (1848–50). Despite his enormous energy, Dumas's extraordinary output (innumerable novels and stories, some ninety plays, ten volumes of memoirs, nineteen volumes of travel impressions, as well as a *Grand Dictionnaire de cuisine*, published posthumously in 1873) was only possible with the help of assistants, copyists, and collaborators. Notable among the latter was Auguste Maquet, who assisted in the creation of a whole series of fictional works, including the most successful romances, all of which were published, however, under Dumas's name alone. Dumas's production methods even led to the charge that he signed works of which he had barely written a word and to the famous barb from Charles Hugo, "Everyone has read Dumas, but nobody has read everything by Dumas, not even Dumas himself." His novels earned him a huge readership in his own time, as well as substantial sums of money, which he habitually squandered with a recklessness, an extravagance, and a joie de vivre that one normally associates with his better-known characters.

As a novelist, Dumas prompted renewed interest in the historical novel, which, inspired by Scott, had been fashionable earlier in the century, but in his works the emphasis shifted from "local color" to plot and action. Though his novels were usually based on chronicles and memoirs (Maquet was a historian) historical accuracy was not one of his major concerns, any more than the authority of the authorship. He preferred to set his historical romances in periods of turbulent upheaval that provided a ready-made basis for dramatic adventures.

While Dumas's plays contributed directly to the Romantic transformation of the theater, his novels exemplify in a flamboyant form the French Romantics' taste for the grand gesture, the spectacular, the excessive, and the heroic. His extraordinarily engaging narrative art has earned him an unrivaled and lasting reputation abroad, where, as he claimed, posterity begins. His romances have transcended the bounds of the specific literary competences and conventions, strictures and tastes of his own times to win over a captivated readership in every land and to lend themselves to the multifarious appropriations of the popular cultures of other ages. As Hugo generously wrote in homage to his rival at the time of his death: "The name of Alexandre Dumas is more than French, it is European; and it is more than European, it is universal."

DAVID BAGULEY

Biography

Born Alexandre Davy de La Pailleteric in Villers-Cotterêts, Aisnes, France, July 24, 1802. Son of Thomas-Alexandre Davy de La Pailleterie (later Dumas), soldier and later general in Napoleon's army. Educated at local school. Articled clerk in lawyers' offices in Villers-Cotterêts and Crépy until 1822. Fathered illegitimate son, the future novelist and playwright Alexandre Dumas *fils*, by Catherine Labay, 1824. Worked in secretariat of the Duke of Orléans, 1822–29; librarian of the Palais Royal, 1829. Entered literary circle of Charles Nodier, 1829. Successful playwright and journalist from 1830s on. Fathered illegitimate daughter by Belle Krelsamer, 1831. Fought in the July Revolution, 1830. Traveled in Switzerland, 1832; in Italy and the Mediterranean, 1834–35 (and again in 1841–42), in Belgium and the Rhine lands, 1838; in Spain and North Africa, 1846. Appointed chevalier, légion d'honneur, 1837. Married Ida Ferrier, 1840 (they separated in 1844). Founded the Théâtre Historique, 1847; took part in the 1848 revolution, editing *La Liberté*, 1848. Founding editor, *La France Nouvelle*, 1848, and *Le Mois*, 1848–50. Declared bankruptcy and fled to Brussels to avoid creditors, 1852; returned to Paris and founded the newspaper *Le Mousquetaire*, 1853–57. Traveled in England, 1857 and Russia, 1858–59. Spent four years in Italy, 1860–64, collaborating with Giuseppe Garibaldi during invasion of Sicily, 1860–61; director of excavations and museums, Naples, 1860–61. Edited *Le Journal de Jeudi*, 1860; *L'indipenente*, Naples, 1860–64. Returned to France, 1864; revived *Le mousquetaire*, 1866–67; editor, *Le D'Artagnan*, 1868, and *Théâtre Journal*, 1868–69. Traveled in Italy, Germany, and Austria, 1866. Awarded Order of Isabella the Catholic (Belgium); Cross of Gustavus Vasa (Sweden); Order of St. John of Jerusalem. Died in Puys, near Dieppe, France, December 5, 1870.

Selected Works

Collections

Les Trois Mousquetaires. Vingt Ans après. Edited by Gilbert Sigaux. Paris: Gallimard, 1989.

Plays

Henri III et sa cour. 1829; translated as *Catherine of Cleves. A Tragic Drama*, 1831. Edited by Fernande Bassan. Paris: Lettres Modernes, 1974.
Antony. 1831; translated into English, 1880. Edited by Fernande Bassan. Paris: Lettres Modernes, 1980.
Kean ou Désordre et génie. 1836; translated as *Kean, or The Genius and the Libertine*, 1847. Adapted by Jean-Paul Sartre as *Kean; or, Disorder and Genius*; translated by Kitty Black. London: Hamilton, 1954.

Novels

Les Trois Mousquetaires. 1844; translated as *The Three Musketeers*, by William Barrow, 1846. Edited by David Coward. Oxford: Oxford University Press, 1991.
Le Comte de Monte-Cristo. 1845; translated as *The Count of Monte Cristo.* Edited by David Coward. Oxford: Oxford University Press, 1990.

Bibliography

Biet, Christian, Jean-Paul Brighelli, and Jean-Luc Rispail. *Alexandre Dumas ou les aventures d'un romancier.* Paris: Gallimard, 1986.
Clouard, Henri. *Alexandre Dumas.* Paris: Albin Michel, 1955.
Hemmings, F. W. J. *Alexandre Dumas. The King of Romance.* London: Hamish Hamilton New York: Scribner's, 1979.
Reed, Frank Wilde, *A Bibliography of Alexandre Dumas Père*, London: Neuhuys, 1933.
Schopp, Claude. *Alexandre Dumas. Le génie de la vie.* Paris: Mazarine, 1985; rev. ed., Paris: Fayard, 1997. Trans.: by A. J. Koch as *Alexandre Dumas. Genius of Life.* New York: Franklin Watts, 1988.
Stowe, Richard S. *Alexandre Dumas Père.* Boston: Twayne, 1976.

DUSSEK, JAN LADISLAV 1760–1812

Bohemian composer and pianist

While he was occasionally called Johann Ladislaus (or Ludwig) and, in spite of the various forms of the surname, Dus'k, Dussik, or Duschek, the more common form during the period, and that most often used by the composer himself, is that of Dussek. One of eight children in a musical family—his father was a well-known composer and organist and the mother a fine harpist—Jan Ladislav Dussek was playing the piano by the age of five and, because of his fine voice, most of his early education was gained in various choir schools, including the New City Gymnasium at Prague (1776–77) and his single term at the University of Prague the following year. He was patronized and employed by a military officer, Count Männer, and traveled to Mechelen in 1779, where he taught the piano. He visited the Low Countries, staying for a year in The Hague, where he taught William V's children. By 1782 he had arrived in Hamburg, his reputation as a brilliant performer preceding him, and met Carl Philipp Emanuel Bach, from whom he may have had lessons. He performed at the court of Catherine II in Saint Petersburg in 1783 and, that same year, became Kapellmeister to the powerful Prince Karl Radziwill in Lithuania, a position he held for two years.

A concert tour of Germany then followed, and included his performance on glass harmonica as well as piano, in Berlin, Frankfurt, and Dresden among other cities. In late 1776 he traveled to Paris, playing before Marie Antoinette and meeting Napoleon; he remained in the French capital as teacher and performer for three years. Dussek's aristocratic patronage and connections made him suspect in the eyes of the Revolutionary regime and, like so many others, including members of the aristocracy themselves, he fled to London in 1789.

Dussek spent the next eleven years becoming a popular performer and a much sought-after teacher. He appeared with Franz Joseph Haydn at the latter's concerts during both his visits to London, and the older composer, with characteristic generosity, told Dussek's father in a letter that he had in Dussek "one of the most upright, moral, and, in music, most eminent of men for a son. I love him just as you do, for he fully deserves it." Haydn hoped that Dussek would be "ever fortunate, which I heartily wish him to be, for his remarkable talents."

In 1792, Dussek married well: his bride, Sophia Corri, was an accomplished (and later famous) singer, pianist, and harpist and the daughter of Domenico Corri, in whose thriving publishing business Dussek soon became a partner, giving him a ready outlet for his compositions. He also had connections with the piano-making firm of Broadwood, and it was due to Dussek's encouragement that the compass of their instruments was increased from five to six octaves. The publishing business, now Corri, Dussek, and Company, slid into bankruptcy, however, and Dussek again fled, abandoning his wife and child and leaving his father-in-law and erstwhile partner to be jailed. The last few months of the century found him in Hamburg again, where he met the violinist-composer Ludwig (Louis) Spohr and the horn player Giovanni Punto, with whom he toured in 1802, visiting his parents in his home town of Cáslav and giving three greatly acclaimed concerts in Prague. It was here that the composer and pianist Jan Vaclav Tomásek wrote a laudatory account of Dussek's playing and stated that he was the first pianist to place the piano sideways on the stage so that the audience could see his profile.

In October 1804 Dussek became Kapellmeister to Prince Louis Ferdinand (Friedrich Christian Ludwig) of Prussia, himself a fine pianist and a good composer who frequently expressed his frustration at the circumstances of his noble birth that required him to pursue a military, as opposed to a musical, career. The two became friends and drinking partners and Spohr, in his autobiography (a very valuable source on all aspects of musical life in the first half of the nineteenth century) writes of their riotous trail around the battlefields of Europe. This life was, however, short-lived, and Louis Ferdinand was fatally wounded commanding the Prussian advance guard at the battle of Saalfeld, October 10, 1806. The tragedy prompted Dussek's celebrated 1806-7 piano sonata in EF-sharp Minor, op. 61, which he entitled *Elégie harmonique sur la mort du Prince Louis Ferdinand de Prusse* (*Harmonic Elegy on the Death of Prince Louis Ferdinand of Prussia*). After a brief appointment with another prince, Dussek traveled to Paris in 1807, where he became pianist to Charles-Maurice de Talleyrand, giving many concerts, often with the virtuoso-violinists Pierre Rode and Pierre Baillot.

His last years were plagued by a problem common among early nineteenth-century musical figures: alcoholism. In Dussek's case this led to obesity (he was almost constantly bedridden during this time) and gout, from which he died in 1812.

Listening to Dussek's mature works, it is difficult to believe that he is a contemporary of Haydn and of Wolfgang Amadeus Mozart, as these pieces are so "unclassical." They conjure up more the world of John Field, Johann Nepomuk Hummel, and Ignaz Moscheles, or even Ludwig van Beethoven and, to an extent, Frédéric Chopin—most of whom were, or can be shown to have been, influenced by Dussek. He was one of the first touring piano composers and the majority of his works are for—or include—the piano and are virtuoso in technique. As has been suggested above, many of the traits associated with later Romanticism are already present: a rich chromatic harmonic vocabulary with daring shifts to more remote keys, passion, virtuosity, sensitivity, occasional extra-musical references, and the kind of Italianate and folksy melodic style that would become standard as the nineteenth century progressed. Although one does not find the predominance of minor-key works so characteristic of later figures, Dussek frequently colors his major-key works with a kind of melancholy, and often incorporates minor-key passages. His choice of the then little-used key of F-sharp minor places his *Elégie harmonique* firmly within the orbit of such works as Hummel's influential sonata (op. 81) in the same key, the introspective slow movement of Beethoven's *Hammerklavier Sonata* (op. 106, in B-flat) or his "Moonlight" Sonata

(op. 27, no. 2 in C-sharp Minor). Dussek's work was much revered in his lifetime, but, as happened with many of the virtuoso composers, soon fell into disfavor after his death. Greater interest has been shown in his music of late, although he continues, unjustly, to remain neglected.

DEREK CAREW

Biography

Born Johann Ladislaus, or Ludwig, Dussek in Cáslav, Bohemia (now in the Czech Republic), February 12, 1760; son of a composer and cathedral organist, he studied piano and organ from an early age, and was a chorister in the Franciscan church at Iglau (now Jihlava) and Kutná Hora. Educated at Jesuit gymnasiums in Iglau and Kutná Hora, at the New City Gymnasium, Prague, 1776–77, and the University of Prague, 1778. Traveled to Malines (now Mechelen) under sponsorship of Austrian army captain Count Männer; moved on to Bergen op Zoom and The Hague, 1779–82. Performed as virtuoso pianist and taught piano to the family of William V. Visited Hamburg, and studied with C. P. E. Bach, 1782. Traveled to Saint Petersburg, 1783: performed at court of Catherine II. Appointed *Kapellmeister* to Prince Karl Radziwill in Lithuania, 1783–84. Undertook a concert tour of Germany, 1784–86. Settled in Paris, 1786–89; fled the French Revolution and settled in London, 1789. Performed in London; appeared with Franz Joseph Haydn on his London visits. Married singer and pianist Sophia Corri (d. 1847), 1792; they had one daughter. Partner in Corri, Dussek, and Company, his father-in-law's music publishing business, 1790s. Fled to Hamburg because of bankruptcy, leaving his wife and daughter in London, 1799. Appeared in concerts in Cáslav and Prague, 1802. Kapellmeister to Prince Louis Ferdinand of Prussia, 1804–6; on his death at the Battle of Saalfield wrote *Elégie harmonique sur le mort du Prince Louis Ferdinand de Prusse*, op. 61, 1806. Employed briefly in the service of Prince Isenburg; moved to Paris as pianist to household of Charles-Maurice de Talleyrand, 1807. Performed and taught in Paris until his death. Died from gout in St Germain-en-Laye, March 20, 1812.

Selected Works

Piano Sonatas
Op. 44 in E-flat ("Farewell Sonata"). 1800.
Op. 64 in A-flat ("La retour à Paris" or "Plus ultra"). 1807.
Op. 77 in F Minor ("L'invocation"). 1812.

Piano Concerti
Op. 40 in B-flat ("Military Concerto"). 1798.
Op. ("The Favorite Concerto"). Circa 1798.
Op. 49 in G Minor. 1801.

Bibliography

Blom, E. "The Prophecies of Dussek." In *Classic Major and Minor.* London, 1958.
Craw, H. A. "A Biography and Thematic Catalog of the Works of J. L. Dussek 1760–1812." Ph.D. diss., University of Southern California, 1964.
Kl'ma, S. V. "Dussek in England." *Music and Letters* 41 (1960).
———. "Dussek in London," *Monthly Musical Record* 90 (1960).
Schiffer, F. L. *Johann Ladislaus Dussek: seine Sonaten und seine Konzerte.* Leipzig, 1914.
Truscott, H. "Dussek and the Concerto," *Music Review* 16 (1955).

DZIADY (FOREFATHERS' EVE) 1823–1832

Verse drama by Adam Mickiewicz

Forefathers' Eve, which has the same status in Poland as *Hamlet* in Anglophone countries, is an enormous work, part lyrical, part dramatic. It consists of two main sections, linked together only tenuously. The first of these, parts 2 and 4, was published in 1823, as part of the second volume of Adam Mickiewicz's *Poezje* (Poetry). Composed mostly in the Lithuanian cities of Vilnius and Kowno, it is often referred to as the *Dziady Wilensko-Kowieńskie* (the *Wilno-Kowno Dziady*). The second portion, part 3, was written after the poet's exile in Dresden. Published in Paris in 1832, it is known as the *Dziady Drezdeńskie* (*Dresden Dziady*). To this, the most powerful portion of the drama, are added seven narrative/lyrical works, the so-called *Ustęp* (*fragment*). We should also mention the brief, fragmentary *Dziady: widowisko* (*Dziady: Spectaculum*), an unfinished dramatic work written on the same theme as that in *Forefathers' Eve* in early 1821, which, although never published during the poet's life, is considered by some scholars to be part 1. The narrative order of the sections, an example of the Romantic love for the fragmentary and irrational, is (1), 2, 4, 3.

The title comes from a semipagan religious ceremony celebrated by the inhabitants of Belorussia, Lithuania, and Poland in honor of their deceased ancestors. Although Forefathers' Eve is usually associated with All Souls' Day, the Polish anthropologist Aleksander Brückner informs us that it was often held several times a year. In his preface to the *Wilno-Kowno* text, Mickiewicz writes: "The common people [gathering to recite spells and hymns under the leadership of a *guslarz* think that with meals, drink, and song they can bring relief to the souls in Purgatory." Mickiewicz himself claimed to have witnessed such midnight celebrations as a boy, at which the spirits of the recently deceased were called forth and interrogated as to how those still living might help them enter paradise.

This calling forth of spirits in dark, lonely chapels and cemeteries seems to be right in the Gothic-Romantic spirit. Yet *Forefathers' Eve* is a particularly Catholic work, and the pious doings of the simple people are shown to be an honest incarnation of the Communion of the Saints. Indeed, parts 2 and 4 of *Forefathers' Eve* are very similar to Dante Alighieri's *Divine Comedy*. The spirits who are called forth, two young children who never tasted bitterness during their life and a young maiden who never gave of herself to any of the men who loved her, both receive some succour from the people they appear to, while also helping them, through their stories, avoid making similar mistakes. Even the sprite of a cruel landowner (the only Hellish spirit to appear), has a warning for the people:

Tak, muszę dręczyć się wiek wiekiem,	Yes, I must bear my pain through age on age,
Sprawiedliwe zrządzenia boże!	How harsh God's just decree, though sage
Bo kto nie był ni razu człowiekiem,	For he who never stooped to be a man
Temu człowiek nic nie pomoże	Hopes not for help from any human hand

Mickiewicz's hero Gustaw makes his appearance at the end of part 2. He appears as an uncontrollable spirit, insistently following a young shepherdess with his love-tormented gaze. It seems that this spirit is the same we meet with in the lyric that opens part 2: *Upiór* (the walking dead). Gustaw has killed himself for love, but the suicide is romantic only to a small degree: in both the Walking Dead and *Forefathers' Eve*, all human actions are seen against the backdrop of eternity. Individuals are judged according to their works, whether they are self- or other-centered. Thus, the narrator of the walking dead suffers, like a lovelorn romantic hero, and at the same time acknowledges the wisdom of God in punishing him for his sin. Likewise, in part 4 (which follows 2), when this same spirit wanders off to a long conversation with his former teacher, a village priest, their talk circles around the ideals of love (the priest was himself once married), but when it comes time for his moment of wisdom, Gustaw warns, "Kto za życia choć raz by ł w niebie / Ten po śmierci nie trafi od razu" ("He who scaled heaven while yet alive / Won't get there quickly after death"). His lessons are: set your sights on the proper goals, do not elevate love for the earthly inhabitant over love for the Creator, and sacrifice selfishness and petty pleasures for the sake of greater things.

This, Gustaw's warning, will be the thesis of the Dresden text, or part 3. The introverted romantic hero becomes the other-centered national hero, worried more about his nation's sufferings than his own broken heart. He does it in dramatic fashion. From the Dresden text, which describes the crushing of patriotic student organizations in Vilnius by the tsarist government, we learn that Gustaw did not die, as we had thought, but has been imprisoned with his companions for their nationalistic activity.

Gustaw becomes Konrad, literally, and the erotic love he formerly bore his shepherdess is now transformed into a patriotic *caritas*. In scene 2, the most well-known soliloquy in Polish literature, known as the "great improvisation," Konrad declares,

Ja i ojczyzna to jedno.	I and the Fatherland am the same.
Nazywam się Milijon—bo za milijony	My name is Million, for the millions' dole
Kocham i cierpię katusze	I love as my own pain.

During this monologue, Konrad's despairing love for his crucified nation attains a fever pitch. He goes so far as to assert his cosubstance as a creator with God himself, to accuse God of fomenting, or at least of permitting, the woes that beset Poland, and, finally, to demand of God "power over souls" such as God has, so that he (Konrad) might make his people happy in a way that even the Lord could not.

The great improvisation has been regarded by generations of commentators as a grand patriotic outburst of heroic despair, and that it is. But such commentators overlook the fact that Konrad is possessed, literally, during the entire rant, and that the scene ends with Konrad's exorcism at the hands of the humble priest, Father Piotr. Mickiewicz destroys the Promethean hero rather than endorsing him. It is interesting that, after the exorcism, Konrad disappears from the play until its very conclusion, when he performs the only heroic act that he is capable of: distributing some meager alms for the physical and spiritual needs of the poor.

The lesson of humility and practical mercy learned by Konrad, plus the ever-present background of eternity, where the ageless struggle of good and evil is played out, lends *Forefathers' Eve* the general, universal eloquence that all great literature shares. This is not to say that it lacks a Polish specific. In the mystical monologue of Father Piotr, for example, his vision of Poland as Christ of the Nations—crucified unjustly but about to resurrect and bring freedom to the downtrodden peoples—is the greatest expression of the Messianistic strain in Polish Romanticism. Indeed, this leitmotiv runs throughout the entire work. Even Gustaw's plea to his priest friend in part 4—that he allow the celebration of the semi-pagan Forefathers' Eve—can be read as the demand of the Poles for cultural, as well as political, autonomy. And, as Poland/Christ is described throughout the dramatic portion of the Dresden text, so too is its chief persecutor, Russia, described in the lyrical fragment with which the book ends. It should be mentioned that the verse "Pomnik Piotra Wielkiego" ("Statue of Peter the Great") spurred Mickiewicz's friend Pushkin to the composition of an angry reply.

Even the Polish specific of the drama has its universal application. Like the "warnings" given to the living by the returning spirits in the earlier parts of the play, Mickiewicz's *Forefathers' Eve* is a parable of tyranny. Thus the poet admonishes the nations of Europe in his introduction to the Dresden text, writing, "And to the merciful nations of Europe, which shed their tears over Poland like the wretched women of Jerusalem over Christ, our nation shall speak only with the words of the Saviour: 'Daughters of Jerusalem, weep not for me, but for yourselves.'"

CHARLES S. KRASZEWSKI

Text

Dziady, parts 2 and 4, 1823; 2d ed., 1829. Part 3, 1832. Part 1, 1860.

Dziady (Forefathers' Eve, Dresden Text). Translated by Charles S. Kraszewski. 2000.

Bibliography

Braun, Kazimierz. "The *Forefathers' Eve:* The Burning Bush of Polish Theater. Some Personal Encounters," *Polish Review*, 43, no. 4 (1998): 397–409.

Fabre, Jean. "Adam Mickiewicz et le romantisme européen." In *Lumières et romantisme: Energie et nostalgie de Rousseau à Mickiewicz*. Paris: Kleinsiech, 1963.

Gille-Maisani, Jean-Charles. *Adam Mickiewicz: poète national de la Pologne: étude psychanalytique et caractérologique*. Montréal: Bellarmin/Paris: Les Belles Lettres, 1988.

Gross, I. G, "Adam Mickiewicz, A European from Nowogrodek," in *East European Politics and Societies* 9, no. 2, (1995): 295.

Janion, Maria. *Gorączka romantyczna*. Warsaw: PIW, 1975.

Jastrun, Mieczysław. *Adam Mickiewicz*. Warsaw: Polonia, 1955.

Kołodziej, Léon. *Adam Mickiewicz au carrefour des romantismes européens, essai sur la pensée du poète*. Aix-en-Provence: Éditions Ophrys, 1966.

Kraszewski, Charles S. *The Romantic Hero and Contemporary Anti-Hero in Polish and Czech Literature: Great Souls and Grey Men*. Lewiston, England: Edwin Mellen Press, 1997.

Kridl, Manfred, ed. *Adam Mickiewicz, Poet of Poland: A Symposium*. New York: Greenwood Press, 1951.

Lednicki, Wacław, ed. *Adam Mickiewicz in World Literature: A Symposium*. Berkeley and Los Angeles: University of California Press, 1956.

Maslowski, Michel. "La structure initiatique des *Aïeux (Dziady)* d' Adam Mickiewicz," *Revue des Etudes Slaves* 57 (1985).

Miłosz, Czesław. *A History of Polish Literature*. Berkeley and Los Angeles: University of California Press 1983.

Mitosek, Zofia, ed. *Adam Mickiewicz aux yeux des Français / textes réunis, établis et présentés avec l'introduction, commentaires, et notes*. Warszawa: PWN, 1992.

Piwinska, Marta. *Legenda romantyczna i szyderczy*. Warsaw: PIW, 1973.

Unesco. *Adam Mickiewicz, 1798–1855; in commemoration of the centenary of his death*. Paris: UNESCO, 1955.

Walc, Jan. *Architekt arki*. Chotomów: Verba, 1991.

Welsh, David J. *Adam Mickiewicz*. New York: Twayne Publishers, 1966.

E

ECHEVERRÍA, ESTEBAN 1805–1851

Argentine poet, writer, and social reformer

When Esteban Echeverría left his native Argentina in 1825 for a five-year stay in France, the South American Wars of Independence had recently ended. Independence had been achieved in 1823, but as Simón Bolívar and others soon realized, the republics of the Americas faced the difficult task of social reorganization. In Argentina, the *unitarios* and *federales* fought for control of the country during the tumultuous period that followed the 1830 Revolución de Mayo (May Revolution, 1810). (The unitarios promoted a centralized government for Argentina; they were identified with metropolitan Buenos Aires and foreign attitudes. The federales were in favor of the independent government of provinces, and so identified with the values of country, religion, and pampa life.) Echeverría returned from France in 1830, and found that Juan Manuel de Rosas, the federal leader, had become Argentina's dictator. For Echeverría, Rosas's rule had changed Argentina beyond recognition, and whatever hopes he had for it seemed impossible: "La patria ya no existía" ("My country no longer existed"). Echeverría would spend the rest of his life writing to reconstruct Argentina in the name of what he believed to be the legacy of Romanticism and the goals of the revolution, "la libertad individual, la libertad civil y la libertad política" ("individual liberty, civil liberty, and political liberty").

In Paris, Echeverría studied literature, economics, and law. He read Lord Byron, Johann Wolfgang von Goethe, Victor Hugo, Johann Christoph Friedrich von Schiller, August Wilhelm von Schlegel, and Madame Anne-Louise-Germaine de Staël, among others. Believing like Victor Hugo that "el romanticismo no es más que el liberalismo en literatura" (Romanticism is nothing more than liberalism in literature), Echeverría saw literary expression as an exercise of the liberties he sought to foment in Argentine society. In "Clasicismo y romanticismo," an essay unpublished during his lifetime, Echeverría examines the place of Argentine literature in the context of European Romanticism. Echeverría saw Romanticism as the aesthetic that allowed for the "originality of the artist": a freedom that would express the recently gained political independence from Europe in cultural terms. Like Andrés Bello, Echeverría called for a poetry based on the experiences and landscapes of the Americas, one which was not imitative of European models.

This idea matures gradually in Echeverría's poetic work. Upon his return to Argentina, he published *Elvira: o la novia argentina* (*Elvira, or the Argentine Bride*, 1832), *Los Consuelos* (*Consolations*, 1834), and *Rimas* (*Rhymes*, 1837), the collection containing "La cautiva" ("The Captive"), Echeverría's perhaps most accomplished and representative poem. Evocative of Samuel Taylor Coleridge's "Rhyme of the Ancient Mariner" and Byronic narratives like *Childe Harold* and *Don Juan*, it narrates the story of María, a white creole woman who, with other women and children, is captured into slavery after an Indian raid on a settlement in the pampas.

"La cautiva" exemplifies Echeverría's poetic program. The pampa desert, "la grandiosa llanura," becomes a site for the sublime, "Que no es dado al vulgo ver" ("that which is not given for the common to see"). The narrator celebrates the nature of this stark landscape, the *pampero* winds, the "yajá" bird and the "quemazón" (fire storm), which correspond to European Romantic aesthetic symbols like the Alps, the nightingale, and the sea. The Indians are identified with the desert that lies "Donde el cristiano atrevido / Jamás estampa la huella" ("Where the brave Christian / never sets foot), and their "savagery" is metonymically signified by the landscape. "La cautiva" enacts on an ideological level the struggle between civilization, represented by Brián and María, and savagery, embodied in the Indians and the desert. Juan Batista Alberdi, Echeverría, Domingo Faustino Sarmiento, and other Argentine intellectuals of the time cast this struggle in terms of their own resistance against Rosas, who was identified with the pampa. Yet political and aesthetic ideologies clash within Echeverría's poem. He laments the massacre of María and her tribe, who are killed in their sleep, and characterizes Indian warriors in the sublime terms he associates with the landscape. The opposition between civilization and savagery collapses as Echeverría finds the sublime in the autochthonous landscape and peoples of Argentina.

The publication of "La cautiva" in 1837 ensured Echeverría's success among the circle of Argentine intellectuals who were mostly *unitarios* and vehemently opposed to Rosas. That same year he gave a series of lectures in a literary salón that primarily served political purposes. In the lectures, published posthumously by his friend and biographer José María Gutiérrez, Echeverría lays out a reading of Argentine and Latin American history after the revolution. Whereas independence ended the state of political childhood in Argentina, conceived here in Hegelian terms, the postrevolutionary period is "la adulta y reflexiva edad de nuestra patria" (the adult and reflexive age of our nation). Independence is not freedom, which remains to be achieved during this new stage of social organization.

These gatherings led to the formation of the Asociación de la Joven Generación Argentina (Association of Argentine Youth) in 1838, which unanimously chose Echeverría as its leader. The association members included the most outstanding intellectuals of Argentina at the time, like Alberdi and Gutiérrez, and two future presidents, Sarmiento and Bartolomé Mitre, who later fought against Rosas in 1851. The association marks a turning point in Echeverría's career; he became increasingly preoccupied with creating a coherent political and cultural platform. His writing turned largely to prose, and to pieces with a decided reformist character. He wrote the two documents that stood as the mission statements of the Asociación: *Dogma socialista* (1838) and *Palabras simbólicas* (*Symbolic Words*, 1838).

In the *Palabras*, Echeverría argues that revolutions throughout the Americas, "como todas las grandes revoluciones del mundo" ("like all great revolutions throughout the world"), overturned tyranny; but declares that though independent, Latin America is not free. As the alternative to tyranny, Echeverría proposes the principles of "fraternidad, igualdad, libertad, asocación" ("fraternity, equality, liberty, association"), and the idea of "progreso indefinido" ("indefinite progress"). He urges Argentine youth to cement society on these principles, which will lead to class equality, the highest attainment of democracy, and the guarantee of political and individual freedom.

The activities of the association captured Rosas's attention, resulting in the persecution and exile of most of its members. In 1840 Echeverría followed Alberdi to Uruguay, where he continued to write political commentary and develop his theories on education. Between 1839 and the early 1840s, Echeverría composed "El matadero" ("The Slaughterhouse"), a *cuadro de costumbres* (sketch of manners) that has secured his literary reputation though it was not published during his lifetime. The story takes place during Lent, when the Catholic Church exercises its "imperio inmaterial sobre las conciencias y estómagos, que en manera alguna pertenecen al individuo" ("hidden power over minds and stomachs, which in no way belong to an individual") and forbids beef, then a staple of the Argentine diet. The scarcity of meat becomes so extreme that "no quedó en el matadero ni un solo ratón vivo de los muchos millares que allí tenían albergue" ("not even a mouse was left alive from the thousands who hid there"). Rosas, who called himself "el Restaurador" (the Restorer), decides to quell the revolutionary grumblings of the populace by striking a bargain with the Church, and allowing some cattle to be slaughtered.

Echeverría describes the environment of the slaughterhouse itself in a Swiftian vein. News that the Restaurador authorizes the slaughter revives even the last moribund rats, and Rosas himself is present when the first head is killed. As the slaughter gets underway, mounted riders police the boys, black servant women, dogs, and seagulls who come to steal whatever they can. The bloody organs of the animals are thrown around as sport and fought over with knives. The scene at the slaughterhouse is a "Simulacro en pequeño . . . del modo bárbaro con que se ventilan en nuestro país las cuestiones y los derechos individuales y sociales" ("A small simulacrum of the barbarous way in which social questions and individual rights are resolved in our country"). The killing continues until a bull charges and escapes. In the confusion, one of the ropes holding the animal decapitates a boy, whose headless body is ignored as the riders run after the bull through the streets of Buenos Aires. Matasiete, the most dexterous of the riders, captures and kills the animal.

The story seems to have come to an end when one of the butchers spots an unitario, and identifies him because of his beard, overcoat, and English saddle, which Rosas had prohibited. Matasiete and others go after the young man, who is hunted like the bull. They bring him before the judge in charge of the slaughterhouse debating what kind of torture might be best for him. The judge calls for scissors, and has his beard styled in the manner of the federales while the men laugh. The symbolic emasculation has no effect on the young man, who remains defiant and denounces the brutality in Rosas's regime. As the riders prepare to strip him for more torture, the young man's suffers an aneurysm as a result of his rage. Blood flows everywhere and stops the morbid anticipation of the butchers. The narrator concludes logically, "por el suceso anterior puede verse a las claras que el foco de la federación estaba en el Matadero" ("it may be seen through the previous incident that the center of the federation was in the slaughterhouse"). Had Echeverría published "El matadero," it is likely that he would have had to pay for it with his life. The unmistakable message of his satire is that Rosas was a butcher who treats the Argentine people like cattle.

Yet Echeverría refrains from the virulence of the satire in "El matadero" in his last works. In 1846, he published the *Manual de enseñanza moral para las escuelas primarias del estado Oriental*, and republished the *Dogma socialista* with a history of the Asociación. He restated many of the principles of the *Dogma* and the *Palabras simbólicas*, and called for the creation of a third party that would combine the best of both federal and unitario principles. He was happy to find that Rosas had critics and enemies who were willing to fight him armed, but he took them to task for not having a social program that they would put in place should Rosas himself call them to govern. Echeverría underscored the importance of accommodating both federalist and centralist tendencies in the new government, because he saw that otherwise Argentina would be doomed to internal strife. After publishing the *Dogma*, Echeverría continued to write and participate in the administration of public schools. In 1849, he finished his last major poem, *Avellaneda*, and became affiliated with the University of Montevideo, but his health began to decline. In 1851, he died of tuberculosis, a year before the end of the Rosista regime.

JOSELYN M. ALMEIDA

Biography

Born in Buenos Aires, September 2, 1805. Educated at the Colegio de Ciencias Morales (College of Moral Sciences), Buenos Aires. Worked as a customs officer, 1823. Moved to Paris; studied law and social sciences; influenced by writing of Johann Wolfgang von Goethe, Victor Hugo, Johann Schiller and others, 1825–30. Returned to Buenos Aires; published a number of works, 1834–39, including *Rimas*, 1837. Founded and led the Asociación de la Joven Generación Argentina (Association of Argentine Youth), 1838. Wrote *El Matadero*, c. 1839 (published 1871). Participated in unsuccessful rebellion against Manuel de Rosas and Argentinian government, 1839; exiled to Montevideo, Uruguay 1840. Cofounder of the Historical and Geographical Institute of Uruguay, 1843. Wrote textbooks for the Uruguayan Ministry of Education, early 1840s; employed by the ministry in schools administration, 1847. Member of the Superior Council of the University of Montevideo, 1849. Died in Montevideo, January 19, 1851.

Selected Works

Dogma socialista. Edited by Alberto Palcos. 1940.
Obras completas de D. Esteban Echeverría. 5 vols. Edited by and with biography by Juan María Gutiérrez. 1951.
La cautiva. El matadero. Edited by Angel Battistessa. 1958.
Prosa literaria. Edited by Roberto Giusti. 1958.
Esteban Echeverría: Obras escogidas. Edited by Beatriz Sarlo and Carlos Altamirano. 1991.

Bibliography

Agosti, Hector P. *Echeverría*. Buenos Aires: Futuro, 1951.
Barreiro, José P. *El espíritu de mayo y el revisionismo histórico*. Buenos Aires: A. Zamora, 1951.
Cháneton, Abel. *Retorno de Echeverría*. Buenos Aires: Ayacucho, 1954.
Furt, Jorge M. *Esteban Echeverría*. Buenos Aires: Colombo, 1938.
Jitrik, Noe. *Esteban Echeverría*. Buenos Aires: Centro Editor de América Latina, 1968.
Kisnernan, Natalio. *Contribución a la bibliografía de Esteban Echeverría* (1805–1955). Buenos Aires: Universidad Nacional, 1960.
Katra, William H. *The Argentine Generation of 1837*. Madison, N.J.: Farleigh Dickinson University Press, 1996.
Mercado, Juan Carlos. *Building a Nation: The Case of Echeverría*. Lanham: University Press of America, 1996.

ECONOMICS

Economics and Romanticism have common roots in Enlightenment moral philosophy and its quest to uncover the principles of human and social behavior. Eighteenth-century economic theory was specifically oriented around issues in agriculture and its relation to statecraft. The French physiocrats, led by François Quesnay, argued that the only true measure of value was land. Mercantilists meanwhile claimed that the wealth of any nation derived from a favorable balance of incoming money over exported goods. Both theories had some residual impact on Romantic political thought; for instance, the environmental consciousness of physiocracy and the social conscience of mercantilism strongly influenced the German economists Johann Gottlieb Fichte and Adam Müller.

As industrialization and capitalism took hold in Europe, economics began to be distinguished from the ethics and politics that define the background of Romanticism. There are, however, important connections to be made between these fields. Though based largely on agricultural statistics, Adam Smith's *An Enquiry into the Nature and Causes of the Wealth of Nations* (1776) dominated economy debate well into the industrial period. Adapting the preliminary insights of Adam Ferguson, David Hume, and Anne-Robert-Jacques Turgot, Smith argued that the foundation for economic growth was the division of labor, a consequence of "the natural propensity to truck, barter, and exchange." Value, Smith claimed, originates in labor, but once commodities begin to be exchanged, this use value would be replaced by a more fluid exchange value. The ratio between these values determined the rate of profits, wages, and trade in the market, which provide the measure of national wealth. These natural exchange forces would ultimately provide for anyone selling or consuming produce or labor in the market, a phenomenon Smith called "the invisible hand." The legislative implications of Smith's liberal theory, however, were somewhat ambiguous. Revolutionary thinkers like William Godwin and Thomas Paine in England and the Marquis de Condorcet, Jean-Baptiste Say, and the Abbé de Sieyes in France held that market individualism would end the archaic despotisms of the old order. Antirevolutionary thinkers, notably Edmund Burke and William Pitt, argued that Smith's liberal economy would preserve the "social contract" by enshrining the necessary disparities between workers and owners in the division of labor.

The most controversial economic work was Thomas Robert Malthus's *Essay on Population* (1798). Malthus asserted that while population increased exponentially, food increased arithmetically. Wars, famines, diseases, and vice were thus necessary and unavoidable. In the second edition of the *Essay* (1803), Malthus further claimed that the horrific effects of overpopulation could be ameliorated through a general campaign of "moral restraint" promoted by national education. Malthus opposed care services for the poor and birth control, arguing that both were contrary to the laws of necessity, for which he was soundly chastised by the likes of Samuel Taylor Coleridge and William Hazlitt. They argued that the moral stability of society could be maintained by reasoned self-consciousness and fellow feeling. Malthus in turn accused both of naïveté. The *Essay on Population* profoundly influenced the development not only of political economy (of which Malthus became the first university chair) but also statistics and legal theory, as well as the utilitarianism of Jeremy Bentham and John Stuart Mill.

Significant advances also came in monetary economics. An extensive network of banks had existed since the seventeenth century. Bills of exchange and other paper monies were readily acceptable in trade, provided they were convertible into gold or silver. The theory of how money worked in relation to the economy as a whole was nevertheless fractious and speculative; even Smith's discussion of money is based largely on Scottish banking. The French revolutionary experiment with an all-paper currency, the *assignat*, was an unmitigated disaster. So when in 1797 the pressures of war, bad harvests, and possible invasion forced the British government to suspend the convertability of paper notes, it was a very controversial move indeed. Some thinkers, including Coleridge, and the prominent banker and evangelist Henry Thornton, defended the suspension on the grounds that confidence in the *virtual* stability of paper was sufficient to defray inflation. Other prominent economists such as Francis Horner and William Huskisson agreed that public confidence was necessary to the stability of commerce, but only through the underlying security of convertible notes would that stability be achieved. Radical thinkers including the Cambridge mathematician William Frend, poets Percy Bysshe Shelley and Robert Southey, journalists William Cobbett and Leigh Hunt, the cartoonist George Cruickshank, and the publisher William Hone argued vociferously that only gold, a product of the earth and human effort, was the natural measure of value. Paper money was essentially a fraud. Despite recurrent inducements to return to convertibility, the British government retained suspension until 1821.

The most important theorist to emerge from the bullion controversy was David Ricardo. A stockbroker by profession, Ricardo was widely regarded as one of the most brilliant thinkers of his generation. His first pamphlet, "The High Price of Bullion" (1809), significantly added to the general understanding of the circulation of paper money in relation to the market in precious metals. After 1811, Ricardo largely abandoned money issues and turned to the larger question of how to solve the age-old problem of value. In *Principles of Political Economy and Taxation* (1817), Ricardo argued that the value of land, apart from the value of any exchangeable commodity, lies in the ratio of how much of it is actually used against how much of lesser quality would need to be used later on, the basis for what economists now call marginal value. A systematic mathematical thinker, Ricardo is regarded as one of the chief pioneers of economic science. No-tably, one of his most important adherents was Thomas De Quincey, who credited the economist with channeling his understanding of abstraction itself. The story of economics and Romanticism represents a bifurcation of science from humanism, though in significant ways this antagonism significantly advanced the development of both.

ALEX DICK

Bibliography

Barrell, John. *The Birth of Pandora and the Division of Knowledge.* London: Macmillan, 1992.

Bladen, Vincent. *From Adam Smith to Maynard Keynes: The Heritage of Political Economy.* Toronto: University of Toronto Press, 1974.

Bowley, Marian. *Studies in the History of Economic Theory before 1870.* London: Macmillan, 1973.

Brown, Vivienne. *Adam Smith's Discourse: Canonicity, Commerce and Conscience.* London: Routledge, 1994.

Connell, Phillip. *Romanticism, Economics, and the Question of Culture.* Oxford: Oxford University Press, 2000.

Fetter, F. W. *The Development of British Monetary Orthodoxy 1797–1875.* Cambridge: Harvard University Press, 1965.

Haakonssen, Knud. *The Science of the Legislator: The Natural Jurisprudence of David Hume and Adam Smith.* Cambridge: Cambridge University Press, 1981.

Heinzelman, Kurt. *The Economics of the Imagination.* Amherst: University of Massachusetts Press, 1980.

Hollander, Samuel. *Classical Economics.* Oxford: Basil Blackwell, 1987.

———. *The Economics of Adam Smith.* Toronto: University of Toronto Press, 1973.

Hutchinson, Terence. *Before Adam Smith: The Emergence of Political Economy, 1662–1776.* Oxford: Basil Blackwell, 1988.

McNally, David. *Against the Market: Political Economy, Market Socialism, and the Marxist Critique.* New York: Verso, 1993.

———. *Political Economy and the Rise of Capitalism: A Reinterpretation.* Berkeley and Los Angeles: University of California Press, 1988.

Meek, Ronald. *Economics and Ideology and Other Essays: Studies in the Development of Economic Thought.* London: Chapman, 1967.

———. *Smith, Marx and After: Ten Essays in the Development of Economic Thought.* London: Chapman and Hall, 1977.

Thompson, James. *Models of Virtue: Eighteenth-Century Political Economy and the Novel.* Durham, N.C.: Duke University Press, 1996.

Winch, Donald. *Riches and Poverty: An Intellectual History of Political Economy in Britain 1750–1834.* Cambridge: Cambridge University Press, 1996.

EDGEWORTH, MARIA 1767–1849

British novelist

From the publication of her *Castle Rackrent* in 1800 until the appearance of Sir Walter Scott's *Waverly* in 1814, Maria Edgeworth was the most popular and respected novelist writing in English. Although she is primarily remembered today for her portraits of Irish nobility and peasantry, Edgeworth's contemporaries regarded her as a versatile novelist capable of working in a variety of genres. Reviewers in England and Scotland praised the Irish writer for her ability to capture the character of her country and for her insights into fashionable society. Scott ac-knowledged the influence of her work on his approach to the historical novel.

Critical assessment of Edgeworth's work has always been colored by her close association with—some would say dominance by—her father, Richard Lovell Edgeworth. A progressive educational theorist, Edgeworth drafted his daughter into service as his literary collaborator. For more than twenty years, the two produced provocative treatises such as *Practical Education* (1798), *Irish Bulls* (1802), and *Essays on Professional Education*

(1809). Much of Maria's fiction was written with a specific didactic intent, especially children's books such as *The Parent's Assistant* (1795) and *Early Lessons* (1801–2). By her own admission, she sought her father's approval of, and advice about, her adult fiction. Giving further impetus to the theory that she depended on him heavily is the fact that, after Richard Edgeworth died in 1817, Maria wrote no major novel for seventeen years.

However, the relationship was not necessarily as stifling as some critics have suggested. Maria, living in Richard Edgeworth's house, became familiar with, and eventually sympathetic toward, the ideas he promoted, the same ideas that shaped the Romantic movement in England and throughout Europe. Richard Edgeworth was a devotee of the educational theories of Jean-Jacques Rousseau. He saw the need for improving the lives of his Irish tenants, whom he treated with respect and a certain degree of benevolence. He did encourage his daughter to use her talents as a novelist toward moralistic and instructional ends. In fairness, though, several Romantic writers possessed a desire to reform humankind through their art (Percy Bysshe Shelley, in his *Defence of Poetry*, wrote that poets are "the unacknowledged legislators of the world"). For the great Romantic writers, however, art was used as a tool of moral improvement only indirectly. Unfortunately, Richard Edgeworth's penchant for didacticism had a decidedly mixed effect on his daughter's fiction. Too frequently in her novels she subordinates plot and characterization to didacticism.

Perhaps because she did not seek advice from her father before writing *Castle Rackrent*, this first book is relatively free of the preachy tone that characterizes much of her later work. Additionally, the book appeared at a propitious time. The genre was little more than a half-century old, but the novel had already garnered certain formulaic qualities that had led to its general dismissal as a vehicle for instruction or enlightenment. No one thus far had equaled Samuel Richardson in psychological analysis, or Henry Fielding in imparting moral education via fiction. Edgeworth's decision to write about the Irish came at a time when interest in Celtic history and legend was growing. Her slim volume on the history of the Rackrent family caught the fancy of many readers, and introduced into literature the subgenre of the regional novel. The four Rackrent gentlemen represent four distinct types of Irish upper-class character. They are appealing or unattractive in proportion to how they treat their neighbors, their servants, and the land and possessions that establish their wealth and their status in the community.

The story is narrated by Thady Quirk, a servant whose presence on the estate throughout four generations of the Rackrents enables him to comment on the strengths and weaknesses of his masters. His naïveté creates a sense of irony, as readers recognize that not one of his four masters is a thoroughly noble figure. Edgeworth's conceit of casting the story as Quirk's memoirs, discovered and prepared by an unnamed editor, appealed to readers of gothic literature, accustomed as they were to the device of the framed tale. The last of the Rackrents, the pitiable Sir Condy, faintly echoes the young hero of an even more popular and influential Romantic novel, Johann Wolfgang von Goethe's *The Sorrows of Young Werther*. In addition, the two novels share a curious characteristic: although they are considered highlights of the respective authors' careers, both novels were inherently rejected by the writers themselves in later works. Goethe never wrote another such overtly Romantic work; he considered his hero too much given to sentimentalism. Edgeworth never again employed the form of *Castle Rackrent*, deciding instead to use devices and methods of mainstream fiction.

More representative of her work is *The Absentee* (1812), a novel that simultaneously explores the English political establishment's treatment of the Irish, and exposes the hypocrisy of London high society. The novel's protagonist, Lord Colambre, initially appears to be a typical upper-class gentleman; a handsome and well-mannered bachelor, he has several female admirers within fashionable society. Unlike other members of the moneyed set, however, he rejects received opinion about both marriage and his responsibilities as an Irish landlord. He rebukes those who would have him remain in London amid the nobility, living comfortably off profits derived from distant estates. He seeks to learn about his impending inheritance firsthand, experiencing the life of the poor Irish peasants who are struggling to meet increasingly excessive demands from agents. His willingness to flaunt traditional social practices and his affinity with the peasantry demonstrate that, at least in part, Edgeworth sympathizes with Romantic principles. Unfortunately, Edgeworth ends with a contrived happy conclusion that results from a series of improbable coincidences; this ending negates the progressive social commentary found earlier in the novel.

Despite her uncertain relationship with progressive politics, feminist critics have found much to praise in Maria Edgeworth's work. Edgeworth had great respect for women of education and intelligence. In many of her novels she presents women of discriminating taste and deep understanding. She does not, however, subscribe to the radical feminism advocated by some of her contemporaries and many later feminists. The character that best embodies radical feminist theory and behavior, Helen Freke in *Belinda* (1801), is portrayed as a threat to the heroine of the novel. Nevertheless, Edgeworth consistently creates female characters presented as equal to men—an idea radical in her time, but one in keeping with Romantic beliefs in the dignity and value of each individual.

LAURENCE W. MAZZENO

Biography

Born at Black Bourton (or Blackbourton), Oxfordshire, January 1, 1767 or 1768. Daughter of educationalist Richard Lovell Edgeworth. Educated at Mrs. Lattuffiere's school, Derby, 1775–80, and Mrs. Devis's school, London, 1781–82. Lived at family estate in Edgeworthstown, County Longford, Ireland, from 1782. Returned with family to England 1791–93. Published *Letters for Literary Ladies*, 1795. Served as her father's companion and literary collaborator, 1795–1817. Published first novel, *Castle Rackrent*, 1800. Traveled in England, France, and Scotland, 1802–3. Declined marriage proposal from Count Abram Niclas Clewberg-Edelcrantz, private secretary to the King of Sweden, 1802. Prepared her father's *Memoirs* for publication after his death in 1817 (published 1820). Traveled to England and Scotland intermittently, 1818–43; Corresponded with and established friendship with Sir Walter Scott; visited him in Scotland, 1823. Traveled to France and Switzerland, 1820–21. Worked to alleviate plight of peasants during Irish famine, 1846. Died at Edgeworthstown, May 22, 1849.

Selected Works

Letters for Literary Ladies. 1795.
The Parent's Assistant; or, Stories for Children. 1796.
Practical Education. 1798.
Castle Rackrent: An Hibernian Tale. 1800. Edited by George Watson and Kathryn J. Kirkpatrick. New York: Oxford Universty Press, 2000.
Moral Tales for Young People. 1801.
Belinda. 1801. Edited by Kathryn J. Kirkpatrick. New York: Oxford University Press, 1999.
Early Lessons. 1801.
Irish Bulls. 1802.
Popular Tales. 1804.
Modern Griselda. 1804.
Leonora. 1806.
Tales of Fashionable Life. First Series, 1809.
Tales of Fashionable Life. Second Series, 1812.
The Absentee. 1812. Edited by Ken Walker and Heidi Thomson. New York: Penguin, 2000.
Patronage. 1814.
Harrington. 1817.
Ormond. 1817. Edited by Claire Connolly. New York: Penguin, 2001.
Comic Dramas. 1817.
Tales and Miscellaneous Pieces. 1825.
Helen. 1834.

Bibliography

Bilger, Audrey. *Laughing Feminism.* Detroit: Wayne State University Press, 1998.
Butler, Marilyn. *Maria Edgeworth: A Biography.* Oxford: Clarendon Press, 1972.
Gilmartin, Sophie. *Ancestry and Narrative in Nineteenth-Century British Literature.* New York: Cambridge University Press, 1998.
Gonda, Caroline. *Reading Daughters' Fictions 1709–1834.* New York: Cambridge University Press, 1996.
Harden, O. E. McW. *Maria Edgeworth.* Boston: Twayne, 1984.
Hollingsworth, Brian. *Maria Edgeworth's Irish Writing.* New York: St. Martin's Press, 1997.
Kowaleski-Wallace, Elizabeth. *Their Father's Daughters.* New York: Oxford University Press, 1991.
McCann, Andrew. *Cultural Politics in the 1790s.* New York: St. Martin's Press, 1999.
Newcomer, James. *Maria Edgeworth, the Novelist, 1767–1849: A Bicentennial Study.* Fort Worth: Texas Christian University Press, 1967.
Owens, Colin, ed. *Family Chronicles: Maria Edgeworth's Castle Rackrent.* Totowa, N.J.: Barnes and Noble, 1987.

EDUCATION

Both pedagogical theory and educational institutions underwent massive transformations during the Romantic era. An unprecedented number of educational treatises appeared in this period, while the educational reforms of the French Revolution focused European attention on the connections between educational systems and political stability. Both conservative and radical reformers attempted to integrate formerly ignored or marginalized groups (such as women or working class adults) into emerging "national" systems of education. The creative literature of the period also bore witness to this unprecedented interest in education, as scenes of educational practice became central to much of Romantic poetry, fiction, and drama. These radical transformations can be tracked by considering three developments: an increasing interest in educational philosophies that centered on children, the proliferation of new educational institutions, and the increasing importance of education to creative literature.

The late eighteenth century was marked by a publishing explosion in the theory and practice of education, as literally hundreds of treatises, essays, and pamphlets devoted to the topic of education appeared. No one set of goals or methodology unified these texts or their authors: some authors considered childrens' education while others focused their efforts on adults; some authors favored national education while others opposed it. Yet almost all of these educational treatises were grounded in one of three basic educational philosophies that dominated the Romantic period: a neo-Lockean position that posited a fundamental malleability of children and the consequent importance of structured environments, a Rousseavian pedagogy that stressed the importance of following the dictates of natural sentiment, or a Christian educational philosophy premised on the innate corruption of children and the need for self-discipline.

While John Locke's *Some Thoughts concerning Education* (1693) was written well before the Romantic period, the theory of education advanced in that book was taken up by a number of Romantic era authors. Locke's educational philosophy was grounded in the theory of knowledge outlined in *An Essay concerning Human Understanding* (1690), where he had argued that all mental ideas were built up from sensations received from the surrounding environment. In *Some Thoughts* he considered the implications of this position for education. Locke argued that "the minds of children [are] as easily turned, this or that way, as water itself," with the result that children's environments could be structured so that they developed into entirely rational beings. Locke's position was adopted by numerous eighteenth- and early-nineteenth-century educational theorists such as the French philosopher Helvetius, British political philosophers William Godwin and Mary Wollstonecraft, and British novelists Maria and Richard Lovell Edgeworth. Radical British social reformer Robert Owen also adopted a neo-Lockean philosophy of education, arguing in *A New View of Society* (1813–16) that "[c]hildren are, without exception, passive and wonderfully contrived compounds; which . . . may be formed collectively to have any human character."

An alternate tradition of educational philosophy, opposed to the neo-Lockean belief that children could be "formed," was initiated by Jean-Jacques Rousseau in *Emile, ou l'education* (*Emile, or On Education*, 1762). Rousseau argued that children were not things of wax, to be molded this way or that, but instead manifested innate reactions that must be encouraged. "[T]he first movements of the human heart are always right," claimed Rousseau, a maxim that did not justify allowing the student free reign, but rather required children to *experience*—rather than simply be instructed in—the consequences of their actions. *Emile* describes the education of a young boy (Emile) and his young mate to be (Sophie), outlining a system in which sentiment, or feeling, guided the pupil. Yet paradoxically, Rousseau also believed that this "natural" system of education required the presence of a highly manipulative governor who structured the child's environment so that the child could experience those natural lessons.

Emile was a flashpoint for controversy, often the subject of attack by critics of all political persuasions, but also adopted by a number of reformers who opposed the Enlightenment stress on "reason" as an absolute value. Religious critics objected to the heterodoxy of the text, while many "enlightened" critics criticized its manipulative system of governance. *Emile* also inspired Mary Wollstonecraft's feminist critique of existing educational structures, for she noted that Rousseau's insistence on separate educational structure for boys and girls *created* the gender inequities that it sought to present as "natural." Yet other reformers enthusiastically embraced Rousseau's philosophy. During the French Revolution, elements of Rousseau's system were explicitly integrated into proposals for new educational systems. In Britain, Thomas Day presented readers with a sympathetic portrait of Rousseau's system in *Sandford and Merton* (1783–89), while in Switzerland, Johann Heinrich Pestalozzi advanced elements of Rousseau's philosophy in *Wie Gertrud ihre Kinder lehrt* (*How Gertrude Teaches Her Children*, 1801), as well as at his school in Yverdon. Elements of Rousseau's insistence on the primacy of natural sentiment are also evident in poet William Wordsworth's various observations on education in his long poem *The Prelude* (1799–1850). Samuel Taylor Coleridge developed a more complicated variant of this philosophy, arguing in various lectures and texts that the primary goal of education was "to educe"—that is, call forth—qualities of the mind only present in potentiality.

British evangelical educational theorists rejected both the neo-Lockean and Rousseauvian philosophies of childhood and education. Most evangelical reformers began with the belief that children were innately corrupt, and the task of education was acknowledge and address, to the extent possible, that original flaw. The mid-eighteenth-century decline of state-sponsored "charity schools" in Britain provided evangelical reformers with a window of opportunity to integrate this philosophy into new forms of Christian pedagogy. Hannah More and Robert Raikes, for example, developed a system of Sunday schools designed to rescue students from their wayward tendencies. Many of these British Christian reformers also understood their goals as sociopolitical, for their pedagogical practices were designed to prevent a perceived flood of atheism and "Jacobinism" from the continent.

While these three theories of education differed radically in their assessment of the child's original nature, they nevertheless agreed on several points. All three understood the primary function of education as the formation of character through the inculcation of "virtue," rather than simply instruction in certain knowledge or skills. All three stressed the need for children to "internalize"—rather than simply learn by rote—their lessons. And all three understood education as a political and social tool for the construction of a virtuous polity.

Paralleling—and in many cases, precipitating—this intense interest in pedagogical theory were radical transformations in educational institutions. Most notable among these changes were an emerging interest in "national" systems of education, and an interest in the education of workers, women, and the poor.

While terms such as *éducation nationale* and *nationale Erziehung* first emerged in the 1760s and 1770s, the French Revolution focused attention on the question of "national" systems of education. During the revolution French reformers reconsidered virtually every aspect of French education, many arguing that a complete and centrally directed reeducation of children and adults was necessary. A system of central schools, designed for children between ages twelve and twenty, was briefly implemented, while adult reeducation often took the form of obligatory attendance of "revolutionary festivals" designed to crush the superstitions of religion and monarchism. This period of open experimentation in educational reform ended with Napolean Bonaparte's dictatorship, but Napolean also continued the effort to develop a national system of education. His imperial university system, for example, provided the foundation for a national system of primary and secondary education that survived in its basic form even after the Bourbon restoration in 1814. Napolean also initiated a reorganization of the German university system, for after conquering Prussia, Napolean closed the universities at Jena and Halle, and William von Humboldt was charged with reorganizing the institutions. Humboldt's unified system of competitive *gymnasia* (high schools) and research-oriented universities still exists in its basic form in Germany today, and was adopted by many American and European universities later in the nineteenth century.

The experiences of France and Germany divided reformers in other countries on the question of national education. So, for example, while Godwin and Wollstonecraft embraced both the goals of the revolution and a neo-Lockean educational philosophy, they disagreed on the wisdom of a centrally-directed system of education. Wollstonecraft encouraged adoption of national education, arguing that it would counteract the "vanity" that often attended a private education. Godwin, on the other hand, argued that government control of education subverted its liberating potential from the start.

While the particulars of French educational reforms were often criticized in other countries, even diehard opponents of the Revolution recognized that political stability and education were intimately connected, and that inclusion of groups formerly ignored or marginalized by educational authorities had to be considered. Hannah More, for example, argued that educating the poor was a national interest, for only a literate lower class could resist Jacobin rhetoric. Through her *Cheap Repository Tracts* (1795–98), she disseminated roughly two million tracts designed to promote Christianity while at the same time teaching "domestic economy" to a lower-class female population assumed to lack this knowledge. Wollstonecraft also focused her attentions on young women, though she hoped to promote political equality among the sexes rather than stave off political change. Orphans and indigenous colonial children became the subjects of the "monitorial" schools developed by Andrew Bell and Joseph Lancaster, in which student monitors—promoted (or demoted) on the basis of merit—observed and disciplined his or her fellows, thereby encouraging students to internalize authority and discipline.

A number of groups and institutions also sought to create forums for adult education. The British Mechanics' Institutes of the 1820s, for example, targeted skilled artisans, disseminating technical knowledge, while the Royal Institution targeted a primarily middle-class audience, popularizing scientific knowledge through series of public lectures. This interest in previously neglected groups was again sociopolitical, for radicals and conservatives alike shared the conviction that violent uprisings could be prevented through directed education.

Creative literature of the Romantic era bears witness to this intense concern with education. Many Romantic-era authors of fiction, poetry, and drama were also authors of educational tracts (Godwin and Wollstonecraft, for example, wrote both educational theory and novels), and much of the creative literature is grounded in a belief that poetic creation could serve as a medium for widespread social change.

Interest in education was apparent in every form and genre of literature, but the novel was an especially acute focal point for debate. The late eighteenth century was marked by an enormous increase in literacy and novel readership, especially among women, a trend that critics of the novel often saw as potentially destructive of "virtue." Some authors such as Elizabeth Inchbald sought to ameliorate the potentially negative effects of the novel form by structuring obvious examples of the consequences of improper education within the plots of novels such as *A Simple Story* (1791). Yet more significantly, both childhood and scenes of education became central to the novel and the question of virtue in ways they had not been before (Richardson's *Pamela* (1740–41) for example, while explicitly designed to inculcate virtue in its readers, was relatively uninterested in Pamela's childhood). A bildungsroman (novel of development), such as Goethe's *Wilhelm Meisters Lehrjahre* (*Wilhelm Meister's Apprenticeship*, 1795–96) emphasized the ways in which a developing individual's environment and experiences become opportunities for character formation. Even gothic novels, ostensibly designed to simply thrill their readers, frequently centered on questions of education; in *The Mysteries of Udolpho* (1794), for example, Ann Radcliffe described her heroine's education in detail. Mary Shelley's neo-Gothic novel *Frankenstein* (1818) also highlights this latent pedagogical theme, for the plot revolves around the education of the central protagonists and narrator. Even Coleridge, generally critical of gothic literature, emphasized the important role of fantastic literature in facilitating a love for "the Great and the Whole."

Important as an awareness of Romantic educational theory and practice is to our understanding of that period, it is equally important for an understanding of the connections between that era and our own. Many, if not most, of our contemporary educational institutions and philosophies emerged during the Romantic era. The national educational system, the goal of universal literacy, a widespread belief in the importance of education to political stability, the importance of continuing "adult" education, and a belief in the fundamental role of imaginative litera-ture in the educational process all date from this period, and continue to serve as foundations for modern educational practice.

ROBERT MITCHELL

See also **Childhood; Children's Literature; Edgeworth, Maria; France: Revolution and Empire; *Frankenstein; or the Modern Prometheus*; Godwin, William; Goethe, Johann Wolfgang von; Humboldt, Wilhelm von; More, Hannah; Owen, Robert; Pestalozzi, Johann Heinrich; Rousseau, Jean-Jacques; Wollstonecraft, Mary**

Bibliography

Adamson, John William. *A Short History of Education.* Cambridge: Cambridge University Press, 1922.

Day, Thomas. *The History of Sandford and Merton.* 3 vols. Edited by Issac Kramnick. New York: Garland, 1977.

Fallon, D. *The German University.* Boulder: Colorado Associated University Press, 1980.

Godwin, William. *The Enquirer: Reflections on Education, Manners and Literature.* New York: Augustus M. Kelly, 1965.

Goethe, Johann Wolfgang von. *Wilhelm Meisters Lehrjahre.* Zurich: Artemis Verlag, 1948. Translated by Eric A. Blackall in cooperation with Victor Lange as *Wilhelm Meister's Apprenticeship.* New York: Suhrkamp, 1989.

Inchbald, Elizabeth. *A Simple Story.* Edited by Jeanette Winterson, London: Pandora, 1987.

More, Hannah. *Cheap Repository Tracts; Entertaining, Moral, and Religious.* 1798.

Owen, Robert. *A New View of Society and other Writings by Robert Owen.* London: Everyman's Library, 1927.

Palmer, R. R. *The Improvement of Humanity: Education and the French Revolution.* Princeton, N.J.: Princeton University Press, 1985.

Pestalozzi, J. H. *Wie Gertrud ihre Kinder lehrt.* Bern: Bey H. Gesner, 1801. Translated by E. Holland Lucy and Frances C. Turner as *How Gertrude Teaches Her Children.* London: Quantum Reprints, 1966.

Radcliffe, Ann. *The Mysteries of Udolpho: A Romance.* London: Oxford, 1970.

Richardson, Alan. *Literature, Education, and Romanticism: Reading as Social Practice, 1780–1832.* Cambridge: Cambridge University Press, 1994.

Shelley, Mary. *Frankenstein; or the Modern Prometheus.* Edited by M. K. Joseph. Oxford: Oxford University Press, 1980.

Silver, Harold. *The Concept of Popular Education: A Study of Ideas and Social Movements in the Early Nineteenth Century.* London: Metheun, 1977.

Snyder, Alice D. *Coleridge on Logic and Learning, with Selections from the Unpublished Manuscripts.* London: Oxford University Press, 1929.

Wollstonecraft, Mary. *A Vindication of the Rights of Woman.* 2d ed. Edited by Carol H. Poston. New York: Norton, 1988.

Wordsworth, William. *The Prelude 1799, 1805, 1850.* Edited by Jonathan Wordsworth, M. H. Abrams, and Stephen Gill. New York: W. W. Norton, 1979.

EICHENDORFF, JOSEPH FREIHERR VON 1788-1857

German poet and novelist

Joseph Freiherr von Eichendorff is the quintessential poet of the German landscape, and his simple, direct lyrics have made him Germany's best-known Romantic poet, not the least thanks to the many song settings of his works by Hugo Wolff and Robert Schumann. Both his prose and his verse are typified by a vivid, musical style whose plangent atmosphere fuses individual subjectivity with images drawn from nature and a mystical apprehension of the divine. He remains enduringly popular, both with other poets and with the general public. For Thomas Mann, his poem *Mondnacht* (*Moonlit Night*) was, quite simply, "die Perle der Perlen" (the pearl of pearls).

Eichendorff was born into a Catholic aristocratic family and spent his youth on the family estate. As intimated in the poem *Abschied* (*Farewell*), the landscape of his homeland and his religious faith provides his later writing with its emotional center. While studying at Heidelberg, he fell under the spell of Johann Joseph von Görres's lectures and of Achim von Arnim and Clemens Brentano's anthology *Des Knaben Wunderhorn* (*The Boy's Magic Horn*, 1805–8). His writing was also profoundly influenced by Johann Wolfgang von Goethe and Novalis and by his close friend, the poet J. J. von Loeben. He shared the German Romantics' delight in literary friendships, hearing Johann Gottlieb Fichte lecture and meeting Arnim, Brentano, and Heinrich von Kleist in Berlin, joining up with Friedrich and Dorothea von Schlegel in Vienna, and later entering the Berlin circle that included Adelbert von Chamisso and Friedrich Heinrich Karl de Fouqué. In his last years, he met Robert and Clara Schumann, and made friends with the young Adalbert Stifter.

Eichendorff's views on poetry appear scattered throughout his works. He summed up his credo in 1846 in *Zur Geschichte der neueren romantischen Poesie in Deutschland* (*On the History of the Recent Romantic Poetry in Germany*), repeating his views in *Geschichte der poetischen Literatur Deutschlands* of 1857 (*History of German Poetic Literature*). Romanticism is seen in terms of a historical dialectic that transcends both what he calls Johann Christoph Friedrich von Schiller's "Christentum ohne Christus" ("Christianity without Christ") and Goethe's "Naturpoesie im höchsten Sinn" ("nature poetry in the highest sense"). Poetry, Eichendorff believes, is "in ihrem Kern selbst religiös" ("at heart itself religious"), and entails "die indirekte, d.h. sinnliche Darstellung des Ewigen" ("the indirect, i.e., sensuous representation of the eternal"). As evidence, he cites his own quatrain, *Wünschelrute* (*Divining Rod*), which modern critics treat as a key to his work: poetry, this little text implies, consists in discovering the *Zauberwort* (magic word) that will awaken the *Lied* (song) that lies dormant in *allen Dingen* (all things). By implication, the divining rod of poetry will lead the reader to the spiritual source that unites man and nature with God. Whereas other German Romantics were Protestants who turned to Catholicism, Eichendorff, while remaining a Catholic, infused his philosophy with German Protestantism and the eighteenth century's natural piety.

In keeping with the "indirect" mode of representation, and echoing Novalis, Eichendorff employs an ambiguous "hieroglyphische Bilderschrift" (hieroglyphic picture writing) throughout his work. In an iconography that closely resembles that of the painter Caspar David Friedrich, these "hieroglyphs," such as fields, trees, woods, rivers, and streams, conjure up evanescent images of indeterminate yet vaguely German, Austrian, and Italian landscapes experienced at morning, noon, evening, dusk, and night, each moment having its own particular mood, from the delight in rebirth at dawn to the gentle awe of a summer twilight. Moments of transition are both dangerous and sublime. In a manner resembling the seventeenth-century emblem, the imagery intimates a higher, spiritual meaning, whereby life on earth, beset by temptations, confusion, and suffering, appears as a journey or pilgrimage toward a divine home.

His first novel, *Ahnung und Gegenwart* (*Premonition and Presence*), written in 1810–12 and published in 1815, is a remarkable achievement which reveals his early mastery of his own, unmistakable style. The novel continues the tradition of the German Romantic *Bildungsroman* and, in the manner of Friedrich von Schlegel's "progressive Universalpoesie" (progressive universal poesie), combines diverse elements—notably, lyrical prose, evocative poems, and politics. Its aim (according to the preface) is to depict the "sultry" and "confused" era prior to the wars of liberation, and to intimate a positive future. His second novel, *Dichter und ihre Gesellen* (*Poets and their Friends*) appeared in 1834, once again reworking the full panoply of Romantic devices, and his third novel, the exotic *Eine Meerfahr* (*A Sea Voyage*) came out posthumously in 1864. Of his several plays, *Die Freier* (*The Wooers*) of 1833 remains the most memorable.

His fairytale novellas are more lucidly structured, such as his best-loved prose work, the delightful *Aus dem Leben eines Taugenichts* (*Memoirs of a Good-for-Nothing*), published jointly with *Das Marmorbild* (*The Marble Statue*) in 1826. The seemingly naive autobiography of the good-for-nothing is in fact steeped in mild irony, which lends the tale an affectionate warmth that is unique in German literature. The plot seemlessly fuses together elements from different genres including the picaresque novel, the *Volksbuch* (popular chapbook), the *Bildungsroman*, the *novelle*, and the fairy tale. Similarly, the hero resembles different types, including the picaro and the wandering minstrel (the original title was *Der neue Troubadour—The Modern Troubadour*). By its "indirect" means of representation, the story's circular plot and memorable songs invoke the importance of religious faith and the ultimate sovereignty of the good. Eichendorff wrote several other fine tales including the realistic *novelle* of 1837, *Das Schloss Dürande* (*Castle Durande*), in which he comes to terms with the French Revolution. The theme is also treated in his great political essay, *Der Adel und die Revolution* (*The Nobility and the Revolution*), in which he sets out his conservative liberal creed, criticizing the past failures of the aristocracy and setting out its challenge, which is to exercise full social responsibility.

Eichendorff collected his poetry in 1837 as *Gedichte* (*Poems*), revised this collection in 1843, published *Neue Gedichte* (*New Poems*) in 1847, and continued to write important, posthumously collected poems thereafter. His simple, even casual manner is accomplished by means of seemingly effortless craftsmanship, as in countless lyrics he combines various traditions and forms, including folk poetry, the ballad, the protestant hymn, the baroque lyric, and the Spanish romance. His nuanced language and rhythms lend a profound ambiguity to his symbolism, and so create a powerful sense of emotional depth. He inspires a wide range of moods, among them joy, nostalgia, and longing: *Der frohe Wandersmann* (*The Happy Wanderer*, English translation 1925, original publication date unknown) conveys a sense of cheerful optimism; *Mondnacht* recalls a mystical response to the merging of heaven and earth at twilight; and *Sehnsucht* (*Yearning*) invokes the central theme of German Romanticism. Other poems dwell on danger, magic, madness, and death, displaying a darker, more threatening side to Eichendorff's work, and his late political sonnets, such as *Deutschlands künftiger Retter* (*Germany's Future Savior*), show his continuing commitment to public affairs. As Fortunato says in *Das Marmorbild*. "Die Kunst . . . bespricht und bändigt die wilden Erdengeister, die aus der Tiefe nach uns langen" ("Art discusses and binds . . . the wild earth spirits that lunge at us from the depths").

JEREMY ADLER

See also **Arnim, Achim von; Brentano, Clemens; Chamisso, Adalbert von; Fouqué, Friedrich Heinrich Karl, Baron de la Motte; Friedrich, Caspar David; Görres, Johann Joseph von; Novalis; Schlegel, Friedrich von**

Biography

Born in Schloss Lubowitz, near Ratibor, Upper Silesia, Germany, March 10, 1788. Son of a Catholic aristocratic family. Educated at Katholisches Gymnasium, Breslau, 1801–04; studied law at the University of Halle, 1805–6, at Heidelberg, 1807–8, and in Vienna, 1810–12. Undertook walking tour in the Harz Mountains, 1805. Visted Paris and Vienna, 1808, and Berlin, 1809–10. Served in volunteer forces during Prussian war of liberation, 1813–15. Dispatch clerk, War Ministry, Berlin, 1815. Married Aloysia (Luise) von Larisch, 1815 (died 1855); they had two sons, three daughters. Wrote the novella *Aus dem Leben eines Taugenichts* (*Memoirs of a Good-for-Nothing*), 1816–25 (published 1826). Entered the Prussian civil service, 1816; assessor, 1819–21; served as government councillor, Danzig, 1821, Ministry of Education and Cultural Affairs, Berlin, 1823 and Königsberg (now Kaliningrad, Russia), 1824; returned to Berlin 1831–44. Retired from service, 1844. Visited Vienna, 1846–47; moved to Neisse, Silesia, to live with his daughter, 1855. Died in Neisse, November 26, 1857.

Selected Works

Fiction

Aus dem Leben eines Taugenichts, 1826. Translated by Ronald Taylor as *Memoirs of a Good-for-Nothing*. 1966.
Das Marmorbild, 1826. Translated as "*The Marble Statue*" by F. E. Pierce. In *Fiction and Fancy of German Romance*. 1927.

Poetry

The Happy Wanderer and Other Poems. Translated by Marjorie Rossy. 1925.

Bibliography

Adorno, Theodor W. "Zum Gedächtnis Eichendorffs." In *Noten zur Literatur*. Frankfurt: Suhrkamp, 1958.
Bormann, Alexander von. *Natura Loquitur. Naturpoesie und emblematische Formel bei Joseph von Eichendorff*. Tübingen: Niemeyer, 1968.
Carrdus, Anna. *Classical Rhetoric and the German Poet, 1620 to the Present: A Study of Opitz, Bürger and Eichendorff*. Oxford: Legenda, 1996.
Flores, Angel, ed. *An Anthology of German Poetry from Hölderlin to Rilke in English*. 1965.
Hughes, G. T. *Aus dem Leben eines Taugenichts*. London: Edward Arnold, 1961.
Mann, Thomas. "*Der Taugenichts*." In *Betrachtuingen eines Unpolitischen*. Berlin, 1918.
Riemen, Alfred. *Ansichten zu Eichendorff. Beiträge der Forschung 1958 bis 1988*. Sigmaringen: Thorbecke, 1988.
Schwarz, Egon. *Joseph von Eichendorff*. Boston: Twayne, 1972.
Seidlin, Oskar. "Eichendorff's Symbolic Language," *PMLA*. 72 (1957): 455–61.
Seidlin, Oskar. *Versuche über Eichendorffi*. Göttingen: Vandenhoeck und Ruprecht, 1965.
Stöcklein, Paul. *Joseph von Eichendorff in Selbstzeugnissen und Bilddokumenten*. Reinbeck bei Hamburg: Rowohlt, 1963.
———, ed. *Eichendorff heute*. 2d ed. Darmstadt: Wissenschaftliche Buchgesellschaft, 1968.

ELECTRICITY AND MAGNETISM

Immanuel Kant famously called Benjamin Franklin the "Modern Prometheus," encouraging contemporaries and critics alike to see in Mary Shelley's subtitle for *Frankenstein* (1818) a deliberate allusion to electricity. As this suggests, electricity and its "sister" science, magnetism, both seemed in the Romantic era to promise great wonders. At various times during this period they were held to be capable of alleviating disease, maintaining good health and longevity, and even of bringing the dead back to life.

Though electricity had been discovered much earlier, it was during this period that natural philosophers felt they had succeeded in taming and using it for their own means. Around 1760, electricity was still described as a "subtle fluid," in the eighteenth-century tradition of "imponderable" elements. In 1745, after the invention of the Leyden jar in Holland, electricity could be stored and the charge that the jar emitted was capable of killing animals. While charging up one such jar during a thunderstorm in 1750, Franklin had chanced to discover that lightning was static electricity. In *The Botanic Garden* (1794–95) Erasmus Darwin described Franklin as an imperial adventurer who invaded the skies and "seized" and "Snatch'd" lightning in order to control it himself. In *The History and Present State of Electricity* (1767), Joseph Priestley represented electricity as a realization of the "sublime." Given the pleasure that the ever-increasing magnificence of electricity afforded, its seemingly unbounded utility and significance to humankind, it seemed to Priestley that it should be placed within this category.

Discovering the relation between electricity and magnetism was a major concern in this period. Electricity could reverse a magnet's polarity or magnetize an otherwise neutral body.

Franklin believed that all matter and space was pervaded by electricity and that the imbalance of internal and external electricity charged a body either negatively or positively. The magnet fascinated German *Naturphilosophie* scientists who spoke of a "conflict of electricity" where contending powers of attraction and repulsion represented the vital force of life itself.

Electrical and magnetic experiments could be replicated easily with little expense or equipment, and provided impressive visual effects. The study of electricity and magnetism became a popular science; the success of itinerant lecturers schooled in the Priestlian tradition testifies to this. The element of theatricality was never far away; Priestley's book contains chapters describing "the Most Entertaining Experiments." Abbé Nollet in France amused Louis XVI by giving an electric shock to 180 guards at Versailles and making them all jump simultaneously.

It was the theatrical nature of demonstrations that allowed quack doctors such as James Graham to take advantage of gullible customers. In his heyday, in the 1770s, he practiced from a large expensive house in London, which he named the Temple of Health. The walls of the entrance hall were lined with crutches supposedly thrown off by patients he had cured. Here he housed the infamous "celestial bed" that purportedly cured infertile couples, and the "magnetic throne" that emitted electrical shocks as treatment for a list of ailments. However, Graham's claims did not extend that far beyond those of other more respectable doctors. Alexander von Humboldt gave himself electric shocks daily to increase longevity. Electricity was viewed by some as a panacea, and its applications extended to cases of palsy, cataracts, circulation, removal of obstructions, chilblains, inflamed eyes, tumors, paralysis, rheumatism, deafness, toothache, and numbness. Magnetism was to produce an even greater public furor, with the notorious medical practice of animal magnetism, or mesmerism.

Luigi Galvani believed he had discovered a new kind of electricity contained within all living bodies that became known as "Galvanism." His experiments with dissected frog's legs encouraged him to believe that animals naturally possessed electricity in their nerves and muscles. The same experiment was tried with live as well as dead animals, both warm- and cold-blooded, and amputated human limbs. When Alessandro Volta repeated Galvani's experiments, he found that the animal's convulsion was due simply to the two different metals coming into contact with each other in a damp environment. He went on to construct the first electrical battery, which did not need to be charged beforehand and continually recharged itself. It was this instrument that Humphry Davy later described as "an alarm-bell to experimenters in every part of Europe," and with which he isolated new metals from their alkalies.

Galvani had been careful not to make grand claims for Galvanism but his nephew, Giovanni Aldini, speculated freely. Aldini argued that "animal electricity" was synonymous with vitality, which he believed remained within the body for some time after death. Controversially, Aldini tested this theory with dead human bodies. In 1752, the so-called Murder Act had been passed in Britain, adding the extra punishment of dissection to that of hanging for the crime of murder. It was this provision that Aldini made use of when he visited England. Aldini's experiments produced terrifying results: "I observed strong contractions in all the muscles of the face, which were contorted in so irregular a manner that they exhibited the appearance of the more horrid grimaces." A number of similar attempts were made to imitate Aldini's successes by British surgeons: in 1803 Dr. Joseph Contadine Carpue attempted unsuccessfully to resurrect the body of the executed murderer Michael Carney.

The period thus began with a sense that Franklin's discoveries had opened the door for others. The lack of knowledge about the powers of electricity meant that it was heralded as the potential cure for all ills. By the end of this era, after the work of many distinguished "electricians" and the exposing of many quack practitioners, the mood was one of triumph.

SHARON RUSTON

Bibliography

John Aldini. *An Account of the Late Improvements in Galvanism, with a series of curious and interesting experiments performed before the commissioners of the French National Institute, and repeated lately in London.* 1803.

Bernard I. Cohen, ed. *Benjamin Franklin's Experiments.* Cambridge, Mass.: Harvard University Library, 1941.

Coley, N. G. "The Animal Chemistry Club: Assistant Society to the Royal Society," *Notes and Records of the Royal Society* 22 (1967): 73–85.

Galvani, Luigi. *De Veribus Elicitatis in Moto Musculari Commentarius.* Translated by Robert Roy Montraville Green, Cambridge Mass.: Elizabeth Licht, 1953.

Porter, Roy. *Health for Sale: Quackery in England.* Manchester: Manchester University Press, 1989.

Priestley, Joseph. *The History and Present State of Electricity, with Original Experiments.* 1767.

Morus, Iwan Rhys. *Frankenstein's Children: Electricity, Exhibition, and Experiment in Early nineteenth-Century London.* Princeton, N.J.: Princeton University Press, 1998.

Volta, Alexander. "Account of some of the discoveries made by Mr. Galvani, of Bologna; with experiments and observations on them," *Philosophical Transactions of the Royal Society of London* 83 (1793): 10–44.

———. "On the electricity excited by the mere contact of conducting substances of different kinds," *Philosophical Transactions of the Royal Society of London* 90 (1800): 403–30.

ELOHIM CREATING ADAM 1795

Color print by William Blake

Elohim Creating Adam is one in a series of color prints on twelve different subjects, this one (like several others) bearing the date 1795 in William Blake's hand. Though Blake made up to three copies of some of the prints in this series, only one copy of *Elohim Creating Adam* is known to exist (this surviving copy is located at the Tate Britain Gallery, London). Evidence suggests that Blake delivered this print to his patron Thomas Butts in September 1805. Differing accounts of Blake's means of production have been offered, but the most convincing is explained in Martin Butlin's definitive catalogue of Blake's paintings and drawings: Blake used a water-based medium that he called "fresco" to paint his design, at least in outline, on millboard, and then, taking a print on paper, Blake used both pen-and-ink and watercolor to finish the image. Butts apparently bought eight of the twelve prints in the series, including *Elohim Creating Adam*. The twelve color prints constitute a series whose unity is partly a matter of visual design and partly of conceptual and thematic content, rather than (as in the biblical watercolors Blake executed for Butts in 1804) a concern with a common text or source. The other color prints (all of them offered for sale by Blake to Dawson Turner in 1818) are *Satan Exulting over Eve, God Judging Adam, Lamech and His Two Wives, Naomi Entreating Ruth and Orpah to Return to the Land, Nebuchadnezzar, Newton, Pity, Hecate, The House of Death, The Good and Evil Angels Struggling for Possession of a Child*, and *Christ Appearing to the Apostles after the Resurrection*.

Accounts of the color print's figurative meanings also vary widely, but there is no doubt that this visually powerful image is a profound expression of some of Blake's most consistent intellectual concerns. Elohim is one of the Hebrew names for God, and it is used in connection with the creation of the world in Genesis. As likewise in Blake's *The Book of Urizen* (1794), which was also produced by the technique of color printing, the biblical myth is appropriated polemically for a harshly critical treatment of patriarchal power. From a philosophical point of view, Blake often (as in this color print) represents the formation of the material world as an error. In "The Marriage of Heaven and Hell" (1793) an aphorism indicates very clearly one level of meaning that is consistently engaged by Blake's use of biblical symbols and myths: "all deities reside in the human breast," though some have taken advantage, enslaved the vulgar, and caused them to forget the purely mental existence of gods. Thus, this print's projection of the god of material creation, hovering malevolently above the tormented man, portrays the nightmare of materialism. In early works including *The Book of Urizen*, and more extensively in his later and longer poetic prophecies (*Vala, or The Four Zoas*, 1795; *Milton*, 1804–8; and *Jerusalem*, 1804–18), Blake uses a variety of imagistic and narrative figures to represent the error of materialism. Often, the doctrine of external and inanimate matter (and therefore mortality) broods threateningly above a vulnerable subject. In addition to *Elohim Creating Adam*, in the same series of color prints that configuration appears also in *Satan Exulting over Eve* and *The House of Death*: a dark error (above) threatens a possibly deluded humanity (below).

This same configuration appears likewise in Blake's watercolor paintings on biblical themes, including *The Great Red Dragon and the Woman Clothed with the Sun* (c. 1805–9), where, as Janet A. Warner points out, the hovering and menacing deity above is clearly satanic in effect. In that painting, as in *Elohim Creating Adam*, the figure above (Elohim) and the figure below (Adam) represent deceptively externalized components of one imagining mind. The gazes upward and downward represent contrasting views, and in this way, according to one school of interpretation, Blake humanizes apocalypse in *The Great Red Dragon* as he demonizes the restraints of material creation in *Elohim Creating Adam*. In contrast to the externalized Elohim, Jesus says in Blake's *Jerusalem*: "Within your bosoms I reside." The delusive exteriority of God and his material creation, in

their fiction of absolute difference, constitute the mortal danger and pain which the design represents. Other visual works in which Blake develops that iconography of an exteriorized and mortal illusion include the frontispiece of *For the Sexes: The Gates of Paradise* (1818), where a worm-like caterpillar hovers over a leafy infant. In plate 6 of *Jerusalem* the specter spreads his batwings above the human artisan who is determined to resist the projection. Blake's engraved *Illustrations to the Book of Job* (1826) use this iconographic positioning as a defining motif on every page: the patriarchal deity is projected like a bad dream over the head of the suffering and innocent (but superstitious and deluded) humanity below. In *Elohim Creating Adam*, the worm encasing the body of Adam reveals the deadliness of the doctrine of a supposedly existent god external to human imagining. With the clarity of a companion piece, *Satan Exulting over Eve*, in the same series of color prints, shows Eve bound in the coils of a serpent while Satan floats above her in flames. Similarly, and much later (certainly after 1804), Britain is represented in the form of a woman trapped in the coils of a worm while the sharply pointed wings of a bat threaten her from above (*Jerusalem*, plate 63).

Early (as in the illuminated poem *America*, 1793) and late (as in *Jerusalem*) Blake's language makes clear the national, political, and social meanings of his apparently biblical and otherwise mythological images. *Elohim Creating Adam* participates in the widespread practice of using biblical iconography as a visual code for political polemics, a practice that was popular especially among political radicals in the period of the Civil War and again in Blake's lifetime. A related design is plate 11 of Blake's picture prophecy "Europe" (1794), in which an easily recognizable George III is portrayed with bat wings, a visual symbol of the oppressive codes imposed by "Kings and Priests." The political engagement of the art is evident in topical reference, whereby the tyrant in the *Elohim Creating Adam* is a representation of the monarch, or whereby "Pitt" is "Behemoth" in Blake's painting *Pitt Guiding Behemoth* (c. 1805), also located in the Tate Gallery. Blake produced this print within a year of the Treason Trials of Thomas Holcroft, John Thelwall, and Horne Tooke, the injustice of which caused Blake's fellow members of the Joseph Johnson circle to write polemical books, including Wil-

William Blake, *Elohim Creating Adam*. Reprinted courtesy of AKG.

liam Godwin's *Cursory Strictures on the Charge Delivered by Lord Chief Justice Eyre to the Grand Jury, October 2, 1794*. In a nation with an established church ("state religion," as Blake sometimes called it), the color print's depiction of the imposition of an oppressive code and of the suffering thus inflicted is quite clear.

Furthermore, as Christopher Z. Hobson has shown, Blake's is an art of social meanings much more than topical reference. Stewart Crehan has explained how, in the color prints of 1795, including *Elohim Creating Adam*, the visual coordinates of upper and lower represent not only the mythological poles of heaven and earth (or heaven and hell), but more substantively the idea of *rulers* and *ruled*. The decalogue imposed by the tyrannical (and fictitious) deity is the "stony law" that in *The Marriage of Heaven and Hell* is "stamp[ed] to dust" by Blake's emblematic representation of political revolution.

TERENCE A. HOAGWOOD

Work

Elohim Creating Adam. Color print, finished in ink and watercolor, 43.1 cm × 53.6 cm, on paper 51.5 cm × 59.5 cm. Tate Gallery, London.

Bibliography

Bindman, David. *Blake as an Artist.* Oxford: Phaidon, 1977.
Butlin, Martin. "The Evolution of Blake's Large Color Prints of 1795," In *William Blake: Essays for S. Foster Damon.* Edited by Alvin H. Rosenfeld. Providence, R.I.: Brown University Press, 1969.
Butlin, Martin. *The Paintings and Drawings of William Blake.* vol. 1. New Haven, Conn.: Yale University Press, 1981.
Butlin, Martin. "The Physicality of William Blake: The Large Color Prints of '1795.'" *Huntington Library Quarterly* 52 (1989): 1–17.
Crehan, Stewart. *Blake in Context.* Dublin: Gill and Macmillan, 1984.
Hoagwood, Terence Allan. *Politics, Philosophy, and the Production of Romantic Texts.* DeKalb: Northern Illinois University Press, 1996.
———. *Prophecy and the Philosophy of Mind: Traditions of Blake and Shelly.* Tuscaloosa: University of Alabama Press, 1985.
Hobson, Christopher Z. *The Chained Boy: Orc and Blake's Idea of Revolution.* London: Associated University Presses, 1999.
Kostelanetz [Mellor], Anne T. "Blake's 1795 Color Prints: An Interpretation." In *William Blake: Essays for S. Foster Damon.* Edited by Alvin H. Rosenfeld. Providence, R.I.: Brown University Press, 1969.
Mee, John. *Dangerous Enthusiasm: William Blake and the Culture of Radicalism.* Oxford: Clarendon Press, 1992.
Morton, A. L. *The Everlasting Gospel: A Study in the Sources of William Blake.* London: Lawrence and Wishart, 1958.
Thompson, E. P. *The Making of the English Working Class.* New York: Vintage, 1966.
———. *Witness against the Beast: William Blake and the Moral Law.* New York: New Press, 1993.

EMERSON, RALPH WALDO 1803–1882

American writer

In 1820, during the second year of his studies at Harvard University, Ralph Waldo Emerson began a journal, one which constitutes the clearest record of the eclectic, eccentric, and individual nature of the self-reliant faith of transcendentalism he ultimately embodied. Before his formal studies at Harvard had begun, Emerson's extensive literary knowledge was guided by his affection for "the good old-fashioned march of Milton or Pope and Dryden," and the "moral strains," wittily evinced, of Joseph Addison, Edmund Burke, Henry Fielding, Samuel Johnson, and Jonathan Swift. It was against this backdrop that Emerson's reaction to the newer schools of English Romantic writing seems predictable, as he "thirsted to abuse the poetical character of Mr. Wordsworth."

However, his early openness to what he perceived as less novel and more "honest" Romantic strains, is evident from his enthusiasm for Lord Byron, who, with "proud feelings of independence imparted the wish not to be governed by the opinions and customs of others but to follow the dictates of his own caprice." Emerson's relationship to his journal symbolizes precisely the path of this Byronic ambition from private desire to public enactment.

Initially a private record of his intellectual debate with a rich and worldwide array of religious, philosophical, and literary traditions, it was measured ultimately against his own sense of an emerging independence of thought. Increasingly Emerson's inner and private world of reflection comes to the fore as the journal provides the basis for the lectures and essays which would determine his public persona. In this ultimate choice of vocation Emerson broke free from the restraints of familial expectation and a life in the ministry, and made his once-private world of thought the basis for public action. Early in those journals he identified a conflict between desire and duty which he would soon resolve, when he stated that "our imaginations of all our mental processes are those to whose impulses we are most alive—to whose pleasures we cling most closely. It is with difficulty and reluctance that man brings himself to exercise the reasoning facilities."

Perry Miller stated in 1940 that the extent to which Emerson's "transcendentalist philosophy emerged out of the American background, of how much of it was not appropriated from foreign sources, is a question that concerns the entire American tradition." Subsequently, Lawrence Buell was at pains to point out that the origin of Emerson's ideas cannot be ascribed wholly either to a native "Puritanism that was discarding the husks of dogma," or to a wanton filching of European and eastern traditions of thought. For six generations Emerson's family had been steeped in the culture of Unitarian liberalism in Boston, Massachusetts, and the growing cosmopolitanism, antisectarianism, and tolerance of this tradition was pushed boldly by Emerson to its logical extreme, an extreme that confounded the need to mediate those very institutions and traditions.

Emerson was also deliberately eclectic in his heterodoxy, so as to shift the ground away from potential ascription of dogmatic statement or affiliations of thought by others. In doing so his emphasis falls on his faith in an idea of selfhood which must retain its capacity to "east itself, and find the sun." Such a phrase reflects Emerson's conscious play on the appeal of nonnative traditions as a means of grounding the self in the here and now. The thought of the "east" must always remain merely a tool for clarification of the self's vision, and must lay no claim over that selfhood, even as it serves to liberate and gives it voice. Emerson's rhetoric must of necessity remain similarly slippery, so as to decentre and undermine, through rhetorical play, dogmatic statement, and fixed definitions.

Similarly, the teacher of self-reliance would immediately place himself in a false position as lecturer and essayist if he was not to encourage the individual to do the groundwork for themselves. Rather than encourage others to follow an "Emerson," as they might any dogma, Emerson insists that "every mind must know the whole lesson for itself—must go over the whole ground. What it does not see, what it does not live, it will not know." For Buell this "tactic" of Emerson's reflects the spirit of his "intellectual nomadism," his own "lifestyle of intellectual self-decentering." His underlying faith is in a selfhood that will take from such oscillations between extremes of thought and ideas, its own path, and so retain its independence of thought and native integrity: "The truth is, you can't find any example that will suit you, nor could, if the whole family of Adam should pass in procession before you, for you are a new work of God."

Thus, a search for native sources of Emerson's inspiration will find that the Unitarian church itself led the way toward a radicalism which transcended a mere emphasis on the inherent benevolence of man, and allowed for the announcement of the altogether more heretical view of "the Divine man." The consequences of Emerson's determined pursuit of this goal (bolstered by the supportive writings of figures such as Thomas Carlyle) were that he resigned his Unitarian ministry, citing his contention of the communion ritual. Such mediation was deemed unnecessary, and indeed the very name of the Christian God he had been in service of was gradually rendered inadequate as Emerson addressed himself and directed others towards a source of innate and worldly power which he termed the "Over-Soul."

Thus Emerson's central, and ultimately revered, place as the embodiment of American Romanticism was not produced in isolated contemplation of his American cultural environment, but was a local adaptation of European models. The important shifts in focus which characterize and differentiate Emerson's vision from its continental precursors includes the extent to which social and religious impositions on the free expression of "Divine man" were to be thwarted. All avenues had to be kept open for the development of an unlimited human potential. The "asthma of the mind" (which Emerson later declared William Wordsworth to be suffering from) was in part a reflection of his sense of the important differentiation between the project for the self embodied in the writings of the Lake school, and his own more ambitious sense of its boundlessness. Society itself could also not be ignored though its influence on the developing soul was seen by Emerson to be pernicious. As Buell observes, "Emersonian self-reliance . . . is a way of defining the individual's participation in—and against—the body politic. Self-reliance sanctions an anarchistic secession of the individual from social constraints, justifying it on the ground of an indwelling God-principle or moral sense that all individuals share." Emerson turned away from the Unitarian ministry in order to exemplify and live out a life of intellectual dissent which he sought to announce and publicize through his lectures and essays.

In 1831 Emerson's wife Ellen died, and in search of solace and renewed vigor he journeyed for the first time to Europe during the following year. He undertook to visit Thomas Carlyle, Samuel Taylor Coleridge, and William Wordsworth, as their work had bolstered his own increasingly vehement questioning. His meeting with Carlyle was particularly fruitful, initiating a famed correspondence and a friendship which would continue for forty years. Emerson's return cemented his conviction to focus on public speaking as he declared his intention to voice "no speech, poem, or book that is not entirely & particularly my work." Such a career as man of letters had few American models, but he was determined to leave "aside all tradition, time, place, circumstance" and engage directly with the genius of the contemporary moment. Emerson also sought intellectual provocation rather than discipleship from his new circle of American friends, who included Bronson Allcott, Margaret Fuller, and Henry David Thoreau. Each was deemed "a sort of beautiful enemy" who would force him to move out from the cloying comfort of intellectual repose.

Just as Emerson sought to oscillate between a commitment to a native expression of contemporary American selfhood and a worldwide eclecticism in knowledge and inspiration, the rhetoric of his essays sought to shift the ground from under familiar connotations and assumptions surrounding such terms as *nature* or *self-reliance*. His first public expression of thought, published anonymously, was his long essay *Nature* (1836). In it he presented his theories as to the origin, present state, and ultimate destiny of man's universe, outlining his belief that the redemption of man's imagination was necessary for the successful reintuiting of God's presence in the world. In 1837 he was invited by the Harvard University chapter of *Phi Beta Kappa* to deliver the annual address to the society at Harvard. In "The American Scholar," self-trust was his hopeful rallying call to the graduates, and the speech was declared by Oliver Wendell Holmes to be an American "intellectual declaration of independence."

Controversy followed when this same self-trust was promoted over the claims of America's own religious institutions in Emerson's address in 1838 to the graduating class at the Harvard Divinity School. Emerson was subsequently banned from speaking at Harvard for thirty years, and declared that the truth of Christ's teachings had been foreclosed and monopolized by modern religion. The tendency towards a cult of the person around Christ needed to be abandoned in favor of a self-trust which needed no mediating institution other than that of man's soul.

Emerson's first collection, *Essays*, appeared in 1841. His journal entries, sermons, and lectures were secularized and reconstituted as each essay examined man's central place as a conduit for empowerment and potential. Further periods of personal tragedy tested and had an impact upon Emerson's positive philosophizing, especially with the death of his beloved son in 1842. In "Experience," published in his second series of *Essays* (1844), a radical skepticism is given full voice as he analyzes the dark side of man's subjectivity. A second trip to Europe in 1847 saw him return with a focus on public events. Prior to the American Civil War, Emerson willingly courted unpopularity in his denunciations of American slavery while he viewed the war itself ultimately as a harsh intellectual and moral restorative "to these languid and dissipated populations." Lecture tours across America ensured Emerson's growing renown in his own lifetime, a fame which increased rapidly to the point of canonization at the time of his death in 1882.

The deification of Emerson as the Sage of Concord by the end of the nineteenth century received its inevitable but concerted backlash. American modernist writers and New Critics in the 1920s and 1930s, such as Irving Babbitt, T. S. Eliot, H. L. Mencken, Allen Tate, and Ivor Winters, reacted against his embodiment of a "genteel" tradition in American philosophy and writing. But this in turn was a critical tag inherited from George Santayana's hugely influential essay on Emerson written in 1911. The 1960s saw the beginning of the publication of Emerson's unexpurgated journals and notebooks, which gradually punctured a reliance on this inherited image and so allowed for his reevaluation and a subsequent resurgence of critical interest.

IAN D. COPESTAKE

Biography

Born in Boston, Massachusetts, May 25, 1803. Son of Rev. William Emerson, Unitarian clergyman and arts patron, and Ruth Haskins. Educated at Boston Public Latin School and Harvard University, 1817–21. Worked as schoolteacher while studying part-time at Harvard Divinity School, 1820s. Licensed as a Unitarian preacher, 1826. Ordained junior pastor of Second Church, Boston (Unitarian); married Ellen Louisa Tucker, 1829. Suffered depression after Ellen's death from tuberculosis, February 1831; resigned from the Unitarian ministry after spiritual crisis, 1832. Made first visit to Europe; met Thomas Carlyle, Samuel Taylor Coleridge, and William Wordsworth, 1832. Returned to the United States, 1833; settled in Concord, Massachusetts, 1834. Married Lydia Jackson, 1835: two sons, two daughters. *Nature* published anonymously, September 1836. Delivered Harvard Divinity School *Address*, July 15, 1838. Leader of the Transcendental Club from 1836; contributor to the club's journal *The Dial*, 1840–44 (editor, 1842–44). *Essays: First Series*, published March 1841. Son Waldo died, 1842. *Essays: Second Series*, published October 1844. Lectured in England, 1847–48; *Representative Men* published, 1849. Active in the abolitionist movement, 1850s. LL.D., Harvard University, 1866. Died in Concord, Massachusetts, April 27, 1882.

Selected Works

Collections

The Collected Works of Ralph Waldo Emerson. 12 vols. Edited by Alfred R. Ferguson, Jean Ferguson Carr, and Douglas E. Wilson. Cambridge, Mass.: Belknap Press of Harvard University Press, 1971.

The Correspondence of Emerson and Carlyle. Edited by Joseph Slater. New York: Columbia University Press, 1964.

The Early Lectures of Ralph Waldo Emerson. 3 vols. Edited by Stephen Whicher, Robert Spiller, and Wallace Williams. Cambridge, Mass.: Belknap Press of Harvard University Press, 1960–72.

Emerson in His Journals. Edited by Joel Porte. Cambridge, Mass.: Belknap Press of Harvard University Press, 1982.

The Journals and Miscellaneous Notebooks of Ralph Waldo Emerson. 16 vols. Edited by William H. Gilman, Alfred R. Ferguson, and Ralph H. Orth. Cambridge: Mass.: Belknap Press of Harvard University Press, 1960–82.

The Letters of Ralph Waldo Emerson. 6 vols. Edited by Ralph L. Rusk. New York: Columbia University Press, 1939.

Selections from Ralph Waldo Emerson. Edited by Stephen Whicher. Boston: Houghton Mifflin, 1957.

Bibliography

Paul, Sherman. *Emerson's Angle of Vision: Man and Nature in American Experience.* Cambridge, Mass.: Harvard University Press, 1952.

Poirier, Richard. *The Renewal of Literature: Emersonian Reflections.* New York: Random House, 1987.

Porte, Joel. *Representative Man: Ralph Waldo Emerson in His Time.* New York: Oxford University Press, 1979.

Porte, Joel, and Sandra Morris, eds. *The Cambridge Companion to Ralph Waldo Emerson.* Cambridge: Cambridge University Press, 1999.

Robinson, David M. *Emerson and the Conduct of Life: Pragmatism and Ethical Purpose in the Later Work.* Philadelphia: University of Pennsylvania Press, 1993.

Rusk, Ralph L. *The Life of Ralph Waldo Emerson.* New York: Charles Scribner, 1949.

Whicher, Stephen E. *Freedom and Fate: An Inner Life of Ralph Waldo Emerson.* Philadelphia: University of Pennsylvania Press, 1953.

Yoder, R. A. *Emerson and the Orphic Poet in America.* Berkeley and Los Angeles: University of California Press, 1978.

EPIC

The epic presents narrative on a vast scale, centering around the actions of a hero of national significance whose deeds have profound consequences for a whole culture. Epics transmitted by oral tradition can be found in preliterate cultures across time and around the world; European folk epics include *El Cid, Le Chanson de Roland* (*The Song of Roland*), and the *Niebelungenlied* (*Song of the Niebelungs*). The foundational epics of the European tradition, the *Iliad* and the *Odyssey* of Homer, probably originated in oral tradition. Virgil's *Aeneid* began the literary tradition of imitating Homer's epics. This tradition continued in the Renaissance with Luiz Camões's *The Lusiads* (1572), Torquato Tasso's *Gerusalemme Liberata* (*Jerusalem Delivered*, 1581); and John Milton's *Paradise Lost* (1667). The epic has frequently been accorded the highest place among literary genres.

Few literary works can, in the strict generic sense adhered to by those listed above, be called epics; even Dante Alighieri's *La divina commedia* (*Divine Comedy*, 1310–14) is not a traditional epic. The epic shares many specific conventions derived from Homer: it involves supernatural "machinery" (divinities, angels, or monsters that participate in the action); it begins, evoking the Muse, *in medias res* (in the middle of relevant events); and the hero eventually tells what came before the start of the narrative in a protracted flashback. Shipwrecks, descents into hell, panoramic views of futurity: the list of such conventions is quite long. The mock epic makes fun of the number of these shared conventions, their often arbitrary and trivial nature, and the effort expended by epic poets to include them all.

Never fitting all these criteria, many Romantic poems show intense awareness of this epic tradition. The Scottish poet James

Macpherson fraudulently published his *Fingal* (1792) as a recently "discovered" traditional epic by the legendary third-century bard Ossian; and Robert Southey pioneered the Romantic epic in England with *Joan of Arc* (1796), on a theme inspired by the French Revolution. Lord Byron would lampoon Southey concerning his prolific composition of epics, but the revolution and the rise and fall of Napoleon Bonaparte inspired an even greater number of epics in France than appeared in England. Edgar Quinet wrote *Napoléon* (1836) and *Prométhée* (*Prometheus*, 1838). Alphonse de Lamartine wrote *Jocelyn* (1836), an intimate epic written in the form of a verse diary, and *La Chute d'un Ange* (*The Fall of an Angel*, 1838). Alfred de Vigny's *Héléna* (1822), an epic in three cantos about the Greek insurrection against the Turks is inspired by Byron; *Eloa* (1824), showing the influence of both Victor Hugo and John Milton, is one of Vigny's finest poems.

Milton's influence on British poets was even stronger. John Keats's *Hyperion: A Fragment* (1819) and *The Fall of Hyperion: A Dream* (1819) are both fragmentary epics that attain briefly to a Miltonic grandeur. William Blake's "epic prophecies," including *Milton* (1804) and *Jerusalem* (1804–20), are always intensely aware of Milton. These poems are far shorter than any conventional epic, but their complex density, internal structuring, and notorious difficulty make them forerunners of such shorter modern epics as T. S. Eliot's *The Waste Land* (1922).

Miltonic epic had entered the German tradition with the great success of Friedrich Gottlieb Klopstock's *Der Messias* (*The Messiah*, 1748–73). But if the mania for epic writing that seized England and France in the period was less visible in Germany, important epic poetry was certainly being written there. Johann Wolfgang von Goethe's *Faust* (1808–32) is a hybrid work that mixes the very genres Goethe and Johann Christoph Friedrich von Schiller took pains to distinguish in their essay "Über epische und dramatische Dichtung" ("On Epic and Dramatic Poetry," 1797); yet *Faust* is as epic a work, in terms of its scope and importance, as the period produced. A less ambitious and more conventional Goethe poem, *Hermann und Dorothea* (1797), anticipates the vernacular language and the subject matter drawn from common life in William Wordsworth's *The Prelude* (1805). *The Prelude*, often cited as the greatest English epic of the period, concerns the growth of the poet's own mind. In its turn it antici-

pates later epics, notably Walt Whitman's *Leaves of Grass* (1855), in its treatment of the epic subject.

The Romantic period gets its name from the influence of Renaissance romances such as Ludovico Ariosto's *Orlando Furioso* (1516)—episodic, allegorical, fantastic variations on the epic form. Edmund Spenser's *Faerie Queene* (1590–95) brought this tradition to English poetry. Such Romantic-era works as Mary Tighe's *Psyche* (1805) are very Spenserian and retain many epic conventions, but more influential were Sir Walter Scott's less derivative verse romances, such as *The Lay of the Last Minstrel* (1805) and *Marmion* (1808). Scott's hugely successful work had a very marked influence on Lord Byron, whose great epic *Don Juan* (1819–24) is at once a wildly funny mock epic and a dark, nihilistic work of genuinely epic stature. Byron would surpass not only Scott, but even Goethe and Wordsworth, as the Romantic writer of epics whose work had the most influence on European poetry, from Vigny to Elizabeth Barrett Browning, whose *Aurora Leigh* (1856) is both attracted and repelled by his influence, to Aleksandr Pushkin, whose masterpiece *Evgeny Onegin* (*Eugene Onegin*, 1833) is thoroughly Byronic.

The novel, often posited as the successor to the epic, aspires at times to the epic tradition. The epic came to have a more pervasive influence via the historical romances of Scott, and in novels that followed, from the greater historical depth of Alessandro Manzoni's *I Promessi Sposi* (*The Betrothed*, 1827) and George Eliot's *Romola* (1863) to the more allegorical style of Herman Melville's *Moby-Dick* (1851).

JOHN M. ANDERSON

Bibliography

Bloom, Harold. "The Internalization of Quest Romance." In *Romanticism and Consciousness*. Edited by Harold Bloom. New York: W. W. Norton, 1970.

Curran, Stuart. *Poetic Form and British Romanticism*. New York: Oxford University Press, 1986.

Calin, William. *A Muse for Heroes: Nine Centuries of the Epic in France*. Toronto: University of Toronto Press, 1983.

Vogler, Thomas A. *Preludes to Vision: The Epic Venture in Blake, Wordsworth, Keats and Hart Crane*. Berkeley and Los Angeles: University of California Press, 1971.

Wilkie, Brian. *Romantic Poets and Epic Tradition*. Madison: University of Wisconsin Press, 1965.

EROICA 1803

Symphony No. 3 by Ludwig van Beethoven

Ludwig van Beethoven's work on the *Eroica* Symphony coincided with a personal crisis brought about by his confrontation of the progressive deterioration of his hearing. He described his anguish in a document now known as the *Heiligenstadt Testament* (1802), in which he confessed his despair, his contemplation of suicide, and his resolve to endure his wretched existence for the sake of his art. Additional evidence that Beethoven experienced a period of artistic reassessment around 1802 appeared in his comments about composing in a "new way" or "an entirely new manner." Beethoven's work on the *Eroica* occurred during this period of psychological struggle and artistic renewal,

1802–3. Thus, the symphony delineated a major turning point in the composer's creative career, marking the emergence of his heroic style. Because of its forcefulness and originality as well as its unprecedented expansion of the genre, the *Eroica* also denoted an important transition between eighteenth-century practices and the Romantic notion of the symphony as an expressive ideal. Repercussions from Beethoven's monumental accomplishment influenced composers, theorists, critics, and aestheticians throughout the nineteenth century.

Beethoven's intended dedication of the *Eroica* to Napoleon Bonaparte captured the imaginations of Romantic writers. A dramatic episode recounted by Ferdinand Ries, in which Beethoven flew into a rage and ripped the title page bearing the name "Buonaparte" upon hearing that Napoleon had proclaimed himself emperor, became a monumental testimony to the composer's abhorrence of tyranny. While the anecdote is credible, it assumed mythological proportions, even though it was not the last incident surrounding the connections between the *Eroica* and Napoleon. At a later date, the words "Intitulata Bonaparte" ("entitled Bonaparte") were erased from Beethoven's manuscript of the title page, though the words "Geschrieben auf Bonaparte" ("written upon Bonaparte") were added in pencil. Three months later, Beethoven wrote to the publisher Breitkopf und Härtel that the symphony was really titled "Bonaparte." Beethoven's apparent ambivalence could have resulted from a variety of circumstances, including his conflict of loyalties between patriotism for Austria and admiration of French republicanism, his scorn for the fickleness of the Viennese public attitude toward Napoleon, his plans to relocate to Paris, Prince Franz Joseph von Lobkowitz's offer of four hundred gulden for the work, and the outbreak of the Franco-Austrian War in 1805. Upon publication in 1806, the symphony was dedicated to Prince Lobkowitz and bore the title *Sinfonia Eroica . . . composta per festeggiare il sovvenire di un grand Uomo* ("*Eroica* Symphony . . . composed to celebrate the memory of a great man").

Beethoven's exposure to French revolutionary music in Vienna influenced the development of his heroic style. The militaristic quality of this music, its overall tone of seriousness and grandeur, and its emphasis on massive sonorities had an impact on Beethoven's music. Michael Broyles has traced the synthesis of French and Viennese sources in Beethoven's orchestral writing during the first decade of the nineteenth century, the period of the *Eroica* and the development of Beethoven's heroic style.

Through the *Eroica*, Beethoven infused the classical symphonic style with aggressive energy, dramatic struggle, and a deep expressiveness characteristic of his emerging heroic style. In so doing, he thoroughly exploited the flexibility of sonata form, expanding that structural process far beyond the boundaries defined by Franz Joseph Haydn and Wolfgang Amadeus Mozart. The massive scale of the first movement transformed the balance and proportions of classical sonata form. Rather than the three-section exposition, development, recapitulation of that formal process, the *Eroica* extended the coda to serve as a fourth major section. Several musical details play a critical role in the expansive plan of the movement. Beginning with the initial presentation of the first theme in the key of E-flat, a C-sharp in the melodic line obscures the strength of tonic as the theme unfolds with an unbalanced phrase structure. The first theme must await the end of the coda for a presentation over clear tonic and dominant harmonies with regular four-bar phrases. Additional widely discussed features within the movement include the introduction of a new theme in the development section and a clash of tonic and dominant harmonies at the close of the development as the horn presents the first theme in tonic before the harmony resolves to the home key for the recapitulation.

Beethoven's interest in Napoleon and French revolutionary music is perhaps most apparent in the slow second movement, entitled *Marcia funebre*. Through allusions to the French funeral march and through the incorporation of such clichés as fanfares, drumrolls, and short runs, Beethoven integrated the French style with Viennese conventions to create an outpouring of grief that transcended both traditions.

The *Eroica* was the first symphony to expand the ternary dance structure characteristic of the third movement to balance the scope of the remainder of the symphony. Innovative features include a delayed confirmation of tonic, a trio section dominated by horns, and an unexpected *alla breve* near the end of the final statement of the scherzo.

The *Eroica* finale has sparked lively commentary not only because of its unique formal design but also because of its origins in the Piano Variations, op.35 (as well as the ballet *The Creatures of Prometheus* and the contradanse). The movement follows a series of variation-like episodes based on two themes—the *Basso del Tema* and a treble theme. Since both themes are varied and elaborated, the movement includes developmental techniques characteristic of sonata procedures. The movement also incorporates fugal elements and a spirited *alla marcia*.

Beethoven wrote hundreds of pages of sketches and drafts for the *Eroica* during 1803 in a single large volume designated Landsberg 6 (known as the *Eroica* sketchbook). Formerly located in the Deutsch Staatsbibliothek in Berlin, the sketches have been housed at the Bibliotéka Jagiellonska in Krakow since World War II. A second set of sketches, the Wielhorsky sketchbook, which appeared in 1962, contains sketches that predate Landsberg 6, with early *Eroica* sketches dating from 1802. Evidence in the Wielhorsky sketchbook has led Lewis Lockwood to argue that the finale of the *Eroica* served as the point of departure for the entire symphony. He has further concluded that both the principal theme of the first movement and the treble theme of the finale originated in the *Basso del Tema*.

Though initial criticism of the *Eroica* complained of its inordinate length, extreme difficulty, and lack of unity, later writers received it more favorably. Following the Romantic tendency to associate music with extramusical events or ideas, writers such as Adolph Bernhard Marx described detailed programs for the symphony, frequently drawing upon metaphors associated with Napoleon, battle scenes, or Homeric heroes. Richard Wagner reflected some of his own aesthetic goals by identifying the *Eroica* with an ideal hero instead of a real person. Other writers focused on psychological interpretations, claiming that Beethoven expressed his inner being or his spirit through his music. Analysts who have sought motivic connections and interrelationships within the symphony reflect a nineteenth- and early-twentieth-century emphasis on organicism and an inner growth process.

As Beethoven composed the *Eroica*, the masterpiece that announced the beginning of his heroic style, he also forged a new symphonic ideal for succeeding generations of Romantic composers. His transformation of the symphony genre was perhaps one of his most striking accomplishments.

RENEE MCCACHREN

Work

Symphony No. 3 (*Eroica*) in E-flat Major, op. 55. Ludwig van Beethoven. Dedicated to Prince Franz Joseph von Lobkowitz. First performed April 7, 1805.

Bibliography

Broyles, Michael. *Beethoven: The Emergence and Evolution of Beethoven's Heroic Style*. New York: Excelsior Music Publishing, 1987.

Burnham, Scott. *Beethoven Hero*. Princeton, N.J.: Princeton University Press, 1995.

———. "On the Programmatic Reception of Beethoven's *Eroica* Symphony." *Beethoven Forum* 1 (1992): 1–24.

Downs, Philip G. "Beethoven's 'New Way' and the *Eroica*," in *The Creative World of Beethoven*. Edited by Paul Henry Lang. New York: W. W. Norton, 1970.

Earp, Lawrence. "Tovey's 'Cloud' in the First Movement of the *Eroica*: An Analysis Based on Sketches for the Development and Coda." *Beethoven Forum* 2 (1993): 55–84.

Floros, Constantin. *Beethovens Eroica und Prometheus-Musik*. Wilhelmshaven: Heinrichshofens Verlag, 1978.

Grove, George. *Beethoven and His Nine Symphonies*. London: Novello, and New York: H. W. Gray, 1896.

Hopkins, Antony. *The Nine Symphonies of Beethoven*. London: Heinemann, and Seattle: University of Washington Press, 1981.

Lockwood, Lewis. *Beethoven: Studies in the Creative Process*. Cambridge, Mass.: Harvard University Press, 1992.

Marx, Adolph Bernhard. "Die Sinfonia eroica und die Idealmusik," in *Ludwig van Beethoven: Leben und Schaffen*. Berlin: O. Janke, 1859.

Meikle, Robert B. "Thematic Transformation in the first Movement of Beethoven's *Eroica* Symphony," *Music Review* 32, no. 3 (1971): 205–18.

Morgan, Robert P. "Coda as Culmination: The First Movement of the 'Eroica' Symphony," in *Music Theory and the Exploration of the Past*. Edited by Christopher Hatch and David W. Bernstein. Chicago: University of Chicago Press, 1993.

Palisca, Claude V. "French Revolutionary Models for Beethoven's *Eroica* Funeral March," in *Music and Context*. Edited by Anne D. Shapiro. Cambridge, Mass.: Cambridge University Press, 1985.

Sipe, Thomas. *Beethoven: Eroica Symphony*. Cambridge: Cambridge University Press, 1998.

Solomon, Maynard. *Beethoven*. New York: Schirmer, 1977.

Tovey, Donald Francis. *Essays in Musical Analysis*. Vol. 1, *Symphonies*. London: Oxford University Press, 1935.

ESPRONCEDA Y DELGADO, JOSÉ DE 1808–1842

Spanish poet and revolutionary

José de Espronceda y Delgado did not radically depart from his neoclassical education until his return from exile in England and France to Madrid after an 1832 amnesty. His early works include an incomplete epic (*Pelayo*) and adaptations of Ossian.

From the mid-1830s onward Espronceda became increasingly radical in both politics and literature. In the former field, his views were not uncharacteristic of the Spanish far left. He enthused about the ideas of the economist Alvaro Flórez Estrada (who argued that since land was not a product of labor, it should not be sold on the open market). In 1840, he helped found the nascent republican movement, and became a member of parliament in 1842.

His explicit utterances about literature were themselves not untypical, emphasizing liberty and a fresh, youthful new mode of writing for the new age. The literary magazine he established with his friends in 1841, *El Pensamiento* (*Thought*), contained reviews very similar to those published elsewhere.

The drastic renewal of his literary style in 1834–35 came against the background of an unorthodox private life; his lover, Teresa, had publicly abandoned her husband and children to be with him, though they in turn were to separate in 1836. Her subsequent death was to haunt him, as is clear from the second canto of his *El diablo mundo* (*The Devil World*, 1840–), dedicated "A Teresa."

The longest of his later works, the frenetic historical novel *Sancho Saldaña* (1834), is notable for its depiction of the eponymous Byronic protagonist and his female counterpart, the increasingly insane Zoraida, torn between extremes of love and evil from which they cannot release themselves.

A taste for the absurd is evident in his short story "La pata de palo" ("The Wooden Leg," 1835). A Hoffmann-like tale of an obsessive fashion for fine wooden legs develops into a playfully comic vision of a man carried across the world in perpetual motion by his new appendage. Detached humor is also central to Espronceda's 1834 play. *Ni el tío ni el sobrino* (*Neither the Uncle nor the Nephew*), which met with critical incomprehension and rejection by Mariano José de Larra. Written with his close friend, Ros de Olano, the play has been more valued by critics of the latter than those of Espronceda. Its puppetlike characterization and hollow versions of sentimental *coups de théâtres* are echoed in the works of another companion, Miguel de los Santos Álvarez.

Indeed, Espronceda's literary strength (and that of those two close friends) lies in violent confrontations with prevailing sensibilities. His greatest achievements in this direction are to be found in his poetry. Perhaps influenced by Victor Hugo as well as by ideas about a typically Spanish literature, Espronceda frequently deploys radical polyphony, shifting rapidly and expressively from one meter or verse length or style to another with powerful rhyming schemes. His verse is often robust and sensual, featuring dynamic narration or discourse, and at times making use of colloquial language. The extreme swings in tone, genre, and subject within *El diablo mundo* have been dubbed polymorphic.

Such dynamism serves to express the energetic verve of the poet's mind and creations as they challenge the reader. A fascination with what might be called "limit cases" emerges with the striking lexis of the songs of 1835 and onward. As Robert Marrast points out, while echoing Pierre Jean de Béranger, Espronceda's beggar is pointedly unsentimentalized, just as his pirate is a voice of freedom unqualified by Byronic loss. The consideration of a prisoner condemned to death examines all perspectives except the man's crime. Most powerfully, the shifting angles of "El verdugo" ("The Executioner," 1835) provide a disconcerting, multidimensional, and all-encompassing assertion of metaphysical as well as social evil. Thomas Lewis's discussion of another poem, "A una estrella" ("To a Star," 1838), shows how the poet's twin identification and distance from the star ends in irresolution.

The long poem *El estudiante de Salamanca* (The Student of Salamanca), published in full in 1840, is a nightmarish vision of a Don Juan figure, Félix, led to his death by a ghostly female who may be his dead, innocent lover Elvira. Critics have emphasized the Promethean aspects of Félix's demand for knowledge and refusal to succumb even at the point of death. More recently, attention has been directed to the parody of Romantic synthesis, redemption, and love deaths in the succubus's fatal kissing of the libertine. It may be argued that the lack of any Byronic loss in the Félix figure emphasizes the absence of contact between two opposing ideals (himself and Elvira). Dialectical thought based on the interplay of such ideals is itself a trap. Such radical musings feature too in "A Jarifa en una orgía" ("To Jarifa in an Orgy," 1840), where an alternative is suggested. Despairing of materialism or spiritual values, the poet seeks love in the arms of the promiscuous Jarifa who has experienced the same disillusionment. Similar sentiments may lie behind the comic but obscene and desensitized Dido and Aeneas fragments, probably a collaboration with Álvarez.

The Faustian epic *El diablo mundo* tells of how an elderly man exhausted by the incomprehensible world has his wish fulfilled and is transformed by a sexualized lady of death into the immortal but absolutely innocent and undressed Adán (Adam). Adán must wander the world forever and rapidly encounters evil. As Ros (to whom the poem is dedicated) points out in the prologue, the work directly echoes Johann Wolfgang von Goethe's *Faust*; it also draws on Lord Byron's *Don Juan*, John Milton's *Paradise Lost*, and the tradition of the innocent in a fallen world. However, the idea behind the work is original. As Ros indicates, unlike in Goethe the Faustian transformation carries no conditions, another example of a limit case. Espronceda directly confronts innocence with the Picaresque world of 1840s Spain (as does Álvarez in *María*), combining, as Thomas E. Lewis suggests, social and metaphysical concerns. Espronceda's Satan, explicitly a projection of the human mind, strikingly dwells on a radical uncertainty about himself and about God. It may be speculated that Espronceda wishes to explore what Ros called the compendium of life once the idea of resolution through dialectical thought had been abandoned. As in a more subdued way in *El estudiante*, the poem's robust Romantic irony helps focus attention on the text's genesis in the poetic mind, here underlined by the strikingly abrupt interpolation of the autobiographical second canto. The poet's death in 1842 meant that the poem was never completed.

ANDREW GINGER

Biography

Born in Almendralejo, Spain, March 25, 1808. Son of Camilo Espronceda, army officer. Educated at the Colegio de San Mateo, Madrid, 1821–23. Cofounded the Academia del Mirto and was founder member of Sociedad Numantina, a political secret society, 1823. Arrested in 1824 and sent to internal exile in the monastery of San Francisco de Gualajara, 1825. Emigrated to Portugal, either because of political harassment or because of desire for adventure, 1827. Possibly met Teresa Mancha for the first time there. Expelled from Portugal; traveled to London, 1827 and began passionate affair with Teresa Mancha, who married Gregorio del Bayo in 1829. Lived in France, 1828–33; participated in the 1830 revolution and the subsequent aborted liberal invasion of Spain. Returned to London, 1832; probably renewed relationship with Teresa. Returned to Spain at political amnesty, 1833; involved with Parnasillo literary group; lived with his mother, installing Teresa in a neighboring house. Joined the Guardia Real but was expelled and sent to internal exile in Cuéllar. Teresa gave birth to a daughter, 1834. Joined the National Militia; arrested and sent into internal exile to Badajoz, 1834. Founding editor of *El Siglo*, 1834, which was shutdown by censors. Founding member of the Ateneo, 1835. Separated from Teresa, 1836. Member of executive committee of the Liceo, 1837; held chair of comparative literature there, 1839. Stood for election for Progressive Liberals in Badajoz, 1838. Teresa died, 1839. Shortly afterward became involved with Carmen de Osorio. Published *El Estudiante de Salamanca*, 1840. Founding member of Republican Party; cofounder of journal *El Pensamiento*; named secretary of legation in Low Countries, 1841. Engaged to marry Bernarda de Beruete, 1842. Took seat in Parliament as a replacement member (*suplente*), 1842. Died, probably from croup, in Madrid, May 23, 1842.

Selected Works

Collections

Poesías de Don José de Espronceda. 1840.
Obras completas. Edited by Jorge Campos. Madrid: Atlas, 1954.
Poesías líricas y fragmentos épicos. Edited by Robert Marrast. Madrid: Castalia, 1970.
El estudiante de Salamanca. El diablo mundo. Edited by Robert Marrast. Madrid: Castalia, 1978.
El estudiante de Salamanca and Other Poems. Edited by Richard Cardwell, London: Taresis, 1980.
El diablo mundo. Poesía. El estudiante de Salamanca. Edited by Jaime Gil de Biedma. Madrid: Alianza, 1987.
El diablo mundo, El pelayo, Poesías. Edited by Domingo Ynduráin. Madrid: Cátedra, 1992.

Prose
Sancho Saldaña. 1834.
"El pato de palo." 1835.
"El ministerio Mendizábal." 1836.

Drama
Niel tío niel sobrlno. 1934.

Poetry
Dates given here are for the complete publication of the poems. In several cases, composition occurred earlier and/or parts of the poems were published earlier.
"El verdugo." 1835.
"A Jarifa en una orgía." 1840.
"A una estrella." 1840.
El estudiante de Salamanca. 1840 (fragments published in preceding years). Translated by C. K. Davies as *The Student of Salamanca*, with introduction by Richard Cardwell. Warminster: Aris and Phillips, 1991.
Pelayo. 1840 (composed 1825–35; fragments published 1835).
El diablo mundo. 1842 (sections published 1840–42).

Bibliography

Bretz, Mary Lee. "Espronceda's *El diablo mundo* and Romantic Irony," *Revista de Estudios Hispánicos* 16 (1982): 257–74.
Casalduero, Joaquín. *Espronceda*. Madrid: Gredos, 1961.
Ginger, Andrew. "Sueños de la razón" and "But I Have Bad Dreams: *El estudiante de Salamanca*," in *Political Revolution and Literary Experiment in the Spanish Romantic Perio (1830–1850)*. Lampeter, Wales: Edwin Mellen Press, 1999.
Ilie, Paul. "Espronceda and the Romantic Grotesque," *Studies in Romanticism* 11 (1972): 94–112.

Larubia Prado, Francisco. "Texto y tiempo en *El estudiante de Salamanca*: La impostura de la historia literaria y del romanticismo español," *Revista Hispánica Moderna* 46 (1993): 5–18.

Lewis, Thomas E. "Contradictory Explanatory Systems in Espronceda's Poetry: The Social Genesis and Structure of *El Diablo Mundo*," *Ideologies and Literature* 4 (1983): 11–45.

Mandrell, James. "The Literary Sublime in Spain: Meléndez Valdés amd Espronceda," *Modern Language Notes* 106 (1991): 294–313.

Marrast, Robert. *Espronceda et son temps*. Paris: Klincksieck, 1975.

Martinengo, Alessandro. *Polimorfismo nel "Diablo mundo" d'Espronceda*. Torino: Bottega d'Erasmo, 1962.

Rees, Margaret. *El estudiante de Salamanca*. London: Grant and Cutler, 1979.

Sebold, Russell P. "El infernal arcano de Félix de Montemar," *Hispanic Review* 46 (1978): 447–64.

Vasari, S. "Aspectos religioso-políticos de la ideología de Espronceda," *Bulletin Hispanique* 82 (1980): 94–149.

ESSAYS: FIRST SERIES 1841

Ralph Waldo Emerson

Ralph Waldo Emerson's first collection of essays was published in March 1841, and contains the following sequence of works: "History," "Self-Reliance," "Compensation," "Spiritual Laws," "Love," "Friendship," "Prudence," "Heroism," "The Over-Soul," "Circles," "Intellect," and "Art." Prior to the volume's publication Emerson described it as merely a "raft" ("only boards and logs tied together"). His dissatisfaction with the work grew from the manner in which it was put together. This presented a conflict with the ideas that the work as a whole sought to express. He continued to revise it for its reprint in 1847, when it gained its more familiar title of *Essays: First Series*.

The material for his collection was garnered from lectures he had given over the previous eight years and entries in the journals which he had begun in 1820. As an enemy of imitation and repetition, and a champion of innovation over recollection, his method of reclaiming material from his past irked and depressed him. What had once been recorded as spontaneous thought now seemed to him rendered deathly by his mechanical trawling of his past. Indeed the first sentence of the opening essay of the volume had been claimed from a source which was five years old. With the exception of "Circles," all the essays had been used in part or in their entirety within lectures. However, the manner in which Emerson respun the many strands of his recorded thought—for no extract from previous sources was repeated verbatim—created a new unity. Indeed, it is the complex symmetries of organization revealing the volume's "vehicle or art," which have been the continuing subject of revealing critical commentary.

The volume derives unity from the fact that the essays as a whole act as something of a guidebook for the culture of the soul. However, a tension is maintained by the essays' celebration of the active will of man and a salutary acknowledgement of the need to remain open to a more passive acceptance of guidance or inspiration. The volume puts forward a belief in a doctrine of self-culture which is justified and promoted as a vital end of human activity. For Emerson, such a belief had been growing ever since his entry into the Unitarian ministry in the mid-1820s. *Essays: First Series* is the fruitful expression of this emergent conviction, apparent in his lectures of the late 1830s. Increasingly, he was led by a strong need to promote a liberating empowerment of the individual against inherited Calvinist notions of innate depravity. With a rationale based on an appeal to man's intuitive knowledge of God's truth, Emerson sought to transcend the restrictions placed on individual thought and conduct by conventional morality, promoting instead a no less vigorous personal responsibility for moral progress. In *Essays* he dealt with the contradictions and pitfalls inherent in such self-reliance, a fact suggested by his interconnection of opposites through the pairings of his essay titles. Thus, he sought to provide a flexible yet uncompromising and practical framework which suggested the possibility of living a life in accordance with spiritual truths.

Essays is a profoundly religious work, and Emerson makes extensive use of religious terms, images, and allusions. However, his extensive revisions indicate a decisive movement in the opposite direction, away from traditional religious references and usage. Thus "God" becomes "the internal ocean," among a variety of other terms, in "Self-Reliance." In transferring active powers away from God the essays reveal the gradual secularization of Emerson's thought and language. Thus, by the late 1830s, Emerson had begun his attempt to break away from conventional religious usage which he had persisted with even in *Nature* (1836), despite its nontraditional and controversial subject matter. He was determined in the *Essays* not to communicate a set of propositions, for such an idea was anathema to a man who despised limitation of thought and action. Instead he sought to encourage and exemplify a specific intellectual attitude and style of thought which his own rhetorical performance was a vital means of conveying.

Emerson's rhetoricism is an integral part of the iconoclastic, self-reliant, yet morally committed intellectual approach he sought to promote. Emerson was influenced in finding his own style and persona by the example of European masters of the essay-writing form, Francis Bacon and Michel Eyquem de Montaigne. In Emerson's work the argument of each essay moves rapidly, bolstered by his iterative use of example and images, creating a snowballing of references via repeated syntactical patterns. Emerson commonly condensed the content of entire lectures into paragraphs. In so doing he sought to emphasize brevity, conciseness in expression, and rapid movement of thought, thereby to achieve a clarity of thought richly textured by his attention to rhetorical devices. The movement and pace variations caused by his control over his prose style demands concentration, even as it looks to sweep the reader on from seeming emphatic or declarative conclusions and summations of thought.

Each essay constitutes a testing ground for the reader's response to a series of intellectual and existential problems, which have as their starting point a familiar and seemingly-fixed definition suggested by the essays' single-word titles. Emerson's exemplary expansion of argument and discussion from these departure points helps to underline the tension between an individual's desire for moral imperatives, and the freedom suggested by the questioning, which Emerson's self-culture sets in motion. The act of self-culture is set within a context of spiritual awareness, which has as its ultimate aim the recognition of "a divine impulse at the core of our being."

The success and controversy of Emerson's volume lies in the offer it makes to become a witness to the immediacy of the divine, through a human agency available to all. The contradictions it explores concern the implications for the moral agencies which Emerson looks to uphold through his appeal to forces of self-reliance. Such a reliance seems to transcend and endanger all notions of restriction, and thus any basis for morality. Emerson's response and defense is made on pragmatic grounds, for his work and thought is as an experimenter: "No facts are to me sacred; none are profane; I simply experiment, an endless seeker, with no Past at my back." If they provoke subsequent actions deemed to be worthy, then the experimentation embodied in his essay writing is justified as a moral act and not one of heresy.

IAN D. COPESTAKE

Text

First published as *Essays.* 1841; reprinted in 1847 as *Essays: First Series.* Reprinted in *The Collected Works of Ralph Waldo Emerson.* vol. 2, *Essays: First Series.* Cambridge, Mass.: Belknap Press of Harvard University Press, 1979.

Bibliography

Bickman, Martin. "'The Turn of His Sentences': The Open Form of Emerson's *Essays: First Series,*" *ESQ: A Journal of the American Renaissance* 34 (1988): 1–2, 59–76.
"Emerson's Strategies of Rhetoric: A Symposium on *Essays: First Series,*" *ESQ: A Journal of the American Renaissance* 69 (1972): 199–297.
Johnson, Glen M. "Emerson's Craft of Revision: The Composition of *Essays* (1841)." In *Ralph Waldo Emerson: A Collection of Critical Essays.* Edited by Lawrence Buell. Englewood Cliffs, N.J.: Prentice-Hall, 1993.
Lauter, Paul. "Emerson's Revisions of Essays (First Series)," *American Literature* 33 (1961): 143–58.
Robinson, David M. "Grace and Works: Emerson's Essays in Theological Perspective." In *American Unitarianism, 1805–1865.* Edited by Conrad Edick Wright. Boston: Northeastern University Press, 1989.
Von Frank, Albert J. "*Essays: First Series* (1841)." In *The Cambridge Companion to Ralph Waldo Emerson.* Edited by Joel Porte and Saundra Morris. Cambridge: Cambridge University Press, 1999.

ETUDES D'ÉXÉCUTION TRANSCENDENTE 1852

Set of piano pieces by Franz Liszt (1811–86)

The study (French *Étude*, German *Studie and Etüde*, Italian *studio*) had traditionally had a didactic function. Before the nineteenth century it was used for pieces that purported to teach specific compositional techniques and aspects of music theory, such as counterpoint or canon. It was also a teaching piece focusing on particular points of instrumental technique and in this guise had a long association with the keyboard, being effectively indistinguishable from forms such as the exercise (Fr. *exercise*, Ger. *Übung*; It. *essercizio*). As time wore on, however, the latter term was increasingly used for the more mechanical, repetitive kind of piece and survived into the nineteenth century in the exercises of Hanon and some of those of Clementi (1752–1832) and Czerny (1791–1857).

The rise of the pianoforte, its enormous popularity and accessibility, and its particular attraction for the well-brought-up young lady as an indicator of her cultural attainments in the middle-class drawing room resulted in a thriving market for instruction manuals for the new instrument and for the music that went with them. Exercises and studies flourished.

However, the piano's capability for tonal gradation by touch alone added a new dimension to the more purely mechanical technique appropriate to its predecessors, the clavichord and the harpsichord, and to the organ, and demanded a new kind of technique. This factor, allied to the early nineteenth century's search for smaller, more individual and intimate, forms focused on the study—as it would also the prelude—as an appropriate form for developing more purely musical, as well as digital, skills.

The French form of the word (*Étude*) was appropriated for this particular manifestation of what was to become part of the literature of the character piece, and which would evolve into the concert study, or étude de concert.

Several composers had pioneered pieces in which one or two particular aspects of piano technique became enshrined in a short piece which would merit performance as a musical as well as a functional entity. Some of J. B. Cramer's (1771–1858) and Moscheles' (1794–1870) studies, the later part of Clementi's *Gradus ad Parnassum* (*Steps to Parnassus*, 1817–26) and those in Hummel's (1778–1837) set of twenty-four (op. 125, 1833) belong to this category. They were all eclipsed, however, by Frédéric Chopin's (1810–49) two sets (twenty-four each) of op. 10 (1833) and op. 25 (1837).

Liszt himself was one of the first to contribute to the literature of the concert study. At the age of thirteen (c. 1824) he began a projected *Étude en 48 exercices dans tous les tons majeurs, et mineurs* (*Study in Forty-Eight Exercises in All the Major and Minor Keys*), of which twelve were written—still an enormous achievement in terms of musical quality and technical acumen for his age. By 1837 he was planning a similar work, twenty-four *Grandes études*, of which, again, only twelve would be completed and which were based on his earlier youthful set; when published in 1839, they were the most difficult ever written, and they remain almost unplayable today. These works in particular fueled the Liszt legend, with its overtones of demonic possession, in a close parallel to the case of Niccolo Paganini (1782–1840), with his set of solo violin *Capricci*, op. 1 (1820).

Liszt produced a new version of the fourth study in 1840 and published it seven years later under the title of *Mazeppa*, altering it to fit the story—used also by Lord Byron and Victor Hugo the Hungarian count lashed to a frenzied horse in punishment for a sexual misdemeanor. Finally, his revision, in terms of texture and a scaling down of technical difficulty, of the other eleven, resulted in the *Douze études d'éxécution transcendente* (*Twelve Transcendental Studies*, 1852) complete with new titles for ten of them (including the retention of *Mazeppa* for the fourth).

The first of the études is entitled *Prélude*, marked *presto* and, as its name suggests, is a short limbering-up exercise in C major. The second, one of the two without a programmatic title, is *molto vivace* in A minor, and has an air of Paganini about it, reinforced by the broken octaves that suggest violin technique. Paganini was a major influence on piano composers at the time of Liszt's first conception of these works, which may well have been an answer to the former's twenty-four solo-violin *Capricci*, which for a long time remained unplayable by anyone but the author. Liszt also paid homage to the violinist in his six *Études d'éxécution transcendente d'après Paganini* of 1838 (published in 1840 and not to be confused with the études under discussion here, in spite of the similarity of the names), five of which are transcriptions for piano of the *Capricci* and the last the well-known set of variations on *La campanella*, from one of Paganini's violin concertos.

The next study, *Paysage* (*Landscape* in F, *poco adagio*), slow moving and relaxed, is a welcome respite from the turmoil of the first two, but we are immediately plunged into the passionate *Mazeppa* (*allegro*, D minor), discussed above. The pianistic effect here is that of Liszt's arch rival Sigismund Thalberg, whose "three-hand" technique divided a middle line (often the melody)

between the thumbs of the hands, with accompanimental textures above and below it.

The fifth étude, *Feux-follets* (*Will o' the Wisps*; *allegretto* in B-flat major) portrays the whimsicality of its subject harmonically as well as in the elusive melody, and the sixth *Vision* (*lento*, G minor) is far more definite and strong than its mystical title would suggest. The heading of the seventh study, *Eroica* (*allegro*, E-flat major) is not a reference to Ludwig van Beethoven's symphony or variations, both of which share its name—and its key—but a more general evocation, reminding us of the later patriotic Liszt and his Hungarian heroics, though folk or national musical traits are not a feature here. The eighth étude, *Wilde Jagd* (*Wild Hunt*: *presto furioso*, C minor), like *Mazeppa*, draws on a common theme of Germanic Romanticism, the night hunt. The ninth *Ricordanza* (*Remembrance*; *andantino*, A-flat major), is the longest of the set and dwells affectionately and, for much of the time, wistfully, on past memories, while the tenth the remaining untitled piece (headed *allegro agitato*, F minor) contrasts passionately, and contains hints of a wild tarantella.

The penultimate piece, *Harmonies du soir* (*Evening Harmonies*; *andantino* in D-flat major), is less taxing for listener and player, but the études end darkly with *Chasse neige* (*Snow Storm*; *andante con moto*, B-flat minor), in which the gloom of a landscape being covered by driving snow is wonderfully evoked.

DEREK CAREW

Work

Collected Edition of Liszt's Works. 34 vols. Leipzig: Breitkopf and Härtel, 1901–36.
Sulyok, I., and I. Mezö, eds. *New Liszt Edition: Complete Works*. Budapest, 1970.

Bibliography

Searle, H. *The Music of Liszt*. Rev. ed. London, 1966.

EURICO, O PRESBÍTERO (EURICO, THE PRIEST) 1844

Historical novel by Alexandre Herculano de Carvalho e Araùjo

To understand the significance of *Eurico, o Presbítero* within Portuguese Romanticism, one must be aware that the novel, and particularly the historical novel, presents itself as a major tool for the systematization of Romantic principles and option, which include the defense of liberty and equality, and affirmation of the individual's capacity for evolution, and the grounding in this capacity of his identity, making him a complete and coherent universe where self-consciousness is a priority. The relevant social perspective posits that the nation is best understood as a dynamic being that possesses a vital energy. It asserts itself and evolves through oppositions and struggles. In *Eurico, o Presbítero* these elements are brought together in a coherent whole, in a hero symbolically endowed with the representation of a group's ideal and, simultaneously, concerning himself as an individual with an uncompromising defense of liberty. Alexandre Herculano's historical narrative follows the models of Alexandre Dumas *pere* and, especially, Sir Walter Scott; everything develops around an individual whose psychology is at the core of the

narrative and for whom the exterior setting is, more often than not, a mere theatrical stage where he is able to present and exhibit his moral options and choices. Exterior action is thus more a consequence of an interior individuality that if correctly assumed, projects itself into the so-called outer world than an element disconnected from the subject's world.

Eurico, o Presbítero was written in 1843, with some of its chapters appearing in a periodical in the same year; it was published as a separate volume in 1844. In the foreword, Herculano confesses his uncertainty regarding the genre of the work, in a typical Romantic gesture that does not, however, erase the historical background of its construction. In addition to a historical aspect, the text also has social and allegorical dimensions. The novel opens at the beginning of the eighth century with the decline of the Visigothic monarchy in the Iberian Peninsula, which paved the way for the Arab invasion, and which in turn led to the creation of the "modern" medieval nations. Thus *Eurico, o Presbítero* emphasizes a period of transition where crises, values, and treason are at the forefront of men's minds and determine the courses of action they choose. Eurico is a solitary priest and a former Visigothic warrior and courtier who, feeling himself to be betrayed in his love for Hermengarda, has chosen to consecrate his life to God. Realizing that his fatherland is about to be invaded and conquered not only by another nation, but also by another religion, he chooses to reappear in public life, although under the mantel of anonymity, becoming the solitary hero (the Black Knight) who is nevertheless unable to prevent treason or indeed the subsequent death of his nation. As he delivers Hermengarda from the conquerors' hands, he has to face the moral question of celibacy in priesthood. Rather than give in to temptation, Eurico sacrifices his life. Hermengarda becomes one of several madwomen in Romantic narratives.

It must be stressed that the historical novel represents, for Herculano, much more than the a longing for a past—though it is also that. This past, in which the hero was transparent and visible to everyone, is seen as a source of hope for the future. The hero is marked physically and morally by "distinctive traits" that underline his radical difference from "the masses" that, nonetheless, he truly represents. It is perhaps for this reason that Eurico, like the other heroes of Herculano's novels and short stories, is essentially being torn by his interior contradictions, in a fight to the death that—even when it projects itself into the outer world—finds its battleground within the subject and his consciousness. Eurico becomes the guiding light of a whole generation (in response to which the critic Vitorino Nemésio coined the term the Eurico complex) and a whole way of writing (Eurico is himself a poet). In this hero we find that the act of self-exclusion from the world (emblematic of Herculano's stance, as well as that of Romantic writers all over Europe), is a symbolic as well as existential gesture. At the beginning of the novel, we meet a Eurico about to re-enter the world, not through the means of his actions in the social world of the court, but through the means of his fighting capacity, a Euricdue to his fighting capacity, which is another form of social action, (as well as,

potentially, another metaphor for the erotic relationship). Nevertheless, what is emphasized in this situation is the fact that such a reentry must be considered as a simulacrum. This is not simply because the Visigothic nation no longer exists (even if it apparently does—the notes of Herculano the historian are, in this respect, revelatory), but also because the entire plot rests upon the notion of treason, and further because Eurico himself, if correctly understood, no longer exists. That part of him that becomes the Black Knight comes to the forefront only as a mask to conceal the warrior who no longer has any right to his own name.

One specific ethic and moral position stems from all these characteristics. It is best considered through the notion of "exhibition." The hero exhibits himself as precisely that, and asserts himself on the world stage through that exhibition—hence, the fundamentally public implication of his private actions. Time becomes a symbolic continuum, a projection of the eternal nature of moral values and ethical stances that stands in marked contrast to the transience of the single individual. It is precisely this individual—the hero—who combines the transitory nature of his personal life and the eternal character of the values that he literally incarnates.

HELENA CARVALHÃO BUESCU

Text

Eurico, o Presbítero. 1844.

Bibliography

Buescu, Helena Carvalhão. "Heróis, romances e histórias: a propósito do Presbítero Eurico." In *A Lua, a Literatura e o Mundo*. Lisbon: Cosmos, 1995.

França, José-Augusto. "Herculano ou a consciência no exílio." In *O Romantismo em Portugal*, vol. 2. Lisbon: Livros Horizonte, 1974.

Lourenço, Eduardo. "Da Literatura como interpretação de Portugal." In *O Labirinto da Saudade*. Lisbon: Publicaçoës Dom Quixote, 1978.

Nemésio, Vitorino. "Dois centenários românticos: Frei Luís de Sousa e Eurico." In *Ondas Médias*. Lisbon: Bertrand, 1945.

EUROPE, 1760–1850: HISTORICAL SURVEY

The period of European history between 1760 and 1850 was dominated by two broad series of events, the French Revolution and the Industrial Revolution, both of which oversaw the emergence and growth of Romanticism. These two phenomena contributed decisively to the most profound structural change of this era: the transformation of Europe from a feudal to a bourgeois society. This transformation is best considered in terms of the political, social, and economic causes and effects of the French and Industrial Revolutions, the growth of nationalism, the kinds of ideological and intellectual struggles emerging from these phenomena, and the response of Romantic thought, much of which was forged in the heat of those struggles. Accounts of this era given by Eric Hobsbawm, Georges Lefebvre, Herbert Marcuse, and others prove especially enlightening, as does the historical material derived from some of the general histories cited in the bibliography.

The French Revolution: Background and Consequences

It would not be an exaggeration to say that the effects of the French Revolution of 1789 are still with us. Historian Hobsbawm has suggested that most political struggles through the nineteenth century up to the present moment have been for or against the principles that were at stake in that revolution. The effect of the revolution was to bring about the destruction of the vast edifice of feudalism that had lasted for centuries. Feudalism had been characterized by a static and localized economy, hereditary privilege, and concentration of power in the hands of monarchy and nobility, together with vast church wealth and influence. Each person was believed to have a fixed place in the allegedly natural and divinely sanctioned order of things.

Essentially, the French Revolution, notes Lefebvre, along with the numerous other revolutions that succeeded it, initiated the displacement of the power of the king and nobility by the power of the bourgeoisie or middle classes that comprised recently appointed nobles, financiers, businessmen, traders, and members of the liberal professions. In addition to the political and economic changes incited by the French Revolution, there was a fundamental change in the thinking of people. The feudal world had been characterized by values of static hierarchy, loyalty, authority, religious faith, and monarchical or oligarchical exercise of power; these values were increasingly displaced by bourgeois ideology, much of which stemmed from Enlightenment thought. Such ideology was predominantly secular, stressing reason, individual experience, efficiency, usefulness, and—above all—political liberalism based on a free rational economy aided by technology and science. Much Romanticism took its initial impetus as a response to the new world created by these vast structural transformations in the realms of politics, economy, philosophy, and aesthetics.

The broad background of the French Revolution was colored by a number of overarching circumstances. The first of these was the rise of absolute monarchies everywhere in Europe during the fourteenth and fifteenth centuries. In England, absolute government was instituted by the Tudor monarchs and continued by the Stuarts, James VI, and Charles I. Their inflated conceptions of monarchy and their attempts to undermine the Parliament eventually resulted in the English Civil War (1642–49) between the supporters of the king and those of Parliament. The latter, led by Oliver Cromwell, were victorious. Charles I was beheaded in 1649 and England was ruled for a short spell by Parliament. However, the so-called Restoration of 1660 placed Charles II upon the throne. In the Glorious Revolution of 1688, William and Mary of Orange were invited to rule England. This series of events put an end to absolute monarchy in England in favor of parliamentary government.

Central Europe and Spain were also under the rule of despots—some more enlightened, such as Frederick II the Great of Prussia (1740–1786) and Joseph II of Austria (1780–90), and others more repressive, such as Catherine the Great of Russia (1762–96), who crushed a serf rebellion in 1773–74. In France, however, the situation was dire. The Bourbon Kings Louis XIV, Louis XV, and Louis XVI (1774–92) took to new extremes the arrogation of power and the instruments of justice. Louis XIV once declared that "*l'etat c 'est moi*" ("the state is me"), and both of his successors professed the divine right of kings. Absolutism as a political theory had been expressed by Jean Bodin (1530–96), who had claimed that the monarch derives his authority from God, as well as by the philosopher Thomas Hobbes (1588–1679) and the Dutch writer Hugo Grotius (1583–1645).

Hence, the French Revolution was in part a reaction against the excesses of absolute government that had grown both in theory and practice since the fourteenth century. Another factor was the economic transformation of society. The fourteenth through the seventeenth centuries witnessed tendencies that would later foster the growth of capitalism: the accumulation of wealth that was invested for profit, the growth of banking and credit facilities, regulated associations of companies and joint-stock companies, the decline of the feudal manufacturing guilds, the growth of new industries such as mining and wool, and the revolutionizing of agricultural methods. These trends were accompanied by economic nationalism, an ethic of competition, and imperialism. By the seventeenth century England,

France, Holland, Italy, Portugal, and Spain, had become imperial powers; trade became a worldwide rather than national or local, phenomenon. By the end of the seventeenth century the bourgeoisie had achieved economic hegemony.

Against this background it can be noted that the more proximate causes of the French Revolution were economic, political, and intellectual. The economic causes were perhaps the most important. Though the middle classes had risen to a dominant economic position, they were without correlative political power; these classes were opposed to the age-old policies of mercantilism, which established monopolies and control of purchase, wages, and prices. Another economic cause was the survival of a feudal system of privileges, whereby the higher clergy and certain classes of nobles monopolized government. Peasants resented the fees and land taxes they were obliged to pay to their lords; and the urban masses suffered greatly from high prices. The political causes included a despotic monarchy and an unsystematic mode of government, finance, taxation, and law. Perhaps the most direct causes were the costly Seven Years' War (1756–63) fought against England and Prussia, and the French involvement in the American War of Independence (1776), which both contributed to the economic bankruptcy of the government.

The intellectual influences stemmed largely from the Enlightenment. The seminal figures of the Enlightenment were the French philosopher René Descartes (1596–1650) and the English mathematician Sir Isaac Newton (1642–1727), who variously promoted the view of a mechanical universe ordered by laws that were scientifically ascertainable. Such a conception eventually displaced the view of the universe as directed by divine providence. In general, the major tendencies of Enlightenment philosophy were toward rationalism, empiricism, pragmatism, and utilitarianism; these tendencies formed the core of liberal-bourgeois thought. Thinkers such as David Hume and John Locke in Britain; Jean le Rond d'Alembert, Denis Diderot, and Voltaire in France; and Gotthold Ephraim Lessing in Germany encouraged more skeptical, rational, and tolerant approaches to religion. The most common approach was deism, which saw divine laws as natural and rational and dismissed all superstition, miracles, and sacraments. The more specific influences on the French Revolution included Locke's *Second Treatise of Civil Government* (1690) which justified the new political system in England that prevailed after the 1688 revolution. Locke condemned despotic monarchy and the absolute sovereignty of parliaments, affirming that the people had a right to resist tyranny. Voltaire advocated an enlightened monarchy or republic governed by the bourgeois classes. Baron Charles-Louis de Secorclat Montesquieu also influenced the first stage of the French Revolution, advancing a liberal theory based on a separation of executive, legislative, and judicial powers. Jean-Jacques Rousseau exerted a powerful impact on the second stage of the Revolution through his theories of democracy, egalitarianism, and the evils of private property, as advocated in his *Social Contract* and *Discourse on the Origin of Inequality*. However, in some ways, Rousseau hardly belongs to the main trends of rationalist Enlightenment thought. Significantly, he is often hailed as the father of Romanticism on account of his exaltation of the state of nature over civilization, and of the emotions and instincts over reason and conventional learning. A final intellectual factor in the background of the revolution was the growth of bourgeois economics that undermined mercantilism, and advocated (with varying qualifications) the doctrine of economic laissez-faire, and labor theories of value.

Many of the aforementioned circumstances came to a head in 1788, a year that yielded poor harvests, government bankruptcy, as well as continued discontent with unpopular taxes and high prices. The French Revolution began with aristocratic unrest with the monarchy and the nobility demanding increase of their privileges; but events were soon controlled by bourgeois interests that shaped the essentially bourgeois nature of the revolution. In the first stage (1789–92) Louis XVI called a meeting in 1789 of the Estates General, a parliamentary body that had been convened only sporadically in the past. The three estates represented there were the clergy, the nobility, and the common people. The third estate, of which the richest and most capable section was the bourgeoisie. This body, led by advocates of bourgeois reform such as Mirabeau and Abbé Sieyes, drafted a new constitution by 1791 and initiated the rationalization of the French economy. This first stage, in which the Bastille was stormed, accomplished the destruction of many surviving feudal privileges, and the secularization of the church through the "Civil Constitution of the Clergy" which mandated that clergy should be elected by the citizens and secularized much church property. It also enacted a Declaration of the Rights of Man, which proclaimed liberty, security, and property as natural rights. The declaration opposed feudal privilege but was not egalitarian in character. The structure of government was not a democracy, but instead a constitutional monarchy in which a propertied oligarchy would govern through a representative assembly. The document was also nationalistic, viewing the source of authority as residing in the nation.

The second phase of the revolution began in August of 1792. It was a more radical phase, involving the masses, whose leaders, such as Georges Jacques Danton, Jean Paul Marat, and Maximilien de Robespierre, were devoted to the egalitarian doctrines of Rousseau. A National Convention was elected, its purpose—which was not achieved—being to draft a new democratic constiution which would include rights and provisions for the poor. France became a republic. In January 1793 Louis XVI was charged with treason and beheaded. France entered into war with, and was defeated by, Austria and Prussia, whose rulers feared the spread of revolutionary ideals. The so-called Reign of Terror (1793–94) was instigated by the executive arm of the National Convention, known as the Committee of Public Safety. This period is usually remembered for its violence and thousands of executions but, as Hobsbawm has pointed out, it was also a period of remarkable achievements. These included the drafting of the first genuinely democratic constitution produced by a modern state (though this was not put into effect), the abolition of all remaining feudal rights, the fixing of maximum prices on grain, the division of large estates to be sold to poorer citizens, the separation of church and state, the abolition of slavery in the French colonies, the expulsion of the invading armies of Prussia and Britain from France, and the relative stabilizing of the French economy.

The National Covention contained a number of factions, the most predominant of whom were the radical Jacobins, led in turn by Danton, Marat, and Robespierre, and the more moderate Girondins who included in their ranks Thomas Paine and the Marquis de Condorcet. Condorcet died after his imprisonment for opposing the violence of the Jacobins. Eventually, the Jacobin leaders suffered the fate they had meted out to others: Marat was assassinated and both Danton and Robespierre were in turn executed.

Robespierre's death in 1794 effectively marks the beginning of the final stage of the revolution. The National convention was now dominated by more moderate leaders who acted in accordance with bourgeois interests. In 1795, the convention drafted a new constitution that was founded on the security of property and restricted voting to wealthy proprietors. Power was vested in a five-man directory. This stage was characterized by profiteering and a great deal of corruption, and the ensuing inflation and economic chaos paved the way for the *coup d'etat* of Napoleon Bonaparte on November 9 (the eighteenth Brumaire), 1799—the date that marks the end of the French Revolution.

The Era of Napoleon

Napoleon had been exalted to the status of a national hero through his success in a French campain against Austria. Eventually, his popularity and military power enabled him to overthrow the French government in 1799 and to become consul; he became Emperor Napoleon I of France in 1804, and his autocratic rule effectively put an end to the liberal ideals of the French Revolution. However, he confirmed and developed certain accomplishments of that revolution, centralizing the government, continuing tax reforms, maintaining the redistribution of vast estates and the abolition of serfdom, and developing the reforms begun by the Revolution in the spheres of education and criminal and civil law (known in their revised form as the Code Napoleon). Some of these legal developments were transported into the legal structures of other countries such as Italy, Prussia, and Switzerland. However, Napoleon undid the revolution's separation of church and state, establishing a Concordat with Pope Pius VII in 1801.

The young G. W. F. Hegel saw Napoleon as a "world-historical" figure. Beyond his administrative reforms, it was Napoleon's military campaigns which ensured him a significant place in effecting historical change. He inherited from revolutionary times a war against Austria, Britain, and Russia, defeating the latter two powers and extending the frontiers of France to encompass most of continental Europe, as well as placing his brothers on the thrones of Naples, Holland, and Westphalia. He had, however, lost to the British in the naval battle at Trafalgar (1805), and more setbacks were on their way. The Spanish revolted in 1808 against his attempt to impose his brother's rule on them; in 1812, Napoleon began what would turn out to be a disastrous campaign against Russia, resulting in the loss of nearly 300,000 troops. This defeat inspired Austria and Prussia, aided by Russia, to renew hostilities with him, and in 1813 he was decisively defeated. The allied forces invaded France and took Paris in the following year. Napoleon was pensioned and sent to the island of Elba, while the allied forces arranged with the French government to restore the Bourbon dynasty with Louis XVIII as a constitutional monarch. Escaping from Elba in 1815, Napoleon returned to France to be greeted once again by loyal peasants and soldiers, many of whom feared a return to the *ancien regime*. Louis XVIII fled before Napoleon took Paris and formed another army. He fought the Battle of Waterloo in Belgium and was crushed by the combined forces of Britain, Holland, and Prussia under the command of the British Duke of Wellington. He was exiled until his death in 1821.

The Congress of Vienna and the Metternich System

In the aftermath of the French Revolution, ideological and political struggles between liberals and conservatives swept through the rest of Europe. The heads or representatives of many powers, including Austria, Britain, Prussia, and Russia, assembled at the Congress of Vienna (1814–15) to decide the future of Europe. The congress was dominated by Klemens von Metternich, the Austrian minister of foreign affairs who had helped forge the alliance that had defeated Napoleon. Metternich was a staunch conservative, determined to return to the status quo before the revolution of 1789. He engineered an agreement whereby the dynasties that had held power in 1789 should be restored and each country should possess again the territories it had held at that time. However, various exceptions were made to this principle, with some of the great powers, such as Britain and Austria, being allowed to retain some of the provinces they had acquired since then. Metternich also fathered a system of alliances (which included Austria, Britain, Prussia, Russia, and subsequently France) whose function was to suppress any violation of the agreed territorial boundaries or any insurrection against the agreed rulers. On two occasions, such suppression was actually enforced, in the uprisings in Sicily and Spain. Liberal movements challenged the conservatives in England, where the Reform Bill of 1832 implemented electoral reforms, enfranchising and establishing the hegemony of the middle class. Bourgeois entrepreneurs also agitated against the Corn Laws, protective tariffs benefiting the landowners; these laws were eventually repealed in 1846. There were uprisings against the restored Bourbon monarch Louis XVIII of France, who was succeeded in 1824 by his even more reactionary brother Charles X.

Intense ideological struggles shook Prussia and Russia also. In response, Metternich enforced in the former a repressive program known as the Carlsbad Decrees (1819) that, in reaction to student unrest, brought the entire university system and the press under strict control and censorship. In Russia, Tsar Alexander I turned from his erstwhile Jacobinistic liberalism, and his successor Nicholas crushed an 1825 revolt led by intellectuals and army officers, imposing a stern regime enforced by secret police.

However, the Metternich system of alliances began to crumble. Britain, primarily for economic motives, withdrew; and Russia violated the alliance's ethic of restoring "legitimate" rulers by supporting the Greek rebellion against Turkey and declaring war on its sultan in 1828. Moreover, several revolutions erupted in Europe in 1830. The first was the July Revolution in France, where bourgeois leaders ousted Charles X and replaced him with Louis-Philippe as head of a constitutional monarchy. The Belgian Netherlands revolted successfully against Dutch rule; and in 1831 Poland's rebellion against Russian rule was quelled severely by Tsar Nicholas I.

The Revolutions of 1848 and the Growth of Nationalism

The French Revolution, whose catchwords were *liberty, fraternity,* and *equality,* had fostered not only the idea of individual rights but also of nationalism, of the obligations of the individual toward a whole society or nation, which was seen as having a specific history, culture, and direction. The revolutions of 1848 were partly inspired by discontent among liberals with reactionary regimes, and were generally fueled by nationalistic sentiment that had taken root everywhere since the French Revolution. In 1848 widespread dissatisfaction with the increasing despotism of Louis-Philippe led to his deposition. France was made a republic and Louis Napoleon Bonaparte (1808–73), nephew of Napoleon I, was elected president by an overwhelming majority. His inherited name appealed to a widespread nationalistic sentiment. A plebiscite held in 1851 empowered him to draft a new constitution, and in 1852 he took the title of Emperor Napoleon III. This so-called second empire lasted until 1870, by which time his popularity had declined, largely as a consequence of his foreign policies. He engaged in the disastrous Franco-Prussian War and was badly defeated. His government was overthrown, and by 1875 a National Assembly inaugurated in France the so-called Third Republic.

Inspired by the 1848 events in France, revolutions also occurred in Austria and Hungary. In the former, Metternich was forced to resign and the emperor obliged to accept a liberal constitution. In 1849 rebels in Hungary formed a liberal government and affirmed the independence of their state. However, these constitutional concessions in both countries were shortly revoked, and the republic in Hungary was abolished. By 1867 an agreement was reached to establish a dual monarchy: while the Austrian Emperor was also King of Hungary, each state was relatively autonomous.

Nationalism was an especially potent force for change in Germany. In the 1848 revolution, liberals forced princes in several German states to grant reforms, and the Frankfurt Assembly was convened with a goal of producing a constitution for a united Germany. The attempt failed, however, and Germany was not united until the deeply conservative prime minister of Prussia, Otto von Bismarck first united the northern German states, and then succeeded through the Franco-Prussian war in rallying the southern German states, to produce a united Germany. Bismarck became chancellor of the newly formed German Empire.

Before 1848, Italy had been similarly composed of a number of small states including the Papal states; Sardinia; the two states of Sicily, and Lombardy and Venetia, which were under Austrian rule; and other territories under Hapsburg dominion. Nationalism in the form of *risorgimento* (the "resurrection" of Italian greatness) played a crucial part here also. In 1848 revolts were organized against Hapsburg rule and everywhere liberal reforms were demanded. In 1858, Lombardy was freed from Austria by a Sardinian army, and in 1860 Giuseppe Garibaldi conquered Sicily and Naples, turning these territories over to Sardinia. In 1861, Victor Emmanuel II was proclaimed King of Italy; Rome itself was annexed as part of the new kingdom in 1870, creating a rift between the papacy and the state.

Nationalism in other parts of Europe arose somewhat later and is beyond the scope of this study. But it may be stated briefly that the Ottoman Empire began to crumble as a result of nationalist uprisings, aided by Russia, in Greece and Serbia (1829), as well as in subject territories such as Bosnia, Bulgaria, and Herzegovina. Further confrontations between Turkey and European powers, as well as a movement for liberal and secular reform in Turkey itself, paved the way for the collapse of the Empire. Nationalism in Russia emerged much later in the century, as a Pan-Slavic movement.

The Industrial Revolutions

The Industrial Revolution, which was given its name by the English and French socialists of the 1820s, is cited by Hobsbawm as "probably the most important event in world history." It is usually divided into two phases, the first stretching from the mid-eighteenth to the mid-nineteenth centuries, and the second phase continuing effectively to the present day. Large-scale industrialization first began in Britain on account of its wealth, its encouragement of private profit, and economic system backed by liberal policies that had ousted the feudal guild system, as well as its colonies andeffective monopoly of the world market. Industrialism spread rapidly, however: by the mid-nineteenth century France and Belgium were engaged in mechanized production; by the end of the nineteenth century Germany had been transformed from an agricultural economy to the greatest industrial power; and industrialization reached Japan and Italy toward the end of the century. The economic transformation of Europe since the fourteenth century had witnessed several technological innovations in many industries such as cotton and iron, culminating in the invention of the steam engine and the large-scale use of coal, along with the development of a factory system using conveyor belts, assembly lines and other techniques of mass production. Cotton manufacture became mechanized through the invention of the spinning jenny in 1767, the power loom in 1785, and the cotton gin in 1792.

The second phase of industrialization was marked by the use of electricity and oil, the development of the iron and steel industries, increased automation, division of labor, and an increasing harnessing of science by industry. The nineteenth century also saw vast improvements in travel with the establishment of improved roads, the railway system, steamships, telecommunications, and cars. Agriculture also became rationally organized and mechanized. More important, as stated earlier, the massively increased wealth of the bourgeoisie sought more outlets for investment in markets that were expanding in both the countries of Europe themselves as a result of increased population and also in the colonies of the European powers. Capital was increasingly dominated by investment, finance, and the formation of vast monopolies, while economic liberalism was gradually displaced by government control, subsidy, and protectionism. By this period, the bourgeois classes had established hegemony and, as Hobsbawm notes the "gods and Kings of the past were powerless before the businessmen and steam-engines of the present."

Notwithstanding its promotion of prosperity and economic expansion, industrialization was not without its social and economic problems, or its political crises. While wages increased, there was large-scale unemployment, partly on account of the use of women and children as cheap labor in factories. Extremely poor working conditions, long hours, and disease increased the misery of the working classes. These flaws in the capitalist economy helped precipitate the European Revolutions of 1848 and the Chartist uprising in Britain (1838–48), which struggled for the implementation of a people's charter demanding universal suffrage, a secret ballot, and salaries as opposed to property qualifications for members of the House of Commons. By the end of the nineteenth century most of the population of Europe was occupied in industrial rather than agricultural labor, embroiled in a crowded, urban way of life. These and other factors gave rise to a new political force, an industrial proletariat that became the main opponent of the recently established hegemony of the new bourgeoisie—the bankers, industrial magnates, and proprietors of factories, railroads, steel works, and mines.

The Struggle between Liberal and Conservative Ideologies

The foregoing political struggles and economic transformations were naturally accompanied by a struggle between liberal and conservative ideologies, between those who wished to advance further the principles behind the French Revolution such as rationalism, individualism, and limited government, and those who wished to return to a prerevolutionary emphasis on tradition, faith, and authority. During the revolution itself, this struggle had expressed itself prominently in the debate between the liberal stateman Edmund Burke and Thomas Paine, one of the moderate members of the National Convention. In his *Reflections of the Revolution in France* (1790) Burke's attack on the revolution was characterized by the usual elements of conservatism: an appeal to the authority of the past and the collective wisdom of tradition as opposed to what he saw as the abstract rationalism of the French Revolutionists; an advocacy of gradual change; and a desire to conserve the essential economic and political fabric of feudalism. Thomas Paine's radicalism, as expressed in his widely influential *Rights of Man* (1791), embraced the central thrust of the new bourgeois ideologies: freedom from the past, from tradition, from convention, and a marked emphasis on the present; and the exaltation of rationalism and individual reasoning. Paine also stressed the natural and divinely sanctioned equality of human beings; finally, he insisted that political authority is neither hereditary nor divinely bestowed, but derives from the people.

This ideological struggle was played out in many spheres, including those of religion, philosophy, literature, and art. Perhaps the most profound general ideological change was the secularization of thinking, consonant with the rationalist and materialist worldview of the bourgeoisie, which imposed its ideological dispositions on society as a whole. The secularization of the educated classes had dated back to the late seventeenth century, what was new to the nineteenth century was the secularization in outlook of the new proletariat. The political and social issues generated by the French Revolution were argued in a secular idiom. For much of the entire nineteenth century, religion was engulfed in debates—with philosophy, science, and the modes of thought generated by an entirely transformed way of life— that often threatened its very foundations. There developed in the 1830s in Germany a school of "higher criticism" devoted to a study of the sources and methods used by the authors of the Bible, often questioning the coherence and historical accuracy of biblical texts. One of the prominent studies in this field was David Strauss's *Life of Jesus* (1835). Later in the century, the Church would face further threats from discoveries in science, particularly those of Charles Darwin. These developments, together with the onslaught of many governments against the wealth, property, legal rights, and temporal power of the church made secularization an institutional as well as an ideological phenomenon. In general, Protestantism fared better than Roman Catholicism in its ability to survive within new social structures, though the century was marked by religious revivals of many types.

The formation of an organized proletariat in the nineteenth century was accompanied and promoted by some important political and economic theories. The liberal-bourgeois economic theories of James Mill, David Ricardo, and Adam Smith had dominated much nineteenth-century thought and practice with their notions of economic individualism, laissez-faire and free competition; these were opposed by thinkers disposed toward representing the interests of the laboring classes, such as the utopian socialists Charles Fourier, who advocated collective ownership of the means of production, Robert Owen, who impugned the profit system as exploiting the labor of the worker, and Claude Henri de Saint-Simon. The most important of the socialist thinkers were Karl Marx and Friedrich Engels, who produced a powerful critique of capitalism, as well as a call for political action in texts such as the *Manifesto of the Communist Party* (1848) and *Capital* (1867). Influenced by the French socialists, English political economists, and the German idealist philosophers such as Hegel, Marx, and Engels developed a materialistic conception of history that saw capitalism as having evolved from a long history of various modes of production, from the ancient slave mode of production through the feudal system, this progression being driven essentially by class conflict. They argued that once technologically assisted capitalist accumulation and world expansion had led to a world of sharply contrasting wealth and poverty and the working classes became conscious of their historical role, capitalism itself would yield to a communism that would do away with private property and base itself on human need rather than the greed of a minority for increasing profit.

It was in the fields of philosophy and literature that Romanticism—as a broad response to Enlightenment, neoclassical, and French Revolutionary ideals—initially took root. In general, this period can best be seen as one in which the major upheavals such as the French Revolution, the Industrial Revolutions, the revolutions of 1830 and 1848, and the growth of nationalism impelled the bourgeois classes toward political, economic, cultural, and ideological hegemony. It was their worldview (broadly, rationalist, empiricist, individualist, utilitarian, and economically liberal) that dominated the thought and practice of this period and spawned various oppositional movements such as socialism, anarchism, cults of irrationalism, and revivals of tradition and religion. Romanticism cannot be placed within any set of these movements, since it effectively spanned them all. While the various developments in Romanticism and its major exponents are treated elsewhere in this volume, a question that might

fruitfully be addressed here is the complex connection of Romanticism to the predominating bourgeois worldview.

As writers such as Eric Hobsbawm, Herbert Marcuse, and Georgy Valentinovich Plekhanov have pointed out, it is too simplistic to view Romanticism in any of its expressions as a straightforward reaction against the prevalent bourgeois worldviews. Some of the Romantics, such as William Blake, Johann Christian Friedrich Hölderlin, and William Wordsworth, initially saw the French Revolution as heralding the dawn of a new era of individual and social liberation. Johann Wolfgang von Goethe and Johann Christoph Friedrich von Schiller in their own ways exalted the struggle for human freedom and mastery of knowledge. Lord, Byron, Heinrich Heine, Victor Hugo, George Sand, and Percy Bysshe Shelley were passionate in their appeals for justice and liberation from oppressive social conventions and political regimes. Underlying nearly all Romantic views of art was an intense individualism based on the authority of experience and—often—a broadly democratic orientation, as well as an optimistic and sometimes utopian belief in progress. In all these aspects, there was some continuity between Enlightenment and Romantic thought.

However, many of the Romantics, including Blake, Byron, Shelley, and Wordsworth, reacted against certain central features of the new bourgeois social and economic order. Appalled by the squalor; the mechanized, competitive routine of the cities; and the moral mediocrity of a bourgeois world given over to what Shelley called the principles of "utility" and "calculation," they turned for spiritual relief to mysticism; to nature; to Rousseauistic dreams of a simple, primitive, and uncorrupted lifestyle that they sometimes located in an idealized period of history such as the Middle Ages. Wordsworth held that the poet should emulate the "language of real life"; he, Blake, and Coleridge exalted the state of childhood and innocence of perception, untainted by conventional education; and many Romantic writers—in tune with growing nationalistic sentiments—revived primitive forms such the folktale and the ballad. *Nature*, for the Romantics, departed from the conception of it held by such neoclassical writers as Alexander Pope, for whom the term signified an eternal unchangable and hierarchical order of the cosmos as well as certain criteria for human thought and behavior. Pope's view had been influenced by notions deriving from Sir Isaac Newton of the universe as a vast machine. For the Romantics, nature was transfigured into a living force and held togther as a unity by the breath of the divine spirit. It was infused with a comprehensive symbolism resting on its profound moral and emotional connection with human subjectivity.

Indeed, perhaps the most fundamental trait of all Romanticism was its shift of emphasis away from classical objectivity toward subjectivity: in the wake of the philosophical systems of Johann Gottlieb Fichte, Friedrich Willhelm Joseph von Schelling, and above all, of Hegel, the worlds of subject and object, self and world, were viewed as mutually constructive processes, human perception playing an active role rather than merely receiving impressions passively from the outside world. Such an emphasis placed a high value on uniqueness, originality, novelty, and exploration of ever-expanding horizons of experience. Moreover, the self that was exalted in Romanticism was a far cry from the self as an atomistic (and economic) unit as premised in bourgeois individualism. The Romantic self was more found, more authentic ego lying beneath the layers of social convention, a self that attempted through principles such as irony to integrate the increasingly fragmented elements of the bourgeois world into a vision of unity; and it was primarily the poet who could achieve such a vision.

The most crucial human faculty for such integration was the imagination, which most Romantics saw as a unifying power—one that could harmonize other strata of human perception, such as sensation and reason. It should be noted that Romanticism is often wrongly characterized as displacing Enlightenment "reason" with emotion, instinct, spontaneity, and imagination. To understand this, it is necessary to recall that much Romantic thought took Immanuel Kant's philosophy (which itself was not at all Romantic) as its starting point—notably, his distinction between phenomena and noumena, his treatment of imagination, and his establishing of a relative autonomy for the category of the aesthetic. Kant's relation to Enlightenment thought was indeed ambivalent inasmuch as he attempted to establish the limitations of reason. Kant declared, however, that the categories of the understanding applied throughout the phenomenal world; his notion of the noumenon is merely a limiting concept, and its actual existence is nothing more than a presupposition of morality and free will. He had, moreover, viewed imagination as a mediating principle that reconciled the deliverances of sensation with the catgeories of the understanding. The Romantics not unlike Hegel (who himself was certainly no Romantic), placed the noumenal realm within the reach of human apprehension and often exalted the function of imagination, viewing it as a vehicle for the attainment of truths beyond the phenomenal world and beyond the reach of reason alone. Hence, Coleridge saw the secondary imagination, peculiar to the poet, as a unifying power that could reconcile general and concrete, universal and particular. Shelley even saw imagination as having a moral function, as a power enabling the self to situate itself within a larger empathetic scheme, as opposed to reason which expressed the selfish constraints of the liberal atomistic self. Hence the relation between Romanticism and the mainstreams of bourgeois thought, which had risen to hegemony on the waves of the Enlightenment, the French Revolution, and the Industrial Revolutions, was deeply ambivalent. Our own era is profoundly pervaded by this ambivalent heritage.

RAFEY M. HABIB

Bibliography

Brewer, John, and Eckhart Hellmuth. *Rethinking Leviathan: The Eighteenth-Century State in Britain and Germany*. London: German Historical Institute and Oxford: Oxford University Press, 1999.

Briggs, Asa. *The Age of Improvement, 1783–1867*. New York: Longman, 2000.

———. *A Social History of England*. London: Weidenfeld and Nicolson, 1983.

Briggs, Asa, and Patricia Clavin. *Modern Europe: 1789–1989*. London: Longman, 1997.

Burns, Edward McNall. *Western Civilizations*. Vol. 2. New York: W. W. Norton, 1973.

Cook, Chris. *The Longman Handbook of Modern European History, 1763–1997*. New York: Addison Wesley Longman, 1997.

Darnton, Robert. *What Was Revolutionary about the French Revolution?* Waco, Tex.: Baylor University Press, 1990.

Doty, Charles Stewart, ed. *The Industrial Revolution*. New York: Holt, Rinehart, and Winston, 1969.

Hanlon, Gregory. *Early Modern Italy, 1550–1800: Three Seasons in European History*. New York: Macmillan, 2000.

Hibbert, Christopher. *The French Revolution*. London: A. Lane, 1980.

Hunt, Lynn Avery. *Politics, Culture, and Class in the French Revolution*. Berkeley and Los Angeles: University of California Press, 1984.

———. *Revolution and Urban Politics in Provincial France: Troyes and Reims, 1786–1790*. Stanford, Calif.: Stanford University Press, 1978.

Hobsbawm, E. J. *The Age of Revolution: Europe, 1789–1848*. London: Abacus, 1977.

Forrest, Alan I. *The French Revolution*. Oxford: Blackwell, 1995.

Lefebvre, Georges. *The French Revolution: From Its Origins to 1793*. Trans. Elizabeth Moss Evanson, London: Routledge and Kegan Paul; New York: Columbia University Press, 1962.

Marcuse, Herbert. *Reason and Revolution: Hegel and the Rise of Social Theory*. Boston: Beacon Press, 1960.

McCraw, Thomas K., ed. *Creating Modern Capitalism: How Entrepreneurs, Companies, and Countries Triumphed in Three Industrial Revolutions*. Cambridge, Mass.: Harvard University Press, 1997.

Roche, Daniel. *France in the Enlightenment*. Trans. Arthur Goldhammer, Cambridge, Mass.: Harvard University Press, 1998.

Royle, Edward. *Modern Britain: A Social History, 1750–1997*. London: E. Arnold, 1997.

Rürup, Reinhard, ed. *The Problem of Revolution in Germany, 1789–1989*. New York: New York University Press, 2000.

Simpson, William, and Martin Jones. *Europe, 1783–1914*. London: Routledge, 2000.

Stearns, Peter N. *The Industrial Revolution in World History*. Boulder, Colo.: Westview Press, 1993.

Taine, Hippolyte Adolphe. *The French Revolution*. New York: Henry Holt, 1878–85.

Welch, David. *Modern European History, 1871–2000: A Documentary Reader*. London: Routledge, 1999.

EVGENII ONEGIN (EUGENE ONEGIN) 1833 (WRITTEN 1823–1831)

Novel in verse by Alexandr Pushkin

Very few Russian books have been as influential as this novel in verse. Inspired partly by Lord Byron's *Don Juan* (1819–24) and *Childe Harold's Pilgrimage* (1812–18), it spawned a whole new generic tradition to which the following belong: *Sashka* (1825–26) by Aleksandr Polezhaev; *Dnevnik devushki* (*The Diary of a Young Woman*, 1840–50), by Evdokiia Rostopchina; *Dvoinaia zhizn* (*A Double Life*, 1848), by Karolina Pavlova; *Svezhee predane* (*A Modern Legend*, 1861–62) by Iakov Polonskii; *Vozmezdie* (*Revenge*, 1910–21), by Aleksandr Blok; and *Spektorskii* (1924–30), by Boris Pasternak. It provided the basis for Pyotr Ilich Tchaikovsky's opera of the same name (1878) and Sergei Prokofiev's literary–musical composition for a reader, a group of actors and a symphonic orchestra (1936), as well as for at least three films, two of them Russian (dir. Vasilii Goncharov, 1911; and dir. Roman Tikhomirov, 1958), and one British (dir. Martha Fiennes, 1999). No less than three books of commentaries on *Eugene Onegin* were produced (by Nikolai Brodskii in 1932, Vladimir Nabokov in 1964, and Iurii Lotman in 1980), all of which went into several editions. Almost 175 years after the publication of its first installment, the presence of the novel in Russian culture was still felt so strongly that the avant-garde poet Dmitrii Prigov found it appropriate to publish his version of the fragments of cantos 5 and 6, under the title *Evgenii Onegin Pushkina* (*Pushkin's Eugene Onegin*, 1998), with all the original adjectives in them replaced either by the word *bezumnyi* (insane) or by *nezemnoi* (unearthly), thus irreverently turning cantos into chants, in mock protest against readers' universal devotion to Pushkin's masterpiece.

Despite the adulation bestowed upon the work, its plot is rather trite. Onegin, a *bon viveur* and dandy who is disenchanted with the high society of Saint Petersburg, goes to a distant country estate to take possession of a large inheritance. There he befriends his neighbors; the poet Lensky, a Romantic; and the Lariny sisters, the superficial Olga and the bookworm Tatyana. Tatyana falls in love with Onegin and naively offers herself to him in a somewhat pathetic letter; he is sensible and noble enough to turn her down. His innocent flirtation with Olga, Lensky's fiancée, leads to a sudden duel between the two male protagonists in which Lensky is killed. Onegin goes on extensive travels and returns to Saint Petersburg to find that Tatyana is a reformed person, a grand dame completely at ease with the high society, married to Onegin's old acquaintance, a prince turned general. Now it is Onegin's turn to fall in love with Tatyana, to write her a passionate letter of confession, and to be rejected—at which point the novel comes to a close.

Although the character of Onegin is undoubtedly modeled on the Byronic hero, and the novel is replete with references to pre-Romantic and Romantic literature (such as *Clarissa* (1747–48) and *Sir Charles Grandison* (1753–54) by Samuel Richardson; *Adolphe* (1806) by Henri-Benjamin Constant de Rebecque; and *René* (1805) by François-Auguste-René, Vicounte de Chateaubriand, as well as occasional nods to Vasilii Zhukovskii's poetry), it is a moot question whether Pushkin's involvement with Romanticism was anything more than a trivial interest in the artistic fashion of the day. It is not even clear whether Pushkin understood with any degree of certainty what Romanticism was about. Thus, while making full use of Romantic cliches in his simulation of Lensky's poetic manner, Pushkin concludes canto 5 with the following, rather puzzling statement: "we call this Romanticism, but I cannot see anything even remotely Romantic in [such verses]." For their part, some contemporary critics, taking advantage of the fact that the Russian word for novel, *roman*, is related to the Russian word for Romantic, *roman(t)ichesky*, and playing on words accordingly, maintained that they could not find much Romanticism in Pushkin's novel (*malo roman(t)icheskogo v romane*). Approximately one hundred years later, Vasilii Sipovskii judiciously pointed out that *Onegin's* early chapters, with their fairly ironic representation of extraordinary individualism, are somewhat closer to the Romantic

tradition than the later ones, which bear a heavy stamp of Realism and enthusiastically focus on the typical and the mundane.

The key to *Eugene Onegin's* enduring appeal lies perhaps not so much in the immediacy of its response to current literary trends, or in its quite unimaginative intrigue, as in the liberating sense of freedom with which the book was written. When Pushkin started working on it, he was not yet completely sure in what direction the novel would lead him. Most of the installments, or cantos (*Eugene Onegin* was published in eight cantos between 1825 and 1832, with the supplementary chapter on Onegin's travels conventionally considered to be canto 9), instead of being preoccupied with character development, are filled with lively conversation about everything and anything, from foreign cuisine and fashions to rural landscape and womanizing. This enabled Vissarion Belinskii to define *Eugene Onegin* as an "encyclopedia of Russian life." To adapt this everyday conversational style to the Russian poetic tradition (which hitherto mostly dealt with lofty topics), Pushkin invented the so-called Onegin stanza (*oneginskaia strofa*), an immensely flexible tetra-iambic fourteen-line form with the AbAbCCddEffEgg rhyming pattern (lowercase letters designating masculine rhymes). Even one hundred years after its invention, the significance of *oneginskaia strofa* was so relevant that the ever subversive Vladimir Nabokov turned it upside down, as AAbCCbDDeeFgFg, in his 1927 "Universitetskaia poema" ("The Student Poem"). In addition, to declare openly his preferred method of free composition, Pushkin introduced the so-called missing stanzas—that is, those for which only a number was supplied, but no text. Partly a deference to the Romantic poetics of fragment, partly in defiance of censorship that demanded changes in some of the stanzas that subsequently "went missing," this provocative device urged the reader to conjecture as to what had been omitted and why. Consequently, the reader was elevated to the status of a coauthor. The device has proven so popular that in both the 1950s and 1980s attempts were made, first by Ivan Gutorov, and then by Viacheslav Cherkasskii and Leonid Timofeev, to publish the "newly discovered" canto 10, which had indeed existed but was destroyed by Pushkin himself, either for political or for artistic reasons (only small remnants of it survived). In 1986, the academic father and son duo of Iurii and Mikhail Lotman convincingly identified the recently presented canto 10 as a hoax, produced in the 1940s or early 1950s. It was attributed to the historian and bibliographer Daniil Alshits, who apparently wrote the piece in a Stalinist labor camp. Undeterred by the well-grounded skepticism of the Lotmans, however, the poet Andrei Chernov at approximately the same time came up with what he termed a "reconstruction" of the destroyed canto. It finally appeared in 1999 in Irkutsk as a book entitled *Sozhzhennaia glava "Evgeniia Onegina"* (*The Burnt Canto of "Eugene Onegin"*). Thus the Russian nation keeps rereading, and at times rewriting, its favorite book.

ANDREI ROGACHEVSKII

See also **Literature; Pushkin, Aleksandr**

Text

Eugene Onegin; first appeared in book form in 1833; translated in excerpts as *A Russian Rake* by Clive Phillipps-Wolley (1883), and in full as *Eugene Oneguine* by T. Spalding (1881). Other attempts included Oliver Elton (1937; revised by A. D. P. Briggs in 1995), Dorothea Prall Radin and George Zinovei Patrick (1937), Babette Deutsch (1943, edited by Avrahm Yarmolinsky), B. Simmons (1950), Walter Arndt (1963), J. Fennel (1964), Eugene M. Kayden (1964), Vladimir Nabokov (1964, with a three-volume commentary; revised in 1975), Charles Johnston (1977), S. D. P. Clough (1988), and James E. Falen (1990). Most recent is a translation by Douglas R. Hofstadter; New York: Basic Books, 1999.

Bibliography

Briggs, Anthony David Peach. *Alexander Pushkin: Eugene Onegin.* Cambridge: Cambridge University Press, 1992.

Chumakov, Iurii Nikelaevich. *"Evgenii Onegin" A. S. Pushkina: V mirestikhotvornogo romana.* Moscow: Izd-vo Moskovskogo universiteta, 1999.

Clayton, J. Douglas. *Ice and Flame: Aleksandr Pushkin's "Eugene Onegin."* Toronto: University of Toronto Press, 1985.

Dalton-Brown, Sally. *Pushkin's "Evgenii Onegin."* Bristol: Bristol Classical Press, 1997.

Dragomiretskaia, Nataliia Vladimirovna. *A. S. Pushkin: Evgenii Onegin: Manifest dialoga-polemiki s romantizmom.* Moscow: Nasledie, 2000.

Hoisington, Sona Stephan, ed. *Russian Views of Pushkin's Eugene Onegin.* Bloomington: Indiana University Press, 1988.

Koshelev, Viacheslav AnatoL'evich. *Onegina vozdushnaia gromada.* Saint Petersburg: Akademicheskii proekt, 1999.

Lotman, Iurii Mikhailovich. *Roman A. S. Pushkina Evgenii Onegin: Kommentarii.* Leningrad: Prosveshchenie, 1980.

Sambeek-Weideli, Beatrice van. *Evgenii Onegin A. S. Pushkina: Bibliografiia.* Bern: Peter Lang, 1990.

———. *Wege eines Meisterwerks: die russische Rezeption von Puskins "Evgenij Onegin."* Bern: Peter Lang, 1990.

F

FANTASY IN C MAJOR, OP. 17 1837

Piano composition by Robert Schumann

The rather tortuous road that Robert Schumann's *Fantasy* had to travel from inception to publication is typical of many of his works. The inspiration for the piece was a letter Schumann reccived from a special committee in Bonn, Ludwig van Beethoven's birthplace, to canvass support for the erection of a monument to the dead composer. It became clear, however, that in terms of financial support the project was flagging, and it was only because of Franz Liszt's personal pledge to make up whatever shortfall there would be that the project came to fulfillment in 1845.

Schumann, who idolized Beethoven, responded enthusiastically, publishing the committee's appeal on the front page of the *Neue Zeitschrift für Music*, a musical periodical he had helped to found and of which he was editor. He also published a long essay, *Monument für Beethoven*, and decided to write a piano piece, some of the royalties from which he would donate to the project. He composed a fantasy entitled *Ruines* (*Ruins*) in June 1836, and in December he added two more movements entitled, respectively, *Trophäen* (*Trophies*) and *Palmen* (*Palms*), while changing the first movement's title to the German *Ruinen*, and calling the whole "A Sonata for Beethoven: Obolus for Beethoven's Monument." After unsuccessfully offering it to several publishers under various names, it was finally published under its present title in 1839.

A fantasy was intended to represent a written-out musical improvisation, overwhelmingly a single-movement piece with loosely connected sections showing free and daring gestures harmonically and in terms of dynamics, much color, and a high degree of virtuosity. Schumann's piece, however, betraying its sonata origins, has three movements, but they run into one another, and he chooses to finish with a slow movement, unorthodox in a sonata. There were precedents for the three-movement fantasy in the work of Felix Mendelssohn; Franz Peter Schubert and Schumann's piece, however, remains a fascinating hybrid, with the improvisational element—so often characteristic of the composer—brought to the foreground.

This work also exemplifies several other of Schumann's preoccupations, particularly his frequent quest for musical stimulus in the extramusical—in this case, the literary. The published score is headed by a quotation (he called it a motto) from one of his favorite writers, Friedrich von Schlegel:

Durch alle Töne tönet	Through all the sounds
Im bunten Erdentraum	in the multihued dream of Earth,
Ein leiser Ton gezogen	there runs a soft drawn-out note
Für den, der heimlich lauschet.	that the secret listener can hear.

It also points to Schumann's love of secret allusions, frequently involving the letters of names that he transliterates into musical notation. There were indeed secrets at this time in his life (the late 1830s)—for example his romance with Clara Wieck, the young piano prodigy, daughter of Schumann's ex–piano teacher Friedrich Wieck. The couple were forbidden all contact, though some clandestine letters did get through thanks to sympathetic friends. The "motto," as Schumann wrote later, refers to Clara and, indeed, the first movement opens with what had become "Clara's Theme," a falling scalic figure that crops up in the compositions of both of the two lovers from this period. The first movement also has a musical quotation from—appropriately enough—Beethoven's song cycle *An die ferne Geleibte* (*To the Distant Beloved*, 1816).

Schumann himself described the first movement to Clara as the most passionate piece he had ever written, "a deep lament for you." It has a wonderfully passionate, dissonant opening whose harmonic buoyancy keeps the listener denied of the expected musical closure for some time. It is in three main sections, the first and last of which have connections suggestive of sonata form (the "exposition," containing two themes, and the "reprise," which recapitulates these with tonal changes, respectively) and the second, the sonata-form "development" section that does, in Schumann's *Fantasy*, fulfill this function to a small extent. Much controversy has surrounded the title Schumann gave to this middle section, "Im Legenden Ton" ("In the Manner of a Legend"), and the fact that it features a change of time-signature from the prevailing four beats per bar to two. Much analytical ink has been spilt on this movement, and it remains a fascinating formal enigma in spite of its utter musical conviction for the listener.

One of the alternative titles Schumann gave the second movement was "Siegesbogen" ("Triumphal March"), and it certainly does suggest such a march in its four-square phrasing and the repetitive, occasionally almost obsessive, dotted rhythms. There is an irresistible reminiscence, in defiance of historical chronology, of jazz rhythms in the syncopations, but also of one of the variations in the finale of Beethoven's last piano sonata, that in C minor (op. 111). This movement is also in three sections, suggesting the earlier symphonic minuet—trio—minuet outline or, its later manifestation as scherzo—trio—scherzo. Here it can be seen as march 1—slightly slower trio— march 2 (based on march 1). The key of the movement is E-flat major, traditionally suggesting strength and determination, and the key of Beethoven's *Eroica* symphony and his *Emperor* Piano Concerto, associations that would, of course, not be lost on Schumann.

The effect of the slow finale has had less to do with its formal enigmas—although these have been addressed—than its emotional aura, calling forth such descriptions as "pure poetry" (Walter Dahms), "a profound benediction" and "a deep, introspective meditation" (Joan Chissell), "[transforming] desire into a projected state of shared intimacy" (Michael P. Steinberg), and "spiritual calm" (Yonty Solomon). The movement does feel imbued with the spirit of late-period Beethoven in its introspection and resignation, but this can also be detected in the stretches of music based on one rhythm, for example the triplet groups or the rhythmic motif of the slightly faster middle section that reappears just before the end. Themes appear to crystallize out of textures and grow from what initially presents itself as accompanimental material; these themes also reappear in middle and bass voices. Clara's own theme is evoked several times, first occurring in the bass a few bars from the opening, and it can also be detected in a truncated, distilled form at the opening and at the end. Her initial reaction to the piece was that it made her "go hot and cold all over," and a week later she wrote to Robert, "I always play the Fantasy with true rapture, and such truly inner delight."

DEREK CAREW

See also **Music, Romantic; Schumann, Robert**

Bibliography

Boettcher, W., ed. *Robert Schumann: Fantasie Opus 17*. Munich, 1987.

Chissell, Joan. *Schumann Piano Music*. London, 1972.

Dale, K. "The Piano Music," in *Schumann: A Symposium*. Edited by Gerald Abraham. London, 1952.

Kahl, W. "Romantic Piano Music: 1830–1850." In *Romanticism (1830–1890)*. Edited by G. Abraham. Vol. 9 of the *New Oxford History of Music*. Oxford: Oxford University Press, 1990.

Marston, N. *Schumann: Fantasie Op. 17*. Cambridge: Cambridge University Press, 1992.

Solomon, Yonty. "Solo Piano Music 1: The Sonatas and Fantasie." In *Robert Schumann: The Man and His Music*. Edited by Alan Walker. London, 1972.

Walker, A. "Schumann, Liszt and the C-Major Fantasie, Op. 17: A eclining Relationship," *Music and Letters* 60 (1979).

FASHION

Fashion is linked to the creation of a nonaristocratic consumer class during the eighteenth century. Initially, this trend in England was associated with social emulation and the middle class's desire to distinguish itself from its superiors and inferiors. With the advent of the popular press, information on consumer goods could be disseminated quickly, emphasizing the perennial principle of change and novelty, which is the essence of fashion.

Since the fifteenth century, costly and cumbersome fashion dolls, called pandoras, disseminated information on fashionable trends. Large, often life-sized, dolls with porcelain faces and movable limbs were used to display the "grande toilette" of official court dress, and smaller ones displayed the latest fashion in negligees or house dresses. At the Versailles court, the ladies accessorized the dolls themselves and sent them to each other. Some were publicly displayed for an admission fee, for example at the Hotel Rambouillet in Paris, and later traveled to the most important European cities. Eventually, collections of illustrations of fashionable clothing (fashion plates) made this information more widely available and paved the way for images in fashion journals.

What distinguishes modern fashion as it emerged during the Romantic period from earlier practices is the nonenforcement of sumptuary laws, the rapid pace of change, and wider availability. Journals played an instrumental role in the accelerated and wider dissemination of information on fashion. As a decidedly modern phenomenon, fashion derived a strong impetus from increased literacy, the periodical press, and the reading revolution of the eighteenth century. The increasing interest in the visual representation of the bourgeoisie in portraits also contributed. The bourgeoisie liked to pose in their domestic fashionable environment, which extended to the body in its dress, coiffure, and accessories. Serious painters, however, argued for a more timeless portraiture and disliked painting people in their fashionable clothes (Joshua Reynolds was a proponent of this view). Bourgeois fashion in portraiture and illustrated fashion journals rendered the self-definition of the middle class visible.

With the immense growth of the periodical press and the formation of a community of middle-class readers, fashion found initially sporadic entrance into almanacs, for example into the 1770 Dresden publication *Almanach de la Toilette et de la Mode* (*Almanac of Attire and Fashion*); four years later the first almanac devoted to fashion, Davault's *Almanach Nouveau ou Recueil des plus Jolies Coeffures a la Mode* (*New Almanac or Collection of the Prettiest Fashionable Hairdos*), appeared. Despite the fact that

Reprinted courtesy of Bildarchiv.

In Erfurt, the first explicit, albeit short-lived, fashion magazine appeared—*Neue Mode und Galanteriezeitung* (1758). In France, the *Courier de la Mode* (1768–70) and in England the *Macaroni and Theatrical Magazine or Monthly Register of Fashions and Diversions of the Times* (1772–73) offered information. As the periodical press became more differentiated and specialized, specific fashion journals emerged, such as the French *Cabinet des Modes* (*Cabinet of Fashions*, 1785–93) and later the *Journal des Dames et des Modes* (*Journal for Ladies and Fashions*, 1798–1839); the German *Hamburger Damen-, Kunst- und Modejournal* (*Hamburg Ladies, Art, and Fashion Journal*, 1783–90) and Bertuch's *Journal des Luxus und der Moden* (*Journal of Luxuries and Fashion*, 1786–1827); the English *The Gallery of Fashion* (1795–1805), succeeded by *La Belle Assemblee or Bell's Court and Fashionable Magazine* (1806–30).

We have to keep in mind that fashion referred to a larger phenomenon than just clothing; it extended to other lifestyle issues such as interior design, luxury goods, pastimes, and customs or practices. Closely linked to the emergence of individualism as a central issue of Romanticism, fashion became a significant socio-aesthetic phenomenon suggestive of the central values of a society shedding its feudal restrictions.

Fashionable consumption is stimulated by a decidedly modern desire for novelty, which is essentially insatiable, requiring an endless chain of new stimuli. Romantic "mentalistic" hedonism, as a child of sentimentality, was no longer dependent merely on physical stimuli but acquired the skill to indulge in imaginary pleasures: the pleasures of reading, day-dreaming, friendship, and romantic love. Fashion exemplified this limitless desire to seek imaginary pleasures. The essential activity of fashionable consumption is not the concrete choice, purchase, or use of commodity items, but the imaginative pursuit of pleasure to which the image associated with the product lends itself. The experience of mentally trying on the clothes depicted in the periodical press, seemed to constitute such an imaginary pleasure. Since the reality does not provide the perfect pleasure encountered in daydreams, each actual purchase leads to disillusionment, which produces the fundamental longing to search for a replacement, a new object of desire. This tension is not only an earmark of the mentality of Romanticism but connects it to the spirit of modern consumerism, which feeds off the same tensions.

Fashion allowed the bourgeoisie to distinguish itself from the strict dress code of absolutism, which situated the body in the hierarchy of the court. The emphasis on naturalness and individuality in middle-class dress served as a means of opposition. At the same time, it dislodged the body from its stable position. But far from offering complete freedom, the selection of fashionable items for dress or the domestic sphere was determined by taste, which became the new yardstick for measuring social identity and individuality in the system of cultural distinctions.

KARIN A. WURST

Bibliography

Bovenschen, Silvia, ed. *Die Listen der Mode*. Frankfurt: Suhrkamp, 1986.

Brewer, John, and Roy Porter, eds. *Consumption and the World of Goods*. London: Routledge, 1993.

Bruford, Walter. *Germany in the Eighteenth Century: The Social Background of the Literary Revival*. Cambridge: Cambridge University Press, 1949.

Germany took the leadership in the fashion press, the undisputed model for fashionable consumption was initially France. The "grand habit" of the French court, with its heavily-boned bodice, and separate, lavishly trimmed skirt and train, influenced all of Europe.

Yet by the arrival of the fashion magazine in the 1780s, the dominance had shifted to England, as the simpler, more functional, and "modern" fashions of the emergent middle class were perceived as desirable; these particularly influenced fashions in the German states. Often, illustrations, the most attractive but also most expensive feature of fashion magazines, were copied outright or only slightly modified in other journals.

The emergence of the fashion journal was accompanied by a more frequent changing of styles and a bewildering array of materials, colors, and silhouettes, ranging from the masculine-looking coated riding dress from England to the gauzy and sheer lightness of the neoclassical chemise dress and seminude fashions from France. With the variety and availability of new materials and the more extensive exchange of ideas, styles also became influenced by fantasy dress (the oriental, the *à la gréque*, the Gothic style).

Campbell, Colin. *The Romantic Ethic and the Spirit of Modern Consumerism*. New York: Blackwell, 1987.

Craik, Jennifer. *The Face of Fashion: Cultural Studies in Fashion*. New York: Routledge, 1994.

Flügel, J. C. *The Psychology of Clothes*. London: Hoarth, 1930.

McCracken, Grant. *Culture and Consumption: New Approaches to the Symbolic Character of Consumer Goods and Activities*. Bloomington: Indiana University Press, 1988.

McKendick, Neil. Introduction. In *The Birth of a Consumer Society: The Commercialization of Eighteenth Century England*. Edited by Neil McKendrick, John Brewer, and J. H. Plumb, London: Hutchinson, 1984; 1–6.

Purdy, Daniel. "Weimar Classicism and the Origins of Consumer Culture." In *Unwrapping Goethe's Weimar: Essays in Cultural Studies and Local Knowledge*. Edited by Burkhard Henke, Susanne Kord, and Simon Richter; Columbia, S.C.: Camden House, 2000.

———. *The Tyranny of Elegance: Consumer Cosmopolitanism in the Era of Goethe*. Baltimore: Johns Hopkins University Press, 1998.

Ribeiro, Aileen. *Dress in Eighteenth-Century Europe, 1715–1789*. London: Batsford, 1984.

———. *A Visual History of Costume: The Eighteenth Century*. London: Batsford, 1983.

Squire, Geoffrey. *Dress and Society 1560–1970*. New York: Viking, 1974.

Veblen, Thorstein. *The Theory of the Leisure Class*. New York: MacMillan, 1899.

Wurst, Karin A. "The Self-Fashioning of the Bourgeoisie in Late Eighteenth-Century German Culture: Bertuch's *Journal des Luxus und der Moden*," *The Germanic Review* 72, no. 3 (1997): 170–82.

FAUST

Part 1, 1808; Part 2, 1832

Drama by Johann Wolfgang von Goethe

Johann Wolfgang von Goethe called his great play "something incommensurable." The scope of the drama extends beyond the essentially theological interests of the traditional Faust story, to encompass an enormous range of social and aesthetic concerns. The earliest impulses for Goethe's reworking of the Faust theme come from the influence of the Sturm und Drang (storm and stress) movement, but he initially encountered the material in popular forms. The first extant printed version of the legend was the chapbook, *Historia des D. Johann Fausten*, published by the Frankfurt printer Johann Spies in 1587. Christopher Marlowe's English version of the Faust tale found its way back to Germany via companies of English touring actors, and, ultimately, into a puppet play that Goethe very likely knew as a boy. The early version of part 1 (generally, though perhaps misleadingly, called the *UrFaust*) already existed as a sequence of scenes when Goethe moved to Weimar in 1775, and this text was preserved in a manuscript transcription by Luise von Göchhausen, rediscovered in 1887. The claim in the early version that "Gefühl ist alles" ("feeling is all"), and the parody of academic life provided by Mephistopheles's encounter with a student, align *Faust* with the antirational impulses of the Sturm und Drang. However, the immediacy of its diction and the irregular lines adopted by Goethe give some measure of the popularity to which his work aspires. The model of folk art or of a restored common culture haunts successive generations of German Romantics: in Part 1 it is seen in the pseudo-Shakespearean crowd scenes of the Easter morning walk and the low comedy of Auerbach's Cellar. This world of integrated faith, ordered social deference, and conviviality serves only to emphasize Faust's exclusion from the coherences that bind it.

In the opening scenes, "Night," Faust stands in his study surrounded by his father's medical paraphernalia and collections. A skull and vial of poison suggest suicide, and subtly reference Hamlet and his infamous question on being. The tragic isolation of the scholar who has lost faith in the academic tradition forces Faust toward a search for self-definition. This anticipates the Romantic fantasy of self-constitution through autopoiesis, which would drive the early Romantic aesthetic in Jena. It is echoed in the artificial man of Mary Shelley's *Frankenstein*. Lord Byron's *Manfred* explicitly takes up Faust's rejection of science and his curse on patience, but allows the central figure to die without the interruption and delay which Goethe contrives. Unlike Marlowe's Dr. Faustus, Goethe's Faust is saved by angelic intervention to pursue a transcendent vision of the eternal feminine. This is ultimately made possible by the crucial change from the traditional pact with the devil to Faust's wager with Mephistopheles that no experience can ever engender full self-knowledge and a simultaneous knowledge of the world.

Faust's flight from dusty scholarship projects an ideal of immediate but unending experience of both nature and the entire range of human emotion. To achieve it, the hero is forced through the rituals of magical rejuvenation, but appears to encounter the real thing in his sudden desire for Margarete, the central focus of the second half of part 1 in the "Gretchen Tragedy." The shift from dalliance to seduction and corruption, and finally to murder and infanticide, makes of this encounter with youthful desire and passion in *Faust* a particularly intense version of a stock dramatic action: the aristocratic seduction of a girl from the lower orders enshrined in the German "bourgeois tragedy" inaugurated by Gotthold Ephraim Lessing. Faust's encounters with the world are "staged" and the drama becomes a series of plays within the play, as Jane Brown has shown. Reminiscences of *Hamlet* and the Book of Job, as of bourgeois tragedy, lend substance within the action to the self-conscious theatricality implied by the "Prelude in the Theater" (where a theater director, a playwright, and an actor discuss the possibilities of the stage) and the "Prologue in Heaven" (where Faust is projected as the focus of a *Welttheater*). This agonizing self-consciousness nags away to suggest, as does Mephistopheles in "Forest and Cavern," that even an encounter with the sublime (not unlike

William Wordsworth's in *The Prelude*) is ultimately self-regarding.

The death of Margarete's mother, brother, and child, and her condemnation at the end of part 1, provide the measure of the tragedy unleashed by Faust's boundless desire for immediate and overwhelming experience in the "little world" of domestic simplicity. The knowledge that Goethe was still working on the second part throughout his life provoked many contemporaries to preempt the sequel, or to provide alternative versions. Where Heinrich Heine's ballet scenario *Faust. Ein Tanzpoem* (1847) emphasizes Faust's sensuality, Christian Dietrich Grabbe's earlier *Don Juan und Faust* recognizes conflicting archetypes, and Nikolaus Lenau's insists on a fundamental pessimism in his hero's suicide. Goethe's hero, on the other hand, strives to reintegrate desire, knowledge, and activity. He traverses the greater world opened up in part 2 as the traveling showman-magician of the Faust book, visiting the court of the Holy Roman Emperor (in fact, Emperor Maximilian I). The empire described by chancellor, treasurer, steward, and general reveals a state on the verge of fiscal collapse and anomie; its early modern context points toward the political strand of the play. What begins in this Act with the devilish invention of paper money is taken up again in the apparent conflict between emperor and antiemperor staged by Mephistopheles in act 4, and concludes in Faust's attempt in act 5 to establish an independent colony on land reclaimed from the sea and granted to him as sovereign territory in return for his "military" support. The collective activity that creates the land in act 5 offers another sense of the common culture and true popularity pursued in various forms by successive Romantic aesthetics in Germany. The hucksters Faust and Mephistopheles can solve the empire's financial crisis in act 1, but paper money is not stable nor founded on real value any more than Helen of Troy can be returned to the stage (in act 1 as a magic trick, in act 3 as a Greek tragic heroine) without suffering from the ambiguity of representation itself.

The necessity of representation no longer simply undermines immediate experience by showing that it is staged, that immediacy is always mediated by consciousness; rather, it suggests that the collaborative efforts of the theater, sketched out in the prelude to part 1 provide the best available model for understanding the collective nature of experience as socially generated.

ANTHONY PHELAN

Text

First Edition
Faust. Ein Fragment. In *Schriften*, vol. 7. 1790.

Critical Edition
Sämtliche Werke, vols. 7.1 and 7.2. Edited by Albrecht Schöne. Frankfurt am Main: Deutscher Klassiker Verlag, 1994.

Translations
Faust, Part One. Translated by Luke David. Oxford: Oxford University Press, 1987.
Faust, Part Two. Translated by Luke David. Oxford: Oxford University Press, 1994.

Bibliography

Atkins, Stuart. *Goethe's Faust: A Literary Analysis.* London: Oxford University Press, 1958.
Bennett, Benjamin. *Goethe's Theory of Poetry: Faust and the Regeneration of Language.* New York: Cornell University Press, 1986.
Boyle, Nicholas. *Faust. Part One.* Cambridge: Cambridge University Press, 1987.
Brown, Jane K. *Goethe's Faust: the German Tragedy.* Ithaca, N.Y.: Cornell University Press, 1986.
Schlaffer, Heinz. *Faust Zweiter Teil. Die Allegorie des 19. Jahrhunderts.* Stuttgart: Metzler, 1981.
Williams, John R. *Goethe's Faust.* London: Allen and Unwin, 1987.
Zabka, Thomas. *Faust II—das Klassische und das Romantische.* Tübingen: Niemeyer, 1993.

FEAR AND TREMBLING: A DIALECTICAL LYRIC (FRYGT OG BÆVEN: DIALECTISK LYRIK) 1843

Johannes de Silentio (John of Silence; pseudonym of Søren Kierkegaard)

Fear and Trembling can be counted as a major work of the Romantic period due to its intense explication of the irrational element in religious faith. Johannes de Silentio, or John of Silence, examines from all angles the story of Abraham and Isaac told in Genesis 22, discovering in Abraham a "knight of faith" whose readiness to accept God's command transcends universal ethical norms for the sake of a higher, religious good. Søren Kierkegaard's usual mask of a pseudonym creates a narrative that allows for some ambiguities, but Abraham's absolute duty to God is argued so forcefully that it is clearly Kierkegaard speaking.

Kierkegaard's disquisition on faith incorporates his vision of three modes open to one in life: the aesthetic, the ethical, and ultimately the religious. It also develops his opposition to certain elements in G. W. F. Hegel's philosophy, and it reflects aspects of his broken engagement to Regine Olsen, and perhaps of his poor relationship with his father. The aesthetic mode emerges most clearly in *Either/Or*, where Kierkegaard pairs it off dialectically with the ethical mode. Each of these stages has its own subtleties, but Patrick Gardiner sees in the aesthetic sensibility a streak of "Romantic *Weltschmerz*," a Byronic hero who "may ascribe his unhappiness to something fixed and unalterable in his character or his environment" and who may feel that "he has been treated badly by other people." This "bad faith," as Jean-Paul Sartre would call it, encourages a "fatalistic or necessitarian viewpoint, [in which] the individual tacitly absolves himself from accountability for his condition as well as from an obligation to do anything about it."

Fear and Trembling goes further, contrasting the ethical mode with the religious in a series of three problemata (the "dialectic" of the subtitle) that follow an opening lyric. Kierkegaard's preface finds him in something of an aesthetic mood, sneering at the too-easy faith of his contemporaries compared to the "old days": "For then faith was a task for a whole lifetime, not a skill thought to be acquired in either days or weeks." He continues in a familiar Romantic lament: "In an age where passion has been done away with for the sake of science [the writer] easily foresees his fate . . ." The preface then ends with a caustic rejection of Hegel's "System," a preview of one of Johannes's dominant themes.

A brief "attunement" narrates four possible scenarios that Abraham might have followed on the mountain in Moriah, and a "speech in praise of Abraham" ends the lyric prelude. The speech begins with a poetic statement of the need for religious faith: "If there were no eternal consciousness in a man, if at the bottom of everything there were only a wild ferment, a power that twisting in dark passions produced everything great or inconsequential; if an unfathomable, insatiable emptiness lay hid beneath everything, what would life be but despair?" This rhetorical question is followed immediately by the bold assertion, "But for that reason it is not so," and all of Kierkegaard's faith ultimately comes down to this conviction that God exists because he has to.

In the "preamble from the heart" that introduces the problemata, Kierkegaard announces his grudge against Hegel with the complaint, "Theology sits all painted at the window courting philosophy's favor, offering philosophy its delights." He also explains that if he, in Abraham's place, were to resign himself to sacrificing Isaac, he would be committing "the greatest falsehood, for my immense resignation would be a substitute for faith." Most important, what constitutes Abraham's faith is his conviction that Isaac would somehow be returned to him, that "even in that moment when the knife gleamed he believed— that God would not demand Isaac." The knight of faith may well appear in the guise of the "bourgeois philistine," but "not the least thing does he do except on the strength of the absurd." These remarks precede several pages on the knight of resignation, a meditation that seems to refer to Kierkegaard's broken relations with Olsen, an act that brought "peace and repose:" "Infinite resignation is the last stage before faith, so that anyone who has not made this movement does not have faith. . . ." There is something poignant about Kierkegaard's remark that "it must be wonderful to get the princess, and yet it is only the knight of faith who is happy. . . ." These are the themes he will pursue in the three problemata.

Problema 1 asks, "Is there a teleological suspension of the ethical?" Or does one ever suspend the accepted ethical norms to achieve some higher telos, or end? The answer is yes, and in doing so one moves on from the ethical mode to the religious. When Kierkegaard begins the problemata by stating, "The ethical as such is the universal" and that the individual must always "abrogate his particularity so as to become the universal," he is expressing the well-known ethical system of Hegel, a philosophy that he must deal with in defining the faith of the religious mode. His explanation of how the individual surpasses the universal to achieve "an absolute relation to the absolute" is, he admits, "a paradox, inaccessible to thought," and it is Abraham who, acting on "the strength of the absurd," most fully embodies this paradox of faith.

The absurd in Abraham's case is his unfaltering conviction that despite the seeming finality of his sacrifice of Isaac, God will return his son to him. In committing himself to the sacrifice, Abraham rejects the demands of the Hegelian universal and plunges into the realm of religious faith. Without mentioning

him by name, Kierkegaard describes the plight of Agamemnon, who had to sacrifice his daughter, Iphigenia, to placate a goddess and fill the sails of the Greek fleet becalmed on its way to Troy. Agamemnon's awful decision, fraught with terrible consequences ten years later, falls far short of the absurd because it is a rational decision made—or so Agamemnon thought—in accordance with the needs of what Hegel would call the universal. Agamemnon thus becomes a "tragic hero," a victim of the universal who virtually defines the term *tragic*. But in his inability to explain or rationalize God's command, Abraham becomes a "knight of faith," and "he who walks the narrow path of faith no one can advise, no one understand."

Problema 2, "Is there an absolute duty to God?" reworks essentially the same arguments, reformulating Hegel to fit Kierkegaard's notion of faith and the absolute. In a representative passage Kerkegaard writes, "Then faith's paradox is this, that the single individual is higher than the universal, that the single individual (to recall a theological distinction less in vogue these days [an apparent glance at Hegel]) determines his relation to the universal through his relation to the absolute, not his relation to the absolute through his relation to the universal." Kierkegaard finds an analogue to his argument in Luke 14:26, which proclaims: "If any man come to me, and hate not his father, and mother, and wife, and children, and brethren, and sisters, yea, and his own life also, he cannot be my disciple." Kierkegaard sneers at "the pious and tender-minded exegete" whose shallow casuistry about this passage "ends up in drivel rather than terror," and he justifies Luke's verb *hate* by insisting that the ethical equivalent of Abraham's ready agreement to kill Isaac is that he hates his son. The entire second problema stresses the terrible loneliness of the knight of faith, "always a witness, never a teacher," unable to communicate his absolute duty to God.

Problema 3, "Was it ethically defensible of Abraham to conceal his purpose from Sarah, from Eleazar, from Isaac?" is bogged down in a tortuous contrast between what Kierkegaard sees as the concealment often demanded in the aesthetic mode and the disclosure common to the ethical. Much of the discussion masks his debate with himself over breaking off his engagement to Regine Olsen, a crisis Kierkegaard figures in his summary of the folktale "Agnete and the Merman." The merman/seducer emerges from the sea to enchant the innocent Agnete, who finds personified in the merman all the passion and mystery she hears in the ocean's roar, but once Agnete accepts him, in "absolute faith," "The ocean roars no more, its wild voice is stilled, nature's passion—which is the merman's strength—deserts him, the sea becomes dead calm." Just so does innocence thwart a seducer. Kierkegaard spins out the possibilities of this tale, following it with the story of Sarah from the apocryphal Book of Tobit, finding in Sarah a real hero for allowing Tobit to marry her even though her previous seven bridegrooms had been stricken to death: "What ethical maturity to take on the responsibility of allowing the loved one such an act of daring!" The narrative continues to circle around familiar assertions about faith, citing Goethe's Faust as one who "knows that the security and happiness people live in are not supported by the power of spirit but can be readily explained as unreflective bliss." Thus is Faust preserving people's illusions, "one more case of an individual wanting to save the universal by his concealment and silence." The third problema engages stimulating moral issues, but it is hard not to think it is concerned more with Kierkegaard and Regine than with Abraham and Isaac.

Alastair Hannay summarizes convincingly Kierkegaard's concern with Abraham and Isaac in *Fear and Trembling*. He writes, "In one respect Kierkegaard was sacrificing Regine, who obviously wanted the marriage; in another he was sacrificing himself, since he obviously wanted Regine; and in yet another he perhaps felt that his whole life had been sacrificed through his father (Abraham?), at least ruined as far as being healthily adapted in mind as well as body to accept the responsibilities and pleasures of family life and a solid job is concerned, and therefore a preparation for some higher mission."

Fear and Trembling is a great work of moral dialectic, and a moving allegory of a personal crisis.

FRANK DAY

Text

Frygt og Bœven: Dialectisk Lyrik. 1843. Translated as *"Fear and Trembling"* by Howard V. Hong and Edna H. Hong; Princeton: Princeton University Press, 1983; and by Alastair Hannay; New York: Penguin, 1986.

Bibliography

Crocker, Sylvia Fleming. "Sacrifice in Kierkegaard's *Fear and Trembling*," *Harvard Theological Review* 68 (1975): 125–39.

Gardiner, Patrick. *Kierkegaard.* New York: Oxford University Press, 1988.

Green, Ronald M. "'Developing' *Fear and Trembling*." In *The Cambridge Companion to Kierkegaard.* Edited by Alastair Hannay and Gordon D. Marino. Cambridge: Cambridge University Press, 1998.

Lowrie, Walter. *Kierkegaard.* London: Oxford University Press, 1938.

Mooney, Edward F. *Knights of Faith and Resignation: Reading Kierkegaard's "Fear and Trembling."* Albany: State University of New York Press, 1990.

Perkins, Robert, ed. *Kierkegaard's "Fear and Trembling": Critical Appraisals.* Tuscaloosa: University of Alabama Press, 1981.

Thompson, Josiah. *Kierkegaard.* London: Gollancz, 1974.

FEMINIST APPROACHES TO ROMANTIC LITERATURE

Feminism has had a significant influence on Romantic criticism since the late 1970s. Feminist approaches to Romantic literature have, for the most part, consisted of two strands. First, the ideals and assumptions that underpin Romanticism, revealed in the writings of the men who constitute the Romantic canon, have been critiqued in order to reveal its masculinist bias. Second, the many women who were writing during the Romantic age have begun to be discovered and discussed. This has led to a project of recanonization, which has manifested itself in a number of recent books, anthologies and collections of essays on Romantic women writers. Romantic recanonization seeks to redress the way in which Romantic scholarship has traditionally restricted itself to a small number of male writers and, subsequently, to a limited range of genres and issues. In introducing women writers to Romantic scholarship, feminist critics have sought to clarify the relationship of women with Romanticism.

The critique of Romanticism as a masculinist ideology has been informed to some extent by French feminist theory, inasmuch as it highlights the inherent maleness of Romanticist poetics as "phallogocentrism" (a term coined by Jacques Derrida to describe Western society's conflation of masculine power with linguistic authority and determinateness). In contrast, much of the work of recovery and recanonization has relied on an Anglo-American "gynocritical" approach, which seeks to unearth and therefore to understand the lives of women and their experiences.

The feminist critique of Romanticism as a masculine and exclusionary poetic practice has centered on the figure of the Romantic poet. Feminist critics emphasize that the Romantic poet possesses a highly developed subjectivity, for the poetic act is construed as the solitary achievement of an individual who understands both himself and his place in the world. Not surprisingly, the poet's position is compared with other traditionally masculine roles, such as the creator, the prophet, the savior, and the legislator. Feminist scholars have argued that the strong sense of self that undergirds this formulation is something that women were not encouraged to develop in the Romantic era. These critics have outlined the ways in which male Romantics, intentionally or otherwise, overwhelmed the female writers in their circle: for example, William Wordsworth effectively silenced his sister Dorothy even as he mined her work for inspiration, while the women in Johann Wolfgang von Goethe's circle were overshadowed by his seemingly unquestionable authority. Women in the Romantic era were disadvantaged by conventional gender expectations whether they were forced to devote time to domestic duties or, more insidiously, undermined by their doubts about the acceptability of their position as writers.

Some critics (for example, Marlon Ross) have suggested that the Romantic emphasis on subjectivity is most clearly manifest in the Romantic poet's desire to control and conquer. The primary contest is often understood as that between the Romantic poet and the great poets of the past. Such an interpretation excludes women, since it reduces the poetic act to a Freudian battle between father and son. More recently, critics have read the Romantic poet's desire for conquest in his encounter with nature. According to this approach, when the Romantic poet draws inspiration from nature, he writes not as a passive receptor of nature's beauty, but as an active perceiver, projecting his own perceptions on to it and appropriating its procreative powers for himself. Most importantly, as in the work of Goethe and Wordsworth, the Romantic poet confronts a feminized nature. Feminist readings of Wordsworthian poetics, such as those by Margaret Homans and Anne Mellor, have pointed out that, although Wordsworth presents nature as a potent maternal and presumably procreative energy, he ultimately envisions himself as subduing and appropriating this energy in order to carry out his own creative acts of poetry writing. In this paradigm, the woman writer, unable to write as the masculine Romantic poet, is also reluctant to identify with a silent and passive feminine nature.

Recently, scholars have argued that the male Romantics further marginalized women by subsuming apparently female characteristics under the Romantic imagination. To use Alan Richardson's theory, Romantic poets effectively "colonized" the traditionally feminine realm of sensibility, ousting women from what could have been their own innovative poetics. The Romantics aligned the poet with the "man of feeling": poets such as Goethe, Novalis, and Wordsworth incorporated this idea into their poetic philosophies, while French Romantic novelists such as François-Auguste-René, Comte de Chateaubriand in *René* (1805) created sensitive and thus emasculated heroes. Even while their work displayed the mark of sentimentality and emotionality, some male Romantics distinguished this from female sensibility, which they denigrated and dismissed. Thus, women were prevented from assuming a masculine sentimentality, while they were, not surprisingly, reluctant to revert to a feminine mode of sensibility.

Hence, feminist critics have suggested that the Romantics sought to silence and appropriate the feminine principle. Not surprisingly, the Romantics have been shown to repeat this pattern of marginalization in their representations of women. Such women are often associated with silence and even death, as are Goethe's inarticulate Mignon (in *Wilhelm Meister's Apprenticeship*, 1821–29), Wordsworth's Lucy and Margaret (in "The Ruined Cottage," 1797), and John Keats's dreamy Madeline (in "The Eve of St Agnes," 1820). Or they are placed outside the familiar, whether as mysterious immortals, as are the temptresses of Keats's "Lamia" and "La Belle Dame sans Merci" (1819), or as exotic nymphs and sirens, as are the various female lovers of Lord Byron's *Don Juan* (1819–24). Even the ideal woman in Romantic literature is often a simple reflection of the ideal man, usually a sister but sometimes a mystical mirror image. Percy Bysshe Shelley's *Revolt of Islam* (1818), for example, imagines the ideal woman Cythna as the feminine version of her brother Laon, while William Blake's writings see woman as a mystical emanation of the ideal human—that is, masculine—form.

Yet, feminist criticism has done more than simply critique Romanticism as a fixed and strictly masculine phenomenon. It has also sought to recover the writings of the many women who published during the Romantic era in Germany, Britain, and France. Attempts have been made to understand better such female authors as Jane Austen, Mary Shelley, Madame Anne-Louise-Germaine de Staël, and Mary Wollstonecraft, and to recontextualize their work within the Romantic tradition. The contributions of those women once regarded as being on the periphery of Romantic circles, such as Caroline von Schelling, Goethe's lover Charlotte von Stein, and Dorothy Wordsworth, are also being reassessed. More recently, however, scholars have brought to light the work of such women as Joanna Baillie, Hannah More, and Helen Maria Williams, once major writers and now less well-known.

One of the more interesting corollaries of Romantic recanonization has been the increasing awareness of generic diversity in the Romantic age. The dramatic successes of a female playwright such as Joanna Baillie, for example, remind us that the Romantic stage was not necessarily the creative vacuum that we may imagine it to be, if we focus merely on the closet dramas of the male Romantics, particularly Byron and Keats. Feminist efforts at recanonization have also shifted attention to literary forms, such as letters, diaries, and conduct books, that have been neglected because of their status as conventionally feminine genres, but have much to say about women's position in the Romantic age. The pedagogical texts of Hannah More, for example, both reflected and shaped the prevailing gender norms of the day; while Dorothy Wordsworth's journal entries demonstrate how effec-

tively Wordsworthian poetics could silence the female. On the other hand, traditionally personal modes of writing can reveal how women subverted gender norms and combined the private with the public: Helen Maria Williams and Mary Wollstonecraft used (among other forms) the letter as a basis for political commentary, while German women writers used their private writings as a forum for discussing aesthetic theories.

lso of interest is the way in which critical discussions of the novel in the Romantic era have expanded in order to take account of the considerable number of women who were writing and reading novels at this time. Critics have noted that the novel, with its emphasis on psychological development and domestic ties, played no small part in the establishment of middle-class family values. Nancy Armstrong's landmark *Desire and Domestic Fiction* (1989) demonstrates how the many novels produced by and for women formed the basis of separate spheres ideology, that is the gendering of the domestic sphere as feminine and the public sphere as masculine. This is evident in women's representations of women; in the way, for example, Jane Austen's heroines find themselves on a trajectory towards marriage and domesticity. In addition, there is now a considerable body of feminist criticism on women's Gothic literature, which reached the height of its popularity in the Romantic age due to writers such as Ann Radcliffe. Much of this criticism argues that women felt increasingly trapped in the domestic sphere and that the Gothic plot, which sees the heroine escaping the confines of a nightmarish castle, is a subversion rather than celebration of the idea of separate spheres.

Significantly, Romantic recanonization, in presenting evidence of successful and popular female writers of the Romantic era, implicitly contradicts that strand of feminist Romanticist scholarship that argues that Romanticism marginalized and thus silenced women. Yet this does not mean that such scholarship is not interested in clarifying the relationship between women and Romanticism. Some critics have paid close attention to the ways in which women have contributed, and indeed helped, to create what we now think of as Romantic ideology. Work on Bettina von Arnim, for example, indicated that she played a central role in developing the art of Romantic conversation in German salons. In British Romanticism, the sonnets of the novelist and poet Charlotte Smith, with their emotionally charged and self-conscious encounters with nature, have been shown to have influenced Wordsworth and his apparently revolutionary poetics. Even where no direct chain of influence may be constructed, as with the coincidence between Baillie's theory of drama in her "Introductory Discourse" to *Plays on the Passions* and Wordsworth's ideas on poetry in *Lyrical Ballads* (1798), such relationships are important because they reveal how both men and women writers were swayed by contemporary currents in thought. Significantly, some work has also been done on the ways in which women critiqued the fundamentals of Romantic ideology. For example, Mary Shelley's *Frankenstein* (1818) has been read as a pointed commentary on the male Romantic's desire to control nature.

However, in addition to remarking on how women writers contributed and responded to "male" or "masculine" Romanticism, much criticism has been devoted to tracing an alternative "female" or "feminine" Romanticism, or at least to studying women and their concerns in isolation from their male counterparts. Such criticism builds on the notion that Romanticism was a predominantly male phenomenon but emphasizes that women, far from silenced, were able to align themselves with a different set of ideas. Often, the term *Romantic* is broadened in this discussion, so that the phrase *Romantic women writers* refers simply to women writers of the Romantic era and not women writers who subscribed to what we commonly understand as Romanticism. Some critics have suggested that a female Romanticism occurred in reaction to mainstream Romanticism. Stuart Curran has used the term *quotidian poetry*, and Anne Mellor has referred to the celebration of the "rational woman," to describe how women writers sought to be defined by the rational and the everyday, in order to counter the transcendence and obscurity privileged by male Romantics. Women writers positioned themselves as rational domestic women, or else created such women among their fictional characters. Overwhelmingly, critics have commented on how women were preoccupied with the home and their position in it, and have seen the increasingly influential notion of separate spheres as the dominant ideology of women writers in the Romantic age. Very recently, however, attempts have been made to recognize the plurality of women's writing rather than to confine it within a single set of beliefs, and other prominent themes in women's writing (for example, revolution and imperialism) are now being explored. Alternative representations of women, such as the deserted woman of Charlotte Smith's sonnets and Felicia Hemans's *Records of Woman* (1828), or the adventurous improvisatrice made popular by Madame de Staël's *Corinne* (1807) and taken up by Letitia Elizabeth Landon, have also emerged.

Feminist approaches to Romantic literature have not been without their risks. For example, the binary of male and female Romanticism could be seen as potentially retrograde to the aims of recanonization, for it facilitates the installation of an alternative female canon, rather than a dismantling, or at least a questioning, of the male Romantic canon. A further problem is the susceptibility of women writers to canonical tokenism. Fortunately, however, recent Romanticist scholarship has shown an awareness of such potential problems. Increasingly, Romanticist criticism is incorporating male and female writers into an exploration of not one but many Romanticisms, and is investigating the gender politics of both male and female authors.

ADELINE JOHNS-PUTRA

See also **Deconstruction and Romantic Literature; Women**

Bibliography

Alexander, Meena. *Women in Romanticism: Mary Wollstonecraft, Dorothy Wordsworth and Mary Shelley.* Basingstoke, England: Macmillan, 1989.

Armstrong, Nancy. *Desire and Domestic Fiction: A Political History of the Novel.* New York: Oxford University Press, 1989.

Ashfield, Andrew, ed. *Romantic Women Poets 1770–1838: An Anthology.* Manchester: Manchester University Press, 1995.

Burroughs, Catherine B. *Closet Stages: Joanna Baillie and the Theater Theory of British Romantic Women Writers.* Philadelphia: University of Pennsylvania Press, 1997.

Curran, Stuart. "Romantic Poetry: The I Altered," in *Romanticism and Feminism.* Edited by Anne K. Mellor. Bloomington: Indiana University Press, 1988.

Ellis, Kate Ferguson. *The Contested Castle: Gothic Novels and the Subversion of Domestic Ideology.* Urbana: University of Illinois Press, 1989.

Feldman, Paula R., and Theresa M. Kelley, eds. *Romantic Women Writers: Voices and Countervoices.* Hanover, N.H.: University Press of New England, 1995.

Goodman, Katherine R., and Edith Waldstein, eds. *In the Shadow of Olympus: German Women Writers around 1800.* Albany: State University of New York Press, 1992.

Homans, Margaret. *Women Writers and Poetic Identity: Dorothy Wordsworth, Emily Brontë, and Emily Dickinson.* Princeton, N.J.: Princeton University Press, 1980.

Jones, Vivien. "Women Writing Revolution: Narratives of History and Sexuality in Wollstonecraft and Williams." In *Beyond Romanticism: New Approaches to Texts and Contexts 1780–1832.* Edited by Stephen Copley and John Whale. London: Routledge, 1992.

Mellor, Anne K. "Possessing Nature: The Female in *Frankenstein.*" In *Romanticism and Feminism.* Edited by Anne K. Mellor. Bloomington: Indiana University Press, 1988.

———. *Romanticism and Gender.* New York: Routledge, 1993.

Rainer, Ulrike. "A Question of Silence: Goethe's Speechless Women." In *Goethes Mignon und ihre Schwestern: Interpretationen und Rezeption.* Edited by Gerhart Hoffmeister. New York: Peter Lang, 1993.

Richardson, Alan. "Romanticism and the Colonization of the Feminine." In *Romanticism and Feminism.* Edited by Anne K. Mellor. Bloomington: Indiana University Press, 1988.

Richardson, Alan, and Sonia Hofkosh, eds. *Romanticism, Race and Imperial Culture, 1780–1834.* Bloomington: Indiana University Press, 1996.

Ross, Marlon B. *The Contours of Masculine Desire: Romanticism and the Rise of Women's Poetry.* New York: Oxford University Press, 1989.

Strand, Mary R. *I/You: Paradoxical Constructions of Self and Other in Early German Romanticism.* New York: Peter Lang, 1998.

Waldstein, Edith. *Bettine von Arnim and the Politics of Romantic Conversation.* Columbia, S.C.: Camden House, 1988.

Waller, Margaret. *The Male Malady: Fictions of Impotence in the French Romantic Novel.* New Brunswick, N.J.: Rutgers University Press, 1993.

Wu, Duncan, ed. *Romantic Women Poets: An Anthology.* Oxford: Blackwell, 1997.

FEUERBACH, LUDWIG 1804–1872

German philosopher

Ludwig Feuerbach is often understood as a more or less transitional figure in German philosophy and social theory, one of several "Left Hegelians" who mediated between the absolute idealism of G. W. F. Hegel and the later dialectical materialism of Karl Marx. Marx himself encouraged this interpretation, suggesting in both *The German Ideology* and the "Theses on Feuerbach" that Feuerbach was a sort of failed materialist, almost—but not quite—able to break free of Hegel's idealism. While there is some validity to this interpretation, it obscures the extent to which Feuerbach developed a distinctive and compelling philosophy of radical humanism, founded on the goal of transforming theology and philosophy into an "anthropology." Feuerbach argued that for humans to fully achieve their individual and species potential, religious faith and doctrine had to be exposed as self-alienations and misrecognitions of human nature.

Feuerbach began his university career in theology, but abandoned this discipline in 1825 to study philosophy with Hegel. While initially enthusiastic about Hegel's philosophical idealism, which held that absolute *Geist* (spirit) realized its inner essence through a process of historical incarnation in matter, Feuerbach eventually came to see Hegel's philosophy as simply another version of religious antagonism to the human world of bodies and feeling. Hints of this movement away from Hegel are evident in Feuerbach's first publication, *Gedanken über Tod und Unsterblichkeit* (*Thoughts on Death and Immortality*, 1830), in which he attempted to reveal that human love and communities in fact contain the elements of infinity and eternity that theologians and philosophers had sought in the realms of religion or "spirit."

Feuerbach published *Gedanken* anonymously, but his authorship was soon discovered, and the anti-Christian tenor of the book effectively negated any possibility of a professorship at Erlangen. (Feuerbach later interpreted resistance to his philosophy as evidence that abstract "philosophical" positions, such as Hegel's, were elaborate—if unconscious—self-deceptions that functioned to maintain social and class interests.) In place of philosophical idealism, Feuerbach began to develop a "sensuous materialism," in which the human species took the place occupied by absolute *Geist* in Hegel's system. Elements of this movement were evident in *Über Philosophie und Christentum* (*On Philosophy and Christianity*, 1839), but the full exposition appeared in Feuerbach's *Das Wesen des Christentums* (*The Essence of Christianity*, 1841).

The fundamental goal of *Das Wesen des Christentums* was to reveal that the supposed attributes of the Christian God and religion were in fact projections of *human* capacities onto a false external image, to which humans then subordinated themselves. Yet Feuerbach also wanted to demonstrate that these misrecognitions of human powers were "motivated" errors, in the sense that they stemmed from valid human needs and desires. Rather than beginning his philosophy, as did Hegel, with "pure Being," Feuerbach's starting point was the material human being, who is defined by desiring, willing, and reasoning, and who constantly needs to relate through consciousness to all other human beings (the "species"). The individual recognizes that, as an individual, he is limited and finite, but also dimly recognizes that as a species he is "absolute." Religion originates in the misrecognition of this relationship between the individual and the species: "Man—this is the mystery of religion—projects his being into objectivity, and then again makes himself an object to this projected image of himself thus converted into a subject." More generally, Feuerbach argued that all theological and philosophical distinctions between, for example, the universal and the particular or the infinite and the finite, were simply misrecognitions of the distinction between the individual and the species. The goal of history, then, was the complete development of human potentialities through the continuing reclamation of human attributes from the "objects" of religion.

Das Wesen des Christenums was predictably attacked by Christian apologists, but was in general well received, and it consolidated Feuerbach's reputation as one of the "Left Hegelians."

This identification of Feuerbach was encouraged in part because his book appeared in the same year as Bruno Bauer's *Kritik der evangelischen Geschichte der* Synoptiker (*Critique of the Synoptic Gospels*, 1841–42) and the second volume of David Friedrich Strauss's *Christliche Glaubenslehre* (*Christian Faith*, 1841–42). All three authors had begun their careers as Hegelians, but had each subsequently developed extremely critical readings of the "illusions" of Christianity. "Left" Hegelianism was thus defined by an attack on religion and an emphasis on social critique, and distinguished from the "Right Hegelians," who employed neo-Hegelian philosophy in a defense of the existing state. Yet while Feuerbach acknowledged the continuities between his work and that of Strauss and Bauer, he objected to the notion that he belonged to any school, and resisted attempts to join formally any Left Hegelian journal or political party, arguing that his work was socially and politically effective in so far as it helped to destroy the religious and philosophical illusions that allowed despotism to hold sway.

While Feuerbach published several interesting works after *Das Wesen des Christentums*, that text established his reputation and his continuing interest to contemporary theologians and philosophy. Moreover, his critique of Christianity and German idealism was positioned within a complicated set of competing traditions, an entanglement that retrospectively seems typically Romantic. His representation of religious doctrine and faith as misrecognized self-alienations of the human essence was in one sense a continuation of the Enlightenment critique of the illusions of "superstition," yet Feuerbach valorized sensuous and material reality in a way that has since become far more associated with Romanticism than the Enlightenment. Moreover, his lifelong obsession with religion, even if in the form of perpetual critique, testified to the much more widespread Romantic-era attempt to mediate between religious tradition and an increasingly secular world. Finally, Feuerbach's radical humanism, while in one sense mediating between German idealism and Marx's political philosophy, also provided an alternative model of social critique, grounded in his belief in the critical value of the destruction of "fantasies" of the imagination.

ROBERT MITCHELL

Biography

Born in Landshut, Bavaria (now Germany), July 28, 1804. Son of the distinguished jurist Paul von Feuerbach. Studied theology at the University of Heidelberg and philosophy at the University of Berlin under G. W. F. Hegel, 1823–25. Received doctorate in philosophy from University of Erlangen, 1828. Worked as *Privatdozent* (private instructor) in philosophy at University of Erlangen, 1828–37. Made three unsuccessful attempts to obtain a salaried professorship at Erlangen; withdrew from academic life; married Bertha Löw, 1837. Published *Das Wesen des Christentums* (*The Essence of Christianity*), 1841. Moved to Rechenberg, near Nuremberg, 1860. Died of a stroke in Rechenberg, September 13, 1872.

Selected Work

Collections

Ludwig Feuerbach's Sämmtliche Werke. 10 vols., 1846–66.
Ludwig Feuerbach's Sämmtliche Werke. Edited by Wilhelm Bolin and Friedrich Jodl. 2d ed., 13 vols., 1959–64.

Gesammelte Werke. Edited by Werner Schuffenhauer, 1967– .
The Fiery Brook: Selected Writings of Ludwig Feuerbach. Edited by Z. Hanfi, 1972.

Philosophy

Gedanken über Tod und Unsterblichkeit. 1830; as *Thoughts on Death and Immortality: From the Papers of a Thinker, along with an Appendix of Theological-Satirical Epigrams*. Translated by James A. Massey, 1980.
Abälard und Heloise. 1834.
Pierre Bayle. 1838.
Über Philosophie und Christenthum. 1839.
Das Wesen des Christenthums. 1841. Translated as *The Essence of Christianity* by George Eliot, 1854.
Grundsätze der Philosophie der Zukunft. 1843; translated as *Principles of the Philosophy of the Future* by Manfred H. Vogel, 1966.

Bibliography

Braun, H. J., H.-M. Sass, W. Schuffenhauer, and F. Tomasoni, eds. *Ludwig Feuerbach und die Philosophie der Zukunft*. Berlin: Akademie Verlag, 1990.
Engels, Friedrich. *Ludwig Feuerbach und der Ausgang der klassischen deutschen Philosophie*. Stuttgart, 1888; translated as *Ludwig Feuerbach and the Outcome of Classical German Philosophy*. New York: C. P. Dutton, 1934.
Harvey, Van A. *Feuerbach and the Interpretation of Religion*. Cambridge: Cambridge University Press, 1995.
Kamenka, E. *The Philosophy of Ludwig Feuerbach*. New York: Praeger, 1970.
Loewith, K. *From Hegel to Nietzsche: The Revolution in Nineteenth Century Thought*. Trans. D. Green. New York: Holt, Rinehart and Winston, 1964.
Wartofsky, M. *Ludwig Feuerbach*. Cambridge: Cambridge University Press, 1977.

FICHTE, JOHANN GOTTLIEB 1762–1814

German philosopher

In his *Biographia Literaria* (1817), Samuel Taylor Coleridge, referring to Immanuel Kant's critical philosophy as the end result of a "revolution in philosophy," acknowledges the influential role of Friedrich Wilhelm Joseph von Schelling, while also noting the relevance of "one or more fundamental ideas which cannot be withheld from Fichte." To appreciate Johann Gottlieb Fichte's impact on Romanticism it is necessary first to understand his contribution to the development of post-Kantian thought.

In his "Declaration Regarding Fichte's *Wissenschaftslehre*" (1799), Kant spoke of his own critical system as "resting on a fully secured foundation, established forever; it will also be indispensable for the noblest ends of humankind in all future ages." Yet this statement indicates Kant's awareness that critical philosophy, the culmination of the Enlightenment in Germany and beyond, was itself gradually becoming the object of critique. One of the earliest and most influential of these critics was Fichte, whose *Versuch einer Kritik aller Offenbarung* (*Attempt at a Critique of All Revelation*, 1792) was, when anonymously published, initially attributed to Kant. But while Fichte began as a Kantian (writing in 1790 that "I am living in a new world, ever since I read the *Critique of Practical Reason*") and a protegé of the "Old Man of Königsberg" (as Johann Wolfgang von Goethe called him), he took seriously the questions about Kantian critical philosophy raised by, among others, Friedrich Heinrich Jacobi, Karl Leonhard Reinhold, and Gottlob Ernst Schulze. For these thinkers, the distinction between the phenomenon (the world as it appears to us) and the noumenon (the world as "thing in itself," or *Ding an sich*) proved to be problematic; Jacobi famously remarked that without the Ding an sich it was impossible to enter Kant's system and, even with it, it was impossible to stay. For his part, Fichte saw it as his task to complete the critical project (despite its founder's belief that this had been done), and he called his system the "doctrine of science," or "science of knowledge"—the *Wissenschaftslehre*. He expounded this system in various treatises, such as *Über den Begriff der Wissenschaftslehre* (*On the Concept of the Science of Knowledge*, 1794); *Grundlage der gesamten Wissenschaftslehre* (*The Basis of the Entire Science of Knowledge*, 1794–95), the *Erste* and *Zweite Einleitung in die Wissenschaftslehre* (*First* and *Second Introduction to the Science of Knowledge*, 1797); and the *Wissenschaftslehre nova methodo* (*The New Method of the Science of Knowledge*, (1797–98). According to Fichte, the Wissenschaftslehre is "the science of all science" (*die Wissenschaft von einer Wissenschaft überhaupt*) and, while the emphasis across these works can be seen to shift, the central concern remains that of giving an account of the relation between the self and the world. In Fichte's terms, the "I" (*Ich*) first "posits" (*setzt*) itself, by means of "intellectual intuition" (*intellektuelle Anschauung*); then it opposes itself with a "not-I" (*Nicht-Ich*). Both "I" and "not-I" proceed to determine each other in a reciprocal manner, anticipating the dialectic associated later with Georg William Fredrich Hegel. The technicalities of the *Wissenschaftslehre* are complex, and the title of Fichte's *Sonnenklarer Bericht an das grössere Publikum über das eigentliche Wesen der neuesten Philosophie: Ein Versuch, die Leser zum Verstehen zu zwingen* (*A Report as Clear as Day for the Wider Public on What Recent Philosophy Is Really About: An Attempt to Force the Readers to Understand*, 1801) illustrates his appreciation of the constant need to explain what was at stake in his philosophy, while Henrik Steffens's account of Fichte's lectures document the difficulty many found in following his expositions. By attempting in *The Science of Knowledge* to uncover "the ground of all experience" and discover "the primordial, absolutely unconditional first principle of all human knowledge," Fichte is *not* arguing a solipsistic case: the "I" of his system is not the individual ego, but the transcendental subject, a necessary structure of all experience. But he *is* arguing in favor of the unconditional freedom (*Freiheit*) of the (transcendental) subject, a metaphysical coin whose other side is "vocation" (*Bestimmung*). The political implications of this notion are reflected in Fichte's claim that his system was "the first system of freedom," which frees itself "from the chains of the *Ding an sich*" just as "that nation [i.e., France] freed humankind from external chains."

Not for nothing, then, did Friedrich von Schlegel claim that the French Revolution, Fichte's *Wissenschaftslehre* and Goethe's *Wilhelm Meister* were "the most powerful trends" (*die grössten Tendenzen*) of the age. Even more explicitly, the *Reden an die deutsche Nation* (*Addresses to the German Nation*, 1808) show how the connection established in the *Wissenschaftslehre* between knowledge and action ("we do not act because we know, but we know, because we are bound [*bestimmt*] to act; practical reason is the root of all reason") both has general implications ("what kind of a philosophy one chooses depends on what kind of a person one is") and, in the specific politicocultural context of the Napoleonic occupation of German lands, carries a nationalist message. As a result, Fichte's political position, like that of some other German Romantics, has been subject to much retrospective criticism. Yet Fichte was never a stranger to controversy. When, as a professor at Jena, he attempted to dissolve rowdy student societies, his windows were smashed in and his wife verbally assaulted on the street. In 1799, following the *Atheismusstreit*, or "atheism controversy," he was dismissed from Jena on the grounds of atheism (Goethe reportedly remarked "one star sets, another rises," but intervened to prevent Fichte being deprived of his professorial title); and his falling out with Schelling (appointed professor of philosophy at Jena University in 1798) was inevitable given their respective philosophical positions and delicate temperaments. Yet his influence on the Jena Romantics (Novalis, Friedrich and August von Schlegel); on Hegal, Friedrich Hölderlin, and Schelling; and on Jean Paul and Ludwig Tieck was immense. For such writers, Fichte's attractiveness, and at the same time his limitation, lay in his perceived insistence on the autonomy of the individual ego (the relationship in Fichte's system between the transcendental "I" and the individual person remains problematic). For Coleridge, in particular, the Wissenschaftslehre . . . "was to add the key-stone of the arch [of the critical philosophy]; and by commencing with an act, instead of a thing or substance, Fichte assuredly gave the first mortal blow to Spinozism, as taught by Spinoza himself; and supplied the idea of a system truly metaphysical, and of a *metaphysique* truly systematic (i.e. having its spring and principle within itself)."

Yet Coleridge critically observed further that "this fundamental idea he overbuilt with a heavy mass of mere notions and psychological acts of arbitrary reflection," with the result that "his theory degenerated into crude *Egoismus*, a boastful and hyperstoic hostility to Nature"—which Schelling would try to correct—"as lifeless, godless and altogether unholy."

In terms of political thought and impact, Fichte's advocacy of the corporate state, the provision of social welfare, and the complete control of external trade in *Der geschlossene Handelstaat* (*The Closed Commercial State*, 1800) anticipated some of the measures later adopted in Bismarck's Prussia. His writings contain important hints about the importance of aesthetics: "The same spirit, through the development of which one becomes aesthetic, must enliven the philosopher"; and he maintained a passionate belief in the ethical significance of pedagogy, declaring it the duty of the scholar to be "a priest of truth" in *Einige Vorlesungen über die Bestimmung des Gelehrten* (*Some Lectures concerning the Vocation of the Scholar*, 1794). (Of "Fichte's notion of the Man of Letters" in this work, Thomas Carlyle wrote that it was "precisely" what he meant by the hero in *On Heroes, Hero-Worship, and the Heroic in History*, 1841.) Although the

Fichte in *Reih'und Glied des Berliner Landsturms* 1813. Reprinted courtesy of Bildarchiv.

mystical overtones of the late work entitled *Die Anweisung zum seligen Leben* (*Instructions for a Blessed Life*, 1806) stand in contrast to *Über den Grund unsers Glaubens an eine göttliche Weltregierung* (*On the Foundation of Our Belief in the Divine Government of the World*, 1798), which led to those charges of atheism, Fichte articulates a deeply Romantic position when, in his *First Introduction*, he writes, "Attend to yourself: turn your attention away from everything that surrounds you and towards your inner life; this is the first demand that philosophy makes of its disciples. Our concern is not with anything that lies outside you, but only with your self."

PAUL BISHOP

Biography

Born in Rammenau, Upper Lusatia, Saxony (now Germany) May 19, 1762. Son of a ribbon weaver. Educated at the Pforta School, 1774–80. Studied theology at University of Jena, 1780–81; then at University of Leipzig, 1781–84; studies were interrupted due to financial hardship. Worked as a *Hauslehrer* (private tutor) 1784–88. Traveled to Zurich, 1788–89; met and became engaged to Johanna Maria Rahn, a niece of Friedrich Klopstock, 1788–90. Returned to Leipzig, then moved to Krokow, near Danzig, as private tutor, 1790–94. Met Immanuel Kant in Königsberg, 1790; renewed engagement to Johanna, 1792; married her, 1793. Appointed to chair of philosophy, University of Jena, 1794; dismissed from professorial post, and moved to Berlin, 1799. Gave public lectures in Berlin, 1804; lecturer at University of Erlangen, 1805, and at Königsberg, 1807. Appointed member of the Bavarian Academy of Sciences, 1808; appointed dean of philosophical faculty of University of Berlin, 1810; Rector of Unversity of Berlin, 1810–12. Contracted typhoid fever from Johanna, working as a volunteer nurse, early 1814. Died of typhus in Berlin, January 29, 1814.

Selected Works

Collections

Sämmtliche Werke. 8 vols. Edited by I. H. Fichte. 1845–46.

Gesamtausgabe der Bayerischen Akademie der Wissenschaften. Edited by Reinhard Lauth, Hans Jacob, Hans Gliwitsky. Stuttgart-Bad Canstatt: F. Frommann, 1962.

Briefwechsel. 2 vols. Edited by Hans Schulz. 1925. Reprinted Hilderheim: G. Olms, 1967.

Early Philosophical Writings. Edited and translated by Daniel Breazeale. Ithaca, NY: Cornell University Press, 1988.

Individual Works

Versuch einer Kritik aller Offenbarung, 1791. Translated as *Attempt at a Critique of All Revelation* by Ganrrett Green. Cambridge: Cambridge University Press, 1978.

Grundlage der gesamten Wissenschaftslehre, 1794 Translated as *Science of Knowledge* by Peter Heath and John Lachs. Cambridge: Cambridge University Press, 1982.

"Über Geist und Buchstab in de Philosophie," written 1794, published 1798. Translated as "On the Spirit and the Letter in Philosophy" by Elizabeth Rubenstein. In *German Aesthetic and Literary Criticism: Kant, Fichte, Schelling, Schopenhauer, Hegel.* Edited by David Simpson. Cambridge: Cambridge University Press, 1984.

Wissenschaftslehre nova methodo, 1797–98. Translated as *Foundations of Transcendental Philosophy* by Daniel Breazeale. Ithaca, N.Y.: Cornell University Press, 1992.

Introductions to the Wissenschaftslehre and Other Writings, 1797–1800. Edited and translated by Daniel Breazeale. Indianapolis: Hackett, 1994.

Die Bestimmung des Menschen 1800. Translated as *The Vocation of Man* by Peter Preuss. Indianapolis: Hackett, 1987.

Reden an die deutsche Nation, 1808. Translated as *Addresses to the German Nation* by R. F. Jones and G. H. Turnbull. Westport, Conn.: Greenwood Press, 1979.

Bibliography

Ashton, Rosemary. *The German Idea: Four English Writers and the Reception of German Thought 1800–1860.* Cambridge: Cambridge University Press, 1980.

Beiser, Frederick C. *The Fate of Reason: German Philosophy from Kant to Fichte.* Cambridge, Mass.: Harvard University Press, 1987.

Betteridge, H. T. "Fichte's Political Ideas: A Retrospect," *German Life and Letters* 14 (1961): 293–304.

Brose, Karl. "Jean Pauls Verhältnis zu Fichte: Ein Beitrag zur Geistesgeschichte," *Deutsche Vierteljahrsschrift* 49 (1975): 66–93.

Henrich, Dieter. "Fichte's Original Insight," *Contemporary German Philosophy* 1 (1982): 5–53.

Hohler, T. P. *Imagination and Reflection: Intersubjectivity—Fichte's Grundlage of 1794.* The Hague: Martinus Nijhoff, 1982.

Jacobs, Wilhelm G. *Johann Gottlieb Fichte mit Selbstzeugnissen und Bilddokumenten dargestellt.* Reinbek bei Hamburg: Rowohlt, 1984.

Janke, Wolfgang. *Fichte: Sein und Reflexion—Grundlagen der kritischen Vernunft.* Berlin: Walter de Gruyter, 1970.

Link, Hannelore. "Zur Fichte Rezeption in der Frühromantik," *Deutsche Vierteljahrsschrift* 52 (1978).

Molnár, Géza von. *Novalis' "Fichte Studies": The Foundations of His Aesthetics.* The Hague: Mouton, 1970.

Neuhouser, Frederick. *Fichte's Theory of Subjectivity.* Cambridge: Cambridge University Press, 1990.

Orsini, Gian N. G. *Coleridge and German Idealism.* Carbondale: Southern Illinois University Press/London: Feffer and Simons, 1969.

Rohs, Peter. *Johann Gottlieb Fichte.* Munich: Verlag C. H. Beck, 1991.

Seidel, George J. *Fichte's Wissenschaftslehre of 1794: A Commentary on Part 1.* West Lafayette, Ind.: Purdue University Research Foundation, 1993.

Seidel, Helmut. *Johann Gottlieb Fichte zur Einführung.* Hamburg: Junius Verlag, 1997.

Sonderband. *Romantik in Deutschland: Ein interdisziplinäres Symposion.* Edited by Richard Brinkmann, Stuttgart: Metzler, 1978.

FICTION: BRITAIN

During the Romantic period, narrative fiction was produced and widely read in both prose and verse. In fact, the 1810s and '20s were a golden age for the narrative poem; since poetry is considered elsewhere in this volume, this study discusses only fiction in prose. Apart from newspapers and magazines, prose fiction was the most widely-read form of print in Britain during the Romantic period. It had a correspondingly large role in expressing and shaping a new national consciousness, and consequently in founding the Romantic nation-state much as we still know it.

Despite this role, fiction also attracted controversy and condemnation. Novels were frequently ridiculed as commercialized and inartistic, disparaged as intellectually and morally corrupting, and condemned as vehicles for subversive ideologies. The importance of the social, cultural, and political role of fiction in Britain was increased by the complex nature of the state—an awkward constitutional union of England (including Wales), Scotland, and Ireland, each with its own history, traditions, culture, and dominant religion. Because fiction was so widely read, however, it could re-create that readership as a national class with a "British" identity.

Romantic fiction contributed to this cultural revolution by its major varieties—the novel of manners, the Gothic romance, the historical novel, and the "national tale." Other forms, partly adapted from these, were less widely read but influential at certain points; they include the overtly political novel, the satirical and burlesque novel, and what may be called the "quasinovel," or novel incorporating nonfictional but culturally respected materials in a fictional framework. Then there was a large mass of chapbook fiction, usually cut-down versions of the novels for the middle and upper classes.

The commonest form of fiction was the novel of manners (or novel of manners, sentiment, and emulation). From it, middle-class readers could learn the "manners" or social conduct appropriate in upper-class and upper-middle-class life. They could learn to have the "sentiments" and "sensibility," or informed, disciplined, sovereign subjectivity, on which modern states and their systems of meritocracy and representative democracy were based. Finally, they could also learn to emulate, or to imitate and ultimately to surpass the historic ruling class, by adopting and practicing an idealized form of middle-class ideology and culture. Because this form of fiction presented much social criticism, it was often satirical, wholly or in part. Leading novelists of manners included Jane Austen, Frances Burney, Charlotte Bury, Maria Edgeworth, Catherine Gore, Caroline Lamb, Charlotte Smith, Robert Plumer Ward, and the "silver-fork" novelists Benjamin Disraeli and Edward Bulwer-Lytton.

The Gothic romance is largely a novel of manners set in distant or exotic times and places; for British readers, these could range from medieval England through southern Europe to the Orient. Like novels of manners, many Gothic romances present social criticism; significantly, the form reached full development during the revolutionary 1790s, in the novels of Matthew Lewis, Ann Radcliffe, and others. Lewis's exotic and libertine Gothic was adapted by Charlotte Dacre, Charles Robert Maturin, and the young Percy Bysshe Shelley. Overtly political Jacobin novelists of the 1790s, such as William Godwin, Elizabeth Inchbald, and Mary Wollstonecraft, adapted elements of Gothic romance. They were followed in the early 1800s by such writers as Caroline Lamb and Marry Shelley, and by such writers as Disraeli and Bulwer-Lytton in the 1830s and 1840s. From about 1800 on, "hack writers" such as Sarah Wilkinson adapted full-length Gothic romances for street literature as severely abridged sixpenny chapbooks. By the 1820s Gothic romance was losing favor with the fashion-conscious reading public, and in the 1830s and 1840s it was absorbed into mass-market fiction, where it today remains prominent, or was adapted in the more literary novels of writers such as the Brontë sisters Charles Dickens.

The historical novel and the national tale were closely related. They often include elements of the Gothic romance and the political novel, but they had a more direct and lasting influence in forming a new national consciousness. The historical novel was pioneered by women such as Sophia Lee, Jane Porter, and Clara Reeve and then developed by Sir Walter Scott and his many imitators in other countries into a major genre of world literature. Historical novels often represent social conflicts of the past as a warning to the present, and suggest that resolution of those conflicts prepared for the emergence of modern national identity, culture, and destiny. In Britain, Scott's form of historical fiction was developed by such writers as Harrison Ainsworth, Bulwer-Lytton, Dickens, Disraeli, and William Makepeace Thackeray.

Unlike the historical novel, the national tale is often set in the present or recent past and deals less with historical events than with regional color and folkways. This form, too, was pioneered in Britain in the 1800s and 1810s by women such as Maria Edgeworth and Sydney Owenson (later Lady Morgan), reinforced by the European success of Madame, Anne-Louis-Germaine de Staël's *Corinne; ou l'Italie* (1807), and developed in the 1820s by men such as John Galt and David Moir. After mid-century the form was adapted by George Eliot, Charles Kingsley, and others into what became the provincial novel. These fictional forms celebrate regional differences within a national culture and identity that supposedly grounds the nation-state.

Some kinds of fiction challenged the formal conventions and cultural and political assumptions of the major Romantic forms, however. Burlesque fiction is the most obvious example. "Anti-Jacobin" novels such as Elizabeth Hamilton's *Memoirs of Modern Philosophers* (1800) mock 1790s political novels of ideas. Eaton Stannard Barrett's *The Heroine* (1813) satirizes the same novels as well as Gothic romance and the national tale. Thomas Love Peacock's novels parody several kinds of Romantic fiction and the Romantic movement generally. James Hogg's *Confessions of a Justified Sinner* (1824), while not a parody, brilliantly exposes the formal artifice and the middle-class cultural assumptions of the historical novel and the national tale. Finally, there was the wide range of quasi-novels, including John Thelwall's *The Peripatetic* (1793), Thomas Frognal Dibdin's *Bibliomania* (1809, 1811, 1842), Thomas Moore's *Lalla Rookh* (1817), John Wilson's "Noctes Ambrosianæ" (published in *Blackwood's*, magazine 1822–35), William Hazlitt's *Liber Amoris* (1823), and Robert Southey's *The Doctor, &c.* (1834–47). These incorporate various nonfiction discourses into novelistic frames for different ends: to reach a wider readership, to raise the novel's literary status or challenge its literary pretensions, to experiment with literary form, or to explore the potential of fiction within the context of the cultural revolution that was Romanticism.

GARY KELLY

Bibliography

Clemit, Pamela. *The Godwinian Novel: The Rational Fictions of Godwin, Brockden Brown, Mary Shelley.* Oxford: Clarendon Press, 1993.

Hollingsworth, Keith. *The Newgate Novel, 1830–1847: Bulwer, Ainsworth, Dickens and Thackeray.* Detroit: Wayne State University Press, 1963.

———. *The English Jacobin Novel 1780–1805.* Oxford: Clarendon Press, 1976.

———. *English Fiction of the Romantic Period 1789–1830.* London and New York: Longman, 1989.

Kiely, Robert. *The Romantic Novel in England.* Cambridge, Mass.: Harvard University Press, 1972.

Rosa, Matthew W. *The Silver-Fork School: Novels of Fashion Preceding Vanity Fair 1901.* Port Washington, N.Y.: Kennikat Press, 1964.

Watson, Nicola J. *Revolution and the Form of the British Novel, 1790–1825: Intercepted Letters, Interrupted Seductions.* Oxford: Clarendon Press, 1994.

FICTION: FRANCE

Historically, French Romantic fiction had a major precursor in Jean-Jacques Rousseau's long epistolary novel of passionate love and protest against the social order: *Julie, ou la nouvelle Héloïse* (*Julie; or, The New Eloise*, 1761), and another in Bernardin de Saint-Pierre's didactic romance *Paul et Virginie* (1787). In contrast, Gustave Flaubert's parody, in *Madame Bovary* (1857), of the sentimental conventions and melodramatic plots characteristic of this genre of literature signaled its decline. Generically complex, French fiction of the period 1800 to 1850 divided into at least five not absolutely separate narrative subgenres:

1. The personal or psychological
2. The philosophicoreligious
3. The historical
4. The popular
5. The *paysan* (country-, or Hardyesque).

Often didactic, as in François-Auguste-René, Vicomte de Chateaubriand's *Génie du christianisme* (*The Beauties of Christianity*, 1802) set in exotic North America, French Romantic fiction also exercised the talents of great novelists like Honoré de Balzac and Stendhal.

Rousseau's novel combined autobiographical elements with the epistolary form in an edifying tale involving a reconciliation of religion and philosophy, a combination exploited to different degrees by many authors of personal or psychological fiction. Chateaubriand's *René* (1802), for instance, as well as documenting the new sensibility, the *mal du siècle* (world-weariness) presented in its eponymous hero, the first of a series of male personifications of Romantic dissatisfaction with contemporary society. Madame Anne-Louise-Germaine de Staël's *Delphine* (1802) created a female figure whose struggles against the conventional view of marriage, religion, and the social inequality of women led to her suicide, disappointed in her personal belief in Romantic love and individuality. Further documentation on the Romantic tendency to melancholy, ennui (chronic boredom), and lassitude is presented by Étienne de Senancour's *Obermann* (1804), another epistolary novel, as plotless as it is misanthropic and misogynistic. In *Corinne, ou l'Italie* (*Corinne, or Italy*, 1807), Madame de Staël created a tale involving the doomed love between her passionate heroine, a Romantic poetess, and a weak, inarticulate Scottish aristocrat who rejects her for domestic bliss with the more conventionally docile Lucile. Henri-Benjamin Constant de Rebecque's *Adolphe* (1816) recounts a love story in which the male lover's weakness prevents him from breaking off an affair with the tempestuous Ellénore, older than himself and the mistress of an aristocrat. The hero's detailed psychological analysis of the unhappiness caused to both parties in the liaison, unhappiness that leads to the heroine's death, makes of *Adolphe* a Romantic paradigm for the kind of sentimental situation that Alexandre Dumas *fils* would exploit, albeit in a different social context, in *La Dame aux camélias* (*The Lady of the Camellias*, 1848), the source of Giuseppe Verdi's opera *La Traviata* (1853). The French personal novel of intimate revelation would blossom in the 1830s in two of Stendhal's great psychological works, *Le Rouge et le Noir* (*The Red and the Black*, 1830) and *La Chartreuse de Parme* (*The Charterhouse of Parma*, 1839), and in Honoré de Balzac's *Le Lys dans la vallée* (*The Lily of the Valley*,

1836). And Alfred de Musset, in the significantly titled *La Confession d'un enfant du siècle* (*The Confession of a Child of the Century*, 1836) provided further autobiographical proof (albeit fictional) of the disillusionment felt by young Romantics with regard to their inglorious post-Napoleonic age.

The didactic tone of much Romantic fiction found early expression in *Atala* and *Les Natchez*, novels originally written as part of Chateaubriand's *Génie du christianisme* stressing the beauty of the Christian religion. In *Atala*, the heroine, a virgin daughter of the Natchez tribe of Louisiana, after being converted to Christianity commits suicide rather than marry Chactas, her Indian suitor, because she misunderstands Christian doctrine. Such unpersuasive apologetics yield in *Les Natchez* to the vision of a hardworking Christian enclave of Natchez Indians led by an idealized priest who falls tragic victim to tribal warfare. In both novels, vivid descriptions of the luxuriant natural environment supplement interest in the human protagonists.

Sir Walter Scott's novels, immediately translated into French upon their publication, provided the principal impetus for the launch of the Romantic novel involving historical events and personages. But before Scott, whose novels did not become known in France until 1814, Chateaubriand's prose epic *Les Martyrs, ou le triomphe de la religion chrétienne* (*The Martyrs, or the Triumph of the Christian Religion*, 1809), recounted the loves of a Greek convert, Eudorus, and a young pagan, Cymodocea, and their subsequent edifying martyrdom in the Roman Colosseum. After Scott, Alfred de Vigny abandoned edification and in *Cinq-Mars* (*The King's Minion*, 1826) presented a ferocious attack on Cardinal Richelieu's usurpation of power during the reign of the weak Louis XIII. He added to the novel's *couleur locale* by recounting, in the manner of a Gothic novel, the story of the accusations of black magic, witchcraft, and demonic possession made in 1637 against Urbain Grandier and the so-called Devils of Loudon, a topic that later inspired French historian Jules Michelet's *La Sorcière* (1862) as well as Aldous Huxley's psychological study *The Devils of Loudun* (1952), and Ken Russell's film *The Devils* (1971). In 1831, Victor Hugo's *Notre-Dame de Paris* helped hugely to reawaken French interest in the Middle Ages, condemned since the neoclassical seventeenth century as unworthy of critical scrutiny. He did so by retelling the "Beauty and the Beast" fairy tale, set in medieval Paris during the reign of Louis XI. Alexandre Dumas *père*'s trilogy of historical novels about the Three Musketeers (*Les Trois Mousquetaires*, 1844; *Vingt ans après*, 1845; and *Le Vicomte de Bragelonne*, 1848–50) chose Louis XIII's reign as the period in which to situate stories of *cape et épée* (cloak and dagger), a decision copied in 1863 by Théophile Gautier in *Le Capitaine Fracasse* (*Captain Fracasse*).

Also written for a popular audience, Eugène Sue's novels *Les Mystères de Paris* (*The Mysteries of Paris*, 1842–43) and *Les Mystères du peuple* (*The Mysteries of the People*, 1849–56) added sensation and excitement to contemporary stories involving mysterious aristocrats living in the Parisian underworld, punishing evil and rewarding virtue, and sharing the people's views on the need for social and democratic reform. Dumas père's *Le Comte de Monte Cristo* (1844–45; *The Count of Monte Cristo*) makes wealth, rather than noble birth, the means by which Edmond Dantès secures revenge against a ruling class of financiers and helps the downtrodden victims of social injustice. And Victor Hugo's *Les Misérables* (1862) similarly places virtue in society's outcasts (an escaped convict, a Parisian street urchin, and a group of young, idealistic revolutionaries) rather than in the representatives of the French political and judicial system.

The novels of country life written by George Sand provide happy endings to stories in which virtuous, but low-born, heroes and heroines achieve their desires despite society's inequalities and injustices. Stolen treasure, in *Le Meunier d'Angibault* (*The Miller of Angibault*, 1845), for instance, makes possible an industrious utopia. In *François le Champi* (*François the Waif*, 1850), partly written in peasant patois, she shows true love triumphing over accidents of birth and fortune. Quite different is Balzac's view of country life in *Les Paysans* (1844), one of the *Scènes de la vie de campagne* (*Scenes of Country Life*) in *La Comédie humaine* (*The Human Comedy*) in which the peasants are depicted as vicious, brutal, and drunken, often the victims of bourgeois moneylenders; unsurprisingly, Balzac's novel attracted the attention of Karl Marx and, later, of Émile Zola.

In *Madam Bovary*, Flaubert satirized particularly the unreality and effusiveness of some romantic fiction, writing, "It was nothing but love affairs, lovers, persecuted ladies fainting in lonely towers, coachmen killed at every stage, horses flogged to death on every page, dark forests, troubled hearts, oaths, sobs, tears and kisses, moonlight sailing, nightingales in the woods, gentlemen as brave as lions, as gentle as lambs, as virtuous as no one is, always immaculately turned out, and weeping like mourners."

ALBERT W. HALSALL

Bibliography

Angenot, Marc. *Le Roman populaire*. Montréal: Presses de l'Université du Québec, 1975.

Cruicksank, John, ed. *French Literature and Its Background*. London: Oxford University Press, 1969.

Fortassier, Rose. *Le Roman du XIXe siècle*. Paris: Presses Universitaires de France, 1982.

Raimond, Michel. *Le Roman depuis la Révolution*. Paris: Armand Colin, 1967.

Rait, A.W. *Life and Letters in France: The Nineteenth Century*. New York: Scribner's, 1965.

Salomon, Pierre. *Le Roman et la nouvelle romantiques*. Paris: Masson, 1970.

Teyssandier, Henri. *Les Formes de la création romanesque à l'époque de Walter Scott et Jane Austen*. Paris: Didier, 1978.

FICTION: GERMANY

German Romantic fiction is extremely diverse and heterogeneous. This is due in part to the successive waves of Romanticism in Germany and their different aims: early or Jena Romanticism, the middle phase of so-called Heidelberg Romanticism, and late Romanticism. A further factor is the span of time covered by the Romantic movement, from the aftermath of the French Revolution in the late 1790s to its final appearances in the work of individual authors like Joseph von Eichendorff and Ludwig Tieck in the late 1820s. Its traces can still be perceived in Heinrich Heine's work and in the transformation of memories and factual documentary from the early Romantic period in Bettina von Arnim's fictional, epistolary "autobiographical" novels based on the lives of her friend Karoline von Günderrode (*Die Günderrode*, 1840) and her brother Clemens Brentano (*Clemens Brentanos Frühlingskranz* [*A Vernal Wreath for Clemens Brentano*], 1844).

German Romantic fiction was strongly influenced by contemporary styles and modes of writing, such as Sentimentalism, the Gothic novel and the epistolary novel. However, works such as Ludwig Tieck's novel *William Lovell* (1796), in which the epistolary form is stretched to a radical perspectivism, or Tieck and Wilhelm Heinrich Wackenroder's collaborative work, the diverse collection of texts on the theme of art in the *Herzensergießungen eines kunstliebenden Klosterbruders* (*Outpourings of an Art-loving Friar*, 1797) already display the impending changes towards a fundamentally new understanding of fiction. A significant influence on subsequent developments was exerted by the reflections on fiction, particularly on the novel, but also on fairy tales and other forms of short prose, set out primarily by Friedrich von Schlegel in the *Athenaeum* (1798–1800), the Jena group's principal organ. In his *Brief über den Roman* (*Letter on the Novel*), which forms one part of the *Gespräch über die Poesie* (*Dialogue on Poetry*) published in 1800 in the *Athenaeum*, Schlegel considers the novel as the principal Romantic genre. The Romantic novel is, according to him, a transgressive genre, in that it encompasses all other genres, and it provides a framework for the dominant aim of Romantic fiction, which is the narrative construction of the lost totality of being, often expressed as the "lost paradise," in absolute and self-reflective poetry. The development of this kind of new aesthetic is to be seen in the context of contemporary idealist philosophy such as Johann Gottlieb Fichte's, Immanuel Kant's, and Friedrich Wilhelm Joseph von Schelling's, as well as in terms of its response to the major political and social changes of the time, which gave rise to a sense of loss, an intensified perception of Dualism and of the impoverishment of human life.

The early Romantics' belief in the unlimited power of imagination to overcome dualistic perceptions of the world on the basis of an assumed unity of human mind, nature, and poetry-generated fiction that thematically examines the quest for the origins of the individual and his/her relation to society, as well as the origins of an undivided world and the connection between this united world and the individual. Principal examples are Novalis's novel *Heinrich von Ofterdingen* (1799/1802), Tieck's *Franz Sternbalds Wanderungen* (1798), and Dorothea Schlegel's *Florentin* (1801). Within early Romantic fiction, attempts at creating a world that transcends the known world lead to a symbolic understanding of the perceivable world.

The main theme of early Romantic fiction, the quest for origins, favors subthemes, such as the "lost paradise" or the myth of Atlantis (Novalis's *Heinrich von Ofterdingen*), childhood as time of innocence (Tieck's *Der blonde Eckbert*, [*Eckbert the Fair*], 1797, and *Die Elfen* [*The Elves*], 1804; Brentano's, *Gockel, Hinkel und Gackeleia* [*The Tale of Gockel, Hinkel and Gackeliah*], 1838), the problems of transition from childhood into adulthood, and the fall of man (Tieck's *Eckbert*, and Eichendorff's,

Das Marmorbild [*The Marble Statue*], 1817). These topics overlap with interest in dreams, the dark side of the human psyche (E. T. A. Hoffmann's *Der Sandmann*, 1816) the supernatural, and the miraculous ("*das Wunderbare*"). The preferred main character of Romantic fiction is the artist, who has the ability to bring about an undivided world: the painter (*Franz Sternbald*, Julius in *Lucinde*, the painters of the *Outpourings* and of the *Phantasien über die Kunst* [*Fantasies on Art*], 1799, by Tieck and Wackenroder), the musician (Tiecks and Wackenroder's Joseph Berglinger in the *Outpourings*, E. T. A. Hoffmann's musicians Gluck, Kreisler, and Krespel), and the poet (*Heinrich von Ofterdingen*). Love and sexuality are other common themes of Romantic fiction, though often appropriated in a wider sense as means of overcoming duality (*Lucinde, Ofterdingen, Sternbald*).

During the course of the Romantic movement's second phase, with its centers in Heidelberg and Berlin, the themes of fiction alter along with political and social changes; characteristic is an increased interest in the collection of folklore (Jakob and Wilhelm Grimm, *Kinder- und Hausmärchen* [*Fairy Tales*], 1812–), and recollecting and re-creating a lost national unity (Arnim). The literary production of the late Romantic phase, represented by individual authors and without a geographical center, is to be considered in the context of the political disillusionment manifest after 1815 (hopes had been raised by the French Revolution). Romantic fiction of the second and third decades of the nineteenth century shows an increasing interest in the individual in crisis; self-divided characters, eccentrics and doppelgangers (E. T. A. Hoffmann, Adalbert von Chamisso's *Peter Schlemihls wundersame Geschichte* [*The Wonderful History of Peter Schlemihl*], 1814) replace those early Romantic characters searching for their past and identity. Related favorite themes are the failed integration of the individual into society (Chamisso, Hoffmann), the experience of being a stranger (Eichendorff), and the role of the artist (Brentano, Hoffmann). "Das Wunderbare," previously the linking element between the two worlds, becomes more and more a confusing, disturbing element that can destroy the mind, particularly in Hoffmann's fiction. The hope for a stable world represented in an ideal Christianity is to be found in the late works of Brentano and Eichendorff.

In much German Romantic fiction, the process of storytelling as part of the process of constructing the self is investigated, whether within the novel as the process of writing the story of one's life (Brentano's *Godwi*, 1801), or within the short prose genres as the process of capturing the particularity of the individual in narrative form (Brentano's *Geschichte vom braven Kasperl und vom schönen Annerl* [*The Story of Just Caspar and Fair Annie*], 1816; E. T. A. Hofmann's *Der goldene Topf* [*The Golden Pot*], 1814).

On a formal level, a distinctive feature of early Romantic fiction is its dissolution of genre boundaries. The expanded genre of the novel, which allows experimentation with the integration of other genres, including theoretical and scientific reflection, becomes the earlier phase's preferred form; most of the Romantic novels remained unfinished, however. Outstanding examples of experimental narrative are Tieck and Wackenroder's *Outpourings* (1797) and Friedrich von Schlegel's *Lucinde* (1799), where the novel is composed of a sequence of varied literary forms, such as letters, allegories, reflections, and idylls. Also notable is Novalis's political reflections in *Glauben und Liebe oder der König und die Königin* [*Faith and Love or The King and the Queen*] of 1798, which consists of a series of fragments, loosely linked

together, introduced by general reflections on the problem of understanding. The other highly esteemed genre of the early Romantic movement is the fairy tale, with its ability to mediate between the real and the unreal. Both novel and fairy tale form the basis of the development of the favorite genres of the middle and later Romantic phases, the short story and the novella. Tieck in particular contributed to the development of the novella in terms of both practice and theory: between 1825 and 1841 he produced roughly thirty novellas and commented also on the novella's unique feature, the *wendepunkt* (turning point).

Also characteristic of the late period of the German Romantic movement is fiction that draws on styles and themes developed during the early phase of the Romantic Era; this is especially evident in the work of Tieck and Eichendorff.

URSULA HUDSON-WIEDENMANN

Selected Works

Overviews/Collections
Fiction and Fantasy of German Romance. Edited by Frederick E. Pierce and Carl F. Schreiber. New York, 1927.
Four Romantic Tales from Nineteenth Century German. Edited and translated by Helene Sher. New York: Ungar, 1975.
The German Classics of the Nineteenth and Twentieth Centuries. vols. 4, 5 and 7. Edited by Kuno Francke and W. G. Howard, New York: AMS Press, 1969.

Individual Authors
Arnim. Bettin von. *The Günderrode*. In Francke and Howard, eds., *German Classics*, vol. 7.
Arnim, Ludwig Achim von. *The Mad Invalid of Fort Ratonneau*. In Sher, ed., *Four Tales*.
Brentano, Clemens. *The Story of Just Caspar and Fair Annie*. In *Sher*, ed., *Four Tales*.
———. *The Tale of Gockel Hinkel and Gacketiah*. Trans. Doris Orgel, New York: Random House, 1961.
Chamisso, Adalbert von. *The Wonderful History of Peter Schlemihl*. In Francke and Howard, eds., *German Classics*, vol. 5.
Eichendorff, Joseph von. "The Marble Statue," in Pierce and Schreiber, eds. *Fiction and Fantasy*.
Grimm, Jakob and Wilhelm. *Fairy Tales*. Translated by E. Taylor. Harmondsworth, England: Penguin, 1971.
Hoffmann, Ernst Theodor Amadeus. *The Tales of Hoffmann*. Translated by R. J. Hollingdale. Harmondsworth: Penguin, 1996.
Klingemann, August. *The Night Watches of Bonaventura*. Bilingual ed. Edited and translated by Gerald Gillespie. Austin: University of Texas Press, 1971.
Novalis [Friedrich Freiherr von Hardenberg]. Various selections in Francke and Howard, eds., *German Classics*, vol. 4.
Schlegel, Friedrich von. *Dialogue on Poetry, and Literary Aphorisms*. Translated by Ernst Behler and Roman Struc. University Park: Pennsylvania University Press, 1968.
Tieck, Ludwig. *The Elves. Fair Eckbert*, and others in Francke and Howard, *German Classics*, vol. 4.
Tieck, Ludwig, and Wilhelm Heinrich, Wackenroder. *Fantasies*. In Pierce and Schreiber, eds. *Fiction and Fantasy*.

Bibliography

Brinkmann, Richard, ed. *Romantik in Deutschland. Ein interdisziplinäres Symposium*. Stuttgart: Metzler, 1978.
Menhennet, Alan. *The Romantic Movement*. London: Croom Helm, 1981.
Neumann, Gerhard. *Romantisches Erzählen*. Würzburg: Königshausen and Neumann, 1995.

Prawer, S. S., ed. *The Romantic Period in Germany*. London: Weidenfeld and Nicholson, 1970.

Schanze, Helmut, ed. *Romantik-Handbuch*. Stuttgart: Kröner, 1994.

Schulz, Gerhard. *Romantik. Geschichte und Begriff*. München: C. H. Beck, 1996.

Stopp, Elisabeth. *German Romantics in Context*. London: Bristol Classical Press, 1992.

Tymms, Ralph. *German Romantic Literature*. London: Methuen, 1955.

Ziolkowski, Theodore. *German Romanticism and Its Institutions*. Princeton, N.J.: Princeton University Press, 1990.

FICTION: UNITED STATES

"In the four quarters of the globe, who reads an American book?" asked Sydney Smith in the *Edinburgh Review* in 1820 as part of a stinging attack on the cultural output of the United States. Partisan and prejudiced though the comment was, it articulated a deficiency that had haunted American authors since the end of the American Revolution. In the early republic, it became a matter of great importance for artists in America to achieve a cultural independence to accompany their political autonomy. It was the oft-expressed wish of nationalistic writers that the American experience and environment should be used as the basis of their literature, to give it a flavor distinct from that of their English forebears and contemporaries. As James Kirke Paulding lamented in 1819, "We have imitated where we might often have excelled; we have overlooked our own rich resources, and sponged upon the exhausted treasury of our impoverished neighbours; we were born rich, and yet have all our lives subsisted by borrowing."

Unfortunately, novel writing and reading were not held in very high regard by the citizens of the new republic. The social climate of the new nation in the aftermath of the revolution was such that men of talent and education who might in more leisurely times devote themselves to literature were engaged in establishing and maintaining the new constitution in its various parts. History was vital, providing models on which society might be based; whereas fiction was a luxury, suitable only to divert women. Much early American fiction, as a result, is concerned with the moral education of women. William Hill Brown's *The Power of Sympathy* (1789) is perhaps the best example of this didactic sentimentalism, borrowed, along with its epistolary form, from the work of Samuel Richardson. *Charlotte Temple* (1791), by Susannah Haswell Rowson, a similarly sentimental tale of warning "for the perusal of the young and thoughtful of the fair sex," was extremely successful upon its publication in America in 1794.

Despite this concern for the virtue of American womanhood, the sentimental novel was too restricted to allow novelists to create a truly American form of writing: a drawing room in Boston might as well be a drawing room in London. One of the most popular narrative forms in colonial America had been the captivity narrative: authentic accounts of white settlers (usually women), taken prisoner by hostile Indians. The captivity was of a uniquely American form; its appeal stemmed directly from its microcosmic reenactment of the initial moment at which European culture encountered the alien environment and people of the new continent. As the eighteenth century progressed, these narratives became increasingly sensational to appeal to a mass audience, and this fictional embellishment of "true" historical accounts indicated a positive direction in which American fiction might progress. Traces of the captivity genre

appear in Ann Eliza Bleeker's *The History of Maria Kittle* (1793), in Gilbert Imlay's *The Emigrants* (1793), and in Rowson's *Reuben and Rachel* (1798); whereas Hugh Henry Brackenridge's *Modern Chivalry* (1792–1815), a picaresque satire of contemporary mores and institutions, owing much to Henry Fielding and Miguel de Cervantes Saavedra, was also set on the Western frontier.

Charles Brockden Brown, often described as the first professional author in America, explained in the preface to his novel *Edgar Huntly* (1799) why he had eschewed traditional European themes and settings to appeal to a specifically American audience: "The incidents of Indian hostility, and the perils of the western wilderness, are far more suitable; and for the native of America to overlook these, would admit of no apology." In this work, and his three other important novels, *Wieland* (1798), *Arthur Mervyn* (1799), and *Ormond* (1799), Brown betrays the influence of William Godwin's *Caleb Williams* (1793), and the Gothicism of Anne Radcliffe; they exhibit a fascination with psychology and scientific phenomena such as ventriloquism and sleepwalking, transferred to an American setting. Although he later abandoned novel writing, he remained a strong advocate for American literary nationalism as a literary editor.

New York was the hub of literary activity during this period; and the most important author to emerge from this literary circle in the early nineteenth century was Washington Irving. Having cut his teeth in collaboration with Paulding and his brother William on the satirical periodical *Salmagundi*, Irving wrote *The History of New York* (1809), as told by his fictional narrator, Diedrich Knickerbocker, in which he satirized contemporary political figures and historical writing. Irving became the first American author to achieve international success with the publication of *The Sketchbook of Geoffrey Crayon, Gent* (1819), but this success was built upon a self-consciously English style borrowed from eighteenth-century writers such as Joseph Addison. William Hazlitt noted that Irving had "*skimmed the cream, and taken off patterns with great skill and cleverness, from our best-known writers. . . .*" The two most famous stories in the collection, "Rip Van Winkle" and "The Legend of Sleepy Hollow," often conceived to be quintessentially American, are actually transplanted German folk tales; and most of the other sketches are whimsical accounts of the author's travels in England.

The first American author to make an international impact using specifically American materials was James Fenimore Cooper, who synthesized the primal appeal of the American captivity narrative with the form of historical novel writing popularized by Sir Walter Scott. The historical novel subsumed the captivity narratives' recurring fear of latent violence in the American landscape into a reassuring master narrative in which the Indians, whether noble or demonic, were doomed to displacement or extinction. It imbued the progress of white civilization with the validating weight of historical inevitability. In a nation with so little history, this type of fiction played a crucial role in helping to define national identity, by mythologizing the defining elements of the American experience: the settlement of the wilderness and the glory of the revolution.

Works of antebellum fiction were often classed, even by the writers themselves, as "romances" rather than "novels," signifying mainly that they were not concerned with the familiar incidents of contemporary life, but with largely historical characters and settings. Cooper's *The Spy* (1821) and the *Leatherstocking Tales* (1823–41) exemplify the genre, but his success sparked many imitators, often with regional or political inflections: William Gilmore Simms's Southern "border romances"; John Pendleton Kennedy's *Horse Shoe Robinson* (1835); Catharine Maria Sedgwick's *Hope Leslie* (1827); and Robert Montgomery Bird's *Nick of the Woods* (1837), to name several of the more prominent works.

The historical romance was also the form chosen by Nathaniel Hawthorne, in whose hands it mutated significantly. A New Englander, Hawthorne's work is preoccupied with the lingering effects of Puritanism on his native region. Introspective and frequently allegorical, it explores the psychological imperatives of guilt and pride. Whereas in Cooper's romances the landscape is described with a pictorial sweep, as a backdrop to the action, in Hawthorne it tends to be a correlative to the dark psychology of his characters. His fictional works in the period were mostly in the short story form (*Twice Told Tales* [1837] and *Tales from the Old Manse* [1846]), but in 1850 he published his most famous novel, *The Scarlet Letter*, a distillation of these prevailing concerns.

Hawthorne's friend and contemporary, Herman Melville, enjoyed a brief period of literary success in the 1840s, during which time he published a series of novels containing the essential ingredients of exotic locations and narratives of adventure. *Typee* (1846), *Omoo* (1847), *Mardi* (1849), *Redburn* (1849), and *White Jacket* (1850) all drew upon Melville's own experiences while sailing the globe in his youth. However, these ostensibly realistic, semi-autobiographical tales evidence Melville's increasingly symbolic turn of mind; *Mardi*, in particular, is heavily allegorical. This tendency in his fiction reached a climax with his acknowledged masterpiece *Moby-Dick* (1851), but the obscurity of his subject discouraged the contemporary reading public.

The other major American fiction writer of the antebellum period was Edgar Allan Poe, even though he only wrote one novel, *The Narrative of Arthur Gordon Pym of Nantucket* (1837). More influential were his short stories. Distinguished by their melancholy, Gothic tone, and highly stylized, often strangely European settings, they reflect Poe's morbid fears and fertile imagination. Often dismissed by his contemporaries due to petty literary jealousies, Poe's work persevered largely through its adoption by European writers; Charles Baudelaire, in particular, was a great admirer.

The struggles of these authors to produce genuine American fiction went largely unrewarded. Publishing conditions in early-nineteenth-century America (particularly uncongenial copyright laws) made it extremely hard for writers to make a living from fiction alone. Although Cooper, Hawthorne, Irving, Melville, and Poe have made it into the traditional canon of American literature, only Cooper and Irving had any major popular success in their lifetimes, and by their death even their reputation had declined. The advent of realism after the Civil War brought with it a new critical approach to fiction writing, causing most early American fiction, and particularly the historical romance, to be undervalued until well into the twentieth century. Indeed, many authors from the period are still awaiting critical resuscitation.

ROWLAND HUGHES

Bibliography

Bell, Michael Davitt. *The Development of American Romance.* Chicago: University of Chicago Press, 1980.
Bradfield, Scott. *Dreaming Revolution: Transgression in the Development of the American Romance.* Iowa City: University of Iowa Press, 1993.
Budick, Emily Miller. *Fiction and Historical Consciousness: The American Romance Tradition.* New Haven, Conn.: Yale University Press, 1989.
Charvat, William. *The Profession of Authorship in America, 1800–1870.* Columbus: Ohio State University Press, 1968.
Clark, Robert. *History, Ideology and Myth in American Fiction, 1823–1852,* London: MacMillan, 1984.
Davidson, Cathy N. *Revolution and the Word: The Rise of the Novel in America.* New York: Oxford University Press, 1986.
Ferguson, Robert A. *The American Enlightenment, 1750–1820.* Cambridge, Mass.: Harvard University Press, 1997.
Gardner, Jared. *Master Plots: Race and the Founding of an American Literature, 1787–1845.* Baltimore: Johns Hopkins University Press, 1998.
Gilmore, Michael T. *American Romanticism in the Market Place.* Chicago: University of Chicago Press, 1985.
Morse, David, *American Romanticism.* Vol. 1, *From Cooper to Hawthorne.* London: Macmillan, 1987.
Spiller, Robert E., ed. *The American Literary Revolution, 1783–1837.* New York: New York University Press, 1969.
Tompkins, Jane. *Sensational Designs: The Cultural Work of American Fiction, 1790–1860.* Oxford: Oxford University Press, 1985.
Vanderbeets, Richard. *The Indian Captivity Narrative: An American Genre.* Lanham, Md.: University Press of America, 1984.

FIDELIO, OP. 72 1805

Opera by Ludwig van Beethoven

Fidelio is Ludwig van Beethoven's only opera, assuring it special standing in the music world. Incorporating the exalted themes of justice, freedom, and love, it contains some of Beethoven's most sublime melodies and most challenging vocal music. The libretto was written by Josef Sonnleithner, Stephan von Breuning, and Georg Treitschke, who based it on a play by Jean-Nicolas Bouilly, *Leonore, ou l'amour conjugal* (*Leonore, or Married Love*). *Fidelio* premiered at the Theater an der Wien in Vienna on November

20, 1805. However, due to the French occupation of Vienna only a week earlier, a weak libretto, and its extraordinary length, the opera was withdrawn after three performances. After being condensed from three acts to two by Beethoven's friend Breuning, *Fidelio* reopened at the Theater an der Wien in 1806. Beethoven closed the opera after two performances, claiming dissatisfaction with the performance. During the following years, he considered several possible librettos for a new opera, none of which ultimately appealed to him. In 1814 Beethoven, by then enjoying critical and popular acclaim, was approached about a revival of *Fidelio*. The libretto was again overhauled, this time by poet and stage director Treitschke, and the revised opera opened in Vienna at the Kärntnertor Theatre on May 23, 1814 with subsequent performances in Prague, Leipzig, Dresden, and Berlin. By the time of the premiere in London (1832) *Fidelio* had a permanent place in the repertoire. Although it has remained on the boards since the 1830s, several important revivals should be noted. In 1905, Richard Strauss led a performance to celebrate the centenary of the first performance. The continuing relevance of the opera's principal themes made it an obvious choice for many European opera houses that reopened following World War II, especially in German-speaking countries, and the 1970 bicentennial of Beethoven's birth prompted many performances.

The opera takes place in Spain, where Florestan is unjustly imprisoned by Don Pizarro, governor of a state prison. Disguising herself as a young man called Fidelio, his devoted wife Leonora is searching for him. She finds work at the prison assisting the jailer Rocco, unwittingly winning the affections of Marcellina, Rocco's daughter. Fidelio's success with Marcellina angers the jealous porter Jacquino, who wants Marcellina for himself. Rocco praises Fidelio's good work and promises to approve a match between Fidelio and Marcellina. Fidelio uses this emotional moment to beg for further responsibility, perhaps tending to the prisoner in the deepest part of the dungeon. Rocco agrees to ask the governor for his consent to the marriage and Fidelio's expanded duties. Brisk march music announces the arrival of the governor, Don Pizarro. After being warned that the minister Don Fernando suspects prisoners are being held unjustly, Don Pizarro decides to silence Florestan immediately. Unable to convince Rocco to carry out the murder, Don Pizarro directs Rocco and Fidelio to dig a grave for Florestan. In a moment alone, Fidelio, or Leonora, voices her determination to find and save her husband. She convinces Rocco to allow the prisoners out of the jail for some fresh air and sunshine. Act 1 ends with a profoundly moving chorus sung by the prisoners hailing the brief moment of freedom and sunlight. When the enraged Don Pizarro discovers the prisoners in the courtyard, the prisoners are sent back to their cells while Pizarro hurries Rocco back to his grave digging.

Act 2 begins with Florestan asking God's help, then singing ecstatically about seeing a vision of his beloved wife, Leonora. As Rocco and Fidelio/Leonora descend to the dungeon, she recognizes Florestan and gives him some wine. Pizarro reveals his identity and prepares to stab Florestan. Leonora intercedes, singing "First kill his wife," thus disclosing her own identity. Pizarro moves toward Florestan again, but hears a trumpet call. As the trumpet sounds again, Jacquino announces that the minister has arrived at the prison. While everyone else rushes out of the dungeon, Leonora and Florestan sing a joyful duet. Marcellina

and Jacquino lead the prisoners to join Don Fernando, his officers, and Don Pizarro. Rocco presents Leonora and the still enchained Florestan and explains their case to the minister. Prison guards take Don Pizarro away, and Don Fernando invites Leonora to remove Florestan's chains. After an acknowledgment of God's mercy and divine justice, the finale ends with the chorus singing a line from Johann Christoph Friedrich von Schiller's *Ode to Joy*, "Let him who has won a fair wife join in our rejoicing."

Beethoven wrote *Fidelio* during his "middle period" or "heroic period," immediately after the innovative *Eroica* Symphony No. 3 in E-Plat Major, op. 55. This is the stylistic period in which Beethoven finds his own voice as an artist and begins expanding and transforming the forms and genres of the classical period. Like other works from this time, *Fidelio* shows Beethoven's ability to use contemporary idioms in new, compelling combinations. *Fidelio* adds to the *opera buffa* vocabulary of Wolfgang Amadeus Mozart some elements of French opera, such as the plot of the "rescue opera" highlighting the ideals of "marital love, of simple fidelity, of devoted heroism, . . . the triumph of good over evil, of freedom over tyranny" (as in, for example, Maria Luigi Cherubini's *Les Deux Journées* [*The Water Carrier*], which Beethoven saw in Vienna in 1803), and melodrama, or spoken words against instrumental background music. He also incorporates compositional technics from past eras, as in the canon at the beginning of act 1, "Mir ist so wunderbar" ("Such strange delight is here"). Richly colored orchestration helps character definition throughout the opera, as in the strings, three French horns, and bassoon that accompany Leonora's aria. Beethoven always made copious revisions, but he labored particularly intensely over *Fidelio*. The overture most often heard today is referred to as the "Fidelio Overture" to distinguish it from the three "Leonora Overtures" rejected before the final version. Beethoven's care was well rewarded. With its plot reflecting the lofty ideals of the French Revolution, the dramatic coherence of the final version, and some of Beethoven's most celestial music, *Fidelio* is still one of the most beloved of all German operas.

ANN SEARS

See also **Beethoven, Ludwig van; Cherubini, Maria Luigi; French Revolution: Its Impact and Importance; Sublime, The**

Work

Fidelio, op. 72. Opera in two acts, libretto written by Josef Sonnleithner, Stephan von Breuning, and Georg Treitschke, based on the play by *Leonore, ou l'amour conjugal* (*Leonore, or Married Love*) by Jean-Nicolas Bouilly. First performance, Vienna, November 20, 1805; second version, 1806; third and final version, 1814.

Bibliography

Forbes, Elizabeth, Basil Deane, and Romain Rolland. *Fidelio: Beethoven*. English National Opera Guide No. 4. Series editor Nicholas John. London: John Calder, 1980.

Marek, George R. *Beethoven: Biography of a Genius*. New York: Funk and Wagnalls, 1969.

Robinson, Paul. *Ludwig van Beethoven: Fidelio*. Cambridge Opera Handbooks. Cambridge: Cambridge University Press, 1996.

Solomon, Maynard. *Beethoven*. 2d. rev. ed. New York: Schirmer, 1998.

FIELD, JOHN 1782–1837

Irish composer and pianist

Born in Dublin of a musical family, John Field had his first music lessons from his grandfather, an organist, and from Tommaso Giordani, an Italian composer who had settled in Dublin. Giordani was responsible for Field's first concert appearance as a pianist at the age of nine, creating a great stir. A year later, the Fields moved to London, John's father becoming a violinist in the orchestra of the Haymarket Theatre while the boy was apprenticed for seven years to Muzio Clementi in the piano-making and publishing firm of Longman and Broderip.

Field's duties, in return for his training, seemed to combine those of a demonstrator and salesman for the patrons who visited the piano warehouse, and Clementi also published some of Field's compositions anonymously. His public concert appearances during these years were few and far between; he played a concerto by Jan Ladislav Dussek (then resident in London) in 1794, and again in 1798. Field's performance of his own first piano concerto at the King's Theatre in February 1799 brought him to the attention of the London musical world, and he was much sought after when his apprenticeship expired the same year. His first opus, a set of three piano sonatas dedicated to Clementi, were published in March 1801.

Clementi embarked on an eight-year tour of Europe in July 1802, the main purpose of which was to publicize his pianos and to secure publishing rights for recent music from composers (Ludwig van Beethoven among them) and publishers. Field accompanied him part of the way, gaining public acclaim in Paris. They reached Saint Petersburg via Vienna in late 1802. Reports were made of Clementi's mistreatment of Field; the violinist-composer Louis Spohr writes of outgrown clothes with sleeves reaching just below the elbows "so that . . . his whole figure appeared awkward and stiff in the highest degree; but as soon as his touching instrumentation began, everything else was forgotten, and one became all ear." The evidence for this has recently been questioned, and it does seem unlikely that the business-conscious Clementi would run the risk of damaging his reputation. On the other hand, Clementi's parsimony was well known, and an article in a Russian journal of 1834 reminds readers of Field walking through the streets in light clothes at twenty-five degrees below zero with a cold.

Such treatment was no doubt a factor in Field's decision to stay in Saint Petersburg when Clementi moved on in 1803, having introduced the younger composer to some important patrons. Field's first concert took place in March 1804 at the Philharmonic Hall, there, including a performance, probably, of his first piano concerto, taking the city by storm and being lionized by the fashionable classes. Aristocratic salons and the homes of the wealthy were opened to him and he attracted many pupils. A concert tour of the northern Russian cities in 1805–6 led to his debut in Moscow on March 2, 1806, where, after a brief affair with her, he married one of his pupils in 1810.

After some years dividing his time between Moscow and Saint Petersburg—during which time he seems to have lived mostly in his patrons' houses—he settled in St. Petersburg for ten years, giving annual concerts and overseeing the first publication of many of his works. During these years he had an illegitimate as well as a legitimate son, but his wife left him shortly after the latter's birth in 1819.

Field moved permanently to Moscow in 1821, where he introduced his (illegitimate) son Leon to the public as a child prodigy and met the composer-pianist Johann Nepomuk Hummel on his tour in 1822. Hummel was at the height of his fame and he and Field had a cordial and healthy respect for each other. In terms of new compositions, the period 1821–31 produced little: Field's love of alcohol began to assume addictive proportions and his eventually terminal cancer began to show itself. He went to London with Leon in 1831; a medical operation there gave some relief, and Leon was reunited with his mother, who died the following year.

During this visit, Field was warmly received by the British capital's musical community, meeting the young William Sterndale Bennett, Felix Mendelssohn, and Ignaz Moscheles. At his public concerts, however, his reception was not as ecstatic as it might have been. Although this is surprising, considering the popularity of his music and his personal fame, it must be seen against the changing backdrop of European pianism, with a new generation of brilliance and bravura, inspired by the violinist Niccolò Paganini. Frédéric Chopin, Franz Liszt, Mendelssohn, and other lesser lights were fresh in the memory of the Paris public during Field's visit. However, his performance of his last major work, the Seventh Piano Concerto, at the Salle du Conservatoire on Christmas Day, 1832, seems to have won over many—even those who preferred the virtuosic work of this younger generation.

Field continued his tour with more success, playing in Toulouse, Marseilles, Lyons, Geneva, and Milan, but by the time he and Leon reached Naples, Field was too ill to play or teach, and languished in a hospital for almost a year, undergoing several further operations. He was claimed by a Russian aristocrat, Rakhmanov, and accompanied his family home to Moscow, having recovered sufficiently to be able to give three concerts in Vienna and spend time as the guest of Carl Czerny.

On his return to Moscow, the deterioration in his appearance and health shocked his friends and must have been apparent in his performance. He composed his last series of nocturnes before his death on January 23, 1837. The contributors to his monument in Vedenskii Cemetery included such figures as Karl Yulevich Davidov, Prince Nikolai Galitzin, and Lev Tolstoy.

It is primarily in Field's contribution to the art of pianism that music's debt to him lies. Although he was as adept as the best of them, his style of playing differed from that of the virtuoso school in its expressive powers and artistic sensitivity. His ability to convey melody in playing of an almost vocal kind earned him the nickname "the singer among pianists," and the "poetic" quality of his performance, a quality much in demand and remarked upon in the early nineteenth century, was always singled out for comment. This may be traced to the fact that he was brought up on the so-called English piano, exemplified in the instruments made in Clementi's firm. This type of piano was distinct from the Viennese piano of the same period in that the heavier action and inefficient damping of the notes facilitated a smooth touch which favored the legato, cantabile (singing) style, particularly effective in slow movements and heard to supreme advantage in Field's own nocturnes.

The Fieldian nocturne is one of the earliest examples of that quintessentially Romantic form, the early-nineteenth-century character piece for piano. Freestanding and nonprogrammatic, it is of medium pace and typically homophonic, with an aria-like melody and a fulsome, often arpeggiated, accompaniment. The genre exploits the tonal and pitch ranges of the piano as well as its capacity for subtle nuance and shading and its ability, through the use of the sustaining pedal, to invest the music with a kind of halo. Field's contribution to pianistic technique in his innovative use of this pedal, both in his performances and in his published compositions, was constantly alluded to and remains significant to the present day. In his preface to his edition of the nocturnes in 1859, Liszt wrote of hearing Field "play, or rather dream, his pieces, wrapt in inspiration, not limiting himself to the written notes, but incessantly inventing new groups wherewith to engarland his melodies." This also points to the contemporary habit of improvisation, at which Field was among the best, and specifically to embellishment in performance.

Field's melody shows the same influences as the other virtuoso composers of the period, a mixture of Italian operatic bel canto and folk or national tunes and dances, especially those Irish and Scottish. The surface simplicity of these—especially in the edited folk songs—allowed for the kind of filigree right-hand decoration so characteristic of piano works of the period.

All of Field's pieces are for, or include, the piano. His seven concertos show that, while not a gifted orchestrator, he could handle the orchestra sensitively; this was sufficient in a period when the orchestra's main function was to color the music and provide an effective foil to the main attraction, the soloist, who would usually be the composer him/herself. His chamber pieces suffer from the fact that they often have the feel of miniature concertos, with the strings in a subordinate role. The Piano Quintet in A-flat, however, is a fine exception, and the works for piano duet, written with consummate understanding of the medium and based on Russian tunes, are among the first "nationalistic" pieces.

Although he lived in a transitional period, it is difficult to think of Field as a transitional figure. All the elements of the early Romantics seem to be present in the early surviving works, written at the end of the eighteenth century. From the very first of the piano concertos, the writing for the soloist is characteristically that of the virtuoso pianist-composers, and his espousal of piano-oriented genres to the exclusion of many of the traditional ones such as the symphonic, the dramatic, the vocal, the sacred, and the nonkeyboard chamber types anticipates Chopin. In his development of the single character-piece, notably the nocturne, and in its unmistakably Romantic aura, Field was an enormous influence on subsequent composers—perhaps surprising, given his location in distant Russia. Direct models for those of Chopin in terms of mood, pianistic layout, and technique, the spirit of Field's compositions is also to be found in Mendelssohn's *Songs without Words* (1830) and in many later nineteenth-century pieces. Field's impact on the Russian nationalists—for example, Mily Balakirev and Mikhail Glinka—can be seen primarily, but not exclusively, in their treatment of their national melodies.

DEREK CAREW

Bibliography

Born, Dublin, July 1782. Studied with Tomasso Giordano and, after moving to London (1793) apprenticed Muzio Clementi, 1793–99. Lived in Russia (Saint Petersburg) 1802–21 with concert tour to northern Russia and Moscow (1805–6). Lived in Moscow 1821–31. Toured to London and Manchester (1831), Paris (1832), southern French cities, Geneva, and Milan, arriving in Naples, 1834. Brought home to Moscow via Vienna in 1835. Died of cancer in Moscow, 1837.

Selected Works

Piano Solo

Seventeen nocturnes; four piano sonatas; fantasies; waltzes.
Variations, including *Kamarinskaya, air russe favori variée* (1809).
Rondos, including *Go to the Devil* (1797) and *Rondo écossais* (1814).

Piano Duets

Air russe variée (1808); *La danse des ours* (1811).

Chamber

Various pieces for piano and strings.

Piano and orchestra

Seven piano concertos.

Bibliography

Branson, D. *John Field and Chopin*. London, 1972.
Flood, W. H. G. *John Field: Inventor of the Nocturne*. Dublin, 1920.
Liszt, Franz. *Über John Fields Nocturne*. Leipzig, 1859.
Marmontel, A. *Les pianistes célèbres*. Tours, 1878.
Piggott, P. *The Life and Music of John Field*. London, 1973.

FLAXMAN, JOHN 1755–1826

British sculptor and designer

John Flaxman was born in 1755, the son of a plaster-cast maker. In 1769 he entered the new Royal Academy School, where he met William Blake, a fellow enthusiast for medieval English art. Among Flaxman's early work there are some introspective self-portraits, including one in which he poses with his hand on a skull, and a series of dark designs on the subject of Thomas Chatterton (the young poet, forger, suicide, and Romantic icon), including a highly gothic vision, *Chatterton Receiving a Bowl of Poison from Despair* (c. 1775–80). Flaxman subsisted by working for Josiah Wedgwood, producing classical bas-relief designs for bowls and portrait medallions of figures such as Captain James Cook, Samuel Johnson, and Sarah Siddons, as well as an exquisite set of Gothic chessmen. He continued to exhibit at the Royal Academy, and eventually gathered enough funds to travel to Italy in 1787, where he remained until 1794. He filled notebooks with drawings of classical and early Italian art, then just becoming fashionable among artists seeking a more "primitive" style.

In 1792, Flaxman was commissioned to provide a series of illustrations for Dante Alighieri's *Divine Comedy*, which he executed in a style of extreme linearity, without modeling or perspective. Among the pictures are many studies of bodily torment, angelic contest, or visionary transcendence, combining a literal appreciation of the text (an important poem for the Romantic period) with a studied version of early Italian art. Another commission led to series of similar illustrations for the Homeric epics; Flaxman's bare outline style was based here on Greek red-figure vases. Many of the scenes illustrate personal virtues such as affection and loyalty, but the narrative also affords Flaxman many instances of violence or torment, which often bear a strong resemblance to allegorical scenes in Blake's epics. In the *Odyssey* (1793) Flaxman gives further rein to an element of gothic fantasy in his depictions of the ghosts and monsters who afflict Odysseus. This element is still more pronounced in Flaxman's drawings for the plays of Aeschylus, especially in the illustrations of the torture of Prometheus.

These drawings, all engraved in a somewhat dry style by Tommaso Piroli, secured for Flaxman a European reputation. Johann Wolfgang von Goethe acknowledged in 1799 that the Dante illustrations had made Flaxman "the idol of the dilettanti" and August Wilhelm von Schlegel in the same year trumpeted the poetic virtues of Flaxman's lucid outlines. The austerity of the drawings appealed to primitivists of Jacques-Louis David's studio, and to the Pre-Raphaelites. Jean-Auguste-Dominique Ingres' *Jupiter and Thetis* (1811) owes much to Flaxman's severe clarity, while Francisco José de Goya Lucientes gives many of Flaxman's motifs a much darker turn. Flaxman himself was rather embarrassed by the success of these drawings, which he intended as models for narrative carvings in bas-relief. Flaxman did little more work of this kind, apart from a series of illustrations to Hesiod (1817), which again include many titanic struggles more familiar from the work of Blake, who did the engraving, softening the impact of the lines with a stipple technique.

While in Rome, Flaxman also received an important commission for the group sculpture *The Fury of Athamas*, which united his opposing interests in domestic virtues and destructive passions. He was also asked to produce a colossal monument to the Earl of Mansfield for Westminster Abbey, and later produced statues of Viscount Horatio Nelson and other British war heroes. But it was the more intimate and reflective monument to the proto-Romantic poet William Collins (in Chichester Cathedral, England) that set the tone for Flaxman's later career; his vision of bas-relief narratives from outline drawings came to be fulfilled through memorial sculptures of pious sensibility. This highlighting of religion and sentiment appealed to Victorian critics, who coined the term "Flaxmanic" to denote a high degree of imagination, sublimity, ideal beauty, and pathos. His subjects include the poetess Mary Tighe, whose poem *Psyche* (1805) influenced Keats and Robert Burns, a poet Flaxman much admired.

He came to have a quasi-industrial practice. Blake described him in 1804 as "a laborious votary of endless work." So regular and obliging was he in business that his wife wrote to William Hayley in 1805 that she wished to see him established in a cottage "where he may employ his talents as he best likes, not cramped by the obstinate will or foolish whim of anyone, but let the world see the inward man." His reputation was confirmed by Hayley's *Essay on Sculpture: In a Series of Epistles to John Flaxman* (1800). In 1810 the Royal Academy instituted the post of professor of sculpture for Flaxman; he fulfilled his duties with meticulous care. In his lectures he inveighed against baroque flashiness, especially as represented by Gian Lorenzo Bernini; his hero is Michaelangelo Buonarroti. But he also recommends early English art, arguing for example that the carvings on Wells Cathedral show "a beautiful simplicity, an irresistible sentiment, and sometimes a grace, excelling more modern productions." In the last years of his life, he returned to large-scale sculptural composition with *Satan Overcome by St. Michael* (1822). Designed to be seen in the round, it represents a writhing, titanic battle in a striking vertical arrangement.

Flaxman combined commercial design with pure antiquity; industrial production with medieval visions; pious spirituality with extreme psychological torment. His career can be clarified through comparison with that of his close contemporary, Blake, whom he tried to help with commissions. In an ecstatic letter of 1800, Blake praises God "that ever I saw Flaxman's face"; he regarded Flaxman as a kind of intermediary between his own visionary existence and the material patronage of Hayley. He calls Flaxman "Dear Sculptor of Eternity" and tells him "You, O Dear Flaxman, are a Sublime Archangel, My Friend & Companion from Eternity," though this vision later dimmed. Both artists were attracted to the high spirituality of Emanuel Swedenborg, both studied early English art, both drew illustrations for Dante, John Milton, and John Burryan's *Pilgrim's Progress*, and both placed great emphasis on clarity of outline. But Flaxman had very little of Blake's self-confident revolutionary vision, retaining an open, cheerful manner quite the opposite of Blake's intense otherworldliness. Flaxman's work, revolutionary as it seemed, was always more accessible than Blake's; he was always closer to classical models than Blake, and more ready than Blake to cooperate with industrial processes. In his association with the Royal Academy and his patriotic monuments, he aligned himself with the state rather than the individual. The "inward man" of his wife's vision remained essentially compromised by engagement with the world.

PAUL BAINES

Biography

Born in York, July 6, 1755. Son of John Flaxman, a plaster-cast manufacturer. The family moved to London, 1756, where he worked in his father's studio and studied classical literature independently. Entered Royal Academy Schools to study sculpture, 1769. Met lifelong friend William Blake; exhibited at Royal Academy annual exhibitions, 1771–73. Worked as designer for Wedgwood, 1775–87. Exhibited design for Thomas Chatterton's tomb at the Royal Academy annual exhibition; commissioned to decorate Josiah Wedgwood's Etruria Hall, 1780. Married Nancy Denman, 1782 (d. 1820). Studied and directed the Wedgwood studio in Rome, 1787–94. Returned to England and established successful sculpture practice in London. Worked on monument to Lord Mansfield at Westminster Abbey, 1795–1810. Elected associate of the Royal Academy, 1797, and fellow, 1800. Appointed first professor of sculpture at the Royal Academy, 1810. Elected member of the Accademia di San Luca, 1816. Died in London, December 9, 1826.

Selected Works

Lectures on Sculpture 1829. Rev. ed. 1838.

Bibliography

Bindman, D., ed. *John Flaxman*. London: Thames & Hudson, 1979.

Constable, W. G. *John Flaxman, 1755–1826*. London: University of London Press, 1927.

Cunningham, A. *The Lives of the Most Eminent British Painters, Sculptors and Architects*. Vol. 3. London: John Murray and A. & R. Spotiswoode, 1830.

Irwin, D. *John Flaxman, 1755–1826: Sculptor, Illustrator, Designer*. London: Cassell Ltd., 1979.

FOHR, CARL PHILIPP 1795–1818

German artist

The brevity of Carl Philipp Fohr's career encourages us to see him as the epitome of the Romantic artist, an unworldly dreamer and wanderer whose creative progress is tragically curtailed. Born in Heidelberg in the heartland of Romantic Germany, Fohr began drawing at a tender age, and although his father arranged for him to take private lessons with a university professor, he liked nothing better than to sketch in the open air. His teenage ramblings through the local Neckar Valley and the forested hills of the Odenwald inspired a set of sketches which were worked up into a watercolor album in 1814.

On one of his excursions, Fohr met a painter named Wilhelm Issel, who offered to be his tutor in Darmstadt, then capital of the Grand Duchy of Hesse; this led to further contacts, notably with Princess Wilhelmine of Hesse. It was she who, delighted by the Neckar watercolors, launched the nineteen-year-old on his career by commissioning an album of views of her home town of Baden-Baden and the nearby Black Forest. The results so pleased her that henceforth she granted Fohr an annual stipend: in turn, he regularly sent her letters and pictures.

In July 1815, Fohr enrolled at the Munich Academy, where he quickly manifested his personal style and independent spirit, occasionally falling foul of the authorities to the point of courting expulsion. His autodidactic approach involved copying master-drawings in the local museum, including those of Albrecht Dürer, and embarking on lengthy sketching tours. In the autumn of 1815, he roamed through the Tyrol and as far south as Padua and Venice, filling his knapsack with studies of peasants in regional costume, townscapes, mountain passes, waterfalls, and clouds. Back in Munich, Fohr was struck by *Heroic Landscape with Rainbow* (1815), a monumental canvas by the Tirolean master of the sublime, Joseph Anton Koch. Another influence was that of a slightly older fellow student, Ludwig Sigismund Ruhl, who had known Achim von Arnim, Clemens Brentano, and Brothers Jacob and Wilhelm Grimm in Kassel and now initiated Fohr into the cult of Germanic folklore and fairy tale. The two enthusiasts copied costumes and furniture from medieval sources and collaborated on illustrations to contemporary tales by Friedrich Heinrich Karl Fouqué and Ludwig Tieck. Ruhl also introduced his friend to oil painting.

In 1816, Fohr returned to Heidelberg and joined the local Burschenschaft, one of the many student societies dedicated to German unification and the ideals of freedom. Its youthful politics found expression in the wearing of pseudomedieval garb and manifestations of contempt for the philistinism of provincial life. Fohr made portraits of many of his circle: one of its leading lights was a young hothead named Adolf Follen who insisted on posing for him in a Teutonic suit of armor.

In the autumn of 1816, Fohr undertook the journey south which had become de rigueur for the aspiring Romantic artist, taking just over a month to hike from Heidelberg to Rome. Here he entered into a lively expatriate culture, befriending the older Koch and joining the clan of the Nazarenes, among them Peter von Cornelius, Johann Friedrich Overbeck, and Philipp Veit. As well as producing architectural studies of Roman monuments, Fohr began work on illustrations to the *Nibelungenlied*, the medieval epic that had become a touchstone of patriotism. Among his best late pencil drawings are portraits of the Nazarenes as they sit drinking, talking, or playing lutes around a table in the Café Greco. Fohr planned a composite engraving of the group: this would doubtless have become its visual manifesto, but he did not live to realize it.

Carl Philipp Fohr. Reprinted courtesy of AKG.

One hot June day in 1818, the twenty-two-year-old took a swim in the fast-flowing Tiber and drowned. Although Fohr's drawings were auctioned off and dispersed, Wilhelm Issel was later able to trace the bulk of the work and deposit it with the Landesmuseum in Darmstadt. Another of Fohr's Darmstadt mentors, Philipp Dieffenbach, published a biography in 1823.

Fohr's remarkable command of line is evident even from his most casual pencil sketches: he had an outstanding ability to move from precise fact to autonomous aesthetic configuration. Acutely observed, the portraits of friends embody a brisk precision which accentuates individuality even in the context of a fashionable Romantic enhancement. The landscapes in ink or watercolor are sensitive to the nuance of hue and tone, and thrive upon effects of atmospheric chiaroscuro. One memorable watercolor is *The Mummelsee* (1814), the depiction of a glacier lake in the Black Forest made harmonious by an overall blue tinge; a penciled inscription cites a local legend about sprites in the watery depths.

It was only during the last three years of his life that Fohr worked in oil. Though he probably never saw anything by the great Caspar David Friedrich, his paintings follow a similar practice in recycling motifs from earlier drawings, melding, for example, Tyrolean prospects with vistas of the Neckar Valley. It is said that *The Waterfalls of Tivoli* (1817) was executed in Koch's studio while Koch worked alongside at his own easel. One may surmise that the older man occasionally dabbed at his junior's canvas; and it is conceivable that Fohr would in due course have responded to this influence and essayed his own approach to the sublime. However, as things stand, the seven surviving oils remain unoriginal exercises in the deployment of idyllic Italianesque pastures or brooding Nordic forests, peopled by stiff figures in archaic costume. Arguably the most striking is *The Knights before the Charcoal Burner's Hut* (1816), a painting on wood illustrating a scene from a popular novel by Fouqué.

Though still a little awkward as a composition, it succeeds in marshalling some bravura effects: much of the image is steeped in inky blackness, yet a shaft of moonlight spotlights a dazzling white horse and the white plumes on a knight's helmet, while in the background the red window of a hut blazes like an unearthly beacon.

ROGER CARDINAL

Biography

Born in Heidelberg, November 26, 1795. Private drawing lessons in Heidelberg, 1808. Sketching tour of Neckar Valley, 1810. Studied in Darmstadt, 1810–14. Sketching tour of Baden, 1814–15. Studied at Munich Academy of the Arts, 1815–16. Hiked from Heidelberg to Rome, 1816. Worked in Rome with Joseph Anton Koch and the Nazarenes, 1816–18. Drowned in a swimming accident in Rome, June 29, 1818.

Bibliography

Andersson, Ulrike, and Annette, Frese. *Carl Philipp Fohr und seine Freunde in Rom*. Heidelberg: Kurpfälzisches Museum, 1995.

Cardinal, Roger. *German Romantics in Context*. London: Studio Vista, 1975.

Dieffenbach, Philipp. *Das Leben des Malers Karl Fohr*. 1823.

Dirkmann, Sigrid. *Carl Philipp Fohr (1795–1818). Studien zu den Landschaften*. Frankfurt am Main: Lang, 1993.

Jensen, Jens Christian. *Carl Philipp Fohr in Heidelberg und im Neckartal*. Karlsruhe: Georg Poensgen, 1968.

Lohmeyer, Karl. *Heidelberger Maler der Romantik*. Heidelberg, 1935.

Märker, Peter, ed. *Carl Philipp Fohr. Romantik—Landschaft und Historie*. Heidelberg: Kehrer, 1995.

Schneider, Arthur von, ed. *Carl Philipp Fohr. Skizzenbuch. Bildniszeichnungen deutscher Künstler in Rom*. Berlin: Gebrüder Mann, 1952.

Schrade, Hubert. *Deutsche Maler der Romantik*. Cologne: Du Mont Schauberg, 1967.

Ziemke, Hans-Joachim, ed. *Karl Philipp Fohr 1795–1818*. Frankfurt am Main: Städelsches Kunstinstitut, 1968.

FOLK LITERATURE: BRITAIN

The study of folk literature in Britain underwent enormous changes in the eighteenth century and during the Romantic period. The title "folk literature" is itself a misnomer, as German and British scholars only started using the term *folk* in the mid-nineteenth century. However, long before a term was applied to it, the study of literature of or by the people became immensely popular. Moreover, there were many ideological and political, as well as aesthetic, motivations that propeled these endeavors. Folk literature encompasses a wide variety of genres, including ballads, songs, romances, tales, fables, myths, legends, ghost stories, hymns, and carols. The Romantic era was concerned not only with recording the efforts of contemporary practitioners, but also in constructing, reviving, and inventing the canons of its ancient literary traditions.

A major component of the interest in folk literature was the revival of the ballad, once seen as the lowest form of literature. Often sold in broadsheets or chapbooks by street vendors, ballads were perceived at best as children's literature, at worst as vulgar and disreputable productions. Throughout the eighteenth century poets as diverse as William Cowper, Mary Wortley Montague, and Johnathan Swift, had composed ballads and attempted to improve the image of the genre. The critic Joseph Addison had raised the profile of ancient ballads in a series of essays in *The Spectator* (1711), and attempts were made throughout the century to suggest that the genre could have positive philosophical and artistic properties as well as negative ones. However, these views were challenged and satirized by many, *A Comment Upon the History of Tom Thumb* (1711) by William Wagstaffe being one early example that criticized the scholarly attention that was placed upon this type of literature.

The appreciation of folk literature gained enormous impetus from James Macpherson's publication in the second half of the century of *Fragments of Ancient Poetry* (1760), *Fingal* (1762), and *Temora* (1763), which drew attention to a putative epic song cycle by the third-century Scottish poet-king Ossian that had ostensibly been preserved by the oral culture of the Scottish

Highlands. Macpherson suggested that native Scottish poetry not only had the same aesthetic importance as classical epics, but that it also could be used to define and draw attention to Scotland's prestigious cultural history. The Ossian texts (their authenticity was ultimately contested) provoked a storm of controversy and directly inspired other collectors throughout Britain and the continent to discover—or invent—competing traditions of indigenous songs. The most notable of these in Britain was Thomas Percy's *The Reliques of Ancient English Poetry* (1765). Percy's work sought to recover, define, and celebrate the English minstrel ballad tradition and differed sharply in relation to Macpherson's as it claimed to be derived from actual printed and manuscript sources. The discussion of the ballad drew attention to questions of literary and national authenticity and underlined tensions that existed within British society between rival groupings. The rising awareness of regional and national cultural identities fueled the desire to maintain Irish, English, Scottish, and Welsh heritage and traditions. Individual poets, such as Robert Burns and Sir Walter Scott, collected or augmented local songs and tunes in their collections of poems. Numerous other anthologists repeated this across the United Kingdom.

Political considerations often lay behind the desire to collect national literatures. In the late eighteenth century the antiquarian Joseph Ritson began to challenge the dominance of conservative antiquarian scholars with the publication of his editions of medieval English romances. His *Select Collection of English Songs* (1783) and *Metrical Romances* (1802) employed more sophisticated editorial methodologies than previous researchers, a fact that Ritson, a Jacobin sympathizer, was keen to express for political as well as academic reasons.

In addition, writers and poets employed the scholarly and antiquarian researches on ballads as raw materials in the composition of their own poetry. Thomas Chatterton gained posthumous notoriety due to his attempts to fabricate the writings of a medieval monk called Thomas Rowley, based on his reading of Geoffrey Chaucer, Thomas Percy's *Reliques*, William Shakespeare and Edmund Spenser. Leading antiquarians of the time, such as Horace Walpole, Thomas Warton, and Percy himself claimed that Chatterton was a forger. However, many others saw the invention and originality inherent in Chatterton's works, as well as the image of genius blighted by lack of public recognition, as extremely positive forces. This stimulated interest in the fragmentary element of literary artifacts, the sentimental reverence for textual relics, the preservation of lost traditions, and the playful editorial framing of supposedly authentic materials, and provided much scope for later Romantic writers to explore in their own works. The first generation of Romantic writers, including Samuel Taylor Coleridge, Robert Southey, and William Wordsworth, were heavily influenced by the ballad tradition and saw in this genre a way to write, as Wordsworth claimed, "in a selection of language really used by men." This allowed them to suggest that the verse and sentiments they were expressing were heightened examples of the rustic speech of Britain and that they themselves were representative voices of their nation. The expansion of literacy levels and the growth of publishing also allowed writers from the lower orders, such as John

Clare, to gain recognition in print. However, the relationships between middle- or upper-class patrons and lower-class poets were often fraught with difficulty, as experienced by, for example, Ann Yearsley and her patron Hannah More.

The ballad's versatility as an instrument of propaganda saw it employed by both reactionary and radical groupings on countless occasions in the turbulent decades of the late eighteenth and early nineteenth centuries. Republican and radical factions, like the United Irishmen in Ireland, used collections of ballads and Gaelic poetry to promote their ideals and attack governmental forces. In many ways ballads and songs were the literary and musical equivalent of Thomas Paine's *Rights of Man* (1791).

During the Romantic period, associations and academies sprang up to try and accomplish the task of preserving and appreciating folk cultures. In addition, the increase in travel and tourism within Britain saw scholars recording local customs, dialect, and folklore. By the middle of the nineteenth century, folk literature was viewed as an integral part of Britain's heritage. No longer the literature of the ignorant and vulgar, it was perceived as an object of academic scrutiny, which could offer patriotic and aesthetic rewards to its consumers.

FRANK FERGUSON

Bibliography

Adams, John R. *The Printed Word and the Common Man: Popular Culture in Ulster, 1700–1900.* Belfast: Institute of Irish Studies, 1987.

Bronson, Bertrand H. *Joseph Ritson, Scholar-at-Arms.* Berkeley and Los Angeles: University of California Press, 1938.

Colley, Linda. *Britons Forging the Nation 1707–1837.* London: Vintage, 1996.

Crawford, Robert, ed. *Robert Burns and Cultural Authority.* Edinburgh: Edinburgh University Press, 1997.

Fowler, David C. *A Literary History of the Popular Ballad.* Durham, N.C.: Duke University Press, 1968.

Friedman, Albert B. *The Ballad Revival.* Chicago: Chicago University Press, 1961.

Gaskill, Howard, ed. *Ossian Revisited.* Edinburgh: Edinburgh University Press, 1991.

Groom, Nick. *The Making of Percy's Reliques.* Oxford: Oxford University Press, 1999.

———. *Thomas Chatterton and Romantic Culture.* Oxford: Oxford University Press, 1999.

Harker, Dave. *Fakesong: The Manufacture of British "Folksong" from 1700 to the Present Day.* Milton Keynes, England: Open University Press, 1985.

Hobsbawm, Eric, and Ranger Terence, eds. *The Invention of Tradition.* Cambridge: Cambridge University Press, 1983.

Newman, Gerald. *The Rise of English Nationalism: A Cultural History 1740–1830.* London: Macmillan, 1997.

Pittock, Murray. *Inventing and Resisting Britain: Cultural Identities in Britain and Ireland, 1685–1789.* London: Macmillan, 1997.

Stafford, Fiona. *The Sublime Savage.* Edinburgh: Edinburgh University Press, 1988.

Thuente, Mary Helen. *The Harp Re-Strung: The United Irishmen and the Rise of Irish Literary Nationalism.* Syracuse, N.Y.: Syracuse University Press, 1994.

Trumpener, Katie. *Bardic Nationalism.* New Haven, Conn.: Yale University Press, 1998.

FOLK LITERATURE: GERMANY

Most of the folk literature that was published in Germany during the Romantic period (after 1800) was intended to contribute to a possible political and cultural unification of Germany. The interest in folk literature in Germany did not, however, initially develop in the nineteenth century. As early as 1760, James Macpherson published the *Fragments of Ancient Poetry* that were supposed to have come from the blind Gaelic bard Ossian. The *Fragments* immediately became very popular throughout Europe. At the time Germany consisted of more than three hundred principalities and the need for a unifying cultural asset, such as the *Fragments* seemed to be for Britain, was great. For this reason the authenticity of the *Fragments* was only of marginal importance.

Johann Gottfried Herder contributed greatly to the popularity of Ossian and the newly discovered interest in folk literature in Germany. He had been collecting folk songs since 1764 and published his collection *Volkslieder (Folk Songs)* in 1778 or 1779. In 1772 Herder published *Briefwechsel über Ossian und die Lieder alter Völker (Letters Regarding Ossian and the Songs of Ancient Peoples)*, in which he explained that the folk songs in his collection were not included because of their age, but because of their origins in cultures that are open to influences from other nations yet simultaneously reflect confidence and pride in their own cultures. This explains why he included poetry by Matthias Claudius, Johann Wolfgang von Goethe, and William Shakespeare in his collection where one might not expect to find them represented. Furthermore, Herder urges his peers to collect these folk songs from the people, so that they may be preserved.

Later the Romantic poets integrated Herder's demands into their concept of *Universalpoesie* (universal poetry). The Romantics, however, got their concept of "folk" and folk literature from their perception of the Middle Ages. The romantic view of the Middle Ages was that this was a time when there was no contrast between art and everyday life and the different German speaking cultural groups lived together in harmony in the Holy Roman Empire. This fascination with the Middle Ages resulted in an interest in medieval fairy tales, legends, and songs that reflected a society that was apparently stable and in harmony with nature, in contrast to the Romantic poets' view of their own society.

In 1805 Clemens Brentano and his friend Achim von Arnim published the first volume of *Des Knaben Wunderhorn* (*The Boy's Magic Horn*), a collection of folk songs from the sixteenth and seventeenth centuries. The songs in this collection are mostly childlike and enchanting in nature and thematize the small bourgeois family that was so highly regarded by the Romantic poets. Also included are many work songs and children's songs. There are also quite a few songs in the collection that are critical of contemporary society and issues, which indicates the social and cultural value of the collection.

In addition to the folk songs that they collected from written sources, they also composed quite a few songs themselves. These additions that they made resulted in some critique on the authenticity of the folk songs in their collection. Goethe responded to this critique in a review of *Des Knaben Wunderhorn* by emphatically rejecting the idea of an "Untersuchung, inwiefern das alles, was uns hier gebracht ist, völlig echt oder mehr oder weniger restauriert sei" ("investigation to determine whether all this that is brought to us here is completely authentic or more or less restored"). In reference to the authors of the collection, Goethe added that "sie werden sich ein Verdienst um die Nation erwerben, wenn sie mitwirken, daß wir eine Geschichte unserer Poesie und poetischen Kultur . . . gründlich, aufrichtig und geistreich erhalten" ("they will do great service for the nation if they contribute to preserving our poetry and our poetic culture thoroughly, honestly, and intelligently"). Goethe was more concerned and impressed with the cultural and political significance of this collection of folk songs than the authenticity of the individual folk songs.

Jakob and Wilhelm Grimm had a different opinion of Brentano and Arnim's collection. They were particularly critical of the authors' approach to collecting, revising, and even including folk songs they had written in the collection. Since the Grimm brothers were such disciplined scholars themselves, they were critical of and doubted the scientific tenability of *Des Knaben Wunderhorn*. In light of their critique of Brentano and Arnim, it is interesting to note that the brothers Grimm revised and edited their own collection of fairy tales, *Kinder- und Hausmärchen* (*Grimms' Fairy Tales*), several times. While they claimed to have gathered these tales from the *Volk* (people), they in fact invited women who were acquainted with their family, to their home and wrote them down there. They did not travel the countryside, collecting these tales from the common people; in fact, many of the tales that they included in their collection were not even of German origin, but rather French.

However, the brothers Grimm may have collected, edited, and revised these tales to suit children, it is clear that this genre was a particularly popular type of folk literature during the Romantic period in Germany. The fairy tale was so popular because it thematized the irrational and fantastic and referred to an undetermined time when mankind lived in harmony with nature. At the same time, however, no genre of literature was as controversial as the fairy tale was during the Romantic period. For example, Jakob and Wilhelm Grimm's collection of fairy tales was very different from the "art" fairy tales that E. T. A. Hoffmann, Novalis, and Ludwig Tieck composed. In contrast to the *Volksmärchen* (folk tales) in the brothers Grimm collection, the *Kunstmärchen* (art fairy tales) written by Hoffmann, Novalis, and Tieck, among others, focus on the psyche of the characters that go off on adventures or overcome impossible odds. In addition, while the Volksmärchen tell of restoring order to a world that was caught up in momentary chaos with anonymous characters as the protagonists, Kunstmärchen usually take places in concrete locations. Hoffmann's fairy tale *Der goldne Topf* (The Golden Pot), for example, takes place in Dresden at the turn of the century.

HEIDE CRAWFORD

Bibliography

Apel, F. *Die Zaubergärten der Phantasie: zur Theorie und Geschichte des Kunstmärchens*. Heidelberg: Winter, 1978.

Lüthi, Max. *Volksmärchen und Volkssage. Zwei Grundformen erzählender Dichtung*. Bern: Francke, 1966.

Poser, T. "Das Märchen." In *Formen der Literatur in Einzeldarstellungen.* Edited by Otto Knörrich. Stuttgart: Kröner, 1991.

Schanze, Helmut, ed. *Romantik—Handbuch.* Tübingen: Alfred Kröner Verlag, 1994.

Tismar, J. *Kunstmärchen.* Stuttgart: Metzler, 1983.

FOLK SONGS

In the early 1880s, the Russian musical critic and journalist Vladimir Stasov wrote that nineteenth-century composers in western Europe had lost interest in the folk song, a form that, in his opinion, had by this time become the province of "musical archeologists." Stasov expressed the opinion that it was in the work of Russian composers that European art music was being resurrected through a fresh infusion of authenticity, and that this was achieved through the use of folk tunes. The folk song, the Russian critic maintained, was "the expression of the spontaneous, unaffected musicality of the people."

While in some respects Stasov's assessment was correct, it nevertheless expressed a biased, narrow view of the situation at hand. Indeed, in Russia the first systematic attempts to collect authentic folk songs, those of Kirsha Danilov, had materialized in the publication, in 1804, of folk song texts from Siberia; this was followed in 1818 by a second edition that included melodies as well. Toward the middle of the century the composer Mikhail Glinka had made ample use of melodic and rhythmic stereotypes characteristic of Russian folk songs, most notably in his opera *Ruslan and Ludmila* (1842). Employing the melodic contours and interval inflections of the folk song was perceived as a patriotic duty by the group of Russian composers known as "The Mighty Five": Milii Balakirev, Alexander Borodin, Cesar Cui, Modest Mussorgsky, and Nicolai Rimski-Korsakov. By the time Stasov was writing his essay, Mussorgsky had quoted several folk tunes in his opera *Boris Godunov* (1868–72; two versions) and Rimski-Korsakov had assembled two collections of folk songs (1875 and 1875–82).

But western Europe had been manifesting an even earlier interest in folk poetry and the folk song, a natural result of the rise of individual European nations as political and cultural entities in the Romantic era. In fact, this phenomenon was an extension of the concept posited in eighteenth-century cultural philosophy—namely, that folk literature and music were the spontaneous expressions of the national soul. This trend was first started in English literature by the antiquarian Thomas Percy, the compiler and editor of the famous *Reliques of Ancient English Poetry* (1765). The anthology initiated the revival of interest in folk poetry, inspiring Romantic poets in both England and Germany, with efforts on the German side deliberately directed toward instilling a sense of national cohesion in a populace divided by numerous geographical borderlines and strong political dissensions.

The German writer, linguist, and cultural philosopher Johann Gottfried Herder coined the term *Volkslied* (folk song) and published the two-volume *Stimmen der Völker in Liedern* (*Voices of the People in Songs,* 1778–79), a comparative anthology of folk songs that met with phenomenal success and was reprinted and reedited at least five times in the following century. A few decades later, the German poets and playwrights Achim von Arnim and Clemens Brentano published their three-volume anthology titled *Des Knaben Wunderhorn* (*The Youth's Magic Horn,*

1806–8). While the collection itself did not include any notated folk-song melodies, individual pieces were set to music by various composers throughout the nineteenth century and beyond, with perhaps the most illustrious example being the fourteen songs for solo voice and orchestra composed toward the close of the century by Gustav Mahler. In the former Polish territories, now partitioned among Austria, Prussia, and Russia, the first methodical steps in field collecting were taken by Oskar Kolberg, who published two large compilations of Polish folk songs (1857 and 1865). On the Finnish side the poet Elias Lönnrot published *Kalevala* (Land of Heroes, 1835), a collection of Finnish folk literature whose component poems he compiled, edited, and arranged so as to confer upon the whole a unity not part of the original.

Romantic composers in general were not direct collectors of folk songs. The material they used was inspired by melodies, rhythms, accentual patterns, and harmonies that could be found in the folk-music repertory of countries such as Germany, Hungary, Poland, and Russia. But the resulting compositions, while preserving the spirit of the original, were highly polished and refined to suit the taste of Western audiences. The "imitation folk songs" in strophic form that constitute a part of the *Lieder* repertoire of Franz Peter Schubert are a good illustration of this model: short, simple, light, and comprised of several stanzas based on identical rhyme and metric schemes set to the same music. Somewhat later in the century, Johannes Brahms wrote some 260 *Lieder* including arrangements of German folk songs, fourteen of which appeared in 1858 and were dedicated to the children of Robert and Clara Schumann. For Brahms, the folk song was the sound ideal, something to be emulated.

Frédéric Chopin's solo polonaises for piano contain (as the name implies) musical reminiscences of his native Poland, but the genre is rather conventional: the polonaise had been around as a form of Western art music for more than a century, and had been polished and refined by generations of composers to the extent that it had become a courtly dance well before Chopin's time. His mazurkas for piano were inspired by Polish folk dances such as the *mazur,* the *oberek,* and the *kujawiak,* but while some of the mazurkas are more closely connected to the music of their folk models, others are the result of Chopin's encapsulation and stylization of the essential elements of the originals. Chopin was, in the eyes of his Parisian audiences and critics, the most eloquent proponent of an elegant, sophisticated "Polishness."

In a similar vein Franz Liszt, the Hungarian-born piano virtuoso and composer, wrote his *National Melodies and Rhapsodies* (later revised and published as *Hungarian Rhapsodies*) after a trip to Pest in 1839. The original sources of Liszt's Hungarian manner can be traced to the indigenous folk genre of the *verbunkos,* a dance based on alternating slow and brisk sections. But Liszt, who barely spoke any Hungarian at all and never had direct contact with the Hungarian peasantry, heard these pieces as they were performed—and transformed—by gypsy orchestras in Budapest.

LUMINITA FLOREA

Bibliography

Arnim, Achim von, and Clemens Brentano. *Des Knaben Wunderhorn* 1874. Edited by H. Rolleke. Stuttgart: Reclam, 1987.

Bellman, Jonathan. *The Style Hongrois in the Music of Western Europe.* Boston: Northeastern University Press, 1993.

Brown, Malcolm H., and Roland John Wiley, eds. *Slavonic and Western Music: Essays for Gerald Abraham.* Ann Arbor, Mich.: University of Michigan Research Press, 1985.

Cui, Cesar. *La musique en Russie.* 1880. Reprint, Leipzig: Zentralantiquariat der DDR, 1974.

Herder, Johann Gottfried. *Stimmen der Völker in Liedern.* Edited by Johann von Müller, 1813. Edited by Christel Kaschel. Leipzig: Reclam, 1968.

Milewski, Barbra. "Chopin's Mazurkas and the Myth of the Folk," *Nineteenth-Century Music* 23 (1999–2000): 113–35.

Taruskin, Richard. *Defining Russia Musically: Historical and Hermeneutical Essays.* Princeton, N.J.: Princeton University Press, 1997.

Vargyas, Lajos. *A magyar nepballada es Europa.* Budapest: Zenemükiado, 1976.

FORSTER, (JOHANN) GEORG(E) (ADAM) 1754–1794

German scientist, philosopher, essayist, and cultural critic

Georg Forster, a natural scientist, philosopher and essayist, was best known for his travel accounts, which balanced scientific observation with *Empfindung* (emotional perception), thus fusing the clinical attitude of the Enlightenment with early Romanticism.

His literary and scientific fame was established instantly, following the publication in English of *A Voyage around the World* (1777) and the subsequent German edition *Reise um die Welt während der Jahre 1772–1775* (1778–80). This text was based on research and accounts undertaken by himself and his father, the pastor, philosopher, and scientist Reinhold Forster, with whom he had participated in Captain James Cook's second expedition to circumnavigate the globe. After the British government barred the older Forster from publishing his findings from the English-sponsored expedition, young Georg took over and beat Cook's team in the race for publication of the project. This early work reflects a philosophical attitude toward the observation of humanity, society, nature, and landscape that reveals the influence of Georges-Louis Leclerq Buffon, who was translated into German by Forster, Carl Linné, and Jean-Jacques Rousseau. *A Voyage* was received enthusiastically by the critics for its poetic description of scientific observations. The text fueled the public's fascination with South Sea Romanticism (*Südseeromantik*), and pioneered a genre of travel description that appealed to the popular predilection for the nature poetry of his day.

During his years as a faculty member at the University of Vilna, Forster produced several important works on botany and anthropology, including the polemical *Noch etwas über die Menschenracen* (*Yet More about the Human Races*, 1786; published in *Teutscher Merkur*). This *Streitschrift* sided with Johann Herder against Immanuel Kant in an ethnological dispute.

After accepting a position as librarian in Mainz, for which Johannes von Müller had recommended him, Forster published an open polemic letter to Gotthold Ephraim Lessing in *Neue Literatur und Völkerkunde* in which he defended Johann Christoph Friedrich von Schiller's neo-Platonism, which the former had criticized in *Fragment eines Briefes an einen deutschen Schriftsteller über Schiller's "Götter Griechenlands"* (*Fragments of a Letter to a German Author regarding Schiller's "Greek Gods,"* 1789). It was in Mainz that Forster's most important work, the *Ansichten vom Niederrhein* (*Views of the Lower Rhine*, 1791–94) was written, which he described in a 1790 letter to his publisher Spener as "mein Empfinden und mein Denken oder Räsonnieren ("my emotional perception and my contemplation or reasoning"). The major body of this text was comprised of travel descriptions in letter form, chronicling his journey with Alexander von Humboldt to France, Germany, and the Netherlands. This work consolidated Forster's reputation as the master of subjective "artistic" observation and description, which had a profound impact on the travel writing and landscape painting of the era. The double entendre of *point of view* and *view*, contained in the semantics of the German word *Ansichten* gave Forster the opportunity to intertwine factual observations with historical analyses as well as philosophical and political opinions. Bound with it were several treatises on the arts that suggest discussions with some of the major figures in aesthetic and art criticism, among them Johann Wolfgang von Goethe, Georg Christoph Lichtenberg, Friedrich and August Wilhelm von Schlegel, and Johann Georg Sulzer. Even though most of the earlier dated assessments on works of art and architecture were written under the spell of Johann Winckelmann, his essay on the Cathedral in Cologne reflects the neo-Gothic revivalist movement in England and was praised by its advocates in Germany, among them Sulpiz Boisserree. Among the texts bound with the *Ansichten* were surveys of Britain's environs as well as those of its art. Its publication in Germany was timely in that it corresponded closely with an interest in British arts and letters that had fostered the Sturm und Drang movement in Germany. Forster's courting of the Romantic concepts of sentimentalism and the sublime reverberate in his "Empfindungen" while in the presence of the neo-Gothic buildings at Oxford University: "Romantische Grösse, schauervolle Stille, lichtscheue Schwermuth und stolzes Bewusstsein füllten die Seele" ("Romantic loftiness, scary silence, melancholy that shied the light, and proud consciousness fill the soul"). Even though most critics have dismissed his comments on art as based on the opinions of others, it is important to remember that Forster was himself an experienced amateur artist; he had provided most of the illustrations for his *Voyage*. His commentaries on landscape painting particularly anticipated, if not influenced, the work of prominent Romantic painters. Forster proposed that landscape painting constitutes "das wesentliche Ziel der Kunst" ("the essential goal of art").

Forster also translated texts from English, such as the east Indian poet Kalidasa's epic *Sakontalo*, which was praised highly by Goethe, Herder, and Friedrich Schiller and August von Schlegel.

As with many liberal intellectuals of his day, the concept of the 1789 French Revolution affected Forster deeply, and he meditated on it in the treatises *Über historische Glaubwürdigkeit* (*About Historical Believability*, 1791) and *Über den gelehrten Zunftzwang* (*About the Restrictions of the Scholarly Profession*, 1792). Highly critical of the conservative Vatican-allied Duke of Mainz, whose oppressive politics were felt especially by the enlightened faculty of the university, Forster advocated the "liberation" of the province by joining revolutionary France. When the duke fled Mainz from the advancing French troops in 1792, Forster became an official member of the German Jakobins and was elected their president in 1793. He was subsequently elected deputy and vice president of the Rhenish-German National Convention, which he represented as a deputy in Paris, after March 1793. The last years of his short life in French exile were dedicated to philosophizing about the ideals of the French Revolution, despite his disillusionment due to the associated carnage. Several texts survived, including *Parisische Umrisse* (*Parisian Sketches*, 1793), *Über die Beziehung der Staatskunst auf das Glück der Menschheit* (*Concerning the Relationship between Governance and the Pursuit of Happiness*, 1794), and the posthumously published *Darstellung der Revolution in Mainz* (*Description of the Revolution in Mainz*, 1843). Even though his sentiments were shared by many of the intellectuals of the time, few joined the French revolutionary ranks as publicly and irreversibly as he did. When the revolutionary army liberated Germany from the aristocracy and gave way to an occupation, national sentiments ran high; many former advocates of the French Revolution turned guerilla fighters against Napoleon Bonaparte and his German puppet governments. Forster was subsequently viewed as the quintessential traitor, and his contribution to the German culture ignored despite a eulogizing essay on his behalf by Friedrich von Schlegel. Even though he was shunned officially, the demand for his *Voyage* and *Ansichten* continued, and may even have been enhanced by his notoriety. These texts were reprinted in new editions that continued to affect the Romantic era.

JOHANN J. K. REUSCH

Biography

Born Johann Georg Adam Forster in Nassenhuben (Mokry Dwór) near Danzig (Gdansk), November 26 or 27, 1754. Educated primarily by his father, Johann Reinhold Forster, Protestant minister and naturalist. Made prolonged excursion to Russia with his father in the services of Catherine II, 1765. Lived in England, 1766–78; worked as translator of travel accounts. Assisted his father as scientific member of James Cook's second circumnavigation of the earth, 1772–75. Returned to Germany; visited the Universities of Anhalt-Dessau, Berlin, Braunschweig, Göttingen, and Kassel, 1776–78; elected member of the Gesellschaft Naturforschender Freunde, Berlin, 1776; received honorary degree from University of Göttingen, 1778. Appointed professor of natural history at the Collegium Carolinum, Kassel; wrote anthropological treatises and moved in Rosicrucian circles, 1778–84. Professor at the University of Vilna (Vilnius), Lithuania, 1784–87. Married Therese Heyne, the daughter of Göttingen classicist Christian Gottlob Heyne, 1785; they had four daughters, two of whom died in infancy. Left academic position in Vilna and returned to Gottingen to participate in planned Russian Pacific expedition, 1787. Appointed librarian at the University of Mainz after cancellation of the expedition, 1788–90. Journeyed with Alexander von Humboldt through northern Europe, 1790. Official member and subsequently president of the Jacobin club in Mainz, 1792–93; deputy and subsequent vice president of the Rhenish-German National Convention in Paris. Died of scurvy and pneumonia in Paris, January 12, 1794.

Selected Works

Werke; sämtliche Schriften, Tagebücher, Briefe. Edited by the Deutsche Akademie der Wissenschaften zu Berlin, 1958–1985.
Die Kasseler Jahre: Texte, Materialien, Dokumente. Edited by Silvia Merz-Horn. 1990.
A Voyage round the World. Edited by Nicholas Thomas and Oliver Berghof, 2000.

Bibliography

Braun, Martin. *"Nichts Menschliches soll mir fremd sein"—Georg Forster und die frühe deutsche Völkerkunde vor dem Hintergrund der klassischen Kulturwissenschaften*. Bonn: Holos, 1991.
Fiedler, Horst. *Georg-Forster Bibliographie 1767–1790*. Berlin: Akademie, 1972.
Fischer, Rotraut. *Reisen als Erfahrungskunst, Georg Forsters "Ansichten vom Niederrhein."* Frankfurt am Main: Hain, 1990.
Forsters Bilder von der Weltumsegelung mit Cook in der Forschungs– und Landesbibliothek Gotha. Gotha: Forschungs– und Landesbibliothek, 1994.
Garber, Jörn, *Wahrnehmung, Konstruktion, Text: Bilder des Wirklichen in Werk Georg Forsters*. Tubingen: Niemeyer, 2000.
Klenke, Claus-Volker. *Georg Forster in interdisziplinärer Perspektive Internationales Georg-Forster-Symposion 1993, Kassel*. Berlin: Akademie Verlag, 1994.
Padberg, Gabriele. *Georg Forster, observateur d'oeuvres d'art: à l'epoque des vues sur le Rhin inferieur*. Paris: Diffusion Les Belles Lettres, 1995.
Peitsch, Helmut. *Georg Forsters "Ansichten vom Niederrhein": zum Problem des Übergangs vom bürgerlichen Humanismus zum revolutionären Demokratismus*. Frankfurt am Main: P. Lang, 1978.
———. *Georg Forster: A History of His Critical Reception*. New York: Lang, 2001.
Rasmussen, Detlev, ed. *Der Weltumsegler und seine Freunde—Georg Forster als gesellschaftlicher Schriftsteller der Goethezeit*. Tübingen: Narr, 1988.
Reichardt, Rolf, ed. *Weltbürger, Europäer, Deutscher, Franke*. Exhibition catalog, Universitätsbibliothek Mainz, January 10–February 27, 1994.
Saine, Thomas P. *Georg Forster*. New York: Twayne, 1972.
Schmied-Kowarzik, Wolfdietrich. *Georg Forster*. Kassel: Gesamthochschul-Bibliothek, 1988.
Schwarz, Astrid. *Georg Forster (1754–1794): Dialektik von Natur Wissenschaft, Anthropologie, Philosophie und Politik in der deutschen Spätoufklärung*. Aachen: Mainz, 1998.
Steiner, Gerhard. *Georg Forster*. Stuttgart: Metzler, 1977.
Strack, Thomas. *Exotische Erfahrung und Intersubjektivität: Reiseberichte im 17 und 18. Jahrhundert: Genregeschichtliche Untersuchung zu Adam Olearius, Hans Egede, Georg Forster*. Paderborn: Igel Verlag Wissenschaft, 1994.
Waetzoldt, Wilhelm. *Deutsche Kunsthistoriker*. Vol. 1. Berlin: Hessling, 1965.

FOSCOLO, UGO 1778–1827

Italian poet and literary critic

E. R. Vincent's definition of Ugo Foscolo as a Byron in reverse is more than a neat summation of the geographic parabola of his life, which began on the Greek island of Zacynthos, then part of Venetian territories, and ended in London. The Greek ideal for which Byron fought and died was in many ways a central element of Foscolo's aspirations, as in his unfinished poem *Le grazie* (*The Graces*, 1822). His intention was to capture the rhythms of Greek poetry in Italian verse, and in his final years he worked on his translation of the *Iliad*. Indeed, Foscolo's life, with his many love affairs and the passionate patriotism that was expressed in actual combat, may seem redolent of a Byronic hero. While there are what might be termed proto-Romantic themes in many of Foscolo's writings, his cultural background, poetics, and mode of expression tend to the neoclassical, with the notable exceptions of the epistolary novel and some of the sonnets.

From an early age, Foscolo was well read in Greek, Latin, and Italian literature, and practiced his craft by doing many translations and composing poems in the style of Vincenzo Monti and Giuseppe Parini. Both his patriotic sentiments and his political naïveté were expressed in the ode he wrote to Napoleon Bonaparte, *A Bonaparte liberatore* (*To Bonaparte the Liberator*, 1796), when he descended into Italy, defeating Austria and her ally, Piedmont. The hopes of political reform for Italy along the lines of the French Revolution were soon dashed, as Napoleon handed over Venice and its territories to Austria in exchange for Belgium. Bitterly disillusioned, Foscolo left Venice for Milan, where he worked on his epistolary novel *Le ultime lettere di Iacopo Ortis* (*The Last Letters of Iacopo Ortis*). This was first published in Bologna in 1799, without the author's consent, under the title *Vera storia di dueamanti infelici* (*The True Story of Two Unhappy Lovers*), and a revised version appeared in Milan in 1802.

The novel owes much to Jean-Jacques Rousseau's *Julie, ou La nouvelle Héloïse* (*Julie: or, the New Eloise*, 1761) and Johann Wolfgang von Goethe's *Die leiden des jungen Werthers* (*The Sorrows of Young Werther*, 1774–87), underpinned by elements of Foscolo's own experiences. The protagonist's suicide is caused by a double disappointment: his love for a young woman promised to another and the loss of his cherished ideals of fatherland, liberty, and justice. Just as Foscolo had left Venice so as not to take the oath of allegiance to Austria, so Ortis chooses suicide rather than compromise with an unacceptable political situation.

Foscolo achieved fame on a European scale with this novel, and in 1803 published two odes and twelve sonnets under the title *Poesie* (Poems). The autobiographical basis of these poems is frequently overlaid with mythological themes, so that the sonnet to his birthplace, "A Zacinto" ("To Zacynthos"), includes references to the birth of Venus and the wanderings of Ulysses. This neoclassical aspect is even more pronounced in the odes, both of which are centered on the deification of a woman, and prefigure *Le grazie*, in which the figures of living women are adored as abstractions, and female beauty is seen as consolation for the ills of human existence.

The four fundamental themes of Foscolo's poetry—death, exile, beauty, and immortality achieved through art—can be detected in his early works, but are seamlessly synthesized in "Dei sepolcri" (*The Tombs*, 1806), the poem on which Foscolo's reputation rests. The poem was inspired by French legislation that was to be extended to Italy, which governed standardization of headstones and inscriptions and prohibited entombment inside churches. While there are echoes from the graveyard poetry of Thomas Gray and Edward Young, Foscolo's poem is written in a quite different vein, not only as his stance is clearly nonreligious, but his central thesis, "a' generosi/giusta di glorie dispensiera è morte" ("a judicious bestower of glory to the bold is death") is precisely the opposite of Gray's line, "The paths of glory lead but to the grave." Having established at the outset that the only afterlife that exists is in the memory of others, in a discourse that illustrates the triumph of imagination over reason, Foscolo argues in favor of the illusion provided by the tomb, which can offer comfort to the individual and patriotic inspiration to the nation. In a series of Pindaric shifts, Foscolo moves from the personal and emotional function of the tomb, through an indictment of the proposed laws, an evocation of the communal burial pit where Parini was interred, to the inspiration provided by the funeral monuments of the famous in Santa Croce in Florence, via the battle of Marathon to Cassandra's prophecy. In the course of the poem, three poets are evoked: Vittorio Alfieri, Homer, and Parini, and the conclusion is that the most lasting monument is literature.

Ugo Foscolo. Reprinted courtesy of Bildarchiv.

The notion of literature as the repository of collective memory and inspiration to patriotic fervor was central to his inaugural lecture on taking up the "chair of eloquence" at Pavia in 1808, *Dell'origine e dell'uffizio della letteratura* (*On the Origin and Office of Literature*), expressed in terms that made his nationalistic tendencies all too explicit, and Napoleon himself advised his removal.

After his voluntary exile to London following the annexing of Lombardy and the Venetian territories to Austria, Foscolo turned his talents to literary criticism and contributed many essays on Italian language and literature to some of the leading journals in Britain. One of his most polemical essays was on the new dramatic school in Italy, an attack on Romantic theory in general and on Alessandro Manzoni's play *Il Conte di Carmagnola* (*The Count of Carmagnola*, 1820) in particular. There was a certain personal rivalry between the two writers, that was exacerbated by Foscolo's umbrage at Manzoni's representation of the doge and senate of Venice in the play.

Neoclassical in formation and Romantic by temperament, Foscolo broke new ground in literary criticism by his application of Giambattista Vico's ideas and is remembered in the Italian context in equal measure as poet, critic, and patriot.

LYNNE PRESS

Biography

Born on Zacynthus, Venetian republic (now Zakynthos, Greece), February 6, 1778, to an Italian father and Greek mother. Educated at Spalato (now Split, Croatia) and Padua; after father's death, moved with family to Venice, around 1792. Associated with literary groups in Venice until 1797. Joined French Army under Napoleon Bonaparte in Bologna, 1797. Moved to Milan; editor of *Il Monitore italiano*, 1798. Fought in the French Army during Austrian and Russian invasion of Italy, 1799; took part in siege of Genoa, 1800. Published the novel *Ultime lettere di Jacopo Ortis*, 1802. Stationed in northern France as Captain of infantry division, 1804–06. Appointed to chair of rhetoric at University of Padua, 1808; after abolition of post by Napoleon, moved to Milan, 1809, and to Florence, 1812. Returned to Milan, 1813. Fled in voluntary exile in Zurich after the Austrian invasion of Italy, 1815; moved to London, 1816. Taught literature and contributed to journals, including *Edinburgh Review* and *Quarterly Review*; lived in relative poverty. Died in London, September 10, 1827.

Selected Works

Edizione nazionale delle opere di Foscolo. 27 vols. Edited by Michele Barbi, 1933.
Opere di Ugo Foscolo. 7th ed. Edited by Mario Puppo, 1977.

Bibliography

Cambon, Glauco. *Ugo Foscolo, Poet of Exile*. Princeton, N.J.: Princeton University Press, 1980.
Carsaniga, Giovanni. "Foscolo." In *The Cambridge History of Italian Literature*. Edited by Peter Brand and Lino Pertile. Cambridge: Cambridge University Press, 1996.
Croce, Benedetto. *European Literature in the Nineteenth Century*. New York: Haskell House, 1967.
Fubini, Mario. *Ugo Foscolo*. Florence: Lanuova Italia, 1962.
Graf, Arturo. *Foscolo, Manzoni, Leopardi*. Turin: Loescher, 1955.
O'Neill, Tom. *Of Virgin Muses and of Love: A Study of Foscolo's "Dei Sepolcri."* Dublin: UCD Foundation for Italian Studies, 1981.
Vincent, E. R. *Ugo Foscolo: An Italian in Regency England*. Cambridge: Cambridge University Press, 1953.

FOUQUÉ, CAROLINE DE LA MOTTE 1774–1831

German writer

Caroline de la Motte Fouqué, née von Briest, doubtless ranks as one of the most prolific women writers of the Romantic period. Born into an old aristocratic Prussian family and married to the more famous author Friedrich de la Motte Fouqué, she belonged both to Romantic intellectual circles and to court society. Over a span of nearly thirty years she published widely in various genres—mainly novels, short stories, and fairy tales—but also didactic, cultural, and social essays (for example, on women's education in *Briefe über Zweck und Richtung weiblicher Bildung*, 1810; Greek mythology in *Briefe über die griechische Mythologie*, 1812; and the history of fashion in *Geschichte der Moden*, 1829). She also published travelogues (*Briefe über Berlin*, 1821, and *Reiseerinnerungen, 1823*). The *Reiseerinnerungen* were the product of a literary collaboration with her novelist husband, with whom she also edited literary almanacs and magazines (for example *Für müssige Stunden*, 1816–1821). Overall her work is strongly influenced by literary fashions and changing styles, and is full of allusions to all kinds of texts, such as epistolary, Gothic, and adventure novels, as well as to the work of individual contemporary authors, including Joseph von Eichendorff, Johann Wolfgang von Goethe, Novalis, Ludwig Tieck, and also her husband, which altogether makes it difficult to classify her oeuvre as sentimental, classicistic, Romantic, or of the early realistic genre.

Thematically, Fouqué's fiction often addresses historical topics. Moreover, she shows an exceptional interest in topics in politics and the latest developments in science and psychology, including the French Revolution (for example, *Die Magie der Natur. Eine Revolutionsgeschichte* [*The Magic of Nature: A Story of the Revolution*, 1812]), the Wars of Liberation (for example *Der Spanier und der Freiwillige in Paris. Eine Geschichte aus dem heiligen Kriege*, 1814; *Edmunds Wege und Irrwege* [*Edmund's Ways and Byways*, 1815]; *Das Heldenmädchen aus der Vendée* [*The Heroic Maiden of the Vendée*, 1816]; and *Die beiden Freunde* [*The Two Friends*, 1824]), the Greek struggle for Independence (*Der letzte der Paläologen*, 1823–24), as well as magnetism and mesmerism (in *Magie der Natur*). These themes are always skillfully interwoven with the dominant themes of her writing: the conflict between individual and society, exemplified in the quest for love, and subsequently the tensions deriving from the inequality of male and female gender roles. Already in her early autobiographical novels—particularly in *Die Frau des Fal-*

kensteins (1810), the novel that made her famous, although it was anonymously published—and also in *Feodora* (1814), Fouqué examined the possibilities of women's emancipation.

The scope of women's roles within society remained for the next two decades the point of reference of most of her writings. As part of this general examination of gender roles, she deals with the topic of the woman soldier in disguise in *The Heroic Maiden of the Vendée* as well as with the then new topic of problems within marriage; fiction is used as a platform for the representation of gender conflict in 1815's *Frauenliebe* (*A Woman's Love*) and the 1829 epistolary novel *Resignation*. Both novels are modeled on Goethe's *Wahlverwandtschaften* (*Elective Affinities*, 1809), where this topic was first treated.

The quality of her fiction (in more than sixty stories and twenty novels) varies quite significantly, possibly due to the financial and therefore time pressures under which she produced them. On the whole, her fictional narrative lacks the complexity and ambiguity, and therefore tension and novelty, of some of her contemporaries' writings. However, Fouqué often shows an intricate and unconventional view on gender issues; while her ultimate conclusion that a woman's role in society is based in motherhood and domesticity appear conventional, it follows her open-minded and fair exploration of quite unconventional possibilities.

In general, the plots of Fouqué's novels provide the framework for dealing with pressing problems concerning gender conflicts as well as political questions, but her novels never reach a conclusion that questions then-acceptable ideas of women's and men's roles in society; nor, in terms of political attitude, do they end on a note other than a moderate conservative one, confirming the attitudes and ideas of her own class, the aristocratic traditionalists. This attitude was recognized and criticized by fellow authors of her day, such as the literary critic and friend of the Fouqués, Karl August Varnhagen von Ense, who in his biographical portrait of Caroline de la Motte Fouqué (published posthumously in 1873) deplores the fact that she had subordinated her original and free-spirited style of writing to her husband's conventional work, and thereby gradually lost the courage and the ability to uphold and fight for her own original and strong views.

The issues that lead current critical discussion of Fouqué's work concern references to other texts and styles of writing and her dual treatment of gender and political issues. Particular interest is paid to some of her essays, which reveal her as a witty and astute writer, especially the 1829 (*Geschichte der Moden*) *History of Fashion*. Here she analyzes recent political history under the guise of a narrative on fashion. On a superficial level, this study is remarkable since it is one of the earliest analytical texts on fashion. But the *History of Fashion* shows the narrative strategy of Fouqué's writing at its best, using the discourse on fashion to evaluate political events censored from public debate.

As one of the most versatile women writers of popular literature, Caroline de la Motte Fouqué deserves to continue to enjoy her recent rediscovery and reconsideration.

URSULA HUDSON-WIEDENMANN

Biography

Born in Berlin, October 7, 1774. Married, in 1791, a Prussian military man; they had three children. After her first husband's suicide, she married Friedrich de la Motte Fouqué in 1803; Salon in Berlin, first publication 1806; wrote and published until 1829; died in Rathenow, her family home, on July 21, 1831.

Selected Works

Ausgewählte Werke. 4 vols. Edited by Petra Kabus. Hildesheim: Olms, 1999.

Bibliography

Arnold de Simine, Silke. "'Verborgener Umgang mit dem Geheimnisvollen.' Caroline de la Motte Fouqué und die Schauerromantik." In *Jahrbuch der Fouqué-Gesellschaft*. Berlin: Weidler, 1999.
Baumgartner, Karin. "Through the Eyes of Fashion: Political Aspects of Fashion in Caroline de la Motte Fouqué's, "Geschichte der Moden," vom Jahre 1785–1829: als Beytrag zur Geschichte der Zeit," *Germanic Review* 72 (1997): 215–30.
Böck, Dorothea. "Caroline de la Motte Fouqué. Sie hätte 'eine deutsche Stael werden können. . . .'" In *"Wen kümmert's, wer spricht." Zur Literatur- und Kulturgeschichte von Frauen aus Ost und West*. Edited by Inge Stephan, Sigrid Weigel, and Kerstin Wilhelm. Köln: Böhlau, 1991.
Kabus, Petra. "Caroline de la Motte Fouqué: 'Resignation.' Ein Roman Zwischen den 'Wahlverwandtschaften' und 'Effi Briest.'" In *Jahrbuch der Fouqué-Gesellschaft*. Berlin: Weidler, 2000.
Kontje, Todd. "Caroline de la Motte Fouqué: Romantic Nationalism Confronts Modernity." In *Women, the Novel, and the German Nation 1771–1871: Domestic Fiction in the Fatherland*. Cambridge: Cambridge University Press, 1998.
Varnhagen von Ense, Karl August. "Karoline von Fouqué." In *Karl August Varnhagen von Ense, Biographien, Ausätze, Skizzen, Fragmente*. Edited by Konrad Feilchenfeldt and Ursula Wiedenmann. Frankfurt: Deutscher Klassiker Verlag, 1990.
Wägenbaur, Birgit. "Romantik für Jedermann. Caroline de la Motte Fouqués Erzählungen." In *Jahrbuch der Fouqué-Gesellschaft*. Berlin: Weidler, 1999.
Wilde, Jean T. *The Romantic Realist: Caroline de la Motte Fouqué*. New York: Bookman Associates, 1955.

FOUQUÉ, FRIEDRICH HEINRICH KARL, BARON DE LA MOTTE 1777–1843

German writer

Friedrich Heinrich Karl, Baron de la Motte Fouqué, was descended from an aristocratic family of Huguenot immigrants. As was customary for a man of his standing, the young Friedrich enjoyed a rounded education that included the study of literature and foreign languages. Despite the humanist tendencies of his youth, he remained drawn to the world of the military throughout his life. His remarkably constant view of the world reflects, in particular, his aristocratic heritage, his close contacts with the army, and his interest in contemporary notions of the Middle Ages as a golden age now long past. Although Fouqué was a prolific author, it is hard to discern a clear pattern of development in either an aesthetic or philosophical sense in his oeuvre. Accordingly, his themes, characters, and settings often strike the reader as interchangeable elements in a *Weltanschauung* (worldview) that remains largely fixed and unchanging.

His novels and short stories present an idealized picture of the Middle Ages together with the central figure of the knight errant, his retinue, and a variety of figures drawn from the world of legend and fairy tale. The encounters between such fantastical figures and the world of ordinary human beings lie at the center of almost all of Fouqué's fiction. But far from leaving us with a harmonious picture of the northern medieval world, Fouqué highlights the tensions and difficulties that ensue from such encounters, thereby underlining the tragic incommensurability of the material world of reality and the metaphysical world of the ideal. It is only a matter of time before his characters are beset by catastrophe and forced to recognize that the world of metaphysical transcendence offers no consolations and may indeed even bring about their destruction. Fouqué's fiction is dominated by the typically Romantic elements of madness, horror, and the demonic and depicts a world in which the individual lacks any sense of orientation or belonging. In a few isolated instances, Fouqué's Romantic fiction does appear to uphold the possibility of transcending the shortcomings of the temporal world, but where this is the case, it borders on the sentimental.

In his day, Fouqué was one of the best known and most popular German Romantic writers and he had a profound influence on his contemporaries. He had personal contact with almost all the leading writers and artists of his generation—including Achim von Arnim, Adalbert von Chamisso, Joseph von Eichendorff, Caspar David Friedrich, Johann Wolfgang von Goethe, Julius Eduard Hitzig, E. T. A. Hoffmann, Wilhelm von Humboldt, Heinrich von Kleist, Adam Müller, Wilhelm Neumann, Philipp Otto Runge, Johann Christoph Friedrich Schiller, August Wilhelm and Friedrich von Schlegel, and Ludwig Tieck—and a number of the above worked with him on joint literary ventures. His collaboration with Hoffmann was to prove particularly fruitful, the latter composing the musical score for an opera based on Fouqué's novella of 1811–14, *Undine*, a work that is often regarded as the first true example of a Romantic opera. Fouqué supplied the libretto, and the set was designed by the well-known architect Friedrich Schinkel. *Undine* is the best known of Fouqué's works and has been translated into many different languages. It has also served as the basis for some thirty operas and its fairytale theme has been adapted in many works of world literature (including Hans Christian Andersen's *The Little Mermaid*, Jean Giraudoux's *Ondine*, and Oscar Wilde's *The Fisherman and His Soul*). The source of Fouqué's inspiration was Paracelsus's *Liber de Nymphis*, a work containing descriptions of a variety of spirits of nature, who, though equipped with all the attributes of a human personality, lack a soul. Only the water sprites—among them, Undine—have the ability to assume human form. Should a water sprite succeed in marrying a human being, he or she will come into possession of a soul; however, should the human partner make disparaging remarks about his or her spouse while in close proximity to water, the latter's soul will be forfeited.

In the course of the novella, Fouqué tells of the beautiful Undine's fateful love for the young knight Huldbrand von

Ringstetten. When bad weather forces the knight to seek refuge in a fisherman's cottage, he encounters the orphan Undine and falls in love with her. (The figure of Undine is modeled on the real life persona of Elisabeth von Breitenbach, with whom Fouqué had become acquainted in 1795 in Minden). Undine lives in close contact with the elemental forces of nature that appear in the form of spirits and goblins, and, above all, in the guise of the raging water spirit Kühleborn. Through her marriage to Huldbrand, Undine, the capricious and headstrong creature of nature, gains a soul and is transformed into a loving—yet suffering—wife. For the naive innocence of her earlier existence is replaced by feelings of guilt and a troubled conscience. Accordingly, we are presented with the typically Romantic dichotomy of spirit (*Geist*) and nature. Kühleborn—who embodies a concept of nature that is not willing to accept human suffering as the inevitable price for being raised to a higher plane of existence—repeatedly tries to come between the lovers. Undine's "human" existence, however, is indeed shaped by suffering, not least when Huldbrand rejects her in favor of her rival, Bertalda. On a boating trip on the Danube he insults Undine and she disappears beneath the waves. Huldbrand is punished in accordance with the laws of the elemental spirits, for when he is at the point of marrying Bertalda, Undine reappears and suffocates her faithless beloved with a final kiss.

Although the essentially tragic nature of the plot lends the story a certain emotional intensity, Fouqué often resorts to the kind of sentimental cliché that, in a more concentrated form, was to detract from his later works. Accordingly, even in *Undine*, he fails to offer the reader the same kind of philosophical depth that we encounter in the fairy-tales by other German Romantic writers such as Hoffman, Novalis, and Tieck.

BIRGIT ROEDER

Biography

Born in Brandenburg an der Havel, February 12, 1777. Joined the Prussian army and takes part in the summer campaigns of the revolutionary wars, 1794. Married Marianne von Schubaert, 1798; the marriage dissolved three years later. Married Caroline von Rochow, 1803, and their residence Gut Nennhausen was established as a meeting place for literary circles; first literary experiments published in Friedrich Schlegel's journal *Europa*. Publication of the dramatic trilogy *Der Held des Nordens*, 1810. Premiere of the opera *Undine* in the Königliches Schauspielhaus in Berlin, 1816. Following the death of Caroline, married Albertine Tode, 1833. Died January 23, 1843, in Berlin.

Selected Works

Werke. Edited by Walther Ziesemer, 1908.
Undine und andere Erzählungen. Edited by Ralph-Rainer Wuthenow, 1978.

Bibliography

Diegmann-Hornig, Katja. *"Sich in die Poesie zu flüchten, wie unantastbare Eilande der Seeligen": Analysen zu ausgewählten Romanen von Friedrich Baron de la Motte Fouqué*. Hildesheim: Olms, 1999.
Dischner, Gisela. "Friedrich de la Motte Fouqué: *'Undine*." In *Romane und Erzählungen der deutschen Romantik*. Edited by P. M. Lützeler, Stuttgart: Reclam, 1981.

"Fouqué und Eichendorff," In *Deutsche National-Litteratur. Historisch-kritische Ausgabe.* Edited by Joseph Kürschner, 1893.

Hofacker, Erich P., Jr. "Friedrich de la Motte Fouqué." In *German Writers in the Age of Goethe, 1789–1832.* Edited by James Hardin and Christoph E. Schweitzer. Detroit: Gale Research, 1989.

Max, Frank R. "Friedrich de la Motte Fouqué." In *Deutsche Dichter. Leben und Werk deutschsprachiger Autoren.* Edited by Gunter E. Grimm and Frank Rainer Max. Stuttgart: Reclam, 1989.

Seibicke, Elisabeth C. *Friedrich Baron de la Motte Fouqué. Krise und Verfall der Spätromantik im Spiegel historisierender Ritterromane.* Munich: Tuduv, 1985.

Stephan, Inge. "Weiblichkeit, Wasser und Tod. Undinen, Melusinen und Wasserfrauen bei Eichendorff und Fouqué." In *Weiblichkeit und Tod in der Literatur.* Edited by Renate Berger and Inge Stephan. Köln: Böhlau, 1987.

Stockinger, Claudia. *Das dramatische Werk Friedrich de la Motte Fouqués. Ein Beitrag zur Geschichte des romantischen Dramas.* Tübingen: Niemeyer, 2000.

FOURIER, CHARLES 1771–1837

French social theorist

Charles Fourier could be defined as a quintessential Romantic; he believed that humans living in equilibrium with nature would be totally content. He was convinced that the social crisis of the early nineteenth century was all in the mind. Human misery existed, not because of economic inequalities, but because the human psyche was inhibited by social norms. When these constraints were removed people would live in harmony, without the need for police, courts of law, or repressive moral codes. Between 1808 and 1827, Fourier wrote three books in which he expounded his theory of how society could advance from social conflict to blissful peace. The first was *Théorie des Quatre Movements* (*The Theory of the Four Movements*, 1808). Like many of his contemporaries, he started from the premise that there were laws governing social relationships parallel to those in the physical world described by Sir Isaac Newton and others. Once understood and implemented, all social ills would melt away. He blamed the social problems of his day on capitalism and marriage—institutions, he argued, that were contrary to nature. No reform of society would work until the worst evil, the lowly status of women, was addressed.

Fourier's solution was to create new, ideal communities, a concept familiar with his contemporaries. His were *phalanges*: experimental, self-governing, share-holding, profit-sharing communal democracies. Each would consist of 1,620 people, representing a perfect balance of combinations of the 300 passions that existed in varying proportions in all humans. The property and buildings of the phalange might be provided by an individual or group. The original owners or investors would maintain their property rights and receive a dividend from the profits each year. The rest of the profits would be shared in a fixed ratio between all the members, with a percentage reserved for mutual aid needs and reinvestment. Fourier always emphasized the economic viability of his proposal. Economies of scale would flow from communal production. The members would hold daily meetings to set agricultural and industrial targets and organize communal work teams. Work would be attractive and enjoyable. All members would be entirely content because they would decide what to do and work would be subdivided so that everyone changed their activity after one hour. Economic and social inequalities would remain, but Fourier argued that this was irrelevant if everyone was achieving their potential.

Not only was all economic activity to be performed communally; so was everything else apart from sleep, which was a solitary function to take place between 10:30 P.M. and 3:30 A.M. The phalange would consist of specially designed communal build-ings for everything from eating to attending the opera. Marriage would disappear. Sexual relations would be fluid and happy; all jealousy, dishonesty, and tensions would evaporate. Children would be reared in communal nurseries by those psychologically best suited to nurture the young. Cooking competitions would be a high point in the social calendar. Meals, prepared and eaten communally, would be gastronomic delights five times daily. Women would then have the opportunity to contribute to the work of the phalange according to their abilities and inclinations.

Fourier always claimed that his ideas were unique and that his thought owed nothing to earlier writers, but this is inaccurate. He knew of Robert Owen's New Lanark experiment and believed that he had much to teach Owen. They met only briefly in 1837, just before Fourier's death. Etienne Cabet also invented a utopian community, Icarie, very different from that of Fourier. Fourier was a lone figure; almost no one read his first book, which he published anonymously and distributed to leading politicians. The deliberate obscurity of his language, the complexities of his semimathematical symbols and arguments, even the idiosyncrasies of irrational pagination and invented vocabulary puzzled his handful of readers. His books read like the minutes of a secret society. He claimed that planets have aromas for long-distance copulation. He believed that in the phalange there would be good-natured lions that would not eat people. Fourier argued that the earth was sick, that its climate was deteriorating, the ice-caps melting, but there was a rescue column of 102 planets moving toward the earth. All this romantic hyperbole may have been just fun for Fourier, but his handful of readers were shocked by his proclamation of sexual freedom and the end of marriage.

In 1822 he published a second major work, *Traité de l'association domestique-agricole* (*Treatise on Domestic Agricultural Association*) revisiting much of the same ground. In 1829 came *Le Nouveau monde industriel et sociétaire* (*The New Industrial World*) and a parallel volume expounding his views on love in such a liberated tone that it remained unpublished until 1999. Each of his books elaborated his original notions with an increasingly familiar absence of continuity or structure. They resemble a stream-of-consciousness approach and seek to retain the reader by a variety of themes, resorting to an increasing range of typefaces to hold the eye.

Fourier might have died known to only a few readers had his ideas not come to the attention of Henri de Saint-Simon, eventually making a considerable impression on his followers, the Saint-Simonians. They adopted his ideas on the liberation of workers and women, but in November 1831 the majority disagreed so violently with their self-imposed leader Prosper Enfantin's call for trial marriage that they broke away to align themselves with Fourier and form a new school of thought. The dominant figure was Victor Considérant, who learned of Fourier's theories when lodging as a high-school student with Fourier's devoted disciple, Clarisse Vigoureux, whose daughter Considérant later married. Fourier's theories were radically toned down by his new followers. Influential women members ensured that marriage and a thoroughly Christian god became cornerstones of a moral, not a "natural," social order. Fourier had always claimed that his essential Romantic dream world was an economically viable program. The Fourierists tried to make it work. An experimental phalange was opened at Condé-sur-Vesgre, near Paris, in 1832, but it collapsed within a year. Subsequently, Fourierists began to focus on state-run public-works programs. They campaigned for the recognition of the obligation of the state to organize work for the jobless and accept the idea that everyone had a right to be found work. Fourierist socialist theory flowed from the pen of Considérant and others in books, pamphlets, a periodical (which began life as Le Phalanstère [1832–49], financed by Vigoureux and edited by Considérant), and the newspaper La Démocratie Pacifique (1843–51). Fourierist ideas diverged so far from those of Fourier that disciples and master were frequently at odds. In the 1840s Fourierists briefly gained worldwide publicity, including in Australia and America. After the failure of socialist reforms in the Second Republic, Considérant and Vigoureux, and indeed Cabet (though separately), participated unsuccessfully in experimental communes. Fourier is still remembered as a quirky idealist, and the Fourierists are hardly remembered at all.

PAMELA PILBEAM

Biography

Born Françoise-Marie-Charles Fourier in Besançon, April 7, 1772. Son of a prosperous cloth merchant, who died while Charles was a child. Initially planned a career as a military engineer but abandoned it for a commercial apprenticeship. Served as an army conscript in the Rhine and Moselle Rivers region. Served commercial apprenticeship as a clerk in Rouen, early 1800s; wrote Théorie des quatre mouvements et des destinées générales, 1808. Worked as a municipal clerk in Lyon, c. 1815–16, and as a cashier in a commercial enterprise in Paris. Died in Paris, October 10, 1837.

Selected Works

Oeuvres complètes de Charles Fourier. 12 vols., facsimile reprints of early editions, 1966–68.
Harmonian Man: Selected Writings of Charles Fourier. Edited by Mark Poster. New York, 1971.
The Theory of the Four Movements. Edited by Gareth Stedman Jones and Ian Patterson. Cambridge University Press, 1996.

Bibliography

Beecher, Jonathan Fourier. The Visionary and His World. Berkely and Los Angeles: University of California Press, 1986.
Beecher, Jonathan and R. Bienvenu. The Utopian Vision of Charles Fourier. Boston, Mass.: Beacon Press, 1971.
Goldstein, L. F. "Early Feminist Themes in French Utopian Socialism: The Saint-Simonians and Fourier," Journal of the History of Ideas 43 (1982): 91–108.
Pilbeam, Pamela. French Socialists before Marx: Workers, Women and the Social Question in France. Teddington, England: Acumen, 2000.

FRAGMENT

The term fragment is used in various archeological, historical, scientific, aesthetic, and philosophical contexts to refer to diverse artifacts, functions, and classificatory categories. In general it connotes something "broken off" (from Latin frangere, to break)—a shard, a part of a whole, something incomplete or unfinished, a remainder. In music, for example, it can describe a motif or "melodic fragment"; in art, a sketch or vignette; in theology, a relic; in archeology or history, a ruin; in literary studies, a range of genres—epitaphs, epigraphs, graffiti, legends, inscriptions, sayings, proverbs, parables, philosophemes, lexias, fables, maxims, aphorisms, pensées (thoughts), epistles, marginalia, interpolations, notes, annotations, and citations.

While some of these brief texts have clearly been produced by accident or historical contingency, others have been created intentionally as fragments, occasional or otherwise. There is a long international tradition of collections of "intentional fragments," many well known from ancient times: the Analects of Confucius, Aesop's Fables, and the fragments of Demophilus and Heraclitus (sixth century B.C.E.), the Old Testament Book of Proverbs and the Aphorisms of Hippocrates (fourth century B.C.E.), the Meditations of Marcus Aurelius (second century C.E.), the writings of the Talmud (fifth century C.E.), and the Koran (seventh century C.E.). Their purpose varies from the mnemonic (in the oral tradition) and pedagogical, to the statement of axioms, principles, and facts of common belief (doxa), to the encapsulation of moral, legal, or social precepts. This tradition continued in the Middle Ages and the Renaissance, with such works as the Fables of Marie de France (1167–89) and François Villon's Ballade des proverbes (Ballade of proverbs, 1460) in France; Francesco Guicciardini's political writings (1512–30) in Italy; and Miguel de Cervantes Saavedra's Don Quixote (1615) in Spain.

In the seventeenth century, the fragment came into its own in France as a literary form, most notably in François, duc de La Rochefoucauld's Reflexions ou sentences et maximes morales (Reflections, or, moral precepts and maxims, 1665) and Blaise Pascal's Pensées (Thoughts, 1670). Three main genres may be identified: the proverb, as in English, usually states a platitude of received belief or opinion; the classical French maxim tends to take the form of a brief, rhythmic, lapidary statement, in which the author ironically critiques an existing state of affairs; and the pensée is similar to the maxim in form, but in general expresses the subjective and individual worldview of the author, based on his or her personal experience.

The classical moralizing fragment evolved primarily in France and Germany during the course of the Romantic Era; in Britain the genre was known from translations of Greek and Roman philosophers, but not taken up, because the fragment form tended to be associated with ambiguity and linguistic trickery. In France, the genre was both preserved and developed by various authors—the Marquis de Vauvenargues (*Reflexions et maxims*, 1746), Sebastien-Roch-Nicholas Chamfort (*Pensées, Maximes et Anecdotes*, 1794), Georg Christoph Lichtenberg (*Aphorismen*, 1799), Jean de La Bruyère (*les Caractères*, 1823), and Joseph Joubert (*Pensées*, 1842)—both through formal and stylistic changes, including complex syntactical and rhetorical effects and puns, and through a thematic shift in emphasis from a coherent and systematic worldview to an ethos based on an atomistic and particular universe. This shift, contemporaneous with the social transformations from transcendental monarchy to participative democracy effected by the French and American Revolutions, was coeval with the development of an alternative epistemology and metaphysics to that of the Encyclopaedists—an alternative grounded in subjectivity, and in the intuitions, feelings and emotions of the individual.

The theorization of such a fragmentary epistemology and metaphysics was developed in Germany, initially in texts such as Johann Wolfgang von Goethe's epistolary novel *Die Leiden des jungen Werther* (*The Sufferings of Young Werther*, 1774) or the fragmentary *Italienische Reise* (*Italian Travels*, 1786–88), and *Maximen und Reflexionen* (*Maxims and Reflections*, 1842). Goethe's understanding of the aphoristic fragment as an appropriate form in which to embody intuitions of nonsystematic knowledge was taken up by the German Romantics based at Jena—in particular, Friedrich von Schlegel, who with his brother August Wilhelm von Schlegel, Novalis, and Friedrich Schleiermacher, coauthored the collection *Fragmente* (*Fragments*, 1798) in the journal *Athenaeum*. However, for Schlegel, author of his own fragmentary novel *Lucinde* (1799), for Novalis, and for the others of the Jena circle, the fragment did not simply serve as an ethical maxim in the Kantian sense, but—on account of its brevity, its potential to be both subjective and objective, and its simultaneous indication and abdication of the totality or whole of which it formed a synecdochic part, "limb," or seminal "pollen grain"—becomes the ideal form in which the genius of language could point to its own limits of signification and transcend them.

In this theorization, the fragment is analogous to what remains after the "breaking of the vessels" in the Eabala of the Jewish mystics; or following the fall of the Tower of Babel in the Old Testament, by which language, which partakes of both the human and the divine, is fragmented into languages requiring translation; or to what is produced in the dissemination of the Tetragrammaton or name of God through material creation: it assumes a theologic-historical aspect within this framework of irrationalism as a site of both memory (as ruin, or trace, of a lost, prelapsarian state)—and anticipation (as a sketch, project, or blueprint for redemption). The theologic-historical situation of the fragment as such is contingent upon the necessary (and yet unrealizable) relation between its two modes of existence—as an autonomous and self-contained entity, a whole in itself; and as a part of a greater unity or totality to which it always points—a relation that is the foundation of what has come to be called "romantic irony."

The German Romantic theorization of the fragment has had broad repercussions in literature, philosophy and theory—in the works of Roland Barthes, Georges Batailles, Walter Benjamin, Maurice Blanchot, Michel Butor, Jacques Derrida, Philippe Lacoue-Labarthe, Lautréamont, Jean-Luc Nancy, Friedrich Nietzsche, and Paul Valéry, among numerous others. The significance of the fragment—which has acquired new articulations through collage, montage, pastiche, and other modes of juxtaposition in theories of "modernism" and "postmodernism"—arises from the fact that it foregrounds the problem of the marginal, relational space *between* fragments, between part and whole, particular and universal, letter and spirit, the material and the transcendental. This differential space—which must be negotiated through the active, totalizing activity of the reader or observer—marks the failure of language to encompass the transcendental in the very moment that it points to its possibility: it is the space of the sublime, of the limits of systematicity, of both loss and desire. It is on this account that, in the theoretical wake of the "death of God" and the "death of the author," the tribulations of the disarticulated and disseminated speaking and thinking subject have today found expression in the fragment as a form stuttering and stammering between language and aphasia, rationalism and madness; a form embodying the social, cultural, political, linguistic crises of our own times.

JOHANN PILLAI

Bibliography

Aitken, Hugh. *The Piece as a Whole: Studies in Holistic Musical Analysis*. Westport, Conn.: Praeger, 1997.

Barthes, Roland. *A Lover's Discourse: Fragments*. Translated by Richard Howard. New York: Hill and Wang/Farrar, Straus and Giroux, 1984.

Blanchot, Maurice. *The Writing of the Disaster*. Translated by Ann Smock. Lincoln: University of Nebraska Press, 1995.

Derrida, Jacques. "Aphorism Countertime." In *Jacques Derrida: Acts of Literature*. Edited by Derek Attridge. New York: Routledge, 1991.

Gasché, Rodolphe. "Foreword: Ideality in Fragmentation." In Friedrich Schlegel, *Philosophical Fragments*. Translated by Peter Firchow. Minneapolis: University of Minnesota Press, 1991.

———. *Of Minimal Things: Studies on the Notion of Relation*, Stanford, Calif.: Stanford University Press, 1999.

Harries, Elizabeth Wanning. *The Unfinished Manner: Essays on the Fragment in the Later Eighteenth Century*. Charlottesville: University Press of Virginia, 1994.

Harter, Deborah A. *Bodies in Pieces: Fantastic Narrative and the Poetics of the Fragment*. Stanford, Calif.: Stanford University Press, 1996.

Lacoue-Labarthe, Philippe, and Jean-Luc Nancy. *The Literary Absolute: The Theory of Literature in German Romanticism*. Translated by Philip Barnard and Cheryl Lester. Albany: State University of New York Press, 1988.

Levinson, Marjorie. *The Romantic Fragment Poem: A Critique of a Form*. Chapel Hill: University of North Carolina Press, 1986.

Lyotard, Jean-François. *The Differend. Phrases in Dispute*. Translated by Georges Van Den Abbecle. Minneapolis: University of Minnesota Press, 1988.

McFarland, Thomas. *Romanticism and the Forms of Ruin: Wordsworth, Coleridge, and Modalities of Fragmentation*. Princeton, N.J.: Princeton University Press, 1981.

Miller, Patricia Cox. "1997 NAPS Presidential Address. 'Differential Networks': Relics and Other Fragments in Late Antiquity," *Journal of Early Christian Studies* 6, no. 1 (1988): 113–38.

FRANCE, 1760 TO THE REVOLUTION

From the perspective of the post-Revolutionary order, the period of 1760–89 is usually portrayed in a negative light; the term *ancien régime* conveys an image of decay, decadence, and decline. Yet this period was also characterized by economic expansion, reforms, and important changes in a host of other areas.

By 1748, France had not only given up the quest for world domination, but also surrendered any title to hegemonic power in Europe. Defeat in the Austrian War of Succession bred a sense of decline that was, by 1763, reinforced yet further. Many believed that France had to adopt the ideas and institutions of their enemy, Britain, if they were to keep their present status or take revenge upon that very nation.

The root cause of the problem for France was that it was economically backward in contrast to Britain. The British had inaugurated an agricultural revolution and from 1760 were beginning to experience an industrial one as well. France's main problem was that its peasantry and its agricultural sector were too large and unproductive. Out of a population of twenty-six million in 1760, some twenty-two million were peasants, and between 1770 and 1790 that number increased by another two million. The majority of these peasants were landless or had plots so small that they could not feed their families or provide a taxable surplus. Taxation was in fact the main difficulty. To uphold its position and fight a series of costly wars against Britain, France needed large tax revenues, but its poverty-stricken peasantry were unable to provide the means.

Many historians have blamed the cost of the French court and the supposedly luxury-loving aristocracy. That group, some 1 to 2 percent of the population, or 400,000 people in total, were in fact not as rich as their British counterparts, mainly because their tenant farmers were poorer. When the state tried to tax them further, it did not increase total revenue considerably, but did antagonize and alienate the royalist order. By 1780 the nobility was as ready to challenge the regime as the middle and lower classes.

What was to be done? This question was being asked more frequently and with ever greater urgency during the decades after the Treaty of Paris in 1763. Many came to believe that the root cause of France's ills was the absolutist monarchy. Once, during the previous century, absolutism had been very effective at mobilizing resources for Louis XIV's wars of expansion and establishing France as the predominant power in western Europe. Now it was seen as an obstacle to much-needed reform and economic liberalization, which would have to be implemented if French power was not to be eroded further.

François de Quesnay, founder of the French school of economists known as the physiocrats, believed that agriculture (not trade) was the foundation of a nation's wealth and economic power. Only the removal of internal trade barriers and the building of roads and canals would stimulate agricultural expansion and modernization. The physiocrats concentrated their call for reforms in the field of economics, while the philosophers (who took a more tolerant and open-minded Enlightenment approach) believed other fields had to be reformed as well. The same levels of toleration, freedom, property rights, and liberalism that prevailed in Britain and the Netherlands had to be intro-duced in order to modernize and stimulate France's moribund economy.

These ideas and the propagation for the introduction of rationalism, humanism, secularization, and scientific thought were presented in seventeen volumes of the *Encyclopédie* (a literary and philosophical enterprise contributed to by various *philosophers*) between 1751 and 1765. The editors and publishers of these volumes, and Jean le Rond d'Alembert and Denis Diderot, questioned every aspect of the established order and its hallowed institutions. The Roman Catholic Church in France was especially castigated as arch reactionary, backward, and a bastion of superstitious practices that prevented the country from being removed from the Middle Ages. Jean-Jacques Rousseau was especially radical and scathing in his anti-religious fulminations.

Neither the philosophers nor the physiocrats created a political movement or any practical suggestions for reforms. But they had won the battles for the hearts and minds of the nobility and the intellectual salons, as shown when Voltaire, another of the radical philosophers, made a triumphal entry into Paris in 1778, having returned from exile. It was, therefore, up to the French ministers to reform and overhaul France's creaking finances. One minister of finance of some brilliance, Anne-Robert-Jacques Turgot, had close links with both reformist groups and had come to the same conclusion. During his years as *intendant* of Limoges (1761–74), he noted that the French peasantry paid over 50 percent of their production in taxes to the state. The tax burden had to be reduced, redistributed, and the entire machinery of state be overhauled. He opposed France's entry into the American War of Liberation as being too costly.

But here Turgot was opposed by Duc de Choiseul and his successor as foreign minister, Charles-Gravier de Vergennes, who believed that the first possible opportunity for revenge against Britain had to be grasped. France was by virtue of its efforts and military successes the real victor of the American war but it was the Americans who reaped the fruits of victory and royalist France that reaped the revolutionary whirlwind. The French performance in that war, which for once led to victory, merits praise and the recognition it deserves. The French navy had been expanded and improved beyond recognition since 1763 and gave a sterling performance against Britain's Royal Navy. It was the ancien régime's finest hour.

It was also the beginning of the end for royalist France. Turgot's warning went unheeded. A rich Swiss banker, Jacques Necker, who had been minister of finance during the war (1776–81), had financed the war through borrowing. But the state had not been solvent since 1741, and had even resorted to peacetime bankruptcies since 1763. Necker may have bought himself some political popularity but at the expense of France's mushrooming national debt. By 1786, 74 percent of the state's revenue was swallowed by the expenses of the armed forces and the servicing of the national debt. In August 1788, the minister of finance declared the state bankrupt, and Necker was summoned. But not even he could solve France's enormous financial and political crisis. France was heading toward revolution due to its thirst for revenge and war against Britain, coupled with its leaders' chronic inability to solve the country's perennial financial problems.

CHRISTER JÖRGENSEN

See also **France, 1815–1852; France: Revolution and Empire; French Revolution: Its Impact and Importance; French Romanticism: Its Literary Legacy**.

Bibliography

Acomb, Frances. *Anglophobia in France, 1763–1789: An Essay in the History of Constitutionalism and Nationalism*. Durham, N.C.: Duke University Press, 1950.

Bailey, Stone. *The Parlement of Paris, 1774–1789*. Chapel Hill: University of North Carolina Press, 1981.

Bosher, J. F. *French Finances, 1770–1795: From Business to Bureaucracy*. Cambridge: Cambridge University Press, 1970.

————. *The Single Duty Project: A Study of the Movement for a French Customs Union in the Eighteenth Century*. London: Athlone Press, 1964.

Dakin, Douglas. *Turgot and the Ancien Régime in France*. London: Methuen, 1939.

Fay, Bernard. *Louis XVI or the End of the World*. Translated by Patrick O'Brian. London: W. H. Allen, 1968.

Hardman, John. *French Politics, 1774–1789: From the Accession of Louis XVI to the Fall of the Bastille*. London: Longman, 1995.

————. *Louis XVI*. New Haven, Conn.: Yale University Press, 1993.

Harris, Robert D. *Necker and the Revolution of 1789*. University Press of America, 1986.

Orville, Murphy T. *Charles Gravier, Comte de Vergennes: French Diplomacy in the Age of Revolution, 1719–1787*. Albany: State University of New York Press, 1982.

Prince, Munro. *Preserving the Monarchy: The Comte de Vergennes, 1774–1787*. Cambridge: Cambridge University Press, 1995.

Van Kley, Dale K. *The Damiens Affair and the Unraveling of the Ancien Régime, 1750–1770*. Princeton, N.J.: Princeton University Press, 1984.

FRANCE, 1815–1852

The French Revolution ended absolute monarchy and noble privilege, but not noble power. Until the mid-nineteenth century, French politics would be dominated by great landed magnates, whether noble or wealthy bourgeois, known as the *grands notables*. The vote was limited to the wealthiest 1 percent of males. However, the years of the Restoration mark an important stage in the consolidation of constitutional government, particularly in opposition to the autocratic pretensions of Charles X after 1824. Brilliant young bourgeois such as Eugène Delacroix, Théodore Géricault, Victor Hugo, Prosper Mérimée, and Stendhal were among those who felt their creativity suffocated by social and political reaction. Many felt a deep nostalgia for the Napoleonic era.

Political opposition coincided with a protracted economic slump. After a decisive liberal electoral victory in July 1830, Charles X introduced severe controls on the press and slashed the electorate. Groups of journalists, printers, and liberal deputies called for resistance. On July 27 barricades were erected in the streets of Paris; in the ensuing three days of fighting (*les Trois Glorieuses*), two thousand insurgents and soldiers were killed. The liberal Louis-Philippe d'Orléans accepted the crown, and the former king was forced to flee the country.

The Revolution of 1830 was also a national revolution. Across the country, peasants and artisans welcomed revolution as a chance to express their grievances and uncertainties. However, hopes for radical change were soon dashed. The Orléanist régime's new charter only offered guarantees against infringement of civil liberties, restored the tricolor as the national flag, and asserted the primacy of parliament over the king.

The Revolution of 1830 resulted in only a slight widening of the electorate, to about 2 percent of adult men. However, the July Monarchy's economic policy marked an important intensification of state intervention to stimulate capitalist enterprise, especially in the railway construction of the 1840s. Overall, industrial production was 30 percent higher in 1835–44 than in the previous decade. While from 1821 to 1846 France's population grew 16 percent to 35.4 million, urban centers grew far more quickly. Most cities, however, continued to be based on small-scale, artisanal production, as in Paris, which grew from 547,000 in 1801 to 1,053,000 in 1851. One of the most striking changes in the language of the labor movement in the years after 1830 is the transition from occupational to class definition. Such changes generated a new, socialist ideology.

The political economy of the July Monarchy also accelerated agricultural change. Specialization in wine making and sugar-beet and cattle raising was facilitated by improved road transport, then the coming of railways. By midcentury the rural population of France had reached its historic peak: the hope of better opportunities elsewhere quickened the rate of rural exodus and in sixteen departments, especially in upland areas, permanent decline had begun.

The education reforms introduced by François Guizot in 1833 increased the number of primary school students from 1.9 million in 1832 to 3.5 million (mostly boys) in 1847. The July Monarchy was also a great age of bourgeois sociability and written culture across the country, despite the régime's tight censorship and control of public gatherings. These years were marked, too, by the expression of a distinctive bourgeois culture in the nature of personal relations; idealized gender roles; the style and function of clothing, furniture, and food; and the practice of leisure and manners. The king personified this culture, with his home-centered routines and bourgeois dress.

The fundamental problem of the July Monarchy was that it could claim legitimacy neither from history, unlike the Bourbons, nor from popular will, unlike resurgent republicans. Bonapartism also became more attractive with the fading of negative memories of 1792–1815 and in contrast with the self-serving, inglorious image of the July Monarchy. The bloody war for annexation in Algeria (begun in 1830) further tarnished its image. Romanticism, which under the Restoration had been championed by François-Auguste-René, Vicomte de Chateaubriand; Alfred Victor Vigny; and other supporters of the régime, now became a language of liberalism and progress for Victor Hugo and Alphonse de Lamartine.

As in 1830, a combination of political opposition, economic crisis, and governmental ineptitude brought the monarchy down. On February 23, 1848, nervous troops fired shots into crowds of protestors. That night barricades were erected all over the city, and Louis-Philippe fled. Crowds invaded the king's chamber and named a republican provisional government. Such action was mirrored in the seizure of power in thousands of towns and villages.

The new government guaranteed subsistence to the urban unemployed through "national workshops" opened in Paris, Marseille, and other cities. It also introduced universal manhood suffrage, and freedom of the press and association. In the colonies, slavery was finally abolished. The collapse of controls on association and the press unleashed the expression of democratic political culture through political clubs and newspapers, including, in 1830, a feminist press.

France's first elections by universal, direct manhood suffrage in April resulted in a conservative Assembly dominated by grands notables. After this assembly decided on June 21 to close the workshops for the unemployed, an unprecedented civil war tore the city in two. The government lost eight hundred troops: at least fifteen hundred insurgents were killed. The composition and ideology of the two sides supports the insight of contemporaries such as Karl Marx and Alexis de Tocqueville that this was a new type of class conflict. The starkness of the social divide inspired a new "realism," exemplified by Gustave Courbet's painting *Burial at Ornans* (1850) and Gustave Flaubert's *L'Education sentimentale* (*Sentimental Education*, 1869).

In the presidential elections of December 10, Louis-Napoleon won a staggering 74 percent of the vote. The reasons for the vote were contradictory: Louis-Napoleon benefited from his uncle's fame, but popular opinion often identified him with the promise of radical social change. However, it soon became apparent that he stood above all for social order.

France again went to the polls in May 1849 in an atmosphere of political polarization and continuing socioeconomic uncertainty. The "party of order" won easily but the left-wing *démocrates-socialistes* gained 35 percent: in parts of the centre and south a "red" countryside had emerged. However, republican hopes for electoral victory in 1852 were dashed by Louis-Napoleon's military coup d'etat on December 2, 1851. Most people welcomed the coup for ending social and political instability. However, in specific areas of southern and central France thousands of peasants and artisans took up arms against it.

This resistance was crushed and a subsequent plebiscite gave *post facto* approval to the coup. The president's new constitution concentrated power in the executive; then, following a second plebiscite in December 1852, he assumed the mantle of emperor and a Second Empire was established. The Second Republic was dead; however, it marked the end of royalist regimes in France and the definitive victory of universal manhood suffrage. The political domination of the grands notables was over.

PETER McPHEE

See also **France, 1760 to the Revolution; France: Revolution and Empire; French Revolution: Its Impact and Importance; French Romanticism: Its Literary Legacy**

Bibliography

Agulhon, M. *The Republican Experiment, 1848–1852.* Cambridge, 1983.

Collingham, H. A. C. *The July Monarchy: A Political History of France, 1830–1848.* New York, 1988.

Gibson, R. *A Social History of French Catholicism, 1789–1914.* London, 1989.

Jardin, A., and A.-J Tudesq. *Restoration and Reaction, 1815–1848.* Cambridge, 1983.

McPhee, P. *A Social History of France, 1780–1880.* London, 1992.

Macgraw, R. *France, 1815–1914: The Bourgeois Century.* London, 1983.

Merriman, J. M. *The Margins of City Life: Explorations on the French Urban Frontier, 1815–1851.* New York, 1991.

Price, R. *A Social History of Nineteenth-Century France.* London, 1987.

FRANCE: REVOLUTION AND EMPIRE

The manifold interpretations of the causes and course of the French Revolution are a reflection of the fact that this event was not distinguished by any unifying, monolithic ideology. Nor was there any single revolutionary figure who might compare with Vladimir Lenin or Mao Zedong in providing the revolution with the kind of unity that marked the Russian and Chinese Revolutions of the twentieth century. In practice and theory, the year 1789 raised more questions than it answered. The revolutionary decade (1789–99) raised political issues that were only partially resolved under the Consulate (1799–1804) and Empire (1804–1814, and 1815). Most lingered until at least the foundation of the Third Republic in the 1870s, and many beyond that.

It was against the context of harvest failure and soaring prices that the politicofiscal crisis that had been present in France since at least the American War of Independence reached a climax. For the peasants who eked out a meager existence from the soil, economic hardship made the continued unequal distribution of fiscal burdens unbearable. The parallel political crisis culminated in May 1789, with the convocation of the Estates General, and its transformation the following month into the National Assembly. Thus was a society of orders rejected in favor of a modern notion of equal citizenship and national sovereignty. The storming of the Bastille by the Parisian mob on July 14 ended the monopoly of violence hitherto held by the state. This monopoly would only be fully reestablished over a decade later by Napoleon Bonaparte.

The extraordinary events (immediately recognised as such by participants and contemporaries) came at the end of a century marked by a philosophical movement, the Enlightenment, defined by Immanuel Kant as "man's emergence from his self-imposed nonage." The Enlightenment had done much to undermine the legitimacy of institutions that failed to adapt to changing opinions and tastes. The French monarchy was one of these institutions, as became apparent after the American War of Independence. This conflict had not only deepened the fiscal crisis, but had brought forth the emergence of a virtuous new republic across the

Atlantic against which the Versailles court appeared all the more decadent (such decadence was also apparent when Versailles was compared to the patriotic virtues of another republic, ancient Rome, as portrayed by artists such as Jacques Louis David). What made the intellectual and cultural developments of the late eighteenth century even more dangerous to the existing order was the concurrent ongoing expansion of the public sphere, in the form of salon culture, Masonic lodges, patriotic clubs, and the press. It was through such institutions that a popularized version of the late Enlightenment (a fusion of the rationalism of Denis Diderot's *Encyclopédie* with Jean-Jacques Rousseau's "return to nature" and proto-Romantic emphasis upon the uniqueness of individual personality and experience) reached a wider audience. As the public sphere expanded, the cultural center shifted from Versailles to Paris. Patriotism was now increasingly (though by no means exclusively) associated with the rising class of nonnoble propertied and professional groups who resented their inferior status within the society of orders.

The events of May, June, and July 1789 marked the beginning, not the end, of a process. Over the following years, the leaders of the Revolution struggled to find a workable constitutional settlement. Initially, at least, Britain served as an inspiration. However, with the constitution of September 1791, something definitely new was created in the form of a document that would serve as a model for all liberal constitutions in the nineteenth century. Yet even before the constitution had been approved, political developments—religious strife sparked by the Civil Constitution of the Clergy (July 1790), the attempted flight of the royal family from France (June 1791), the massacre of republicans on the Champs de Mars (July 1791) and deteriorating international situation—made the preferred, moderate option of a constitutional monarchy practically unworkable.

At least in cultural terms, the gains of the early revolutionary years can be judged more positively. Press freedom, which had been one of the frequent demands in the *cahiers de doléances*, was in practice guaranteed from May/June 1789, and in theory according to article 11 of the Declaration of the Rights of Man and the Citizen (August 1789). This declared, "The free communication of ideas and opinions is one of the most precious rights of man; every citizen may therefore speak, write and print freely, with the exception of cases where this liberty is abused, as will be determined by the law." In practice, freedom of expression lasted until the summer of 1792. Subsequent press laws reflected the vicissitudes of the revolution.

The revolution entered a more radical phase in the summer of 1792. The outbreak of the first revolutionary war in April 1792 aggravated fear of internal conspiracy. This fear manifested itself in violence (the storming of the Tuileries in August 1792; prison massacres in September 1792). At the same time, press freedom ended with the suppression of royalist journals (August 12, 1792) and state sponsorship for "patriotic publications." The constitutional monarchy was finally put out of its misery with the establishment of the republic (September 22, 1792). This new regime confronted domestic and foreign emergency with fanaticism and severity (the Reign of Terror, 1793–94). The Law of Suspects (September 17, 1793) decreed the arrest of those who through their words, whether written or spoken, showed themselves to be enemies of liberty and friends of tyranny. The opposition press ceased to exist in Paris.

Culturally, this phase of the revolution is less associated with great reflective works and more with swiftly produced pamphlets and journals, the composition of revolutionary songs (most famously, the *Marseillaise*) and with the great revolutionary festivities choreographed by David. At the same time, Paris embarked upon a campaign to eliminate local cultures on the grounds that they were "feudal." Instead, the center attempted to enforce a republican "standard high culture" on the provinces, thus opening a century-long campaign to transform peasants into an acceptable French citizenry. Back in revolutionary Paris, each political faction and associated journal attempted to employ poets and writers for their respective causes but, as later under Napoleon's Empire, the most talented failed to flourish under compulsion. In any case, works needed to be produced quickly to avoid being overtaken by events, and this required a different kind of talent. Political activism and the written word merged, as writers became political missionaries and politicians (for example, Georges-Jacques Danton, Camille Desmoulins, Jean-Paul Marat, and Maximilien de Robespierre) themselves became men of letters. Writers and artists also shared the same risks as politicians, as demonstrated by the guillotining of France's most promising poet, André Chénier (July 25, 1794), for criticizing the excesses of the Terror. Not surprisingly under these circumstances, the best French literature of this period was produced not in the maelstrom of Paris, but on the margins and more specifically, among the *émigrés* (those who left France after 1789 to escape the Revolution). It was in emigration that Chateaubriand began his literary career, with his *Essai sur les revolutions*, a critique of revolutionary actions, if not revolutionary ideals. Other émigrés included Madame Anne-Louise-Germaine de Staël, who produced an important early liberal statement on the Revolution, *Considérations sur la Révolution*, and Joseph de Maistre, with his more wide-ranging philosophical condemnation of both revolutionary acts and principles, *Considérations sur la France*. Two other works that might be mentioned in this context are Sabatier de Castres's *Pensées et observations morales et politiques* and Portalis's *De l'usage et de l'abus de l'esprit philosophique*, written in the same circumstances and both representing the beginnings of a broader reaction against the Enlightenment. The emigration had a wider significance still, in that it encouraged cross-fertilization between French and non-French European culture. States of mind associated with early Romanticism—introspection, solitude, the sentimental, the importance of the "self"—were inherent in the emigration.

The fury of the Terror ended abruptly with the overthrow of Robespierre (July 27–28, 1794). There followed the Directory (1795–99), an unstable regime that, to its detractors, was marked primarily by corruption. Recently rehabilitated by historians, the Directory can be seen as the first sustained, large-scale attempt at a liberal, constitutional, democratic republican government in Europe. In cultural and educational terms, some of its achievements were quite impressive. For example, it was during the Directory that the Institut de France was forged out of a collection of moribund institutions. The Écoles centrals, with their radical curriculum, were also a product of this period, though they were soon to founder on conservative hostility. The main intellectual group of this period were the so-called Ideologues, ensconced in their power base in the class of moral and political sciences within the Institut de France. In many respects, the *Ideologues* can be seen as a continuation of the encyclopedist tradition, though they went beyond this. In much of the literature, the Ideologues are dismissed as representing a rather sterile phase, falling chronologically between the stools of Enlightenment and Romanticism. This view is sustainable only if Romanticism is considered as the anti-Enlightenment. If, conversely, the connections between the two are stressed, and Romanticism is interpreted as stemming from the Enlightenment (albeit with fundamental modifications and revisions), then the Ideologues can be seen as an important link. Arguably, Marie François Xavier Bichat (histology), Pierre Jean Georges Cabamis (physics and philosophy), Antoine Louis Claude Destutt de Tracy (philosophy), Joseph Marie, Baron de Gérando (philosophy), Philippe, Pinel (psychiatry), Pierre-Louis Roederer (jurisprudence and political thought), Emile Joseph Sieyès (political thought), and Constantin François Chasseboeuf, Comte de Volney (philosophy) collectively contributed to the development of a more complex, organic conception of society and the individual in this period. While they strove to apply the same rigorous scientific method to the social sciences as had been done previously to the natural sciences, their thought undoubtedly contributed to a reevaluation of philosophical and cultural theories that went beyond the Enlightenment.

The Directory finally succumbed to one of the many coups that plagued its existence in November 1799, when Napoleon Bonaparte seized power and instituted the Consulate. The majority of the French, weary of a decade of turmoil, welcomed the prospect of stability. The new regime, though socially exclusive in its policies, appeared ideologically inclusive, ready to embrace all apart from those on the extreme left and right. The Ideologues—some of whom played a prominent role in Napoleon's coup—as well as liberals and moderate royalists initially supported the new regime. However, while Napoleon had previously attempted to associate himself with France's leading intellectuals, in power he became increasingly irritated by their advice and criticisms. He was annoyed at the Ideologues (now "*misérables metaphysicians*") attacks against the concordat with the Catholic Church as well as other policies, and retaliated by eliminating their base of power in the Tribunate, dissolving the class of moral and political sciences in the Institut, buying others off with important positions and drowning the remainder in a flood of decorations and honors.

Others, of a royalist or liberal inclination, were horrified by such arbitrary acts as the kidnap and execution of the Duc d'Enghien (1804), an event that led Chateaubriand to break with the regime. More fundamentally, Napoleonic cultural authoritarianism, though it did not prevent painters, sculptors, and architects from capturing the heroism and glory associated with the regime, did alienate the most talented writers of this period, including François-Auguste-Reué, Vicomte de Chateaubriand, Henri-Benjamin Constant de Rebecque, Etionne Pivert de Senancour, and Madame de Staël. It would take a new generation of writers, one that had not fully experienced the empire (1804–14/15) but only the mediocrity of the Restoration (1815–30) and July Monarchy (1830–48), to employ their pens in sustaining the Napoleonic legend.

MICHAEL ROWE

Bibliography

Baker, Keith. *Inventing the French Revolution: Essays on French Political Culture in the Eighteenth Century*. Cambridge: Cambridge University Press, 1990.

Bergeron, Louis. *France under Napoleon*. Trans. by R. R. Palmer. Princeton, N.J.: Princeton University Press, 1981.

Chartier, Roger. *The Cultural Origins of the French Revolution*. Translated by Lydia G. Cochrane. Durham, N.C.: Duke University Press, 1991.

Darnton, Robert. *The Literary Underground of the Old Regime*. Cambridge Mass.: Harvard University Press, 1991.

Doyle, William. *Oxford History of the French Revolution*. Oxford: Clarendon Press, 1989.

Hesse, Carla. *Publishing and Cultural Politics in Revolutionary Paris*. Berkeley and Los Angeles: University of California Press, 1991.

Hunt, Lynn. *Politics, Culture and Class in the French Revolution*. Berkeley and Los Angeles: University of California Press, 1984.

Kennedy, Emmet. *A Cultural History of the French Revolution*. New Haven, Conn.: Yale University Press, 1989.

Lefebvre, Georges. *The Thermidorians and the Directory*. Translated by Robert Baldick. London: Routledge and Kegan Paul, 1965.

Ozouf, Mona. *Festivals of the French Revolution*. Translated by Alan Sheridan. Cambridge, Mass.: Harvard University Press, 1988.

Sutherland, D. M. G. *France, 1789–1815: Revolution and Counter-Revolution*. London: Fontana Press, 1985.

Woloch, Isser. *The New Regime: Transformations of the French Civic Order, 1789–1820s*. New York: W. W. Norton, 1994.

FRANKENSTEIN; OR, THE MODERN PROMETHEUS 1818

Novel by Mary Shelley

Frankenstein is the first, most influential, and arguably most innovative of the seven novels written by Mary Shelley. It is one of the most important Gothic fictions and has been described as the first work that can legitimately be classified as science fiction. This tale of the destructive force unleashed on society by a science that divides itself from nature and abjures responsibility for its creations has inspired a host of dramatic, literary and, in the twentieth century, filmic imitations and recensions. It is the source of one of the key, shaping myths of modern culture, in which a scientist, in pursuit of truth, but unaware of the desires that drive his quest, inadvertently destroys the society of which he is part.

In her introduction to the revised edition of *Frankenstein*, published in 1831, Shelley famously traces the book's origin to an evening she and her husband, Percy Bysshe Shelley, spent with Lord Byron and his physician, John Polidori in the Villa Diodati on the shores of Lake Léman near Geneva. Enthused by *Fantasmagoriana, ou Recueil d'Histoires d'Apparitions de Spectres, Revenans, Fantômes, etc.* (1812), a volume of German ghost stories translated into French by J. B. B. Eyriès, Byron proposed that they create their own. Although her companions soon began to write, Mary Shelley's inspiration stalled. Ghost stories may have been a necessary, but were clearly not a sufficient catalyst for the creation of *Frankenstein*.

Shelley found the proximate cause of her story in contemporary scientific theories and debates about "the principle of life," mediated at the Villa Diodati in part by conversations between Byron and Percy Shelley. These conversions, Mary Shelley notes, referred to the experiments of Erasmus Darwin and the theories of Luigi Galvani. The latter had argued in *De Veribus Electricitatis in Motu Musculari Commentarius* (*Commentary on the Effect of Electricity on Muscular Motion*, 1791) for the existence of a subtle fluid—animal electricity—that was the source of animal motion and of life. The former argued in *The Temple of Nature or the Origin of Society* (1803) that life began by "spontaneous birth" and, in *Zoonomia* (1794–6), that "one and the same kind of living filament is and has been the cause of all organic life." Perhaps, Byron and Percy Shelley speculated, if "the principal of life" could be identified, then a corpse might be reanimated or a "creature might be manufactured, brought together, and endued with vital warmth." Such speculations prompted the vivid dream that, Shelley claims, was the beginning of *Frankenstein*: "I saw the pale student of unhallowed arts kneeling beside the thing he had put together. I saw the hideous phantasm of a man stretched out, and then, on the working of some powerful engine, show signs of life, and stir with an uneasy, half-vital motion." This convergence of contemporary science with the conventions and preoccupations of Gothic fiction animates Mary Shelley's *Frankenstein*.

In early Gothic fictions, horror is often generated by the sense that the present is in thrall to a murderous past. Against this past Gothic novels routinely invoke the protection offered by an enlightened, paternal protector and the moral values represented by the heroine of sensibility. In strong contrast, *Frankenstein* depicts a horror that emerges from the present, from the successful attempt by Victor Frankenstein to infuse "life into an inanimate body." Moreover, though Shelley poses the paternal family as a possible counterweight to the excesses of science, it proves helpless against Victor's monster. The figure who should act as paternal protector (Victor) produces the monster who destroys the heroine of sensibility (Elizabeth). In more traditional Gothic fictions one can find both "real" and illusory monsters. In *Frankenstein* the creature is "real," but his monstrosity emerges only when Victor refuses to nurture and protect his creation. Victor once dreamed of pouring "a torrent of light into our dark world"; the product of this dream, rejected by his maker, becomes his murderous double, destroying those who should constitute his family.

Through the use of dreams to reveal internal psychological states, writing that at key moments suggests unconscious motivation, and a narrative told from multiple points of view, Shelley coordinates her critique of masculinist science with an account of the social and sexual relations that attend it. Central to this account is the relation between Victor's quest to discover "the principle of life" and his troubled relations with the feminine. Victor's journey to Ingolstadt divides him from the feminine and introduces him to the all-male world of the university. Moreover, as recent critics have observed, in attempting to "bestow animation upon lifeless matter," Victor hopes to make the production of new life independent of the feminine. Rather than escaping the feminine, however, it returns as the unconscious, parodic sub-text to his actions: in the enclosed, womblike space of his study, in a parody of the process of gestation, he gives form to a living being.

Victor's creation of new life also puts in male hands a creative power usually associated with God. To the extent that it is successful, this appropriation turns nature (now understood as representing a divine order) into culture, an order created by and subject to "man." Victor Frankenstein is in this regard, as the book's subtitle suggests, the modern Prometheus: he has stolen a creative spark that properly belongs to God. This correspondence links the book to conservative critiques of the French Revolution and to debates about what constitutes true monstrosity.

For conservative writers such as Edmund Burke, the French revolutionaries had produced a monstrous jumble of elements, from which they were attempting to create a new order. They are like children, Burke writes in *Reflections on the Revolution in France* (1790), who have rashly hacked their "aged parent in pieces, and put him in the kettle of magicians, in hopes that by their poisonous weeds, and wild incantations, they may regenerate the paternal constitution, and renovate their father's life." This description closely parallels Victor's attempt to create new life from material collected from "the dissecting room and the slaughter-house." Seen in this light, it is no doubt significant that Victor's monstrous work of creation occurs in Ingolstadt, the city identified by anti-Jacobins as the source of the conspiracy that culminated in the French revolution. The scientist in Shelley's *Frankenstein*, and the revolutionary seen in Burke's *Reflections*, are ultimately destroyed by their own creations. The monster draws Frankenstein to his death in the frozen wastes of the Arctic. In the Terror, many of the revolutionaries were destroyed by their own creation.

In *Frankenstein*, Victor destroys the female mate he had begun to create for the monster, fearful that they would procreate and, eventually, overrun the earth. The novel itself, a volume Shelley described as her "hideous progeny," was hampered by no analogous interdiction. It has spawned a voluminous secondary criticism and been followed by numerous stage and film adaptations—most notably, James Whale's *Frankenstein* (1931) and *Bride of Frankenstein* (1935), starring Boris Karloff as the monster. Recent developments in genetic engineering ensure the continuing relevance of Shelley's novel, making it likely that we will see further literary and filmic children of *Frankenstein*.

PETER OTTO

Text

Frankenstein; or, The Modern Prometheus. First edition published anonymously, in three volumes, 1818. A two-volume second edition, with authorship now attributed to Mary Shelley, was published in 1823; a third edition, substantially revised by Shelley, was published in 1831.

Bibliography

Baldick, Chris. *In Frankenstein's Shadow: Myth, Monstrosity and Nineteenth-Century Writing.* Oxford: Oxford University Press, 1987.

Bann, Stephen, ed. *Frankenstein, Creation, and Monstrosity.* London: Reaktion, 1994.

Botting, Fred. *Frankenstein: Mary Shelley.* Basingstoke, England: Macmillan, 1995.

Ellis, Kate Ferguson. *Gothic Novels and the Subversion of Domestic Ideology.* Urbana: University of Illinois Press, 1989.

Forry, Steven Earl. *Hideous Progenies: Dramatizations of "Frankenstein" from Mary Shelley to the Present.* Philadelphia: University of Pennsylvania Press, 1990.

Levine, George, and U. C. Knoepflmacher. *The Endurance of "Frankenstein": Essays on Mary Shelley's Novel.* Berkeley and Los Angeles: University of California Press, 1979.

Lowe-Evans, Mary, ed. *Critical Essays on Mary Wollstonecraft Shelley.* New York: G. K. Hall, 1998.

Thornburg, Mary K. Patterson. *The Monster in the Mirror: Gender and the Sentimental/Gothic Myth in "Frankenstein".* Ann Arbor, Mich.: UMI Research Press, 1987.

Veeder, William. *Mary Shelley and Frankenstein: The Fate of Androgyny.* Chicago: University of Chicago Press, 1986.

FRANZ STERNBALDS WANDERUNGEN (THE TRAVELS OF FRANZ STERNBALD) 1798

Novel by Ludwig Tieck

"Der erste Roman seit Cervantes der romantisch ist" (The first romantic novel since Cervantes): so Ludwig Tieck's Romantic contemporary Friedrich Schlegel described *Franz Sternbalds Wanderungen*. What was it about this incomplete, and much criticized, novel that captured the nascent Romantic spirit in Germany and exerted such an influence on later Romantic fiction? Following the tradition of the *Bildungsroman* and of Johann Wolfgang von Goethe's *Wilhelm Meisters Lehrjahre* (*Wilhelm Meister's Apprenticeship*, 1824) in particular, *Sternbald* portrays a journey of self-discovery, but uses it as the springboard for a picaresque novel in which romantic *Wanderlust* becomes an end in itself and plot dissolves into multifarious adventures, evocative atmosphere, and lyrical poetry. Time and geography are relativized as the Romantic author indulges his subjective imagination and sends his hero meandering capriciously from Germany to Holland to Italy in a poeticized sixteenth century. It was these features of *Sternbald* that made it a model for artist novels such as Dorothea Schlegel's *Florentin* (1801) and Novalis's *Heinrich von Ofterdingen* (1802), and eventually for the narratives of Joseph von Eichendorff—especially his novel *Ahnung und Gegenwart* (*Premonition and Present*, 1819) and the celebrated short story "Aus dem Leben eines Taugenichts" ("Memoirs of a Good-for-Nothing," 1826), in both of which journeying without destination performs a thematic function.

The first part of the novel opens as Franz Sternbald and his friend Sebastian, both apprentices of Albrecht Dürer in Nuremberg, say their farewells before Franz's departure on his journeyman's travels. In its hagiographic portrayal of Dürer and other contemporary artists, the novel seems at first to be a narrative extension of the reflections and anecdotes in the *Herzensergiessungen eines kunstliebenden Klosterbruders* (*Outpourings of an Art-Loving Friar*) which Tieck had composed two years earlier in collaboration with Wilhelm Heinrich Wackenroder. Indeed, Tieck stated that Wackenroder had played a significant part in planning *Sternbald*. In both works there is more than a hint of nationalism in the idealization of "old German" art as an embodiment of godfearing probity. This emphasis continues as Franz meets the Dutch painters Lucas van Leyden and Quentin Metsys and witnesses the meeting between Dürer and van Leyden in 1521. Yet this apparently historical novel, set in the workshops of painters in northern Europe during the Renaissance, soon undergoes an unexpected metamorphosis.

Even in the opening chapters, the focus of attention begins to turn from Franz's artistic vocation to the mysterious circumstances surrounding his parentage and to the identity of a fair lady whom he fleetingly encounters. The traditions of the romance take over. On a voyage from Leiden to Antwerp, Franz meets the minstrel Rudolf Florestan and with him sets off on a series of travels through the Low Countries and up the Rhine, accompanied for some time by a pair of lovable vagabonds, Ludoviko and Roderigo, and along the way entering into a bewildering succession of exploits with aristocratic damsels, monks in disguise, and hermits. Romantic and even erotic involvements and intrigues abound. Again and again the characters break into song. All sense of a purposeful itinerary is lost, and references to artistic matters become merely sporadic. It is only in the last four chapters of the second part of the novel, hundreds of pages later, that Franz is suddenly found in Florence in the midst of a group of Italian painters and rediscovers his career as an artist.

The abruptness of Franz's arrival in Italy is not the only disconcerting feature of this brief final section. Initially he seems to have rejected the way of life and view of art he had professed in Nuremberg. Apparently betraying his commitment to Dürer's devout values and staid domesticity, Franz now enters unashamedly upon a bohemian and dissolute lifestyle in which the practice of art seems synonymous with indulgence in wine, women, and song. In the very last chapter, following a move to Rome, there is another *volte-face*: moved by the sight of Michelangelo's *Last Judgment*, Franz expresses repentance over his loss of direction and a renewed commitment to the artistic and personal ideals of Dürer, as if by way of reward finding the elusive woman he has sought since the start of his travels. Franz's last-minute conversion has not convinced critics, and the impression remains of a novel that is deeply self-contradictory. Jeffrey L. Sammons, who believes that *Sternbald* as a whole lacks thematic discipline, notes, "The speed of the concluding scene is more than breathtaking; it is a final disappointment." Against this background it is hardly surprising that Tieck failed in his repeated attempts to produce a third part of the novel later in his life, although the fragmentary beginning of a continuation has survived. Following the death of Wackenroder and shifts in Tieck's own literary interests, the mood of the opening sections of the novel could not be recovered.

The appeal of *Sternbald* to Tieck's Romantic contemporaries in a sense lay in its very contradictoriness. It presents a spectrum of mutually incompatible Romantic role models: the saintly artist devoted to his art, the bohemian spurning bourgeois restrictions, the artist divided in himself and guilty over his lack of social utility, the carefree troubadour, the restless itinerant attracted by the lure of the South and the exotic in general. It proclaims the Romantic belief in the artist as visionary, the mediator of hieroglyphics of the divine, and from it Philipp Otto

Runge derived a new conception of symbolic landscape painting; but simultaneously it creates an ideal of spontaneous poetic existence unencumbered by any such lofty mission. Friedrich Schlegel wrote in the journal *Das Athenäum* that in *Sternbald* "der romantische Geist scheint angenehm über sich selbst zu fantasiren" ("the Romantic spirit seems congenially to indulge in fantasies about itself"). Tieck's novel was all things to all Romantics. Perhaps its most lasting influence, however, was exercised in conjunction with the *Herzensergiessungen*: together the two works gave rise to a cult of "old German" religious painting that was famously condemned by Goethe in as "sternbaldisirende Unwesen" ("Sternbaldizing mischief") and later led to the Nazarene movement. From there its influence was to extend to the Pre-Raphaelites in Britain.

RICHARD LITTLEJOHNS

Text

Franz Sternbalds Wanderungen, in two parts, 1798; 2d rev. ed. as vol. 14 of Tieck's *Schriften*. 1843. Revision of the 1st ed. by Alfred Anger. Stuttgart: Reclam 1966. Revision of the 2d ed. by Marianne Thalmann in Tieck's *Werke*, vol. 1: *Frühe Erzählungen und Romane*. Munich: Winkler 1963; fragment of a third part published by Richard Alewyn in *Jahrbuch des Freien Deutschen Hochstifts*, 1962.

Bibliography

Behler, Ernst. *German Romantic Literary Theory*, Cambridge University Press, 1993: 248–59.

Kahn, Robert L. "Tieck's *Franz Sternbalds Wanderungen* and Novalis's *Heinrich von Ofterdingen*," *Studies in Romanticism* 7 (1967–68): 40–64.

Lillyman, William J. *Reality's Dark Dream: The Narrative Fiction of Ludwig Tieck*. Berlin: de Gruyter, 1979.

Mornin, Edward. "Art and Alienation in Tieck's *Franz Sternbalds Wanderungen*," *Modern Language Notes* 94 (1979): 510–23.

Paulin, Roger. *Ludwig Tieck: A Literary Biography*. Oxford: Clarendon Press, 1985.

Sammons, Jeffrey L. "Tieck's *Sternbald*: the Loss of Thematic Control", *Studies in Romanticism* 5 (1965–66): 30–43.

FRATERNITY

In the eighteenth-century dictionaries of Samuel Johnson and others, *fraternity* denoted brotherly relations between family, social groups and peoples, often bearing a Christian or Masonic connotation. The advent of the French Revolution, however, heralded a new importance for the concept in European Romanticism.

Revolutionary France politicized fraternity, with two conceptual strands emerging. The first reflects the jubilant initial responses of the French masses to the Revolution. In 1789 the feeling of fraternity embodied the "emotionally empowering quality of moral obligation spontaneously assumed in relation to equals." This egalitarian emotion became reinforced in public oaths and festivals, as well as in speeches and sermons throughout France. In this heady atmosphere, moreover, the idea of fraternity became an aspiration, and many Revolutionaries looked forward to the imminent realization of a potentially all-embracing universal affection.

In nineteenth-century France, this positive vision of fraternity would influence both artistic and political movements. Fraternity's egalitarian ideal helped to generate new artistic brotherhoods, such as that which emerged from Jacques-Louis David's studio in the 1790s, as well as the later Nazarene and Pre-Raphaelite brotherhoods. The communal organization of these groups challenged the authoritarian structure of the academies and offered European artists the opportunity of thriving without state or royal patronage. Such brotherhoods reflected in artistic circles fraternity's growing role in French socialist theory and practice. In political theory, fraternity came to represent a spirit of cooperation and association in opposition to capitalist exploitation. Charles Fourier (1772–1837) used the concept to justify the setting up of small, self-supporting voluntary communities or *philanstères*, whose members would live in social amity through mutual cooperation. "Fourierism" in turn influenced the many fraternal associations which sprang up among the French peasantry in the mid-nineteenth century.

The Revolution, however, also created another, more disturbing fraternity. With the onset of the Terror in 1793, the concept was increasingly used to divide, rather than unite, social groups. The activity of "fraternization" came to refer to specific procedures by which the Revolutionary leaders excluded the Girondins and other political moderates. In the name of fraternity, activists would seek brotherly help from other comrades forcefully to exclude unwanted groups from sectional meetings. In this way, fraternity under Maximilien de Robespierre became associated with violence, encapsulated in the popular slogan "Fraternity or death."

The two strands of Revolutionary fraternity quickly colored English political and poetic discourse. An inclusivist fraternity became a self-conscious part of the radical community's ideology, and helped to justify its advocacy of universal suffrage and an end to the war with France. Oaths of friendship and brotherhood characterized the tavern meetings of the Corresponding societies of the 1790s, as well as the letters these societies exchanged. British liberal enthusiasm for fraternity in the mid-1790s was exemplified by Samuel Taylor Coleridge and William Wordsworth. In his poetry, Wordsworth uses fraternity on at least two levels: as the bond uniting all human beings, and as the amity linking man and man in Wordsworth's ideal community. In these years he consistently invokes these concepts to highlight social injustices. In *Adventures on Salisbury Plain* (1795) he celebrates the welcoming atmosphere of a rustic tavern as expressive of the spirit of fraternity embodied in those oppressed by the ruling classes. By way of contrast, the poet condemns war as a disruption of man's natural brotherhood.

By 1798, however, counter-revolutionary forces were attempting to appropriate fraternity for themselves. Politically conservative voices, notably the weekly *Anti-Jacobin* (1797–98), viewed the inclusivist fraternity of Wordsworth and his ilk as encouraging a pacifism that was tantamount to treason. For them, fraternity was a term that should unite English patriots in the war against France. English disillusionment with the Revolution, as well as the domestic backlash, led many to reassess the idea of fraternity. For Wordsworth in *The Prelude* (1805), and Percy Bysshe Shelley and Thomas De Quincey after him, the Romantic consciousness of fraternity increasingly becomes tested against visions of social disintegration and images of nightmare, in which writers describe lost souls or maimed bodies and faces. Wordsworth's encounter with a prostitute in *The Prelude* becomes archetypal: the poet acknowledges this symbol of an alienated society while hoping to translate his disturbing vision into the basis for a dialogue with his fellow men, and implicitly invoking fraternity's latent ideal.

At the same time, Revolutionary fraternity remained a Christian idea, one that comes to have a profound influence on nineteenth-century artistic communities in Britain, Europe, and the United States. The foremost visionary theorist of Christian fraternity in the postrevolutionary years is William Blake. For Blake the idea of brotherhood is connected with the immanence of God, his who reveals himself through the spirit of Christ that men bear within themselves as imagination. In this way, Blake, like the New Testament itself, grounds fraternity in the notion that men are "brethren in Christ" (Col. 1:2). In *Jerusalem* (1804–18), the culmination of his thinking on fraternity, Blake argues that in the awakened state of Imagination or "Eden," brotherhood prevails. Because fraternity represents man's essential nature, so in his fallen state of alienation, Blake contends, both man and the nation ("Albion") remain alive only in a minimal sense. The fraternal state can be realized through the annihilation of selfhood. Jesus Christ represents for Blake the archetypal figure of self-sacrifice, and people imitate him in sacrificing themselves for another, particularly through forgiveness of sins.

In the 1790s, Coleridge harnessed the rhetoric of Christian fraternity for politically radical ends. In *Religious Musings* (1794–97), he uses the notion of the consubstantiality of men with God-as-man to envision a universal brotherhood based on mankind's profound common identity. Coleridge attempts to ground his idealism in actual social projects. During 1794–95, he and Robert Southey proposed establishing a Christian commune in North America. Central to this community of "Pantisocracy" would be its political egalitarianism and abolition of individual property, which, Coleridge argued, would allow the Pantisocrats' natural fraternity to flourish. Although the scheme did not materialize, such artistic fraternities grounded in religious and spiritual ideals became increasingly popular on the Continent, in particular, with the Nazarenes, the Ancients, the Nabis and the Visionists. Self-consciously organizing themselves as religious confraternities, these artistic groups attempted to realize a spiritual ideal of brotherhood, and to recreate, while living in monasteries and convents the mindset of sanctified groups like Christ and the apostles.

In the nineteenth century, many European concepts of fraternity become transposed to American soil. The novels of James Fenimore Cooper (1789–1851) continue the Rousseauean quest for fraternity in nature and the simple, spontaneous relations among men freed from urban society. The Transcendentalist movement, moreover, extended religious ideas of brotherhood into doctrines of "cosmic fraternity" and a "universal soul," as in Walt Whitman's poem "The Sleepers" (1855). In American Romanticism, however, fraternity proved as elusive an ideal as it had in Europe. In Cooper's novels, fraternity dwells ever westward, pushing the frontier so far that the utopia threatens to become extinguished altogether.

GURION TAUSSIG

Bibliography

Baker, Alan R. H. *Fraternity among the French Peasantry: Sociability and Voluntary Associations in the Loire Valley, 1815–1914.* Cambridge: Cambridge University Press, 1999.

Baker, Felicity. "Rousseau's Oath and Revolutionary Fraternity: 1789 and Today," *Romance Quarterly* 38 (1991): 273–87.

Ferber, Michael. *The Social Vision of William Blake.* Princeton, N.J.: Princeton University Press, 1985.

Hamill, Paul, "Other People's Faces: The English Romantics and the Paradox of Fraternity," *Studies in Romanticism* 17 (1978): 465–82.

McWilliams, Wilson Carey. *The Idea of Fraternity in America.* Berkeley and Los Angeles: University of California Press, 1973.

Morovitz, Laura, and William Vaughan, eds. *Artistic Brotherhoods in the Nineteenth Century.* Burlington, Vt.: Ashgate, 2000.

Ozouf, Mona. "Fraternity," in *A Critical Dictionary of the French Revolution.* Edited by François Furet and Mona Ozouf. Translated by Arthur Goldhammer. Cambridge, Mass.: Belknap Press of Harvard University Press, 1989.

Wuscher, Hermann J. *Liberty, Equality and Fraternity in Wordsworth 1791–1800.* Uppsala: University of Uppsala, 1980.

DER FREISCHÜTZ 1821

Opera by Carl Maria von Weber

The Freeshooter is not a very satisfactory translation of *Der Freischütz*. The second element in the title certainly refers to a shooter or, as might be said, a marksman, but "free" does not adequately convey the notions behind the opera; perhaps *The Magic Bullets* would be the best solution. As early as about 1810, Carl Maria von Weber, then in his mid-twenties, read a tale in *Das Gespesterbuch*, a recently published collection of ghost stories by J. A. Apel and F. Laun, and considered turning it into an opera. He was not alone in this: at least three other composers had taken up a theme well suited to the taste of the age before Weber settled down to serious work on it some seven years later after taking up his post as musical director of the German Opera House at Dresden. Weber enlisted the aid of the minor poet Johann Friedrich Kind to draft the libretto of what was originally called *Der Probeschuss* (*The Trial Shot*). Progress was slow because Weber was encumbered by his professional duties, was in ill health, and there were many changes in plan. In 1819, he persuaded the director of the rebuilt Schauspielhaus in Berlin to mount his opera, at that time called *Die Jägerbraut* (*The Hunter's Bride*), but it was not until June 18, 1821, that the premier took place.

Starting quietly, the substantial overture introduces many of the major musical ideas that are taken up later and sets the mood for the opera. Act 1, set in the Bohemian forest in the seventeenth century, brings on stage a chorus of peasants who are enjoying a shooting competition. The prowess of Kilian wins praise, while Max is mocked for his lack of skill. The mood darkens, and the two men are prevented from coming to blows by the arrival of Cuno, the chief forester. His daughter Agathe is the object of Max's affections, but, Cuno explains, he will not be allowed to marry her unless he satisfies the traditional test to succeed him as chief forester unless he is more successful in the shooting trials that will be held on the morrow. Learning this makes Max take all the more seriously what another forester, Caspar, has been saying: it is a matter of invoking the black arts. As the act continues with folk scenes of singing and dancing, Caspar convinces Max that he really can help by lending him his gun to shoot at an eagle that is flying by at a great height; the efficacy of the magic bullet is proved as the bird falls at his feet.

Act 2 is divided into two contrasting sections. The first, set in Cuno's house, is a scene of comfortable domestic contentment, and interest focuses on Agathe as she and her young cousin Ännchen hang up again a portrait of one of Cuno's ancestors that has fallen down and discuss marital prospects. Max arrives, only to tell Agathe that he must go into the forest to pick up a deer that he has shot near the Wolf's Glen. The very name of the place terrifies her, but Agathe soon recovers her high spirits.

The second part of act 2 takes us to the Wolf's Glen in the dead of the night. The scene has been carefully prepared both dramatically and musically, and for the first production Carl Gropius ensured that the stage set should also contribute to a sense of Gothic horror. Caspar conjures Samiel and arranges a quasi-Faustian bargain: Caspar shall have a further supply of magic bullets, but the seventh shall claim another victim for Samiel.

A forest glade is the setting for the first part of act 3. Max has already impressed the hunting party with his accurate shooting, but Caspar, who declines to hand over more bullets, plainly plans mischief. The scene changes to Agathe's room, and a sense of doom alternates with a feeling of elation as she prepares for her wedding. Ottokar, the ruling prince, is present for the final confrontations. Celebrations nearly turn to tragedy, but a hermit emerges to ensure a happy ending. Caspar is slain, Max must purge his sins by waiting a year before he marries, and the opera ends in rejoicing.

Der Freischütz plainly met the mood of the times when it was first produced. The folktale with its German setting made a welcome contrast with the more usual classical fare, and the combination of Gothic horror with homely personal emotions was all the more attractive because of the conventional conclusion with the good and the pure triumphing over evil. Attention was naturally drawn to the powerful and original Wolf's Glen scene, yet the scenes of popular festivities and those involving Agathe, even if she sometimes seems to revert to Italianate styles for her more extended arias, were also appealing in the apparent simplicity in an age that was exploring ways of profiting in art music from the quite recent rediscovery of folk song. Weber's employment of horns to convey a sense of hunting in the forest is as effective as his use of melodrama (i.e., a speaking voice over a musical accompaniment) in the Wolf's Glen, and the identification of certain harmonies with particular characters and themes is on the whole very successful.

At its premiere *Der Freischütz* was hailed as an outstanding achievement in Romantic opera. It was soon heard in all the major European opera houses. Weber had, however, adopted the popular German form a *Singspiel*, linking the sung numbers with passages of spoken dialogue. This was not acceptable in other countries, at least not with a serious subject, and recitatives had to be specially composed. Encouraged by the reception of *Der Freischütz*, Weber continued to experiment with Romantic opera, but never again with the same success.

CHRISTOPHER SMITH

Bibliography

Warrack, John. *Carl Maria von Weber*. London: Hamish Hamilton, 1968.
Weber, Carl Maria von. *Writings on Music*. Translated by Martin Cooper, Cambridge: Cambridge University Press, 1981.

FRENCH REVOLUTION: ITS IMPACT AND IMPORTANCE

No event in modern history has shaped our present world as much as the French Revolution and its aftermath. The values and principles of modern life and most aspects of contemporary society were born during the revolutionary era. At one stroke the *ancien régime* across most of Europe was either overturned or seriously challenged. The revolution also, indirectly, gave birth to the Romantic age and movement which came to challenge the restored monarchies, religious beliefs, and conservative principles of Clemens Lothar Wenzel Metternich's European order.

Probably the greatest legacy of the Revolution to most Europeans, whose livelihood depended upon agriculture, was the ending of the feudal dues and serfdom that had shackled the peasantry. This wasteful system of organization had, at least in western and central Europe, been replaced by the middle part of the nineteenth century by commercial farming which enabled the agricultural sector to produce a surplus to feed the ever growing cities. In other parts of Europe and the world, such as Latin America, the Ottoman Empire, and Russia, similar reforms came much later in the century—in Russia, as late as 1863. In France, ironically, the creation of an independent and prosperous peasantry as proprietors and producers retarded the country's industrial development during the nineteenth century.

The other great development in a positive direction for the great mass of the world's population and of great practical value was the ending of slavery early on in the revolution. Although in 1802 Napoleon Bonaparte was to reverse this decision despite strong advice to the contrary the momentum toward complete abolition in the Western world had been set. By 1804 the Republic of Haiti (formerly the French slave and sugar producing colony of Saint Domingue) had not only abolished slavery, but was North America's second independent state. Britain outlawed the slave trade three years later, and by 1848 both Britain and France had outlawed slavery in their colonies and collaborated to stop the exportation of slaves from the west coast of Africa. The United States, too, After a long and savage civil war, ended slavery in 1865, followed (finally) in 1891 by Brazil.

Thus two vital institutions that had underpinned the economic and social order of the ancien régime had been eradicated. A new capitalist system of free trade and enterprise, based upon the belief in the strong and inspired individual, personified by the "self-made man," was being established. Merit, not birth, was to decide the fate of the individual. The postrevolutionary years were the golden era of the utilitarians, led by Jeremy Bentham and James Mill. Led by such brilliant economists such as Thomas Malthus and David Ricardo, the science of political economy grew in prestige and importance in the field of learning.

Both these trends had their roots in the Enlightenment and were a consequence of the growing secularization in society since the seventeenth century. Secularization was entirely at odds with the intrusive doctrines of the established churches, which saw it, quite rightly, as undermining the church's authority in society. In France, and every part of Europe touched by the Revolution, secularization was accelerated and deepened. All institutions, especially the Catholic Church, seen as supporting the ancien régime were either crushed outright or modified to survive in the social and political climate. Although individual Catholics' rights were trampled, other religious minorities such as the European Jews were given greater rights during the revolution and by Napoleon.

The above benefits to society have to be qualified and set against some major negative developments. One of the most dangerous and erroneous was the French revolutionary notion that their revolution was both universally popular and applicable. Anyone opposing its principles were therefore seen as, at best, misguided or more commonly as an outright enemy of progress. Such enemies deserved to be crushed. This extreme standpoint was espoused by the first of lamentably many totalitarian parties: the Jacobins. Led during the Terror (1792–94) by Jacques Danton and Maximilien Robespierre, the Jacobins crushed their enemies within with every political mean of intimidation and terror available. Abroad the spread of the revolution was facilitated by the advances of the French revolutionary armies underpinned by mass conscription and the first modern war economy. Both were organized by General Lazare Carnot. This new army of egalitarian conscripts were led by officers whose commands had been given on the basis not only of party patronage, but also upon simple merit. Nowhere in the new order was advancement by merit and talent as well rewarded as in the French revolutionary and Napoleonic armies.

The French Revolution not only spawned the modern nation state in Europe, but also the new centralized and bureaucratically efficient state. A state with a nation in arms that could go on fighting for over two decades in the first proper world war. Nationalists in the Balkans (1804, 1821–31, 1875–78), Ireland (1798, 1803), and Poland (1830–31, 1863) were to follow the French example in an attempt to redraw the map of Europe. But the revolution was a global phenomena with great consequences outside the confines of this small continent. Under cover of war and using the excuse of a potential French threat to her empire, Britain not only conquered the Cape (South Africa), which was to create the Boer problem, but also established, after General Sir Arthur Wellesley's victories, the modern British Empire in India. Britain's worldwide dominance was thus established during and after the Napoleonic War and lasted until the end of the nineteenth century. Yet no continent besides Europe was as dramatically transformed by the revolution as South America. Here the example of Haiti and France, coupled with Spain's military and economic weaknesses, encouraged a series of uprisings from Mexico in the north to Rio de la Plata (Argentina) in the south. Following the example of Don Francisco de Miranda's failed 1806 invasion of the Spanish Main (Venezuela), leaders such as Simon Bolivar, Morales, O'Higgins, and San Martin managed to liberate the entire Spanish speaking part of the continent by 1825. In Brazil, Napoleon's invasion and occupation of Portugal in 1807 forced the ruler, Don John, to seek refuge in Rio de Janeiro. In 1822 he became emperor of an independent Brazilian state.

In the fields of science and literature this turbulent period proved fertile ground for changes. Literature in Europe, including Britain exemplified by Jane Austen and Lord Byron's works, flourished, and both Russia and the Unites States became part of the European cultural sphere for the first time. While the sculptural arts were not as flourishing as before 1789, those of painting triumphed with the works of John Constable, Jacques-Louis David, and J. M. W. Turner, to mention a few. Musical compositions flourished also with works of genius by Ludwig von Beethoven, Frédéric Chopin, Wolfgang Amadeus Mozart, and Robert Schumann.

There was now an identifiable national sense of culture, and the use of the vernacular at the expense of Latin and French was growing. The experiences of the revolutionary era did not hamper the use of French which remained the language of diplomacy, culture, the European elite, and polite society. In this field, as in others, the question was if one was to continue to ape Paris (after what had occurred there in the past) or to develop a national culture using ones native tongue? The younger generation of Romantics were inclined, given that their intense dislike of the postrevolutionary and conservative regimes of the Restoration under Metternich, to have a most naive and positive view of the revolution. The older generation, with the revolution's excesses in fresh memory and Napoleon's abuses of power in mind, were less enthusiastic about events after 1789.

Whatever the loss of political prestige, colonial territory, and military reputation, France kept its predominance not only in the arts but even more so in the sciences too. Through the

The Storming of the Bastille, 14th July 1789 (based on the accounts of Lieutenant Cholat). Reprinted courtesy of AKG.

creation and expansion of the polytechnics France kept the lead in such fields as chemistry, engineering, and mathematics. Prussia, badly beaten by Napoleon in 1806, carried out a serious program of educational reform that included technical high schools and the establishment of a National University in Berlin. After 1815, several other countries on the Continent followed Prussia's example, and in Britain, where there was not the same role for the state, this was amply compensated by industrialists' philanthropy.

CHRISTER JÖRGENSEN

Bibliography

Chandler, David. *The Campaigns of Napoleon*. London: Weidenfeld and Nicolson, 1990.

Doyle, William. *The Origins of the French Revolution*. Oxford: Oxford University Press, 1987.

———. *The Oxford History of the French Revolution*. Oxford: Oxford University Press, 1990.

Duffy, Michael. *Soldiers, Sugar and Sea Power: The British Expeditions to the West Indies and the War against Revolutionary France*. Oxford: Clarendon Press, 1987.

Hobsbawn, Eric J. *The Age of Revolution. Europe 1789–1848*. London: Weidenfeld and Nicolson, 1962.

Roider, Karl. *Baron Thugut and Austria's Response to the French Revolution*. Princeton, N.J.: Princeton University Press, 1987.

Rude, George. *Revolutionary Europé 1783–1815*. London: Fontana Press, 1985.

Schama, Simon. *Patriots and Liberators. Revolution in the Netherlands 1780–1813*. New York: Vintage, 1992.

Sutherland, D. M. G., *France 1789–1815. Revolution and Counterrevolution*. London: Fontana Press, 1985.

Tilly, Charles. *European Revolutions, 1492–1992*. Oxford: Blackwell, 1992.

FRENCH ROMANTICISM: ITS LITERARY LEGACY

From the 1820s to the 1850s, Romanticism dominated French literature. During these three decades, the strands of the pre-Romantic era, often intertwined with the late Enlightenment, became more pronounced, while new generations of artists dared to use innovative means of expression to convey their feelings and perceptions. For this new wave to happen, however, there also needed to be an acknowledgement of a need for renewal, and whom this should affect. This theme would remain a leitmotiv of French Romanticism's legacy. Among the educated classes, writers who met to theorize about the new wave generally felt that rather than a series of theoretical arguments, the public would be better served (and convinced) by a masterpiece. Alphonse Marie Louis de Lamartine's *Méditations* of 1820 became the starting point of the perception of French Romanticism. However, the author refused to become engaged in debates which split the Romantics into two wings, namely the conservative one, led by François-Auguste-René, Vicomte de Chateaubriand and speaking through its journal *Le Conservateur*; and liberals who expressed themselves through *Le Constitutionel*. Both sides tended to oppose themselves based on political preference and the adoption of classicist form, even though all were equally curious about Romantic ideas coming from abroad. A third group appeared in 1823, speaking through *La Muse française*, and seeking a middle ground between the two sides by arguing for the need to judge works based on their literary quality alone. This group evolved into a salon organized by Charles Nodier, at which Victor Hugo established his leadership. Yet the *Muse* group, drawing on Catholics and royalists, faced constant tensions with the liberals, who regrouped themselves in 1824 around *Le Globe* and the leadership of Stendhal. By the late 1820s, however, an agreement came about on building together the Romantic movement. The theories accompanying its development included the need to break with the rules of classicist literature as established under Louis XIV; a need to restitute a world closer to reality; and to develop a national style, using themes from the country's history separate from Roman, Greek, or other influences. Poetry, as Victor Hugo argued in 1822, was to become intimate, moving away from the typology of ideas expressed towards an examination of the ideas in themselves.

In the 1830s, French Romanticism was at its peak. In both literature and the arts, its advocates felt that it would shift social and cultural paradigms in such a way that history would be changed, the way the French Revolution had broken with the past. Conceiving a specifically Romantic philosophy, several thinkers came to believe that Romantic genius should not only enjoy special rights, but accomplish a series of duties. In so doing, however, they created a paradox. Whereas freedom was advocated for the technique of artistry, it was also abandoned when the purpose of the art form came up. Many—with the exception of Théophile Gautier and Alfred de Musset—felt that their mission was no longer moral, but now social and humanitarian. Instead of art for art's sake, art for the people was to become the new standard, one which assumed the writer was invested with a vision that only he could communicate to the masses. This also reflected the notion of an evolution of history associated with the contemporary period. Politically, this translated into a conciliation with the past rather than a rejection of it.

Indeed, many sympathizers felt that an outright rejection of the rationalist Enlightenment was insufficient to properly define the romantic movement, since their social concerns matched more closely those of the era leading to the French Revolution than those of the Restoration. By 1848, Romantics were closer to liberals than they were to conservatives. In so doing, however, some also rebelled against what they perceived as a conservative misuse of religion and advocated to a purer form of religious feeling perhaps through popular spontaneity.

This call for freedom from rules made romanticism not just the bastion of genius with a social mission, but also, ironically, of popular feeling. To reach it, poets would have to shed the old rules of the academies, and in so doing, they would sow the seeds of symbolism, which would appear after the Revolution of 1848 and the short-lived Second Republic. Then, the Romantic ideals of revolution would come to an end, but not their their influence on literature. Prose, for example, came to be seen as an intrinsic part of the artful expression rather than merely a support for it. This enrichment gave new dimensions to the symbolist wave of poetry, as exemplified by Charles Baudelaire.

Beaudelaire is sometimes considered to have defined a second romantic wave that rejected a special role for poets as vanguards of an improved humanity. Other historians suggest that the disillusionment of Romanticism offered a straight path to Realism, as exemplified by Champfleury's *Chien-Caillou* (1845), which argued the need to base art in what was *observable*, not beautiful. Yet the difference between the two movements was sometimes hard to determine; Baudelaire himself argued, in his *Salon de 1846*, that Romanticism was less about the choice of subjects or in the exact truth, but in how one felt, adding a decade later that any good poet was always a realist.

In fact, a further strand, the naturalist, also played a role in the evolution of the literary canon by suggesting that careful observation of nature may in fact awaken specific feelings, a notion that Honoré de Balzac would years later credit as a key to his inspiration. Indeed, through his *La Comédie humaine*, he assembled a moral world based on his understanding of the physical one. In other words, the application of analogy took over in the mid-nineteenth century, and played a role in symbolist works. Landscapes became bases of descriptions of inner feelings, but all of reality became associated with a moral significance. In other words, centering onto one's own feelings to reconstruct perceptions of the two worlds represented a further evolution of Romanticism and constituted a pre-announcement of Freudian theories of the unconscious and of the surrealist movement! After all, father of psychoanalysis Sigmund Freud cites Wilhelm Jensen's *Gradiva* (1903), a German work that was inspired by Théophile Gautier's *Arria Marcella* (1852).

Parallel to the naturalist wave, a tendency to dismiss the historical novel (especially in its classicist dimensions) became more pronounced, as can be seen through the works of Emile Zola and his followers. Yet the very freedoms early Romantics had advocated meant that their successors would use such claims to resurrect the historical narrative. As evidenced through the publication of several such series (like the publisher Armand Collin's *Bibliothèque de romans historiques*), the genre did well. A primary factor in this resurrection wasn't just a new evolution of aesthetic tastes, but the peculiar situation of France's Third Republic (1871–1940), which craved historical situations as a basis for social and political debate. Through these works, a reappearance of older historical themes became common. Few of these works, however, were great classics, but their popular appeal also reflects how Romanticism had become part of a mass culture associated with the second Industrial Revolution. A second kind of historical novel brought further the romantic ideal of escapism, replacing the travel narrative with a historical analogy. Finally, a third kind of historical novel took up the issue of *fin-de-siècle* pessimism through the recreation of certain historical epochs, like the decline of the roman empire. Together though, all three types exhibited a clear link to early French romanticism, even though critics sometimes chose to reject any such relationship, partly because of the popular appeal (and resulting lower quality) of many such novels.

Such disagreements over the evolving nature of Romanticism and its offspring takes another turn when evaluated through the work of Marcel Proust. As a primary representative of Romantic modernity (some have even called him a reactionary modernist), the author of *A la recherche du temps perdu* (*Remembrance of Things Past*) suggests, in fact, that the only unity that could harmonize the linkage between the moral and physical universes came through intimate feelings. His association of Venice with the notion of pain offers a perfect illustration of Romantic modernity, one that calls for harsh truths to be told but also for the emphasis of personal notions over generic ones. This particular expression of the French Romantic aesthetic, one that also played on the notion of nostalgia and memory, also made clear that while French Romanticism had hoped to be revolutionary, its protagonists in fact acted as reformers who made it evolve into a new literary tradition.

GUILLAUME DE SYON

See also **France, 1760 to the Revolution; France, 1815–1852; France: Revolution and Empire; French Revolution: Its Impact and Importance**

Bibliography

Brix, Michel. *Le romantisme français.* Louvain: Peeters, 1999.

Crossley, Ceri. *French Historians and Romaticism: Thierry, Guizot, the Saint-Simonians, Quinet, Michelet.* London: Routledge, 1993.

Fraisse, Luc. *L'Esthétique de Marcel Proust.* Paris: Sedes, 1995.

Malinowski, Wiesllaw Mateusz. *Le roman historique en France après le romantisme, 1870–1914.* Poznan: Wydanictwo Naukowe UAM, 1989.

Rosen, Charles, and Henri Zerner. *Romanticism and Realism: The Mythology of Nineteenth-Century Art.* New York: Viking, 1984.

Rosenthal, Léon. *Du romantisme au réalisme. Essai sur l'évolution de la peinture en France de 1830 à 1848*, 1914. Paris: Macula, 1987.

Tieghem, Philippe, van. *Le romantisme français.* Paris: Presses Universitaires de France, 1999 (first published 1944).

FRIEDRICH, CASPAR DAVID 1774–1840

German landscape painter

The foremost artist of German Romanticism devoted practically his entire career to painting landscapes. As a technician, Caspar David Friedrich devised alluring atmospheric effects of luminosity and mistiness; as a delineator of real-life scenes, he combined mimetic fidelity with poetic enhancement; and as a manipulator of symbols, he worked out a unique idiom of spiritual suggestion.

Friedrich was born in the Hanseatic harbor town of Greifswald on the southern rim of the Baltic, just by the large offshore island of Ruegen. His family was devoutly Protestant. His childhood was marked by two calamities, the death of his mother when he was seven, and the drowning of a younger brother in a skating accident when he was thirteen. These traumas have often been linked to the depressive tendencies which were to plague his adult life.

In his teens, Friedrich took private drawing lessons from a teacher at Greifswald University, Johann Gottfried Quistorp, who encouraged him to make pencil-and-pen sketches in the open air. Friedrich speedily developed a passion for the local coastline, with its desolate strands and windswept horizons punctuated by sailing ships. It is thought that his personal way of seeing the natural world was first shaped by contact with Quistorp's friend Gotthard Ludwig Kosegarten. This theologian and poet was renowned for his *Uferpredigten*, mystical sermons that he gave, and then later published, about the Ruegen seashore. Inspired by Johann Georg Hamann and Johann Gottfried von Herder, Kosegarten saw nature as a revelation of the divine, and assigned to the artist the role of mediator between this world and the next. In his verses, he also projected a mythic nationalism onto the Nordic landscape, identifying such things as oak groves and Neolithic burial sites as tokens of Germany's noble past. Friedrich's subsequent friendship with the Swedish philosopher and poet Thomas Thorild, a librarian at Greifswald University, was particularly decisive. Thorild envisaged nature less in Christian than in pantheistic terms, and saw the true artist as one who drew not on technical prowess, but on emotional authenticity. By the end of the eighteenth century, such associations were integral to the creative ethos of Romanticism. Friedrich was quite clearly attuned to the Zeitgeist, although, in their ideological projections, his drawings and paintings betray an unmistakable individualism, not to say idiosyncrasy.

When in 1794 Friedrich enrolled at the Copenhagen Academy of Art, he had already begun to disengage himself from the strictures of formal training and of obeisance to past masters. By early 1798 he had left Copenhagen and journeyed via Berlin to Dresden. The great Baroque city on the Elbe had long been a locus of artistic excellence, with its museums, gardens, and architectural treasures dating back to the Habsburg dynasty. Yet now it had assumed a fresh identity as the epicenter of Romantic creativity, associated with such figures as Heinrich von Kleist, Novalis, Gotthilf Heinrich Schubert, (whose celebrated lectures were published in 1808 as *Ansichten von der Nachtseite der Naturwissenschaften* [*Remarks on the Night-Side of the Natural Sciences*], and Ludwig Tieck. Contemporary Dresden culture was equally receptive to the attractions of landscape art and of the local countryside, and this prompted Friedrich's decision to settle in the city. He was to remain there for the rest of his life, joining the Dresden Academy in 1816 and taking a wife in 1818.

The slightly younger artist Philipp Otto Runge had similarly studied in Copenhagen before moving to Dresden in 1801. Friedrich had previously met Runge in Greifswald, yet a friendship never developed, and, despite a mutual interest in nature mysticism and the ideas of Kosegarten, their creative practices diverged quite markedly, with Runge inclining to allegorical figure painting and symmetrical ornamentation. In general, though, Friedrich's relations with younger Romantics were always cordial. He befriended the painter and physician Carl Gustav Carus, who in 1831 published *Neun Briefe über Landschaftsmalerei* (*Nine Letters on Landscape Painting*) as a treatise indebted to both Friedrich and Runge. Friedrich's closest friend and disciple was the Norwegian Johann Christian Claussen Dahl, who lodged permanently in Friedrich's house and often exhibited with him. Friedrich also acted as mentor to the young painter Ernst Ferdinand Oehme, insisting on imparting not technical advice but a spiritual outlook.

By the mid–1820s, signs of mental aberration had begun to emerge, with Friedrich exhibiting depressive and paranoid symptoms and accusing his wife of infidelity. As a physician, Carus offered therapy, but was rejected. In 1835 a stroke left Friedrich partially incapacitated, although he managed to continue working until his death, reverting to the small-scale watercolor and sepia formats of his early years.

Friedrich's first major oil painting caused a great controversy. *The Cross in the Mountains* (1807–08) was commissioned as an altarpiece for a private chapel and depicts a crucifix upon an alpine summit which is emphatically outlined against a sunset. The work outraged the reactionary critic Friedrich Basil von Ramdohr, who panned it in a review for the *Zeitung für die elegante Welt* (*Journal for the Elegant Classes*) in 1809. Ramdohr's classical eye was offended by the image's giddy viewpoint as well as the dramatic singularization of the mountain peak. Such anticlassical innovations announced Friedrich's commitment to a Romantic style of expression.

For all his avowed piety, Friedrich was no churchgoer, preferring to commune directly with the natural world, which he treated as a book of symbols pertaining to a Protestant narrative of life, suffering, death, and redemption. To lay bare the world's sacred inscriptions, he presented his landscapes and seascapes from striking angles and lit their surfaces so as to elicit their latent connotations. One specialist, Helmut Börsch-Supan, has seen Friedrich's pictures in terms of a strict repertoire of overt Christian symbols. On the other hand, the artist's often shadowy and misted prospects appear saturated with an undefined paganism or pantheism, with natural features such as broken trees or jagged rocks functioning as uncanny portents, replete with nameless emotionality.

Friedrich's art registers an obvious affinity with wild and inhospitable places—the empty beaches and moorlands of his native Pomerania, the dark mountains of the Harz region, and the uninhabited ranges of the Riesengebirge east of Dresden. A stubborn preference for Nordic scenes seems to have dissuaded him from ever visiting the Alps, while his refusal to find time for an Italian journey—seen as mandatory by most contemporary artists—may be explained in terms of an entrenched gloominess and asperity of character. Some commentators posit a direct connection between his morbid psyche and his predilection for snowscapes and desolate shores. Friedrich's almost unbearably bleak canvas *The Sea of Ice* (1823–25) was inspired by a real-life catastrophe, a shipwreck in the Arctic wastes; yet it prompts speculation as an oblique reminiscence of his brother's death in the ice or as an involuntary confession of emotional paralysis.

Friedrich was a highly competent draftsman, and his early sketchbooks testify to a fascination with motifs ranging from Gothic ruins to the rigging of Baltic sailing vessels, along with stark geological features and the intricacies of plants and trees. Apart from the occasional bird he hardly acknowledges the presence of wildlife, though he does admit human figures into his otherwise ultrastill tableaux. During the three decades of his life in Dresden, he made half a dozen major journeys to the Baltic, revisiting not only his home town, but other local sites such as the monastery at Eldena and the island of Ruegen, with its bizarre chalk formations. The masterly oil *The Chalk Cliffs at Ruegen* was completed in the Dresden studio in late 1818, following that summer's honeymoon trip to the island. It portrays three human figures on the grassy brink of a cliff, with columns of chalk jutting up from below against an expanse of blue sea and sky which reaches up to the overarching boughs of two trees. Tiny sailboats can be seen out at sea. The man on the right, his back turned to us, is perhaps the artist himself, lost in contemplation of a magical vista in which white chalk, blue water, and green foliage meet in a timeless transfiguration, a pictorial enactment of what Novalis saw as the "romanticization" of the world.

By inserting figures into his settings Friedrich seems less intent upon enlivening them or marking their scale than upon directing the viewer's gaze towards their metaphysical dimension. One of his most characteristic ploys is to stick a pair of pensive wanderers in front of an outlook, portraying them from behind and as if mesmerized. By contagion, as it were, their raptness incites the viewer to participate in the spectacle of the sublime. In the programmatic *The Wanderer above the Sea of Mist* (c. 1818), a lone mountaineer (probably an idealized self-projection) strikes a pose on a summit and gazes out at an oceanic turmoil of mists and protruding crags, an Ossianic prospect designed to evoke the challenge of that Absolute posited in the *Naturphilosophie* of Johann Gottlieb Fichte and Friedrich Wilhelm Joseph von Schelling. Such a painting translates the Romantic urge to test boundaries, to transcend present reality, to summon up an internal cosmos complementary to the outer one.

Commentators have rightly drawn attention to the imprint on Friedrich's imagery of a somewhat naive and impulsive patriotism. As a young man in the 1800s, Friedrich had deeply resented French imperialism and harbored a yearning for Germany's defunct grandeur. Gotthilf Heinrich Schubert recorded a conversation with Friedrich in around 1806, at the height of Napoleon's ascendancy, when the painter voiced his francophobia and, pointing to one of his paintings (since lost) that showed an eagle soaring above a sea of mist, made a long speech about Germanic pride and defiance. A painting of 1813–14 called *The Chasseur in the Forest* shows a French cavalry officer, alone and without his horse, standing in front of a forbidding forest; in the foreground, a raven perches on a tree stump. Contemporary viewers could hardly have missed the reference to Napoleon's disastrous Russian campaign. Remembering Kosegarten, Friedrich often uses oak trees or Gothic ruins as Germanic allusions. His fondness for Neolithic burial sites, usually collapsed dolmens encircled by trees and snow, suggests a kind of lurking tribalism. The artist specifically portrayed the graves of national heroes like Ulrich von Hutten or Arminius, the latter being the legendary freedom fighter who had resisted the Romans and in whose honor Heinrich von Kleist composed *Die Hermannsschlacht* (*The Battle of Arminius*, 1808), a dramatic text said to have been recited in Friedrich's studio. Throughout his life, Friedrich nurtured the same quirky, brooding patriotism even when censorship obliged him to tone down his allusions. One persistent and idiosyncratic motif is the ritualistic costume of his male figures, who sport heavy archaic berets and dark overcoats: in this way, long after the suppression of the *Burschenschaften* (the student leagues), Friedrich continued to register his solidarity with their response to Ernst Moritz Arndt's nationalistic call of 1814 to wear authentic "German" costume.

Well before his death Friedrich's reputation had begun to fade, and by the end of the nineteenth century he was all but forgotten. The modern appreciation of his work dates from 1906, when a major retrospective was held at the Nationalgalerie in Berlin. Thereafter, his popularity has grown at a steady pace,

with the result that his landscape imagery is now a familiar component of popular Western culture, as witness its relentless and indiscriminate recycling on posters and paperbacks. Central to its appeal is a kind of hypnotic attraction which owes much to Friedrich's talent for compositional drama and intense chiaroscuro. Not unlike the American luminist painter Frederic Edwin Church, Friedrich seems never to hold back from hyperbole in his approach to the sublime, with the result that some latter-day viewers dismiss his grandiose sunsets and mountain peaks as indigestible kitsch. Even so, his best work achieves a notable synthesis of the observed and the visionary, and may be counted one of the most distinctive artistic expressions of the Romantic era.

ROGER CARDINAL

Biography

Born in Greifswald, Pomerania, September 5, 1774. Studied at Copenhagen Art Academy, 1794–98. Moved to Dresden, 1798. First of several extensive visits to Ruegen, 1801. Met Philipp Otto Runge in Greifswald, 1801. Visited Northern Bohemia in 1807–08, the Riesengebirge in 1810, and the Harz in 1811. Joined Dresden Academy, 1816. Married in 1818. Gave lessons to several younger artists from 1820. Dahl resided in his house from 1823. First signs of depressive illness, 1824. Suffered a stroke, 1835. After several years of mental deterioration, died in Dresden, May 7, 1840.

Bibliography

Bauer, Fritz. *Caspar David Friedrich—ein Maler der Romantik.* Stuttgart, 1961.

Becker, Ingeborg Agnesia. *Caspar David Friedrich. Leben und Werk.* Stuttgart: Belser, 1983.

Bernhard, Marianne, ed. *Caspar David Friedrich: Das gesamte graphische Werk.* Hersching, n.d.

Blühm, Andreas, ed. *The Passage of Time: Philipp Otto Runge, Caspar David Friedrich.* Zwolle: Waanders, 1996.

Börsch-Supan, Helmut, and Karl Wilhelm Jähnig. *Caspar David Friedrich. Gemälde, Druckgraphik und bildmässige Zeichnungen.* Munich: Prestel, 1973.

———. *Caspar David Friedrich.* 4th ed. London: Thames and Hudson, 1987.

Brion, Marcel. *Peinture romantique.* Paris: Albin Michel, 1967.

Carus, Carl Gustav. *Briefe über Landschaftsmalerei.* Heidelberg: Lambert Schneider, 1972.

Dufour-Kowalska, Gabrielle. *Caspar David Friedrich aux sources de l'imaginaire romantique.* Lausanne: L'Age d'Homme, 1992.

Eimer, Gerhard. *Caspar David Friedrich. Auge und Landschaft.* Frankfurt am Main: Insel, 1974.

Emmrich, Irma. *Caspar David Friedrich.* Weimar, 1964.

Fiege, Gertrud. *Caspar David Friedrich in Selbstzeugnissen und Bilddokumenten.* Reinbek bei Hamburg: Rowohlt, 1977.

Grundmann, Günther. *Das Riesengebirge in der Malerei der Romantik,* 1924. Reprinted Munich, 1958.

Grütter, Tina. *Caspar David Friedrich (1774–1840). Bedeutung seiner Gesteinsdarstellungen.* Berlin: Dietrich-Reimer, 1986.

Hinz, Sigrid. *Caspar David Friedrich in Briefen und Bekenntnissen.* Berlin, 1984.

Hofmann, Werner. *Caspar David Friedrich.* London: Thames and Hudson, 2001.

———, ed. *Caspar David Friedrich 1774–1840.* Munich: Prestel, 1974.

Hofstätter, Hans, ed. *Caspar David Friedrich. Das gesamte graphische Werk.* 2 vol. Munich: Rogner und Bernhard, 1974.

Jensen, Jens Christian. *Caspar David Friedrich. Leben und Werk.* Cologne: Dumont Schauberg, 1974.

Koerner, Joseph Leo. *Caspar David Friedrich and the Subject of Landscape.* London: Reaktion and New Haven, Conn.: Yale University Press, 1990.

Krieger, Peter, ed. *Caspar David Friedrich. Die Werke aus der Nationalgalerie Berlin Staatliche Museen Preussischer Kulturbesitz.* Berlin: Nationalgalerie, 1985.

Landsberg, Madeleine. "Caspar David Friedrich, peintre de l'angoisse romantique," *Minotaure* 12–13 (1939).

Nemitz, Fritz. *Caspar David Friedrich. Die unendliche Landschaft.* Munich: F. Bruckmann, 1938.

Rewald, Sabine, ed. *The Romantic Vision of Caspar David Friedrich. Paintings and Drawings from the USSR.* New York: Metropolitan Museum of Art, 1990.

Rosenblum, Robert. *Modern Painting and the Northern Romantic Tradition: Friedrich to Rothko.* New York: Harper and Row, 1975.

Schmid, Wieland. *Caspar David Friedrich.* Cologne: DuMont Schauberg, 1992; English edn., New York: Abrams, 1995.

Vaughan, William. *German Romantic Painting.* 2nd ed. New Haven Conn.: Yale University Press, 1994.

Vaughan, William, Helmut Börsch-Supan, and Hans Joachim Neidhart. *Caspar David Friedrich 1774–1840.* London: Tate Gallery, 1972.

Wolfradt, Willi. *C. D. Friedrich und die Landschaft der Romantik.* Berlin, 1924.

Zschoche, Herrmann. *Caspar David Friedrich auf Rügen.* Amsterdam: Verlag der Kunst, 1998.

———. *Caspar David Friedrich im Harz.* Amsterdam: Verlag der Kunst, 2000.

FULLER, SARAH MARGARET 1810–1850

American writer and journalist

Among American women of the Romantic era, none was more quintessentially Romantic than Margaret Fuller. Deeply inspired by the German Romantic emphasis upon self-development and the French Romantic example of sensual feminism (as embodied by George Sand), Fuller wrote the first major feminist work in America. Her landmark *Woman in the Nineteenth Century* (1845), argued that women must fulfill themselves as individuals, not as subordinates to men. She wrote, "We would have every arbitrary barrier thrown down. We would have every path laid open to woman as freely as to man . . . let them be sea-captains, if you will. I do not doubt there are women well fitted for such office." Fuller edited the transcendentalist journal the *Dial* for two years before turning it over to her close friend Ralph Waldo Emerson, the great popularizer and interpreter of European Romanticism in America. But, departing from Emerson's American Romantic emphasis upon quietistic, individual self-exploration, Fuller's Romanticism developed more upon the line of the European model of social activism.

Fuller was the oldest of eight children; her father, a Harvard University–educated lawyer and stern New England puritan, believed women were intellectual equals of men and educated Fuller accordingly. She undertook a rigorous regimen of classical studies, later contending that the strain of these drills was the cause of the nightmares, headaches, and general nervousness that she suffered all her life. However, this thorough training did enable her to form lasting intellectual and emotional friendships with a number of young Harvard scholars and with the members of the transcendentalist circle.

Her father died when she was twenty-five, and she became the de facto head of the family, an obligation that forced her to become a schoolteacher. In 1836, she arranged a meeting with Emerson, whom she had been wanting to meet for some time, and she was delighted by their intellectual exchange. Fuller and Emerson were central figures of the transcendentalist movement. While the members' interests were remarkably diverse, they shared a common commitment to discovering the divinity within the soul and a broad impetus to be one's truest self. Her most significant contribution to this movement was as the first editor of the *Dial*, from 1840–42, but during this period she also published *Conversations with Goethe in the Last Years of His Life* (1839) and *Gunderöde* (1842).

In 1839–44, Fuller began what would prove to be an extraordinarily popular series of "conversations," or seminars for women. Each conversation was devoted to a philosophical question; Fuller would first elicit from the participants their ideas and would then expound her views, in a style that seemed to awaken in each listener a sense of her own potentialities. In the July 1843 issue of the *Dial*, she published a long essay, "The Great Lawsuit: Man versus Men: Woman versus Women" arguing that preventing women's self-development had had a deleterious effect upon the entire human race. A year later she expanded the essay into the book *Woman in the Nineteenth Century* (1845), her most significant piece of writing. In it Fuller addresses the question of gender essentialism, conceding that woman's nature is distinct from that of men, but arguing that aspects of both genders appear in all people. There is no wholly masculine man, she says, nor any wholly feminine woman, and the failure to allow people access to their full, true natures imprisoned both genders in unnaturally rigid roles. This work had a galvanizing effect on many American women, playing an important role in the social ferment that led to the first women's rights conventions.

After publishing a travel narrative, *Summer on the Lakes*, which grew out of a trip to the Midwest in the summer of 1843, Fuller began a career as the first self-supporting female member of the working press. Horace Greeley, editor of the *New York Tribune*, hired Fuller to write literary criticism and to report on social conditions. She addressed the plight of abandoned women, female convicts, immigrants, African Americans, the blind, and the insane, and she opposed such issues as the war in Mexico, southern slavery, northern prejudice, and capital punishment. In 1846, some of her essays and journalistic pieces were collected in *Papers on Literature and Art*. While in New

York Fuller fell in love with James Nathan, a German Jew; but he left the city in 1845.

Fuller's encounters with poverty and widespread social neglect in New York began a transformation in her consciousness from self-oriented idealist in the Emersonian vein to socially oriented realist and revolutionary activist. Experiences in Europe reinforced this new direction. In August 1846, Fuller sailed for Europe, where she worked as foreign correspondent for the *Tribune*. England shocked Fuller, who noted, "Poverty in England has terrors of which I never dreamed at home," and she was bitterly disappointed that such earlier heroes as Thomas Carlyle and William Wordsworth espoused tepid politics that ignored urgent appeals for social justice rising from the streets. However, Fuller made other, more revolutionary friends, including Giuseppe Mazzini and Adam Mickiewicz. In Paris, she also met George Sand, whose model of sexually liberated womanhood she admired. Inspired by Sand, Fuller was ready to explore and develop her sexual side. The opportunity soon arose in Rome with Giovanni Angelo Ossoli. A few months later Fuller was pregnant, with no one in whom she could confide, and marriage was out of the question because of opposition from Ossoli's family. After retreating to the Rieti, in the countryside, Fuller gave birth to a son.

Fuller left the baby with a wet nurse and returned to Rome in late November, to report on the extraordinary political events unfolding there. Like her friend Mazzini, Fuller promoted Italian unification. Under growing anti-Catholic pressure, the pope fled Rome, and in early 1849 the republic was established under Giuseppe Garibaldi. However, this republican experiment was short-lived. In July 1849, French forces defeated the republicans, and restored the pope to power. During the struggle for Rome, Fuller directed a hospital and, with Ossoli, played an active role in the siege.

Fuller returned to Rieti to to find that her nurse, believing the baby had been abandoned, was allowing it to starve. Ossoli and Fuller took their child to Florence, and in May 1850, decided to return to the United States to seek a publisher for her history of the Italian Revolution, which she had written following the fall of Rome.

They set sail from Livorno, reaching the waters off Fire Island, where the ship struck a sandbar offshore and slowly sank. Fuller's body was never found; the manuscript was also lost.

Fuller's deeply shocked friends mourned her lavishly, and William Ellery Channing, James Freeman Clarke, and Ralph Waldo Emerson produced an edition of her *Memoirs* in 1852. Their edition not only sanitized her private life, however, but minimized the quality and significance of her writing and her activism. It is only recently that the scandal of her sexuality has died down sufficiently to enable readers to hear the powerful and iconoclastic voice of this great American writer.

MARIANNE NOBLE

Biography

Born in Cambridgeport, Massachusetts, May 23, 1810. Eldest of nine children of Timothy Fuller, a lawyer and legislator, and Margaret Crane Fuller. Educated by her father and later at a finishing school in Groton, Connecticut. After her father's death in 1835, took charge of her younger siblings and supported the family financially. Taught at Bronson Alcott's experimental Temple School, Boston, 1836–37 and at the Greene Street School, Providence, Rhode Island, 1837–39. Published translation of *Eckermann's Conversations with Goethe*, 1839. Led "conversation" classes in Boston and Cambridge, 1839–1844. Met the writer Ralph Waldo Emerson and became significant figure in the transcendentalist movement. Cofounded and edited the *Dial*, a transcendentalist journal, 1840–42. Published *Summer on the Lakes*, 1844. Appointed literary critic of Horace Greeley's newspaper, the New York *Tribune*, 1844. Published *Woman in the Nineteenth Century*, 1845. Relationship with James Nathan in New York, 1845–46. Traveled to Europe, 1846. Worked as foreign correspondent for New York *Tribune* in England, Paris, and Italy, 1846–50. Started relationship with Giovanni Angelo Marchese Ossoli in Rome, 1847; gave birth to son, 1848, and possibly married Ossoli, 1849. Supported the revolution in Rome and wrote account of the history of the Roman Republic, 1848–1849. After the republic was suppressed, fled to Florence and sailed with Ossoli and son for America, May 1850. Died with Ossoli and son in shipwreck off Fire Island, coastal New York, July 19, 1850.

Selected Works

Summer on the Lakes, 1844. Edited by Susan Belasco Smith. Reprint, Urbana: University of Illinois Press, 1991.
Woman in the Nineteenth Century, 1845. Edited by Larry J. Reynolds; New York: W. W. Norton, 1998.
Papers on Literature and Art, 1846.
Memoirs of Margaret Fuller Ossoli. Edited by Ralph Waldo Emerson, William Ellery Channing, and James Freeman Clarke, 1852; reprint, 2 vols., New York: Burt Franklin, 1972.
The Essential Margaret Fuller. Edited by Jeffrey Steele. New Brunswick, N.J.: Rutgers University Press, 1992.

Bibliography

Blanchard, Paula. *Margaret Fuller: From Transcendentalism to Revolution*. New York: Delacorte, 1978.
Buell, Lawrence. *Literary Transcendentalism: Style and Vision in the American Renaissance*. Ithaca, N.Y.: Cornell University Press, 1973.
Capper, Charles. *Margaret Fuller: An American Romantic Life*. Vol. 1, *The Private Years*. New York: Oxford University Press, 1992.
Chevigny, Bell Gale. *The Woman and the Myth: Margaret Fuller's Life and Writings*. Rev. ed. Boston: Northeastern University Press, 1994.
Douglas, Ann. *The Feminization of American Culture*. New York, Alfred A. Knopf, 1977.
Kolodny, Annette. "Inventing a Feminist Discourse: Rhetoric and Resistance in Margaret Fuller's *Woman in the Nineteenth Century*," *New Literary History* 25 (1994): 355–82.
Myerson, Joel, ed. *Critical Essays on Margaret Fuller*. Boston: K. Hall, 1980.
Reynolds, Larry J. *European Revolutions and the Literary Renaissance*. New Haven, Conn.: Yale University Press, 1988.
von Mehren, Joan. *Minerva and the Muse: A Life of Fuller*. Amherst: University of Massachusetts Press, 1994.
Zwarg, Christina. *Feminist Conversations: Fuller, Emerson, and the Play of Reading*. Ithaca, N.Y.: Cornell University Press, 1995.

FUR TRADERS DESCENDING THE MISSOURI 1845

Painting by George Caleb Bingham

The frontier wilderness has always been an intensely Romantic source of creative inspiration and mythology in American culture. Michel Guillaume Jean de Crèvecoeur, the Frenchman who lived in America from 1759 till 1790 and wrote under the name J. Hector Saint Jean Crèvecoeur, penned *Letters from an American Farmer*, describing the gradual movement west from such coastal cities as Boston, Charleston, and New York, to the more primitive settlements of the Midwest, and finally on to the frontier. In answering his own question, "What is an American?" Crèvecoeur included those adventurous native-born conquistadors who prepared the forests and prairies for the advancing merchants, preachers, and schoolmarms: the trappers, traders, hunters, and mountain men. The frontier theme, with its noble savages and hardy pioneers, has long been integral to American art and literature, as well as formalized in American scholarship by Frederick Jackson Turner.

Thus, when George Caleb Bingham exhibited *Fur Traders Descending the Missouri* in 1845, he tapped into a vital source for the American imagination. Many of these men on the margins of civilization spent their winters in the mountains tending their traps and living with Indians, paddling in the spring down rivers like the Platte and the Missouri to settlements where they sold their winter's harvest of pelts. The title by which Bingham's first masterpiece is now known is actually a euphemism, concealing the relationship stated in the original title, *French Trader and His Half-Breed Son*. The new title takes the Old World out of the picture, although it was the French who initiated the fur trade in the New World, and it makes the relationship of the two men more palatable to genteel viewers. The new title was a wise marketing move. Moreover, the new title emphasizes the romantic associations surrounding the Missouri River, described by Levis Thomas and J. C. Wild as "the Nile of the New World, for it more nearly resembles that famous stream, than any other river in the Western Hemisphere, and, like the Nile it rises periodically and suddenly and inundates a large tract of country." Bingham himself said in a letter that "surely [the Missouri] is the greatest river in the world, except the Nile." Commenting on associations with the Nile, Nancy Rash has remarked, that "Even the mysterious animal in the prow, on whose species critics still cannot agree, may allude to a river of another ancient civilization. It sits like a jackal in the prow of the Egyptian boat of the dead, evoking the Nile, to which the Missouri River was often compared. . . ." *Fur Traders on the Missouri* was followed by a series of splendid riverboat paintings that soon inspired Bingham's sobriquet as the "Missouri Artist." The new paintings are vivid and exuberant, but they record contemporary river life rather than the rich history behind *Fur Traders*.

When Bingham sent *Fur Traders* to the American Art Union in 1845, it was accompanied by two landscapes and *Indian Figure—Concealed Enemy*, a depiction of an Osage brave with a rifle peering over a bluff at the river below. Henry Adams has observantly suggested that *Fur Traders* and *Concealed Enemy* are pendants. They were painted at the same time, are the same size, and, seen together, portray a popular theme: the Indian and frontiersman as adversaries. Adams notes that, in 1844,

Bingham had painted for a Whig convention in Missouri a series of banners (all now lost but known from newspaper descriptions) representing, in effect, Indian savagery confronted by the advance of civilization, a representation revealing, Adams says, Bingham's own "emotional sympathies." Adams's claim that *Fur Traders* "describes different aspects of the progression towards civilization as one scans the composition from left to right" may advance his thesis too boldly, but his reading of the painting as a pendant to *Concealed Enemy* remains original and stimulating.

Bingham's works abound in allusions and borrowings. *Concealed Enemy* clearly owes a lot to one of J. C. Wild's lithographs included in *The Valley of the Mississippi Illustrated* (1841), and both Adams and Rash spell out the similarities in *Concealed Enemy* to the landscape mode of Claude Lorraine and in *Fur Traders* to that of Salvator Rosa. The Claudian mode, "calm, atmospheric," and the Salvatoran, "rugged and blasted," in Rash's words, work together to create a satisfying complementariness for the two paintings. Charles Collins identifies another possible inspiration for *Fur Traders* in Charles Deas's *The Trapper and His Family* (1845), and Rash points to the parallels in the postures of Bingham's figures and the seated Christ and Peter in Raphael's *Miraculous Draught of Fishes* (c. 1514).

Parallels and influences aside, *Fur Traders Descending the Missouri* remains a gorgeous rendition of Romantic atmosphere and landscape. The placid river surface, with its carefully painted mirror images, merges into a sky suffused with rosy light to create a setting in which the two men and their captive mascot in the prow seem right at home in the barely explored New World. Just what animal the "mascot" represents has occasioned much pseudozoological commentary, with a bear cub probably leading the parade of a fox, a cat, and even an owl on to Bingham's ark. The later, less skillful *The Trappers' Return* (1851)

George Caleb Bingham, *Fur Traders Descending the Missouri*. Reprinted courtesy of the Bridgeman Art Library.

may not definitively establish the bear cub at the helm but it at least eliminates the owl and reshapes the ark as clearly a pirogue, or boat fashioned from a hollowed-out log.

Fur Traders Descending the Missouri ranks with James Fenimore Cooper's Leatherstocking Tales, his five novels chronicling the American frontier in the person of the Deerslayer Natty Bumppo, as a contribution to the American myth of the frontier.

The New World glows in Bingham's vision, although it perhaps may be a fallen paradise, when its implications regarding the concealed enemy are fully realized. But the vision painted on the canvas remains a Romantic Eden, still only slightly blurred in Americans' imaginative re-creation of their past.

FRANK DAY

Work

Fur Traders Descending the Missouri. 1845. Oil on canvas, 74.3 × 92.2 cm. Metropolitan Museum of Art, New York.

Bibliography

Adams, Henry. "A New Interpretation of Bingham's *Fur Traders*," *The Art Bulletin*, 65 (1983): 675–80.

Bloch, E. Maurice. *George Caleb Bingham: The Evolution of an Artist*. 2 vols. Berkeley and Los Angeles: University of California Press, 1967.

———. *The Paintings of George Caleb Bingham: A Catalogue Raisonné*. Columbia: University of Missouri Press, 1986.

Collins, Charles D. "A Source for Bingham's *Fur Traders Descending the Missouri*," *Art Bulletin* 66 (1984): 678–81.

Demos, John. "George Caleb Bingham: The Artist as Social Historian," *American Quarterly* 17 (1965): 218–28.

Glanz, Dawn. *How the West Was Drawn: American Art and the Settling of the Frontier*. Ann Arbor: University of Michigan Press, 1982.

McDermott, James F. *George Caleb Bingham: River Portraitist*. Norman: University of Oklahoma Press, 1959.

Rash, Nancy. *The Paintings and Politics of George Caleb Bingham*. New Haven, Conn.: Yale University Press, 1991.

Rogers, Meyric R. *Four American Painters: George Caleb Bingham, Winslow Homer, Thomas Eakins, Albert P. Ryder*. New York: Arno Press, 1970.

Rusk, Fern. *George Caleb Bingham: The Missouri Artist*. Jefferson City, Mo.: Hugh Stephens, 1917.

Shapiro, Michael Edward, Barbara Groseclose, Elizabeth Johns, Paul C. Nagel, and John Wilmerding. *George Caleb Bingham*. New York: Abrams, for the Saint Louis Art Museum, 1990.

Sunder, John E. *The Fur Trade on the Upper Missouri, 1840–1865*. Norman: University of Oklahoma Press, 1965.

Thomas, Lewis F., and J. C. Wild. *The Valley of the Mississippi Illustrated*, 1841. Reprint St. Louis: Joseph Garnier, 1948.

Tyler, Ron. *American Frontier Life: Early Western Painting and Prints*. New York: Abbeville Press, 1987.

FUSELI, HENRY 1741–1825

Swiss-born painter

Though one of the foremost painters of the Romantic period working in England, Fuseli's original intellectual background was in art history, philosophy, theology, and literature. His early critical influences included the neoclassical ideas of Anton Raphael Mengs and Johann Joachim Winckelmann while his literary interests lay in the works of Dante Alighieri, Homer, John Milton, William Shakespeare, and the *Nibelungenlied*. Ordained as a Zwinglian minister in 1761, Fuseli was forced to leave Switzerland in 1762 and traveled in Germany with his friend Johann Kaspar Lavater, the future writer on physiognomy. Arriving in London in 1764, he established himself as a professional writer. His earliest published works were a translation into English of Winckelmann's *Gedanken über die Nachahmung der griechischen Werke in der Malerei und Bildhauerkunst* (*Reflections on the Paintings and Sculptures of the Greeks*, 1765), followed by *Remarks on the Writings and Conduct of J.-J. Rousseau* (1767), whom he had met in Paris the previous year. He also wrote essays and reviews, often anonymously, many of which remain unidentified. In London he was drawn to the theater, particularly the performances of David Garrick. Naturally this intellectual legacy revealed itself in his art, a medium to which he turned in the mid-1760s following the encouragement of Joshua Reynolds. This legacy is seen most dramatically in the famous works depicting scenes from Shakespeare, such as *The Three Witches* (1783), *Lady Macbeth Sleepwalking* (1784), and *Titania and Bottom* (1790). A man of great intelligence and strong, sometimes tempestuous, character, he was equally unafraid to paint subjects of his own invention, and one of these, *The Nightmare* (1781), is his most famous and helped establish his contemporary reputation.

The early influence of Mengs and Winckelmann was rejected by Fuseli during his eight-year residence in Italy from 1770, during which time he was greatly impressed by Rome's classical statuary and the works of the mannerist movement. It was Michelangelo, however, and his frescoes in the Sistine Chapel, that had the strongest influence on the growth of Fuseli the painter. Developing his own distinctive style focused on the figure in dramatic, theatrical poses, he became the center of a group of artists in Rome. By 1773 his work was being acclaimed as the painterly correlate of the German literary Sturm und Drang (storm and stress) movement. Lavater proclaimed, "He is everything in extremes—always an original; his look is lightning, his word a thunderstorm; his jest is death, his revenge, hell." Lavater's attempts to interest Fuseli in the work of Johann Gottfried von Herder and Johann Wolfgang von Goethe seemingly failed, though on reading a defense of the image in poetry in one of Fuseli's letters, Goethe observed, "What fire and fury the man has in him!" He was equally impressed by Fuseli's drawings and paintings, which he saw in Zurich in 1779, purchasing some himself. Goethe initially expressed a keen interest in collaborating with Fuseli, but by the end of the century was criticizing him for "addressing himself to the imagination," which he thought was the preserve of the poet: "With Fuseli, poetry and painting are always at war with one another . . . one values him as a poet, but as a plastic artist he always makes his audience impatient."

Henry Fuseli, *Satan and the Birth of Sin*. Reprinted courtesy of AKG.

Fuseli's interest in the fantastic and the dreamlike has led him to be bracketed with William Blake. The two men became friends around 1787, and Blake made some powerful engravings from Fuseli's work. Blake famously described Fuseli as the only man "[w]ho did not make me almost spew," and Fuseli's iconoclastic sayings provided the inspiration for Blake's aphoristic proclamations in *The Marriage of Heaven and Hell* (1793). Fuseli's attempts in 1799 to launch an illustrated Milton Gallery in emulation of the printer John Boydell's Shakespeare Gallery, though a financial failure, was a likely inspiration for Blake's comparable project. But following the events of the French Revolution the formerly rationalist Fuseli became increasingly conservative, and more distanced from the political Blake. This is evidenced in Fuseli's acceptance (against Reynold's wishes) into the Royal Academy in 1790, an institute which he had formerly criticized as a promoter of mediocrity.

Despite his prominence in the Romantic period, Fuseli's style and art criticism as revealed in his lectures to the Royal Academy was fundamentally classicist, and not Romantic. While he believed genius "discovers new materials of nature or combines the known with novelty," it was talent which "arranges, cultivates, [and] polishes the discoveries of genius." Blake, by contrast, expressed the opinion that "Talent thinks, genius sees." In pri-

vate, Fuseli reflected in 1796 that though Blake "thinks he has a great deal of invention," yet "fancy is the end not the means in his designs."

Inaccurately claimed by Sidney Colvin in 1873 as "the first of the Romantics," Fuseli's work had a mixed reception among other Romantic writers and artists of the period. Fuseli read and enjoyed the works of Lord Byron and William Cowper, and Mary Wollstonecraft fell in love with the painter. But William Hazlitt and Leigh Hunt were both strong critics of his work, and his technique came under attack for its "faulty" colouring and gloomy shadowing. His drawings were often better received, however. Erasmus Darwin, whose poem "Botanical Garden" Fuseli helped to illustrate, wrote how the "daring pencil of Fuseli transports us beyond the boundaries of nature, and ravishes us with the charm of the most interesting novelty."

DAVID HAYCOCK

Biography

Born Johann Heinrich Füssli in Zurich, February, 6 1741. Son of Johann Caspar Füssli, painter and art critic. Studied theology and ordained into the Zwinglian ministry, 1761; left Switzerland, 1762 and toured Germany; studied art in Berlin, 1763. Visited London, 1764; worked as a translator; encouraged by Joshua Reynolds to abandon philosophy and theology and become a painter. Studied art in Rome, 1770–78. Returned to Zurich, 1778; met and fell in love with Anna Landolt; returned to settle permanently in London after unsuccessful courtship, 1779. Met and formed friendship with William Blake, around 1787. Married Sophia Rawlins, 1788. Achieved artistic recognition with his painting *Nightmare* (1781) after its exhibition at the Royal Academy, 1789. Worked for John Boydell's Shakespeare Gallery, 1789. Elected an associate member of the Royal Academy, 1790; professor of painting at the Royal Academy, 1799; keeper of the Royal Academy, 1804. Died in London, April 16, 1825.

Bibliography

Knowles, John. *The Life and Writings of Henry Fuseli, Esq.* 3 vols. London: H. Colbun and R. Bentley, 1831.

Mason, Eudo Colecestra. *The Mind of Henry Fuseli: Selections from his Writings with an Introductory Essay.* London: Routledge and Paul, 1951.

Powell, Nicolas. *The Drawings of Henry Fuseli.* London: Faber and Faber, 1951.

Pressly, Nancy L. *The Fuseli Circle in Rome: Early Romantic Art of the 1770s.* New Haven, Conn.: Yale University Press, 1979.

Schiff, Gert. *Johann Heinrich Füssli: Oeuvrekatalog.* Zurich: 2 vols. Verlag Berichthaus, 1973.

———. *Henry Fuseli.* London and Hamburg: Tate Gallery Publication, 1975.

Tomory, Peter. *The Life and Art of Henry Fuseli.* London: Thomas and Hudsen, 1972.

G

GAINSBOROUGH, THOMAS 1727–1788

British painter

Since Thomas Gainsborough died early in the Romantic period, he could perhaps be considered at best a pre-Romantic, possessed of some influence on the ideas and practice of Romanticism, particularly if Romanticism is regarded as a movement based in feeling as opposed to the intellect; Gainsborough was not a thinker, nor involved in any intellectual movement in art. He was not trained formally in the classical tradition, and he did not, as was the custom, visit Italy to study the ancient and Renaissance artists. Precociously gifted, he began working in London at the age of thirteen with a French rococo engraver, Hubert Gravelot.

Sir Joshua Reynolds, the doyen of British painters of the late eighteenth century and intellectual arbiter of English art, rather despaired of Gainsborough. Reynolds, as president of the Royal Academy, spoke of Gainsborough shortly after his death, in his fourteenth annual address to that body (December 19, 1788) in a way that shows why Gainsborough is sometimes considered a harbinger of the Romantic movement. Reynolds acknowledged Gainsborough's success, but deplored his lack of serious ambition. He admitted that Gainsborough's work with landscapes and simple human subjects was excellent, but declared that his skill with such subjects was consistent with his lack of education, in particular his lack of Italian study. Reynolds made a point of gently criticizing the loose painting, the unfinished nature of Gainsborough's works, the "scratches and marks," the uncouth and shapeless appearance of his canvas when viewed closely; he admitted, however, that such messiness miraculously resolved itself at a distance, and conceded that it made for a "lightness" that worked well for modest subjects.

However, despite his technical faults, Gainsborough was one of the most popular portrait painters of the late eighteenth century, and the greatest exponent of the French rococo in England. His gift for expressing playful, elegant beauty was part of his Romantic inclination. The exploration of character is also one of the main ambitions of Romantic artists. Gainsborough's portraits are evocations of charm, intense beauty, and sometimes human fragility, as seen in *The Painter's Daughters Chasing a Butterfly* (1757–58), although occasionally a deeper attempt at character was successful, for example in *Mary, Duchess of Montagu* (1768).

Gainsborough's greater contribution lies in his landscapes. From early on, he sketched landscapes, aware that such work was in itself of no interest to the public, although they seemed to manifest an enthusiasm for the same if produced by continental artists. The English painter was confined almost solely to portraiture, and Gainsborough had great success in this area. He often used the English countryside as a background for his portraits, with considerable shaping and styling, in a lively, spontaneous rendering that some of his contemporaries considered much too informal and unfinished. He developed an immediately recognizable idyllic England, inhabited by his subjects lounging dreamily in elegant dress before softly defined masses of foliage and clouds, a style exemplified in the portrait of *Lady Brisco* (1776). Occasionally he would vary the topic to celebrate the life of simple rural folk, as in *The Cottage Door* (1780). He constantly complained about having to do portraits to make a living, although it must be said that his landscape backgrounds, always highly stylized and clearly identifiable as artistic renderings, were much appreciated. He made countless studies of nature, which he often gave to friends. Nature might sometimes be tender, sometimes stormy, often poetic, but always based clearly on the English countryside. By the late 1760s, his landscapes and the wooded backgrounds of his portraits began to show an increasing Romanticism. There are also a few paintings of mountain scenes, notably *Woody Mountain Landscape* (1783), that hint at the more intense contemplation of the sublime aspects of nature. Gainsborough's developing interest in a rougher natural order was expressed with sketch-like informality; these paintings were contemplated by the Romantic landscape painters, and later by the Impressionists.

Always a successful painter of children, he developed a line of paintings in his later years that he called "fancy pictures," mainly studies of rural children, such as *A Peasant Girl Gathering Sticks* (1772). These were subsequently to ally him to the rural themes of the Romantic poet William Wordsworth.

It is, perhaps, best to think of Gainsborough not as a painter committed to the expression of Romantic principles, but as a painter of pictures full of powerfully emotive settings and handsome, sometimes beautiful, people, rendered in rich colours and expressive of human feeling. Much of this can be traced back to the confluent influences on him of Dutch landscape art (particularly that by Salomon van Ruisdael), rococo elegance and sophistication, the colourism and swagger of Anthony van Dyck and Peter Paul Rubens, and the sentimental urchins of Bartolomé Murillo.

CHARLES PULLEN

Biography

Born in Sudbury, Suffolk; baptized May 14, 1727. Youngest son of John Gainsborough, wool worker. Trained and worked in studio of engraver Hubert Gravelot in London, 1740–c. 1747. Married Margaret Burr, illegitimate daughter of the Duke of Beaufort, 1746; they had two daughters. Returned to Sudbury; settled in Ipswich as a portrait and landscape painter, 1752. Moved to Bath, 1759. Established fashionable portrait studio in Bath; met and became friend of actor David Garrick. Exhibited in London regularly, 1760s onward. Invited to become a foundation member of the Royal Academy in London, 1768. Settled in Pall Mall, London, 1774. First royal portrait commission, 1781. After disagreement with the Royal Academy, refused to exhibit there after 1784. Died in London, August 2, 1788.

Bibliography

Crown, P. "Portraits and Fancy Pictures by Gainsborough and Reynolds: Contrasting Images of Childhood," *British Journal for Eighteenth-Century Studies* 7 (1984): 159–67.

Hawes, Louis. *Presences of Nature: British Landscape 1780–1830.* New Haven, Conn.: Yale Center for British Art, 1982.

Hayes, John. *The Landscape Paintings of Thomas Gainsborough.* London: Philip Wilson, 1983.

Millar, Oliver. *Thomas Gainsborough.* New York: Harper and Brothers, 1949.

Paulson, Ronald. "A Metaphysics of the Countryside," *Times Literary Supplement* (1983): 283–84.

Pevsner, Nikolaus. *The Englishness of English Art.* London: Penguin, 1964.

Quennell, Peter. *Romantic England: Writing and Painting 1717–1851.* London: Weidenfeld and Nicolson, 1970.

Reynolds, Sir Joshua. *Fifteen Discourses Delivered in the Royal Academy.* London: J. M. Dent, 1960.

Rosenthal, Michael. *The Art of Thomas Gainsborough.* New Haven, Conn.: Yale University Press, 1999.

Waterhouse, Ellis. *British Painting in the Eighteenth Century.* London: The British Council, 1958.

———. *Gainsborough.* London: Spring Books, 1958.

Woodall, Mary Woodall. *Gainsborough.* London: Blandford Press, 1970.

GALT, JOHN 1779–1839

Scottish novelist

Often ranked as a minor literary figure and a "provincial" writer, and generally overshadowed by Sir Walter Scott, John Galt produced a series of works that made an original contribution to the development of early-nineteenth-century fiction. His novels, and particularly the so-called Tales of the West, celebrated the rural world of western Scotland by narrating stories of local events and characters and by making use of Scottish vernacular. His depiction of Scottish society derived much of its sociological insight from the Scottish Enlightenment but, in many respects, also engaged with the Romantic interest in primitivism.

Galt became a writer almost by accident, and throughout his life his career as novelist was often interrupted in favor of mercantile pursuits. Until at least 1819, he seemed destined for an undistinguished career as a hack writer, trying his hand at virtually everything, including two travel books, drawn from his journey through the Mediterranean of 1809–11, during which he met Lord Byron; biographies of Cardinal Wolsey and Benjamin West; a volume of plays; a number of schoolbooks; plus poetry, articles, and tales for various periodicals.

It was a series of tales serialized in the *Blackwood's Edinburgh Magazine*, published with no great pretension from June 1820 to February 1821, which provided Galt with his first rewarding literary venture. *The Ayrshire Legatees*, published in book form in June 1821, appeared as letters written by a Scottish minister, the Reverend Zacariah Pringle, and his family to their Scottish friends, relating their impressions on their first visit to London. Galt's work presented from a personal perspective the sense of estrangement and disorientation of a Scot moving from a primitive and backward society to the modernity and progress of the capital.

Annals of the Parish (1821) heralded Galt's most productive phase and, in its subject, style, and language, set a pattern for all his works for the following two years. The main elements of *Annals* were drawn from Galt's own boyhood experiences, and centered around the environment of his native Ayrshire. Micah Balwhidder, a country curate, gives a series of brief yearly accounts on the life of the parish of Dalmailing (the first of Galt's fictitious settings, which echoed the places of his youth) from 1760 to 1810. The history of humble, ordinary characters and small-scale events in a provincial setting is cast against the background of Scotland's recent past, but Galt's characters are always aware of external, far-reaching events such as the American War or the French Revolution.

As he later wrote in his *Autobiography* (1833), Galt aimed at writing not novels but "theoretical histories of society" (2: 220). He was very interested in the dynamics of social change, and his works depict Scottish rural society at a time of drastic transformation. The chronicles of his Scottish characters cover the late eighteenth and early nineteenth centuries, the period of the Industrial Revolution, commercial expansion, and agricultural and political reforms. During this period, the poor and provincial life of Scotland was evolving into a more modern society. Significantly, Galt's writing was so vivid and convincing in its realism that historians such as G. M. Trevelyan and Eric Hobsbawm have cited *Annals of the Parish* as a primary reference for the extent of social and economic change undergone by Scotland at the turn of the century. As novels, Galt's "theoretical histories" generally lack a proper plot, as Galt himself acknowledged. Yet what makes them more significant as novels is Galt's linguistic skills and the humor and comic characteristics of many of his subjects.

The Provost (1822) follows Galt's characteristic first-person format, but this time the focus is on local politics. The protagonist, James Pawkie, is an able country politician who exerts control over the small community of Gudetown, which is none other than Irvine, Galt's own birthplace. *The Entail* (1822), again with a plot set in Scotland, has a much darker mood than both *Annals* and *The Provost*, and touches on certain core aspects of Romantic sensibility more than any other of Galt's works.

The fictions of Balwhidder and Pawkie, although subjective and unremittingly self-centered, ultimately express a realistic and "common sense" narrative, to the point that many readers believed them to be real-life accounts. On the other hand, the narration of *The Entail* centers on the psychological portrait of the obsessive Claud Walkinshaw, who struggles all his life to regain the family lands and to entail them to his descendents. The portrait of Claud's egocentricity and moral indifference was Galt's version of the solipsism of Manfred and the other Byronic heroes. Galt, however, condemns Claud's greed and obsession and eventually, after his death, his widow, Leddy Grippy, emerges as a lively and spontaneous figure, gifted with good sense and sparkling humor. Not surprisingly, *The Entail* was Galt's most admired work. It won the unconditional praise of Samuel Taylor Coleridge and Walter Scott, while Byron was reduced to tears and judged Galt's portrait of Leddy Grippy one of the most original women figures in the history of literature.

Ringan Gilhaize (1823), written mainly as a response to Scott's harsh treatment of the Scottish Covenanters in *Old Mortality*, was the first of a cycle of historical novels, but Galt's fortunes were on the wane, and his later novels, some of which dealt with Canada, where he lived for most of the late 1820s, are now forgotten. Of note is his biography *Life of Byron* (1830), which significantly avoided the posthumous hostility affecting Byron's reputation.

Seen in the context of contemporary Scottish and English fiction, Galt's novels contribute an original dimension of small-scale domesticity set within an informed context of wider social and historical change. His use of Scottish vernacular has often made his novels difficult to read for most non-Scottish readers, but at the time the popularity he gained was such that for a short period he was Scott's most formidable rival in the field of Scottish fiction. The Tales of the West were accused of vulgarity by Scott, Margaret Oliphant, and Francis Jeffrey, the editor of the *Edinburgh Review* who leveled a similar charge at William Wordsworth and the Lake Poets. Indeed, while Galt's avowed realism and moralism have problematized his status as a typical Romantic writer, his use of the Scots language, his nationalistic

overtones, and the often tragicomic qualities of his characters grant him a privileged place in Romantic prose fiction.

MASSIMILIANO DEMATA

Biography

Born in Irvine, Ayrshire, May 2, 1779. Son of a sea-captain. Educated at Irvine Grammar School and at schools in Greenock. Worked as a clerk at Greenock Customs House, 1796, and for James Miller and Company, Greenock, 1796–1804. Moved to London, 1804; studied law at Lincoln's Inn. Began working as a magazine writer; engaged in business ventures in London, 1805–8. Declared bankrupt, 1808. Traveled on commercial commission to the Mediterranean and the Near East, 1809–11; met Lord Byron. Worked as agent for a merchant in Gibraltar, 1812–13. Married Elizabeth Tilloch, 1813: three sons. Editor, *Political Review*, London, 1812 and *New British Theatre* monthly, London, 1814–15. Traveled to France and the Netherlands on commercial business, 1814. Contributor, *Blackwood's Magazine*, from 1819. Secretary, Royal Caledonian Society, 1815. London lobbyist for Edinburgh and Glasgow Union Canal Company, 1819–20, and later for other Scottish commercial enterprises. Achieved literary success with Tales of the West, most of which published by Blackwood, 1820–23. Employed in several failed commercial speculations. Moved to Canada in 1826, as secretary and later superintendent to the Canada Land Company, a settlement organization formed for the purchase of crown land. Opened passage through forest between Lakes Huron and Erie; founded town of Guelph, Upper Canada (now Ontario), 1827. Dismissed and imprisoned for debt after his return to England, 1829. Resumed literary career, including writing novels based on his Canadian experiences. Editor, *The Courier* newspaper, London, 1830; contributor, *Fraser's Magazine*, from 1830. Returned to Greenock, 1834. Died in Greenock, April 11, 1839.

Selected Works

The Ayrshire Legatees. 1821.
Annals of the Parish. 1821.
Sir Andrew Wylie, of That Ilk. 1822.
The Provost. 1822.
The Entail, or, the Lairds of Grippy. 1822.
Ringan Gilhaize; or, the Covenanters. 1823.
The Last of the Lairds. 1826. Reprinted from the original manuscript. Edited by Ian A. Gordon. Edinburgh: Scottish Academic Press, 1976.
Life of Byron. 1830.
The Member. 1832.

Bibliography

Costain, Keith M. "Theoretical History and the Novel: The Scottish Fiction of John Galt," *English Literary History*, 43 (1976): 342–65.
Costain, Keith M. "The Spirit of the Age and the Scottish Fiction of John Galt," *The Wordsworth Circle* (1980): 98–106.
Frykman, Eryk. *John Galt's Scottish Stories, 1820–1823*. Uppsala: Uppsala Lundequistska Bokhandeln, 1959.
Gardiner, Marguerite Countess of Blessington, *Conversations of Lord Byron with the Countess of Blessington*, London, 1834.
Gordon, Ian A. *John Galt. The Life of a Writer*. Edinburgh: Oliver & Boyd, 1972.
Hart, Francis Russell. "John Galt." In *The Scottish Novel: A Critical Survey*. London: John Murray, 1978.

Lyell, Frank Hallam. *A Study of the Novels of John Galt*. Princeton, N.J.: Princeton University Press, 1942.

Scottish Literary Journal, 8, no. 1 (1981); special Galt issue.

Scottish Literary Journal, 24, no. 1 (1997); special Scott and Galt issue.

Whatley, Chistopher A., ed. *John Galt 1779–1979*. Edinburgh: Ramsay Head, 1979.

GARCÍA GUTIÉRREZ, ANTONIO 1813–1884

Spanish dramatist

Antonio García Gutiérrez was a poet as well as a dramatist, but his real achievements lie in the theater, for which he also translated French plays and wrote librettos for *zarzuela* (musical comedies).

His 1836 play *El trovador* (*The Troubadour*), later adapted to the opera by Giuseppe Verdi, was famously the first occasion on which a Spanish author was called to the stage to receive applause. The work follows Ángel de Saavedra (Duque de Rivas) *Don Alvaro* in its multiple verse meters modeled on golden-age drama combined with sections of prose. This flexible and diverse expressivity is reinforced by the extension of the traditional three acts to the French five, each of which has an emblematic title after the fashion of Victor Hugo. No act passes without a scene change. The author's dynamically organic approach to the theater, influenced by August Wilhelm von Schlegel, is seen most strikingly in the radical division into two storylines: though her tale is mentioned briefly earlier, the key figure of Azucena, the gypsy, does not appear until act III. In a pattern of broken mirroring, when the two plots do come together at the end, the two women who love Manrique (his supposed mother Azucena and his lover Leonor) manage not to meet within a single prison cell, and Manrique dies alone, ignorant of the connection between the two stories even as Azucena reveals the truth. The play thus projects an image of shattered unity and split identity, its fragmented form expressing the impossibility, even in a *liebestod* of the kind seen in Hugo's *Hernani*, of reintegration or synthesis of its alienated parts.

Critics have tended to stress the centrality of revenge, the resonant backdrop of a civil war (so relevant to Spain in the 1830s), and a cruel destiny that brings down the lovers even as they defy religious order in the name of love. Such interpretations connect the latter issue to the *mal du siècle*. However, the play is richer than that: Leonor, for example, seems never to resolve her tormented relationship with religion. Manrique, the troubadour, a symbol of liberty and the poetic sublime, both loves and torments the two women in his divided loyalties and ambitions. Much of the effect of the play resides in the poignant emotional torture to which they subject each other amid contingent events, according to what was called Christian tragedy. Action on stage, lengthy soliloquies, and metaphysical reflection are consequently curtailed to focus on interpersonal relationships. Even the obsessive concern with pictorial detail in Saavedra is reduced to a focus on emblematic elements in staging. Azucena's final, ambiguous cry "¡Ya estás vengada!" ("Now you are avenged!") summarizes the resonance beyond defined meaning that is central to the work. It is an emotional effect of darkly suggestive indeterminacy (what contemporaries tended to call *vaguedad*, vagueness) that the fractured drama conveys.

As the plot develops, the story of Azucena and her mother is told no less than four times, once in a haunting, indeterminate dream, focusing attention on the effect of telling tales of horror. Perhaps García Gutiérrez's point is that rather than just enjoying the thrills as the servants at the start do, or being pursued by images that incite revenge and fear like Azucena and Manrique, the audience should adopt a more poetic attitude of emotive contemplation. This appears to be the author's first response to concerns that the disturbing effects of Romantic drama might corrupt the audience, and his first vision of how to transcend its indeterminacies. From the outset, the play was praised by critics for its lyrical qualities. The author casts his dark creation in relatively simple but affective language as the emotional mood swings develop, particularly favoring the lilting effect of short lines with close, emphasized rhyme, counterbalanced with assonantal short lines, and prose (often for sinister or "low-life" scenes), exploding into longer verse lines only on two occasions of violent torment and in the final words.

Several of García Gutiérrez's subsequent plays develop elements seen in *El trovador* without ever equaling the work: the role of revenge, haunting images of the past, and passion set against a backdrop of civil war. *El Paje* (*The Page*, 1837) unfurls in turbulent twists and turns of mutual emotional torture a double story of illicit love, featuring unintentional incestuous lust and a parallel longing for a lost mother that takes on Oedipal overtones. The ambiguities are limited to an extent by the page's parents' recognition of the consequences of their passion in the protagonist's death, and by the latter's inability to kill his own mother. Perhaps again responding to critics' concerns about disturbing content and effects, García Gutiérrez strengthens the framework of progressive liberal values in *El Rey Monje* (*The Monk King*, 1837) and *El encubierto de Valencia* (*Concealed in Valencia*, 1840). However, the former work remained sufficiently disturbing to provoke outrage from the leftist critic Jacinto de Salas y Quiroga. The tyrannical protagonist, a victim of sexual frustration, is still loved by his enemy's daughter, and a turbulent confession scene in which they declare their feelings raises unresolved questions about virtue and desire. Even in the 1840 play, in which values are clearer, there remains something unsettling in the way María is forced to choose between her virtuous father and the tyrannical, wicked lover she seeks to forgive.

Simón Bocanegra (1843), again the source of a Verdi opera, is García Gutiérrez's most audacious attempt to resolve the recurrent tension between a guiding framework and dynamic, indeterminate exploration of overpowering emotions. The haunting image from the past is given physical form in a frenetic prologue which looms over the play, with pictorial detail and violent use of light and shadow. The protagonist is caught in uncertain ground between politics and sexual desire in a world of ambitions, contingency, and mortality. He becomes Dux in order to realize his illicit love and free Genova, but finds only a corpse when he is declared leader. Some twenty-four years later, haunted by guilt, and obliged to hide his feelings, but a hero of the people, Simón finds his life invaded by the consequences of his past in a plot of complex twists and turns that leads his daughter's lover to plot his death and his enemies to conspire to poison him. In subtle comparison and contrast to Hugo, the last moments see his enemy (Fiesco) realize the full horror of what he has done, but, at the same time, the very pattern of events that consume Simón leads to the final union in love of Simón, his daughter, her lover, and Fiesco. García Gutiérrez seeks thus to transcend the disturbing passions without denying their complexities, but the changes of heart involved are perhaps too abrupt to convince. The versification is highly dynamic, shifting meter and rhyme with action and tone, with passionate long verse lines erupting only once in the course of each of the first three acts, before taking their position at the climactic ends of acts 3 and 4. The final moments settle into lyrical, close-rhyming short lines.

García Gutiérrez's fairly prolific output continued into later life, most notably with the politically resonant dramas *Venganza catalana* (*Catalan Revenge*, 1864) and *Juan Lorenzo* (1865).

ANDREW GINGER

Biography

Born in Chiclana, Cádiz, Spain, July 5, 1813. Son of an artisan family. Studied medicine 1830–32, until closure of universities by absolutist government. Traveled to Madrid on foot, 1833. Involved in Parnasillo literary group. Worked as translator of Augustine Eugène Scribe and Alexandre Dumas; joined the army in 1836. Deserted in order to attend première of *El trovador*, March 1836, but pardoned by the Ministry of War and allowed to resign his military post. Worked as dramatist; suffered from depression and poverty. Went to Latin America, 1844. Worked with *Gaceta oficial* in Cuba, 1844–46; worked for a number of newspapers in Mexico, also publishing plays, 1846–50. Returned to Spain and worked mainly as librettist for zarzuelas as well as continuing to write plays. Held Spanish government post in London, 1855–58. Named Comendador de la Orden de Carlos III, 1856. Elected academician of the Real Academia Española, 1861. Joined Progressive Liberal Party, 1864. Collection of his works published in homage to him by Real Academia and friends, 1866. Supported Revolution of 1868; appointed consul in Bayonne, then in Genoa, 1869–72. Awarded Gran Cruz de la Orden de María Victoria. Made director of Museo Arqueológico, Madrid, 1872. Died of a stroke in Madrid, August 26, 1886.

Selected Works

Collections
Obras escogidas. 1866.

Plays
El trovador. 1836.
El Paje. 1837.
El rey monje. 1839.
El encubierto de Valencia. 1840.
Simón Bocanegra. 1843.
Los hijos del tío Tronera. 1846.
El trovador New version, in verse only. 1851.
Venganza catalana. 1864.
Juan Lorenzo. 1865.

Poetry
Poesías. 1840.
Luz y tinieblas: Poesías sagradas y profanas. 1842.
"¡Abajo los borbones!" With music by Emilio Arrieta. 1868.

Bibliography

Adams, Nicholson. *The Romantic Dramas of García Gutiérrez*. New York: Instituto de las Españas, 1922.
Díaz Larios, Luis F. Introduction to edition of *El trovador* and *Simón Bocanegra*. Barcelona: Planeta, 1989.
Gies, David. *The Theatre in Nineteenth-Century Spain*. Cambridge: Cambridge University Press, 1994.
Irango, Carmen. *Antonio García Gutiérrez*. Boston: Twayne, 1980.
Johnson, Jerry L. "Azucena: Sinister or Pathetic?" *Romance Notes* 12 (1970): 114–18.
Picoche, J. Introduction to edition of *El trovador*. Madrid: Alhambra, 1972.
Ruiz Silva, Carlos. Introduction to edition of *El trovador*. Madrid: Cátedra, 1994.
San Vicente, Félix. "La evolución de García Gutiérrez, Hartzenbusch, Gil y Zárate." In *Historia de la literatura española: Siglo XIX*. Edited by Guillermo Carnero. Madrid: Espasa-Calpe, 1997.
Shaw, Donald. "*El trovador* y Antonio García Gutiérrez." In *Historia de la literatura española: Siglo XIX*. Edited by Guillermo Carnero. Madrid: Espasa-Calpe, 1997.
Villarnovo, A. "Poética del sonido en *El trovador*," *Revista de literatura* (1986): 101–13.

GARRETT, JOÃO BAPTISTA DA SILVA LEITÃO DE ALMEIDA 1799–1854

Portuguese poet, novelist, dramatist, and critic

Almeida Garrett should be considered, along with Alexandre Herculano de Carvalho e Araùjo, one of the major figures in Portuguese Romanticism, both in terms of his artistic output and his symbolic resonance. His siding with the liberals in the political aftermath of the Peninsular Wars, his extraordinary capacities as a public speaker, his knowledge of both classical and modern literatures (English, French, German, Spanish, and Italian), and his constant and intense literary production (as a novelist, poet, dramatist, essayist, critic, and founder of several periodicals) all contribute to his central place in Portuguese cultural life in the first half of the nineteenth century. Garrett was an intellectual whose literary work combines aesthetic quality with civic power of intervention. Thus, he truly embodies the ideal of the Romantic writer.

As a university student, Garrett distinguished himself by writing plays in the philosophical tradition with a strong ethical objective (1822; *Catão; Mérope*, published 1841). He also published, in 1821, *O Retrato de Vénus* (*Venus' Portrait*), an essay on painting which attacked censorship as immoral and materialistic.

Garrett's fervent liberalism forced him to go into exile, thus his subsequent works were published outside Portugal, first in Paris and then in London. These are *Camões* (1825), *Dona Branca* (1826), *Adozinda* (1828), *Lírica de João Mínimo* (*Lyrics of João Mínimo*, 1829), *Tratado da Educação* (*Treatise on Education*, 1829). The works already display aspects of the qualities fully evident in his mature writing: an intellectual curiosity and literary experimentation evidenced by the use of various genres, including lyrical poetry (*Lírica*), the Romantic narrative poem (*Camões, Dona Branca*), the pedagogical essay (*Tratado*), and the first written version of traditional, Portuguese, oral literature (*Adozinda*) (later on expanded by the publication of his *Romanceiro* [1843–51, 3 vols.]). These early works also exhibit that particularly significant blend of different literary and cultural traditions which characterize Garrett, from the neoclassical to the specifically Iberian. He also displayed the Romantic interest in popular traditions, as well as its affirmation of a specific political, social, and cultural position. This period is one of critical development for Garrett as a writer.

After his return to Portugal in 1836, until his untimely death in 1854, Garrett produced a mature body of work in several literary genres that would set the pattern for several trends important to Portugal's literary evolution. Drama was the genre in which Garrett had already produced his major juvenile works. Over the course of five years he wrote three major plays (in addition to other, more minor ones): *Um Auto de Gil Vicente* (*An "Auto" by Gil Vicente*, 1838), *O Alfageme de Santarém* (*The Swordmaker of Santarém*, 1842), and *Frei Luís de Sousa* (*Friar Luís de Sousa*, 1843). All three address one of Garrett's major concerns: that of the interplay between national and personal identities, explored through historical settings and historical (and symbolic) figures. In *Um Auto*, this is done through the mediation of the major Portuguese dramatist of the Renaissance, Gil Vicente; in *O Alfageme*, the same effect stems from his choice of the temporal setting of the political crisis of 1383–85 in which Portugal almost lost its independence. But it is by far *Frei Luís de Sousa* that deserves the most serious and sustained critical attention, beginning with its famous theoretical preface, in which Garrett explains the particular blend of classical tragedy and contemporary drama that characterizes this play. Its poetical, symbolical, and historical density must be emphasized. The play is set during the Castilian domination of Portugal in the seventeenth century (staging a nation that is, then, a collective specter). The ghostly presence of the poet Luis Vaz de Camões, by name and from readings from the epic poem *The Lusiads*, echoes the ghost of the lost king, Dom Sebastião. Other key plot developments and figures include: the story of an involuntary adultery and betrayal, catching in its net the "ghost" returned from the dead (Dom João, former husband of Dona Madalena); the couple who became such at the presumption of Dom João's death (Dona Madalena and Manuel de Sousa Coutinho); their daughter Maria, whose consumption will inevitably lead to her death; and Telmo, the servant who helped to bring up both Dom João and Maria, now torn by his loyalty to both. All share a sense of guilt independent of the facts at hand, and it is this pervasive "guilty innocence" that characterizes the climate woven by this play, a major Romantic achievement.

With regard to prose fiction, Garrett published *O Arco de Sant'Ana* (*Sant'Ana's Arch*, two volumes; 1845 and 1851) and *Viagens na Minha Terra* (*Travels in My Homeland*, 1846), and left an incomplete novel, *Helena*, unpublished. *Viagens* is certainly the most influential Romantic Portuguese novel, both laying the foundation for modern Portuguese prose fiction and illustrating it in its most paradigmatic form. The work is complex in composition, displaying the intensity and the brio of Romantic irony. Garrett's prose combines classical and erudite traditions with verbal invention, effective dialogue, and an openness to orality, both on a lexical and a syntactical level. The intricacy of its structure is influenced by Miguel de Cervantes Saavedra and Laurence Sterne. *O Arco* is an example of another successful tradition of the Romantic novel: the historical novel, following here in the wake of Victor Hugo. The story is set in the fourteenth century (although admittedly echoing nineteenth century problems such as oppression and dictatorship), and involves an intended abduction and rape of a town girl by the Bishop of Porto, which promptly triggers the appearance of the hero Vasco in a fight where he is given no quarter. By the conclusion, this confrontation is recognized as a confrontation with his own father. The Romantic overtones of the story, another tale of family-as-problem (as in *Frei Luís* and *Viagens*), are underscored by its political implications, namely an anticlericalism that, in the Romantic tradition, Garrett combines with profound religious sentiments.

Garrett was a lyrical poet from the very beginning of his literary career. But the two collections that ensured his fame, *Flores sem Fruto* (*Fruitless Flowers*, 1845) and *Folhas Caídas* (*Fallen Leaves*, 1853) are also from this later period. In these collected poems, the passionate and erotic dimension of Garrett's writing reveals itself at its fullest, in a poetic diction that still echoes, particularly in the first collection, some of his early poems, but is here combined with a versatile and innovative approach to traditional rhyme, meter, and sources of inspiration.

HELENA CARVALHÃO BUESCU

Biography

Born 1799 in Porto. After receiving a solid classical education, attended Universidade de Coimbra (1816), where he completed a degree in law (1820). In 1824, after a reactionary "coup," he was obliged to exile himself in England and France. Choosing the liberal side in the civil war, and taking an active part in it, found himself at the center of the political scene after 1834, and built a career as a public figure, man of politics, and writer. Sent as a diplomat to Brussels (1834), then became a member of Parliament in Portugal (1837), and general inspector of theaters (1838). Was made viscount (1851), and a year later became minister of Foreign Affairs. Died 1854 in Lisboa.

Selected Works

Frei Luís de Sousa, 1843. Lisboa: Ed. Comunicação, 1982.
    Translated as *"Brother Luiz de Sousa" of Viscount de Almeida Garrett* by Edgar Prestage. London: Elkin Matthews, 1909.
    Translated as *The Pilgrim* (*Frei Luís de Sousa*) by Nicholas G. Round. Forthcoming.
Flores sem Fruto, 1845, and *Folhas Caídas*, 1853. Critical edition by R. A. Lawton. Paris: PUF, 1975.
Viagens na Minha Terra. 1846. Lisboa, Ed. Estampa, 1983.
    Translated as *Travels in My Homeland* by John M. Parker. London: Peter Owen/UNESCO, 1987.

Bibliography

Amorim, Gomes de. *Garrett. Memórias Biográficas*. 3 vols. Lisboa: 1881–83.

Buescu, Helena Carvalhão. *Incidências do Olhar: Percepção e Representação*. Lisboa: Editorial Camisho, 1990.

Coelho, Jacinto do Prado. *A Letra e o Leitor*. Lisboa: Moraes Editores, 1969.

Lawton, R. A. *Almeida Garrett: L'Intime Contrainte*. Paris: Didier, 1966.

Mendes, Vítor. *Almeida Garrett: Crise na Representação das "Viagens na Minha Terra."* Lisboa: Editorial Cosmos, 1999.

Monteiro, Ofélia Paiva. *A Formação de Almeida Garrett: Experiência e Criação*. 2 vols. Coimbra: Centro de Estudos Românicos, 1971.

Raitt, Lia Noémia Correia. *Garrett and the English Muse*. London, Tamesis Books, 1983.

Reis, Carlos. *Introdução ao Estudo das "Viagens na Minha Terra."* Coimbra: Livreria Almedira, 1987.

Rocha, Andrée Crabbé. *O Teatro de Garrett*. Coimbra: Tipografia Atlântida, 1954.

GAUTIER, THÉOPHILE 1811–1872

French poet, novelist, and critic

Gautier's unfinished *Histoire du romantisme* (*A History of Romanticism*, 1874) reflects his involvement with the movement in 1830 and his lifelong admiration for Victor Hugo. His *Poésies* (*Poems*, 1830) were influenced by Victor Hugo and Alphonse de Lamartine, but the Byronic verse narrative *Albertus* (1832) parodies the Romantic taste for the macabre, and the satirical stories of *Les Jeunes France* (1833) mock Romantic excess. He swiftly rejected the Romantic doctrine of poetry as the servant of social progress, and developed a detached style in *La Comédie de la mort* (*The Comedy of Death*, 1838) and *España* (*Spain*, 1845). *Émaux et Camées* (*Enamels and Cameos*, 1852–72), written in octosyllables rather than the grander alexandrine favored by the Romantics, shows him turning to restrained description, but still commited to Romantic themes: "Affinités secrètes. Madrigal panthéiste" ("Secret Affinities," 1849) reflects the Romantic notion of the interrelatedness of phenomena, which is also the subject of Charles Baudelaire's sonnet "Correspondances." "Le Château du Souvenir" ("The Castle of Remembrance," 1861) evokes Gautier's prominent role in support of Hugo at the first night of *Hernani*, when he sported his famous "pourpoint de satin rose" (pink satin doublet), also called his "gilet rouge" (red waistcoat). However, "L'Art" (Ars Victrix, 1857) anticipating Parnassianism, exhorts the poet to emulate the formal precision of the sculptor and the enamelist; "Le Poème de la femme. Marbre de Paros" ("The Poem of Woman. Parian Marble," 1849) celebrates the sculptural beauty of the female body; "Symphonie en blanc majeur" ("Symphony in White," 1849) is a virtuoso piece on images of whiteness and their connotations; "Bûchers et tombeaux" ("Pyres and Tombs," 1858), defining Christianity as a negative force, shows a growing commitment to the classical ideal.

In the 1830s, Gautier was attracted to the Romantic theory of "la fraternité des arts" (the brotherhood of the arts), which stressed the interrelationship between painting, music, and literature, and by the exoticism of orientalist painters such as Prosper Marilhat and Alexandre Decamps. This influenced his experimentation in verse and prose with *transpositions d'art* (literary representations of artworks) and his constant use of visual allusions and cultural references that represent reality through artistic stereotypes. Gautier's remark, quoted Edmond and Jules de Goncourts, "Toute ma valeur . . ., c'est que je suis un homme pour qui le monde visible existe" ("All my worth . . ., it is that I am a man for whom the visible world exists"), suggests that beautiful and enduring forms, with no practical utility, are our only consolation in an impermanent world, and echoes the "art for art's sake" doctrine first elaborated in the prefaces to *Albertus* (1832) and *Mademoiselle de Maupin* (1835). Gautier's cult of physical beauty has a metaphysical dimension, art being the quest for immortality. He also argued that beauty and morality are intimately associated: "Le torse de Vénus est plus moral que toute l'œuvre de Hogarth" ("The torso of Venus is more moral than all of Hogarth's work"). Such ideas impressed Algernon Charles Swinburne and Oscar Wilde.

Baudelaire thought Gautier's greatest originality was in the "nouvelle poétique" (poetic novella). In fantastic tales like *La Cafetière* (*The Coffee Pot*, 1831), *La Morte Amoureuse* (*The Dead in Love*, 1836), *Arria Marcella* (1852), and *Spirite* (1865), Gautier treats the Romantic theme of love beyond the grave in terms showing his indebtedness to Achim von Arnim, Johann Wolfgang von Goethe, E. T. A. Hoffmann, Washington Irving, Edgar Allan Poe, and Sir Walter Scott. Exotic stories of distant lands and times, like *Une nuit de Cléopâtre* (*One of Cleopatra's Nights*, 1838), *Le Roi Candaule* (King Candaules, 1844), or *Le Pavillon sur l'eau* (*The Water Pavilion*, 1846) are a form of Romantic escapism, while the semiautobiographical *La Pipe d'opium* (*The Opium Pipe*, 1838) and *Le Club des Haschischins* (*The Hashish Club*, 1846) record experimentation with drugs and mingle irony and metaphysical anguish.

Romantic themes are also present in his novels. In *Mademoiselle de Maupin* (1835), Albert is the archetypal victim of the *mal du siècle* (turn-of-the-century world-weariness). *Fortunio* (1837) is a hedonistic rejection of the modern world. *Militona* (1847), set in Spain, is a tale of passion that exploits the Romantic cult of local color. *Le Roman de la momie* (*The Romance of a Mummy*, 1858), a story of doomed love in ancient Egypt, emulates the Romantic historical novel, combining archaeological reconstruction and the supernatural, and influenced Gustave Flaubert's *Salammbô* (1862). *Le Capitaine Fracasse* (*Captain Fracasse*, 1863) is a romanticized version of Paul Scarron's *Le Roman comique* (1651–57), which uses pastiche and parody to reconstruct the age of Louis XIII.

Gautier's contributions to theater are fanciful. *Une larme du diable* (*The Devil's Tear*, 1839) is a verse parody of a mystery play, with echoes of Goethe's *Faust*. *Le Tricorne enchanté* (*The Magic Hat*, 1845) is an ironic pastiche of Molière. *La Fausse Conversion* (*The Bogus Conversion*, 1846) is a satirical *proverbe*

Théophile Gautier (1811–72), caricature. Reprinted courtesy of Roger-Viollet.

set in the eighteenth century, and *Pierrot posthume* (*Posthumous Pierrot*, 1847) is inspired by the *commedia dell'arte*. The ballet scenarios *Giselle* (1841), *La Péri* (*The Fairy*, 1843), and *Sacountala* (1858), exploit stock Romantic motifs and exotic settings.

Predilection for the picturesque, at the expense of social comment, is apparent in his travel books: *Tra los montes (Voyage en Espagne)* (*Wanderings in Spain*, 1843), *Italia (Voyage en Italie)* (*Travels in Italy*, 1852), *Constantinople* (1853), and *Voyage en Russie* (*Travels in Russia*, 1866). *Tableaux de Siège. Paris 1870–71* (*Paris Besieged*, 1871) is a masterpiece of elegiac description in which aestheticism and conservatism coalesce.

Most of Gautier's output consists of newspaper articles on theater, literature, ballet, music (he was an early supporter of Richard Wagner), and art, the most influential being those on the annual Salon. Though criticized by Eugène Delacroix as unduly descriptive, his art criticism is subtly evaluative and shows his complex attitude towards neoclassicism and Romanticism. Accepting Goethe's notion of the microcosm (the personal vision that informs an artist's work), he championed the Romantic individualism of Delacroix but also the work of Jean-Auguste-Dominique Ingres, which shunned the academic neoclassicism of Jacques-Louis David and echoed the true classicism

of the ancients. Gautier's aesthetics was based on the continuity of great art since the time of the Greeks, and on the disinterested pursuit of beauty. His rejection of Gustave Courbet, Édouard Manet, and realism suggests both fidelity to Romanticism and adherence to the classical ideal. He disliked French neoclassicial tragedy of the seventeenth century, preferring, in *Les Grotesques* (1844) the "irregular" or "baroque" poets of that period. His social circle included Honoré de Balzac, Baudelaire, Flaubert, the Goncourts, Princess Mathilde, Gerard de Nerval, and Madame Sabatier, and he knew all the leading artists and composers of his day. A voluminous correspondence reveals a pivotal figure in Parisian cultural life from 1830 to 1870. A 1873 anthology in his honor, *Le Tombeau de Théophile Gautier* includes poems by Hugo, Leconte de Lisle, Stéphane Mallarmé, and Swinburne.

PETER WHYTE

Biography

Born Pierre-Jules Théophile Gautier in Tarbes, France, August 31, 1811. Moved to Paris with his family, 1814. Educated in Paris at the Collège Louis-le-Grand and the Collège Charlemagne, 1822–29. Met and began a lifelong friendship with the poet Gérard de Nerval; introduced by Nerval and Petrus Borel to Victor Hugo, 1829. Studied painting in studio of Louis-Édouard Rioult, 1828–29. Abandoned artistic career for writing, 1830. Participated in famous "battle" at the first performance of Hugo's *Hernani*, February 1830. Member of the Petit Cénacle literary group with Borel and others, early 1830s. Lived bohemian life in the impasse du Doyenné, Paris, 1834–36. Published the novel *Madame de Maupin*, 1835; forced by financial necessity to pursue a career in arts journalism from 1836. Fathered a son (Théophile, known as "Toto") with Eugénie Fort, 1836. Contributed regularly to *La Presse* (1836–55) and *Le Moniteur universel* (1855–68). Also wrote for *Le Figaro, Ariel, La France Littéraire*; codirector of the *Revue de Paris*, 1851, and editor of *L'Artiste*, 1856–59. Traveled to Belgium and Holland with Gérard de Nerval, 1836, and to Spain with Eugène Piot, 1840. Named chevalier of the Légion d'honneur, 1842. Traveled to Algeria, 1845. Maintained long-term relationship with opera singer Ernesta Grisi: two daughters, born 1845 and 1847. Traveled to Constantinople, Athens, and Venice, 1852. Named officier of the Légion d'honneur, 1858. Traveled to Russia, 1858–59. Traveled frequently to Geneva to visit Ernesta and his children. Gave regular financial support to his two younger, unmarried sisters, particularly after the death of their father, 1854. Liaisons with a number of women, including Marie Mattei, whom he met in London, 1849; harbored idealized passion for ballerina Carlotta Grisi, Ernesta's sister, inspiration for *Spirite* (1865), c. 1840–70. Appointed librarian to Princess Mathilde, 1868. Attempted election to the Académie française several times unsuccessfully, 1865–69. Traveled to Egypt for the inauguration of the Suez Canal, 1869. Died of heart failure in Neuilly-sur-Seine, France, October 23, 1872.

Selected Works

Collections
The Works of Théophile Gautier. 24 vols. Translated by Frederick Sumichrast. 1900–1902.
Poésies complètes. 3 vols. Edited by René Jasinski. 1970.
Œuvres complètes. 11 vols. 1978.

Correspondance générale. 12 vols. Edited by Claudine
Lacoste-Veysseyre and Pierre Laubriet. 1985–2000.
L'Œuvre fantastique. 2 vols. Edited by Michel Crouzet. 1992.
Critique d'art: Extraits des Salons (1833–1872). Edited by
Marie-Hélène Girard. 1994.
Œuvres: Choix de romans et de contes. Edited by Paolo Tortonese.
1995.
Paris et les Parisiens. Edited by Claudine Lacoste. 1996.
Romans, contes et nouvelles. 2 vols. Edited by Perre Laubriet,
Jean-Claude Bruon, Jean-Claude Fizaine, Claudine Lacoste, and
Peter Whyte. 2002.

Poetry
Poésies. 1830. Edited by Harry Cockerham. 1973.
Poésies complètes de Théophile Gautier. 1845. Published as *Poésies
complètes.* Rev. ed. 2 vols. Edited by Maurice Dreyfous.
1875–76.
Émaux et Camées. 1852. Definitive edition, 1872. Edited by
Madeleine Cottin. 1968.

Fiction
Les Jeunes France. 1833. Published as *Œuvres humoristiques. Les
Jeunes-France.* Rev. ed. 1851. Edited by Michel Crouzet. 1995.
Mademoiselle de Maupin: Double Amour. 2 vols. 1835. Published as
Mademoiselle de Maupin. Rev. ed. 1845. Translated anonymously
as *Mademoiselle de Maupin: A Romance of Love and Passion.* 1887.
Translated as *Mademoiselle de Maupin,* by Joanna Richardson,
1981; edited by Jacques Robichez. 1979.
Nouvelles. 1845. Published as *Fortunio et autres nouvelles.* Edited by
Claudine Lacoste. 1979.
Romans et contes. 1863. Edited by Anne Bouchard. 1979.
Le Roman de la momie. 1858. Translated as *The Romance of a
Mummy* by Anne Toppan Wood, 1863; edited by Marc
Eigeldinger. 1985.
Le Capitaine Fracasse. 1863. Translated as *Captain Fracasse* by Ellen
Murray Beam, 1880; edited by Antoine Adam. 1972.
Spirite: Nouvelle fantastique. 1866. Translated: anonymously as
Spirite, a Fantasy. 1877; edited by Marc Eigeldinger, 1970; edited
by Pierre Laubriet. 1978.

Drama
Théâtre: mystère, comédies et ballets. 1872. Rev. ed. 1882.

Travel Books
Zigzags. 1845. Published as *Caprices et Zigzags.* Rev. ed. 1852.
Tra los montes. 2 vols. 1843. Published as *Voyage en Espagne.* Rev.
ed. 1845. Edited by Patrick Berthier. 1981.
Italia. 1852. Published as *Voyage en Italie.* Rev. ed. 1875. Edited by
Marie-Hélène Girard. 1997.
Constantinople. 1853. Translated as *Constantinople of Today* by R. H.
Gould, 1854; edited by Sarga Moussa. 1990.
Voyage en Russie. 2 vols. 1866. Translated as *A Winter in Russia* by
M. M. Ripley, 1874; edited by Francine-Dominque Liechtenhan.
1990.
Loin de Paris. 1865.
Quand on voyage. 1865.
Tableaux de siège. 1871. Translated as *Paris Besieged* by Frederick
Sumichrast. 1902.
L'Orient. 2 vols. 1877.
Voyage en Égypte. Edited by Paolo Tortonese. 1991.

Voyage pittoresque en Algérie. Edited by Madeleine Cottin. 1973.
Published as *Voyage en Algérie.* Edited by Denise Brahimi. 1989.

Criticism
Les Grotesques. 1844. Translated as *The Grotesques* by Frederick
Sumichrast, 1900; edited by Cecilia Rizza. 1986.
Les Beaux-Arts en Europe. 2 vols. 1855–56.
L'Art moderne. 1856.
Histoire de l'art dramatique en France depuis vingt-cinq ans. 6 vols.
1858–59.
Histoire du romantisme. 1874. Translated as *A History of
Romanticism.* Translated by Frederick Sumichrast. 1902.
Portraits contemporains. 1874.
Portraits et souvenirs littéraires. 1892.
La Musique. 1911.

Bibliography

Binney, Edwin. *Les Ballets de Théophile Gautier.* Paris: Nizet, 1965.
Book-Senninger, Claude. *Théophile Gautier, auteur dramatique.* Paris:
Nizet, 1972.
Court-Pérez, Françoise. *Gautier, un romantique ironique: Sur l'esprit
de Gautier.* Paris: Champion, 1998.
Delvaille, Bernard. *Théophile Gautier.* Paris: Seghers, 1968.
Dillingham, Louise Bulkley. *The Creative Imagination of Théophile
Gautier: A Study in Literary Psychology.* Princeton, N.J.:
Psychological Review Company, 1927.
Gosselin Schick, Constance. *Seductive Resistance: The Poetry of
Théophile Gautier.* Amsterdam: Rodopi, 1994.
Grant, Richard B. *Théophile Gautier.* Boston: Twayne, 1975.
Jasinski, René. *Les Années romantiques de Théophile Gautier.* Paris:
Vuibert, 1929.
Lovenjoul, Charles de Spoelberch de. *Histoire de Œuvres de
Théophile Gautier* (1887). 2 vols. Geneva: Slatkine Reprints,
1968.
Matoré, Georges. *Le Vocabulaire et la société sous Louis-Philippe.*
Geneva: Droz, 1951.
Richer, Jean. *Études et recherches sur Théophile Gautier prosateur.*
Paris: Nizet, 1981.
Rizza, Cecilia. *Théophile Gautier: critico letterario.* Turin:
Giappichelle, 1971.
Savalle, Joseph. *Travestis, métamorphoses, dédoublements: Essai sur
l'œuvre romanesque de Théophile Gautier.* Paris: Minard, 1981.
Schapira, Marie-Claude. *Le Regard de Narcisse: Romans et contes de
Théophile Gautier.* Lyon: Presses Universitaires de Lyon, 1984.
Senninger, Claude. *Théophile Gautier: Une vie, une œuvre.* Paris:
SEDES, 1994.
Snell, Robert. *Théophile Gautier: A Romantic Critic of the Visual Arts.*
Oxford: Clarendon Press, 1982.
Spencer, Michael. *The Art Criticism of Théophile Gautier.* Geneva:
Droz, 1969.
Tennant, P. E. *Théophile Gautier.* London: Athlone Press, 1975.
Tortonese, Paolo. *La Vie extérieure: Essai sur l'œuvre narrative de
Théophile Gautier.* Paris: Lettres Modernes, 1992.
Voisin, Marcel. *Le Soleil et la nuit: L'Imaginaire dans l'œuvre de
Théophile Gautier.* Brussels: Éditions de l'Université de Bruxellcs,
1981.
Whyte, Peter. *Théophile Gautier: conteur fantastique et merveilleux.*
Durham: Durham Modern Languages Series, 1996.

GAY APPROACHES TO THE ROMANTIC PERIOD

As homosexual men of the mid-nineteenth century began to speak to and write among themselves about their sense of otherness, they often associated their own experiences with those of earlier cultural and historical figures, at times by making lists of male couples or male lovers of other men or boys. This identification, not just with other individuals but even with other types, effectively amounts to a cumulative approach to homosexuality, avoiding distinctions. Anthologies of homosexual literature have been the most visible signs of this tendency. Considered as bibliographies, they are, perhaps, the best starting point for the study of homosexuality in the Romantic period.

In *Ioläus: An Anthology of Friendship* (1902), Edward Carpenter lists as being significant in this respect Johann Winckelmann's letters, Johann Wolfgang von Goethe's comments on Winckelmann's work, August von Platen, Richard Wagner's letters about Ludwig II of Bavaria and about ancient Greek civilization, Lord Byron, Percy Bysshe Shelley on friendship, Alfred, Lord Tennyson's *In Memoriam*, Robert Browning's "May and Death," and Ralph Waldo Emerson and Henry David Thoreau. In his second edition (1906), he adds Johann Christoph Friedrich von Schiller's *Don Karlos*, Frederick the Great's poems, Johann Gottfried von Herder on Greek friendship, Elisar von Kupffer on ethics and politics, and Ludwig II's letters to Richard Wagner. This eclectic selection, mixing literary texts with other ephemera, forms the rudimentary basis of the twentieth-century gay reader's view of homosexuality in the Romantic period. It has subsequently been updated with more extensive lists.

For instance, Cecile Beurdeley's *L'Amour Bleu* (1977) has Winckelmann, Jean-Jacques Rousseau (the account of a sexual assault from the *Confessions*), the Marquis de Sade, Goethe, William Beckford, and an assortment of paintings by Elisar von Kupffer. Stephen Coote's *Penguin Book of Homosexual Verse* (1983) includes selections from Thomas Gray, Charles Churchill, Anna Seward, Goethe, Wordsworth on the Ladies of Llangollen (two Irish women with an ambiguous relationship who defied convention to live together in Llangollen, Wales, in the late eighteenth and early nineteenth centuries), Byron, Platen, Aleksandr Pushkin, Tennyson, and Thoreau. Wolfgang Popp's *Mannerliebe* (1992) includes a section of Platen at the start of a chapter tellingly entitled "Männerfreundschaft—homosexuell?" ("Male Friendship: homosexual?"). Lillian Faderman's *Chloe Plus Olivia* (1994) has the Ladies of Llangollen, Anna Seward, Maria Edgeworth, and Anne Lister. Gregory Woods's *History of Gay Literature* (1998) corrals its main information on the Romantic period into chapters on the English elegiac tradition, the development of libertine literature into the Gothic novel, the European novel (Théophile Gautier, Honoré de Balzac), and the American renaissance.

Such inventories of homoerotic texts had also been compiled by writers in the Romantic period itself and before, but these early lists tended to consist solely of Greek and Latin materials. Thus, the anonymous author of *Don Leon* (apocryphally attributed to Lord Byron) invokes Plato, Socrates, Plutarch, Virgil, and Horace in defense of his own sexual and emotional orientation.

Gay critics of the twentieth century have variously engaged in biographical approaches concerning the relationships between certain poets and their male lovers or intimate friends, purely textual reappraisals, rereading texts in the light of contemporary practice, and more complex theoretical reconceptualizations of how the eighteenth and nineteenth centuries lived and represented what are now thought of as sexualities and sexual identities. If the category Romanticism is itself a retrospective construction, hardly less so is the concept of Gay Romanticism.

The first and finest of the gay liberationist reappraisals of Romanticism was Louis Crompton's *Byron and Greek Love* (1985), which located Byron's bisexuality in the context of English antisodomite hysteria, setting against the court records and accounts of the pillory and the gallows the unpublished papers of Jeremy Bentham, who was working his way toward a tolerant account of the place of homosexual relationships in the wider social fabric.

In the 1990s, such reappraisals slowed due to gay studies' strict adherence to a post-Foucauldian, constructionist line asserting that only "homosexuality" as definition was the beginning of homosexuality proper; in other words, that homosexuality did not begin until it was named, in the 1860s. Before that time, it was argued, men thought of their sexual acts as discrete from matters of personal identity. In many respects, this theoretical purism has inhibited the study of single-sex relationships in any period prior to the mid-nineteenth century. Following on from this tendency, Eve Kosofsky Sedgwick's work theorizing the unstable boundaries between the homosexual and what she called the "homosocial" stemmed from initial research into Gothic fiction. For Sedgwick, "The Gothic novel crystallized for English audiences the terms of a dialectic between male homosexuality and homophobia, in which homophobia appeared thematically in paranoid plots."

The problem of the "homosocial" as a concept in gay studies is that, like a gas, it may expand to fill any space, edging "homoeroticism" and "homosexuality" out of view, especially when used to refer to a prefeminist universe in which all male–male social interactions are seen as being more valuable than those between men and women, let alone those between women and women. To describe male interactions as "homosocial" is virtually tautological. The most influential of the more recent anti-constructionist historians is Rictor Norton, for whom "homosociality is little more than homosexuality with a fig leaf." He argues that "The evidence of history points to repression rather than construction as the shaping force of queer identity and culture." These are the principles behind Norton's researches into the working-class "molly" subcultures of urban England in the eighteenth and early nineteenth centuries (where cross-dressing and homosexual acts were allowed). He even goes so far as to call them a "gay subculture."

Influential subsequent criticism includes George Haggerty's insistence on the reassertion of the concept of love in the work of Thomas Gray, William Beckford, and Horace Walpole. Haggerty insists on the legitimacy of gay studies' interrogation of such men's "friendships": there is a place, he argues, between the friendships of heterosexual men and the sexual acts of homosexual men, which cannot merely be categorized as friendship rendered extreme by the unusually tender sensitivities of the poetically inclined. He implies that those critics who reduce male love to the safer equanimity of mere friendship are doing no less a disservice to the complex truth than gay critics who want to read homosexuality into the faintest sign of comradeship.

GREGORY WOODS

See also **Homosexuality**

Bibliography

Beurdeley, Cecile, ed. *L'Amour Bleu*. Fribourg: Office du Livre, 1977.

Carpenter, Edward, ed. *Anthology of Friendship: Ioläus*. London: Allen and Unwin, 1906.

Coote, Stephen, ed. *The Penguin Book of Homosexual Verse*. Harmondsworth, England: Penguin, 1983.

Crompton, Louis. *Byron and Greek Love: Homophobia in Nineteenth-Century England*. Berkeley and Los Angeles: University of California Press, 1985.

Faderman, Lillian, ed. *Chloe Plus Olivia: An Anthology of Lesbian Literature from the Seventeenth Century to the Present*. New York: Viking, 1994.

Haggerty, George E. *Men in Love: Masculinity and Sexuality in the Eighteenth Century*. New York: Columbia University Press, 1999.

Hammond, Paul. *Love between Men in English Literature*. London: Macmillan, 1996.

Norton, Rictor. *Mother Clap's Molly House: The Gay Subculture in England, 1700–1830*. London: GMP, 1992.

———. *The Myth of the Modern Homosexual: Queer History and the Search for Cultural Unity*. London: Cassell, 1997.

Popp, Wolfgang. *Männerliebe: Homosexualität und Literatur*. Stuttgart: Metzler, 1992.

Sedgwick, Eve Kosofsky. *Between Men: English Literature and Male Homosocial Desire*. New York: Columbia University Press, 1985.

Woods, Gregory. *A History of Gay Literature: The Male Tradition*. New Haven, Conn.: Yale University Press, 1998.

GENDER

The philosopher Jean-Jacques Rousseau, arguably the first of the Romantics, describes in his educational tract *Émile* (1762) the faltering attempts of a young girl to learn to write. She practices repeatedly the formation of the letter *O* and is absorbed in her task until she catches sight of herself writing in a mirror. She is appalled by her awkward posture and her pained expression of concentration; she finds herself ugly in the act of writing and abandons her task.

A certain ideology of gender is in operation in this extract. It appears that learning and femininity are antithetical; the girl is disconcerted by the extent to which the act of writing renders her unattractive and unwomanly. Rousseau posits this concern as natural: it is to be expected that girls will cultivate beauty over intellect, since the former is valued more highly in a woman. *Émile* conforms to, and perpetuates, a certain eighteenth-century understanding of gender. The female personality, as Rousseau describes it, is passive and malleable; women exist not for their own sake, but for the sake of others whom they must please. In his influential sentimental fiction, *Julie, ou La Nouvelle Héloïse* (*Julie, or the New Eloise*, 1761), gender is presented in similar terms. The heroine renounces sexual desire to become the ideal, domesticated Christian wife and mother. *La Nouvelle Héloïse* has been termed the original Romantic novel.

In many respects, representations and constructions of gender in the Romantic era continued to conform to Rousseau's depiction of masculine and feminine identity, in terms of female self-renunciation and masculine self-assertion. Indeed, such conceptualizations of gender came to be consolidated by the Romantic interest in, and emphasis upon, the aesthetic of the sublime. The sublime is a deeply gendered aesthetic. It was defined most influentially by Edmund Burke's *Enquiry into the Origins of our Ideas of the Sublime and the Beautiful* (1757) as always "some modification of power." Its antithesis is beauty, a quality defined in terms of delicacy, weakness, and submissiveness, explicitly feminized by Burke. Beauty is to be loved on account of its weakness and not admired on account of its strength. Beauty is thus the aesthetic equivalent of that which is, in cultural terms, properly feminine.

Aesthetic conceptualizations of the sublime and the beautiful are important to an understanding of Romantic constructions and representations gender. The sublime poses an intellectual and physical challenge to the Romantic philosopher and artist; in rising to that challenge, the subject is assured of his own transcendental self-identity. Immanuel Kant's division of the sublime into the "mathematical" and the "dynamical" in the *Critique of Judgment* (1790) conceives of the sublime in terms of immeasurable greatness and the intellectual effort that this demands of the subject, an effort that guarantees rational and transcendental subjectivity. The depiction of sublime landscape, in particular, may be seen as an attempt to guarantee the sublime qualities of the Romantic artist himself. In Johann Christoph Friedrich von Schiller's poem "The Walk" (1795), the poet transcends a familiar domestic environment so as to encounter the savage splendor of the sublime:

> Before me, heaven
> With all its Far-Unbounded!—one blue hill
> Ending the gradual world—in vapour!
> Where I stand upon the montain summit, lo,
> As sink its sides precipitous before me

Schiller's poem evokes Casper David Friedrich's 1818 painting *The Wanderer Above the Sea*. The wanderer stands on the summit of a mountain, with his back to the viewer, facing a typically Romantic sublime scene. Through the presence of this solitary male explorer, the sublime landscape on which he gazes is figured implicitly as male territory. If humanity figures at all in Romantic landscape painting, it tends to figure as masculine (for example, see Thomas Cole's *Salvator Rosa Sketching Banditti* [c. 1832–40]; Henry Fuseli's *View of Niagara Falls* [c. 1776]; William Henry Bartlett's *View below Table Rock* [1837]; and Casper David Friedrich's *The Monk by the Sea* [1809]). The sublime landscape is a frontier accessible, insofar as it is accessible, only to the male. Artistic representations of femininity seem incompatible with representations of sublime power, and women in art continued to be associated with beauty rather than sublimity. Moreover, women as artists tended to conform to, rather than subvert, this association, preferring on the whole pastoral landscape and portraiture to an engagement with the sublime in nature.

Representations of gender in poetry and prose tended to operate according to a similar paradigm. In the work of the English Romantic poets, the sublime is, as in the work of Johann Christoph Friedrich von Schiller, implicitly masculine, and Romantic masculinity itself is, in a sense, sublime. In the work of both male and female writers the feminine continued to be associated with beauty and domesticity. This is evident particularly in the Romantic-era novel, which incorporated many elements of eighteenth-century sentimental fiction, including its Rousseauesque depictions of masculinity and femininity. However, certain women writers were not averse to challenging conventional representations of gender, nor to appropriating "masculine" discourses in a way that confronted rigid categorizations of writers in terms of their gender identity. Female poets in England and Germany engaged with the sublime (for example, Karoline von Günderode Felicia Hemans and Helen Maria Williams). The heroines of fiction by Mary Hays, Elizabeth Inchbald, Charlotte Smith, and Mary Wollstonecraft in England and, in France, Madame Anne-Louise-Germaine de Staël, were often women capable of appreciating the sublime and who possessed certain "masculine" characteristics (reason, strength, and fortitude) that aligned them more with the sublime than the beautiful. Madame de Staël's *Delphine* (1802) portrays a woman of extraordinary energy, a female Werther in many respects stronger and more passionate that Johann Wolfgang von Goethe's own protagonist. In the later Romantic period, the novels of George Sand championed the right of women to defy conventional gender stereotypes, and Sand's own unconventional life, like that of Wollstonecraft in England, was in many respects a challenge to those stereotypes. And like Emily Brontë in England, Rosalla Castro in Spain also explored, later in the Romantic period, the dark, sublime aspect of extreme human passion in both men and women.

Moreover, male gender identity in the Romantic era did not always correspond to the stereotype of sublime masculinity; gender identity was not so fixed that masculinity necessarily excluded, in art and life, qualities associated with the feminine. To some degree, the feminized eighteenth-century "man of feeling" lived on in a new form, as Goethe's Werther (in *The Sorrows of Young Werther*, 1774), the archetypal "feminine" male Romantic hero. John Keats's rejection of the Wordsworthian cult of "self" has been well-documented, and the "feminine" elements in his work explored. Samuel Taylor Coleridge's ambiguous representations of gender in the poem *Christabel* (1816), and the scandalized contemporary response to that work, suggest a certain anxiety as to gender identity and its representation in art. As Karen Swann observes, Coleridge and his poem were denigrated as somehow "feminine"; the poem was an "old woman's story" and its author "unmanly."

Indeed, what appears to characterize Romantic conceptualizations and representations of gender is a certain instability of "masculine" and "feminine" subject positions. The fluidity of gender as a social construct became apparent. Wollstonecraft's polemical essays of the 1790s are possibly the first texts to deal with the eighteenth-century ideal of femininity as a damaging social construct. In her two *Vindications* (*Vindication of the Rights of Men*, 1790; *Vindication of the Rights of Women*, 1792), Wollstonecraft engages with Burke and Rousseau, positing both men

as irrational, hysterical, "feminine" figures while appropriating for herself a learned, rational, "masculine" style of argument. In Friedrich von Schlegel's novel *Lucinde* (1799), the masculinity and femininity of the heroine and her lover appear interchangeable; and Lucinde herself is, in many respects, a liberated woman, defying cultural norms and confounding conventional Romantic representations of femininity by men. The novel is arguably one of the few contributions by a male Romantic writer to the literature of feminism. Meanwhile, one thing that emerges out of Rousseau's *Confessions* (1765–70) is the impossibility of attributing to the author an unequivocally "masculine" identity. This classic text of early Romanticism in many ways affirms its author's status as a victim and, indeed, the increasing presence within Romanticism of the male-as-victim undermines to some degree the ideology of gender that the period seems otherwise to promote. Suffering masculinity becomes a potent theme within Romantic literature, from Goethe's *Werther* to Keats's *La Belle Dame Sans Merci* and Alphonse de Lamartine's *Méditations Poétiques* (both published in 1820).

A similar departure from conventional representations of male gender identity is observable, though to a lesser extent, in Romantic painting. Jacques Louis David produced a famous set of paintings glorifying the Napoleonic wars and asserting an ideal of male military heroism. In the work of Théodore Géricault and Delacroix, however, the emphasis shifts from triumphant heroism to suffering and defeat. Delacroix's *The Massacre at Chios* (1824) and *The Death of Sardanapule* (1827) depict the horror, not glory, of war. In Géricault's the *Wounded Cuirassier* (1814), a defeated soldier drags himself injured away from the field, his vulnerability emphasized by descending clouds and the rising smoke of battle. While masculinity is ennobled, rather than "feminized" through suffering in these works, the paintings nevertheless suggest that the Romantic hero is often as likely to appear as a wounded man of sorrows as a solitary genius rising to the challenge of the sublime.

Romantic criticism, however, has not traditionally sought to interrogate and problematize questions of gender to any great extent. Indeed, late-twentieth-century critics have contended that such stereotypical assumptions in relation to gender as appear in the work of Burke, Rousseau, and the later Romantics, have shaped our very understanding of the term "Romanticism." Romanticism is itself a deeply gendered discourse, defined historically as a masculine phenomenon. Hence, it may be seen as no coincidence that, until the late twentieth century, the Romantic canon was restricted to the work of men, since to define the Romantic subject is in a sense to define what it means to be male at this historical moment: self-sufficient, creative, transcendental, and sublime. Moreover, to perceive Romanticism as a "masculine phenomenon" raises questions as to the relation between gender and genre in the Romantic period and in Romantic criticism since that period. The six great British Romantics are male poets. Within British Romanticism, poetry has generally been placed in opposition to prose fiction and privileged in relation to it. The novel in the Romantic era was deemed to be a feminine mode of writing, constructed as the proper domain of the female author at a time when female authorship was still tainted with a certain cultural impropriety. Romantic poetry, meanwhile, provided the serious male writer with a genre sufficiently elevated to explore themes that transcended the mundane, domestic concerns of the novel. The Romantic poet is thus the intellectual equivalent of Friedrich's wanderer above the sea, rising out of a domesticated, feminized environment and into the region of the sublime. Romantic criticism has arguably perpetuated this assumption through its willingness to regard Romantic poetry as a vehicle through which the supremacy of the imagination could assert itself in the act of literary creation. This act of artistic self-assertion is implicitly a "masculine phenomenon," bound up as it is with a deeply-gendered eighteenth-century notion of the sublime. Romantic poetry and Romantic criticism have thus been shown to partake of a certain ideology of gender that can be traced back to Burke's *Enquiry* and Rousseau's *Émile*.

Ultimately, however, it is impossible to approach the question of gender in this period without acknowledging its fluidity and instability. Such diverse representations of masculinity as appear, for example, in Goethe's *Werther*, Lord Byron's *Manfred* (1817), and Percy Bysshe Shelley's *Alastor* (1816), suggest that masculinity is not a fixed category; it is as likely to manifest beauty and sensibility as sublimity and raw power. Similarly, the heroines of Jane Austen, Emily Brontë, and Madame de Staël are united in at least one respect: they frustrate any straightforward equation of femininity with passivity and an anti-intellectual sensibility. In the poetry and prose of women, particularly, the gendered dichotomy between Romantic male transcendence and feminine domesticity breaks down, leading to the emergence of what Anne Mellor has termed a "feminine Romantic ideology" premised upon a belief in the capacity for transcendence of both men and women, given an equality of education and experience. Thus, a consideration of the representation of gender in the Romantic era leads to an engagement with the gender politics of the period, to the frustrated ambitions of the heroines of Mary Hays and Elizabeth Inchbald, to Friedrich von Schlegel's calls for the equality of women and to Mary Wollstonecraft's insistent demand for a "revolution in female manners" to counteract the pernicious effect of the Rousseauesque ideology of gender.

The question of gender can no longer be regarded as peripheral to Romantic studies. The relation of gender to the politics and art of the Romantic period is complex, and a variety of fresh critical perspectives have emerged in relation to it in recent decades. Indeed, given the longstanding critical tendency to regard Romanticism as gendered male, it would seem that any engagement with the issue of gender within this context is fundamentally likely to challenge what we understand by the term *Romanticism*.

SUSAN CHAPLIN

Bibliography

Cox, Philip. *Gender, Genre and the Romantic Poets*. Manchester, U.K.: Manchester University Press, 1996.

Cranston, Maurice. *The Romantic Movement*. Oxford: Blackwell, 1994.

Jacobus, Mary. *Romanticism, Writing and Sexual Difference: Essays on the Prelude*. Oxford: Clarendon Press, 1989.

Janowitz, Anne. *Romanticism and Gender: Essays and Studies*. London: D. S. Brewer, 1998.

Labbe, Jaqueline. *Romantic Visualities: Landscape, Gender and Romanticism*. London: Macmillan, 1998.

Mellor, Anne K. *Romanticism and Gender*. London: Routledge, 1993.

Ross, Marlon B. *The Contours of Masculine Desire: Romanticism and the Rise of Women's Poetry*. Oxford: Oxford University Press, 1989.

GENIUS

The *Oxford English Dictionary*'s earliest example of the word *genius* in the sense of "native intellectual power of an exalted type" dates from 1749, and it was during the middle and later years of the eighteenth century that this term began to be used, first in Britain and then in Germany, to denote that combination of original creative power and transcendent or uncommon insight which we particularly associate with Romanticism. From the 1770s onward, indeed, genius is so often used in combination with the idea of an organically shaping imagination that the two qualities or capacities cannot easily be separated. As with so many aspects of Romanticism—including many traditionally attributed to German sources—however, this meaning is clearly anticipated in Mark Akenside's *Pleasures of Imagination* (1744), which notably calls on "Some heav'nly genius, whose unclouded thoughts / Attain that secret harmony which blends / Th'aetherial spirit with its mold of clay" to teach the poet how God or nature enables us to discover that the physical world is ultimately an expression of our own imaginative powers. Samuel Johnson's *Dictionary* of 1775, however, resists connecting genius with imagination (let alone the imagination which, in Akenside, first creates and then reveals the significance of physical nature), going no further than to define genius as "Mental powers or faculties" (albeit the faculties of a *man* of genius are defined as "superiour"). Similarly with regard to imagination, Johnson is distinctly reserved, defining it as "the power of forming ideal pictures" or "the power of representing things absent to oneself or others." Akenside's use of these terms, however, is echoed in the work of the Scottish philosopher Alexander Gerard, whose *Essay on Genius* (1774) specifically associates this quality with an organically shaping imagination which imitates the creativity of nature, anticipating the better-known theories of Samuel Taylor Coleridge and Friedrich Wilhelm Joseph von Schelling. Akenside's pioneering work had been translated into German as early as 1756; yet Gerard's work, which was translated in 1776, perhaps exercised a wider influence on German thinkers of the late eighteenth century, and was received with particular enthusiasm by Immanuel Kant's contemporary, J. N. Tetens, who in turn was read by Kant himself, as well as by Coleridge and Schelling. Tetens's influence on Romantic theories of imagination (especially those of Coleridge) was extensive, and like Gerard he regarded genius as consisting chiefly in the possession of an unusual degree of this power. It was the arch-Romantic Schelling, however, who (chiefly in his *System of Transcendental Idealism*, 1800) added to these organicist theories the view of genius and imagination as reflecting a divine creative power in their capacity to reestablish the original unity of self and other, or the conscious and unconscious minds, which he called "the Absolute." In addition, Schelling was distinctive in describing these powers (particularly as manifested in the work of art) as uniquely facilitating the resolution of that problem that philosophy itself could never overcome—namely, how to reconcile the free production of our own ideas and interpretations with the seemingly objective facts of the world around us. It is in this leap of thought that we find the seeds of so many Romantic (and later nineteenth-century) authors' fascination with the unity of mind and nature, and the ability to discover one's own thoughts and feelings reflected in the world around us. Hence, also, the widespread Romantic view of genius, whether manifested in the creative arts themselves, or in philosophy, science, and politics, as consisting in the power to make a leap of imagination which overcomes the problems others have found insuperable. Even Schelling's celebration of the power of imaginative genius to rediscover the unity of mind and nature, however, can be seen as echoing Akenside's original combination of Neo platonism with organicist theories of imagination; yet Schelling explores and celebrates this power more vigorously than any other Romantic, and encapsulates the vision of transcendent genius which was later adopted and emulated by poets from Coleridge to John Keats and beyond. Coleridge is the chief British advocate of this organicist and Neo platonic theory, and his explorations of it in prose and poetry are among the most vivid expressions of this Romantic trend. As in Gerard, however, it is William Shakespeare whom Coleridge sees as most vividly exemplifying this capacity to create, from one's imagination, a world no less vivid and complex than that formed by the divine creative power. In addition, Coleridge echoes not only Gerard, but also Étienne Bonnot de Condillac, Kant, and others in contrasting genius with the lesser quality of "talent," or "the comparative facility of acquiring, arranging, and applying the stock furnished by others," and whose secondary status is thus analogous to that of "fancy" in its relation to "imagination." Coleridge's distinction between "absolute genius" (or the genius manifested in artistic creativity) and "commanding genius" (or that expressed in politics and practical activity) is not so clearly derived from earlier thinkers, albeit some critics locate its origin in Johann Christoph Friedrich von Schiller. As Coleridge's connection of "commanding genius" with the evils of Napoleon suggests, however, in many later Romantic authors the importance of genius lies partly in its association with a transcendent individualism that pursues its own course, whether for good or ill, and is often ambiguously associated with the transgressive qualities of so many Gothic antiheroes. Feminist critics in particular have highlighted the evils which Mary Shelley implicitly associated with this power and its manifestations in the Romantic poets she knew so well; and we should not ignore the extent to which Lord Byron's stance of heroic individualism, which led to his near-deification by contemporaries including Johann Wolfgang von Goethe, echoes or seeks to emulate the qualities of genius described by earlier Romantic theorists.

DAVID VALLINS

Bibliography

Akenside, Mark. *The Poetical Works of Mark Akenside.* Edited by Robin Dix. Madison, N.J.: Associated University Presses, 1996.

Coleridge, S. T. *Biographia Literaria.* 2 vols. Edited by James Engell and W. Jackson Bate. Princeton, N.J.: Princeton University Press, 1983.

———. *The Friend.* 2 vols. Edited by Barbara E. Rooke. Princeton, N.J.: Princeton University Press, 1969.

Engell, James. *The Creative Imagination: Enlightenment to Romanticism.* Cambridge, Mass.: Harvard University Press, 1981.

Johnson, Samuel. *A Dictionary of the English Language.* 2 vols. London, 1775.

Mellor, Anne K. *Mary Shelley: Her Life, Her Fiction, Her Monsters.* London: Routledge, 1988.

Schelling, F. W. J. *System of Transcendental Idealism.* Translated by Peter Heath. Charlottesville: University of Virginia Press, 1978.

Simpson, David, ed. *German Aesthetic and Literary Criticism: Kant, Fichte, Schelling, Schopenhauer, Hegel.* Cambridge: Cambridge University Press, 1984.

Wheeler, Kathleen, ed. *German Aesthetic and Literary Criticism: The Romantic Ironists and Goethe.* Cambridge: Cambridge University Press, 1984.

GEOFFROY SAINT-HILAIRE, ETIENNE 1772–1844

Etienne Geoffroy Saint-Hilaire was France's foremost Romantic biologist. His struggle with the doyen of French biology, his friend and rival Georges Cuvier, attracted enormous interest in France and Europe, both within and beyond the scientific community.

One of the many bright young men forging careers in revolutionary Paris, Geoffroy Saint-Hilaire received a professorship at the Paris Museum of Natural History in 1793. He was partly responsible for convincing Cuvier, another ambitious young scientist, to come to Paris in 1795. (Even after he and Cuvier became bitter rivals, he considered his bringing Cuvier to Paris one of the great achievements of his life.) The two lived together briefly and collaborated on five natural history papers. They parted in 1798 when Geoffroy Saint-Hilaire accepted, and Cuvier declined, a position in Napoleon Bonaparte's expedition to Egypt. Geoffroy Saint-Hilaire's time in Egypt was very productive. His study of Egyptian fish led him to compare the skeletons of fish with those of other vertebrates. Belief in the "unity of plan"—the idea that all vertebrates, and ultimately all animals, are variations on a single design—marked all of Geoffroy Saint-Hilaire's subsequent scientific work. Intellectually, the source for this idea was Count de Buffon's *Histoire Naturelle* (1849–88; 36 vols.), of which Geoffroy Saint-Hilaire was a great admirer. He found many parallels, or "homologies" between fish skeletons and those of mammals, but the question of the bones of the osculum (the fish's gill cover) vexed him. There seemed to be no obvious parallel in the human skull.

Geoffroy Saint-Hilaire wished to make anatomy philosophical, to go beyond merely accumulating facts about various creatures. His fondness for grand theory, and an encounter with some electric fish, led him in his last days in Egypt to devise a unified theory of the physical universe in terms of forces and fluids, a theory which he never seems to have entirely abandoned. On his return to France in 1802, he found French natural history dominated by Cuvier, who was suspicious of both grand theory and the idea of a universal plan of design for all animals. Geoffroy Saint-Hilaire set forth his own views, and opposed Cuvier's, in *Philosophical Anatomy* (1818). He asserted that all vertebrates had fundamentally the same skeletal system, and that each part had a parallel on all other creatures. He solved the problem of the osculum by paralleling it with the bones of the mammalian ear. In the 1820s, Geoffroy Saint-Hilaire expanded this parallelism to invertebrate creatures, finding parallels between the exoskeletons of insects and the skeletons of mammals, for example. This was an unmistakable challenge to Cuvier, who had divided all animals into four completely independent classes. It also led to an alliance between Geoffroy Saint-Hilaire and his followers, the "philosophical anatomists," and the German naturephilosophers (proponents of the school of thought known as *Naturphilosophie*), who had arrived at similar conclusions by a somewhat different route. As early as 1817, Geoffroy Saint-Hilaire's work had been published in German nature-philosophy journals. He adopted from the nature-philosopher Lorenz Oken the idea that the skull is composed of fused vertebrae. Despite the benefits of this alliance in spreading "philosophical anatomy" in Germany, association with what Cuvier and other French scientists saw as mysticism left Geoffroy Saint-Hilaire vulnerable to attack.

During the 1820s, Geoffroy Saint-Hilaire also engaged in teratology, the study of monsters, which he was one of the first to integrate into a general biological theory. He hoped to create a classification scheme for human and animal monsters that would emphasize commonalities in the body parts deformed and the ways they were deformed. He actually attempted to create monstrous birds from eggs, either by surgically interfering with the mother or by exposing the eggs to extreme conditions. This was not successful in advancing knowledge. Some of his writings from this period touch on evolution, but unlike his friend Jean Lamarck, he never made it a major feature of his biological theory.

The tension between Geoffroy Saint-Hilaire and Cuvier peaked in 1830. Two obscure provincial naturalists submitted a paper supporting the "philosophical anatomist" position by arguing that the arrangement of the organs of mollusks was homologous to that of vertebrates. In reporting the paper to the Academy of Sciences, Geoffroy Saint-Hilaire repeated and ridiculed a passage from one of Cuvier's writings on cephalopods, without mentioning the author's name. Cuvier's reply, expounding on the differences between cephalopod and vertebrate anatomy, was generally considered to be an accurate and worthy response by his and Geoffroy Saint-Hilaire's scientific peers. But opinion was different outside the scientific community. Geoffroy Saint-Hilaire carried the argument into the public realm, appealing to a broader audience with an account of the controversy, *Principles of Zoological Philosophy* (1830). Geoffroy Saint-Hilaire presented himself and his views in Romantic terms, as a rebel standing against the scientific despotism of Cuvier, a role that made him a hero, particularly of anticlericals and politi-

cal leftists. Pamphlets and dramas presented him as a true philosopher and friend of man, while Cuvier was presented as a pedant and corrupt politician. Johann Wolfgang von Goethe, who admired Geoffroy Saint-Hilaire, published two articles in his support, and considered the conflict between the two French scientists a more significant event than the French Political Revolution of 1830. Prominent Romantic figures who supported Geoffroy Saint-Hilaire included George Sand, who corresponded with him; Edgar Quinet; and Honoré de Balzac; who dedicated the second edition of *Pere Goriot* (1842) to him.

The immediate conflict ended with Cuvier's death in 1832. Geoffroy Saint-Hilaire made an effort to take his place as the leader of French biology and as permanent secretary of the Academy of Sciences, but this attempt was unsuccessful due to his age and failing powers. He began delivering long-winded and obscure essays expounding a universal system of natural philosophy based on the idea, which he never fully explained, of "self for self": presumably based on the notion of self-attraction as a universal principle. He successfully toured Germany, whose scientific culture he extolled over that of France. His funeral in 1844 was a great occasion, attended by thousands, including Victor Hugo.

WILLIAM BURNS

Biography

Born in Étampes, France, April 15, 1772. Graduated in law, 1790. Studied medicine under Louis Daubenton; also studied sciences at the Collège du Cardinal Lemoine, Paris. Superintendent, cabinet of zoology, Jardin des Plantes, Paris, 1793; chair of zoology, French National Museum of Natural History, 1793–1844. Collaborated with Georges Cuvier on natural history papers, 1795–98. Participated in scientific expedition attached to Napoleon's Egyptian invasion, 1798–1801. Married Pauline Briere de Mondetour, 1804; they had three children. Admitted to the Académie des Sciences, 1807. Appointed professor of zoology at the University of Paris, 1809. Representative for Étampes in the National Assembly during the Hundred Days, 1815. Engaged in major scientific debate with Cuvier, 1830–32. Died in Paris, June 19, 1844.

Selected Works

Philosophie Anatomique, 1818.
Essai de Classification des Monstres Paris, 1821.
Principes de Philosophie Zoologique dicutes en mars 1830 a l'Academie Paris, 1830.
Catalogue des Mammiferes du Museum Paris, 1903.

Bibliography

Appel, Toby A. *The Cuvier-Geoffroy Debate: French Biology in the Decades before Darwin*. New York: Oxford University Press, 1987.
Geoffroy Saint Hilaire, Isidore. *Vie, Travaux et Doctrine Scientifique D'Etienne Geoffroy Saint-Hilaire*. 1847.
Le Guyader, Herve. *Geoffroy Saint-Hilaire: Un Naturaliste Visionnaire*. Paris: Belin, 1998.

GÉRARD, FRANÇOIS-PASCAL-SIMON 1770–1837

French painter

As a member of the first generation of artists to train with Jacques-Louis David, François-Pascal-Simon Gérard might be expected to have developed a version of his master's innovative classicism, which was first fully revealed in the *Oath of the Horatii*, exhibited in 1785 (a mere year before Gérard joined David's studio). As Gérard reached maturity, however, the French Revolution intervened; it was an event significant enough to shift the focus of David himself, let alone that of a young and unestablished artist. Gérard's first important independent works were, therefore, contingent upon the complicated and fluctuating circumstances of the early 1790s. In 1794, he entered a government-sponsored competition that called for depictions of significant recent events. His entry, *The French People Demanding the Overthrow of the Tyrant on 10 August 1792*, shows the Paris populace entering the National Assembly in search of Louis XVI and his family, who had sought sanctuary there. The revolutionary legislators become incoherent in the face of the armed mob, whose ugly mood is specified by a banner atop a pike reading "Plus de roi" ("No more kings"). This is a turbulent image, albeit guided by David's *Oath of the Tennis Court* (1791), but it is either reportage or historical re-creation, hardly essential Romanticism.

Left more to his own devices, Gérard did, unsurprisingly, emulate the classical vein pioneered by David and produced his best-known work, *Cupid and Psyche*, in 1798. This may now seem merely a glossy piece of vapid eroticism, with the undeniably attractive and largely naked young couple set against a simplified landscape background. It appears more resonant, however, when put into context. In the late 1790s, David's studio was dominated by a group of students known as the Méditateurs. Extreme radicals, they sought an art even more purified than their master's, which they characterized as "rococo." All contemporary artists suffered abuse at their hands, with the exception of Gérard, whom they characterized as "naive"—a term of approbation for them. The "Méditateurs" distanced themselves from society, deliberately adopting outlandish clothes and practicing quasi-occult rites (both distinctly Romantic traits). Gérard did not consciously encourage this group, but their slightly later work has strong stylistic affinities with *Cupid and Psyche*. Unwittingly, he may have been a role model for a group that has been characterized as constituting the first bohemians.

Gérard's early prominence is indicated by a commission in 1800 from Bonaparte, installed as first consul in the previous year, to illustrate a theme from Ossian. Now little considered outside specialist circles, the Ossianic sagas were very popular at the time and were particularly loved by Bonaparte. Initially presented as "translated" by James Macpherson, and in fact largely written by him, they weave tales of Nordic heroes, who stood for some as equal counterparts to the classical heroes of Homer. Gérard's painting, completed in 1801, is conventionally titled *Ossian Evoking the Spirits on the Banks of the Lora to the Sound of his Harp*. A misty, moonlit landscape reveals the bard Ossian by the river's edge, leaning over his harp; behind him are the ghostly figures of the warriors and maidens who people his poetry. As James Rubin has pertinently suggested, it is unclear whether these figures are the emanations of Ossian's poetic imagination, or whether by contrast they provide inspiration. Hence the doubts about the accuracy of the conventional title, not traceable back to the artist himself. There is no doubt about the fundamentally nonclassical nature of the picture. Gérard's work generally looks highly polished, but one contemporary critic described this work as "an impassioned sketch in flight from his brushes." This unusual analysis suggests the playful, the unspecific, the Romantic. The most crucial element was again recognized by a contemporary, who wrote, "The best aspect is not to have chosen an isolated episode from Ossian's life but to have focused on a general aspect which can indicate a whole system." In other words, Gérard is attempting to visualize Ossian's complete poetic practice, a massive and genuinely Romantic aspiration.

Gérard's early work indicates that he was far from being merely a follower of David. He negotiated his own path through strange regions—notably, the far north of the Ossianic world—but this was not to be his natural habitat. As he developed he became known as the painter of king and the king of painters, for his socially illustrious portrait clientele and for the wealth that they provided. His portrait practice was indeed formidable, encompassing the pomp of the court and the enduring sexual allure of society beauties (particularly *Mme Récamier*, 1805). He continued occasionally, however, to work in other genres. In 1819, he produced *Corinne at Cape Miseno*, illustrating an episode from Madame Anne-Louise-Germaine de Staël's novel *Corinne, ou l'Italie* (1807). The eponymous poet-heroine holds a lyre, akin to Ossian's harp, and like him indicates uncertainty as to the nature of poetic inspiration. Corinne's vacant expression, however, and the clumsy placement of the other figures, seriously compromise the coherence of the work.

Gérard had considerable success in 1828 with a rare venture into religious painting. *Saint Thérésa* was produced for the Infirmerie de Marie-Thérèse, a Parisian hospice supported by the social elite, including François-Auguste-René, Vicomte de Chateaubriand's wife. Shown in a public exhibition prior to its installation in the hospice chapel, it was favorably reviewed. One critic wrote that the saint "is far outside of herself; she is already in heaven." Anyone imagining, however, the eroticoreligious ecstasy of Gian Lorenzo Bernini's *Saint Theresa* will be sorely disappointed. In the painting, a young nun kneels awkwardly against a column with an equivocal expression even less convincing than Corinne's. A more judicious critic saw the work as an accurate reflection of the religious ideals of the aristocratic inhabitants of the Faubourg Saint-Germain—hardly making it a paradigm of Romanticism.

It would not be fair to say that Gérard lost his way; rather, he found it. We might want to applaud his ambition in taking on the daunting subject of poetic inspiration in 1800 via his *Ossian* canvas. But there was no guaranteed market for probing work of this nature during the Napoleonic period. Flattering Napoleon's officers and officials, and their wives and mistresses, was a surer way to success. Gérard did make later attempts to come to terms with the emerging new aesthetic (Eugène Delacroix's first public exhibit, *The Barque of Dante*, was shown in

1822 at the same exhibition as a replica of *Corinne*) but perhaps without real commitment. He was not, then, a Romantic painter as such, but showed at the outset of his career, a breadth of imagination of which many Romantics would have been proud.

ED LILLEY

Biography

Born in Rome, May 4, 1770, where his father was a diplomat. Returned with his family to France in 1782 and attended the studios of, (successively) the sculptor Augustin Pajou and the painter Nicolas-Guy Brenet before switching to that of Jacques-Louis David in 1786. Competed unsuccessfully for the Prix de Rome organized by the Royal Academy of Painting and Sculpture, in 1789 but visited Italy 1790–91. The latter year saw his first exhibit at the Paris Salon. On the death of his mother in 1793, Gérard married her younger sister. He was made a member of the Légion d'Honneur in 1802, the year of its institution, and thereafter gained many distinctions. Named First Painter to the Empress Josephine in 1806, he became professor at the Ecole des Beaux-Arts in 1811. King Louis XVIII made him his "First Painter" in 1817 and created him baron in 1819. He found equal favour with King Louis-Philippe after the 1830 Revolution, receiving prestigious commissions for decorating Versailles. He died in Paris on January 11, 1837.

Selected Works

Le Peuple français demandant la destitution du tyran à la journée du 10 août 1792. 1794–95. Graphite, pen, and wash on paper, 67 cm × 92 cm. Musée du Louvre, Paris.
Psyché et l'Amour. 1798. Oil on canvas, 186 cm × 132 cm. Exhibited at the Paris Salon 1798. Musée du Louvre, Paris.
Portrait de Mme Récamier. 1805. Oil on canvas, 225 cm × 148 cm. Now in the Musée Carnavalet, Paris.
Ossian évoque les fantômes au son de la harpe sur les bords du Lora. Oil on canvas, 184 cm × 194 cm. Now in the Kunsthalle, Hamburg. The original is lost, and the details herein refer to a version painted by Gérard around 1810.
Corinne au Cap Misène. 1819. Oil on canvas, 256 cm × 277 cm. Musée des Beaux-Arts, Lyon.
Saint Theresa (Sainte Thérèse). 1828. Oil on canvas, 172 cm × 96 cm. Infirmerie Marie-Thérèse, Paris.

Bibliography

Crow, Thomas. *Emulation: Making Artists for Revolutionary France*. New Haven, Conn.: Yale University Press, 1995.
French Painting 1774–1830: The Age of Revolution. Exhibition catalog. Paris: Grand Palais/Detroit: Institute of Arts/New York: Metropolitan Museum of Art, 1974–5.
Gérard, Henri. *Correspondance de François Gérard*. Paris: Lainé, 1867.
———. *Lettres adressées au baron François Gérard*. Paris: Quantin, 1886.
Honour, Hugh. *Romanticism*. London: Allen Lane, 1979.
Hubert, Gérard. "L'Ossian de François Gérard et ses variants," *La Revue du Louvre* 17 (1967): 239–48.
Lenormant, Charles. *François Gérard, peintre d'histoire: essai de biographie et de critique*. 2d ed. Paris: René, 1847.
Levitine, George. *The Dawn of Bohemianism*. University Park: Pennsylvania State University Press, 1978.
Rubin, James. "New Documents on the Méditateurs: Baron Gérard, Mantegna, and French Romanticism circa 1800," *Burlington Magazine* 117 (1975): 785–90.
Rubin, James. "Gérard's Painting of 'Ossian' as an Allegory of Inspired Art," *Studies in Romanticism* 15 (1976): 383–94.
Spencer-Longhurst, Paul. "Gérard, François (-Pascal-Simon)" *The Dictionary of Art*. Vol. 12. Edited by Jane Turner. London: Macmillan, 1996.

GÉRICAULT, JEAN LOUIS ANDRÉ THÉODORE 1791–1824

French painter and graphic artist

Born to an elite family of Royalist sympathies, Jean Louis André Théodore Géricault passed his short life within the era of neoclassical painting; his work, however, embodies the formal characteristics and emotional spirit of Romanticism that assumed definite shape under Eugène Delacroix. Géricault's anatomical studies, portraits of the insane, and translations of contemporary events embody the spirit of individuality and heroism that became hallmark characteristics of Romanticism, the movement that triumphed at the Paris Salon of 1824.

Géricault attended the Lycée Impérial, but left there in 1808. He found two masters, Carle Vernet and Pierre-Narcisse Guérin. Vernet, a painter of horses and hunting scenes, seems to have influenced Géricault's handling of landscape, while Guérin's classical modeling of the figure and explicit gestures with a clean, linear style, are given a Romantic sensibility in Géricault's later figural compositions.

To review his career is to consider also his working method. Three sketchbooks (a sketchbook of 1808, the Zoubaloff sketchbook in the Louvre, and a piecemeal sketchbook in the Art Institute of Chicago) bear witness to the genesis of many of Géricault's compositions. He frequented the Louvre, which had recently been filled with masterpieces from Italy, Flanders, Germany, and Spain. At the Louvre, he studied works by Titian, Raphael, Caravagio, Nicolas Poussin, Peter Paul Rubens, Anthony van Dyck, and Rembrandt von Rijn. On tour of Italy, he was fascinated by Michelangelo's handling as well as the diversity of form in classical sculptures. Thus, he intended to emulate the abundance of energy he perceived through close examination of such figural compositions.

He offered his *Charging Chasseur* for debut at the Paris Salon in 1812. Featuring a presumably anonymous rider on horseback engaged in a heroic charge on the battlefield, the painting shows his emancipation from Guérin's classical teaching and his adoption of the heroism of Rubens and van Dyck. The painting was awarded the highest honor. By contrast, his Salon entry in 1814, *Wounded Cuirassier*, was unfavorably received. Against the background of the empire's decline and the First Restoration, the painting presented the transformation of the heroic military figure from a charging, powerful force into a lonely, defeated individual immersed, rather, in melancholic heroism.

After a visit to Italy that yielded three landscapes, genre scenes, and ample interaction with antique inspiration, Géricault's interest became quasi-journalistic in 1818 as he absorbed his interests in specific events that dominated French opinion through popular press and lithographs. One such event was the murder case known as the Fualdès Affair, concerning a politician who suffered a tragic, cruel, and savage death the previous year. He completed a series of drawings for the *Murder of Fualdès* (1818), and abandoned this subject to take up that of another genuine horror story, the sinking of a ship, *Medusa*, off the coast of West Africa.

To capture the tragedy of the dying survivors of a contemporary shipwreck, Géricault involved himself in meticulous study. He had a small replica of the raft built by the ship's carpenter, went to Dieppe to study the natural conditions such as waves, clouds, and sky, explored the dissecting rooms at hospitals to witness the physical characteristics of extreme deprivation, and examined severed limbs and heads of executed persons.

Entitled *The Raft of the Medusa*, the finished painting debuted at the Salon in 1819, where Guérin, Géricault's former teacher, marveled at it. Jean-Auguste-Dominique Ingres, however,—proponent of the classical school of painting—found it repellent, fearing that it would corrupt the young students of the academy, who might view it and try to imitate its violence and labored technique. The idealized figures and realistic agony, when accompanied by fiery color silhouetted by tempestuous shadows, graphic detail, and powerful emotion, aroused a storm of controversy between neoclassical and Romantic artists. The work remained unsold upon the close of the exhibition, but Géricault took it to England, where it was on view at the Egyptian Hall in Piccadilly, among other places, and received favorable review in *The London Times*.

While in England Géricault experimented with lithography; he also continued to paint, adopting refined subjects such as ladies in the park and horse racing (*Epsom Derby of 1821*), as well as mundane subjects including a factory, a public hanging, and the urban poor. His last years were extremely productive, during which he painted portraits of patients afflicted with delusions or monomanias that demonstrate the predilection of romantic artists with derangement, neuroses, and inner struggles.

Throughout his career, Géricault posed a dialogue with other artists. *The Raft of the Medusa*, for example, echoes Michelangelo's *Last Judgment*, which features tragic groups in both contemplative and writhing poses. Géricault emulated Caravaggio, whose plastic forms and sharp chiaroscuro are evident in *The Raft of the Medusa* and its rudimentary studies with subtle, warm tones that also invoke Rubens. Among his contemporaries, Géricault admired Antoine-Jean Gros. His handling of animals and genre scenes, beautifully exhibited in the monumental landscapes and the lithographs, are indebted to James Ward, George Morland, and David Wilkie.

Yet, throughout Géricault's work runs a thread of psychic darkness that exudes Romantic sensibilities of tension, mobility, and desperation. From his early military compositions and his representation of tragic human suffering to his abundant output in his last three years, Géricault's career was marked by sustained representation of action and emotional condition that reflect his colorful, energetic subjects that reject, to a large degree, the balanced, idealized harmonic compositions of many classical (often academic) painters. Nonetheless, his works, as Walter Friedlaender has noted, capture the essence not of particular heroes, but of heroism; that is, the heroic endurance of the anonymous, suffering at the hands of fate and their fellow men. Géricault lends them a pathos and passion attained neither by his predecessors nor by his contemporaries.

JUILEE DECKER

Biography

Born in Rouen, September 26, 1791. Training under Carle Vernet, 1808, and Pierre-Narcisse Guérin, 1810. Self-guided study at the Louvre, 1811–12. Entry to Salon, *Charging Chasseur*, 1812. Entry to Salon, *Wounded Cuirassier*, 1814. Joined royalist forces acting as the King's bodyguards, 1814–16. Study in Italy, 1816–17. Salon entry, *The Raft of the Medusa*, 1819. Visit to England, where he took up lithography, 1820. Portraits of the insane, 1821–23. Died January 26, 1824.

Bibliography

Bazin, Germain. *Théodore Géricault: Etude critique, documents, et catalogue raisonné*. 5 vols. Paris: Bibliothèque des Arts, 1987–92.

Berger, Klaus. *Géricault and His Work*. Translated by Winslow Ames. Lawrence: University of Kansas Press, 1955.

Clément, Charles. *Géricault, etude biographique et critique*. Paris: Didier, 1879. Revised and updated edition *Géricault: a Biographical and Critical Study with a Catalogue Raisonné of the Master's Works*. New York: Da Capo, 1974.

Delteil, Loys. *Théodore Géricault (Le Peintre-Graveur illustré)*. Vol. 17. Paris: Loys Delleil (chez e'antetur) 1924.

Eitner, Lorenz. *Géricault, His Life and Work*. London: Orbis, 1983.

Friedlaender, Walter. *David to Delacroix*. Translated by Robert Goldwater. Cambridge, Mass.: Harvard University Press, 1952.

Stranahan, C. H. *A History of French Painting from its Earliest to its Latest Practice including an account of the French Academy of Painting, its salons schools of instruction and regulations*. 1888.

Thuillier, Jacques. Introduction to *Tout l'oeuvre peint de Géricault*. Paris: Flammarion, 1991.

GERMAN IDEALISM: ITS PHILOSOPHICAL LEGACY

The era of German Idealism began with Immanuel Kant and ended with G. W. F. Hegel. The influence of Hegelian Idealism (especially in its materialist reformulation by Karl Marx) has profoundly affected the historical development of social, political, and cultural thought in the twentieth century. German Idealism, in its post-Kantian Romantic formulation, had a lasting impact on the development of later continental European philosophy, most especially in the notions of subjectivity in the movements of modern existentialist philosophy and postmodern structuralist/deconstructionist thought.

The reception of Hegel's historicism in the nineteenth century was divided into two camps, the so-called conservative right, or "old," and the radical left, or "young," Hegelians. The former were of the opinion that the (often repressive) political systems of that time in Europe were the true realization of the Hegelian *Geist* (spirit/mind) in its progression through history. The latter group believed that the realization of the Geist had not yet occurred, and that radical political and social change was necessary. The Young Hegelians were atheists and anarchists, and included important individuals such as Ludwig Feuerbach and Max Stirner.

Karl Marx, along with Friedrich Engels, was one of the radical Young Hegelians; he turned Hegelian Idealism on its head and reinterpreted the dialectical progress of the Hegelian Geist through history (thesis–antithesis–synthesis) in strictly materialist–economic terms; that is, that the conditions of material reality determined the progress of humanity or the Geist in history and not vice versa. Industrial capitalism had emerged as the antithesis to agrarian barter economies and was destined to be opposed by the advent of its antithesis, socialism, Marx's Romantic vision of an equitable ideal society. He thereby introduced, both literally and figuratively, a revolutionary spirit of change that spread throughout the world. The socialist–communist revolutions in Russia and China, and in numerous other countries as well, have profoundly affected the course of modern history.

The influence of Hegelianism on modern thought, most especially in the areas of political–historical philosophy and aesthetics, can be seen in most subsequent German schools of thought, in the teachings of Bernard Bosanquet and F.H. Bradley at British universities, and in the work of Benedetto Croce and Giovanni Gentile in Italy. Hegel's metaphysical notion of the Geist as progress in history became transformed into an issue of political ideologies and was used to justify both leftist and rightist sociopolitical agendas, specifically in the justification of totalitarian government control. Karl Popper, in his important 1962 work *The Open Society and its Enemies*, sought to blame the twin evils of modern communism (in the former Soviet Union and in China) and fascism (in its Second-World-War German and Italian manifestations) on these perversions of Hegelianism.

Among the post-Kantian idealist thinkers, which included important figures such as Johann Gottlieb Fichte and Friedrich Wilhelm Joseph von Schelling, was that of Arthur Schopenhauer. Kant's fundamental insight—that there is a difference between reality as it is objectively and as it is subjectively constructed by mind—had created a seemingly unbridgeable division between consciousness and world. Schopenhauer's revision of the Kantian duality of noumenon and phenomenon as the *Wille und Vorstellung* ("will and its representation") became fashionable after 1848; it injected a dimension of irrationality and pessimism into the emerging nineteenth-century spirit of optimistic positivism and the Hegelian belief in the progress of science. For the dour Schopenhauer, reality as it truly is (the Kantian "thing in itself") is will, a metaphysical life force or striving that is absolute, amoral, and nonrational. The will seeks only to perpetuate itself in unending cycles of creation and destruction that are without any final goal or teleology other than its own self-assertion. In a sense, Schopenhauer's thought is a metaphysical counterpart to the Darwinian scientific vision of biological evolution in the process of genetics and natural selection. The individual human being has meaning only as a tool through which the will asserts itself, and he/she can find peace only in a "Buddhistic" stilling (or quietism) of the individual's will (or "desire") or in the Romantic transcendence (or escape) afforded by the disinterestedness inherent in aesthetic experience. This bleak view of nature contributed to the modern, post-Romantic experience of alienation and to the aesthetic philosophy of modernism in the arts.

Friedrich Nietzsche—considered, along with Søren Kierkegaard, to be one of the founders of modern existential thought—conceived much of his work as a response to Schopenhauerian pessimism, as an attempt to overcome, with "joyful wisdom," the nihilism and "enervation" of the will to live (or the impulse to suicide) that is implicit in Schopenhauer's profoundly atheistic vision of the individual's existence as a source of unlimited suffering. In a universe that is without divine providence, only absolute contingency rules, and the task of creating existential meaning becomes for Nietzsche a uniquely human and heroic enterprise (of the "superman" or *Übermensch*), most especially through creation in the *Wille zur Macht* ("will to power"). In a world where there is a perceived gap between consciousness and reality, there is also a profound experience of alienation and a turn toward irrationalism (for Nietzsche, the "Dionysian") as a distrust of reason and science. Nietzsche's examination of Western culture found that what passes for truth is often a product of language, especially metaphor, that has become reified. With its rejection of all rationalist absolutes, existentialism thereby proposes a radically irrational post-Romantic vision of the individual as the sole criterion of "existential" truth.

Later existentialist thinkers (for example, Martin Heidegger and Karl Jaspers in Germany, and Albert Camus and Jean-Paul Sartre in France) sought to explore the consequences of atheism, irrationalism, and alienation in terms of philosophical discourse and in moral and social behavior. Dismissing all previous Western metaphysics (including Kant), Heidegger turned to the quasi-religious thought of the pre-Socratic Greeks (for example Heraclitus) in order to examine what has become the alienation of the modern age from "being" (*Sein*), the fundamental ground of nothingness from which human existence (*Dasein*) springs. Sartre's doctrine that "existence preceeds essence" set out for the individual the radical task of creating (through free choice) meaning when there are no *a priori* truths with which he/she can identify. Religious existentialists such as Karl Barth, Nicholas Berdyaev, and Martin Buber followed the example of Kierkegaard's "leap of faith" and examined the problem of spiritual belief in a universe in which the divinity is seemingly silent.

THOMAS F. BARRY

Bibliography

Acton, H. B. "Hegelian Political and Religious Ideas." *Dictionary of the History of Ideas*. Vol. 2. Edited by Philip H. Wiener. New York: Scribner's, 1973. 407–16.

Ameriks, Karl, ed. *Cambridge Companion to German Idealism*. Cambridge Companions to Philosophy series. Cambridge: Cambridge University Press, 2001.

Barrett, William. *Irrational Man: A Study in Existential Philosophy*. New York: Doubleday, 1958.

Fairlamb, Horace L. *Critical Conditions: Postmodernism and the Question of Foundations*. Cambridge: Cambridge University Press, 1994.

Löwith, Karl. *From Hegel to Nietzsche*. New York: Holt, Rinehart and Winston, 1964.

Manfred, Frank. *What is Neostructuralism?* Translated by Sabine Wilke and Richard Gray. Minneapolis: University of Minnesota Press, 1989.

GERMAN ROMANTICISM: ITS LITERARY LEGACY

German Romanticism greatly influenced the development of later nineteenth and twentieth century literature in Europe and the United States. The German Bildungsroman, or novel of education, of the Romantic era (notably by Christoph Martin Wieland and Johann Wolfgang von Goethe), for example, influenced later American writers such as Herman Melville and Philip Roth. As the poetic realism of mid-nineteenth century German literature evolved into the positivistic social realism of naturalism, there was also a corresponding countermovement at the end of the nineteenth century toward the interiority (the inner world of dreams, visions, and intuitions) that had characterized earlier Romantic literature. Some of the most famous German authors of the twentieth century are associated with this post-Romantic trend. Hermann Hesse's novels of mystical inwardness and Eastern-tinged spirituality are most clearly indebted to the Romantic period. Likewise, an Thomas Mann owes much to German idealism, especially to Arthur Schopenhauer and Friedrich Nietzsche, and to Romantic themes of the transcendence of art and the decadence of the artist versus the vitality of the bourgeois. For some authors, however, this literary trend—in the spirit of Sigmund Freud and his early followers—was more valuable in the context of a psychological exploration of the nature of consciousness and subjectivity. This period has been variously called *impressionism* (after the painting style), *neoclassicism*, and *neo-Romanticism*. The last term in German is *Neuromantik*, which is also a wordplay on *neuro*, suggesting the nerves and nervous system that first intrigued Freud. The Viennese writer Arthur Schnitzler, for example, wrote plays and stories that probed the nature of desire and the unconscious with such a degree of psychological acumen that Freud was prompted to call the writer his "alter ego." At this time, psychologically oriented narrative techniques such as stream of consciousness emerged in European literature.

The high valuation of art and the artist in Romantic literature was intensified around the turn of the century in the so-called art for art's sake (*l'art pour l'art*) movement. Oscar Wilde was its most visible adherent in British literature. The early poetry of Rainer Maria Rilke evolved from Romantic themes into a mature symbolic lyric that influenced the evolution of the modernist poetic sensibility in Europe and America. Writers such as William Carlos Williams and J. D. Salinger were keen admirers of Rilke's work. The esoteric lyric of Stefan George and the early writings of the young Viennese Hugo von Hofmannsthal explored the themes of aestheticism and the decadent-elitist artist.

The legacy of German Romanticism is most clearly evident in the German expressionist movement and the genesis of twentieth-century modernism in the arts. Early expressionist writers (the poet Georg Heym and the dramatist Carl Sternheim, for example) posited ecstatic emotion as the primal source of experience, and they have been compared in this regard to the German pre-Romantic Sturm und Drang (storm and stress) movement. The Romantic themes of the isolation of the artist from bourgeois society and the darker side of subjectivity (as an abyss of madness) are also common to these German expressionist writers. The impact of Immanuel Kant's idealistic philosophy, especially his aesthetics, on the development of modern art is enormous. Liberated from the need to produce a mimetic or a didactic art, and operating in a domain of the complete autonomy of consciousness (with the aesthetic, as opposed to the logical, attributes of language), the modernist literary artist was given, in the Kantian framework, the absolute freedom to create according to the dictates of the inner self and the idiosyncratic rules of the creative imagination. The result is an art that is variously surreal, abstract, and highly subjective. The inventory of poetic imagery, for example, became at times rather recondite and self-conscious, as in T. S. Eliot and Ezra Pound, or even esoteric and hermetic, as in the work of the Austrian poet Georg Trakl. The effect of this new aesthetic freedom was felt not only in literature but also in the visual arts (the Abstract Expressionism of the American painter Jackson Pollock, for example) and in music, as in the atonal abstract compositions of Arnold Schoenberg.

The German Expressionist writer who most clearly incorporates the aesthetic freedom inherited from the age of Romanticism and who remains undoubtedly the most influential of modernist prose writers is the lonely figure from Prague, Franz Kafka. He took the highly personal images of his own inner (and deeply conflicted) dream life and presented them as if they were objective realities, thereby producing a highly powerful and surreal body of fiction that has been of immeasurable influence on generations of later writers within and without Germany. A short list of Kafka's literary progeny might include names such as Kobo Abe W. H. Auden, Italo Calvino, and Philip Roth. Kafka's psychological fiction of the alienated self must also be seen in the context of the two most important intellectual movements of the modern era: the Freudian examination of the psyche and the existential vision of the self. Both of these perspectives have their roots in the literature of the Romantic era and its exploration of feeling and subjectivity as modes of knowledge.

Both the Freudian and existential perspectives explore the nature of human subjectivity, and they have had a considerable impact on the literature of the modern and postmodern eras. The fiction of the Swiss writer Max Frisch owes much to post-Romantic existentialist trends of the 1950s and 1960s. Despite the radical political movements of the 1960s in German-speaking nations, some authors of the 1970s took up post-Romantic concerns in what was termed the movement of "New Subjectivity" (*Neue Subjektivität*). Austrian writers such as Thomas Bernhard and Peter Handke turned towards the exploration of existential subjectivity and the isolation of the self in the artist. Handke was also especially influenced by postmodern developments in structuralism and in the manner in which language and linguistic signs structure perception of reality.

THOMAS F. BARRY

Bibliography

Batts, Michael S., Anthony W. Riley, and Heinz Wetzel, eds. *Echoes and Influences of German Romanticism: Essays in Honour of Hans Eichner*. New York: Peter Lang, 1987.

Bernd, Clifford A., Ingeborg Henderson, and Winder McConnell, eds. *Romanticism and Beyond: A Festschrift for John F. Fetzer*. California Studies in German and European Romanticism and in the Age of Goethe. Vol. 2. New York: Peter Lang, 1996.

Kipperman, Mark. *Beyond Enchantment: German Idealism and English Romantic Poetry*. Pittsburgh: University of Pennsylvania Press, 1986.

Seyhan, Azade. *Representation and Its Discontents: The Critical Legacy of German Romanticism*. Berkeley and Los Angeles: University of California Press, 1992.

Sokel, Walter H. *The Writer in Extremis: Expressionism in Twentieth-Century German Literature*. Stanford, Calif.: Stanford University Press, 1959.

GERMANY: CULTURAL SURVEY

In Germany, the era under consideration here was dominated by the rise and fall of Romanticism, a period generally defined by literary historians as beginning in the 1790s and ending in the 1830s, marked by the publication of Johann Wolfgang von Goethe's novel *Wilhelm Meister* (1795) and the deaths of Georg William Friedrich Hegel (1831) and Goethe (1832). The period is divided into an early and a late movement, a separation based more on generation, geography, and differences in approaches to literature and philosophy than on chronology, though Napoleon's invasion and the end of the Holy Roman Empire (1806) also serve as a dividing line between the two movements.

The term *Romantic*, with its derivative *romantisieren* (to render Romantic) has need of further definition. Rooted in at least two separate traditions, its immediate background places it within a nonclassical, nonestablished literary convention, a form of *littera vulgaris* that derived its impetus from an oral tradition, based on folklore. In this context the term can be traced back to French and Spanish romance, as defined by Samuel Johnson, and revived in a fanciful, chimerical, and sentimental style in England, from where it reached Germany. These trends, established in Germany during the Sturm und Drang (1770–90) movement, were associated with Johann Gottfried von Herder's concept of *Volk* and were stimulated by the Ossian phenomenon and a bardic tradition, harking back to the Middle Ages, particularly to legends surrounding Roland and the Arthurian Knights. Friedrich von Schlegel reappraised this tradition by referring specifically to "the older moderns, in Shakespeare, Cervantes, in Italian poetry, in that age of knights, love and fairy-tales in which the thing itself and the word for it originated." The young Goethe (*Götz von Berlichingen*, 1773; *Urfaust*, 1775; *Egmont*, 1787) and Faust, Part One 1808 and the young Friedrich Schiller (*Die Räuber* [*The Robbers*, 1781]; *Kabale und Liebe*, [*Love and Intrigue*, 1784]) form part of this tradition.

A separate but related origin of the term *Romantic* derived from a new depiction of nature in landscape painting, of rugged mountains, ancient ruins, and turbulent skies, often placed in contrast to scenes of pious contemplation in a Mediterranean setting. Literature borrowed from such paintings the topos *locus amoenis*, a compilation and intensification of opposites, indicating a critical turning point as the protagonist pursues his quest or yearning toward some higher aim. In *Heinrich von Ofterdingen* (1802), Novalis uses the term *Romantic* several times, denoting the chivalry of the Middle Ages, a period that established itself "between a period of cruel barbarism and a cultured, wise and opulent age." He also depicts the magic of the Orient as the land of poetry, a desire for the reconciliation of opposing natural forces, pilgrimage and heroic battles, and Romantic encounters where innocence and the "irresistible force of sweet passion and youthfulness" are consumed in a *Liebesrausch* (ecstasy of love). This second origin of the term strengthens the symbolical element, so that the symbol can fuse diverse elements and emotions, while at the same time affording them intellectual reflection. In this manner the Romantic image becomes sublimated, dissolves into emotion, and dematerializes; it becomes part of a mystical anticipation of the Golden Age that, in its transcendental infinity, evades permanence and completeness. Novalis described the art of "Romanticizing" as a "qualitative calculation involving powers," whereby a less important element is identified with a more important one: "The common object is given a higher significance, the ordinary gains a mysterious appearance, the familiar the dignity of the unknown, the finite is given the glow of infinity." Within the terms of such a mathematical analogy, the process will lead toward a hyperbolic infinity. Attempts to endow it with a spurious completeness or permanence must be countered through irony, an operation that, according to Schlegel, must destroy all semblance of perfection in order to keep alive "the irreconcilable conflict between the absolute and the conditionally presupposed."

The early Romantic movement distinguished itself in the realms of literature and philosophy; major achievements in fine art and music were to follow later. One of the first to develop a concept of art that was closely associated with landscape painting was Wilhelm Heinrich Wackenroder, whose *Confessions of an Art-Loving Friar* (1797) attempted to revitalize the Italian Renaissance, especially the luminosity and religious piety of Raphael. Wackenroder composed his own "landscapes in words," with a "pale sky, wide paradisiacal prospects, through which a refreshing breath of air moves in playful mood." These landscapes, with their many facets, were reflected in the heart of the narrator, filling his soul "with the grace and power of the Almighty, far more effectively than can be expressed in the language of words."

The early Romantic generation, centered first at the University of Jena and later at Berlin, focused on the writers, Novalis, Friedrich and August Wilhelm Schlegel, and Ludwig Tieck, the philosophers Johann Gottlieb Fichte and Friedrich Wilhelm Joseph von Schelling, the theologian Friedrich Daniel Ernst Schleiermacher, and the physicist Johann Wilhelm Ritter. It originated with the friendship between Novalis and Friedrich Schlegel (1792) and ended in 1804, when Schlegel moved first to Paris, then to Cologne, while his brother, accompanied by Madame Anne-Louise-Germaine de Staël, moved to Lake Geneva. Friedrich Schlegel's statement of the "three tendencies of the age," the effects of the French Revolution, Fichte's doctrine of knowledge, and Goethe's *Wilhelm Meister*, provides a useful introduction to this epoch. The French Revolution was considered primarily not as a political event but as representing the end of an era, new beginnings in literature and philosophy, and above all, a rebellion against a neoclassical straitjacket, which had enforced the supremacy of reason over emotion. In Germany, however, there was no outright battle of the books, but rather a dialogue between the neoclassical and the Romantic positions, as illustrated by the manner in which Fichte continued Immanuel Kant's philosophy. Far from rejecting Kant's "Copernican revolution" as "a reversal of the common manner of thinking," Fichte took the revolution further, with the ego achieving complete freedom or self-determination through a liberation from all the alienating barriers of the objective world. Where Kant's "revolution" was still arrested by the "thing-in-itself," some form of absolute objectivity, Fichte overcame this "remnant" of objectivity, describing it as nothing in itself and rendering it instead into a creation of the ego.

Another aspect of Fichte's philosophy, already evident in his *Vocation of the Scholar* (1794), defined the acquisition of knowledge as a process unachievable in the here and now "as long as man is to remain man and is not supposed to become God." Such ideas demanded an essential openness that was most adequately expressed in the literary form of the fragment, a witty, epigrammatic style of writing much used by Novalis and Friedrich Schlegel, either in aphoristic form or as an ongoing dialogue on a given subject. It also manifested itself in the open, inconclusive endings of many Romantic novels, although these could be occasioned by other, largely biographical, factors.

The third of Schlegel's "tendencies" refers to Goethe's *Wilhelm Meister*. Its definition as a bildungsroman (a novel centered on the moral and intellectual development of the main character, generally a youth) is misleading in this context, placing too much emphasis on social and economic aspects at the expense of the generic novelty of this form of fiction. The romance, established by Miguel de Cervantes Saavedra, had fallen into decline until taken up by Jonathan Swift, Laurence Sterne, and Henry Fielding as a rival to the novel. *Meister* was built on these earlier attempts, and comparisons with the Homeric epos indicate its revolutionary new perspective. Goethe's romance alternates between prose and poetry, narration and reflection, and achieves an encyclopedic quality that transforms such fiction into a "scientific Bible." The most truly outstanding Romantic quality of *Meister* lies in its subjective perspective. Whereas Homer's epics remain distant and detached, devoid of passion or irony, Goethe's *Meister*, and virtually all subsequent Romantic novels, pushes against these epic conventions, just as Fichte's rejection of the "thing in itself" removed the last vestiges of authorial objectivity. As Friedrich Schlegel observed, the new Romantic perspective was the very opposite to the epic style, in that it sought to reveal "the influences of the subjective mood" in their totality, as the author gives full rein to irony while relinquishing seriousness. With reference to his own concept of a "progressive universal poetry," Schlegel praised Goethe's "overall coherence," which opened new vistas and mirrored individual images, so that "every book opens with a new scene and a new world . . . and with vital energy absorbs into its own being what the previous book has yielded." The term *arabesque* was employed by Romantics to describe this technique, a concept first employed in a literary context by Goethe and further developed by Friedrich von Schlegel and Philipp Otto Runge. It describes the dissolution of rigid form and its transformation into other forms. Schlegel equates arabesque with chaos, with intentional openness, with the novel's interrelationship with other literary genres. The employment of irony and the arabesque in a work ensures its essential openness, symptomatic of the Romantic yearning for infinity. Schlegel defines irony as containing and arousing "a feeling of indissoluble antagonism between the absolute and the relative, between the impossibility and the necessity of complete communication. It is the freest of all licenses, for by its means one transcends oneself."

Goethe's *Meister* was, however, only a starting point for the new genre. While sharing Friedrich Schlegel's admiration for *Meister*, Novalis went much further in his criticism, maintaining that *Meister* was no more than a "satire against poetry." He described it as modern, but not Romantic, since he felt that the miraculous elements in the novel were no more than poetry and enthusiasm, ultimately sacrificed to economic necessity in a bourgeois world. Novalis conceived *Heinrich von Ofterdingen* as "anti-*Meister*," as a progression from novel to fairy tale, the apotheosis of the miraculous. Heinrich would surpass the respected and admired poet-magician (Klingsohr), a portrait of Goethe.

Most novelists of the early Romantic movement followed in the tradition of Goethe, but sought to exceed him in their employment of the miraculous and the progression toward infinity. The treatment of the infinite allows for a distinction between a Utopian and a nihilistic model. The former achieves the transformation into infinity, either by evolving to the level of a fairy tale or by ending in fragmentary form (*Sternbald*), leaving the reader to anticipate a future Golden Age. The nihilistic model ends in despair and dejection at the failure to reach the chiliastic Utopia; examples are Tieck's *William Lovell* (1795) and the anonymous publication *Nachtwachen des Bonaventura* (1804), both depicting the hero's psychological disintegration and descent into crime or insanity.

The later Romantic movement differs from its predecessor, often to the point of rendering earlier aspirations absurd or by moving toward the bourgeois milieu of the *Biedermeier*. The Peace of Basle (1795) afforded Prussia a decade of tranquillity in the midst of a tempestuous Europe, but the later generation experienced French invasion and the wars of liberation. In geographical terms, the focus moved south, first to Heidelberg, then to Munich and Vienna, while the Swabian school established itself in Stuttgart and Tübingen, preoccupied with folklore and a scholarly examination of the Middle Ages. This change of location coincided with a move away from philosophical experimentation toward greater orthodoxy in philosophy and religion. H. A. Korff states that, where the earlier period had converted religion into "the image of its own philosophical spirituality," the later movement "shifted the emphasis from the creative freedom of the spirit towards an uncreative commitment to tradition." This change is best illustrated with reference to religion, the role of the artist, and a new understanding of the Middle Ages. It should be seen as an organic development rather than as a deliberate countermovement.

In attempting to assimilate the mysticism of Jakob Böhme, transcendental philosophy lost its subjective nature. For Schelling, the human spirit had its origin in the divine spirit, which reveals itself to the world through man. The divine idea, revealed in nature, led Schelling to conclude that nature is the spirit made visible, just as the spirit is invisible nature. This philosophy of identity reconciles opposing forces and culminates in contemplative religiosity. Joseph von Eichendorff expressed this philosophy in one of his most memorable poems, "Schläft ein Lied in allen Dingen" ("A Song is Asleep in All Things," 1835), suggesting that poetry is dormant in everything and this secret is revealed to us when we discover the "magic word." Catholicism now became the dominant religion, evident in many conversions

(Adam Müller, Friedrich Schegel, Zacharias Werner) and a return to Catholic dogma in writers such as Achim von Arnim Clemens Brentano, and Joseph Johann von Görres. Eichendorff's novels celebrated this new religiosity; his *Ahnung und Gegenwart* (1815) amounted to a fundamental criticism of the French Revolution. The author presents two alternative solutions: either abandon Europe by emigration to America, or embrace the contemplative monastic life. In *Dichter und ihre Gesellen* (1834), Eichendorff rejects the earlier Romantic role of the artist, with the priesthood now offering the only true alternative to secular life. The artist genius is no longer perceived as "second maker" or "mediator" between God and man, but is increasingly perceived as a vulnerable, tragic figure. The young poet Otto in *Dichter und ihre Gesellen*, lost in subjective abstraction, becomes increasingly estranged from society, finding final consolation as he dies in the arms of a young maiden. Eichendorff's history of literature culminated in a partial condemnation of Romanticism, insofar as man's captivity in the sensuous is concerned. He compared Romanticism to a rocket, lifting off into the firmament, only to explode within a short time and disintegrate into a thousand pieces. He proposed that literature should always return "to its religious center," and rejected its intellectual luster and subjectivity. Tieck's novella *Der junge Tischlermeister* (1836) advocated the reconciliation of artist and artisan, integrating both within the corporate society that we associate with Biedermeier. A revised approach toward classical antiquity is related to the new Catholic dogmatism and the Biedermeier lifestyle. The celebration of the beauty of the nude body, rediscovered by Winckelmann and celebrated by Heinrich Heine as "sensualism," is now rejected as destructively dangerous. Contrasted with the image of Madonna and child, the Venus figure became a symbol of self-love and eroticism.

The Middle Ages, too, lost some of their Romantic aura and were explored in a more scholarly fashion. Jacob and Wilhelm Grimm, Johann Ludwig Uhland, and other scholars of *Germanistik* (the study of German literature, history, law, and civilization) edited the works of the *Minnesänger* (German troubadours) and writers of Arthurian romance, together with fairy tales, Germanic mythology, folklore, and documents associated with Germanic law. This appreciation of medieval history occurred during the Napoleonic wars, a time of national awakening. Fichte's *Addresses to the German Nation* (1808), promoting a patriotic education, were later frequently distorted into chauvinistic, anti-Western sentiments (those of Ernst Moritz Arndt, Friedrich Ludwig Jahn, and of Heinrich von Kleist). Interest in folklore led to a new understanding of the *Märchen* (generic term for "fairytale"), evident in the brothers Grimm's collection (1812) and in the ironic witticism of Clemens Brentano and E. T. A. Hoffmann. Arnim and Brentano's collection *Des Knaben Wunderhorn* (1806–8) influenced a new type of lyrical poetry that borrowed its traditional rhyme and rhythm to express a yearning for union with nature and the past (Eichendorff), sentiments of isolation (Brentano), and national identity (Arnim, Uhland).

Music and the visual arts are more difficult to categorize. Philosophers and writers have recognized the centrality of music as the most powerful means of expressing irrational forces and heightened subjectivity. Wackenroder's art-loving friar considered it "a kind of intellectual activity," and Hoffmann declared music "the most Romantic of all the arts ... for its subject is the Eternal." In music "we leave behind all *precise* emotions in order to surrender ourselves to an ineffable yearning." While music historians may count composers from Ludwig van Beethoven to Gustav Mahler, Richard Wagner, and Hugo Philipp Jakob Wolf, as Romantics, the present analysis will focus on Franz Peter Schubert, Robert Alexander Schumann, and Carl Maria von Weber. These composers were less interested in the grand forms of neoclassicism and instead sought inspiration in the spiritual unity of their personal experience and in subjective vision. The *Lied* (song), often to piano accompaniment, gave pride of place to the human voice and full rein to subjective, personal emotion. Schubert chose to set ballads and lyrical poems by Eichendorff, Goethe, and Heine, wishing to break down the barriers between the arts by giving music an often thematic emotionalism that sought to interpret the written word. His "Unfinished Symphony" expresses the longing for a future, still unattainable, Golden Age. He composed instrumental music for small groups, favoring intimate personal expression over cosmic sensation. Adopting folk melodies and dance tunes, Weber's opera *Der Freischütz* (*The Freeshooter*, 1821) explored folklore and superstition, the mysterious and the supernatural, while exposing strong German national sentiments. Enhancing these themes are hunting horns and woodwind instruments, which also feature in Hoffmann's opera *Undine* (1816). This more narrowly defined musical period of Romanticism ends with Schumann, whose symphonic work received many stimuli from contemporary literature but already points toward a more realistic age.

The visual arts gained much of their theoretical inspiration from Wackenroder and Friedrich Schlegel, in particular from Schlegel's essay "General Principles on the Art of Painting" (1803). Art was conceived of as a divine language, leading to religious piety. Whereas Wackenroder extolled the painters of the Renaissance, notably Raphael, Schlegel praised those of the German Middle Ages whose work combined profound religiosity with naive originality. Philipp Otto Runge's theoretical writings, profoundly influenced by Jakob Böhme, Novalis, and Ludwig Tieck, emphasized the "hieroglyphic" nature of art. His characteristic compositions of flowers and children exhibit a pronounced arabesque style, rich in allegory. Best known is his cycle *Die Tageszeiten* (*Times of Day*, 1809), of which only *Der Morgen* was completed; his numerous portraits are also important for their depiction of the nature of children and of ordinary people, but he valued these less. The most quintessentially Romantic artist was Caspar David Friedrich, who, together with Philipp Otto Runge and Ludwig Tieck, established Dresden as a center for German Romantic art. Friedrich introduced a new concept of landscape painting which sought to explore the inner, symbolic character of landscape. His *Tetschen Altar* (1808) caused a major controversy when neoclassical art critics accused him of allowing landscape to usurp the place of religion, and of a lack of realism. Friedrich painted all his landscapes in his studio, where he experimented much with sepia sketches. His use of color was limited to dark greens, misty greys, and chalky whites, and among his favorite motifs were stormy seas, icy wastelands, and mountains, with symbolic significance in his ruined churches, gnarled trees, and shipwrecks. Friedrich believed that the artist should paint "what he sees in himself"; this introverted subjectivity is evident in the perspective of his figures, who do not confront the spectator but gaze into the interior of the picture, allowing the spectator to share some mysterious experience. His *Monk by the Sea*

(1810) engendered a literary debate among Arnim, Brentano, and Kleist, who felt its impact was so strong and immediate that it seemed that one's eyelids had been cut off. Some of Friedrich's work expressed the new nationalist sentiments, with decaying oak trees representing the parlous condition of Germany.

Italy became another center for Romantic—painters, particularly Rome, where, in the 1820s and 1830s, the Nazarenes attempted to revive the religious art of the Middle Ages. They also followed the theories of Schlegel and Wackenroder and formed the St. Luke Brotherhood in an endeavor to live in accordance with medieval religiosity. Prominent among them were Franz Pforr and Johann Friedrich Overbeck, followed later by Peter von Cornelius and Carl Philipp Fohr. Although most of their work concentrated on religious themes, they were also preoccupied with Germanic mythology and the early Middle Ages.

While it is impossible to convey the overall cultural achievements of Romanticism so briefly, herein, it is nevertheless possible to suggest that this movement laid the intellectual foundations for a profound exploration of religious emotions, an appreciation of German history and folklore, and a yearning for a future chiliastic Golden Age. Several periods have since returned to the Romantics, though not always to a successful understanding of this German tradition of irrationalism.

HANS-JOACHIM HAHN

Bibliography

Behler, Ernst. *German Romantic Literary Theory*. Cambridge: Cambridge University Press, 1993.

Bohrer, Karl Heinz. *Die Kritik der Romantik: Der Verdacht der Philosophie gegen die literarische Moderne*. Frankfurt am Main: Suhrkamp, 1989.

Bowie, Andrew. *From Romanticism to Critical Theory: The Philosophy of German Literary Theory*. London: Routledge, 1997.

Brinkmann, Richard, ed. *Romantik in Deutschland: Ein interdisziplinäres Symposium*. Stuttgart: Metzler, 1978.

Brown, Marshall. *The Shape of German Romanticism*. Ithaca, N.Y.: Cornell University Press, 1979.

Frank, Manfred. *Einführung in die frühromantische Ästhetik*. Frankfurt am Main: Suhrkamp, 1989.

Huch, Ricarda. *Die Romantik: Blütezeit, Ausbreitung und Verfall*. 2 vols. Tübingen: R. Wunderlich, 1951.

Hughes, G. T. *Romantic German Literature*. London: Edward Arnold, 1979.

Korff, H. A. *Geist der Goethezeit*. 7th ed. Vols. 3 and 4. Leipzig: Koehler and Amelang, 1974.

Menhennet, Alan. *The Romantic Movement*. London: Croom Helm, 1981.

Paulin, Roger. *German Romanticism*. Manchester: John Rylands University Library, 1989.

Pikulik, Lothar. *Frühromantik, Epoche-Werke-Wirkung*. Munich: Verlag C. H. Beck, 1992.

Prawer, Siegbert, ed. *The Romantic Period in Germany*. London: Weidenfeld and Nicolson, 1970.

Vaughan, William, Peter Wegmann, Matthias Wohlgemut, and Franz Zelger. *Caspar David Friedrich to Ferdinand Holder, a romantic tradition*, trans. by M. Russell. Berlin, 1965.

Ziolkowski, Theodore. *German Romanticism and its Institutions*. Princeton, N.J. Princeton University Press, 1990.

GERMANY: HISTORICAL SURVEY

The period 1760–1850 is a broader historical span than traditionally considered when discussing German Romanticism, and as such it is necessary to examine precursors and aftermaths to the movement. By the mid-eighteenth century, Germany had recovered from the ravages of the Thirty Years' War (1618–48), and although the Holy Roman Empire had by then lost its political significance through its division into hundreds of individual states, two major central European powers began to emerge from within it. The Austrian Empire under the Habsburg Dynasty remained the titular holder of the imperial crown, while in 1701, Prussia, under the Hohenzollerns, had attained the status of a kingdom. Throughout the period under discussion we notice a gravitational shift from Austria to Prussia and from Catholicism to Protestantism, accompanied by similar trends in literature and art, but not yet in music. Literature, philosophy, and art began to be dominated by the Protestant north, and cognate changes were to affect education, politics, and the economy. These changes in the cultural and intellectual climate were, in general, emancipatory in that they entailed a struggle against the prevailing tendencies of a feudal, supranational political order, the dictate of French rationalism, and the repression of national and indigenous traditions.

During this epoch, Germany remained a preindustrialized country, with more than 80 percent of its population living on the land. The agrarian reforms at the beginning of the nineteenth century initiated modernization in agricultural methods, improving productivity so that the population growth could be sustained, but also producing a new, increasingly mobile agrarian proletariat which moved into towns in search of work. With less than 5 percent of the population reaching the age of sixty-five and fewer than half reaching marital age, life expectancy was low. Child mortality was particularly high, and many who survived were orphaned or taken into foster care. As mortality rates exceeded birth rates, towns could only grow through the influx of migrants. Around 1820 most German towns were still very small, hardly exceeding a few thousand inhabitants. The few urban centers were notoriously filthy and noxious. An English traveler to Berlin in the 1830s observed that in front of the royal palace was "a stinking, festering gutter, rank with bubbles of a putrid effervescence." Vienna was exceptional in being the best-lit and best-paved of all Germanic cities, which facilitated easier transport; it also enjoyed the most comprehensive entertainment, offering opera, many theaters, ballrooms, numerous coffee houses, and the Prater (Viennese amusement park with its big wheel as chief attraction). Vienna was also notable for its medical provision and care for unmarried mothers, but as with other regional capitals, it was unable to escape economic depression and an alarming increase in its proletariat population. Social life in general, but particularly in the smaller and medium-sized towns, was based on a strictly observed corporate order. Those born into a small privileged elite constituted the top of this pyramid, followed by citizens with wide-ranging rights, as opposed to the *Schutzbürger* (denizens) with restricted rights, and a proletariat with virtually no rights whatsoever. Watching jealously over this corporate order were the guilds, consisting of master craftsmen, journeymen, and apprentices, all struggling to achieve independence.

This system of privileges was mirrored in academic circles, with a hierarchy requiring that learned titles, dress codes, and a plethora of social niceties be meticulously observed. Townspeople earned their living as artisans, shopkeepers, and domestic servants, while a large proportion of the more eminent citizenry occupied positions within the extensive administration, at either the local, princely, ecclesiastical, or imperial level. As Madame Anne-Louise-Germaine de Staël observed in 1813, Germany was "an aristocratic federation" without a capital or a center for the development of a public mind. But while she considered this fragmentation to be damaging to Germany's political aspirations she also found it to be most beneficial in providing a climate in which genius and the power of the imagination might soar to greater heights. Literature and metaphysics flourished within "some kind of mild, peaceful anarchy, permitting everyone to unfold his individual opinions entirely unhindered." However, Staël also noted the sluggish pace of ordinary life: "Nobody is ever in a hurry, obstacles are to be found everywhere and the exclamation 'that is impossible!' is heard in Germany a hundred times more often than in France."

This state of affairs was encapsulated in the caricature figure of the "deutsche Michel," a narrow-minded, sleepy character who huddles beside the stove in his nightcap, watching the world go by, preferring travelers' tales to any prospect of undertaking an actual journey. These apathetic responses to daily concerns can be traced to the restrictive dominance of the guilds, an army of civil servants, and the thousands of customs posts that impeded traffic and commerce. Some improvement to economic and social life came about through the introduction of the Prussian, later the German, Customs Union (from 1834 onwards), which attempted to remove this host of "advisors, bureaucrats, aides, chancelleries, clerks, registries." The abolition of tariffs (1871) proved to be an important milestone toward the eventual unification of Germany; it also encouraged home industries and stimulated an economic infrastructure that would in time lead to the large-scale construction of railways and canals. While mining in general and coal production in particular were still lamentably underdeveloped, certain writers of the time (Johann Wolfgang von Goethe, Novalis) still found literary inspiration in the topics of mining, engineering, and road construction. However, the Romantic period came to an end with industrialization, as illustrated in Heinrich Heine's poem "Horse and Donkey" (1844), in which the steam engine has finally ousted the Romantic knight on horseback.

In the field of literature and arts, France's linguistic and cultural hegemony, though still powerful, was on the wane. The German language began to liberate itself from its intricate, latinate *Kanzleistil* (bureaucratic German), and, influenced by the religious revival of Protestant pietism and the philosophy of the Enlightenment, a more subtle and sophisticated language began to emerge, capable of expressing both the philosophical complexities of rationalism and the emotional nuances of a new subjectivity. While culture was still dominated by the princely courts and the churches, many German universities were gaining in importance. Serving once more as a witness, Madame de Staël

commented that, notably in the Protestant north, academic opportunities were better than anywhere else in the world, and suggested that scholarship in particular was highly acclaimed, though unfortunately limited to theoretical knowledge. She nevertheless praised German philology as the foundation of all learning and applauded the incomparable depth and wealth of literary studies.

A German public mind began to develop in the universities, with those of Berlin and Jena soon taking the lead. Although these early moves were not yet based on the political concept of the nation-state, at least in broad cultural terms they stimulated the gradual formation of a national consciousness. In literature, Gotthold Ephraim Lessing searched for a new dramatic style more relevant to the concerns of the middle classes; he also developed literary forms that gave greater expression to the experiences and feelings of ordinary citizens. Johann Gottfried von Herder built on the religious convictions and theory of language as formulated by Johann Georg Hamann, who had reversed rationalist understanding of the Socratic search for truth and challenged literary convention by invoking the superior insight of the genius figure. Herder also benefited from the international revival of folklore, which he promoted in order to develop not only a new awareness of language and style, but also to illustrate the anthropological understanding of language as that element which could best achieve a genuine national awareness. Central to this fertile cultural climate was the development of the notion of the genius as a "favorite of nature" (Immanuel Kant). The period from 1770 to 1830 is referred to in Germany as *Geniezeit* ("the age of the genius"), denoting its most important period in the spheres of philosophy and literature. Kant's philosophy provided the foundation for a new ethics, making the individual central to all social and public concerns, establishing an epistemology based on individual knowledge and on categories which defined the limitations of the human intellect. While building on Kant's philosophy, Johann Gottlieb Fichte sublimated all ethical and objective categories into subjective action, thereby gaining freedom and self-determination for the individual. The exceptional literary achievements of Goethe and Johann Christoph Friedrich von Schiller, while too comprehensive for consideration within one specific literary period, provided groundbreaking stimuli for the new art form of Romanticism.

Beyond the immediate concerns of literature and art, the period is one of tumultuous change. The Holy Roman Empire of the German nation was in no way what it proclaimed to be; it was a ramshackle powerless bureaucracy that excluded huge areas where German was the native language (Prussia) and including others where the dominant language and culture was not German (Bohemia). Several of the empire's princes were "foreigners," such as the English monarch who, as elector of Hanover, was instrumental in appointing the emperor. The many hundreds of individual states comprised a motley collection, ranging from medium-sized European states to insignificant, semiautonomous statelets. Scattered among them were numerous ecclesiastical territories and fifty-one imperial cities, ranging in influence from the economic powerhouse of Hamburg to minor towns with less than ten thousand inhabitants, owing their status entirely to history. The French Revolution of 1789, described by Friedrich von Schlegel as one of the three great "tendencies" of the age, signaled a new social and political order in Germany, and resulted in the abolition of the old feudal order. Following Napoleon Bonaparte's victory over Austria and Prussia (1805), Francis II renounced the imperial crown (1806). This political decision had been preceded by the Final Recess (1803; *Reichsdeputationshauptschluss*), whereby all ecclesiastical and imperial territory was abolished and awarded to those southern German states who had surrendered territory left of the Rhine to France. In 1806 Napoleon established the Rhenish Confederation, linking the southern and central German states in a close alliance with France.

This period of great uncertainty spelled political humiliation for Germany, but was by the same token also a period of fundamental regeneration. Following the humiliating Treaty of Tilsit with France (1807), the Prussian reform movement (1807–9) was initiated by Freiherr Heinrich Friedrich Karl von Stein and continued by Karl August von Hardenberg. It brought about the liberation of peasants from serfdom and removed the autonomy of the guilds. Citizens, who for the first time enjoyed a measure of local self-government, experienced a new sense of civic pride. The introduction of compulsory military service and the fostering of a popular patriotism helped to democratize the army. The movement was often described as a "revolution from above" and also instituted a wholesale reform of the education system, begun by Karl Wilhelm von Humboldt and completed by Johann Gottlieb Fichte and Friedrich Daniel Ernst Schleiermacher. While these reforms were initially limited to Prussia, they subsequently transformed the whole country, establishing Prussia's claim to leadership within Germany. Comparable to these reforms were those introduced in the south and west of Germany, based on the Code Napoléon. They had a significant modernizing and liberalizing effect in establishing a civil law that was to benefit the nascent middle classes. The Wars of Liberation (1812–15), instigated by Prussian military reformers and initially against the wishes of the Prussian monarch, culminated in Napoleon's defeat in 1815. Despite the fact that the war produced some internecine confrontation between German forces, with Saxony and the southern German states fighting on Napoleon's side, it nevertheless had a decisive, unifying, and patriotic impact on Germany, almost the equivalent of a revolutionary *levée en masse*. Many patriotic poets took up arms in the "battle of the nations" at Leipzig, while the newly formed student fraternity alliance Burschenschaften, established in 1815, symbolized the new spirit of liberal nationalism. Unfortunately, the modernizing potential of these wars was curtailed by the establishment of the Holy Alliance (1815), a reactionary federation of the crowned heads of Russia, Austria, and Prussia, formed during the Vienna Congress, whose illiberal policies sought to turn the clock back to prerevolutionary days.

These political changes had a twofold effect on the arts. Some writers and philosophers withdrew from public life to focus on lofty abstraction, religious themes, and transcendental philosophy, but also (e.g., G. W. F. Hegel) on the philosophy of state that encompassed all human activity within an established monarchic order. On the other hand, the liberating and emancipatory forces that had been unleashed could not be silenced, and found expression either in satire or political criticism, as well as finding themselves suppressed or persecuted by censorship. The burgeoning newspaper industry, although liberal in tendency, did little more than report cultural events. The Karlsbad Decrees (1819) ushered in a reactionary decade; the press and the universities were strictly monitored. Patriotic student fraternities were prohibited and university professors were dismissed on suspicion of demagogic activities, among them brothers Jakob and Wilhelm Grimm and the poets August Heinrich Hoffmann von Fallersleben and Johann Ludwig Uhland. Censorship and political surveillance at first stifled further liberal and nationalist activities, but later, in the aftermath of the French July Revolution (1830), created a climate of political opposition, culminating in the revolutions of 1848.

In the more narrowly defined terms of German Romanticism, the post-1815 period in general exhibits a return to conventional religiosity, particularly to Catholic dogmatism (Joseph von Eichendorff, Friedrich von Schlegel) or, alternatively, to an increasingly illiberal form of nationalism (Johann Arndt, Jacob Grimm, and Friedrich Ludwig Jahn). The latter movement inspired the development of *Germanistik* (German studies), defined as an endeavor to reveal Germany's past in all her cultural tendencies, especially in law, mythology, and philology. A comprehensive inventory of the German Middle Ages was attempted, eventually leading to a more speculative interest in Germanic mythology and in Scandinavian myths (Edda), developments which increasingly distanced German intellectual life from the western European tradition of the Enlightenment.

France's July Revolution of 1830, together with the deaths of Hegel (1831) and Goethe (1832), marked the end of German idealism and, by convention, the end of Romantic literature. In art and music the Romantic period continued for another decade with the paintings of Caspar David Friedrich and the music of Robert Schumann (and, to a certain degree, that of Richard Wagner). The period following the July Revolution is usually referred to as the German "pre-March" era in that it anticipated the March Revolutions of 1848. The political upheavals of 1848 saw the fall of several governments, the establishment of constitutional monarchies, and the formation of a first all-German National Assembly at the Paulskirche in Frankfurt. This elected body created a set of basic laws reflecting the liberal and democratic spirit of the time, which remains the basis for Germany's current constitution. However, it failed to achieve national unification, and the resurgence of Austria and Prussia signaled a decline of democratic liberalism in the face of a new reactionary nationalism, reflected in the conflict with Denmark over Schleswig-Holstein and, on a wider European scale, over Posen. The revolutionary forces in Germany had failed to forge links with their fellow revolutionaries in France, while the forces of reaction were able to take advantage of a disunited opposition and regrouped to suppress all progressive elements. Contemporary political tensions reflected the philosophical debate: the Hegelian school split into a political Left and a more orthodox conservative Right. The former attacked religious orthodoxy (the theologian David Friedrich Strauss, the philosopher Ludwig Feuerbach, and the poets Freiligrath, Heine, and Herwegh) as well as, the Ancien régime as exemplified by Klemens Fürst von Metternich's Vienna and the general absence of a modern, liberal society. The conservatives, usually confined within the orthodoxy of the universities, had a lower public profile. In general, however, we observe a growing radical rejection of philosophical idealism and an advance towards material realism. An emphasis on power, in its mechanical (Ludwig Büchner), economical (Karl Marx), and political (Johann Julius Hecker, Gustav Struve) dimensions was noticeable. It became manifest in the 1848–49 revolutions, leading to the overthrow of Metternich's reactionary, semifeudal system, and to the adoption of the first German constitution. It also led to a growing nationalism that was based on *Realpolitik*, the principle that "might is right".

HANS-JOACHIM HAHN

Bibliography

Blackbourn, David. *The Fontana History of Germany 1780–1918: The Long Nineteenth Century*. London: Fontana Press, 1997.

Gagliardo, John G. *Reich and Nation: The Holy Roman Empire as Idea and Reality 1763–1806*. Bloomington: University of Indiana Press, 1980.

Hahn, Hans-Joachim. *1848/49: The Revolutions in the German-speaking Countries*. London: Pearson Education, 2001.

Sagarra, Eda. *A Social History of Germany 1648–1914*. London: Methuen, 1977.

Sheehan, James J. *German History 1770–1866*. Oxford: Clarendon Press, 1998.

Staël, Germaine de. *De l'Allemagne*. Paris: Hacheth, 1958/9.

GILLRAY, JAMES 1757–1815

English caricaturist

Born in London in 1757, James Gillray was the son of an army man who, losing an arm at the Battle of Fontenoy during the War of the Austrian Succession, was a pensioner of Chelsea Hospital and sexton to the Moravian cemetery. Gillray was raised in the Moravian religion, an offshoot of Swedenborgianism and Methodism, which instilled in him a belief in the inherent moral and sexual corruption of humanity and the worthlessness of secular life. Gillray began his career as a letter engraver, but he quickly grew bored with this, and ran away to join a troupe of strolling players. After some years of hardship, he left the troupe and, returning to London, joined the Royal Academy. In 1784 he published some uncommissioned, engraved illustrations of Oliver Goldsmith's *Deserted Village*. While his academy training qualified him to produce fine works, Gillray turned to caricature, and—inspired by William Hogarth—to the study of contemporary politics and morals. In his early career he worked for a variety of print sellers, but by 1791 had committed himself exclusively, artistically, and, presumably, personally, to Hannah Humphrey, with whom he shared a shop and home at 27 Saint James's Street. He continued engraving until the mid-1790s, and in 1792 he traveled to France and Flanders with his friend and landscape artist Phillipe Jacques Loutherbourg, to collect materials for Loutherbourg's works.

Stylistically, Gillray's caricatures are busy, dynamic designs. First appearances are often deceptive, as background details and border figures often complicate the seeming simplicity of his subject. The prints meld personal satire with visual and literary symbolism with great ease and effect. His crowd scenes, which bear the influence of Hogarth, demonstrate his facility for detailed observation of human expression and gesture, and show a mass of figures engaged in a range of politically charged and social attitudes and behavior. His figures are drawn in bold, confident line, and the detail in gesture, expression, proportion, and movement exaggerate the conventions of figure drawing that Gillray learned at the Royal Academy. Gillray also pays careful attention to the titles of his prints, revealing a talent for verbal, as well as visual, satire.

As a political satirist, Gillray was both prolific and popular. He was, early on, a political mercenary: the subjects and loyalties of his morally ambiguous, often violent and sexually charged vision were diverse, and he often ridiculed what he was supposed to be celebrating. The American Revolution enabled him to flex his political muscles and provided him with a visual vocabulary to express his political, moral, and social values. In 1780, he attacked "no popery" rioters; in 1784, William Pitt and the government; and, during his most fertile period, the French Revolution decade, he derided royalty, loyalists, and radicals alike: *The Dagger Scene, or the Plot Discovered* (1792) lampooned the famous moment when Edmund Burke, author of *Reflections on the Revolution in France* (1790), produced a dagger in the House of Commons as a prop to one of his frequent and dramatic anti-Jacobin tirades. Gillray's caricatures of the Revolution and the Anglo-Gallic wars are polemical, contrasting images of British security, wealth, and plenty with French anarchy, violence, and poverty. Images such as *French Liberty, British Slavery* (1792) satirize the supposed virtues of Republican life. Gillray also delighted in depicting England after the invasion of French Jacobins: indeed, these images, exemplified by *Promis'd Horrors of the French INVASION—or—Forcible Reasons for Negotiating a Regicide Peace* (1796) often did not contain visual references to the French at all, and featured only domestic political figures; these, including Charles James Fox, William Pitt, the king and queen, and the prince regent, show Gillray's extraordinary facility for detailed, readily recognizable, personal satire. He was frequently a merciless critic of the Hanoverians, stripping them of their royal mystique and showing them as deeply flawed, greedy commoners: *A New Way to Pay the National Debt* (1786) shows the royal family emerging from the Treasury, their pockets overflowing; *Sin, Death and the Devil* (1792) shows Queen Charlotte grasping at Pitt's genitals, seizing the "root" of political power during her husband's madness (just one instance of Gillray's tendency to mark political corruption with sexual promiscuity); and in a series of prints, Gillray caricatures George III as "Farmer George," a rural simpleton out of his depth in the world of political machinations.

The 1790s also saw Gillray introduce John Bull, the phlegmatic, dim-witted yet stoic symbol of the common British man. Bull embodied the kind of naive, honest patriotism promoted in Hannah More's book of conservative fables, *Village Politics* (1790). Prints such as *Alecto and Her Train at the Gate of Pandemonium—or—the Recruiting Sergeant enlisting JOHN BULL into the Revolution Service* (1791) feature the simple British man resisting the temptations of the French Republicans and opposition Whigs. This embodiment of enduring loyalism remains the single consistently positive figure of Gillray's oeuvre and, along with Gillray's anti-Gallicism, remains one of the few political constants in his pragmatic, often paradoxical, career.

The mid- to late 1790s consolidated Gillray's allegiances to Tory politics and culture, forming close ties with George Canning and his conservative circle and contributing to *The Anti-Jacobin Review* (1798–1821). In 1797 Canning arranged for Gillray to receive a government pension of £200, an odd arrangement considering Gillray's tendency to criticize domestic politics, and in 1798 Gillray provided illustrations for Canning's poem *New Morality*. The anti-Gallicism that had marked his antirevolution satires continued in his celebrated series of caricatures of Napoleon Bonaparte, whom Gillray represented as "Little Boney," a spoiled child dwarfed by his oversized boots and military hat.

Gillray was notorious for what his Victorian biographers would call an intemperate life. In 1807, his faculties began to deteriorate, apparently the consequence of manic depression, and by 1810 he had become insane. His friend and publisher Hannah Humphrey cared for him in her home until his death on June 1, 1815.

MICHELLE CALLANDER

Biography

Born in London, August 13, 1756. Son of James Gillray, an invalid army officer living at Chelsea Royal Hospital. Educated at Moravian Academy, Bedford. Apprenticed to a letter engraver; left to join troupe of strolling players, early 1770s. Returned to London, 1775; began selling engravings to print shops. Entered Royal Academy Schools, 1778. Established a portrait studio in Soho with little success; concentrated on political caricature from early 1780s on. Sold prints exclusively in publisher Hannah Humphrey's print shop, Old Bond Street, from, 1791 on; lived above Humphrey's shop, moving with her to premises in New Bond Street, 1794 and Saint James's Street, 1797. Traveled to France and Flanders with the artist Philippe Jacques de Loutherberg, 1792. Met George Canning, 1795; contributed to Canning's journal *The Anti-Jacobin Review*, 1790s. Published the etching *The Plum Pudding in Danger*, 1805. Began to lose sight, 1806. Became depressed and suffered from mental deterioration, eventually becoming insane; attempted suicide, 1811. Cared for by Hannah Humphrey until his death. Died in London, June 1, 1815.

Bibliography

Bryan, M. *Dictionary of Painters and Engravers*. New ed. 2 vols. 1886.

Dabundo, Laura, ed. *Encyclopaedia of Romanticism: Culture in Britain, 1780s–1830s*. New York: Garland, 1992.

Hill, Draper. *Mr Gillray: The Caricaturist*. London: Phaidon, 1965.

Knight, C. *The English Encyclopaedia*. 7 vols. 1856.

McCalman, Iain, ed. *The Oxford Companion to Romanticism and the Age of Revolution*. Oxford: Oxford University Press, 1999.

Newman, Gerald, ed. *Britain in the Hanoverian Age, 1714–1837*. New York: Garland, 1997.

Redgrave, S. *A Dictionary of Artists of the English School*. 1878.

Wood, Marcus. *Radical Satire and Print Culture, 1790–1822*. Oxford: Clarendon Press, 1994.

GIRODET DE ROUSSY-TRIOSON, ANNE-LOUIS 1767–1824

French painter

Anne-Louis Girodet was an immensely gifted, learned, and complex painter whose relationship with Romanticism is significant but fraught. His skilled and careful draftsmanship and his training have led many to see him firmly in the context of Davidian neoclassicism, and throughout his career he remained deeply indebted to this background. It is also true that Girodet himself was intolerant and hostile toward the emerging generation of Romantic painters by the time of his troubled old age in the 1820s. However, in a turbulent career, Girodet painted the images most readily associated with early Romanticism in French visual art, the *Endymion* and the *Entombment of Atala*. Furthermore, his willful originality, his deliberate departure from the ideals and preferred subject matter of the neoclassical school, his fascination with landscape, his inventive and often troubling use of light and darkness, as well as the intense religiosity of tone of many of his canvases, anticipate much Romantic art.

Girodet's work is indelibly stamped with the impression of his time in David's studio. Between 1786 and 1789, Girodet's engagement with the ideas and personalities of David's atelier was intense and tempestuous. In these years of intense creative activity, as well as of personal and political turmoil, Girodet also produced a deposition that was not only remarkable for capturing an intense religiosity so at odds with the lack of enthusiasm for religious subjects endemic in David's studio but also a profoundly influential painting not only for Girodet's own later *Atala* but also on David's great picture of secular martyrdom, the *Death of Marat* (1793).

It was, however, *The Sleep of Endymion* (1791) that established Girodet as a significant and innovative talent. He stated at the time that the painting took him far from the style and tone of his master, David; and indeed, commentators have seen the painting as a challenge to, even a refutation of, Davidian practice and philosophy as well as a rapturous, sexually charged anticipation of Romantic ecstasy in nature. The moon bath of the languorous Endymion, and indeed his softly articulated yet overextended, even androgynous, male body were self-consciously "original" conceptions, and together with the ostentatious sfumato, echoes of Corregio, and neobaroque chiaroscuro, added up to something radically other than the dominant strain of stoic clarity or virtuous neoclassicism.

If the reception of the *Endymion* marked a high point, Girodet's subsequent career in Italy was problematic and patchy, but significant in its anticipation of the myth of the struggles of the Romantic artist. Pursued by increasingly hostile Italian authorities in Rome and Venice, imprisoned for a time, suffering from tubucular illness, Girodet continued to mold a particular self-image, producing a remarkable self-portrait (1795), which was defiant in its disguise of personal suffering and its creation of a bohemian self-image.

Girodet's gift for accomplished, complex, and creative portraiture was most firmly established in the portrait of Jean-Baptiste Bellay (1797). In this picture, intellectual ideas and ideals and delight in human physicality again combine, but this time in more celebratory and less troubling ways. Bellay was the Jacobin deputy from Saint-Domingue (present-day Haiti) who was still a member of the lower house under the Directory. A former slave, he had bought his freedom, and after a military career he was elected to the Convention in 1793. Girodet portrays Bellay leaning confidently on the plinth of an imaginary bust of the Abbé Raynal, the recently deceased philosophe whose *Histoire des deux-Indes* (1770) had promulgated ideas of popular sovereignty and opposed slavery. While modern commentators sometimes see Girodet as falling into clichés of extra-European sexual potency in his representation of the pronounced genitalia of Bellay, this is in fact far less striking than the composition of the portrait, which linked the two figures both physically and physiognomically, thus refusing the colonizing division between Western intellect and black physicality and giving elevated, intellectual, and sophisticated status to its subject, who is the equal of all he surveys.

However, Girodet's next public brush with portraiture was to be far more problematic. Asked to portray a famous society actress, Madamoiselle Lange, he prepared the portrait for the 1799 Salon. However, in response to disparaging remarks made by Lange's entourage, Girodet removed and destroyed the portrait, and replaced it with a bizarre, highly learned allegorical attack on the actress, *The New Danaï* (1799). The picture caused a scandal that ended the career of the actress but also rebounded negatively on the artist.

This paved the way for one of Girodet's most complex and hallucinatory compositions, the *Apotheosis of French Heroes who Died for the Country during the War for Liberty* (1800–), which demonstrated the extent of Girodet's engagement with James Macpherson's pseudo-bard, Ossian, and his ability to create complex and overextended allegorical canvases of baroque complexity. Critics at the time thought it the fruits of a delirious mind, and David saw it as further evidence that Girodet was mad. Girodet's interest in Ossian produced other work such as his *Death of Malvina* (c. 1802) and his illustrations of the *Poems of Ossian*.

More successful was the *Scène de Déluge* (1806), whose monumental scale, limited number of figures, and more accessible subject made for a more positive critical reaction. However, the canvas is still an original and disturbing one whose subject is biblical in feel but not specific in narrative source. It is notable due to the distinctly, yet subtly, antagonistic relationship between the father and son it portrays. Uncomplicated filial piety on the model of the Anaeas gives way to an atmosphere of unspoken struggle between father and son, and this is indicative of the wider transformation from the exempla of virtue to sites of violent conflict that marked the history painting of French Romanticism.

The greatest success of Girodet's later career came with the *Funeral of Atala*, which was exhibited at the Salon of 1808. This was the canvas that most unambiguously associated his work with contemporary Romantic currents; its success was due to a combination of striking simplicity of composition, overt religios-

ity, and an ability to dramatize in paint the climactic scenes familiar to the readers of that contemporary literature in vogue.

However, ambitious public history painting was not to be a significant feature of the remaining years of Girodet's career. Preoccupied with commissions for decorative paintings at Compiègne, and with the thirty-six portraits of Napoleon in imperial robes (of which he completed twenty-six), and wealthy following the death of his benefactor and surrogate father, he dedicated his time to portraits, and increasingly to literary endeavors such as his long poem *Le Peintre* (*The Painter*).

Girodet's final attempt at a new foray into large-scale historical painting, the 1819 *Pygmalion and Galatea*. received negative critical and popular reception. Perhaps his last great legacy to Romanticism was posthumous. After the artist's death in 1824, Pierre-Antoine Coupin edited three volumes of Girodet's correspondence and writings, thus helping to create a mythical artistic personality, and tying interpretation of the work to the publicly known facts of the artist's life. This was the beginning of a kind of mythologizing that built up a central Romantic paradigm, one still prevalent today. In this sense it is fitting that Girodet should have had dedicated to him what was, to all intents and purposes, one of the first one-artist museums, in his native town of Montargis, a museum that remains a crucial center for the study of the artist's work.

MARK LEDBURY

Biography

Born in Montargis 1767; orphaned early, he became surrogate son and tutee of the Doctor Trioson; early demonstration of talent led to enrollment in Jacques-Louis David's studio in Paris c. 1785; involved in cheating scandal while competing for the Prix de Rome in 1787; finally won prize in 1789 and traveled to Rome; became embroiled in Revolutionary tensions at the Academie de France; was imprisoned, fled to Naples, and became ill; returned to Paris 1796; painted Bellay and illustrated luxury edition of Virgil; scandal of *The New Danaë* disgraced him, 1799; failure of *Ossian Receiving the French Heroes* (1802) rescued by *Deluge Scene* (1806) and *Entombment of Atala* (1808); received large commission for thirty-six portraits of Napoleon (1812), only completed twenty-six, failure of *Pygmalion and Galatea* (1819); in permanent poor health, he divided his time between Montargis and Paris. Died Paris 1824.

Selected Works

Joseph Recognised by His Brothers. 1789. École Nationale Supérieure des Beaux-Arts, Paris.
Pietà (or *Deposition*). 1790. Church of Montesquieu-Volvestre, Volvestre.
The Sleep of Endymion. 1791. Louvre, Paris.
Hippocrates Refusing the Gifts of Artaxerxes. 1792. University of Paris, Faculty of Medicine, Paris.
Self Portrait. 1795. Château, Versailles.
Portrait of Jean-Baptiste Bellay. 1797. Château, Versailles.
Mlle Lange as Danaë. 1799. Institute of Arts, Minneapolis.
Apotheosis of the French Heroes. 1800–1802. Château, Malmaison.
Deluge Scene. 1806. Louvre, Paris.
Entombment of Atala. 1808. Louvre, Paris.
The Revolt at Cairo. 1810. Château, Versailles.
Pygmalion and Galatea. 1819. Château, Dampierre.

Bibliography

Brown, Stephanie. "Girodet: A Contradictory Career." Ph.D. diss., University of London, 1980.

Coupin, Pierre-Antoine, ed. *Oeuvres Posthumes de Girodet-Trioson, peintre d'histoire*. 2 vols. Paris: 1829. (This includes Girodet's poem *Le Peintre*.)

Crow, Thomas. *Emulation: Making Artists For Revolutionary France*. New Haven, Conn.: Yale University Press, 1995.

Levitine, George. *Girodet-Trioson: An Iconographical Study*. New York: 1978.

MacGregor, Neil. "Girodet's poem *Le Peintre*," *Oxford Art Journal* 4 no. 1 (1981): 26–30.

Pruvost-Auzas, Jaqueline, ed. *Girodet*. Exhibition catalog. Montargis: Musée Girodet, 1967.

Stafford, Barbara. "Les Météores de Girodet," *Revue de l'art* 46 (1979): 46–51.

Toussaint, Hélène, ed. *Ossian*. Exhibition catalog. Paris: Grand Palais, 1974.

GIRTIN, THOMAS 1775–1802

English painter

Thomas Girtin's short life began and ended in the middle of the Romantic era. He began his career as a topographic painter and draftsman in the tradition of Paul Sandby, and ended it combining the topographer's dedication to the individuality of place with the artist's expression of self in his rendering of atmospheric effects. Girtin, with J. M. W. Turner, is credited with founding the English watercolor school, in which watercolor is used as an expressive medium rather than as one dedicated exclusively to documenting the landscape. Turner and Girtin, born two months apart in 1775, worked together for Dr. Thomas Monro for three years copying the watercolors of John Robert Cozens among others in Monro's possession. As a result, exploration of their formative years is typically linked, taking into consideration their early apprenticeship to topographic artists, the influence of Dr. Monro as their patron, the artists they copied for him, and their influence on each other. While both are central to the English watercolor tradition, their ambitions differed significantly; and given that Turner outlived Girtin by forty-nine years, his direct influence as an artist and teacher reached several generations beyond Girtin.

In eighteenth-century England, the changing conception of the landscape made it a subject worthy of both artist and patron. Discussion of theories of the picturesque, beautiful, and sublime, as well as the power of association with a place, made landscape a centerpiece of aesthetic theory and practice. As a result, landscape was no longer deemed a minor subject; rather, it became the primary vehicle for the exploration of aesthetic theory. Girtin was among the leaders of this exploration in watercolor.

Girtin was apprenticed to the topographic painter Edward Dayes, and through him became acquainted with his first patron James Moore, a linen draper and antiquarian. Moore traveled throughout Britain sketching abbeys, priories, and castles as part of the research for his publications about historic buildings in England, Scotland, and Wales. He employed Dayes and Girtin to transform his sketches into the watercolors that would be used to illustrate his books. Initially Girtin traveled through Moore; later he traveled with Moore, making sketches and finished paintings on their tour through the Midlands. By the mid-1790s, when Girtin's relationship with Moore appears to have ended, he had not yet achieved his mature style; however, his relationship with Moore illustrates his transition from the topographic draftsman who produced tinted or stained drawings from another's original, to the independent artist who created finished watercolor paintings from his own authentic experience of place.

Following his association with Moore, Girtin began his work for Monro and met Monro's fellow collector, John Henderson, who similarly employed him to copy paintings from his collection by Canaletto, Giovanni Battista Piranesi, and Thomas Hearne, among others. Canaletto's influence on Girtin is apparent in his approach to the urban landscape in works such as *Eidometropolis* David Girtin's panoramic view of London. Girtin borrowed the concept of the large-scale panoramic view from Robert Barker's popular panoramas depicting Edinburgh and London. *Eidometropolis* was well received when it was exhibited in 1802. One contemporary viewer writing in the *Monthly Magazine*, October 1802, remarked on the harmony and variety of atmospheric effects. *Eidometropolis*, now lost, is known only from watercolor sketches and contemporary accounts.

Girtin was aided in capturing atmospheric effects by technical advances in the medium. The topographer's monochromatic tinted drawing, though evocative, could not stand up to the strong colors that oil painting made possible. As a result, watercolor artists sought to combine the depth of color of oils with the translucence that made watercolor so appealing. Girtin for example, expanded upon Cozens's technique through his use of warm colors and textured paper to produce contrast. Additionally, watercolor artists including Girtin began to scrape and reserve parts of the paper to create highlights.

In 1799 Girtin was among the founders of the "Brothers," also known as the Girtin Sketching Club. Another member, Louis Francia, noted on the reverse of a work from the first evening's meeting that the "small and select society of Young Painters under the title (as I give it) of the Brothers met for the purpose of establishing by practice a school of Historic Landscape, the subjects being designs from poetick passages." The group's members were professional watercolor artists not amateurs, whose creative spirit, inspired by the poetry of contemporaries such as William Cowper and William Wordsworth, could be expressed through the architectural ruins of past generations. Watercolor was the ideal medium to capture the immediacy of the artist's response to the passage read by the evening's host, just as it was to capture the fleeting effects of sunlight and rain.

Girtin died shortly after his return from a six-month stay in Paris, possibly from asthma or another respiratory ailment. The cause of his death may be linked to his practice of sketching or painting outdoors regardless of the weather, in order to enable him to capture the fleeting effects of light and shadow as the sky changed. Girtin may be understood as heroic in his dedication to the authentic representation of the passage of time, through his combination of atmospheric change with the human presence in the landscape. Paintings such as *Guisborough Priory*, Yorkshire (1801) or *Bolton Abbey*, Yorkshire (1800) illustrate his ability to render the contrasting light and dark of the shadow and sky, that at once verify his experience of that moment and suggest the passage of time and human vulnerability in the crumbling architecture.

In his short life, Girtin influenced the formation of the English watercolor school as a professional practitioner of the medium. He taught the medium, and his vision of a poetic landscape that could only be captured in watercolor, to both professionals and amateurs. Among his followers were John Sell Cotman and the drawing master John Varley, and through Varley, David Cox. Girtin's methods were widely disseminated by Varley and Cox.

KATHLEEN L. BUTLER

Biography

Born in Southwark, England, February 18, 1775. Apprenticed to the painter Edward Dayes from 1789 until approximately 1791 or 1792. Began to exhibit at the Royal Academy in London, 1794, and did so regularly until his death. Married Mary Ann Borrett October 16, 1800, their son Thomas Calvert Girtin, born December 10, 1801. In Paris, 1802; *Eidometropolis* is exhibited. Died November 9, 1802.

Bibliography

Bayard, Jane. *Works of Splendor and Imagination: The Exhibition Watercolour, 1770–1870.* New Haven, Conn.: Yale Center for British Art, 1981.

Clarke, Michael. *The Tempting Prospect: A Social History of English Watercolours.* London: Colonnade Books, 1981.

Girtin, Thomas, and David Loshak. *The Art of Thomas Girtin.* London: Adam and Charles Black, 1954.

Guillemard, F. N. H. "Girtin's Sketching Club," *The Connoisseur* 58, no. 252 (1922): 189–95.

Hardie, Martin. *Watercolour Painting in Britain II: The Romantic Period.* London: B. T. Batsford, 1967.

Hawcroft, Francis W. *Watercolours by Thomas Girtin.* Mancester: Whitworth Art Gallery, 1975.

Mayne, Jonathan. *Thomas Girtin.* Leigh-on-Sea, U.K.: F. Lewis, 1949.

Morris, Susan. *Thomas Girtin, 1775–1802.* New Haven, Conn.: Yale Center for British Art, 1986.

Smith, Greg. *Thomas Girtin: The Art of Watercolour.* London: Tate Publishing, 2002.

Stanton, Lindsay. *British Landscape Watercolours, 1600–1800.* Cambridge: Cambridge University Press, 1985.

Wilton, Andrew. *British Watercolours 1750–1850.* Oxford: Phaidon, 1977.

Wilton, Andrew, and Anne Lyles. *The Great Age of British Watercolours, 1750–1880.* Munich: Prestal-Verlag, 1993.

GISELLE, OU LES WILIS 1841

Ballet by Jean Coralli and Jules Perrot

Giselle, ou Les Wilis (Giselle, or The Wilis) is the most famous ballet of the Romantic era, and is generally considered to be the finest. It has come to be known as the *Hamlet* of the ballet world, with ballerinas aspiring to the title role, one that makes great demands on technique and dramatic talent. The fusion of the music, set, costumes, and choreography produces an impressive evocation of a favorite Romantic theme, that of man's desire to escape into an otherworldly realm. But this is not the only way in which *Giselle* appealed to the Romantic zeitgeist. Although medieval settings were not uncommon, a physically and emotionally frail heroine who goes mad was a favorite Romantic theme. And the importance of dancing itself could be seen to reflect Théophile Gautier's notion of art for art's sake, and prefigures the ascendancy of dancing in ballet. It is, however, Giselle's transition between peasant maiden and ethereal wili that makes *Giselle* rather different from its Romantic ballet predecessors and progeny. And the relatively prominent role of Albrecht stands alone in an era where the *premier danseur* was often relegated to supporting the ballerina.

Giselle owed its creation to Théophile Gautier, who was inspired by a story in Heinrich Heine's *De l'Allemagne* (1835). Heine relates the Slavic legend of betrothed girls who have died before their wedding day and return as wilis to dance in the moonlight, taking revenge on men by dancing them to their death. There has been much controversy regarding the authorship of *Giselle*, but it seems that while Jules-Henir Vernoy de Saint-Georges may well have written act 1, it is probable that Gautier penned act 2, influenced also by Victor Hugo's poem "Les Fantômes."

At curtain rise we see a medieval rustic village on the Rhine at harvest time. Giselle has fallen in love with Count Albrecht, whom she believes to be the peasant Loys. While they dance together, Loys convinces her of his love, although Giselle's he-loves-me-he-loves-me-not game has suggested otherwise. Giselle's mother Berthe is roused by the villagers' dancing and reproaches them, relating the fate of those who loved to dance too much and reminding Giselle of her weak heart. A hunting party, including the Duke of Courland and his daughter Bathilde, arrives; Bathilde enjoys Giselle's dancing and gives her a necklace. During the celebrations, when Giselle is crowned harvest queen, Hilarion, who is in love with Giselle, unmasks Loys/Albrecht by presenting his nobleman's sword. Bathilde recognizes her fiancé and, heartbroken at this disclosure, Giselle loses her reason, tries to stab herself with Albrecht's sword, and dies at his feet.

In act 2 the curtain rises on a misty forest where Giselle is buried. Myrtha, Queen of the Wilis, dances in a beautiful, flowing, yet soulless way as she calls forth the other wilis and summons Giselle's spirit to join this band of vampire-like brides to be. Hilarion enters, only to be surrounded by the wilis, who relentlessly force him to dance. Utterly exhausted, he is passed down a diagonal line of wilis until they cast him into the lake. A disconsolate Albrecht appears to place flowers on Giselle's tomb, and an irate Myrtha commands him to dance until he dies. Giselle pleads vainly on his behalf. Giselle and Albrecht dance together and, just as he is about to yield to sheer exhaustion, dawn breaks and the wilis' power diminishes. They vanish, and Giselle returns to her grave and leaves Albrecht, desolate and exhausted, but alive.

Although the basic plot has remained the same, there have been many other variations over the years. In some productions Giselle dies of a weak heart, and sometimes Bathilde appears at the end to reclaim Albrecht: thus the dark, mysterious, supernatural forces give way to the ordinary, real world again at daybreak. In most modern stagings, however, the curtain falls on Albrecht alone.

One of the characteristics that distinguishes *Giselle* is the originality of the music. Although Adolphe Adam's original score has been altered—sections by Friedrich Burgmüller have also been added and removed —the music is wonderfully effective in the theater and complements the action much better than the music in *La Sylphide* had done. Adam uses a leitmotif system to highlight the dramatic developments on stage. Giselle's descent into madness is particularly well portrayed: her dramatic theme is repeated there in a slower, more fragmentary fashion.

Pierre Ciceri's set also heightened the contrast between the ordered, realistic, medieval German village in act 1 and the overgrown, dark forest by a lake in act 2. This transition was clearly visible in Paul Lormier's costumes too: the colourful peasant costumes of act 1 become long, flowing, white dresses in act 2.

Although choreography was officially credited to Jean Coralli, ballet master at the Paris Opéra, it is generally accepted that, while Coralli was responsible for the ensemble dances, Giselle's dances were almost certainly choreographed by Jules Perrot, teacher and lover of Carlotta Grisi, the first Giselle. The fact that dancing is Giselle's passion and the wilis' method of exacting revenge doubtless enabled the choreographers to communicate much of the action through the medium of dance itself. Giselle's madness is effectively conveyed as she tries unsuccessfully to reenact the steps of her joyful *pas de deux* with Loys. The contrast between the earthly character dancing of act 1—reminiscent of Fanny Elssler—and the ethereal, flowing, and graceful dancing of act 2—eminiscent of Marie Taglioni—is striking.

As Susan Au notes, *Giselle* inspired many contemporaries, including William Moncrieff's *Giselle, or The Phantom Night Dancers* (1841), George Soane and Edward James Loder's opera *The Night Dancers* (1846), and Alcide Joseph Lorentz's series of caricatures, *Grise-aile*, which appeared in *La Revue Philipar* in 1842. The Jean Coralli/Jules Perrot choreography has been successfully staged by Anton Dolin, Mikhail Fokine, Serge Lifar, Marius Petipa, Marie Rambert, and Nikolai Sergeyev, among others. Modernized versions are surprisingly rare, with only a creole version by the Dance Theatre of Harlem in 1984, and Mats Ek's adaptation for the Culberg Ballet (1982), in which act 2 is set in a lunatic asylum.

Giselle has been considered as embodying the quintessence of Romanticism, depicting both disillusionment with this world and the search for a new ideal. Whether *Giselle* is interpreted as a story of the universality and transcendence of love, as a love story inextricably linked to the contemporary sociopolitical situation, as Sally Banes suggests, or as the story of an *homme fatal*, this does little to affect its ongoing popularity. This success surely attests to its quality and ability to evince not only the intrinsic nature of the Romantic sensibility, but also to develop so that it might still have relevance in a post-Romantic age.

SHONA M. ALLAN

Work

Giselle, ou Les Wilis, 1841. Ballet in two acts. Choreography by Jean Coralli and Jules Perrot. Music by Adolphe Adam and Friedrich Burgmüller. Libretto by Jules-Henri Vernoy de Saint-Georges and Théophile Gautier. Set by Pierre Ciceri and costumes by Paul Lormier. First production at the Théâtre de l'Academie Royale de Musique, Paris, on June 28, 1841, with Carlotta Grisi (Giselle), Lucien Petipa (Loys/Albrecht), Adèle Dumilâtre (Myrtha, Queen of the Wilis), and Jean Coralli (Hilarion).

Bibliography

Alderson, Evan. "Ballet as Ideology: *Giselle*, Act II," *Dance Chronicle* 10, no. 3 (1987): 290–304.

Aschengreen, Erik. "The Beautiful Danger: Facets of the Romantic Ballet," New York: Dance Perspectives, 1974. Translated by Patricia N. McAndrew, *Dance Perspectives* 58 (1974).

Au, Susan. "*Giselle*." In *International Encyclopedia of Dance*. Vol. 3. pp. 177–84. Edited by Selma Jeanne Cohen. Oxford: Oxford University Press, 1998.

Banes, Sally. *Dancing Women: Female Bodies on Stage*. London: Routledge, 1998.

Beaumont, Cyril W. *The Ballet Called Giselle*. London: Dance Books, 1988.

———. *Complete Book of Ballets*. London: Putnam, 1937.

Binney, Edwin 3rd. *Les Ballets de Théophile Gautier* Paris: Nizet, 1965.

———. "Gautier, Théophileo" in *International Encyclopedia of Dance*. Vol. 3. pp 122–23. Edited by Selma Jeanne Cohen. Oxford: Oxford University Press, 1998.

Bonynge, Richard. "Adam, Adolphe." In *International Encyclopedia of Dance*. Vol. 1. pp. 9–11. Edited by Selma Jeanne Cohen. Oxford: Oxford University Press, 1998.

Foster, Susan Leigh. *Choreography and Narrative: Ballet's Staging of Story and Desire*. Bloomington: Indiana University Press, 1996.

Grant, Richard B. *Théophile Gautier*. Boston: Twayne, 1975.

Guest, Ivor. "Perrot, Jules." In *International Encyclopedia of Dance*. Vol. 5. pp. 134–42. Edited by Selma Jeanne Cohen. Oxford: Oxford University Press, 1998.

———. *The Romantic Ballet in Paris*. 2nd ed. London: Dance Books, 1980.

Mason, Francis, ed. *Balanchine's Complete Stories of the Great Ballets*. Garden City, N.Y.: Doubleday, 1954.

Poesio, Giannandrea. "*Giselle*: Part II," *The Dancing Times* 84 (1994): 563–73.

GLINKA, MIKHAIL IVANOVICH 1804–1857

Russian composer

Mikhail Ivanovich Glinka is often described as an amateur composer, and that is correct in a literal sense: belonging to the minor nobility and quite comfortably off, he did not undertake a regular course of musical instruction and, although he readily accepted payment when it was offered, he was not dependent on music for his livelihood. From early childhood, however, he was enthralled by music. His musical education, though unsystematic, began early and continued intermittently throughout his life. Playing the piano, he had just three lessons with John Field and continued his studies under one of his pupils; on leaving the Noble Boarding School in Saint Petersburg, he performed Johann Nepomuk Hummel's A-Minor Piano Concerto, later venturing to play it in the presence of the composer. A tenor who took singing seriously, Glinka opened his own composing career with songs and variations on the popular classics of the day. Due to a restless disposition and a weak constitution (which was probably undermined rather than strengthened by treatment at the various spas he visited), he traveled widely across Europe. At home and on journeys to Germany, Italy, France, and Spain he seized every opportunity to broaden his musical knowledge and to familiarize himself with the entire repertory from Christoph Willibald Gluck to Gaetano Donizetti. The consequence was eclecticism, combining Russian elements with techniques and styles derived from the most highly rated composers of the day. Glinka is sometimes denigrated for not adopting a more thoroughly Russian manner, but the criticism is unjust. In the first half of the nineteenth century musical tastes in Moscow, and particularly Saint Petersburg, were both cosmopolitan and conservative, and Glinka was wise (and probably not unhappy) to present nationalist innovation along with a good deal of imitation of the styles that he and his public already knew well.

Though Glinka composed songs and instrumental works, he is remembered above all for two operas. The first, premiered with great success in 1836, is *A Life for the Tsar*. It was originally called *Ivan Susanin*, which was the title of an earlier, far less successful work (with music by Catterino Cavos and text by Alexander Shokhovsku), of which an adaptation was known in the Stalinist period. Several poets contributed to the libretto set by Glinka: V. A. Zhukovsky suggested the theme, but left most of the drafting to Y. F. Rozen, V. Sologub, and N. V. Kulkol'nik. The action of the opera takes place in 1613 at the time of the "Troubles," a key moment in Russian history, and shows how Polish efforts to prevent the accession to power of the Romanov dynasty were thwarted by the stoic self-sacrifice of Susanin. Appropriately a bass of great range and force, Susanin is a simple peasant who is obliged by his sense of duty to forfeit the idyllic charms of village life. After the female chorus has welcomed spring in act 1, thoughts turn to the forthcoming marriage of Antonida, Susanin's daughter; prospects seem good when her fiancée, the tenor Sobinin, arrives to report that the cause of the Romanovs is advancing. Act 2 provides a great contrast. Set in the Polish headquarters and portraying an elegant ball, it creates atmosphere almost exclusively with polonaises, krakowiaks, and other Polish dances; only at the end does the mood change when plans are made to kidnap the tsar-elect. The idyll is reestablished in Act 3, back in the village, where Vanya, an orphan who is Susanin's ward, sings of his happy existence. Designed to show the talents of the sensational contralto Anna Vorobieva, the role also reflects the fashion of male roles written for female singers, while completing the traditional quartet of soloists. Preparations for Antonida's wedding are interrupted by the arrival of Polish troops, who seize Susanin: he must, they insist, guide them to the fleeing tsar, though he makes it plain to the villagers (and the audience) that he will not.

Act 4 is in three sections, each providing fine opportunities for solo singing. In the first, Sobinin encourages the exhausted peasants to march on; in the second, Vanya arrives to raise the alarm at the monastery where the tsar has taken refuge; and in the third, in the depths of the forest, Susanin is slain for having led the Poles astray. The epilogue makes its impact primarily though spectacle and the pealing of bells. Vanya, Sobinin, and his bride have come to the Kremlin; as they witness the apotheosis of the tsar, a mute role but a majestic and mystic presence, they realize that Susanin's death has been worthwhile.

A Life for the Tsar was well received by Nicholas I and Russian audiences. Though Glinka disapproved of Carl Maria von Weber's harmonic language, Luszt was right to insist on the affinities between the two, and *A Life* may be seen as a Russian development from *Der Freischütz*. *A Life* showed the way for later Russian opera composers, and was also the first Russian work to win a European reputation.

Ruslan and Lyudmila, premiered in Saint Petersburg in 1842, has a libretto devised by Glinka and a number of collaborators on the basis of a fairy tale written in 1820 by Alexander Pushkin, with whom the composer had been on friendly terms before Pushkin's fatal duel in 1837. After a lively overture that has become a popular concert piece, the opera opens at a wedding feast in the hall of the Prince of Kiev. The bride, Lyudmila, is kidnapped, and the remainder of the opera portrays Ruslan's endeavors to release her. Leisurely pacing undermines the delights of this romance of wizardry and chivalrous adventure.

CHRISTOPHER SMITH

Biography

Born June 1, 1802 into minor noblility at Novospasskoye (now called Glinka) near Smolensk. Spent infancy and early childhood with grandmother. In 1810, returned to parents and often heard uncle's serf orchestra. In 1817 moved to Saint Petersburg to attend Noble Boarding School; heard much music, took piano lessons with John Field and one of his pupils. Left school in 1822; civil service post, but could not settle. In 1823 to Causcasus, visited spas in vain effort to restore health. 1824–28, back in Saint Petersburg; met Pushkin and writers; some composition. To Italy in 1830, in company of Nikolay Ivanov, a tenor at the Imperial chapel. In 1833, traveled to Vienna and Berlin. Returned to Russia, 1834. Married in 1835. In 1836, successful premiere of *A Life for the Tsar*. Appointed Kapellmeister of Imperial choir, 1837. Marital problems 1841. Somewhat unsuccessful premiere of *Ruslan and Lyudmila*, 1842. To Paris in 1844; met Hector Berlioz; traveled to Spain and wrote music evoking the country. In 1848 returned to Saint Petersburg. Final years, in ill health, in Russia, Poland, and Germany. Died in Berlin, January 15, 1857.

Selected Works

Glinka, M. I. *Memoirs*. Translated by Richard B. Mudge. Norman: University of Oklahoma, 1963.

Bibliography

Abraham, Gerald. "Michael Glinka." Edited by M. D. Calvorocessi and Gerald Abraham. London: Duckworth, 1936. 13–64.
Brown, David. "Mikhail Glinka." In *Russian Masters*. The New Grove Series, vol. 1. London: Macmillan, 1980. 1–44.

GODWIN, WILLIAM 1756–1836

British political philosopher, novelist, and biographer

For a brief period during the 1790s William Godwin was the most celebrated English writer of his day. His *Political Justice* gave him fame and notoriety in equal measure; as a radical political philosopher, he was at the center of a circle of thinkers that included Thomas Paine and Horne Tooke, and as such was sought out by Samuel Taylor Coleridge and William Wordsworth, both of whom incorporated Godwinian ideas into their writings. Later, Godwin's anarchistic views were to be shared by an admiring Percy Bysshe Shelley (who eloped with Godwin's daughter, Mary), and Godwinian influence can be seen in several of Shelley's works of the period between 1817 and 1819. As a philosopher, Godwin is one of the founding fathers of British radicalism, a quintessential Enlightenment figure believing in progress through reason. As a major novelist, he is notable as an early proponent of the psychological novel, and his *Caleb Williams* is an important precursor of detective fiction, influencing Edgar Allan Poe. His biography of his first wife Mary Wollestonecraft, *Memoirs of the Author of a Vindication of the Rights of Woman*, remains a model of candor.

Godwin began his literary career in the 1780 with a *History of the Life of William Pitt, Earl of Chatham* (1783), three short novels (*Italian Letters, Damon and Delia*, and *Imogen*, all 1784), and numerous political and religious pamphlets. The *Life of Chatham* is written from a Whiggish perspective, but maintains a judicious detachment; the novels are all romances, and develop the vigorous style and literary strategy of fictionalized history that were to become characteristic of Godwin's mature novels. His reputation was secured by *An Enquiry concerning Political Justice* (1793), a relatively late response to the debates initiated by the French Revolution. By this time Godwin had abandoned both his early Whiggism and his Christianity, and the result is the first anarchist work to be written in the English language. The central tenet of the book is that in a state of nature, Man is inherently rational, an idea borrowed from Jean-Jacques Rousseau; however, unlike Rousseau, Godwin maintains that political justice will be attained if all individual men follow the dictates of this reason, rather than nature as such, in all of their actions. This leads to the doctrine of perfectibility, whereby the human race enters a state of perpetual improvement, as the adoption of reason takes over and spreads throughout the populace. The state and its instrument, the law, can be allowed to diminish proportionately to the increase in the universal application of the law of reason. In this way, Godwin's philosophy is an important precursor to the utilitarianism of Jeremy Bentham and John Stuart Mill.

The publication of *Political Justice* made Godwin an instant celebrity: although prohibitively expensive, it became widely disseminated through "corresponding societies," whose members clubbed together to purchase it and arranged public readings. It was against this background that Godwin wrote his *Cursory Strictures* (1794), demonstrating the unconstitutionality and internal incoherence of charges of treason leveled against four political writers and corresponding society organizers. Godwin's pamphlet was instrumental in securing their acquittal.

At the height of his fame, Godwin published *Things as they Are; or the Adventures of Caleb Williams* (1794), which was written ostensibly in order to present his political views in an accessible form to a wider public, and specifically to criticize the judicial system of the time and the state of the prisons. However, the novel is more properly celebrated as an adventure novel, as an early example of detective fiction, and as a psychological novel. It tells the tale of a robust, naive young man, Caleb, who discovers a guilty secret of his refined, worldly wise patron Squire Falkland (a prototype of the Byronic hero), and who for his pains is persecuted through the remorseless pursuit of Falkland's agent, Grimes. Caleb has his life ruined through the burden of the knowledge he carries, and yet in a surprising reversal at the end, both Caleb and Falkland insist to one another that they themselves are the guilty ones and that the other party is innocent.

The novel marks a departure in Godwin's thinking insofar as the characters are shown to have virtues and vices distributed between them. Falkland carries with him the arbitrary tyranny of the aristocracy condemned in *Political Justice*, and yet he also embodies all of that book's rationalism, enabling him to recognize his own fatal flaw at the end. Caleb, meanwhile, achieves heroic status despite being as impulsive as he is rational. This new allowance for a place for emotion in Godwin's philosophy was expanded through the influence of Mary Wollstonecraft, whom Godwin met in 1796 and married the following year. When Mary died later in 1797 as a consequece of giving birth to the future Mary W. Shelley, Godwin was moved to write his *Memoir of the Author of the Vindication of the Rights of Woman* (1798). Applying *Political Justice*'s doctrine of "sincerity," this was an explicit account, with unapologetic descriptions of Mary's unconventional conduct, such as her cohabiting out of wedlock with the father of her first child, and her being four months pregnant before marrying Godwin. Despite flirting with poor taste, the book reveals Godwin to be a "new man of feeling" (to quote the subtitle of his novel *Fleetwood*, 1805), and this is reflected in changes he made to *Political Justice* for its third edition (1798).

Godwin paints a more idealized portrait of Mary Wollstonecraft in his second great novel, *St. Leon: A Tale of the Sixteenth Century* (1799), where she appears as the eponymous protagonist's wife Marguerite. This novel tells of an essentially good man who, as in *Caleb Williams*, has his life ruined by the acquisition of forbidden knowledge, in this case, the philosopher's stone and the elixir of life. Setting out with the best of intentions to improve the lot of ordinary people through his newfound wealth, he succeeds only in precipitating a series of calamities, and heaping ignominy upon himself, until he finally comes to realize that his great gifts are, in fact, poison chalices.

In the 1800s Godwin found that, despite good sales of his monumental *Life of Chaucer* (1803), his expenditure was exceeding his income, and in 1805 he decided to sustain himself by founding, with his second wife Mary Jane Clairmont, a children's publishing house, the Juvenile Library. For the next nineteen years Godwin published a number of children's books written by himself (under the pseudonym Edward Baldwin) and his friends, including Charles and Mary Lamb's *Tales from Shakespeare* (1807). In his histories for children, as in his *History of the Commonwealth of England* (1824–28) for adults, Godwin is always keen to extract a moral from his narrative. This is also true of his further novels: *Mandeville* (1817), *Cloudesley* (1830), and *Deloraine* (1833) are each tales of a hero who suffers a downfall through a flaw in character or an impulsive act, and who then shares his remorse with the reader. Nor was Godwin done with political philosophy; in 1820 he published a comprehensive reply to Malthus, *Of Population*, which retained *Political Justice*'s faith in man as rational and worthy of resisting natural controls on population such as disease and famine. But it is as an innovative and influential political philosopher and novelist of the 1790s that Godwin continues to be remembered and read.

Karl Simms

See also **Britain: Cultural Survey; Britain: Historical Survey; Children's Literature; Fiction: Britain; Gothic Fiction; Hero; Individualism; Liberty; Poe, Edgar Allan; Political Thought; Progress; Rationalism and Irrationalism; Shelley, Mary Wollstonecraft; Shelley, Percy Bysshe; Sincerity; Wollstonecraft, Mary; Women**

Biography

Born Wisbech, Cambridgeshire, March 3, 1756. Lived at Debenham, Suffolk, 1758–60, and at Guestwick, Norfolk, 1760–63. Educated at Akers' School, Hindolveston, Norfolk, 1764–67 and 1770–71, and at the Old Meeting House, Norwich, 1767–70 and 1771. Assistant schoolmaster, Akers' School, 1771–73. Attended Hoxton Dissenting Academy, 1773–78. Independent candidate minister at Ware, Hertfordshire, 1778–79; at Stowmarket, Suffolk, 1779–82; and at Beaconsfield, Buckinghamshire, 1782–83, but failed to be ordained. Writer in London, 1782, and from 1783. Married Mary Wollstonecraft, 1797; birth of daughter Mary, and widowed the same year. Married Mary Jane Clairmont, 1801; birth of son William, 1802. Proprietor of the Juvenile Library, 1805–25; office keeper and yeoman usher in the Receipt of the Exchequer, 1833–35. Died of a fever, London, April 7, 1836.

Selected Works

Collections
Collected Novels and Memoirs. 8 vols. Edited by Mark Philp, Pamela Clemit, and Maurice Hindle. 1992.
Political and Philosophical Writings. 7 vols. Edited by Mark Philp, Pamela Clemit, and Martin Fitzpatrick. 1993.

Political Writings
An Enquiry concerning Political Justice, and its influence on General Virtue and Happiness, 1794; revised editions 1796 and 1798. Edited by Mark Philp in *Political and Philosophical Writings*, vols. 3 and 4. 1993.
Cursory Strictures on the Charge delivered by Lord Chief Justice Eyre to the Grand Jury, October 2, 1794, 1794. Edited by Mark Philp in *Political and Philosophical Writings*, vol, 2. 1993.
Of Population. An Enquiry concerning the Power of Increase in the Numbers of Mankind, being an Answer to Mr Malthus's Essay on that Subject, 1820. Edited by Mark Philp in *Political and Philosophical Writings*, vol. 2. 1993.

Novels
Italian Letters: or, the History of the Count de St Julian, 1784. Edited by Pamela Clemit in *Collected Novels and Memoirs*, vol. 2. 1992.
Damon and Delia: A Tale, 1784. Edited by Pamela Clemit in *Collected Novels and Memoirs*, vol. 2. 1992.
Imogen: A Pastoral Romance, 1784. Edited by Pamela Clemit in *Collected Novels and Memoirs*, vol. 2. 1992.
Things as they Are; or, the Adventures of Caleb Williams, 1794. Edited by Pamela Clemit in *Collected Novels and Memoirs*, vol. 3. 1992.
St. Leon: A Tale of the Sixteenth Century, 1799. Edited by Pamela Clemit in *Collected Novels and Memoirs*, vol. 4. 1992.
Fleetwood: or, the New Man of Feeling, 1805. Edited by Pamela Clemit in *Collected Novels and Memoirs*, vol. 5. 1992.
Mandeville. A Tale of the Seventeenth Century in England, 1817. Edited by Pamela Clemit in *Collected Novels and Memoirs*, vol. 6. 1992.
Cloudesley: A Tale, 1830. Edited by Maurice Hindle in *Collected Novels and Memoirs*, vol. 7. 1992.
Deloraine, 1833. Edited by Maurice Hindle in *Collected Novels and Memoirs*, vol. 8. 1992.

Biography and History
The History of the Life of William Pitt, Earl of Chatham, 1783. Edited by Martin Fitzpatrick in *Political and Philosophical Writings*, vol. 1. 1993.
Memoirs of the Author of a Vindication of the Rights of Woman, 1798. Edited by Mark Philp in *Collected Novels and Memoirs*, vol. 1. 1992.
Life of Geoffrey Chaucer, the Early English Poet, including the Memoirs of his Near Friend and Kinsman, John of Gaunt, Duke of Lancaster: With Sketches of the Manners, Opinions, Arts and Literature of England in the Fourteenth Century. 2 vols. 1803; rev. ed., 2 vols. 1804.
History of the Commonwealth of England from its Commencement to the Restoration of Charles the Second. 4 vols. 1824–28.

Bibliography
Clemit, Pamela. *The Godwinian Novel: The Rational Fictions of Godwin, Brockden Brown, Mary Shelley.* Oxford: Clarendon Press, 1993.

Hill-Miller, Katherine C. *"My Hideous Progeny:" Mary Shelley, William Godwin, and the Father-Daughter Relationship.* Newark: University of Delaware Press, 1995.

Marshall, Peter H. *William Godwin.* New Haven, Conn.: Yale University Press, 1984.

Myers, Mitzi. "Godwin's *Memoirs of Wollstonecraft*: The Shaping of Self and Subject," *Studies in Romanticism* 20, no. 3 (1981): 299–316.

Philp, Mark. *Godwin's Political Justice.* London: Duckworth, 1986.

Pollin, Burton R. "Poe and Godwin," *Nineteenth-Century Fiction* 20 (1965): 237–53.

Scheuermann, Mona. "From Mind to Society: *Caleb Williams* as a Psychological Novel," *Dutch Quarterly Review of Anglo-American Letters* 7 (1977): 115–27.

St. Clair, William. "William Godwin as Children's Bookseller." In *Children and Their Books: A Celebration of the Work of Iona and Peter Opie.* Edited by Gillian Avery and Julia Briggs. Oxford: Clarendon Press, 1989.

GOETHE, JOHANN WOLFGANG VON 1749–1832

German poet, novelist, playwright, and natural philosopher

Born in 1749 in Frankfurt am Main to a leading town councillor, Johann Caspar Goethe, and his second wife, Catharina Elisabeth, Johann Wolfgang von Goethe wrote in one of his later poems: "From my father I get my stature, / The serious conduct of life; / From my mother, my cheerful nature, / The desire for telling stories." The autobiographical work *Aus meinem Leben: Dichtung und Wahrheit* (*From My Life: Poetry and Truth*, 1811–33) offers a personal account of Goethe's life from his birth to his decision to go to Weimar in 1775, and provides information on the historical background (including the Seven Years War) to his early years, his study at the universities of Leipzig and Strasbourg, the seminal influence on him of Johann Gottfried Herder and Adam Friedrich Oeser, and his early sweethearts (including Friederike Brion, Charlotte Buff, and Lili Schönemann). Goethe's early works in the years 1766 to 1786 (the play *Götz von Berlichingen mit der eisernen Hand* [*Götz of Berlichingen with the Iron Hand*, 1773]; the novel *Die Leiden des jungen Werthers* [*The Sorrows of Young Werther*, 1774]; and such poems as "Prometheus" and "Wanderers Sturmlied" ["Wanderer's Storm-Song,"]) are characteristic of the Sturm und Drang (storm and stress) movement.

Following the invitation from Duke Carl August to come to Weimar, Goethe was subsequently appointed to the ducal cabinet. His works in the years 1786 to 1800, particularly following his visit to Italy (1786–88), an account of which is offered in his *Italienische Reise* (*Italian Journey*, 1816–17), can be categorized, albeit problematically, as "classical": *Iphigenie auf Tauris* (*Iphigenia on Tauris*, 1787), *Torquato Tasso* (1789), and the later work, *Faust* (eventually published in two parts in 1808 and 1832). Goethe's novels, *Wilhelm Meisters Lehrjahre* (*Wilhelm Meister's Years of Apprenticeship*, 1795–96), *Die Wahlverwandtschaften Elective Affinities*, 1809), and *Wilhelm Meisters Wanderjahre* (*Wilhelm Meister's Years of Travel*, 1821 and 1829) represent a shift toward, and consolidation of, the style of his later writings. Entertaining through many of these years a difficult and possibly Platonic relationship with Charlotte von Stein, Goethe began his more openly erotic relationship with Christiane Vulpius in 1788, and she lived with him openly before their marriage in 1806 (she died in 1816). In the cycle of poems *West-östlicher Divan* (*West-Eastern Divan*, 1819), Goethe's love for Marianne von Willemer, who also contributed to the collection, can be detected, and the three poems collected under the title *Trilogie der Leidenschaft* (*Trilogy of Passion*, written 1823–24, published 1825–27) reflect the love of the seventy-four-year-old Goethe for the nineteen-year-old Ulrike von Levetzow, to whom he (unsuccessfully) proposed marriage. In addition to his works as a lyric and epic poet, dramatist, novelist, and literary critic, Goethe wrote monographs on such scientific fields as botany (*Versuch die Metamorphose der Pflanzen zu erklären* [*Attempt to Explain the Metamorphosis of Plants*, 1790] and optics (*Zur Farbenlehre* [*Theory of Colors*, 1810]) allegedly, his last words before his death in 1832 were "More light."

Thanks in part to his reception, first in France and then in the rest of Europe via Madame Anne-Louise-Germaine de Staël's *De l'Allemagne* (*Germany*, 1810), and in Britain via Thomas Carlyle's translation of *Wilhelm Meister* (1824–27) and Matthew Arnold's enthusiastic acclaim, Goethe is still frequently characterized outside German-speaking Europe as a Romantic writer; yet his attitude to Romanticism was complex and deeply ambivalent. As Goethe remarked to Johann Peter Eckermann on April 2 1829, recorded the following remark made on April 2, 1829, "The 'classical' I call *healthy* and the 'romantic' I call *sick*. The *Nibelungenlied* is as classical as Homer, for both are healthy and vigorous. Most of what is produced today is not romantic, because it is new, but because it is weak, morbid, and sick; and what is old is not classical *because* it is old, but because it is strong, fresh, joyful, and healthy. If we distinguish between 'classical' and 'romantic' according to these qualities, we will have got everything sorted out."

In the light of this famous remark, which served as the starting point for Friedrich Nietzsche's critique of Romanticism, it might come as a surprise to learn that Goethe was initially favorably disposed toward many of the early German Romantics. After all, only about twenty kilometers away from Weimar lies Jena, one of the early centers of German Romanticism, where Johann Gottlieb Fichte was appointed professor in 1794; the brothers August Wilhelm and Friedrich von Schlegel and August's wife Caroline Michaelis arrived in 1796, Ludwig Tieck in 1799, and Novalis in 1790; and Friedrich Wilhelm Joseph von Schelling was appointed Fichte's successor in 1798. In the journal *Das Athenäum*, founded and edited by the Schlegels, much praise was lavished on Goethe. For example, in the unfinished essay "Über Goethes 'Meister'" ("On Goethe's *Meister*," 1798), Friedrich von Schlegel expressed great admiration for the novel as expressing one of the most powerful tendencies of modernity, and his *Gespräch über die Poesie* (*Dialogue on Poetry*, 1800) included a section entitled "Versuch über den verschiedenen Sti in Goethes früheren und späteren Werken" ("Essay on the Different Style in Goethe's Earlier and Later Works"), acclaiming *Wilhelm Meister* as a unique manifestation of "the spirit of antiquity" in "modern guise," "opening a new, unending perspective on what appears to be the highest task of the entire art of poetry, the harmony of the classical and the romantic." Yet the latent irony contained within such apparent enthusiasm emerges when Schlegel's reception is compared with that of Novalis, who in 1797 described Goethe as "the true governor of the poetic spirit on earth," but in 1800 bitterly and polemically described *Wilhelm Meister* as "a Candide, set up against poetry." Indeed, Tieck's *Franz Sternbalds Wanderungen* (*The Wanderings of Franz Sternbald*, 1798) and Novalis's own *Heinrich von Ofterdingen* (1802) can be understood as works directed against *Wilhelm Meister*. And although Schlegel wrote in *Athenäum* that "the French Revolution, Fichte's *Wissenschaftslehre* and Goethe's *Meister* are the most powerful trends of the age," he privately noted in an unpublished sketch, "But all three are, after all, only trends not being properly carried out."

In another conversation with Eckermann of March 21, 1830, Goethe went so far as to claim for himself and Johann Christoph Friedrich von Schiller the invention of the "Classical–Romantic" distinction:

> The distinction between Classical and Romantic poetry, which is now spread over the world and causes so much argument and division, originally started with Schiller and me. I held to the maxim of the objective method in poetry and wanted this alone to be valid. But Schiller, who worked quite subjectively, considered his way to be the right one and, to defend himself against me, wrote the treatise on naive and sentimental poetry [*Über naïve und sentimentalische Dichtung*, 1795–96]. He proved to me that I was, against my will, romantic and that my *Iphigenie* was, through the prevalence of feeling, by no means as classical and in the antique spirit as one might have supposed. The Schlegels took up this idea and carried it further, so that it has now been diffused over the entire world, and now everybody is talking about Classicism and Romanticism, of which nobody fifty years ago would have thought.

The reference to the naive and the sentimental provides an important clue as to one of the major differences at stake between the Weimar Classicists and the Romantics (in Jena, and elsewhere, too). In his celebrated essay, Schiller postulated a contrast between a past era in the history of the mind—when the individual lived in a "naive" (Schiller), "objective" (Goethe), or "immediate" (G. W. F.) relation to the world—and the present (modern) era, when consciousness and reflection mean our relation to the world is a "sentimental," "subjective," or "mediated." By the same token, the difference between Classicism and Romanticism can be seen in their respective attitudes to the past and the present. For both maintained a deep interest in and admired the art of antiquity. Thus Goethe praised Homer and, in Italy, absorbed the culture of ancient Rome; in "Die Götter Griechenlands" ("The Gods of Greece," 1788 and 1793) Schiller exclaimed, "Beautiful world, where are you? Come back again, / Sweet blossoming youthfulness of nature!" Equally, in *Über das Studium der griechischen Kunst* (*On the Study of Greek Poetry*, 1797), Friedrich Schlegel urged "the modern poet, who strives for real art," to "dedicate

himself to pure Greekness." But if, for Schiller, "Greekness" could be defined in the *Xenien* as "common sense and moderation and clarity" and the ideals of antiquity revived in the modern age, then, for the Romantics, these ideals were to remain just that, and hence their yearning for the "beyond" rather than the here and now, their cultivation of the fragment rather than the classical whole. So whereas Goethe wrote that "Only in limitation does the master reveal himself, / And the law alone can give us freedom" ("Natur und Kunst" ["Nature and Art," 1800–1802]), Schlegel argued that "Romantic poetry is a progressive universal poetry . . . embracing all that is poetic, from the greatest art system that enfolds further systems, down to the sigh, the kiss uttered in artless song by the child creating its own poetry." In 1802, the painter Philipp Otto Runge wrote, "We are no longer Greeks, we can no longer feel that wholeness when we see their perfect works of art, even less produce such works, and why should we make the effort to produce something mediocre?" Yet the center of Schiller's argument had been that "the [poetic] *ideal*, in which a perfected art returns to nature" corresponded to the sentimental, in which the naive feeling for nature was united with reflective understanding: if the loss of wholeness was real, so was, for Weimar classicism, the possibility of its temporary reinstatement through art.

In addition to these differences of artistic principle and practice, Goethe and the Romantics differed also in political and personal respects. Nearly all the Romantics regarded the French Revolution with approval, whereas Goethe, "no friend to the revolutionary mob," "hate[d] every violent overthrow, because as much good is destroyed as is gained by it," as he noted in an 1825 conversation with Eckermann. And while Goethe worked in close collaboration with Schiller from 1794 until the latter's death in 1805, the author of "Würde der Frauen" ("Dignity of Women," 1796) and "Das Lied von der Glocke" ("The Song of the Bell," 1800) was a frequent target of Romantic ridicule, a ridicule restrained only by the desire to retain Goethe's support.

Throughout the first few decades of the nineteenth century, Goethe remained a reference point for the Romantics, if only as a foil against which to register differences. As Heinrich Heine put it in *Die Romantische Schule* (*The Romantic School*, 1836), "One no longer spoke of Romanticism and classical poetry, but about Goethe, on and on about Goethe." Indeed, Heine's attitude to Goethe—"Nature wanted to know how it looked, and it created Goethe," (*Reise von München nach Genua* [*Journey from Munich to Genua*, 1828])—was as shot through with self-confessed ambivalence as his attitude toward Romanticism itself. Goethe and Schiller themselves disagreed (for example, about the direction taken by the first *Wilhelm Meister* novel), and neither believed in the actual revival of ancient Greece, but argued instead for the validity of classical aesthetic criteria. The rifts within Weimar (especially between Goethe and Herder) were just as strong as those between Weimar and Jena. Therefore, Goethe's strictures against the "sickness" of Romanticism can be seen to target not just contemporary artistic developments in Germany but rather a perennial problem. Cutting through the knot of the *querelle des anciens et des modernes* (quarrel between the ancients and the moderns), ultimately they are directed against the notion that the "modernity" of a work of art may be gauged by the extent to which it deals with anything "weak, morbid, and sick." Rather, as Goethe wrote to Johann Heinrich Voss on January 26, 1804, "everything that is excellent is *eo ipso* classical, whatever kind of genre it is." And arguably "postmodernism," with its belief in the "crisis of representation," its emphasis on the aporia, the simulacrum, on perpetual deferral and playfulness, represents a continuation of the Romantic doctrines of incompleteness, fragmentariness, and infinite yearning. Commenting on December 16, 1829 on the presence of both classical and Romantic elements in the early acts of *Faust II*, Goethe went on to note, "The French are now beginning to think about these things in the right way. 'They are both equally good,' they say, 'both classical and romantic, it all depends on using these forms with common sense and being excellent. Because it's possible to be absurd in both, and then one is as worthless as the other.' I think That is well thought and well said, and we may be content with it for a while."

PAUL BISHOP

Biography

Born in Frankfurt am Main, August 28, 1749. Studied law at University of Leipzig 1765–68, and University of Strasbourg, 1770–71; obtained law degree, 1771. Practiced law in Frankfurt, 1771–72, and Wetzlar, 1772. Published *Die Leiden des jungen Werthers* (The Sorrows of Young Werther), 1774. Moved to Weimar and served at court of Duke Carl August in a number of official capacities, 1775–1817. Journeyed with the Duke to Switzerland, 1779. Elevated to nobility, 1782. Traveled to Italy, 1786–88. Lived with Christine Vulpius from 1788 (died 1816); married her, 1806: one son. General supervisor for arts and sciences, 1788, and director of court theaters, 1791–1817. Witnessed invasion of imperial troops in France, 1792–93. Collaborated closely with the writer Johann Schiller, 1794–1805: co-edited journal *Xenien* with Schiller, 1796–97. Edited *Die Propyläen* with J. H. Meyer, 1798–1800. Conducted two meetings with Napoleon Bonaparte in Erfurt and Weimar, 1808. Became chancellor of the University of Jena in 1809. Edited *Zur Naturwissenschaft*, 1817–24. Son August died, 1830. Died in Weimar, March 22, 1832.

Selected Works

Collections

Werke (Weimarer Ausgabe). Edited on behalf of Grossherzogin Sophie von Sachsen. 133 vols. 1887–1919. Available as CD-ROM. Cambridge: Chadwyck-Healey, 1985

Die Schriften zur Naturwissenschaft. Edited on behalf of the Deutsche Akademie der Naturforscher (Leopoldina). Abteilung I: *Texte.* 11 vols. Weimar: H. Böhlaus Nachfolger, 1947–70.

Werke (Hamburger Ausgabe). 14 vols. Edited by Erich Trunz. Hamburg: Christian Wegner, 1948–60. Reprint, Munich: C. H. Beck, 1981.

Der junge Goethe. 6 vols. Edited by Hanna Fischer-Lamberg. Berlin: Walter de Gruyter, 1963–74.

Goethe's Collected Works. 12 vols. Edited by Christopher Middleton, Stuart Atkins, John Gearey, Thomas P. Saine, Jeffrey L. Sammons, Cyrus Hamlin, Frank Ryder, Eric A. Blackall, Victor Lange, Jane K. Brown, David E. Wellbery, Douglas Miller Translated by Michael Hamburger, David Luke, Christopher Middleton, John Frederick Nims, Vernon Watkins, Stuart Atkins, Ellen von Nardroff and Ernest H. von Nardroff, Robert R. Heitner, Robert M. Browning, Cyrus Hamlin, Frank Ryder, Hunter Hannum, Jan van Heurck, Krishna Winston, Victor Lange, Judith Ryan, Douglas Miller. Cambridge, Mass.: Suhrkamp/Insel Publishers Boston, 1983–89.

Sämtliche Werke (Frankfurter Ausgabe). Edited by Dieter Borchmeyer. Frankfurt am Main: Deutscher Klassiker Verlag, 1985–.

Sämtliche Werke nach Epochen seines Schaffens (Münchener Ausgabe). 21 vols. Edited by Karl Richter. Munich: C. Hanser, 1985–98.

Der junge Goethe in seiner Zeit. 2 vols. Edited by Karl Eibl, Fotis Jannidis, and Marianne Willems. Available as CD-ROM. Frankfurt am Main: Insel, 1998.

Poetry

West-östlicher Divan, 1819. Edited by Max Rychner, 1952. Translated as *West-Eastern Divan.* By John Whaley. London: Wolff, 1974. Bilingual edition, translated as *Poems of the West and East.* Berlin and New York: Peter Lang, 1998.

Goethes Gedichte in zeitlicher Folge. Edited by Heinz Nicolai. Frankfurt am Main: Insel, 1982.

Erotic Poems. Bilingual edition, translated by David Luke. Oxford and New York: Oxford University Press 1997.

Selected Poetry. Bilingual edition, translated by David Luke. London: Libris, 1999.

Plays

Frühes Theater, 1771–1828. Edited by Dieter Borchmeyer. Frankfurt am Main: Insel, 1982.

Faust: *Der Tragödie erster Teil.* 1808. Translated as *Faust: Part One* by David Luke. Oxford: Oxford University Press, 1987.

Faust: *Der Tragödie zweiter teil*, 1832. Translated as *Faust: Part Two* by David Luke. Oxford/New York: Oxford University Press, 1994.

Faust: *A Tragedy.* 2nd ed. Translated by Walter Arndt. Edited by Cyrus Hamlin. New York: W. W. Norton, 2001.

Novels

Dies Lieden des jungens Werthers, 1774. Revised 1787. Translated as *The Sorrow of Young Werther* by Michael Hulse. London/New York: Penguin, 1989.

Wilhelm Meisters Lehrjahre, 1795–96; translated as *Wilhelm Meister's Apprenticeship* by Thomas Carlyle, 1824. *Wilhelm Meisters Wanderjahre*, 1821; translated as *Wilhelm Meister's Apprenticeship* by Thomas Carlyle, 1827. Both volumes revised and combined as *Wilhelm Meister's Apprenticeship and Travels*, 1865.

Die Wahlverwandtschafte, 1809. Translated as *Elective Affinities* by David Constantine. Oxford/New York: Oxford University Press, 1994.

Other

Italienische Reise, 1816–17 and 1819–28. Translated as *Italian Journey, 1786–1788* by W. H. Auden and Elizabeth Mayer, London: Collins; New York: Pantheon Books, 1962; see also *The Flight to Italy: Diary and Selected Letters*, edited and translated by T. J. Reed, Oxford/New York: Oxford University Press, 1999.

Gespräche mit Goethe, transcribed by *Johann Peter Eckermann.* Vols. 1–2, 1836. Vol. 3, 1848. Translated: *Conversations of Goethe with Eckermann and Soret* by John Oxenford. Edited by J. K. Moorhead. 2 vols. 1850. 1930. Reprinted, as *Conversations of Goethe with Johann Peter Eckermann*, New York: Da Capo Press, 1998.

Maximen und Reflexionen, edited by Max Hecker, 1907. Edited and translated as *Maximen und Reflexionen: A Selection* by R. H. Stephenson, 1986. Translated as *Maxims and Reflections.* by Elisabeth Stopp, edited by Peter Hutchinson, London/New York: Penguin Books, 1998.

Briefe, edited by Karl Robert Mandelkow and Bodo Morawe. 4 vols. 1962–67. *Briefe an Goethe*, edited by Karl Robert Mandelkow. 2 vols. 1965–69. Reprinted together as *Goethes Briefe und Briefe an Goethe.* Munich: Beck/Deutscher Taschenbuch Verlag, 1988.

Bibliography

Bishop, Paul, ed. *A Companion to Goethe's "Faust" Parts I and II.* Rochester, N.Y.: Camden House, 2001.

Bishop, Paul, and R. H. Stephenson, eds. *Goethe 2000.* Leeds: Maney, 2000.

Boyle, Nicholas. *Goethe: The Poet and the Age.* Vol. 1, *The Poetry of Desire (1749–1790).* Oxford: Clarendon Press, 1991. Vol 2, *Revolution and Renunciation (1790–1803).* Oxford: Clarendon Press, 2000.

Dobel, Richard, ed. *Lexikon der Goethe-Zitate.* 1968. Reprinted Munich: Deutscher Taschenbuch Verlag, 1995.

Gray, Ronald. *Goethe the Alchemist: A Study of Alchemical Symbolism in Goethe's Literary and Scientific Works.* Cambridge: Cambridge University Press, 1952.

———. *Poems of Goethe.* Cambridge: Cambridge University Press, 1966.

Kommerell, Max. *Gedanken über Gedichte.* Frankfurt am Main: Vittorio Klostermann, 1943.

Lewes, George Henry. *The Life and Works of Goethe.* London: David Nutt, 1855.

Otto, Regine, and Bernd Witte, eds. *Goethe-Handbuch in vier Bänden.* 5 vols. in 6. Stuttgart: Metzler, 1996–99.

Simpson, James. *Goethe and Patriarchy: Faust and the Fates of Desire.* Oxford: Legenda, 1998.

Staiger, Emil. *Goethe.* 3 vols. Zurich: Artemis, 1952–59.

Stephenson, R. H. *Goethe's Wisdom Literature: A Study in Aesthetic Transmutation.* Bern: Peter Lang, 1983.

Stephenson, R. H. *Goethe's Conception of Knowledge and Science.* Edinburgh: Edinburgh University Press, 1995.

Trevelyan, Humphrey. *Goethe and the Greeks.* Cambridge: Cambridge University Press, 1942.

Wellbery, David E. *The Specular Moment: Goethe's Early Lyric and the Beginnings of Romanticism.* Stanford, Calif.: Stanford University Press, 1996.

Wilkinson, Elizabeth M., ed. *Goethe Revisited.* London: John Calder, 1983.

Wilkinson, Elizabeth M., and L. A. Willoughby. *Goethe: Poet and Thinker.* London: Edward Arnold, 1962.

Wilpert, Gero von. *Goethe-Lexikon.* Stuttgart: Alfred Kröner Verlag, 1998.

GOGOL, NIKOLAI VASILIEVICH 1809–1852

Russian prose writer and dramatist

As nineteenth-century Russia's greatest comic/satiric writer and author of its first real novel, Nikolai Vasilievich Gogol has influenced many generations of Russian writers. Though his themes and character types recur in the work of scores of Russian writers, his greatest contribution lies in his extraordinary mastery of the Russian language. Unlike the clear prose of his contemporary, Aleksandr Pushkin, Gogol's "ornamental" style draws attention to itself as it intrudes into the narrative. At times his prose may be polysyllabically inelegant and grotesquely farcical; it can also rise to rhetorically rich poetic heights, especially with its sound play and rhythms. Passages of his prose can even be scanned like poetry. He employs many tropes and figures of speech, predominantly similes which are often Homeric in scope.

Gogol's first two collections, *Vechera na khutore bliz Dikanki I and II* (*Evenings on a Farm near Dikanka* 1 and 2, 1831 and 1832) incorporate all of his stylistic hallmarks in tales that satisfied the public's interest in local color and "exotic" settings, which he described with lyric virtuosity. Set in Gogol's native Ukraine, the stories offered Russians a glimpse into Ukrainian customs, folk tales, and superstitions. The intrusion of the supernatural world into daily life, in the form of the devil and other evil spirits, forms the core of several of the stories, and introduces a theme basic to all of Gogol's writing: the source of evil in the world. The plots revolve around love intrigue, trickery, deception, magic, confrontation with horror, and the eternal struggle between good and evil. A local beekeeper, Rudy Panko, supposedly collected the tales and provides the necessary framing device employed at the time. Of the eight stories, two are generally considered the best of the collections: "Strashnaya mest'" ("A Terrible Vengeance") and "Ivan Fyodorovich Shponka i ego tyotushka" ("Ivan Fyodorovich Shponka and His Auntie"). The utter evil in the first manifests itself in acts of murder, infanticide, and incest that result from an ancient curse; the comic absurdity

of the second arises from inverted gender stereotyping that has offered Freudian critics much to ponder.

The *Dikanka* stories did much to obliterate the failure of Gogol's attempt at a narrative poem, *Gants Kyukhelgarten* (*Hans Küchelgarten*, 1929), a pallid conglomerate of borrowings from Johann Voss, Lord Byron; François-Auguste-René, Vicourte Chateaubriand; Kyukhelbeker; Thomas Moore; Pushkin, and Vasilii Zhukovskii. So negative was its critical reception that Gogol burned all remaining copies and fled the country. After the success of the *Dikanka* tales, Gogol also set his next collection, *Mirgorod* (1835), in the Ukraine, although with a only narrator more objective than Rudy Panko (though the last tale is presumably his). The four stories in *Mirgorod* offer a variety of genre lacking in the earlier works: "Starosvetskie pomeshchiki" ("Old World Landowners"), is a nostalgic idyll of a vanishing way of life; "Taras Bulba," is an epic, historical novella about the Cossacks; "Viy," is a horror story featuring a terrifyingly evil creature; and "Povest' o tom, kak possorilsya Ivan Ivanovich s Ivanom Nikiforovichem" ("A Tale of How Ivan Ivanovich Quarrelled with Ivan Nikiforovich") is a comic rendering of the absurd lengths to which the two Ivans take a petty disagreement. After *Mirgorod* Gogol moves the locale of his works to Saint Petersburg, a city known for its own brand of absurdity and dreamlike fantasy.

Arabeski (*Arabesques*, 1835) brings together stories, fictional fragments, and essays on topics as diverse as art, history, pedagogy, literature, and geography. Three stories, "Zapiski sumasshedshego" ("Diary of a Madman"), "Nevsky Prospect," and the Hoffmannesque "Portret" ("The Portrait," extensively revised in 1842), according to Donald Fanger, form a cycle more unified than anything that came before, with each story leading to the vision of a city "absurd, fantastic, dehumanized" as a result of Europeanization and modernization. Other themes in the works include the destruction of the ideal, the danger of false impressions, pure art versus commercial success, and bureaucracy's deadly effect on human aspirations. In these stories Saint Petersburg becomes a main character, as it does in an uncollected story, "Nos" ("The Nose," 1836) about a man who awakens one morning to find his nose missing. In the last and best known of his Saint Petersburg stories, "Shinel" ("The Overcoat," 1842), the protagonist is a caricature with a ridiculous name—Akakii Akakievich; yet he serves as a prototype of a Gogolian "dead soul." The themes of "The Overcoat" bring new depth to Gogol's writing: Christian love and brotherhood, ethical and moral values, social consciousness, and a sense of what truly matters in life. The stylistic tension between comedy and pathos gives form to the multilayered meanings of the text.

In the play *Revizor* (*The Inspector General*, 1836), Gogol travels away from the capital city to the provincial Russian countryside, where mistaken identity and the ensuing chaos reveal humankind's petty vices. The play's final "dumb scene" draws the audience into full participation with the characters and thus symbolically extends the scope of the play beyond Russia's borders. Gogol directed his satire not specifically at Russia, but at the human condition. However, a story of the same year, "Koliaska" ("The Carriage"), exposes the boredom of Russian country life and the shallow existence of its inhabitants while prefiguring the essential Russia of *Dead Souls*.

At Pushkin's suggestion, Gogol undertook a project that ultimately combined elements of Miguel de Cervantes Saavedra's picaresqueness, Dante Alighieri's *Divine Comedy*, and Laurence Sterne's narrative devices; it was the novel *Myortvye dushi* (*Dead Souls*, 1842), which he called a *poema* (narrative poem). The main character, Chichikov, goes about the countryside buying up dead serfs (known as souls in Russia) who are still listed on census rolls. Gogol's exposé of deception, *poshlost'* (crass, vulgar materialism), and spiritual death leads the reader to conclude that the real "dead souls" of the novel are not the deceased serfs, but the living characters.

In his didactic work, *Vybrannye mesta iz perepiski s druziami* (*Selected Passages from Correspondence with Friends*, 1847), a compilation of articles, homilies, and personal confessions, Gogol expounds on themes that were long close to his heart: the writer as prophet, his self-image as messiah, literature's spiritual mission, Russia's cultural identity as a religiously orthodox nation, and the righteousness of Nicholas I's policy of "Official Nationalism." This book outraged the liberal critics, chief among whom was Vissarion Grigoryevich Belinskii, whose infamous "Letter to Gogol" voiced his disappointment in the author he had consistently misread as a social critic of Russia's ills.

Critics have a difficult time placing Gogol in a particular movement. His contemporaries put him in the "Natural school," a term that eventually became synonymous—at least for Belinskii—with realism. Some of his stories have Romantic themes—especially the Saint Petersburg tales—but Gogol is not a Romantic in the true sense. If Gogol is a realist, he is his own peculiar brand. By using everyday details to describe fantasy and dream worlds and somehow make them seem real, he created a school that can only be called "Gogolian."

CHRISTINE A. RYDEL

Biography

Born Nikolai Vasilyevich Gogol in Sorochintsy, Ukraine, March 19, (April 1) 1809. Attended boarding school in Poltova, 1819–21, and the High School for Advanced Study in Nezhin, 1821–28. Moved to Saint Petersburg, 1828. Civil servant in Saint Petersburg, 1829–31; history teacher at Patriotic Institute for daughters of the nobility, Saint Petersburg, and private tutor, 1831–34. Assistant professor of history, at University of Saint Petersburg, 1834–35. Met Pushkin, Zhukovskii, and other leading literary figures. Visited Germany, Switzerland, and France, 1836; Italy, 1837–39. Started work on *Myortvye dushi* (*Dead Souls*), 1837. Traveled in Western Europe and throughout Russia, 1839–48. Met Father Matvei Konstantinovsky, future spiritual advisor, 1847. Visited Palestine, 1848. Resettled in Russia, 1849. Under influence of Konstantinovsky, stopped writing and burned manuscript of second volume of *Myortvye dushi*; began fast that led to death, 1852. Died in Moscow, February 21, (March 4) 1852.

Selected Works

Collections
Sochineniya. 4 vols. 1842.
The Collected Works. 6 vols. Translated by Constance Garnett. 1922–28.
Polnoe sobranie sochineniy. 14 vols. Edited by N. L. Meshcheryakov and V. V. Gippius. 1937–52.
The Collected Tales and Plays. Constance Garnett translations, edited and revised by Leonard J. Kent. 1964.

Nikolai Vasilievich Gogol. Reprinted courtesy of Bildarchiv.

The Theater of Nikolai Gogol: Plays and Selected Writings. Translated by Milton Ehre and Fruma Gottschalk. 1980.

The Complete Tales of Nikolai Gogol. 2 vols. Edited by Leonard J. Kent. 1985.

Prose Fiction

Vechera na khutore bliz Dikanki. 2 vols. 1831–32.

Arabeski. Raznye sochineniyu. 2 vols. 1835. Translated as *Arabesques* by Alexander R. Tulloch. 1985.

Mirgorod. 2 vols. 1835.

Pokhozhdeniya Chichikova, ili Myortvye dushi. Poema. Part I, 1842; Part II, 1855.

Chichikov's Journey, or, Home Life in Russia. Translated as *Dead Souls* by Bernard Guilbert Guerney, 1942; reprinted, 1948. Rev. ed. 1996.

Other

Gants Kyukhel'garten. Idiliya v kartinakh, as V. Alov. 1829. In *Hanz Kuechelgarten, Leaving the Theater, and Other Works*. Edited by Ronald Meyer. 1990.

Revizor. 1836.

Vybrannye mesta iz perepiski s druz'iami. 1847. Translated as *Selected Passages from Correspondence With Friends* by Jesse Zeldin. 1969.

Razmyshleniya o bozhestvennoy liturgii (*Thoughts about the Divine Liturgy*). 1857.

Pis'ma (Letters). Edited by V. I. Shenrok. 1901.

Letters of Nikolai Gogol. Edited by Carl R. Proffer. Translated by Carl R. Proffer and Vera Krivoshein. 1967.

Pis'ma. 2 vols. Edited by S. I. Mashinsky and M. B. Khrapchenko. 1988.

Bibliography

Bernstein, Lina. *Gogol's Last Book: The Architectonics of "Selected Passages from Correspondences With Friends."* Birmingham, England: Department of Russian Language and Literature, University of Birmingham, 1994.

Debreczeny, Paul. *Nikolay Gogol and His Contemporary Critics*. Philadelphia: American Philosophical Society, 1966.

Erlich, Victor. *Gogol*. New Haven, Conn.: Yale University Press, 1980, 1969.

Fanger, Donald. *The Creation of Nikolai Gogol*. Cambridge, Mass.: Belknap Press of Harvard University Press, 1979.

Frantz, Philip E., comp. and ed. *Gogol: A Bibliography*. Ann Arbor, Mich.: Ardis, 1989.

Fusso, Susanne. *Designing "Dead Souls": An Anatomy of Disorder in Gogol*. Stanford, Calif.: Stanford University Press, 1993.

Fusso, Susanne, and Priscilla Meyer, eds. *Essays on Gogol: Logos and the Russian Word*. Evanston, Ill.: Northwestern University Press, 1994, 1992.

Karlinsky, Simon. *The Sexual Labyrinth of Nikolai Gogol*. Cambridge, Mass.: Harvard University Press, 1976.

Magarshack, David. *Gogol: A Life*. London: Faber and Faber, 1956.

Maguire, Robert A. *Exploring Gogol*. Stanford: Stanford University Press, 1994.

———. *Gogol From the Twentieth Century: Eleven Essays*. Princeton, N.J.: Princeton University Press, 1976, 1974.

Nabokov, Vladimir. *Nikolai Gogol*. New York: New Directions, 1944.

Peace, Richard A. *The Enigma of Gogol: An Examination of the Writings of N. V. Gogol and Their Place in the Russian Literary Tradition*. Cambridge: Cambridge University Press, 1981.

Proffer, Carl R. *The Simile and Gogol's "Dead Souls."* The Hague: Mouton, 1968.

Rancour-Laferriere, Daniel. *Out From Under Gogol's Overcoat*. Ann Arbor, Mich.: Ardis, 1982.

Setchkarev, Vsevolod. *Gogol: His Life and Works*. London: Owen, 1966.

Shapiro, Gavriel. *Nikolai Gogol and the Baroque Cultural Heritage*. University Park: Pennsylvania State University Press, 1993.

Terts, Abram. *V teni Gogolya*. Paris: Sintaksis, 1981.

Veresaev, V. V. *Gogol' v zhizni*. Moscow: Moskovskiy rabochiy, 1990.

———. *Etyudy o stile Gogolya*. Leningrad: Akademiya, 1929.

Vinoarndov, V. *Gogol i natural'naya shkola*. Leningrad: Obrazovanie, 1925.

Woodward, James B. *Gogol's Dead Souls*. Princeton, N.J.: Princeton University Press, 1978.

———. *The Symbolic Art of Gogol: Essays on His Short Fiction*. Columbus, Ohio: Slavica, 1982.

Zeldin, Jesse. *Nikolai Gogol's Quest for Beauty: An Exploration into His Works*. Lawrence: Regents Press of Kansas, 1978.

GÓMEZ DE AVELLANEDA, GERTRUDIS 1814–1873

Cuban-Spanish poet, dramatist, and prose writer

The Romantic literary movement in Spain began around 1835, but it was not until the 1840s, at the peak of the Romantic movement and during the first wave of liberal reform, that women began to assert themselves as writers. Gertrudis Gómez de Avellaneda was a central figure in the Spanish Romantic period. Although she was born and educated in Cuba, she lived in Spain during her most productive years; her work appears in both Cuban and Spanish anthologies. Gómez de Avellaneda belongs to the first generation of Hispanic women writers who developed their writing under the influence of the Romantic cult of subjectivity. She stands out among the Romantics by making the issue of gender a central component of her creative writing; her definition of the Romantic paradigm of the self is also notable. Her desire for personal independence encouraged her to defy conventional society by voicing emancipatory ideas on marriage, divorce, and the traditional views of women in her work. Gómez de Avellaneda's writing was influenced by the liberal trends of Romanticism, and has direct and interesting implications for feminism.

Her prolific career as a writer spanned more than thirty years, consisting of a large collection of poetry, six novels, several plays, a collection of short stories (*Leyendas*) and two series of journalistic essays on women entitled "La mujer" ("The Woman") and "Galería de mujeres célebres" ("Gallery of Famous Women"). Gómez de Avellaneda was first recognized as a poet in Madrid in the early 1840s. Although her poems do not appear to be explicitly preoccupied with gender, they undoubtedly bear witness to her attempts to represent female identity in the numerous strategies she used to personify her poetic "I." An eloquent example is the first poem that opens her collection *Poesías*, "Al partir" ("On Departure," 1836), anticipating the social and cultural polarities that divide the lyrical Romantic self. Other poems such as "A la poesía" ("To poetry," 1841), "Despedida a la Señora D.G.C. de V." ("Farewell to Lady D.G.C. de V," 1841), "El porqué de la insconstancia" ("The Reasons for Inconsistency," mid-1840s) and the later poem "Romance contestando a otro de una señorita" ("Ballad in Response to One by a Young Lady," 1850) display Gómez de Avellaneda's constant attempt to praise the authority of the lyrical feminine voice as a means of challenging the misogynist definition of womanhood. The words of Gómez de Avellaneda's contemporary and friend, the Spanish writer Nicomedes Pastor Díaz, are an indication of the obstacles to come in Gómez de Avellaneda's career as a woman writer in a male-dominated culture: "[S]ome have accused the verses in question of lacking the mildness and tenderness that apparently should be the distinctive character of poetry written by the fair sex." Gómez de Avellaneda's poetry can be read not only as questioning the Romantic concept of self, but also as attempting to merge the cultural definitions of the feminine and the emerging female lyrical subject. In so doing, the poet undertakes a search for a cultural acceptance of her autonomous Romantic self.

After 1845, Gómez de Avellaneda continued to be a prolific writer, but her poetic creativity was now directed toward popular drama. She wrote several plays, both tragedies and comedies, that were staged in the most famous theaters of Madrid. These included *Munio Alfonso* (1844), *Egilona* (1845), *Saúl* (1849), *Baltasar* (1858) and comedies such as *La hija de las Flores* (*The Daughter of the Flowers*, 1852), and *La aventurera* (*The Adventuress*, 1853). The plays reveal concerns with the major philosophical currents of the Romantic period of freedom, morality, and justice. Gómez de Avellaneda often projects women characters into the center of her dramatic works, thereby revealing and exploring the difficulties of expressing female subjectivity in a male literary tradition. Her victimized female figures represent the socially marginalized protagonists that are such a feature of Romantic literature in general. However, although her plays and poetry both express feminist ideas to some extent, it is in Gómez de Avellaneda's novels that these concerns are expressed most consistently. The women depicted eloquently articulate her dilemma as a writer seeking alternative voices through which to express her identity as a woman. Gómez de Avellaneda wrote six novels: *Sab* (1841), *Dos mujeres* (*Two women*, 1842), *Espatolino* (1844), *Guatimozín* (1846), *Dolores* (1851), and *El artista barquero* (*The Boatman Artist*, 1861). All six novels represent, to a greater or lesser degree, a contribution to gender-oriented and feminist ideas, but *Sab* and *Dos mujeres*, stand out in this respect. Published at the peak of Spanish Romanticism, their female characters display the Romantic proclivity for personal autonomy and subjectivity. In *Sab*, Gómez de Avellaneda uses the dialectical relationship between Spanish Romanticism and liberal ideology to establish an analogy between the positions of women and slaves. Slavery is used as a trope to emphasize women's marginality, a theme which is repeated and treated more explicitly in her other early novel *Dos mujeres*.

Dos mujeres was published very soon after *Sab*. Here Gómez de Avellaneda resorts to a more direct approach, because the use of far less explicit strategies in *Sab* had not protected her from criticism. *Dos mujeres* presents with considerable realism the constraints under which male-female relations are conducted in a patriarchal culture. It reveals a more liberated female voice, unafraid to express opinions in a society that condemns her act of writing. Gómez de Avellaneda's efforts to develop fully her cultural critique were constantly frustrated by the society she attacked. Both *Sab* and *Dos mujeres* were banned in Cuba as dangerously immoral, the former because it contained what were considered to be subversive doctrines that were critical of the system of slavery in Cuba and therefore of the prevailing morals, and the latter because it was deemed to have an immoral content. Gómez de Avellaneda struggled to make her views known through her fiction to the extent that she was described by a male contemporary, Bretón de los Herreros, with the statement, "Es mucho hombre esta mujer" ("She is very much a man, this woman").

In many ways, Gómez de Avellaneda's own life was a constant pursuit of personal emancipation although whether she achieved it is not clear. She led an atypical life for a woman of her class and time: she defied conventional patriarchal culture by refusing an arranged marriage, indulged in love affairs, and had an illegitimate child. She thus not only filled her writing with sentiments concerning nonconformity in a repressive and conventional society, she also rebelled against established social canons in her personal life. Despite being a successful writer, Gómez de Avellaneda suffered discrimination in her male-dominated world. At the pinnacle of her literary career, in 1853, she applied for a vacant seat at the Spanish Royal Academy and was rejected for no reason other than that of her gender. Nevertheless, Gómez de Avellaneda was ultimately not defeated by the patriarchal society that she had so often attacked. The incident with the Academy drove her to an even more overt and combative expression of the feminism she had expressed so many times, covertly and "conventionally" through her fictional characters. As a result she now openly promulgated her emancipated ideas in the literary magazine *Album Cubano de lo Bueno y lo Bello*, which she founded and edited after her return to Cuba in 1860, although it only survived for six months. Its twelve issues included her polemical article series "La mujer," in which she set forth arguments that attempted to prove the merits of her sex demanded the right of equality, and even expressing the superiority of women's talents and intellects.

Although during her lifetime Gómez de Avellaneda was acclaimed as the greatest female writer of Spanish literature, she was largely forgotten for many years after her death. However, in the last fifteen years there has been a revival of interest in the Cuban-Spanish author. Gómez de Avellaneda's writings subvert and redefine the textual tradition from which her work evolved, and are unquestionably a source of inspiration for women writers who attempt to enter the male-dominated literary establishment. As a nineteenth-century feminist pioneer in Hispanic culture, she bravely attempted to challenge the discriminatory society in which she lived, and her success should guarantee not only her critical acclaim but also a place at the forefront of Hispanic Romantic literature and feminist thought.

BRÍGIDA PASTOR

Selected Works

Dos mujeres. 4 vols. 1842.
"La mujer," In *Album cubano de lo Bueno y lo Bello (Revista quincenal de moral, literatura, bellas artes y modas)*. 1860.
Devocionario nuevo y completísmo en prosa y verso. 1867.
Obras literarias. 5 vols. 1869–71.

Cartas inéditas y documentos relativos a su vida en Cuba de 1859 a 1864. Edited by José Augusto Escoto. Matanzas: La Pluma de Oro, 1912.

Autobiografía y cartas, with a prologue and an obituary by Lorenzo Cruz de Fuentes, Madrid: Imprenta Helénica, 1914.

Gertrudis Gómez de Avellaneda. Biography, bibliography, iconography, including many letters, unpublished and published, written by Avellaneda, and her memoirs. Edited by Domingo Figarola-Caneda. Madrid: Sociedad Española de Librería, 1929.

Poesías selectas por Gertrudis Gómez de Avellaneda. Edited by Benito Varela Jácome, Barcelona: Bruguera, 1968.

Sab. With a prologue by Mary Cruz. La Habana: Instituto Cubano del Libro, 1973.

Sab and Autobiography. (Critical edition). Translated by Nina M. Scott. Austin: University of Texas Press, 1993.

Bibliography

Alzaga, Florinda. *La Avellaneda: Intensidad y Vanguardia*. Miami: Ediciones Universal, 1997.

Alzate Cadavid, Carolina. *Desviación y verdad. La re-escritura en Arenas y Avellaneda*. Boulder, Colo.: Society of Spanish and Spanish American Studies, 1999.

Araújo, Nara. *El alfiler y la mariposa*. La Habana: Editorial Letras Cubanas, 1997.

Bravo-Villasante, Carmen. "Las corrientes sociales del Romanticismo en la obra de la Avellaneda," *Cuadernos Hispanoamericanos* 75–76 (1968): 771–75.

———. *Una vida romántica: La Avellaneda*. Barcelona: Editora y Distribuidora Hispano-Americana, 1967.

Cabrera, Rosa M., and Gladys B. Zaldívar. *Homenaje a Gertrudis Gómez de Avellaneda, memorias del simposio en el centenario de su muerte*. Miami: Ediciones Universal, 1981.

Gold, Janet. "The Feminine Bond: Vitmization and Beyond in the Novels of Gertrudis Gómez de Avellaneda," *Letras Femeninas* 15 (1989): 83–90.

Gonzales Ascorra, Martha. *La evolución de la conciencia femenina a través de las novelas de Gertrudis Gómez de Avellaneda, Soledad Acosta de Samper y Mercedes Cabello de Carbonera*. New York: Peter Lang, 1997.

Guerra, Lucía. "Estrategias femeninas en la elaboración del sujeto romántico en la obra de Gertrudis Gómez de Avellaneda," *Revista Iberoamericana* 132–33 (1985): 707–22.

Harter. Hugh. *Gertrudis Gómez de Avellaneda*. Boston: Twayne, 1981.

Kirkpatrick, Susan. *Las Románticas: Women Writers and Subjectivity in Spain, 1835–1850*. Berkeley and Los Angeles: University of California Press, 1989.

Kirkpatrick, Susan. "Gómez de Avellaneda's *Sab*: Gendering the Liberal Romantic Subject." In *In the Feminine Mode: Essays on Hispanic Women Writers*. Edited by Noël Valis and Carol Maier. Lewisburgh/Penn.: Bucknell University Press/Associated Universities Presses, 1990.

Marco, Concha de. *Las escritoras: La mujer del Romanticismo*. 3 vols. León: Everest, 1969.

Pastor, Brígida. "Cuba's Covert Cultural Critique: The Feminist Writings of Gertrudis Gómez de Avellaneda," *Romance Quarterly* 43 (1995): 178–89.

———. "A Romantic Life in Novel Fiction: The Early Career and Works of Gertrudis Gómez de Avellaneda," *Bulletin of Hispanic Studies* 75 (1998): 169–81.

Picón Garfield, Evelyn. *Poder y sexualidad: El discurso de Gertrudis Gómez de Avellaneda*. Amsterdam: Rodopi, 1993.

Rexach, Rosario. "La Avellaneda como escritora romántica," *Anales de la Literatura Latinoamericana* 2–3 (1973–4): 241–54.

Williams, Lorna V. "The Feminized Slave in Gómez de Avellaneda's *Sab* (1841)" *Revista de Estudios Hispánicos*, 27 (1993): 3–17.

GÖRRES, JOHANN JOSEPH VON 1776–1848

German man of letters

The casual observer may be forgiven for imagining that Johann Joseph von Görres lived around half a dozen distinct lives in rapid succession. He was by turns an enlightened thinker, a revolutionary, an educationalist, a politician, an editor, an academic, and an apologist of mysticism who became a passionate champion of rights for Catholics. There are obvious contradictions in the positions he adopted during his career, which, like that of so many other Romantics, spanned the difficult transitional period from the French Revolution to the upheavals of 1848. His collected works are unstructured and fragmentary, and it is not hard to understand why this man, who mocked religion and yet was fascinated by Christian mysticism, who saw himself as liberal and in the end deferred to the pope and believed in strengthening the Habsburg monarchy, could have appeared to some as a beacon of wisdom and as "the greatest figure in the annals of German Catholicism" (Alexander Dru), while others saw him as little more than a turncoat with outdated and potentially sinister mystic propensities. Germany's leading satirist of the day, Heinrich Heine, spoke of "the tonsured hyena" and portrayed him as a kind of living Tower of Babel, in which a hundred internal voices call out to each other without being able to make themselves understood.

There are, by contrast, a number of fixed points in his life that could be said to provide a veneer of consistency. A democrat with a clear vision of justice, Görres held a firm belief in equality and self-determination. These are constants, as is his lasting opposition to tyranny, hypocrisy, and falsehood. He was largely self-taught, and tended to write even some of his longer treatises during extended moments of inspiration, which may help to explain their lack of structure and clarity. The platform from which he operated most effectively in this respect was the press, and he could be said to have invented political journalism in Germany. During the Wars of Liberation, the clarion call of his influential journal *Rheinischer Merkur* (which he founded in 1814) was heard above the confused voices of the various parties, and even Napoleon had to acknowledge its effect. His criticism of the incapacity of the many autocratic governments of his day reached its apex in *Teutschland und die Revolution* (*Germany and the Revolution*, 1819), which reflects the discontent of those who hoped that victory over France would be followed by a new flowering of democracy. This pamphlet so outraged the Prussian administration that it led to a warrant for his arrest and to his subsequent withdrawal to France and Switzerland. Two years later Görres published *Europa und die Revolution* (*Europe and* the Revolution), which began to mark a return to Christianity. Here, he rebuked the governments of Europe for ignoring the popular desire for religious experience. From then on, he moved steadily towards the study of myth and mysticism, taking as his point of departure the traditions of the Middle Ages and the Orient, which he saw as related. In his characteristically intuitive account of the origins of statehood, he envisaged the "primeval state" (Urstaat) as having been located in Persia or Afghanistan, and argued against the view that individual social units had come into being separately. In this respect, Görres theory of history is similar to Johann Wolfgang von Goethe's "metamorphic" inquiries into the origins of plants and animals. His approach to folk poetry, which he did much to popularize, was to strike a balance between Achim von Arnim's and Clemens Brentano's imaginative empathy and the Jacob and Wilhelm Grimm's meticulous recording of data, the consequence of which was that it was rejected by both parties.

His position as professor of history at Munich (1829–48) remains the most controversial phase of his career. His views on history became increasingly influenced by his faith, and he did not shrink from attacking what he saw as perilous evidence of paganism in the Prussian state. While his previous period as a teacher at the University of Heidelberg (1806–8) had been successful (Joseph von Eichendorff speaks of the Görres's Heidelberg lectures as resembling "magnificent nocturnal thunderstorms that awaken and inspire"), he was now less than totally convincing in his attempts to argue, on a largely intuitive basis, that world history was the product of transcendental conflicts between good and evil. The lectures and writings of this period may have stimulated debate and led to greater political awareness in church circles, but the amount of effort expended on demonstrating the existence and credibility of the supernatural was excessive. Görres's distinctions between divine, natural, and diabolical mysticism are not unrelated to the Romantic endeavor to integrate natural and revelatory experiences. His celebration of the medieval period as an unending springtime in which church and state were harmoniously integrated is similarly open to question, though echoed by members of the Romantic school. The medieval mystics were the subject of the major work of his maturity, Die christliche Mystik (The Christian Mystic, 1836–42), which arose directly out of his lectures at Munich.

In effect, Görres's attempts at achieving syntheses between apparent opposites recall the line of thinking pioneered by Novalis. In one of his essays, he attempted to present St. Francis of Assisi as a troubadour. His understanding of mysticism was likewise idiosyncratic, embracing the study of medicine, mythology, history, and theology. It is possible that Görres's propensity to mysticism was influenced by accounts of the Romantic poet Clemens Brentano's experiences watching over a stigmatized nun, Anna Katharina Emmerick, in Dülmen; both men turned to Roman Catholicism in their old age and remained in close contact with one another.

Many of his theories not only seem thoroughly abstruse by present-day standards, but seemed so to many in his own time, when they failed to satisfy either the traditional theological faction or the modern skeptics. To envisage church and monarchy moving towards a new synthesis was, as Karl Gutzkow pointed out, to ignore the inevitable waning of two increasingly irrelevant institutions. Görres lacked self-criticism and remained a dilettante in scientific matters, frequently having recourse to inspiration at a time when the natural sciences were recognizing the need for practical and verifiable experimentation. His thought processes were associative rather than systematic, and he reached his insights by serendipitous analogies rather than through rational deductions. But he also helped to further the cause of democracy at a time when it was vulnerable, stimulated public debate of artistic as well as ethical topics, and strove to bring the cultural concerns of German Catholics into the public arena. After his death, the so-called Görres-Gesellschaft, a society formed in 1876 by his supporters, continued to pursue what they took to be his aims.

OSMAN DURRANI

Biography

Born in Koblenz, January 25, 1776, Görres was the son of a timber merchant. Between 1801 and 1814 he taught physics at schools in Koblenz, with a short interlude as lecturer at the University of Heidelberg in 1806–8. Here he espoused the cause of Romanticism and became familiar with many of its leading lights, especially von Arnim, Brentano, and Eichendorff. Under the influence of Romanticism, he took an interest in the folk poetry and Middle Ages. Through his call for German unity and support of the Austrian emperor, Görres made himself increasingly unpopular in German circles, and lived in exile in Switzerland and Strasbourg for much of the 1820s. He returned to become Professor of History at Munich on the recommendation of King Ludwig I of Bavaria in 1829, a post he held for twenty years. From then on was an important figure in the struggle for equality for Roman Catholics, committed to defend their rights. Became "von Görres" in 1839. Died Munich, January 29, 1848.

Selected Works

"Der allgemeine Frieden." 1797.
"Resultate meiner Sendung nach Paris." 1800.
"Aphorismen über die Kunst." 1802.
"Glauben und Wissen." 1805.
Die teutschen Volksbücher. 1807.
"Wachstum der Historie." 1808.
Mythengeschichte der asiatischen Welt. 1810.
"Reflexionen über den Fall Deutschlands und die Bedingungen seiner Wiedergeburt." 1810.
"Deutschlands künftige Verfassung." 1816.
Die altdeutschen Volks- und Meisterlieder. 1817.
"Teutschland und die Revolution." 1819.
"Europa und die Revolution." 1821.
Die christliche Mystik, 4 vols., 1836–42; 5 vols., 1879–80.
"Athanasius." 1838.

Editions

Frühwald, Wolfgang, ed. Joseph Görres: Ausgewählte Werke. 2 vols. Freiburg/Br: Herder, 1978.
Schellberg, Wilhelm, ed. Josef von Görres' Ausgewählte Werke und Briefe. 2 vols. Kempten: Kösel, 1911.
Schellberg, Wilhelm, Adolf Dyroff, Leo Just, and Heribert Raab, eds. Joseph Görres Gesammelte Schriften. Paderborn: Schöningh (begun 1926; in progress).

Translations

Josef Görres. "Germany and the Revolution" (1819), in Metternich's Europe. Edited by Mack Walker. London: Macmillan, 1968.

Bibliography

Dru, Alexander. *The Contribution of German Catholicism*. New York: Hawthorn, 1963.

Habel, Reinhardt. *Joseph Görres: Studien über den Zusammenhang von Natur, Geschichte und Mythos in seinen Schriften*. Wiesbaden: Steiner, 1960.

Habersack, Hermann. "*Joseph von Görres: Grundlinien seiner Gestalt.*" Ph.D. diss., University of Würzburg, 1931.

Körber, Esther-Beate. *Görres und die Revolution: Wandlungen ihres Begriffs und ihrer Wertung in seinem politischen Weltbild 1793 bis 1819*. Husum: Matthiesen, 1986.

Portmann-Tinguely, Albert. *Romantik und Krieg: eine Untersuchung zum Bild des Krieges bei deutschen Romantikern und "Freiheitssängern": Adam Müller, Joseph Görres, Friedrich Schlegel, Achim von Arnim, Max von Schenkendorf und Theodor Körner*. Fribourg, Switzerland: Fribourg University Press, 1989.

Pourrat, Pierre. *Christian Spirituality*. London: Burns, Oates, 1922.

Raab, Heribert, ed. *Joseph Görres, ein Leben für Freiheit und Recht: Auswahl aus seinem Werk, Urteile von Zeitgenossen, Einführung und Bibliographie*. Paderborn: Schöningh, 1978.

Raab, Heribert. "Joseph Görres." In *Deutsche Dichter der Romantik. Ihr Leben und Werk*. 2nd ed. Edited by Benno von Wiese. Berlin: Schmidt, 1983. 409–438.

Saitschick, Robert. *Joseph Görres und die abendländische Kultur*. Olten: Walter, 1953.

Schultz, Franz. *Joseph Görres als Herausgeber, Litterarhistoriker, Kritiker im Zusammenhange mit der jüngeren Romantik*. Berlin: Mayer and Mayer, 1902. Reprinted New York, 1967.

Schultz, Hartwig. *Clemens Brentano und Joseph Görres: Anmerkungen zur Biographie einer Freundschaft*. Koblenz: Plato, 1981.

Stopp, E. "Joseph Görres' Metaphorical Thinking." In *Literaturwissenschaft und Geistesgeschichte: Festschrift für Richard Brinkmann*. Edited by Brummack Jürgen, et al. Tübingen: Niemeyer, 1981. 371–86.

Vanden Heuvel, Jon. *A German Life in the Age of Revolution: Joseph Görres, 1776–1848*. Washington, D.C.: Catholic University of America Press, 2001.

Wacker, Bernd. *Revolution und Offenbarung: Das Spätwerk (1824–48) von Joseph Görres*. Mainz: Matthias Grünewald, 1990.

Wibbelt, Augustin. *Joseph von Görres als Litterarhistoriker*. Cologne: Bachem, 1899.

GOTHIC FICTION

The term "*Gothic fiction*" refers to a literary form popular in the period between the publication of Horace Walpole's *The Castle of Otranto* in 1764 (the second edition was subtitled "A Gothic Story") and Charles Maturin's *Melmoth the Wanderer* in 1820. Walpole's novel is commonly thought to have inaugurated the genre, inspiring a host of imitators, while *Melmoth the Wanderer* represents the culmination, although certainly not the conclusion, of this tradition. Gothic fiction can also be understood in a broader sense, to refer to fiction of the nineteenth century, and fiction and film of the twentieth century, that repeats or transforms many of the stock motifs and preoccupations of the Gothic.

A list of the major writers that shaped the genre would include William Beckford, Charlotte Dacre, William Godwin, Matthew Lewis, Charles Maturin, Ann Radcliffe, Clara Reeve, Mary Shelley, and Horace Walpole; however, these writers are only the most well-known of those who in the last two decades of the eighteenth century and first decades of the nineteenth century wrote many hundreds of Gothic works.

Gothic fiction provided a vehicle and language for writing about the dark, irrational elements of experience and of the mind. It explored extreme mental states characterized by guilt, panic, fear, anxiety, obsession, paranoia, and claustrophobia, while frequently also attempting to assuage them by, for example, concluding with the discovery of the hero's or the heroine's true origin, identity, inheritance, or family. In so doing, Gothic fiction registered the anxieties and vulnerabilities, along with the hopes, of a culture in upheaval from the American and the French Revolutions, as well as the Industrial Revolution. This context explains in part the preoccupation of Gothic writers with the psychology of transgression and the possibilities of rebellion.

The publication of Matthew Lewis's *The Monk* (1796) and Ann Radcliffe's *The Mysteries of Udolpho* (1794) provided the paradigms for two contrasting streams of this protean genre: terror and horror gothic. As Radcliffe explains in the prologue to *Gaston de Blondeville*, published posthumously in 1826, terror and horror are opposites that have radically different effects on the reader. In the latter, disturbing events are described in minute, appalling detail. In the former, such events are left in significant part to the reader's imagination, which consequently must work to construe events from the hints given by the narrator. Consequently, Radcliffe argues, where the second "contracts, freezes, and nearly annihilates" the faculties, the first "awakens" the mind "to a high degree of life."

The Monk and *The Mysteries of Udolpho* also provide the primary instances of, in the parlance of contemporary criticism, feminine and masculine Gothic. In the former, the male protagonist is locked in an oedipal struggle with the past (often pictured as a monastic or feudal institution). In opposition to a barbarous past and supernatural horrors, these works advance the egalitarian ethos they associate with friendship between men and the values represented by the paternal family. In contrast, for feminine gothic the source of terror is often the paternal home. It arises from the possibility that the paternal protector may be untrustworthy or, worse, a villain. These novels trace the heroine's gradual discovery of her origins and her growing knowledge of the forces that confine her. In the course of this journey of discovery, the novel's supernatural horrors are discovered to be figments of the imagination, products of the heroine's disempowerment. As these contrasts might suggest, masculine gothic typically arouses horror, while feminine gothic prompts terror.

It is important to remember that both feminine and masculine gothic could be written by writers of either gender. Indeed, many writers, such as Charlotte Dacre in *Zafloya, or The Moor* (1806) or Mary Shelley in *Frankenstein; or The Modern Prometheus* (1818), drew on both of these modes. Moreover, Gothic works are more diverse than this binary opposition suggests. The genre also includes the oriental Gothic, the domestic Gothic, Gothic melodrama, the monastic shocker, the sentimental Gothic, and Gothic history, to mention only the most significant of the subgenres. In addition, these works spawned some remarkable parodies, such as Jane Austen's *Northanger Abbey* (1818) and Thomas Love Peacock's *Nightmare Abbey* (1818) and *Gryll Grange* (1860–61).

Walpole's *The Castle of Otranto* displays the conjunction of two very different ways of making sense of the world: the unreasonable, superstitious world of the Middle Ages and the enlightened world of the present, where reason appears to govern reality. This conjunction established what might be described as the "formula" of Gothic fiction: the conjunction of a detestable, alien "other" and the everyday, reasonable world. Rather than being able simply to divide one from the other, works of Gothic fiction derive much of their energy and horror from the sense that the alien cannot once and for all be divided from the familiar. This is why Gothic literature is fascinated by doubles that torment the self and, inverting this trope, why they are often preoccupied by the trauma of "live" burial: its heroes and heroines routinely find themselves locked within a nightmare world (the prisons of the Inquisition, a ruinous castle, the crypt of a monastery). This elementary "formula" is used to explore a startling variety of anxieties. Perhaps the enlightened world will be unable to divide itself from the barbarous past, the domestic family is a place of violence rather than refuge, the work of the scientist or the monk disguises a monstrous sexuality, the self houses a monstrous nature, and so on.

Until the 1960s, many accounts of Gothic works itemized the conventions that they often hold in common: persecuted lovers, villains intent on imprisoning the trembling heroine, gloomy ruins, monastic institutions, subterranean passages, dreams, visionary states, ghosts, unnatural parents, murders, indecipherable manuscripts, and so on. Indeed, according to some critics, once you have read one work of Gothic fiction you have read them all. Nevertheless, one of the paradoxes of Gothic fiction is that while being one of the most conventional of all genres, it is also one of the most innovative, prolific, and influential. It is the most important genre of Romantic fiction, while also being an important precursor of the modern detective story, the psychological novel, and even the historical novel.

Recent criticism has explored its relation to "dark" Romanticism, mapped its uncanny prefiguration of many of the insights of Freudian psychology, traced its development in the nineteenth and twentieth centuries, and used it to explore the plight of women in the paternal cultures of modernity. In contemporary culture, the Gothic tradition continues to spawn new, often surprising, literary children.

PETER OTTO

Bibliography

Bruhm, Steven. *Gothic Bodies: The Politics of Pain in Romantic Fiction*. Philadelphia: University of Pennsylvania Press, 1994.

Carroll, Noël. *The Philosophy of Horror, or Paradoxes of the Heart*. New York: Routledge, 1990.

Clery, E. J. *The Rise of Supernatural Fiction, 1762–1800*. Cambridge: Cambridge University Press, 1995.

Cottom, Daniel. *The Civilized Imagination: A Study of Ann Radcliffe, Jane Austen and Sir Walter Scott*. Cambridge: Cambridge University Press, 1985.

DeLamotte, Eugenia C. *Perils of the Night: A Feminist Study of Nineteenth-century Gothic*. Oxford: Oxford University Press, 1990.

Ellis, Kate Ferguson. *The Contested Castle: Gothic Novels and the Subversion of Domestic Ideology*. Urbana: University of Illinois Press, 1989.

Fleenor, Juliann E., ed. *The Female Gothic*. Montréal: Eden Press, 1983.

Graham, Kenneth W. *Gothic Fictions: Prohibition/Transgression*. New York: AMS Press, 1989.

Grixti, Joseph. *Terrors of Uncertainty: The Cultural Contexts of Horror Fiction*. London, New York: Routledge, 1989.

Haggerty, George E. *Gothic Fiction/Gothic Form*. University Park: Pennsylvania State University Press, 1989.

Kiely, Robert. *The Romantic Novel in England*. Cambridge, Mass.: Harvard University Press, 1972.

Miles, Robert. *Gothic Writing, 1750–1820: A Genealogy*. London: Routledge, 1993.

Punter, David. *The Literature of Terror: A History of Gothic Fictions from 1765 to the Present Day*. London: Longmans, 1980.

Sedgwick, Eve Kosofsky. *The Coherence of Gothic Conventions*. New York: Methuen, 1986.

Williams, Anne. *Art of Darkness: A Poetics of Gothic*. Chicago: University of Chicago Press, 1995.

GOTHIC REVIVAL

During the Renaissance, *Gothic* became a pejorative label for all things barbarous. In a model of history probably first posited by Petrarch and developed and disseminated by Italian humanists, there were two epochs of cultural excellence: the classical and their own, which were separated by a terrible period of ignorance and barbarism, the Dark and Middle Ages. The Germanic invaders, the Goths, were held to be largely responsible for this cultural catastrophe. François Rabelais employed the term *Gothic* to describe a vulgar literary style, not reflecting Greek and Latin scholarship, and the most influential condemnation of all things Gothic can be found in Giorgio Vasari's *Lives of the Architects, Painters and Sculptors* (1550), wherein medieval architecture is designated simply as German and rejected as disorderly, overdecorative, and poorly constructed, the antithesis of the universally accepted classical style. By the early seventeenth century, the use of the term *German* was discarded in this context (Germany having long since embraced the classical ideal); scholars employed the adjective "Gothic" in their polemics instead.

It was the English who laid the foundations of a reevaluation that would later spread to the continent. Parliamentarians, quoting Tacitus, argued that representative government was in fact not a product of classical antiquity, but of the German tribes; the "Gothic polity" therefore represented free institutions and was opposed to tyranny and privilege. In art, the true Gothic revival began in England with a gradual shift in the crucial, classicist-dominated concept of nature, as writers (influenced by the new vogue for landscape gardening), began to champion irregularity and variety as "natural," an idea eventually falling under the banner of the "picturesque." The related aesthetic concept of the (nonclassical) sublime in opposition to the (classical) beautiful suggested that nature in its highest (sublime) form was free of the constraints of the classical. This trend toward aesthetic relativism in England resulted in the pre-Romantic "Gothic mood," which is most famously characterized by the fiction of Horace Walpole and the papier-mâché decoration of Strawberry Hill, his country seat in Twickenham, and is well-known as the form which dominated Victorian English architecture through the work of such influential figures as the prolific Sir George Gilbert Scott, his pupil George Edmund Street, the high-churchman William Butterfield, and the obsessive genius Augustus Welby Northmore Pugin.

In 1751, Bishop Warburton had argued, without a shred of evidence, that the Goths had worshipped in sacred groves, developing an organic style for their shrines, giving them the appearance of an avenue of trees, an analogy developed by Johann Wolfgang von Goethe in his *Von deuscher Baukunst* (*On German Architecture*, 1773), which records his response to seeing Strasbourg Cathedral, which he likens to a "tree of God." This was a Romantic manifesto to German Gothicists, but Goethe had been more interested in the cathedral's architect, Erwin von Steinbach, than in its relationship to medieval Christian tradition. This wider aspect of Gothic architecture was soon explored by, among others, Wilhelm Heinse, who described Milan Cathedral as "the most glorious symbol of the Christian religion I have ever seen"; and by Friedrich Wilhelm von Schlegel, who also propagated the belief that Gothic architecture was a tangible expression of the infinite (Schlegel, like Pugin, was a converted Roman Catholic). In addition, in 1835, Johannes Wetter laid out the true principles of the Gothic structural system for the first time in his guide to Mainz Cathedral. German enthusiasm for such architecture led to Cologne Cathedral being completed according to the original thirteenth-century plans in 1842, the King of Prussia laying the foundation stone.

No other country, however, committed itself to the Gothic with the passion of England. The hallmark of German historicism was actually the *Rundbogenstil* ("round-arched style," rather than the Gothic pointed), derived from a synthesis of early Christian, Byzantine, German, Italian Romanesque, and Italian Renaissance style. Germany was one of the first countries to rid its system of the past, and was an early exponent of functionalism (although Gothic style remains in expressionism). French architecture largely resisted Gothic style in the eighteenth-century, turning instead to classicism (which can be seen in the work of its great architect Ange-Jacques Gabriel) and neoclassicism, signaling a new attitude to antiquity in which a Roman regularity of style was combined with the structural lightness of Gothic (perfectly represented by Jacques Germain Soufflot's Panthéon [1757–90], with a Wren-inspired dome resting upon Gothic piers). Toward the end of the century, young architects moved towards radical experimentation inspired by classicism and the theories of Giovanni Battista Piranesi. There was a certain Romanticism in the *jardin anglais*, such as the Bagatelle (1778) in Paris by François-Joseph Bélanger, but the trend was rather neo-Gothic, with the Gothic and the classical interacting throughout the nineteenth century. The chapel of Louis XVIII at Dreux (1816–22), for example, was originally classical, but when it was enlarged in 1832 it became Gothic. The most committed French Gothicist was Eugène-Emmanuel Viollet-le-Duc, who analyzed the style in his *Dictionnaire raisonné de l architecture française* (1854–68). Viollet-le-Duc saw the Gothic style as the product of a secular civilization succeeding the religious domination of the Middle Ages, based on a rational construction which employed the system of rib vault, flying buttress, and buttress. The ribs are a skeleton, and its influence is apparent in the Eiffel Tower and in the work of Baron Victor Horta in Brussels; his theories also inspired some inconclusive medieval revivalism in Russia.

Even in the United States, where the classical tradition was highly influential, the Gothic style had some effect on church design. Notable Gothic churches include Grace Church, New York (James Renwick, 1846); the Church of the Holy Trinity, Brooklyn (Richard Upjohn, 1841–46); and the National Cathedral, Washington D.C. (designed by George Frederick Bodley in 1907 and finally completed in 1990). "Carpenter's Gothic," an eighteenth-century English term, is also applied to nineteenth-century American wooden buildings with exterior Gothic motifs. Other significant international examples of the Gothic revival are the Rijksmuseum, Amsterdam (Petrus Josephus Hubertus, Cuypers, 1877–85); the Vienna Town Hall (Friedrich von Schmidt, 1872–83); and the Houses of Parliament, Budapest (Imre Steindl, 1839–1902).

STEPHEN CARVER

Bibliography

Andrews, W. *Architecture in America: A Photographic History.* London, 1960.

Clark, Kenneth. *The Gothic Revival: An Essay in the History of Taste.* London: Constable, 1928.

Condit, C. W. *American Building Art: The Nineteenth Century.* New York, 1960.

Ferriday, P., ed. *Victorian Architecture.* London, 1963.

Fitch, J. M. *American Building.* 2 vols. New York, 1966–72.

Giedion, S. *Space, Time and Architecture: The Growth of a New Tradition.* 4th ed. Cambridge, Mass.: Harvard University Press, 1963.

———. *Spätbarocker und Romantischer Klassizismus.* Munich, 1922.

Hamlin, T. *Greek Revival Architecture in America.* New York, 1944.

Hautecoeur, L. *Histoire de l'architecture classique en France*, vols. 5, 6, and 7. Paris, 1953, 1955, and 1957.

Hitchcock, H. R. *Architecture: nineteenth and twentieth Centuries.* 2d ed. London, 1963.

———. *Early Victorian Architecture in Britain.* 2 vols. New Haven, Conn.: Yale University Press, 1954.

Hughes, Robert. *American Visions: The Epic History of Art in America.* New York, 1997.

Jordy, W. *American Buildings and their Architects.* Garden City, N.Y., 1972.

Kimball, *Domestic Architecture of the American Colonies and of the Early Republic.* New York, 1922.

Macaulay, James. *The Gothic Revival 1745–1845.* London: Blackie, 1975.

Morrison, Hugh. *Early American Architecture.* New York: 1952.

Murray, Peter, and Linda Murray. *The Oxford Companion to Christian Art and Architecture.* Oxford: Oxford University Press, 1998.

Muthesius, S. *The High Victorian Movement in Architecture.* London, 1972.

Pevsner, Nikolaus. *An Outline of European Architecture.* 7th ed. London: Penguin, 1990.

———. *Pioneers of Modern Design.* 2nd ed. London: Penguin, 1991.

———. *Some Architectural Writers of the Nineteenth Century.* Oxford: Oxford University Press, 1972.

Pugin, Austus Welby Northmore. *Contrasts; or, A Parallel Between the Noble Edifices of the Fourteenth and Fifteenth Centuries, and Similar Buildings of the Present Day; Shewing the Present Decay of Taste: Accompanied by Appropriate Text.* 1836.

Rosenau, H., ed. *Boulée's Treatise on Architecture.* London, 1953.

Stanton, Phoebe. *Pugin.* London: Thames and Hudson, 1971.

Watkin, David. *English Architecture.* London: Thames and Hudson, 1978.

GÖTTINGER HAIN

The university town of Göttingen in the early 1770s was not the most obvious place for a literary renaissance. However, a group of students and young men came together here for a short time to give new impetus to cultural life and poetry in Germany. This group became known as the Göttinger Hain (or Göttingen Grove League). They were led by Heinrich Christian Boie, an experienced and well-read critic who edited most of the volumes of the *Göttinger Musenalmanach*, a literary journal, and encouraged young talent.

The founder members of the group were Johann Heinrich Voss, who gave the group its name, became its active leader, and took over the editorship of the *Almanach* in 1775; L. P. Hahn; Ludwig Heinrich Christoph Hölty; J. M. and G. D. Miller; and J. T. L. Wehrs. Its foundation was ceremonious and spontaneous. While on a walk together on the night of September 12, 1772, these young men joined hands in the moonlight around an oak tree and swore eternal friendship: "Der Bund ist ewig." Mutual support, honesty, and openness were to be their watchwords. Others to be associated with the group were C. F. Cramer, Count C. A. Haugwitz, and the dramatist Johann Anton Leisewitz, and Counts C. and F. L. Stolberg.

These men were inspired by the poetry of Friedrich Gottlieb Klopstock, who visited them, whose poetry they read at meetings, and whose birthday they ceremoniously celebrated together in 1772. While exalting Klopstock as bardic they denigrated the poetic output of Christoph Martin Wieland as decadent, rococo, and Francophilic. The most fertile period of poetic production for the Göttinger Hain was the winter and spring of 1773, and the 1774 Almanach contained contributions by Klopstock as well as by Gottfried August Bürger, Matthias Claudius, Johann Wolfgang von Goethe, and Johann Gottfried von Herder.

The values of the Göttinger Hain were those of the emerging middle classes in Germany. Many of the group's members had a background in theology. They attacked despotism and cherished freedom and love of their own country. They pursued happiness and virtue with religious zeal and aspired to a more natural form of life.

Still, their poetry is learned, allusive, sometimes playful, and shows sophistication of form. Ancient models remained important to them: the ode, the elegy, the idyll, the hymn. Some, like Voss, were notable translators of Homer. They also turned to English poetry, Hölty translating Thomas Gray's *Elegy*. Klopstock was an important bridging figure for them between the ancient and the modern; they built on his legacy and continued his efforts to achieve suppleness of expression in the German language. They also cultivated indigenous forms such as the ballad, the romance, and the Lied. Their consciousness of German traditions was important to them, and chimed with the efforts of Herder and others in this direction.

However, by the mid-1770s the group had faded. When Goethe later looked back on his association with members of the group in his autobiography, *Dichtung und Wahrheit* (*Poetry and Truth*, 1811–22), it was the diversity of their literary activities and the various directions in which they went after the group's dissolution that he found worthy of note. Several of its members left their mark on German literature: Voss and Hölty on poetry, Leisewitz on drama, and J. M. Miller on the novel.

There are direct lines of influence from the Göttinger Hain to Romanticism in Germany (for example, in August von Platen's odes we find echoes of Hölty), but the group's significance for later developments should be seen in broader terms, as a stage in the gradual move away from a style of poetry that was rhetorical or gallant to one in which subjective emotions and the bond between individuals came to the fore. Like the Sturm und Drang (storm and stress) movement, with which it coincided, the group's publications and lifestyle were another important symptom of the reaction to rationalism and convention.

J. D. GUTHRIE

Bibliography

Behrens, Jürgen. "Der Göttinger Hainbund." In *Sturm und Drang: Ausstellung im Frankfurter Goethe-Museum*. Edited by Christoph Perels. Frankfurt am Main: Freies Deutsches Hochstift, 1988.

Cothran, Bettina Kluth. "Ludwig Christoph Hölty (1748–1776)." In *German Writers from the Enlightenment to Sturm und Drang*. Edited by James Hardin and Christoph E. Schweizer. *Dictionary of Literary Biography*, vol. 97. Detroit: Gale Research, 1990.

Alfred Kelletat, ed. *Der Göttinger Hain*. Stuttgart: Reclam, 1979.

McNight, Phillip S. "Heinrich Christian Boie (1744–1806)." *Dictionary of Literary Biography*, vol. 94. Defroit: Gale Research.

Schneider, Ferdinand Josef. *Die deutsche Dichtung der Geniezeit*. Stuttgart: Metzler, 1952.

GOUNOD, CHARLES 1818–1893

French composer

A prolific composer of the mid-to-late nineteenth century, Charles Gounod seems to be more popular with performers and listeners than with scholars. His music has been out of fashion with the professional musical community for most of the last seventy-five years. Nevertheless, his achievements as a composer are substantial. Today he is best known for two works: the song *Ave Maria* (1889), which is a melody composed above the accompaniment of Johann Sebastian Bach's C-Major Prelude from the first book of *The Well-Tempered Clavier*; and his opera *Faust* (1856–59). Gounod was a complex man with a volatile personality, a prolific composer in many genres, a conductor, and a central figure in the cultural life of France during the second half of the nineteenth century.

Based on contemporary reports, Gounod had a complex and contradictory personality. Fanny Mendelssohn Henzel met the young Gounod in Rome (during his residency at the French

Academy resulting from the Prix de Rome); she attested to a person who was a series of opposites and contradictions founded on quick changes of mood. He demonstrated characteristics of being detached, thoughtful, contemplative, excitable, charming, mystical, and unrestrained. His religious beliefs played an important part in his life; his faith and the Catholic Church seem to have been stabilizing forces through the periods of tumultuous swings of temperament that plagued him throughout his life.

Gounod's musical style is eclectic and influenced by numerous musical sources. In addition to the French music being written during his musically formative years, Gounod's style seems to have been influenced by such diverse composers as Ludwig Felix Mendelssohn, Giovanni Pierluigi da Palestrina, and Robert Schumann. Various aspects of these influences would appear in Gounod's works several decades after his first acquaintance with the music of these composers. It appears that Gounod's mature style was fully developed between 1856 and 1859, the period when he was working on *Faust*. After his success with *Faust*, Gounod did not greatly modify his overall style. For example, he was not affected greatly by the compositions of Richard Wagner; and unlike numerous of his contemporaries, he did not attempt to incorporate major mainstays of Wagner's style into his work.

One of the foundations of Gounod's style is his eclecticism. This may be found in various aspects of the different genres in which he composed. For example, in his church music, two of his frequently employed styles were distinctly different. Some of his religious choral music is written in a strict a cappella style incorporating white-note notation of the *stile antico* derived from the works of Palestrina. Usually these works were of fairly conservative harmonic design, remaining in the diatonic harmonic idiom with occasional wanderings of sections into distantly related keys. Another of Gounod's a cappella styles included his own kind of nineteenth-century chromaticism, and was usually based on a Gregorian melody. Eclecticism can be observed in Gounod's first opera *Sapho* (1851); here, he combines and juxtaposes several different styles to create his own stylistic statement. These include a combination of a Gluckian eighteenth-century foundational style with Italian-style ensemble composition and the salon song, a favorite French idiom. This resulted in a lyrical, intimate, and simple structure.

Melody is the main stylistic component in the composer's vocal music. In fact, his operas and French secular songs emerge as the vessel of various specific details of his musical style. The relationship between verbal texts and the rhythm of the melodic writing is important to the understanding of Gounod's melodic style. This style was frequently configured by rhythmic writing that is cast about the expressive subtlety of the text. Interestingly, most of his melodies are primarily syllabic. He does not seem to be interested in vocal virtuosity, as demonstrated in the relatively modest melodic figuration incorporated in his melodic writing. While Gounod opposed the stereotypical French melodic style of standard phrase lengths, strong melodic and rhythmic emphasis on the first beat of the measure, and the employment of standard cadential formulae, there are numerous instances of the composer employing these techniques. Also, he composed melodies that are flexible and develop in a spontaneous fashion. This latter type of writing is accomplished within a framework of regular phrase lengths, and results, in melodies that have an inclination to make the meter ambiguous by the use of duration accents on weak beats.

Gounod's harmonic language was in the vein of mid-nineteenth-century harmonic writing by French composers. His use of chromaticism emerges in some of his early songs. The technique of his tonal writing shows mastery, and demonstrates a sophisticated and gracious character, and he showed originality in the tonal progressions which led to cadences. Gounod did not become influenced by the progressive harmonic vocabulary of Richard Wagner; rather, he remained within the mainstream of Romantic tonality with the incorporation of chromaticism that is stylistically based on French contemporaries such as Cesar Franck.

It is difficult to separate Gounod's rhythmic writing from his melodic writing, and in turn the setting of text and melody. Early songs demonstrate his facility for moving among the various types of rhythmic accent to accurately align the melodic rhythm with the rhythmic nature of French texts. He cleverly utilized the various types of accent (agogic, metric, and accents of register) for specific poignant results.

Gounod's instrumental music, which is less prominent in his oeuvre, displays the same eclecticism. In his First Symphony, particularly in the second movement, there is evidence of the influence of Mendelssohn's style, while in the Second Symphony the ideas of Beethoven can be discerned. Gounod was not known as an innovator in orchestration. However, the inclusion of uncommon instruments and specific effects may be found in the incidental music for *Ulysse* (1881). His orchestral writing is characterized by its conservative use of color, its transparent clarity, and its fineness. He employs a type of contrapuntal writing which is a model of clarity and demonstrates a textural design that interweaves solo winds within the context of the larger orchestral composition.

Listeners and fellow musicians of the era were impressed by his preference for elegance over harsh realistic effects and uncontrolled emotion. Additionally, he was known for the musical and lyrical grandeur of his compositions, which contemporary audiences found gripping.

JEFFREY WASSON

Biography

Born in Paris on June 18, 1818. He began piano study with his mother. A graduate of the Lycée St.-Louis, he took music (composition) lessons from the famed Czech composer Antoine Reicha (1770–1836). In 1836, he began his studies at the Paris Conservatory, and in 1837 he was the one of two winners of the second Prix de Rome. Gounod won the Prix de Rome in 1839. He resided in Rome (1829–42) and Vienna (1842–43). During this sojourn he met Felix Mendelssohn and his sister Fanny Mendelssohn Henzcl. Returning to Paris, he acquired the title *maître de chapelle* at the *Séminaire des Missions étrangères*. He studied for the priesthood during the years 1846–48, but did not pursue ordination. He married Anna Zimmermann, the daughter of his former piano teacher Pierre-Joseph-Guillaume Zimmermann. The 1850s and 1860s were his most prolific and important years of composition. In 1852, he was appointed conductor of the male chorus of *L'Orphéon de la ville de Paris*. He left Paris for London in 1870, to avoid the Franco-Prussian War, and continued to reside there until 1874. During the 1880s his compositional focus returned to sacred music. He died in Saint Cloud on October 18, 1893.

Selected Works

Musical Compositions (summarized by category)

Ten operas, the most important of which are *Faust* (1856–59) and *Roméo et Juliette* (1865–71).

Seven theatrical works of incidental music and *opéra comique*.

An extensive list of Latin liturgical choral works, in the manner of motets.

Twenty-one masses, including two Requiems.

Twenty-three sacred or semireligious choral work in French and English.

Ten oratorios and cantatas.

Thirty-two solo sacred and semireligious songs, mostly with piano or organ accompaniments. There are texts in French, English and Latin, the most well known of which is his *Ave Maria melody*, written on Bach's C-Major Prelude from the *Well-Tempered Clavier*.

Twenty-three secular part songs, several of which exist in different versions.

Eleven vocal duets.

A great number of secular solo songs, mostly with piano accompaniments.

Numerous parts songs and some solo songs for children, mostly unaccompanied, some published as solo songs with piano accompaniment.

Thirteen works for orchestra, including two symphonies

Fifteen works for chamber ensembles of diverse scoring.

Many works for piano; some exist in both two and four hand versions, others exist in orchestral versions.

Three works for organ.

Writings

Autobiographie et articles sur la routine en matière d' art. Edited by Georgina Weldon. London, 1875.

"Memoires d'un artist," *Revue de Paris*. Vol. 2, 3–4, 1895. Translated as *Charles Grounod: Autobiographical Reminiscence, with Family Letters and Notes of Music* 1896. This enlarged English version includes unpublished material such as letters and lectures.

Memoirs of An Artist: an Autobiography. Translated by Annette Crocker. 1895. This appears to be an American edition of the *Autobiographical Reminiscence* listed above.

Bibliography

Busser, Henri. *Charles Gounod*. Lyon: Editions et imprimeries du sud-est, 1961.

Curtiss, Mina. "Gounod before Faust," *Musical Quarterly* 38 (1952): 48–67.

Demuth, Norman. *Introduction to the Music of Gounod*. London: Dobson, 1950.

Harding, James. *Gounod*. New York: Stein and Day Publishers (London: Allen and Unwin), 1973.

Hopkinson, Cecil. "Notes on the Earliest Editions of Gounod's *Faust*." In *Festschrift for Otto Eric Deutsch*. Edited by Walter Gerstenberg, Jan LaRue, and Wolfgang Rehm. Kassel and New York: Barenreiter Verlag, 1963.

Huebner, Steven. *The Operas of Charles Gounod*. Oxford: Clarendon Press of Oxford University Press, 1990.

———. "Gounod." In *The New Grove Dictionary of Music and Musicians*. 2d ed. Vol. 10. Edited by Stanley Sadie and John Tryell. New York: Grove Dictionaries, 2000.

Reicha, Anton. *Treatise on Melody*. Translated by Peter Landey. Hillsdale, N.Y.: Pendragon Press, 2000.

Wright, Leslie A. "Gounod and Bizet: a Study in Musical Paternity," *Journal of Musicological Research* 13 (1993): 31–48.

GOYA Y LUCIENTES, FRANCISCO JOSÉ DE 1746–1828

Spanish painter

Francisco José de Goya y Lucientes's life and work might at first seem emblematic of the career of the Romantic artist, given the variety of roles he may embody: an antiacademic, antiestablishment rebel, a man of passion whose relationship with female sitters was sometimes carnal, a chronicler of the life of the pueblo, a lone genius in constant ill health, an artistic guerrilla ending his life in exile. All these personae are features of a biographical myth of Goya, constructed out of some facts and the many silences of the documentary record surrounding the artist. In recent years, many of the individual aspects of this myth have been reexamined critically in the light of new evidence, and we have been forced to rethink or reject some cherished notions of the artist.

However, what remains is a body of work astonishing in its variety and accomplishment, which remains central to an understanding of Romanticism in the visual arts. Goya's output is of a richness and diversity that distinguish him not only from all his contemporaries in Spain, but from almost every practicing artist in Europe in his period. An accomplished and original portraitist, a bold religious painter and creator of complex allegories, he was equally adept at creating large-scale decorative cartoons and intimate cabinet pictures. He was a fresco painter of brilliance and originality, a printmaker whose unique vision still fascinates and perplexes viewers and commentators, and a draughtsman of rare skill.

More important than his technical brilliance and variety, however, is Goya's pictorial imagination, which seemed to find inspiration in the age-old, indigenous traditions of his native land which painters had neglected or spurned, and in the ferment of international modernity with its new landscape of ideas, wars, follies, and hubris.

Goya's first significant learning experiences were under the Aragonese painter José Luzàn. After a self-funded visit to Rome he returned to Saragossa and won a commission for religious frescoes for the church of Our Lady of the Pillar, which demonstrated an already developed facility with the technique. It was his move to Madrid in 1774 (and his marriage to the sister of most distinguished living Aragonese painter, Francisco Bayeu) that launched his career. The series of illustrations he created for the Palace of El Pardo (1776–78) demonstrated Goya's gift for color, movement, and pastoral drama. At the same time, Goya made a series of engravings after paintings after Velasquez that demonstrated the importance of his engagement with Velasquez and his understanding of the multiplicity and depth of the artist.

The traces of the study of Velasquez, as well as the tastes and imperatives of ecclesiastical and academic patrons, shaped Goya's set piece for the Real Academia de Belles Artes de San Fernando (the Spanish Academy), the *Crucified Christ* (1780). This was Goya's point of entry into the academic ranks, and it showed him to be sensitive to indigenous Spanish models of intense piety. It must be remembered that, whatever his marked self-proclaimed originality in invention and his often unorthodox views and techniques, Goya remained a loyal exhibitor and contributor to the exhibitions and to the life of the Spanish Academy well into the 1800s.

Goya's facility and skill in fresco painting were amply demonstrated in his commissions for the *Queen of the Martyrs* fresco in the Church of Our Lady of the Pillar in Sarragosa (1780–81). As well, in the 1780s, the artist began to develop his talents as a portraitist; the most striking of the portraits of this period are those of key patrons such as the Duke and Duchess of Osuna (1785–86) and the mysterious, quasi-symbolic portraits such as that of the child Manuel Osorio de Zuñiga (c. 1788).

All these portraits and religious commissions point to an artist of talent and originality integrated into traditional systems of patronage. In the 1780s the boldness and vision of the painter start to emerge. In his response to the Duke of Osuna's commission for the chapel of their ancestor, Fransisco de Borja, Goya painted monsters haunting the deathbed of a sinner (*Saint Francis Borgia at the Deathbed of an Impenitent*); this interest in the monstrous, the supernatural, and in incarnations of evil more generally was to be constant in his later work.

Goya fell seriously ill in late 1792; his malady nearly killed him, and left him profoundly deaf. Much comment has focused on the transformation of the artist at this point from court painter to visionary. This is too simplistic, however; although he was forced by ill health to give up his role as director of painting at the Spanish Academy, the intensity and scope of Goya's work for the court and academy actually increased after this point, and he continued to exhibit there. However, it is true that shortly after his illness he produced a remarkable series of cabinet pictures (on tinplate) that evidenced an interest in subjects such as bullfighting, street trading, popular theater, and the physiognomy and behavior of the insane (see for example the *Corral de Locos* [*Courtyard with Lunatics*, 1794]), these seem far removed in mood and intensity from his treatment of popular pastimes in his illustrations, and they foreshadow the *Caprichos*.

Goya returned to Andalusia in 1796–97, and it was during this visit that he stayed with the recently widowed Duquesa de Alba at her estate in Sanlúcar. This produced the famous and enigmatic portrait of the Duchess (1797) that has fueled so much speculation, but also the album now known as the Sanlúcar album, in which ludic and erotic subjects feature prominently. The energy, complexity, and sensitivity of Goya as a draftsman are also evident in the near contemporary album now known as the Madrid album (now dispersed). Here, though, the drawings show a development from Maja and Majo themes and other subjects familiar from the tapestry illustrations to drawings far more satirical, venomous, and violent in tone and content. In a series of numbered drawings, customs, religion, and social and sexual commerce are all viewed witheringly and represented via caricature and visual satire.

Out of these satirical drawings grew the *Caprichos* (*Caprices*), drawn between 1797 and 1799 and published in 1799. Perhaps no other series has attracted so much comment, as these are seen as indication of both the enlightened critique of Spanish religious, social, and popular custom, and as a sign of an intense imagination. It has been pointed out that they made little public impact at the time of their publication; notwithstanding, they remain remarkable both for their visual boldness, their unusual range of subject matter (monsters, violence, sexual commerce, and superstitious and carnival ritual feature prominently, as do satirical images of clergy), and for their density of allusion. It is clear that Goya was to some extent influenced in the creation of these engravings by his relationships with intellectuals and writers such as Moratín and Jovellanos, and that through them he became acquainted with the politically engaged caricatures of the British tradition. However, as the copperplates were purchased by the crown in return for a pension, we must perhaps temper our view of the politically radical nature of the series. *The Sleep of Reason Produces Monsters*, the famous Capricho number 43, divides the satirical engravings from those inspired by emblem books, popular imagery, and the artist's imagination, which are populated by more supernatural elements. This image, which (perhaps despite itself) has been used as both evidence of Goya's rejection of Enlightenment and his embrace of it, is a striking symbolic portrayal of the struggle between reason and imagination and between order and the monstrous that was central to his own creative impulses (and, it might be argued, to the "enlightenment project" more generally).

But while the *Caprichos* allow us a glimpse of Goya's private struggles, his public duties and commissions continued throughout the 1790s. One of his notable triumphs was the decoration of the church of St. Antonio de la Florida Madrid (completed 1798).

In 1799 Goya became first painter to the king, a title that brought him recognition and financial security. He painted several court portraits, most famous of which is *The Family of Charles IV* (1800–1801). The portrait is sometimes seen as deliberately subversive of its subject, but is better seen as daring in its refusal of physiognomic idealism and its flattening of the picture space. The favored minister Manuel Godoy became a particularly important patron of Goya, and the artist portrayed him in swaggering military-intellectual guise at the height of his glory, in the wake of the defeat of Portugal, in 1801.

Goya did no more royal portraits until 1808, but worked regularly for Godoy. Sometime before 1808, he created two of his most notorious images, the *Naked Maja* (c. 1798) and the *Clothed Maja* (c. 1806–8?) for Godoy, and these became touchstones of the erotic imaginations of nineteenth-century Romanticism. They found only the smallest of audiences at the moment of their conception, however, and were not regarded as having much artistic worth. Fascinating, even alluring, as they are for our age, it remains true that the are anomalies within Goya's ouevre, and their myth relies on the absence of documentation about subject, reason for commission, or even firm date of completion.

The turbulent events of 1808 that toppled the Regime of Carlos IV and Godoy and brought effective French domination of Spain, included a popular uprising on May 2, 1808. Goya worked for both the new, "puppet" regime of Fernando VII and for its French masters; this counters the persistent notion of Goya as patriotic realist.

Perhaps that reputation rests most firmly on the *Second of May* and the *Third of May* (both 1814). These were explicitly mythologizing paintings for the consumption of a conservative, patriotic public, painted for money; but the *Third of May* in particular retains great power, as it exploits popular and political imagery, as well as a claustrophobic compression of space, to make vivid a sense of fierce struggle between oppressor and oppressed. But, as commentators have shown, these images were conceived as part of a re-creation in myth rather than a documentary depiction, of what had been a far from heroic popular uprising. They never had a wide audience, as they were, it seems, confined to storage for most of the early years of their existence.

The formally striking series of etchings, the *Tauromaquia*, was published in 1816, by which time Goya had been (it seems) summoned to explain his Maja paintings in front of the Inquisition. He seems to have circumvented any sanction, though, and his painted output was limited to portraits, of friends, patrons, and himself. In 1819, at the age of seventy-three, Goya bought a country house and decorated it with a series of frescoes that have become known as the *Black Paintings* (from 1821 on: *Saturn, Judith and Holophernes, Duel with Cudgels, The Great He-Goat*). The peculiar technique, which involved the direct painting of oil onto the plaster, and the obsessions with grim violence, age, pain, and the rituals of popular superstition, have made these paintings famous, seen as the product of an isolated but vivid imagination, and portents of the hold which the violent and the supernatural were to gain over the Romantic imagination.

Goya's final years were spent in a self-imposed semiexile in Bordeaux, where he preferred to live with a group of Spanish liberals. His late work includes some striking portraits (such as that of his grandson, Mariano) and figure paintings, and two albums of drawings in which Goya's imaginative engagement with witchcraft, aging, madness, and love was as powerfully and economically represented as in any of his earlier drawings.

Goya also continued and deepened his interest in the new technique of lithography, producing the extraordinary series the *Bulls of Bordeaux* in 1825. According to eyewitnesses, Goya worked directly on the stone, using techniques that showed his appetite for innovative and energetic technique undiminished at the age of eighty.

It was through his graphic work that Goya's posthumous reputation grew. In France, key aesthetic and poetic figures of the Romantic movement, such as Théophile Gautier and Charles Baudelaire, wrote enthusiastically of Goya's etchings and lithographs. Subsequent generations of artists and writers became similarly enthused, and Goya's influence over the realist generation, Édouard Manet, and the modernists (especially Pablo Picasso), as well as the postmodernist generations (for example, Jake and Dinos Chapman), is perhaps more tangible than that of any other artist of his generation.

MARK LEDBURY

Biography

Born, Fuendetodos, 1746. Apprenticed to the Painter José Luzán Martinez in Saragossa, 1758–61. First of his unsuccessful attempts to obtain a scholarship to the Royal Academy, Madrid, 1763 (tried again 1766). Visited Rome, 1770–71. Received commission for vault in Cathedral in Saragossa, 1771–72. Married Josepha Bayeu, sister of Ramon and Francisco, 1773. First tapestry illustrations, 1774. Elected member of Spanish Royal Academy of Fine Arts on the strength of *Christ on the Cross*, May 1780. Completed Regina Martyrum frescoes at Cathedral in Saragossa, 1781. Birth of Javier Goya (only son to survive him), 1784. Appointed deputy director of Royal Academy 1785. Appointed painter to the king, 1786. Named court painter by Charles IV, 1789. Visited Cadiz, where he fell seriously ill, 1792. Returned to Madrid, permanently deaf, 1793. Appointed director of painting at the Royal Academy, 1795. Traveled to Andalusia once again, and stayed with the Duchess of Alba at Sanlúcar, 1796. Began work on *Los Caprichos*, and resigned from the Royal Academy on account of his deafness, 1797. Painted frescoes of St. Antonio de la Florida, 1798. *Caprichos* published as he was appointed first court painter, 1799. Finished *The Family of Charles IV*, June 1801. Death of Duchess of Alba, 1802. Journeyed to Saragossa between the two sieges of the city by Napoleonic troops, 1808. Commissioned by city of Madrid to paint allegorical portrait of Joseph Bonaparte, 1809. First *Desastres de la Guerra* etchings, 1810. Began relationship with Leocadia Weiss, 1811. Painted the *Second of May 1808* and the *Third of May 1808*, 1814. Indicted by the Inquisition for obscenity, 1815. Published the *Tauromachia* engravings, 1816. Completed *Desastres* 1820. Began the decoration of his country villa with paintings now known as the *Black Paintings*, 1821. Escaping a wave of persecution of liberals, traveled to France "to take the waters," and remained there with Leocadia Weiss and her children, 1824. Returned to Madrid and gained from Ferdinand VII both a release from his duties and a pension, 1826. Died in Bordeaux, 1828.

Selected Works

The Duke of Osuna and his Family. c. 1786. Prado, Madrid.
Self-Portrait. 1794. Musée Goya, Castres.
The Duchess of Alba. 1796. Hispanic Society of America, New York.
Portrait of Doctor Peyral. c. 1796. National Gallery, London.
The Field of San Isidro. 1797. Prado, Madrid.
The Miracle of Saint Anthony. Frescoes for the Cupola of San Antonio de la Florida. 1798.
Portrait of Gaspar Melchior de Jovellanos. 1798. Prado, Madrid.
Naked Maja and Clothed Maja. c. 1795–1800. Prado, Madrid.
Los Capricho, 1799.
The Family of Charles IV. 1800–1801. Prado, Madrid.
Godoy as Commander in the War of the Oranges. 1801. San Fernando Academy, Madrid.
The Diasters of War, created c. 1813–20; published 1863.
Second of May 1808. 1814. Prado, Madrid.
Third of May 1808. 1814. Prado, Madrid.
Madhouse. c. 1816. San Fernando Academy, Madrid.
Mural Paintings from La Quinta del Sordo ("The Black Paintings"), including *The Laughing Woman, The Old Monk,* all c. 1819. Prado, Madrid.
Los Disparats, 1820–27.

Bibliography

Batice, Jeannine. *Goya.* Paris, 1992.
Gassier, Pierre. *The Drawings of Goya.* 2 vols. New York, 1973.
Gassier, Pierre, and Juliet Wilson-Bareau. *The Life and Work of Francisco Goya, with a Catalogue Raisonné of the Paintings, Drawings and Engravings.* New York and London, 1971. Rev. ed. 1980.
Glendinning, Nigel. *Goya and His Critics.* New Haven, Conn.: Yale University Press, 1977.

Guidol, José. *Goya 1746–1828: Biography, Analytical Study and Catalogue of his Paintings.* Barcelona, 1984.

Harris, Tomás. *Goya: Engravings and Lithographs.* Oxford, 1964.

Luna, J., ed. *Goya 250 Aniversario.* Exhibition catalog. Madrid, 1996.

Malraux, André. *Saturn: An Essay on Goya.* Oxford, 1957.

Pérez Sánchez, Alphonso E., and Julian Gállego. *Goya: The Complete Etchings and Lithographs.* Munich, 1995.

Symmons, Sarah. *Goya.* Oxford, 1999.

Tomlinson, Janis. *Francisco Goya Y Lucientes 1746–1828.* London, 1994.

Yriarte, Charles de. *Goya: Sa biographie, les fresques, les toiles, les tapisseries, les eaux-fortes et la catalogue de l'oeuvre.* Paris, 1867.

GRABBE, CHRISTIAN DIETRICH 1801–1836

German playwright

Christian Dietrich Grabbe's early years as the son of the head prison warder in small-town Detmold left an indelible mark on his personality. For many years Grabbe felt slighted by people, and throughout his life he would be troubled by a sense of inferiority. A very gifted child, Grabbe attended the local school; from there he moved on to Leipzig University, where he studied law. He later continued his studies at Berlin University. He abandoned his formal education to train, unsuccessfully, as an actor, but soon returned to the university and eventually graduated. Grabbe took on a position as *Militärauditeur* (a military legal clerk) in his native Detmold. His first book was published in 1827 and included a number of his early plays, as well as a programatic essay entitled "Über die Shakespearo-Manie" ("On the Shakespeare-Mania"), in which he criticized the Romantics for idealizing William Shakespeare. However, faced with the same alternative as other contemporary playwrights—that is, having to choose between Shakespeare's epic theater and Johann Christoph Friedrich von Schiller's classicist theater—Grabbe would as often decide in favor of Shakespeare's more flexible form as against it. Such ambivalence is a central characteristic of Grabbe's oeuvre.

Grabbe's first play, *Herzog Theodor von Gothland* (*Duke Theodor of Gothland*, 1827), takes the occasion of a premodern, violent dispute between already Christianized Swedes and pagan Finns to present life as governed by brutality, heroism, and insatiable passions. Grieved by the death of one brother and deceived by the workings of his malicious enemy, the African Berdoa, into believing his other brother responsible, Gothland takes murderous revenge. When he later learns of his error, he does not repent, but commits further villainy in pursuit of his rival Berdoa. Due to its length, its unpolished dialogue, some improbable developments, and its extreme nature, the play remains rather unstageable.

Grabbe's comedy *Scherz, Satire, Ironie und tiefere Bedeutung* (*Jest, Satire, Irony and Deeper Significance: A Comedy in Three Acts*, 1827) is a continuation and rebuttal of the literary comedy (*Literaturkomödie*) of the German Sturm und Drang (storm and stress) movement and such early Romantic plays as Ludwig Tieck's *Der gestiefelte Kater* (*Puss-in-Boots*, 1797). Engaging in a general attack upon the church, the intelligentsia, the aristocracy, and the government during German Restoration, and simultaneously chastising the bland works of art during this era, Grabbe employs realistic, farcical, stereotypical, and absurd elements in this play. In a cast that even features the author himself, the devil succinctly expresses Grabbe's own sentiments when he describes life as *ein mittelmässiges Lustspiel* (*a mediocre comedy*) and compares hell favorably with heaven. The play's ironic tendency extends to itself and thus is an early example of metafictional narrative, predating postmodernity's tendency toward doubt and absurdity. Indeed, the work clearly deconstructs all transcendental or metaphysical beliefs.

The year 1829 saw the production of Grabbe's *Don Juan und Faust* in Detmold, the only play to be performed during Grabbe's lifetime. In the play, Grabbe attempts to combine the two stories of Don Juan and Faust. Although the two protagonists' love of Donna Anna establishes a thematic link, the play's success is questionable. The popular Romantic theme of the Gothic makes a brief appearance in the figure of Anna's slain father. Eventually, both Faust, seeking ultimate wisdom, and Don Juan, seeking countless affairs, are thwarted in their endeavors.

Grabbe only completed two of a planned cycle of eight Hohenstaufen plays: *Kaiser Friedrich Barbarossa* (1829) and *Kaiser Heinrich der Sechste* (1830). The plays were an answer to his own demand for a national German drama. In both plays, Grabbe's nihilistic belief in an apersonal history forms a sharp contrast to the monumental glorification of his heroes. During the 1930s, Nazi Germany appropriated the idealizing and nationalistic tone of Grabbe's historical plays, as well as the proto-Nietzschean propagation of his larger-than-life heroes. Grabbe's dramas were turned into propaganda for the alleged need of the people to follow strong leadership. The last work Grabbe finished was the historical play *Hermannsschlacht* (1838). An epic portrait of Hermann's victorious battle (9 C.E.) against the Roman general Varus, the play presents the German leader in almost superhuman grandeur, fighting for a liberated and united Germany—as did some of Grabbe's contemporaries, the authors of *Junges Deutschland* (*Young Germany*). The earlier historical tragedy *Hannibal* (1835) includes similar criticism of contemporary politics, but also derives much of its energy from Grabbe's personal situation. Embittered by life, his own lack of professional recognition, and by the recent failure of his marriage, Grabbe idealizes Hannibal's greatness and contrasts it negatively with the mediocrity of the people surrounding him. Hannibal eventually succumbs to this conflict.

With *Napoleon oder die hundert Tage* (*Napoleon or the Hundred Days*, 1831) Grabbe presents his most impressive and, from a dramatic point of view, most original historical play. The author portrays his protagonist as being both a brutal tyrant and a mythological hero. Napoleon Bonaparte's reactionary despotism, the nobility's complacency, and the desolation among the general population serve as a critique of Grabbe's own time. In the rise and fall of Napoleon, Grabbe once again emphasizes the absurdity and arbitrariness of history. Misanthropically, he further casts mankind as ruled by base instincts, unless being guided by a heroic leader.

After the 1834 dismissal from his clerical job, Grabbe first moved to Frankfurt, the literary center at the time, then attempted to start upon a theatrical career in Düsseldorf. Unfortunately, his plan to work with theater director Karl Immermann eventually failed. Literary success never materialized for Grabbe, despite a promising start. However, the painful realization that the theater of his day shunned his work freed Grabbe to indulge in formal experimentation. Ironically, it was his innovative dramatic technique that would eventually lead to his lasting fame. Not until the twentieth century was the playwright rightfully understood as a precursor of the modern epic theater. Grabbe's influence on the Weimar theater and, later, on Berthold Brecht was significant. The 1918 stage debut in Munich of Hanns Johst's play about Grabbe, entitled *Der Einsame* (*The Lonely Man*), inspired Brecht to write his first play, *Baal*.

GERD BAYER

Selected Works

Werke und Briefe: Historisch-kritische Gesamtausgabe in sechs Bänden. Editor. Akademie der Wissenschaften in Göttingen, bearbeitet von Alfred Bergmann. Emsdetten: Lechte, 1960–73.
Jest, Satire, Irony and Deeper Significance: A Comedy in Three Acts. Translated and introduced by Maurice Edwards. New York: F. Ungar, 1966.

Bibliography

Cowen, Roy C. *Christian Dietrich Grabbe.* New York: Twayne, 1972.
———. *Christian Dietrich Grabbe: Dramatiker ungelöster Widersprüche.* Bielefeld: Aisthesis, 1998.
Ehrlich, Lothar. *Christian Dietrich Grabbe: Leben, Werk, Wirkung.* Berlin: Akademie, 1983.
Freund, Winfried, ed. *Grabbes Gegenentwürfe: Neue Deutungen seiner Dramen.* Munich: Fink, 1986.
Kopp, Detlev, ed. *Christian Dietrich Grabbe: Ein Dramatiker der Moderne.* Bielefeld: Aisthesis, 1996.
Löb, Ladislaus. *Christian Dietrich Grabbe.* Stuttgart: Metzler, 1996.
Nicholls, Roger A. *The Dramas of Christian Dietrich Grabbe.* The Hague: Mouton, 1969.

GRAVEYARD POETS

Graveyard poets was a term retrospectively applied by nineteenth- and early-twentieth-century critics to a group of poets writing in the early and mid-eighteenth century whose work ostensibly demonstrated a unity of purpose both in its exploration of the substance and the effects of "melancholy" on mankind, and in its consideration of the larger implications of human mortality in general. The poets of what was, on occasion, argued to have constituted an entirely distinctive Graveyard "school" of writing were said to have composed quietly reflective and meditative verses; their poems were more often than not dramatically set within the context of some actual burial ground or churchyard. Authors writing in this mode were thought to have anticipated the work of the first generation of Romantic poets, both in their concern for the meditations of a solitary individual and in their obsession with the gothic aspect of the Romantic imagination.

Thomas Parnell, whose *Night-Piece on Death* was initially printed in 1721, was considered by many to have constituted the first significant adherent of this supposed school. The speaker of Parnell's lines abandons his seemingly pointless, scholarly studies instead to wander and contemplate among "a place of graves." His meditations on the brevity and instability of human existence lead him within less than a hundred verse lines to conclude that "Death's but a path that we must trod, / If man would ever pass to God." The Oxford-educated Edward Young began publishing his much lengthier, blank verse consideration of similar subjects—*The Complaint, or Night Thoughts on Life, Death, and Immortality*—in 1742. In lines that would eventually amount to the meditations of nine *Nights* in all, Young expatiates on

> Th'importance of contemplating the tomb;
> Why men decline it; suicide's foul birth;
> The various kinds of grief; the faults of age;

> And death's dread character . . .

Young's emphatic concern elsewhere in the poem with his own, particular fate, however—as opposed to the general condition of mankind—works to make his poem, as the early twentieth-century critic Amy Reed argued, "essentially a rejection of the optimistic philosophy of Shaftesbury and Pope, and a reaction against the doctrine of the unimportance of the individual."

The works of other "Graveyard poets," however, were likely to be far more orthodox in sentiment. The self-consciously religious and moral considerations of the Scotish divinity student Robert Blair, for example, were first given voice in 1743 in his *The Grave.* The conclusion of Blair's poem emphasizes the doctrinal truth of the fact that the Son of God has defeated death, and reiterates the familiar paradox that death is the path to eternal life; the body of Blair's poem, however, dwells with a kind of fascinated horror on the gravestones, skeletons, skulls, and epitaphs that constitute the landscape of the graveyard. Describing a schoolboy passing through the "lone churchyard at night," for example, Blair writes,

> Sudden he starts, and hears, or thinks he hears,
> The sound of something purring at his heels;
> Full fast he flies, and dare not look behind him,
> Till out of breath he overtakes his fellows;
> Who gather round, and wonder at the tale
> Of horrid apparition, tall and ghastly,
> That walks at dead of night, or takes his stand
> O'er some new-opened grave, and (strange to tell!)
> Evanishes at crowing of the cock.

Other poets whose work might be said to have participated in the graveyard school would most notably include John Dyer (*Grongar Hill*), Matthew Green (*The Spleen*), William Whitehead (*The Enthusiast: An Ode*), and Lady Winchelsea (*Nocturnal Reverie*). European poems sometimes described as participating in the genre would include the German von Creutz's *Die Gräber*, and the Italian poet Pindemonte's *I Sepulcri*.

The postulation of a distinctive thematically and topographically-obsessed group of writers by the critics of the early twentieth century, however, can to some extent be seen merely as part of a larger attempt to form some kind of aesthetic genealogy so as to account for the otherwise close to inexplicable popularity of the work that was invariably said to have constituted the school's greatest achievement: Thomas Gray's *Elegy Written in a Country Church-Yard* (1751). Gray's *Elegy* had been memorably praised in its own era by Samuel Johnson for its success in articulating "images which find a mirrour in every mind, and with sentiments to which every bosom returned an echo." The *Elegy* emphasized both the universality of death and the irresistible impulse toward commemoration and human memory. As Gray's elegist memorably asked his readers

> For who, to dumb forgetfulness a prey,
> This pleasing, anxious being e'er resign'd,
> Left the warm precincts of the cheerful day,
> Nor cast one longing, ling'ring look behind?
>
> On some fond breast the parting soul relies,

> Some pious drops the closing eye requires;
> E'en from the tomb the voice of nature cries,
> E'en in our ashes live their wonted fires.

The suggestion that there had been a "school" of poets whose work logically built on past achievements, and which itself testified to the persistence of isolation and melancholy as legitimate poetic subjects, was thus one attempt to explain the seemingly universal and transcendent claims of the *Elegy*. Critics in the late twentieth century, however, tended to question the efficacy of a terminology that with benefit of hindsight alone appeared to bestow some sense of unity and development on the otherwise often wildly idiosyncratic poets and poetic subjects of the mid-eighteenth century.

ROBERT L. MACK

Bibliography

Draper, J. W. *The Funeral Elegy and the Rise of English Romanticism.* 1929.

Reed, Amy. *The Background of Gray's Elegy: A Study in the Taste for Melancholy Poetry, 1700–1751.* New York: Russell and Russell, 1924; 1962.

Rothstein, Eric. *Restoration and Eighteenth-Century Poetry, 1660–1780.* Boston: Routledge & Kegan Paul, 1981.

Sickel, E. M. *The Gloomy Egoist.* 1932.

GREECE: CULTURAL AND HISTORICAL SURVEY

Romanticism as a literary and cultural movement was practically unknown among educated Greeks before the revolution against the Ottoman empire that broke out in March 1821. With the exception of Adamandios Korais, whose vision of a nation-state defined by language and tradition may have been influenced by Johann Gottfried von Herder, the horizons of Greek writers and thinkers before 1821 were determined very largely by the European, and particularly French, Enlightenment.

The war of independence in the 1820s brought Romanticism to Greece in the person of Lord Byron, who died there in 1824, and of the many idealistic young men from Europe and America, known as Philhellenes, who flocked to Greece to take part in the struggle. It was the Philhellenes, and those educated Greeks who appealed to them for help, who turned an inchoate rebellion into an international crusade that by 1834 had established the first new nation of modern Europe, with a European head of state (King Otho of Bavaria), and its capital at Athens. The nation-state that became established then, and its self-definition as the racial, linguistic, and cultural descendant of the Greek civilization of antiquity, were both products of Romanticism.

In literature, the Romantic belief in national self-determination was celebrated as early as 1823 by Dionysios Solomos and 1824 by Andreas Kalvos, poets who had benefited from the Italian-dominated culture of the Ionian Islands. A more systematic involvement with the poetry and philosophy of German Romanticism begins with Solomos, in Corfu, during the 1830s. Had this reclusive aristocrat chosen to publish the fragmentary works that resulted, the course of Greek literature in the nineteenth century might have been very different. As it was, Solomos's most important work emerged only posthumously; and by this time the baton had passed from the Ionian Islands to Athens. There, Panayotis Soutsos and Alexandros Rizos Rangavis, émigrés from the Greek intellectual elite of Constantinople, established a more superficial but lasting form of engagement with literary Romanticism.

Even today the term *Greek Romanticism* is most often used in a restricted sense, to group together the minor literature of the period 1830–80 that these writers inaugurated. Poetry during this period tends to be either, on the large scale, nationalistic and grandiose, or, in shorter, lyric mode, elegiac and languorous; the predominant models being, respectively, Lord Byron and Alphonse de Lamartine. Prose fiction at this time is "Romantic" in a double sense: not only does it follow in the footsteps of Johann Wolfgang von Goethe, Victor Hugo, and (later) Walter Scott; it is also predicated on a deliberate revival of the Hellenistic novels of idealized love that had been written in Greek more than a millennium and a half before.

In Greece the concept, derived from Herder, of a nation as a homogenous group bound together by the "traditions of a people" soon prevailed. The immediate and visible traditions of the Greeks, in this sense, were language and the Orthodox Church. A third was the dogma of direct continuity from the civilization of the fifth century B.C.E. At first, Greek writers and thinkers celebrated their newfound freedom as the rebirth of an ancient civilization, and ignored the many centuries between. Korais followed Edward Gibbon in disparaging the medieval civilization of Byzantium, even though its religion and language were those of the Greeks of his day. During the 1830s, Byzantine as well as Ottoman monuments in Athens were indiscriminately pulled down, in the effort to create a cityscape that would express the perception of an ancient civilization revived without a break.

The neoclassical architecture of nineteenth-century Athens has earned few admirers. Most of the architects before the 1880s were not themselves Greek, but the vision they expressed of the modern Greek capital both helped to define and consolidate the Greek sense of identity at the time, and gave visible form to the way in which official Greek culture saw itself. The strictly neoclassical forms adopted contradict only superficially the underlying Romanticism of the period: for these foreign architects, and the prominent citizens for whom they worked, the "traditions" of the modern Greek people were those of *ancient* Greece. So to build using neoclassical forms was actually no less a manifestation of Romanticism than were the wild neo-Gothic fantasies of some German architecture of the same period.

The discovery of traditions closer in time began only in the second half of the nineteenth century. Only then, just as other peoples in Europe were buttressing their contemporary sense of identity by reinventing the Middle Ages, and through the study and dissemination of folklore, did Greek writers and thinkers begin seriously to assimilate indigenous folklore and to rehabilitate Byzantine civilization. Landmarks in this process were the publication, respectively, of Spyridon Zambelios's *Asmata demotika tes Ellados* (*Folk Songs of Greece*) in Corfu in 1852, and of the five-volume *Istoria tou ellenikou ethnous* (*History of the Greek Nation*) by Konstantinos Paparrigopoulos between 1860 and 1875.

These developments, in turn, were highly influential in literature during the last years of the nineteenth century. Poets such as Georgios Drosinis and Kostis Palamas began to exploit the common roots of their language and culture in their poems. At the same time, fiction by Andreas Karkavitsas, Alexandros Papadiamandis, G. M. Vizyinos, and many others brought to an urban readership a vivid portrayal of life in traditional rural communities. This development, known in Greek as *ethography*, is equivalent to *costumbrismo* in Spanish literature and *verismo* in Italian fiction and opera; ethography favors a blend of folklore and realism. Although some of the underlying preoccupations of this fiction are clearly grounded in Romantic conceptions of nation and tradition, the style and plots are more often vigorously realist.

Greek Romanticism, although the term itself is mostly out of favor today, was the formative phase of both a national literature and the nation itself. The distinctive ways in which Greeks absorbed the ideas and practices of European Romanticism add up to a complex and crucial phase of modern Greek history, and also contributed to Romanticism some of its least expected manifestations, including the buildings of the Athens Academy, the visionary poetic fragments of Solomos, and the haunting tales of island life in Skiathos by Papadiamandis.

RODERICK BEATON

Bibliography

Beaton, Roderick. *An Introduction to Modern Greek Literature*. 2nd ed., revised and expanded. Oxford: Oxford University Press, 1999.

———. "Romanticism in Greece." In *Romanticism in National Context*. Edited by R. Porter and M. Teich. Cambridge: Cambridge University Press, 1988.

Clogg, Richard. *A Concise History of Greece*. 2nd ed. Cambridge: Cambridge University Press, 2002.

Constantinides, Elizabeth. "Toward a Redefinition of Greek Romanticism," *Journal of Modern Greek Studies* 3 (1985): 121–36.

Dimaras, K. Th. *Ellinikos Romantismos*. Athens: Ermis, 1982.

Herzfeld, Michael. *Ours Once More: Folklore, Ideology and the Making of Modern Greece*. 2d ed. New York: Pella, 1986.

Politis, Alexis. *Romantika Chronia: ideologies kai nootropies sten Ellada tou 1830–1880*. Athens: E. M. N. E.-Mnemon, 1993.

GRIBOEDOV, ALEKSANDR SERGEEVICH 1795–1829

Russian writer

A distinctive Russian writer and a talented diplomat, Aleksandr Sergeevich Griboedov went down in the history of literature as the author of the immortal comedy *Gore ot uma* (*Woe from Wit*, 1824). Although Griboedov's creative heritage does not end here, his other comedies and verses are relatively trivial and negligible. His early plays *Molodye suprugi* (*The Young Spouses*, 1815); *Student* (1817; first published in full in 1889 as *The Student*, together with Pavel Katenin); *Svoia sem'ia, ili zamuzhniaia nevesta* (*His Own Family, or a Married Bride*, 1817; together with Aleksandr Shakhovskoi); *Pritvornaia nevernost'* (*Pretended Infidelity*, 1818; together with Andrei Zhandr); and *Proba intermedii* (*An Attempt at an Interlude*, 1818) fully employ the literary techniques and aesthetic principles of the mainstream Russian drama represented by the works of N. I. Khmel'nitskii, Shakhovskoi, and Mikhail Zagoskin. At the beginning of the nineteenth century, Russian drama was still based on the model developed by the classicists, and the repertoire of Russian theater consisted mostly of this sort of production. The playwrights of that time were particularly interested in comedies, so the classical comedy not only survived over the first decades of the nineteenth century, but had a revival.

Griboedov's comedies *The Young Spouses, Pretended Infidelity* (both based on the plots of famous French comedies: *Le secret du ménage* by A.F. Crenzé de Lesser and *Les fausses infidelités* by Nicolas-Thomas Barthe), and *His Own Family, or a Married Bride*, were successfully performed in Saint Petersburg and Moscow, although his later comedy *Kto brat, kto sestra, ili obman za obmanom* (*Who's Brother, Who's Sister, or, Deception after Deception*, 1823; with Petr Viazemskii) was first staged in Moscow and failed. *Woe from Wit* marked the period of Griboedov's devotion to the genre of comedy, but all his tragedies and dramas of the 1820s remained unfinished. Perhaps the most interesting of these is *Gruzinskaia noch'* (*A Georgian Night*, 1826–27), based on an episode from Georgian history. This can be considered as a proof of his interest in exotic stories, something common to Romantics. Griboedov's attention to Romantic stories is also revealed in the fragment of the poem *Kal'ianchi* (published in 1838), which the Russian Romantic poet Vil'gel'm Kiukhel'beker compared to Lord Byron's *Childe Harold's Pilgrimage*. Some of the other verses also illustrate Griboedov's devotion to Romanticism, although his talent was not fully implemented in poetry. Griboedov's critical essays, travel notes, and letters are also of significant interest to literary experts, as they show the author as an original historian, ethnographer, linguist, and literary critic. A person of many talents, Griboedov was also a gifted musician, though he never took music seriously. Two waltzes he composed occupy an important place in his creative works.

Completed in 1824, the famous comedy *Woe from Wit* (also known in translations as *The Misfortune of Being Clever, The Disadvantages of Being Clever, Wit Works Woe, The Woes of Wit, Distress from Cleverness, The Mischief of Being Clever*) was never published in Griboebov's lifetime. It first appeared as late as 1831 in a German translation, and a Russian edition followed two years later. The comedy was found offensive in Russia, and the first legal, uncensored, edition came out only in 1862. As the comedy was not approved, theater performances of the play were also banned, and Griboedov could enjoy only some episodes of his work, staged by amateur companies. Although unpublished and excluded from the official repertoire, the comedy became well known due to the manuscripts being distributed in literary circles. The influence of *Woe from Wit* was so significant that some thirty years later Evdokia Rostopchina wrote her own comedy with the same characters: *Vozvrat Chatskogo v Moskvu, ili vstrecha znakonykh lits posle dvadtsatipiatiletnei razluki* (*Chatskii is Back in Moscow, or a Meeting of Acquaintances after Twenty-Five Years*, 1856).

Griboedov's play adheres to the canons of classical comedy in its composition, dramatic conflict, and characters. Like his predecessors Denis Fonvisin and Molière, Griboedov uses meaningful names (Famusov: famous; Sofiia: wise; Molchalin: silent) and long monologues, and he constructs the play around a love story (three men aspire to the hand of one girl, Sofiia Famusova). Moreover, Griboedov follows the unities of time, place, and action, and finally presents a satirical portrait of the contemporary society. However, a close examination would suggest that the comedy employs literary techniques developed also by Romanticism and realism. The characters certainly possess a greater degree of individuality than they were supposed to have under classicism. In D. S. Mirsky's words, "they are persons, but they are also types—archetypes or quintessences of humanity, endowed with all we have in life and individuality, but endowed also with a super-individual existence." The main character Chatskii is a Romantic figure, who is struggling against the entire world. He inveighs against the world and society, having no positive program of his own. Moreover, he is preoccupied by his love and irritated by total misunderstanding on Sofiia's part, so he tries to take revenge on anyone he sees. It is clear that Chatskii's ideas do not reflect, and are not wholly approved by, Griboedov's principles; a more realistic approach to art and its aims is suggested in the play. A story that started as an amusing comedy ends as a drama; Chatskii is banished from society, Sofiia's match is broken and her illusions are destroyed, and those who were meant to be satirically criticized remain in power. Such a combination of techniques and approaches demonstrates the unique nature of Griboedov's style. This was not fully recognized by Aleksandr Pushkin, who denounced Chatskii for the lack of "wit," as "the first evidence that a man is smart as his

Aleksandr Sergeevich Griboedov. Reprinted courtesy of AKG.

awareness of whom he is talking to." In Pushkin's opinion, the main character of *Woe from Wit* was wasting his eloquence in front of people who were not even capable of seeing the point of his censure. Such a contradiction can only manifest itself when the classical form of the comedy no longer prevails over its content.

Although not completely satisfied with the characters, Pushkin predicted a long life for the natural and colloquial language of the comedy. *Woe from Wit* is written in rhymed verse, in iambic lines (also heavily exploited in Russian Romantic poetry) of various length, conveying a genuinely conversational atmosphere. By virtue of the groundbreaking features of this work, Griboedov occupies in Russian literature a place next to Pushkin and Mikhail Lermontov.

EKATERINA ROGATCHEVSKAIA

Biography

Born in Moscow, January 4 (15), 1795 (1794 or 1790, according to some sources) to a family of Russian nobility. Studied at the Boarding School for the Nobility; then Moscow University, 1806–12. Graduated in law, 1812. Joined the Moscow Hussars, serving in White Russia, 1812–16. Appointed to Ministry of Foreign Affairs, Saint Petersburg, 1816; secretary of the Russian mission at the Persian court, Tehera, 1819–21. Wrote the comedy *Gore ot uma* (*Woe from Wit*), 1822–24. Diplomatic secretary to General A. P. Ermolov in Tiflis, 1823–25. Moved to Georgia, 1825. Arrested and held for connection with the Decembrists after the uprising; 1825–26. Returned to Caucasus, 1826. Prepared the text of the Treaty of Turkmanchai; appointed Russian minister in Teheran, 1828. Killed during the storming of the Russian embassy, Teheran, January 30 (February, 11) 1829.

Selected Works

The Woes of Wit

Gore ot uma. Edited by N. K. Piksanov and A. L. Grishunin. 2nd ed. Moscow: Nauka, 1987. *Gore ot uma*. Edited by Richard Peace, notes by D. P. Costello. London: Bristol Classical Press, 1995. Translated as *The Woes of Wit*, by Alan Shaw. Tenafly, N.J.: Hermitage, 1992. Translated as: *Distress from Cleverness* by Beatrice Yusem. New York: Effect, 1993.

Collections

Polnoe sobranie sochinenii. Edited by Ars. I. Vvedensky. Saint Petersburg: A. F. Marks, 1892.

Izbrannye proizvedeniya. Leningrad: Sovetskií pisatel, 1961.

Sochineniia. Edited by S. A. Fomichev. Moscow: Khudozhestvennaia Literatura, 1988.

Polnoe sobranie sochinenii v trekh tomakh. Edited by S. A. Fomichev *et al*. Saint Petersburg: Notabene 1995.

Bibliography

A. S. Griboedov v vospominaniiakh sovremennikov. Moscow: Khudozhestvennaia Literatura, 1980.

Fomichev, Sergei A. ed. *A. S. Griboyedov: khmel'nitskii sbornik*. Smolensk: SGU 1998.

Grishunin, Aleksandr L., V. M. Markovich, and L. S. Melikhova. "A. S. Griboedov." In *Russkie pisateli 1800–1917, biograficheskii slovar'*. Moscow: G-K, Bol'shaia Rossiiskaia Entsiklopedia. Fiant, 1992.

Harden, Evelyn J. *The Murder of Griboedov: New Materials*. Brimingham: Birmingham Slavonic Monographs, 1979.

Karinsky, S. *Russian Drama from Its Beginnings to the Age of Pushkin*. Berkeley and Los Angeles: University of California Press, 1985.

Krasnov, Petr S. et al. *A. S. Griboedov: zhizn' i tvorchestvo*. Moscow: Russkaia Kniga, 1994.

Mirsky, Dmitrii A. *A History of Russian Literature*. London: E. Benn, 1927.

Orlov, Vladimir. *Griboedov: ocherk zhizni i tvorchestva*. Leningrad: Prosveshchenie, 1967.

Timrot, Aleksandr D. *V miatezhnye gody: Griboedov v krugu dekabristov*. Moscow: Moskovskii Rabochii 1976.

GRILLPARZER, FRANZ 1791–1872

Austrian dramatist

Franz Grillparzer was sometimes called the "German Shakespeare," and he compared himself, perhaps somewhat immodestly, to the great German writers Johann Wolfgang von Goethe and Johann Christoph Friedrich von Schiller. He is considered neither a purely Romantic writer (although he belongs chronologically to this period), nor a complete realist, and is usually included by literary historians in the so-called Biedermeier period (named after the Biedermeier style of furniture), which extended from the 1815 Congress of Vienna to the March Revolutions of 1848. The Biedermeier style in painting and literature emphasized an inward turn to romanticized idylls of bourgeois family life and idealized natural landscapes, an escape from the political and social turmoil that plagued central European nations after Napoleon's defeat at Waterloo. At a time when the German-language literary scene was dominated by names like Goethe and Schiller, Grillparzer sought to establish a uniquely Austrian literary sensibility based upon the qualities (modesty, common sense, and genuine emotions) that he considered to be typically Austrian. He attempted to create an Austrian identity by striking a fine balance between the disparate peoples and nationalistic elements that threatened the stability of the Austro-Hungarian empire and an idealized romantic myth of the great Habsburg family dynasty who ruled this vast domain and in whose court he worked for most of his life. The psychological problem of identity, both on a personal level (he hated his own family name, for example) and on a national plane, seems to recur throughout his writings.

His first major dramatic work *Die Ahnfrau: Ein Trauerspiel in fünf Aufzügen* (*The Ancestress: A Dramatic Sketch*) premièred in Vienna on January 31, 1817 at the Theater an der Wien. It combines elements of the Gothic horror genre, the classical fate tragedy (such as Sophocles' *Oedipus the King*), and the ghost-and-robber stories that were so popular in later Romantic literature. The protagonist, Jaromir, does not know his own true identity and unwittingly returns to his family's Bohemian castle as a thief. He ends up falling in love with his sister and murdering his own father, echoing the plot, elements of the Sophocles play. Anxiously harried by the vengeful image of a family ancestress he sees in a mirror, Jaromir finally learns his true fate and must accept all that he has done. The psychological dimensions (existential anxiety and self-knowledge) of this early Grillparzer play lend depth to the contrived plot, and seem to foreshadow the insights of the later Viennese depth psychologist Sigmund Freud. His next drama, *Sappho*, deals with the Romantic theme of the identity of the artist. It first performed at the Viennese Burgtheater on April 21, 1818, and its success prompted Grillparzer's appointment as court playwright. The aging Greek poetess Sappho misinterprets the attentions of a young man named Pharon, believing he is in love with her as a woman, when in fact he is merely an admirer of her poetry. She becomes jealous when the boy turns to a young woman, and kills herself when she realizes the truth. Grillparzer plays here with the Romantic theme of the pure artist versus the normal bourgeois; the true artist must sacrifice his or her emotional life to the lonely demands of creation. The theme of the tortured artist/intellectual recurs in post-Romantic German writers such as Thomas Mann and Hermann Hesse.

Grillparzer's next work is a three-part dramatic poem, *Das goldene Vliess* (*The Golden Fleece*, 1821), which also deals with a plot from classical literature, the story of the Greek hero Jason and Medea, the barbarian woman he marries and than abandons in order to go on his quest for the golden fleece. Medea becomes insane, and in a terrible act of revenge she kills their children. Grillparzer illustrates here another central Romantic theme, namely the power of the emotions as expressed in concepts of the rational and civilized (the ancient Greeks) versus the irrational and barbaric (the noble savage). Jason leaves his family in order to pursue an ideal of honor, a concept that is intangible and abstract. He must sublimate his emotions in order to serve this abstract intellectual notion, an action that is required by civilization. Medea, as a barbarian, gives free rein to her powerful emotions and acts upon irrational impulse, thereby destroying herself and all that she loves. This is an example of the darker side of the Romantic literary theme of the primacy of the emotions: sometimes they lead to the abandonment of all reason and thus to the destruction of the self. Grillparzer deliberately seeks to destroy the literary image of harmonious balance in ancient Greek culture as projected by the eighteenth-century neoclassical tradition.

Grillparzer's historical dramas were highly controversial. His 1825 *König Ottokar's Glück und Ende* (*King Ottokar's Rise and Fall*) deals with the beginnings of the Habsburg dynasty, but was censored because its plot evoked sensitive feelings about Austria's recent defeat by Napoleon. It was only performed after the emperor gave his permission. In 1826 Grillparzer returned to classical myth and the psychology of the individual's passion with his *Des Meeres und der Liebe Wellen* (*Hero and Leander*), adopting the Romantic theme of the destructive power of love. His 1834 drama *Der Traum ein Leben* (*A Dream is Life*) treats the Biedermeier theme of the idyllic bourgeois life in the story of Rustan, who escapes his humdrum existence into an escapist fantasy of action that becomes so violent that he gladly returns to his boring but peaceful middle-class world.

Although a dramatist, Grillparzer is also well known for one work of prose fiction, the 1847 novella *Der arme Spielmann* (*The Poor Musician*), generally considered to be one of the masterpieces of German realism. In the framed narrative, a dramatist who has depleted his imaginative powers searches for new material in real life, and so narrates the story of the poor and untalented street fiddler named Jakob, a social loner who lives a sad life of continual disappointments on the margins of society and who perishes finally in a River Danube flood. In Jakob's own mind his art is a sacred activity, but he is ironically unaware that his music is in fact terrible. In this clearly autobiographical tale, Grillparzer voices his own doubts about the limits of his creative abilities and of the Romantic imagination, as well as his lifelong feelings of alienation in the bourgeois society of the Biedermeier era.

THOMAS F. BARRY

Biography

Born in Vienna, January 15, 1791, son of a lawyer. Educated at Anna-Gymnasium, Vienna, 1800–1807. Studied law at the University of Vienna, 1807–11. Tutor in law studies to nephew of Graf von Seilern, 1812; unpaid assistant at court library, 1813. Embarked on government service: clerk in department of revenue, 1814–18; clerk in treasury, 1818. Appointed court dramaturg, 1818. Mother committed suicide, 1819. Traveled to Italy, 1819; traveled to Germany and met Goethe in Weimar, 1823. His tragedy *Des Meeres und der Liebe Wellen* (*The Waves of Sea and Love*) published, 1831. Appointed director of the court archives, 1832. Withdrew from literary life, 1838; retired from official service with the title of court counselor, 1856. Founder member of the Austrian Academy of Sciences, 1847. Made a member of the Herrenhaus (upper house, Austrian parliament), 1861. Awarded honorary doctorate, University of Leipzig, 1859. Died in Vienna, January 21, 1872.

Selected Works

Plays

Die Ahnfrau: Ein Trauerspiel in fünf Aufzügen, 1817. Translated *The Ancestress: A Dramatic Sketch* by Letitia Elizabeth Landon. 1828.

Sappho: Trauerspiel in fünf Aufzügen. 1818. Translated *Sappho: A Tragedy in Five Acts* by John Bramsen. 1820.

Das goldene Vliess: Dramatisches Gedicht in drei Abtheilungen. 1821. Translated *The Golden Fleece* by Arthur Burkhard. Yarmouth Port, Mass.: Register, 1942.

König Ottokar's Glück und Ende: Trauerspiel in fünf Aufzügen, 1825. Translated *Ottokar: His Rise and Fall* by Henry H. Stevens. Yarmouth Port, Mass.: Register 1938.

Des Meeres und der Liebe Wellen: Trauerspiel in fünf Aufzügen. 1826. Translated *Hero and Leander* by Henry H. Stevens. Yarmouth Port, Mass.: Register, 1938.

Ein treuer Diener seines Herrn: Trauerspiel in fünf Aufzügen. 1830. Translated 1830 *A Faithful Servant of His Master* by Arthur Burkhard. Yarmouth Port, Mass.: Register, 1938.

Der Traum ein Leben: Dramatisches Märchen in vier Aufzügen. 1834. Translated *A Dream is Life* by Henry H. Stevens. Yarmouth Port, Mass.: Register, 1946.

Weh dem, der lügt! Lustspiel in fünf Aufzügen. 1840. Translated *Thou Shalt Not Lie* by Henry H. Stevens. Yarmouth Port, Mass.: Register, 1939.

Novel

Der arme Spielmann 1847. Translated *The Poor Fiddler* by Alexander and Elizabeth Henderson, New York: Ungar, 1967.

Bibliography

Roe, Ian F. "An Introduction to the Major Works of Franz Grillparzer, 1791–1872, German Dramatist and Poet." In *Studies in German Language and Literature*. Vol. 7. New York: Edwin Mellen Press, 1991.

———. "Franz Grillparzer: A Century of Criticism." In *Studies in German Literature, Linguistics, and Culture*. Columbia, S.C.: Camden House, 1995.

Seeba, Hinrich C. "Franz Grillparzer." In Nineteen Century German Authors to 1840. pp. 123–33. Edited by James Hardin and Siegfried Mews. *Dictionary of Literary Biography*. Detroit: Gale Research, 1993.

Thompson, Bruce, and Mark G. Ward. *Essays on Grillparzer*. Hull, England: Hull University German Department, 1981.

Thompson, Bruce. *Franz Grillparzer*. Boston: Twayne, 1981.

Wagner, Eva. "An Analysis of Franz Grillparzer's Dramas: Fate, Guilt, and Tragedy." In *Studies in German Language and Literature*. Vol. 10. New York: Edwin Mellen Press, 1992.

Yates, Douglas. *Franz Grillparzer: A Critical Biography*. Oxford: Blackwell, 1946.

Yates, W. E. *Grillparzer: A Critical Introduction*. Cambridge: Cambridge University Press, 1972.

GRIMM, JAKOB LUDWIG CARL 1785–1863, AND WILHELM KARL 1786–1859

German philologists, ethnographers, editors

Jakob and Wilhelm Grimm have had an enormous impact on the development of modern German studies, in the areas of language, literature, and culture. Their work as researchers and editors in the fields of Germanic linguistics and philology, medieval literary texts, folklore, and mythology set the foundations for our understanding of German linguistic cultures. Their *Deutsches Wörterbuch* (*German Dictionary*) is recognized as the standard work on the historical development and the usage of the German language. Their well-known collection of German fairy tales, *Kinder und Hausmärchen* (*Grimms' Fairy Tales*), has been translated into numerous languages and has become part of the literary canon of world culture.

The first edition of the collection of fairy tales was published in 1812 and contained eighty four tales. In the preface, the two Grimm brothers asserted their belief that the stories represent a Germanic oral folk tradition that had remained unchanged over centuries. Although this assertion is not really true—the stories they published had undergone numerous changes and transformations over the years and many had been previously printed—their work introduced important notions of ethnographic and anthropological research to both scholars and to the general public. The collection contains several story types, ranging from literary fairy and traditional morality tales, adaptations of creation or cosmological myths, to magic and burlesque tales. The figures in the stories are often portrayed in terms of binary oppositions such as good/bad, hardworking/lazy, or beautiful/ugly, a structure universally typical of such oral tales in a variety of world cultures. Some readers of the Grimm collection view the stories in Jungian archetypal terms—that is, as representative of universal human qualities and attitudes. Wilhelm Grimm, a more gifted storyteller than Jakob, was more involved in the editing of subsequent editions, and he attempted to include more genuine folk tales. Scholarly notes sought to examine the stories in an ethnographic mode—that is, the variant forms of the tales and their distribution throughout German speaking lands. He also put together ten smaller editions (with illustrations from the Grimms' younger brother, Ludwig Emil) which were intended for children.

The two brothers also produced, from 1816 to 1818, a two-volume collection of Germanic legends, *Deutsche Sagen* (*The German Legends of the Brothers Grimm*). Both these scholarly works (on traditional fairy tales and legends) can be seen as key texts of the German Romantic movement. They supported the Romantic belief that the spirit of the common, rural people (*das Volk*) was closer to true nature and therefore more vital and real than the overly rationalized knowledge of sophisticated urban society that remained divorced from nature.

Jakob and Wilhelm also edited, in 1812, two important documents of older German literature: the heroic poem *Das Lied von Hildebrandt und Hadubrand* (*The Song of Hildebrand und Hadubrand*) and *Das Weissenbrunner Gebet* (*The Weissenbrunner Prayer*). Their editorial work contributed greatly to the beginnings of the academic study of medieval German literature and

of the historical development of the German language. Their 1826 collection of Irish stories translated into German, *Irische Elfenmärchen* (*Irish Folktales*), was their last collaborative effort.

Jakob Grimm went on to produce further important works on the history of the German language and its culture. His volumes on a systematic historical grammar of the language, *Deutsche Grammatik* (*German Grammar*), published from 1819 to 1837, were a tremendous contribution to the history of the language. His 1835 work on Germanic mythology, *Deutsche Mythologie* (*Teutonic Mythology*), was also an important discussion of folklore theory. Jakob's 1848 *Geschichte der deutschen Sprache* (*History of the German Language*) continued his scholarly exploration of the historical development of German. Perhaps his greatest achievement as an editor, with the assistance of Wilhelm and many others, was his work on the first four volumes of the *Deutsches Wörterbuch* (*German Dictionary*), published between 1854 and 1861, a project of monumental scale (finally completed in 1960), comparable in importance to the *Oxford English Dictionary*. Jakob Grimm considered the German language the single most important factor that culturally (and therefore also, politically) unified the disparate kingdoms and principalities that made up the lands of Germany, often speaking of it in connection with the naïve nationalistic ideas of the "German people" (das deutsche Volk) and the "fatherland" (das Vaterland). This simplistic nationalism inherent in much of nineteenth-century German Romanticism (in Johann Gottlieb Fichte, for example) would later come to be exploited by the fascist political ideologies of Adolph Hitler's National Socialism.

Wilhelm Grimm enjoyed translating foreign literature into German, and published in 1813 *Drei altschottische Lieder* (*Three Old Scottish Songs*). He also worked on older German literature, publishing in 1829 *Die deutsche Heldensage* (*The German Heroic Epic*). Like his brother Jakob, he also edited a number of medieval German texts, including *Vridankes Bescheidenheit* (*Freidank's Wisdom*) in 1834 and *Ruolandes liet* (*The Song of Roland*) in 1838.

Both Jakob and Wilhelm had been granted professorships at Göttingen University in 1830. The decade of the 1830s was a politically turbulent and unstable period in European history as the liberal, revolutionary forces that had been awakened during the Napoleonic era were being vigorously suppressed by conservative, reactionary regimes. In June 1837, Ernst August II became ruler of Hannover and immediately invalidated the rather liberal constitution that had been approved by his predecessor Wilhelm IV. The faculty of Göttingen University protested vociferously and seven professors, including Jakob and Wilhelm Grimm, were dismissed. The "Göttingen Seven" became somewhat of a liberal *cause célèbre* throughout Germany.

THOMAS F. BARRY

Biography

Jakob Grimm

Born Jakob Ludwig Carl Grimm in Hanau, Hesse-Kassel (Germany), January 4, 1785. Son of Philipp Wilhelm Grimm, lawyer and town clerk in Hanau, later justiciary in Steinau. Educated at Kassel Lyceum; studied law at University of Marburg, 1802. Met writers Clemens Brentano and Friedrich Karl von Savigny. Traveled to Paris as researcher to Savigny, 1805. Secretary to War Office, Kassel, 1806–8; private librarian to King Jérôme Bonaparte of Westphalia, 1808–14; *auditeur* of the Conseil d'État, 1809. Traveled to Paris and took part in Congress of Vienna as secretary to Hessian delegation, 1814–15. Secretary to electoral library, Kassel, 1816. Collected folk songs with Wilhelm for the collection of Achim von Arnim and Clemens Brentano; co-editor, with brother Wilhelm, *Altdeutsche Wälder*, 1813–16. Published first edition of *Kinder und Hausmärchen* (known as *Grimms' Fairy Tales*) with brother Wilhelm, 1812. Published *Deutsche Grammatik (German Grammar)*, 1819–37. Librarian and professor at University of Göttingen, 1829–37. Wrote *Deutsche Mythologie*, 1830s. Dismissed from university post for political reasons; exiled to Kassel, 1837–40. Moved to Berlin to lecture at the University as member of Berlin Royal Academy of Sciences on invitation of King of Prussia, Frederick William IV, 1841. Lived in Berlin with Wilhelm and his family until his death, writing and lecturing. President, Conferences of Germanists, Frankfurt am Main, 1846, Lubeck, 1847; elected to the Frankfurt parliament, 1848. Received Order of Merit, 1842. Traveled widely throughout Europe on scientific expeditions, 1840s–63. Collaborated with Wilhelm Grimm on the German dictionary *Deutsches Wörterbuch*, from 1854 on. Died in Berlin, September 20, 1863.

Wilhelm Grimm

Born Wilhelm Karl Grimm in Hanau, Hesse-Kassel (Germany), February 24, 1786. Son of Philipp Wilhelm Grimm, lawyer and town clerk in Hanau, later justiciary in Steinau. Educated at Kassel Lyceum; studied law at the University of Marburg, 1803–6. Published first edition of *Kinder und Hausmärchen* (known as *Grimms' Fairy Tales*) with brother Jakob, 1812. Coeditor, with brother Jakob, of *Altdeutsche Wälder*, 1813–16. Assistant librarian, electoral library, Kassel, 1814–29. Married Henriette Dorothea Wild, 1825; they had one daughter, three sons. Professor at University of Göttingen, 1830–37; dismissed from post for political reasons. Lived in exile in Kassel, 1837–40. Moved to Berlin to lecture at the university as member of Berlin Royal Academy of Sciences on invitation of King of Prussia, Frederick William IV, 1841. Collaborated with Jakob Grimm on the German dictionary *Deutsches Wörterbuch*, from 1854 on. Died December 16, 1859.

Selected Works

Grimm, Jakob and Wilhelm. *Kinder und Hausmärchen*. 1812–15. Translated as *German Popular Stories* by Edgar Taylor. 1823–26. Translated as *The Complete Grimms' Fairy Tales* by various translators. 1976, and as *The Complete Grimms' Fairy Tales* by various translators. New York: Grammercy, 1993.

Grimm, Jakob and Wilhelm. *Deutsche Sagen*. 1816–18. Translated as *The German Legends of the Brothers Grimm* by Donald Ward. Philadelphia: Institute for Human Issues, 1981.

Grimm, Jakob. *Deutsche Grammatik*. 1819–37.

Grimm, Jakob. *Deutsche Mythologie*. 1835. Translated as *Teutonic Mythology* by James Steven Stallybrass. 1883–85.

Grimm, Jakob. *Geschichte der deutschen Sprache*. 1848.

Grimm, Wilhelm and Jakob, et al. *Deutsches Wörterbuch*. 1854–61.

Grimm, Wilhelm and Jakob, eds. *Die beiden ältesten deutschen Gedichte aus dem achten Jahrhundert: Das Lied von Hildebrandt und Hadubrand und das Weissenbrunner Gebet*. 1812.

Grimm, Wilhelm and Jakob, eds. *Altdeutsche Wälder*. 1813–16.

Grimm, Wilhelm. *Die deutsche Heldensage*. 1829.

Bibliography

Bottigheimer, Ruth. *Grimms' Bad Girls and Bold Boys: The Moral and Social Vision of the Tales*. New Haven, Conn.: Yale University Press, 1987.

———. "Jacob Grimm." In *German Writers in the Age of Goethe 1789–1832*. Edited by James Hardin and Christoph E. Schweitzer. *Dictionary of Literary Biography*. Vol. 90. Detroit: Gale Research, 1989: 100–107.

———. "Wilhelm Grimm." In *German Writers in the Age of Goethe 1789–1832*. Edited by James Hardin and Christoph E. Schweitzer. *Dictionary of Literary Biography*. Vol. 90. Detroit: Gale Research, 1989: 108–13.

Peppard, Murray B. *Paths through the Forest: A Biography of the Brothers Grimm*. New York: Holt, Rinehart, and Winston, 1971.

Tatar, Maria. *The Hard Facts of the Grimms' Fairy Tales*. Princeton, N.J.: Princeton University Press, 1987.

Zipes, Jack. *The Brothers Grimm*. London: Routledge, 1988.

GROS, ANTOINE-JEAN 1771–1835

French painter

Born in Paris to two painters of miniatures, Antoine-Jean Gros entered the studio of Jacques-Louis David in 1785. In this year, David had astounded the art world of France with the exhibition of his *Oath of the Horatii*, often considered a paradigm of the neoclassical style in painting. During his time with David (1785–87), and at the Académie Royale de Peinture et de Sculpture (1787–93), where David's presence was inescapable, Gros became steeped in neoclassicism, though his most original works are those in which he pulls away from David's influence. It was his attempt to return to an austere neoclassicism, at David's prompting, that enfeebled Gros's last works. Writing from his exile in Brussels following the fall of Napoleon in 1815, David asked, "Are you still determined to paint a big history picture? I feel sure that you are. You love your art too much to continue with feeble subjects, with contingent pictures." The "contingent pictures" were Gros's vast canvases devoted to Napoleonic subjects, works that ensured his reputation and that associate him firmly, if not completely, with Romanticism.

Following his apprenticeship, Gros, like many of his ambitious young contemporaries, wished to complete his education with a visit to Italy. He left France in 1793, but was unable to visit the normal destination for artists, Rome, because of hostility there towards the French in the wake of the 1789 Revolution. He remained in northern Italy and had a momentous meeting in 1796 with then General Napoleon Bonaparte, recently arrived as commander-in-chief of the Army of Italy. Napoleon took to the young painter, who subsequently produced a canvas showing the dashing young general grabbing a flag and rushing forward to encourage his troops at The Battle of Arcola, November 15–17, 1796. Following Gros's return from Italy in 1800, the picture was shown at the Paris Salon exhibition of the following year. Eugène Delacroix was to call *Bonaparte at Arcola* "the living image of heroism," and it remains one of the most vibrant depictions of the man. At the same time, David produced an equestrian portrait, *Bonaparte Crossing the Great Saint Bernard Pass* (1800), where he deserted his classical style to the extent of showing Bonaparte in contemporary dress. The theatrical pose of Napoleon on a rearing horse (he actually rode a mule) is, however, rather conventional and unconvincing beside Gros's riveting image of Napoleon's aquiline profile turned back towards his troops as he brandishes his flag at the enemy in front. This was a new, Romantic manner of producing military painting, showing the determination of the commander in action, not the calm demeanor of the assured victor, as was more usual.

Gros was to become Napoleon's favorite chronicler, with perhaps his greatest success coming from his first large-scale commission, the *Plague House at Jaffa* (1804). Napoleon accompanied by his officers, touches the bubo (inflamed, swollen lymph node) of a plague victim with his bare hand in a hospital established in the courtyard of a mosque. French soldiers and exotically garbed Egyptians are both represented as plague ridden, and the setting, together with the local color of the indigenous inhabitants, make this an early example of Orientalism, a cultural phenomenon with strong links to Romanticism. The concentration on the despair of the sick, together with the inventiveness of Gros as regards the setting (the hospital was actually housed in a Greek Orthodox monastery), ties the massive canvas in with Romanticism itself. But it would be wrong to use this epithet unreservedly. The reason behind the commission was to counteract rumors that Napoleon had ordered the poisoning of the patients, which may have been the case. The motive was, therefore, propaganda, to replace a negative image of Bonaparte with one showing him as fearless, concerned, and perhaps even able to cure the plague by his mere touch. Such manipulative intent hardly fits in with the unfettered imaginative ethos expected of Romanticism. Whatever the verdict on the motivation of the painting, it was enormously admired by Gros's colleagues, who staged a banquet in his honor.

Gros illustrated many other episodes from the Napoleonic saga, including the *Battle of the Pyramids* (1810) and the *Interview between Napoleon and Francis II of Austria* (1812). These works are relatively conventional, but the *Battle of Eylau* (1808), showing a frozen plain in Silesia rather than the burning heat of Egypt, vies with *Jaffa* as his most convincing Napoleonic epic. Again the image reeks of propaganda, with Napoleon admitting in exile that he had only commissioned it to counteract rumors that the French had not actually won the battle. Delacroix memorably described it, noting, "This sinister painting, made up of a hundred paintings, seems to command the eye and the mind from all sides at once; yet it is nothing but a frame for the sublime figure of Napoleon." The astute Delacroix realized that the central aim of the work was to show Napoleon compassionate among carnage; but other, powerful messages escape from the "frame." The lowest register, at the eye level of spectators,

is filled with chilling, and chilled, corpses. No matter how sorrowful and commanding Napoleon may appear, the results of his megalomaniac invasion policy are underlined by Gros. This is an intensely complex painting, its value as propaganda subverted by its subtext of suffering.

Gros was an extremely successful artist, patronized by the Restoration monarchs as he had been by Napoleon. In his later years, he was a thriving portrait painter and also attempted to fulfil his master David's demands that he produce history pictures. For instance, his *Bacchus and Ariadne* (1821) is a feeble example of the neoclassical erotic, with two vapid half-length nudes against a landscape background. For reinforcement of his connection with Romanticism, it makes sense to return to his early years and to an ostensibly classical painting, *Sappho at Leucadia*, shown at the Salon of 1801 in company with *Bonaparte at Arcola*. The Greek poet is shown about to throw herself into the sea, in despair at the lack of reciprocation by her lover, Phaon. Although classical in subject, the painting transgresses the expectations of that style by being set in the gloomy night and in focusing on the despair of the heroine. A contemporary critic writing in the *Journal de Paris* furnished an analysis which positions the painting firmly at the center of Romanticism. "There is more of poetry than of truth in this painting: the setting is romantic, the color idealized. The subject could be presented in this manner to the imagination, but never to the eyes."

This fascinating comment indicates uncertainty about the very possibility of a Romantic aesthetic in French painting in 1801. Imaginative, poetic concepts could be envisaged mentally, it is suggested, but not realized on canvas. Later artists, Delacroix and Théodore Géricault for example, arguably resolved this problem, partly through their knowledge of Gros's work, but this equivocation was something that remained with Gros himself throughout his career. His Napoleonic pictures are too tied to the demands of propaganda to achieve the freedom of true Romanticism, and his continued acknowledgement of the classical precepts of his forceful master David suggest too much a spirit of compromise. His work in general lacks the bravura confidence in composition of an artist like Géricault, or the brilliance in color combination of a Delacroix. The contemporary subjects of his Napoleonic scenes are an important move away from the tradition of painting scenes from antiquity, but these works are relatively staid in technique. Yet *Sappho*, as was presciently realized at the time of its first exhibition, was a portent of possible developments; and the sketch for *Bonaparte at Arcola*, lacking the need for high finish of the final version, has a freedom of execution and a general dynamism that bespeak the Romantic sensibility.

ED LILLEY

Biography

Born in Paris, March 16, 1771; his parents were both miniaturists. Studied with his father; then apprenticed in the studio of Jacques-Louis David, 1785, later study at the Académie Royale de Peinture et de Sculpture, Paris, in 1787. Traveled in Italy, 1793–1800. Met Napoleon Bonaparte, 1796; traveled with French army to Arcole and with Napoleon on other campaigns. Returned to France, 1800. Married the artist Augustine Defresne, 1809. Named chevalier, Légion d'honneur, 1808.

Commissioned by Napoleon to decorate the cupola of the Panthéon in Paris, 1812. Elected to the Institut de France, 1815. Served as head of Jacques-Louis David's studio during David's exile after fall of Naploeon, 1815. Created a baron by Charles X, 1824, after the completion of the Panthéon cupola. Became depressive and melancholic in later life. Committed suicide by drowning himself in the Seine at Meudon, June 25, 1835.

Selected Works

Bonaparte at Arcola (sketch). c. 1801. Oil on canvas, 72 cm × 59 cm. Louvre, Paris.

Bonaparte at Arcola (*Bonaparte à Arcole*). 1801. Oil on canvas, 131 cm × 94 cm. Musée National du Château, Versailles.

Sappho at Leucadia (*Sapho à Leucate*). 1801. Oil on canvas, 122 cm × 100 cm. Musée Baron-Gérard, Bayeux.

The Plague House at Jaffa (*Les Pestiférés de Jaffa*). 1804. Oil on canvas, 532 cm × 720 cm. Louvre, Paris.

The Battle of Eylau (*La Bataille d'Eylau*). 1808. Oil on canvas, 533 cm × 800 cm. Louvre, Paris.

Battle of the Pyramids (*Bonaparte harangue ses troupes avant la Bataille des Pyramides*). 1810. Oil on canvas, 385 cm × 511 cm. Musée National du Château, Versailles.

Interview between Napoleon and Francis II of Austria (*Entrevue de Napoléon 1er et de l'Empereur d'Autriche François II*). 1812. Oil on canvas, 384 cm × 532 cm. Musée National du Château, Versailles.

Bacchus and Ariadne (*Bacchus et Ariane*). 1822. Oil on canvas, 85 cm × 100 cm. Phoenix Art Museum, Phoenix, Arizona.

Bibliography

Delacroix, Eugène, *Oeuvres littéraires*. Paris: G. Crès, 1923.

Delestre, J. B. *Gros et ses ouvrages*. 1845; 2d ed. as *Gros, sa vie et ses ouvrages*. Paris: Veuve Jules Renouard, 1867.

Herbert, Robert. "Baron Gros's Napoleon and Voltaire's Henri IV." In *The Artist and the Writer in France*. Edited by Francis Haskell, Anthony Levi, and Robert Shakleton. Oxford: Oxford University Press, 1974.

O'Brien, David. "Antoine-Jean Gros in Italy." *Burlington* 137 (1995): 651–60.

Prendergast, Christopher. *Napoleon and History Painting: Antoine-Jean Gros's "La Bataille d'Eylau."* Oxford: Oxford University Press, 1997.

Tripier Le Franc, J. *Histoire de la vie et de la mort du Baron Gros*. Paris: Martin, 1880.

Whiteley, Jon. Entry on "Gros, Antoine-Jean." In *The Dictionary of Art*. Vol. 13. Edited by Jane Turner. London: Macmillan, 1996.

GRUNDTVIG, NIKOLAI FREDERIK SEVERIN 1783–1872

Danish priest and writer

It is difficult to overestimate Nikolai Frederik Severin Grundtvig's influence on the cultural life of Denmark, both in the course of his own long life and for succeeding generations of Danes. The sheer volume of his writings—an estimated 140 volumes if all of it were printed—is rivaled only by their scope; Grundtvig was a priest, theologian, historian, philosopher, scholar of mythology, politician, and poet. Perhaps because one particular aspect of Grundtvig's legacy has taken on such a tangible form, in the shape of the "folk schools" movement which took inspiration from his educational and mythological teachings, his aesthetic achievements as a poet have sometimes been overlooked.

To an extent, Grundtvig's work escapes classification, because the unique persona he created for himself seems to supersede any of the literary or philosophical benchmarks against which the various movements of the nineteenth century can be measured. His career has been described as a series of revelations, with each new direction offering a new means to achieve the same ends: a solution to the mystery of human existence, and a national and religious renewal based on *folkelighed*. This, the central focus of Grundtvig's thinking, is an untranslatable Danish noun, expressing a rootedness in the history and soil of the motherland, but without the negative connotations of the English *folk* or the German *Volk*.

Grundtvig's relationship to German Romanticism is problematic. There is little doubt that he, like his contemporary Adam Oehlenschläger, was affected by the lectures on natural philosophy of Henrik Steffens, but it was not until the 1820s that Grundtvig came to assimilate this philosophy. Grundtvig's diaries from his time on the island Langeland, as a young tutor

and pastor, reveal his struggle to reconcile his Christian worldview with the "German Rebellion," as he called it. While on the island, he fell in love with Constance Leth, the married lady of the house, and suffered agonies of despair and ecstasy, fueled by his reading of German Romantic poetry, an experience which effectively ended his brief flirtation with the tail end of eighteenth-century rationalism. Was Grundtvig, then, "converted" to Romanticism on Langeland? The answer seems to be "no." His main objection was the Romantic striving for totality and its tendency to pantheism, for this ran counter to his Lutheran training.

Grundtvig's Romantic readings on Langeland, however, initiated the studies in Norse mythology which were to dominate his life's work. His early writings are largely interpretations of mythology in the light of contemporary events; for example, *Nordens Mytologi* (*Northern Mythology*, 1808) and *Optrin af Kæmpelivets Undergang i Nord* (*Scenes from the Fall of the Giants in the North*, 1809). From 1815 to 1823, Grundtvig translated the great medieval Nordic historians Snorre Sturluson and Saxo Grammaticus into Danish, as well as the Old English epic poem *Beowulf*. In so doing, he brought *folkesproget*, the language of the Danish farming classes, into the national canon, just as, later on, he would their culture.

Grundtvig posits his own view of history in *Kort Begreb af Verdens Krønike i Sammenhæng* (*Brief Summary of the World Chronicle in Context*, 1812): the driving force of history is the faith and actions of civilizations. Just as Novalis looked forward to a golden age for the world, so too did Grundtvig, his admirer, write of *Gyldenaaret*, the golden year, a wonderful time of popular and Christian awakening initiated by God. At this time, he was also attacking the "rationalism" of certain Danish theologians, and the poem *Paaske-Lilien* (*The Easter Lily*, 1817), describes a contemporary revival of Christianity. However, the key revelation that allowed Grundtvig to connect history, the church, and the people was *det levende Ord*, the "living word"; the inexorable development of the church and of society stemming from the lived experience of the community over generations, and from their oral *Vexel-virkning*, or interaction.

The poem *Nyaars-morgen* (*New Year's Morning*) was published in 1824, and is considered to be one of the highlights of Danish literary history. It is a work of astounding fantasy and metaphor, of cosmic proportions, encompassing the history of the nation, the Bible, and of Grundtvig himself, and attempting to synthesize the Norse world view with the Christian. Shortly afterwards an "incomparable realization" (*mageløse Opdagelse*) struck Grundtvig: the basis of the Christian Church on Earth should be baptism and the Eucharist, rather than the absolute authority of the Bible.

Three visits to England between 1829 and 1831 exposed Grundtvig to laissez-faire liberalism and inspired him to develop his pedagogical theories. He now realized that it was possible to separate his dual roles as Christian priest and as historian, and began to focus on the project of "schools for life," useful education through the living word. His new *Nordens Mythologi* (*The Mythology of the North*, 1832) is a manifesto for cultural freedom and renewal: "Frihed for *Loke* saavelsom for *Thor*, / Frihed for *Ordet* i Verdenen ny / . . . *Frihed* for Alt hvad der stammer fra *Aand*" (Freedom for *Loke* as well as for *Thor*, / Freedom for *the Word* in the new world / . . . *Freedom* for everything that comes from the *spirit*). Grundtvig then worked on a new *Haandbog i Verdens-historien* (*Handbook on the History of the World*, 1833–43), in the confidence that a Christian worldview would not now besmirch his impartiality: "I have gradually learned to differentiate sharply between *Church* and *School*, *Belief* and *Knowledge*, *temporal* and *eternal*."

Song was considered an essential aspect of the living word. Grundtvig's collection of psalms, *Sang-Værk til den Danske Kirke* (*Songs for the Danish Church*, 1837–41) includes psalms old and new, from various traditions. Here, we see the *vexel-virkning* (interaction) of his mastery of vocabulary with his down-to-earth language; the mysteries of Christianity are imbued with a prophetic, Nordic glory and a domestic familiarity. These hymns are meant to inspire communion, not the fear of God.

That the Danish State Church in 1849, in line with the new constitution, changed its name to *Folkekirken*, the People's Church, is largely due to Grundtvig's influence. His faith in the folk as a prerequisite for the church necessitated a national program of education, self-help, and cultural renewal, which he pursued through his folk schools; his educational *Vennemøder* (meetings of friends), attended by royalty, the working classes, and even by women; and his series of lectures. This political and cultural program, like much of his literary output, is basically rooted in the national Romantic tradition, broadly defined.

What sets Grundtvig apart is his attempt to synthesize this tradition with a reworking of the Lutheranism of his forefathers.

CLAIRE THOMSON

Biography

Born in Udby, near Vordingborg, Denmark, September 8, 1783. Educated privately and later at the Latin School, Århus. Studied theology at the University of Copenhagen, 1800–1803. Took position as a domestic tutor at Egeløkke on Langeland, 1805. Studied at Valkendorfs Kollegium, 1808. Ordained, against his will, as assistant priest in his father's parish and subsequently underwent a religious crisis, 1810. Unable to find a permanent position after criticizing leading Danish theologians, he gave up the ministry in 1815. From then on he concentrated on philosophy, history, and poetry. Received an annual stipend from King Frederik VI from 1817, married Lise Blicher, 1818. Wrote and published journal *Danne-Virke* 1816–19. Appointed to Our Saviour's Church, Copenhagen, 1822–26; resigned when his preaching was censored. Visited England three times, 1829–31; stayed at Cambridge University. Appointed priest at Vartov Hospital Church, 1839. First Folk High School, inspired by his writing, established at Rødding, 1844. Elected to the Constitutional Assembly; independent member of Danish Parliament from 1848. Published journal *Danskeren*, 1848–51. Married Ane Marie Elise Carlsen, 1851 (she died 1854). Married Countess Asta Krag-Juel-Vind-Frijs, 1858. Created Lutheran Bishop, 1861. Died in Copenhagen, September 2, 1872.

Selected Works

Nordens Mytologi. 1808.
Optrin af Kæmpelivets Undergang i Nord. 1809.
Kort Begreb af Verdens Krønike i Sammenhæng. 1812.
Paaske-Lilien. 1817.
Nyaars-Morgen. 1824.
Nordens Mytologi, new version. 1832.
Haandbog i Verdens-historien. 3 vols. 1833–43.
Sang-Værk til den danske Kirke. 2 vols. 1837–41.

Bibliography

Borish, Steven M. *The Land of the Living: The Danish Folk High Schools and Denmark's Non-Violent Path to Modernization.* Nevada City, Calif.: Blue Dolphin, 1991.

Borum, Poul. *Digteren Grundtvig.* Copenhagen: Gyldendal, 1983.

Jensen, Niels Lyhne, ed. *A Grundtvig Anthology.* Cambridge: James Clarke Viby; Denmark: Centrum, 1984.

Knudsen, Johannes, ed. *Selected Writings.* Philadelphia: Fortress Press, 1976.

Scharling, C. I. *Grundtvig og Romantiken, Belyst ved Grundtvigs Forhold til Schelling.* Copenhagen: Gyldendal, Nordisk Forlag, 1947.

Thaning, Kaj. *N. F. S. Grundtvig.* Copenhagen: Det Danske Selskab, 1972.

Thodberg, Christian, and Anders Pontoppidan Thyssen, eds. *N. F. S. Grundtvig: Tradition and Renewal.* Copenhagen: Det Danske Selskab, 1983.

GUILLAUME TELL (WILLIAM TELL) 1829

Opera by Gioacchino Antonio Rossini

There are two operatic settings of the William Tell story. The first, by Grétry, to a libretto by Michel-Jean Sedaine (after a play by Antoine-Marin Lemierre) was performed at the Comédie-Italienne on April 9, 1791. It portrays the revolutionary topic with considerable power and technical innovation, and held the stage for a number of years. Although revised in 1828 and staged to vie with Gioacchino Antonio Rossini's opera, the latter, based on Johann Christoph Friedrich von Schiller's play, soon eclipsed the earlier work.

Schiller was a major influence on the aesthetics and drama of the Romantic period in Germany. For the most part his dramas are concerned with moral and political freedom, and this melded well with the concerns and endeavors of the Romantic movement. His dramas also had a considerable influence on serious opera during the nineteenth century. At least five of his dramas were treated operatically—some of them several times— by such other distinguished composers as Gaetano Donizetti, Zdenko Fibich, Pyotr Ilich Tchaikovsky, and Giuseppe Verdi.

Wilhelm Tell (1804) dramatizes the struggle of the Swiss to free themselves from Austrian rule. The plot is complex, the characterization distinguished. A shepherd, Leuthold, kills an Austrian soldier who had tried to abduct his daughter. His escape is helped by Tell. Arnold, the son of Melchthal, is in love with the daughter of the tyrannical Austrian governor, Gessler. Arnold finally joins the rebels when his father is imprisoned and killed by the Austrians. In the market square, Gessler demands demeaning obeisance from the Swiss. When Tell and his son Jemmy refuse, Gessler imposes a dangerous test of skill: Tell, using a bow and arrow, must strike an apple placed on his son's head. He does this successfully. After further complications, the Swiss rebel, and Gessler dies from an arrow shot by Tell.

This is the plot of the great climax of Rossini's career in which he drew together all the best components of both the Italian and the French musical theater of his time. The libretto was crafted by Étienne de Jouy, the regular poet of the Paris Opéra. The rather colorless and bland text which he produced was revised by Hippolyte-Louis-Florent Bis and further refinements were added by Adolphe Crémieux and Armand Marrast—and by Rossini himself. It still took Rossini five months to write the score—far longer than was his custom. Avoiding his tested techniques, Rossini strove to articulate the grandeur and power of the subject, rather than its melodramatic set pieces. The subject required, both on the political and the personal level, the huge formal advances Rossini had developed throughout his career—especially during his final years in Naples. The larger-scale units Rossini had created in his late Italian operas now found a dramatically valid theatrical space. He also rearticulated his treatment of the text, using carefully crafted French-derived dramatic declamation that was engineered to the precise needs of the text, a text that Rossini himself shaped and critically examined down to the level of every syllable.

Exceptional is Rossini's treatment of the chorus. Although he had already raised the function of this derided element of Italian opera, in *Guillaume Tell* it achieves far greater stature, becoming a major protagonist and an important articulator of the drama. In act I, while complying with the French requirement of including ballet within opera, Rossini fuses this with the chorus in dances and choral interludes which portray the people and rural habitat of the Swiss—an idealization of a people at one with nature. Again, at the end of the opera they are central: in their magnificent hymn to the rising sun and to national liberty, they *are* the work's apotheosis. At a technical level also, Rossini is innovative, as well as dramatically expressive. In act II he divides the chorus into three groups to represent the three separate groups of men from Unterwald, Schwyz, and Uri. In act III the chorus is used to embody the downtrodden and disruptive town mob that confronts the tyrant Gessler.

Rossini's treatment of the soloists and the orchestra are also distinctive. Having a larger orchestra, substantial scenic resources, and a large company of carefully chosen singers at the Paris Opéra allowed Rossini to vary his ensembles and solos to reflect both character and dramatic allegiance, and to create tours de forces of orchestration. Notable examples are the famous (or, through its abuse by advertisers, notorious) four-movement, programmatic overture; Mathilde's romance "Sombre forêt"; the trio for Walter, Tell, and Arnold in Act II; and the cabaletta of Arnold's Act IV aria "Asil héréditaire." In all these settings, Rossini took the greatest care with his French prosody and with French theatrical practice. He even selected an ensemble of singers who could deliver the florid Italian bel canto style as well as the French declamatory one, so that he could select the style most suited to each dramatic situation.

The first performance of *Guillaume Tell* took place on August 3, 1829, and was received coldly. The Parisian audience expected a Rossini of bravura pieces. Instead they were confronted with a simplification of musical line and strong dramatic procedures. Florid utterance (so much loved by the Italians and expected by the French) was banished in favor of a sharpened declamation and a more realistic characterization. Here was a radical Romantic work, rich in pathos, in delicately shaped romantic idylls, and in powerful dramatic tensions. A further innovation was the use of Swiss folk songs (such as a *ranz des vaches*) to typify

Guillaume Tell. Reprinted courtesy of the Lebrecht Collection.

the nationalistic elements of the drama. Although many later composers would follow this practice in characterizing individual groups of people, it did not appeal to the Parisians of the premiere. Notwithstanding this cool response, this is an opera of the greatest importance in which Rossini opened the way to a new era of Romantic music drama. Grand opera in France (and Italy) owed a great deal to this, Rossini's final stage work. Giacomo Meyerbeer and the other composers of French grand opera admired the work greatly and further developed the use of the chorus and Rossini's pictorial effects. This opera also influenced Hector Berlioz and Richard Wagner, both of whom radically reformed the content and procedures of Romantic opera.

BENEDICT SARNAKER

See also **Berlioz, Hector; Meyerbeer, Giacomo; Rossini, Giocchino Antonio; Wagner, Richard**

Bibliography

Berlioz, Hector. "Guillaume Tell," *Gazette musicale* 1 (1834): (English translation in *Source Readings in Music History.* Edited by O. Strunk. New York: W. W. Norton 1950.)

Cametti, Alberto. "Il 'Guglielmo Tell' e le slue prime rappresetazioni in Italia," *Rivista musicale italiana* 6 (1899): 580.

Cohen, H. R., ed. *The Original Staging Manual for Twelve Parisian Operatic Premières.* New York: Stuyvesant, 1991.

Gerhard, A. "Incantesimo o specchio dei costumi: un'estetica dell' opera del librettista di *Guillaume Tell.*" In *Bolletino del Centro rossiniano di studi.* Pesaro, 1987, 45–60.

Gui, Vittorio. "Si naturale o la naturale a proposito del Guglielmo Tell," *Musica d'oggi* 13 (1926).

L'avant-scène opéra. 118 (1989). Special.

Porter, Andrew. "William Tell," *Opera* 9 (1958): 145–50.

vander Straeten, Edmond. *La mélodie populaire dans l'opéra "Guillaume Tell" de Rosslini.* 1879.

GÜNDERRODE, KAROLINE VON 1780–1806

German poet

Karoline von Günderrode remains to this day one of the most intriguing figures of the German Romantic period. The life and work of this young poet who, for several years, hovered on the periphery of the Clemens Brentano circle of friends, and who committed suicide at the age of twenty-six, continues to fascinate writers and critics alike. In 1840 Bettina von Arnim published a novel, *Die Günderrode*, as a memorial to her friend, and eminent critics such as Geneviève Bianquis, Marcel Brion, and Margarete Susman returned time and again to the Günderrode enigma. More recently, Christa Wolf has reinterpreted her life and work in modern feminist terms.

Yet—outwardly at least—Karoline von Günderrode's life, except for its dramatic end, was uneventful and even conventional. She was born in Karlsruhe, the eldest of six children of Hektor von Günderrode, a court official, and his wife Sophie, a talented poet and scholar who dedicated much of her time to the education of her children. After the death of Hektor in 1787, the family became increasingly impoverished and when Karoline was seventeen years old, her mother persuaded her, no doubt for financial reasons, to enter the evangelical retreat for highborn ladies of Cronstetten-Hynsperg in Frankfurt. The young poet, who, in her teenage years, had enjoyed great social and intellectual freedom, and whose spiritual inclinations were pantheistic rather than Christian Protestant, found the restrictive routine and oppressive intellectual atmosphere of her new environment virtually intolerable. However, she did succeed in establishing and maintaining a stimulating circle of friends whom she would visit frequently. She belonged to a generation of young German intellectuals who, early on, had been inspired by the ideals of the French Revolution and the heroic figure of the young Napoleon, but who came to maturity in an atmosphere of repressive conservatism with which German society at large countered the challenge of the new age. Being of aristocratic descent, female, and poor, she suffered more than most through the strictures that her status imposed on her. The tension between a perceived ideal and the "murderous normality" of everyday life became

for her a source of existential torment. In 1801 she wrote: "How many times have I had the unfeminine desire to rush into battle and to die in combat.—Why was I not born a man!"

One of her frequent laments concerns the fact that true heroism, and heroic death in particular, were things of the past and could now only be recreated in dreams or in artistic expression. A passionate admirer of Euripides and Sophocles, she felt herself to be "Greek in her soul," but she also read with abandon the works of Tiberius Hemsterhuys, Johann Gottfried von Herder, Novalis, Friedrich Wilhelm Joseph von Schelling, Friedrich Daniel Ernst Schleiermacher, and especially Ossian; and some of her poems, such as "Der Knabe und das Vergissmeinnicht" ("The Boy and the Forget-me-not," date unknown) have clearly been influenced by Johann Wolfgang von Goethe. Those who met her noted, with varying degrees of admiration or unease, her extraordinary erudition, her uncompromising idealism, and her total remoteness from everyday concerns. In 1804 she published *Gedichte und Phantasien* (*Poems and Fantasies*), which was followed, a year later, by *Poetische Fragmente* (*Poetical Fragments*). Both are slim volumes containing poems and short dramatic texts which bear witness to her fascination with grand historical and mythological figures from Mohammed and Attila to Narcissus, Don Juan, and Ossian's Darthula. Here, as in the many poems which remained unpublished during her lifetime, the twin themes of love and death are dominant.

Günderrode became involved with three men in quick succession, and each was unsuitable in a different way. She first formed an attachment to Friedrich Carl von Savigny, at that time a serious and uncommunicative young student of law, a kind of "Doric column" as she humorously called him, who, alarmed by the vehemence of the young girl's feelings, rejected her in favor of Bettina von Arnim's more easygoing sister Gunda. Günderrode then had a moment of intense infatuation with Bettina's mercurial brother Clemens Brentano, who, for a time, enjoyed toying with the young woman's emotions. Finally she succumbed to the passionate wooing of Friedrich Creuzer, a married professor of ancient history and mythology at Heidelberg, who perceived in her his classical ideal in female form.

During the two years of her involvement with Creuzer, Günderrode wrote *Melete* (1806), a collection of poems and poetic prose, in which she returns with increased intensity to her characteristic preoccupations of love and self-sacrifice. A dominant figure here is Adonis, the youth who, loved by the goddess Aphrodite, becomes transfigured in death, while the poem "Die Malabarischen Witwen" ("The Widows of Malabar") culminates with "death becomes the sweet feast of love." *Melete* was clearly written for Creuzer, yet these poems are not so much about the love for one particular man, than about the poet's fascination with the destructive nature of love itself. Creuzer was deeply impressed by *Melete*, and in February 1806 he succeeded in selling it to the publishers Zimmer & Mohr on Karoline's behalf. For some time he had been trying to find a way to divorce his devoted wife Sophie so as to be free to marry Karoline. However, he eventually decided instead to break off his relationship with Günderrode. On July 26, 1806, a letter in which he told a friend of this final decision fell into Karoline's hands. Without a word to anyone she walked down to the banks of the Rhine and stabbed herself through the heart with the dagger she had been carrying for some time. For her shocked contemporaries, as well as for subsequent generations, Karoline von Günderrode became a figure in which the Romantic spirit was seen to have found its most pure and awesome expression.

AGNÈS CARDINAL

Biography

Born in Karlsruhe, February 11, 1780. Educated at home by her mother. Entered the Protestant retreat for young ladies of Cronstett-Hynsperg in Frankfurt 1797. Suicide July 26, 1806, in Winkel am Rhein.

Selected Works

Gedichte und Phantasien. Hamburg: Hermann, 1804.
Poetische Fragmente. Frankfurt: Wilmans. 1805.
Melete. 1806. (The publication was stopped by Friedrich Creuzer after Günderrode's death. First published in its entirety, Berlin: Harritz, 1906.)
Gesammelte Werke. 3 vols. Edited by Leopold Hirschberg. Berlin: Goldschmidt-Gabrielli, 1920–22.
Sämtliche Werke und Ausgewählte Studien: Historisch-Kritische Ausgabe. 3 vols. Edited by Walter Morgenthaler. Basel: Stroemfeld/Frankfurt: Roter Stern, 1990–91.

Bibliography

Bianquis, Geneviève. *Amours en Allemagne*. Paris: Hachette, 1961.
———. *Caroline de Günderode 1780–1806*. Paris: Alcan, 1910.
Brion, Marcel. *L'Allemagne Romantique*. Paris: Albin Michel, 1962.
Susman, Margarete. *Frauen der Romantik*. Jena: Eugen Diederichs, 1929.
Wolf, Christa. *Karoline von Günderode: Der Schatten eines Traumes*. Berlin: Der Morgen, 1979.
———. *Kein Ort: Nirgends*. Berlin: Aufbau, 1979. Translated as *No Place on Earth* by Jan van Heurck. London: Virago, 1992.

H

HALÉVY, JACQUES FRANÇOIS 1799–1862

French composer

Although his music has been largely neglected since the nineteenth century, Jacques François Halévy was one of the leading composers of French grand opera from 1830 to 1850. Commonly known as Fromental Halévy, the composer was father-in-law to Georges Bizet and the uncle of Ludovic Halévy, one of the librettists for Bizet's celebrated *Carmen*. In addition to forty operas, Halévy composed ballets, cantatas, solo songs, and keyboard works. A lifelong interest in his Jewish heritage led Halévy to oversee the publication of the first professional synagogue music in nineteenth-century France. Along with his contemporaries Daniel Auber and Giacomo Meyerbeer, Halévy helped to establish the style of French opera that would remain in place for several decades under the leadership of Louis Véron at the Paris Opéra. Only two of his operas, *La Juive* and *L'Éclair*, have survived in the repertory into the twentieth century, and only *La Juive* is still performed, although such productions are rare. The crucial role of Eléazar in *La Juive* has been a favorite of several celebrated tenors, including Enrico Caruso.

Born in Paris to Jewish parents, Halévy entered the prestigious Paris Conservatoire in 1811 to study with Luigi Cherubini, an important relationship for Halévy both personally and professionally. He also studied with Berton and Méhul. During his student days, Halévy traveled to Italy and Austria, where he eventually met Beethoven.

In 1819, Halévy won the Prix de Rome prize for composition and wrote several works during this period, including the finale for the Italian opera *Don Curzio*. From 1826 to 1829 Halévy served as *chef du chant* at the Théâtre Italien and later held the same position at the Paris Opera. He began teaching at the Paris Conservatoire in 1827, where his pupils included Camille Saint-Saëns, Bizet, and Charles Gounod. Regarded by some pupils as an ineffective teacher, Halévy played an important role in the musical development of several significant French composers. Halévy's first major success was *Le Dilettante d'Avignon*

(*The Dilettante of Avignon*), which premiered at the Paris Opéra-Comique in 1829.

The success of *La Juive* catapulted the composer to the heights of French culture. *La Juive*, with libretto by Scribe, was one of many Halévy operas based on religious subject matter and one of the most frequently performed French operas of the nineteenth century. Preceding Meyerbeer's equally famous *Les Huguenots* by one year, *La Juive* exhibits striking similarities with the Meyerbeer work, including a plot concerning a man who kills his female enemy only to learn that she is his own child, and the French grand opera conglomeration of static tableaux, elaborate staging, and conflict between opposing groups. Other ingredients of French grand opera evident in *La Juive* include large block choruses, fondness for exotic locales, and huge ensemble finales. By 1886, *La Juive* had marked its five hundredth Parisian performance. The success of *La Juive* soon led to performances of the work outside Paris, including New Orleans (1844), New York (1845), and London (1846).

The year 1835 also saw the premiere of *L'Éclair*, an opera that along with *Juive* secured Halévy's reputation. His later operas differed little from their predecessors, and in his final years Halévy devoted much of his energy to memoirs and writings, collected in a two-volume series of *Souvenirs et portraits* and posthumous *Derniers souvenirs et portraits*. The reason for the relative neglect of Halévy's music after 1850 is largely a matter of changing tastes. As French audiences began to demand more realism in stage works, the static tableaux and improbable plots of Halévy began to fall out of favor. Another contributing favor was the enormous cost and effort required to stage these operas.

While Halévy has been the subject of much criticism, especially regarding the repetitiveness of his music, his works mirror the *zeitgeist* of the period, an era where celebration of *le merveilleux* (the marvelous) was paramount. The esteem with which he was held by the French public was clearly evident at his elaborate funeral, with fifteen thousand mourners in attendance. *La Juive* and many other works by Halévy exhibit his impressive command of orchestration, lyricism, and dramatic expression.

KEITH E. CLIFTON

Biography

Born Jacques-François Fromentin-Elias Levy in Paris, May 27, 1799. Family name changed to Halévy, 1807. Son of Elias Levy, Jewish scholar and poet, and Julie, née Meyer. Enrolled at the Paris Conservatoire, 1810. Studied with Luigi Cherubini from 1811. Won second prize in the Prix de Rome, 1816 and 1817; first prize, 1819. Studied in Rome, 1820–22 and in Vienna, 1822. Taught at the Paris Conservatoire as professor of harmony and accompaniment from 1827 to 1833; of counterpoint and fugue from 1833 to 1840; and of composition from 1840, on. Students included composers Georges Bizet, Charles Gounod, and Camille Saint-Saëns. *Chef du chant* at the Théâtre Italien, 1826–29, and at the Paris Opéra, 1829–45. Completed thirty-two operas, 1819–58, of which only *La Juive* and *L'Éclair* have survived in the repertory. Elected to the Institut de France, 1835. Married Léonie Rodrigues, 1842. Secretary of the Institut de France, 1854. Died in Nice, France, March 17, 1862.

Selected Works

Operas

L'Artisan, 1827.
Le Roi et le batelier, 1827.
Le Dilettante d'Avignon, 1829.
La Langue musicale, 1830.
Les Souvenirs de Lafleur, 1833.
La Juive, 1835.
L'Éclair, 1835.
Guido et Ginevra, 1838, rev. ed., 1840.
Le Drapier, 1840.
La Reine de Cyphere, 1841.
Le Lazzarone, ou le bien vient en dormant, 1844.
Les Mousquetaires de la reine, 1846.

Le Val D'Andorre, 1848.
La Tempestà, 1848.
Le Juif errant, 1852.
Jaguarita l'Indienne, 1855.
La Magicienne, 1858.

Vocal Cantatas and Solo Vocal Works
Les derniers Moments du Tasse, 1816.
La mort d'Adonis, 1817.
Herminie, 1819.
Les Plages du Nil, 1846.
Italie, 1859.

Works for Voice and Orchestra
Marche funèbre et de Profundis, 1820.
Prométhée enchainé, 1849.
Ave verum, 1850.
Messe de l'Orphéon, 1851 (two movements completed by Halévy, the rest by Adam and Clapisson).

Instrumental Works
Ouverture for orchestra, 1822.
Les Cendres de Napoléan for military band, 1840.
La tombola, scherzo dramatique for piano, 1859.

Bibliography

Barbier, Patrick. *Opera in Paris: 1800–1850: A Lively History.* Translated by Robert Louma. Portland, Or.: Amadeus Press, 1995.

Baron, J. H. "A Golden Age for Jewish Composers in Paris: 1820–1865," *Musica Judaica* 12 (1991–92): 30–51.

Hallman, D. R. "The French Grand Opera 'La Juive' (1835): A Socio-Historical Study." Ph.D. dissertation. City University of New York, 1995.

Lacombe, Hervé. *The Keys to French Opera in the Nineteenth Century.* Translated by Edward Schneider. Berkeley and Los Angeles: University of California Press, 2001.

MacDonald, Hugh. "Fromental Halévy." In *The New Grove Dictionary of Music and Musicians*, 2d ed. Edited by Stanley Sadie. New York: Grove's Dictionaries, 2000.

HALLGRÍMSSON, JÓNAS 1807–1845

Icelandic poet

Jónas Hallgrímsson, a natural scientist by education and profession, is the single most influential poet of modern Icelandic literature. According to Dick Ringler, "His work transformed the literary sensibility of his countrymen, reshaped the language of their poetry and prose, opened their eyes to the beauty of their land and its natural features, and accelerated their determination to achieve political independence." Along with the other members of the group associated with the periodical *Fjölnir* (issued 1835–39 and 1843–1846), Hallgrímsson defined Icelandic national Romanticism for decades to come, and after his premature death became its poetical icon. When Iceland gained full independence from Denmark in 1918 and became a republic in 1944 (it had been a province in the Danish state since the late fourteenth century), Hallgrímsson's poetry gradually lost some of its political and iconic status. But this also made it possible to revalue his contribution to Icelandic literature and culture on less nationalistic grounds than before, and the last decades have seen renewed interest in his poetry, both public and scholarly. Attention has especially been drawn to the final phase of Hallgrímsson's poetical activity, when he moved away from nationalistic and medieval motives toward a more personal kind of poetry, modern in diction and elegantly balanced between dark broodings and a Romantic irony, which shows the growing effect Heinrich Heine had on him.

According to Stephán Einarsson, "Romanticism in Germany and Denmark, the wave of liberalism caused by the July revolution in 1830, and the nationalism in Eggert Ólafsson's *Poems* (1832) all combined to mould Jónas." Hallgrímsson burst into bloom as a poet when he left Iceland for Denmark to study at the University in Copenhagen. He made his name with masterfully crafted panorama poems that reimagined the glory of Commonwealth Iceland and juxtaposed it with the present lethargy of the Icelandic nation ("Ísland," "Iceland," 1835; and "Gunnarshólmi," "Gunnar's Holm, 1837"—the latter based on a famous incident described in the medieval Saga of Burnt Njal). As he did so, Hallgrímsson introduced classical meters into Icelandic literature, such as the hexameter and the pentameter, along with Romantic (originally medieval and Renaissance) meters like the terza rima and the ottava rima, although the *fornyrðoislag*, which Hallgrímmson based on the Old Norse Eddic poems, was his favorite meter. Later he was to introduce the sonnet and the triolet to his fellow countrymen, using these meters with great virtuosity in poems full of longing for his love, an Icelandic girl, and his own native valley ("Ég bið aðo heilsa!," "I send greetings!"; and "Dalvísa" and "Valley Song," both written in Sorø, Sjaelland, in 1844), which he had to love from afar, feeling estranged as he did in Denmark during the last years of his life. Using another Eddic meter, *ljóðoaháttur*, he wrote "Ferðoalok" (1845, "Journey's End"), an elevated love poem, which also alludes to the end of Hallgrímsson's life journey, as he seems to have been haunted by thoughts of impending doom.

Nature is always prominent in Hallgrímsson's poetry, especially its more pleasing aspects, but also its sublime elements, as in his description of a volcanic eruption in the tour poem "Fjalliðo Skjaldbreiðour" (1841; "Mount Broadshield"). "Hulduljóðo" (1841–45; "Lay of Hulda") is an ambitious but unfinished nature poem in the tradition of the pastoral elegy. It is dedicated to the memory of Eggert Ólafsson, a natural scientist and poet, whom Hallgrímson considered to be his great predecessor. His pronounced admiration for Eggert, a man of the Enlightenment, shows that Hallgrímsson's interests were not exclusively Romantic, as also is evident in the Fjölnir group's declaration that their periodical was committed to "usefulness, beauty, truth" and "everything that is good and moral," indicating Enlightenment values as well as Romantic ones. Nature, formerly a benign force and presence to the poet and the natural scientist, becomes hostile in Hallgrímsson's late poems, written with a Heine-like twist of the traditional loco-descriptive genre ("Annes og eyjar" ["Capes and Islands"], 1844–45).

A versatile writer, Hallgrímson was able to produce with equal ease short stories ("Grasaferðo" ["Gathering Highland Moss"], dating from around 1836 and considered to be the first short story written by an Icelander), *Reisebilder* like those that Heine was famous for (1836, "Salthólmsferðo"), *Kunstmärchen* in the fashion of Hans Christian Andersen ("Fífill og hunangsfluga" ["The Dandelion and the Bee"]), Gothic tales ("Stúlkan í turninum" ["The Girl in the Tower"]), and mock-heroic pieces ("Gamanbréf til kunningja" ["The Queen Goes Visiting"]), a humorous description of Queen Victoria's state visit to France in 1843. He furthermore wrote scathing critical reviews, a famous example being the one he delivered in *Fjölnir* (1837) against the poetical genre known as *rímur*, which had been popular in Iceland for hundreds of years until Hallgrímson criticized them from an artistic point of view, thereby indirectly offering his own aesthetic manifesto. This versatility also shows in his poetry, for he had many distinct strings in his harp, ranging from elegy (1841; "Bjarni Thorarensen", Jónas's tribute to the first Icelandic Romantic) to convivial festive songs ("Borðosálmur" ["Table Hymn"], 1839). He also tried his hand at translation (Adalbert von Chamisso, Horace, Johann Christoph Friedrich von Schiller, and especially Heine), sometimes rendering his originals so freely that they should be seen less as conventional translations and more as independent variations on a given theme.

SVEINN YNGVI EGILSSON

Biography

Born, probably November 16, 1807, in Öxnadalur, a valley in the Eyjafjörðour region in north central Iceland; studied at the Latin School at Bessastaðoir, south of Reykjavík on the Álftanes Peninsula, 1823–29. Worked as secretary to the magistrate in Reykjavík, 1829–32. Studied at the University in Copenhagen, 1832–38, first law and then natural sciences, finishing his studies by taking examinations in mineralogy and geology. Traveled extensively around Iceland, 1839–42, in spite of ill health, working on a scientific description of the geography and the natural history of the island. Continued working on this project in Copenhagen 1842–43, at Sorø in Sjælland, 1843–44, and again in Copenhagen 1844–45 (he did not live to bring it to a conclusion). Coedited the periodical *Fjölnir* 1835–39 and 1843–45; its final issue, 1846 (printed in 1847), was devoted to Hallgrímsson writings. Died May 26, 1845.

Selected Works

Ritverk Jónasar Hallgrímssonar. 4 vols. Edited by Haukur Hannesson, Páll Valsson, and Sveinn Yngvi Egilsson. Reykjavík: Svart á hvítu, 1989.

Bibliography

Egilsson, Sveinn Yngvi. *Arfur og umbylting: Rannsókn á íslenskri rómantík.* Reykjavík: Reykjavíkur Akademían and Hiðo íslenska bókmenntafélag, 1999.
Einarsson, Stefán. *A History of Icelandic Literature.* New York: Johns Hopkins University Press for the American Scandinavian Foundation, 1957.
Pétursson, Hannes. *Kvæðoafylgsni: Um skáldskap eftir Jónas Hallgrímsson.* Reykjavík: Iðounn, 1979.
Ringler, Dick. *Bard of Iceland: Jónas Hallgrímsson, Poet and Scientist.* Madison: University of Wisconsin Press, 2002.
Valsson, Páll. *Jónas Hallgrímsson: Ævisaga.* Reykjavík: Mál og menning, 1999.

HAMANN, JOHANN GEORG 1730-1788

German philosopher and theologian

The epithet "Magus of the North" was coined for Johann Georg Hamann by Karl Friedrich von Moser in 1763, as an expression of endearment and admiration. It was quickly adopted by Hamann's circle of friends, and eventually it became a persona that Hamann was pleased to assume. *North* alludes to Hamann's residence in Königsberg in the northeastern part of central Europe, but *magus* in this instance has to be differentiated from *magician* and explicated more thoroughly. It alludes to Hamann's essay "Die Magi aus Morgenlande" ("The Wise Men of the East"), published in *Kreuzzüge des Philologen* (*Crusades of a Philologian*, 1762). The term is, therefore, not a reference to pagan magic but is firmly anchored in Christianity. By using *magus* in reference to Hamann, Moser equates Hamann's religious insight with that of the three Wise Men following the Star of Bethlehem. Despite living during the height of the Enlightenment and having Immanuel Kant as a close friend, Hamann tenaciously clung to his religious faith. He eventually gained recognition as a representative of a countercurrent in the German Enlightenment, which in time influenced the Sturm und Drang (storm and stress) and early German Romanticism (also known as Jena Romanticism).

Like Kant, Hamann was raised in the Pietist tradition; unlike Kant, however, this particular strain of Lutheran Protestantism, with its emphasis on personal faith as individual experience, the Bible as the Word of God, and its opposition to secularization, remained an important part of Hamann's writing. In his childhood, Pietism and Enlightenment coexisted peacefully in his mind, but during a trip to London in 1757 Hamann fell into a deep spiritual crisis from which he was reawakened to religion by a rigorous regime of Bible reading. The immediate result of this crisis was a number of texts about his spiritual health, collectively referred to as the *Londoner Schriften* (*London Texts*, 1758); the long-term result was that Hamann turned his back on the kind of exclusively secular and rationalistic thinking that defined and dominated the Enlightenment in Europe.

It is an unfortunate myth that after 1757 Hamann turned his back on enlightened rationalism in order to embrace irrationalism. It is true that he refused to accept that "reine Vernunft" (pure rational thought) was capable of solving all of life's mysteries. It is also true that he disagreed violently with the deist and atheist aspects of Enlightenment thought. However, it was purity, not rationalism, that troubled him. Hamann read the writings of Francis Bacon and David Hume with great delight and cleverly merged some of their concepts with his own. Hamann was a syncretist and so his thought easily encompassed Hume's atheist notion of belief within his own definition of religious faith in God. Indeed, one of the strongest arguments against Hamann's irrationalism is that his notion of faith is deeply indebted to Humean belief, Hamann arguing that Hume had effectively established the limits of reason. Hamann consciously exploits the semantic shift that the English word *belief* undergoes when it is translated into German, because in German *Glaube* is both belief and faith. Unlike Thomas the Doubter, whose insufficient faith drove him to ask for proof of Christ's resurrection, Hamann does not place belief in opposition to

knowledge, but makes it a prerequisite of knowledge. Hamann believes that reason alone is insufficient to prove the existence of the external world, thus using Hume's secular belief in the guise of religious faith to understand our place in the world.

The myth of Hamann's irrationalism has its roots in the difficulty of Hamann's style, which is so complex and allusive that even his most devoted disciple, Johann Gottfried Herder, sometimes despaired. At times even Hamann had to admit that it was difficult to reconstruct the meaning of his own writings, often saying that now only God understood what he had written. The Hamannian style is deliberately created out of the frequent use of rhetorical figures such as paronomasia, antonomasia, and metaschematism (interweaving of quotations with his own text), all of which require direct personal involvement by the reader in order to understand Hamann's indirect form of communication, making his style a threshold to knowledge that can only be crossed by those willing to demonstrate their dedication.

Hamann's style is filled with puns, private jokes, biblical allusions, and wide-ranging quotes from Classical to contemporary literature, philosophy, history, and theology. This interwoven text is a landmark in the art of quoting because in Hamann's text, quotes are not primarily used as reference to support a line of argumentation. A delicate irony is achieved by carefully juxtaposing the meaning of a quote with the context in which the quote is placed. Hamann's citational technique is remarkable because it harks forward to Romantic irony as defined by Friedrich von Schlegel (married to Dorothea Mendelssohn, the daughter of Moses Mendelssohn, who despite his adherence to a rationalistic view of the Enlightenment was in regular correspondence with Hamann). It can even be argued that Hamann's notion of text is a harbinger of Roland Barthes's notion of an authorless text. Even though Hamann would have disagreed passionately with the atheistic implications embedded in Barthes's textual ideas, his ironic use of interwoven quotations is strikingly similar to the Barthesian concept of text as "a tissue of quotations drawn from innumerable centres of culture."

In the words of one of Hamann's most famous metaphors, this irony is like mold and as such not visible to everyone. The irony only reveals itself to those whose affection for Hamann induces them to make an effort to understand him, as will only someone who makes the effort to look at mold through a microscope be able to see the tiny forest inside. This metaphor is taken from a small treatise called *Sokratische Denkwürdigkeiten* (*Socratic Memorabilia*, 1759) in which Hamann also describes this hermeneutical process with the metaphor that his thoughts are spread out on a number of islands and only those readers who are able to "swim" from one thought to the next are granted comprehension of his text.

In contrast to Herder, who wrote a prize essay on the origin of language in 1772 "Abhandlung über den ursprung der sprache" ("Essay On the Origin of Language"), Hamann could not accept the premise that language was an achievement of gradual human development. He believed that language was a vehicle of God's condescension to man. This idea is part of Hamann's overall theory that God reveals himself every day in everything (the

Book of Nature topos) and that God is the author of the text of Creation to which the Bible is the key. This insistence on divine, and not developmental, origin of language gives Hamann the philosophical freedom necessary to claim, in *Aesthetica in Nuce* (1762), "Poetry is the mother-tongue of the human race; as gardening is older than farming: painting,—than writing: song—than declamation: parables—than arguments: bartering—than commerce." So, even though Hamann and Herder disagree about the origin of language, Hamann's insistence on the primordial status of poetry supports Herder's underlying Lutheran-inspired premise that it is the word that shapes the concept and not vice versa.

Although not read by a wide readership in his own lifetime, the eminent few who did read Hamann recognized him as a gifted thinker. However, in a twist of fate, the man who inspired, befriended, and corresponded with Herder, Kant, Johann Wolfgang von Goethe, Moses Mendelssohn, Friedrich Heinrich Jacobi, Johann Lavater, and countless others was outshone by his disciples and his influence on his famous friends was soon forgotten. As the nineteenth century progressed, thinkers such as Georg William Friedrich Hegel and Søren Kierkegaard would read Hamann, but it was not until the twentieth century that Hamann was recognized as a subtle but clearly identifiable source of influence. Today, Hamann is studied and acknowledged as an important thinker whose personality and written work have had a profound influence on literary history and theory, philosophy, linguistics, and theology.

HENRIETTE B. STAVIS

Biography

Born in Königsberg, East Prussia (now Kaliningrad, Russia), August 27, 1730. Eldest son of Johann Hamann and Maria Magdalene Hamann (née Nuppenau). Studied law, philosophy, and theology at Albertus University, Königsberg, 1746–52; did not graduate. Collaborated on the women's journal *Daphne*, 1840s. Private tutor in Latvia, 1752–56. Employed in Riga in a commercial role by the Berens company; traveled to London on an unsuccessful business mission for Berens, 1757. Returned to Riga, 1757–59. Lived at his father's house, Königsberg, 1759–63; wrote *Sokratische Denkwurdigkeiten* and *Aesthetica in nuce*. Took Johann Gottfried Herder as pupil, 1863. Embarked on relationship with future common-law wife Anna Regina Schu-

macher, a household servant of his father's, 1763. Had four children from 1769 onward. Editor of a Königsberg newspaper, 1764–79. Traveled to Frankfurt to seek employment, later moving to Berlin, 1764. Secretary, diplomatic mission to Warsaw, 1765–67. Translator, Prussian excise administration, 1767–77. Superintendent of a bonded warehouse, 1777–87. Traveled to Westphalia to visit Friedrich Heinrich Jacobi and the Princess Amalia von Gallitzin, 1787. Became ill while staying in Westphalia; attempted unsuccessfully to return to Königsberg. Died in Münster, Germany, June 21, 1788.

Selected Works

Sokratische Denkwürdigkeiten and Aesthetica in Nuce, edited by Sven-Aage Jørgensen. Stuttgart: Phillipp Reclam, Jun., 1968.
Londoner Schriften, 1758, edited by Oswald Bayer and Bernd Weißenborn. Munich: Book, 1993.
Briefwechsel, 1751–1785, edited by Walther Ziesemer and Arthur Henkel. Wiesbaden: Insol, 1955–1965.
Sämtliche Werke, 1757–1788, edited by Josef Nadler. Halle: Niemeyer, 1949.

Bibliography

Barthes, Roland. "The Death of the Author." In *Image—Music—Text*. Translated by Stephen Heath. New York: Hill and Wang, 1977.
Berlin, Isaiah. *The Magus of the North: J. G. Hamann and the Origins of Modern Irrationalism*. London: Fontana Press, 1994.
Blanke, Fritz, and Lothar Schreiner, ed. *Johann Georg Hamanns Hauptschriften erklärt*. Gütersloh: Bertelsmann Verlag, 1956.
Dickson, Gwen Griffith. *Johann Georg Hamann's Relational Metacriticism*. Berlin: De Gruyter, 1995.
Friedemann, Fritsch. *Communicatio idiomatum: Zur Bedeutung einer christologischen Bestimmung für das Denken Johann Georg Hamanns*. Berlin: De Gruyter, 1999.
Gajek, Bernhard. *Johann Georg Hamann und England: Hamann und die englischsprachige Aufklärung*. Frankfurt: Lang, 1996.
Jørgensen, Sven-Aage. *Johann Georg Hamann*. Stuttgart: Metzlersche Verlagsbuchhandlung, 1976.
Nadler, Josef. *Johann Georg Hamann, 1730–1788: Der Zeuge des Corpus Mysticum*. Salzburg: Müller Verlag, 1949.
O'Flaherty, James C. *Hamann's Socratic Memorabilia: A Translation and Commentary*. Baltimore, Md.: Johns Hopkins University Press, 1967.
Swain, Charles. "Hamann and the Philosophy of David Hume," *Journal of the History of Philosophy* 5 (1967): 343–51.

DAS HAMMERKLAVIER (PIANO SONATA NO. 29, OP. 106)

Ludwig van Beethoven

Written in 1818, *Das Hammerklavier* constitutes the twenty-ninth work in Ludwig van Beethoven's oeuvre of thirty-two sonatas. Historically, it was the greatest sonata to date, and in terms of sheer length and musical content has arguably never been surpassed. Likewise, its physical demands test the limits of human technique, setting the standard for great virtuosic works of later Romantic composers. Just as Beethoven's Ninth Symphony cast a decades-long shadow over subsequent symphonists, the extent to which the *Hammerklavier* influenced sonata writing cannot be overestimated. The most obvious example of this con-

cerns the opening of Johannes Brahms's Piano Sonata, op. 1, which unabashedly quotes from it. Even before the completion of *Das Hammerklavier* Beethoven himself recognized the significance of this work. In the summer of 1818, during one of his customary walks in the countryside around Vienna, the composer told his pupil Carl Czerny that he was in the process of writing a sonata, one which he declared would be his "greatest."

The title *Hammerklavier*, unlike that of most other sonatas by Beethoven (such as "Moonlight" or "Appassionata"), derives directly from the composer himself, who directed that the title page of the work read: "Grosse Sonate für das Hammer-Klavier" ("Grand Sonata for the Pianoforte"). The fact that this work is known simply by the contemporary German word for the instrument on which it is played illustrates the then rarity of using the German language within musical circles, whether regarding the title of works or expression markings within individual works. In a letter of 1817 to the publisher Steiner, Beethoven even felt the need to make his intentions explicit in this respect, humorously evoking legal language: "we are . . . hereby resolved that from henceforth on all our works, on which the title is German, instead of pianoforte *Hammerklavier* shall be used." Although Beethoven's aversion in later years to using the traditional musical language of Italian can be traced back to his patriotism in the face of the Napoleonic Wars, his subsequent consistency in using German, regarding both the titles of works and markings within musical works, clearly originates in the need to express his emotions as accurately as possible. Perhaps the most telling example is found in the heading to the finale of his Piano Sonata, op. 109, which was written two years after *Das Hammerklavier*: "Gesangvoll, mit innigster Empfindung" (songful, with innermost feeling). In contrast to the emotion-filled German, Beethoven's Italian translation simply reads: "Andante molto cantabile ed espressivo."

The *Hammerklavier* sonata consists of four movements, the sum total of which approaches forty-five minutes in performance:

1. A fast sonata-form allegro
2. A fast scherzo
3. A slow adagio
4. A finale composed of a slow introduction followed by a fast allegro that draws on contrapuntal "fugato" elements

The pianist and scholar Paul Badura Skoda has remarked on the symmetry between the movements of *Das Hammerklavier*. Both "cornerstones"—that is, the first and last movements—reflect one another with their unbounded strength and rhythmic energy. Also noteworthy is a common interest in polyphony and counterpoint (the musical technique that dominated the Baroque era, in which two or more independent musical lines closely interact and intertwine with each other), distilled as a fugue in the finale and found in the first movement in more isolated passages. For instance, in the quiet phrases following the sonata's huge opening chords, musical elements reminiscent of a Bach chorale are clearly audible. In other passages of the first movement Beethoven introduces repetitive figures that are realized fully only in the fugue. This illustrates two fundamental Romantic features in music: the involvement of so-called cyclic elements (in which motifs common to two or more movements of a sonata help the work to cohere as a whole, not just as a collection of individual movements) and in the evocation of a Baroque style during selected passages. Although it might seem contradictory to assert that the presence of fugal elements can be indicative of a Romantic style, such practices are found in all of Beethoven's late sonatas (from op. 101 to op. 111) as well as in the major works of both conservative and progressive composers of the mid-nineteenth century (such as Brahms's Piano Concerto no. 1 and Franz Liszt's Piano Sonata in B Minor). Another typically Romantic feature of the sonata's structure is the fact that Beethoven reverses the traditional order of inner movements within a four-movement sonata design. By placing the weightier slow movement after the scherzo, Beethoven shifts the *Schwerpunkt* (emphasis) toward of the end of the sonata, thus ensuring that the dramatic momentum of the work as a whole carries through effectively into the finale.

Although op. 106 has received due recognition since the second quarter of the nineteenth century, in Beethoven's day no other sonata did more to alienate the composer from the musical public, who found the content of its mammoth dimensions beyond their comprehension. The fact that *Das Hammerklavier* is a superlative work in virtually every sense did little to help make it accessible to the amateur musicians for whom, during the late eighteenth century, most piano sonatas were intended. Only an accomplished virtuoso is capable of breathing life into this sonata, but in such hands the work serves as a consummate vehicle to express the whole gamut of emotions. Many, if not most, of Beethoven's late works drew the same kind of criticism: that he had become "difficult," abandoning the traditional ideal of classical beauty and turning instead to the exaltation of "newness" for its own sake. Of course, the need of composers and other artists to find something new, to attempt to surpass previous achievements or outdo their colleagues, took root in the nineteenth century as part of Romantic tradition—a tradition that has continued to thrive until the present day.

TALLIS BARKER

See also **Beethoven, Ludwig van; Music, Romantic**

Bibliography

Dahlhaus, C., A. Riethmüller, and A. Ringer, eds. *Beethoven: Interpretationen seiner Werke*. Laaber, 1994.

Drake, Kenneth. *The Sonatas of Beethoven as he Played and Taught Them*. Cincinnati, 1972.

Kinderman, William. *Beethoven*. Oxford, 1995.

Kunze, Stefan. *Ludwig van Beethoven: Die Werke im Spiegel seiner Zeit. Gesammelte Konzertberichte und Rezensionen bis 1830*. Regensburg, 1987.

Newman, William. *Beethoven on Beethoven*. New York, 1989.

———. "Some 19-century Consequences of Beethoven's 'Hammerklavier' Sonata, opus 106," *Piano Quarterly* 67 (1969): 12; 68 (1969): 12.

Tovey, Donald. *A Companion to Beethoven's Pianoforte Sonatas*. London, 1935.

Uhde, Jürgen. *Beethovens Klaviermusik*. Stuttgart, 1990.

HAPPINESS

The pursuit of happiness, famously listed as an unalienable right in the American Declaration of Independence (1776), was a serious quest in the eighteenth century. Rationalist assaults on religious, social, and moral prejudices opened up the prospect of a secular happiness blessed by reason and nature. Happiness as spontaneous social harmony joined other definitions that emphasized individual, material welfare or an inner state, and contested the stoical contentment counselled by former moralists. Classical ideas of the happy man, which involve rural retirement from the cares of public life, gave way to a new social idea; Horace's farm was exchanged for Samuel Taylor Coleridge's pantisocracy, an example designed to change the world. Exploration revealed primitive societies with harmonious, hedonistic lifestyles unrestrained by European codes of morality, such as the Tahitians who fascinated Denis Diderot. The philosophic historian John Millar granted that the poets' version of the pastoral golden age might have some truth, and Mary Wollstonecraft sought such a Rousseauesque state in the valleys of Norway. America lured immigrants with prospects of material prosperity and a life of rational freedom amid the beauty and bounty of its natural wonders. Natural and social evils which had checked early Utopian hopes seemed to be less inevitable as Enlightenment science advanced in understanding and control of the environment, and political wisdom placed good government above warfare and extension of empire.

In Britain, a millennialist spirit particularly widespread among Dissenters read God's will into the greater diffusion of happiness. Richard Price and Wollstonecraft rejected the plenum theories that regarded the system of society as a whole and insisted on the greatest happiness of every individual member. Wollstonecraft particularly maintained that the poor had a right to more happiness than present society granted them. Both social and natural progress were foreseen in protoevolutionary ideas popularized by Coleridge, Erasmus Darwin, David Hartley, and Joseph Priestley in which nature, permeated by the deity's creative power, was progressing to perfection and happiness in every form of life. Letitia Barbauld and William Blake poetically depicted divine power which sustained a universe of joy, and Blake forecast revolutionary change from an improvement in sensual enjoyment. The Rousseauistic union of primitivism and progress is evident in William Godwin, Thomas Paine, and Percy Bysshe Shelley as they educe the natural principles of society and justice from the mere coexistence of human beings. As Coleridge enthused in his Godwinian phase, justice is here synonymous with happiness as the highest happiness is found in the pleasure of benevolence. The pleasure of benevolence was a major topic of the movement of sensibility and was developed importantly by William Hazlitt, John Keats, and Shelley. Jeremy Bentham's individualistic and materialistic analysis of pleasure stands out as notably unsentimental, especially in his recognition of the pleasures of malevolence.

The failure of Revolutionary hopes and the French wars brought a profound revaluation of happiness. Coleridge's "France: an Ode" (1798) renounced political prospects to find happiness in a paradisiacal, imaginative relationship with nature and God. The Coleridgean happiness of the creative imagination has been compared to Johann Christoph Friedrich von Schiller's idea of aesthetic education developing a sublime humanity. William Wordsworth appealed to the primal principle of pleasure as the basis of life and even of knowledge, but it is pleasure as an overbalance against the miseries of existence. Wordsworth's imagination is often directed toward future social reformation but under a more gradualist, religious discipline. In *The Excursion* (1814), he criticized Voltaire's *Candide* (1759) as the product of a scoffer writing off the possibility of social happiness as well as mocking religion.

The child as the representative of healthy, spontaneous happiness remained important to Wordsworth and Coleridge, but growth was seen as a necessary process of loss as well as gain, especially in Wordsworth's "Ode: Intimations of Immortality" (1802–4). Rousseauesque educational ideas gave way to more socializing disciplines, especially under the growing influence of evangelicalism. Maria Edgeworth and Richard Lovel planned to educate children for happiness in life, but it was a morally guarded happiness confined to a domestic setting and carefully defined against social notions of success. The later Romantics mocked the hypocritical morality of British society, but their cult of the pagan, sensuous south only brought them disrepute and exile. Keats's ecstatic imaginative experience of intensity is shadowed by the consciousness of transitoriness and the schooling of an identity in a woeful vale of soulmaking. Shelley's equally ecstatic ideal of love, the merging of the self in social harmony, entails a self-ironizing submission to the spirit of the age. Lord Byron, exploiting his image of the libertine aristocrat in the high tide of Regency dissipation, delivers a verdict of vanity and Dead Sea fruits, with nostalgic glimpses of unsustainable Tahitian paradises in "The Island" (1823) and the Haidee episode of "Don Juan" (1819–24).

The pursuit of social happiness continued into the nineteenth century under the auspices of Benthamite utilitarianism and Owenism. Robert Owen offered pantisocracy on a global scale, maintaining a faith in natural cooperation rather than artificial traditions or industrial exploitation. His system, stressing the Enlightenment connection of happiness, reason, and virtue, relied upon the formation of character by rationalistic education, and was too restrictive for Fourierists, who aimed to turn even men's vices to social use. Utilitarianism, while attacking privilege in the cause of maximizing happiness, accepted Thomas Malthus's ideas and his limitation of happiness by vice and misery among the overproductive lower class. The happiness of the greatest number required the workhouse to be a deterrent to indigence in the new Poor Law of 1834, but the beneficent aims of the Benthamites were seen in penal reform, public health measures, and factory regulations. However, the connection of personal happiness with social happiness was strained in their administrative labors. John Stuart Mill was one of the first to describe a loss of faith in the harmony of self, society, and nature that constituted the Romantic idea of happiness, a condition widely shared later in the century under the influence of Darwinism. Departing from Bentham's assertion of the equivalence of all sources of pleasure, Mill nevertheless looked on Romantic pleasures in nature, art, and music as privatized commodities, technologies of the self rather than an inspirational source of universal renovation.

CHRIS JONES

Bibliography

Abrams, Meyer Howard. *Natural Supernaturalism*. London: Oxford University Press, 1971.

Becker, Carl L. *The Heavenly City of the 18th Century Philosophers*. New Haven, Conn.: Yale University Press, 1932. Reprinted 1959.

Bentham, Jeremy. *An Introduction to The Principles of Morals and Legislation*. Edited by J. H. Burns and H. L. A. Hart. Oxford: Clarendon, 1996.

Butler, Marilyn. *Romantics, Rebels and Reactionaries*. Oxford: Oxford University Press, 1981.

Cox, Jeffrey N. *Poetry and Politics in the Cockney School*. Cambridge: Cambridge University Press, 1998.

Deane, Seamus. *The French Revolution and Enlightenment in England, 1789–1832*. Cambridge, Mass.: Harvard University Press, 1988.

Harrison, J. F. C. *Robert Owen and the Owenites in Britain and America*. London: Routledge, 1969.

Jones, Chris. *Radical Sensibility*. London: Routledge, 1993.

Lockridge, Laurence S. *The Ethics of Romanticism*. Cambridge: Cambridge University Press, 1989.

Lovejoy, A. O. *The Great Chain of Being*. Cambridge, Mass.: Harvard University Press, 1936.

Mill, John Stuart. *Autobiography*. London: Penguin, 1989.

Philp, Mark. *Godwin's Political Justice*. London: Duckworth, 1986.

Piper, Herbert Walter. *The Active Universe*. London: Athlone Press, 1962.

Richardson, Alan. *Literature, Education, and Romanticism*. Cambridge: Cambridge University Press, 1994.

Thomas, William. *The Philosophic Radicals*. Oxford: Clarendon Press, 1979.

Whitney, Lois. *Primitivism and the Idea of Progress*. Baltimore: Johns Hopkins University Press, 1934.

HARTZENBUSCH, JUAN EUGENIO 1806–1888

Spanish playwright

Juan Eugenio Hartzenbusch wrote at the height of Spanish Romanticism. It may be argued that in general he did not add anything new to the literary culture of his time, that his achievements were already present in other works such as the Duke of Rivas's *Don Álvaro o la fuerza del sino* (*Don Alvaro or the Force of Fate*, 1832, rev. ed. 1835) or Antonio Gutiérrez's *El trovador* (*The Troubadour*, 1836). His history dramas are marked by complexity and a preference for striking effects. Consequently, his characters tend to be stereotyped, so as to place more emphasis on the primacy of plot.

Besides his history dramas, Hartzenbusch wrote fantasy comedies. He makes a conscious use of irony in them, which allows them to retain some freshness and readability for readers today. Appropriate proportions of humor, fantasy, and morality mark them as less typically Romantic and more classical, in the broad sense of the term. He also published a number of prose works, including narrative sketches, a collection of tales, and a collection of legends in verse, and is also known for his work as a literary critic—especially for his writings on the Spanish golden age, and more specifically, on Spanish playwrights.

The staging of *Los amantes de Teruel* (*The Lovers from Teruel*, 1837), his best and most acclaimed drama, brought him sudden fame and prominence in the Spanish Romantic cultural milieu. The play was performed for the first time in Madrid on January 19, 1837. It was subsequently to be rewritten several times. Hartzenbusch began writing it in 1834, but abandoned the project when he noticed its similarities with Mariano José de Larra's *Macías* (1834). In 1836, he again turned his attentions to *Los amantes*. He continued to revise the play extensively; indeed, the changes made in 1849 were so drastic that some critics argue that, at this stage, it became essentially an entirely new play. The revisions made at this point include the removal of an act, the assignment of new names to some characters, and the addition of new settings. It has been suggested that by 1849, the fervor for Romanticism had cooled, and thus Hartzenbusch downplayed the more Romantic aspects of the play in favor of more classical characteristics.

The plot is based on a Spanish legend of two lovers, Diego Marcilla and Isabel de Segura, who cannot marry each other, because he is poor. Isabel's father decrees that Diego can only marry his daughter if he can amass a fortune within a set period of time. Having become rich, Diego returns when the period of time has passed, only to see that Isabel is marrying another man. Heartbroken, he dies. The legend had been adapted by other authors, but Hartzenbusch manages to offer a newly Romantic version, dominated by the primacy of pure love, a lack of psychological complexity among the characters, and the presence of Romanctic dramatic conventions (an absence of the three units common to classical works, use of both prose and verse, and use of different types of verse). Hartzenbusch suffered criticism from some of his contemporaries for departing from factual history in *Los amantes de Teruel*. However, the playwright argued that his play was not history but a creative literary work. He defended the artist's right to recast historical individuals and events for creative and artistic purposes. It has been much debated whether Victor Hugo's history plays influenced Hartzenbusch. Regardless, it should be noted that previous Spanish dramatists, such as the Duke of Rivas, Antonio García, and especially José Zorrila had written dramas which also blended Spanish history and legend; it is likely Hartzenbusch had them in mind when writing *Los amantes de Teruel*.

After the success of *Los amantes*, he wrote other plays in which love is the dominant force dictating the characters' actions. *Doña Mencía o la boda en la Inquisición* (*Mrs. Mencia or the Wedding During Inquisition*, 1838) is a bizarre play geared toward an audience used to morbid or Gothic plots. Although it is rarely appreciated nowadays, it was a great success when first performed. *La jura en Santa Gadea* (*The Oath in Santa Gadea*, 1845), another loosely historical work, was written in the manner of ancient Spanish dramas. *Alfonso el Casto* (*Chaste Alfonso*, 1841), which also centers on the theme of love, exhibits the excesses that also, unfortunately, burden the above-mentioned works.

SANTIAGO RODRÍGUEZ GUERRERO-STRACHAN

Biography

Born in Madrid, September 6, 1806. Son of a German cabinet-maker and Spanish mother. Fled from Spanish court as a consequence of the War of Independence; returned in 1815. Educated at the Jesuit San Isidro School, Madrid, 1818–22. Because of the family's liberal political allegiance, their property was confiscated by the monarchy. Worked in his father's cabinetmaking workshop, including helping to complete commission for work on the Senate building, Madrid; also studied literature and translated and adapted plays. Wrote for the newspaper *La Gaceta* in Madrid, 1834–38 and for the government newspaper *Diario de Sesiones del Congreso* from 1838. Published *Los Amantes de Teruel*, 1837. Married María Morgue; after her early death, married Salvadora Hirnat. Worked in the National Library, Madrid, 1844–75. Director of the National Library from 1862 on. Director, Escuela Normal de Madrid, from 1854. Member of the Real Academia Española, 1847; Died in Madrid, August 2, 1880.

Selected Works

Collections

Ensayos poéticos y artículos en prosa, literarios y de costumbres. 1843.
Obras escogidas, prólogo de Eugenio de Ochoa. 1850.
Obras escogidas, edición alemana dirigida por el autor. Prólogo de Antonio Ferrer del Río. 1863.

Drama

Los amantes de Teruel. 1836. Rev. ed., 1849.

Bibliography

Iranzo, Carmen. *Juan Eugenio Hartzenbusch.* Boston: Twayne, 1978.
Picoche, Jean Louis. *Los Amantes de Teruel.* Paris: Centre de Recherches Hispaniques, 1970.

HASKALAH

Haskalah (Enlightenment) derives from the Hebrew verb *le-haskil* (to enlighten), and its practitioners are termed *maskilim* (enlightened ones). Haskalah was both an intellectual movement closely aligned with the *Aufklärung* (German Enlightenment) and a practice of deliberate Jewish cultural revision. In its broadest definition, Haskalah required the combination of secular, especially scientific, knowledge and cultural cultivation with a purified Jewish knowledge and continued Jewish legal observance. Haskalah flowered in Berlin in the second half of the eighteenth century under the conspicuous leadership of Moses Mendelssohn, and subsequently spread eastward into Habsburg Galicia and then through Lithuania and into the Jewish communities in Russia's Pale of Settlement. The Haskalah movement faced opposition from both anti-Semitic gentiles and Orthodox Jewish traditionalists.

It became an ideological and cultural support to emancipation and was a precondition of such later secular Jewish movements as Zionism (the effort to relocate Jewish culture and population to Israel); autonomism (the effort to secure the rights of national and ethnic autonomy for Jewish populations in eastern Europe); and Bundism (a Yiddish-language social democracy that combined Marxism with respect for Jewish interests and ethnicity). These ideologies resulted in part from disappointed maskilic hopes for gentile magnanimity toward a modernized Jewry. Its advent in the Prussia of Frederick the Great (1740–86) has both particular and general causes. The particular cause was the arrival of the fourteen-year-old Mendelssohn in Berlin in 1743, where he continued his talmudic studies and fell under the influence of Israel Zamosc. Zamosc was as versed in natural science as in the Torah and was a leader in the *musar* (ethics) movement that, in its attacks on talmudic casuistry and its concomitant appeals for intellectual and moral improvement, anticipated haskalah.

The general cause was the uncertain, ambiguous status of Jews in Frederick's Prussia. He invited Enlightenment thinkers such as Voltaire to his capital and granted religious toleration; yet, he was overtly anti-Semitic and, in any case, had no wish to share power with society or to emancipate the Jews. (Jews were already freer in England than in Prussia, and soon would be freer in France). The Jews' uncertain position was itself a cause for haskalah: only intellectual production could offer any prospect for Jewish integration into Prussian society. Since culture became the theater of German-Jewish strivings, it is not surprising that nineteenth-century German Jews rather one-sidedly allied with Germany's *Gebildeten*, the (gentile) German cultured elite.

Mendelssohn was the cynosure of the haskalah's first generation. His descendants, notably including his grandson Felix Mendelssohn, would convert to Christianity as a means to social promotion, but Mendelssohn was steadfastly observant. His project was a purified Judaism that was uncompromising, yet congruent with the Enlightenment's ideal of natural religion. Thus, he authored such celebrated philosophical works as the *Philosophical Dialogues* (1755), *Metaphysical Evidence* (1763), and *Phaedon* (1767). Each of these impressed gentile readers and helped him toward his famous friendship with the dramatist and critic Gotthold Ephraim Lessing, who had Mendelssohn in mind when writing his play *Nathan der Weise* (*Nathan the Wise*).

Characteristically, Mendelssohn did not abandon Judaism for cosmopolitan culture. On the contrary, he publicly defended Judaism against the skeptical attacks of Johann Caspar Lavater in the 1770s; inspired Christian Wilhelm Dohm to defend the Jews of Alsace in his controversial *On the Civic Improvement of the Jews*; and wrote his moving defense of authentic Judaism, *Jerusalem in 1782–1783*. He also sought to improve Jewish piety by translating the Pentateuch, with the help of Solomon Dubno, into a high German written in Hebrew characters, with a Hebrew commentary (*Bi'ur*) jointly authored with other authorities.

Of course, haskalah was greater than Mendelssohn, and expanded beyond Berlin. In Mendelssohn's moral weekly, *Qohelet Musar*, haskalah began to acquire a new medium in a revivified Hebrew. Hebrew journals, such as *ha Me'asef* (*The Gatherer*, founded in 1784 by *maskilim* in Königsberg) promised to spread the haskalah far more widely. As it spread eastward, haskalah preserved some common features. First, it treasured Hebrew as a language of Jewish expression, though its proponents were normally fluent in the local gentile cultural language. Second, it balanced between religious traditionalism and secularism, while seeking to instil Jewish cultural pride.

In later generations, maskilim varied their programs according to local conditions. Thus, in Galicia, maskilim satirized the obscurantism of an entrenched Hasidism, while the brilliant Nachman Krochmal sought a philosophical synthesis in his post-humously published (1851) *Moreh Nevukhim ha-Zeman* (*Guide to the Perplexed of Our Time*). Krochmal adapted the title of Maimonides's classic to address the doubts of Germanophone Jews, whose Judaism was challenged by German idealism. In Russian lands, haskalah was often a program for intellectual modernization, notably in improved, nonrabbinic schools.

ROBERT SOUTHARD

Bibliography

Pelli, Moshe. *The Age of Haskalah: Studies in Hebrew Literature of the Enlightenment in Germany.* Leiden: Brill, 1979.
Zinberg, Israel. *A History of Jewish Literature*, vol. 8. Cleveland: Case Western Reserve University, 1976.

HAUFF, WILHELM 1802–1827

German prose writer

Wilhelm Hauff is usually associated with a loosely defined "school" of Swabian poets that includes Justinus Kerner, Eduard Mörike, Gustav Schwab, and Ludwig Uhland. Hauff spent practically the whole of his short life in his native region, establishing a reputation as the author of *Märchen* (fairy tales) before turning to more ambitious fictions in which fantasy and whimsicality in the Romantic vein are offset by a gradual shift toward realism.

Hauff's father having died when he was only six, his mother pointed him toward an ecclesiastical career. Educated at schools in Tübingen and Blaubeuren, the young Hauff read widely, absorbing the plays of Johann Christoph Friedrich von Schiller and Johann Wolfgang von Goethe as well as foreign classics by writers like Henry Fielding and Oliver Goldsmith. In 1820, he enrolled at the University of Tübingen to study theology, philosophy, and literature. He was ordained as a Protestant pastor in 1824, but never practiced. For a while he was private tutor to the children of a family in Stuttgart, for whom he made up fairy stories. The publication of these met with acclaim, and this emboldened him to take up writing full-time: in the space of the two years left to him he produced a prolific body of work, and in 1826 ventured on an eight-month journey through France and northern Germany to bask in his renown and to visit such luminaries as Friedrich Heinrich Karl Fouqué and Ludwig Tieck. On his return to Stuttgart, he was appointed literary editor of the local daily newspaper. In the spring of 1827 Hauff married his cousin Luise and fathered a daughter; but before the year was out, he had succumbed to a fatal fever, just before his twenty-fifth birthday and a few days after the birth of his child. Uhland and Schwab each wrote an elegy on his untimely end; the latter went on to edit his complete works in 1830, with a long biographical introduction.

Still regularly reprinted in popular editions, Hauff's fairy tales originally came out as *Märchenalmanache* (*Fairy Tales*) between 1825 and 1828. The early tales are pastiches of the *Arabian Nights* and take place in an unreal and marvelous Orient; later, Hauff took his cue from Jakob and Wilhelm Grimm and shifted his settings to Germany, even making explicit regional references. Thus the story "Das Wirtshaus im Spessart" ("The Hostelry in the Spessart") is set in the gloomy Spessart Forest west of Würzburg, supposedly the haunt of robbers; while the intercalated tale "Das kalte Herz" ("The Cold Heart") opens with some folksy banter about the eccentricities and superstitions of the inhabitants of the Black Forest.

Hauff's stories and novellas sometimes affect a wry other-worldliness reminiscent of Jean Paul; yet this soon gives way to a more down-to-earth approach. Thus the jovial *Phantasien im Bremer Rathskeller* (*Fantasies in the Council Cellar of Bremen*, 1827) and the tragic *Die Bettlerin vom Pont des Arts* (*The Woman Beggar of the Pont des Arts*, 1828) are firmly located in, respectively, Bremen and Paris, both of which the author had prospected on his 1826 journey. Focusing upon an historical figure from the early eighteenth century, the novella *Jud Süss* (*The Jew Süss*, 1827) charts the rise and fall of Josef Süss-Oppenheimer, the corrupt finance minister of the duchy of Württemberg, who was executed for treason in 1738. Perhaps Hauff's most accomplished novella is *Das Bild des Kaisers* (*The Portrait of the Emperor*), which was issued posthumously in 1828. It deals with the political disillusionment of young liberals in contemporary Swabia, where a reactionary regime had held sway since the fall of Napoleon. Hauff's orchestration of debates with multiple voices opens up a sociopolitical perspective upon immediate circumstances, in a way already suggestive of a post-Romantic sensibility.

However, Hauff's reputation as a fiction writer rests primarily upon the ultra-Romantic *Lichtenstein* (*The Banished: A Swabian Historical Tale*, 1826), named after a ruined castle on a crag in the Schwäbische Alb. (The castle was rebuilt in 1839 as a consequence of the novel's popularity). Enthused by Walter Scott's visions of the past, Hauff had dug up a remote yet emotive subject, the life and times of the sixteenth-century Duke Ulrich von Württemberg. His narrative of heroic battles and political upheaval is played out within an idealized Swabia of hills and forests stretching between the source of the Danube and the Rhine. As in most Romantic excursions into the historical, documentary veracity is much embellished by the imaginary, so that actual topography and place names mingle with invented local color and folkloric touches, such as the dialect conversations of peasants and mercenaries. In effect, Hauff converts the ancient province of Swabia into a utopian myth, as he half-acknowledges in his subtitle, "a Romantic legend."

The satirical novel *Mittheilungen aus den Memoiren des Satan* (*Memoirs of Satan*, 1826–27) bears traces of the influence of

E. T. A. Hoffmann. It is an episodic yarn that casts the devil as an inquisitive tourist who journeys through contemporary Germany to encounter a succession of social types, portrayed in caricature. Hauff's taste for playful satire prompted a further novel, *Der Mann im Monde* (*The Man in the Moon*, 1826), which parodied the mawkish style of a best-selling contemporary novelist from Berlin and was even issued under his pen name, Heinrich Clauren. When the latter (in reality Karl Heun) hit back with a successful lawsuit, Hauff had to pay a fine, but he still had the last word by publishing a scathing sermon about the whole affair.

In 1827, Hauff made a trip to Austria to research a novel about the events of 1809 and 1810, when Andreas Hofer had led armed resistance to the Bavarian army of occupation imposed by Napoleon. In 1810 the Tyrolean revolt was crushed, and Hofer was shot. It may be that the novelist would have broken fresh ground here by dealing with violent events still present in popular memory, but he died before realizing this project. His mature and altogether tougher outlook notwithstanding, Hauff still tends to be stereotyped as a minor but "pure" Romantic, and many remember him only for the handful of sentimental poems he composed in the folk idiom. The best of these, "Morgenrot" ("Red Sky at Morning", 1828), was adapted from a Swabian folk song, and then reabsorbed into the cultural heritage as an "authentic" work of popular genius.

ROGER CARDINAL

Biography

Born in Stuttgart, November 29, 1802. Studied theology at Tübingen Seminary, 1820–24. Private tutor in Stuttgart, 1824–26. Major journey to Paris, Brussels, Antwerp, Kassel, Bremen, Hamburg, Berlin, and Dresden, 1826. Literary editor of Stuttgart's daily newspaper, 1827. Married, 1827. Traveled to the Tirol, 1827. Died of a "nervous fever" in Stuttgart, November 18, 1827.

Selected Works

Märchenalmanache, 1826–28. Translated as *Fairy Tales* by J. Emerson and others. London: Jonathan Cape, 1971.

Lichtenstein. Romantische Sage aus der württembergischen Geschichte, 1826. Translated as *The Banished: A Swabian Historical Tale* anonymously. 1839.

Mittheilunger aus den Memoiren des Satan [*Memoirs of Satan*, 1826–27.

Das Bild des Kaisers, 1828. Translated. *The Portrait of the Emperor* anonymously. 1845.

Novellen, 3 vols., 1828.

Phantasien und Skizzen, 1828.

Sämtliche Schriften. 36 vols., Edited by Gustav Schwab. 1830.

Bibliography

Beckman, Sabine. *Wilhelm Hauff. Seine Märchenalmanache als zyklische Kompositionen*. Bonn: Bouvier, 1976.

Bloch, Ernst. *Literarische Aufsätze*. Frankfurt: Suhrkamp, 1965.

Hofmann, Hans. *Wilhelm Hauff. Eine nach neuen Quellen bearbeitete Darstellung seines Werdegangs*. Eschborn: Klotz, 1998.

Martini, Fritz. "Wilhelm Hauff." In *Deutsche Dichter der Romantik. Ihr Leben und Werk*. 2d rev. Edited by Benno von Wicsz. Berlin: Erich Schmidt, 1971.

———. *Wilhelm Hauff und der Lichtenstein. Marbacher Magazin* no. 18. Marbach: Schillergesellschaft, 1999.

———. *Wilhelm Hauff, der Verfasser des "Lichtenstein." Chronik seines Lebens und Werkes*. Stuttgart: Fleischauer and Spohn, 1981.

Spiekerkötter, G. "Lebensbild." In *Werke*. vol. 3. Wilhelm Hauff. Munich: Bong, 1961.

HAWTHORNE, NATHANIEL 1804–1864

American novelist and short story writer

Along with his contemporary, Herman Melville, Nathaniel Hawthorne's considerable literary skills, his fascination with questions of morality, and his keen sense of psychological insight made him one of the foremost writers of Romantic narrative fiction of early nineteenth-century America. That he was a Romantic is not only apparent in the *Romance* subtitle appended to many of his works but also in his commitment to art and imagination (as opposed to science and reason) as a mode of knowing true reality, although this dedication may entail the isolation of the Romantic artist from the practical world of everyday bourgeois society. Since he believed that all truth is to be found in emotion and intuition, he discounted the verisimilar spirit of realistic fiction and felt that the reality depicted in his fiction must remain true to his inner vision. His writing therefore tends to the allegorical and symbolic.

Hawthorne lived at home with his mother after he graduated from college, and it was there that he wrote his first novel, *Fanshawe*, which he published at his own expense in 1828. Bearing the influence of Walter Scott, it was a failure and he later destroyed as many copies as he could find. *Twice-Told Tales* (1837), a collection of short stories and his second published work, received critical praise from authors such as Henry Wadsworth Longfellow and Edgar Allan Poe. The stories reflect Hawthorne's interest in the history and daily life of the New England area. One of the stories, "Dr. Heidegger's Experiment," treats an unusually modern theme that concerned Hawthorne throughout his career: his criticism of science and its moral implications. He felt that the reality presented in scientific studies gave only a limited and one-sided view of human existence. The Romantic domain of the ineffable, including the emotions, the artistic imagination, and the spiritual, could simply not be accounted for in the discourse of scientists. The manipulation of life (ultimately of divine and sacred origin) in scientific experiment carried for the fundamentally conservative Hawthorne a frightening and dubious implication for human morality. For Hawthorne, the scientist fails to strike a proper balance between intellect and emotion. The criticism of science as the attempt to control nature is a favorite Romantic theme that can be found in works as diverse as Johann Wolfgang von Goethe's *Faust* (1808–32) and Mary Shelley's *Frankenstein* (1818).

The *Mosses from the Old Manse* collection of 1846 contains the widely read early masterpiece "Young Goodman Brown," an allegorical tale originally written in 1828 and 1829 that deals with two other favorite Hawthorne themes: the seventeenth-century New England Puritan's strict code of morality and sin and its repressive effects in the shame and guilt that follow. As some readers have argued, this story of a young man's dreamlike encounter with evil in the depths of a dark forest shows an uncanny foreshadowing of the depth psychology that Freud would seek to formulate sixty years later. The Puritan village, with its rigid moral code, suggests the strict dictates of the personality's conscience or superego and the forest, with its sinful "Black Mass" seems to depict the individual's darker side in the unconscious mind or id. Brown learns of his darker side but remains unable to accept it, to reconcile it with his life within the community, thus condemned to living his life in social isolation and inner shame.

Several of the stories from *Mosses from the Old Manse* treat another of Hawthorne's favorite psychological themes: obsession with perfection. In "The Birthmark" and "Rappaccini's Daughter," the subject is again the scientist who seeks to control life. Aylmer in the former story is obsessed with the perfection of his wife's beauty and tragically cannot recognize his human limitations. Dr. Rappaccini in the latter story uses science in a vain Faustian attempt to surpass nature: to create a new Eden with his garden of beautiful but also highly toxic plants. The scientist's daughter has been raised to live in this deadly world as a new Eve, but in the end this project that is inimical to life fails as it must. Hawthorne's science stories read in some ways as precursors to the genre of modern science fiction. The artist who is obsessed with perfect beauty is a related Romantic theme, which is treated in the story "The Artist of the Beautiful." The artist Owen Warland pursues the abstract ideal of a perfected beauty, but his spiritual quest only results in his isolation from life. The alienation of the artist from the everyday bourgeois world represents a major thematic complex in Romantic and post-Romantic literature in writers such as E. T. A. Hoffmann and Thomas Mann.

Hawthorne's best-known work, the short novel *The Scarlet Letter* (1850), takes up the same themes of sin, repression, and secret guilt in the Puritan village of Salem, Massachusetts, in the story of the adulteress Hester Prynne. Hawthorne is critical of the stern Puritan spirit that casts moral issues in simple black and white when human motives and behaviors are more often ambiguous in real life. Such an unforgiving and rigid moral code also represses the natural impulses in the individual—what he called "the truth of the human heart"—and produces unnecessary tragedy in sin and guilt. Here Hawthorne's defense of the natural impulse over the rigidity of moral doctrine links him to the heart of the Romantic movement and to individuals such as Jean-Jacques Rousseau and Goethe.

Hawthorne's interest in the psychology of the individual and the symbolic-allegorical bent of his writing helped to define the genre of the short story for generations of later American authors.

His portraits of the culture and history of the northeastern United States where he was born and spent his life—most especially his view of the influence of the Puritan settlers with their strict and unyielding moral code—have given readers insight into the early origins of the American psyche. Finally, Hawthorne's espousal of feeling and intuition as legitimate modes of perceiving human existence and his criticism of the growing nineteenth-century turn to science and empiricism as the sole means of describing reality gave a defining impetus to the American Romantic movement.

THOMAS F. BARRY

Biography

Born Nathaniel Hathorne in Salem, Massachusetts, July 4, 1804. son of Captain Nathaniel Hathorne and Elizabeth Clarke, née Manning. Educated at Samuel Archer School, Salem, 1819. Studied at Bowdoin College, Brunswick, Maine, 1821–25. Magazine editor in Boston, 1836. Measurer, Boston Customs House, 1839–40. Invested in the Brook Farm Commune, West Roxbury, Massachusetts; lived there, 1841–42. Married Sophia Peabody, 1842: two daughters, one son. Lived in Concord, 1842–45. Met Ralph Waldo Emerson and Henry David Thoreau, early 1840s. Surveyor, Salem Customs House, 1845–49. Lived in Lenox, Massachusetts, 1850–51, and West Newton, Massachusetts, 1851. Published *The Scarlet Letter*, 1850. Met Herman Melville, 1850. U.S. consul in Liverpool, England, 1853–57. Lived in Italy, 1858–59 and in England, 1859–60. Died in Concord, Massachusetts (or Plymouth, New Hampshire?), May 19, 1864.

Selected Works

Novels and Other Fiction
Fanshawe: A Tale. 1828.
Twice-Told Tales. 1837.
Mosses from the Old Manse. 1846.
The Scarlet Letter: A Romance. 1850.
The House of the Seven Gables: A Romance. 1851.
The Blithedale Romance. 1852.
The Marble Faun. 1860.

Bibliography

Baym, Nina. *The Shape of Hawthorne's Career*. Ithaca, N.Y.: Cornell University Press, 1976.
Bell, Michael Davitt. *Hawthorne and the Historical Romance of New England*. Princeton, N.J.: Princeton University Press, 1971.
Bell, Millicent. *Hawthorne's View of the Artist*. Albany: State University of New York Press, 1962.
Bloom, Harold and William Golding, eds. *Nathaniel Hawthorne*. Modern Critical Views. Philadelphia, Penn.: Chelsea House, 1990.
Dunne, Michael, ed. *Hawthorne's Narrative Strategies*. Jackson: University Press of Mississippi, 1995.
Mellow, James R. *Nathaniel Hawthorne in His Times*. Baltimore: Johns Hopkins University Press, 1998.
Mitchell, Thomas R. *Hawthorne's Fuller Mystery*. Amherst: University of Massachusetts Press, 1998.

HAYDN, FRANZ JOSEPH 1732–1809

Austro-German composer

In at least one important respect, Franz Joseph Haydn's career foreshadows the path carved out by the early Romantics in that he made music a vehicle for transmitting a range of emotional qualities, from the earthy humor of the "Gypsy rondo" to the sublimity of the "Emperor" quartet, a concept lying beyond the power of mere words to describe. For most of his life, Haydn was a paid employee and little more than a servant, supplying music to order for a succession of princely patrons, notably the Esterházy family. From 1779, however, the role of servant became more and more notional. Haydn's works had begun to attract widespread critical notice, and from this date his contacts with the wider musical scene across Europe grew ever more intimate, a circumstance reflected in the much looser terms of his revised contract of employment with the Esterházy family. His works were increasingly disseminated in print from the 1770s (frequently by more than one publisher simultaneously) in Vienna, Paris, Berlin, Amsterdam, London, and elsewhere. Commissions from public musical societies, such as the Société de la loge Olympique in Paris, for whom Haydn composed the so-called Paris symphonies between 1785 and 1786, affirmed his changing status as a musician whose talents were recognized not merely by his employer, but on a European stage where cultural life was transforming into something that was a focus for civic aspirations (as witness, for instance, the evolution of the Gesellschaft der Musikfreunde in Vienna, or the Gewandhaus in Leipzig). Thus, before Ludwig van Beethoven (Haydn's pupil) made the crucial escape from a network of patronage toward the freelance existence of an individual for whom music (or painting, or literature) was a means of personal expression, Haydn had made such a transition possible.

Haydn's output was vast, covering just about every genre then cultivated. Critical consideration of his achievement has typically focused on his mature symphonies and string quartets, although his operatic and sacred vocal output was extensive and important, culminating perhaps in the late masses: "concert" settings of the Kyrie, Gloria, Credo, Sanctus, Benedictus, and Agnus Dei, which, by about 1800, had shed much of their original liturgical background and which were written on the command of Prince Anton Esterházy in celebration of the name-day of Princess Maria Hermenegild yearly from 1796 to 1802. Haydn is commonly said to have been the "father of the string quartet," though he did not actually invent that genre. In his hands, the instrumental genres of sonata, quartet, piano trio, and symphony (though not concerto, perhaps because Haydn, unlike Wolfgang Amadeus Mozart or Beethoven, was not himself a skilled player on the piano or violin) were raised to a degree of sophistication unimaginable in about 1760. By the end of Haydn's career any one of these could encapsulate the profound, a circumstance that is quite difficult to grasp retrospectively in the light of, say, Beethoven's late quartets, the piano sonatas of Franz Schubert or the symphonies of Gustav Mahler. It was Haydn's achievement to transform what had initially been genres for domestic consumption in a purely amateur context into something of artistic significance. In particular, in his hands the symphony and string quartet escaped their original locale of *divertissements* for the entertainment of a princely or ecclesiastical employer, attaining instead the status of "public" genres, performed by professionals in civic settings before a paying audience and disseminated in print across a wide geographical area. Such transformations led sometimes to a redefining of generic limits. For instance, the op. 71 and op. 74 sets, written for Count Apponyi in 1793 and published respectively in 1795 and 1796, were specifically designed for professional performance, being presented by the Salomon Quartet in Johann Peter Salomon's 1794 concert series during Haydn's second visit to London; they adopt gestures more typically encountered in Haydn's later symphonies, including features such as the slow introductions to op. 71 no. 2 and op. 74 no. 3, which are quite rare in Haydn's earlier quartets and imply that their communicative process involves an essential measure of interaction with an audience. In such works, Haydn routinely played with the expectations of his listeners (sometimes comically, as in the famous slow movement of the "Surprise" symphony). Indeed, the audience became a vital ingredient in the representation of such works, a situation in which the composer assumes a role rather different from the cool detachment so typical of musical Classicism.

Haydn is somehow personified in his music, which now transcends mere technical and structural boundaries, speaking a language of individual expression, of something lying beyond the notes themselves, a conception of music that was soon to become central to Romanticism. His quartets and symphonies gradually acquired an iconic cultural status, in which they are viewed as timeless exemplars, objects of aesthetic enquiry whose identity lay in sharp contrast to notions of locally and temporally confined *Gebrauchmusik* ("house music") that had characterized appreciations of his earlier output in both genres. This transformation is noticeable, too, in critical responses to Haydn's published output.

Two common themes running through reviews of Haydn's published string quartets that appeared in German periodical literature during the last quarter of the eighteenth century are the acknowledgment of his preeminence among European composers (indeed, Haydn is arguably the first composer to have secured a Europe-wide reputation), and the association between the use of remote, sometimes chromatic melody or harmony and genius, a category that emerges strongly in aesthetics in the later eighteenth century, stressing the individual personality of the artist, an essentially Romantic concept. According to a 1782 review of his op. 33 string quartets in the *Hamburgischer Correspondent*, "[Haydn is] an inexhaustible genius who appears to exceed himself in each new work that he publishes." This certainly captures the esteem in which the composer was held toward the end of his life. By contrast, during the nineteenth and early twentieth centuries the sentimental image of "Papa Haydn" characterized the reception history of his music, especially when set alongside that of Mozart and Beethoven. Since World War II, that imbalance has been redressed, notably through the scholarly work of H. C. Robbins Landon and Jens Peter Larsen.

JOHN IRVING

Biography

Born in Rohrau, Lower Austria (now Romania) March 31, 1732. Son of Mathias Haydn, a master wheelwright, and Anna Maria, Haydn, née Koller, a cook. Educated at the *Capell Hauss* (choir school) at the Stephansdom (St. Stephen's Cathedral), Vienna, 1740–49. Dismissed from St. Stephen's when his voice changed. Engaged in freelance teaching and further training in Vienna, 1750–58. Musical director to Count Karl Morzin in Vienna, 1759–61. Married Maria Anna Aloysia Apollonia Keller (d. 1800), 1760. Entered service of Esterhazy princes Pál Antal (Paul Anton), Miklós (Nicolaus), Antal (Anton), and Miklós (Nicolaus) II, 1761–1809: *Kapellmeister* (musical director) at the Esterházy court at Eisenstadt, near Vienna, from 1766 and later at the Esterháza castle near Lake Neusiedl (now in Hungary). Romantic involvement with Luigia Polzelli, Italian singer at the Esterházy court, for many years. Probably met Wolfgang Amadeus Mozart, 1782–83. Traveled to England by arrangement of Johann Peter Salomon, 1791–92 and 1794; awarded honorary degree by Oxford University, 1791. Gave lessons to Beethoven in Vienna, 1792. Continued working for the Esterházy court at Eisenstadt and in Vienna until his retirement due to ill health, 1802. Died in Vienna, May 31, 1809.

Selected Works

String Quartets

op. 20. 1772.
op. 33. 1781.
op. 50. 1787.
op. 74. 1793.
op. 76. 1797.
op. 77. 1799.

Symphonies

nos. 6–8. 1761.
no. 26. 1770.
no. 49. 1768.
nos. 82–7. 1785–86.
nos. 93–104. 1791–95.

Masses

In tempori belli. 1796.
Nelson. 1798.
Theresienmesse. 1799.

Oratorios

The Creation. 1796–98.
The Seasons. 1799–1800.

Bibliography

Joseph Haydn Gesammelte Briefe und Aufzeichnungen. Unter Benützung der Quellensammlung von H. C. Robbins Landon. Herausgegeben und erläutet von Dénes Bartha Kassel: Bärenreiter, 1965

Hughes, R. *Haydn.* 5th ed. London: Dent, 1975.

Robbins Landon, H. C. *Haydn: Chronicle and Works.* 5 vols. London: Thames and Hudson, 1976–80.

Sisman, E., ed., *Haydn and His World.* Princeton, N.J.: Princeton University Press, 1997.

HAZLITT, WILLIAM 1778–1830

English essayist, critic, metaphysician, and polemicist

William Hazlitt's career was framed by two French revolutions, for he "set out in life with the French Revolution" of 1789, and he died just six weeks after the July Revolution of 1830 that witnessed the final overthrow of the Bourbons. His commitment to the political and social ideals of these revolutions never wavered. He was a belligerently determined and often isolated enemy of cant, tyranny, and injustice, attacking the many arbitrary exercises of political power, and deriding the evasions and ambiguities of youthful idols such as Samuel Taylor Coleridge and William Wordsworth. A brilliant stylist, Hazlitt wrote on topics ranging from art and aesthetics to economics, moral theory, and the novel. He made great claims for the disinterested powers of the imagination, but his finest essays are rooted in the passions of his own personality.

Hazlitt had an uncertain start. He began as a painter, exhibiting at the Royal Academy in 1802, and producing the most well-known portrait of his close friend *Charles Lamb* (in the manner of Titian) in 1804. He then switched to metaphysics, and published his first book, *An Essay on the Principles of Human Action*, in 1805. The work denounced the rational egotism of "modern philosophy" and argued that there is a natural benevolence in the human mind that overturned Hobbesian notions of innate and necessary selfishness. His concerns then became more explicitly political. In his *Reply to the Essay on Population*

(1807) he attacked Thomas Malthus, whose doctrines on population presented the lot of the poor as "natural" and "inevitable," and seemed to offer a scientific justification for complacency and the brutal inequalities of the status quo. That same year, in *The Eloquence of the British Senate*, Hazlitt engaged for the first time with the political legacy of his archconservative antagonist Edmund Burke. Remarkably, in this instance he celebrated Burke for his powerful prose style and his immense comprehension of human nature, but in later essays he recanted and damned him as a champion of legitimacy, who "strewed the flowers of his style over the rotten carcass of corruption" ("Arguing in a Circle," 1823). Hazlitt's two very different views highlight one of the central paradoxes of his work: his fascination with the power of the imagination, and his intense commitment to political reform.

In 1812 Hazlitt began to write for the *Morning Chronicle* (1789–1865), and over the next fifteen years he became primarily a periodical writer, producing scores of essays for the leading liberal journals of the age, including Leigh Hunt's *Examiner* (1808–81), the *Edinburgh Review, London Magazine* (1820–29), and *New Monthly Magazine* (1814–84). The range, force, and immediacy of these essays is remarkable, and reveal Hazlitt as vitally responsive to the key figures, events, and issues of his age. He was in the lecture hall listening to Coleridge, or delivering his own series of lectures on literature and philosophy, many of which he collected and issued in book form. He was among the first to review new publications by Lord Byron, Samuel Taylor Coleridge, Walter Savage Landor, Thomas Moore, Mary Shelley, and William Wordsworth. He frequented art galleries, provincial inns, and London coffee houses, poring over newspapers, arguing with friends, championing reform, and defending Napoleon Bonaparte. He featured regularly in the Tory press as one of the marked men of *Blackwood's Magazine's* "Cockney school," and he lashed back with equal ferocity. He socialized with John Keats, who cited his "depth of Taste" as one of "three things to rejoice at in this Age." He went to boxing matches and the theater. He reported from parliament on the machinations of Lord Castlereagh, Lord Liverpool, George Canning, and other senior Tory officials. He wrote on utilitarians and Methodists, philosophy and the law, the Elgin marbles, patronage and authorship, republicanism and kingship, the periodical press, Walter Scott's *Waverley* (1814), reason and imagination, hero worship, the people, the pleasure of hating, and much else. He then collected these essays in volumes such as *The Round Table* (1817), *Political Essays* (1819), *Table Talk* (1821–2), *The Spirit of the Age* (1825), and *The Plain Speaker* (1826). Nowhere are the central concerns of the Romantic era more vigorously confronted, debated, and assessed.

In 1823, Hazlitt published perhaps the most remarkable autobiography of the age, *Liber Amoris*. He had always had an uneasy relationship with women, and the book is a thinly veiled fictional account of his infatuation with Sarah Walker, the teenage daughter of his landlord. The forty-two-year-old Hazlitt first met Walker in August 1820, and within days he was obsessed, relentlessly idealizing her but tortured by sexual desire and the knowledge that she had lips "as common as the stairs." He soon divorced his wife of fourteen years, only to find that Walker had been seeing other men all along. *Liber Amoris* stands in a line of Romantic confessional prose that includes Samuel Taylor Coleridge's *Biographia Literaria* (1817), Thomas De Quincey's *Confessions of an English Opium-Eater* (1821), and Stendhal's *De l'amour* (1822), while its full title (*Liber Amoris; or, the New Pygmalion*) taps into the recent success of Mary Shelley's *Frankenstein; or, the Modern Prometheus* (1818). Hazlitt's raw exposé of his own mania was a gift to the assassins of the Tory press, who read the book as confirmation of the degradation and debilitation bound to result from a commitment to radical politics. But Hazlitt was always the unflinching analyst of his own passions, and he seems to have needed the book to vent an intensity of emotion that was pushing him toward mental collapse.

In his later years Hazlitt produced an account of his travels through France and Italy, and his Boswellian *Conversations with James Northcote* (1830). Much of his energy, however, was devoted to his four-volume *Life of Napoleon* (1828–30), which he considered to be his most important work. In it he defiantly upheld the beliefs of a lifetime: Napoleon Bonaparte is celebrated as "the child and champion" of the French Revolution, reform is insisted upon as just and necessary, the Tories are denigrated as unfeeling mediocrities, and Waterloo is lamented as the disastrous triumph of privilege over merit and courage. Hazlitt died in penury shortly after the final two volumes appeared. In De Quincey's words, he had "placed himself in collision from the first with all the interests that were in the sunshine of this world." But sunshine or not, Hazlitt had spent his entire career saying what he wanted to say; his famous last words were, "Well, I've had a happy life."

ROBERT MORRISON

Biography

Born in Maidstone, Kent, 1778; family moved to America, 1783–87. Attended New Unitarian College at Hackney in London, 1793–95. Met Samuel Taylor Coleridge and William Wordsworth, and reads *Lyrical Ballads* in manuscript, 1798. Undertook a commission to copy old masters in the Louvre, 1802. Visited Wordsworth and Coleridge in the Lake District, but was forced to flee because of a sexual scandal, 1803. Met Charles and Mary Lamb, 1804. Married Sarah Stoddart 1808; birth of son William, 1811. Delivered first series of public lectures and began to write for the *Morning Chronicle*, 1812. Met John Keats, and published *The Round Table* and *Characters of Shakespear's Plays*, 1817. Attacked by *Blackwood's Magazine* as a member of the "Cockney school," 1818. Met Sarah Walker, 1820. Published the first volume of *Table Talk* essays, 1821. Divorced his wife, 1822. Published *Liber Amoris*, 1823. Married Isabella Bridgewater and met Stendhal, 1824. Separated from Isabella, 1827. Published *The Life of Napoleon*, 1828–30. Died September 18, 1830.

Selected Works

The Complete Works of William Hazlitt. 21 vols. Edited by P. P. Howe. London: Dent, 1930–34.

William Bewick, *Hazlitt*. Reprinted courtesy of AKG.

William Hazlitt: Selected Writings. Edited by Jon Cook. Oxford: Oxford University Press, 1991.

The Selected Writings of William Hazlitt. 9 vols. Edited by Duncan Wu. London: Pickering and Chatto, 1998.

Letters

The Letters of William Hazlitt. Edited by Herschel M. Sikes, Willard Hallam Bonner, and Gerald Lahey. New York, 1978.

"William Hazlitt to his Publishers, Friends, and Creditors: Twenty-Seven New Holograph Letters," edited by Charles E. Robinson, *Keats-Shelley Review* 2 (1987): 1–47.

Bibliography

Albrecht, W. P. *Hazlitt and the Creative Imagination.* Lawrence: University of Kansas Press, 1965.

Baker, Herschel. *William Hazlitt.* Cambridge, Mass.: Harvard University Press, 1962.

Barrell, John. *The Political Theory of Painting from Reynolds to Hazlitt.* New Haven, Conn.: Yale University Press, 1986.

Bate, Jonathan. "The Example of Hazlitt." In *Shakespearean Constitutions.* Oxford: Oxford University Press, 1989. 127–201.

Bate, W. J. "William Hazlitt." In *Criticism: the Major Texts.* New York: Harcourt, Brace, 1952. 281–92.

Bloom, Harold, ed. *William Hazlitt.* New York: Chelsea House, 1986.

Bromwich, David. *Hazlitt: The Mind of a Critic.* Oxford: Oxford University Press, 1983.

Burroughs, Catherine. "Acting in the Closet: A Feminist Performance of Hazlitt's *Liber Amoris* and Keats's *Otho the Great*," *European Romantic Review* 2 (1992): 125–44.

Butler, Marilyn. "Satire and the Images of Self in the Romantic Period: the Long Tradition of Hazlitt's *Liber Amoris*," *Yearbook of English Studies* 14 (1984): 209–25.

Eagleton, Terry. "William Hazlitt: An Empiricist Radical," *New Blackfriars* 54 (1973): 108–17.

Houck, James A. *William Hazlitt: A Reference Guide.* Boston: Hall, 1977.

Jack, Ian. "The Critic: William Hazlitt." In *Keats and the Mirror of Art.* Oxford: Oxford University Press, 1967. 58–75.

Jones, Stanley. *Hazlitt: A Life.* Oxford: Oxford University Press, 1989.

Kinnaird, John. *William Hazlitt: Critic of Power.* New York: Columbia University Press, 1978.

Mahoney, John L. *The Logic of Passion.* New York: Fordham University Press, 1981.

Morrison, Robert. "Essayists of the Romantic Period: De Quincey, Hazlitt, Hunt, and Lamb." In *Literature of the Romantic Period: A Bibliographical Guide.* Edited by O'Neill Michael. Oxford: Oxford University Press, 1998. 341–63.

Natarahan, Uttara. *Hazlitt and the Reach of Sense.* Oxford: Clarendon Press, 1998.

Park, Roy. *Hazlitt and the Spirit of the Age.* Oxford: Oxford University Press, 1971.

Paulin, Tom. *The Day-Star of Liberty: William Hazlitt's Radical Style.* London: Faber, 1998.

Ready, Robert. *Hazlitt at Table.* Rutherford, N.J.: Fairleigh Dickinson University Press, 1981.

Schneider, Elisabeth. *The Aesthetics of William Hazlitt.* Philadelphia: University of Pennsylvania, 1933.

Uphaus, Robert W. *William Hazlitt.* Boston: Twayne, 1985.

Wardle, Ralph M. *Hazlitt.* Lincoln: University of Nebraska Press, 1971.

HEBBEL, FRIEDRICH 1813–1863

German dramatist

Friedrich Hebbel is considered by many critics to be the greatest German dramatist of the nineteenth-century Biedermeier period, which followed the age of Johann Wolfgang von Goethe and Johann Christoph Friedrich von Schiller. His gift for dramatic dialogue and his insight into his characters' psychological processes produced stage works of great power. Hebbel's works can be considered Romantic in that they were informed by abstract concepts of historical process that he had gleaned from his readings of the idealist philosopher G. W. F. Hegel, whose progressive ideas dominated academic discussion during the first half of the nineteenth century. For Hebbel, the genre of drama is to be considered philosophical discourse that been realized in action upon the stage.

In his first play, *Judith* (1841), Hebbel uses a biblical story, that of Holofernes the general and the Jewish Judith of Bethulia. Judith secretly loves this handsome and powerful enemy of her people and is placed in a tragic dilemma when she is called upon to assassinate him. She does, somewhat reluctantly, kill him when he rapes her and tells her people they should kill her too if she becomes pregnant. Judith sacrifices herself so that the monotheism of the Jews may prevail over pagan polytheism. She serves as a tool of historical progress. The innocent victim (usually female) who suffers at the hands of a self-willed and egotistical individual (usually male) who places himself in opposition to the forces of history forms the core dramatic scenario of Hebbel's plays. From the point of view of the individual, Hebbel's vision of history is rather grim and echoes in this regard the Romantic pessimism found in the idealistic philosophy of Arthur Schopenhauer.

In the essay "Mein Wort über das Drama" ("My View on the Drama," 1843) and in the introductory forward to his first great drama, *Maria Magdalene* (1844), Hebbel explained how his dramas were to be viewed in the light of Hegelian aesthetics. Hegel's philosophy of the dialectic is inherently dramatic in that the historical unfolding of the *Geist* (absolute spirit) procedes from the inescapable conflict of thesis and antithesis that results in the resolution of the synthesis. Hegel discussed the great tragedies of ancient Greece as artistic illustrations of this historical process. Likewise, the middle-class tragedy *Maria Magdalene* seeks to dramatize the conflict between the traditional bourgeois patriarchal world view of the inflexible Meister Anton and that of an emerging nineteenth-century social and political liberalism, a clash that results in the suicide of Anton's daughter Klara, who has internalized the outmoded and spiritually bankrupt values of her father. As Hegel had argued, the individual, here both Meister Anton and Klara, must inevitably be sacrificed in the vast sweep of humanity's historical progress. Immense guilt emerges when the individual places his or her self-will against the impersonal movement of history, which in this abstracted Hegelian and Romantic view becomes itself a dramatic protagonist on the stage. With its contemporary and realistic social milieu, *Maria Magdalene* proved to be the most successful of Hebbel's dramas.

In the 1850 tragedy *Herodes und Mariamne*, Hebbel returns to a love story from ancient biblical history, that of Herod, who had been appointed king of Judea by the Romans, and Mariamne of the royal house of the Jewish Maccabees, opposed to Roman rule. He orders her death should he not return from a perilous journey and she is so outraged by his lack of trust in her love that she decides to kill herself as a means of revenge. After her death, Herod learns of her innocence and is devastated. Here again is the Hegelian dialectic realized in dramatic form: the pagan Romans in conflict with the monotheistic Jews. The play ends with the advent of the three kings heralding the birth of the Christ child, a synthesis that promises a more humane and tolerant future for mankind.

The tragedy *Agnes Bernauer* of 1855 treats an actual event from fifteenth-century Bavarian history—namely, the marriage of Albrecht, the son of Duke Ernst, to the beautiful Agnes Bernauer, the daughter of a commoner from Augsburg. Albrecht's father fears that Agnes' rightful claims to the Bavarian throne might cause social upheaval in the future, so he has her drowned while his son is away. When Albrecht learns of the treachery, he wages war against his father, who finally abdicates and retreats to a monastery. Hebbel's vision is again of an individual, Agnes, who must be sacrificed in favor of a greater historical vision of social peace.

The 1856 verse tragedy *Gyges und sein Ring* (*Gyges and His Ring*) is considered to be Hebbel's last great work and was his attempt to revive the style of the French classical theater. Again there is a woman, Rhodope, who must sacrifice herself because a powerful male figure, King Kaudaules, has violated the customs of his society in a vain attempt to be "modern" before the historical time for social change had come. The play conveys Hebbel's criticism of what he felt were prematurely progressive political and social changes that had occurred in Austria during the revolution of 1848.

Hebbel is also known for the literary controversy that sprung up between himself and the contemporary Austrian Biedermeier author Adalbert Stifter. The latter, a conservative prose writer, believed that social change occurred slowly and undramatically as it does in the evolutionary processes of nature, and not in momentous historical confrontations as Hebbel's dramas depicted. Although the dialogue and social milieu of Hebbel's plays are realistic, the dramatic view that informs them is highly abstracted and philosophical, depicting tragic individuals and historical events in the grand sweep of a Romantic vision that owes much to the idealism of Hegel.

THOMAS F. BARRY

Biography

Born in Wesselburen, Holstein, Denmark (now Germany), March 18, 1813. Son of a mason, he was brought up in poor circumstances. Worked to support family as bailiff's clerk and messenger after his father died, 1827. Published first poetry and founded literary circle in Hamburg, early 1830s; supported financially by Elise Lensing, a seamstress, with whom he lived. Studied law at the Universities of Heidelberg and Munich, 1836–39. Returned to Hamburg as an invalid, also suffering from financial problems. Lived in Copenhagen, 1842. Traveled to Paris and Italy, sponsored by the Danish king, 1843–44. Received doctorate in philosophy from the University of Erlangen, 1844. Lived in Vienna from 1845 on. Married Viennese actress Christine Enghaus, 1846. Suffered from rheumatic fever in later life. Published *Gyges und sein Ring* (*Gyges and his Ring*), 1854. Honorary court librarian, Weimar, 1863. Awarded Schiller Prize, 1863. Died in Vienna, December 13, 1863.

Selected Works

Plays

Judith: Eine Tragödie in fünf Akten, 1841. Translated as *Judith: A Tragedy in Five Acts*. Translated by Carl van Doren: 1914.

Maria Magdalene: Ein bürgerliches Trauerspiel in drei Acten. Nebst einem Vorwort, das Verhältnis der dramatischen Kunst zur Zeit und verwandte Puncte, 1844. Translated as *Maria Magdalena* by Paul Bernard Thomas, 1914.

Herodes und Mariamne: Eine Tragödie in fünf Akten, 1850. Translated as *Herod and Mariamne: A Tragedy in Five Acts* by Edith Isaacs and Kurt Rahlson, 1912.

Agnes Bernauer: Ein deutsches Trauerspiel in fünf Aufzügen, 1855. Translated as *Agnes Bernauer: A German Tragedy in Five Acts* by Logen Pattee, 1909.

Gyges und sein Ring: Eine Tragödie in fünf Acten, 1856. Translated as *Gyges and His Ring*. Translated by L. H. Allen, 1914.

Essay

"Mein Wort über das Drama!: Eine Erwiderung an Professor Heiberg in Kopenhagen," 1843. Translated as "My View on the Drama" by Moody Campbell, 1922.

Bibliography

Alt, Tilo A. "Friedrich Hebbel." In *Dictionary of Literary Biography*, vol. 129: *Nineteenth-Century German Writers, 1841–1900*. Edited by James Hardin and Siegfried Mews. Detroit: Gale Research, 1993. 131–42.

Flygt, Sten. *Friedrich Hebbel*. New York: Twayne, 1968.

Garland, Mary. *Hebbel's Prose Tragedies: An Investigation of the Aesthetic Aspect of Hebbel's Dramatic Language*. Anglica Germanica, series 2. Cambridge: Cambridge University Press, 1973.

Niven, W. John. *The Reception of Friedrich Hebbel in Germany in the Era of National Socialism*. Stuttgart: Heinz, 1984.

THE "HEBRIDES" OVERTURE, OP. 29 1832

Musical composition by Felix Mendelssohn

The visit of the twenty-year-old Felix Mendelssohn to Britain in 1829 marked the culmination of a period of educating and cultivating his precocious genius. It was also the start of a relationship with the British musical public that was hardly less fruitful for him than it was beneficial for his admirers. After making a great impression in London, he went on to Scotland with his friend Karl Klingemann, a junior Hanoverian diplomat, and after a stay in Edinburgh, they toured the Highlands and Islands and journeyed by paddle steamer to the island of Staffa (to the west of Mull, which is itself west of Oban).

In making an excursion to Staffa, Mendelssohn and his companion were following what over the previous three-quarters of a century had become fashionable, a northern variant on the classic "grand tour." Since the 1745 Jacobite Rising, Scotland had claimed more attention on account of its picturesque scenery and stirring history, reflections of which were sought in its music and literature. In 1772, visiting a site that the locals did not appreciate, the famous explorer Joseph Banks hailed the wonder of Staffa's huge vertical columns of volcanic basalt and its great cave echoing the incessant undulations of the waves: "Compared to this what are the cathedrals and palaces built by men! mere models or playthings." Thomas Pennant promptly inserted an account of Banks's discovery in his *Tour of Scotland and to the Hebrides*; henceforth Staffa figured on the itinerary of enterprising travelers. The development of associations of Ossian (an ancient Celtic poet, whose poems were deemed to have been the work of James Macpherson) with Staffa added to the interest of the spot. Among those attracted to the island were Samuel Johnson (who could not, however, reach land because of bad weather), Thomas Campbell, Walter Scott, John Keats, and Joseph Mallord William Turner.

Once he recovered from a bout of seasickness, Mendelssohn responded to the Hebrides first with a pen-and-ink drawing dated August 7, 1829. Soon after, though, in a letter written in Tobermory, Mull, and bearing the same date, Mendelssohn noted the opening of what was to become an orchestral evocation of the scenery he had seen. There were, however, many stages between this initial, apparently spontaneous inspiration, and the finished work, which was in fact completed in Rome. There were also changes to its title, with Ossianic connections being made more specific, possibly without Mendelssohn's authority. The manuscript score of December 11, 1830, entitled "Ouvertüre zur einsamen Insel" ("Overture: The Lonely Island") was succeeded only five days later by a full score called *Die Hebriden*. Two years later *Overture to the Isles of Fingal* became the preferred title among English music lovers. Uncertainty was not resolved when, after the publication of the orchestral parts in 1834 under the name *Die Hebriden*, the full score appeared a year later as *Die Fingals-Höhle* (*Fingal's Cave*).

Problems over nomenclature make it more difficult, given the nonspecificity of musical language, to identify Ossianic elements in the score, even if the rousing trumpet calls, for example, may be suggestive of a call to war. What appears to be beyond question is that Mendelssohn is evoking solely with instrumental sound a vivid, yet never literal or onomatopoeic, image of the sea as it surges with constant restless movement in recurrent yet ever-changing patterns, and with infinite resources of power. As well as referring to a prime Romantic site (and, if the Ossianic link is admitted, to a major Romantic myth), the celebration of the sea, an element generally judged abhorrent in earlier epochs, also reflects changing sensibilities.

The employment of orchestral means for the interpretation of a specific, unusual natural scene is an effort by Mendelssohn to move beyond both absolute music and also such highly conventionalized events as battle pieces and pastoral idylls, to create works that crossed generic boundaries. The "Hebrides" Overture also marks a step forward from Mendelssohn's previous practice, which had been to take literary texts as a starting point, as with his "A Midsummer Night's Dream" Overture. In 1826 the composer was entitled to assume that the public, in Germany as well as other countries, knew the Shakespearean comedy and was thus able to respond to his evocation of its spirit. By the same token, audiences in Germany, if not elsewhere, were familiar with the lyric by Johann Wolfgang von Goethe that is the inspiration for the "Calm Sea and Prosperous Voyage" Overture of 1828. The consequence of Mendelssohn's turning away from literary models is a liberation from obligations to fulfill certain prior expectations, and a movement toward music as a direct personal reflection of the phenomenon presented, without the mediation of another work of art or its creator. As the overture developed into the tone-poem (most notably in the work of Hector Berlioz and Franz Liszt), the tradition of reinterpreting literature or works of art in music would remain strong, but subsequent composers, such as Bedrich Smetana and Claude Debussy, would have great successes in following more progressive trends initiated by the "Hebrides" Overture.

Approximately ten minutes long, the "Hebrides" is scored for a full, but not exceptionally large, orchestra, with the usual strings complemented, supplemented, and given additional color by double woodwinds, two horns, two trombones, and timpani. From the outset an insistent falling figure in quavers enlivened with a single rising semiquaver is heard again and again at different pitches, as the double basses establish B minor as the basic key. Beginning quietly, the music swells, to fade away again, while the initial theme recurs. Brass and timpani contribute to climaxes, just as the strings also have great moments. Surges are repeated, but not identically, and at the end the falling phrase returns, like the eternal motion of the seas.

CHRISTOPHER SMITH

See also **Mendelssohn-Bartholdy, Jakob Ludwig Felix; Music, Romantic**

Bibliography

Crum, Margaret. *Felix Mendelssohn Bartholdy*. Oxford: Bodleian Library, 1972. Mendelssohn's sketch of the Hebrides is reproduced as Plate 12.

MacCulloch, Donald B. *Staffa*. Newton Abbot, U.K.: David and Charles, 1978.

Radcliffe, Philip. *Mendelssohn*. London: Dent, 1954.

Todd, R. Larry. *Mendelssohn: "The Hebrides" and Other Overtures*. Cambridge: Cambridge University Press, 1993.

HEGEL, GEORG WILHELM FRIEDRICH 1770–1831

German philosopher

Georg Wilhelm Friedrich Hegel was the greatest systematic philosopher of the early nineteenth century, but his relationship with the Romanticism that was flowering in Germany was always ambiguous and ambivalent. He famously abused some of his well-known Romantic colleagues, such as Friedrich Heinrich Jacobi and Friedrich Wilhelm Joseph von Schelling, and he found a ferocious antagonist in Arthur Schopenhauer, who competed with Hegel (without success) by scheduling his lectures at the same time at the University of Berlin. But Schelling was at one time Hegel's roommate at Tübingen and later his mentor, and both were strongly influenced by their mutual friend, Friedrich Hölderlin, the brilliant lyrical poet; they were also great admirers of Johann Wolfgang von Goethe.

Even though he rejected Romanticism, Hegel was equally ambiguous and ambivalent about the Enlightenment, or *Aufklärung*, in Germany. He was an avid follower of Immanuel Kant (one of the main defenders of the Enlightenment in Germany), and as a young man he was enthusiastic about the French Revolution: he and other students at the Tübingen seminary danced around a "liberty tree" singing the Marseillaise and reciting Johann Christoph Friedrich von Schiller's "An die Freude" ("Ode to Joy," 1785). But he particularly disliked the businesslike and spiritless "utilitarian" thinking of the English Enlightenment, and he much preferred the spiritual atmosphere of German Romanticism. Nevertheless, he was not particularly religious, nor could he accurately be called a Romantic, although his influence on both religious thought and Romanticism was considerable.

Hegel is most famous for his "system," which appeared in full through several versions of his *Encyklopädie der philosophischen Wissenschaften in Grundrisse* (*Encyclopedia of the Philosophical Sciences*, 1820–30). But Hegel's systematic philosophy had many incarnations, beginning in his Jena lecture notes of 1803. The most substantial versions of the system were to be found in two gigantic tomes (which originally were intended to be parts of a single work), the *Die Phänomenologie des Geistes* (*Phenomenology of Spirit*, 1807), and the *Wissenschaft der Logik* (*Science of Logic*, 1816). The Phenomenology was reputedly finished just as Napoleon reached the height of his power at the battle of Jena, where Hegel was teaching. But in the wake of Napoleon Bonaparte, Hegel envisioned the birth of a new world, which he announced in the preface of *Phenomenology* (and to his classes), writing, "We find ourselves in an important epoch, in a fermentation, in which Spirit has made a great leap forward, has gone beyond its previous concrete form and acquired a new one. . . . A new emergence of Spirit is at hand; philosophy must be the first to hail its appearance and recognize it."

Perhaps never has an esoteric philosophy book been more self-conscious in its expression of the times. Indeed, the whole subject matter of *Phenomenology* is the ultimate liberation and final unification of the human spirit. Fifteen years later, with Napoleon gone and Europe in the midst of "the Reaction," Hegel would lament in the preface of his *Grundlinien der Philosophie des Rechts oder Naturrecht und Staatswissenschaft im Grundrisse* (*Philosophy of Right and Law*, 1820–21) that the philosophical owl flies only at night, and then paints its "grey on grey,"

a gloomy phrase taken straight out of Goethe's *Faust*. The influence of *The Phenomenology of Spirit* in philosophy would be as profound and as enduring as Napoleon's bold ventures in European history, both in terms of its impact and the reactions it engendered. It is Immanuel Kant whose "Copernican revolution" is usually compared in its far-reaching effects to the upheaval in France, but it is Hegel who deserves credit for consolidating and spreading that revolution. If Heinrich Heine could compare Kant to Maximilien de Robespierre, then Hegel, with comparable philosophical hyperbole, deserves comparison to Napoleon. (In 1806, on seeing Napoleon enter Jena after the crushing defeat of German forces at the battle of Jena, Hegel famously referred to him as the "World Spirit [*Weltgeist*] . . . astride a horse.")

Hegel began studying and writing philosophy soon after Kant had redefined the philosophical world, just as Europe was entering the turbulent new century. As a young man Hegel was educated in the Tübingen seminary, although he seemed to have little religious ambition or theological talent. In fact, his first philosophical essays were somewhat blasphemous attacks on Christianity, including "The Life of Jesus," which went out of its way to make Jesus into an ordinary moralist who in his Sermon on the Mount espoused Kant's categorical imperative. As a student, however, Hegel entertained the idea of inventing a new religion that stressed our unity with nature, a "synthesis of nature and spirit" drawn from the ancient Greeks and crudely formulated with great poetic flair by Hölderlin. Hölderlin was without doubt one of the poetic geniuses of his generation and a powerful influence on young Hegel. Drawing not only from the ancient Greeks but from the Romantic culture that surrounded them, Hölderlin and later Hegel promulgated a grand metaphor of effusion, cosmic spirit making itself known to us and to itself throughout all of nature, in human history and, most clearly of all, in poetry and the "spiritual sciences."

Their younger friend Schelling had already converted that metaphor into philosophical currency by 1795, and when Hegel finally decided to turn to serious philosophy just after the turn of the new century, it was with the encouragement and sponsorship of his friend Schelling. He sought and obtained the teaching position at Jena, and, in sharp contrast to the clear polemical tone of his earlier, "antitheological" essays, he began to write philosophy in a terse, academic style. Hegel joined Schelling in his bold attempt to forge a new form of philosophy, following Kant and the radical neo-Kantian Johann Gottlieb Fichte. Together, Schelling and Hegel published a journal, the *Critical Journal of Philosophy*. Hegel's first professional essay was a comparison of the philosophies of Fichte and Schelling, making clear the superiority of the latter. For several years, Hegel was dimly known in the German philosophical world only as a disciple of Schelling. For his first teaching job at Jena, he toyed with "the system" in his lectures and developed the basis of his moral and political theories. Then, in 1806, he wrote *The Phenomenology of Spirit*.

Hegel's original intentions and initial approach to the *Phenomenology* were rather modest and for the most part derivative of earlier efforts by Fichte and Schelling to "complete Kant's system," a unified and all-encompassing "science" of philosophy. But according to Fichte, Schelling, and then Hegel, Kant had failed to show the unity of human experience. Moreover, Kant's notorious conception of the *Ding an sich* (the thing in itself), while central to his philosophy and the key to his division between the phenomenal world of knowledge and the noumenal world of free will, morality, and religion, was greeted by these post-Kantians as a mistake, a serious flaw that threatened to undermine the whole critical enterprise. Hegel's response was that we can achieve "absolute knowledge"—that is, the integrated all-encompassing system to which Kant had aspired.

In the Tübingen seminary, Hegel, Schelling, and Hölderlin had dreamed of a new religion. They despised much of their theological training, dismissing it. They had deep misgivings about German culture as well, torn between the cosmopolitan clarity and free thinking of the French and British Enlightenment (represented in Germany by Kant) and the Romantic nationalism mixed with mysticism that marked the German reaction to the Enlightenment. Although his early essays had been clumsy attempts to revise and reconcile Christianity with Greek folk religion, insisting that religions are particular to a people and a time, it nevertheless makes sense to speak of religion in general, and of certain universal features that all religions and peoples have in common. Hegel insists that "the aim and essence of all true religion, and our religion included, is human morality." He finds fault with the idea that God and man are separate and distinct, in which God is infinitely superior and we are merely his servants. He also finds fault with the distinctions between and separation of reason and the passions, theology and faith, theory and practice. And here we find the seeds of two of the most dramatic and central themes of the *Phenomenology*, the grand conception of *Geist* (Spirit) as immanent God incorporating us all, and the all-important place of local customs and affections in ethics.

One can understand in this the political as well as ontological imagery that pervades Hegel's philosophy. Hegel is not an individualist. In the *Phenomenology* he comments that much less should be thought of and expected of the individual, and in his later *Vorlesungen über die Philosophie der Geschichte* (*Lectures on the Philosophy of History*, 1837) he famously tells us that even the greatest individuals follow unwittingly "the cunning of reason" and find themselves pawns in the hands of a larger fate, a dramatic idea that is embodied in flesh and blood in Lev Tolstoy's account of Napoleon's Russian campaign in *War and Peace* (1865–69). One can imagine Hegel, envisioning the great battles of that war in which hundreds of thousands of undifferentiated "individuals" in identical uniforms moved in waves and slaughtered one another for the sake of larger, dimly understood ideas and loyalties (his own brother, Ludwig, died during Napoleon's ill-fated Russian campaign). So viewed, the individual does indeed count for very little, and it is the larger movement of humankind that comes into focus instead. And yet, Hegel is no fascist—regardless of whatever ideas or inspiration Benito Mussolini and his kind may have drawn from him. Hegel insists on this larger view of human history but nevertheless claims throughout his work that the ultimate aim and result of that history has been human freedom and respect for the individual. But it is the individual as an aspect of Geist that impresses him, not the ontologically isolated and autonomous individual of He-

gel's liberal predecessors. Geist is a cosmic self that pervades and ultimately embraces us all.

In his later lectures, this insight becomes the centerpiece of Hegel's philosophy, as he traces the origins and development of the various religions, the course of human history, and the evolution of philosophy itself. Religion, as he had recognized in his early essays, was not abstract dogma but the expression of basic human needs and tendencies, and these are not to be found whole in any single religion but in the interplay and development of religions. Nevertheless, the ultimate purpose of all religions is finally recognized only in philosophy, with the concept of Geist. Human history, he later writes, may appear to be a "slaughterbench" on which whole nations as well as millions of individuals are butchered. But to one who "looks with a rational eye," Hegel argues, "history in turn presents its rational aspect," and that rational aspect is the realization of Geist. The history of humanity, brutal as it has been, nevertheless displays an ineluctable sense of progress and increasing freedom (whether or not Hegel also believed in the "end of history," a final fulfilment of that freedom in all its forms). Finally, Hegel teaches us not to see the history of philosophy as merely competing answers to the same ill-formed questions but rather as a growth of ideas that have developed out of the conflicts and confrontations of the past. The name of this process of confrontation and improvement, as everyone knows, is dialectic.

And yet, Hegel's *Phenomenology* is not history such as one later finds in Karl Marx and Friedrich Engels. To be sure, various movements in philosophy are traced in more or less historical order in the first few chapters of the book, and there are bits of actual history spread through the later sections. But one also notes with some consternation that the Greeks are discussed after the moderns, and Sophocles after the Stoics. One would be hard-pressed to formulate a historical interpretation that would account for such chronological oddities. What *Phenomenology* is doing, therefore, is not tracing the actual order of the development of various "forms of consciousness" in history but rather ordering them and playing them against one another in such a way that we see how they fit and how they conflict and how a more adequate way of thinking may emerge. Dialectic is not just development but a mode of argument, and the order of *Phenomenology* is not just a demolition derby, a process of elimination and the survival of the fittest, but a *teleology*, a genuine progression from less adequate ways of thinking to more adequate and more comprehensive and, finally, to the most comprehensive way of all.

ROBERT C. SOLOMON

Biography

Born in Stuttgart, August 27, 1770. Son of Georg Ludwig Hegel, minor civil servant at the court of the Duchy of Württemberg. Educated at a grammar school in Stuttgart until 1788. Studied theology at the Tübinger Stift (University of Tübingen seminary), 1788–93. Met and established friendship with Goethe. Tutor in Berne, 1793–96 and in Frankfurt am Main, 1793–1801. Received small inheritance after father's death, 1799. Unsalaried private lecturer, then professor, University of Jena, 1801–1806. Left Jena after French occupation; editor of Catholic newspaper *Bamburger Zeitung* in Bavaria, 1807. Fathered a son, Ludwig, 1807. Headmaster, Nuremberg Gymnasium,

1808–16. Married Marie von Tucher, 1811; they had one daughter who died shortly after birth and two sons. Professor, University of Heidelberg, 1816–18. First Son Ludwig joined the family, 1816. Appointed to chair of philosophy, University of Berlin, 1818; held that position until his death. Appointed to the Royal Academic Board of Examiners, Brandenburg, working on reform of the Prussian education system, 1821. Died of cholera in Berlin, November 14, 1831.

Selected Writings

Die Phänomenologie des Geistes, 1807. Translated as *The Phenomenology of Spirit* by J. B. Baillie. 2 vols. 1910.

Wissenschaft der Logik. 2 vols., 1812–16. Translated as *Hegel's Science of Logic* by W. H. Johnston and L. G. Struthers, 1929.

Encyklopädie der philosophischen Wissenschaften im Grundrisse, 1817; 2d ed., 1827. Translated as *The Logic of Hegel, Translated from the Encyclopaedia of the Philosophical Sciences* by William Wallace, 1874.

Grundlinien der Philosophie des Rechts, oder Naturrecht und Staatswissenschaft im Grundrisse, 1821. Translated as *Hegel's Philosophy of Right* by T. M. Knox, 1952.

Vorlesungen über die Philosophie der Geschichte, 1837. Translated as *Lectures on the Philosophy of World History* by H. B. Nisbet, 1975.

Bibliography

Althaus, Horst. *Hegel: An Intellectual Biography*. Cambridge: Polity Press, 2000.

Findlay, J. N. *Hegel: A Re-examination*. London: Allen and Unwin, 1958.

Harris, H. S. *Hegel's Development*. Oxford: Clarendon Press, 1972.

Inwood, Michael. *A Hegel Dictionary*. Oxford: Blackwell, 1992.

Kaufmann, Walter. *Hegel: A Reinterpretation*. Notre Dame, Ind.: University of Notre Dame, 1978.

Mills, Patricia J., ed. *Feminist Interpretations of G. W. F. Hegel*. College Park, Penn.: Pennsylvania State University Press, 1996.

Pinkard, Terry P. *Hegel: A Biography*. Cambridge: Cambridge University Press, 2000.

Pippin, Robert B. *Hegel's Idealism, The Satisfactions of Self-Consciousness*. Cambridge: Cambridge University Press, 1989.

Singer, Peter. *Hegel*. Oxford: Oxford University Press, 1983.

Taylor, Charles. *Hegel*. Cambridge: Cambridge University Press, 2000.

HEINE, HEINRICH 1797–1856

German poet

Heinrich Heine's life and work spans the period from the Romantics, through Junges Deutschland (Young Germany) and Vormärz (anticipation of the March revolution of 1848), and into the later phases of the Biedermeier era and realism. It is not only the changing contexts of his work that make it difficult to assign him to a particular movement; in many ways he is instrumental in defining the changing styles of the day. The critical essay *Die Romantische Schule* (*The Romantic School*, 1836), for example, was an early attempt to give popular coherence to the various writers grouped under the name of Romanticism. Often critical of Romantic writing and its styles, Heine recognized himself in the term *romantique défroqué* (defrocked Romantic). In the autobiographical *Geständnisse* (*Confessions*, 1854), he claims "with me the old lyric German school closed, while at the same time the new school, the modern German lyric, was inaugurated by me." In his critical essays, Heine identifies the Romantic medievalism as backward-looking and antimodern: conversely, he argues, a classicism common to Johann Wolgang von Goethe and Napoleon Bonaparte is the true mark of historical progress. When Heine returns to Romantic themes and forms in his later poetry, it is to demonstrate his nostalgia for its exhausted imagery and the continuing contemporary significance, for political reasons, of its interests in folksong, myth, and legend.

Heine identified *das Ende der Kunstperiode* (the end of the period of art) with Goethe's death. This acknowledges the unavoidable dominance of the older poet in the earlier part of Heine's career, as well as his own allegiance to Goethe. In his critical competition with the *Tendenzdichter* (tendentious) political poets of the Vormärz, by contrast, he defines and then transcends a current propagandist style through the ironic deployment of Romantic themes and the Romantic poetics of mood. Like many contemporaries, such as Christian Dietrich Grabbe in Germany or Stendhal in France, he saw in the passing of great figures like Goethe or Napoleon the end of a heroic age, which was succeeded by mediocrity.

Whatever his ostensible theme, Heine constantly writes about himself. His first public successes, the *Reisebilder* (*Pictures of Travel*, 1826–31), create within the loose framework of the travelogue a half-fictional and half-autobiographical persona who returns in different guises and disguises throughout his work. This personal dimension of Heine's writing attracted both prurient curiosity and sharp criticism among contemporaries and subsequent readers alike. The first collections of *Reisebilder* (1826, 1830) established Heine's reputation as a master of comic ridicule, often condemned as frivolity; the poems collected in *Buch der Lieder* (*Book of Songs*, 1827) yielded his image as a poet of unrequited love and inner self-division (so-called *Zerrissenheit*). This Byronic pose came to be the target of his satire in the unusual free-verse poems of his cycle *Der Nordsee* (*The North Sea*, 1826–27).

Despite converting to Lutheranism, Heine was unable, as a Jew, to find suitable employment in public administration or the universities. In response to the July revolution, he moved to Paris in May 1831 and became both a high-profile exile moving in the literary circles of the French capital and an acute commentator on its cultural and political life. When his health finally collapsed in 1848 and he was left bedridden, a third image of Heine was constructed by his visitors and by Heine himself: that of a man who courageously endured his *Matratzengruft* (mattress grave) with his mind and spirits intact.

Three issues have dominated critical discussion of Heine's work: the extent and significance of the autobiographical element in his writings, the nature of his political commitments, and the extent to which his response to political censorship, on the one hand, and pressure to conform to the party line of radical liberalism, on the other, can be successfully deciphered as a coherent discourse. The poems of *Buch der Lieder* parade themselves as the product of unrequited love, supposedly first for his Hamburg cousin Amalie and then for her sister Therese. The chronological inconsistency of this explanation was demonstrated by William Rose. The poems are now seen as variations on a Petrarchan theme; the carefully arranged illusion of autobiography that they create explores the conventions of the *Erlebnislyrik* (lyric of experience) as defined by Goethe's love poetry and his novel *Die Leiden des jungen Werther* (*The Sorrows of Young Werther*, 1774). In reworking the conventional terms of individual experience, however, *Buch der Lieder* also measures Heine's sense of exclusion from the social world of the grand bourgeoisie in Hamburg; Heine's Jewish origins also excluded him from the public world of politics and the academy.

If social criticism is nevertheless marginal to Heine's early poetry, political questions are both implicit and explicit in *Neue Gedichte* (*New Poems*, 1844). After poems recalling the sarcastic-sentimental mixture of the first collection, the sequences entitled "Verschiedene" ("Sundry Women") consider a more modern, Parisian eroticism, but they testify, above all, to Heine's engagement with the fleshly and emancipationist materialism of Claude-Henri de Saint-Simon. In the "Zeitgedichte" ("Poems of the Times") section, Heine develops a political aesthetic designed to drum up opposition to Prussian authoritarianism without giving way to the "vague and unproductive pathos" (preface to *Atta Troll*) that he detected in the work of his contemporaries. The verse satire *Atta Troll: Ein Sommernachtstraum* (*Atta Troll: A Midsummer Night's Dream*, 1847), like its companion piece *Deutschland: Ein Wintermärchen* (*Germany: A Winter's Tale*, 1844), makes fun of the liberal aspirations and national sentiments of the Vormärz poets. Heine resists their attempts to convert political belief into poetic allegory, a form that he particularly subverts in *Atta Troll*. According to Heine, the freedom to which they aspire is not to be found in the generalized political slogans of the struggle against feudalism, but it can be preserved for the time being in the utopian space of poetry itself. In his later poetry, *Romanzero* (1851) and the posthumous *Gedichte 1853 und 1854* (*Poems, 1853 and 1854*), Heine again reworks traditional forms he had exploited before, but uses the romance and the historical ballad to express the disappointment of radical expectations after 1848, and the apostasy of other writers on the left. In these works, Heine locates himself and his bedridden existence in relation to the disenchantments of modern urban life in Paris, "the world capital of light"; the late poems on the biblical Lazarus theme indicate a searching and critical engagement with religious thought and feeling.

An analysis of religious ideas laid the foundation for Heine's two critical books on German literature and thought. *Die Romantische Schule* and *Zur Geschichte der Religion und Philosophie in Deutschland* (*On the History of Religion and Philosophy in Germany*, 1835) constitute a progressive account of the state of German intellectual life that responds to Madame Anne-Louise-Germaine de Staël's *De l'Allemagne* (*On Germany*, 1810). Heine identifies in Christianity (and Judaism) the oppressive principle of "spiritualism," which, in elevating the soul, condemns the flesh; against this principle, he sets the Greek "sensualism" that vindicates the full and physical rights of humanity. According to Heine, German thought has progressed through the religious and philosophical revolutions of the Reformation and idealism; what must now complete the development is the social and political revolution. In literary terms, the two principles are realized in Romanticism, with its allegorical view of reality, and, by contrast, in the Classical ideal of immediate and fully realized individuality, which Heine also identifies with the experience of modernity. Its heroes are Martin Luther, who liberated thought; Gotthold Ephraim Lessing, who promoted the Enlightenment critique of religion; and Johann Heinrich Voss, who polemicized against the wave of Romantic conversions to Roman Catholicism.

Heine was determined to mediate between German thought and French social action, and his Paris journalism, in *Französische Zustände* (*French Affairs*, 1832) and *Französische Maler* (*French Painters*, 1833), reported on cultural and political developments in France. Like almost all of Heine's writing, his accounts of French and German culture and politics encountered the restrictions of censorship. In 1835, a decree of the Bundestagsbeschluss (German Federal Parliament) banned his works along with those of "Das junge Deutschland" (Young Germany), and in Prussia all his writings, past and future, were banned. Heine quickly responded to this situation by developing techniques of self-censorship and an indirect discourse that invites the reader to recognize an "esoteric" meaning in the most harmless details. In *Die Harzreise* (*The Harz Journey*, 1826), for example, the narrow "philistine" world of the German bourgeoisie is contrasted with a true freedom found in nature, which politicizes the Romantic cliché. Subsequent *Reisebilder* are more explicit in their celebration of Napoleon as the representative of revolutionary politics, in *Ideen: Das Buch Le Grand* (*Ideas: The Book of Le Grand*, 1827) or in the polemics of Heine's response to August Graf von Platen's anti-Semitic attack on his work, or in *Die Bäder von Lucca* (*The Baths at Lucca*, 1830). In the latter, Heine's vicious remarks about Platen's homosexuality are designed as a broader attack on Bavarian aristocracy and clericalism. In later journalism on the culture and politics of Paris, collected as *Lutezia* (1854), as in his earlier writings on Berlin, London, and Paris, Heine generates a complex web of allusion, inviting his readers to observe successive attempts to give allegorical meaning to the cultural life of the city, and to read these signs of the times for themselves.

The memoir *Ludwig Börne: Eine Denkschrift* (*Ludwig Börne: Portrait of a Revolutionist*, 1840) returns to the contrasts of the spiritual and the sensual (under the guise of the Nazarenic and Hellenic). Shortly after the death of the radical journalist Ludwig Börne in 1837, Heine responded with extraordinary virtuosity to the exiled republican's criticism that he was not a true patriot and that mere talent overwhelmed any moral character in his work. Within the range of Heine's prose, from his largely unsuccessful attempts at fiction such as *Der Rabbi von Bacherach* (1826–40) through the *Reisebilder*, to his critical essays and journalism, the Börne book draws together themes of exile and marginalization, while its structure and rhetoric brilliantly transcend the limitations of what passed for liberal politics in the Vormärz.

The many settings by Robert Schumann and Johannes Brahms, among others, of poems from the "Lyrisches Intermezzo" ("Lyric Intermezzo") and "Heimkehr" ("The Homecoming") sections of *Buch der Lieder* have sustained Heine's reception. Since the 1960s, however, it has been the later poetry, and particularly *Romanzero*, that has held critical attention. This collection and the later and posthumous poems reveal remarkable affinities with the work of younger contemporaries such as Baudelaire. As the huge editorial efforts of the Düsseldorf edition are assimilated, Heine's significance in relation to the politics of modern urban experience in Paris and his profound exploration of the relations between Judaism and modernity have both been underlined. Heine wanted to be thought of as the "first man of the [nineteenth] century," and he cheerfully modified the date of his birth (to December 31, 1799) to accommodate this desire: the extraordinary political and satirical finesse of his writing will continue to guarantee his central position as the first truly *modern* author writing in the German language.

ANTHONY PHELAN

Biography

Born in Düsseldorf, probably December 13, 1797. Apprenticed to a banking house and to a grocery dealer, Frankfurt, 1815. Worked in his uncle's bank, Hamburg, 1816. Ran a textile business, 1818–19. Studied law, University of Bonn, 1819–20, University of Berlin, 1821–24, and University of Göttingen, 1820–21 and 1824–25. Doctor of law, University of Göttingen, 1825. Worked as a writer in Lüneberg and Hamburg, 1825–27. Coeditor, *Neue Allgemeine Politische Annalen*, Munich, 1827–28. In Italy, 1828; in Hamburg and Berlin, 1829–31; in Paris from 1831. Correspondent for *Augsburg Allgemeine Zeitung*. Died February 17, 1856.

Selected Works

Collections
Briefe. Edited by Friedrich Hirth. 6 vols., 1950–51.
Historisch-kritische Gesamtausgabe der Werke. Edited by Manfred Windfuhr. 16 vols., 1973–97.
Selected Works. Translated by Helen M. Mustard and Max Knight, 1973.
The Complete Poems of Heinrich Heine. Edited and translated by Hal Draper. 1982.
Selected Prose. Edited and translated by Ritchie Robertson. 1993.

Poetry
Buch der Lieder, 1827; rev. ed., 1844. Translated as *Book of Songs* by J. E. Wallis. 1856.

Neue Gedichte, 1844; rev. ed., 1851. Translated as *New Poems* by Margaret Armour. 1910.
Deutschland: Ein Wintermärchen, 1844. Translated as *Germany: A Winter's Tale*. In *The Complete Poems of Heinrich Heine*. Edited and translated by Hal Draper. 1982.
Atta Troll: Ein Sommernachtstraum, 1847. Translated as *Atta Troll: A Midsummer Night's Dream* by Thomas Selby Egan, in *Atta Troll and Other Poems*, 1876.
Romanzero, 1851. Translated as *Romancero* by Margaret Armour. 1905.
Gedichte 1853 und 1854. 1854.

Other
Reisebilder (includes *Die Harzreise; Ideen: Das Buch Le Grand; Die Bäder von Lucca*). 4 vols., 1826–31. Translated as *Pictures of Travel* by Charles Godfrey Leland. 1855.
Französische Zustände, 1832. Translated as *French Affairs*, 1889.
Französische Maler, 1833. Translated as *French Painters*, 1833.
Zur Geschichte der neueren schönen Literatur in Deutschland, 1833. Translated as *The Romantic School* by S. L. Fleishman. 1882.
Zur Geschichte der Religion und Philosophie in Deutschland, 1835. Translated as *On the History of Religion and Philosophy in Germany*, 1835.
Ludwig Börne: Eine Denkschrift, 1840. Translated as *Ludwig Börne: Portrait of a Revolutionist* by T. S. Egan. 1881.
Geständnisse, 1854. Translated as *Confessions*, 1854.
Lutezia, 1854.

Bibliography

Altenhofer, Norbert. *Die Verlorene Augensprache: Über Heinrich Heine*. Edited by Volker Bohn. Frankfurt: Insel, 1993.
Bayerdörfer, Hans-Peter. "Politische Ballade: Zu den 'Historien' in Heines Romanzero," *Deutsche Vierteljahrsschrift* 46 (1972).
Höhn, Gerhard. *Heine-Handbuch: Zeit, Person, Werk*. Stuttgart: Metzler, 1987.
Reeves, Nigel. *Heinrich Heine: Poetry and Politics*. London: Oxford University Press, Rev. ed., 1997.
Robertson, Ritchie. *Heine*. London: Halban/New York: Grove Press, 1988.
Rose, William. *The Early Love Poetry of Heinrich Heine: An Inquiry into Poetic Inspiration*. Oxford: Clarendon Press, 1962.
Sammons, Jeffrey L. *Heinrich Heine: The Elusive Poet*. New Haven, Conn.: Yale University Press, 1969.
Sammons, Jeffrey L. *Heinrich Heine: A Modern Biography*. Princeton, N.J.: Princeton University Press, 1979.

HEINRICH VON OFTERDINGEN 1802

Novel by Novalis

Novalis began this fragmentary novel, a key work in German Romanticism, in November 1799. Part 1, "Die Erwartung" ("Expectation"), was finished in early April 1800; Part 2, "Die Erfüllung" ("Fulfillment"), remained unfinished. As sketched out in *Berliner Papiere*, it was to contain seven chapters, of which only a few introductory pages of the first chapter were completed before his death. His friend Ludwig Tieck produced a slightly enlarged version of Novalis's outline.

Novalis conceived the theme for his novel in response to Johann Wolfgang von Goethe's *Wilhelm Meister*, a bildungsroman that he admired both for its variety and profound under-

standing of human nature, but ultimately rejected as the product of a rationalism that destroyed the essentially Romantic qualities of the poetic and the miraculous, sacrificing art to commerce. Novalis's *Ofterdingen* can, therefore, be regarded as an "anti-*Meister*" novel while still retaining most of the features of the bildungsroman, a genre that dominated nineteenth- and early twentieth-century German literature. Whereas for Goethe, the protagonist engaged in art as a prelude to a bourgeois career, thereby moving from the aesthetic to the ethical, in accordance with Weimar classicism, Novalis portrays his hero as the perfect poet. The "original" Afterdingen was a mythical figure who featured with medieval Germany's most famous poets in the *Sänger-krieg* (poetry contest) at Wartburg Castle in about 1205.

The narrative structure of the novel employs different styles and registers. The actual story is told in simple, descriptive language, but is interspersed with several digressive episodes that lend the novel its encyclopedic nature. Among these are dreams: prophetic by nature, they are a "divine gift on our pilgrimage to the holy grave." Heinrich's first dream thus foretells the plot of part 1, while the second dream anticipates Mathilde's death and entry into the golden land of paradise, where he will join her and enjoy eternal life in perfect harmony with animals, plants, and inorganic nature. The interspersed poems either complete passages of high poetic intensity, as at the conclusion of the Atlantis story, or symbolize some festive climax, as in the celebrations at Augsburg. Of a more philosophical nature, the essays are often concerned with poetry or the secrets of life; some have an allegorical function, as in the passage in which the mining of gold is compared to a mystical, religious redemption, the "incarcerated metal" liberated from the worthless rubble.

The Romantic dimension of *Ofterdingen* becomes apparent in its profoundly reflective nature, in the manner in which it intensifies external, sensuous experiences, reflecting Novalis's own observation that while "we dream of journeys into the universe," that universe is actually within us; "The depths of our spirit are unknown to us.—The secret path leads into the interior. Eternity and its worlds, the past and the future, are within us or nowhere. The external world is the shadow world, it casts its shadow into the world of light . . ." This early fragment unlocks the essence of the novel. Traveling is a vital means of gaining experience in every *Bildungsroman*, but in *Ofterdingen* the journey becomes a quest for something magical that cannot be attained in this world. It will, ultimately, lead to reconciliation between the finite and infinity and transform history into *Heilsgeschichte*, as the return to a golden age. The novel must be read at different levels, each new level providing further depth and philosophical significance. Starting in the puritanical north, the physical journey leads from Eisenach and the Wartburg, venue of the medieval singing contest but also Luther's stronghold, down to Augsburg in the sensuous, Catholic south, with the intention of returning north. The poetic journey, however, becomes a process of self-discovery, a kind of cosmic understanding, as revealed in chapter 5, where a concealed door opens into a soaring cathedral with vistas into past and future, an experience soon after intensified as personal insight into the Book of Life. Like all bildungsromanes, *Ofterdingen* centers on key human experiences such as journey, meeting of strangers, experience of art and love, and *Bildungsgespräch* (learned discourse). In *Ofterdingen*, however, these experiences are of a more profound, cosmological nature. The journey itself proceeds in nine stages, each comprising one chapter. Several of these go beyond space and time, however, either in the hero's unconscious dreams, or as digressions into fairy tales, explorations of the inorganic world, or philosophical discourses on poetry, philosophy, and life. Love and poetry are the two forces that inspire all action, their anticipated reconciliation will finally overcome all the obstacles of our finite world and will project the novel into the world of *Astralis* where, as the opening poem of part 2 suggests, Heinrich and Mathilde will be united in celestial bliss, in a life after death. It is in the nature of such a journey that the novel does not de-velop by linear progression, but advances in a hyperbolic motion, described by Friedrich von Schlegel as "progressive Universalpoesie."

Heinrich's journey begins in the company of merchants who acquaint him with the nature of poetry. This is done in two steps, first through the Arion allegory, taken from the Orpheus myth, and then intensified in the fairy tale of Atlantis. Here, as in most other instances, the author employs a dialectic argument: whereas Arion reconciles man and beast through poetry, the Atlantis story unites the poet with the scientist, the hermit in his solitude with the king in the splendor of his court. Chapters 4 and 5 intensify this complexity by harmonizing the oriental allure of Islam with the martial fervor of Christian crusaders and by unifying the cosmic knowledge of the geologist-miner (who himself brings together the organic and the inorganic) with Count Hohenzollern, whose pilgrimage reconciled history with religion. Chapter 6 features the arrival at Augsburg, thereby terminating the physical journey. Heinrich has gained insight into the "world in its vast and varied dimensions" and reached the maturity necessary for his meeting with the poet Klingsohr. This meeting is prefaced by a typology of man, distinguishing between two life forms, the *vita activa* and the *vita contemplativa*. The latter, in typically Romantic spirit, represents the life of the poet, leading back to the process of internalization. The name Klingsohr is a reference to the Wartburg poetry contest, where the magician Klingsohr assisted Afterdingen during the competition. More significant, however, are certain similarities between Klingsohr and Goethe. Goethe's physiognomy, his interest in colors, and his concept of poetry are transposed onto Klingsohr. Klingsohr/Goethe is thus described as the greatest living poet, who will be surpassed by Heinrich/Novalis through his truly cosmic and universal poetry.

In accordance with Novalis's view that the hero "is the organ of the poet in the novel," in whose "vicinity . . . poetry will erupt spontaneously," Heinrich is depicted as a passive hero, a kind of catalyst who can transform the world from a prosaic into an ennobled, poetic state. Chapters 6 through 9 are devoted to poetry and to Heinrich's manifestation as a poet; they begin with the festivities celebrating the bacchanalian qualities of wine and the youthful, loving charm of girls. Poetry and love become reconciled, symbolically presented in the figures of Klingsohr and his daughter Mathilde, who appeared to Heinrich in his first dream as the magical blue flower. These celebrations will "open his dumb lips," bestowing on him poetic and prophetic gifts. Allusions to the Pentecostal experience and the sun turned into darkness anticipate Heinrich's vocation as a Romantic poet. They also serve as prelude to Klingsohr's fairy tale and to part 2 of the novel, where, as foretold in Heinrich's second dream, Mathilde's death and transportation into the world of Astralis indicate that the true poet will triumph over death and—as *Mittler* (mediator)—lead us to eternal life. Concluding part 1, Klingsohr's fairy tale provides an allegorical illustration of this poetic and eternal life. It is modeled on Goethe's *Märchen*, but employs motifs from many other literary sources. Essentially a story of redemption, it is comparable, albeit on a much higher level, to the *Sleeping Beauty* pattern in that it celebrates the liberation of forces confined within a crystal palace, under the spell of the scribe's rational tyranny, threatened by death but eventually freed by the symbiosis of poetry and love. Ranging "from heaven, through the world, right down to hell," its cosmic nature is comparable to Goethe's *Faust*.

HANS-JOACHIM HAHN

Work

Heinrich von Ofterdingen. In *Schriften. Die Werke Friedrich von Hardenbergs. Nach den Handschriften ergänzte, erweiterte und verbesserte Auflage*. Edited by Paul Kluckhohn and Richard Samuel. Vol. 1, *Das dichterische Werk*. 3d ed., 1977. Translated as *Henry von Ofterdingen: A Novel* by Pamela Hilty, 1964.

Bibliography

Barrack, Charles M. "Conscience in *Heinrich von Ofterdingen*: Novalis' Metaphysic of the Poet," *Germanic Review* 46 (1971): 257–84.

Hauer, Berhard E. "Die Todesthematik in *Wilhelm Meisters Lehrjahre* und *Heinrich von Ofterdingen*," *Euphorion* 79 (1985): 182–206.

Mähl, Hans-Joachim. "Friedrich von Hardenberg (Novalis)." In *Deutsche Dichter der Romantik. Ihr Leben und Werk*. Edited by Benno von Wiese. 2d ed. Berlin: Schmidt Verlag, 1983.

Pikulik, Lothar. *Frühromantik, Epoche—Werk—Wirkung*. Munich: Beck, 1992.

Ritzenhoff, Ursula, ed. *Erläuterungen und Dokumente. Novalis (Friedrich von Hardenberg) Heinrich von Ofterdingen*. Stuttgart: Reclam, 1988.

Stadler, Ulrich. "Novalis: *Heinrich von Ofterdingen* (1802)." In *Romane und Erzählungen der Deutschen Romantik. Neue Interpretationen*. Edited by Paul Michael Lützeler. Stuttgart: Reclam, 1981.

Uerlings, Herbert. *Friedrich von Hardenberg, Genannt Novalis. Werk und Forschung*. Stuttgart: Metzler, 1991.

White, John J. "Novalis' *Heinrich von Ofterdingen* and the Aesthetics of 'Offenbarung'," *Publications of the English Goethe Society* 52 (1983): 90–119.

HEMANS, FELICIA 1793–1835

English poet and dramatist

Felicia Hemans was the most widely read female poet in the nineteenth-century English-speaking world. The fact that her work promoted a moderate liberalism shared by the broadly middle-class reading public encouraged her popularity. Her intellectual and social background in the English provincial and commercial Enlightenment, combined with a cosmopolitan European cultural perspective derived from her mother, enabled her to fashion a distinctive poetic voice while still an adolescent. She relentlessly refashioned that voice over a literary career of three decades that ran from the 1810s to the 1830s, addressing the prolonged global crisis of the Napoleonic Wars and their aftermath of conservative restoration and liberal revolt. After her death, she continued to appeal to a reading public living through the formation of modern liberal states in Britain, Europe, and beyond.

Hemans began her career conventionally enough. Her first volume, *Poems* (1808), was published by subscription and most of the verse was domestic, belletristic, and personal, as would be expected at that time from a young female writer. The book was dedicated to the Prince of Wales, however (at that time the associate of reformist Whigs), and among the subscribers were members of the English Midlands Enlightenment (leading figures of commercial, cultural, and political reform in Britain). Her second volume, *England and Spain; or Valour and Patriotism* (1808), turned to decidedly more public issues and celebrates the Iberian Peninsular war against Napoleon Bonaparte's armies in Spain, where two of her brothers served in the British army. The poem takes up themes of late eighteenth-century public verse written by women, deploring the necessity for war, defending the national and imperial cause, and anticipating the advent of peace and prosperity. *The Domestic Affections, and Other Poems* (1812) continues this convergence of acceptably "feminine" domestic and humanitarian themes with public issues that would otherwise be considered unfeminine.

After her marriage in 1812, Hemans turned to even more ambitious subjects and forms, addressing the post-Napoleonic situation of Britain and Europe in long historical-reflective poems, again linking acceptably feminine matter with great and pressing public questions. "The Restoration of the Works of Art to Italy" (1816) and "Modern Greece: A Poem" (1817) deal, respectively, with the return of Italian artworks looted by Napoleon and Britain's acquisition of the ancient Greek Parthenon marbles. The poems do so in the light of two thousand years of European cultural history, culminating in the emergence of Britain as the global superpower.

The arts were a conventionally acceptable subject for a woman writer, but Hemans takes the theme into a domain normally considered unfeminine: contemporary politics. Her ambition was signaled by a new publisher, John Murray, who had put out the works of Lord Byron and other prominent Romantic writers. She continued to follow public events in Britain, Europe, and elsewhere with intense interest, supporting moderate reform and liberal constitutionalism. She also continued to expand on post-Napoleonic themes of history as a spectacle of male-dominated ambition, conflict, and mass death, implying that feminization of history would create a better future. Finally, she continued to explore various poetic forms, including the historical narrative verse in "Tales, and Historic Scenes" (1819); the reflective verse essay in "The Sceptic" (1820) and "Dartmoor" (1821); verse drama in *The Siege of Valencia* (1823) and *The Vespers of Palermo* (1823); and translations and imitations of folk poetry as the new national voice of the people in *Translations from Camoens, and Other Poets* (1818) and *A Selection of Welsh Melodies* (1822).

By now she was an established poet, though critics persistently read her as a distinctly "feminine" poet and cited this as both her strength and her limitation. Hemans did play to this reading, both to pursue feminization of the public, political sphere and to maximize her earnings. She followed with fascination the fate of liberal revolts in Spain and Latin America and the Greek War of Independence from Turkey. She eagerly took up German Romantic literature in its struggle to form nation-states in the German-speaking lands and as an example to other peoples. She also began contributing poetry to the liberal *New Monthly Magazine* (1821–36). Hemans's moderate liberal ideology also made her poetry increasingly popular in the United States. In 1825 she published "The Forest Sanctuary," which she considered her best work. It is a retrospective poetic monologue by a sixteenth-century Spanish conquistador and Roman Catholic who became Protestant and sought exile in the American wilderness. The poem brings together Hemans's interest in the historical clash of empires and belief systems, and the narrator represents, as a figure of the past, a feminized, liberal citizen for the future.

Several factors then led Hemans to become more personal in her poetry, including her growing celebrity as a specifically feminine poet, her concern over increasing social conflict in Britain, and personal family losses. Throughout her career she addressed the topic of death, treating it paradoxically as a source of personal meaning in the aftermath of the Revolutionary and Napoleonic era of apparently meaningless mass death. She also moved to another publisher, William Blackwood, proprietor of the conservative though widely read (and high-paying) *Blackwood's Magazine*, where she now published most of her lyrics. She published *Records of Woman: With Other Poems* (1828), shorter poems in the fashionable (and also high-paying) literary annuals, or gift books, and volumes collecting her personal lyrics: *Songs of the Affections* (1830) and *Scenes and Hymns of Life, with Other Religious Poems* (1834). Her *Poetical Remains* was published posthumously in 1836. In this last phase of her literary career she presented female characters from history or fiction heroically resisting the destructiveness of masculine history, and increasingly she wrote in her own voice, presenting herself as an exemplary liberal subject of the future.

Hemans's literary reputation declined after her death, especially with male critics, while women writers continued to respect her as a pioneer and the middle class reading public continued to buy her poems in successive editions, until the early twentieth century and the demise of Victorian liberalism. At that point she ceased to be read seriously, and only recently, with feminist criticism and scholarship, has she begun to reemerge from obscurity.

GARY KELLY

Biography

Born Felicia Dorothea Browne in Liverpool, September 25, 1793, second daughter and fourth child of six, to a merchant father and a mother of Italian and Austrian extraction. Father's business failed and family moved to North Wales. Educated at home. Married Captain Alfred Hemans, veteran of Iberian Peninsular war, in 1812, and bore five sons. Her husband left for Italy in 1818 and did not return. Supported herself and her family by her literary earnings. Died in Dublin on May 16, 1835.

Selected Works

Collection
The Works of Mrs. Hemans. 7 vols., 1841.

Poetry
Poems. 1808.
England and Spain; or Valour and Patriotism. 1808.
The Domestic Affections, and Other Poems. 1812.
The Restoration of the Works of Art to Italy: A Poem. 1816.
Modern Greece: A Poem. 1817.
Translations from Camoens, and Other Poets, with Original Poetry. 1818.
Tales, and Historic Scenes, in Verse. 1819.
The Sceptic; A Poem. 1820.
Stanzas to the Memory of the Late King. 1820.
Wallace's Invocation to Bruce. 1820.
Dartmoor; A Poem. 1821.
A Selection of Welsh Melodies, with Symphonies and Accompaniments By John Parry, and Characteristic Words By Mrs. Hemans. 1822.
The Siege of Valencia: A Dramatic Poem; The Last Constantine: with Other Poems. 1823.
The Vespers of Palermo: A Tragedy, in Five Acts. 1823.
The Forest Sanctuary: and Other Poems. 1825.
Hymns for Childhood. 1827.
Records of Woman: with Other Poems. 1828.
Songs of the Affections, with Other Poems. 1830.
Hymns on the Works of Nature, for the Use of Children. 1833.
National Lyrics, and Songs for Music. 1834.
Scenes and Hymns of Life, with Other Religious Poems. 1834.
Songs of the Affections. 1835.
Poetical Remains of the Late Mrs. Hemans. 1836.

Bibliography

Clarke, Norma. *Ambitious Heights: Writing, Friendship, Love—The Jewsbury Sisters, Felicia Hemans, and Jane Welsh Carlyle.* London: Routledge, 1990.

Chorley, Henry F. *Memorials of Mrs. Hemans with Illustrations of Her Literary Character from Her Private Correspondence.* 2d ed. 2 vols. London: Saunders and Otley, 1837.

Feldman, Paula R. "The Poet and the Profits: Felicia Hemans and the Literary Marketplace," *Keats-Shelley Journal* 46 (1997): 148–76.

Feldman, Paula R., and Theresa M. Kelley, eds. *Romantic Women Writers: Voices and Countervoices.* Hanover, N.H.: University Press of New England, 1995.

Hughes, Harriet Mary Browne. "Memoir of the Life and Writings of Mrs. Hemans." In *The Works of Mrs Hemans.* 7 vols. Edinburgh and London: William Blackwood and Sons, 1841.

Linkin, Harriet Kramer, and Stephen C. Behrendt, eds. *Romanticism and Women Poets: Opening the Doors of Reception.* Lexington: University Press of Kentucky, 1999.

McGann, Jerome. *The Poetics of Sensibility: A Revolution in Literary Style.* Oxford: Clarendon Press, 1996.

Mellor, Anne K. *Romanticism and Gender.* New York: Routledge, 1993.

Ross, Marlon. *The Contours of Masculine Desire: Romanticism and the Rise of Women's Poetry.* Oxford: Oxford University Press, 1989.

Trinder, Peter. *Mrs. Hemans.* Cardiff: University of Wales Press, 1984.

Wilson, Carol Shiner, and Joel Hafner, eds. *Re-Visioning Romanticism: British Women Writers, 1776–1837.* Philadelphia: University of Pennsylvania Press, 1994.

HERCULANO, ALEXANDRE 1810-1877

Portuguese poet, novelist, historian, and critic

Alexandre Herculano was, along with João Baptista de Almeida Garrett, one of the founding figures of Portuguese Romanticism, one of its emblems, and indeed its moral consciousness embodied in one man. This was a role that he performed throughout his life, maintaining a coherent attitude in political, cultural, and literary life that made him shun public honors but also brought him wide recognition as a moral leader through a large part of the nineteenth century.

Herculano's ideology must be considered fundamental in the sense that it determined his actions, whether the active part he took fighting for the liberals in the civil war in his early twenties; his unceasing defense of liberty as the driving force of society, connecting it with qualities such as moral vitality and with historical periods such as the Middle Ages; the profound religious sentiment he maintained, even while strenuously battling against the conservative forces of a reactionary clergy; or the way his narrative plots reflect his ideological stance, with liberty embodied in a striving and often doomed hero.

He began his literary career as a contributor to a periodical, *Repositório Literário*, right after the victory of liberalism in Portugal (1834), while he held a post at the public library of Porto. He published several articles on critical, theoretical, and aesthetic issues, and demonstrated a solid literary knowledge deriving mainly from English and German sources. His two first books, however, were little engaged with the main trends he pursued afterward: *A Voz do Profeta* (1836), a kind of prophetic lament in the wake of Felicité de Lamennais's *Paroles d'un Croyant*, presenting a poetic voice that, expressing itself in a highly literary prose, really must be considered as a metonym for the romantic poet, charged with a transcendental though social mission in an immanent universe, as Percy Bysshe Shelley intended; and *A Harpa do Crente* (1838), his only book of lyrical poetry, later expanded (1850) under the title *Poesias*. In it we find a poetic diction quite apart from the main current of the Portuguese lyrical tradition, closely related to conceptual thought, echoing Luiz Vaz de Camões and prefiguring such very different poets as the romantic Antero Tarquínio de Quental and the modernist Fernando Pessoa. The choice of long lines, poetically and rhetorically charged, serves an aesthetic project of expression whose basic characteristics center around religious sentiment manifested through contemplation and meditation upon a natural scene; social sentiment, directly related to a consciousness of (literal and symbolic) exile, a moral solitude that distances the poet from corruption and compromises; and the moral and ethical integrity he displays, and which becomes his most distinctive feature.

Herculano then moved into the realm of narrative. First, through his prose fiction, between 1839 and 1844 he published in a periodical a series of short stories that appeared in 1851 under the title *Lendas e Narrativas*. Mainly constituted by short stories of historical inspiration, this series must be considered the seed from which the historical novel sprang, producing in the subsequent decades a great number of titles. The majority of these short stories must also be related to the historical work in which Herculano was engaged around the same period (this is especially true for texts such as "A Dama Pé-de-Cabra," "Arras por foro de Espanha," and "A Abóbada"), though we also find more contemporary examples that should be mentioned for their presentation of new (and not fully explored) characteristics: "De Jersey a Granville," an episode connected to Herculano's experience of exile, and "O Pároco de Aldeia," a story set in a country village where the practical and humorous rector functions as a symbolic and ritualistic presence.

All the other short stories combine the characteristics Herculano will express, at greater length, in his historical novels, also at least partly prepublished as "feuilletons" in different periodicals: *Eurico, o Presbítero* (1844), *O Monge de Cister* (1848), and *O Bobo* (1878, posthumous). All of them follow the example set mainly by Walter Scott, stressing moments of social transition where crisis suddenly becomes unavoidable and fostering the appearance of "real individuals." One should also note the profound dynamism that such a characterization brings forth. In *Eurico*, the temporal setting is the beginning of the eighth century, during the invasion of the Iberian Peninsula by the Arabs, which put an end to the Visigothic monarchy; in *O Monge* we are barely at the beginning of the second dynasty of the Portuguese monarchy, after the crisis of 1383–85; institutions are still finding a way to establish themselves in a new society, which symbolically represents the end of the vital Middle Ages and the beginning of the new centralized and authoritarian rule of modern times; and in *O Bobo* it is truly the birth of a nation that is portrayed in the middle of the twelfth century, through the political and symbolic rivalry between mother and son, from which Portugal will be born as an independent country—but in this novel one should also stress the importance of the figure who gives the novel its title: the court jester, in front of whose eyes the political and individual episodes unfold.

Such transitional moments, typically grounded in different periods of the Middle Ages, underscore the importance of national symbolism, converging into a theory of the novel which endows it with a distinctive ethical as well as aesthetical resonance. Against this historical setting, and playing an active role in it through the interweaving of plot connections, the individual story unfolds, centered around a normally forbidden or impossible love. The relationship between both plots (personal and historical) is, of course, the hero, fighting for liberty and to avenge different forms of betrayal—both the real symbol of national identity and, at the same time, the one who distinguishes himself from the crowd.

The historical works form another part of Herculano's literary career that cannot be overlooked, both because of their intrinsic value and because they represent the beginning of modern historiography in Portugal. Throughout his life Herculano fostered his interest in history, especially of the Middle Ages. Besides having had a post as second librarian in the public library of Porto, he was subsequently appointed director of the National Archives; in both posts he took active steps to prevent the disappearance of historical documents. He also collected historical materials from all over the country, later published under the title *Portugaliae Monumenta Historica*; and he wrote several books on Portuguese history: *Cartas sobre a História de Portugal* (1842), conceived on Augustin Thierry's model, in which he lays the ground for a critical historiography; *História de Portugal* (4 vols., 1846–53); and several other titles, such as *Da Origem e Estabelecimento da Inquisi-*

ção em Portugal (3 vols., 1854–59) (*History of the Origin and Establishment of the Inquisition in Portugal*) and *A Reacção Ultramontana em Portugal* (1857). In all his historical work he continuously reaffirms his liberal thought, stressing the communitarian and antiabsolutist roots of medieval society and institutions, but also making him a declared enemy of all forms of reactionism in the political and religious fields. This standpoint accounts for the different polemics in which he became involved—and from which he never flinched—at different points in his lifetime. In 1850, for example, because of his dismissal of mythical narratives considered until then as historical documents, about the divine origin of Portuguese monarchy; and in 1865, in his proposal for civil marriage alongside religious marriage. With regards to his historical oeuvre, Herculano's major work is *História de Portugal*, where for the first time a history of the institutions, and not only of political facts and individuals, is achieved.

HELENA BUESCU

Biography

Born Alexandre Herculano de Carvalho e Araújo in Lisbon, March 28, 1810. Studied humanities and literature; forced into exile in England and France after unsuccessful rebellion against Dom Miguel in Portugal, 1831. Returned to Portugal with army of victorious Liberal leader, Dom Pedro, 1832. Worked at public library, Porto; contributed to the periodical *Repositório Literário*, from 1834. Librarian at the Royal Library of Ajuda, 1839. Elected to the *cortes* (parliament), 1840. Withdrew from political life after establishment of the Costa Cabral regime, 1841. Participated in the regeneration movement and overthrow of the Cabral government, 1851. Engaged in political journalism, 1850s; participated in the writing of the first Portuguese Civil Code. Wrote *Da Origem e Estabelecimento da Inquisição em Portugal* (*Origin and Establishment of the Inquisition in Portugal* 1854–59). Withdrew to his farm in Vale de Lobos, near Santarém, 1856. Died in Santarém, September 13, 1877.

Selected Works

Poetry
Poesias. 1850.

Fiction
Eurico, o Presbítero. 1844.
O Monge de Cister. 1848.
Lendas e Narrativas. 1851.
O Bobo. 1878; posthumous.

Translation
History of the Origin and Establishment of the Inquisition in Portugal. Translated by John C. Branner. Stanford, Cal.: Stanford University Press, 1926.

Bibliography

Alexandre Herculano à Luz do Nosso Tempo. Lisboa: Academia Portuguesa de História, 1977.
Bernstein, Harry. *Alexandre Herculano (1810–1877), Portugal's Prime Historian and Historical Novelist*. Paris: Fundação Calouste Gulbenkian, 1983.
Buescu, Ana Isabel. *O Milagre de Ourique e a História de Portugal de Alexandre Herculano—Uma Polémica Oitocentista*. Lisbon: INIC, 1980.
França, José-Augusto. "Herculano ou a Consciência no Exílio." In *O Romantismo em Portugal*. vol. 2. Lisbon: Livros Horizonte, 1974.
Moser, Gerd. *Les Romantiques Portugais et l'Allemagne*. Paris: Jouve, 1939.
———. *A Mocidade de Herculano*. 2 vols. Lisbon: Bertrand, 1978.
Nemésio, Vitorino. *Relações Francesas do Romantismo Português*. Coimbra: 1936.
Pires, António Machado. "A Expressão do Sagrado na *Harpa do Crente* de Herculano." In *Estética do Romantismo em Portugal*. Lisbon: Grémio Literário, 1974.
Saraiva, António José. *Herculano e o Liberalismo em Portugal*. Lisbon: Bertrand, 1977.

HERDER, JOHANN GOTTFRIED 1744–1803

German critic, theologian, and philosopher

While Johann Gottfried Herder reacted against the rationalism, cosmopolitanism and universalism that were central facets of the thought of the Enlightenment, he was essentially an eclectic thinker whose contribution to the history of thought was a unique synthesis of ideas from diverse sources. Although Herder rejected the notion, central to eighteenth-century neo-Classicism, of the art and literature of antiquity as a benchmark against which to evaluate that of other periods and as an ideal to be imitated, it was Johann Joachim Winckelmann's insight that "Greek art was the product of the physical and cultural environment of Greece" on which Herder's view of history, like that of Charles-Louis Montesquieu before him, was premised. Similarly, while Herder's conception of religion as individual intuition of "the infinite being" who exists "everywhere in the world, and everywhere unmeasured, whole and indivisible," represented a departure from his pietist upbringing and a reaction against the abstract conception of God espoused by the deists, it

reflected his Spinozist sympathies. In his avowal of direct sensory experience as vital, Herder drew on the empiricism of thinkers like John Locke and Anthony Ashley Cooper, third Earl of Shaftesbury; and his celebration of primitive cultures as superior to their modern counterparts was not merely a product of his friendship with Johann Georg Hamann, but of the profound influence of Jean-Jacques Rousseau's thought on his own.

As a pastor who held posts in the Lutheran Church at Riga (1767–69), Bückeburg (1771–76), and Weimar (1776–1803), Herder retained faith in aspects of orthodox religion throughout his life. This is illustrated by his defense of Genesis in the *Älteste Urkunde des Menschengeschlechts* (*Oldest Document of the Human Race*, 1774–76) as a valid account of the story of the Creation based on the early Hebrews' sensory experience of nature. This was informed by his conception of religious experience as sentient and emotive and of the workings of nature as a manifestation of God's benevolence—aspects of his thought that were also fundamental to pietism. That in the same text Herder endorsed the evolutionary theories—developed in the wake of the scientific discoveries of Galileo and Isaac Newton—as a modern expression of religious consciousness no less valid than Genesis lent his conception of religion a secular and rational dimension that was reminiscent of Deism. However the central tenet of his religious thought—that spiritual experience is vital, immediate experience of the world "built on the witness of the senses and not merely of the higher mental powers; upon faith, that embraces all powers"—was not merely a reaction against the theological dogma of the church, but against the secularity and rationality of the Enlightenment. The pantheistic weltanschauung voiced by Herder, which culminated in the open declaration of his Spinozist sympathies in the 1780s, was fundamental to the attempt, shared by thinkers of the *Sturm und Drang* movement, to recover a spiritual dimension to human experience, and fundamental to the different facets of Herder's thought.

Herder's pantheism underpinned his organic conception of nationhood as that which evolves from the physical geography and "climate" of a country. He maintained that the culture and sense of collective consciousness of any people is shaped by their environment, and that its development is fostered by the preservation of small communities and localized traditions that inspire in the individual a feeling of belonging to their homeland. He valued most highly domestic and family ties, and the natural bonds that develop among individuals in a small group as the ideal basis for the communal existence of human beings in harmony with nature.

Herder was opposed to the formation of political states presided over by monarchs and emperors who sought, with their absolute power, to instill in their subjects a sense of national identity (with disregard for the sanctity of local traditions) and superiority to other nation-states. Herder accorded equal status to the culture of every nation, as a product of its environment and, while seeking to foster patriotism, he fiercely condemned political nationalism as the origin of war and imperialism. Thus, as Isaiah Berlin notes, "Herder was no nationalist: he supposed that different cultures could and should flourish fruitfully side by side like so many peaceful flowers in the great human garden."

Herder's condemnation of the universalism of French philosophers resulted in the strong anti-French polemic that pervades his writings. He criticized their invocation of the authority of reason as a yardstick with which to evaluate the merits of different cultures, and their promotion of the art and literature of classical antiquity as an ideal to be imitated, which for Herder constituted a betrayal of their own national identity.

Herder also rejected the gradualist view of history, voiced by Bernard le Bovier de Fontenelle and Voltaire among others, as the continual progress toward perfection that was equated with the progress of reason. As an influential exponent of historical relativism, Herder maintained that every epoch must be evaluated on its own terms as a stage in the development of a culture. Herder followed Rousseau, however, in defending the superiority of primitive cultures to their modern counterparts on the grounds that while modern man subjugated his sensory experience to his rational conceptualization of the world, thus alienating himself from nature; primitive man was "the more barbarous, that is, the more alive, the more free, the closer to the senses."

Herder's organic weltanschauung, his historical relativism, and primitivism all informed his aesthetic thought. The corollary

Friedrich Rehberg, *Johann Gottfried Herder*. Reprinted courtesy of AKG.

of his rejection of the art and literature of antiquity as an ideal to be imitated was his defense of that which was a genuine expression of the cultural milieu in which it was created. This was reflected in his enthusiasm for *Volkspoesie* (popular poetry), as "the impression of the nation's heart, a living grammar, the best dictionary and natural history of the people" of all periods, which resulted in the publication of his collection of German Volkspoesie in 1778 and 1789. However, Herder expressed a preference for the language and literature of early societies, as an expression of the unity of man's immediate sensory experience and rational conception of the world, and condemned the "artificial, scientific manner of thinking, speaking, and writing" that evolved in the eighteenth century, and resulted in "poetry about subject-matter that gives us nothing to think about, still less to sense, and even less to imagine."

In conceiving literature and art as an expression of the human spirit, and therefore as the counterpart of nature, the aesthetic appreciation of which facilitates spiritual experience, Herder articulated a central tenet of Romantic aesthetics. Similarly, in emphasizing the necessity for empathy with the zeitgeist in which a work was created as a prerequisite for aesthetic appreciation and understanding, Herder expressed a view fundamental to Romantic hermeneutics, the most influential exponent of which was Friedrich Ernst Daniel Schleiermacher. Indeed in his avowal of pantheism, in his primitivism and historicism, in the nationalism incipient in his writings, as well as in his aesthetic and hermeneutic thought, Herder was essentially a proto-Romantic thinker.

ABIGAIL CHANTLER

Biography

Born in Mohrungen, East Prussia, August 25, 1744. Studied theology at Königsberg University. 1762–64. Taught at the Domschule (cathedral school) in Riga, 1764–67. Ordained, 1767. Minister in Lutheran Church at Riga, 1767–69. Traveled to France, staying in Nantes and Paris, 1769–70. Tutor and traveling companion of Prince of Holstein-Gottorp, 1770–71. Chief pastor, and subsequently superintendent, at Court of Bückeburg, 1771–76. Married Caroline Flachsland, 1773. General superintendent of Lutheran Church at Weimar, 1776–1803. Died December 18, 1803.

Selected Works

Abhandlung über den Ursprung der Sprache, 1771. Translated as *Essay on the Origin of Language* by John H. Moran and Alexander Gode. In *On the Origin of Language*. (Chicago: University of Chicago Press, 1966.

Auszug aus einem Briefwechsel über Ossian und die Lieder alter Völker, 1773. Translated as *Extract from a Correspondence on Ossian and the Songs of Ancient Peoples* by H. B. Nisbet. In *German Aesthetic and Literary Criticism: Winckelmann, Lessing, Hamann, Herder, Schiller, Goethe*. Cambridge: Cambridge University Press, 1985.

"Shakespeare," 1773. Translation "Shakespeare." Translated by H. B. Nisbet. In *German Aesthetic and Literary Criticism: Winckelmann, Lessing, Hamann, Herder, Schiller, Goethe*. Cambridge: Cambridge University Press, 1985.

Ideen zur Philosophie der Geschichte der Menschheit, 1784–91. Translated as *Outlines of a Philosophy of the History of Man* by T. O. Churchill. New York: Bergnar Publishers, 1966.

Gott: Einige Gespräche, 1787. Translated as *God: Some Conversations* by Frederick H, Burkhardt. New York: Veritas Press, 1940.

J. G. Herder on Social and Political Culture. Translated and edited by F. M. Barnard. Cambridge, Cambridge University Press 1969.

Briefe: Gesamtausgabe, 1763–1803. Edited by Karl-Heinz Hahn, Wilhelm Dobbek, and Günter Arnold. 9 vols. Weimar: Bölan. 1977–88.

Werke. Edited by Ulrich Gaier. 10 vols. Frankfort am Main: Deutscher Klassiker Verlag, 1985–2000.

Johann Gottfried Herder: Selected Early Works 1764–1767: Addresses, Essays, and Drafts; Fragments on Recent German Literature. Edited by Ernst A. Menze and Karl Menges. Translated by Ernst A. Menze and Michael Palma. University Park: Pennsylvania State University Press, 1992.

Against Pure Reason: Writings on Religion, Language, and History. Edited and translated by Maria Bunge. (Minneapolis: Fortress Press, 1993.

On World History: An Anthology. Edited by Hans Adler and Ernst A. Menze. Translated by Ernst A. Menze and Michael Palma. New York & London: M. E. Sharpe, 1997.

Bibliography

Barnard, F. M. *Self-Direction and Political Legitimacy: Rousseau and Herder*. Oxford: Clarendon Press, 1988.

Berlin, Isaiah. "Herder and the Enlightenment." In *Aspects of the Eighteenth Century*. Edited by Earl R. Wasserman. Baltimore, Md.: Johns Hopkins University Press, 1965.

———. *Against the Current: Essays in the History of Ideas*. Edited by Henry Hardy. London: Pimlico, 1979.

———. *The Roots of Romanticism*. Edited by Henry Hardy. London: Chatto and Windus, 1999.

———. *Three Critics of the Enlightenment: Vico, Hamann, Herder*. Edited by Henry Hardy. London: Pimlico, 2000.

Bernd, Fischer. *Das Eigene und das Eigentliche: Klopstock, Herder, Fichte, Kleist: Episoden aus der Konstruktionsgeschichte nationaler Intentionalitäten*. Berlin: Schmidt, 1995.

Bollacher, Martin, ed. *Johann Gottfried Herder: Geschichte und Kultur*. Würzburg: Königshausen und Neumann, 1994.

Chamberlain, Timothy J., ed. *Eighteenth Century German Criticism*. New York: Continuum, 1992.

Clark, Robert T. *Herder: His Life and Thought*. Berkeley and Los Angeles: University of California Press, 1955.

Critchfield, Richard, and Wulf Koepke, eds. *Eighteenth-Century German Authors and Their Aesthetic Theories: Literature and the Other Arts*. Columbia, S.C.: Camden House, 1988.

Dietze, Walter. *Johann Gottfried Herder: Abriß seines Lebens und Schaffens*. Berlin: Aufbau, 1983.

Ergang, Robert Reinhold. *Herder and the Foundations of German Nationalism*. New York: Octagon, 1966.

Fasel, Christoph. *Herder und das klassische Weimar: Kultur und Gesellschaft 1789–1803*. New York: Peter Lang, 1988.

Gaier, Ulrich. *Herders Sprachphilosophie und Erkenntniskritik*. Stuttgart: Frommann-Holzboog, 1988.

Gaycken, Hans-Jürgen, ed. *Johann Gottfried Herder und seine zeitgenössischen Kritiker Herder-Kritik in der "Allgemeine Deutschen Bibliothek."* Bern: Peter Lang, 1985.

Gesche, Astrid. *Johann Gottfried Herder: Sprache und die Natur des Menschen*. Würzburg: Königshausen und Neumann, 1993.

Gilles, Alexander. *Herder*. Oxford: Basil Blackwell, 1945.

Günter, Arnold. *Johann Gottfried Herder*. Leipzig: Bibliographisches Institut, 1988.

Haym, Rudolf. *Herder nach seinem Leben und seinen Werken dargestellt*. 2 vols. Berlin: Aufbau, 1958.

Heizmann, Bertold. *Ursprünglichkeit und Reflexion: Die "poetische Ästhetik" des jungen Herder im Zusammenhang der Geschichtsphilosophie und Anthropologie des 18. Jahrhunderts*. New York: Peter Lang, 1981.

Heinz, Marion. *Sensualistischer Idealismus: Untersuchungen zur Erkenntnistheorie (und Metaphysik) des jungen Herder (1763–1778)*. Hamburg: Meiner, 1994.

———, ed. *Herder und die Philosophie des deutschen Idealismus*. Amsterdam: Rodopi, 1997.

Iggers, Georg G. *The German Conception of History: The National Tradition of Historical Thought from Herder to the Present*. Middletown, Conn.: Wesleyan University Press, 1983.

Kelley, Donald R. *Faces of History: Historical Inquiry from Herodotus to Herder*. New Haven, Conn.: Yale University Press, 1998.

Koepke, Wulf. *Johann Gottfried Herder*. Boston: Twayne, 1987.

———, ed. *Johann Gottfried Herder: Academic Disciplines and the Pursuit of Knowledge*. Columbia, S.C.: Camden House, 1996.

———, ed. *Johann Gottfried Herder: Innovator throughout the Ages*. Bonn: Bouvier, 1982.

———, ed. *Johann Gottfried Herder: Language, History, and the Enlightenment*. Columbia, S.C.: Camden House, 1990.

Leventhal, Robert S. *The Disciplines of Interpretation: Lessing, Herder, Schlegel and Hermeneutics in Germany 1750–1800*. Berlin: Walter de Gruyter, 1994.

Morton, Michael. *Herder and the Poetics of Thought: Unity and Diversity in "On Diligence in Several Languages."* University Park: Pennsylvania State University Press, 1989.

Mueller-Vollmer, Kurt, ed. *Herder Today: Contributions from the International Herder Conference, November 5–8, 1987, Stanford, California*. Berlin: Walter de Gruyter, 1990.

Nisbet, H. B. *Herder and the Philosophy and History of Science*. Cambridge: Modern Humanities Research Association, 1970.

———, ed. *German Aesthetic and Literary Criticism: Winckelmann, Lessing, Hamann, Herder, Schiller, Goethe*. Cambridge: Cambridge University Press, 1985.

Norton, Robert E. *Herder's Aesthetics and the European Enlightenment.* Ithaca, N.Y.: Cornell University Press, 1991.

Pascal, Roy. *The German Sturm und Drang.* Manchester: Manchester University Press, 1953.

Reill, Peter Hanns. *The German Enlightenment and the Rise of Historicism.* Berkeley and Los Angeles: University of California Press, 1975.

Rose, Ulrich. *Poesie als Praxis: Jean Paul, Herder und Jacobi im Diskurs der Aufklärung.* Wiesbaden: Deutscher Universitäts-Verlag, 1990.

Sauder, Gerhard, ed. *Johann Gottfried Herder, 1744–1803.* Hamburg: Felix Meiner, 1987.

Schnur, Harald. *Schleiermachers Hermeneutik und ihre Vorgeschichte im 18 Jahrhundert: Studien zur Bibelauslegung, zu Hamann, Herder und F. Schlegel.* Stuttgart: Verlag J. B. Metzler, 1994.

Waniek, Erdmann. "Johann Gottfried Herder." In *Dictionary of Literary Biography*, vol. 97, *German Writers from the Enlightenment to Sturm und Drang, 1720–1764.* Edited by James Hardin and Christoph E. Schweitzer. New York: Gale, 1990.

HEREDIA, JOSÉ MARÍA DE 1803–1839

Cuban poet

José María de Heredia stands as one of—if not the—most important Cuban poets of the Romantic age. He was the most popular Spanish American writer in Europe during his lifetime. Despite his weaknesses as a poet, he has never been denied his genius. His poetry is so truthful, and so full of passion and lyrical impetus, that its place in the canon of Romantic literature is assured.

Heredia was a precocious poet. At the age of eighteen, while in Mexico, he wrote and published the ode "España libre" ("Free Spain," 1820) and the "Himno patriótico al restablecimiento de la Constitución" ("Patriotic Hymn to the Restoration of the Constitution," 1820). He then collected his works in three notebooks and wrote what has been considered his best poem, "En el teocalli de Cholula" (1820; "On the Teocalli of Cholula"). His poetic career can be divided into three periods. The first covers the eight years from his childhood to early youth (up to 1820) and is closely linked to his experiences in Venezuela, Cuba, and Mexico. Three types of poetry are found at this time: civil poetry, love poetry, and philosophical and moral poetry. The first type deals with the independence of Latin American countries from the point of view of a person who regards himself as Spanish; it is not surprising, then, that Heredia views the fighters for independence as outlaws, or that he wrote poems to colonialist military leaders and to the Spanish king Ferdinand VII. His love poetry, written in a neoclassical mode, arises from his experiences in Cuba; although he was frustrated in his personal romantic life, he ultimately produced a number of interesting love poems that were published in 1825. The third type of poetry was also published in 1825.

The second period began in 1821, with his return to Cuba. At this point his nationalism began to develop. Cuba was the country in which he first fell in love, and this was a stimulus for the shaping of his patriotic sentiment. The death of his father also played a role in his growing nationalism. There are only a few nationalistic poems: "La estrella de Cuba" ("The Star of Cuba," 1823), "A Emilia" ("To Emilia," 1824), "Proyectos" ("Projects," 1824), "Oda" ("Ode," 1825), "Himno del desterrado" ("Hymn for the Exile," 1825) and "Vuelta al Sur" ("Back to the South," 1825).

The third poetic period began in 1825, when Heredia moved to Mexico. He did not forget Cuba, but he developed a great love for his newly adopted home. The poetry of this era is more mature, and displays a higher level of virtuosity. The freshness and youthful enthusiasm of his earlier work had, however, faded. In 1932, he collaborated in the publication of his collected poems in two volumes. The first volume included his love poems and poems written in the manner of other poets. The second included the philosophical and descriptive poems, his versions of James Macpherson's false Ossian works, and patriotic poems on Cuba and the freedom of other countries.

His education was primarily classical; he preferred Latin poets, though in a later stage he widened the scope of his readings to Spanish and French neo-Classical writers and the Romantics Ossian, Lord Byron, François-Auguste-Réné de Chataeubriand, Alphonse Marie Louis Lamartine, Victor Hugo, and Ugo Foscolo. Heredia accomplished a union between neoclassical and Romantic ideals. His Romanticism is that of the search and longing for freedom, both political and literary. To this extent, his poetry comes directly from his life.

"En el teocalli de Cuba" and "Niágara" (1824) are his two most important poems. His poetry lasts both because of the subject matter and because of the intimate sentiment inherent in the compositions. Nature is clearly depicted in the fashion of the Romantic Age and mirrors his spiritual state. The poet praises America's natural wealth. Heredia chooses the moment of sunset as the appropriate setting for his meditations. The night, however, is not a mere natural phenomenon; rather, it is tinged with mystery. Heredia's fascination with the Aztec ruins has to be included among the Romantic features of his work. These ruins stand in for those classical figures that are present in so many Romantic European poems. There should be little doubt that one of the most interesting features is the ghostly atmosphere at Anáhuac.

The Cuban environment is reflected in the landscape in "Niágara," for which Heredia states his admiration. The distance provides the poem with the desperate idea of mortality. Nostalgia is a present feature in his poem and becomes more present with the passing of time. Everything in it points to the painful idea of failure, and to death, despite the conviction of permanence. This is expressed in the awareness of the value of his poetry, and in the capacity of poetry for timeless permanence.

The most prominent Romantic feature in Heredia is the ever-present involvement of his life in his poetry, as well as the dark notes of death, melancholy and gloominess that pervade his writings.

SANTIAGO RODRÍGUEZ GUERRERO STRACHAN

Biography

Born in Cuba, December 31, 1803. Lived in Cuba, Mexico, and Venezuela. Solicitor, and member of the revolutionary secret society Cabaleros racionales (Rational Gentlemen). Became a member of the armed forces. Exiled for political reasons in New York and Mexico. Died May 7, 1839.

Selected Works

Poesía lírica. 1893.
Poesías del ciudadano. 1872.
Obras poéticas. Edited by Antonio Bachiller y Morales. 1875.
Poesías, dicursos y otras cartas. 2 vols Edited by María Lacoste de Arufe. La Habana: Cultural, 1939.
Poesías completas. 2 vols. Edited by E. Roig de Leuchsenring. La Habana: Municipio de la Habana, 1940–41.
Poesías, La Habana: Consejo Nacional de Cultura, 1965.

Bibliography

Alonso, Amado, and Julio Caillet-Bois. "Heredia como Crítico Literario," *Revista Cubana* 15 (1941): 54–62.
Balaguer, Joaquín. *Heredia.* Santiago, Dominican Republic: El Diario, 1939.
Carilla, Emilio. "La Prosa de José María Heredia," *Boletín de la Academia Argentina de Letras* 14 (1945): 667–84.
Fontanella, Lee. "José María Heredia: A Case for Critical Inclusivism," *Revista Hispánica Moderna* 37 (1972–73): 162–79.
González, Manuel Pedro. *José María Heredia, Primogénito del Romanticismo Hispano.* México City: El Colegio de México, 1955.
Ibrovats, Miodrag. *José María Heredia. Sa Vie, Son Oeuvre.* Paris: Les Presses Français, 1923.
Lens y de Vera, Eduardo Félix. *Heredia y Martí: Dos Grandes Figuras de la Lírica Cubana.* Havana: Selecta, 1954.
Silvestri, Laura. "José María Heredia: L'esotismo come presa di cosncienza," *Letterature d'America* (1983): 5–32.
Souza, Raymond D. "José María Heredia. The Poet and the Ideal of Liberty," *Revista de Estudios Hispánicos* 1 (1971): 31–38.

HERMENEUTICS

Although hermeneutics, the science or art of interpretation, can be traced back to the classical and Judaic origins of Western civilization, it is generally agreed that it was during the Romantic period that modern interest in it developed, with Friedrich Schleiermacher being regarded as the founder of modern hermeneutics. The problem at the center of hermeneutics is that although texts written in the past may survive and may still be understandable at a linguistic level, their authors and the historical and cultural context that produced them no longer exist. It is not enough merely to read these texts; they require interpretation as well. Reading and interpretation therefore become inseparable. Schleiermacher, one of the founders of modern Protestant theology as well as of hermeneutics, would have been well aware of how central the Bible was to the question of interpretation, since how it should be read was crucial to Christian, especially Protestant, doctrine. However, a major reason why he is regarded as the founder of modern hermeneutics is that he extended hermeneutics beyond the sphere of religion so that it could be applied to the interpretation of texts in a more general sense.

Why should modern hermeneutics have emerged in the Romantic period? It is significant that the historical novel also emerged during the Romantic period, notably in the fiction of Walter Scott. It can be argued that a new conception of the relation between past and present underlies both hermeneutics and the historical novel. Although the Enlightenment is generally associated with modernity, the conception of history held by eighteenth-century historians was one in which the past was judged by the standards of the present. As Hugh Trevor-Roper notes, "The achievement of the great eighteenth-century historians was immense . . . But their philosophy was essentially linear, and their weakness was a lack of sympathy with the past." He adds, "To see the past in its own terms; to deduce it directly from its spontaneous records, widely defined—that is, from its literature, its traditions, its mythology, its portraiture, as well as from its public documents, to respect its autonomy, to sympa-thise with its coherent assumptions, and at the same time not to surrender to mere nostalgia or lose one's position in the present—this requires a nice balance of imagination and realism."

What distinguished the Romantic conception of the past from that of the Enlightenment was that for significant Romantic figures the past was different in a fundamental way from the present. It had its own integrity and could not simply be judged in terms of the present. It thus had to be understood in terms of its difference, and this required that it be interpreted rather than merely "read."

Schleiermacher was not the only Romantic thinker concerned with hermeneutics. Two contemporaries of Schleiermacher were the philologists Friedrich August Wolf and Friedrich Ast; both were interested in hermeneutic questions from a philological point of view. In 1808, Ast published a work entitled *Basic Elements of Grammar, Hermeneutics, and Criticism.* In this work Ast argues that three elements are necessary to understand texts of earlier eras: 1) a historical understanding of their content; 2) a grammatical understanding of the language and style of these texts; 3) a spiritual understanding of the *Geist,* or total culture, of which the author and these texts are the product. "For every passage that needs explication," he notes, "one must first ask what the letter is stating; secondly, how it is stating it, what meaning the statement has, what significance it occupies in the text; thirdly, what the idea of the whole or of the spirit is, as that unity from which the letter emanated and into which it seeks to return. Without the meaning, the letter is dead and unintelligible. To be sure, the meaning without the spirit is in itself intelligible, but it has an individual or atomistic meaning which has no basis and no purpose without the spirit."

Schleiermacher's major contribution was to make "understanding" (*Verstehen*) central to hermeneutic theory by directing attention away from the difficulties of reading texts because they might contain corruptions to the question of the conditions necessary before it was possible to understand such texts. Interpretation was therefore theorized. Understanding, he argued, had two essential aspects: the grammatical and the psychological (or, as he called it, the "technical"), and by implication this applied not merely to the interpretation of texts that were the product of past eras but also to interpretation in the present. Before one could understand any utterance, spoken or written, one must understand the structure of the linguistic system of which it is a product (the grammatical aspect). But since such an utterance was also a human product, it must be understood in relation to the life of the person who created the utterance (the psychological aspect). Psychological interpretation consists of two methods, which he calls the "divinatory" and the "comparative." He notes, "By leading the interpreter to transform himself, so to speak, into the author, the divinatory method seeks to gain an immediate comprehension of the author as an individual. The comparative method proceeds by subsuming the author under a general type. It then tries to find his distinctive traits by comparing him with the others of the same general type. Divinatory knowledge is the feminine strength in knowing people; comparative knowledge the masculine."

The need for the divinatory implies that neither spoken nor written language on their own gives one access to true meaning and that misunderstanding is the norm. The hermeneutic project for Schleiermacher, therefore, is directed at the thought that lies "behind language."

Schleiermacher's hermeneutics has been influential on those who favor historical and intentionalist criticism. E. D. Hirsch, probably the leading proponent of intentionalist criticism, for example, quotes approvingly the following statement by Schleiermacher: "Everything in a given text which requires fuller interpretation must be explained and determined and deter-mined exclusively from the linguistic domain common to the author and his original public." However, one of the major modern hermeneutic theorists, Hans-Georg Gadamer, who was much influenced by Heidegger, is critical of what he calls "Romantic hermeneutics." For Gadamer, it is not only impossible but undesirable to try to exclude the historical and temporal situation of the interpreter. For him, understanding the past involves a "fusion of horizons" in which an identification takes place between the perspective of the reader in the present and the historical perspective of the text. This is perhaps a further development of Romantic hermeneutics rather than a radical break from it.

K. M. NEWTON

Bibliography

Bruns, Gerald L. *Hermeneutics Ancient and Modern*. New Haven, Conn.: Yale University Press, 1992.
Grondin, Jean. *Introduction to Philosophical Hermeneutics*. Translated by Joel Weinsheimer. New Haven, Conn.: Yale University Press, 1994.
Hirsch, E. D. "Three Dimensions of Hermeneutics," *New Literary History* 3 (1971–72): 245–61.
Mueller–Vollmer, Kurt, ed. *The Hermeneutics Reader: Texts of the German Tradition from the Enlightenment to the Present*. Oxford: Basil Blackwell, 1986.
Ormiston, Gayle L. and Alan D. Schrift eds. *The Hermeneutic Tradition: From Ast to Ricoeur*. Albany: SUNY Press, 1990.
Schleiermacher, Friedrich. *Hermeneutics and Criticism and Other Writings*. Translated and edited by Andrew Bowie. Cambridge: Cambridge University Press, 1998.
Trevor-Roper, Hugh. "Sir Walter Scott and History," *The Listener* (August 19, 1971): 225–32.

HERNANI OU L'HONNEUR CASTILLAN (HERNANI, OR CASTILIAN HONOR) 1830

Play by Victor Hugo

After the excitement aroused in 1827 by the preface to his drama *Cromwell* (which could not be staged), Victor Hugo was still without a play with which to launch his career as a Romantic dramatist. Between August 29 and September 24, 1829, he wrote the five acts in alexandrine verse of *Hernani ou l'honneur castillan* (*Hernani, or Castilian Honor*). The play premiered at the Comédie Française on February 25, 1830 and provoked the "battle" between the young Romantics and their opponents during many of the play's first thirty-nine performances. Its success ensured that the Romantic drama, with its Shakespearean mixture of comic and tragic themes and actions, would replace the generic purity and Classical "rules" of neo-Classical tragedy as the dominant dramatic paradigm in France then and thereafter.

The action of *Hernani* may best be approached by reference to its subtitle, which encapsulates the contrasting yet interwoven propositions in the plot's logic. *Castilian Honor* corresponds to the suprahuman constraint that in *Notre-Dame de Paris* (*The Hunchback of Notre Dame*), the novel Hugo wrote in the same year as *Hernani*, is called ΑΝΑΓΚΗ (fatality). In *Notre Dame*, Claude Frollo's fatal sexual desire for Esmeralda kills her, himself, and her protector, Quasimodo. In *Hernani*, Don Ruy Gomez's absolute subjection to the honor of his house causes his own death and those of Doña Sol and Hernani, her bandit lover. Castilian honor explains why Gomez is ready to protect Hernani, his hated rival for the hand of his niece, even at the risk of his own death or her abduction as hostage by Don Carlos, the king of Spain. Castilian honor explains why in act 5, despite being pardoned, restored to his lands and titles, and married to Doña Sol by Don Carlos, newly-elected Holy Roman Emperor, Hernani drinks poison at his own marriage feast. Having himself abused Gomez's trust and hospitality in act 3 and sworn an oath to give his own life in exchange for the right to avenge his father by killing Don Carlos, Hernani cannot face the shame of breaking his oath, and so dies. Doña Sol, unable to understand or sympathize with such a male or macho principle, pleads with him to reject male honor in favor of female happiness and so ignore Gomez's sarcastic gibes, but to no avail. Hernani, bent entirely on vengeance, is unable to overcome the fatal power of honor, symbolized in the plot by his death pact with Gomez; bloodlust is stronger than sexual passion or desire for conjugal bliss. And so the lovers achieve the *Liebestod* (love death) that represents the unhappy ending characteristic of French Romantic drama.

Hugo's opponents have traditionally argued that the "psychology" of characters in the French neo-Classical theater represents those plays' most "obvious" (and therefore unable to be attacked) value. Such critics dismissed Hugo's Romantic characters as "incoherent," the kind of personages whose actions reveal no underlying plot logic. Jean Massin, arguing against such dismissive accounts, proposes that the type of psychological activity revealed in Hugo's dramatic works, far from being "Cartesian," or rationalistic, derives from his understanding of what we now call "depth psychology" (*la psychologie des profondeurs*). Massin contends that the superficial incoherence in the characters of Hugo's heroes should be read as evidence of the kind of unconscious, inexplicable motivations we meet in dreams, and that psychologists identify with repressed memories, desires, or other psychic activities. The action of Hugo's Romantic dramas, he therefore concludes, is "symbolic." According to this interpretation, Hugo's characters personify values, impulses, and conflicts in a secret world where appearances do not correspond to realities. Hugo's world is, however, open to scrutiny if one possesses the right key. For Massin, Anne Ubersfeld, J. Seebacher, and many of the other contributors to the chronological edition of Hugo's complete works, the key allowing one to decode their meaning is the psychoanalytical interpretation of his life. Hugo's fictional works display to the cognoscenti his deepest and most carefully hidden inhibitions, his unconscious desires and repulsions.

On the other hand, formalist critics treat the plays, novels, and poems as something other than disguised or unconscious autobiography on Hugo's part. For example, rather than proposing alle-

gorical interpretations of the plays, formalists offer descriptions of their dramatic functioning. They explain verisimilitude, for instance, in terms of generic rather than "real-life," or rationalistic, constraints. For such critics, Hugo's characters offer an audience satisfaction of a specifically literary kind, deriving from an audience's informed appreciation of the author's treatment of the relevant literary codes. Hernani, for them, is a Romantic hero, whose reactions must be understood without reference to nonliterary models. The playwright's skill should therefore be judged on his rhetorical ability to convince certain actors and audiences to sympathize with his characters to the point of overlooking any actions which, rationally, they would find incredible.

Related to the formalist approach is the view that Romantic experiments resulted in a nonmimetic or "anti-illusionist" type of drama. Using this criterion, Frederick Burwick clearly distinguishes Hugo's dramas from neo-Classical theater, first by explaining the theory behind them: "On the one hand," he notes, "there is the theatre as the mirror of life that imitates reality and exploits the illusion of the proscenium arch as invisible fourth wall to the stage setting. On the other hand, there is the theatre of myth and ritual, of allegory and masque, which makes no attempt at verisimilitude." Hugo's characters, he argues, should not be judged by their "truth-to-life" but rather by their ability to personify Romantic irony. This self-reflexive type of reference to the action as a dramatic performance is both illusion-shattering and illusion-creating. He writes, "In the drama, the characters are caught up in their own illusory perceptions, and they 'escape' only to remind the audience that they are acting . . . this act of 'falling out of the role' ('*aus der Rolle fallen*') reinforces rather than disrupts the spontaneity of stage illusion. If a character falls out of one role, after all, he inevitably falls into another."

In *Hernani*, Hugo's hero "falls out of role" thanks to a dramatized change of identity brought about by his disguise as a bandit, and subsequent recognition. Burwick's distinction and the criterion upon which it is based, should, if remembered, encourage us to see Hugo's characters as Romantic archetypes like Johann Wolfgang von Goethe's Faust or Richard Wagner's legendary figures, and so reduce the temptation to treat them as mimetic representations of "real people."

ALBERT W. HALSALL

Work

Hernani, ou l'honneur castillan, 1830. Translated as *Hernani* by Frederick L. Slous and Camilla Crosland. In *Three Plays by Victor Hugo*. New York: Howard Fertig, 1995.

Bibliography

Burwick, Frederick. "Stage Illusion and the Stage Designs of Goethe and Hugo," *Word and Image* 4, nos. 3 and 4 (1988): 692–718.

Halsall, Albert W. *Victor Hugo and the Romantic Drama*. Toronto: University of Toronto Press, 1998.

Hugi, Hermann. *Les Drames de V. Hugo expliqués par la psychanalyse*. Bern: Buch und Kunstdruckerei, 1930.

Massin, Jean. *Hernani*, "Présentation." In Hugo, V. *Oeuvres complètes*, vol. 3. General editor, Jean Massin. Paris: Le Club Français du Livre, 1966–71.

Ubersfeld, Anne. *Le Roi et le bouffon*. Paris: Corti, 1974.

———. *Le Roman d'Hernani*. Paris: Comédie Française-Mercure de France, 1985.

"Les Romains escheveles a la 1re representation d'*Hernani*." Reprinted courtesy of AKG.

HERO

In May 1840, the historian and social commentator Thomas Carlyle delivered a series of six public lectures that he published one year later under the title of *On Heroes, Hero-Worship, and the Heroic in History*. In it he bemoaned what he saw as the devastating negativity of Enlightenment Europe: "The Eighteenth was a *Sceptical* Century; . . . Perhaps, in few centuries since the world began, was a life of Heroism more difficult for a Man. That was not an age of Faith,—an age of Heroes! The very possibility of Heroism had been, as it were, formally abnegated in the minds of all. Heroism was gone forever; Triviality, Formulism and Commonplace were come forever . . . An effete world; wherein Wonder, Greatness, Godhood could not dwell." Romanticism, on the other hand, sought the recovery and redefinition of heroism.

A hero is at once an individual and an exemplary figure who, as an expression of the finest achievement of his tribe or state, and more generally of the human race, represents a collective dream of self-transcendence, and not infrequently a deep nostalgia, the celebration of a simpler, nobler world that has since been lost. In the classical period, the hero was a figure of myth and literature who was larger than life: more valiant, physically stronger, more honorable than his peers. That one of his parents was divine is suggestive of this superiority: "An excellence beyond human scale," to quote Aristotle in his *Nicomachean Ethics*, "something heroic and divine, which may be illustrated by the phrase Homer makes Priam regarding Hector to express his signal excellence, 'He seemed the son of a god, not of mortal man.'" For this reason, as the English poet John Dryden wrote in the dedication prefixed to his translation of the *Aeneid* (1697), the "heroic poem, truly such, is undoubtedly the greatest work which the soul of man is capable to perform."

The closest Dryden himself and many other seventeenth- and eighteenth-century writers came to the heroic remained indirect, however: translation and, paradoxically, the mock heroic, which like all satire held only a comparatively modest place in the strict hierarchy of literary genres maintained by neo-Classical theory. Moreover, if the mock heroic suggested that contemporary society was incommensurate with an heroic world that was grand in action and gesture, masculine, martial, and mythicoreligious, it also betrayed an awareness that heroic sentiments and values were somehow inappropriate to the modern world, if not inherently absurd. The truth is that the ancient values of physical prowess and military glory, of honor or saving "face" and other public virtues, were coming under severe scrutiny at the end of the seventeenth century. If military heroism survived with the wars that made it necessary, it was considered by many to be anomalous in a Christian state. The poet John Oldham summed up Enlightenment skepticism about the heroic when he dismissed the archetypal heroic poem, Homer's *The Iliad*, as "*Grecian* Bullies fighting for a Whore."

To restore a dignity to human aspiration, the Romantics attempted to rescue the heroic from the combined assault of Cartesian rationalism, Christian pacificism, and Enlightenment historicism. Already by 1801, John Thelwall could write of a "press teeming, and, perhaps the public already satiated with national heroics," as epic poetry reached something of an epidemic. From James Macpherson's *Ossian* in the 1760s to Richard Wagner's operatic *Ring* cycle a hundred years later, artists sought their heroes in the fashionable Celtic, Germanic, and Norse mythologies at critical moments in the emergence of one form of nationalism after another. In some cases—as with Carlyle and Wagner—hero worship also becomes an aggressive defense against what contemporary commentators saw as the oppressive egalitarianism of a mass society, threatening the heroic freedom of an inherited or spiritual aristocracy.

Yet it was not just from the past that Romantic culture sought its heroes and not just in literature, music, and the fine arts that heroes could be found. A developing mass culture of magazines and newspapers, published prints and popular ballads, reaching an ever-expanding public, encouraged the commercialization of the hero. In politics, the revolutionary decade of the 1790s threw up a number of contemporary heroes and martyrs like the Polish freedom fighter Kosiuszko, the French revolutionary Jean Paul Marat and Haitian revolutionary Toussaint L'Ouverture. During the opening years of the new century, cults grew up around Lord Nelson and Napoleon Bonaparte in war and around Lord Byron in the arts. Indeed, Byron probably did more than any other writer to encourage the taste for heroes and heroic adventures (and for himself as hero) in *Childe Harold's Pilgrimage* (1811–18) and his poetic tales, elaborating from the brooding, aristocratic villain-heroes of the Gothic novelists a brand of hero all his own. On the other hand, Byron also exposed the brutality beneath the stylization of the ancient epic in his late essay in the mock heroic *Don Juan* (1819–24).

The mention of Byron reminds us that another kind or other kinds of hero can be seen as emerging during the Romantic era, as Classical heroism is brought out of the battlefield and into the social and cultural arena. Carlyle celebrated the "Hero as Poet" (Dante, William Shakespeare), and announced the advent of "the Hero as Man of Letters" (Samuel Johnson, Jean-Jacques Rousseau), a "Great Soul living apart in that anomalous manner; endeavouring to speak-forth the inspiration that was in him by Printed Books." The degree of contemporary recognition of these new culture heroes can be measured by the number of those ancillary forms that since the eighteenth century have made up the new cult of the artist, and particularly of the writer: such as biographies, recollections, and gossip.

Under the influence of Romantic notions of the creative imagination and of genius, the Romantic artist-as-hero was seen to undertake the psychic equivalent of the traditional heroic (or chivalric) pilgrimage. And the gap between the heroic ideal and the real that was such fertile ground for the eighteenth-century satirist and the moral novelist became the site for what Friedrich von Schlegel called Romantic irony: an awareness that art's expressive or representational means are necessarily incommensurate with the transcendental idea it strives to comprehend, involving for the artist an heroic *Sehnsucht* (yearning after the absolute) and tragic exasperation.

WILLIAM CHRISTIE

Bibliography

Bowra, C. M. *Heroic Poetry*. London: Macmillan, 1952.
Carlyle, Thomas. *On Heroes and Hero-Worship, and the Heroic in History*. London: Oxford University Press, 1904.
Dundes, Alan, Lord Raglan, and Otto Rank. *In Quest of the Hero*. Princeton, N.J.: Princeton University Press, 1990.
Furst, Lillian. *Romanticism in Perspective: A Comparative Study of Aspects of the Romantic Movements in England, France and Germany*. 2d ed. London: Methuen, 1979.
Hoffmeister, Gerhart. *European Romanticism: Literary Cross-Currents, Modes, and Models*. Detroit: Wayne State University Press, 1990.
Kermode, Frank. *Romantic Image*. London: Collins, 1971.
Schenk, H. G. *The Mind of the European Romantics: An Essay in Cultural History*. Oxford, and New York: Oxford University Press, 1979.

A HERO OF OUR TIME (GEROY NASHEGO VREMENI) 1840

Novel by Mikhail Lermontov

A Hero of Our Time by Mikhail Lermontov is commonly recognized as one of the classic novels of Russian nineteenth-century literature. Written by the author at the age of twenty-six and published only one year before his death in a duel in 1841, the novel became a significant event in Russian fiction and made Lermontov known to the world.

This work has several claims to fame. Its revolutionary form made a valuable contribution to the development of the Russian novel that had been initiated by Nikolay Mikhaylovich Karamzin and Aleksandr Pushkin. The specific structure, experiments with chronology, and inventive narration are complemented by a vivid depiction of the main character—Grigorii Pechorin, a Byronic and demonically attractive figure who is supposed to represent the post-Decembrist generation of Russian noblemen. Despite the author's romantic outlook, *A Hero of Our Time* contains strong elements of psychological realism that made it possible for some critics to call this work the first psychological novel in Russian literature.

Although fully original, the novel reflects certain literary influences experienced by Lermontov. The first place among these is undoubtedly occupied by Byronic Romanticism. The Russian author constantly compared his lyrical alter ego to the great English poet and his characters, and as Pechorin is in many ways very close to the lyrical hero created by Lermontov, the references to Byron's works are quite obvious in the novel. However, Byron's influence was not the only one. *A Hero of Our Time* appeared in the period when the entire tradition of semiautobiographic novels, centered around the main figure—a young man portrayed as one of those who personify certain notable contemporary features—was being established in the West. Apart from Byron's *Childe Harold's Pilgrimage* (1812–18), which was greatly popular in Russia from the early nineteenth century on, Lermontov was inspired by Benjamin Constant de Rebecque's *Adolphe* (1816; Russian translation by Prince P. A. Viazemsky) and Alfred de Musset's *Confession d'un Enfant du Siécle* (*Confessions of a Son of the Century*, 1836). Both novels use confession as a means of introduction, and the analysis of the main character following the tradition of Jean-Jacques Rousseau. Lermontov's novel continues this trend.

In the list of the Russian sources of the novel, Pushkin's *Eugene Onegin* (1833) should occupy the first place. Lermontov made this explicit when he decided to name his main character Pechorin. For the Russian aristocracy the family name *Onegin* sounded bizarre and unnatural, as it did not resemble any of the typical surnames of the Russian gentry. This was certainly done on purpose to distance the literary character from real life. Pushkin named Onegin after a large northern river (Onega), and Lermontov followed this model and named his after the river Pechora, located in the same region as Onega. Pushkin's influence could be also seen in the image of Maxim Maximych, as this figure is sometimes compared to Samson Vyrin in Pushkin's *The Station Master*. This type of character was labeled "a little man" by the nineteenth-century Russian critics. The Caucasian topic treated in works by A. A. Marlinsky and in Pushkin's *The Caucasian Captive* is also heavily exploited by Lermontov in *A Hero of Our Time*.

Among other references to Russian and foreign fiction that seem to be important to the author—as they indicate his Romantic background—the following influences should be noted: Johann Wolfgang Goethe's *Wilhelm Meisters Lehrjahre* (*Wilhelm Meister's Apprenticeship*, 1796); the literary circle of young French poets close to Victor Hugo who called themselves the Young France; the poem *Undina* (1831–36), V. A. Zhukovsky's translation of the novel in prose *Undine: eine Erzählung* (*Undine: A Narrative*) written by Baron de la Motte Fouqué; other Zhukovsky poems, such as *Eolova Arfa*; works by Torquato Tasso; *The Vampyre* by John William Polidori; and *Old Mortality* and *St. Ronan's Well* by Walter Scott.

A Hero of Our Time consists of five individual stories with their own plots, all of which deal with an army officer, Pechorin. The action takes place mostly in the Caucasus Mountains in the early 1830s and lasts approximately five years. The preface to the book is followed by the novellas *Bela* and *Maxim Maximych*, which form the first part of the novel. These stories are presented by the narrator, also an army officer, who is traveling through the Caucasus. The form of the travel notes used for the first two stories places the narrator among other important male characters of the novel. The narrator meets an old officer, Maximych, who was a commander of a Caucasian fortress when Pechorin served there. Maximych is the first to tell the narrator and the readers about Pechorin and the unfortunate fate of Bela, a Circassian girl who was abducted by Pechorin. As Lermontov deals with the double narration, the structure of Bela becomes quite sophisticated. In *Maxim Maximych* the narrator makes his own impression of the main character while witnessing Pechorin's chance meeting with his former commander. The second part of the book is called *Pechorin's Diary* and consists of the introduction to the diary, *Taman, Princess Mary*, and *The Fatalist*, in which Pechorin speaks for himself.

Initially Lermontov did not envisage these individual stories as a complex book, and *Bela, The Fatalist,* and *Taman* were published separately in the journal *Otechestvennye zapiski* (*Notes of the Fatherland*) in 1839 and 1840. Probably the idea of uniting these stories into a novel occurred to Lermontov when the novellas were in press, because in 1840 *A Hero of Our Time* appeared as a separate edition nearly in its final form (only the preface was added later, in 1841).

Chronologically the events of Pechorin's life should be told in an entirely different order from the novel. On his way from St. Petersburg to the Caucasus, the new place of his military service, Pechorin stops in the small town of Taman in the Crimea, where he happens to be tossed "into the peaceful midst" of "honest smugglers" (*Taman*). After a military operation, he takes rest at the Piatigorsk spa where he flirts with Princess Mary and eventually kills a young officer Grushnitsky in a duel. As a punishment, Pechorin is banished to a small fortress in Chechnya where he first meets Maxim Maximych and continues his diary (the final piece of *Princess Mary*). While doing his stint in the fortress Pechorin spends a fortnight in a Cossack settlement where he witnesses an incident with one Vulich, who puts his life at risk in a Russian Roulette–like game (*The Fatalist*). When back in the fort he abducts Bela and after her death moves to Georgia. Five years later Maxim Maximych and the narrator bump into Pechorin on his way to Persia (*Maxim Maximych*). Some time later the narrator learns that Pechorin has died. This information provides him with an excuse to publish Pechorin's diary.

Lermontov's experiments with different styles of narration and nonchronological order gave him an opportunity to portray his "hero" from different angles and constantly shift the focus of his analysis of Pechorin's individuality. Maxim Maximych is a kind, modest, and sincere person, but he is too simple and naïve to understand Pechorin's emotional life. The Bela incident told by Maximych intrigues the reader, as it shows only the surface of things, tells about the actions of the character and does not help to learn much about the underlying reasons for Pechorin's behavior. The narrator is a more experienced and keen observer than Maximych, and that is proved by the portrait of Pechorin presented by the narrator. Each detail of this portrait tells more about Pechorin's state of mind and psyche, rather than about his physical appearance. Eventually the form of the diary enables Lermontov to reveal all the contradictions in Pechorin's character and to make an attempt to explain them. When compared to previous literary portraits that had existed in Russian literature this one should be considered as a true innovation in fiction.

The other male and female characters in the novel revolve around Pechorin. Pechorin is too organic and natural to keep pretenses, and therefore he finds himself in conflict with his social milieu. On the other hand, his demonic energy cannot fit well with the simplicity of natural life because his mentality is too sophisticated. Thus Pechorin's life is depicted as a series of meetings with different people who represent various outlooks and life styles, equally unacceptable for Pechorin. Such an impossibility to harmonize his wishes, thoughts, and emotions is additionally emphasized by yet another Romantic feature in the novel, the problem of correlation of fate and free will that is treated in *Taman, Princess Mary*, and especially in *The Fatalist*.

Among other merits of this novel Lermontov's Romantic irony should be mentioned; it is still being discussed by contemporary critics and scholars.

EKATERINA ROGATCHEVSKAIA

See also **Hero; Irony; Romantic; Lermontov, Mikhail Yurievich; Russia: Cultural Survey; Russia: Historical Survey**

Work

Geroy nashego vremeni: 1840.
Translated as *A Hero of Our Time*. Translated by Paul Foote. Harmondsworth, England: Penguin, 1966.

Bibliography

Barratt, Andrew, and Antony David Briggs. *A Wicked Irony: The Rhetoric of Lermontov's "A Hero of Our Time."* Bristol: Bristol Classical Press, 1989.
Eikhenbaum, Boris Mikhailovich. *Lermontov: A Study in Literary-Historical Evolution*. Translated by Ray Parrott and Harry Weber. Ann Arbor, Mich.: Ardis, 1981.
Gilroy, Marie. *The Ironic Vision of Lermontov's "A Hero of Our Time."* Birmingham Slavonic Monographs 19. Birmingham: Birmingham University Press, 1989.
Manuilov, Viktor Andronikovich. *Roman M. Iu. Lermontova "Geroi nashego vremeni." Kommentarii*. Leningrad: Prosveshchenie, 1975.
Reid, Robert. *Lermontov's A Hero of Our Time*. Bristol: Bristol Classical Press, 1997.

HERZEN, ALEKSANDR IVANOVICH 1812–1870

Russian writer and journalist

First as a member of the Stankevich Circle, which arose at Moscow University not long after he enrolled in 1829, and then as the founding member of a parallel circle, Aleksandr Ivanovich Herzen studied and absorbed the works of the German idealist philosophers (G. W. F. Hegel, Friedrich Wilhelm Joseph von Schelling, Johann Christoph Friedrich von Schiller) and of the utopian socialists. These influences were to affect his fiction, all of which was written before his departure from Russia in 1847, as well as his widely varied essays. Herzen came to occupy a special place among Russian intellectuals of the nineteenth century; even as he gained early recognition as a prose writer he emerged as the prolific author of essays on literary issues, philosophy, history, the social system, and the role of the individual in a political order. Although he spent the last twenty-three years of his life outside Russia, his writings continued to have an enormous impact on liberal and radical thought in Russia. Despite Herzen's sharp differences with the more extreme revolutionaries of the 1860s, his ideas were instrumental in setting a course for the social activism that ultimately led to the overthrow of the tsarist government.

As Monica Partridge has shown, Herzen's first literary efforts, which were composed in the summer of 1833 and remained unpublished by him, display an autobiographical thrust and an elevated literary language that derives from his acquaintance with the writings of Johann Wolfgang von Goethe, Jean Paul, Jean-Jacques Rousseau, and Schiller. While some of his early stories reveal a greater affinity for the emerging realist tradition in Russian literature, the first story that he actually published, *Legenda* (*A Legend*, 1836) contains an allegorical elaboration of Claude Henri de Saint-Simon's ideas against the background of a Russian saint's life. A strong autobiographical element combined with the influence of E. T. A. Hoffmann marks the story *Elena* (1837), in which the ironic narrative persona, deriving no doubt from Nikolai Gogol, gets the story off to a promising start; however, the tale is soon overwhelmed by its improbably fantastic plot, melodramatic turns, and the constant striving for effect. After these early experiments, Herzen gradually moves away from Russian Romanticism and toward the more realistic writing that characterizes his other stories as well as his novel *Kto vinovat?* (*Who Is to Blame?*, 1847). The novel focuses on a series of characters who serve to illustrate the actual social issues and ideas of the day (and for this very reason Vissarion Belinskii, who brought to Russian literary criticism the notion that literature needed to reflect a nation's development, maneuvered to have the work published in his own journal). If the novel as a whole belongs more to the emerging realistic tradition, the central figure, Vladimir Beltov, nonetheless reflects the influences of Romanticism. As a boy Beltov is educated by a Swiss tutor who is enamored of Rousseau and passes on to Vladimir a sense of noble ideals but little ability to deal with or understand Russian reality. Beltov grows up to be one of the lost souls (or "superfluous people," to use the term popularized by an Ivan Turgenev story) who live in disharmony with the world around them; he sees the failings of society's conventions, which stand in contrast to his noble ideals, but his weakness and indecisiveness prevent him from challenging the social order.

Herzen's impatience with the Romantic outlook was already apparent several years earlier, in the essay "Diletanty-romantiki" (*Romantic Dilettantes*, 1843), which comprises a section of his *Diletantizm v nauke* (*Dilettantism in Science*, 1843–46). Here he contrasts Classical empiricism and interest in nature with Romantic mysticism and avoidance of the real world. Herzen's own interests were turning more and more to a direct engagement with social and political issues, and it is perhaps for this reason that he did not write any more fiction after his departure from Russia.

However, if Herzen rejected what he perceived as the Romantic (and hence ineffectual, disengaged) persona, his readings of the German idealists, as well as of the utopian socialists, came to have an ongoing effect on his outlook. His *Dilettantism in Science* reflects, as Martin Malia has pointed out, Herzen's discovery of Hegel, who inspired the emphasis on the need to overcome illusion in order to gain an understanding of the world as it is. Herzen also adopted Hegel's notion of the dialectic, not only discerning an evolution from one historical moment to the next, but also coming to realize that everything must be viewed against its relation to the given historical phase: phenomena and ideas are not inherently good or bad, true or false, but take on qualities relative to the time in which they appear. These Hegelian notions provide the basis for Herzen's own philosophy of history, as set forth in his *Pis'ma ob izuchenii prirody* (*Letters on the Study of Nature*, 1845).

Interestingly, Herzen's efforts to study the world around him and his rejection of the Romantic persona were accompanied by a rediscovery of Schiller, and in particular of the later philosophical works. Like Schiller, Herzen emphasizes the importance of moral freedom for the individual. Thus in *S togo berega* (*From the Other Shore*, 1847–50), which in part reflects Herzen's response to the failure of the 1848 revolution in Europe, he finds that people's willingness to follow imposed systems of awards and punishments signifies mediocrity and an acceptance of the status quo; to gain freedom people have to declare independence from such external dictates and create a moral order on their own.

Herzen's views on history and morality were closely linked to his calls for social action, which grew more from his reading of the French utopian socialists, including Charles Fourier and Pierre Joseph Proudhon, as well as of English thinkers, and were of course shaped by his observations while in Russia and then of the revolutions of 1848 in Europe. In *Russkii narod i sotsializm* (*The Russian People and Socialism*, 1851), among other works, he expressed what is ultimately a Romantic faith in the common people and saw them as the backbone of a nascent revolutionary movement. Like the Slavophiles, with whom he was often in sharp disagreement, he saw "collectivism" as inherent to Russian peasant society and the village commune as the first stage in the development of a new social order. Besides his commentaries on Russia, which were to inspire the powerful oppositional forces that developed over the second half of the nineteenth century, he composed works, such as *Robert Owen* (1861), in which he pondered more generally, sometimes with hopeful optimism but at others despairingly, on the structure of the state, on human nature, and on ways to establish the order that would give the fullest rein to individual aspirations.

Herzen's masterpiece, and the work by which he remains best known today, is *Byloe i dumy* (*My Past and Thoughts*, 1852–68). Using his autobiography as the structural link, Herzen weaves together historical observations, sociopolitical commentary, and philosophical ruminations to create an enormously rich source of information on nineteenth-century intellectual life, as well as a fitting monument to his own encyclopedic interests and restless desire to help create a better world.

BARRY P. SCHERR

Biography

Born in Moscow, March 25, 1812, to Ivan Yakovlev, a wealthy member of the Russian gentry, and Luiza Haag. Studied natural sciences at Moscow University, 1829–34. With his cousin and friend Nikolai Ogaryov, established a philosophical circle, where works of the German Romantics and of the utopian socialists were read and discussed. Circle suppressed, 1834; Herzen imprisoned, then exiled to Perm, Vyatka (1835–37), and Vladimir, 1838–40. Married Natalya Zakharina, daughter of one of his uncles, 1838; their first son born, 1839. Returned to Moscow and then Saint Petersburg, wrote for the journal *Otechestvennye zapiski*, and, as a result of his writings was exiled to Novgorod, 1841–43. Allowed to return to Moscow, then used inheritance from his father to leave Russia, 1847. Spent time in Paris and Geneva, became Swiss citizen, 1851. Mother and a son died in a shipwreck, 1851; wife died 1852. Settled in London, 1852, and founded journal *The Bell*. Left England in 1865 and traveled throughout Europe; died in Paris of pneumonia on January 21, 1870.

Selected Works

Collections

Sobranie sochineniy. 30 vols., Moscow: Akademiya nauk SSSR, 1954–64.
Selected Philosophical Works. Translated by Lev Navrozov. Moscow: Foreign Languages Publishing House, 1956.

Essays

Diletantizm v nauke, 1843–46. Translated as *Dilettantism in Science* by James P. Scanlan. In: *Russian Philosophy.* New York: Quadrangle Books, 1965.
Pis'ma ob izuchenii prirody, 1845. Translated as *Letters on the Study of Nature* by Lev Navrozov. In *Selected Philosophical Works.* Moscow: Foreign Languages Publishing House, 1956.
S togo berega, 1847–50. Translated as *From the Other Shore* by Moura Budberg and *Russkii marod i sotsializm,* 1851. Translated as *The Russian People and Socialism: An Open Letter to Jules Michelet* by Richard Wollheim. Published together in one volume. New York: G. Braziller, 1956.
Pis'ma iz Frantsii i Italii, 1847–51. Translated as *Letters from France and Italy, 1847–1851* by Judith Zimmerman. Pittsburgh: University of Pittsburgh Press, 1995.
Kontsy i nachala, 1860. Translated as *Ends and Beginnings* by Constance Garnett. Edited by Aileen Kelly. New York: Oxford University Press, 1985.
Robert Owen, 1861. Extract translated by W. J. Leatherbarrow and D. C. Offord. In: *A Documentary History of Russian Thought.* Ann Arbor: Ardis, 1987.
Byloe i dumy, 1852–68. Translated as *My Past and Thoughts* by Humphrey Higgins. 4 vols. New York: Knopf, 1968.

K staromu tovarishchu, 1869. Translated as *To an Old Comrade* by Lev Navrozov. In *Selected Philosophical Works.* Moscow: Foreign Languages Publishing House, 1956.

Fiction

Legenda, 1836.
Elena, 1837.
Kto vinovat?, 1847. Translated as *Who Is to Blame?* by Michael R. Katz. Ithaca: Cornell University Press, 1984.

Bibliography

Acton, Edward. *Alexander Herzen and the Role of the Intellectual Revolutionary.* Cambridge: Cambridge University Press, 1979.
Berlin, Isaiah. *Russian Thinkers.* New York: Viking, 1978.
Carr, E. H. *The Romantic Exiles: A Nineteenth-Century Portrait Gallery.* New York, Frederick A. Stokes, 1933.
Copleston, Frederick. *Philosophy in Russia: From Herzen to Lenin and Berdyaev.* Notre Dame, Ind.: University of Notre Dame Press, 1986.
Kelly, Aileen M. *Toward Another Shore: Russian Thinkers between Necessity and Chance.* New Haven, Conn.: Yale University Press, 1998.
Kelly, Aileen M. *Views from the Other Shore: Essays on Herzen, Chekhov, and Bakhtin.* New Haven, Conn.: Yale University Press, 1999.
Malia, Martin. *Alexander Herzen and the Birth of Russian Socialism, 1812–1855.* Cambridge, Mass.: Harvard University Press, 1961.
Partridge, Monica, ed. *Alexander Herzen and European Culture: Proceedings of an International Symposium, Nottingham and London, 6–12th September 1982.* Nottingham: Astra Press, 1985.
———. *Alexander Herzen: Collected Studies.* 2d ed., Nottingham: Astra Press, 1993.
Rzhevsky, Nicholas. *Russian Literature and Ideology: Herzen, Dostoevsky Leontiev, Tolstoy, Fadeyev.* Urbana: University of Illinois Press, 1983.

HESS, MOSES 1812–1875

German-Jewish journalist and historian

Moses Hess was born in Bonn to a religiously observant Jewish family. He never apostatized, but he did insist that the destiny of the Jews had to be seen in political, not religious, terms. In his *Sacred History of Mankind*, he foretold Jewish disappearance amid historical progress, and in his *Final Judgment on the Old Social World* (1851) he remarked on the isolation to which history had condemned the Jews. These were not his major themes, however. Hess was famous in the nineteenth century first as a socialist, whom Karl Marx attacked for drawing too heavily on allegedly Utopian French social theory. In fact, Hess saw moral will as more important than social forces in driving history. Marx's strictures condemned Hess to obscurity. Police harassment, after his agitations in Germany in 1848 and 1849, led to his exile in Paris after 1853. Hess's reputation improved as humanistic socialists of the late 1950s returned to studying him. Nevertheless, he is best known as a forerunner of Zionism, even though the founders of political Zionism discovered his work only after the Zionist movement was already in being. With his *Rome and Jerusalem* (1862), Hess announced a decision to return "to my people" and became the first proponent of a national

Jewish nation-state in Palestine. His work was immediately celebrated and attacked. Its call for a Jewish national commonwealth distinguished Hess' political Zionism from both the cultural Zionism of Nachman Krochmal and the religious Zionism of Rabbi Zwi Hirsch Kalischer of Thorn. In 1862, Kalischer wrote *drishat Tsiyyon* (*The Need[s] of Zion*), in which he argued that the messiah would come after, not before, large numbers of Jews settled in the Holy Land. The Jewish historian Heinrich Graetz shared Hess's work with Kalischer.

Graetz was greatly impressed by Hess's rambling, book-length essay. Hess had decided to write the book during the 1859 and 1860 war of Italian unification, and did much of the writing between late 1860 and April 1861. He was an outsider with unconventional ideas, so his approaches to publishers met repeated refusal. His friend Berthold Auerbach refused to help because he was "a German Jew, a German" in Germany, the "homeland of intellect." Hess's previous publisher, Otto Wigand, was even less encouraging. Abraham Goldschmidt in Leipzig liked the work but would not publish it. However, Graetz admired Hess's train of thought and found him a publisher.

Graetz expected the essay to start the needed "ferment" in the current situation and to provoke a "vigorous polemic." His own eleven-volume *History of the Jews*, which began to appear in 1853, by no means anticipated renewed interest in Jewish statehood, so his support of Hess is evidence of his own delight in intellectual contestation. Hess must have been surprised and flattered at the attention. He also convinced Hess to change the title from *Rebirth of Israel* or *Springtime of Peoples* to *Rome and Jerusalem* (1862). This title rhetorically links the city of the proposed Jewish state with the central historic and ancient city in a country undergoing its own means of transformation and unification at the time.

Hess was an autodidact, inspired by Benedict de Spinoza's writings. He cited the pragmatic Hegelianism of the Polish emigré August von Cieszkowski when setting Jewish history in the context of a progressive world history that moved toward socialist transformation. He argued this case in *The Holy Family* (1837) and, differently, in *The European Triarchy* (1841). Hess began *Holy Family* with the stories of the Pentateuch and he foresaw a future international triumph of the Torah; even in his socialist years, Hess was thinking ahead to Israel. History began with the Jews and would conclude in a higher Judaism, while gentile nations such as Germany would be bypassed. His *Rome and Jerusalem* made the nation-state the means to this end.

Thus, he found intellectual support in Graetz. In his foreword to *Rome and Jerusalem*, Hess approvingly quoted "the foremost modern Jewish historian, Graetz," noting, "The history of post-talmudic times therefore always had a *national* character; in no sense is it merely religious or ecclesiastical history (*Kirchengeschichte*). As the history of a people (*Volksstammes*), Jewish history is far from being a mere literary history or religious history . . . on the contrary, the literature and the religious development, just like the high flown martyrology are . . . only individual moments in the course of its history (*einzelne Momente in seinem Geschictsverlaufe*) which do not constitute its essence." Hess saw in Graetz a valuable ally against the German Jewish "Reformers" who severed the "political from the religious," and who saw in scriptural and talmudic "life source" (*Lebensborn*) only an occasion for "accommodation for ever-changing temporal circumstances." He did not want "rigid orthodoxy," but the "superficial rationalism" of the reformers promised desertion of Judaism. Both could be avoided with what Graetz offered, namely "submergence in the national essence of Judaism" (*nationale Wesen des Judenthums*).

Hess also admitted his debt to Graetz in the sixth letter of *Rome and Jerusalem*. After noting signs of increased Jewish national self-esteem, Hess called Graetz's history "epoch-making" because it could win "the hearts of our people [*Volkes*] for its heroes and martyrs" and "overcome shallow, christianizing spiritualism." With this statement, Hess identified the great idea that was latent in Graetz's histories. If the Jews were indeed a people with an unbroken national past, then they could have, *must* have, a national future. There was no acceptable alternative, Hess believed, because anti-Semitism had proven ineradicable. His earlier hopes for assimilation into an improving human race no longer seemed practical or achievable.

Rome and Jerusalem was an impressive book, but Hess did not further develop the ideas he expressed there. After 1862 his interest in Judaism waned somewhat. He returned to socialist work and the study of natural science before his death at Paris in 1875.

ROBERT SOUTHARD

Bibliography

Laqueur, Walter. *A History of Zionism*. New York: Schocken, 1972.

Michael, Reuven. *Heinrich Graetz. Tagebuch und Briefe*. Tübingen: Leo Doeck Institute, 1977.

Silberner, Eduard. *Moses Hess. Die Geschichte seines Lebens*. Leiden: Brill, 1966.

Zlocisti, Theodro. *Moses Hess*. Berlin, 1921.

HISTOIRE DE FRANCE (THE HISTORY OF FRANCE) 1833–1844, 1855–1867

Study by Jules Michelet

The History of France is the major work of the finest French historian of the period, Jules Michelet, who was to French Romantic historiography what Victor Hugo was to French Romantic poetry and what Eugène Delacroix was to French Romantic painting. Unlike many of his Romantic peers, Michelet did not yield to the elegiac mood, but rather adopted an optimistic outlook in his historical publications, conceiving his mission as a historian at the time of the July Revolution, when he concluded that the people were history's motive force. The first volumes of *The History of France* were written in 1833, when Michelet, having been named head of the historical division of the National Archives in 1831, had access to incomparably rich documentation related to French history. These initial volumes illustrate the historian's theory that history should be a resurrection of a nation's entire life. The work is remarkable in its exhaustive treatment of French geography and every aspect of French culture and social institutions, including religion, philosophy, and language. Enriched by reference to previously unpublished sources (in contradistinction to the works of contemporary historians like Amédée and Augustin Thierry and François Guizot) Michelet's *History of France* shows the influence of Victor Cousin, Johann Gottfried von Herder, and Giambattista Vico in its tendency to fashion immense syntheses. Michelet views French history as a broad movement toward unification and centralization beginning not with the reign of Charlemagne, seen as emblematic of foreign intervention, but with those of medieval kings, such as St. Louis and Louis XI, and with the miraculous intervention of Joan of Arc. But the synthesizing sweep of Michelet's narrative, enlivened by a colorful style that betrays a Romantic imagination emotionally involved and seeking the dramatic and spectacular, rings less true in the parts of *The History of France* composed after 1851. Here Michelet, writing of the Renaissance and the Reformation (having written, in the interim, *Histoire de la Révolution* [*A History of the Revolution*,

1847–53]) is guided not by principles of impartiality, but by the impulse to judge kings and clergy mainly on the basis of their opposition to the ideals of the French Revolution, now conceived as the realization, however imperfect, of a kind of social justice. In other words, Michelet appears to politicize history, to consider it from the biased perspective of partisanship.

Whatever the unevenness of *The History of France*, and whatever the failings of a methodology eventually turned to the service of a personal conception of the proper thrust of human activity, the work is most noteworthy because of the historian's determination to establish a style of historical evocation that breaks fully with the techniques of conventional narration; that, whatever the dangers of a subjective, interpretive approach, seeks (as Michelet says in the preface of 1833) to make the "papers" of historical documentation come to life by representing the actors of the drama of history as creatures of flesh and blood, by probing with his imagination the depths of their psyches. In the process, Michelet discovers, as reflected in the later preface of 1869, that France has created itself, and that the development of a nation is not reducible to a single, monolithic factor like race but a result of the complex nature of a people. In fact, it is Michelet's attention to the people, and his attempt, however frustrated, to report accurately and faithfully in his account their language as well as their sentiments, that give a new dimension to historical writing.

The first six volumes of *The History of France*, published between 1833 and 1844, take the reader from the origins of France through the reign of Louis XI. Although Michelet initially pays tribute to historians such as the Thierrys, Jean-Charles-Léonard de Sismondi, and Guizot (whose influence on his work he would disclaim in subsequent volumes), it is quickly apparent that his approach is significantly different from theirs. An early example of this difference is the *Tableau de la France*, in volume 2, book 3. Here Michelet is concerned not only with the examination of the geography of France but with the exploration of those unique features that make up the French genius (perhaps it would not be too bold to say the French *soul*), France emerging as a person, the notion of *patrie* or homeland evolving from this sense of the "personal" distinction of being French. Another example of Michelet's originality is the manner in which he treats Joan of Arc. The peasant girl and savior of France, evoked in volume 5, book 10, is for Michelet—as she is for other historians of the period, such as Henri Martin and Guizot—the embodiment of France. But, for Michelet, Joan of Arc is the *perfect* embodiment of France, in that she is selflessly devoted to her homeland, an absolutely pure contributor to the ideal of French unity and centralization, which goes a long way toward explaining the historian's description of her in Romantic terms both of saintliness and of legend. Joan's stature in Michelet's eyes is more clearly defined by contrast with the other leaders of France he discusses in his study of the medieval period. St. Louis and Louis XI are monarchs whom Michelet praises for advancing the cause of French unity and centralization, but he does so excusing or rationalizing in the process their extermination of feudal rights. In the case of the latter king, Michelet's overall positive assessment is at odds with that of his favorite novelist, Walter Scott, who excoriated Louis XI in his novel *Quentin Durward* (1823). With Joan there is nothing to excuse or rationalize. The reference to Scott is relevant in another regard: Michelet is the novelist of history, introducing us into the conscience of his "characters" and highlighting for us the most symbolic of their gestures, as when, the flame touching her, Joan asks for holy water then, insisting her voices were from God, cries "Jesus" as she expires.

The part of *The History of France* published between 1855 and 1867, comprising eleven volumes covering the sixteenth, seventeenth, and eighteenth centuries, is the bitter fruit of Michelet's academic and intellectual experience after 1838, the year in which he was named professor of history and ethics at the Collège de France. Influenced by the liberal thinking of Edgar Quinet and Adam Mickiewicz, and now considering it his mission to promulgate democratic ideas, Michelet became incensed with the vehement criticism directed against the university, and against himself in particular, in Catholic circles. He was first optimistic about the revolution of 1848 and then profoundly disillusioned by its failure (a consequence of which was, with Louis-Napoleon's coup d'état, the loss of his position at the Collège de France). The convergence of these factors led to a new attitude on the part of the historian regarding the Catholic Church and the monarchy. The former, lauded in the earlier volumes for its association, during the Middle Ages, with the principle of liberty and for its protection and consolation of the disinherited and downtrodden, now becomes the enemy of liberty and thus of the people, an enemy severely judged by a Michelet who has since become the ardent historian of the French Revolution and is now seeing the church through its lens. Michelet's hostility toward the monarchy is fully manifest in his evaluation of Louis XIV and the two kings who came after him. As for the reign of Louis XIV, even its artistic splendor is challenged. Michelet acknowledges that, as a youth, his models were Pierre Corneille, Jean de La Fontaine, Molière, and Blaise Pascal, but, he adds, nothing in their writing rises to the level of Greek drama, Dante Alighieri, François Rabelais, or William Shakespeare. Moreover, in any event, says Michelet, indulging in the metaphorical flourishes he enjoys, Louis XIV is the burial ground for a world; like his Versailles palace, he faces the sunset.

If Michelet is often unfair and partial, converting this part of his *History of France* into a personal religious and political statement, what nevertheless emerges obviously to his credit is his impassioned defense of liberty transformed into a basic historical perspective. History is, for Michelet, not only the resurrection of the past in its multifaceted reality but a chronicle, imbued with all the optimism of the Enlightenment's notion of progress, of the heroic struggle and eventual triumph of human liberty. It is the irrefutable demonstration that, if France created France, it is because man is his own Prometheus, finally prevailing over the "fatalities" of human existence. What is perhaps less obvious and more "modern" is that, whatever the distortions of Michelet's partisan point of view, he appears to have keenly understood the complexities and ironies of the way in which power functions, and how progress results at times, paradoxically, from the most devious, even the most selfish designs of heads of state.

NORMAN ARAUJO

Work

Histoire de France. 17 vols., 1833–67. Translated as *The History of France* by G. H. Smith. 2 vols. 1845–47.

Bibliography

Barthes, Roland. *Michelet par lui-même*. Paris: Le Seuil, 1954.

Haac, Oscar A. "The Literature of History: Michelet's Middle Ages," *Nineteenth-Century French Studies* 4 (1976): 162–68.

Haac, Oscar A. *Jules Michelet*. Boston: Twayne, 1982.

Kippur, Stephen A. *Jules Michelet: A Study of Mind and Sensibility*. Albany: State University of New York Press, 1981.

Mitzman, Arthur. *Michelet ou la subversion du passé*. Paris: La Boutique de l'histoire, 1999.

Remaud, Olivier. *Michelet: La Magistrature de l'histoire*. Paris: Éditions Michalon, 1998.

Rudler, Gustave. *Michelet historien de Jeanne d'Arc*. Paris: Presses Universitaires, 1925–26.

HISTORIOGRAPHY: BRITAIN

The era of British Romanticism saw a dramatic change in the way that writers conceived and represented the historical past. Among the most significant transformations occurring in this period is the emergence of a new role for historical writing itself, conceived less as a kind of "teaching by example," and more as a way of representing the peculiarity of specific epochs and of the individuals whose lives were shaped by them. In late eighteenth-century Britain, history emerged as a popular subject in its own right, and the lively market in these years for historical work of all kinds reflects the emergence of history in this period as both a popular and a philosophical concern.

For many readers of the late eighteenth century, David Hume's *History of England* (1754–62) represented the highest pinnacle of the historian's art. Although Hume is better known today for the philosophical work written earlier in his career, he established a reputation as England's preeminent historian with the publication of this work. *The History of England* looked back to the political ferment preceding the Restoration of 1688, and commemorated the establishment of peace and prosperity in England. Much as he had done earlier in essays such as "Of the Rise and Progress of the Arts and Sciences" (1742), Hume heaped praise on the growth of English commercial society, particularly on what he saw as that society's ability to stimulate intellectual activity, to promote a healthy spirit of competition, and to spread ever greater networks of politeness and civility across the globe. Thus Hume offered a mode of historiography that catered to the needs of a credit economy that depended for its prosperity upon the image of a stable and largely secular future.

Hume's *History* must be understood in relation to a historiographical discourse emerging in Scotland at this time. This ambitious genre of historical writing was known as "philosophical" or "conjectural" history, and numbered John Millar, William Robertson, and Adam Smith among its practitioners. It sought to chart the history of human civilizations as they advanced between historical stages characterized most often by the dominant form of property ownership: from hunting to herding to agriculture to commerce. While Charles-Louis Montesquieu is frequently credited as the first such practitioner of this philosophical history, it was well suited to appeal to the Scots, whose nation was thrust into a period of rapid modernization following the ill-fated Stuart revolt of 1744 and 1745 against the Hanoverian throne. Though Hume generally looked with optimism upon the progress of commercial society, not all historians were as sanguine about the ameliorating effects of that progress. In the most popular of the conjectural histories, Adam Ferguson's *Essay on the History of Civil Society* (1767), Ferguson concluded that the progress of commercial society would diminish rather than enhance the manly and competitive spirit that invigorated most republics, leaving both the republic and its citizens effeminate, languorous, and helpless in the face of aggression from abroad.

An important influence on later historical thinkers such as Karl Marx, Ferguson's *Essay* represents an early version of a critique of modernization that we frequently associate with Romantic thought and literature. In the philosophical history of the late eighteenth century, William Wordsworth had a basis to claim, in his preface to the *Lyrical Ballads* (1798), that "a multitude of causes unknown to former times"—among them the French Revolution and the rapid growth of England's cities—were "acting with a combined force . . . to reduce [the mind] to a state of almost savage torpor." While Jean-Jacques Rousseau had popularized a similar dialectic of civility and savagery in the *Discourse on the Origins of Inequality among Men* (1754), British philosophical historians located this dialectic in a determinate historical context rather than in society or human nature in general.

Despite such emphases on the particularity of historical epochs, historians were acutely sensitive to kinships among different moments of the historical past, frequently insisting on a historical logic that repeated itself from age to age. The historiographical premise that empires were subject to the same laws of growth and decay as organic forms found its most profound elaboration in Edward Gibbon's *Decline and Fall of the Roman Empire* (1776–88), which provided readers with an ample basis for comparing ancient empires to contemporary ones. Several decades after the publication of Gibbon's work, Lord Byron revisited its argument in famous lines from *Childe Harold's Pilgrimage* (1812–18):

> There is a moral in all human tales;
> Tis but the same rehearsal of the past,
> First Freedom, and then Glory—when that fails,
> Wealth, vice, corruption—barbarism at last.

Byron's dyspeptic historical vision unites the four-stages theory of social progress with Gibbon's history of an empire's decline and fall.

In addition to narrating the history of empires, British historical writing was deeply invested in accounts of individual historical "characters"; indeed, most histories of this period reflect an understanding of the reciprocal and mutually determining relationship between public and private affairs. Through the late eighteenth and ninteenth centuries, there emerges a conception of private life as uniquely representative of the customs and manners of a particular historical epoch. The fascination with

individuals as historical "types"—what in German, and especially Hegelian thought, is known as the concept of the "world-historical individual"—would culminate in ninteenth-century England with Thomas Carlyle's famous definition of history as "the essence of innumerable biographies." Yet Carlyle's sense of the importance of heroic individuals, strongly indebted to German historiography, surely intensified in light of his apprehension that such individuals were rarely to be found in the present. In his famous essay "Signs of the Times" (1829), Carlyle delivered a searing critique of what he saw as the thorough mechanization of English life, the product not only of the emergent Industrial Revolution but of a people who had lamentably perfected "the great art of adapting means to ends." Carlyle's own masterpiece of historical writing, his mammoth account of the French Revolution (1837), is enriched by detailed descriptions of many of the principal players in Revolutionary events, yet heroes are conspicuously absent.

This explosion of interest in the private lives of historical actors finds a significant parallel in an emergent conception of literature as a legitimate form of "making history" in its own right. In his essay "On History and Romance" (1797), William Godwin claimed priority for fiction over history on the grounds that it is better able to represent the private as well as public lives of historical figures. Many writers of the Romantic period shared this idea that by telling the history of the individual, one might best capture the spirit of the age that created that individual. In the enormously popular *Waverley* novels (1814–25), Wal-ter Scott pioneered the notion of a "passive hero" whose relative lack of a strong personality makes him the ideal figure through which to represent the force of historical circumstances upon the individual character. Scott's portrait of Edward Waverley, torn between competing sides of the 1745 rebellion, is the best-known Romantic depiction of an individual determined by historical events in which he himself participates and to a limited extent creates. In poetry, the same principle finds an expression in Percy Bysshe Shelley's insistence (from the preface to *Prometheus Unbound* [1819]) that "[p]oets . . . are in one sense the creators and in another the creations of their age."

NOEL JACKSON

Bibliography

Bann, Stephen. *Romanticism and the Rise of History*. New York: Twayne, 1995.

Chandler, James K. *England in 1819: The Politics of Literary Culture and the Case of Romantic Historicism*. Chicago: University of Chicago Press, 1998.

Philipson, Nicholas T. *Hume*. New York: St. Martin's Press, 1989.

Phillips, Mark Salber. *Society and Sentiment: Genres of Historical Writing, 1740–1820*. Princeton, N.J.: Princeton University Press, 2000.

Pocock, J. G. A. *Virtue, Commerce, and History: Essays on Political Thought and History, Chiefly in the Eighteenth Century*. Cambridge: Cambridge University Press, 1985.

Rigney, Ann. *Imperfect Histories: The Elusive Past and the Legacy of Romantic Historicism*. Ithaca, N.Y.: Cornell University Press, 2001.

HISTORIOGRAPHY: FRANCE

With the advent of Romanticism, history ceased to be the province of antiquarians and became, in the words of Stephen Bann, "a flood that overrode all disciplinary barriers and finally, when the barriers became no longer easy to perceive, became a substratum to almost every type of cultural activity." The fascination of Romanticism with history expressed more than a desire for reconnection with the past. In the wake of the French Revolution, a number of guiding ideas that had sustained eighteenth-century thought were called into question. Romanticism challenged the universalism of Enlightenment thought, its belief in empirical science, and its confidence in the ability of human reason to build a better world. Romanticism rehabilitated religion, attributed value to the imagination, and questioned the claims of Enlightenment liberalism. Traumatic events such as the French Revolution and the collapse of the Napoleonic Empire encouraged a reassessment not just of the recent past but of universal history. A common complaint made by the Romantics regarding Enlightenment historians was that the latter had restricted their investigations to providing a bare relation of the facts, whereas in reality events needed to be understood in relation to the unfolding of a greater purpose. The Romantic view of history was metaphysical. It went beyond Enlightenment notions of perfectibility and proposed a theory of progress which grounded the interpretation of art, society, and language in a general notion of development. Usually this sense of development was related to the notion of an inwardness seeking outward expression. History was held to be made by humans, but it was viewed as the expression of something greater: the collective spirit of humankind, the national essence, or the divine ideal.

The first half of the nineteenth century saw the emergence of a number of philosophies whose goal was social reconstruction. These philosophies primarily concerned themselves with the question: how could society be rebuilt and reorganized in the wake of the French Revolution? Historiography played a crucial role in this process of coming to terms with the consequences of 1789. Was the Revolution an aberration, or was it the outcome of a logical process of development? The debate concerned the whole of Europe, but not surprisingly it was felt most acutely in France. For the people of France, the Revolution had problematized the relationship between past and present. The revolutionaries had proclaimed their intention to abolish the past, to begin anew, to create a radically new type of human being. They considered that little of value could emerge from a national past which had been dominated by church and monarchy; it was far better to entrust humankind's development to a progressive, future-oriented reason. However, the descent of the revolution into violence and repression caused many in France to reassess their earlier willingness to embrace social change. The early nineteenth century was marked by a nostalgia for an idealized prerevolutionary world, stabilized by Catholicism and founded upon fixed social hierarchies. According to counterrevolutionary thinkers such as Joseph de Maistre, the revolution had been caused by the sinful individualism generated by the freethinking, skeptical Enlightenment. Counterrevolutionary writers rejected

Enlightenment views of history and of human nature, and placed their trust instead in tradition and revelation. They believed that only by turning to divine providence could the meaning of history be understood. The liberals, as political opponents of the traditionalists, responded to these arguments by constructing a new historiography which justified 1789 and legitimated change, understood as progress. The liberal interpretation took hold during the Restoration and marked a change in attitude on the left. During the Napoleonic Empire those thinkers who had continued to defend the cause of Enlightenment liberalism were disinclined to place much value on historical knowledge, which they considered to be unsure and unreliable. After 1815 it was the liberal historians, the most celebrated being Jacques-Nicolas-Augustin Thierry and François-Pierre-Guillaume Guizot, who rehabilitated history so as to serve as a weapon against the ultraconservatives while remaining in tune with the spirit of the post-Revolutionary cultural configuration. Thierry's best-known works were his *Lettres sur l'histoire de France* (*Letters on the History of France*, 1827) and *Histoire de la conquête de l'Angleterre par les Normands* (*History of the Conquest of England by the Normans*, 1825). Guizot's key texts were his *Essais sur l'histoire de France* (*Essays on the History of France*, 1823), *Histoire de la civilisation en Europe* (*History of Civilization in Europe*, 1828), and *Histoire de la civilisation en France depuis la chute de l'Empire romain* (*History of Civilization in France Since the Fall of the Roman Empire*, 1829–30).

The liberal historians distanced themselves from abstract political theory and argued instead that political ideas needed to be grounded in history. They emphasized the extent to which the driving forces that moved history were collective, that religions, beliefs, and ideas were responsible for change. However, their objective remained the defense of key liberal freedoms and the rights of the individual. To this end they understood that it was essential for them to reclaim history as a field of knowledge from the counterrevolutionary Right. This was done in several ways. First, traditional overviews of French history were contested as inaccurate, unscholarly, and biased; old-fashioned works were denounced as propaganda written in support of the former ruling order. Second, once the French national past had been rescued from the forces of the Right it was reinterpreted in terms of a history of conflict and struggle in which the Third Estate played the role of the central protagonist. Third, the meaning of the Revolution itself was revised and the sequence of events represented in a manner which, while in no way siding with egalitarianism or with Jacobin tyranny, nevertheless endowed 1789 with an air of inevitability. This move was undertaken by the liberal historians François-Auguste-Marie Mignet and Adolphe-Louis Thiers who, during the Restoration, published histories of the revolution that scandalized many readers by apparently justifying evil in the name of an amoral historical determinism. Fourth, liberal historians put into play a dynamic principle that explained the process of change over the centuries and lent a pattern to the succession of events. Thierry focused on class conflict and the relations between victorious and conquered peoples. Guizot emphasized the role played by ideas tracing the roots of European civilization to three elements: the Germanic idea of independence, the Christian sense of inward spiritual life, and the Roman ideas of empire and municipal freedoms.

It must be emphasized that for the Romantics, history was perceived as an exciting new science which unlocked the meaning of the past and perhaps gave access to the future. In this way, social regeneration and construction of a utopian future rested on the application of Claude-Henri de Saint-Simon's understanding of history's movement in terms of organic and critical periods. What distinguished the new science of history was the quest to discover the laws that governed historical change. This preoccupation was shared by many historians and philosophers of history during the Romantic era. Parallels were often drawn between history and recent developments in comparative anatomy, embryology and physiology. In his *Introduction à la science de l'histoire ou science du développement de l'humanité* (*Introduction to the Science of History or Science of the Development of Humankind*, 1833) Philippe-Joseph-Benjamin Buchez went so far as to claim that progress in history could be understood as a mathematical series. Societies were not fixed entities; rather, they resembled living organisms, evolving in time and possessing their own internal necessity and life cycle. History-as-science mastered the past and legitimated speculation about the future. Hadn't Auguste-Marie-François Comte considered that every science had prediction as its goal? There were, not unsurprisingly, as many visions of the future as there were scientific explanations of the past. Liberal history endorsed middle class freedoms and lent legitimation to the postrevolutionary nation state. Guizot's view was that the laws which governed progress appeared to be congruent with the development of reason, truth, justice, and right. Moreover, the rationality of European history was held to correspond to the intentions of divine providence. History justified the liberal nation and any potential threat posed by individualism was contained, limited by the concept of civilization, which emphasized the social dimension. For such liberals the message was clear: French history taught that France needed a constitutional monarchy, a moderate system of government that united the monarchical principle with effective but limited representative institutions. For Thierry and Guizot, the July Monarchy seemed to be the logical culmination of French history.

According to Guizot, the work of historians comprised three stages. First they dissected the body of history, and then they described how the different organs were connected, and finally they revitalized the past, representing it as living reality. Jules Michelet went further and viewed history as the integral resurrection of the past. Romantic historiography had serious pretensions to scientific method: the publication of documents, reliance on archival material, and the elaboration of protocols that lent substance to the constitution of the discipline as a fullfledged profession. However, the writing of history went beyond science because the successful historian openly drew on the power of the imagination; Thierry spoke of the gift of second sight. Writing history became an act of re-creation that at times brought into question the lines of demarcation between history and literature, truth and fiction. Amable-Guillaume-Prosper Barante's *Histoire des Ducs de Bourgogne* (*History of the Dukes of Burgundy*, 1824–26) made a strong appeal to a readership that enjoyed the historical novels of the day. Romantic history struck a chord with the reading public because, as with Romantic literature, it placed emphasis on conflict, violence, and local color. History, like literature, set out to make the past present. Moreover, Romantic historiography, like Romantic art, grounded meaning in a transcendent ideal. History contained more than events, because behind events lay ideas and collective forces. Michelet's

Histoire de France (*History of France*, 1833–67) possessed a genuinely epic dimension grounded in a powerful use of symbol and metaphor. History could be viewed as a form of revelation. In certain instances Romanticism elevated the historian or the philosopher of history to the status of priest, interpreting the past, explaining God's intentions to men.

The two major foreign influences on the development of French historiography were Johann Gottfried von Herder and Giambattista Vico, who were translated by Jules Michelet and Edgar Quinet. In the 1820s Michelet and Quinet's political sympathies lay with the liberal opposition. However, both men became disillusioned with the July Monarchy and dissatisfied with the liberal reading of the national past that lent an intellectual validation to Orleanism. Michelet and Quinet took history in a more radical direction, aligning it with the popular forces that had initiated the French Revolution, but were still excluded from power in the time of the July Monarchy. Over the course of the 1830s and 1840s Michelet made the French people ("le peuple") very much the collective subject of his narrative. Human history was represented as an aspect of an eternal struggle between spirit and matter that generated meaning, purpose, and direction. At the same time, Michelet insisted on the need for historians to situate history in relation to geography. In Michelet's eyes, France was a religion. Christianity had failed, and he urged a return to the revolutionary values that alone would ensure a national renaissance. By the 1840s French historiography had become focused on the history of the revolution. The various competing ideologies (socialist, communist, reformist, republican) produced their key texts on this theme, the most celebrated being Alphonse Marie-Louise de Lamartine's *Histoire des Girondins* (*History of the Girondists*, 1847), Esquiros's *Histoire des Montagnards* (*History of the Mountain*, 1847), and Jules Michelet's *Histoire de la Révolution française* (*History of the French Revolution*, 1847–53).

The 1848 Revolution and the advent of the Second Empire had a significant impact on historical writing in France. Eventually there emerged a new form of positivist history that distrusted literary qualities and aspired to something akin to scientific objectivity. In the wake of 1848, Alexis de Tocqueville undertook his classic reassessment of the relationship between the ancien régime and the revolution. Now even some Republicans began to challenge the myth of the revolution that had been fostered by Romantic historiography. In the light of Louis-Napoleon's coup d'état, was it reasonable any longer for those on the left to claim that the Revolution of 1789 had been a success? In 1865 Quinet published *La Révolution*, which dared to question the orthodox republican interpretation of the Revolution. However, there was more at stake in this than the need to reappraise the meaning of 1789. The demythologizing impulse went deeper, because it subjected to critical analysis the general sense of determinism and inevitability that had underpinned the metaphysical pretensions of much nineteenth-century French historiography.

CERI CROSSLEY

Bibliography

Bann, Stephen. *The Clothing of Clio: A Study of the Representation of History in the Nineteenth Century Britain and France*. Cambridge: Cambridge University Press, 1984.

————. *Romanticism and the Rise of History*. New York: Twayne, 1995.

Barzun, Jacques. "Romantic Historiography as a Political Force in France," *Journal of the History of Ideas* (1941): 318–29.

Bernard, Claudie. *Le Passé recomposé. Le roman historique français du dix-neuvième siècle*. Paris: Hachette, 1996.

Crossley, Ceri. *French Historians and Romanticism: Thierry, Guizot, the Saint-Simonians, Quinet, Michelet*. London: Routledge, 1993.

Den Boer, Pim. *History as a Profession: The Study of History in France 1818–1914*. Princeton, N.J.: Princeton University Press, 1998.

Ehrard, Jean, and Guy Palmade. *L'Histoire*. Paris: Colin, 1964.

Engel-Janosi, Friedrich. *Four Studies in French Romantic Historical Writing*. Baltimore, Md.: Johns Hopkins University Press, 1955.

Gérard, Alice. *La Révolution française, mythes et interprétations 1789–1970*. Paris: Flammarion, 1970.

Glencross, Michael. *Reconstructing Camelot. French Romantic Medievalism and the Arthurian Tradition*. Cambridge: D. S. Brewer, 1995.

Gossman, Lionel. *Between History and Literature*. Cambridge, Mass.: Harvard University Press, 1990.

Johnson, Douglas. *Guizot: Aspects of French History 1787–1874*. London: Routledge and Kegan Paul, 1963.

Leterrier, Sophie-Anne. *Le XIXe siècle historien*. Paris: Belin, 1997.

Mellon, Stanley. *The Political Uses of History*. Stanford, Calif.: Stanford University Press, 1958.

Moreau, Pierre. *L'Histoire en France au XIXe siècle*. Paris: Les Belles Lettres, 1935.

Roanvallon, Pierre. *Le Moment Guizot*. Paris: Gallimard, 1985.

Reizov, Boris. *L'Historiographie romantique française*. Moscow: Editions en Langues Etrangeres, n.d. [1962].

Walch, Jean. *Les Maîtres de l'histoire 1815–1850*. Geneva: Slatkine, 1986.

White, Hayden. *Metahistory: The Historical Imagination in nineteenth-Century Europe*. Baltimore: Johns Hopkins University Press, 1973.

HISTORIOGRAPHY: GERMANY

The century between 1750 and 1850 has been described by Reinhart Koselleck as a *Sattelzeit*, a period of transition during which the foundations of modern society were laid. A concept of history was developed that saw all things past as part of a uniform process, leading from pragmatism as the essential paradigm of Enlightenment historiography to nineteenth-century historicism. In reconstructing this process of transformation, historians have recently underlined the breaks between the pre- and post–1789 periods and established that contemporaries had already perceived this age not as a self-contained unit, but rather as one phase in a number of intellectual changes. Especially as regards theoretical positions, historiography after 1800 distanced itself from eighteenth-century pragmatism and its didactic intentions and retreated into a distinct objectivism, which was followed by a more subjective theory of history only after the revolution of 1848. These supposed breaks were, however, not as clear-cut as they may seem in retrospect, and, especially in the second half of the nineteenth century, politically engaged historians such as Johann Gustav Droysen and Heinrich von Sybel were still closely bound to the intellectual roots of Hegelian and Humboldtian philosophy.

German historiography in the late eighteenth century was clearly dominated by trends set by the famous Göttingen historians Johann Christoph Gatterer and A. L. von Schlözer, but also by Johann Friedrich Böhmer, C. G. Heyne, Johann David Michaelis, Johann Stephan Pütter, and Ludwig Timotheus von Spittler. Gatterer's impact lay in his rediscovery of world history as a serious subject, to which he, in his *Abriss der Universalhistorie* (*Outline of Universal History*, 1765), contributed a theoretical basis that lasted until Leopold von Ranke addressed similar questions in his world-historical studies. Further, Gatterer helped to promote history as a professional discipline. He called for the institutionalization of the historical sciences, and expressed his epistemological ideas about what the historian's task was in newly founded journals such as the *Historisches Journal* (1772–81). Unlike Gatterer's, Schlözer's studies are characterized by a wide-ranging interest in geographical, ethnological, social, and linguistic aspects of universal history, thereby broadening historiography and including cultural aspects as well as those from the life sciences. This diversity was new to German historiography, and the use of an approach based on a history of the bourgeoisie's emancipation rather than a court-oriented hagiography mirrored the influence of revolutionary ideas before, during, and after the French Revolution.

German philosophers also played an important role in contributing new philosophical ideas to historical thought. Immanuel Kant and Gotthold Ephraim Lessing, though holding different views on the idea of historical progress and, in connection with this, on the development of moral standards, influenced historical writing insofar as they introduced to it the philosophical method based on argument and evidence. In his influential *Ideen zur Philosophie der Geschichte der Menschheit* (*Outlines of a Philosophy of the History of Man*, 1784–91), Johann Gottfried Herder was the first to use the concept of *Verstehen* (empathy) and to connect it with historical interpretation. In contrast to Kant, he emphasized that thought and language were inseparable, and that for the study of a people's history and culture a knowledge of its language was indispensable. History and language formed a natural process, and according to Herder, they progressed toward humanitarian improvement. Consequently, the Enlightenment was historicized as a stage within the organic and progressive development of universal history.

Few literary figures were as important as Johann Christoph Friedrich von Schiller in forming a bridge between Enlightenment historiography and historicism. Generally still regarded more as a poet than as a historian, Schiller had a deep interest in universal history and has only recently been discovered as a mediator of ideas between Schlözer and Wilhelm von Humboldt. Understanding history as art, he wanted to write both for specialists and for a broader public, as seen in his works on the Netherlands breaking away from Spain and on the Thirty Years War. Schiller prompted the systematic evaluation of the question of whether history was an art or a science.

Johann Gottlieb Fichte, G. W. F. Hegel, Friedrich Wilhelm Joseph von Schelling, and other philosophers of German idealism went further in systematizing history as a dialectically related continuum of different stages. Past and present formed a logical unit when brought into a relationship with each other by man's reason. In Fichte's view, and particularly so under the impact of the French Revolution, history also had the task of formulating the goal of freedom, both of the individual and the nation. But with the advent of a more politically orientated philosophy and historiography at the turn of the century, the individual will and the collective will of the nation were no longer as clearly distinguished as they had been before 1789. In fact, the nation, or state, seen as an ethical entity, was ranked above the individual and the idea of the social contract. From this Fichte and Hegel concluded that nations pursued their own destiny, possessed their own particular historical laws, and were distinguished from each other by the role of the *Weltgeist* (spirit of the age) in the different stages of history.

In contrast to this teleological, idealist position, historicism as formulated by Humboldt, Friedrich Karl von Savigny, and, most notably, by Barthold Georg Niebuhr and Ranke, set out to emphasize the significance of each particular age, the uniqueness of its culture, and its independence from previous and subsequent periods. Each age was *unmittelbar zu Gott* (immediate to God) as Ranke put it, implying that there was not necessarily a teleological link between past, present, and future. However, the understanding of the past, or an accurate empathy for it, could help as a guide to the present if the historian could identify historical trends that were part of a continuity. The association between the heritage of the past and the political and cultural needs of the present was demonstrated most obviously in what Ranke and the following generation of Prussian historians focused on: the power of the nation-state. This could best be studied by using an "objective" method and concentrating on primary sources in political and diplomatic archives. Although Ranke and German historicism achieved an almost unsurpassable position in the history of nineteenth-century historiography, historians such as Jacob Burckhardt tried to shift the balance toward a history more orientated by culture, and intellectuals such as Karl Marx emphasized the social and economic dimensions of the past. Yet nation and state continued to play a central role in German historiography, and universal perspectives, which had been so popular and dominant in the late eighteenth century, were only sporadically pursued, characteristically enough by Ranke himself in his old age.

BENEDIKT STUCHTEY

Bibliography

Blanke, Horst Walter, and Dirk Fleischer, eds. *Theoretiker der deutschen Aufklärungshistorie.* 2 vols. Stuttgart: Frommann-Holzboog, 1990.

Blanke, Horst Walter, and Jörn Rüsen, eds. *Von der Aufklärung zum Historismus: Zum Strukturwandel des historischen Denkens.* Paderborn: Schöningh, 1984.

Fulda, Daniel. *Wissenschaft aus Kunst: Die Entstehung der modernen deutschen Geschichtsschreibung, 1760–1860.* Berlin: Walter de Gruyter, 1996.

Hardtwig, Wolfgang. "Die Verwissenschaftlichung der Geschichtsschreibung zwischen Aufklärung und Historismus." In *Geschichtskultur und Wissenschaft.* Munich: DTV, 1990.

Iggers, Georg G. "The University of Göttingen, 1760–1800, and the Transformation of Historical Scholarship," *Storia della Storiografia* 2 (1982): 11–37.

Jordan, Stefan. *Geschichtstheorie in der ersten Hälfte des 19. Jahrhunderts. Die Schwellenzeit zwischen Pragmatismus und Klassischem Historismus.* Frankfurt: Campus, 1999.

Muhlack, Ulrich. *Geschichtswissenschaft im Humanismus und in der Aufklärung. Die Vorgeschichte des Historismus.* Munich: Beck, 1991.

Reill, Peter Hanns. *The German Enlightenment and the Rise of Historicism.* Berkeley and Los Angeles: University of California Press, 1975.

Stuchtey, Benedikt, and Peter Wende, eds. *British and German Historiography, 1750–1950: Traditions, Perceptions, and Transfers.* Oxford: Oxford University Press, 2000.

HISTORIOGRAPHY: UNITED STATES

Puritan historiography, as illustrated by Edward Johnson and Cotton Mather, embraced a providential view of history consistent with John Winthrop's "city upon a hill" philosophy and William Bradford's *History of Plymouth Plantation, 1606–1646* (1630–54). It endorsed the Calvinist belief that God had preordained a New Jerusalem in the American wilderness and that his people were destined to play a role in its establishment and millenial unfolding. The "task of the historian," as Michael Kraus and Davis D. Joyce observe, was "not to entertain the reader but to discover his people's place in God's plan for the universe." Even as Enlightenment historians such as Voltaire revealed the role of human agency in historical events, Puritan doctrinal biases persisted in New England histories and contributed to the distinctly nationalist and Romantic impulses of post-revolutionary historiography.

After 1776, chronicles and historical writing by David Ramsay, Mercy Otis Warren, and other writers of American history, both at the state and national levels, espoused a unique sense of nationalism, with Ramsay, for example, proclaiming in his *History of the American Revolution* (1789) that America's purpose was to assert the "rights of man" and promote the virtues of republicanism. Despite self-conscious attempts by colonial historians such as Thomas Prince and Hannah Adams to infuse rationalist "objectivity" into historical narratives, early American historical writing continued to turn to the "chosen people" myth and its attendant millenial or typological images. Jeremy Belknap's attempts, for instance, to acknowledge the role of bias in historical writing and to embrace a rationalist ethos in his *History of New Hampshire* (1784) still relied on the "providence of the supreme ruler" and assumptions of national destiny. Indeed, in the 1780s and 1790s an increasingly intense sense of nationalism contributed to the view of history as not only a record of great men's lives but as a vehicle for instilling republican values.

If, as Hayden White remarks, late Enlightenment ideas about reason, natural laws, and progress entered a period in which Europeans disagreed about the "proper *attitude* with which to approach the study of history" and moved toward "empathy as a method of historical inquiry," American intellectuals and historians also engaged in debate about historical meaning and its moral or literary appeal. Despite the ways in which histories by Edward Gibbon, David Hume, and William Robertson helped popularize historical writing in America, and aside from the manner in which Johann Gottfried Herder, Johann Christoph Friedrich von Schiller, and the historical romances of Walter Scott also contributed to an American appetite for Romantic history writing, American intellectuals such as Charles Brockden Brown questioned the meaning and function of history. Brown debated the differences between "history" and "romance" and commented in his magazine essays on the fictive dimensions of historical narrative. Essays such as "Walstein's School of History" (1799), "The Difference between History and Romance" (1800), and "Modes of Historical Writing" (1806) record a highly self-conscious and critical enquiry into the motivations behind and cultural effects of Romantic historiography.

Just as the eighteenth century ended with a limited but intense enquiry into the fictive nature of historical writing, so nineteenth-century European and American historiography found itself deeply influenced by the historiographical ideas of German historian Leopold von Ranke. Ranke's emphasis on archival research and historical documentation and authenticity led to a view of history that anchored itself in archival evidence yet focused on the struggle of individual nations and "the hand of God." Influenced by German notions of historical progress and purpose, American historians such as George Bancroft proceeded to inaugurate a Romantic tradition of history writing. To be sure, the historical writing of Washington Irving and Richard Hildreth variously employed irony and scientific objectivity in ways that were less boisterous or nationalistic and offer evidence of a less self-congratulatory style amid the exuberant Romantic historiography of the nineteenth century; but beginning with Bancroft, the histories of John Motley, Francis Parkman, William H. Prescott, and Jared Sparks each contain progressive ideologies that exalt American democracy and idealism, or used the rhetoric of national redemption to interpret events and their meaning.

Bancroft's *History of the United States from the Discovery of the Continent* (1834–74), for instance, turned to the dialectical philosophy of G. W. F. Hegel and German idealism of Herder to describe the progressive unfolding of American history. Like his Puritan forefathers, Bancroft sought to explain the development and role of the United States as an agent of providence in spreading freedom. Unlike them, however, his moral interpretation of historical events or incidents tended to be more intuitive, teleological, and certain of universal progress. Similarly, just as Bancroft's history took the American frontier into account, Prescott's *The Conquest of Mexico* (1843) and its history of the Spanish empire in sixteenth-century America also focused on Anglo-American struggles in the wilderness and related events in elevated fashion. His broad but in-depth use of original source material, however, distinguished his history writing from that of other historians.

If Henry Adams wrote history as a way of remembering the past, focusing specifically on the presidential administrations of Thomas Jefferson and James Madison, Parkman would become perhaps the most original historian, writing about the American struggle for control of the continent in almost epic terms. Parkman's *History of the Conspiracy of Pontiac* (1851) and *The Jesuits in North America in the Seventeenth Century* (1867) detail the struggle between France and England for control of the North American continent. While he slanted this contest as an Anglo-Protestant victory over Catholic authoritarianism and savage Indians, his narrative comes alive with vivid, episodic action and dramatic detail, providing lasting images of marching men, dying Jesuit martyrs, and various individual characters.

In sum, the elevated, Romantic style of writing that came to dominate nineteenth-century American historiography was nationalist in origin. From the Puritan belief in divine Providence to patriotic histories such as Parkman's, American historical writers, with few exceptions, constructed a history of America that was highly idealistic in its assumptions about individual morality, national progress, and American destiny.

MARK L. KAMRATH

Bibliography

Appleby, Joyce, Lynn Hunt, and Margaret Jacob. *Telling the Truth about History.* New York: W. W. Norton, 1994.

Baym, Nina. *American Women Writers and the Work of History, 1790–1860.* New Brunswick, N.J.: Rutgers University Press, 1995.

Calcott, George H. *History in the United States 1800–1860.* Baltimore: Johns Hopkins University Press, 1970.

Kraus, Michael, and Davis D. Joyce. *The Writing of American History.* rev. ed., Norman: University of Oklahoma Press, 1985.

Levin, David. *History as Romantic Art: Bancroft, Prescott, Motley, and Parkman.* New York: AMS Press, 1967.

Wish, Harvey. *The American Historian: A Social-Intellectual History of the Writing of the American Past.* New York: Oxford University Press, 1960.

HISTORY PAINTING: BRITAIN

Britain had developed no strong native tradition of history painting by the eighteenth century, but when the Royal Academy in London was founded in 1768, members were drawn into the intellectual debate about its nature and significance, a debate that had dominated academic discourse throughout Europe since the Renaissance. One of the basic requirements of a history painting, as defined by Alberti, was a morally improving subject that could both instruct and please, allowing a full interpretation and display of the noblest human emotions and illustrating the best in human aspirations. The subject matter was not limited strictly to Classical, ancient, or modern history, but could encompass religious, mythological or literary themes. The human figure in action or thought was an essential component, and was to be studied carefully from life. The composition was to be fully conceived before work on the final canvas, preferably on a grand scale, was undertaken.

Joshua Reynolds, first president of the Royal Academy, absorbed these ideas with enthusiasm and promulgated them in his influential series of fifteen *Discourses*, delivered to the academy between 1769 and 1790 at the annual prize-giving ceremonies. A hierarchy of subject matter that gave preeminence to paintings which involved the human figure in heroic action was embraced by the Royal Academy. Historical or Shakespearean titles were set as examination pieces in the annual competition for premium awards.

The essential requirement to succeed in history painting was a correct understanding of human anatomy in action. As it was not possible to obtain systematic tuition in life drawing in Britain until the late eighteenth century, study in Rome was encouraged. The painter Gavin Hamilton settled in Rome in 1752. His chief project in history painting, which took him over a quarter of a century to complete, was the execution of two major series of large Homeric subjects. These heroic scenes were subsequently engraved by Domenico Cunego, under Hamilton's own direction, and the prints were circulated throughout Europe. Their neoclassical vision and ambitious scope proved profoundly influential on the next generation of history painters. The American Benjamin West spent three formative years in Rome, from 1760 to 1763, before establishing himself in London. He became one of the most innovative and successful painters of Classical sub-

jects and achieved more royal commissions than any British contemporary. Later he illustrated the exploits of contemporary heroes like Nelson and Wolfe. The Irishman James Barry was a proponent of noble subjects from antiquity, although he was an intense Romantic by temperament and acknowledged no antipathy between the classical and the modern subject. He met the Scots Alexander and John Runciman in Rome. The Runciman brothers, like West and Barry, had been supported in their studies by enlightened patrons. Alexander returned to Scotland in 1771, determined to paint the history of his own country, and began in 1772 by decorating the main Hall at Penicuik House, Midlothian, for John Clerk, with a series of vigorous and dramatic scenes from Ossian. (These have since been destroyed by fire.) Angelica Kaufmann, on the other hand, very shrewdly assessed contemporary public opinion, and achieved remarkable success by specializing in Classical subjects that featured heroines, like Penelope, who exemplified acceptable feminine virtues.

John Mortimer had remained in Britain and gained recognition with his highly imaginative, pioneering subjects from Classical literature and Shakespeare. Others were not so fortunate in selling their work. On his return from Rome, Barry spent seven years of his life executing a series of six huge canvases, at his own cost. These were on the theme of the *Progress of Human Culture* from the Golden Age of Greece to imagined improvements to commerce and the arts under enlightened patronage. Barry was an imaginative and gifted artist but his mantle as champion of history painting fell to a lesser artist: Benjamin Robert Haydon. Haydon tried to revive history painting in the grand style in his *Assassination of Dentatus* (1806–1809). He won a premium at the British Institution and his patrons were patient, but his pictures, like the *Judgment of Solomon* (1812–1814) or *Christ's Entry into Jerusalem* (1814–1820) were too large scale for most country houses, did not sell, and proved his ruin. His championing of the Elgin Marbles as touchstones for good taste, and his evidence that these Classical works were based on a study of life models, are of far more continuing importance to art historians than his own paintings.

Artists who turned to modern subjects were more successful in finding sponsors. The subject was initially limited to dramatic incidents of war or commemorations of important events. The most famous was the *Death of General Wolfe* (1770), by Benjamin West, which recorded the demise of a modern hero using the compositional formula of a pieta, with the addition of modern dress and an exotic Indian figures. *The Death of Major Pearson* (1783) by John Singleton Copley was a more exciting modern history painting, showing active combat on a grand scale.

Throughout the period under discussion the major problem experienced by history painters was the lack of patronage in Britain for serious subject paintings. In the seventeenth century the monarchy had employed foreign artists to decorate palaces in London and Edinburgh with allegorical and historical scenes, but there was a dearth of commissions for British history painters. In the eighteenth century, wars with America and France stimulated some interest in paintings of national heroes and military engagements. George IV, however, who was very interested in painting and, as regent, had led fashionable taste in Britain, had a strong personal preference for detailed genre paintings. It was private entrepreneurs such as James Boydell who were more successful in popularizing historical subjects. His lavish *Boydell Shakespeare Gallery*, executed between 1786 and 1789, was intended to stimulate a national appetite for serious compositions. It comprised a series of 150 works, engraved and published as *A collection of Prints from Pictures Painted for the Purpose of Illustrating the Dramatic Works of Shakspeare by the Artists of Great Britain*. This project engaged many major eighteenth-century history painters, such as Henry Fuseli, Angelica Kaufmann, and George Romney, and achieved wide circulation.

Some artists tried to adapt history painting to the national taste. David Allan's *Hector Taking Leave of Andromache* (1773) won a prize at the Academy in Rome over all his Italian rivals, because of his sympathetic interpretation of the Classical text. When he returned to Scotland, he tried to extend the scope of history painting to include subjects illustrating the effects of world events on ordinary people. His preface (dedicated to Gavin Hamilton) to the 1788 illustrated edition of the Jacobite pastoral poem by Alan Ramsay, *The Gentle Shepherd*, claimed that high moral virtues necessary in history painting were demonstrated throughout all levels of society. It was David Wilkie, however,

who successfully brought the ordinary citizen into the repertoire of history painting. His *Chelsea Pensioners Reading the Waterloo Gazette* (1816–22) portrayed the intensity of human reaction to news of international importance. The painting had an unprecedented success when it was exhibited. Wilkie had applied the principles of studying profound human emotions from life to ordinary people and changed the definition of heroism and history painting. Later he sought out popular modern history subjects in Spain and Ireland, and personally supervised a series of high quality engravings of his paintings of contemporary events. These achieved a wide circulation of his ideas, thus popularizing the idiom, and enabling the next generation of Pre-Raphaelites to develop the definition of history painting.

PATRICIA CAMPBELL

Bibliography

Agnew, Thomas. *Victorian Painting: 1837–1887*. London: 1961.

Boase, T. *English Art 1800–1870*. Oxford: Clarendon Press, 1959.

Cunningham, Allan. *The Life of Sir David Wilkie R. A., 1785–1841*. London, 1843.

Cummings, Frederick, Robert Rosenblum, and Staley Allen. *Romantic Art in Britain: Paintings and Drawings 1760–1860*. Philadelphia, 1968.

Farington, Joseph. *The Farington Diary*. 8 vols. Edited by Fames Greig. London, 1923–28.

Holloway, James. *Patrons and Painters: Art in Scotland 1650–1760*. Edinburgh: Trustees of the National Galleries of Scotland, 1989.

Irwin, David, and Francina Irwin. *Scottish Painters at Home and Abroad, 1700–1900*. Faber and Faber, 1975.

Macmillan, Duncan. *Scottish Painting, 1460–1990*. Mainstream Press, 1990.

Reynolds, Joshua. *Discourses on Art*. Edited by Robert Wark. 1959.

Ruskin, John. *The Works of John Ruskin*. 39 vols. Edited by E. T. Cook and Alexander Wedderburn. London: 1903–28.

Santaniello, A. E. *The Boydell Shakespeare Prints*. New York: Arno Press, 1979.

Tolley, Thomas. *Painting the Canon's Roar*. Ashgate, 2001.

Vaughan, W. *British Painting, The Golden Age*. London: 1999.

Waterhouse, Ellis. *Painting in Britain 1530–1790*. Pelican History of Art, Yale, 1994.

Wind, E. "The Revolution of History Painting," *Journal of the Warburg Institute*, 2 (1938): 116–27.

HISTORY PAINTING: GERMANY

Given the emphasis on the private and imaginative nature of the artist's vision, we might assume that records of factual events and locations would not feature prominently in German Romantic art. Yet they did, for reasons that stemmed from a positive approach to the Middle Ages no less than from a popular desire to see Germany occupy a central place among the nations of Europe. These two aspirations are related. Medieval Germany had wielded influence on the international stage as the custodian of the Holy Roman Empire; and when, in the eighteenth century, the struggle for national recognition was fought out on a cultural and on a political plane, the Middle Ages were, paradoxically, felt by many to point forward to a long-overdue revival.

Johann Wolfgang von Goethe, who eventually became the declared enemy of the Romantic school in Germany, penned an early appreciation of Gothic art that was to foreshadow key

positions of the later Romantics. His essay *Von deutscher Baukunst* (*On German Architecture*, 1772) takes Strasbourg Cathedral as its example and praises Gothic architecture as a supreme achievement of the human spirit. This new, dynamic attitude to history was to gain ground during the following decades and supplant both the fanciful Baroque and the austere neoclassical style.

Before long, history painting in Germany was to become overtly patriotic and adopt an almost unwavering focus on the medieval period. Naive piety, celebrated as *Kunstfrömmigkeit* in Wackenroder's seminal *Herzensergiessungen eines kunstliebenden Klosterbruders* (*Outpourings from the Heart by an Art-loving Friar*, 1797), was recognized as important and led to the widespread adoption of a simple, childlike presentation. Friedrich von

Schlegel's *Dritter Nachtrag alter Gemälde* (*Third Supplement on Ancient Paintings*) advised artists to concentrate on traditional German themes and Christian symbols. Novalis was also insistent that Europe must return to its Christian roots if the chaotic spirit of modernity, latterly exemplified by the French Revolution, was to be overcome. This simultaneously backward- and forward-looking ethos lives on in Karl Friedrich Schinkel's 1815 canvases *Medieval City on a River* and *Gothic Church on a Rock by the Sea*. In the former it is a rainbow, in the second a low-lying sun that illuminates the scene and gives the depicted building the aura of a national symbol.

Caspar David Friedrich may not have painted scenes from German history, but even his somber landscapes are not devoid of a patriotic subtext. The solitary oak tree he so often places in the midst of a bleak landscape is invariably a reminder of Germany's isolation and latent strength. The dark, sinister *Man and Woman Contemplating the Moon* (1818–25) may seem devoid of contemporary connotations, but the antique (*altdeutsch*) clothing worn by the couple suggests at least tacit support for the nationalist faction.

The artists who had the greatest impact in the first quarter of the nineteenth century were the Nazarenes. They imitated the Flemish and Italian masters and invoked a simple world in which spiritual values triumphed over rationalism and sectarianism. In their work, there is no place for the harsher aspects of war as observed in some of Antoine-Jean Gros's studies of Napoleon Bonaparte or in Goya's brutal firing-squads of 1808. Instead, the German canvases of the period take on a grandiose naïveté that was intended to stimulate enthusiasm for the pan-Germanic cause. Peter von Cornelius's illustrations of *Faust* and *The Lay of the Nibelungs* were much admired; historical subjects included the conversion of the Germanic tribes to Christianity by Saint Boniface, the defeat of the Romans by the Germanic leader Arminius, the campaigns of Charlemagne and the Emperors of the high medieval period.

The Nazarene Franz Pforr treated *The Entry of Rudolf von Habsburg into Basle in 1273*, 1810 in a consciously archaic style that was intended to give the impression that it had been painted in the thirteenth rather than in the nineteenth century. The towering frescoes designed by Alfred Rethel and completed by his assistant Josef Kehren for the Coronation Hall in Aachen's Town Hall (1847–52) were based on meticulous studies, as the surviving sketches show, and psychological verisimilitude is not absent from them, but they, too, communicate a glorified view of the Middle Ages that is far removed from verifiable reality. Charlemagne the all-conquering hero sweeps aside Arabs, Lombards, Saxons, and simultaneously lays the permanent foundations for a Christian empire that will exceed anything the Romans created. Political figures were not the only icons in this reevaluation of the period: the minstrels' contest that Moritz von Schwind painted for Wartburg Castle (1854–55) had a similarly epic breadth and a clear orientation toward a golden age of chivalry-cum-poetry that stands in deliberate counterpoint to the modern age of reason.

The Romantic transfiguration of the medieval period owes its simplistic perspective to the masters of medieval art whose celebratory style the Romantics set out to emulate, but imaging post-Reformation Germany was to become problematic for them. The reformist zeal of Jan Hus and Martin Luther reveals itself powerfully in Carl Friedrich Lessing's work, nowhere more so than in *Die Hussitenpredigt* (*Hus Preaching*, 1836). The Düssel-dorf school, under its director Wilhelm von Schadow, was among the first to eschew the energetic monumentalism of Rethel's battle scenes and turn instead to subjects drawn from recent history. Gradually, a more oblique perspective gained ground. It has been argued that Wilhelm Joseph Heine's *Criminals at Church* (1837) is a cryptic tribute to the imprisoned priest Friedrich Ludwig Weidig. It was left to Adolph Menzel, whose *Gustav Adolph Greets his Wife outside Hanau Castle* (1847) had shown the warrior king not on the battlefield but locked in a conjugal embrace, to introduce a new tone of scepticism when imaging the recent past. *Night Attack at Hochkirch 1758*, 1856) is a grim record of an event that ended not in victory but in defeat. Menzel's most celebrated painting of Frederick is also his most cynical: *The Flute Concert of Frederick the Great at Sanssouci* (1852) shows the king, in the artist's own words, "standing there like a shop assistant playing the recorder to his mum on Sunday." German history painting did not come of age until it moved away from the pseudo-medieval spectacular to develop searching and increasingly critical approaches to the nation's more recent figureheads.

OSMAN DURRANI

Bibliography

Belting, Hans. *The Germans and their Art: A Troublesome Relationship*. Translated by Scott Kleager. New Haven, Conn.: Yale University Press, 1998.

Bowron, Edgar Peters. *Romantics, Realists, Revolutionaries*. Munich: Prestel, 2000.

Brieger, Peter. *Deutsche Geschichtsmalerei des 19. Jahrhunderts*. Berlin: Deutscher Kunstverlag, 1930.

Brown, David Blayney. *Romanticism*. London: Phaidon, 2001.

Foster-Hahn, Françoise. "Adolph Menzel's 'Daguerrotypical' Image of Frederick the Great: A Liberal Bourgeois Interpretation of German History," *Art Bulletin* 59, no. 1 (1977).

Foster-Hahn, Françoise, Claude Keisch, Peter-Klaus Schuster, and Angelika Wesenberg, eds. *Spirit of an Age: Nineteenth-Century Paintings from the Nationalgalerie, Berlin*. London: National Gallery, 2001.

Grimschitz, Bruno. *Deutsche Bildnisse von Runge bis Menzel*. Vienna: Frick 1941.

Haskell, Francis. *History and its Images: Art and the Interpretation of the Past*. New Haven, Conn.: Yale University Press, 1993.

Hemingway, Andrew, and William Vaughan. *Art in Bourgeois Society 1790–1850*. Cambridge: University Press, 1998.

Hofmann, Werner. *Das entzweite Jahrhundert. Kunst von 1750 bis 1830*. Munich: Beck, 1995.

———. *Wie deutsch ist deutsche Kunst? Eine Streitschrift*. Leipzig: Seemann, 1999.

Koetschau, Karl. *Alfred Rethels Kunst vor dem Hintergrund der Historienmalerei seiner Zeit*. Düsseldorf: Verlag des Kunstvereins für die Rheinlande und Westfalen, 1929.

Oellers, Adam C. *Alfred Rethel: die Karlsfresken im Aachener Rathaus und die Ölstudien im Museum Burg Frankenberg*. Aachen: Suermondt-Ludwig-Museum, 1987.

Paret, Peter. *Art as History: Episodes in the Culture and Politics of Nineteenth-Century Germany*. Princeton, N.J.: Princeton University Press, 1988.

Preising, Dagmar, ed. *Alfred Rethel (1816–1859), Zeichnungen und Ölstudien, Suermondt-Ludwig-Museum, 2. August bis 15. September 1991*. Aachen: Museen der Stadt Aachen, 1991.

Scholz, Robert. *Volk, Nation, Geschichte. Deutsche historische Kunst im 19. Jahrhundert*. Rosenheim: Deutsche Verlagsgesellschaft, 1980.

HOFFMANN, ERNST THEODOR (WILHELM) AMADEUS 1776–1822

German writer

In the popular consciousness, Ernst Theodor (Wilhelm) Amadeus Hoffmann is almost exclusively associated with his *Tales*, an image which has been reinforced by Jacques Offenbach's portrait in his operetta *The Tales of Hoffmann*. Hoffmann himself would certainly have wished his musical achievements to be accorded as much importance, and though posterity would probably not agree, they should certainly not be ignored. For a period of about six years (1808–14) he devoted himself almost exclusively to the practical and professional side of the art, working at the Bamberg theater as a jack of all trades: a director, stage designer, and even applying his considerable talents as a draftsman and painter to the stage scenery. At the same time he composed a huge number of musical compositions, mostly in the popular form of the *Singspiel*, but also in the larger format of the increasingly important genre of Romantic opera (*Der Trank der Unsterblichkeit*, [*The Drink of Immortality*, 1808] and *Aurora, eine grosse romantische Oper* [*A Grand Romantic Opera*, 1811–12]). It was in Bamberg too that the first plans were made for his most ambitious and attractive opera, *Undine. Eine Zaubereroper* (*A Magic Opera*, 1816), based on the *Märchen* of the same name by a fellow Romantic and friend of Hoffmann's, Friedrich de la Motte Fouqué. It was a tale of the close but tragic relationship that exists between the human world and the supernatural. Hoffmann's music in *Undine*, although clearly deferential toward Wolfgang Amadeus Mozart and Ludwig van Beethoven, maintains a powerful dramatic momentum of its own: the ensembles and choruses are deftly handled and so too is the orchestration, especially in the writing for woodwinds, which were becoming a feature of German opera. When the opera was eventually performed in Berlin in 1816 (the sets were built by the great architect and painter Karl Friedrich Schinkel) it achieved considerable success and was the subject of an enthusiastic review by Carl Maria von Weber. Ironically, it was Weber's *Der Freischütz* (*The Freeshooter*, 1821) that represents a further considerable step along the path of Romantic opera, with its powerfully atmospheric, spine-chilling presentation of the supernatural, which would supplant Hoffmann's opera in the public mind. Hoffmann's deep and abiding commitment to music, which among all his varied professional and artistic activities remained his primary passion, had a lasting effect on his literary works, both as a recurring theme and as a starting point for theoretical discussions about the relationship between the different art forms, in, for example, his essay "Der Dichter und der Komponist" ("The Word and the Composer").

In privileging themes dealing with the supernatural in his prose tales as well, Hoffmann was able to call on the recent publication of Jakob and Wilhelm Grimm's collection of folktales *Kinder- und Hausmärchen* (*Domestic and Children's Fairy Tales*, 1812–15). These unvarnished, ostensibly "authentic" narratives, based on the oral tradition of an unsophisticated people (*Volk*), were transformed by Hoffmann into highly sophisticated explorations of the inner world of the imagination, most particularly that of the creative individual, often placed in a modern, early nineteenth-century society whose values were consolidating to an alarming degree around a dull philistinism and a growing materialism. The early masterpiece in this mode, "Der Goldne Topf" (*The Golden Pot*, 1813–14), from the collection entitled *Fantasiestücke*, is subtitled "Ein Märchen aus der neuen Zeit" ("A Modern-Day Fairy Tale") and presents the view that the talented individual may extricate himself from this dismal prospect, given the right direction and propitious circumstances. Thus the tale operates at two different levels between which the hero, a young poet Anselmus, oscillates. One is a mythological world where magical transformations can take place, suggested by a subtext and narrative derived from the "Genesis" story and blended with an eclectic amalgam of "Oriental" motifs assembled by the author. These focus on the "magic pot" of the title, which is fought over by the forces of good and evil, with good eventually triumphing. The other focuses on solid, middle-class characters set in contemporary Dresden, where comfort, respectability, and social status represent the highest good. Not all Hoffmann's *Märchen* are so optimistic or lighthearted, however. "Der Sandmann" ("The Sandman," 1815), taken from the collection entitled *Nachtstücke*, features an introspective and obsessive hero, Nathaniel, an aspiring poet whose childhood has been blighted by indifferent parents and the effect of a fairy tale told by his nurse on his overactive imagination. This concerns the sandman, who feeds his bird children the eyes of humans. The grotesque and horrific effects of this story (in which Hoffmann spares the reader none of the gruesome details) and the emphasis on human eyes will affect every aspect of Nathaniel's future life, his relations with his family and his devoted girlfriend Clara. The malevolence of the "dark powers" that are unleashed on the human mind by the supernatural produces in the reader a sense of inevitability and impending doom, culminating in the dramatic climax when Nathaniel flings himself from a church tower to his death. Other notable examples of Hoffmann's use of the *Märchen* form include *Nussknacker und Mäusekönig* (*The Nutcracker and the Mouse-King*, 1816), a delightful presentation of the supernatural viewed from a child's perspective at Christmas, though not without serious undertones (unlike the familiar version popularized by Pyotr Illich Tchaikovsky's ballet), and *Meister Floh* (*Master Flea*, 1822) in which the supernatural plays a liberating role in promoting the development of latent forces in the individual which had been repressed in childhood. This work also introduces a contemporary dimension, indeed uncomfortably so, since Hoffmann inserts an episode (the "Knarrpanti" section) which is a thinly disguised satire on the mishandling of a legal case in which he himself was directly involved as a judge and member of a special commission. The commission was called on to adjudicate on subversive, demagogic activities in the increasingly reactionary political climate that had spread from Klemens Fürst von Metternich's Austria to Prussia after 1815. The incident raises the issue of literary censorship at the time and reveals Hoffmann's own boldness in stepping beyond the limits fixed on tolerance and free speech. After copies of the work had been seized prior to publication, he was required to withdraw this section.

Many of Hoffmann's *Tales* were first published in journals and later assembled in collections such as the *Fantasiestücke* and *Nachtstücke*. A more elaborate presentational device was employed for the large collection of tales assembled under the title of *Die Serapionsbrüder*. Inspired by the foundation of a literary society in Berlin, called the Seraphinenorden, to which celebrated Romantic writers such as Fouqué and Adalbert von Chamisso as well as Hoffmann himself belonged, he created a fictional equivalent, changing the name to "Serapionsbrüderschaft." The literary inspiration for this device came from Ludwig Tieck's then recent collection of tales *Phantasus* (1812–14), but Hoffmann developed its possibilities far beyond Tieck's rather conventional base. It became a repository for many of his theoretical views, including ideas about the interrelationship of literature, music, and the visual arts in a clear anticipation of what would later, in the hands of Richard Wagner, come to be termed the *Gesamtkunstwerk*, or "complete artwork." At the same time, the framework provides the reader with a multitude of perspectives on the stories themselves. The members of the brotherhood present what they term the "Serapiontic" principle as a yardstick by which to judge the tales, and the lively debates which ensue as each and every story in the collection is subjected to scrutiny under this heading give Hoffmann tremendous scope to present his literary credo, albeit one that itself is pervaded with irony. The "principle" touches on three important facets of his narrative art. First, the rendering of the external world in clear and plastic terms ("plastische Rundung"). Second, using it as a lever ("Hebel") on which to raise up an imaginative structure, thereby converting the realm of external observation into a world of inner vision ("inneres Schauen"), and third, the ironic detachment the artist brings to bear on the creation as a whole, and his awareness of the fundamental "Duplizität des Seins" (duplicity of all being) that underlies all things. Tales such as "Die Bergwerke zu Falun" ("The Mines of Falun" 1819), "Die Fermate" ("The Fermata" 1815), "Der Artushof" ("The Artushof" 1817), and "Doge und Dogaresse" ("Doge and Dogaresse" 1817) all provide excellent examples, but the principle is not restricted in its application and can be seen at work across the entire range of Hoffmann's prose writings.

Hoffmann's oeuvre includes two novels, each occupying an important position. The first of these, *Die Elixiere des Teufels* (*The Devil's Elixir*, 1815–16), operates to some extent within the tradition of the gothic novel, and openly reflects the influence of Matthew Lewis's *The Monk* (1796). It focuses on the criminal personality that is so often a feature of this tradition; in this case it is embodied in the divided psychological makeup of the monk Medardus. To externalize this inner conflict, Hoffmann makes brilliant use of the Doppelgänger device, which in turn opens up a supernatural dimension and points to the existence of a malevolent fate that is working its way through various generations of the Medarduss family. At the same time, however, through the theme of love the novel raises the possibility of a redemptive force at work on human affairs. These themes, which themselves are not unfamiliar in the Gothic tradition, are given added depth and ambiguity by Hoffmann's use of multiple perspectives (prefaces, documents, and letters) and emerge as another extension of his interest in, and insight into, the psychology of the creative mind and its vulnerability.

Lebensansichten des Katers Murr (*Life and Opinions of the Tomcat*, 1820–21) features the artist figure more directly through the character of Kreisler, a composer and *Kapellmeister* (director of music) who is an alter ego and a paradigm of the Romantic artist and who appears in other works by Hoffmann (for example, in *Kreisleriana*). This complex novel is unfinished and comprises two distinct, but interconnected, narratives that are set side by side: an autobiography in the form of a satire on literary pretensions, presented from the standpoint of a braggart tomcat and would-be literary genius, and sections of a biography of the cat's master, Meister Abraham, torn out at random by the cat for his own literary effusions. The biography focuses as much on Meister Abraham's close friend, Kreisler, the artist whose uncompromising dedication to his art and longing for love and understanding fall foul of the intrigues and inanities of court life. In this extravaganza, traces of the whimsy of Laurence Sterne (an author particularly favored by Hoffmann) are to be detected, but the impact of the whole (or such as is complete) comes from its ironic interplay of comic and tragic registers—a duality at the heart of Hoffmann's outlook on life.

In the nineteenth century, judgments on Hoffmann's writings often failed to move beyond speculations on his reasons for favoring fantastic and bizarre themes, as for example Walter Scott's infamous but influential remarks that they are the product of an "immoderate use of opium" (for which, according to the response of Charles Baudelaire, alcohol was substituted, albeit with more approval). However, in the early twentieth century new perspectives were opened up by Sigmund Freud's famous essay "Des Unleim lichs" ("The Uncanny," 1919) which leans heavily on an analysis of *Der Sandmann*. Here, Nathaniel's obsessions are identified with a clinical condition that Freud terms the "castration complex," which can be seen as a manifestation of the workings of the unconscious. The psychoanalytical approach to Hoffmann's prose writings continued to provide a rich vein of interpretation and gave impetus to modernist interpretations of his work. More recent critical focus has been on the self-reflexivity of Hoffmann's narrative methods, the multiple perspectivism and general complexity and virtuosity of his techniques and, in particular, his irony. These main lines of investigation have further confirmed the range, depth, and endless appeal of his oeuvre and his position as a leading figure in German Romanticism.

HILDA M. BROWN

Biography

Born in Königsberg, East Prussia, January 24, 1776. Studied at the University of Königsberg, 1792–95; bar studies, 1795 ("Auskultator") and 1798 (" Referendar"). 1800, appointment as assessor at the Obergericht, Posen (Posznan). Appointment as "Regierungsrat" annulled because of satirical caricatures of town dignitaries, 1802; transferred in disgrace to Plock, where he composed several musical works, including chamber music and a Mass in D. Transferred to Warsaw, 1804, many compositions. In 1806, the French marched into Warsaw, and Hoffmann refused to take the oath of allegiance to Napoleon Bonaparte. Accepted offer from Graf Soden to become director of music in the Bamberg theater, 1808; started to use the name "Amadeus" out of veneration for Mozart; worked as a composer of Singspiele and as theater architect and designer. First published tale, "Ritter Gluck," 1809. Left Bamberg for Dresden, where he visited the battlefield, 1813; later left for Leipzig (both cities under Allied bombardment). Employed by Joseph Seconda as director of his opera troupe. Returned to Berlin, 1814, eventually reemployed as a judge for the Supreme Court; started to write in earnest, *Tales* and musical reviews. First performance of *Undine* at the Königliches Schauspielhaus, Berlin, 1816; in 1817, the theater burned down. Served on special commission set up to investigate subversive activities and the involvement in the student movement of "Turnvater Jahn," 1819–21. The "Hoffmann-case" copies of *Meister Floh* seized and Hoffmann cross-examined, 1821. Died of an undiagnosed illness whose main symptom was a spinal paralysis, June 25, 1822.

Selected Works

Fantasiestücke in Callots Manier. 1813.
Nachtstücke. 1816–17.
Die Elixiere des Teufels. 1815–16.
Die Serapionsbrüder. 1819–21.

Lebensansichten des Katers Murr, 1820–21. Translated as *Life and Opinions of the Tomcat*. Introduction by Jeremy Adler; translation by Anthea Boli. Harmondsworth: Penguin, 1999.
The Golden Pot and Other Tales. Translated by Ritchie Robertson. Oxford: World's Classics, 1992.

Bibliography

Charlton, David, ed. *E. T. A. Hoffman's Musical Writings.* Cambridge: Cambridge University Press, 1989.
Hewett-Thayer, Harvey W. *Hoffmann: Author of the "Tales."* Princeton, N.J.: Princeton University Press, 1948.
Köhn, Lothar. *Vieldeutige Welt. Studien zur Struktur der Erzählungen bei E. T. A. Hoffmann.* Tübingen: Niemeyer, 1966.
Kremer, Detlef. *E. T. A. Hoffmann. Erzählungen und Romane.* Berlin: Erich Schmidt, 1999.
Schnapp, Friedrich, ed. *Der Musiker E. T. A. Hoffmann. Selbstzeugnisse, Dokumente und zeitgenössische Urteile.* Hildesheim: Gerstenberg Verlag, 1981.
Segebrecht, Wulf. *Autobiographie und Dichtung, Eine Studie zum Werk E. T. A. Hoffmanns.* Stuttgart: J. B. Metzlerssche Verlagsbuchhandlung, 1967.

HOGG, JAMES 1770–1835

Scottish poet and novelist

Born in Ettrick to a poor Scottish-border farming family and having enjoyed no substantial formal education, James Hogg became one of the most important Scottish Romantic vernacular poets and writers after Robert Burns and Allan Ramsay. In 1814, Lord Byron wrote in a letter to John Murray that Hogg was "surely . . . a man of great powers," and other friends and admirers included Walter Scott and William Wordsworth. Having worked as a herdsman and laborer from boyhood, he first published his own verse in 1794. In 1797, he heard Robert Burns's poetry for the first time, a decisive moment in his life. He claimed that after this event "I wept, and always thought with myself—what is to heed me from succeeding Burns . . . But then I wept again because I could not write. However, I resolved to be a poet, and to follow in the steps of Burns."

Though this claim contains clear shades of Romantic self-fashioning, it is correct that Hogg was largely self-educated. Though (untruthfully) claiming to avoid books so as to retain his originality, his literary influences included Henry Fielding, Oliver Goldsmith, Alexander Pope, and Jonathan Swift, as well as the Classical pastoral poetry of Virgil as translated by John Dryden. Around 1801, he met Scott for the first time, who was then collecting material for his *Minstrelsy of the Scottish Border*, the first volumes of which appeared in 1802. Though the two became lifelong friends, Hogg was disappointed by Scott's imitation ballads. His ambition was to produce original Scottish verse, in which he was no doubt assisted by his mother, whom in a letter to Scott he described as "a living miscellany of old songs."

Having settled in Edinburgh in 1810 with a view to establishing a literary career, he began publishing a weekly journal, the *Spy*, but it failed after a year. A large part of his readership had been lost after he published a risqué prose tale, and he wrote in his editorial to the remaining few how the "learned, the enlightened, and polite circles of this flourishing metropolis, disdained to be either amused or instructed by the ebulitions of humble genius." In 1813, George Goldie published Hogg's *The Queen's Wake*, a long, historical verse narrative in the style popularized by Byron and Scott. It was met with broad critical acclaim and made Hogg's name, and he became known popularly as "the Ettrick Shepherd." There were, however, those suspicious of his poetic gift. The poet James Gray wrote that "it was impossible that a work possessing so high and so varied excellencies could be produced by a man who had actually spent the greater part of his life in the character of a shepherd." *The Queen's Wake* was followed by other long poems (including the visionary *The Pilgrims of the Sun* in 1815), as well as sketches, tales, and articles published in various periodicals. None of these met with similar success. In 1817, he became one of the leading figures in the establishment of the Tory *Blackwood's Edinburgh Magazine*, but the internecine wranglings of the city's literary community cost him dearly. The magazine's "Noctes Ambrosianae," begun in 1822, unfairly presented Hogg in the role of "the Shepherd" as what one friend called a "boozing buffoon." Hogg reflected in later life that "I know I have always been looked on as an intruder," a fact not helped by his conceited sense of his own genius.

From his first poem published anonymously in the *Scots Magazine* in 1794 (an account of a young man who accidentally seduces his girlfriend's mother) much of Hogg's work developed the theme of characters who fall from a state of initial confidence into one of confusion and catastrophe. This is most obvious in his masterpiece, *The Private Memoirs and Confessions of a Justified Sinner*, first published anonymously in 1824. The book was not highly regarded by contemporary critics, *The Westminster Review* described it as "an experiment intended to ascertain how far the English public will allow itself to be insulted." Nevertheless, it has proved to be by far Hogg's most enduring work. Unlike earlier novels, such as *The Brownie of Bodsbeck* (1818), which were imitative of Scott's style, *The Private Memoirs* was largely original, though echoes of E. T. A. Hoffmann have been noted. An edition of Hoffmann's *Die Elixiere des Teufels* (*The Devil's Elixir*), translated by a friend of Hogg's, was published in the same month as *The Private Memoirs*. Hogg's novel is a subtly structured narrative (some critics have said satire) on Calvinist religion and the encompassing power of evil. It features a doppelganger and the devil in the identity of the mysterious Gil-Martin, who persuades an illegitimate young man to murder his older brother. *The Private Memoirs* was so superior to Hogg's previous novels that it was again claimed by critics that he must have had literary assistance. It was suggested that his friend J. G. Lockhart, novelist and editor of *Blackwood's*, had a hand in the writing. This claim has been much disputed, and remains unproven.

Hogg's career was throughout hampered by poverty and financial misfortune. Despite the assistance of wealthy patrons, he suffered numerous setbacks in his efforts to establish himself either as a poet or a tenant farmer. Though enjoying fame in his lifetime, and being read and praised in Europe and America, Hogg's reputation did not endure after his death.

DAVID HAYCOCK

Biography

Born Ettrick, Selkirkshire, Scotland, in late 1770. Working as a shepherd and farm laborer, began writing poetry in 1793. His first work was published in the *Scots Magazine* in 1794 and his first success was with the recruiting song *Donald M'Donald* in 1800. The first volume of his own verse, *Scottish Pastorals, Poems, Songs, &c.*, published in 1801, and a collection of his early ballads, *The Mountain Bard*, in 1807. Bankrupted in 1809 following attempts to become a tenant farmer, settled in Edinburgh to pursue a literary career, 1810; made his name in 1813 with his historical poem *The Queen's Wake*. Leased farm at Eltrive Lake, rent-free, from the Duke of Buccleuch, 1815. Married Margaret Phillips, 1820. Visited London, well received by the literary community, 1832. Biographical memoir, *The Domestic Manners and Private Life of Sir Walter Scott*, published, 1834. Died November 21, 1835.

Selected Writings

The Private Memoirs and Confessions of a Justified Sinner, 1824. Edited and with an introduction by John Carey. 1981.
The Works of the Ettrick Shepherd. Edited by Thomas Thompson. 2 vols. 1865.

Bibliography

Batho, Edith C. *The Ettrick Shepherd*. Cambridge, 1927.
Gifford, Douglas. *James Hogg: The Ramsay Head Press*. Edinburgh, 1976.
Groves, David. *James Hogg: The Growth of a Writer*. Edinburgh: Scottish Academic Press, 1988.
Simpson, Louis. *James Hogg: A Critical Study*. Edinburgh: Oliver and Boyd, 1962.

HÖLDERLIN, JOHANN CHRISTIAN FRIEDRICH 1770–1843

German poet

(Johann Christian) Friedrich Hölderlin is not among the first group of writers usually classified as German Romantics by literary historians, but he is of the Romantics' generation. Affinities to other kinds of Romanticism are suggested by the year of his birth, which he shares, probably not coincidentally, with Ludwig van Beethoven, G. W. F. Hegel, and William Wordsworth. In that wider context, Hölderlin appears as a Romantic, but despite being much more a product of his times than was once thought, he remains significantly different from any other contemporary and was never part of a group. In 1799 he wrote some notes setting out the aims for a journal he intended to found that seem to reject the style of August Wilhelm and Friedrich Schlegel's *Athenäum*, even though his general plans were close to theirs and he had written some short aphoristic prose akin to Novalis's in *Blütenstaub*. On the other hand, Hölderlin's late odes, or the novel *Hyperion* (2 vols., 1797 and 1799), fulfill Friedrich Schlegel's requirements for "transcendental poetry" more nearly than anything written by the German Romantics proper. He can thus be seen, as Walter Benjamin suggested in *Der Begriff der Kunstkritik in der deutschen Romantik* (*The Concept of Criticism in German Romanticism*, 1919), as simultaneously peripheral to German Romanticism and at its center. Johann Gottlieb Fichte, whose lectures he attended in Jena in 1795, was important to his development, and some of his earliest works (essay fragments) are philosophical. In the wider context, there are affinities between *Hyperion* and Wordsworth's *The Prelude*, and arguably between the composition of his hymns and that of Beethoven's symphonies and quartets, though with neither of these juxtapositions is any direct influence implied. It was the later German Romantics who were the first readers not personally acquainted with Hölderlin to recognize his quality, though Bettina and Achim von Arnim, Clemens Brentano, and others were equally fascinated by the figure of the poet in his madness in Tübingen.

Hölderlin began writing early, but all of his important work was produced after the French Revolution. The release of hope the Revolution brought about can be felt and traced in the workings of his poetry, and it forms part of the matter of *Hyperion*, of the unfinished tragedy *Der Tod des Empedokles* (*The Death of Empedocles*, 1797–1800), and of many individual poems, but always obliquely, as allegory, allusion, quotation, or cipher (in the poetry often as thunder). Learning to see references to the Revolution in Hölderlin is part of learning to read him. His understanding of it, and of what it meant to live in revolutionary or postrevolutionary times, shaped all his thinking, from the historical to the poetological. He saw the present he lived in as a period of transition, hastened and intensified by the Revolution and its consequences, which were being worked out in the acts and thoughts of his contemporaries. An unfinished essay, usually known as "Das Werden im Vergehen" ("On the Process of Becoming in Passing Away," 1799–1800) or by its opening words "Das untergehende Vaterland . . ." ("The declining country . . ."), pays close attention to the transitional nature of the present and its possibilities. Hölderlin treats the present as a turning point, as a continually self-renewing moment between past and future where an old world is dissolving and a new one is coming into form. Those two processes, dissolution and formation, are in reality one process, so that what is felt as disintegration, as ending, can also be understood as the arrival of the new, as beginning. The turmoil and confusion that is the postrevolutionary present can be countered by presenting it as a process of becoming, and this is the job of poetry, to aid the transition by clarifying the times and pointing forward, mindful of the identity of "Untergang oder Übergang" (decline or transition). The aim is to see the marvelous opening of possibility that lies at the point *in between*, when fixity has become flux, "in the state between being and not-being possibility everywhere becomes real." Poetry should enable the drawing of a new coherence from the incoherence by remembering past forms and projecting future ones. Poetry as Hölderlin understands and practices it belongs to the period of transition, the time in between; arrived at, a new ideal constellation, a world fit to be lived in, would render it superfluous.

The focus of memory in all of Hölderlin's writings is ancient Greece. In the mythographical fictions of his poems, and most clearly and systematically in the elegy *Brot und Wein* (*Bread and Wine*) the transitional period began, or began to be felt, with the passing of Christ, who as the last of the gods inaugurated a historical nighttime. Hölderlin saw classical civilization as the most fulfilled realization of human life in history, when it was "full of divine sense." He was the most fervent and eloquent Hellenist of his age. The Greek achievement represented an absolute ideal, but its main force came from the fact that it had existed on earth and was thus proof that a full life was possible. Its example condemned life as it was now lived, but also gave the stimulus necessary to create a better one. This operates in Hölderlin's poetry through the conjuring up of poignant images of life in Greek antiquity that are then undercut and revealed as illusory, thus generating a longing which the poem itself cannot satisfy. The effect of the eighteenth-century landscape in *Hyperion* works similarly: it is radiant with loss, expressive in its beauty of both the existence and the disappearance of fulfilment.

Hölderlin's understanding of Greece was also religious, for there the gods had been immanent in human affairs. The future state he hoped for—and which for a time he, like others of his generation, believed was imminent—was also to be religious in nature, it would be consecrated from outside. But that could only happen once the world was prepared and receptive; a fit world would not be brought about by an outside force but would, by its nature, summon the gods into itself. Hölderlin did not believe in what he called "positive revelation." The shifting of possibilities that marked the present, the continuous forming and undoing of different constellations, made by its variousness the likelihood of manifestation, of the right constellation's being found, greater. This principle can also be observed in Hölderlin's

manuscripts, in the undermining and disruption of finished forms to achieve fuller expressiveness.

Hölderlin trained for the Church at the protestant *Stift* (seminary) in Tübingen, where his fellow students included Hegel and, five years younger but very precocious, Friedrich Wilhelm Joseph von Schelling. Like them, he avoided entering the Church, at first by remaining outside Württemberg, and worked instead toward the "invisible Church" of the coming fulfilment. His early poems were written under the influence of Friedrich Schiller, whom he idealized and with whom his relationship was always fraught, though Schiller encouraged him and published some of his earlier poems in his journals along with an important early fragment of *Hyperion*. Hölderlin's mature poetry was written in three main forms, in or derived from Classical measures: the ode, the elegy, and the hymn. The important precedent for the use of Greek meter in German was Friedrich Gottlieb Klopstock, whom Hölderlin admired even after most other German influences had waned, but by far the strongest model for his poetic practice, particularly in the hymns, was Pindar, most of whose Olympian and Pythian hymns he translated in 1800 while in Homburg. This eccentric but very deliberate translation, which transposed the Greek original word for word, together with the essays written at about the same time to investigate the workings of poetry and genre and the strenuous but eventually abandoned efforts to complete his political tragedy *Empedokles*, seem to have brought about a change in Hölderlin's writing and got for him the language he needed to write his best poems. Before 1800 there was much good work, including the ode "Mein Eigentum" ("What I own") the whole of *Hyperion*, and the "Diotima" poems written for Susette Gontard, the wife of his employer in Frankfurt, but after 1800 every word he wrote, including those in letters, had a necessity about it, and essential conviction of sense and tone, that puts Hölderlin among the very greatest European poets. For about three years (1800–1803) he worked on poems of great complexity and formal perfection, such as "Heimkunft" ("Homecoming"), "Patmos, Andenken" ("Remembrance"), and "Der Ister." Thereafter, the new demands he made of poetry, and perhaps also the demands made on him by his impending madness, meant that few poems were completed, and his return to and undoing of poems which had already formally reached a perfection indicates a dissatisfaction with the implications of finished form. The fragments and fragment-like poems he continued to write have an intensity and luminosity greater than before but lack the scope and coherence of the completed poems, which are themselves always aware of their fictive status and constantly unsettle the evocations of fullness they devise.

Hölderlin continued to write despite the onset of insanity (1806–1807), but poems of a quite different kind, rhymed and in fixed nonclassical meters, focused mainly on the passage of the seasons and on what he could see from his window. These poems have a static quality, but from them images of great clarity and transparency emerge. Some of them he wrote at the request of his visitors (he had by then become a curiosity as a mad poet in his "tower"), and signed "Scardanelli," with strange dates.

Hölderlin published little in his lifetime, and his stature only became evident with the first full edition of his works begun by Norbert von Hellingrath in 1913. He saw *Hyperion* through the press, as well as his translations *Die Trauerspiele des Sophokles* (*The Tragedies of Sophocles*, 2 vols., 1804), consist-

F. K. Hiemer, *Friedrich Hölderlin*, 1792. Reprinted courtesy of Bildarchiv.

learned something of from his experience of southern France. Today, the translations, of searing beauty and power, are recognized as exemplary and belong at the center of Hölderlin's *oeuvre*. He provided them with notes of extreme difficulty and originality, always pushing at the limits of understanding, exploring theories of tragedy, translation, and history. Analogous are the late *Pindar-Fragmente* (*Pindar Fragments*, 1804), which add prose continuations to translated snippets of Pindar and in so doing invent a new genre.

Hölderlin is supreme as a poet, but his novel stands in its own right, his translations are unique, and he contributed to philosophy, too, in part through his stimulation of Hegel but also in texts now seen as key to German idealism. The implications of the now nearly complete Frankfurt edition, which presents the reader with the full complexity of the manuscripts, are just beginning to be responded to, but his modernity and importance have long been clear.

CHARLIE LOUTH

Biography

Born in Lauffen am Neckar, Swabia, March 20, 1770. Sent to monastery school in Denkendorf, 1784–86, and Maulbronn, 1786–88. Studied at the theological seminary (*Stift*) in Tübingen, 1788–93. Worked as a private tutor in Waltershausen, Jena, and Weimar, 1794. Studied in Jena, 1795. Tutor in Frankfurt, 1795–98. Freelance writer in Homburg, 1798–1800, then in Nürtingen and Stuttgart. Tutor in Hauptwil, Switzerland and in Bordeaux, 1801–2. At home in Nürtingen, 1802–4. Court librarian (a sinecure) in Homburg, 1804–6. Consigned as mad to clinic in Tübingen, 1806. Cared for by a cabinet-maker's family in Tübingen from 1807 on. Died in Tübingen, June 7, 1843.

Selected Works

Collections
Sämtliche Werke, edited by Friedrich Beissner and Adolf Beck, 8 vols, Stuttgart: Kohlhammer, 1943–85.
Sämtliche Werke. Edited by D. E. Sattler, planned as 20 vols. with 3 supplements. Frankfurt am Main: Stroemfeld/Roter Stern, 1975–
.

Poetry
Gedichte. Edited by Gustav Schwab and Ludwig Uhland. 1826.
Poems and Fragments. Translated by Michael Hamburger. 3d. London: Anvil, 1994.
Selected Poems. Translated by David Constantine. 2d ed. Newcastle-upon-Tyne: Bloodaxe, 1996.

Other
Hyperion oder der Eremit in Griechenland. 2 vols., 1797–99. Translated as *Hyperion, or The Hermit in Greece* by Willard R. Trask. New York and London: Signet, 1965.
Die Trauerspiele des Sophocles. 2 vols., 1804. Translated as *Hölderlin's Sophocles: Oedipus and Antigone*. Translated by David Constantine. Newcastle-upon-Tyne: Bloodaxe, 2001.
The Poet's Vocation: Selections from Letters of Hölderlin, Rimbaud, and Hart Crane. Edited and translated by William Burford and Christopher Middleton, 1968. Austin, Texas.
"The Ground of the Empedocles" and "On the Process of Becoming in Passing Away." Translated by Jeremy Adler. *Comparative Criticism* 7 (1985): 157–72.

ing of *Antigone* and *Oedipus the King* and meant to be completed by versions of the other tragedies, but no edition of his poems appeared apart from the unauthorized *Gedichte* (*Poems*, 1826) prepared by Gustav Schwab and Ludwig Uhland and seriously incomplete and faulty. Though some appeared in periodicals (over seventy between 1791 and 1808, not all with Hölderlin's knowledge), many important poems remained unpublished until the twentieth century. A significant group of nine difficult poems was published in an annual in 1805 under the title *Nachtgesänge* (*Night Songs*). These poems overtly counter contemporary taste and must have met with very little understanding. From quite early on, Hölderlin saw himself as writing for posterity and was aware, as he put it in a note introducing the hymn "Friedensfeier" ("Celebration of Peace"), that his language would be thought "too unconventional."

The Sophocles translations opposed taste even more than the poems and were taken as conclusive proof that their author had lost his mind. According to a famous anecdote Schiller roared with laughter on hearing passages read to him by Heinrich Voss, whose father's versions of Homer had inaugurated the kind of translation Hölderlin radicalized. Hölderlin himself explained to his publisher that he was trying to bring out the "Oriental" element of Greekness that Sophocles had been forced to deny and which Hölderlin thought he had

Bibliography

Bertaux, Pierre. *Friedrich Hölderlin*. Frankfurt am Main: Suhrkamp, 1978.

Constantine, David. *Hölderlin*. Oxford, U.K.: Oxford University Press, 1988.

———. *The Significance of Locality in the Poetry of Friedrich Hölderlin*. London: Modern Humanities Research Association, 1979.

Grunert, Mark. *Die Poesie des Übergangs: Hölderlins späte Dichtung im Horizont von Friedrich Schegels Konzept der "Transzendentalpoesie."* Tübingen: Niemeyer, 1995.

Henrich, Dieter. *Der Grund im Bewußtsein: Untersuchungen zu Hölderlins Denken (1794–1795)*. Stuttgart: Klett, 1992.

Louth, Charlie. *Hölderlin and the Dynamics of Translation*. Oxford, U.K.: Legenda, 1998.

Santner, Eric L. *Friedrich Hölderlin: Narrative Vigilance and the Poetic Imagination*. New Brunswick, N.J.: Rutgers University Press, 1986.

Schmidt, Jochen, ed., *Über Hölderlin*. Frankfurt am Main: Insel, 1970.

Seifert, Albrecht. *Untersuchungen zu Hölderlins Pindar-Rezeption*. Munich: Fink, 1982.

Szondi, Peter. *Hölderlin-Studien: Mit einem Traktat über philologische Erkenntnis*. Frankfurt am Main: Suhrkamp, 1970.

Wackwitz, Stephan. *Friedrich Hölderlin*. Stuttgart: Metzler, 1985.

HOLMES, OLIVER WENDELL 1809–1894

American physician and writer

Oliver Wendell Holmes had virtually none of the fiery mysticism associated with the Romantic era, nor its meditative solitude, nor its revolutionary solidarity with members of oppressed groups. On the contrary, he was politically rather conservative and socially gregarious. Holmes was involved in the club life of the New England intellectual aristocracy, associating with such figures as William Cullen Bryant, Ralph Waldo Emerson, Nathaniel Hawthorne, William Dean Howells, Henry Wadsworth Longfellow, and John Greenleaf Whittier. His most renowned poems were treasured in the United States and abroad for their wit and for their encapsulation of cherished ideals.

Holmes was, by his own description, a quintessential Boston Brahmin. The eldest son of Mary Wendell and Abiel Holmes, orthodox Calvinist minister of the First Congregational Church in Cambridge, Holmes was educated at Cambridgeport, where Richard Henry Dana and Margaret Fuller were among his schoolmates. At fifteen, he attended Phillips Academy, in Andover. Holmes was a member of the class of 1829 at Harvard University, where he began developing a reputation as a poet. A year after graduation, during law studies, he wrote "Old Ironsides," a patriotic paean to the historic U.S. frigate *Constitution*. The boat had been slated for demolition, but it was rescued by the patriotic sentiment aroused by the poem, which was printed first in the *Boston Daily Advertiser* in 1830, copied nationwide, and even scattered about the capital in handbill form.

In 1831, Holmes abandoned law for medicine in Boston and Paris. At the time, training in Paris emphasized a practical and scientific approach that was unfamiliar in America. Although he practiced medicine for ten years, his real gifts lay in teaching and writing about it. He wrote prize-winning medical essays in 1836 and 1837, cofounded the Tremont Medical School, where he taught pathology and physiology and later also surgical anatomy; and worked as a professor of anatomy and physiology at Dartmouth College until his marriage to Amelia Lee Jackson in 1840.

Holmes's greatest contribution to medical writing came in 1843 when he published, in the *New England Quarterly Journal of Medicine and Surgery*, "The Contagiousness of Puerperal Fever" (also called "childbed fever"). Doctors had tended to see the disease as an unpredictable complication of childbirth, but Holmes accurately demonstrated its infectious nature, and confronted American members of his own profession with their role in transmitting the illness. This work was vilified in pamphlets by leading Philadelphia obstetricians. In 1847, Holmes was made Parkman Professor of Anatomy and Physiology in the Medical School of Harvard University, a position he retained for thirty-five years; he also served as the school's dean. He was an extraordinarily gifted lecturer, attracting huge classes with lectures informed by vivid anecdotes and witty wordplay. Although as an administrator he seemed to be progressive by supporting admissions for African Americans and women, in fact he backed down when challenged by other members of the medical school. He was mostly a lifelong conservative and antiabolitionist who changed his opinion on the subject only with the outbreak of the Civil War.

Holmes was one of the leading members of the Saturday Club, an exclusive weekly gathering of intellectual glitterati that included Louis Agassiz, Richard Henry Dana, Ralph Waldo Emerson, Henry Wadsworth Longfellow, James Russell Lowell, and Benjamin Pierce as regulars and welcomed such visitors as James T. Fields, Bret Harte, Nathaniel Hawthorne, and Harriet Beecher Stowe. Holmes was renowned for his gifts of conversation and wit. As Annie Fields later recalled, "He was king of the dinner-table during a large part of the century. . . . How incomparable his gift of conversation was, it will be difficult, probably impossible, for anyone to understand who had never known him. It was not that he was wiser, or wittier, or more profound, or more radiant with humor, than some other distinguished men . . . but with Dr. Holmes sunshine and gayety came into the room." The club was formed in 1856; many of its members founded the *Atlantic Monthly* (1857), with Lowell as editor. Lowell agreed to head the project on condition that Holmes be secured as a regular contributor. In the *Atlantic Monthly*, Holmes inaugurated an extremely popular series of conversational essays entitled "The Autocrat of the Breakfast-Table." Beginning with the sentence "I was just going to say, when I was interrupted," the speaker converses in a simple and fresh way with other residents at his Boston boarding house, offering wisdom, humor, anecdotes, epigrams, and chat. The pieces often concluded with an original poem; some of Holmes's best—including "The Chambered Nautilus" (1858) and "The Deacon's Masterpiece, or the Wonderful One-Hoss-Shay" (1858)—appeared first in this manner. These were followed by a more serious and less successful series, *The Professor at the Breakfast-Table* (1860), *The Poet at the Breakfast-Table* (1872), and *Over the Teacups* (1891). Holmes continued to publish poetry throughout his life, in book volumes from 1847 to 1887.

Holmes also wrote three novels that took advantage of his medical knowledge. All three were case studies of abnormal psychic or physiological states. The first, *Elsie Venner* (1861), traces the fate of a girl who suffers from the long-lasting ill-effects of a snakebite that her mother experienced during her pregnancy. Holmes said that he wrote it to "test the doctrine of original sin" and the notion of "inherited moral responsibility," a perspective that limited its popularity when it appeared in 1861. *The Guardian Angel* (1867) also examines its heroine's ancestral psychological inheritance, while *A Moral Antipathy* (1885) concerns the psychology of a man who is afraid of women. Holmes also wrote two biographies, a life of the historian John Lothrop Motley (1878) and a memoir of Ralph Waldo Emerson (1884), written shortly after his death.

In 1848, Holmes built a cottage on an inherited estate in Pittsfield, Massachusetts, which was a popular retreat for many of the important American authors of the era, among them Hawthorne and Herman Melville. In 1850, he participated in an ascent of nearby Monument Mountain that has since become renowned because it gathered together so many of the important literary figures of the day: Evert Duyckinck, James T. Fields, Nathaniel Hawthorne, Cornelius Matthews, Herman Melville, Henry Dwight Sedgwick, and several women whose names we do not know.

Holmes did not originally support abolitionism, but once the Civil War began, with his son's enlistment into the Union Army, he changed his mind. His son was wounded at three battles, and after going to find him Holmes described the journey in "My Search after the Captain," (*Atlantic Monthly*, 1862)—much to his son's displeasure. Indeed, relations remained strained between the father and the son who later went on to national renown as a justice of the U.S. Supreme Court.

Holmes visited Europe with his daughter in the summer of 1886. In England, he was heartily welcomed and royally entertained. He received honorary degrees from Cambridge, Edinburgh, and Oxford. He continued to publish in the *Atlantic Monthly* throughout his long life. He died at home in 1894, and was mourned throughout America and Europe.

MARIANNE NOBLE

Biography

Born August 29, 1809, Cambridge, Massachusetts. Studied at Harvard University, 1825–29, studied medicine in Paris, April 1833–October 1835. Practiced medicine for ten years, taught anatomy for two years at Dartmouth College. Published article on the contagiousness of puerperal fever, 1843. Professor of anatomy and physiology at Harvard, 1847–82. Dean of the Harvard Medical School, 1847–53. Also worked as an author. Published "Old Ironsides," 1830. Began publishing "Breakfast-Table" papers in *The Atlantic Monthly*, 1857, and subsequently published *The Autocrat of the Breakfast-Table*, 1858; *The Professor at the Breakfast-Table*, 1860; *The Poet at the Breakfast-Table*, 1872; and *Over the Teacups*, 1891. He published three novels: *Elsie Venner*, 1861; *The Guardian Angel*, 1867; and *A Moral Antipathy*, 1885. Died in Cambridge, October 7, 1894.

Selected Works

The *Complete Poetical Works of Oliver Wendell Holmes*. Boston: Houghton Mifflin, 1887.
Morse, John T. *The Life and Letters of Oliver Wendell Holmes*. 2 vols. Boston: Houghton Mifflin, 1896.
The Complete Works of Oliver Wendell Holmes. Boston: Houghton Mifflin, 1909.

Bibliography

Dalke, Anne. "Economics, or the Bosom Serpent: Oliver Wendell Holmes' Elsie Venner: A Romance of Destiny," *American Transcendental Quarterly* 2, no. 1 (1988): 57–68.
Gougeon, Len. "Holmes's Emerson and the Conservative Critique of Realism," *South Atlantic Review* 59, no. 1 (1994): 107–25.
Hallissy, Margaret. "Poisonous Creature: Holmes's *Elsie Venner*," *Studies in the Novel* 17, no. 4 (1985): 406–19.
Hoyt, Edwin P. *The Improper Bostonian: Dr. Oliver Wendell Holmes*. New York: Morrow, 1979.
Menikoff, Barry. "Oliver Wendell Holmes." In *Fifteen American Authors before 1900: Bibliographical Essays on Research and Criticism*. Edited by Earl N. Harbert and Robert A. Rees. Madison: University of Wisconsin Press, 1984. 281–305.
Parker, Gail T. "Sex, Sentiment, and Oliver Wendell Holmes," *Women's Studies—An Interdisciplinary Journal* 1 (1972): 47–64.
Thrailkill, Jane F. "Killing Them Softly: Childbed Fever and the Novel," *American Literature* 71, no. 4 (1999): 679–707.
Tilton, Eleanor M. *The Poetical Works of Oliver Wendell Holmes*. Boston: Houghton Mifflin, 1975.
Traister, Bryce. "Sentimental Medicine: Oliver Wendell Holmes and the Construction of Masculinity," *Studies in American Fiction* 27, no. 2 (1999): 205–27.

HOMOSEXUALITY

By the end of the Enlightenment, sexuality had become a suitable matter for philosophical enquiry. In a series of lectures on ethics delivered to his male students at Königsberg between 1756 and 1794, Immanuel Kant warned against involvement in fornication, adultery, masturbation, bestiality, prostitution, and sexual activity with a member of the same sex. It was thought that only heterosexual intercourse within marriage avoided the animalistic and objectifying tendencies of desire. Among other thinkers who gradually expressed greater tolerance of sexual diversity were the jurist and reformist philosopher Cesare Beccaria, Jeremy Bentham, Charles-Louis Montesquieu, and Voltaire. The penal code adopted by the Constituent Assembly of Revolutionary France in 1791 omitted sodomy from the catalog of offences, a decision that the Code Napoléon reaffirmed in 1810. Yet antisodomite hysteria was at its height in England during the same period. The death penalty for sodomy was not abolished in England and Wales until 1861 (though no executions were carried out after 1836).

Jeremy Bentham's unpublished papers include hundreds of pages on the topic of homosexuality. Bentham argued that homosexuality is neither unnatural nor immoral. Appealing to both Classical culture and the anthropological work of his contemporaries in an attempt to undermine the case for the execution of sodomites, he put the blame for the irrational hatred of homosexual men on superstition (the fear of divine vengeance), hypocrisy (immoral men's need to make themselves appear virtuous by attacking the habits of others), and a rabidly irresponsible popular press.

While reading Plato's *Phaedrus* in 1818, Percy Bysshe Shelley wrote "A Discourse on the Manners of the Ancient Greeks Relative to the Subject of Love," in which he displays a familiarity with the homosexual passages in Catullus, Horace, Juvenal, Lucretius, Martial, Suetonius and Vergil. (He also refers to William Shakespeare's sonnets in this context.) For the most part, Shelley's essay speaks approvingly of the platonic aspect of male-male love; but he also acknowledges that such relationships in Greece did often have a sexual element. Since he cannot believe that the more refined of Greek lovers could possibly have indulged in the abomination of anal intercourse, he assumes that their sexual activities consisted of less violating pleasures. William Blake, too, was developing an acceptance of same-sex relations, in theory at least, as a radical response to what he saw as the oppressive and hypocritical antihomosexual operations of state-sponsored Christianity.

Generally, it was travel that brought homosexuality into open discussion. Many northern Europeans had their assumptions challenged when faced with sexual practices in southern Europe during the traditional "grand tour." The Islamic Middle East was seen to have inherited the traditions of ancient Greek pederasty; while Greece, with its ruins becoming an increasingly popular destination, came to be seen as a less alien, European version of the Middle East. Major Eastern texts on homoerotic themes started to be read in new translations, such as Antoine Galland's translation of *The Thousand and One Nights* into French (1704–17) and William Jones's translation of Hafiz of Shiraz into English (1772). Archaeology, too, was shedding light on ancient cultural practices. Johann Joachim Winckelmann's visits to Pompeii, Herculaneum and Paestum in 1755 led to his intermittently homoerotic critical writings. Famously, Johann Wolfgang von Goethe's trips to Italy in 1786 through 1788 and 1790 and Gustave Flaubert's visit to Cairo in 1849 through 1850 both included observations of homosexual activities. Moreover, the accumulative instincts of homosexual aesthetes like Frederick the Great of Prussia and Gustav III of Sweden were gradually making ancient homoerotic art available for viewing in northern Europe.

The Gothic fiction of homosexual and bisexual men like Matthew "Monk" Lewis, William Beckford, and Horace Walpole generally had its source in travel. Beckford, the richest man in England, lived as an outcast from society on his Fonthill estate after rumors of his relationship with his younger cousin William "Kitty" Courtenay were deliberately leaked to the press in 1784. Although he continued to travel abroad, and to court foreign boys, the wall with which he surrounded Fonthill became the physical embodiment of his defensive response to the English hostility to sodomy. The extravagant possibilities of the Gothic saw expression in the camp architectural follies of Beckford at Fonthill and Walpole at Strawberry Hill.

The elegiac tradition in English poetry continued to celebrate an intense love between men for which the term "friendship" was adequate only in its respectability and restraint. Following the precedent of John Milton's *Lycidas*, Shelley's *Adonais* accessed the resources of Greek pastoral mythology as a way of responding to John Keats's death in 1821. Later, in *In Memoriam* (1850), Alfred, Lord Tennyson characterized his grief at the death of Arthur Henry Hallam in 1833 as a widowhood from which he would never recover.

Lord Byron's career begins with sentimental love poems referring to younger boys at Harrow school. He wrote a sequence of elegies to John Edleston, with whom he had fallen in love while at Cambridge University, disguised as the female "Thyrza." Although there followed in England the celebrated relationships with Lady Caroline Lamb and his half-sister Augusta Leigh, and his unhappy marriage to Annabella Milbanke, Byron ultimately left the country under threat of scandalous revelations about sodomy and incest. After the relative stability of a relationship with Teresa Guiccioli in Italy, in 1823 Byron answered the call to arms in Greece. There, in the last months of his life, he fell in love with a fifteen-year-old boy called Lukas, whom he took on as his page. This unrequited affair is dealt with in the lines beginning "On This Day I Complete My Thirty Sixth Year" and "Love and Death."

Not subjected to anything like the same publicity as sodomy, lesbianism was far less visible. Lesbian writing was confined to the "ephemera" of private journals and letters, where women recorded their love for each other. The best known of these include the diaries of Eleanor Butler and Anne Lister. Mary Wollstonecraft's *Mary: A Fiction* (1788) was the first published book in English by a woman on love between women. Some of the sonnets of Anna Seward refer to women she loved, including the so-called "Ladies of Llangollen" who were considered so unusual in their domestic cohabitation as to become a genteel cultural tourist attraction. However, neither their one bed nor the self-evidence of their love for each other seems ever to have been publicly understood as carnal. Wordsworth, for example, called them "Sisters in love."

The period's most unequivocal representations of same-sex love occur among the characters of French fiction. In Théophile Gautier's *Mademoiselle de Maupin* (1835), indeterminate and disguised gender demonstrates the sheer contingency of sexual object choice. Later, Honoré de Balzac creates the master criminal Vautrin who, in several novels but principally in *Lest Illusions* (1837–43), shows a propensity for sentimental friendships with high-born youths which mask more carnal desires.

In the visual arts, neoclassicism allowed, in representations of pre-Christian civilizations, a certain amount of homoerotic imagery. In France, Jacques-Louis David painted several great canvases depicting male lovers in ancient Greece, starting with the *Funeral of Patroclus* (1779) with its weeping figure of the bereft Achilles. His *Death of Socrates* (1787) combined the themes of public virtue and personal beauty in a manner characteristic of post-revolutionary France. And David's *Leonidas at Thermopylae* (1800–14) shows the Spartan general surrounded by his doomed troops in varying stages of undress and embracing as they ready themselves for battle. David's pupil Jean-Auguste-Dominique Ingres also depicted such scenes, as in his painting *Achilles and Patroclus*, which won the Prix de Rome in 1801.

Théodore Géricault produced countless academic studies of the male nude without recourse to the classical world as justification, and in the great canvas of 1819, *The Raft of the Medusa*, he built up a complex composition of active and passive male bodies to demonstrate the proximity of the extremes of hope and despair. Géricault's many studies for this masterpiece fetishize the male body, alive or dead, fragmented or intact, with an unprecedented degree of detailed intensity.

GREGORY WOODS

Bibliography

Aldrich, Robert. *The Seduction of the Mediterranean: Writing, Art and Homosexual Fantasy.* London: Routledge, 1993.

Faderman, Lillian. *Surpassing the Love of Men: Romantic Friendship and Love Between Women from the Renaissance to the Present.* New York: Morrow, 1981.

Hammond, Paul. *Love between Men in English Literature.* London: Macmillan, 1996.

Hobson, Christopher Z. *Blake and Homosexuality.* London: Palgrave, 2001.

Merrick, Jeffrey, and Bryant T. Ragan, Jr., eds. *Homosexuality in Early Modern France: A Documentary Collection.* Oxford: Oxford University Press, 2001.

Saslow, James M. *Pictures and Passions: A History of Homosexuality in the Visual Arts.* New York: Viking, 1999.

Summers, Claude J., ed. *The Gay and Lesbian Literary Heritage: A Reader's Companion to the Writers and their Works, from Antiquity to the Present.* New York: Henry Holt, 1995.

Woods, Gregory. *A History of Gay Literature: The Male Tradition.* New Haven, Conn.: Yale University Press, 1998.

HOOD, THOMAS 1799–1845

English poet, cartoonist, novelist, and editor

Thomas Hood's distinct talent and claim to fame throughout the 1820s and 1830s is no traditional Romantic sensibility, but rather a large body of comic verse, comprised of poem after poem of social satire laced with outrageous and sometimes silly verbal play. His cartoon illustrations for many of these, especially in the annuals he edited, supply perverse textual supplements and visual puns. The wit, both verbal and visual, often makes a grim farce of the vulnerability of the human body to catastrophe, especially in the violence of war. With overt compassion for the victimized body, Hood turned his poetry, in the last decade of his life (as his health was being eroded by tuberculosis) to the agonies of poverty and dehumanizing labor. "The Song of the Shirt" (1843)—a sensation when, against strong advice, it appeared in the Christmas issue of the comic magazine *Punch*—won international fame (Engels commented on it), and "The Bridge of Sighs" (1844; based on an attempted suicide that had been reported in the *Times* throughout the spring of that year) was admired by Edgar Allan Poe and Charles Baudelaire, and has proved a perennial anthology favorite.

Hood's first endeavors displayed intermittent Romantic tendencies of a Keatsian temper, in subjects, themes, and even phrasings. Yet even in this phase, Hood could not resist using puns and wordplay. Near the close of a long "Ode to Melancholy" (1827), he writes: "Even the bright extremes of joy / Bring on conclusions of disgust, / Like the sweet blossoms of the May, / Whose fragrance ends in must" (113–16). Some readers enjoy the extra verbal senses of *May* and *must*; others have been put off by the tonal rupture—the random grammatical jest of punning these nouns into verbs as a way of enforcing the grimly deterministic wit. As the occasion suggests, Hood's wit is frequently animated by an obsession with the inevitability and pervasiveness of death. Most of his immediate family died of consumption by the time he was twenty-one, and throughout his life his health was often quite poor, and at best precarious. His son Tom later said that as a boy he thought one of the advantages of being an adult was that one could spit blood. Hood lived longer than most consumptives of his day (Keats died at age twenty-five). Even his comic verse is typically sharpened by a vivid imagination of death and a mordant wit about its ghastly events.

William Thackeray, in "On a Joke I Once Heard from the Late Thomas Hood" (1863), gives a portrait of the poet as a young man: "I quite remember his pale face; he was thin and deaf, and very silent; he scarcely opened his lips during the dinner, and he made one pun." Although other fine poets are (in)famous punsters (Lord Byron, William Shakespeare) and other fine punsters sometimes poets (Lewis Carroll, Edward Lear), Hood's imagination is devoted to punning, especially its morbid events. The word becomes double, splitting in two, often as a body is being dismembered (a shipwrecked, shark-mauled sailor hails his lamenting Sally: "But now, adieu—a long adieu! / I've solved death's awful riddle, / And would say more, but I am doomed / To break off in the middle!" (37–40). "A double meaning shows double sense," Hood winks in his pun-propelled epic "Miss Kilmansegg and her Precious Leg: A Golden Legend" (1840). Deploying such verbal shifts and densities, Hood's comic verse often treats early romantic themes to farce or morbid humor or, as in "Miss Kilmansegg," infuses potentially serious subjects with mocking jeremiad to generate a sharp and hilarious satire on life in the material world.

Such effects may jar even sympathetic readers. "It is difficult to see why a man like Hood, who wrote with energy when he was roused, should have produced so much verse of a trivial and undirected verbal ingenuity," William Empson laments in *Seven Types of Ambiguity*, suspecting Hood of punning in order "to back away from the echoes and implications of words, to distract your attention by insisting on his ingenuity so that you can escape from sinking into meaning." Poe, who adored "Fair Ines" (1823) and "The Bridge of Sighs," found the sinking into puns "painful": "they are the hypochondriac's struggle at mirth—the grinnings of the death's head"—that betray the "peculiar genius . . . of vivid *Fancy* impelled by Hypochondriasis." Poe could allow a pun only in a mode of "richest *grotesquerie*; impressing the imaginative reader with remarkable force, as if by a new phase of the ideal," but Hood honored no such self-imposed boundaries. It is utterly telling of the man who said "I have to be a lively Hood for a livelihood" that his death is marked doubly, by the poignant stanzas, "Farewell, Life!" (1845) and by his remark that he was dying really "to please the undertaker, who wished to urn a lively Hood." G. K. Chesterton remarked, "The tragic necessity of puns tautened and hardened Hood's genius," and had in mind such sober punning as "Sewing at once with a double thread / A shroud as well as a shirt" and "Oh! God! that bread should be so dear, / And flesh and blood so cheap" ("The Song of the Shirt"); the tender pathos of "We thought her dying when she slept, / And sleeping when she died" ("The Death-Bed," 1831); and even the grimly comic "A cannon-ball took off his legs, / So he laid down his arms" ("Faithless Nelly Gray," 1826).

As Chesterton recognized, Hood's wordplay and punning radiate from a sensibility that could also abandon such play, to tune a music of haunting moods, whether of supernatural possession, elegy, or social anger. In the 1840s, he was writing a poetry of passionate protest on behalf of socially oppressed classes. "The Lay of the Labourer" (1844) and "The Workhouse Clock: An Allegory" (1844) were sparked by reports of workers' plights in the *Times*, as was the tragic elegy "The Bridge of Sighs." "The Song of the Shirt," in deadening mechanical rhymes, became his most famous poem. After it appeared in *Punch*, it "ran through the land like wildfire," and tripled the magazine's circulation. For a monument to Hood at Kensal Green Cemetery—with a crest, designed by Hood, of a heart pierced with a needle, threaded with tears—among the sums that poured in were pittances from working-class towns, the costly gifts of the poor, the dressmakers, and needlewomen. Hood's self-chosen epitaph was "He sang the Song of the Shirt."

SUSAN J. WOLFSON

Biography

Born May 23, 1799 in Poultry, City of London. Living in Islington, 1811, father and brother died. Left school to support his family, as a clerk in London (1813), then as an engraver (1814). Went to Dundee for health and began publishing satirical rhymes. Returned to London in 1817 to work as an engraver until 1821, when he became a subeditor for *London Magazine* (until 1823) and frequent contributor. Mother died in 1821 and he became sole support for his sisters. Engaged in 1822 to Jane Reynolds (1794–1847), marrying in 1825, the same year he published *Odes and Addresses to Great People* with Jane's brother, John Hamilton Reynolds (a success, seeing three editions in one year). Contributed to *New Monthly Magazine* from 1826 on. The birth and death of a daughter in 1827 inspired Charles Lamb's *Ode on an Infant Dying as Soon Born*. Convalesced in Brighton from a severe attack of rheumatic fever in 1828. Edited *The Gem* (a Christmas annual) in 1829 and published *Eugene Aram* in it. Daughter Frances Freeling born in 1830 (d. 1878). Published and edited *Comic Annual* (until 1842) and contributed most of its literary pieces. Sought better health by moving in 1832 to a country house in Essex, which proved a financial burden; wrote his three-volume novel *Tylney Hall* as a moneymaker. Suffered setbacks in his health and severe financial losses in 1834 with the collapse of his engraving firm in 1834 and a break with his publisher. Son Tom born 1835 (d. 1874). Went to Coblenz, Germany, to escape debts and repair his finances; his family soon joined him as his health worsened. Supported T. N. Talford's efforts to reform copyright law with a series of letters to the *Athenaeum* (1836). The Hoods moved to Ostend, 1838, and he published his monthly magazine, *Hood's Own: Or, Laughter from Year to Year*. Returned to London in 1840, published an autobiographical memoir, and edited *New Monthly Magazine* (1841–43). Received a grant from the Royal Literary Fund in 1841 and a civil pension in 1844. In 1844 founded *Hood's Magazine and Comic Miscellany* and edited it until just a few weeks before his death, in Hampstead, from a lingering illness (tuberculosis aggravated by influenza), May 3, 1845. Buried at Kensal Green.

Selected Works

"Fair Ine," 1823.
Odes and Addresses to Great People (with John Hamilton Reynolds), 1825.
"Faithless Nelly Gray," 1826.
Whims and Oddities, First Series, 1826, 2nd ed., 1827.
Whims and Oddities, Second Series, 1827, 2nd ed., 1829.
The Plea of the Midsummer Fairies, Hero and Leander, Lycus the Centaur, and Other Poems, 1827.
The Last Man, 1827.
The Epping Hunt, 1829.
Comic Melodies, 1830.
The Dream of Eugene Aram, The Murderer, 1830.
"The Death-Bed," 1831.
Tylney Hall, 1834.
Up the Rhine, 1840.
Miss Kilmansegg and Her Precious Leg, 1840.
The Song of the Shirt, 1843.
The Bridge of Sighs, 1844.
"The Lay of the Labourer," 1844.
"The Workhouse Clock: An Allegory," 1844.
Whimsicalities, 1844.
"Farewell, Life!" 1845.

Collections

The Works of Thomas Hood, 11 vols. Edited by Thomas Hood, Jr. and Frances Freeling Broderip. 1882–84.

The Complete Poetical Works of Thomas Hood. Edited by Walter
Jerrold. London: Oxford University Press, 1906.
Selected Poems of Thomas Hood. Edited by John Clubbe. Cambridge,
Mass.: Harvard University Press, 1970.
Selected Poems of Hood, Praed, and Beddoes. Edited by Susan J.
Wolfson and Peter J. Manning. Harmondsworth, England:
Penguin, 2000. University of Pittsburgh Press, 2001.

Letters and Biography
Broderip, Frances Freeling. *Memorials of Thomas Hood: Collected,
Arranged, and Edited by his Daughter, With a Preface and Notes by
his Son*, 1860.
Clubbe, John. *Victorian Forerunner: The Later Career of Hood.*
Durham, N.C.: Duke University Press, 1968.

Jerrold, Walter. *Thomas Hood: His Life and Times.* London: Oxford
University Press, 1909.
Morgan, Peter F., ed. *The Letters of Thomas Hood.* Toronto:
University of Toronto Press, 1973.
Reid, John C. *Thomas Hood.* London: Routledge and Kegan Paul,
1963.

Bibliography

Brander, Laurence. *Thomas Hood.* London: Longmans, 1963.
Henkle, Roger B. "Comedy as Commodity: Thomas Hood's Poetry
of Class Desire," *Victorian Poetry* 26 (1988): 301–18.

A HORSE FRIGHTENED BY A LION 1770

Painting by George Stubbs

The subject of *A Horse Frightened by a Lion* is one that George Stubbs returned to at different points in his career, and in different media, including oils, mezzotint, and enamel on a ceramic base (a speciality of Stubbs's), while similar horses are rendered by him in reliefs for the ceramicist Josiah Wedgwood. At least a dozen reinterpretations of this, and the allied subject of the horse with the lion attacking it by savaging its back, have survived, and there is evidence of more that have not, pointing to the popularity of the image with Stubbs's aristocratic and bourgeois public.

The first version was painted for Charles, second Marquis of Rockingham, at some point in the 1760s. The source of this and the subsequent images has been disputed, in ways that can be mapped onto critical dispute as to whether Stubbs is properly seen as a proto-Romantic or a neoclassical painter. He returned from a journey to Rome in the 1750s and said (according to his biographer Ozias Humphrey) that he had wanted in Italy to test whether "nature as and is always superior to art whether Greek or Roman, and having received this conviction he immediately resolved upon returning home." This either supports, or is the source of, a report in the *Sporting Magazine* of 1808 stating that the series is based on an event that Stubbs witnessed in Italy. But it can be equally plausibly argued that Stubbs's starting point was a celebrated marble statue of the same subject, currently in the Museo del Palazzo dei Conservatori in Rome, and often quoted by Roman painters of the seventeenth century.

The art-historical dispute might be easily resolved if we recall that Stubbs's starting point was scientific, and it is in this context, rather than that of Romantic pantheism, that we must understand his use of the term *nature*. And in this context, there is no conflict between classical art and "the real" if, as in the case of the Roman marble, Stubbs could see that the ancient sculptor had recorded the muscle groups, the poses and the actions of the heads of the animals in a way that made them more accessible for study than they could possibly be in reality. Stubbs's major project when he returned from Rome to Liverpool was to begin the series of plates, based on his own dissections, that were later to be collected as *The Anatomy of the Horse* (the work had to be done in the obscure Humberside village of Horkstow, in order to escape public suspicion and distaste: Enlightenment scienti-

cism was in conflict with emerging sensibility . . . and then again, there was the smell). Though he did not immediately find a publisher when he took the resulting drawings to London in 1759, he found a vast and affluent market in devotees of horseracing and hunting, both then at their highest peak of development and cultural prestige. The commissions that resulted from this launched a provincial and self-directed artist into a highly lucrative career.

The earlier picture, like the later ones, contains no human presence; the drama is entirely between the two animals. A painting now in the Yale University Art Gallery, *Horse Attacked by a Lion*, is identical in size (40″ × 50″) and in date (1770) to the *Horse Frightened by a Lion* now in the Walker Art Gallery, Liverpool, with a similar horse in exactly the same place in the composition; the two may well have been conceived of as a diptych, in which case the major difference—the rougher (in strictly classical terms, more "horrid") state of the foliage and the stormy sky in *Horse Attacked*, as opposed to the blue sky of

George Stubbs, *A Horse Frightened by a Lion*. Reprinted courtesy of The Bridgeman Art Library.

Horse Frightened—suggests that in this case, at least, Stubbs is using the environment of the encounter expressively.

This, and the very absence of the human, allows us to read the painting proto-Romantically, as a nonhuman drama standing in for intensely human emotions of panic and fear. Though the horse scarcely looks like a wild horse, it is riderless, and bears no traces of the human civilization which must have bred it; has it escaped from society into the more dangerous space of wilderness? Another way in which the image is readable as on a cusp between the neo-Classical and the Romantic is in the Platonic sense of the horse as passion controlled, in an assertion of the truly human, by reason. Here the horse may be about to pay the penalty for its escape. And the horses' intense whiteness, in both these pictures set off by the dark and earthy browns of the landscape, speaks both of Classical marble, and of the spectral, the hallucinatory.

Horse Frightened by a Lion, in its treatment of the lion, both supports and subverts a reading of the painting as a projection of human passion. That here Stubbs focuses on the moment *before* the attack captures us in a moment of empathy, rather than in placing us in a safely voyeuristic relation to a gladiatorial spectacle. But the lion itself is scarcely frightening; he emerges from the shadows, behind and a little below the rock on which

the horse. Like Classical statuary, he is poised, but we see only his face, which looks old and rather tired; perhaps Stubbs worked from a lazy, semitame menagerie beast. Furthermore, the lion looks past the horse, directly at the spectator, and as his face is full on, it is tempting to read it's expression anthropomorphically. It seems to be establishing kinship with the human viewer; the horse occupying the space between is splendidly, enigmatically, alien, but the lion faces the viewer, another compromised, inefficient predator, with a look that is almost humorous. As in so much of Stubbs's work, precise scientific attention to the object produces an image that is resonant precisely because it offers no commentary or context for itself. The lion, in the end, keeps its own counsel.

EDWARD BURNS

Work

A Horse Frightened by a Lion, 1770. Oil on canvas, 40″ × 50″. The Walker Art Gallery, Liverpool.

Bibliography

Stubbs, George. *Anatomy of the Horse*. London: J. A. Allen, 1965.
Taylor, Basil, "George Stubbs: The Lion and Horse Theme," *Burlington Magazine* 107: 81– .
———. *Stubbs*. London: Phaidon, 1971.

HOUDON, JEAN-ANTOINE 1741–1828

French sculptor

Jean-Antoine Houdon was the most versatile and varied French sculptor of the eighteenth century, representing the best in traditional Classicism and innovative Romanticism. Common to both approaches was his commitment to anatomical veracity. He ran a large workshop, trained employee technicians in an experimental bronze casting foundry, taught generations of student pupils at the Academy and Institute of France, and executed commissions for the German court and the American government. He knew and portrayed many of the major figures of the Enlightenment—statesmen, artists, and intellectuals—and was profoundly influenced by the ideas of Denis Diderot and Jean-Jacques Rousseau in his representation of a proto-Romantic "sensibility."

Although he did not come from a family of artists, Houdon grew up among the French Academy's elite group of prizewinners preparing for study at Rome at the Ecole des Élèves Protégés, where his father was concierge from 1749. His education at the academy was strictly Classical: his *Morceau de reception* (1777) was a Classical subject, *Morpheus*. His period of work coincides with the neo-Classical movement and some of his funerary monuments incorporate classical motifs; however he seems to have been able to temper his work to accommodate changes in the prevailing taste. Throughout his life he offered clients a choice from three types of portrait: representation *à l'antique* in Classical dress, a depiction in fashionable French dress or a type intermediate to these, in which every reference to contemporary life is carefully avoided. He used all three types to represent Voltaire. The same variety can be seen in his subjects, which range from monumental funerary works, through allegorical statues to portraits, and his materials, which include terracotta, plaster,

marble, and bronze. From 1782 he lived next to the Paris city foundry and his greatest boast was that he had revived the languishing art of bronze casting in France. He established a foundry of his own at 195 rue du Faubourg Sainte-Honoré, manned by technicians he had personally trained, as well as a separate studio for portrait work where he employed professional modellers to copy his designs. He was extremely prolific and proud to unite the skills of sculptor and bronze caster in his own person.

Houdon's claim to have studied nature all his life is supported by the two paintings by Louis-Léopold Boilly of *Houdon in His Studio*, painted late in Houdon's life in 1804 and 1808. These show him still working directly from the sitter and teaching from the life model, with one of his earliest designs, his famous anatomical figure *L'Ecorche*, prominently displayed. Versions of this literal study of musculature based on dissected corpses were produced by Houdon throughout his life, and they were used in many teaching academies in Europe to demonstrate anatomy in the drawing sessions. It is not only the precise realism that gives force to the figure in an age of enquiry so much as the dramatic authority of the pose, with arm outstretched in command.

Perhaps the most overtly Romantic of all Houdon's portraits is that commissioned by the singer Sophie Arnould. She is shown in her starring role of Iphiginia (1775), from Christoph Willibald Gluck's opera, at the intense moment when, dressed for sacrifice with the attributes of Diana in her hair, eyes raised to heaven, she implores the gods for clemency. A series of thirty plaster versions was commissioned in addition to the marble; they are now exhibited in the Louvre.

Houdon produced a series of six portraits of contemporary French philosophers, and his 1771 portrait bust of the encyclopedist Diderot, full of spirit, without wig or coat, was probably solicited by the artist rather than commissioned by the sitter. Diderot thought it an excellent likeness and became friendly with Houdon during the sittings. Diderot, who enjoyed advising artists and who was accustomed to propose complete programs for complex funerary monuments, seems to have influenced Houdon's terracotta sketch for the Tomb of Prince Alexander Mikhailovitch Galitzin (1777). The moment of death is shown when life's vanities, virtues, and vices become irrelevant and the prince is left with "only Virtue to console him and Friendship to miss him": the effect of the design is an impressive mixture of pathos and fortitude. Smaller projects on the theme of death that were executed in the same year, such as the marble *Dead Thrush* and the plaster *Eagle Attacking a Deer* share similar sentiment and foreshadow the work of Antoine-Louis Barye.

It is in his portrait busts that Houdon anticipates the Romantic movement of the nineteenth century. His marble *Madame Adelaide, Aunt of Louis XVI (1777)* is almost shocking in the uncompromising portrayal of her unlovely but intellectual features. Only the Scottish painter-philosopher Allan Ramsay had insisted more deliberately on depicting the individual features of society women—however irregular they might be. Houdon's search for particularity was usually less ruthless, but in the case of Mirabeau (1791) the sitter's pockmarked skin is prominently featured. Movement, animation, vivacity, and personality—all the features claimed by Stendhal as appropriate qualities for a modern hero or heroine—are introduced by Houdon in a development of the vigorous busts of the seventeenth-century sculptor Gian Lorenzo Bernini, whose work he must have known in Rome. Like Bernini, Houdon concentrated on lights and shadows in the eye sockets to achieve maximum effect of vivacity, cutting a deep recess to represent the pupil and leaving a spicule of marble at the surface level to reflect light. Like Bernini in his *Constanza Buonarelli* (1635), Houdon distinguished specific textures such as the softness of hair and skin, excelling in his portrayal of a unique personality in the bust *Madame Houdon* (1787).

In some cases, such as *The Kiss* (1778), it is difficult to decide whether the feeling of the sculpture is more rococo or Romantic, but in the later figure of *Hiver* (*Winter*, 1787) the little terracotta version in the Louvre known as *La Petite Frileuse*, which is totally nude, represents the sensation of being cold more naturalistically than the more famous and more titillating marble versions. In the versions of his famous *Diana Chasseresse*, first conceived in 1776 and cast in bronze in 1790, the argument is balanced between neoclassicism and realism. This subject had many classical prototypes but Houdon's goddess is shown completely nude with and clear outward signs of female genitalia. The statue was initially considered too shocking to exhibit and the naturalistic vulval vent on the Louvre bronze version was sealed up.

The strong emphasis on individuality and animation in Houdon's work fell temporarily out of favor during the early years of the nineteenth century when Antonio Canova's reputation was at its height and neoclassicism was the favored style. He continued to receive commissions, even from Napoleon Bonaparte, and his brilliant handling of marble continued to be admired by patrons in Russia, Germany, and the United States.

PATRICIA CAMPBELL

Biography

Born at Versailles, March 25, 1741. Enrolled in the French Academy of Painting and Sculpture, 1756, and studied under Rene-Michel Slodz, Jean-Baptiste Lemoyne, and Jean-Baptiste Pigalle. Attained first prize in Sculpture, 1761. Enrolled at the École des Élèves Protégés 1761–64, then studied in Rome until 1768, returning to Paris in November, when he was elected agree of the Academy. Learned bronze-casting techniques in the 1770s. Visited German court at Saxe-Gotha in 1771 and 1773. Traveled with two technicians to the United States in 1785. Married Marie-Ange-Cecile Langlois on July 1, 1786 and had three daughters: Sabine 1787, Anne-Ange 1788, and Claudine 1790. After the suppression of the academy he renounced his academic titles; he was appointed to the Institute of France and held a sale of works from his studio in the Biblioteque du Roi in 1795. Moved to the old College Mazarin in 1801. Created Chevalier of the Legion of Honor by Napoleon in 1803 and professor of the Institute of France in 1805. Last exhibited in 1814. Wife died in 1823. King of Prussia visited his studio, 1824. Houdon died on July 15, 1828.

Bibliography

Arnason, H. H. *Sculpture by Houdon*. Worcester, Mass., 1964.

Bresc-Bautier, Genevieve. "Fonderie et ateliers du Poule." In *Rue du Faubourg Saint-Honore*. Paris, 1994. 373–77.

Dierks, Hermann. *Houdon's Leben und Werke*. 1887.

Gaborit, Jean-Rene. *Sculpture Francaise II—Renaissance et temps Modernes*. Paris: Musee du Louvre, 1998. 421–34.

Giacometti, Georges. *Le statuaire Jean-Antoine Houdon et son epoque (1741–1828)*. 3 vols. Paris, 1918–19.

"Houdon fondeur," in *La Revue du Louvre et des Musees de France* 4 (1975): 242–47.

Houdon, sa vie et son oeuvre. Paris, 1964.

"Is Houdon a Neo-classical sculptor?," "Houdon and his Models," and "Houdon: Funerary and Mythological Works," in *Feuillets* 5, nos. 2, 3, and 4.

La vie et l'oeuvre do Houdon. 2 vols. Paris, 1928.

Lami, Stanislas. *Dictionnaire des Sculpteurs de l'ecole francaise en dix-huitieme siecle*. Vol 1. Paris, 1910. 408–36.

Mansfeld, Heinz, "Der Bildhauer Jean-Antoine Houdon. Seine Zeit, sein Werk in Deutchland." Ph.D. diss. Deutche Akademie der Kunste. Berlin, 1955.

Reau, Louis. *Houdon, biograpnie critique*. Paris: 1930.

Scherf, Guilhem. *Houdon. Diane chasseresse*. Paris: Musée du Louvre, 2000.

The Sculptures of Houdon. London: Phaidon, 1975.

Vitry, Paul. "La Diane et l'Apollon de Houdon," in *Les Arts* 61 (1907): 9–16.

HUET, PAUL 1803–1869

French landscape artist

Paul Huet rejected the academic precepts of his neo-Classical training and, receptive to depictions of nature by his contemporaries the Romantic poets, he inaugurated a new direction for French landscape painting that would prove to be a decisive influence on the later, more naturalistic Barbizon school. More generally, he may be said to have given landscape painting an independence that allowed it to become the preeminent genre in nineteenth-century French painting. From the outset, his work was firmly identified with the new Romantic aesthetic and was thus subjected to the strictures of the artistic establishment. The sympathetic critic Gustave Planche was appalled that Huet did not receive even a "mention" at the Paris Salon of 1831. Yet despite the fact that his art went on to attract the admiration of Charles Baudelaire and Théophile Gautier (the eventual author of his obituary), Huet's reputation was on the wane for much of his lifetime, largely as a result of having remained faithful to a sensibility that would soon seem outmoded in a century ever more preoccupied with the real.

Although Huet was engaged from the outset in bold and independent exercises in the depiction of natural settings, his manner was profoundly affected by the discovery of the oil paintings of John Constable, whose *Haywain* (1821) caused a stir at the Salon of 1824. But if, like his friend Jean-Baptiste Isabey, he marveled at the technical inventiveness that permitted the English painter to depict with such finesse the effect of light on the landscape, he was by no means a simple imitator of Constable's manner. His son would later attempt to differentiate the two artists by proclaiming Huet the melancholic painter of autumn and Constable the exuberant painter of summer. Prior to 1824, he had already traveled in Normandy with Richard Parkes Bonington. So close in manner were the watercolors produced by the two friends that attribution has sometimes proved difficult.

Huet's output (oils, watercolors, and drawings) was largely devoted to the depiction of the same familiar landscapes. Although he painted and sketched in the south of France and made the occasional trip to other Mediterranean countries, it was to Compiègne, the Forest of Fontainebleau, and the countryside around Paris that his artistic eye would inevitably return, attentive as he was to seasonal and atmospheric change (he claimed to have a visual memory of every bush in the park at Saint-Cloud). It was his practice to make vivid and expressive sketches which he would then work up into often large-scale paintings in oil.

Huet sought to enter into contact with the grandeur of nature. His compositions typically feature thick forests, steep rocks, and trees intertwined or otherwise yielding to stormy conditions. Human figures, if present at all, are tiny, vulnerable beings struggling against turbulent enivronmental forces. Buildings often retain a certain Gothic dimension, thereby contributing to the sense of mystery or foreboding. His landscapes reveal a dedication to authentic observation combined with a sensitivity to poetic effects, which he felt it was the artist's duty to heighten.

In 1830, Charles-Augustin Sainte-Beuve (and not, as Hugh Honour has stated, Philippe Burty, who was simply using Sainte-Beuve's essay as a preface to his own account of Huet's work) saw Huet's aesthetic prefigured in a passage in E. T. A. Hoffmann's tale, "The Jesuit Church in G." (1819), where the painter Berthold is given a homily that reads, "To seize nature in its most profound expression, in its most intimate sense, in that thought which elevates all beings towards a more sublime life, is the holy mission of all the arts ... Is a simple, exact copy of nature ever able to realize such an aim? How miserable, awkward and forced is the inscription in a foreign tongue copied by a scribe who comprehends it not ... ! So it is that certain landscapes are no more than correct copies of an original written in a foreign tongue. ... The painter who is initiated in the divine secrets of art hears the voice of nature recounting its infinite mysteries through the trees, plants, flowers, waters and mountains. There comes upon him, in the manner of the spirit of God, the gift of transporting into his works his own feelings." Huet himself saw the artist's mission as being to express his personal sensibility, which in his own case he considered to consist of a "nervous affection."

Early in his career, Huet was one of the artists who provided scenes for the Diorama Montesquieu (later destroyed in the fire that engulfed the Gaîté theatre). Sainte-Beuve recalls in this connection a bird's-eye view of Rouen and a depiction of the Château d'Arques, forty feet long. Huet is also said to be the painter of the landscape background in Ferdinand-Victor-Eugène Delacroix's portrait *Baron Schwiter* (1826) and also his *Le Christ au Jardin des Oliviers (Agony in the Garden*, 1826). Huet painted eight decorative panels for the sitting room of a private property in Normandy, first shown at the Salon of 1859. He was also a lithographer, etcher, and engraver on wood, and as such was a contributor to a number of volumes, including the Curmer edition of Jacques-Henri Bernardin de Saint-Pierre's *Paul et Virginie* (1788), the elder Alexandre Dumas *Isabel de Bavière* (1830), and the Petrus Borel translation of Daniel Defoe's *Robinson Crusoe*. He became a member of the Society of Painter-Etchers in 1863.

More generally, Huet was a leading proponent of the early Romantic movement and a friend of such writers as Théophile Gautier, Victor Hugo (who acquired one of his paintings in 1831), Charles-Augustin Sainte-Beuve, Alfred-Victor de Vigny, Théophile Gautier, and the historian Jules Michelet. For such individuals, art was a means of promoting a liberal revolution at a time when the restored Bourbon monarchy was seen as inimical to the arts as well as to individual liberties. With them, and together with his fellow artists Ferdinand-Victor-Eugène Delacroix and Eugène Devéria, Huet was a member of the "holy battalion of Shakespearean supporters" (Armand de Pontmartin) that formed ranks at the Café Voltaire before making its entrance at the epoch-making English performance of *Hamlet* at the Odéon in 1827. On February 12, 1830, he participated in the still noisier first night of *Hernani*, which was later seen as a prelude to the July Revolution—which event found Huet alongside Dumas *père* on the barricades (as reported in a letter to Baudelaire, September 2, 1868). He would later recall, regarding the events of 1830, "The younger generation seemed to emerge from its long period of exhaustion . . . Drawn by an irresistible desire for liberty, it rushed to the very sources of life in order to sample the beautiful and the good." Outraged by Louis-Philippe's repressive measures in the face of republican opposition, he produced for *La Caricature* in 1832 a lithograph entitled "Amnesty," in which he starkly evoked those republicans who, following the riot at General Lamarque's funeral, had either been executed or had died in prison, and were therefore unable to benefit from the proposed amnesty. It was with some justification that Daumier dubbed him "le paysagiste patriote."

Huet's better-known paintings include: *Inondation à Saint-Cloud (Flood at Saint-Cloud*, 1855); *Le Château d'Arques (Arques Castle*, 1838–39); *Grande Marée d'équinoxe aux environs de Honfleur (Spring Tide near Honfleur*, 1861); *Le Bois de La Haye (Wood in the Hague*, 1866); *Fontainebleau. Les Chasseurs (Forest of Fontainebleau: Hunters*, c.1866); and the early *Intérieur de forêt, Maison de garde, (Guardian's House in the Forest of Compiègne*, 1826). He considered his most representative picture to be *Fourré de la forêt (Woodland Freshness: Forest Thicket*, 1847–55); it was refused by the 1855 Salon jury but was nonetheless on view, having been hung by Delacroix in the midst of his own exhibitions. His finest painting, however, is usually considered to be *Les Ruines du châttau de Pierrefonds (The Ruins of the Château of Pierrefonds*), a composition that dates from the last year or two of his life and demonstrates that Constable's influence never left him. It was one of a pair of canvasses, the other (*Le Châttau de Pirrefonds [The Château of Pierrefonds*, 1867]) being of the castle as restored for Napoleon III by Eugène-Emmanuel Viollet-le-Duc. It depicts the ruined castle in a dramatic storm and memorably captures the effect of the wind on the lowering clouds, the spindly birch trees, and the characteristically tiny figure of the peasant girl making her way home, in addition to the more theatrical effects occasioned by a flash of sunlight on both the ruins and the surrounding landscape. Its slightly earlier companion piece has been interpreted as a tribute to the Emperor's restoration of a "functioning feudal hierarchy."

MICHAEL TILBY

Biography

Born in Paris, October 3, 1803. Schooling in Paris. Drawing lessons with Deltil, a former pupil of David. Spells in the studios of Guérin and Gros, 1818–19. Exhibited with various Paris dealers; friendship with Delacroix and Bonington, 1822. Exhibited for first time at the Paris Salon, 1827. Present at first night of Victor Hugo's *Hernani*; participated in July Revolution, 1830. Involvement in republican politics, 1831. Painted with Théodore Rousseau in Honflcur, 1835 (they later fell out). Teacher of Duchess of Orleans, 1837. Studied Classical art in Rome, 1842. Gold medal at the Salon; fought against the June Revolution, 1848. Painted in forest of Fontainebleau for first time, 1849. Napoleon III's coup d'état rekindled his republicanism, 1851 (though he would later become reconciled to the new regime). Showed at Exposition Universelle (special medal), 1855. Delivered oration at Delacroix's funeral, 1863. Exhibited at Exposition Universelle, 1867. Died in Paris, January 8, 1869.

Bibliography

Boyé, Maurice-Pierre. *La Mêlée romantique.* Paris: Julliard, 1946.
Burty, Philippe. "Paul Huet." In *Maîtres et petits maîtres.* 1869.
Gautier, Théophile. *Les Beaux-Arts en Europe 1855.* 2d series. 1856.
———. *Exposition de 1859.* Edited by Wolfgang Drost and Ulrike Henninges. Heidelberg: Carl Winter, 1992.
Honour, Hugh. *Romanticism.* London: Allen Lane, 1979.
House, John, *Landscapes of France: Impressionism and its Rivals.* London: Hayward Gallery, 1995.
Huet, René Paul. *Paul Huet (1803–1869) d'après ses notes, sa correspondance, ses contemporains.* Paris: H. Laurens, 1911.
Miquel, Pierre. *Paul Huet, de l'aube romantique à l'aube impressioniste.* Sceaux: Editions de la Martinelle, 1962.
Paul Huet (1803–1869). Rouen: Musée des Beaux-Arts, 1965.
Sainte-Beuve, Charles-Augustin. "Paul Huet." In *Portraits contemporains.* vol. 2. 1869.
Séché, Léon. *Le Cénacle de Joseph Delorme, 1827–1830.* 2 vols. Paris: Mercure de France, 1912.
Tilby, Michael. "The Romantic Landscapes of Joseph Delorme and Paul Huet." In *Essays in Memory of Michael Parkinson and Janine Dakyns.* Edited by Christopher Smith. Norwich: University of East Anglia, 1996.

HUGO, VICTOR MARIE 1802–1885

French poet, novelist, dramatist, and critic

Victor Marie Hugo's success in three literary genres (poetry, novel, and drama) makes him the principal Romantic writer in the France of his time and thereafter. In addition, his critical writings—from the preface he appended to his drama *Cromwell* in 1827, to his essay on the Romantic genius and its avatars, *William Shakespeare*, completed in 1864—defined his vision of French Romanticism both aesthetically and politically. In the preface, pleading for "the liberty of art against the despotism of [all] systems, codes, and rules," Hugo anticipated his well-known declaration, made during the rehearsals for *Hernani* in January 1830, on what, for him, constituted the new Romanticism, which is "simply *Liberalism* in literature. . . . Liberty in art, liberty in society, that is the dual goal toward which all consequent and logical minds must tend; that is the dual banner under

which, with the exception of some few minds (which one day will see more clearly), the whole of today's youth, so strongly and patiently rallies." Nothing, perhaps, better confirms the essentially social nature of Hugo's literary values than this kind of definition. Thirty-four years later, forced into exile because of his preference for a liberal democracy over imperial despotism, and having moved further to the political Left, Hugo's definition of Romanticism shows the ideology that gave rise to *Les Misérables* (1862): "The Revolution closed one century and opened another," he writes. "After the political revolution, a literary and social revolution took place . . . Romanticism and socialism, it has been said with hostility, but with accuracy, are the same thing." Hugo's campaigns—on behalf of the poor, in favor of social justice, against kings and their wars, and against capital punishment—fill not only his political speeches made in the French Chamber of Deputies or at the Lausanne peace conference of 1869, but find central expression in his literary works. It is this fact, coupled, of course, with his ability to express his social ideas in strikingly original literary form, that assured his works' popularity in his own time and subsequently and that characterizes him as the principal French Romantic writer.

But Hugo's literary and political development also illustrates Romanticism's rejection of Classical logic in favor of paradox, oxymoron, and contradiction in terms. In his first critical writings, in *le Conservateur littéraire*, a review he edited in 1820 and 1821 with his two brothers, Abel and Eugène, he reserved his praise for Classical poetry and tragedy; just as in his own first odes he celebrated the French monarch Henri IV and deplored the death of the Duc de Berry, stabbed by a Bonapartist in 1820. In so doing, Hugo revealed the influence of his royalist mother, Sophie, and went against his father Léopold, who, thanks to his exploits as a soldier of Napoleon Bonaparte, had attained the rank of count in the Imperial nobility. He would heal this split in his loyalties by a typically Romantic paradox: Napoleon would become, in his eyes, the logical embodiment of the French Revolution, liberator of Europe from the old monarchies, the personification of French "glory."

In literature, he performed the same about-face early in his career, rejecting French neo-Classical doctrines stipulating imitation of Classical models, decorum, generic purity of tone, and the "noble style" and preferring to celebrate instead the originality of nineteenth-century geniuses like himself who would overturn the old "rules," in so doing creating a new vision combining sublime and grotesque, comic and tragic themes, and expressed in a new kind of alexandrine verse: "the old poetry was descriptive, the new will be alive," he wrote. As to the novel, it was to be historical, "dramatic," and popular in the style of Walter Scott in that it was to bring France's past back to life; it would also be Gothic in its horrors, as in Hugo's *Han d'Islande* (*Hans of Iceland*, 1823), and essentially didactic. Reviewing, in 1823, the newly published French translation of Scott's *Quentin Durward*, he asked rhetorically what should be the novelist's intention, answering, "To express, in an interesting tale, some useful truth." So much the better then if, as in *Le Dernier jour d'un condamné à mort* (*The Last Day of a Condemned Man*, 1829), the condemned man's "journal" might arouse public indignation against the death penalty, or, as in *Notre-Dame de Paris* (*The Hunchback of Notre-Dame*, 1830), the hunchback's tragic history might alert the French people to the need to repair the dilapidation of their medieval monuments. By the time he completed *Les Misérables* in 1862, exiled in Guernsey, he had become the champion of the poor and unjustly treated underclass, creating in Jean Valjean, the reformed thief and escaped convict, a secular saint whose charity contrasts with the cruelty and social inequities of nineteenth-century France. His last three novels also mix historical themes, incidents, and characters with melodramatic fiction. *Les Travailleurs de la mer* (*The Toilers of the Sea*, 1866), *L'Homme qui rit* (*The Man Who Laughs*, 1869), and *Quatrevingt-treize* (*Ninety-Three*, 1874), recount, respectively, the adventure of the Guernseyman Gilliat in saving the engine of a sunken ship; the campaign, led by Gwynplaine the orphan deformed by his kidnappers, to reduce aristocratic privilege in the England of Queen Anne; and the war between revolutionary and royalist forces in Brittany during the Terror.

In his dramas, too, he championed—in both poetry and prose—the causes of women married to unfaithful and violent husbands—as in *Angelo, tyran de Padoue* (*Angelo*, 1835)—and the "people" against the ruling class—in *Ruy Blas* (1838). But Hugo's main contribution to Romantic drama in France lay in his rejection of Classical, Greco-Roman myths. Instead, he and his fellow Romantic dramatist, Alexandre Dumas *père*, chose as subject matter medieval, Renaissance, and seventeenth-century Spanish, French, Italian, English, or German historical events and personages that they then sensationalized, while claiming to respect contemporary "local color." So, Hugo's *Le Roi s'amuse* (*The King's Fool*, 1832) showed François I as sexual predator seducing his courtiers' wives; the play was banned by the public censor in consequence. *Lucrèce Borgia* (*Lucretia Borgia*, 1832), his greatest financial success, dramatized that Renaissance lady's reputation for committing incest and as poisoner. *Marie Tudor* (*Mary Tudor*, 1833), and *Torquemada* (1869) exploited popular myths concerning the cruelty of "Bloody Mary" and the bloodlust of the founder of the Spanish Inquisition. *Les Burgraves* (*The Burgraves*, 1843), which concluded his success as a Romantic dramatist, pitted legendary Holy Roman Emperor Frederick Babarossa against bandits preying, from their mountain lairs, upon travelers on the Rhine River. Giuseppe Verdi appreciated fully the larger-than-life nature of Hugo's dramas, basing his grand operas *Ernani* (1844) and *Rigoletto* (1851), on *Hernani* and *le Roi s'amuse*.

Romantic self-revelation, as opposed to Classical restraint in such matters (as Molière said, "[Writing about] oneself is detestable"), characterizes almost all of the twenty-five collections of verse he published between the *Odes et ballades* (*Odes and Ballads*, 1818–28) and *Océan*, published posthumously in 1942. In *Feuilles d'automne* (*Autumn Leaves*, 1831), *les Contemplations* (*Contemplations*, 1856), and *l'Art d'être grand-père* (*The Art of Being a Grandfather*, 1877), for instance, he recounts lyrically the principal events of his family life with the climax attained in "A Villequier," a poem detailing his personal grief at the death of his daughter Léopoldine and her husband of six months in a boating accident on the Seine. In other collections, he details the highs and lows of his emotional, intellectual, and religious life: musings on the conflict between the sensitive soul and everyday society (*les Chants du crépuscule*; *Songs of Twilight*, 1838), on the functions of poetry and the role of the Romantic poet (*les Rayons et les ombres*; *Sunbeams and Shadows*, 1840), and on his metaphysical and mystical speculations about the Divine (*Dieu*; *God*, 1891) and the devil (the Milton-like *la Fin de Satan*; *The End of Satan*, 1886). His political triumphs and disasters brought forth his long poem mythologizing Napoleon Bonaparte (*le Retour de l'empereur*; *The Emperor's Return*, 1840), as well as a vicious polemic against the great man's unworthy descendant whom Hugo considered his personal enemy, Napoleon III (*Châtiments*; *Punishments*, 1853). And his own, and his family's, involvement in the tragic events in France during the Franco-Prussian War and Commune of 1870 and 1871 ensures that the interest of *l'Année terrible* (*The Terrible Year*, 1872) is as much personal as national. Finally, his "little epics," forming the three volumes of *la Légende des siècles* (*The Legend of the Centuries*, 1883), present his personal philosophical history of humanity's rise from barbarism to the happy future state it was to attain, he believed, in the twentieth century. Throughout his life, his practice of French fixed and free-verse forms, the breadth and variety of his subject matter, and his forging of a poetic rhetoric, at once adhering to the rules he developed for the new prosody and censuring no topic as indecorous, made him the greatest, as well as the most popular, French Romantic poet.

Throughout his career, Hugo pursued the didactic end he expressed repeatedly. In his final critical works, *Utilité du Beau* (*The Usefulness of Beauty*, 1863–64), and *William Shakespeare* (which contains a section entitled "le Beau serviteur du vrai," or "Beauty, the Servant of Truth"), he showed how his Romantic ideal differed from that of Théophile Gautier and the Parnassian poets who succeeded the Romantics in France: "Art for art's sake may be fine, but art for the sake of progress is finer still."

ALBERT W. HALSALL

Biography

Born in Besançon, February 26, 1802. During the disunion and infidelities of his parents, Victor sided with his mother, 1802–18. Victor, his brothers, Abel and Eugène, and their mother Sophie traveled to Spain to visit General Leopold Hugo, now Comte de Sigüenza, 1811–12. Hugo attended the College of Nobles in Madrid, 1812–18. Attended classes at the Feuillantines and Cordier boarding schools and at the Collège Louis-le-Grand, 1818. Victor's parents, Leopold and Sophie separated. Brother Eugène's first signs of mental imbalance. Hugo married Adèle Foucher on October 12; Eugène's mental breakdown followed shortly after, 1822. Birth of Léopoldine Hugo, 1824. Made chevalier de la Légion d'honneur; attended coronation of Charles X in Rheims, 1825. Birth of Charles Hugo, 1826.

C. Motter, *Victor Hugo*. Reprinted courtesy of Bildarchiv Preussischer Kulturbesitz.

[François-]Victor, Hugo's second son born 1828. Refused Charles X's offer of seat on Council of State; Sainte-Beuve declared his love for Adèle, Hugo's wife. Birth of Adèle, Hugo's daughter, 1830. Began liaison with Juliette Drouet, 1833. Elected to the Academy, 1841. Léopoldine married Charles Vacquerie; both drowned at Villequier, 1843. Peer of France, 1844. Elected to Legislative Assembly and president of the International Peace Conference, 1849. Member of the committee resisting coup d'état; December 11, began his exile from France, 1851. At Marine Terrace, Jersey; expelled, 1852–55. Bought Hauteville House, St. Peter Port, Guernsey; Juliette settled nearby, 1856. Adèle Hugo returns to Paris; François-Victor publishes translation of *Shakespeare*. Suffered nearly fatal bout of anthrax, 1858. Refused political amnesty offered by Napoleon III; tried to save the life of John Brown, 1859. Established, at his own expense, a weekly meal for poor children in Guernsey, 1862. Returned to Paris and national acclaim, 1870. Elected to National Assembly; resigns; Charles Hugo dies; in Brussels, Hugo offered asylum to members of the Paris Commune, 1871. Elected senator, 1876. Suffered stroke; convalescing in Guernsey with Juliette, June 1878. Died of pneumonia in Paris; National funeral, burial in the Panthéon, May 22, 1885.

Selected Works

Collections

Oeuvres complètes. Edited by Jacques Seebacher and Guy Rosa. 16 vols. Paris: le Club français du livre, 1985–90.
Théâtre complet. Edited by J.-J. Thierry and Josette Mélèze. 2 vols. Paris: Gallimard, 1963–64.

Plays

Hernani, 1830. Translated as *Hernani*. In: *Three Plays by Victor Hugo*; translated by Camilla Crosland and Frederick L. Slous. New York: Howard Fertig, 1995.
Le Roi s'amuse, 1832. Translated as *The King Amuses Himself* by Frederick L. Slous and Mrs. Newton (Camilla) Crosland. In: *Three Plays by Victor Hugo*. New York: Howard Fertig, 1995.
Ruy Blas, 1838. Translated by Frederick L. Slous and Mrs. Newton (Camilla) Crosland, In: *Three Plays by Victor Hugo*. New York: Howard Fertig, 1995.
Torquemada. Edition critique par John J. Jane. Lanham, Md., University Press of America, 1989.

Novels

Notre-Dame de Paris—1482, 1831. Translated as *The Hunchback of Notre-Dame* by Frederic Shoberl. London: Richard Bentley, 1833. Translated as *Notre-Dame de Paris* by Alban Krailsheimer. Oxford: Oxford University Press, 1993.
Les Misérables, 1862. Translated by Lascelles Wraxall. London: Hurst and Blackett, 1862.

Criticism

Préface de "Cromwell," 1827. Edited by Pierre Grosclaude. Paris: Larousse, 1949.
William Shakespeare, 1864. Translated by Melville B. Anderson. Chicago: M.C. McClurg & Co., 1887.

Bibliography

Brombert, Victor. *Victor Hugo and the Visionary Novel*. Cambridge, Mass.: Harvard University Press, 1984.
Halsall, Albert W. *Victor Hugo et l'art de convaincre. Le récit hugolien: rhétorique, argumentation, persuasion*. Montréal: Éditions Balzac, 1995.

———. *Victor Hugo and the Romantic Drama*. Toronto: University of Toronto Press, 1998.

Ireson, John, C. *Victor Hugo, A Companion to his Poetry*. Oxford, Clarendon Press, 1997.

Laster, Arnaud. *Pleins Feux sur Victor Hugo*. Paris: Comédie-française, 1981.

Nash, Suzanne. *Les Contemplations of Victor Hugo: An Allegory of the Creative Process*. Princeton N.J.: Princeton University Press, 1982.

Robb, Graham. *Victor Hugo*. London: Picador, 1997.

Tieghem, Philippe van. *Dictionnaire Victor Hugo*. Paris: Larousse, 1970.

Ubersfeld, Anne. *Le Drame romantique*. Paris: Éditions Belin, 1993.

LES HUGUENOTS 1836

Opera by Giacomo Meyerbeer

Les Huguenots, by the German composer Giacomo Meyerbeer, is one of the most celebrated examples of French grand opera, featuring spectacular special effects, a large chorus, and seven demanding principal roles. Set during the period of conflict between Catholics and Calvinist Protestants (Huguenots) in sixteenth-century France, it depicts the unleashing of the St. Bartholomew's Day Massacre of three thousand Huguenots in Paris on the night of August 23, 1572.

In 1832, Meyerbeer signed a contract with the director of the Paris Opéra, Louis Véron, for a new opera, then entitled *Léonore, ou La Sainte Barthélemy* (*Leonora, or St. Bartholomew*). It has been claimed that the librettist Eugène Scribe modeled his plot on Prosper Mérimée's novel *Chronique du règne de Charles IX* (*Chronicle of the Reign of Charles IX*, 1829), which in turn provided material for Ferdinand Hérold's popular opéra comique *Le pré aux clercs* (1832), but this has since been discounted as a significant source. Creation of the opera was marked by disagreements between the collaborators. Much of the music had been drafted before Meyerbeer decided on substantial revisions during a visit to Italy in 1834. A previous collaborator, Gaetano Rossi, provided Italian verse for these parts, but back in Paris Scribe was unhappy to work on these contributions, so Meyerbeer turned to another writer, Émile Deschamps. Further modifications and substantial cuts were made during rehearsal, mainly prompted by Véron and by the censor.

A classic grand opera, it is set in five acts, involving spectacular visual effects and striking tableaux, and integrating the private love of a Catholic (Valentine) and a Protestant (Raoul) with the political conflict between the religious groups. In the first act, the Catholic Comte de Nevers has, in a spirit of reconciliation between the two sides, invited Raoul to a banquet. Raoul describes how he has rescued and fallen in love with a mysterious woman, who he then sees talking to Nevers. He assumes she must be his mistress, though in fact she is Valentine, daughter of the Catholic leader St. Bris, who is engaged to Nevers.

In act 2 the king's sister Marguerite de Valois tries to bring peace by proposing the marriage of Raoul and Valentine. Raoul agrees, without knowing who Valentine is, and the Catholics and Huguenots celebrate the proposed union. But when Raoul meets Valentine, he recognizes her as Nevers' supposed mistress and rejects her. In act 3 Valentine overhears St. Bris and Nevers plotting to ambush Raoul, and warns him. Marguerite arrives and a duel between St. Bris and Raoul is averted, but St. Bris is horrified to learn of his daughter's act of betrayal. Marguerite explains to Raoul that Valentine and Nevers are engaged, against Valentine's will, which calms his jealousy. In act 4, however,

the marriage between Valentine and Nevers takes place, and after visiting her for the last time, Raoul resolves to kill himself. But as he is leaving the leading Catholic noblemen arrive, and Valentine hides him. He overhears St. Bris instructing the nobles about the massacre of Huguenots that is to take place that night at midnight. He rushes off to warn his colleagues.

When act 5 opens, the massacre is underway. Nevers has been killed, and Valentine renounces Catholicism and joins Raoul. The couple, together with Raoul's old retainer Marcel, face death together in a spirit of defiance and optimism. When the three are challenged by Catholic soldiers, St. Bris gives the order to fire, realizing too late that his daughter is among them. The lovers die, and the massacre continues.

Meyerbeer employs a number of techniques to suggest the political tensions underlying the story, build suspense, and create a sense of real horror. Key to the dramatic effects of grand opera in general, and *Les Huguenots* in particular, are the imaginative use of the chorus and careful juxtaposition of contrasting musical styles. At the beginning of act 3, the chorus is divided into conflicting groups: first Parisian citizens enjoying their Sunday afternoon, next a band of Huguenot soldiers who sing an unaccompanied Huguenot warlike song, then Valentine's bridal procession of young girls who sing a prayer. Marcel interrupts the procession. Finally, all three choruses sing simultaneously. The mounting tension is palpable, and dissipated only by the arrival of a group of gypsies. Layering and juxtaposition suggest, in a concise and dramatic way, the latent tensions that are about to come to the surface.

The chorus is used again to striking effect in act 4. When St. Bris has issued his instructions for the massacre, a trio of monks arrives to bless the swords, in what has become the most notorious scene in the opera. Their calm chanting belies the words of their exhortation to destroy the enemy, before the chorus responds energetically with "Frappons" ("Let's strike"). This violent passage modulates abruptly with each repetition of the phrase and concludes with cries of "anathema," at which point trumpet fanfares launch a final and still more frenetic *allegro furioso* during which the men rush to the front of the stage wielding their swords. This scene has been viewed as a crystallization of mob violence, one that both refers back to the Terror after the French Revolution and points forward to fears about the underclasses in a modern city—although this is a mob of noblemen. Musically, it is a strikingly innovative and dramatic use of the chorus. Rather than simply repeating what the soloist sings, in a conventional static number, the chorus drives the action forward, with a dynamism that projects us into the next act.

In the penultimate scene of the opera, Meyerbeer uses the chorus in a further innovative and highly effective fashion, this time offstage and juxtaposed with the onstage main characters. The chorale tune "Ein' feste Burg ist unser Gott" stands as a symbol for the Huguenots in the opera, and here acquires central importance. Women taking shelter from the Catholics are heard singing it offstage in a church, but they are interrupted repeatedly by the sound of gunfire and shouting and finally fall silent. The chorale tune then transfers to the three onstage characters facing the marauders: the tension is gradually ratcheted up with each hearing of the chorale tune: each fragment is slightly faster and the key is gradually raised (from E flat to F to G to A). The chorale thus stands for the systematic reduction of the Huguenot faith to fragments, transferring from the chorus to the remaining individuals.

The opera illustrates Meyerbeer's interest in defining distinct musical personalities and evolving a continuous musicodramatic structure that communicates, directly and forthrightly, the horror of such a historical episode.

SARAH HIBBERD

See also **Meyerbeer, Giacomo**

Work

Les Huguenots. 1836.

Bibliography

Gerhard, Anselm. *The Urbanization of Opera: Music Theater in Paris in the Nineteenth Century.* Chicago: University of Chicago Press, 1998.

DIE HÜLSENBECKSCHEN KINDER (THE HÜLSENBECK CHILDREN) 1805–1806

Painting by Philipp Otto Runge

Die Hülsenbeckschen Kinder is one in a series of intimate oil portraits of family and friends made by Philipp Otto Runge between 1804 and 1810. The subjects here are the three children of a friend, his brother's business partner Friedrich August Hülsenbeck: from right to left Maria (age five), August (age four), and Friedrich (age two). They are seen at play together by the garden of their parents' house in the village of Eimsbüttel, now a suburb of Hamburg. Maria and August hold the shaft of a low wooden handcart in which Friedrich reclines. In the background, across meadows, the Hamburg skyline with its four church spires can be made out, "with the garden and Hamburg, all of it, a portrait," as Runge wrote in November 1805 soon after beginning the work. Yet the finished picture, for all its semblance of bourgeois domesticity, is anything but a Biedermeier genre painting.

Despite the infant faces, it is difficult to grasp that the children are little more than toddlers. They dominate the picture and appear out of scale, dwarfing the garden fence and, even allowing for perspective, the house behind them. As spectators, we do not look down at them but find ourselves at their eye level and abruptly close to them, experiencing existence from their perspective, literally and metaphorically. What we witness in this children's domain is an undisturbed idyll of uncorrupted innocence, spontaneous play, and sibling cohesion. In a preliminary drawing Runge had included a sketchy female figure emerging from the house, but now the childhood paradise is not compromised even by this one adult presence. The three children are outside the fence, beyond the domesticated garden, implying that their serenity can only arise without parental influence. The adult world of work with its utilitarian pressures, represented by farmsteads and a dye works discernible above the fence, is banished into the distance, shut off behind a hedge, fields, and a row of trees. Urban society is no threat to the naturalness of these children. The sunflower bush seems almost a fourth member of their group, manifesting their unity with organic nature: its three flowers parallel the three children in the bloom of youth, while the two-year-old, the least integrated into the social order, grasps the bush tightly

by a stem. Writing to his fiancée in 1803 Runge had spoken of children living in a state of paradise as being "blissful, not knowing themselves," uncontaminated by learning, which necessarily entailed sin; but, he went on, adults nostalgically longed to revert "to childhood, to ourselves, to paradise, to God." *Die Hülsenbeckschen Kinder* fulfills this wish: we participate in a Rousseauesque celebration of the innocence of presocietal mankind, a Garden of Eden within sight of nineteenth-century Hamburg.

This idyll is not merely anthropological: it enjoys metaphysical endorsement. The shadows in the foreground and the pink tinges in the sky above the fence indicate that the sun has not long risen. In Runge's *Tageszeiten* (*Times of Day*) cycle of drawings, first conceived three years earlier, *Morgen* shows a symbolic sunrise: each dawn represents a divine reconstitution of the earth in unsullied form, a repetition of the Creation. In *Die Hülsenbeckschen Kinder*, too, the new dawn corresponds to, and corroborates, the primal innocence of the children. The children themselves are beatified by sunlight, their faces irradiated preternaturally. As in another portrait of a four-year-old by Runge, *Die Kleine Perthes* (*Perthes's Little Girl*, painted in 1805 immediately before the Hülsenbeck portrait), even the children's clothing seems infused with solar radiance. They are illuminated by what Robert Rosenblum terms "a kind of secular sanctification." The intense sunlight, as in J. M. W. Turner's paintings, has metaphysical significance: in typically Romantic fashion Runge uses it to lend transcendent luminosity to the earthly children he converts into symbols. In the color versions of *Morgen* that Runge later produced a newborn baby lies similarly resplendent in a pool of light, significantly replicating the naked infant Christ in Die Ruhe der Flucht (*Resting on the Flight*), that Runge also painted in 1805.

The idyll of *Die Hülsenbeckschen Kinder* does, however, contain the implication of its own termination. The children are not shown playing some random game but are evidently pretending to depart on a journey. August in the middle waves a riding crop as if to set horses in motion, his brother's little handcart representing a carriage which the two older siblings are about

Philipp Otto Runge, *Die Hülsenbeckschen Kinder*, Reprinted courtesy of The Bridgeman Art Library.

to tug away out of the picture. Symbolically they are setting off on the journey of life, the eldest of the children departing first. Yet the journey into adulthood is in terms of Runge's symbolism also the journey into original sin, into corrupted social reality, into utilitarian activity, away from pristine dawn into compro-

mised daytime, the same movement as in the daily cycle portrayed in the *Tageszeiten*. The five-year-old leads the way because she is the most conscious, the most socialized. Her outstretched hand represents less a gesture of protection or affection than an exhortation to the baby to release the sunflower stem by which he still clings to nature and to stop thus retarding their communal departure. His resistance is futile, however, because the journey into adult degeneration is inevitable. Untainted childhood, like the dawn, is a momentary state which begins to pass at the instant of its inception. Ludwig Tieck, whose writing Runge admired, had made his narrator in the fairy story *Der blonde Eckbert* (*Fair Eckbert*, 1797) remark, "[I]t is a misfortune for human beings that they only acquire understanding at the cost of losing the innocence of their soul." Precisely this tragic dilemma is demonstrated in *Die Hülsenbeckschen Kinder*, a snapshot of the brief moment when childhood remains intact. What appears at first to be naturalistic portraiture turns out to be an exercise in Romantic myth-making.

RICHARD LITTLEJOHNS

Work

Die Hülsenbeckschen Kinder. 1805–6. Oil on canvas, 131.5 cm × 143.5 cm. Kunsthalle, Hamburg.

Bibliography

Rosenblum, Robert. *The Romantic Child. From Runge to Sendak*. London: Thames and Hudson, 1988.
Traeger, Jörg. *Die Hülsenbeckschen Kinder*. Frankfurt am Main: Insel, 1987.

HUMBOLDT, ALEXANDER VON 1769–1859

German natural scientist and explorer

Born into a wealthy Prussian noble family, Alexander von Humboldt and his equally famous brother Wilhelm were privately educated before they attended university. After studying the natural sciences and mining engineering, Alexander von Humboldt entered the Prussian civil service as a junior mining official (1792–96) while preparing himself for his great expedition to Central and South America (1799–1804). This was the first expedition that served neither economic nor political purposes but solely scientific ones, and that brought to Europe knowledge about parts of the world that had been conquered but were not really known. It laid the foundations for his worldwide reputation as one of the greatest philosophical scientists and explorers with an almost universal range of interests and scientific skills. Formed by the humanitarian and Romantic ideals of Weimar Classicism, Humboldt, with the French botanist Aimé Bonpland, traveled through the places today known as Venezuela, Cuba, Colombia, Ecuador, Peru, and Mexico, and returned via the United States to Europe. On meeting Simon Bolivar and Thomas Jefferson, he became a great critic of slavery and the missionary movement. Until 1827 he chose to live in Paris, the then capital of science, where, with Joseph-Louis Gay-Lussac, he carried out analytical experiments with gasses and was in close contact with Victor Hugo and Honoré de Balzac. He was then convinced by the Prussian king, Frederick William III,

to go to Berlin and deliver his widely acclaimed lectures on the physical description of the world. On the invitation of Tsar Nicholas I, Humboldt undertook a second great expedition in 1829, with Gustav Rose and Christian Gottfried Ehrenberg, which took them to the Asiatic parts of Russia close to the Chinese border (Ural, Altai, Caspian Sea). A consequence of this was the foundation and organization of a worldwide network of geomagnetic observation stations that Humboldt initiated with Carl Friedrich Gauss. Back in Berlin in 1830 he set out to write his late work, *Kosmos. Entwurf einer physikalischen Weltbeschreibung*, (*Kosmos. Description of the Physical Universe*), a summary of his knowledge of the physical universe, which became a best-seller in his own time (1845–62).

While *Kosmos* certainly consolidated Humboldt's position as a natural scientist who could transmit the results of his research to the general public or to specialists equally well, other works of his could claim to be among the most important studies in the library of the natural sciences between Isaac Newton and Albert Einstein. In what could be called the greatest travel journal ever written, the *Voyage aux régions équinoxiales du nouveau continent*, in thirty-six volumes (1805–34), Humboldt describes his phytogeographical, climatological, geophysical, geological, zoological, and oceanographical observations. In combination with ecological considerations, he also discussed anthropological, ethnological, archaeological, and philological problems, and he was particularly interested in the history and the institutions of Mexico and Cuba. With the help of newly developed precise measuring instruments, Humboldt was the first scientist to undertake an ecological investigation of the landscape, measure the height of mountains (Chimborazo), determine the exact geographical positions of towns, and measure the temperatures of the "Humboldt Current" in the South Pacific that flows north along the coasts of Chile and Peru. However, it was primarily the material he collected that has made Humboldt's work so relevant to the present day: the major outcome of his scientific expeditions was the sheer amount of material containing answers to questions not yet asked. The result is not a theory of nature but a great atlas, a collection of diverse maps with all possible data. The unity of Humboldt's examination of nature is best reflected in the uniformity of the archives he built up with all its potential for drawing comparisons and establishing relationships. The natural scientist Humboldt was an outstanding figure among his contemporaries. For example, he maintained a friendship with Johann Wolfgang von Goethe, who mentioned Humboldt in his novel *Die Wahlverwandtschaften* (*Elective Affinities, 1809*).

In recent years there has been a remarkable renaissance of interest in Humboldt, which reflects the continuing acceptance of his work by scholars and the general public alike. His particular way of handling research projects and presenting the results of his research, his concept of nature, his understanding of his profession as lying between a scientific and an almost philosophical comprehension of nature have considerable attraction for a modern readership. His scholarly texts are highly readable and written in an instructive and lucid style. Humboldt built up an extensive international network of correspondents with whom he exchanged all sorts of information, data, and recommendations for new scientific reading. Between the late 1780s and his death in 1859, Humboldt received more than 100,000 letters, and he probably wrote no less than 50,000. Humboldt wrote many of his publications in French, and they were then translated into German and other languages. (He himself spoke eleven languages.) After he moved to Berlin, his house became a center of worldwide scholarship for the last thirty years of his life.

Often considered his most important work, *Kosmos* presents Humboldt's complex program against the background of the knowledge of the natural sciences to bring together as many facts as possible about the organic and the inorganic world. Nature in its entirety was moved and animated by inner forces thereby constructing a harmonious and orderly system which he termed "cosmos." To understand and appreciate this system the scientist had to do more than just compile data and develop subdisciplines. Rather, the inner connection between the general and the particular needed to be elaborated in order to make nature's uniformity visible in its complexity. The description of the physical universe (the subtitle of *Kosmos*) was thus an examination and description of everything that had once been created, whether organic or inorganic, within the existing entirety of nature. Scholars have called this concept of science "Humboldtian science," pointing to the fact that Humboldt did not envisage a holistic or encyclopedic study of nature, but wanted to follow up the connections between individual natural phenomena. He paid special attention to a multitude of measuring

instruments to enable the data to be continuously compared. This was the objective, systematic-empirical aspect of Humboldtian science, but equally important for Humboldt was the aesthetic element in the perception of nature. Here the Romantic influence of his age becomes apparent. Acquiring knowledge of the subject of study was one aspect; the other was a love for it, a side often neglected in descriptions of Humboldtian science. With his contemporary Carl Ritter, Humboldt can certainly be called the confounder of scientific geography. Both men wanted to show the close relationship between nature and humankind, while Ritter emphasized the work of God, revealing the influence of Johann Heinrich Pestalozzi.

Further, Humboldt stressed the historicity of nature and of man's knowledge of it. Empirical change in nature therefore followed historical laws no less than man's understanding of it. Consequently, he wrote on the social, ethnological, and historical issues affecting the countries he visited (examples are *Essai politique sur le royaume de La Nouvelle-Espagne* [1811] and *Essai politique sur l'île de Cuba* [1825]). He analyzed demographic structures, the administration, trade, culture, and history. Humboldt clearly saw a close connection between the natural conditions of a country and the social, economic, and political state of its population. In contrast to Henrik Steffens, however, who was a propagator of German idealism and the Romantic spirit in Denmark, Humboldt did not write novellas. In sum, Humboldt was among the first scientists to think in liberal terms before the dawn of liberalism, to work in an interdisciplinary way before the invention of the different scientific disciplines, and to fight for a postcolonial political world system before the dissolution of the empires. While keeping in touch with the universalist tradition of the eighteenth century, he paved the way for the scientific innovations of the nineteenth century.

BENEDIKT STUCHTEY

Selected Works

Alexander von Humboldt: Studienausgabe. 7 vols. Edited by Hanno Beck. Darmstadt: Wissenschaftliche Buchgesellschaft, 1989–97.

Alexander von Humboldt: Aus meinem Leben. Autobiographische Bekenntnisse. Edited by Kurt-R Biermann. Munich: Beck, 1989.

Alexander von Humboldt: Reise in die Äquinoktial-Gegenden des Neuen Kontinents. 2 vols. Edited by Ottmar Ette. Frankfurt: Insel, 1999.

Alexander von Humboldt: Über das Universum. Die Kosmos-Vorträge 1827/28 in der Berliner Singakademie. Edited by Jürgen Hamel and Klaus H. Tiemann. Frankfurt: Insel, 1993.

Alexander von Humboldt: Briefe aus Amerika, 1799–1804. Edited by Ulrike Moheit. Berlin: Akademie, 1993.

Alexander von Humboldt: Über die Freiheit des Menschen. Auf der Suche nach Wahrheit. Edited by Manfred Osten. Frankfurt: Insel, 1999.

Alexander von Humboldt: Die Wiederentdeckung der Neuen Welt. Erstmals zusammengestellt aus dem unvollendeten Reisebericht und den Reisetagebüchern. Edited by Paul K. Schäfer. Munich: Hanser, 1992.

Bibliography

Beck, Hanno. *Alexander von Humboldt.* 2 vols. Wiesbaden: Steiner, 1959–61.

Daum, Andreas. "Alexander von Humboldt, die Natur als 'Kosmos' und die Suche nach Einheit. Zur Geschichte von Wissen und seiner Wirkung als Raumgeschichte," *Berichte zur Wissenschaftsgeschichte* 23 (2000): 243–68.

Fiedler, H. and Ulrike Leitner. *Beschreibendes Verzeichnis der selbständigen Schriften Alexander von Humboldts*. Berlin: Akademie, 2000.

Hein, Wolfgang-Hagen, ed. *Alexander von Humboldt: Leben und Werk*. Frankfurt am Main: Weisbecker, 1985.

Humboldt, Alexander von, *Netzwerke des Wissens*. Catalogue of the exhibition *Haus der Kulturen der Welt, Berlin, 6. Juni bis 15. August 1999, und Kunst- und Ausstellungshalle der Bundesrepublik Deutschland, Bonn, 15. September bis 9. Januar 2000*. Bonn/Berlin, 1999.

Kellner, Lotte. *Alexander von Humboldt*. London: Oxford University Press, 1963.

Krätz, Otto. *Alexander von Humboldt: Wissenschaftler, Weltbürger, Revolutionär*, Munich: Callwey, 1997.

Minguet, Charles. *Alexandre de Humboldt: Historien et géographe de l'Amérique espagnole 1799–1804*. Paris: L'Harmattan, 1997.

Nicolson, Malcolm. "Alexander von Humboldt, Humboldtian Science and the Origins of the Study of Vegetation," *History of Science* 25 (1987): 167–94.

Osterhammel, Jürgen. "Alexander von Humboldt: Historiker der Gesellschaft, Historiker der Natur," *Archiv für Kulturgeschichte* 81 (1999): 105–31.

Raphael, Lutz. "Freiheit und Wohlstand der Nationen. Alexander von Humboldts Analysen der politischen Zustände Amerikas und das politische Denken seiner Zeit," *Historische Zeitschrift* 260 (1995): 749–76.

Web Site

Alexander von Humboldt on the Internet, a joint project of the University of Potsdam and the Haus der Kulturen der Welt. http://www.uni.potsdam.de/u/romanistik/humboldt/index.html.

HUMBOLDT, WILHELM VON 1767–1835

German philosopher, politician, and educator

Wilhelm von Humboldt was a member of a noble family of Reichsritter, answerable directly to the German emperor. He was brought up and privately educated on the family estate at Tegel near Potsdam, where one of his tutors was Joachim Campe, a famous pedagogue of the late Enlightenment. His early study included the writings of Gottfried Wilhelm Leibniz and Christian Wolff. Following his university studies at Frankfurton on der, Oder and Göttingen, he moved into a circle of famous philosophers and men of letters, among them Georg Forster, philologist and explorer, the Romantic scholar and translator August Wilhelm von Schlegel, and the pietist writer Friedrich Heinrich Jacobi. He came to know Johann Wolfgang von Goethe well and formed a close friendship with Johann Christoph Friedrich von Schiller. In 1789 he traveled to Paris, spending much of his time in art galleries, while apparently oblivious to the immediate impact of the French Revolution. Humboldt traveled widely both within Germany and abroad to France, Spain, and Italy. From 1801 to 1808 he was Prussian envoy in Rome. He returned to Berlin on his appointment by Freiherr von Stein as Director of Education at the Prussian Ministry of the Interior. His sixteen-month tenure of this post was to affect the whole concept of German education until well into the twentieth century. From 1810 to 1819 he served the Prussian government in several different capacities, including envoy to London and to Vienna, where he represented Prussia during the Vienna Congress. In 1819 he resigned from public service, partly because of disagreements with the increasingly reactionary Karl August, Prince von Hardenberg, and retired to his estate in Tegel, where he devoted himself to writing and to language studies.

Humboldt should not primarily be considered within the narrower German confines of the Romantic period, but should rather be seen as one of the major representatives of neo-Classicism. It is, therefore, essential to begin by defining those aspects of his life which can be associated with the Romantic era and those which ran counter to the German Romantic spirit. Humboldt's Romantic tendencies can be seen in his views on individualism and on the close interrelationship between the individual and his environment, in his passionate interest in language studies, and in his association with Freiherr von Stein's Prussian reform movement. This particular association marked his involvement in a growing interest in Germany's cultural unification. His political liberalism and a preference for classical Greek over Germanic mythology saw him opposed to his Romantic contemporaries. Humboldt will always be remembered for his outstanding contributions to German thought.

His early reputation for political liberalism, often neglected today, was established with his 1792 publication *Versuch, die Grenzen der Wirksamkeit des Staates zu bestimmen* (*The Sphere and Duties of Government*). In this study, he applied his personal experience of the French Revolution to consider the state merely as a necessary evil, with no positive impact on social welfare and education beyond providing the essential means for an optimal environment. Within such a liberal climate individuals would develop "inner energies" and "active virtues," progressing toward self-perfection by an unfolding of all human potential. While this actual process of education has much in common with Romantic ideas of self-perfection and with the Fichtean interrelationship of Ego and Non-Ego, Humboldt's perception of the role of the state stands in stark contrast to that of G. W. F. Hegel and many other Romantic philosophers. He was much closer to the Romantics, however, in his views on a future German nation-state, though they probably did not share his belief that the German Confederation would "compose a unity through their tribal relationships and language."

Disregarding prevailing rationalist opinion, Humboldt wished to shift education away from its instrumentalist, vocational priorities and give it an entirely student-centered, individualist direction. His views, both on education and on language learning, were influenced by his particular interest in comparative anthropology. His many travels abroad and his knowledge of well over forty languages afforded him new insights into the different characteristics of peoples, and more specifically into the development of individuals, to promote the optimal conditions under which personal talent can achieve its fullest potential. He shared the neo-Classical belief that the unfolding of individuality is based on the dialectical process of a realization of all human faculties, which simultaneously provides a universal worldview. This harmonious unfolding of our physical, mental, and spiritual individuality, bound up with a general understanding of the "world," is free of any consideration of utilitarianism or vocational purpose; a process described as totality. In contrast to the sixteenth-century humanist tradition, based on ancient Roman culture, Humboldt embraced classical Greece, to emphasize harmonious, all-encompassing beauty over rational clarity and self-discipline. His desire for an "all-round human education" takes priority over "the necessities of life or an individual's occupation." While August Wilhelm von Schlegel shared Humboldt's passion for ancient Greece, he considered that the harmony enjoyed by the Greek civilization was impossible for modern man, who is aware of a gulf between his own existence and infinity. Since knowledge of ancient Greek culture was seen as a precondition for universal self-perfection, Humboldt required every pupil, regardless of his potential, to learn Classical Greek, "for knowledge of language, even incomplete, always illuminates the mind and exercises the memory and the imagination." University education, too, rather than being limited to a proscribed curriculum, was to be allowed to promote scholarship, enabling the individual to achieve personal maturity in "solitude and freedom"—in an environment free from economic or social pressures. Research was seen as a Socratic dialogue, intent on opening our minds to the eternal pursuit of truth, regardless of any outcome other than that of developing the human character.

Humboldt's understanding of language has much in common with Johann Gottfried Herder's anthropological views, though Herder and the later Romantics tended to lay greater emphasis on national characteristics associated with language learning. They did, however, share the belief that, through a command of languages, individuals would achieve both versatility and unity, experience harmony between the self and the other, and become appreciative of the totality of truth and beauty. In *Latium und Hellas* (*Roman Italy and Classical Greece*, 1807), Humboldt compared the single word to the individual, and language, "the sum of all words," to the national or cultural community. The study of languages therefore alerts us to "the analogy between man and the world in general as well as to each nation in particular." Language studies are "a compliment of our thought processes," as language "assumes the twofold nature of world and man," in mutual exchange and interchange. In contrast to Romantic thought, Humboldt was not concerned with man's teleological transcendence toward a golden age of self-perfection, but saw human perfection realized in the here and now, in the continual achievement of *humanitas*, a concept described by Goethe as the "beauty of man." Friedrich and August Wilhelm von Schlegel shared this neo-Classical notion of self-perfection and moderation, though they were the exception within a more narrowly defined German concept of Romanticism. Humboldt's promotion of universality in a purpose-free system of education, his emphasis on the primacy of beauty and his belief in language as an instrument for universal understanding, may have been partly shared by the Romantic generation, but his ideas should not be placed within the actual confines of the Romantic worldview.

Hans-Joachim Hahn

Biography

Born in Potsdam, June 22, 1767. Studied law at the Prussian universities of Frankfurt/Oder and Göttingen; employed at the Berlin Supreme Court, 1790–91, while privately pursuing his interests in philosophy and philology and entering circle of notable writers and philosophers. Contributed to Schiller's journal *Die Horen*, 1794–97. Served as Prussian Envoy in Rome, 1802–1808. Recalled by Freiherr von Stein to take charge of Office of Cultural and Educational Affairs, a department of the Prussian Ministry of the Interior. Appointed minister of state in 1810. Represented Prussian interests at the Congress of Vienna. Member of the German Territorial Commission at Frankfurt, 1816–17, followed by assignment as envoy to London. Attempted to continue the Stein reform program as minister for corporate and communal affairs, 1819, but opposed Carlsbad Decrees and resigned from public service to continue his language studies. Died April 8, 1835 in Tegel.

Selected Works

Gesammelte Schriften. 17 vols. Edited by the Königlich Preußische Akademie der Wissenschaften. 1903–36; reprint Berlin Walter de Gruyter, 1968.
Werke in fünf Bänden. Edited by Andreas Flitner and Klaus Giel. Stuttgart: J.G. Colta, 1960–81.

Translations

The Sphere and Duties of Government. Translated by Joseph Coulthard. London: Chapman, 1854.
On Language: the Diversity of Human Language Structure and its Influence on the Mental Development of Mankind. Translasted by

"Wilhelm von Humboldt in seinem Arbeitszimmer im Schloß Tegel." Reprinted courtesy of Bildarchiv Preussischer Kulfurbesitz.

Peter Lauchlan Heath. Cambridge.: Cambridge University Press, 1988.

Bibliography

Bollnow, Otto Friedrich. *Die Pädagogik der deutschen Romantik.* Stuttgart: Kohlhammer, 1952.

Bruford, W. H. *The German Tradition of Self-Cultivation. "Bildung" from Humboldt to Thomas Mann.* Cambridge: Cambridge University Press, 1975.

Menze, Clemens. *Wilhelm von Humboldts Lehre und Bild vom Menschen.* Ratingen: Henn, 1965.

Spranger, Eduard. *Wilhelm von Humboldtund die Humanitätsidee.* 3d ed. Tübingen: Niemeyer, 1965.

HUMMEL, JOHANN NEPOMUK 1778–1837

Austrian composer, pianist, and conductor

Johann Nepomuk Hummel's fluctuating status is typical of similar figures active in periods that were dominated by a handful of "greats." During, and for some years after, his productive life he was a household name throughout Europe, much revered as a composer, pianist, teacher, and, in a period that expected such skills from its composer-performers, as an improviser, second perhaps only to Ludwig van Beethoven before the latter's increasing deafness put an end to his performing career. Then followed a period that saw a decline in his reputation for the rest of the nineteenth and the first half of the twentieth century, succeeded by a reappraisal beginning in the 1960s, leading to performances and recordings of his most important works.

Born in Pressburg, now Bratislava, Hummel was a prodigy, playing the violin and piano by the age of six. Two years later, in 1786, the family moved to Vienna when his father, Johannes, was appointed director of the Theater auf der Wieden, which would later see the triumphal first performance of Wolfgang Amadeus Mozart's *Die Zauberflöte* (*The Magic Flute*, 1791). Within a very short time, Mozart heard the boy and was so impressed that he offered to teach him free of charge, and Hummel moved into Mozart's house, staying for two years. Mozart was also instrumental in arranging Hummel's first public appearances, at the age of eight.

As Mozart's father had done, Johannes Hummel took his son on a concert tour lasting for four years. The first stop was Prague, where they met Jan Ladislav Dussek, followed by many cities, including Berlin, Hanover, Hamburg, and Copenhagen, before they settled for three months in Edinburgh, where both taught and young Johann improved his English. After concerts in Durham and Cambridge, they arrived in London, and Hummel played a Mozart piano concerto and a sonata of his own in the Hanover Square Rooms on May 5, 1792, to much acclaim. Further progress southward in Europe was checked by the revolutionary wars, and father and son spent two months in the Hague, where the latter performed weekly for the Prince of Orange.

On their return to Vienna, a period of self-improvement began. Hummel studied with the most famous and respected teachers in Europe: counterpoint with Johann Georg Albrechtsberger; vocal composition, aesthetics, and philosophy with Antonio Salieri; and organ with Franz Joseph Haydn, who had been kind to the boy in London and who counseled against too much organ practice, which might be to the detriment of his piano playing. Beethoven, among others, also studied with this triumvirate and caused a great stir on his appearance in Vienna, giving pause to many a composer-performer, Hummel included.

Haydn himself recommended Hummel for his old post of *Kapellmeister* to Prince Nikolaus Esterházy at the palace of Eisenstadt, although Haydn retained the honorary title and Hummel was called *Konzertmeister*; most of his religious and dramatic works belong to this period. Outside interests, however, became increasingly important to Hummel and, like his illustrious predecessor, Vienna and the wider world began to attract. His contract was terminated in 1811 and he moved back to Vienna, laying the foundation for his compositional career with music for piano and chamber ensembles.

He married a well-known singer, Elisabeth Röckl, in 1813, and it was no doubt her affinity with the public stage that persuaded her that Hummel should revitalize his pianistic career. There could hardly have been a better place or time for such a venture than Austria in the 1810s, with the Congress of Vienna in full swing and most of the nobility of Europe present in need of nightly entertainment. A tour of Germany in 1816 brought fame and money and, aware of the need for financial stability for his young family, Hummel accepted the Kapellmeistership at Stuttgart.

Similar problems to those at Eisenstadt soon reasserted themselves: little or no time to compose and practice, and great difficulty in acquiring leave for concert tours. In November 1818, Hummel accepted the post of grand-ducal Kapellmeister at Weimar. His contract included three months' leave for touring each year and, as a Catholic, absolved him from the customary obligation to compose, or otherwise become involved in, Protestant religious music. The appointment was quite a coup for a young composer-performer; Weimar included in its crown such musical jewels as Johann Sebastian Bach, Johann Gottfried Walther, and, later, Franz Liszt and Richard Strauss, as well as such literary figures as Johann Gottfried Herder, Christoph Martin Wieland, and Johann Wolfgang von Goethe, who, like Hummel, remained there until the end of his life.

From this time on, Hummel divided his time among composing, performing, his lenient duties in Weimar, and touring. He met the pianist-composer John Field in Russia in 1822 and Frédéric François Chopin in Poland, and was at Beethoven's bedside shortly before his death in 1827. He was one of the pallbearers at Beethoven's state funeral and improvised memorably on themes from Beethoven's works at the memorial concert. He died in 1837 and is buried in Weimar.

Hummel's life coincided with the first great age of the international virtuoso composer and the ubiquity of the piano as a very affordable domestic instrument, the center of the middle-class drawing room and its entertainments. This popularity in turn led to a drastic increase in the publication of music for piano and this, together with teaching and, when possible, performing, was the mainstay of the nineteenth-century composer's income, handsomely replacing eighteenth-century aristocratic patronage.

Hummel's compositional style revolves around the piano, upon which he made his international reputation as a performer and for which he wrote most of his best works. In particular, the influence of his pianistic improvisation, which was generally recognized as being of the very best during his heyday, can be seen in many of his works. It was inevitable that a composer-performer with a wide variety of audiences in different countries should produce the required potboilers: variation sets, fantasies, rondos on popular tunes, and concertos. The better composers, however, imbued such pieces with greater worth (the expressions "science" and "learning" crop up frequently in criticism) while retaining their mass appeal, and at the same time added to the more traditionally respectable genres, such as the mass, oratorio, opera, string quartet, piano trio, duo sonata, solo sonata, and symphony. Hummel contributed to all of these with the exception of the last, his only attempt at this form remaining in an unfinished manuscript. Together with those of Franz Peter Schubert, his masses, especially the Mass in E-Flat, are regarded as being among the best examples of the genre, while several of the piano sonatas occupy an important place in the early Romantic literature. (The influence of, for example, the F-sharp Minor op. 81, can be discerned in the work of Robert Alexander Schumann, who spent a year learning to play this sonata; Felix Mendelssohn; and the young Johannes Brahms, whose own first sonata in the same key is clearly modeled upon that of the older composer).

Hummel's transitional status, as the main transmitter of the Viennese classical style in a form that made it acceptable to the nineteenth century, belies the many early Romantic gestures that abound and were recognized and accepted by the younger Romantics. It was to Hummel, at the time the best teacher in Europe, that the young Schumann wrote for composition lessons, settling in the end for advice and encouragement. Chopin, several times, mentioned him together with Haydn and Mozart as one of the greats, and Schubert dedicated his last three sonatas to him; the dedication was altered posthumously by his publisher after Hummel had left Vienna.

Widely respected as a conductor, Hummel is also an important figure in the history of copyright law and a prime mover in canvassing support from composers for fairer conditions for those writing and performing music, the dying Beethoven among them. His music is belatedly enjoying a revival.

DEREK CAREW

Biography

Born in Pressburg (now Bratislava), November 14, 1778. Moved to Vienna, 1886, and studied with Mozart (1886–88), giving his first public concert there in 1889. Concert tour with his father (Austria, Germany, Denmark, Scotland, England, and the Netherlands, including Hummel's first publications), 1789–93. Vienna, 1793–1804, studying with Haydn, Salieri, and Albrechtsberger, and meeting Beethoven. 1804, Appointed *Konzertmeister* to Prince Nikolaus Esterházy, succeeding Haydn on the latter's recommendation. Contract terminated in 1811, returned to Vienna, married. Concert tour of Germany and appointment as Kapellmeister in Stuttgart, 1816. Resigned 1818 and accepted *Kapellmeistership* at Weimar in January 1819. Tour of Russia, 1822; visit to the dying Beethoven, 1827, tours of Poland, 1828, and Paris, and London, 1830. Two more tours to London, 1831 and 1833, and to Vienna, 1834. Died in Weimar, October 17, 1837.

Selected Works

Piano Solo

Sonatas; many sets of variations (including those on "God Save The King" [1804], and on a theme from Gluck's *Armide* [1811–15]); Fantasies, Potpourris, Rondos (including Adagio, Variations and Rondo on "The Pretty Polly" [c. 1817]); 24 Etudes Op. 125 (1833).

Orchestral

Variations and concertos for piano and orchestra (in C [c. 1811], in E (1814), A minor (c. 1816), B minor (1819), A flat (1827) and F (1833). Mandolin concerto in G (1799) and trumpet concerto in E flat (1803). Many sets of dances and incidental music to plays; ballets and pantomimes.

Pedagogical

Ausführlich theoretisch-practische Anweisung zum Piano-forte Spiel. 1822–85.

Bibliography

Benyovszky, K. *Hummel und seine Vatersdtadt*. Bratislava, 1937.
———. *J. N. Hummel: der Mensch und Künstler*. Bratislava, 1934.
Davis, R. "The music of J. N. Hummel, its Derivation and Development," *Music Review* 26 (1969): 169.
Sachs, J. "Hummel and the Pirates: the Struggle for Musical Copyright," *Musical Quarterly* 59 (1973): 31.
———. *Kapellmeister Hummel in England and France*. Detroit, 1977.

HUNGARY: CULTURAL SURVEY

Hungarian Romanticism began during a period known as the reform era, the main objectives of which were counteracting the absolutist policies of the Hapsburg rulers and securing, through modernization, more autonomy for Hungary within the Austrian empire. It was the Hungarian nobility who, at meetings of the Hungarian Diet between 1825 and 1840, forged the policies of reform, often hindered by Vienna. At the initial stage, it was the example of aristocrats such as Count István Széchenyi offering his annual income toward the foundation of the Hungarian Academy of Sciences that gave an enormous boost to cultural development. Széchenyi also excelled as an author of treatises on economics and was a practical reformer, but in the second period of the reform era his cautious policies were superseded by the liberal democrats of the journal *Pesti Hirlap*

(*Journal of Pest*), edited by the great orator and statesman Lajos Kossuth. Both Széchenyi and Kossuth were Romantic characters, in different ways, and the reform era was the result of their (often competing) efforts to steer Hungary toward a more "Western" model of society.

Literature

Culturally, Hungary was rather decentered in the first two decades of the nineteenth century. There was no proper cultural center and the greatest literary figure of the period, Ferenc Kazinczy, a Classicist both by taste and temperament, lived on his estate in Eastern Hungary and kept in touch with other writers by correspondence. While he contributed significantly to the language reform that prepared the ground for the Romantics, by the 1820s his literary judgment was challenged by two playwrights: József Katona, author of the historical play *Bánk bán* (*Banus Bank*, 1833) which took its theme from a conflict in the thirteenth century between the king and the nobility that ended with the queen's murder; and by Károly Kisfaludy. While Katona's talent was not recognized by fellow writers or by the theatergoing public, Kisfaludy, (brother of Sándor Kisfaludy, a popular sentimental poet), was more fortunate: his first play, staged in 1819, *A tatárok Magyarországon* (*Mongols in Hungary*) was highly successful and brought him instant fame. Yet it was not so much his historical plays (of which the critics think most highly of *Iréne*, 1820), but his launching of the literary journal *Aurora* in 1821 that earned him the title of "the father of Hungarian Romanticism." The circle around *Aurora*, which included the poet Mihály Vörösmarty, the critic József Bajza, and the literary historian Ferenc Toldy, fought the decisive literary battles that finally led to the acceptance of Romantic taste and ideals among the Hungarian reading public.

As in the theater, in poetry national ideals prevailed. These were interpreted differently by writers involved in the Romantic movement: the first ambition of the poets was to create a "national epic" and Vörösmarty's grand epic poem written in hexameters, *Zalán futása* (*The Flight of Zalán*, 1825) is often regarded as the first important achievement of Hungarian Romanticism. This poem, like many later works by the same author, uses mythical and fabulous elements in conjuring up pictures of the Hungarian Conquest, but its enchanting lyrical interludes capture the imagination. Vörösmarty wrote a number of successful shorter poetic tales, but he is most revered for his lyrical verse, which evolved from a quiet patriotism and wistful love poetry toward a somber, philosophical tone addressing universal themes, as seen, for example, in the poems "Szózat" ("Appeal," 1848) and "Vén cigány" ("The Old Gypsy," 1854). He translated two plays by William Shakespeare into Hungarian and wrote melodramas that are now seldom performed; however, his charming verse play based on a fairy tale, *Csongor és Tunde* (*Csongor and Tunde*, 1831) has been read and performed ever since its first publication. It is "the unparalleled beauty of the language" rather than dramatic tension that makes this play successful.

Among the literary critics, Ferenc Kölcsey stands out as an original thinker. In his seminal essay "National Traditions" (1826) he put forward a view which found full justification only a few decades later, namely that Hungarian Romanticism, if it wanted to preserve its national characteristics, should turn toward folk literature. While trying to use certain folk elements in his poetry, Kölcsey as a poet is now remembered for some intensely pessimistic patriotic poems, including a grand inventory of national woes entitled "Himnusz" ("Hymn," 1823), the first stanza of which later became, with Ferenc Erkel's music, Hungary's national anthem.

It was during the early 1840s that Hungarian poetry began to follow Kölcsey's recommendation. A great poetic talent, Sándor Petöfi appeared, who simplified and at the same time transformed the original Romantic message. Lord Byron's generation still believed in the supreme right of the individual to challenge all worldly powers; the second generation of European Romantics in certain countries tried to assert the rights of the people above all and fashion a role for the individual to lead the popular struggle for freedom and independence. Petöfi is a representative of a kind of "populist" Romanticism that is often mistaken for realism; in fact, one could be a realist in short descriptive pieces and a Romantic in lyrical outpourings of one's soul. Petöfi wrote the fairy tale of a narrative poem *János vitéz* (*John the Hero*, 1844), which recounts the dazzling career of a simple shepherd boy turned into victorious Hussar who finally finds happiness with his resurrected lover in Fairyland. The chief value esteemed by poets at this time was love, but soon freedom joined it with compelling force, Petöfi asserting in a short emblematic poem that he would sacrifice his life for love, but he would give away his love for liberty. In fact, Petöfi followed this program, the Byronesque unity of life and poetry by being a leading force in the March, 1848 revolution. He died on the battlefield of Segesvár (now Şigishoara in Romania) a year later. He even foretold the manner of his death in the poem ("I'm Troubled by One Thought,") a perfect example of wish-fulfilment by a revolutionary Romantic.

The journals *Aurora* and then *Athenaeum* (the latter edited by Bajza) paved the way for political journalism in Hungary during the Romantic period. After the discontinuation of *Athenaeum* in 1843, the field was taken up by a number of "fashion journals" that published literary works. In the reform era both drama and poetry developed rapidly; prose lagged behind somewhat. Though Károly Kisfaludy wrote historical novels at this time, it was only András Fáy and even more Miklós Jósika who made an impact on the reading public. Jósika followed Walter Scott in his historical novels, of which *Abafi* (*The Son of Aba*, 1836) is thought of most highly. The two greatest Romantic novelists in Hungary appeared a few years later, namely József Eötvös and Mór Jókai. As a young man, Eötvös traveled extensively throughout Western Europe, hence the cosmopolitan choice for the heroes of his first novel *A karthausi* (*The Carthusian*, 1839–41). It is the story of Gustave, a young French nobleman who finds no happiness in love and who finally becomes a Carthusian monk to make up for his sins. According to one critic, in this book Eötvös "overcame the Byronic-Romantic melancholy of his generation." Of his later novels, *A falu jegyzöje* (*The Village Notary*, 1845) has the best construction and is generally more realistic than Romantic, with a strong dose of social criticism addressed to Hungarian society. As for Jókai, his pre-1848 writing, mostly modeled on Victor Hugo, is inferior to his later work, of which *Egy magyar nábob* (*A Hungarian Nabob*, 1853–54) was the first success with the public. It was followed by a string of Romantic novels and stories, many of which were promptly translated into German and English, although it was only with *Az aranyember* (*The Man with the Golden Touch*, 1872) that Jókai managed to create the perfect Utopia of Romantic escapism. Jókai, called on occasion "the great story-teller," played a didactic part, too: the public at large learned much about Hungarian as well as world history from his colorful, adventurous, and beautifully written novels.

Music

The two main exponents of Hungarian Romanticism in music were born almost at the same time, but their musical interests and career showed marked differences. Ferenc Erkel came from a family of musicians and played the organ and the piano as a child. He studied in Pozsony (now Bratislava) and conducted his first concerts (with a nonprofessional orchestra) at Kolozsvár (now Cluj in Romania) in 1833 and 1834. From 1835, he conducted at Pest-Buda, where in 1837 he became the chief conductor of the new National Theater. Erkel is regarded as the pioneer of the opera in Hungary and the creator of its national repertory. While influenced by German and Italian composers of the period, Erkel used typically Hungarian melodies and musical motifs, such as the *verbunkos* (traditional army recruiting dance) in his work, which includes *Hunyadi László* (*Laszlo Hunyadi*, 1844), an opera in four acts, and *Bánk bán* (*Banus Bank*, 1861) an opera based on József Katona's tragedy. His later operas were less significant, although from 1875 to 1886 Erkel was director of the Hungarian Music Academy in Budapest. He composed music to the Hungarian national anthem as well as Vörösmarty's "Szózat," Hungary's "second anthem." Although he did incorporate foreign elements into his music, Erkel, together with Franz Liszt, did most to develop the nineteenth-century Hungarian musical idiom.

Franz Liszt, composer and pianist, was born in Raiding (Doborján) in the region of Burgenland, which was part of historical Hungary but since 1918 has belonged to Austria: while he is claimed by German historians of music, Liszt always emphatically referred to his nationality as Hungarian. He was a child prodigy who gave his first concert at the age of nine. From 1821, he studied music in Vienna under Carl Czerny and Antonio Salieri, but in 1832 he moved to Paris, his home for the next few years. From 1838 to 1847, he lived the life of the cosmopolitan musician travelling from country to country, then from 1848 to 1861 he was director of the court musicians in Weimar, later on he lived in Rome, Budapest, and Weimar. Liszt, considered the greatest virtuoso of the day, started out as a composer for the piano in the 1840s and, while he composed twenty Hungarian rhapsodies (1851–86), most of his music for this instrument is international in character. This is largely true for his orchestral music, of which perhaps the *Faust Symphony* (1853–61) and his piano concertos are the best known. His choral music, however, particularly after 1860, shows a strong Hungarian orientation. This includes *The Legend of St. Elizabeth* (1862) and the *Magyar Koronázási Mise* (*Hungarian Coronation Mass*, 1867), which he composed to celebrate the compromise between Austria and Hungary and the coronation of Franz Joseph as King of Hungary. Among his compositions, perhaps the Hungarian rhapsodies have the most Romantic character; his music has been criticized for its "over-rhetorical style" but much praised for its richness and variety. Liszt played an important role in stimulating musical life in Hungary, particularly in the second half of the nineteenth century.

Visual Arts

Although the building of the Hungarian National Museum was completed by the Classical architect Mihály Pollack as early as 1847, no royal academy or national gallery existed in Hungary in the first half of the nineteenth century. Most Hungarian artists studied abroad during this period: the sculptor István Ferenczy in Rome, where he became Bertel Thorwaldsen's stone-carver assistant, and the painters Károly Markó and Miklós Barabás in Italy and Vienna, respectively. Markó, a skilful classico-Romantic landscape painter, lived most of his life in Italy and had but little influence on the development of Hungarian painting. Barabás, whose career took off during the age of reform, became the most popular portraitist of the period, his work including such celebrities as Count István Széchenyi and the poet Sándor Petőfi. His style was "simple and objective, somewhat reminiscent of Viennese Biedermeier." As for Ferenczy, he had a number of commissions after his return from Italy, but none of his major plans (notably the establishment of a school for sculptors) came to fruition and he died a frustrated man.

National Romanticism in Hungarian painting began to flourish only after the War of Independence of 1848 and 1849. Its main exponent was László Madarász, a veteran of that war who later studied art in Vienna and decided to devote his art to "programmatic" painting inasmuch as he chose his subjects almost exclusively from Hungarian history. In 1856, Madarász went to Paris to study and it was there that he painted *Lamenting over László Hunyadi*, which in 1861 was awarded the Gold Medal of the French State. Another highly acclaimed canvas of Madarász's was *The Parting of Zrinyi and Frangepán in the Wiener Neustadt Prison* (1864), which hangs in the Hungarian National Gallery.

The other outstanding Hungarian Romantic painter, Mihály Zichy, reached fame outside Hungary. After studies in Vienna, in 1847 he was invited to Russia. By this time Zichy embraced Romantic themes, as shown by *The Life-Boat* (1847), which is similar to Théodore Géricault's famous *Raft of the Medusa* (1819). In Russia, he first worked as drawing master for an aristocratic family, but soon gained the position of official painter to the imperial court, which he held for several decades. Zichy was a virtuoso graphic artist and painter working mostly in watercolors; Théophile Gautier called him in a review a "monster of a genius." In 1874, Zichy moved to Paris where he lived for five years before eventually returning to Russia. His highly individual, allegorical, and symbolic style did not influence his Hungarian contemporaries, and he is mainly known in Hungary for his fine illustrations of the work of the Hungarian writers Sándor Petőfi, János Arany, and Imre Madách, and the Russian Romantic poet Mikhail Lermontov.

GEORGE GÖMÖRI

Bibliography

Bárány, George. *Stephen Széchenyi and the Awakening of Hungarian Nationalism, 1791–1841*. Princeton, N.J.: Princeton University Press, 1968.

Czigány, Lóránt. *The Oxford History of Hungarian Literature.* Oxford: Clarendon Press, 1984.

Jones, Mervyn, D. *Five Hungarian Writers.* Oxford: Clarendon Press, 1966.

Kampis, Antal. *The History of Art in Hungary.* London; Collet's, 1966.

Legány, Dezso. *Liszt and His Country.* Budapest: Corvina Press, 1983.

Reményi, Joseph. *Hungarian Writers and Literature.* New Brunswick N.J.: Rutgers University Press, 1964.

Searle, H. *The Music of Liszt.* London, 1954.

Sötér, István, ed. *A magyar irodalom története.* vol. III. Budapest: Akadémiai kiadó, 1965.

Szabolcsi, Bence. *A XIX század magyar romantikus zenéje.* Budapest: Zenemukiadó, 1951.

Tóth, Dezsö. *Vörösmarty Mihály.* 2nd ed. Budapest: Akadémiai kiadó, 1974.

Vardy, Steven Béla. *Baron Joseph Eötvös: A Literary Biography.* Boulder, Colo.: East European Monographs 214/Atlantic Studies on Society in Change no. 52, 1987.

HUNGARY: HISTORICAL SURVEY

When discussing Hungarian history in the context of the Romantic movement, one has to go back further than the beginnings of literary Romanticism. The assumption of the throne by Francis I in 1792 ushered in the age of "royal absolutism," though this age, lasting until 1848, can be subdivided into periods from the French wars to the Age of Reform, and from 1825 to the revolution and War of Independence. This division is due to the changing economic circumstances of the Hungarian nobility as well as to the growing cultural awareness of Hungary's "backwardness" as Austria's supplier of wheat and raw materials. At any rate, during the first period the Habsburgs took off the agenda the internal reform of Hungary (the county system of administration continued to function undisturbed), and in exchange they got recruits and food supplies for the wars against Napoleon Bonaparte. At the same time, strict censorship was imposed on all publications. Nonetheless, in 1806 a Hungarian-language newspaper, *Hazai tudósitások* (*Reports from the Homeland*) began to appear in Pest. Since during the first years of its publication the newspaper was not allowed to print any political news from abroad, it concentrated on the promotion of Hungarian culture and literature. Cultivation of the Magyar tongue, greatly increased after Johann Gottfried Herder's ominous "prophecy" (that the Hungarian language might disappear in the future, absorbed by the large German and Slav population of the kingdom of Hungary), while "apolitical" in the short run, still played an important role in preparing the Age of Reform. In fact, the language reform movement (*nyelvujítás*), directed, mostly through correspondence, by ex-political prisoner Ferenc Kazinczy, enriched the Hungarian language with thousands of new words and enhanced the development of both literature and the scientific language. However, as George Barany points out, Kazinczy's movement ultimately promoted Hungarian cultural nationalism which opposed both the "multinational patriotism" of old Hungary based on the use of Latin as well as the budding cultural nationalism of the national minorities.

The compromise between the Hungarian nobility and the Hapsburg ruler was first broken by the currency reform of 1811, about which Vienna failed to consult the Hungarian Diet, though Hungary "was expected to shoulder almost one half of the state's debt and to double her contribution in taxes." When the Diet refused to approve this, Francis I dissolved the Diet and continued to rule by decree, appointing royal commissioners who forced his will upon the (theoretically autonomous) counties. War expenses led to the devaluation of Austrian currency in 1816, which, understandably, further undermined confidence in the government. Military intervention in Italy in 1820 and 1821 were also deeply unpopular in Hungary, which was compelled to provide recruits and burdened with further taxes. Many counties refused to obey, and it was widespread discontent with Vienna's policies that made Francis I listen to the advice of his chancellor, Clemens Metternich, regarding the convocation of a new Diet in 1825.

The Hungarian Diet at that time consisted of two chambers. In the lower chamber sat representatives of the nobility, the clergy, and the chartered or free royal cities. In contrast to England, these deputies, by and large, had to abide with the instructions of their constituents. Most members of the upper chamber were high state officials, bishops, rich magnates, or persons who attended by royal invitation. Sometimes the two chambers had joint sessions chaired by the Palatine. In the Diet there were no political parties in the modern sense of the word, and deputies would not concede defeat if there was a simple majority against them; much depended on the maneuvering of the presiding personalities. Even if an agreement was reached, it could be disputed on the basis of the "evaluation of the votes" and it was not until the 1830s that the principle of following the will of the majority was accepted in legislation.

While the Diet of 1823 through 1825 ended in a legislative stalemate between king and country, it provided a symbolic breakthrough in the development of Hungarian culture. A young captain of the Hussars, Count István Széchenyi, offered one year's income of his estates (estimated later at sixty thousand florins) toward the foundation of an institution to propagate "the national idiom." This declaration set in motion offers by other rich landowners that, taken together, led to the establishment of the Hungarian Academy of Sciences (in 1830 Széchenyi became its first vice president). Széchenyi's first book, *Hitel* (*Credit*), published in 1830, described the backwardness of feudal Hungary, in a forthright manner attacking the "law on entail" as the primary cause for the country's poverty. Modernization depended on credit, and credit could be achieved only if certain laws, and with them the attitude to labor, was changed. Széchenyi aimed at raising domestic consumption and did not advocate radical political change, but his recommendations pointed toward the unavoidable liberation of the serfs and a change over from feudal despondence and inefficiency to a different mode of production.

The publication of *Hitel* was praised as "a patriotic deed" by other reformers (notably József Eotvos), but also provoked sharp antagonism among conservatives. The debate centered on taxation—that is, whether the landowning nobility ought to pay taxes on its hereditary lands, thereby shifting the tax burden, which fell mostly on the peasantry. While Széchenyi was hoping for a "spiritual rejuvenation" of the aristocracy (in his view the "natural" leaders of the nation), his ideas were taken up by the landed gentry and it was representatives of this social group who began to dominate the Diet of 1832 through 1836. At this Diet (held in Pozsony/Pressburg, now Bratislava in Slovakia), the so-called Dietal Youth, mostly liberal-minded law students, began to play a role by providing a kind of audience to the proceedings. One of their numbers, the representative of two absent magnates at the Diet, Lajos Kossuth, made a particular impact—he became editor of a hand-copied bulletin called *Országgyülési tudósítások* (*Dietal Reports*) which was sent out to the counties and turned into a powerful weapon in influencing public opinion. Metternich resented the strength of the liberal opposition of the Diet and instructed his police to arrest some leaders of Dietal Youth for "political sedition." This did not mean, however, an end to the program of Széchenyi (which was partly supported by Vienna): administrative and economic reform in Hungary for the benefit of the towns. In 1833 Széchenyi was appointed royal commissioner in charge of improving Danube navigation, and he also proceeded with his plans to build a permanent stone bridge between Buda and Pest with the help of two Scottish engineers.

In 1835 Francis I died and his successor, Ferdinand V, slowly agreed to the continuation of reforms in Hungary. This became apparent at the end of the Diet of 1839 and 1840, which passed a law that allowed individual serfs to pay money for manumission compensation and decided to prepare a new penal code on the basis of the best foreign examples. This Diet also lifted restrictions placed on Jews, who could now own real estate or pursue any kind of trade or profession. In the spring of 1840, political amnesty was declared and the mood of Magyar-speaking Hungarians was very optimistic. In the same year a law was passed that replaced Latin with Magyar as the official language of all legislation and administration in Hungary, with the exemption of Croatia (which traditionally had had semiautonomy).

As Széchenyi had foreseen, the language issue became an important sticking point between the Hungarian majority of the kingdom of Hungary and its ethnic minorities. (The term *majority* is relative, for in 1840 only about forty percent of Hungary's population spoke Magyar as its first language.) Magyar nationalism in fact disregarded the increasing claims of ethnic Slovaks and Romanians for cultural autonomy; while resisting Austrian centralism and German as the lingua franca of the Hapsburg empire, Hungarians paid scant attention to the counterclaims of other nationalities living on the same territory. While this led to serious problems in 1848 and 1849, in the earlier 1840s the issue was by and large ignored by most Hungarian liberals.

If the period of 1825 through 1840 "belonged" to István Széchenyi, the 1840s were prime times for Lajos Kossuth. Having been released from jail, in 1841 he launched the newspaper *Pesti Hirlap* (*Journal of Pest*) which became a powerful force in shaping public opinion. Kossuth was a liberal who realized that because of the absence of a proper Hungarian urban middle class, it was the landed gentry who would have to promote the course of constitutional and economic reform, even if this meant the loss of some of their privileges. In Kossuth's view, no rapid industrial development was possible in Hungary until Vienna

agreed to the modification of internal tariffs within the empire. This was raised at the Diet of 1843 and 1844 but was rejected by the imperial authorities. It was after this that the Chamber of Deputies passed a resolution supporting the newly founded National Protective Association which encouraged the public to buy mostly Hungarian-produced goods.

While Kossuth, who had a partly Slav background and as a result was accused by A. J. P. Taylor of exhibiting "a cocksureness alien to the Hungarian caution," advocated radical reforms, Széchenyi tried to avoid a fatal clash that might lead to a break with Austria. In 1845 he published a book denouncing Kossuth's nationalism and his social "radicalism," but *Kelet népe* (*People of the Orient*) had a much less enthusiastic reception than any of the great reformer's previous works. Even those liberals who opposed the county system of administration (the so-called centralists) could not subscribe to Széchenyi's accusations, which coincided with Metternich's administrative counteroffensive. In 1844 a Hungarian chancery was established in Vienna which then sent centrally appointed and well-paid administrators to the Hungarian counties. The administrators enforced control through threats and bribery and prepared the ground for the 1847 elections to the Diet which produced a victory for the conservatives. By this time Kossuth had given up editorship of *Pesti Hirlap* but edited another newspaper and was as influential in shaping liberal opinion as ever. The opposition manifesto which he drew up in June 1847, with the help of the more moderate Ferenc Deák, was a document of sweeping reform that the Diet of 1847 and 1848 was still reluctant to embrace—until developments abroad and in Pest-Buda finally forced its hand.

One of the major demands of the opposition manifesto was the request to the king to appoint "a genuine national ministry responsible to a parliament." Once news of the French Revolution reached Vienna, Kossuth realized that the moment was ripe to stress that demand. On March 3, 1848, he submitted to the lower chamber of the parliament (in session at Pozsony/Pressburg) a draft address to the crown that reworded the opposition's program with a special emphasis on responsible government. This was accepted by the lower chamber by acclamation, but before it could be presented to the upper chamber revolution broke out in Vienna. Metternich resigned and with him the conservative Hungarian vice chancellor Gyorgy Apponyi. This, and the March 15 revolution in Pest led by young writers, poets, and law students, frightened the magnates of the upper chamber, who accepted the address that was then taken to Vienna by a deputation. Ferdinand I, fearing Hungary's complete secession from the empire, yielded to the "wishes of the nation" and appointed Lajos Batthyány, a liberal magnate, to form a Hungarian government. This first government of 1848 included all the best available political talents, alongside Ferenc Deák, József Eotvos, Lajos Kossuth, and István Széchenyi.

The so-called April Laws of 1848, which codified the victory of the reform movement, meant that Hungary became a limited monarchy, with a bicameral parliament—the Lower House to be elected on a wide suffrage. Taxation became universal, the serfs were liberated, freedom of the press and assembly were guaranteed. As for the "national" demands, Hungary's union with Transylvania was enacted, subject to the consent of the Transylvanian Diet. Altogether, the April Laws were the culmination of the Age of Reform, a huge step forward in Hungary's modernization. While the outcome of the following War of Independence (in fact provoked by Vienna going back on its previous concessions) was a setback in the enactment of these laws, some of them were not annulled by the post-1849 centralizing administration, and all of them were incorporated in the 1867 compromise between Austria and Hungary that made the joint monarchy possible.

GEORGE GÖMÖRI

Bibliography

Bárány, George. "The Age of Royal Absolutism, 1790–1848." In *A History of Hungary*. Edited by F. Peter Sugar. London: Tauris, 1990.

———. *Stephen Széchenyi and the Awakening of Hungarian Nationalism*. Princeton N.J.: Princeton University Press, 1968.

Bödy, Paul. *Joseph Eötvös and the Modernization of Hungary*. New York: Brooklyn College Press, 1985.

Deák, István. *The Lawful Revolution, Louis Kossuth and the Hungarians 1848–49*. New York: Columbia University Press, 1979.

Király, Béla. *Ferenc Deák*. Boston: Twayne, 1975.

Macartney, C. A. *Hungary: A Short History*. Edinburgh: University of Edinburgh Press, 1962.

Várdy, Steven Bela. *Baron Joseph Eötvös (1813–1871): A Literary Biography*. Boulder, Colo.: East European Monographs, 214/Atlantic Studies on Society in Change no. 52, 1987.

Wagner, Francis, S. "Széchenyi and the Nationality Problem in the Habsburg Empire," *Journal of Central European Affairs* 20, no. 3, (196): 289–311.

HUNT, LEIGH 1784-1859

English essayist, poet, critic, editor, and journalist

Leigh Hunt is best known as a lighthearted essayist and a minor associate of Lord Byron, William Hazlitt, John Keats, and Mary and Percy Bysshe Shelley. He was, however, an important poet, critic, editor, and journalist in his own right. Many critics argue that Hunt inspired the poetic experiments and political ideals that define later Romanticism. "Poetry," Hunt believed, "is imaginative passion," emphasizing that by *passion* he also meant *suffering*. Passionate poetry inspires in readers deep feelings of sympathy. From such feelings of sympathy there emerges a communal solidarity that can counter oppressive social forms. Intense feeling is a familiar motif of Romanticism; for Hunt it has overt political implications.

Hunt established the radical journal the *Examiner* in 1808 with his brother John. Decrying arbitrary government and promoting liberal Enlightenment, the *Examiner* became the most important reformist journal of its day. It also became a vehicle for the emerging generation of urban poets and critics. Poems by Shelley and Keats, and essays by Hazlitt and Charles Lamb flanked editorials on political injustice. This contiguity of poetry and polemic provides strong evidence for the political impulse of Romanticism.

In February 1812, the Hunts published a scathing description of the Prince Regent. The government successfully sued for libel. The brothers were sentenced to pay £500 each and to serve two years imprisonment in separate prisons. Leigh turned his two-room cell in Horsemonger Lane Gaol into a literary salon. Frequent visitors included prominent members of the liberal opposition and the Romantic literati from Jeremy Bentham, Henry Brougham (who had defended the Hunts) and Francis Burdett, to Byron, Maria Edgeworth, Benjamin Haydon, and Tom Moore.

Hunt's prison experience revealed to him how passion and sympathy might intersect with political protest. After his release, he sought to bring that experience to poetry. For instance, Hunt was a champion of the sonnet. In "To Hampstead" (1815) and the collection *Foliage* (1818), he demonstrated how the compressed sonnet form could produce feelings so intense as to inspire an expansive cathartic release. In *The Story of Rimini* (1816), he developed this method in an epic of forbidden love.

From Dante Alighieri's *Inferno*, Hunt took the story of Paolo and Francesca, two doomed lovers whose erotic passions fly in the face of the customs of arranged marriage and political honor. Much of the poem is a vehicle for the expressive power of poetry itself. Loaded with images of natural restlessness and weighted with lugubrious adjectives, the poem invokes the sensuality it espouses. Hunt's ambitions in *Rimini* were not strictly literary. He intended the poem to be read as an allegory for his personal struggle against political oppression.

The Story of Rimini was derided for its motifs of lust and rebellion. It inspired a series of vociferous reviews in *Blackwood's London Magazine* entitled "The Cockney School," which pilloried Hunt for his social pretensions, poetic vulgarity, and lack of Classical learning. Hunt was not deterred; he published a rejoinder in *The Examiner*. In the same vein, Hunt adapted aristocratic poetical forms, like the sonnet and the epic, to ironic liberal political ends. *The Descent of Liberty* (1816) depicted Napoleon Bonaparte, with his republican pretensions, as a doomed tyrant, and celebrated the genuine spirit of liberty as a powerfully emotional force emerging from the experience of oppression.

While they are no doubt important to an understanding of the social context of Romanticism, Hunt's "radical" politics should not be overstressed. Hunt's poetics and politics, while seemingly dangerous, were nevertheless based on an ideal of comfortable domestic life. Such views clashed with the intellectual impulses of his friends. Relinquishing the editorship of *The Examiner* in 1821 at the height of his literary reputation, Hunt took his family to Italy to join Byron and Shelley and begin a new journal, the *Liberal*. Hunt arrived at Leghorn on July 1, 1822, only one week before Shelley drowned. Byron soon became bored with what he regarded as Hunt's affected sensibility. Without Shelley's mediation, the relationship between the domestic Hunt and the tempestuous Byron became anxious and strained. The *Liberal* lasted only four issues. After his return from Italy, Hunt published an unusually frank and rather embittered memoir of Byron's London heydays, *Lord Byron and Some of His Contemporaries* (1828). Contrary to Hunt's expectation, the public received the memoir as a scandalous betrayal of a cult hero by a jealous rival.

Hunt worked as a journalist and editor well into the 1830s. After the 1832 Reform Bill achieved many of Hunt's political hopes, his writings became more staid and reflective. In that year, he published a spiritual manifesto, *Christianism*. He subsequently revised and expanded *Christianism*, later releasing it as *Religion of the Heart* (1853). Hunt's religious views stress what he called "natural piety," a somewhat watered-down version of his poetics. In these views, every individual is blessed with the ability to imagine divine consolation for the tribulations of life. These imaginings lead to a confident sense of individual purpose that can be channeled into benevolent acts. Neither of Hunt's two texts garnered much public favor, and he is instead best remembered in his later life for his memoirs, editions, and criticism. Among many other works, his *Autobiography* and the essay *An Answer to the Question What is Poetry?* (both 1844) represent crucial defenses of the Romantic zeitgeist. Unfortunately, Hunt's most enduring claim to fame is his appearance in Charles Dickens's *Bleak House* (1853) as the self-proclaimed child of nature, Harold Skimpole. As parodic as it appears to be, Dickens's depiction of Hunt as a man of light and feeling in the shadow of arbitrary law reveals precisely the kind of polemical energy that Hunt sought in his poetry.

ALEX DICK

Biography

Born James Leigh Hunt October 19, 1784. He was educated at Christ's Hospital in London where he was exposed both to the rigors of an archaic Classical education system attuning itself to utilitarian enterprise and to the literary heritage of Great Britain: Geoffrey Chaucer, John Milton, William Shakespeare, and Edmund Spenser. In 1809, Hunt married Marianne Kent. They had eleven children; seven reached maturity. For a brief time, their home in the Vale of Health near Hampstead became a meeting place for young artists and thinkers, all under the auspices of Hunt's own publications. The Hunt family would never achieve the domestic harmony that Hunt himself idolized in his writings. Dogged by poverty even into their middle and old age, they were forced to move from home to home, throughout London and the south of England. Their youngest son Vincent died in 1852. Marianne Hunt became bedridden and died five years later. Hunt died peacefully in 1859 in a friend's house in Putney.

Selected Works

The Examiner: A Weekly Paper on Politics, Literature, Music, and the Fine Arts. 1808–21.
The Feast of the Poets, with Notes, and Other Pieces in Verse, by the Editor of the Examiner. 1814.
The Descent of Liberty: A Mask. 1815.
Foliage; or, Poems Original and Translated. 1818.
The Liberal. 1822–23.
Lord Byron and Some of his Contemporaries; with Recollections of the Author's Life, and of his Visit to Italy. 1828.
Imagination and Fancy; or Selections from the English Poets Illustrative of Those First Requisites of their Art, with Markings of the Best Passages, Critical Notices of the Writers, and an Essay in Answer to the Question, "What is Poetry?" 1844.
The Correspondence of Leigh Hunt. 2 vols. Edited by Thornton Hunt. 1862.
The Autobiography of Leigh Hunt. Edited by J. E. Morpurgo. London: Cresset Press, 1949.
The Complete Works of Leigh Hunt. Edited by Michael-Eberle Sinatra. London: Pickering and Chatto, 2002.

Bibliography

Blainey, Ann. *Immortal Boy: A Portrait of Leigh Hunt.* New York: St. Martin's Press, 1985.
Cox, Jeffrey. *Poetry and Politics in the Cockney School: Keats, Shelley, Hunt and Their Circle.* Cambridge: Cambridge University Press, 1998.
Gates, Eleanor, ed. *Leigh Hunt: A Life in Letters.* Essex, Conn.: Falls River, 1998.
Kucich, Greg. " 'The Wit in the Dungeon': Leigh Hunt and the Insolent Politics of Cockney Coteries." *ERR* 10, No. 2 (Spring 1999): 242–53.
Wheatley, Kim. "The *Blackwood's* Attacks on Leigh Hunt." *Nineteenth-Century Literature,* 47 (1992): 1–31.
Wu, Duncan. "Leigh Hunt's 'Cockney Aesthetics.' " *Keats-Shelley Review* 10 (1996): 77–97.

HYMNEN AN DIE NACHT (HYMNS TO THE NIGHT), 1800

Poem by Novalis

This cycle of six hymnal poems comprises a key Romantic work that should be read as Novalis's attempt to create a universal vision. Inspired by the death of his fiancée, Sophie von Kühn, it expresses the poet's personal religion, influenced by his pietist background, and the theology of Friedrich Schleiermacher and Johann Gottfried von Herder's *Paramythien*. In the *Hymnen* Novalis responds to the challenge of the Enlightenment, endorsing Edward Young's *Night Thoughts* (1742–45) as an early criticism of pure rationalism and further extending the argument by including a critique of the cosmology of Johann Christoph Friedrich von Schiller and Friedrich Hölderlin.

The *Hymnen* were first published in August 1800 in the journal *Athenaeum* under their present title, despite the fact that Novalis had asked for the term *hymns* to be dropped. They were printed largely in prose form with rhyming verse introduced into parts 4 and 5 and part 6 printed entirely in verse. This format lends the work a dramatic character, allowing also for a rhythmic variation and a movement between a meditative, cerebral style and emotional ecstasy. The *Athenaeum* version (succeeding an earlier all-verse manuscript) corresponds to the Romantic ambition of an encyclopedic grasp of universal totality and its synthesis with the poetic subject, described by Novalis as the composition of a "scientific Bible."

The poem's cosmic vision begins with the praise of the sun as source of life and ends with a "longing for death," as redemption from personal isolation and acceptance of eternal night. As the womb of life, night will restore us to our eternal father, overcoming history as time, so as to enter the Golden Age, a prelapsarian ageless state of innocence. The mystical *coincidentia oppositorum* provides an important structural element, manifest in the reconciliation of opposites, partly as an upward force defying gravity or, in more metaphorical form, as the transformation of sunlight into darkness, of the Christ figure into the Virgin Mary, or as the purification of the physical world into the astral spirit. Sexual love becomes part of a cosmic life force; divine love, in its all-embracing, unifying nature, is experienced as a mystical union between the individual and cosmic totality and is afforded poetic expression through ecstatic verse. Such transformation is also evident in Friedrich von Hardenberg's pen name Novalis ("a newfound land").

A detailed analysis of the poems cannot be undertaken here; certain observations on their basic structure must suffice. The initial praise of light, associated with the rationalist *principium indivuationis*, becomes subsumed by night as the "womb of life." Ecstatic dream images celebrate night as the eternal loving mother, a force that will transubstantiate the individual into the universal, thus abolishing the confines of space and time. The twin brother figures *hypnos* and *thanatos*, sleep and death, now become reconciled, replacing the Classical image of death as the genius figure with the inverted torch, a rigid statue that could never resolve the problem of death, with the true Christ figure whose resurrection overcame death. The third part, based on the poet's personal experience of the death of his fiancée, bears a close similarity to his contemporary diary entries. Traditionally, this part, which relates Novalis's vision at Sophie's graveside of her transformation into some kind of astral body, has been given too much prominence; it should be interpreted as an integral part of the whole poem. Faith and love are felt to urge each other on, elevating the poet and his beloved into the company of Christ, her grave becoming the holy tomb and their love transformed into divine love. The graveside epiphany celebrates the newborn spirit and its celestial eternity, voluptuous love turns into a mystical longing for death, returning us to the origins of all life. Part 5 presents the poem's philosophical climax, as Novalis takes issue with Schiller and the neo-Classical tradition. More recent interpretations seem to suggest that the contrast between them is less pronounced, in that both poets search for an artistic solution to the death problem. However, whereas in *Götter Griechenlands*, (*The Gods of Greece*) Schiller laments the retreat of the ancient gods in the face of the monotheistic Christian religion, Novalis refutes this argument by indicating that antiquity could not resolve the problem of death. Just as daylight reduces everything to individual shapes and entities, so the genius-death figure of Greek antiquity, by its very clarity, denies the mystical union with the universe. In Novalis's poem the mysterious singer intensifies the function of the ancient poet, now presented as mediator, capable of reconciling life in this world with the Christian promise of eternal life, thereby giving art a new function. His new message finds expression in the lines "In everlasting life death found its goal, / For thou art Death and thou first makest us whole." The ecstatic style is left behind as the final hymn completes the poetic cycle. Life is conceived in conventional metaphors as a pilgrimage, the "longing for death" brings the expectation of eternal life, reuniting light and darkness, the female with the male principle. The poem concludes with the great revelation of the totality of life: intimately Christian, it is more emotional confession than orthodox theology, presenting a cosmic vision, the apotheosis of poetry, love, and victory over death.

HANS-JOACHIM HAHN

Work

Hymen an die Nacht, edited by August Wilhelm and Friedrich von Schlegel. First printed in *Athenaeum* 3, no. 2 (1800): 188–204. Subsequent edition in *Schriften. Die Werke Friedrich von Hardenbergs. Nach den Handschriften ergänzte, erweiterte und verbesserte Auflage*. Edited by Paul Kluckhohn and Richard Samuel. vol. 1: *Das dichterische Werk*. 3rd ed. 1977. Stuttgart: Kohlhammer. Translated as *Hymns to the Night; Spiritual Songs* by George MacDonald. 1992.

Bibliography

Davis, William Stephen. " 'Menschwerdung des Menschen': Poetry and Truth in Hardenberg's Hymnen an die Nacht and the Journal of 1797," in *Athenäum, Jahrbuch für Romantik* 4 (1994): 239–59.

Frye, Lawrence O. "Spatial Imagery in Novalis' *Hymnen an die Nacht*," *Deutsche Vierteljahrsschrift für Literaturwissenschaft und Geistesgeschichte* 41 (1967): 568–91.

Pfaff, Peter. "Geschichte und Dichtung in den *Hymnen an die Nacht* des Novalis," in *Text und Kontext* 8 (1980): 88–106.

Timm, Hermann. *Die heilige Revolution. Das religiöse Totalitätskonzept der Frühromantik. Schleiermacher—Novalis—Friedrich Schlegel*. Frankfurt: Syndikat, 1978.

Uerlings, Herbert. *Friedrich von Hardenberg, Genannt Novalis. Werk und Forschung*. Stuttgart: Metzler, 1991. 277–320.

HYPERION ODER DER EREMIT IN GRIECHENLAND (HYPERION, OR THE HERMIT IN GREECE) 1797, 1799

Novel by Johann Christian Friedrich Hölderlin

Friedrich Hölderlin's only novel was published in two volumes in 1797 and 1799. A second edition came out in 1822, and an important fragment from an earlier version appeared in Johann Christoph Friedrich Schiller's magazine *Neue Thalia* in 1794. What little recognition Hölderlin had in his lifetime rested largely on *Hyperion*. (The cabinetmaker who took him into his household and cared for him during the second half of his life had read and admired it.) In the seven years or so he spent working on it, the book went through many versions, including a metrical one, but in its final form it is a novel in letters, like Johann Wolfgang Goethe's *Die Leiden des Lungen Werther* (*The Sorrows of Young Werther*) in that the correspondence is all in one direction. Hyperion, a young Greek, recounts his life to a German friend, Bellarmin. Progressing in his story, Hyperion registers its effects on himself as he tells it, so that the letters braid together two sometimes indistinguishable strands: one narrative, one reflective and critical.

An early reviewer called the book a "lyric poem," and this uncertainty about its genre persists. The language is never merely descriptive, nor does it ever simply roll the story onwards. It sustains a level of intensity that derives from experience refracted through the mind of a narrator who is still deeply affected by what he relates. The model of the recollecting mind Hölderlin's complex narrative provides is similar to William Wordsworth's account in the preface to the 1800 *Lyrical Ballads*, in which "the emotion is contemplated till by a species of reaction [. . .] tranquillity gradually disappears, and an emotion, similar to that which was before the subject of contemplation, is gradually produced, and does itself actually exist in the mind." Only since *Hyperion* is a piece of narrative prose, with a development that includes a process of learning, toward the end Hyperion arrives at a kind of tranquillity that survives the dangerous confrontation with emotion through the recognition of a pattern to his life and to life as a whole.

The novel is set in Greece around 1770, when the Greeks joined the Russians in an unsuccessful uprising against the rule of the Turks. These events are so presented that they can be read as a loose allegory of the French Revolution, and Hyperion takes part in the rebellion in volume two in an attempt to win "space on earth" for the "new Church," the "theocracy of beauty" which he has begun to realize in his private life and wants to embody in a republic worthy of Pericles's Athens. This is part of what Hyperion, at Bellarmin's request, begins to relate in the novel's third letter. He has just returned from Germany in a depressed state, with regrets and the desire to withdraw as what the subtitle styles a "hermit," first on the Isthmus of Corinth and later on the island of Salamis. These places, together with the other Greek localities rendered in detail throughout (Hölderlin made good use of travel accounts), have a similar effect on him to his memories and are, in fact, with their ruins and half-buried statuary, a kind of memory of ancient Greece. They both soothe and exacerbate, inspire and condemn.

The memories themselves are constructed around encounters of rising intensity with three figures, and each encounter, as also with certain landscapes, has an erotic quality. The first is Adamas, an older man who instructs Hyperion in his heritage and tours the Classical sites with him, instilling a longing for the regeneration of his country. In Alabanda he meets someone who is more of an equal and with whom such regeneration seems possible, but they part bitterly when it turns out that Alabanda belongs to a secret society that aims to bring change through terror and violence. The third figure is Diotima, in whom Hyperion sees the embodiment of the ideal, a manifestation of the absolute in the world. She is the confirmation that all his longings and hopes can be satisfied: "It was there, the Absolute, in this sphere of human nature and things it was there. I no longer ask where it is; it was in the world, it can return." But it is also

Diotima who urges him to realize the fulfilment and unity they have achieved together in a wider sphere, to become a "teacher of our people," and the second volume deals with Hyperion's attempts to follow this injunction. The participation in the uprising, for which Hyperion rejoins forces with Alabanda, is, for Hyperion, a wrong course, and it ends not just in failure but brings on Diotima's fading and death when Hyperion in his disappointment decides to renounce her and die in battle. The true course is then the one represented by the letters themselves, which realize Hyperion's transition from hermit-like withdrawal and resignation to engagement with the world as a writer. Like Wordsworth's *Prelude*, the last letter takes us to the point immediately preceding the writing of the first letter, in a kind of circularity which is a spiral rather than a closed ring.

This structure perfectly articulates the novel's preoccupations, which are largely philosophical and were taken up later by G. W. F. Hegel. *Hyperion* identifies and embodies a principle of "opening and closing," of "issue and return," and it is Hyperion's recognition of this pattern that allows him to recover his life and look back on the loss and pain of it as necessary for its moments of fulfilment. "It is in the course of change that we represent perfection," Diotima says. The relating of literary and philosophical concerns, specifically touched on in the novel's preface and in a discussion in the last letter of the first volume, brings Hölderlin close to other Romantics such as Friedrich von Schlegel and Novalis. The problem of division the novel confronts is both accepted as an enabling power and momentarily overcome in the form itself. Hölderlin's intention was that this process should be reduplicated in the reader.

CHARLIE LOUTH

Work

Hyperion oder Der Eremit in Griechenland. Vol. 1, 1797; vol. 2, 1799; republished in one volume, 1822. Translated as *Hyperion, or The Hermit in Greece* by Willard R. Trask. New York and London: Signet, 1965.

Bibliography

Abrams, M. H. *Natural Supernaturalism: Tradition and Revolution in Romantic Literature*. New York: W. W. Norton, 1971.
Constantine, David. *Hölderlin*. Oxford: Oxford University Press, 1988.
Gaskill, Howard. *Hölderlin's Hyperion*. Durham: University of Durham, 1984.
Hamlin, Cyrus. "The Poetics of Self-Consciousness in European Romanticism: Hölderlin's *Hyperion* and Wordsworth's *Prelude*," *Genre* 6 (1973): 142–77.
Ryan, Lawrence. "Hölderlins *Hyperion*: Ein 'romantischer' Roman?" In *Über Hölderlin*. Edited by Jochen Schmidt. Frankfurt: Insel, 1970.
———. *Hölderlins "Hyperion": Exzentrische Bahn und Dichterberuf*. Stuttgart: Metzler, 1965.

See also **Alfieri, Vittorio; art and Medievalism; Foscolo, Ugo; Greece: Cultural and Historical Survey; Literature; Nationalism; Orientalism: Literature and Scholarsip;**

I

IMAGE AND METAPHOR

Jerome J. McGann's intellectually courageous attempt to anthologize *The New Oxford Book of Romantic Period Verse* capaciously and chronologically in 1993 so that it presented complicated, interwoven, and often contradictory strands of Romantic verse began by evoking the extreme critical difficulty of summarizing the shifting forms of Romanticism's "figures of imaginative desire." John Keats's "Ode on a Grecian Urn" may offer powerfully versed yet figurally elusive articulations for strange modes of longing circulating through the verse of the era. If McGann's suggestion that Romantic period images and metaphors may be forged "under the sign of longing" for beauty, truth, the sublime, the artificial, the natural, the liberatory, the just, the regional, the oriental, the demotic, the exotic, the gendered, the unsexed, the earthy ordinary, or the strange and fantastic shapes of lost or alternative worlds, then an important key for unlocking the emotive power and intellectual logic of imagery and metaphors during the Romantic era might well be on offer.

Keats's "On First Looking into Chapman's Homer" (1816) powerfully renews the classic trope of the book as world and reinvigorates the Petrarchan or Miltonic sonnet. Its stunningly memorable last line ("Silent, upon a peak in Darien") offers an arresting image or visual figure of imaginative desire that stands emblematic of the power and logic of Romantic figuration. Keats elaborates in the octave of the sonnet the conceit of reading poetic tales as voyaging in "the realms of gold" until he hearkens unto the "loud and bold" speech of Chapman's "deep-brow'd Homer," opening a new world of articulate discovery. Keats's articulation of the felt emotive power of this moment of discovery in the sestet shifts abruptly the ground of the initial conceit onto a silent reading of skies, not books, for a hint of further worlds seen by telescopists or Spanish conquistadors. Reading poetry becomes a metaphor of imaginative longing, not for tales of old, but unknown, unseen, and highly elusive realms opened by "wild surmise." The Keatsian voyager longs for the unseen and longs to be elevated, stunned, brought up short, and paradoxically rendered or figured speechless in the quest for his de-

sire. That grammatically disjunctive yet emotively elevated figure upon which Keats's sonnet concludes renders a terse, powerful, exotic image of Romantic desire—an image of longing without a constant object, turning from the bounded worlds of classical figures and forms toward the unprecedented.

Even a Romantic era poet strongly wedded to Augustan age poetic forms and discursive strategies such as Lord Byron often reveals this tendency in figuration and imagery in his longer versifications. For instance, in stanzas 37 to 39 of *Don Juan*'s canto 13 (1823), Byron notoriously calls attention to his self-conscious delight in refiguration once a prior figure has been overextended: "I'll have another figure in a trice." A frozen bottle of champagne will still harbor "a liquid glassful" of "that immortal rain" at its center, "hidden nectar under a cold presence" available in its delightfully concentrated strength to the drinker "past all price." Byron beautifully elaborates this figure much in keeping with the discursive practices of neoclassical and Augustan conceits, but he overextends the image of the frozen bottle of champagne to become "a North-West Passage / Unto the glowing India of the soul" in the third stanza. A clever yet neoclassical image of "immortal" pleasure becomes abruptly and unexpectedly an extended, elusive figure of imaginative desire linking up with "Parry's efforts" to find and open the frozen northern Pole as a shorter route to the goods of "glowing India." Byron projects his well-wrought figure into new territory and desires until its own abrupt loss in the thought that "if the Pole's not open, but all frost, / (A chance still) tis a voyage or vessel lost." Byron's halted voyager is less sublime than Keats's or than Wordsworth's stunned listener in "The Solitary Reaper" (1807), but the approach to imagery and figuration is significantly similar. Byron's wild surmise pushes his figural choice "beyond all price" into a powerful, exotic image of longing without a constant object. Like Keats, Byron turns from the bounded worlds of Augustan figures toward unexplored territories of desire.

This approach to Romantic uses of image and metaphor captures an insistent pattern of Romantic era discourse on figural language. Contemporaneous writers and philosophers who wrote on image and metaphor often articulate postneoclassical conceptions of literary figuration that involve the transgression of classical models, forms, figures, and habits of imaginative invention. However, this discourse on imagery and metaphor neither conforms to the "high Romantic argument" of an imaginative desire for transcendence, especially self-conscious transcendence of nature, that forms the backbone of M. H. Abrams's, Harold Bloom's, Geoffrey Hartman's, and Thomas Weiskel's readings of Romanticism, nor parrots the "New Romantic Historicism" that trivializes the motives of Romantic era verse as simply so many figurative displacements of debates regarding patriotism and rebellion (Linda Colley, Kelvin Everest, Murray Pittock, etc.). Keats's metaphor of autumn's "Conspiring" with a "Close bosom-friend," "the maturing sun," in his last ode "To Autumn" (1820), for instance, should not be read merely as a figure for Peterloo Massacre–era political conspiracy, as Nick Roe does in the epilogue to *John Keats and the Culture of Dissent* (1997). The metaphor of a mutual conspiracy between the natural power of the sun, personified as male, and the earthly labors of the "Season of mists and mellow fruitfulness," personified as an indulgent farm worker and articulated in the imagery of the ode as neither male nor female but indifferently androgynous, embodies a mood of richness, ripeness, and relaxation from the torments of bodily desire ("Where are the songs of Spring?"). Neither transcendence nor displacement is figured forth. There is, nevertheless, an emotively powerful figure of imaginative desire "sitting careless on [the] granary floor" of the ode's conspiratorial personifications—namely, an unsexed, vaguely androgynous image of human contentment as the embodied center of natural rhythms, songs, and breathings. The imagery of "To Autumn" conspires to body forth a figure of imaginative contentment that exceeds gendered constancy and transgresses human sexual delimitation and self-division.

Novalis's famous fragment 481 from *Studies in the Visual Arts* (1798) encapsulates this sense of Romantic era imagery: "Everything Visible cleaves to the Invisible—the Audible to the Inaudible—the Palpable to the Impalpable. Perhaps the Thinkable to the Unthinkable—The *telescope* is an *artificial, invisible organ*." The emotive power and intellectual logic of imagery is articulated as a set of sensual and rational contradictions. Romantic figuration "cleaves to" or desires inconstant, ineffable objects; it watches pacific skies, imagines arctic passages, or personifies autumnal ripeness more as ends in themselves than as allegories or emblems of intended significations or hypothecated values. Novalis's telescope becomes a metaphor of seeing and feeling differently. It is a machined instrument for studying the visible and palpable at the edges of the known world, but becomes also an extension of human powers of sensation and cognition. It probes unknown and unprecedented realms within and through itself. Transgression and contradiction carry meaning in this metaphor: a visual image of seeing intimates sense beyond embodied perception (See also Caraher).

Such a perspective on imagery and figuration may be seen in Immanuel Kant, whose writings on aesthetics, taste, judgment, and the fine arts often reflect residual neoclassical concern for standards and norms rather than the aesthetics of transgression and contradiction typically found in Novalis, Friedrich von Schlegel, Karl Solger, and Ludwig Tieck. When Kant theorizes the "ideal of beauty" in the famous seventeenth section of "Ana-

lytic of the Beautiful" of his *Critique of Judgment* (1790) he offers "a psychological explanation" for the way in which "the imagination" can produce a gestalt-like image of "the stature of a beautiful man" through the concatenation of "a great number of images (perhaps the whole thousand) [that] fall on one another." For Kant this dynamic mental process embodies how we settle upon norms or functional images of human beauty from culture to culture, whether we live under the "empirical conditions" of "a Negro," "a white man, a Chinaman" or "a European." However, Kant's ideal of beauty "floats among all the variously different intuitions of individuals, which nature takes as archetype in her productions of the same species, but which appears not to be fully reached in an individual case." Such an ideal is intimated in the figure of Polycletus's *Spearbearer*, but ineffably escapes containment in such a consummate object of attention. The archetypal form of beauty is intimated as some unknown, uncharted, genetic code of the species. We may construct images of the stature of beautiful beings, but for Kant the ideal form of our figures of imaginative desire ineffably escape us into a mode of natural production swimming beyond our ken. So it is with Kant on the sublime in the twenty-fifth section of the *Critique*: we produce figures of the absolutely boundless that escape the reckoning of our "telescopes" and "microscopes" and offer tantalizing images and metaphors of the human mental ability of "*surpassing every standard of sense*." Like Byron, the English poet to whom the Prussian thinker is seldom compared, Kant images "a glowing India of the soul," and like Keats, "a wild surmise" beyond absolute reckoning.

Even G. W. F. Hegel's ideal of the beauty of art in *Aesthetics: Lectures on Fine Art* limns this sense of a Romantic power and logic for "figures of imaginative desire." Hegel attends closely to the genres, rhythms, and modes of diction of poetic expression; yet the mode of imagery in Romantic epic, lyric, and drama—especially in the work of Johann Wolfgang von Goethe and Johann Christoph Friedrich von Schiller—arrests his attention. Classical art is characterized for Hegel by the "concrete universal" which embodies the spirit or mind of humankind in the well-contoured, anthropomorphic forms of sculpture, dance, and drama. However, Romantic poetry works to set the spirit "free" of the imagined concretions of word, image, and metaphor toward "the prose of thought." That is to say, Hegel theorizes Romantic figuration striving to free beauty from the constraints of anthropomorphic imagery and set it on the road toward philosophy. Romantic images cancel or negate their "concrete" sensuousness in the pursuit of an ideal of beauty that ineffably lies beyond them.

Later critical commentaries on the nature of the Romantic image, such as W. H. Auden's *The Enchafed Flood*, Frank Kermode's *Romantic Image*, and William K. Wimsatt Jr.'s *The Verbal Icon*, tend to neglect Hegel's pointed transgression of the "concrete universal," in his characterization of Romantic figuration, in the interests of restituting some version of it as the model for understanding Romantic era poetic images. Curiously enough, Samuel Taylor Coleridge's opportunistic definitions of "the imagination" and "a poem" in the thirteenth and fourteenth chapters of *Biographia Literaria* (1817) tend to provide the impetus. Coleridge's notion of the "secondary imagination" broadly characterizes the inventive power of the poetic image maker who "dissolves, diffuses, dissipates in order to recreate" or "struggles to idealize and to unify" materials which the "primary imagination," "the living power and prime agent of all human perception," provides. By implication images are sensuous particulars remade to form a new unity, one echoing "the eternal act of creation" informing our human form. The "poem" for Coleridge accordingly emphasizes the organic unity of such imagined particulars, "which mutually support and explain each other," and which bear the diffusing and unifying power of the poet's imaginative force. The notion of the image and metaphoric figuration recede into the background; the "esemplastic" power of the imagination and the construction of the poem as unified "symbol" become dominant—so dominant that Thomas Carlyle in *Sartor Resartus* (1831) and Ralph Waldo Emerson in "Circles" (1840) and "The Poet" (1843) hypothesize the symbol and symbolism as the hallmarks of the Romantic imagination, rather than examine the Romantic turn in figuration noted largely by earlier German writers.

However, Coleridge's poetic practice often subverts, even countermands, his attempts at theory and poetics. *Kubla Khan* (1816) is a fragmentary poem and, despite its various doublings and repetitions, struggles to sustain its powerfully evocative opening image of Xanadu's "pleasure-dome." It is an image built upon a "deep romantic chasm" that subverts even as it is being evoked. The rhetoric and imagery of the poem's first thirty lines oscillate precariously between constructing an Oriental garden of sunny, earthly delights and a Gothic nightscape of moaning subterranean earth and unholy hauntings ("woman wailing for her demon-lover"). Coleridge articulates "a miracle of rare device," a figure of imaginative desire, founded and foundering on its own contradictions. The "pleasure-dome" exists as a bold figure of poetic image-making, as a metaphor of Coleridge's "secondary imagination," and only can be kept aloft as long as the poet feeds "on honey-dew" and imbibes "the milk of Paradise." John Livingston Lowes's wild fantasia on archival materials and sources in *The Road to Xanadu* never serves to mask the fact that "the sleeping images" which invite the critic to speculate on the poet's mental states and the strange byways of "imagination" ultimately do not unify—that is, they intimate an ineffable figure of imaginative desire, the exotic lost dreamworld of Coleridge.

Mary Tighe images forth a comparable "stately pleasure-dome" in "the splendid dome" or the Palace of Love that Psyche enters in search of her sleeping male beloved. Tighe's *Psyche* (1805) recycles the classical tale of Cupid and Psyche, channeled through Spenserian pastoralism and prosody, but resisting circumscription within neoclassical protocols for image and metaphor. Like Coleridge, Tighe devises an image of rare device to bring Psyche's wanderings toward an exotic abode of heightened pleasure. Love's "splendid dome" in canto 2 of *Psyche* appears to be both the sleeping chamber of the god and suggestively the sleeping head of the desiring heroine. Psyche "hangs enamoured

o-er the Deity" until she drops her "fatal lamp" and startles love or the dream-image of ineffable beauty away. Psyche is another halted traveler brought to the brink of a strange new world only to disclose to readers of Romantic figuration not simply an image of tragic loss, but a distinctively Romantic era image of longing without a constant object.

Romantic era writers did not theorize as much about imagery and metaphor as classical and neoclassical writers. For the former, "imagination" and the "symbol" seemed more worth commentary. However, Romantic era figurative practice often coalesced with the "strange seas of thought" in those philosophers such as Kant, Hegel, and Novalis, who did transgress neoclassical norms for modeling imaginative figuration in the interests of tracking the play of desire seeking unprecedented, uncharted, even contradictory realms.

BRIAN CARAHER

Bibliography

Auden, W. H. *The Enchafed Flood.* Charlottesville: University of Virginia Press, 1950.

Caraher, Brian G. "Metaphor as Contradiction: A Grammar and Epistemology of Poetic Metaphor." *Intimate Conflict: Contradiction in Literary and Philosophical Discourse.* Ed. Brian G. Caraher. Albany: State University of New York Press, 1992. 155–80.

Carlyle, Thomas. *Sartor Resartus: The Life and Opinions of Herr Teufelsdrockh. In Three Books.* London: Chapman and Hall, 1871.

Emerson, Ralph Waldo. "Circles" and "The Poet." In *The Collected Works of Ralph Waldo Emerson.* 5 vols. Cambridge, Mass.: Harvard University Press, 1971.

Hartman, Geoffrey H. *Wordsworth's Poetry, 1787–1814.* New Haven, Conn.: Yale University Press, 1964.

Hegel, G. W. F. *Aesthetics: Lectures on Fine Arts.* 2 vols. Translated by Thomas Malcolm Knox. Oxford: Clarendon Press, 1975.

Kant, Immanuel. *Critique of Judgment.* 2nd ed., rev. Translated by John Henry Bernard. New York: Hafner, 1931.

Kermode, Frank. *Romantic Image.* London: Routledge and Kegan Paul, 1957.

Lowes, John Livingston. *The Road to Xanadu: A Study in the Ways of the Imagination.* Rev. ed. London: Constable, 1930.

McGann, Jerome J. Introduction to *The New Oxford Book of Romantic Period Verse.* Edited by Jerome J. McGann. Oxford: Oxford University Press, 1993.

Novalis. "Studies in the Visual Arts" (1798). In *German Aesthetic and Literary Criticism: The Romantic Ironists and Goethe.* Edited by Kathleen Wheeler. Cambridge: Cambridge University Press, 1984.

Roe, Nicholas. Epilogue to *John Keats and the Culture of Dissent.* Oxford: Oxford University Press, 1997. 230–67.

Wimsatt, William K., Jr. "The Structure of Romantic Nature Imagery." *The Verbal Icon.* Frankfort: University of Kentucky Press, 1954.

IMAGINATION

Although imagination is one of the most important terms in the discourse of Romanticism, there is among Romantic writers no consensus on its precise nature or the extent of its powers. According to Samuel Taylor Coleridge, the "synthetic and magical power" of the poet's imagination "brings the whole soul of man into activity, diffusing a tone and spirit of unity." Novalis calls the productive imagination "the *summum bonum*"; Percy Bysshe Shelley describes it as a gateway into "the invisible nature of man"; and for John Keats, "Imagination and its empyreal reflection is the same as human Life and its spiritual repetition."

Yet Lord Byron describes imagination and invention as "the two commonest of qualities: an Irish peasant with a little whiskey in his head will imagine and invent more than would furnish forth a modern poem"; and Thomas De Quincey draws a close correspondence between imaginative visions and those furnished by opium. These widely differing views, however, take as their locus the Romantic claim that imagination is a fundamentally productive rather than merely reproductive power, the ultimate source of nature, literature, and the self.

One of the earliest, clearly Romantic accounts of the imagination can be found in William Blake's "There is No Natural Religion" (c. 1794, although the plates may have first been etched c. 1788), a series of aphoristic propositions which lead to the claim that "If it were not for the Poetic or Prophetic character, the Philosophic & Experimental would soon be at the ratio of all things. & stand still, unable to do other than repeat the same dull round over again."

This conclusion is developed in the last two pages of the work, which provide contrasting images of reason and imagination. The latter is represented by a roughly sketched, human figure reclining on a mound of earth. Beams of light stream from his head, as if this son were also a sun, soon to rise into the sky. The rising son/sun is accompanied by what at first sight would seem an orthodox assertion that "God becomes as we are, that we may be as he is." The Christian doctrines of incarnation and atonement are, however, here radically revised by the belief that, as Blake writes in his annotations to George Berkeley's *Siris*, "Man is all Imagination God is Man & exists in us & we in him." In other words, the imagination is proof of the identity of God and Man: it allows us (like Jesus) to rise from imaginative death and become (like God) creators of new ideas, things, and even worlds.

In contrast, reason is depicted earlier in the annotations as an aged man, kneeling beneath the overarching branches of a tree. In this claustrophobic space, he bends over to measure a triangle inscribed on the ground. Reason is contained and absorbed by a world that it can divide, classify, sometimes even control, but not fundamentally change. Blind to the ultimate source of his life, the scientist mistakes for objective reality a world created by the imagination.

Blake develops this contrast between reason and imagination in graphic works such as "Glad Day" (1794) and "Newton" (1795), and in mythological characters such as Urizen ("your reason") and Los (the fallen imagination). The imagination emerges as the creator of the entire perceptual world, along with the materials, categories, and forms with which reason works. In religious thought, reason was often aligned with the divine, in part because it contemplates matters (God, immortality, the soul) which exceed temporal experience. For Blake, however, it is the imagination that allows us to glimpse the deepest source of life. As he writes in *A Vision of the Last Judgment* (c. 1809–10), "I assert for My self that I do not behold the Outward Creation & that to me it is hindrance & not Action it is as the Dirt upon my feet No part of Me. What it will be Questiond When the Sun rises do you not see a round Disk of fire somewhat like a Guinea O no no I see an Innumerable company of the Heavenly host crying Holy Holy Holy is the Lord God Almighty I question not my Corporeal or Vegetative eye any more than I would Question a Window concerning a Sight I look thro it & not with it." In passages and images such as these, Blake

inverts views commonly held in the eighteenth and nineteenth centuries, of the relative merits of reason and the imagination. For materialist and empiricist philosophers, reason was the true faculty of knowledge, while the imagination was confined to the re-presentation and association of ideas and images drawn from experience. If not governed by reason, the imagination's ability to associate ideas could be a potent source of error, superstition, and even madness. The mad are those who have, as John Locke argues in *An Essay Concerning Human Understanding* (1690), "by the violence of their imaginations . . . taken their fancies for realities." Emancipation is, therefore, commonly linked with reason rather than imagination. "Sapere aude! 'Have courage to use your own reason!'—that is the motto of enlightenment," writes Immanuel Kant in Beantwortung der Frage: Was ist Aufklärung? (An Answer to the Question: "What is Enlightenment?" 1784).

Despite this valorization of reason, eighteenth-century philosophers analyzed in considerable detail aspects of the mind's creative powers, in particular its capacity to associate ideas. This culminates in David Hume's *Treatise of Human Nature* (1739) and *Enquiry Concerning Human Understanding* (1748), David Hartley's *Observations on Man* (1749), and Alexander Gerard's "An Essay on Genius" (1774). A still more profound creative power was suggested by Berkeley's idealist philosophy, as elaborated in *A Treatise concerning the Principles of Human Knowledge* (1710, 1734); the Third Earl of Shaftesbury's Neoplatonic account of aesthetics in *Characteristics of Men, Manners, Opinions, and Times* (1711); and the transcendental philosophy of Immanuel Kant, developed in his three Critiques: *Kritik der reinen Vernunft* (*Critique of Pure Reason*, 1781; a substantially revised second edition was published in 1787), *Kritik der praktischen Vernunft* (*Critique of Practical Reason*, 1788), and *Kritik der Urtheilskraft* (*Critique of Judgment*, 1790). Of these eighteenth-century developments, the thought of Kant exerted the strongest influence on Romantic accounts of imagination.

In *Critique of Pure Reason*, Kant distinguishes between the productive and the reproductive (or empirical) imagination. Where the latter, working according to the laws of association, calls to mind an earlier perception, the former operates according to principles that are prior to experience, spontaneously synthesizing the manifold of sense impressions into forms that can be recognized by the understanding. Although the freedom of the productive imagination is circumscribed (it is able only to shape the manifold of sense impressions in accordance with the categories of the understanding), it nevertheless, particularly in the first edition of *Critique of Pure Reason*, plays a key role in establishing the preconditions for, and so shaping rather than merely re-presenting, experience. The imagination, writes Kant, is "a blind but indispensable function of the soul, without which we should have no knowledge whatsoever, but of which we are scarcely ever conscious." This remarkable "art concealed within the depths of the human soul" brings into relation sensibility and understanding, the faculty through which "objects are given to us" and the faculty through which "they are thought."

In his *Critique of Judgment*, Kant introduces a third imagination—the aesthetic imagination. This is also a productive rather than merely reproductive power, yet it enjoys a freedom not extended to the productive imagination. It produces objects that, while they must take the form of a "possible intuition" (otherwise they could not be the object of sensuous perception), and to that extent must be in harmony with the laws of the understanding, are not confined to the sensory objects found in nature. The aesthetic imagination is therefore both productive and original. In Kant's words, it is the "originator of arbitrary forms of possible intuitions" and, therefore, "a powerful agent for creating, as it were, a second nature out of the material supplied to it by actual nature."

Kant's account of the productive, mediating, and creative roles of the imagination were developed in German idealism. These ideas also exerted a powerful influence on German Romantics such as Johann Wolfgang von Goethe, Friedrich Hölderlin, Novalis, and Friedrich von Schlegel. Such writers complete the transition, implied by Kant's thought, from an eighteenth-century artistic practice based on imitation and an aesthetic theory preoccupied by questions of taste, to a Romantic aesthetics centred on imagination, genius, originality, and art.

Among English Romantics, Kant directly and profoundly influenced the work of Samuel Taylor Coleridge and Thomas De Quincey, who in turn provided a powerful vehicle for the dissemination of Kantian and post-Kantian ideas in England. Romanticism's most famous definition of the imagination, found in the thirteenth chapter of Coleridge's *Biographia Literaria* (1817), is clearly inflected by (although not able to be reduced to) Kantian and post-Kantian accounts of this faculty. Coleridge's distinction between imagination and fancy parallels Kant's discrimination between productive and reproductive imagination. Fancy, like "the ordinary memory," has no other counters to play with but "fixities and definites": it must "receive all its materials ready made from the law of association." In contrast, the imagination is a truly productive and creative power: "It dissolves, diffuses, dissipates, in order to re-create; or where this process is rendered impossible, yet still, at all events, it struggles to idealize and to unify." Like Kant, Coleridge also divides the productive imagination between an activity that blindly shapes experience and one that coexists "with the conscious will." The former, the primary imagination, is "the living power and prime agent of all human perception." The latter, the secondary imagination, is most clearly seen in the creation of works of art. Drawing on Friedrich Wilhelm Joseph von Schelling, Coleridge claims a remarkable correspondence, certainly not anticipated by Kant, between the varieties of human imagination and God's creative power: the secondary imagination (active in the production of art) is an "echo" of the primary imagination ("the living power and prime agent of all human perception"), which in turn repeats "in the finite mind . . . the eternal act of creation."

Romantic writers did not, of course, require a program in Kantian metaphysics to discover the Romantic imagination. Indeed, to take Kant as a template for Romantic thought on this topic can be misleading. Blake's account of imagination draws on and dramatically transforms elements not of Kant's philosophy, but of nonconformist religious traditions, the work of Jacob Boehme and neoplatonism. It is also shaped by the strength of Blake's reaction against empiricist and associationist accounts of the mind. Or, to take another example, Keats draws on both religious and Platonic traditions when he compares the imagination to "Adam's dream" of Eve, recounted by John Milton in *Paradise Lost* (1667). Adam's dream was coterminous with Eve's creation by God: when Adam awoke, he therefore "found it truth." By the same token, Keats argues that "What the imagina-

tion seizes as Beauty must be truth—whether it existed before or not."

The belief that the individual's imagination is the site of creative powers once thought to belong exclusively to God suggests that culture, perhaps even nature, is contingent. It fosters the belief that the world can be transformed by human imagination *and*, as a perhaps inevitable counterpart of the first, an awareness of the distance between the ideal world of the imagination and the real. The former is the keynote of Percy Bysshe Shelley's *A Defence of Poetry* (1822), although its rhetoric relies on the latter. As Shelley writes, "All things exist as they are perceived; at least in relation to the percipient. 'The mind is its own place, and of itself can make a Heaven of Hell, a Hell of Heaven.' But poetry defeats the curse which binds us to be subjected to the accident of surrounding impressions . . . It creates anew the universe."

The contingent nature of the external world, and its distance from the universe of the imagination, are prominent themes of the German *Frühromantik* (Early Romantics). Schelling strikes a characteristic tone when he writes in his *System des transcendentalen Idealismus* (*System of Transcendental Idealism*, 1800),

> Each splendid painting owes, as it were, its genesis to a removal of the invisible barrier dividing the real from the ideal world, and is no more than the gateway, through which come forth complete the shapes and scenes of that world of fantasy that gleams but imperfectly through the real.

This tension between imagined and "real" worlds, present disorder and the promise of future order, allows the Romantic subject-in-process to appear. Moreover, the aim of Schelling's philosophy, like the poetry of Novalis, is to bring internal and external worlds into relation by uncovering their common source in the productive imagination.

The faculty that opens us to desired worlds *and* reveals our innermost nature also connects us to human others, through mimesis and sympathy. Keats famously declared that the poet has no identity because he is continually imagining himself in the place of "some other Body." In his *Defence of Poetry* (1821), Shelley associates imagination with "love; or a going out of our own nature, and an identification of ourselves with the beautiful which exists in thought, action, or person, not our own." The imagination is also a unifying power that enables the poet, Wordsworth claims in the preface to his *Lyrical Ballads* (1802), to bind "together by passion and knowledge the vast empire of human society, as it is spread over the whole earth, and over all time." It plays a similar role within the individual, where its "synthetic and magical power" brings the faculties into harmony with each other.

The imagination is the cornerstone of Romantic ideas concerning health, education, and even morality and philosophy. Many of the most important Romantic poems, such as Coleridge's "The Rime of the Ancient Mariner" (1798) and Wordsworth's *The Prelude* (1805, 1850) are "crisis" poems, in which mental health is regained through a return to the imagination. Reversing the relations of traditional pedagogy, Wordsworth declares that "The Child is father of the Man": rather than being tutored by age, education involves the gradual unfolding of the child's imaginative potential. And morality becomes in the hands of the Romantics a matter of "life" rather than precepts. Novalis, for example, defines "Moral feeling" as "the feeling of absolutely *creative* power, of productive freedom." Even for the philosopher, "Art is paramount" because, as Schelling contends, "it opens to him, as it were, the holy of holies," the source of life in the productive imagination.

Most important, ideas about the nature of the imagination strongly influence Romantic literary practices, underwriting, to cite only a few examples: the Romantic valuation of the lyric over the epic; penchant for the fragment and extempore effusion; revision of the natural sublime; and experiments with biography. The Romantic imagination also supports a set of hierarchies (organic/mechanical; genius/talent; poetry/prose; symbol/allegory) and literary values (spontaneity; intensity; unity) that exerted a powerful influence on Romantic literary criticism. Rather than being a product of conscious intention, the Romantics believe that literature arises spontaneously from sources deep within the self.

"But what is the Romantic imagination?" one may still be inclined to ask. It is significant that Coleridge's definition of the imagination in the thirteenth chapter of *Biographia Literaria* is often cited as evidence of the Romantic failure to provide more than indirect evidence of this faculty. Coleridge is able to provide no more than a fragment of the comprehensive deduction and definition of the imagination which, he rather disingenuously tells his readers, he has withheld on the advice of a friend, not because it was incorrect, but because it was too long and likely to retard sales.

The Romantic imagination can, of course, be the subject of an only indirect presentation because, as the purported source of the human world, it cannot itself be produced. It is, therefore, always vulnerable to the charge that its visions represent an escape from the real rather than a return to its source. This is Thomas Love Peacock's argument in "The Four Ages of Poetry" (1821), where he claims that the Lake Poets (Coleridge, Robert Southey, and Wordsworth), "remaining studiously ignorant of history, society, and human nature, cultivated the phantasy only at the expence of the memory and the reason." De Quincey develops an analogous, though more equivocal, case in *Confessions of an English Opium Eater* (1821), where the purportedly "vital" powers of imagination are mimed by the "artificial" powers of opium. This debate is repeated in the late twentieth century in the struggle between "innocent" and "suspicious" accounts of the Romantic imagination, represented respectively by the work of M. H. Abrams and Paul De Man.

Traditional accounts of the Romantic imagination often tell a heroic story of the discovery by the Romantics of a previously unrecognized faculty. More recent criticism focuses on the ways in which the Romantic imagination is itself a cultural product, inflected by class, gender, and history. The Romantic imagination has played a key role in some of the most important cultural movements of the nineteenth and twentieth centuries. It remains a key term within the Romantic discourse that still influences Romantic studies, literary criticism, and critical debate in general.

PETER OTTO

Bibliography

Abrams, M. H. *The Mirror and the Lamp: Romantic Theory and the Critical Tradition.* Oxford: Oxford University Press, 1953.

Brann, Eva T. H. *The World of the Imagination: Sum and Substance.* Lanham, Md.: Rowman and Littlefield, 1991.

Cocking, J. M. *Imagination: A Study in the History of Ideas.* London: Routledge, 1991.

De Man, Paul. *The Rhetoric of Romanticism.* New York: Columbia University Press, 1984.

Engell, James. *The Creative Imagination: Enlightenment to Romanticism.* Cambridge, Mass.: Harvard University Press, 1981.

Furst, Lilian R. *Romanticism in Perspective: A Comparative Study of Aspects of the Romantic Movements in England, France and Germany.* London: Macmillan, 1969.

Kearney, Richard. *The Wake of Imagination: Ideas of Creativity in Western Culture.* London: Hutchinson, 1988.

McGann, Jerome J. *The Romantic Ideology: A Critical Investigation.* Chicago: University of Chicago Press, 1983.

Pyle, Forest. *The Ideology of Imagination: Subject and Society in the Discourse of Romanticism.* Stanford, Calif.: Stanford University Press, 1995.

Schulte-Sasse, Jochen and Haynes Horne, eds. *Theory as Practice: A Critical Anthology of Early German Romantic Writings.* Minneapolis: University of Minnesota Press, 1997.

Warnock, Mary. *Imagination.* London: Faber and Faber, 1976.

Whale, John C. *Imagination under Pressure, 1789–1832: Aesthetics, Politics, and Utility.* New York: Cambridge University Press, 2000.

IN MEMORIAM A.H.H. 1850

Poem by Alfred, Lord Tennyson

The occasion for Alfred, Lord Tennyson's greatest elegy was the death of his closest friend, Arthur Henry Hallam, who died of a brain aneurysm in Vienna in September 1833. News reached England on September 28, and Tennyson was "prostrated" with grief. He began writing poems to articulate his sorrow in October 1833, and continued doing so throughout the 1830s and 1840s. Some of these poems adopted blank verse or dramatic monologue forms ("Tithonus," "Ulysses") but many were lyrics written in formally distinctive four-line stanzas. Tennyson continued charting the shifting terrain of his bereavement over the course of the next seventeen years, with the working title of *Elegies*.

Whether, or at how early a stage, Tennyson decided that he was writing one long poem rather than a collection of small ones is unclear. The work was finally published in 1850, appearing anonymously, perhaps because the painfully intimate nature of much of the poetry made Tennyson disinclined to reveal himself to a public that had (up to that point) been rather hostile to his verse.

In Memoriam is an arrangement of 133 lyrics (131 sections plus a prologue and an epilogue), some as short as three stanzas long, some as long as thirty-three, all with the same rhyme-scheme (*abba*). The whole thing charts what the first stanza of the first lyric calls the "stepping-stones" of continuing experience, the movement of the mind and spirit out of the blackest depression occasioned by the death of a loved one and toward a state of acceptance and healing. Tennyson himself once discussed the structure of the poem as tripartite, and cited Dante Alighieri, noting, "It was meant to be a kind of *Divina Commedia*, ending with happiness. The sections were written at many different places, and as the phases of our intercourse came to my memory and suggested them. I did not write them with any view to weaving them into a whole, or with any view of publication, until I found that I had written so many. The different moods of sorrow as in a drama are dramatically given, and my conviction that fear, doubts, and suffering will find answer and relief comes from Faith in a God of Love."

It is tempting to read this as a firm statement of structural intent, but very few critics have seen *In Memoriam* as a satisfyingly unified poem. Christopher Ricks is of the opinion that it "evades the proper responsibilities of the long poem," that its mode of operation is "weaving, not growing or building." We need not take this judgment as pejorative: this formal fragmentation effectively expresses the subject. Tennyson may model himself on a unified, Dantean journey through grief, purgatory, and to acceptance; but in place of Dantean epic unity he constellates a restless series of circular, circling lyric moments. In place of the onward thrust of Dante's *terza rima*, Tennyson's *abba* stanzas circle back to their original rhyme, constantly setting out (*ab*) only to return (*ba*). There certainly is an overall drift to the poem, taking it away from the bleakest intensities of Tennyson's first grief and toward a more contemplative state of mind, but few critics have been convinced that the famous statement "it is better to have loved and lost / Than never to have loved at all" carries any conclusive emotional force.

There are several senses in which this is a poem about loss. The primary sense, of course, is the loss of Hallam himself, the death which occasions this elegy. But there is another loss in this poem, a more paradoxical one: the loss of language. This is paradoxical because, of course, the poem exists as language; without language it could not be. But it is a recurring theme of *In Memoriam* that language is insufficient to its task when it comes to articulating the enormity of Tennyson's grief. This inadequacy leads to the state where it is not possible to *say* anything; all that remains is a howl, a cry of grief. This is expressed most famously in the last quatrain of lyric 54:

So runs my dream: but what am I?
An infant crying in the night:
An infant crying for the light:
And with no language but the cry.

This records that Tennyson "cried like a baby" when he heard of Hallam's death; but it also reminds us that the Latin *infans* means "without speech," and postulates grief as a return to the inarticulacy of childhood. This is what Isobel Armstrong calls "the great complexity and incipient collapse of *In Memoriam*, which is called 'a contradiction on the tongue' [lyric 125]."

There in turn reflects another, broader cultural loss recorded in the poem as well: the loss of religious and metaphysical certainty. Tennyson's grief unpicks his religious foundation; the allegorical figure of Sorrow speaks to him of the world as a hollow, godless show; as in lyric 3 we read:

"The stars," she whispers, "blindly run;
A web is woven across the sky;
From out waste places comes a cry,
And murmurs from the dying sun:
"And all the phantom, Nature, stands—
With all the music in her tone,
A hollow echo of my own,—
A hollow form with empty hands."

This can be taken as the more Victorian element of the poem: a repeated worrying at questions of religious faith and doubt, particularly in the light of contemporary scientific discoveries. The pitiful description in lyric 56 of man as deluded in his belief in God, a creature

Who trusted God was love indeed
And love Creation's final law—
Tho' Nature, red in tooth and claw
With ravine, shrieked against his creed

is ultimately contradicted by the poem's conclusion, but tends to stay with the reader. Similarly, the pious invocation of God at beginning and end is undercut by the sensuality with which the poet recalls the dead love object, his "dearest" who "can be clasped no more" and whose loss has left him "widowed." Ultimately, the poem's attempts to step past a Byronic fascination with the moral hollowness of the universe and a Keatsian sensuality into a more severe Victorian space do not carry through, and *In Memoriam* remains a deeply Romantic work.

ADAM ROBERTS

Text

In Memoriam A.H.H. In *Tennyson.* Oxford Authors series. Oxford: Oxford University Press, 2000.

Bibliography

Armstrong, Isobel. *Victorian Poetry: Poetry, Poetics and Politics.* London: Routledge, 1993.

Bloom, Harold. *The Ringers in the Tower: Studies in Romantic Tradition.* Chicago: University of Chicago Press, 1971.

Bradley, A. C. *A Commentary on Tennyson's "In Memoriam."* London: Macmillan, 1901.

Eliot, T. S. "In Memoriam" 1936. In *Selected Prose of T. S. Eliot.* Edited by Frank Kermode. London: Faber, 1987.

Ricks, Christopher. *Tennyson.* 2d ed. London: Macmillan, 1989.

Shaw, Marion, "*In Memoriam* and Popular Religious Poetry," *Victorian Poetry* 15 (1977):1–8.

Sinfield, Alan. *Alfred Tennyson.* Rereading Literature series. Oxford: Blackwell, 1986.

Tennyson, Hallam. *Alfred, Lord Tennyson: A Memoir.* 2 vols. London: 1897.

INCHBALD, ELIZABETH 1753–1821

English actress, playwright, and novelist

Elizabeth Inchbald's reputation now rests mostly on her two novels, but in her day she was known as an accomplished, if never quite triumphant, actress, and, primarily, as the author of many highly successful comedies.

Her ambition to become an actress manifested itself very early, despite the fact that she had a stutter. Born into a Catholic farming family in Suffolk, Elizabeth Simpson was only sixteen years old when she began to pester the manager of Norwich's patent theater for a part. Her brother became an actor in the Bury Saint Edmunds Theatre Royal; disappointed in her own thespian strivings, she ran away to London in April 1772. Like so many of the would-be stars that today arrive in Hollywood, she was then unable to find work and became prey to various theatrical managers and hangers-on who were attracted by her youth and beauty. It seems likely that she married Joseph Inchbald, whom she had met on her one previous visit to London, in order to secure her freedom from this unwanted attention. Inchbald, also a Catholic, was twice the age of his nineteen-year-old wife, and already an established actor. He provided Elizabeth with the entrée to the theater that she craved, and in September 1772, three months after her wedding, she made her professional debut in Bristol as Cordelia opposite his Lear.

Touring the provinces was still regarded as the standard route to gaining a successful career on the London stage, and Inchbald and her husband played several seasons in Scotland, and then in Liverpool and Canterbury, before taking work in 1777 with the most important provincial company, run by Tate Wilkinson in Yorkshire. It was during this time that Inchbald met and became friendly with Sarah Siddons and her brother John Philip Kemble. They too were Catholics, and Kemble in particular was to remain close to Inchbald throughout her life. Joseph Inchbald died suddenly in June 1779, and although Wilkinson invited Inchbald to stay on with him, she was anxious to make her debut in London. She did this in October 1780 in Thomas Harris's company, and she continued to alternate between winter seasons with him at Covent Garden and summer seasons with George Colman's company at the Little Theatre, Haymarket. She played mostly secondary roles, except when she returned to the provinces.

Both Harris and Colman rejected her first attempts at writing drama, but *The Mogul Tale* was accepted for the Little Theatre in 1784. It was successfully performed that summer with Inchbald herself in the cast. In her second play, *I'll Tell You What* (1785), Inchbald did not take a part, and as her plays became more successful she phased out her acting, taking her final role in 1789. She wrote twenty-one plays between 1784 and 1805. Eleven were original, and the rest were free adaptations from French texts. Almost all were rather conventional comedies, revolving around mistaken identities and prolonged misunderstandings, and populated by traditional "type" characters such as Lord Rakeland, Mr. Placid, or Sir George Splendourville. Yet the plays benefit from fresh and sprightly dialogue, and they are sometimes interesting for their political alignment. Disparities of wealth and the dangers of prejudice and tyranny are presented, and the plays generally manifest Romantic, humanitarian, liberal principles, very much like those of August Ferdinand Friedrich von Kotzebue, several of whose plays Inchbald translated via the French. (Perhaps her most famous drama was *Lover's Vows*, from Kotzebue's *Das Kind der Liebe*, which appears in Jane Austen's *Mansfield Park*.) Inchbald attempted one tragedy, *The Massacre* (1792). As it was ostensibly set in sixteenth-century France but clearly dealing with the developing French Revolution, Inchbald suppressed the work just as it was going to press. It has generally been thought that this was because she felt it too radical for the political climate then prevailing. In fact, even the most wary anti-Jacobin would have found little amiss in a play which displayed no obvious Jacobin sympathies and simply condemns bigotry and violence.

Inchbald's novels have also sometimes been considered Jacobin works. Certainly she was on close terms with leading literary radicals in London in the early 1790s. She counted William Godwin and Thomas Holcroft among her friends, both of whom commented on drafts of her *Simple Story* (and both of whom proposed marriage to her). She also knew Amelia Opie, Mary Robinson, and Mary Wollstonecraft (who called her "Mrs. Perfection"). Yet, *A Simple Story* is not really a political novel, nor has its continuing popularity been based on its claim to be the first English Catholic novel. Rather, the novel is successful because of the way in which Inchbald allows the reader to gain insight into the developing psychological state of her characters through their interaction and conversation with others. As well as being stylistically elegant, *A Simple Story* is unique in its format, the final two volumes picking up the story of the first part of the novel seventeen years later. This may have resulted from Inchbald joining together two different narratives. The version rejected for publication in 1777 probably consisted only of the first half of the novel she reworked for its eventual publication in 1791.

Inchbald's second novel, *Nature and Art* (1796), was more overtly ideological. It tells the story of two brothers and their two sons. While one son receives the worldly education which he can use to rise through the ranks of the judiciary, the other grows up in Africa, virtually a "noble savage." When he returns to Britain, he cannot help but expose the hypocrisy of society by comparing the pure, natural environment he has come from with Britain's corrupt institutions. Around this, Inchbald wove a plot that rammed the point home: corruption must lead to unhappiness. Clearly the novel owed much to the ideas of Godwin and to Jean-Jacques Rousseau's *Émile*.

In her later life Inchbald's reputation as a dramatist was such that she was invited to edit and introduce several substantial anthologies of plays and to become a critic for the fledgling *Quarterly Review* (she declined). She was one of the most successful women writers of the age, earning as much as £900 for a single play. Investing wisely and living economically, she was able to retire from writing with an ample annual income and to leave £5,000 to her heirs. Her work guaranteed her the independence which she had coveted from her youth and jealously maintained throughout her adult life.

M. O. GRENBY

Biography

Born Elizabeth Simpson in Standingfield (now Stanningfield), Suffolk on October 15, 1753, one of nine children of John and Mary (née Rushbrook) Simpson, owners of a moderate farm. No formal education outside the home; unsuccessfully sought employment at theaters in Norwich and Bury Saint Edmunds, 1769–72; ran away to London, April 1772, and sought employment as an actress; married Joseph Inchbald, June 1772, and immediately secured her first professional role in Bristol; toured Scotland as part of Thomas Digges's company, 1772–76; in France, July and August 1776; acted in Liverpool and Canterbury from October 1776, and with Tate Wilkinson's company in Yorkshire from October 1777; death of Joseph Inchbald, June 1779; debut on London stage, October 1780, and continued acting in London and the provinces until 1789; permanently living in London from 1783; her first play performed July 1784 and published 1786; eighteen further plays performed and published, 1784–1805; *A Simple Story* published 1791; *The Massacre* suppressed, 1792; *Nature and Art* published 1796; wrote prefaces to 125 plays in *The British Theatre* series, 1806–9; selected the plays to be included in *Modern Theatre* and *Collection of Farces and Afterpieces*, 1809. Died August 1, 1821.

Selected Works

The Mogul Tale. Performed 1784, published 1786.
I'll Tell You What. Performed 1785, published 1786.
The Widow's Vow. 1786.
Such Things Are. Performed 1787, published 1788.
The Child of Nature. 1788.
The Married Man. 1789.
Next Door Neighbours. 1791.
A Simple Story. 1791.
The Massacre. Written 1792, published 1833 in James Boaden, *Memoirs of Mrs. Inchbald.*
Everyone Has His Fault. 1793.
The Wedding Day. 1794.
Nature and Art. 1796.
Wives as They Were, and Maids as They Are. 1797.
Lovers' Vows. 1798.
The Wise Men of the East. 1799.
To Marry or Not to Marry. 1805.
Prefaces to *The British Theatre*. 25 vols. 1806–9.

Bibliography

Boaden, James, ed. *Memoirs of Mrs. Inchbald: including her Familiar Correspondence with the most distinguished persons of her time. To which are added The Massacre, and A Case of Conscience; now first published from her autograph copies.* London: Richard Bentley, 1833.

Joughin, G. Louis. *An Inchbald Bibliography.* Reprinted from *The University of Texas Studies in English* 14 (1934).

Kelly, Gary. *The English Jacobin Novel 1780–1805.* Oxford: Clarendon Press, 1976.

Littlewood, S. R. *Elizabeth Inchbald and Her Circle: The Life Story of a Charming Woman (1753–1821).* London: Daniel O'Conner, 1921.

Manvell, Roger. *Elizabeth Inchbald: England's Principal Woman Dramatist and Independent Woman of Letters in Eighteenth Century London. A Biographical Study.* Lanham, Md.: University Press of America, 1987.

INDIVIDUALISM

The first use of an equivalent term to *individualism* in any European language was probably by French opponents of the ideology of individuality, being appropriated from 1815 onward by those on the left and the right as a term of abuse. *Individualisme* has still, in fact, a predominantly pejorative implication in French today. This is witness to the fact that, despite the positive connotations in twentieth-century English-speaking culture of the concepts reified by individualism ("the individual" and "individuality" as personal uniqueness realized within society), the prickliness of the Romantic period's philosophical grounding of these concepts has since been lost. In order to construct a system of individualism that contained the positive connotations of individuality without destroying community or order, and despite the common assumption that Romanticism raised the individual genius to a new status, this conceptual grounding is often characterized by defensive paradox, or else by optimistic but highly abstracted and unstable dialectic.

Twentieth-century observers have usually distinguished Romantic individualism from the emphasis on self-reliance and equality of opportunity to be found in eighteenth-century bourgeois economic and social thinking. The shift can be understood either as a modification, an attempt by the Romantics to render dry and unlovely economic individualism expressive and attractive; or it can be seen as a more radical break, a new philosophy that grew up in opposition to the dehumanizing effects of economic and utilitarian rationalism. But the eighteenth-century legacy, even if it resulted in an ideology where individuals are responsible for their own ends in society, was never quite as simple as that. The kind of thinking, especially in Britain, for which Bernard de Mandeville laid the groundwork and which Adam Smith theorized systematically—that if every individual maximizes their own economic utility it will have a largely beneficial economic and social effect for any nation—is problematized when one puts *The Wealth of Nations* (1776) alongside Smith's other works, particularly the *Theory of Moral Sentiments* (1763). In his moral philosophy, the individual is postulated on real and imagined reciprocal observation of his activity, particularly by reference to the "impartial spectator," an imagined figure that judges the actions of each individuals and, by giving each individual an objective yardstick, defines that individual's subjectivity. This construction gives an intimation of the later complex dialectical construction of the subject. Other constructions of the individual in the British empiricist traditions are similarly unstable; for example, David Hume's famous comparison of consciousness to a theater in which different images come and go (*A Treatise of Human Nature*, 1739–40), or David Hartley's psychology of association and materialist vibration in *Observations on Man* (1749). The French Enlightenment similarly theorized and looked forward to the economic and social emancipation of self-reliant individuals in a meritocratic society; yet when it reached more searching expression in the works of Jean-Jacques Rousseau, the individuated subject as manifested by systematic revelation of consciousness is dependent on others for definition and is caught in a diabolic, cyclical action of suspicion and recrimination, as it so often is in *The Confessions* (1782). The division and choice between being "all for oneself, or all for others," as he says in *Emile, or Of Education* (1762), is a contradiction that cannot so easily be resolved, despite the attempts of the political economists.

Such a contradiction was carried into the French Revolution as tension between its bourgeois proponents and its more radical tendencies. The first wished simply to do away with aristocratic privileges and increase the suffrage so that the individual could better participate in a more reasonable society. But its more radical tendencies required of the citizen total submission to the general will by a total disclosure of "private" affairs to the public gaze, to the extent that the self-reliant individual is dissipated into the public arena and the public good; Maximilien de Robespierre was the statesman who best exemplifies this Rousseauesque condition.

The revolutionary and Napoleonic conquests of 1795–1814, no matter how far they strayed from some of the principles of the French Revolution in the imperial phase, did temporarily sweep away the old aristocratic privileges, giving certain groups a taste of economic self-determination and legal equality in Italy, Germany, and Spain. The republican and Napoleonic victories up until 1815 did have the effect of spreading legal reform so that individuals in Italy and Germany got a taste of equality before the law. In Restoration France, the term *individuality* was used derisively by the reactionary "ultra" royalists to refer to a dangerous, antisocial tendency that would lead to the destruction of stable ties in traditional communities. French liberal thought, as in Henri-Benjamin Constant de Robecque and Alexis de Tocqueville, saw the affirmation of individuality as a dangerous retreat into a private world away from the public sphere, and the Utopian socialist Pierre-Joseph Proudhon saw individuality as something threatened by the power of capital, but that could be affirmed in any significant sense only after collective action had destroyed capitalism's construal of individualism.

In Britain, the reaction in the 1790s was led by Edmund Burke, who expounded in a series of pamphlets his view of society as a system of natural deference to authority according to each person's predefined place in that society, rather than as a contract or series of contracts between citizens who participate in these agreements in their particular and complex ways. After the bliss of the revolution had lost its luster, Romantics in Britain increasingly associated economic and democratic individualism with the worst ills of the modern world; Samual Taylor Coleridge and William Wordsworth stressed the importance of the traditional structures of rural communities in fostering the emancipated subject in their earlier writing, but slid into a highly reactionary position of supporting traditional hierarchies while extolling the virtues of the individual genius in the poetic, but not the civic, realm. In Britain this was a way of supplementing the harsher aspects of the dominant Utilitarianism and Contractarianism with a softer, personal space in which authentic individuality could be fulfilled. Liberal political writers such as John Stuart Mill responded to the romantic desire for individual subjectivity by constructing systems that attempted to reconcile the demands of increasingly complex society and economic production with personal liberty and autonomy.

Meanwhile, Immanuel Kant had been making the transcendental deduction, and it was perhaps in the German lands and the critical tradition that the most important developments in the philosophy and politics of the individual took place. In his *Critique of Pure Reason* (1781) Kant attempted to establish the objectivity of our world without, unlike René Descartes, reference to anything other than one's own subjectivity by claiming that certain categories of knowledge were the necessary forms for knowledge to be possible in any intelligible world. Subjectivity, or the "I"-producing "transcendental unity of apperception" is not an experience (as in empiricism), but instead is *presupposed* by experience. This would theoretically have provided a sound basis for objective knowledge and individual action, and Kant followed this up, at least in the early part of his career, by championing individual freedom in political and religious matters, as against relying on received doctrines, which he saw in typical Enlightenment style as a process of growing up, or as "Man's quitting the nonage." However, the transcendental deduction, in the end, has in its turn to be taken on trust, and our world is not a world of things as entities, but terms standing proxy for the unrealizable idea of perspectiveless knowledge. This unrealizable aspect of Kant's philosophy is borne out in his two later *Critiques*. The *Critique of Practical Reason* (1788) is an attempt to establish a system that will generate immutable moral laws for individual behavior. It starts with the antinomy that, on the one hand, ethics implies choice which implies individual freedom (a statement of individual freedom); and on the other, men are but part of nature and as such are always in "chains of ineluctable necessity." This contradiction is not really resolved by Kant; at times he comes very close to arguing that one has only to *think* of oneself as free in order to *be* free, or at any rate one has to entertain and believe such a fiction in order for any kind of ethical life to be possible. This informs his prescriptions for making categorical imperatives in ethics, by which the individual, who still thinks of himself as free, is to abstract from all personal interest in making moral decisions in order to imagine himself as a universal legislator whose laws would apply in all cases. Although he goes on to say that the freedom of each individual is one principle that such a legislator would uphold, Kant's ethics are founded on an aesthetic of universal order, and in the order of this moral life humanity gets a glimpse of a higher level of being that looks toward the deity to which it is responsible. Kant's final major work, the *Critique of Judgment* (1790), which deals with aesthetics and subjectivity, begins similarly with an antinomy centering around the contradiction of individual uniqueness against universal validity; aesthetic judgments are particular to the taste of each individual, but the fact that we try to justify our judgments to our peers suggests that they should have a general claim on all people. In a work of great complexity and obscurity, even more so than his other writings, Kant attempts to resolve this contradiction, as elsewhere, through slightly uneasy accommodations of individual particularity dissipating into a universal generality. When we hear music, for example, its harmony and unity are perceptions of us because it is our imagination and understanding at play that make such a synthesis; however, the perceptions are not arbitrary, because they are based on a disposition which is common to all rational beings. We get pleasure from contemplation of the form of the beautiful object, which is also the form of the harmonious workings of nature. Sometimes we are confronted with the contradiction in a more acute way, and we glimpse an impersonal, transcendental realm, in the wake of a perception whose *formlessness* overwhelms us into transcending the limits of our own perceptual experience to encounter something absolute, in a judgment that Kant calls "the sublime." As with epistemology and ethics, so with aesthetics; the paradoxes inherent to individualism result in the dissipation of the self's judgment into a premonition of theology; for reasons that were partly political, no doubt, but partly organic to his thought, Kant increasingly accepted the authoritarianism of the Prussian state.

Those following Kant in the critical tradition were unhappy with the uneasy accommodations he so often made, and attempted to formulate a more sophisticated concept of individualism as uniqueness (*Einzigkeit*) in opposition to that of individual self-determination (*Einzelheit*). In *The Limits of State Action* (1792) Wilhelm von Humboldt sees the old state as the main constraint to the fulfillment of individuality. However, he forged out a new way of thinking about society not as a contractual arrangement between individuals with essentially divergent interests but as an organism, building in the good society out of the material of individuals, who are themselves ever expanding toward infinity, to create social and state institutions to embody the Whole. Meanwhile, Friedrich von Schlegel, in a different strand of the idealist tradition, used the concept of irony to mediate between individual interest and the universal or "Absolute." On a more theoretical level, G. W. F. Hegel, in the *Phenomenology of Mind* (1807), based selfhood on a dialectical process of development between nature and mind that would be synthesized into Absolute Being. This kind of thought led in Germany to a particularly strong conjunction of liberalism with nationalism in the 1848 revolutions, because by then liberals there had begun using the term *Individualismus* as a desirable, characteristically German quality that combined particularity and uniqueness with a plausible vision of community.

Such paradoxes were reflected and transformed in the Arts, and during the Romantic period the idea gained ground of the artist as unique individual genius who was at once eccentric to or removed from society *and* the sage critic of it. The rejection or modification of the empiricist model of experience as the basis of knowledge gave a greater prestige to the Imagination, the faculty of the individual psyche that generates knowledge and beauty from within; this enabled art to be formulated, in a way of thinking that still predominates today, as *self-expression*, the revelation of a subjectivity rather than mimetic reproduction. Most obviously this meant that in literature, music, and the visual arts practitioners moved away from the set of classical rules that prescribed form, subject, composition, and harmony of elements. As in the political and philosophical problematics

already surveyed, however, this supposed emphasis on artistic individual expression masked a more complex reality. British Romanticism, as has been said, began to see individualism in the political realm as dangerous and tending to break down traditional social bonds, to which it often looked back nostalgically, even while affirming the individual imagination in the personal and aesthetic realm. The social eccentricity of artistic production thus became the basis of its claims to truth. In the later British Romantics individuality often took an ironic twist, anxieties over individualism leading such as Lord Byron to create ironic heroes like Don Juan, or indeed himself as celebrity and political proponent, as temporarily magnificent, yet comical and absurd, and thus capable of occupying an impossible position. On the continent, where liberals were struggling against the reimposition of the old privileges and systems of government by an unstable conservative coalition led by the Austrian statesman Klemens Wenzel Nepomuk Lothar Metternich, it was perhaps easier to appropriate the figure of the individual artistic genius to the struggles for economic and social liberty, and for national unification in Germany and Italy, but this again relied on the paradox of the artist's individual detachedness from society legitimizing his claims to truth.

If economic and political liberalism was to develop during this period, it required a convincing armory of philosophical and cultural constructions of autonomous individuality that could nevertheless function in society. The great fear of pan-European conservatism, for which the Austrian foreign minister and chancellor was the figurehead, was that such individualism would tear traditional social ties apart. When they began to appropriate individualist strategies into their own ideology, it was the Left, for whom Karl Marx is dominant, that brought out the contradictions inherent in the philosophy of the individual, which nevertheless remain largely concealed in public discourse today.

PETER HOWELL

Bibliography

Bygrave, Stephen. *Romantic Egotism: Coleridge and the Self.* Basingstoke, England: Macmillan, 1986.

Izenberg, Gerald N. *Impossible Individuality: Romanticism, Revolution, and the Origins of Modern Selfhood, 1787–1802.* Princeton, N.J.: Princeton University Press, 1992.

Lukes, Steven. *Individualism.* Oxford: Blackwell, 1973.

Macpherson, C. B. *The Political Theory of Possessive Individualism.* Oxford: Oxford University Press, 1962.

McGann, Jerome J. *The Romantic Ideology: A Critical Investigation.* Chicago: Chicago University Press, 1983.

Porter, Roy, ed. *Rewriting the Self: Histories from the Renaissance to the Present Day.* London: Routledge, 1997.

Simmel, Georg. *The Sociology of Georg Simmel.* Edited by K. H. Wolff. New York: Free Press of Glencoe, 1950.

Taylor, Charles. *Sources of the Self: The Making of Modern Identity.* Cambridge: Cambridge University Press, 1989.

Whale, John. *Imagination Under Pressure, 1789–1832: Aesthetics, Politics, Utility.* Cambridge: Cambridge University Press, 2000.

INDUSTRIAL REVOLUTION

The Romantic era saw a series of economic and technological changes, originally and principally in England, which were later designated by the term *Industrial Revolution*. The first to refer to English industrialization as a "revolution" was the French economist Adolphe Blanqui, in 1827; the concept was based on a parallel between the concurrent British economic and technological revolution and the French political one. Many economic historians have questioned the appropriateness of the term, pointing out that the economic changes were gradual rather than sudden or revolutionary; nevertheless, it is clear that their cumulative effect was great. Before industrialization, a majority of the labor force worked in agriculture. This had ceased to be true in England by 1850, and the rest of Western and Central Europe was following the same trend, as was the northeastern United States.

In order for the Industrial Revolution to begin in late eighteenth-century England, a number of conditions were necessary. The most basic was the existence of natural resources. England was well-supplied with coal and iron. England was also a society with a high degree of aggregate wealth, a rich society by premodern standards. There was a surplus of capital available for investment; a developed system of capital markets made it relatively easy to get capital to entrepreneurs through joint-stock companies and other financial arrangements. The British dominated the seas, and their colonial empire was exploited as a source of cheap raw materials and as captive markets (although the direct contribution of colonial capital was limited: little tax revenue derived from the colonies went directly into manufacturing). England also possessed a technologically-astute population of mechanics and engineers with some training in Newtonian physics. Very little of this, however, had been imparted by the formal education system. Rather, technical knowledge was disseminated through informal courses and lectures at coffeehouses, Masonic lodges, and other venues outside the formal educational system. These presentations often involved demonstrations with complex mechanical devices. Newtonian science took on a more practical cast in England than in France or elsewhere in Europe. Eighteenth-century English natural philosophers did not draw distinctions between pure and applied science. Its relatively efficient and consolidated agricultural system, combined with the also-common dispossessed status of many smallholders, meant that England, unlike many European nations, did not have a peasantry bound to the land. The nation's agricultural sector was oriented toward market, rather than subsistence, production. This market orientation, coupled with the rapid English population growth of the eighteenth century, created a large surplus work force, primed to work in various industrial fields.

The initial industrial development occurred primarily in textiles, particularly cotton (so-called light industry). Historians now question the once commonly held assumption that cotton was absolutely central to the British industrial revolution; nevertheless, despite reconsiderations, what remains certain was that cotton was important to the greater Industrial Revolution. Expansion within the textile industry was initially possible due to technical and organizational innovations in spinning and weaving, including the spinning mule, the spinning jenny, the power loom, and the steam engine. The quantity of raw cotton imported into Great Britain grew from 11 million pounds in 1785 to 588 million pounds in 1850; the output of cloth rose from 40 million to 2,025 million square yards. This was an export-oriented trade, and efficient to the degree that, despite Napoleon Bonaparte's attempts to block British goods from reaching the European continent, even the French army was clothing soldiers in English cotton cloth. In addition to Europe, colonial markets were important, as were exports to India and Africa. After it gained independence from Spain and Portugal, Latin America virtually became an economic colony of Britain throughout the eighteenth and nineteenth centuries. Even the United States continued to be a major market for British manufactured goods after the American Revolution.

The relation of the Industrial Revolution to Romanticism is complex. There was an admiring Romantic response to the massive quantitative increase in human control over nature which industrialization represented, culminating in the famous statement of Karl Marx, in his *Communist Manifesto* (1848), that the bourgeoisie had been the first to demonstrate what human activity could bring about. This positive response to a perceived increase in humankind's domination over nature control was accentuated in the so-called railway era, generally acknowledged as beginning in the second quarter of the nineteenth century (the first public railroad beginning service in Britain in 1825). The railroad made material and technological progress clearly obvious, and dramatically changed the way people related to space and time. It had a cultural impact far exceeding that of previous industrial developments.

However, despite the Romantic admiration of the human achievement that industrialization represented, there was also repulsion, based primarily on aesthetic factors, such as the unattractive factories and polluted waters that resulted. There was also a Romantic reaction against the exploitation of industrial workers, and the materialistic vulgarity of industrial leaders and developers. William Blake spoke of "dark satanic mills." Friedrich Engels's *The Condition of the Working Class in England* (1845), a study of the northern industrial center of Manchester, emphasized the squalor and danger industrial workers faced. Many foreign visitors remarked on the disparity between the wealth of industry leaders and the poverty of industrial workers. Native English individuals also noted the negative aspects of the Industrial Revolution. Charles Dickens, for example, made the imaginary industrial city of Coketown the symbol of both physical and mental repression and degradation in *Hard Times*, while his industrialist Bounderby represents the selfishness and arrogance of the factory owners. The Romantic embrace of nature, medievalism, and the past can be seen as a reaction against industrialization, representing as they do an ostensibly simpler, healthier way of life that is gone.

WILLIAM BURNS

Bibliography

Clark, Anna. *The Struggle for the Breeches: Gender and the Making of the British Working Class*. Berkeley and Los Angeles: University of California Press, 1995.

Jacob, Margaret C. *Scientific Culture and the Making of the Industrial West*. New York: Oxford University Press, 1997.

Landes, David S. *The Unbound Prometheus: Technological Change and Industrian Development in Western Europe from 1750 to the Present.* London: Cambridge University Press, 1969.

Marcus, Stephen. *Engels, Manchester and the Working Class.* New York: Random House, 1974.

Mokyr, Joel, ed. *The British Industrial Revolution: An Economic Perspective.* 2d ed. Boulder: Westview Press, 1998.

Teich, Mikulas, and Roy Porter, eds. *The Industrial Revolution in National Context: Europe and the U.S.A.* Cambridge: Cambridge University Press, 1996.

Thompson, E. P. *The Making of the English Working Class.* New York: Pantheon, 1963.

Williams, Raymond. *Culture and Society, 1780–1950.* London: Chatto and Windus, 1960.

INGEMANN, BERNHARD SEVERIN 1789–1862

Danish writer

Bernhard Severin Ingemann is best remembered for his historical novels and for his psalms and songs, and in both these genres he pursued his oft-stated aim of national rebirth and communion. In the case of Ingemann's novels, Denmark's historical figures and events are brought to life in a style owing much to the historical works of Sir Walter Scott; in singing Ingemann's psalms and songs, Danes came together as a nation at home, in church, and at school to raise their voices in praise of God and of the national nature and way of life.

Ingemann was an incredibly prolific writer, and turned his hand to every imaginable genre, producing over forty volumes of writings by the time of his death. A nonexhaustive categorization of his writings would include tragedy, comedy, satire, memoirs, fairy tales, and dissertations on various subjects including theology, astrology, natural philosophy, and mythology. As has often been commented, Ingemann's development as a writer follows a strikingly similar pattern to that of his contemporaries, including Adam Oehlenschläger: a poor boy shows intellectual promise and gains a university education, participates in the defense of Copenhagen under bombardment, begins to write poetry bearing all the hallmarks of universal Romanticism, spends some years visiting the leading lights of German Romantic literature, begins to channel his writing toward a form of national idealism, and displays an increasingly inward-looking concern with a Christianity grounded in the twin Biedermeier ideals of the family home and the nation.

Ingemann's first collection of poetry, *Digte* (1811–12; Poems), and his first few dramas, reveal a creativity very much in tune with the spirit of the times. The young Ingemann, as he later reveals in his memoirs *Tilbageblik* (*Looking Back*, 1863), was enthused by the reaction against rationalism, and determined to imbue his poetry with a supernatural and idealist spirit. But the recurring dialectical themes in Ingemann's works are also caught up in the social issues of the times: his poetry, drama, and, later, his Romantic novels problematize, first, the duality of good and evil; second, the nature of romantic love and the interaction of the sexes; and third, the management of the role of the individual as a participant in the collective, that is, the nation.

Ingemann's turn-of-the-century generation was raised in a society centering on the sanctity of family life, in which new strictures were placed on the sexual mores of earlier times. The problems stemming from the dualism of carnal versus spiritual love are thematized in his early dramas, very few of which were ever staged. The plot of *Løveridderen* (*The Knight of the Lion*, 1816), for example, attributes the transgressions of (near-) incest, patricide, and matricide to one accursed medieval knight, who is forced to haunt the scene of his crimes ever after. In his *skæbnedramaer* (dramas of fate), chastity is usually rewarded, and often it is a sexual transgression of some kind that initiates the tribulations. In *Blanca* (1815), the most successful of Ingemann's early dramas, as well as in many of his early poems, only in death can the souls of the lovers be united.

De sorte Riddere (*The Black Knights*, 1814) also recommends the same sublimation of carnal love, but this particular epic is an example of Ingemann's increasing engagement with his own times and his own personal experience, albeit transported to a timeless, mystical setting. Here, the hero Viduvelt and his band of helpers must first free the realm of Ungerland from the spell of a troll, the incarnation of Evil, before returning home to fight that same evil in the shape of Ridder Rød, the Red Knight. This work also explores Ingemann's conception of the mutually rewarding relationship between male and female, in the shape of the poet couple Theobald and Seraphine, who, quite literally, can only make sweet music together. But neither can the parallels with the international situation Ingemann had experienced as a young man be ignored; Ridder Rød, then, has been interpreted as representative of the psychological angst felt by a generation in the throes of social and religious liberation, but also as an allegory for the all-conquering figure of Napoleon which still stalked the Danish psychological landscape.

Ingemann took up the same themes, to more critical and popular acclaim, in *Reinald Underbarnet* (*Reinald the Wonder Child*, 1816), and two decades later in *Holger Danske. Et Digt i Fem Sangkredse* (*Holger the Dane: A Poem in Five Song Cycles*, 1837).

It is a commonplace to point to the influence of Scott on Ingemann; indeed, Ingemann explicitly acknowledged Scott as the master of the historical novel. As elsewhere in Europe, the 1820s and 1830s saw a great popular breakthrough in Denmark for prose writing. It was Ingemann's aim to reach a wide reading public in order to disseminate the ideals of national unity in a period of limited democratic reform, of which he disapproved.

At Nikolai Frederik Severin Grundtvig's suggestion, Ingemann wrote a suite of romances—four novels book-ended by two verse epics—between 1824 and 1836, describing the fall and rise of the Danish kingdom in the Middle Ages. In a sense, Ingemann's interpretation of history was radically out of tune with the times; the autarchic system of government his novels seem to defend was soon to come to a peaceful end. But in their color, detail, and psychological complexity, they weave a beguiling tapestry out of the events and characters of Danish history. As Ingemann wrote in his preface to *Prins Otto af Danmark* (1835), "That a number of events are essentially factually true makes them not at all, in my opinion, unpoetic, for History and human life encompass all the riches of poetry and ideas."

Some of Ingemann's prose writing was more avant-garde and inspired by the work of E. T. A. Hoffmann. Ingemann's collections of fairy tales and stories, such as *Nye Eventyr og Fortællinger* (New Fairytales and Stories, 1847), which often have a macabre undercurrent, should be seen in this light. Quite a different attempt at generic innovation is the four-volume novel *Landsbybørnene* (*The Children of the Village*, 1852), which applies the principles of the historical novel to the present day. Here, too, there are traces of Hoffmann's influence; we see the recurring *dobbeltgænger* figure, the dark side of the decent Danish hero; but the overriding message of this novel is, again, inextricably linked to the situation of war Denmark again found itself in, and thus the necessity of sacrifice for the fatherland.

Ingemann's name is also closely associated with the Academy at Sorø, a school specializing in modern languages and natural sciences, where he taught Danish language and literature and served as director from 1842 until its closure in 1849. One lasting legacy of Ingemann's time at the academy is the body of psalms and popular songs he wrote for the school and for the wider public. His most famous are *Morgensange for Børn* (*Morning Songs for Children*, 1837) and *Syv Aftensange* (*Seven Evening Songs*, 1838), many of which are still sung and enjoyed today wherever Danes gather. Their charm lies not least in the close collaboration of the poet with the composer C. E. F. Weyse, whose music perfectly suits the naïveté and intimacy of Ingemann's poetry. Ingemann's particular conception of Christianity was thus disseminated into Danish homes, and into the schools of subsequent generations.

CLAIRE THOMSON

Biography

Born Torkildstrup, on Falster Island, Denmark, May 28, 1789, the son of a pastor, and the youngest of nine children. In 1806 he started, but never finished, studies in Theology. Having published several works, he undertook, with financial support from the king, his travels in Europe 1818–19. Visited Tieck, as a substitute for E. T. A. Hoffmann, but deliberately avoided Goethe, for whom he felt antipathy. Marriage to Lucie, a minor painter, in 1822 (no children). Teaching at Sorø Akademi, 1822–49; Director, 1842–49. Died Sorø, 1864.

Selected Works

Digte. 1811.
Procne. 1813.
De sorte Riddere. 1814.
Blanca. 1815.
Reinald Underbarnet. 1816.
Løveridderen. 1816.
Waldemar den Store og hans Mænd. 1824.
Valdemar Seier. 1826. Translated as *Waldemar surnamed Seir, or the Victorious* by Jane Frances Chapman. 1841.
Erik Menveds Barndom. 1828. Translated as *The Childhood of King Erik Menved: An Historical Romance* by J. Kesson. 1846.
Kong Erik og de Fredløse. 1833. Translated as *King Erik and the Outlaws, or, the Throne, the Church and the People* by Jane Frances Chapman. 1843.
Prins Otto af Danmark. 1835.
Dronning Margrethe. 1836.
Holger Danske. Et Digt i Fem Sangkredse. 1837.
Morgensange for Børn. 1837.
Syv Aftensange. 1838.
Nye Eventyr og Fortællinger. 1847.
Fire nye Fortællinger. 1850.
Landsbybørnene. En Nytidsroman. 1852.
Tankebreve fra en Afdød. 1855.
Tilbageblik paa mit Liv og min Forfattervirksomhed fra 1811–1837. Edited and introduced by I. Galskjøt. 1863.

Bibliography

Dreyer, Kirsten, ed. *H.C. Andersens brevveksling med Lucie og B.S. Ingemann* 3 vols. Copenhagen: Museum Tusculanums Forlag, Københavns Universitet, 1997–98.

Gjesing, Knud Bjarne. "Den indre revolte. B.S. Ingemann, "Sphinxen." In *Læsninger i Dansk Litteratur*, vol. 2. Edited by Povl Schmidt, Anne-Marie Mai, Finn Hauberg-Mortensen, Inger-Lise Hjort-Vetlesen. Odense: Odense Universitetsforlag, 1998.

Langballe, Carl. *B.S. Ingemann. Et Digterbillede i ny Belysning.* Copenhagen: Gyldendal Nordisk Forlag, 1949.

Rossell, Sven H., ed. *A History of Danish Literature.* Lincoln: University of Nebraska Press, 1992.

———. "Midnight Songs and Churchyard Ballads: The Other Ingemann." In *Vänbok. Festgabe für Otto Gschwantler.* Edited by Imbi Sooman. Vienna: VWGÖ, 1990.

INGRES, JEAN-AUGUSTE-DOMINIQUE 1780–1867

French painter

To speak of Jean-Auguste-Dominique Ingres in the context of Romanticism may seem perverse or contradictory; after all, histories of French painting depict Ingres as the antithesis of the arch-Romantic Eugène Delacroix. Throughout an exceptionally long career in which he was able to witness the lighting of the fuse of Romanticism in the visual arts, the incandescence of its explosion, and the damp fizzle of its final embers, Ingres seemed to remain a rigid and dogmatic classicist, holding firm against the tide, insisting on the values that defined French Academic teaching, and thus isolating himself from the main currents of painting in France in his epoch.

It is true that Ingres remained staunchly loyal to a set of beliefs and practices which are at first glance far removed from those we now associate with the Romantics. He did much to revivify the academic tradition in France, particularly in his role as Director of the French Academy in Rome (1834–41), and his insistence on the primacy of line over color, and on the importance of studious imitation in his teaching of his many pupils, did much to prolong the life of a doctrine that might otherwise have proved less resistant to the challenge of new currents in painting.

It is also true that Ingres was hostile to novelty, and to what he regarded as ugliness in the work of his contemporaries. Urging the removal of Théodore Gericault's *Raft of the Medusa* from the Louvre, he wrote, "I don't want anything to do with the *Medusa* or those operating-theater canvases that show nothing of man but the corpse, which represent only the ugly, the hideous." He was fastidious in his allegiance to the imitation of the ancients and in his belief that novelty was a sham. But his sweeping and damning indictments of key aspects of the Romantic imagination (the search for novelty, the exploration of the suffering body and soul, etc.) are part of the self-constructed persona of an artist whose work, in its very complexity, defies doctrinal pigeonholing, and is often difficult to dissociate from the movements and tendencies of European Romanticism in the visual arts, music, and literature. When we examine Ingres's luxurious *Odalisques* (*Grand Odalisque*, 1814; *Odalisque with Slave*, 1839–40), with their rhythmically contorted abstract anatomies, their joyous surface opulence, and their deep undercurrents of material and sexual fantasy, we must acknowledge how closely these are related to the exotic and erotic fantasies of his Romantic peers, from Gérard de Nerval to Delacroix. Some of his intimate portraits painted against landscape backgrounds, such as that of the Painter François-Marius Granet reveal, despite their rigorous order, a restless excitement very much based in the intense youthful experience of the Italian landscape, and a command of color that is reminiscent, in form and in mood, of some contemporary German painting and of the fusion of loaded landscape, intensity of artistic fellow feeling, and personal dynamism that was so crucial to Romantic portraiture (as for example, in Anne-Louis Girodet de Roussy-Trioson's *Portrait of Chateaubriand*, c. 1809).

However, it must be remembered that Ingres saw himself first and foremost as a history painter, and it is in this genre that we can most fruitfully investigate Ingres's complex relationship with European Romanticism. From his earliest precocious education at the Academy School in Toulouse, Ingres's skills as a draftsman and his ambitions to continue a grand tradition of historical painting were evident. These would remain with him throughout his life. The story of Ingres's development as a history painter really begins, though, with his period of study in Paris, and specifically in the Atelier of Jacques-Louis David after 1797. For here, Ingres was not only under the tutelage of the preeminent history painter in France, but also in the ambit of the group of young student artists known as the Barbus, who were engaged on a quest for extreme purification of the neoclassical style by recourse to Greek vase painting and Italian primitive art, and were responsible for a model of that brotherhood ethic that was the germ of the crucial concept of bohemian artistic society so crucial to Romanticism from the Nazarenes to the Pre-Raphaelites.

Ironically, given Ingres's own oft-stated aversion to the search for innovation, it was the perception of radical archaism and search for novelty for its own sake that offended critics of, for example, the overt and courageous primitivism of *Paulo et Francesca da Rimini*—a picture that, in its references to Dante Alighieri and the medieval world, its pictorial allusions to Flemish and Italian primitives, and its peculiar mixture of chivalrous decorum and erotic sensuality, can be readily associated with key Romantic currents in literature and the arts.

This particular mixture of sexuality and respectability, and of archaism and the contemporary, is central to other historical compositions by Ingres, including *Roger et Angelica* and *Antiochus et Stratonice*, subjects to which Ingres returned again and again in the course of his long career. In the latter subject, despair, forbidden love, illness, and passion are as important to Ingres's version as is the noble gesture of Seleceus in according his wife to his son. It might be argued that the dramas of sensuality, violence, and death are as central to the composition of Ingres's seemingly austere and temperate historical canvases as they are to the more obviously passionate paintings of Delacroix.

The disciplined opulence and brilliant draftsmanship of his remarkable portraits established Ingres as a master of line, and thus as an opposite to the colorist Delacroix. But the patience and discipline associated with the line, and with Ingres, often belie an intensity and expressivity (for example, in the snaking imploring physicality of Thetis in *Jupiter and Thetis* or the libidinous fantasy of the *Turkish Bath*, which must make us rethink the traditional association in Ingres's work between line and disciplined regularity.

Furthermore, Ingres's astonishingly meticulous preparation for large-scale projects (such as his *Age of Gold* at Dampierre, which include up to four hundred preparatory drawings, oil sketches, etc.), though indebted to that studious approach which marked the École des Beaux-Arts, was also itself an obsessive activity, a search not for a certain and sure ideal, but for an elusive vision of perfection, which, as he said in 1822, forced him to measure his own lack and insufficiency.

Perhaps for this reason, Ingres's career was underpinned by a persistent counterpoint in which self-assured creativity and discipline competed with the dispiriting downbeat of criticism, rejection, and self-abnegation. This career path, and the studied peculiarity of Ingres's large-scale work, means that we cannot see Ingres as the serene and untroubled apogee of a particular tradition, or in studied opposition to Romanticism and modern currents in painting. Indeed, he was an influence on and inspiration to many key modern artists, including Pablo Picasso (in whose *Guernica*, among other canvases, Ingres's extended anatomies are evoked for expressive effect) and Henri Matisse. It seems that, like these artists, both the public, who flocked to a recent exhibition of his portraits, and art historians are now rediscovering an artist of immense talent, whose complexities and contradictions seem to point to the tensions inherent in the relationship between French classicism and European Romanticism and modernity.

MARK LEDBURY

Biography

Born in Montauban on August 29, 1780, the son of a sculptor and painter; entered the studio of Jacques Louis David in Paris in 1797; won the Prix de Rome in 1801 for his painting *The Ambassadors of Agamemnon*. From 1806 to 1820 he painted in Rome. His pictures were received coolly by critics in Salons from 1806 to 1819. In 1820 left Rome for Florence. On his return to Paris, Ingres won great acclaim with *The Vow of Louis XIII* (1820), commissioned for the Cathedral of Montauban and exhibited in the Salon in 1824. Painted *The Apotheosis of Homer* (1827) for a ceiling in the Louvre in Paris. Angered by the poor reception given his *Martyrdom of Saint Symphorian* Ingres left Paris to direct the French Academy at Rome (1834–41). Given the rank of commander of the Legion of Honour in 1845. Settled in Dampierre and began the ultimately unfinished *Age of Gold* and *Age of Iron* commission for the Duc de Luynes. In the Universal Exhibition of Paris in 1855, both he and Delacroix awarded gold medals; major exhibition of his work in 1861. Elected a Senator in 1862. Died in Paris on January 14, 1867.

Selected Works

The Ambassadors of Agamemnon in the Tent of Achilles. 1801. Ecole des Beaux-Arts, Paris.
Portrait of Mme Philibert Rivière. c. 1805. Louvre, Paris.
Portrait of Mlle Rivière. 1805. Louvre, Paris.
Portrait of François-Marius Granet. c. 1807 Musée Granet, Aix en Provence.
Valpinçon Bather. 1808. Louvre, Paris.
Oedipus and the Sphinx. 1808–27. Louvre, Paris.
Jupiter and Thetis. 1811. Musée Granet, Aix en Provence.
The Dream of Ossian. 1813. Musée Ingres, Montauban.
Grande Odalisque. 1814. Louvre, Paris.
Paolo and Francesca. 1819. Musée des Beaux-Arts, Angers.
The Vow of Louis XIII. 1824. Cathedral, Montauban.
The Apotheosis of Homer. 1827. Louvre, Paris.
Portrait of Louis-François Bertin. 1832. Louvre, Paris.
Roger and Angelica. c. 1839 National Gallery, London.
Odalisque with Slave. 1839–40. Fogg Art Museum, Cambridge, Massachusetts.
Antiochus and Stratonice. 1839. Musée Condé, Chantilly.
Portrait of Mme Moitessier, Seated. 1856. National Gallery, London.
The Golden Age. Replica of 1862 version. Fogg Art Museum, Cambridge, Massachusetts.
The Turkish Bath. 1863. Louvre, Paris.

Bibliography

Duval, Amaury. *L'Atelier d'Ingres*. Paris, 1993.
Connisbee, Philip, and Gary Tinterow, eds. *Portraits by Ingres: Image of an Epoch*. Exhibition catalog. New York, 1999.
Condon, P., ed. *In Pursuit of Perfection: The Art of J-A-D Ingres*. Exhibition catalog. Louisville, 1984.
Ingres, J. A. D. *Ecrits sur l'art*. Paris, 1947.
Lapauze, Henri. *Ingres: Sa vie, son oeuvre*. 1911.
Levitine, George. *The Dawn of Bohemianism*. University Park: Pennsylvania State University Press, 1978.
Ockman, Carol. *Ingres Eroticised Bodies: Rethinking the Serpentine Line*. New Haven, Conn.: Yale University Press, 1995.
Rifkin, Adrian. *Ingres Then, and Now*. London: 2000.
Rifkin, Adrian, ed. *Fingering Ingres*. Oxford: Blackwells, 2001.
Rosenblum, Robert. *Jean-Auguste Dominique Ingres*. 1967.
Siegfried, Susan. "Ingres and His Critics 1806–1824." Ph.D. diss., Harvard University, 1980.
Ternois, Daniel. *Ingres*. Paris, 1980.
Vigne, Georges. *Ingres*. (Translated by John Goodman. New York, 1995.
Wildenstein, Daniel. *The Paintings of J-A-D Ingres*. Rev. ed. London, 1956.

IRELAND: HISTORICAL SURVEY

In the Romantic era, Ireland was an arena of fierce political struggle. Catholics and liberal Protestants challenged the Protestant ascendancy, Protestant Dissenters fought for equal status with Anglican members of the "Church of Ireland," and Protestant and Catholic Irish people fought for a loosening of British control and sometimes outright independence. Challenges to British rule began during the American Revolution. A militia movement, the Irish Volunteers, was created in 1778, ostensibly to defend against French attack. The Volunteers were a Protestant force with gentry leadership, posing no threat to the Irish social order, but advocating greater liberty for Ireland. The Irish Parliament was made legally independent of the British Parliament in 1782. Catholics also demanded political rights with some success. Laws against Catholic religious organization (largely dead issues anyway) were repealed, and Catholics were allowed to open schools and hold land on the same terms as Protestants.

The French Revolution and revolutionary wars radicalized Irish politics. The Irish Catholic population was a source of military manpower for Britain, while the French saw Ireland as Britain's weak point. Political Catholics and Northern Irish Presbyterian dissenters, along with some disaffected Anglicans, came together in 1791 in a radical secret society, the United Irishmen, led by the Dublin Protestant lawyer Theobald Wolfe Tone (1763–98). The United Irishmen agitated for an independent republic free from English control. They also advocated manhood suffrage, equal electoral districts, and annual Parlia-

ments. The United Irishmen published dozens of newspapers and hundreds of pamphlets.

Lack of unity contributed to the failure of the United Irishmen. The gap between Catholic and Protestant in Ireland was widening with the formation of militant sectarian groups, the Catholic Defenders and the Protestant Orange Order. Alliances the United Irishmen formed with France and the Defenders were rejected by many Protestants, and by the latter part of the decade few Protestants were involved in the group. Nor were all Catholics supporters: many Catholic prelates preferred Protestant rule to domination by anticlerical and republican France, and even excommunicated Catholic members of the United Irishmen and the Defenders. A French invasion in 1796 was prevented by bad weather. Another small French invasion led to a rising in 1798 defeated by the British general Lord Charles Cornwallis (1738–1805). Tone was captured and sentenced to die as a common criminal, a fate he avoided by cutting his throat.

The British government, led by Prime Minister William Pitt (1759–1806), sought to base British–Irish relations on a combination of violent repression of revolution with a conservative alliance between the Protestant rulers and the leading and wealthiest Irish Catholics. Pitt encouraged the Irish parliament to pass a Catholic relief act in 1793, which gave Catholics the right to vote on the same economic basis as Protestants and to hold office in the civil and military administration of Ireland, but not to stand for Parliament or serve at the very top level, such as Lord Lieutenant or general in the army. The 1798 revolt convinced Pitt that the Irish Protestants were no longer able to control the island in the English interest, and the best solution was to unite Britain and Ireland. The Act of Union in 1801 created the United Kingdom, with one Parliament sitting at Westminster. Some Irish lords and Church of Ireland bishops were admitted to the House of Lords. The Union aroused widespread resentment, but it accelerated British recruiting. Hundreds of thousands of Irishmen served in the British army during the wars.

George III refused to allow Pitt's plan to complete the policy of union by allowing Catholics to stand for Parliament to pass. Many Irish Catholics resented the combination of union and nonemancipation. Catholic emancipation would ultimately be brought about by Irish Catholics themselves. The leader most identified with Catholic emancipation was a Catholic lawyer, Daniel O'Connell (1775–1847). O'Connell founded a nonviolent political movement for Catholic Emancipation. One of the first modern political movements, O'Connell's Catholic Association had a mass membership, central control by a party leader, a central fund contributed and collected by party activists, a network of election agents (often Catholic priests), a party press, and electoral pledges that could be viewed as a party platform.

The Catholic Association started supporting Parliamentary candidates in by-elections. In 1828 O'Connell himself won one overwhelmingly. O'Connell had made the refusal to take the anti-Catholic oath required for all members of the United Kingdom parliament a key point in his campaign. The government, fearing a massive Irish insurrection, hurriedly passed Catholic emancipation in 1829, although at the same time it raised the monetary qualifications for Irish voters. Although both Irish and British Catholics could now serve in Parliament, there were actually fewer Catholic voters in Ireland itself. Nonetheless, this was seen as a great personal triumph for O'Connell.

O'Connell's last years were dominated by the unsuccessful struggle to repeal the Union. He died shortly after his release from prison, where he had been held on a charge of sedition. Leadership of Irish politics passed in the 1840s to less adept and more ideological politicians, Romantic nationalists known collectively as "young Ireland." Unlike O'Connell, Young Ireland, whose first leading members were the Protestant Thomas Davis and the Catholics John Blake Dillon and Charles Gavan Duffy, was willing to contemplate the use of violence. They were also cultural nationalists who supported the preservation of the Irish language, and whose newspaper, the *Nation*, founded in 1842, published much political poetry on Irish history. Young Irelanders launched an abortive revolution in 1848.

The late 1840s in Ireland were dominated by famine, triggered by a failure of the potato crop and compounded by the indifference or incompetence of the British government. About a million died of starvation or malnutrition-related diseases, and another million emigrated. The Irish population has never fully recovered to pre-famine levels. Emigration led to the creation of the Irish diaspora in Britain ("the nearest place that wasn't Ireland"), the United States, and the areas of white settlement in the British Empire—particularly Australia. This population would become a potent source of support for Irish nationalism.

WILLIAM BURNS

Bibliography

Elliott, Marianne. *Wolfe Tone: Prophet of Irish Independence*. New Haven, Conn.: Yale University Press, 1989.

Lydon, James. *The Making of Ireland: From Ancient Times to the Present*. London: Routledge, 1998.

Macdonagh, Oliver. *The Emancipist: Daniel O'Connell, 1830–49*. London: Weidenfeld and Nicolson, 1989.

———. *The Hereditary Bondsman: Daniel O'Connell, 1775–1829*. London: Weidenfeld and Nicolson, 1988.

McDowell, R. B. *Ireland in the Age of Imperialism and Revolution, 1760–1801*. Oxford: Clarendon Press, 1979.

Mokyr, Joel. *Why Ireland Starved: A Quantitative and Analytical History of the Irish Economy, 1800–1850*. London: Allen and Unwin, 1983.

Molony, John N. *A Soul Came into Ireland: Thomas Davis 1814–1845: A Biography*. Templeogue, Dublin: Geography Publications, 1995.

Smyth, Jim. *The Men of No Property: Irish Radicals and Popular Politics in the Late Eighteenth Century*. New York: St. Martin's Press, 1992.

IRONY, ROMANTIC

Although there are numerous textbook definitions of Romantic irony, this notion cannot be separated from the convoluted history of irony in general, which appears in the Western tradition in contexts ranging from literary stylistics, philosophical discourse (metaphysics and ethics in particular), religion and mystical theology to historiography and literary theory. A survey of these contexts—threads from all of which converge in the period of Romanticism—leads inevitably to the conclusion that Romantic irony should not be considered as a term or a concept, or as something that can be defined precisely—and in particular, that it is something far more complex than a mere figure of speech or stylistic device—because it appears and serves as nothing other than the trace or mark of the failure of linguistic conceptualization or definition, and indeed, of representation in general.

Philosophical and Rhetorical Contexts

In the classical tradition, the chiasmic formulations of Heraclitus—"[one] cannot step twice into the same river, nor can one grasp any mortal substance in a stable condition, but it scatters and again gathers; it forms and dissolves, and approaches and departs"; "The lord whose oracle is in Delphi neither declares nor conceals, but gives a sign"—provide a starting point by representing a universe based on flux, where all things are in a state of constant transformation and cannot be pinned down. In such a universe of irony, the medium of a message from the divine to the human realm is the sign, which neither reveals nor conceals its meaning, leaving it open to interpretation.

As it is developed in the works of Plato and in Aristotelean treatises, irony comes to take on a negative sense—the Greek word *eironeia* means "dissimulation," or an affectation of ignorance used to provoke an antagonist—as the concealment of the intended meaning of a sign. Thus Socrates is an *eiron* or "dissembler," one who says less than he means, and, through his "naive" questions hollows out and negates the discourse of his interlocutors. For Aristotle, irony is associated with understatement (*litotes*) or the use of a word or phrase in a sense contrary to its usual meaning (*antiphrasis*); in the works of his contemporaries, Demosthenes and Theophrastus, the *eiron* appears as a liar who avoids responsibility by understating his abilities.

During the Roman period, largely on account of its treatment by Cicero and Quintilian, the ethical sense of the word "irony" gradually gives way to an almost exclusively rhetorical usage: saying something contrary, in varying degrees, to what one means, or saying something different. As a result of the influence of these and other theorists of rhetoric in the Middle Ages and the Renaissance, irony appears in handbooks and treatises as a close counterpart, or a subspecies of allegory (the etymological sense of which is literally "to speak something other" [*allos* + *agoreuein*]), and it is used to describe logical contraries such as *negatio* (denial or contradiction) and *praeteritio* (omission).

Through the sixteenth and seventeenth centuries the senses of "irony" multiply until, in the early eighteenth century, it becomes a general term used to encompass or characterize a large variety of literary and dramatic figures, tropes, and genres, including sarcasm, satire, parody, farce, caricature, burlesque, and the lampoon. In Spain its implications are played out in the works of Miguel de Cervantes Saavedra; in France, in the comedies of Molière, the pamphlets of Nicolas Boileau-Despréaux, and the satirical works of Voltaire; and in Britain, in the works of Daniel Defoe, Henry Fielding, Alexander Pope, Laurence Sterne, and Jonathan Swift. The term comes to be associated with "wit," and is used in a range of compounds, including *comic irony, dramatic irony, tragic irony*, and the *irony of fate*; toward the end of the eighteenth century, however, irony takes a new turn beyond rhetoric, and is developed by the German Romantics, Friedrich von Schlegel in particular, into the philosophical theory of what has come to be called Romantic irony.

Theological and Mystical Contexts

This new direction in the representation of irony must be understood in the context of trends in theological mysticism (the Cabbala, Behmenism) on the one hand, and concomitant developments in rational philosophy (Fichtean and Kantian idealism) and the physical sciences (alchemy and analytical chemistry) on the other.

The early Christian Gnostics believed that the god of the Bible, one of several lesser gods or "archons" created by the true God, was essentially evil, as revealed by his prohibition of the fruit of the tree of knowledge in the Garden of Eden, with the purpose of keeping man in a state of ignorance. The serpent, by tempting Eve, kindled in man the fire of the true God, the spark of divinity, which seeks to grow to fulfillment through self-knowledge.

The "divine spark" of the true God inheres in all things, which were created out of the four elements (earth, air, fire, and water), and so there is an exact analogical relationship between all things in the microcosm (the human realm) and the macrocosm (the divine realm of the true God, or the world spirit). Thus, for example, the divine spark within all metals comes to be associated with gold, the purest and most incorruptible; and all metals grow in the earth like seeds, until they realize their full potential as gold. The search for a catalyst—the "philosophers' stone" or "elixir of life"—that could speed up this transformation in metals became the principle quest of the alchemists; material benefits aside, this quest was understood to be "esoteric" or spiritual, culminating in the self-realization and immortality of the alchemist.

By the end of the eighteenth century, such currents of mystical and alchemical thought—which appeared in the writings of Renaissance and Enlightenment natural philosophers and scholars from Robert Fludd and Isaac Newton in England to Jakob Böhme, Johann Wolfgang von Goethe, and Gottfried Wilhelm Leibniz in Germany—were gradually coming into conflict with the rationality of Kantian epistemology on the one hand, and developments in the new analytical chemistry on the other. It is at this point of crisis that the theory of Romantic irony, as it is known today, emerged in Germany.

The Theory of Romantic Irony

It is of some importance to distinguish between Romanticisms when discussing irony. The term *Romantic* may refer to different time frames and concepts; for example, in Britain it has tended to characterize poetry, while in Germany it is associated with the novel (*Roman*) and also alludes to medieval romance. Also, the use of the word *irony* may vary in different national traditions, even between individuals within a given national tradition.

There are moments, however, in English and American Romanticism that point to the conception of Romantic irony as it developed in Germany. Among the English Romantics, John Keats, with his notion of "negative capability" ("when a man is capable of being in uncertainties, mysteries, doubts, without any irritable reaching after fact and reason") comes close to its antirational sensibility; while Samuel Taylor Coleridge, influenced by the German Romantics as well as the rationalists and the Behmenist tradition, indicates, in his treatment of "imagination," the relation of microcosm and macrocosm, or part and whole, to the creative act: "The primary IMAGINATION . . . [is] a repetition in the finite mind of the eternal act of creation in the infinite I AM." The American Romantic, Edgar Allan Poe, suggests another dimension—that of transgression—in his understanding of "perverseness," which he defines as a "perpetual inclination, in the teeth of our best judgment, to violate that which is *Law*, merely because we understand it to be such[;] . . . [an] unfathomable longing of the soul *to vex itself*—to offer violence to its own nature. . . ."

In Germany, the idea of Romantic irony is associated with a group of writers and philosophers, including August Wilhelm von Schlegel, Karl Solger, and Ludwig Tieck, who were based in the town of Jena, but its most important theorizations, which bring together the mystical–theological, rhetorical–philosophical, and rational traditions, appear in three short texts by Friedrich von Schlegel.

In "*Kritische Fragmente*" 42 ("Critical Fragment 42," 1797; published in *Lyceum*), Schlegel suggests that irony might be defined "as logical beauty, for wherever something becomes philosophized . . . and yet not completely systematically, there should one accomplish irony and call for it." Irony is thus something that operates on the limits of a system; it marks breaches or gaps in the boundaries of a system which prevent its closure. Later in the same fragment, irony is characterized as "transcendental buffoonery," with the implication that it marks the relation between the internal, transcendental meaning of the system, and its external manifestation as stylistic or literary form.

In another key text, his essay "*Über die Unverständlichkeit*" ("On Incomprehensibility," 1800; published in *Athenaeum*), Schlegel attempts to "draw attention to the fact that among philosophical words—which often in their texts . . . confuse everything and exert the invisible force of the World-Spirit even on him who does not want to recognize it—there must be a secret brotherhood." Arguing that the communication of (Platonic, mystical) ideas or truths in language is impossible—because the "brotherhood" of these ideas underlies language and constantly bursts through, perversely rupturing and subverting any intention to communicate through them by means of language—Schlegel reconfigures irony in three ways.

First, on the textual level, irony reveals this relation between the spirit and the letter, or more generally, the world spirit and language, the macrocosm and the microcosm. The stylistic and rhetorical play of language that we call irony is thus simply the superficial, external rhetorical manifestation of irony proper, which indicates the subversive relation between the universal, secret brotherhood of the world spirit and the local, specific system of human language.

Second, irony operates on the level of the individual, because the individual spirit is a metonymic, microcosmic part or element, whose human limitations prevent him (or "her," complex gender issues in Schlegel notwithstanding) from participating in the whole of the world spirit. In theory, the individual who succeeded in transcending the limits of language and realizing the whole within himself would become the paradigm of the prophet/hierophant/artist, one whose words are by definition incomprehensible, except to kindred spirits. (Many of the texts produced by Schlegel and his colleagues thus take the form of collections of "fragments," each of which is a whole in itself, but also stands as a part, a metonymy for the totalization of the collection as a whole, as a system. The spaces, or gaps between the fragments, represent the ironic disjunction between the totality of meaning and the fragmentation of its expression in language. Other texts, such as Schlegel's novel *Lucinde* [1799], are composed of a "Babel," or mixture of genres, pointing to a theoretical moment when all languages might be unified in a single, universal language.)

Third, irony is to be thought of not simply in relation to the spatial relations of a system, but also temporally, on the hermeneutic or interpretive plane of history, considered as a system. On this temporal plane, the end, or closure, of history (and irony) would be the achievement of an absolute and transparent "real language," which would transcend the limitations of human language. Here Schlegel incorporates elements of Johann Gottlieb Fichte's extension to Immanuel Kant's critical philosophy in the principle of a transcendental, collective ego or "I," which strives infinitely to realize itself, through the tensions pos-

ited within it as an opposition between the self (the "finite I") and other (the "finite non-I"). The quest for this moment is analogous to the quest for the philosophers' stone; its attainment would be a moment of total self-revelation. But such an eschatological moment is unattainable, for the end of irony is itself ironized—this is what Schlegel calls the "irony of irony"—and so irony is to be understood, finally, *within* human history, as arousing "a feeling of the insoluble antagonism of the absolutely unlimited and the absolutely limited, of the impossibility and the necessity of a complete communication"—in other words, as a "perpetual self-parody."

It is for this reason that in a short, much quoted text, Schlegel's posthumously published "Philosophical Fragment 668" (c. 1800), we read that "irony is a permanent parabasis." The Greek word *parabasis* literally means "a stepping beyond": in the New Testament it is translated as "sin" or "transgression"; and in the Attic Old Comedy (fifth century B.C.E.) it referred to a moment in a play where the action was suspended or interrupted, and the chorus stepped forward to the edge of the stage, removed their masks, and verbally abused members of the audience, *ad hominem* and as a whole. This characterization suggests, in fine, that Romantic irony must be thought of as an endless transgression or suspension of closure, including the closure of its own definition; as the mark of the necessity and yet the ultimate impossibility of an absolutely totalizing system; as simultaneously the necessity and the impossibility of the end of human history as the history of reading.

The Aftermath of Romantic Irony

Schlegel's theory of irony deeply influenced his colleagues and contemporaries, who incorporated aspects of it in their own work. His brother August Wilhelm popularized some of the ideas in his "*Vorksungen über dramatische Kunst und Literatur*" ("Lectures on Dramatic Art and Literature," 1808); irony came to be understood, in the later works of his colleague Solger, as the fundamental principle of all art. The theory of irony was brought to England by the efforts of the Hegelian scholar Heinrich Heine; and Bishop Connop Thirlwall, Tieck's translator, contributed to its dissemination with his essay ("On the Irony of Empedocles" (1833). Romantic irony was attacked by G. W. F. Hegel for its endless deferral of tragic closure; it received a more sympathetic treatment in Søren Kierkegaard's thesis on *The Concept of Irony, with Constant Reference to Socrates* (1848), although Kierkegaard's characterization of it as a "concept" ironically indicates a fundamental misinterpretation of Schlegelian irony.

By the turn of the nineteenth century, irony in various forms had become central to the works of such writers as Charles Baudelaire, Henry James, Gustave Flaubert, and Anatole France, and in the early twentieth century it became associated both with critical distance and with paradoxes intrinsic to language, through a kind of aestheticization of the Heraclitean flux: in the discourse of Anglo-American "new criticism" it appears in various guises as ambiguity (William Empson), tension (Allen Tate), paradox (I. A. Richards, Cleanth Brooks), depersonalization (T. S. Eliot), or stable irony (Wayne Booth); in Russian formalism it appears as defamilarization (Viktor Schklovskii) or the ambivalence of the carnivalesque (Mikhail Bakhtin).

While the stylistic and rhetorical senses of irony continued to hold sway in literary criticism during the late twentieth century (in the work of Stanley Fish and Linda Hutcheon, for example), a rethinking of Romantic irony that began in the 1930s in the writings of Schlegel's most sympathetic reader, Walter Benjamin, saw a return, in some areas of literary theory, to the original philosophical discussion initiated at Jena. Schlegelian Romantic irony was resurrected as "the rhetoric of temporality" in the metacritical texts of Paul de Man; as "différance" in the philosophy of Jacques Derrida; and as "permanent parabasis" in the deconstructive criticism of J. Hillis Miller. More recently, the work of Philippe Lacoue-Labarthe and Jean-Luc Nancy has attempted to reinstate romantic irony as a philosophical concept; and its relation to mystical theology and idealism has emerged in the writings of Werner Hamacher. At the dawn of the twenty-first century—and in keeping with the very nature of romantic irony—no end is sight.

JOHANN PILLAI

Bibliography

Behler, Ernst. *Klassische Ironie, Romantische Ironie Tragische Ironie.* Darmstadt: Wissenschaftliche Buchgesellschaft, 1972.

Benjamin, Walter. "The Concept of Criticism in German Romanticism." In *Selected Writings. Vol. I: 1913–1926.* Edited by Marcus Bullock and Michael W. Jennings. Cambridge, Mass.: Belknap Press of Harvard University Press, 1996.

Debus, Allen G. *The Chemical Philosophy: Paracelsian Science and Medicine in the Sixteenth and Seventeenth Centuries.* Vols. 1 and 2. New York: Science History Publications/Neale Watson Academic Publications, 1977.

De Man, Paul. "The Concept of Irony." In *Aesthetic Ideology.* Edited by Andrzej Warminski. *Theory and History of Literature,* vol. 65. Minneapolis: University of Minnesota Press, 1996.

———. "The Rhetoric of Temporality." In *Blindness and Insight: Essays in the Rhetoric of Contemporary Criticism.* Minneapolis: University of Minnesota Press, 1983.

Derrida, Jacques. *Dissemination.* Translated by Barbara Johnson. Chicago: University of Chicago Press, 1981.

Fish, Stanley. "Short People Got No Reason to Live: Reading Irony." In *Doing What Comes Naturally: Change, Rhetoric, and the Practice of Theory in Literary and Legal Studies.* Durham, N.C.: Duke University Press, 1989.

Hamacher, Werner. "Der Satz der Gattung: Friedrich Schlegels poetologische Umsetzung von Fichtes unbedingtem Grundsatz," *Modern Language Notes* 95 (1980): 1155–80.

Handwerk, Gary. *Irony and Ethics in Narrative: From Schlegel to Lacan.* New Haven, Conn.: Yale University Press, 1985.

Heraclitus. "The Fragments." In *The Art and Thought of Heraclitus: An Edition of the Fragments with Translation and Commentary.* Edited by Charles H. Kahn. Cambridge: Cambridge University Press, 1983.

Hutcheon, Linda. *Irony's Edge: The Theory and Politics of Irony.* New York: Routledge, 1995.

Kierkegaard, Søren. *The Concept of Irony, with Constant Reference to Socrates.* Translated by Lee M. Capel. London: Collins, 1966.

Lacoue-Labarthe, Philippe, and Jean-Luc Nancy. *The Literary Absolute: The Theory of Literature in German Romanticism.* Translated by Philip Barnard and Cheryl Lester. Albany, N.Y.: State University of New York Press, 1988.

Miller, J. Hillis. *Fiction and Repetition: Seven English Novels.* Cambridge, Mass: Harvard University Press, 1982.

Muecke, D. C. *The Compass of Irony.* London: Methuen, 1970.

Schaefer, Albert, ed. *Ironie und Dichtung.* Munich: C. H. Beck, 1970.

Schlegel, Friedrich. *Friedrich Schlegel's Lucinde and the Fragments.* Translated by Peter Firchow. Minneapolis: University of Minnesota Press, 1971.

Seligmann, Kurt. *Magic, Supernaturalism and Religion: A History of Magic and its Influence on Western Civilization.* New York: Grosset and Dunlap, 1968.

Strohschneider-Kohrs, Ingrid. *Die romantische Ironie in Theorie und Gestaltung.* Tübingen: Max Niemeyer Verlag, 1977.

IRVING, WASHINGTON 1783–1859

American writer, essayist, biographer, and historian

It is widely accepted that Washington Irving was the first professional American writer. Irving was named after George Washington and he grew up with the new nation. Although he was not as radical in forging an American literary identity as later Romantics such as Ralph Waldo Emerson and Walt Whitman, Irving developed European literary models to address the social and political issues emerging in the post-Revolutionary America. The relationship between Europe and America is explored throughout his work, from the folk tales published in *The Sketch Book of Geoffrey Crayon, Gent* (1819–20) to his chronicle *A History of the Life and Voyages of Christopher Columbus* (1828), and his late biography of *George Washington* (1855–59). He wrote his major work in the first half of the nineteenth century, but his style is characterized by eighteenth-century gentility, and his interest in publishing work under pseudonyms is distinctly Augustan: for example, his early newspaper sketches were published under the name Jonathan Oldstyle, Gent, and his satirical *A History of New York from the Beginning of the World to the End of the Dutch Dynasty* (1809) is presented by the phlegmatic Dutch character Diedrich Knickerbocker (who later features in *The Sketch Book*). The view of Irving as an "oldstyle" writer suggests a backward-looking perspective, with which his views on contemporary American democracy are unfavorably contrasted. However, although the social trajectory of his writing may be conservative, Irving was eager to experiment with literary form. He avoided the novel (which at the time had no tradition in America) in favor of the serial, the sketch, and the history, which seemed better suited to his subject matter. His fiction offered the contemporary reader the delight of storytelling released from pedagogic constraint, while his histories helped to sustain the patriotism of a new nation deeply interested in its origins.

Debates continue as to whether Irving's style was a direct copy of Sir Walter Scott and Oliver Goldsmith (the latter of whom he wrote an acclaimed biography in 1849), or whether he was successful in refashioning an English literary idiom and skillful in his adaptation of European folktales to deal directly with questions of American national identity. His transatlantic journeys—in 1815 to England, in 1822 to France and Spain, and then later as an American diplomat in Europe—reveal his interest in combining the cultural fruits of two continents. This shuttling back and forth between the old and new worlds is expressed most clearly in his explanatory piece "The Author's Account of Himself," published in *The Sketch Book*. Here, Irving venerates European tradition for containing "the masterpieces of art, the refinements of highly-cultivated society, the quaint peculiarities of ancient and local custom," but he also expresses his intense admiration of the unspoiled qualities of the American landscape: "her mighty lakes, like oceans of liquid silver; her mountains, with their bright aerial tints; her valleys, teeming with wild fertility." Such descriptions embody Irving's Romantic conception of nature. Nature, however, is not always a fixed image in his work. The critic Richard Dorson identifies at least two symbolic functions of landscape in Irving's writing: the "Earthly Paradise" and the "Howling Wilderness." Irving's stories are more domesticated than James Fenimore Cooper's frontier tales and prefigure the American Romantic split between Emerson's divine conception of "Nature" imbued with the benevolent spirit of "the Over-Soul" and the macabre and, at times, malignant Gothic world portrayed by Charles Brockden Brown and Edgar Allan Poe. However, Irving is never as extreme as Emerson or Poe, adopting a stylistic middle ground that is better described as "picturesque" rather than Romantic or Gothic.

Many of the picturesque tales in *The Sketch Book* are set within the region of New York and the Hudson River. The tales attempt to blend the magical with the commonplace, foreshadowing Henry David Thoreau's Romantic argument that the strange actually exists close at hand if one looks carefully enough. Elsewhere, however, Irving adopts more clearly the form of the traveler's tale to deal with foreign legends. The traveler's tale is a major strain in Euro-American writing that can be traced back to Christopher Columbus's letters to the Spanish Court, in which the merchant sailor elaborated his anthropological discoveries in poetic language. For example, Irving's collection of tales *The Alhambra* (1835) offers the reader a mixture of cultural insight into the Andalusian people with an opportunity to "linger and loiter" with him in Granada "until we gradually become familiar with all its localities." Irving is as much interested in challenging false representations of the Spanish landscape by offering the reader firsthand emotional impressions, although he is aware that the reader, raised on the understanding that fiction should serve primarily as instruction, may think his work has been "too much made up of dreams." This balance between imparting pleasure and widening the reader's experience of alternative cultures distances Irving's work from the moral instruction of puritan writing, and aligns him more closely with a Romantic aesthetic in which the reader is invited to reassess cultural value.

Irving's critical reputation has fluctuated since the publication of *The Sketch Book*. In the early 1820s, English and American reviewers praised his work for being "full of imagination, and embellished with a delicacy of feeling," complemented by an emotional appeal unsurpassed at the time. However, from early on he also had detractors: William Hazlitt, in *The Spirit of the Age* (1825), argued that Irving had capitulated to "the tempting bait of European popularity," while Emerson claimed that the picturesque mode was a chief weakness of his work. Although Irving is often lionized for introducing "festive comedy" to American writing and for pioneering internationalist themes, others have criticized him for relying too heavily on secondary sources, for ignoring or stereotyping women, or for his tendency to repeat his old themes in new disguises. Despite these complaints, his exuberant descriptions of nature and his interest in the origins of a national sensibility have secured Irving a central place in nineteenth-century American Romanticism.

MARTIN HALLIWELL

Biography

Born in New York City, April 3, 1783, the youngest of eleven children, to Scottish father and mother of English descent. Entered Hugh Masterton's law office, 1799; became a clerk and published letters in the Morning Chronicle under pseudonym "Jonathan Oldstyle, Gent," 1803. Visited Europe on "grand tour," 1804–6. Passed the bar and entered New York society, 1806. Fell in love with Matilda Hoffman, 1807, who died of consumption in 1809. Made partner in family import business, 1810. Served on Canadian front in 1812 war. Traveled to England, 1815–18, where he met Walter Scott in London, 1817. Lived in Paris, 1820–21; traveled in Germany, 1822. Relationship with Emily Foster, 1823. Traveled in France and began study of Spanish culture, 1825. Appointed American Legation in Madrid; settled in Alhambra, 1829. Awarded honorary Doctorate of Civil Law at Oxford, 1831. Returned to America, 1832. Became adviser to Martin Van Buren, 1835; appointed Minister to the Court of Spain, 1842–45; presented to Queen Victoria in London and King Louis Philippe in Paris, 1845. Supported Spanish possession of Cuba, 1845. Died November 28, 1859.

Selected Works

Collection
The Works of Washington Irving. 21 vols. 1860–61.

Individual Works

Salmagundi, The Whim-Whams and Opinions of Launcelot Longstaff (with James Kirke Paulding and William Harving). 1807–08.
A History of New York from the Beginning of the World to the End of the Dutch Dynasty, by Diedrich Knickerbocker. 1809.
The Sketch Book of Geoffrey Crayon, Gent. 1819–20.
Bracebridge Hall. 1822.
Tales of a Traveller. 1824.
A History of the Life and Voyages of Columbus. 1828.
A Chronicle of the Conquest of Granada. 1829.
The Alhambra. 1832.
Astoria, or Anecdotes of an Enterprise Beyond the Rocky Mountains. 1836.
Adventures of Captain Bonneville, U.S.A. 1837.
Oliver Goldsmith: A Biography. 1849.
A Book of the Hudson. 1849.
Mahomet and His Successors. 1850.
Life of George Washington. 1856–59.

Bibliography

Bowden, Mary Weatherspoon. *Washington Irving.* Boston: Twayne, 1981.
Bradbury, Malcolm. "Storied Associations: Washington Irving Goes to Europe." In *Dangerous Pilgrimages: Trans-Atlantic Mythologies and the Novel.* London: Penguin, 1996.
Brodwin, Stanley, ed. *The Old and New World Romanticism of Washington Irving.* New York: Greenwood Press, 1986.

Brooks, Van Wyck. *The World of Washington Irving*. London: Dent, 1945.

Fetterly, Judith. *The Resisting Reader*. Bloomington: Indiana University Press, 1978.

Hoffman, Daniel. "Irving's Use of American Folklore in 'The Legend of Sleepy Hollow'," *PMLA* 68 (1953): 425–35.

Putnam, George Haven. *Washington Irving: His Life and Work*. New York: Putnam, 1903.

Roth, Martin. *Comedy and America: The Lost World of Washington Irving*. Port Washington, N.Y.: Kennikat Press, 1976.

Rubin-Dorsky, Jeffrey. *Adrift in the Old World*. Chicago: University of Chicago Press, 1988.

Springer, Haskell. *Washington Irving: A Reference Guide*. Boston: G. K. Hall, 1976.

Tuttleton, James W. *Washington Irving: The Critical Reception*. New York: AMS Press, 1989.

Wagennecht, Edward. *Washington Irving: Moderation Displayed*. New York: Oxford University Press, 1962.

Williams, Stanley T. *The Life of Washington Irving*. New York: Oxford University Press, 1935.

IVANOV, ALEXANDER ANDREYEVICH 1806–1858

Russian painter

The purification of the soul, or the invocation of the spirit of a golden age, lay at the heart of Alexander Andreyevich Ivanov's lifelong artistic quest. In the formation of his mature worldview, two individuals stand out as seminal influences: Nikolai Rozhalin and Friedrich Overbeck. The first, the translator of Johann Wolfgang von Goethe's *Sorrows of Young Werther* (1774) into Russian and a student of Friedrich Wilhelm Joseph von Schelling, stimulated the neo-Pythagoreanist tendency in Ivanov. Their association took place in Rome during the painter's early Italian period, coinciding specifically with his production of *Apollo, Hyacinthus and Cyparissus Practicing Music and Song*, 1831–34. This is a painting about the inspired, harmonic union of the divine and mortal. Its naked Hellenist trinity is wrapped in nature as an allegory of the three stages on the path to perfection. The goal of this process appears achievable through a Schelling-like synthesis of the ideal and real, and through a "soul realization" made possible by music and poetry. The antique sculptural qualities of the three shepherds are unified, their individual poses and color tones suggesting that they also represent the joining of a new or future Russia to the cultural hegemony of Greece and Italy. While working on *Apollo*, Ivanov wrote to Rozhalin, acknowledging his role as mentor: "I am indebted to you for my understanding of life, and for the relationship that my art has with its source, the soul." Yet, although it is often interpreted as a statement of his early intoxication with Italy and its classical heritage, the painting already contains suggestions of his subsequent rejection of pagan antiquity and immersion in the Bible. For its subject is also metamorphosis, and before Ivanov completed it, the tubercular Rozhalin left Rome and died. So a shadow falls across Apollo's inspired face, his lyre is abandoned in a tree, and Ivanov adds the boys' tragic attributes, the discus and dead stag, that will bring about their transformation into flowers and trees of sorrow. The painting becomes a memorial to his friend's Hellenist Romanticism.

Despite the fact that *Apollo* remained unfinished, it heralded an abiding interest in depictions of adolescent male nudes in nature in Ivanov's work of the late 1840s and 1850s. Typically, the boys in this series sunbathe, sometimes alone, sometimes in small groups. For Ivanov this is far from idle recreation, for he imbues his figures with a tension and pensiveness that suggests sensitivity to, and union with, each other and their environment. Through such identity of the human with earth, sky, and light, he strove to express his syncretic conception of ideal beauty and truth. This coincided with a variety of contemporaneous plein-air landscapes, whose focus moved from isolated boulders or olive branches to elongated coastal scenes and the glowing *Annueba gopoza* (via Appia) (*Appian Way at Sunset*, 1845). In choosing unexpectedly low or high viewpoints for these scenes, Ivanov conjoins the intimate with the universal to convey his sense of evolving, infinite, and powerful nature.

The presence of the experience of nature in Ivanov's work is actually complemented and ordered in a very specific way by his quality of "mythopoetic construction," so that, as Mikhail Allenov has perceived, "rather than being a mythographer he becomes a perspicacious historiographer of nature." The epithet "the Russian Nazarene" can be legitimately applied to him. Decrying the falsities of current academic trends, he lived an ascetic life in Rome, striving for a spiritual revival in, and through, painting. He was a disciple of Overbeck, whose art and judgment he revered as the most significant of all his contemporaries, particularly after the death of Rozhalin.

The evolution of Ivanov's religious orientation and messianic goals was emphatically expressed in *The Appearance of the Messiah* (1833–57) and a cycle of biblical sketches from the 1850s. The works are testament to his intense grappling with fundamental questions of human existence and meaning. This turn toward the scriptures derived from a profound desire to effect redemptive psychological and social transformation. In keeping

Alexander Andreyevich Ivanov. *The Appearance of the Messiah*. Reprinted courtesy of AKG.

with Schelling, he believed this to be achievable through the visible reconciliation of alternatives, most particularly of the ideal and real. *The Appearance of the Messiah*, the product of twenty-five years of labor, is a panorama of values. As this multifigured composition synthesizes episodes from the gospels, so it gathers together different peoples, belief systems, traditions, cycles of nature, and styles of art. It encapsulates the test of faith that Ivanov constantly put before himself, the artist-thinker, and contemporary society. Among the collated, animated huddles of people appear John the Baptist, the apostles Andrew and John, pharisees, slaves, servants, soldiers, and sceptics. The figure closest to Christ appears to have the features of Nikolai Gogol, while a beggar in the shade resembles Ivanov. The viewer is invited to actively join the crowd, to be as engaged as they with the coming of Christ. The circle of life is also represented through the treatment of nature. Over John the Baptist's group the trees change from the young olives on the right to the decaying branches on the left. And balancing this, the rocks grow from small half-submerged boulders at bottom left to undulating mountains in the background. Integrating a careful selection of multiple sources, including life studies, classical Roman sculpture, Renaissance models, and Byzantine frescoes, the composition of Ivanov's figures moves dramatically upwards and backwards from the depiction of age and youth emerging from the River Jordan at lower left, to the spiritual apparition of Christ, whose centralized presence unifies earth and sky, foreground and background.

Upon commencing work on *Appearance of the Messiah* Ivanov had iterated his vision as follows: "Now thanks to mathematics we are unfettering ourselves from those chains with which our new scribes and Pharisees have darkened the light of revelation and inspiration . . . The soul which is mathematically formed and which is perfect in its morality is the goal of Creation . . . Our calling now is, through the sciences, to bring humanity to spiritual perfection, to usher in a 'Golden Age.'" (Ivanov, *For Discussion with Rozhalin*, c. 1833)

However, while working on the monumental composition he struggled with his own faith and artistic concerns. His doubts stemmed partly from the failure of the 1848 revolutions, the onset of what Isaiah Berlin calls the "darkest hour in the night of Russian obscurantism," the propagation of positivism, and his reading of David Strauss's "blasphemous" *Life of Jesus* (1835). The painting lost its initial meaning; Christ's appearance was diminished, and, together with individuals in the crowd, assumed a distinctly ambiguous aspect. Concurrent with these changes, Ivanov transferred his attention away from the *Messiah* to his idea, following Strauss, of a temple of heaven and humanity. He produced scores of drawings and watercolors, anticipating the construction in Moscow of a building dedicated to the history and reconciliation of world beliefs. He envisaged two tiers of frescoes depicting the historical sacred landscapes and personages of the Holy Land. Ultimately the watercolors he produced were mainly fatalistic, small-scale miracle images which anticipated qualities of the ensuing Byzantine revivalist and symbolist movements. Finally, Ivanov had abandoned his attempts to assimilate the real and the ideal. Instead, he expressed pure spiritual presence through fleeting, melodic figures dematerialized through the use of transparency and an enveloping mysterious radiance.

JEREMY HOWARD

Selected Works

Appearance of the Messiah, 1833–57.

Biography

Born in Saint Petersburg, July 16 (28), 1806. Studied at the Saint Petersburg Academy of Arts under his father, Andrey Ivanov, and under Alexey Yegorov, 1817–28. Lived in Italy, mainly in Rome, 1831–58. Appointed Academician in 1836. Died, apparently of cholera, possibly by suicide, in Saint Petersburg, July 3 (15), 1858.

Bibliography

Allenov, Mikhail. *Aleksandr Ivanov*. Moscow: Trilistnik, 1997.
———. *Aleksandr Andreyevich Ivanov: Zhizn"i Tvorchestvo*. 2 vols. Moscow: Iskusstvo, 1956.
Barooshian, Vahan. *The Art of Liberation: Alexander A. Ivanov*. London: University Press of America, 1987.
Zagyanskaya, Galina. *Peyzazhi Aleksandra Ivanova*. Moscow: Iskusstvo, 1976.

J

JACOBI, FRIEDRICH HEINRICH 1743-1819

German philosopher and novelist

Friedrich Heinrich Jacobi, or Fritz, as he was known by his contemporaries, is an anomalous figure in German cultural history. He cannot be classified easily as a philosopher or a novelist, as a rationalist or an irrationalist, as a liberal or a conservative, as an intellectual or an anti-intellectual—yet he was in some measure all of these. His literary career (as a novelist) and his political career (as a senior civil servant) were both short-lived, the former frustrated by the hostile reception of his two novels, the latter by official resistance to his advocacy of free trade. A perspicacious philosophical critic rather than a significant original thinker, Jacobi undermined the Enlightenment dogma of the autonomy of human reason while seeking to establish a philosophical grounding for religious faith. He is best known now, as he was in his own time, for having initiated or exacerbated acrimonious philosophical controversies over the philosophies of Johann Gottlieb Fichte, Gotthold Ephraim, Lessing, and Friedrich Wilhelm Schelling. Yet however much his philosophical and political views set him at odds with his contemporaries, Jacobi was fully engaged with German and French intellectual life in the last decades of the eighteenth century. Throughout the 1770s and 1780s his family estate at Pempelfort (near Düsseldorf) was visited by numerous literary and philosophical figures, including Denis Diderot, Johann Wolfgang von Goethe, Johann Georg Hamann, Frans Hemsterhuis, Johann Gottfried Herder, Wilhelm von Humbolt, Johann Kaspar Lavater, and Christoph Martin Wieland.

Jacobi's thought was shaped above all by his pietistic upbringing, by his reading of Baruch de Spinoza and Immanuel Kant, and by his encounters with Goethe in 1774 and with Lessing in 1780. The sentimentalism and introspective subjectivism characteristic of Pietism (a radical Lutheran movement that emphasized personal devotion to God, prayer, self-examination, and charitable acts) are evident in his novels, early versions of which were published serially in *Der Teutsche Merkur* (*The Ger-*

man Mercury), a literary review founded in 1773 by Wieland with Jacobi's assistance. Both *Eduard Allwills Papiere* (*Eduard Allwill's Papers*, 1775–76), written in epistolary form after the example of Goethe's *Leiden des jungen Werthers* (*The Sorrows of Young Werther*, 1774) and *Woldemar: Eine Seltenheit aus der Naturgeschichte* (*Woldemar: A Curiosity of Natural History*, 1779) epitomize the literature of sensibility (*Empfindsamkeit*), an outgrowth of Pietism, in their celebration of friendship, love, and emotionalism. Each novel centers on a contrasting pair of characters: a selfless, caring woman and a self-centered, impulsive man. Jacobi's critique of the Sturm und Drang cult of individualism manifests itself in the fact that Allwill and Woldemar are led to the verge of despair by their narcissism and lack of moral grounding, and can be saved only by learning humility and accepting love. While Goethe's public ridicule of *Woldemar* (which included nailing a copy of the novel to a tree) deeply offended Jacobi and discouraged him from pursuing his literary career, Lessing's private praise of it provided the pretext for Jacobi to visit Lessing in July 1780, a few months before the latter's death.

According to Jacobi's report, the authenticity (as opposed to the accuracy) of which has never been seriously questioned, Lessing admitted to him that he rejected "the orthodox concepts of divinity" and affirmed that "there is no other philosophy than Spinoza's philosophy." Because he considered Spinoza's dogmatic rationalism to be fatalistic, and hence fundamentally atheistic, Jacobi was profoundly disturbed by Lessing's endorsement of the Dutch philosopher, which he brought to the attention of Lessing's friend Moses Mendelssohn in 1783 in a correspondence that quickly became clouded by mutual misunderstandings and recriminations. Fearing that Mendelssohn would publish his own account of Lessing's thought without properly acknowledging his Spinozism, Jacobi hastily published *Über die Lehre des Spinoza* (*Concerning the Doctrine of Spinoza*) in 1785. Along with a transcript of his conversations with Lessing, reflections on the nature of Spinozism, and his letters to Mendelssohn, Jacobi included in the book—without permission—Mendelssohn's letters to him and Goethe's previously unpublished poem *Prometheus*, the manuscript of which Jacobi had shown Lessing and thereby elicited his affirmation of Spinoza. Since Spinozism was commonly regarded as equivalent to atheism, Jacobi's revelation about the widely admired Lessing generated a heated controversy, known as the *Pantheismusstreit*, which lasted nearly a decade and involved Hamann, Herder, Goethe, Kant, and Mendelssohn, among others. An unintended consequence of Jacobi's book, which appeared in an expanded edition in 1789, was to focus the attention of his younger contemporaries on the attractions of Spinoza's philosophy and of pantheism generally.

Jacobi's primary concern in the *Pantheismusstreit* was neither Lessing nor Spinoza, but rationalism itself. For Jacobi, Spinoza's philosophy was an exemplar of rationalism in its assumption of the universal applicability of the principle of sufficient reason. If, according to that principle, every cause has an identifiable prior cause, then a consistent rationalism must be deterministic and fatalistic, for it is incompatible with the belief in a self-caused God and the freedom of the will. What rationalism cannot supply is a grounding for its demonstrations: this, Jacobi insisted, requires an act of faith. But, paradoxically, he also sought to justify his *salto mortale* ("mortal leap") by arguing that religious beliefs are self-evidently true, like mathematical axioms. Stung by the resulting accusations that he was "an enemy of reason, a preacher of blind faith" ("ein Vernunftfeind . . . ein Prediger des blinden Glaubens"), he published a dialogue, *David Hume über den Glaube* (*David Hume on Faith*, 1787), in which he drew on Hume and Thomas Reid to defend his insistence on the dependence of reason on faith, specifically in establishing causal connections between objects of perception. In a supplement to the dialogue, he criticized Kant for assuming that there are things in themselves (*Dinge an sich*) while denying that we can have knowledge of anything but phenomena: "*without* that presupposition [of the thing in itself] I could not enter into the [Kantian] system, and *with* it I could not remain within it."

Jacobi's criticism of Kant strongly influenced the subsequent development of German idealism in the philosophies of Fichte, Hegel, and Schelling. But Jacobi himself, in *Jacobi an Fichte* (*Jacobi to Fichte*, 1799) and *Von den göttlichen Dingen und ihrer Offenbarung* (*On Divine Things and Their Revelation*, 1811), caustically rejected first Fichte's theory of knowledge (*Wissenschaftslehre*) and then Schelling's philosophy of identity (*Identitätsphilosophie*) as merely disguised forms of Spinozism. The latter attack provoked an equally fierce response from Schelling and cost Jacobi his long (if difficult) friendship with Goethe. By the time of his death Jacobi was an isolated figure, his genuine contributions to philosophy overshadowed by his ad hominem polemics.

NICHOLAS HALMI

See also **Fichte, Johann Gottlieb; German Idealism: Its Philosophical Legacy; Germany: Cultural Survey; Goethe, Johann Wolfgang von; Hamann, Johann Georg; Kant, Immanuel; Lessing, Gotthold Ephraim; Mendelssohn, Moses; Religion:**

Germany; Schelling, Friedrich Wilhelm Joseph von; Sensibility; Sturm und Drang; Wieland, Christoph Martin.

Biography

Born in Düsseldorf, January 25, 1743. Briefly apprenticed to a merchant in Frankfurt, 1759. Studied science and philosophy under Georges Louis Le Sage in Geneva for three years. Returned to Düsseldorf to take over his father's sugar factory, 1764, and married Elisabeth (Betty) von Clermont (who died in 1784). Gave up control of the family business, 1772. Served as a civil administrator in the Duchy of Jülich-Berg, 1773–79, and briefly as a privy councillor in Bavaria, 1779. Left the Rhineland for Wandsbeck and then Eutin to avoid the advancing French army, 1794; Moved to Munich, 1805, to join the new Bavarian Academy of Sciences, and was elected its first president. Retired, 1812; oversaw the publication of his collected works, 1812–19. Died in Munich, March 10, 1819.

Selected Works

Collections

Werke. Edited by Friedrich Köppen and Friedrich Roth. 6 vols. (in 7). 1812–25.

Werke: Gesamtausgabe. Edited by Klaus Hammacher and Walter Jaeschke. 3 vols. to date. Hamburg: Meiner, 1998–.

Briefwechsel: Gesamtausgabe. Edited by Michael Brüggen and Siegfried Sudhof. 5 vols. to date. Stuttgart: Frommann, 1981–.

The Main Philosophical Writings and the Novel "Allwill." Translated by Gorgio di Giovanni. Montreal: McGill-Queens University Press, 1994.

Friedrich Heinrich Jacobi: Dokumente zu Leben und Werk. Edited by Michael Brüggen, Heinz Gockel, and Peter-Paul Schneider. 2 vols. to date. Stuttgart: Frommann, 1989–.

Philosophical Writings

Über die Lehre des Spinoza in Briefen an den Herrn Moses Mendelssohn. 1785; Rev. ed. 1789; further edited by Marion Lauschke. Hamburg: Meiner, 2000. Translated as *Concerning the Doctrine of Spinoza in Letters to Herr Moses Mendelssohn* by Gorgio di Giovanni. In *The Main Philosophical Writings and the Novel "Allwill."* Montreal: McGill-Queen's University Press, 1994.

Friedrich Heinrich Jacobi wider Mendelssohns Beschuldigung betreffend die Briefe über die Lehre des Spinozas. 1786.

David Hume über den Glauben, oder Idealismus und Realismus. 1787. Translated as *David Hume on Faith, or Idealism and Realism.* Gorgio di Giovanni. In *The Main Philosophical Writings and the Novel "Allwill."* Montreal: McGill-Queen's University Press, 1994.

Jacobi an Fichte. 1799. Translated as *Jacobi to Fichte.* Giorgio di Giovanni. In *The Main Philosophical Writings and the Novel "Allwill."* Montreal: McGill-Queen's University Press, 1994.

Von den göttlichen Dingen und ihrer Offenbarung. 1811; Rev. ed. 1822.

Die Hauptschriften zum Pantheismusstreit zwischen Jacobi und Mendelssohn. Edited by Heinrich Scholz. 1916. Translated as *The Spinoza Conversations between Lessing and Jacobi,* translated by G. Vallée, J. B. Lawson, and C. G. Chapple. Lanham: University Press of America, 1988.

Fiction

Eduard Allwills Papiere, published serially in *Isis* (1775) and *Der Teutsche Merkur* (1776).

First published in book form as *Eduard Allwills Briefsammlung,* 1792; Rev. ed. 1826. Edited by U. Terpstra, 1957. Translated as

Edward Allwill's Collection of Letters. Translated by Giorgio di Giovanni. In *The Main Philosophical Writings and the Novel "Allwill."* Montreal: McGill-Queen's University Press, 1994.

Freundschaft und Liebe, published serially in *Der Teutsche Merkur* (1777). First published in book form as *Woldemar: eine Seltenheit aus der Naturgeschichte,* 1779. Rev. eds. 1794, 1799, and 1826.

Bibliography

Altmann, Alexander. *Moses Mendelssohn: A Biographical Study.* London: Routledge, 1973.

Beck, Lewis White. *Early German Philosophy.* Cambridge, Mass.: Harvard University Press, 1969.

Beiser, Frederick C. *The Fate of Reason: German Philosophy from Kant to Fichte.* Cambridge, Mass.: Harvard University Press, 1987.

Bollow, Otto F. *Die Lebensphilosophie F. H. Jacobis.* Stuttgart: Kohlhammer, 1933.

Giovanni, Giorgio di. Introduction to Friedrich Hernrich Jacobi, *The Main Philosophical Writings and the Novel "Allwill."* Montreal: McGill-Queen's University Press, 1994.

Goethe, Johann Wolfgang. *From My Life.* Translated by Robert R. Heitner. New York: Suhrkamp, 1987.

Hammacher, Klaus. *Die Philosophie Friedrich Heinrich Jacobis.* Munich: Fink, 1969.

Lévy-Bruhl, Lucien. *La Philosophie de Jacobi.* Paris: Alcan, 1894.

McFarland, Thomas. *Coleridge and the Pantheist Tradition.* Oxford: Clarendon Press, 1969.

Scholz, Heinrich. "Einleitung." In *Die Hauptschriften zum Pantheismusstreit zwischen Jacobi und Mendelssohn.* Berlin: Reuther, 1916.

Weischedel, Wilhelm. *Jacobi und Schelling: eine philosophisch-theologische Kontroverse.* Darmstadt: Wissenschaftlich, 1969.

JANE EYRE 1847

Novel by Charlotte Brontë

Jane Eyre is one of the most outstanding novels of late Romanticism. It is doubtful that Charlotte Brontë considered herself a Romantic author, but there is no doubt that her novel displays a wide array of Romantic themes, concepts, and modes. It was written in the final years of the period and acquired an immense popularity immediately, as several reprints of the work confirm. Histories of literature tend to include it within the Victorian movement, which might be appropriate to a chronological extent, but some central features such as the main character, the use of the autobiography or use of the Gothic conventions make it advisable to label it as Romantic.

The novel is divided into three sections. The first part is the story of Jane Eyre's childhood; she lives with her aunt, Mrs. Reed, and then in a charitable school, Lowood Asylum. The second part narrates her stay at Mr. Rochester's house as a governess; the mixture of Romantic love and Gothic horror stands as its most important feature, though Jane Eyre's strong and truthful feelings have to be pointed out as well. The third section tells how she refuses marriage to a clergyman, only to eventually marry Rochester.

The subtitle of the novel indicates that it is an autobiography, which is not true, as Jane Eyre is a fictional character constructed by Brontë. The autobiographical mode emphasizes introspection, however, and an attention to individual psychology. It enables the narrator to describe Jane Eyre's vital development from a unique, individualized perspective, a concern central to Romantic narratives.

The novel has been considered religious in two senses: it portrays characters who hold Christian faith, and it adapts the language and forms of Christianity to the author's own literary purposes. The heroines of the novel find inspiration and release in spiritual experiences which cannot be expressed within the limits of religious orthodoxy; this creates an ambiguity in the general interpretation of the novel that has given way to varied feminist interpretations. *Jane Eyre* can be included within the Puritan tradition of English literature, along with John Bunyan's *The Pilgrim's Progress* and *Grace Abounding to the Chief of Sinners* or Milton's *Paradise Lost*, while simultaneously challenging the assumptions of that tradition.

The centrality of Romantic concerns in Jane Eyre should not be dismissed. Nevertheless, the use of the Gothic narrative mode, or more accurately the "New Gothic" as Heilman calls it, indicates the relevance of the work to the Romantic period. There are, however, some distinctive features that set Jane Eyre apart from the mainstream of Gothic literature, including the comic modifications or the lack of transcendence in terms of material reality. It is a more modern Gothic work, in which rationalist explanations can be given for the supernatural events that take place in the narrative. This links *Jane Eyre* to Edgar Allan Poe's or E. T. A. Hoffmann's stories.

Jane Eyre is out of step with the social standards of her time. She exemplifies the Romantic hero who is seeking the place she is meant to inhabit in society; she can even be considered as a Byronic character in the sense that she opposes society's dictates, leaning upon her own subjective interpretations as the only standard with which she measures the world. Rochester is presented as her opposite. His literary heritage can be traced back to Milton's Satan; in this sense he is also Byronic, but from the opposite, evil side.

Contemporary critical reaction to *Jane Eyre* was favorable. The critic George Lewes praised it as "the best novel of the season." The novel was reprinted three times within six months. It has been analyzed and read from different points of view and with a variety of approaches, which have generally emphasized the importance of the autobiographical mode, the psychoanalytic elements, and the feminist issues at stake in the novel. Motherhood, sexuality, and identity, the latter a postmodern concern not specific to feminist criticism, have been explored in the text. The social situation of the female writer in the nineteenth century has been given appropriate attention, *Jane Eyre* being an extraordinary case study because of its artistry and the role that the Brontë sisters played in their period (compared to other female novelists such as Elizabeth Gaskell or George Eliot). Probably this is the most fruitful trend of criticism of late, partly because of the topic of the novel and its portrayal of social dictates, partly because of the importance of contextual examinations of literary works.

In the nineteenth and twentieth centuries *Jane Eyre* served directly or indirectly as a model for other female writers. Jean Rhys made use of the plot for her novel *Wide Sargasso Sea*; writers including Adrienne Rich and Virginia Woolf have written essays commending *Jane Eyre*.

SANTIAGO RODRÍGUEZ GUERRERO-STRACHAN

Text

Jane Eyre, 1847. Numerous reprints since then, among those by Clarendon Press, 1969 and by W. W. Norton, 1971.

Bibliography

Allot, Miariam, ed. *The Brontës: the Critical Heritage.* London: Routledge and Kegan Paul, 1974.
———. *Charlotte Brontë: "Jane Eyre" and "Villette."* London: Macmillan, 1973.

Boumelha, Penny. *Charlotte Brontë.* Hemel Hempstead: Harvester Wheatsheaf, 1990.
Chase, Karen. *Eros and Psyche: The Representation of Personality in Charlotte Brontë, Charles Dickens and George Eliot.* London: Methuen, 1984.
Eagleton, Terry. *Myths of Power: A Marxist Study of the Brontës.* London: Macmillan, 1975.
Gilbert, Sandran, and Sara Gubar. *The Madwoman in the Attic: The Woman Writer and the Nineteenth-Century Literary Imagination.* New Haven, Conn.: Yale University Press, 1979.
Heilman, Robert. "Charlotte Brontë's 'New' Gothic." In *From Jane Austen to Joseph Conrad.* Edited by R. C. Rathburn and M. Steinmann Jr. Minneapolis: University of Minnesota Press, 1958.
Peters, Margot. *Unquiet Soul: A Biography of Charlotte Brontë.* London: Hodder and Stoughton, 1975.
Showalter, Elaine. *A Literature of Their Own: British Women Novelists from Brontë to Lessing.* London: Virago, 1982.
Tayler, Irene. *Holy Ghosts: The Male Muses of Emily and Charlotte Brontë.* New York: Columbia University Press, 1990.
Tromly, Annette. *The Cover of the Mask: The Autobiographers in Charlotte Brontë's Fiction.* Victoria, B.C.: English Literary Studies, University of Victoria, 1982.
Yaeger, Patricia. *Honey-Mad Women: Emancipatory Strategies in Women's Writings.* New York: Columbia University Press, 1988.

JÁNOS VITÉZ

Poem by Sándor Petöfi

Sándor Petöfi wrote a narrative poem entitled *János vitéz* (Sir John) in 1844. This poem, written in the "Hungarian alexandrine" (twelve-syllable lines) and divided into twenty-seven cantos, was an instant success when published in 1845. Petöfi's success was largely due to the ease of versification: rhymes in it occurred as naturally as in a village narrator's speech. The story itself was a typical folktale in which realistic and fantastic elements blended effortlessly, the storyline itself ascending from a native Hungarian scene to a universal Fairyland with a strong Hungarian colouring.

János vitéz consists of three parts. The first one (cantos 1–6) is characterized by intense realism. The hero Kukoricza Jancsi (Johnny Maize), a foundling shepherd boy, is in love with Iluska, a beautiful fair-haired orphan whose stepmother is as cruel to her as Jancsi's foster-father to him. The lovers usually meet at a brook where Iluska is washing clothes and Jancsi is grazing the sheep entrusted to him by his foster father. In a sunny summer afternoon they forget about their respective duties and enjoy the secret meeting, but are interrupted by the appearance of Iluska's stepmother (an old witch-like figure), anxious to find out why the girl is late in returning with the linen. She wildly abuses the young lovers; to make things worse, Jancsi discovers that his flock is gone. For his negligence his foster father drives him out of the house and, after a pathetic farewell to his beloved, Jancsi sets forth into the world.

In part two (cantos 7–17) neither realism nor the time factor is any longer relevant. Johnny becomes a hero in a world which is gradually changed into a timeless supernatural place. After an episode in a desolate forest (in a robbers' hideout) ending in Johnny's escape, the young man joins the army. As early as in the eighteenth century this was the only chance for a village boy to prove himself; later on Hungarian hussar veterans were known to tell fanciful stories about their exploits on faraway battlefields. Joining up with the hussars was therefore a realistic choice for a village lad like Johnny, but what follows leads us into the realm of fantasy. These particular hussars are on their way to defend France against Turkish invaders. After many incredible adventures Jancsi not only slays the Turkish general, but rescues the daughter of the King of France. In gratitude, her hand is offered to the brave hussar, but his devotion to his old lover is unflagging: he politely declines the offer. Having listened to Johnny's story, neither the King nor his daughter are offended; the King knights him (that is how he becomes János vitéz or Sir John), sending him on his way in a ship laden with gold and jewels. While on the homeward journey a storm wrecks his ship and John loses his treasure; he escapes with his life saved by a griffin.

After this fabulous episode another "realistic" element is introduced that thoroughly shocks our hero—upon the return to his village he finds Iluska dead and buried. He plucks a rose from her grave and sets out again, to continue his wanderings in the world. It is now, in the third part of the poem (cantos 18–27) that the narrative transports the reader into a supernatural world peopled by giants, witches, and fairies. Here John, according to the rules set in the folktales, overcomes a series of obstacles and reaches Fairyland, having crossed a sea which surrounds the world. This feat is done with the help of a giant who carries him over the sea; in the middle of the boundless sea there is an island, the island of the blessed, Fairyland. Sir John first has to defeat three monsters who guard the gates of Fairyland. Once there, for a moment he contemplates suicide: the bliss of others reminds him of his lost love. He throws the rose picked from Iluska's grave into a lake in the middle of

Fairyland that turns out to be the "water of life"—it resurrects the dead Iluska. The poem ends with the happy reunion of the lovers, who are duly elected as king and queen of Fairyland by the fairies enchanted by the young pair's beauty.

While D. Mervyn Jones finds *János vitéz* influenced by Mihály Vörösmarty's Romantic works, especially the *Valley of the Fairies*, clearly Petőfi's achievement lies in the masterful blending of realism and fantasy in a work which is accessible to any literate reader, including young children. In this "heroic folk poem" he managed to bridge the gap between "high" and "low" culture, the world of the Romantic imagination and oral folk tradition. The narrative is not only fanciful but full of humorous detail, and the poem ends on an "upbeat note" which, however, can be interpreted in two ways. Lóránt Czigány believes that with the description of Fairyland "Petőfi came to the conclusion that the only happiness which is available to mankind is love." The other possible interpretation is a more pessimistic one: that perfect love can be achieved *only in Fairyland*—that is, in our fantasies.

János vitéz has enjoyed great popularity ever since 1845. After numerous editions of the work itself, in 1904 it was adapted to the stage as a musical drama by Jenő Heltai, Károly Bakonyi and the composer Pongrác Kacsóh. In 1973 a full-length Hungarian animated film version was produced by Marcell Jankovics.

LÓRÁNT CZIGÁNY AND GEORGE GÖMÖRI

Bibliography

Basa Molnár, Enikö. *Sándor Petöfi*. Twayne: Boston, 1980.

JEWS

Romanticism could not be nearly as useful and beneficial for the Jews as the Enlightenment had been. In fact, the Jews played only a marginal role in the Romantic movement, although European authors employed the Jewish theme in works of literature. The lack of any direct Jewish involvement occurred because the ideology of Romanticism, with its emphasis on the poet's creative harnessing of divine power and idealization of the folk, was inconsistent with the Jews' political needs and intellectual tradition, at least as they understood them. In Central and Eastern Europe, where civil rights for the Jews were not entirely available, the great majority of the Jews were left out of the rarefied elite culture of the capitals. Moreover, for those Jews permitted entrance into elite salons, such as those in Berlin, conversion to Christianity was a familiar result, as the example of Rachel Varnhagen von Ense or the children of Moses Mendelsohn show. In contrast to Romanticism, the previous epoch, the Enlightenment and its embodiment in the French Revolution, had brought equal rights for the Jews in France and an extension of their rights in most of the German-speaking states.

The Romantic idea of the individual genius and the philistine rabble was not a paradigm particularly applicable to the Jews. After all, Jewish creativity had its foundation in collective learning. Few Jewish writers could valorize insanity as a source for artistic creativity, since in the Jewish tradition reason and argumentation (*pilpul*) were highly valued. Granted there were some positive images of irrationality in the Bible, such as King David's Psalms and the "Song of Songs," but Jewish mysticism was considered by cultured Jews as a reflection of the "uneducated" Jewish masses and therefore crass and debased. Romanticism's emphasis on sentiment, intense feeling, the exotic, and the uncivilized were also unfamiliar to the Jewish masses of Eastern Europe, for whom Romantic notions of love and eroticism, boredom and ennui, were entirely foreign.

The view of the folk as the embodiment of the traditional and true characteristics of the nation held dangers for the Jews of Europe. As Johann Gottfried von Herder's ideas of the nation grew more popular, minorities in Europe found themselves facing hostility, since now these peoples were not merely strange but also acted as a potentially harmful presence, a scar on the nation's purity.

If interpreted properly, the Romantic ideology could adequately embrace the Jewish experience. After all, Jewish history and the Jewish people certainly embodied the concepts of tradition, antiquity, creative individuality, and divine force. Some European writers, such as Lord Byron, in his series of poems entitled "Jewish Melodies" (1814–15), understood the power of the Jewish theme as the expression of failed revolution, unjustified suffering, and proud defiance. The Polish poet Adam Mickewicz saw in the oppressed Polish people, their very identity seemingly obliterated by foreign occupation, the "Christ among nations." He looked to the Jews as a model for the Poles: the Poles were also a "chosen" people. The French writer Eugene Sue used the Jews as the subject of a historical novel, *Le juif errant* (*The Wandering Jew*, 1844–45).

For the Jews themselves, the realization that the Jewish people had their own proper history and tradition, and that these subjects could become the object of serious study, did not take hold until the 1820s with the formation of the Society for the Culture and Science of the Jews (*Wissenschaft des Judentums*) in 1819. Among the leading figures of this movement were Edward Gans, Immanuel Wohnwill, (pseudonym, Wolf), and Leopold Zunz. But one should realize that the *Wissenschaft des Judentums* was a small movement and, moreover, that it had only slim connections with Romanticism. The desire to cultivate national self-consciousness was only a secondary goal, while primarily these writers wanted to spread enlightenment, to awaken the Jews to secular culture.

Surprisingly, it occurred to no one at the time that the Jews did not need to look to the distant past to recreate their own folk tradition, since the Jewish masses of Russia and eastern Europe were right at hand. Moreover, while only a century old, the Hasidic movement connected itself to a living tradition of intense religious meditation, the supernatural and irrational. Hasidism valorized folk culture, Jews used the folk language, Yiddish, as their means of communication and education, and they cultivated folk dance, story-telling, music, and magic. The Hasidic leader, the *tsaddik*, saw himself as a divine representative of God himself. Even more than the Orthodox purists, the *mitnagdim*, the Hasidic Jews were hostile to modern life and critical of the Enlightenment values of political equality and civil rights.

Unfortunately, Jews of the time were unable to notice the similarities between the Herderian Romantic ideals and Hasidism. Those who potentially could have drawn parallels were enlightened Jews for whom their Hasidic brethren were an embarrassment. It was not until the last quarter of the nineteenth century that historians and writers began to see the remarkable national creative impulse at the heart of Hasidism.

In terms of European Christian attitudes toward the Jews, Romanticism brought a conservative backlash against the universalism of the Enlightenment. Whereas previously—so the Enlightenment ideology had it—Jews as individual citizens could be included into the body politic, European Romantics viewed them in a dualistic manner: they were either the biblical heroes of the ancient world, oppressed but defiant, or in the present, members of an inferior and potentially dangerous culture who should either be converted to Christianity or at least educated in "modern" values. In the German territories Christian religious practices influenced the Jews, leading to the development of the Jewish reform movement (Meyer). In other situations, Jews converted purely for material gain. For example, Heinrich Heine considered conversion a useful "entrance ticket" into European culture.

It was only in the 1840s that a Europeanized Jew, Moses Hess, first came to the conclusion that Jewish national culture could alone provide positive elements for the creation of national identity. But even then Hess's ideas were too far ahead of his time. The world, it seems, caught up only towards the end of the nineteenth century, when it became unavoidably clear that many European countries, intolerant of their Jewish neighbors, relied on rhetoric that came into fashion during Romanticism to exclude the Jews from taking part in national political and economic life.

BRIAN HOROWITZ

Bibliography

Hertzburg, Arthur. *The French Enlightenment and the Jews.* New York: Columbia University Press, 1968.

Hess, Moses. *The Revival of Israel: Athens and Jerusalem, the Last Nationalist Question.* Translated by Meyer Waxman. Lincoln: University of Nebraska Press, 1995.

Katz, Jacob. *Out of the Ghetto: The Social Background of Jewish Emancipation 1770–1870.* Cambridge, Mass.: Harvard University Press, 1973.

Meyer, Michael A. *Response to Modernity: A History of the Reform Movement in Judaism.* New York: Oxford University Press, 1988.

Sholem, Gershom. "The Science of Judaism—Then and Now." In *The Messianic Idea in Judaism.* Translated by Michael A. Meyer. New York: Schoeken, 1971.

JÓKAI, MÓR (MAURUS) 1825–1904

Hungarian writer and journalist

Mór Jókai was a talented writer who achieved great popularity during his lifetime. This was due both to his talent for strong, appealing storytelling and his promotion of national Romanticism. His long lifespan afforded him opportunities to continually realign himself within the evolving political context of the period. In a sense he never departed from the liberal protestant traditions of his family in Komárom (a port on the River Danube), and it was his good fortune that he could take part in (and later commemorate) the 1848 revolution, which propelled Hungary toward modern development.

The young Jókai had ambitions as a playwright; he regarded the play *A zsidó fiú* (*The Jewish Boy*, 1843), a tragedy written in iambics, as his first mature literary work. In fact, literary history assigns that role to *Hétköznapok* (*Weekdays*), a novel modeled on Eugene Sue and Victor Hugo and published in 1846. This novel, while certainly imaginative, has been described by Lóránt Czigány as "extravagant," and while well received by the readers, Jókai was still searching for his most suitable form of expression. This he found after 1849, with a series of historical novels and sketches, published in rapid succession. During this period (which lasted till 1865) his writing focused on two broad themes: the distant past of Hungary (the "Turkish" novels), and its very recent past (the age of reform and the War of Independence). The "Turkish novels," the first of which is *Erdély aranykora* (*Amid the Wild Carpathians*, 1852), are typically Romantic evocations of national and individual conflicts against the background of the sixteenth and the seventeenth centuries, with few attempts made at psychological introspection. Jókai is clearly fascinated by outstanding individuals such as Ali, Pasha of Janina, the chief hero of the exciting and fast-paced *Janicsárok végnapjai* (*The Lion of Janina*, 1854). However, in presenting Ali's drama, Jókai finds it difficult to curb his buoyant imagination. In the 1850s Hungary was ruled directly from Vienna, and Hungarian society, by and large, refused to cooperate with Bach's centralistic government. Jókai's "Turkish" novels created a comfortable venue for national escapism. (Lóránt Czigány notes that these novels were still popular abroad at the beginning of the twentieth century).

There is less exoticism and more Hungarian local color in novels *Egy magyar nábob* (*A Hungarian Nabob*, 1853–54) and its sequel *Kárpáthy Zoltán* (*Zoltan Karpathy*, 1854–55). In fact, the first of these opens with the description of the *puszta* (according to the English translator, R. Nisbet Bain, "a wide-spreading heath"), thus setting the Romantic story against the background of Sánder Petofi's poems. The nabob in question is John Kárpáthy, a wealthy Hungarian magnate, who, having lived the carefree life of a heavy-drinking and womanizing aristocrat, marries a young middle-class woman and begets a son, Zoltán. After the 1825 diet (which is generally regarded as the beginning of the age of reform), both old Kárpáthy and other members of his class become socially conscious individuals who are now bent on improving living conditions and promoting culture in their country. The negative character in *Egy magyar nábob* is Count Abellino (alias Béla), the nabob's cosmopolitan nephew who spends most of his time in Parisian casinos and whose greed, which motivates him to plot a means of gaining the nabob's wealth for himself, makes him contest his uncle's will, which favors Zoltán. Zoltán is the idealized representative of the new generation which will struggle for a more just, independent Hungary, not yet achieved in 1848–49, but in part realized in the Compromise of 1867. While these novels are undoubtedly Romantic in their composition and in the characterization of the main heroes, they also have many humorous, realistic aspects, and capture the reader with their colorful and interesting narratives.

During the years following the Compromise, Jókai continued his national Romantic cycle with *A koszivu ember fiai* (*The Baron's Sons*, 1869), a novel of romance and intrigue about the adventures of the three Baradlay brothers before and during the 1848–49 War of Independence. *A fekete gyémántok* (*Black Diamonds*, 1872) introduces Iván Berend, an entrepreneur. Berend is an engineer and an inventor who owns a coal mine at Bondavár, but he is also one of Jókai's superheroes—a war veteran who fought as a hussar in the War of Independence, a great public speaker, and an impeccable gentleman who also loves the simple folk of his own country. Berend succeeds in spite of his difficulties with numerous domestic and foreign pressure groups, which include the clergy as well as influential financial circles. Natural disasters and bold utopian thinking about the future of society (foreseeing unbridled technological progress) are part of *Black Diamonds*, the influence of which was felt even half a century later when Stefan Zeromski, the Polish novelist, wrote *Przedwiosnie* (*Early Spring*), the chief character of which is seduced by a vision of "glass houses" as foreseen by Berend, Jókai's fictional voice. This is, incidentally, the first of Jókai's novels that is critical of the speculation and financial manipulation that already characterized capitalism in the second half of the nineteenth century.

If *Fekete gyémántok* contained some elements of science fiction, Jókai's next project created the first specimen of the genre on Hungarian soil. *A jovo század regénye* (*Novel of the Next Century*, 1872–74) is a bold vision of the second half of the twentieth century, based on the interpolation of expected technological advances and political perspectives. The central hero is David Tatrangi, a Hungarian Sekler from Transylvania whose discovery, a glass-like substance called *ichor*, allows him to build flying machines. These play a decisive role in the wars fought between Austria–Hungary (a symbol of civilized Europe), and a Russia first taken over by the "nihilists" and then ruled with an iron fist by President Madame Alexandra, who eventually restores the monarchy. The capital for the mass production of Tatrangi's airplanes is provided by an African-American banker, Mr. Severus, who later betrays his partner for the sake of the bewitching Tsaritsa. Jókai's description of a massive air battle over Lake Baykal may have been the very first of its kind in any language, but what is even more ambitious and astonishing is his dream of creating a society that outlaws war and social injustice, a society of plenty which is threatened at the end of the book by the approach of a comet. In the end the comet does not hit the earth but it does land on the moon, creating another planet subsequently named "Pax."

A jovo század regénye is an example of Romantic science fiction. In Jókai's novel the main heroes have extraordinary qualities: Tatrangi is not only honest, intelligent, a good husband, and an incredibly versatile person, but he also has a political foresight that is almost uncanny. Madame Alexandra ("Sasha") is another exceptional individual, a beautiful but evil "superwoman" whose pride and obsession with power drive her to inhuman deeds (for example, the massacre of a vast number of Russians in her counter-revolutionary coup). While Jókai's visions of the future include ideas that today may seem naive or slightly ridiculous, several are amazingly accurate, and the highly readable narratives illustrate the skill of this brilliant storyteller.

If *The Novel of the Next Century* envisioned a collective utopia, *Az arany ember* (*The Golden Man*, 1873; translated as *Timár's Two Worlds*) was motivated by the middle-aged Jákai's individual utopia, the wish to escape to an earthly paradise of peace and harmony. His hero, the Danube skipper Mihály Timár, becomes a rich citizen of Komárom thanks to the treasure of Ali Chorbadjee, a Turkish refugee; he also becomes the guardian of the Turk's daughter Timea and eventually marries her. Timea is grateful to Timár but is not really in love with him; after many adventures, Timár finds happiness with Noemi, a simple, loving young woman on a nameless island in the Danube. While the concept of *Az arany ember* is still Romantic and some of the minor figures are classified according to the good-versus-evil dichotomy of earlier Jókai heroes, the character of Timár is much more complex; his feelings of guilt and conflict between duty and pleasure lend credibility to his psychological profile. The novel's duality (some realistic descriptions of Danube trade and contemporary corruption scandals and the psychological realism of Timár's character on the one hand, and the escapism of Timár's final choice on the other) may be what most appealed to readers and, indeed, *Az arany ember* remains one of Jókai's most popular novels.

Both Hungarian and foreign history provided ample material for Jókai's imagination. He produced novels popular in English-speaking countries such as *Névtelen vár* (*The Nameless Castle*, 1877) and *Szabadság a hó alatt* (*Freedom Under the Snow*, 1880; translated as *The Green Book*). The latter, which deals with the Decembrist conspiracy in Russia and includes purely imaginary elements (for example, Alexander Pushkin saving the life of the tsar's daughter), was so well-received in England that it was published in no less than six editions by the end of the nineteenth century and prompted a *Daily Telegraph* critic to rank the Hungarian author with the elder Alexandre Dumas. Another historical novel was *A locsei fehér asszony* (*The White Lady of Locse*, 1884–85), set at the time of the War of Independence of 1703–11. As in many previous Jókai novels, love, treason, and revenge play an important part in the shaping of historical events.

The changing world affected the aging Jókai. In some of his later novels he makes more use of realism. One of his less popular works is *Rab Ráby* (*Ráby in Jail*, 1879) which deals with the clash between the reforming Habsburg King Joseph II and the Hungarian nobility of the time, and which criticizes the anachronistic rules based on counties that characterized the administrative system. In the novel *A gazdag szegények* (*The Rich Poor*, 1890) Jókai turns his attention to a social class hitherto neglected in his fiction: the urban poor living in the Budapest suburbs, whose values are often preferable to those of the rich. Nevertheless, critics point out that during the last fifteen years of his career, Jókai's prose became repetitive and lacked new ideas. Nonetheless, his success is phenomenal in terms of the number of books published and read: the "national edition" of his works (1894–98) ran to 100 volumes, including poems, short stories, and plays. As a playwright, while scoring fleeting successes with some historical plays—*A szigetvári vértanuk* (*The Martyrs of Szigetvár*, 1860) and *Levente* (1897)—he fared best with stage adaptations of his most popular novels. His autobiographical sketches and reminiscences were published in 1904 under the title *Onmagáról* (*On Himself*) with an introduction by Zsolt Beothy.

Jókai's style has been described as musical and sonorous. In his early works he preferred long sentences with numerous subordinate clauses, rhetorical questions, and exclamations. Later he employed what Czigány calls "the natural rhythm of colloquial speech," also excelling in descriptions of nature and natural phenomena. While his style is peppered with foreign expressions (some of the historical novels with Latin phrases), he is the first Hungarian prose writer (alongside with József Báró Eötvös) to naturally blend new words created by the language reform with traditional expressions. He also uses dialect to great effect. Known as the "great storyteller," Jókai influenced generations of Hungarian writers, and (though often criticized for his "boundless optimism"), left an indelible mark on Hungarian national consciousness.

GEORGE GÖMÖRI

Biography

Born in Komárom, February 18, 1825 to a wealthy noble family; his father was a lawyer. He was educated first in the Reformed Protestant school of his native town, then between 1835 and 1837 in Pozsony (Pressburg, now Bratislava in Slovakia) to learn German. He began his higher education in the Reformed College of Pápa, where he met Petöfi and read his first published short story in the College's literary circle. Jókai studied law at Kecskemét (1824–44), but having passed his final examination in 1846 at Pest, he stopped practicing law. He always regarded 1845 as the beginning of his career as a writer (he wrote his first play in that year). In July 1847 he became editor of the review *Eletképek* (*Life Sketches*), which he turned into a mouthpiece of democratic liberal ideas. Already in 1846 he joined the Society of Ten (a group of young radical writers) and, consequently, became one of the leaders of the revolution of March 15, 1848. He married the actress Róza Laborfalvi in the summer of 1848, which led to a quarrel with his family. During the War of Independence he fled to Debrecen with the Kossuth government in early 1849 and edited there the moderate journal *Esti Lapok* (*Evening Journal*). After the military defeat of the Hungarian Army in August 1849 he went into hiding for a while, but his wife managed to get him a letter of safe conduct from Komárom that enabled Jókai to return to Pest as early as the turn of 1849–50. He became a popular journalist and writer in the 1850s, contributing to many journals and editing some of them (*Nagy Tukor*, 1856; *Ustokos*, 1858; *A Hon*; 1863). He was elected a member of the Academy of Sciences in 1858 and of the Kisfaludy Society in 1860. He was elected parliamentary deputy in 1861 and continued to serve as a member of Parliament from 1865 to 1896 in the (from 1867) governing party of Kálmán Tisza. At the request of Prince Rudolf he became a member of the editorial board of the publication *The Austro-Hungarian Monarchy in Pictures and Writing* (1887–1901). In 1886 his wife died; he then married Bella Grosz, a much younger woman, in 1899. His fifty-year jubilee as a writer was a national event, celebrated by the publication of his collected works in one hundred volumes (1894–98). In 1897 he became a member of the upper chamber. In 1900, during the Great Exposition in Paris, he was given a warm reception by French writers. He continued writing to his death on May 4, 1904. He was buried in the National Pantheon in Budapest; his funeral was attended by thousands of mourners.

Selected works

Osszes muvei. Vols 1–100. Budapest, 1894–98.
Hátrahagyott muvei. Vols 1–10. Budapest, 1912.
Osszes muvei. Vols 1–98. Edited by Lengyel Dénes and Miklós Nagy. Budapest, 1962.

Bibliography

Czigány, Lóránt. "Jókai's Popularity in Victorian England." In *The New Hungarian Quarterly* (1975).
———. *The Oxford History of Hungarian Literature*. Oxford: Clarendon Press, 1984.
Gomori, Gyorgy. "A jovo század regénye—a századvég nézetébol." In *Az új század Kuszobén*. Hollandiai Mikes Kelemen Kor/Jelenkor: Pécs, 1998. 87–102.
Mikszáth, Kálmán. *Jókai élete és kora*. Budapest: Muvelt Nép, 1954.
Nagy, Miklós. *Jókai*. Budapest, 1968.
Reményi, József. "Mór Jókai, Romancer, 1825–1904." In *Hungarian Writers and Literature*. New Brunswick, N.J.: Rutgers University Press, 165–77.
Sotér, István. *Jókai Mór*. Budapest: Franklin, 1941.

JOURNALS AND PERIODICALS: GERMANY

The division of Germany in the eighteenth century into some 300 separate states, of which nearly forty still existed in 1850, prejudiced the production of journals no less than other features of cultural life. The absence of unified intellectual activity focused on a metropolitan center prompted repeated attempts to found a journal with national appeal as a forum for supraprovincial information and debate. The same political fragmentation, however, frustrated such attempts and condemned most journals to limited circulation and a brief lifespan. They remained mainly the outlets of local literary coteries or particular political groupings. *Das Athenäum*, the most celebrated of Romantic journals, lasted only two years (1798–1800) and drew its contributors almost entirely from the Schlegel circle in Jena.

Moreover, German journals of the time, in their anxiety to overcome intellectual isolation, tended to the cerebral rather than the entertaining, offering philosophical essays and aesthetic or political theorizing at least as much as creative fiction or literary reviews.

The first attempt to institute a national journal was made by Christoph Martin Wieland with his quarterly *Teutsche Merkur* (*German Mercury*), founded in 1773 in the up-and-coming cultural center of Weimar, although the journal exerted significant influence only in the 1780s. Wieland serialized some of his own works but also included contributions by Johann Gottfried Herder, Johann Wolfgang von Goethe, and Johann Christoph Friedrich von Schiller, and a series of influential essays by Karl

Leonhard Reinhold popularizing Kantian philosophy. In Jena, linked administratively and intellectually to neighboring Weimar, the *Allgemeine Literatur-Zeitung* (*General Journal of Literature*) was founded in 1785 by Christian Gottfried Schütz. This journal, appearing at six-week intervals, also propagated Kantian thought and in the 1790s published contributions by Johann Gottlieb Fichte and the rising generation of Romantics, especially August Wilhelm and Friedrich Schlegel.

Weimar and Jena were between 1794 and 1805 the setting for the classicism of Goethe and Schiller, which triggered a whole series of almanacs, calendars, and journals. Goethe edited two periodicals devoted to art history and theory: the *Propyläen*, which proclaimed a strict neoclassicism but survived only from 1798 to 1800; and *Über Kunst und Altertum* (*On Art and Antiquity*), founded in 1814, which denounced the religious art of the Nazarene painters and the generally pro-Catholic tendencies of later Romanticism in Germany. The most important journal of classicism was Schiller's *Die Horen* (*The Horae*, named for the Greek goddesses of order, justice, and peace), appearing monthly and carrying not only poetry by Goethe, Schiller, and Johann Christian Friedrich Hölderlin but also Schiller's treatise "Über naive und sentimentalische Dichtung" (On Naive and Reflective Poetry) and his "Über die ästhetische Erziehung des Menschen" (On the Aesthetic Education of Man). The declared aim of *Die Horen* was to avoid discussion of immediate political issues, and this impracticable and controversial restriction, together with the abstruse content of the journal, led to its termination in 1797 after only three years.

Meanwhile in Berlin the Enlightenment continued to set the intellectual tone. Its leading journals were Friedrich Nicolai's *Allgemeine Deutsche Bibliothek* (*General German Library*) (1765–1806), an organ for literary reviews from a rigidly rationalist perspective, and the *Berlinische Monatsschrift* (*Berlin Monthly*), edited by Friedrich Gedike and Johann Erich Biester from 1783 to 1796 and containing instructive pieces on a variety of topical issues by authors such as Moses Mendelssohn and Immanuel Kant. The 1790s saw a proliferation of political journals given over to the polemics which had excited Schiller's distaste: from the anti-revolutionary camp publications such as *Eudämonia*, published in Leipzig from 1795 to 1798 by reactionaries who attributed the upheaval in France to the influence of the Enlightenment, and on the pro-revolutionary side Jacobin magazines such as Andreas Georg Friedrich Rebmann's *Die Geissel* (*The Scourge*), appearing in Altona and then Mainz from 1797 to 1799. In Berlin the most important pro-revolutionary journal was *Deutschland*, edited by the composer Johann Friedrich Reichardt, which in the one year of its existence (1796) contained extracts from works by Friedrich Schlegel and Wilhelm Heinrich Wackenroder. Reichardt replaced it with the *Lyceum der schönen Künste* (*Lyceum of the Fine Arts*), also lasting only 12 months and including further politically progressive pieces by Schlegel and also his first collection of Romantic aphorisms.

Aphorisms or "fragments," as Schlegel entitled them, were a striking feature of *Das Athenäum*, launched by the Schlegels in 1798 after the disappearance of the *Lyceum* and the loss to August Wilhelm of his outlets in both *Die Horen* and the *Allgemeine Literatur-Zeitung* following a dispute with Schiller. The aphorisms—one group composed by various authors, one group exclusively by Friedrich Schlegel (*Ideen* [*Ideas*]), and one by Novalis (*Blütenstaub* [*Pollen*])—were provocative, open-ended *aperçus* on a variety of political, social, and aesthetic issues and encapsulated key Romantic doctrines. *Athenäum* Fragment 116 offers a famous definition of Romanticism: "Romantic Poesy is a universal progressive poesy." Equally important in the *Athenäum* were a prescient theory of the novel and the enunciation of the concept of Romantic Irony as an instrument of intellectual agility. After the end of the *Athenäum* in 1800 and Friedrich Schlegel's move to Paris, he published *Europa* (1803–5), a journal devoted mainly to art history and especially to the painting of the Renaissance and the Middle Ages, which he idealized from an increasingly religious perspective.

The vehicle for German Romanticism in its middle phase in Heidelberg was the *Zeitung für Einsiedler* (*Journal for Hermits*), edited by Achim von Arnim with the collaboration of Clemens Brentano and Joseph Görres. In a period of military humiliation (hence the retreat into "hermitage") it counter-attacked by emphasizing the German cultural tradition, its concentration on older German literature and legend making the brothers Grimm obvious contributors. It survived for barely a year (1808). Among the many other Romantic periodicals, two equally short-lived journals edited by Heinrich von Kleist, an author close to the Romantics but not allied with them, deserve mention: *Phöbus* (1808), published in Dresden and co-edited by Adam Müller; and the *Berliner Abendblätter* (1810–11; *Berlin Evening Paper*), the first German daily newspaper. Both manifested conservative and patriotic tendencies.

The Restoration period in Germany after 1815 was marked by a plethora of generally mediocre journals devoted to reviewing and the publication of occasional poetry, such as the *Morgenblatt für gebildete Stände* (1807–65; *Morning Paper for the Educated Classes*), published in Stuttgart, and the *Abendzeitung* (*Evening Journal*), edited in Dresden and in the 1820s numbering Ludwig Tieck among its contributors. Heinrich Heine placed his poems in such journals. Yet the problem for journal editors in Germany was unchanged: despite the growing middle-class readership, the division of Germany prevented national impact, the more so since absolutism was reinforced after 1819 by repressive censorship. It was not until the 1848 revolutions were imminent that German periodicals tackled major national issues, and even then from abroad: in 1844 in Paris Karl Marx and Arnold Ruge published their *Deutsch-Französische Jahrbücher* (*German-French Yearbooks*).

RICHARD LITTLEJOHNS

Bibliography

Behler, Ernst. *Die Zeitschriften der Brüder Schlegel*. Darmstadt: Wissenschaftliche Buchgesellschaft, 1983.

Bobeth, Johannes. *Die Zeitschriften der Romantik*. Leipzig: Haessel, 1911 (reprint Hildesheim and New York: Olms, 1970).

Hocks, Paul and Schmidt, Peter. *Literarische und politische Zeitschriften 1789–1805*. Stuttgart: Metzler, 1975.

JOURNALS AND PERIODICALS: JEWISH

Jewish journalism began as an effect of the Jewish Enlightenment. As Moses Mendelssohn sought to purify and modernize Judaism under the influence of the European Enlightenment, he also adopted Enlightenment modes of expression. A case in point was the 1755 launching of *Kohelet Musar* (*The Moralist*, 1755), which was a moral weekly in the tradition of *The Spectator* (1711–present), and which was the first instance of Hebrew-language journalism. *Ha-Me'asef* (*Collection*), which began publication in 1783 in Königsberg, shortly followed by *Sulamith* (*Maid of Shulim*), was influenced by *Kohelet Musar*, but—as its title, *The Gatherer* suggested—offered a greater variety of articles. The writers were chiefly *maskilim* ("The enlightened"—that is, partisans, or *haskalah*) who wrote for each other and their young followers. These journals sometimes included current events, but they were not yet newspapers. The Jewish press expressed the concerns of specific communities and also created unity among communities in different countries. In Western and Central Europe, these papers were written in the local national vernacular. Although their circulations were inevitably small, these journals reached far wider readerships than their Hebrew predecessors (or than such scholarly vernacular journals as Leopold Zunz's short-lived *Zeitschrift für die Wissenschaft des Judenthums* (*Journal of Jewish Scholarship*, 1822–23).

The appearance of Jewish newspapers coincided with, and gained strength from, the Damascus Affair of 1840, when a Capuchin priest disappeared in Damascus. First, the Damascus Christians, then the local authorities, accused Jews of murdering him for ritual purposes, and several damascene Jews were seized and tortured. These events scandalized liberal Europe and, naturally enough, horrified Europe's Jews. Reports of these events quickly spread through the European press, and became the dominant news items in Jewish papers, which now became the means to bring relevant news to Jewish homes.

The first, and most influential newspaper predated the Damascus Affair. This was the *Allgemeine Zeitung des Judenthums* (*General Newspaper*), established in 1837 at Magdeburg under the editorship of the moderate Reform rabbi, Ludwig Philippsohn. The *Allgemeine Zeitung* reported heavily on Jewish affairs in Germany, and also on new settlements in the land of Israel. In 1840, Julius Fürth at Leipzig created a rival paper, *Der Orient* (*The East*). This was more scholarly than the *Allgemeine Zeitung*, and only survived until 1852. Fürth's experiment with a weekly *Sabbath-Blatt* (*Sabbath Page*, 1842) that reported on cultural events, however, was successful and inspired a more popular German-Jewish press. German-Jewish readers demanded a higher standard from their monthly press, from which two early examples stand out. In 1839 the reformer Mendel Hess started publishing *Der Israelit des neunzehnten Jahrhunderts* (*The Jew of the Nineteenth Century*), to which Samuel Enboch replied in 1845 with the neo-orthodox *Der treue Zionswächter* (*The Faithful Guardian of Zion*).

London's *Jewish Chronicle* reported news in considerable detail and achieved high prestige and influence. It first appeared in 1841, and had to be revived in 1844, but in 1847 began to appear as a weekly. Along with reporting political news of special interest to Jewish readers, it urged English Jews toward an informed Jewish observancy. The *Archives Israélites de France* (1840) began to appear in Paris under the editorship of Samuel Cahen, a biblical scholar. Its editorial line was close to Philippsohn's in the *Allgemeine Zeitung*, though the *Archives* was a weekly, not a daily, and had a low circulation.

Jewish newspapers appeared later in Eastern-Central Europe, initially with *Haskalah*-style Hebrew as the language of choice (later in the nineteenth century, Yiddish, newly reworked as a literary language, became the dominant language for eastern-European Jewish journalism). The major Hebrew-language papers were *ha-Maggid* (*The Herald*), founded in 1856 in Lyck, Prussia; and *ha-Melitz* (*The Advocate*) and *ha-Carmel*, which were founded in 1860 in Odessa and Vilna, respectively.

The mere act of adapting the formerly holy tongue of Hebrew to the needs of journalism was a controversial innovation. These journals were also programmatic, and existed to further cultural change among their readers. For example, the Galician *maskilim* Joseph Perl and Isaac Erter created *he-Haluz* (*The Pioneer*, [1852]; a noun later favored by Zionists) aimed at unchanging religious tradition. Suggestively, their editors liked to name them after dawn. Thus, in 1860 the *maskilim* created the *Razsvet* (*Dawn*, 1861) as a Russian-language Jewish journal. Similarly, *Ha-Tsefirah* (*The Dawn*), launched by the Society for the Promotion of Culture among Jews, began publication in Warsaw in 1862. Finally, in 1868 Perez Smolenskin started his journal *ha-Shahar* (*The Dawn*) to promote autoemancipation.

These papers, especially those published in languages other than Hebrew or Yiddish, showed the progress of Jewish acculturation produced by full (England and France) or partial (Germany and Russia) emancipation. However, the acculturation overall was only partial, since Jews felt a need for their own press to comment on specifically Jewish events or, alternately, on gentile events seen in a Jewish light. A further effect of increased Jewish acculturation was the growing number of Jewish journalists publishing or writing in the general press. Significantly, important press agencies, such as Reuters in England and Wolff's in Germany, were founded by Jews. Some point to the cosmopolitanism of Jews as an aid to their journalism; Henri de Blowitz, for example, was a correspondent for *The Times* (London) and, as such, invented the newspaper interview.

ROBERT SOUTHARD

Bibliography

Ettinger, Schmuel. "The Modern Period." In *A History of the Jewish People*. Edited by H. H. ben-Sasson. Cambridge, Mass.: Harvard University Press, 1974.

Gilon, Meir. *Kohelet Musar shel Mendelssohn*. 1979.

Mevorah, B. "Ikvoteiha shel 'alilat damesek be hitpathuta shel ha-'itonut ha-yehudit ba-shanim 1840–1846." *Zion* 23–24, nos. 1–2 (1958–59): 46–65.

Meyer, Michel. "Jewish Self-Understanding." In *German Jewish History in Modern Times*. Vol. 2. *Emancipation and Acculturation: 1780–1871*. Edited by Michael Meyer. New York: Columbia University Press, 1997.

JOURNALS AND PERIODICALS: RUSSIA

Journalism in Russia does not have a long tradition. The early eighteenth century saw sporadic publication of journals and newspapers. Many of the journals were privately printed in small editions for friends; others were academic in nature and therefore limited in scope. The situation began to change when Catherine the Great took up the ideas of the French Enlightenment and decided that Russia needed satirical journals in the manner of Joseph Addison and Sir Richard Steele's *Tatler* (1709–11) and *Spectator* (1711–12). In 1769 she founded her own journal, *Vsyakaya Vsyachina* (*All Sorts and Sundries*), in which she set the tone of "satire with a smile" directed at moral vices. However, when other satirical journals used "satire with a sting" to criticize specific issues, such as serfdom, Catherine responded by closing them. The government came down most heavily on journalists in 1774 after the Pugachev Rebellion. The Masonic spirit of some of the publications also displeased Catherine.

The most notable of the journalists who suffered heavily from Catherine's retreat from Enlightenment ideals, Nikolai Novikov, nevertheless managed to publish four journals until the measures of 1774 effectively silenced the satiric press. Novikov continued his publishing and journalistic activities until his arrest in 1792. Under the directorship of Princess Ekaterina Dashkova, *Sobesednik Lyubiteley Rossiiskogo Slova* (*Interlocutor of Lovers of the Russian Word*, 1783–84), the organ of the Academy of Sciences, also managed to survive and publish the leading writers of the day. In addition, Nikolai Karamzin became active in journalism in the 1790s. His almanacs (*Aglaya*, 1794–95, and *Aonidy*, 1796–99) and journal, *Moskovskiy zhurnal* (*Moscow Journal*, 1791–92) helped to popularize sentimentalism in Russia. *Moskovskiy zhurnal* was the first journal to separate its contents into sections, and the forerunner of the "thick journals" that became the most popular venue for all of the major writers of the nineteenth century. From 1802–4 Karamzin also edited the highly professional journal *Vestnik Evropy* (1802–30; *Herald of Europe*).

Almanacs played a major role in Russian literary life of the nineteenth century; almost 500 were published between 1800 and 1850. Most of them had limited runs, some appearing only once. Four of the most important almanacs championed various forms of Romanticism. Edited by the Decembrists Aleksandr Bestuzhev-Marlinskii and Kondratii Ryleev, *Polyarnaya Zvezda* (1823–25; *Polar Star*) advocated civic Romanticism and nationalistic literature. It published belles-lettres as well as criticism, with Marlinskii's annual surveys, "Glances at Russian Literature," one of its most noteworthy features. *Mnemozyne* (*Mnemosyne*, 1824–25; 4 vols.) provided a platform for the German idealistic Romanticism of the Liubomudry (Lovers of Wisdom) society. The editors, Vil'gel'm Kyukhel'beker and Vladimir Odoevskii, published original Russian literature rather than translations. Sympathetic to European Romanticism and Karamzin's language reforms, *Severnye Tsvety* (*Northern Flowers*, 1825–32; 8 vols.) best represents the state of Russian literature of this period. Anton Del'vig edited the elegant, beautifully illustrated volumes; Orest Somov, the chief theoretician of Russian Romanticism, coedited the final five. Egor' Alad'in's *Nevskiy Al'manakh* (*Nevsky Almanac*, 1825–33) modeled itself on *Polyarnaya Zvezda* and published Romantic prose and poetry. This popular illustrated periodical enjoyed commercial but not critical success.

The journals of the time also expressed the political and literary biases of the editorial boards and thus became a forum for polemical debate. The nature of the polemics changed over the years: Karamzin's language reforms versus Alexandr Semenovich Shishkov's linguistic conservatism, Romanticism versus neoclassicism, Westernizers versus Slavophiles, conservatives versus radicals. Sometimes the orientation of individual journals changed with different editors. For example, the sentimental/Romantic bias of *Vestnik Evropy* gradually took on an anti-Romantic slant through five editorships. Nikolai Polevoy's liberal *Moskovskiy Telegraf* (*Moscow Telegraph*, 1825–34) backed Romanticism and published many European Romantics. A true "encyclopedic" journal, it had sections on a wide range of subjects from literature and the arts to agriculture and economics. It was closed after publishing a negative review of a play staged under the patronage of the tsar.

The *Liubomudry* backed Mikhail Pogodin's *Moskovskiy Vestnik* (*Moscow Herald*, 1827–30) with its German Romantic slant. At first the journal was strong in literature; when it narrowed its focus to history, it lost readers and eventually closed. Nikolai Nadezhdin billed his *Teleskop* (*Telescope*, 1831–36) as a "journal of contemporary enlightenment." Both Westernizers and Slavophiles contributed to this progressive journal, and Vissarion Belinskii published his influential *Literaturnye mechtaniya* (*Literary reveries*) in a supplement, *Molva* (*Rumor*). The government closed *Teleskop* after it published Petr Chaadaev's controversial "Philosophical Letter."

With the literary historian and poet Stepan Shevyrev, Pogodin edited *Moskvitianin* (*The Muscovite*, 1841–56), a Slavophile journal of literature and history that stood for "Official Nationalism" and stressed the religious and moral nature of Russia. Another "patriotic" journal, *Syn Otechestva* (*Son of the Fatherland*, 1812–52), flourished under the editorial guidance of the leaders of the so-called viper press (Faddei Bulgarin, Nikolai Grech, and Osip Senkovskii), and the financial backing of the publisher, Aleksandr Smirdin. It began as a historical–political journal, then added literature in 1818; it declined in the 1830s–40s. Within the pages of the journal, Bulgarin, Grech, and Senkovsky carried on polemical debates with almost everyone. The editors received the sobriquet of "viper" because they were generally perceived as government lackeys.

Smirdin also financed the most commercially-successful journal of the age, *Biblioteka Dlya Chteniya* (*The Reading Library*, 1834–65), edited by Senkovsky and Grech. The journal attracted the best talent in Russia and did much to popularize Russian literature; it also published much translated literature. The variety of its offerings appealed to a large readership. Alexandr Pushkin's journal, *Sovremennik* (*The Contemporary*, 1836–66), challenged the supremacy of *Biblioteka Dlya Chteniya*. In *Sovremennik*, Pushkin and his friends simply wanted to publish good literature. Though ostensibly nonpolitical in orientation, the journal championed Enlightenment ideals over Official Nationalism. After Pushkin's death in 1837, his friends Petr Vyazemskii, Vasilii Zhukovskii, Vladimir Odoevskii, Andrey Kraevskii, and Petr Pletnyov became the editors, with Pletnyov in complete control from 1838–46. When Ivan Panaev and Nikolai Nekrasov (who became editor) purchased *Sovremennik* in 1846, they made it the voice of the progressives and Russia's leading literary journal until it closed. After Kraevskii left *Sovremennik*, he founded *Otechestvennye Zapiski* (*Notes of the Fatherland*, 1839–84), a scholarly literary journal whose Western stance challenged prevailing conservatism. With Belinskii as its leading critic until his death in 1848, *Otechestvennye Zapiski* championed realism over outmoded Romanticism.

Newspapers did not gain the wide currency of the journals, although two deserve mention because they symbolize the evolution of Russian journalism in the nineteenth century: Del'vig and Somov's *Literaturnaya Gazeta* (*Literary Gazette*, 1830–31) and Bulgarin and Grech's *Severnaya Pchela* (*Northern Bee*, 1825–62). *Literaturnaya Gazeta* published only literature of the highest quality, but failed because of low readership. On the other hand, *Severnaya Pchela* survived mainly because of political patronage, but it also catered to the changing tastes of the reading public. *Literaturnaya Gazeta* offered its outmoded aristocratic idealism and refined literary taste to an audience made up mostly of bureaucrats and petty officials whose plebeian tastes demanded bombastic nationalism and accessible prose. They found both in publications like *Severnaya Pchela*.

CHRISTINE A. RYDEL

Bibliography

Babaeva, E. G., and B. I. Esin. *Russkaya zhurnalistika i literatura XIX v. Sbornik statei*. Moscow: Moskovskiy gosudarstvenny universitet, 1979.

Berezina, V. G., et. al. *Istoriya russkoy zhurnalistiki XIII-XIX vekov*. 3d corrected ed. Edited by A. V. Zapadov. Moscow: Vysshaya shkola, 1973.

Boyer, Arline. "A Description of Selected Periodicals in the First Half of the Nineteenth Century." *Russian Literature Triquarterly* 3 (1972): 465–73.

Lemke, M. K. *Ocherki po istorii russkoy tsenzury i zhurnalistiki XIX stoletiya*, 1904. Reprint, The Hague: Mouton, 1970.

Marker, Gary. *Publishing, Printing, and the Origins of Intellectual Life in Russia, 1700–1800*. Princeton, N.J.: Princeton University Press, 1985.

Martinsen, Deborah A., ed. *Literary Journals in Imperial Russia*. Cambridge: Cambridge University Press, 1997.

Smirnov-Sokol'skiy, A. I. *Russkie literaturnye al'manakhi i sborniki XVIII-XIX vv.* Moscow: Izdatel'stvo "Kniga," 1965.

Stan'ko, A. I. *Russkie gazety pervoy poloviny XIX veka*. Rostov: Izdatel'stvo Rostovskogo universiteta, 1969.

JOURNALS AND PERIODICALS: UNITED STATES

In the first part of Benjamin Franklin's *Autobiography* (1791), we see eighteenth-century American print culture in miniature. Here Franklin describes his apprenticeship to his printer brother James; James's imprisonment (June 12–July 7, 1722) for printing a piece found offensive by the Massachusetts Assembly; Franklin's own anonymous submissions to his brother's paper; and Franklin's employment in the rundown printshop operated by Keimer. In one memorable passage, Franklin describes Keimer's shortage of letters of type, noting, "there was no Letter Founder in America. I had seen Types cast at James's in London . . . I now contriv'd a Mold . . . struck the Matrices in Lead, and thus supplied in a pretty tolerable way all Deficiencies. I also engrav'd several Things on occasion. I made the Ink, I was Warehouse-man and everything." While Franklin's own youthful experience had already shown him that not all printers ran their business on such precarious foundations as Keimer, the story highlights an important facet of journal and periodical production—indeed, of all print culture—in colonial America. Publications were frequently the product of small, localized businesses. Publishers ran the risk of being censored by government. And for every skilled printer such as Franklin, there was a Keimer who had little notion of any international standard of professionalism to which his productions might aspire. The catalyst driving both the expansion and professionalization of American print culture was the American Revolution, during which journals and periodicals declared their partisanship through the ballads, engravings, and stories they carried. Prior to the revolution, however, and following the cessation of hostilities between Britain and America in 1783, periodicals reflect a burgeoning intellectual scene in which an intelligentsia seeks to transform a colonized periphery of empire into a series of cosmopolitan centres with their own rich cultural lives.

In the early part of the eighteenth century, colonial printers generally worked in the service of the lower house of colonial legislatures. The expectation was that their journals and periodicals would serve to make known the broad outlines of state policy, but ephemeral print culture was not expected to comment on the perceived rights and wrongs of government policy; indeed, parliamentary rulings on libel effectively restricted that which could be reported and the manner in which reports could be written up. Other forms of printing and publishing were often simply not viable. An analysis by Cynthia and Gregory Stiverson of the book trade in Virginia from the mid-eighteenth century shows that publishing books in the Chesapeake region would have been commercial suicide, when one volume of Tobias Smollett's *History* would have cost a carpenter—"one of the highest-paid laborers in colonial Virginia"—about three months' wages. Nor were literacy rates in states dependent on a thinly spread population (for example, the tobacco-based economy of Virginia) high enough or concentrated enough to make local print industries an option. Those in colonial America who wished to read and be read might subscribe to the London-based *Gentleman's* magazine; gain their knowledge of scientific developments from the imported *Philosophical Transactions of the Royal Society*, or support the increasingly sophisticated *Maryland Gazette*; while the publication of poems in the *American Mercury* and *Pennsylvania Gazette* suggests a self-consciously "literary" readership.

The Revolution of 1776 and the disquiet that preceded it demonstrated the power of American periodicals and journals to form and give voice to the public mood. Franklin was already aware of the power of the press and the importance of an engaging style that he had employed to great effect in his immensely influential *Poor Richard's Almanac* (1733), filled with maxims for achieving wealth and promoting hard work. From the first stirrings of unrest expressed about the notorious Stamp Act of 1765, papers such as the *New York Gazette* turned political actions into homespun allegory that did not patronize any level of reader. So the *New York Gazette* makes political actions in Westminster understandable to average readers in New York State through the story of John Bull's marriage of his daughter, Lady North American Liberty, to Toleration. Liberty's dowry is a tract of land that she names after herself. But despite Liberty's marriage, Commerce has his beady eye upon her, and Mrs. John Bull, seeing the foolishness of the original match "determined to . . . destroy her Daughter, disavow her Son-in-Law, make slaves of all their Children and Servants." This is a far cry from early colonial printers' inability to comment on government policy. In the 1770s and 1780s, overt political comment and partisanship is at its height in the American press. Ballads directed against Westminster politicians and policies can be shown to be shared rapidly among titles such as the *Freeman's Journal*; the *Massachusetts Spy, or Thomas's Boston Journal* (later the *Massachusetts Spy, or American Oracle of Liberty*); the *New-Hampshire Gazette*; the *Norwich Packet*; the *Pennsylvania Gazette*; the *Pennsylvania Packet*; the *Providence Gazette*, and the *Virginia Gazette*.

To chart the date of publication of any single ballad among a group of these publications is to gain a sense of the speed with which information traveled and propaganda was disseminated in Revolutionary America. When peace was finally concluded in 1783, a prototypical "information highway" had been formed down the eastern seaboard, signaling an increasingly diverse print culture and an increasingly ordered means of distributing printed material. British-based periodicals and journals would continue to be popular imports, but they now competed for readers' attentions alongside publications printed nearer home, and more interested in a distinct American readership.

GLYNIS RIDLEY

Bibliography

Copeland, David A. *Colonial American Newspapers: Character and Content*. Newark: University of Delaware Press, 1997.
———. *Debating the Issues in Colonial Newspapers: Primary Documents on Events of the Period*. Westport, Conn.: Greenwood, 2000.
Humphrey, Carol Sue. *The Press of the Young Republic, 1783–1833*. Westport, Conn.: Greenwood, 1996.
Sloan, William David, and Julie Hedgepath Williams. *The Early American Press, 1690–1783*. Westport, Conn.: Greenwood, 1994.
Smith, Jeffrey A. *Printers and Press Freedom: The Ideology of Early American Journalism*. New York: Oxford University Press, 1988.

JOURNAL OF EUGÈNE DELACROIX 1822–1824, 1847–1863

The Journal of Eugène Delacroix is one of the key documents of the Romantic movement, ranking alongside Berlioz's *Memoirs* for its passion, observations on contemporary society, and absorption with the self and the mysteries of the creative process.

Delacroix first kept his journal from September 3, 1822 until October 5, 1824 when, for no apparent reason, he suddenly stopped. He did not begin it again until January 1847 and then continued until June 22, 1863, less than two months before his death. Unfortunately the journal for 1848 is lost—it is traditionally said to have been left by Delacroix in a horse-drawn carriage when returning to Paris from his country house at Champrosay.

The form and content of the two portions of the journal reflect the changed priorities and maturation that took place between the ages of twenty-six and forty-eight. The earlier journal is the chronicle of a fashionable young man trying to live a full social life on a limited budget. As such, it records meetings with friends, meals, visits to concerts and plays, gives detailed accounts of expenditure on food, paint, and materials, as well as technical notes, discussions of paintings seen, and plans for future reading. A good proportion of the early journal is also concerned with love affairs, flirtations with servant girls and maids, and casual, paid sex with his models.

The second journal is much more concerned with theoretical matters and Delacroix's response to the art of his times; it also contains the notes for the *Dictionary of the Fine Arts*, which he planned but never completed. This concern with public pronouncements dates from 1857 following his election to the Institut on January 10 of that year. As well as containing more substantial subject matter, the later journal is also physically more imposing, written in tall household account ledgers, rather than on pasted-in scraps of paper.

Delacroix began his journal with a declaration of his intention to preserve the truth that reads, "I am carrying out my plan; formulated so many times, of writing a journal. My keenest wish is not to lose sight of the fact that I am only writing for myself alone; thus I will be truthful, I hope, and I will become the better for it. These pages will reproach me for my instability." Significantly, Delacroix started the work on the eighth anniversary of the death of his mother, and although he did not mention this on the entry for that day, two days later he confided: "May her spirit always be near me as I write, and may nothing I put into it cause her to blush for her son!"

A regular reader of the personal writings of past figures as varied as Marcus Aurelius, Giovanni Giacomo Casanova, and Michel Montaigne, Delacroix was also very familiar with the work of the Enlightenment author and philosopher Jean-Jacques Rousseau. In fact, the beginning of his journal has echoes of Rousseau's own Confessions, written around 1766–70 and first published in 1782. As Rousseau then wrote, "I am commencing an undertaking, hitherto without precedent and which will never find an imitator. I desire to set before my fellows a man in all the truth of nature; and this man shall be myself."

Yet despite Delacroix's initial promise, it is soon apparent that there is a considerable amount of self-censorship, and the reader does not get the impression of a voyeur penetrating the innermost private thoughts of the author.

In making the decision to keep a journal, Delacroix was participating in a trend toward personal and self-investigative writing that had gathered momentum at the end of the eighteenth century. Thanks to the uncertainties of the Revolution and the Napoleonic Wars, there had been a shift from a universal response to events and phenomena to an individual and subjective attitude. When the world could not be explained by simple cause and effect, many writers turned inwards for solace and explanation, and the confession and the journal replaced the historical survey or novel written in the third person.

Delacroix saw the keeping of a journal as a way of preserving the past and also of giving order to his life. He noted, "The future is all black. The past that has not been preserved is the same. Can I pass a day without sleeping and without eating! That is for the body. But my mind and the record of my soul, all that will be annihilated, because I do not want to owe what remains of them to the obligation of writing. On the contrary, nothing is better than the doing of a little chore that recurs daily." More important still, the discipline of the journal was also proof of the productive use of time, whereby the deadly menace of ennui was banished and time was given value and meaning by the act of recording thought.

The later journal has more philosophical reflections on art and aesthetics, and underpins Delacroix's insistence on the differences between literature and art. He always felt that painting was superior to the written word because of its variety and complexity, and its ability to leave elements to the viewer's imagination. Literature, by contrast, demanded constant attention and delivered only a few key ideas; painting was more immediate and yet more suggestive because, in Delacroix's opinion, a bridge was formed between the mind of artist and the mind of the spectator. The *Journal*'s lack of narrative structure, its noncumulative nature, and its complexity also coincided with Delacroix's particular views on pictorial values.

Delacroix deeply invested himself in the later journal, and the self he described within its pages shaped his attitudes to life and became the dominant aspect of his autobiography. His self-absorption in the journal confirmed a trend that had begun in the 1830s, that of a retreat into himself and an incessant desire to work. Although the product of considerable labor, Delacroix did not want the journal published in his lifetime, though he did lend portions to the critic Théophile Silvestre as material for an essay of 1854.

There have been some notable studies on the content and style of the journal G. P. Mras has painstakingly tracked down the sources of Delacroix's theories from Renaissance and Enlightenment authors, and believed Delacroix considered painting akin to music in their common ability to render the intangible tangible. M. Hanoosh sees the brevity and autonomy of individual *Journal* entries as intimately connected to the characteristics of Delacroix's painting rather than the conventions of literature, and thus a vindication of his ultimate belief that painting was superior. A. Laruc examines the *Journal* from a literary standpoint and considers it an exercise in the genre of Romantic melancholy.

SIMON LEE

Text

Delacroix, E. *Journal 1822–1863*. Preface by Hubert Damisch, with an introduction and notes by André Joubin. Rev. ed. Paris: Régis Labourdette, 1996.

Bibliography

Hanoosh, Michele. *Painting and the Journal of Eugène Delacroix*. Princeton, N.J.: Princeton University Press, 1995.

Larue, Anne. *Romantisme et Mélancolie: Le Journal de Delacroix*. Paris: Honoré Champion, 1998.

Mras, George P. *Eugène Delacroix's Theory of Art*. Princeton, N.J.: Princeton University Press, 1966.

JOVELLANOS, GASPAR MELCHOR DE 1744–1811

Spanish writer

Along with Benito Jerónimo Feijoo, Gaspar Melchor de Jovellanos is considered one of the primary figures of the Spanish Enlightenment. An erudite and prolific man, Jovellanos pursued various artistic and intellectual endeavors. His reputation rests on his contributions to various fields rather than on special merit in any single genre. He was a creative writer and literary critic; he also wrote on aesthetics, educational theory, political philosophy, economics, and public administration. Francisco José de Goya y Lucientes, a friend of Jovellanos, captures Jovellanos's seriousness of purpose in a painting completed in 1798. Now in Madrid's El Prado, the portrait shows an elegantly dressed and pensive Jovellanos in front of a desk, holding an open book on his lap. A statue of Minerva, goddess of knowledge, rests on top of the desk among the books and papers.

Were a unifying thread discernable in Jovellanos' work—spanning as it did many subjects and genres—it would be the urge to discard outmoded norms with the intent to improve, even perfect, aesthetic forms, ideas, and institutions. In this respect, Jovellanos is a committed proponent of the ideals of the Enlightenment. What sets him apart from many of his Spanish contemporaries is, on the one hand, the sheer volume of his writings, and on the other, his active involvement in many of the pressing issues of his day.

Less clear is Jovellanos's reputation as a pre-Romantic, which has been argued for by a number of literary historians. It has been pointed out, for example, that his work contains elements that predefine the Romantic canon, such as his use of history as inspiration, appreciation of nature, concern for the less privileged, and promotion of direct, spontaneous, and accessible language. Jovellanos's reputation as a champion of neoclassicism, however, remains unchallenged, as does his standing as a leading exponent of rationalist thinking as understood in the second half of the eighteenth century.

Jovellanos wrote poetry, drama, and prose. His poetic output, notwithstanding a few exceptions, is well-executed and technically proficient but devoid of qualities necessary to secure him a leading place among the poets of his generation. The same may be said of his dramatic works: while not entirely forgotten, they have elicited little interest and infrequent staging. His prose work (his essays and reports in particular) have contributed to his reputation more significantly, and the problems he examined, such as rural underdevelopment and unequal wealth distribution, remain relevant today.

Like many of his contemporaries, Jovellanos subscribed to Ignacio de Luzán's critique of Baroque aesthetics, as expressed in *La Poética* (*Poetics*, 1737). As the principal theorist of neoclassicism in Spain, Luzán insisted on the preeminence of order in art, not inspiration, and the need to abide by set precepts and rules in writing. In his exposition of literary principles, Luzán emphasized the instructive role of art; the unities of time, place, and action in dramatic compositions; and the importance of maintaining the purity of individual literary genres. Luzán also believed in the value of history, Spanish history in particular, as a worthy subject of dramatic plots.

Jovellanos's first play, the tragedy *Pelayo* (1769), faithfully implements many of Luzán's precepts. Performed in 1782 and published posthumously in 1832, *Pelayo* combines official history and unsubstantiated apocrypha as it relates the aftermath of the Muslim conquest of the Iberian Peninsula in the early eighth century. The drama derives its name from one of its characters, the noble Pelayo, the national hero credited with the first Christian victory against the Muslims and the beginning of the Castilian reconquest. The action takes place in Gijón, a city in Asturias that was Jovellanos's birthplace and the birthplace of the Castilian *Reconquista*. *Pelayo* is written in verse, in a form known as *romance* heroico (eleven-syllable verses rhymed in even-numbered lines). A second stage effort, the more popular *El delincuente honrado* (*The Honorable Culprit*, 1773) was written in prose, performed the following year, and published by the author in 1787. The play explores the fate of Torcuato, an innocent man victimized by unjust laws. Torcuato's fate highlights an important social theme deemed instructive to an audience. *El delincuente* was translated into several European languages, and enjoyed some popularity in Europe and America into the 1840s.

Jovellanos began writing poetry early in life, yet remained modest and apologetic about his interest in verse; in fact, he burned many of his early compositions, and only fifty two poems have survived. Influenced by Luzán's views, Jovellanos wrote lyric poems, satires, and epistles, among other verse. The best known titles are the verse epistles "Carta de Jovino a sus amigos salmantinos" ("Letter from Jovino to his Salamancan Friends," 1776), in which he dispenses literary advice to a group of contemporary poets from the Salamanca School; "Epístola de Jovino a Anfriso" ("Epistle from Jovino to Anfriso," 1779), which explores the tension between memory and emotion on the one hand and the desire for a peaceful and contemplative life on the other; "Canto guerrero para los asurianos" ("Asturian Battle Hymn," 1810), a patriotic piece encouraging resistance to Napoleon; and two satires (1767, 1786; known separately as the first satire and the second satire or collectively as *A Arnesto* [*To Arnesto*]), published in the influential periodical *El Censor* in 1786 and 1787, in which Jovellanos laments the moral lassitude of men and women of the Spanish aristocracy. In true neoclassical fashion, these compositions contain their share of latinized names, allusions to classical mythology, nymphs and muses in particular, and poetic pseudonyms.

Jovellanos's prose works cemented his reputation to a greater extent than his creative writing as the leading figure of the Spanish Enlightenment. In the course of his career he became a member of several academies and societies, the elite institutions of the Enlightenment (e.g., the Economic Society of Madrid, 1778; the Academies of History and Fine Arts, 1780; the Academy of Canon Law, 1782; the Royal Spanish Academy and Royal Commission on Commerce, Currency and Mines, 1783; the Academy of Public Law, 1785).

Jovellanos's prose is varied and extensive. Among the better-known titles is *Informe en el expediente de ley agraria* (*Report on the Agrarian Law*, 1794) in which he criticizes the damaging effects of primogeniture and the concentration of property in the hands of the church. The report was placed on the Index of Forbidden Books in 1825. His *Memoria sobre el arreglo de la policía de espectáculos y diversiones públicas, y sobre su origen en España* (*Report on the Regulation of Spectacles and Public Entertainments and on their Origin in Spain*, 1790) urges the abolition of outdated legislation pertaining to popular entertainment. His *Memoria en defensa de la Junta Central* (*Report on the Defense of the Junta Central*, 1811) is part political memoir, part treatise on good government. There are several additional works, some of them extensive, on education, art, and architecture, as well as numerous speeches on politics, art, education, geography, and economics.

CLARA ESTOW

Biography

Born in Gijón, Asturias, January 5, 1744. Studied canon law at the Universities of Oviedo, Osma, and Avila from 1757 on and received a degree in canon law from the University of Alcalá de Henares in 1764. Appointed criminal magistrate in Seville in 1768 and in Madrid in 1778; in 1780, appointed to the Council of Military Orders; exiled to Asturias in 1790; appointed Ambassador to Russia in 1797, but appointment rescinded and named minister of justice instead. Relieved of the ministry in 1798 and sent to Asturias. Arrested in 1801 and sent to Majorca until 1808, when he became a member of the Junta Central. Junta Central is dissolved in 1810; on November 27, 1811 Jovellanos died of pneumonia in Puerto de Vega (Asturias).

Selected Works

Collections
Obras en prosa. Edited by José Caso González: 1969.
Poesía; teatro; Prosa. Edited by José Luis Abellán: 1979.
Poesía; teatro; Prosa literaria. Edited by John H. Polt, Madrid: 1993.

Individual Works
A Arnesto. 1786 and 1767.
Canto guerrero para los asuriauos. 1810.

Bibliography

Caso González, José M. *Jovellanos*. Barcelona: Ariel, 1998.
Fernández Fernández, José Luis. *Jovellanos: antropología y teoría de la sociedad*. Madrid: UPCO, 1991.
Fernández Sanz, Amable. *Gaspar de Jovellanos: 1744–1811*. Madrid: Ediciones del Orto, 1995.
Helman, Edith. *Jovellanos y Goya*. Madrid: Taurus, 1970.
Polt, John H. R. *Jovellanos and his English Sources: Economic, Philosophical, and Political Writings*. Philadelphia: American Philosophical Society, 1964.
———. *Gaspar Melchor de Jovellanos*. New York: Twayne, 1971.

JUDAISM 1760–1850

Major changes in Jewish demography were under way during the years 1760–1850. At the start of the eighteenth century, there were about one million Jews in the world, and the numbers of Sephardic (formerly Spanish) and Ashkenazic (northern European) Jews were roughly equal. By 1800, the total had increased to two and a half million Jews, with Ashkenazic numbers increasing more rapidly and outpacing concurrent gentile population growth (by 1880, on the eve of large-scale migration to the Americas, there would be about seven million Jews). The direction of Jewish migration changed as well. In consequence of late medieval expulsions, by 1750 most Jews lived either in the Ottoman Empire or the Polish–Lithuanian Republic, with smaller communities in western cities. Before 1850, migrations westward and from villages into cities had begun and later increased.

Major changes in Jewish self-conception and legal arrangements accompanied population growth. Jews defined themselves as living *b' galut* (in exile) since the destruction of the Second Temple by the Romans in 70 C.E. They lived in legal ambiguity. On the one hand, they possessed their own comprehensive body of law, or *halakha*, and enjoyed varying degrees of self-administration wherever they were allowed to reside. On the other hand, they were sovereign nowhere. Their privilege of residence, which rarely permitted ownership of land, was restricted and easily revocable by the gentile authorities. They existed precariously in fetid, overcrowded ghettos or tiny eastern *shtetlach* (small towns) or on Polish estates, and had little protection against abuse.

The rabbis taught that *dina de-malkhuta dina* (the law of the land is the law). Jews were bound by their own law to obey gentile laws except when those commanded apostasy, murder, or sexual pollution. Therefore, in 1750, Jews were scattered in disparate communities and were tolerated as visitors in, rather than civic members of, the several gentile states where they resided. They also were linguistically distinct: Hebrew and Aramaic were the holy languages of male-dominated legal study and worship. There were also Jewish languages for everyday affairs. In northern Europe ordinary dealings might occur in Yiddish, a Germanic language written in Hebrew characters whose literary flowering would occur later in the nineteenth century. In sephardic lands Jews spoke Judaismo, a descendant of medieval Spanish, and more colloquial than the liturgical Ladino. These were also written in Hebrew block characters.

This period saw the beginning and the uneven, partial progress of the problematic legal and social process termed "Jewish emancipation." Eventually, the emancipation drew on the discourses of rights and citizenries that informed late-eighteenth-century democratic revolutions. Even earlier, mercantilistic ideas of rational exploitation of people and resources had occasioned some amelioration of Jews' legal conditions. The Austrian emperor Joseph II's Toleranzpatent (Edict of Toleration, 1782) is a case in point. Because the first modern Jewish social scientists were German Jews, German Jewish history is often treated as normative. That is a little misleading. In the German states, Jewish emancipation began during Napoleonic occupation and accompanied other social reforms undertaken

to defeat him. By 1850, emancipation was complete nowhere, much less uncontested. By contrast, continual ad hoc decisions and enactments ended most restrictions on the smaller, and less self-conscious, Jewish population of England.

France also varied from the Germanic pattern. As a result of legal enactments during the revolutionary and Napoleonic periods, the once discrete Jewish communities of France had French citizens of the "Mosaic persuasion" as their descendants. They changed from an ethnicity to a community of belief. Another pattern of change appeared in the Russian Pale of Settlement (formerly Polish–Lithuanian lands to which most Russian Jews were confined by law). Institutions of Jewish self-governance, already in disrepair before the Partitions of Poland in 1772, 1793, and 1795, were abolished, and harsh measures including the drafting of Jewish youngsters into the army, and the modernization of Jewish education, were undertaken against the Jews. Jews successfully withstood these pressures, though they underwent profound changes that were largely visible in the second half of the nineteenth century. It is a mistake to see changes imposed by Russian authorities as entirely negative in intent and effect.

In any event, emancipation was not welcomed as a self-evident good by all Jews; Jewish conservatives recognized the threat that it posed to Jewish legal observance. Questions of how to accommodate legal changes—and, relatedly, of how to take advantage of new possibilities without ceasing to be Jewish—drove Jewish intellectual change in central and western Europe. In Germany, Jewish denominationalism came as a long-term consequence of the *haskalah* (the Jewish enlightenment). In addition, as German Jews joined the middle class, women increasingly set the tone of domestic religious observance. Reform Judaism appeared as an effort to modernize traditional Jewish liturgy and to reconceive Jewish theology in modernity. Thus, Jews in Hamburg in 1818 built what they called a "temple" and introduced organ music into services. In North America, in an independent movement, Jews in Charleston, South Carolina, founded a "Reformed Society." Reform's intellectual leaders were Samuel Holdheim, who sought sweeping or "radical change," and the more measured and scholarly Abraham Geiger. Zacharias Frankel was also engaged in reform, but he sought only changes that could be continuous with older traditions. His "historical school" is the inspiration of what became Conservative Judaism. Hungarian Jewish Reform, normally termed "neologue" Judaism, combined theological modernization with continued voluntary observance of Jewish law. If Reform was a departure from traditional Judaism, so was "neo-Orthodoxy," pioneered by Samson Raphael Hirsch. In response to Reform, he argued that law and tradition were unchangeable and authoritative; however, modernization in profession, dress, and education were necessary. Hirsch was not alone. In Hamburg Isaac Bernays, and the talmudist Ya'aqov Ettlinger in Mannheim, modified liturgy while maintaining legal orthodoxy.

Most Jews lived farther east, in Austrian Galicia and the Russian pale of settlement. Denominalization did not occur there, but another departure from earlier tradition did. A *Hasid* was a "pious one," and *Hasidism* is the name given to the movement of religious enthusiasm started about 1750 in southeastern Poland by Rabbi Yisra'el ben Eli'ezer, the *baal shem tov* ("master of the good name"). He wandered in Podolia, Volhynia, and Galicia, and won adherents while he worked wonders. He devised a new mysticism that he passed orally to his followers. His student, Dov Ber of Mezhirech, institutionalized the Hasidic movement. Hasidism asked Jews to seek *da'at* ("mindfulness") as a means of reuniting with divine truth. This dispensed with formal legal training, at least for ordinary Jews. Therefore it was an attack on traditional Jewish leaders of wealth and talmudic learning. Ordinary Hasidim were not self-sufficient, however, and needed a *tsaddik* ("righteous man," often honored as a rebbe) who was not merely learned and righteous but also might have special access to the divine. Eventually, *tsaddikim* might form rabbinic dynasties for various Hasidic communities. Hasidism spread rapidly among eastern European Jews, though not in Lithuania where it provoked the countermovement of the *mitnagdim* ("opponents") led by Eliahu ben Shlomo Zalman, the *gaon* of Vilna, who objected to the unlearned and unseemly popular quality of Hasidic practice and to its undue celebration of its leaders.

ROBERT SOUTHARD

Bibliography

Ben Sasson, H. H., ed. *A History of the Jewish People.* Cambridge, Mass.: Harvard, 1976.

Birnbaum, Pierre, and Ira Katznelson, eds. *Paths of Emancipation: Jews, States, and Citizenship.* Princeton, N.J.: Princeton University Press, 1995.

Diner, Hasia. *A Time for Gathering: The Second Immigration 1820–1880.* Baltimore: Johns Hopkins University Press, 1992.

Feldman, David. *Englishmen and Jews: Social Relations and Political Culture.* New Haven, Conn.: Yale University Press, 1994.

Greenberg, Louis. *The Jews in Russia: The Struggle for Emancipation.* 2 vols. New York: Schocken, 1976.

Harris, Jay M. *How Do We Know This? Midrash and the Fragmentation of Modern Judaism.* Albany: State University of New York Press, 1995.

Hertz, Aleksander. *The Jews in Polish Culture.* Evanston, Ill.: Northwestern University Press, 1988.

Hertzberg, Arthur. *The French Enlightenment and the Jews.* New York: Columbia, 1970.

Hundert, Gershon. *The Jews in a Polish Private Town: The Jews in Opatów in the Eighteenth Century.* Baltimore: Johns Hopkins University Press, 1992.

Hyman, Paula E. *The Jews of Modern France.* Berkeley, Calif., 1998.

Katz, Jacob. *Out of the Ghetto.* New York: Schocken, 1973.

Meyer, Michael. *Response to Modernity.* Oxford and New York: Oxford University Press, 1988.

———, ed. *German Jewish History in Modern Times.* Vols. 1 and 2. New York: Columbia University Press, 1996.

Sachar, Howard M. *The Course of Modern Jewish History.* Rev. ed. New York: Vintage, 1990.

Sorkin, David. *The Transformation of German Jewry.* Oxford: Oxford University Press, 1987.

Stanislawsky, Michael. *Tsar Nicholas I and the Jews: The Transformation of Jewish Society in Russia 1825–1855.* Philadelphia: JPS, 1983.

Vital, David. *A People Apart: The Jews of Europe 1789–1939.* Oxford: Oxford University Press, 1999.

JULIE, OU LA NOUVELLE HÉLOÏSE 1761

Novel by Jean-Jacques Rousseau

Julie, ou la nouvelle Héloïse (*Julie, or the New Heloise*) takes its title from the tumultuous history surrounding the medieval lovers Pierre Abélard and Heloise. Jean-Jacques Rousseau reinvents this story of forbidden love for an eighteenth-century reading public eager to indulge in spontaneous feelings and authentic sensibilities. After 1760, even the decadent aristocracy began to consider alternatives to the cynicism associated with love and marriage, in which one party was bound to win or lose in a merciless but ingenious game. *Julie* turned the tide in the direction of pathos or unabashed sentimentality, though French fiction had, in general, carried with it the moralizing features and stylistic fluidity that Rousseau inherited from the neoclassical tradition. However, Charles-Augustin de Sainte-Beuve noted in Rousseau textures and tonal qualities not seen before in the French language; he also emphasized the overwhelming response of female readership to *Julie*, which broke new ground in eighteenth-century French culture.

Rousseau's deliberate choice to philosophize in letters represents an attempt to capitalize on the development of the novel or "le genre romanesque"—laid down by earlier practitioners such as Madame de Lafayette (Rousseau apparently modeled his confession scene on her *Princesse de Clèves*, 1678), the Abbé Prévost, especially his *Manon Lescaut and Cleveland* (1731) and his leadership role in the translation of Samuel Richardson's novels into French; the works of Pierre Marivaux (1730s) and Marie-Jeanne Riccoboni (1750s and 1760s); Madame de Grafigny's *Lettres péruviennes* (1747); and a few translations of English authors such as Daniel Defoe and Jonathan Swift.

Even though *Julie* articulates some of the social distinctions raised in these works, it went one step further in introducing a kinetic abundance of dramatic qualities (catastrophes, deaths, ruin, banishment, betrayal, and disappointment) that forces the reader to respond emotionally to what Frederick C. Green called the "first Romantic novel" because Romanticism advocates the individual's right to develop the ego as nature allows, over and against institutionalized prohibitions, particularly those associated with love and marriage. Rousseau's assertion that "everywhere in society the heart is in contradiction with the law" forms the basis of his breakaway thinking of the 1750s, when he distanced himself from friends and colleagues among "les philosophes," generalist thinkers who relied upon scientific data, rationalist motifs, "Iles bienséances" of order and refined taste, and cool detachment to promote a deist worldview. Rousseau's appeal to raw emotion and full-blown sentimentality galvanized a readership ready to submit to "delicious suffering" and "the happiness of tears"—terms later adopted by the German Sturm und Drang movement, which was in many respects a Rousseauistic cult.

A similar response, especially among female readers in England and Germany, suggests that Europe had accepted a new rhetorical mode contextualized in sentimental fiction: a suspension of disbelief that implicates the reader in the tales of the protagonists, as if the reader participates as an accomplice in the genuine saga of true people experiencing heightened emotions in realistic situations. Yet, novels written in the late eighteenth century do not anticipate the later capacious Romanticism of the nineteenth century, which cuts across social classes, with characters of timeless interest and an intense analysis of socioeconomic and political conditions. Even though Rousseau was deeply concerned with the preservation of social order through marriage and family, Saint-Preux is a forerunner of that lonely Byronic figure in a majestic landscape driven by disordered passions and irreconcilable principles, much like Stendhal's hero Julien Sorel in *Le Rouge et le Noir* (*The Red and the Black*, 1830).

Even a cursory reading of *Julie* reveals an elevated tone and hyperbolic language, particularly in letters written by Saint-Preux during his exile from Julie. The description of mountain scenery is one of the first in French literature, and in it the reader is accosted by elements of the sublime:

> continuelles extases torrents des plus délicieux sentiments la magnificence, la majeste de l'ensemble qui ravit les sens . . . je ne sais quel caractère grand et sublime . . . des régions éthérées . . . tous les désirs trop vifs s'émoussent . . . une émotion légère et douce . . . la grandeur, la beauté, de milles étonnants spectacles—a profondeur de ces abîmes . . . ces chansons de vieilles romances.

This revolution in overt sentimentality was well-received (*Julie* went through seventy editions between 1761 and 1800) except among Enlightenment authors, who saw it as a pale imitation of Samuel Richardson's *Clarissa* (1747–48), weighted down by implausible characters and sententious moralizing. Certainly Julie could never be the paragon that Clarissa represents, but her views on education, religion, country living, and the division of labor are not without merit. However, a modern reader cannot help but observe that Wolmar and Julie manage their domestic affairs with the same precision as a Swiss clock; thus they do not interact with each other or with their estate employees any more than the hands of the clock relate with its inner mechanisms. Furthermore, this long and complex epistolary novel expends a great deal of energy justifying the benefits of life in a rural setting while the interlocutors remain *indoors* at their writing desks in order to explain in voluminous letters emotions stimulated by the great *outdoors*.

When compared with *Clarissa*, Rousseau's attempt to "remove" Julie from the novel seems contrived; her death, the result of a fever that comes after she saves her son from drowning, represents a form of mental euthanasia or self-imposed closure given that her love for Saint-Preux has never diminished. It is ironic that Clarissa can never go home again and Julie can never leave home. Julie is a composite sketch based on experiences in Rousseau's life, notably his formative years as protégé to Madame de Warens in the Duchy of Savoy (1731–41), and his infatuation with Sophie d'Houdetot and with Zulietta, a mysterious courtesan who enchanted him while he served as secretary to the French Ambassador to Venice (1743–44).

Even though Julie and Saint-Preux exemplify the Protestant ethic, a Catholic pattern carried over from Rousseau's conversion experiences (born a Protestant, he converted to Catholicism, only to convert back to Protestantism) is evident in the relationship of the two lovers: guilt, remorse, confession, renunciation, rehabilitation, and canonization, and in Rousseau's autobiography.

In the final analysis, Rousseau offers not so much a critique of European institutions but an attempt to endow them with greater potentialities. He examines all the issues associated with human progress—the valuation of children, political and religious tolerance, parity of gender esteem, natural rights, and pacifism—as an alternative to war. The younger generation was deeply impressed, and it is not surprising that one of the last visitors welcomed to Ermenonville in 1778 was a young lawyer named Maximilien de Robespierre. Madame Anne-Louise-Germaine de Staël commented, "All the veils of the heart have been rent." The classic mode of restraint, order, reason, and form began to fade. Hence Johann Wolfgang von Goethe's observation, "With Voltaire a world ends; with Rousseau a world begins." *Julie, ou la nouvelle Héloïse* engages all the faculties: sensation, logic, poetry, philosophy, and nature. This may be its greatest legacy.

ROBERT J. FRAIL

Text

Julie, ou la nouvelle Héloïse, Lettres de deux amants, recueillies et publiées par J.-J. Rousseau. 1761. Translated as *Julie or the New Héloïse.* by Judith H. McDowell. University Park: Pennsylvania State University Press, 1968. Translated as *Julie and Emile* by Jo-Ann E. McEachern. Oxford: Voltaire Foundation, 2001.

Bibliography

Arico, Santo. *Rousseau's Art of Persuasion in "La Nouvelle Héloïse."* Lanham, Md.: University Press of America, 1994.

Blum, Carol. *Rousseau and the Republic of Virtue: The Language of Politics in the French Revolution.* Ithaca, N.Y.: Cornell University Press, 1989.

Cranston, Maurice. *The Solitary Self: Jean-Jacques Rousseau in Exile and Adversity.* Chicago: University of Chicago Press, 1997.

Ellis, Madeleine. *"Julie, ou la Nouvelle Héloïse": A Synthesis of Rousseau's Thought (1749–1759).* Toronto: University of Toronto Press, 1949.

Fabry, Anne Srabian de. *Études autour de "La Nouvelle Héloïse."* Sherbrooke, Canada: Éditions Naaman, 1977.

Hamilton, James. F. *Rousseau's Theory of Literature: The Poetics of Art and Nature.* York, S.C.: French literature Publications, 1979.

Jones, James. *"La Nouvelle Héloïse": Rousseau and Utopia.* Geneva: Droz, 1977.

Mall, Laurence. *Origines et Retraites dans La Nouvelle Héloïse.* New York: Peter Lang, 1997.

McEachern, Jo-Ann E., ed. *Bibliography of "Julie, ou la nouvelle Héloïse" to 1800.* Oxford: Voltaire Foundation, 1993.

Morley, John. *Rousseau and His Era.* Kessinger, 1996.

Swenson, James. *On Jean-Jacques Rousseau Considered as One of the First Authors of the Revolution.* Stanford, Calif.: Stanford University Press, 2000.

Trouille, Mary. *Sexual Politics in the Enlightenment: Women Writers Read Rousseau.* Albany: State University of New York Press, 1997.

Vance, C. M. "The Extravagant Shepherd: A Study of the Pastoral Vision in Rousseau's 'Nouvelle Héloïse'," *Studies in Voltaire and the Eighteenth Century* 105 (1973).

JUNGES DEUTSCHLAND

The group of authors known collectively as Junges Deutschland (Young Germany) were never artistically homogeneous, and hardly mutually friendly. The movement lasted from 1830 to 1840 and was followed by the decidedly more revolutionary Vormärz. Both Junges Deutschland and Vormärz disappear as literary movements after the disillusioning effects of the 1848 revolution. Despite the apparent lack of literary homogeneity within Junges Deutschland, the fact that one can speak at all of a literary movement is largely due to the official (if largely inefficient) ban on the works of Karl Ferdinand Gutzkow, Heinrich Heine, Heinrich Laube, Theodor Mundt, and Ludolf Wienbarg that the German Bundestag declared on December 10, 1835. The official document based its decision on the authors' alleged attack on Christianity, their denigration of the social status quo, and their destruction of decency and morality. In a scathing attack, the writer Wolfgang Menzel accused Gutzkow's novel *Wally, die Zweiflerin* (*Wally the Doubter*, 1835) of blasphemy, frivolity, and antinational tendencies. Already worried about liberalism taking away much of its power, the government readily adopted Menzel's arguments. In retrospect, the repercussions against these writers seem rather exaggerated. They coincide, however, with a time when the Austrian conservative statesman Klemens von Metternich, the Prussian leaders, and others increased censorship and spying into private correspondence, both as a reaction to the July Revolution and as a means to protect their system of particularism against the idea of a single, centrally administered national state. The term *Young Germany* is sometimes used more widely to refer to all writing of the period that deviates from the ideologically more conformist and contemporary literary movement Biedermeier. The term *Junges Deutschland* appears in Ludolf Wienbarg's dedication of his *Ästhetische Feldzüge* (*Aesthetic Campaign*, 1834). This early manifesto propagates the idea of *littérature engagée* that Junges Deutschland shared with related movements in France (*La jeune France*), Italy (*La giovina Italia*), and Switzerland (*Das junge Europa*).

The decade starting in 1825 also saw the deaths of a significant number of great German thinkers: Jean Paul, Johann Wolfgang von Goethe, Georg Wilhelm Friedrich Hegel, Karl Wilhelm von Humboldt, and Friedrich von Schlegel. The feeling of cultural melancholia—known as *Weltschmerz* and caused by the gloomy sense that an era had ended, yet no identifiable future had announced itself—was a strong presence in most works of art. The new generation of writers was viewed as young, perhaps too young to follow their predecessors. The authors themselves did not so much feel as epigones, but rather saw an historical chance for change. The contemporary political situation certainly seemed to support such a view. However, the recent opening of aesthetic was disadvantageous, since much energy was spent in establishing artistic prominence and not enough went into developing a literary program. The imminence of the historical moment finds its reflection in the use of a new programatic vocabulary. For Laube, the word *modern* incorporated the idea of the contemporary, and stressed the prevalence of a new feeling or zeitgeist. For Mundt, similar ideas motivated the choice of the word *Bewegung* (movement), with its implications of renovation and progress. In general, the authors of Junges Deutschland opposed religious orthodoxy, political conservatism, unnecessary adherence to conventions, and, above all, the dubious idealism of German Romanticism. From the perspective of literary history, Junges Deutschland is a period of transition from a Romantic-idealistic to a modern-realistic paradigm of aesthetic production. However, it is less for aesthetic reasons, and more for its ideological motivations, that the literature of Junges Deutschland is still studied. The single most influential political inspiration for the movement was the 1830 July Revolution in Paris.

What the authors of Young Germany had in common was above all a programmatic mission, combined with a sense of political urgency. One concern of the Young Germans was to express their sense of societal stagnation, as well as to propose remedies. In addition to demanding freedom of speech, they also proposed that literature had to be politically engaged, the carrier of serious thoughts and rational criticism. Literature also should be concerned with educating readers instead of being superficial entertainment. Biedermeier's orientation toward the personal realm was highly criticized. Other issues of the Young German writers were the upheaval of the absolutist state and the dogmatic church, as well as the promotion of social justice and women's emancipation. In short, they were at odds with much, if not all, of their contemporary political and aesthetic environment. The existence of a sense of literary crisis became obvious in their search for the ideal medium in which to express themselves: drama, poetry, essays, and other forms were all used, and they were even in some cases blended and redefined. However, despite their shared goals, the Young Germans never aspired to a single aesthetic movement with one consistent form of expression. In fact, they were constantly attacking each other's work, often for good reasons. Many authors were somewhat blind to their own flaws, while accusing their fellow writers of not addressing the important issues, or of doing so by applying inappropriate means. Indeed, the Young Germans' hastily composed prose is often inaccessible and convoluted. Such deficiencies can be explained by the sense of political urgency and by the pressing deadlines of journals and daily publications, the authors' principal outlets. They were aware that following the German periods of *Klassik* (the use of this term goes back to Laube) and of Romanticism, art had to redefine itself. Two seminal and programmatic works of Young Germany were written by authors who belonged to an earlier generation:

Ludwig Börne's *Briefe aus Paris* (*Letters from Paris*, 1830–34) demanded political activism in artistic writing; Heinrich Heine in *Die romantische Schule* (*The Romantic School*, 1836) criticized the reactionary tendencies of late Romanticists; his *Reisebilder* (*Pictures of Travel*, 1826–31) included essayistic polemics against the workings of the German state. Börne and Heine were more the intellectual and artistic forefathers of the movement rather than active participants. Heine's name was added to the official ban at the very last moment, but he was soon pardoned. So were almost all of the other writers by the end of the 1830s.

GERD BAYER

Bibliography

Dietze, Walter. *Junges Deutschland und deutsche Klassik: Zur Ästhetik und Literaturtheorie des Vormärz.* Berlin: Rütten und Loening, 1962.

Houben, H. H. *Jungdeutscher Sturm und Drang.* Leipzig: Brockhaus, 1911.

Koopmann, Helmut. *Das junge Deutschland: Eine Einführung.* Darmstadt: Wissenschaftliche Buchgesellschaft, 1993.

Mattenklott, Gert, and Klaus R. Scherpe, eds. *Demokratisch-revolutionäre Literatur in Deutschland.* Kronberg, Taunus: Scriptor Verlag, 1974.

Sammons, Jeffrey L. *Six Essays on the Young German Novel.* Chapel Hill: University of North Carolina Press, 1975.

K

KALEVALA 1835, 1849

Finnish National Epic collected and compiled by Elias Lönnrot and other folklorists

When the *Kalevala* (Land of Heroes) appeared in 1835, Finland was an autonomous Grand Duchy of Russia (a designation it received in 1809), having previously been a province of Sweden since the Middle Ages. Swedish functioned as the language of government, administration, and education, and consequently the Finnish language occupied a position of low status: it was the language of the peasantry, with a sparse written tradition restricted mainly to a few religious and legal texts, although the New Testament had been translated as early as 1548 and the Bible as a whole in 1642. The ideals of national Romanticism, however, took root at the university in Turku (Åbo) from the late eighteenth century and, reinforced by the level of autonomy permitted by Imperial Russia, led to a growth in national consciousness which had the development of the Finnish language and Finnish-language culture as a prime aim. The publication of the *Kalevala* marked the perhaps decisive step forward in the process whereby Finnish achieved the status of an official language in 1863.

The *Kalevala* is an epic poem compiled and constructed from the great body of ancient Karelian folk songs collected from oral tradition by Elias Lönnrot (1804–84) during a series of collecting trips mainly in the years after 1828. Lönnrot's own background and career is an integral part of the myth. A Finnish speaker, son of a poor tailor in Samatti in southern Finland, Elias's hunger for learning was such that by his own and his parents' efforts he went on to the University of Turku to study medicine. He became part of the group of nationally-oriented scholars and, while continuing to study and later practice medicine, he collected over a million lines of oral song. After publishing four booklets of collected songs between 1829 and 1831, the first edition of his *Kalevala* appeared in 1835 and consisted of some 12,000 lines. A new, much expanded, version of 22,000 lines, based on the fruits of further collecting trips and on contributions by other folklorists (notably D. E. D. Europaeus), was

published in 1849, and it is this "new" *Kalevala* that is considered to be the standard text. Lönnrot was appointed Professor of Finnish Literature in Helsinki in 1853. It should perhaps be emphasized that the *Kalevala* is Lönnrot's creation in that, although he himself composed less than 3 percent of the lines, mainly in the form of linking passages, nothing like the completed *Kalevala* had existed in oral tradition. He cut, pasted, conflated, and adapted sections and episodes from the songs of many singers in order, as he explicitly wrote, to provide the Finns "with something corresponding to the Icelandic *Edda*" or "if not to Homer, at least to Hesiod." At the same time he standardized the language of the poem, producing a normalized language out of the disparate dialects of the original songs.

The *Kalevala* consists of fifty cantos. It opens with the creation of the world and the birth of the wise and supernaturally powerful Väinämöinen, master of the magical music of the *kantele* (harp), and it closes with his departure to make way for a new ruler, whose coming marks the end of the pagan era and the arrival of Christianity. Between these points we are told of how the blacksmith Ilmarinen forges the obscure and mysterious *sampo*, an object that brings wealth and good fortune to those who possess it; but it is also a source of conflict and is ultimately destroyed. We meet, too, a third major figure, the charming, womanizing warrior Lemminkäinen, who shares many adventures with Väinämöinen and Ilmarinen, and whose death and resurrection play a central role. The underlying theme of the epic is the conflict between the people of Kalevala and their enemies, the people of the dark northern realm of Pohjola, who steal and hide the sun, the moon, and fire. The people of Kalevala are finally victorious.

The meter of the *Kalevala*—unrhymed, nonstrophic, trochaic tetrameters with much use of alliteration—is of great antiquity among the Baltic peoples and is likely to be best known to

English speakers as the meter that Longfellow used for his *Hiawatha* after reading a German translation of the Finnish epic. The effect of the meter is displayed well in Kirby's translation, the opening lines of which are:

> I am driven by my longing,
> And my understanding urges
> That I should commence my singing,
> And begin my recitation.
> I will sing the people's legends,
> And the ballads of the nation.
> To my mouth the words are flowing,
> And the words are gently falling,
> Quickly as my tongue can shape them,
> And between my teeth emerging.

The role of the *Kalevala* as the central culturoliterary icon of Finnish consciousness, nation building, and identity is difficult to overstate, whether viewed from a national or an international perspective. In music, themes from the *Kalevala* provide the inspiration behind many of the best-known works of Jean Sibelius (*The Swan of Tuonela*, the *Kullervo Symphony*, the *Lemminkäinen Suite*, etc.) and Robert Kajanus (*Aino, Kullervo's Death*, etc.). In the visual arts, the paintings and illustrations of Akseli Gallen-Kallela (*The Aino Myth, Lemminkäinen's Mother, The Forging of the Sampo*, etc.) are lodged in the visual imagination of most readers coming to the poem. On a more mundane level, there is a Kalevala Day (February 28), and Kalevalaic names are used as personal and place-names; they are also employed to brand and market everything from insurance to jewelry. Outside Finland, the *Kalevala* has been translated into fifty languages, in many cases with more than one version in a single language.

PETER GRAVES

Work

First Edition
Kalevala. 1835; Expanded, now standard, edition, 1849.

Selected
Selections from the Kalevala. Translated from a German version by J. A. Porter. New York, 1868.
The Kalevala, the Epic Poem of Finland. Translated by John Martin Crawford. New York: Alden, 1889.
The Kalevala. Translated by W. F. Kirby. London: Everyman, 1907. (New edition with introduction by Michael H. Branch. London: Athlone Press, 1985.)
The Kalevala: Epic of the Finnish People. Translated by Eino Friberg, edited and introduced by George C. Schoolfield. Helsinki: Otava, 1988.
The Kalevala: An Epic Poem after Oral Tradition. Translated and introduced by Keith Bosley. Oxford: Oxford University Press, 1989.

Bibliography

Asplund, Anneli, and Ulla Lipponen, ed. *The Birth of the Kalevala*. Helsinki: Finnish Literature Society, 1985.
DuBois, Thomas A. *Finnish Folk Poetry and the Kalevala*. New York: Garland, 1995.
Henko, Lauri, ed. *Religion, Myth and Folklore in the World's Epics: the Kalevala and its Predecessors*. Berlin: Mouton de Gruyter, 1990.
Jones, Michael Owen, ed. *The World of the Kalevala: Essays in Celebration of the 150 Year Jubilee*. Los Angeles: UCLA Folklore and Mythology Publications, 1987.
Moyne, Ernest John. *Hiawatha and Kalevala: A Study of the Relationship between the "Indian Edda" and the Finnish Epic*. Helsinki: 1963.
Oinas, Felix J. *Studies in Finnish Folklore: Homage to the Kalevala*. Bloomington: Indiana University Press, 1985.
Pentikäinen, Julia Y. *Kalevala Mythology*. Bloomington: Indiana University Press, 1989.
Puranen, Rauni, ed. *The Kalevala Abroad: Translations and Foreign Language Adaptations of the Kalevala*. Helsinki: Suomalaisen Kirjallisuudenseura, 1985.

KALVOS, ANDREAS 1792–1869

Greek poet

Andreas Kalvos today ranks close behind Dionysios Solomos as the second "national" poet of modern Greece. This reputation rests on the two books of odes, ten in each, that he published while the Greek war of independence was at its height, and were evidently addressed to European philhellenes. *I Lyra* (*The Lyre*, 1824) was published in Geneva, while a French translation appeared in Paris the same year; its successor *Lyrika* (*Lyrics*, 1826) came out in a bilingual Greek and French edition in Paris. These poems have been linked to Romanticism on account of their passionate espousal of the cause of national self-determination, their sometimes daring lyrical imagery, and the way in which they cumulatively exalt the poet's calling. Greek criticism, however, has never accepted Kalvos into the fold of "Greek Romanticism"; the extreme formality of the odes, their use of an artificial, archaizing form of the Greek language, the prevalence in them of abstract personifications, and the austere impersonality of all

but two of them are characteristics which have been invoked to place Kalvos instead in the eighteenth-century neoclassical tradition.

One of the few personal touches in the odes is to be found in the first, "O Filopatris" ("The Patriot"). Here Kalvos invokes his native island of Zakynthos and (in ornate, neoclassical style, substituting ancient names for modern) the travels that have taken him away to Italy, France, and England. "Death," the poem, concludes, "is sweet only when we sleep in our native land." It was not until 1960, almost a century after his death, that Kalvos's remains were returned from Lincolnshire, where he died, to Greece and reburied in Zakynthos, in a specially built vault alongside his compatriot, Solomos.

Kalvos left Zakynthos before the age of ten. In Italy, he entered the service of the writer Ugo Foscolo. During the period 1812 to 1818, which was spent mostly in Italy, he wrote three neoclassical tragedies in Italian, which he himself seems to have valued highly, although they made no impact in Italy and have only become the object of study by scholars whose starting point is Kalvos's poetry in Greek. With Foscolo, he traveled to England, where the two men quarreled and parted company for good. A short-lived marriage in London in 1818 ended in tragedy when his wife and their infant daughter died. In London, between 1818 and 1820, Kalvos supported himself by giving Italian lessons and translating biblical texts for the British and Foreign Bible Society. It is not known whether Kalvos became a Protestant, but his strong interest in the Anglican Church and its literature dates from this period.

Perhaps during his time with Foscolo, and certainly after his departure from England, Kalvos was actively involved with the Carbonari (members of a secret society dedicated to bringing about liberal reforms) in Florence, from where he was expelled in 1821. Modern scholarship is divided on whether Kalvos's decisive turn to writing poetry in his native Greek was a response to the outbreak of the war of independence in the same year, or the culmination of a process that had begun much earlier, with his earliest poems and his tragedies in Italian. In 1820, he had already translated the Psalms of David into the same form of modern Greek as he used in his odes. Though he left no political writing other than his odes, it is evident that, at least until 1826, Kalvos's political sympathies were notably radical, and not confined to Greece. This alone is a strong factor linking Kalvos, and his odes, with the Romantic movement.

After 1826, Kalvos wrote no more original work in Greek (his last verses in Italian date from 1831). After the publication of his second volume of odes in 1826, he announced his intention to subordinate words to action and take up arms in Greece. He appears to have been so shocked at what he encountered there, that after a few months at Nafplion, the provisional capital, he retired to the safety of Corfu (then a British protectorate).

In Corfu, Kalvos worked intermittently for the Ionian Academy, founded by Lord Guilford, but his austerely unbending temperament seems to have made him difficult to work with, and he frequently had to rely on private tuition for an income. Although for a little over twenty years Kalvos lived in the same small town as Solomos, there is no certain evidence that the two "national poets of modern Greece" were even acquainted. Kalvos seems to have chosen a lonely path in his life; the high-minded sentiments and heroic refusal to compromise that are so resoundingly celebrated in the odes may have transferred poorly to the realities of daily life. Whatever the cause, like many Romantic poets, Kalvos "burned out" early.

In Kalvos's odes, the formal characteristics of neoclassicism serve a purpose which brings him closer to the Romantic movement. This is evident, first of all, in the generic term he uses. An *ode*, for his Western contemporaries, meant simply an emotionally highly charged piece, often in an elaborate verse form. For Kalvos, it means something much more specific: *The Lyre* begins with an epigraph from the ancient lyric poet Pindar that reminds us that the ode in Greece in the sixth century B.C.E. had been a special form of highly elaborated song, specially composed to celebrate the victors in the Olympic games and other contests. Pindar's odes use mythology to highlight the human virtues that the ancient Greeks sought to promote through the games, and originally they were sung to the accompaniment of the lyre, during the ceremony when the laurel crowns were given to the victors. If Pindar sang to celebrate the victory of athletes in the games, and to extol the moral and physical attributes of the winner, then Kalvos set himself to do the same thing for the victors (as he fervently believed they would be) in the Greek war of independence, and similarly to extol the ancient virtues he associated with the modern cause.

RODERICK BEATON

Biography

Born in Zakynthos (Zante), spring 1792. Between 1800 and 1802 left Zakynthos with his father and brother, for Italy; mostly self-educated in Livorno, Italy, 1802–11; met Ugo Foscolo in Florence, August 1812; worked for Foscolo as secretary and tutor to friends, spending time in Florence, London, and Zurich, 1812–19. Married Maria Theresa Thomas, 1818; they had one daughter (both mother and daughter died soon afterwards). Left London for Florence, 1820; expelled from Florence for political activity, established himself in Geneva, 1821–24. Moved to Paris, 1824. Second book of odes published. Left Paris for Nafplion, Greece, 1826. Settled in Corfu, August 1826; supported himself by teaching, intermittently at the Ionian Academy, Corfu, 1826–52. Moved definitively to England, 1852; married Charlotte Augusta Wadam, 1853; settled with his wife at her educational establishment in Louth, Lincolnshire, 1855. Died there of pneumonia, November 1869.

Selected Works

Collection
Odai. Edited by F. M. Pontani, 1970. Translated as *Odes*. Translated by George Dandoulakis, 1998.

Poetry
I Lyra. 1824.
Lyrika. 1826.

Bibliography

Bouvier, Bertrand. "Calvos in Geneva." In *Modern Greek Writers*. Edited by Edmund Keeley and Peter Bien. Princeton: Princeton University Press, 1972.

Ricks, David. "The Progress of Poesy: Kalvos, Gray and the Revival of Ancient Literary Language," *Modern Greek Studies (Australia and New Zealand)* 4 (1996): 111–132.

Sherrard, Philip. "Andreas Kalvos and the Eighteenth-Century Ethos," *Byzantine and Modern Greek Studies* 1 (1975): 175–206.

Vayenas, Nasos. *I Odes tou Kalvou: ekloyi kritikon keimenon*. Heraklion: Crete University Press, 1992.

Vitti, Mario. *O Kalvos ke i epoche tou [Kalvos and his Era]*. Athens: Stigmi, 1995.

KANT, IMMANUEL 1724–1804

German philosopher

Immanuel Kant is an important—perhaps *the* most important—German idealist thinker, and arguably one of the most difficult German philosophers to read. Born to a Prussian mother and a father of Scottish roots, Kant was raised in a Christian pietist household and never left his home city. He lived simply in a small room with only a bed, table, and chair. A lifelong bachelor, he maintained a sober and disciplined lifestyle with a strong sense of personal and civic duty. He took a stroll in the company of his servant Lampe every day regardless of the weather. Kant was so precise in his habits that it was said the citizens of Königsberg could set their clocks by the time of the professor's daily walk. The regularity of his everyday life is indicative of the carefully detailed and rigorously logical argumentation of his philosophical writings, which makes them such dense, difficult reading. It is most certainly ironic that this disciplined and reserved professor initiated a revolution in philosophy so radical that it has been compared to the French Revolution in its impact on the age.

Kant's initial studies were in the areas of mathematics and physics (what was then called "natural philosophy") and his first treatise was on the works of Sir Isaac Newton. He was also influenced by the earlier German Enlightenment thinkers Gottfried Leibniz and Christian Wolff, who both struggled to reconcile the discoveries of the newly emerging sciences with the concepts of traditional religion. At this time, Kant was also reading David Hume and the British empirical philosopher John Locke. He became interested in the subfield of philosophy called epistemology, which deals with how the mind or consciousness comes to know objective reality, or the external world. One of his objectives was to establish a rational basis for science and mathematics in light of Humean skepticism. He looked at Locke's theory of the mind of the infant as a tabula rasa, a blank slate or blackboard upon which experience is written. The newborn's mind receives sense data from the object world as experience, which it then organizes and interprets according to subjective categories that are suggested by the senses, thereby presumably creating a more or less accurate representation of external reality as it is. In Locke's theory, the mind is a passive agent that simply responds to the external world. The locus or source of our understanding of reality is squarely in the objective world that has been created by God.

In his *Kritik der reinen Vernunft* (*Critique of Pure Reason*, 1781), Kant made a radical revision of Locke's epistemological model. Kant termed his insight his "Copernican revolution" in epistemology after the Polish astronomer Nicolaus Copernicus, who had argued against the medieval view of the universe that placed the earth at the center of the solar system. Copernicus posited the sun as the center and thereby radically changed mankind's view of itself in the universe. Kant suggested that our mind is not merely a passive blank slate upon which reality imposes or inscribes itself, but it rather actively formulates what we perceive to be reality. He called this perceived reality the *phenomenon*, or the *phenomenal world*. Our mind constructs this reality through fundamental categories of perception and understanding that are a priori (existing prior to experience) or inherent to our consciousness—categories as basic as time, space, causality, and totality. The phenomenal reality we perceive is produced by the activity of our own mind, and all human minds share these fundamental attributes. It is important to remember here that Kant does not assert that absolute reality does not exist independent of the mind, only that we cannot perceive it without the categories of understanding that make up our reason. The world as it really is, called the *noumenon*, or the *Ding an sich* (thing in itself), only is unknowable to the mind, since we can never transcend the categories of our understanding. Time and space are imposed upon the noumenal world by our consciousness, and we cannot know if or how they really exist independently of the mind. In Kant's theory of transcendental idealism, the mind does not conform to the world (as in Locke's model), but rather the world conforms to the mind. Science and mathematics are only possible because their structures and laws exist a priori to experience, prior to the data provided by the senses. Scientific knowledge is valid with respect to the perceived universe (Kant successfully defended science from skepticism), but it can make no valid claims concerning reality as it may exist independent of mind. His argument for an idealistic philosophy breaches the long-standing dualism between mind and matter in a radical manner. It has been argued that Kantian thought broaches the problem of perspectivism or relativism (truth is a function of point of view) by claiming that knowledge of an absolute reality is unattainable, and that it thus opens up a veritable abyss of subjectivity that heralds the alienation of consciousness from the world that marks the sensibility of the modern era in twentieth-century philosophies such as existentialism and deconstructionism.

What, then, was the significance of the Kantian "Copernican revolution" for the Romantic era? His understanding of how we perceive reality introduces a profound subjectivism and perspectivism to the late eighteenth-century worldview, which is broadly reflected in the art and culture of the time. That perceived reality is subjectively constructed or "created" places importance on the inner world of the mind: on the emotions, intuitions, visions, dreams, and, above all, on the creative imagination. This was a pivotal shift from the Enlightenment valuation of reason as the sole mode of knowing an objective reality. Romantic art became the domain of the exploration and depiction of interiority, of human subjectivity, as a valid mode of perception. It is in this aspect that Kant can be termed the father of Romanticism. His subjectivism also suggests that human truth is not an absolute grounded in the world created by a knowable divinity, but rather is a function of the mind's perspective. Since the noumenon is unknowable, so is the idea of a God whose will and purpose is knowable to human understanding: absolute truth (and a divine basis for morality) cannot be established with certainty. The Kantian insight effectively demolished all previously asserted rational proofs for the existence of God, a fact that caused Kant's work to be banned for a time in his native land as an expression of atheism. The German writer Heinrich von Kleist supposedly suffered a "Kant crisis" over this loss of a basis for absolute certainty, a problem which is reflected in his writings and which contributed to his mental breakdown and suicide.

Kant sought to address this problem in his *Kritik der praktischen Vernunft* (Critique of Practical Reason, 1788) with his notion of the "categorical imperative." Moral behavior is established by reason prior to experience and is made practical in action through choice when this "practical reason" is linked to the act of willing. This is, in a sense, a Kantian version of the perennial golden rule, a moral duty, which suggests that we should all act in such a way that our behavior can be held up as a maxim or rule for all, that all human beings must always be treated as ends and never as means to an end. We perform this moral duty by an assertion of our capacity to will, which is autonomous or free, over our emotions, instincts, or inclinations, which are bound by natural necessity. True morality is evidenced in individuals who act morally solely for the sake of duty and not for some kind of reward or from the demands of physical necessity. Johann Christoph Friedrich von Schiller's mature dramas of the Romantic sublime, for example, took their starting point from this inherently dramatic inner conflict of the autonomy of the free will or self-imposed duty over the inclinations in Kantian Idealism.

Kant's *Kritik der Urteilskraft* (*Critique of Judgment*, 1790) deals with questions of beauty and purpose in nature. It profoundly influenced the formulation of Romantic art and aesthetic theory, and indeed much of later twentieth-century modernism as well. Art and the imagination—the "aesthetic idea" as distinct from the logical-analytical concepts of the sciences—function, like the autonomous will, in a completely self-governing and subjective realm, free from both the physical necessity (nature) and moral duty (divine law) that usually define the boundaries of the human spirit. The truths of science and mathematics are appropriate only to the domain of perceived reality, whereas the truths of art and the imagination, and the truths of religion as well, refer to another, quite different, field of human experience that is not bound by sense data. The Romantic artist may therefore give free creative reign to his or her imaginative subjectivity as a mode of knowing reality. He or she is also freed from any obligation to produce a realistic or verisimilar depiction of reality (the classical dictate of mimesis) since the noumenon or reality as it truly is remains unknowable. Almost all of the Romantics still emphatically believed that an ultimate union with some intuitive conception of the noumenon as "nature" or the "divine" was possible, most especially in the domains of aesthetic and spiritual perception; Kant's writings, however, remained ambiguous on this point. The creation of aesthetic form was, in any case, no longer to be dictated solely by reality but by the power of the artist's imagination. The creative human mind as the supreme agent of knowing is certainly Kant's greatest contribution to the Romantic movement and to later philosophical thought. Since the will of the divinity is also unknowable, then the artist is likewise relieved of the ethical duty of producing morally didactic works or art that reveals the nature of divine will.

Within this aesthetic domain of absolute freedom, the human imagination reigns supreme and the artist becomes somewhat of a creative divinity within a "universe" of his or her own conception. Art as the sole province of human autonomy is thus justified as an end in and of itself, and the artist serves as a kind of religious seer figure. The artist is discussed here as being a "genius," often a solitary individual, isolated from bourgeois society, who lives and creates on his or her own terms. Weimar "neoclassicist" Schiller took up Kantian ideas in a number of his own philosophical writings on aesthetics, the most notable being his *Über die ästhetische Erziehung des Menschen* (On the Aesthetic Education of Man, 1795), in which he argues that art (and the act of aesthetic contemplation) as a disinterested and harmonious union of nature and spirit (or feeling and form) educates mankind to a state of moral autonomy and spiritual freedom. German Romantic writers such as Novalis and Ludwig Tieck, who were in revolt against rationalist/neoclassical aesthetics, also embraced both the artistic freedom and the illustrious station of the artist implicit in Kant's idealism. The German Schillerist Romantic movement quickly spread to England, France, and the United States, to writers ranging from Charles Baudelaire, Samuel Taylor Coleridge, and William Wordsworth, to Edgar Allan Poe. With this exalted self-justification of artistic creation as imaginative freedom, art assumed a privileged position as a mode of perception unique to human experience.

Kant's ideas signaled the end of the empiricism and skepticism that had marked traditional Enlightenment thought, and introduced a new transcendental rationalism that presented a radically different picture of reality. His philosophical thought formed the starting point for the philosophies of later Romantic-Idealist (or post-Kantian) thinkers such as Johann Gottlieb Fichte, G. W. F. Hegel, Friedrich Wilhelm Joseph von Schelling, Friedrich Daniel Ernst Schleiermacher, and Arthur Schopenhauer. Kant's works were read by many of the German Romantic writers (including Novalis and Heinrich von Kleist), and were therefore influential in the formulation of Romantic literary theory and practice both in Germany and abroad, most especially among the English Romantics, notably Coleridge and Thomas De Quincey.

Thomas F. Barry

Biography

Born in Königsberg, East Prussia 1724. Studied at the University of Königsberg. Lecturer at University of Königsberg 1755–70; Professor of Logic and Philosophy at University of Königsberg 1770–1804. Died in Königsberg, 1804.

Selected Works

Die Kritik der reinen Vernunft. 1781. Translated as *Critique of Pure Reason* by Paul Guyer. Cambridge: Cambridge University Press, 1999.

Prolegomena zu einer Metaphysik der Zukunft. 1783. Translated as *The Prologemena to any Future Metaphysics* by P. Carus. Revised by L. W. Beck. 1950.

Die Kritik der praktischen Vernunft. 1788. Translated as *Critique of Practical Reason* by Lewis White Beck. New York: MacMillan, 1992 or Mary Gregor. Cambridge: Cambridge University Press, 1997.

Die Kritik der Urteilskraft, 1790. Translated as *Critique of the Power of Judgment* by Eric Matthews. Cambridge: Cambridge University Press, 2002.

Bibliography

Allison, Henry E. *Idealism and Freedom: Essays on Kant's Theoretical and Practical Philosophy.* Cambridge: Cambridge University Press, 1996.

Beck, Lewis White. *A Commentary on Kant's Critique of Practical Reason.* Chicago: University of Chicago Press, 1996.

Cassirer, Ernst, et al. *Kant's Life and Thought,* New Haven, Conn.: Yale University Press, 1981.

Gardner, Sebastian. *Routledge Philosophy Guidebook to Kant and the Critique of Pure Reason,* London: Routledge 1999.

Guyer, Paul, ed. *The Cambridge Companion to Kant.* Cambridge Companions to Philosophers series. Cambridge: Cambridge University Press, 1992.

Klemme, Heiner, and Manfred Kuehn, eds. *Immanuel Kant.* International Library of Critical Essays in the History of Philosophy. Aldershot, U.K.: Ashgate Publishing, 1998.

Schott, Robin May, ed. *Feminist Interpretations of Immanuel Kant* (Re-Reading the Canon). University Park: Pennsylvania State University Press, 1997.

Smith, Norman Kemp. *A Commentary to Kant's Critique of Pure Reason.* Atlantic Highlands, N.J.: Humanities Press International, 1991.

KARADZIC, VUK STEFANOVIC 1787–1864

Serbian poet and language reformer

Unknown as he is to the general public in the Western world, Vuk Stefanovic Karadzic's linguistic and literary legacy casts a long shadow over the Balkans. The Serbs see Vuk (as they call him) as the founder of their modern language and written culture, as important a national founding figure as the princely rulers of the 1820s and 1830s. Other Balkan peoples are less charitable. To them, Vuk is the founder of Serbian nationalism and stepfather of the idea of a greater Serbia.

Vuk's disability—a lame leg—was an exceptional burden in a society that valued physical fitness and military prowess. Yet that leg proved a blessing in disguise, since it forced the young Vuk to prove himself as a scholar instead. A decisive turning point in Vuk's life and that of Serbia was the uprising in 1804: having tired finally of Turkish misrule, by 1810 the Serbs had driven their former masters from the area around Belgrade. Vuk was unfit for military service and instead served as secretary to the Serb brigand leaders Hajduk Curcija and Hajduk Veljko. His experiences during this phase of the Serbian War of Independence gave rise to his books *The First Year of the War against the Dahijas* (1828) and the *Lives of the Serbian Marshals* (1829). With their war against Russia ending in 1812, the Turks invaded Serbia, and Vuk, like many other Serbs, was forced to flee to safety in the Austrian Empire.

Vuk made his way to Vienna, where he had the good fortune to meet a highly placed Slovene, Jenaj Kopitar, who worked as imperial librarian and censor. Until his death in 1844, Kopitar was to remain a good friend, mentor, and protector.

With Kopitar's support and encouragement, Vuk collected and published his most famous works, the Serbian Songs. *The First and Second Books of Songs and Poetry* were published in Vienna during 1814–15. Kopitar hoped these publications would be a way of harnessing the Serbs to Austria rather than Russia. Never a supporter or advocate of Kopitar's Austro-Slav ideals, Vuk nevertheless benefited from the imperial censor's support. He was also assisted by Jakob Grimm's favorable reviews in various German literary journals; this support was as crucial as that of Kopitar, since it exposed Vuk to the German market and literary world. The publication of another book, *The Third Book of Songs and Poetry,* in Leipzig in 1823, was directly assisted by Grimm.

These books made Vuk famous and put Serbia on the cultural map of Europe for the first time since the Middle Ages. By the 1830s Vuk's *Songs* had been translated into English, French, and German. In the west the Greek uprising (1821–29) had increased interest in the Balkans and its "exotic" culture. To

Vuk it seemed that the Greeks had overshadowed the Serbs' earlier and more "heroic" uprising with their own. Despite his enlightened view on other peoples such as the Turks, Vuk remained, unfortunately, anti-Greek.

Back in Vuk's homeland, Serbian hope had increased under the leadership of the ruthless and able Prince Milos Obrenovic, who drove the Turks from Serbia for the second and final time. Vuk heeded a call from the prince to return, and served for two short periods as a Serbian official. In 1820–21 Vuk was secretary to the prince and general official. During his second stint (1830–31), he served as chief magistrate in Belgrade and president of the committee to draw up a Serbian constitution. All but the

Vuk Stefanovic Karadzic. Reprinted courtesy of AKG.

coterie surrounding the prince appreciated Vuk's hard work, integrity, and honesty, which stood in sharp contrast to that of most Serbian officials.

Disgusted and disillusioned with the prince's increasingly despotic and corrupt regime, Vuk left his post, vowing never to be a bureaucrat again. Until his death in 1860, Vuk's relationship with Prince Milos remained tempestuous. Despite his "Letter to Milos Obrenovic" (composed and sent in 1832 but only published in 1842), Vuk remained a staunch supporter of the Obrenovic dynasty and received a generous pension from the Prince. Vuk had a less turbulent relationship with the ruler of Montenegro, the Prince-Bishop Petar II Njegos of Montenegro, a scholar and poet in his own right. During a journey to Montenegro in 1834, Vuk met and befriended the charismatic and fascinating Prince. Vuk concluded that the Serbs and Montenegrians were of the same stock and that they had everything to gain from closer bonds of friendship and cooperation.

Whatever his views about the princely rulers of Serbia, Vuk remained a devoted patriot ever eager to sing the praises of his homeland and increase its fame and reputation abroad. His record of contribution to the writing of Serbia's history was far from unimpressive; there are the *History of Contemporary Serbia* (1828), *Serbian Popular Tales* (1850), *Specimens of the Slavonic–Serbian Language* (1857), and *Governing Council of Serbia in Karadjordje's Time* (1857). Vuk also made vital contributions to Lepold Ranke's *The Serbian Revolution* (1828) which, in addition to few other works, put Serbia on the map of Europe and into the consciousness of Europeans in general.

In contemporary Serbia, however, Vuk is primarily remembered not as historian, writer, or song collector, but as architect of the modern Serb language and national identity. Vuk quite rightly saw one of his most important tasks as popularizing the Serbian language as a prelude to the implementation of a modern education system that would lead to literacy and progress in other fields. The alphabet of Church Slavonic was seen by many Serbs as holy but Vuk believed it was entirely unsuitable for the purposes of mass education and had to be simplified until it suited his purposes. He published a Serbian *Grammar* (1815), *Dictionary* (1818), and *Calendar* (1825) and a translation of the New Testament (1847) using his new, improved alphabet.

His orthographic and linguistic ideas provoked an uproar among the Serbs, both in Srem (inside Austria) and in Serbia proper. Conservatives railed against the "vulgarization" of their ancient language while the Serb Orthodox Church spearheaded the attacks upon Vuk's work that its hierarchy saw as pure blasphemy. Vuk rose to the occasion and attacked his opponents savagely. In the end his sensible ideas and simplifications won the day.

By the time of his death (1864), Vuk could look back at a long and productive life. His linguistic ideas had become accepted as the norm among Serbs, while his *Songs* not only served as a historical memory for a reborn nation, but had brought him fame among his European peers. He had also won his struggle against poverty. Unfortunately Vuk died before Serbia became fully independent and the Turkish flag was finally lowered in his long-suffering homeland.

CHRISTER JÖRGENSEN

Biography

Born in western Serbia in October 1787. Attended the Monastery School at Tronosa (1795–98), worked on family farm (1798–1804), and served as military secretary to illiterate Hajduk Curcija (1804–5). Continued studies at Karlovici, Belgrade, and Budapest (1805–10). Returned to Serbia and served as military secretary to Hajduk Veljko (1810–13), but forced to flee when Turks invaded Serbia. Met Kopitar in Vienna (1813); published first book in 1814; married Anna Kraus (1818); visited Russia (1819), and served as administrator in Belgrade (1820–21). Met Grimm and Goethe during trip to Germany (1822). Received pension during 1832–39. Traveled with Prince Michael Obrenovic (son of Milos) to Serbia in 1844 and linked with Illyrian movement, which sought coalition among all southern Slavs, whatever their religious or historical differences. Traveled in Serbia for further songs, 1860–63, returned to family in Vienna and died in 1864.

Selected Works

Selected Historical and Critical Writings and Letters. 3 vols. Edited by Djuro Gavela. Belgrade: Srpska Knjizevnost, 1962.

Zivoti Srpskih Vojvoda. Edited by Golub Dobrasinovic. Belgrade, 1963.

Raskovnik: Proza iz Recnika. Edited by Radomir Kostantinovic. Belgrade: Prosveta, 1964.

Vuk Karadzic o Srpskoj narodnoj poeziji. Edited by Borivoje Marinkovic: Belgrade: Prosveta, 1964.

Susretis Vukom. Edited by Golub Dobrasinovic and Borivoje Marinkovic.

Vuk Stefanovic Karadzic, Selected Works. Belgrade: Narodna Knijga, 1964.

Vukovi Zapisi. Edited by Vojislav Djuric. Belgrad: Srpska Knjizevna Zadruga, 1964.

Songs of the Serbian People: From the Collections of Vuk Karadzic. Edited by Milne Holton and Vasa D. Mihailovich. Pittsburgh: University of Pittsburgh Press, 1997.

Bibliography

Anzulovic, Branimir. *Heavenly Serbia: from Myth to Genocide*. London: Hurst, 1999.

Bojic, Vera. *Jakob Grimm und Vuk Karadzic*. Munich: Sagner, 1976.

Chester, Pamela, and Sibelan Forrester. *Engendering Slavic Literatures*. Bloomington: Indiana University Press, 1996.

Curcija-Prodanovic, N. *Yugoslav Folk Tales*. Oxford: Oxford University Press, 1960.

Dragnich, Alexander N. *Serbia's Historical Heritage*. Boulder, Colo.: East European Monographs, 1994.

———. *Serbs and Croats*. New York: Harcourt Brace Jovanovich, 1992.

Erlich, Vera. *Family in Transition: a Study of Three Hundred Yugoslav Villages (1937–1940)*. Princeton; N.J.: Princeton University Press, 1966.

Festschrift: Vuk Stefanovitch Karadzic. Vienna: Österreichers Ost und Sudeuropainstution, 1987.

Gordon-Fischer, Laura. *Marko Songs from Hercegovina a Century after Karadzic*. New York: Garland, 1990.

Hafner, Stanislaus. *Vuk Stefanovich Karadzic 1787–1864*. Vienna: Österreicher Akademie der Wissenschaft, 1989.

Hopf, Claudia. *Sprachnationalismus in Serbien udn Griechenland: theoretische Grundlagen sowie en Vergleich von Vuk Stefanovich Karadzic und Adamtinos Korais*. Wiesbaden: Harassowitz, 1997.

Judah, Tim. *The Serbs: History, Myth and the Destruction of Yugoslavia.* New Haven, Conn.: Yale University Press, 1996.

Karanovich, Milenko. *The Development of Education in Serbia and Emergence of its Intelligentsia (1838–1858).* New York: Columbia University Press, 1995.

Köpf, Peter. *Karadzic: Die Schande Europas.* Dusseldorf: Econ Taschenbuch Verlag, 1995.

Lowe, D. H. *The Ballads of Marko Kraljevic.* Cambridge: Cambridge University Press, 1922.

Novak, Viktor. *Vuk i Hrvati.* Belgrade: Naucno Delo, 1967.

Popovic, Miodrag. *Vuk Stefanovic Karadzic.* Belgrade: Nolit Press, 1964.

Rootham, Helen. *Kossovo: a Translation of the Heroic Songs of the Serbs.* London: Blackwell, 1920.

Simic, Charles. *The Horse Has Six Legs: An Anthology of Serbian Poetry.* Saint Paul, Minn.: Greywolf Press, 1992.

Stojanovic, Ljubomir. *Zivot I rad Vuka Stefanovica Karadzica* Belgrade, 1924.

Vuk Stefanovich Symposium: Sprache, Literature, Folklore. Wiesbaden: Harassowitz, 1989.

Wilson, Duncan. *The Life and Times of Vuk Stefanovitch Karadzic 1787–1864: Literacy, Literature, and National Independence in Serbia,* 1970. (Reprint: Ann Arbor, Mich.: Michigan University Slavic Publications, 1986.)

KARAMZIN, NIKOLAI MIKHAILOVICH 1766–1826

Russian poet, historian, and journalist

Nikolai Mikhailovich Karamzin can rightly be described as Russia's first man of letters. His work as a poet, author of fiction, literary critic, cultural and linguistic theorist, and historian made a lasting mark on Russian literature, and had an immediate impact on his contemporaries and on the younger generation of authors, particularly Aleksandr Pushkin. The wide range of his accomplishments is tribute to his ceaseless engagement with European intellectual movements, and to his ambition for Russia's rapid achievement of cultural parity with the West.

In 1783, Karamzin began his career as a poet with an early publication of a translation of an idyll by Salomon Gessner, a poet whose version of pastoral and personal philanthropy exercised a conspicuous influence on Karamzin's poetry. Translation was to be a mainstay of the modernization of Russian secular literature. Karamzin's introduction to literary and Masonic circles in Saint Petersburg bore fruit in a number of works, including a translation of Albert Haller's pietistic poem "O proiskhozhdenii ala" ("On the Origin of Evil," 1785); at the same time he collaborated with the important publisher Nikolai Novikov on the journal *Destskoe chtenie dlia serdtsa i razuma* (*Juvenile Reading for the Heart and Mind,* 1787–89), and it was in this periodical that he published his original story "Evgenii i Iulia" ("Eugene and Julia," 1789), the first of a series of influential sentimental tales that display the influence of Johann Wolfgang von Goethe, Jean-Jacques Rousseau, and Christoph Martin Wieland. There is no evidence to prove his direct involvement, but Karamzin was interested in Freemasonry as one of a series of moral philosophies, at least until his return from a trip to Europe in 1791.

His time in Saint Petersburg coincided with a new spirit of innovation in Russian literary and cultural history, and Karamzin took advantage of this openness to Western thought and taste by reading widely in the Enlightenment literature of the time. His poems and stories are synchronous with European movements, but the full extent of his engagement with Western thinkers and ideas becomes most important in his *Pisma russkogo puteshestvennika* (*Letters of a Russian Traveler,* 1797). A milestone in the development of Russian narrative prose, Karamzin's fictional account of his travels to England, France, Germany, and Switzerland follows an itinerary of intellectual exploration organized, at least in part, according to a series of interviews with the key thinkers of the day: his Russian traveler meets Christian Fürchtegott Gellert, Immanuel Kant, Johann Lavater, and numerous other figures. At the same time, the *Letters* comprise a type of bildungsroman. Heavily influenced by the techniques of the novel as well as the travelogue, the letters are consciously crafted performances and projections of a narrative persona, whose behavior changes not only according to his immediate social environment, but as a reflection of his changing literary sensibility. Numerous letters feature embedded, self-contained tales written in the style of the Gothic, or in the style of Ossianic romanticism, or drawing on the Rousseauian novel of sensibility. At the same time, a number of letters articulate a view of history, imbued with the spirit of Johann Gottfried von Herder, that affirm both the individual identity of national cultures and an optimism about the progress of civilization in Europe and in Russia. What is most striking about the *Letters,* however, is their implicit view of the Russian traveler as a full-fledged European, whose understanding of Western culture and command of the codes of politeness testify to a profound shift in the Russian sensibility.

The traveler also witnesses the early days of the French Revolution, and Karamzin returned to a less tolerant Russia, where Catherine II's fearful reaction led to the confiscation of books, imprisonment of Russian philosophers such as Nikolai Novikov and Aleksandr Radishchev, persecution of Freemasons, and more active censorship. His own faith in the progress of history and universal enlightenment seems to have suffered a severe blow, and this new spirit of skepticism is played out in a number of stories, most notably the Gothic fantasy "Ostrov Borngolm" ("The Isle of Bornholm," 1794), in which a tale of incest has been read as an allegory for the unnatural violence and unreason of political revolution. The epistolary sequence "Melodor to Filaret" and "Filaret to Melador" (1795) stages a debate about the course of history in terms of a reasoned exchange of views, but the overall impression is that belief in the sustainability of an age of reason has declined. Despite increasing pessimism about events abroad and in Russia, in the 1790s Karamzin made his mark as the publisher of a number of journals, which became the vehicle for his literary reviews and a showcase for poetic talent. Under his editorship the *Moskovskii zhurnal* (*Moscow Journal*), the almanac *Aglai,* and the *Vestnick Evropy* (*Herald of Europe*) began to publish high-quality poetry and fiction, and represent the first Russian attempt not only to write for a larger readership, but also to create that readership beyond the elite, aristocratic circles of the capital and to shape its literary taste. It is in the stories published in these journals, including his most famous work *Bednaia Liza* (*Poor Liza*, 1792), that Karamzin also demonstrated his influential view of literary language as an approximation of the well-educated speech one would hear in the salon. Given the prevalence of French in his circles, the advocacy of an elegant Russian unmarred by old-fashioned Slavonicisms and distinguished by a more fluent syntax was a crucial development. As late as the 1810s and 1820s, schools of writers continued to debate Karamzin's ideas, which had in fact taken hold very quickly.

In 1801, Karamzin returned to journalistic activity as editor of the *Herald of Europe* and the *Pantheon of Foreign Belles-Lettres*, and published a further series of fictions, the surface simplicity of which masked complex ideas about his philosophy of history. These views on the laws of history and the uniqueness of national histories were to find an outlet in Karamzin's greatest labor, his *Istoriia gosudarstva rossiiskogo* (*History of the Russian State*, 1818). Based on pioneering analysis of medieval documentary material, Karamzin's work proceeds through the sequence of princely biographies until the foundation of the Romanov dynasty in 1613. His faith in progress seems to have been transmuted into an acceptance of the providential historiography of the French Romantic school. The development of the state of Muscovy as a great empire is consequently seen as inevitable and in teleological terms. This narrative of the rise of absolutism was confirmed in the infamous, secret memorandum on Russia that Karamzin gave the tsar in 1811 (published abroad in 1861). Karamzin's views had a tangible impact on the Decembrist political movement, which fiercely disputed Karamzin's belief in the inevitability of the autocracy; and on Aleksandr Pushkin, whose Romantic, Shakespearean drama *Boris Godunov* (1831) took issue with Karamzin's *History*, but was nonetheless dedicated to his memory.

ANDREW KAHN

Biography

Born into the provincial gentry in Mikhailovsk, Simbirsk province, December 12, 1766. Educated at private boarding schools there and in Moscow, 1775–81, where he learned French and German. Brief period of service in the Guards in Saint Petersburg. First literary work published 1783. Brief correspondence with Lavater. After a year in Simbirsk, moved to Moscow, became a member of the literary circle of Nikolai Novikov, and may have participated in Masonic activities, 1785. Traveled to Germany, Switzerland, France, and England, 1789–90. Career as writer, editor, journalist, and poet in Moscow, 1791–1803. Married 1801, widowed in 1802, remarried in 1804. Appointed imperial historiographer, 1803; began historical research and writing, 1804–16, and then published his pioneering history of Russia. Moved to Saint Petersburg, 1816. Elected to the Russian Academy, 1818. Died in Saint Petersburg, June 2, 1826.

Selected Works

Izbrannye sochineniia. 2 vols. Khudozh. literatura, 1964.
Polnoe sobranie stikhotvorenii. Moscow: Biblioteka Poeta, 1966.
Sochineniia. 2 vols. Leningrad, 1984.
Pis'ma russkogo puteshestvennika. Leningrad: Nauka, 1984.
Istoriia gosudarstva rossiiskogo. 12 vols. Saint Petersburg, 1818–29, with numerous reprints. Voennaia t.p. Glav. Shtaba.
Selected Prose of N. M. Karamzin. Translated with an introduction by Henry M. Nebel, Jr. Evanston: Northwestern University Press, 1969.
Letters of a Russian Traveller. A translation, with an essay on *Karamzin's discourses of Enlightenment* by Andrew Kahn (Oxford: Voltaire Foundation, 2003).

Bibliography

Anderson, Roger A. *N. M. Karamzin's Prose: The Teller in the Tale*. Houston: Cordovan Press, 1974.
Black, Joseph L. *Essays on Karamzin: Russian Man-of-Letters, Political Thinker, Historian, 1766–1826*. The Hague: Mouton, 1975.
Cross, Anthony G. *N. M. Karamzin: A Study of His Literary Career (1782–1803)*. Carbondale, Ill.: Southern Illinois University Press, 1971.
Hammarberg, Gitta. *From the Idyll to the Novel: Karamzin's Sentimentalist Prose*. Cambridge: Cambridge University Press, 1991.
Kahn, Andrew. "Politeness and Its Discontents in Karamzin's Letters of a Russian Traveller (1797)." In *L'Invitation au voyage: Studies in Honour of Peter France*. Oxford: Voltaire Foundation, 2000.
Kotchetkova, Natalya. *Nikolay Karamzin*. Boston: Twayne, 1975.
Lotman, Iurii M. *Karamzin*. Saint Petersburg: Saint Peterburg-Iskusstvo, 1997.

KAUFFMANN, ANGELIKA 1741–1807

Swiss painter

In 1781 the Danish ambassador in London famously wrote that "the whole world is angelicamad." He was referring to the contemporary craze in English high society for the portrait painting of Angelika Kauffmann (both forename and surname occur in more than one spelling); yet his bon mot could be taken as a motto for her career as a whole, during which she achieved recognition and popularity throughout Europe in both artistic and literary circles. Born in Switzerland of an Austrian father, she completed her education and her training as an artist in Italy before moving to England in her early twenties. In Italy she had been influenced by Anton Raphael Mengs and Johann Joachim Winckelmann, the prophets of neo-classicism in German painting, whereas in London she exploited the fashion for portraits in the style of Thomas Gainsborough and Sir Joshua Reynolds. Returning to Rome in the 1780s, she developed contacts with the group of artists surrounding Johann Wolfgang von Goethe during his Italian journey. Despite her roots in the cultural traditions of the eighteenth century, she also associated with important representatives of pre-Romanticism, such as the painter Henry Fuseli, the Sturm und Drang authors Johann Gottfried Herder and Johann Kaspar Lavater, and the religious poet Friedrich Gottlieb Klopstock.

During her lifetime Kauffmann produced approximately five hundred portraits. Her first commissions were executed when she was twelve years old, traveling through Italy as a child prodigy, and from this period there are also juvenile self-portraits. The breakthrough came, however, in 1764 in Rome, when she painted Winckelmann's portrait. Despite the stylized portrayal of a classical scholar sunk in posed reflection, contemporaries testified to the impressive facial likeness. By this time Kauffmann was painting English travelers on their "grand tours," including Lord Exeter and John Parker (later Lord Boringdon and one of her most prominent sponsors). She also drew the artists Nathaniel Dance and Benjamin West, the former of whom fell in love with Kauffmann and painted a striking portrait of her; and in 1765 her portrait of David Garrick was sent for exhibition in England. There were now lucrative opportunities for Kauffmann in London, and she settled there in 1766. She met Joshua Reynolds, becoming his friend and collaborator: they painted portraits of each other and were together involved in the founding of the Royal Academy of Arts in London. Kauffmann also gained royal patronage, completing portraits of Princess Augusta and her sister-in-law Queen Charlotte. Numerous portraits of aristocrats followed, including Lord Althorp, the Earl of Ely, the Duchess of Richmond, and Marchioness Townshend. Later in her career, after returning to Italy, Kauffmann was commissioned to portray members of several European royal families: the King of Naples, Prince Poniatowski of Poland, and Crown Prince Ludwig of Bavaria. In general her portraits betray her neoclassicist training, although sometimes with rococo touches or sentimental prettifying of their subjects. At the same time an authentic and often intimate impression of individuals emerges. Her pictures of Garrick, in which the actor appears without background, leaning informally over the back of a chair, and of Goethe, shown as a sensitive young genius despite his thirty-eight years of age and ministerial career, indicate a new and more introverted Romantic mode of portraiture.

Despite the commercial success of her portraits, Kauffmann's background in neo-classicism generally led her to regard history painting as the most important genre. A floridly baroque style with opulent colors gradually gave way, in her history paintings of the 1780s, to the more austere classicism of David and the French school. She drew her subject matter from Greek and Roman mythology and frequently from Homer, but also from Roman history (Antony and Cleopatra being a favorite subject). During her residence in London, she painted scenes from older periods of English history and thus made a significant contribution to the developing Gothic revival. In 1788 John Boydell commissioned two pictures from her for his *Gallery* of illustrations to the works of William Shakespeare: *Two Gentlemen of Verona*, act 5, scene 3; and *Troilus and Cressida*, act 5, scene 2. In Kauffmann's later years in Rome, biblical subjects came to the fore in her work, especially after she received commissions from ecclesiastical patrons close to the pope. Many of her paintings are allegorical, featuring classical deities such as Hebe, or muses such as Clio. One particularly significant allegorical work is *Selbstbildnis am Scheidewege zwischen Musik und Malerei* (*Self-Portrait at the Crossroads between Music and Painting*, 1792), in which her own youthful wavering between the two arts is represented by female figures who clutch a musical score and a

palette, respectively, and seek to lead her in opposite directions. A similar approach characterizes the four ceiling panels (1781, now in Burlington House) that she painted for Somerset House, the new home of the Royal Academy: *Invention, Composition, Design* and *Colour*, each personified as a female muse. She was also much in demand for designs for internal decorative work and furnishing in English stately homes.

Following her marriage to the painter Antonio Zucchi and their migration to Italy in 1781, Kauffmann's salon became a focal point for the artistic community in Rome, including a circle of German painters (including Friedrich Bury, Johann Heinrich Lips, and Wilhelm Tischbein) and writers such as Karl Philipp Moritz in which Goethe moved during his stay in Italy from 1786 to 1788. Goethe accompanied her to galleries and took drawing lessons from her, later describing her with affection in his *Italienische Reise* (*Italian Journey*) and corresponding with her for some years after his return to Germany. In the winter of 1788–89 she entertained a visiting party of Goethe's Weimar acquaintances, including the Duchess of Weimar and the cultural historian Herder, both of whom sat for portraits. Kauffmann's enthusiasm for Goethe and his work is reflected in the illustrations to the play *Egmont* that she supplied for his collected *Schriften* in 1788.

In some respects, Kauffmann constitutes an embodiment of the eighteenth-century ideal of the "schöne Seele" ("beautiful soul"), a serene individual balancing her artistic vocation and her material needs without apparent friction. At the same time, she can be seen as a modern woman successful in her own right, independent of male sponsors. From her youth she pursued her career with professionalism and a regime of hard work, managing her income and her artistic commissions with aplomb, and achieving financial security before and outside her marriage to Zucchi. However traditional much of her artistic production may have been, she nevertheless represents the type of cosmopolitan and emancipated woman which the Romantic generation admired.

RICHARD LITTLEJOHNS

Biography

Born October 30, 1741 in Chur, Switzerland. Lived, 1752–54, in Como (then part of the Austrian Empire). Toured Italy, based in Milan, 1754–57. Returned to her father's home area in the Vorarlberg, Austria, 1757–58. Toured Italy again, 1758–62. In Florence, 1762–63; in Rome, 1763–66; in London, 1766–81. Married "Count de Horn," who turned out to be a confidence trickster, 1767: marriage annulled after four months. Founder member of British Royal Academy of Arts, 1768. Involved in scandal surrounding Nathaniel Hone's painting *The Conjuror*, which she alleged contains a scurrilous portrayal of her, 1775. Married the painter Antonio Zucchi and returned to Italy, initially to Venice, 1781. Settled in Rome, 1782. Visited in her studio by Emperor Joseph II of Austria, who commissioned two history paintings from her, 1784. Developed friendship with Goethe, 1786–88 and received other visitors from Weimar, notably Herder, 1788–89. Died in Rome November 5, 1807.

Selected Works

Bildnis Johann Joachim Winckelmann, 1764. Oil, 97.2 cm × 71 cm. Kunsthaus, Zurich.

of the past and the future, while speaking of the
Other actors are continually thinking of their sum-
throughout a play. Kean delivers himself up to the ins
ing, without a shadow of a thought about any thing
feels his being as deeply as Wordsworth. . . . We will
more."

EDWARD B

Biography

Born, to unknown parents, most probably Edmund Kean and
Nancy Carey, 1787. First appearance on stage, at Drury Lane,
as Robin in Shakespeare's *The Merry Wives of Windsor*, 1796.
First recorded performing comic roles in small companies on
provincial tours, 1804. Appeared in a season at the Haymarket
Theatre, 1806. Discovered and contracted to the Drury Lane
Theatre; established a preeminent Shakespearean career, 1813.
Died in debt, after a number of illnesses and accidents on stage
had disrupted his acting career, 1833.

Bibliography

Bate, Jonathan. *The Romantics on Shakespeare*. London: Penguin,
  1992.
Highfill, Philip H., et al. *A Biographical Dictionary of Actors,
  Actresses, Musicians, Dancers, Managers and other Stage Personnel
  in London, 1660–1800*. Carbondale: Southern Illinois University
  Press.
Hillebrand, Harold Newcombe. *Edmund Kean*. New York:
  Columbia University Press, 1933.
Hogan, Charles Beecher. *Shakespeare in the Theatre 1701–1800*.
  Oxford: Clarendon Press, 1957.

of
uel
ents
ponse
Kean is
ts from
mes pro-
him act,
o not think
llo." Hazlitt,
mpathies very
he people, and
can do all that
ent that parallels
s Richard III that
of Hazlitt's remark
lanus did not really
the "electric shocks"
compensate for what
ortcomings and a per-
is very sense of a man of
pushing against the limits
at moved and excited his
Keats is the most eloquent,
s passage in poetry is full of
l. . . . The sensual life of verse
an. . . . There is an indescribable
feel that the utterer is thinking

KEATS, JOHN 1795–1821

English poet

1795, John Keats, the son of the head
nn, lost his father when he was eight years
when he was fourteen. His younger brother
December 1, 1818, nursed during his final
mself, who had also watched over his mother
ying. The poet would later die of turberculosis,
e that claimed the lives of his mother and Tom,
ebruary 23, 1821. His last few months are painful
te as Keats lived out what he called his "posthumous
n Italy, where he had sailed, accompanied by the
seph Severn, in search of a more hospitable climate.
me sensitivity to loss, always apparent, resulted in a
ken assertion about Fanny Brawne, the woman he loved
m he had lived next door at Wentworth Place in Hamp-
toward the end of 1819 and much of 1820, and whom he
eft behind in England): "I eternally see her figure eternally
shing." At the same time, his courage, in evidence through-
t his life ("he would at all hazards," his brother George would
rite, "defend the oppressed"), shows itself at the end in his
ympathy with the overburdened Joseph Severn who looked after
im, and in his capacity to joke, as when he signs off his last
ter with the self-deprecating remark: "I can scarcely bid you
d bye even in a letter. I always made an awkward bow."

As a student at Guy's Hospital from 1815–16, where he
trained successfully to be an apothecary, Keats would have witnessed, as a dresser to the surgeons, frequent sights of severe
suffering, as patients underwent surgery without anaesthetics.
His personal and professional knowledge of pain, suffering, and
mortality helps to explain the extraordinary complexity and
depth of the body of poetry which he produced in his short
career. The poetry stands in a dialectical relationship to the somber knowledge aforementioned, since it displays a relish for life
that is exuberant yet tragically aware. The development of Keats
from the youthful poet championed by Leigh Hunt in 1817 to
the author of the major odes and narrative poems has been the
subject of much critical investigation. This investigation usually
and necessarily follows in the wake of Keats's own self-scrutiny,
traced in his brilliant letters, which contain a wealth of information about his evolving sense of poetry. In them we move from
his early preference for instinct over reason when he proclaims
(in November 1817) to Benjamin Bailey, "O for a Life of Sensations rather than of Thoughts!", to his later view of life as "the
vale of Soul-making," a redefinition of the Christian idea of life
as a vale of tears, that looks ahead to existentialism in its emphasis
on life as a process of acquiring identity through experience.
"Do you not see," he asks in this second letter, "how necessary

602 KEAN, EDMUND

of Romantic individualism, and a powerful reimagination... Shakespeare, which they respected as equal to their own. Sa... Taylor Coleridge was less enthusiastic, and his com... (recorded as *Table Talk*, in 1836) give us the mixed re... that might well have been copies from himself. His rapid desce... original; but he copies from himself, though some... the hyper-tragic to the infra-colloquial, though some... ductive of great effect, are often unreasonable. To s... is like reading Shakspeare by flashes of lightning. I... him thorough-bred gentleman enough to play Oth... a less conservative writer and one with political s... different from Coleridge's, called Kean "one of... what might be termed a *radical* performer. H... may become a man of our infirmity"; a com... Byron's remark in his diary after seeing Kea... this Richard was "a man." But the contex... was his observation that the role of Cori... suit the actor; what he has called elsewhere... of Kean's performances did not always... were, in conventional terms, physical... ceived lack of "aristocratic" quality. T... high intelligence and quick sensitivity... of his "given" identity is surely w... distinguished admirers, of whom... having once written, "A melodio... pleasures both sensual and spirit... springs warm from the lips of K... gusto in his voice, by which w...

The true parents of the great Ro... have never been established, a fact w... speculation that he was, perhaps, an illeg... tocracy. His birth date, and so his exact a... His ethnicity was also debated (it was suspec... least partially Jewish). This, like so much in his... public image, set him apart from his great riva... respectable dynasty of Kemble and Siddons. Kean... former of charismatic individualism and fierce natura... whose shorter stature and more demotic style of speech... movement was often contrasted by critics with Kemble's aris... cratic bearing and grace of gesture. In roles like Hamlet or Coriolanus, his performances were, for this reason, controversial, though still widely admired; the tragic roles most clearly identified with him were those of the outsider figures Richard III and Othello.

His stage debut was at the Drury Lane Theatre in 1796, playing the role of Robin in William Shakespeare's *The Merry Wives of Windsor*. If one takes his birth date as 1789 (the date given by the actress Miss Tidswell, who looked after him as a child, and whom he sometimes suspected might have been his mother), then he was seven—a fact that in itself makes the earlier date of 1787 more likely. Kean tended to move the date forward as he aged (as seems to still be the way with actors and actresses). His childhood and youth are mysterious due to the myth making undertaken by himself and his admirers, but it can be established that he was acting in a provincial touring company in 1804, having taken the name Carey from another, probably more likely, identification of his birth mother. His major role at this time was as Harlequin, a popular import into English pantomime from the Italian *commedia del'arte*. He returned to London in 1806 to play servants and minor juveniles in a season at the Haymarket Theatre, then the third most important theater after Drury Lane and Covent Garden. This established a pattern of frustration and ambition, as Kean's sense of his own talent and need for preeminence grew. "Look at the little man," one

...sel... create... work in... ever, he sc... Shylock in Sh... III, following t... established both h... the Kembles at Cove... would remain at the cor... especially in Ireland and... broiled, despite his immens... drink and debt. In his place... London theater, but of British cult... virtue not only of his iconic presence... reinterpretation of the protagonists he... of stage business to animate them, whic... to call a moment in his Hamlet "the fine... was ever made on Shakespeare."

The admiration of literary figures like Lord L... Hazlitt, and John Keats have fixed Kean's reputa... modern reader, and confirmed that his acting was an...

Born on October 3... ostler at a London i... old and his mother... Tom would die o... weeks by John h... while she was d... the same disea... in Rome on... to contempl... existence"... painter Jo... His extre... heartbro... (to wh... stead... had... van... ou...

aristocratic circles of the capital and to shape its literary taste. It is in the stories published in these journals, including his most famous work *Bednaia Liza* (*Poor Liza*, 1792), that Karamzin also demonstrated his influential view of literary language as an approximation of the well-educated speech one would hear in the salon. Given the prevalence of French in his circles, the advocacy of an elegant Russian unmarred by old-fashioned Slavonicisms and distinguished by a more fluent syntax was a crucial development. As late as the 1810s and 1820s, schools of writers continued to debate Karamzin's ideas, which had in fact taken hold very quickly.

In 1801, Karamzin returned to journalistic activity as editor of the *Herald of Europe* and the *Pantheon of Foreign Belles-Lettres*, and published a further series of fictions, the surface simplicity of which masked complex ideas about his philosophy of history. These views on the laws of history and the uniqueness of national histories were to find an outlet in Karamzin's greatest labor, his *Istoriia gosudarstva rossiiskogo* (*History of the Russian State*, 1818). Based on pioneering analysis of medieval documentary material, Karamzin's work proceeds through the sequence of princely biographies until the foundation of the Romanov dynasty in 1613. His faith in progress seems to have been transmuted into an acceptance of the providential historiography of the French Romantic school. The development of the state of Muscovy as a great empire is consequently seen as inevitable and in teleological terms. This narrative of the rise of absolutism was confirmed in the infamous, secret memorandum on Russia that Karamzin gave the tsar in 1811 (published abroad in 1861). Karamzin's views had a tangible impact on the Decembrist political movement, which fiercely disputed Karamzin's belief in the inevitability of the autocracy; and on Aleksandr Pushkin, whose Romantic, Shakespearean drama *Boris Godunov* (1831) took issue with Karamzin's *History*, but was nonetheless dedicated to his memory.

ANDREW KAHN

Biography

Born into the provincial gentry in Mikhailovsk, Simbirsk province, December 12, 1766. Educated at private boarding schools there and in Moscow, 1775–81, where he learned French and German. Brief period of service in the Guards in Saint Petersburg. First literary work published 1783. Brief correspondence with Lavater. After a year in Simbirsk, moved to Moscow, became a member of the literary circle of Nikolai Novikov, and may have participated in Masonic activities, 1785. Traveled to Germany, Switzerland, France, and England, 1789–90. Career as writer, editor, journalist, and poet in Moscow, 1791–1803. Married 1801, widowed in 1802, remarried in 1804. Appointed imperial historiographer, 1803; began historical research and writing, 1804–16, and then published his pioneering history of Russia. Moved to Saint Petersburg, 1816. Elected to the Russian Academy, 1818. Died in Saint Petersburg, June 2, 1826.

Selected Works

Izbrannye sochineniia. 2 vols. Khudozh. literatura, 1964.
Polnoe sobranie stikhotvorenii. Moscow: Biblioteka Poeta, 1966.
Sochineniia. 2 vols. Leningrad, 1984.
Pis'ma russkogo puteshestvennika. Leningrad: Nauka, 1984.
Istoriia gosudarstva rossiiskogo. 12 vols. Saint Petersburg, 1818–29, with numerous reprints. Voennaia t.p. Glav. Shtaba.
Selected Prose of N. M. Karamzin. Translated with an introduction by Henry M. Nebel, Jr. Evanston: Northwestern University Press, 1969.
Letters of a Russian Traveller. A translation, with an essay on *Karamzin's discourses of Enlightenment* by Andrew Kahn (Oxford: Voltaire Foundation, 2003).

Bibliography

Anderson, Roger A. *N. M. Karamzin's Prose: The Teller in the Tale.* Houston: Cordovan Press, 1974.
Black, Joseph L. *Essays on Karamzin: Russian Man-of-Letters, Political Thinker, Historian, 1766–1826.* The Hague: Mouton, 1975.
Cross, Anthony G. *N. M. Karamzin: A Study of His Literary Career (1782–1803).* Carbondale, Ill.: Southern Illinois University Press, 1971.
Hammarberg, Gitta. *From the Idyll to the Novel: Karamzin's Sentimentalist Prose.* Cambridge: Cambridge University Press, 1991.
Kahn, Andrew. "Politeness and Its Discontents in Karamzin's Letters of a Russian Traveller (1797)." In *L'Invitation au voyage: Studies in Honour of Peter France.* Oxford: Voltaire Foundation, 2000.
Kotchetkova, Natalya. *Nikolay Karamzin.* Boston: Twayne, 1975.
Lotman, Iurii M. *Karamzin.* Saint Petersburg: Saint Peterburg-Iskusstvo, 1997.

KAUFFMANN, ANGELIKA 1741–1807

Swiss painter

In 1781 the Danish ambassador in London famously wrote that "the whole world is angelicamad." He was referring to the contemporary craze in English high society for the portrait painting of Angelika Kauffmann (both forename and surname occur in more than one spelling); yet his bon mot could be taken as a motto for her career as a whole, during which she achieved recognition and popularity throughout Europe in both artistic and literary circles. Born in Switzerland of an Austrian father, she completed her education and her training as an artist in Italy before moving to England in her early twenties. In Italy she had been influenced by Anton Raphael Mengs and Johann Joachim Winckelmann, the prophets of neo-classicism in German painting, whereas in London she exploited the fashion for portraits in the style of Thomas Gainsborough and Sir Joshua Reynolds. Returning to Rome in the 1780s, she developed contacts with the group of artists surrounding Johann Wolfgang von Goethe during his Italian journey. Despite her roots in the cultural traditions of the eighteenth century, she also associated with important representatives of pre-Romanticism, such as the painter Henry Fuseli, the Sturm und Drang authors Johann Gottfried Herder and Johann Kaspar Lavater, and the religious poet Friedrich Gottlieb Klopstock.

During her lifetime Kauffmann produced approximately five hundred portraits. Her first commissions were executed when she was twelve years old, traveling through Italy as a child prodigy, and from this period there are also juvenile self-portraits. The breakthrough came, however, in 1764 in Rome, when she painted Winckelmann's portrait. Despite the stylized portrayal of a classical scholar sunk in posed reflection, contemporaries testified to the impressive facial likeness. By this time Kauffmann was painting English travelers on their "grand tours," including Lord Exeter and John Parker (later Lord Boringdon and one of her most prominent sponsors). She also drew the artists Nathaniel Dance and Benjamin West, the former of whom fell in love with Kauffmann and painted a striking portrait of her; and in 1765 her portrait of David Garrick was sent for exhibition in England. There were now lucrative opportunities for Kauffmann in London, and she settled there in 1766. She met Joshua Reynolds, becoming his friend and collaborator: they painted portraits of each other and were together involved in the founding of the Royal Academy of Arts in London. Kauffmann also gained royal patronage, completing portraits of Princess Augusta and her sister-in-law Queen Charlotte. Numerous portraits of aristocrats followed, including Lord Althorp, the Earl of Ely, the Duchess of Richmond, and Marchioness Townshend. Later in her career, after returning to Italy, Kauffmann was commissioned to portray members of several European royal families: the King of Naples, Prince Poniatowski of Poland, and Crown Prince Ludwig of Bavaria. In general her portraits betray her neoclassicist training, although sometimes with rococo touches or sentimental prettifying of their subjects. At the same time an authentic and often intimate impression of individuals emerges. Her pictures of Garrick, in which the actor appears without background, leaning informally over the back of a chair, and of Goethe, shown as a sensitive young genius despite his thirty-eight years of age and ministerial career, indicate a new and more introverted Romantic mode of portraiture.

Despite the commercial success of her portraits, Kauffmann's background in neo-classicism generally led her to regard history painting as the most important genre. A floridly baroque style with opulent colors gradually gave way, in her history paintings of the 1780s, to the more austere classicism of David and the French school. She drew her subject matter from Greek and Roman mythology and frequently from Homer, but also from Roman history (Antony and Cleopatra being a favorite subject). During her residence in London, she painted scenes from older periods of English history and thus made a significant contribution to the developing Gothic revival. In 1788 John Boydell commissioned two pictures from her for his *Gallery* of illustrations to the works of William Shakespeare: *Two Gentlemen of Verona*, act 5, scene 3; and *Troilus and Cressida*, act 5, scene 2. In Kauffmann's later years in Rome, biblical subjects came to the fore in her work, especially after she received commissions from ecclesiastical patrons close to the pope. Many of her paintings are allegorical, featuring classical deities such as Hebe, or muses such as Clio. One particularly significant allegorical work is *Selbstbildnis am Scheidewege zwischen Musik und Malerei (Self-Portrait at the Crossroads between Music and Painting*, 1792), in which her own youthful wavering between the two arts is represented by female figures who clutch a musical score and a palette, respectively, and seek to lead her in opposite directions. A similar approach characterizes the four ceiling panels (1781, now in Burlington House) that she painted for Somerset House, the new home of the Royal Academy: *Invention, Composition, Design* and *Colour*, each personified as a female muse. She was also much in demand for designs for internal decorative work and furnishing in English stately homes.

Following her marriage to the painter Antonio Zucchi and their migration to Italy in 1781, Kauffmann's salon became a focal point for the artistic community in Rome, including a circle of German painters (including Friedrich Bury, Johann Heinrich Lips, and Wilhelm Tischbein) and writers such as Karl Philipp Moritz in which Goethe moved during his stay in Italy from 1786 to 1788. Goethe accompanied her to galleries and took drawing lessons from her, later describing her with affection in his *Italienische Reise (Italian Journey)* and corresponding with her for some years after his return to Germany. In the winter of 1788–89 she entertained a visiting party of Goethe's Weimar acquaintances, including the Duchess of Weimar and the cultural historian Herder, both of whom sat for portraits. Kauffmann's enthusiasm for Goethe and his work is reflected in the illustrations to the play *Egmont* that she supplied for his collected *Schriften* in 1788.

In some respects, Kauffmann constitutes an embodiment of the eighteenth-century ideal of the "schöne Seele" ("beautiful soul"), a serene individual balancing her artistic vocation and her material needs without apparent friction. At the same time, she can be seen as a modern woman successful in her own right, independent of male sponsors. From her youth she pursued her career with professionalism and a regime of hard work, managing her income and her artistic commissions with aplomb, and achieving financial security before and outside her marriage to Zucchi. However traditional much of her artistic production may have been, she nevertheless represents the type of cosmopolitan and emancipated woman which the Romantic generation admired.

RICHARD LITTLEJOHNS

Biography

Born October 30, 1741 in Chur, Switzerland. Lived, 1752–54, in Como (then part of the Austrian Empire). Toured Italy, based in Milan, 1754–57. Returned to her father's home area in the Vorarlberg, Austria, 1757–58. Toured Italy again, 1758–62. In Florence, 1762–63; in Rome, 1763–66; in London, 1766–81. Married "Count de Horn," who turned out to be a confidence trickster, 1767: marriage annulled after four months. Founder member of British Royal Academy of Arts, 1768. Involved in scandal surrounding Nathaniel Hone's painting *The Conjuror*, which she alleged contains a scurrilous portrayal of her, 1775. Married the painter Antonio Zucchi and returned to Italy, initially to Venice, 1781. Settled in Rome, 1782. Visited in her studio by Emperor Joseph II of Austria, who commissioned two history paintings from her, 1784. Developed friendship with Goethe, 1786–88 and received other visitors from Weimar, notably Herder, 1788–89. Died in Rome November 5, 1807.

Selected Works

Bildnis Johann Joachim Winckelmann, 1764. Oil, 97.2 cm × 71 cm. Kunsthaus, Zurich.

Bacchus entdeckt die von Theseus verlassene Ariadne auf Naxos, 1764. Oil, 166 cm × 125 cm. Amt der Landeshauptstadt, Bregenz.

Portrait of Sir Joshua Reynolds, 1767. Oil, 127 cm × 101 cm. Saltram House, Plymouth.

The Parting of Hector and Andromache, 1768. Oil, 134 cm × 176 cm. Saltram House, Plymouth.

Bildnis Johann Wolfgang von Goethe. 1787. Oil, 63.5 cm × 51.5 cm. Goethe-Nationalmuseum, Goethewohnhaus. Weimar.

The Two Gentlemen of Verona—Valentine, Proteus, Silvia and Julia in the Forest. 1788. Oil, 161.9 cm × 222.3 cm. Davis Museum, Wellesley College Museum, Wellesley.

Bildnis Gräfin Catherine Skawronska, 1789. Oil, 158 cm × 122 cm. Germanisches Nationalmuseum, Nuremberg.

Bildnis Johann Gottfried Herder, 1791. Oil, 63.7 cm × 52.1 cm. Goethe-Museum, Frankfurt.

Selbstbildnis am Scheideweg zwischen Musik und Malerei, 1792. Oil, 151 cm × 212 cm. Puschkin-Museum, Moscow.

Christus und die Samariterin am Brunnen, 1796. Oil, 123.5 cm × 158.5 cm. Neue Pinakothek, Munich.

Bibliography

Baumgärtel, Bettina, ed. *Angelika Kauffmann.* Ostfildern-Ruit: Hatje, 1998.

Manners, Lady Victoria, and G. C. Williamson. *Angelica Kauffmann: Her Life and Works.* London: John Lane, 1924.

Mayer, Dorothy Moulton. *Angelica Kauffmann.* Gerrards Cross, England: Colin Smythe, 1972.

Pape, Walter, and Frederick Burwick. eds. *The Boydell Shakespeare Gallery.* Bottrop: Pomp, 1996.

Roworth, Wendy Wassyng, ed. *Angelica Kauffman: A Continental Artist in Georgian England.* London: Reaktion, 1992.

Thurnher, Eugen, ed. *Angelika Kauffmann und die deutsche Dichtung.* Bregenz: Russ, 1966.

KEAN, EDMUND c. 1787–1833

English actor

The true parents of the great Romantic actor Edmund Kean have never been established, a fact which allowed him to fuel speculation that he was, perhaps, an illegitimate son of the aristocracy. His birth date, and so his exact age, is still unknown. His ethnicity was also debated (it was suspected he might be at least partially Jewish). This, like so much in his acting style and public image, set him apart from his great rivals, the highly respectable dynasty of Kemble and Siddons. Kean was a performer of charismatic individualism and fierce natural energy, whose shorter stature and more demotic style of speech and movement was often contrasted by critics with Kemble's aristocratic bearing and grace of gesture. In roles like Hamlet or Coriolanus, his performances were, for this reason, controversial, though still widely admired; the tragic roles most clearly identified with him were those of the outsider figures Richard III and Othello.

His stage debut was at the Drury Lane Theatre in 1796, playing the role of Robin in William Shakespeare's *The Merry Wives of Windsor.* If one takes his birth date as 1789 (the date given by the actress Miss Tidswell, who looked after him as a child, and whom he sometimes suspected might have been his mother), then he was seven—a fact that in itself makes the earlier date of 1787 more likely. Kean tended to move the date forward as he aged (as seems to still be the way with actors and actresses). His childhood and youth are mysterious due to the myth making undertaken by himself and his admirers, but it can be established that he was acting in a provincial touring company in 1804, having taken the name Carey from another, probably more likely, identification of his birth mother. His major role at this time was as Harlequin, a popular import into English pantomime from the Italian *commedia del'arte.* He returned to London in 1806 to play servants and minor juveniles in a season at the Haymarket Theatre, then the third most important theater after Drury Lane and Covent Garden. This established a pattern of frustration and ambition, as Kean's sense of his own talent and need for preeminence grew. "Look at the little man," one

of his fellow actors is supposed to have said of him in a very minor role; "he's trying to act; he's trying to make a part of Carney!" He returned to provincial touring, largely in Wales and Ireland, and acquired a reputation for temperamental behavior and showy semicomic acting, often in "wild man" or "noble savage" roles, where his energy, ambiguous ethnicity (probably another myth), and gift for movement were exploited in a contemporary taste for the exotic. He married the actress Mary Chambers in 1808; the marriage was an only intermittently happy and often bewildering experience for the bride. It also put pressure on Kean to solve the problem of his always chaotic finances.

Things seemed to improve when, in 1813, a talent scout from Drury Lane spotted him in one of his "savage" roles, but contractual difficulties and Kean's habitual combination of high self-esteem, impulsive fictionalizing, and lack of business sense created a situation which stranded him and his family without work in London for several months. Later in the season, however, he scored public and critical success with performances of Shylock in Shakespeare's *The Merchant of Venice* and of Richard III, following them with Othello and with Hamlet. He thus established both himself and the theater as powerful rivals of the Kembles at Covent Garden, and established the roles that would remain at the core of his repertoire. He toured extensively, especially in Ireland and America, until he died in 1833, embroiled, despite his immense success, in the old problems of drink and debt. Yet his place was at the center not only of London theater, but of British cultural life, and he occupied it by virtue not only of his iconic presence, but through a spontaneous reinterpretation of the protagonists he played, and an invention of stage business to animate them, which led William Hazlitt to call a moment in his Hamlet "the finest commentary that was ever made on Shakespeare."

The admiration of literary figures like Lord Byron, William Hazlitt, and John Keats have fixed Kean's reputation for the modern reader, and confirmed that his acting was an expression

of Romantic individualism, and a powerful reimagination of Shakespeare, which they respected as equal to their own. Samuel Taylor Coleridge was less enthusiastic, and his comments (recorded as *Table Talk*, in 1836) give us the mixed response that might well have been more general, as he wrote, "Kean is original; but he copies from himself. His rapid descents from the hyper-tragic to the infra-colloquial, though sometimes productive of great effect, are often unreasonable. To see him act, is like reading Shakspeare by flashes of lightning. I do not think him thorough-bred gentleman enough to play Othello." Hazlitt, a less conservative writer and one with political sympathies very different from Coleridge's, called Kean "one of the people, and what might be termed a *radical* performer. He can do all that may become a man of our infirmity"; a comment that parallels Byron's remark in his diary after seeing Kean's Richard III that this Richard was "a *man*." But the context of Hazlitt's remark was his observation that the role of Coriolanus did not really suit the actor; what he has called elsewhere the "electric shocks" of Kean's performances did not always compensate for what were, in conventional terms, physical shortcomings and a perceived lack of "aristocratic" quality. This very sense of a man of high intelligence and quick sensitivity pushing against the limits of his "given" identity is surely what moved and excited his distinguished admirers, of whom Keats is the most eloquent, having once written, "A melodious passage in poetry is full of pleasures both sensual and spiritual. . . . The sensual life of verse springs warm from the lips of Kean. . . . There is an indescribable gusto in his voice, by which we feel that the utterer is thinking of the past and the future, while speaking of the instant. . . . Other actors are continually thinking of their sum-total effect throughout a play. Kean delivers himself up to the instant feeling, without a shadow of a thought about any thing else. He feels his being as deeply as Wordsworth. . . . We will say no more."

EDWARD BURNS

Biography

Born, to unknown parents, most probably Edmund Kean and Nancy Carey, 1787. First appearance on stage, at Drury Lane, as Robin in Shakespeare's *The Merry Wives of Windsor*, 1796. First recorded performing comic roles in small companies on provincial tours, 1804. Appeared in a season at the Haymarket Theatre, 1806. Discovered and contracted to the Drury Lane Theatre; established a preeminent Shakespearean career, 1813. Died in debt, after a number of illnesses and accidents on stage had disrupted his acting career, 1833.

Bibliography

Bate, Jonathan. *The Romantics on Shakespeare*. London: Penguin, 1992.

Highfill, Philip H., et al. *A Biographical Dictionary of Actors, Actresses, Musicians, Dancers, Managers and other Stage Personnel in London, 1660–1800*. Carbondale: Southern Illinois University Press.

Hillebrand, Harold Newcombe. *Edmund Kean*. New York: Columbia University Press, 1933.

Hogan, Charles Beecher. *Shakespeare in the Theatre 1701–1800*. Oxford: Clarendon Press, 1957.

KEATS, JOHN 1795–1821

English poet

Born on October 31, 1795, John Keats, the son of the head ostler at a London inn, lost his father when he was eight years old and his mother when he was fourteen. His younger brother Tom would die on December 1, 1818, nursed during his final weeks by John himself, who had also watched over his mother while she was dying. The poet would later die of turberculosis, the same disease that claimed the lives of his mother and Tom, in Rome on February 23, 1821. His last few months are painful to contemplate as Keats lived out what he called his "posthumous existence" in Italy, where he had sailed, accompanied by the painter Joseph Severn, in search of a more hospitable climate. His extreme sensitivity to loss, always apparent, resulted in a heartbroken assertion about Fanny Brawne, the woman he loved (to whom he had lived next door at Wentworth Place in Hampstead toward the end of 1819 and much of 1820, and whom he had left behind in England): "I eternally see her figure eternally vanishing." At the same time, his courage, in evidence throughout his life ("he would at all hazards," his brother George would write, "defend the oppressed"), shows itself at the end in his sympathy with the overburdened Joseph Severn who looked after him, and in his capacity to joke, as when he signs off his last letter with the self-deprecating remark: "I can scarcely bid you good bye even in a letter. I always made an awkward bow."

As a student at Guy's Hospital from 1815–16, where he trained successfully to be an apothecary, Keats would have witnessed, as a dresser to the surgeons, frequent sights of severe suffering, as patients underwent surgery without anaesthetics. His personal and professional knowledge of pain, suffering, and mortality helps to explain the extraordinary complexity and depth of the body of poetry which he produced in his short career. The poetry stands in a dialectical relationship to the somber knowledge aforementioned, since it displays a relish for life that is exuberant yet tragically aware. The development of Keats from the youthful poet championed by Leigh Hunt in 1817 to the author of the major odes and narrative poems has been the subject of much critical investigation. This investigation usually and necessarily follows in the wake of Keats's own self-scrutiny, traced in his brilliant letters, which contain a wealth of information about his evolving sense of poetry. In them we move from his early preference for instinct over reason when he proclaims (in November 1817) to Benjamin Bailey, "O for a Life of Sensations rather than of Thoughts!", to his later view of life as "the vale of Soul-making," a redefinition of the Christian idea of life as a vale of tears, that looks ahead to existentialism in its emphasis on life as a process of acquiring identity through experience. "Do you not see," he asks in this second letter, "how necessary

a World of Pains and troubles is to school an intelligence and make it a soul?" It would oversimplify to see Keats's development in linear terms; in the 1817 letter to Bailey, he imagines "a complex Mind—one that is imaginative and at the same time careful of its fruits," which describes well the poetic intelligence found in his best work. But Keats's poetic career has seemed especially significant to many readers for the evidence it gives of a continual striving toward "truth" and "beauty," two abstractions identified as identical, with a certain dramatic irony (the identification is made by an artwork), at the close of "Ode on a Grecian Urn" (1820). That these abstractions can come into conflict troubled Keats, to the benefit of his poetry, and led him to develop an aesthetic that places value on "intensity": "The excellence of every Art is its intensity, capable of making all disagreeables evaporate, from their being in close proximity with Beauty & Truth—Examine King Lear," he wrote in a letter, "& you will find this exemplified throughout." The choice of William Shakespeare as an exemplary figure is in keeping with Keats's admiration for the author whose picture he was delighted to find in a boarding house on the Isle of Wight in April 1817 where he went to write *Endymion*, his first major long poem. With the picture installed in his room, he asked his friend, the painter Benjamin Robert Haydon, "Is it too daring to fancy Shakespeare [the] Presider?" Though Keats's attempts to write plays (*Otho the Great* [1819–20] and the unfinished *King Stephen*) do not indicate a Shakespearean dramatic talent, there are parallels to be traced between Keats and Shakespeare in their gift of sympathy with others and their ability to convey thought through sensuous imagery.

Keats's view of history and culture was typically Romantic in its concern with evolution and becoming, and the recent view of him as politically radical, eloquently articulated by Nicholas Roe and others, gains support from the fact that he was educated at Enfield School (1803–11), a dissenting academy, where he made friends with the headmaster's son, Charles Cowden Clarke, who is praised in a verse letter for having "upheld the veil from Clio's beauty, / And pointed out the patriot's stern duty." Yet if Keats expressed a trust in "the general and gregarious advance of intellect," admiring William Wordsworth as "deeper than Milton" because of this advance, he also recognized that his own "poetical Character" differed from "the wordsworthian or egotistical sublime." What appealed to Keats was "negative capability," the ability to live "in uncertainties, Mysteries, doubts, without any irritable reaching after fact & reason." This quality, attributed by Keats to Shakespeare, lies close to the heart of his own finest work. As a result, Keats can prove hard to align with any one position or ideological stance. In contrast to Percy Bysshe Shelley (whom Keats knew through Leigh Hunt and who was the author of *Adonais*, 1821, an elegy for Keats that praises his poetic genius but subscribes to a sentimental view of him as easily broken by the rough-and-tumble of literary warfare), Keats seems at crucial moments in his work to be skeptical of utopian thought (this is not to deny Shelley's own skepticism about his most ardent desires). Although Keats's commitment to the "Liberal side of the Question," as he put it, is observable—especially in his earlier work, which earned the mocking contempt of Tory reviewers—the politics of many poems, particularly in his 1820 volume are, at best, implicit.

Keats's first volume, *Poems*, appeared in 1817, after he made the decision to be a poet rather than an apothecary. It owes much to the encouragement and example of Hunt, to whom the volume is dedicated. Keats derives from Hunt a jauntily conversational use of the couplet, an unguarded readiness to assert his love of literature and a strong regard for the values of friendship and for what in one sonnet he calls "the social thought." But the volume is distinctively Keatsian in the rich sensuousness of its language and in its fascination with the vocation of poetry. For the former, one might consider the close of an otherwise forgettable sonnet when Keats rejects social charm and writes, "My ear is open like a greedy shark / To catch the tunings of a voice divine." For the latter, one might cite the extended "Sleep and Poetry," among the finest poems in the collection, and of great interest for its developing understanding of poetry, not merely as a catalogue of "luxuries", but as "a friend / To soothe the cares and lift the thoughts of man."

Subsequent work would subject this ideal to severe testing. Keats began to turn away from Hunt and the Hampstead set, deliberately seeking a degree of independence in the composition of *Endymion*, which was written in a variety of places, including Margate and Oxford. Over four thousand lines in length, the four books of *Endymion* constitute a "trial of Invention" that, like Shelley's *Alastor* (1816), explores the relationship between ideal and human love. The poem, written in heroic couplets that reveal a greater depth and strength than is apparent in the 1817 volume, answers Shelley's tragic vision. Endymion, haunted in his highly erotic dreams by Cynthia, the goddess of the moon, learns to feel for others such as the "*lovers tempest-tossed*" in book 3 (whom he saves), and he is finally rewarded when the goddess and a mortal Indian maid turn out to be one and the same. That there is an element of wish fulfillment here is evident, and later work both shapes great poetry out of wish fulfilment and subjects that impulse to scrutiny; examples include "The Eve of St. Agnes," composed in January 1819 after a visit to Bedhampton with his close friend Charles Armitage Brown, and "Ode to a Nightingale," written a few months later. The latter poem finishes by questioning the value of the experience recorded in the ode "Was it a vision, or a waking dream?" and it manages at once to celebrate the imagination's capacity for escape, redefinition, and transformation (the terms blend and blur) and to interrogate the validity of its flights. In so doing, the poem manages to encapsulate the qualities of honesty, unpredictability, surrender to impulse, and technical inventiveness that make Keats an important Romantic poet.

Though his letters convey a strong sense that this eager, humorous, and generous young man was a delightful companion, they communicate more than anything his fervent desire to develop as a poet. His walking tour of Scotland and the Lake District, undertaken in late June 1818 with Brown after his brother George and sister-in-law Georgiana had left for America, would, he hoped, enable him to "load me with grander Mountains, and strengthen more my reach in Poetry." In his knapsack he had a three-volume edition of Henry Cary's translation of Dante Alighieri's *Divine Comedy* (1321). Characteristically, this work is put to use by Keats, whose responsiveness to great writing was acute, and a Dantean influence is clearly and beneficially present in "The Fall of Hyperion," a revised version of the fragment "Hyperion." "The Fall" was not published until 1857, but it represents Keats's profoundest investigation of poetry and its connection-cum-contrast with "dream," partly reasserting, through Moneta (the narrator's stern, admonitory muse), the poet's duty to be "a sage, / A humanist, physician to all men."

Joseph Severn, *John Keats*. Reprinted courtesy of AKG.

"Hyperion," a fragment placed at the end of Keats's third and last collection to appear in his lifetime, *Lamia, Isabella, The Eve of St Agnes, and other Poems* (1820), is the culmination of his efforts to adapt Greek mythology to contemporary concerns. A Romantic reworking of John Milton's *Paradise Lost* (1665), it cost Keats a great deal of labor and contains much of his most substantial thinking about the role of suffering in life and the nature of cultural change. It is in the great odes, however—composed in April and May 1819—that Keats produced his most original work and has exerted most influence as a poet. With their fluid exploration of contraries, these poems serve as models and points of departure for lyrics such as William Butler Yeats's "Sailing to Byzantium" (1928) and "Byzantium" (1933). In them, Keats writes his own version of the poetry he sensed was required by his age, a poetry of the mind's and imagination's inner debates, cut off from "the simple worship" of a less complex era: a poetry caught up in the dilemma of living without dogmatic belief yet feeling, like Ruth in "Ode to a Nightingale," "sick for home." "To Autumn" represents the nearest cure in Keats's poetry to such homesickness. Written in October 1819, it accepts, with stoical serenity and responsive gratitude, the perishable, impermanent gifts of being alive.

As already suggested, Keats's influence on subsequent poets from Alfred, Lord Tennyson to Amy Clampitt (the author of *Voyages*, a fine poetic meditation on Keats's life and work) has been immense. The sensuousness that underpins the religious raptures of Gerard Manley Hopkins is deeply indebted for its expression to the young Romantic poet; so, too, is the lyric

debate found in many twentieth- and twenty-first-century poets, such as Elizabeth Bishop or Derek Mahon. Keats's earthbound humanism constitutes one of his distinctive legacies to later poets, a legacy realized most productively in the work of Wallace Stevens in poems such as "Sunday Morning" (1915), which spells out the world view implicit in Keats's *To Autumn*: "We live in an old chaos of the sun, / Or old dependency of day and night," our condition "unsponsored" and "free." The exercise of creative freedom, in full awareness of the burdens of such freedom, accounts for Keats's centrality in English Romantic poetry.

MICHAEL O'NEILL

See also **Lamia, Isabella, The Eve of St Agnes, and Other Poems; Poetry: Britain**

Biography

Born at the Swan and Hoop Livery Stables, Moorfields, October 31, 1795; death of his father, April 16, 1804; burial of his mother, March 20, 1810. Attended Enfield School, 1803–11. Apprenticed as surgeon to Thomas Hammond in Edmonton, 1811; entered Guy's Hospital as a student, October 1, 1815; passed examination at Apothecaries Hall, July 25, 1816. Met Benjamin Robert Haydon, Leigh Hunt, and John Hamilton Reynolds, 1816. *Poems* published on March 3, 1817; *Endymion* published in April 1818. Began walking tour of Scotland and the Lake District, June 1818, returning to Hampstead in 1818 because of severe cold and sore throat. Met Fanny Brawne before the end of November 1818. Death of Tom Keats, December 1, 1818. Moved into Wentworth Place, Hampstead, with Charles Armitage Brown, December 1818; wrote most of his finest poetry between January 1819 ("The Eve of St Agnes") and September 1819 (when he gave up "The Fall of Hyperion"), including the spring or great odes (April/March), and traveled a fair amount, to the Isle of Wight (June to September), and to Winchester (September to October), returning to Wentworth Place, where he lived next door to Fanny Brawne (November), to whom he was engaged by the end of December. Had haemorrhage, February 3, 1820. Last volume published in July of that year. Sailed to Italy with Joseph Severn in September 1820; his ship was held in quarantine at Naples, October 21–31. Lived in Rome at the Piazza di Spagna from November 15. Died in Rome, February 23, 1821, and buried in the Protestant Cemetery in Rome, February 26.

Selected Works

The Poems of John Keats. Edited by Miriam Allott. London: Longman, 1970.
The Poems of John Keats. Edited by Jack Stillinger. London: Heinemann, 1978.
John Keats: The Complete Poems. 3d ed. Edited by John Barnard. Harmondsworth, England: Penguin, 1988.
Selected Poems: John Keats. Edited by Nicholas Roe. London: Dent, 1995.

Bibliography

Aske, Martin. *Keats and Hellenism*. Cambridge: Cambridge University Press, 1985.
Barnard, John. *John Keats*, Cambridge: Cambridge University Press, 1987.

Bate, W. J. *John Keats*. Cambridge, Mass.: Harvard University Press, 1963.

Bayley, John. "Keats and Reality," *Proceedings of the British Academy* 48 (1962): 91–125.

Bennett, Andrew. *Keats, Narrative, and Audience*. Cambridge: Cambridge University Press, 1994.

Cox, Jeffrey N. *Poetry and Politics in the Cockney School: Keats, Shelley, Hunt and their Circle*. Cambridge: Cambridge University Press, 1998.

Levinson, Marjorie. *Keats' Life of Allegory*. Oxford: Blackwell, 1988.

McFarland, Thomas. *The Masks of Keats: The Endeavour of a Poet*. Oxford: Oxford University Press, 2000.

O'Neill, Michael. *Romanticism and the Self-Conscious Poem*. Oxford: Oxford University Press, 1997.

———, ed. *Keats: Bicentenary Readings*. Edinburgh: Edinburgh University Press, 1997.

Ricks, Christopher. *Keats and Embarrassment*. Oxford: Oxford University Press, 1974.

Roe, Nicholas. *John Keats and the Culture of Dissent*. Oxford: Oxford University Press, 1997.

———, ed. *Keats and History*. Cambridge: Cambridge University Press, 1995.

Ryan, Robert M., and Ronald A. Sharp, eds. *The Persistence of Poetry: Bicentennial Essays on Keats*. Amerherst, Mass.: University of Massachusetts Press, 1998.

Sperry, Stuart M. *Keats the Poet*. Princeton, N.J.: Princeton University Press, 1973.

Vendler, Helen. *The Odes of John Keats*. Cambridge, Mass.: Harvard University Press, 1983.

Waldoff, Leon. *Keats and the Silent Work of Imagination*. Urbana: University of Illinois Press, 1985.

Wolfson, Susan J. *The Questioning Presence: Wordsworth, Keats, and the Interrogative Mode*. Ithaca, N.Y.: Cornell University Press, 1986.

Woof, Robert, and Stephen Hebron. *John Keats*. Grasmere: Wordsworth Trust, 1995.

KERNER, JUSTINUS ANDREAS CHRISTIAN 1786–1862

German physician and writer

Justinus Kerner was born in the Swabian town of Ludwigsburg, in the Württemberg region. After a false start as an apprentice cabinetmaker, he was able to enroll as a medical student at Tübingen, where, in 1806, he was briefly entrusted with the care of the aging and demented Johann Christian Friedrich Hölderlin. (With his poet friends Gustav Schwab and Ludwig Uhland he would later collaborate on the first edition of Hölderlin's poems, published in 1826.)

In 1808, Kerner graduated as a doctor, having completed a thesis on the functioning of the ear. Yet he was equally a practicing poet, and enthusiast of Achim von Arnim and Clemens Brentano's *Wunderhorn* anthology of folk songs. Hiking home to Ludwigsburg, he composed "Wanderlied" ("Wayfaring Song") and fancied he had witnessed the poem's spontaneous entry into popular lore when a passing apprentice overheard him singing the words and begged to be taught them. (The poem was set to music by Robert Schumann in 1840.)

In 1809–10 Kerner devoted a year to rounding off his education through travel. He chose to tour Germany rather than Italy or France, being particularly drawn to medieval towns like Frankfurt, Göttingen, and Hannover. As well as enhancing his clinical training through short-term hospital appointments, Kerner made it his business to make contact with the luminaries of contemporary culture: in Hamburg, he met the painter Philipp Otto Runge; in Berlin, the writers Adalbert von Chamisso and Friedrich Heinrich Karl Fouqué, and in Vienna, the writer Friedrich Schlegel and his wife Dorothea, and the composer Ludwig van Beethoven. By 1810 Kerner was back in his native Swabia, setting up a medical practice in Wildbad in the Black Forest before moving to Welzheim in 1812 and finally to Weinsberg, near Heilbronn, in 1819. Here he spent the rest of his career as a general practitioner, all the while developing a reputation as a pioneering researcher into the paranormal.

Kerner had married in 1813, and, once settled in Weinsberg, he devoted himself to hospitality on a grand scale, even enlarging his house to accommodate a stream of guests which included scientists, artists, aristocrats, apprentices, clergymen, and peasants, as well as writers from near and far: the poets of the so-called Swabian school (such as Karl August Varnhagen von Ense, Wilhelm Hauff, Eduard Mörike, and Ludwig Uhland), Gustav Schwab, the mystic theologian Franz Baader, and the Austrian poet Nikolaus Lenau, whom he briefly treated for depression. After Kerner's death, his son Theobald would take over the establishment and write a memoir about it; today the *Kernerhaus* is a museum.

As a doctor Kerner was solicitous and methodical, keeping careful records of his patients' symptoms and treatments. He is credited with the discovery of botulism, having tracked down the cause of several deaths to the consumption of contaminated smoked sausage. Yet from the 1820s onward, his expertise reached beyond physical ailments to embrace both psychological and spiritual aspects of human experience. He became a participant in a growing movement in psychiatry that sought to tackle mental illness by so-called moral treatment. Spearheaded by the Englishman William Tuke and the Frenchman Jean Étienne Dominique Esquirol, this movement sought to make a humane appeal to those turbulent passions which were thought to provoke psychic derangement. Like Esquirol, Kerner ran a therapeutic community and is said to have often had as many as a dozen patients living in his house. He encouraged them to socialize with his other guests, play games, listen to music, and take walks in the countryside.

As an exponent of Romantic medicine, Kerner shared the views of his fellow Romantics Carl Gustav Carus and Gotthilf Heinrich Schubert, positing a link between physical and psychic impulses, and thus seeing bodily symptoms and even organic defects as potentially curable through spiritual means. He explained "deviant" behaviors like somnambulism and epilepsy in terms of a person's susceptibility to latent influences in the natural world. As a Romantic, Kerner entirely accepted the notion that dreams voice impalpable truths. He further averred that women rather than men are the true mediators, since they are subject to nature's promptings and given to spontaneous intuitions and prophetic utterances. Kerner's thinking embraced occultism, spiritualism, astrology, and what we would nowadays call parapsychology; and he was a partisan of the doctrine of animal magnetism introduced by Franz Anton Mesmer. (Mesmer happened also to be Swabian, and Kerner wrote the first biography on him in 1856.)

Kerner's favorite therapeutic technique was hypnosis, or what he called the "magnetic cure." It involved not only making passes to induce a trance but also stroking the patient's limbs. His reputation as a caring therapist modulated into that of a kind of magus capable of dispelling demonic influences. Many contemporaries still envisaged madness in terms of possession, equating therapy with exorcism. One of Kerner's cures involved a young girl supposedly possessed by a murderous monk dead several centuries before. It is said that he spoke of being accompanied on his night rounds by the ghosts of patients whom he had been unable to save. Another anecdote relates how he soothed a raving lunatic by playing a Jew's harp, a variant on Mesmer's use of the glass harp. (It may be noted that the link between music and visionary experience was a significant part of the German Romantic aesthetic, and a central theme in the writings of E. T. A. Hoffmann, himself well versed in psychiatry.)

Kerner's best-known work, *Die Seherin von Prevorst* (*The Seer of Prevorst*, 1829), is reminiscent of Clemens Brentano's observations of the Catholic mystic Katharina Emmerich. Kerner's half-analytical, half-lyrical case study focuses upon an uneducated woman, Friederike Hauffe, who was a clairvoyant and somnambulist. She was said to be seized by trembling if she looked at the moon; she could hear the ringing of unearthly bells and perceived an immortal blue flame in the eyes of animals. For two years she remained Kerner's revered and somewhat disquieting house-guest until her death in 1829.

Among Kerner's literary works are poems that capture the artless grace of the folk song, albeit in a more melancholic vein redolent of undefined longings and frustrations. "Der Wanderer in der Sägemühle" ("The Wayfarer in the Saw-Mill"), in which a wayfarer contemplates the sawing of the timber that will form his own coffin, is said to have been the favorite poem of Franz Kafka. The early novel *Reiseschatten, Von dem Schattenspieler Luchs* (*Travel Shadows, By the Shadow-Player Luchs*, 1811) is a loose compendium of travel sketches, poems, and even a play, based on Kerner's tour of 1809–10. In later life, he published a memoir of his early years entitled *Das Bilderbuch aus meiner Knabenzeit* (*Picture Book of my Boyhood*, 1849).

A final eccentricity is a work composed in 1857 but not published until after Kerner's death. *Kleksographien* (*Ink-Blot Images*, 1890) is an album of drawings produced by spilling ink onto a sheet of paper and then folding it. Ostensibly, the resulting configurations are bereft of subject matter and authorial intention, yet Kerner's "explanations" in verse confidently identify butterflies, scarabs, and hieroglyphs and propose a link with ancient Egypt. Intriguingly, this document anticipates the Rorschach Test, introduced in 1921 as a diagnostic tool by the Swiss psychiatrist Hermann Rorschach. It also foreshadows the experiments in pictorial automatism conducted in the 1920s by the Paris surrealists, who were similarly fascinated by aberrant psychic states and, ignorant of Kerner (though not of Sigmund Freud), saw unconscious process as the key to a fuller understanding of the human organism.

ROGER CARDINAL

Biography

Born in Ludwigsburg, September 18, 1786. Medical studies at Tübingen University, 1804–08. Tour of Germany, 1809–10. Began lifelong career as a doctor, 1810. Married, 1813. Kept open house for friends and mental patients from 1818. Treated the disturbed clairvoyant Friederike Hauffe, 1827–29. Edited *Magikon*, a journal about paranormal phenomena, 1840–53. Died in Weinsberg after succumbing to influenza, February 21, 1862.

Selected Works

Gedichte. 1826.
Die Seherin von Prevorst. Eröffnungen über das innere Leben des Menschen und über das Hereinragen einer Geisterwelt in die unsere. 1829. Translated as *The Seer of Prevorst. Disclosures about the Inner Life of Man and the Projection of a Spirit World into Our Own* anonymously, 1845.
Das Bilderbuch aus meiner Knabenzeit. 1849.
Lyrische Gedichte. 1854.
Magikon. Archiv für Beobachtungen aus dem Gebiete der Geisterkunde und des magnetischen und magischen Lebens nebst andern Zugaben für Freunde des Innern. 5 vols. 1840–53.
Franz Anton Mesmer aus Schwaben, Entdecker des thierischen Magnetismus. 1856.
Kleksographien. Hadesbilder kleksographisch entstanden und in Versen erläutert. 1890.
Ausgewählte Werke. Edited by G. Grimm. Stutlgart: Reclan, 1981.

Bibliography

Grüsser, Otto-Joachim. *Justinus Kerner 1786–1862: Arzt-Poet-Geisterseher.* Berlin: Springer, 1987.
Huch, Ricarda. *Die Romantik: Blütezeit, Ausbreitung und Verfall.* Tübingen: Rainer Wunderlich, 1951.
Jennings, Lee B. *Justinus Kerners Weg nach Weinsberg.* Columbia, S.C.: Camden House, 1983.
Kerner, Theobald. *Das Kernerhaus und seine Gäste* (1894). Heilbronn: Eugen Salzer, 1964.
Peters, Uwe Henrik. *Studies in German Romantic Psychiatry: Justinus Kerner as a Psychiatric Practitioner. E. T. A. Hoffmann as a Psychiatric Theorist.* London: Institute of Germanic Studies, 1990.
Pfäfflin, Friedrich, and Reinhard Tgahrt, eds. *Justinus Kerner Dichter und Arzt 1786–1862* Rev. 2d. ed., Marbach am Neckar: Deutsche Schillergesellschaft, 1990.
Schott, H, ed. *Medizin und Romantik: Justinus Kerner als Arzt und Seelenforscher.* Weinsberg: Stadt Weinsberg and Justinus-Kerner-Verein, 2nd ed., 1998.
Spranger, Peter. *Der Geiger von Gmünd: Justinus Kerner und die Geschichte einer Legende.* Schwäbisch Gmünd: Stadtarchiv, 1980.

KERSTING, GEORG FRIEDRICH 1785–1847

German artist

Georg Friedrich Kersting did not produce a large body of work, but his elegant little paintings radiate an inner life that connect them to the core of German Romantic thought even while approaching the boundaries of a Biedermeier aesthetic. He spent the most fruitful years of his career in Dresden, surrounded by a circle of friends who constituted that city's teeming reservoir of intellectual, literary, and artistic talent, and produced there a majority of the works on which his reputation rests. While he also painted a few history and landscape paintings, still-lifes, numerous portraits, and a series of genre scenes of children, his greatest contribution to German painting of the early half of the nineteenth century was the introspective articulation of a self-contained bourgeois space.

Like Caspar David Friedrich and Philipp Otto Runge before him, Kersting left a small northern German hometown that offered little by way of artistic stimulation in order to take advantage of the free schooling offered by the Royal Danish Academy of Fine Arts in Copenhagen. There he acquired a style typical for students coming out of that school, distinguished by compositional clarity and a crisp, linear precision. His facility in drawing, for which he won a silver medal at the Academy, underpins all of his paintings, although his refined sense of color application gives the expressive force to his work. He demonstrates a studied attention to detail without being overly fussy, and a superb feel for nuances of light and shadow that enlivens even the quietest of his paintings.

In Dresden, where he moved after completing his training, Kersting quickly became close to Caspar David Friedrich, whom he accompanied in 1810 on a trip through the Riesengebirge, and whose portrait, *Caspar David Friedrich in seinem Atelier,* (*Caspar David Friedrich in his Studio*, 1811), he submitted as his first entry (along with a pendant portrait of Gerhard von Kügelgen) to the annual exhibition of the Dresden Academy. The older artist wielded a decided influence upon the younger one, but the opposite may also have been true, for Kersting is rumored to have executed the figures in several of Friedrich's paintings. At first glance, Kersting's modest images of a complacent, middle-class existence contained within the geometric confines of a simple yet comfortable room seem to be the antithesis of Friedrich's open, sublime landscapes, with their ambitious claims to spiritual transcendence and their ponderous figures reflecting upon a nature of which they are no longer a part. But beyond stylistic similarities in both artists' linear handling of paint, Kersting's work also shares with Friedrich's a common goal, namely the visualization of an inwardness that is indicative of a deeply rooted Pietistic ethic.

Kersting portrays solitary figures who are utterly absorbed in their activities, unaware of being observed, as in the paintings *lesender Mann beim Lampenlicht* (*Elegant Reader*, 1814) or *Die Stickerin* (*The Embroiderer*, 1812). Prescribed gender roles announce the separation of men's and women's spheres in the home: men read, write, and think; while women sew, embroider, and perform music. The linear fastidiousness of the rooms they occupy is only slightly offset by the assortment of carefully observed objects placed around the figures, subtly defining their essence (for example, the books, letters, and small female portrait in *Lesender Mann beim Lampenlicht* or the wreath-covered male portrait, guitar, and sheet music in *Die Stickerin*). In their isolation of a single activity, these images are clearly related to seventeenth-century Dutch interior painting, without, however, the latter's tendency towards an acute verisimilitude in the rendering of object surface. Kersting himself saw a larger meaning in his work, in its pursuit of universal truths through the depiction of the specific.

The contentedness of these intimate scenes, in which the relationship between figure and environment is never less than harmonious, gives no indication of the upheavals taking place in the outside world in the years during and after the Napoleonic occupation of Germany, or of the disappointment experienced in the wake of failed hopes for political reform. Such images are suggestive of a withdrawal to an internal world of erudition and refinement, an assertion of the stabilizing and protective nature of the enclosed private sphere regardless of what chaos and disillusionment may exist in the public one.

Kersting himself had participated in the Wars of Liberation, as a member of the Lützower Freikorps (Voluntary Corps), and after his tour of duty he composed a pair of pendants as tributes to three of his fallen comrades, including the poet Theodor

Georg Friedrich Kersting, *Lesender bei Lampenlicht*. Reprinted courtesy of Bildarchiv.

Körner. *Auf Vorposten* (*On Sentry Duty*) and *Die Kranzwinderin* (*Woman Winding Wreaths*—both 1815—are set symbolically in a dark, Teutonic forest of oak trees. The first is a group portrait of men in uniform conceived as a vignette from daily soldier life; in *Die Kranzwinderin* they have disappeared, becoming only carved names on the trees, as a young woman in white makes wreaths in their honor. Still, although set outdoors and imbued with conspicuous patriotic sentiment, the two works maintain Kersting's inclination toward intimacy and function more as personal mementos of lost friends than as public monuments to fallen heroes.

Through the artist Louise Seidler, the model for *Die Stickerin*, Kersting was introduced to Johann Wolfgang von Goethe, who took a personal interest in his work, helping him to sell several paintings. From a family of very modest means, Kersting needed to find a steady income to survive, but his work as a genre and portrait painter did not recommend him for a professorship at the Dresden Academy. Although small genre paintings were more readily collectable by the general population than large history paintings, Kersting had no prospect of survival as an independent artist in Dresden. He found it necessary in 1815 to take a position as a drawing teacher to a royal family in Warsaw, and after three years returned to Saxony to become the artistic director of the royal porcelain manufactory at Meissen, which he held for almost thirty years. While solving his financial difficulties, the move compromised his career as a fine artist, leaving him little time for his own projects. While he continued to paint interior scenes, many of his later works are less intense in their introspective nature and succumb more quickly to Biedermeier-like sentiment in their narrative effect. In the years after his death, Kersting gradually faded into obscurity, until his rediscovery in the early twentieth century once again placed him amid the spirited circle of Dresden Romantics.

MARGARET DOYLE

Biography

Born October 24, 1785 in Güstrow. Studied at the Royal Academy in Copenhagen, 1805–8; moved to Dresden, 1808. Accompanied Caspar David Friedrich on trip through the Riesengebirge 1810. Met Goethe for first time 1813; sold *Die Stickerin* to Duke Karl August Goethe, 1813. Entered Lützower Freikorps and honored with Iron Cross, 1813. Drawing teacher for children of Princess Sapieha in Warsaw 1815–18; artistic director of painting department at the Royal Porcelain Manufactury in Meissen 1818–47. Died of stroke July 1, 1847.

Bibliography

Gärtner, Hannelore. *Georg Friedrich Kersting*. Leipzig: Seemann, 1988.

"Georg Friedrich Kersting 1785–1847." In *Proceedings of Fifth Greifswalder Romanticism Conference.* (Special issue of *Wissenschaftliche Zeitschrift der Ernst-Moritz-Arndt-Universität Greifswald* 35, nos. 3–4, (1986).

Koch, Ira, Werner Schell, and Bärbel Kovalevsk. "Das Gesicht ist der edelste Sinn . . ." *Georg Friedrich Kersting: zur Porträtkunst.* Güstrow: Museum der Stadt, 1997.

Schnell, Werner. *Georg Friedrich Kersting (1785–1847): das zeichnerische und malerische Werk.* Berlin: Deutsche Verlag für Kunstwissenschaft, 1994.

Vriesen, Gustav. *Die innenraumbilder Georg Friedrich Kerstings.* Berlin: Deutscher Verein für Kunstwissenschaft, 1935.

KHOMYAKOV, ALEKSEY STEPANOVICH 1804–1860

Russian poet, playwright, critic, journalist, theologian

Whether in the fields of literature, philosophy, or theology, Aleksey Stepanovich Khomyakov passionately pursued his mission as an apologist for the Russian Orthodox Church, which he viewed as the foundation of Russia's unique culture and history. He believed that Russia had a divine mission to bring salvation to the world and that only Russia could fulfill this task because Russian Orthodoxy was the one true church. He became one of the founders of the Slavophile movement that espoused harmony among the Slavs united in the love of Christ, with Russia at their head, and expressed his views in articles, poetry, and historical tragedies.

While Khomyakov was in Paris studying painting (1825–26), he wrote the first of his two historical tragedies, *Ermak*, an immature drama in verse, in which first appeared the themes that became a mainstay of his poetry and plays: patriotism, pride in Russia's divine destiny, idealism, chaste love, and nobility of thought and deed. *Ermak* was staged in 1827 and subsequently published in 1832. Khomyakov's next play, *Dmitriy Samozvanets* (*Dmitry the Pretender*, 1833), set during Russia's "Troubles" at the beginning of the seventeenth century, before the Romanovs ascended the throne, was a platform for the rudimentary ideas that would evolve into the Slavophile agenda.

Khomyakov's early poems, like the plays, were filled with the spirit of Romanticism. "Poèt" (1827) defines the poet as an intermediary between God and humankind who speaks in a divine voice as he breathes life into the earth. In this and other poems like "Son" ("The Dream," 1828), "Zhavoronok, orel, i poèt" ("Lark, Eagle, and Poet," 1833), and "Vdokhnovenie" ("Inspiration," 1828), a vision of the poet as an eternal, divine, tragic character emerges. Khomyakov's idealism extends to his view of women, whom he admires and respects. The love poems of the 1830s depict a lover who is passionate, but also chaste and restrained. Various women inspired lyrics such as "Priznanie" ("Recognition," 1830), "Inostranke" ("To a Foreigner," 1832); and "Kogda glyazhu, kak chisto i zerkal'no tvoe chelo ("When I See How Pure and Smooth Your Brow," 1834). "Lampada nochnaya gorela" ("A night lamp burns"), a poem he wrote to his wife after their 1836 marriage, hints at the almost divine love he feels for her: a *lampada* is the light one burns in front of a holy icon.

Most critics agree that Khomyakov wrote the best religious poems in Russia, mainly because of the noble simplicity and sincerity of feeling. "Truzhennik" ("The Laborer") encapsulates how he sees himself as he toils in the fields of the Lord: he is a tireless plowman who will break the hard ground to plant the seeds of God's word until the job is done. Khomyakov displays the same single-mindedness in his political and historical poems, but with a different message. "Orel" ("The Eagle," 1832) puts forth an idea that dominates all of Khomyakov's poems and theoretical works: all Slavs must unite under the wings of the Russian eagle. During the Crimean War Khomyakov reaffirmed Russia's mission, but called on the nation to repent for its sins, because Russia could fulfill its destiny only with a pure heart, in the two 1854 poems "Rossiya" ("Russia") and "Raskayavshayasya Rossiya" ("Repentant Russia").

At the urging of his friends, Khomyakov directed his main energies away from poetry and in 1838 began to write articles that articulated the Slavophile position. In that year he began a journal that was to elucidate his philosophy of history; he faithfully wrote in that diary daily until he died. In 1839, Khomyakov read his essay "O starom i novom" ("About the Old and the New"), which expanded in prose the ideas of his poem "To Russia." This essay and Ivan Kireevsky's "Otvet Khomyakovu" ("Answer to Khomyakov," 1839) brought together the ideas that would give birth to the Slavophile movement. Three articles best express his views about Russia's relationship with the West: "Mnenie inostrantsev o Rossii" ("The Foreigners' View of Russia," 1845), "Mnenie russkikh ob inostrankakh" ("The Russians' View of Foreigners," 1846), and "O vozmozhnosti russkoi khudozhestvennoi shkoly" ("About the Possibility of a Russian School of Art," 1847). Each article states that Russia does not need the West, with its superficial culture and destructive influences. On the other hand, Russia's own distinctive history and essential values, as well as its authentic art that originated with the people, can gain the respect of Western Europe.

Between 1844 and 1855, Khomyakov corresponded with an English friend, William Palmer, about Russian Orthodoxy and its possible reunion with the Anglican Church. The correspondence helped him formulate his ideas about orthodoxy, which he developed in his theological writings. In his numerous articles he over and again tries to clarify the idea of "Church" as a "living organism of love and truth." The Russian Orthodox Church alone could unite "individuality and freedom in the principle of Christian love." This free union in the love of Christ was the essence of the term that was the bedrock of the Slavophile philosophy; *sobornost'*.

Between 1839 and the early 1840s, Khomyakov worked on his first theological treatise "O Tserkvi" ("About the Church"; originally titled "Tserkov' odna" ["There is Only One Church"]; published 1864), in which he explained his concept of sobornost'. Here he also voiced the first of his many condemnations of the Roman Catholic Church, whose members he saw as "rejected children." The animosity he felt for the Church of Rome, and especially for the Jesuits, never abated, but rather grew stronger with the passing years. In fact, some of his final articles give full voice to his chauvinistic defense of Russian Orthodoxy. All three

had the same name, "Neskol'ko slov pravoslavnogo khristianina o zapadnykh veroispovedaniiakh" ("A Few Words of an Orthodox Christian About Western Confessions," 1853, 1855, 1858). In these articles Khomyakov attacks the pope, sees Western religions as a revolt against divine dogma, defends the Russian Orthodox Church as the true Church because only it has sobornost', and reaffirms Russia's divine mission.

Khomyakov also wrote articles on other topics, such as England's political system, agricultural conditions, and reforms; Mikhail Ivanovich Glinka's opera *A Life for the Tsar* and the birth of Russian music; Aristotle's pernicious influence on Western culture; and the errors of G. W. F. Hegel. He spent his last productive years working as a journalist, organizing the publication of Vladimir Dal's dictionary, editing letters of Nikolai Mikhailovich Karamzin and Aleksander Sergeevich Griboedov and folk songs from the collection of Petr Kireevsky, and translating the Epistles to the Galatians and the Ephesians. Posterity remembers Khomyakov best, however, as a brilliant polemicist, the formulator of Slavophile philosophy, and a lucid apologist for the Orthodox Church. Though he wrote without the sanction of the church and his theological works were not published until 1879, Khomyakov was Russia's first modern theologian, whose views have continued to influence subsequent Russian religious philosophers.

CHRISTINE A. RYDEL

Biography

Born May 1, 1804 in Moscow; educated at home by private tutors. In 1815 family moved to Saint Petersburg; 1817, returned to Moscow, where his tutoring continued. 1822, enlisted in army; 1825–26, studied painting in Paris; 1826 returned home via Italy, Switzerland, Slavic areas of Austro-Hungarian Empire. In 1828 posted to Bulgaria during Russo-Turkish War; 1829, returned to Russia. 1836, married Katerina Mikhaylovna Yazykov; 1847, family trip to Europe. In 1852, death of wife. Died of cholera in 1860 and buried in Moscow at the Donskoy Monastery.

Selected Works

Collections
Stikhotvoreniya A. S. Khomiakova. 1861.
Sochineniya. 4 vols. vol. 1, 1861; vol. 2, 1867, vols. 3–4, 1872.
Polnoe sobranie sochineniy. 8 vols. 1900–11.
Stikhotvoreniye i dramy. 1969.
Sochinenie v dvukh tomakh. 2 vols. 1994.

Books
Ermak, tragediya v pyati deystviyakh, v stikhakh. 1832.
Dmitriy Samozvanets: Tragediyakh v pyati deystviyakh. 1833.
Quelques mots sur les communions occidentales, à l'occasion d'une brochure de M. Laurentie. 1853, under the pseudonym Ignotus.
Sravnenie russkikh slov s sanskritskimi. 1856.

Bibliography

Baron, Pierre. *Un theologien laic orthodoxe russe au XIXe siecle: Alexis Stepanovich Khomiakov (1804–1860). Son ecclesiologie expose et critique.* Rome: Pont. Institutum Orientalium Studiorum, 1940.
Berdyaev, Nikolai Aleksandrovich. *A. S. Khomyakov.* Moscow: Put', 1912.

Bolshakoff, Serge. *The Doctrine of the Unity of the Church in the Works of Khomiakov and Moehler*. London: Society for Promoting Christian Knowledge. 1946.

Christoff, Peter K. *An Introduction to Nineteenth-Century Russian Slavophilism: A. S. Khomiakov*. Vol. 1. s'Gravenhage: Mouton, 1961.

Gratieux, Albert. 2 vols. *A. S. Khomiakov et le mouvement slavophile*. Paris: Editions du cerf, 1939.

McNally, Raymond. "Chaadaev vs. Khomiakov in the late 1830s and 1840s," *Journal of the History of Ideas* 27 (1966): 73–91.

Riasanovsky, Nicholas V. "Khomiakov and *Sobornost'*." In *Continuity and Change in Russian and Soviet Thought*. Edited by Ernest J. Simmons. Cambridge, Mass.: Harvard University Press, 1955.

———. *Russia and The West in the Teaching of the Slavophiles*. Cambridge, Mass.: Harvard University Press, 1952.

KIERKEGAARD, SØREN 1813–1855

Danish philosopher and theologian

Almost all of Søren Kierkegaard's work is written directly or indirectly in response to G. W. F. Hegel. Although he admired Friedrich Wilhelm Joseph von Schelling and attended his lectures, Kierkegaard lived in a state of relative intellectual isolation in Denmark, where philosophy in the mid-nineteenth century was dominated by Hegelianism, and religion by the Church of Denmark. Kierkegaard was of the view that the church had lost touch with its Lutheran origins, and in response he sought to reassert the claims of the individual in the face of Hegelian systematizing. Although Kierkegaard follows Hegel in adopting dialectics as a method of proceeding, his conclusions are entirely different: he sees the individual as being in direct relation to God (what Hegel calls the "absolute"), rather than having to approach God mediated through the community at large (the "universal") or its representative, the state. Although a prolific writer of sermons, or "upbuilding discourses," it is through his pseudonymous "ironic" works that Kierkegaard is now best known. But the aim in all of his works is the same: to move from a position of complexity to one of simplicity, restoring faith, as opposed to Hegel's intellect, as the ground for theological and philosophical enquiry.

Kierkegaard's first substantial work was his thesis for his master's degree, *Um Begrebet Ironi med Statigt Hensyn til Socrates* (*The Concept of Irony with Continual Reference to Socrates*, 1841), that was to establish his own ironic style for the rest of his career. According to Kierkegaard, Socrates lived an ironic life, allowing blatant sophisms and errors in thinking to be attributed to him, so that the true thought of Socrates must be worked out by whoever examines his life, rather than necessarily by taking everything he says at face value. In each of his own major works Kierkegaard was to present a pseudonymous author who similarly would not necessarily speak the truth as such, but from whom something could be learnt by the example of the character's life and personality, even if that is a negative example. Kierkegaard's readers are thus put into the position of having to work out the truth for themselves, rather than be directly instructed.

At the completion of his thesis Kierkegaard suffered a personal crisis. Realizing that to take a place in civil society with a wife and children would not be consistent with his own religious and philosophical objections to "the universal," Kierkegaard broke off his engagement to Regine Olsen in order to dedicate himself entirely to writing, although he was to remain in love with her for the rest of his life. The themes of a turning point in life, of sacrifice, of the paradox of behaving properly to another by doing her harm, of the self-inflicted wound, and of

being true to oneself, are all ones that come to dominate the major texts of Kierkegaard's most productive period, 1843–45: *Either/Or, Repetition, Fear and Trembling, The Concept of Anxiety*, and *Stages on Life's Way*.

Enten-Eller (*Either/Or*, 1843) presents two opposing pseudonymous authors, "A" and "B." "A" is intellectually dazzling in his style, but is governed by despair. His essays are mainly on the theme of seduction; his final diaries reveal him to have been a seducer himself. Hegel thought the "unhappy consciousness" to be governed by the alienation of the individual from the process of world history, but the example of "A" shows that this Hegelian universalism is an ideal which no individual can attain anyway. Despair, meanwhile, is dominated by personal time, not by history; it consists in having only bad memories, and of having given up hope of those things which are attainable. This is further illustrated by "A"'s stories: for example, the story of Elvira and Don Juan reveals the paradox that Elvira must take refuge in the memory of Don Juan's love, to save herself from the despair that this memory of love has precipitated. "A"'s diary, meanwhile, in its presentation of his detail-oriented and calculating personality, suggests that, contra Hegel, the development of intellect does not of itself bring one closer to God.

"B"'s personality, by contrast, is more soberly consistent. If the attraction of seduction is that it provides a constant representation of first love, then marriage is just as appealing insofar as that sensation can be enjoyed just as well with one person as with a succession of seducees. Meanwhile, erotic love as an aesthetic experience leads to despair, since it militates against continuity in life. The aesthete despairs because ultimately he is alone.

Gentagelsen (*Repetition*, 1843) and "In Vino Veritas" (the principal part of *Stadier paa Livets Vej* (*Stages on Life's Way*, 1845) continue to develop the theme of personal memory as determining a person's outlook on life. According to *Repetition*, the melancholic personality, which results from unrequited love, is dominated by recollection, which is opposed to memory: recollection is defined by loss, whereas memories are of things preserved. One who is dominated by such recollections lives life in a state of false mourning, lamenting over a loss of something never held in the first place. Remembrance, on the other hand, requires a stronger personality to stand up to the apprehension of losing what is remembered. Repetition is the ideal that gives constancy to life, and this can only be achieved through remembering what is repeated. "In Vino Veritas" follows a very similar analysis to arrive at the opposite conclusion. It asserts that recollection is a more valuable asset than remembering, precisely be-

H. B. Hansen, *Sören Aabye Kierkegaard*. Reprinted courtesy of AKG.

cause what is remembered can be forgotten, whereas what is recollected cannot be. The point is that life is not about the number of things accomplished in it, since they can all be forgotten—it is about the ideal through which a person brought about those events, which will always be available to be recollected. It is for the reader to decide which of these two texts is the more "ironic."

Frygt og Bæven (*Fear and Trembling*, 1843) is dominated by analyses of the story of Abraham. The principal characteristic of Abraham for Kierkegaard is that he is not an intellectual: turning Hegel on his head, faith alone is sufficient for him, and he comes closer to God not through reason, but through flying in the face of the rational. Consequently, Abraham's relationship with the absolute is his alone, and is not mediated through the community or the universal. But since Abraham's faith is absolute, he is led into a paradoxical position, because he loves both Isaac and God out of all proportion. In obeying both of God's commandments, to sacrifice Isaac and not to kill, he becomes incomprehensible to reason. The paradox is resolved through the passage of time, Abraham's journey being neither too long nor too short. Kierkegaard's point is to counter Hegel's claim that for there to be goodness, the ethical cannot be suspended. For Hegel, ethics consists of duty, and in turn this is duty to the Universal. Kierkegaard does not deny this, but points out that Abraham simply has no relation to the Universal, and so the question of his ethical duty does not apply. Faith is prior to ethical considerations because it is a matter between the individual and God alone.

Kierkegaard develops this "philosophy of paradox" in *Begrebet Angest* (*The Concept of Anxiety*, 1844), which is likewise an attempt to define faith, this time through considering the concept of sin, positing a Lutheran alternative to the Catholic concept of hereditary sin. According to Kierkegaard, what is inherited is the disposition to sin, not sinfulness as such. The disposition to sin is to sinfulness what anxiety is to fear: the possibility of sinning is always there, but is not necessarily actualized. Being innocent does not save one from anxiety in so far as anxiety is the contemplation of the possibility of falling into sin at a future date. But anxiety is also positive in that it is an education into the art of the possible, which is why animals cannot suffer it—only humans can distinguish what *may* happen from what *will* happen. Like faith, anxiety is a disposition that is held prior to the positing of existence.

In 1844–45 Kierkegaard published what he intended to be his last philosophical works, *Philosophiste Emøler eller en Emøle Philosophie* (*Philosophical Fragments or a Fragment of Philosophy*) and *Øffløttende Øbidenskabelig Efterskrift til de Philosophiste Emøler* (*Concluding Unscientific Postscript to Philosophical Fragments*). *Philosophical Fragments* continues the disquisition into the paradox of faith. The "absolute paradox" of thought is that either God does not exist, in which case it would be impossible to demonstrate His existence, or He does exist, in which case there is no need to demonstrate it. Kierkegaard sees God as a Socratic teacher, known not through His existence as such, but through His works. These works, though, invite trust in God, rather than demonstrate His existence. Whoever entertains the possibility of the nonexistence of God is already denying the existence of God through betraying that trust. Belief in God is an assumption, a matter of faith, not of demonstration. The *Concluding Unscientific Postscript* compares the historical truth of Christianity with its "subjective" truth. Kierkegaard argues that subjectivity is the highest form of truth, and that this truth is arrived at not through reason, but through the silent acceptance of faith prior to any thought whatever. Once again, faith is a ground of existence, not something which existence subsequently discovers. Life is paradoxical in the spiritual trial it presents—the whole of life is a "dialectical contradiction" within the demand that faith be grounded on the acceptance of Christ, who is both a historical and temporal figure, and the opening into eternity. The Christian is faced with the paradox of his faith in the eternal being based on the temporal, but the unreasonableness of this is precisely why Christianity is an act of faith.

Kierkegaard wished to emulate Socrates by being among the ordinary people rather than the intellectuals of Copenhagen, and so had resolved to retire from writing to become a rural pastor. However, a second major life-crisis was to alter this plan. He saw it as his duty to destroy *The Corsair*, a scurrilous satirical journal that, through its libels, was bringing the morality of the Danish literary scene into disrepute. Kierkegaard thought himself bigger than the journal, and invited it to attack him. This it did, but in a personally abusive and ridiculing manner, rather than through intellectual debate. As a result, Kierkegaard was unable to go out in the street in Copenhagen for some two years without being insulted and occasionally threatened with violence. Although eventually the paper folded, he found the affair a humbling experience, and it spurred him on to a second phase of writing, motivated both out of atonement for the sin of pride in his own Christian superiority, and out of a perceived necessity to reform the public morals of contemporary Denmark.

The most significant work of this second phase of Kierkegaard's writing is *Sygdommen til Døden* (*Sickness unto Death*, 1849), which returns to the theme of despair, here characterized as the hopelessness of not even being able to die. Kierkegaard finds this a "contradiction": despair is a sickness of the self that entails both dying and not dying, a perpetual state of dying. Being alive itself becomes the torment of the person in despair, so that despair becomes "jacked up" into despair at its own despair. In this way despair becomes despair of the eternal's ability to be of help, which is a sin. Contrary to Hegel, who saw sin merely as a negation of the good, Kierkegaard sees sin as a position reached when one refuses to will to be oneself even when God has granted us this ability. The cycle of despair can only be broken by willing to be oneself outside of despair, which means being an individual and not following the crowd. Most people are in a state of sin, not because of some great crime they have committed, but because they do not have the freedom of spirit to follow their own way.

During his lifetime Kierkegaard was virtually unknown outside Denmark. His reputation grew when he was translated into German in the 1920s and 1930s, and his notion of the originariness of faith was a major influence on the Christian existentialists Karl Jaspers and Gabriel Marcel. His parables of seduction became an inspiration for Jean-Paul Sartre's famous model of "bad faith" in *Being and Nothingness* (1956). More recently, Kierkegaard has become important to philosophers of the "new ethics" in his identification of paradox as fundamental to the understanding of existence. He is now recognized as one of the nineteenth century's most important philosophers, anticipating Friedrich Nietzsche in his promotion of the Romantic individual over the universalism of Hegel's rational system.

KARL SIMMS

See also **Concept of Dread; German Idealism: Its Philosophical Legacy; Hegel, Georg Wilhelm Friedrich; Individualism; Irony, Romantic; Rationalism and Irrationalism; Schelling, Friedrich Wilhelm Joseph von; Self and Subjectivity**

Biography

Born in Copenhagen, May 5, 1813. Attended School of Civic Virtue, Copenhagen, 1821–30; studied theology, University of Copenhagen, 1830–37, 1838–40; taught Latin at School of Civic Virtue 1837–38; studied for M.A. in theology, University of Copenhagen, 1840–41. Engaged to Regine Olsen 1840; broke off engagement 1841. Writer in Copenhagen 1841–55. Died, possibly of infection of the lungs, November 11, 1855.

Selected Works

Collections

Samleder Vaerker. Edited by A. B. Drachmann, J. L. Heiberg, and H. O. Lange, revised by P. P. Rohde. 20 vols. 1962–64.

Kierkegaard Anthology. Edited by Robert Bretall, 1973.
Kierkegaard's Writings. Edited by Howard V. Hong and Edna H. Hong. 26 vols. 1980–2000.
Essential Kierkegaard. Translated and edited by Howard V. Hong and Edna H. Hong, 2000.
Selections from the Writings of Kierkegaard. Translated by L. M. Hollander, edited by Alan Brown, 2000.
The Kierkegaard Reader. Edited by Jonathan Rée and Jane Chamberlain, 2001.

Individual Works

Um Begrebet Ironi med Statigt Hensyn til Socrates. 1841. Translated as *The Concept of Irony with Continual Reference to Socrates* by H. V. Hong and E. H. Hong, 1990.
Enten-Eller. 1843. Translated as *Either/Or,* by Howard V. Hong and Edna H. Hong. 2 vols. 1988.
Gentagelsen. 1843. Translated as *Repetition.* In *Fear and Trembling/Repetition.* by Edna H. Hong and Howard V. Hong, 1983.
Frygt og Bæven. 1843. Translated as *Fear and Trembling.* In *Fear and Trembling/Repetition.* by Edna H. Hong and Howard V. Hong, 1983.
Begrebet Angest. 1844. Translated as *The Concept of Anxiety.* by R. Thomte, 1980.
Stadier paa Livets Vej. 1845. Translated as *Stages on Life's Way* by Howard V. Hong and Edna H. Hong, 1988.
Philosophiste Emøler eller en Emøle Philosophie. 1844. Translated as *Philosophical Fragments, or a Fragment of Philosophy.* In *Philosophical Fragments, or a Fragment of Philosophy/Johannes Climacus, or De amnibus dubitandum est.* Translated by Edna H. Hong and Howard V. Hong, 1985.
Øffløttende Øbidenskabelig Efterskrift til de Philosophiste Emøler. 1845. Translated as *Concluding Unscientific Postscript to Philosophical Fragments* by Howard V. Hong and Edna H. Hong. 2 vols. 1992.
Sygdommen til Døden. 1849. Translated as *Sickness unto Death* by Edna H. Hong and Howard V. Hong, 1980.

Bibliography

Daise, Benjamin. *Kierkegaard's Socratic Act.* Macon, Ga.: Mercer University Press, 2000.
Gardiner, Patrick. *Kierkegaard.* Oxford: Oxford University Press, 1988.
Hannay, Alastair. *Kierkegaard.* London: Routledge, 1982.
——, ed. *Cambridge Companion to Kierkegaard.* Cambridge: Cambridge University Press, 1998.
Lowrie, Walter. *Kierkegaard.* London: Oxford University Press, 1938.
Matustik, Martin Joseph, and Merold Westphal, ed. *Kierkegaard in Post/Modernity.* Bloomington: Indiana University Press.
Rée, Jonathan, and Jane Chamberlain, eds. *Kierkegaard: A Critical Reader.* Oxford: Blackwell, 1997.
Stack, George G. *Kierkegaard's Existential Ethics.* Aldershot: Gregg Revivals, 1992.
Weston, Michael. *Kierkegaard and Modern Continental Philosophy: An Introduction.* London: Routledge, 1994.

KLEIST, BERND HEINRICH WILHELM VON 1777–1811

German playwright and writer

To include Bernd Heinrich Wilhelm von Kleist under the rubric of *Romantic* seems at first highly problematic, for this idiosyncratic author lacks many of the attributes associated with the movement. He worked largely alone, and never in the "symphilosophierenden" (cophilosophizing) groups in Jena, Berlin, or Heidelberg. His work lacks any religious or transcendental aura. Nostalgia for the past or childhood do not figure in his oeuvre. Yet the pervasive distancing irony found everywhere in his work is, despite the very real humor, less like the Enlightenment's corrective mockery of reason gone awry than the Romantically ironic anxiety about the very possibility of meaning and knowledge. Kleist lived a short life of many crises, the most famous being the so-called *Kantkrise* (Kant Crisis) of March 1801, when he wrote to his fiancée Wilhelmine von Zenge that recent reading in philosophy (presumably Kant) had led him to realize the contingent nature of all human knowledge. "If all humans had green glasses instead of eyes," he wrote, "they would have to judge that all objects viewed with these were green—and they would never be able to decide whether their eyes showed them things as they are or whether they added to things which belonged not to the objects but to their eyes. Thus it is with our understanding. We cannot decide whether that which we call truth is truly true, or whether it just seems so to us."

With this, Kleist leaves the Enlightenment behind and joins the Romantic age, or so tradition has it. Yet this scion of an established family of the Prussian aristocratic *Junkertum* (military aristocracy) had already committed an unheard-of offense by leaving his post as an officer in the Prussian Army (which he had joined at the age of fifteen) two years earlier, and he would continue creating crises for himself. At one point he considered moving (with Wilhelmine) to an island on Lake Thun to become a farmer. Later he alienated potential literary allies in Berlin, Dresden, and Weimar by preemptive attacks on them. He burned and could never retrieve what might have been his best work, the tragedy *Robert Guiskard*, which survives only in a fragment reconstructed from memory. Kleist managed to be imprisoned at least twice on charges of espionage; and finally, he ended his life in a dramatic double suicide.

Kleist's writing activity spans from approximately 1802 until his death in November 1811. He has left us with eight plays and fragments of plays, eight stories (*Erzählungen*), several essays, a wealth of anecdotes, and some 230 letters. Furthermore, he founded a short-lived literary journal, *Phöbus* (*Phoebus*, in which many of his stories and plays first appeared) in 1807, and also the first daily newspaper, the even shorter-lived *Berliner Abendblätter* (*Berlin Evening Pages*, October 1810–March 1811), for which he wrote original pieces or summarized material read in other papers.

Kleist considered himself primarily a playwright, and indeed his contribution here is both wide-ranging and unique. In his first play to be performed publicly, *Der zerbrochene Krug* (*The Broken Jug*, 1808), Kleist brings a realistic vigor (and bawdy humor) to the language, which was unusual enough to be misunderstood in the stilted climate of Johann Wolfgang von Goethe's Weimar, leading to a disastrous performance in March 1808 for which Kleist never forgave Goethe. In the very early *Die Familie Schroffenstein* (*The Schroffenstein Family*, 1803) and the later *Das Kätchen von Heilbronn* (*Katherine of Heilbronn*, 1810), popular dramatic forms such as the *Rührstück* (melodrama), *Familiengemälde* (domestic drama), and *bürgerliches Trauerspiel* (domestic tragedy) are experimented with and simultaneously deconstructed. In the aftermath of the French occupation of Prussia after the defeat at Jena in 1806, Kleist's patriotic fervor produced *Die Hermannsschlacht* (*Armenius's Battle*, 1821) and, not without a good deal of distancing irony from the ideas of manly soldiery, *Prinz Friedrich vom Homburg* (*Prince Friedrich of Homburg*, 1821). However, the most unusual of Kleist's plays is the unstageable *Penthesilea* (1808), in which the original Greek heroic legend is transformed into a truly bizarre tale of sexual passion (with a shocking turn toward cannibalism at the end).

The modern reader is perhaps more intrigued by Kleist's fiction, though for him, the necessity to curry favor with a public ill-disposed to watch his plays was a disappointment. The narrative style is truly unique, with an almost journalistic listing of facts and occurrences in a rapid, relentless manner. Goethe had said that the novella genre should begin with an *unerhörte Begebenheit* (unheard-of circumstance) and develop from there, and Kleist's stories often fulfill this prerequisite admirably, as the characters certainly do find themselves in bizarre circumstances for which nothing in their previous experience has prepared them. The uncanny mixture of the distanced reporting style with deeply felt emotional crises, narrated without an ounce of sentimentality, creates an unusual atmosphere in the stories. Incredibly, the most outrageous, violent, and terrifying situations are depicted with a humor that is both lighthearted and macabre.

There is not so much a development of ideas running through Kleist's work as a repeated return to the same basic scenarios, each time with some difference. Characters in the plays and stories are continually confronted with crises of knowledge caused by one of a series of recurring events or conflicts. These are either a case of mistaken identity, a scenario in which a character is revealed as drastically different than previously thought, or an episode in which a character is forced to recognize a hitherto denied aspect of his personality or the world. Alkmene (in *Amphitryon*, 1807) discovers that the man she has been sleeping with is not her own husband but the god Jupiter in disguise, while the lead character in *Marquise von O. . .* (1810–11) finds that the heroic officer who rescued her in battle is in fact her rapist. Antonio Piachi in *Der Findling* (*The Foundling*, 1811) must admit that his son Nicolo is a cruel and vicious traitor. Josephe and Jeronimo in *Das Erdbeben in Chili* (*Earthquake in Chile*, 1810–11) find that a church full of devout Christians is also a violent and vindictive mob, and that the extraordinary chain of events (including natural disasters and examples of human kindness) that seems to have saved them from punishment for their illicit relationship has not done so after all, since they die at the conclusion.

Language proves a tricky matter: in the *Marquise von O . . .* the Count simply cannot express what he needs to say, and yet

Heinrich von Kleist. Reprinted courtesy of Bildarchiv.

in *Der zerbrochene Krug* Judge Adam reveals more than he means to and incriminates himself in his courtroom through constant slips of the tongue. Truth and reality seem for Kleist to be a compromise and convention in the best of times: recurring phrases in his stories and plays include "die gebrechliche Einrichtung der Welt" ("the fragile construction or organization of the world"); "eine Umwälzung der Ordnung" ("a radical revolution of the order of things"); and "eine neue Ordnung" ("a new order of things"). The order, so fragile and susceptible to being overthrown, is an arbitrary construct. Stories and plays end in conditional statements (*Das Erdbeben in Chili* ends with "it was almost as if he would have to be happy") or ambiguous exclamations (Alkmene's "Ach!" when she realizes the god Jupiter is leaving her with her mortal husband).

Though he had the support of the established writer Christoph Martin Wieland, and a few friends such as Adam Müller, most contemporaries considered Kleist a writer who wrote gratuitously violent and sexual fiction and drama. In the later nineteenth century, his patriotic work (*Prinz Friedrich vom Homburg, Die Hermannsschlacht*) was appreciated, as were *Das Kätchen von Heilbronn* and *Die Marquise von O . . .* for the paeans to feminine virtue they were perceived to include. Under the Third Reich, a selective and delicate approach was taken to Kleist's work; the violent and vulgar aspects of his work were carefully examined and considered before his work was made available. Existential critics rehabilitated the author in close readings which reveled in the work's ambiguity. They discovered thematic unity in binary oppositions such as emotion/reason, head/heart, and active/passive, and considered topics such as

the *Erkenntnisproblematik* (the problematizing of the cognitive process) and *Bewusstseinskritik* (the criticism of consciousness). More recently, some critics have investigated Kleist's work in the contexts of class and of humor. A significant number of psychoanalytic interpretations of the work, made since the 1970s, have forced reconsiderations of to the nature of his work. Most recently, the self-deconstructive aspects and gender ambiguity of Kleist's works have been investigated. In all, he proves a truly multifaceted author whose life and works remain the subject of speculation.

LAURA MARTIN

Biography

Born October 18, 1777, in Frankfurt an der Oder. Corporal in the Prussian Army 1792–1799. Studied physics, mathematics, and cultural history at the University of Frankfurt an der Oder for one year, 1799–1800. Traveled frequently through Germany and to France and Switzerland, 1799–1803. Held several jobs, including a technical deputation in 1800, and began writing in 1802. Arrested as a spy by the French, 1803. Returned to Berlin and entered civil service, 1804; sent to Königsberg, 1805–1806. Arrested again as a spy and imprisoned in Fort de Joux and Chalon, January–April, 1807. Returned to Dresden, August 1807; founded the monthly journal *Phöbus* in December 1807 (it lasted until February 1809). Traveled extensively, ending back in Berlin for good in February 1810. Founded first daily newspaper, the *Berliner Abendblätter*, October 1810 (it lasted until March 1811). Committed double suicide by first shooting the terminally ill Henriette Vogel though the heart, then himself through the head at Wannsee, a lake near Potsdam, November 21, 1811.

Selected Works

Primary
Sämtliche Werke und Briefe. 2 vols. Edited by Helmut Sembdner. Munich: Deutsche Taschenbuchverlag, 1984.
Sämtliche Werke und Briefe. 4 vols. Edited by Ilse-Marie Barth. Frankfurt am Main: Deutscher Klassiker Verlag, 1987–97.

Translations
Selected Writings. Translated by David Constantine. London: J. M. Dent, 1997.
Five Plays. Translated by Martin Greenberg. New Haven, Conn.: Yale University Press, 1988.
Three Plays. Translated by Noel Clark. London: Oberon, 2000.
Three Major Plays. Translated by Carl R. Mueller. Hanover, New Hampshire: Smith & Kraw, 2000.
The Marquise of O. . . and Other Stories. New York: Penguin, 1978.

Bibliography

Allan, Séan. *The Plays of Heinrich von Kleist: Ideals and Illusions.* Cambridge: Cambridge University Press, 1996.
Brahm, Otto. *Das Leben Heinrich von Kleists.* 4th rev. ed. Berlin: Fleischel, 1911.
Brown, Hilda Meldrum. *Heinrich von Kleist: The Ambiguity of Art and the Necessity of Form.* Oxford: Clarendon Press, 1998.
Cixous, Hélène. "Grace and Innocence: Heinrich von Kleist." In *Readings: The Poetics of Blanchot, Joyce, Kafka, Kleist, Lispector and Tsvetayeva.* Edited, translated, and with an introduction by Verena Andermatt Conley. New York: Harvester Wheatsheaf, 1992.

Dietrick, Linda. *Prisons and Idylls: Studies in Heinrich von Kleist's Fictional World*. Frankfurt: Lang, 1985.

Dyer, Denys. *The Stories of Kleist: A Critical Study*. London: Duckworth/New York: Holmes and Meier, 1977.

Ellis, John M. *Heinrich von Kleist: Studies in the Character and Meaning of His Writings*. Chapel Hill: University of North Carolina Press, 1979.

Fischer, Bernd. *Ironische Metaphysik: Die Erzählungen Heinriche von Kleists*. Munich: Fink, 1988.

Gelus, Marjorie. "Patriarchy's Fragile Boundaries under Siege: Three Stories of Heinrich von Kleist," *Women in German Yearbook* 10 (1995): 59–82.

Horn, Peter. *Heinrich von Kleists Erzählungen: Eine Einführung*. Regensburg: Scriptor Verlag, 1978.

Kreutzer, Hans Joachim. *Die dichterische Entwicklung Heinrichs von Kleist*. Berlin: E. Schmidt, 1968.

Maass, Joachim. *Kleist: A Biography*. Translated by Ralph Manheim. New York: Farrar, Straus and Giroux, 1983.

Moering, Michael. *Witz und Ironie in der Prosa Heinrich von Kleists*. Munchen: Fink, 1972.

Müller-Seidel, Walter. *Versehen und Verkennen: Eine Studie über Heinrich von Kleist*. Cologne: Böhlau, 1967.

Sembnder, Helmut. *Heinrich von Kleists Nachruhm: eine Wirkungsgeschichte in Dokumenten*. Munich: Deutscher Taschenbuch Verlag, 1996.

Stahl, E. L. *Heinrich von Kleists Dramas*. Oxford: Blackwell, 1948.

Stephens, Anthony. *Heinrich von Kleist: The Dramas and Stories*. Oxford: Berg, 1994.

KLENZE, LEO VON 1784–1864

German architect, painter, and writer

Though less well-known now than his Berlin counterpart and friend Karl Friedrich Schinkel, Leo von Klenze was an equally significant exponent of Greek Revival architecture, and his public buildings in Munich transformed the architectural character of the Bavarian capital no less dramatically than Schinkel's work transformed that of the Prussian capital. Uncompromising in his theoretical insistence that ancient Greece provided the sole model of architectural perfection, Klenze was more flexible in practice, in part out of the necessity (about which he complained bitterly in his private journals) of accommodating his royal patron, Ludwig I. His oeuvre is thus more stylistically varied than his reputation as a neoclassicist par excellence would suggest: not only classical Greek and Roman but Egyptian, Romanesque, Renaissance Italian, and even Gothic inspirations are evident in his exterior designs, while the influence of the contemporary French Empire style is dominant in his interiors. As Achim von Arnim observed in 1829, "If Schinkel has more talent, originality, and artistic sense than Klenze, which no one will deny, there dwells in Klenze on the other hand a greater power to submit himself to external circumstances." Precisely that power enabled him to oversee Bavaria's state building programs for nearly three decades while making uniquely distinguished contributions to them.

Klenze's inclination to classicism reflects the influence of Aloys Hirt, his teacher at the Berliner Bauakademie, who found in ancient Greece his ideal of a functionalist architecture, and of Jean-Nicolas-Louis Durand, whose rationalist theory of design (which subordinated form to function and rejected rococo decorative excess) he encountered in Paris in 1803. His first publication (1805), a design for a monument to Martin Luther modeled on the Pantheon and Friedrich Gilly's proposed monument to Frederick the Great (1797), promoted Durand's criteria of appropriateness, economy, and utility. Though not built, this early design anticipates Klenze's later realized projects in its appropriation of classical form for a German nationalistic purpose.

Klenze's first executed project, a theater on the grounds of the Wilhelmshöhe palace in Kassel (1809–13), was commissioned by Napoleon Bonaparte's brother Jérôme, who had appointed Klenze as court architect shortly after assuming the throne of the newly created Westphalian kingdom in 1807. In 1813, after Jérôme had fled Westphalia, Klenze traveled to Munich and Vienna in search of a new patron, to whom his new project of a monument to the post-Napoleonic peace (*Monument à la pacification de l'Europe*, 1814)—again derivative of Gilly's monument to Frederick the Great—might appeal. Although he found no patron at the Congress of Vienna, his interview with Bavaria's Crown Prince (later King) Ludwig in Munich in February 1814 resulted in an eventual offer of employment and an invitation to submit a competition design for a Glyptothek, or museum of ancient sculpture, "in the classical style." Rejecting the advice of his academic jury, Ludwig awarded the commission to Klenze, who quickly mastered the skill of outmaneuvering rival architects in satisfying Ludwig's desire to turn Munich into a European cultural centre with museums and monuments worthy of Rome's.

As built, the Glyptothek (1816–30), an ensemble of vaulted galleries entered through an Ionic portico and arranged around a square courtyard, in fact makes limited use of Greek forms. Klenze's assimilation of Johann Joachim Winckelmann's *Geschichte der Kunst des Alterthums* (*History of Ancient Art*, 1764) manifested itself in his arrangement of galleries according to historical period, proceeding clockwise from the Egyptian Room to the Roman Room, and his interest in polychromy found expression in the interior decoration (destroyed in the Second World War and unfortunately not restored) of green and violet marble walls, elaborately gilt cornices, and brightly painted coffered ceilings. In front of the building he planned a suitably monumental square, the Königsplatz, in which his vast Doric gateway, the Propyläen, was erected in 1854–60 to commemorate the Greek war of independence. (After Ludwig's son Otto was made king of Greece in 1832, Klenze traveled to Athens on a diplomatic mission and developed plans for protecting the ancient monuments and constructing new buildings, though only a Roman Catholic cathedral was executed to his design.)

Klenze's plan to redevelop Munich's Ludwigstrasse, worked out in secret with the crown prince, proceeded less smoothly, since Ludwig envisioned a street lined with large Italianate palaces, while Klenze preferred more modest and liberally fenestrated designs derived from fifteenth-century Florence. In the event Klenze had to compromise, concealing multiple dwellings behind unified façades and disguising the Odeon concert hall (1826–28) as a palace corresponding to the one he had already designed for Ludwig's brother-in-law (Leuchtenbergpalais, 1817–21). Conflicts with Ludwig are also evident in the neo-Romanesque Court Church of All Saints (1826–37), in which Klenze tried to reconcile his own preference for a schema of simple geometric forms with the prince's insistence on a stylistic amalgam of St. Mark's in Venice and the Palatine Chapel in Palermo.

Where Klenze had a freer hand, his buildings were far more successful. He claimed in 1830 that his design of the Italianate Pinakothek (the state picture gallery, built 1826–36) followed entirely from the demands of arranging, lighting, and protecting the collections: the result, which was widely acclaimed and imitated, was a sequence of top-lit main galleries flanked on the north by small cabinets and on the south by a long loggia. (He later incorporated design elements from this museum and the Glyptothek into the neoclassical New Hermitage Museum, built 1842–52.) His later public monuments returned to neoclassical style, Friedrich Gilly and the Parthenon providing the inspiration for the Walhalla (1830–42), a Doric temple built atop a three-tiered plinth on a spectacular site above the River Danube near Regensburg. The polychromatic marbled interior, intended for displaying busts of eminent Germans and undamaged in the war, not only recalls the Glyptothek's interior, but attests to Klenze's interest in the contemporary debate about polychromy in ancient Greek architecture and sculpture. Like the Ruhmeshalle (Bavarian Hall of Fame, 1843–53) in Munich, a U-shaped Doric colonnade remarkably similar in form to the then-unknown altar at Pergamum, and the Befreiungshalle (Liberation Hall, 1843–63) near Kelheim, a vast stone cylinder surmounted by a Doric colonnade, the Walhalla demonstrated definitively that neoclassical styles could be used to promote German nationalism no less effectively, perhaps even more so, than the Gothic styles promoted by some Romantic writers—a lesson not lost on Albert Speer a century later.

NICHOLAS HALMI

Biography

Born in Schladen (near Brunswick), February 28, 1784. Studied architecture under David Gilly and Aloys Hirt, Berlin, 1800–1803. Visited Paris, 1803. Appointed court architect by Jérôme Bonaparte, 1808. Visited Italy, 1806–7. Married Felicitas Blangini and fled Kassel after Westphalia's dissolution, 1813. Met Crown Prince Ludwig in Munich, 1814. In Vienna and Paris, 1814–15. Moved permanently to Munich at Ludwig's behest; visited Italy with Ludwig, 1818 and 1823–24. Appointed privy councillor, 1818; appointed director of the Bavarian Building Authority, 1830. Visited Greece, 1834. Visited Belgium, England and France, to inspect railways, 1836. Traveled to Russia for the first of seven visits, 1839. Relieved of directorship of the Bavarian Building Authority, 1843; received Gold Medal of the Royal Institute of British Architects, 1851. Died in Munich, January 27, 1864.

Selected Works

Buildings (with dates of completion)
Hoftheater Schloss Wilhelmshöhe, Kassel. 1813.
Ludwigstrasse (redevelopment), Munich. 1817–30.
Leuchtenbergpalais, Munich. 1821.
Odeon, Munich. 1826.
Glyptothek, Munich. 1830; exterior restored to original appearance after World War II.
Königsbau Residenz, Munich. 1834; restored 1980ff.
(Alte) Pinaktothek, Munich. 1836; restored after World War II.
Allerheiligen-Hofkirche Residenz, Munich. 1837; restored 1986ff.
Walhalla, near Regensburg. 1842.
Festsaalbau Residenz, Munich. 1842.
New Hermitage Museum, Saint Petersburg. 1852.
Ruhmeshalle, Munich. 1853.
Propyläen, Munich. 1862.
Befreiungshalle, near Kelheim. 1863.
Cathedral of St. Dionysius, Athens. 1887.

Writings
Entwurf zu einem Denkmal für Dr. Martin Luther. 1805.
Projet de monument à la pacification de l'Europe. 1814.
Anweisung zur Architektur des christlichen Kultus. 1822. (Rev. ed 1834. Edited by Adrian von Buttlar: Nördlingen: Uhl, 1990.
Tempel des olympischen Jupiter von Agrigent. 1827.
Sammlung architektonischer Entwürfe. 10 vols. 1830–50. Edited by Florian Hufnagl. Worms: Werner, 1983.
Aphoristische Bemerkungen, gesammelt auf seiner Reise nach Griechenland. 1838.
Die Walhalla in artistischer und technischer Beziehung. 1843.

Bibliography

Buttlar, Adrian von. *Leo von Klenze: Leben, Werk, Vision.* Munich: Beck, 1999.
Hederer, Oswald. *Leo von Klenze.* Munich: Callwey, 1964.
Irwin, David. *Neoclassicism.* London: Thames and Hudson, 1997.
Lieb, Norbert, and Florian Hufnagl. *Leo von Klenze: Gemälde und Zeichnungen.* Munich: Callwey, 1979.
Nerdinger, Winfried, ed. *Klassizismus in Bayern, Schwaben und Franken: Architekturzeichnungen 1775–1825.* Munich: Stadtmuseum, 1980.
———, ed. *Leo von Klenze: Architekt zwischen Kunst und Hof.* Munich: Prestel, 2000.
Watkin, David, and Tilman Mellinghof. *German Architecture and the Classical Ideal.* London: Thames and Hudson, 1987.

KLOPSTOCK, FRIEDRICH GOTTLIEB 1724–1803

German poet

The poetry of Friedrich Gottlieb Klopstock inaugurated a new era in German literature, and had a pronounced effect on modern European poetry. Through his literary theory, his odes, hymns, plays, and above all through his celebrated verse epic *Der Messias* (The Messiah), which went through no less than six editions in English alone (1763–1826), Klopstock both forged an original poetic idiom and created a range of models that were emulated by later poets. In public life, he lent a new dignity to the poet's profession. The unique power he accorded to the imagination contributed to the popularity of the sentimental mode, which became a key feature of European Romanticism. As a result, almost every subsequent phase in German literature reveals his influence, from Johann Wolfgang von Goethe's Sturm und Drang lyrics to Friedrich Hölderlin's classical verse, Novalis's Romantic symbolism, and Friedrich Nietzsche's dithyrambs. His impact continued into modernism, affecting both Stefan George's emphasis on poetic recitation and Rainer Maria Rilke's sublime style in the *Duineser Elegien* (Duino Elegies), as well as the more muted tone employed by later twentieth-century poets, notably Franz Baermann Steiner and Johannes Bobrowski. On the other hand, the limitations of his abstractions were soon recognized, and in Christian Dietrich Grabbe's play *Scherz, Satire, Ironie und tiefere Bedeutung* (*Fun, Satire, Irony and Deeper Meaning*), the devil reads Klopstock's *Der Messias* to send himself to sleep.

Klopstock first conceived *Der Messias* in 1742 at the age of seventeen and set out his poetic mission in his farewell speech at school in 1745. The first three—and by far the most influential—cantos appeared in the literary journal *Bremer Beiträge* in 1748, and Klopstock completed the work in 1773 when he finished the remarkable twentieth canto. The final, revised, and corrected version appeared in 1799–1800. Inspired by the epic tradition of Homer and Virgil, and especially by John Milton's Christian epic *Paradise Lost*, Klopstock's magnum opus focuses on Christ's passion and culminates in a grand evocation of the Last Judgment. Symmetrically constructed, the poem devotes the first ten cantos to Christ's suffering and the last ten to celebration. The theme, announced in the opening lines, is "der sündigen Menschheit Erlösung" (the salvation of sinful mankind). Christ is understood as the "Gottmensch" (God-Man) or "Mittler" (mediator) who achieves the gradual union of creation with God.

In form and ideas, the poem effects a powerful synthesis of humanist learning, apparent in its fluent, evocative use of rhetoric and the classical hexameter, and orthodox Christian tradition, rooted in the Bible. The worldview also owes much to neo-Platonism, while the emotionalism is indebted to pietism; Enlightenment optimism adds a further, distinctly unorthodox trait. Most notably, the second canto prefigures the forgiveness of a devil, Abbadona, because of his virtue, and this intimation is fulfilled at the end. Less concrete than the work of Homer, less vivid than that of Milton, Klopstock's *Der Messias* is a spiritual epic, related in tone to the prophetic writings of Christopher Smart and William Blake. Set simultaneously in the infinite space of the Copernican universe, typified by its plurality of worlds, and in the no less unbounded realm of the mind, the poem sonorously rouses and moves the reader "Gott zu denken" (to think God), elevating human emotion into an ineffable, heavenly sphere, illuminated by the divine "Urlicht" (original light).

Klopstock's personality exercised a considerable influence. Invited to Zurich as the author of *Der Messias* by Johann Georg Bodmer, his host was shocked by his worldliness, but he became a cult figure among the young, notably the poets of the Göttinger Hain (Göttingen Glade) group. His love of skating was legendary, and his poem "Der Eislauf" ("Skating," 1764) inaugurated a literary fashion that left its mark on William Wordsworth's *Prelude* and culminated in the grand skating scene in Lev Tolstoy's *Anna Karenina*. In later life, he was elected an honorary citizen of the new French Republic, which he supported, but subsequently revoked his allegiance in the poem "Mein Irrtum" ("My Mistake," 1793).

Klopstock's views on language, poetry, and other topics feature in a series of major essays which crystallize his literary and linguistic credo. In *Von der Darstellung* (*On Representation*, 1779), he lends preeminence to *Leben* (life) as the chief principle of art, while cognate themes figure in *Von der Sprache der Poesie* (*On the Language of Poetry*, 1758) and *Von der Nachahmung des griechischen Sylbenmasses im Deutschen* (*On Imitating Greek Verse-Forms in German*, 1755). His chief theoretical work, *Die deutsche Gelehrtenrepublik* (*The German Intellectual Republic*), published in 1774, sets out the principles for a German republic of letters.

Klopstock's shorter poems, the odes and hymns first collected as *Oden* (*Odes*, 1771), probably constitute his finest achievement. The briefest are pure lyrics, notably the affectingly simple love poem "Das Rosenband" (The Rose Band, 1753), and two elegiac pieces: "Die frühen Gräber" (The Early Graves, 1764) and "Die Sommernacht" (The Summer Night, 1766). Such verses express the poet's mood in masterly rhythms and clear, yet suggestive language. The great odes are more ambitious, exhibiting complex structures and a dazzling linguistic boldness, as in the religious poem "An Gott" (To God, 1752), with its brilliant opening lines, "Ein stiller Schauer deiner Allgegenwart/ Erschüttert, Gott! mich . . ." (A still tremor of your omnipresence/Shatters, God! me . . .), or the memorable ode that entwines the themes of friendship and nature, "Der Zürchersee" (The Lake of Zurich, 1750). Apart from nature, friendship, and religion, the other major themes of Klopstock's odes are love and death, the latter being understood in poems like "An Fanny" (To Fanny, 1748) as a positive state in which separated lovers will be rejoined, and the soul will be united with God. There are also poems on history, politics, and war. In sum, the odes constitute the first fully successful verse written in classical meters in the German language. Klopstock took this technical inventiveness with unrhymed verse a stage further in six hymns in free rhythms, which initiate the tradition of European free verse. In the best known, first published as "Das Landleben" (Country Life, 1759) and revised as "Die Frühlingsfeier" (Spring Celebration, 1771) the poet speaks as a contemporary psalmist who bears witness to God's presence in a thunderstorm, which he treats vividly as an overwhelming but deeply uplifting manifestation of the sublime.

JEREMY ADLER

Biography

Born in Quedlinburg, Saxony, July 2, 1724. Attended the Gymnasium at Quedlinburg 1736–39, and the Prince's School, Pforta, 1739–45. Studied theology and philosophy at the Universities of Jena (1745–46) and Leipzig (1746–48). Worked as a private tutor in Langensalsza, Saxony, 1748–50. Visited Zurich in 1750. Lived in Denmark from 1751, where King Frederick V awarded him a life pension to complete *Der Messias*. Moved to Hamburg in 1770. Married Margarete (Meta) Moller in 1754, who died in 1758, and Johanna Elisabeth von Winthem in 1791. Died in Hamburg, March 14, 1803.

Selected Works

Poetry

Der Messias, 1748–1800. Translated in part as *The Messiah* by Mary Collyer and Joseph Collyer, 1763; translated by Solomon Hallings, 1810; translated by Thomas Raffles, 1814; translated by G. H. C. Egestorff, 1821–22; translated by Catherine Head, 1826.
Oden, 1771. Translated as *Odes of Klopstock from 1747 to 1780* by William Nind. 1848.

Plays

Der Tod Adams, 1757. Translated as *The Death of Adam* by Robert Lloyd. 1763.
Salomo, 1764. Translated as *Solomon* Robert Huish. 1809.

Letters and Memoirs

Memoirs of Frederick and Margaret Klopstock. Translated by Elizabeth Smith. 1808.

Klopstock und seine Freunde: Briefwechsel der Familie Klopstock unter sich, und zwischen dieser Familie, Gleim, Schmidt, Fanny, Meta und andern Freunden. 2 vols. Edited by Klamer Schmidt. 1810. Translated as *Klopstock and His Friends. A Series of Family Letters, Written between the Years 1750 and 1803* by Elizabeth Ogilvy. 1814.

Bibliography

Bjorklund, Beth, "Klopstock's Poetic Innovations: The Emergence of German as a Prosodic Language," *Germanic Review* 56 (1981).
Blackall, Eric. *The Emergence of German as a Literary Language 1770–1775*. Cambridge: Cambridge University Press, 1959; 2nd ed., Ithaca, N.Y.: Cornell University Press, 1978.
Hellmuth, Hans-Heinrich. *Metrische Erfindung und metrische Theorie bei Klopstock*. Munich: Fink, 1973.
Hilliard, Kevin. *Philosophy, Letters, and the Fine Arts in Klopstock's Thought*. London: Institute of Germanic Studies, University of London, 1987.
Kaiser, Gerhard. *Klopstock: Religion und Dichtung*. 2d ed. Kronberg/Ts, 1975.
Kohl, Katrin. *Rhetoric, the Bible, and the Origins of Free Verse*. Berlin: de Gruyter, 1995.
———. *Friedrich Gottlieb Klopstock*. Stuttgart: Metzler, 2000.
Lee, Meredith. *Displacing Authority: Goethe's Poetic Reception of Klopstock*. Heidelberg: Winter, 1999.
Murat, Jean. *Klopstock: Les thèmes principaux de son oeuvre*. Paris, 1959.
Pape, Helmuth. *Klopstock: Die "Sprache des Herzens" neu entdeckt. Die Befreiung des Lesers aus seiner emotionalen Unmündigkeit: Idee und Wirklichkeit dichterischer Existenz um 1750*. Frankfurt: Lang, 1998.
Schneider, Karl Ludwig. *Klopstock und die Erneuerung der deutschen Dichtersprache im achtzehnten Jahrhundert*. Heidelberg, 1960.
Werner, Hans-Georg. *Friedrich Gottlieb Klopstock: Werk und Wirkung*. Berlin: Akademie, 1978.

KØBKE, CHRISTEN SCHIELLERUP 1810–1848

Danish painter

Christen Schiellerup Købke was a pioneer of Scandinavian plein-air painting. During the first half of the nineteenth century, several of his artistic contemporaries, who had also been trained at the Royal Academy of Fine Arts in Copenhagen, decided to reject the literary and historic motifs of academic painting. Købke followed suit, choosing to focus on portraits and landscapes, or in a wider sense on nature itself—something that, with the arrival of Romanticism, presented challenges of perception that were hitherto unknown. Købke's career covers no more than twenty years, during the first ten of which (c. 1828–38) he worked as a landscape painter within a geographically restricted, Danish circle of motifs. However, his descriptions of nature from the following years (c. 1838–48) are based on impressions drawn from German Romantic landscape painting and the artist's acquaintance with Italy.

Købke was introduced to plein-air studies by his teacher Christoffer Wilhelm Eckersberg. Following studies in Paris and Rome, Eckersberg took up the post of professor at the Royal Academy in Copenhagen in 1818. Although Købke was admitted to the Academy in 1822, he did not begin to study under Eckersberg until 1828. The core of Eckersberg's teaching, which was to prove immensely important to an entire generation of Danish painters, was the plein-air study, which, drawing from nature and depicting an existing reality, provided the basis for a type of landscape painting that aimed to achieve a balance between naturalism and the ideal. With nature study as the starting point, the ideal picture could be created, the "basic picture," which according to Eckersberg was the true purpose of art. In Friedrich Wilhelm Joseph von Schelling's philosophy of nature, held much in esteem by Eckersberg, it is argued that nature is a divinity in itself: Schelling's theories are based on the idea of shared identity between nature, God, and the perfect pictorial composition. Eckersberg did more than teach his pupils how to paint from nature; he impressed on them also his view of the artist as a free and independent individual, which was that "[t]he intellectual activity of the artist, his individuality, belongs to himself. Fully according to his own inclinations, he may choose to make such things as he finds most appealing, moving or interesting, the subject of his illustrated work." This was Eckersberg's dictum. Købke chose landscapes, portraits, and representations of architecture. The lack of drama in Danish nature was compensated for by his remarkably precise feeling for composition, along with his striking ability to describe the atmosphere of a landscape as well as the effect of light on the motif. Typically, Købke found his motifs in the areas surrounding his birthplace at the citadel of Copenhagen and later his residence on the outskirts of the city. The results were peaceful, nondramatic landscapes, their composition determined by architecture and the distribution of light and shadow, with horizontal and vertical lines playing against each other. In all of his work, Købke builds a firm picture structure, in which the principal lines of the landscape run parallel to the picture plane. Often, a drawbridge, a citadel gate, a fence, or a roof ridge are his simple means of creating spatiality within a composition. Seemingly random sections of a motif or a framed view are chosen—this might be, for example, a landscape viewed from an interior through an open window or door, a compositional resource much favored among Romantic artists such as Caspar David Friedrich.

Købke received further inspiration from another influential professor at the Royal Academy in Copenhagen, the art historian Nicls Laurits Høyen. In his national-Romantic program proposed during the 1830s and 1840s, Høyen argued for the development of a Scandinavian tradition of national art. He called on artists to make Denmark's scenery and historic monuments the subjects of their art, in order to establish a Nordic genre of landscape painting fit to replace the classic Italian tradition. Influenced by Høyen's doctrine, Købke worked in the early 1830s on motifs recommended by the professor, including Danish medieval cathedrals and the castle architecture of the Renaissance. In spite of its small size, *The Transept of Aarhus Cathedral* (1830) is an excellent depiction of a corner of a church interior, in particular the way in which the light falls through the windows onto the whitewashed surfaces of the church walls. During the mid-1830s, Købke painted a series of melancholic evocative landscapes, their titles indicating the circumstances under which they were painted—the time of day, the particular season, and thus the very cycle of nature. When choosing the Renaissance castle of Frederiksborg north of Copenhagen as his motif, Købke sets the scene in a quiet summer's evening after sunset. By doing so, the scenery has come to play almost as great a part as the actual castle. The building is outlined against the evening sky and mirrored in the calm, clear waters of the lake. This motif exudes a lyrical atmosphere that may appeal to the spectator's more Romantic sentiments. *Frederiksborg Castle in the Evening Light* (1835) and *Autumn Landscape: Frederiksborg Castle in the Middle Distance* (c. 1835) are without doubt influenced by the Romantic landscape paintings of Dresden, represented by Caspar David Friedrich and Norwegian-born artist Johann Christian Dahl. Titles such as *Autumn Landscape* suggest an emphasis on the season rather than the location. Critic Robert Rosenblum likens Købke's paintings from this period to contemporary work by Jean-Baptiste-Camille Corot, noting, "They both approach these venerable buildings as if they almost stumbled upon them by accident and were indifferent to their weighty histories." Købke made plein-air studies, observing nature directly, painted quick oil sketches while the motif was still in front of him, and then executed the final painting in his studio. These are sober descriptions, populated not by hermits, knights, or monks, but by decent citizens, contemporaries of the artist.

The studies are usually deserted, as figures would be added to the final paintings.

As a portrait painter, Købke painted artist colleagues and portraits of peasants as well as members of his own family, although he produced only very few pieces of commissioned work. The portrait of Købke's artist friend and mentor, *Portrait of the Sculptor Johann Ernst Frend* (c. 1838), represents a striking tribute to the genius of Romantic art. It also symbolizes the greatest dilemma of the time, the choice between two sources of inspiration—classical antiquity versus Norse ancient history and mythology. Købke depicts the sculptor as pondering; wearing his artist's smock, he is deep in thought as he sits before his statuette of Odin, the Norse god. The interior, which is the sculptor's own home, is decorated in the style of a Pompeian mural.

Although he was advised against it, Købke went to Italy for a period of study during 1838–40. The scenery surrounding Naples and Capri inspired him to paint a number of monumental—though hardly sublime—landscapes related to Italian landscape paintings by contemporary German artists such as Karl Blechen and Carl Rottmann, as well as the Austrian Joseph Rebell. Light plein-air sketches of rocks, waves crashing over rocky shores, studies of clouds and atmospheric phenomena "painted from nature"—that is, taken on location—were later transferred to large canvases, as idealistic landscapes with figures added back in the artist's studio in Copenhagen. One example is *Motif from Capri Shortly after the Rising of the Sun* (1843).

In 1844, Købke's application for membership of the Royal Academy in Copenhagen was rejected. Whenever Købke's art does touch upon the powerful forces of nature, it reflects the notion of the sublime. Hence, viewed against the background of Købke's earlier oeuvre, the tone of his later works may seem slightly false.

METTE BLIGAARD

Biography

Born in Copenhagen May 26, 1810. Admitted as a student to the Royal Academy in Copenhagen, 1822. Pupil of Christoffer Wilhelm Eckersberg 1828–33. Awarded the Academy's silver medal, 1833. Travels to Berlin, Dresden, and Munich, 1838; Italy (Venice, Rome, Sorrento, Capri, Pompeii, and Florence), 1838–40. Refused membership in the Royal Academy in Copenhagen, 1844. Died February 7, 1848.

Selected Works

The Transept of Aarhus Cathedral. 1830. Statens Museum for Kunst, Copenhagen.
View from the Grain Loft in the Citadel. 1831. Statens Museum for Kunst, Copenhagen.
Portrait of the Landscape Painter Frederik Sødring. 1832. Den Hirschprungske Samling, Copenhagen.
The North Gate of the Citadel, Copenhagen. 1834. Ny Carlsberg Glyptotek, Copenhagen.
Autumn Landscape, Frederiksborg Castle in the Middle Distance. c. 1835. Ny Carlsberg Glyptotek, Copenhagen.
Frederiksborg Castle Seen from the North West. 1836. Statens Museum for Kunst, Copenhagen.
View of a Street in a Copenhagen Suburb. Morning Light. 1836. Statens Museum for Kunst, Copenhagen.
Portrait of the Sculptor Hermann Ernst Freund. 1838. Royal Academy of Fine Arts, Copenhagen.

Autumn Morning on Lake Sortedam. 1838. Ny Carlsberg Glyptotek, Copenhagen.
Motif from Capri after Sunrise. c. 1843. Statens Museum for Kunst, Copenhagen.

Bibliography

Gunnarsson, Torsten. "The Beginning of Open-air Oil-sketching in Scandinavia." *Nationalmuseum Bulletin* 9, no. 2 (1985).

Johnston, Catherine, et al. *Baltic Light: Early Open-Air Painting in Denmark and North Germany.* New Haven, Conn.: Yale University Press, 1999.

Kent, Neil. "Christen Købke's Drawings: Assessing a Little-known Master," *Apollo* 1993, 175–77.

Monrad, Kasper, ed. *Danish Painting: The Golden Age.* London: National Gallery, 1984.

———, ed. *The Golden Age of Danish Painting.* Los Angeles: 1993.

Nørregård-Nielsen, Hans Edvard. *Christen Købke.* Copenhagen, 1996.

———. *Købke og Kastellet.* Copenhagen, 1981.

Nørregård-Nielsen, Hans Edvard, and Kasper Monrad, eds. *Christen Købke 1810–1848.* Exhib. cat. Copenhagen: Statens Museum for Kunst, 1996.

Schwartz, Sanchez. *Christen Købke.* New York, 1992.

KOCH, JOSEPH ANTON 1768–1839

German landscape painter

A primary practitioner of "heroic" landscape painting, Joseph Anton Koch was the Romantic era's heir to the grand tradition of Claude Lorrain and Nicolas Poussin. Even as he worked within the boundaries of classical landscape, however, Koch expanded them under the influence of Romantic thought. Throughout his artistic career, depictions of conventional themes that correspond entirely to the academic concept of landscape painting's noblest aspirations are infused with a passion for the spectacle of nature. This Romantic inflection is manifest in his inclination for topographic specificity and in the clarity of his brushwork, which makes every single leaf visible and notable, and replaces the moderating action of atmospheric perspective with an almost surreal focus on distant terrain, as in *Berner Oberland* (*Bernese Oberland*, 1816). While large-scale, orderly paintings such as *Heroische Landschaft mit dem Dankopfer Noahs* (*Heroic Landscape with the Sacrifice of Noah*, 1803) and *Heroische Landschaft mit Regenbogen* (*Heroic Landscape with Rainbow*, 1815) seem the very epitome of the academic doctrine that idealized the biblical land of the Mediterranean and the noble countryside of Virgil and Homer, Koch also broke away from the orthodoxy of the south to paint the wild Alpine landscape of his Tyrolean youth. At times he could wallow in the depths of the aesthetics of the sublime as he did in the later painting *Macbeth und die Hexen* (*Macbeth and the Witches*, 1835), in which the frightening forces of nature synchronize with the dark powers wielded by a trio of raging sorceresses. The idealization of the Middle Ages and Renaissance that entranced so many German Romantics found its way into his work at an early point in his career. Besides William Shakespeare, Koch was consumed with a passion for Dante Alighieri and Ossian. But above all, it was the mountain landscape that captured his artistic imagination, and he turned to it repeatedly, whether in depicting the sublime northern vista or the ideal southern countryside.

Koch's deeply-rooted attachment to nature, born of a youth spent in the Tyrol performing shepherd's duty, has become the stuff of his artistic legend. The sketches of the scenery he made while tending to his flock were given to the Bishop of Augsburg, who took an interest in the boy and saw to it that he received the beginnings of a proper artistic education. In Stuttgart, where he was sent to study, the young Koch rebelled against the stric-

tures of academic training and embraced the cause of liberty espoused by the French Revolution. He finally fled the school and, after an itinerant year, headed to Switzerland, where he rediscovered the beauty of the Alps and produced a large number of studies from nature that would serve as the basis for paintings throughout his career. A grant from an English patron allowed him to tour Italy, and he ultimately landed in Rome, where he came under the influence of the neoclassical painter Asmus Jakob Carstens and briefly set aside landscape painting to concentrate on figural composition. While Koch eventually returned to the subject matter dearest to him—nature—Carstens's work left a visible imprint on his own. His mature style displays a heightened sense of grandeur, a lucid pictorial structure, and a crispness of line that to a large extent can be attributed to this encounter. In Rome, Koch also befriended the artist Christian Rheinhart, whose vision of nature closely mirrored his own, and together the two would set the standards for heroic landscape painting for German artists of the nineteenth century.

Koch's impassioned reaction to mountains and other dramatic scenery reveals him to be a product of late eighteenth-century Sturm und Drang culture, which transformed the perceived experience of the sublime in nature from a confrontation with terror and danger into a positive encounter that moved the soul and stirred emotions. In Koch's case, such scenery often was associated with the concept of liberty: one rousing passage in his diaries describes how a particular strip of unruly terrain along the Rhine caused him to feel the strength necessary to rise up against despotism in defense of human liberty. Switzerland, which he called "the land of freedom," provided him with some of the most sensational views, one of which was of the Schmadribach Falls in the Bernese Oberland, a spectacular waterfall that inspired several paintings. In the imposing early *Schmadribachfall* (1805/11), diverse layers of earth are piled on top of each other, tracing the origins and course of a river from the snow-capped mountain peaks to the waterfall that crashes through a strapping mass of rocks, slowed down by a dense evergreen forest and finally culminating in the docile flow winding through a peaceful valley. It is at once a realistic and an artificial image, both a product of intense observation of the geological components and processes of nature and a manufactured composition springing from an artist's mind—a combination of the real and the ideal that is at the heart of Koch's aesthetic.

KOGĂLNICEANU, MIHAIL 1817–1891

Moldavian writer

A Moldavian nobleman's son and (initially) protégé of the Prince Mihai Sturdza (r. 1834–49), Mihail Kogălniceanu was sent to be educated in France with the prince's sons in 1834, but soon had to move to Berlin at the order of the Russian government, who held a protectorate over Moldavia and feared these young men would become contaminated by French revolutionary ideas. At Berlin, Kogălniceanu met Alexander von Humboldt, heard Leopold von Ranke's lectures, and in 1837 published three precocious early works. *Histoire de la Valachie, de la Moldavie et des Valaques transdanubiens* and *Moldau und Wallachei. Romanische oder Wallachische Sprache und Literatur* constitute remarkable early attempts at synthesis, contouring the historical and literary traditions of the Romanians in modern critical forms and in Western languages; while his *Esquisse sur l'histoire, les mœurs et la langue des Cigains* widely influenced European scholarship on the Roma.

On his return to Iaşi in 1838, Kogălniceanu was eager to establish modern cultural institutions and entered into conflict with the authorities over the leasing of a printing press and the founding of new journals. In 1840 he became a codirector of the Moldavian National Theater; three years later he delivered his famous "Speech on the Opening of the Course in National History" at the then recently founded (1835) Academy (a course that was shortly to be closed down by order of the authorities). In 1846 he produced the first edition of the Moldavian chronicles of the sixteenth to eighteenth centuries, which he reedited in 1874 in Latin script. These historiographical efforts were crucial in grafting into Romanian culture a conception of history based on organic evolutionism, ideas that Kogălniceanu derived largely from his German masters. This became a paradigmatic model for Romanians in the 1848 revolution and in the nationalist drive to independence and unity as a whole.

However, Kogălniceanu's importance as a promoter of Romanticism rests on the journals he edited on his return to Iaşi in 1840: *Dacia litterară* (*Literary Dacia*, 1840) and *Propăşirea* (*Progress*, 1844), with which he further challenged the literary and political status quo. The introduction to the former is one of the key programmatic documents of Romanian Romanticism. Kogălniceanu insisted on the need for an original national literature, both in terms of Romanian subject matter and by introducing questions of a national style; he also advocated the preservation of folk traditions against the prevailing currents imitating Western literary forms. Kogălniceanu can also be credited with the consecration of the idea of literature as an autonomous field of cultural activity, although this was a paradoxical process: literature was claimed as innocent and apolitical, so as to appease the censors, but at the same time was constructed as a field of moral value, and so gained political capital.

In *Dacia litterară*, Kogălniceanu also sought to promote the national unity of the Romanians by soliciting material from co-nationals in other provinces. He published key works by others (Costache Negruzzi's Sir Walter Scott–derived historical novella *Alecsandru Lăpuşneanu*; [*Sketches by Alecsandri*]) and his own literary criticism and attempts at fiction, which were slight and heavily dependent on the popular French *physiologies littéraires*, but paved the way for the development of the Romanian novel.

In and after 1848, Kogălniceanu wrote few literary works, but was active as a journalist and statesman, enacting the emancipation of the peasantry in 1864 and acting as Romanian Foreign Minister in the "Eastern Crisis" of 1877–78. He died in Paris, but was buried in Iaşi: in a Romantic gesture imitating the funeral of Baron von Stein, the Prussian emancipator of the peasantry, his body was borne by peasants to the Moldavian capital all the way from the railway station on the Austrian frontier.

ALEXANDER DRACE-FRANCIS

Biography

Born 1817. Sent to France for education, 1834. Published *Histoire de la Valachie, de la Moldavie et des Valaques transdanubiens*, and *Moldau und Wallachei: Romanische oder Wallachische Sprache und Literatur*, 1837. Returned to Iaşi, 1838. Became a codirector of the Moldavian National Theater, and edited *Dacia litterară*. 1840, edited *Propăşirea*, 1844. Produced the first edition of the Moldavian chronicles of the sixteenth–eighteenth centuries, 1846. Romanian Foreign Minister in the Eastern Crisis, 1877–78. Died, 1891.

Selected Works

Opere, books 1 and 2. Bucureşti: Academia Română, 1974–76.

Bibliography

Al. Zub. *Mihail Kogălniceanu*. Bucarest: Enciclopedică, 1984. (In French.)

Jelavich, Barbara. "Mihail Kogălniceanu as historian and politician." In *Historians as Nation-Builders*. Dennis Deletant and Harry Hanak, eds. London: Macmillan, 1988. 87–106.

Kogălniceanu, Mihail, ed. *Fragments tirés des chroniques moldaves et valaques*. Parts I-II. Iaşi: Feuille Communale, 1846.

Despite his interest in scientific explications of the natural world—his favorite book next to the Bible was Anton Friedrich Büsching's *Neue Erdbeschreibung* (*New Description of the Earth*), an eighteenth-century standard on geography—and his insistence upon firsthand observation of it, Koch rejected the idea that mere imitation of nature could be art. Instead, he strove to paint the poetic in nature, an ideal that echoed theories about landscape imagery put forth by the influential Rome-based art critic C. L. Fernow. If Koch did not see poetry in the outdoor scenery around him, he nevertheless would produce it indoors on his canvas. "Art must give what nature does not have," he wrote; "only then is it creative."

While northern German artists produced one type of stark, melancholic Romantic nature, Koch's notion of romantic, as seen in a landscape he so designated (see *Wasserfall bei Subiaco* [*Waterfall at Subiaco*, 1813]) bordered on the sentimental. In its saturated composition, the painting presents all manner of delights for the eye: a young peasant couple, bathers, and a shepherd with flock dispersed throughout a complex arrangement of rugged mountains, earth-colored buildings nestled in gentle hills below, and a small, placid waterfall. Koch believed that only living beings imparted idea to the landscape painting, never reaching the point, as did some Romantic artists like Caspar David Friedrich, at which he felt a depiction of the natural world devoid of human intervention could stand alone as a meaningful work or attain an ideal character. Yet, although he remained conservative in his belief in the ultimate hierarchy of human narrative over the accompanying scenery in a landscape painting, he often imbued his naturalistic nature with a thrilling brawniness that overshadows the figures lending the pretext to the works.

With the exception of a few years spent in Vienna (in protest of the French occupation of the Eternal City), Rome became Koch's permanent home. His looming presence led him to act as doyen to the many *Deutsch-Römer* (German Romans), and in the late 1820s he was invited to join several Nazarene artists in creating a series of frescoes in a Roman villa, the Casino Massimo, where he illustrated scenes from Dante's *Divine Comedy*. During his lifetime, despite the irritation expressed by some critics at the hardness of his painterly touch, Koch's work generally was recognized as a monumental contribution to the art of the day. He wielded a decided influence upon younger artists such as Julius Schnorr von Carolsfeld, Carl Philipp Fohr, and Ludwig Richter; and his vision of nature, held up as ideal by the very academies whose pedagogy he had so despised, helped to shape the practice of German landscape painting production for decades to come.

MARGARET DOYLE

Biography

Born July 27, 1768 in Obergibeln bei Elbigenalp. First artistic training, 1782–83; began studies in Augsburg, 1784; attended Hohe Karlsschule in Stuttgart 1785–91; school honors, 1788 89. Traveled in and around Strasbourg, 1791; in Switzerland 1792–94; in Italy, 1795. Married Cassandra Ranaldi, 1806 birth of daughter Helena, 1811. In Rome to 1812; sojourn in Vienna, 1812–15. Birth of son Camillus, 1814. Won prize at annual Munich exhibition, 1814. Returned to Rome permanently, 1815. Birth of son Augosto, 1817. Published memoirs, *Moderne Kunstchronik*. 1834. Died January 12, 1839 in Rome of effects of stroke.

Selected Works

Heroische Landschaft mit dem Dankopfer Noahs, 1803. Oil on canvas, 86 cm × 116 cm. Städelsches Kunstinstitut, Frankfurt.

Heroische Landschaft mit Regenbogen, 1804/1815. Oil on canvas, 188 cm × 171.2 cm. Bayerische Staatsgemäldesammlungen, Neue Pinakothek, Munich.

Der Schmadribachfall (first version), 1805/1811. Oil on canvas, 123 cm × 93.5 cm. Museum der bildenden Künste, Leipzig.

Wasserfall bei Subiaco, 1813. Oil on canvas, 58 cm × 68 cm. Nationalgalerie, Staatliche Museen Preußischer Kulturbesitz, Berlin.

Berner Oberland, 1816. Oil on canvas, 101 cm × 134 cm. Staatliche Kunstsammlungen, Gemäldegalerie Neue Meister, Dresden.

Die Wasserfall von Tivoli, 1818/1823. Oil on canvas, 104 cm × 148 cm. Österreichische Galerie Belvedere, Vienna.

Der Schmadribachfall (third version). 1821/22. Oil on canvas, 131.8 cm × 110 cm. Neue Pinakothek, Munich.

Scenes from Dante's La Divina Commedia (*Divine Comedy*), 1825–1828. Four frescoes. Casino Massimo, Rome.

Heroische Landschaft mit Ruth und Boas. 1826/27. Oil on canvas, 105 cm × 151 cm. Tiroler Landesmuseum Ferdinandeum, Innsbruck.

Macbeth und die Hexen, 1835. Oil on canvas, 115 cm × 155.5 cm. Kunstmuseum, Basel.

Bibliography

Czymmek, Götz, Ekkehard Mai, and Albert Schug. *Heroismus und Idylle: Formen der Landschaft um 1800 bei Jacob Philipp Hackert, Joseph Anton Koch und Johann Christian Reinhart*. Cologne: Wallraft-Richartz-Museum, 1984.

Frank, Hilmar. *Joseph Anton Koch: Der Schmadribachfall*. Frankfurt: Taschen, 1995.

Goldfarb, Hilliard T. "Defining 'Naive and Sentimental' Landscape, Schiller, Hackert, Koch, and the Romantic Experience," *Bulletin of the Cleveland Museum of Art* 69, no. 9 (1982): 282–96.

Holst, Christian von. *Joseph Anton Koch 1768–1839*. Stuttgart: Edition Cantz, 1989.

Koch, Joseph Anton. *Moderne Kunstchronik*. 1834. Edited and expanded by Hilmar Frank. Leipzig: G. Kiepenheuer, 1984.

Lutterotti, Otto R. von *Joseph Anton Koch 1768–1839 Leben und Werk*. Vienna: Herold Verlag, 1985.

Mitchell, Timothy F. *Art and Science in German Landscape Painting 1770–1840*. Oxford: Clarendon Press, 1993.

Vaughan, William. *German Romantic Painting*. New Haven, Conn.: Yale University Press, 1980.

KORAÏS, ADAMANTIOS 1748–1833

Greek scholar, essayist, and language reformer

Often considered the last, and most influential, representative of the Greek Enlightenment, Adamantios Koraïs straddled the huge shift in European perceptions that took place during his long life. A self-taught classical scholar who declined a chair at the Collège de France, Koraïs was a prolific essayist, correspondent, and pamphleteer who lived for much of his life in Paris. He made a distinctive contribution to the ideological construction of the Greek nation-state, which came into being in 1821, and to the causes of Greek education and language reform. It is the first of these, principally, that links him with the Romantic movement.

Koraïs was probably the first to equate the idea of Greek emancipation from Ottoman rule with the nineteenth-century model of the nation-state. Although he was not a systematic thinker, and the sources and development of his ideas are not always easy to trace, Koraïs defined both nation and language in terms that recall those of Johann Gottfried von Herder.

For Koraïs, the key to national self-determination was language ("The language is the nation," he wrote in 1829), and some of his statements about language, as an inalienable inheritance, for example, are close to the spirit of Herder and Romanticism. It was their language that defined the Greeks of his day; Koraïs insisted that the modern Greek language was the precious and distinctive, biological descendant of ancient Greek. The prestige of ancient Greek in Europe was high at this time. While neoclassicists upheld Greek (and Latin) models for imitation, Koraïs was the first to stake the claim to this inheritance in the Herderian terms of the "traditions of a people," terms which have been standard in Greece ever since.

Koraïs was no mere chauvinist, however. He was uncompromising in his demands, directed toward his compatriots, that they should deserve this inheritance and be seen to do so. To this end, he embarked on a series of publications, subsidized by wealthy businessmen, the Zosimas brothers of Ionnina, and circulated throughout the Greek-speaking communities of the Ottoman empire, in which he urged on the Greek people two things: education in the classical past and in modern political ideas, and reform of the Greek language.

Koraïs, although he had left his native Smyrna as a young man, was vividly aware that the Greek speakers of his day did not share his own erudition. Untutored as they were, with little knowledge of the ancient Greek heritage and less interest in it, they were in no condition to press the special claim that Koraïs had conceived for them. As he saw it, two thousand years of barbarism and slavery had to be eradicated before the Greek nation could take its rightful place alongside the nations of Europe. Active though he was in promoting the cause of national independence among Greeks of the Ottoman empire, Koraïs was taken by surprise by the uprising of 1821, and his first reaction was to condemn it as premature.

Koraïs's program of linguistic reform was part of the same strategy, and here lies the fundamental contradiction at the heart of his work, and also of its later reception. The spoken Greek of his day was no more recognizable to a classically trained European as the descendant of the language of Periclean Athens than were the longshoremen of Smyrna as the descendants of Pericles himself. Koraïs was well aware of this, and it was for this strategic purpose that he set himself to elaborate, over the last thirty years of his life, an ever more demanding set of reforms to the "inalienable heritage" that was the Greek language. Koraïs did not believe, as some still did, at this time and later, that it was possible to resurrect the dead language of classical antiquity. The starting point of his linguistic reforms was the spoken language, whose properties he saw in biological terms that bring him close to Romanticism. But in order to fulfill the (also Romantic) ideal of national self-determination, Koraïs saw it as necessary to "correct and embellish" this rude, spontaneous tongue, so as to make its organic link to its ancient counterpart both evident and irrefutable.

The result was that Koraïs's very considerable authority among Greeks, once the nation-state came into existence, was thrown behind the dead hand of an archaizing tendency that swept Greek education, civic life, and much of literature for almost a century. This form of the language came to be known by the term *katharevousa* (literally; "[language] undergoing purification"), a term not used by Koraïs himself, but from the 1830s onwards inextricably linked with his name and prestige. Ever since then, Koraïs's reputation has been contradictory. He is the ideological "father of the Greek nation"; but he is also the arbiter of an artificially imposed language which, as the poet Solomos protested in 1824, "has not been spoken, is not spoken, and never will be spoken."

Koraïs's many writings consist of letters (which include vivid accounts of the Terror in postrevolutionary France); a small number of vibrant patriotic poems and pamphlets, printed and distributed anonymously or under a pseudonym during the period of Napoleon Bonaparte's campaigns in the eastern Mediterranean, and again after 1821; the series of prefaces to his own editions of ancient Greek texts; and a short autobiography, written at the end of his life. He is sometimes credited with a novel, *Papatrechas*, but it was not until 1842 that an editor thought to gather the lightly fictionalized prefaces to Homer in which the character Papatrechas appears, and present them to the public in this way. In 1804, Koraïs coined the modern Greek word for novel, a genre which he pointed out had been initiated by Greek writers in the early centuries of the common era.

RODERICK BEATON

Biography

Born in Smyrna, Ottoman empire (modern Izmir, Turkey), the son of a merchant from Chios, April 17, 1748. Sent by his father to work in a business house in Amsterdam, 1771; returned to Smyrna, 1777. Studied Medicine at Montpellier, 1782; established himself permanently in Paris, 1788. Actively supported Napoleon's Mediterranean operations and urged Greeks to rise against Ottoman rule, 1801–4. First set out his views on the Greek language, 1804. Embarked on the series of editions of ancient Greek works with long prefaces, *Greek Library*, 1807. Declined the offer of a chair at the Collège de France, 1814. Died in Paris, April 6, 1833.

Selected Works

Collections

Epistolai. Edited by Nikolaos M. Damalas. 4 vols. 1885–86.
Koray's Letters Written from Paris, 1788–92. Translated and edited by P. Ralli. 1898.

Essays and Academic Writing

Adelfiki Didaskalia pros tou evriskomenous kata pasan tin Othomanikin epikrateian Graikous. 1798.
Mémoire sur l'état actuel de la civilisation dans la Grèce. 1803.
Peri ton Ellinikon Sumferonton dialogos dyo Graikon. 1825.
Elliniki Vivliothiki. 8 vols. 1805–14.
Atakta. 4 vols. 1828–32.
O Papatrechas. 1842.

Bibliography

Beaton, Roderick. "Koraes, Toynbee and the Modern Greek Heritage," *Byzantine and Modern Greek Studies* 15 (1991): 1–18.
Chaconas, S. G. *Adamantios Korais: A Study in Greek Nationalism*. 1942. Reprinted New York: AMS Press, 1968.
Clogg, Richard, ed. *The Movement for Greek Independence, 1770–1821: A Collection of Documents*. London: Macmillan, 1976.
Henderson, G. P. *The Revival of Greek Thought: 1620–1830*. Albany: State University of New York Press, 1970.
Jeffreys, Michael. "Adamantios Koraes: Language and Revolution." In *Culture and Nationalism in Nineteenth-Century Eastern Europe*. Edited by R. Sussex and J. C. Eade. Columbus, Ohio: Slavica, 1985.

KORDIAN

Play by Juliusz Słowacki

Kordian (1834), a play by Polish Romantic playwright Juliusz Słowacki, is probably the best historical play by this prolific and ingenious Polish poet. It was written soon after the Polish uprising of 1830–31 and the war of Independence with Russia that ended in Polish defeat. Instead of describing or properly analyzing the events of the near past, Słowacki creates a Romantic myth based partly on his own autobiography, partly on a symbolic Hamlet-like figure. In some respects, Słowacki clearly attempted to compete with Adam Mickiewicz's *Dziady* (Forefathers' Eve, 1823), which also balances autobiographical elements alongside fantastic and miraculous ones. Słowacki's rivalry with the older poet is suggested also by the subtitle, *First Part of a Trilogy*. Mickiewicz's play went by the full title *Forefathers Eve, Part 3*, but no earlier parts of the play exist. The same goes for *Kordian: First Part of a Trilogy*, which is a singular work. Also, like Mickiewicz's play, the structure of *Kordian* is not particularly coherent.

A play in three acts, *Kordian* begins with two introductory scenes before act 1: "Przygotowanie" ("Preparation"), and "prolog" ("Prologue"). "Preparation" presents a bizarre scene at night in the Carpathian Mountains on the eve of the nineteenth century. A sorcerer, Satan, and other diabolical figures concoct a brew in a large cauldron from which various figures emerge. Various allusions make clear that some of them are contemporary figures, such as the Polish statesmen Czartoryski and Lelewel, as well as the failed "dictator" of 1831, Krukowiecki. Słowacki himself speaks in the mysterious "Prologue": "Give me ashes encased in a national urn / I shall resurrect people from those ashes. . . ." This request projects a kind of national hero in the shape of Kordian, whose name is probably derived from the Latin word for heart, *cor*. The road to Kordian's acceptance of this proposed role is quite long and full of detours. In act 1, we see Kordian as an adolescent, grieving over the suicide of his best friend. At this stage he is without a guiding idea; indeed, in the very first monologue Kordian sighs, "God! Take off this swallow-like anxiety from my heart / Fill my life with a spirit and prophesise a goal for the soul." This wish, however, will not be fulfilled in act 1, which ends with Kordian's attempt to shoot himself because of his unrequited love for Laura. His attempt fails and he recovers, reappearing in act 2, "A Wanderer."

If act 1 showed Kordian the adolescent dreamer, act 2 presents a young man's search for truth and life's meaning. It begins with scenes in England: the first one is a conversation with a guard in Saint James' Park, and the second a monologue on the white cliffs of Dover where the hero is reading (suitably) *King Lear* and pays tribute to William Shakespeare's genius. The next scene is a villa in Italy, where Kordian finds out how little the affection of his girlfriend Violetta is worth. From here, rather unexpectedly, we move to Rome, where the Pope receives Kordian personally and gives him "good advice" similar to the encyclical message of Pope Gregory XVI in 1830 ("Let the Poles pray, respect the Tsar and keep up their faith . . ."), which is angrily rejected by Kordian. The next scene in this act takes place on Mont Blanc, a favorite spot for Romantic wanderings after Lord Byron, but here Kordian is transformed from a cosmopolitan individual into a patriot in the spirit of self-sacrificing knighthood. His "great thought" rejects Mickiewicz's recipe for national resistance, for he sees Poland as "the Winkelried of nations" (Arnold Winkelried being a Swiss hero who intercepted the enemy in a mountain gorge and gave his life for his country, not unlike Leonidas). At the end of act 2, Kordian is picked up by a cloud and miraculously dropped in Poland.

It is really act 3, "The Coronation Plot," that constitutes the most interesting part of the play. It consists of ten scenes, the first three of which take place in front of the Royal Palace and in the Warsaw Cathedral in 1829, the new tsar now being crowned as the king of Poland. In these scenes Słowacki shows both the opportunism of the people (they are happy to celebrate the coronation of a foreign oppressor) and their hidden revolutionary potential (in the song of an unknown person: "Wine has to be changed into blood / You have to drink transformed wine!"). The unknown person (*Nieznajomy*) may be identical to Kordian, and it is he who appears in scene 4, when the plotters hold a secret meeting, as an officer cadet who will be posted that night to guard the tsar's sleep. In spite of the hesitation of the majority of the plotters, Kordian volunteers to assassinate the tsar, to "take upon himself this crime" if it saves Poland. In scene 5, Kordian struggles in vain with two powerful spirits, Imagination and Fear, though in the end it is not them who prevent the planned murder but a devil who appears from nowhere only to utter two very revealing lines: "I was choking the Tsar—and I would have killed him / But in his sleep he looks so much like my father." In other words in Kordian's mind the murder would be equivalent to a kind of patricide (significantly, Dr. Bécu, Słowacki's stepfather, was a collaborator with the tsarist authorities at the time of the Vilno reprisals of 1824). Kordian faints on the doorstep of the tsar, who is awakened by the noise and commands him to be taken away with the instruction that "if he is not mad he should be shot dead." This command is changed by the Grand Duke Constantine, who is very proud of his Polish soldiers. Kordian, as one of the soldiers, manages to jump over the fixed bayonets of a row of soldiers to save his life. Even after this deed he is to be executed for treason. A high degree of suspense surrounds Kordian's fate until the very last scene of the play, when the tsar's aide de-camp arrives with a letter of clemency halting the execution.

Kordian is written in rhymed thirteen-syllable line verse, which Słowacki handles with great skill, though some of his characters' monologues are often embarassingly long. The play has large crowd scenes—not unlike *Forefathers' Eve*, and Zygmunt Krasiński's *The Undivine Comedy* (1835) and makes use both of the abnormal and the supernatural: act 3, scene 6, for example, takes place in a lunatic asylum. Kordian's final temptation is to lose faith in all that he had fought for, to admit that his radical democratic ideals are far detached from reality and devoid of all practical value. In a great monologue in act 3, scene 8, he curses the people for their "pettiness" and disloyalty to the patriotic cause; but then he is a failed Romantic hero who pre-

pares himself for death in one way or another. *Kordian* therefore shows not only the contradiction between the individual and his community, but also the antinomy of thought and deed, idea and reality.

First published anonymously in France in 1834 and appreciated properly only by Krasiński, *Kordian* reached the Polish stage many years later: it was first performed in 1899 in Kracow and its Warsaw premier had to wait until 1916. Since then it has been in the repertory of Polish theater, with some memorable productions by Leon Schiller in the 1930s.

GEORGE GÖMÖRI

Text

Kordian. Published anonymously, 1834. Republished in a ten-volume edition of Juliusz Słowacki's work edited by B. Gubrynowicz and W. Hahn, 1909. Subsequently republished in *Dziela wszystkie*. 17 vols. Edited by J. Kleiner and J. Floryan, 1952–76.

Bibliography

Bizan, M., and P. Hertz. *Głosy do "Kordiana."* 2nd ed. Warsaw: PIW, 1972.
Kleiner, Juliusz. *Słowacki*. Wroclaw: Ossolineum, 1972.
Kridl, Manfred. *Antagonizm wieszczów*. Warsaw, 1925.
Makowski, S. *"Kordian" Juliusza Słowackiego*. 2d ed. Warsaw, 1976.
Maciejewski, Jaroslaw. *Dramatyczna trylogia*. Poznan, 1961.
Milosz, Czeslaw. *The History of Polish Literature*. London: Colliers-Macmillan, 1969.
Ujejski, Józef. "Juliusza Slowackiego 'Kordian,'" *Księga pamiątkowa . . . Słowackiego*.

KRASIŃSKI, ZYGMUNT (SPIRIDION PRAWDZICKI) 1812–1859

Polish poet and dramatist

Like all of the Polish Romanticists, Zygmunt Krasiński was born into a country with no independent political status, and this played a decisive role in his development, both as a poet and as a man. Poland had steadily declined since the Renaissance, when the Polish–Lithuanian Commonwealth was the largest territorial entity in Europe, through growing dependence on the stronger empires which surrounded it, to the nadir of its fortunes in 1795: a complete loss of independence. Poles were to consider themselves either Austrians, Germans, or Russians. For most Poles, this was an intolerable situation. The sacredness of Poland, and the overriding importance of regaining its independence, were to become the central themes of Polish art at least until the nation's political rebirth in 1918. What was clear and easily acceptable to most, however, was to be complicated and problematical for Krasiński, caught between, as he liked to put it, "drogim ojcem a drogą ojczyzną" ("my dear father, and my dear fatherland").

The most nobly born of the Polish Romanticists, Krasiński was allied by birth to the twelve most powerful families in Poland. His father Wincenty (1782–1858) was a general, and hosted one of the most brilliant literary salons in Warsaw. It is he that Adam Mickiewicz gently satirizes as the "General" in the Warsaw salon scenes in the Dresden *Dziady* (1823; Forefathers' Eve). Although he had fought alongside Napoleon, Wicnety Krasiński entered the service of the tsar after the French

emperor's fall, eventually rising to a cabinet position and at one time serving as viceroy for the Russian-occupied Kingdom of Poland. This allowed him to retain his family's magnate status, but it proved a source of some embarrassment for his son. Most of the entire nation was filled with a patriotic longing for independence, waiting only for the appropriate moment to rise up against the tsar and evict the Russians from Poland. Yet, as much as Zygmunt sympathized with these sentiments, striking against the Russians would mean aiming a blow at his father, and he was reluctant to do this.

In 1829, his refusal to join his fellow university students in an antigovernment protest that directly concerned his father led to his public shaming by the students, his withdrawal from the University of Warsaw, and his first trip abroad, to continue his studies in Geneva. He returned to Poland three years later, at his father's insistence. In 1832, he was presented to the tsar in Saint Petersburg, under the presumption that he would take a civil service career. However, this time his personal feelings prevailed and, pleading illness, he received the tsar's permission for a passport. He left home again, never to return.

Yet his father cast a long shadow. Some ten years after this audience, he obeyed his parent's wishes in breaking off a romance with Delfina Potocka and married Eliza Branicka instead. Whether or not his marriage to Eliza was a successful one, his love for Delfina was sublimated into an ideal "spiritual marriage" to a "mystical sister." By the same token, the influence of his in-laws is said to have strengthened his penchant for political conservatism and traditional Roman Catholicism.

Krasiński was weakened by the chronic illnesses that beset him since their first onset in Saint Petersburg, and they may have become more acute and wasting as a result of his constant mental struggles with his domineering father. He died in Paris in 1859, one year after his father's death.

In short, Krasiński is something of a tragic figure. He was unable to remain unaffected by the revolutionary zeitgeist infecting his nation, yet he was too loving a son to effect a break from his tsar-allied father. This tension between his overbearing, conservative father and his natural inclinations to revolutionary patriotism is the prism through which Krasiński's development and works must be considered.

Although it would be unfair to say that Krasiński's fate depends on the *Nie-boska komedia* (*The Undivine Comedy*, 1835), this drama is his greatest and most recognizable work. Along with Adam Mickiewicz's *Dziady* (*Forefathers' Eve*) it is one of the two great works of Polish "monumental" drama, and, with Juliusz Słowacki's *Kordian* (1834), one of the key works dealing with the failed November Uprising of 1830–31. However, Krasiński writes about politics in a much more universal way than either Mickiewicz or Słowacki. Rather than dealing with the Polish uprising per se, *Nie-boska komedia* looks ahead prophetically to the vicious class struggles which were to characterize the Marxist years of the European twentieth century. Neither of his protagonists (the harsh noble Count Henryk and the revolutionary leader Pankracy) are portrayed as heroes at the conclusion of the work; only Christ can bring true peace and justice to the suffering peoples of the earth. Thus, the work ends, not with the triumph of the unstoppable democratic hordes that overrun the Count's men, but with the apocalyptic triumph of the Cross. Pankracy, shielding his eyes from the bright advent, cries out "Galilaee, vicisti!", the words of the dying Julian the Apostate.

Besides this political aspect, *Nie-boska komedia* also has an interesting aesthetic side. Part 1 attacks especially the unreal, otherworldly tendencies of idealistic Romanticism. Henryk, whom we first meet as a poet, becomes so overwhelmed in his Fichtean world of poetic creation that he destroys his real family for the sake of a phantom-maiden "Poesie." With harsh sarcasm, Krasiński characterizes this "ideal woman" as the corpse of a whore, sent into the very real world by Hell, to wreak havoc with this "great soul."

Much more blatantly political and Poland-oriented is *Irydion* (Son of the Rainbow, 1836), Krasiński's other great drama, and this despite the fact that the action is set in ancient Rome during the reign of the depraved Caesar Heliogabalus. Irydion is a young Greek full of hatred for the Romans who have enslaved his nation. The Romans here are an obvious symbol of Russia, and the Greeks a symbol of the Poles (a historical allegory that Cyprian Kamil Norwid was to make use of later in his long narrative poem "Quidam" [1863]). Irydion leads a revolutionary group consisting of Greeks, slaves, plebians, barbarians, and even some impatient Christians, but the revolt fails to succeed, mainly because Irydion is motivated by hatred. True victory over Rome will only come with the weapons of Christ: love for one's enemies and patience under persecution. In this way, Krasiński criticizes the November insurrectionists yet still holds out hope for the future. In the epilogue of the play, God gives Irydion an odd penance: he is to be born again, later, in a "ziemia mogił i krzyżów" ('land of gravemounds and crosses," i.e., Poland) where, "after a long period of martyrdom I will send the dawn / . . . / promised to all people from the summit of Golgotha—freedom!"

As important a dramatist as he is, Krasiński is not known for his lyric poetry. Indeed, he more than once confessed his lyric impotence, most eloquently in the verse "Bóg mi odmówił tej anielskiej miary / Bez której ludziom nic zda się poeta" ("God has denied me that angelic measure / Without which one cannot be called a poet"). In the nineteenth century, Krasiński was hailed, alongside Mickiewicz and Słowacki, as the third "national bard" (*wieszcz*). Twentieth century critics, however, have generally pointed out that Krasiński does not possess the breadth of vision of his two compatriots, and his lack of brilliance in more than one genre has led many to reevaluate his status. On the other hand, while his lyric output is not quite in the same league as that of Mickiewicz and Słowacki, two longer, philosophical poems are often read and commented upon as touchstones of Krasiński's political conservatism.

First, *Przedświt* (*Predawn*, 1841–43), is a quasi-messianistic work that sets forth the somewhat (by then) hackneyed thesis of Poland as the "Christ of the nations." As Czesław Miłosz puts it, this somewhat Hegelian work "idolised the division of mankind into nations as necessary and predetermined by God, likening these divisions to the parts of an immense chorus. Viewed in such a light, the partition of Poland became a crime againt humanity." Still, the sufferings undergone by Poland were to "redeem" mankind and usher in a new era of universal justice. Interestingly enough, only the Polish aristocracy is singled out by the poet as the conduit of this "grace" as, among all Poles, their characteristics of leadership and willing suffering on behalf of others through the ages liken them most to Christ. This outlook cannot be interpreted as blue-blooded triumphalism. Krasiński sees nobility as a burden rather than an exclusive badge of honor. This sort of caste-conscious thinking did not go down well in a Poland which was rapidly reshaping itself into a more inclusive democratic ideal, in which class distinctions were to play a much smaller role than they had in the past.

But Krasiński held firmly to his conservatism. It is evident once more in the *Psalmy przyszłości* (*Psalms of the Future*, 1845). In Krasiński's defense, he was moved to extreme glorification of the nobility by fear. Henryk Kamieński's political pamphlet *O prawdach żywotnych narodu polskiego* (*On the Vital Truths of the Polish Nation*, 1844) suggested arming the peasantry for a campaign of partisan violence (in which the aristocracy would also have a role to play, though not necessarily the leading one). Gustaw Ehrenberg's poem "Szlachta w roku 1831" ("The Nobility in 1831," 1836) openly calls for the slaughter of the nobility at the hands of the peasants for their unwillingness to join the revolutionary ranks during the November Uprising: Krasiński passionately pleads, in response, "Jeden tylko, jeden cud: / Z szlachtą polską polski lud, / Jak dwa chóry jedno pienie!" ("One, only one miracle: / The Polish people along with the Polish nobility / Like two choirs singing the same song!") Later, he compares the peasantry to a dead, gigantic body that can only be properly vivified when the "spirit" of the nobility enters into it to animate and guide it. In 1846, one year after the poem was published, the peasantry of Galicja rose up and turned on the nobility of the Austrian sector, slaughtering many. Terrified,

Krasiński looked upon this horrible event as the fulfillment of Ehrenberg's poem, and the prophetic vision of the class struggle he had himself described in *The Undivine Comedy*. It was in this context that he reluctantly referred to himself as *Kassandra tych dni* ("the Cassandra of these days").

Such is the extent of Krasiński's important literary opus. Mention might also be made of three novels, written in his youth. *Grób rodziny Reichstalów*, (*The Reichstal Family Grave*, 1828) is a novel of horrors in the Gothic style, and *Władysław Herman i jego dwór* (*Władysław Herman and His Court*, 1830) with *Agaj-Han* (1834) are historical novels in the style of Sir Walter Scott. Despite some fine descriptive, not to say poetic, writing, especially in *Agaj-Han*, these works are rarely read by nonspecialists.

Much more important are Krasiński's letters. Along with those of Juiliusz Słowacki, they constitute the main trunk of Polish Romantic epistolary literature. Some seven hundred letters remain from literally thousands that he had written over the years to his beloved Delfina Potocka. Also important is his correspondence with his English friend Henry Reeve, and those addressed to the philosopher August Cieszkowski, whose cyclic idea of history and the near approach of the final perfect age of blessedness had a direct influence on Krasiński.

CHARLES S. KRASZEWSKI

Biography

Born in Paris, February 19, 1812 to a noble Polish family. In 1829 he left the University of Warsaw for political reasons. After studying at the University of Geneva, he was called home in 1832 and formally presented to the tsar. Receiving an exit passport, he left Poland and the rest of his life was to be spent in Western Europe, chiefly in France, Switzerland, and Italy. In 1843 occurred the arranged marriage with Eliza Branicka, which dashed his hopes of consummating a love match with his lifelong correspondent Delfina Potocka. From 1848 on his health was to decline rapidly. He spent time in Baden, Heidelburg, and France seeking a congenial climate and cure; he died in Paris, February 23, 1859.

Selected works

Polish
Krasiński, Zygmunt. *Dzieła Literackie*. Warsaw: PIW, 1973.

English and Other Languages
Correspondance de Sigismond Krasiński et de Henry Reeve. Preface by Joseph Kallenbach. Paris: C. Delagrave, 1902.
The Un-Divine Comedy. Translated by Harriette E. Kennedy and Zofia Umińska. Preface by G. K. Chesterton. Introduction by Arthur Górski. London: G. G. Harrap, 1924.
Krasiński, Zygmunt. *Prealba, e Il figlio delle ombre*. Translated by Carlo Verdiani. Firenze: La Nuova Italia, 1950.
Segel, Harold B. *Polish Romantic Drama: Three Plays in English Translation*. Ithaca, N.Y.: Cornell University Press, 1977.
Krasiński, Zygmunt. *The Undivine Comedy*. Translated by Charles S. Kraszewski. Lehman, Penn.: Libella Veritatis, 1999.

Bibliography

Günther, Władysław. *Krasiński żywy*. London: B. Świderski, 1959.
Jakubowski, Jan Z. *Europejskie związki literatury Polskiej*. Warsaw: PIW, 1969.
Janion, Maria. *Gorączka romantyczna*. Warsaw: PIW, 1975.
Kleiner, Juliusz. *Zygmunt Krasiński: studia*. Warsaw: PWN, 1998.
Kraszewski, Charles S. *The Romantic Hero and Contemporary Anti-Hero in Polish and Czech Literature: Great Souls and Grey Men*. Lewiston, England: Edwin Mellen, 1998.
Lednicki, Waclaw, ed. *Zygmunt Krasinski, Romantic Universalist: An International Tribute*. New York: Polish Institute of Arts and Sciences in America, 1964.
Marek, Edmond. *La comédie non-divine de Zygmunt Krasinski: réflexions sur un drame romantique*. Lille: Club culturel franco-polonais "Polonia-Nord," 1998.
———. *Zygmunt Krasinski et sa vision de la Pologne et de l'Europe*. Lille: Club culturel "Polonia-Nord," 1995.
Piwińska, Marta. *Legenda romantyczna i szyderczy*. Warsaw: PIW, 1973.

KROCHMAL, NACHMAN 1785-1840

Austrian Jewish scholar

Born in the predominantly Jewish Brody region in Austrian Galicia, Nachman Krochmal, also known as "RaNak," or Rabbi Nachman Krochmal, demonstrated the limitations of *haskalah* (the Jewish enlightenment) in the territories taken by Austria in the first partition of Poland in 1772. Krochmal's father was a merchant who often traveled to Germany and who knew Moses Mendelssohn. Brody became a center of Galician haskalah, and Krochmal personally knew such figures as Mendel Lefin. Although Joseph II's *Toleranzpatent* (Edict of Toleration, 1782) made it easier for Jews to be economically productive, the new law also included harsh "reformatory" provisions that ended Jewish communal autonomy and enforced the use of German rather than Hebrew or Yiddish. The consequent linguistic Germanization of educated Jews opened them to the influence of the Berlin haskalah, but set them apart from the largely Hasidic Jewish masses, even while it continued their estrangement from their Polish neighbors. Krochmal's education reflected this ambivalence: he was first trained thoroughly in Talmudic study, but he later taught himself German and French rather than Polish, Latin, and Arabic in order to study modern and medieval philosophy. Though he left Brody first for Zolkiew and later for Tarnopol, he never left Galicia. Hence, his exploration of Enlightenment ideas was entirely cerebral and solitary; Galicia offered no opportunities for membership in gentile cultural institutions.

Krochmal enjoyed little success either in business or, despite his impressive Jewish learning, as a community leader and rabbi. He became a struggling single parent after his wife's death in 1826, and with his health in severe decline after 1836 he worked hard to complete his philosophical masterpiece, the *Moreh Nevukhei ha-Zeman* (*Guide to the Perplexed of the Age*). The work was incomplete at Krochmal's death in 1840, and had to be edited posthumously for publication by Leopold Zunz; it appeared in Hebrew in 1851, under the title given it by Krochmal. As the title suggests, the work was modeled on Moses Maimonides' synthesis; Krochmal was a devoted student of the medieval Jewish rabbi and philosopher. Nevertheless, he considered Maimonides' conception of God inadequate to human needs, and therefore corrected it with neo-Platonic ideas derived from Maimonides' predecessor Abraham ibn Ezra and his successor Moses Nahmanides. The choice of title was not merely intellectual respect. Krochmal sought to demonstrate that Jewish tradition could survive modernity without fundamental change, but also without ignorant obscurantism. He wrote to guide faithful, observant Jews intent on living a renewed Judaism.

The means to Jewish renewal was Jewish celebration of Jewish philosophy. Krochmal's intent was to demonstrate the intellectual superiority of Judaism to the philosophical legacy of Immanuel Kant and G. W. F. Hegel. In general, Krochmal considered their philosophical syntheses to be triumphalist Protestantism disguised as universal philosophy. These were dangerous to Judaism because, in an updated version of the Christian dismissal of Judaism as a superceded belief system, they relativized Jewish learning as a long-bypassed intellectual accomplishment. In particular, Krochmal wished to rebut Kant's dismissal of teleology by positing internal final causes present in human beings since creation: all creation serves a hierarchy of causes. This was a philosophical vindication of the teleology offered by traditional Judaism. He responded to Hegel by faulting the identification of Protestant Christianity with absolute religion; and sought instead to find the admitted insights of German philosophy in Jewish writings, so that Judaism seemed the genuinely absolute religion. His argument was both a defense against the continual Christian denigration of Judaism as mere legalism and a defense of Judaism against historical relativism.

Krochmal therefore embraced Jewish triumphal, whose tendency appeared in his periodization of Jewish history. In the *Moreh Nevukhei*, he posited three completed ages of Jewish spiritual progress. The first began in the age of the biblical patriarchs and ended with the destruction of the first Temple in 586 B.C.E. The second endured until the suppression of the bar Kokhba revolt in 135 C.E. The third embraced the elaboration of rabbinic thought and medieval Jewish history more generally. It is possible, but by no means certain, that Krochmal believed that a fourth age had begun in his own time. Scholars have variously attributed Krochmal's historical theory to the influences of Hege, Johann Gottfried Herder, Gotthold Ephraim Lessing, or Giambattista Vico, but this search for specific intellectual influences has not proved fruitful. Surely Krochmal borrowed from various sources to create his version of an organic progress of Jewish spirit. He is original in applying this triumphalism to the Jewish nation in its defense against relativism. He believed that, unlike other religions, Judaism had arrived originally at an absolute conception of God. Therefore, Jews were safe against historical change in a way that other religious groups were not: they had a history, but their history was one of progressively discovering the implications of a truth already conferred.

This meant that Krochmal had to respond to recent, chiefly German-Jewish, critiques of the authenticity of Jewish law that rabbis derived in the Talmud from a supposed "oral Torah" recorded and construed only in Krochmal's third age of Judaism. Krochmal tried to answer their doubts by borrowing from the conservative legal theorist Friedrich Karl von Savigny who, unlike legal idealists, believed that legal change occurred through organic development of existing laws rather than through idealist legislation. Krochmal invoked Savigny to suggest that all written codes coexisted with a body of oral law that supplied the required standards of exegesis. This did not imply the original imperfection of the Torah. On the contrary, all legal systems required continual novel applications and interpretations. This position in no way contradicted Krochmal's insistence on the originally absolute nature of Judaism. The truth of Judaism was eternal, but in history Jews progressively understood and discovered differing aspects of that truth. This fact accounts for Krochmal's immense influence on conservative scholars of Judaism. This influence is clearest in the work of Hanokh Albeck, Zacharias Frankel, and Isaac Hirsh Weiss.

ROBERT SOUTHARD

Biography

Born in Brody, Galicia, in 1785. He married Sarah Haberman and moved to Zolkiew, near Lvov in 1798, and in 1803 began to learn German. In 1808 illness forced him to move to Lvov. After his wife's death in 1826, he moved to Tarnopol, then back to Brody, where he wrote the *Moreh* between 1836 and his death in 1840.

Bibliography

Harris, Jay M. *Nachman Krochmal: Guiding the Perplexed of the Modern Age*. New York: New York University Press, 1991.

Katz, Jacob. *Out of the Ghetto*. New York: Schocken, 1973.

Mahler, Raphael. *Hasidism and the Jewish Enlightenment*. Philadelphia: JPS, 1988.

Meyer, Michael. *Origins of the Modern Jew*. Detroit: Wayne State University Press, 1967.

Rotenstreich, Nathan. *Jews and German Philosophy: The Polemics of Emancipation*. New York: Schocken, 1984.

KUBLA KHAN 1816

Poem by Samuel Taylor Coleridge

Samuel Taylor Coleridge's fantastical, opium-induced, fifty-four-line poem *Kubla Khan: Or a Vision in a Dream. A Fragment* was first published in 1816 in a short collection with the other unfinished poems *Christabel, A Vision*, and *The Pains of Sleep*. By 1816 Coleridge was under pressure from friends and critics to publish, but he did not feel certain that these works merited publication. In his preface to "Kubla Khan," which is almost as famous as the poem itself, he wrote that he had only published it "at the request of a poet of great and deserved celebrity." This refers to Lord Byron, and it was Byron's publisher, John Murray, who brought out the collection with Byron's assistance. Coleridge added in his preface that "as far as the Author's own opinions are concerned," the poem was appearing "rather as a psychological curiosity, than on the grounds of any supposed *poetic merits.*"

He further explained that *Kubla Khan* had been written in the summer of 1797, when he had been living in Somerset and collaborating closely with Wordsworth. He had been out walking alone when, taken suddenly ill, he "had retired to a lonely farm-house between Porlock and Linton." He had then taken an anodyne (i.e., opium) to cure what he described elsewhere as an attack of dysentery. Coleridge then fell for three hours into a "profound sleep . . . in which all the images [of the poem] rose up before him as *things* . . . without any sensation of consciousness or effort." Before falling asleep he had been reading a collection of travel accounts compiled in the early seventeenth century by the London clergyman Samuel Purchas, known as Purchas's *Pilgrimage.* Purchas had written there of *Xanada,* where "*Cublai Can* built a stately Pallace," a magic walled summer kingdom. Upon waking, Coleridge began writing down what he thought would be two or three hundred lines of poetry, but his task was interrupted by a call away to business. When he returned to his room later, he found he was unable to recall what he had intended to write.

Inspired by Purchas, Coleridge's opening lines are some of the most remarkable in English Romantic poetry:

In Xanadu did Kubla Khan
A stately pleasure-dome decree:
Where Alph, the sacred river, ran
Through caverns measureless to man
Down to a sunless sea.

Fed by his reading of Purchas's travel accounts, as well as the influences of John Milton and William Shakespeare, Coleridge succeeds in evoking an exotic Eastern landscape like nothing he had ever physically seen. But despite Byron's efforts, the critics did not receive this collection of fragments well. *Christabel* was largely derided, while *Kubla Khan* received little comment, with William Hazlitt declaring that the poem "only shews that Mr Coleridge can write better *nonsense* verses than any man in England. It is not a poem, but a musical composition." The *Edinburgh Review,* meanwhile, called it "one of the most notable pieces of impertinence of which the press has lately been guilty; and one of the boldest experiments that has yet been made on the patience or understanding of the public." The poet's estranged wife exclaimed, "Oh! when will he ever give his friends anything but pain?"

Doubt has been cast on Coleridge's account of the composition of his poem, in particular by Molly Lefebure, who questioned the poet's claim that it was written at this time or in the manner described. Certainly, there is no reference to the poem in Coleridge's letters, nor those of his friends, prior to around 1810. But Richard Holmes has written that in his reflections on the fragmentary work, Coleridge opened up "the whole question of the creative impulse in startling new ways." Furthermore, Coleridge's fellow opium eater, Thomas De Quincey, in 1821 described similar exotic, drug-induced visions of Asia in his *Confessions of an English Opium Eater.* De Quincey's work, which in its first edition alluded anonymously to Coleridge ("one celebrated man of the present day"), spoke of "oriental dreams, which always filled me with such amazement at the monstrous scenery, that horror seemed absorbed, for a while, in sheer astonishment." *Kubla Khan* has become the apotheosis of the Romantic era's opium dream, a fragmentary vision itself fragmented in its series of regressing visions. Yet two of the very reasons for which it was derided at the time, its unfinished aspect and its apparent meaninglessness, have become two of its most engaging features in critical terms. The poem's evoked landscape has thus inevitably been open to numerous critical interpretations: it has been seen as an Edenic paradise ruled over by the all-seeing Khan, or alternatively as a false paradise, an Eden after the Fall, with Khan as its failed genius. Psychological interpretations have also been drawn, which take into consideration the turbulence of the poet's chaotic inner life.

DAVID HAYCOCK

See also **Coleridge, Samuel Taylor; Poetry: Britain**

Bibliography

De Quincey, Thomas. *Confessions of an English Opium Eater and Other Writings.* Oxford: Oxford University Press, 1985.

Holmes, Richard. *Coleridge: Early Visions.* London: Hodder and Stoughton, 1989.

Jordan, Frank. *The English Romantic Poets: A Review of Research and Criticism.* New York: Modern Language Association of America, 1985.

Lefebure, Molly. *Samuel Taylor Coleridge: A Bondage of Opium.* London: Quartet Books, 1977.

Lowes, J. Livingstone. *The Road to Xanadu: A Study in the Ways of the Imagination.* Cambridge, Mass., 1927.

McFarland, Thomas. *Romanticism and the Forms of Ruin: Wordsworth, Coleridge and Modalities of Fragmentation.* Princeton, 1981.

Schneider, Elisabeth. *Coleridge, Opium and "Kubla Khan."* Chicago, 1953.

Skeat, T. C. "Kubla Khan," *British Museum Quarterly* 26 (1962–63): 77–83.